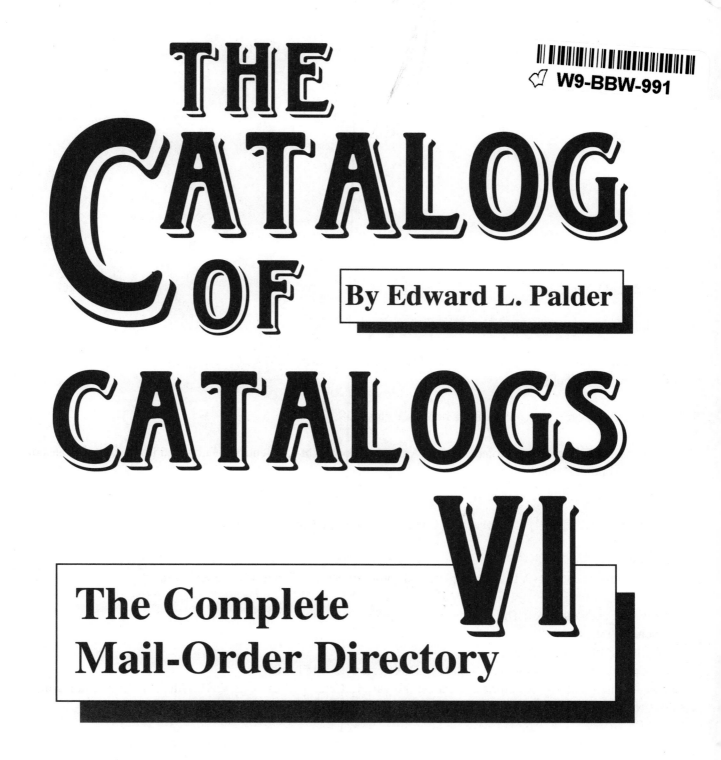

# THE CATALOG OF CATALOGS VI

By Edward L. Palder

## The Complete Mail-Order Directory

WOODBINE HOUSE • 1999

Sixth Edition

Published by Woodbine House, 6510 Bells Mill Road, Bethesda, MD 20817. 800-843-7323.
http://www.woodbinehouse.com

For information on ordering copies of this book, see page 569.



**Library of Congress Cataloging-in-Publication Data**

Palder, Edward L.
The catalog of catalogs VI : the complete mail-order directory / Edward L. Palder. – 6th ed.
p. cm.
Rev. and updated ed. of: The catalog of catalogs V.
Includes indexes.
ISBN 1-890627-08-9 (pbk.)
1. Commercial catalogs—United States—Directories. 2. Mail-order business—United States—Directories. I. Palder, Edward L. Catalog of catalogs V. II. Title. III. Title: Catalog of catalogs 6. IV. Title: Catalog of catalogs six.
HF5466.P35 1999
381'.142'029473—dc21 98-55354
CIP

Manufactured in the United States of America

10 9 8 7 6 5 4 3 2 1

# TABLE OF CONTENTS 

# ❖ INTRODUCTION 

Catalog shopping is said to be ideally suited to the way people live today. In fact, two out of three Americans shop by mail at least occasionally, according to the Direct Marketing Association. It's easy to understand why, considering the potential savings in:

- **time** (you can tell at a glance whether a particular catalog has the styles, sizes, or products you are looking for, then complete a purchase in minutes without having to fight crowds, wait in long lines, or search for a parking spot at local stores);
- **money** (you can comparison shop in stores thousands of miles apart without even leaving home);
- **aggravation** (you can shop when it's convenient for you, without having to drag kids along or get a babysitter).

Wouldn't it be great if you could save even more of these kinds of drains on your time, energy, and emotional well-being? You can, with the **Catalog of Catalogs VI.** The **Catalog of Catalogs VI** is designed to help the average catalog shopper streamline the process of shopping by mail. It will enable you to quickly zero in on companies that sell exactly what you're looking for, and also to find out how to prevent or resolve mail order problems. And if you happen to simply enjoy catalog shopping for its own sake, the **Catalog of Catalogs VI** will point the way to hundreds of catalogs from companies big and small, specializing in an almost undreamed-of variety of products.

The **Catalog of Catalogs VI** contains listings for about 15,000 different retailers, wholesalers, and manufacturers in the United States and Canada, grouped into about 900 subject areas. That's about 1,000 more listings than in the previous edition. The **Catalog of Catalogs VI** not only includes companies with catalogs, but also companies that will send free or low-cost information about particular brands of merchandise, or lists of nearby dealers who carry those brands. As in previous editions, companies that offer a variety of products sometimes appear in more than one category. The number of double listings, however, has been kept to a minimum, so that as many different companies as possible could be included. New in this edition, web sites and e-mail addresses are included in company listings where available. All companies listed in the **Catalog of Catalogs,** however, offer print catalogs or product information in addition to any product information that might be available on web sites. To ensure that this directory is equally useful to readers with and without Internet access, there are no companies listed that have online catalogs only.

**The Catalog of Catalogs VI** gives you one of the widest possible selections of merchandise to choose from. Retail stores order their inventories from many of the same companies whose catalogs are listed in this book, but stores only have room to display a few items. When you browse through a catalog, you get to see all the possibilities. What's more, you can often save yourself a bundle in the process. First, if you don't live in the state where the mail-order company is based, you might not have to pay sales tax. (A few states have entered into reciprocal arrangements with other states and require that sales tax be paid even on catalog orders.) Second, since mail-order houses don't have to pay for fancy window displays or expensive floor space, they often pass their savings on to you, the catalog shopper.

## Making *The Catalog of Catalogs* Work for You

**The Catalog of Catalogs VI** is a directory for obtaining catalogs and information, not an order catalog. The information given is intended to help you determine which catalogs you would like to have and how to get them.

Many of the catalogs, brochures, price lists, and information packets in **The Catalog of Catalogs VI** are free. In fact, if a company has a web site, you can often view their catalog online for no charge. If you prefer to receive printed information, you can request free information by calling the phone number in the catalog description or by sending in a postcard. Some mail-order companies ask that a business-size, self-addressed, stamped envelope (SASE) accompany requests for catalogs or other information. When this is the case, you'll find the notation "with SASE" immediately following the address in the catalog listing. If there's a charge for a catalog, you'll also find this information right after the address—with information about how much of the charge, if any, is refundable after you place an order.

No matter what the charge for a catalog is, *never send cash through the mail.* Pay by money order or personal check. That way, if you don't receive the information you requested, you'll have proof of your payment. Not that this is likely to happen. In compiling this new edition of **The Catalog of Catalogs,** I reviewed all of the listings in the fifth edition to verify they were still in business, and that their addresses hadn't changed. I sent at least one letter to each company—whether a repeat or new listing—and requested that they verify the information I had on file. However, merchants do go out of business, change their names, combine with other companies, or move to new addresses without notifying the Post Office. In addition, if you are using this book several years after its publication date, you are bound to run into listings—especially of small businesses—that are no longer accurate. I therefore apologize in advance should any of your requests for information go unanswered.

I'm continually updating the information in **The Catalog of Catalogs,** so if any of your catalog requests are returned as undeliverable, I invite you to send me the returned correspondence and any other information available. If I have a more recent address, I'll send it to you. Your requests for this information should be sent to:

Edward L. Palder
The Catalog of Catalogs
P.O. Box 6590
Silver Spring, MD 20906-6590
E-mail: catalogs@erols.com

Please do not send requests for copies of **The Catalog of Catalogs** to this address. Instead, please see the ordering information on page 569.

One final note about ordering catalogs: try to be patient. Catalogs are usually mailed fourth class, and delivery can take from two to three weeks. Possible delays can occur when companies are revising or reprinting their catalogs, and some companies process catalog requests only once or twice a month. Remember, too, that some companies *will not send the information requested unless a SASE is enclosed.*

## Finding the Catalogs You Need

Catalogs in **The Catalog of Catalogs VI** are grouped according to subject matter. For example, all catalogs of musical instruments are listed in the *Musical Instruments* section, and all food catalogs appear in the *Foods* section. Long sections are further divided into subsections. The *Musical Instruments* section, for example, is subdivided into the categories of Accordians; Folk & Traditional Instruments; Guitars & Other Stringed Instruments; Harmonicas; Keyboard Instruments; Percussion Instruments; and Wind Instruments. In the *Foods* section, catalogs featuring Cakes & Cookies; Maple Syrup; Meats; and other types of food are grouped together.

Within **The Catalog of Catalogs VI,** subjects are listed alphabetically, from *Air Compressors* to *Yoga.* Within each subject area, I've listed catalogs alphabetically by company name. *Silver Eagle Creations* comes before *Silver Nugget,* and so on. Please note that when a company name begins with a personal name, it is alphabetized by last name, instead of first name. For example, *Earl May Seeds & Nursery Company*, is alphabetized as though it began with an "M" instead of an "E"; *L.L. Bean* is alphabetized as if it began with a "B." Also, names that include numerals are alphabetized as though the numerals were spelled out.

You can find catalogs within **The Catalog of Catalogs VI** two ways: 1) under a company's name, or 2) according to the type of product sold. To locate the catalog of a company whose name you already know, simply turn to the Corporate Index near the end of the book. This index lists the names of company listed in **The Catalog of Catalogs VI,** alphabetized according to the rules outlined above. Sometimes a company is listed more than once because it carries several different types of products. To locate catalogs that offer a specific type of product, check the Table of Contents first. Like the book as a whole, the Table of Contents is arranged alphabetically by subject. So if you were looking for catalogs of pet supplies, you'd turn to the "P's" in the Table of Contents to find the page number you needed.

If you can't find exactly what you're looking for in the Table of Contents, turn to the Subject Index at the very back of the book. Here I've listed topics under as many alternate names as I could think of—for example, the words "dishes" and "plates" will refer you to the pages listing suppliers of china. Through cross references ("see also's") the Subject

Index can also direct you to related topics you might otherwise overlook. For instance, the listing for *Greeting Cards* instructs you to see also *Birth Announcements* and *Wedding Invitations.*

# Your Mail-Order Rights

Shopping by mail can be fun and adventuresome, but it's not entirely without its hassles. Although I made every effort to ensure that **The Catalog of Catalogs VI** includes only reputable merchants, sometimes your catalog orders may be damaged in transit, fail to live up to your expectations, take too long to be delivered, or never arrive. Fortunately, in each of these instances, you can take steps to get a refund, repairs, or replacement.

## Packages Damaged in Transit

Let's start with the simplest situation. If something you've ordered arrives with obvious damage to the package, write "refused" on the wrapper and return it unopened. Don't sign for it if it arrives insured, registered, certified, or C.O.D., or you'll have to pay the return postage. If you don't discover that your merchandise is damaged until you've opened the package, repackage it with a note describing the problem. Then mail it back by certified or insured mail and wait for the company to send you a free replacement.

## Unsatisfactory Merchandise

What if something you ordered breaks soon *after* it arrives, or is unsatisfactory for other reasons (it's the wrong size, shoddily made, or completely different from the description in the catalog)? In this case, your next step depends on the exchange policy of the company you ordered from. Many companies allow you to return unsatisfactory merchandise within thirty days after purchase; others offer unconditional money-back guarantees for the lifetime of their products. Check a company's warranty policies *before you buy.* A bargain is no bargain if it comes without a guarantee. Consult the catalog for the company's return policies and for any special procedures to be followed when returning merchandise for a replacement or refund.

If the company has no stated returns policy, don't give up. Noted consumer activist David Horowitz recommends that you send back the unsatisfactory item with a letter explaining why you're disappointed, a copy of your proof of purchase (cancelled check, money order, or credit card statement), and a copy of the original ad. If you don't receive a reply within two weeks, place a collect call to the president of the company to ask what action he or she intends to take. (Horowitz notes that you may not get through to the president, but should at least find out his or her name.) If your phone call doesn't resolve your problem, write a letter to the president informing him that you'll contact the deputy chief postal inspector in his region if you don't get a refund or replacement in seven days. Then do what you said you would. Bring copies of your letters and proof of purchase to the local post office and fill out a Consumer Service form. Your postmaster will turn the matter over to the postal inspectors and the Post Office Consumer Advocate for investigation of possible fraud.

As an alternative to involving the post office, you can also register a complaint with the Mail Order Action Line (MOAL) of the Direct Marketing Association. The MOAL acts as an intermediary between consumers and companies that sell products through the mail, over the phone, or over the Internet. You can contact the MOAL by sending a written description of the dispute, together with photocopies of cancelled checks or other relevant documents, to: Mail Order Action Line, Direct Marketing Association, 1111 19th Street, NW, Suite 1100, Washington, DC 20036.

## Delayed or Missing Orders

What if your order never arrives? What if you wait days or weeks longer than the delivery time promised in the catalog and still no package? Under the Mail or Telephone Order Merchandise Rule of the Federal Trade Commission, you can take immediate recourse. This rule requires a company to ship your order within the time promised in its ad or within thirty days of receiving your order and payment. In case of delay, the merchant must notify you of the new shipment date. If the new date is more than thirty days later than the original date, you can cancel your order (in writing) for a full refund. If the new date is less than thirty days later, you can still cancel for a refund, but if you don't respond, it means that you accept the new date. In either case, it is advisable to send your reply by registered or certified mail so you have a return receipt to show that your letter was delivered.

The merchant must refund your money within ten days of receiving your cancellation (or notify your credit card company within one billing cycle to credit your account). If the merchant does not give you a refund, credit, or the merchandise, take or send a copy of your letter and proof of payment to the: Mail Order Action Line, Direct Marketing Association, 1111 19th St. NW, Suite 1100, Washington, DC 20036. If the merchant is a member of the DMA, the Association can pressure the merchant to refund your money.

### Preventing and Reducing Problems

I hope you don't run into any of the problems described above, but on the off chance that you might, there are several precautions that can make resolution of problems easier. When in doubt about a product, contact the merchant *before you buy* for information about warranties, exchange policies, missing facts, or unbelievable claims. Also make sure you fill out the order form accurately and completely, and enclose all shipping and handling charges requested by the company. And finally, always pay by check, money order, or credit card so you have proof of payment. Keep a record of the name and address of the company, the merchandise ordered, the date you placed the order, the name of the publication in which the merchandise was described, and the number of your money order or check.

## A Word about Shopping Online

This edition of the **Catalog of Catalogs** includes web sites for about a third of the companies listed. The web site addresses are underlined and appear in italics at the end of listings. Please note that to dial up a web site, you will need to type **http://** in front of the address given in this book. Be aware that companies switch web sites even more frequently than they change addresses, and they don't always leave a forwarding address at their old web site. If you encounter this problem, the easiest solution is to call the company and ask for their new web site.

You will find that no two web sites are designed quite the same. Some companies choose to display only a sample of their products, with contact phone numbers or e-mail addresses for requesting more information. Other companies display the same information that is in their print catalogs on their web sites, and may or may not allow orders to be placed over the Internet. Still other companies offer special deals that may be available only to customers who visit their web site, or informational articles of interest to their customers. If you are intrigued by a company's listing in the **Catalog of Catalogs,** it is often well worth your effort to check out the company's web site.

If you have not previously ordered products online, you may be concerned about how safe it is to send personal information out over the Internet. In truth, ordering online is as safe as ordering through the mail, so long as you observe a few simple precautions. The Federal Trade Commission (FTC) recommends that you follow these steps:

- **Use a secure browser.** Your browser is the software such as Microsoft Internet Explorer or Netscape that enables you to connect to web sites and explore the Internet. Secure browsers scramble credit card numbers and other personal information that you send over the Internet. Generally, if you try to place an order using a browser that is not secure, you will get a message letting you know that your browser is not secure, and asking you if you wish to proceed with your order.

- **Shop with companies you know.** If you are unsure about a company's reputation or the quality of its products, request a paper catalog before you order.

- **Keep your password(s) private.** Before you place an order over the Internet, companies will usually ask you to choose a password that you will use whenever you are placing an order with them or inquiring about your account. Do not choose an obvious password such as your birth date. Be creative and come up with something that is meaningful to you alone.

- **Pay by credit or charge card.** If you do, you will be protected by the Fair Credit Billing Act. This gives you certain rights to dispute erroneous charges and withhold payment. It also usually limits your liability to $50 if an unauthorized user makes purchases using your credit card number.

- **Keep a record.** Print out a copy of your order and confirmation number when your online order is complete.

Like other companies, those that do business over the Internet are required to abide by the Mail or Telephone Order Merchandise Rule. That is, you must receive your order within 30 days, unless you are informed up front that there will be a delay.

For more information on placing orders over the Internet, unsolicited e-mail, or other Internet subjects, visit the FTC's web site at http://www.ftc.gov/ (no period). You can also request print copies of the FTC's publications about the Internet by contacting the Consumer Response Center, Federal Trade Commission, Washington, DC 20580; 202-FTC-HELP. If you are plagued by junk e-mail, particularly e-mail that you suspect is fraudulent, you can contact the National Fraud Information Center for help and information at P.O. Box 65868, Washington, DC 20035; 800-876-7060. You can also report fraudulent e-mail through the NFIC's web site at http://www.fraud.org (no period).

## Let the World Come to You

Now that you know the ground rules of mail-order shopping **The Catalog of Catalogs** way, why not take a moment to glance through the Table of Contents and Subject Index? I hope you will not only find what you are looking for, but also hundreds of other teasers you'll want to send away for. Don't resist the urge! Ordering by mail is by far the easiest, most convenient, and most cost-effective way I know of to shop. It can also be highly addictive, as the long-suffering mail carrier who delivers all my catalogs and packages can attest. But don't worry. In the event you ever want to break the habit of catalog shopping, you can have your name removed from many merchants' mailing lists by contacting the Mail Preference Service, Direct Marketing Association, P.O. Box 9008, Farmingdale, NY 11735-9008. So, sit back and take advantage of all **The Catalog of Catalogs VI** has to offer you. Send away for what you want, and let the world come to you.

## AIR COMPRESSORS

**Campbell Hausfeld,** 100 Production Dr., Harrison, OH 45030: Free information ◆ Air compressors, pneumatic tools, and paint sprayers. 800-543-8622; 13-367-4811 (in OH). www.grizzlyimports.com/campair.html

**Coleman Powermate Compressors,** 118 W. Rock St., P.O. Box 206, Springfield, MN 56087: Free information ◆ Air compressors. 800-445-1805.

**DeVilbiss,** 213 Industrial Dr., Jackson, TN 38301: Free brochure ◆ Air compressors and air-operated tools. 800-888-2468; 901-423-7931 (in TN).

**Stanley-Bostitch Inc.,** Briggs Dr., East Greenwich, RI 02818: Free information ◆ Air compressors. 800-556-6696. www.stanleyworks.com

## AIR CONDITIONERS & CONTROLS

**Barnett Inc.,** 333 Lenox Ave., Jacksonville, FL 32254: Free catalog ◆ Plumbing, HVAC, hardware, and electrical products. 904-384-6530. www.bntt.com

**Carrier Corp.,** Box 408, Syracuse, NY 13221: Free information ◆ Furnaces, heat pumps, and air conditioners. 800-227-7437. www.carrier.com

**G.E. Appliances,** General Electric Company, Appliance Park, Louisville, KY 40225: Free information ◆ Air conditioners and heat pumps. 800-626-2000. www.ge.com

**Hunter Fan Company,** 2500 Fisco Ave., Memphis, TN 38114: Brochure $1 ◆ Programmable thermostats. 901-745-9222. www.hunterfan.com

**Sanyo Fisher Service Corp.,** 1411 W. 190th St., Ste. 800, Gardena, CA 90248: Free information with a long SASE ◆ Ductless split system air conditioners.

**Thomas Industries Inc.,** 1419 Illinois Ave., Sheboygan, WI 53082: Free information ◆ Air conditioners. 414-457-4891.

## AIR PURIFIERS

**Advanced AirCare Inc.,** 281 Delsea Dr., Sewell, NJ 08080: Free brochure ◆ Systems for improving air quality. 800-304-9301. advanced@jersey.net

**Air-Care,** Division DPL Enterprises Inc., 5115 S. Industrial Rd., Ste. 506, Las Vegas, NV 89118: Free catalog ◆ Air cleaning equipment for indoor settings. 800-322-9919; 702-736-4063 (in NV). Info@Air-Care.com

**Austin Air Systems Ltd.,** 701 Seneca St., Buffalo, NY 14210: Free information ◆ Air cleaners for the home. 800-724-8403. www.austinair.com

**Carrier Corp.,** Box 408, Syracuse, NY 13221: Free information ◆ Electronic air cleaners. 800-227-7437. www.carrier.com

**Des Champs Laboratories Inc.,** 66 Okner Pkwy., Livingston, NJ 07039: Free list of retail sources ◆ Heat recovery ventilation systems for indoor air pollution. 540-291-1111. www.thomasregister.com/olc/deschamps

**Environtrol Corp.,** 12015 Manchester Rd., St. Louis, MO 63130: Free catalog ◆ Air purification systems for use at home, work, or during travel. 800-423-1982; 314-966-6686 (in MO).

**HealthWay,** P.O. Box 2729, Syracuse, NY 13220: Free brochure ◆ Micro-processor controlled air purifiers for the home and office. 315-463-0240.

**Hepalta Purified Air Inc.,** 16406 117th Ave., Edmonton, Alberta, Canada T5M 3W2: Free brochure ◆ Free-standing, central, or portable air filter systems. 800-268-7485. www.breatheasy.com

**Honeywell Inc.,** Customer Assistance Center, P.O. Box 524, Minneapolis, MN 55440: Free information ◆ Electronic air cleaners. 800-345-6770. www.honeywell.com

**IEP Air Cleaners,** 27 Sunnyside Rd., Scotia, NY 12302: Free information ◆ Air cleaners for the home.

**Isolate Inc.,** P.O. Box 40794, Houston, TX 77240: Free information ◆ Air cleaners for the home. 713-937-9393. www.isolate.com

**Kool-O-Matic Corp.,** P.O. Box 310, 1831 Terminal Rd., Niles, MI 49120: Free information ◆ Attic space ventilators with thermostat and humidifier controls. Also room and whole-house variable speed ventilation systems. 616-683-2600.

**Nortec Industries,** Box 698, Ogdensburg, NY 13669: Free information ◆ Home air filters. 315-425-1255.

**Priorities,** 70 Walnut St., Wellesley, MA 02181: Free catalog ◆ Air filter systems for allergy relief and a healthy home environment. 800-553-5398. getrelief@priorities.com

**Sanyo Fisher Service Corp.,** 1411 W. 190th St., Ste. 800, Gardena, CA 90248: Free information with long SASE ◆ Electrostatic air cleaner/ionizer with a smoke sensor.

## AIRCRAFT & AERO ACTIVITIES

### Aircraft Kits (Fixed Wing Powered)

**Aircraft Technologies,** 4265 Lilburn Ind. Way, Lilburn, GA 3027: Free information ◆ Two-person side-by-side low-wing aircraft. 770-806-9098.

**Avid Aircraft,** P.O. Box 728, Caldwell, ID 83606: Information $13 (specify model) ◆ Two-place high-wing aircraft and three-place amphibian. 208-454-2600. www.avidair.com

**CGS Aviation Inc.,** P.O. Box 470635, Broadview Hts., OH 44147: Information packet $10 ◆ High-wing ultralight aircraft. 216-632-1424. www.cgsaviation.com

**Classic Composites LLC,** 15425 Dayton Pike, Box 716, Sale Creek, TN 37373: Brochure and video $28 ◆ Four-person canard. 423-332-8300.

**Composite Companions Inc.,** 15425 Dayton Pike, Sale Creek, TN 37373: Free information ◆ Four-place canard airframe in a pre-molded quick-build kit. 423-332-8300. www.glassic.com

**Europa Aviation,** 3400 Airfield Dr. West, Lakeland, FL 33811: Information package $25 ◆ Two-place low-wing aircraft. 941-647-5355. europa@gate.net

**Falconar AVIA,** 7739 81st Ave., Edmonton, Alberta, Canada T6C 0V4: Information $10 (specify model) ◆ One and two-place low-wing aircraft and two-place low-wing amphibian. 403-465-2024.

**Fisher Aero Corp.,** 7118 SR 335, Portsmouth, OH 45662: Information $8 (specify model) ◆ One and two-place biplanes and two-place side-by-side high-wing aircraft. 614-820-2219.

**Fisher Flying Products Inc.,** P.O. Box 468, Edgeley, ND 58433: Information $5 (specify model) ◆ Two-place biplane and one and two-place high-wing or one-place low-wing aircraft. 701-493-2286. www.fisherflying.com

**Flightstar,** P.O. Box 760, Ellington, CT 06029: Free brochure ◆ One and two-place high-wing ultralight aircraft. 860-875-8185.

**Golden Circle Air Inc.,** 10 Ellefson Dr., Box 676, De Soto, IA 50069: Information packet $5 ◆ Two-person side-by-side ultralight. 515-834-2225.

**Hipp's Superbird's Inc.,** P.O. Box 266, Saluda, NC 28773: Information $5 ◆ One-place high-wing aircraft. 704-749-3986.

**Innovation Engineering Inc.,** Davenport Municipal Airport, 8970 Harrison, Davenport, IA 52804: Information $5 ◆ Pusher-type two-place high-wing aircraft. 319-386-6966.

**Keuthan Aircraft Corp.,** 910 Airport Rd., Merritt Island, FL 32952: Free information ◆ Two-place side-by-side amphibian. 407-459-3200.

**Kolb Company Inc.,** RD 3, Box 38, Phoenixville, PA 19460: Information $5 ◆ One and two-place high-wing aircraft. 610-948-4136. www.kolbaircraft.com

**Laron Aviation Technologies,** P.O. Box 5026, Borger, TX 79008: Information $10 ◆ One and two-place high-wing aircraft. 806-273-8513. www.thebook.com/laronaviation

**Leading Edge Air Foils Inc.,** 8242 Cessna Dr., Peyton, CO 80831: Catalog $6.95 ◆ One and two-place open-cockpit biplane. 719-683-5323. www.leadingedge-airfoils.com

**Light Miniature Aircraft,** 19695 NW 80th Dr., Okeechobee, FL 34972: Information $7.50 (specify model) ◆ One and two-place high-wing aircraft. 941-467-0933.

**Lockwood Aircraft Corp.,** 280-B Hendricks Way, Sebring, FL 33870: Information $20 ◆ Two place twin-engine pusher-type utility sport plane. 941-655-4242.

**Loehle Aviation Inc.,** 380 Shipmans Creek Rd., Wartrace, TN 37183: Information $10 (specify model) ◆ One-place low-wing and high-wing aircraft. 615-857-3419. loehle@edge.net

**Merlin Aircraft Inc.,** 509 Airport Rd., Muskegon, MI 49441: Information $10 (specify model) ◆ Two-place pontoon and two-place high-wing aircraft. 616-798-1622.

**Mirage Aircraft Inc.,** 1091 W. Sahara Palms Dr., Tucson, AZ 85704: Brochure $7.50 ◆ Two-person low-wing aircraft. 520-797-2161.

**Murphy Aircraft Manufacturing Ltd.,** 8155-K Aitken Rd., Chilliwack, British Columbia, Canada V2R 4H5: Information $20 (specify model) ◆ Two-place biplane, two-place pontoon aircraft, and two and four-place high-wing monoplanes. 604-792-5855. www.murphyair.com

**Mustang Aeronautics,** 1470 Temple City, Troy, MI 48084: Information packet $10 ◆ Easy-to-build two-person aircraft. 810-589-9277. MustAir@wwnet.com

**Neico Aviation Inc.,** 2244 Airport Way, Redmond, OR 97756: Information $15 (specify model) ◆ Two and four-place low-wing aircraft. 541-923-2244.

**Barney Oldfield Aircraft Company,** P.O. Box 228, Needham, MA 02192: Information $10 (specify model) ◆ One and two-place biplanes. 781-444-5480.

**Osprey Aircraft,** 3741 El Ricon Way, Sacramento, CA 95864: Information $15 (specify model) ◆ Pusher-type two-place amphibian and two-place low-wing aircraft. 916-483-3004.

**Phantom Sport Airplane,** P.O. Box 249, Southern Pines, NC 28388: Brochure $2 ◆ One-place high-wing amphibian. 910-947-4744.

**Preceptor Aircraft,** 1230 Shepard St., Hendersonville, NC 28792: Information $5 ◆ Two-place high-wing airplane with folding wings. 704-697-8284.

**Progressive Aerodyne,** 520 Clifton St., Orlando, FL 32808: Information $2 ◆ Two-place pusher-type high-wing amphibian. 407-292-3700.

**Quad City Ultralight Aircraft,** 201-939-0252, Moline, IL 61266: Information $5 (specify model) ◆ One and two-place high-wing aircraft. 309-764-3515. daveatqcu@aol.com

**Quicksilver Enterprises,** P.O. Box 1572, Temecula, CA 92390: Information $6 (specify model) ◆ One and two-place high-wing aircraft with tricycle landing gear. 909-676-6886.

**Quikkit,** 9002 Summer Glen, Dallas, TX 75243: Information and video $22.50 ◆ Two-place amphibian. 972-349-0462.

**Rand-Robinson Engineering Inc.,** 15641 Product Ln., Huntington Beach, CA 92649: Information $8 (specify model) ◆ One and two-place low-wing aircraft. 714-898-3811. pilot@fly-kr.com

**Rans Company,** 4600 Hwy. 183 Alternate, Hays, KS 67601: Catalog $15 (specify model) ◆ Two-place low-wing and one and two-place high-wing aircraft. 913-625-6346.

**Skystar Aircraft Corp.,** 100 N. Kings Rd., Nampa, ID 83687: Information $15 ◆ Two-place high-wing aircraft. 800-554-8369. www.skystar.com

**Spencer Amphibian Aircraft,** P.O. Box 327, Kansas, IL 61933: Information $10 ◆ Four-place amphibian. 217-948-5505.

**Stoddard-Hamilton Aircraft Inc.,** 18701 58th Ave. NE, Arlington, WA 98223: Information $25 (specify model) ◆ Two-place low-wing and high-wing aircraft. 360-435-8533. glasair@stoddard-hamilton.com

**Stolp Starduster Corp.,** 4301 Twining Flabob Airport, Riverside, CA 95209: Information $5 (specify model) ◆ One and two-place biplanes. 909-686-7943.

**TEAM Inc.,** 10790 Ivy Bluff Rd., Bradyville, TN 37026: Information $5 (specify model) ◆ One-place mid and high-wing aircraft. 615-765-5397. www.tval.com/TEAM

**Titan Aircraft,** 2730 Walter Main Rd., Geneva, OH 44041: Information $10 ◆ Pusher-type one and two-place high-wing aircraft. 216-466-0602.

**Tri-R Technologies,** 1114 E. 5th St., Oxnard, CA 93030: Information $10 ◆ Two-place low-wing sport airplane. 805-385-3680.

**Van's Aircraft Inc.,** P.O. Box 160, North Plains, OR 97133: Information $8 (specify model) ◆ One and two-place low-wing aircraft. 503-647-5117. www.vansaircraft.com

**Velocity Aircraft,** 200 W. Airport Rd., Sebastian, FL 32958: Information $29.50 ◆ Four-place canard pusher-type airplane. 561-589-1860. www.velocityaircraft.com

**Viking Aircraft Inc.,** P.O. Box 646, Elkhorn, WI 53121: Information $10 ◆ Two-place low-wing and canard aircraft. 414-723-1048. viking@pensys.com

**Zenith Aircraft Company,** P.O. Box 650, Mexico, MO 65265: Information $15 (specify model) ◆ Two-place low and high-wing aircraft. 573-581-9000. www.zenithair.com

## Aircraft Kits (Helicopters & Gyroplanes)

**Air Command International Inc.,** 702 Cooper Dr., P.O. Box 1345, Wylie, TX 75098: Information $12.50 ◆ Gyroplanes. 214-442-6694.

**Barnett Rotorcraft,** 4307 Olivehurst Ave., Olivehurst, CA 95961: Information $15 (specify model) ◆ One and two-place gyroplanes. 916-742-7416.

**Ken Brock Manufacturing,** 11852 Western Ave., Stanton, CA 90680: Information $7 ◆ One-place gyroplane and parts. 714-898-4366.

**Canadian Home Rotors Inc.,** P.O. Box 370, Ear Falls, Ontario, Canada P0V 1T0: Free information ◆ Two-place helicopter kit. 807-222-2474.

**Revolution Helicopter Corp.,** 1905 W. Jesse James Rd., Excelsior Springs, MO 64024: Information $15 ◆ Easy-to-assemble one-place helicopter. 800-637-6867. www.revolutionhelicopter.com

**Robinson Helicopter Company,** 2901 Airport Dr., Torrance, CA 90505: Free information ◆ One-place helicopter. 562-539-0508.

**Rotary Air Force Inc.,** Box 1236, Kindersley, Saskatchewan, Canada S0L 1S0: Information $12 ◆ Cross-country gyroplane. 306-463-6030. www.raf2000.com

**RotorWay International,** 4140 Mercury Way, Chandler, AZ 85226: Brochure $15 (specify model) ◆ One and two-place gyroplanes. 602-961-1001. www.rotorway.com

**Sport Copter,** Scappoose Airport, 34012 N. Honeyman Rd., Scappoose, OR 97056: Information $12 (specify model) ◆ Ultralight one-place and two-place gyroplanes. 503-543-7000.

**Star Aviation Inc.,** 821 Lone Star Dr., New Braunfels, TX 78130: Information $15 ◆ Easy-to-build helicopter kit. 210-608-9001.

**Vertical Aviation Technologies Inc.,** P.O. Box 2527, Sanford, FL 32772: Information $15 ◆ Easy-to-build sport helicopter. 407-322-9488.

**Vortech Inc.,** P.O. Box 511, Fallston, MD 21047: Information $10 ◆ One-place ultra-compact helicopter. 410-337-0212. www.webcom.com/neatstuf/helio

## Aircraft Kits (Sailplanes & Motorgliders)

**Falconar AVIA,** 7739 81st Ave., Edmonton, Alberta, Canada T6C 0V4: Information $10 ◆ One-place sailplane. 403-465-2024.

**Group Genesis Inc.,** 1530 Pole Lake Rd., Marion, OH 43302: Information $10 ◆ One-place sailplane. 614-387-9464.

**Marske Aircraft,** 975 Loire Valley Dr., Marion, OH 43302: Information $8 (specify model) ◆ One-place high and mid-wing sailplanes. 614-389-3776.

## Aircraft Recovery Systems & Para-Gear

**Body Sport USA,** 1621 Oak Ave., St. Helena, CA 94574: Free information ◆ Clothing for skydivers. 800-586-7784. www.bodysportusa.com

**BRS Parachutes,** 1845 Henry Ave., South St. Paul, MN 55075: Free information ◆ Emergency parachutes for sport planes. 612-875-8185.

**D.L.T. Designs,** P.O. Box 934, Angwin, CA 94508: Free information ◆ Skydiving jump suits. 707-965-1126.

**Para-Gear Equipment Company Inc.,** 3839 W. Oakton St., Skokie, IL 60076: Catalog $2 ◆ Sport parachuting equipment. 800-323-0437; 847-679-5905 (in IL). info@para-gear.com

**The PD Source Inc.,** P.O. Box 185, DeLand, FL 32721: Free information ◆ Instruments, clothing, videos, helmets, and skydiving equipment. 800-222-0482. www.pdsource.com

**Precision Aerodynamics Inc.,** P.O. Box 691, Dunlap, TX 37327: Free information ◆ Skydiving equipment. 423-949-4688. www.precision.aerodynamics.com

**Square One Parachute Sales & Service,** 425 W. Rider St., Perris, CA 92571: Free information ◆ Skydiving gear. 800-877-7191. www.square1.com

**Sunshine Factory,** 38529 5th Ave., Zephyrhills, FL 33540: Free information ◆ Parachuting gear. 800-266-1883; 813-788-9831 (in FL). sunshine-factory@msn.com

## Avionics & Communications Equipment

**Aircraft Spruce & Specialty,** 225 Airport Circle, Corona, CA 91720: Catalog $5 ◆ Avionics equipment. 800-824-1930; 714-870-7551 (in CA). www.aircraft-spruce.com

**AirStar Sales,** 2251 Shady Willow Ln., Brentwood, CA 94513: Catalog $5 ◆ Avionics and radio equipment. 800-AIRSTAR.

**Airwich Avionics Inc.,** 1611 S. Eisenhower, Wichita, KS 67209: Free brochure ◆ Used and repaired avionics equipment. 316-942-8721.

**AlliedSignal General Aviation Avionics,** 400 N. Rogers Rd., Olathe, KS 66062: Free information ◆ Instrument displays, flight controls, and communications, navigation, and identification systems. 913-768-3000.

**American Avionics Inc.,** 7675 Perimeter Rd. South, Seattle, WA 98108: Free brochure ◆ New and used avionics equipment. 800-518-5858; 206-767-9781 (in WA). www.americanavionics.com

**Avion Research Corp.,** 1022 W. Maude Ave., Ste. 102, Sunnyvale, CA 94086: Free brochure ◆ Replacement aircraft instrument panels, glare shields, and control wheels. 408-738-1690. www.avion.com

**Century Instrument Corp.,** 4440 Southeast Blvd., Wichita, KS 67210: Free catalog ◆ Rebuilt avionics equipment. 800-733-0116; 316-683-7571 (in KS).

**Chief Aircraft Inc.,** 1301 Brookside Blvd., Grants Pass, OR 97526: Free information ◆ Avionics, communication, and other equipment. 800-447-3408. www.chiefaircraft.com

**David Clark Company Inc.,** 360 Franklin St., Box 15054, Worcester, MA 01615: Free information ◆ Aircraft intercom and communications equipment. 508-756-6216.

**DayStar Avionics,** 1150 Airport Dr., Burlington International Airport, South Burlington, VT 05403: Free information ◆ Avionics equipment. 802-862-8900.

**Eventide Avionics,** One Alsan Way, Little Ferry, NJ 07643: Free information ◆ Avionics equipment. 201-641-1200.

## Flight Planning Software

**Jeppesen,** 55 Inverness Dr. East, Englewood, CO 80112: Free information ◆ Flight planning and training, logging and record-keeping, moving map software, and marine navigation software. 800-628-4640. jeppesen.com

**Flightcom,** 7340 SW Durham Rd., Portland, OR 97224: Free information ◆ Communications equipment. 800-432-4342. www.flight/com.com

**Flytec,** 14020 NW 23rd Ave., Gainesville, FL 32606: Free information ◆ Flight instruments. 800-662-2449. usaflytec@aol.com

**Marv Golden Discount Sales Inc.,** 8690 Aero Dr., San Diego, CA 92123: Free catalog ◆ Headsets and other equipment. 800-348-0014. www.marvgolden.com

**Gulf-Coast Avionics,** 4243 N. Westshore Blvd., Tampa International Airport, Tampa, FL 33614: Free catalog ◆ Ready-to-install custom instrument panels for kit planes and avionics equipment. 800-474-9714; 813-879-9714 (in FL). www.gulf-coast-avionics.com

**Horizon Instruments Inc.,** 556 S. Saint College Blvd., Fullerton, CA 92631: Free information ◆ Compact high-visibility engine instruments. 800-541-8128. members.aol.com/horizonins

**ICOM America,** 2380 116th Ave. NE, Bellevue, WA 98004: Free list of retail sources ◆ Avionics equipment. 800-999-9877. www.icomamerica.com

**IIMorrow,** 2345 Turner Rd. South, Salem, OR 97302: Free information ◆ Avionics equipment. 800-525-6726. www.iimorrow.com

**J.P. Instruments,** P.O. Box 7033, Huntington Beach, CA 92615: Free information ◆ Engine instrumentation with miniature gauges. 714-557-5434. www.jpinstruments.com

**Leading Edge Air Foils Inc.,** 8242 Cessna Dr., Peyton, CO 80831: Catalog $6.95 ◆ Avionics instruments. 719-683-5323. www.leadingedge-airfoils.com

**Microflight Products Inc.,** 16141 Pine Ridge Rd., Fort Myers, FL 33908: Catalog $3 ◆ Communication systems, instruments, and avionics equipment. 800-247-6955.

**Narco Avionics,** 270 Commerce Dr., Fort Washington, PA 19034: Free information ◆ Avionics equipment. 215-643-2900.

**Northstar Avionics,** 30 Sudbury Rd., Acton, MA 01720: Free information ◆ Avionics equipment. 800-628-4487. www.northstarcmc.com

**Pacific Coast Avionics,** 22783 Airport Rd., Aurora, OR 97002: Free information ◆ Avionics instruments. 800-353-0370; 503-678-6242 (in OR). pca@pacavionic.com

**PS Engineering,** 9800 Martel Rd., Lenoir City, TN 37771: Free information ◆ Aircraft intercoms. 423-988-9800.

**RMS Technology Inc.,** 124 Berkley, P.O. Box 249, Molalla, OR 97038: Free information ◆ Flight planning and moving map software. 800-533-3211. www.RMSTek.com

**San-Val Discount,** 7444 Valjean Ave., Van Nuys, CA 91406: Free information ◆ Aircraft accessories, avionics equipment, and pilot supplies. 818-786-8274.

**Sennheiser Electronics,** P.O. Box 987, Old Lyme, CT 06371: Free information ◆ Headsets and other communications equipment. 203-434-9190 (voice/TDD). www.sennheiserusa.com/2

**Sigtronics,** 822 N. Dodsworth Ave., Covina, CA 91724: Free information ◆ Voice-activated panel-mounted intercom with automatic squelch. Also other communications equipment. 626-915-1993. www.aviation-rha.com/SIGTRO~1.HTM

**SkySports,** Hangar 1, LindenAirport, Linden, MI 48451: Free catalog ◆ Instruments, avionics, and accessories for sport and ultralight aircraft. 800-AIR-STUF. airstuff.com

**Vision Microsystems Inc.,** 4071 Hannegan Rd., St. T, Bellingham, WA 98226: Free information ◆ Engine monitoring system with easy-to-read graphics and digital readout. 360-714-8203.

## Hang Gliding, Powered Parachutes & Trikes

**AeroImports,** 501 W. San Juan Ave., Phoenix, AZ 85013: Free information ◆ Powered parachutes with trikes. 602-285-4094.

**AirBorne USA,** P.O. Box 579, Asotin, WA 99402: Free information ◆ Powered parachutes with trikes. 509-243-4988.

**Ascending Parachutes International,** 1341 E. 5150 South, Ogden, UT 84403: Free information ◆ Powered parachutes. 801-479-FLY1.

**British School of Paragliding,** P.O. Box 50382, Henderson, NV 89016: Free information ◆ Powered parachutes. 702-896-6000.

**Buckeye Powered Parachutes Inc.,** 16111 Linden Rd., Argos, IN 46501: Information $5 ◆ Powered parachutes. 219-892-5566.

**EASYUP,** 1089 Medford Center, Medford, OR 97504: Free information ◆ Backpack-powered parachutes.

**Fletcher's Ultralights,** 2165 Xavier Ave., Turlock, CA 95380: Free information ◆ Powered parachutes with trikes. 209-667-4397.

**Harmening's High Flyers Inc.,** Powerized Parachutes, 15487 State Rt. 72, Genoa, IL 60135: Video $15 ◆ One and two-person powered parachutes. 815-784-5876.

**Kemmeries Aviation,** 8710 W. Carefree Hwy., Peoria, AZ 85382: Free information ◆ Powered parachutes with trikes. 602-566-8026. www.sportplanes.com/kemries.htm

**Para-Flyer,** 3510 County Rd. 63, Rosharon, TX 77583: Free information ◆ Powered parachutes with trikes. 713-369-2441.

**Paramarketing Inc.,** 237 South, Oyster Bay, NY 11771: Free information ◆ Powered parachutes. 516-922-1032. www.paramotor.com

**ParaPlane International,** 68 Stacy Haines Rd., Medford, NJ 08055: Free information ◆ Two-person powered parachute. 609-261-1234.

**Parascender Technologies Inc.,** 1040 E. Carroll St., Kissimmee, FL 34744: Free information; video $20 ◆ One-person powered parachute. 407-935-0775. www.iag.net/~para

**Paratrek Flying Club,** 121366 Poplar Rd., Auburn, CA 95602: Free information ◆ Powered parachutes. 916-995-8676.

**Personal Flight Inc.,** 1819 Central Ave. South, Kent, WA 98032: Free information ◆ Backpack-powered parachutes. 800-685-8238. www.personalflight.com

**Phoenix Industries Inc.,** 738 Maple Ave., Southampton, NJ 08008: Free information ◆ Powered parachutes. 609-267-7088. www.paraflyer.com

**Raisner Aircraft Depot,** 8242 Cessna Dr., Peyton, CO 80831: Free information ◆ Powered parachutes with trikes. 719-683-4357. info@leadingedge-airfoils.com

**Six-Chuter Inc.,** P.O. Box 8331, Yakima, WA 98903: Free information ◆ Sky-riding aero-chute for one and two-persons. 509-966-8211.

## Parts & Tools

**Aircraft Spruce & Specialty,** 225 Airport Circle, Corona, CA 91720: Catalog $5 ◆ Tools, construction materials, instruments, engines, pilot supplies, and books. 800-824-1930; 714-870-7551 (in CA). www.aircraft-spruce.com

**Aircraft Tool & Supply,** 1000 Old US 23, Oscoda, MI 48750: Free information ◆ Test equipment, sheet metal, tools, and fasteners. 800-248-0638; 517-739-1447 (in MI). www.aircraft-tool.com

**Alexander Aeroplane Company Inc.,** P.O. Box 909, Griffin, GA 30224: Free catalog ◆ Aircraft building supplies. 800-831-2949. www.aircraft-spruce.com

**California Power Systems Inc.,** 790 139th Ave., San Leandro, CA 94578: Catalog $6.95 ◆ Ultralight aircraft parts. 800-247-9653. www.800-airwolf.com

**Leading Edge Air Foils Inc.,** 8242 Cessna Dr., Peyton, CO 80831: Catalog $6.95 ◆ Aircraft building materials, hardware, tools, engines and propellers, and books. 719-683-5323. www.leadingedge-airfoils.com

**Wil Neubert Aircraft Supply,** 1488 St. Rt. 162, Sprakers, NY 12166: Catalog $5 (refundable) ◆ Avionics equipment, engines, radios and antennas, aircraft components, engine mounts, hardware, and batteries. 518-922-5830.

**Poly Fiber Aircraft Coatings,** P.O. Box 3129, Riverside, CA 92519: Free information ◆ Fabric for covering aircraft. 800-362-3490. www.polyfiber.com

**San-Val Discount,** 7444 Valjean Ave., Van Nuys, CA 91406: Free information ◆ Aircraft accessories, avionics equipment, and pilot supplies. 818-786-8274.

**Tuthill Corp.,** Cablecraft Division, 4401 S. Orchard St., P.O. Box 11372, Tacoma, WA 98411: Free brochure ◆ Control cables for home built aircraft. 206-475-1080.

**U.S. Industrial Tool & Supply Company,** 15101 Cleat St., Plymouth, MI 48170: Free information ◆ Aircraft building tools. 313-455-3388. www.ustool.com

**USATCO Tools,** U.S. Airtool International, 60 Fleetwood Ct., Ronkonkoma, NY 11779: Free brochure ◆ Aircraft tools. 516-471-3300.

**Wag-Aero Group of Aircraft Services,** 1216 North Rd., P.O. Box 181, Lyons, WI 53148: Free information ◆ Avionics equipment, engines, and tools. 800-558-6868. wagaero-sales@wagaero.com

**White Industries Inc.,** P.O. Box 198, Bates City, MO 64011: Free information ◆ Used aircraft parts. 800-821-7733. white-ind@microlink.net

**Wicks Aircraft Supply,** 410 Pine St., Highland, IL 62249: Catalog $5 ◆ Tools, construction materials, instruments, fabric, engines, and propellers. 800-221-9425; 618-654-7447 (in IL). www.wicks.com/aircraft

## Pilot Supplies & Equipment

**Aerox Oxygen Systems,** 200 Dillon Rd., Hilton Head Island, SC 29926: Free brochure ◆ Oxygen systems. 800-237-6902; 843-681-5221 (in SC). www.aerox.com

**Aircraft Industries Inc.,** P.O. Drawer W, 27238 May St., Edwardsburg, MI 49112: Free information ◆ Portable oxygen systems. 800-253-0800. www.skyox.com

**Aircraft Spruce & Specialty,** 225 Airport Circle, Corona, CA 91720: Catalog $5 ◆ Tools, construction materials, instruments, engines, fabrics, flight equipment, and books. 800-824-1930; 714-870-7551 (in CA). www.aircraft-spruce.com

**Aviation Book Company,** 7201 Perimeter Rd. S, Ste. C, Seattle, WA 98108: Free catalog ◆ Books, videos, pilot supplies, clothing, and gifts. 800-423-2708. www.aviationbook.com

**Butler Parachute Systems Inc.,** 1820 London Ave. NW, P.O. Box 6098, Roanoke, VA 24017: Catalog $2 ◆ Parachute systems. 540-342-2501.

**Citizen Watch Company of America,** 1200 Wall St. West, Lyndhurst, NJ 07071: Free information ◆ Professional diving watches and sports, flight, yachting, and windsurfer chronographs. 201-438-8150.

**Flight Products International Inc.,** P.O. Box 1558, Kalispell, MT 59901: Free information ◆ Cockpit equipment. 800-526-1231.

**Marv Golden Discount Sales Inc.,** 8690 Aero Dr., San Diego, CA 92123: Free catalog ◆ Pilot supplies. 800-348-0014. www.marvgolden.com

**Gulf Coast Avionics,** 4243 N. Westboro Blvd., Tampa International Airport, Tampa, FL 33614: Free catalog ◆ Avionics and pilot supplies. 800-474-9714. www.gulf-coast-avionics.com

**Mountain High Equipment & Supply Company,** 516 12th Ave., Salt Lake City, UT 84103: Free information ◆ Electronic-on-demand oxygen system. 800-468-8185. mtn-high.com/

**National Parachute Industries,** 47 E. Main St., Box 1000, Flemington, NJ 08822: Free brochure ◆ Parachute systems. 800-526-5946. www.nationalparachute.com

**Pilot Supplies,** 4243 N. Westshore Blvd., Tampa International Airport, Tampa, FL 33614: Free catalog ◆ Pilot supplies. 800-474-9714; 813-879-9714 (in FL). www.gulf-coast-avionics.com

**San-Val Discount,** 7444 Valjean Ave., Van Nuys, CA 91406: Free information ◆ Aircraft accessories, avionics equipment, and pilot gear. 818-786-8274.

**Schweizer Aircraft Corp.,** P.O. Box 147, Elmira, NY 14902: Free list ◆ Glider flight equipment and books. 607-739-3821.

**Sporty's Pilot Shop,** Clermont Airport, Batavia, OH 45103: Free catalog ◆ Flight equipment. 800-543-8633. www.sportys-catalogs.com

**Strong Enterprises,** 11236 Satellite Blvd., Orlando, FL 32837: Free catalog ◆ Emergency parachutes. 407-859-9317.

**Watkins Aviation Inc.,** 15770 Midway Rd., Hanger #6, Dallas, TX 75244: Free information ◆ United States military and civilian flight clothing. 972-934-0033

# ALARM SYSTEMS, LOCKS, & REMOTE CONTROL EQUIPMENT

**Active Electronics,** 11 Cummings Park, Woburn, MA 01801: Free information ◆ Multi-purpose alarm systems. 800-677-8899. www.future.ca

**Ademco,** 180 Michael Dr., Syosset, NY 11791: Free information ◆ Multi-purpose alarm systems. 800-573-0154. www.ademco.com

**ADT Security Systems,** 300 Interpace Pkwy., Parsippany, NJ 07054: Free list of retail sources ◆ Burglar alarm systems. 800-ADT-4636. www.adt.com

**Advanced Security,** 2964 Peachtree Rd., Atlanta, GA 30305: Catalog $1 ◆ Burglar and fire alarm systems. 800-241-0267. www.ussecassoc.com

**Advanced Services,** Home Automation Products, 32 Court St., Box 3871, Plymouth, MA 02361: Free catalog ◆ Remote and automatic controls for lights, appliances, and audio/video equipment in homes and offices. 800-263-8608; 508-747-5598 (in MA). www.asihome.com

**Alpan Inc.,** 50 Commerce Dr., Trumbull, CT 06611: Free information ◆ Compact infrared motion activated alarm. 800-972-2112.

**ATV Research Inc.,** 1301 Broadway, P.O. Box 620, Dakota City, NE 68731: Catalog $3 ◆ Closed circuit surveillance systems. 402-987-3771. www.atvresearch.com

**Automated Voice Systems,** 17059 El Cajon Ave., Yorba Linda, CA 92886: Free catalog ◆ Voice activated control systems. 714-524-4488. www.mastervoice.com

**Boston Lock & Safe Company,** 30 Lincoln St., Brighton, MA 02135: Free information ◆ Alarms, locks, and safes. 617-787-3400.

**CC TV Corp.,** 280 Huyler St., South Hackensack, NJ 07606: Free information ◆ Closed circuit cameras for TVs. 800-221-2240. gbc@sentrol.com

**Chelsea Industries International,** 304 Main Ave., Ste. 384, Norwalk, CT 06851: Free catalog ◆ Security systems accessories. 800-544-1165; 203-845-0338 (in CT). www.chelseacorp.com

**Dakota Alert Inc.,** Box 130, Elk Point, SD 57025: Free information ◆ Wireless driveway alarms. 605-356-2772.

**DFE Communications Corp.,** 1522 W. Main St., Oklahoma City, OK 73106: Free information ◆ "Touch 'n Talk" entry access systems. 800-822-4TNT.

**Digi-Key Corp.,** 701 Brooks Ave. South, P.O. Box 677, Thief River Falls, MN 56701: Free information ◆ Multi-purpose alarm systems. 800-344-4539. www.digikey.com

**Doorking,** 120 Glasgow Ave., Inglewood, CA 90301: Free information ◆ Telephone entry and access control systems. 800-826-7493. www.doorking.com

**Dynamic Living Inc.,** P.O. Box 370249, West Hartford, CT 06137: Free catalog ◆ Easy-to-install remote controls for lights and appliances, other aids for hard-to-do tasks, and more. 888-940-0605. www.dynamic-living.com

**Fyrnetics Inc.,** 1055 Stevenson Ct., Roselle, IL 60172: Free information ◆ Burglar and smoke alarm systems with selective control options. 800-654-7665. fyrnetics@aol.com

**Genie,** 190 Main St., Hackensack, NJ 07601: Free information ◆ Multi-purpose alarm systems. 800-638-9636. www.genie.com

**HAI Home Automation Inc.,** 5725 Powell St., Ste. A, New Orleans, LA 70123: Free brochure ◆ Security and home automation controllers. 800-229-7256. www.homeauto.com

**Heathkit Educational Systems,** 455 Riverview Dr., Benton Harbor, MI 49022: Free catalog ◆ Easy-to-install home security, entertainment, and automation equipment. 800-253-0570. www.heathkit.com

**Herbach & Rademan,** 16 Roland Ave., Mt. Laurel, NJ 08054: Free catalog ◆ Multi-purpose alarm systems. 609-802-0422. www.herbach.com

**Home Automated Living,** 14311 Old Columbia Pike, Burtonsville, MD 20866: Free list of retail sources ◆ Voice activated home automation system. 301-879-2305. www.automatedliving.com

**Home Automation Systems Inc.,** 17171 Daimler St., Irvine, CA 92614: Free catalog ◆ Easy-to-install home automation control and security systems. 800-242-7329. www.smarthome.com

**Home Controls Inc.,** 7626 Miramar Rd., Ste. 3300, San Diego, CA 92126: Free information ◆ Security and home automation equipment. 800-266-8765. www.homecontrols.com

**Interactive Technologies Inc.,** 2266 N. 2nd St., St. Paul, MN 55109: Free information ◆ Telephone home security systems. 612-777-2690.

**JDS Technologies,** 16750 W. Bernardo Dr., San Diego, CA 92127: Free information ◆ Telephone home security systems and remote controls for computers, lights, and other devices. 800-983-5537; 619-487-8787 (in CA). www.jdstechnologies.com/index.html

**Lutron Lighting Controls,** 7200 Suter Rd., Coopersburg, PA 18036: Free information ◆ Button-operated door jamb and lighting controls. 800-523-9466; 610-282-3800 (in PA). www.lutron.com

**Makita USA Inc.,** Drapery Opener Division, 14930 Northam St., La Mirada, CA 90638: Free information ◆ Automatic drapery opener. 800-4-MAKITA.

**Maple Chase Company,** 2820 Thatcher Rd., Downer's Grove, IL 60515: Free information ◆ Alarm and security equipment. 708-963-1550.

**Miltronics Mfg. Inc.,** 95 Krif Rd., Keene, NH 03431: Free information ◆ Infrared motion sensor operated transmitter and receiver for a wireless driveway alert system. 800-828-9089. www.miltronics.com

**Mountain West Alarm Supply Company,** Alpha Omega Security Group Inc., 9405 E. Doubletree Ranch Rd., Scottsdale, AZ 85258: Catalog $1 ◆ Burglar and fire-protection security systems. 800-528-6169; 602-971-1200 (in AZ). mountainwest@earthlink.net

**Mouser Electronics,** P.O. Box 699, Mansfield, TX 76063: Free catalog ◆ Multi-purpose alarm systems. 800-992-9943. www.mouser.com

**National Fire Protection Association,** 1 Batterymarch Park, P.O. Box 9101, Quincy, MA 02269: Free catalog ◆ Multi-purpose alarm systems. 800-344-3555. www.nfpa.org

**The National Locksmith,** 1533 Burgundy Pkwy., Streamwood, IL 60107: Free information ◆ Multi-purpose alarm systems. 630-837-2044.

**NuTone Inc.,** P.O. Box 1580, Cincinnati, OH 45201: Catalog $3 ◆ Video door-answering system with voice transmission over telephones and a wireless security system that can be zone programmed. 800-543-8687. www.nutone.com

**Paladin Electronics,** 19425 Soledad Cyn Rd., Ste. 333, Canyon Country, CA 91351: Free information ◆ Talking security systems and motion sensors. 805-251-8725.

**Preso-Matic Keyless Locks,** 237 Coastline Rd., Sanford, FL 32771: Free information ◆ Keyless entry locks. 800-269-4234. campbell@parkave.net

**Radio Shack,** Division Tandy Corp., 1500 One Tandy Center, Fort Worth, TX 76102: Free information ◆ Easy-to-install burglar and fire alarm system for homes. Will work with an automatic message dialer. 817-390-3011. www.radioshack.com

**Sentinel Systems Inc.,** 1620 Kipling St., Lakewood, CO 80215: Free information ◆ Home security systems. 800-456-9955. www.sentinelsystems.com

**Siemens Solar Industries,** P.O. Box 6032, Camarillo, CA 93120: Free information ◆ Solar-powered motion sensor light. 800-272-6765. www.siemenssolar.com

**Small Parts,** P.O. Box 4650, Miami Lakes, FL 33014: Free information ◆ Multi-purpose alarm systems. 800-220-4242. www.smallparts.com

**Stanley Door Systems,** 1225 E. Maple Rd., Troy, MI 48083: Free information ◆ Automobile remote control for house lights. 800-521-2752.

**Street Smart Security,** 7147 University Ave., La Mesa, CA 91941: Free information ◆ Remote control receivers for security and other applications. 800-908-4737. www.vanet.com/sss

**Tane Alarm Products,** 24740 Jerico Tnpk., Floral Park, NY 11001: Free information ◆ Multi-purpose alarm systems. 800-852-5050.

**Video Surveillance Corp.,** 1050 E. 14th St., Brooklyn, NY 11230: Free information ◆ Surveillance TV cameras. 718-258-1310.

**X-10 USA Inc.,** 91 Ruckman Rd., Box 420, Closter, NJ 07624: Free information ◆ Controls for lighting and appliances, security systems, personal assistance, and entertainment systems. 201-784-9700. www.x10.com

## ALL-TERRAIN VEHICLES (ATVS) & SAND BUGGIES

**American Honda Motor Company Inc.,** 1919 Torrance Blvd., Torrance, CA 90501: Free list of retail sources) ◆ All-terrain vehicles. 562-783-2000.

**DG Performance Specialties Inc.,** 1220 La Loma Circle, Anaheim, CA 92806: Free catalog ◆ Performance parts and accessories for all-terrain vehicles and personal watercraft. 800-854-9134; 714-630-5471 (in CA).

**Intraser Inc.,** 428 N. La Cienega Blvd., Los Angeles, CA 90048: Free information ◆ New and pre-owned motorcycles, ATVs, snowmobiles, trailers, personal water vehicles, and small boats. 213-652-6966.

**Kawasaki Motors Corp.,** 9950 Jeronimo Rd., Irvine, CA 92619: Free list of retail sources ◆ Motorcycles, ATVs, and accessories. 714-770-0400. www.kawasaki.com

**Maier Manufacturing USA,** 416 Crown Point Circle, Grass Valley, CA 95945: Free catalog ◆ Road and dirt motorcycle and all-terrain vehicle fairings, fenders, panel covers, and accessories. 800-336-2437; 916-272-9036 (in CA) www.maiermfg.com

**Recreatives Industries Inc.,** 60 Depot St., Buffalo, NY 14206: Free information ◆ Two and 4-passenger six-wheel drive amphibious all-terrain vehicle. 800-255-2511. www.maxatus.com

**Sand Buggy Supply Company,** 13055 Rosecrans Ave., Santa Fe Springs, CA 90670: Free list of retail sources ◆ Sand buggies. 562-921-3719.

**Bob Traceys World of Cycles,** 604 Narrows Run Rd., Moon Township, PA 15108: Free information ◆ Suzuki parts for dirt and street bikes, ATVs, and watercraft. 800-860-0686. www.partswarehouse.com

**Weekend Warrior Company,** 1614 E. Holt Blvd., Ontario, CA 91761: Free list of retail sources ◆ All-terrain vehicles. 800-500-9914.

**Yamaha Motor Corp.,** P.O. Box 6555, Cypress, CA 90630: Free list of retail sources ◆ All-terrain vehicles. 800-526-6650. www.yamahausa.com

## ANTIQUES & REPRODUCTIONS

### Antique & Art Restoration

**A & H Brass & Supply,** 126 W. Main St., Johnson City, TN 37604: Catalog $2 ◆ Restoration supplies. 800-638-4252; 423-928-8220 (in TN).

**Antique & Art Restoration by Wiebold,** 413 Terrace Park, Cincinnati, OH 45174: Free brochure ◆ Restoration services for antiques and art objects. 800-321-2541. wiebold@eos.net

**Fredi W. Boese, Master Artist,** 96 Rt. 17M, Harriman, NY 10926: Free information ◆ Porcelain and ceramics restoration. 800-755-0417; 914-783-4438. fredi@frediboese.com

**Certified Restoration Service,** 2378 Linwood Ave., Naples, FL 34112: Free information ◆ Porcelain art restoration services. 888-PORCELN.

**Estes-Simmons Silverplating Ltd.,** 1050 Northside Dr. NW, Atlanta, GA 30318: Free brochure ◆ Silver repair and plating. 800-645-4193. info@estes-simmons.com

**Fine Art Restoration,** RFD 2, Box 1440, Brooks, ME 04921: Free information ◆ Restoration services for paintings. 207-722-3464.

**Gone Hollywood,** 172 Bella Vista Ave., Belvedere, CA 94920: Free information ◆ Movie poster restoration. 415-435-1929.

**J & K Curios,** 2950 SW Persimmon Ln., Dunnellon, FL 34431: Free information ◆ Museum-quality restoration of porcelain, pottery, and art objects. 352-465-0756.

**Johnson Music Company,** P.O. Box 615, Mt. Airy, NC 27030: Brochure $2 ◆ Reed organ restoration and custom bellows recovering. 919-320-2212.

**A. Ludwig Klein & Son Inc.,** P.O. Box 145, Harleysville, PA 19438: Free brochure ◆ Porcelain and glass restoration. 215-256-9004.

**Old World Restorations,** 347 Stanley Ave., Cincinnati, OH 45226: Free catalog ◆ Antique and art restoration. 513-321-1911.

**Poster Restoration Studio,** 7466 Beverly Blvd., Ste. 205, Los Angeles, CA 90036: Free information ◆ Restoration services for posters. 213-934-4219.

**Senti-Metal Silver Restoration Company,** 1919 Memory Ln., Columbus, OH 43209: Free information ◆ Silver heirlooms restoration. 800-345-8112. www.antique/SentiMetal.com

**Van Dyke Supply Company,** Box 278, Woonsocket, SD 57385: Catalog $1 ◆ Hardware, hardwoods, curved glass, trim, and supplies for restoring antiques. 800-843-3320. www.vandyke.com

### Antiques & Reproductions

**Bargain John's Antiques,** 700 S. Washington, P.O. Box 705, Lexington, NE 68850: Free information ◆ Antique furniture.

**Benedikt & Salmon Record Rarities,** 3020 Meade Ave., San Diego, CA 92116: Free catalog, indicate choice of (1) autographs and rare books, (2) classical, (3) jazz, big bands, and blues, and (4) personalities, soundtracks and country music ◆ Early phonographs and cylinders, autographed memorabilia and rare books in music and the performing arts, and hard-to-find phonograph recordings from 1890 to date. 619-281-3345. rarerecords@groupweb.com

**Warren Blake, Old Science Books,** 308 Hadley Dr., Trumbull, CT 06611: Catalog $1 ◆ Hard-to-find astronomy books and prints. 203-459-0820.

**Joan Bogart,** P.O. Box 265, Rockville Centre, NY 11571: Brochure $5 ◆ Authentic antiques. 516-764-5712.

**Bootleggers Nostalgia,** P.O. Box 165, South Hadley, MA 01075: Free list ◆ Pub jug collectibles. 413-533-0419.

**The Bugle Call,** Robert C. Trownsell, 1241 Ellis St., Bensenville, IL 60106: Free information ◆ Military antiques. Specializes in shoulder straps. 630-350-1116. www.infinitiv.com/BugleCall

**The Bushwacker Militaria,** P.O. Box 966, Black Mountain, NC 28711: Price list $3 ◆ Spanish American, WWI, WWII, United States, and German military antiques and collectibles. 704-669-4603.

**Chinese Porcelain Company,** 475 Park Ave., New York, NY 10022: Free information ◆ Chinese porcelain antiques. 212-838-7744. cpco@msn.com

**Chuctanunda Antique Company,** 1 Fourth Ave., Amsterdam, NY 12010: Catalog $1 ◆ French and European enamel graniteware, from 1880 to 1940. 518-843-3983. www.enameledware.com

**Circa Antiques,** 374 Atlantic Ave., Brooklyn, NY 11217: Free information ◆ American furniture from the 19th-century. 718-596-1866.

**Civil War Antiques,** David W. Taylor, Box 87, Sylvania, OH 43560: Catalog subscription $10 ◆ Civil War antiques. 419-882-5547.

**Civil War Antiquities,** P.O. Box 1411, Delaware, OH 43015: Free catalog ◆ Civil War collectibles. 614-363-1862. www.civilwarantiquities.com

**Gordon S. Converse & Company,** Spread Eagle Village, Stratfords, PA 19087: Free catalog ◆ Antique clocks. 800-789-1001. www.pond.com/~gfc

**The Country House,** 805 E. Main St., Salisbury, MD 21804: Catalog $3 ◆ Antique reproductions and other gifts. 800-331-3602. www.thecountryhouse.com

**Dovetail Antiques,** 474 White Pine Rd., Columbus, NJ 08022: Catalog $5 ◆ Antique wicker furniture. 609-298-5245.

**Dubrow Antiques,** P.O. Box 128, Bayside, NY 11361: Free information ◆ American-style 19th-century furniture. 718-767-9758.

**Bill Egleston Inc.,** 509 Brentwood Rd., Marshalltown, IA 50158: Free price list ◆ Stone carvings. 800-798-4579.

**N. Flayderman & Company Inc.,** P.O. Box 2446, Fort Lauderdale, FL 33303: Catalog $10 ◆ Antique guns, swords, knives, and western, nautical, and military memorabilia. 305-761-8855.

**4x1 Imports Inc.,** 5873 Day Rd., Cincinnati, OH 45251: Catalog $8 (refundable) ◆ Nostalgic tin advertising signs. 513-385-8185.

**Games People Played,** P.O. Box 1540, 17 James Ln., Pinedale, WY 82941: Catalog $4 ◆ Antique replica game boards and signs. 307-367-2502.

**Gasoline Alley,** 6501 20th NE, Seattle, WA 98115: Free information with long SASE ◆ Baseball and football collectibles and toys, from 1875 to 1975. 206-524-1606. www.gasolinealleyantiques.com

**The Gemmary Rare Books & Antique Scientific Instruments,** P.O. Box 2560, Fallbrook, CA 92088: Mineralogy book catalog $2, science book catalog $2 ◆ Specializes in out-of-print books on mineralogy that include mining, jewelry, and meteorites; science books that include physics, microscopy, and scientific instruments. 760-728-3321. www.gemmary.com/rcb

**Governor's Antiques & Architectural Materials Ltd.,** 6240 Meadowbridge Rd., Mechanicsville, VA 23111: Free catalog ◆ Original and reproduction 18th and 19th-century furnishings and antique architectural building materials. 804-746-1030.

**Grace Galleries Inc.,** Box 2488, Brunswick, ME 04011: Free information (specify items wanted) ◆ Original antique maps, prints, sea charts, and cartographic books. 207-729-1329.

**Hake's Americana,** P.O. Box 1444, York, PA 17405: Catalog $7.50 ◆ Americana and collectibles. 717-848-1333. www.hakes.com

**Herman Military Antiques,** P.O. Box 5091, Chatsworth, CA 91313: Free list with long SASE ◆ American, German, and Japanese military antiques from World War I and II. 818-718-0682. BBH1122@aol.com

**Hoosier-Peddler,** Dave Harris, 5400 S. Webster St., Kokomo, IN 46902: Price list $2 ◆ Banks, Walt Disney collectibles, wind-up, character, and other toys. 765-453-6172.

**Hornung Art,** 32 E. Charlotte Ave., Cincinnati, OH 45215: Free information ◆ Art, antiques, and miniature figures. 513-761-8518. www.hornungart.com

**Imelda,** 16960 S.R. 12 East., Findlay, OH 45840: Free catalog ◆ Antiques, Victorian furniture, and cast aluminum lighting. 800-483-7105; 419-424-1722 (in OH).

**It's A Dog's Life,** 308 Signal Dr., Rossville, GA 30741: Free information with long SASE (specify breed of dog) ◆ Antique prints, books, and figurines. 706-866-7729. dogslife1@mindspring.com

**Jacques Noel Jacobsen,** 60 Manor Rd., Ste. 300, Staten Island, NY 10310: Catalog $10 ◆ Military insignia, weapons, photos and paintings, band instruments, and Native American and western collectibles. 718-981-0973.

**Jukebox Junction,** 203 4th, Cumming, IA 50061: Catalog $2.50 ◆ Antique jukeboxes. 515-981-4019.

**Lake Forest Antiquarians,** P.O. Box 841, Lake Forest, IL 60045: Free catalog ◆ English and Continental silver and antiques. 847-234-1990.

**Leonard's Antiques,** 600 Taunton Creek, Seekonk, MA 02771: Catalog $4 ◆ Original and reproduction antique beds. 508-336-8585.

**Little Bat's Trading Post,** 123 Main St., Crawford, NE 69339: Catalog $10 ◆ Antique firearms, Old West collectibles, and militaria. 308-665-1900.

**Melton's Antique Dolls,** 4201 Indian River Rd., Chesapeake, VA 23325: Free information with long SASE ◆ Antique dolls. 804-420-9226.

**Miltech,** P.O. Box 322, Los Altos, CA 94023: Catalog $1 ◆ Hand-restored original vintage firearms. 415-948-3500.

**Neon Clock,** 246 W. 3rd Ave., New Lenox, IL 60451: Free information ◆ Antique neon clocks. 815-485-5573.

**19th Century America,** 3603 Johnson St., Lafayette, LA 70503: Information $1 ◆ American and Victorian furniture and accessories, from 1840 to 1890. 318-988-1020.

**Ogan Antiques Ltd.,** P.O. Box 14831, North Palm Beach, FL 33408: Catalog $10 ◆ Antique firearms. 407-844-2434.

**Osceola Antiques,** 117 Cascade St., P.O. Box 297, Osceola, WI 54020: Free information ◆ Antique furniture. 715-294-2886. oscantiq@centuryinter.net

**The Picket Post,** 602 Caroline St., Fredericksburg, VA 22401: Catalog $10 (3 issues) ◆ Civil War antiques. 703-371-7703.

**Pittsburgh Antique Company,** 143 West College St., Canonsburg, PA 15317: Free brochure ◆ Gas fixtures, early electric chandeliers, other period lighting, mantels, doors, hardware, newel posts, columns, ornamental iron, and architectural antiques. 412-222-8586. PPAC@city-net.com6

**Anne Powell Ltd.,** P.O. Box 3060, Stuart, FL 34995: Catalog $5 ◆ Needlework supplies and one-of-a-kind antique sewing tools. 407-287-3007. www.annepowellltd.com

**Quester Maritime Gallery,** P.O. Box 446, Stonington, CT 06378: Catalog $10 ◆ Marine art and antiques. 860-535-3860.

**Radiomania Catalog,** Mark V. Stein, 2109 Carterdale Rd., Baltimore, MD 21209: Catalog $5 ◆ Collectible antique radios. 410-466-2814. www.machineage.com/radiomania

**M.S. Rau,** 630 Royal St., New Orleans, LA 70130: Catalog $5 ◆ Antiques from the 19th-century. 800-544-9440. bmark.com/rau.antiques

**Eugene & Ellen Reno,** Box 191, Lawrence, MA 01842: Free information ◆ Cut and depression glass, other glassware, dolls and toys, miniatures, jewelry, sterling silver, china, and antiques. 603-898-7426 (do not call after 7 PM).

**Samurai Antiques,** 229 Santa Ynez Ct., Santa Barbara, CA 93103: Price list $1 with long SASE ◆ Japanese antique Samurai, Emperor, and Empress dolls. 805-965-9688.

**Setnik's in Time Again,** 815 Sutter St., Folsom, CA 95630: Free information ◆ Restored American Victorian furniture, European and American clocks, and accessories. 916-985-2390.

**Asher Shahar,** P.O. Box 640684, North Miami, FL 33164: Catalog $3 ◆ Reproduction Tiffany lamps.

**So Rare Galleries,** Triangle Bldg., Ste. 504, 701 Smithfield St., Pittsburgh, PA 15222: Free catalog ◆ Fine and decorative art from the 19th-century. 800-260-2909; 412-281-5150 (in PA). www.so-rare.com

**Southampton Antiques,** 172 College Hwy., Rt. 10, Southampton, MA 01073: Video catalog $25 ◆ Antique American oak and Victorian furniture. 413-527-1022.

**A Summer Place,** 37 Boston St., Guilford, CT 06437: Free information ◆ Antique wicker furniture. 203-453-5153.

**Dave Taylor Civil War Antiques,** Box 87, Sylvania, OH 43560: Catalog $8 ◆ Guns, swords, uniforms, insignia, flags. drums, photographs, letters, diaries, autographs, and antique memorabilia. 419-878-8355.

**Tesseract Early Scientific Instruments,** Box 151, Hastings-On-Hudson, NY 10706: Catalog $5 ◆ Antique scientific and medical instruments and books. 914-478-2594.

**Time & Tide,** 56 Byram Rd., P.O. Box 156, Point Pleasant, PA 18950: Free information ◆ Imported French antique furniture and clocks. 215-297-5854.

**Wartime Collectables,** P.O. Box 165, Camden, SC 29020: Catalog subscription $12 (8 issues) ◆ Military antiques. 803-424-5273.

**Watertower Pines,** Rt. 1 South, Kennebunk, ME 04043: Free information ◆ Kerosene, gas, and early electric lighting. 207-985-6868.

**Mary Webster Frames,** 12 Edwards St., Binghamton, NY 13905: Free information ◆ Antique picture frames. 607-722-1483.

## APPLIANCES

### Manufacturers

**Amana Refrigeration,** 2800 220th Trail, Amana, IA 52204: Free information ◆ Refrigerators. 800-843-0304.

**Asko Appliances,** 1161 Executive Dr. West, Richardson, TX 75081: Free information ◆ Household appliances. 800-367-2444. www.askousa.com

**Black & Decker,** 6 Armstrong Rd., Shelton, CT 06484: Free information ◆ Small appliances. 800-544-6986. www.blackandecker.com

**Braun Appliances,** 400 Unicorn Park Dr., Woburn, MA 01801: Free information ◆ Small appliances. 800-272-8622.

**Custom Fireplaces,** 1611 E. Spring St., Cookeville, TN 38506: Catalog $4 ◆ Antique-styled electric and gas ranges, coordinated refrigerators, and wall ovens. 615-526-8181.

**Dacor Appliances,** 950 S. Raymond Ave., Pasadena, CA 91109: Free information ◆ Household appliances. 800-793-00933. dacorworld@dacorappl.com

**Dynamic Cooking Systems,** 5800 Skylab Rd., Huntington Beach, CA 92647: Free catalog ◆ Outdoor gas grills and professional gas ranges for commercial settings. 800-433-8466. www.dcs-range.com

**Frigidaire Company,** 6000 Perimeter Rd., Dublin, OH 43017: Free information ◆ Refrigerators, freezers, dishwashers, and other appliances. 800-374-4432. www.frigidaire.com

**G.E. Appliances,** General Electric Company, Appliance Park, Louisville, KY 40225: Free information ◆ Electric cooktop stoves, microwave ovens, dishwashers, refrigerators, freezers, washers and dryers, and small appliances. 800-626-2000. www.ge.com

**In-Sink-Erator,** Emerson Electric Company, 4700 21st St., Racine, WI 53406: Free information ◆ Dishwashers and appliances. 800-558-5712. www.insinkerator.com

**Jenn-Air Company,** 3035 Shadeland Ave., Indianapolis, IN 46226: Free information ◆ Cooktop stoves, dishwashers, ranges, and range hoods. 800-536-6247. www.jennair.com

**Kelvinator,** 6000 Perimeter Dr., Dublin, OH 43017: Free information ◆ Appliances. 800-843-0304.

**KitchenAid Inc.,** 750 Monte Rd., Benton Harbor, MI 49022: Free information ◆ Cooktop stoves, dishwashers, range hoods, small appliances, wall ovens, washing machines and dryers, and refrigerators. 800-422-1230 (large appliances); 800-541-6390 (counter-top appliances). www.KitchenAid.com

**Magic Chef,** 3035 N. Shadeland Ave., Indianapolis, IN 46226: Free information ◆ Electric cooktop stoves, wall ovens, refrigerators, and dishwashers. 800-536-6247. www.jennair.com

**Panasonic,** Panasonic Way, Secaucus, NJ 07094: Free list of retail sources ◆ Microwave ovens. 201-348-7000. www.panasonic.com

**Sanyo Fisher Service Corp.,** 1411 W. 190th St., Ste. 800, Gardena, CA 90248: Free information with long SASE ◆ Under-the-counter refrigerators, microwave ovens, portable laundry washers and dryers, and other electronics.

**Sharp Electronics,** Sharp Plaza, Mahwah, NJ 07496: Free information ◆ Microwave ovens. 800-BE-SHARP. www.sharp-usa.com

**Tappan,** 6000 Perimeter Dr., Dublin, OH 43017: Free information ◆ Electric cooktop stoves, ranges, and dishwashers. 800-537-5530.

**Thermador/Waste King,** 5119 District Blvd., Los Angeles, CA 90040: Free information ◆ Electric and gas cooktop stoves, ranges, wall ovens, and other appliances. 800-656-9226. www.thermador.com

**Vent-A-Hood Company,** P.O. Box 830426, Richardson, TX 75083: Free information ◆ Range hoods. 972-235-5201.

**Viking Range Corp.,** 111 Front St., Greenwood, MS 38930: Free list of retail sources ◆ Gas ranges, range hoods, and cooktop stoves. 888-845-4641. www.viking-range.com

**Waring Products,** 283 Main St., New Hartford, CT 06057: Free information ◆ Small appliances. 860-379-0731.

**Whirlpool Corp.,** 2000 M63 North, Benton Harbor, MI 49022: Free information ◆ Electric cooktop stoves, wall ovens, dishwashers, refrigerators, and freezers. 800-253-1301. www.whirlpool.com

### Retailers

**Bernie's Discount Center Inc.,** 821 6th Ave., New York, NY 10001: Catalog $1 (refundable) ◆ Video equipment, telephones and answering machines, and large and small appliances. 212-564-8582.

**Bondy Export Corp.,** 40 Canal St., New York, NY 10002: Free information with long SASE ◆ Large and small appliances, cameras, video equipment TVs, office machines and typewriters, and luggage. 212-925-7785.

**Dial-A-Brand Inc.,** 57 S. Main St., Freeport, NY 11520: Free information with long SASE ◆ TVs, large and small appliances, and video equipment. 516-378-9694.

**Foto Electric Supply Company,** 31 Essex St., New York, NY 10002: Free information ◆ Appliances. 212-673-5222. www.fotoelectric.com

**Harry's Discounts & Appliances Corp.,** 8701 18th Ave., Brooklyn, NY 11214: Free information with long SASE ◆ Electronics and appliances. 718-236-3507.

**LVT Price Quote Hotline Inc.,** Box 444, Commack, NY 11725: Free information (specify items and manufacturer's model number) ◆ Large and small appliances, office equipment, telephones and fax machines, word processors, and other nationally advertised products. 888-CALL-LVT; 516-234-8884 (in NY). members.aol.com/calllvt

**Percy's Inc.,** 19 Glennie St., Worcester, MA 01605: Free information ◆ Appliances and electronics. 508-755-5334.

**Richlund Sales,** 75695 Hwy. 1053, Kentwood, LA 70444: Free information ◆ Ice-maker, central vacuum system, trash compactor, rear vision camera, electric heating equipment, combination washer and dryer, and other appliances for recreational vehicles. 504-229-4922.

## APPLIQUES & OTHER PATTERNS

**Bee Hive,** 12413 Tomanet, Austin, TX 78758: Catalog $2 (refundable) ◆ Iron-on transfer printing. 512-836-4424.

**Creative Uniques Inc.,** RR 3, Box 390, Linton, IN 47441: Catalog $2 ◆ Easy-to-apply creative appliques. 812-847-7780.

**Jehlor Fantasy Fabrics,** 730 Andover Park West, Seattle, WA 98188: Catalog $5 ◆ Bridal fabrics, appliques, trim, and jewelry-style decorative sew-on notions. 206-575-8250.

**Lace Corner,** P.O. Box 1224, Weaverville, CA 96093: Catalog $3 (refundable with $25 order) ◆ Ruffled flat lace, ribbons, and appliques. 530-623-3586.

**Laube's Stretch & Sew Fabrics,** 609 W. 98th St., Bloomington, MN 55420: Catalog $1 with long SASE ◆ Applique kits. 612-884-7321.

**Southwest Decoratives,** 191 Bighorn Ridge NE, Albuquerque, NM 87122: Catalog $3 ◆ Quilt patterns and kits, applique patterns and kits, cross-stitch charts and kits, and stenciling supplies. 505-856-9585. www.swdecoratives.com

**Sugar Petals,** 209 Astrid Dr., Pleasant Hill, CA 94523: Free information ◆ Appliques. 510-934-2462.

## AQUATIC FITNESS & SPORTS

**BSN Sports,** P.O. Box 7726, Dallas, TX 75209: Free information ◆ Archery, aquatic fitness, baseball, basketball, boxing, field hockey, football, weight-lifting, and other sports equipment. 800-527-7510; 972-484-9484 (in TX). www.bsnsports.com

**E.Z. Enterprises,** 205 D Exeter Rd., London, Ontario, Canada N6L 1A4: Free information ◆ Lightweight aquatic basketball and water polo goals. 519-472-5261.

## ARCHERY & BOW HUNTING

**Aimpoint,** 420 W. Main St., Geneseo, IL 61254: Free brochure ◆ Archery equipment. 309-944-1702. www.aimpointusa.com

**Ames Industries,** 3631 Interlake Ave. N., Seattle, WA 98103: Free information ◆ All-weather targets. 206-633-0404.

**B & J Archery,** P.O. Box 8461, Jacksonville, TX 75766: Information $2 ◆ Longbows for hunting and recreational shooting. 903-586-0715. bows21cjim@tyler.net

**Barnett International,** P.O. Box 934, Odessa, FL 33556: Free information ◆ Arrow holders, bow cases, quivers, bows, and sights. 800-237-4507; 813-920-2241 (in FL). www.barnettcrossbows.com

**Bay Archery Sales,** 2713 W. Center Ave., Essexviille, MI 48706: Free catalog ◆ Camping and backpacking equipment and survival supplies. 517-894-5800.

**Bear Archery Inc.,** 4600 SW 41st Blvd., Gainesville, FL 32608: Free information ◆ Arrows, arrow-making components, bows, sights, and targets. 800-874-4603; 352-376-2327 (in FL). www.thebowman.com

**Besherse Brothers,** 1032 Old Elkton Pike, Frankenwing, TN 38459: Catalog $2 ◆ Bowhunting equipment. 615-732-4277.

**Black Widow Custom Bows,** 1201 Eaglecrest, P.O. Box 2100, Nixa, MO 65714: Free information ◆ Bows. 417-725-3113. www.archery.net/blackwidow

**Bohning Company Ltd.,** 7361 N. Seven Mile Rd., Lake City, MI 49651: Free information ◆ Archery equipment, arrows, and arrow-making components. 800-253-0136. www.bohning.com

**Bow Works,** P.O. Box 1803, Hurst, TX 76053: Free catalog ◆ Bow-making supplies and woodworking tools. 817-285-8000.

**Bowhunters Discount Warehouse Inc.,** P.O. Box 158, Wellsville, PA 17365: Free catalog ◆ Rifles, game calls, targets, camouflage clothing, and hunting, bow hunting, archery, and camping equipment. 800-735-BOWS. www.bowhunterswarehouse.com

**Jim Brackenbury Inc.,** 8326 SE 252nd Ave., Gresham, OR 97080: Brochure $1 ◆ Custom takedown and longbows. 503-666-1667.

**Bracklyn Archery,** 4400 Stillman Blvd., Tuscaloosa, AL 35401: Free information ◆ Archery targets. 205-345-2697.

**Browning Company,** Dept. C006, One Browning Pl., Morgan, UT 84050: Catalog $2 ◆ Arm guards, arrow holders, gloves, point sharpeners, scents and lures, quivers, tabs, wax, bows, arrows, arrow-making components, and sights. 800-333-3288. www.browning.com

**BSN Sports,** P.O. Box 7726, Dallas, TX 75209: Free information ◆ Archery, aquatic fitness, baseball, basketball, boxing, field hockey, football, weight-lifting, and other sports equipment. 800-527-7510; 972-484-9484 (in TX). www.bsnsports.com

**Bud K Worldwide,** P.O. Box 2768, Moultrie, GA 31776: Free catalog ◆ Mini crossbows and arrows. 800-543-5061. www.budkww.com

**Butler's Bowhunting,** 163 Bear River Dr., Evanston, WY 82930: Free catalog ◆ Bowhunting supplies. 307-789-4982.

**Carron Net Company,** 1623 17th St., P.O. Box 177, Two Rivers, WI 54241: Free information ◆ Archery, baseball, basketball, gymnasium and climbing, football, racquetball, soccer, tennis, and volleyball equipment. 800-558-7768; 414-793-2217 (in WI). sales@carronnet.com

**J.K. Chastain,** 490 S. Queen St., Lakewood, CO 80226: Free information ◆ Custom-made longbows and recurves. 303-989-1120. members.aol.com/jkchastain

**Cheaper than Dirt,** 2536 NE Loop 820, Fort Worth, TX 76106: Free catalog ◆ Holsters and cases, scopes, survival supplies, gunsmith and cleaning supplies, clothing, hunting and camping gear, and archery, crossbow, and shotgun equipment. 888-625-3848. www.cheaperthandirt.com

**Darton Archery,** 3540 Darton Rd., Hale, MI 48739: Free catalog ◆ Bow hunting equipment. 517-728-4231. www.dartonarchery.com

**Delta Industries,** 117 E. Kenwood St., Reinbeck, IA 50669: Free information ◆ Life-size 3-dimensional archery targets and penetrating arrowheads. 800-708-0673. www.delphiglass.com

**Doskocil Manufacturing Company,** P.O. Box 1246, Arlington, TX 76004: Free information ◆ Gun and bow cases. 817-467-5116.

**Dynasty Custom Bows,** 738 Maple St., Colon, MI 49040: Free brochure ◆ Handcrafted one-piece and takedown bows. 616-432-3732.

**Easton,** 5040 W. Harold Gatty Dr., Salt Lake City, UT 84116: Free list of retail sources ◆ Arrow shafts. 801-539-1400.

**F/S Discount Arrows and Supplies,** 2852 Walnut, Unit A2, Tustin, CA 92782: Free catalog ◆ Arrow-making supplies and tools. 800-824-8261. www.vpm.com/fsarchery

**Flex-Fletch Products,** 1840 Chandler Ave., St. Paul, MN 55113: Free information ◆ Arrows. 612-488-4948.

**The Footed Shaft,** 5510 North Hwy. 63, Rochester, MN 55906: Catalog $1 (refundable) ◆ Archery equipment. 507-288-7581.

**Gander Mountain (Cabela's),** One Cabela Dr., Sidney, ME 69160: Free catalog ◆ Archery equipment. 800-237-4444. www.cabelas.com

**Great Northern Longbow Company,** P.O. Box 777, Nashville, MI 49073: Brochure $1 ◆ Archery equipment. 517-852-0820.

**James Greene Archery Products,** 2179 Yellow Banks Rd., North Wilkesboro, NC 28659: Free information ◆ Bow cases. 910-670-2188.

**High Country Archery,** P.O. Box 1269, 312 Industrial Park Rd., Dunlap, TN 37327: Free information ◆ Archery equipment. 423-949-5000.

**Howard Hill Archery,** Craig & Evie Ekin, 248 Canyon Creek Rd., Hamilton, MT 59840: Free information ◆ Recurves, longbows, and accessories. 406-363-1359.

**Horton Manufacturing Company,** 484 Tacoma Ave., Tallmadge, OH 44278: Free information ◆ Crossbow hunting equipment. 330-633-0305.

**Hoyt USA,** 543 N. Neil Armstrong Rd., Salt Lake City, UT 84116: Free information ◆ Bows, cases, stabilizers, strings, quivers, slings, sights, arrows, and arrow-making supplies. 801-363-2990. www.hoytusa.com

**Jennings Archery,** Catalog Department, 4600 SW 41st Blvd., Gainesville, FL 32608: Catalog $2 (request list of retail sources) ◆ Hunting bows. www.jenarch.com/request.html

**Kolpin Manufacturing Inc.,** 205 Depot St., Fox Lake, WI 53933: Free information ◆ Arm guards, arrow holders, bow cases, gloves, tabs, and arrow-making components. 920-928-3118.

**Kustom King Arrows,** 1260 E. 86th Pl., Merrillville, IN 46410: Free catalog ◆ Archery supplies. Includes tapered wood arrows. 219-769-6640.

**Leal's Archery Sights,** 62 Liberty St., East Taunton, MA 02718: Free information ◆ Archery hunting sights. 508-824-7274.

**Martin Archery,** Rt. 5, Box 127, Walla Walla, WA 99362: Free information ◆ Bow cases. 509-529-2554. www.martinarchery.com

**McKenzie Taxidermy Supply,** P.O. Box 480, Granite Quarry, NC 28072: Free catalog ◆ Natural-looking 3-D life-like animal targets. 800-279-7985. mckenziep@infoave.net

**McPherson Archery,** P.O. Box 327, Brewton Industrial Park, Brewton, AL 36427: Free information ◆ Bows. 334-867-8980.

**Miami Valley Outdoor Products,** 800 S. Downing St., Piqua, OH 45356: Free information ◆ Bow and arrow cases. 937-773-9477.

**Monarch Longbow Company Inc.,** 184 N. Milnor Lake Rd., Troy, MT 59935: Brochure $1 ◆ Handcrafted longbows.

**Mountaineer Archery Inc.,** 4340 Terrace Ave., Huntington, WV 25722: Free information ◆ Archery equipment. 304-525-9222.

**O.H. Mullen Sales Inc.,** 9928 Rd. 171, Oakwood, OH 45873: Free information ◆ Bows and strings, arm guards, arrow holders, cases, strings, stabilizers, gloves, nock locks, point sharpeners, quivers, racks, scents and lures, slings, tabs, arrows, arrow-making components, sights, and targets. 800-258-6625.

**New Archery Products Corp.,** 7500 Industrial Dr., Forest Park, IL 60130: Free information ◆ Arrows for bow hunting. 800-323-1279; 708-488-2500 (in IL). www.nap.corp.com

**Oneida Labs Inc.,** P.O. Box 68, Phoenix, NY 13135: Brochure $2 ◆ Bow hunting equipment. 315-695-2741.

**Papa D's Discount Archery Outlet,** P.O. Box 80712, Lansing, MI 48908: Free information ◆ Archery equipment and accessories. 888-790-1480. www.PAPAD.com

**PSE Catalog Inet,** 2727 N. Fairview, Tucson, AZ 85705: Catalog $2 ◆ Bows and archery accessories. 520-884-9065. www.pse-archery.com/html/psecatalog.html

**Rocky Mountain Archery,** 79 Burke Loop, Silver City, NM 88061: Free brochure ◆ Handcrafted longbows and recurves. 505-388-4734.

**Sauk Trail Archery,** 13960 Kildare Ave., Crestwood, IL 60445: Catalog $2 (refundable) ◆ Handcrafted bows. 708-489-9780.

**Saunders Archery Company,** P.O. Box 476, Columbus, NE 68601: Free information ◆ Arm guards, arrow holders, cases, strings, stabilizers, gloves, nock locks, point sharpeners, quivers, scents and lures, slings, tools, arrows, arrow-making components, sights, and targets. 800-228-1408; 402-564-7176 (in NE). sausa@megavision.com

**Scout Mountain Equipment Inc.,** 556 S. Main St., Pocatello, ID 83204: Free information ◆ Target sights. 208-232-5656.

**Silver Arrow Archery,** 106 Foredway Ext., Derry, NH 03038: Catalog $2 ◆ Custom bows. 603-434-0569.

**Spence's Targets,** 3056 E. Lincoln Hwy., Lynnwood, IL 60411: Free information ◆ Multi-layered foam animal targets. 708-758-9144.

**Spot Target Decoys,** 1637 Westhaven Blvd., Jackson, MS 39209: Free information ◆ Anatomically accurate animal decoy targets. 800-748-8765; 601-922-8212 (in MS).

**Stillwater Archery,** P.O. Box 992, Harrison, MI 48625: Brochure $1 ◆ Laminated longbows, recurves, and Osage self-bows. 810-539-6333.

**Three Rivers Archery Supply,** P.O. Box 517, Ashley, IN 46705: Catalog $2 ◆ Archery equipment. 219-587-9501. steve@3riversarchery.com

**Timberline Archery Products,** P.O. Box 333, Lewiston, ID 83501: Free catalog ◆ Archery equipment. 208-746-2708.

**Wes Wallace Custom Bows,** 21420 S. Upper Highland Rd., Beaver Creek, OR 97004: Free brochure ◆ Custom takedown recurves and longbows. 503-632-7365.

**Xi Compound Bows & Accessories,** P.O. Box 889, Evansville, IN 47706: Free catalog ◆ Archery equipment. 812-467-1200.

# ART SUPPLIES & EQUIPMENT

## Airbrush Equipment & Supplies

**Alvin & Company Inc.,** P.O. Box 188, Windsor, CT 06095: Free catalog ◆ Airbrush equipment and supplies. 800-444-2584. www.alvinco.com

**Badger Air-Brush Company,** 9128 W. Belmont Ave., Franklin Park, IL 60131: Brochure $1 ◆ Airbrushes. 800-247-2787. www.badger-airbrush.com

**Bear Air,** 15 Tech Circle, Natick, MA 01760: Free catalog ◆ Airbrushing equipment and supplies. 800-BearAir. www.bearair.com

**Binks Manufacturing Company,** 9201 Belmont Ave., Franklin Park, IL 60131: Free catalog ◆ Airbrush systems and accessories. 847-671-3000.

**Dick Blick Company,** P.O. Box 1267, Galesburg, IL 61402: Catalog $1 ◆ Books, videos, airbrushes, and printing, drafting, and commercial art supplies. 800-447-8192. www.artmaterials.com

**Decart Inc.,** P.O. Box 309, Morrisville, VT 05661: Free list of retail sources ◆ Fabric paints and dyes for use with airbrushes, water-base enamels and paints for transfer techniques, and glass crafting, silk-screening, and craft supplies. 802-888-4217.

**Dixie Art Supplies,** 2612 Jefferson Hwy., New Orleans, LA 70121: Free catalog ◆ Airbrush equipment. 800-783-2612. artdixie@aol.com

**Nasco,** 901 Janesville Ave., Fort Atkinson, WI 53538: Free catalog ◆ Paints, brushes, airbrushes, pastels and crayons, drawing and drafting equipment, and craft supplies. 800-558-9595. www.nascofa.com

**Paasche Airbrush Company,** 7440 W. Lawrence Ave., Harwood Heights, IL 60656: Free information ◆ Airbrushing and spraying equipment. 773-867-9191.

**Salis International Inc.,** 4093 N. 28th Way, Hollywood, FL 33020: Free information ◆ Airbrush acrylic and fluorescent colors. 800-843-8293; 954-921-6971 (in FL). www.docmartins.com

**Thayer & Chandler,** 28835 N. Herky Dr., Lake Bluff, IL 60044: Free brochure ◆ Airbrushes. 800-548-9307; 847-816-1611 (in IL).

## Graphic Art Supplies

**Aiko's Art Materials Import,** 3347 N. Clark St., Chicago, IL 60657: Catalog $1.50 ◆ Japanese handmade paper, Oriental art supplies, and fabric dyes. 312-404-5600.

**Alvin & Company Inc.,** P.O. Box 188, Windsor, CT 06095: Free catalog ◆ Art supplies for artists, drafters, engineers, and surveyors. 800-444-2584. www.alvinco.com

**Anco Wood Specialties Inc.,** 7108 80th St., Glendale, NY 11385: Free information ◆ Easels. 800-262-6963; 718-326-2023 (in NY).

**Art Essential of New York Ltd.,** 3 Cross St., Suffern, NY 10901: Free catalog ◆ Tools, how-to videos, and gold, silver, and other metal leafs in sheets and rolls. 800-283-5323.

**Art Express,** P.O. Box 21662, Columbia, SC 29221: Catalog $3.50 ◆ Art supplies. 800-535-5908. www.artxpress.com

**Art Supply Warehouse,** 5325 Departure Dr., Raleigh, NC 27616: Catalog $2 ◆ Art supplies. 800-995-6778; 919-878-5077 (in NC). www.aswexpress.com

**Artisan Santa Fe Inc.,** 717 Canyon Rd., Santa Fe, NM 87501: Free catalog ◆ Art supplies. 800-331-6375. www.artsupply@artisan-santafe.com

**Artists' Connection,** 600 Rt. 1 South, Iselin, NJ 08830: Free catalog ◆ Art supplies. 800-851-9333. www.artistconnect.com

**Artograph Inc.,** 2838 Vicksburg Ln. North, Minneapolis, MN 55447: Free list of retail sources ◆ Projector that enlarges and reduces opaque compositions, photographs, drawings, and other illustrations. 888-975-9555. www.artograph.com

**ASW Express,** 5325 Departure Dr., Raleigh, NC 27616: Free catalog ◆ Art supplies and equipment. 800-995-6778. www.aswexpress.com

**Atelier,** 205 Bucky Dr., Lititz, PA 17543: Free information ◆ Acrylics. 800-257-8278. info@chroma-inc.com

**Benbow Chemical Packaging Inc.,** 935 E. Hiawatha Blvd., Syracuse, NY 13208: Free information ◆ Dry pigments. 315-474-8236.

**Best Moulding Frames,** 102 Alameda Rd., Albuquerque, NM 87114: Free information ◆ Wood studio furniture. 505-897-1365.

**Black Market Art Materials,** 1925 9th St., Berkeley, CA 94710: Free information ◆ Art supplies and equipment. 800-624-ARTS.

**Dick Blick Company,** P.O. Box 1267, Galesburg, IL 61402: Catalog $1 ◆ Books, videos, airbrushes, and printing, drafting, and commercial art supplies. 800-447-8192. www.artmaterials.com

**Arthur Brown & Bros. Inc.,** 2 W. 46th St., New York, NY 10036: Catalog $3 ◆ Art supplies. 800-772-7367. www.artbrown.com

**Stan Brown's Arts & Crafts Inc.,** 13435 NE Whitaker Way, Portland, OR 97230: Catalog $3.50 ◆ Art supplies and books. 800-547-5531; 503-257-0559 (in OR). sbrown4207@aol.com

**Charrette Art Supplies,** P.O. Box 4010, Woburn, MA 01888: Catalog $7.50 ◆ Art and design supplies and equipment. 800-367-3729. www.charrette.com

**Chaselle Inc.,** 101 Almgren Dr., Agawam, MA 01001: Catalog $4 ◆ Books, ceramics molds and kilns, sculpture equipment, and art, silk-screening, and craft supplies. 800-628-9608. www.schoolspecialty.com

**Chatham Art Distributors,** P.O. Box 3851, Frederick, MD 21705: Free information ◆ Art supplies and books. 800-822-4747.

**Cheap Joe's Art Stuff,** 374 Industrial Park Rd., Boone, NC 28607: Free catalog ◆ Art supplies and drawing accessories. 800-257-0874. www.artscape.com/cheapjoe

**Chroma Acrylics Inc.,** 205 Bucky Dr., Lititz, PA 17543: Free information ◆ Acrylic polymer emulsion-base gesso for fine and decorative art and wildfowl painting. 800-257-8278; 717-626-8866 (in PA). info@chroma-inc.com

**Columbia Omnicorp,** 14 W. 33rd St., New York, NY 10001: Free catalog ◆ Office and computer supplies, furniture, and artist materials. 212-279-6161.

**Commercial Art Supplies,** 935 Erie Blvd. East, Syracuse, NY 13210: Price list $3 ◆ Fabric dyeing, silk-screening, and marbling supplies. 800-669-2787.

**Conrad Machine Company,** 1525 S. Warner, Whitehall, MI 49461: Free catalog ◆ Etching and lithography presses. 616-893-7455.

**Createx Colors,** 14 Airport Park Rd., East Granby, CT 06026: Free list of retail sources ◆ Permanent liquid dyes, pure pigments, and pearlescent, iridescent, acrylic, and other fabric colors. 800-243-2712. www.easelart.com

**Crown Art Products,** 90 Dayton Ave., Passaic, NJ 07055: Free catalog ◆ Silk-screening supplies. 201-777-6010.

**Da Vinci Paint Company,** 11 Goodyear St., Irvine, CA 92718: Free information ◆ Permanent pigment paints, oils, watercolors, acrylics, and gouache.

**Decart Inc.,** P.O. Box 309, Morrisville, VT 05661: Free list of retail sources ◆ Fabric paints and dyes for use with airbrushes, water-base enamels and paints for transfer techniques, and glass crafting, silk-screening, and craft supplies. 802-888-4217.

**Delta Technical Coatings,** 2550 Pellissier Pl., Whittier, CA 90601: Free catalog ◆ Acrylics, oils, casein paints, and paint sticks. 800-423-4135; 562-686-0678 (in CA). www.deltacrafts.com

**Dickerson Press Company,** P.O. Box 8, South Haven, MI 49090: Free information ◆ Etching and lithography presses in manual and electric models. Also a press that prints intaglio, relief, lithographs, stone, plate, and other medias. 616-637-4251.

**Gregory D. Dorrance Company,** 1063 Oak Hill Ave., Attleboro, MA 02703: Free information ◆ Decoy-making and art supplies, tools, and wood for carving. 508-222-6255.

**Dove Brushes,** 280 Terrace Rd., Tarpon Springs, FL 34689: Catalog $2.50 ◆ Art supplies. 800-334-3683; 813-934-5283 (in FL). www.dovebrushes.com

**The Duck Blind,** 8709 Gull Rd., Richland, MI 49083: Free catalog ◆ Carving and art supplies, books, and wood. 800-852-7352.

**Duncan Enterprises,** 5673 E. Shields Ave., Fresno, CA 93727: Free list of retail sources ◆ Fabric paints, outline writers, and glitter dispensers. 800-438-6226; 209-291-4444 (in CA). www.duncan-enterprises.com

**The Easel Connection,** 2820 Sunset Ln., Henderson, KY 42420: Free information ◆ Easels and other art supplies. 800-916-2278. easel@gate.net

**Ebersole Lapidary Supply,** 11417 West Hwy. 54, Wichita, KS 67209: Catalog $2 ◆ Shells, lapidary equipment, and supplies for art, calligraphy, jewelry design, and clock-making. 316-722-4771.

**Essex House,** P.O. Box 8684, Prairie Village, KS 66208: Free information ◆ Art supplies. 800-581-0949. www.i-netmall.com/shops/essex

**Fairgate Rule Company Inc.,** 22 Adams Ave., P.O. Box 278, Cold Spring, NY 10516: Free catalog ◆ Rulers, other measuring devices, stencils, and drawing aids. 800-431-2180; 914-265-3677 (in NY).

**The Fine Gold Leaf People,** Art Essentials, Three Cross St., Suffern, NY 10901: Free information ◆ Genuine, imitation, and variegated sheets and rolls of metallic foil. Also brushes, supplies, and books. 800-283-5323.

**Flax Artist Materials,** 240 Valley Dr., Brisbane, CA 94005: Free catalog ◆ Supplies for artists, architects, drafters, and sign painters. 800-547-7778. www.flaxart.com

**Fletcher-Lee & Company,** P.O. Box 626, Elk Grove Village, IL 60009: Free information ◆ Acrylic paints and art supplies. 800-468-2897; 708-766-8888 (in IL). www.artsupplystore.com

**Foster Manufacturing Company,** 414 N. 13th St., Philadelphia, PA 19108: Free catalog ◆ Equipment and storage cabinets for graphic artists. 800-523-4855; 215-625-0500 (in PA).

**A.I. Friedman Art Supplies,** 44 W. 18th St., New York, NY 10011: Catalog $5 ◆ Art supplies. 212-243-9000.

**Frisk Products (USA) Inc.,** 5240 Snapfinger Park Dr., Ste. 115, Decatur, GA 30035: Free information ◆ Graphic art supplies. 770-593-0031.

**Gamblin,** P.O. Box 625, Portland, OR 97207: Free list of retail sources ◆ Oil paints, oil painting mediums, and etching inks. 503-228-9763. www.gamblincolors.com

**Gold Leaf & Metallic Powders,** 74 Trinity Pl., Ste. 1200, New York, NY 10006: Free information ◆ Genuine and composition leaf in rolls, sheets, and books. Also supplies and tools. 800-322-0323; 212-267-4900 (in NY).

**Graphic Chemical & Ink Company,** P.O. Box 27, Villa Park, IL 60181: Free catalog ◆ Print-making supplies for etching, block printing, lithography, and other reproduction processes. 630-832-6004.

**J.L. Hammett Company,** P.O. Box 9057, Braintree, MA 02184: Free catalog ◆ Art supplies. 781-848-1000.

**Russell Harrington Cutlery Inc.,** 44 Green River St., Southbridge, MA 01550: Free information ◆ Mat cutters. 508-765-0201. www.russell-harrington.com

**Hearlihy & Company,** 714 W. Columbia St., Springfield, OH 45504: Free catalog ◆ Art supplies and drafting furniture. 800-622-1000. www.hearlihy.com

**Hofcraft,** P.O. Box 72, Grand Haven, MI 49417: Catalog $4 ◆ How-to art books, brushes, dyes, paints, and handcrafted wood items. 800-828-0359. www.hofcraft.com

**HK Holbein Inc.,** Box 555, Williston, VT 05495: Catalog $7 ◆ Artist paints and colors. 800-682-6686. www.holbeinhk.com

**Houston Art Inc.,** 10770 Moss Ridge Rd., Houston, TX 77043: Free catalog ◆ Art and craft supplies. 800-272-3804. www.houstonart.com

**Christian J. Hummul Company,** P.O. Box 1093, Hunt Valley, MD 21030: Free catalog ◆ Carving tools, art supplies, and how-to-books. 800-762-0235. www.bcpl.net/~rzajac/index.html

**The Italian Art Store,** 84 Maple Ave., Morristown, NJ 07960: Free catalog ◆ Art supplies. 800-643-6440.

**Janovic/Plaza Inc.,** 30-35 Thomson Ave., Long Island City, NY 11101: Catalog $4.95 ◆ Supplies and accessories for art, tole and decorative painting, and other crafts. 800-772-4381. www.janovic.com

**Jerry's Artarama Inc.,** P.O. Box 58638, Raleigh, NC 27658: Catalog $2 ◆ Art supplies. 800-U-ARTIST; 919-878-6782 (in NC). www.jerrycatalog.com

**Kalish Brushes,** 43 Parkside Dr., East Hanover, NJ 07936: Free information ◆ Handmade watercolor brushes. 800-322-5254. brushes@worldnet.att.net

**Krylon,** 31500 Solon Rd., Solon, OH 44139: Free information ◆ Textured paints that make wood, metal, plastic, ceramic, and other surfaces look like stone. 800-797-3332.

**Learning How,** 8895 McGaw Rd., Ste. 200, Columbia, MD 21045: Free brochure ◆ Art materials and educational supplies. 800-675-7627; 410-381-0828 (in MD).

**Loew-Cornell Inc.,** 563 Chestnut Ave., Teaneck, NJ 07666: Free brochure ◆ Brushes for all mediums and surfaces. 201-836-7070. loewcornel@aol.com

**Logan Graphic Products,** 1100 Brown St., Wauconda, IL 60084: Free information ◆ Mat cutter with optional accessories. 800-331-6232. www.artproducts.com

**Martin Universal Design,** 4444 Lawton Ave., Detroit, MI 48208: Free information ◆ Studio furniture. 800-366-7337.

**Marx Brush Manufacturing Company Inc.,** 130 Beckwith Ave., Paterson, NJ 07503: Catalog $2 ◆ Brushes. 800-654-6279. symfau@aol.com

**The Napa Valley Art Store,** 1041 Lincoln Ave., Napa, CA 94558: Free catalog ◆ Art supplies. 800-648-6696.

**Nasco,** 901 Janesville Ave., Fort Atkinson, WI 53538: Free catalog ◆ Paints, brushes, airbrushes, pastels and crayons, drawing and drafting equipment, and craft supplies. 800-558-9595. www.nascofa.com

**Naz-Dar Company,** 1087 N. North Branch St., Chicago, IL 60622: Free catalog ◆ Graphic art and silk-screening equipment. 312-943-8215.

**New York Central Art Supply Company,** 62 3rd Ave., New York, NY 10003: Free information ◆ Art supplies. 212-473-7705.

**Nova Color,** 5894 Blackwelder St., Culver City, CA 90232: Free price list ◆ Pearls, metallic supplies, and acrylic paints. 213-870-6000.

**Omnicorp,** 14 W. 33rd St., New York, NY 10001: Free catalog ◆ Art supplies, drafting materials, ink jet and toner cartridges, and more. 212-279-6161. www.columbiaomni.com

**Otts Art Supplies,** 102 Hungate Dr., Greenville, NC 27858: Free catalog ◆ Art, calligraphy, and drawing supplies. 800-356-3289. www.otts.com

**Pearl Paint,** P.O. Box 946, Smithtown, NY 11787: Catalog $1 ◆ Art supplies. 800-451-7327. www.pearlpaint.com

**Perma Colors,** 226 E. Tremont St., Charlotte, NC 28203: Free catalog ◆ Dry pigment colors, other paint mediums, and supplies. 800-365-2656. members.aol.com/Animalia/index.html

**Plaid Enterprises,** P.O. Box 7600, Norcross, GA 30091: Free information ◆ Acrylic paints and art supplies. 770-923-8200.

**Jack Richeson & Company Inc.,** 557 Marcella Dr., Kimberly, WI 54136: Free list of retail sources ◆ Brushes and studio furniture. 800-233-2404. www.richesonart.com

**Safco Products Company,** 9300 Research Center Rd. West, New Hope, MN 55428: Free information ◆ Storage and filing systems and studio furniture. 888-971-6225.

**Sargent Art Inc.,** 100 E. Diamond Ave., Hazleton, PA 18201: Free information ◆ Crayons, powdered and liquid tempera, water colors, and finger paints. 717-454-3596.

**Sax Arts & Crafts,** P.O. Box 51710, New Berlin, WI 51710: Free catalog ◆ Art supplies. 800-323-0388. www.saxarts.com

**Heinz Scharff Brushes,** P.O. Box 746, Fayetteville, GA 30214: Free catalog ◆ Brushes for tole, chinaware, and decorative painting. 770-461-2200. www.artbrush.com

**Seaway Artist Supplies,** 135 Broadway, Marine City, MI 48039: Free catalog ◆ Oil and water colors, gouache, acrylics, fabric paints, and more. 800-968-1862. www.lukasamerica.com

**Sepp Leaf Products Inc.,** 381 Park Ave. South, New York, NY 10016: Free information ◆ Gold and palladium leaf, rolled gold, tools, and kits. 800-971-7377. www.seppleaf.com

**Sinopia,** 229 Valencia St., San Francisco, CA 94103: Free catalog ◆ Pigments and materials for restoration, interior design, and fine arts. 415-621-2898. www.sinopia.com

**Daniel Smith Art Supplies Inc.,** 4150 1st Ave. South, Seattle, WA 98134: Catalog $5 (refundable) ◆ Art and framing supplies, studio equipment and furniture, and books. 800-426-6740. www.danielsmith.com

**Sunshine Discount Crafts,** 12335 62nd St. North, Largo, FL 33773: Free catalog ◆ Modeling clays and accessories, art supplies, beads, tole and decorative painting supplies, and more. 800-720-2878. www.sunshinecrafts.com

**M. Swift & Sons Inc.,** 10 Love Ln., Hartford, CT 06141: Free information ◆ Silver, palladium, aluminum, and composite gold leaf for decorating and restoring artwork and surfaces. 800-628-0380.

**Tara Materials Inc.,** P.O. Box 646, Lawrenceville, GA 30246: Free information ◆ Artist canvasses. 770-963-5256.

**Technical Papers Corp.,** P.O. Box 546, Dedham, MA 02027: Free catalog ◆ Sheets and rolls of handmade rice paper in prints and solid and multi-colors for all types of artistic printing, including block printing, etching, lithography, and silk-screening. 781-461-1111. www.technicalpapers.com

**Testrite Instrument Company Inc.,** 135 Monroe St., Newark, NJ 07105: Free catalog ◆ Lightweight aluminum and chrome-steel easels, portable light boxes, photography equipment, and opaque projectors. 973-589-6767. www.testrite.com

**Texas Art Supply Company,** 2001 Montrose Blvd., Houston, TX 77006: Catalog $5 ◆ Furniture for the artist. 800-888-9278. www.texasart.com

**Torrington Brush Works Inc.,** P.O. Box 56, Torrington, CT 06790: Free catalog ◆ Brushes and accessories. 860-482-3517.

**United Art & Education,** Box 9219, Fort Wayne, IN 46899: Free catalog ◆ Art supplies. 800-322-3247.

**Utrecht Art & Drafting Supply,** 33 35th St., Brooklyn, NY 11232: Free catalog ◆ Art, sculpture, and print-making supplies. 718-768-2525.

**Visual Systems Company Inc.,** 1596 Rockville Pike, Rockville, MD 20852: Free catalog ◆ Art and drawing supplies. 800-368-2803; 301-770-0500 (in MD).

**Wehrung & Billmeier Company,** 1924 Eddy St., Chicago, IL 60657: Free information ◆ Gilding supplies. 773-472-1544.

**Yasutomo & Company,** 490 Eccles Ave., South San Francisco, CA 94080: Free list of retail sources ◆ Easy-to-blend and apply oil pastels. 415-737-8888.

**Zim's Inc.,** 4370 S. 300 West, Salt Lake City, UT 84107: Catalog $10 (refundable) ◆ Craft and painting supplies. 801-268-9859.

## Modeling & Casting Supplies

**Abatron,** 5501 95th Ave., Kenosha, WI 53144: Free information ◆ Mold-making supplies. 800-445-1754; 414-653-2000 (in WI). www.abatron.com

**Ace Resin,** 7481 E. 30th St., Tucson, AZ 85710: Free information ◆ Casting and molding kit. 520-886-8051.

**Aluminite Corp.,** 225 Parsons St., Kalamazoo, MI 49007: Free information ◆ Fast-setting liquid casting plastic. 616-342-1259.

**American Art Clay Company Inc.,** 4717 W. 16th St., Indianapolis, IN 46222: Free catalog ◆ Modeling and self-hardening clay, paper mache, casting compounds, mold-making materials, acrylics, fabric dyes, fillers and patching compounds, wood stains, and metallic finishes. 800-374-1600; 317-244-6871 (in IN). www.amaco.com

**Johnson Atelier,** 50 Princeton-Hightstown Rd., Ste. L, Princeton Junction, NJ 08550: Free catalog ◆ Sculpture and casting supplies. Also carving tools for wood and stone. 800-732-7203. jasacs@aol.com

**Bare-Metal Foil Company,** P.O. Box 82, Farmington, MI 48332: Catalog $2.50 ◆ Quick-setting molding materials and adhesive-backed chrome, black chrome, gold, matte aluminum, and copper foil sheets. 248-477-0813.

**Belmont Metals Inc.,** 330 Belmont Ave., Brooklyn, NY 11207: Free information ◆ Non-ferrous metals for making sculptures. 718-342-4900.

**Castaldo,** 120 Constitution Blvd., Franklin, MA 02038: Free information ◆ Jewelry molding rubber. 508-520-1666.

**Castcraft,** P.O. Box 17000, Memphis, TN 38187: Free information ◆ How-to information, rubber and plastic materials, and mold-making and casting supplies. 901-682-0961. www.castcraft.com

**Castolite,** 4915 Dean, Woodstock, IL 60098: Catalog $3 ◆ Casting resins, mold-making supplies, and how-to books. 815-338-4670.

**Cementex Latex Corp.,** 121 Varick St., New York, NY 10013: Free catalog ◆ Molds and liquid rubber. 800-782-9056; 212-741-1770 (in NY). www.cementex.com

**Chaselle Inc.,** 101 Almgren Dr., Agawam, MA 01001: Catalog $4 ◆ Books, ceramics molds and kilns, sculpture equipment, and art, silk-screening, and craft supplies. 800-628-8608. www.schoolspecialty.com

**Chavant Inc.,** 42 West St., Red Bank, NJ 07701: Free information ◆ Water-base clay for sculpting at room temperature. 908-842-6272.

**Clay Factory of Escondido,** P.O. Box 460598, Escondido, CA 92046: Free information ◆ Modeling materials. 800-243-3466. www.clayfactoryinc.com

**Colorado Alabaster Supply,** 1507 N. College Ave., Fort Collins, CO 80524: Free brochure ◆ Alabaster stone for carving, hand tools, finishing supplies, and books. 970-221-0723.

**Concrete Machinery Company,** P.O. Box 99, Hickory, NC 28603: Information $10 ◆ Supplies and aluminum molds for making ornamental concrete items. 704-322-7710.

**Creative Paperclay Company,** 1800 S. Robertson Blvd., Ste. 907, Los Angeles, CA 90035: Free information ◆ Air hardening sculpting material. 213-839-0466.

**Gerlachs of Lecha,** P.O. Box 213, Emmaus, PA 18049: Catalog $2.25 ◆ Paper sculpting kits. 610-965-9181.

**Gold's Artworks Inc.,** 2100 N. Pine St., Lumberton, NC 28358: Free catalog with long SASE ◆ Paper-making pigments and chemicals, pulp materials, kits, and supplies. 800-356-2306; 910-739-9605 (in NC).

**Great Lakes Clay & Supply Company,** 120 S. Lincoln Ave., Carpentersville, IL 60110: Free catalog ◆ Sculpting and modeling compounds, tools, and studio equipment. 800-258-8796; 847-551-1070 (in IL) www.greatclay.com

**Handcraft Designs Inc.,** 63 E. Broad St., Hatfield, PA 19440: Free information with long SASE ◆ Molds, tools, modeling material, and how-to books for use with polymer and air-drying clays. 800-523-2430; 215-855-3022 (in PA). hdclays@aol.com

**Montoya/MAS International Inc.,** 435 Southern Blvd., West Palm Beach, FL 33405: Catalog $3 ◆ Bronze casting (lost wax process), mold-making, polishing and stone finishing, and alabaster, steatite, soapstone, marble, and onyx carving stones. 800-682-8665; 561-832-4401 (in FL). home.att.net/~montoya-mas

**Nasco,** 901 Janesville Ave., Fort Atkinson, WI 53538: Free catalog ◆ Modeling materials, non-firing and firing clays, tools, molds, and craft supplies. 800-558-9595. www.nascofa.com

**Polyform Products Company,** 1901 Estes Ave., Elk Grove Village, IL 60009: Free information ◆ Shatter and chip-proof ceramic-like sculpting compound, paints, glazes, tools, and modeling sets.

**Polymer Clay Express,** 25-5 Broad St., Ste. 242, Freehold, NJ 07728: Catalog $1 ◆ Modeling compounds and clays. 732-431-1390. PolyExp@aol.com

**Sculpture House,** 155 W. 26th St., New York, NY 10001: Catalog $2 ◆ Sculpting tools, modeling and mold-making accessories, and supplies. 212-645-9430.

**Smooth-On,** 1000 Valley Rd., Gillette, NJ 07933: Free information ◆ Liquid plastic compounds. 800-766-6841; 908-647-5800 (in NJ). www.smooth-on.com

**Sunshine Discount Crafts,** 12335 62nd St. North, Largo, FL 33773: Free catalog ◆ Modeling clays and accessories, art supplies, beads, tole and decorative painting supplies, and more. 800-720-2878. www.sunshinecrafts.com

**Sutton Supply Company,** 215 McLin Creek Rd. North, Conover, NC 28613: Free information ◆ Casting glue gelatin. 704-464-8297.

**TBF Inc.,** P.O. Box 80126, Phoenix, AZ 85060: Free brochure ◆ Fimo modeling supplies and accessories. 800-492-0806; 602-392-0806 (in AZ). www.fimo-usa.com

**United States Gypsum Company,** Industrial Products Division, P.O. Box 6721, Chicago, IL 60680: Free list of retail sources ◆ Plaster for molding. 800-487-4431. bpayne@usp.com

**Vagabond Corp.,** P.O. Box 39, Warner Springs, CA 92086: Free information ◆ Casting supplies. 619-782-3136.

**Wee Folk Creations,** 18476 Natchez Ave., Prior Lake, MN 55372: Free catalog ◆ How-to videos and books on molding with clay, tools, accessories, and supplies. 888-933-3655. www.weefolk.com

**Wisconsin Fibrecraft Inc.,** P.O. Box 465, Sullivan, WI 53178: Free brochure ◆ Paper mache forms for decoration. 800-645-7857; 414-593-8336 (in WI).

## ARTHRITIS AIDS

**adaptAbility,** P.O. Box 515, Colchester, CT 06415: Free catalog ◆ Mobility, grooming, dressing, bathing, eating and cooking aids; exercise and therapy games; and adaptive home aids for arthritis sufferers. 800-288-9941. service@snswwide.com

**Danmar Products Inc.,** 221 Jackson Industrial Dr., Ann Arbor, MI 48103: Free brochure ◆ Easy-to-hold utensil handles and arthritis aids. 800-783-1998; 313-761-1990 (in MI).

**Fashion Ease,** Division M & M Health Care, 1541 60th St., Brooklyn, NY 11219: Free catalog ◆ Clothing with Velcro closures, wheelchair attachments, and incontinence supplies. 800-221-8929; 718-871-8188 (in NY). www.fashionease.com

**Maxi-Aids,** P.O. Box 3209, Farmingdale, NY 11735: Free catalog ◆ Communications devices, eating and kitchen aids, dressing aids, wheelchair accessories, and more. 800-522-6294. sales@maxiaids.com

**Miles Kimball Company,** 41 W. 8th Ave., Oshkosh, WI 54906: Free catalog ◆ Assistive devices and aids for people with arthritis and physical disabilities. 800-546-2255. www.mileskimball.com

**W.R. Medical Electronics Company,** 123 N. 2nd St., Stillwater, MN 55082: Free information ◆ Drug-free paraffin-heat therapy system for arthritis pain relief, joint stiffness, inflammation, and muscle spasms. 800-321-6387. www.wrmed.com

## ARTWORK

### Posters, Paintings, Prints, & Other Art Forms

**A & K Historical Art,** 12 Kilburn Ave., Huntington Station, NY 11746: Free information ◆ Limited edition historical art. 800-286-3884.

**American Print Gallery,** P.O. Box 4477, Gettysburg, PA 17325: Information $1 ◆ Military art prints and note cards. 800-448-1863. www.mkunstler.com

**American Royal Arts Corp.,** 123 Frost St., Ste. 201, Westbury, NY 11590: Free catalog ◆ Original and limited edition animation art. 800-888-9449; 516-997-2220 (in NY). www.ara-animation.com

**Animation Art Resources,** 118 N. 3rd St., Philadelphia, PA 19106: Free information (specify interests) ◆ Disney, Warner Brothers, Hanna Barbera, and other studio cels. 800-269-1009; 215-925-2009 (in PA). www.netaxs.com/~animart

**The Animation Celection,** 1002 Prospect St., La Jolla, CA 92037: Free catalog ◆ Animation art collectibles. 800-223-5328. www.animationcelection.com

**The Animation Company,** 19806 N. 4th St., Phoenix, AZ 85024: Free catalog ◆ Animated artwork from Disney, Warner Brothers, Hanna Barbera, and other studios. 888-222-0332.

**Animation Station,** P.O. Box 270701, San Diego, CA 92198: Free information ◆ Collectible animation cels and drawings. 619-485-5844.

**Art in Action,** 1052 S. Moon Lake Dr., Eveleth, MN 55734: Free catalog ◆ Framed reproductions of original paintings on canvas. 800-701-4278.

**Art-Toons,** P.O. Box 670600, Northfield, OH 44067: Free catalog ◆ Animated art for collectors. 888-468-2655; 330-468-2655 (in OH).

**Artisans Gallery,** P.O. Box 256, Mentone, AL 35984: Free information ◆ Original folk art. 256-634-4037. www.folkartisans.com

**Artist Roost,** 3520 N. Swan St., Silver City, NM 88061: Free brochure ◆ Aviation art and note cards. 505-538-8814.

**Artistic Judaic Promotions,** 4990 S. Lafayette Ln., Englewood, CO 80110: Free information ◆ Handmade jewelry, Judaica, art, and ketubot. 303-789-3879. ajpi@ixnetcom.com

**Artrock Posters,** 1155 Mission St., San Francisco, CA 94103: Free catalog ◆ Original rock concert posters, T-shirts, books, and memorabilia. 415-255-7390.

**Arts & Designs of Japan,** Box 22075, San Francisco, CA 94122: Catalog $10 ◆ 18th through the 20th-century Japanese woodblock prints. 415-759-6233. www.artsanddesignsjapan.com

**Ascalon Studios,** 115 Atlantic Ave., Berlin, NJ 08009: Free brochure ◆ Synagogue art. 609-768-3779.

**The Astronomical Society of the Pacific,** 390 Ashton Ave., San Francisco, CA 94112: Free catalog ◆ Posters of the cosmos. 800-962-3412. www.aspsky.org

**B & R Gallery,** 17720 Sierra Hwy., Canyon Country, CA 91351: Free brochure ◆ Limited edition western theme prints and other works of art. 800-255-6498; 805-298-2038 (in CA). www.bnr-art.com

**Virginia Bader Fine Arts,** John Wayne Orange County Airport, 19531 Campus Dr., Ste. 19, Santa Ana, CA 92707: Catalog $5 ◆ Aviation art. 800-328-5826. www.virginiabader.com

**Barker Animation,** 1188 Highland Ave., Cheshire, CT 06410: Free catalog ◆ Animation art. 800-995-CELS; 203-272-CELS (in CT). www.barkeranimation.com

**Bayshore Graphics,** 2058 NW Miami Ct., Miami, FL 33127: Free brochure ◆ Aviation art. 800-576-0154.

**The Big Image,** P.O. Box 1121, Grants Pass, OR 97526: Free information ◆ Full color photo transfers to canvas. 541-474-0854.

**Brana Fine Arts,** 15332 Antioch St., #108, Pacific Palisades, CA 90272: Free information ◆ Salvadore Dali prints. 800-275-DALI. www.daligallery.com

**Breedlove Enterprises,** P.O. Box 538, Bolivar, OH 44612: Free information ◆ Limited edition, numbered, and signed Civil War lithographs. 800-221-1863.

**Bill & Kathy Brewer,** 203 Asbury Ave., Greenville, IL 62246: Price list $2 ◆ Reproductions and restoration of Plains Indian (Native American) art. 618-664-3384.

**Brush Strokes,** 19312 Haviland Dr., South Bend, IN 46637: Brochure $3 ◆ Signed and numbered limited editions of reproduction prints of oil paintings with optional framing. 219-277-5414.

**Buchanan Aviation Art,** 56 S. Broad St., Milford, CT 06460: Free catalog ◆ Aviation art. 800-659-4174; 203-876-0560 (in CT).

**Buck Hill Associates,** P.O. Box 4736, Queensbury, NY 12804: Free catalog ◆ Posters, handbills, historical documents, and other Americana.

**Cartoon Art Unlimited,** 379 Belmont Ave., Haledon, NJ 07508: Free catalog ◆ Animation art. 800-966-TOON; 201-942-1003 (in NJ).

**The Cartoon Company,** Crown Center Shops, 2nd Floor, 2450 Grand Ave., Kansas City, MO 64108: Free catalog ◆ Vintage cels and drawings from Disney, Warner Brothers, and other major studios. 816-842-3300.

**Cherokee National Museum Gift Shop,** P.O. Box 515, TSA-LA-GI, Tahlequah, OK 74464: Free price list with long SASE ◆ Original paintings, prints, sculptures, and Native American crafts and art. 918-456-6007.

**Christian Book Distributors,** P.O. Box 7000, Peabody, MA 01961: Free catalog ◆ Religious-theme Christian artwork and books. 978-977-5050. www.chrbook.com

**Cincinnati Art Museum,** Eden Park Dr., Cincinnati, OH 45202: Free catalog ◆ Reproductions of posters, postcards, and museum collectibles. 513-721-5204.

**Stan Clark Military Books,** 915 Fairview Ave., Gettysburg, PA 17325: Catalog $2 ◆ Civil War prints. 717-337-1728.

**Classic Aerographs,** 1764 Montecito Circle, Livermore, CA 94550: Free brochure ◆ Aviation art. 510-443-0299.

**The Cricket Gallery,** 5525 Glen Errol Rd., Atlanta, GA 30327: Free catalog ◆ Vintage and contemporary animation cels, drawings, and Disney backgrounds. 800-BUY-CELS.

**The CSA Galleries Prints,** 2150 Northwoods Blvd., North Charleston, SC 29406: Catalog $5 (refundable) ◆ Civil War Confederate-related art prints. 800-256-1861; 803-818-2009 (in SC). www.csagalleries.com

**The Decoy,** P.O. Box 3652, Carmel, CA 93921: Free brochure ◆ Handcarved wood birds, antique decoys, limited edition prints, and original art. 800-332-6988. decoy1881.aol.com

**Decoys & Wildlife Gallery,** 55 Bridge St., Frenchtown, NJ 08825: Free catalog ◆ Limited edition fine art prints, books, and works of art in porcelain. Custom framing available. 908-996-6501.

**Déja-Vu Enterprises Inc.,** 1029 Westwood Blvd., Los Angeles, CA 90024: Free catalog ◆ Autographed movie star photos, original movie posters, and lobby cards from silent film days to the present. 310-443-5280. DEJAVU@EARTHLINK.NET

**DeRus Fine Art,** 9100 Artesia Blvd., Bellflower, CA 90706: Free list ◆ Art books and 19th and early 20th-century artwork. 310-920-1312.

**Design Evolution,** P.O. Box 341, Boulder, CO 80306: Free information ◆ Original movie posters from the 1930s, 1940s, and 1950s. 888-779-3337.

**Designs Etc.,** P.O. Box 1586, Middleburg, VA 20118: Free brochure ◆ Framed postage stamp art. 800-STAMPS-8.

**Eagle Editions Ltd.,** P.O. Box 580, Hamilton, MT 59840: Free brochure ◆ Aviation art. 800-255-1830; 406-363-5415 (in MT). www.eagle-editions.com

**European Tradition,** P.O. Box 01-0055, Miami, FL 33101: Catalog $5 (refundable) ◆ Victorian-style paintings, prints, and mirrors. 305-371-4474.

**Filmart's Cartoon World,** 362 New York Ave., Huntington, Long Island, NY 11743: Free catalog ◆ Vintage and contemporary animation art from most major studios. 800-ART-CELS. celworld@aol.com

**Wally Findlay Gallery,** 188 E. Walton Pl., Chicago, IL 60611: Free information ◆ Original paintings. 312-649-1500. www.artnet.com/wfindlay-il.html

**Fine Art Impressions,** 5115 Excelsior Blvd., #204, Minneapolis, MN 55416: Free catalog ◆ Oil-on-canvas art reproductions of famous masterpiece works. 800-279-4278. www.masterscollection.com

**Finetoon Cartoon Art,** 2427 Bissonnet, Houston, TX 77005: Free newsletter and list ◆ Cartoon art from Disney, Warner Brothers, Hanna-Barbera, and other animation studios. 888-487-0447. www.finetoon.com

**Framing Fox Art Gallery,** P.O. Box 679, Lebanon, NJ 08833: Free information with long SASE ◆ Civil War prints. 800-237-6077.

**Galerie Robin,** P.O. Box 42275, Cincinnati, OH 45242: Free information ◆ Limited edition art prints. 800-635-8279. www.judaica-online.com

**Gallery Lainzberg,** 222 3rd St. SE, Ste. 200, Cedar Rapids, IA 52401: Catalog $4.95 ◆ Serigraphs, other animation art from most major studios, and limited edition, classic, and modern production cels. 800-678-4608. lainzberg.com

**Gallery 247,** 814 Merrick Rd., Baldwin, NY 11510: Free brochure ◆ Collectible plates and prints. 516-868-4800.

**Gartlan USA Inc.,** 575 Rt. 73N, Ste. A-6, West Berlin, NJ 08091: Free catalog ◆ Autographed limited edition collector plates, figurines, ceramic trading cards, and lithographs featuring athletes and entertainers. 609-753-9280. www.gartlanusa.com

**Gifted Images Gallery,** P.O. Box 34, Baldwin, NY 11510: Free catalog ◆ Animation art. 800-726-6708; 516-536-6886 (in NY).

**Glass Art,** 1435 Hopkins Rd., Williamsville, NY 14221: Free catalog ◆ Original glass art paintings. 800-335-9350; 716-689-2417 (in NY). www.glassartisans.com

**Ari Gradus,** 414 7th St., Brooklyn, NY 11215: Free catalog ◆ Original serigraphs, lithographs, and paintings. 718-768-6688.

**The Greatest Scapes,** 1613 Hawthorne St., Pittsburgh, PA 15201: Free catalog ◆ Framed art reproductions. 800-786-3022.

**The Greenwich Workshop Inc.,** P.O. Box 875, Shelton, CT 06484: Free information ◆ Fantasy, wilderness, western, exotic lands, aviation themes, and other limited edition prints. 800-243-4246. www.thegreenwichworkshop.com

**Gremlin Animation,** P.O. Box 1787, Manchester Center, VT 05255: Catalog $3 ◆ Vintage and modern animation art. 800-541-CART. www.thegremlin.com

**Grossman Art Brokerage,** 30345 LaBrea Ct., Franklin, MI 48025: Free information ◆ Collectible artwork. 800-332-1278.

**Guarisco Gallery,** 2828 Pennsylvania Ave. NW, Washington, DC 20007: Catalog $10 ◆ European, British, and American 19th-century paintings. 202-333-8533.

**Guide Dog Foundation for the Blind,** 371 E. Jericho Tnpk., Smithtown, NY 11787: Free catalog ◆ Limited edition guide dog prints, holiday cards, mugs, mats, key rings, stationery, pet accessories, and gifts. 800-443-8372. www.guidedog.org

**Halibar Company,** P.O. Box 608, Chatfield, MN 55923: Catalog $2 (refundable) ◆ Screen-printed silhouettes. 800-848-0130.

**Harringtons Ink,** 11011 N. Granville Rd., Mequon, WI 53097: Free brochure ◆ Nostalgic America rendered in acrylics. 414-242-2099.

**Harvest Gallery Inc.,** 1527 Beverly Dr., Wichita Falls, TX 76309: Free brochure ◆ Limited edition prints. 800-545-8231.

**Heirloom Editions,** Box 520-B, Rt. 4, Carthage, MO 64836: Catalog $4 ◆ Lithographs, greeting cards, stickers, miniatures, stationery, framed prints, turn-of-the-century art, and paper collectibles. 800-725-0725.

**Heritage Aviation Art,** 12819 SE 38th St., #211, Bellevue, WA 98005: Catalog $5 (refundable) ◆ Paintings, prints, posters, and art by aviation artists. 800-331-9044; 206-747-7429 (in WA).

**Heritage Historical Prints Inc.,** 3772 Angelton Ct., Burtonsville, MD 20866: Free information ◆ Antique prints, engravings, and fine art. 800-890-4566; 301-890-4566 (in MD). www.heritageprints.com

**Hornung Art,** 32 E. Charlotte Ave., Cincinnati, OH 45215: Free information ◆ Art, antiques, and miniature figures. 513-761-8518. www.hornungart.com

**Intergalactic Trading Company,** P.O. Box 521516, Longwood, FL 32752: Free catalog ◆ Movie posters and related material. 800-383-0727. sales@intergalactictrading.com

**J's Gallery & Frame Shoppe,** 406 E. Broadway, Eagle Grove, IA 50533: Free information ◆ Collectible prints. 800-448-1861; 515-448-4012 (in IA). www.netins.net/showcase/art

**Kennedy Galleries,** 730 5th Ave., New York, NY 10019: Catalog $5 ◆ Prints and other artwork. 212-541-9600. Kennedydygal@aol.com

**Leona King Gallery,** 7171 Main, Scottsdale, AZ 85251: Free information ◆ Serigraphs, glicees, other artwork, and limited edition prints. 800-227-2589; 602-945-1209 (in AZ). www.kinggalleries.com

**Leslie Levy Fine Art,** 1505 N. Hayden Rd., Scottsdale, AZ 85257: Free information ◆ Contemporary American paintings, drawings, and sculptures. 800-765-2787; 602-945-8491 (in AZ). www.leslielevy.com

**Liros Gallery Inc.,** Main St., Blue Hill, ME 04614: Free catalog ◆ Art prints and paintings. 800-287-5370; 207-374-5370 (in ME). www.media1.hypernet.com/liros.html

**Map Appeal Inc.,** 1402 Pine Ave., Ste. 827, Niagara Falls, NY 14301: Free brochure ◆ Earth and sky satellite photographs. 800-363-0938; 905-627-2462 (in NY). www.mapappeal.com

**Ben Marra Studios,** 310 1st Ave. South, Seattle, WA 98104: Free information ◆ Photographs that capture the authentic pride and spirituality of today's Native Americans. 800-624-1940. benmarra@halcyon.com

**The Masters' Collection,** 40 Scitico Rd., Somersville, CT 06072: Catalog $5 ◆ Art replicas on canvas of the world's masterpieces. 860-749-2281. www.MastersCollection.com

**Nedra Matteucci Fenn Galrie,** 1075 Paseo de Peralta, Santa Fe, NM 87501: Free information ◆ Historical American art and contemporary Southwestern paintings and sculpture. 505-982-4631.

**Meehan Military Posters,** P.O. Box 477, New York, NY 10028: Catalog $10 ◆ Original authentic World War I and II posters. 212-734-5683. www.posterfair.com/nm/storefront.htm

**Metropolitan Museum of Art,** Special Service Office, Middle Village, NY 11381: Free catalog ◆ Porcelain, ceramics and glass, scarves, shawls, neckties, books, jewelry, and original lithographs, prints, and graphics from around the world. 800-662-3397. www.metmuseum.org

**Motorhead Art & Collectibles,** 1917 Dumas Circle NE, Tacoma, WA 98422: Catalog $5 ◆ Automotive art prints and collectibles, scale model cars and kits, and books. 800-859-0164.

**Moulton Gallery Inc.,** 12262 SW 131st Ave., Miami, FL 33186: Free brochure ◆ Limited edition contemporary paintings and 3-dimensional art renditions. 305-233-5714.

**Mt. Nebo Gallery,** Grandma Moses Rd., P.O. Box 94, Eagle Bridge, NY 12057: Free catalog ◆ Limited edition lithographs, prints, serigraphs, and etchings by Will Moses. 800-328-6326.

**Museum Editions of New York Ltd.,** 434 Greenwich St., New York, NY 10013: Catalog $5 ◆ Reproductions of contemporary to modern posters. 212-431-1913.

**Name That Toon,** 28 Mountain View Ave., San Rafael, CA 94901: Free brochure ◆ Advertising animation art. Available framed and matted. 800-550-5202; 415-456-3452 (in CA). www.namethattoon.com

**Jeanne Nash Studio,** 974 Marlin Dr., Jupiter, FL 33458: Free information ◆ Watercolors, embossings, and limited edition prints. 561-575-2030.

**National Archives & Records Administration,** National Archives Books, Washington, DC 20408: Free brochure ◆ Historic patriotic posters and postcards. 202-523-3164.

**Nostalgia Decorating Company,** 3 Birchwood Dr., Mountain Top, PA 18707: Brochure $2 ◆ Framed or unframed turn-of-the-century prints. 717-788-4017.

**Novagraphics,** P.O. Box 37197, Tucson, AZ 85740: Catalog $3 ◆ Astronomy and space-theme artwork and greeting cards. 800-727-6682. www.novaspace.com

**Old Glory Gallery & Frame Shop,** 2966 Park Hill Dr., Fort Worth, TX 76109: Free list ◆ Civil War prints. 800-731-0060; 817-923-5576 (in TX).

**Old Grange Graphics,** 1590 Reed Rd., West Trenton, NJ 08628: Catalog $6 (refundable) ◆ Prints and canvas replicas of folk art in large and miniature sizes. 800-282-7776.

**The Old Print Gallery,** 1220 31st St. NW, Washington, DC 20007: Catalog $3 ◆ Prints and maps from the 18th and 19th-century. 202-965-1818.

**Original Print Collectors Group Ltd.,** 88 Astor Square, Rhinebeck, NY 12572: Free catalog ◆ Numbered, signed, and framed original limited edition prints, serigraphs, etchings, and lithographs. 800-556-6200.

**Osbourne-Schneider Enterprises Inc.,** Stay Tooned! Animation Art, P.O. Box 139, Honeoye Falls, NY 14472: Free information ◆ Animation, comic, and other cartoon-related collectible art. 716-624-1580.

**Pendleton Cowgirl Company,** P.O. Box 19474, Portland, OR 97280: Catalog $2 ◆ Classic western theme T-shirts, lithographs, note cards, and calendars. 503-977-0292.

**Posters of Santa Fe,** 111 E. Palace Ave., Santa Fe, NM 87501: Free catalog ◆ Art posters. 800-827-6745. www.ssun.com/posters

**PosterWorld,** P.O. Box 1180, Concord, MA 01742: Free catalog ◆ Reproduction posters for decorating and art collecting. 508-369-9088.

**Presentations Gallery,** 200 Lexington Ave., New York, NY 10016: Free information ◆ Contemporary synagogue art, furniture, memorial renditions, and recognition gifts. 212-481-8181.

**Quality Collectables,** 71 S. Mast St., Goffstown, NH 03045: Free information ◆ Limited edition figurines and statues, signed plates and lithographs, and sports art. 800-422-6514. mattmo@aol.com

**Steven S. Raab,** P.O. Box 471, Ardmore, PA 19003: Catalog $5 ◆ Autographs, signed books and photos, old newspapers, World War I posters, and historic memorabilia. 610-446-6193. www.raabautographs.com

**Red Fox Fine Art,** 7 N. Liberty St., Middleburg, VA 22117: Catalog $5 ◆ Sculptures and 19th-century animal and sports paintings. 540-687-5780.

**Red Lancer,** P.O. Box 8056, Mesa, AZ 85214: Catalog $6 ◆ Original 19th-century military art, rare books, Victorian campaign medals and helmets, toy soldiers, and other collectibles. 602-964-9667.

**The Norman Rockwell Museum,** P.O. Box 308, Stockbridge, MA 01262: Catalog $1 ◆ Prints, books about Norman Rockwell, and other reproductions of artwork by Americas's favorite illustrator. 800-742-9450. www.nrm.org

**Ronin Gallery,** 605 Madison Ave., New York, NY 10022: Catalog $6 ◆ Contemporary prints, 19th-century masks, netsuke, wood, and other Japanese art. Also 18th, 19th, and 20th-century woodblock prints. 212-688-0188.

**Salzer's,** 5801 Valentine Rd., Ventura, CA 93003: Free information ◆ Vintage concert posters. 805-639-2169.

**Shadow Box,** 655 Saratoga Ave., San Jose, CA 95129: Free catalog ◆ Art reproductions. 800-551-5285. www.shadow-box.com

**Sisters of St. Joseph of LaGrange,** Ministry of the Arts, 1515 W. Ogden Ave., LaGrange Park, IL 60526: Free catalog ◆ Religious/spiritual art. Includes posters, calendars, art prints, greeting cards, and paper sculptures. 708-354-9200. www.ministryofthearts.org

**Sports Memorabilia Etc.,** 11841 Ventura Blvd., Studio City, CA 91604: Free information ◆ Autographed lithographs, signed plates, figurines, plaques, and baseball and other sports cards. 800-995-0650. sports1@earthlink.net

**Starland Collector's Gallery,** P.O. Box 622, Los Olivos, CA 93441: Catalog $2.50 ◆ Sports cards, movie posters, original comic art, and hard-to-find movies. 805-688-8300.

**The Stokes Collection,** Box 1420, Pebble Beach, CA 93953: Catalog $7.50 ◆ Limited edition aviation art lithographs and reproductions on canvas. 800-359-4644. www.stokescollection.com

**Drew Strouble's Cat-A-Log,** 539 Avenida Del Norte, Sarasota, FL 34242: Free information ◆ Fine art for cat lovers. 800-349-MEOW. www.catmandrew.com

**Studio II,** P.O. Box 1274, Orange, VA 22960: Brochure $1 ◆ Original limited edition watercolors, oil paintings, and lithographs. 540-854-7828.

**John Tackett Galleries,** 1616 Holt St., Fort Worth, TX 76103: Free catalog ◆ Aviation art prints, T-shirts, and computer screen savers with over 25 full-color images for Windows. 800-243-1661.

**Taggart Galleries,** 48 E 73rd St., New York, NY 10021: Free information ◆ American paintings from the 19th and 20th-century and contemporary realism art. 212-628-4000. taggartnyc@aol.com

**Thoroughbred Racing Catalog,** P.O. Box 610, Warsaw, VA 22572: Free catalog ◆ Calendars and limited edition prints with pictures of famous racing horses and horse-decorated mailboxes, doormats, sweatshirts and T-shirts, mugs and glasses, jewelry, and wall clocks. 800-777-RACE. www.thoroughbred-racing.com

**True Reproductions,** Box 21, 155 Tycos Rd., Toronto, Ontario, Canada M6B 1W6: Catalog $2 ◆ Reproduction World War II posters.

**Vintage Animation Gallery,** 1404 3rd St. Promenade, Santa Monica, CA 90401: Free information ◆ Original animation art, from the 1940s, 1950s, and 1960s. 310-393-8666.

**Vladimir Arts U.S.A. Inc.,** 5401 Portage Rd., Kalamazoo, MI 49002: Free information ◆ Original oils, acrylics, watercolors, and graphics. 800-676-8523; 616-383-0032 (in MI). www.vladimir.com

**Willitts Designs,** 1129 Industrial Ave., Petaluma, CA 94952: Free information ◆ Collectible movie cels. 800-358-9184. www.willitts.com

**Thelma Winter,** 8260 E. Eden Rd., Eden, NY 14057: Free brochure ◆ Limited edition original paintings in pen, ink, and watercolors. 716-992-4277.

**Worlds of Wonder,** P.O. Box 814-CS, McLean, VA 22101: Free catalog ◆ Framed (unless indicated otherwise) science fiction, fantasy, and horror artwork. 703-847-4251. www.wow-art.com

**Yanoff International,** 18949 Centerville Creek Rd., Caledone, Ontario, Canada L0N 1E0: Free catalog ◆ Original posters. 905-584-9398. ww3w.yanoff.com

## Sculptures, Carvings, & Castings

**American Bronze Foundry,** 1650 E. Lake Mary Blvd., Sanford, FL 32773: Catalog $10 (refundable) ◆ Artist bronze and silver castings (limited edition sculpture and replicas). 800-881-8090; 407-328-8090 (in FL). www.americanbronze.com

**Arrow Gems & Minerals Inc.,** 9827 Cave Creek Rd., Phoenix, AZ 85020: Free catalog ◆ Pewter figurines. 602-997-6373.

**Ballard Designs,** 1670 DeFoor Ave. NE, Atlanta, GA 30318: Catalog $3 ◆ Sculptured castings, furniture, lamps, decorative and fireplace accessories, garden and landscaping items, frames, and pictures. 800-367-2810. www.ballard-designs.com

**Henry Bonnard Bronze Company,** 1490 S. Hwy. 17-92, Longwood, FL 32750: Free catalog ◆ Bronze statuary with optional marble bases. 800-521-3179. www.bronzesculpturesusa.com

**Cherokee National Museum Gift Shop,** P.O. Box 515, TSA-LA-GI, Tahlequah, OK 74464: Free price list with long SASE ◆ Original paintings, prints, sculptures, baskets, and Native American arts and crafts. 918-456-6007.

**Churchills,** Twelve Oaks Mall, Novi, MI 48377: Free information ◆ Art collectibles and plates. 800-388-1141.

**Dakota Craftsman,** P.O. Box 845, Custer, SD 57730: Free information ◆ Lamp stands, animals, and art made from recycled antlers. 505-673-2112.

**Dewey Graff Fine Art Inc.,** 6005 Idylwood Dr., Edina, MN 55436: Free catalog ◆ Fine art acrylic sculptures. 800-935-8182; 612-935-2289 (in MN). www.deweygfa.com

**DR Sports,** 1275 Bloomfield Ave., Bldg. 6, Unit 34, Fairfield, NJ 07004: Free information ◆ Major and minor league baseball card sets. Also other sports cards and figurines, plates, and ceramics and pewter collectibles. 973-227-6547.

**Duncan Royale,** 1141 S. Acacia Ave., Fullerton, CA 92631: Free information ◆ Sculptured figurines. 800-366-4646. www.duncanroyale.com

**Eleganza Ltd.,** Magnolia Village, 3217 W. Smith, Seattle, WA 98199: Catalog $6 ◆ Handcrafted sculptures. 206-283-0609. www.eleganza.com

**Enesco Corp.,** 1 Enesco Plaza, Elk Grove Village, IL 60007: Free list of retail sources ◆ Figurines, sculptures, ornaments, Barbie dolls, and gifts. www.enesco.com

**David Epstein Sports Collectibles,** 6 Robin Rd., Edison, NJ 08820: Free information ◆ Figurines, plates, lithographs, and other porcelain sports figurines. 800-343-1256; 908-549-4648 (in NJ). dmepstein@aol.com

**European Imports & Gifts,** Oak Mill Mall, 7900 N. Milwaukee Ave., Niles, IL 60648: Free information ◆ Art, porcelains, Christmas ornaments, and pewter. 847-967-5253.

**Excalibur Bronze Sculpture Foundry,** 85 Adams St., Brooklyn, NY 11201: Catalog $10 (refundable) ◆ Bronze sculptures. 718-522-3330.

**Fellowship Foundry Pewtersmiths,** 1605 Abram Ct., San Leandro, CA 94577: Free catalog ◆ Goblets, sculptures, switchplates, jewelry, cups and steins, glassware and crystal, and pewter gifts. 510-352-0935.

**Gallery Northwest,** P.O. Box 1747, Shelton, WA 98584: Free brochure ◆ Original wood sculptures. 360-427-5693. www.halcyon.com/cjlew/rscott/rs.html

**Giust Gallery,** 1920 Washington St., Boston, MA 02118: Catalog $5 ◆ Replicas of classical sculptures from major European museums. 617-445-3800.

**Goebel Inc.,** Goebel Plaza, P.O. Box 10, Pennington, NJ 08534: Free information ◆ Miniature sculptures of characters from Walt Disney's animated film classics. 800-366-4632. www.mihummel.com

**Guys Cats,** Box 1339, Avalon, CA 90704: Free information ◆ Wire cat sculptures. 800-392-9037.

**Enoch Kelley Haney Art Gallery,** P.O. Box 72, Seminole, OK 74868: Free brochure with long SASE ◆ Original paintings and prints, sculptures, and carvings. 405-382-3369.

**Historical Sculptures,** P.O. Box 141, Cairo, NY 12413: Free brochure ◆ Bronze historical sculptures. 518-622-3508.

**Hollow Tree Hand-carved Collectibles,** 98 Adams St., Westborough, MA 01581: Free brochure ◆ Handcarved and acrylic handpainted basswood sculptures. 508-366-8777.

**Images In Steel,** P.O. Box 288, Clyde Park, MT 59018: Catalog $2 (refundable) ◆ Weather vanes, fireplace screens, furniture, and custom and western art handcrafted from plate steel. 800-511-1324; 406-686-4166 (in MT).

**Imagine That,** 5903 Queens Chapel, Hyattsville, MD 20782: Free information ◆ Sculptures, figurines, and art objects. 800-223-5903.

**Imperial Manufacturing,** 14502 Resort Ln., Lakewood, WI 54138: Free catalog ◆ Pewter figurines. 715-276-7865.

**Jay "Bird" Jones,** 520 Pine Oaks Rd., Colorado Springs, CO 80926: Catalog $10 (refundable); brochure $1 ◆ Antler chairs, lamps, chandeliers, and carvings. 719-527-1845.

**Jems Inc.,** 2293 Aurora Rd., Melbourne, FL 32935: Free price list ◆ Gem trees and wire-crafting supplies, tumbled gemstones, figurines, and jewelry-making supplies. 407-254-5600.

**Will Kirkpatrick Decoys,** 124 Forest Ave., Hudson, MA 01749: Catalog $3 ◆ Authentic reproductions of works by early carvers. 800-505-7841. www.kirkpatrickdecoy.com

**Leslie Levy Fine Art,** 1505 N. Hayden Rd., Scottsdale, AZ 85257: Free information ◆ Contemporary American paintings, drawings, and sculptures. 800-283-ARTS; 602-947-2925 (in AZ). www.leslielevy.com

**MAX-CAST,** 611 B. Ave., P.O. Box 662, Kalona, IA 52247: Free brochure ◆ Sculptures and custom casting in iron, aluminum, and bronze. 319-656-5365.

**Miller Import Company,** 300 Mac Ln., Keasbey, NJ 08832: Free list of retail sources ◆ Giuseppe Armani religious figurines. 800-3-ARMANI. www.the-society.com

**Munyon & Sons,** 1119 Waverly Hills Dr., Thousand Oaks, CA 91360: Free catalog ◆ Reproductions of Remington bronzes. 800-289-2850.

**Netsales,** 5815 Cozzens St., San Diego, CA 92122: Free catalog ◆ Remington bronzes, Charles Russell and western classics, and classical, wildlife, equestrian, art deco, and other statuary. 619-457-0277. www.sirbronze.com

**Red Fox Fine Art,** 7 N. Liberty St., Middleburg, VA 22117: Catalog $5 ◆ Sculptures and 19th-century animal and sports paintings. 540-687-5780.

**Regency Portrait Sculpture,** Box 105, Venango, PA 16440: Free brochure ◆ Portrait busts made from photographs. 814-398-4864.

**Renaissance Marketing,** 24181 S. Tamiani Trail, Bonita Springs, FL 34134: Free catalog ◆ Bronze sculptures and collectible art glass. 941-495-6033.

**Rostand Fine Jewelers,** 8349 Foothill Blvd., Sunland, CA 91040: Free information ◆ Lladro porcelain. 800-222-9208; 818-352-7814 (in CA).

**Sculpture Concepts,** 5388 E. Burris Rd., Loma Rica, CA 95901: Free catalog ◆ Sculptured products for use as awards and gifts, specializing in custom designs. 800-800-5950; 916-742-7070 (in CA). www.sculptureconcepts.com

**Sun Foundry,** 299 S. Lake St., Burbank. CA 91502: Catalog $10 ◆ Bronze sculptures. 800-367-3479. www.sunbronze.com

**3DPolitics,** 1907 N. Mendell, Chicago, IL 60622: Free catalog ◆ Cast stone and bronze sculptures of Civil War leaders and other persons. 773-862-5744. www.shoga.wwa.com/~3DPOLIT

**Weston's Limited Editions,** 17A Park Rd., Eatontown, NJ 07724: Brochure $1 ◆ African-American figurines. 800-526-2391. www.westonsltd.com

**Windy Meadows Pottery Ltd.,** 1036 Valley Rd., Knoxville, MD 21758: Free brochure ◆ Detailed stonewear buildings. 800-527-6274.

**Wood Carvings by Ted Nichols,** Noah's Ark, 2909 Old Ocean City Rd., Salisbury, MD 21801: Catalog $1 ◆ Handcarved and painted wood carvings. 410-546-9522.

**Zola Art & Crafts,** 3810 Borland Circle, Anchorage, AK 99517: Free brochure ◆ Handcarved moose bone carvings of ten centuries-old Eskimo life styles. 907-248-4399.

## ASTROLOGY

**ACS Publications Inc.,** P.O. Box 34487, San Diego, CA 92163: Free information ◆ Books on astrology, Tarot reading, psychic understanding, nutrition, healing, and channeling. 619-297-9203.

**A.R.E. Press,** 68th & Atlantic Ave., P.O. Box 656, Virginia Beach, VA 23451: Free catalog ◆ Study aids for research and personal enlightenment. Also charts for determining astrology horoscopes. 888-723-1112. www.edgarcayce.com

**Astro Communications Services Inc.,** 5521 Ruffin Rd., San Diego, CA 92123: Free catalog ◆ Astrology books and software. 800-888-9983. sales@astrocom.com

**Astrology Bookstore,** P.O. Box 77511, Seattle, WA 98177: Free catalog ◆ Astrology books and supplies. 206-526-8906. www.astrologyetal.com

**The Astrology Center of America,** 714 Baca St., P.O. Box 10170, Santa Fe, NM 87504: Free catalog ◆ New and hard-to-find books on astrology. 800-475-2272. www.astroamerica.com

**Aurora Press,** P.O. Box 573, Santa Fe, NM 87504: Free catalog ◆ Books on astrology and yoga. 505-363-4393.

**Cosmic Patterns,** 6212 NW 43rd St., Ste.B, Gainesville, FL 32653: Catalog $3 ◆ Kepler astrology program. 352-373-1504. kepler@patterns.com

## ASTRONOMY

### Astrophotography

**Adirondack Video Astronomy,** 35 Stephanie Ln., Queensbury, NY 12804: Free information ◆ Video and CCD imaging equipment. 888-799-0107. www.ourworld.compuserve.com/homepages/AVAastro

**Apogee Instruments Inc.,** 3340 N. Country Club, Ste. 103, Tucson, AZ 85716: Free information ◆ CCD digital imaging systems. 520-326-3600.

**Astro-Physics,** 11250 Forest Hills Rd., Rockford, IL 61115: Free information ◆ Refractors, equatorial mountings, visual and photographic accessories, and instruments for observers and astrophotographers. 815-282-1513.

**Axiom Research Inc.,** 2450 E. Speedway, Ste. 3, Tucson, AZ 85719: Free information ◆ Astronomy image-processing software. 520-791-2864.

**Electrim Corp.,** 356 Wall St., Princeton, NJ 08540: Free information ◆ Electronic imaging equipment. 609-683-5546.

**Murnaghan Instruments,** 1781 Primrose Ln., West Palm Beach, FL 33414: Free catalog ◆ CCD imaging equipment. 561-795-2201. murni@bix.com

**SBIG Astronomical Instruments,** Santa Barbara Instrument Group, 1482 E. Valley Rd., P.O. Box 50437, Santa Barbara, CA 93150: Free catalog ◆ Color imaging equipment. 805-969-1851. www.sbig.com

**Schuler Astro-Imaging,** P.O. Box 307, Sudbury, MA 01776: Free information ◆ Filters for CCD imaging. 978-443-2037.

**Spectra Astronomy,** 6631 Wilbur Ave., Ste. 30, Reseda, CA 91335: Free catalog ◆ Astrophotography and telescopic equipment for beginning and advanced astronomers. 800-735-1352. www.rahul.net/resource/spectra

**TAURUS Technologies,** P.O. Box 14, Woodstown, NJ 08098: Free information ◆ Astrophotography systems. 609-769-4509.

## Observatories & Planetariums

**Ash Manufacturing Company Inc.,** Box 312, Plainfield, IL 60544: Free catalog ◆ Mechanical and electrical-operated observatory domes from 10 to 36 feet in diameter. 815-436-9403.

**Learning Technologies Inc.,** 40 Cameron Ave., Somerville, MA 02144: Free catalog ◆ Portable planetarium system. 800-537-8703. starlab@starlab.com

**Minolta,** 101 Williams Dr., Ramsey, NJ 07446: Free information ◆ Planetariums. 201-825-4000. www.minolta.com

**Observa-Dome Laboratories Inc.,** 371 Commerce Park Dr., Jackson, MS 39213: Free information ◆ Domes for amateur astronomers and professional tracking, research, communications, and defense systems. 800-647-5364; 601-982-3333 (in MS). odl@misnet.com

**Prometheus Books,** 59 John Glenn Dr., Amherst, NY 14228: Free information ◆ Books on astronomy, astrology, and other subjects. 800-421-0351. www.prometheusbooks.com

**Seiler Instrument,** 170 E. Kirkham Ave., St. Louis, MO 63119: Free information ◆ Planetariums and accessories. 800-726-8805.

**Technical Innovations Inc.,** 22500 Old Hundred Rd., Barnesville, MD 20838: Free brochure ◆ Easy-to-assemble observatories for amateur astronomers. 301-972-8040. www.homedome.com

## Software

**The Astronomical Society of the Pacific,** 390 Ashton Ave., San Francisco, CA 94112: Free catalog ◆ Software and CD-ROMs for Macintosh and PC computers. 800-962-3412. www.aspsky.org

**Astrosoft,** Division Astronomics, 2401 Tee Circle, Ste. 106, Norman, OK 73069: Free information ◆ Observing software. 405-364-0858.

**Carina Software,** 12919 Alcosta Blvd., San Ramon, CA 94543: Free information ◆ Astronomy software for Macintosh computers. 510-355-1266.

**David Chandler Software,** P.O. Box 309, La Verne, CA 91750: Free information ◆ Custom star charts for PCs. 909-988-5678.

**Etlon Software,** 2250 Parkview Dr., Longmont, CO 80501: Free information ◆ Macintosh software that shows the planets, stars, moon, and sky summaries. 303-702-9274.

**Farpoint Research,** 10932 Hasty Ave., Downey, CA 90241: Free information ◆ PC software that shows the stars, planets, and all-known comets and asteroids. 310-861-6606.

**Logos Software,** 110 Bagot St., Kingston, Ontario, Canada K7L 3E5: Free information ◆ Macintosh software that displays many comets, asteroids, and the planets with their moons.

**Maxis Software,** Electronic Arts, 1450 Fashion Island Blvd., San Mateo, CA 94404: Free information ◆ Astronomy software. 800-245-4525; 415-573-7111 (in CA). www.maxis.com

**Project Pluto Software,** 168 Ridge Rd., Bowdoinham, ME 04008: Free information ◆ Windows and DOS star charts for PCs. 800-777-5886; 207-666-5750 (in ME). www.projectpluto.com

**The Sky Astronomy Software,** 912 12th St., Golden, CO 80401: Free information ◆ Windows 95 astronomy software. 800-843-7599. www.bisque.com

**Software Bisque,** 912 12th St., Golden, CO 80401: Free information ◆ Astronomy software. 800-843-7599. www.bisque.com

**Software Systems Consulting,** 615 S. El Camino Rd., San Clemente, CA 92672: Free catalog ◆ Weather satellite imaging software for PCs connected to shortwave or other radio equipment. 714-498-5784. www.ssccorp.com

**Stellar Software,** P.O. Box 10183, Berkeley, CA 94709: Free information ◆ Astronomy software for PCs and the Macintosh. 510-845-8405.

**Virtual Reality Labs Inc.,** 2945 McMillan Ave., San Luis Obispo, CA 93401: Free catalog ◆ Astronomy software for Macintosh and PC computers. 800-829-8754; 805-545-8515 (in CA).

**Willmann-Bell Inc.,** P.O. Box 35025, Richmond, VA 23235: Catalog $1 ◆ Astronomy software. 804-320-7016. www.willbell.com

**Zephyr Services,** 1900 Murray Ave., Pittsburgh, PA 15217: Free catalog ◆ Astronomy software for PCs and Macintosh computers. 412-422-6600. www.zephyrs.com

## Telescopes & Accessories

**AB Engineering,** 5822 Kruse Dr., Fort Wayne, IN 46818: Free information ◆ Professional telescopes for research, education, and serious amateur observatories. 219-489-2845.

**Adorama,** 42 W. 18th St., New York, NY 10011: Catalog $3 ◆ Telescopes, telescope-making supplies, photographic equipment, audiovisual aids, mounts, charts and star maps, books, and binoculars. 212-741-0466. goadorama@aol.com

**Analytical Scientific,** 11049 Bandera Rd., San Antonio, TX 78250: Catalog $3 (refundable) ◆ Telescopes. 830-684-7373. analyticalscientific@compuserve.com

**Apogee Inc.,** P.O. Box 136, Union, IL 60180: Free catalog ◆ Surplus astronomy and other optical equipment. 815-923-1602. Apogee@mc.net

**Astro-Physics,** 11250 Forest Hills Rd., Rockford, IL 61115: Free information ◆ Refractors, equatorial mountings, visual and photographic accessories, and instruments for observers and astrophotographers. 815-282-1513.

**The Astronomical Society of the Pacific,** 390 Ashton Ave., San Francisco, CA 94112: Free catalog ◆ Astronomy teaching and observing aids. 800-962-3412. www.aspsky.org

**Astronomics,** 2401 Tee Circle, Ste. 106, Norman, OK 73069: Free information ◆ Astronomy equipment. 405-364-0858. www.astronomics.com

**The Astronomy Shoppe,** 15836 N. Cave Creek Rd., Phoenix, AZ 85032: Free information with long SASE ◆ Telescopes, maps and star charts, and books. 602-971-3170.

**AstroSystems Inc.,** 5348 Ocotillo Ct., Johnstown, CO 80534: Free catalog ◆ Telescope kits, components, and accessories. 970-587-5838. www.fril.com/~astrosys

**Ball Photo Supply Company,** 85 Tunnel Rd., Asheville, NC 28805: Free information ◆ Telescopes, spotting scopes, camera equipment, binoculars, eyepieces, and accessories. 704-252-2443.

**Bausch & Lomb,** 9200 Cody, Overland Park, KS 66214: Free list of retail sources ◆ Telescopes. 800-423-3537. www.bushnell.com

**Berger Brothers Camera Exchange,** 209 Broadway, Amityville, NY 11701: Free information ◆ Telescopes, telescope-making supplies, audiovisual aids, photographic equipment, mounts, charts and star maps, books, and binoculars. 800-262-4160; 516-264-4160 (in NY). www.berger-bros.com

**Brite Sky,** Rivers Camera Shop, 454 Central Ave., Dover, NH 03820: Free information ◆ Astronomy equipment, accessories, and cleaning fluid for lenses. 800-245-7963. rivers@tlc.net

**Byers Company,** 29001 W. Hwy. 58, Barstow, CA 92311: Information $2 ◆ Telescope drives, custom-designed instruments, and other equipment. 619-256-2377.

**California Telescope Company,** P.O. Box 1338, Burbank, CA 91507: Catalog $5 ◆ Telescopes, telescope-making supplies, audiovisual aids, photographic equipment, computer software, charts and star maps, books, and binoculars. 818-505-8424.

**Camera Bug Ltd.,** 1799 Briarcliff Rd., Atlanta, GA 30306: Free information ◆ Telescopes, binoculars, spotting scopes, and accessories. 404-873-4513. cam_bug@msn.com

**Captain's Nautical Supplies,** 2500 15th Ave. West, Seattle, WA 98119: Free information ◆ Telescopes and accessories. 800-448-2278; 206-283-7242 (in WA). captainsnautical@msn.com

**CC Sales/Camera Corner,** 2273 S. Church St., Burlington, NC 27215: Free information ◆ Telescopes and accessories. 800-868-2462. info@camcor.com

**Celestron International,** 2385 Columbia St., Torrance, CA 90503: Catalog $2 ◆ Telescopes. 562-328-9560. www.celestron.com

**City Camera,** P.O. Box 721172, Berkley, MI 48072: Free information ◆ Telescopes.

**Cosmic Connection Telescopes,** 32 Ashgrove Blvd., Brandon, Manitoba, Canada R7B 1C2: Free information ◆ Telescopes. 204-727-3111.

**Coulter Optical Company,** Division Murnaghan Instruments, 1781 Primrose Ln., West Palm Beach, FL 33414: Free information ◆ Telescopes, mirrors, and mounts. 561-795-2201. murni@bix.com

**Cutler of New England,** P.O. Box 1083, Northampton, MA 01061: Free brochure ◆ Handcrafted telescopes. 800-947-8854. www.cutlerofnewengland.com

**Davilyn Corp.,** 13406 Saticoy St., North Hollywood, CA 91605: Free information ◆ Star drives and declination motors. 800-235-6222; 818-787-3334 (in CA). www.Davilyn.com/Electronics

**Daystar Filter Corp.,** P.O. Box 5110, Diamond Bar, CA 91765: Free catalog ◆ Filters. 909-591-4673.

**DFM Engineering Inc.,** 1035 Delaware Ave., Unit D, Longmont, CO 80501: Brochure $4 ◆ Computer-controlled telescopes. 303-678-8143. www.csn.net/~dfm42

**Dino Productions,** P.O. Box 3004, Englewood, CO 80155: Free catalog ◆ Fossils, rocks and minerals, ecology and oceanography equipment, and chemistry, general science, astronomy, and biology supplies. 303-741-1587. www.dinoproductions.com

**Dover Photo Supply,** 26 E. Blackwell St., Dover, NJ 07801: Free information ◆ Telescopes and accessories. 201-366-0994.

**Eagle Optics,** 2120 W. Greenview Dr., #4, Middleton, WI 53562: Free catalog ◆ Binoculars, telescopes, and accessories. 608-836-6568. www.eagleoptics.com

**Earth & Sky Adventure Products,** 2382 Leptis Circle, Morgan Hill, CA 95037: Free information ◆ Telescopes, refractors, and accessories. 408-778-1695. www.astrosales.com

**Edmund Scientific Company,** Edscorp Bldg., Barrington, NJ 08007: Free catalog ◆ Telescopes, telescope-making supplies, audiovisual aids, photographic equipment, charts and star maps, domes, books, and binoculars. 609-547-8880. www.edsci.com

**Efstonscience Inc.,** 3350 Dufferin St., Toronto, Ontario, Canada M6A 3A4: Catalog $6 ◆ Telescopes, telescope-making supplies, audiovisual aids, books, cameras, computers and software, and planetariums. 416-787-4581. www.efstonscience.com

**Equatorial Platforms,** 11065 Peaceful Valley Rd., Nevada City, CA 95969: Brochure $2 ◆ Equatorial platforms with computer controls. 916-265-3183. www.Astronomy-Mall.com

**Focus Camera,** 4419 13th Ave., Brooklyn, NY 11219: Free information ◆ Telescopes, audiovisual aids, photographic equipment, and binoculars. 718-437-8810. orders@focuscamera.com

**Fraunhofer Systems Company,** 12115 Magnolia Blvd., North Hollywood, CA 91607: Catalog $5 ◆ Custom refracting telescope systems.

**Galaxy Optics,** P.O. Box 2045, Buena Vista, CO 81211: Catalog $2 ◆ Telescope-making supplies and Newtonian optics. 719-395-8242.

**Harrison Astronomy,** 2574 Granville St., Vancouver, British Columbia, Canada V6H 3C8: Free information ◆ Telescopes and accessories, binoculars, microscopes, magnifiers, meteorological instruments, and books. 604-737-4303.

**Edwin Hirsch,** Egret Isle Terrace, Lake Worth, FL 33467: Free brochure ◆ Telescopes and accessories. 561-641-28511. Astronomy-Mall.com

**International Optics Ltd.,** P.O. Box 6475, Nashua, NH 03063: Free information ◆ Telescopes. 603-595-7978. Astronomy-Mall.com

**J.M.B. Inc.,** 20762 Richard, Trenton, MI 48183: Free information ◆ Glass solar filters and other optics. 313-675-3490.

**Jim's Mobile Inc.,** 810 Quail St., Unit E, Lakewood, CO 80215: Video catalog $10 (refundable with $100 purchase) ◆ Dedicated computers with object databases, telescope-to-PC links, focusing motors, push and snap-on declination motors, drive controls, locking easels, telescopes, software, and other astronomy equipment. 303-233-5353.

**JSL Perpetual Technology,** P.O. Box 51, Willard, UT 84340: Free catalog ◆ Telescopes and accessories. 801-723-5568.

**Jim Kendrick Studio,** 2775 Dundas St. West, Toronto, Ontario, Canada M6P 1Y4: Free information ◆ Heating systems for telescopes, binoculars, and cameras. 416-762-7946. kendrick-studio.com

**Khan Scope Center,** 3243 Dufferin St., Toronto, Ontario, Canada M6A 2T2: Free price list ◆ Telescopes, telescope-making supplies, binoculars, audiovisual aids, books, photographic equipment, computers and software, and planetariums. 416-783-4140. www.khanscope.com

**La Maison de l'Astronomie,** 7974 Rue St-Hubert, Montreal, Quebec, Canada H2R 2P3: Free catalog ◆ Telescopes and accessories. 514-279-0063. rlotte@InterLink.NET

**Light Speed Telescopes Inc.,** 3991 Weld County Rd. 18, Erie, CO 80516: Brochure $2 ◆ Easy-to-set up car-transportable and clock-driven equatorial mounted telescope. 303-678-9547.

**Los Angeles Optical Company,** 4870 Lankershim Blvd., North Hollywood, CA 91601: Free information ◆ Telescopes, books, maps and charts, filters, and photographic equipment. 818-762-2206.

**Lumicon,** 2111 Research Dr., Livermore, CA 94550: Free catalog ◆ Telescopes, binoculars, eye pieces and filters, mirrors and lenses, mounts, star maps and atlases, computers and software, and photographic equipment. 510-447-9570. www.Astronomy-Mall.com/Lumicon

**Meade Instruments Corp.,** 16542 Millikan Ave., Irvine, CA 92714: Catalog $3 (request list of retail sources) ◆ Telescopes, spotting scopes, and telephoto lenses. 714-556-2291. www.meade.com

**F.C. Meichsner Company,** 182 Lincoln St., Boston, MA 02111: Free information ◆ Telescopes, antique instruments, photographic equipment, charts and star maps, books, and binoculars. 800-321-8439. www.meichsner.com

**MMI Corp.,** P.O. Box 19907, Baltimore, MD 21211: Catalog $2 ◆ Portable planetariums, 35mm slides, videos, celestial globes, computer software, laser disks, teaching manuals, and telescopes. 410-366-1222. members.aol.com/mmicorp

**National Camera Exchange,** 9300 Olson Memorial Hwy., Golden Valley, MN 55427: Free information ◆ Telescopes, audiovisual aids, photographic equipment, charts and star maps, books, and binoculars. 888-873-1979; 612-591-5175 (in MN). usedcameras@natcam.com

**New Mexico Astronomical,** 834 N. Gabaldon Rd., Belen, NM 87002: Free information ◆ Telescopes. 505-864-2953.

**Newport Glass Works Ltd.,** 2044-D Placentia Ave., Costa Mesa, CA 92627: Free catalog ◆ Telescopes and components. 714-642-9980. www.newportglass.com

**Nurnberg Scientific,** 6310 SW Virginia Ave., Portland, OR 97201: Free information ◆ Telescopes. 503-246-8297.

**Obsession Telescopes,** P.O. Box 804, Lake Mills, WI 53551: Brochure $2; video and brochure $5 ◆ Portable 15, 18, 20, 25, or 30-inch alt-azimuth telescopes. 414-648-2328. obsessiontscp@globaldialog.com

**Oceanside Photo & Telescope,** 1024 Mission Ave., Oceanside, CA 92054: Free information ◆ Telescopes and accessories. 800-483-6287; 619-722-3348 (in CA). www.optcorp.com

**Optec Inc.,** 199 Smith St., Lowell, MI 49331: Free information ◆ Photometers with easy-to-use controls. 616-897-9351. info@optecinc.com

**Orion Telescope & Binocular Center,** P.O. Box 1815, Santa Cruz, CA 95061: Free catalog ◆ Telescopes, photographic equipment, charts and star maps, books, science supplies, and binoculars. 800-447-1001. www.oriontel.com

**Palomar Optical Supply,** P.O. Box 1310, Wildomar, CA 92595: Catalog $2 ◆ Mirror-making kits, pyrex blanks, grinding and polishing compounds, primary and elliptical mirrors, and supplies. 909-631-2835.

**Parks Optical Company,** 679 Easy St., Simi Valley, CA 93065: Catalog $3 ◆ Telescopes and optical equipment. 805-522-6722.

**Perceptor,** Brownsville Junction Plaza, Box 38, Ste. 201, Schomberg, Ontario, Canada L0G 1T0: Free information ◆ Telescopes, telescope-making supplies, mounts, audiovisual aids, books, cameras, computers and software, planetariums, and binoculars. 905-939-2313.

**Pocono Mountain Optics,** 104 North Pocono 502 Plaza, Moscow, PA 18444: Catalog $6 ◆ Binoculars, sighting scopes, new and used telescopes, telescope-making supplies, charts and star maps, photographic supplies, and books. 800-569-4323; 717-842-1500 (in PA). pocmtnop@ptdprlog.net

**QSP Optical Technology,** 1712 Newport Circle, Santa Ana, CA 92705: Free information ◆ Optical coatings for mirrors. www.QSPtech.com

**Quadrant Engineering Inc.,** 10138 Commercial Ave., Penn Valley, CA 95946: Free information ◆ Equatorial mounts with computer control systems. 916-432-5285.

**Questar,** P.O. Box 59, New Hope, PA 18938: Catalog $4 ◆ Telescopes and accessories. 215-862-5277.

**Redlich Optical,** 711 W. Broad St., Falls Church, VA 22046: Free information with long SASE ◆ Telescopes, telescope-making equipment, binoculars, books, cameras, photographic supplies, computers and software, star maps, and atlases. 703-241-4077.

**Rex's Astro Stuff,** 63 Observatory Ln., Dover, AR 72837: Free catalog ◆ Telescopes, binoculars, and accessories. Includes new and used equipment, books, posters, star charts, meteorites, and meteorite jewelry. 501-331-3773.

**Rivers Camera Shop,** 454 Central Ave., Dover, NH 03820: Free information ◆ Astronomy equipment and accessories. 800-245-7963. rivers@tlc.net

**Scope City,** P.O. Box 440, Simi Valley, CA 93065: Catalog $7 (refundable) ◆ Telescopes, telescope-making supplies, photographic equipment, books, and binoculars. 805-522-6646.

**Shutan Camera & Video,** 312 W. Randolph, Chicago, IL 60606: Free catalog ◆ Telescopes, telescope-making supplies, photographic equipment, charts and star maps, binoculars, video accessories, and other electronics. 800-621-2248; 312-332-2000 (in IL). www.shutan.com

**Sirius Instruments,** 141 N. Charles St., Villa Park, IL 60181: Free information ◆ CCD cameras for non-motorized telescopes. 800-288-CWIP; 630-782-5819 (in IL). www.htennant.com/sirius

**Sky Designs,** 4100 Felps Dr., Colleyville, TX 76034: Free catalog ◆ Portable telescopes. 817-581-9878.

**Sky Optics,** 4031 Fairview St., Burlington, Ontario, Canada L7L 2A4: Free information ◆ Telescopes, binoculars, eyepieces, CCDs, books, software, and accessories. 905-631-9944. www.worldchat.com/commercial/skyoptics

**Sky Valley Scopes,** 9215 Mero Rd., Snohomish, WA 98290: Free brochure ◆ Custom built 12 to 18-inch telescopes. 360-794-7757.

**Sovietski Collection,** P.O. Box 81347, San Diego, CA 92138: Free information ◆ Reflector telescopes, other optics, timepieces, space memorabilia, and more. 800-442-0002. www.sovietski.com

**Spectra Astronomy,** 6631 Wilbur Ave., Ste. 30, Reseda, CA 91335: Free catalog ◆ Astrophotography and telescopic equipment for beginning and advanced astronomers. 800-735-1352. www.rahul.net/resource/spectra

**Stano Components,** P.O. Box 2048, Carson City, NV 89702: Catalog $4 ◆ Night-vision optical equipment. 702-246-5281.

**Star Instruments,** P.O. Box 597, Flagstaff, AZ 86002: Catalog $2 ◆ Custom optics for amateurs and professionals. 602-774-9177.

**Star-Liner Company,** 6118 E. 34th St., Tucson, AZ 85711: Catalog $14 ◆ Telescopes, from a 6-inch amateur to 24-inch observatory models. 520-795-3361.

**Stargazer Steve,** Steve Dodson, 1752 Rutherglen Cres., Sudbury, Ontario, Canada P3A 2K3: Free brochure ◆ Newtonian reflecting telescopes and accessories. 705-566-1314. stargazr@isys.ca

**Starsplitter Telescopes,** 3228 Rikkard Dr., Thousand Oaks, CA 91362: Free information ◆ Complete telescope systems or custom built using your optics. 805-493-2489. STRSPLTR@AOL.com

**Starry Messenger,** P.O. Box 6552, Ithaca, NY 14851: Free information ◆ Used telescopes and accessories. 201-992-6865.

**Stellar-Vision & Astronomy Shop,** 1835 S. Alvernon, Tucson, AZ 85711: Free information ◆ New and used equipment. 520-571-0877. www.theriver.com/stellar_vision

**Surplus Shack,** 407 US Rt. 222, Blandon, PA 19510: Free information ◆ Surplus optics and electronics equipment. 888-88-SHACK; 610-926-9226 (in PA). www.SurplusShack.com

**Swift Instruments Inc.,** 952 Dorchester Ave., Boston, MA 02125: Free list of retail sources ◆ Telescopes, weather instruments, binoculars, and other optics. 800-446-1115; 617-436-2960 (in MA). www.swift-optics.com

**TECH2000,** 3349 SR99 S, Monroeville, OH 44847: Free brochure ◆ Drive system for home-built and commercial telescopes for loads up to 250 pounds. 419-465-2997. www.accnorwalk.com/~tddi/tech2000

**Tectron Telescopes,** 2111 Whitfield Park Dr., Sarasota, FL 34243: Free catalog ◆ Easy-to-set-up Dobsonian telescopes. 941-758-9890.

**Tele Vue Optics,** 100 Rt. 59, Suffern, NY 10901: Catalog $3 ◆ Telescopes and optical equipment. 914-357-9522. esource@resource-intl.com

**Telescope & Binocular Center,** P.O. Box 1815, Santa Cruz, CA 95061: Free catalog ◆ Telescopes, binoculars, and accessories. 800-447-1001. www.oriontel.com

**Texas Nautical Repair Company,** 3110 S. Shepherd, Houston, TX 77098: Free catalog ◆ Portable camera mounting and tracking systems, telescopes, science equipment, star maps, and atlases. 713-529-3551. www.lsstnr.com

**Thousand Oaks Optical,** Box 4813, Thousand Oaks, CA 91359: Free brochure ◆ Solar filters and astronomy equipment. 805-491-3642.

**Roger W. Tuthill Inc.,** 11 Tanglewood Dr., Mountainside, NJ 07092: Free catalog with 9x12 SASE with four 1st class stamps ◆ Telescopes, audiovisual aids, telescope-making supplies, photographic equipment, books, and binoculars. 800-223-1063.

**Unitron Inc.,** 170 Wilbur Pl., P.O. Box 469, Bohemia, NY 11716: Free catalog ◆ Telescopes, spotting scopes, binoculars, and other optical instruments. 516-589-6666.

**University Optics,** P.O. Box 1205, Ann Arbor, MI 48106: Free catalog ◆ Telescopes and telescope-making parts, CCD camera kits, eyepieces, binoculars, and astronomy publications. 800-521-2828. www.universityoptics.com

**VERNONscope & Company,** 5 Ithaca Rd., Candor, NY 13743: Catalog $3 ◆ Portable telescopes. 607-659-7000.

**Vista Instrument Company,** P.O. Box 1919, Santa Maria, CA 93454: Catalog $2 ◆ Precision camera tracker with optional accessories. 800-552-9170.

**Ward's Natural Science,** P.O. Box 92912, 5100 W. Henrietta Rd., Rochester, NY 14692: Earth science catalog $10; biology catalog $15; middle school catalog $10 ◆ Telescopes, telescope-making supplies, binoculars, audiovisual aids, books, computers and software, planetariums, and meteorites. 800-962-2660. www.wardsci.com

**What In The World,** P.O. Box 1767, Lake Arrowhead, CA 92352: Free information ◆ Telescopes, cameras, weather stations, binoculars, and accessories. 909-337-5080. www.whatintheworld.com

**Wholesale Optics Division,** 59 Mine Hill Rd., New Milford, CT 06776: Catalog $10 (refundable) ◆ Telescopes, telescope-making supplies, photographic equipment, computer software, science supplies, books, and binoculars. 860-355-3132. www.astroptx.com/~astroptx

**Willmann-Bell Inc.,** P.O. Box 35025, Richmond, VA 23235: Catalog $1 ◆ Telescopes and books. 804-320-7016. www.willbell.com

**Wolf Camera,** 1055 S. Tamiami Trail, Sarasota, FL 34236: Free information ◆ New and used telescopes, binoculars, filters, parts, and software. 941-366-7484. www.wolfcamera.com

**Woodland Hills Camera,** 5348 Topanga Cyn. Blvd., Woodland Hills, CA 91364: Free information ◆ Telescopes and accessories. 888-427-8766.

## AUTOGRAPHS

**A & K Sports Collectibles,** 106 Galway Tr., Moore, SC 29369: Free list ◆ Autographed and other sports collectibles. 864-576-1942.

**Alexander Autographs Inc.,** 100 Melrose Ave., Greenwich, CT 06830: Free catalog ◆ Collectible autographs. 203-622-8444.

**Alfie's Autographs of Hollywood,** 8424 Santa Monica Blvd., #500, West Hollywood, CA 90069: Catalog $9 plus $3 shipping ◆ Autographed 8x10 color glossies of Hollywood celebrities. 213-650-7508.

**Michael J. Amenta Autographs,** P.O. Box 618, Merrick, NY 11566: Free catalog with long SASE ◆ Autographs by entertainment personalities, sports figures, astronauts, and others. 516-868-9208.

**American Heritage Autographs & Collectibles,** 4514 Den Haag Rd., Warrenton, VA 20187: Free information (specify interests) ◆ Americana autographs and scarce collectibles. 540-341-7300.

**American Historical Guild,** 17 Firelight, Ste. 100, Dix Hills, NY 11746: Catalog $2 ◆ Original letters and documents by world leaders, scientists, authors, composers, artists, and others.800-544-1947;516-621-3051 (in NY).

**Ray Anthony Autograph Company,** 9363 Santa Monica Blvd., Ste. 212, Beverly Hills, CA 90210: Catalog $8 ◆ Autographed letters, albums, books, photographs, and documents. 800-626-3393. beverlyhills@earthlink.net

**Authentic Cinema Collectibles,** 7726 Girard St., La Jolla, CA 92037: Free information ◆ Autographs, posters, lobby cards, and memorabilia. 619-551-9886.

**Autograph Outlet,** Susan Sanders Wadopian, 3 Ellenwood Dr., Asheville, NC 28804: Free catalog with long SASE ◆ Autographs. 704-253-5202.

**Autographs On-Line,** 3603 N. Las Vegas Blvd., #116, Las Vegas, NV 89115: Free information ◆ Autographed sports cards and photographs. 702-657-8152. www.n-link.com/~autograph

**Robert F. Batchelder,** 1 W. Butler Ave., Ambler, PA 19001: Free catalog ◆ Letters, documents, and manuscripts. 215-643-1430.

**Benedikt & Salmon Record Rarities,** 3020 Meade Ave., San Diego, CA 92116: Free catalog, indicate choice of (1) autographs and rare books, (2) classical, (3) jazz, big bands, and blues and (4) personalities, soundtracks, and country music ◆ Autographed memorabilia and rare books in music and the performing arts, hard-to-find rare phonograph recordings, from 1890 to date, and antique phonographs and cylinders for collectors. 619-281-3345. rarerecords@groupweb.com

**Walter R. Benjamin, Autographs,** P.O. Box 255, Hunter, NY 12442: Catalog subscription $10 ◆ Letters and documents from historical, literature, musical, and scientific areas. 518-263-4133.

**The Best of Baseball & All Sports Inc.,** 980 Broadway, Ste. 624, Thornwood, NY 10594: Free information (enclose want list) ◆ Sports collectibles. 914-769-6707.

**Beverly Hills Autographs,** 9363 Santa Monica Blvd., Ste. 212, Beverly Hills, CA 90210: Catalog $8 ◆ Autographed letters, albums, books, photographs, and documents. 800-626-3393. beverlyhills@earthlink.net

**John Blumenthal Autographs,** 2853 Rikkard Dr., Thousand Oaks, CA 91362: Catalog $2 ◆ Autographs and signed photographs and letters. 805-493-5070.

**Broadway Rick's Strike Zone,** 1840 N. Federal Hwy., Boynton Beach, FL 33435: Free information with long SASE ◆ Autographed sports memorabilia, sports cards, and collectibles. 800-344-9103; 561-364-0453 (in FL).

**Celebrity Autographs of Southern California,** 1999 W. Arrow Rt., Upland, CA 91786: Free catalog ◆ Collectible autographs with certificate of authenticity. 909-982-3622. www.autographs.com

**Champion Sports Collectables Inc.,** 702 W. Las Tunas, San Gabriel, CA 91776: Free information ◆ Autographed sports memorabilia, sports and non-sports cards, and collecting supplies. 800-522-4267. www.championcollectables.com

**Classic Rarities & Company,** P.O. Drawer 29109, Lincoln, NE 68529: Free catalog ◆ Autographed letters and documents. 402-467-2948.

**Daniel Cohen,** 24 The Links Rd. #120, Willowdale, Ontario, Canada M2P 1T6: Free catalog ◆ Autographs, Hollywood and television collectibles, and music memorabilia. 416-222-0232. dcohen@danielcohen.com

**Bob Colip,** 120 Scarborough Circle, Noblesville, IN 46060: Free catalog with long SASE ◆ Autographed celebrity photographs. 317-877-5145.

**The Dance Mart,** P.O. Box 994, Teaneck, NJ 07666: Free catalog with long SASE ◆ Rare books, magazines, autographed material, and other dance collectibles. 201-833-4176.

**Nelson Deedle,** P.O. Box 5358, Scottsdale, AZ 85261: Free catalog ◆ Autographed celebrity photographs. 602-905-7019.

**Déja-Vu Enterprises Inc.,** 1029 Westwood Blvd., Los Angeles, CA 90024: Free catalog ◆ Autographed movie star photos, original movie posters, and lobby cards from silent film days to the present. 310-443-5280. DEJAVU@EARTHLINK.NET

**Joseph A. Dermont,** 13 Arthur St., P.O. Box 654, Onset, MA 02558: Free catalog ◆ Literary first editions and autographs. 508-295-4760. jdermont@interloc.com

**A. Lovell Elliott,** 940 Crescent Beach Rd., Vero Beach, FL 32963: Free information ◆ Autographed letters, photos, and documents. 561-234-1034.

**Elmer's Nostalgia Inc.,** 3 Putnam St., Sanford, ME 04073: Free catalog with long SASE and two 1st class stamps ◆ Entertainment, political, historical, literary, and pop culture autographs and memorabilia. 207-324-2166.

**Empire State Sports Memorabilia & Collectibles Inc.,** 331 Cochran Pl., Valley Stream, NY 11581: Free information ◆ Baseball and other sports cards, autographs, and memorabilia. 516-791-9091.

**Executive Collectibles Gallery Inc.,** 3444 Via Lido, Newport Beach, CA 92663: Free information ◆ Contemporary and vintage autographs. 714-673-1742.

**Dan Farek,** Box 1212, Bellaire, TX 77402: Free list ◆ Medals from worldwide sources. Also military autographs, photographs, and other military collectibles.

**G & P Autographs International,** P.O. Box 2082, Middletown, NY 10940: Free information (enclose want list) ◆ Signed photos and postcards, rock and pop memorabilia, autographs, and other collectibles. 914-343-3362.

**Robert Gentry,** P.O. Box 850, Many, LA 71449: Free list ◆ Country music albums, 78 and 45 rpm records, autographs, movie posters, books and magazines, press kits, and collectibles. 318-256-2886.

**Golden State Autographs,** P.O. Box 14776, Albuquerque, NM 87191: Free information with long SASE ◆ Autographs from all fields. 505-293-7407.

**Brian & Maria Green,** P.O. Box 1816, Kernersville, NC 27285: Free price list ◆ Civil War autographs, letters, diaries, and collectibles. 336-993-5100.

**Roger Gross Ltd.,** 225 E. 57th St., New York, NY 10022: Free list ◆ Autographs, books, memorabilia, and unsigned photographs of opera stars. 212-759-2892. www.padaweb.org/rgross

**Jim Hayes,** Box 12560, James Island, SC 29422: Catalog subscription $6 ◆ Autographs from the Civil and Revolutionary war periods. 803-795-0732.

**Heroes & Legends,** P.O. Box 9088, Calabasas, CA 91372: Free catalog ◆ Autographs and memorabilia. 818-346-9220. www.heroesandlegends.net

**History Brokers,** P.O. Box 136, Rialto, CA 92377: Free information (enclose want list) ◆ Movie-related autographs from 1900 to date and original movie posters. 909-877-5536.

**History Makers Inc.,** 4040 E. 82nd St., Indianapolis, IN 46250: Catalog $3 ◆ Original letters and documents, photographs, and rare books signed by famous people from all fields. 800-424-9259.

**Hollywood Legends,** 6621 Hollywood Blvd., Hollywood, CA 90028: Free information ◆ Celebrity autographs from the early days of Hollywood to the present. 213-962-7411.

**Houle Rare Books & Autographs,** 7260 Beverly Blvd., Los Angeles, CA 90036: Catalog $5 ◆ Autographs in all fields. 213-937-5858.

**Jeanne Hoyt Autographs,** P.O. Box 1517, Rohnert Park, CA 94927: Free catalog ◆ Autographs from all areas. 707-584-4077.

**Hummerdude's,** P.O. Box 4348, Dunellan, NJ 08812: Catalog $4 ◆ Celebrity photos, posters, and autographs. 732-424-9367.

**The I.P.A. Network,** 231 E. Alessandro Blvd., Riverside, CA 92508: Free information (enclose want list) ◆ Signed photos and autographed collectibles. 909-789-0405.

**Michael E. Johnson & Associates,** 862 Thomas Ave., San Diego, CA 92109: Free catalog ◆ Collectible autographs and publications. 619-483-8632.

**Kohl's Celebrity Gallery,** 1840 N. Federal Hwy., Boynton Beach, FL 33435: Catalog $5 ◆ Autographs and vintage sports memorabilia.800-344-9103; 561-364-0453 (in FL).

**La Scala Autographs Inc.,** P.O. Box 715, Pennington, NJ 08534: Free catalog ◆ Celebrity autographs. 800-622-2705.

**Lame Duck Books,**90 Moraine St., Jamaica Plain, MA 02130: Free catalog ◆ Signed books, autographs, manuscripts, photos, and art. 617-522-6657. LameDuckBk@aol.com

**Robert A. LeGresley,** P.O. Box 1199, Lawrence, KS 66044: Free catalog with long SASE ◆ Autographs, signed letters, photographs, and original comic art. 913-749-5458.

**Les Perline & Company,** 2 Gannett Dr., Ste. 200, White Plains, NY 10604: Free catalog ◆ Historic autographs, documents, and manuscripts. 800-567-2014; 914-273-2910 (in NY). perlineco@aol.com

**Blake LeVine Autographs,** 954 Lexington Ave., Ste. 99, New York, NY 10021: Free catalog ◆ Autographs by theatrical performers, political figures, and others. 212-737-9038.

**Abraham Lincoln Book Shop,** 357 W. Chicago Ave., Chicago, IL 60610: Catalog $10 (2-year subscription) ◆ New and used books, autographed letters, prints, oils, photographs, Lincolniana, and United States Civil War and Presidential documents. 312-944-3085.

**William Linehan Autographs,** Box 1225, Concord, NH 03301: Catalog $3 ◆ Autographs and costumes of movie stars. 603-224-7226.

**Lone Star Autographs,** P.O. Box 500, Kaufman, TX 75142: Free catalog ◆ Books signed or owned by Presidents and First Ladies and autographed letters, documents, and photographs, from the Civil War, movie stars, scientific community, authors, musicians, astronauts, military greats, and politicians. 972-932-6050.

**Richard MacCallum,** 866 Auburn Ct., Highland Park, IL 60035: Free information (enclose want list) ◆ Autographed matted pieces from all areas of history, sports, world leaders, art, and motion pictures. 847-432-7942.

**Joseph M. Maddalena,** 345 N. Maple Dr., Ste. 202, Beverly Hills, CA 90210: Free information ◆ Letters, photos, documents, signed books, and memorabilia from presidents, statesmen, movie stars, scientists, authors, inventors, and others. 800-942-8856.

**Main Street Fine Books & Manuscripts,** 206 N. Main St., Galena, IL 61036: Free information ◆ American literature and Civil War collectibles. Also Grant, Lincolniana, Illinoisana, and autographed memorabilia. 815-777-3749.

**Menig's Memorabilia,** 517 Manor, Peotone, IL 60468: Free catalog ◆ Civil War autographs, newspapers, and documents. 708-258-9487.

**Moody's Collectables,** 319 Wake Forest Dr., Warner Robins, GA 31093: Free catalog ◆ Autographed sports collectibles. 800-779-4024.

**J.B. Muns, Bookseller,** 1162 Shattuck Ave., Berkeley, CA 94707: Price list $1 ◆ Autographs by classical singers, musicians, and composers. 510-525-2420.

**Nate's Autographs,** 1015 Gayley Ave., Los Angeles, CA 90024: Catalog subscription $24 (4 issues) ◆ Autographs and memorabilia by entertainers, presidents, and historic, air and space, science, and sports personalities. 310-575-3851.

**Odyssey Auctions Inc.,** 510-A South Corona Mall, Corona, CA 91719: Catalog $20 ◆ Movie memorabilia and autographed letters, manuscripts, photographs, and documents from the arts and sciences to politics and entertainment stars. 800-996-3977. OdysGroup@aol.com

**Olde Soldier Books Inc.,** 18779 N. Frederick Ave., Gaithersburg, MD 20879: Free information ◆ Civil War books, documents, autographs, prints, and Americana. 301-963-2929. Warbooks@erols.com

**The Opera Box,** P.O. Box 994, Teaneck, NJ 07666: Free catalog ◆ Rare books, magazines, autographs, and opera collectibles. 201-833-4176.

**Deborah Perry Autographs,** P.O. Box 6449, Glendale, AZ 85312: Free catalog ◆ Signed celebrity photos. 602-842-8050.

**Bob Pivoroff,** 3629 Ransdom Pl., Alexandria, VA 22306: Free catalog ◆ Classic rock, metal, alternative, country, pop, and jazz star autographs. 703-768-3565.

**Cordelia & Tom Platt Autographs,** 2805 E. Oakland Blvd., Fort Lauderdale, FL 33306: Free catalog ◆ Autographs in all categories. 954-564-2002.

**Premiere Space Editions,** P.O. Box 580056, Houston, TX 77258: Free information ◆ NASA Apollo Program autographed astronomy memorabilia. 713-270-5878. www.premierespace.com

**Profiles in History,** 345 N. Maple Dr., Ste. 202, Beverly Hills, CA 90210: Free information ◆ Historical autographs. 800-942-8856.

**The Queen's Shilling,** 14 Loudoun St. SE, Leesburg, VA 22075: Catalog $3 ◆ Autographs and old, rare, and antiquarian books on military history. 703-779-4669.

**R & R Enterprises,** 3 Chestnut Dr., Bedford, NH 03110: Free catalog ◆ Autographs of movie, television, sport, music, and history personalities. 800-937-3880; 603-471-0808 (in NH).

**Steven S. Raab,** P.O. Box 471, Ardmore, PA 19003: Catalog $5 ◆ Autographs, signed books and photos, historic newspapers, World War I posters, and memorabilia. 610-446-6193. www.raabautographs.com

**Max Rambod Autographs,** 10449 Ashton Ave., Los Angeles, CA 90024: Catalog $2 ◆ Signed letters and autographs. 310-475-4535.

**Ramparts Inc.,** P.O. Box 9429, Dayton, OH 45409: Free catalog ◆ Authentic signed photos. 800-463-1932.

**Joseph Rubinfine,** 505 S. Flagler Dr., Ste. 1301, West Palm Beach, FL 33401: Free catalog with long SASE ◆ American historical autographs. 561-659-7077.

**Safka & Bareis, Autographs,** P.O. Box 886, Forest Hills, NY 11375: Free catalog ◆ Signed photos, letters, and autographs by opera, music, and movie entertainers. 718-263-2276.

**H. Drew Sanchez,** P.O. Box 2618, Apple Valley, CA 92307: Free catalog ◆ Cartoon art and autographs by entertainers and personalities. 619-242-7523.

**Schenker Promotions,** 13B Chestnut Ct., Brielle, NJ 08730: Free information ◆ Autographed sports photographs and memorabilia. 201-791-1675.

**The Score Board Inc.,** 1951 Old Cuthbert Rd., Cherry Hill, NJ 08034: Free information ◆ Autographed sports memorabilia. 800-327-4145; 609-354-9000 (in NJ).

**Seaport Autographs,** 6 Brandon Ln., Mystic, CT 06355: Free catalog ◆ Autographed letters, manuscripts, and documents. 860-572-8441.

**Searle's Autographs,** P.O. Box 9369, Asheville, NC 28814: Free list ◆ Autographs of television, movie, and theater personalities. 704-258-8096.

**Philip Sears Disney Collectibles,** 1457 Avon Terrace, Los Angeles, CA 90026: Free catalog ◆ Walt Disney autographs, animation art, and memorabilia. 213-666-3740.

**Fred Senese,** P.O. Box 310, Brockton, MA 02403: Free catalog ◆ Entertainment, sports, political, literary, and historical autographs. 508-586-1796.

**R.M. Smythe,** 26 Broadway, New York, NY 10004: Catalog $15 ◆ Obsolete stocks and bonds, bank notes, and autographs. 800-622-1880; 212-943-1880 (in NY).

**SportsCards Plus,** 28221 Crown Valley Pkwy., Laguna Niguel, CA 92677: Catalog $1 ◆ Sports cards, autographs, and sports memorabilia. 800-350-2273. www.sportscardsplus.com

**Stampede Investments,** 1533 River Rd., Wisconsin Dells, WI 53965: Free catalog ◆ Fine books, autographs, and historical artifacts. 608-579-6805.

**Stan's Sports Memorabilia Inc.,** 14 Washburn Pl., Caldwell, NJ 07006: Free catalog ◆ Signed sports memorabilia and photos. 201-228-5257.

**Star Shots,** 5389 Bearup St., Port Charlotte, FL 33981: Free catalog ◆ Celebrity autographs. 941-697-6935. www.star-shots.com

**Starr Autographs,** 5360 SE Ruether Rd., Oak Grove, OR 97267: Free catalog ◆ Entertainment and sports celebrity autographs. 503-659-3333.

**Startifacts,** 3101 E. Hennepin Ave., Minneapolis, MN 55412: Free catalog ◆ Authentic signed memorabilia. 612-331-6454.

**Georgia Terry, Autographs,** 840 NE Cochran Ave., Gresham, OR 97030: Free catalog ◆ Autographs by entertainment personalities. 503-667-0950.

**Truly Unique Collectibles,** P.O. Box 29, Suffern, NY 10901: Free catalog ◆ Sports and entertainment autographs. 800-382-3075. www.uniquecollectibles.com

**Mark Vardakis Autographs,** Box 1430, Coventry, RI 02816: Catalog $2 ◆ Autographs, paper Americana, pre-1900 stocks, and bonds and checks. 800-342-0301; 401-823-8440 (in RI). sigking@aol.com

**Walk of Fame Autographs,** P.O. Box 1026, DeLand, FL 32721: Free catalog ◆ Autographs by past and present Hollywood and TV celebrities and super models. 904-943-9500.

**Walls of Fame Autographs,** P.O. Box 1053, Neptune, NJ 07753: Free catalog ◆ Music, television, Hollywood, historic, sports, and celebrity autographs from other areas. 732-988-0315.

**Wex Rex Records & Collectibles,** 280 Worcester Rd., Framingham, MA 01701: Catalog $3 ◆ Autographs, movie and TV show character toys, and collectibles. 508-620-6181.

## AUTOMOTIVE PARTS & ACCESSORIES

### Automotive Art & Gifts

**Antique Car Paintings,** 6889 Fairwood, Dearborn Heights, MI 48127: Free information ◆ Color prints, ink illustrations, and original art. 313-274-7774.

**Auto Art by Paul G. McLaughlin,** 2720 Tennessee NE, Albuquerque, NM 87110: Free information ◆ Pen and ink, pencil, oil, and watercolor automotive art. 505-296-2554.

**Auto Cards Inc.,** P.O. Box 452, Stuart, FL 34996: Brochure $2 ◆ All-occasion and Christmas cards for auto enthusiasts, featuring classic 5.0 Mustangs, Corvettes from 1955 to 1956, and 1957 Chevrolets. 561-287-6970.

**Auto Motif Inc.,** 2941 Atlanta Rd., Smyrna, GA 30080: Catalog $3 ◆ Books, prints, puzzles, models, office accessories, lamps, original art, posters, and other gifts with an automotive theme. 800-367-1161. automotif@juno.com

**Automobilia Collectibles,** Division Lustron Industries, 18 Windgate Dr., New City, NY 10956: Free catalog ◆ 1:43 scale diecast models of historic European race cars and classics. 914-639-6806. lustron@worldnet.att.net

**Automotive Emporium,** 280 Preston Forest Village, Dallas, TX 75230: Free information with long SASE ◆ Automotive books and original literature, art and memorabilia, miniatures, and bronze sculptures. 972-361-1969.

**Autosaurus,** 5225 Pooks Hill Rd., Ste. 1421N, Bethesda, MD 20814: Free information ◆ Automotive art, books, models, clothes, posters, memorabilia, and gifts. 800-269-7221; 301-942-1500. www.vintageautos.com

**Benkin & Company,** 14 E. Main St., Tipp City, OH 45371: Free information ◆ Automotive collectibles. 937-667-5975.

**Car Collectables,** 32 White Birch Rd., Madison, CT 06443: Free brochure ◆ Christmas cards, note cards, and gifts with an automotive theme. 203-245-7299.

**Comet Products,** 101-B Cherry Parke, Cherry Hill, NJ 08002: Catalog $3 ◆ Car grille emblem badges and car-related gifts. 609-795-4810.

**Gearbox Grannie's,** 5161 Wolpen-Pleasant Hill Rd., Milford, OH 45150: Free catalog ◆ Specialty tools, books, gifts, and collectibles. 800-831-6137. www.trimparts.com

**Gee Gee Studios Inc.,** 6636 S. Apache Dr., Littleton, CO 80120: Catalog $2 (refundable) ◆ Original pen and ink drawings and numbered lithographs of famous cars. 303-794-2788.

**The Haley Motorsports Collection,** P.O. Box 1957, St. Peters, MO 63376: Free catalog ◆ Limited edition prints, apparel, die-cast models, books, and other gifts. 314-441-2541.

**Hemmings Bookshelf,** P.O. Box 76-S14945, Bennington, VT 05201: Free information ◆ Automotive books and gifts for car lovers. 800-227-4373. www.hemmings.com

**International Auto Parts Inc.,** Rt. 29 North, P.O. Box 9036, Charlottesville, VA 22906: Catalog $2 ◆ Travel and auto accessories, safety items, collectibles, and clothing. 800-726-0555; 804-973-0555 (in VA). www.international-auto.com

**Jesser's Classic Keys,** 26 West St., Akron, OH 44303: Free information ◆ Western style, 18k gold plated belt buckles with a choice of 100 different emblems to match cars, trucks, or motorcycles. 330-376-8181.

**JMJ Automobilia,** P.O. Box 156, Princeton Junction, NJ 08550: Free catalog ◆ Racing memorabilia and collectibles. 609-275-5174. www.JMJAuto.com

**Merchandising Incentives Corp.,** 352 Oliver Dr., Troy, MI 48084: Catalog $3 ◆ Chevrolet and Ford licensed gifts and collectibles. 810-362-5060.

**Motor Cars International,** 528 N. Prince Ln., Springfield, MO 65802: Free catalog ◆ Gifts for the Lamborghini owner, car care products, and sport utility vehicle accessories. 800-977-9707. www.motorcars-intl.com

**Motorhead Art & Collectibles,** 1917 Dumas Circle NE, Tacoma, WA 98422: Catalog $5 ◆ Automotive art prints and collectibles, scale model cars and kits, and books. 800-859-0164.

**Nostalgia Unlimited,** P.O. Box 291563, Port Orange, FL 32129: Catalog $1 ◆ Automotive nostalgia. 800-843-3487. www.nostalgia-unlimited.com

**Past Gas,** 308 Willard St., Cocoa, FL 32922: Catalog $1 ◆ Automotive memorabilia. 407-636-0449.

**Pelham Prints,** 2819 N. 3rd St., Clinton, IA 52732: Free information ◆ Note cards, antique and classic automotive art, and pen and ink drawings. 319-242-0280.

**Time Passages Ltd.,** P.O. Box 65596, West Des Moines, IA 50265: Free catalog ◆ Globes, globe frames, pump parts, decals, signs, literature, novelty gifts, and other memorabilia. 800-383-8888.

**Universal Tire Company,** 987 Stony Battery Rd., Lancaster, PA 17601: Free catalog ◆ Lucas electric parts, wheel hardware, moldings, antique and classic tires, and other automotive memorabilia. 800-233-3827. www.universaltire.com

**Weber's Nostalgia Supermarket,** 6611 Anglin Dr., Fort Worth, TX 76119: Catalog $4 (refundable) ◆ Gas globes, gas pump restoration supplies, car models, photographs, posters, and automotive gifts. 817-534-6611.

## Automotive Batteries & Chargers

**The Antique Auto Battery Manufacturing Company,** 2320 Old Mill Rd., Hudson, OH 44236: Free information ◆ Automotive batteries. 800-426-7580; 216-425-2395 (in OH). www.classicar.com/vendors/antibat/antibat.htm

**Deltran Corp.,** 801 US Hwy. 92 East, DeLand, FL 32724: Free information ◆ Battery chargers. 904-736-7900.

**New Castle Battery Mfg. Company,** 3601 Wilmington Rd., P.O. Box 5040, New Castle, PA 16105: Free information ◆ Antique and classic reproduction batteries for the Chevrolet, Chrysler, Ford, and Mustang. 800-622-6733; 412-658-5501 (in PA). www.turbostart.com

## Body Repair Parts

**Auto Body Specialties Inc.,** Rt. 66, P.O. Box 455, Middlefield, CT 06455: Catalog $5 ◆ Reproduction and original quarter panels, fenders, repair panels, grilles, bumpers, and carpets for 1950 to 1986 American and foreign cars, pickups, and vans. 860-346-4989.

**Bill's Speed Shop,** 13951 Millersburg Rd., Navarre, OH 44662: Free information ◆ Hard-to-find panels for older cars and current models. 330-832-9403.

**Hoffman Automotive Distributor,** US Hwy. 1, Box 818, Hilliard, FL 32046: Free information ◆ NOS and reproduction body parts for 1955 to 1972 Chevrolets and 1968 to 1972 Mustangs. 904-845-4421.

**Howell's Sheetmetal Company,** P.O. Box 792, Nederland, TX 77627: Free information ◆ Body panels and reproduction sheet metal for 1909 to 1940 Fords. 409-727-1999.

**Made-Rite Auto Body Products Inc.,** 869 E. 140th St., Cleveland, OH 44110: Free information ◆ Steel replacement panels for cars, pickups, and vans. 216-681-2535.

**Mill Supply,** 3241 19801 Miles, Cleveland, OH 44128: Catalog $4 ◆ Steel replacement panels, tools, and body shop equipment for most United States cars, vans, pickups, and foreign cars. 800-888-5072; 440-241-5072 (in OH). www.millsupply.com

**MPC Classics,** 2100 E. Main St., #4A, Grand Prairie, TX 75050: Free catalog ◆ Mid-1964 to 1973 original, reproduction, and used interiors, exteriors, sheet metal, and parts for Mustangs. 800-888-1672. www.mpcclassics.com

**Raybuck Autobody Parts,** RD 4, Box 170, Punxsutawney, PA 15767: Free information ◆ Reproduction body parts for Jeeps, vans, and pickups. 814-938-5248. www.raybuck.com

**Rootlieb Inc.,** P.O. Box 1829, Turlock, CA 95381: Free catalog ◆ Hoods, fenders, running boards, splash aprons, and other parts for older Ford and Chevrolet cars. 209-632-2203.

**Scarborough Faire,** 1151 Main St., Pawtucket, RI 02860: Catalog $3 (specify year and car) ◆ Body repair panels for most cars. 401-724-4200.

**Surplus Supply Company,** Box 9047, Akron, OH 44305: Catalog $3 ◆ Body repair panels for 1957 to 1996 Ford pickups, 1961 to 1991 Ford vans, and 1949 to 1968 Chevrolets. 330-825-3900.

**Vintage Vehicles Inc.,** 8190 20th Dr., Wautoma, WI 54982: Free information ◆ Automotive interior and exterior stainless moldings, beauty rings, head and taillights, radiator shells, and hubcaps. 414-787-2656.

**West Coast Sheetmetal,** 219 S. 20th St., San Jose, CA 95116: Free information ◆ Body parts for American cars, from the 1950s to 1980s. 408-286-6537.

## Books & Miscellaneous Publications

**ADP Parts Service,** 14800 28th Ave. North, Plymouth, MN 55447: Free information ◆ Reference parts interchange manuals, from the 1920s and later. 800-825-0644. www.hollander-auto-parts.com

**Antique Auto Literature & Keys,** 1100 Shady Oaks, Ann Arbor, MI 48103: Free information ◆ Shop manuals, sales catalogs, and keys and locks for cars, from 1900 to 1960. 313-761-2490.

**Applegate & Applegate,** Box 260, Annville, PA 17003: Free information ◆ Sales literature, owner manuals, tune-up charts, and photographs. 717-964-2350.

**Auto Literature Outlet,** 527 Hwy. 431 South, Boaz, AL 35957: Free information with long SASE (enclose want list) ◆ Shop and owner manuals, showroom literature, and memorabilia. 256-593-4111.

**The Auto Review,** P.O. Box 510, Florissant, MO 63032: Free information ◆ Books and information on antique and classic car history and restoration. 314-355-3609.

**Auto World Books,** P.O. Box 562, Camarillo, CA 93011: Free information with long SASE ◆ Automobile, truck, and motorcycle books, service manuals, and back issues of magazines. 805-987-5570.

**Automotive Information Clearinghouse,** P.O. Box 1746, La Mesa, CA 92041: Free information with long SASE ◆ Original domestic and foreign automobile shop and parts manuals. 619-447-7200.

**Caliber Motors Inc.,** 5395 E. La Palma Ave., Anaheim Hills, CA 92807: Free information ◆ Mercedes-Benz parts, shop, and owner manuals. 800-252-6877. www.mercedes-net.com/dealer/caliber

**Car Books,** 1660 93rd Ln. NE, Minneapolis, MN 55449: Free information ◆ Automotive books and manuals. 800-642-3289.

**Chewning's Auto Literature Ltd.,** 2011 Elm Tree Terrace, Buford, GA 30518: Free information (specify year and car) ◆ Shop and owner automotive manuals, parts, and sales catalogs. 770-945-9795.

**Classic Motorbooks,** P.O. Box 1, Osceola, WI 54020: Free catalog ◆ Automotive books. 800-826-6600. www.motorbooks.com

**Crank'en Hope Publications,** 461 Sloan Alley, Blairsville, PA 15717: Free catalog ◆ Cadillac manuals and illustrated parts books. 412-459-8853.

**Dragich Auto Literature,** 1660 93rd Ln. NE, Minneapolis, MN 55434: Free catalog ◆ Original and reproduction automotive books and manuals. 612-786-3925.

**The Evergreen Press,** 9 Camino Arroyo Pl., Palm Desert, CA 92260: Free information with long SASE ◆ Reference books on Fords (Model A, T, and pre-war V-8), Chevrolets, Volkswagens, Thunderbirds, Mustangs, Falcons, Corvettes, and Camaros. 213-510-1700.

**Faxon Auto Literature,** 3901 Carter Ave., Riverside, CA 92501: Free information ◆ Automotive factory manuals and literature. 800-458-2734.

**Justin Hartley Publisher,** 17 Fox Meadow Ln., West Hartford, CT 06107: Free information ◆ Cadillac and LaSalle service books, from 1902 to 1995. 860-523-0056.

**Bob Johnson's Auto Literature,** 21 Blandin Ave., Framingham, MA 01701: Free information ◆ Automotive shop and interchange manuals and literature. 508-872-9173.

**Rudy R. Koch,** P.O. Box 291, Chester Heights, PA 19017: Free information with long SASE (specify year of manual) ◆ New and original manuals for Chevrolets, Corvettes, Camaros, Chevelles, and Monte Carlos. 610-459-8721.

**Lloyds Literature,** P.O. Box 491, Newbury, OH 44065: Free information with long SASE ◆ Shop and owner manuals, parts and data books, dealer albums, sales brochures, service bulletins, and other publications. 800-292-2665; 216-338-1527 (in OH).

**Ken McGee Holdings Inc.,** 232 Britannia Rd. West, Goderich, Ontario, Canada N7A 2B9: Free information with long SASE ◆ Factory original manuals, brochures, dealer books, and other publications. 519-524-5821.

**McLellan's Automotive History,** 9111 Longstaff Dr., Houston, TX 77031: Free catalog ◆ Sales literature, out-of-print books, dealer albums and books, magazines, and memorabilia. 713-772-3285.

**Walter Miller,** 6710 Brooklawn Pkwy., Syracuse, NY 13211: Free information ◆ Original repair and owner manuals, sales brochures, and parts books for domestic and foreign cars. 315-432-8282.

**Mission Viejo Imports,** 28701 Marquerite Pkwy., Mission Viejo, CA 92692: Free information ◆ Parts, accessories, gifts, tools, technical literature, service information, and owner manuals. 800-842-3769.

**Motorbooks International,** P.O. Box 1, Osceola, WI 54020: Free catalog ◆ Automotive books. 800-826-6600. www.motorbooks.com

**Parts of the Past,** P.O. Box 602, Waukesha, WI 53187: Free information with long SASE (enclose want list) ◆ Owner and shop manuals and other automotive literature for cars and trucks, from the 1930s to 1990s. 414-679-4212.

**Portrayal Press,** P.O. Box 1190, Andover, NJ 07821: Catalog $3 ◆ Books and manuals for early Jeeps, military vehicles, and trucks. 973-579-5781. www.portrayal.com

**Schiff European Automotive Literature Inc.,** 373 Richmond St., Providence, RI 02903: Free information with long SASE ◆ European and Japanese automotive publications. 401-453-5370.

**Pete Sharp,** P.O. Box 1689, Glendale, CA 91209: Free information ◆ Shop manuals. 818-956-1559.

**Douglas Vogel,** 1100 Shady Oaks, Ann Arbor, MI 48103: Free information with long SASE (enclose want list) ◆ Shop manuals, from 1920 to 1995. 313-761-2490.

## Bumpers

**The Bumper Boyz,** 2435 E. 54th St., Los Angeles, CA 90058: Free information ◆ Reconditioned bumpers for General Motors, Ford, Chrysler, and foreign cars. 800-995-1703; 213-587-8976 (in CA).

**Hanlon Plating Company,** 925 E. 4th St., Richmond, VA 23224: Free information ◆ Bumper repair services. 804-233-2021.

## Car Floor Mats

**MacNeil Automotive Products Ltd.,** 2435 Wisconsin St., Downers Grove, IL 60515: Free information ◆ Mats for most domestic and imported cars. 800-441-6287. www.macneilauto.com

**USA Parts Supply Ltd.,** 8505 Euclid Ave., Manassas, VA 22111: Free catalog ◆ Floor mats for Cadillacs, from 1949 to 1985. 703-335-1935.

## Carriers & Racks

**Allsop,** P.O. Box 23, Bellingham, WA 98227: Free information ◆ Nordic skis and poles, boot trees, and carriers. 360-426-4303; 206-734-9090 (in WA).

**Canyon Sports Racks,** P.O. Box 502175, San Diego, CA 92150: Free information ◆ Easy-to-set up and break down watersports equipment carrier for trucks. 800-414-9019. www.ourworld.compuserve.com/homepages/canyon_sr

**Car Racks Direct,** 80 Danbury Rd., Wilton, CT 06897: Free list ◆ Automobile multi-purpose storage box and rack systems for bicycles, skis and snowboards, and water sports equipment. 800-722-5734. www.outdoorsports.com

**Collins Ski Products Inc.,** P.O. Box 11, Bergenfield, NJ 07621: Free brochure ◆ Ski carriers, goggles, and ski poles and locks. 800-526-0369; 201-384-6060 (in NJ).

**D & R Industries,** 7111 Capitol Dr., Lincolnwood, IL 60645: Free information ◆ Car-mounted bicycle racks, child carriers, horns, lamps, locks, packs and bags, reflectors and speedometers, tires and tubes, and helmets. 800-323-2852; 847-677-3200 (in IL). www.champdealers.com

**Graber,** 5253 Verona Rd., Madison, WI 53711: Free list of retail sources ◆ Bicycle, ski, and snowboard carriers. Also cargo containers and accessories. 800-783-7257. www.saris-products.com

**Highland Group Industries,** 31200 Solon Rd., Solon, OH 44139: Free catalog ◆ Towing and travel accessories, tie-downs, and car top carriers for bicycles and skis. 216-498-0001.

**Hike-A-Bike Inc.,** 2706 S. Willow Ave., Fresno, CA 93725: Free information ◆ Easy-to-install automobile-mounted carrier for up to four bicycles. 800-541-4453.

**K & S Products,** 13071 Madrone Forest Dr., Nevada City, CA 95959: Free brochure ◆ Bike racks for inside installation in a sport utility vehicle, van, pickup, or trailer. 800-986-8000. www.timesync.com/ks

**Mirage Truck Racks,** 10 Harte Circle, Williston, VT 05495: Free information ◆ Easy and fast to set up adjustable carrier rack. Folds when not in use and can be stored in a carrying case. 800-272-5362.

**North Shore Inc.,** 4 Fourth St., Hood River, OR 97031: Free catalog ◆ Canoe and kayak paddles, equipment, and transporting systems. 541-386-1980.

**Pedal Pusher Ski & Sport,** 658 Easton Rd., Rt. 611, Horsham, PA 19044: Free catalog ◆ Bicycles, frames, components, tools, clothing, and car carry-all racks. 215-672-0202.

**Piper Sport Racks,** 1160 Industrial Rd., Ste. 6, San Carlos, CA 94070: Free catalog ◆ Bicycle, snowboard, and ski racks for cars. 415-598-0858.

**Primex of California,** P.O. Box 505, Benicia, CA 94510: Catalog $5 ◆ Kayak and canoe carrier, helmets, gloves, face-savers, sailing rigs, and repair supplies. 800-422-2482. primex@castles.com

**Scooter Tote,** Divisiom Thamesford Holdings, 45 Seaview Dr., Port Moody, British Columbia, Canada V3H 1N8: Free brochure ◆ Scooter transporter for cars. 604-931-8168.

**Sports Rack,** 2401 Arden Way, Sacramento, CA 95825: Free catalog ◆ Automotive roof and rear racks, truck carriers, car camping equipment, and sport trailers. 916-648-9200. www.sportsrack.com

**Technic Tool Corp.,** P.O. Box 1406, Lewiston, ID 83501: Free list of retail sources ◆ Car carrier rack system for sports equipment, canoes, kayaks, surfboards, sailboards, or rubber rafts. 800-243-9592.

**Thule Car Rack Systems,** 42 Silvermine Rd., Seymour, CT 06483: Free catalog ◆ Automobile multi-purpose storage box and carrier systems. 800-783-4160. www.thulerack.com

**Tip Top Mobility,** Box 5009, Minot, ND 58702: Free information ◆ Battery-operated car top wheelchair carrier. 800-735-5958. www.minot.com/~tiptop

**White Water Express,** 1330 Main St., Venice, CA 90291: Free information ◆ Custom built kayak, canoe, raft, windsurfer, and other equipment carrier. 310-820-1103.

**Worldwide Engineering Inc.,** 3240 N. Delaware St., Chandler, AZ 85225: Free information ◆ Automatic and semi-automatic fold-up wheelchair and scooter carrier for automotive vehicles. 800-848-3433. wwmoblift1@aol.com

**Yakima,** 1385 8th, Arcata, CA 95521: Free catalog ◆ Racks for bicycles, skis, and other equipment. Also luggage carriers. 707-826-8000.

## Dash Sets

**Dash Specialists,** 1910 Redbud Ln., Medford, OR 97504: Free information ◆ Domestic and imported dashes. 541-776-0049.

**Just Dashes,** 5941 Lemona Ave., Van Nuys, CA 91411: Catalog $3 ◆ Restored and reproduction dash pads, door panels, and other interior parts for foreign and domestic cars. 800-247-3274; 818-780-9005 (in CA). www.justdashes.com

**Prestige Autowood & Trim,** 140 N. Harrison Ave., Campbell, CA 95008: Free information ◆ Automotive wood dash sets.

## Dollies

**Kingsbury Dolly Company Inc.,** 128 Kingsbury Rd., Walpole, NH 03608: Free information ◆ Car dollies. 800-413-6559.

**NMW Products,** 35 Orlando Dr., Raritan, NJ 08869: Free information ◆ Car dollies. 908-526-3800.

## Exhaust Systems & Mufflers

**Borla East,** 600A Lincoln Blvd., Middlesex, NJ 08846: Free information ◆ Stainless steel exhaust systems for Mercedes-Benz, Rolls Royce, Bentley, Jaguar, and other cars. 908-469-9666.

**Classic Exhaust,** 182 Industrial Pkwy., Cleveland, GA 30528: Free information ◆ Exhaust systems. 706-865-5433.

**Vetus Denouden Inc.,** P.O. Box 8712, Baltimore, MD 21240: Free catalog ◆ Exhaust system parts and accessories. 410-712-0760. www.vetus.com

**Hooker Headers,** 1024 W. Brooks St., P.O. Box 4030, Ontario, CA 91761: Free information ◆ Automotive exhaust systems and accessories. 909-983-5871.

**Kanter Auto Parts,** 76 Monroe St., Boonton, NJ 07005: Free catalog ◆ Heavy-duty replacement exhaust systems for most cars, from 1909 to 1970. 973-334-9575. www.kanter.com

**John Kepich Exhaust Inc.,** 17370 Alico Center Rd., Fort Myers, FL 33912: Free information ◆ Heavy-duty stainless steel exhaust systems. 800-365-5764.

**King & Queen Mufflers,** Box 423, Plumsteadville, PA 18949: Free information ◆ NOS exhaust system parts for cars and trucks, 1926 and later. 215-766-8699.

**TimeValve Mfg. Company,** P.O. Box 161, Plainfield, CT 06374: Free information ◆ Stainless steel exhaust systems for the Mercedes-Benz. 800-243-1170.

## Garage Floor Mats

**Billie Inc.,** P.O. Box 207, Fairfax Station, VA 22039: Free information ◆ Individual mats and cut-off rolls. 800-878-6328.

## Gas (Fuel) Tanks

**Bill Hirsch,** 396 Littleton Ave., Newark, NJ 07103: Free information ◆ Gas tank sealers. 800-828-2061; 201-642-2404 (in NJ). www.hirschauto.com

**Resto Motive Laboratories Inc.,** P.O. Box 1235, Morristown, NJ 07962: Free information ◆ Fuel tank repair kits. 800-457-6715; 201-887-1999 (in NJ). www.por15.com

**Restoration Preservation Products,** 45 Cissel Dr., North East, MD 21901: Free catalog ◆ Gas tanks and parts, restoration products, and services for classic and muscle cars. 410-658-5700.

**Transfer Flow Inc.,** 1444 Fortress St., Chico, CA 95926: Free catalog ◆ Auxiliary fuel tanks, combination fuel tanks, and tool storage systems. 800-826-5776. www.transferflow.com

## Glass Windshields & Windows

**Bob's Classic Auto Glass,** 21170 Hwy. 36, Blachly, OR 97412: Free information ◆ Auto glass for most American cars, from 1920 to 1960. 800-624-2130.

**Buchingers,** Rt. 34 West, Earville, IL 60518: Free information ◆ Windshields and side and back windows, for 1940 to 1970 cars. 815-246-8224.

**Iowa Glass,** 425 8th Ave. SE, Cedar Rapids, IA 52401: Free information ◆ Hard-to-find windshields for most pre-1960 cars. 800-747-2005.

**Lo-Can Glass International,** 693 McGrath Hwy., P.O. Box 45248, Somerville, MA 02145: Free information ◆ Hard-to-find glass for old and new cars. 800-345-9595; 617-396-9595 (in MA).

**OEM Glass Inc.,** P.O. Box 362, Rt. 9 East, Bloomington, IL 61702: Free information ◆ Glass for 1920 to 1976 cars and trucks. 309-662-2122.

## Headlights & Headlight Covers

**Albrico Auto & Truck Parts,** P.O. Box 3179, Camarillo, CA 93010: Free information ◆ Lamp assembly components. 805-482-9792.

**Donald I. Axelrod,** 35 Timson St., Lynn, MA 01902: Catalog $2 ◆ Headlights, headlight lenses, and parts. 781-598-0523.

**High Performance Bulbs,** 7057 Driftwood, Fenton, MI 48430: Free information ◆ Headlights. 800-414-BULB. www.jazconcept.com

## License Plates

**Norman D'Amico,** 44 Middle Rd., Clarksburg, MA 01247: Free information ◆ License plates for all years from all countries. 413-663-6886.

**Darryl's License Plates,** 266 Main St., Duryea, PA 18642: Free information ◆ License plate restoration. 717-451-1600.

**Richard Diehl,** 5965 W. Colgate Pl., Denver, CO 80227: Free list with long SASE ◆ License plates from most states, Canada, and foreign countries. 303-985-7481.

**Eurosign Metalwerke Inc.,** 1469 Bank Rd., Margate, FL 33063: Free information ◆ Antique license plate replicas. 954-979-1448.

**Richard Hulburt,** 27 West St., Greenfield, MA 01301: Free information with long SASE (enclose want list) ◆ License plates from United States, Canada, and foreign countries, from 1930 to 1980. 413-773-3235.

**Bob Lint Motor Shop,** P.O. Box 87, Danville, KS 67036: Inventory list $2 ◆ Old license plates. 316-962-5247.

## Locks & Keys

**Antique Auto Literature & Keys,** 1100 Shady Oaks, Ann Arbor, MI 48103: Free information ◆ Shop manuals, sales catalogs, and keys and locks for cars from 1900 to 1960. 313-761-2490.

**Autotec,** 12915 Eastbrook Pl., Brookfield, WI 53005: Free information ◆ Re-coding, repairs, and key-making for domestic and foreign cars. 414-797-9988.

**Jesser's Classic Keys,** 26 West St., Akron, OH 44303: Free information ◆ NOS classic emblem keys. 330-376-8181.

**Mito Corp.,** 54847 County Rd. 17, Elkhart, IN 46516: Free information ◆ Electronic rear view mirror and remote keyless entry systems. 800-433-6486. www.mitocorp.com

**Performance Years Classic Locks,** 320 Elm Ave., North Whale, PA 19454: Free information ◆ Automotive locks and keys, from the 1950s to 1970s. 215-699-6681.

## Miscellaneous Repairs

**Instrument Services Inc.,** 11765 Main St., Roscoe, IL 61073: Free information ◆ Auto clock repairs. 800-558-BORG; 815-623-2993 (in IL).

**Just Dashes,** 5941 Lemona Ave., Van Nuys, CA 91411: Catalog $3 ◆ Restored and reproduction dash pads, door panels, and other interior parts for foreign and domestic cars. 800-247-3274; 818-780-9005 (in CA). www.justdashes.com

**Vintage Radio Restorations,** 900 Crestview Dr., Newberg, OR 97132: Free information ◆ Automobile radios restored to factory specifications. 503-538-2392.

## Paint & Touch-Up Supplies

**EagleOne,** P.O. Box 4246, Carlsbad, CA 92018: Free information ◆ Do-it-yourself detailing kits. 800-432-4531.

**Bill Hirsch,** 396 Littleton Ave., Newark, NJ 07103: Free information ◆ High-temperature engine enamels for spray or brush application. 800-828-2061; 973-642-2404 (in NJ). www.hirschauto.com

## Parts for All Makes & Models

**A-1 Auto Wrecking,** 13818 Pacific Ave., Tacoma, WA 98444: Free information ◆ Brake drums, axles, transmission parts, wheels, and parts for old cars. 253-537-3445.

**All-American Parts Distributor,** 1646 NE 148th St., North Miami, FL 33181: Free catalog ◆ Engine, transmission, tune-up, and replacement parts for all makes and models. 800-886-6115; 305-949-9424 (in FL).

**Alley Auto Parts,** Rt. 2, Box 551, Immokalee, FL 33934: Inventory list $4 ◆ Parts for cars and trucks, from 1948 to 1975. 813-657-3541.

**Alotta Auto Parts,** 8426 Upper Miamisburg Rd., Miamisburg, OH 45342: Free information ◆ NOS used car and light truck parts, from the 1950s to 1960s. 513-866-1849.

**American Performance Products,** 675 S. Industry Rd., Cocoa, FL 32926: Catalog $6 ◆ New, used, NOS, and reproduction parts for AMX, Javelin, Jeep, Wagoneer, and other AMC cars. 407-632-8299.

**Antique Auto Parts,** P.O. Box 64, Elkview, WV 25071: Free information ◆ Parts for most cars, from 1935 to 1969. 304-965-1821.

**Antique Auto Parts Cellar,** P.O. Box 3, South Weymouth, MA 02190: Free information with long SASE ◆ NOS and reproduction mechanical parts for most cars, from 1909 to 1965. 781-335-1579.

**Auto Body Specialties Inc.,** Rt. 66, P.O. Box 455, Middlefield, CT 06455: Catalog $5 ◆ Reproduction and original quarter panels, fenders, repair panels, grilles, bumpers, and carpets for 1950 to 1986 American and foreign cars, pickups, and vans. 860-346-4989.

**Bartnik Sales & Service,** 6524 Van Dyke, Cass City, MI 48726: Free information ◆ Parts for cars and trucks, from 1960 to 1970. 517-872-3541.

**Beckers Auto Salvage,** 3221 73rd St., Atkins, IA 52206: Free information ◆ Parts for AMC, Ford, Studebaker, Edsel, Chevrolet, and other cars. 319-446-7141.

**Big Ben's Used Cars & Salvage,** Hwy. 79 East, Fordyce, AR 71742: Free information ◆ Used parts for 1975 and older cars. 870-352-7423.

**Bill's Auto Parts,** 310 7th Ave., Newport, MN 55055: Free information ◆ Used parts for all makes and models, from the 1930s to 1980s. 612-459-9733. www.billsauto.8M.com

**Bob's Auto Parts,** 6390 N. Lapeer Rd., Fostoria, MI 48435: Free information with long SASE ◆ Parts for most 1930 to 1970 cars. 517-793-7500.

**Bradley Auto Inc.,** 2026 County Rd. A, West Bend, WI 53095: Free information ◆ Parts for American cars, imports, and light duty trucks, 1975 and later. 414-334-4653.

**Bryant's Auto Parts,** 1406 Warrington Ave., Danville, IL 61832: Free information with long SASE ◆ Parts for most 1939 to 1988 cars. 217-442-0858.

**Burlington Foreign Car Parts Inc.,** 1863 Shelburne Rd., Shelburne, VT 05482: Free information ◆ Parts for imported and domestic cars. 800-343-3033.

**Canfield Motors,** 22-24 Main, New Waverly, IN 46961: Free information ◆ Parts for American cars, 1940 and later. 219-722-3230.

**Canyon Classics,** P.O. Box 1111, Black Canyon City, AZ 85324: Free information ◆ Used truck and auto parts for the Cadillac, Ford, Lincoln, and Mercury. 800-571-1488. www.dzat.com

**CBS Performance Automotive,** 2605-A W. Colorado Ave., Colorado Springs, CO 80904: Free information ◆ Solid-state electronic breaker-less ignition system for 1960 to 1972 Chrysler, 1957 to 1974 General Motors, and 1957 to 1974 Ford cars. 800-685-1492. www.inovatec.com/cbsauto

**Cedar Auto Parts,** 1100 Syndicate St., Jordan, MN 55352: Free information ◆ Parts for cars, from 1949 to current models. 800-755-3266.

**Cherry Auto Parts,** 5650 N. Detroit Ave., Toledo, OH 43612: Free brochure ◆ Used and rebuilt parts for foreign cars. 419-476-7222.

**Chuck's Used Auto Parts,** 4722 St. Barnabas Rd., Marlow Heights, MD 20748: Free information ◆ Parts for General Motors early and late model cars and trucks. 301-423-0007.

**Classic Auto Air Mfg. Company,** 2020 W. Kennedy Blvd., Tampa, FL 33606: Free catalog ◆ Air-conditioning systems and parts for pre-1973 General Motors auto temperature control systems. 813-251-4994.

**Classic Ford Sales,** P.O. Box 60, East Dixfield, ME 04227: Free information ◆ Parts for the 1949 to 1972 Comet, Cougar, Falcon, Fairlane, Lincoln, Mercury, Mustang, and Thunderbird cars. 207-562-4443.

**Classic Tube,** 80 Rotech Dr., Lancaster, NY 14086: Catalog $1 ◆ Brake, fuel, and transmission lines for collector cars and trucks. 800-882-3711; 716-759-1800 (in NY) www.classictube.com

**Del-Car Auto Wrecking,** 6650 Harlem Rd., P.O. Box 157, Westerville, OH 43081: Free information ◆ Parts for cars and trucks, from 1965 to 1992. 614-882-0220.

**Doc's Auto Parts,** 38708 Fisk Lake Rd., Paw Paw, MI 49079: Free information ◆ Parts for most cars, from 1930 to 1970. 616-657-5268.

**Don's Antique Auto Parts,** 37337 Niles Blvd., Fremont, CA 94536: Free information ◆ Parts, up to 1954, for most cars and trucks. 415-792-4390.

**E & J Used Auto & Truck Parts,** 315 31st Ave., P.O. Box 6007, Rock Island, IL 61204: Free information ◆ Parts for 1940 to 1987 American and foreign cars and trucks. 800-728-7686; 309-788-7686 (in IL).

**East End Auto Parts,** 75 10th Ave. East, Box 183, Dickinson, ND 58601: Inventory list $5 ◆ Parts for 1940 to 1980 Chevrolets, Fords, Dodges, and foreign cars. 701-225-4206.

**Eastern Nebraska Auto Recyclers,** P.O. Box 266, Elmwood, NE 68349: Free information ◆ Parts for cars, from late 1940 to 1980. 402-994-4555.

**Easy Jack & Sons Auto Parts,** 2725 S. Milford Lake Rd., Junction City, KS 66441: Free information ◆ Used parts, from 1912 to 1982. 913-238-7541.

**Eaton Detroit Spring,** 1555 Michigan, Detroit, MI 48216: Free information ◆ Springs, U-bolts, shackles, and parts for most American cars and trucks. 810-963-3839.

**Egge Machine Company,** 8403 Allport, Santa Fe Springs, CA 90670: Catalog $2 ◆ Parts for older American cars. 800-866-EGGE; 562-945-3419 (in CA). www.egge.com

**Ferrill's Auto Parts Inc.,** 18306 Hwy. 99, Lynnwood, WA 98037: Free information ◆ Parts for American cars, from 1970 to 1985. 206-778-3147.

**Fitz Auto Parts,** 24000 Hwy. 9, Woodinville, WA 98072: Free information ◆ Parts for Ford, General Motors, Chrysler, AMC, and some European and Japanese cars. 206-483-1212.

**Flathead Salvage & Storage,** 495 Hwy. 82, Box 128, Somers, MT 59932: Free information ◆ Parts for most cars, from 1932 to 1950 and 1970 to current year. 406-857-3791.

**Fleetline Automotive,** P.O. Box 291, Highland, NY 12528: Free information ◆ Parts for Chevrolet cars and trucks, Corvairs, Novas, Camaros, Chevelles, Buicks, Pontiacs, Cadillacs, and Oldsmobiles. 914-691-9228.

**Fort Auto Parts,** P.O. Box 4528, Huachuca City, AZ 85616: Free information ◆ Parts for most cars, from 1923 to 1973. 520-456-9082.

**Ron Francis Wire Works,** 167 Keystone Rd., Chester, PA 19013: Free catalog ◆ Custom wiring kits for street rods, trucks, and muscle cars. 800-NEAT-STF. www.wire-works.com

**Golden Sands Salvage,** 501 Airport Rd., Boscobel, WI 53805: Free information: Parts for most cars, from the 1930s to 1970s. 608-375-5353.

**Marc B. Greenwald,** 6644 San Fernando Rd., Glendale, CA 91201: Free information ◆ Parts for Lamborghini, Maserati, Ferrari, Fiat, and other Italian cars. 818-956-7933.

**Hidden Valley Auto Parts,** 21046 N. Rio Bravo Rd., Maricopa, AZ 85239: Free information with long SASE (specify parts wanted) ◆ Used antique and classic parts for American and foreign cars. 520-568-2945.

**Wayne Hood,** 228 Revell Rd., Grenada, MS 38901: Free information ◆ NOS parts for cars, from the 1930s to the 1960s. 601-227-8426.

**J & B Auto Parts Inc.,** 17105 E. Hwy. 50, Orlando, FL 32820: Free information with long SASE ◆ Parts for most makes and models of American and foreign cars and trucks. 407-568-2131.

**J & M Vintage Auto,** P.O. Box 297, Goodman, MO 64843: Free information ◆ Parts for 1930 to 1968 cars. 417-364-7203.

**Jess Auto Supply Company,** 119 Market, Wilmington, DE 19801: Free information ◆ Parts for cars, from 1940 to 1990. Does not have body parts. 302-654-6021.

**Joblot Automotive,** Ford Part Specialists, 98-11 211th St., Queens Village, NY 11429: Catalog $2 ◆ Parts for 1928 to 1948 Ford cars and trucks. 800-221-0172; 718-468-8585 (in NY).

**Just Dashes,** 5941 Lemona Ave., Van Nuys, CA 91411: Catalog $3 ◆ Dash pads, arm rests, door panels, consoles, head rests, and vinyl restored parts for domestic and imported cars. 800-247-3274; 818-780-9005 (in CA). www.justdashes.com

**Kalend's Auto Wrecking,** 8237 East Hwy. 26, Stockton, CA 95215: Free information with long SASE ◆ Parts for 1978 to 1988 foreign and domestic cars. 209-931-0929.

**Kanter Auto Parts,** 76 Monroe St., Boonton, NJ 07005: Free catalog ◆ Automotive parts. 973-334-9575. www.kanter.com

**Kelsey Auto Salvage,** Rt. 2, Iowa Falls, IA 50126: Free information with long SASE ◆ Parts for 1948 to 1981 American cars. 515-648-9086.

**Meier Auto Salvage,** RR 1, Sioux City, IA 51108: Free information ◆ Automotive parts, from 1935 to 1988. 712-239-1344.

**Gus Miller,** Rt. 2, Box 217, Heyworth, IL 61745: Free information with long SASE ◆ Parts for 1940 to 1950 cars. 309-473-2979.

**Art Morrison Enterprises,** 5301 8th St. East, Fife, WA 98424: Catalog $5 (refundable) ◆ Drag car racing suspension components. 206-922-7188.

**Nash Auto Parts,** Pump Rd., Weedsport, NY 13166: Free information ◆ NOS and 1920 to 1975 parts. 800-272-6274.

**North End Auto Wrecking Inc.,** 55 W. 32nd St., Dubuque, IA 52001: Free information with long SASE ◆ Parts for late model cars. 319-556-0044.

**Northern Auto Parts Warehouse,** 613 Water St., P.O. Box 3147, Sioux City, IA 51102: Free catalog ◆ Automotive parts, accessories, hardware, and tools. 800-831-0884. www.naparts.com

**Northern Tire & Auto Sales,** N. 8219 Hwy. 51, Irma, WI 54442: Free information with long SASE ◆ Parts for most cars, from the 1920s to the 1970s. 715-453-5050.

**Old Car City USA,** 3098 Hwy. 411 NE, White, GA 30184: Video catalog $19.95 ◆ Parts for cars, from 1969 and later. 770-382-6141.

**Olympic Imported Parts Corp.,** 5172 Eisenhower Ave., Alexandria, VA 22304: Free list of retail sources ◆ Exhaust systems, mufflers, clutch kits, ignition parts, other remanufactured parts and accessories, tools, and more for imported and domestic cars. 800-370-0041. www.forparts.com

**Options Auto Salon,** 337 W. Cerritos Ave., Glendale, CA 91204: Catalog $5 ◆ Options and accessories for late model Japanese imports. 800-678-2886.

**Pacific Auto Accessories,** 5882 Machine Dr., Huntington Beach, CA 92649: Brochure $3 ◆ Easy-to-install ground effect styling parts for most cars, trucks, and sport utility vehicles. 714-891-3669.

**M. Parker Autoworks Inc.,** 150 Cooper Rd., West Berlin, NJ 08091: Free information ◆ Automotive wiring accessories and supplies for 1955 to 1975 General Motors cars and trucks. 609-753-0350.

**Pearson's Auto Dismantling & Used Cars,** 2343 Hwy. 49, Mariposa, CA 95338: Free information with long SASE (enclose want list) ◆ Parts for 1959 and older cars. 209-742-7442.

**Performance Automotive Warehouse,** 8966 Mason Ave., Chatsworth, CA 91311: Catalog $5 ◆ Stock, performance, and racing engine parts. 818-998-6000.

**Performance Corner,** 150 Engineers Rd., Hauppage, NY 11788: Catalog $3 ◆ High-performance automotive and truck parts and accessories. 516-348-4493.

**Petry's Junk Yard Inc.,** 800 Gorsuch Rd., Westminster, MD 21157: Free information with long SASE ◆ Parts for most cars, from 1940 to 1970. 410-876-3233.

**Porter Auto Repair & Salvage,** Rt. 1, Box 180, Park River, ND 58270: Free information ◆ Parts for Fords, Chevrolets, Dodges, Oldsmobiles, Buicks, Pontiacs, pickups, and trucks, from 1950 to 1975. 701-284-6517.

**Power Brake Exchange,** 260 Phelan Ave., San Jose, CA 95112: Free information ◆ Rebuilt power brakes for domestic and foreign cars. 408-292-1305; 800-232-8866 (in CA).

**Quanta Restoration Products,** 743 Telegraph Rd., Rising Sun, MD 21911: Free catalog ◆ Restoration parts and accessories for antique, classic, and muscle cars. 410-658-5700. www.quantaproducts.com

**Restoration Preservation Products,** 45 Cissel Dr., North East, MD 21901: Free catalog ◆ Gas tanks and restoration products and services for classic and muscle cars. 410-658-5700.

**Restoration Specialties & Supply Inc.,** P.O. Box 328, Windber, PA 15963: Catalog $3.50 ◆ Restoration parts and accessories, from 1920 to 1970. 814-467-9842.

**Ron's Auto Salvage,** RR 2, Box 54, Allison, IA 50602: Free information ◆ Parts for most cars, from 1949 to 1977. 319-267-2871.

**Donald E. Schneider Marinette & Menominee,** RR 1, N7340 Miles Rd., Porterfield, WI 54159: Free information ◆ NOS parts for 1930 to 1969 trucks and cars. 715-732-4958.

**Seward Auto Salvage Inc.,** 2506 Vincent Rd., Milton, WI 53563: Free information with long SASE ◆ Parts for American and foreign cars, from 1946 to 1986. 608-752-5166.

**Bill Shank Auto Parts,** 14648 Promise Rd., Noblesville, IN 46060: Free information with long SASE ◆ Parts for 1948 to 1988 cars. 317-776-0080.

**Sherman & Associates Inc.,** 28460 Groesbeck, Roseville, MI 48066: Catalog $5 ◆ Reproduction parts and panels for classic car and truck restorations. 810-774-8297.

**Sil's Foreign Auto Parts Inc.,** 1498 Spur Dr. South, Islip, NY 11751: Free information with long SASE ◆ Parts for late model European and Japanese cars. 516-581-7624.

**Sleepy Eye Salvage Company,** RR 4, Box 60, Sleepy Eye, MN 56085: Free information ◆ Parts for 1937 to 1977 cars. 507-794-3005.

**Speedway Motors,** P.O. Box 81906, Lincoln, NE 68501: Catalog $5 ◆ Restoration and performance parts. 402-474-4411.

**Stainless Steel Brakes Corp.,** 11470 Main Rd., Clarence, NJ 14031: Free information ◆ Stainless steel brake components for most domestic and foreign cars. 800-448-7722; 716-759-8666 (in NY). www.stainlesssteelbrakes.com

**Lynn H. Steele Rubber Products,** 6180 Hwy. 150 East, Denver, NC 28037: Catalog $2 (specify car) ◆ Reproduction rubber parts for Cadillacs, Pontiacs, Buicks, Chevrolets, Chryslers, Oldsmobiles, Packards, and General Motors trucks. 800-544-8665; 704-483-9343 (in NC).

**Stevens Auto Wrecking,** 160 Freeman Rd., Charlton, MA 01507: Free information with long SASE ◆ Parts for early and late model cars and trucks. 888-382-5941.

**Summit Racing Equipment,** P.O. Box 909, Akron, OH 44309: Catalog $3 ◆ Performance automobile parts. 800-230-3030; 330-630-3030 (in OH). www.summitracing.com

**Sunrise Auto Sales & Salvage,** Rt. 3, Box 6, Aero Ave., Lake City, FL 32055: Free information ◆ Parts for most cars, from the 1950s through early 1970s. 904-755-1810.

**Super Auto Parts,** 6162 Lapeer Rd., Clyde, MI 48049: Free information ◆ Automotive parts, from 1950 to 1980. 810-982-6895.

**TABCO,** 11655 Chillcothe Rd., Chesterland, OH 44026: Catalog $5 (refundable) ◆ Steel repair parts for cars, vans, and trucks. 216-729-5151.

**Umatilla Auto Salvage,** 19714 Saltsdale Rd., Umatilla, FL 32784: Free information ◆ Parts for most cars, from the 1950s to 1970s. 352-669-6363.

**Van's Auto Salvage,** N3147 Center Rd., Waupun, WI 53963: Free information with long SASE ◆ Parts for most cars, from 1947 to 1976. 414-324-2481.

**Vintage Auto Parts Inc.,** 24300 Woodinville-Snohomish Hwy., Woodinville, WA 98072: Free information ◆ Parts, from 1916 to 1970, for American trucks and cars. 800-426-5911. vintageinc.@aol.com

**Vintage Automotive,** P.O. Box 958, 2290 N. 18th East, Mountain Home, ID 83647: Free information ◆ Parts for most cars prior to 1970. 208-587-3743.

**Vogt's Parts Barn,** 2239 Old Westminster Pike, Finksburg, MD 21048: Free information ◆ Parts for most cars, from 1935 to 1990.

**White Post Restorations,** One Old Car Dr., White Post, VA 22663: Free information ◆ Sleeved and rebuilt brake systems. 540-837-1140.

**J.C. Whitney & Company,** 1 JC Whitney Way, P.O. Box 3000, Chicago, IL 61301: Free catalog ◆ Hard-to-find items and custom-fit accessories. 312-431-6102. www.jcwhitneyusa.com

**Wiese Auto Recycling Inc.,** West 1421 Hwy. TW, Theresa, WI 53091: Free information ◆ Parts for most cars, from the 1960s to the present. 414-488-3030.

**Leo Winakor & Sons Inc.,** 470 Forsyth Rd., Salem, CT 06420: Free information ◆ Parts for most cars, from 1930 through 1981. 203-859-0471.

**Windy Hill Auto Parts,** 9200 240th Ave. NE, New London, MN 56273: Free information ◆ Parts for American cars and trucks, from 1915 to 1990. Most parts pre-1968. 320-354-2201.

**Winnicks Auto Sales & Parts,** P.O. Box 476, Shamokin, PA 17872: Free information with long SASE ◆ Parts for American and imported cars and trucks. Also Ford and Chevrolet engines. 717-648-6857.

**Wiseman's Auto Salvage,** 900 W. Cottonwood Ln., Casa Grande, AZ 85222: Free information with long SASE ◆ Parts for 1930 to 1970 cars. 520-836-7960.

**Woller Auto Parts Inc.,** 8227 Rd. South, Lamar, CO 81052: Free information ◆ Parts for 1955 to 1984 domestic cars and pickups. 719-336-2108.

**Zeb's Salvage,** N3181 Bernitt Rd., Tigerton, WI 54486: Free information ◆ Parts for most cars, from the 1930s to 1970s. 715-754-5885.

## Parts for Specific Makes & Models

### ACURA

**Alpharetta Auto Parts Inc.,** 5770 Hwy. 9 North, Alpharetta, GA 30201: Free information ◆ Used Acura parts. 800-494-PART; 770-475-1929 (in GA). www.alphauto.com

**King Motorsports,** 105 E. Main St., Sullivan, WI 53178: Catalog $5 ◆ Acura parts and accessories. 414-593-2800.

**Rancho Cordova Specialized Recyclers,** 3688 Omec Circle, Rancho Cordova, CA 95742: Free information ◆ Used, new, rebuilt, and aftermarket parts. 800-999-9499; 916-638-3311 (in CA).

**Worldwide Auto Parts,** Rt. 38, Maple Shade, NJ 08052: Free information ◆ Factory parts. 800-500-PART; 800-887-9999 (in NJ). www.wwparts.com

### ALFA-ROMEO

**Alfa Heaven Inc.,** 2698 Nolan Rd., Aniwa, WI 54408: Free information ◆ Alfa-Romeo parts, from 1975 to current models. 715-449-2141.

**Algar Enterprises Inc.,** 1234 Lancaster Ave., P.O. Box 167, Rosemont, PA 19010: Free information ◆ Alfa-Romeo parts. 800-441-9824; 215-527-1100 (in PA).

**Beach Imports,** 30 Auto Center Dr., Tustin, CA 92782: Free information ◆ Alfa-Romeo parts. 800-777-4895.

**Bobcor Motors,** 247 Passaic St., Maywood, NJ 07607: Catalog $6 ◆ Alfa-Romeo performance parts. 800-526-0337.

**Centerline Products,** Box 1466, 4715 N. Broadway, Boulder, CO 80306: Free information ◆ New and used Alfa-Romeo parts. 303-447-0239.

**Concours Cars of Colorado Ltd.,** 2414 W. Cucharras St., Colorado Springs, CO 80904: Free information ◆ Accessories and parts for the Alfa-Romeo, BMW, Jaguar, and Volvo. 719-473-6288.

**Ereminas Imports Inc.,** P.O. Box 1214, Torrington, CT 06790: Catalog $3 ◆ Alfa-Romeo parts. 203-496-9800.

**International Auto Parts Inc.,** Rt. 29 North, P.O. Box 9036, Charlottesville, VA 22906: Catalog $2 ◆ Replacement, restoration, and performance parts for the Alfa-Romeo. 800-726-726-0555; 804-973-0555 (in VA). www.international-auto.com

**Italian Car,** P.O. Box 515, West Linn, OR 97068: Free catalog ◆ Parts, tools, and accessories. 503-655-9811. www.rogue.northwest.com/~cndent

**Momentum Alfa-Romeo,** 10002 Southwest Freeway, Houston, TX 77074: Free information ◆ Alfa-Romeo parts and accessories. 800-234-1063.

**Orion Motors Inc.,** 10722 Jones Rd., Houston, TX 77065: Free information ◆ Alfa-Romeo parts. 800-736-6410; 713-894-1982 (in TX).

**Prestige Imports,** 14800 Biscayne Blvd., North Miami Beach, FL 33181: Free information ◆ Alfa-Romeo parts. 305-944-1800.

### AMC

**Blaser's Auto,** 3200 48th Ave., Moline, IL 61265: Free information ◆ AMC parts, from 1946 to 1987. 309-764-3571.

**Doc & Jessie's Auto Parts,** 6 Holly Blvd., Scotia, NY 12302: Free list with long SASE ◆ Hard-to-find parts and accessories for 1954 to 1975 AMC cars. 518-346-8553.

**For Ramblers Only,** 2324 SE 34th Ave., Portland, OR 97214: Free information ◆ Parts and accessories for 1958 to 1969 Ramblers and AMC cars. 503-232-0497.

**Kennedy American Inc.,** 7100 State Rt. 142 SE, West Jefferson, OH 43162: Free information ◆ New, used, and reproduction parts for AMC, AMX, Javelin, Jeep, and Rambler cars, from 1950 and later. 614-879-7283.

**Garth B. Peterson,** 122 N. Conklin Rd., Veradale, WA 99037: Free information ◆ NOS and used 1930 to 1970 parts for AMC, Hudson, and Nash cars. 509-926-4620.

**Wymer Classic AMC,** 340 N. Justice St., Fremont, OH 43420: Free information ◆ NOS and used 1958 to 1982 parts for the AMC, Nash, and Rambler. 419-332-4291.

### AMPHICAR

**Gordon Imports Inc.,** 14330 Iseli Rd., Santa Fe Springs, CA 90670: Free information ◆ Amphicar parts, all years. 562-802-1608.

### AMX

**American Parts Depot,** 409 N. Main St., West Manchester, OH 45382: Catalog $5 ◆ New, used, reproduction, and NOS parts. 937-678-7249.

**American Performance Products,** 681 S. Industry Rd., Cocoa, FL 32926: Catalog $6 ◆ AMX parts. 407-632-8299.

**AMX Connection,** 19641 Victory Blvd., Reseda, CA 91335: Catalog $10 ◆ NOS and used AMX parts, from 1968 to 1970. 818-344-4639.

**Kennedy American Inc.,** 7100 State Rt. 142 SE, West Jefferson, OH 43162: Free information ◆ New, used, and reproduction parts for AMC, AMX, Javelin, Jeep, and Rambler cars, from 1950 and later. 614-879-7283.

**Webb's Classic Auto Parts,** 5084 W. State Rd. 114, Huntington, IN 46750: Free information with long SASE ◆ AMX and Javelin parts. 219-344-1714.

**Year One Inc.,** P.O. Box 129, Tucker, GA 30085: Catalog $5 ◆ New, used, and reproduction AMX restoration parts. 800-932-7663; 770-493-6568 (in GA).

### ANTIQUE & CLASSIC CARS

**A-1 Auto Wrecking,** 13818 Pacific Ave., Tacoma, WA 98444: Free information ◆ Parts for older cars. 253-537-3445.

**B & W Antique Auto Parts,** 4653 Guide Meridian Rd., Bellingham, WA 98226: Catalog $5 (specify year and model) ◆ Antique Ford parts. 800-561-4622.

**Egge Machine Company,** 8403 Allport, Santa Fe Springs, CA 90670: Catalog $2 ◆ Parts for older cars. 800-866-EGGE; 562-945-3419 (in CA). www.egge.com

**Gowen Auto Works,** Rt. 2, P.O. Box 249, Coffeyville, KS 67337: Free information ◆ Antique and classic parts, from the 1910s to 1970s. Mostly engine, brake, and suspension parts. 316-251-4237.

**Bob Lint Motor Shop,** P.O. Box 87, Danville, KS 67036: Inventory list $2 ◆ Collectible license plates and parts for early Fords, Chevrolets, Pontiacs, Plymouths, Dodges, and Buicks. 316-962-5247.

**PRO Antique Auto Parts,** 50 King Spring Rd., Windsor Locks, CT 06096: Catalog $3 ◆ Restoration parts for antique cars. 860-623-0070.

### ASTON MARTIN

**Aston Martin of Cincinnati,** 220 Mill St., Milford, OH 45150: Free information ◆ Aston Martin parts. 937-831-7100.

**Steelwings Automotive Parts,** 229 Railroad Dr., Ivyland, PA 18974: Free information ◆ Pre-war to current parts for the Aston Martin. 215-322-7420.

### AUBURN

**Auburn's West,** 3202 NE 185th St., Seattle, WA 98155: Free catalog ◆ New and used parts, from 1934 to 1936. 206-364-1163.

**W.H. Lucarelli,** 14 Hawthorne Ct., Wheeling, WV 26003: Free information ◆ Parts for 1931 to 1933 and 1935 to 1936 Auburns. 304-232-8906.

### AUDI

**EEC Auto Parts Group,** 2732 Navajo Rd., El Cajon, CA 92020: Free information ◆ New original and remanufactured parts and accessories for the Audi, BMW, Mercedes-Benz, Porsche, Saab, Volkswagen, and Volvo. 800-259-1125.

**Euromeister,** 19507 Yuma St., Castro Valley, CA 94546: Catalog $4.95 ◆ Audi parts and accessories. 800-581-3327.

**European Parts Specialists Ltd.,** P.O. Box 6783, Santa Barbara, CA 93160: Free information ◆ Parts and accessories for the Audi. 805-683-4020.

**Parts Hotline,** 10385 Central Ave., Montclair, CA 91763: Free information with long SASE ◆ Audi parts. 800-637-4662.

**Rancho Cordova Specialized Recyclers,** 3688 Omec Circle, Rancho Cordova, CA 95742: Free information ◆ Used, new, rebuilt, and aftermarket parts. 800-999-9499; 916-638-3311 (in CA).

**Sonnen Motors,** 601 Francisco Blvd. East, San Rafael, CA 94901: Free information ◆ Genuine factory parts and accessories. 800-543-7626; 415-456-9040 (in CA).

**Valley Motors,** 3203 Bragg Blvd., Fayetteville, NC 28303: Free information ◆ Audi parts. 800-264-3203.

## AUSTIN

**Austin Works,** 229 3rd St., Manhattan Beach, CA 90266: Free information ◆ Parts for the English Austin, from 1947 to 1953. 310-372-7985.

**Kip Motor Company Inc.,** 13325 Denton Dr., Dallas, TX 75234: Free catalog (specify car) ◆ Parts for the Austin, English Ford, Sunbeam, and other British cars. 972-243-0440.

**Midtown Auto,** 212 Burnet Ave., Syracuse, NY 13203: Free information ◆ New, used, and rebuilt sheet metal, transmission, engine, brake, and electrical parts for the Austin, MG, Triumph, and Jaguar. 315-476-9421.

## AUSTIN-HEALEY

**The Austin Healey Store,** 122 Sheldon St., El Segundo, CA 90245: Free information ◆ New and used parts. 800-HEALEYS; 310-640-3782 (in CA).

**BMC Classics,** 828 N. Dixie Hwy., New Smyrna Beach, FL 32168: Free information ◆ Parts for the Austin-Healey, Jaguar, Mercedes-Benz, Porsche, and Triumph, from the 1950s to 1970s. 904-426-6405.

**British Miles,** 9278 Old E. Tyburn Rd., Morrisville, PA 19067: Catalog $5 ◆ Austin-Healey parts. 215-736-9300. www.britishmiles.com

**Engel Imports,** 5850 Stadium Dr., Kalamazoo, MI 49009: Free information ◆ Jaguar, MG, Triumph, Rover, and Austin-Healey parts, from the 1950s to the current year. 800-253-4080.

**English Car Spares Ltd.,** 345 Branch Rd SW, Alpharetta, GA 30201: Free information ◆ Austin-Healey parts. 800-241-1916; 770-475-2662 (in GA).

**Hemphill's Healey Haven,** 4 Winters Ln., Baltimore, MD 21228: Free information ◆ New and used parts. 800-9-HEALEY.

**Mini Mania,** 31 Winsor St., Milpitas, CA 95035: Free information ◆ Parts for the Morris Minor, MG, Mini Cooper, and Austin-Healey Sprite. 800-946-2642; 408-942-5595 (in CA). www.minimania.com

**Moss Motors Ltd.,** 440 Rutherford St., Goleta, CA 93117: Free catalog (specify model) ◆ Hard-to-find Austin-Healey parts. 800-MOSS-USA; 805-681-3400 (in CA). www.mossmotors.com

**Sports & Classics,** 512 Boston Post Rd., Darien, CT 06820: Catalog $5 ◆ Restoration, engine, electrical, and body parts for the Austin-Healey. 203-655-8731.

**Victory Autoservices,** Box 5060, RR 1, West Baldwin, ME 04091: Free information ◆ Post-1946 parts for the Austin-Healey, Jaguar, MG, and Triumph. 207-625-4581.

## AVANTI

**Newman & Altman Inc.,** P.O. Box 4276, South Bend, IN 46634: Catalog $5 ◆ Avanti parts. 800-722-4295. www.newman-altman.com

**Nostalgic Motor Cars,** 47400 Avante Dr., Wixom, MI 48393: Free information ◆ NOS, new original, and other replacement parts, from 1963 to 1985. 800-AVANTI-X.

**Penn Auto Sales,** Dr. Roger Penn, 7115 Leesburg Pike, #113, Falls Church, VA 22043: Free information ◆ Avanti parts, from 1963 to 1991. 703-538-4388.

**Southwest Avanti,** 915 W. Hatcher, Phoenix, AZ 85021: Free information with long SASE ◆ Avanti parts, from 1963 to 1991. 602-943-6587.

## BEL AIR

**J.R.'s Chevy Parts,** 478 Moe Rd., Clifton Park, NY 12065: Catalog $3 (specify car) ◆ Parts for 1965 to 1979 Chevrolets, Bel Airs, Biscaynes, Caprices, and Impalas. 518-383-5512.

## BENTLEY

**Bassett Classic Restoration,** 2616 Sharon St., Kenner, LA 70062: Free information ◆ Bentley parts. 504-469-2982.

**Carriage House Motor Cars Ltd.,** 25 Railroad Ave., Greenwich, CT 06830: Free information ◆ Rolls-Royce and Bentley parts. 800-883-2462.

**Classic Auto Air Mfg. Company,** 2020 W. Kennedy Blvd., Tampa, FL 33606: Free catalog ◆ Air-conditioning systems and parts for 1949 to 1969 Bentleys. 813-251-4994.

**The Enthusiasts Shop,** P.O. Box 80471, Baton Rouge, LA 70898: Free information ◆ Pre-war Bentley parts. 504-928-7456.

**Foreign Motors West,** 253 N. Main St., Natick, MA 01760: Free information ◆ Factory-new parts for the Silver Shadow and postwar Rolls-Royces and Bentleys. 800-338-3198.

**Tony Handler's Inc.,** 2028 Cotner Ave., Los Angeles, CA 90025: Free information ◆ Used parts for post-war Bentleys and Rolls-Royces. 310-473-7773.

**Oregon Crewe Cutters Inc.,** 1665 Redwood Ave., Grants Pass, OR 97527: Free information ◆ Post-war Bentley and Rolls-Royce parts. 541-479-5663.

**Powers Parts Inc.,** 425 Pine Ave., P.O. Box 796, Anna Maria, FL 34216: Free information ◆ New and used parts for Bentleys and Rolls-Royces, from 1933-1939. 941-778-7270.

**Proper Motor Cars Inc.,** 1811 11th Ave. North, St. Petersburg, FL 33713: Free information ◆ Parts for Rolls-Royces, Bentleys, Citroens, and the Ferrari. 813-821-8883.

**Replacement Parts Company,** P.O. Box 152, Villa Rica, GA 30180: Free information ◆ Rolls-Royce and Bentley replacement parts. 770-459-0040.

**Rolls Royce of Beverly Hills,** 11401 W. Pico Blvd., Los Angeles, CA 90064: Free information ◆ Rolls-Royce and Bentley parts. 800-321-9792; 310-477-4262 (in CA).

**Teddy's Garage,** 8530 Louise Ave., Northridge, CA 91325: Free information ◆ Pre-1966 parts for Rolls-Royce and Bentley cars. 818-341-0505.

## BISCAYNE

**J.R.'s Chevy Parts,** 478 Moe Rd., Clifton Park, NY 12065: Catalog $3 (specify car) ◆ Parts for 1965 to 1979 Chevrolets, Bel Airs, Biscaynes, Caprices, and Impalas. 518-383-5512.

## BMW

**Alpharetta Auto Parts Inc.,** 5770 Hwy. 9 North, Alpharetta, GA 30201: Free information ◆ Used BMW parts. 800-494-PART; 770-475-1929 (in GA). www.alphauto.com

**The Auto Works,** 846 NW 8th Ave., Fort Lauderdale, FL 33311: Free information ◆ Used BMW parts. 800-377-2520.

**Bavarian Autosport,** 275 Constitution Ave., Portsmouth, NH 03801: Catalog $3 ◆ BMW parts. 800-535-2002. www.bavauto.com

**The Best Source,** 389 Fort Salonga Rd., Northport, NY 11768: Catalog $5 ◆ BMW parts. 800-537-8248.

**BMP Design,** 3208 Park Center Dr., Tyler, TX 75701: Catalog $5 ◆ BMW parts. 800-648-7278.

**Concours Cars of Colorado Ltd.,** 2414 W. Cucharras St., Colorado Springs, CO 80904: Free information ◆ Accessories and parts for the Alfa-Romeo, BMW, Jaguar, and Volvo. 719-473-6288.

**CSI BMW,** 1100 S. Raymond Ave., Fullerton, CA 92831: Free information ◆ New and used BMW parts. 714-879-7955.

**EEC Auto Parts Group,** 2732 Navajo Rd., El Cajon, CA 92020: Free information ◆ New original and remanufactured parts and accessories for the Audi, BMW, Mercedes-Benz, Porsche, Saab, Volkswagen, and Volvo. 800-259-1125.

**Electrodyne Inc.,** 4750 Eisenhower Ave., P.O. Box 9670, Alexandria, VA 22304: Catalog $3 ◆ BMW parts. 800-658-8850; 703-823-0202 (in VA).

**Euromeister,** 19507 Yuma St., Castro Valley, CA 94546: Catalog $4.95 ◆ BMW parts and accessories. 800-581-3327.

**European Parts Specialists Ltd.,** P.O. Box 6783, Santa Barbara, CA 93160: Free information ◆ Parts and accessories for the BMW. 805-683-4020.

**Foreign Motors West,** 253 N. Main St., Natick, MA 01760: Free information ◆ BMW parts for all years and models. 800-338-3198.

**Greenfield Imported Car Parts,** 335 High St., Greenfield, MA 01301: Free information ◆ BMW parts and accessories. 413-774-2819.

**Hoffman BMW Parts,** 425 Bloomfield Ave., Bloomfield, NJ 07003: Free information ◆ BMW parts. 800-238-8373.

**Maximillian Importing Company,** 606 Maiden Choice, Baltimore, MD 21228: Free information ◆ BMW parts. 410-744-2697.

**Motorcars Ltd.,** 8101 Hempstead, Houston, TX 77008: Free information ◆ Used and new Jaguar, MG, Range Rover, BMW, Triumph, and Rolls-Royce parts. 800-338-5238.

**Perfect Plastics Industries Inc.,** 14th St., Bldg. 201, New Kensington, PA 15068: Free information ◆ BMW body parts. 800-229-3568; 412-339-3568 (in PA).

**Rancho Cordova Specialized Recyclers,** 3688 Omec Circle, Rancho Cordova, CA 95742: Free information ◆ Used, new, rebuilt, and aftermarket parts. 800-999-9499; 916-638-3311 (in CA).

**Stephen's Auto Works,** 433 Meadow Rd., Kings Park, NY 11754: Free information ◆ Mechanical parts for the BMW, Mercedes-Benz, and Porsche. 516-544-1114.

**Worldwide Auto Parts,** Rt. 38, Maple Shade, NJ 08052: Free information ◆ Factory parts. 800-500-PART; 800-887-9999 (in NJ). www.wwparts.com

## BRICKLIN

**Bob's Brickyard Inc.,** 399 Washington St., Brighton, MI 48116: Free information ◆ Parts for 1974 to 1975 Bricklin cars. 810-229-5302.

**The Gullwing Garage Ltd.,** 5 Cimorelli Dr., New Windsor, NY 12553: Free information ◆ Parts for 1974, 1975, and 1976 Bricklin cars. 914-561-0019.

## BRITISH SPORTS CARS

**British Car Specialists,** 2060 N. Wilson Way, Stockton, CA 95205: Catalog $2 ◆ MG, Jaguar, Triumph, and Austin-Healey parts. 209-948-8767.

**British Miles,** 9278 Old E. Tyburn Rd., Morrisville, PA 19067: Catalog $5 ◆ MG, Triumph, Austin-Healey, and Jaguar parts. 215-736-9300. www.britishmiles.com

**FASPEC British Parts,** 1036 SE Stark St., Portland, OR 97214: Free catalog (specify MGA/MGB, Sprite-Midget, or Austin-Healey) ◆ New and used parts. 800-547-8788; 503-232-1232 (in OR).

**Kip Motor Company Inc.,** 13325 Denton Dr., Dallas, TX 75234: Free catalog (specify car) ◆ Parts and manuals for British sports cars. 972-243-0440.

**Mini Mania,** 31 Winsor St., Milpitas, CA 95035: Free catalog ◆ Parts for the Morris Minor, Mini Cooper, Austin Sprite, and MG Midget. 800-946-2642; 408-942-5595 (in CA) www.minimania.com

**Moss Motors Ltd.,** 440 Rutherford St., Goleta, CA 93117: Free catalog (specify model) ◆ Hard-to-find parts for British sports cars. 800-MOSS-USA; 805-681-3400 (in CA). www.mossmotors.com

**Perfect Plastics Industries Inc.,** 14th St., Bldg. 201, New Kensington, PA 15068: Free information ◆ Body parts for MGA, MGB, Midget, Austin-Healey, and Triumph TR-4 and TR-6. 800-229-3568; 412-339-3568 (in PA).

**Scarborough Faire,** 1151 Main St., Pawtucket, RI 02860: Catalog $3 (specify year and car) ◆ Parts for the MGB, MGA, Austin-Healey, and Sprite. 401-724-4200.

**Sports & Classics,** 512 Boston Post Rd., Darien, CT 06820: Catalog $5 ◆ Restoration, engine, electrical, and body parts. 203-655-8731.

**TS Imported Automotive,** 404 Basinger Rd., Pandora, OH 45877: Catalog $2 (refundable) ◆ New, used, and NOS parts for British cars. 800-543-6648.

**Victoria British Ltd.,** P.O. Box 14991, Lenexa, KS 66215: Free catalog ◆ Original and reproduction Austin-Healey and other British sports car parts. 800-255-0088.

## BRONCO

**Auto Krafters Inc.,** P.O. Box 8, Broadway, VA 22815: Catalog $3 (specify year) ◆ New, used, and reproduction parts, from 1966 to 1977. 540-896-5910. www.autokrafters.com

**Bronco Parts,** 8169 Alpine Ave., Sacramento, CA 95826: Catalog $2 ◆ New and used Bronco parts, accessories, and restoration supplies, from 1966 to 1977. 916-737-9264.

**Midland Automotive Products,** Rt. 1, Box 27, Midland City, AL 36350: Free information ◆ Reproduction and new Bronco parts and accessories. 334-983-1212.

**New England Mustang,** 1830 Barnum Ave., Bridgeport, CT 06610: Catalog $3 ◆ Bronco parts, from 1966 to 1977. 203-333-7454.

**Obsolete Ford Parts Company,** 311 E. Washington Ave., Nashville, GA 31639: Catalog $4 (specify year) ◆ Parts for 1966 to 1972 Broncos. 912-686-2470.

**Obsolete Ford Parts Inc. (Oklahoma City),** 8701 South I-35, Oklahoma City, OK 73149: Catalog $3 (specify year) ◆ Parts for 1948 to 1972 Broncos. 405-631-3933.

## BUGATTI

**Italian Car,** P.O. Box 515, West Linn, OR 97068: Free catalog ◆ Parts, tools, and accessories. 503-655-9811. www.rogue.northwest.com/~cndent

## BUICK

**Bob's Automobilia,** Box 2119, Atascadero, CA 93423: Catalog $4 ◆ Parts, rubber, literature, upholstery fabrics, and hardware for 1919 to 1953 Buicks. 805-434-2963.

**Boyer's Restorations,** 1348 Carlisle Pike, Hanover, PA 17331: Free information ◆ New, used, and reproduction parts, from 1937 to 1974. 717-632-0670.

**Buick Bonery,** 6970 Stamper Way, Sacramento, CA 95828: Free information ◆ New, used, and reproduction Buick parts, from 1936 to 1975. 916-381-5271.

**The Buick Farm,** 4143 W. Hwy. 166, Carrollton, GA 30116: Catalog $2 ◆ Parts for postwar Buicks, 1950 to 1975. 770-214-0145.

**The Buick Nut-Joe Krepps,** 2486 Pacer Ln. South, Cocoa, FL 32926: Free information ◆ Reproduction 1928 to 1955 Buick parts. 407-636-8777.

**Buick Specialist,** P.O. Box 5368, Kent, WA 98064: Catalog $4 ◆ Buick parts, from 1946 to 1963. 253-852-0584.

**Cars Inc.,** Pearl St., P.O. Box 5, Neshanic Station, NJ 08853: Catalog $3 (specify year) ◆ New, used, and reproduction parts for 1935 to 1975 Buicks. 908-369-3666.

**Classic Buicks Inc.,** 4632 Riverside Dr., Chino, CA 91710: Catalog $5 ◆ New, used, and reproduction parts for 1946 to 1975 Buicks. 909-591-0283.

**Collector Car Parts,** P.O. Box 6732, Rockford, IL 61125: Free information ◆ Parts for Buick, Cadillac, Chrysler, Duesenberg, and Packard cars. 815-229-1236.

**Cooper's Vintage Auto Parts,** 121 E. Linden Ave., Burbank, CA 91502: Free information ◆ Vintage parts for Buicks. 818-567-4140.

**Fannaly's Auto Exchange,** P.O. Box 23, Ponchatoula, LA 70454: Free information ◆ Parts for 1939 to 1975 Buicks. 504-386-3714.

**GM Muscle Car Parts Inc.,** 10345 75th Ave., Palos Hills, IL 60465: Free information ◆ Buick parts, from 1964 to 1987. 708-599-2277.

**Kanter Auto Parts,** 76 Monroe St., Boonton, NJ 07005: Free catalog ◆ Parts for Buicks. 973-334-9575. www.kanter.com

**LES Auto Parts,** P.O. Box 81, Dayton, NJ 08810: Free information ◆ NOS parts, from 1950 to 1985, for Impalas, Chevelles, Novas, Camaros, Pontiacs, Buicks, and Oldsmobiles. 414-526-3411.

**Poston Enterprises,** 206 N. Main St., Atmore, AL 36502: Catalog $2 ◆ Buick Skylark performance and restoration parts. 334-368-8577.

**PRO Antique Auto Parts,** 50 King Spring Rd., Windsor Locks, CT 06096: Catalog $3 ◆ New parts for 1929 to 1964 Buicks. 860-623-0070.

**Russel Toyota,** 6700 Baltimore National Tnpk., Baltimore, MD 21228: Free information ◆ Buick, Mazda, Subaru, and Toyota parts. 800-638-8401.

**Speedway Automotive,** 2300 W. Broadway, Phoenix, AZ 85041: Free information with long SASE ◆ Buick parts, from 1961 to 1987. 602-276-0090.

**Swanson's,** 3574 Western Ave., Sacramento, CA 95838: Free information ◆ Vintage parts and accessories, from 1938 to 1948. 916-646-0430.

**Terrill Machine Inc.,** Rt. 2, Box 61, DeLeon, TX 76444: Free information with long SASE ◆ Engine overhaul parts for Buicks, from 1937 to 1958. 817-893-2610.

**Worldwide Auto Parts,** Rt. 38, Maple Shade, NJ 08052: Free information ◆ Factory parts. 800-500-PART; 800-887-9999 (in NJ). www.wwparts.com

**Year One Inc.,** P.O. Box 129, Tucker, GA 30085: Catalog $5 ◆ New, used, and reproduction Skylark restoration parts. 800-932-7663; 770-493-6568 (in GA).

## CADILLAC

**Aabar's Cadillac & Lincoln Salvage,** 9700 NE 23rd, Oklahoma City, OK 73141: Free information with long SASE ◆ Cadillac and Lincoln parts, from 1939 and later. 405-769-3318.

**Akerman Old Cadillac Parts,** 19 Gulf Rd., Box 107, Sanbornton, NH 03269: Free information with long SASE ◆ NOS and used Cadillac parts, from the 1930s to the 1970s. 800-487-3903.

**All Cadillacs of the 40's,** 12811 Foothill Blvd., Sylmar, CA 91342: Catalog $2 ◆ Used, original, NOS, and reproduction 1940 to 1950 parts and accessories. 800-808-1147. uniglobe@netport.com

**Binder's Auto Restoration & Salvage,** P.O. Box 1144, Palmer, AK 99645: Free information ◆ Parts for Cadillacs, from 1960 to the present. 907-745-4670.

**Cadillac Crazy,** P.O. Box 343, Boyce, VA 22620: Free information ◆ NOS and used 1963 to 1978 Cadillac parts. 703-665-2027.

**Cadillac King Inc.,** 9840 San Fernando Rd., Pacoima, CA 91331: Free information with long SASE ◆ New, used, and rebuilt Cadillac parts. 818-890-0621.

**Cadillac Parts & Cars Limited,** 46 Hardy, Sparks, NV 89431: Free information ◆ New, used, and reproduction Cadillac parts, from 1938 to 1980. Also manuals and other literature. 702-826-8363.

**Cadillac USA Parts Supply,** 8505 Euclid Ave., Manassas, VA 22111: Free catalog ◆ Cadillac parts, from 1949 to 1985. 703-335-1935.

**California Collectors' Classics,** P.O. Box 2281, Irwindale, CA 91706: Free information ◆ Parts, from 1961 to 1985, for the Cadillac, Lincoln, and Thunderbird. 818-962-6696.

**Collector Car Parts,** P.O. Box 6732, Rockford, IL 61125: Free information ◆ Parts for Buick, Cadillac, Chrysler, Duesenberg, and Packard cars. 815-229-1236.

**Continental Enterprises,** 1673 Cary Rd., Kelowna, British Columbia, Canada V1X 2C1: Information $2 ◆ Cadillac dress-up accessory kits, from 1949 to 1993. 604-763-7727.

**Cooper's Vintage Auto Parts,** 121 E. Linden Ave., Burbank, CA 91502: Free information ◆ Vintage parts for Cadillacs. 818-567-4140.

**Fannaly's Auto Exchange,** P.O. Box 23, Ponchatoula, LA 70454: Free information ◆ Parts for 1939 to 1974 Cadillacs. 504-386-3714.

**F.E.N. Enterprises,** P.O. Box 1559, Wappingers Falls, NY 12590: Free catalog (specify year and model) ◆ New, used, and reproduction parts. 914-462-5094.

**Ted M. Holcombe Cadillac Parts,** 2933 Century Ln., Bensalem, PA 19020: Free information ◆ NOS, used, and reproduction Cadillac parts, from 1949 to 1983. 215-245-4560.

**Honest John's Caddy Corner,** P.O. Box 741, Justin, TX 76247: Free information ◆ NOS, rebuilt, and reproduction Cadillac parts, from 1941 to 1981. 940-648-3330.

**Kanter Auto Parts,** 76 Monroe St., Boonton, NJ 07005: Free catalog ◆ Parts for Cadillacs. 973-334-9575. www.kanter.com

**McVey's,** 5040 Antioch, Merriam, KS 66203: Catalog $4 ◆ Cadillac parts and accessories, from 1936 to 1970. 913-722-0707.

**PRO Antique Auto Parts,** 50 King Spring Rd., Windsor Locks, CT 06096: Catalog $3 ◆ New parts for 1929 to 1964 Cadillacs. 860-623-0070.

**Sam Quinn Cadillac Parts,** Box 837, Estacada, OR 97023: Free information ◆ Cadillac and LaSalle parts, from 1937 to 1977. 503-637-3852.

**Rancho Cordova Specialized Recyclers,** 3688 Omec Circle, Rancho Cordova, CA 95742: Free information ◆ Used, new, rebuilt, and aftermarket parts. 800-999-9499; 916-638-3311 (in CA).

**Robinson's Auto Sales,** 200 New York Ave., New Castle, IN 47362: Free information ◆ Parts for 1960 to 1970 models. 765-529-7603.

**Selco Restoration,** 9315 FM 359, Richmond, TX 77469: Free information ◆ Restoration parts for 1930 to 1960 Cadillacs. 713-342-9751.

**Silverstate Cadillac Parts,** P.O. Box 2161, Sparks, NV 89432: Free information ◆ NOS Cadillac parts, from 1932 to 1982. 702-331-7252.

**Lynn H. Steele Rubber Products,** 6180 Hwy. 150 East, Denver, NC 28037: Catalog $2 (specify car) ◆ Reproduction rubber parts for Cadillacs and LaSalles. 800-544-8665; 704-483-9343 (in NC).

**Terrill Machine Inc.,** Rt. 2, Box 61, DeLeon, TX 76444: Free information with long SASE ◆ Engine overhaul parts for Cadillacs, from 1936 to 1962. 817-893-2610.

**USA Parts Supply Ltd.,** 8505 Euclid Ave., Manassas, VA 22111: Free catalog ◆ New, rebuilt, and reproduction Cadillac parts, from 1949 to 1985. Also decals, books, and accessories. 703-335-1935.

**Worldwide Auto Parts,** Rt. 38, Maple Shade, NJ 08052: Free information ◆ Factory parts. 800-500-PART; 800-887-9999 (in NJ). www.wwparts.com

## CAMARO

**American Auto & Truck Dismantlers,** 12172 Truman St., San Fernando, CA 91340: Free information ◆ Parts for General Motors trucks, 1955 to 1957 Chevrolets, 1967 to 1989 Camaros, and 1964 to 1972 Chevelles. 818-365-3908.

**Auto Heaven,** 103 W. Allen St., Bloomington, IN 47403: Free information ◆ Parts for 1967 to 1969 models. 800-777-0297; 812-332-9401 (in IN).

**Camaro Connection,** 139 Cortland St., Lindenhurst, NY 11757: Free information with long SASE ◆ NOS and reproduction parts for 1967 to 1988 Camaros. Also sheet metal, interiors, electrical items, and decals. 800-835-8301.

**Camaro-Heaven,** 64 River St., Rochester, NH 03867: Free information ◆ New and used Camaro and Firebird parts. 800-CAMARO-1.

**Camaro Parts Network,** 1090 W. Bagley Rd., Cleveland, OH 44017: Free price list ◆ Camaro parts. 216-234-1188.

**Camaro Specialties,** 112 Elm St., East Aurora, NY 14052: Catalog $1 ◆ New, used, NOS, and reproduction parts for 1967 to 1972 Camaros. 716-652-7086.

**Camaroland,** 3840 Finley Ave., Santa Rosa, CA 95407: Free information ◆ New and used parts. 707-568-7022.

**Chevy Parts Warehouse,** 13545 Sycamore Ave., San Martin, CA 95046: Free information ◆ Parts for 1955 to 1966 Chevrolets, 1947 to 1972 pickups, 1964 to 1972 Chevelles and El Caminos, 1962 to 1974 Novas, and 1967 to 1973 Camaros. 408-683-2438.

**Chevyland,** 3667 Recycle Rd., Rancho Cordova, CA 95742: Catalog $4 ◆ Camaro parts and accessories. 800-624-6490; 800-624-8756 (in CA).

**Chicago Muscle Car Parts,** 912 E. Burnett Rd., Island Lake, IL 60042: Catalog $5 (refundable) ◆ New and used Camaro parts, from 1967 to 1981. 847-526-2200.

**Classic Industries,** 17832 Gothard St., Huntington Beach, CA 92647: Catalog $5 ◆ Camaro parts and accessories. 800-854-1280.

**Competition Automotive Inc.,** 2095 West Shore Rd., Warwick, RI 02886: Free information ◆ Restoration supplies. 401-739-6262.

**CPX-Doug Martz,** P.O. Box 223, Butler, WI 53007: Free information ◆ Chevrolet, Camaro, Chevelle, El Camino, Monte Carlo, and Nova parts, from 1955 to 1975. 414-463-2277.

**D & R Classic Automotive,** 30 W. 255 Calumet Ave., Warrenville, IL 60555: Free price list ◆ Camaro parts. 630-393-0009.

**Desert Muscle Cars,** 2853 N. Stone Ave., Tucson, AZ 85705: Free information ◆ Restoration parts and supplies for 1955 to 1970 Chevrolets, 1967 to 1981 Camaros, 1964 to 1972 Chevelles, and 1947 to 1972 Chevrolet trucks. 520-882-3010.

**FireAro Restoration Parts Company,** 935 Hedge Dr., Mississauga, Ontario, Canada L4Y 1E9: Free information ◆ Camaro and Firebird parts and accessories, from 1967 to 1972. 905-277-3230.

**Harmon's Inc.,** P.O. Box 100, Hwy. 27 North, Geneva, IN 46740: Free catalog ◆ Camaro restoration parts, from 1967 to 1980. 219-368-7221. www.harmons.com

**J & M Auto Parts,** P.O. Box 778, Pelham, NH 03076: Price list $1 (specify year) ◆ NOS, new, and reproduction 1967 to 1972 Camaro parts. 603-635-3866.

**Kanter Auto Parts,** 76 Monroe St., Boonton, NJ 07005: Free catalog ◆ Camaro parts. 973-334-9575. www.kanter.com

**LES Auto Parts,** P.O. Box 81, Dayton, NJ 08810: Free information ◆ NOS parts, from 1950 to 1985, for Impalas, Chevelles, Novas, Camaros, Pontiacs, Buicks, and Oldsmobiles. 414-526-3411.

**Martz Classic Chevy Parts,** RD 1, Box 199B, Thomasville, PA 17364: Free catalog (specify year) ◆ NOS and reproduction parts, from 1967 to 1981. 717-225-1655.

**National Parts Depot,** 3101 SW 40th Blvd., Gainesville, FL 32608: Free catalog ◆ Camaro parts and accessories, from 1967 to 1981. 800-874-7595; 352-378-2473 (in FL).

**Obsolete Chevrolet Parts Company,** P.O. Box 68, Nashville, GA 31639: Catalog $3 (specify year) ◆ Camaro reproduction parts, from 1962 to 1972. 912-686-5812.

**Ole Chevy Store,** Division T & N Manufacturing Company, 2509 S. Cannon Blvd., Kannapolis, NC 28083: Free information ◆ Parts for Camaros. 704-938-2923.

**The Paddock Inc.,** 221 W. Main, Knightstown, IN 46148: Catalog $1 ◆ Camaro parts. 800-428-4319.

**Rick's First Generation,** 120 Commerce Blvd., Bogart, GA 30622: Catalog $3 ◆ Used, rare, and discontinued parts for 1967 to 1969 Camaros. 800-359-7717.

**Southwestern Classics,** 1230 Dan Gould Dr., Arlington, TX 76017: Free catalog ◆ New, used, remanufactured, and hard-to-find parts and accessories for 1967 to 1973 Camaros. 800-346-7362; 817-477-1322 (in TX).

**Super Sport Restoration Parts Inc.,** 7138 Maddox Rd., Lithonia, GA 30058: Free information ◆ Camaro, Chevy II, Nova, and Chevelle parts. 404-482-9219.

**Tom's Obsolete Chevy Parts,** 14 Delta Dr., Pawtucket, RI 02860: Catalog $2 ◆ Camaro parts, from 1955 to 1972. 401-723-7580.

**Volunteer State Chevy Parts,** Hwy. 41 South, Greenbrier, TN 37073: Catalog $5 (specify year) ◆ Camaro parts. 615-643-4583.

**Year One Inc.,** P.O. Box 129, Tucker, GA 30085: Catalog $5 ◆ New, used, and reproduction Camaro restoration parts. 800-932-7663; 770-493-6568 (in GA).

## CAPRI

**Dobi Capri Catalog,** 320 Thor Pl., Brea, CA 92621: Catalog $2 ◆ Capri parts. 714-529-1977.

## CAPRICE

**JR's Chevy Parts,** 478 Moe Rd., Clifton Park, NY 12065: Catalog $3 (specify car) ◆ Parts for 1965 to 1979 Chevrolets, Bel Airs, Biscaynes, Caprices, and Impalas. 518-383-5512.

**Old Car Parts,** 109 N. 15th St., Box 184, Clear Lake, IA 50428: Catalog $3.75 (specify year) ◆ NOS, new, and reproduction Caprice parts, from 1965 to 1970. 515-357-5510.

## CHECKER

**Blackheart Enterprises Ltd.,** 65 S. Service Rd., Plainview, NY 11803: Free information with long SASE (specify parts wanted) ◆ NOS Checker taxicab parts. 516-935-6249.

**Pollard Company,** Joe Pollard, 9331 Johnell Rd., Chatsworth, CA 91311: Free information with long SASE (specify parts wanted) ◆ Parts for Checker sedans and station wagons, from 1960 to 1982. 818-999-1485.

**Turnpike Center,** 495 North St., Middletown, NY 10940: Free information ◆ Parts for Checker taxicabs, from 1960 to 1982. 914-457-1898.

## CHEVELLE

**American Auto & Truck Dismantlers,** 12172 Truman St., San Fernando, CA 91340: Free information ◆ Parts for General Motors trucks, 1955 to 1957 Chevrolets, 1967 to 1989 Camaros, and 1964 to 1972 Chevelles. 818-365-3908.

**Ausley's Chevelle Parts,** 300 S. Main St., Graham, NC 27253: Catalog $2 ◆ Chevelle parts. 910-228-6701.

**Chevelle Shop,** 739 N. Batavia, Orange, CA 92868: Catalog $3 ◆ Chevelle and El Camino parts, 1964 to 1972. 714-771-7878.

**Chevy Parts Warehouse,** 13545 Sycamore Ave., San Martin, CA 95046: Free information ◆ Parts for 1955 to 1966 Chevrolets, 1947 to 1972 pickups, 1964 to 1972 Chevelles and El Caminos, 1962 to 1974 Novas, and 1967 to 1973 Camaros. 408-683-2438.

**Chicago Muscle Car Parts,** 912 E. Burnett Rd., Island Lake, IL 60042: Catalog $5 (refundable) ◆ New and used Chevelle parts, from 1964 to 1972. 847-526-2200.

**CPX-Doug Martz,** P.O. Box 223, Butler, WI 53007: Free information ◆ Chevrolet, Camaro, Chevelle, El Camino, Monte Carlo, and Nova parts, from 1955 to 1975. 414-463-2277.

**D & R Classic Automotive,** 30 W. 255 Calumet Ave., Warrenville, IL 60555: Free price list ◆ Chevelle parts. 630-393-0009.

**Danchuk Manufacturing Inc.,** 3201 S. Standard Ave., Santa Ana, CA 92705: Catalog $4 ◆ Parts for 1964 to 1972 Chevelles. 800-854-6911; 714-751-1957 (in CA).

**Desert Muscle Cars,** 2853 N. Stone Ave., Tucson, AZ 85705: Free information ◆ Restoration parts and supplies for 1955 to 1970 Chevrolets, 1967 to 1981 Camaros, 1964 to 1972 Chevelles, and 1947 to 1972 Chevrolet trucks. 520-882-3010.

**Harmon's Inc.,** P.O. Box 100, Hwy. 27 North, Geneva, IN 46740: Free catalog ◆ Chevelle restoration parts, from 1947 to 1980. 219-368-7221. www.harmons.com

**J & M Auto Parts,** P.O. Box 778, Pelham, NH 03076: Price list $1 (specify year) ◆ NOS, new, and reproduction 1964 to 1972 Chevelle parts. 603-635-3866.

**Kanter Auto Parts,** 76 Monroe St., Boonton, NJ 07005: Free catalog ◆ Chevelle parts. 973-334-9575. www.kanter.com

**LES Auto Parts,** P.O. Box 81, Dayton, NJ 08810: Free information ◆ NOS parts, from 1950 to 1985, for Impalas, Chevelles, Novas, Camaros, Pontiacs, Buicks, and Oldsmobiles. 414-526-3411.

**Martz Classic Chevy Parts,** RD 1, Box 199 B, Thomasville, PA 17364: Free catalog (specify year) ◆ Chevelle NOS and reproduction parts, from 1964 to 1972. 717-225-1655.

**Muscle Factory,** 2031 E Via Burton, Anaheim, CA 92806: Free catalog ◆ Chevelle parts, from 1964 to 1972. 800-762-0317; 714-635-2314 (in CA).

**National Parts Depot,** 3101 SW 40th Blvd., Gainesville, FL 32608: Free catalog ◆ Chevelle parts and accessories, from 1964 to 1972. 800-874-7595; 352-378-2473 (in FL).

**Obsolete Chevrolet Parts Company,** P.O. Box 68, Nashville, GA 31639: Catalog $3 (specify year) ◆ Chevelle reproduction parts, from 1962 to 1972. 912-686-5812.

**Ole Chevy Store,** Division T & N Manufacturing Company, 2509 S. Cannon Blvd., Kannapolis, NC 28083: Free information ◆ Parts for Chevelles. 704-938-2923.

**Original Parts Group Inc.,** 17892 Gothard St., Huntington Beach, CA 92647: Catalog $4 ◆ Chevelle parts. 800-243-8355.

**The Paddock Inc.,** 221 W. Main, Knightstown, IN 46148: Catalog $1 ◆ Chevelle parts. 800-428-4319.

**Paddock West Inc.,** 1663 Plum Ln., P.O. Box 8547, Redlands, CA 92375: Free information ◆ Parts and accessories for 1964 to 1977 Chevelles. 800-854-8532.

**Southwestern Classics,** 1230 Dan Gould Dr., Arlington, TX 76017: Free catalog ◆ New, used, remanufactured, and hard-to-find parts and accessories for 1964 to 1972 Chevelles. 800-346-7362; 817-477-1322 (in TX).

**Super Sport Restoration Parts Inc.,** 7138 Maddox Rd., Lithonia, GA 30058: Free information ◆ Parts for the Chevelle, Chevy II, Nova, and Camaro. 770-482-9219.

**Tom's Obsolete Chevy Parts,** 14 Delta Dr., Pawtucket, RI 02860: Catalog $2 ◆ Chevelle parts, from 1955 to 1972. 401-723-7580.

**True Connections,** 8829 Pembroke, Riverside, CA 92503: Free information ◆ NOS, reproduction, and previously installed parts for 1964 to 1972 Chevelles. 909-688-6040.

**Volunteer State Chevy Parts,** Hwy. 41 South, Greenbrier, TN 37073: Catalog $5 (specify year) ◆ Chevelle parts. 615-643-4583.

**Ted Williams,** 5615 Rt. 45, Box A, Lisbon, OH 44432: Free catalog ◆ Restoration parts for 1964 to 1972 Chevelles. 216-424-9413. www.c.boss.com/tw/tedshome.htm

**Year One Inc.,** P.O. Box 129, Tucker, GA 30085: Catalog $5 ◆ New, used, and reproduction Chevelle restoration parts. 800-932-7663; 770-493-6568 (in GA).

## CHEVETTE

**Year One Inc.,** P.O. Box 129, Tucker, GA 30085: Catalog $5 ◆ New, used, and reproduction Chevette restoration parts. 800-932-7663; 770-493-6568 (in GA).

## CHEVROLET

**Adler's Antique Autos Inc.,** 801 New York Rt. 43, Stephentown, NY 12168: Free information ◆ Parts for Chevrolet cars and trucks, from 1930 to 1970. 518-733-5749.

**Allchevy Auto Parts,** 4999 Vanden Rd., Vacaville, CA 95667: Free information ◆ Parts for 1955 to 1993 Chevrolet cars and trucks. 707-437-5466.

**American Auto & Truck Dismantlers,** 12172 Truman St., San Fernando, CA 91340: Free information ◆ Parts for General Motors trucks, 1955 to 1957 Chevrolets, 1967 to 1989 Camaros, and 1964 to 1972 Chevelles. 818-365-3908.

**American Classic Automotive,** P.O. Box 50286, Denton, TX 76206: Catalog $4 (specify year) ◆ Chevrolet car and GMC truck parts, from 1936 to 1959 and 1960 to 1972. 940-497-2456.

**B & W Antique Auto Parts,** 4653 Guide Meridian Rd., Bellingham, WA 98226: Catalog $5 (specify year and model) ◆ Chevrolet parts, 1935 to 1976. 800-561-4622.

**Big Boy Accessories,** 581 Kenbridge Dr., Carson, CA 90746: Free information ◆ Chevrolet parts, from 1958 to 1968. 310-324-4787.

**C & P Chevy Parts,** Box 348, Kulpsville, PA 19443: Catalog $3 ◆ New and restoration parts for 1955 to 1957 Chevrolet cars. 800-235-2475.

**C.A.R.S. Inc.,** 1964 W. 11 Mile Rd., Berkley, MI 48072: Catalog $4 ◆ Parts for 1955 to 1972 Bel-Airs, Impalas, Camaros, Novas, and Chevelles. 800-235-2475.

**C.A.R.S. Inc. West,** 525 S. Raymond Ave., Fullerton, CA 92631: Catalog $4 ◆ Parts for 1955 to 1972 Bel-Airs, Impalas, Camaros, Novas, and Chevelles. 800-451-1955.

**Car Shop,** 739 N. Batavia, Orange, CA 92868: Catalog $3 ◆ Chevrolet parts, from 1955 to 1957. 714-771-6432.

**John Chambers Vintage Chevrolet,** P.O. Box 35068, Phoenix, AZ 85069: Catalog $2 ◆ Chevrolet parts, from 1955 to 1957. 602-934-CHEV.

**Chev's of the 40's,** 2027 B St., Washougal, WA 98671: Catalog $3.75 ◆ Chevrolet parts, from 1937 to 1954. 800-999-2438.

**Chevy Parts Warehouse,** 13545 Sycamore Ave., San Martin, CA 95046: Free information ◆ Parts for 1955 to 1966 Chevrolets, 1947 to 1972 pickups, 1964 to 1972 Chevelles and El Caminos, 1962 to 1974 Novas, and 1967 to 1973 Camaros. 408-683-2438.

**Ciadella,** 3116 S. 52nd St., Tempe, AZ 85282: Free information ◆ Reproduction Chevrolet interiors. 602-968-4179.

**Classic Auto Parts Inc. (Chevrolet),** 8723 S. Interstate 35, Oklahoma City, OK 73149: Catalog $2 ◆ Chevrolet parts, from 1932 to 1972. 405-631-4400.

**Cliff's Classic Chevrolet Parts Company,** 619 SE 202nd, P.O. Box 16739, Portland, OR 97216: Catalog $5 ◆ Used, new, and reproduction parts for 1955 to 1957 Chevrolets. 503-667-4329.

**Continental Enterprises,** 1673 Cary Rd., Kelowna, British Columbia, Canada V1X 2C1: Information $2 ◆ Chevrolet dress-up accessory kits, from 1949 to 1993. 604-763-7727.

**Grady Cox,** 480 Utah St., Avery, TX 75554: Free information with long SASE (enclose want list) ◆ New, used, and reproduction 1929 to 1932 Chevrolet parts. 903-684-4172.

**CPX-Doug Martz,** P.O. Box 223, Butler, WI 53007: Free information ◆ Chevrolet, Camaro, Chevelle, El Camino, Monte Carlo, and Nova parts, from 1955 to 1975. 414-463-2277.

**Danchuk Manufacturing Inc.,** 3201 S. Standard Ave., Santa Ana, CA 92705: Catalog $4 ◆ Parts for 1955 to 1957 Chevrolets. 800-854-6911; 714-751-1957 (in CA).

**Desert Muscle Cars,** 2853 N. Stone Ave., Tucson, AZ 85705: Free information ◆ Restoration parts and supplies for 1955 to 1970 Chevrolets, 1967 to 1981 Camaros, 1964 to 1972 Chevelles, and 1947 to 1972 Chevrolet trucks. 520-882-3010.

**Doug's Auto Parts,** Hwy. 59 North, Box 811, Marshall, MN 56258: Free information ◆ Chevrolet parts, from 1937 to 1969. 507-537-1487.

**Mike Drago Chevrolet Parts,** 141 E. Saint Joseph St., Easton, PA 18042: Catalog $3 ◆ NOS, reproduction, and used Chevrolet parts, from 1955 to 1957. 610-252-5701.

**East Coast Chevy,** 4154A Skyron Dr., Doylestown, PA 18901: Catalog $4 ◆ Parts for 1955, 1956, and 1957 Chevrolets. Also parts for 1958 to 1970 cars (catalog $2). 215-348-5568.

**Edmonds Old Car Parts,** 307 E. Pearl, P.O. Box 303, McLouth, KS 66054: Free information ◆ Chevrolet parts, from 1928 to 1957. 913-796-6415.

**Fiberglass & Wood Company,** Rt. 3, Box 385, Nashville, GA 31639: Catalog $4 (specify year) ◆ Chevrolet parts, from 1927 to 1957. 912-686-3838.

**Fifties Forever,** 206 Division Ave., Garfield, NJ 07026: Free information ◆ New, used, and NOS parts for 1955 to 1957 Chevrolets. 201-478-1306.

**The Filling Station,** 990 S. 2nd St., Lebanon, OR 97355: Catalog $5 ◆ Reproduction parts for 1929 to 1954 Chevrolets and 1929 to 1972 trucks. 800-841-6622.

**Fleetline Automotive,** P.O. Box 291, Highland, NY 12528: Free information ◆ Parts for 1935 to 1975 Chevrolet cars and trucks. 914-691-9228.

**Garton's Auto,** 401 N. 5th St., Millville, NJ 08332: Free information with long SASE (specify car) ◆ Fenders, grilles, trim, ornaments, mechanical, chassis, and other 1929 to 1960 Chevrolet parts. 609-825-3618.

**GM Muscle Car Parts Inc.,** 10345 75th Ave., Palos Hills, IL 60465: Free information ◆ Chevrolet parts, from 1964 to 1987. 708-599-2277.

**H & H Classic Parts,** 12325 Hwy. 72 West, Bentonville, AR 72712: Catalog $4 ◆ Parts for 1955 to 1957 Chevrolets. 501-787-5575.

**Harmon's Inc.,** P.O. Box 100, Hwy. 27 North, Geneva, IN 46740: Free catalog ◆ Chevrolet restoration parts, from 1955 to 1972. 219-368-7221. www.harmons.com

**J & M Auto Parts,** P.O. Box 778, Pelham, NH 03076: Price list $1 (specify year) ◆ NOS, new, and reproduction 1955 to 1972 Chevrolet parts. 603-635-3866.

**JR's Chevy Parts,** 478 Moe Rd., Clifton Park, NY 12065: Catalog $3 (specify car) ◆ Parts for 1965 to 1979 Chevrolets, Bel Airs, Biscaynes, Caprices, and Impalas. 518-383-5512.

**Kanter Auto Parts,** 76 Monroe St., Boonton, NJ 07005: Free catalog ◆ Parts for 1955 to 1986 Chevrolets. 973-334-9575. www.kanter.com

**W.L. Walley Mansfield,** Box 237, 526 E. 2nd, Blue Springs, NE 68318: Free information ◆ Chevrolet parts, from 1925 to 1948; Dodge parts, from 1920 to 1926; and Ford parts, from 1914 to 1948. Also NOS and used parts for Model T and A Fords. 402-645-3546.

**Martz Classic Chevy Parts,** RD 1, Box 199B, Thomasville, PA 17364: Free catalog (specify year) ◆ NOS and reproduction 1955 to 1970 Chevrolet parts. 717-225-1655.

**Merv's Classic Chevy Parts,** 1330 Washington, Iowa Falls, IA 50126: Free information ◆ Used, reproduction, and NOS parts for 1955 to 1957 Chevrolets and 1967 to 1972 Chevrolet pickups. 515-648-3168.

**Modern Performance Classics,** 1127 W. Collins, Orange, CA 92667: Free information ◆ NOS, reproduction, and used Nova and Chevy II parts. 800-457-NOVA.

**Dick Moffit's Chevy Parts,** 1821 Columbus Ave., Springfield, OH 45503: Catalog $4 (specify year) ◆ Chevrolet parts, from 1928 to 1972. 937-325-7861.

**National Chevy Association,** 947 Arcade St., St. Paul, MN 55106: Catalog $5 ◆ New, used, and NOS parts, from 1953 to 1954. 612-778-9522.

**North Yale Auto Parts,** Rt. 1, Box 707, Sperry, OK 74073: Free information ◆ Chevrolet parts, from the 1960s to 1980s. 800-256-6927; 918-288-7218 (in OK).

**Obsolete Chevrolet Parts Company,** P.O. Box 68, Nashville, GA 31639: Catalog $3 (specify year) ◆ Reproduction parts for 1929 to 1954, 1955 to 1957, and 1958 to 1970 cars. 912-686-5812.

**Ohio Valley Street Parts,** 7021 Harrison Ave., Cincinnati, OH 45247: Catalog $3 ◆ Chevrolet restoration parts, from 1937 to 1954. 513-353-3113.

**Ol' 55 Chevy Parts,** 4154-A Skyron Dr., Doylestown, PA 18901: Catalog $4 ◆ Chevrolet parts, from 1955, 1956, and 1957. 215-348-5568.

**Old Car Parts,** 109 N. 15th St., Box 184, Clear Lake, IA 50428: Catalog $3.75 (specify year) ◆ NOS, new, and reproduction Chevrolet parts, from 1930 to 1970. 515-357-5510.

**Ole Chevy Store,** Division T & N Manufacturing Company, 2509 S. Cannon Blvd., Kannapolis, NC 28083: Free information ◆ Parts for 1937 to 1958 Chevrolets. 704-938-2923.

**Paddock West Inc.,** 1663 Plum Ln., P.O. Box 8547, Redlands, CA 92375: Free information ◆ Parts and accessories for 1955 to 1957 Chevrolets. 800-854-8532.

**Pioneer Classic Auto Inc.,** 2111 W. Deer Valley Rd., Phoenix, AZ 85027: Catalog $4 (specify year) ◆ New and used parts for 1955 to 1972 Chevrolets. 602-993-5999.

**PRO Antique Auto Parts,** 50 King Spring Rd., Windsor Locks, CT 06096: Catalog $3 ◆ New parts for 1929 to 1964 Chevrolets. 860-623-0070.

**Rancho Cordova Specialized Recyclers,** 3688 Omec Circle, Rancho Cordova, CA 95742: Free information ◆ Used, new, rebuilt, and aftermarket parts. 800-999-9499; 916-638-3311 (in CA).

**SC Automotive,** 409 Super Sport Ln., Rt. 3, Box 9, New Ulm, MN 56073: Free catalog ◆ Chevrolet parts. 800-62-SS-409.

**Southwestern Classics,** 1230 Dan Gould Dr., Arlington, TX 76017: Free catalog ◆ New, used, and re-manufactured parts and accessories for 1961 to 1970 Chevrolets. 800-346-7362; 817-477-1322 (in TX).

**Super Sport Restoration Parts Inc.,** 7138 Maddox Rd., Lithonia, GA 30058: Free information ◆ Parts for the Chevy II, Nova, Chevelle, and Camaro. 770-482-9219.

**Terrill Machine Inc.,** Rt. 2, Box 61, DeLeon, TX 76444: Free information with long SASE ◆ Engine overhaul parts for Chevrolets, from 1929 to 1951. 817-893-2610.

**Tom's Obsolete Chevy Parts,** 14 Delta Dr., Pawtucket, RI 02860: Catalog $2 ◆ Chevrolet parts, from 1955 to 1972. 401-723-7580.

**Volunteer State Chevy Parts,** Hwy. 41 South, Greenbrier, TN 37073: Catalog $5 (specify year) ◆ Chevrolet parts, from 1955 to 1957. 615-643-4583.

**Winnicks Auto Sales & Parts,** P.O. Box 476, Shamokin, PA 17872: Free information with long SASE ◆ Ford and Chevrolet engines and parts for American and imported cars and trucks. 717-648-6857.

**Worldwide Auto Parts,** Rt. 38, Maple Shade, NJ 08052: Free information ◆ Factory parts. 800-500-PART; 800-887-9999 (in NJ). www.wwparts.com

**Year One Inc.,** P.O. Box 129, Tucker, GA 30085: Catalog $5 ◆ New, used, and reproduction Nova and Chevy II restoration parts. 800-932-7663; 770-493-6568 (in GA).

## CHRYSLER

**Andy Bernbaum Auto Parts,** 315 Franklin St., Newton, MA 02158: Catalog $4 ◆ Chrysler parts. 617-244-1118.

**Collector Car Parts,** P.O. Box 6732, Rockford, IL 61125: Free information ◆ Parts for Buick, Cadillac, Chrysler, Duesenberg, and Packard cars. 815-229-1236.

**Vin Devers of Sylvania,** 5570 Monroe St., Sylvania, OH 43560: Catalog $5 (refundable) ◆ MOPAR accessories. 800-887-5921.

**Hardens Muscle Car World,** P.O. Box 306, Lexington, MO 64067: Catalog $4 ◆ NOS, reproduction, and used Chrysler parts. 800-633-4690.

**Imperial Motors,** 2165 Spencer Creek Rd., Campobello, SC 29322: Free information ◆ Chrysler, Plymouth, and Dodge parts. 864-895-3474.

**Mid-South Auto Sales,** 2700 Neiman Industrial Dr., Winston-Salem, NC 27103: Free information ◆ Chrysler parts and accessories. 336-768-6251.

**Mike's Auto Parts,** Box 358, Ridgeland, MS 39157: Free information with long SASE ◆ Chrysler parts. 601-856-7214.

**Mitchell Motor Parts Inc.,** 1601 Thraikill Rd., Grove City, OH 43123: Free information with long SASE ◆ Chrysler parts, from 1928 to the present. 614-875-4919.

**North Yale Auto Parts,** Rt. 1, Box 707, Sperry, OK 74073: Free information ◆ Parts for Chrysler cars, 1977 and later. 800-256-6927; 918-288-7218 (in OK).

**PRO Antique Auto Parts,** 50 King Spring Rd., Windsor Locks, CT 06096: Catalog $3 ◆ New parts for 1929 to 1964 Chrysler cars. 860-623-0070.

**Rancho Cordova Specialized Recyclers,** 3688 Omec Circle, Rancho Cordova, CA 95742: Free information ◆ Used, new, rebuilt, and aftermarket parts. 800-999-9499; 916-638-3311 (in CA).

**Roberts Motor Parts,** 17 Prospect St., West Newbury, MA 01985: Catalog $4 ◆ Parts for Chrysler cars. 978-363-5881.

**Terrill Machine Inc.,** Rt. 2, Box 61, DeLeon, TX 76444: Free information with long SASE ◆ Engine overhaul parts for Chryslers, from 1937 to 1954. 817-893-2610.

**Worldwide Auto Parts,** Rt. 38, Maple Shade, NJ 08052: Free information ◆ Factory parts. 800-500-PART; 800-887-9999 (in NJ). www.wwparts.com

## CITROEN

**Proper Motor Cars Inc.,** 1811 11th Ave. North, St. Petersburg, FL 33713: Free information ◆ Parts for Rolls-Royces, Bentleys, Citroens, and the Ferrari. 813-821-8883.

## COBRA

**Cobra Restorers,** 3099 Carter, Kenesaw, GA 30144: Catalog $5 ◆ Parts for Cobra cars. 404-427-0020.

**Contemporary Classic Motor Car Company,** 115 Hoyt Ave., Mamaroneck, NY 10543: Catalog $5 ◆ Cobra parts. 914-381-5678.

## COMET

**Dennis Carpenter Reproductions,** P.O. Box 26398, Charlotte, NC 28221: Catalog $3 (specify year) ◆ Rubber parts for 1960 to 1970 Comets. 219-335-2425.

**Bob Cook Classic Auto Parts,** 2055 Van Cleave Rd., P.O. Box 600, Murray, KY 42071: Catalog $6 ◆ Reproduction parts for the 1956 to 1972 Comet. 800-486-1137; 502-753-4000 (in KY).

**Jim Dottling's Vintage,** 728 E. Dunlap, Phoenix, AZ 85020: Catalog $3 ◆ Parts for the Falcon, Comet, and Fairlane. 800-TTT-BIRD.

**Highway Classics,** 949 N. Cataract Ave., San Dimas, CA 91773: Catalog $3 ◆ Comet parts and accessories, from 1960 to 1970. 909-592-8819.

**Dale King Obsolete Parts Inc.,** P.O. Box 1099, Liberty, KY 42539: Free information ◆ NOS and reproduction Comet parts. 606-787-5031.

**Northwest Classic Falcons,** 1964 NW Pettygrove, Portland, OR 97209: Parts list $2 ◆ Used, new, reproduction, and NOS Comet parts, from 1960 to 1970. 503-241-9454.

**Obsolete Ford Parts Inc. (Oklahoma City),** 8701 South I-35, Oklahoma City, OK 73149: Catalog $3 (specify year) ◆ Parts for 1949 to 1972 Comets. 405-631-3933.

**Thunderbird & Falcon Connections,** 728 E. Dunlap, Phoenix, AZ 85020: Free information ◆ Used Thunderbird, Falcon, Fairlane, and Comet parts. 800-888-BIRD; 602-997-9285 (in AZ).

## CORVAIR

**Clark's Corvair Parts Inc.,** Rt. 2, Shelburne Falls, MA 01370: Catalog $5 ◆ Corvair parts. 413-625-9776. www.clarkscorvair.com

**Corvair Underground,** P.O. Box 339, Dundee, OR 97115: Catalog $5 ◆ New, used, reproduction, and rebuilt Corvair parts. 800-825-VAIR.

**Robinson's Auto Sales,** 200 New York Ave., New Castle, IN 47362: Free information ◆ Parts for 1960 to 1970 models. 765-529-7603.

**Southwest Corvair,** 32 E. Raymond St., Phoenix, AZ 85040: Free catalog ◆ Used Corvair parts. 602-268-5968.

## CORVETTE

**Andover Corvette,** P.O. Box 3143, Laurel, MD 20709: Free catalog (specify year) ◆ Parts for 1963 to 1967, 1968 to 1972, 1973 to 1977, and 1978 to 1982 Corvettes. 410-381-6700. www.andauto.com

**Auto Accessories of America,** Rt. 322, Box 427, Boalsburg, PA 16827: Catalog $5 ◆ Corvette accessories and parts. 800-458-3475.

**B & W Antique Auto Parts,** 4653 Guide Meridian Rd., Bellingham, WA 98226: Catalog $5 (specify year and model) ◆ Corvette parts, 1953 to 1996. 800-561-4622.

**Blue Ribbon Products Ltd.,** 4965 Old House Trail NE, Atlanta, GA 30342: Free catalog ◆ Corvette parts, from 1956 to 1967. 404-843-8414.

**Chevyland,** 3667 Recycle Rd., Rancho Cordova, CA 95742: Catalog $4 ◆ Corvette parts and accessories. 800-624-6490; 800-624-8756 (in CA).

**Chicago Corvette Supply,** 7322 S. Archer Ave., Justice, IL 60458: Catalog $3 ◆ New and reproduction parts for 1953 to 1982 Corvettes. 800-872-2446; 847-458-2500 (in IL).

**Corvette Central,** 5865 Sawyer Rd., Sawyer, MI 49125: Catalog $4 ◆ New, used, and reproduction parts for 1953 to 1982 Corvettes. 616-426-3342.

**Corvette Pacifica,** P.O. Box 2360, Atascadero, CA 93423: Free catalog ◆ Parts for 1953 to 1997 Corvettes. 800-488-7671.

**Corvette Rubber Company,** 10640 W. Cadillac Rd., Cadillac, MI 49601: Free catalog (specify year) ◆ Rubber parts and weatherstripping for 1953 to 1993 Corvettes. 616-779-2888.

**Corvette Specialties of MD,** 1912 Liberty St., Eldersburg, MD 21784: Free information ◆ New, used, and reproduction Corvette parts. 410-795-3180.

**Eckler's Corvette Parts & Accessories,** P.O. Box 5637, Titusville, FL 32783: Catalog $5 ◆ Corvette restoration parts and accessories, from 1953 to 1996. 800-327-4868.

**J.B.'s Corvette Supplies,** 1256 E. 10th St., Bronx, NY 10460: Catalog $5 ◆ Corvette parts. 800-874-6019; 718-823-3100 (in NY).

**Kanter Auto Parts,** 76 Monroe St., Boonton, NJ 07005: Free catalog ◆ Corvette parts, from 1963 to 1982. 973-334-9575. www.kanter.com

**Long Island Corvette Supply Inc.,** 1445 Strong Ave., Copiague, NY 11726: Catalog $3 ◆ Corvette parts, from 1963 to 1967. 516-225-3000.

**Mid America Designs Inc.,** P.O. Box 1368, Effingham, IL 62401: Catalog $5 ◆ Corvette replacement and performance parts. 800-500-8388.

**Paragon Reproductions Inc.,** 8040 S. Jennings Rd., Swartz Creek, MI 48473: Free information ◆ Corvette restoration parts. 810-655-4641.

**Rik's Unlimited,** 3758 Hwy. 18 South, Morganton, NC 28655: Catalog $2 ◆ Corvette parts and accessories, from 1963 to 1982. 704-433-6506.

**Stoudt Auto Sales,** 1350 Carbon St., Reading, PA 19601: Catalog $3 ◆ Corvette parts, from 1953 to 1994. 610-374-4856.

**Vette JD,** 9833 Alondra Blvd., Bellflower, CA 90706: Free information ◆ Used parts and fiber glass accessories. 800-838-8353.

**Zip Products,** 8067 Fast Lane, Mechanicsville, VA 23111: Catalog $3 ◆ Corvette restoration parts. 804-746-2290.

## COUGAR

**Auto Krafters Inc.,** P.O. Box 8, Broadway, VA 22815: Catalog $3 (specify year) ◆ New, used, and reproduction parts, from 1967 to 1973. 540-896-5910. www.autokrafters.com

**Bob Cook Classic Auto Parts,** 2055 Van Cleave Rd., P.O. Box 600, Murray, KY 42071: Catalog $6 ◆ Reproduction parts for the 1953 to 1973 Cougar. 800-486-1137; 502-753-4000 (in KY).

**Highway Classics,** 949 N. Cataract Ave., San Dimas, CA 91773: Catalog $3 ◆ Cougar parts and accessories, from 1967 to 1973. 909-592-8819.

**Dale King Obsolete Parts Inc.,** P.O. Box 1099, Liberty, KY 42539: Free information ◆ NOS and reproduction Cougar parts. 606-787-5031.

**Midland Automotive Products,** Rt. 1, Box 27, Midland City, AL 36350: Free information ◆ Reproduction and new Cougar parts and accessories. 334-983-1212.

**Mustangs Unlimited,** 185 Adams St., Manchester, CT 06040: Catalog $3 (specify year) ◆ Cougar parts. 800-243-7278.

## CROSLEY

**Edwards Crosley Parts,** P.O. Box 632, Mansfield, OH 44901: Free information with long SASE (specify parts wanted) ◆ Crosley parts. 419-589-5767.

## CUTLASS

**Chicago Muscle Car Parts,** 912 E. Burnett Rd., Island Lake, IL 60042: Catalog $5 (refundable) ◆ New and used Cutlass parts, from 1964 to 1972. 847-526-2200.

**Year One Inc.,** P.O. Box 129, Tucker, GA 30085: Catalog $5 ◆ New, used, and reproduction Cutlass restoration parts. 800-932-7663; 770-493-6568 (in GA).

## DATSUN (NISSAN)

**Dobi Datsun Catalog,** 320 Thor Pl., Brea, CA 92621: Catalog $2 ◆ Replacement parts for the Datsun Z, 200SX, and 510. 714-529-1977.

**Motorsport,** 1139 W. Collins Ave., Orange, CA 92667: Free catalog ◆ Parts for the Datsun Z and ZX. 800-633-6331.

**Perfect Plastics Industries Inc.,** 14th St., Bldg. 201, New Kensington, PA 15068: Free information ◆ Body parts for the Datsun Z. 800-229-3568; 412-339-3568 (in PA).

**Rancho Cordova Specialized Recyclers,** 3688 Omec Circle, Rancho Cordova, CA 95742: Free information ◆ Used, new, rebuilt, and aftermarket parts. 800-999-9499; 916-638-3311 (in CA).

## DELOREAN

**Delorean One,** 20229 Nordhoff St., Chatsworth, CA 91311: Free information ◆ Delorean parts. 818-341-1796.

**P.J. Grady Delorean,** 118 Montauk Hwy., West Sayville, NY 11796: Free information ◆ DeLorean parts. 516-589-6224.

## DESOTO

**Andy Bernbaum Auto Parts,** 315 Franklin St., Newton, MA 02158: Catalog $4 ◆ Parts for the DeSoto. 617-244-1118.

**Mike's Auto Parts,** Box 358, Ridgeland, MS 39157: Free information with long SASE ◆ DeSoto parts. 601-856-7214.

**Mitchell Motor Parts Inc.,** 1601 Thraikill Rd., Grove City, OH 43123: Free information with long SASE ◆ DeSoto parts, from 1928 to the present. 614-875-4919.

**PRO Antique Auto Parts,** 50 King Spring Rd., Windsor Locks, CT 06096: Catalog $3 ◆ New parts for 1929 to 1964 DeSotos. 860-623-0070.

**Roberts Motor Parts,** 17 Prospect St., West Newbury, MA 01985: Catalog $4 ◆ Parts for DeSotos. 978-363-5881.

**Terrill Machine Inc.,** Rt. 2, Box 61, DeLeon, TX 76444: Free information with long SASE ◆ Engine overhaul parts for DeSotos, from 1937 to 1954. 817-893-2610.

## DETOMASO PANTERRA

**Collectors Choice,** 6400 Springfield Lodi Rd., Dane, WI 53529: Free information ◆ Parts for the DeTomaso Panterra, Shelby, Ferrari, Jaguar, and Rolls-Royce. 608-849-9878.

**Panterra Performance Center,** 1856 N. Park St., Castle Rock, CO 80104: Free information ◆ DeTomaso Panterra parts. 303-660-9897.

## DODGE

**Andy Bernbaum Auto Parts,** 315 Franklin St., Newton, MA 02158: Catalog $4 ◆ Parts for Dodge cars. 617-244-1118.

**Hardens Muscle Car World,** P.O. Box 306, Lexington, MO 64067: Catalog $4 ◆ NOS, reproduction, and used Dodge parts. 800-633-4690.

**Imperial Motors,** 2165 Spencer Creek Rd., Campobello, SC 29322: Free information ◆ Chrysler, Plymouth, and Dodge parts. 864-895-3474.

**Jim's Auto Parts,** 40 Lowell Rd., P.O. Box 908, Salem, NH 03079: Catalog $7 ◆ Hard-to-find original NOS and reproduction restoration Dodge and Plymouth parts, from 1963 to 1976.

**Koller Dodge,** 1565 W. Ogden Ave., Naperville, IL 60540: Catalog $7 ◆ Dodge restoration parts. 630-355-3411.

**Jim Mallars,** 5931 Glen St., Stockton, CA 95207: Free information ◆ New and used parts for 1915 to 1928 4-cylinder Dodge cars. 209-477-1702.

**W.L. Walley Mansfield,** Box 237, 526 E. 2nd, Blue Springs, NE 68318: Free information ◆ Chevrolet parts, from 1925 to 1948; Dodge parts, from 1920 to 1926; and Ford parts, from 1914 to 1948. Also NOS and used parts for Model T and A Fords. 402-645-3546.

**Mid-South Auto Sales,** 2700 Neiman Industrial Dr., Winston-Salem, NC 27103: Free information ◆ Dodge parts and accessories. 336-768-6251.

**Mike's Auto Parts,** Box 358, Ridgeland, MS 39157: Free information with long SASE ◆ Dodge parts. 601-856-7214.

**Mitchell Motor Parts Inc.,** 1601 Thraikill Rd., Grove City, OH 43123: Free information with long SASE ◆ Dodge parts, from 1928 to the present. 614-875-4919.

**Paddock West Inc.,** 1663 Plum Ln., P.O. Box 8547, Redlands, CA 92375: Free information ◆ Parts and accessories for 1962 to 1974 Dodges. 800-854-8532.

**PRO Antique Auto Parts,** 50 King Spring Rd., Windsor Locks, CT 06096: Catalog $3 ◆ New parts for 1929 to 1964 Dodge cars. 860-623-0070.

**Rancho Cordova Specialized Recyclers,** 3688 Omec Circle, Rancho Cordova, CA 95742: Free information ◆ Used, new, rebuilt, and aftermarket parts. 800-999-9499; 916-638-3311 (in CA).

**Roberts Motor Parts,** 17 Prospect St., West Newbury, MA 01985: Catalog $4 ◆ Dodge parts. 978-363-5881.

**Terrill Machine Inc.,** Rt. 2, Box 61, DeLeon, TX 76444: Free information with long SASE ◆ Engine overhaul parts for Dodges, from 1937 to 1954. 817-893-2610.

**Vintage Power Wagons Inc.,** 302 S. 7th St., Fairfield, IA 52556: Free information ◆ Parts for 1939 to 1970 Dodge Power Wagons. 515-472-4665.

**Worldwide Auto Parts,** Rt. 38, Maple Shade, NJ 08052: Free information ◆ Factory parts. 800-500-PART; 800-887-9999 (in NJ). www.wwparts.com

**Year One Inc.,** P.O. Box 129, Tucker, GA 30085: Catalog $5 ◆ New, used, and reproduction Dodge restoration parts. 800-932-7663; 770-493-6568 (in GA).

## DUESENBERG

**Collector Car Parts,** P.O. Box 6732, Rockford, IL 61125: Free information ◆ Parts for Buick, Cadillac, Chrysler, Duesenberg, and Packard cars. 815-229-1236.

## EDSEL

**B & W Antique Auto Parts,** 4653 Guide Meridian Rd., Bellingham, WA 98226: Catalog $5 (specify year and model) ◆ Edsel parts, 1958 to 1960. 800-561-4622.

**Beckers Auto Salvage,** 3221 73rd St., Atkins, IA 52206: Free information ◆ Parts for Edsel cars. 319-446-7141.

**Bob Cook Classic Auto Parts,** 2055 Van Cleave Rd., P.O. Box 600, Murray, KY 42071: Catalog $6 ◆ Reproduction parts for 1958 to 1960 Edsels. 800-486-1137; 502-753-4000 (in KY).

## EL CAMINO

**Chevelle Shop,** 739 N. Batavia, Orange, CA 92868: Catalog $3 ◆ Chevelle and El Camino parts, from 1964 to 1972. 714-771-7878.

**Chevy Parts Warehouse,** 13545 Sycamore Ave., San Martin, CA 95046: Free information ◆ Parts for 1955 to 1966 Chevrolets, 1947 to 1972 pickups, 1964 to 1972 Chevelles and El Caminos, 1962 to 1974 Novas, and 1967 to 1973 Camaros. 408-683-2438.

**Chevyland,** 3667 Recycle Rd., Rancho Cordova, CA 95742: Catalog $4 ◆ El Camino parts and accessories. 800-624-6490; 800-624-8756 (in CA).

**CPX-Doug Martz,** P.O. Box 223, Butler, WI 53007: Free information ◆ Chevrolet, Camaro, Chevelle, El Camino, Monte Carlo, and Nova parts, from 1955 to 1975. 414-463-2277.

**Danchuk Manufacturing Inc.,** 3201 S. Standard Ave., Santa Ana, CA 92705: Catalog $4 ◆ Parts for the 1964 to 1972 El Camino. 800-854-6911; 714-751-1957 (in CA).

**Muscle Factory,** 2031 E Via Burton, Anaheim, CA 92806: Free catalog ◆ El Camino parts, from 1964 to 1972. 800-762-0317; 714-635-2314 (in CA).

**Original Parts Group Inc.,** 17892 Gothard St., Huntington Beach, CA 92647: Catalog $4 ◆ El Camino parts. 800-243-8355.

**Southwestern Classics,** 1230 Dan Gould Dr., Arlington, TX 76017: Free catalog ◆ New, used, remanufactured, and hard-to-find parts and accessories for 1964 to 1972 El Caminos. 800-346-7362; 817-477-1322 (in TX).

**Ted Williams,** 5615 Rt. 45, Box A, Lisbon, OH 44432: Free catalog ◆ Restoration parts for 1964 to 1972 El Caminos. 216-424-9413. www.c.boss.com/tw/tedshome.htm

**Year One Inc.,** P.O. Box 129, Tucker, GA 30085: Catalog $5 ◆ New, used, and reproduction El Camino restoration parts. 800-932-7663; 770-493-6568 (in GA).

## ENGLISH FORD

**Anglia Obsolete,** 1311 York Dr., Vista, CA 92084: Free information ◆ New, used, and reproduction parts for English Fords. 619-630-3136.

**Dave Bean Engineering Inc.,** 636 E. Saint Charles St., San Andreas, CA 95249: Catalog $6 ◆ Parts for the English Ford. 209-754-5802.

**Kip Motor Company Inc.,** 13325 Denton Dr., Dallas, TX 75234: Free catalog (specify car) ◆ Parts for the Austin, English Ford, Sunbeam, and other British cars. 972-243-0440.

**Weld-N-Fab Performance,** P.O. Box 356, Norwalk, IA 50211: Free information ◆ Parts for 1948 to 1952 English Fords. 515-981-4928.

## ESSEX

**Kenneth Fogarty,** Anson Valley Rd., New Vineyard, ME 04956: Free information with long SASE (specify parts wanted) ◆ Essex parts, from 1919 to 1933. 207-652-2210.

**K-Gap Automotive Parts,** P.O. Box 3065, Santa Fe Springs, CA 90670: Catalog $2 (refundable) ◆ Reproduction Hudson and Essex parts.

## FAIRLANE

**Auto Krafters Inc.,** P.O. Box 8, Broadway, VA 22815: Catalog $3 (specify year) ◆ New, used, and reproduction parts for 1962 to 1971 Fairlanes. 540-896-5910. www.autokrafters.com

**B & W Antique Auto Parts,** 4653 Guide Meridian Rd., Bellingham, WA 98226: Catalog $5 (specify year and model) ◆ Fairlane parts, 1955 to 1971. 800-561-4622.

**Dennis Carpenter Reproductions,** P.O. Box 26398, Charlotte, NC 28221: Catalog $3 (specify year) ◆ Rubber parts for 1962 to 1971 Fairlanes. 219-335-2425.

**Bob Cook Classic Auto Parts,** 2055 Van Cleave Rd., P.O. Box 600, Murray, KY 42071: Catalog $6 ◆ Reproduction parts for 1960 to 1972 Fairlanes. 800-486-1137; 502-753-4000 (in KY).

**Dearborn Classics,** P.O. Box 1248, Sunset Beach, CA 90742: Catalog $4 ◆ Fairlane parts and accessories. 562-372-3175.

**Jim Dottling's Vintage,** 728 E. Dunlap, Phoenix, AZ 85020: Catalog $3 ◆ Parts for the Falcon, Comet, and Fairlane. 800-TTT-BIRD.

**Ford Parts Specialists,** 98-11 211th St., Queens Village, NY 11429: Catalog $2 (specify year) ◆ Parts for 1949 to 1969 Fairlanes. 212-468-8585.

**Ford Parts Store,** P.O. Box 226, Bryan, OH 43506: Catalog $2 ◆ Fairlane parts. 419-636-2475.

**Highway Classics,** 949 N. Cataract Ave., San Dimas, CA 91773: Catalog $3 ◆ Fairlane parts and accessories, from 1962. 909-592-8819.

**Joblot Automotive,** 98-11 211th St., Queens Village, NY 11429: Catalog $2 ◆ Parts for 1949 to 1969 Fairlanes. 800-221-0172; 718-468-8585 (in NY).

**Dale King Obsolete Parts Inc.,** P.O. Box 1099, Liberty, KY 42539: Free information ◆ NOS and reproduction Fairlane parts. 606-787-5031.

**Melvin's Classic Ford Parts Inc.,** 2526 Panola, Lithonia, GA 30058: Free information ◆ Parts for 1962 to 1979 Fairlanes. 770-981-2357.

**Midland Automotive Products,** Rt. 1, Box 27, Midland City, AL 36350: Free information ◆ Reproduction and new Fairlane parts and accessories. 334-983-1212.

**Obsolete Ford Parts Company,** 311 E. Washington Ave., Nashville, GA 31639: Catalog $4 (specify year) ◆ Parts for 1962 to 1971 Fairlanes. 912-686-2470.

**Obsolete Ford Parts Inc. (Oklahoma City),** 8701 South I-35, Oklahoma City, OK 73149: Catalog $3 (specify year) ◆ Parts for 1960 to 1972 Fairlanes. 405-631-3933.

**Thunderbird & Falcon Connections,** 728 E. Dunlap, Phoenix, AZ 85020: Free information ◆ Used Thunderbird, Falcon, Fairlane, and Comet parts. 800-888-BIRD; 602-997-9285 (in AZ).

## FALCON

**Auto Krafters Inc.,** P.O. Box 8, Broadway, VA 22815: Catalog $3 (specify year) ◆ New, used, and reproduction parts for 1960 to 1970 Falcons. 540-896-5910. www.autokrafters.com

**B & W Antique Auto Parts,** 4653 Guide Meridian Rd., Bellingham, WA 98226: Catalog $5 (specify year and model) ◆ Falcon parts, 1960 to 1970. 800-561-4622.

**Dennis Carpenter Reproductions,** P.O. Box 26398, Charlotte, NC 28221: Catalog $3 (specify year) ◆ Rubber parts for 1960 to 1970 Falcons. 219-335-2425.

**Bob Cook Classic Auto Parts,** 2055 Van Cleave Rd., P.O. Box 600, Murray, KY 42071: Catalog $6 ◆ Reproduction parts for 1960 to 1972 Falcons. 800-486-1137; 502-753-4000 (in KY).

**Dearborn Classics,** P.O. Box 1248, Sunset Beach, CA 90742: Catalog $4 ◆ Falcon parts. 562-372-3175.

**Jim Dottling's Vintage,** 728 E. Dunlap, Phoenix, AZ 85020: Catalog $3 ◆ Parts for the Falcon, Comet, and Fairlane. 800-TTT-BIRD.

**Fabulous Falcons,** 18 W. Peoria, Paola, KS 66071: Free information ◆ Reproduction, new, and used parts for the Falcon, Ranchero, Sprint, Ranchero, and other Ford cars. 800-850-2699.

**Ford Parts Specialists,** 98-11 211th St., Queens Village, NY 11429: Catalog $2 (specify year) ◆ Falcon parts, 1949 to 1969. 212-468-8585.

**Highway Classics,** 949 N. Cataract Ave., San Dimas, CA 91773: Catalog $3 ◆ Falcon parts and accessories, from 1960 to 1970. 909-592-8819.

**Joblot Automotive,** 98-11 211th St., Queens Village, NY 11429: Catalog $2 ◆ Parts for 1949 to 1969 Falcons. 800-221-0172; 718-468-8585 (in NY).

**Dale King Obsolete Parts Inc.,** P.O. Box 1099, Liberty, KY 42539: Free information ◆ NOS and reproduction Falcon parts. 606-787-5031.

**Melvin's Classic Ford Parts Inc.,** 2526 Panola, Lithonia, GA 30058: Free information ◆ Parts for 1960 to mid-1970 Falcons. 770-981-2357.

**Midland Automotive Products,** Rt. 1, Box 27, Midland City, AL 36350: Free information ◆ Reproduction and new Falcon parts and accessories. 334-983-1212.

**Northwest Classic Falcons,** 1964 NW Pettygrove, Portland, OR 97209: Parts list $2 ◆ Hard-to-find new, used, and reproduction 1960 to 1970 Falcon parts. 503-241-9454.

**Obsolete Ford Parts Company,** 311 E. Washington Ave., Nashville, GA 31639: Catalog $4 (specify year) ◆ NOS and reproduction parts for 1960 to 1970 Falcons. 912-686-2470.

**Obsolete Ford Parts Inc. (Oklahoma City),** 8701 South I-35, Oklahoma City, OK 73149: Catalog $3 (specify year) ◆ Parts for 1960 to 1972 Falcons. 405-631-3933.

**Thunderbird & Falcon Connections,** 728 E. Dunlap, Phoenix, AZ 85020: Free information ◆ Used Thunderbird, Falcon, Fairlane, and Comet parts. 800-888-BIRD; 602-997-9285 (in AZ).

## FERRARI

**Alfa Ricambi,** 6644 San Fernando Rd., Glendale, CA 91201: Free information ◆ Parts for the Ferrari. 818-956-7933.

**Algar Enterprises Inc.,** 1234 Lancaster Ave., P.O. Box 167, Rosemont, PA 19010: Free information ◆ Ferrari parts. 800-441-9824; 215-527-1100 (in PA).

**AW Imports,** P.O. Box 5300, Somerset, NJ 08875: Free information ◆ Maserati and Ferrari parts. 908-249-2177.

**Collectors Choice,** 6400 Springfield Lodi Rd., Dane, WI 53529: Free information ◆ Parts for the DeTomaso Panterra, Shelby, Ferrari, Jaguar, and Rolls-Royce. 608-849-9878.

**Marc B. Greenwald,** 6644 San Fernando Rd., Glendale, CA 91201: Free information ◆ Parts for Lamborghini, Maserati, Ferrari, Fiat, and other Italian cars. 818-956-7933.

**International Auto Parts Inc.,** Rt. 29 North, P.O. Box 9036, Charlottesville, VA 22906: Free catalog ◆ Ferrari parts. 800-726-0555; 804-973-0555 (in VA). www.international-auto.com

**Italian Car,** P.O. Box 515, West Linn, OR 97068: Free catalog ◆ Parts, tools, and accessories. 503-655-9811. www.rogue.northwest.com/~cndent

**Partsource,** 32 Harden Ave., Camden, ME 04843: Free information ◆ Ferrari parts, from 1949 to 1991. 207-236-9791.

**Peninsula Imports,** 3749 Harlem, Buffalo, NY 14215: Free catalog ◆ Ferrari parts. 800-999-1209.

**Proper Motor Cars Inc.,** 1811 11th Ave. North, St. Petersburg, FL 33713: Free information ◆ Parts for Rolls-Royces, Bentleys, Citroens, and the Ferrari. 813-821-8883.

**Shelton Sports Cars,** 5750 N. Federal Hwy., Fort Lauderdale, FL 33308: Free information ◆ Ferrari parts and accessories. 800-448-6777.

**Special Interest Car Parts,** 1340 Hartford Ave., Johnston, RI 02919: Free catalog ◆ Ferrari parts. 800-556-7496.

## FIAT

**Bayless Inc.,** 1111 Via Bayless, Marietta, GA 30066: Catalog $4 ◆ High-performance replacement parts. 770-928-1446.

**Caribou Imports Inc.,** 23151 Alcade Dr., Laguna Hills, CA 92653: Catalog $5 ◆ Fiat parts. 714-770-3136.

**Celiberti Motors,** P.O. Box 561, Forestville, CA 95436: Free information ◆ Fiat parts.

**Marc B. Greenwald,** 6644 San Fernando Rd., Glendale, CA 91201: Free information ◆ Parts for Lamborghini, Maserati, Ferrari, Fiat, and other Italian cars. 818-956-7933.

**International Auto Parts Inc.,** Rt. 29 North, P.O. Box 9036, Charlottesville, VA 22906: Free catalog ◆ Replacement and restoration parts and performance accessories. 800-726-0555; 804-973-0555 (in VA). www.international-auto.com

**Italian Car,** P.O. Box 515, West Linn, OR 97068: Free catalog ◆ Parts, tools, and accessories. 503-655-9811. www.rogue.northwest.com/~cndent

**Orion Motors Inc.,** 10722 Jones Rd., Houston, TX 77065: Free information ◆ Fiat parts. 800-736-6410; 713-894-1982 (in TX).

**Peninsula Imports,** 3749 Harlem, Buffalo, NY 14215: Free catalog ◆ Fiat parts. 800-999-1209.

**Perfect Plastics Industries Inc.,** 14th St., Bldg. 201, New Kensington, PA 15068: Free information ◆ Body parts for the Fiat. 800-229-3568; 412-339-3568 (in PA).

## FIERO

**Green's Obsolete Parts,** 9 June St., Pepperell, MA 01463: Free parts list ◆ NOS and used 1940 to 1981 Fiero parts. 978-433-9363.

## FIREBIRD

**Ames Performance Engineering,** Bonney Rd., Marlborough, NH 03455: Free catalog ◆ Firebird parts. 800-421-2637.

**Auto Heaven,** 103 W. Allen St., Bloomington, IN 47403: Free information ◆ Parts for 1967 to 1969 Firebirds. 800-777-0297; 812-332-9401 (in IN).

**Camaro-Heaven,** 64 River St., Rochester, NH 03867: Free information ◆ New and used Camaro and Firebird parts. 800-CAMARO-1.

**Camaro Parts Network,** 1090 W. Bagley Rd., Cleveland, OH 44017: Free price list ◆ Firebird parts. 216-234-1188.

**Camaro Specialties,** 112 Elm St., East Aurora, NY 14052: Catalog $1 ◆ New, used, NOS, and reproduction parts for 1967 to 1972 Firebirds. 716-652-7086.

**Chicago Muscle Car Parts,** 912 E. Burnett Rd., Island Lake, IL 60042: Catalog $5 (refundable) ◆ New and used Firebird parts, from 1967 to 1981. 847-526-2200.

**Classic Industries,** 17832 Gothard St., Huntington Beach, CA 92647: Catalog $5 ◆ Firebird and Trans-AM parts and accessories. 800-854-1280.

**Competition Automotive Inc.,** 2095 West Shore Dr., Warwick, RI 02886: Free information ◆ Restoration supplies. 401-739-6262.

**D & R Classic Automotive,** 30 W. 255 Calumet Ave., Warrenville, IL 60555: Free price list ◆ Firebird parts. 630-393-0009.

**FireAro Restoration Parts Company,** 935 Hedge Dr., Mississauga, Ontario, Canada L4Y 1E9: Free information ◆ Camaro and Firebird parts and accessories, from 1967 to 1972. 905-277-3230.

**Green's Obsolete Parts,** 9 June St., Pepperell, MA 01463: Free parts list ◆ NOS and used 1940 to 1981 Firebird parts. 978-433-9363.

**The Paddock Inc.,** 221 W. Main, Knightstown, IN 46148: Catalog $1 ◆ Firebird parts. 800-428-4319.

**Paddock West Inc.,** 1663 Plum Ln., P.O. Box 8547, Redlands, CA 92375: Free information ◆ Parts and accessories for 1967 to 1995 Firebirds. 800-854-8532.

**Triangle Automotive,** P.O. Box 2293, Arcadia, CA 91077: Free information ◆ Restoration parts and accessories. 626-357-2377.

**Year One Inc.,** P.O. Box 129, Tucker, GA 30085: Catalog $5 ◆ New, used, and reproduction Firebird restoration parts. 800-932-7663; 770-493-6568 (in GA).

## FORD

**Ace Antique Automotive,** P.O. Box 81021, San Diego, CA 92138: Free information ◆ Ford parts, 1928 to 1973. 619-702-9084.

**Auto Krafters Inc.,** P.O. Box 8, Broadway, VA 22815: Catalog $3 (specify year) ◆ New, used, and reproduction Ford parts, from 1960 to 1970. 540-896-5910. www.autokrafters.com

**B & W Antique Auto Parts,** 4653 Guide Meridian Rd., Bellingham, WA 98226: Catalog $5 (specify year and model) ◆ Antique Ford parts, 1928 to 1953. 800-561-4622.

**C & G Early Ford Parts,** 1941 Commercial St., Escondido, CA 92029: Catalog $6 ◆ Reproduction parts for 1932 to 1956 Ford cars and trucks. 619-740-2400.

**Dennis Carpenter Reproductions,** P.O. Box 26398, Charlotte, NC 28221: Catalog $3 (specify year) ◆ Rubber parts for 1932 to 1964 Fords. 219-335-2425.

**Concours Parts & Accessories,** 3563 Numancia St., P.O. Box 1210, Santa Ynez, CA 93460: Catalog $4 ◆ Ford parts, from 1949 to 1966. 805-688-7795.

**Continental Enterprises,** 1673 Cary Rd., Kelowna, British Columbia, Canada V1X 2C1: Information $2 ◆ Ford dress-up accessory kits, from 1949 to 1993. 604-763-7727.

**Bob Cook Classic Auto Parts,** 2055 Van Cleave Rd., P.O. Box 600, Murray, KY 42071: Catalog $6 ◆ Carpet, sheet metal, and new, obsolete, and reproduction parts for 1960 to 1972 Fords. 800-486-1137; 502-753-4000 (in KY).

**Tony Copeland Auto Parts,** 1617 21st St., Lewiston, ID 83501: Free information ◆ New and used Ford, Mercury, and Lincoln parts. 800-821-8174.

**Mike Dennis, Nebraska Mail Order,** 1845 S. 48th St., Lincoln, NE 68506: Free information with long SASE ◆ Mercury parts, from 1939 to 1965. Also used and NOS Ford parts, from 1926 to 1970. 402-489-3036.

**Doug's Auto Parts,** Hwy. 59 North, Box 811, Marshall, MN 56258: Free information ◆ Ford parts, from 1932 to 1948. 507-537-1487.

**Bob Drake Reproductions Inc.,** 1819 NW Washington Blvd., Grants Pass, OR 97526: Catalog $5 (specify model) ◆ Reproduction Ford car and pickup parts. 800-221-3673.

**Early Ford Parts,** 2948 Summer Ave., Memphis, TN 38112: Catalog $4 (specify year and model) ◆ New parts for 1928 to 1969 Ford cars and 1928 to 1972 Ford pickup trucks. 901-323-2179.

**Ford Parts Store,** P.O. Box 226, Bryan, OH 43506: Catalog $2 ◆ Ford parts. 419-636-2475.

**Ford USA Parts Supply,** 9020 A Euclid Ave., Manassas, VA 20110: Free catalog ◆ Parts for full-size Fords, from 1949 to 1972. 703-257-4382.

**Lou Fusz Toyota,** 10725 Manchester, St. Louis, MO 63122: Catalog $4 ◆ Ford parts and accessories. 800-325-9581. loufusz@stlnet.com

**Garton's Auto,** 401 N. 5th St., Millville, NJ 08332: Free information with long SASE (specify car) ◆ Fenders, grilles, trim, ornaments, mechanical, chassis, and other 1932 to 1975 Ford parts. 609-825-3618.

**Joblot Automotive,** 98-11 211th St., Queens Village, NY 11429: Catalog $2 ◆ Parts for cars and trucks, from 1949 to 1969. 800-221-0172; 718-468-8585 (in NY).

**Kanter Auto Parts,** 76 Monroe St., Boonton, NJ 07005: Free catalog ◆ Parts for Fords, from 1932 to 1953. 973-334-9575. www.kanter.com

**Kenroy Ford Parts,** 2 Folwell Ln., Mullica Hill, NJ 08062: Free information ◆ NOS parts for Ford, Mercury, Lincoln, Thunderbird, and Mustang cars. Also for Ford trucks. 609-478-2527.

**Dale King Obsolete Parts Inc.,** P.O. Box 1099, Liberty, KY 42539: Free information ◆ NOS and reproduction Ford parts. 606-787-5031.

**Lakeview Vintage Ford Parts,** P.O. Box 95, Skaneateles, NY 13152: Free information ◆ Reproduction parts for 1928 to 1948 Ford cars. 315-685-7414.

**Mac's Antique Auto Parts,** P.O. Box 238, Lockport, NY 14095: Free catalog ◆ Parts for 1928 to 1931 Model A; 1909 to 1927 Model T; and early Ford V-8s, from 1932 to 1948. 800-777-0948; 716-433-1500 (in NY).

**W.L. Walley Mansfield,** Box 237, 526 E. 2nd, Blue Springs, NE 68318: Free information ◆ Chevrolet parts, from 1925 to 1948; Dodge parts, from 1920 to 1926; and Ford parts, from 1914 to 1948. Also NOS and used parts for Model T and A Fords. 402-645-3546.

**Medicine Bow Motors Inc.,** 343 One Horse Creek Rd., Florence, MT 59833: Free information ◆ Parts for 1928 to 1948 Fords. 406-273-0002.

**Midland Automotive Products,** Rt. 1, Box 27, Midland City, AL 36350: Free information ◆ Reproduction and new Ford parts and accessories. 334-983-1212.

**Miller Obsolete Parts,** 1329 Campus Dr., Vestal, NY 13850: Free information ◆ NOS parts from 1950 to the 1980s, for Ford, Lincoln, and Mercury cars. 607-722-5371.

**Mustangs Unlimited,** 185 Adams St., Manchester, CT 06040: Catalog $3 (specify year) ◆ Ford performance parts, from 1965 to 1973. 800-243-7278.

**Myers Model A Ford & Mustang Parts,** 17103 Sterling Rd., Williamsport, MD 21795: Free information with long SASE ◆ Model A and T parts. Also for Fords up to 1948 and Mustang cars. 301-582-2478.

**North Yale Auto Parts,** Rt. 1, Box 707, Sperry, OK 74073: Free information ◆ Parts for 1977 and later Fords. 800-256-6927; 918-288-7218 (in OK).

**NOS Only,** 414 Umbarger Rd., Unit E, San Jose, CA 95111: Free information ◆ Obsolete and new, 1955 to current year, Ford, Lincoln, and Mercury parts. 408-227-2353.

**Obsolete Ford Parts Company,** 311 E. Washington Ave., Nashville, GA 31639: Catalog $4 (specify year) ◆ Ford NOS and reproduction parts from 1949 to 1959 and 1960 to 1964. 912-686-2470.

**Obsolete Ford Parts Inc. (Oklahoma City),** 8701 South I-35, Oklahoma City, OK 73149: Catalog $3 (specify year) ◆ Ford parts, from 1928 to 1932. 405-631-3933.

**Papke Enterprises,** 16178 Shasta St., Fountain Valley, CA 92708: Catalog $4 ◆ Parts for 1949 to 1951 Fords. Some 1952 to 1953 parts available. 714-839-3050.

**PRO Antique Auto Parts,** 50 King Spring Rd., Windsor Locks, CT 06096: Catalog $3 ◆ New parts for 1928 to 1964 Fords. 860-623-0070.

**Rancho Cordova Specialized Recyclers,** 3688 Omec Circle, Rancho Cordova, CA 95742: Free information ◆ Used, new, rebuilt, and aftermarket parts. 800-999-9499; 916-638-3311 (in CA).

**Dick Spadaro Early Ford Reproductions,** P.O. Box 617, 6599 Rt. 158, Sharps Rd., Altamont, NY 12009: Catalog $4 ◆ Ford parts, from 1932 to 1948. 518-861-5367.

**T-Bird Nest,** 2550 E. Southlake Rd., Southlake, TX 76092: Free information ◆ New parts for 1928 to 1959 Fords. 817-481-1776.

**Tee-Bird Products Inc.,** P.O. Box 728, Exton, PA 19341: Catalog $3 ◆ Ford car parts, from 1955 to 1956. 610-363-1725.

**Winnicks Auto Sales & Parts,** P.O. Box 476, Shamokin, PA 17872: Free information with long SASE ◆ Ford and Chevrolet engines and parts for American and imported cars and trucks. 717-648-6857.

**Worldwide Auto Parts,** Rt. 38, Maple Shade, NJ 08052: Free information ◆ Factory parts. 800-500-PART; 800-887-9999 (in NJ). www.wwparts.com

## FRAZER

**Wayne's Auto Salvage,** RR 3, Box 41, Winner, SD 57580: Free information ◆ Frazer parts. 605-842-2054.

## GALAXIE

**B & W Antique Auto Parts,** 4653 Guide Meridian Rd., Bellingham, WA 98226: Catalog $5 (specify year and model) ◆ Galaxie parts, 1960 to 1964. 800-561-4622.

**Dennis Carpenter Reproductions,** P.O. Box 26398, Charlotte, NC 28221: Catalog $3 (specify year) ◆ Rubber parts for 1960 to 1964 Galaxies. 219-335-2425.

**Bob Cook Classic Auto Parts,** 2055 Van Cleave Rd., P.O. Box 600, Murray, KY 42071: Catalog $6 ◆ Reproduction parts for 1960 to 1972 Galaxies. 800-486-1137; 502-753-4000 (in KY).

**Greg Donahue,** 12900 S. Betty Point, Floral City, FL 34436: Catalog $5 ◆ Reproduction and NOS 1963 to 1964 Galaxie parts. 904-344-4329.

**Joblot Automotive,** 98-11 211th St., Queens Village, NY 11429: Catalog $2 ◆ Parts for 1949 to 1969 Galaxies. 800-221-0172; 718-468-8585 (in NY).

## GMC

**Rancho Cordova Specialized Recyclers,** 3688 Omec Circle, Rancho Cordova, CA 95742: Free information ◆ Used, new, rebuilt, and aftermarket parts. 800-999-9499; 916-638-3311 (in CA).

**Worldwide Auto Parts,** Rt. 38, Maple Shade, NJ 08052: Free information ◆ Factory parts. 800-500-PART; 800-887-9999 (in NJ). www.wwparts.com

## GTO

**Ames Performance Engineering,** Bonney Rd., Marlborough, NH 03455: Free catalog ◆ GTO parts. 800-421-2637.

**Chicago Muscle Car Parts,** 912 E. Burnett Rd., Island Lake, IL 60042: Catalog $5 (refundable) ◆ New and used GTO parts, from 1964 to 1972. 847-526-2200.

**Obsolete Ford Parts Inc. (Oklahoma City),** 8701 South I-35, Oklahoma City, OK 73149: Catalog $3 (specify year) ◆ Ford parts, from 1928 to 1932. 405-631-3933.

**Original Parts Group Inc.,** 17892 Gothard St., Huntington Beach, CA 92647: Catalog $4 ◆ Chevelle parts. 800-243-8355.

**The Paddock Inc.,** 221 W. Main, Knightstown IN 46148: Catalog $1 ◆ GTO parts. 800-428-4319.

**Triangle Automotive,** P.O. Box 2293, Arcadia, CA 91077: Free information ◆ Restoration parts and accessories. 626-357-2377.

**Year One Inc.,** P.O. Box 129, Tucker, GA 30085: Catalog $5 ◆ New, used, and reproduction GTO restoration parts. 800-932-7663; 770-493-6568 (in GA).

## HONDA

**Alpharetta Auto Parts Inc.,** 5770 Hwy. 9 North, Alpharetta, GA 30201: Free information ◆ Used Honda parts. 800-494-PART; 770-475-1929 (in GA). www.alphauto.com

**Dobi Honda Catalog,** 320 Thor Pl., Brea, CA 92621: Catalog $2 ◆ Honda parts. 714-529-1977.

**King Motorsports,** 105 E. Main St., Sullivan, WI 53178: Catalog $5 ◆ Honda parts and accessories. 414-593-2800.

**Steve Millen Sports Cars,** 3176 Airway, Costa Mesa, CA 92626: Free catalog ◆ Performance parts for the Nissan, Honda, and Toyota. 714-540-9154.

**Rancho Cordova Specialized Recyclers,** 3688 Omec Circle, Rancho Cordova, CA 95742: Free information ◆ Used, new, rebuilt, and aftermarket parts. 800-999-9499; 916-638-3311 (in CA).

**Worldwide Auto Parts,** Rt. 38, Maple Shade, NJ 08052: Free information ◆ Factory parts. 800-500-PART; 800-887-9999 (in NJ). www.wwparts.com

## HUDSON

**Wm. Albright's Vintage Coach,** 16593 Arrow Blvd., Fontana, CA 92335: Free information with long SASE (specify parts wanted) ◆ NOS and reproduction parts. 909-823-9168.

**K-Gap Automotive Parts,** P.O. Box 3065, Santa Fe Springs, CA 90670: Catalog $2 (refundable) ◆ Reproduction Hudson and Essex parts.

**Garth B. Peterson,** 122 N. Conklin Rd., Veradale, WA 99037: Free information ◆ NOS and used 1930 to 1970 parts for AMC, Hudson, and Nash cars. 509-926-4620.

**Wayne's Auto Salvage,** RR 3, Box 41, Winner, SD 57580: Free information ◆ Hudson parts. 605-842-2054.

## HYUNDAI

**Peninsula Imports,** 3749 Harlem, Buffalo, NY 14215: Free catalog ◆ Hyundai parts. 800-999-1209.

## IMPALA

**Camaro Parts Network,** 1090 W. Bagley Rd., Cleveland, OH 44017: Free price list ◆ Impala parts, from 1962 to 1974. 216-234-1188.

**Hubbard's Impala,** 3116 Tucker St. Ext., Burlington, NC 27215: Catalog $3 ◆ Impala parts. 336-227-1589.

**Impala Bob's,** 9006 E. Fannin, Mesa, AZ 85207: Catalog $6 ◆ Restoration parts for 1958 to 1975 Impalas. 800-464-2527.

**JR's Chevy Parts,** 478 Moe Rd., Clifton Park, NY 12065: Catalog $3 (specify car) ◆ Parts for 1965 to 1979 Chevrolets, Bel Airs, Biscaynes, Caprices, and Impalas. 518-383-5512.

**LES Auto Parts,** P.O. Box 81, Dayton, NJ 08810: Free information ◆ NOS parts, from 1950 to 1985, for Impalas, Chevelles, Novas, Camaros, Pontiacs, Buicks, and Oldsmobiles. 414-526-3411.

**Old Car Parts,** 109 N. 15th St., Box 184, Clear Lake, IA 50428: Catalog $3.75 (specify year) ◆ NOS, new, and reproduction Impala parts, from 1965 to 1970. 515-357-5510.

**Paddock West Inc.,** 1663 Plum Ln., P.O. Box 8547, Redlands, CA 92375: Free information ◆ Parts and accessories for 1958 to 1976 Impalas. 800-854-8532.

**Sinclair's Impala Parts,** 3324 Westover Dr., Danville, VA 24541: Catalog $2 ◆ Impala parts and accessories. 804-685-2337.

**Tom's Obsolete Chevy Parts,** 14 Delta Dr., Pawtucket, RI 02860: Catalog $2 ◆ Impala parts, from 1955 to 1972. 401-723-7580.

## INFINITY

**Rancho Cordova Specialized Recyclers,** 3688 Omec Circle, Rancho Cordova, CA 95742: Free information ◆ Used, new, rebuilt, and aftermarket parts. 800-999-9499; 916-638-3311 (in CA).

## JAGUAR

**G.W. Bartlett Company,** 1912 Granville Ave., Muncie, IN 47303: Free catalog ◆ Interior restoration parts. 800-338-8034.

**Bassett's Jaguar Inc.,** P.O. Box 245, Wyoming, RI 02898: Free catalog ◆ Jaguar parts. 401-539-3010.

**Bluff City British Cars,** 1810 Getwell, Memphis, TN 38111: Free information ◆ Parts for Jaguars. 800-621-0227; 901-743-4422 (in TN).

**BMC Classics,** 828 N. Dixie Hwy., New Smyrna Beach, FL 32168: Free information ◆ Parts for the Austin-Healey, Jaguar, Mercedes-Benz, Porsche, and Triumph, from the 1950s to 1970s. 904-426-6405.

**British Auto Parts Inc.,** 93256 Holland, Marcola, OR 97454: Free information ◆ New, used, and rebuilt MG, Triumph, and Jaguar parts. 541-933-2880.

**British Auto/USA,** 92 Londonberry Tnpk., Manchester, NH 03104: Catalog $4 ◆ Restoration parts and accessories. 603-622-1050.

**British Parts International,** 8101 Hempstead, Houston, TX 77008: Free information ◆ Jaguar parts. 800-231-6563.

**British Parts Northwest,** 4105 SE Lafayette Hwy., Dayton, OR 97114: Catalog $2.50 ◆ Jaguar parts. 503-864-2001.

**British Vintages Inc.,** 1115 Toro St., San Luis Obispo, CA 93401: Catalog $3 ◆ New, used, and reproduction Jaguar parts, 1948 and later. 800-350-JAGS.

**Collectors Choice,** 6400 Springfield Lodi Rd., Dane, WI 53529: Free information ◆ Parts for the DeTomaso Panterra, Shelby, Ferrari, Jaguar, and Rolls-Royce. 608-849-9878.

**Concours Cars of Colorado Ltd.,** 2414 W. Cucharras St., Colorado Springs, CO 80904: Free information ◆ Accessories and parts for the Alfa-Romeo, BMW, Jaguar, and Volvo. 719-473-6288.

**Coventry West,** 5936-A Peachtree Rd., Atlanta, GA 30341: Free information ◆ Remanufactured Jaguar parts. 800-331-2193; 770-451-3839 (in GA).

**Engel Imports,** 5850 Stadium Dr., Kalamazoo, MI 49009: Free information ◆ Jaguar, MG, Triumph, Rover, and Austin-Healey parts, from the 1950s to the current year. 800-253-4080.

**English Car Spares Ltd.,** 345 Branch Rd SW, Alpharetta, GA 30201: Free information ◆ Jaguar parts. 800-241-1916; 770-475-2662 (in GA).

**Exotic Car Parts,** 923 N. Central Ave., Upland, CA 91786: Free information ◆ Parts for Jaguar XK120 and MKVII to XJ6 and XJS. 800-231-3588.

**Jaguar & SAAB of Troy,** 1815 Maplelawn, Troy, MI 48084: Free catalog ◆ Parts for the Jaguar. 800-832-5839; 810-643-7894 (in MI).

**Jaguar Heaven,** 1433 Tillie Lewis Dr., Stockton, CA 95206: Free information ◆ Used Jaguar parts. 209-942-4524.

**Jaguar Motor Works,** 3701 Longview Dr., Atlanta, GA 30341: Free information ◆ New, used, and rebuilt parts for XJ6 and XJS Jaguars. 800-331-2193; 770-451-4921 (in GA).

**Midtown Auto,** 212 Burnet Ave., Syracuse, NY 13203: Free information ◆ New, used, and rebuilt sheet metal, transmission, engine, brake, and electrical parts for the Austin, MG, Triumph, and Jaguar. 315-476-9421.

**Moore Jaguar,** 14116 Manchester, St. Louis, MO 63011: Free information ◆ Jaguar parts. 800-JAG-PART; 314-394-0900 (in MO).

**Moss Motors Ltd.,** 440 Rutherford St., Goleta, CA 93117: Free catalog (specify model) ◆ Hard-to-find parts for Jaguars. 800-MOSS-USA; 805-681-3400 (in CA). www.mossmotors.com

**Motorcars Ltd.,** 8101 Hempstead, Houston, TX 77008: Free information ◆ Used and new Jaguar, MG, Range Rover, BMW, Triumph, and Rolls-Royce parts. 800-338-5238.

**Peninsula Imports,** 3749 Harlem, Buffalo, NY 14215: Free catalog ◆ Jaguar parts. 800-999-1209.

**Special Interest Car Parts,** 1340 Hartford Ave., Johnston, RI 02919: Free catalog ◆ Parts for 1948 to 1988 Jaguars. 800-556-7496.

**Sports & Classics,** 512 Boston Post Rd., Darien, CT 06820: Catalog $5 ◆ Parts and accessories for the XK 120, 140, 150, and XKE Jaguar. 203-655-8731.

**Terry's Jaguar Parts,** 117 E. Smith St., Benton, IL 62812: Free catalog ◆ High-performance Jaguar parts. 800-851-9438. www.terrysjag.com

**Bill Tracy,** 4050 Red Rock Ln., Sarasota, FL 34231: Free information ◆ XK120, XK140, and XK150 Jaguar parts. 941-924-9523.

**Vicarage Jaguars,** 3952 Douglas Rd., Miami, FL 33133: Free information (specify parts wanted) ◆ Restoration parts and upgrades for postwar Jaguars. 305-444-8759.

**Victory Autoservices,** Box 5060, RR 1, West Baldwin, ME 04091: Free information ◆ Post-1946 parts for the Austin-Healey, Jaguar, MG, and Triumph. 207-625-4581.

**Welsh Jaguar Enterprises Inc.,** P.O. Box 4130, Steubenville, OH 43952: Free catalog ◆ New and used parts for XX-120 to XJ40 Jaguars. 800-875-5247; 614-282-8649 (in OH). www.classicar.com/vendors/welshjag/welshjag/htm

**Ed West CARS,** 1941 Jan Marie Pl., Tustin, CA 92680: Parts list $2 (specify year and car) ◆ New, used, and reproduction XK120, 140, 150 and Mark I, II, VII, VIII, and IX Jaguar parts. 714-832-2688.

**XK's Unlimited,** 850 Fiero Ln., San Luis Obispo, CA 93401: Catalog $6 ◆ Parts for Jaguars, from 1948 to 1994. 800-445-JAGS.

### JAVELIN

**American Parts Depot,** 409 N. Main St., West Manchester, OH 45382: Catalog $5 ◆ New, used, reproduction, and NOS parts. 937-678-7249.

**American Performance Products,** 681 S. Industry Rd., Cocoa, FL 32926: Catalog $6 ◆ Javelin parts. 407-632-8299.

**Kennedy American Inc.,** 7100 State Rt. 142 SE, West Jefferson, OH 32162: Free information ◆ New, used, and reproduction parts for AMC, AMX, Javelin, Jeep, and Rambler cars, from 1950 and later. 614-879-7283.

**Webb's Classic Auto Parts,** 5084 W. State Rd. 114, Huntington, IN 46750: Free information with long SASE ◆ AMX and Javelin parts. 219-344-1714.

### JEEP

**American Performance Products,** 681 S. Industry Rd., Cocoa, FL 32926: Catalog $6 ◆ Jeep parts. 407-632-8299.

**Army Jeep Parts,** P.O. Box 1006, Canal Bristol, PA 19007: Free information ◆ Military Jeep parts. 215-788-6012.

**Paul Barry,** 6152 Cazadero Hwy., P.O. Box 364, Cazadero, CA 95421: Free information ◆ Parts for Willys Overland Jeeps and trucks. 707-632-5590.

**Daryl Bensinger,** 2442 Main St., Narvon, PA 17555: Free information ◆ Parts for military Jeeps and trucks. 610-286-9545.

**Four Wheel Drive Hardware Inc.,** P.O. Box 57, 44488 State Rt. 14, Columbiana, OH 44408: Catalog $3.50 ◆ Parts and accessories for Jeeps. 800-333-5535. www.4wd.com

**J.A.T. Design Inc.,** 11232-3 St. Johns Industrial Pkwy., Jacksonville, FL 32246: Free catalog ◆ Jeep Cherokee and Grand Cherokee accessories. 904-642-0044.

**JD's Off-Road & Performance,** 740 N. Bedford Rd., Bedford Hills, NY 10507: Free information ◆ Jeep accessories. 800-884-JEEP; 914-666-5337 (in NY).

**Kennedy American Inc.,** 7100 State Rt. 142 SE, West Jefferson, OH 43162: Free information ◆ New, used, and reproduction parts for AMC, AMX, Javelin, Jeep, and Rambler cars, from 1950 and later. 614-879-7283.

**Obsolete Jeep & Willys Parts,** 6110 17th St. East, Bradenton, FL 34203: Free information ◆ New, used, rebuilt, and NOS parts. 941-756-7844.

**Quadratec,** 5125 West Chester Pike, Edgemont, PA 19028: Catalog $3 ◆ Mechanical and performance parts for Jeep Wranglers. 800-745-5337.

**Leon Rosser Jeep/Eagle,** P.O. Box 1185, Bessemer, AL 35021: Free information ◆ Jeep parts. 800-633-4724.

**Sports & Classics,** 512 Boston Post Rd., Darien, CT 06820: Catalog $5 ◆ Restoration, engine, electrical, and body parts. 203-655-8731.

**Willy's Jeep Parts,** P.O. Box 4189, Yuma, AZ 85366: Free information ◆ Jeep parts, owner manuals, parts lists, and shop manuals. 800-4-WILLYS.

### JENSEN

**Dave Bean Engineering Inc.,** 636 E. Saint Charles St., San Andreas, CA 95249: Catalog $6 ◆ Jensen parts. 209-754-5802.

**Delta Motorsports Inc.,** 2724 E. Bell Rd., Phoenix, AZ 85032: Free catalog ◆ Jensen factory parts. 602-265-8026.

### KAISER-FRAZER

**Fannaly's Auto Exchange,** P.O. Box 23, Ponchatoula, LA 70454: Free information ◆ A limited selection of Kaiser-Frazer parts. 504-386-3714.

**K-F-D Services Inc.,** HC 65, Box 49, Altonah, UT 84002: Free information ◆ Kaiser-Frazer restoration parts. 801-454-3098.

**Wayne's Auto Salvage,** RR 3, Box 41, Winner, SD 57580: Free information ◆ Kaiser parts. 605-842-2054.

**Zeug's K-F Parts,** 1435 Moreno Dr., Simi Valley, CA 93063: Parts list $2 ◆ NOS and used Kaiser-Frazer, Henry J, and Kaiser-Darrin parts. 805-718-7722.

### KARMANN GHIA

**Karmann Ghia Parts & Restoration,** 355 Harriet St., Ventura, CA 93001: Free catalog ◆ Replacement parts and restoration accessories. 805-652-1974. www.karmannghia.com

### LAMBORGHINI

**Marc B. Greenwald,** 6644 San Fernando Rd., Glendale, CA 91201: Free information ◆ Parts for Lamborghini, Maserati, Ferrari, Fiat, and other Italian cars. 818-956-7933.

**Italian Car,** P.O. Box 515, West Linn, OR 97068: Free catalog ◆ Parts, tools, and accessories. 503-655-9811. www.rogue.northwest.com/~cndent

**Peninsula Imports,** 3749 Harlem, Buffalo, NY 14215: Free catalog ◆ Lamborghini parts. 800-999-1209.

**Prestige Imports,** 14800 Biscayne Blvd., North Miami Beach, FL 33181: Free information ◆ Lamborghini parts. 305-944-1800.

**Sports & Classics,** 512 Boston Post Rd., Darien, CT 06820: Catalog $5 ◆ Parts and accessories for the Lamborghini. 203-655-8731.

### LANCIA

**Alfa Ricambi,** 6644 San Fernando Rd., Glendale, CA 91201: Free information ◆ Parts for the Lancia. 818-956-7933.

**Bayless Inc.,** 1111 Via Bayless, Marietta, GA 30066: Catalog $4 ◆ Replacement parts. 770-928-1446.

**Caribou Imports Inc.,** 23151 Alcade Dr., Laguna Hills, CA 92653: Catalog $5 ◆ Lancia parts. 714-770-3136.

**Celiberti Motors,** P.O. Box 561, Forestville, CA 95436: Free information ◆ Lancia parts.

**International Auto Parts Inc.,** Rt. 29 North, P.O. Box 9036, Charlottesville, VA 22906: Catalog $2 ◆ Replacement, restoration, and performance parts for the Lancia. 800-726-0555; 804-973-0555 (in VA). www.international-auto.com

**Italian Car,** P.O. Box 515, West Linn, OR 97068: Free catalog ◆ Parts, tools, and accessories. 503-655-9811. www.rogue.northwest.com/~cndent

### LASALLE

**Classic Auto Parts,** 550 Industrial Dr., Carmel, IN 46032: Free information ◆ Genuine classic LaSalle parts, from 1928 to 1941. 317-844-8154.

**McVey's,** 5040 Antioch, Merriam, KS 66203: Catalog $4 ◆ LaSalle parts and accessories, from 1936 to 1970. 913-722-0707.

**Sam Quinn Cadillac Parts,** Box 837, Estacada, OR 97023: Free information ◆ Cadillac and LaSalle parts, from 1937 to 1977. 503-637-3852.

### LE MANS

**Ames Performance Engineering,** Bonney Rd., Marlborough, NH 03455: Free catalog ◆ Le Mans parts, 1964 to 1977. 800-421-2637.

**Chicago Muscle Car Parts,** 912 E. Burnett Rd., Island Lake, IL 60042: Catalog $5 (refundable) ◆ New and used Le Mans parts, from 1964 to 1972. 847-526-2200.

**Original Parts Group Inc.,** 17892 Gothard St., Huntington Beach, CA 92647: Catalog $4 ◆ Le Mans parts. 800-243-8355.

**Triangle Automotive,** P.O. Box 2293, Arcadia, CA 91077: Free information ◆ Restoration parts and accessories. 626-357-2377.

**Year One Inc.,** P.O. Box 129, Tucker, GA 30085: Catalog $5 ◆ New, used, and reproduction Firebird restoration parts. 800-932-7663; 770-493-6568 (in GA).

### LEXUS

**Rancho Cordova Specialized Recyclers,** 3688 Omec Circle, Rancho Cordova, CA 95742: Free information ◆ Used, new, rebuilt, and aftermarket parts. 800-999-9499; 916-638-3311 (in CA).

### LINCOLN

**Aabar's Cadillac & Lincoln Salvage,** 9700 NE 23rd, Oklahoma City, OK 73141: Free information with long SASE ◆ Lincoln and Cadillac parts, from 1939 and later. 405-769-3318.

**Auto Parts Exchange,** P.O. Box 736, Reading, PA 19603: Free information ◆ NOS and used parts for 1953 to 1979 Lincolns and 1958 to 1979 Thunderbirds. 610-372-2813.

**Baker's Auto Inc.,** Rt. 44, Putnam, CT 06260: Free information ◆ Lincoln parts, from 1961 to 1979. 860-928-7614.

**California Collectors' Classics,** P.O. Box 2281, Irwindale, CA 91706: Free information ◆ Parts, from 1961 to 1985, for the Cadillac, Lincoln, and Thunderbird. 818-962-6696.

**Classic Cars Unlimited,** P.O. Box 249, Lakeshore, MS 39558: Catalog $3 (specify year) ◆ Lincoln parts, from 1960 to 1976. 800-543-8691; 601-467-9633 (in MS).

**Classique Cars Unlimited,** 5 Turkey Bayou Rd., P.O. Box 249, Lakeshore, MS 39558: Parts list $5 ◆ Lincoln parts, from 1958 to 1988. 601-467-9633.

**Continental Enterprises,** 1673 Cary Rd., Kelowna, British Columbia, Canada V1X 2C1: Information $2 ◆ Lincoln dress-up accessory kits, from 1949 to 1993. 604-763-7727.

**Bob Cook Classic Auto Parts,** 2055 Van Cleave Rd., P.O. Box 600, Murray, KY 42071: Catalog $6 ◆ Reproduction parts for 1960 to 1972 Lincolns. 800-486-1137; 502-753-4000 (in KY).

**Tony Copeland Auto Parts,** 1617 21st St., Lewiston, ID 83501: Free information ◆ New and used Ford, Mercury, and Lincoln parts. 800-821-8174.

**Buzz De Clerck,** 41760 Utica Rd., Sterling Heights, MI 48313: Free information ◆ Lincoln Continental new and used parts, from 1969 to 1971. 810-731-0765.

**Fannaly's Auto Exchange,** P.O. Box 23, Ponchatoula, LA 70454: Free information ◆ Parts for 1946 to 1956 Lincolns. 504-386-3714.

**Hommel Automotive Parts,** 933 Osage Rd., Pittsburgh, PA 15243: Free information ◆ Used, NOS, and reproduction parts for 1941 to 1948 Lincoln Continentals. 412-279-8884.

**The Lincoln Factory,** 3636 Scheuneman Rd., Gemlake, MN 55110: Free information ◆ Lincoln 1936 to 1948 parts. 612-426-8001.

**Lincoln Land Inc.,** 1928 Sherwood St., Clearwater, FL 34625: Free information ◆ Lincoln parts. 813-531-5351; 813-446-2193 (in FL).

**Lincoln Parts International,** 707 E. 4th St., Bldg. G, Perris, CA 92570: Free catalog ◆ Lincoln 1961 to 1980 parts. 909-657-5588.

**Mainly Convertibles,** 13805 Hillsborough Ave., Tampa, FL 33635: Free information ◆ Parts for sedans, coupes, and convertibles, from the 1950s and 1960s. 813-855-6869.

**MARK II Parts,** 5225 Canyon Crest Dr., Riverside, CA 92507: Catalog $2 ◆ MARK II and Lincoln parts, from 1956 to 1957. 909-686-2752.

**Miller Obsolete Parts,** 1329 Campus Dr., Vestal, NY 13850: Free information ◆ NOS parts from 1950 to the 1980s, for Ford, Lincoln, and Mercury cars. 607-722-5371.

**Narragansett Reproductions,** 107 Woodville Rd., P.O. Box 51, Wood River Junction, RI 02894: Catalog $2 (specify car) ◆ Parts for 1936 to 1948 Lincolns, 1956 to 1957 Lincoln Continentals, and the Lincoln Zephyr. 401-364-3839.

**NOS Only,** 414 Umbarger Rd., Unit E, San Jose, CA 95111: Free information ◆ Obsolete and new, 1955 to current year, Ford, Lincoln, and Mercury parts. 408-227-2353.

**Rancho Cordova Specialized Recyclers,** 3688 Omec Circle, Rancho Cordova, CA 95742: Free information ◆ Used, new, rebuilt, and aftermarket parts. 800-999-9499; 916-638-3311 (in CA).

**Jack Rosen,** 5525 Canyon Crest Dr., Riverside, CA 92507: Catalog $2 ◆ New, reproduction, rebuilt, and used Mark II and some post-1965 Lincoln parts. 909-686-2752.

**Worldwide Auto Parts,** Rt. 38, Maple Shade, NJ 08052: Free information ◆ Factory parts. 800-500-PART; 800-887-9999 (in NJ). www.wwparts.com

## LOTUS

**Dave Bean Engineering Inc.,** 636 E. Saint Charles St., San Andreas, CA 95249: Catalog $6 ◆ Lotus parts. 209-754-5802.

**Italian Car,** P.O. Box 515, West Linn, OR 97068: Free catalog ◆ Parts, tools, and accessories. 503-655-9811. www.rogue.northwest.com/~cndent

**Prestige Imports,** 14800 Biscayne Blvd., North Miami Beach, FL 33181: Free information ◆ Lotus parts. 305-944-1800.

**Tingle's Lotus Center,** 1615 Shawsheen St., #8, Tewksbury, MA 01876: Free information ◆ Lotus parts. 978-851-8370.

## MASERATI

**Algar Enterprises Inc.,** 1234 Lancaster Ave., P.O. Box 167, Rosemont, PA 19010: Free information ◆ Maserati parts. 800-441-9824; 215-527-1100 (in PA).

**AW Imports,** P.O. Box 5300, Somerset, NJ 08875: Free information ◆ Maserati and Ferrari parts. 908-249-2177.

**Beach Imports,** 30 Auto Center Dr., Tustin, CA 92782: Free information ◆ Maserati parts. 800-777-4895.

**Caribou Imports Inc.,** 23151 Alcade Dr., Laguna Hills, CA 92653: Catalog $5 ◆ Maserati parts. 714-770-3136.

**Celiberti Motors,** P.O. Box 561, Forestville, CA 95436: Free information ◆ Maserati parts.

**Marc B. Greenwald,** 6644 San Fernando Rd., Glendale, CA 91201: Free information ◆ Parts for Lamborghini, Maserati, Ferrari, Fiat, and other Italian cars. 818-956-7933.

**International Auto Parts Inc.,** Rt. 29 North, P.O. Box 9036, Charlottesville, VA 22906: Catalog $2 ◆ Replacement, restoration, and performance parts for the Maserati. 800-726-0555; 804-973-0555 (in VA). www.international-auto.com

**Italian Car,** P.O. Box 515, West Linn, OR 97068: Free catalog ◆ Parts, tools, and accessories. 503-655-9811. www.rogue.northwest.com/~cndent

**Maserati Automobiles Inc.,** 1501 S. Caton Ave., Baltimore, MD 21227: Free information ◆ Maserati parts. 410-646-6400.

**Peninsula Imports,** 3749 Harlem, Buffalo, NY 14215: Free catalog ◆ Maserati parts. 800-999-1209.

## MAVERICK

**Auto Krafters Inc.,** P.O. Box 8, Broadway, VA 22815: Catalog $3 (specify year) ◆ New, used, and reproduction parts, from 1970 to 1977. 540-896-5910. www.autokrafters.com

**The Maverick Connection,** 137 Valley Dr., Ripley, WV 25271: Free information ◆ Parts for 1970 to 1977 Ford Mavericks and Mercury Comets. 800-889-9322; 304-372-7825 (in WV).

## MAZDA

**Dobi Mazda Catalog,** 320 Thor Pl., Brea, CA 92621: Catalog $2 ◆ Parts for the Mazda Rx7 and GLC. 714-529-1977.

**Racing Beat Inc.,** 1291 Hancock St., Anaheim, CA 92807: Catalog $7 ◆ Performance and appearance accessories for Mazda RX-7 and Miata cars. 714-779-8677. www.racingbeat.com

**Rancho Cordova Specialized Recyclers,** 3688 Omec Circle, Rancho Cordova, CA 95742: Free information ◆ Used, new, rebuilt, and aftermarket parts. 800-999-9499; 916-638-3311 (in CA).

**Russel Toyota,** 6700 Baltimore National Tnpk., Baltimore, MD 21228: Free information ◆ Buick, Mazda, Subaru, and Toyota parts. 800-638-8401.

**Worldwide Auto Parts,** Rt. 38, Maple Shade, NJ 08052: Free information ◆ Factory parts. 800-500-PART; 800-887-9999 (in NJ). www.wwparts.com

## MERCEDES-BENZ

**Aase Brothers Inc.,** 701 E. Cypress St., Anaheim, CA 92805: Free information ◆ Mercedes-Benz parts. 800-444-7444; 714-956-2419 (in CA).

**Atlanta Stuttgart Auto Parts,** 1200 Menlo Dr., Atlanta, GA 30318: Free information ◆ Used Mercedes-Benz parts. 770-351-4811.

**ATVM Automotive Parts,** P.O. Box B, Aberdeen, MD 21001: Free information with long SASE ◆ Mercedes-Benz parts, from 1934 to 1972. 410-575-7115. ATVM@PRODIGY.NET

**Blitzen Enterprises Inc.,** 8341 East Evans Rd., Ste. 104, Scottsdale, AZ 85260: Free information ◆ Mercedes-Benz parts. 888-254-8936.

**BMC Classics,** 828 N. Dixie Hwy., New Smyrna Beach, FL 32168: Free information ◆ Parts for the Austin-Healey, Jaguar, Mercedes-Benz, Porsche, and Triumph, from the 1950s to 1970s. 904-426-6405.

**Caliber Motors Inc.,** 5395 E. La Palma Ave., Anaheim Hills, CA 92807: Free information ◆ Mercedes-Benz parts, shop, and owner manuals. 800-252-6877. www.mercedes-net.com/dealer/caliber

**Embee Parts,** 4000 Lee Rd., Smyrna, GA 30080: Free information ◆ Mercedes-Benz parts, from 1934 to 1988. 770-434-5686.

**Euromeister,** 19507 Yuma St., Castro Valley, CA 94546: Catalog $4.95 ◆ Mercedes-Benz parts and accessories. 800-581-3327.

**European Parts Specialists Ltd.,** P.O. Box 6783, Santa Barbara, CA 93160: Free information ◆ Parts and accessories for the Mercedes-Benz. 805-683-4020.

**Fletcher-Jones Motor Cars,** 1001 Quail St., Newport Beach, CA 92660: Free information ◆ Replacement parts for the Mercedes-Benz. 800-328-3095; 714-832-4421 (in CA).

**IMPCO Inc.,** 5300 Glenmont Dr., Houston, TX 77081: Free catalog ◆ Original 1977 to 1985 Mercedes-Benz parts. 800-243-1220.

**IPCO Inc.,** 250 Buxton Ct., Lilburn, GA 30247: Free information ◆ Original Mercedes-Benz parts. 800-635-8590; 770-381-1114 (in GA).

**K & K Mfg. Inc.,** 951 Nine Mile Rd., Sparta, MI 49345: Free catalog ◆ Parts for the 190SL, 230SL, 280SL, and 450SL. 616-784-4286.

**Metro Motors,** 9377 Autoplex St., Montclair, CA 91763: Free information ◆ Parts and accessories for the Mercedes-Benz. 800-446-5703.

**Miller's Incorporated,** 7412 Count Circle, Huntington Beach, CA 92647: Catalog $5 ◆ Replacement parts for the 1950, 1960, and 1970 Mercedes-Benz. 800-538-4222.

**Mission Viejo Imports,** 28701 Marquerite Pkwy., Mission Viejo, CA 92692: Free information ◆ Parts, accessories, gifts, tools, technical literature, service information, and owner manuals. 800-842-3769.

**Paul's Autohaus Inc.,** 233 N. Pleasant St., P.O. Box 978, Amherst, MA 01004: Free catalog ◆ Parts for classic and vintage Mercedes-Benz cars. 800-406-9736.

**Star Quality,** One Alley Rd., LaGrangeville, NY 12540: Free catalog ◆ Parts for 190SL, 230SL, 250SL, and 280SL Mercedes-Benz. 914-223-5385.

**Stephen's Auto Works,** 433 Meadow Rd., Kings Park, NY 11754: Free information ◆ Mechanical parts for the BMW, Mercedes-Benz, and Porsche. 516-544-1114.

**Thoroughbred Coach Builders,** P.O. Box 171, Mount Dora, FL 32757: Information package $10 ◆ Mercedes-Benz reproduction parts. 352-735-4607.

**Valley Motors,** 3203 Bragg Blvd., Fayetteville, NC 28303: Free information ◆ Mercedes-Benz parts. 800-264-3203.

## MERCURY

**B & W Antique Auto Parts,** 4653 Guide Meridian Rd., Bellingham, WA 98226: Catalog $5 (specify year and model) ◆ Antique Mercury parts, 1928 to 1953. 800-561-4622.

**Continental Enterprises,** 1673 Cary Rd., Kelowna, British Columbia, Canada V1X 2C1: Information $2 ◆ Mercury dress-up accessory kits, from 1949 to 1993. 604-763-7727.

**Bob Cook Classic Auto Parts,** 2055 Van Cleave Rd., P.O. Box 600, Murray, KY 42071: Catalog $6 ◆ Reproduction parts for the 1956 to 1972 Mercury. 800-486-1137; 502-753-4000 (in KY).

**Tony Copeland Auto Parts,** 1617 21st St., Lewiston, ID 83501: Free information ◆ New and used Ford, Mercury, and Lincoln parts. 800-821-8174.

**Mike Dennis, Nebraska Mail Order,** 1845 S. 48th St., Lincoln, NE 68506: Free information with long SASE ◆ Mercury parts, from 1939 to 1965. Also used and NOS Ford parts, from 1926 to 1970. 402-489-3036.

**Early Ford Parts,** 2948 Summer Ave., Memphis, TN 38112: Catalog $4 (specify year and model) ◆ Ford and Mercury parts, 1932 to 1959. 901-323-2179.

**Garton's Auto,** 401 N. 5th St., Millville, NJ 08332: Free information with long SASE (specify car) ◆ Fenders, grilles, trim, ornaments, mechanical, chassis, and other 1932 to 1975 Mercury parts. 609-825-3618.

**Kenroy Ford Parts,** 2 Folwell Ln., Mullica Hill, NJ 08062: Free information ◆ NOS parts for Ford, Mercury, Lincoln, Thunderbird, and Mustang cars. Also for Ford trucks. 609-478-2527.

**Dale King Obsolete Parts Inc.,** P.O. Box 1099, Liberty, KY 42539: Free information ◆ NOS and reproduction Mercury parts. 606-787-5031.

**The Maverick Connection,** 137 Valley Dr., Ripley, WV 25271: Free information ◆ Parts for 1970 to 1977 Ford Mavericks and Mercury Comets. 800-889-9322; 304-372-7825 (in WV).

**Miller Obsolete Parts,** 1329 Campus Dr., Vestal, NY 13850: Free information ◆ NOS parts from 1950 to the 1980s, for Ford, Lincoln, and Mercury cars. 607-722-5371.

**Mustangs Unlimited,** 185 Adams St., Manchester, CT 06040: Catalog $3 (specify year) ◆ Cougar reproduction and original restoration parts, from 1965 to 1973. 800-243-7278.

**NOS Only,** 414 Umbarger Rd., Unit E, San Jose, CA 95111: Free information ◆ Obsolete and new, 1955 to current year, Ford, Lincoln, and Mercury parts. 408-227-2353.

**Obsolete Ford Parts (Oklahoma City),** 8701 South I-35, Oklahoma City, OK 73149: Catalog $3 (specify year) ◆ Parts for 1949 to 1972 Mercury cars. 405-631-3933.

**Papke Enterprises,** 16178 Shasta St., Fountain Valley, CA 92708: Catalog $4 ◆ Parts for 1949 to 1951 Mercury cars. 714-843-6969.

**PRO Antique Auto Parts,** 50 King Spring Rd., Windsor Locks, CT 06096: Catalog $3 ◆ New parts for the 1928 to 1964 Mercury. 860-623-0070.

**Rancho Cordova Specialized Recyclers,** 3688 Omec Circle, Rancho Cordova, CA 95742: Free information ◆ Used, new, rebuilt, and aftermarket parts. 800-999-9499; 916-638-3311 (in CA).

**Worldwide Auto Parts,** Rt. 38, Maple Shade, NJ 08052: Free information ◆ Factory parts. 800-500-PART; 800-887-9999 (in NJ). www.wwparts.com

## METEOR

**Bob Cook Classic Auto Parts,** 2055 Van Cleave Rd., P.O. Box 600, Murray, KY 42071: Catalog $6 ◆ Reproduction parts for the 1956 to 1964 Meteor. 800-486-1137; 502-753-4000 (in KY).

## MG & MGB

**Abingdon Spares Ltd.,** South St., P.O. Box 37, Walpole, NH 03608: Catalog $6 ◆ MG parts. 800-225-0251.

**Aurora Auto Wrecking Inc.,** 9217 Aurora Ave. North, Seattle, WA 98103: Free information ◆ New, used, and rebuilt MG parts. 800-426-6464.

**Brit-Tek Ltd.,** 12 Parmenter Rd., Londonberry, NH 03053: Free catalog ◆ Performance and restoration parts. 800-255-5883.

**British Auto Parts Inc.,** 93256 Holland, Marcola, OR 97454: Free information ◆ New, used, and rebuilt MG, Triumph, and Jaguar parts. 541-933-2880.

**British Miles,** 9278 Old E. Tyburn Rd., Morrisville, PA 19067: Catalog $5 ◆ Reconditioned and new MG parts. 215-736-9300. www.britishmiles.com

**Dobi MGB Catalog,** 320 Thor Pl., Brea, CA 92621: Catalog $2 ◆ Parts for MGB cars. 714-529-1977.

**Engel Imports,** 5850 Stadium Dr., Kalamazoo, MI 49009: Free information ◆ Jaguar, MG, Triumph, Rover, and Austin-Healey parts, from the 1950s to the current year. 800-253-4080.

**English Car Spares Ltd.,** 345 Branch Rd SW, Alpharetta, GA 30201: Free information ◆ MG parts. 800-241-1916; 770-475-2662 (in GA).

**M & G Vintage Auto,** 265 Rt. 17, Box 226, Tuxedo Park, NY 10987: Free information ◆ Parts for the MGA, MGB, and MGT. 914-753-5900.

**Midtown Auto,** 212 Burnet Ave., Syracuse, NY 13203: Free information ◆ New, used, and rebuilt sheet metal, transmission, engine, brake, and electrical parts for the Austin, MG, Triumph, and Jaguar. 315-476-9421.

**Mini Mania,** 31 Winsor St., Milpitas, CA 95035: Free information ◆ Parts for the Morris Minor, MG, Mini Cooper, and Austin-Healey Sprite. 800-946-2642; 408-942-5595 (in CA). www.minimania.com

**Moss Motors Ltd.,** 440 Rutherford St., Goleta, CA 93117, CA 93116: Free catalog (specify model) ◆ MG parts. 800-MOSS-USA; 805-681-3400 (in CA). www.mossmotors.com

**Northwest Import Parts,** 10042 SW Balmer, Portland, OR 97219: Information $1 ◆ Parts for the MGB, MGA, and Midget. 503-245-3806.

**O'Connor Classic Autos,** 2569 Scott Blvd., Santa Clara, CA 95050: Free information ◆ New and used MG parts. 408-727-0430.

**Peninsula Imports,** 3749 Harlem, Buffalo, NY 14215: Free catalog ◆ MG parts. 800-999-1209.

**Scarborough Faire,** 1151 Main St., Pawtucket, RI 02860: Catalog $3 (specify year) ◆ MGB body repair parts and panels. 401-724-4200.

**Seven Enterprises Ltd.,** 716 Bluecrab Rd., Newport News, VA 23606: Free information ◆ MGB parts, from 1962 to 1980. 800-992-7007.

**Special Interest Car Parts,** 1340 Hartford Ave., Johnston, RI 02919: Free catalog ◆ MG parts. 800-556-7496.

**Sports & Classics,** 512 Boston Post Rd., Darien, CT 06820: Catalog $5 ◆ Restoration, engine, electrical, and body parts. 203-655-8731.

**Victoria British Ltd.,** P.O. Box 14991, Lenexa, KS 66215: Free catalog ◆ Original, replacement, and reproduction parts for the MG and other British sports cars. 800-255-0088.

**Victory Autoservices,** Box 5060, RR 1, West Baldwin, ME 04091: Free information ◆ Post-1946 parts for the Austin-Healey, Jaguar, MG, and Triumph. 207-625-4581.

## MIATA

**Racing Beat Inc.,** 1291 Hancock St., Anaheim, CA 92807: Catalog $7 ◆ Bolt-on performance and appearance accessories for Mazda RX-7 and Miata cars. 714-779-8677. www.racingbeat.com

## MINI COOPER

**Mini Mania,** 31 Winsor St., Milpitas, CA 95035: Free information ◆ Parts for the Morris Minor, MG, Mini Cooper, and Austin-Healey Sprite. 800-946-2642; 408-942-5595 (in CA). www.minimania.com

## MITSUBISHI

**Peninsula Imports,** 3749 Harlem, Buffalo, NY 14215: Free catalog ◆ Mitsubishi parts. 800-999-1209.

**Rancho Cordova Specialized Recyclers,** 3688 Omec Circle, Rancho Cordova, CA 95742: Free information ◆ Used, new, rebuilt, and aftermarket parts. 800-999-9499; 916-638-3311 (in CA).

## MODEL A & MODEL T FORDS

**Ace Antique Automotive,** P.O. Box 81021, San Diego, CA 92138: Free information ◆ Ford parts, 1928 to 1973. 619-702-9084.

**Antique Auto Parts et al,** 9103 E. Garvey Ave., Rosemead, CA 91770: Free information with long SASE (enclose want list) ◆ Parts and accessories for 1903 to 1931 cars and trucks. 818-288-2121.

**Antique Auto Parts of Kentucky,** P.O. Box 23070, Lexington, KY 40523: Free information ◆ Model A parts. 606-272-7602.

**Bob's Antique Auto Parts,** P.O. Box 2523, Rockford, IL 61132: Catalog $2 ◆ Ford Model T parts. 815-633-7244.

**Bratton's Antique Ford Parts,** 9410 Watkins Rd., Gaithersburg, MD 20879: Free catalog ◆ Parts for the Model A Ford. 301-253-1929.

**Car-Line Manufacturing & Distributor Inc.,** 1250 Gulf St., P.O. Box 1192, Beaumont, TX 77701: Catalog $2 ◆ Wood, sheet metal, engine, and chassis parts for Ford Model T, A, and V8 cars. 409-833-9757.

**Classic Wood Manufacturing,** 1006 N. Raleigh St., Greensboro, NC 27405: Free information ◆ Kiln-dried ash wood kits. 336-691-1344.

**Chuck & Judy Cubel,** P.O. Box 278, Superior, AZ 83273: Free information (specify year) ◆ Wood replacement parts. 520-689-2734.

**Ford Parts Specialists,** 98-11 211th St., Queens Village, NY 11419: Free catalog (specify year) ◆ Ford Model A and T parts. 718-468-8585.

**Freeman's Garage,** 19 Freeman St., Norton, MA 02766: Free information ◆ Model A parts, from 1928 to 1931. 508-285-6500.

**Funk's Antique Auto Parts,** 330 Industry Dr., P.O. Box 8208, Carlisle, OH 45005: Catalog $3 ◆ Parts for Ford Model A and early V8 cars. 513-746-1113.

**Gaslight Auto Parts Inc.,** P.O. Box 291, Urbana, OH 43078: Catalog $2 ◆ Replacement parts for the Ford Model A and T. 937-652-2145.

**Good Old Days Garage Inc.,** 2340 Farley Pl., Birmingham, AL 35226: Free brochure ◆ Model A and T engines. 205-822-4569.

**Harry's Early Ford Parts,** 6090 Crater Lake Ave., Unit F, Central Point, OR 97502: Free catalog ◆ Model A parts, from 1928 to 1931. 800-833-2580.

**Lang's Old Car Parts,** 202 School St., Winchedon, MA 01475: Catalog $1 ◆ Ford Model T reproduction parts, from 1909 to 1927. 800-872-7871.

**LeBaron Bonney Company,** P.O. Box 8, Amesbury, MA 01913: Catalog $1 ◆ Interiors, seat upholstery, panels and headlining, top kits and assemblies for 1928 to 1931 Fords. 800-221-5408.

**Mac's Antique Auto Parts,** P.O. Box 238, Lockport, NY 14094: Free catalog ◆ Parts for 1928 to 1931 Model A, 1909 to 1927 Model T, and 1932-1948 Ford V-8. 800-777-0948; 716-433-1500 (in NY).

**W.L. Walley Mansfield,** Box 237, 526 E. 2nd, Blue Springs, NE 68318: Free information ◆ Chevrolet parts, from 1925 to 1948; Dodge parts, from 1920 to 1926; and Ford parts, from 1914 to 1948. Also NOS and used parts for Model T and A Fords. 402-645-3546.

**McInnes Antique Auto,** P.O. Box 653, Niagara-on-the-Lake, Ontario, Canada L0S 1J0: Free price list ◆ Ford parts, 1909 to 1931. 905-468-7779.

**Mike's "A" Ford-able Parts,** 1930 Patrick Rd., Dacula, GA 30211: Free catalog ◆ Rebuilt Ford Model A engines and parts. 800-732-6453.

**Myers Model A Ford & Mustang Parts,** 17103 Sterling Rd., Williamsport, MD 21795: Free information with long SASE ◆ Model A and T parts. Also for Fords up to 1948 and Mustang cars. 301-582-2478.

**Obsolete Ford Parts Inc. (Oklahoma City),** 8701 South I-35, Oklahoma City, OK 73149: Catalog $3 (specify year and car) ◆ Model A and T parts. 405-631-3933.

**Rootlieb Inc.,** P.O. Box 1829, Turlock, CA 95381: Free catalog ◆ Sheet metal parts for early vintage Ford cars. 209-632-2203.

**Sacramento Vintage Ford Parts Inc.,** 4675 Aldona Ln., Sacramento, CA 95841: Catalog $5 ◆ Model T parts, from 1909 to 1927 and Model A parts, from 1928 to 1931. 916-489-3444.

**Smith & Jones Antique Parts,** 1 Biloxi Square, West Columbia, SC 29170: Catalog $2 ◆ Reproduction Ford parts, from 1909 to 1931. 803-822-8500.

**Snyder's Antique Auto Parts,** 12925 Woodworth Rd., New Springfield, OH 44443: Catalog $1 ◆ Model T parts, 1909 to 1927 and Model A parts, 1928 to 1931. 216-519-5313.

**Tin Lizzie Antique Auto Parts,** 1549 Ellinwood, Des Plaines, IL 60016: Catalog $3 ◆ Antique Ford parts, from 1928 to 1931. 847-298-7889.

## MONTE CARLO

**Chicago Muscle Car Parts,** 912 E. Burnett Rd., Island Lake, IL 60042: Catalog $5 (refundable) ◆ New and used Firebird parts, from 1964 to 1972. 847-526-2200.

**CPX-Doug Martz,** P.O. Box 223, Butler, WI 53007: Free information ◆ Chevrolet, Camaro, Chevelle, El Camino, Monte Carlo, and Nova parts, from 1955 to 1975. 414-463-2277.

**Harmon's Inc.,** P.O. Box 100, Hwy. 27 North, Geneva, IN 46740: Free catalog ◆ Monte Carlo restoration parts, from 1970 to 1977. 219-368-7221. www.harmons.com

**Original Parts Group Inc.,** 17892 Gothard St., Huntington Beach, CA 92647: Catalog $4 ◆ Monte Carlo parts. 800-243-8355.

**Paddock West Inc.,** 1663 Plum Ln., P.O. Box 8547, Redlands, CA 92375: Free information ◆ Parts and accessories for 1970 to 1977 Monte Carlos. 800-854-8532.

**The Parts Place,** 950 Paramount Pkwy., Batavia, IL 60510: Free information ◆ Monte Carlo parts, from 1963 to 1977. 630-879-1600.

**Year One Inc.,** P.O. Box 129, Tucker, GA 30085: Catalog $5 ◆ New, used, and reproduction Monte Carlo restoration parts. 800-932-7663; 770-493-6568 (in GA).

## MONTEGO

**Bob Cook Classic Auto Parts,** 2055 Van Cleave Rd., P.O. Box 600, Murray, KY 42071: Catalog $6 ◆ Reproduction parts for the 1960 to 1972 Montego. 800-486-1137; 502-753-4000 (in KY).

## MORGAN

**Cantab Motors Ltd.,** Valley Industrial Park, 12 E. Richardson Ln., Purceville, VA 20132: Free information ◆ Parts and accessories. 540-338-2211.

**Isis Imports Ltd.,** P.O. Box 2290, Gateway Station, San Francisco, CA 94126: Free information ◆ Morgan parts. 415-433-1344.

**Olde World Restorations,** 2727 Philmont Ave., Ste. 350, Huntington Valley, PA 19006: Free information ◆ Morgan parts. 215-947-8720.

## MORRIS MINOR

**Mini Mania,** 31 Winsor St., Milpitas, CA 95035: Free information ◆ Parts for the Morris Minor, MG, Mini Cooper, and Austin-Healey Sprite. 800-946-2642; 408-942-5595 (in CA). www.minimania.com

## MUSTANG

**Tom Adams,** 13211 N. 103rd Ave., Sun City, AZ 85351: Free information ◆ NOS parts from mid-1964 to 1967. 602-933-1777.

**Andy's Classic Mustangs,** 18502 E. Sprague, Greenacres, WA 99016: Free information ◆ Mustang parts, 1965 and later. 509-924-9824.

**Auto Krafters Inc.,** P.O. Box 8, Broadway, VA 22815: Catalog $3 (specify year) ◆ New, used, and reproduction parts for 1965 to 1973 Mustangs. 540-896-5910. ww.autokrafters.com

**B & W Antique Auto Parts,** 4653 Guide Meridian Rd., Bellingham, WA 98226: Catalog $5 (specify year and model) ◆ Mustang parts, from 1964 to 1973. 800-561-4622.

**Branda Shelby & Mustang Parts,** 1434 E. Pleasant Valley Blvd., Altoona, PA 16602: Catalog $3 ◆ Mustang parts. 800-458-3477; 814-942-1869 (in PA).

**California Pony Cars,** 1906 Quaker Ridge Pl., Ontario, CA 91761: Free information ◆ High-performance Mustang parts, mid-1964 to 1973. 909-923-2804.

**Canadian Mustang,** 1844 78th Ave., Surrey, British Columbia, Canada V3W 8E7: Catalog $3 ◆ Mustang parts, from 1965 to 1973. 604-594-2425.

**Central Jersey Mustang,** 36 Craig St., Edison, NJ 08817: Free information ◆ New and used Mustang parts, from mid-1964 to 1970. 908-572-3939.

**CJ Pony Parts Inc.,** 7441-B Rd., Allentown Blvd., PA 17112: Free information ◆ Mustang parts, from 1964 to 1973. 800-888-6473; 717-657-9252 (in PA).

**Classic Auto Air Mfg. Company,** 2020 W. Kennedy Blvd., Tampa, FL 33606: Free catalog ◆ Air-conditioning systems and parts for 1965 to 1973 Mustangs. 813-251-4994.

**Classic Mustang,** 24 Robert Porter Rd., Southington, CT 06489: Catalog $3 ◆ Mustang parts, from 1965 to 1973. 800-243-2742.

**Classic Mustang Parts of Oklahoma,** 8801 S. I-35, Oklahoma City, OK 73149: Catalog $5 ◆ Mid-1964 to 1973 Mustang parts. 405-631-1400.

**Bob Cook Classic Auto Parts,** 2055 Van Cleave Rd., P.O. Box 600, Murray, KY 42071: Catalog $6 ◆ Reproduction parts for 1964 to 1973 Mustangs. 800-486-1137; 502-753-4000 (in KY).

**Dallas Mustang Parts,** 10720 Sandhill Rd., Dallas, TX 75238: Free catalog ◆ Mustang parts. 800-527-1223.

**Florida Mustang Inc.,** 1219 Dixie Cutoff Rd., Stuart, FL 34994: Catalog $3 ◆ NOS, reproduction, new, and used mid-1964 to 1997 Mustang parts and accessories. Also literature. 561-288-4068.

**Glazier's Mustang Barn Inc.,** 531 Wambold Rd., Souderton, PA 18964: Free catalog ◆ Mustang and Shelby parts, from mid-1964 to 1973. 800-523-6708.

**Highway Classics,** 949 N. Cataract Ave., San Dimas, CA 91773: Catalog $3 ◆ Mustang parts and accessories, from 1965 to 1973. 909-592-8819.

**Joblot Automotive,** 98-11 211th St., Queens Village, NY 11429: Catalog $2 ◆ Parts for 1949 to 1969 Mustangs. 800-221-0172; 718-468-8585 (in NY).

**John's Mustang,** 5234 Glenmont Dr., Houston, TX 77081: Free catalog ◆ Mustang parts and accessories, from 1965 to 1973. 713-668-5646.

**Dale King Obsolete Parts Inc.,** P.O. Box 1099, Liberty, KY 42539: Free information ◆ NOS and reproduction Mustang parts. 606-787-5031.

**Larry's Thunderbird & Mustang Parts,** 511 S. Raymond Ave., Fullerton, CA 92631: Catalog $2 ◆ New and used parts for 1958 to 1956 Mustangs. 800-854-0393; 714-871-6432 (in CA).

**Midland Automotive Products,** Rt. 1, Box 27, Midland City, AL 36350: Free information ◆ Reproduction and new Mustang parts and accessories. 334-983-1212.

**Mostly Mustang's Inc.,** 55 Alling St., Hamden, CT 06517: Free catalog ◆ New, used, and reproduction Mustang parts. 203-562-8804.

**MPC Classics,** 2100 E. Main St., #4A, Grand Prairie, TX 75050: Free catalog ◆ Mid-1964 to 1973 original, reproduction, and used interiors, exteriors, sheet metal, and parts for Mustangs. 800-888-1672. www.mpcclassics.com

**Mustang Corral,** Box 242, Edwardsville, IL 62065: Free information with long SASE ◆ New and used parts for 1965 to 1973 Mustangs. 800-327-2897.

**Mustang of Chicago,** 1321 W. Irving Park Rd., Bensenville, IL 60106: Catalog $4 ◆ New and used Mustang parts, from 1965 to 1991. 630-860-7077.

**Mustang Parts Corral of Texas,** 2100 E. Main, Ste. 4A, Grand Prairie, TX 75050: Free catalog ◆ Mustang parts. 800-888-1672.

**Mustang Specialties,** 308 Washington Ave., Nutley, NJ 07110: Free information ◆ Reproduction and other parts for mid-1964 to 1973 Mustangs. 201-661-3001.

**Mustangs & More,** 2065 Sperry Ave., Ventura, CA 93003: Free catalog ◆ New and reproduction parts, from mid-1964 to 1973. 800-356-6573.

**Mustangs Unlimited,** 185 Adams St., Manchester, CT 06040: Catalog $3 (specify year} ◆ Performance parts for the Mustang and Shelby, 1965 to 1973 and Mustang parts, 1974 to present. 800-243-7278.

**Myers Model A Ford & Mustang Parts,** 17103 Sterling Rd., Williamsport, MD 21795: Free information with long SASE ◆ Model A and T parts. Also for Fords up to 1948 and Mustang cars. 301-582-2478.

**National Parts Depot,** 3101 SW 40th Blvd., Gainesville, FL 32608: Free catalog ◆ Mustang parts and accessories, from 1965 to 1973. 800-874-7595; 352-378-2473 (in FL).

**The Paddock Inc.,** 221 W. Main, Knightstown, IN 46148: Catalog $1 ◆ Mustang parts. 800-428-4319.

**Greg Purdy's Mustang Supply,** P.O. Box 784, Forest Hill, MD 21050: Free information ◆ Used, new, NOS, and obsolete 1965 to 1973 Mustang parts. 410-836-5991.

**PV Antique & Classic Ford,** 1688 Main St., Tewksbury, MA 01876: Free information ◆ Mid-1964 to 1973 Mustang accessories and parts. 978-851-9159.

**Stillwell's Obsolete Car Parts,** 1617 Wedeking Ave., Evansville, IN 47711: Free information ◆ NOS and reproduction 1965 to 1973 Mustang parts. 812-425-4794.

**Texas Mustang Parts,** 5774 S. University Park Dr., Waco, TX 76706: Free catalog ◆ New and reproduction parts for 1965 to 1973 Mustangs. 254-662-2789.

**Virginia Classic Mustang Inc.,** P.O. Box 487, Broadway, VA 22815: Catalog $3 ◆ Mustang parts, from mid-1964 to 1973. 540-896-2695.

## NASH

**Blaser's Auto,** 3200 48th Ave., Moline, IL 61265: Free information ◆ Nash parts. 309-764-3571.

**Charles Chambers Parts,** Box 60, HC 64, Goldthwaite, TX 76844: Free information with long SASE ◆ Nash parts.

**Lucky Lee Lott,** 800 E. Diana St., Tampa, FL 33604: Free information ◆ Nash parts, from 1902 to 1958. 813-238-5408.

**Garth B. Peterson,** 122 N. Conklin Rd., Veradale, WA 99037: Free information ◆ NOS and used 1930 to 1970 parts for AMC, Hudson, and Nash cars. 509-926-4620.

**Treasure Chest Sales,** 413 Montgomery, Jackson, MI 49202: Free information ◆ Nash NOS and used parts. 517-787-1475.

**Wayne's Auto Salvage,** RR 3, Box 41, Winner, SD 57580: Free information ◆ Nash parts. 605-842-2054.

**Webb's Classic Auto Parts,** 5084 W. State Rd. 114, Huntington, IN 46750: Free information with long SASE ◆ Nash parts. 219-344-1714.

**Harold Wenner,** 5449 Tannery Rd., Schnecksville, PA 18078: Free information ◆ Nash parts 610-799-5419.

## NISSAN

**Steve Millen Sports Cars,** 3176 Airway, Costa Mesa, CA 92626: Free catalog ◆ Performance parts for the Nissan, Honda, and Toyota. 714-540-9154.

**Peninsula Imports,** 3749 Harlem, Buffalo, NY 14215: Free catalog ◆ Nissan parts. 800-999-1209.

**Rancho Cordova Specialized Recyclers,** 3688 Omec Circle, Rancho Cordova, CA 95742: Free information ◆ Used, new, rebuilt, and aftermarket parts. 800-999-9499; 916-638-3311 (in CA).

**Worldwide Auto Parts,** Rt. 38, Maple Shade, NJ 08052: Free information ◆ Factory parts. 800-500-PART; 800-887-9999 (in NJ). www.wwparts.com

## NOVA & CHEVY II

**Camaro Parts Network,** 1090 W. Bagley Rd., Cleveland, OH 44017: Free price list ◆ Nova and Chevy II parts, from 1962 to 1974. 216-234-1188.

**Chevy Parts Warehouse,** 13545 Sycamore Ave., San Martin, CA 95046: Free information ◆ Parts for 1955 to 1966 Chevrolets, 1947 to 1972 pickups, 1964 to 1972 Chevelles and El Caminos, 1962 to 1974 Novas, and 1967 to 1973 Camaros. 408-683-2438.

**Chevyland,** 3667 Recycle Rd., Rancho Cordova, CA 95742: Catalog $4 ◆ Nova parts and accessories. 800-624-6490; 800-624-8756 (in CA).

**Chicago Muscle Car Parts,** 912 E. Burnett Rd., Island Lake, IL 60042: Catalog $5 (refundable) ◆ New and used Firebird parts, from 1967 to 1981. 847-526-2200.

**Classic Industries,** 17832 Gothard St., Huntington Beach, CA 92647: Catalog $5 ◆ Nova parts and accessories. 800-854-1280.

**CPX-Doug Martz,** P.O. Box 223, Butler, WI 53007: Free information ◆ Chevrolet, Camaro, Chevelle, El Camino, Monte Carlo, and Nova parts, from 1955 to 1975. 414-463-2277.

**D & R Classic Automotive,** 30 W. 255 Calumet Ave., Warrenville, IL 60555: Free price list ◆ Nova parts. 630-393-0009.

**Harmon's Inc.,** P.O. Box 100, Hwy. 27 North, Geneva, IN 46740: Free catalog ◆ Nova restoration parts, from 1962 to 1972. 219-368-7221. www.harmons.com

**J & M Auto Parts,** P.O. Box 778, Pelham, NH 03076: Price list $1 (specify year) ◆ NOS, new, and reproduction 1962 to 1972 Nova parts. 603-635-3866.

**J & W Nova Parts,** 8253 Mt. Cross Rd., Danville, VA 24540: Free catalog ◆ Nova parts and accessories. 804-685-4310.

**Kanter Auto Parts,** 76 Monroe St., Boonton, NJ 07005: Free catalog ◆ Nova and Chevy II parts. 973-334-9575. www.kanter.com

**LES Auto Parts,** P.O. Box 81, Dayton, NJ 08810: Free information ◆ NOS parts, from 1950 to 1985, for Impalas, Chevelles, Novas, Camaros, Pontiacs, Buicks, and Oldsmobiles. 414-526-3411.

**Martz Classic Chevy Parts,** RD 1, Box 199 B, Thomasville, PA 17364: Free catalog (specify year) ◆ NOS and reproduction parts, from 1962 to 1974. 717-225-1655.

**Modern Performance Classics,** 1127 W. Collins, Orange, CA 92667: Free information ◆ NOS, reproduction, and used Nova and Chevy II parts. 800-457-NOVA.

**Ole Chevy Store,** Division T & N Manufacturing Company, 2509 S. Cannon Blvd., Kannapolis, NC 28083: Free information ◆ Parts for the Chevy II and Nova. 704-938-2923.

**Paddock West Inc.,** 1663 Plum Ln., P.O. Box 8547, Redlands, CA 92375: Free information ◆ Parts and accessories for 1962 to 1979 Novas. 800-854-8532.

**The Parts Place,** 950 Paramount Pkwy., Batavia, IL 60510: Free information ◆ Nova parts, from 1963 to 1977. 630-879-1600.

**SC Automotive,** 409 Super Sport Ln., Rt. 3, Box 9, New Ulm, MN 56073: Free catalog ◆ Nova parts. 800-62-SS-409.

**Lyn Smith Nova Parts,** 1104 Countryside Ln., Pontiac, IL 61764: Free information ◆ New, used, and reproduction 1962 to 1967 Nova parts. 815-844-7852.

**Southwestern Classics,** 1230 Dan Gould Dr., Arlington, TX 76017: Free catalog ◆ New, used, remanufactured, and hard-to-find parts and accessories for 1962 to 1974 Novas and the Chevy II. 800-346-7362; 817-477-1322 (in TX).

**Super Sport Restoration Parts Inc.,** 7138 Maddox Rd., Lithonia, GA 30058: Free information ◆ Parts for the Nova, Chevy II, Chevelle, and Camaro. 770-482-9219.

**Tom's Obsolete Chevy Parts,** 14 Delta Dr., Pawtucket, RI 02860: Catalog $2 ◆ Nova parts, from 1955 to 1972. 401-723-7580.

**Volunteer State Chevy Parts,** Hwy. 41 South, Greenbrier, TN 37073: Catalog $5 (specify year) ◆ Chevy II parts. 615-643-4583.

**Ted Williams,** 5615 Rt. 45, Box A, Lisbon, OH 44432: Free catalog ◆ Chevy II and Nova restoration parts, from 1962 to 1972. 216-424-9413. www.c.boss.com/tw/tedshome.htm

**Year One Inc.,** P.O. Box 129, Tucker, GA 30085: Catalog $5 ◆ New, used, and reproduction Nova and Chevy II restoration parts. 800-932-7663; 770-493-6568 (in GA).

## OLDSMOBILE

**Brothers Automotive Products,** 7275 W. 162nd St., #103, Stilwell, KS 66085: Catalog $5 ◆ Parts for the Oldsmobile Cutlass. 913-851-7986. www.oldsparts.com

**Cooper's Vintage Auto Parts,** 121 E. Linden Ave., Burbank, CA 91502: Free information ◆ Vintage Oldsmobile parts. 818-567-4140.

**Fusick Automotive Products,** P.O. Box 655, East Windsor, CT 06088: Catalog $5 (specify car) ◆ Parts for Oldsmobiles, from 1935 to 1960 and 1961-1975. Also Cutlass 1961 to 1977 parts. 860-623-1589.

**GM Muscle Car Parts Inc.,** 10345 75th Ave., Palos Hills, IL 60465: Free information ◆ Oldsmobile parts, from 1964 to 1987. 708-599-2277.

**LES Auto Parts,** P.O. Box 81, Dayton, NJ 08810: Free information ◆ NOS parts, from 1950 to 1985, for Impalas, Chevelles, Novas, Camaros, Pontiacs, Buicks, and Oldsmobiles. 414-526-3411.

**J. Miller Restoration,** Rt. 2, Box 281, Buchanan, TN 38222: Free information ◆ Oldsmobile parts. 901-642-5937.

**Clayton T. Nelson,** Box 259, Warrenville, IL 60555: Free information ◆ NOS parts for Oldsmobiles, from the 1940s to mid-1970s. 708-369-6589.

**Oldsmobile USA Parts Supply,** 8505 Euclid Ave., Manassas, VA 22111: Free catalog ◆ New, rebuilt, and reproduction parts for 1941 to 1975 Oldsmobiles. 703-335-1935.

**Paddock West Inc.,** 1663 Plum Ln., P.O. Box 8547, Redlands, CA 92375: Free information ◆ Parts and accessories for the 1964 to 1977 Cutlass. 800-854-8532.

**The Parts Place,** 950 Paramount Pkwy., Batavia, IL 60510: Free information ◆ Cutlass parts and accessories. 630-879-1600.

**PRO Antique Auto Parts,** 50 King Spring Rd., Windsor Locks, CT 06096: Catalog $3 ◆ New parts for 1929 to 1964 Oldsmobiles. 860-623-0070.

**Terrill Machine Inc.,** Rt. 2, Box 61, DeLeon, TX 76444: Free information with long SASE ◆ Engine overhaul parts for Oldsmobiles, from 1937 to 1960. 817-893-2610.

**Worldwide Auto Parts,** Rt. 38, Maple Shade, NJ 08052: Free information ◆ Factory parts. 800-500-PART; 800-887-9999 (in NJ). www.wwparts.com

## OPEL

**Opel GT Source,** 8030 Remmet Ave., Canoga Park, CA 91304: Catalog $4 ◆ Opel parts, from 1968 to 1973. 818-992-7776.

**Opel Parts & Service Inc.,** 3961 S. Military Hwy., Chesapeake, VA 23321: Free information ◆ Reproduction, NOS, used, and rebuilt Opel parts, from 1957 to 1975. 757-487-3851.

**Opels Unlimited,** 871 E. Lambert Rd., La Habra, CA 90631: Free information ◆ Opel parts, from 1960 to current models. 562-690-1051.

## PACKARD

**Gary Brinton's Antique Auto Parts,** 6826 SW McVey Ave., Redmond, OR 97756: Catalog $1 ◆ New and used 1920 to 1956 Packard parts. 541-548-3483.

**Classic Auto Parts,** 550 Industrial Dr., Carmel, IN 46032: Free information ◆ Genuine Packard parts, from 1928 to 1941. 317-844-8154.

**Classic Cars,** 1 Maple Terrace, Hibernia, NJ 07842: Free information ◆ Parts for Packard cars, 1928 to 1942. 201-627-1975.

**Collector Car Parts,** P.O. Box 6732, Rockford, IL 61125: Free information ◆ Parts for Buick, Cadillac, Chrysler, Duesenberg, and Packard cars. 815-229-1236.

**Fannaly's Auto Exchange,** P.O. Box 23, Ponchatoula, LA 70454: Free information ◆ Parts for 1946 to 1956 Packards. 504-386-3714.

**Kanter Auto Parts,** 76 Monroe St., Boonton, NJ 07005: Free catalog ◆ Used and reproduction parts for rebuilding Packards. 973-334-9575. www.kanter.com

**Max Merritt Auto,** P.O. Box 10, Franklin, IN 46131: Free information ◆ NOS and reproduction Packard parts and accessories. 317-736-6233.

**Packard Farm,** 97 N. 150 West, Greenfield, IN 46140: Free information ◆ Engine and transmission parts and exhaust systems. 317-462-3124.

**Packard Friends Garage,** 1 Packard Pl., Welcome Center Exit 1, Rt. 4, Fair Haven, VT 05743: Free information ◆ Reproduction and NOS Packard parts. 802-265-7969.

**Packard Store,** 9 Hall Hill Rd., Sterling, CT 06377: Free information ◆ Packard parts for all models. 860-564-5345.

**Patrician Industries Inc.,** 11869 Wilfred St., Dearborn, MI 48213: Free information (specify parts wanted) ◆ New and used parts. 810-839-0200.

**Steve's Studebaker-Packard,** 2287 2nd St., Napa, CA 94559: Free information with long SASE ◆ Packard parts, from 1951 to 1956. 707-255-8945.

**Terrill Machine Inc.,** Rt. 2, Box 61, DeLeon, TX 76444: Free information with long SASE ◆ Engine overhaul parts for 1935 to 1956 Packards. 817-893-2610.

**John Ulrich,** 450 Silver Ave., San Francisco, CA 94112: Free information ◆ NOS and used parts, from 1928 to 1956.

**Tom Vagnini,** 58 Anthony Rd., RR 3, Pittsfield, MA 01201: Free information ◆ Used Packard parts, from 1923 to 1931.

## PANTERA

**Mostly Mustang's Inc.,** 55 Alling St., Hamden, CT 06517: Free catalog ◆ New, used, and reproduction Pantera parts. 203-562-8804.

## PEUGEOT

**Foreign Motors West,** 253 N. Main St., Natick, MA 01760: Free information ◆ Peugeot parts for all years and models. 800-338-3198.

**Stamford Peugeot,** 107 Myrtle Ave., Stamford, CT 06902: Free information ◆ Peugeot parts. 800-281-8658; 203-359-2266 (in CT).

## PIERCE ARROW

**Classic Auto Parts,** 550 Industrial Dr., Carmel, IN 46032: Free information ◆ Genuine classic Pierce Arrow parts, from 1928 to 1941. 317-844-8154.

## PLYMOUTH

**Arcadia Parts Locating,** 8294 Allport Ave., Santa Fe Springs, CA 90670: Free information ◆ New, used, and reproduction parts, from 1966 to 1973. 310-698-8067.

**Andy Bernbaum Auto Parts,** 315 Franklin St., Newton, MA 02158: Catalog $4 ◆ Parts for Plymouth cars. 617-244-1118.

**Hardens Muscle Car World,** P.O. Box 306, Lexington, MO 64067: Catalog $4 ◆ NOS, reproduction, and used Plymouth parts. 800-633-4690.

**Imperial Motors,** 2165 Spencer Creek Rd., Campobello, SC 29322: Free information ◆ Chrysler, Plymouth, and Dodge parts. 864-895-3474.

**Jim's Auto Parts,** 40 Lowell Rd., P.O. Box 908, Salem, NH 03079: Catalog $7 ◆ Hard-to-find original NOS and reproduction restoration Dodge and Plymouth parts, from 1963 to 1976.

**Mid-South Auto Sales,** 2700 Neiman Industrial Dr., Winston-Salem, NC 27103: Free information ◆ Plymouth parts and accessories. 336-768-6251.

**Mike's Auto Parts,** Box 358, Ridgeland, MS 39157: Free information with long SASE ◆ Plymouth parts. 601-856-7214.

**Mitchell Motor Parts Inc.,** 1601 Thraikill Rd., Grove City, OH 43123: Free information with long SASE ◆ Plymouth parts, from 1928 to the present. 614-875-4919.

**Clayton T. Nelson,** Box 259, Warrenville, IL 60555: Free information ◆ NOS Oldsmobile and MoPar Plymouth parts, late 1940s to mid-1970s. 708-369-6589.

**Paddock West Inc.,** 1663 Plum Ln., P.O. Box 8547, Redlands, CA 92375: Free information ◆ Parts and accessories for 1962 to 1974 Plymouths. 800-854-8532.

**PRO Antique Auto Parts,** 50 King Spring Rd., Windsor Locks, CT 06906: Catalog $3 ◆ New parts for 1929 to 1934 Plymouths. 860-623-0070.

**Roberts Motor Parts,** 17 Prospect St., West Newbury, MA 01985: Catalog $4 ◆ Parts for Plymouth cars. 978-363-5881.

**Terrill Machine Inc.,** Rt. 2, Box 61, DeLeon, TX 76444: Free information with long SASE ◆ Engine overhaul parts for Plymouths, from 1933 to 1952. 817-893-2610.

**Year One Inc.,** P.O. Box 129, Tucker, GA 30085: Catalog $5 ◆ New, used, and reproduction Plymouth restoration parts. 800-932-7663; 770-493-6568 (in GA).

## PONTIAC

**Ames Performance Engineering,** Bonney Rd., Marlborough, NH 03455: Free catalog ◆ Pontiac parts, from 1955 to 1977. 800-421-2637.

**Bethel Goat Farm,** 85 N. 27th St., San Jose, CA 95116: Free information ◆ New, used original, and reproduction parts for GTO, LeMans, and Tempest cars. 408-295-7611.

**Bill's Birds,** 1021 Commack Rd., Dix Hills, NY 11746: Catalog $3 ◆ Pontiac parts and accessories. 516-667-3853.

**Boneyard Stan,** 218 N. 69th Ave., Phoenix, AZ 85043: Free information ◆ Pontiac parts, from 1950 to the 1980s. 602-936-8045.

**Continental Enterprises,** 1673 Cary Rd., Kelowna, British Columbia, Canada V1X 2C1: Information $2 ◆ Dress-up accessory kits for Pontiacs, from 1949 to 1993. 604-763-7727.

**GM Muscle Car Parts Inc.,** 10345 75th Ave., Palos Hills, IL 60465: Free information ◆ Pontiac parts, from 1964 to 1987. 708-599-2277.

**Green's Obsolete Parts,** 9 June St., Pepperell, MA 01463: Free parts list ◆ NOS and used 1940 to 1981 Pontiac parts. 978-433-9363.

**Kurt Kelsey,** Antique Pontiac Parts, 14083 P Ave., Iowa Falls, IA 50126: Free information ◆ Antique and obsolete Pontiac parts. 515-648-9086.

**LES Auto Parts,** P.O. Box 81, Dayton, NJ 08810: Free information ◆ NOS parts, from 1950 to 1985, for Impalas, Chevelles, Novas, Camaros, Pontiacs, Buicks, and Oldsmobiles. 414-526-3411.

**Original Parts Group Inc.,** 17892 Gothard St., Huntington Beach, CA 92647: Catalog $4 ◆ Parts for the LeMans and Tempest. 800-243-8355.

**Performance Years Pontiac,** 320 Elm Ave., North Wales, PA 19454: Free information ◆ Parts for 1964 to 1974 GTO, 1967 to 1981 Firebird, 1962 to 1977 Grand Prix, and other models. 800-542-7278.

**PRO Antique Auto Parts,** 50 King Spring Rd., Windsor Locks, CT 06096: Catalog $3 ◆ New parts for 1929 to 1964 Pontiacs. 860-623-0070.

**Terrill Machine Inc.,** Rt. 2, Box 61, DeLeon, TX 76444: Free information with long SASE ◆ Engine overhaul parts for Pontiacs, from 1937 to 1956. 817-893-2610.

**Worldwide Auto Parts,** Rt. 38, Maple Shade, NJ 08052: Free information ◆ Factory parts. 800-500-PART; 800-887-9999 (in NJ). www.wwparts.com

## PORSCHE

**Aase Brothers Inc.,** 701 E. Cypress St., Anaheim, CA 92805: Free information ◆ Porsche parts. 800-444-7444; 714-956-2419 (in CA).

**Automotion,** 193 Commercial St., Sunnyvale, CA 94086: Catalog $4 (refundable) ◆ Porsche parts and accessories. 800-777-8881. www.automotion.com

**Best Deal Porsche,** 8171 Monroe, Stanton, CA 90680: Free information ◆ New, used, and reproduction parts for 1953 to 1986 models. 800-354-9202.

**BMC Classics,** 828 N. Dixie Hwy., New Smyrna Beach, FL 32168: Free information ◆ Parts for the Austin-Healey, Jaguar, Mercedes-Benz, Porsche, and Triumph, from the 1950s to 1970s. 904-426-6405.

**EEC Auto Parts Group,** 2732 Navajo Rd., El Cajon, CA 92020: Free information ◆ New original and remanufactured parts and accessories for the Audi, BMW, Mercedes-Benz, Porsche, Saab, Volkswagen, and Volvo. 800-259-1125.

**Euromeister,** 19507 Yuma St., Castro Valley, CA 94546: Catalog $4.95 ◆ Porsche parts and accessories. 800-581-3327.

**928 International,** 2900-D E. Miraloma Ave., Anaheim, CA 92806: Free brochure ◆ Parts and accessories. 714-632-9288.

**Par-Porsche Specialists,** 310 Main St., New Rochelle, NY 10801: Free information ◆ New and used Porsche parts and accessories. 914-637-8800.

**Parts Hotline,** 10385 Central Ave., Montclair, CA 91763: Free information with long SASE ◆ Porsche parts. 800-637-4662.

**Performance Products,** 7658 Haskell Ave., Van Nuys, CA 91406: Catalog $4 ◆ Parts and tools for Porsche cars. 800-423-3173; 818-787-7500 (in CA). www.performanceproducts.com

**Special Interest Car Parts,** 1340 Hartford Ave., Johnston, RI 02919: Free catalog ◆ Parts and accessories for the Porsche. 800-556-7496.

**Stephen's Auto Works,** 433 Meadow Rd., Kings Park, NY 11754: Free information ◆ Mechanical parts for the BMW, Mercedes-Benz, and Porsche. 516-544-1114.

**Stoddard Imported Cars Inc.,** 38845 Mentor Ave., Willoughby, OH 44094: Catalog $5 ◆ Restoration parts for the Porsche. 800-342-1414; 216-951-1040 (in OH). www.stoddard.com

**Tweeks,** 8148 Woodland Dr., Indianapolis, IN 46278: Free catalog ◆ Porsche restoration, performance, and mechanical parts.

**Valley Motors,** 3203 Bragg Blvd., Fayetteville, NC 28303: Free information ◆ Porsche parts. 800-264-3203.

## RAMBLER

**All American Rambler,** 11661 Martens River Circle, Fountain Valley, CA 92708: Free information ◆ Rambler parts, from 1958 to 1963. 714-662-7200.

**American Parts Depot,** 409 N. Main St., West Manchester, OH 45382: Catalog $5 ◆ Rambler and AMC parts. 937-678-7249.

**Blaser's Auto,** 3200 48th Ave., Moline, IL 61265: Free information ◆ Rambler parts, from 1946 to 1987. 309-764-3571.

**For Ramblers Only,** 2324 SE 34th Ave., Portland, OR 97214: Free information ◆ Parts and accessories for 1958 to 1969 Ramblers and AMC cars. 503-232-0497.

**Doug Galvin Rambler Parts,** 7559 Passalis Ln., Sacramento, CA 95829: Free information ◆ New and used Rambler parts, 1958 to 1988. 916-689-3356.

**Kennedy American Inc.,** 7100 State Rt. 142 SE, West Jefferson, OH 43162: Free information ◆ New, used, and reproduction parts for AMC, AMX, Javelin, Jeep, and Rambler cars, from 1950 and later. 614-879-7283.

**Webb's Classic Auto Parts,** 5084 W. State Rd. 114, Huntington, IN 46750: Free information with long SASE ◆ Parts for Rambler and AMC cars, 1950 and later. 219-344-1714.

## RANCHERO

**Dearborn Classics,** P.O. Box 1248, Sunset Beach, CA 90742: Catalog $4 ◆ Ranchero parts. 562-372-3175.

**Highway Classics,** 949 N. Cataract Ave., San Dimas, CA 91773: Catalog $3 ◆ Ranchero parts and accessories, from 1960 to 1979. 909-592-8818.

## RENAULT

**British Auto/USA,** 92 Londonberry Tnpk., Manchester, NH 03104: Catalog $4 ◆ Restoration parts and accessories. 603-622-1050.

**4-CV Service,** 3301 Shetland Rd., Beavercreek, OH 45434: Free information with long SASE ◆ NOS and used parts and accessories.

**PF Engineering,** 4529 San Fernando Rd., Glendale, CA 91204: Free information with long SASE ◆ Renault parts and accessories. 818-244-2498.

## ROLLS-ROYCE

**Albers Rolls-Royce,** 360 S. 1st St., Zionsville, IN 46077: Free information ◆ Rolls-Royce parts. 317-873-2360.

**Carriage House Motor Cars Ltd.,** 25 Railroad Ave., Greenwich, CT 06830: Free information ◆ Rolls-Royce and Bentley parts. 800-883-2462.

**Classic Auto Air Mfg. Company,** 2020 W. Kennedy Blvd., Tampa, FL 33606: Free catalog ◆ Air-conditioning systems and parts for 1949 to 1969 Rolls-Royces. 813-251-4994.

**Collectors Choice,** 6400 Springfield Lodi Rd., Dane, WI 53529: Free information ◆ Parts for the DeTomaso Panterra, Shelby, Ferrari, Jaguar, and Rolls-Royce. 608-849-9878.

**Foreign Motors West,** 253 N. Main St., Natick, MA 01760: Free information ◆ Factory-new parts for the Silver Shadow and postwar Rolls-Royces and Bentleys. 800-338-3198.

**Tony Handler's Inc.,** 2028 Cotner Ave., Los Angeles, CA 90025: Free information ◆ Used parts for post-war Bentleys and Rolls-Royces. 310-473-7773.

**Joe L. Jordan,** 2615 Waugh Dr., Houston, TX 77006: Free information ◆ Rolls-Royce parts, from 1956 to 1965. 713-680-3181.

**Motorcars Ltd.,** 8101 Hempstead, Houston, TX 77008: Free information ◆ Used and new Jaguar, MG, Range Rover, BMW, Triumph, and Rolls-Royce parts. 800-338-5238.

**Oregon Crewe Cutters Inc.,** 1665 Redwood Ave., Grants Pass, OR 97527: Free information ◆ Post-war Bentley and Rolls-Royce parts. 541-479-5663.

**Powers Parts Inc.,** 425 Pine Ave., P.O. Box 796, Anna Maria, FL 34216: Free information ◆ New and used parts for Bentleys and Rolls-Royces, from 1933-1939. 941-778-7270.

**Proper Motor Cars Inc.,** 1811 11th Ave. North, St. Petersburg, FL 33713: Free information ◆ Parts for Rolls-Royces, Bentleys, Citroens, and the Ferrari. 813-821-8883.

**Replacement Parts Company,** P.O. Box 152, Villa Rica, GA 30180: Free information ◆ Rolls-Royce and Bentley replacement parts. 770-459-0040.

**Rolls-Royce of Beverly Hills,** 11401 W. Pico Blvd., West Los Angeles, CA 90064: Free information ◆ Rolls-Royce and Bentley parts. 800-321-9792; 310-477-4262 (in CA).

**Teddy's Garage,** 8530 Louise Ave., Northridge, CA 91325: Free information ◆ Pre-1966 parts for Rolls-Royce and Bentley cars. 818-341-0505.

## ROVER

**Atlantic British Parts,** P.O. Box 110, Mechanicsville, NY 12118: Free catalog ◆ Parts for the Rover. 800-533-2210.

**Bluff City British Cars,** 1810 Getwell, Memphis, TN 38111: Free information ◆ Parts for the Range Rover. 800-621-0227; 901-743-4422 (in TN).

**The British Northwest Land-Rover Company,** 1043 Kaiser Rd. SW, Olympia, WA 98512: Free information ◆ New, rebuilt, and used parts for Land-Rovers. 360-866-2254.

**British Pacific Ltd.,** 3317 Burton Ave., Burbank, CA 91504: Free information ◆ Land Rover parts. 800-554-3825.

**Engel Imports,** 5850 Stadium Dr., Kalamazoo, MI 49009: Free information ◆ Jaguar, MG, Triumph, Rover, and Austin-Healey parts, from the 1950s to the current year. 800-253-4080.

**Foreign Motors West,** 253 N. Main St., Natick, MA 01760: Free information ◆ Land Rover parts for all years and models. 800-338-3198.

**Motorcars Ltd.,** 8101 Hempstead, Houston, TX 77008: Free information ◆ Used and new Jaguar, MG, Range Rover, BMW, Triumph, and Rolls-Royce parts. 800-338-5238.

**Rovers North,** 1319 VT Rt. 128, Box 61, Westford, VT 05494: Free information ◆ Factory and some aftermarket Land Rover parts. 802-879-0032.

**Rovers West,** 940 S. Warren, Unit 143, Tucson, AZ 85719: Free information ◆ Parts for the Rover Sedan, Range Rover, Land Rover, and other models. 520-670-9377.

**Spectral Kinetics,** 17 Church St., Garnerville, NY 10923: Free information ◆ Range Rover parts. 914-947-3126.

## SAAB

**African Specialists Ltd.,** P.O. Box 6783, Santa Barbara, CA 93160: Free information ◆ Parts and accessories for the SAAB. 805-683-4020.

**EEC Auto Parts Group,** 2732 Navajo Rd., El Cajon, CA 92020: Free information ◆ New original and remanufactured parts and accessories for the Audi, BMW, Mercedes-Benz, Porsche, Saab, Volkswagen, and Volvo. 800-259-1125.

**English Car Spares Ltd.,** 345 Branch Rd. SW, Alpharetta, GA 30201: Free information ◆ Saab parts. 800-241-1916; 770-475-2662 (in GA).

**Jaguar & SAAB of Troy,** 1815 Maplelawn, Troy, MI 48084: Free catalog ◆ Parts for the SAAB. 800-832-5839; 810-643-7894 (in MI).

**Peninsula Imports,** 3749 Harlem, Buffalo, NY 14215: Free catalog ◆ Saab parts. 800-999-1209.

**Rancho Cordova Specialized Recyclers,** 3688 Omec Circle, Rancho Cordova, CA 95742: Free information ◆ Used, new, rebuilt, and aftermarket parts. 800-999-9499; 916-638-3311 (in CA).

## SATURN

**Rancho Cordova Specialized Recyclers,** 3688 Omec Circle, Rancho Cordova, CA 95742: Free information ◆ Used, new, rebuilt, and aftermarket parts. 800-999-9499; 916-638-3311 (in CA).

## SHELBY

**Branda Shelby & Mustang Parts,** 1434 E. Pleasant Valley Blvd., Altoona, PA 16602: Catalog $3 ◆ Shelby parts. 800-458-3477; 814-942-1869 (in PA).

**Cobra Restorers,** 3099 Carter, Kenesaw, GA 30144: Catalog $5 ◆ Parts for the Shelby. 404-427-0020.

**Collectors Choice,** 6400 Springfield Lodi Rd., Dane, WI 53529: Free information ◆ Parts for the DeTomaso Panterra, Shelby, Ferrari, Jaguar, and Rolls-Royce. 608-849-9878.

**Glazier's Mustang Barn Inc.,** 531 Wambold Rd., Souderton, PA 18964: Free catalog ◆ Mustang and Shelby parts, from mid-1964 to 1973. 215-723-9674.

**Mostly Mustang's Inc.,** 55 Alling St., Hamden, CT 06517: Free catalog ◆ New, used, and reproduction Shelby parts. 203-562-8804.

**Mustangs Unlimited,** 185 Adams St., Manchester, CT 06040: Catalog $3 (specify year) ◆ Shelby parts. 800-243-7278.

## SKYLARK

**Chicago Muscle Car Parts,** 912 E. Burnett Rd., Island Lake, IL 60042: Catalog $5 (refundable) ◆ New and used Skylark parts, from 1964 to 1972. 847-526-2200.

## SPITFIRE

**British Parts Northwest,** 4105 SE Lafayette Hwy., Dayton, OR 97114: Catalog $2.50 ◆ Spitfire parts. 503-864-2001.

## STEARNS-KNIGHT

**Arthur W. Aseltine,** 18215 Challenge Cut-Off Rd., Forbestown, CA 95941: Free information with long SASE (specify parts wanted) ◆ Hard-to-find parts. 916-675-2773.

## STERLING

**Bluff City British Cars,** 1810 Getwell, Memphis, TN 38111: Free information ◆ Parts for the Sterling. 800-621-0227; 901-743-4422 (in TN).

**Jaguar & SAAB of Troy,** 1815 Maplelawn, Troy, MI 48084: Free catalog ◆ Parts for the Sterling. 800-832-5839; 810-643-7894 (in MI).

**Rancho Cordova Specialized Recyclers,** 3688 Omec Circle, Rancho Cordova, CA 95742: Free information ◆ Used, new, rebuilt, and aftermarket parts. 800-999-9499; 916-638-3311 (in CA).

## STUDEBAKER

**Beckers Auto Salvage,** 3221 73rd St., Atkins, IA 52206: Free information ◆ Parts for Studebakers. 319-446-7141.

**Dakota Studebaker Parts,** 39408 280th St., Armour, SD 57313: Free information ◆ Parts for cars, pickups, and trucks, from 1936 to 1964. 605-724-2527.

**Dennis DuPont,** 77 Island Pond Rd., Derry, NH 03038: Free information ◆ NOS and used Studebaker parts, from the mid-1930s to 1966. 603-434-9290.

**Jim's Auto Sales,** Rt. 2, Inman, KS 67546: Free information ◆ Studebaker parts, from 1935 to 1966. 316-585-6648.

**Newman & Altman Inc.,** P.O. Box 4276, South Bend, IN 46634: Catalog $5 ◆ Studebaker parts and accessories, for 1947 to 1966 cars and trucks. 800-722-4295. www.newman-altman.com

**Packard Farm,** 97 N 150 West, Greenfield, IN 46140: Free information ◆ Studebaker engine and transmission parts and exhaust systems. 317-462-3124.

**Phil's Studebaker,** 11250 Harrison Rd., Osceola, IN 46561: Free information ◆ NOS, reproduction, and used Studebaker parts, from 1947 to 1966. 219-674-0084.

**Steve's Studebaker-Packard,** 2287 2nd St., Napa, CA 94559: Free information with long SASE ◆ Studebaker parts, from 1953 to 1966. 707-255-8945.

**Tucker's Auto Salvage,** RD 1, Box 29A, Burke, NY 12917: Free information ◆ Studebaker NOS and used parts. 518-483-5478.

**Wayne's Auto Salvage,** RR 3, Box 41, Winner, SD 57580: Free information ◆ Studebaker parts. 605-842-2054.

## SUBARU

**Parts Hotline,** 10385 Central Ave., Montclair, CA 91763: Free information with long SASE ◆ Subaru parts. 800-637-4662.

**Russel Toyota,** 6700 Baltimore National Tnpk., Baltimore, MD 21228: Free information ◆ Buick, Mazda, Subaru, and Toyota parts. 800-638-8401.

**Stamford Subaru,** 107 Myrtle Ave., Stamford, CT 06902: Free information ◆ Subaru parts and accessories. 800-281-8658; 203-359-2266 (in CT).

## SUNBEAM

**Classic Sunbeam Auto Parts,** 2 Tavano Rd., Ossining, NY 10562: Free catalog ◆ Parts for 1959 to 1967 Alpines and Tigers. 800-23-SUN-BEAM; 914-941-8673 (in NY).

**Kip Motor Company Inc.,** 13325 Denton Dr., Dallas, TX 75234: Free catalog (specify car) ◆ Parts for the Austin, English Ford, Sunbeam, and other British cars. 972-243-0440.

**Moss Motors Ltd.,** 440 Rutherford St., Goleta, CA 93117: Free catalog (specify model) ◆ Parts for the Sunbeam. 800-MOSS-USA; 805-681-3400 (in CA). www.mossmotors.com

**Sunbeam Specialties,** P.O. Box 771, Los Gatos, CA 95031: Free catalog ◆ Parts for 1959 to 1968 Tigers and Alpines. 408-371-1642.

**Victoria British Ltd.,** P.O. Box 14991, Lenexa, KS 66285: Free catalog ◆ Sunbeam parts. 800-255-0088.

## TEMPEST

**Original Parts Group Inc.,** 17892 Gothard St., Huntington Beach, CA 92647: Catalog $4 ◆ Tempest parts. 800-243-8355.

## THUNDERBIRD

**Auto Krafters Inc.,** P.O. Box 8, Broadway, VA 22815: Catalog $3 (specify year) ◆ New, used, and reproduction parts, from 1958 to 1976. 540-896-5910. www.autokrafters.com/

**Auto Parts Exchange,** P.O. Box 736, Reading, PA 19603: Free information ◆ NOS and used parts for 1953 to 1979 Lincolns and 1958 to 1979 Thunderbirds. 610-372-2813.

**B & W Antique Auto Parts,** 4653 Guide Meridian Rd., Bellingham, WA 98226: Catalog $5 (specify year and model) ◆ Thunderbird parts, 1955 to 1966. 800-561-4622.

**Bird Nest,** P.O. Box 14865, Portland, OR 97293: Free catalog ◆ New, NOS, used, reproduction, and rebuilt 1958 to 1966 Thunderbird parts. 800-232-6378. www.tbirdparts.com

**Bob's T-Birds,** 5397 NE 14th Ave., Fort Lauderdale, FL 33334: Free information with long SASE ◆ New and used parts. 954-491-6652.

**California Collectors' Classics,** P.O. Box 2281, Irwindale, CA 91706: Free information ◆ Parts, from 1961 to 1985, for the Cadillac, Lincoln, and Thunderbird. 818-962-6696.

**Dennis Carpenter Reproductions,** P.O. Box 26398, Charlotte, NC 28221: Catalog $3 (specify year) ◆ Rubber parts for 1958 to 1966 Thunderbirds. 219-335-2425.

**Classic Auto Supply Company Inc.,** 795 High St., P.O. Box 850, Coshocton, OH 43812: Catalog $1 ◆ Parts for 1955 to 1957 Thunderbirds. 800-374-0914.

**Classique Cars Unlimited,** 5 Turkey Bayou Rd., P.O. Box 249, Lakeshore, MS 39558: Parts list $5 ◆ Thunderbird parts, from 1958 to 1988. 601-467-9633.

**Concours Parts & Accessories,** 3563 Numancia St., P.O. Box 1210, Santa Ynez, CA 93460: Catalog $4 ◆ Thunderbird 1955 to 1957 parts. 805-688-7795.

**Continental Enterprises,** 1673 Cary Rd., Kelowna, British Columbia, Canada V1X 2C1: Information $2 ◆ Thunderbird dress-up accessory kits, from 1949 to 1993. 604-763-7727.

**Bob Cook Classic Auto Parts,** 2055 Van Cleave Rd., P.O. Box 600, Murray, KY 42071: Catalog $6 ◆ Reproduction parts for 1958 to 1960, 1961 to 1964, 1965 to 1966, and 1967 to 1972 Thunderbirds. 800-486-1137; 502-753-4000 (in KY).

**Buzz De Clerck,** 41760 Utica Rd., Sterling Heights, MI 48313: Free information ◆ New and used Thunderbird parts, from 1969 to 1971. 810-731-0765.

**Ford Parts Specialists,** 98-11 211th St., Queens Village, NY 11429: Free catalog (specify year) ◆ Thunderbird parts, 1955 to 1966. 718-468-8585.

**Hollywood Classic Motorcars Inc.,** 363 Ansin Blvd., Hallandale, FL 33009: Free information ◆ Used 1958 to 1966 Thunderbird parts. 800-235-2444; 954-454-4641 (in FL).

**Joblot Automotive,** 98-11 211th St., Queens Village, NY 11429: Catalog $2 ◆ Parts for 1949 to 1969 Thunderbirds. 800-221-0172; 718-468-8585 (in NY).

**Larry's Thunderbird & Mustang Parts,** 511 S. Raymond Ave., Fullerton, CA 92631: Catalog $2 ◆ New and used 1955 to 1957 parts for Thunderbirds. 800-854-0393; 714-871-6432 (in CA).

**LeBaron Bonney Company,** P.O. Box 8, Amesbury, MA 01913: Catalog $1 ◆ Thunderbird parts. 800-221-5408.

**Lincoln Parts International,** 707 E. 4th St., Bldg. G, Perris, CA 92570: Free information ◆ Thunderbird parts, from 1972 to 1979. 909-657-5588.

**Midland Automotive Products,** Rt. 1, Box 27, Midland City, AL 36350: Free information ◆ Reproduction and new Thunderbird parts and accessories. 334-983-1212.

**Muck Motor Sales,** 10 Campbell Blvd., Buffalo, NY 14068: Free information ◆ Thunderbird parts and accessories. 800-228-6825.

**National Parts Depot,** 3101 SW 40th Blvd., Gainesville, FL 32608: Free catalog ◆ Thunderbird parts and accessories, from 1955 to 1957. 800-874-7595; 352-378-2473 (in FL).

**Nicks T-Birds,** 14649 Lanark St., Unit B, Panorama City, CA 91402: Free catalog (specify year) ◆ Thunderbird parts, from 1958 to 1960, 1961 to 1963, and 1964 to 1966. 800-669-1961.

**Obsolete Ford Parts Inc. (Oklahoma City),** 8701 South I-35, Oklahoma City, OK 73149: Catalog $3 (specify year) ◆ Parts for 1949 to 1959 and 1960 to 1972 Thunderbirds. 405-631-3933.

**Sunyaks,** P.O. Box 498, Bound Brook, NJ 08805: Free information ◆ NOS and restored hard-to-find Thunderbird parts, from 1955 to 1957. 908-356-0600.

**T-Bird Nest,** 2550 E. Southlake Rd., Southlake, TX 76092: Free information ◆ Thunderbird parts, from 1958 to 1966. 817-481-1776.

**The T-Bird Sanctuary,** 9997 SW Avery, Tualatin, OR 97062: Catalog $5 ◆ Parts for 1958 to 1976 Thunderbirds. 503-692-9848.

**Tee-Bird Products Inc.,** Box 728, Exton, PA 19341: Catalog $3 ◆ Parts for 1955 to 1957 Thunderbirds. 610-363-1725.

**Thunderbird & Falcon Connections,** 728 E. Dunlap, Phoenix, AZ 85020: Free information ◆ Used Thunderbird, Falcon, Fairlane, and Comet parts. 800-888-BIRD; 602-997-9285 (in AZ).

**Thunderbird Center,** 23610 John R., Hazel Park, MI 48030: Free catalog ◆ Upholstery, sheet metal, weatherstripping, and new, used, NOS, and reproduction parts for 1956 to 1957 Thunderbirds. 810-548-1721.

**Thunderbird Headquarters,** 1080 Detroit Ave., Concord, CA 94518: Free catalog ◆ Thunderbird parts, from 1955 to 1957. 800-227-2174; 800-642-2405 (in CA).

**Thunderbird Parts & Restoration,** 5844 Goodrich Rd., Clarence Center, NY 14032: Free information ◆ NOS, reproduction, used, and re-manufactured parts. 800-289-2473; 716-741-2866 (in NY).

**Thunderbirds East,** 140 Wilmington-West Chester Pike, Chadds Ford, PA 19317: Free information ◆ New and used parts for 1955 to 1957 Thunderbirds. 610-358-1021.

**Thunderbirds USA Parts Supply,** 3621 Resource Dr., Tuscaloosa, AL 35401: Free catalog ◆ 1955 to 1957 Thunderbird upholstery, decals, radios, books, and NOS, used, and reproduction parts. 800-842-5557; 205-758-5557 (in AL).

## TORINO

**Auto Krafters Inc.,** P.O. Box 8, Broadway, VA 22815: Catalog $3 (specify year) ◆ New, used, and reproduction parts for 1962 to 1971 Torinos. 540-896-5910. www.autokrafters.com

**Dennis Carpenter Reproductions,** P.O. Box 26398, Charlotte, NC 28221: Catalog $3 ◆ Rubber parts for 1962 to 1971 Torinos. 219-335-2425.

**Bob Cook Classic Auto Parts,** 2055 Van Cleave Rd., P.O. Box 600, Murray, KY 42071: Catalog $6 ◆ Reproduction parts for the 1960 to 1972 Torino. 800-486-1137; 502-753-4000 (in KY).

**Dearborn Classics,** P.O. Box 1248, Sunset Beach, CA 90742: Catalog $4 ◆ Torino parts and accessories. 562-372-3175.

**Ford Parts Store,** P.O. Box 226, Bryan, OH 43506: Catalog $2 ◆ Torino parts. 419-636-2475.

**Highway Classics,** 949 N. Cataract Ave., San Dimas, CA 91773: Catalog $3 ◆ Torino parts and accessories. 909-592-8818.

**Melvin's Classic Ford Parts Inc.,** 2526 Panola., Lithonia, GA 30058: Free information ◆ Parts for the 1962 to 1979 Torino. 770-981-2357.

**Obsolete Ford Parts Inc. (Oklahoma City),** 8701 South I-35, Oklahoma City, OK 73149: Catalog $3 (specify year) ◆ Parts and accessories for 1962 to 1972 Torinos. 405-631-3933.

## TOYOTA

**Dobi Toyota Catalog,** 320 Thor Pl., Brea, CA 92621: Catalog $2 ◆ Replacement parts for the Toyota Celica and Corolla. 714-529-1977.

**Lou Fusz Toyota,** 10725 Manchester, St. Louis, MO 63122: Catalog $4 ◆ Toyota parts and accessories. 800-325-9581. loufusz@stlnet.com

**Impact Parts,** Glen Wild Rd., Glen Wild, NY 12738: Catalog $1 ◆ Parts for the Toyota. 800-431-3400; 914-434-3338 (in NY). www.impactparts.com

**Jaguar & SAAB of Troy,** 1815 Maplelawn, Troy, MI 48084: Free catalog ◆ Parts for the Toyota. 800-832-5839; 810-643-7894 (in MI).

**Steve Millen Sports Cars,** 3176 Airway, Costa Mesa, CA 92626: Free catalog ◆ Performance parts for the Nissan, Honda, and Toyota. 714-540-9154.

**Newark Toyota,** 1344 Marrows Rd., Newark, DE 19711: Free information ◆ Toyota parts and accessories. 800-537-4510.

**Rancho Cordova Specialized Recyclers,** 3688 Omec Circle, Rancho Cordova, CA 95742: Free information ◆ Used, new, rebuilt, and aftermarket parts. 800-999-9499; 916-638-3311 (in CA).

**Russel Toyota,** 6700 Baltimore National Tnpk., Baltimore, MD 21228: Free information ◆ Buick, Mazda, Subaru, and Toyota parts. 800-638-8401.

**Worldwide Auto Parts,** Rt. 38, Maple Shade, NJ 08052: Free information ◆ Factory parts. 800-500-PART; 800-887-9999 (in NJ). www.wwparts.com

## TRIUMPH

**Aurora Auto Wrecking Inc.,** 9217 Aurora Ave. North, Seattle, WA 98103: Free information ◆ New, used, and rebuilt Triumph parts. 800-426-6464.

**BMC Classics,** 828 N. Dixie Hwy., New Smyrna Beach, FL 32168: Free information ◆ Parts for the Austin-Healey, Jaguar, Mercedes-Benz, Porsche, and Triumph, from the 1950s to 1970s. 904-426-6405.

**British Auto Parts Inc.,** 93256 Holland, Marcola, OR 97454: Free information ◆ New, used, and rebuilt MG, Triumph, and Jaguar parts. 541-933-2880.

**British Miles,** 9278 Old E. Tyburn Rd., Morrisville, PA 19067: Catalog $5 ◆ Reconditioned and new Triumph parts. 215-736-9300. www.britishmiles.com

**British Parts Northwest,** 4105 SE Lafayette Hwy., Dayton, OR 97114: Catalog $2.50 ◆ Triumph parts. 503-864-2001.

**Engel Imports,** 5850 Stadium Dr., Kalamazoo, MI 49009: Free information ◆ Jaguar, MG, Triumph, Rover, and Austin-Healey parts, from the 1950s to the current year. 800-253-4080.

**English Car Spares Ltd.,** 345 Branch Rd. SW, Alpharetta, GA 30201: Free information ◆ Triumph parts. 800-241-1916; 770-475-2662 (in GA).

**Midtown Auto,** 212 Burnet Ave., Syracuse, NY 13203: Free information ◆ New, used, and rebuilt sheet metal, transmission, engine, brake, and electrical parts for the Austin, MG, Triumph, and Jaguar. 315-476-9421.

**Moss Motors Ltd.,** 440 Rutherford St., Goleta, CA 93117: Free catalog (specify model) ◆ Triumph parts. 800-MOSS-USA; 805-681-3400 (in CA). www.mossmotors.com

**Motorcars Ltd.,** 8101 Hempstead, Houston, TX 77008: Free information ◆ Used and new Jaguar, MG, Range Rover, BMW, Triumph, and Rolls-Royce parts. 800-338-5238.

**Peninsula Imports,** 3749 Harlem, Buffalo, NY 14215: Free catalog ◆ Triumph parts. 800-999-1209.

**Roadster Factory,** P.O. Box 332, Armagh, PA 15920: Free catalog ◆ Parts for the Triumph, TR2 through TR8, Spitfire, and GT6. 800-283-3723.

**Special Interest Car Parts,** 1340 Hartford Ave., Johnston, RI 02919: Free catalog ◆ Parts and accessories for Triumphs. 800-556-7496.

**Sports & Classics,** 512 Boston Post Rd., Darien, CT 06820: Catalog $5 ◆ Restoration, engine, electrical, and body parts. 203-655-8731.

**Victoria British Ltd.,** P.O. Box 14991, Lenexa, KS 66215: Free catalog ◆ Original, replacement, and reproduction parts for the Triumph and other British sports cars. 800-255-0088.

**Victory Autoservices,** Box 5060, RR 1, West Baldwin, ME 04091: Free information ◆ Post-1946 parts for the Austin-Healey, Jaguar, MG, and Triumph. 207-625-4581.

## VENTURA

**Ames Performance Engineering,** Bonney Rd., Marlborough, NH 03455: Free catalog ◆ Ventura parts, from 1971 to 1974. 800-421-2637.

## VOLKSWAGEN

**African Specialists Ltd.,** P.O. Box 6783, Santa Barbara, CA 93160: Free information ◆ Parts and accessories for the Volkswagen. 805-683-4020.

**EEC Auto Parts Group,** 2732 Navajo Rd., El Cajon, CA 92020: Free information ◆ New original and remanufactured parts and accessories for the Audi, BMW, Mercedes-Benz, Porsche, Saab, Volkswagen, and Volvo. 800-259-1125.

**Electro Automotive,** P.O. Box 1113, Felton, CA 95018: Catalog $5 ◆ Bolt-in kit for converting a gas or diesel Rabbit to electricity. 408-429-1989.

**Euromeister,** 19507 Yuma St., Castro Valley, CA 94546: Catalog $4.95 ◆ Volkswagen parts and accessories. 800-581-3327.

**JBUGS Car & Truck Depot,** 14222 Prairie Ave., Hawthorne, CA 90250: Free information ◆ New and used parts and accessories. 310-978-0926.

**Rancho Cordova Specialized Recyclers,** 3688 Omec Circle, Rancho Cordova, CA 95742: Free information ◆ Used, new, rebuilt, and aftermarket parts. 800-999-9499; 916-638-3311 (in CA).

**Rocky Mountain Motorworks,** 1003 Tamarac Pkwy., Woodland Park, CO 80863: Free catalog ◆ Restoration parts. 800-544-1066.

**Sonnen Motors,** 601 Francisco Blvd. East, San Rafael, CA 94901: Free information ◆ Genuine factory parts and accessories. 800-543-7626; 415-456-9040 (in CA).

## VOLVO

**African Specialists Ltd.,** P.O. Box 6783, Santa Barbara, CA 93160: Free information ◆ Parts and accessories for the Volvo. 805-683-4020.

**Beechmont Volvo,** 8639 Beechmont Ave., Cincinnati, OH 45255: Free catalog ◆ Volvo parts. 800-255-3601.

**Brentwood Volvo,** 7700 Manchester Rd., St. Louis, MO 63143: Free information ◆ Volvo parts. 800-844-9502.

**Concours Cars of Colorado Ltd.,** 2414 W. Cucharras St., Colorado Springs, CO 80904: Free information ◆ Accessories and parts for the Alfa-Romeo, BMW, Jaguar, and Volvo. 719-473-6288.

**EEC Auto Parts Group,** 2732 Navajo Rd., El Cajon, CA 92020: Free information ◆ New original and remanufactured parts and accessories for the Audi, BMW, Mercedes-Benz, Porsche, Saab, Volkswagen, and Volvo. 800-259-1125.

**English Car Spares Ltd.,** 345 Branch Rd. SW, Alpharetta, GA 30201: Free information ◆ Volvo parts. 800-241-1916; 770-475-2662 (in GA).

**Euromeister,** 19507 Yuma St., Castro Valley, CA 94546: Catalog $4.95 ◆ Volvo parts and accessories. 800-581-3327.

**European Parts Specialists Ltd.,** P.O. Box 6783, Santa Barbara, CA 93160: Free information ◆ Parts and accessories for the Volvo. 805-683-4020.

**Foreign Autotech,** 3225 Sunset Ln., Hatboro, PA 19040: Free information ◆ Volvo 1800 parts. 215-441-4421.

**Impact Parts,** Glen Wild Rd., Glen Wild, NY 12738: Catalog $1 ◆ Parts for the Volvo. 800-431-3400; 914-434-3338 (in NY). www.impactparts.com

**Rancho Cordova Specialized Recyclers,** 3688 Omec Circle, Rancho Cordova, CA 95742: Free information ◆ Used, new, rebuilt, and aftermarket parts. 800-999-9499; 916-638-3311 (in CA).

**Stamford Volvo,** 107 Myrtle Ave., Stamford, CT 06902: Free information ◆ Genuine Volvo parts. 800-281-8658; 203-359-2266 (in CT).

**Swedish Classics,** P.O. Box 557, Oxford, MD 21654: Catalog $5 (specify model) ◆ Original Volvo parts and accessories. 410-226-5183.

**Voluparts,** 751 Trabert Ave., Atlanta, GA 30318: Free information ◆ New and used Volvo parts. 404-352-3402.

### WILLYS

**Obsolete Jeep & Willys Parts,** 6110 17th St. East, Bradenton, FL 34203: Free information ◆ New, used, rebuilt, and NOS parts. 941-756-7844.

### YUGO

**Orion Motors Inc.,** 10722 Jones Rd., Houston, TX 77065: Free information ◆ Yugo parts and accessories. 800-736-6410; 713-894-1982 (in TX).

## Pickup Storage Boxes

**Creative Technologies,** Box 248, Kenmare, ND 58746: Free information ◆ Pickup storage boxes. 800-543-1218.

## Plating

**A & A Plating,** 9400 E. Wilson Rd., Independence, MO 64053: Free information ◆ Custom plating. 800-747-9914.

**Bison Plating Inc.,** 600 Sherman Ave., Adell, WI 53001: Free information ◆ Copper, nickel, and chrome metal plating. 800-843-3023; 414-994-4013 (in WI).

**Burns Binnert Plating Inc.,** 412 Clifford Ave., Rochester, NY 14621: Free information ◆ Chrome plating, die-cast repairs and refinishing, polishing, and buffing. 716-342-5180.

**Castle Metal Finishing,** Ron McGilvray, 15 Broad St., Hudson, MA 01749: Free information ◆ Chrome restoration plating. 978-562-7294.

**CoTech Plating,** 130 Malaga Way, Brentwood, CA 94513: Free information ◆ Plastic re-chroming services.

**Custom Chrome Inc.,** 117 Elk St., Rock Springs, WY 82901: Free information ◆ Restoration plating. 307-362-1504.

**Custom Chrome Plating,** 963 Mechanic St., P.O. Box 125, Grafton, OH 44044: Free information ◆ Chrome, nickel, and copper plating. 440-926-3116.

**Custom Plating,** 3030 Alta Ridge Way, Snellville, GA 30278: Free information ◆ Chrome plating. 770-736-1118.

**Graves Plating Company,** Industrial Park, P.O. Box 1052, Florence, AL 35631: Free information ◆ Chrome, nickel, brass, and gold plating. 205-764-9487.

**International Chromium Plating Company,** 2 Addison Pl., Providence, RI 02909: Free information ◆ Custom chrome plating of marine, motorcycle, and auto hardware. Also nickel, zinc, and cadmium plating. 401-421-0205.

**J & P Custom Plating,** Box 16, 807 N. Meridian St., Portland, IN 47371: Free information ◆ Copper, nickel, chrome, and brass plating. 219-726-9696.

**King's Bumper Company Inc.,** 1 Ontario Ave., New Hartford, NY 13413: Free information ◆ Chrome plating. 315-732-8988.

**Ron Monte Triple Chrome Plate,** 25 Roseland Ave., Caldwell, NJ 07006: Free information ◆ Copper, nickel, chrome, brass, and silver plating. 201-226-6184.

**Paul's Chrome Plating Inc.,** 341 Mars-Valencia Rd., Mars, PA 16046: Free information ◆ Plating and pot metal restoration. 800-245-8679; 412-625-3135 (in PA). www.igateway.com/mall/special/chrome/index.htm

**Pot Metal Restorations,** 4794 Woodlane Circle, Tallahassee, FL 32303: Free brochure ◆ Pitless pot metal chrome plating. 904-562-3847.

**Speed & Sport Chrome Plating,** 404 Broadway, Houston, TX 77012: Free information ◆ Chrome plating, specializing in antique automobile parts. 713-921-0235.

**Verne's Chrome Plating,** 1559 El Segundo Blvd., Gardena, CA 90249: Free information ◆ Chrome plating and polishing. 310-754-4126.

## Radar Detectors (Manufacturers)

**Cincinnati Microwave,** One Microwave Plaza, Cincinnati, OH 45249: Free information ◆ Micro and standard-size radar detectors. 800-543-1608. www.cnmw.com

**Cobra,** 6500 W. Cortland St., Chicago, IL 60707: Free information ◆ Micro, remote, and standard-size radar detectors. 800-COBRA-22.

**Escort Detectors,** 5200 Fields-Ertel Rd., Cincinnati, OH 45249: Free information ◆ Radar and laser detectors. 800-433-3487.

**K-40 Electronics,** 1500 Executive Dr., Elgin, IL 60123: Free brochure ◆ Radar detectors. 800-323-5608. www.k40.com

**Kortesis Marketing Ent.,** P.O. Box 460543, Aurora, CO 80046: Free brochure ◆ Laser/radar jammer and detector combination. 303-548-3995.

**Radar Sales,** 5640 International Pkwy., Minneapolis, MN 55428: Free catalog ◆ Radar equipment for sports testing and speed enforcement. 888-782-5537.

**Radar U.S.A.,** 1749 Golf Rd., Mt. Prospect, IL 60056: Free information ◆ Radar units and accessories. 800-777-6570; 847-350-0201 (in IL).

**Radio Shack,** Division Tandy Corp., One Tandy Center, Fort Worth, TX 76102: Free information ◆ Mini, remote, and standard-size radar detectors. 817-390-3011. www.radioshack.com

**Valentine Research Inc.,** 10280 Alliance Rd., Cincinnati, OH 45242: Free information ◆ Radar locator, radar locator with laser detection, and concealed display modules. 513-984-8900.

## Radar Detectors (Retailers)

**ComputAbility Consumer Electronics,** P.O. Box 17882, Milwaukee, WI 53217: Free catalog ◆ Radar detectors. 800-558-0003. www.computability.com/csh.html

**Radar U.S.A.,** 1749 Golf Rd., Mt. Prospect, IL 60056: Free information ◆ Radar detectors. 800-777-6570; 847-350-0201 (in IL).

**S.B.H. Enterprises,** 1678 53rd St., Brooklyn, NY 11204: Free information ◆ Radar detectors. 800-451-5851; 718-438-1027 (in NY).

## Radiators

**Brassworks/Flowkooler,** 289 Prado Rd., San Luis Obispo, CA 93401: Free information ◆ Handcrafted rebuilt and duplicated radiators, from the 1890 to 1957. 800-342-6759.

**Kassa's Parts & Accessories,** 3277 Staunton Rd., Edwardsville, IL 62025: Free information ◆ Reproduction radiators, from 1955 to 1992. 618-656-8359.

**Glen Ray Radiators Inc.,** 2105 6th St., Wausau, WI 54401: Free information ◆ Rebuilds and re-cores radiators. 914-691-7020.

## Ramps & Lifts

**Access to Recreation Inc.,** 8 Sandra Ct., Newbury Park, CA 91320: Free catalog ◆ Ramps for scooters and wheelchairs. Includes permanent, tri-fold, threshold, and roll-up models. 800-634-4351.

**Backyard Buddy Corp.,** P.O. Box 5104, Niles, OH 44446: Free information ◆ Hydraulic-powered lifts for standard wheelbase cars and trucks. 800-837-9353.

**Highland Group Industries,** 31200 Solon Rd., Solon, OH 44139: Free catalog ◆ Towing and travel accessories, tie-downs, and car top, bike, and ski carriers. 216-498-0001.

**Stinger Inc.,** 1375 17th Ave., McPherson, KS 67460: Free information ◆ Lifts for commercial parking and residential use. 800-854-4850; 316-241-5580 (in KS).

**Tru-Cut Automotive,** P.O. Box 1240, Salem, OH 44460: Free information ◆ Car ramp extensions that prevent slipping or digging into asphalt or earth. 800-634-7267.

## Replica & Conversion Kits

### ALLARD

**Hardy Motors,** P.O. Box 1302, Bonita, CA 91908: Brochure $5 ◆ Reproduction car kits. 619-421-5920.

### AUBURN

**The Classic Factory,** 1454 E. 9th St., Pomona, CA 91766: Information $3 ◆ Replica car kits. 909-629-5968.

### BRADLEY GT

**Sun Ray Products Corp.,** 8017 Ranchers Rd., Minneapolis, MN 55432: Free brochure ◆ Replica car kits. 612-780-0774.

### COBRA

**Antique & Collectible Autos Inc.,** 35 Dole St., Buffalo, NY 14210: Brochure $1 ◆ Replica car kits. 800-245-1310; 716-825-3990 (in NY).

**Bennett Automotive,** 3385 Enterprise, Hayward, CA 94545: Free brochure ◆ Reproduction car kits. 510-782-0705.

**Classic Roadsters,** 1617 Main Ave., Fargo, ND 58103: Free brochure ◆ Easy-to-assemble Cobra kit. 800-373-9000.

**Contemporary Classic Motor Car Company,** 115 Hoyt Ave., Mamaroneck, NY 10543: Catalog $5 ◆ Replica car kits. 914-381-5678.

**ERA Replica Automobiles,** 608 E. Main St., New Britain, CT 06051: Information $10 ◆ Replica car kits. 860-224-0253.

**Everett-Morrison Motorcars,** 5137 W. Clifton St., Tampa, FL 33634: Brochure $5 ◆ Replica car kits. 813-887-5885.

**Hi-Tech Motorsports,** 2204 W. Southern Ave., Tempe, AZ 85282: Free catalog ◆ Cobra kits. 602-431-9400.

**MidStates Classic Cars,** 835 W. Grant, P.O. Box 427, Hooper, NE 68031: Catalog $5 ◆ Replica car kits. 402-654-2772.

**Shell Valley Motors,** Rt. 1, Box 69, Platte Center, NE 68653: Free information ◆ Replica car kits. 888-246-0300.

**Unique Motorcars Inc.,** 230 E. Broad St., Gadsden, AL 35903: Brochure $5 ◆ Reproduction car kits. 256-546-3708.

**West Coast Cobra,** 6785 16 Mile Rd., Sterling Heights, MI 48077: Information $5 ◆ Replica car kits. 810-736-7274.

### CORVETTE

**Beck Development,** 1531 W. 13th St., Upland, CA 91786: Free information ◆ Replica car kits. 909-981-3840.

**D & D Corvette,** 1985 Manchester Rd., Akron, OH 44314: Information $5 ◆ Replica car kits. 330-745-2544.

### FERRARI

**Corson Motorcars Ltd.,** P.O. Box 41396, Phoenix, AZ 85080: Brochure $5 ◆ Replica car kits. 602-375-2544.

### FIERO

**American Fiberbodies International,** P.O. Box 726, Xenia, OH 45385: Information $10 ◆ Body package for any stock Fiero. 937-372-5938.

**Fiero Conversions Inc.,** 3410 Walker Rd., Windsor, Ontario, Canada N8W 3S3: Information $5 ◆ Body and aerodynamic conversion accessories. 519-972-4989.

**Fiero Plus,** 12 Banner Rd., Nepean, Ontario, Canada K2H 5T2: Catalog $7 ◆ Body conversion kits. 613-596-6269.

**Mac's Auto Body,** 4427 Maygog Rd., Sarasota, FL 34233: Information $5 ◆ Body kits. 941-921-4420.

### FORD

**Antique & Collectible Autos Inc.,** 35 Dole St., Buffalo, NY 14210: Brochure $1 ◆ Replica car kits. 800-245-1310; 716-825-3990 (in NY).

### JAGUAR

**Antique & Collectible Autos Inc.,** 35 Dole St., Buffalo, NY 14210: Brochure $1 ◆ Replica car kits. 800-245-1310; 716-825-3990 (in NY).

**Braden River Engineering,** 2604 Manatee Ave. East, Bradenton, FL 34208: Free information ◆ Body conversion kits. 941-747-6146.

### MAZDA

**Design Energy Inc.,** 414 N. Salsipuedes, Santa Barbara, CA 93103: Information $5 ◆ Body conversion kits. 805-965-5115.

### PORSCHE

**Beck Development,** 1531 W. 13th St., Upland, CA 91786: Free information ◆ Reproduction car kits. 909-981-3840.

### SEBRING MX

**Classic Roadsters,** 1617 Main Ave., Fargo, ND 58103: Free brochure ◆ Easy-to-assemble kit. 800-373-9000.

### SPECIALTY CARS

**BGW Spectre Ltd.,** 2534 Woodland Park Dr., Delafield, WI 53018: Free information ◆ Fiberglass car kits with optional custom components. 414-646-4884. bgwhttwe@execpc.com

**Euro-Works,** 3771 Eileen Rd., Dayton, OH 45429: Information $5 ◆ Sports car kit. 937-293-6834.

**Exotic Illusions,** Rear 347 Main St., Dickson City, PA 18519: Information $5 ◆ Replica car kits. 717-383-1206.

**I.F.G. Cars,** 15740 El Prado Rd., Chino, CA 91710: Information $3 with long SASE ◆ Sports car kits. 909-597-4110.

**Sun Valley Autotech,** 13802 N. Scottsdale Rd., Scottsdale, AZ 85254: Free information ◆ Easy-to-build car for the street, off-road, and sand driving. Uses Volkswagen parts. 602-991-8975.

**Warlock Designs,** 15740 El Prado Rd., Unit B, Chino, CA 91710: Free information ◆ Phantom VT car kit. 909-597-3621.

### TOYOTA

**Aeroform,** 6300 St. John Ave., Kansas City, MO 64123: Information $5 ◆ Reproduction car kits. 800-345-2376.

### VOLKSWAGEN

**Archway Import Auto Parts Inc.,** 1900 Telegraph Rd., St. Louis, MO 63125: Catalog $3.95 ◆ Parts for Volkswagen kit cars. 314-638-7700.

### WILLYS

**Antique & Collectible Autos Inc.,** 35 Dole St., Buffalo, NY 14210: Brochure $1 ◆ Replica car kits. 800-245-1310; 716-825-3990 (in NY).

## Replica & Conversion Parts & Accessories

**CB Performance Parts,** 1715 N. Farmersville, Farmersville, CA 93223: Catalog $5 ◆ Kit car accessories and high-tech parts. 800-274-8337; 209-733-8222 (in CA).

**Heidt's Hot Rod Shop,** 1345 N. Old Rand Rd., Wauconda, FL 60084: Free catalog ◆ Front suspension kits. 800-841-8188; 847-487-0150 (in IL). www.heidts.com

**Hi-Tech Motorsports,** 2204 W. Southern Ave., Tempe, AZ 85282: Free catalog ◆ Cobra accessories. 602-431-9400.

**Moto-Lita/Finish Line,** 2601 S. Bayshore Dr., Ste. 700, Miami, FL 33133: Free brochure ◆ Parts and steering wheels for most custom and kit cars. 305-854-4585.

**Smiths Instruments,** 850 Fiero Ln., San Luis Obispo, CA 93401: Free catalog ◆ Replica gauges. 800-444-5247.

**Speedway Motors,** P.O. Box 81906, Lincoln, NE 68501: Catalog $5 ◆ Kit car parts and accessories. 402-474-4411.

**Total Performance Inc.,** 400 S. Orchard, Wallingford, CT 06492: Catalog $5 ◆ Components and accessories. 800-243-6740.

## Rubber Parts & Weatherstripping

**A & M Soffseal Inc.,** 104 May Dr., Harrison OH 45030: Catalog $3 (request list of retail sources) ◆ Weatherstripping and rubber detail parts for 1955 and later General Motors cars and 1962 to 1974 Chrysler Performance A, B, and E bodies. 800-426-0902.

**Dennis Carpenter Reproductions,** P.O. Box 26398, Charlotte, NC 28221: Catalog $3 (specify year) ◆ Rubber parts for 1932 to 1964 Fords, 1958 to 1966 Thunderbirds, and 1960 to 1965 Falcons. 219-335-2425.

**Gateway Reproductions,** 411 High Gear Dr., Winfield, MO 63389: Free catalog ◆ Rubber parts for most American cars. 800-437-8787.

**Karr Rubber Mfg.,** 133 Lolita St., El Segundo, CA 90245: Catalog $5 ◆ Reproduction rubber extrusions. 800-955-5277; 310-322-1993 (in CA).

**Metro Moulded Parts Inc.,** 11610 Jay St., P.O. Box 33130, Minneapolis, MN 55433: Catalog $3 ◆ Rubber reproduction parts for most American and foreign cars and trucks, from 1929 to 1970. 800-878-2237.

**Lynn H. Steele Rubber Products,** 6180 Hwy. 150 East, Denver, NC 28037: Catalog $2 (specify car) ◆ Reproduction rubber parts for Cadillac, Packard, Chrysler, Chevrolet, Buick, Oldsmobile, and Pontiac cars and Chevrolet trucks. 800-544-8665; 704-483-9343 (in NC).

## Runningboards & Fenders

**Fibreglas Unlimited,** Box 41198, St. Petersburg, FL 33743: Free list ◆ Front and rear fenders. 813-345-2647.

**J & J Enterprises,** 5498 Mission Blvd., Ontario, CA 91762: Free catalog ◆ Running boards. 800-367-4961; 909-628-5679 (in CA). www.j-jent.com

**L & L Antique Auto Trim,** 403 Spruce, Box 177, Pierce City, MO 65723: Free information (specify type of car and model) ◆ Reproduction of original runningboard moldings. 417-476-2871.

**R & R Fiberglass,** 4850 Wilson Dr., Cleveland, TN 37312: Free price list ◆ Fenders and runningboards. 423-476-2270.

## Seat & Body Covers

**A-Cover,** Mark Savran, 965 W. River St., Milford, CT 06460: Free information ◆ Instant car storage garage with double zipper front and solid back panel. 800-426-8004.

**Anything Car Covers Ltd.,** 11431 Santa Monica, West Los Angeles, CA 90025: Free information ◆ Car covers for small, medium, and large cars. Also for most vans and trucks. 800-445-4048.

**Autoxtra California,** 1624 Wilshire Blvd., Santa Monica, CA 90403: Free information ◆ Custom fit car covers, 1918 to 1996. 800-331-9872. autoxtra@earthlink.NET

**Beverly Hills Motoring Accessories,** 200 S. Robertson Blvd., Beverly Hills, CA 90211: Free catalog ◆ Car covers. 800-421-0911; 562-657-4800 (in CA).

**Boulevard Motoring Accessories,** 7033 Topanga Canyon Blvd., Canoga Park, CA 91303: Catalog $3 ◆ Sheepskin seat covers, car covers, and automotive accessories. 800-325-0022; 818-883-9696 (in CA).

**California Car Cover Company,** 9525 DeSoto Ave., Chatsworth, CA 91311: Free information ◆ Custom fit car covers. 800-423-5525.

**Canvas Shoppe Inc.,** 3198½ S. Dye Rd., Flint, MI 48507: Free catalog ◆ Lightweight water-resistant car covers. 800-345-3670.

**Car Cover Pros,** 11431 Santa Monica Blvd., West Los Angeles, CA 90025: Free brochure ◆ Car covers. 800-221-9872.

**CarCovers USA,** 200 S. Robertson, Beverly Hills, CA 90211: Free information ◆ Car covers. 800-872-6837.

**Classic Motoring Accessories,** 146 W. Pomona Ave., Monrovia, CA 91016: Catalog $3 ◆ Car covers. 800-327-3045.

**Cover-Up Enterprises,** 1444 Manor Ln., Blue Bell, PA 19422: Free information ◆ Covers for most cars, trucks, vans, motorcycles, and other automotive vehicles. 800-268-3757.

**Fleetfoot Industries,** 2680 Blake St., Denver, CO 80205: Catalog $3.50 (refundable) ◆ Front end covers for cars and trucks. 800-503-2727.

**Bill Hirsch,** 396 Littleton Ave., Newark, NJ 07103: Free information ◆ Car covers and convertible tops. 800-828-2061; 973-642-2404 (in NJ). www.hirschauto.com

**Kanter Auto Parts,** 76 Monroe St., Boonton, NJ 07005: Free catalog ◆ Fitted seat cover and upholstery kits for most American cars, from 1932 to 1980. 973-334-9575. www.kanter.com

**MacNeil Automotive Products Ltd.,** 2435 Wisconsin St., Downers Grove, IL 60515: Free information ◆ Seat covers and floor mats. 800-441-6287. www.macneilauto.com

**McCullough's Automotive Products,** 15102 Bolsa Chica St., Huntington Beach, CA 92649: Free information ◆ Car covers, convertible tops, carpets, and upholstery sets. 800-395-9624; 714-897-9768 (in CA).

**Multisheep,** 646 S. Hauser Blvd., Los Angeles, CA 90036: Free information ◆ Sheepskin seat covers for most cars. 800-532-1222.

**New England Auto Accessories Inc.,** 2984 E. Main St., Waterbury, CT 06705: Catalog $3 ◆ Car and sheepskin seat covers and accessories. 800-732-2761; 203-573-1504 (in CT).

**Pine Ridge Enterprise,** 13165 Center Rd., Bath, MI 48808: Free brochure ◆ Easy-to-use dust-free car and motorcycle covers. 800-522-7224.

**Superior Seat Covers,** 2954 NW 72nd Ave., Miami, FL 33122: Free information ◆ Easy-to-install seat covers. 800-2-COVERS.

## Seats

**Keiper-Recaro Inc.,** 905 W. Maple Rd., Clawson, MI 48017: Free information ◆ Orthopaedically designed car seats. 800-873-2276.

**PAR Seating Specialists,** 310 Main St., New Rochelle, NY 10802: Free catalog ◆ Office chairs and automotive seats. 800-367-7270.

**ProAm, The Seat Warehouse,** 6125 Richmond, Houston, TX 77057: Free catalog ◆ Car seats. 800-847-5712.

**Relaxo-Back Inc.,** P.O. Box 2613, Anderson, IN 46018: Free information ◆ Form-fitting auxiliary seat that can be used to relieve lower back pain. 800-527-5496.

## Security Systems (Manufacturers)

**American Autosecurity Equipment,** 236 E. Star of India Ln., Carson, CA 90746: Free brochure ◆ Do-it-yourself car alarms. 310-538-4670.

**Auto Page,** 1815 W. 205th St., Ste. 101, Torrance, CA 90501: Free information ◆ Automotive security systems. 800-423-6687.

**Autotech Distributing Inc.,** 4291 Holland Rd., Ste. 576, Virginia Beach, VA 23452: Free brochure ◆ A plug-in anti-theft system with optional under the dash or dash mount, with removable 16-pin plug. Disarms 2 electrical or electronic circuits for full anti-theft protection. 757-631-8222.

**Avitrol Technologies Inc.,** 1535 Barclay Blvd., Buffalo Grove, IL 60089: Free brochure ◆ Vehicle security systems and accessories, keyless entry aids, and remote energy starters. 800-253-0334; 847-215-2233 (in IL).

**Kenwood,** P.O. Box 22745, Long Beach, CA 90801: Free information ◆ Automotive security systems. 800-536-9663. www.kenwood.net

**Radio Shack,** Division Tandy Corp., One Tandy Center, Fort Worth, TX 76102: Free information ◆ Automotive security systems. 817-390-3011. www.radioshack.com

**Sansui USA,** 200 Metroplex Dr., Edison, NJ 08817: Free information ◆ Automotive security systems. 732-460-9710.

**Wolo Manufacturing Corp.,** 1 Saxwood St., Deer Park, NY 11729: Free list of retail sources ◆ Electronic-operated security/alarm system with a key-lock. 800-991-9656.

## Security Systems (Retailers)

**Grant Products,** 700 Allen Ave., Glendale, CA 91201: Catalog $3 ◆ Steering wheels, covers, and security products. 800-952-6947; 213-849-3171 (in CA).

**Spectre Security Systems,** 843 Dumont Pl., #22, Rochester Hills, MI 48307: Free information ◆ Home and automotive security systems. 248-652-8117.

## Steering Wheels

**Automotive Specialties,** 11240 E. Sligh Ave., Seffner, FL 33584: Free information ◆ Steering wheel restorations. 800-676-1928.

**Bighorn Sheepskin Company,** 4810 Hwy. 90 East, San Antonio, TX 78219: Free information ◆ Sheepskin steering wheel covers. 800-992-1650.

**J.B. Donaldson Company,** 2533 W. Cypress St., Phoenix, AZ 85009: Brochure $2 (specify year) ◆ Recast steering wheels. 602-278-4505.

**Grant Products,** 700 Allen Ave., Glendale, CA 91201: Catalog $3 ◆ Steering wheels, covers, and security products. 800-952-6947; 213-849-3171 (in CA).

**Moto-Lita Inc.,** 503 Corporate Square, 1500 NW 62nd St., Fort Lauderdale, FL 33309: Free brochure ◆ Steering wheels for most American, European, Japanese, custom and kit cars, and sport trucks. 305-776-2748.

**Bill Peters,** 41 Vassar Pl., Rockville Centre, NY 11570: Free information with long SASE ◆ Steering wheel restoration services. 516-766-8397.

## Stereo Equipment (Manufacturers)

**Aiwa America Inc.,** 800 Corporate Dr., Mahwah, NJ 07430: Free information ◆ Stereo receivers. 800-289-2492. www.aiwa.com

**Alpine Electronics of America,** 19145 Gramercy Pl., Torrance, CA 90505: Free list of retail sources ◆ Car audio and navigation systems. 800-ALPINE-1. www.alpine1.com

**Blaupunkt,** 2800 S. 25th Ave., Broadview, IL 60153: Free information ◆ Stereo receivers. 630-865-5200.

**Clarion Corp. of America,** 661 W. Redondo Beach Blvd., Gardena, CA 90247: Free information ◆ Sound systems. 800-487-9007.

**Denon America,** 222 New Rd., Parsippany, NJ 07054: Free information ◆ Stereo receivers. 201-575-7810.

**Fujitsu America,** 2801 Telecom Pkwy., Richardson, TX 75082: Free information ◆ Stereo receivers. 800-955-9926.

**Harman/Kardon,** 250 Crossways Park Dr., Woodbury, NY 11797: Free information ◆ Audio and stereo in-dash receivers and cassette tuners, amplifiers, and other equipment. 800-645-7484. www.harmankardon.com

**Hitachi Sales Corp.,** Customer Service, 3890 Steve Reynolds Blvd., Norcross, GA 30093: Free information ◆ Stereo receivers. 800-241-6558.

**Jensen,** 25 Tri-State International Office Center, #400, Lincolnshire, IL 60069: Free information ◆ Stereo receivers. 800-677-6863.

**JVC,** 41 Slater Dr., Elmwood Park, NJ 07407: Free information ◆ Stereo receivers. 800-252-5722. www.jvc-america.com

**Kenwood,** P.O. Box 22745, Long Beach, CA 90801: Free information ◆ Audio and stereo sound systems. 800-536-9663. www.kenwood.net

**Marantz America Inc.,** 440 Medinah Rd., Roselle, IL 60172: Free information ◆ Stereo receivers. 630-307-3100. www.marantz.com

**Mitsubishi Electronics,** 5757 Plaza Dr., Cypress, CA 90630: Free information ◆ Stereo receivers. 800-843-2515.

**Panasonic,** Panasonic Way, Secaucus, NJ 07094: Free information ◆ Stereo receivers. 201-348-7000. www.panasonic.com

**Pioneer Technologies,** P.O. Box 1760, Long Beach, CA 90801: Free information ◆ Stereo receivers. 800-746-6337. www.pioneerelectronics.com

**Radio Shack,** Division Tandy Corp., One Tandy Center, Fort Worth, TX 76102: Free information ◆ Stereo receivers. 817-390-3011. www.radioshack.com

**Sansui USA,** 200 Metroplex Dr., Edison, NJ 08817: Free information ◆ Audio and stereo sound systems and removable cassette receivers. 732-460-9710.

**Sanyo Fisher,** P.O. Box 2329, Chatsworth, CA 91313: Free information ◆ Stereo receivers. 818-998-7322.

**Sharp Electronics,** Sharp Plaza, Mahwah, NJ 07496: Free information ◆ Stereo receivers. 800-BE-SHARP. www.sharp-usa.com

**Sherwood,** 14830 Alondra Blvd., La Mirada, CA 90638: Free information ◆ Stereo receivers. 800-962-3203.

**Sony Consumer Products,** 1 Sony Dr., Park Ridge, NJ 07656: Free information ◆ Stereo receivers. 201-930-1000. www.sony.com

**Technics,** One Panasonic Way, Secaucus, NJ 07094: Free list of retail sources ◆ Stereo receivers. 201-348-7000. www.panasonic.com

**Toshiba,** 82 Totowa Rd., Wayne, NJ 07470: Free information ◆ Stereo receivers. 201-628-8000. www.toshiba.com/tacp

**Yamaha,** P.O. Box 6660, Buena Park, CA 90620: Free information ◆ Audio and stereo receivers. 800-492-6242. www.yamaha-motor.com

## Stereo Equipment (Retailers)

**The Classic Car Radio,** 2718 Koper Dr., Sterling Heights, MI 48310: Free information ◆ Radios with FM conversion. 810-977-7979.

**Crutchfield,** 1 Crutchfield Park, Charlottesville, VA 22906: Free catalog ◆ Stereo equipment. 800-955-9009. www.crutchfield.com

**Crystal Sonics,** 1638 S. Central Ave., Glendale, CA 91204: Catalog $2 ◆ Stereo equipment. 800-545-7310; 818-240-7310 (in CA).

**Custom Autosound,** 808 W. Vermont Ave., Anaheim, CA 92805: Free catalog ◆ Custom radios for classic cars and trucks with no modifications to original dash opening. 800-888-8637.

**S.B.H. Enterprises,** 1678 53rd St., Brooklyn, NY 11204: Free information ◆ Radar detectors and car stereo systems. 800-451-5851; 718-438-1027 (in NY).

**The Sound Approach,** 6067 Jericho Tnpk., Commack, NY 11725: Free information ◆ Home electronics and car audio systems. 800-368-2344.

**Sound Move Inc.,** 217 S. Main St., Elkhart, IN 46516: Free information ◆ Easy-to-install in-dash radios for classic cars and trucks. 800-901-0222. www.soundmove.com

**Wholesale Connection,** 361 Charles St., West Hempstead, NY 11552: Free information ◆ Camcorders, other video accessories, and audio, car stereo, and home theater equipment. 800-967-5588.

## Tires

**Antique Automotive Accessories,** P.O. Box 19041, Topeka, KS 66619: Free information ◆ Radial tires for classic cars. 800-742-6777.

**Classic Tires of America Inc.,** 1075 Old Farm Rd., Middletown, PA 17057: Free information ◆ Tires. 717-944-7650.

**Coker Tires,** 1317 Chestnut St., Chattanooga, TN 37402: Free catalog ◆ Original tires. 800-251-6336; 423-265-6368 (in TN). www.coker.com

**Discount Tire Direct,** 7333 E. Helm Dr., Scottsdale, AZ 85260: Free information (specify car) ◆ Tires and wheels for most domestic and imported cars. 800-790-6444.

**Euro-Tire Inc.,** 500 Rt. 46, Fairfield, NJ 07004: Free catalog ◆ European tires, light alloy wheels, and shock absorbers. 800-631-0080; 201-575-0080 (in NJ).

**Exotic Tires International,** 161 LaSalle Rd., Oak Ridge, TN 37830: Free information ◆ Tires. 800-729-0367. www.exotictires.com

**Kelsey Tire Inc.,** Box 564, Camdenton, MO 65020: Free information ◆ Tires and tubes for vintage automobiles. 800-325-0091.

**Lucas Automotive,** 2850 Temple Ave., Long Beach, CA 90806: Free catalog ◆ Antique and classic tires. 800-952-4333.

**Snyder's Antique Auto Parts,** 12925 Woodworth Rd., New Springfield, OH 44443: Catalog $1 ◆ Tires. 216-519-5313.

**Ken Thorpe,** P.O. Box 230244, Portland, OR 97233: Free information ◆ Tires. 503-590-8550.

**Tire Rack,** 771 W. Chippewa Ave., South Bend, IN 46614: Brochure $3 (specify car) ◆ Tires and wheels for most domestic and imported cars. 888-370-8473; 219-287-2345 (in IN). www.tirerack.com

**Universal Tire Company,** 987 Stony Battery Rd., Lancaster, PA 17601: Free list of retail sources ◆ Antique and classic tires and wheel hardware. 800-233-3827. www.universaltire.com

**Vintage Tire,** 25700 Solan Rd., Bedford Heights, OH 44146: Free information ◆ Tires. 800-225-8473.

**Wallace W. Wade Specialty Tires,** P.O. Box 560906, Dallas, TX 75356: Free information ◆ Antique and classic automobile tires. 800-666-TYRE; 972-688-0091 (in TX).

**Willies Antique Tires,** 5257 W. Diversey Ave., Chicago, IL 60639: Free price list ◆ Tires for antique cars. 773-622-4037.

## Tools

**A & I Supply,** 401 Radio City Dr., North Pekin, IL 61554: Free catalog ◆ Electric and air-operated tools, special-purpose tools, welders, and compressors. 800-260-2647.

**Daytona Manufacturing,** 1821 Holsonback Dr., Daytona Beach, FL 32117: Free information ◆ Welding equipment. 800-331-9353.

**Eastwood Company,** 580 Lancaster Ave., P.O. Box 3014, Malvern, PA 19355: Free catalog ◆ Welding tools, rust removers, sand blasting equipment, body repair tools, pin striping equipment, and buffing supplies. 800-343-9353. www.ewab.com

**Gearbox Grannie's,** 5161 Wolpen-Pleasant Hill Rd., Milford, OH 45150: Free catalog ◆ Specialty tools, books, gifts, and collectibles. 800-831-6137. www.trimparts.com

**Griot's Garage,** 3500-A 20th St. East, Tacoma, WA 98424: Free catalog ◆ Automotive tools, storage cabinets, workbenches, and diagnostic equipment. 800-345-5789.

**Harbor Freight Tools,** 3491 Mission Oaks Blvd., Camarillo, CA 93011: Free catalog ◆ Tools and accessories. 800-444-3353. www.harborfreight.com

**HTP America Inc.,** 261 Woodwork Ln., Palatine, IL 60067: Free information ◆ Welding equipment. 800-USA-WELD.

**Production Tool Supply of Ohio,** 10801 Brookpark Rd., Cleveland, OH 44130: Free catalog ◆ Hand and power tools, shop supplies, and accessories. 800-362-0142; 216-265-0000 (in OH).

**Skyway Tool Company,** 1401 Mangrove Ave., Chico, CA 95926: Free information ◆ Tools. 915-891-1495.

**Tip Tools & Equipment,** P.O. Box 649, Canfield, OH 44406: Free catalog ◆ Automotive power tools. 800-321-9260. www.tiptools.com

**Tools Plus,** 167 North Rd., Troy, OH 45373: Free information ◆ Pressure-type sandblasters. 800-288-6829; 513-339-6829 (in OH).

## Trailers & Recreational Vehicles

**Atwood Mobile Products,** 4750 Hiawatha Dr., Rockford, IL 61103: Free information ◆ Trailers, appliances, engineered components, and systems for recreational vehicles and boats. 815-877-5700.

**Camper's Choice,** 502 4th St. NW, P.O. Box 1546, Red Bay, AL 35582: Free catalog ◆ Trailer accessories and outdoor camping equipment. 800-833-6713. www.caperschoice.com

**Casita Travel Trailers,** 3030 S. McKinney, Rice, TX 75155: Free brochure ◆ All-fiberglass self-contained trailers. 800-442-9986.

**Chinook Motorhomes,** P.O. Box 2589, Yakima, WA 98907: Free list of retail sources ◆ Motorhomes. 800-552-8886.

**Classic Manufacturing,** 21900 US 12, Sturgis, MI 49091: Free brochure ◆ Race car, cargo, and other trailers. 616-651-9319.

**Coachmen Recreational Vehicle Company,** P.O. Box 30, Middlebury, IN 46540: Free information ◆ Fifth wheels and travel trailers. 219-825-5821.

**Correct Craft,** 6100 S. Orange Ave., Orlando, FL 32809: Free information ◆ Boat trailers. 800-346-2092; 407-855-4141 (in FL).

**D & D Trailers Inc.,** 100 Lexington Ave., Trenton, NJ 08618: Free information ◆ Custom built car transporters and utility trailers. 609-771-0001.

**Fleetwood Enterprises Inc.,** P.O. Box 92919, Milwaukee, WI 53202: Free list of retail sources ◆ Mini-vans and recreational vehicles. 800-444-4905.

**Glen-L Trailers,** 9152 Rosecrans, Box 1804, Bellflower, CA 90706: Catalog $1 ◆ Plans and kits for campers and travel trailers. 562-630-6258.

**Hi-Lo Trailer Company,** 145 Elm St., Butler, OH 44822: Free information ◆ Folding travel trailers. 800-337-6482.

**Highland Group Industries,** 31200 Solon Rd., Solon, OH 44139: Free catalog ◆ Towing and travel accessories, tie-downs, and car top, bike, and ski carriers. 216-498-0001.

**Holiday Rambler Corp.,** P.O. Box 465, Wakarusa, IN 46573: Free information ◆ Motor homes. 219-862-7211.

**Intraser Inc.,** 428 N. La Cienega Blvd., Los Angeles, CA 90048: Free information ◆ New and pre-owned motorcycles, ATVs, snowmobiles, trailers, personal water vehicles, and small boats. 213-652-6966.

**Lazy B Trailer Sales Inc.,** 6040 State Rt. 45, Bristoville, OH 44402: Free information ◆ Automotive trailers. 800-424-5110; 330-889-2353 (in OH). www.lazybtrailera.com

**Omnifac Corp.,** 1700 E. Whipp Rd., Dayton, OH 45440: Free information ◆ Battery and AC monitors and polarity indicators, bilge pump monitors, and electronic digital clocks for recreational vehicles and on-board boats. 937-434-8400.

**Overlander Outfitters,** 5592 Buckingham, Dr., Huntington Beach, CA 92649: Catalog $4 ◆ Sport utility equipment and accessories. 800-288-4068. www.overlander.com

**Pierce Sales,** Rt. 1, Box 3A, Henrietta, TX 76365: Catalog $1 ◆ Cargo, runabouts, horse and stock trailers, and truck beds. 940-538-5646.

**Play-Mor Trailers Inc.,** P.O. Box 128, Westphalia, MO 65085: Free information ◆ Multi-purpose recreational vehicles. 573-455-2322.

**Richlund Sales,** 75695 Hwy. 1053, Kentwood, LA 70444: Free information ◆ Icemaker, central vacuum system, trash compactor, rear vision camera, electric heat equipment, combination washer-dryer, and other recreational vehicle appliances. 504-229-4922.

**S & H Trailer Manufacturing Company,** 800 Industrial Dr., Madill, OK 73446: Free information ◆ Recreational vehicles and horse, cargo, utility, and carryall trailers with optional features. 405-795-5577.

**Scamp Eveland's Inc.,** Box 2, Backus, MN 56435: Free brochure ◆ Trailers. 800-346-4962; 800-432-3749 (in MN).

**Silverado Trailers,** 632 Shelley St., Springfield, OR 97477: Free list of retail sources ◆ Living quarters, horse, and combination trailers. 800-644-7155. www.silveradotrailers.com

**Sooner Trailers,** 1515 McCurdy, Duncan, OK 73533: Free information ◆ Horse trailers. 405-255-6979. www.soonertrailers.com

**Sunnybrook RV Inc.,** 11756 County Rd. 14, Middlebury, IN 46540: Free information ◆ Recreational vehicles. 219-825-5250.

**Teton Homes,** P.O. Box 2349, Mills, WY 82644: Free information ◆ Fifth wheel motorhomes. 307-235-1525.

**Trailer World,** P.O. Box 1687, Bowling Green, KY 42102: Free catalog ◆ Enclosed and open car trailers, vendor trailers, and parts. 800-872-2833; 502-843-4587 (in KY).

**Trailers of New England,** Rt. 20, Palmer, MA 01069: Free information ◆ Wells Cargo and open car trailers. 800-628-9982; 413-289-1211 (in MA).

**Trailex,** 60 Industrial Park Dr., P.O. Box 553, Canfield, OH 44406: Free brochure ◆ Boat trailers. 800-282-5042.

**Transport Designs Inc.,** 240 Streibeigh Ln., Montoursville, PA 17754: Free information ◆ Enclosed car trailers. 717-368-1403.

**Veri-Lite Inc.,** 22540 Pine Creek Rd., P.O. Box 339, Elkhart, IN 46515: Free information ◆ Truck campers. 219-295-8313.

**Wells Cargo Inc.,** P.O. Box 728-1178, Elkhart, IN 46514: Free information ◆ Concession, car, and display trailers. 800-348-7553. www.wellscargo.com

## Truck Parts

**Accessoryland Truckin' Supplies,** Hwy. 151 & 61 South, 10723 Rt. 61, Dubuque, IA 52003: Free information ◆ NOS, reproduction, and used accessories and parts for Chevrolet and GMC trucks, from the 1930s to the present. 319-556-5482.

**Alley Auto Parts,** Rt. 2, Box 551, Immokalee, FL 33934: Inventory list $4 ◆ Parts for cars and trucks, from 1948 to 1975. 813-657-3541.

**Alotta Auto Parts,** 8426 Upper Miamisburg Rd., Miamisburg, OH 45342: Free information ◆ NOS, used car, and light truck parts, from the 1950s to 1960s. 513-866-1849.

**American Auto & Truck Dismantlers,** 12172 Truman St., San Fernando, CA 91340: Free information ◆ Parts for General Motors trucks, 1955 to 1957 Chevrolets, 1967 to 1989 Camaros, and 1964 to 1972 Chevelles. 818-365-3908.

**American Classic Truck Parts Inc.,** P.O. Box 50286, Denton, TX 76206: Catalog $4 (specify year) ◆ Chevrolet and GMC truck parts, from 1936 to 1959 and 1960 to 1972. 940-365-9786.

**Antique Auto Parts et al,** 9103 E. Garvey Ave., Rosemead, CA 91770: Free information with long SASE (enclose want list) ◆ Parts and accessories for 1903 to 1931 cars and trucks. 818-288-2121.

**Auto Body Specialties Inc.,** Rt. 66, P.O. Box 455, Middlefield, CT 06455: Catalog $5 ◆ Ford, Chevrolet, and Dodge truck body parts, from 1949 to 1992. 860-346-4989.

**B & T Truck Parts,** P.O. Box 799, Siloam Springs, AR 72761: Catalog $4 ◆ Chevrolet and GMC truck parts, from 1960 to 1966. 501-524-5959.

**B & W Antique Auto Parts,** 4653 Guide Meridian Rd., Bellingham, WA 98226: Catalog $5 (specify year and model) ◆ Chevrolet and GMC truck parts, 1936 to 1972. 800-561-4622.

**Paul Barry,** 6152 Cazadero Hwy., P.O. Box 364, Cazadero, CA 95421: Free information ◆ Parts for Willys Overland Jeeps and trucks. 707-632-5590.

**Bartnik Sales & Service,** 6524 Van Dyke, Cass City, MI 48726: Free information ◆ Parts for trucks and cars, from 1960 to 1970. 517-872-3541.

**Daryl Bensinger,** 2442 Main St., Narvon, PA 17555: Free information ◆ Parts for military Jeeps and trucks. 610-286-9545.

**Andy Bernbaum Auto Parts,** 315 Franklin St., Newton, MA 02158: Catalog $4 ◆ Parts for Dodge and Plymouth trucks. 617-244-1118.

**Brothers Truck Parts,** 5670 Schaefer Ave., Unit G, Chino, CA 91708: Catalog $4 ◆ Chevrolet and GMC truck parts, from 1947 to 1972. 800-977-2767.

**C & P Chevy Parts,** Box 348, Kulpsville, PA 19443: Catalog $3 ◆ Restoration supplies for 1955 to 1959 Chevrolet trucks. 800-235-2475.

**Canyon Classics,** P.O. Box 1111, Black Canyon City, AZ 85324: Free information ◆ Used truck and auto parts for the Cadillac, Ford, Lincoln, and Mercury. 800-571-1488. www.dzat.com

**Carolina Classics,** 624 E. Geer St., Durham, NC 27701: Catalog $3 ◆ Ford truck parts, from 1948 to 1966. 919-682-4211.

**Dennis Carpenter Reproductions,** P.O. Box 26398, Charlotte, NC 28221: Catalog $3 (specify year) ◆ Parts for Ford pickups. 219-335-2425.

**Jim Carter Antique Truck Parts,** 1500 E. Alton, Independence, MO 64055: Catalog $2.50 ◆ Chevrolet and GMC truck parts, from 1934 to 1972. 800-336-1913; 816-833-1913 (in MO).

**Chev's of the 40's,** 2027 B St., Washougal, WA 98671: Catalog $3.75 ◆ Parts for Chevrolet trucks, from 1937 to 1954. 800-999-2438.

**Chevy Duty Pickup Parts,** 4319 NW Gateway, Kansas City, MO 64150: Catalog $3 ◆ Restoration supplies for 1947 to 1972 Chevrolet and GMC pickups. 816-741-8029.

**Chevy Parts Warehouse,** 13545 Sycamore Ave., San Martin, CA 95046: Free information ◆ Parts for 1955 to 1966 Chevrolets, 1947 to 1972 pickups, 1964 to 1972 Chevelles and El Caminos, 1962 to 1974 Novas, and 1967 to 1973 Camaros. 408-683-2438.

**Chevyland,** 3667 Recycle Rd., Rancho Cordova, CA 95742: Catalog $4 ◆ Chevrolet truck parts and accessories, from 1967 to 1972. 800-624-6490; 800-624-8756 (in CA).

**Classic Tube,** 80 Rotech Dr., Lancaster, NY 14086: Catalog $1 ◆ Brake, fuel, and transmission lines for collector cars and trucks. 800-TUBES-1; 716-759-1800 (in NY).

**Cliff's Classic Chevrolet Parts Company,** 619 SE 202nd, P.O. Box 16739, Portland, OR 97216: Catalog $5 ◆ Used, new, and reproduction parts for 1955 to 1959 Chevrolet trucks. 503-667-4329.

**Concours Parts & Accessories,** 3563 Numancia St., P.O. Box 1210, Santa Ynez, CA 93460: Catalog $4 ◆ Parts for 1948 to 1966 Ford trucks. 805-688-7795.

**Dakota Studebaker Parts,** 39408 280th St., Armour, SD 57313: Free information ◆ Parts for cars, pickups, and trucks, from 1936 to 1964. 605-724-2527.

**Dearborn Classics,** P.O. Box 1248, Sunset Beach, CA 90742: Catalog $4 ◆ Ford Ranchero parts and accessories. 562-372-3175.

**Desert Muscle Cars,** 2853 N. Stone Ave., Tucson, AZ 85705: Free information ◆ Restoration parts and supplies for 1955 to 1970 Chevrolets, 1967 to 1981 Camaros, 1964 to 1972 Chevelles, and 1947 to 1972 Chevrolet trucks. 520-882-3010.

**Desert Valley Auto Parts,** 22500 N. 21st Ave., Phoenix, AZ 85027: Free information ◆ Hard-to-find and classic car parts, from the 1950s to 1980s. 602-780-8024.

**Don's Antique Auto Parts,** 37337 Niles Blvd., Fremont, CA 94536: Free information ◆ Parts, up to 1954, for most cars and trucks. 415-792-4390.

**Doug's Auto Parts,** Hwy. 59 North, Box 811, Marshall, MN 56258: Free information ◆ Ford truck parts, from 1932 to 1948. 507-537-1487.

**E & J Used Auto & Truck Parts,** 315 31st Ave., P.O. Box 6007, Rock Island, IL 61204: Free information ◆ Parts for most American and foreign cars and trucks, from 1940 to 1987. 800-728-7686; 309-788-7686 (in IL).

**Eaton Detroit Spring,** 1555 Michigan, Detroit, MI 48216: Free information ◆ Springs, U-bolts, shackles, and parts for most American cars and trucks. 810-963-3839.

**Fiberglass & Wood Company,** RR 2, Box 2150, Nashville, GA 31639: Catalog $4 (specify year) ◆ Chevrolet and GMC truck parts, from 1934 to 1984. 912-686-3838.

**Gilbert's Early Chevy Pickup Parts,** 470 RD 1 North, P.O. Box 1316, Chino Valley, AZ 86323: Catalog $2 (specify year) ◆ Chevrolet and GMC pickup parts, from 1947 to 1966. 602-636-5337.

**Golden State Pickup Parts,** P.O. Box 1019, Santa Ynez, CA 93460: Catalog $8.95 (specify year) ◆ Chevrolet and GMC truck parts, from 1947 to 1954, 1955 to 1966, 1967 to 1972, and 1973 to 1987. 800-235-5717;805-686-2020 (in CA).

**Harmon's Inc.,** P.O. Box 100, Hwy. 27 North, Geneva, IN 46740: Free catalog ◆ Chevrolet truck restoration parts, from 1947 to 1980. 219-368-7221. www.harmons.com

**Heavy Chevy Truck Parts,** P.O. Box 650, Siloam Springs, AR 72761: Catalog $2 ◆ Parts for 1948 to 1959 GMC and Chevrolet trucks. 800-317-2277; 501-524-9575 (in AR).

**Bruce Horkey Cabinetry,** Rt. 4, Box 188, Windom, MN 56101: Catalog $2 ◆ Wood and other parts for 1934 to 1992 Chevrolet, 1939 to 1985 Dodge, and 1928 to 1992 Ford pickups. 507-831-5625.

**J & J Enterprises,** 5498 Mission Blvd., Ontario, CA 91762: Free catalog ◆ Handcrafted stainless and chrome accessories for light trucks and sport utilities. 800-367-4961; 909-628-5679 (in CA). www.j-jent.com

**Joblot Automotive,** 98-11 211th St., Queens Village, NY 11429: Catalog $2 ◆ Parts for 1928 to 1948 Ford cars and trucks. 800-221-0172; 718-468-8585 (in NY).

**Kenroy Ford Parts,** 2 Folwell Ln., Mullica Hill, NJ 08062: Free information ◆ NOS parts for Ford, Mercury, Lincoln, Thunderbird, and Mustang cars. Also for Ford trucks. 609-478-2527.

**Dale King Obsolete Parts Inc.,** P.O. Box 1099, Liberty, KY 42539: Free information ◆ NOS and reproduction Ford truck parts. 606-787-5031.

**Lakeview Vintage Ford Parts,** P.O. Box 95, Skaneateles, NY 13152: Free information ◆ Reproduction parts for 1928 to 1960 Ford pickups. 315-685-7414.

**LMC Truck,** P.O. Box 14991, Lenexa, KS 66285: Free catalog (specify year) ◆ Chevrolet truck parts and accessories, from 1947 to 1959, 1960 to 1972, and 1973 to 1987. 800-222-5664.

**Ron Manes,** 9904 E. 63rd Terrace, Raytown, MO 64133: Free information ◆ Parts for 1967 to 1972 Chevy and GMC trucks. 816-358-6745.

**Merv's Classic Chevy Parts,** 1330 Washington, Iowa Falls, IA 50126: Free information ◆ Used, reproduction, and NOS parts for 1955 to 1957 Chevrolets and 1967 to 1972 Chevrolet pickups. 515-648-3168.

**Midland Automotive Products,** Rt. 1, Box 27, Midland City, AL 36350: Free information ◆ Reproduction and new Ford truck parts and accessories. 334-983-1212.

**Obsolete Chevrolet Parts Company,** P.O. Box 68, Nashville, GA 31639: Catalog $3 (specify year) ◆ Reproduction Chevrolet truck parts, from 1929 to 1959 and 1960 to 1972. 912-686-5812.

**Obsolete Ford Parts Company,** 311 E. Washington Ave., Nashville, GA 31639: Catalog $3 (specify year) ◆ Ford pickup parts for 1948 to 1956 and 1957 to 1972. 912-686-5812.

**Ole Chevy Store,** Division T & N Manufacturing Company, 2509 S. Cannon Blvd., Kannapolis, NC 28083: Free information ◆ Parts for 1947 to 1972 Chevrolet trucks. 704-938-2923.

**Performance Corner,** 150 Engineers Rd., Hauppage, NY 11788: Catalog $3 ◆ High performance automotive parts and truck accessories. 516-348-4493.

**Pioneer Classic Auto Inc.,** 2111 W. Deer Valley Rd., Phoenix, AZ 85027: Catalog $4 (specify year) ◆ New and used parts for 1947 to 1972 Chevrolet pickups. 602-993-5999.

**Roberts Motor Parts,** 17 Prospect St., West Newbury, MA 01985: Catalog $4 ◆ Chevrolet and GMC truck parts. 978-363-5881.

**Donald E. Schneider Marinette & Menominee,** RR 1, N7340 Miles Rd., Porterfield, WI 54159: Free information ◆ NOS parts for 1930 to 1969 trucks and cars. 715-732-4958.

**Sherman & Associates Inc.,** 28460 Groesbeck, Roseville, MI 48066: Catalog $5 ◆ Reproduction parts and panels for classic car and truck restorations. 810-774-8297.

**O.B. Smith Chevy Parts,** P.O. Box 11703, Lexington, KY 40577: Catalog $3 ◆ Parts for 1947 to 1972 Chevrolet trucks. 606-253-1957.

**Don Sumner-The Truck Shop,** P.O. Box 5035, 102 W. Marion Ave., Nashville, GA 31639: Catalog $5 ◆ Chevy and GMC truck parts, from 1927 to 1987. 800-245-0556.

**The Truck Shop,** 104 W. Marion Ave., P.O. Box 5035, Nashville, GA 31639: Catalog $3 ◆ Chevrolet truck parts from 1947 to 1954; 1955 to 1966; 1967 to 1972; and 1973 to 1980. 912-686-3833.

**Truck Shop Parts,** 739 N. Batavia, Orange, CA 92868: Catalog $3 (specify year) ◆ Parts for Chevrolet trucks, from 1947 to 1954, 1955 to 1966, and 1967 to 1972. 714-771-7871.

**Vintage Auto Parts Inc.,** 24300 Woodinville-Snohomish Hwy., Woodinville, WA 98072: Free information ◆ Parts, from 1916 to 1970, for American trucks and cars. 800-426-5911. vintageinc.@aol.com

**Vintage Ford & Chevrolet Parts of Arizona,** 3427 E. McDowell, Phoenix, AZ 85008: Ford catalog $2; Free Chevrolet price sheet ◆ Parts for 1948 to 1966 Fords and 1947 to 1972 Chevrolet trucks. 602-275-7990.

**Bill Wales,** 143 Center, Carleton, MI 48117: Free catalog with two 1st class stamps ◆ Chevrolet truck parts, from 1936 to 1972. 313-654-8836.

## Upholstery, Carpets & Tops

**ABC Auto Upholstery & Top Company,** 1634 Church St., Philadelphia, PA 19124: Free information ◆ Upholstery kits for 1954 to 1959 Fords. 215-289-0555.

**Auto Custom Carpets Inc.,** P.O. Box 1350, 1429 Noble St., Anniston, AL 36202: Free information ◆ Original-style carpets for General Motors, Chrysler, and Ford cars and trucks. 800-633-2358.

**G.W. Bartlett Company,** 1912 Granville Ave., Muncie, IN 47303: Free catalog ◆ Interior restoration parts. 800-338-8034.

**BAS Ltd. USA,** 250 H St., Unit 8110, Blaine, WA 98231: Free information ◆ Jaguar interiors. 800-661-5377.

**Carpet King,** P.O. Box 16303, Columbus, OH 43216: Free information ◆ Reproduction molded carpets. 800-826-4279.

**Denning Automotive,** P.O. Box 28, Springfield, NJ 07081: Catalog $5 ◆ Convertible top and carpet sets. 973-379-2335.

**Hampton Coach,** P.O. Box 6, Amesbury, MA 01913: Free information ◆ Upholstery and top kits. 888-388-8726.

**Bill Hirsch,** 396 Littleton Ave., Newark, NJ 07103: Free information ◆ Car covers and convertible tops. 800-828-2061; 973-642-2404 (in NJ). www.hirschauto.com

**Hydro-E-Lectric,** 48 Appleton, Auburn, MA 01501: Free information ◆ Top and window parts. 800-343-4261.

**Kanter Auto Parts,** 76 Monroe St., Boonton, NJ 07005: Free catalog ◆ Interior parts and accessories. 973-334-9575. www.kanter.com

**Al Knoch Interiors,** 130 Montoya Rd., El Paso, TX 79932: Free information ◆ Seat covers, carpet, door panels, convertible tops, and interiors for the Camaro, Corvette, and Pontiac Firebird. 800-880-8080.

**LeBaron Bonney Company,** P.O. Box 8, Amesbury, MA 01913: Catalog $1 ◆ Upholstery materials for antique, classic, and special interest cars. 800-221-5408.

**Legendary Auto Interiors Ltd.,** 121 W. Shore Blvd., Newark, NJ 14513: Catalog $5 ◆ Reproduction seat upholstery, door panels, and interior and exterior trim for 1957 to 1980 Chrysler, Dodge, and Plymouth cars. 800-363-8804.

**McCullough's Automotive Products,** 15102 Bolsa Chica St., Huntington Beach, CA 92649: Free information ◆ Car covers, convertible tops, carpets, and upholstery sets. 800-395-9624; 714-897-9768 (in CA).

**Midland Automotive Products,** Rt. 1, Box 27, Midland City, AL 36350: Free information ◆ Chevrolet carpeting, truck mats, landau tops, and convertible top pads. 334-983-1212.

**Original Auto Interiors,** 7869 Trumble Rd., Columbus, MI 48063: Catalog $2 ◆ Upholstery fabrics and original molded carpet sets. 810-727-2486.

**Original Interiors,** 6343 Seaview Ave. NW, Seattle, WA 98107: Free information ◆ NOS and OEM upholstery sets and restoration parts for the Falcon, Comet, and Ranchero. 800-400-6531.

**SMS Auto Fabrics,** 2325 SE 10th Ave., Portland, OR 97214: Free information ◆ Auto upholstery fabrics. 503-234-1175.

**Winross Restorations Upholstery Shop**, 2060 O'Neil Rd., Macedon, NY 14502: Free information ◆ Upholstery for antique automobiles. 315-986-7368.

**World Upholstery & Trim,** P.O. Box 4857, Thousand Oaks, CA 91359: Free information (specify model and year) ◆ Head liners, seat upholstery, and carpets for European cars. 800-222-9577.

## Wheels, Hubcaps, & Wheelcovers

**Agape Auto,** 2825 Selzer, Evansville, IN 47712: Free information ◆ Wheel covers from 1949 to 1980 and fender skirts from 1935 to 1972. 812-423-7332.

**Appleton Garage,** P.O. Box B, West Rockport, ME 04865: Free information ◆ New and used hubcaps and wheelcovers. 207-594-2062.

**Burr Nyberg Screw-On Hubcaps,** 200 Union Blvd., #425, Denver, CO 80228: Free information ◆ Reproduction screw-on hubcaps made from original patterns or drawings.

**Coker Tires,** 1317 Chestnut St., Chattanooga, TN 37402: Free catalog ◆ New wheels for muscle cars. 800-251-6336; 423-265-6368 (in TN). www.coker.com

**Dayton Wheel Products,** 1147 S. Broadway St., Dayton, OH 45408: Free information ◆ Wire wheels. 800-862-6000; 513-461-1707 (in OH).

**Discount Tire Direct,** 7333 E. Helm Dr., Scottsdale, AZ 85260: Free information (specify car) ◆ Tires and wheels for most domestic and imported cars. 800-790-6444.

**Early Wheel Company,** P.O. Box 1438, Santa Ynez, CA 93460: Free information ◆ Hubcaps and chromed or ready-to-paint wheels. 805-688-1187.

**Freedom Design Wheels,** 4750 Eisenhower Ave., Alexandria, VA 22034: Brochure $1 ◆ Special-designed wheels. 800-296-1792; 703-823-5606 (in VA).

**Giant Auto Wreckers Inc.,** 23944 Pine St., Newhall, CA 91321: Free information ◆ Used hubcaps and wheelcovers. 805-259-4678.

**House of Hubcaps,** 20034 Pacific Hwy. South, Seattle, WA 98198: Free information ◆ New and used hubcaps. 800-825-9715; 206-824-5040 (in WA).

**HRE Performance Wheels,** 2540 Pioneer Ave., Vista, CA 92083: Free information ◆ Aluminum wheels. 619-941-2008.

**Hubcap Capital,** P.O. Box 21949, Carson City, NV 89721: Free information with long SASE (specify items wanted) ◆ Hubcaps. 702-246-0220.

**Hubcap Jack Inc.,** 1330 Market St., Linwood, PA 19061: Free information ◆ Hubcaps and wheelcovers for cars, trucks, imports, and classics. 610-485-1155.

**The Hubcap & Wheel Store,** Rt. 22 & 4th St., Easton, PA 18042: Free information ◆ Used wheels and wheelcovers, from 1946 to 1995. 800-HUBCAPS.

**Motorsport Specialties Inc.,** 435A W. 4th St., Quarryville, PA 17566: Free information ◆ Wheels. 800-621-8408. www.usacomp.com

**Specialty Wheels Inc.,** 34566 SE Gunderson Rd., Sandy, OR 97055: Free information ◆ Reproduction and remanufactured wheels. 503-668-4793.

**Tire Rack,** 771 W. Chippewa Ave., South Bend, IN 46614: Brochure $3 (specify car) ◆ Tires and wheels for most domestic and imported cars. 888-370-8473; 219-287-2345 (in IN). www.tirerack.com

**Vintage Vehicles Inc.,** 8190 20th Dr., Wautoma, WI 54982: Free information ◆ Interior and exterior auto stainless moldings, beauty rings, head and taillights, radiator shells, and hubcaps. 414-787-2656.

**Wheel Repair Service Inc.,** 317 Southbridge St., Auburn, MA 01501: Free information ◆ Hubcaps and wheel covers for most cars, street rods, and replicas. Also wire spoke, alloy, and steel disc wheels. 508-832-4949.

**Wheel Vintiques,** 5468 E. Lamona, Fresno, CA 93727: Free information ◆ Wheels. 209-251-6957.

**Wheelcovers - Robinson's Auto Sales,** 200 New York Ave., New Castle, IN 47362: Free information ◆ Hubcaps, wheel covers, hubcap sets, and NOS and used parts. 765-529-7603.

## AWARDS & TROPHIES

**Alden Galleries,** 387 Washington St., Boston, MA 02108: Free catalog ◆ Personalized engraving and thermal printing on awards and plaques. 617-426-8222.

**Arnolds for Awards,** 3971 Durock Rd., Shingle Springs, CA 95682: Free information ◆ Recognition and promotional awards. 916-677-0623. arnolds@spider.lloyd.com

**Atelier Bernard Chaudron Inc.,** 2449 Chemin de l'Ile, Val-David, Quebec, Canada J0T 2N0: Free catalog ◆ Functional and artistic pewter, lamps, trophies, medals, sculptures, murals, and commissioned work. 819-322-3944.

**Award Company of America,** P.O. Box 2029, Tuscaloosa, AL 35403: Free brochure ◆ Plaques, acrylic awards, recognition certificates, badges, and awards. 800-633-2021.

**Award Pros,** 4175 US Rt. 1 South, Monmouth Junction, NJ 08852: Free catalog ◆ Trophies, plaques, advertising specialties, and imprinted activewear. 908-274-2255.

**Bale Company,** 222 Public St., Box 6400, Providence, RI 02940: Free catalog ◆ Pins, class and club school rings, academic and scholastic medals, athletic medals, novelties and charms, and other awards. 800-822-5350. www.bale.com

**Captain's Emporium,** 7855 Gross Point Rd., Skokie, IL 60077: Free information ◆ Trophies and gifts. 847-675-5411.

**Chicago Trophy & Awards Company,** 3255 N. Milwaukee Ave., Chicago, IL 60618: Free catalog ◆ Trophies and plaques. 800-621-8826; 312-685-8200 (in IL). award1@interaccess.com

**Classic Medallics,** 2-15 Borden Ave., Long Island City, NY 11101: Free information ◆ Letters, ribbons, cups, medals, emblems, pins, plaques, and other awards. 800-221-1348; 718-392-5410 (in NY). www.classic-medallics.com

**Cornette Ribbon & Trophy Company,** 850 Dunbar Ave., Oldsmar, FL 34677: Free catalog ◆ Ribbons, awards, and trophies. 800-869-0234; 813-854-2824 (in FL).

**Crown Trophy,** 1 Odell Plaza, Yonkers, NY 10701: Free information ◆ Letters, ribbons, cups, emblems, pins, plaques, and other awards. 800-227-1557; 914-963-0005 (in NY). www.crowntrophy.com

**Custom Glass Etching,** 1139 E. Las Tunas Dr., San Gabriel, CA 91776: Free catalog ◆ Personalized crystal glass awards, gifts, wedding gifts, and promotional products. 626-287-3775.

**Dern Trophy Corp.,** 267 Broad St., Westerville, OH 43081: Free catalog ◆ Trophies and plaques. 800-848-3988.

**Dinn Bros.,** 68 Winter St., P.O. Box 111, Holyoke, MA 01041: Free catalog ◆ Trophies, cups, medals, desk sets, hollowware items, and plaques. 413-536-3816. sales@dinntrophy.com

**Emblem & Badge Inc.,** P.O. Box 6226, Providence, RI 02940: Free information ◆ Trophies, trophy cases, plaques, medals, pins, and ribbons. 800-875-5444; 401-331-5444 (in RI). www.recognition.com

**Fantastic Glass,** 909 Walnut St., Emporia, KS 66801: Free catalog ◆ Carved glass awards and specialty gifts. 316-343-4877. www.Fantasticglass.com

**Feather's Plaques & Awards,** P.O. Box 84, 101 Market St., Newburg, WV 26410: Free catalog ◆ Cast bronze national register and award plaques. Also medallions with a choice of materials and finishes. 304-892-4501.

**Hodges Badge Company Inc.,** 1170 E. Main, Portsmouth, RI 02871: Free catalog ◆ Brass medals with gold, silver and copper/bronze finish. Also award certificates. 800-556-2440. www.hodgesbadge.com

**Lane 4 Awards,** P.O. Box 451591, Sunrise, FL 33345: Free catalog ◆ Embroidered emblems, medals, pins, ribbons, and trophies. 954-742-8609. lane4@interpoint.net

**Logo USA,** P.O. Box 2070, Cottonwood, CA 96022: Free information ◆ Customized logo watches, both casual and corporate. Also logo desk and wall clocks. 800-655-3364; 530-347-9178 (in CA). www.logousa.com

**Music Stand,** 1 Music Stand Plaza, 66 Benning St., West Lebanon, OH 03784: Free catalog ◆ Trophies, plaques, and certificates. 800-717-7010. www.musicstand.com

**Successories Inc.,** 919 Springer Dr., Lombard, IL 60148: Free catalog ◆ Awards for promotion of individual and team excellence. 800-535-2773. www.successories.com

**Sun State Trophy Supply,** 1090 Rainer Dr., Altamonte Springs, FL 32714: Free catalog ◆ Trophies and plaques. 800-327-2020; 407-788-0600 (in FL). www.ispace.com/Sunstate

**Trophyland USA Inc.,** 7001 W. 20th Ave., Hialeah, FL 33014: Free catalog ◆ Awards for incentive programs, athletic events, and other competitions. 800-432-3528; 305-823-4830 (in FL). www.trophyland.com

**Victorian House,** 1203 Columbus Circle, Janesville, WI 53545: Brochure $1 ◆ Victorian-style certificates with optional calligraphy. 800-597-8378.

**Volk Corp.,** 23936 Industrial Park Dr., Farmington Hills, MI 48335: Free information ◆ Award ribbons. 800-521-6799; 248-477-6700 (in MI).

**Whippoorwill Crafts,** 126 S. Market St., Boston, MA 02109: Free information ◆ Imaginative crafts customized for awards. 800-860-9551; 617-523-5149 (in MA).

## AWNINGS & PATIO COVERS

**Inter Trade Inc.,** 3175 Fujita St., Torrance, CA 90505: Free information ◆ Indoor-operated patio covers and awnings for protection from heat, sun, cold, rain, and noise. 310-515-7177.

**International E-Z UP Inc.,** 1601 Iowa Ave., Riverside, CA 92507: Free information ◆ Easy-to-set-up spring-loaded center pole shelter/canopy. 909-781-0586.

**JIL Industries Inc.,** 184 Charles St., Malden, MA 02148: Free brochure ◆ Retractable deck and patio awnings. 800-876-2340. www.sunsetter.com

**Pease Industries Inc.,** 7100 Dixie Hwy., Fairfield, OH 45014: Information $1 ◆ Retractable arm awning with optional wind sensor for automatic closing and sun sensor that opens the awning. 800-883-6677. www.peasedoor.com

**PYC Awnings,** 1111 Talbot St., St. Michaels, MD 21663: Free information ◆ Window, door, and retractable awnings. 800-933-6936; 410-822-9302 (in MD). www.willoworks.com/pya

**Shade & Comfort Company,** P.O. Box 1808, Centralia, IL 62801: Free information ◆ Patio covers, window awnings, porch curtains, and other coverings. 800-442-7423.

**The Sunsetter Awning,** JIL Industries, 184 Charles St., Malden, MA 02148: Free information ◆ Retractable awnings for decks and patios. 800-876-8060. www.sunsetter.com

## BABY CARE

**Abracadabra Maternity,** 4411 San Mateo Blvd. NE, Ste. J, Albuquerque, NM 87109: Free information ◆ Maternity clothing and accessories for new mothers and mothers-to-be. Includes casual to professional, swimsuits, exercise wear, nursing tops, pajamas, other fashions, nursing accessories, and baby care items. 505-881-6820.

**After the Stork,** 4311 Fulcrum Way, Rio Rancho, NM 87124: Free catalog ◆ Natural fiber clothing, records, tapes, books, and toys for children, from birth to age 7. 800-333-5437.

**Angel Fluff Diaper Company,** P.O. Box 1131, Lewisburg, TN 37091: Free catalog ◆ Pre-folded 100 percent cotton diapers. 800-996-2644.

**As A Little Child,** 10701 W. 80th Ave., Arvada, CO 80005: Free information ◆ Breathable and waterproof Gore-Tex fabric diaper covers. 303-456-1880.

**Audio-Therapy Innovations Inc.,** P.O. Box 550, Colorado Springs, CO 80901: Free information ◆ Rhythmic audio cassettes that help relax children and adults and aid in their going to sleep. 719-473-0100.

**Baby Bunz & Company,** P.O. Box 113, Lynden, WA 98264: Catalog $1 ◆ Diapering and layette supplies. 800-676-4559.

**The Baby Jogger Company,** P.O. Box 2189, Yakima, WA 98902: Free brochure ◆ Baby joggers for exercise fun. 800-241-1848; 509-457-0925 (in WA). www.babyjogger.com

**Baby Wrap Products Inc.,** P.O. Box 100584, Denver, CO 80250: Free brochure ◆ Strapless baby carrier. 800-432-0494; 303-757-5564 (in CO).

**BabyTown,** 1730 NE 92nd St., Seattle, WA 98115: Free brochure ◆ Cotton diapers, pull-up and training pants, liners and inserts, denim diaper bag, and other accessories. 800-957-2749.

**Babyworks,** 11725 NW West Rd., Portland, OR 97229: Free catalog ◆ Environmentally-kind diapers, diaper covers and bags, blankets, pads, and other baby products. 800-422-2910. www.babyworks.com

**Biobottoms,** 617-C 2nd St., Petaluma, CA 04952: Free catalog ◆ Cotton diapers and wool covers. 800-766-1254; 707-778-7152 (in CA). www.biobottoms.com

**Born To Love,** 5775 Yonge St., 8th Floor, North York, Ontario, Canada M2M 4J1: Free catalog ◆ Natural baby care products. 416-226-9520. born2luv@idirect.com

**The Bumpa Bed Company,** 2609 River Rd., P.O. Box 2189, Yakima, WA 98907: Free brochure ◆ Crib mattresses. 800-241-1848; 509-457-0825 (in WA).

**Caring Products International Inc.,** 200 1st Ave. West, Ste. 200, Seattle, WA 98119: Free information ◆ Toilet training products. 800-333-5379; 206-282-6040 (in WA). www.caringproducts.com

**Carry Me Inc.,** 130 E Grand Ave., Escondido, CA 92025: Free information ◆ Baby carriers.

**Child Secure,** P.O. Box 34462, Bethesda, MD 20827: Free brochure ◆ Strollers, high chairs, car seats, baby backpacks, jogging strollers, and other baby security products. 800-450-6530.

**Citikids,** 152 Clement St., San Francisco, CA 94118: Free information ◆ Children's furniture, car seats, strollers, carriers, clothing, and baby care items. 415-752-3837.

**Diaperaps,** 9760 Owensmouth Ave., Chatsworth, CA 91311: Free brochure ◆ Cotton outer layer and polyfoam-protected diaper covers. 800-477-3424.

**Double Trouble,** P.O. Box 464, Midway City, CA 92655: Free catalog ◆ Baby care items, birth announcements, party accessories, and other items for twins. 800-966-TWIN.

**Earthwise Basics,** 8716 Park Lane South, Ste. 3C, Woodhaven, NY 11421: Free brochure ◆ Prefolded diapers, all-in-one diapers, and covers.800-791-3957; 718-846-7434 (in NY).

**Ecobaby,** 1475 N. Cuyamaca, El Cajon, CA 92020: Free catalog ◆ Organic and natural fiber clothes, bedding, toys, and diapering products. 888-ECOBABY; 619-596-7450 (in CA). www.ecobaby.com

**Hand in Hand,** Catalogue Center, 100 Plaza Dr., Secaucus, NJ 07094: Free catalog ◆ Books, toys and games, car seat time occupiers, furniture, bathroom accessories, car seats, housewares and hardware, health aids, and other products that help nurture, teach, and protect children. 800-872-9745. hihcatalog@aol.com

**Mommy's Little Helpers,** 9250 Watson Rd., St. Louis, MO 63126: Free catalog ◆ Sling carriers, breast-feeding apparel, diapers, and supplies.

**Mother-ease,** 6391 Walmore Rd., Niagara Falls, NY 14304: Free catalog ◆ Fitted cotton terry diapers and waterproof diaper covers. 800-416-1475.

**Motherwear Diapers,** 320 Riverside Dr., Northampton, MA 01061: Free brochure ◆ Contour-shaped diapers, covers, and easy-access clothing for nursing mothers. 800-633-0303.

**Murphy Diaper System,** 24 Sullivan Ave., Newton, MA 02164: Free brochure ◆ Pre-folded diapers. 617-244-6238.

**The Natural Baby Company,** 7835 Freedom Ave. NW, North Canton, OH 44720: Free information ◆ Diapering and medical products, wood toys, cotton clothes, and alternative products. 800-388-BABY.

**The Natural Bedroom,** P.O. Box 2048, Sebastopol, CA 95472: Free information ◆ Natural fiber baby's bedding. 800-365-6563.

**The Natural Nursery,** Division Bright Future Futon Company, 3120 Central Ave. SE, Albuquerque, NM 87106: Free information ◆ Organic cotton and wool bedding alternatives. 505-232-9667.

**The New Native,** P.O. Box 247, Davenport, CA 95017: Free brochure ◆ Baby carrier for newborns through 35 pounds. Can be worn front or back. 800-646-1682.

**The Nurtured Baby,** Rt. 2, Box 327, Walstonburg, NC 27888: Free catalog ◆ Cloth diapers and other baby care aids. 800-462-2293.

**One Step Ahead,** P.O. Box 517, Lake Bluff, IL 60044: Free catalog ◆ Baby items for use when traveling, feeding, at bath time, and for security. 800-950-5120. osacatalog@aol.com

**Organic Cotton Alternatives,** 3120 Central Ave. SE, Albuquerque, NM 87106: Free information ◆ Organic cotton and wool bedding in a woven bassinet. 505-268-9738.

**JCPenney Catalog,** P.O. Box 675, Milwaukee, WI 53201: Free information ◆ Nursery furniture, bedding, strollers, car seats, and other baby care items. 800-222-6161. www.jcpenney.com/shopping

**Peg Perego U.S.A. Inc.,** 3625 Independence Dr., Fort Wayne, IN 46818: Free list of retail sources) ♦ Baby strollers with easy-to-handle maneuverability, nursery furniture, high chairs, and walk and play walkers. 219-482-8191.

**Perfectly Safe,** 7835 Freedom Ave. NW, North Canton, OH 44720: Free catalog ♦ Safety items for children age 3 to 6. 800-837-5437.

**Petterson Infant Products,** 189 Dadson Row, Flin Flon, Manitoba, Canada R8A 0C8: Free information ♦ Easy-on and off five-position baby carrier for birth to three years. 800-665-3957.

**Pleasant Company,** P.O. Box 620190, Middleton, WI 53562: Free catalog ♦ Bassinets, diaper bags, bunting, and knits for newborns and infants. 800-845-0005. www.americangirl.com

**RAD Enterprises,** P.O. Box 23, Barons, Alberta, Canada T0L 0G0: Free brochure ♦ Personalized baby blankets. 403-757-2140.

**Right Start Catalog,** Right Start Plaza, 5334 Sterling Center Dr., Westlake Village, CA 91361: Catalog $2 ♦ Car seats, clothing, educational toys, and shopping carts that convert into strollers. 800-548-8531.

**Rubens & Marble Inc.,** P.O. Box 14900, Chicago, IL 60614: Free brochure with long SASE ♦ Stretch stay-up diapers with elastic ends. 773-348-6200.

**Runabout,** 8025 SW 185th, Aloha, OR 97007: Free information ♦ Baby strollers. 800-832-2376.

**Tender Treasures,** 39882 SW Dixon Mill Rd., Gaston, OR 97119: Free brochure ♦ Diapers. 503-985-3228.

**Tot Tenders Inc.,** 14260 Garden Rd., Bldg. 99, Poway, CA 92064: Free information ♦ Baby carrier for twins. 800-634-6870.

**Tough Traveler,** 1012 State St., Schenectady, NY 12307: Free catalog ♦ Baby carriers. 800-468-6844. www.toughtraveler.com/tt

**Twincerely Yours,** 748 Lake Ave., Clermont, FL 34711: Free catalog with long SASE ♦ Gifts, novelties, and T-shirts for twins and their families. 352-394-5493.

**The Uptown Nursery,** 1601 Mt. Rushmore Dr., Rapid City, SD 57701: Free catalog ♦ Heirloom round crib bedding, cribs, and accessories. 888-545-2742.

**Wee Bees,** P.O. Box 712, Littleton, CO 80160: Free information ♦ Diapers that absorb and diaper covers that stay dry. 303-794-0966.

## BADGES & BUTTONS

**AD-BADGE Company Inc.,** 18905 NE 5th Ave., Miami, FL 33179: Free information ♦ Easy-to-operate button-making machine and supplies. 800-780-6441; 305-652-8957 (in FL).

**B & K Buttons,** 16 S. Detroit St., Xenia, OH 45385: Free information ♦ Custom buttons. 800-223-4392.

**Badge-A-Minit Ltd.,** Box 800, LaSalle, IL 61301: Free catalog ♦ Badge-making machine, supplies, and beginner's starter kit for making badges and pin-back buttons. 800-223-4103. www.badgeaminit.com

**Be-In Buttons,** Box 35593, Houston, TX 77235: Catalog $1 ♦ Presidential and other buttons.

**Bob's Old Badges,** 1621 S. 120th Ave., Hershey, MI 49639: Catalog $3 ♦ Recreated western sheriff, U.S. Marshall, Texas Ranger, Pony Express, Wells Fargo, railroad, and other badges of the past. 616-734-5491. www.rosemart.com

**Bold Concepts,** 1501 Broadway, Ste. 1808, New York, NY 10036: Free information ♦ Political buttons. 212-764-6330.

**Frontier Lassix,** P.O. Drawer 1865, Magnolia, AR 71753: Free information ♦ Reproduction silver plated badges worn by Old West lawmen. 501-234-7402.

**KA-MO Engravers,** P.O. Box 30337, Albuquerque, NM 87190: Free catalog ♦ Badges for square and round dancers. 800-352-5266; 505-883-4963 (in NM).

**Lifton Studio Inc.,** 121 S. 6th St., Stillwater, MN 55082: Catalog $5 ♦ Authentic reproduction of Old West and nickel-plated badges from America's history. 612-439-7208.

**Micro Plastics,** Box 847, Rifle, CO 81650: Free information ♦ Custom club badges. 970-625-1718.

**Nasco,** 901 Janesville Ave., Fort Atkinson, WI 53538: Free catalog ♦ Badge-making equipment and supplies. 800-558-9595. www.nascofa.com

**N.G. Slater Corp.,** 220 W. 19th St., New York, NY 10011: Free catalog ♦ Equipment for making buttons. 212-924-3133. 800-848-4621. www.ngslater.com

**Spartan Products Inc.,** 12427 Foothill Blvd., Sylmar, CA 91342: Free catalog ♦ Equipment and supplies for souvenir, identification, and promotional photo buttons. 800-288-3948; 818-899-2626 (in CA).

**Veach Foil Accessories,** 37007 S. Oak St., Kennewick, WA 99337: Free information ♦ Gold stamping and photo button-making machines, pens, and supplies. 800-523-9944. www.veachco.com

## BADMINTON

**AC Badminton,** 37 Atlantic View Dr., Lawrencetown, NS, Canada B2Z 1R4: Free brochure ♦ Badminton racquets, bags, shuttlecocks, nets, and sets. 902-434-4282.

**Asby Sports Inc.,** 392 N. Capitol Ave., San Jose, CA 95133: Free catalog ♦ Badminton racquets. 800-995-ASBY. asby@sj.bigger.net

**Bauer Sports,** 150 Ocean Rd., Greenland, NH 03840: Free list of retail sources ♦ Nets, posts, racquets, strings, shuttlecocks, and sets. 800-362-3146. www.bauer.com

**Century Sports Inc.,** Lakewood Industrial Park, 1995 Rutgers University Blvd., Box 2035, Lakewood, NJ 08701: Free information ♦ Nets, posts, shuttlecocks, and racquets. 800-526-7548; 732-905-4422 (in NJ).

**Douglas Sport Nets & Equipment Company,** 3441 S. 11th Ave., P.O. Box 393, Eldridge, IA 52748: Free information ♦ Nets, posts, and sets. 800-553-8907; 319-285-4162 (in IA).

**Franklin Sports Industries Inc.,** 17 Campanelli Pkwy., P.O. Box 508, Stoughton, MA 02072: Free information ♦ Nets, posts, racquets, strings, shuttlecocks, and sets. 800-426-7700. www.eisnerbros.com

**General Sportcraft Company,** 140 Woodbine Rd., Bergenfield, NJ 07621: Free information ♦ Nets, posts, sets, racquets, strings, and shuttlecocks. 201-384-4242.

**Indian Industries Inc.,** P.O. Box 889, Evansville, IN 47706: Free catalog ♦ Nets, posts, racquets, strings, shuttlecocks, and sets. 800-457-3373; 812-467-1200 (in IN).

**Louisville Badminton Supply,** 1313 Lyndon Ln., Ste. 103, Louisville, KY 40222: Free brochure ♦ Racquets, shuttlecocks, bags, covers, books, and other supplies. 502-426-3219.

**Dick Martin Sports Inc.,** 181 E. Union Ave., P.O. Box 7381, East Rutherford, NJ 07073: Free information ♦ Nets, posts, racquets, strings, and sets. 800-221-1993; 201-438-5255 (in NJ).

**Neat Nets Inc.,** P.O. Box 0091, Youngwood, PA 15607: Free brochure ♦ Self-contained retractable net system. 800-257-5250.

**Olympia Sports,** P.O. Box 1941, Ann Arbor, MI 48106: Free information ♦ Shuttlecocks, racquets, and sets. 800-521-2832. www.wolverinesports.com

**Park & Sun Inc.,** 2150 S. Tejon St. South, Englewood, CO 80110: Free information ♦ Nets, posts, and sets. 800-776-7275.

**Porter Athletic Equipment Company,** 2500 S. 25th Ave., Broadview, IL 60153: Free information ♦ Nets, posts, racquets, sets, and shuttlecocks. 630-338-2000.

**San Diego Badminton Supply,** P.O. Box 232494, Encinitas, CA 92023: Free information ♦ Badminton racquets, equipment, shuttlecocks, and accessories. 888-223-6468. www.squash.net

**Spalding Sports Worldwide,** 425 Meadow St., P.O. Box 901, Chicopee, MA 01201: Free list of retail sources ♦ Nets, posts, racquets, strings, shuttlecocks, cases, covers, grips, presses, and sets. 800-225-6601. www.spalding.com

**Sport Fun Inc.,** 4621 Sperry St., Los Angeles, CA 90039: Free information ♦ Nets, posts, racquets, strings, shuttlecocks, and sets. 800-423-2597; 213-245-7530 (in CA).

**Sportime,** Customer Service, 1 Sportime Way, Atlanta, GA 30340: Free information ♦ Nets, posts, shuttlecocks, racquets, and sets. 800-444-5700; 770-449-5700 (in GA).

**Worldwide Games,** P.O. Box 517, Colchester, CT 06415: Free catalog ♦ Equipment for badminton, horseshoes, and boccie. 800-888-0987. www.worldwidegames.com

**WWW.Shuttles.com Inc.,** 16200 NE 13th Ave., North Miami Beach, FL 33162: Free brochure ♦ Badminton shuttlecocks. 305-949-0556. www.shuttles.com

**Yonex Corp.,** 3520 Challenger St., Torrance, CA 90503: Free list of retail sources ♦ Racquets, strings, and shuttlecocks. 800-44-YONEX.

## BALLOONS

**Anagram International Inc.,** 7700 Anagram Dr., Minneapolis, MN 55344: Free list of retail sources ♦ Balloons with birthday messages and one-of-a-kind designs. 800-554-4711; 612-949-5665 (in MN).

**Balloon Printing Company,** P.O. Box 150, Rankin, PA 15104: Free information ♦ Imprinted balloons. 800-533-5221.

**Balloons For You,** 2152 Chennault, Carrollton, TX 75006: Free information ♦ Balloons. 800-636-4887.

**Clown City,** 6 Salem Market Pl., Salem, CT 06420: Catalog $2 ♦ Balloons and clown supplies. 203-889-1000.

**Clown Heaven,** 4792 Old State Rd. 37 South, Martinsville, IN 46152: Catalog $3 ♦ Balloons, make-up, puppets, wigs, ministry and gospel items, novelties, magic, clown props, and books. 317-342-6888.

**Dewey's Good News Balloons,** 1202 Wildwood, Deer Park, TX 77536: Free catalog ♦ Gospel clown supplies and balloon books. 281-479-2759. balloonz@flash.net

**Flowers Inc. Balloons,** 325 Cleveland Rd., Bogart, GA 30622: Free catalog ♦ Balloons and gifts. 800-241-2094; 706-548-1588 (in GA). www.flowersincballoons.com

**Gayla Balloons,** P.O. Box 920800, Houston, TX 77292: Free catalog ♦ Balloons for the balloon artist. 800-327-9513. www.asisupplier.com/gayla

**La Rock's Fun & Magic Outlet,** 3847 Rosehaven Dr., Charlotte, NC 28205: Catalog $3 ♦ Clown and balloon how-to books, balloons, balloon sculpture kits, juggling supplies, and magic equipment. 704-563-9300. larocks1@aol.com

**Mecca Magic Inc.,** 49 Dodd St., Bloomfield, NJ 07003: Catalog $10 ♦ Balloons, theatrical make-up, clown equipment, magic, costumes and wigs, puppets, ventriloquism equipment, and juggling supplies. 201-429-7597. meccamagic@meccamagic.com

**More Than Balloons Inc.,** 2409 Ravendale Ct., Kissimmee, FL 34758: Free information ♦ Regular balloons, balloons for making sculptures, how-to books, balloon accessories, and magic. 800-BALUNES.

**Morris Costumes,** 3108 Monroe Rd., Charlotte, NC 28205: Catalog $20 ♦ Balloons, costumes, clown props, masks, joke items, magic tricks, special effects, novelties, and books. 704-332-3304.

**T. Myers Magic Inc.,** 1509 Parker Bend, Austin, TX 78734: Free catalog ♦ Balloons and balloon-sculpting supplies. Also clown make-up, stickers, temporary tattoos, and magic. 800-648-6221; 512-263-2375 (in TX). TMyersMagi@aol.com

**Novelties Unlimited,** 410 W. 21st St., Norfolk, VA 23517: Catalog $5 ♦ Balloons, magic tricks, party decorations, make-up, clown supplies, props, and gags. 757-622-0344.

**Paradise Products,** P.O. Box 568, El Cerrito, CA 94530: Catalog $2 ♦ Balloons. 510-524-8300.

**Ed Rohr Company,** 3323 Darlington Rd., Toledo, OH 43606: Free information ♦ Compact self-contained balloon inflator in an ultra-light-weight shoulder pack. 419-536-7495.

**Sally Distributors,** 4100 Quebec Ave. North, Minneapolis, MN 55427: Free information ♦ Party supplies and decorations. Includes holiday theme items, balloons, gift wrap, small toys, novelties, children's games, headwear, and tissue bells. 800-472-5597; 612-533-7100 (in MN).

**Sparkle's Entertainment Express,** Jan Lovell, 152 N. Water St., Gallatin, TN 37066: Product list $1 ♦ Make-up, costumes and clown shoes, balloons, juggling and magic equipment, puppets, books, and other supplies. 615-452-9755.

**Suburban Balloon & Helium,** 31735 Vine St., Willowick, OH 44094: Free information ♦ Remote and stationary helium or nitrogen filling stations with hose, connectors, and crimping tool. 800-572-0100.

**Wyco Props,** 8344 Yecker Ave., Kansas City, KS 66109: Free information ♦ Battery-operated balloon pump. Comes with a charger and car lighter adapter. 913-788-9338. www.wycoprops.com

## BANKS

**American American Classics Unlimited,** Frank Troll, President, P.O. Box 192, Oak Lawn, IL 60454: Catalog $1 ♦ Promotional model cars and banks, collectible automobilia, other cars, and kits. 708-424-9223.

**Asheville Diecast,** 1434 Brevard Rd., Asheville, NC 28806: Free information ♦ Die-cast collectible banks, signs, and vehicle replicas. 800-343-4685. www.asheville-diecast.com

**Gateway Toys,** Ron & Nancy Russell, 2390 Riverbluff, Arnold, MO 63010: Free price list with long SASE ♦ Ertl banks. 314-296-2765.

**Homestead Collectibles,** P.O. Box 173, Mill Hall, PA 17751: Information $1 ♦ Die-cast metal, Ertl, and airplane banks. 717-726-3597. jturner@cub.kcnet.org

**B. Huhn,** 432 S. Gore Ave., St. Louis, MO 63119: Free list with 1st class stamp ♦ Collectible banks.

**Dan Iannotti,** 212 W. Hickory Grove, Bloomfield, MI 48302: Price list $3 ♦ Mechanical cast-iron banks. 810-335-5042.

**Kenzel Toys,** 3623 Cambria-Wilson Rd., Wilson, NY 14172: List $1 with long SASE ♦ Collectible banks. 716-751-9392.

**Midwest Toys,** P.O. Box 56, Kimmswick, MO 63053: Free list with long SASE ♦ Banks. 314-464-1685.

**Pit Stop Racing Collectibles,** 415 N. Main St., Ste. 106, Euless, TX 76039: Free list ♦ Collectible die-cast model cars and banks. 817-354-7657. WWW.PITSTOPRACING.com

**R & B Collectibles,** P.O. Box 406, Frenchtown, NJ 08825: Free list with long SASE ♦ Hard-to-find collectible banks. 908-996-2141.

**R.P. Company,** P.O. Box 3020, Boscawen, NH 03303: Catalog $1 ♦ Limited edition historical postal coin banks. 603-796-2200.

**Rural America Toy Collectibles,** 2488 Omega Rd., Delhi, IA 52223: Free information with long SASE ♦ Banks, farm toys, and collectibles. 319-926-2479.

**Vicars Toy Heaven,** 9080 Pelham, Taylor, MI 48180: Price list $1 ♦ Ertl banks. 313-291-9000.

## BARBECUE GRILLS & SMOKE-COOKING OVENS

**Armitage Hardware,** 925 W. Armitage, Chicago, IL 60614: Free information ♦ Weber grills and accessories. 888-GO-WEBER.

**B-West Outdoor Specialties,** 2425 N. Huachuca, Tucson, AZ 85745: Free information ♦ Outdoor cookware and barbecue equipment. 800-293-7855; 520-628-1990 (in AZ).

**Bar-B-Que Specialties,** 3881 Southwest Fwy., Houston, TX 77027: Free brochure ♦ Hibachi pots, stands, cooking tools, and barbecuing accessories. 800-370-8211.

**Char-Broil,** Grill Lovers Catalog, 7100 Jamesson Rd., Midland, GA 31820: Free catalog ♦ Grills, outdoor furniture, barbecue cookers, and seasonings, spices, and condiments. 800-241-8981. www.grilllovers.com

**Cookshack,** 2304 N. Ash St., Ponca City, OK 74601: Free catalog ♦ Barbecue and smoke-cooking ovens for homes and retail establishments. 800-423-0698.

**Grill Parts Distributors,** 6150 49th St. North, St. Petersburg, FL 33709: Free catalog ♦ Parts and accessories for grills, smoking chips, cookbooks, and rotisserie kits. 800-447-4557; 800-282-4513 (in FL). www.gasgrills.com

**Hasty-Bake,** P.O. Box 471285, Tulsa, OK 74147: Free catalog ♦ Gourmet foods, charcoal ovens, and grill accessories. 800-426-6836. www.webczar.com.hastybake

**The Iron Works,** P.O. Box 578, 4974 Bird Dr., Stockbridge, MI 49285: Free catalog ◆ Custom outdoor cooking equipment. 517-851-8889.

**Klose Bar-B-Que Pits,** 2214½ W. 34th St., Houston, TX 77018: Free catalog ◆ Adjustable grills with fireboxes. 800-487-7487. www.bbqpits.com

**Morrone Company,** 465 Albert St., Macon, GA 31206: Free information ◆ Portable cooker with cast-iron gas burner. 800-826-8863.

**Weber Grills & Accessories,** The BBQ Pit, 925 W. Armitage, Chicago, IL 60614: Free catalog ◆ Gas and charcoal barbecues and accessories. 888-GO-WEBER.

## BARBERSHOP MUSIC & HARMONY

**SPEBSQSA,** 6315 3rd Ave., Kenosho, WI 53143: Free catalog ◆ CDs, tapes, videos, apparel, pitch pipes, instructional materials, barbershop quartet and chorus arrangements, chapter awards, and more. 800-876-SING.

**Sweet Adelines International,** P.O. Box 470168, Tulsa, OK 74147: Free catalog ◆ Sheet music, choral arrangements, pitch pipes, books, jewelry, presentation supplies, and more. 800-992-1444. www.sweetadelineintl.org

## BASEBALL & SOFTBALL

### Clothing

**Don Alleson Athletic,** 2921 Brighton-Henrietta Town Line Rd., Rochester, NY 14623: Free information ◆ Uniforms. 800-641-0041; 716-272-0606 (in NY).

**Alpha Shirt Company,** 401 E. Hunting Park Ave., Philadelphia, PA 19124: Free information ◆ Caps, jackets, and shorts. 800-523-4585; 215-291-0300 (in PA).

**Austin Sportsgear,** 621 Liberty St., Jackson, MI 49203: Free information ◆ Caps, pants, shorts, and uniforms. 800-999-7543; 517-784-1120 (in MI).

**Baseball Express,** P.O. Box 792310, San Antonio, TX 78279: Free catalog ◆ Baseball and softball equipment and clothing. 800-937-4824. www.baseballexp.com

**Betlin Manufacturing,** 1445 Marion Rd., Columbus, OH 43207: Free information ◆ Uniforms and undershirts. 614-443-0248.

**Bike Athletic Company,** P.O. Box 666, Knoxville, TN 37901: Free information ◆ Uniforms and undershirts. 800-251-9230. www.bike-athletic.com

**Bomark Sportswear,** P.O. Box 2068, Belair, TX 77402: Free information ◆ Caps and uniforms. 800-231-3351.

**Bristol Athletic,** 700-726 Shelby St., Bristol, TN 37621: Free information ◆ Basketball, baseball and softball, football, track, volleyball, and lacrosse uniforms for men, women, and youths. 800-336-8775; 615-968-4140 (in TN).

**Champion Products Inc.,** 475 Corporate Square Dr., Winston-Salem, NC 27105: Free information ◆ Uniforms, undershirts, and footwear.

**DeLong,** 733 Broad St., P.O. Box 189, Grinnell, IA 50112: Free information ◆ Uniforms, caps, and undershirts. 800-733-5664; 515-236-3106 (in IA).

**Direct Sports,** P.O. Box 497, 1720 Curve Rd., Pearlsburg, VA 24134: Free catalog ◆ Equipment, shoes, and clothing. 800-456-0072. www.directsports.com

**Eastbay,** P.O. Box 8066, Wausau, WI 54402: Free catalog ◆ Shoes and clothing. 800-826-2205. www.eastbay.com

**Ebbets Field Flannels,** Box 19865, Seattle, WA 98109: Free catalog ◆ Historic baseball apparel. 800-377-9777.

**Empire Sporting Goods Manufacturing Company,** 443 Broadway, New York, NY 10013: Free information ◆ Uniforms, caps, undershirts, and socks. 800-221-3455; 212-966-0880 (in NY).

**Fab Knit Manufacturing Company,** Division Anderson Industries, 1415 N. 4th St., Waco, TX 76707: Free information ◆ Caps, uniforms, and undershirts. 800-333-4111; 817-752-2511 (in TX).

**Georgia Tees Inc.,** 4200 McEver Industrial Dr., Box Tee, Achworth, GA 30101: Free information ◆ Caps. 800-553-0021; 404-974-0040 (in GA). gateddie@aol.com

**Jewel & Company Inc.,** 9601 Apollo Dr., Landover, MD 20705: Free information ◆ Caps and jackets. 800-638-8583; 301-925-6200 (in MD). www.jewellandco.com

**Majestic Athletic Wear,** 636 Pen Argyl St., Pen Argyl, PA 18072: Free information ◆ Uniforms, caps, and undershirts. 800-955-8555; 610-863-6161 (in PA).

**Markwort Sporting Goods,** 4300 Forest Park Ave., St. Louis, MO 63108: Catalog $8 (request list of retail sources) ◆ Clothing and equipment. 800-669-6626; 314-652-3757 (in MO).

**Matrix Group Ltd.,** 1536 S. Missouri Ave., Clearwater, FL 34616: Free information ◆ Caps. 800-370-9300.

**Mitchell & Ness Nostalgia Company,** 1229 Walnut St., Philadelphia, PA 19107: Free information ◆ Vintage major league team uniforms. 800-483-6377; 215-592-6512 (in PA). Mness1@aol.com

**Movin USA,** 7411 W. Boston, Ste. 1, Chandler, AZ 85225: Free information ◆ Caps and shorts. 800-445-6684.

**New South Athletic Company Inc.,** 301 E. Main, P.O. Box 604, Dallas, NC 28034: Free information ◆ Shoes, uniforms, caps, undershirts, and socks. 800-438-9934; 704-922-1557 (in NC).

**JCPenney Catalog,** P.O. Box 675, Milwaukee, WI 53201: Free information ◆ Athletic clothing and equipment. 800-222-6161. www.jcpenney.com/shopping

**The Perfect Game,** 11025 Elm St., Omaha, NE 68144: Free catalog ◆ Baseball and softball equipment and uniforms. 888-444-6227.

**Puma USA Inc.,** 147 Centre St., Brockton, MA 02403: Free information with long SASE ◆ Shoes and other athletic clothing. 800-662-7862. www.puma.com

**Saucony/Hyde,** 13 Centennial Dr., Peabody, MA 01961: Free list of retail sources ◆ Shoes. 800-365-7282.

**Sportsprint Inc.,** 6197 Bermuda Rd., St. Louis, MO 63135: Catalog $5 ◆ Uniforms, caps, and socks. 800-325-4858. www.biteStL.com/sportsprint

**Star Struck,** P.O. Box 308, Bethel, CT 06801: Free catalog ◆ Fitted caps and jerseys. 800-908-4637; 877-THE-GAME (in CT). www.starstruck.com

**Title 9 Sports,** 5743 Landregan St., Emeryville, CA 94608: Free catalog ◆ Women's clothing created by and for women. 510-655-5999. thefolks@title9sports.com

**Venus Knitting Mills Inc.,** 140 Spring St., Murray Hill, NJ 07974: Free information ◆ Uniforms, caps, socks, and undershirts. 800-955-4200; 908-464-2400 (in NJ).

**Wilson Sporting Goods,** 8700 Bryn Mawr, Chicago, IL 60631: Free information ◆ Caps and socks. 800-946-6060; 773-714-6400 (in IL). www.wilsonsports.com

### Equipment

**ATEC,** 10 Greg St., Sparks, NV 89431: Free information ◆ Baseballs and softballs, field equipment, pitching machines, training aids, and bags for balls, bats, and uniforms. 800-755-5100; 702-352-2800 (in NV).

**The Athletic Connection,** 1901 Diplomat, Dallas, TX 75234: Free information ◆ Bat and ball bags, bats, baseballs and softballs, field equipment, protective gear, helmets, and pitching machines. 800-527-0871; 972-243-1446 (in TX).

**Ballwall,** 5 Flint Ave., Larchmont, NY 10538: Free brochure ◆ Indoor and outdoor backstop training wall for sports that use a ball. 800-966-1190; 914-833-0390 (in NY).

**Baseball Express,** P.O. Box 792310, San Antonio, TX 78279: Free catalog ◆ Baseball and softball equipment and clothing. 800-937-4824. www.baseballexp.com

**Bauer Sports,** 150 Ocean Rd., Greenland, NH 03840: Free list of retail sources ◆ Softballs and baseballs, bats, field equipment, mitts and gloves, protective gear, and bags for bats, balls, and uniforms. 800-362-3146. www.bauer.com

**Beacon Ballfields,** P.O. Box 45557, Madison, WI 53744: Free catalog ◆ Baseball, football, and soccer field equipment. 800-747-5985; 608-274-5985 (in WI).

**Dick Bixler Sports Inc.,** Woodring Airport, Rt. 5, Box 41, Enid, OK 73701: Free brochure ◆ Indoor/outdoor training machine for catching, pitching, fielding grounders, batting, and more. 800-494-0072.

**BSN Sports,** P.O. Box 7726, Dallas, TX 75209: Free information ◆ Equipment for archery, aquatic fitness, baseball, basketball, boxing, field hockey, football, weight lifting, and other sports. 800-527-7510; 972-484-9484 (in TX). www.bsnsports.com

**Carron Net Company,** 1623 17th St., P.O. Box 177, Two Rivers, WI 54241: Free information ◆ Archery, baseball, basketball, gymnasium and climbing, football, racquetball, soccer, tennis, and volleyball equipment. 800-558-7768; 414-793-2217 (in WI). sales@carronnet.com

**Dalco Athletic,** P.O. Box 550220, Dallas, TX 75355: Free information ◆ Baseballs and softballs, bats, helmets, catcher masks, chest protectors, and gloves and mitts. 800-288-3252; 972-494-1455 (in TX). www.dalcoathletic.com

**Decatur Electronics Inc.,** 715 Bright St., Decatur, IL 62522: Free information ◆ Ball speed radar gun. 800-428-4315.

**Diamond King Sports,** 852 Elmwood Rd., #269, Lansing, MI 48917: Free brochure ◆ Professional leather gloves. 800-826-1464.

**Direct Sports,** P.O. Box 497, 1720 Curve Rd., Pearlsburg, VA 24134: Free catalog ◆ Equipment, shoes, and clothing. 800-456-0072. www.directsports.com

**Douglas Sport Nets & Equipment Company,** 3441 S. 11th Ave., P.O. Box 393, Eldridge, IA 52748: Free information ◆ Baseball equipment. 800-553-8907; 319-285-4162 (in IA).

**Dudley Sports Company,** 521 Meadow St., Chicopee, MA 01021: Free information ◆ Baseballs and softballs. 800-523-5387; 413-536-1200 (in MA).

**Flaghouse Sports Equipment,** 601 Flaghouse Dr., Hasbrouck Heights, NJ 07604: Free catalog ◆ Baseball equipment. 800-793-7900. www.flaghouse.com

**Gared Sports Inc.,** 1107 Mullanphy St., St. Louis, MO 63106: Free information ◆ Baseball equipment. 800-325-2682.

**Hillerich & Bradsby Company Inc.,** P.O. Box 35700, Louisville, KY 40232: Free list of retail sources ◆ Baseball and softball bats, gloves, and other equipment. 800-282-2287.

**Jayfro Corp.,** Unified Sports Inc., 976 Hartford Tnpk., P.O. Box 400, Waterford, CT 06385: Free catalog ◆ Safety protectors, batting tees, mats, baseball and softball practice cages, batting cubicles, and backstops. 860-447-3001.

**Kelley Baseball,** 2001 E. Randol Mill Rd., Ste. 101, Arlington, TX 76011: Free brochure ◆ Professional gloves, batting gloves, training aids, sport supports, sunglasses, and baseballs. Also softball equipment. 800-652-6602. www.kelleybaseball.com

**King Sports Inc.,** 1230 Johnson Ferry Rd., Ste. J-60, Marietta, GA 30068: Free information ◆ Fishing, golf, baseball, and basketball equipment. 800-344-1480.

**Korney Board Aids Inc.,** P.O. Box 264, 312 Harrison Ave., Roxton, TX 75477: Free catalog ◆ Coaching and training aids. 800-842-7772.

**Markwort Sporting Goods,** 4300 Forest Park Ave., St. Louis, MO 63108: Catalog $8 (request list of retail sources) ◆ Baseballs and softballs, bats, batting gloves and helmets, catcher masks, chest protectors, and gloves and mitts. 800-669-6626; 314-652-3757 (in MO).

**Dick Martin Sports Inc.,** 181 E. Union Ave., P.O. Box 7381, East Rutherford, NJ 07073: Free information ◆ Bat bags, baseballs and softballs, gloves, and protective gear. 800-221-1993; 201-438-5255 (in NJ).

**Master Pitching Machine,** 4200 NE Birmingham Rd., Kansas City, MO 64117: Free information ◆ Pitching machine with simulated pitcher wind up and delivery actions. 800-878-8228.

**Memphis Net & Twine Company Inc.,** 2481 Matthews Ave., P.O. Box 80331, Memphis, TN 38108: Free catalog ◆ Cages and backstops, soccer nets, tennis windscreens, pitching machines, protector and miscellaneous nets for other sports, and sports accessories. 800-238-6380. memnet@netten.net

**Nocona Athletic Goods Company,** P.O. Box 329, Nocona, TX 76255: Free catalog ◆ Baseball equipment. 817-825-3326.

**Osborne Innovative Products Inc.,** 2221 2nd St., Enumclaw, WA 98022: Free information ◆ Baseball and softball equipment. Includes multi-use and pitcher safety screens, hitting tees, batting cages, pitching machines, and nets. 800-325-7238; 360-825-4299 (in WA). www.oipsports.com

**The Perfect Game,** 11025 Elm St., Omaha, NE 68144: Free catalog ◆ Baseball and softball equipment and uniforms. 888-444-6227.

**Progressive Fitness Inc.,** 8 Independence Way, Southampton, NJ 08088: Free information ◆ Baseball throwing simulator. 888-FAST-ARM.

**ProHoop,** 7623 Champlons Ct., Wichita, KS 67226: Free brochure ◆ Shot training and auto-rebounding shooting system. 888-ONE-HOOP.

**Radar Sales,** 5640 International Pkwy., Minneapolis, MN 55428: Free catalog ◆ Radar equipment for sports testing and speed enforcement. 888-782-5537.

**Rawlings Sporting Goods,** 1859 Impertech Dr., Fenton, MO 63026: Free list of retail sources ◆ Baseballs, bats, mitts and gloves, protective gear, and bags for balls, mitts, and uniforms. 800-426-3334. www.rawlings.com

**Riddell Inc.,** 3670 N. Milwaukee Ave., Chicago, IL 60641: Free information ◆ Baseballs and softballs, gloves and mitts, and protective gear. 800-445-7344; 773-794-1994 (in IL).

**SGD Company Inc.,** P.O. Box 8410, Akron, OH 44320: Free information ◆ Baseball and softball equipment. 330-239-2828. www.sgdgolf.com

**Sportime,** Customer Service, 1 Sporting Way, Atlanta, GA 30340: Free information ◆ Bats and bags for balls and bats, protective gear, and helmets. 800-444-5700; 770-449-5700 (in GA).

**Sports Tutor,** 2612 W. Burbank Blvd., Burbank, CA 91505: Free brochure ◆ No cage required, batting tutor for fast balls and curves. 800-448-8867. www.sportstutor.com

**SSK America Inc.,** 21136 S. Wilmington Ave., Ste. 220, Long Beach, CA 90810: Free information ◆ Bats, gloves, and score books. 800-421-2674; 562-549-2762 (in CA).

**Steele's Sports Company,** 5197 W. 137th, Brook Park, OH 44142: Free information ◆ Softball and baseball equipment. 800-367-7114; 216-267-5300 (in OH). www.steelexlt-boyat.com

**Tennessee Sports Company,** P.O. Box 310, 2102 N. Jackson St., Tullahoma, TN 37388: Free information ◆ Softball and baseball bats for youths and adults. 615-455-7765.

**Wolvering Sports,** P.O. Box 1941, Ann Arbor, MI 48106: Catalog $1 ◆ Baseball, basketball, field hockey, soccer, football, other athletic, and recreation equipment. 313-761-5691.

## BASKETBALL

### Clothing

**Don Alleson Athletic,** 2921 Brighton-Henrietta Town Line Rd., Rochester, NY 14623: Free information ◆ Uniforms and warm-up clothing. 800-641-0041; 716-272-0606 (in NY).

**Austin Sportsgear,** 621 Liberty St., Jackson, MI 49203: Free information ◆ Uniforms. 800-999-7543; 517-784-1120 (in MI).

**Betlin Manufacturing,** 1445 Marion Rd., Columbus, OH 43207: Free information ◆ Uniforms, warm-up jackets, and pants. 614-443-0248.

**Boast Inc.,** Box 10176, Riviera Beach, FL 33419: Free information ◆ Uniforms and warm-up clothing. 800-327-7666; 561-848-1096 (in FL).

**Bristol Athletic,** 700-726 Shelby St., Bristol, TN 37621: Free information ◆ Basketball, baseball and softball, football, track, volleyball, and lacrosse uniforms for men, women, and youths. 800-336-8775; 615-968-4140 (in TN).

**Champion Products Inc.,** 475 Corporate Square Dr., Winston-Salem, NC 27105: Free information ♦ Uniforms, warm-up jackets, pants, socks, and shoes.

**Eastbay,** P.O. Box 8066, Wausau, WI 54402: Free catalog ♦ Shoes and clothing. 800-826-2205. www.eastbay.com

**Empire Sporting Goods Manufacturing Company,** 443 Broadway, New York, NY 10013: Free information ♦ Uniforms, warm-up jackets, pants, socks, and wristbands. 800-221-3455; 212-966-0880 (in NY).

**GeorGI-Sports,** P.O. Box 1107, Lancaster, PA 17603: Free information ♦ Uniforms, warm-up jackets, pants, and socks. 800-338-2527; 717-291-8924 (in PA).

**Letrell Sports,** 3004 Industrial Pkwy. West, Knoxville, TN 37921: Free information ♦ Uniforms and warm-up clothing. 800-325-3975; 615-546-8070 (in TN).

**Lotto Sports,** 1900 Surveyor Blvd., Carrollton, TX 75006: Free information ♦ Shoes. 800-527-5126; 972-416-4003 (in TX).

**Majestic Athletic Wear,** 636 Pen Argyl St., Pen Argyl, PA 18072: Free information ♦ Uniforms and warm-up clothing. 800-955-8555; 610-863-6161 (in PA).

**JCPenney Catalog,** P.O. Box 675, Milwaukee, WI 53201: Free information ♦ Athletic clothing and equipment. 800-222-6161. www.jcpenney.com/shopping

**Pony Sports & Leisure,** 2801 Red Dog Dr., Knoxville, TN 37914: Free information ♦ Shoes, socks, and sweat bands. 423-546-4703.

**Puma USA Inc.,** 147 Centre St., Brockton, MA 02403: Free information with long SASE ♦ Warm-up jackets, pants, wristbands, shoes, and socks. 800-662-7862. www.puma.com

**Shaffer Sportswear,** 224 N. Washington, Neosho, MO 64850: Free information ♦ Uniforms and warm-up clothing. 417-451-9444.

**Southland Athletic,** P.O. Box 280, Terrell, TX 75160: Free list of retail sources ♦ Uniforms, warm-up jackets, and pants. 800-527-7637; 972-563-3321 (in TX).

**Spalding Sports Worldwide,** 425 Meadow St., P.O. Box 901, Chicopee, MA 01021: Free list of retail sources ♦ Uniforms, warm-up jackets, pants, wristbands, socks, shoes, and equipment. 800-225-6601. www.spalding.com

**Star Struck,** P.O. Box 308, Bethel, CT 06801: Free catalog ♦ Fitted caps and jerseys. 800-908-4637; 877-THE-GAME (in CT). www.starstruck.com

### Equipment

**Amko Inc.,** P.O. Box 5809, Huntsville, AL 35814: Free information ♦ Basketballs. 800-289-2656; 205-851-7080 (in AL).

**The Athletic Connection,** 1901 Diplomat, Dallas, TX 75234: Free information ♦ Backboards, basketballs, and nets. 800-527-0871; 972-243-1446 (in TX).

**Bauer Sports,** 150 Ocean Rd., Greenland, NH 03840: Free list of retail sources ♦ Basketballs, ball carriers, goals, nets, knee braces, pads and guards, supporters, and whistles. 800-362-3146. www.bauer.com

**Bike Athletic Company,** P.O. Box 666, Knoxville, TN 37901: Free information ♦ Pads and guards, supporters, and knee braces. 800-251-9230. www.bike-athletic.com

**Bison Basketball Equipment,** 603 L St., Lincoln, NE 68508: Free list of retail sources ♦ Basketball equipment. 800-247-7668.

**BSN Sports,** P.O. Box 7726, Dallas, TX 75209: Free information ♦ Equipment for archery, aquatic fitness, baseball, basketball, boxing, field hockey, football, weight lifting, and other sports. 800-527-7510; 972-484-9484 (in TX). www.bsnsports.com

**Carron Net Company,** 1623 17th St., P.O. Box 177, Two Rivers, WI 54241: Free information ♦ Archery, baseball, basketball, gymnasium and climbing, football, racquetball, soccer, tennis, and volleyball equipment. 800-558-7768; 414-793-2217 (in WI). sales@carronnet.com

**Cramer Products Inc.,** P.O. Box 1001, Gardner, KS 66030: Free information ♦ Knee braces, pads, and guards. 800-345-2231; 913-884-7511 (in KS).

**Escalade Sports,** P.O. Box 889, Evansville, IN 47706: Free catalog ♦ Backboards and nets. 800-457-3373; 812-467-1200 (in IN).

**Flaghouse Sports Equipment,** 601 Flaghouse Dr., Hasbrouck Heights, NJ 07604: Free catalog ♦ Basketball equipment. 800-793-7900. www.flaghouse.com

**Franklin Sports Industries Inc.,** 17 Campanelli Pkwy., P.O. Box 508, Stoughton, MA 02072: Free information ♦ Pads, guards, miscellaneous equipment, and basketballs. 800-426-7700. www.eisnerbros.com

**Gared Sports Inc.,** 1107 Mullanphy St., St. Louis, MO 63106: Free information ♦ Basketball equipment. 800-325-2682.

**Gopher Sport,** 2929 Park Dr., Owatonna, MN 55060: Free information ♦ Equipment and accessories for basketball, football, soccer, track and field, and other net games. 800-533-0446; 507-451-7470 (in MN).

**Grid Inc.,** NDL Products, 4031 NE 12th Terrace, Oakland Park, FL 33334: Free information ♦ Supporters, knee braces, pads, and guards. 800-843-3021.

**Holabird Sports Discounters,** 9220 Pulaski Hwy., Baltimore, MD 21220: Free catalog ♦ Equipment and clothing for basketball, tennis, running and jogging, golf, exercising, and racquetball. 410-687-6400. www.holabirdsports.com

**Indian Industries Inc.,** P.O. Box 889, Evansville, IN 47706: Free catalog ♦ Backboards, nets, and poles. 800-457-3373; 812-467-1200 (in IN).

**Jayfro Corp.,** Unified Sports Inc., 976 Hartford Tnpk., P.O. Box 400, Waterford, CT 06385: Free catalog ♦ Backboards, post and portable standards, and goals. 860-447-3001.

**M.W. Kasch Company,** 5401 W. Donges Bay Rd., Mequon, WI 53092: Free information ♦ Basketballs, backboards, goals, nets, and basketball sets. 414-242-5000.

**Porter Athletic Equipment Company,** 2500 S. 25th Ave., Broadview, IL 60153: Free information ♦ Backboards, basketballs, goals, and nets. 630-338-2000.

**Rawlings Sporting Goods,** 1859 Impertech Dr., Fenton, MO 63026: Free list of retail sources ♦ Basketballs, nets, and score books. 800-426-3334. www.rawlings.com

**Riddell Inc.,** 3670 N. Milwaukee Ave., Chicago, IL 60641: Free information ♦ Basketballs and nets. 800-445-7344; 773-794-1994 (in IL).

**Spalding Sports Worldwide,** 425 Meadow St., P.O. Box 901, Chicopee, MA 01021: Free list of retail sources ♦ Basketballs, other equipment, uniforms, warm-up jackets and pants, wristbands, socks, and shoes. 800-225-6601. www.spalding.com

**Sporting Edge,** 11042 Outpost Dr., North Potomac, MD 20878: Free catalog ♦ Basketball and volleyball equipment. 301-424-2762.

**Sportime,** Customer Service, 1 Sporting Way, Atlanta, GA 30340: Free information ♦ Backboards, basketballs, and nets. 800-444-5700; 770-449-5700 (in GA).

**Sportline of Hilton Head Ltd.,** Heritage Plaza, Pope Ave., Hilton Head, SC 29928: Free information ♦ Basketballs. 888-996-8855. www.hiltonhead9.com/sportline

**TC Sports,** 7251 Ford Hwy., Tecumseh, MI 49286: Free information ♦ Backboards and nets. 800-523-1498; 517-451-5221 (in MI).

**The Training Camp,** c/o Genesis Direct, 100 Plaza Dr., Secaucus, NJ 07094: Free catalog ♦ Basketball, football, golf, hockey, and soccer training aids for children. 800-873-8263. care@GenesisDirect.com

**Venus Knitting Mills Inc.,** 140 Spring St., Murray Hill, NJ 07974: Free information ♦ Basketballs, nets, and score books. 800-955-4200; 908-464-2400 (in NJ).

**Wolvering Sports,** P.O. Box 1941, Ann Arbor, MI 48106: Catalog $1 ♦ Baseball, basketball, field hockey, soccer, football, other athletic, and recreation equipment. 313-761-5691.

## BASKETS

**Allen's Basketworks,** 11008 SE Main St., Milwaukie, OR 97222: Catalog $2 ♦ Basket-making supplies. 503-238-6384.

**Ashwood Basket Corp.,** 375 Union St., Peterborough, NH 03458: Free catalog ◆ Handcrafted baskets. 800-463-6233.

**Atkinson's Country House,** 2775 Riniel Rd., Lennon, MI 48449: Free catalog ◆ Basket-making supplies. 800-832-3071; 810-621-4947 (in MI). www.sandyatkinson.com

**Bamboo & Rattan Works Inc.,** 470 Oberlin Ave. South, Lakewood, NJ 08701: Free information ◆ Rattan, cords, chair cane, matting, and bamboo, flat, and round reeds. 800-4-BAMBOO.

**Basket Beginnings,** 25 W. Tioga St., Tunkhannock, PA 18657: Free price list ◆ Basket-making and fiber art supplies. 800-82-FIBER.

**Basket Maker's Catalog,** GH Productions, P.O. Box 621, Scottsville, KY 42164: Free catalog ◆ Basket-making and chair caning supplies including reed, cane, books, tools, handles, kits, and more. 502-237-4821. www.basketmakerscatalog.com

**Basketville Inc.,** Main St., P.O. Box 710, Putney, VT 05364: Catalog $2 ◆ Ready-to-finish baskets. 800-258-4553. www.basketville.com

**Braid-Aid,** 466 Washington St., Pembroke, MA 02359: Catalog $4 ◆ Braided rug kits and braiding accessories, wool by the pound or yard, and hooking, basket-making, shirret, spinning, and weaving supplies. 781-826-2560.

**P.L. Butte Baskets,** 44 W. Park Ave., Long Beach, NY 11561: Free list of retail sources ◆ Basket-making and caning supplies. 800-289-1049. www.PLButte.com

**C & D Baskets,** 170 Turkey Ln., Livermore, ME 04253: Free list ◆ Basket-making supplies. 207-897-6043.

**Cane & Basket Supply Company,** 1283 S. Cochran, Los Angeles, CA 90019: Catalog $2 ◆ Fiber and genuine rush, Danish seat cord, raffia, rattan, sea grass, hoops and handles, other supplies, and flat, oval, and round reeds. 800-468-3966.

**Caning Shop,** 926 Gilman St., Berkeley, CA 94710: Catalog $2 (refundable) ◆ Supplies and how-to books for basket-making and chair-weaving. 800-544-3373.

**Carib-America Inc.,** 10160 Fisher Ave., Tampa, FL 33619: Free brochure ◆ Baskets. 800-783-0812.

**Carolina Basketry,** 2703 Hwy. 70 East, New Bern, NC 28560: Free catalog ◆ Basket weaving and caning supplies. 252-637-6290. www.clearlight.com/baskets

**Connecticut Cane & Reed Company,** P.O. Box 762, Manchester, CT 06040: Catalog 50¢ ◆ Caning and basket-making supplies. 860-646-6586.

**Country Seat,** 1013 Old Philly Pike, Kempton, PA 19529: Free catalog with long SASE and three 1st class stamps ◆ How-to books and basket-making and chair-caning supplies. 610-756-6124. www.countryseat.com

**Earth Guild,** 33 Haywood St., Asheville, NC 28801: Catalog $3 ◆ Basket-making, weaving, spinning, dyeing, pottery, woodcarving, hand and machine knitting, rug-making, netting, and chair-caning supplies. 800-327-8448. www.earthguild.com

**Frank's Cane & Rush Supply,** 7252 Heil Ave., Huntington Beach, CA 92647: Free information ◆ Wood parts, tools, cane and rush, and other basket-making and seat-weaving supplies. 714-847-0707.

**GH Productions,** 521 E. Walnut St., Scottsville, KY 42164: Catalog $1 (refundable) ◆ Basket-making supplies. 800-526-1630.

**The Gibbs Company,** 606 6th St., Canton, OH 44702: Free catalog ◆ Basket-making supplies. 800-775-4426; 330-455-5344 (in OH).

**Gundula's & Peerless Rattan & Reed,** 624 S. Burnett Rd., Springfield, OH 45505: Catalog $1.50 ◆ Caning supplies. 937-323-7353. www.weavenet.com

**In a Hand Basket,** 2808 Winston St., Bloomington, IN 47401: Catalog $5 (refundable) ◆ Basket-making supplies and kits. 812-333-1817. www.inahandbasket.com

**Jonathan Kline Black Ash Baskets,** 5066 Mott Evans Rd., Trumansburg, NY 14886: Brochure $2 ◆ Traditional handmade black ash baskets. 607-387-5718.

**John E. McGuire Basket Supply,** 398 S. Main St., Geneva, NY 14456: Free price list with two 1st class stamps ◆ Basket-making supplies and tools. 315-781-1251.

**Michigan Cane Supply,** 5348 N. Riverview Dr., Kalamazoo, MI 49004: List $1 ◆ Chair cane, rush, and basket-weaving supplies. 616-282-5461.

**Nasco,** 901 Janesville Ave., Fort Atkinson, WI 53538: Free catalog ◆ Basket-making supplies. 800-558-9595. www.nascofa.com

**New England Basket Company,** P.O. Box 1335, North Falmouth, MA 02556: Catalog $3 ◆ Bamboo trays, picnic hampers, and rustic rattan, country-style, and willow baskets. 800-524-4484; 508-295-8298 (in MA).

**Susi Nuss, Basketmaker,** 5 Steele Crossing Rd., Bolton, CT 06043: Brochure $2 ◆ Handmade reproduction 19th-century baskets. 860-646-3876.

**Alice Ogden,** 48 Old Hillsboro Rd., Henniker, NH 03242: Free brochure with long SASE ◆ Black ash baskets. 603-428-7849.

**Ozark Basketry Supply,** P.O. Box 599, Fayetteville, AR 72702: Catalog $1 ◆ Books, basket-making kits, chair cane, dyes, hoops, and handles. 501-442-9292.

**J. Page Basketry,** 820 Albee Rd. West, Nokomis, FL 34275: Catalog $2 (refundable) ◆ Basket-making, wheat-weaving, and pine needle crafting supplies. Also tools, books, dried and preserved flowers, and herbs. 941-485-6730.

**Peacock Crate Factory,** 1511 S. Jackson St., Jacksonville, TX 75766: Catalog $2 ◆ Ready-to-finish and use baskets. 800-666-5647.

**Peerless Rattan at the Wrap n Post,** 624 S. Burnett Rd., Springfield, OH 45505: Free information ◆ Chair caning and basket weaving supplies. 937-323-7353. www.weavenet.com

**H.H. Perkins Company,** 10 S. Bradley Rd., Woodbridge, CT 06525: Free catalog ◆ Basket-making, seat-weaving, and macrame supplies. Also books and how-to instructions. 800-462-6660.

**Plymouth Reed & Cane,** 1200 W. Ann Arbor Rd., Plymouth, MI 48170: Brochure $1 ◆ Reed, cane, fiber rush, handles, hoops, kits, dyes, tools, books, and other basket-making and chair-caning materials. 734-455-2150.

**Restoration Products,** 3191 West, 975 South, Fairmount, IN 46928: Free catalog ◆ Basket-making supplies and books. 800-562-5291.

**Royalwood Ltd.,** 517 Woodville Rd., Mansfield, OH 44907: Catalog $1 ◆ Caning and basket-making supplies, tools, kits, and dyes. 800-526-1630; 419-526-1630 (in OH). www.bright.net/~royalwood

**Snapvent Company,** 147 W. Baxter Ave., Knoxville, TN 37917: Free price list with long SASE ◆ Basket-making and chair-caning supplies. 423-523-6784.

**V.I. Reed & Cane,** Rt. 5, Box 632, Rogers, AR 72756: Free catalog ◆ Flat and round reeds, smoked reed, cane, hoops, handles, raffia, dyes, and basket-weaving kits. 800-852-0025. www.basketweaving.com

**Weaving Works,** 4717 Brooklyn Ave. NE, Seattle, WA 98105: Catalog $4.50 ◆ Basket-making supplies, looms, spinning wheels, yarns and fibers, hand and machine-knitting supplies, dyes, and how-to books. 206-524-1221.

**Donna Weber,** DW Baskets, 64 Blotz Rd., Washington, MA 01223: Free catalog ◆ Hand-woven country baskets, kits, and supplies. 413-655-8601.

**West Rindge Baskets Inc.,** 47 W. Main St., Rindge, NH 03461: Free brochure ◆ Hand-woven New England-style baskets. 603-899-2231.

**Martha Wetherbee Basket Shop,** 171 Eastman Hill Rd., Sanbornton, NH 03269: Catalog $3 ◆ Hand-woven and pounded brown ash Shaker basket reproductions. 603-286-8927.

**Woven Spirit Basketry,** 635 N. Tamiami Trail, Nokomis, FL 34275: Free catalog ◆ Basket-making tools and supplies. 800-697-6730; 941-485-6730 (in FL).

**Stephen Zeh, Basketmaker,** P.O. Box 381, Temple, ME 04984: Catalog $2 ◆ Hand-split and woven traditional brown ash baskets in Native American, Shaker, and other styles. 207-778-2351.

## BATHROOM FIXTURES & ACCESSORIES

**A-Ball Plumbing Supply,** 1703 W. Burnside St., Portland, OR 97209: Free catalog ◆ Nostalgic and contemporary plumbing fixtures and supplies. 800-228-0134. www.a-ball.com

**The Adaptive Design Shop,** 12847 Point Pleasant Dr., Fairfax, VA 22033: Free brochure ◆ Toilet supports and combination bath and shower chairs for children and adults. 800-351-2327.

**Alumax,** P.O. Box 40, Magnolia, AR 71753: Free information ◆ Bathroom fixtures and shower enclosures. 800-643-1514.

**American Standard Inc.,** P.O. Box 6820, Piscataway, NJ 08855: Free information ◆ Whirlpool tubs with molded headrest and grab bars, toilets, and other bathroom fixtures. 800-524-9797.

**Antique Treasures,** 19 Buckingham Plantation Dr., Bluffton, SC 29910: Catalog $3 (request list of retail sources) ◆ Wholesale supplier of home accents in the antique style for dealers only. 800-422-9982. www.antiquehardware.com

**Aqua Glass Corp.,** P.O. Box 412, Industrial Park, Adamsville, TN 38310: Free list of retail sources ◆ Whirlpool baths, combination steam showers, lavatories, wall surrounds, and shower floors. 800-238-3940; 901-632-0911 (in TN). www.aquaglass.com

**Baldwin Hardware Corp.,** P.O. Box 15048, Reading, PA 19612: Bathroom accessories brochure 75¢, fixtures brochure $3, door hardware brochure 75¢, hardware brochure 75¢ ◆ Brass dead bolts, other door hardware, and bathroom accessories and fixtures. 800-566-1986.

**Barnett Inc.,** 333 Lenox Ave., Jacksonville, FL 32254: Free catalog ◆ Plumbing, HVAC, hardware, and electrical products. 904-384-6530. www.bntt.com

**Bathroom Machineries,** 495 Main St., Murphys, CA 95247: Catalog $3 ◆ Early American and Victorian-style antique and reproduction bathroom fixtures. 209-728-2031. www.deabath.com

**Baths from the Past,** 83 E. Water St., Rockland, MA 02370: Catalog $5 ◆ Designer Victorian and traditional bathroom fixtures and plumbing accessories. 800-697-3871; 781-871-8530 (in MA).

**Bidematic,** 282 Westward Dr., Miami Springs, FL 33166: Free brochure ◆ Easy-to-install cold or hot and cold water adaptable bidet system for toilets. 305-888-8898. AcquaLib@bellsouth.net

**Biolet Composting Toilet,** Damonmill Square, Concord, MA 01742: Free list of retail sources ◆ Plumbing-free and self-contained biological toilet system. 800-5-BIOLET.

**Bona Decorative Hardware,** 3073 Madison Rd., Cincinnati, OH 45209: Price list $2 ◆ English and French-style bathroom fittings and accessories, cabinet and door hardware, and fireplace tools. 513-321-7877.

**Brass Menagerie,** 524 Saint Louis St., New Orleans, LA 70130: Free information with long SASE (specify items wanted) ◆ Plumbing, bathroom fixtures, and hardware. 504-524-0921.

**Briggs Industries,** 4350 W. Cypress, Ste. 800, Tampa, FL 33607: Free information ◆ Acrylic one-piece tub-shower combination units and multi-jet whirlpool tubs. 813-878-0178.

**Country Plumbing,** 5042 7th St., Carpinteria, CA 93013: Free information ◆ Antique and new plumbing supplies. 805-684-8685.

**Decorum Inc.,** 231 Commercial St., Portland, ME 04101: Free information ◆ Decorative hardware, custom lighting, old-style bathroom fixtures, and accessories. 207-775-3346.

**Dimestore Cowboys,** 407 2nd St. SW, Albuquerque, NM 87102: Catalog $7 ◆ Door sets, cabinet pulls, shutters, bathroom accessories, curtain rods and rings, and hardware. 505-244-1493.

**Eljer Plumbingware,** 17120 Dallas Pkwy., Ste. 205, Dallas, TX 75248: Free information ◆ Bathroom accessories in chrome and polished brass, frame-free shower doors, and designer tubs with multi jets. 800-4898-4048.

**Equiparts,** 817 Main St., Pittsburgh, PA 15215: Free information ◆ Vintage plumbing, heating, and electrical parts. 800-442-6622.

**The Faucet Factory,** 19 Thompson St., Winchester, MA 01890: Free catalog ◆ Designer solid cast brass fixtures in polished, untreated brass, and other optional finishes. 800-270-0028. www.faucetfactory.com

**Fiat Tubs, Showers & Steam Baths,** 1235 Hartrey Ave., Evanston, IL 60202: Free information ◆ Multi-jet tubs, showers, whirlpools, and steam baths. 847-864-7600.

**Granite Lake Pottery Inc.,** Rt. 9, P.O. Box 236, Munsonville, NH 03457: Free catalog ◆ Handcrafted stoneware sinks, accessories, and tile. 800-443-9908.

**Häfele America Company,** 3901 Cheyenne Dr., Archdale, NC 27263: Free information ◆ Folding shower seat and textured grab bars. 919-889-2322.

**Hansgrohe Inc.,** 1465 Ventura Dr., Cumming, GA 30130: Catalog $3 ◆ Faucets, massaging and hand showers, make-up/shaving mirrors, and other accessories. 770-844-7414.

**Hardware, Bath & More,** 20830 Coolidge Hwy., Oak Park, MI 48237: Free information ◆ Decorative hardware, plumbing, and light fixtures. 800-760-3278. www.h-b-m.com

**Home Decorators Collection,** 8920 Pershall Rd., Hazelwood, MO 63042: Free catalog ◆ Oak, high-glazed porcelain, chrome and brass, and wicker bathroom accessories. 800-240-6047.

**Interbath Inc.,** 665 N. Baldwin Park Blvd., City of Industry, CA 91748: Free list of retail sources ◆ Shower head attachments. 800-800-2132.

**Kallista,** 2701 Merced St., San Leandro, CA 94577: Free list of retail sources ◆ Claw foot bathroom tub, other fixtures, and accessories. 510-895-6990.

**Kohler Company,** 444 Highland Dr., Kohler, WI 53044: Catalog $3 ◆ Solid brass faucets and other plumbing fixtures, bathroom tubs and toilets, and low threshold shower stalls for wheelchair accessibility. 800-220-2291. www.kohlerco.com

**Liette International,** 243 Fleet St., New Bern, NC 28562: Free information ◆ Victorian-style bathroom accessories. 919-636-0972.

**Lyons Industries,** P.O. Box 88, Dowagiac, MI 49047: Free information ◆ Whirlpools for space-saving corner installation with optional walls and shatter-proof folding shower stall doors. 800-458-9036.

**MAC the Antique Plumber,** 6325 Elvas Ave., Sacramento, CA 95819: Catalog $6 (refundable) ◆ Antique plumbing fixtures. 916-454-4507.

**Nexton Industries Inc.,** 51 S. 1st St., Brooklyn, NY 11211: Free information ◆ Brass decorative hardware and bathroom accessories. 718-599-3837.

**Northstar Acrylic Designs,** P.O. Box 370350, Denver, CO 80237: Catalog $15 ◆ Victorian and contemporary whirlpool bathtubs, Victorian-style acrylic drop-in sinks, shower and lavatory faucets, and acrylic shower bases. 888-225-8827; 303-337-0688 (in CO). www.northstarcrylics.com

**Old Smithy Shop,** 195 Rt. 13, Brookline, NH 03055: Catalog $3 ◆ Hand-forged reproduction colonial hardware, fireplace equipment, curtain accessories, and bathroom fixtures. 603-672-4113.

**Ole Fashion Things,** 402 SW Evangeline Thwy., Lafayette, LA 70501: Catalog $6 ◆ Antique clawfoot bathtubs, bathtub faucets, and shower assemblies. Tub drains and supplies. Bath accessories. 318-234-4800.

**Paragon Products,** P.O. Box 14914, Scottsdale, AZ 85267: Catalog $4.50 (refundable) ◆ Faucets and fixtures, sinks, pedestals, whirlpools, and other bathroom accessories. 800-232-8238. www.800afaucet.com

**Plastic Creations,** 1023 S. Hamilton St., Dalton, GA 30720: Free brochure ◆ Acrylic whirlpool baths. 800-868-0254.

**Potterton-Myson**, Myson Inc., 20 Lincoln St., Essex Junction, VT 05452: Free list of retail sources ◆ Towel warmers. 802-879-1170.

**Research Products,** 2639 Andjon, Dallas, TX 75220: Free brochure ◆ Self-contained INCINOLET electric, non-polluting, and water-less toilet that incinerates waste to clean ash. 800-527-5551.

**Restoration Works Inc.,** P.O. Box 486, Buffalo, NY 14205: Catalog $3 ◆ Plumbing fixtures, bathroom accessories, ceiling medallions and trims, furniture, and hardware. 716-856-6400.

**Robern Inc.,** 7 Wood Ave., Bristol, PA 19007: Free list of retail sources ◆ Bathroom mirrors and cabinets. 215-826-9800.

**Roy Electric Company,** 22 Elm St., Westfield, NJ 07090: Free catalog ◆ Antique plumbing fixtures. 800-366-3347; 908-317-4665 (in NJ).

**Sancor Envirolet,** 140-30 Milner Ave., Scarborough, Ontario, Canada M1S 3R3: Free brochure ◆ Composting waterless and low-water toilet systems. 800-387-5126; 800-387-5245 (in Canada).

**The Sink Factory,** 2140 San Pablo Ave., Berkeley, CA 94702: Catalog $3 ◆ Traditional oval and round porcelain basins, from the classic styles of 1880 to the 1930s. 510-540-8193.

**Sonoma Woodworks Inc.,** 1285 S. Cloverdale Blvd., Cloverdale, CA 95425: Brochure $1 ◆ High-tank pull-chain toilets, solid oak cabinets, and medicine and vanity cabinets. 800-659-9003.

**Sterling Plumbing Group,** 2900 Golf Rd., Rolling Meadows, IL 60008: Free information ◆ Faucets in fired-on epoxy colors, chrome, and polished brass. 800-895-4774.

**Studio Workshop,** 2808 Tucker St., Omaha, NE 68112: Catalog $2 ◆ Solid oak bathroom accessories. 800-383-7072.

**Sunflower Showerhead Company,** P.O. Box 4218, Seattle, WA 98104: Free information ◆ Traditional, big face, and rust-proof showerheads. Nickel, brass, chrome, and gold finishes available. 206-722-1232. www.deweyusa.com/deweyusa

**Sunrise Specialty Company,** 5540 Doyle St., Emeryville, CA 94608: Catalog $2 ◆ Reproduction Victorian-style bathroom fixtures. 510-654-1794.

**Sussman Automatic,** 43-20 34th St., Long Island City, NY 11101: Free information ◆ Equipment to convert shower stalls into steam rooms. 800-238-3535.

**Swan Corp.,** 1 City Centre, St. Louis, MO 63101: Free information ◆ Shower enclosures. 314-231-8148.

**Touch of Class Catalog,** 1905 N. Van Buren St., Huntingburg, IN 47542: Free catalog ◆ Bathroom accessories, comforters, pillows and shams, window treatments, towels and rugs, and nightwear and robes for men, women, and children. 800-457-7456.

**Ultra Baths Inc.,** 1200 chemin Industriel, Bernières-St-Nicolas, Quebec, Canada G7A 1B1: Free brochure ◆ Water-operated thermo massagers and optional accessories for bath tubs. 800-463-2187 (in United States and Canada).

**Ultraflo,** P.O. Box 2294, 310 Industrial Ln., Sandusky, OH 44870: Free brochure ◆ Push-button temperature-controlled plumbing systems. 419-626-8182. www.ultraflo.com

## BATHROOM SCALES

**Frontgate,** 2800 Henkle Dr., Lebanon, OH 45036: Free catalog ◆ Bathroom scales, housewares, and kitchen accessories. 800-626-6488. www.frontgate.com

**One Step Ahead,** P.O. Box 517, Lake Bluff, IL 60044: Free catalog ◆ Bathroom scales and baby items for use when traveling, feeding, and at bath time. 800-950-5120. osacatalog@aol.com

**JCPenney Catalog,** P.O. Box 675, Milwaukee, WI 53201: Free information ◆ Bathroom scales. 800-222-6161. www.jcpenney.com/shopping

**Spiegel,** P.O. Box 182563, Columbus, OH 43218: Free catalog ◆ Bathroom scales. 800-345-4500. www.spiegel.com

## BATTERIES & CHARGERS

**Accessory Source,** 1864 48th St., Brooklyn, NY 11204: Free information ◆ Batteries for video equipment, video tapes, microphones, editors, mixers, and other equipment. 800-723-6633; 718-435-0343 (in NY).

**Battery Biz,** 31352 Via Colinas, Ste. 104, Westlake Village, CA 91362: Free catalog ◆ Batteries. 800-848-6782. www.battery-biz.com

**Battery-Tech Inc.,** 800 S. Broadway, Hicksville, NY 11801: Free catalog ◆ Replacement batteries. 800-442-4275; 516-496-9520 (in NY).

**Cunard Associates,** RD 6, Box 104, Bedford, PA 15522: Free catalog ◆ Batteries, battery packs, and battery rebuilding services. 814-623-7000. www.users.aol.com/PrimeCell

**Falkner Enterprises,** P.O. Box 1378, Ottuma, IA 52501: Free information ◆ Batteries for radios and cellular telephones. 515-683-7621.

**Halon Marketing Inc.,** P.O. Box 203, Thorndale, PA 19372: Free information ◆ Charger for lead-acid and gel batteries. 800-343-9763.

**Motorcycle Accessory Warehouse,** 3620 Jeannine Dr., Colorado Springs, CO 80917: Free information ◆ Tires, helmets, batteries, seats, saddlebags, and sportswear. 800-241-2222. maw@iex.net

**New Castle Battery Mfg. Company,** 3601 Wilmington Rd., P.O. Box 5040, New Castle, PA 16105: Free information ◆ Storage batteries. 800-622-6733; 412-658-5501 (in PA). www.turbostart.com

**1-800-Batteries,** 2301 Robb Dr., Reno, NV 89523: Free catalog ◆ Batteries for laptops, cellular phones, camcorders, and other equipment. 800-228-8374. www.1800Batteries.com

**SR Batteries Inc.,** Box 287, Bellport, NY 11713: Information $3 ◆ Batteries for model airplanes. 516-286-0079.

**Sunshine Camera and Video,** 1562 Coney Island Ave., Brooklyn, NY 11230: Free information ◆ Computers, memory upgrades, fax modems, carrying cases, mouse devices, batteries, video equipment, and other electronics. 800-331-2661; 718-692-4140 (in NY).

**Technical Inc.,** 301 Central Park Dr., Sanford, FL 32771: Free catalog ◆ Lead acid, lithium, and other batteries for laptops, camcorders, cellular phones, and other equipment. 800-346-0601.

**Thrifty Distributors,** 641 W. Lancaster Ave., Frazer, PA 19355: Free catalog ◆ Video cameras, editing equipment, batteries, wireless microphones, lights, and accessories. 800-342-3610.

**TNR Technical Inc.,** 301 Central Park Dr., Sanford, FL 32771: Free information ◆ Sealed lead acid, lithium, and other batteries. 800-346-0601.

**W & W Associates,** 800 S. Broadway, Hicksville, NY 11801: Free information ◆ Batteries and chargers. 800-221-0732; 516-942-0011 (in NY). www.wwassociates.com

**E.H. Yost & Company,** 2211-D Parview Rd., Middleton, WI 53562: Free catalog ◆ Batteries for radios, computers, and other equipment. 608-631-3443. ehyost@midplains.net

## BEAD CRAFTING

**Alpha Supply,** P.O. Box 2133, Bremerton, WA 98310: Catalog $7 ◆ Beads, engraving and jewelry-making tools, and supplies. 800-257-4211; 360-373-3302 (in WA).

**Ambush Wholesale Beads & Findings,** P.O. Box 144, Worcester, MA 01613: Catalog $1 ◆ Charms, beads, findings, and jewelry-making supplies.

**B. Rush Apple Company,** 3855 W. Kennedy Blvd., Tampa, FL 33609: Free price list ◆ Gemstone, cloisonne, and Swarovski crystal beads. 813-870-3180.

**ARA Imports,** P.O. Box 41054, Brecksville, OH 44141: Catalog $1 ◆ Semi-precious beads, fresh water pearls, precious metal beads, and findings. 440-838-1372.

**Arizona Gems & Crystals,** 1705 W. 14th Dr., Safford, AZ 85546: Free catalog ◆ Arizona fire agate, beads, cabochons, findings, silver, jewelry kits, rough and slabs, and supplies. 800-657-6263.

**Arizona Gems & Minerals Inc.,** 6370 East Hwy. 69, Prescott Valley, AZ 86314: Catalog $4 ◆ Chip beads, other beads and findings, silversmithing and lapidary tools, jewelry-making supplies, and mineral specimens. 602-772-6443.

**Art to Wear,** 5 Crescent Pl. South, St. Petersburg, FL 33711: Catalog $1 ♦ Beads, bead-stringing supplies, findings, and tools. 272-867-3711.

**B & J Rock Shop,** 14744 Manchester Rd., Ballwin, MO 63011: Catalog $3 ♦ Rockhounding equipment, beads, quartz crystals, imported and domestic gemstones, and jewelry-making and bead-stringing supplies. 314-394-4567.

**Bally Bead Company,** 2304 Ridge Rd., Rockwall TX 75087: Catalog $4.95 (refundable) ♦ Beads and findings. 800-543-0280; 972-771-4515 (in TX). www.ballybead.com

**Banasch,** 2810 Highland Ave., Cincinnati, OH 45212: Free catalog ♦ Beads, pearls, sewing notions, and buttons. 800-543-0355; 513-731-2040 (in OH).

**Bead Boppers,** 3924 S. Meridian, Puyallup, WA 98373: Catalog $2.50 (refundable) ♦ Beads and findings, tools, charms, seed beads, leather, supplies, and books. 888-848-3880. www.ibrowse.com/boppers

**The Bead Gallery,** 3963 Main St., Amherst, NY 14226: Free information ♦ Czech glass, Swarovski crystal, African trade, semi-precious, seed beads, charms, and books. 888-BEAD-125; 716-836-6775 (in NY). www.beadgallery.com

**The Bead Shop,** 10222 Warwick Blvd., Newport News, VA 23601: Catalog $2 ♦ Beads, charms, findings, and craft supplies. 757-245-5844.

**Bead Source,** 7047 Reseda Blvd., Reseda, CA 91335: Catalog $11 ♦ Beads, Austrian crystals, Peruvian beads, findings, and appliques. 818-708-0972.

**Bead Warehouse,** 4 Meadowlake Dr., Mendon, VT 05701: Free catalog ♦ Beads, books, tools, clay, necklace and earring kits, and other craft items. 800-736-0781.

**Bead World,** 4931 Prospect NE, Albuquerque, NM 87110: Catalog $2 ♦ Beads, findings and supplies, and leather cord. 505-884-3133.

**Beada Beada,** 4262 N. Woodward Ave., Royal Oak, MI 48073: Free catalog ♦ Beads, bead-stringing supplies, and findings. 248-549-1005.

**Beadbox Inc.,** 10135 E. Via Linda, Scottsdale, AZ 85258: Catalog $5 ♦ Beads from worldwide sources and jewelry kits. 800-232-3269.

**Beadman Enterprises,** 27195 Duffy Rd., Sedro-Woolley, WA 98284: Catalog $3 (refundable) ♦ All types and sizes of beads, findings, and specialty items. beadman@cnw.com

**Beads Galore International Inc.,** 2123 S. Priest, Tempe, AZ 85282: Catalog $5 (refundable) ♦ Beads and bead-stringing supplies. 800-424-9577. www.beadsgalore.com

**Beadtrader,** 2750 S. Broadway, Englewood, CO 80110: Free catalog ♦ Beads from Africa, India, Europe, the Orient, and North and South America. 800-805-BEAD.

**Beadworks,** 149 Water St., Norwalk, CT 06854: Catalog $7.95 ♦ Glass, ceramic, porcelain, pearl, stone, and other beads. 800-232-3761. www.beadworks.com

**BeadZip,** 2316 Sarah Ln., Falls Church, VA 22043: Catalog $5 (refundable) ♦ Beads from around the world. 703-849-8463. www.catalogmall.com/scripts/tame.exe/beadzip/index.tam

**Beyond Beadery,** P.O. Box 460, Rollinsville, CO 80474: Catalog $2 ♦ * Looms, findings, needles and thread, and Czechoslovakian, Japanese, and Austrian crystal beads. 800-840-5548. members.aol.com/beyondbead

**Bourget Bros.,** 1636 11th St., Santa Monica, CA 90404: Catalog $5 ♦ Beads, bead-stringing and jewelry-making supplies, and tools. 800-828-3024. www.bourgetbros.com

**Bovis Bead Company,** P.O. Box 13345, Tucson, AZ 85732: Catalog $5 ♦ French glass beads and Native American craft supplies. 520-318-9512.

**Bucks County Classic,** 73 Coventry Ln., Longhorn, PA 19047: Catalog $2 ♦ Cabochons, fresh water pearls, findings, and gemstone, Chinese cloisonne, Austrian crystal, stone, and metal beads. 800-942-GEMS. www.xmission.com/~arts

**Caravan Beads,** 449 Forest Ave., Portland, ME 04101: Free price list ♦ Japanese Delica, seed and fringe beads, triangles, and more. 800-230-8941. www.caravanbeads.com

**Charlie's Rock Shop,** P.O. Box 399, Penrose, CO 81240: Catalog $3 (refundable) ♦ Beads, bead-stringing and jewelry-making supplies, jewelry boxes, and faceted gemstones. 719-372-0117.

**Columbine Beads,** 2723 Lock Haven Dr., Ijamsville, MD 21754: Sample newsletter catalog $3.50 ♦ Japanese, Czech, other glass beads, and supplies. 301-865-5047.

**Copper Coyote Beads Ltd.,** 9430 E. Golf Links, #286, Tucson, AZ 85730: Catalog $2 ♦ Japanese seed beads and Delicas; bead-related books; graph paper. 520-722-8440. www.coppercoyote.com

**The Cracker Box,** P.O. Box 413, Solebury, PA 18963: Catalog $4.50 ♦ Bead-crafting kits. 215-862-2100.

**Creations by Lauren,** 921 Rosilee Ln., Rapid City, SD 57701: Catalog $2 (refundable) ♦ Custom handmade beaded clothing and accessories in traditional Native American style. Also moccasins, knife cases, war shirts, dresses, and other crafts.

**Creative Castle,** 2321 Michael Dr., Newbury Park, CA 91320: Free catalog ♦ Bead-making jewelry kits. 805-499-1377. www.creativecastle.com

**Dawn's Hide & Bead Away,** 521 E. Washington St., Iowa City, IA 52240: Free catalog ♦ Tools, jewelry wire, necklace findings, gemstones, beads, supplies, and accessories. 319-338-1566.

**Discount Bead House,** P.O. Box 186, The Plains, OH 45780: Catalog $5 ♦ Seed beads, findings, and tools. 800-793-7592.

**Double Joy Beads,** 7119 E. Sahuaro Dr., Scottsdale, AZ 85254: Catalog $1 ♦ Copper beads and findings. 602-998-4495.

**E & W Imports Inc.,** P.O. Box 15703, Tampa, FL 33684: Price list $3.50 ♦ Gemstone, cloisonne, and Austrian crystal beads and 14k findings. 813-885-1138. www.wp.com/E&WImports

**Eagle Feather Trading Post,** 168 W. 12th St., Ogden, UT 84404: Catalog $3.50 ♦ Beading and Native American craft supplies, beads and bead-stringing kits, and how-to beading and craft books. 801-393-3991.

**Ebersole Lapidary Supply Inc.,** 11417 West Hwy. 54, Wichita, KS 67209: Catalog $5 ♦ Beads, bead-stringing supplies, carving materials, tools, findings, mountings, cabochons and rocks, and jewelry kits. 316-722-4771.

**Enterprise Art,** P.O. Box 2918, Largo, FL 33779: Free catalog ♦ Beads from around the world, bead and jewelry-making kits, and craft and jewelry-making supplies. 800-366-2218. www.enterpriseart.com

**Evening Star Designs,** 69 Coolidge Ave., Haverhill, MA 01832: Catalog $3 ♦ Antique Christmas to Zuni-style fetish animal beads. 800-666-3562.

**Exclusive Imports,** 451 E. 58th Ave., Box 415, Denver, CO 80216: Free catalog ♦ Imported beads from the Czech Republic. 800-520-0550.

**Fire Mountain Gems,** 28195 Redwood Hwy., Cave Junction, OR 97523: Catalog $3 ♦ Beads, findings, tools, and bead-stringing and jewelry-making supplies. 800-423-2319. www.firemtn.com

**Renee Foxx Beads by Mail,** 196 Valley St., Pembroke, MA 02359: Free catalog with long SASE and two 1st class stamps ♦ Rare and unusual beads.

**Frantz Bead Company,** E. 1222 Sunset Hill Rd., Shelton, WA 98584: Catalog $6 ♦ Glass bead-making supplies, handmade glass beads from India and Thailand, other beads, and findings. 800-839-6712. frantzbead@olywa.net

**Garden of Beadin',** P.O. Box 1535, Redway, CA 95560: Catalog $3 ♦ Seed beads, crystals, semi-precious gemstones, books, and bead-stringing supplies. 800-232-3588. www.a1server.com/beadluv

**Gem-O-Rama Inc.,** 150 Recreation Park Dr., Hingham, MA 02043: Free catalog ♦ Beads and bead-stringing supplies. 781-749-8250.

**General Bead San Diego,** 317 National City Blvd., National City, CA 91950: Catalog $4 ♦ Imported Japanese seed beads. 619-336-0100. www.genbead.com

**Hardies,** P.O. Box 1920, Quartzsite, AZ 85346: Catalog $3 (refundable) ◆ Czech, seed, handmade glass, and other beads. Also findings, buckles, bolas, Native American jewelry, gems, rocks, and books. 800-962-2775; 520-927-6381 (in AZ). Ahardies@aol.com

**Hedgehog Handworks,** P.O. Box 45384, Westchester, CA 90045: Catalog $5 ◆ Semi-precious beads, sewing notions, gold and silver threads, and needlecraft, embroidery, and other craft supplies. 888-670-6040; 310-670-6040 (in CA).

**Hirsch Designs,** 7000 N. 16th St., Ste. 120-181, Phoenix, AZ 85020: Catalog $3 ◆ Delica and antique beads. 602-861-2961.

**Jay's of Tucson Inc.,** 4621 E. Speedway Blvd., Tucson, AZ 85712: Catalog $5 (refundable) ◆ Findings, crafts, gifts, Navajo rugs, sand paintings, Taos moccasins, drums, and Navajo, Hopi, and Zuni jewelry. Also Czech, seed, pony, Peruvian, and other beads. 602-294-3397.

**Audrey S. Johnston,** Dixie Village Shopping Center, Gastonia, NC 28052: Free information ◆ Antique pendants and African trade, Venetian glass, Old Nagaland, and precious and semi-precious beads. 704-866-8776.

**Judybeads,** 255 Old Ford Rd., New Paltz, NY 12561: Free price list ◆ Japanese beads. 914-255-7207.

**Victor H. Levy Inc.,** 1355 S. Flower St., Los Angeles, CA 90015: Catalog $5 ◆ Rocailles, shells, jewelry-making supplies, and seed, bone, fancy, and other beads. 800-421-8021; 213-749-8247 (in CA).

**Morning Light Emporium,** Roxy Grinnell, P.O. Box 1155, Paronia, CO 81428: Free catalog ◆ Beads and jewelry-making supplies. 800-392-0365. www.wic.net/mle/mle.htm

**National Supply Inc.,** 9666 Olive Blvd., Ste. 145, St. Louis, MO 63132: Catalog $4 (refundable) ◆ Beads, jewelry findings, tools, crafts, and supplies. 800-221-9032; 314-567-1928 (in MO). www.nationalsupply.com

**New England International Gems,** 188 Pollard St., Billerica, MA 01862: Free catalog ◆ Beads and beading supplies. 978-863-8331.

**Optional Extras,** P.O. Box 8550, Burlington, VT 05402: Catalog $2 ◆ Jewelry findings and beads from worldwide sources. 800-736-0781.

**Ornamental Resources Inc.,** P.O. Box 3010, Idaho Springs, CO 80452: Catalog $15 ◆ Rare, old, and vintage glass and metal beads. Also glass pendants and stones, plastic beads, ceramic items, and beading supplies. 800-876-6762. www.ornabead.com

**Out On A Whim,** 121 E. Cotati Ave., Cotati, CA 94931: Free information ◆ Imported beads, glass beads, semi-precious stones, jewelry findings and supplies, and beading accessories. 707-664-8343.

**Peninsula Bead & Supply,** 5166 Moorpark Ave., San Jose, CA 95129: Catalog $5 ◆ Glass and Austrian crystal, horn, metal, and bone beads. 408-253-6434.

**The Peruvian Bead Company,** 1601 Callens Rd., Ventura, CA 93003: Catalog $2 ◆ Handpainted ceramic and hemp jewelry kits. 800-333-7378. www.perubead.com

**Promenade Le Bead Shop,** 1970 13th St., Boulder, CO 80302: Catalog $2.50 (refundable) ◆ Beads, bead-crafting kits, and books. 303-440-4807.

**Rising Arrow Beads,** 265 Sobrante Way, Sunnyvale, CA 94086: Catalog $1 ◆ Native American beads and supplies. 408-732-2001.

**Riviera Lapidary Supply,** 50898 7th St., Box 40, Riviera, TX 78379: Catalog $3 ◆ Beads, bead-stringing supplies and kits, shells, petrified wood products, cabochons, slabs, cabbing rough, gemstones, and crystals. 512-296-3958.

**San Francisco Arts & Crafts,** 1592 Union St., #174, San Francisco, CA 94123: Catalog $3 ◆ Czech glass beads. 707-935-6756.

**Marvin Schwab,** 2740 Garfield Ave., Silver Spring, MD 20910: Catalog $3.50 ◆ Beads, bead-crafting supplies, and findings. 301-565-0487. beadware@erols.com

**Scottsdale Bead Supply,** 3625 N. Martial Way, Scottsdale, AZ 85251: Free information ◆ Bali and Israel silver, Native American and Czech glass, Japanese replicas, Austrian crystal, and other beads. 602-945-5988.

**Shepherds,** 2802 Juan St., #14, San Diego, CA 92110: Catalog $2 ◆ Japanese seed beads and beading components. 619-297-4110.

**Shipwreck Beads Inc.,** 2727 Westmoor Ct., Olympia, WA 98502: Catalog $4 ◆ Beads, bead-stringing supplies, and findings. 360-754-2323. www.shipwreck-beads.com

**Sioux Trading Post Inc.,** 415 6th St., Rapid City, SD 57701: Catalog $2 ◆ Beads and beadwork. 800-456-3394. www.prairieedge.com

**Soho South,** P.O. Box 1324, Cullman, AL 35056: Catalog $2.50 (refundable) ◆ Beads and findings, fabric dyes and paints, silk scarves and fabrics, and marbling supplies. 256-739-6114. soho@airnet.net

**South Pacific Wholesale Company,** Rt. 2, P.O. Box 249, East Montpelier, VT 05651: Free price list ◆ Beads, findings, semi-precious gemstone settings, gold and silver bracelets, necklaces, and earrings. 800-338-2162. sopacvt@aol.com

**Southwest America,** 1506 Wyoming NE, Albuquerque, NM 87112: Brochure $1 ◆ Tiny antique seed beads to large ornamental varieties. 505-299-1856.

**Stone Design,** 123 Sandrah Dr., Orange, MA 01364: Catalog $2 ◆ Beads. 978-544-6998.

**Sunshine Discount Crafts,** 12335 62nd St. North, Largo, FL 33773: Free catalog ◆ Modeling clays and accessories, art supplies, beads, tole and decorative painting supplies, and more. 800-720-2878. www.sunshinecrafts.com

**Today's Vintage Designs,** 436 W. Broadway, SoHo, NY 10012: Catalog $2 (refundable) ◆ Venetian glass, antique, Czech crystal, and metal beads. Also supplies. 212-925-6342.

**TSI Jewelry Supply,** 101 Nickerson St., Seattle, WA 98109: Free catalog ◆ Jewelry-making tools and supplies. 800-426-9984. www.Tsijeweltools.com

**Veon Creations,** 3565 State Rd. V, De Soto, MO 63020: Catalog $4 ◆ Beads, gemstones, pearls, findings and jewelry-making supplies. 314-586-5377.

**Wale Apparatus Company Inc.,** 400 Front St., P.O. Box D, Hellertown, PA 18055: Catalog $5 ◆ Bead-making and artistic glass working equipment and supplies. 800-334-WALE; 610-838-7047 (in PA).

## BEAR MAKING & CLOTHING

**Animal Crackers Patterns,** 1404 Peyton, Los Lunas, NM 87031: Catalog $2 ◆ Kits, supplies, and patterns for easy-to-make stuffed toys, bears, and other animals. 505-865-7218.

**Bear Clawset,** 27 Palermo Walk, Long Beach, CA 90803: Catalog $2 ◆ Bear-making supplies. 562-434-8077.

**Bear Hugs,** 7 Cooper Ave., Marlton, NJ 08053: Free information ◆ Bears and bear clothing. 800-MR-BEARS.

**By Diane,** 1126 Ivon Ave., Endicott, NY 13760: Catalog $3 ◆ Furs and mohair, growlers, squeakers, music boxes, noses, eyes, joint sets, and patterns for bears, soft toys, and puppets. 607-754-0391.

**CR's Crafts,** Box 8, Leland, IA 50453: Catalog $2 ◆ Doll and bear-making supplies, new jointed bears, electronic melody units, kits, patterns, and crafting items. 515-567-3652. www.crscrafts.com

**Edinburgh Imports Inc.,** P.O. Box 340, Newbury Park, CA 91319: Free catalog with two 1st class stamps ◆ Bear-making supplies. 800-EDINBRG; 805-376-1700 (in CA). www.edinburgh.com

**Intercal,** 1760 Monrovia, Ste. A-17, Costa Mesa, CA 92627: Free information with two 1st class stamps ◆ Imported mohair, alpaca, woven synthetics, glass eyes, wool felt, and other bear-making supplies. 714-645-9396.

**Itty Bitty Small Originals & Pattern Company,** 3116 Thorn St., San Diego, CA 92104: Catalog $3 ◆ Miniature teddy bear patterns and kits. 619-282-4404.

**Miniature Teddy Bear Kits,** Emily Farmer, P.O. Box 2911, Sanford, NC 27330: Catalog $3 ◆ Miniature teddy bear kits.

**Monterey Outlet Store,** 1725 E. Delavan Dr., Janesville, WI 53545: Sample swatches $5 ◆ Knitted deep pile fur fabrics. 800-432-9959; 608-754-8309 (in WI). www.montereyoutlet.com

**Spare Bear Parts,** P.O. Box 56, Interlochen, MI 49643: Catalog $1.75 ◆ Bear-making supplies, patterns, and kits. 616-276-7915. www.SpareBear.com

**Tailormade Togs for Teddy Bears,** 4037 161st St. SE, Bellevue, WA 98006: Catalog $4 ◆ Clothing pattern catalog for teddy bears. 206-644-4469.

**Teddies N' Tole,** Earlene Vaughn, 16324 Langfield Ave., Ceritos, CA 90701: Catalog $1.50; fabric samples $6 ◆ Supplies for miniature bears. 262-926-0778.

**Teddys by Tracy,** 32 Pikehall Pl., Baltimore, MD 21236: Catalog $5 (refundable with first $10 order) ◆ Bear fabrics, eyes, kits, silk and organdy ribbons, and other supplies. 410-529-2418.

**Tender Heart Treasures Ltd.,** 10525 J St., Omaha, NE 68127: Free catalog ◆ Clothing and accessories for bears and dolls. 800-443-1367. www.tenderheart.com

**Unicorn Studios,** 424 Blount Ave., Knoxville, TN 37920: Catalog $1 ◆ Easy-to-install windup and electronic music box movements, winking light units, and voices for dolls and bears. 423-573-1863. www.imox.com/unicorn

## BEARS

**Animal Haus Ltd.,** 7784 Montgomery Rd., Cincinnati, OH 45236: Free catalog with four 1st class stamps ◆ Bears. 513-984-9955.

**Anything Goes Inc.,** 9801 Gulf Dr., Anna Maria, FL 34216: Quarterly newsletter $2 ◆ Antique and collectible bears. 800-780-2327; 813-778-4456 (in FL).

**Dottie Ayers,** 22 E. 24th St., Baltimore, MD 21218: Free information ◆ Antique bears. 410-366-7010.

**Bear Hugs,** 7 Cooper Ave., Marlton, NJ 08053: Free information ◆ Bears and bear clothing. 800-MR-BEARS.

**Bear In Mind Inc.,** 53 Bradford St., Concord, MA 01742: Catalog $1 ◆ Exclusive handcrafted bears and other collectibles. 978-369-1167.

**Bear Pawse,** 502 S. Montezuma, Prescott, AZ 86303: Catalog $6 ◆ Bears. 520-445-3800.

**Beardeaux Barn,** 8907 Warner Ave., Ste. 166, Huntington Beach, CA 92647: Catalog $4 (specify patterns or bears) ◆ Artist bears, bear-related items, and bear-making supplies. 714-842-4460.

**Bears Everywhere,** 703 Caroline St., Fredericksburg, VA 22401: Free information ◆ One-of-a-kind exclusive editions and other collectible bears. 540-371-8484.

**The Bears of Bruton Street,** 107 Bruton St., Wilson, NC 27893: Free information with long SASE ◆ Bears. 800-488-BEAR.

**Bears 'N Things,** 1491 Bacon Rd., Albion, NY 14411: Monthly list (annual subscription) $10 ◆ Artist bears. 716-589-4066.

**Bears 'n Wares,** 312 Bridge St., New Cumberland, PA 17070: Brochure $2 ◆ Bears. 717-774-1261.

**The Bears To Go,** 525 Cedar Hill Ave., Wyckoff, NJ 07481: Free information ◆ Collectible and retired bears. 201-444-9133.

**Campbell's Collectibles,** 10971 Four Seasons Pl., Crown Point, IN 46307: Free information with long SASE ◆ Collectible bears. 219-988-3615.

**Laura Caruso,** The Country Bear, 10465 Big Hand Rd., Columbus Twp., MI 48063: Catalog $5 ◆ Artist bears. 810-727-1737.

**Christy's Bears,** Buckingham Green, #202, Buckingham, PA 18912: Free information with long SASE ◆ Bears. 215-794-5840.

**Collector's Corner Bears,** P.O. Box 816, Grand Haven, MI 49417: Newsletter $20 (annual subscription) ◆ New and retired collectible bears. 616-846-0876.

**Country Etc.,** 135 W. Plymouth Ave., DeLand, FL 32720: Free brochure ◆ Bear accessories. 800-538-1753.

**CR's Crafts,** Box 8, Leland, IA 50453: Catalog $2 ◆ Doll and bear-making supplies, new jointed bears, electronic melody units, kits, patterns, and crafting items. 515-567-3652. www.crscrafts.com

**Crafts by Pat,** 194 Grove St., Reading, MA 01867: Free catalog ◆ Afghans, dressed teddy bears, all-occasion wreaths, baskets, and other crafts. 781-944-1294.

**Cynthia's Country Store,** The Wellington Mall, 12794 W. First Hill Blvd., Ste. 15A, West Palm Beach, FL 33414: Catalog $15 ◆ Collectible bears. 561-793-0554.

**Di's Vintage Bear Collection**, 3754 Kipling, Berkley, MI 48072: Brochure $2 ◆ Collectible vintage bears. 248-547-0769.

**Divine Little Delights,** P.O. Box 167, Grant, FL 32949: Free brochure with long SASE ◆ Miniature teddy bears and stuffed animals. 407-725-5270.

**The Doll House,** 18 S. Broadway, Edmond, OK 73034: Free information ◆ Limited edition bears. 405-348-9895.

**dolls 'n bearland,** 15001 N. Hayden Rd., Ste. 104, Scottsdale, AZ 85260: Free catalog with two 1st class stamps ◆ Collectible dolls and teddy bears. 800-359-9541. www.dollsnbearland.com

**Dollsville Dolls & Bearsville Bears,** 292 N. Palm Canyon Dr., Palm Springs, CA 92262: Catalog $2 ◆ Bears. 800-225-2327. www.dollsville.com

**Enchanted Doll House,** Rt. 7A, RR 1, Box 2535, Manchester Center, VT 05255: Catalog $2 ◆ Bears, toys, and dolls. 802-362-1327.

**Ernie's Toyland,** 1012 6th St., Ste. 120, Yuba City, CA 95901: Free information ◆ Manufactured, limited edition, and discontinued bears. 800-367-1233. www.erniestoyland.com

**FairyTales Inc.,** 3 S. Park Ave., Lombard, IL 60148: Catalog $2 ◆ Artist and other bears and plush toys. 800-495-6973. www.fairytalesnbears.com

**Gift World,** 2392 Locust St., Portage, IN 46368: Brochure $2 ◆ Registered limited edition collector bears. 800-847-4450; 219-763-2408 (in IN).

**GiGi's Dolls & Sherry's Teddy Bears Inc.,** 6029 N. Northwest Hwy., Chicago, IL 60631: Free catalog ◆ Bears, dolls, plush toys, and miniatures. 773-594-1540.

**Groves Quality Collectibles,** 204 N. Main St., Bluffton, OH 45817: Catalog $5 ◆ Bears, dolls, and toys. 419-358-8559. members.aol.com/ grovescoll

**Gund Bears,** P.O. Box H, Edison, NJ 08818: Free brochure ◆ Collectible bears.

**Harper General Store,** RD 2, Box 512, Annville, PA 17003: Newsletter (6 issues $10) ◆ Antique bears. 717-865-3456.

**It's A Zoo,** 3009 W. Magnolia Blvd., Burbank, CA 91505: Free information ◆ Artist and manufactured bears. 818-842-5534.

**Cindy Kalnow Bears,** 658 W. Willow St., Chicago, IL 60614: Photos $2 ◆ Heirloom teddy bears. 312-587-3252.

**Ladybug Garden,** 3805 Lakeview Dr., Elizabeth, IN 47117: Color photos $2; free brochure with long SASE ◆ Collectible artist bears. 812-969-3840.

**Lane's Toyland & Gifts,** 720 Realtor Ave., Texarkana, AR 75502: Free catalog ◆ Collectible bears. 800-421-8697.

**Tammie Lawrence,** 717 Dakota St., Holton, KS 66436: Information $3 ◆ Authentic antique reproductions. 913-364-4256.

**Lexin Inc.,** Nice Stuff, 148 W. 132nd St., Los Angeles, CA 90061: Free brochure ◆ Bears. 310-329-7568.

**Littlethings,** 129 Main St., Irvington, NY 10533: Free list with long SASE ◆ Bears, dollhouses, miniatures, furniture, miniature paintings, and other collectibles. 914-591-9150.

**Marj's Doll Sanctuary,** 5238 Plainfield Ave. NE, Grand Rapids, MI 49505: Catalog $1 ◆ Bears and dolls. 616-361-0054. marjsdolls@compuserve.com

**Mary D's Dolls & Bears & Such,** 423-431 3rd St., Osseo, MN 55369: Catalog $2 ◆ Collectible bears. 612-424-4375.

**My Kind of Bear,** Kathy Nearing, 38 Montague St., Binghamton, NY 13901: Free brochure with long SASE ◆ Limited edition artist bears. 607-648-6122.

**North American Bear Company,** 401 N. Wabash, Ste. 500, Chicago, IL 60610: Free information with long SASE ◆ Bears. 312-329-0020.

**The Old Game Store,** Rt. 11, Manchester, VT 05254: Free information with long SASE ◆ Games, puzzles, collectible teddy bears, and toys. 802-362-2756.

**Old-Timers Antiques,** 3717 S. Dixie Hwy., West Palm Beach, FL 33405: Free list with long SASE ◆ New and older Steiff bears. Also discontinued and limited editions. 561-832-5141.

**The Paper Place & Doll Place,** 212 S. River, Holland, MI 49423: Catalog $3 (refundable) ◆ Collectible bears and dolls. 616-392-7776.

**Parlor Bears,** 1423 NW Hwy. 101, Lincoln City, OR 97367: Free information ◆ Artist bears. 541-994-2082.

**Playhouse,** Mary Radbill, 4512 Eden St., Philadelphia, PA 19114: Free catalog ◆ Artist dolls, bears, and accessories. 215-632-4606.

**Romerhaus Creations,** 951 S. Alvord Blvd., Evansville, IN 47714: Catalog $10 ◆ Miniature bears. 812-473-7277.

**Rose's Doll House Store,** 6572 Lover's Ln., Milwaukee, WI 53132: Free catalog ◆ Bears, dolls, and dollhouse furnishings and miniatures. 800-926-9093; 414-529-3020 (in WI).

**Sara's Bears & Gifts,** 173 S. Yonge St., Ormond Beach, FL 32174: Free video catalog ◆ Current and retired bears. 800-988-4073.

**Shirley's Doll House,** 971 N. Milwaukee Ave., Wheeling, IL 60090: Free information with long SASE ◆ Bears and dolls, doll-making supplies, dollhouse furniture, and collectibles. 847-537-1632.

**The Teddy Bear Emporium,** 51 N. Broad St., Lititz, PA 17543: Free information with long SASE ◆ Bears. 800-598-6853; 717-626-TEDI (in PA).

**Teddy Bears To Go,** 897 W. Park Ave., Cobblestone Village, Ocean, NJ 07712: Free information ◆ Over 400 different teddy bears. 800-284-BEAR; 493-4455 (in Monmouth County).

**Teddies R' Friends,** 2467 Fairview Rd., American Falls, ID 83211: Photos $7 ◆ Collectible artist bears. 208-226-2171.

**Teddytown U.S.A.,** 73 White Bridge Rd., Nashville, TN 37205: Free information ◆ Bears. 615-356-2484.

**Tide-Rider Inc.,** P.O. Box 429, Oakdale, CA 95361: Free information ◆ Handmade bears and stuffed animals from Merrythought Iron Bridge in Great Britain. 209-848-4420.

**Today's Treasures,** 655 73rd St., Niagara Falls, NY 14304: Catalog $3 (refundable) ◆ Collector dolls and bears. 716-283-1726.

**Toy Shoppe,** 11632 Busy St., Richmond, VA 23236: Free information ◆ Collectible dolls and bears. 800-447-7995.

**Toy Village,** 3105 W. Saginaw, Lansing, MI 48917: Free information ◆ Toys, dolls, bears, and collectibles. 517-323-1145.

**Vermont Teddy Bear Company,** US Rt. 7, Shelburne Rd., Shelburne, VT 05482: Free information with long SASE ◆ Bears. 800-829-BEAR; 802-985-3001 (in VT). www.vtbear.com

**Worldly Bear Company,** P.O. Box 430, Greenfield, MA 01302: Catalog $3 ◆ Collectible bears. 413-774-4590.

# BEDDING

## Comforters & Bed Coverings

**Antique Quilt Source,** 385 Springview Rd., Carlisle, PA 17013: Catalog $7 ◆ Antique quilts. 717-245-2054.

**Barton-Sharpe Ltd.,** 66 Crosby St., New York, NY 10012: Free information ◆ Reproduction 18th and 19th-century furniture, lighting, bedding, stoneware, and decorative items. 212-925-9562.

**The Bed Rizer,** 736 Federal St., Davenport, IA 52803: Free information ◆ Bed elevating legs, bed ruffles, and matching accessories. 800-321-9447. www.bedrizer.com

**The Blanket Brigade,** Dale & Dona Harrison, P.O. Box 534, Kunkleton, PA 18058: Catalog $2 ◆ Men and women's leather and cloth clothing. Also imported Witney blankets from England. 610-381-4400. www.blanketbrigade.com

**Carter Canopies,** P.O. Box 808, Troutman, NC 28166: Brochure $1 ◆ Hand-tied cotton fishnet canopies, dust ruffles, coverlets, and other country-style bedroom furnishings. 800-538-4071. www.carter-canopies.com

**Chambers,** Mail Order Dept., P.O. Box 7841, San Francisco, CA 94120: Free catalog ◆ Bed and bath furnishings. 800-334-1254.

**Choices,** 1000 Lake St., Oak Park, IL 60301: Brochure $2 ◆ Handmade 100 percent cotton yarn quilts with bonded cotton batting, quilted tote bags, and pillow shams. 708-386-6555.

**The Company Store,** 500 Company Store Rd., LaCrosse, WI 54601: Free catalog ◆ Linens, mattress pads, down-filled pillows, comforters, and outerwear. 800-289-8508. info@thecompanystore.com

**Laura Copenhaver Industries Inc.,** P.O. Box 149, Marion, VA 24354: Free brochure ◆ Handmade quilts, coverlets, hand-tied canopies, and curtains. 800-227-6797.

**Cuddledown of Maine,** 312 Canco Rd., Portland, ME 04103: Free catalog ◆ Down and feather/down comforters, sheets, sleepwear, mattress pads, throw pillows, flannel bedding, and nursery items. 800-323-6793. www.cuddledown.com

**Dewey Trading Company,** 53 Old Santa Fe Trail, Santa Fe, NM 87501: Free brochure ◆ Blankets with designs that are a tribute to Native Americans and western artists. 800-444-9665. www.deweytradingcom

**Domestications,** Hanover Direct Pennsylvaniia Inc., Hanover, PA 17333-0001: Free catalog ◆ Comforters, sheets, pillows, blankets, bedspreads, throws, solid and lace tablecloths, mini blinds, shower curtains, and bathroom accessories. 717-633-3313.

**Donna's Custom Canopies,** 123 Lomax St., Boone, NC 28607: Brochure $1 with long SASE ◆ Cotton hand-tied canopies, throw pillows, and down-filled comforters. 828-262-1631.

**Down Home Comforts,** P.O. Box 2281, West Brattleboro, VT 05303: Brochure $1 ◆ New and re-made down comforters, pillows, and featherbeds. 802-688-3780.

**Down Home Factory Outlet,** 85 Rt. 46 West, Totowa, NJ 07512: Free catalog ◆ Comforters, pillows, and other bedding. 800-ALL-DOWN.

**Eldridge Textile Company,** 17 E. 37th St., New York, NY 10016: Catalog $3 (refundable) ◆ Blankets, sheets, towels, comforters, bedspreads, rugs, and pillows. 212-576-2991. www.eldridgetextile.com

**Family Heirloom Weavers,** 775 Meadowview Dr., Red Lion, PA 17356: Catalog $3 ◆ Coverlets woven in the tradition of Pennsylvania German weavers in the early 1800s. 717-246-2431.

**Feathered Friends Mail Order,** 1415 10th Ave., Seattle, WA 98122: Free information ◆ Down comforters and robes, slip covers, pillows, shams, dust ruffles, and flannel sheets. 206-328-0887. www.halcyon.com/featherd/

**Freedom Quilting Bee,** Rt. 1, P.O. Box 43-A, Alberta, AL 36720: Free information ◆ Handmade quilts. 334-573-2225.

**G & K Enterprises,** 1408 Glenwood Ave., Greensboro, NC 27403: Free information ◆ Throws and pillows with a western motif. 336-275-0049.

**Garnet Hill,** 231 Main St., Franconia, NH 03580: Free catalog ◆ Natural fiber linens and sheets, blankets, comforters, and clothing. 800-622-6216.

**Gazebo of New York,** 114 E. 57th St., New York, NY 10022: Catalog $6 ◆ Patchwork quilts and hand-woven rag, hooked, and braided rugs. 212-832-7077.

**The Horchow Collection,** P.O. Box 620048, Dallas, TX 75262: Free catalog ◆ Linens, bed coverings, and home accessories. 800-395-5397. www.neimanmarcus.com

**JANICE Corp.,** 198 Hwy. 46, Budd Lake, NJ 07828: Free catalog ♦ Allergy-free women and men's clothing, towels, bathroom accessories, quilts, linens, personal grooming aids, hats, gloves, and scarves. 800-JANICES.

**Kelmscott Farm,** Box 356, Lincolnville, ME 04849: Catalog $5 ♦ Blankets and other bed coverings. 800-545-9363.

**Landau Woolens,** 102 Nassau St., Princeton, NJ 08542: Free catalog ♦ Machine washable wool blankets. 800-257-9445.

**Leron,** 750 Madison Ave., New York, NY 10021: Free catalog ♦ Linens, towels, pillows and covers, and imported handkerchiefs with optional monogramming for men and women. 212-249-3188.

**Linen & Lace,** 4 Lafayette, Washington, MO 63090: Catalog $2 ♦ Bed ruffles, canopies, and curtains. 800-332-5223.

**The Linen Source,** 5401 Hangar Ct., P.O. Box 31151, Tampa, FL 33631: Free catalog ♦ Bedroom ensembles, linens, pillows, and curtains. 800-431-2620.

**Marle Miller,** P.O. Box 968, Rt. 30, Dorset, VT 05251: Catalog $7 ♦ Antique-style quilts. 802-867-5969.

**Missouri Breaks Industries,** Quilt Brochure, HCR 64, Box 52, Timber Lake, SD 57656: Free brochure ♦ Original Sioux Native American star quilts. 605-865-3418.

**Quilts Unlimited,** 1023 Emmet St., Charlottesville, VA 22903: Catalog $6 ♦ Antique and new crib quilts. 804-979-8110.

**Rocky Mountain Tanners Inc.,** 2331 W. Hampden Ave., #146, Englewood, CO 80110: Brochure $2 ♦ Elk and deer leather throws for beds, couches, and chairs. 303-761-1049.

**St. Peter Woolen Mill,** 101 W. Broadway, St. Peter, MN 56082: Free information ♦ Wool comforters and mattress pads. 800-208-9822. www.woolenmill.com

**Star Quilts,** P.O. Box 8542, Fort Worth, TX 76124: Free information ♦ Hand-quilted and appliqued quilts. 817-654-1782.

**Strouds,** P.O. Box 4209, Anaheim, CA 92803: Free list of retail sources) ♦ Comforters, other bedding, pillows and linens, and more. 800-STROUDS.

**The Uptown Nursery,** 1601 Mt. Rushmore Dr., Rapid City, SD 57701: Free catalog ♦ Heirloom round crib bedding and accessories. 888-545-2742.

**The Village Weaver,** P.O. Box 71, Dillard, GA 30537: Brochure $2 ♦ Hand-woven Tartan blankets. 706-746-2287.

**Warm Things,** 180 Paul Dr., San Rafael, CA 94903: Free catalog ♦ Down quilts, pillows, and quilt covers. 415-472-2154.

**Western Trading Post,** P.O. Box 9070, Denver, CO 80209: Catalog $3 ♦ Blankets, Navajo wool rugs, and Eagle-design bed throws. 303-777-7750.

**Yankee Pride,** 29 Parkside Circle, Braintree, MA 02184: Catalog $3 (refundable) ♦ Handcrafted quilts, comforters, bedspreads, and hand-braided, hooked wool, and rag rugs. 800-848-7610. www.yankee-pride.com

### Pillows & Sheets

**Bedroom Secrets,** P.O. Box 529, Fremont, NE 68025: Catalog $2 ♦ Linens for the bath and bed. 800-955-2559.

**Celestial Silks,** P.O. Box 824, Fairfield, IA 52556: Free information ♦ In-stock and custom-made silk sheets, pillowcases, silk-filled comforters, and silk lingerie. 515-472-9062.

**The Company Store,** 500 Company Store Rd., LaCrosse, WI 54601: Free catalog ♦ Down-filled pillows and comforters, linens, mattress pads, and outerwear. 800-289-8508. info@thecompanystore.com

**Cuddledown of Maine,** 312 Canco Rd., Portland, ME 04103: Free catalog ♦ Down and feather/down comforters, sheets, sleepwear, mattress pads, throw pillows, flannel bedding, and nursery items. 800-323-6793. www.cuddledown.com

**Domestications,** Hanover Direct Pennsylvaniia Inc., Hanover, PA 17333-0001: Free catalog ♦ Comforters, sheets, pillows, blankets, bedspreads, throws, solid and lace tablecloths, mini blinds, shower curtains, and bathroom accessories. 717-633-3313.

**Down Home Comforts,** P.O. Box 2281, West Brattleboro, VT 05303: Brochure $1 ♦ New and re-made down comforters, pillows, and featherbeds. 802-688-3780.

**Down Home Factory Outlet,** 85 Rt. 46 West, Totowa, NJ 07512: Free catalog ♦ Comforters, pillows, and other bedding. 800-ALL-DOWN.

**Ecobaby,** 1475 N. Cuyamaca, El Cajon, CA 92020: Free catalog ♦ Organic and natural fiber clothes, bedding, toys, and diapering products. 888-ECOBABY; 619-596-7450 (in CA). www.ecobaby.com

**Eldridge Textile Company,** 277 Grand St., New York, NY 10002: Catalog $3 (refundable) ♦ Blankets, sheets, towels, comforters, bedspreads, rugs, and pillows. 212-925-1523.

**Feathered Friends Mail Order,** 1415 10th Ave., Seattle, WA 9812: Free information ♦ Down comforters and robes, slip covers, pillows, shams, dust ruffles, and flannel sheets. 206-328-0887. www.halcyon.com/featherd

**G & K Enterprises,** 1408 Glenwood Ave., Greensboro, NC 27403: Free information ♦ Throws and pillows with a western motif. 336-275-0049.

**Garnet Hill,** 231 Main St., Franconia, NH 03580: Free catalog ♦ Natural fiber linens and sheets, blankets, and comforters. 800-622-6216.

**The Horchow Collection,** P.O. Box 620048, Dallas, TX 75262: Free catalog ♦ Linens, bed coverings, and accessories. 800-395-5397. www.neimanmarcus.com

**JANICE Corp.,** 198 Hwy. 46, Budd Lake, NJ 07828: Free catalog ♦ Allergy-free women and men's clothing, towels, bathroom accessories, quilts, linens, personal grooming aids, hats, gloves, and scarves. 800-JANICES.

**Johnson Woolen Mills Inc.,** P.O. Box 12, Johnson, VT 05656: Free brochure ♦ Woolen outerwear for men, women, and children. Also blankets, underwear, and sweaters. 802-635-2271.

**Leron,** 750 Madison Ave., New York, NY 10021: Free catalog ♦ Linens, towels, pillows and covers, and imported handkerchiefs with optional monogramming for men and women. 212-249-3188.

**Harris Levy,** 278 Grand St., New York, NY 10002: Free catalog ♦ Linens for tables, beds, and bathrooms. 800-221-7750; 212-226-3102 (in NY).

**The Linen Source,** 5401 Hangar Ct., P.O. Box 31151, Tampa, FL 33631: Free catalog ♦ Linens, pillows, curtains, and bedroom ensembles. 800-431-2620.

**The Natural Bedroom,** P.O. Box 2048, Sebastopol, CA 95472: Free information ♦ Natural fiber baby's bedding. 800-365-6563.

**Palmetto Linen Company,** 50 Palmetto Bay Rd., Hilton Head, SC 29928: Free information ♦ Sheets and matching dust ruffles, bath towels, blankets, comforters, pillows, tablecloths, place mats, and shower curtains. 800-972-7442.

**Primarily Pillows,** 86 Rt. 32 South, New Paltz, NY 12518: Free catalog ♦ Designer pillows. 914-534-5296.

**Rue de France,** 78 Thames St., Newport, RI 02840: Catalog $3 ♦ Pillows, tablecloths and runners, and lace curtains. 800-777-0998.

**Strouds,** P.O. Box 4209, Anaheim, CA 92803: Free list of retail sources ♦ Comforters, other bedding, pillows and linens, and more. 800-STROUDS.

**Warm Things,** 180 Paul Dr., San Rafael, CA 94903: Free catalog ♦ Down quilts, pillows, and quilt covers. 415-472-2154.

## BEEKEEPING

**Alberta Honey Producers Co-operative Ltd.,** Box 3909, Spruce Grove, Alberta, Canada T7X 3B1: Free information ♦ Beekeeping equipment. 403-962-5667.

**Archia's Floral & Plants,** 712 S. Ohio, Sedalia, MO 65301: Free catalog ♦ Vegetable and flower seeds, gardening supplies, nursery stock, and beekeeping equipment. 816-826-4000.

**Bear River Honey Company,** P.O. Box 782, Wheatland, CA 95692: Free information ◆ Carniolans and Italian queen bees. 916-633-4789.

**Betterbee-Meadery Inc.,** RR 4, Box 4070, Greenwich, NY 12834: Free information ◆ Beekeeping supplies. 518-692-9669.

**Blossomland Supply,** 6680 Pokagon, Berrien Center, MI 49102: Free catalog ◆ Beekeeping equipment and supplies. 800-637-5262; 616-473-3917 (in MI).

**Bob Brandi Honey,** 1518 Paradise Ln., Los Banos, CA 93635: Free information ◆ Package bees, queens, bulk bees, and nucs. 209-826-1240.

**Brushy Mountain Bee Farm,** P.O. Box 135, Moravian Falls, NC 28654: Free catalog ◆ Gloves and protective clothing, equipment for processing honey, books, videos, and other beekeeping supplies. 800-BEESWAX.

**Buzzing By Apiaries,** 2570 Royal Circle, Chico, CA 95973: Free information ◆ Package bees and queens. 916-343-7466.

**Cowen Manufacturing Company,** P.O. Box 399, Parowan, UT 84761: Free information ◆ Extracting equipment. 800-477-3338.

**Dadant & Sons Inc.,** 51 S. 2nd St., Hamilton, IL 62341: Free catalog ◆ Honey extracting equipment, honey containers, beeswax foundation and plasticell, woodenware, and queen and package bees. 800-220-8325. www.dadant.com

**Draper's Super-Bee Apiaries Inc.,** RD 1, Box 2744, Eugene, OR 97402: Free information ◆ Beekeeping supplies, honey and bee products, and videos. 800-233-4273; 717-537-2381 (in OR).

**Friesen Honey Farms Inc.,** 8099 Rd. 29, Glenn, CA 95943: Free information ◆ Italian package bees and queens. 916-934-4944.

**John Foster Apiaries,** P.O. Box 699, Esparto, CA 95627: Free information ◆ Queen bees. 916-787-3044.

**Glenn Apiaries,** P.O. Box 2737, Fallbrook, CA 92088: Free information ◆ Italian and Carnolian queen bees. 760-728-3731.

**Glorybee Foods Inc.,** P.O. Box 2744, Eugene, OR 97402: Free catalog ◆ Beekeeping and honey processing supplies, honey, honey-prepared foods, and gift assortments. 800-456-7923; 541-689-0913 (in OR). www.glorybee.com

**Hardeman Apiaries,** P.O. Box 214, Mt. Vernon, GA 30445: Free price list ◆ Italian package and queen bees. 912-583-2710.

**Harrell & Sons Inc.,** P.O. Box 215, Hayneville, AL 36040: Free information ◆ Italian package bees and queens. 334-548-2313.

**Heitkam's Honey Bees,** 25815 Post Ave., Orland, CA 95963: Free price list ◆ Queen bees. 916-865-9562.

**Hel-le Bee Farm,** P.O. Box 315, Monticello, FL 32345: Free information ◆ Italian queen bees. 904-997-4511.

**Hendrix Apiaries,** Rt. 6, Box 120, West Point, MS 39773: Free information ◆ Italian queen bees. 601-494-7271.

**Homan Honey Farms,** 793 Hwy. 45 A, Shannon, MS 38868: Free price list ◆ Queen and package bees. 601-767-3960.

**The Walter T. Kelley Company Inc.,** P.O. Box 240, Clarkson, KY 42726: Free catalog ◆ Beekeeping supplies. 502-242-2012.

**C.F. Koehnen & Sons Inc.,** 3131 Hwy. 45, Glenn, CA 95943: Free brochure ◆ Italian package and queen bees. 916-891-5216.

**Kona Queen Company,** P.O. Box 768, Captain Cook, HI 96704: Free information ◆ Italian queen bees. 808-328-9016.

**Lapp's Bee Supply Center,** Box 460, 500 S. Main St., Reeseville, WI 53579: Free information ◆ Package bees, fructose, beeswax, glass accessories, honey, and woodenware. 800-321-1960; 920-927-3848 (in WI).

**Lohman Apiaries,** 6437 Wagner Rd., Arbuckle, CA 95912: Free information ◆ Queen and package bees. 916-476-2322.

**Mann Lake Supply,** 501 S. 1st St., Hackensack, MN 56452: Free catalog ◆ Beekeeping and honey production equipment, protective clothing, and candle molds. 800-233-6663. www.mannlakeltd.com

**Maxant Industries Inc.,** P.O. Box 454, Ayer, MA 01432: Catalog $1 ◆ Honey processing equipment. 978-772-0576.

**McCary Apiaries,** P.O. Box 87, Buckatunna, MS 39322: Free information ◆ Queen bees. 601-648-2747.

**Mid-Continent Agrimarketing Inc.,** 1465 N. Winchester, Overland Park, KS 66061: Free catalog ◆ Beekeeping and candle-making supplies. 800-547-1392; 913-768-8967 (in KS).

**Miksa Honey Farm,** David & Linda Miksa, 13404 Honeycomb Rd., Groveland, FL 34736: Free information ◆ Queens, cells, and nucs. 352-429-3447.

**Miller Wood Products,** P.O. Box 2414, White City, OH 97503: Free information ◆ Woodenware. 800-827-9266.

**Millry Bee Company,** Rt. 2, Box 90, Millry, AL 36558: Free information ◆ Three-banded Italian queens and package bees. 334-846-2662.

**Morris Family Apiaries,** 305 W. Tollison St., Baxley, GA 31513: Free information ◆ Italian queen bees. 912-367-0638.

**Norman Bee Farm,** P.O. Box 26, Ramer, AL 36069: Free information ◆ Italian bees and queens. 334-562-3354.

**Homer E. Park,** P.O. Box 38, Palo Cedro, CA 96073: Free information ◆ Italian queen bees. 916-547-3391.

**Pendell Apiaries,** Frank & Sheri Pendell, P.O. Box 148, Stonyford, CA 95979: Free information ◆ Italian queens and package bees. 916-963-3062.

**Plantation Bee Company,** P.O. Box 24559, St. Simons Island, GA 31522: Free information ◆ Bees. 912-634-1884.

**Powell Apiaries,** 4140 County Rd. KK, Orland, CA 95963: Free information ◆ Italian package bees and queens, hives, and beekeeping supplies. 916-865-3346.

**Presley Apiaries,** 2205 Day Rd., Gilroy, CA 95020: Free information ◆ Italian queen bees. 408-848-8886.

**A.I. Root Company,** P.O. Box 706, Medina, OH 44258: Free catalog ◆ Hives, protective clothing and gloves, tools, honey-processing equipment, books, videos, smokers, and beekeeping supplies. 800-289-7668. www.airoot.com

**Rossman Apiaries Inc.,** P.O. Box 905, Moultrie, GA 31768: Free catalog ◆ Package bees and queens, beekeeping supplies, and starter kit for beginners. 800-333-7677.

**Ruhl Bee Supply,** 12713 NE Whitaker Way, Portland, OR 97230: Free catalog ◆ Beekeeping and extracting supplies. 503-256-4231.

**Southwestern Ohio Hive Parts Company,** 52 Marco Ln., Centerville, OH 45458: Free information ◆ Beekeeping supplies. 800-765-5112. www.MeMerrell.com

**Spell Bee Company,** 425 Patterson Rd., Baxley, GA 31513: Free information ◆ Italian queens. 912-367-9352.

**Strachan Apiaries Inc.,** 2522 Tierra Buena Rd., Yuba City, CA 95993: Free information ◆ Queen bees. 916-674-3881.

**Taber's Honey Bee Genetics,** P.O. Box 1672, Vacaville, CA 95696: Free brochure ◆ Queens and package bees. 707-449-0440.

**Tollett Apiaries,** 8700 Honey Ln., Millville, CA 96062: Free information ◆ Italian package bees and queens. 916-547-3387.

**Binford Weaver Apiaries Inc.,** Rt. 1, Box 256, Navasota, TX 77868: Free information ◆ Queen and package bees. Also honey. 409-825-7312. www.ipt.com/bweaver

**The Wilbanks Apiaries,** P.O. Box 12, Claxton, GA 30417: Free information ◆ Package bees and queens. 912-739-4820.

**Wooten Golden Queens,** 11189 Deschutes Rd., Palo Cedro, CA 96073: Free information ◆ Queen bees and nucs. 916-549-3555.

**York Bee Company,** P.O. Box 307, Jesup, GA 31545: Free information ◆ Starline, midnight, Italian, package, and queen bees. 912-427-7311.

## BEER CANS & STEINS

**Anheuser-Busch Inc.,** P.O. Box 503015, St. Louis, MO 63150: Free catalog ◆ Heirloom Budweiser and other collectible plates and steins. Also gifts for men and women. 800-325-9665. www.Budshop.com

**Beverage Containers Museum,** 1055 Ridgecrest Dr., Millersville, TN 37072: Free catalog ◆ Beer and soda cans, signs, trays, glasses, steins, bottle caps, and other reproduction and original nostalgic collectibles. 615-859-5236. www.gono.com

**Classic Carolina Collection,** 1502 N. 23rd St., Wilmington, NC 28405: Free catalog ◆ Limited edition steins and tankards with history, sports, entertainment, notable individuals, and anniversary themes. 800-457-9700.

**Fellowship Foundry Pewtersmiths,** 1605 Abram Ct., San Leandro, CA 94577: Free catalog ◆ Goblets, sculptures, switch plates, jewelry, cups and steins, glassware and crystal, and other pewter gifts. 510-352-0935.

**Flash Collectables,** 560 N. Moorpark Rd., Thousand Oaks, CA 91360: Free brochure ◆ Collectible current and retired American and German steins. 805-499-9222. members.aol.com/flashcoll

**Gene's Can Shop,** 27 State Rt. 34, Martville, NY 13111: Free catalog with one 1st class stamp ◆ Hard-to-find United States, Canadian, and foreign beer cans. 315-564-6699.

**Global Specialty Imports Inc.,** 8711 Shipwatch Dr., Wilmington, NC 28412: Free brochure ◆ Unique collectible beer cans. 910-791-3035.

**Charlie Golden Jr.,** 345 S. Sterley St., Shillington, PA 19607: United States list $2, foreign list $3, both lists $4.50 ◆ Beer cans from the United States and foreign countries. 610-777-7078.

**House of Tyrol,** P.O. Box 909, 66 E. Kytle St., Cleveland, GA 30528: Free catalog ◆ Musical cuckoo clocks, steins, crystal, porcelain, lamps, music boxes, pillows, knitted items, decor accessories, bar accessories, collector plates, pewter, tapestries, cards, Alpine hat pins, Christmas decorations, and folk music videos. 800-241-5404.

**Kaiser Bill's,** Horse & Ducky Platz, P.O. Box 177, Helen, GA 30545: Free catalog ◆ Collector steins. 800-922-2182; 706-878-2182 (in GA). www.kaiserbills.com

**Chester J. Kilanowicz,** 5446 Rockwood Rd., Columbus, OH 43229: List $1 ◆ Beer cans. 614-888-0917.

**Sam's Steins & Collectables,** 2207 Lincoln Hwy East, Lancaster, PA 17602: Free catalog with two 1st class stamps ◆ Collectible steins. 800-608-BREW; 717-394-6404 (in PA). SAMSSTEINS@MSN.com

**Sellek Industries Inc.,** 9547 Brenda Dr., P.O. Box 290, Roscoe, IL 61073: Free brochure ◆ Sports and professional-theme beer steins for collectors. 800-369-7287.

**Thomas Stein Exchange,** 11111 Kingsley Rd., #154, Dallas, TX 75238: Free price list ◆ Collectible steins. 972-341-6133,

## BELLY DANCING

**Artemis Imports,** P.O. Box 68, Pacific Grove, CA 93950: Catalog $3 ◆ Belly dancer costume patterns, supplies, books, and more. 831-373-4113.

**Audrena's International Bazaar,** 9720 South Mason Ave., Oak Lawn, IL 60453: Free information ◆ Supplies for amateur and professional middle eastern dancers. 800-327-3406.

**Baladi Boutique,** 16416 Myers Ct., Clermont, FL 34711: Free information ◆ Handmade belly dancing costumes. 407-656-7524.

**Kathleen Barrett,** 5032 W. Willow Hwy., Lansing, MI 48917: Free catalog ◆ Costumes, jewelry, headpieces, and other accessories. 517-323-8014. LadiJoi@aol.com

**Chandra's Dance Extravaganza,** 6706 NW 18th Ave., Gainesville, FL 32605: Catalog $2 ◆ Belly dancing costumes, jewelry, and supplies. 800-790-2102; 352-332-9080 (in FL). www.chandras.com

**Cost Less,** 1710 University Ave., Berkeley CA 94703: Catalog $2 ◆ Coin, mirror, and crystal belly dancing costumes. 510-548-2800. www.costlesscostumes.com

**Distant Caravans,** P.O. Box 5254, Reno, NV 89513: Catalog $1 ◆ Belly dancing jewelry, music, clothing, drums, lanterns, and other accessories. 702-746-0416. www.distantcaravans.com

**Turquoise International,** 22830 Califa St., Woodland Hills, CA 91367: Free brochure ◆ Hand-beaded Egyptian fringe, beaded hip sashes, silk veils, caftans, video tapes, and audio cassettes. 800-548-9422; 818-999-5542 (in CA).

## BICYCLES & ACCESSORIES

### Bicycles

**American Cycle Express,** 223 Main St., P.O. Box 155, Binghamton, NY 13905: Free information ◆ Bicycles, accessories and parts, and clothing. 607-777-1223. www.americancycle.com

**AngleTech Cycles,** 318 N. Hwy. 67, P.O. Box 1893, Woodland Park, CO 80863: Catalog $2 ◆ Recumbent, special needs, and women's bicycles. 800-793-3038. www.angletechcycles.com

**Matthew Assenmacher Bikes,** 8053 Miller Rd., Swartz Creek, MI 48473: Free information ◆ Mountain and tandem bicycles. 810-635-7844. www.tir.com/~ride531

**Bianchi USA,** 2371 Cabot Blvd., Hayward, CA 94545: Free information ◆ Racing, mountain, and city bicycles. 800-431-0006; 510-264-1001 (in CA). www.bianchi.it

**Bicycle Corp. of America,** 2811 Brodhead Rd., Bethlehem, PA 18017: Free information ◆ Mountain bicycles. 800-225-2453. www.titan-hyper.com

**Bike E,** 5460 SW Philomath Blvd., Corvallis, OR 97333: Free list of retail sources ◆ Bicycles for comfort riding and accessories. 800-231-3136; 541-753-9747 (in OR). www.bikee.com

**Bike Empire,** 12630 Poway Rd., Poway, CA 92064: Free catalog ◆ Bicycles, components, and accessories. 800-896-4913; 619-679-0306 (in CA). www.bikeempire.com

**Bike Nashbar,** 4111 Simon Rd., P.O. Box 3449, Youngstown OH 44512: Free catalog ◆ Racing, sport-touring, touring, and mountain bicycles. 800-627-4227. www.nashbar.com

**Bilenky Cycle Works,** 5319 N. 2nd St., Philadelphia, PA 19120: Free information ◆ Tandem bicycles. 800-213-6388. www.bilenky.com/hack.html

**Bontrager Cycles,** 104 Bronson St., Santa Cruz, CA 95062: Free information ◆ Bicycles for adults. 800-509-7433. www.bontrager.com

**Burley Design Cooperative,** 4020 Stewart Rd., Eugene, OR 97402: Free list of retail sources ◆ Tandems, other bicycles, and folding bike trailers for children. 541-687-1644. www.burley.com

**Cambria Bicycle Outfitter,** 2164 Center St., Cambria, CA 93428: Free brochure ◆ Bicycles, frames, parts, and accessories. Also features closeouts. 888-WE-RIDE-Z. www.cambriabike.com

**Cannondale Corp.,** 16 Trowbridge Dr., Bethel, CT 06801: Free list of retail sources ◆ Racing, sport-touring, and touring bicycles. 800-BIKE-USA. www.cannondale.com

**Charger Electric Bicycles,** 222 E. Huntington Dr., Monrovia, CA 91016: Free information ◆ Electric power-assisted bicycles. 818-357-9983. www.charger.com

**The Colorado Cyclist,** 3970 E. Bijou St., Colorado Springs, CO 80909: Free catalog ◆ Bicycles, bicycle components, tools and accessories, and men and women's clothing. 800-688-8600; 719-591-4040 (in CO). www.colcyc.com

**Cycles LaMoure,** 613 SE Jackson, Roseburg, OR 97470: Free information ◆ Handcrafted custom frames, frame repair and painting, custom brazing, and accessories. 503-957-1020. steve@sandmachine.com

**Cyclops Bicycles,** 740 Waddington Dr., Unit 3, Vernon, British Columbia, Canada V1T 9E9: Free brochure ◆ Custom handbuilt road, triathlon, and mountain bicycles. 604-545-5644. www.mindlink.bc.ca/cyclops

**Dan's Competition,** 613 E. 4th St., Mt. Vernon, IN 47620: Information $2 ◆ Bicycles, accessories and parts, and clothing. 812-838-2691. doachs@gac.edu

**Davidson Cycle,** 2116 Western Ave., Seattle, WA 98121: Free information ◆ Mountain, tandem, and women's bicycles. 800-292-5374. www.davidsoncycles.com

**Dean Ultimate Bicycles,** P.O. Box 470, Boulder, CO 80301: Free information ◆ Full-suspension bicycles. 970-530-3091.

**DiamondBack Bicycles,** 4030 Via Pescador, Camarillo, CA 93012: Catalog $2 (request list of retail sources) ◆ Off-road and mountain bicycles for adults and youths. 800-776-7641. www.diamondback.com

**Erickson Cycles,** 6119 Brooklyn NE, Seattle, WA 98115: Free information ◆ Mountain, tandem, women's, track, and touring bicycles. 206-524-7731.

**Excel Sports Boulder,** 2045 32nd St., Boulder, CO 80301: Free catalog ◆ Bicycle computers, off-road equipment, bicycle frame sets, tires, and tubes. 800-627-6664. www.excelsports.com

**Fisher Bicycles,** 801 W. Madison, Waterloo, WI 53594: Free list of retail sources ◆ Mountain bicycles and accessories. 414-478-3532. www.fisherbikes/com

**Free Agent Bicycles,** 1264 E. Walnut St., Carson, CA 90746: Catalog $1 ◆ Bicycles for adults. 310-632-7173.

**Fuji America,** 118 Bauer Dr., Oakland, NJ 07436: Free information ◆ Racing, sport-touring, touring, mountain, and city bicycles. 800-631-8474; 201-337-1700 (in NJ). www.fujibike.com

**Steve Garn,** Brew Racing Frames, 1733 Sutherland Rd., Creston, NC 28615: Free information ◆ Racing, touring, sport-touring, hybrid, track, and mountain bicycle frames.

**Giant Bicycle Company,** 475 Apra St., Rancho Dominguez, CA 90220: Free catalog ◆ Racing, mountain, and city bicycles. 800-874-4268; 310-609-3340 (in CA). www.giant-bicycle.com

**Gita Sporting Goods,** 12600 Steele Creek Rd., Charlotte, NC 28273: Free information ◆ Racing and track bicycles. 800-729-4482.

**Bruce Gordon Cycles,** 613 2nd St., Petaluma, CA 94952: Free information ◆ Frames and bicycles. 707-762-5601. www.bgcycles.com

**GT Bicycles,** 2001 E. Dyer Rd., Santa Ana, CA 92705: Free information ◆ Mountain bicycles. 800-RID-EAGT. www.gtbicycles.com

**Haverich Ortho-Sport Inc.,** 67 Emerald St., Keene, NH 03431: Free information ◆ Specialized bicycles, tricycles, and tandems with specially designed accessories to meet most needs. 603-358-0438.

**Havnoonian,** 1901 S. 19th St., Philadelphia, PA 19148: Free catalog ◆ Custom carbon fiber, titanium, steel, and metal matrix frames. 215-334-8500.

**HH Racing Group,** 1901 S. 13th St., Philadelphia, PA 19148: Free information ◆ Racing, touring, tandem, and track bicycles. 215-334-8500.

**Hoffman Bikes,** P.O. Box 130172, Edmond, OK 73013: Catalog $2 ◆ Bicycles for adults. 405-528-4130. www2.hoffmanbikes.com

**Holland Cycles,** 3735 Kenora Dr., Spring Valley, CA 91977: Free information ◆ Racing, track, tandem, triathlon, and time-trial bicycle frames. 619-469-1772. www.hollandsbicycles.com

**Ibis Cycles,** P.O. Box 275, Sebastopol, CA 95473: Free information ◆ Mountain and tandem bicycles. 707-829-5615. www.ibiscycles.com

**Intense Cycles,** 18273 Grand Ave., Lake Elsinore, CA 92530: Free list of retail sources ◆ Mountain bicycles. 909-678-4576.

**International Pro,** 15 W. Franklin, Bellbrook, OH 45305: Free information ◆ Custom steel road bicycles and old-fashioned wire spoked wheels. 800-875-8467.

**Iron Horse Bicycles,** 6570 E. Rogers Circle, Boca Raton, FL 33487: Free information ◆ Mountain bicycles. 800-645-5477. www.ironhorsebikes.com

**Jamis Bicycles,** P.O. Box 100, Northvale, NJ 07647: Free information ◆ Off-road and mountain bicycles. 800-222-0570.

**Jig Enterprises,** P.O. Box 448, Pismo Beach, CA 93448: Free brochure ◆ Engine kits for powering skateboards and bicycles, safety gear, and accessories. 805-473-6997.

**Kestrel/Sandpoint Design Inc.,** 185 Westridge Rd., Watsonville, CA 95076: Free list of retail sources ◆ Mountain bicycles. 408-724-9079. www.kestrel.usa.com

**Kinesis USA Inc.,** 2690 NW Nicolai St., Portland, OR 97210: Free information ◆ Aluminum frame bicycles. 503-294-1012.

**KHS Bicycles,** 1264 E. Walnut St., Carson, CA 90746: Free information ◆ Mountain and hybrid bicycles. 310-632-7173. www.khsbicycles.com

**Kona Mountain Bikes,** 2455 Salashan, Ferndale, WA 98248: Free information ◆ Mountain bicycles. 360-366-0951. www.konaworld.com

**Lippy Bikes,** 60265 Fuagarwee Circle, Bend, OR 97702: Free information ◆ Tandem bicycles. 541-389-2503.

**Litespeed Titanium Bicycles,** P.O. Box 22666, Chattanooga, TN 37422: Free information ◆ Bicycles. 423-238-5530. www.litespeed.com

**Mac's Motor Sports,** P.O. Box 7190, Wesley Chapel, FL 33544: Free information ◆ Motorized scooters and bicycles. Also folding bikes. 813-973-7108.

**Marin Mountain Bikes,** 16 Mary St., San Rafael, CA 94901: Free information ◆ Mountain bicycles. 800-222-7557. www.marinbikes.com

**Marinoni USA Inc.,** P.O. Box 187, Bakersfield, VT 05441: Free information ◆ Racing bicycles. 802-827-3647. Marinoni@sover.net

**McMahon Full Suspension,** 4195 Carpinteria Ave., Carpinteria, CA 93013: Free information ◆ Bicycle frames and components. 805-684-7398. www.mrcbikes.com

**Mongoose Bicycles,** 3400 Kashiwa St., Torrance, CA 90505: Catalog $3 ◆ Lightweight fitness exercise and mountain bicycles. 562-539-8860. www.mongoose.com

**Montague Bicycle Company,** P.O. Box 381118, Cambridge, MA 02238: Free information ◆ Mountain, hybrid, and tandem folding bicycles. 800-736-5348. www.montagueco.com

**Morgan's Cycle & Fitness,** 2509 Sunset Ave., Rocky Mount, NC 27804: Free information ◆ Recumbent bicycles. 919-443-4480. www.bikeroute.com/MorganCycle

**Mt. Constance Mountain Shoppe,** 1550 NE Riddell Rd., Bremerton, WA 98310: Free catalog ◆ Outdoor equipment, in-line skates, and accessories for mountain bikes. 360-377-0668. MTSHOPPE@MOUNTAINSHOPPE.com

**Nobilette Cycles,** 1616 S. Horseshoe Circle, Longmont, CO 80501: Free information ◆ Custom bicycle frames and ready-to-use bicycles for racing and touring. Also tandems and tricycles. 303-772-8139.

**Norco Products USA Inc.,** 7950 Enterprise St., Burnaby, British Columbia, Canada V5A 1V7: Free information ◆ Racing, sport-touring, mountain, and city bicycles. 206-251-9370. www.norco.com/core.html

**Nytro Hi-Tech Bicycles,** 940 1st St., Encinatas, CA 92024: Free information ◆ Bicycles and accessories. 619-632-0006.

**O'Neil's Bicycle Shop,** 1094 Main St., Worcester, MA 01603: Free catalog ◆ Bicycles, parts and accessories, and clothing. 800-638-6344; 508-798-0084 (in MA). www.oneils.com

**Ochsner International,** 246 Marquardt Dr., Wheeling, IL 60090: Free information ◆ Racing, mountain, and trail bicycles. 312-286-3111.

**One-Off Titanium,** 221 Pine St., Florence, MA 01060: Free information ◆ Racing, touring, sport-touring, hybrid, track, mountain, tandem, and recumbent bicycle frames. 413-585-5913.

**Online Sports,** 13692 W. Virginia Dr., Ste. 101, Lakewood, CO 80228: Free information ◆ Skis, snowboards, bindings, clothing, mountain bikes, and roller blades. 303-980-4014.

**Panasonic Bicycle Division,** Panasonic Way, Secaucus, NJ 07094: Free information ◆ Racing, sport-touring, touring, and mountain bicycles. 201-348-5375. www.panasonic.com

**Price Point,** 1442 W. 135th St., Gardena, CA 90249: Free catalog ◆ Bicycles, parts and accessories, and clothing. 800-774-2376. www.pricepoint.com

**R & A Cycles Inc.,** 105 5th Ave., Brooklyn, NY 11217: Free information with long SASE ◆ Bicycles and frames. 718-636-5242.

**Raleigh Cycle Company of America,** 22710 72nd Ave. South, Kent, WA 98032: Free information ♦ Racing, sport-touring, and mountain bicycles. 800-222-5527; 206-656-0126 (in WA).

**Red Rose Imports,** 418 N. Charlotte St., Lancaster, PA 17603: Free list of retail sources ♦ Imported Italian steel and titanium bicycles. 717-397-0951.

**Redline Bicycles,** 7620 S. 192nd St., Kent, WA 98032: Catalog $3 ♦ Bicycles for adults and juniors. 206-251-1516. www.redlinebicycles.com

**Rhoades Car,** 125 Rhoades Ln., Hendersonville, TN 37075: Free information ♦ Easy-to-pedal 4-wheel bicycles for 1, 2, and 4-persons. 800-974-6233. www.rhoadesinfo.com

**Rideable Bicycle Replicas Inc.,** 2329 Eagle Ave., Alameda, CA 94501: Free brochure ♦ Hi-wheel bicycles, rickshaw cycle with 2-passenger trailer and optional electric motor assistance, and other replica bicycles. 510-769-0980. www.hiwheel.com

**Ritchey Design,** 860 Hurlingame Ave., Redwood City, CA 94063: Free information ♦ Mountain, racing, and tandem bicycles. 415-368-4018. www.ritcheylogic.com

**Rock N' Roll Cycles,** P.O. Box 1558, Levelland, TX 79336: Free information ♦ Single riders, tandems, and hand-and-foot-powered cycles with optional seat configurations and custom-fitting for individual needs. 800-654-9664. www.rocknrollcycles.com

**Romic Cycle Company,** 4434 Steffani Ln., Houston, TX 77041: Free information ♦ Custom racing, touring, and sport-touring bicycles. 713-466-7806.

**Ross Bicycles USA,** 51 Executive Blvd., Farmingdale, NY 11735: Free information ♦ Mountain and hybrid bicycles. 800-338-7677; 516-249-6000 (in NY).

**Ryan Recumbent Cycles,** 99 R Washington St., Melrose, MA 02176: Free information ♦ Recumbent bicycles and tandems. 781-979-0072. www.ryancycles.com

**Richard Sachs Cycles,** P.O. Box 194, Chester, CT 06412: Free information ♦ Road racing bicycles. 860-526-2059.

**Salsa Bicycles,** 611 2nd St., Petaluma, CA 94952: Free information ♦ Bicycle frames, components, and clothing. 707-762-8191. www.SalsaCycles.com

**Santana Cycles Inc.,** P.O. Box 206, La Verne, CA 91750: Free information ♦ Tandem bicycles. 909-596-7570. Santanainc@aol.com

**Schwinn Bicycle Company,** 1690 38th St., Boulder, CO 80301: Free information with long SASE ♦ Racing, mountain, tandem, and city bicycles. Also trailers for children. 303-939-0100. www.schwinn.com

**Scott USA,** 5775 Arapahoe Ave., Boulder, CO 80304: Free information ♦ Mountain bicycles. 303-473-9609.

**SE Racing,** 190 Bosstick Blvd., San Marcos, CA 92069: Brochure $3 ♦ Racing bicycles. 619-598-4170. www.se-racing.com

**Sidetrak Inc.,** 774 Industry Dr., Seattle, WA 98188: Free catalog ♦ Bicycle parts and accessories. 206-575-0335. www.sidetrak.com

**Specialized Bicycle Components,** 15130 Concord Circle, Morgan Hill, CA 95037: Free information ♦ Racing and mountain bicycles. 800-245-3462; 408-779-6229 (in CA). www.specialized.com

**Spectrum Cycles,** 1190 Dorney Rd., Breinigsville PA 18031: Free information ♦ Frames and bicycles. 610-398-1986. www.spectrum-cycles.com

**Summit Mountain Bikes,** 4209 California Ave., Norco, CA 91760: Free catalog ♦ Mountain bicycles and frames. 909-279-8133.

**Supergo Bike Shops,** 501 Broadway, Santa Monica, CA 90401: Free information ♦ New and used bicycles and accessories. 800-326-2453. www.supergo.com

**Teel Inc.,** 567 Commerce St., Franklin Lakes, NJ 07417: Information $3 ♦ Frame and fork sets.

**Terry Precision Bicycles,** 1704 Wayneport Rd., Macedon, NY 14502: Free information ♦ Bicycles, apparel, and accessories for women. 800-289-8379; 315-986-2103 (in NY). www.terrybicycles.com

**Ti Cycles,** 824 Post Ave., Seattle, WA 98104: Free brochure ♦ Custom titanium and steel bicycles. 206-624-9697. www.ticycles.com

**Treads, Bicycle Outfitters,** 16981 E. Iliff Ave., Aurora, CO 80013: Free catalog ♦ Clothing, gloves, parts, and accessories. 800-587-3237. TREADS@TREADS.com

**Trek Bicycle Corp.,** 801 W. Madison St., P.O. Box 183, Waterloo, WI 53594: Free list of retail sources ♦ Racing, sport-touring, touring, mountain, city bicycles, and accessories. 800-369-8735. www.trekbikes.com

**UNIVEGA,** 3030 Walnut Ave., Long Beach, CA 90807: Free information ♦ Mountain, road, and tandem bicycles. 888-UNIVEGA. www.univega.com

**Veltec Sports Inc.,** 1793 Catalina St., Sand City, CA 93955: Free information ♦ Racing bicycles, parts, and accessories. 800-578-5790. www.sidiusa.com

**Ted Wojcik,** 6 Gigante Dr., Hampstead, NH 03841: Free information ♦ Mountain, road, sport, hybrid, tandem, and track bicycles. 603-329-8057. www.tedwojcik.com

**World Class Cycles,** 11 Dewey Rd., Commack, NY 11725: Free information ♦ Custom built frame sets for road, track, and touring bicycles. 516-543-1835.

**ZAP Power Systems,** 117 Morris St., Sebastopol, CA 95472: Free brochure ♦ Full-size electric and folding bicycles. 800-251-4555. www.zapbikes.com

## Bicycles (Folding)

**Avon Marine,** 11215 Young River Ave., Fountain Valley, CA 92708: Free catalog ♦ Folding bicycles. 800-854-7595; 714-444-9244 (in CA). www.avonmarine.com

**Brompton Folding Bicycles,** C.M. Wasson Company, 423 Chaucer St., Palo Alto, CA 94301: Free list of retail sources ♦ Custom adjustable English-made folding bicycles. 415-321-0808. www.bromptonbike.com

**Burley Design Cooperative,** 4020 Stewart Rd., Eugene, OR 97402: Free list of retail sources ♦ Tandems, other bicycles, and folding bike trailers for children. 541-687-1644. www.burley.com

**Caribike USA Inc.,** 6980 Aragon Circle, #5, Buena Park, CA 90620: Free brochure ♦ Innovative folding bicycles. 714-523-4535. www.caribike.com

**Dahon California,** 833 Meridian St., Duarte, CA 91010: Free information ♦ Folding bicycles. 818-305-5264. www.dahon.com

**DiBlasi of America,** 2633 Lantana Rd., Lantana, FL 33642: Free information ♦ Folding motor bike. 561-963-1189. www.diblasi.com

**Mac's Motor Sports,** P.O. Box 7190, Wesley Chapel, FL 33544: Free information ♦ Motorized scooters and bicycles. Also folding bikes. 813-973-7108.

**Marbel Associates,** Terratran Bicycles, 1819 Timberlake Dr., Delaware, OH 43015: Free information ♦ Folding motor bikes and motors for custom fitting. 740-548-5561. www.terratran.com

**Montague Bicycle Company,** P.O. Box 381118, Cambridge, MA 02238: Free information ♦ Mountain, hybrid, and tandem folding bicycles. 800-736-5348. www.montagueco.com

**C.M. Wasson Company,** 423 Chaucer St., Palo Alto, CA 94301: Free brochure ♦ Brompton folding bicycles. 415-321-0808. www.bromptonbike.com

**ZAP Power Systems,** 117 Morris St., Sebastopol, CA 95472: Free brochure ♦ Full-size electric and folding bicycles. 800-251-4555. www.zapbikes.com

## Clothing

**Branford Bike,** 1074 Main St., Branford, CT 06405: Free catalog ♦ Frames, parts and accessories, tires and tubes, team clothing, cycling gloves, socks, caps, and headbands. 203-488-0482. www.branfordbike.com

**Canari Cycle Wear,** 10025 Huennekens St., San Diego, CA 92121: Free information ♦ Winter apparel for bikers. 800-929-2925; 619-455-8245 (in CA). www.sportsx.com/canari/7161.html

**Cannondale Corp.,** 16 Trowbridge Dr., Bethel, CT 06801: Free list of retail sources ◆ Jackets and tights for women. Also frame and saddle bags. 800-BIKE-USA. www.cannondale.com

**Dan's Competition,** 613 E. 4th St., Mt. Vernon, IN 47620: Information $2 ◆ Bicycles, accessories and parts, and clothing. 812-838-2691. doachs@gac.edu

**The Finals Inc.,** 21 Minisink Ave., Port Jervis, NY 12771: Free catalog ◆ Bicycling, aerobic, swimming, running, and exercise clothing. 800-345-3485. www.thefinals.com

**Pearl Izumi,** 620 Compton St., Brownfield, CO 80020: Free information ◆ Wind-resistant tights and jerseys with zippers for easy removal of the front panel. 800-877-7080. www.pearlizumi.com

**Kucharik Bicycle Clothing,** 1745 W. 182nd St., Gardena, CA 90248: Free information ◆ Winter clothing. 310-538-4611.

**O'Neil's Bicycle Shop,** 1094 Main St., Worcester, MA 01603: Free catalog ◆ Bicycles, parts and accessories, and clothing. 800-638-6344; 508-798-0084 (in MA). www.oneils.com

**Pace Sportswear,** 15422 Assembly Ln., Huntington Beach, CA 92849: Free catalog ◆ Custom cycling sportswear. 800-762-7223. sales@pacesportswear.com

**Performance Bicycle Shop,** P.O. Box 2741, Chapel Hill, NC 27514: Free catalog ◆ Clothing, frames, bicycles and parts, and frame and saddle bags. 800-727-2433. www.performancebike.com

**Price Point,** 1442 W. 135th St., Gardena, CA 90249: Free catalog ◆ Bicycles, parts and accessories, and clothing. 800-774-2376. www.pricepoint.com

**Puma USA Inc.,** 147 Centre St., Brockton, MA 02403: Free information with long SASE ◆ Clothing, shoes, and gloves. 800-662-7862. www.puma.com

**Salsa Bicycles,** 611 2nd St., Petaluma, CA 94952: Free information ◆ Bicycle frames, components, and clothing. 707-762-8191. www.SalsaCycles.com

**ZOIC Core Clothing,** 2415 3rd St., #230, San Francisco, CA 94107: Free list of retail sources ◆ Clothing for men and women bikers. 800-241-WEAR. www.zoic.com

## Parts & Accessories

**Adventure Cycling Association,** P.O. Box 8308, 150 E. Pine St., Missoula, MT 59807: Free catalog ◆ Maps and gear for cyclists. 800-721-8719. www.adv-cycling.org

**American Cycle Express,** 223 Main St., P.O. Box 155, Binghamton, NY 13905: Free information ◆ Parts and accessories. 607-777-1223. www.americancycle.com

**Avocet Inc.,** P.O. Box 120, Palo Alto, CA 94302: Free information with long SASE ◆ Bike computer that measures speed, distance, and time. 800-227-8346; 650-321-8501 (in CA). www.avocet.com

**Bell Sports Inc.,** 6350 San Ignacio Ave., San Jose, CA 95119: Free catalog ◆ Bicycle racks, cages, pumps, work stands, trainers, and cycling bags. 800-776-5677. answer_desk@bellsport.com

**Bicycle Parking Systems Inc.,** 6 Antares Dr., Phase II, Unit #10B, Nepean, Ontario, Canada K2E 8A9: Free information ◆ Vertical and horizontal bicycle parking racks. 613-226-6452. www.bikeup.com

**Bike Box,** 1729 E. Commercial Blvd., Ste. 290, Fort Lauderdale, FL 33334: Free information ◆ Bicycle travel box. 800-900-1663. www.bikebox.com

**Bike Nashbar,** 4111 Simon Rd., P.O. Box 3449, Youngstown OH 44512: Free catalog ◆ Bicycles, components, and saddlebags. 800-627-4227. www.nashbar.com

**The Bike Source,** 17777 Main St., Irvine, CA 92714: Free information ◆ Mountain bicycles, parts, and accessories. 714-622-8103. www.bikesource.com

**Bike Tight,** P.O. Box 3242, Paso Robles, CA 93447: Free information ◆ Bicycle transporter for cars. 800-247-3843. www.biketight.com/index.html

**Bikecentennial,** P.O. Box 8308, Missoula, MT 59802: Free catalog ◆ Maps, books, and gear for the adventure cyclist. 800-721-8719. www.adv-cycling.org

**Branford Bike,** 1074 Main St., Branford, CT 06405: Free catalog ◆ Frames, parts and accessories, tires and tubes, team clothing, cycling gloves, socks, caps, and headbands. 203-488-0482. www.branfordbike.com

**Brule Mountain Gear,** 1385 Klock Rd., Aylmer, Quebec. Canada J9H 5E1: Free brochure ◆ Bicycles and backpacks. 819-685-9163. www.panpack.com

**Burley Design Cooperative,** 4020 Stewart Rd., Eugene, OR 97402: Free list of retail sources ◆ Bike trailers for children. Comes with chest harness, seat belt, and roll bar. 541-687-1644. www.burley.com

**Cosmopolitan Motors Inc.,** 301 Jacksonville Rd., Hatboro, PA 19040: Free information ◆ Bicycle locks, packs and bags, tires, and other accessories for bicycles and mopeds. 800-523-2522; 215-672-9100 (in PA). www.full-motion-net.com/cosmo

**D & R Industries,** 7111 Capitol Dr., Lincolnwood, IL 60645: Free information ◆ Car-mounted bicycle racks, child carriers, horns, lamps, locks, packs and bags, reflectors, speedometers, tires and tubes, and helmets. 800-323-2852; 847-677-3200 (in IL). www.champdealers.com

**Dan's Competition,** 613 E. 4th St., Mt. Vernon, IN 47620: Information $2 ◆ Bicycles, accessories and parts, and clothing. 812-838-2691. doachs@gac.edu

**Eastpak,** 50 Rogers Rd., P.O. Box 8232, Ward Hill, MA 01835: Free list of retail sources ◆ Frame and saddle bags. 978-373-1581.

**Ecko Helmets,** 111 W. 7th St., Silver City, NM 88061: Free information ◆ Helmets. 505-388-8080.

**Excel Sports Boulder,** 2045 32nd St., Boulder, CO 80301: Free catalog ◆ Bicycle computers, off-road equipment, bicycle frame sets, tires, and tubes. 800-627-6664. www.excelsports.com

**Fairfield Processing Corp.,** P.O. Box 1130, Danbury, CT 06813: Free information ◆ Lightweight folding bicycle fairing. 800-980-8000; 203-371-1901 (in CT). www.poly-fil.com

**Frankford Bicycle Company,** 964 N. State St., Girard, OH 44420: Free catalog ◆ Bicycle components and accessories. 800-621-3593; 330-545-0392 (in OH).

**Giro Sport Designs,** 380 Encinal, Santa Cruz, CA 95060: Free information ◆ Lightweight foam helmets. 800-294-6098. www.giro.com

**Hammer Helmets,** 3619 NW 124th Ave., Coral Springs, FL 33065: Free information ◆ Helmets. 954-340-3501.

**Innovations in Cycling Inc.,** 2700 E. Bilby Rd., Tucson, AZ 85706: Free information ◆ Emergency tire inflator. 520-295-3936.

**Jenson USA,** 580 W. Central Ave., Ste A, Brea, CA 92821: Free information ◆ Custom mountain bicycles and road bicycle accessories. 800-577-8720. www.jensonusa.com

**Loose Screws,** 12225 Hwy. 66, Ashland, OR 97520: Free catalog ◆ Small parts for bicycles. 541-488-4800. www.loosescrews.com

**Macaw Helmets,** 4105 Indus Way, Riverside, CA 92503: Free information ◆ Helmets. 800-355-6229.

**Madden Mountaineering,** 2400 Central Ave., Boulder, CO 80301: Free catalog ◆ Frame and saddle bags. 303-442-5828. www.maddenusa.com

**Nightsun Performance Lighting,** 995 S. Fair Oaks Ave., Pasadena, CA 91105: Free list of retail sources ◆ Dual-beam light systems. 818-799-5074. www.night-sun.com

**O'Neil's Bicycle Shop,** 1094 Main St., Worcester, MA 01603: Free catalog ◆ Bicycles, parts and accessories, and clothing. 800-638-6344; 508-798-0084 (in MA). www.oneils.com

**Overland Equipment,** 2145 Park Ave., Ste. 4, Chico, CA 95928: Free catalog ◆ Frame and saddle bags and backpacks. 800-487-8851.

**Park Tool Company,** 6 Long Lake Rd., St. Paul, MN 55115: Free brochure ◆ Tool kits and accessories. 612-777-6868. www.parktool.com

**Pedal Pusher Ski & Sport,** 658 Easton Rd., Rt. 611, Horsham, PA 19044: Free catalog ◆ Bicycles, frames, components, tools, clothing, and car carry-all. 215-672-0202.

**Performance Bicycle Shop,** P.O. Box 2741, Chapel Hill, NC 27514: Free catalog ◆ Clothing, frames, bicycles and parts, and frame and saddle bags. 800-727-2433. www.performancebike.com

**Phat Tire,** 14237 Inwood Rd., Farmer's Branch, TX 75244: Free information ◆ Tires, wheels, frames, parts, and accessories. 800-742-8682. www.phattire.com

**Price Point,** 1442 W. 135th St., Gardena, CA 90249: Free catalog ◆ Bicycles, parts and accessories, and clothing. 800-774-2376. www.pricepoint.com

**REI Recreational Equipment Company,** Sumner, WA 98352: Free catalog ◆ Frame and saddle bags. 800-426-4840. www.rei.com

**Sachs Bicycle Components,** 4980 E. Landon Dr., Anaheim, CA 92807: Catalog $2 ◆ Bicycle components. 714-701-0254. www.sachs-bike.com/index2.htm

**Schwinn Bicycle Company,** 1690 38th St., Boulder, CO 80301: Free information with long SASE ◆ Bicycle computer that measures current and maximum speeds, trip distance, odometer readings, and cadence. 303-939-0100. www.schwinn.com

**Specialized Bicycle Components,** 15130 Concord Circle, Morgan Hill, CA 95037: Free information ◆ Frame and saddle bags. 800-245-3462; 408-779-6229 (in CA). www.specialized.com

**Syncros,** 975 Vernon Dr., Vancouver, British Columbia, Canada V6A 3P2: Free brochure ◆ Mountain bicycle parts and accessories. 604-253-5204. www.syncros.com

**Teel Inc.,** 567 Commerce St., Franklin Lake, NJ 07417: Information $3 ◆ Bicycle frames.

**Third Hand,** 12225 Hwy. 66, Ashland, OR 97520: Free catalog ◆ Bicycle repair tools, repair stands, parts, and how-to books. 541-488-4800. www.thethirdhand.com

**Treads, Bicycle Outfitters,** 16981 E. Iliff Ave., Aurora, CO 80013: Free catalog ◆ Clothing, gloves, parts, and accessories. 800-587-3237. TREADS@TREADS.com

**Ultimate Bicycle Support,** P.O. Box 470, Fort Collins, CO 80522: Free information ◆ Bicycle storage and repair stands. 970-493-4488.

**Vigor Sports,** 13929 Equitble Rd., Cerritos, CA 90703: Free catalog ◆ Helmets and other protection gear. 310-407-1013. www.hjc-chatterbox.com

**VistaLite (Bell Sports),** 6350 San Ignacio Ave., San Jose, CA 95119: Free information ◆ Easy-to-install halogen lights. 800-776-5677. www.bellsports.com

**Wallingford Bicycle Parts,** P.O. Box 31775, Seattle, WA 98103: Free catalog ◆ Saddles, saddlebags, fenders, tools, and other accessories. 888-731-3537. www.wallbike.com

**Wheel World,** 22718 Ventura Blvd., Woodland Hills, CA 91364: Free information ◆ Bicycle components and accessories. 818-224-2044.

**Xtrskin,** 115 Hawkins Rd., Fort Walton Beach, FL 32547: Free information ◆ Helmets and other protection gear. 904-864-4243.

## Tandems

**Burley Design Cooperative,** 4020 Stewart Rd., Eugene, OR 97402: Free list of retail sources ◆ Tandems, other bicycles, and folding bike trailers for children. 541-687-1644. www.burley.com

**Haverich Ortho-Sport Inc.,** 67 Emerald St., Keene, NH 03431: Free information ◆ Bicycles, tricycles, and tandems with specially designed accessories to meet every need. 603-358-0438.

**Montague Bicycle Company,** P.O. Box 381118, Cambridge, MA 02238: Free information ◆ Folding tandems. 800-736-5348. www.montagueco.com

**Rock N' Roll Cycles,** P.O. Box 1558, Levelland, TX 79336: Free information ◆ Single riders, tandems, and hand-and-foot-powered cycles with optional seat configurations and custom-fitting for individual needs. 800-654-9664. www.rocknrollcycles.com

**Ryan Recumbent Cycles,** 99 R Washington St., Melrose, MA 02176: Free information ◆ Recumbent bicycles and tandems. 781-979-0072. www.ryancycles.com

**Tandems East,** 86 Gwynwood Dr., Pittsgrove, NJ 08318: Free catalog ◆ Tandem bicycles, parts, and accessories. 609-451-5104. www.tandemseast.com

**Tandems Limited,** Jack & Susan Goertz, 2220 Vanessa Dr., Birmingham, AL 35242: Free information ◆ Tandems, parts, and accessories. 205-991-5519. www.tandemsltd.com

**Totally Tandems Inc.,** P.O. Box 1661, Marshalltown, IA 50158: Free catalog ◆ Tandem bicycles, parts, and accessories. 800-255-0576. ttandems@adiis.net

## Trailers (Bicycle & Children Carriers)

**Alley-Cat Cycles,** P.O. Box 1242, San Carlos, CA 94070: Free information ◆ Trailer bicycles. 800-257-0662.

**B.O.B. Universal Headquarters,** 3641 Sacramento Dr., #3, San Luis Obispo, CA 93401: Free brochure ◆ Bicycle trailers. 805-541-2554.

**Bicycler Evolution,** 985 Irving Rd., Eugene, OR 97404: Free brochure ◆ Bicycle trailers. 800-357-2773; 541-688-2773 (in IA). www.rio.com/~bsi/brev

**Blue Sky Cycle Carts,** P.O. Box 5788, Bend, OR 97708: Free information ◆ Bicycle trailers for carrying larger children and adults with disabilities. 800-669-1753. www.BlueSkyCycleCarts.com

**Burley Design Cooperative,** 4080 Stewart Rd., Eugene, OR 97402: Free brochure ◆ Bike trailers for children, with chest harness, seat belt, and roll bar. 503-687-1644. www.burley.com

**Cycle Components,** P.O. Box 3480, La Habra, CA 90632: Free information ◆ Children's bicycle trailer-carrier. 800-247-9754.

**Equinox Industries Inc.,** P.O. Box 674, Cottage Grove, OR 97424: Free brochure ◆ Lightweight bicycle trailers. 800-942-7895. www.efn.org/~equinox

**Fresh Aire Trailer Works,** 216 N. Hazel, Ames, IA 50010: Free catalog with two 1st class stamps ◆ Bicycle utility trailers. 515-233-6120. members.aol.com/FATrailers

**Schwinn Bicycle Company,** 1690 38th St., Boulder, CO 80301: Free information with long SASE ◆ Racing, mountain, tandem, and city bicycles. Also trailers for children. 303-939-0100. www.schwinn.com

## Tricycles

**Mary Arnold Toys,** 962 Lexington Ave., New York, NY 10021: Free catalog ◆ Tricycles. 212-744-8510.

**Back to Basics Toys,** 1 Memory Ln., Ridgely, MD 21685: Free catalog ◆ Tricycles. 800-356-5360. www.backtobasicstoys.com

**Childcraft,** 250 College Park, P.O. Box 1811, Peoria, IL 61656: Free catalog ◆ Tricycles. 800-631-5657.

**Haverich Ortho-Sport Inc.,** 67 Emerald St., Keene, NH 03431: Free information ◆ Bicycles, tricycles, and tandems with specially designed accessories to meet every need. 603-358-0438.

**Mobileation,** 445 E. 87th St., Ste 4, New York, NY 10128: Free catalog ◆ Mobile interactive riding toys for children. Includes electric and gasoline-engine cars, battery operated and pedal driven vehicles, ride-on toys for toddlers and infants, tricycles, bikes, scooters, seesaws, build-them-yourself pedal car kits, and handcrafted rocking horses. 888-88-MOBILE; 212-426-8074 (in NY). service@mobileation.com

**One Step Ahead,** P.O. Box 517, Lake Bluff, IL 60044: Free catalog ◆ Tricycles. 800-950-5120. osacatalog@aol.com

**Viewpoint Mfg. Inc.,** P.O. Box 108, Spanish Fork, UT 84660: Free information ◆ Therapeutic tricycle for children with special needs. 800-798-2430.

## Unicycles

**Dekker Service Inc.,** 5433 116th Ave. SE, Bellevue, WA 98006: Free brochure ◆ Pashley unicycles. 425-641-9639. www.eskimo.com/~mdekker

**Teresa & Sem Unicycles,** P.O. Box 40353, Redford, MI 48240: Free brochure ♦ Unicycles and other juggling accessories. 313-537-8175. members.aol.com/semcycle

## BILLIARDS

**Adam Custom Cues,** 25 Hutcheson Pl., Lynbrook, NY 11563: Free information ♦ Pool cues. 800-645-2162; 516-593-5050 (in NY).

**Ajay Leisure Products Inc.,** 1501 E. Wisconsin St., Delavan, WI 53115: Free list of retail sources ♦ Billiards balls, bridges, chalk, cues and cases. 800-558-3276; 414-728-5521 (in WI).

**Atlas Billiard Supplies,** 3721 W. Chase Ave., Skokie, IL 60076: Free catalog ♦ Billiard supplies and equipment. 800-283-7845. www.cuestick.com

**Billiard Pro Shop,** 9160 US Hwy. 64, Ste. 5, Arlington, TN 38002: Free information ♦ Cues, cases, and billiards tables. 800-365-4776.

**Black Boar,** 5110 College Ave., College Park, MD 20740: Free information ♦ Handcrafted pool cues. 301-277-3236.

**Bruns Manufacturing Ltd.,** 10110 State Rt. 13, Huron, OH 44839: Free information ♦ Billiards tables, cues, and accessories. 419-433-6137.

**Compleat Gamester,** 350 Moody St., Waltham, MA 02154: Free information ♦ Juggling, dart, and billiard supplies. 800-698-9505. www.compgames.com

**Connelly Billiard Manufacturing,** 2540 E. Grant Rd., Tucson, AZ 85716: Free information ♦ Billiards tables. 520-881-5503.

**Creative Inventions,** 9142-44 Jordan Ave., Chatsworth, CA 91311: Free information ♦ Cues, cue-making equipment, and cases. 800-388-5132; 818-727-7966 (in CA).

**The Cue Tender Company,** P.O. Box 924, Ojai, CA 93024: Free information ♦ Handcrafted wood cue holder that attaches to tables. 805-646-7508.

**D & R Industries,** 7111 Capitol Dr., Lincolnwood, IL 60645: Free information ♦ Billiards balls, bridges, chalk, cues and cases, and racks. 800-323-2852; 847-677-3200 (in IL). www.champdealers.com

**Dart Mart Inc.,** 2255 Computer Ave., Willow Grove, PA 19090: Free information ♦ Billiards equipment. 800-423-3220; 215-830-0501 (in PA).

**Discount Cues & Cases,** 170 Koontz Ln., #135, Carson City, NV 89701: Free catalog ♦ Cues and cases. 800-693-8736.

**Dufferin Inc.,** 1514 St. Paul Ave., Gurnee, IL 60031: Free information ♦ Pool cues. 847-244-4762.

**Escalade Sports,** P.O. Box 889, Evansville, IN 47706: Free catalog ♦ Pool tables. 800-457-3373; 812-467-1200 (in IN).

**Giuseppe,** 6920 Knott Ave., Buena Park, CA 90620: Free information ♦ Custom cue cases. 800-432-4382.

**Hercek Fine Billiard Cues,** 1352 Armour Blvd., Mundelein, IL 60060: Free brochure ♦ Custom cues with optional leather wraps and inlays. 847-680-7498.

**Indian Industries Inc.,** P.O. Box 889, Evansville, IN 47706: Free catalog ♦ Racks and cues. 800-457-3373; 812-467-1200 (in IN).

**International Billiards Inc.,** 2311 Washington Ave., Houston, TX 77007: Free information ♦ Billiards balls, bridges, chalk, cues and cases, and racks. 800-255-6386; 713-869-3237 (in TX).

**J-S Sales Company Inc.,** 5 S. Fulton Ave., Mt. Vernon, NY 10550: Free information ♦ Billiards balls, bridges, chalk, cues and cases, non-slate and slate tables, and racks. 800-431-2944; 914-668-8051 (in NY).

**Kasson Game Tables,** 11 Commerce Rd., Babbitt, MN 55706: Free information ♦ Billiards tables. 218-827-3701.

**The Henry W.T. Mali & Company,** 257 Park Ave. South, New York, NY 10010: Free information ♦ Cues. 800-223-6468; 212-475-4960 (in NY). www.mali.cues.com

**Mueller Sporting Goods Inc.,** 4825 S. 16th, Lincoln, NE 68512: Free catalog ♦ Billiards and dart supplies. 800-925-7665. www.Mueller-Sporting-Goods.com

**Murrey & Sons Company Inc.,** Billiard & Recreation Manufacturing Division, 14150 S. Figueroa St., Los Angeles, CA 90061: Free information ♦ Tables, cues and cases, and accessories. 310-323-1752.

**Owl Darts,** 1001 SW Adams, Peoria, IL 61602: Free catalog ♦ Billiards supplies and darts. 800-832-7871.

**Pennray Billiard & Recreational Products,** 7847 N. Calswell Ave., Niles, IL 60714: Free catalog ♦ Darts, billiards, and soccer equipment. 800-523-8934. www.wicothesource.com

**Playmaster,** 76 N. 625 West, Bountiful, UT 84010: Free catalog ♦ Billiard and game tables. 801-298-7665.

**Porcupine Inc.,** P.O. Box 588, Meridianville, AL 35759: Free price list ♦ Cues and accessories. 800-232-3654. www.rackem.com

**Prathers Custom Cue Parts Inc.,** P.O. Box 7, Mooreland, OK 73852: Free information ♦ Cue building components. 405-994-2414. www.prathercue.com

**Saunier-Wilhem Company,** 3216 5th Ave., Pittsburgh, PA 15213: Free catalog ♦ Equipment and accessories for bowling, billiards, darts, table tennis, and shuffleboard. Also board games. 412-621-4350.

**Schmelke Manufacturing Company,** 1879 28th Ave., Rice Lake, WI 54868: Free information ♦ Pool cue cases. 715-234-6553.

**The Schuler Cue,** 540 W. Colfax St., #2, Palatine, IL 60067: Free brochure ♦ Handcrafted pool and billiard cues. 847-776-7769. www.schulercue.com

**Showcase Custom Cues,** Division Showcase Billiards, 12031 Tejon St., Westminster, CO 80234: Free information ♦ Custom-made cues. 800-783-7849.

**Sporty's Preferred Living Catalog,** Clermont Airport, Batavia, OH 45103: Free catalog ♦ Billiards tables complete with balls, rack, bridge, and cues. 800-543-8633. www.sportys-catalogs.com

**Tom's Q Stix,** 4111 Dudley, Lincoln, NE 68503: Free information ♦ Cues, cases, tips, and accessories. 402-466-1077.

**Trusty Enterprises Inc.,** 2453 Rosemead, South El Monte, CA 91733: Free catalog ♦ Cues and cases. 800-222-2174.

**Universal Bowling, Golf & Billiard Supplies,** 619 S. Wabash Ave., Chicago, IL 60605: Free catalog ♦ Billiards supplies. 800-523-3037. www.universal-bowling.com

**Valley Recreation Products Inc.,** P.O. Box 656, Bay City, MI 48707: Free information ♦ Cues. 800-248-2837; 517-892-4536 (in MI).

**Viking Cue Mfg.,** 2710 Syene Rd., Madison, WI 53713: Free catalog ♦ Billiard cues and accessories. 608-271-5155. www.vikingcue.com

**Wa-Mac Inc.,** P.O. Box 128, Carlstadt, NJ 07410: Free information ♦ Billiards balls, bridges, chalk, cues and cases, and racks. 800-447-5673; 201-438-7200 (in NJ).

**World of Leisure Manufacturing Company,** 13504 Phantom St., Victorville, CA 92394: Free list of retail sources ♦ Billiards balls, bridges, chalk, cues and cases, and racks. 619-246-3790.

## BINOCULARS & ACCESSORIES

**Adorama,** 42 W. 18th St., New York, NY 10011: Catalog $3 ♦ Binoculars and telescope equipment. 212-741-0466. goadorama@aol.com

**Armchair Sailor Bookstore,** 543 Thames St., Newport, RI 02840: Free information ♦ Binoculars. 800-292-4278; 401-847-4252 (in RI). www.seabooks.com

**Astronomics,** 2401 Tee Circle, Ste. 106, Norman, OK 73069: Free information ♦ Binoculars. 405-364-0858. www.astronomics.com

**Ball Photo Supply Company,** 85 Tunnel Rd., Asheville, NC 28805: Free information ♦ Telescopes, spotting scopes, camera equipment, binoculars, eyepieces, and accessories. 704-252-2443.

**Bausch & Lomb,** 9200 Cody, Overland Park, KS 66214: Free list of retail sources ♦ Binoculars. 800-423-3537. www.bushnell.com

**Beckson Marine,** 165 Holland Ave., Bridgeport, CT 06605: Catalog $3.25 ◆ Binoculars. 203-333-1412. www.beckson.com

**Berger Brothers Camera Exchange,** 209 Broadway, Amityville, NY 11701: Free information ◆ Binoculars. 800-262-4160; 516-264-4160 (in NY). www.berger-bros.com

**Binocular City,** 811 Hwy. 13, Diamond Jims Mall, Mendola Heights, MN 55118: Free information ◆ Binoculars, spotting scopes, and rifle scopes. 800-473-1621.

**The Bushnell Corp.,** 9200 Cody, Overland Park, KS 66214: Free information ◆ Binoculars and spotting scopes. 800-423-3537. www.bushnell.com

**California Telescope Company,** P.O. Box 1338, Burbank, CA 91507: Catalog $5 ◆ Binoculars. 818-505-8424.

**Camera Bug Ltd.,** 1799 Briarcliff Rd., Atlanta, GA 30306: Free information ◆ Telescopes, binoculars, spotting scopes, and accessories. 404-873-4513. cam_bug@msn.com

**Camera Corner of Iowa,** 3523 Eastern Ave., Davenport, IA 52807: Free information ◆ Camera equipment and binoculars. 800-762-4282.

**Celestron International,** 2835 Columbia St., Torrance, CA 90503: Catalog $2 ◆ Binoculars. 562-328-9560. www.celestron.com

**The Chartroom,** Chase, Leavitt & Company, 10 Dana St., Portland, ME 04112: Free information ◆ Marine binoculars. 800-638-8906; 207-772-3751 (in ME).

**Chinon America Inc.,** 1065 Bristol Rd., Mountainside, NJ 07092: Free information ◆ Binoculars. 908-654-0404.

**Christophers Ltd.,** 2401 Tee Circle, Ste. 106, Norman, OK 73069: Free information ◆ Binoculars. 800-356-6603.

**City Camera,** P.O. Box 721172, Berkley, MI 48072: Free information ◆ Binoculars and spotting scopes.

**Compass Industries,** 104 E. 25th St., New York, NY 10010: Free information ◆ Binoculars. 800-221-9904.

**Eagle Optics,** 2120 W. Greenview Dr., #4, Middleton, WI 53562: Free catalog ◆ Binoculars, telescopes, and accessories. 608-836-6568. www.eagleoptics.com

**Edmund Scientific Company,** Edscorp Bldg., Barrington, NJ 08007: Free catalog ◆ Binoculars, telescopes, and other educational and science equipment. 609-547-8880. www.edsci.com

**Europtik Ltd.,** P.O. Box 319, Dunmore, PA 18509: Free information ◆ Binoculars and rifle scopes. 717-347-6049. www.europtik.com

**Eye-1 Optics,** 1525 Xenia Ave., Yellow Springs, OH 45387: Free information ◆ Binoculars and spotting scopes. 800-800-EYE-1.

**Focus Camera,** 4419 13th Ave., Brooklyn, NY 11219: Free information ◆ Binoculars. 718-437-8810. orders@focuscamera.com

**Fujinon,** 10 High Point Dr., Wayne, NJ 07470: Free information ◆ Binoculars. 201-633-5600.

**Harrison Astronomy,** 2574 Granville St., Vancouver, British Columbia, Canada V6H 3C8: Free information ◆ Telescopes and accessories, binoculars, microscopes, magnifiers, meteorological instruments, and books. 604-737-4303.

**Helix,** 310 S. Racine, Chicago, IL 60607: Free catalog ◆ Binoculars. 800-33-HELIX; 312-421-6000 (in IL). helixuw@aol.com

**HP Marketing Group,** 16 Chapin Rd., Pine Brook, NJ 07058: Free information ◆ Binoculars. 732-808-9010.

**InteliOptics**, Division Brunton Company, 620 E. Monroe, Riverton, WY 82501: Free brochure ◆ Binoculars with an integrated microprocessor for precision range finding and data interpretation. 307-856-6559.

**Internet Telescope Exchange,** 7151 Market St., Wilmington, NC 28405: Free catalog ◆ Night vision scopes, goggles, binoculars, and other optical accessories. 416-663-6963. www.europtik.com

**ITT Night Vision,** 7671 Enon Dr., Roanoke, VA 24019: Free list of retail sources ◆ Night vision optical viewer. 800-448-8678. www.ittnightvision.com

**Jim Kendrick Studio,** 2775 Dundas St. West, Toronto, Ontario, Canada M6P 1Y4: Free information ◆ Heating system for telescopes, binoculars, and cameras. 416-762-7946. www.kendrick-studio.com

**Khan Scope Center,** 3243 Dufferin St., Toronto, Ontario, Canada M6A 2T2: Free price list ◆ Telescopes, telescope-making supplies, binoculars, audiovisual aids, books, photographic equipment, computers and software, and planetariums. 416-783-4140. www.khanscope.com

**Leica Camera Inc.,** 156 Ludlow St., Northvale, NJ 07647: Free information ◆ Binoculars and camera equipment. 800-222-0118. www.leica-camera-usa.com

**Leupold & Stevens Inc.,** P.O. Box 688, Beaverton, OR 97075: Free list of retail sources ◆ Binoculars. 800-929-4949. www.leupstv.com/gidealer.html

**Lumicon,** 2111 Research Dr., Livermore, CA 94550: Free catalog ◆ Binoculars. 510-447-9570. www.Astronomy-Mall.com/Lumicon

**Meade Instruments Corp.,** 16542 Millikan Ave., Irvine, CA 92714: Catalog $3 (request list of retail sources) ◆ Binoculars. 714-556-2291. www.meade.com

**F.C. Meichsner Company,** 182 Lincoln St., Boston, MA 02111: Free information ◆ Binoculars. 800-321-8439. www.meichsner.com

**Minolta,** 101 Williams Dr., Ramsey, NJ 07446: Free information ◆ Binoculars. 201-825-4000. www.minolta.com

**National Camera Exchange,** 9300 Olson Memorial Hwy., Golden Valley, MN 55427: Free information ◆ Binoculars and spotting scopes. 888-873-1979; 612-591-5175 (in MN). usedcameras@natcam.com

**Nautac,** 3176 SE Dixie Hwy., Stuart, FL 34997: Free information ◆ Binoculars. 407-220-2320.

**Nikon Photo,** 1300 Walt Whitman Rd., Melville, NY 11747: Free information ◆ Binoculars. 516-547-4200. www.nikonusa.com

**Orion Telescope & Binocular Center,** P.O. Box 1815, Santa Cruz, CA 95061: Free catalog ◆ Telescopes, photographic equipment, charts and star maps, books, science supplies, and binoculars. 800-447-1001. www.oriontel.com

**Parks Optical Company,** 679 Easy St., Simi Valley, CA 93065: Catalog $3 ◆ Binoculars. 805-522-6722.

**Pentax Corp.,** 35 Inverness Dr. East, Englewood, CO 80112: Free information ◆ Binoculars, cameras, lenses, and other optical equipment. 303-799-8000. www.pentax.com

**Perceptor,** Brownsville Junction Plaza, Box 38, Ste. 201, Schomberg, Ontario, Canada L0G 1T0: Free information ◆ Binoculars. 905-939-2313.

**Pioneer Research,** 216 Haddon Ave., Westmont, NJ 08108: Free information ◆ Binoculars. 800-257-7742; 609-854-2424 (in NJ). www.pioneer-research.com

**Pocono Mountain Optics,** 104 North Pocono 502 Plaza, Moscow, PA 18444: Catalog $6 ◆ Binoculars, sighting scopes, new and used telescopes, telescope-making supplies, charts and star maps, photographic supplies, and books. 800-569-4323; 717-842-1500 (in PA). pocmtnop@ptdprlog.net

**Redlich Optical,** 711 W. Broad St., Falls Church, VA 22046: Free information with long SASE ◆ Binoculars, spotting scopes, and telescopes. 703-241-4077.

**Rex's Astro Stuff,** 63 Observatory Ln., Dover, AR 72837: Free catalog ◆ Telescopes, binoculars, and accessories. 501-331-3773.

**Ricoh Consumer Products Group,** 475 Lillard Dr., Sparks, NV 89434: Free brochure ◆ Binoculars. 800-225-1899. www.ricohcpg.com

**Scope City,** P.O. Box 440, Simi Valley, CA 93065: Catalog $7 (refundable) ◆ Binoculars. 805-522-6646.

**Selsi Binoculars,** P.O. Box 10, Midland Park, NJ 07432: Free information ◆ Binoculars.

**Shutan Camera & Video,** 312 W. Randolph, Chicago, IL 60606: Free catalog ◆ Binoculars. 800-621-2248; 312-332-2000 (in IL). www.shutan.com

**Simmons Outdoor Company,** 201 Plantation Oak, Thomasville, GA 31792: Catalog $2 ◆ Binoculars. 912-227-9053.

**Sky Optics,** 4031 Fairview St., Burlington, Ontario, Canada L7L 2A4: Free information ◆ Telescopes, binoculars, eyepieces, CCDs, books, software, and accessories. 905-631-9944. www.worldchat.com/commercial/skyoptics

**Stano Components,** P.O. Box 2048, Carson City, NV 89702: Catalog $4 ◆ Night-vision optical equipment. 702-246-5281.

**Steiner Binoculars,** c/o Pioneer Research Inc., 216 Haddon Ave., Westmont, NJ 08108: Free information ◆ Binoculars. 800-257-7742. www.pioneer-research.com

**Swarovski Optik,** One Wholesale Way, Cranston, RI 02920: Free information ◆ Binoculars. 800-426-3089.

**Swift Instruments Inc.,** 952 Dorchester Ave., Boston, MA 02125: Free list of retail sources ◆ Binoculars, cases, and camera-adaptable spotting scopes. 800-446-1115; 617-436-2960 (in MA). www.swift-optics.com

**Tamron Industries Inc.,** 125 Schmitt Blvd., Farmingdale, NY 11735: Free brochure ◆ Binoculars and spotting scopes that can be adapted for camera use as an ultra-telescopic zoom lens. 516-694-8700. www.tamron.com

**Tasco Sales Inc.,** Box 520080, Miami, FL 22152: Free information ◆ Binoculars and other optical equipment. 305-591-3670.

**Telescope & Binocular Center,** P.O. Box 1815, Santa Cruz, CA 95061: Free catalog ◆ Telescopes, binoculars, and accessories. 800-447-1001. www.oriontel.com

**Tokina Optical Corp.,** 1512 Kona Dr., Rancho Dominguez, CA 90220: Free information ◆ Binoculars. 800-421-1141. www.thkphoto.com

**Roger W. Tuthill Inc.,** 11 Tanglewood Ln., Mountainside, NJ 07092: Free catalog with 9x12 SASE with four 1st class stamps ◆ Binoculars. 800-223-1063.

**Unitron Inc.,** 170 Wilbur Pl., P.O. Box 469, Bohemia, NY 11716: Free catalog ◆ Binoculars. 516-589-6666.

**University Optics,** P.O. Box 1205, Ann Arbor, MI 48106: Free catalog ◆ Binoculars. 800-521-2828. www.universityoptics.com

**Virgo Astronomics,** 608 Falconbridge Dr., Ste. 46, Joppa, MD 21085: Free catalog ◆ Mounting stand for all sizes of binoculars. 410-679-7055. www.Astronomy-Mall.com

**Vivitar Corp.,** 1280 Rancho Conejo Blvd., Newbury Park, CA 91320: Free brochure ◆ Binoculars. 805-498-7008. www.vivitarcorp.com

**Ward's Natural Science,** P.O. Box 92912, 5100 W. Henrietta Rd., Rochester, NY 14692: Earth science catalog $10; biology catalog $15; middle school catalog $10 ◆ Binoculars, optical science equipment, other laboratory equipment, and supplies. 800-962-2660. www.wardsci.com

**What In The World,** P.O. Box 1767, Lake Arrowhead, CA 92352: Free information ◆ Telescopes, cameras, weather stations, binoculars, and accessories. 909-337-5080. www.whatintheworld.com

**Wholesale Optics Division,** 59 Mine Hill Rd., New Milford, CT 06776: Catalog $10 (refundable) ◆ Telescopes, telescope-making supplies, photographic equipment, computer software, science supplies, books, and binoculars. 860-355-3132. www.astroptx.com/~astroptx

**WilsonTrace Distribution,** 1808 Sportsman Ln., Huntsville, AL 35816: Free catalog ◆ Reloading equipment, scopes, sportshooting rifles, binoculars, and accessories. 800-494-5397. www.wileyoutdoorsports.com

**Wolf Camera,** 1055 S. Tamiami Trail, Sarasota, FL 34236: Free information ◆ New and used telescopes, binoculars, filters, parts, and software. 941-366-7484. www.wolfcamera.com

**World Photo & Video,** 225 Liberty St., New York, NY 10281: Free information ◆ New and used photography equipment, binoculars, camcorders, and electronics. 212-945-7415.

**Zeiss Optical Inc.,** 1015 Commerce St., Petersburg, VA 23803: Free brochure ◆ Binoculars. 800-338-2984.

## BIRD FEEDERS & HOUSES

**Animal Environments,** 1954 Kellogg Ave., Carlsbad, CA 92008: Free information ◆ Environmentally designed cages. 619-438-4442. www.animalenvironments.com

**Anyone Can Whistle,** 323 Wall St., Kingston, NY 12401: Free catalog ◆ Bird feeders, wind chimes, and other musical gifts. 800-435-8863. anyonecan@chimes.com

**Avian Accents,** P.O. Box 109, Troy, IL 62294: Free information ◆ Hardwood bird cages. 618-667-2243.

**B & B Nurseries,** Box 1057, Morrisville, VT 05661: Free information ◆ Handcrafted feeders, houses, and baths. 800-724-7284.

**The Backyard Sanctuary Company,** 133 River Rd., Cos Cob, CT 06807: Free information ◆ Handcrafted copper bird feeders. 800-247-3735.

**Best Feeders Inc.,** P.O. Box 998, Poteet, TX 78065: Free list of retail sources ◆ Hummingbird feeders and accessories. 800-772-3604.

**Bird City USA,** 14715 Live Oak Dr., Panama City Beach, FL 32413: Free information ◆ Wrought iron and regular exotic bird cages, toys, and toy parts. 850-233-3006. www.birdcity.com

**Birding Concepts,** 4929 Wren Dr., Appleton, WI 54915: Free information ◆ Wild bird feeders and seed. 800-269-4450.

**Brushy Mountain Bee Farm,** P.O. Box 135, Moravian Falls, NC 28654: Free catalog ◆ Birdhouses, feeders, and beekeeping supplies. 800-BEESWAX.

**C & S Products Company Inc.,** Box 848, Fort Dodge, IA 50501: Free catalog ◆ Suet products and feeders. 515-955-5605.

**California Cageworks Corp.,** 3314 Burton Ave., Burbank, CA 91504: Free information ◆ Animal enclosures, breeding cages, walk-in aviaries, other all-purpose cages, and accessories. 626-843-6283.

**The Clarion Martin House,** 733 Mansion Rd., Winfield, MO 63389: Free information ◆ Purple martin house with telescoping pole. 800-845-9178.

**Country Lane Rustic Wood Products,** 166 Bailey Pond Rd., Voluntown, CT 06384: Free information ◆ Handcrafted cedar birdhouses and feeders. 860-564-5682.

**Droll Yankees Inc.,** 27 Mill Rd., Foster, RI 02825: Free catalog ◆ Bird feeders. 800-352-9164.

**Duncraft,** 102 Fisherville Rd., Concord, NH 03303: Free catalog ◆ Wild bird supplies, squirrel-proof feeders, birdhouses, bird baths, and books. 800-763-7878. www.duncraft.com

**The Edisonville Woodshop,** 1916 Edisonville Rd., Strasburg, PA 17579: Brochure $1 ◆ Handcrafted all-wood mailboxes and bird feeders. 717-687-0116.

**1891 Originals,** P.O. Box 9505, Canton, OH 44711: Brochure $1 (refundable) ◆ Antique reproduction nesting boxes. 800-381-BIRD.

**Feather Creek,** P.O. Box 379, Moncure, NC 27559: Free information ◆ Birdhouses. 919-542-0240.

**Frey Ltd.,** 4680 Pell Dr., Sacramento, CA 95838: Free brochure ◆ Space-efficient cages and accessories for bird owners with space for one cage. 916-922-3202.

**Hammer's Wire & Wood,** P.O. Box 205, Judson, TX 75660: Free information ◆ Handcrafted birdhouses. 800-227-8841; 903-663-1145 (in TX).

**Humming Bird Hollow Designs,** 2137 Kerr Rd., Sevierville, TN 37876: Brochure $1 ◆ Birdhouses and feeders. 888-831-2235.

**Hyde Bird Feeder Company,** 56 Felton St., P.O. Box 168, Waltham, MA 02254: Free catalog ◆ Bird feeders and wild bird food. 781-893-6780.

**Inglebrook Forges,** 2001 Gladstone, #D, Glendora, CA 91740: Free information ◆ Bird cages. 909-599-0933.

**King's Cages,** 145 Sherwood Ave., Farmingdale, NY 11735: Free information ◆ Bird cages. 516-777-7300.

**The Kinsman Company,** River Rd., Point Pleasant, PA 18950: Free catalog ◆ Thatched English birdhouses. 800-733-4146.

**Lady Slipper Designs,** RR 3, Box 556, Bemidji, MN 56601: Free information with long SASE ◆ Birdhouses. 800-950-5903.

**Laurel Arts Pottery,** 125 Lost Laurel Ln., Union Mills, NC 28167: Free brochure ◆ Handmade and painted signed stoneware birdhouses. 704-286-4862.

**Mac Industries,** 8125 South I-35, Oklahoma City, OK 73149: Brochure $1 ◆ Traditional and colonial-style Martin houses with galvanized steel telescoping and perch poles, stops, and weather vane. 800-654-4970.

**Made in Colorado,** 4840 W. 29th Ave., Denver, CO 80212: Free brochure ◆ Hummingbird feeders. 800-272-1046; 303-480-9050 (in CO). www.madeincolorado.com

**McCoy's Arts & Crafts,** 706 E. Sprague, Spokane, WA 99202: Brochure $2 ◆ Decorated or undecorated wood birdhouses. 800-456-5005.

**The Nature Products Company,** Yawgoo Pond Rd., West Kingston, RI 02892: Free information ◆ Hummingbird and butterfly feeders. 800-556-7670.

**Nature's Nest,** 1551 Barwise, Wichita, KS 67214: Free information ◆ Gazebo bird feeder. 800-268-9240.

**Orchard Crafts,** P.O. Box 1, Wallingford, VT 05773: Free information ◆ Birdhouses and feeders. 802-775-6667.

**Parrot Paradise,** 22701 Wood St., St. Clair Shores, MI 48080: Free brochure ◆ Wrought iron cages and supplies for parrots. 800-472-7768; 810-776-3595 (in MI).

**Plow & Hearth,** P.O. Box 5000, Madison, VA 22727: Free catalog ◆ Outdoor furniture, birdhouses and feeders, bird baths, and gardening tools. 800-627-1712. peggy@plowhearth.com

**Safeguard Products Inc.,** P.O. Box 8, New Holland, PA 17557: Free catalog ◆ Exotic bird and parrot breeding and flight cages. 800-433-1819.

**Somerset,** 5456 SE International Way, Portland, OR 97222: Catalog $5 (refundable) ◆ Handcrafted birdhouses. 800-225-3870.

**UPCO,** P.O. Box 969, St. Joseph, MO 64502: Free catalog ◆ Cages, birdseed, books, toys, and remedies for birds. 800-444-8651. www.upco.com

**Web Cage Inc.,** 1250 Greenleaf Ave., Elk Grove Village, IL 60007: Free information ◆ Cages for amazon, standard, and large macaws. 847-228-1403. www.webcage.com

**Wild Bird Supplies,** 4815 Oak St., Crystal Lake, IL 60012: Free catalog ◆ Feeders, birdhouses and baths, birdseed mixes, and books on bird care. 815-455-4020.

## BIRTH ANNOUNCEMENTS

**Baby Face,** P.O. Box 12410, Portland, OR 97212: Free brochure ◆ Personalized birth announcements. 800-553-1412.

**Babygram Service Center,** 201 Main St., Ste. 1955, Fort Worth, TX 76102: Free brochure ◆ Photographic birth announcements. 800-345-BABY.

**ColorFast Laser Press,** P.O. Box 75217, Oklahoma City, OK 73147: Free information ◆ Custom printed birth announcements. 888-211-2999.

**Especially For You,** 6000 Medrock Bridge Pkwy., Alpharetta, GA 30202: Free information ◆ Birth announcements and invitations for christenings, weddings, bridal showers, anniversary celebrations, special occasions, and parties for children, adolescents, and adults. 770-623-6077.

**H & F Announcements,** 9219 Quivira Rd., Overland Park, KS 66215: Free catalog ◆ Birth announcements and children's party invitations. 800-289-1560. www.hfproducts.com

**Heart Thoughts Cards,** 6200 E. Central, Ste. 100, Wichita, KS 67208: Free brochure ◆ Birth announcements and thank-you notes. 800-670-4224. www.heart-thoughts.com

**Knapp Printing,** 5635 Planet Ave., Toledo, OH 43623: Free information ◆ Custom printed birth annoucements. 800-773-4546. members.aol.com/KnappPrint

**Naptime Productions,** 525 Highland Dr., Rossford, OH 43460: Free information ◆ Baby announcements, shower invitations, Christmas cards, and baby items. 419-666-3742. members.aol.com/naptimeTwo

**NewBaby Announcements,** P.O. Box 812600, Chicago, IL 60681: Free information ◆ Baby announcements, gift certificates, and gifts. 800-500-1204; 312-251-4414 (in IL).

**New Kids,** c/o connect.ad, 11823 Raintree Dr., Panama City, FL 32404: Free information ◆ Birth annoucements.

**The Personal Touch,** 19 Forest Dr., Flemington, NJ 08822: Free information ◆ Personalized birth announcements. 800-488-8404.

**Pride & Joy Announcements,** 5415 Kendall St., Boise, ID 83706: Free catalog ◆ Birth announcements. 800-657-6404.

**Stork Ave.,** 1500 S. Dixie Hwy., Ste. 300, Coral Gables, FL 33146: Free brochure ◆ Birth annoucements and invitations for christenings and baby showers. 800-863-5747. www.storkavenue.com

## BLACKSMITHING

**Airco Welding Supplies,** 1411 E. Michigan, Jackson, MI 49203: Free information ◆ Blacksmithing supplies. 517-784-8177.

**Amsterdam Blacksmith Supply,** 185 Amsterdam Rd., New Holland, PA 17557: Free information ◆ Blacksmithing supplies. 717-354-3186.

**Armstrong Brothers Tool Company,** 5200 W. Armstrong Ave., Chicago, IL 60646: Free information ◆ Blacksmithing supplies. 312-763-3333.

**Centaur Forge Ltd.,** P.O. Box 340, Burlington, WI 53105: Catalog $5 (refundable) ◆ Blacksmithing equipment. 414-763-9175.

**Cumberland General Store,** #1 Hwy. 68, Crossville, TN 38555: Catalog $4 ◆ Blacksmithing equipment, hand pumps, windmills, wood cooking ranges, gardening tools, cast-iron wares, farm bells, buggies, harnesses, and other equipment. 800-334-4640. www.cumberlandgeneral.com

**Mankel Blacksmith Shop,** P.O. Box 29, Cannonsburg, MI 49317: Free information ◆ Forging equipment. 616-874-6955.

**NC Tool Company,** 6568 Hunt Dr., Pleasant Garden, NC 27313: Free information ◆ Equipment for blacksmiths and farriers. 800-446-6498.

## BLOCK PRINTING

**Cutbill & Company,** 274 Sherman Ave. North, Hamilton, Ontario, Canada L8L 6N6: Free catalog ◆ Block printing supplies and kits. 905-547-8525.

**Graphic Chemical & Ink Company,** P.O. Box 27, Villa Park, IL 60181: Free catalog ◆ Print-making supplies for etching, block printing, lithography, and other reproduction processes. 630-832-6004.

**Technical Papers Corp.,** P.O. Box 546, Dedham, MA 02027: Free catalog ◆ Sheets and rolls of handmade rice paper in prints and solid and multi-colors for all types of artistic printing, including block printing, etching, lithography, and silk-screening. 781-461-1111. www.technicalpapers.com

## BLOWGUNS

**Blowguns Northwest,** P.O. Box 5441, Lynnwood, WA 98046: Free price list ◆ Blowguns for hunting and target shooting, blowgun cases, darts, quivers, and targets. 888-774-0124. www.blowgunsnw.com

## BLUEPRINTING SUPPLIES

**Blueprint-Printables,** 1400-A Marsten Rd., Burlingame, CA 94010: Catalog $3 ◆ Fabrics, T-shirts, and blueprinting kits. 800-356-0445.

# BOATS & BOATING

## Boating Apparel & Safety Gear

**ACR Electronics,** 5757 Ravenswood Rd., Fort Lauderdale, FL 33312: Free information ◆ Safety and survival equipment. 954-981-3333. www.acrelectronics.com

**Atlantis,** 30 Barnet Blvd., New Bedford, MA 02745: Free catalog ◆ Foul weather gear and clothing for yachtsmen and fishermen. 508-995-7000.

**L.L. Bean,** Casco St., Freeport, ME 04032: Free catalog ◆ Safety apparel, foul weather gear, and deck shoes. 800-221-4221. www.llbean.com

**Cal-June,** 5238 Vineland Ave., North Hollywood, CA 91609: Free information ◆ Safety apparel and equipment. 818-761-3516. email@jim-buoy.com

**Clavey River Equipment,** 607 2nd St., P.O. Box 180, Petaluma, CA 94953: Free catalog ◆ Inflatable boats, oars and paddles, rowing frames, dry bags, life vests, clothing, and other river sports equipment. 800-832-4226; 707-766-8070 (in CA). www.clavey.com

**Colorado Kayak,** P.O. Box 1, Nathrop, CO 81236: Free catalog ◆ Men and women's clothing. 888-265-2925. www.coloradokayakusa.com

**Commodore Uniform & Nautical Supplies,** 335 Lower County Rd., Harwichport, MA 02646: Free information ◆ Boating uniforms, insignia, and flags. 800-438-8643; 508-430-7877 (in MA). www.capecod.com/allenharbor

**Datrex,** P.O. Box 1150, Kinder, LA 70648: Free information ◆ Safety and survival gear. 800-828-1131. www.datrex.com

**Defender Industries Inc.,** 42 Great Neck Rd., Waterford, CT 06385: Free catalog ◆ Clothing, life vests, foul weather gear, and marine supplies. 800-435-7180; 860-701-3415 (in CT). defenderus@aol.com

**Fireboy/Xintex,** P.O. Box 152, Grand Rapids, MI 49502: Free information ◆ Fire extinguishers for boats. 616-454-8337. www.fireboy-xintex.com

**Fletcher-Barnhardt & White,** 1211 S. Tyron St., Charlotte, NC 28203: Free catalog ◆ Sportswear. 800-543-5453.

**Givens Marine Survival,** 548 Main St., Tiverton, RI 02878: Free information ◆ Safety and survival gear. 800-328-8050; 401-624-7900 (in RI). www.givensliferafts.com

**Halotech Inc.,** P.O. Box 5102, Center Square, Blue Bell, PA 19422: Free information ◆ Emergency radio beacons. 610-275-8359.

**Hellamarine,** 201 Kelly Dr., Peachtree City, GA 30269: Free information ◆ Handheld searchlights, navigation and interior lamps, halogen floodlights, and other lamps. 800-247-5924; 770-631-7500(in GA).

**High Seas Foul Weather Gear,** 880 Corporate Woods Pkwy., Vernon Hills, IL 60061: Free list of retail sources ◆ Clothing for the outdoors. 847-913-1100. smartgear@hssc.com

**Johnson Sails Inc.,** P.O. Box 20926, St. Petersburg, FL 33702: Free catalog ◆ Overboard rescue system, safety harnesses, emergency position indicating beacons, and other equipment. 800-234-3220; 813-577-3220 (in FL). www.jsisail.com

**JSI Esprit,** 417 10th Ave. West, Palmetto, FL 34221: Free catalog ◆ Overboard rescue system, safety harnesses, emergency position indicating beacons, and other equipment. 941-729-5119.

**Kokatat,** 5350 Ericson Way, Arcata, CA 95521: Free information ◆ Waterproof and breathable water sportswear. 800-225-9749; 707-822-7621 (in CA).

**Life Raft & Survival Equipment,** 3 Maritime Dr., Portsmouth, RI 02871: Free information ◆ Inflatable life jackets. 800-451-2127; 401-683-0307 (in RI). www.lrse.com

**Mariner Resource,** 405 Main St., Unit 6, Port Washington, NY 11050: Free information ◆ Boating clothing and safety gear. 800-645-6516.

**Maximum Whitewater Performance,** 6211 Ridge Dr., Bethesda, MD 20816: Free catalog ◆ Boats, paddles, clothing, and safety gear. 301-229-4304. dhearnc1@aol.com

**Mustang Survival,** 3870 Mustang Way, Bellingham, WA 98226: Free information ◆ Survival flotation clothing for protection against hypothermia and overboard accidents. 800-526-0532; 360-676-1782 (in WA). mustang@mustangsurvival.com

**Northwest Outdoor Center,** 2100 Westlake Ave. North, Seattle, WA 98109: Free catalog ◆ Kayak gear, safety and rescue equipment, clothing, and books. 800-683-0637.

**O-S Systems,** The Drysuit People, 33550 SE Santosh, P.O. Box 864, Scappoose, OR 97056: Free information ◆ Men and women's clothing. 503-543-3126.

**Patagonia,** 8550 White Fir St., Reno, NV 89523: Free catalog ◆ Sportswear and foul weather clothing. 800-638-6464. www.patagonia.com

**Peconic Paddler,** 89 Peconic Ave., Riverhead, NY 11901: Free information ◆ Canoes, kayaks, rowing shells, paddles, life jackets, and dry suits. 516-727-9895.

**Port Supply/Lifesling,** 500 Westridge Dr., Watsonville, CA 95076: Free information ◆ Overboard rescue system. 800-621-6885; 408-728-4417 (in CA).

**RapidStyle,** 4124 Howard Ave., Kensington, MD 20895: Free list of retail sources ◆ Gear, clothing, and accessories for paddlers. 301-564-0459.

**Safety Flag Company of America,** P.O. Box 1088, Pawtucket, RI 02862: Free catalog ◆ Flags, vests, belts, and marine safety equipment. 401-722-0900.

**Seda Products,** 926 Coolidge Ave., National City, CA 91950: Free catalog ◆ Kayaks and canoes, life vests, and paddles. 619-336-2444.

**Smallwoods Yachtwear,** 1001 SE 17th St., Fort Lauderdale, FL 33316: Free catalog ◆ Uniforms for boating and casual sportswear. 800-771-2283. www.smallwoods.com

**SMR Technologies Inc.,** 1420 Wolf Creek Trail, P.O. Box 326, Sharon Center, OH 44274: Free list of retail sources ◆ Life rafts with emergency equipment. 330-239-1000.

**Stohlquist WaterWare,** P.O. Box 3059, Buena Vista, CO 81211: Free catalog ◆ Rescue accessories and clothing. 800-635-3565. www.stohlquistwaterware.com

**Survival Products Inc.,** 5614 SW 25th St., Hollywood, FL 33023: Free information ◆ Emergency life rafts. 954-966-7329.

**Survival Safety Engineering Inc.,** 321 Naval Base Rd., Norfolk, VA 23505: Free information ◆ Collision-avoidance radar detector. 804-480-5508. sse@norfolk.infi.net

**Survival Technologies Group,** 304-B Miller Rd., Apollo Beach, FL 33572: Free information ◆ Safety and survival gear. 800-525-2747; 813-645-5586 (in FL).

**Switlik Parachute,** 1325 E. State St., Trenton, NJ 08609: Free information ◆ Safety and survival products. 609-587-3300. www.switlik.com

**Varigas International Inc.,** P.O. Box 489, Timonium, MD 21094: Free information ◆ Radar reflector. 410-252-3026. varigas@erols.com

## Boat-Building Kits & Plans

**Benford Design Group,** P.O. Box 447, St. Michaels, MD 21663: Catalog $15.95 ◆ Traditional cruising boat designs for professional and amateur construction. 410-745-3235.

**The Boat Place,** 2906 Hunt St., Lansing, MI 48906: Free information ◆ Epoxy supplies for do-it-yourself boat builders. Also sail and power boat kits. 517-487-3642. www.theboatplace.com

**Boat Plans International,** P.O. Box 18000, Boulder, CO 80308: Catalog $24.95 ◆ Boat plans. 303-932-6874.

**Britannia Boats Ltd.,** P.O. Box 5033, Annapolis, MD 21403: Free information ◆ Boat-building plans for easy-to-understand amateur construction. 410-267-5922. www.britanniaboats.com

**Chesapeake Light Craft,** 1805 George Ave., Annapolis, MD 21401: Free brochure ◆ Kits, plans, and finished wood kayaks. 410-267-0137. www.by-the-sea.com/clc.html

**ClarkCraft Boat Company,** 16-30 Aqualane, Tonawanda, NY 14150: Catalog $5 ◆ Power and sailboat kits, plans, and hardware. 716-873-2640. www.clarkcraft.com

**Arch Davis Designs,** P.O. Box 119, Morrill, ME 04952: Information package $7 ◆ Kits for boat construction by the average home builder. Includes a choice of sailing rigs. 800-357-8091.

**Bruce Farr & Associates,** 613 3rd St., P.O. Box 4964, Annapolis, MD 21403: Free information ◆ Plans for amateur and professional sailboat construction. 410-267-0780. 71054.1441@compuserve.com

**Feather Canoes Inc.,** 3080 N. Washington Blvd., Sarasota, FL 34234: Free information ◆ Boat kits. 941-355-6736.

**J. Gengler Boat Design,** Rt. 2, Box 209, Plainfield, WI 54966: Free information ◆ Fishing skiffs. 715-335-4802.

**Glen-L Marine Designs,** 9152 Rosecrans, Box 1804, Bellflower, CA 90706: Catalog $5 ◆ Marine hardware, boat-building supplies, and kits for canoes, kayaks, dinghies, and other boats. 562-630-6258. boatkit@aol.com

**Great Lakes Boat Building Company,** 7066 103rd Ave., South Haven, MI 49090: Information $3 ◆ Boat kits. 616-637-6805.

**Ken Hankinson Associates,** P.O. Box 272, Hayden Lake, ID 83835: Catalog $6 ◆ Boat plans, patterns, kits, and supplies. 208-772-5547. www.boatdesigns.com

**Jordan Wood Boats,** P.O. Box 194, South Beach, OR 97366: Information $3 ◆ Easy-to-build boats. 541-867-3141.

**King Boat Works,** P.O. Box 234, Putney, VT 05346: Information $5 ◆ Shells for 1, 2, 4, and 6-persons. 802-387-5373.

**Laughing Loon,** Rob Macks, 833 W. Colrain Rd., Greenfield, MA 01301: Catalog $5 ◆ Custom canoes, kayaks, and building plans. 413-773-5375.

**Monfort Associates,** Division Aladdin Products, RR 2, Wiscasset, ME 04578: Catalog $5.95 ◆ Boat plans and kits. 207-882-5504.

**The Newfound Woodworks Inc.,** RFD 2, Box 850, Bristol, NH 03222: Free information ◆ Canoe kits, books, plans, supplies, and accessories. 603-744-6872. www.newfound.com

**Parker Marine Enterprises,** P.O. Box 4102, Key West, FL 33041: Catalog of cruising sailboat designs $15 ◆ Traditional and contemporary boat designs. 305-292-1570.

**David Pecci Carpentry,** 4 Patricia Dr., Topsham, ME 04086: Free information ◆ Dinghy kit. 207-729-3997.

**Bruce Roberts Design,** P.O. Box 1086, Severna Park, MD 21146: Free information ◆ Boat plans. 410-268-4611.

**Nick Schade,** 104 S. 2nd Ave., Taftville, CT 06380: Information $2 ◆ Kayak kits, plans, and finished boats. 860-887-5847.

**Stillwater Boats,** 16700 Norwood Rd., Sandy Spring, MD 20860: Free catalog ◆ Easy-to-build rounded bilge boats. 301-774-5737.

**Stimson Marine Inc.,** RR 1, Box 524, River Rd., Boothbay, ME 04537: Brochure $2 ◆ Boat lumber and building plans. 207-633-7252.

**Tri-Star Trimarans,** P.O. Box 286, Venice, CA 90291: Free information ◆ Boat plans. 310-396-6154.

**Wayland Marine,** Ron Mueller, P.O. Box 4330, Bellingham, WA 98227: Free catalog ◆ Boat kits. 360-738-8059.

**Windward Designs,** 794 Creekview Rd., Severna Park, MD 21146: Plans catalog $10 ◆ Easy-to-build skiffs, daysailers, shallow-draft sharpies, and cruisers. 800-376-3152.

**The Wooden Boat Shop,** 1007 NE Boat St., Seattle, WA 98105: Catalog $3 ◆ Easy-to-build skiff kit. 206-634-3600. www.halcyon.com/wbs

**WoodenBoat Books,** P.O. Box 78, Brooklin, ME 04616: Free information ◆ Wood racing shell kit. 800-273-SHIP. www.woodenboat.com

**Woodrow Inc., Ray Heater,** P.O. Box 19954, Portland, OR 97280: Free information ◆ Wood/epoxy river boats and easy-to-assemble kits. 503-244-3608.

## Canoes, Kayaks, & Paddles

**Aire,** P.O. Box 3412, Boise, ID 83703: Free catalog ◆ Self-bailing inflatable touring kayaks. 208-344-7506.

**Alder Creek Boat Works,** 10511 Joslin Rd., Remsen, NY 13438: Catalog $3 (refundable) ◆ Wood canoes. 315-831-5321.

**Alumacraft Boat Company,** 315 W. St. Julien St., St. Peter, MN 56082: Free information ◆ Aluminum canoes. 507-931-1050.

**American Traders Classic Canoes,** 627 Barton Rd., Greenfield, MA 01301: Free catalog ◆ Wood canoes. 800-782-7816.

**Aqua-Bound Technology Ltd.,** 9520 192nd St., Surrey, British Columbia, Canada V4N 3R9: Free information ◆ Sea cruising and touring kayak paddles. 604-882-2052.

**Baidarka Boats,** Box 6001, Sitka, AK 99835: Free catalog ◆ Folding kayaks. 907-747-8996.

**Baldwin Boat Company,** RFD 2, Box 268, Orrington, ME 04474: Free information ◆ Kayaks. 207-825-4439.

**Bear Creek Canoe,** Box 1638, Rt. 11, Limerick, ME 04048: Free information ◆ Handbuilt recreational canoes. 207-793-2005.

**Betsie Bay Kayak,** P.O. Box 1706, Frankfort, MI 49635: Free information ◆ Composite fiberglass and wood/epoxy kayaks. 616-352-7774.

**L.L. Bean,** Casco St., Freeport, ME 04032: Free catalog ◆ Boating and outdoor equipment and canoes. 800-221-4221. www.llbean.com

**Bell Canoe Works,** 25355 Hwy. 169 South, Zimmerman, MN 55398: Information $1 ◆ Kevylar, fiberglass, and graphite canoes. 612-856-2231.

**Bending Branches Paddles,** 812 Prospect Ct., Osceola, WI 54020: Free information ◆ Straight shaft, bent shaft, and kayak paddles. 715-755-3405.

**Black Bart Paddles,** 5830 US 45 South, Bruce Crossing, MI 49912: Free information ◆ Ultralight graphite paddles for racing, cruising, and whitewater. 906-927-3405.

**Blue Hole Canoes,** 18079 James Madison Hwy., Gordonsville, VA 22942: Free brochure ◆ Canoes. 540-832-7855.

**The Boundary Waters Catalog,** 105 N. Central Ave., Ely, MN 55731: Free catalog ◆ Canoeing, skiing, camping, and winter gear. 800-223-6565. www.piragis.com

**BSD,** Rt. 1, Box 131, Red Oak, VA 23964: Information $2 ◆ Sail rigs and outriggers for kayaks and canoes. 804-735-8262.

**Camp Canoe & Paddle Manufacturing,** 9 Averill, Otego, NY 13825: Free information ◆ Kayak and canoe paddles. 607-988-6842.

**Carlisle Paddles,** P.O. Box 488, Grayling, MI 49738: Free information ◆ Kayak paddles. 800-258-0290.

**Caviness Woodworking Company,** P.O. Box 710, Calhoun City, MS 38916: Free information ◆ Paddles and oars. 800-626-5195; 601-628-5195 (in MS).

**Chesapeake Light Craft,** 1805 George Ave., Annapolis, MD 21401: Free brochure ◆ Kits, plans, and finished wood kayaks. 410-267-0137. www.by-the-sea.com/clc.html

**Clavey River Equipment,** 607 2nd St., P.O. Box 180, Petaluma, CA 94953: Free catalog ◆ Inflatable boats, oars and paddles, rowing frames, dry bags, life vests, clothing, and other river sports equipment. 800-832-4226; 707-766-8070 (in CA). www.clavey.com

**William Clements, Boat Builder,** P.O. Box 87, North Billerica, MA 01862: Catalog $3 ◆ Classic cruising boats, double-paddle and decked sailing canoes, and canoe yawls. 978-663-3103.

**Collinsville Canoe & Kayak,** Rt. 179, P.O. Box 336, Collinsville, CT 06022: Free information ◆ Canoes, kayaks, and accessories. 860-693-6977. www.cckstore.com

**Cricket Paddles,** 17530 W. Hwy. 50, Salida, CO 81201: Free brochure ◆ Whitewater and canoe touring paddles. 800-243-0586. cricketd@csn.net

**Current Adventures,** 1800 Twitchell Rd., Placerville, CA 95667: Free information ◆ Surf kayaks. 916-642-9755.

**Current Designs,** 10124 McDonald Park Rd., Sidney, British Columbia, Canada V8L 3X9: Free catalog ◆ Touring kayaks. 604-655-1822.

**Dagger Canoe Company,** P.O. Box 1500, Harriman, TN 37748: Free catalog ◆ Canoes, kayaks, and sit-on-tops. 423-882-0404. www.dagger.com/dagger.html

**Duluth Pack,** 357 Canal Park Dr., Duluth, MN 55802: Free catalog ◆ Traditional canvas canoe packs and luggage. 800-849-4489. www.duluthpacks.com

**Easy Rider Canoe & Kayak Company,** P.O. Box 88108, Seattle, WA 98138: Catalog $5 ◆ Single and double-seating sea kayaks and canoes, rowing trainers, and paddles. 206-228-3633.

**Ecomarine Ocean Kayak Center,** 1668 Duranleau St., Vancouver, British Columbia, Canada V6H 3S4: Free brochure ◆ Folding kayaks and kits. 604-689-7575.

**Eddyline Kayak Works,** 1344 Ashten Rd., Burlington, WA 98223: Free catalog ◆ Kayaks and paddles. 800-788-3634.

**Englehart Products Inc.,** 10420 Kinsman Rd., P.O. Box 377, Newbury, OH 44065: Free information ◆ Sea and touring kayaks. 216-564-5565.

**Essentials for Paddlers,** P.O. Box 3059, Buena Vista, CO 81211: Free catalog ◆ Equipment for paddlers. 888-CO-KAYAK.

**Essex Industries,** Box 374, Mineville, NY 12956: Free catalog ◆ Portable and easy-to-store canoe seats and accessories. 518-942-6671.

**European Inflatable Kayaks,** 180 W. Dayton, Ste. 202, Edmonds, WA 98020: Free brochure ◆ Inflatable touring kayaks. 206-776-1171.

**Feathercraft Kayaks,** 4-1244 Cartwright St., Vancouver, British Columbia, Canada V6H 3R8: Free brochure ◆ Lightweight folding kayaks. 604-681-8437. www.feathercraft.com

**Fletcher Canoes,** Box 1321, Atikokan, Ontario, Canada P0T 1C0: Free information ◆ Custom built cedar/canvas canoes. 800-996-9935.

**Gillespie Paddles,** 1283 Harris Rd., Webster, NY 14580: Free information ◆ Kayak and canoe paddles. 716-872-1723.

**Gillies Canoes & Kayaks,** Margaretville, Nova Scotia, Canada B0S 1N0: Free information ◆ High-performance canoes and kayaks. 902-825-3725.

**Great Canadian Canoe Company,** Rt. 146, Sutton, MA 01590: Free catalog ◆ Lightweight canoes. 508-865-0010.

**Great River Outfitters,** 4180 Elizabeth Lake Rd., Waterford, MI 48328: Catalog $1 (request list of retail sources) ◆ Sea and white water kayaks. 248-683-4770.

**Grey Owl Paddle Company,** 62 Cowansview Rd., Cambridge, Ontario, Canada N1R 7N3: Free catalog ◆ Paddles. 519-622-0001.

**Headwaters,** 139 Cardiff Valley Rd., Rockwood, TN 37854: Free information ◆ Kayak and canoe equipment for flat or whitewater. 423-354-4944.

**Hydra Tuf Lite Kayaks,** 5061 S. National Dr., Knoxville, TN 37914: Catalog $5 ◆ Touring kayaks for lakes, rivers, and the open sea. 800-537-8888.

**Hyside Inflatables,** P.O. Box Z, Kernville, CA 93238: Free information ◆ Kayaks, catarafts, and rafts. 800-868-5987.

**Impex International Inc.,** 1107 Station Rd., Bellport, NY 11713: Free information ◆ Kayaks. 516-286-1988.

**Island Falls Canoe,** Jerry Stelmok, RFD 3, Box 76, Dover-Foxcroft, ME 04426: Free catalog ◆ Custom-built canoes. 207-564-7612.

**Jersey Paddler,** Rt. 88 West, Brick, NJ 08724: Free information ◆ Canoes and kayaks. 732-458-5777.

**Keel Haulers Outfitters,** 30940 Lorain Rd., North Olmsted, OH 44070: Free catalog ◆ Canoes, kayaks, safety gear, clothing and wet suits, and outdoor equipment. 216-779-4545.

**Ketter Canoeing,** 101 79th Ave. North, Minneapolis, MN 55444: Free information ◆ Canoes and paddles. 612-560-3840.

**Kiwi Kayak Company,** P.O. Box 1140, Windsor, CA 95492: Free information ◆ Two-seat kayaks and other models. 800-K-4-KAYAK.

**Klepper America,** 168 Kinderkamack Rd., Park Ridge, NJ 07656: Free list of retail sources ◆ Folding boats and kayaks. 800-323-3525.

**Lee's Value Right Inc.,** P.O. Box 19346, Minneapolis, MN 55419: Free information ◆ Touring kayak paddles. 800-758-1720.

**Mad River Canoe Inc.,** P.O. Box 610, Waitsfield, VT 05673: Free catalog ◆ Canoes for navigating rivers, rapids, and pleasure boating. 800-843-8985. madriver@madriver.com

**Mariner Kayaks,** 2134 Westlake North, Seattle, WA 98109: Free information ◆ Kayaks. 206-284-8404.

**Kevin Martin Boatbuilder,** Box 441, RFD 1, Epping, NH 03042: Free information ◆ Solo and sailing canoes, runabouts, lobster boats, daysailers, and other small boats. 603-679-5153.

**Maximum Whitewater Performance,** 6211 Ridge Dr., Bethesda, MD 20816: Free catalog ◆ Racing and other boats, paddles, clothing, and safety gear. 301-229-4304. dhearnc1@aol.com

**Mermaid Stabilizers,** P.O. Box 1072, North Battleford, Sask, Canada S9A 3E6: Free information ◆ Canoe and windsurfing stabilizers and sails. 800-215-5307. www.w2d.com/mermaid

**Merrimack Canoe Company,** 202 Harper Ave., Crossville, TN 38555: Free information ◆ Fiberglass canoes. 615-484-4556.

**Mid-Canada Fiberglass Ltd.,** Box 1599, New Liskeard, Ontario, Canada P0J 1P0: Free list of retail sources ◆ Fiberglass, Kevlar, and Royalex canoes. 705-647-6549.

**Middle Path Boats,** Box 8881, Pittsburgh, PA 15221: Brochure $2 ◆ Wood/epoxy composite-constructed solo and tandem canoes and rowing cruisers. 412-247-4860.

**Mitchell Paddles Inc.,** RD 2, P.O. Box 922, Canaan, NH 03741: Free information ◆ Canoe and kayak paddles and dry suits. 603-523-7004.

**Mohawk Canoes,** 963 North Hwy. 427, Longwood, FL 32750: Free information ◆ Solo and tandem canoes. Also paddles. 800-686-6429.

**Mountain Surf,** P.O. Box 70, Friendsville, MD 21531: Free catalog ◆ Equipment and accessories. 301-746-5389.

**Navarro Canoe Company,** 225 Rogue River Pkwy., Talent, OR 97540: Free information ◆ Lightweight canoes. 541-512-9447.

**Necky Kayaks Ltd.,** 1100 Riverside Rd., Abbotsford, British Columbia, Canada V25 7P1: Free information ◆ Touring kayaks. 604-850-1206.

**New Wave Kayak Products,** 2535 Roundtop Rd., Middletown, PA 17057: Free catalog ◆ Cruising and racing kayaks, paddles, and helmets. 717-944-6320. newkayak@aol.com

**New York Kayak Company,** P.O. Box 2011, New York, NY 10011: Free information ◆ Folding kayaks. 800-KAYAK-99. NYKayak@spacelab.net

**The Newfound Woodworks Inc.,** RFD 2, Box 850, Bristol, NH 03222: Free information ◆ Canoe kits, books, plans, supplies, and accessories. 603-744-6872. www.newfound.com

**Nimbus Paddles,** 4915 Chilsolm St., Delta, British Columbia, Canada V4K 2K6: Free information ◆ Touring, whitewater kayak, and recreational canoe paddles. 604-940-1957.

**North Shore Inc.,** 4 Fourth St., Hood River, OR 97031: Free catalog ◆ Canoe and kayak paddles, other equipment, and transporting systems. 541-386-1980.

**Northwest Kayaks,** 15145 NE 90th, Redmond, WA 98052: Free information ◆ Handcrafted kayaks. 800-648-8908; 425-869-1107 (in WA). www.nwkayaks.com

**Northwest Outdoor Center,** 2100 Westlake Ave. North, Seattle, WA 98109: Free catalog ◆ Kayak equipment, safety and rescue equipment, clothing, and books. 800-683-0637.

**Northwoods Canoe Company,** 336 Range Rd., Atkinson, ME 04426: Catalog $1 ◆ Canoes.

**Nova Craft Canoe,** 183 Exeter Rd., London, Ontario, Canada N6L 1A4: Free catalog ◆ Whitewater kayaks. 519-652-3649.

**NW Outdoor Center on Lake Union,** 2100 Westlake North, Seattle, WA 98109: Free catalog ◆ Kayaking supplies. 800-683-0637.

**Oak Orchard Canoe,** 2133 Eagle Harbor Rd., Waterport, NY 14571: Catalog $2 (specify canoes, kayaks, or accessories) ◆ Canoes, kayaks, and accessories. 716-586-5990.

**Ocean Kayak Inc.,** 1920 Main St., Ferndale, WA 98248: Free list of retail sources ◆ Ocean kayaks and clothing. 800-8-KAYAKS.

**Old Town Canoe Company,** 58 Middle St., Old Town, ME 04468: Free catalog ◆ Canoes. 800-595-4400.

**Osagian Canoes Inc.,** 27067 Hwy. 5, Lebanon, MO 65536: Free brochure ◆ Aluminum and plastic canoes, trailers and haulers, and accessories. 877-637-3000. www.osagian-canoes.com

**Pacific Water Sports,** 16055 Pacific Hwy. South, Seattle, WA 98188: Brochure $2 ◆ Kayaks and paddles. 206-246-9385. www.pwskayaks.com

**Pakboats,** P.O. Box 700, Enfield, NH 03748: Free information ◆ Folding canoes. 603-632-7654.

**Peconic Paddler,** 89 Peconic Ave., Riverhead, NY 11901: Free information ◆ Canoes, kayaks, rowing shells, sea kayaks, paddles, life jackets, and dry suits. 516-727-9895.

**Perception,** 111 Kayaker Way, Easley, SC 29642: Free information ◆ Kayaks for river running. 800-262-0268. www.kayaker.com

**Piragis Northwoods Company,** 105 N. Central Ave., Ely, MN 55731: Catalog $2 ◆ Canoes, boating gear, boats, videos and tapes, and trail foods. 800-223-6565. www.piragis.com

**Primex of California,** P.O. Box 505, Benicia, CA 94510: Catalog $5 ◆ Kayak and canoe carrier, helmets, gloves, face-savers, sailing rigs, and repair supplies. 800-422-2482. primex@castles.com

**Pygmy Boat Company,** P.O. Box 1529, Port Townsend, WA 98368: Catalog $3 ◆ Kayak and rowing skiff kits. 360-385-6143.

**Rapidstyle,** 4124 Howard Ave., Kensington, MD 20895: Free list of retail sources ◆ Gear for paddlers. 301-564-0459.

**RGP Composites,** 3223 C St., Ste. 9, Auburn, WA 98002: Free information ◆ Whitewater, slalom, touring, canoe, racing, and recreation paddles. 253-939-4420.

**Rutabaga,** 220 W. Broadway, Madison, WI 53716: Free information ◆ Canoes and kayaks. 800-I-PADDLE.

**Savage River Works,** 1832 Dry Run Rd., Swanten, MD 21561: Free information ◆ Touring, cruising, sport, and racing canoes. 301-245-4327.

**Sawbill Canoe Outfitters,** Box 2127, Tofte, MN 55615: Free information ◆ Canoe outfitters. 218-387-1360. www.sawbill.com

**Sawyer Composite Products,** P.O. Box 459, Oscoda, MI 48750: Free information ◆ Handcrafted composite canoes. 517-739-9181.

**Sawyer Paddles & Oars,** 299 Rogue River Pkwy., Talent, OR 97540: Free information ◆ Wood paddles and oars with solid fiberglass tips. 503-535-3606.

**Seairsports,** 20443 Main St., San Diego, CA 92113: Free information ◆ Fullback, three-quarterback, halfback, and quarterback seats for sit-on-top kayaks or canoes and accessories. 619-230-1167.

**Seavivor,** 576 Arlington Ave., Des Plaines, IL 60016: Catalog $3 ◆ Folding kayaks. 847-297-5953. www.seavivor.com

**Seda Products,** 926 Coolidge Ave., National City, CA 91950: Free catalog ◆ Kayaks and canoes, life vests, and paddles. 619-336-2444.

**Sevylor USA,** 6651 E. 26th St., Los Angeles, CA 90040: Free information ◆ Inflatable boats, canoes, kayaks, dinghies, paddles, and oars. 213-727-6013.

**Shaw & Tenney,** P.O. Box 213, Orono, ME 04473: Free catalog ◆ Oars and paddles. 207-866-4867.

**Shearwater Boats,** 22 Soundview Dr., Stamford, CT 06902: Free catalog ◆ Wood-epoxy canoes, sea kayaks, and paddles. 203-359-6431.

**Sierra South Mountain Sports,** Box Y, Kernville, CA 93238: Free catalog ◆ Whitewater and recreational kayaks and paddle sports equipment. 800-376-7303.

**SOAR Inflatables,** 20 Healdsburg Ave., Healdsburg, CA 95448: Free information ◆ Solo and tandem inflatable canoes. 707-433-5599. www.soar1.com

**Southern Exposure Sea Kayaks,** P.O. Box 4530, Tequesta, FL 33469: Free information ◆ Sea kayaks. 561-575-4530.

**Splashdance,** Hwy. 85 South, Niceville, FL 32578: Free information ◆ Fiberglass sea kayaks. 904-678-1637.

**Suncoast Sea Kayaks,** 10900 Oakhurst Rd., Largo, FL 33774: Free catalog ◆ Regular and folding kayaks, paddles, and accessories. 813-595-3220.

**Swift Canoe & Kayak,** RR 1, Oxtongue Ln., Dwight, Ontario, Canada P0A 1H0: Free catalog ◆ Fiberglass, Kevlar, and Royalex canoes and kayaks. 705-635-1167. www.swiftcanoe.com

**Tubbs Snowshoe Company (Canoes),** 52 River Rd., Box 207, Stowe, VT 05672: Free information ◆ Lightweight fiberglass canoes. 802-253-7398.

**Under Cover,** P.O. Box 609, Hyannis, MA 02601: Free brochure ◆ Canoe and kayak travel and storage covers. 800-275-2580.

**Valhalla Surf Ski Products,** 4724 Renex Pl., San Diego, CA 92117: Free information ◆ Easy handling kayaks. 619-569-1395.

**Wave Sports Inc.,** P.O. Box 5207, Steamboat Springs, CO 80477: Free list of retail sources ◆ White water kayaks. 970-736-0080.

**We-No-Nah Canoes,** Box 247, Winona, MN 55987: Free catalog ◆ Canoes for whitewater and flatwater boating and racing. 507-454-5430. wenonah@luminet.net

**Werner Paddles,** P.O. Box 1139, Sultan, WA 98294: Free information ◆ Paddles for canoes and kayaks. 800-275-3311.

**Western Canoeing Inc.,** Box 115, Abbotsford, British Columbia, Canada V2S 4N8: Information $1 ◆ Kayaking and canoeing equipment. 604-853-9320.

**Western Folding Kayak Center,** 6155 Mt. Aukum Rd., Somerset, CA 95684: Free information ◆ Folding kayaks. 916-626-8647.

**Wilderness Systems,** 1110 Surrett Dr., High Point, NC 27260: Free list of retail sources ◆ Kayaks, accessories, and sail rigs for kayaks. 336-883-7410. www.wildsys.com

**Wildwasser Sport USA Inc.,** P.O. Box 4617, Boulder, CO 80306: Free information ◆ Racing, touring, and whitewater kayaks and accessories. 303-444-2336.

**ZuZu Paddle Company,** P.O. Box 957, Flagstaff, AZ 86002: Free information ◆ Wood kayak paddles. 520-774-6535. www.zuzupaddles.com

## Catamarans

**Murrays Catamarans,** P.O. Box 490, Carpinteria, CA 93014: Free list of retail sources ◆ Catamarans, factory parts, books, and videos. 800-788-8964. www.murrays.com

## Hovercraft

**Neoteric Hovercraft Inc.,** 1649 Tippecanoe St., Terre Haute, IN 47807: Catalog $11 ◆ 4-passenger light hovercraft for pleasure and rescue. Also kits. 812-234-1120. hovercraft@delphi.com

**Oregon Hovercraft,** 27612 Crow Rd., Eugene, OR 97402: Free information ◆ Quick build kits for cruising or high performance craft. Will also custom build and features hard-to-find or unique components. 541-345-6083. www.continet.com/hovercraft

**Universal Hovercraft,** Box 281, 1204 3rd St., Cordova, IL 61242: Catalog $2 ◆ Plans, parts. and kits for easy-to-build hovercraft. 309-654-2588. www.bews.com/hover

## Inflatable Boats

**Aire,** P.O. Box 3412, Boise, ID 83703: Free catalog ◆ Self-bailing inflatable touring kayaks. 208-344-7506.

**Altco Trading International,** 6 Macaulay St. East, Hamilton, Ontario, Canada L8L 8B1: Free information ◆ Soft and rigid bottom inflatable dinghies. 905-521-1061.

**APEX Inflatable,** 919-A Bay Ridge Rd., Annapolis, MD 21403: Free catalog ◆ Inflatable boats. 800-422-5977; 410-267-0850 (in MD).

**Avon Marine,** 11215 Young River Ave., Fountain Valley, CA 92708: Free catalog ◆ Inflatable boats. 800-854-7595; 714-444-9244 (in CA). www.avonmarine.com

**Berry Scuba Company,** 6674 Northwest Hwy., Chicago, IL 60631: Free catalog ◆ Inflatable boats, watches, clothing, skin diving and scuba equipment, diving lights, and underwater cameras. 800-621-6019; 312-763-1626 (in IL).

**Bombard,** Thompson Creek Rd., P.O. Box 400, Stevensville, MD 21666: Free information • Inflatable boats. 410-643-4141.

**Caribe Inflatables USA,** 14372 SW 139th Ct., #7, Miami, FL 33186: Free list of retail sources • Inflatable boats. 305-253-4822. www.wwtelco.com/~caribe

**Clavey River Equipment,** 607 2nd St., P.O. Box 180, Petaluma, CA 94953: Free catalog • Inflatable boats, oars and paddles, rowing frames, dry bags, life vests, clothing, and other river sports equipment. 800-832-4226; 707-766-8070 (in CA). www.clavey.com

**Coleman Outdoor Products Inc.,** P.O. Box 2931, Wichita, KS 67201: Free catalog • Inflatable boats, canoes, and dinghies. 800-835-3278. www.coleman.com

**Custom Inflatable Boats Inc.,** P.O. Box 80, Rt. 1, Albrightr, WV 26519: Free information • Inflatable watercraft. 800-673-3537.

**Down River Equipment Company,** 12100 W. 52nd Ave., Wheatridge, CO 80033: Free catalog • Whitewater inflatables and accessories. 303-467-9489.

**European Inflatable Kayaks,** 180 W. Dayton, Ste. 202, Edmonds, WA 98020: Free brochure • Inflatable touring kayaks. 206-776-1171.

**Grabner Inflatables,** 9702 Gayton Rd., Ste. 153, Richmond, VA 23233: Free catalog • Easy-to-transport inflatables. 800-360-2365.

**Innova Kayaks,** 180 W. Dayton, Ste. 202, Edmonds, WA 98020: Free information • Inflatable touring and whitwater kayaks. 425-776-1171. www.innovakayak.com

**Jumbo Inflatables,** Division Sevylor USA, 1931 SW 14th St., Portland, OR 97201: Free information • Inflatable boats for river and sea kayaking. 503-274-2313. jumbo@teleport.com

**Kirby Kraft,** Box 582, Seachelt, British Columbia, Canada V0N 3A0: Free information • Folding fiberglass rigid bottom inflatable. 614-885-2695.

**Nautica International,** 6135 NW 167th St., Miami, FL 33015: Free information • Rigid inflatable boats. 305-556-5554. www.nauticaintl.com

**Northwest River Supplies Inc.,** 2009 S. Maine, Moscow, ID 83843: Free catalog • Inflatable boats. 800-635-5202. nrs@moscow.com

**Novurania Inflatable Boats,** 4775 NW 132nd St., Miami, FL 33054: Free information • Inflatable boats. 305-685-2464.

**Quicksilver Inflatables,** Mercury Marine, c/o Maritz, 1365 N. Highway Dr., Fenton, MO 63099: Free catalog • Easy-to-tow and stow inflatable boats. 800-552-3882. www.mercurymarine.com

**Sea Eagle,** 200 Wilson St., Port Jefferson Station, NY 11776: Free brochure • Inflatable boats that can be used as fishing platforms, motor runabouts, or yacht tenders. 800-852-0925. www.seaeagle.com

**Sevylor USA,** 6651 E. 26th St., Los Angeles, CA 90040: Free information • Inflatable boats, canoes, kayaks, dinghies, paddles, and oars. 213-727-6013.

**SOAR Inflatable,** 3152 Cherokee St., St. Louis, MO 63118: Free information • Solo and tandem inflatable canoes. 314-776-6994.

**Star Inflatable Boats,** 232 Banks Rd., Travelers Rest, SC 29690: Free information • Inflatable river boats. 864-836-2800.

**West Marine Products,** P.O. Box 50070, Watsonville, CA 95077: Free catalog • Inflatable boats, electronics, fishing equipment, navigation software, and other boating supplies. 800-538-0775. www.westmarine.com

**Wing Inflatable Boats,** P.O. Box 279, Arcata, CA 95518: Free information • Rafts, kayaks, and catarafts. 707-826-2887. www.wing.com

**Zodiac of North America,** Thompson Creek Rd., Box 400, Stevensville, MD 21666: Free information • Inflatable boats. 410-643-4141. www.zodiac.com

## Life Rafts

**Dunlop-Beaufort,** 12351 Bridgeport Rd., Richmond, BD, Canada V6V 1J4: Free list of retail sources • Life rafts. 604-278-3221. www.dbcmarine.com

**Givens Marine Survival,** 548 Main St., Tiverton, RI 02878: Free information • Life rafts. 800-328-8050; 401-624-7900 (in RI). www.givensliferafts.com

## Miscellaneous Boats & Surfing Skis

**The Anchorage,** 65 Miller St., Warren, RI 02885: Free information • Rigid dinghies. 401-245-3300.

**BayCraft Inc.,** 1911 Navco Rd., Mobile, AL 36605: Free information • Wood boats.

**Boats & Gear,** 51 E. Lowe, Fairfield, IA 52556: Catalog $1 • Features the folding Porta-Bote, dollies, seats, outboard motors, canopies, and accessories. 515-472-7758.

**Brooklin Boat Yard,** P.O. Box 143, Brooklin, ME 04616: Free information • Custom boats. 207-359-2236.

**Castlecraft,** P.O. Box 3, Braidwood, IL 60408: Free information • Canoes, sailboats, and accessories. 815-458-3590.

**William Clements, Boat Builder,** P.O. Box 87, North Billerica, MA 01862: Catalog $3 • Classic cruising boats, double-paddle and decked sailing canoes, and canoe yawls. 978-663-3103.

**Covey Island Boatworks,** Petite Riviere, Lunenburg County, Nova Scotia, Canada B0J 2P0: Free information • Wood and epoxy power and sailing yachts. 902-688-2843. covey@fox.nstn.ca

**Fletcher Boats Inc.,** 292 Wellman Rd., Port Angeles, WA 98363: Free information • Inboard and outboard mahogany runabouts. 360-452-8430.

**Folbot Inc.,** P.O. Box 70877, Charleston, SC 29415: Free catalog • Boat kits and sail, power, paddle wheel, and folding boats. 800-528-9592. www.folbot.com

**Freedom Boatworks,** P.O. Box 511, Baraboo, WI 53913: Free information • Mahogany runabouts. 608-356-5861.

**Futura Surf Skis,** 730 W. 19th St., National City, CA 92050: Free brochure • Surfing skis. 619-474-8382.

**Grand-Craft,** 430 W. 21st St., Holland, MI 49423: Free information • Mahogany runabouts. 616-396-5450.

**Hill's Boat Yard,** Little Cranberry Island, Islesford, ME 04646: Free information • Skiffs and tenders for oars and sails. 207-244-7150.

**Hyde Drift Boats,** 1520 Pancheri Dr., Idaho Falls, ID 83402: Free brochure • Drift boats for fishermen. 800-444-4933.

**Intraser Inc.,** 428 N. La Cienega Blvd., Los Angeles, CA 90048: Free information • New and pre-owned motorcycles, ATVs, snowmobiles, trailers, personal water vehicles, and small boats. 213-652-6966.

**JW Outfitters,** 169 Balboa, San Marcos, CA 92069: Free information • Pontoon boats with optional operating systems. 760-471-2171.

**Little Boat Shop,** P.O. Box 1406, Mattapoisett, MA 02739: Free information • Custom built small rowing and sailing crafts. 508-758-3988.

**Lowell's Boat Shop,** 459 Main St., Amesbury, MA 01913: Brochure $2 • Wood boats. 978-388-0162.

**Marine Railway Inc.,** Gannon & Benjamin, P.O. Box 1095, Beach Rd., Vineyard Haven, MA 02568: Free information • Traditionally-built custom boats. 508-693-4658.

**Marshall Marine Corp.,** Box P-266, South Dartmouth, MA 02748: Free information • Catboats. 508-994-0414.

**Kevin Martin Boatbuilder,** Box 441, RFD 1, Epping, NH 03042: Free information • Solo and sailing canoes, runabouts, lobster boats, daysailers, and other small boats. 603-679-5153.

**Maximum Whitewater Performance,** 6211 Ridge Dr., Bethesda, MD 20816: Free catalog • Racing and other boats, paddles, clothing, and safety gear. 301-229-4304. dhearnc1@aol.com

**Middle Path Boats,** Box 8881, Pittsburgh, PA 15221: Brochure $2 • Wood/epoxy composite-constructed solo and tandem canoes and rowing cruisers. 412-247-4860.

**Nexus Marine Corp.,** 333 Falkenburg Rd., Bldg. B-221, Tampa, FL 33619: Brochure $3 • Custom power and sailboats. 813-654-1799. www.nexmar@ix.netcom.com

**Norton Boat Works,** 535 Commercial, Green Lake, WI 54941: Free information ◆ Ready-to-use ice boats, parts, kits, and plans. 920-294-6813.

**David Nutt Boatbuilder Inc.,** Box 320, Rt. 27, West Southport, ME 04576: Free information ◆ Custom built boats. 207-633-6009.

**Ostercraft Inc.,** 10727 SE Knapp Circle, Portland, OR 97266: Free information ◆ All-mahogany runabouts. 503-761-6693.

**Pakboats,** P.O. Box 700, Enfield, NH 03748: Free information ◆ General boating and whitewater boats that fold and can be carried in one bag. 603-632-7654.

**Hans Pedersen & Sons,** 165 W. Front St., Keyport, NJ 07735: Free information ◆ Custom wood boats up to 45 feet. 908-264-0971.

**Porta-Bote International,** 1074 Independence Ave., Mountain View, CA 94043: Free information ◆ Folding boats. 800-227-8882; 650-961-5334 (in CA). www.porta-bote.com

**Richard S. Pulsifer,** Boatbuilder, 642 Mere Point Rd., Brunswick, ME 04011: Brochure $5 ◆ Handcrafted diesel-powered small boats. 207-725-5457.

**Spring Creek Watercraft,** 13764 NW Klahanie Pl., Bremerton, WA 98312: Free catalog ◆ Lightweight fiberglass constructed fishing boat. 800-840-7726.

**Stauter Boat Works,** 4549 Clearview Dr., Mobile, AL 36619: Free information ◆ Wood boats. 334-666-1152.

**Greg Tatman Wooden Boats,** 1075 Clearwater Ln., Springfield, OR 97478: Free catalog ◆ Easy-to-assemble drift boats. 541-746-5287.

**Van Dam Wood Craft,** 970 E. Division St., Boyne City, MI 49712: Free information ◆ Custom wood boats. 616-582-2323.

**Water Otter,** 112 Freeze Ln., Hamilton, MT 59840: Free information ◆ One-person fishing boat. 406-363-2398.

**Chris White Designs Inc.,** 5 Smith's Way, South Dartmouth, MA 02748: Design portfolio $10 ◆ Cruising catamarans. 508-636-6111.

## Rowing Boats & Shells

**Alden Ocean Shells Inc.,** P.O. Box 368, Eliot, ME 03903: Free catalog ◆ Rowing boats, ocean shells, sliding seat rowing skiff kit, accessories, and more. 800-477-1507. www.rowonline.com/alden

**Durham Boat Company,** 220 Newmarket Rd., Durham, NH 03824: Free information ◆ Rowing equipment and hardware, wood and composite shells, oars, clothes, books, and videos. 603-659-7575.

**Johannsen Boat Works,** P.O. Box 7048, Vero Beach, FL 32961: Free information ◆ Rowing and sailing dinghies. 800-869-0773. www.trinka.com

**Little River Marine,** P.O. Box 986, Gainesville, FL 32602: Free information ◆ Rowing shells. 800-247-4591; 352-378-5025 (in FL). www.gnv.fdt.net/~it/rivr

**MAAS Rowing Shells,** 1319 Canal Blvd., Richmond, CA 94804: Free brochure ◆ Open water rowing shells. 510-232-1612.

**Pygmy Boat Company,** P.O. Box 1529, Port Townsend, WA 98368: Catalog $3 ◆ Kayak and rowing skiff kits. 360-385-6143.

## Sailboats & Supplies

**Bacon & Associates,** P.O. Box 3150, Annapolis, MD 21403: Free information ◆ Sailboat hardware and equipment. 410-263-4880. www.bacon-sails.com

**Bainbridge International,** 255 Revere St., Canton, MA 02021: Free information ◆ Sail cloth. 800-422-5684; 781-821-2600 (in MA). www.sailcloth.com

**Benjamin River Marine Inc.,** Rt. 175, Brooklin, ME 04616: Free information ◆ Handcrafted classic sailing boats. 207-359-2244.

**Bohndell Sails,** Commercial St., Rockport, ME 04856: Free information ◆ Sails, rigging, life lines, and canvas. 207-236-3549.

**Cruising Direct Sails,** 200 Highpoint Ave., Portsmouth, RI 02871: Free information ◆ Easy-to-measure sails sold direct from factory. 401-683-2160. www.cd.northsails.com

**Dwyer Aluminum Mast Company Inc.,** 2 Commerce Dr., North Branford, CT 06471: Free information ◆ Sailboat masts, booms, rigging, and hardware. 203-484-0419. www.csiworld.com/dwyer

**E & B Discount Marine,** 201 Meadow Rd., Edison, NJ 08818: Free catalog ◆ Power and sailboat equipment. 800-533-5007. www.ebmarine.com

**Forespar Products,** 22322 Gilberto, Rancho Santa Margarita, CA 92688: Free catalog ◆ Rigging and hardware. 714-858-8820. www.forespar.com

**Gambell & Hunter Sailmakers,** 16 Limerock St., Camden, ME 04843: Free information ◆ Sails and rigging. 207-236-3561.

**Goldbergs' Marine,** 201 Meadow Rd., Edison, NJ 08818: Free catalog ◆ Power and sailboat equipment. 800-BOA-TING.

**Hacker Boat Company,** Rt. 9 North, Silver Bay, NY 12874: Free information ◆ Custom-built boats with seating and size options. 518-543-6731.

**Hild Sails,** 225 Fordham St., P.O. Box 207, City Island, NY 10464: Free catalog ◆ Sails. 212-885-2255.

**Hill's Boat Yard,** Little Cranberry Island, Islesford, ME 04646: Free information ◆ Skiffs and tenders for oars and sails. 207-244-7150.

**Hood Sailmakers,** 58 Fore St., Portland, ME 04102: Free information ◆ Sailcloth, sail-making supplies, sail kits, and bosun chairs. 207-828-0003.

**Johannsen Boat Works,** P.O. Box 7048, Vero Beach, FL 32961: Free information ◆ Rowing and sailing dinghies. 800-869-0773. www.trinka.com

**JSI Esprit,** 417 10th Ave. West, Palmetto, FL 34221: Free catalog ◆ Sails, equipment, spars, rigging, canvas, and cushions. 941-729-5119.

**JSI-The Sailing Source,** P.O. Box 20926, St. Petersburg, FL 33702: Free catalog ◆ Sails, spars, rigging, canvas, cushions, and other equipment. 800-234-3220. www.jsisail.com

**Ludlow Boat Works,** RR 4, Pecketts Landing, Kempville, Ontario, Canada K0G 1J0: Free information ◆ Ready-to-sail boats. 613-258-4270.

**M & E Marine Supply Company,** P.O. Box 601, Camden, NJ 08101: Catalog $2 ◆ Power and sailboat equipment. 800-541-6501. www.memarine.com

**Kevin Martin Boatbuilder,** Box 441, RFD 1, Epping, NH 03042: Free information ◆ Solo and sailing canoes, runabouts, lobster boats, daysailers, and other small boats. 603-679-5153.

**Nexus Marine Corp.,** 333 Falkenburg Rd., Bldg. B-221, Tampa, FL 33619: Brochure $3 ◆ Custom power and sailboats. 813-654-1799. www.nexmar@ix.netcom.com

**Pease Boatworks,** 43 Eliphanets Ln., Chatham, MA 02633: Free information ◆ Handcrafted classic sailboats. 508-432-8112.

**The Rigging Company,** 1 Maritime Dr., Portsmouth, RI 02871: Catalog $2 ◆ Sailboat rigging and tools. 800-322-1525; 401-683-1525 (in RI).

**Sailrite,** 305 W. Van Buren, P.O. Box 987, Columbia City, IN 46725: Free catalog ◆ Sail-making supplies. 800-348-2769; 219-244-6715 (in IN). www.sailrite.com

**Sailsource,** P.O. Box 655, Nyack, NY 10960: Free information ◆ Used sails. 800-268-9510; 914-268-9758 (in NY). sailbroker@aol.com

**Skipper Marine Electronics Inc.,** 1511 Reidel Dr., Mundelein, IL 60060: Free catalog ◆ Sailboat instruments. 800-SKIPPER; 847-566-1800 (in IL).

**Tackle Shack,** 7801 66th St. North, Pinellas, Park, FL 33781: Free catalog ◆ New and used small sailboats and accessories. 800-537-6099. www.FunOnWater.com

**West Marine Products,** P.O. Box 50070, Watsonville, CA 95077: Free catalog ◆ Power and sailboat equipment. 800-538-0775. www.westmarine.com

**Whitehall Reproductions,** Box 1141, Commercial Station, Victoria, British Columbia, Canada V8W 2T6: Free brochure ◆ Handcrafted classic rowing and sailboats. 800-663-7481. www.whitehallrow.com

**Nathaniel S. Wilson, Sailmaker,** Lincoln St., P.O. Box 71, East Boothbay, ME 04544: Free information ◆ Hand-finished sails. 207-633-5071.

## General Supplies & Equipment

**A & B Industries Inc.,** 1160-A Industrial Ave., Petaluma, CA 94952: Free list of retail sources ◆ Marine hardware for power and sailboats. 707-765-6200.

**Aamstrand Corp.,** 629 Grove, Manteno, IL 60950: Free information ◆ Anchor, winch, and general rigging ropes. 800-338-0557; 815-468-2100 (in IL). www.aamstrand.com

**ABI Inc.,** 1160 Industrial Ave., Petaluma, CA 94952: Free catalog ◆ Marine hardware for power and sail boats. 707-765-6200. abi3@ix.netcom.com

**Atwood Mobile Products,** 4750 Hiawatha Dr., Rockford, IL 61103: Free information ◆ Appliances and engineered components and systems for recreational vehicles and boats. 815-877-5700.

**Avon Marine,** 11215 Young River Ave., Fountain Valley, CA 92708: Free catalog ◆ Anchors, barometers, bilge pumps, ropes, and other equipment. 800-854-7595; 714-444-9244 (in CA). www.avonmarine.com

**Barkley Sound Marine,** 3073 Vanhorne Rd., Qualicum Beach, British Columbia, Canada V9K 1X3: Free information ◆ Custom-made and in-stock solid or laminated straight and spoon blade spruce oars. 250-752-5115.

**Basic Designs,** P.O. Box 1498, St. Cloud, MN 56303: Free information ◆ Plastic collapsible boarding ladders. 800-328-3208.

**Beckson Marine,** 165 Holland Ave., Bridgeport, CT 06605: Catalog $3.25 ◆ Marine equipment and accessories. 203-333-1412. www.beckson.com

**Berkeley Inc.,** 1900 18th St., Spirit Lake, IA 51360: Free catalog ◆ Bilge pumps, compasses, boating cables, and rigging, anchor, winch, and other ropes. 800-237-5539; 712-336-1520 (in IA).

**Boat/U.S.,** 880 S. Pickett St., Alexandria, VA 22304: Free catalog ◆ Boating equipment. 800-937-2628.

**Boulter Plywood Corp.,** 24 Broadway, Somerville, MA 02145: Free catalog ◆ Plywood and hardwood lumber for building boats. 617-666-1340.

**Canor Plarex,** P.O. Box 33765, Seattle, WA 98133: Free information ◆ Folding anchors. 206-365-3006.

**Classic Canoes,** 627 Baron Rd., Greenfield, MA 01301: Free information ◆ Easy-to-use folding boat walker. 800-782-7816; 413-773-9631 (in MA).

**Clavey River Equipment,** 607 2nd St., P.O. Box 180, Petaluma, CA 94953: Free catalog ◆ Inflatable boats, oars and paddles, rowing frames, dry bags, life vests, clothing, and other river sports equipment. 800-832-4226; 707-766-8070 (in CA). www.clavey.com

**William Clements, Boat Builder,** P.O. Box 87, North Billerica, MA 01862: Catalog $3 ◆ Wood boat and canoe restoration supplies. 508-663-3103.

**Maurice L. Condon Company,** 252 Ferris Ave., White Plains, NY 10603: Catalog $2 ◆ Boat-building lumber. 914-946-4111.

**Creative Marine Products,** P.O. Box 2120, 243 John R. Junkin Dr., Natchez, MS 39121: Free catalog ◆ Marine products and accessories. 800-824-0355. www.creativemarine.com

**Crook & Crook,** 2795 SW 27th Ave., P.O. Box 109, Miami, FL 33133: Free catalog ◆ Boating gear. 305-854-0005.

**Cruising Equipment,** 5245 Shilshole Ave., Seattle, WA 98107: Free information ◆ Battery monitors. 206-782-8100. www.cruisingequip.com

**Davis Anchors,** 18519 E. Valley Hwy., Kent, WA 98032: Free information ◆ Galvanized carbon-manganese or stainless steel anchors. 800-328-4770; 425-251-4922 (in WA). talonind@wolfenet.com

**Defender Industries Inc.,** 42 Great Neck Rd., Waterford, CT 06385: Free catalog ◆ Clothing, life vests, foul weather gear, and marine supplies. 800-435-7180; 860-701-3415 (in CT). defenderus@aol.com

**Durham Boat Company,** 220 Newmarket Rd., Durham, NH 03824: Free information ◆ Rowing equipment, marine hardware, wood and composite shells, oars, clothes, books, and videos. 603-659-7575.

**E & B Discount Marine,** 201 Meadow Rd., Edison, NJ 08818: Free catalog ◆ Power and sailboat equipment. 800-533-5007. www.ebmarine.com

**Edensaw Woods Ltd.,** 211 Seton Rd., Port Townsend, WA 98368: Free information ◆ Boat lumber and marine plywood. 800-745-3336; 360-385-7878 (in WA). www.olympus.net/biz/edensaw/index.htm

**Edson International,** 146 Duchaine Blvd., New Bedford, MA 02745: Free catalog ◆ Power and sail steering systems and accessories, boat davits, radar towers, pumps, and other equipment. 508-995-9711. www.edsonintl.com

**Electra Marine,** 610 Merrick Rd., Lynnbrook, NY 11563: Catalog $2 ◆ Marine equipment. 516-599-5375.

**Essex Industries,** Box 374, Mineville, NY 12956: Free catalog ◆ Portable and easy-to-store canoe seats and accessories. 518-942-6671.

**Euromar,** 22 Tame Buck Rd., Wolcott, CT 06716: Free information ◆ Hydraulic, telescoping, and folding gangways. 203-879-0702. euromar@snet.net

**Fiberglass Coatings Inc.,** 3201 28th St. North, St. Petersburg, FL 33713: Free catalog ◆ Composite materials and supplies. Includes resins, glass, fillers, and other hard-to-find products. 800-272-7890; 727-327-8117 (in FL). www.fgci.com

**Flounder Bay Boat Lumber Company,** 1019 3rd St., Anacortes, WA 98221: Free information ◆ Boat-building kits snd supplies. 800-228-4691. www.flounderbay.com

**Freeport Marine Supply Company,** 47 W. Merrick Rd., Freeport, NY 11520: Free catalog ◆ Marine equipment, boating accessories, and optical aids. 800-645-2565; 516-379-2610 (in NY). www.freeportmarine.com

**Gander Mountain (Cabela's),** 812 13th Ave., Sidney, ME 69160: Free catalog ◆ Boating equipment. 800-237-4444. www.cabelas.com

**Garelick Mfg. Company,** 644 2nd St., P.O. Box 8, St. Paul Park, MN 55071: Free catalog ◆ Boarding ladders and steps, boat seats, deck chairs and tables, outboard motor accessories, and other marine equipment. 612-459-9795. www.garelickmfg.com

**Glenwood Marine,** 1627 W. El Segundo Blvd., Gardena, CA 90249: Catalog $3 ◆ Marine hardware. 213-757-3141.

**Goldbergs' Marine,** 201 Meadow Rd., Edison, NJ 08818: Free catalog ◆ Power and sailboat equipment. 800-BOA-TING.

**Grove Boat-Lift,** P.O. Box 8095, Fresno, CA 93727: Free information ◆ Easy-to-use boat lift. 800-447-5115; 209-251-5115 (in CA).

**Hamilton Marine Inc.,** US Rt. 1, Searsport, ME 04974: Free catalog ◆ Marine hardware, navigation and safety gear, and other equipment. 800-639-2715; 207-548-6302 (in ME). www.hamiltonmarine.com

**Ken Hankinson Associates,** P.O. Box 272, Hayden Lake, ID 83835: Catalog $6 ◆ Boat plans, patterns, kits, and supplies. 208-772-5547. www.boatdesigns.com

**The Harbor Sales Company Inc.,** 1401 Russell St., Baltimore, MD 21230: Information $1 ◆ Boat-building lumber. 800-345-1712.

**Hudson Marine Plywoods,** P.O. Box 1184, Elkhart, IN 46515: Free information ◆ Flooring, decking boards, marine plywood, and other lumber. 219-262-3666.

**Idea Development Company,** 83 Idea Pl., Sequim, WA 98382: Free catalog ◆ Trolling equipment, water ski storage holders, launching wheels, small boat dollies, bumpers and line shock absorbers, and other accessories. 800-854-6480. www.happyidea.com

**Imtra,** 30 Barnet Blvd., New Bedford, MA 02745: Free information ◆ Anchors. 508-995-7000.

**Jamestown Distributors,** P.O. Box 348, Jamestown, RI 02835: Free catalog ◆ Boat-building supplies, marine fasteners, and tools. 800-423-0030.

**Johnson Sails Inc.,** P.O. Box 20926, St. Petersburg, FL 33742: Free catalog ◆ Sails, equipment, spars, rigging, canvas, and cushions. 800-234-3220; 813-577-3220 (in FL). www.jsisail.com

**JSI Esprit,** 417 10th Ave. West, Palmetto, FL 34221: Free catalog ◆ Sails, spars, rigging, canvas, cushions, and equipment. 941-729-5119.

**M & E Marine Supply Company,** P.O. Box 601, Camden, NJ 08101: Catalog $2 ◆ Power and sailboat equipment. 800-541-6501. www.memarine.com

**Marinetics Corp.,** P.O. Box 2676, Newport Beach, CA 92663: Free information ◆ Electrical power systems, distribution panels, alert and alarm systems, and other equipment. 800-762-1414; 714-646-8889 (in CA). www.marinetics.com

**Maritime Wood Products Corp.,** The Teak Connection, 3361 SE Slater St., Stuart FL 34997: Free catalog ◆ Teak furnishings and boat-building supplies. 561-287-2919.

**Marshall Design,** P.O. Box 2789, Poulsbo, WA 98370: Free information ◆ Outboard motor and gear hoist. 800-823-3417.

**Matrix Desalination Inc.,** 3295 SW 11th Ave., Fort Lauderdale, FL 33315: Free information ◆ Desalinization equipment. 954-524-5120.

**Nautica International,** 6135 NW 167th St., Miami, FL 33015: Free information ◆ Safety and survival gear. 305-556-5554. www.nauticaintl.com

**New England Ropes,** 848 Airport Rd., Fall River, MA 02720: Free information ◆ High-strength and easy-to-splice polyester ropes. 800-333-6679; 508-678-8200 (in MA). www.neropes.com

**New Found Metals Inc.,** 240 Airport Rd., Port Townsend, WA 98368: Catalog $3 ◆ Silicon and manganese-bronze marine hardware. 360-385-3315.

**Offshore Marine Products Inc.,** 510 Long Meadow Dr., Salisbury, NC 28144: Free brochure ◆ Davits for inflatable boats and dinghies. 704-636-6558.

**Overton's Sports Center Inc.,** P.O. Box 8228, Greenville, NC 27835: Free catalog ◆ Boating accessories. 800-334-6541. custserv@overtonsonline.com

**Peconic Paddler,** 89 Peconic Ave., Riverhead, NY 11901: Free information ◆ Canoes, kayaks, rowing shells, sea kayaks, paddles, life jackets, and dry suits. 516-727-9895.

**Piragis Northwoods Company,** 105 N. Central Ave., Ely, MN 55731: Catalog $2 ◆ Canoes, boating gear, boats, videos and tapes, and trail foods. 800-223-6565. www.piragis.com

**C. Plath,** 222 Severn Ave., Annapolis, MD 21403: Free list of retail sources ◆ Marine instruments, other electronics, navigation gear, books, and accessories. 410-263-6700.

**Roloff Manufacturing,** P.O. Box 7002, Kaukauna, WI 54130: Free information ◆ Anchors. 414-766-3501.

**Rule Industries Inc.,** Cape Ann Industrial Park, Gloucester, MA 01930: Free information ◆ Compasses, anchors, pumps, and other equipment. 978-281-0573.

**Sawyer Paddles & Oars,** 299 Rogue River Pkwy., Talent, OR 97540: Free information ◆ Wood paddles and oars with solid fiberglass tips. 503-535-3606.

**Seitech Marine Products Inc.,** 52 Maritime Dr., Portsmouth, RI 02871: Free information ◆ Launching dolly for any kind of dinghies. 401-683-6898. www.paw.com/sail/seitech

**Shaw & Tenney,** P.O. Box 213, Orono, ME 04473: Free catalog ◆ Handcrafted paddles and oars. 207-866-4867.

**Spring Creek Outfitters Inc.,** P.O. Box 246, 5714 Mineral Ave., Mountain Iron, MN 55768: Free catalog ◆ Canoe accessories. 800-937-8881.

**SSI Boating Accessories,** P.O. Box 99, Hollywood, MD 20636: Free catalog ◆ Boating and sport fishing equipment. 301-373-2372.

**Stimson Marine Inc.,** RR 1, Box 524, River Rd., Boothbay, ME 04537: Brochure $2 ◆ Boat lumber and building plans. 207-633-7252.

**Suncor Marine & Industrial,** 7 Riverside Dr., Pembroke, MA 02359: Free information ◆ Anchors. 800-394-2222; 781-829-8899 (in MA). www.suncormarine.com

**Super Dock Products,** RR 2, Box 37, Center Harbor, NH 03228: Free catalog ◆ Dock rafts and docks, hardware, and accessories. 603-253-4000.

**Fred Tebb & Sons Inc.,** 1906 Marc St., P.O. Box 2235, Tacoma, WA 98401: Free information ◆ Sitka spruce for masts and spars, canoes, and oars. 253-272-4107.

**Travaco Labs/ITW Philadelphia Resins,** 130 Commerce Dr., Montgomeryville, PA 18936: Free catalog ◆ Boat repair supplies. 215-855-8450.

**Value Carpets Inc.,** Marine Division, 1802 Murray Ave., Dalton, GA 30721: Free information ◆ Do-it-yourself replacement carpet kits for boats. 800-634-3702.

**Vetus-Denouden Inc.,** P.O. Box 8712, Baltimore, MD 21240: Free catalog ◆ Boating accessories and equipment. 410-712-0740. www.vetus.com

**Voyageur,** P.O. Box 207, Waitsfield, VT 05673: Free catalog ◆ Waterproof bags, packs, camera bags, storage and flotation systems, and other performance canoe and kayak gear. 800-843-8985.

**West Marine Products,** P.O. Box 50070, Watsonville, CA 95077: Free catalog ◆ Power and sailboat equipment. 800-538-0775. www.westmarine.com

**West Wind Hardwood Inc.,** P.O. Box 2205, Sidney, British Columbia, Canada V8L 3S8: Free catalog ◆ Hardwoods, softwoods, marine grade plywood, other plywoods, and boat lumber. 800-667-2275.

**The Wooden Boat Shop,** 1007 NE Boat St., Seattle, WA 98105: Catalog $3 ◆ Tools, building supplies, and accessories. 206-634-3600. www.halcyon.com/wbs

## Instruments & Electronics

**Alpha Marine Systems,** 1125 12th Ave. NW, B-3, Issaquah, WA 98027: Free information ◆ Autopilots and compasses. 800-257-4225.

**Apelco Marine Electronics,** 676 Island Pond Rd., Manchester, NH 03109: Free information ◆ Communications equipment, navigation gear, marine instruments, and other electronics. 800-539-5539. www.raytheon.com

**Aqua Meter Instrument Corp.,** Rule industries, Cape Ann Industrial Park, Gloucester, MA 01930: Free catalog ◆ Navigation gear and other electronics. 978-272-7400.

**Armchair Sailor Bookstore,** 543 Thames St., Newport, RI 02840: Free information ◆ Navigation aids. 800-292-4278; 401-847-4252 (in RI). www.seabooks.com

**Autohelm,** 676 Island Pond Rd., Manchester, NH 03109: Free information ◆ Weather and marine instruments, compasses and autopilots, and navigation and electronics gear. 800-539-5539. www.raymarine.com

**Baker, Lyman & Company,** 3220 South I-10 Service Rd., Metairie, LA 70001: Free information ◆ Navigation aids. 800-535-6956; 504-831-3685 (in LA). www.chartinteractive.com

**Captain's Nautical Supplies,** 2500 15th Ave. West, Seattle, WA 98119: Free information ◆ Charts, books, compasses, sextants, clocks, barometers, and other equipment. 800-448-2278; 206-283-7242 (in WA). captainsnautical@msn.com

**Cassens & Plath of U.S. Inc.,** 3220 S. I-10 Service Rd., Metairie, LA 70001: Free brochure ◆ Sextants. 800-535-6956; 504-831-3685 (in LA).

**Celestaire,** 416 S. Pershing, Wichita, KS 67218: Free information ◆ Navigation instruments and books. 800-727-9785; 316-686-9785 (in KS). www.celestaire.com

**Citizen Watch Company of America,** 1200 Wall St. West, Lyndhurst, NJ 07071: Free information ◆ Professional diving watches and sports, flight, yachting, and windsurfer chronographs. 201-438-8150.

**Datamarine,** 7030 220th SW., Mountlake Terrace, WA 98043: Free information ◆ Electronic charting equipment. 206-771-2182. www.sea-dmi.com

**Davis Instruments,** 3465 Diablo Ave., Hayward, CA 94545: Free information ◆ Weather and marine instruments, compasses, and navigation and electronics gear. 800-678-3669. www.davisnet.com

**Eagle Electronics,** P.O. Box 669, Catoosa, OK 74015: Free information ◆ Navigation gear and other marine instruments. 800-324-1354. www.eaglesonar.com

**Furuno USA,** 271 Harbor Way, South San Francisco, CA 94083: Free information ◆ Marine instruments, communications equipment, navigation and electronics gear, compasses, and alarm systems. 415-873-9393. www.FurunoUSA.com

**Garmin,** 1200 E. 151st St., Olathe, KS 66062: Free list of retail sources ◆ Communications, navigation equipment, handheld plotter, and other electronics. 800-800-1020; 913-397-8200 (in KS).

**ICOM America,** 2380 116th Ave. NE, Bellevue, WA 98004: Free list of retail sources ◆ Marine instruments, compasses, navigation and electronics gear, and communications equipment. 800-999-9877. www.icomamerica.com

**InfoCenter Inc.,** Forestville, MD 20753: Free catalog ◆ Navigation equipment and services; sextants and accessories, handheld computers, and PC software. 800-852-0649; 301-420-2468 (in MD).

**KVH Industries Inc.,** 110 Enterprise Center, Middletown, RI 02842: Brochure $1 ◆ Handheld pocket-size compasses, Weather and marine instruments, navigation equipment, and electronics gear. 401-847-3327.

**Landfall Navigation,** 354 W. Putnam Ave., Greenwich, CT 06830: Free information ◆ Navigation equipment. 800-841-2219. www.landfallnav.com

**Leica GPS,** 23868 Hawthorne Blvd., Torrance, CA 90505: Free information ◆ Navigation instruments. 562-791-5300. www.leica-gps.com

**Lowrance Electronics,** 12000 E. Skelly Dr., Tulsa, OK 74128: Free list of retail sources ◆ Marine instruments and electronics. 800-324-4737. www.lowrance.com

**Magellan Systems Corp.,** 960 Overland Ct., San Dimas, CA 91773: Free list of retail sources ◆ Navigation and communications equipment, compasses, and other electronics. 800-669-4477. www.magellangps.com

**Marine Electronics,** P.O. Box 1597, Nags Head, NC 27959: Free information ◆ Marine electronics. 800-654-9251; 919-441-1360 (in NC). www.meob.com

**Marisystems Inc.,** 77 Tosca Dr., Stoughton, MA 02072: Free information ◆ Battery-operated tide and current information indicator. 781-341-3611.

**Maryland Nautical Sales Inc.,** 1400 E. Clement St., Baltimore, MD 21230: Free information ◆ Nautical books and videos, clocks, barometers, binoculars, sextants, compasses, and other equipment. 800-596-SAIL.

**Maximum Inc.,** 30 Barnet Blvd., New Bedford, MA 02745: Free catalog ◆ Weather and marine instruments. 508-995-7000. maximum@imtra.com

**Micrologic Electronics,** 9174 Deering, Chatsworth, CA 91311: Free information ◆ Navigation, other electronics, and communications equipment. 818-998-1216.

**Morad Electronics,** 1125 NW 46th St., Seattle, WA 98107: Free information ◆ Antennas. 206-789-2525.

**Navico Inc.,** 10701 Belcher Rd., Ste. 128, Largo, FL 34643: Free information ◆ Weather and marine instruments, compasses and autopilots, and communications equipment. 813-524-1555.

**Netcraft Company,** P.O. Box 5510, Toledo, OH 43613: Free catalog ◆ Marine electronics, fishing rods, reels, rod and lure-building components, and fly-tying supplies. 419-472-9826.

**Northstar Technologies,** 30 Sudbury Rd., Acton, MA 01720: Free information ◆ Electronic charting equipment. 800-628-4487. www.northstarcmc.com

**Ocean Electronics,** P.O. Box 90, Bufford, GA 30518: Free catalog ◆ Marine electronics. 770-271-5753. www.randomc.com/~oceanel

**Ockam Instruments,** 26 Higgins Dr., Milford, CT 06460: Free information ◆ Weather and marine instruments and navigation gear. 203-877-7453. www.ockam.com

**Omnifac Corp.,** 1700 E. Whipp Rd., Dayton, OH 45440: Free information ◆ Battery and AC monitors and polarity indicators, bilge pump monitors, electronic digital clocks, and on-board boat electrical systems. 937-434-8400.

**C. Plath,** 222 Severn Ave., Annapolis, MD 21403: Free list of retail sources ◆ Marine instruments, other electronics, navigation gear, books, and accessories. 410-263-6700.

**Radio-Holland Group,** 8943 Gulf Freeway, Houston, TX 77017: Free information ◆ Alarm systems, other electronics, marine instruments, and communications equipment. 713-943-3325.

**Raytheon Marine Company,** 676 Island Pond Rd., Manchester, NH 03109: Free information ◆ Navigation and electronics gear, communications equipment, and alarm systems. 800-539-5539. www.raymarine.com

**Ritchie Compasses,** 243 Oak St., Pembroke, MA 02359: Free catalog ◆ Compasses. 781-826-5131.

**Si-Tex Marine Electronics,** 11001 Roosevelt Blvd., Ste. 800, St. Petersburg, FL 34716: Free information ◆ Autopilots, navigation and electronics gear, communications equipment, and alarm systems. 813-576-5734. www.si-tex.com

**Signet Marine,** 505 Van Ness Ave., Torrance, CA 90501: Free information ◆ Analog and digital instruments. 310-320-4349.

**Simerl Instruments,** 528 Epping Forest Rd., Annapolis, MD 21401: Free brochure ◆ Weather instruments. 410-849-8667.

**Skipper Marine Electronics Inc.,** 1511 Reidel Dr., Mundelein, IL 60060: Free catalog ◆ Navigation systems, radar, autopilots, and marine electronics. 800-SKIPPER; 847-566-1800 (in IL).

**Sperry Marine,** 1070 Seminole Trail, Charlottesville, VA 22901: Free information ◆ Weather and marine instruments, compasses and autopilots, and navigation and electronics gear. 804-974-2000.

**SR Instruments,** 600 Young St., Tonawanda, NY 14150: Free information ◆ Weather and marine instruments. 800-654-6360; 716-693-5977 (in NY).

**Trimble Navigation,** 645 N. Mary Ave., Sunnyvale, CA 94086: Free information ◆ Navigation and communications equipment and other electronics. 800-827-2424; 408-481-8000 (in CA). www.trimble.com

**Vetus-Denouden Inc.,** P.O. Box 8712, Baltimore, MD 21230: Free catalog ◆ Wind/weather forecasting equipment for boats. 410-712-0740. www.vetus.com

**W-H Autopilots,** 150 Madrone Ln. North, Bainbridge Island, WA 98110: Free information ◆ Autopilots for power and sailboats. 206-780-2175. pilotwhale@worldnet.atl.net

**Yazaki-VDO Marine,** 188 Brooke Rd., Winchester, VA 22604: Free information ◆ Weather and marine instruments, compasses, and navigation and electronics gear. 540-665-0100.

## Nautical Books & Software, Videos & Gifts

**American Booksellers,** 102 W. 11th St., Aberdeen, WA 98520: Free catalog ◆ Used and rare maritime books. 360-532-2099.

**Bluewater Books & Charts,** 1481 SE 17th St. Causeway, Fort Lauderdale, FL 33316: Catalog $4.95 ◆ Nautical books, charts, and software. 800-942-2583; 954-768-0846 (in FL). www.bluewaterweb.com

**Captain's Emporium,** 7855 Gross Point Rd., Skokie, IL 60077: Free information ◆ Trophies and gifts. 847-675-5411.

**Captn. Jack's Software Source,** P.O. Box 65119, Port Ludlow, WA 98365: Free information ◆ Electronic charting and nautical software. 888-227-5225. www.capjack.com

**Caysoft,** 62 Maritime Dr., Portsmouth, RI 02871: Free catalog ◆ Marine software and electronic charts. 401-683-3520.

**International Marine,** Division McGraw Hill, P.O. Box 548, Black Lick, OH 43004: Free catalog ◆ Nautical books. 800-262-4729. www.mcgraw-hill.com

**Jeppesen,** 55 Inverness Dr. East, Englewood, CO 80112: Free information ◆ Flight planning and training, logging and record-keeping, moving map software, and marine navigation software. 800-628-4640. www.jeppesen.com

**Johnson Sails Inc.,** P.O. Box 20926, St. Petersburg, FL 33702: Free catalog ◆ Nautical gifts. 800-234-3220; 813-577-3220 (in FL). www.jsisail.com

**JSI Esprit,** 417 10th Ave. West, Palmetto, FL 34221: Free catalog ◆ Nautical gifts. 941-729-5119

**The Maritime Store,** 2905 Hyde St. Pier, San Francisco, CA 94109: Free catalog ◆ Maritime maps, greeting cards, boat models, children's and maritime books, and gifts. 415-775-BOOK.

**Maryland Nautical Sales Inc.,** 1400 E. Clement St., Baltimore, MD 21230: Free information ◆ Nautical books and videos, clocks, barometers, binoculars, sextants, compasses, and other equipment. 800-596-SAIL.

**Moby Dick Marine Specialties,** 21 William St., New Bedford, MA 02740: Catalog $5 ◆ Nautical gifts, accessories, and scrimshaw. 800-343-8044.

**The Nautical Book Catalog,** P.O. Box F, Ringoes, NJ 08551: Free catalog ◆ Marine education and technical books. 800-297-7617. www.boatbooks.com

**Nautical Software,** 14657 SW Teal Blvd., Beaverton, OR 97007: Free information ◆ Windows tides and currents software for PCs. 503-579-1414. www.tides.com

**Naval Institute Press,** Customer Service, 2062 Generals Hwy., Annapolis, MD 21401: Free catalog ◆ Books on navigation, seamanship, naval history, ships, and aircraft. 800-233-8764. www.usni.org

**Pilothouse,** 1600 S. Delaware Ave., Philadelphia, PA 19148: Free information ◆ Nautical books and charts. 800-407-4568.

**Preston's,** Main Street Wharf, Greenport, NY 11944: Free catalog ◆ Ship's wheels, clocks and bells, tavern signs, harpoons, binoculars, nautical lamps, caps and sweaters, antique maps, glassware, and marine paintings. 800-836-1165.

**Resolution Mapping Inc.,** One Riverside Dr., Andover, MA 01810: Free information ◆ Nautical mapping and charting software for PCs. 978-933-3000. www.maptech.com

**Ship's Hatch,** 10376 Main St., Fairfax, VA 22030: Brochure $1 ◆ Military patches, pins and insignia, official USN ship ball caps, ship's clocks, military and hatch cover tables, nautical and military gifts, jewelry, lamps, lanterns, ship's wheels, jewelry boxes, and plaques. 703-691-1670.

**Somerset Publishing Company Inc.,** 307 Bradford Pkwy., Syracuse, NY 13224: Free information ◆ Celestial navigation software. 315-446-0614.

**Starboard Software,** Box 1462, Royal Oak, MI 48068: Free information ◆ Boating navigation software for PCs and the Macintosh. 810-545-9928.

**J. Tuttle Maritime Books,** 18098 Laurel Crest, Madison, WI 53705: Free catalog ◆ Out-of-print books about the sea, ships, and sailors. 608-238-7245.

**The Wilderness Collection,** 716 Delaware Ct., Lawton, MI 49065: Free catalog ◆ New and used books about canoeing and wilderness travel. 616-624-4410.

**Wind in the Rigging,** 125 E. Main St., P.O. Box 323, Port Washington, WI 53074: Free catalog ◆ Nautical gifts and gear. 800-236-7444; 414-284-3494 (in WI). www.discoverusa.com/wi/windrig

**WoodenBoat Books,** P.O. Box 78, Brooklin, ME 04616: Free catalog ◆ Books about boats. 800-273-SHIP. www.woodenboat.com

## BOCCIE

**Sport Fun Inc.,** 4621 Sperry St., Los Angeles, CA 90039: Free information ◆ Boccie sets. 800-423-2597; 213-245-7530 (in CA).

**Venus Knitting Mills Inc.,** 140 Spring St., Murray Hill, NJ 07974: Free information ◆ Boccie sets. 800-955-4200; 908-464-2400 (in NJ).

**Worldwide Games,** P.O. Box 517, Colchester, CT 06415: Free catalog ◆ Equipment for badminton, horseshoes, and boccie. 800-888-0987. www.worldwidegames.com

## BOOK REPAIR & BINDING

**Bohemian Brigade Bookshop & Publishers,** 7347 Middlebrook Pike, Knoxville, TN 37909: Free information ◆ Bindery, conservation, and book repair services. 615-694-8227. www.aimsinc.com/cwmedbooks

**The Bookbinder's Warehouse,** 31 Division St., Keyport, NJ 07735: Free catalog ◆ Bookbinding supplies and equipment. 908-264-0306.

**BookMakers,** 6001 66th Ave., Ste. 101, Riverdale, MD 20737: Free catalog ◆ Supplies and equipment for hand bookbinding, book and paper conservation, and book arts. 301-459-3384.

**Library Binding Company,** 2900 Franklin Ave., Waco, TX 76710: Free price list ◆ Bookbinding and restoration services for rare books. 800-792-3352.

**John Neal, Bookseller,** 1833 Spring Garden St., Greensboro, NC 27403: Free information ◆ Calligraphy and marbling supplies, books on arts and crafts, and bookbinding services. 800-369-9598; 336-272-6139 (in NC). www.JohnNealBooks.com

**Talas,** 568 Broadway, New York, NY 10012: Catalog $5 ◆ Bookbinding supplies. 212-219-0735.

## BOOK SEARCH SERVICES

**K.S. Alden Books,** 511 W. Fairmount Ave., State College, PA 16801: Free information ◆ Book search services. 800-359-8848.

**American Indian Books & Relics,** P.O. Box 16175, Huntsville, AL 35802: Free information with long SASE ◆ Search service for books about Native Americans. 256-881-6727.

**Avonlea Books,** P.O. Box 74, White Plains, NY 10602: Free information ◆ Book search service for out-of-print books. 800-423-0622; 914-946-5923 (in NY). www.bushkin.com

**Better Book Getter,** 310 Riverside Dr., #202, New York, NY 10025: Free information ◆ Hard-to-find and out-of-print book search services. 800-804-3956. bettgett@concentric.net

**Michael Dennis Cohan, Bookseller,** 502 W. Alder St., Missoula, MT 59802: Free catalog ◆ Search service for books on geology, mining, and related subjects. 406-721-7379.

**Hard-to-Find Needlework Books,** 96 Roundwood Rd., Newton, MA 02164: Catalog $1 ◆ Search services for hard-to-find and rare books on needle crafts. 617-969-0942. hardtofind@needleworkbooks.com

**Heritage Book Search,** College Highway, P.O. Box 48, Southampton, MA 01073: Free information ◆ Book search services. 413-527-5200. sales@heritagebks.com

**Richard A. LaPosta,** 154 Robindale Dr., Kensington, CT 06037: Information $1 ◆ Searches for out-of-print, first editions, and other Civil War books. 860-828-0921.

**The Military Bookman,** 29 E. 93rd St., New York, NY 10128: Free information ◆ Search service for military, naval, and aviation out-of-print and rare books. 212-348-1280. www.militarybookman.com

**NightinGale Resources, Books for Cooks,** P.O. Box 322, Cold Spring, NY 10516: Free catalog with SASE ◆ Non-text Judaica, children's books, cookbooks. 914-265-3282.

**R.H. Pettit,** Viewpoint Company, 41 Union Square West, New York, NY 10003: Free information ◆ Book search services. 212-242-5478.

**Reed Books,** 107 20th St., Birmingham, AL 35233: Free information ◆ Book search services. 205-326-4460. JimReedBooks@compuserve.com

**Michael Sober Booksearch,** 60 Sutton Pl. South, New York, NY 10022: Free information ◆ Book search services. 800-729-1880. msober@att.net

**Thaddeus Books,** 4404 NE Going, Portland, OR 97218: Free information ◆ Worldwide book search service. 503-281-6689. symbol@teleport.com

**The Wayward Bookman,** 3 Main St., Wales, MA 01081: Free information ◆ Book search services. 413-245-6210.

## BOOKKEEPING & ACCOUNTING SUPPLIES

**Accountants Supply House,** 301 Grove Rd., Thorofare, NJ 08086: Free catalog ◆ Stationery and envelopes, forms and labels, adding machines, shipping materials, disk storage cabinets, typewriter and data processing ribbons, office furniture, and other supplies. 800-342-5274.

**HG Professional Forms Company,** 2000 California St., Omaha, NE 68102: Free catalog ◆ Pre-printed forms, accounting and office supplies, record-keeping systems, and computer paper. 800-228-1493. www.hgproforms.com

**Medical Arts Press,** 8500 Wyoming Ave. North, Minneapolis, MN 55445: Free catalog ◆ Forms for medical and dental professions. 612-493-7300.

## BOOKPLATES & BOOKMARKS

**Bookplate Ink,** P.O. Box 187, Yellow Springs, OH 45387: Free brochure ◆ Self-adhesive imprinted personalized bookplates. 888-823-3608; 937-767-7373 (in OH). www.ysnews.com

**Creations by Elaine,** 6253 W. 74th St., Box 2001, Bedford Park, IL 60499: Free catalog ◆ Art motif bookmarks. 800-323-1208. www.catalogs.order.com/co/index.html

**Walter Drake & Sons,** Drake Bldg., Colorado Springs, CO 80940: Free catalog ◆ Bookmarks, personalized stationery, toys, household items, clothing, decor and office accessories, and other items. 800-525-9291. amyconnors@wdrake.com

**Kidstamps,** P.O. Box 18699, Cleveland Heights, OH 44118: Catalog $3 ◆ Bookplates. 800-727-5437. www.kidstamps.com

**Lixx Labelsz,** 2619 14th St. SW, P.O. Box 32055, Calgary, Alberta, Canada T2T 5X0: Catalog $4 ◆ Labels and bookmarks that combine wildlife designs, calligraphy, eco-action, and recycling. 403-245-2331.

## BOOKS

### Bargain Books

**The Bargain Book Warehouse,** P.O. Box 8515, Ukiah, CA 95482: Free catalog ◆ Popular fiction paperbacks and hardcovers. 800-301-7567. www.bargainbookwarehouse.com

**Barnes & Noble,** Books By Mail, 1 Pond Rd., Rockleigh, NJ 07647: Free catalog ◆ Bargain books, videos, and records. 800-843-2665. www.barnesandnoble.com

**Critics' Choice Video,** P.O. Box 749, Itasca, IL 60143: Free catalog ◆ Books, records, and video cassettes. 800-544-9852. www.ccvideo.com

**Daedalus Books Inc.,** 4601 Decatur St., Hyattsville, MD 20781: Free information ◆ Publisher overstocks and remainders. 800-944-8879. www.daedalus-books.com

**Edward R. Hamilton, Bookseller,** 5014 Oak, Falls Village, CT 06031: Free catalog ◆ Overstocks, remainders, imports, and reprints from major publishers. www.hamiltonbook.com

### Children's Books

**Advocacy Press,** P.O. Box 236, Santa Barbara, CA 93102: Free information ◆ Books for children and young adults on gender equity, career planning, problem solving, personal planning, life skills, self-esteem, and self-awareness. 800-676-1480.

**Astor Books,** 62 Cooper Square, New York, NY 10003: Free catalog ◆ Children's books. 212-777-3700.

**Bellerophon Books,** P.O. Box 21307, Santa Barbara, CA 93121: Free catalog ◆ Art and history coloring books for children. 800-253-9943.

**Cedco Publishing Company,** 100 Pelican Way, San Rafael, CA 94901: Free catalog ◆ Books and calendars for children, adults, and recording wedding memories. 800-233-2624. www.cedco.com

**Cheshire Cat Children's Books,** 5512 Connecticut Ave. NW, Washington, DC 20015: Free information ◆ Books, records, and tapes. 202-244-3956.

**Children's Book Press,** 246 1st St., San Francisco, CA 94105: Free information ◆ Multi-cultural and bilingual picture books and audio cassettes for children. 415-995-2200.

**Chinaberry Book Service,** 2780 Via Orange Way, Ste. B, Spring Valley, CA 91978: Free catalog ◆ Books and music for children and adults. 800-776-2242.

**Christian Book Distributors,** P.O. Box 7000, Peabody, MA 01961: Free catalog ◆ Christian books. 978-977-5050. www.chrbook.com

**DK Family Learning,** 7800 Southland Blvd., Ste. 200, Orlando, FL 32809: Free catalog ◆ Learning-books, CDs, and videos for children and adults. 800-DK-BOOK-1.

**Dover Publications Inc.,** 31 East 2nd St., Mineola, NY 11501: Free catalog ◆ Children's classics, cut-and-assemble and coloring books, paper dolls and stickers, and other educational activity books. 516-294-7000.

**The Evergreen Press,** 9 Camino Arroyo Pl., Palm Desert, CA 92260: Free information with long SASE ◆ Adult and children's books, greeting cards, book marks and bookplates, wedding certificates, calendars, ornaments, paper dolls, postcards, and 19th and early 20th-century paper memorabilia. 213-510-1700.

**Free Spirit Publishing Inc.,** 400 1st Ave. North, Ste. 616, Minneapolis, MN 55401: Free information ◆ Nonfiction, psychology and self-help materials for and about gifted, talented, and creative young people, their parents, and teachers. 800-735-7323. www.freespirit.com

**W.H. Freeman & Company,** 41 Madison Ave., New York, NY 10010: Free information ◆ Adult and children's books on science, computers, and other subjects. 800-877-5351. www.whfreeman.com

**JHAB Services,** P.O. Box 972742, Miami, FL 33197: Free brochure ◆ Children's personalized books. 888-321-3266; 305-253-7541 (in FL).

**Klutz Press,** 2121 Staunton Ct., Palo Alto, CA 94306: Free information ◆ How-to, fun, and song books for children. 650-424-0739. www.klutz.com

**The Maritime Store,** 2905 Hyde St. Pier, San Francisco, CA 94109: Free catalog ◆ Maritime maps, greeting cards, boat models, children's and maritime books, and gifts. 415-775-BOOK.

**Metacom Inc.,** 5353 Nathan Ln., Plymouth, MN 55442: Free catalog ◆ Golden Age Radio programs, comedy super stars of past years, famous radio plays, foreign language cassettes, coloring books with stories, and read-along books and cassettes for teaching children to read. 800-328-0108. AlC4Radio2@aol.com

**The Mind's Eye,** P.O. Box 6547, Chelmsford, MA 01824: Free catalog ◆ Children's favorites and classics, military intrigue, mystery, horror, science fiction, adventure, drama, history, comedy, poetry, and self-improvement books, audio cassettes, and CD-ROMs. 800-949-3333.

**Music for Little People,** P.O. Box 1460, Redway, CA 95560: Free catalog ◆ Stories and books, favorite songs, lullabies, nature stories, folk music, classical music, and other children's music cassettes and videos. 800-346-4445.

**Village StoryTapes,** 937 Midpine Way, P.O. Box 1440, Sebastopol, CA 95473: Free catalog ◆ Fiction, self-improvement and learning, drama and poetry, mystery, for children, science fiction, and other abridged and unabridged readings of books. 800-238-8273. www.storytapes.com

**Warren Publishing House Inc.,** P.O. Box 2250, Everett, WA 98203: Free catalog ◆ Children's story books and resources with activities for teachers, parents, and librarians. 800-773-7240.

### General Books & Manuscripts

**A & C Books,** P.O. Box 1050, Dubuque, IA 52004: Free information ◆ Reference books for collectors. 800-334-7165.

**A.R.C. Books,** P.O. Box 2, Carlisle, MA 01741: Free information ◆ Books for collectors of antique radios. 978-371-0512.

**A.R.E. Press,** 68th & Atlantic Ave., P.O. Box 656, Virginia Beach, VA 23451: Free catalog ◆ Study aids for reseach and personal enlightenment. Also charts for determining astrology horoscopes. 888-723-1112. www.edgarcayce.com

**Abenaki Publishers,** 126 North St., P.O. Box 4100, Bennington, VT 05201: Free information ◆ Books on fishing. 802-447-2471.

**Harry N. Abrams Inc.,** 100 5th Ave., New York, NY 10011: Free information ◆ Art, how-to craft, food and wine, architecture, science, folk art, and pictorial non-fiction books. 212-206-7715. www.abramsbooks.com

**Academic Press Inc.,** 6277 Sea Harbor Dr., Orlando, FL 32887: Free catalog ◆ Scientific and technical books. 800-321-5068. ap@acad.com8

**Addison-Wesley Publishing Company,** One Jacob Way, Reading, MA 01867: Free catalog ◆ Books about computers, child care and health, biographies, children's activities, psychology, current affairs, and business. 781-944-3700. www2.awl.com/corp/corpcomm/contact.html

**Advanstar Communications,** 7500 Old Oak Blvd., Cleveland, OH 44130: Free information ◆ PC graphics and video books. 800-598-6008. www.advanstar.com

**Adventurous Traveler Bookstore,** P.O. Box 64769, Burlington, VT 05406: Free catalog ◆ New, used, and rare books and maps on hiking, climbing, kayaking, diving, mountaineering, exploration, and travel. 800-282-3963; 802-860-6776 (in VT). www.atb-rarebooks.com

**Jamey Aebersold Jazz Inc.,** P.O. Box 1244, New Albany, IN 47151: Free catalog ◆ Books on music and musical instruments.

**Air Age Publishing,** 251 Danbury Rd., Wilton, CT 06897: Free information ◆ Books on model boating. 800-243-6685; 203-834-2900 (in CT).

**Airbrush Magazine,** 3676 Cosby Hwy., Cosby, TN 37722: Free information ◆ Books on airbrushing. 800-910-4891. www.airbrushmagazine.com

**Alpine Publications,** P.O. Box 7027, Loveland, CO 80537: Free catalog ◆ Books on horses, dogs, mules, and llamas. 800-777-7257.

**Alter Years,** 3749 E. Colorado Blvd., Pasadena, CA 91107: Catalog $5 ◆ Underpinnings and accessories, costume-making supplies, over 1000 costume reference books, and patterns. 818-585-2994.

**Amadeus Press,** 133 SW 2nd Ave., Ste. 450, Portland, OR 97204: Free catalog ◆ Books on classical music and opera. 800-327-5680. www.amadeuspress.com

**American Booksellers,** 102 W. 11th St., Aberdeen, WA 98520: Free catalog ◆ Used and rare maritime books. 360-532-2099.

**American Botanical Council,** P.O. Box 201660, Austin, TX 78720: Free information ◆ Books on herbs and herbal medicine. 800-373-7105. custsserv@herbalgram.org

**American Diabetes Association,** Order Fulfillment Dept., P.O. Box 930850, Atlanta, GA 31193: Free information ◆ Recipe and general diabetes information books for diabetics and professionals. 800-232-6733. www.diabetes.org

**American Homeowners Foundation,** 5776 Little Falls Rd., Arlington, VA 22213: Free catalog ◆ Books on real estate, home improvement, and new home construction. 703-536-7776.

**American Indian Books & Relics,** P.O. Box 16175, Huntsville, AL 35802: Free information with long SASE ◆ Books on Native Americans and their relics. 256-881-6727.

**American Map Corp.,** 46-35 54th Rd., Maspeth, NY 11378: Free information ◆ Bilingual dictionaries, travel guides and atlases, travel language aids, maps, and other educational publications. 718-784-0055.

**American Radio Relay League,** 225 Main St., Newington, CT 06111: Free information ◆ Books on how to become a HAM radio operator, get a license, learn Morse code, organize equipment, how to operate and set up equipment, and other topics. 888-277-5289; 860-594-0250 (in CT). www.arrl.org

**Andy's Front Hall,** P.O. Box 307, Wormer Rd., Voorheesville, NY 12186: Free catalog ◆ Books and music for and about folk, traditional, and acoustic sounds. 800-759-1775; 518-765-4193 (in NY). members.aol.com/fronthal

**The Anglers Art,** P.O. Box 148, Plainfield, PA 17081: Free catalog ◆ Books on fishing. 800-848-1020.

**Antique Collectors Club,** Market St. Industrial Park, Wappingers Falls, NY 12590: Free brochure ◆ Books on antiques, fine art, and other collectibles. 800-252-5231. www.antiquecc.com

**Aperture Foundation Inc.,** 20 E. 23rd St., New York, NY 10010: Free information ◆ Fine art and photography books. 800-929-2323; 212-505-5555 (in NY).

**Apollo Books,** 250 W. 57th St., Ste. 811, New York, NY 10107: Free catalog ◆ Reference books and price guides for fine art, antiques, and gardening. 800-431-5003.

**Art Book Services,** Market St. Industrial Park, Wappingers Falls, NY 12590: Free brochure ◆ Books about antiques, fine art, and other collectibles. 800-247-9955. www.artbookservices.com

**Artemis Imports,** P.O. Box 68, Pacific Grove, CA 93950: Free catalog ◆ Books about the Middle East. 408-373-4113. www.artemisimports.com

**The Artist Magazine Bookshelf,** 1507 Dana Ave., Cincinnati, OH 45207: Free information ◆ Books for artists. 800-289-0963.

**Asian World of Martial Arts,** 11601 Caroline Rd., Philadelphia, PA 19154: Catalog $5 ◆ Training and protective equipment, weapons, uniforms, belts, books, and videos. 800-345-2962. www.awma.com

**The Astrology Center of America,** 714 Baca St., P.O. Box 10170, Santa Fe, NM 87504: Free catalog ◆ New and hard-to-find books on astrology. 800-475-2272. www.astroamerica.com

**Audio-Forum,** 96 Broad St., Guilford, CT 06437: Free catalog ◆ Self-instruction foreign language courses. 800-448-7671; 203-453-9794 (in CT). 74537.550@compuserve.com

**Audubon Publishing Company,** One Glamore Ct., Smithtown, NY 11787: Free information ◆ Books about birds. 800-359-2473.

**August House Publishers Inc.,** P.O. Box 3223, Little Rock, AR 72203: Free information ◆ Story teller books. 501-372-5450.

**Aunt Clowney's Warehouse,** P.O. Box 1444, Corona, CA 91718: Free catalog with two 1st class stamps ◆ Books on clowning. 909-273-0900. auntc@empirenet.com

**Aurora Press,** P.O. Box 573, Santa Fe, NM 87504: Free catalog ◆ Books on astrology and yoga. 505-363-4393.

**Australian Catalogue Company,** 7605 Welborn St., Raleigh, NC 27615: Free catalog ◆ Books about Australia. 800-808-0938. www.aussiecatalog.com

**The Auto Review,** P.O. Box 510, Florissant, MO 63032: Free information ◆ Books and information on antique and classic car history and restoration. 314-355-3609.

**Autograph Collector,** 510 S. Corona Mall, Corona, CA 91720: Free information ◆ Books on autographs and autograph collecting. 800-395-1359. OdysGroup@aol.com

**Aviation Book Company,** 7201 Perimeter Rd. S, Ste. C, Seattle, WA 98108: Free catalog ◆ Books, videos, pilot supplies, clothing, and gifts. 800-423-2708. www.aviationbook.com

**Gary Backman Books,** 1005 Woodland Dr., Santa Paula, CA 93060: Free catalog ◆ Hunting, firearms and shooting, waterfowl, fly fishing, and other books. 805-525-2647.

**Bailey Craftsman Supply,** P.O. Box 276, Fulton, MO 65251: Free information ◆ How-to books on metal-working and fabrication. 573-642-5998. www.baileycraft.com

**The Baird Company,** P.O. Box 7240, Moreno Valley, CA 92552: Free catalog ◆ Police insignia and other collectibles. Also books on law enforcement, crime, and the military. 909-943-4180. bairdco@aol.com

**Bantam Doubleday Dell Publishing Group Inc.,** 1540 Broadway, New York, NY 10036: Free catalog ◆ Fiction and non-fiction books. 212-354-6500. www.bdd.com

**Bantam Doubleday Dell Travel Books,** 1540 Broadway, New York, NY 10036: Free information ◆ Travel guidebooks, atlases, and other books. 212-354-6500. www.bdd.com

**Bantam Electronic Publishing,** 1540 Broadway, New York, NY 10036: Free information ◆ Computer books. 212-354-6500. www.bdd.com

**Baron/Barclay Bridge Supplies,** 3600 Chamberlain Ln., Ste. 320, Louisville, KY 40241: Free catalog ◆ Bridge supplies and how-to books. 800-274-2221. www.baronbarclay.com

**Barron's Educational Series,** 250 Wireless Blvd., Hauppage, NY 11788: Free catalog ◆ Educational books. 800-645-3476.

**Bas Bleu,** 515 Mean St. NW, Atlanta, GA 30318: Free information ◆ A bookstore for women. 800-433-1155.

**Basic Books Inc.,** Division HarperCollins, 10 E. 53rd St., New York, NY 10022: Free catalog ◆ Books on psychology, business, history, science, political science, women's studies, and other subjects. 212-207-7057. www.harpercollins.com

**Bear & Company Publishing,** P.O. Box 2860, Santa Fe, NM 87504: Free catalog ◆ New age, Native American, spirituality and alternative health, and divination systems books. 505-983-5968.

**Berkshire House Publishers,** 480 Pleasant St., Ste. 5, Lee, MA 01238: Free information ◆ Travel, recreation, self-help, crafts, psychology, and cooking books. 800-321-8526. www.berkshirehouse.com

**Better Homes & Gardens Books,** 1716 Locust St., Des Moines, IA 50309: Free information with long SASE ◆ Books on cooking, gardening, how-to, crafts, and other subjects. 800-678-8091.

**Betterway Books,** 1507 Dana Ave., Cincinnati, OH 45207: Free catalog ◆ Woodworking books. 800-289-0963.

**Beyond Beadery,** P.O. Box 460, Rollinsville, CO 80474: Catalog $2 ◆ * How-to books on working with beads. 800-840-5548. members.aol.com/beyondbead

**Bicycle Books Inc.,** 1282 7th Ave., San Francisco, CA 94122: Free information ◆ Books about bicycles, touring guides, health and fitness, mountain biking, racing, and other topics. 415-665-8214.

**Myron J. Biggar Group,** P.O. Box 239, 65 S. Broad St., Nazareth, PA 18064: Free brochure ◆ Books on O gauge model train repairs, restoration, and for beginners. 610-759-0406. members.aol.com/Ogaugerwy/OGR.html

**Bird Watcher's Digest,** P.O. Box 110, Marietta, OH 45750: Free information ◆ Books on birds. 800-879-2473. www.petersononline.com/birds

**Warren Blake, Old Science Books,** 308 Hadley Dr., Trumbull, CT 06611: Catalog $1 ◆ Hard-to-find old-to-early astronomy books and prints. 203-459-0820.

**Bloomington Wholesale Garden Supply,** 7854 N. Hwy. 37, Bloomington, IN 47404: Free information ◆ Books on hydroponic gardening. 800-316-1306. www.wormsway.com

**Bluewater Books & Charts,** 1481 SE 17th St. Causeway, Fort Lauderdale, FL 33316: Catalog $4.95 ◆ Nautical books, charts, and software. 800-942-2583; 954-768-0846 (in FL). www.bluewaterweb.com

**Blystone's Books,** 2132 Delaware Ave., Pittsburgh, PA 15218: Free information ◆ Hard-to-find books for toy collectors. 412-371-3511.

**Bohemian Brigade Bookshop & Publishers,** 7347 Middlebrook Pike, Knoxville, TN 37909: Free information ◆ First edition and out-of-print Civil War books. Includes hard-to-find titles and popular reprints. 615-694-8227. www.aimsinc.com/cwmedbooks

**The Bold Strummer Ltd.,** 20 Turkey Hill Circle, P.O. Box 2037, Westport, CT 06880: Catalog $1 (refundable) ◆ Books on music and musical instruments. 203-259-3021. BSTRUMMER@aol.com

**The Book Mailer,** P.O. Box 1273, Helena, MT 59624: Free information ◆ Fly fishing books. 800-874-4171.

**Book Sales Inc.,** 114 Northfield Ave., Edison, NJ 08818: Free catalog ◆ Books on Americana, Civil War, fine arts, military, photography, religion, travel, humor, health, cooking, and crafts. 908-225-0530.

**The Book Stable,** 5326 Tomahawk Trail, Fort Wayne, IN 46897: Free catalog ◆ Books on horses and other equine information. 800-274-2665. www.bookstable.com

**BookBound,** Box 2376, East Hampton, NY 11937: Free information ◆ Can supply any book in print, from new releases to classics. 800-959-7323; 516-267-6425 (in NY).

**Books for Educators Inc.,** 17051 SE 272nd St., Ste. 18, Kent, WA 98042: Free catalog ◆ Books for educators. 253-630-6908. www.books4edu.com

**The Bookshelf,** P.O. Box 6925, Ventura, CA 93006: Free information ◆ Books on metalsmithing.

**Bowling's Bookstore,** 200 S. Michigan Ave., Ste. 1430, Chicago, IL 60604: Free information ◆ Books and videos on bowling. 800-521-BOWL. www.bowlingsbookstore.com

**Brandenburg Historical,** P.O. Box 1574, Rutherford, NJ 07070: Catalog $2 ◆ German military collectibles, from 1900 to the present. Also books and German military music on CDs.

**Brandy Station Bookshelf,** P.O. Box 1863, Harrah, OK 73045: Free catalog ◆ New, rare, and out-of-print Civil War books. 405-964-5730.

**Brew Pot,** 13031 11th St., Old Bowie, MD 20715: Free catalog ◆ Books on home-brewing and wine-making. 301-805-6799.

**The Bridge World,** 717 White Plains Rd., Ste. 106, Scarsdale, NY 10583: Free catalog ◆ Bridge books, magazines, computer software for Windows, games, and accessories. 914-725-6712. www.bridgeworld.com

**Broadfoot Publishing Company,** 1907 Buena Vista Circle, Wilmington, NC 28405: Free catalog ◆ Books about the Civil War. 910-686-4816. www.broadfoot.wilmington.net

**Broadway Play Publishing Inc.,** 56 E. 81st St., New York, NY 10028: Free catalog ◆ Full-length contemporary American plays. Also some musicals and one-act plays. 212-772-8334. www.BroadwayPlayPubl.com

**Brooklyn Botanic Garden,** Attention: Plants & Gardens, 1000 Washington Ave., Brooklyn, NY 11225: Free brochure ◆ Gardening books and videos. 718-941-4044. www.bbg.org

**Brooks Books,** P.O. Box 21473, Concord, CA 94521: Free catalog ◆ Books on botany and ornamental horticulture. 925-672-4566. brooksbk@interloc.com

**Butterworth-Heinemann Books,** Attention: Order Department, 2647 Waterfront Parkway E. Dr., Indianapolis, IN 46214: Free catalog ◆ Books on electronics and other technical subjects. 800-428-7267. www.bh.com

**C & T Publishing/Fox Hill Workshop,** P.O. Box 1456, Lafayette, CA 94549: Free catalog ◆ Books on quilting, color, doll-making, dying, embroidery, ethnic textiles, fabric painting, and wearable art. 800-284-1114. www.ctpub.com/~ctpub

**Caboose Hobbies,** 500 S. Broadway, Denver, CO 80209: Free information ◆ Fiction, nonfiction, and how-to books on model trains. 303-777-6766. www.caboosehobbies.com

**Calibre Press Inc.,** 666 Dundee Rd., Ste. 1607, Northbrook, IL 60062: Free catalog ◆ Law enforcement videos, books, and survival products. 800-323-0037; 847-498-5680 (in IL).

**Cambridge University Press,** 40 W. 20th St., New York, NY 10011: Free catalog ◆ Reference and academic books. 800-872-7423. www.cup.org

**Capability's Books,** 2379 Hwy. 46, Deer Park, WI 54007: Catalog $1 ◆ Books for gardeners. 800-247-8154.

**Career Publishing Inc.,** 905 Allanson Rd., Mundelein, IL 60060: Free brochure ◆ Spelling, home repair, sewing, quotation dictionary, legal matters, medical adviser, and other how-to books. 847-949-0011.

**Cedco Publishing Company,** 100 Pelican Way, San Rafael, CA 94901: Free catalog ◆ Books and calendars for children, adults, and recording wedding memories. 800-233-2624. www.cedco.com

**Tony Chachere's Creole Foods,** P.O. Box 1687, Opelousas, LA 70571: Free brochure ◆ Cajun country specialties and Cajun and Creole cookbooks. 800-551-9066. www.cajunspice.com/index.html

**Charlesbridge Publishing,** 85 Main St., Watertown, MA 02172: Free catalog ◆ Nature, science, and multi-cultural books. 617-926-0329. www.charlesbridge.com

**Charington House,** P.O. Box 9661, Bradenton, FL 34206: Catalog $2 ◆ Children's books from all publishers, picture books, multi-cultural, special needs, and multimedia. 941-746-3326. charington@worldnet.att.net

**Chautauqua Inc.,** 1627 Marion Ave., Durham, NC 27705: Free information ◆ Books about beer. 800-977-BEER.

**Cheertime U.S.A.,** P.O. Box 2844, Edmond, OK 73083: Free brochure ◆ How-to books, cassettes, and videos on cheerleading. 405-359-1231.

**Chelsea House Publishers,** 1974 Sproul Rd., Ste. 400, Broomall, PA 19008: Free catalog ◆ Non-fiction books for children and young adults. 800-848-BOOK.

**Chessler Books,** P.O. Box 399, Kittredge, CO 80457: Free catalog ◆ New, used, and rare books on mountaineering. 800-654-8502; 303-670-0093 (in CO). chesslerbk@aol.com

**The Chessworks Studio,** David Weinstock, 6253 36th Ave. NE, Seattle, WA 98115: Free catalog ◆ Chess accessories, software, contemporary chess books, and rare and hard-to-find chess books. 206-526-8116. www.chessmate.com

**China Books & Periodicals Inc.,** 2929 24th St., San Francisco, CA 94110: Free catalog ◆ Books and periodicals from and about China since 1960. 415-282-2994. www.chinabooks.com

**Chivalry Sports,** P.O. Box 18904, Tucson, AZ 85731: Free catalog ◆ Medieval, renaissance, and fantasy costumes, gifts, and books. 800-730-5464. www.RenStore.com

**Chronicle Books,** 275 5th St., San Francisco, CA 94103: Free information ◆ Books about cooking and food, art and photography, architecture, nature, travel, and history. 800-722-6657. www.chronbooks.com

**Civil War Antiquities,** P.O. Box 1411, Delaware, OH 43015: Free catalog ◆ Books about the Civil War. 740-363-1862. www.civilwarantiquities.com

**Stan Clark Military Books,** 915 Fairview Ave., Gettysburg, PA 17325: Catalog $2 ◆ Civil War books. 717-337-1728.

**Classic Motorbooks,** P.O. Box 1, Osceola, WI 54020: Free catalog ◆ Automotive books. 800-826-6600. www.motorbooks.com

**Classical Numismatic Group Inc.,** P.O. Box 479, Lancaster, PA 17608: Free list ◆ Books on Greek, Roman, Byzantine, medieval, foreign, and British coins. 717-390-9194.

**Cliff's Notes Inc.,** P.O. Box 80728, Lincoln, NE 68501: Free information ◆ Study aids and test preparation guides. 800-228-4078; 402-423-5050 (in NE).

**Coin World Books,** P.O. Box 150, Sidney, OH 45365: Free information ◆ Books on coin collecting. 800-253-4555.

**Collector Books,** P.O. Box 3009, Paducah, KY 42002: Free catalog ◆ Books on antiques, depression glassware, pottery, toys, dolls, teddy bears, thimbles, and other collectibles. 800-626-5420.

**The Collector's Book Source,** 1 Corporate Dr., Grantsville, MD 21536: Free catalog ◆ Books on dolls and teddy bears. 800-554-1447.

**The College Board,** 45 Columbus Ave., New York, NY 10023: Free information ◆ Books that help students and their families in the transition from high school to college and college to work. 212-713-8000.

**Colonial House Publishers,** P.O. Box 609, Enka, NC 28728: Free information ◆ Postcard price guides. 704-667-1427. Jmashb0735@aol.com

**Columbia Trading Company,** 1 Barnstable Rd., Hyannis, MA 02601: Free catalog ◆ Used and rare nautical antiques, marine art, books, and gifts. 508-778-2929. www.by-the-sea.com/nautical

**Columbia University Press,** 562 W. 113th St., New York, NY 10025: Free catalog ◆ Scholarly and general interest books. 212-666-1000. www.cc.columbia.edu/cu/cup

**The Complete Traveler of Overland Park,** 7321 W. 80th St., Overland Park, KS 66204: Free catalog ◆ Maps, travel books, travel accessories, and luggage. 888-862-0888. www.completetrav.com

**The Complete Traveller Bookstore,** 199 Madison Ave., New York, NY 10016: Free catalog ◆ Travel guides and destination books. 212-685-9007. completetraveller@worldnet.att.net

**Congressional Quarterly Inc.,** 1414 22nd St. NW, Washington, DC 20037: Free information ◆ Books on government, political science, current affairs, and the Congress. 202-887-8600.

**Consumer Information Center,** Pueblo, CO 81003: Free catalog ◆ United States Government books and pamphlets for consumers. 888-8-PUEBLO. www.pueblo.gsa.gov

**Consumer Reports Books,** 101 Truman Ave., Yonkers, NY 10703: Free catalog ◆ Books on consumer information and advice on goods, services, health, personal finances, and other topics. 914-378-2903.

**The Cookbook Collection Inc.,** 2500 E. 195th St., Belton, MO 64012: Free catalog ◆ Classic regional and community cookbooks. 816-322-2122. www.cookbookstore.com

**The Cookbook Store,** 850 Yonge St., Toronto, Ontario, Canada M4W 2H1: Free information ◆ Cookbooks for professionals and the home chef. 800-268-6018. www.cook-book.com

**Copper Coyote Beads Ltd.,** 9430 E. Golf Links, #286, Tucson, AZ 85730: Catalog $2 ◆ Japanese seed beads, Czech pressed glass beads, beading supplies, and how-to books on bead crafting. 520-722-8440. www.coppercoyote.com

**The Cotton Patch,** 3405 Hall Ln., Lafayette, CA 94549: Catalog $8 ($5 refundable) ◆ Quilting books. 800-835-4418. CottonPa@aol.com

**Cowboy Shopper,** P.O. Box 6459, Santa Fe, NM 87502: Free catalog with SASE ◆ Source for cowboy books, gear, events, and organizations. 505-995-0102. zon@nets.com

**CQ Communications Inc.,** 76 N. Broadway, Hicksville, NY 11801: Free information ◆ Books and videos for radio amateurs. 800-853-9797. members.aol.com/cqmagazine

**Craig Manuscripts,** P.O. Box 3909, Newport, RI 02840: Free catalog ◆ Original colonial manuscripts from 18th-century America. 401-841-8478.

**John S. Craig,** P.O. Box 1637, Torrington, CT 06790: Free information ◆ Hard-to-find instruction books for photography equipment. Also other photographic literature. 860-496-9791. john@craigcamera.com

**Creative Homeowner Press,** 24 Park Way, Upper Saddle River, NJ 07458: Free information ◆ How-to books on home improvement and repair. 800-631-7795.

**Creative Stitches,** P.O. Box 89, Bountiful, UT 84011: Free information ◆ How-to books on machine embroidery, quilting, and other related crafts. 800-748-5144.

**Culinary Arts Ltd.,** P.O. Box 2157, Lake Oswego, OR 97035: Free information ◆ Specialty books on cooking, party giving, wines and liqueurs, and other gourmet topics. 503-639-4549. Cartsltd@aol.com

**Culinary Collections,** P.O. Box 1823, Winter Park, FL 32790: Free catalog ◆ Calendars, cookbooks, and stationery. 407-647-6765. www.netcom.com/~sgridley

**Curriculum Associates,** P.O. Box 2001, North Billerica, MA 01862: Free catalog ◆ Assessment and instruction books for teachers, test-prep/study skills aids, student books and teacher guides, and other educational materials. 800-225-0248; 978-667-8000 (in MA). www.curriculumassociates.com

**Da Capo Press,** 233 Spring St., New York, NY 10013: Free information ◆ Classic military paperbacks. 800-321-0050.

**Dagefore Publishing,** 122 S. 29th St., Lincoln, NE 68510: Free catalog ◆ Books, featuring regional, history, biography, and poetry. 800-216-8794; 402-475-1123 (in NE). www.dageforde.com

**Darrow Production Company,** P.O. Box 1457, El Reno, OK 73036: Free information ◆ Decorative painting books. 405-422-5727.

**The Dartmouth Bookstore,** 33 S. Main St., Hanover, NH 03755: Free catalog ◆ Classic books on philosophy, psychology, history, fiction, poetry, and other subjects. 800-624-8800; 603-643-3616 (in NH). www.dartbook.com

**Charles Davis,** Box 547, Wenham, MA 01984: Free price list ◆ United States, ancient, and British numismatic books, catalogs, and periodicals. 978-468-2933.

**Daw Books Inc.,** 375 Hudson St., New York, NY 10014: Free catalog ◆ Science fiction, fantasy, and horror books. 800-253-6476.

**DBI Books/Krause Publications,** 700 E. State St., Iola, WI 54990: Catalog $2 ◆ Books on guns. 715-445-2214. www.krause.com

**Dealers Choice Books,** P.O. Box 710, Land O'Lakes, FL 34639: Free information ◆ Art reference books. 800-278-2637; 813-996-6599 (in FL). www.art-amer.com

**Cy Decosse Incorporated,** 5900 Green Oak Dr., Minnetonka, MN 55343: Free information ◆ How-to books on cooking, sewing, hunting, and fishing. 800-328-3895.

**Defender Industries Inc.,** 42 Great Neck Rd., Waterford, CT 06385: Free catalog ◆ Clothing, books, life vests, foul weather gear, and marine supplies. 800-435-7180; 860-701-3415 (in CT). defenderus@aol.com

**Deltiologists of America,** P.O. Box 8, Norwoods, PA 19074: Price list $1 ◆ Postcard reference books. 610-486-8572.

**Demos Publications,** 386 Park Ave. South, New York, NY 10016: Free catalog ◆ Health resources for people with disabilities and chronic disease. 800-532-8663; 212-683-0072 (in NY).

**DeRus Fine Art,** 9100 Artesia Blvd., Bellflower, CA 90706: Free list ◆ Art from the 19th and early 20th century. Also fine art books. 310-920-1312.

**Design Originals,** 2425 Cullen St., Fort Worth, TX 76107: Free information ◆ How-to books on making rag rugs, baskets, wood and fabric items, cross stitching, and other crafts. 800-877-7820.

**Dollmasters,** P.O. Box 2319, Annapolis, MD 21404: Catalog $5 ◆ Nostalgic gifts and collectibles that celebrate yesterday's childhood. Also doll clothing and reference books. 800-966-3655; 410-224-4386 (in MD). www.ea.net/dollmasters

**Dos Tejedoras,** Fiber Arts Publications, P.O. Box 14238, St. Paul, MN 55114: Catalog $2.50 ◆ Books for knitters, weavers, and ethnic textile lovers. 612-646-7445.

**Dover Publications Inc.,** 31 E. 2nd St., Mineola, NY 11501: Free catalog ◆ Books on arts and crafts, business, hobbies, architecture, science, juvenile interests, health, fiction, and other subjects. 516-294-7000.

**Dragon Door Publications,** P.O. Box 4381, St. Paul, MN 55104: Free catalog ◆ Books, videos, audio cassettes, and special reports on health, self-defense, and healing systems. 800-899-5111; 651-645-0517 (in MN). www.dragondoor.com

**Dubrow Antiques,** P.O. Box 128, Bayside, NY 11361: Free information ◆ Out-of-print books on decorative arts and furniture. 718-767-9758.

**Durham's Antiques,** 909 26th St. NW, Washington, DC 20037: Catalog $5 ◆ Jukebox service manuals and other books on coin-operated machines. 202-338-1342.

**Eagle Feather Trading Post,** 168 W. 12th St., Ogden, UT 84404: Catalog $3.50 ◆ Beading and Indian (Native American) craft supplies, beads, and how-to beading and craft books. 801-393-3991.

**East Coast Prospecting & Mining Supplies,** Rt. 3, Box 321-J, Ellijay, GA 30540: Catalog $3 ◆ How-to books on mining and prospecting. 706-276-4433.

**East Earth Trade Winds,** P.O. Box 493151, 1620 E. Cypress Ave., Ste. 8, Redding, CA 96049: Catalog $1 ◆ Books on traditional Chinese herbs. 800-258-6878. www.snowcrest.net/eetw

**Eastman Kodak Company,** Information Center, 343 State St., Rochester, NY 14650: Free information ◆ Photography books. 800-242-2424. www.kodak.com

**The Easton Press,** 47 Richards Ave., P.O. Box 5706, Norwalk, CT 06860: Free catalog ◆ The world's greatest books with leather binding and 22k gold accents. 800-409-4629.

**Effective Learning Systems Inc.,** 5255 Edina Industrial Blvd., Edina, MN 55439: Free catalog ◆ Self-improvement books on weight control, stress relief, health and healing, and inner peace and happiness. 800-966-5683.

**Eisers,** 360 Kiwanis Blvd., P.O. Box 159, Hazleton, PA 18201: Free list of retail sources ◆ Books and manuals on horses. 800-526-6987. www.eisers.com

**Electronic Technology Today Inc.,** P.O. Box 240, Massapequa Park, NY 11762: Free information ◆ Books on electronics.

**Empire Publishing,** P.O. Box 717, Madison, NC 27025: Catalog $3 (refundable) ◆ Comedy, action, western, drama, glamour, and classic TV star photographs and books. 336-427-5850.

**Alan Ende,** 40 Morrow Ave., Scarsdale, NY 10583: List $3 ◆ Ventriloquist figures, accessories, and vintage magic books. 914-961-7066.

**Eureka Gardening Collection,** 5586 Quail Creek Dr., Granite Falls, NC 28630: Free information ◆ Reference books on daylilies, irises, hostas, and other perennials. 704-396-6107. www.users.twave.net/eureka

**The Evergreen Press,** 9 Camino Arroyo Pl., Palm Desert, CA 92260: Free information with long SASE ◆ Adult and children's books, greeting cards, book marks and bookplates, wedding certificates, calendars, ornaments, paper dolls, postcards, and 19th and early 20th-century paper memorabilia. 213-510-1700.

**Fabricators & Manufacturers Association International,** Attn: Books, P.O. Box 626, Rockford, IL 61105: Free information ◆ How-to books on metal-working and fabrication. 815-399-8700. www.fmametalfab.org

**Falcon,** P.O. Box 1718, Helena, MT 59624: Free catalog ◆ Cookbooks and books on western adventure and lifestyles, human interest, and cowboy poetry. 800-582-2665.

**FAMA Books,** P.O. Box 487, Sierra Madre, CA 91025: Free information ◆ Books about tropical fish. 800-523-1736; 818-355-1476 (in CA). rcmcorp@aol.com

**FarPointer Sports Corp.,** P.O. Box 702618, Tulsa, OK 74170: Free information ◆ Books, videos, audio cassettes, and software products covering training, coaching, motivational and skills improvement, and other sports-related subjects. 918-587-6477.

**Farnsworth Military Gallery,** 401 Baltimore St., Gettysburg, PA 17325: Free information ◆ Art prints and new, used, and rare Civil War books. 717-334-8838.

**Fascinating Folds,** P.O. Box 10070, Glendale, AZ 85318: Catalog $1 ◆ Supplies, kits, and how-to books on origami. 800-968-2418. www.fascinating-folds.com

**Fielding Worldwide Inc.,** 308 S. Catalina Ave., Redondo Beach, CA 90277: Free information ◆ Travel guides. 800-FEW-2-GUIDE.

**Firefighters Bookstore,** 18281 Gothard St., #105, Huntington Beach, CA 92648: Free catalog ◆ Books, software, and videos for firefighters. 714-375-4888. www.firebooks.com

**First Corps Books,** 42 Eastgrove Ct., Columbia, SC 29212: Catalog $2 ◆ Out-of-print and new books about the Civil War. 803-781-2709. FirstCorps@msn.com

**Fiskars Corp.,** 7811 W. Stewart Ave., Wausau, WI 54401: Free list of retail sources ◆ Paper crafting project books and supplies. 715-842-2091. www.fiskars.com

**Five Star Publications,** P.O. Box 6698, Chandler, AZ 85246: Free catalog ◆ Books on ethnic foods, cooking, household help, and current issues. 602-940-8182. www.fivestarsupport.com

**The Floating Drydock,** c/o General Delivery, Kresgeville, PA 18333: Free catalog ◆ Plans, kits, books, fittings, other supplies, and accessories about the US Navy from the World War II era. www.usbusiness.com/drydock

**Floyd's Record Shop,** P.O. Drawer 10, Ville Platte, LA 70586: Catalog $1 (refundable) ◆ Cajun and Creole music, books, videos, and T-shirts. 318-363-2184. www.floydsrecords.com

**The Fly Box,** 1293 NE 3rd St., Bend, OR 97701: Catalog $1 ◆ Books on fly fishing. 541-388-3330. flybox@empnet.com

**Fodor's Travel Publications Inc.,** 201 E. 50th St., New York, NY 10022: Free information ◆ Travel books. 212-572-8784. www.fodors.com

**Forsythe Travel Library Inc.,** P.O. Box 2975, Shawnee Mission, KS 66201: Free brochure ◆ Travel books, maps, and other publications. 800-367-7984; 913-384-3440 (in KS). www.raileurope.com

**Forum Publishing Company,** 383 E. Main St., Centerport, NY 11721: Catalog $1 ◆ Business start-up, expansion, diversification, mail order, legal, and other books for business activities. 800-635-7654. www.forum123.com

**Four Winds Trading Company,** 635 S. Broadway, Ste. E, Boulder, CO 80303: Free catalog ◆ Traditional and contemporary Native American music and books. 800-456-5444; 303-499-4484 (in CO). Fourwinds-Trading.com

**W.H. Freeman & Company,** Von Holtzbrinck Publishing Services, 16365 James Madison Hwy., Gordonsville, VA 22942: Free information ◆ Adult and children's books on science, computers, and other areas. 800-330-8477. www.whfreeman.com

**Samuel French Catalog,** 45 W. 25th St., New York, NY 10010: Catalog $4.50 ◆ Scripts for plays and other theatrical productions. 212-206-8990. www.samuelfrench.com

**Samuel French Trade,** 7623 Sunset Blvd., Hollywood, CA 90046: Free catalog ◆ Books about the film industry. 213-876-0570. www.samuelfrench.com

**Fulcrum Publishing,** 350 Indiana St., Ste. 350, Golden, CO 80401: Free catalog ◆ Books on a variety of subjects. 800-992-2908. www.fulcrum-books.com

**Fun Publishing Company,** 3322 Erie Ave., Cincinnati, OH 45208: Free information ◆ Soft toys for children ages 1 to 3, books for children in kindergarten and 1st grade, and ages 2 to 4, 5 to 6, and 7 to 8. Also music items for children age 3 to adults, and special books for teachers. 513-533-3636.

**Gambler's Book Shop,** 630 S. 11th, Las Vegas, NV 89101: Free catalog ◆ Books and computer software on gambling. 800-522-1777. www.gamblersbook.com

**Gateways,** P.O. Box 1706, Oijai, CA 93024: Free catalog ◆ Books on self-improvement, relaxation, health and healing, creativity, stress reduction, and other life-style self-improvement subjects. 800-477-8908. www.gateways411.com

**Paul Gaudette Books,** 2050 E. 17th St., Tucson, AZ 85719: Catalog $2 ◆ Aviation, military, and naval history books. 800-874-3097.

**Robert Gavora Bookseller,** 4514 E. Burnside St., Portland, OR 97215: Free catalog ◆ First edition science fiction, horror, and mystery books. 503-236-1516. rgavora@teleport.com

**Gemstone Press,** P.O. Box 237, Woodstock, VT 05091: Free catalog ◆ Books for the consumer, hobbyist, investor, and retail trade on buying, identifying, selling, and enjoying jewelry and gems. 802-457-4000.

**Genealogical Publishing Company,** 1001 N. Calvert St., Baltimore, MD 21202: Free catalog ◆ Books on genealogy. 800-296-6687. www.genealogical.com

**The General's Books,** Blue & Gray Magazine, 522 Norton Rd., Columbus, OH 43228: Free catalog ◆ Civil War books. 614-870-1861.

**Robert Gentry,** P.O. Box 850, Many, LA 71449: Free list ◆ Country music albums, 78 and 45 rpm records, autographs, movie posters, books and magazines, press kits, and other collectibles. 318-256-2886.

**Getty Trust Publications,** Distribution Center, Dept. TSC8, P.O. Box 49659, Los Angeles, CA 90049: Free catalog ◆ Books on the arts and humanities. 800-223-3431. www.getty.edu/publications

**David Ginn Magic,** 4387 St. Michaels Dr., Lilburn, GA 30247: Catalog $10 ◆ Books, props, and how-to-do magic on videos for magicians and clowns. 770-923-1899.

**Glass Crafters,** 398 Interstate Ct., Sarasota, FL 34240: Catalog $3 ◆ Stained glass crafting books. 800-422-4552. www.glasscrafters.com

**The Globe Corner Bookstore,** 28 Church St., Cambridge, MA 02138: Free information ◆ Travel books and maps for the traveler. 800-358-6013. info@gcb.com

**Globe Pequot Press,** P.O. Box 833, 6 Business Park Rd., Old Saybrook, CT 06475: Free catalog ◆ Travel guides, cookbooks, outdoor recreation, how-to, and nature books. 800-243-0495. www.globe-pequot.com

**Gluten-Free Pantry,** P.O. Box 840, Glastonbury, CT 06033: Free information ◆ Gluten-free cookbooks. 800-291-8386. www.glutenfree.com

**Golden West Publishers,** 4113 N. Longview, Phoenix, AZ 85024: Free catalog ◆ Cookbooks and books on western adventure and lifestyles, western humor, and human interest. 800-658-5830.

**GORP,** P.O. Box 3016, Everett, WA 98206: Free catalog ◆ Over 3000 maps, guidebooks, handbooks, videos, CD-ROMs, and more on the outdoors. 888-994-4677. www.gorp.com

**Gotham Book Mart,** 41 W. 47th St., New York, NY 10036: Free information ◆ Postcard reference books. 212-719-4448.

**Orville J. Grady,** 6602 Military Ave., Omaha, NE 68104: Free information ◆ New and out-of-print numismatic literature. 800-295-4846; 402-558-6782 (in NE).

**Graywolf Press,** 2402 University Ave., Ste. 203, St. Paul, MN 55114: Free catalog ◆ New books and reprints of poetry, fiction, and nonfiction. 612-641-0077. www.graywolfpress.org

**Great Chefs Television,** P.O. Box 56757, New Orleans, LA 70156: Free information ◆ Great Chef cookbooks. 800-321-1499. www.greatchefs.com

**Great Christian Books,** 229 S. Bridge St., P.O. Box 8000, Elkton, MD 21922: Free catalog ◆ Bibles, commentaries, language tools, cookbooks, home schooling books, bible study software, and bible video games. 800-775-5422. www.GreatChristianBooks.com

**Green Gate Books,** P.O. Box 989, Lima, OH 45802: Free catalog ◆ Books on antiques and collectibles. 800-228-3816; 419-222-3816 (in OH). www.greengatebooks.com

**Green Horizons,** 145 Scenic Hill Rd., Kerrville, TX 78028: Free brochure ◆ Books on wildflowers, herbs, grasses, fruits and vegetables, trees, shrubs, and woody vines. 210-257-5141.

**Green House Books,** Jeanne Mance, 4068 St. Laurent, P.O. Box 42051, Montreal, Quebec City, Canada H2W 2T3: Free catalog ◆ Books for children and teens. 800-834-8608.

**Greystone's History & Emporium Gallery,** 461 Baltimore St., Gettysburg, PA 17325: Free brochure ◆ Movies, military documentaries, miniatures, Civil War books, and other collectibles. 717-338-0631. WWW.GREYSTONEONLINE.com

**Gulf Publishing Company,** Book Division, P.O. Box 2608, Houston, TX 77252: Free information ◆ Camping guides, cookbooks, and books on travel, snorkeling, gardening, business, and other subjects. 713-520-4444.

**H & R Magic Books,** 3702 Cyril Dr., Humble, TX 77396: Catalog $3 ◆ Old and new magic books and magazines. 281-454-7219.

**Hammond Incorporated,** 515 Valley St., Maplewood, NJ 07040: Free information ◆ Maps and prints, travel guides, road atlases, adult and juvenile references, and books on business. 201-763-6000. www.hammondmap.com

**The Hannum Company,** Box 1505, Ardmore, OK 73402: Free information ◆ Used, rare, and out-of-print books on prospecting, localities, minerals, gems, fossils, geology, mining, archeology, and meteorites. 580-223-4826. www.hannum.cc

**Hard-to-Find Needlework Books,** 96 Roundwood Rd., Newton, MA 02164: Catalog $1 ◆ Search services for hard-to-find and rare books on needle crafts. 617-969-0942. hardtofind@needleworkbooks.com

**HarperCollins,** 10 E. 53rd St., New York, NY 10022: Free catalog ◆ Books for preschool children through young adult, fiction and nonfiction for adults, cookbooks, business titles, religion, and other subjects. 212-207-7000. www.harpercollins.com

**The Haworth Press Inc.,** 10 Alice St., Binghamton, NY 13904: Free catalog ◆ Books and journals on psychotherapy and mental health. 800-342-9678. www.haworthpressinc.com

**Hays Electronics,** P.O. Box 26848, Prescott Valley, AZ 86312: Free catalog ◆ Metal detectors, maps, and books on prospecting, mining, and relic hunting. 800-699-2624.

**Hazelden Foundation,** 15251 Pleasant Valley Rd., P.O. Box 176, Center City, MN 55012: Free catalog ◆ Psychology, self-help, chemical dependency, gambling addiction, self-esteem, compulsive eating disorders, and spirituality books. 800-328-9000. www.hazelden.org

**Heimburger House Publishing Company,** 7236 W. Madison St., Forest Park, IL 60130: Catalog $1 ◆ Books on model and prototype railroads, cooking, history, humor, and Walt Disney. 708-366-1973.

**Hemmings Bookshelf,** P.O. Box 76-S14945, Bennington, VT 05201: Free information ◆ Automotive books and specialty gifts for car buffs. 800-227-4373. www.hemmings.com

**Herb Products Company,** P.O. Box 898, 11012 Magnolia Blvd., North Hollywood, CA 91603: Free price list ◆ Books on herbs and their uses. 818-761-0351. www.herbproducts.com

**The Herb Quarterly,** Box 689, San Anselmo, CA 94979: Free information ◆ Books on herbs. 800-371-HERB.

**Heritage Books Inc.,** 1540 E. Pointer Ridge Place, Ste. 207, Bowie, MD 20716: Free catalog ◆ Books on history, genealogy, and Early American life. 301-390-7709. www.heritagebooks.com

**Heritage Map Museum,** P.O. Box 412, Lititz, PA 17543: Free information ◆ Antique maps and books. 800-432-8183; 717-626-5002 (in PA). www.carto.com

**Herzinger & Company,** 2821 NE 65th Ave., Vancouver, WA 98661: Free catalog ◆ Books on antiques, collectibles, and art. 800-428-2670.

**Hey Enterprises,** 2100 Hwy. 35, Old Mill Plaza, Sea Girt, NJ 08750: Free catalog ◆ Postcards, rare books, and other collectibles. 908-974-8855.

**Higginson Books,** 14 Derby Square, Salem, MA 01970: Catalog $3 ◆ Genealogies, how-to guides, and local histories. 978-745-7170.

**High-Grade Publications,** P.O. Box 20904, Cheyenne, WY 82003: Catalog $1 ◆ Books and maps on treasure hunting, gold locations, lost mines, ghost towns, gems and minerals, and geology. 307-634-8835.

**High-Lonesome Books,** P.O. Box 878, Silver City, NM 88062: Free catalog ◆ New, used, rare, and out-of-print books on the outdoors, homesteading, hunting, fishing, and other subjects. 505-388-3763.

**High View Publications,** P.O. Box 51967, Pacific Grove, CA 93950: Free catalog ◆ Chinese martial arts books and videos. 408-622-0789.

**Highsmith Multicultural Bookstore,** P.O. Box 800, Fort Atkinson, WI 53538: Free information ◆ Multi-cultural books about Native and African-Americans. 800-558-2110.

**HighText Publications Inc.,** P.O. Box 1489, Solana Beach, CA 92075: Free catalog ◆ Books about radios, scanners, antennas, and shortwave listening. 619-793-4141. www.hightext-publications.com

**Highwood Bookshop,** 10381 E. Shady Ln., Suttons Bay, MI 49682: Free catalog with two 1st class stamps (specify interest) ◆ Back issues of outdoor activities, fishing, and hunting publications, from the late 1800s to the present. 616-271-3898. www.traversecity.com/highwood

**Himalayan Institute Press,** RR 1, Box 405, Honesdale, PA 18431: Free information ◆ Books and audio tapes on physical, psychological health and well-being, spiritual growth though meditation, and other yoga practices. 800-822-4547. www.himalayaninstitute.org

**Historic Aviation,** 1401 Kings Wood Rd., Eagan, MN 55122: Free catalog ◆ History, biography, classic, humor, and aviation books and videos. 800-225-5575.

**Hobby House Press Inc.,** 1 Corporate Dr., Grantsville, MD 21536: Free information ◆ Books on dolls, teddy bears, postcards, costumes, and crafts. 800-554-1447. hobbyhouse@aol.com

**Peter M. Holmes Books,** 3112 Fremont Ave. South, Minneapolis, MN 55408: Catalog $2 ◆ Rare and out-of-print books. 612-827-0461.

**Home Buyer Publications Inc.,** 4451 Brookfield Corporate Dr., Ste. 101, P.O. Box 220039, Chantilly, VA 22022: Free information ◆ Books on how to build log homes. 800-826-3893; 703-222-9411 (in VA). www.timberframehomes.com

**Home Planners Inc.,** 3275 W. Ina Rd., Ste. 110, Tucson, AZ 85741: Catalog $2 ◆ Books on home planning, architectural design, landscaping, and remodeling. 800-848-2550. www.homeplanners.com

**The Home Shop Machinist Magazine,** P.O. Box 629, Traverse City, MI 49685: Free information ◆ Home shop how-to books on metalworking. 800-447-7367.

**Honda Martial Arts Supply,** 120 W. 30th St., New York, NY 10001: Free catalog ◆ Books about martial arts. 212-620-4050. www.hondamartialarts.com

**Horse Prints,** 6300 Sparta-Conesus Town Line Rd., Conesus, NY 14435: Free brochure ◆ How-to and books about horses. 800-276-9026.

**Horticulture Book Department,** Customer Service Center, 1476 Massachusetts Ave., North Adams, MA 01247: Free information ◆ Gardening books. 800-704-6781.

**The House of Musical Traditions,** 7040 Carroll Ave., Takoma Park, MD 20912; Free catalog ◆ Folk music books and recordings. 800-540-3794; 301-270-9090 (in metro DC area). www.hmtrad.com/index.html

**House of White Birches,** 306 E. Parr Rd., Berne, IN 46711: Free catalog ◆ Books on crafts and hobbies.

**How-To-Do-It Book Shop,** 1608 Sansom St., Philadelphia, PA 19103: Free catalog ◆ Hundreds of books on how to do hundreds of different things. 888-836-4822; 215-563-1516 (in PA). www.how2doit.net

**Howell Book House Inc.,** MacMillan Publishing Company, Attention: Order Dept., 201 W. 103rd St., Indianapolis, IN 46290: Free catalog ◆ Books about dogs, cats, birds, horses, and other animals. 800-428-5331. www.superlibrary.com

**Hudson Hills Press,** 230 5th Ave., Ste. 1308, New York, NY 10001: Free information ◆ Books on photography and fine art. 212-889-3090.

**Hughes Books,** P.O. Box 840237, New Orleans, LA 70184: Catalog $3 (3 issues) ◆ Old and rare Civil War books. 504-948-2427. HUGHESBOOK@AOL.com

**Human Kinetics,** P.O. Box 5076, Champaign, IL 61825: Free information ◆ Sport and physical fitness books. 800-747-4457. www.humankinetics.com

**Humanities Press International Inc.,** 165 1st Ave., Atlantic Highlands, NJ 07716: Free catalog ◆ Books that focus on radical social and political theory, European history, and the history and philosophy of science. 732-872-1441. www.humanitiespress.com

**Hunter Publishing Inc.,** 130 Campus Dr., Edison, NJ 08818: Free information ◆ Travel guides, language cassette courses, and maps. 800-255-0343. www.hunterpublishing.com

**I.D.S.A. Books,** P.O. Box 1457, Piqua, OH 45356: Free list ◆ Firearms books. 513-773-4203.

**ICS Books Inc.,** 1370 E. 86th Pl., Merrillville, IN 46410: Free list ◆ Books on outdoor lifestyles, narratives, how-to, medical care, humor, and other activities. 800-541-7323. www.icsbooks.com

**IDG Books Worldwide Inc.,** 7260 Shadeland Station, Ste. 100, Indianapolis, IN 46256: Free information ◆ Computer books. 800-762-2974. www.idgbooks.com

**Imagiknit Ltd.,** 2586 Yonge St., Toronto, Ontario, Canada M4P 2J3: Catalog $4.50 ◆ Yarns, how-to books on knitting, and kits. 800-318-9426.

**Impact Publishers,** P.O. Box 910, San Luis Obispo, CA 93406: Free catalog ◆ Self-help books. 805-543-5911. www.impactpublishers.com

**Independent Publishers Group,** 814 N. Franklin St., Chicago, IL 60610: Free catalog ◆ Adult, young adult, and children's books. 800-888-4741. www.ipgbook.com

**Indiana Berry & Plant Company,** 5218 W. 500 South, Huntingburg, IN 47542: Free catalog ◆ Books on how-to-cultivate berry plants. 800-295-2226; 812-683-3055 (in IN).

**Inner Traditions International,** One Park St., Rochester, VT 05767: Free catalog ◆ Books on alternative health, aromatherapy, spirituality, and metaphysics. 802-767-3174. www.gotoit.com

**Intel Corp.,** 2200 Mission College Blvd., Santa Clara, CA 95052: Free catalog ◆ Computer books. 408-765-1709. www.intel.com

**International Fabric Collection,** 3445 W. Lake Rd., Erie, PA 16505: Catalog $3 ◆ Quilting and embroidery books and fabrics from Italy, India, Japan, Holland, Africa, and other worldwide sources. 800-462-3891; 814-838-0740 (in PA). www.intfab.com

**International Marine,** Division McGraw Hill, P.O. Box 548, Black Lick, OH 43004: Free catalog ◆ Nautical books. 800-262-4729. www.mcgraw-hill.com

**International Press Publications Inc.,** 90 Nolan Ct., #21, Markham, Ontario, Canada L3R 4L9: Free information ◆ Books on career guidance, general health, history and politics. dictionaries, travel, business, sports, Internet, arts and entertainment, and more. 905-946-9588. www.interlog.com/~ipp

**International Universities Press Inc.,** 59 Boston Post Rd., Box 1524, Madison, CT 06443: Free catalog ◆ Books on mental health for professionals. 800-835-3487.

**Interweave Press,** 201 E. 4th St., Loveland, CO 80537: Free catalog ◆ Books on basket-making, weaving and spinning, sweater designing, hand and machine knitting, rug-weaving, tapestry-making, fabric-designing and sewing, and spinning wheels. 800-645-3675. www.interweave.com

**Iranbooks Inc.,** 8014 Old Georgetown Rd., Bethesda, MD 20814: Catalog $3 ◆ Persian and English books about Iran. 301-718-8188. www.iranbooks.com

**Irish American Book Company,** 6309 Monarch Park Pl., Niwot, CO 80503: Free catalog ◆ Books about Ireland and the Irish people. 800-452-7113; 303-530-1352 (in CO).

**Janus Books,** P.O. Box 40787, Tucson, AZ 85717: Free catalog ◆ Fine and first editions of detective, mystery, and suspense fiction. 800-986-1165; 520-881-8192 (in AZ). www.janusbooks.com

**Jessica's Biscuit,** The Cookook People, P.O. Box 301, Newtonville, MA 02160: Free catalog ◆ Cookbooks. 800-878-4254. www.jessicas.com

**Johns Hopkins University Press,** 2715 N. Charles St., Baltimore, MD 21218: Free catalog ◆ Books on a variety of subjects. 800-537-5487. www.jhu.edu/~jhupress

**Jope's Bonsai Nursery,** P.O. Box 594, Wenham, MA 01984: Catalog $2 ◆ Books on bonsai. 978-468-2249.

**Kamper's Kettle,** 2165 Bruneau Dr., Boise, ID 83709: Free catalog ◆ Outdoor cooking tables and accessories, ovens, cast-iron cookware, Dutch ovens, accessories, and books and videos on cooking with Dutch ovens. 800-860-1100; 208-377-0344 (in ID). Kampers@RMC.NET

**KDM Books,** P.O. Box 2122, Ventura, CA 93002: Free list ◆ Books for doll and teddy bear collectors.

**Kedco Homebrew & Wine Supply,** 564 Smith St., Farmingdale, NY 11735: Free brochure ◆ Wine accessories, beer and wine making supplies, books and videos, and wine racks, cellars and cabinets. 800-654-9988; 516-454-7800 (in NY).

**Keepsake Quilting,** Rt. 25B, P.O. Box 1618, Centre Harbor, NH 03226: Free catalog ◆ Quilting books and accessories, patterns, notions, fabrics, scrap bags, and batting. 800-865-9458. www.keepsakequilting.com

**Kennel Vet Corp.,** P.O. Box 523, Laurel, DE 19956: Catalog $1 (refundable) ◆ Books about dogs, cats, birds, and horses. 800-782-0627. www.KennelVet.com

**Paul E. Kisselburg,** 665 Wildwood, Stillwater, MN 55082: Free catalog ◆ Military history World War II books. 612-439-1884.

**Knife World Books,** P.O. Box 3395, Knoxville, TN 37927: Free information ◆ Books on how-to and all-about knives. 800-828-7751. www.knifeworld.com

**Knollwood Books,** P.O. Box 197, Oregon, WI 53575: Free catalog ◆ Rare, hard-to-find, and out-of-print books on astronomy, meteorology, space exploration, rocketry, and related fields. 608-835-8861. www.knollwoodbooks.com

**Kodansha America Inc.,** 114 5th Ave., New York, NY 10011: Free information ◆ Books in English from and about Japan. 800-788-6262. www.kodansha.co.jp/index_e.html

**George Frederick Kolbe,** P.O. Drawer 3100, Crestline, CA 92325: Free information ◆ Rare titles and other books on virtually any numismatic topic. 909-338-6527.

**Krause Publications,** 700 E. State St., Iola, WI 54990: Catalog $2 ◆ Books on hobbies, records, collectibles, and the outdoors. 800-258-0929. www.krause.com

**Krieger Publishing Company,** 1725 Krieger Ln., Malabar, FL 32950: Free information ◆ Books on reptiles and other exotic pets. 407-724-9542. info@krieger-pub.com

**La Rock's Fun & Magic Outlet,** 3847 Rosehaven Dr., Charlotte, NC 28205: Catalog $3 ◆ Clown and balloon how-to books, balloons, balloon sculpture kits, juggling supplies, and magic equipment. 704-563-9300. larocks1@aol.com

**Lacis,** 3163 Adeline St., Berkeley, CA 94703: Catalog $5 ◆ Books on fabrics, costumes, needle crafts, and beading. 510-843-7178. www.lacis.com

**Lancer Militaria,** P.O. Box 886, Mt. Ida, AR 71957: Catalog $2 ◆ Military books. 870-867-2232. www.warbooks.com

**Langenscheidt Publishers,** 46-35 54th Rd., Maspeth, NY 11378: Free catalog ◆ Foreign language dictionaries, skills building texts, children's books, language phrase cards, and electronic translators. 718-784-0055.

**Lapidary Journal Book & Video Sellers,** 60 Chestnut Ave., Devon, PA 19333: Free information ◆ Lapidary and jewelry-making books. 800-676-4367. www.lapidaryjournal.com

**Lark Books,** P.O. Box 2580, Asheville, NC 28802: Free catalog ◆ Kits, books on arts and crafts, and gifts. 800-284-3388. www.larkbooks.com

**Lark in the Morning,** P.O. Box 1176, Mendocino, CA 95460: Free catalog ◆ Hard-to-find musical instruments, books about music, CDs, cassettes, and videos. 707-964-5569. larkinam@larkinam.com

**The Las Vegas Insider,** P.O. Box 1185, Chino Valley, AZ 86323: Free information ◆ How-to books on Las Vegas casinos. 520-636-1649.

**Leisure Arts,** Consumer Service, P.O. Box 5595, Little Rock, AR 72215: Catalog $2 ◆ Cookbooks. 501-771-1006.

**Alan Levine Movie & Book Collectibles,** P.O. Box 1577, Bloomfield, NJ 07003: Catalog $5 ◆ Books on old-time movie posters, lobby cards, and old radio, television, and movie magazines. 973-743-5288.

**Light Impressions,** 439 Monroe Ave., P.O. Box 940, Rochester, NY 14607: Free catalog ◆ Books on photography and supplies for archival storage of negatives and prints. 800-828-6216. www.lightimpressionsdirect.com

**Linden Publishing Company Inc.,** 336 W. Bedford, Ste. 107, Fresno, CA 93711: Free catalog ◆ New and out-of-print books and videos on woodworking. 800-345-4447. www.lindenpub.com

**Lindsay Publications Inc.,** P.O. Box 538, Bradley, IL 60915: Catalog $1 ◆ Metal working books. 815-935-5353. www.lindsaybks.com

**Live Steam Magazine,** P.O. Box 629, Traverse City, MI 49685: Free information ◆ Books on machine shop practice and live steam train models. 800-447-7367. www.largescale.com

**Log Homes Books,** 20 Academy St., Norwalk, CT 06850: Free information ◆ Books on log home building. 800-435-4032.

**Lonely Planet Publications,** 155 Filbert St., Ste. 251, Oakland, CA 94607: Free booklist ◆ Guidebooks for worldwide destinations. 800-275-8555.

**Louisiana State University Press,** 102 French House, Baton Rouge, LA 70893: Free catalog ◆ Books about the Civil War and scholarly subjects. 504-388-6666.

**Lucidity Institute,** 2555 Park Blvd., Ste 2, Palo Alto, CA 94306: Free catalog ◆ Yoga books, tapes, and biofeedback devices. 800-465-8243. www.lucidity.com

**J.K. Lutherie Guitars,** 11115 Sand Run, Harrison, OH 45030: Free catalog ◆ Vintage guitar parts, new and vintage accessories, catalogs and other literature, guitar magazines, and out-of-print guitar books. 800-344-8880; 513-353-3320 (in OH). www.jklutherie.com

**MacMillan Computer Publishing,** Attention Order Dept., 201 W. 103rd St., Indianapolis, IN 46290: Free catalog ◆ Computer books. 800-428-5331. www.superlibrary.com

**MacMillan Publishing Company,** Attention Order Dept., 201 W. 103rd St., Indianapolis, IN 46290: Free catalog ◆ Fiction and nonfiction books for children and adults. 800-428-5331. www.superlibrary.com

**The Mail Order Catalog on Healthy Cooking,** Box 180, Summertown, TN 38483: Free catalog ◆ Books on vegetarian cooking, other health food cookbooks, nutrition, health care, Native American traditions, animal issues, and other subjects. 800-695-2241; 615-964-2241 (in TN). www.healthy-eating.com

**Mainly Shades,** One Hundred Gray Rd., Falmouth, ME 04105: Catalog $3 ◆ Lampshade crafting supplies and how-to books. 800-624-6359. www.maineguide.com/maineshade

**Mallery Press,** 4206 Sheraton Dr., Flint, MI 48532: Free information ◆ How-to quilt-making books. 800-A-STITCH.

**Man at Arms Bookshelf,** P.O. Box 460, Lincoln, RI 02865: Free information ◆ Books on antique and other famous guns. Includes the Civil War, other major military conflicts, and infantry weapons. 800-999-4697.

**Manderley Romance Books,** P.O. Box 8515, Ukiah, CA 95482: Free catalog ◆ Books for women. 800-301-7546. www.manderleybooks.com

**Manny's Woodworkers Place,** 555 S. Broadway, Lexington, KY 40508: Free information ◆ Woodworking books and videos. 606-255-8444. www.mannyswoodbooks.com

**The Maritime Store,** 2905 Hyde St. Pier, San Francisco, CA 94109: Free catalog ◆ Maritime maps, greeting cards, boat models, children's and maritime books, and gifts. 415-775-BOOK.

**Martingale & Company,** P.O. Box 118, Bothell, WA 98041: Free catalog ◆ Books on quilts and crafts. 800-426-3126. www.patchwork.com

**Maryland Reptile Farm,** 109 W. Cherry Hill Rd., Reistertown, MD 21136: Free catalog with long SASE ◆ Herps supplies and books on reptiles. 410-526-4184.

**Bill Mason Books,** 104 N. 7th St., Morehead City, NC 28557: Free catalog ◆ Rare, new, and used books. Also prints and Civil War, Western Americana, and other military and nautical collectibles. 919-247-6161. bmasonbks@collectorsnet.com

**Mass-C Enterprises,** 3102 Barus St., Valdese, NC 28690: Free catalog ◆ Books on marketing, public relations, advertising, and other business topics for small business owners. 828-874-0521.

**McLellan's Automotive History,** 9111 Longstaff Dr., Houston, TX 77031: Free catalog ◆ Sales literature, out-of-print books, dealer albums and books, magazines and programs, and memorabilia. 713-772-3285.

**Mel Bay Publications Inc.,** 4 Industrial Dr., Pacific, MO 63069: Free catalog ◆ How-to-play and other music books. 800-8-MELBAY.

**Merriam-Webster Inc.,** P.O. Box 281, Springfield, MA 01102: Free brochure ◆ Dictionaries and reference books. 800-201-5029. www.m-w.com

**Meyerbooks Publisher,** P.O. Box 427, Glenwood, IL 60425: Catalog 50¢ ◆ Books on herbs, herbal recipes. health, and Americana. 708-757-4950.

**Microsoft Press,** One Microsoft Way, Redmond, WA 98052: Free information ◆ Books on computers. 800-227-4679. www.microsoft.com

**The Midas Touch,** 15 Thorncliffe Park Dr., Ste. 412, Toronto, Ontario, Canada M4H 1H6: Catalog $6 ◆ Metal detectors and accessories, prospecting tools, water hunting equipment, and books on treasure hunting. 416-467-6016.

**The Military Bookman,** 29 E. 93rd St., New York, NY 10128: Free information with long SASE ◆ Military, naval, and aviation out-of-print and rare books. 212-348-1280. www.militarybookman.com

**The Mind's Eye,** P.O. Box 6547, Chelmsford, MA 01824: Free catalog ◆ Children's favorites and classics, military intrigue, mystery, horror, science fiction, adventure, drama, history, comedy, poetry, and self-improvement books, audio cassettes, and CD-ROMs. 800-949-3333.

**Minnesota Clay USA,** 8001 Grand Ave. South, Bloomington, MN 55420: Free catalog ◆ Books on ceramics and pottery crafts. 800-252-9872; 612-884-9101 (in MN). mnclayus@mn.com

**Miss Roben's,** P.O. Box 1434, Frederick, MD 21702: Free catalog ◆ Gluten and wheat-free mixes for breads, cakes, cookies, and pizza and pie crusts. Also baking supplies for cooking from scratch and books. 800-891-0083. www.jagunet.com/~msrobens

**The MIT Press,** 5 Cambridge Center, Cambridge, MA 02142: Free catalog ◆ Books on a variety of subjects. 800-356-0343. www.mitpress.mit.edu/staff.html

**Morningside Bookshop,** 260 Oak St., Dayton, OH 45401: Catalog $4 ◆ Reprints and original Civil War books. 800-648-9710. www.morningsidebooks.com

**Motorbooks International,** P.O. Box 1, Osceola, WI 54020: Free catalog ◆ Automotive, motorcycle, aviation, and other books. 800-826-6600. www.motorbooks.com

**The Mt. Sterling Rebel,** P.O. Box 481, Mt. Sterling, KY 40353: Catalog 45 (annual subscription)* Rare, used, and out-of-print Civil War books. 606-498-5821.

**Mountain Heritage Crafters,** 601 Quail Dr., Bluefield, VA 24605: Free catalog ◆ Carving tools and how-to books. 540-322-5921. www.mhc-online.com

**Mountain Press Publishing Company,** P.O. Box 2399, Missoula, MT 59806: Free catalog ◆ Geology books, outdoor guides, and history titles. 800-234-5308. www.mtnpress.com

**The Mountaineers Books,** 300 3rd Ave. West, Seattle, WA 98119: Free information ◆ Books about the outdoors, hiking, bicycling, skiing, mountaineering, nature, and conservation. 800-284-8554. clubmail@mountaineers.org

**Murrays Catamarans,** P.O. Box 490, Carpinteria, CA 93014: Free list of retail sources ◆ Catamarans, factory parts, books, and videos. 800-788-8964. www.murrays.com

**Music Books Plus,** 23 Hannover Dr., #7, St. Catharines, Ontario, Canada L2W 2A3: Free catalog ◆ Books, instructional videos, audio cassettes, CD-ROMs, computer software, and other music-related items. 800-265-8481. www.musicbooksplus.com

**Mysteries by Mail,** P.O. Box 8515, Ukiah, CA 95482: Free catalog ◆ Mystery books. 800-722-0726. www.mysteriesbymail.com

**National Fire Protection Association,** 1 Batterymarch Park, P.O. Box 9101, Quincy, MA 02269: Free catalog ◆ Fire safety books, products, and services from the National Fire Protection Association. 800-344-3555. www.nfpa.org

**National Geographic Society,** 1145 17th St. NW, Washington, DC 20036: Free catalog ◆ Books on geography, history, archeology, science, and industry. 800-225-5647. www.nationalgeographic.com/main.html

**National Wildlife Federation,** P.O. Box 9004, Winchester, VA 22604: Free catalog ◆ Books, holiday cards, and gifts. 800-477-5560. www.nwf.org

**National Yiddish Book Center,** 48 Woodbridge St., South Hadley, MA 01075: Free information ◆ Books on Judaic subjects. 413-535-1303.

**The Nautical Book Catalog,** P.O. Box F, Ringoes, NJ 08551: Free catalog ◆ Marine education and technical books. 800-297-7617. www.boatbooks.com

**Naval Institute Press,** Customer Service, 2062 Generals Hwy., Annapolis, MD 21401: Free catalog ◆ Books on navigation, seamanship, naval history, ships, and aircraft. 800-233-8764. www.usni.org

**John Neal, Bookseller,** 1833 Spring Garden St., Greensboro, NC 27403: Free information ◆ Calligraphy and marbling supplies, books on arts and crafts, and bookbinding services. 800-369-9598; 336-272-6139 (in NC). www.JohnNealBooks.com

**The Needlework Attic,** 4706 Bethesda Ave., Bethesda, MD 20814: Free information ◆ How-to books on knitting and yarns. 301-652-8688.

**New England Cheesemaking Supply Company,** P.O. Box 85, Ashfield, MA 01330: Catalog $1 ◆ Supplies and how-to books for making and using cheese, butter, yogurt, and buttermilk. 413-628-3808. www.cheesemaking.com

**New England Wildflower Society,** 180 Hemenway Rd., Framingham, MA 01701: Free catalog with long SASE and two 1st class stamps ◆ Books on wildflowers and their propagation. 508-877-7630.

**New Harbinger Publications,** 5674 Shattuck Ave., Oakland, CA 94609: Free catalog ◆ Self-help psychology books and other health publications. 800-748-6273. www.newharbinger.com

**New Moon Gardening Books,** P.O. Box 1027, Corvallis, OR 97339: Free list ◆ Indoor and outdoor gardening books. 800-888-6785.

**The New Orleans School of Cooking and Louisiana General Store,** The Jackson Brewery, 620 Decatur St., New Orleans, LA 70130: Free catalog ◆ New Orleans specialties and cookbooks. 800-237-4841. www.nosoc.com

**New Wireless Pioneers,** Jim & Felicia Kreuzer, P.O. Box 398, Elma, NY 14059: Free information ◆ Books, magazines, and other literature on antique radios. 716-681-3186.

**NightinGale Resources, Books for Cooks,** P.O. Box 322, Cold Spring, NY 10516: Catalog $3 ◆ Out-of-print, rare, and current cookbooks. 914-753-5383.

**Nolo Press,** 950 Parker St., Berkeley, CA 94710: Free catalog ◆ Self-help law books and computer software. 800-992-6656. www.nolo.com

**The Noontide Press,** P.O. Box 2719, Newport Beach, CA 92659: Free catalog ◆ Books, audiotapes, and videos on social, political, economic, and historical taboos of the modern age. 714-631-1490.

**The Norman Rockwell Museum,** P.O. Box 308, Stockbridge, MA 01262: Free catalog ◆ Prints, books about Norman Rockwell, and reproductions of artworks by Americas's favorite illustrator. 800-742-9450. www.nrm.org

**North Light Books,** 1507 Dana Ave., Cincinnati, OH 45207: Free information ◆ Art and graphic design books. 800-289-0963.

**Northland Publishing,** P.O. Box 1389, Flagstaff, AZ 86002: Free catalog ◆ Cookbooks and books on western adventure and lifestyles, general equine subjects, and cowboy poetry. 800-346-3257; 520-774-5251 (in AZ). www.northlandpub.com

**NorthStar L.L.C.,** 119 Minnis Circle, Milpitas, CA 95035: Free information ◆ Self-development, self-help, positive thibking, and other instructional and motivational audio recordings, videos, books, and more. 800-565-8713. www.gonorthstar.com

**Numismatic Arts of Santa Fe,** P.O. Box 9712, Santa Fe, NM 87504: Catalog $5 ◆ Antiquarian and out-of-print numismatic and philatelic books in all languages. 505-982-8792.

**Nurture,** P.O. Box 1527, Palo Alto, CA 94302: Catalog $2 ◆ Books for parents and others. 800-519-3420; 650-323-9191 (in CA).

**O'Reilly & Associates,** 103 Morris St., Sebastopol, CA 95472: Free information ◆ How-to books on using E-mail and other computer areas. 800-998-9938; 707-829-0515 (in CA). www.oreilly.com/oreilly/contact.html

**Ohara Publications Inc.,** P.O. Box 918, Santa Clarita, CA 91380: Free information ◆ Books on martial arts. 800-423-2874. www.blackbeltmag.com/email

**Old-House Bookshop,** Two Main St., Gloucester, MA 01930: Free catalog ◆ How-to books on home styles, furniture, gardening, and period settings for rooms. 800-931-2931. www.frii.com/~phouka/ren books.html

**Old Tech-Books & Things,** John V. Terrey, P.O. Box 803, Carlisle, MA 01741: Free information (specify subject areas) ◆ Early technical books and collectible apparatus. 978-371-2231.

**Olde Soldier Books Inc.,** 18779 N. Frederick Ave., Gaithersburg, MD 20879: Free information ◆ Civil War books, documents, autographs, prints, manuscripts, photographs, and other Americana. 301-963-2929. Warbooks@erols.com

**Online Press Inc.,** 14320 NE 21st St., Bellevue, WA 98007: Free information ◆ Quick-course computer training books. 206-641-3434.

**The Opera Box,** P.O. Box 994, Teaneck, NJ 07666: Free catalog ◆ Rare books about the opera. 201-833-4176.

**Opera World,** Box 800, Concord, MA 01742: Free catalog ◆ Videos, laser discs, CDs, and books on the opera. 800-99-OPERA. www.operaworld.com

**Osceola Antiques,** 117 Cascade St., P.O. Box 297, Osceola, WI 54020: Free information ◆ Books on antiques and collectibles. 715-294-2886. oscantiq@centuryinter.net

**Out-Door Books East,** 3240 Sylvan Ln., Ellicott City, MD 21043: Free catalog ◆ Vacation guide books for the Eastern United States, from Maine to Florida. 410-465-7213.

**The Overlook Connection,** P.O. Box 526, Woodstock, GA 30188: Catalog $1 ◆ Books, audio cassettes, and magazines on horror, science fiction, fantasy, and mystery. 770-926-1762. www.overlookconnection.com

**Oxfam Publishing,** c/o Humanities Press, 165 1st Ave., Atlantic Highlands, NJ 07716: Free catalog ◆ Books and resource materials to educate the world's poor in their struggle against hunger and exploitation. 908-872-1441. www.humanitiespress.com

**Oxmoor House,** P.O. Box 2463, Birmingham, AL 35201: Free catalog ◆ Books for everyone. 205-877-6000.

**Pachart Publishing House,** P.O. Box 35549, Tucson, AZ 85704: Free catalog ◆ Astronomy and astrophysics books. 520-297-4797.

**Pequeno Press,** P.O. Box 1711, Bisbee, AZ 85603: Catalog $2 ◆ Cast paper and handmade paper-covered basketry vessels. 520-432-5924.

**Peri Lithon Books,** Box 9996, San Diego, CA 92169: Catalog $2 ◆ Out-of-print, rare, and other books about gemstones, minerals, fossils, jewelry, and geology. 619-488-6904.

**Piccadilly Books,** P.O. Box 25203, Colorado Springs, CO 80936: Free catalog ◆ Books on magic, clowning, juggling, puppetry, and balloon art. 719-550-9887.

**Pictorial Histories Publishing Company,** 713 S. 3rd St., Missoula, MT 59801: Free catalog ◆ Military books. 406-549-8488.

**Pieces of History,** P.O. Box 4470, Cave Creek, AZ 85331: Catalog $2 ◆ Military history books. 602-488-1377.

**Pilothouse,** 1600 S. Delaware Ave., Philadelphia, PA 19148: Free information ◆ Nautical books and charts. 800-407-4568.

**The Planetary Society,** 65 N. Catalina Ave., Pasadena, CA 91106: Free brochure ◆ Astronomy books, videos, and slide sets. 626-793-1675.

**Planetree Health Resource Center,** 2040 Webster St., San Francisco, CA 94115: Free catalog ◆ Books and tapes on aging, animal health, and various medical conditions. 415-923-3680.

**Bud Plant Comic Art,** P.O. Box 1689, Grass Valley, CA 95945: Catalog $3 ◆ Graphic novels, comic strip collections, history of comics and comic creators, limited editions, prints, and other comic book-related material. 916-273-2166. www.budplant.com

**Plum Choices Inc.,** 15204-100 Ave., Edmonton, Alberta, Canada T5P 0K4: Free information ◆ Business and motivational books on tape. 403-414-0264.

**Popular Topics Publications,** 741 N. Countyline St., Fostoria, OH 44830: Free brochure ◆ Books on computer fundamentals, Windows, MS-DOS, and networking. 419-435-6868.

**Port In A Storm Bookstore,** Main St., Rt. 102, Mount Desert, ME 04660: Free information ◆ Books and music. 800-694-4114.

**Portrayal Press,** P.O. Box 1190, Andover, NJ 07821: Catalog $3 ◆ Hard-to-find books on 20th-century subjects. 973-579-5781. www.portrayal.com

**The Potters Shop,** 31 Thorpe Rd., Needham Heights, MA 02194: Free catalog ◆ Books on pottery and ceramics. 781-449-7687.

**Pro-Action Sports Inc.,** P.O. Box 26657, Los Angeles, CA 90026: Free information ◆ Books and videos on martial arts. 888-567-7789.

**Pro-Mack South,** 940 W. Apache Trail, Apache Junction, AZ 85220: Catalog $3 ◆ How-to books on metal detecting and prospecting. 800-722-6463.

**Prometheus Books,** 59 John Glenn Dr., Amherst, NY 14228: Free information ◆ Books on astronomy, astrology, and other subjects. 800-421-0351. www.prometheusbooks.com

**Prompt Publications,** Attention: Order Department, 2647 Waterfront Parkway East Dr., Indianapolis, IN 46214: Free catalog ◆ Books on electronics. 800-428-7267. csmgr@in.net

**Pruett Publishing Company,** 2928 Pearl St., Boulder, CO 80301: Free catalog ◆ Books about the history and people of the American West, outdoor adventures, railroads, cooking, and horticulture. 303-449-4919. Books@tatteredcover.com

**Publications International Ltd.,** Customer Service, 7373 N. Cicero Ave., Lincolnwood, IL 60646: Free catalog ◆ Cookbooks and books on automobiles, sports, lifestyles, entertainment, consumer information, crafts and hobbies, and health. 847-676-3502.

**Puett Electronics,** Antique Radio Division, P.O. Box 28572, Dallas, TX 75228: Catalog $5 (refundable with $20 order) ◆ Reprinted antique radio publications, from 1902 to the 1960s. 214-321-0927.

**QUE Corp.,** 135 South Mt. Zion Rd., Lebanon, IN 46052: Free information ◆ Computer books. 800-428-5331. www.superlibrary.com

**The Queen's Shilling,** 14 Loudoun St. SE, Leesburg, VA 22075: Catalog $3 ◆ Autographs and old and rare books on military history. 703-779-4669.

**R & R Books,** 4447 E. Lake Rd., Livonia, NY 14487: Free information ◆ Books on Civil War weapons. 716-346-2577.

**Radio Bookstore,** P.O. Box 209, Rindge, NH 03461: Free catalog ◆ Books about radios and shortwave listening. 800-457-7373. www.radiobooks.com

**Rainbow Gardens Bookshop,** 1444 E. Taylor St., Vista, CA 92084: Catalog $2 ◆ Books on gardening, plants, greenhouse propagation, and related subjects. 760-758-4290. www.cactus-mall.com/rainbow_bookshop

**Rainy Day Books,** P.O. Box 775, Fitzwilliam, NH 03447: Free list ◆ Books on radio and related technologies. 603-585-3448.

**Randall International,** P.O. Box 1656, Orange, CA 92856: Free catalog ◆ Books for decorating professionals. 800-882-8907; 714-771-8488 (in CA). www.randallintl.com

**Random House,** 201 E. 50th St., New York, NY 10022: Free catalog ◆ Calendars, travel guides, books for children and adults, and other publications. 212-572-2120. www.randomhouse.com

**Reader's Digest,** P.O. Box 107, Pleasantville, NY 10571: Free catalog ◆ Books on gardening, crafts and hobbies, travel, science and nature, cooking, health, history, geography, religion, and archeology. 914-241-7445. www.readersdigest.com

**Reel World,** 130 Garth Rd., Ste. 154, Scarsdale, NY 10583: Catalog $3 ◆ Rare books. 914-722-4333.

**Reiter's Scientific & Professional Books,** 2021 K St. NW, Washington, DC 20006: Free catalog ◆ Electronics, architecture, biology, mathematics, medicine and health, communications, and other scientific and professional books. 800-591-7894; 202-223-3327 (in Metro DC area). www.reiters.com

**Research Unlimited,** 210 N. Mary St., Ames, NE 68621: Free catalog ◆ Books about the Civil War, gems, ghost towns, history, maps and mining, Old West, self-help subjects, treasure how-to's, and other topics. 402-721-8588.

**Roberts Rinehart Publishers,** 6309 Monarch Place Park, Niwot, CO 80503: Free information ◆ Books about natural history, Native Americans, and the west. Also videos, CDs, and books about Ireland history and culture. 800-352-1985. www.robertsrinehart.com

**Robinson's Harp Shop,** P.O. Box 161, 33908 Mount Laguna Dr., Mount Laguna, CA 91948: Free catalog ◆ How-to books on harps. 619-473-8556.

**The Rock Barrell,** 13650 Floyd Rd., Dallas, TX 75243: Free catalog ◆ How-to books on jewelry making and design. 972-231-4809.

**Rockbridge Publishing Company,** P.O. Box 351, Berryville, VA 22611: Free information ◆ New books and reprints from other small presses. 800-473-3943. cwpub@visuallink.com

**Rodale Books,** Box 8, Emmaus, PA 18099: Free information ◆ Gardening books. 610-967-5171. www.rodalepress.com

**Mary Roehr Books & Videos,** 500 Saddlerock Circle, Sedona, AZ 86336: Free catalog ◆ How-to books, videos, and supplies on sewing and tailoring. 800-291-6764.

**Ron's Books,** P.O. Box 714, Harrison, NY 10528: Free information ◆ Books and videos on trains. 914-967-7541.

**Ryon's Saddle & Ranch Supplies,** 2601 N. Main, Fort Worth, TX 76106: Free catalog ◆ Books on training horses and general equine subjects. 800-725-7966. www.luskey.com

**Ryukyu Imports Inc.,** 5005 Merriam Dr., Olathe, KS 66203: Free price list ◆ Books on martial arts. 913-782-3920. www.ryukyu.com

**S.A.E. Historical Book Series,** 400 Commonwealth Dr., Warrendale, PA 15096: Free brochure ◆ Books on automotive history. 412-776-4841.

**Howard W. Sams & Company,** Attention: Order Department, 2647 Waterfront Parkway E. Dr., Indianapolis, IN 46214: Free catalog ◆ Books on electronics and technical subjects. 800-428-7267. www.hwsams.com

**Saratoga Soldier Shop & Military Bookstore,** Curtis Industrial Park, Ballston Spa, NY 12020: Catalog $6 ◆ Civil War miniatures and books. 518-885-1497.

**The Scholar's Bookshelf,** 110 Melrich Rd., Cranbury, NJ 08512: Free catalog ◆ Old and new World War II books. 800-817-9993.

**Schoolhouse Press,** 6899 Cary Bluff, Pittsville, WI 54466: Catalog $5 ◆ Knitting books, how-to videos, kits, and knitting tools. 715-884-2799.

**Schoolmasters Science,** 745 State Circle, Box 1941, Ann Arbor, MI 48106: Catalog $2 ◆ Books and interactive CD-ROMs on science and science fair projects. 800-521-2832. www.schoolmasters.com

**Scott Publications,** 30595 Eight Mile, Livonia, MI 48152: Free catalog ◆ Books for the ceramist, china painter, and doll-maker. 800-458-8237; 313-477-6650 (in MI).

**Sharon & Gayle Publications,** 133 W. 10th St., Covington, KY 41011: Catalog $2 (refundable) ◆ How-to books on decorative art and tole painting. Also pattern packets. 606-291-0784.

**Jackie Shaw Studio Inc.,** 733 Peaks St., Bedford, VA 24523: Catalog $2 ◆ Craft books. 540-586-5732. www.jackieshaw.com

**R.L. Shep Publications,** P.O. Box 2706, Fort Bragg, CA 95437: Catalog $2.50 ◆ Books on cloth and related subjects. 707-964-8662. fsbks@mcn.org

**Ship to Shore Inc.,** 10500 Mount Holly Rd., Charlotte, NC 28214: Free brochure ◆ Caribbean-style recipe cookbooks. 704-392-4777.

**Shutterbug Store,** 5211 S. Washington Ave., Titusville, FL 32780: Free information ◆ Books on photography. 800-677-5212. www.shutterbug.net

**Sierra Club Books,** 85 2nd St., 2nd Floor, San Francisco, CA 94105: Free catalog ◆ Books about ecology, natural history, environment, wildlife, outdoor activities, and nature photography. 800-935-1056. www.sierraclub.org/books

**Silvercat Publications,** 4070 Goldfinch St., San Diego, CA 92103: Free brochure ◆ Non-fiction and quality of life books. 619-299-6774.

**Skipjack Press Inc.,** 637 Drexel Ave., Drexel Hill, PA 19026: Free information ◆ Books on blacksmithing. 610-284-7693.

**Sky Publishing Corp.,** 49 Bay State Rd., Cambridge, MA 02138: Free information ◆ Astronomy books, posters, and videos. 800-253-0245. www.skypub.com

**K.B. Slocum Books,** P.O. Box 10998, Austin, TX 78766: Free catalog ◆ Treasure-hunting books and old city, county, state, and military maps. 800-521-4451.

**Small Press Distribution Inc.,** 1341 7th St., Berkeley, CA 94710: Free catalog ◆ Poetry, critical-cultural studies, fiction, and other books. 510-524-1668. spd@spdbookd.org

**Samuel Patrick Smith,** P.O. Box 787, Eustis, FL 32727: Free catalog ◆ How-to books on theatrical marketing, writing letters, entertaining children, performing better on the stage, advertising, and other topics. 800-810-0722. spspub@aol.com

**Soda Creek Press,** P.O. Box 8515, Ukiah, CA 95482: Free catalog ◆ Mysteries, romances, and bargain books. 800-722-0726. www.sodacreekpress.com

**Softpro Software Books,** 112 Mall Rd., Burlington, MA 01803: Free catalog ◆ How-to and teach-yourself books on software. 781-273-2919. books@softpro.com

**Special Needs Project,** 3463 State St., #282, Santa Barbara, CA 93105: Free catalog ◆ Books about disabilities and disability related topics. 800-333-6867. www.specialneeds.com

**Specialty Books Company,** P.O. Box 616, Croton-on-Hudson, NY 10520: Catalog $1 ◆ Books on wine, wine regions, wine and travel, wine and food, and other wine-related subjects. 800-274-4816. Kellgren@aol.com

**Spice Merchant,** P.O. Box 524, Jackson Hole, WY 83001: Free catalog ◆ Books on Oriental cooking. 800-551-5999. www.emall.com/spice

**Sporting Clays Books & Videos,** 5211 S. Washington Ave., Titusville, FL 32780: Free information ◆ Sporting clays, books, and videos. 407-268-5010.

**SportsProducts.com,** P.O. Box 702618, Tulsa, OK 74170: Free information ◆ Sports instructional videos, books, and software for professional and amateur youth coaches and players. 800-926-5892. www.sportsproducts.com

**Sporty's Pilot Shop,** Clermont Airport, Batavia, OH 45103: Free catalog ◆ Aircraft pilot training books. 800-543-8633. www.sportys-catalogs.com

**Springer-Verlag New York,** 175 5th Ave., New York, NY 10010: Free information ◆ Books on medicine and science. 212-460-1500. www.springer-ny.com

**Springhouse Direct,** P.O. Box 10613, Des Moines, IA 50336: Free catalog ◆ Books on nursing and health. 800-666-5597. www.springnet.com

**Stackpole Books,** 5067 Ritter Rd., Mechanicsburg, PA 17055: Free catalog ◆ Outdoor and adventure books. 800-732-3669. www.stackpolebooks.com

**StageStep,** 2000 Hamilton St., Philadelphia, PA 19130: Free catalog ◆ Dance, theater, film, music, and fitness books, videos, and CDs. 800-523-0960. www.stagestep.com

**Stampede Investments,** 1533 River Rd., Wisconsin Dells, WI 53965: Free catalog ◆ Fine books, autographs, and other historical artifacts. 608-579-6805.

**State House Press,** P.O. Box 15247, Austin, TX 78761: Free information ◆ Books on the Civil War. 800-421-3378.

**Sterling Publishing Company Inc.,** 387 Park Ave. South, New York, NY 10016: Free catalog ◆ Books on body building, hobbies, crafts, occult, herbs and gardening, science, cooking, health, sports, music, theater, and self-defense. 212-532-7160.

**Storey's How-To Books for Country Living,** 105 Schoolhouse Rd., Pownal, VT 05261: Free information ◆ How to books on crafts, gardening, animals, woodworking and building, cooking, nature, beer and wine, and the outdoors. 800-441-5700.

**Strand Book Store,** 828 Broadway, New York, NY 10003: Free catalog ◆ New and used books in most fields of interest. 212-473-1452. strand@strandbooks.com

**Straw into Gold,** 3006 San Pablo Ave., Berkeley, CA 94702: Catalog $2 with long SASE and two 1st class stamps ◆ Ready-to-spin alpaca and books for spinners, weavers, and knitters. 510-548-5241. www.straw.com/sig

**Sun Mountain Books,** P.O. Box 743, Virginia City, NV 89440: Catalog $3 (refundable) ◆ Western books, videos, and cassettes.

**Sysko's Books,** 30 W. Main St., P.O. Box 6, Benton, WI 53803: Free catalog ◆ Basketball books and videos. 800-932-2534. www.bbhighway.com/store/Products/catalog.asp

**Tab Books Inc.,** Division McGraw Hill, P.O. Box 548, Black Lick, OH 43004: Free catalog ◆ How-to books on electronics, computers, aviation, science, hobbies, automobiles, crafts, and other subjects. 800-262-4729. www.mcgraw-hill.com/

**Tara Publications,** P.O. Box 707, Owings Mills, MD 21117: Free catalog ◆ Jewish music books, cassettes, CDs, and videos. 800-TARA-400; 410-654-0880 (in MD). www.jewishmusic.com

**Target Communications,** 7626 W. Donges Bay Rd., Mequon, WI 53097: Free information ◆ Books for hunters and shooters. 800-324-3337. www.americaoutdoors.com/target/index.html

**The Taunton Press,** 63 S. Main St., P.O. Box 5506, Newtown, CT 06470: Free information ◆ Books, videos, and magazines on sewing, fabrics and patterns, gardening, woodworking, and other crafts. 800-888-8286. www.taunton.com

**Taxidermy Today Magazine,** 119 Gadsden St., Chester, SC 29706: Free information ◆ Taxidermy books. 800-851-7955. ttoday@infoave.net

**Technical Analysis Inc.,** 4757 California Ave. SW, Seattle, WA 98116: Free information ◆ How-to-understand books on stocks and commodities. 800-832-4642. www.traders.com

**The Textile Museum Shop,** 2320 S St. NW, Washington, DC 20008: Free catalog ◆ Books on rugs, textiles, and related craft techniques. 202-667-0441.

**That Patchwork Place,** P.O. Box 118, Bothell, WA 98041: Free information ◆ Quilting books. 800-426-3126. www.patchwork.com

**Thomas Publications,** P.O. Box 3031, Gettysburg, PA 17325: Free catalog ◆ Civil War books. 800-840-6782; 717-3434-1921 (in PA). www.civilwarreader.com/thomas

**C. Clayton Thompson,** P.O. Box 5033, Pleasanton, CA 94566: Free information ◆ Civil War books, CDs, cassettes, regimental histories, and other ephemera. 925-462-5211. members.aol.com/greatbooks

**Timber Frame Homes,** Home Buyer Publications Inc., P.O. Box 5361, Pittsfield, MA 01203: Free information ◆ How-to books on timber frame homes. 800-850-7279. www.timberframehomes.com

**Timber Press,** 133 SW 2nd Ave., Ste. 450, Portland, OR 97204: Free catalog ◆ Books for gardeners, horticulturists, and botanists. 800-327-5680. www.timber-press.com

**Timeless Books,** P.O. Box 3543, Spokane, WA 99220: Free catalog ◆ Books, audiotapes, and videos on yoga, Buddhism, and Eastern philosophy. 800-251-9273. www.timeless.org

**TimesPast,** P.O. Box 1, Osceola, WI 54020: Free catalog ◆ Books on nostalgic America, collectibles, and items from the past. 800-826-6600. www.motorbooks.com

**TKD Enterprises Inc.,** 1423 18th St., Bettendorf, IA 52722: Free information ◆ Martial arts books and videos. 800-388-5966.

**The Tool Chest,** 45 Emerson Plaza East, Emerson, NJ 07630: Catalog $2 (refundable) ◆ Books for the home craftsman. 800-617-TOOLS.

**Tools for Exploration,** 9755 Independence Ave., Chatsworth, CA 91311: Free catalog ◆ Self-improvement books, tapes, machines, and other products. 888-748-6657; 818-885-9090 (in CA). www.toolsforexploration.com

**TOPAZ-Mineral Exploration,** 1605 Hillcrest, Grand Haven, MI 49417: Catalog $1 ◆ Antiquarian books on natural sciences, geology, mining, archaeology, and more. 616-842-3506. www.topazexpl.com

**James Townsend & Son Inc.,** 133 N. 1st St., P.O. Box 415, Pierceton, IN 46562: Catalog $2 ◆ Costuming, textile, cooking, music, and other books. 800-338-1665.

**Trafalgar Square Publishing,** P.O. Box 257, North Pomfret, VT 05053: Free catalog ◆ Books on gardening, crafts, and equestrian how-to. 800-423-4525.

**Travel Keys Books,** Order Desk, P.O. Box 160691, Sacramento, CA 95816: Free information ◆ Travel guides. 916-452-5200.

**Travelers Bookstore,** 22 W. 52nd St., New York, NY 10019: Catalog $2 ◆ Maps and books on travel, adventure, student opportunities, trekking, hiking, biking, kayaking, and mountaineering. 800-755-8728; 212-664-0995 (in NY).

**Turtle Press,** P.O. Box 290206, Wethersfield, CT 06129: Free catalog ◆ Books on martial arts. 800-77-TURTL. www.turtlepress.com

**Tuttle Antiquarian Books Inc.,** 28 S. Main St., Rutland, VT 05701: Free catalog ◆ Books and pamphlets of interest to historians, researchers, and collectors. 802-773-8229. tuttbook@interloc.com

**J. Tuttle Maritime Books,** 18098 Laurel Crest, Madison, WI 53705: Free catalog ◆ Out-of-print books about the sea, ships, and sailors. 608-238-7245.

**U.S. Chess Federation,** 3054 NYS Rt. 9W, New Windsor, NY 12553: Free catalog ◆ Conventional and computer chess sets, books, timers, and competition supplies. 800-388-KING. www.uschess.org

**U.S. Government Printing Office,** Free Business Catalog, Stop SM, Washington, DC 20401: Free catalog ◆ Best-selling Federal government publications.

**Unicorn Books & Crafts Inc.,** 1338 Ross St., Petaluma, CA 94954: Catalog $3 ◆ Books on basketry, color, costumes, dolls, dyeing, embroidery, fabric decoration, historic and ethnic textiles, jewelry, knitting and crochet, lace, machine knitting, paper-crafting, rug hooking, sewing, weaving, and spinning. 800-289-9276; 707-762-3362 (in CA).

**Uniquity,** P.O. Box 10, Galt, CA 95632: Free catalog ◆ Books, games, and more for child health, therapy, and anger release. 800-521-7771. uniquity@lodinet.com

**United Broadcasting,** Tefford Hotel, 3 River St., White Springs, FL 32096: Free catalog ◆ Books for everyone. 800-888-9999. www.audionet.com

**United Ostomy Association,** 19772 Mac Arthur Blvd., Ste. 200, Irvine, CA 92612: Free information ◆ Books that dispel anxiety and encourage positive approaches to healing and coping with ostomies. 800-826-0826. www.uoa.org

**United States Holocaust Memorial Museum Shop,** P.O. Box 92420, Washington, DC 20090: Free catalog ◆ Books, memoirs, and Holocaust studies for adults and younger readers. 800-259-9998.

**United Synagogue Book Service,** 155 5th Ave., New York, NY 10010: Free information ◆ Books on Judaism. 212-533-7800.

**VCH Publishers Inc.,** 605 3rd Ave., New York, NY 10158: Free catalog ◆ Science books. 800-367-8249. www.wiley.com

**Viking Folk Art Publications Inc.,** 301 16th Ave. SE, Waseca, MN 56093: Free information ◆ Decorative painting books. 507-835-8009. www.viking-publications.com

**Wagon Wheel Records & Books,** 17191 Corbina Ln., #203, Huntington Beach, CA 92649: Free catalog ◆ Square dancing records and books. 714-846-8169.

**Warner-Crivellaro,** 1855 Weaversville Rd., Allentown, PA 18103: Free information ◆ How-to books on stained glass crafting and supplies. 800-523-4242; 610-264-1100 (in PA). www.warner-criv.com

**Del & Jean Warren,** P.O. Box 364, Liberty, MO 64068: Catalog $6 ◆ Civil War era historic books and patterns, jewelry and accessories, underpinnings, uniforms and accouterments, black powder rifles, and shooting supplies. 816-781-9473. Jamescntry@aol.com

**T.E. Warth Esq., Automotive Books,** 15 Lumberyard Shops, Marine on St. Croix, MN 55047: Free information ◆ Rare and out-of-print automotive books. 612-433-5744.

**Watson-Guptill Publications,** 1515 Broadway, New York, NY 10036: Free information ◆ How-to books on decorative painting, silk painting, and marbling techniques. 800-ART-TIPS.

**Gary Wayner Books,** 1002 Glenn Blvd. SW, Fort Payne, AL 35967: Free catalog ◆ Natural history books. 205-845-7828.

**The Weaver's Place,** 75 Mellor Ave., Baltimore, MD 21228: Free information ◆ Japanese braiding equipment and books. 410-788-7262.

**Web-sters Handspinners, Weavers & Knitters,** 11 N. Main St., Ashland, OR 97520: Free catalog ◆ Designer yarns, books, and tools. 800-482-9801.

**Wee Folk Creations,** 18476 Natchez Ave., Prior Lake, MN 55372: Free catalog ◆ How-to videos and books on molding with clay, tools, accessories, and supplies. 888-933-3655. www.weefolk.com

**Barbara Weindling,** P.O. Box 368, Bridgewater, CT 06752: Catalog $2 ◆ Out-of-print and hard-to-find cookbooks.

**Samuel Weiser Inc.,** Box 612, York Beach, ME 03910: Free catalog ◆ Books on Eastern philosophy and other teachings. 207-363-4393.

**Western Horseman Books,** P.O. Box 7980, Colorado Springs, CO 80933: Free information ◆ Books on horsemanship and training, barrel racing, team and calf roping, reining, cutting, health problems, and horse breaking and shoeing. 800-874-6774. www.westernhorseman.com

**Western Publishing Company Inc.,** 444 Madison Ave., New York, NY 10022: Free catalog ◆ Golden Field Guides on birds, reptiles, rocks and minerals, seashells, astronomy, trees, insects, fishes, fossils, and weather. 212-688-4500.

**Ivan Whillock Studio,** 122 NE 1st Ave., Faribault, MN 55021: Free catalog ◆ Woodcarving tools, supplies, how-to books, and kits. 800-882-9379; 507-334-8306 (in MN). www.whillock.com

**Whitehorse Press,** P.O. Box 60, North Conway, NH 03860: Free information ◆ Books and videos on motorcycle touring, maintenance, history, performance, restoration, and riding techniques. 800-531-1133. www.whitehorsepress.com/catalog.htm

**Whole Person Associates,** 210 W. Michigan, Duluth, MN 55802: Free catalog ◆ Self-improvement books and videos on wellness promotion, stress management, and relaxation. 800-247-6789. www.wholeperson.com

**Wicwas Press,** P.O. Box 817, Cheshire, CT 06410: Free information ◆ Beekeeping books. 203-250-7575. ljconnor@aol.com

**The Wilderness Collection,** 716 Delaware Ct., Lawton, MI 49065: Free catalog ◆ New and used books about canoeing and wilderness travel. 616-624-4410.

**Wilderness Press,** 2440 Bancroft Way., Berkeley, CA 94704: Free catalog ◆ Hiking guides and other books. 800-443-7227. www.wildernesspress.com

**Willmann-Bell Inc.,** P.O. Box 35025, Richmond, VA 23235: Catalog $1 ◆ Astronomy books. 804-320-7016. www.willbell.com

**Windmill Publishing Company,** 2147 Windmill View Rd., El Cajon, CA 92020: Free information ◆ Books on antiques, Victorian items, and other collectibles.

**Wine Appreciation Guild,** 360 Swift Ave., Ste. 34, San Francisco, CA 94080: Free information ◆ Wine cellars, racks, accessories, and books. 800-231-9463.

**Wine Art,** 5890 N. Keystone Ave., Indianapolis, IN 46220: Free catalog ◆ How to books on wine, beer, and liqueur-making at home. 800-255-5090; 317-546-9940 (in IN).

**The Wine Trader,** P.O. Box 1598, Carson City, NV 89702: Free information ◆ Books about wine. 800-845-9463. winetrader@aol.com

**Wolfe Publishing Company,** 6471 Airpark Dr., Prescott, AZ 86301: Free catalog ◆ Sporting books. 800-899-7810. wolfspub@bslnet.com

**Woodbine House,** 6510 Bells Mill Rd., Bethesda, MD 20817: Free catalog ◆ Consumer reference books and The Special Needs Collection on disabilities for parents, educators, and medical professionals. 800-843-7323; 301-897-3570 (in MD). www.woodbinehouse.com

**Wooden Porch Books,** Rt. 1, Box 262, Middlebourne, WV 26149: Catalog $3 ◆ Books on fiber arts and related subjects. 304-386-4434.

**WoodenBoat Books,** P.O. Box 78, Brooklin, ME 04616: Free information ◆ Calendars, posters, prints, and books about wood boats. 800-273-SHIP. www.woodenboat.com

**Woodland Publishing Inc.,** P.O. Box 160, Pleasant Grove, UT 84062: Free catalog ◆ Books on health through natural means. 800-777-2665. woodland@itsnet.com

**Sylvia Woods Harp Center,** P.O. Box 816, Montrose, CA 91021: Free catalog ◆ Harps, recordings, books, harp-theme jewelry, and gifts. 800-272-4277; 818-956-1363 (in CA). www.harpcenter.com

**Woodworkers' Discount Books & Videos,** 735 Sunrise Ct., Woodland Park, CO 80863: Free catalog ◆ How-to books and videos on woodworking. 800-378-4060. www.discount-books.com

**The Woolery,** RD 1, Genoa, NY 13071: Catalog $2 ◆ Books on spinning, weaving, knitting, and dyeing. 315-497-1542. jive@woolery.com

**Wooly Knits,** 6728 Lowell Ave., McLean, VA 22101: Catalog $5 (12 issues) ◆ Designer yarns, unusual buttons, needle craft kits, how-to knitting books, and needlework supplies. 703-448-9665. www.woolyknits.com

**Workman Publishing Company Inc.,** 708 Broadway, New York, NY 10003: Free catalog ◆ Cooking, food and wine, travel, homes and gardens, space, humor, exercise and health, pregnancy and babies, sports and television, games, hobbies and handicrafts, computers, and children's books. 800-722-7202; 212-254-5900 (in NY). www.workmanweb.com

**Write Stuff Syndicate Inc.,** 1515 SE 4th Ave., Fort Lauderdale, FL 33316: Free brochure ◆ Hardbound coffee table books and classic boat calendars. 954-462-6657. www.writestuffbooks.com

**Writer's Digest Books,** 1507 Dana Ave., Cincinnati, OH 45207: Free catalog ◆ Self-help and how-to books for writers, fine and graphic artists, songwriters, musicians, photographers, homemakers, and children. 800-289-0963.

**Written Heritage,** P.O. Box 1390, Folsom, LA 70437: Free catalog ◆ American Indian (Native American) books and videos. 800-301-8009; 504-796-5433 (in LA). www.whisperingwind.com

**Yarn Barn,** 930 Massachusetts, Box 334, Lawrence, KS 66044: Free catalog ◆ Fiber books, patterns, yarns, and more. 800-468-0035. yarnbarn@idir.net

**YMAA Publication Center,** 38 Hyde Park Ave., Jamaica Plain, MA 02130: Free catalog ◆ Martial arts books, videos, clothing, and music. 800-669-8892. www.ymaa.com/pubcenter.html

**Yoga Journal's Book & Tape Source,** 2054 University Ave., Berkeley, CA 94704: Free information ◆ Books, audio cassettes, and videos on yoga. 800-359-YOGA. BookandTape@yogajournal.com

**Zed Books,** c/o Humanities Press, 165 1st Ave., Atlantic Highlands, NJ 07716: Free catalog ◆ Books on Third World sustainable development, environmental issues, gender, self-empowerment, and cultural studies. 908-872-1441. www.humanitiespress.com

**Zenith Books,** P.O. Box 1, Osceola, WI 54020: Free catalog ◆ Books about ragwings, supersonic spy planes, and other aircraft. Also calendars and videos on military aircraft, plastic and radio control modeling, warplanes, and aviation history. 800-826-6600. www.motorbooks.com

**Zephyr Press,** P.O. Box 66006, Tucson, AZ 85728: Free catalog ◆ Activities for teachers looking for new ways of teaching for all ways of learning. 800-232-2187. www.zephyrpress.com/OrderCatalog.html

**Zon International Publishing Company,** P.O. Box 6459, Santa Fe, NM 87502: Catalog $2.50 ◆ Guides and books about carousels, cowboy antiques, and other collectibles. 800-266-5767.

## Large-Print & Braille Books

**American Printing House for the Blind,** 1839 Frankfort Ave., P.O. Box 6085, Louisville, KY 40206: Free catalog ◆ Accessible large-print and braille books for visually impaired people. 800-223-1839; 502-895-2405 (in KY). www.aph.org

**The William A. Thomas Braille Bookstore,** Division Braille International Inc., 3290 SE Slater St., Stuart, FL 34997: Free catalog ◆ Books in braille and large-print. 800-336-3142. www.gate.net/~braille

**Thorndike Press,** P.O. Box 159, Thorndike, ME 04986: Free catalog ◆ Large-print books. 800-257-5157. www.sscp.com

## Religious Books & Software

**American Bible Sales,** 870 S. Anaheim Blvd., Anaheim, CA 92805: Free information ◆ King James, New International, and New American Standard Bible software for the Macintosh. 800-535-5131.

**Augsburg Fortress Publishers,** 426 S. 5th St., Minneapolis, MN 55415: Free catalog ◆ Books, curriculum materials, music, gifts, audiovisuals, and ecclesiastical arts items. 800-328-4648; 612-330-3341 (in MN). www.augusburgfortress.org

**Baker Book House,** 1830 Breton Rd. SE, Grand Rapids, MI 49506: Free catalog ◆ Religious books for the home, church, and school. 616-942-9880. www.bakerbooks.com

**Behrman House Publishers Inc.,** 235 Watchung Ave., West Orange, NJ 07052: Free information ◆ Books on Jewish subjects for children and adults. 800-221-2755. www.behrmanhouse.com

**Bible Research Systems,** 2013 Wells Branch Pkwy., Ste. 304, Austin, TX 78728: Free brochure ◆ Bible education software for PCs and Macintosh computers. 800-423-1228. www.brs-inc.com/bible

**BibleSoft,** 22014 7th Ave. South, Seattle, WA 98198: Free information ◆ Windows and DOS bible-study software. 800-995-9058.

**Catholics United for the Faith Inc.,** Books and Tapes by Mail, 827 N. 4th St., Steubenville, OH 43952: Free catalog ◆ Catholic books and audio cassettes. 800-693-2484.

**Christian Book Distributors,** P.O. Box 7000, Peabody, MA 01961: Free catalog ◆ Books, bibles, videos, computer software, music items for children and adults, and artwork. 978-977-5050. www.chrbook.com

**Cokesbury,** Division United Methodist Publishing House, 201 8th Ave. South, P.O. Box 801, Nashville, TN 37202: Free information ◆ Bibles and bible reference books, bible study and Christian education books, fund-raising programs, gifts and casual clothing, choir apparel, church and clergy supplies, and church furniture. 800-672-1789. webservant@umph.org

**Dharma Publishing,** 2910 San Pablo Ave., Berkeley, CA 94702: Free information ◆ Books and art reproductions on Tibet meditation. 800-873-4276. www.nyingma.org

**Eborn Books,** P.O. Box 2093, Peoria, AZ 85380: Free catalog ◆ Used, rare, and out-of-print Mormon books. 602-979-2624. www.bibliofind.com

**God's World Books,** P.O. Box 2330, Asheville, NC 28802: Free catalog ◆ Selected books from Christian and secular publishers. 800-951-2665.

**Gospel Advocate Bookstores,** Order Dept., 1006 Elm Hill Pike, Nashville, TN 37210: Free catalog ◆ Bibles, Christian books, and magazines. 800-251-8446.

**Great Christian Books,** 229 S. Bridge St., P.O. Box 8000, Elkton, MD 21922: Free catalog ◆ Bibles, commentaries, language tools, cookbooks, home schooling books, bible study software, and bible video games. 800-775-5422. www.GreatChristianBooks.com

**Immaculata Bookstore,** P.O. Box 159, St. Mary's, KS 66536: Free catalog ◆ Educational books, and music tapes, CD-ROMs, full score music books of great composers, and other Catholic books and publications. 913-437-2409. www.immaculata.com

**Jewish Publication Society,** 1930 Chestnut St., Philadelphia, PA 19103: Free information ◆ Books about Judaica. 800-234-3151.

**Kar-Ben Copies Inc.,** 6800 Tildenwood Ln., Rockville, MD 20852: Free catalog ◆ Judaic books and cassettes. 800-452-7236. www.karben.com

**The Liturgical Press,** St. John's Abbey, Box 7500, Collegeville, MN 56321: Free information ◆ Catholic and general Christian books on scripture, theology, and liturgy. 800-858-5450. www.litpress.org/index.html

**Living the Good News Inc.,** 600 Grant St., Ste. 400, Denver, CO 80203: Free catalog ◆ Lutheran, Catholic, Episcopal, and other Christian education materials for parishes, schools, and families. 303-832-4427.

**Thomas Nelson Publishers,** P.O. Box 140300, Nashville, TN 37214: Free catalog ◆ Christian books, bibles, audio and video recordings, and music. 800-933-9673. www.nelsonworddirect.com

**The Neumann Press,** Rt. 2, Box 30, Long Prairie, MN 56347: Free catalog ◆ Catholic book publisher, orthodox, traditional, homeschool. 320-732-6358. www.rea-alp.com/~neumann

**Orbis Books,** P.O. Box 308, Maryknoll, NY 10545: Free catalog ◆ Religious books. 914-941-7636. www.maryknoll.org/orbis/mklorbhp.htm

**Precept Ministries,** P.O. Box 182218, Chattanooga, TN 37422: Free catalog ◆ Religious books, audio cassettes, and videos. 423-894-3277. www.precept.org

**Quest Books,** Theosophical Publishing House, 306 W. Geneva Rd., P.O. Box 270, Wheaton, IL 60189: Free catalog ◆ Spiritual growth, trans-personal psychology, world religions, and other books. 800-669-9425. www.theosophical.org/pubhouse.html

**Tan Books & Publishers Inc.,** P.O. Box 424, Rockford, IL 61105: Free catalog ◆ Catholic books. 800-437-5876. www.theosophical.org/pubhouse.html

**Torah Educational Software,** Developers of ArtScroll's Multimedia Educational, 21 Main St., Monsey, NY 10952: Free information ◆ Judaic educational software on CD-ROMs for PCs and Macintosh computers. 914-356-1485. www.jewishsoftware.com

**Unique Multicultural Playthings,** 1723 Rosewood Ave., Louisville, KY 40204: Free catalog ◆ Jewish books, games, and videos. 502-451-2293.

**Zondervan DirectSource,** P.O. Box 668, Holmes, PA 19043: Free information ◆ Bibles and religious books. 800-876-7335. www.zondervan.com

### Used & Rare Books

**Adventurous Traveler Bookstore,** P.O. Box 64769, Burlington, VT 05406: Free catalog ◆ New, used, and rare books on mountaineering and exploration. 800-282-3963; 802-860-6776 (in VT). www.atb-rarebooks.com

**Benedikt & Salmon Record Rarities,** 3020 Meade Ave., San Diego, CA 92116: Free catalog, indicate choice of (1) rare books and autographs, (2) classical, (3) jazz, big bands, and blues and (4) personalities, soundtracks, and country music ◆ Autographed memorabilia and rare books on music and the performing arts, antique phonographs and cylinders, and rare recordings from the 1890s to date. 619-281-3345. rarerecords@groupweb.com

**Between the Covers-Rare Books Inc.,** 35 W. Maple Ave., Mercantile, NJ 08109: Free catalog ◆ First editions, African-American literature and history, and other rare books. 609-665-2284. www.betweenthecovers.com

**Books in Transit,** 2830 Case Way, Turlock, CA 95382: Free catalog ◆ Hard-to-find used and out-of-print books on knitting and needlecrafting, painting, jewelry-making, woodworking, papermaking, and other arts and crafts. 209-632-6984.

**Bradbury Books & Beyond,** Dan & Jobeth Bradbury, 3318 Karnes Blvd., Kansas City, MO 64111: List $3 ◆ Out-of-print and used books on magic for magicians and its allied arts. 816-531-2468. www.bradburybooks.com

**Michael Dennis Cohan, Bookseller,** 502 W. Alder St., Missoula, MT 59802: Free catalog ◆ Out-of-print and rare books on geology, mining, and related subjects. 406-721-7379.

**Joseph A. Dermont,** 13 Arthur St., P.O. Box 654, Onset, MA 02558: Free catalog ◆ Literary first editions and autographs. 508-295-4760. jdermont@interloc.com

**David E. Doremus Books,** 100 Hillside Ave., Arlington, MA 02174: Catalog subscription $2 ◆ Used and rare Civil War books. 781-646-0892.

**Editions,** Boiceville, NY 12412: Catalog $2 ◆ Used, old, and rare books. 914-657-7000. www.nleditions.com

**The Electronic Magic Store,** Library Services Inc., 1498-M Reistertown Rd., #337, Baltimore, MD 21208: Free catalog ◆ New and used magic books and videos. 888-622-7376; 410-358-8889 (in MD). emagic@universe.digex.net

**The Gemmary Rare Books & Antique Scientific Instruments,** P.O. Box 2560, Fallbrook, CA 92088: Mineralogy book catalog $2, science book catalog $2 ◆ Specializes in out-of-print books on mineralogy that include mining, jewelry, and meteorites; science books that include physics, microscopy, and scientific instruments. 760-728-3321. www.gemmary.com/rcb

**Haslam's Book Store,** 2025 Central Ave., St. Petersburg, FL 33713: Free information ◆ Out-of-print and used books.

**Joslin Hall Rare Books,** P.O. Box 516, Concord, MA 01742: Free catalog ◆ Rare books. Includes acquisitions from the 17th and 18th-century and other books. 978-371-3101. www.joslinhall.com

**Just Good Books,** P.O. Box 232, Belgrade, MT 59714: Free catalog ◆ New, used, out-of-print, and rare sporting books. 800-207-0799. www.justgoodbooks.com

**John W. Knott, Bookseller,** 8453 Early Bud Way, Laurel, MD 20723: Free information ◆ First edition science fiction, fantasy, and horror books. 301-317-8427.

**Lame Duck Books,** 90 Moraine St., Jamaica Plain, MA 02130: Free catalog ◆ Signed books, autographs, manuscripts, photos, and art. 617-522-6657. LameDuckBk@aol.com

**Last Seen Reading,** Bonnie & David Pollard, P.O. Box 1423, Palo Alto, CA 94302: Free list ◆ Hard-to-find used books. 415-321-3348.

**Ken Lopez-Bookseller,** 51 Huntington Rd., Hadley, MA 01035: Free catalog ◆ Literary first editions in individual titles or collections. Specializes in Latin American literature, the Vietnam War, and the 1960s. 413-584-4827. www.lopezbooks.com

**M & S Rare Books Inc.,** P.O. Box 2594, East Side Station, Providence, RI 02906: Free catalog ◆ Rare literature, and other books on thought, reform, and history. 401-421-1050.

**Robert A. Madle,** 4406 Bestor Dr., Rockville, MD 20853: Catalog $3 ◆ Science fiction and fantasy magazines and books, from 1900 to present. 301-460-4712.

**Marcher Books,** 6204 N. Vermont, Oklahoma City, OK 73112: Free catalog ◆ Rare and out-of-print American history books.

**McGowan Book Company,** 39 Kimberly Dr., Durham, NC 27707: Catalog $3 ◆ Rare and out-of-print Civil War books. 800-449-8406. www.mcgowanbooks.com

**David Meyer Magic Books,** P.O. Box 427, Glenwood, IL 60425: Catalog $2 ◆ New and old books on magic. 708-757-4950.

**George Robert Minkoff Inc.,** 26 Rowe Rd., Alford, MA 01230: Free catalog ◆ Rare books. 413-528-4575.

**Ms. Information,** P.O. Box 262, El Granada, CA 94018: Free catalog ◆ Out-of-print, new, and used books about antiques and collectibles. 650-726-1367. msinfo@coastside.net

**Old Hickory Bookshop Ltd.,** 20225 New Hampshire Ave., Brinklow, MD 20862: Free catalog ◆ Used medical books. 301-924-2225.

**Peddler's Wagon,** Box 109, Lamar, MO 64759: Needlework list $3; quilting list $3; rugs list $1 ◆ Out-of-print and pre-owned books. 417-682-3734.

**Bud Plant Illustrated Books,** P.O. Box 1689, Grass Valley, CA 95945: Catalog $3 ◆ Rare and out-of-print children's books, art monographs, and history of book illustrating. Also books about comics, comic strips, and their creators. 916-273-2166. www.budplant.com

**Wallace D. Pratt, Bookseller,** 1801 Gough St., Ste. 304, San Francisco, CA 94109: Free catalog ◆ Out-of-print and rare books about the Civil War, Indian Wars, American Revolution, World War I and II, and miscellaneous military history. 415-673-0178.

**Red Lancer,** P.O. Box 8056, Mesa, AZ 85214: Catalog $6 ◆ Rare books, Victorian-era campaign medals and helmets, toy soldiers, and original 19th-century military art. 602-964-9667.

**William Reese Company,** 409 Temple St., New Haven, CT 06511: Free catalog ◆ Rare books, other literature, and Americana. 203-789-8081. www.reeseco.com/

**Peter L. Stern & Company,** 355 Boylston St., 2nd Floor, Boston, MA 02116: Free catalog ◆ Rare and collectible science fiction, fantasy, Arthur Conan Doyle and Sherlock Holmes, and American and English literature. Includes signed and inscribed books. 617-421-1880.

**Tuttle Antiquarian Books Inc.,** 28 S. Main St., Rutland, VT 05701: Free catalog ◆ Books on family histories and other miscellany. 802-773-8229.

**Unicorn Books & Crafts Inc.,** 1338 Ross St., Petaluma, CA 94954: Catalog $3 ◆ Books on basketry, color, costumes, dolls, dyeing, embroidery, fabric decoration, historic and ethnic textiles, jewelry, knitting and crochet, lace, machine knitting, paper-crafting, rug hooking, sewing, weaving, and spinning. 800-289-9276; 707-762-3362 (in CA).

## BOOKS ON TAPE

**Ash Grove Audiobook Exchange,** P.O. Box 2647, Silverdale, WA 98383: Free information ◆ Books recorded on tape. 800-697-6797.

**Audio Editions, Books on Cassette,** P.O. Box 6930, Auburn, CA 95604: Free catalog ◆ Best sellers and all-time favorites, books for young people, classics, drama and poetry, languages, books on cassettes, and personal growth, business, and management titles. 800-231-4261. www.audioeditions.com

**B & B Audio Inc.,** 3175 Commercial Ave., #107-B, Northbrook, IL 60062: Free catalog ◆ Mysteries, westerns, biographies, history, military, self-help, children's, non-fiction, and general fiction audio books. 847-562-9516. www.bandbaudio.com

**Blackstone Audio Books,** P.O. Box 969, Ashland, OR 97520: Free catalog ◆ Unabridged books on audio cassettes. 800-729-2665. www.blackstoneaudio.com

**Books on Tape Inc.,** P.O. Box 7900, Newport Beach, CA 92658: Free catalog ◆ Books recorded on cassettes. 800-626-3333. www.booksontape.com

**Bookcassette Sales,** 1704 Eaton Dr., P.O. Box 481, Grand Haven, MI 49417: Free catalog ◆ Best selling titles in unabridged and bridged format for adults and children. 800-222-3225. sales@brillianceaudio.com

**Jim Cin Recordings,** P.O. Box 536, Portsmouth, RI 02871: Free brochure ◆ Classic audio books and stories on cassettes. 800-538-3034.

**Dragon Door Publications,** P.O. Box 4381, St. Paul, MN 55104: Free catalog ◆ Books, videos, audio cassettes, and special reports on health, self-defense, and healing systems. 800-899-5111; 651-645-0517 (in MN). www.dragondoor.com

**Himalayan Institute Press,** RR 1, Box 405, Honesdale, PA 18431: Free information ◆ Books and audio cassettes on physical, psychological health and well-being, spiritual growth though meditation, and other yoga practices. 800-822-4547. www.himalayaninstitute.org

**Listening Library Inc.,** One Park Ave., Old Greenwich, CT 06870: Free catalog ◆ Listening books (cassettes) for adults and children. 203-637-3616. www.listeninglib.com

**Recorded Books Inc.,** 270 Skipjack Rd., Prince Frederick, MD 20678: Free catalog ◆ Unabridged books on cassettes. 800-638-1304. www.recordedbooks.com

**Frank Schaffer Publications Inc.,** 23740 Hawthorne Blvd., P.O. Box 2853, Torrance, CA 90509: Free information ◆ Children's books on tape, resources for teachers, and other educational aids. 800-421-5565.

**Sounds True Audio,** 413 S. Arthur Ave., Louisville, CO 80027: Free catalog ◆ Audio and video recordings on personal discovery, relationships, sacred music of the world, homeopathy, psychology, health and healing, and other life-related topics. 800-333-9185. info@soundstrue.com

## BOOMERANGS

**Boomerang Man,** 1806 N. 3rd St., Monroe, LA 71201: Free catalog ◆ Contest and sport boomerangs. 318-325-8157. BMANRICH@iAMERICA.NET

**Colorado Boomerangs,** 2530 S. Ouray Way, Aurora, CO 80013: Free catalog ◆ Boomerangs in 23 styles. Also night rangs and leftys. 800-35-RANGS; 303-671-6878 (in CO). www.coloradoboomerangs.com

**Brian Dube Inc.,** 520 Broadway, 3rd Floor, New York, NY 10012: Free catalog ◆ Juggling equipment, boomerangs, yo-yo's, and books. 212-941-0060. www.dube.com

**Ford Flyers Boomerang,** 7205 Cherokee Rd., Richmond, VA 23225: Free information ◆ Handcrafted boomerangs. 804-272-8192.

**Gel Boomerangs,** 2124 Kittredge St., Box 61, Berkeley, CA 94704: Free brochure ◆ Handcrafted boomerangs for beginners, intermediate to expert throwers, and competitions. 800-GEL-8220; 510-658-2469 (in CA).

**Infinite Illusions,** P.O. Box 2584, Tallahassee, FL 32316: Free information ◆ Juggling supplies, boomerangs, and yo-yo's. 800-548-6724; 904-385-6463. www.yoyoguy.com

**Into the Wind/Kites,** 1408 Pearl St., Boulder, CO 80302: Free catalog ◆ Kites, windsocks, flags, and boomerangs. 800-204-5483. www.intothewind.com

**What's Up Kites,** 4500 Chagrin River Rd., Chagrin Falls, OH 44022: Free list of retail sources ◆ Boomerangs, kites, air toys, and books. 216-247-4222.

**The Wright Life,** 200 Linden, Fort Collins, CO 80524: Free catalog ◆ Frisbees (flying discs), skateboards, snowboards, in-line skates, boomerangs, stunt kites, juggling equipment, and more. 800-321-8833. www.wrightlife.com

## BOWLING

### Clothing

**Converse Inc.,** 1 Fordham Rd., North Reading, MA 01864: Free information ◆ Shoes. 800-428-2667; 781-664-1100 (in MA).

**Eastern Bowling/Hy-Line Inc.,** 4717 Stenton Ave., Philadelphia, PA 19144: Free information ◆ Shoes. 800-523-0140; 215-438-9000 (in PA).

**King Louie International,** 13500 15th St., Grandview, MO 64030: Free information ◆ Jackets, shirts, and blouses. 800-521-5212; 816-765-5212 (in MO).

**National Sporting Goods Corp.,** 25 Brighton Ave., Passaic, NJ 07055: Free information ◆ Shoes. 201-779-2323.

**Nike Footwear Inc.,** One Bowerman Dr., Beaverton, OR 97005: Free list of retail sources ◆ Shoes, shirts, blouses, and bowling ball bags. 800-344-6453. www.nike.com

**Saucony/Hyde,** 13 Centennial Dr., Peabody, MA 01961: Free list of retail sources ◆ Shoes. 800-365-7282.

**Shaffer Sportswear,** 224 N. Washington, Neosho, MO 64850: Free information ◆ Jackets and shirts. 417-451-9444.

**Universal Bowling, Golf & Billiard Supplies,** 619 S. Wabash Ave., Chicago, IL 60605: Free catalog ◆ Shirts, one and two-ball bags, and women's shoes. 800-523-3037. www.universal-bowling.com

**Wa-Mac Inc.,** P.O. Box 128, Carlstadt, NJ 07410: Free information ◆ Shoes, gloves, bowling ball and shoe bags, grips, novelties, and towels. 800-447-5673; 201-438-7200 (in NJ).

**Windjammer,** 525 N. Main St., Bangor, PA 18013: Free information ◆ Jackets, shirts, T-shirts, sweat suits, and other sportswear. 800-441-6958; 610-588-0626 (in PA).

**Wolverine Boots & Shoes,** 9341 Courtland Dr. NE, Rockford, MI 49351: Free list of retail sources ◆ Shoes. 800-543-2668.

### Equipment

**Access to Recreation Inc.,** 8 Sandra Ct., Newbury Park, CA 91320: Free catalog ◆ Adaptive bowling equipment for the disabled. 800-634-4351.

**Ajay Leisure Products Inc.,** 1501 E. Wisconsin St., Delavan, WI 53115: Free list of retail sources ◆ Bowling ball bags, grips, novelties, and towels. 800-558-3276; 414-728-5521 (in WI).

**Bowling's Bookstore,** 200 S. Michigan Ave., Ste. 1430, Chicago, IL 60604: Free information ◆ Books and videos on bowling. 800-521-BOWL. www.bowlingsbookstore.com

**Ebonite International Inc.,** 1813 W. 7th St., Box 746, Hopkinsville, KY 42240: Free information ◆ Bags, balls, and wrist supports. 800-626-8350; 502-886-5261 (in KY).

**J-S Sales Company Inc.,** 5 S. Fulton Ave., Mt. Vernon, NY 10550: Free information ◆ Bowling ball bags, grips, towels, and novelties. 800-431-2944; 914-668-8051 (in NY).

**KR Industries Inc.,** 1200 S. 54th Ave., Cicero, IL 60650: Free information ◆ Bags. 800-621-6097.

**Master Industries Inc.,** 17222 Von Karman Ave., Irvine, CA 92713: Free information ◆ Bags, balls, grips, novelties, and towels. 800-854-3794; 714-660-0644 (in CA).

**Nike Footwear Inc.,** One Bowerman Dr., Beaverton, OR 97005: Free list of retail sources ◆ Bowling ball bags, shoes, shirts, and blouses. 800-344-6453. www.nike.com

**Saunier-Wilhem Company,** 3216 5th Ave., Pittsburgh, PA 15213: Free catalog ◆ Equipment and accessories for bowling, billiards, darts, table tennis, shuffleboard, and board games. 412-621-4350.

**Skor-Mor Company,** Bowling Division, P.O. Box 346, Dickinson, ND 58602: Catalog $2 ◆ Bowling equipment and accessories. 800-635-2695. www.ctctel.com/SKORMOR

**Sports Technologies Inc.,** 2923 Industrial Dr., Sanford, NC 27330: Free information ◆ Bags, balls, and accessories. 800-322-3962; 919-776-9544 (in NC).

**Storm Products Company,** 165 S. 8th West, P.O. Box 212, Brigham City, UT 84302: Free brochure ◆ Bowling balls and accessories. 801-723-0403.

**Universal Bowling, Golf & Billiard Supplies,** 619 S. Wabash Ave., Chicago, IL 60605: Free catalog ◆ Bowling equipment. 800-523-3037. www.universal-bowling.com

**Universal Trav-Ler,** 359 Wales Ave., Bronx, NY 10454: Free information ◆ Bowling ball and shoe bags. 800-833-3026; 718-993-7100 (in NY).

**Wa-Mac Inc.,** P.O. Box 128, Carlstadt, NJ 07410: Free information ◆ Bowling ball and shoe bags, grips, novelties, towels, shoes, and gloves. 800-447-5673; 201-438-7200 (in NJ).

## BOXING

### Clothing

**Adidas USA,** 5675 N. Blackstock Rd., Spartanburg, SC 29303: Free list of retail sources ◆ Shoes. 800-423-4327. www.adidas.com

**Betlin Manufacturing,** 1445 Marion Rd., Columbus, OH 43207: Free information ◆ Robes and trunks. 614-443-0248.

**Butwin Sportwear Company,** 3401 Spring St. NE, Minneapolis, MN 55413: Free information ◆ Robes. 800-328-1445.

**Converse Inc.,** 1 Fordham Rd., North Reading, MA 01864: Free information ◆ Shoes. 800-428-2667; 781-664-1100 (in MA).

**Eisner Brothers,** 75 Essex St., New York, NY 10002: Free information ◆ Trunks. 800-426-7700; 212-475-6868 (in NY). www.eisnerbros.com

**Faber Brothers,** 4141 S. Pulaski Rd., Chicago, IL 60632: Free information ◆ Bags, gloves, head guards, and clothing. 773-376-9300.

**Franklin Sports Industries Inc.,** 17 Campanelli Pkwy., P.O. Box 508, Stoughton, MA 02072: Free information ◆ Bags and gloves. 800-426-7700.

**G & S Sporting Goods,** 43 Essex St., New York, NY 10002: Free price list ◆ Trunks, robes, gloves, training equipment, and protective gear. 212-777-7590.

**Genesport Industries Ltd.,** Hokkaido Karate Equipment Manufacturing Company, 150 King St., Montreal, Quebec, Canada H3C 2P3: Free information ◆ Robes, shoes, trunks, punching bags, skip ropes, and boxing rings. 514-861-1856.

**Markwort Sporting Goods,** 4300 Forest Park Ave., St. Louis, MO 63108: Catalog $8 (request list of retail sources) ◆ Bags, gloves, and head guards. 800-669-6626; 314-652-3757 (in MO).

**Otomix,** 3691 Lenawee Ave., Los Angeles, CA 90016: Free information ◆ Fitness clothing, shoes, and martial arts equipment. 800-701-7867. www.otomix.com

**Pony Sports & Leisure,** 2801 Red Dog Dr., Knoxville, TN 37914: Free information ◆ Shoes, socks, and sweat bands. 423-546-4703.

**Tuf-Wear USA,** P.O. Box 239, Sidney, NE 69162: Free information ◆ Robes, shoes, and trunks. 800-445-5210; 308-254-4011 (in NE).

### Equipment

**Bauer Sports,** 150 Ocean Rd., Greenland, NH 03840: Free list of retail sources ◆ Punching bags and skip ropes. 800-362-3146. www.bauer.com

**BSN Sports,** P.O. Box 7726, Dallas, TX 75209: Free information ◆ Equipment for archery, aquatic fitness, baseball, basketball, boxing, field hockey, football, weight lifting, and other sports. 800-527-7510; 972-484-9484 (in TX). www.bsnsports.com

**Everlast Sports Manufacturing Corp.,** 750 E. 132nd St., Bronx, NY 10454: Free information ◆ Punching bags, boxing rings, skip ropes, gloves, head guards, helmets, and tooth and mouth protectors. 800-221-8777; 718-993-0100 (in NY).

**Faber Brothers,** 4141 S. Pulaski Rd., Chicago, IL 60632: Free information ◆ Bags, gloves, head guards, and clothing. 773-376-9300.

**G & S Sporting Goods,** 43 Essex St., New York, NY 10002: Free price list ◆ Trunks, robes, gloves, training equipment, and protective gear. 212-777-7590.

**Genesport Industries Ltd.,** Hokkaido Karate Equipment Manufacturing Company, 150 King St., Montreal, Quebec, Canada H3C 2P3: Free information ◆ Punching bags, skip ropes, boxing rings, robes, shoes, trunks, gloves, head guards, helmets, and tooth and mouth protectors. 514-861-1856.

**Gladiator Sports,** 3499 Cowes Mewes, Woodbridge, VA 22193: Free information ◆ Gloves, protective gear, punching bags, and dummies. 703-878-9434.

**The Innovative Solutions Company,** P.O. Box 658, 817 W. Broad St., Bethlehem, PA 18016: Free information ◆ Self-supporting multi-station boxing workout machine, bag gloves, hand wraps, and jump ropes. 888-INNOSOL.

**Ivanko Barbell Company,** P.O. Box 1470, San Pedro, CA 90731: Free list of retail sources ◆ Punching bags and skip ropes. 800-247-9044; 310-514-1155 (in CA). www.advmax.com/ivanko

**Macho Products Inc.,** 10045 102nd Terrace, Sebastian, FL 32958: Free catalog ◆ Equipment and clothing. 800-327-6812; 561-388-9892 (in FL).

**NDL Products Inc.,** 4031 NE 12th Terrace, Oakland Park, FL 33334: Free information ◆ Punching bags and skip ropes. 800-843-3021.

**Ringside,** P.O. Box 14171, Lenexa, KS 66285: Free catalog ◆ Boxing equipment, clothing, and training aids. 800-KARATE-1; 913-888-1719 (in KS). www.ringside.com

## BRAID CRAFTING

**Distlefink Designs Inc.,** Box 358, Pelham, NY 10803: Free brochure ◆ Tools, books, accessories, and fabrics for braid-crafting.

## BREAD MAKING

**Burnt Cabins Grist Mill,** Cowans Gap Rd., Burnt Cabins, PA 17215: Free brochure ◆ Old-fashioned buckwheat and wheat flour, roasted and regular cornmeal, and pancake and muffin mixes. 717-987-3244.

**Genie's Kitchen,** 150 Magic Ln., Box 456, Wibaux, MT 59353: Free information ◆ Low-fat and no cholesterol muffin mixes. 800-276-5259.

**The Gluten-Free Pantry,** P.O. Box 840, Glastonbury, CT 06033: Free catalog ◆ Easy-to-make wheat-free and gluten-free gourmet bread and cake baking mixes. 800-291-8386. www.glutenfree.com

**HeartyMix Company,** 1231 Madison Hill Rd., Rahway, NJ 07065: Free catalog ◆ Mixes for bread machines. 732-382-3010.

**The J.B. Dough Company,** 5600 E. Napier, Benton Harbor, MI 49022: Free price list ◆ Mixes for automatic bread machines. 800-528-6222. jbdough@jbdough.com

**The King Arthur Flour Baker's Catalog,** P.O. Box 876, Norwich, VT 05055: Free information ◆ Sourdough starter for bread, pancakes, biscuits, and cakes. 800-827-6836. www.kingarthurflour.com

**R.F. Nature Farm Foods Inc.,** 925 S St., Lincoln, NE 68508: Free list of retail sources ◆ All-natural bread mixes for bread machines and oven-baking. 800-222-FARM; 402-474-7576 (in NE).

**Wanda's Nature Farm Foods,** 925 S St., Lincoln, NE 68508: Free catalog ◆ All-natural bread, muffin, pancake, waffle, and double-chocolate cake mixes. 800-222-FARM. naturefarmfood@aol.com

## BRIDGE

**Baron/Barclay Bridge Supplies,** 3600 Chamberlain Ln., Ste. 230, Louisville, KY 40201: Free catalog ◆ Bridge supplies and books. 800-274-2221. www.baronbarclay.com

**The Bridge World,** 717 White Plains Rd., Ste. 106, Scarsdale, NY 10583: Free catalog ◆ Bridge books, magazines, computer software for Windows, games, and accessories. 914-725-6712. www.bridgeworld.com

**Great Games Products,** 8804 Chalon Dr., Bethesda, MD 20817: Free brochure ◆ Mouse-supported computer bridge games for DOS 2.0 or higher, Windows, and the Macinosh. 800-GAMES-4-U.

## BRUSHES

**Ace Wire Brush Company Inc.,** 30 Henry St., Brooklyn, NY 11201: Free brochure ◆ Brushes and brooms. 718-624-8032.

**Fuller Direct,** One Fuller Way, Great Band, KS 67530: Free catalog ◆ Brooms and brushes, space-saving organizers, and other home aids. 800-522-0499.

**Home Trends,** 1450 Lyell Ave., Rochester, NY 14606: Free catalog ◆ Cleaning supplies, energy-saving devices, lighting equipment, pest control, brushes, vacuums and accessories, and more. 716-254-6520. home@eznet.net

## BULLETIN & CHALKBOARDS

**Bangor Cork Company Inc.,** William & D Streets, Pen Argyl, PA 18072: Free catalog ◆ Cork bulletin, marker, and chalkboards. 610-863-9041.

**Business & Institutional Furniture Company,** P.O. Box 92039, Milwaukee, WI 53202: Free catalog ◆ Office and institutional furniture. 800-558-8662.

**Flaghouse Furniture Express,** 601 Flaghouse Dr., Hasbrouck Heights, NJ 07604: Free catalog ◆ Bulletin and chalkboards and other office furnishings. 800-793-7900. www.flaghouse.com

**Memindex Inc.,** 149 Carter St., P.O. Box 20566, Rochester, NY 14602: Free catalog ◆ Organizational tools for scheduling, planning, and controlling time. 716-342-7740.

**Office Depot Inc.,** 2200 Old Germantown Rd., Delray Beach, FL 33445: Free catalog ◆ Bulletin and chalkboards, office supplies, and furniture. 800-685-8800. www.officedepot.com

**Staples Inc.,** P.O. Box 5173, Westborough, MA 01581: Free catalog ◆ Office furniture, drafting equipment, fax machines, typewriters, and supplies. 800-333-3330. www.staples.com

## BUMPER STICKERS

**A Graphic Edge,** 1313 Simpson Way, Ste. F, Escondido, CA 92029: Free brochure ◆ Dimensional signs, bumper stickers, and decals. 760-735-8494.

**Idiot Ink Bumper Stickers,** P.O. Box 9368, Colorado Springs, CO 80932: Free brochure ◆ Full-color vinyl bumper stickers. 719-632-6877. www.idiot-ink.com

**Lancer Label,** 301 S. 74th St., Omaha, NE 68114: Free catalog ◆ Bumper stickers and labels in rolls, sheets, and pinfeed for computers. 800-228-7074.

**Prestige Promotions,** 4875 White Bear Pkwy., White Bear Lake, MN 55110: Free information ◆ Pens, coffee mugs, calendars, and bumper stickers. 800-328-9351.

**Royal Graphics Inc.,** 3117 N. Front St., Philadelphia, PA 19133: Free information ◆ Bumper stickers, posters, and show cards. 215-739-8282.

**N.G. Slater Corp.,** 220 W. 19th St., New York, NY 10011: Free catalog ◆ Advertising novelties, T-shirts, clips and pins, ID cards, bumper stickers, and equipment for making imprinted buttons. 212-924-3133.

## BUSINESS & CALLING CARDS, ID CARDS, & CARD CASES

**Advanced Products,** 11201 Hindry Ave., Los Angeles, CA 90045: Free catalog ◆ Plastic ID cards, calendars, and Rolodex cards. 800-421-2858.

**Artistic Greetings Catalog,** P.O. Box 1050, Elmira, NY 14902: Catalog $2 ◆ Business cards, memo and informal note cards, and personalized stationery. 800-733-6313. www.artisticgreetings.com

**Beaver Prints,** 305 Main St., Bellwood, PA 16617: Free information ◆ Business cards, matching brochures, stationery, postcards, and more. 814-742-6070.

**Arthur Blank & Company Inc.,** 225 Rivermoor St., Boston, MA 02132: Free information ◆ Plastic credit, ID, membership, and other cards. 800-776-7333; 617-325-9600 (in MA).

**The Business Book,** P.O. Box 1393, Hagerstown, MD 21741: Free catalog ◆ Pressure sensitive labels, stampers, personalized business envelopes and stationery, speed letters, memo pads, business cards and forms, greeting cards, books, and other office supplies. 800-558-0220.

**Business Envelopes,** P.O. Box 517, Thorofare, NJ 08086: Free catalog ◆ Business cards, imprinted envelopes, forms, stationery, and labels. 800-275-4400.

**CardCo,** 3525 Ryder St., Santa Clara, CA 95051: Free price list ◆ Business cards. 408-732-7526.

**Cowens,** 215 NE 59th St., Miami, FL 33137: Free information ◆ Vinyl card cases. 800-442-0244.

**Day-Timers,** One Day-Timer Plaza, Allentown, PA 18195: Free catalog ◆ Business cards, stationery, forms, and office supplies. 800-225-5005. www.daytimer.com

**Enfield Stationers,** Olympia Sales, 215 Moody Rd., Enfield, CT 06082: Free catalog ◆ Greeting cards, calendars, and gifts. 860-749-0751.

**Grayarc,** P.O. Box 2944, Hartford, CT 06104: Free catalog ◆ Stationery, business cards, forms, labels, and envelopes. 800-562-5468.

**The Great American Printing Company,** P.O. Box 80459, Rancho Santa Margarita, CA 92688: Free brochure ◆ Custom and personalized colored photo business cards. 800-440-2368. www.gapco.com

**Heirloom Editions,** Box 520-B, Rt. 4, Carthage, MO 64836: Catalog $4 ◆ Victorian-style calling cards. 800-725-0725.

**Jackson Marketing Products,** Brownsville Rd., Mt. Vernon, IL 62864: Free information ◆ Business cards and supplies for making rubber stamps. 800-STAMP-CALL.

**Lee's Company Inc.,** 1717 N. Bayshore Dr., Unit 4145, Miami, FL 33132: Free information ◆ Photo business cards. 800-LEES-023.

**NEBS Inc.,** 500 Main St., Groton, MA 01471: Free catalog ◆ Computerized and manual business forms, stationery, labels, checks, business cards, and supplies. 800-367-6327. www.nebs.com

**The Personal Marketing Company,** Lasting Impressions Business Cards, P.O. Box 656, Shawnee Mission, KS 66201: Free information ◆ Full-color business cards. 800-458-8245.

**Photo Card Specialists Inc.,** 1726 Westgate Rd., Eau Claire, WI 54703: Free information ◆ Full-color photo business cards. 800-727-4488; 715-839-9102 (in WI).

**Photo Images,** 554 Park Dr., Jackson, MS 39208: Free information ◆ Photo business cards. 800-637-1440.

**Pronto Business Cards,** Box 548, Safety Harbor, FL 34695: Free catalog ◆ Raised business cards. 813-726-8120.

**Silver Image Photographics,** 3102 Vestal Pkwy. East, Vestal, NY 13850: Free information ◆ Custom photo and color business cards, enlargements, and poster prints. 607-797-8795.

**Smalltown Printing Service,** 67000 E. CR38, Byers, CO 80103: Free catalog ◆ Rodeo and western-theme business cards. Available with personal photographs. 303-929-8982.

**ZIP Business Cards,** P.O. Box 935, Norwalk, OH 44857: Free information ◆ Thermographed business cards in wholesale quantities. 800-882-6757.

## BUTTER CHURNS

**Lehman Hardware & Appliances Inc.,** P.O. Box 41, Kidron, OH 44636: Catalog $2 ◆ Butter churns. 330-857-5757. GetLehmans@aol.com

**Mills River Industries,** 824 Locust St., Hendersonville, NC 28792: Catalog $1 ◆ Butter churns and other decorative accents for the home. 704-697-9778.

**Zimmerman Handcrafts,** 254 E. Main St., Leola, PA 17540: Brochure $1 ◆ Butter churns, country-style decorative items, and traditional crafts. 800-267-5689.

## BUTTERFLIES & OTHER INSECTS

**Brown's Edgewood Gardens,** 2611 Corrine Dr., Orlando, FL 32803: Catalog $3 ◆ Butterfly-attracting plants, herbs, and organic gardening products. 407-896-3203.

**The Butterfly Gallery Inc.,** 1304 Poppyseed Dr., New Brighton, MN 55112: Free information ◆ Butterfly-raising kits. 612-717-0115. tbgallery@usa.net

**Flutterbies,** 447 Stanley Plaza Blvd., Newark, DE 19173: Free brochure ◆ Live Monarch butterflies for celebrating special occasions. 302-455-1833.

**The Nature Products Company,** Yawgoo Pond Rd., West Kingston, RI 02892: Free information ◆ Hummingbird and butterfly feeders. 800-556-7670.

**Young Entomologists' Society Inc.,** 1915 Peggy Pl., Lansing, MI 48910: Free catalog ◆ Butterflies, entomology supplies, and kits. 517-887-0499.

# CABINETS

## Bathroom Cabinets

**Decorá,** P.O. Box 420, Jasper, IN 47547: Free information ◆ Bathroom cabinets, knobs, and pulls. 812-634-2288. www.decora.com

**NuTone Inc.,** P.O. Box 1580, Cincinnati, OH 45201: Catalog $3 ◆ Bathroom cabinets, other fixtures, and accessories. 800-543-8687. www.nutone.com

**Omega Too,** 2204 San Pablo Ave., Berkeley, CA 94702: Free information ◆ Wood medicine cabinets. 510-843-3636.

**Sonoma Woodworks Inc.,** 1285 S. Cloverdale Blvd., Cloverdale, CA 95425: Brochure $1 ◆ Medicine and vanity cabinets, high-tank pull chain toilets, and bathroom furniture. 800-659-9003.

## General Purpose Cabinets

**Campbell Cabinets,** 116 Barber St., Bath, PA 18014: Brochure $1. 610-837-7775.

**Craftsmen in Wood,** 5441 W. Hadley St., Phoenix, AZ 85043: Catalog $8. 602-278-8054.

**Iberia Millwork,** P.O. Box 12139, New Iberia, LA 70562: Free information. 318-365-8129.

**The Kennebec Company**, One Front St., Bath, ME 04530: Portfolio $10. 207-443-2131.

**Specialty Woodworks,** P.O. Box 1450, Hamilton, MT 59840: Catalog $7. 406-363-6353. www.montana.com/specialtywoodworks

**Vintage Pine Company,** P.O. Box 85, Prospect, VA 23960: Free information ◆ Custom heart-pine cabinets. 804-248-9102.

## Kitchen Cabinets

**Aristokraft,** P.O. Box 3513, Evansville, IN 47734: Planning kit $7.95. 812-482-2527. www.aristokraft.com

**CrownPoint Cabinetry,** 153 Charlestown Rd., P.O. Box 1560, Claremont, NH 03743: Free information. 800-999-4994.

**Crystal Cabinet Works Inc.,** 1100 Crystal Dr., Princeton, MN 55371: Free list of retail sources. 612-389-4187.

**Decorá,** 1 Aristocraft Sq., Jasper, IN 47547: Free information. 812-634-2288. www.decora.com

**Fieldstone Cabinetry Inc.,** P.O. Box 109, Northwood, IA 50459: Free information. 800-339-5369.

**Haas Cabinet Company Inc.,** 625 W. Utica St., Sellersburg, IN 47172: Free information. 800-457-6458.

**Heritage Custom Kitchens,** 215 Diller Ave., New Holland, PA 17557: Free information. 717-354-4011.

**Hirsh Company,** 8051 Central Ave., Skokie, IL 60076: Free information. 847-673-6610.

**HomeCrest Corp.,** P.O. Box 595, Goshen, IN 46526: Free information. 800-346-4852.

**The Kennebec Company,** One Front St., Bath, ME 04530: Portfolio $10. 207-443-2131.

**Kitchen Kompact Inc.,** P.O. Box 868, Jeffersonville, IN 47131: Free information. 812-282-6681.

**KraftMaid Cabinetry Inc.,** 16052 Industrial Pkwy., P.O. Box 1055, Middlefield, OH 44062: Catalog $4. 800-495-1990. www.kraftmaid.com

**Merillat Industries Inc.,** P.O. Box 1946, Adrian, MI 49221: Free information. 800-624-1250. www.merillat.com

**Plain 'n Fancy Kitchens,** P.O. Box 519, Schaefferstown, PA 17088: Free information. 800-447-9006.

**Rutt Custom Cabinetry,** P.O. Box 129, Goodville, PA 17528: Catalog $7 (request list of retail sources). 800-420-7888. www.rutt1.com

**Triangle Pacific Corp.,** 16803 Dallas Pkwy., Dallas, TX 75266: Free information. 972-931-3000.

**Wellborn Cabinet Inc.,** P.O. Box 1210, Ashland, AL 36251: Free list of retail sources. 800-336-8040.

**Wilsonart,** P.O. Box 6110, Temple, TX 76503: Free information. 800-710-8846. www.wilsonart.com

**Wood-Hu Kitchens Inc.,** 343 Manley St., West Bridgewater, MA 02379: Free information. 800-343-7919; 508-586-8050 (in MA).

**Wood-Mode Cabinets,** 1 Second St., Kreamer, PA 17833: Free information. 717-374-2711. www.wood-mode.com

## Kits & Parts

**Cabinet Factory Inc.,** 2600 Hemstock St., La Crosse, WI 54603: Free brochure ◆ Finished or unfinished drawers and doors. 800-237-1326.

# CALCULATORS

**Fidelity Products Company,** P.O. Box 155, Minneapolis, MN 55440: Free catalog ◆ Calculators, office equipment, and supplies. 800-328-3034; 612-526-6500 (in MN).

**Office Depot Inc.,** 2200 Old Germantown Rd., Delray Beach, FL 33445: Free catalog ◆ Calculators, office equipment, and supplies. 800-685-8800. www.officedepot.com

**Quill Office Supplies,** 100 Schelter Rd., Lincolnshire, IL 60197: Free catalog ◆ Calculators, computers and peripherals, office equipment, and supplies. 800-789-1331. www.quillcorp.com

**Reliable Home Office,** P.O. Box 1502, Ottawa, IL 61350: Catalog $2 ◆ Calculators, computer accessories and furniture, filing and storage systems, fax machines, and office supplies. 800-326-6230.

**Staples Inc.,** P.O. Box 5173, Westborough, MA 01581: Free catalog ◆ Calculators, office supplies, furniture, computer accessories, drafting equipment, fax machines, and typewriters. 800-333-3330. www.staples.com

**Viking Office Products,** 13809 S. Figueroa St., P.O. Box 61144, Los Angeles, CA 90061: Free catalog ◆ Office equipment, calculators, and supplies. 800-421-1222. www.VikingOP.com

**Wholesale Electronic Supply Inc.,** Education Division, 2809 Ross Ave., Dallas, TX 75201: Free catalog ◆ Calculators and accessories. 800-880-9400; 972-969-9400 (in TX).

# CALENDARS

**Accents,** 215 Moody Rd., Enfield, CT 06083: Free catalog ◆ Greeting cards, calendars, and gifts. 800-357-1000.

**Angler's Catalog Company,** P.O. Box 161, Twin Falls, ID 83303: Free catalog ◆ Gifts and calendars for the fly fisherman. 800-657-8040; 208-735-8755 (in ID). anglecat@micron.net

**Candid Calendars,** 10498 Loveland-Madeira Rd., Loveland, OH 45140; Free information ◆ Personalized photo calendars, puzzles, coasters, hats, mouse pads, neckties, aprons, and more. 800-328-8415; 513-583-0883 (in OH). www.candidcalendars.com

**Cedco Publishing Company,** 100 Pelican Way, San Rafael, CA 94901: Free catalog ◆ Calendars and date and other memorandum-style books. 800-233-2624. www.cedco.com

**Christian Book Distributors,** P.O. Box 7000, Peabody, MA 01961: Free catalog ◆ Religious-theme calendars. 978-977-5050. www.chrbook.com

**Culinary Collections,** P.O. Box 1823, Winter Park, FL 32790: Free catalog ◆ Calendars, cookbooks, and stationery. 407-647-6765. www.netcom.com/~sgridley

**Down East Books & Gifts,** P.O. Box 679, Camden, ME 04843: Free catalog ◆ Calendars, books, and crafts from Maine and New England. 800-766-1670.

**Enfield Stationers,** Olympia Sales, 215 Moody Rd., Enfield, CT 06082: Free catalog ◆ Greeting cards, calendars, and gifts. 860-749-0751.

**G & K Enterprises,** 1408 Glenwood Ave., Greensboro, NC 27403: Free information ◆ Calendars and all-occasion and Christmas greeting cards with a western theme. 336-275-0049.

**Heirloom Editions,** Box 520-B, Rt. 4, Carthage, MO 64836: Catalog $4 ◆ Lithographs, greeting cards, stickers, miniatures, stationery, framed prints, and turn-of-the-century art and paper collectibles. 800-725-0725.

**Kar-Ben Copies Inc.,** 6800 Tildenwood Ln., Rockville, MD 20852: Free catalog ◆ Calendars. 800-452-7236. www.karben.com

**Lang Companies,** P.O. Box 55, Delafield, WI 53018: Catalog $1 ◆ Country-style calendars, boxed note cards, and greeting cards. 800-967-3399. www.lang.com

**Main Street Press,** P.O. Box 126, Delafield, WI 53018: Catalog $1 ◆ Wall calendars, boxed greeting cards, note cards and pads, and stationery. 414-646-8511.

**National Wildlife Federation,** P.O. Box 9004, Winchester, VA 22604: Free catalog ◆ Nature-theme calendars and holiday cards. 800-477-5560. www.nwf.org

**Naval Institute Press,** Customer Service, 2062 Generals Hwy., Annapolis, MD 21401: Free catalog ◆ Calendars. 800-233-8764. www.usni.org

**Petprints Inc.,** P.O. Box 643, Corona Del Mar, CA 92625: Free information ◆ Calendars with pictures of pets. 800-738-2257; 714-444-1944 (in CA). www.petprints.com

**Pomegranate Calendars & Books,** Box 6099, Rohnert Park, CA 94927: Free catalog ◆ Wall, mini, pocket, wallet, and poster calendars. 800-227-1428; 707-586-5500 (in CA).

**Posty Cards,** 1600 Olive St., Kansas City, MO 64127: Free catalog ◆ Calendars and greeting and birthday cards. 800-554-5018. www.postycards.com

**N. Schumann Publisher Inc.,** P.O. Box 504, East Boothbay, ME 04544: Free information ◆ Original poster calendars and prints and note cards adapted from past calendars. Also children's posters for classroom and home use. 888-383-6027. www.nikkischumann.com

**Ronnie Sellers Productions Inc.,** P.O. Box 71, Kennebunk, ME 04043: Free catalog ◆ Humor, theme, specialty design, cause-related, and portobello picture calendars. 800-625-3386.

**Sormani Calendars Inc.,** P.O. Box 6059, Chelsea, MA 02150: Free catalog ◆ Photo illustrated calendars. 800-321-9327; 617-387-7300 (in MA).

**Thoroughbred Racing Catalog,** P.O. Box 610, Warsaw, VA 22572: Free catalog ◆ Calendars and limited edition prints with pictures of famous racing horses and horse-decorated mailboxes, doormats, sweatshirts and T-shirts, mugs and glasses, jewelry, and wall clocks. 800-777-RACE. www.thoroughbred-racing.com

**Tide-Mark Press Ltd.,** P.O. Box 280311, East Hartford, CT 06128: Catalog $2 ◆ Calendars and desk diaries. 800-338-2508. tide860@aol.com

**Write Stuff Syndicate Inc.,** 1515 SE 4th Ave., Fort Lauderdale, FL 33316: Free brochure ◆ Hardbound coffee table books and classic boat calendars. 954-462-6657. www.writestuffbooks.com

**Zenith Books,** P.O. Box 1, Osceola, WI 54020: Free catalog ◆ Calendars, books, and videos about aviation. 800-826-6600. www.motorbooks.com

## CALLIGRAPHY

**American Stationery Company,** 100 Park Ave., Peru, IN 46970: Free catalog ◆ Regular and calligraphy stationery, wedding invitations, note cards and personal memos, envelopes, and postcards. 800-822-2577.

**Ken Brown Studio,** P.O. Box 22, McKinney, TX 75069: Catalog $1 ◆ Calligraphy supplies and engraving equipment . 800-654-6100. www.kenbrownink.com

**Bugei Trading Company,** 1070 Commerce St., Ste. I, San Marcos, CA 92069: Catalog $5 ◆ Products from the feudal era of the Samurai. Includes Japanese swords, calligraphy supplies, and instructional videos. 800-437-0125.

**Creative Calligraphy,** 1600 E. Lincoln Hwy., P.O. Box 943, De Kalb, IL 60115: Catalog $2 ◆ Framed personal remembrances and family heirloom collectibles. 800-545-3928; 815-756-6900 (in IL).

**Ebersole Arts & Crafts Supply,** 11417 West Hwy. 54, Wichita, KS 67209: Catalog $5 ◆ Calligraphy and art supplies. 316-722-4771.

**Hunt Manufacturing Company,** 2005 Market St., Philadelphia, PA 19103: Free information ◆ Fountain pens and sets, nibs, inks, and calligraphy papers, markers, and kits. 800-765-5669.

**Literary Calligraphy,** 5326 White House Rd., Moneta, VA 24121: Catalog $2 ◆ Framed literary calligraphy gifts. 800-261-6325. susanloy@rev.net

**Nasco,** 901 Janesville Ave., Fort Atkinson, WI 53538: Free catalog ◆ Calligraphy supplies and greeting cards. 800-558-9595. www.nascofa.com

**John Neal, Bookseller,** 1833 Spring Garden St., Greensboro, NC 27403: Free information ◆ Calligraphy and marbling supplies, books on arts and crafts, and bookbinding services. 800-369-9598; 336-272-6139 (in NC). www.JohnNealBooks.com

**Otts Art Supplies,** 102 Hungate Dr., Greenville, NC 27858: Free catalog ◆ Art, calligraphy, and drawing supplies. 800-356-3280. www.otts.com

**Paper & Ink Books,** P.O. Box 35, 3 N. 2nd St., Woodsboro, MD 21798: Free catalog ◆ Calligraphy books and supplies. 301-898-7991.

**Pendragon,** P.O. Box 1995, Arlington Heights, IL 60006: Catalog $2 ◆ Calligraphy supplies. 800-775-7367.

**Victorian House,** 1203 Columbus Circle, Janesville, WI 53545: Brochure $1 ◆ Victorian-style certificates with optional calligraphy. 800-597-8378.

## CAMCORDERS & ACCESSORIES

### Manufacturers

**Allsop,** P.O. Box 23, Bellingham, WA 98227: Free information ◆ Camcorders. 800-426-4303; 360-734-9090 (in WA).

**AMI Corp.,** P.O. Box 27682, Denver, CO 80227: Free information ◆ Camcorders and accessories. Also computer and audio and video equipment. 800-325-0853.

**Azden Corp.,** 147 New Hyde Park Rd., Franklin Square, NY 11016: Free information ◆ Camcorders, headphones, and electronics. 516-328-7500.

**Canon,** One Canon Plaza, Lake Success, NY 11042: Free information ◆ Cassette players, camcorders, and electronics. 516-488-6700. www.usa.canon.com

**Casio,** P.O. Box 7000, Dover, NJ 07801: Free information ◆ Camcorders. 973-361-5400. www.casio-usa.com

**Chinon America Inc.,** 1065 Bristol Rd., Mountainside, NJ 07092: Free information ◆ Camcorders. 908-654-0404.

**Discwasher,** 2950 Lake Emma Rd., Lake Mary, FL 32746: Free information ◆ Camcorders. 800-325-0573.

**Eastman Kodak Company,** Kodak Information Center, 343 State St., Rochester, NY 14650: Free information ◆ Camcorders. 800-242-2424. www.kodak.com

**Emerson Radio Corp.,** 9 Entin Rd., Parsippany, NJ 07054: Free information ◆ Camcorders, monitors, receivers, cassette and CD players, and TVs. 201-884-5800.

**Hitachi Sales Corp.,** Customer Service, 3890 Steve Reynolds Blvd., Norcross, GA 30093: Free information ◆ Cassette and CD players, camcorders, TVs, and electronics. 800-241-6558.

**JVC,** 41 Slater Dr., Elmwood Park, NJ 07407: Free information ◆ CD and cassette players, camcorders, receivers, amplifiers, TVs, and headphones. 800-252-5722. www.jvc-america.com

**Minolta,** 101 Williams Dr., Ramsey, NJ 07446: Free information ◆ Cassette players and camcorders. 201-825-4000. www.minolta.com

**Mitsubishi Electronics,** 5757 Plaza Dr., Cypress, CA 90630: Free information ◆ Audio and video systems, cassette and CD players, camcorders, and TVs. 800-843-2515.

**NEC Technologies,** 1250 N. Arlington Heights Rd., Itasca, IL 60143: Free information ◆ Speakers, CD and cassette players, receivers, amplifiers, TVs, camcorders, and electronics. 800-284-4484. www.nec.com

**Olympus Corp.,** 2 Corporate Center Dr., Melville, NY 11747: Free information ◆ Camcorders. 800-221-3000. www.olympusamerica.com

**Panasonic,** Panasonic Way, Secaucus, NJ 07094: Free list of retail sources ◆ Audio and video systems, cassette and CD players, TVs, camcorders, headphones, and electronics. 201-348-7000. www.panasonic.com

**Pentax Corp.,** 35 Inverness Dr. East, Englewood, CO 80112: Free information ◆ Cassette players, camcorders, and electronics. 303-799-8000. www.pentax.com

**Radio Shack,** Division Tandy Corp., One Tandy Center, Fort Worth, TX 76102: Free information ◆ Cassette and CD players, camcorders, universal remotes, computers, and electronics. 817-390-3011. www.radioshack.com

**RCA Sales Corp.,** Thomson Consumer Electronics, P.O. Box 1976, Indianapolis, IN 46206: Free information ◆ Audio and video systems, cassette and CD players, TVs, camcorders, and electronics. 800-336-1900.

**Ricoh Consumer Products Group,** 475 Lillard Dr., Sparks, NV 89434: Free brochure ◆ Camcorders. 800-225-1899. www.ricohcpg.com

**Sanyo Fisher,** P.O. Box 2329, Chatsworth, CA 91313: Free information ◆ Cassette and CD players, camcorders, TVs, and electronics. 818-998-7322.

**Sharp Electronics,** Sharp Plaza, Mahwah, NJ 07496: Free information ◆ Cassette and CD players, camcorders, TVs, and electronics. 800-BE-SHARP. www.sharp-usa.com

**Sony Consumer Products,** 1 Sony Dr., Park Ridge, NJ 07656: Free information with long SASE ◆ Camcorders, speakers, CD and cassette players, headphones, and electronics. 201-930-1000. www.sony.com

## Retailers

**Abe's of Maine Camera & Electronics,** 1957 Coney Island Ave., Brooklyn, NY 11223: Free information ◆ Video and photography equipment, camcorders, and accessories. 800-531-2237. ABEMAINE@aol.com

**Accessory Source,** 1864 48th St., Brooklyn, NY 11204: Free information ◆ Batteries, video tapes, microphones, editors and mixers, and other equipment. 800-723-6633; 718-435-0343 (in NY).

**Audio Video Center,** 490 2nd Street Pike, Southampton, PA 18966: Free information ◆ Camcorders and audio components. 800-220-6510; 215-942-2242 (in PA).

**B & H Photo-Video,** 420 9th Ave., New York, NY 10001: Catalog $3.95 ◆ Photographic and video equipment and camcorders. 800-947-9903; 212-444-5001 (in NY). www.bhphotovideo.com

**Beach Photo & Video Inc.,** 604 Main St., Daytona Beach, FL 32118: Free information ◆ Video equipment and camcorders. 904-252-0577. www.beachphoto.com

**Bel Air Camera & Video,** 1025 Westwood Blvd., Los Angeles, CA 90024: Free information ◆ Photographic equipment and video cameras. 800-200-4999.

**Berger Brothers Camera Exchange,** 209 Broadway, Amityville, NY 11701: Free information ◆ Camcorders and accessories. 800-262-4160; 516-264-4160 (in NY). www.berger-bros.com

**Cam America,** 7403 18th Ave., Brooklyn, NY 11204: Free information ◆ Camcorders and accessories. 800-667-8878. www.camamerica.com

**Camera City Inc.,** 342 Kings Hwy., Brooklyn, NY 11223: Free information ◆ Camcorders and accessories. 800-896-2626.

**Camera Sound of Pennsylvania,** 1104 Chestnut St., Philadelphia, PA 19107: Free information ◆ Camcorders, VCRs, editing equipment, and electronics. 800-477-0022; 215-627-1080 (in PA).

**Camera World,** 1809 Commonwealth Ave., Charlotte, NC 28205: Catalog $1 ◆ Video equipment, camcorders, and photography equipment. 800-868-3686; 704-375-8453 (in NC). www.cameraworld.com

**Camera World of Oregon,** 700 NW 55th Ave., Portland, OR 97213: Free information ◆ Camcorders and tapes. 800-729-8937; 503-227-6008 (in OR). www.cameraworld.com

**Coast to Coast,** 2570 86th St., Brooklyn, NY 11214: Free information ◆ Camcorders, video editing equipment, receivers, CD and cassette players, and other equipment. 800-788-5555. www.coasttocoastcamera.com

**Colonel Video & Audio,** 10765 Kingspoint Dr., Houston, TX 77075: Free information ◆ Video and audio editing equipment, camcorders, and accessories. 713-910-1776.

**Data Vision,** 445 5th Ave., New York, NY 10016: Free information ◆ Video cameras and editing equipment. 888-888-2087; 212-689-1111 (in NY). www.datavis.com

**Division of Video Necessities,** 1546 Coney Island Ave., Brooklyn, NY 11230: Free information ◆ Audio, video, multi-system, and home theater equipment. 800-228-8480.

**Electronic Mailbox,** 10-12 Charles St., Glen Cove, NY 11542: Free information ◆ Camcorder, video, and production accessories. 800-323-2325. www.videoguys.com

**Electronic Wholesalers,** 1166 Hamburg Tnpk., Wayne, NJ 07470: Free information ◆ Camcorders, TVs, cassette players, audio and video receivers, CD and laser players, and telephones. 201-696-6531. www.samans.com

**Executive Digital & Imaging Corp.,** 60 Broadway, Brooklyn, NY 11211: Free information ◆ Cameras, camcorders, video equipment, VCRs, and accessories. 888-5-EXECUTIVE.

**Family Photo & Video,** 1957 Coney Island Ave., Brooklyn, NY 11257: Free information ◆ Cameras, camcorders, video equipment, VCRs, and accessories. 800-405-7468; 718-645-1298 (in NY).

**Free Trade Photo Video,** 4718 18th Ave., Brooklyn, NY 11204: Free information ◆ Cameras, camcorders, video equipment, VCRs, and accessories. 800-234-8813; 718-633-6890 (in NY). www.freetradephoto.com

**Genesis Camera Inc.,** 814 W. Lancaster Ave., Bryn Mawr, PA 19010: Free information ◆ Audio, video, and photographic equipment. 800-575-9977; 610-527-5260 (in PA). GENESIS@DVOL.com

**Global Video,** 1104 Chestnut St., Philadelphia, PA 19107: Free information ◆ Video cameras and editing equipment. 800-211-4101.

**Hunt's Photo & Video,** 100 Main St., Melrose, MA 02176: Free information ◆ Camcorders and accessories. 800-924-8682. www.wbhunt.com

**K.P. Pro Video Inc.,** 87-07 Jamaica Ave., Woodhaven, NY 11421: Free information ◆ Used and new equipment. 800-670-6555.

**Marine Park Camera & Video Inc.,** 3126 Ave. U, Brooklyn, NY 11229: Free information ◆ Video equipment and VCRs. 800-360-1722; 718-891-1878 (in NY).

**Markertek Video Supply,** 4 High St., Saugerties, NY 12477: Free catalog ◆ Video equipment. 800-522-2025.

**Mission Service Supply,** 4565 Cypress St., West Monroe, LA 71291: Free catalog ◆ Camcorders, video systems, and accessories. 800-352-7222; 318-397-2755 (in LA).

**New West Electronics,** 4120 Meridian, Bellingham, WA 98226: Free information ◆ VCRs, camcorders, TVs and monitors, disk players, audio components and speakers, and electronics. 800-488-8877.

**Newtech Video & Computers,** 350 7th Ave., New York, NY 10001: Free information ◆ Video equipment, computers and peripherals, software, cellular phones, fax machines, and office equipment. 800-554-9747.

**Paramount Video & Photo,** 260 W. Swedesford Rd., Berwyn, PA 19312: Free information ◆ Camcorders and accessories. 800-477-0330.

**Philly's Camera,** 27 S. 11th St., Philadelphia, PA 19107: Free information ◆ Camcorders and accessories. 215-922-5130.

**Photo-Video,** 420 8th Ave., New York, NY 10001: Catalog $3.95 ◆ Photographic and video equipment and camcorders. 800-947-9960; 212-444-6660 (in NY). www.bhphotovideo.com

**Prime Time Video & Cameras,** 1104 Chestnut St., Philadelphia, PA 19107: Free information ◆ Video cameras and editing equipment. 800-477-8445.

**Profeel Video,** 42 Main St., Monsey, NY 10952: Free information ◆ Video cameras and editing equipment. 914-425-2070.

**Professional Video Warehouse,** 575 SE Ashley Pl., Grants Pass, OR 97526: Free information ◆ Video equipment. 800-736-6677.

**The Right Spirit Corp.,** 118 S. Westshore Blvd., Ste. 231, Tampa, FL 33609: Free information ◆ Underwater video camera housing. 800-269-6867.

**Samman's Electronics,** 1166 Hamburg Tnpk., Wayne, NJ 07470: Free information ◆ Camcorders, home theater systems, and accessories. 800-AUDIO-93.

**Sixth Avenue Electronics,** Rt. 22 West, Springfield, NJ 07081: Free information ◆ Video and audio equipment, TVs, monitors, camcorders, laser players, and electronics. 201-467-0100.

**Smile Photo & Video,** 29 W. 35th St., New York, NY 10001: Free information ◆ Photography and video equipment. 212-967-5900.

**Sound City,** 45 Indian Lane East, Towaco, NJ 07082: Free information ◆ Audio and video equipment, cassette and CD players, camcorders, TVs, processors, fax machines, telephones, and electronics. 800-432-0007; 973-263-6060 (in NJ). www.soundcity.com

**The Southern Advantage Company,** 8108 Idlewild Rd., #794, Charlotte, NC 28212: Free information ◆ Camcorders, VCRs, home audio equipment, videonics accessories, and other electronics. 800-632-6076. www.southernadvantage.com

**Sunshine Camera and Video,** 1562 Coney Island Ave., Brooklyn, NY 11230: Free information ◆ Computers, memory upgrades, fax modems, carrying cases, mouse devices, batteries, video equipment, and other electronics. 800-331-2661; 718-692-4140 (in NY).

**Supreme Camera & Video,** 1562 Coney Island Ave., Brooklyn, NY 11230: Free information ◆ Video editing equipment. 800-332-2661; 718-692-4140 (in NY).

**Thrifty Distributors,** 641 W. Lancaster Ave., Frazer, PA 19355: Free catalog ◆ Video cameras, editing equipment, batteries, wireless microphones, lights, and accessories. 800-342-3610.

**Tri-State Camera,** 650 6th Ave., New York, NY 10011: Free information ◆ Audio and video equipment and cassettes, camcorders, fax machines, and accessories. 800-221-1926; 212-633-2290 (in NY). tscamvid@aol.com

**Universal Video & Camera,** 1104 Chestnut St., Philadelphia, PA 19107: Free information ◆ Video cameras and editing equipment. 800-477-1003.

**Video Direct Distributors,** 116 Production Dr., Yorktown, VA 23693: Free catalog ◆ Video and audio equipment, TVs, monitors, camcorders, microphones, carrying cases, and electronics. 800-368-5020.

**Video Discount Warehouse,** 203 Commack Rd., Ste. 152, Commack, NY 11725: Free information ◆ Camcorders and accessories. 800-301-0028; 516-543-4398 (in NY).

**Video Innovators,** P.O. Box 4130, Frisco, CO 80443: Free information ◆ Camcorders and support equipment. 800-872-2636.

**Video Plus,** 6533 Roosevelt Blvd., Philadelphia, PA 19149: Free information ◆ Camcorders, VCRs, home audio and videonic equipment, and other electronics. 800-226-6784.

**Videonics,** 1370 Dell Ave., Campbell, CA 95008: Free list of retail sources ◆ Video editing equipment. 800-338-EDIT.

**Vidicomp Inc.,** 10988 Wilcrest, Houston, TX 77099: Free information ◆ Video cameras and editing equipment. 800-263-8211.

**Wholesale Connection,** 361 Charles St., West Hampstead, NY 11552: Free information ◆ Camcorders, video accessories, and audio, car stereos, and home theater equipment. 800-967-5588.

**World Photo & Video,** 225 Liberty St., New York, NY 10281: Free information ◆ New and used photography equipment, binoculars, camcorders, and electronics. 212-945-7415.

**World Trade Video,** 295 Greenwich St., Ste. 360, New York, NY 10007: Free information ◆ Camcorders and accessories. 800-253-2639.

**Worldwide Photo, Video & Electronics,** 203 US Hwy. 22, Greenbrook, NJ 08812: Free information ◆ Cameras, video equipment, camcorders, VCRs, and accessories. 800-995-6800. WWPVE@AOL.com

### Video Editing Equipment

**Accessory Source,** 1864 48th St., Brooklyn, NY 11204: Free information ◆ Batteries, video tapes, microphones, editors and mixers, and other equipment. 800-723-6633; 718-435-0343 (in NY).

**Colonel Video & Audio,** 10765 Kingspoint Dr., Houston, TX 77075: Free information ◆ Video and audio editing equipment. 713-910-1776.

**CrystalGraphics,** 3350 Scott Blvd., Ste. 1114, Santa Clara, CA 95054: Free information ◆ Windows 3-D animation titling software. 408-496-6175. www.crystalgraphics.com

**Energetic Music,** P.O. Box 84583, Seattle, WA 98124: Free catalog ◆ Royalty-free production music CDs and cassettes. 800-323-2972.

**Fast Electronic U.S. Inc.,** 393 Vintage Park Dr., Foster City, CA 94404: Free information ◆ Desktop video production software for PCs. 800-249-FAST.

**FutureVideo,** 28 Argonaut, Aliso Viejo, CA 92656: Free information ◆ Windows video editing software. 800-346-5254; 714-770-4416 (in CA).

**NRG Research Inc.,** 233 Rogue River Hwy., Ste. 1144, Grants Pass, OR 97527: Free catalog ◆ Video editing equipment and accessories. 800-753-0357.

**Planet Electronics,** P.O. Box 251446, West Bloomfield, MI 48325: Free catalog ◆ Computer-controlled editing software for PCs. 800-542-8811.

**Studio 1 Productions,** 1524 County Line Rd., York Springs, PA 17372: Free catalog ◆ Video editing equipment and accessories. 717-528-8374.

**Video-Cam Productions,** 3264 W. Stephens Pl., Chandler, AZ 85226: Free information ◆ Video editing equipment and accessories. 800-564-1865.

**Videonics,** 1370 Dell Ave., Campbell, CA 95008: Free list of retail sources ◆ Editing equipment. 800-338-EDIT.

**The Winstead Corp.,** 10901 Hampshire Ave. South, Minneapolis, MN 55438: Free catalog ◆ Video support systems. 612-944-9050.

## CAMPING & BACKPACKING

### Clothing & Shoes

**ActionDirect,** P.O. Box 830760, Miami, FL 33283: Free catalog ◆ Gear and clothing for outdoor activities. 800-667-4191. www.action-direct.com

**Adidas USA,** 5675 N. Blackstock Rd., Spartanburg, SC 29303: Free list of retail sources ◆ Hiking and climbing shoes. 800-423-4327. www.adidas.com

**Alpina Sports Corp.,** P.O. Box 24, Hanover, NH 03755: Free list of retail sources ◆ Hiking and climbing shoes. 800-4-ALPINA. www.alpinasports.com

**Alpine Adventures,** 7012 S. 300 East, Midvale, UT 84047: Free catalog ◆ Outdoor apparel and camping gear. 801-561-1592. rich@alpine-adventures.com

**American Camper,** 14760 Santa Fe Trail Dr., Lenexa, KS 66215: Free list of retail sources ◆ Camouflage clothing and backpacks. 800-315-2267. www.americancamper.com

**Asolo Boots,** Nordica Sportsystems, P.O. Box 800, Williston, VT 05495: Free list of retail sources ◆ Outdoor footwear. 800-892-2668. www.asolo.com

**B-West Outdoor Specialties,** 2425 N. Huachuca, Tucson, AZ 85745: Free catalog ◆ Backpacks, shoes and boots, and outdoor accessories. 800-293-7855; 520-628-1990 (in AZ).

**Eddie Bauer,** P.O. Box 182639, Columbus, OH 43218: Free catalog ◆ Men and women's active and casual clothes, footwear, and goose down outerwear. 800-426-8020. www.ebauer.com

**L.L. Bean,** Casco St., Freeport, ME 04032: Free catalog ◆ Clothing for hiking, camping, fishing, sports, and other outdoor activities. 800-221-4221. www.llbean.com

**Brigade Quartermasters Inc.,** 1025 Cobb International Blvd., Kennesaw, GA 30144: Free catalog ◆ Clothing, rainwear, and camping gear. 800-338-4327. www.actiongear.com

**Browning Company,** Dept. C006, One Browning Pl., Morgan, UT 84050: Catalog $2 ◆ Clothing, rainwear, and hiking shoes. 800-333-3288. www.browning.com

**Campmor,** P.O. Box 700, Saddle River, NJ 07458: Free catalog ◆ Outdoor clothing and equipment for climbing, camping, hiking, backpacking, and biking. 800-226-7667. www.campmor.com

**Climb High Inc.,** 1861 Shelburne Rd., Shelburne, VT 05482: Free catalog ◆ Boots and clothing, carabineers, ropes, backpacks, sleeping bags, and equipment. 802-985-5056. www.climbhigh.com

**Coleman Outdoor Products Inc.,** P.O. Box 2931, Wichita, KS 67201: Free catalog ◆ Clothing, hiking and climbing shoes, and equipment. 800-835-3278. www.coleman.com

**Damart,** 3 Front St., Rollinsford, NH 03805: Free information ◆ Thermal underwear for men and women. 800-258-7300. www.damartusa.com

**Danner Shoe Manufacturing Company,** 12722 NE Airport Way, Portland, OR 97230: Free catalog ◆ Climbing and hiking boots. 800-345-0430. www.danner.com

**Dorfman-Pacific,** P.O. Box 213005, Stockton, CA 95213: Free information ◆ Clothing and rainwear. 800-367-3626; 209-982-1400 (in CA).

**Fabiano Shoe Company,** 850 Summer St., South Boston, MA 02127: Free information with long SASE ◆ Insulated hiking and climbing shoes. 617-268-5625. info@fabiano.com

**Garmont USA Inc.,** Adams Park, 75 Boyer Circle, Williston, VT 05495: Free information ◆ Boots, backpacks, and hiking poles. 800-343-5200.

**Gorilla & Sons,** P.O. Box 2309, Bellingham, WA 98227: Free catalog ◆ Outdoor apparel and equipment. 800-246-7455.

**Hi-Tec Sports USA Inc.,** 4801 Stoddard Rd., Modesto, CA 95356: Free list of retail sources ◆ Hiking and climbing boots. 800-521-1698. www.hi-tec.com

**Hiker's Hut,** 99 Main St., Littleton, NH 03561: Free information ◆ Boots and footwear. 603-444-6532.

**Integral Designs,** 5516 3rd St., Calgary, Alberta, Canada T2H 1J9: Free catalog ◆ Sleeping bags, tents, and outerwear. 403-640-1445. www.integraldesigns.com

**La Sportiva USA,** 3280 Pearl St., Boulder, CO 80301: Free list of retail sources ◆ Climbing and hiking boots. 303-442-7541. www.sportiva.com/sportiva

**Legends Footwear,** 14450 Chambers Rd., Tustin, CA 92780: Free catalog ◆ Climbing and hiking boots. 800-948-7245.

**Leisure Outlet,** 953 Towes Pl., Santa Cruz, CA 95062: Free catalog ◆ Camping equipment and clothing. 800-322-1460. duraprod@aol.com

**Lowe Alpine,** P.O. Box 1449, Broomfield, CO 80038: Free list of retail sources ◆ Outdoor clothing, mountaineering fleecewear, and backpacks. 303-465-0522. www.lowealpine.com

**Martin Archery,** Rt. 5, Box 127, Walla Walla, WA 99362: Free information ◆ Hiking shoes. 509-529-2554. www.martinarchery.com

**Merrell Footwear,** 9345 Cortland Dr. NE, Rockford, MI 49351: Free list of retail sources ◆ Outdoor footwear. 888-637-70001. www.merrellboot.com

**Moonstone Mountaineering,** 5350 Ericson Way, Arcata, CA 95521: Free information ◆ Clothing, sleeping bags, and accessories. 800-822-2985. Moonstone@AOL.com

**Mt. Constance Mountain Shoppe,** 1550 NE Riddell Rd., Bremerton, WA 98310: Free catalog ◆ Outdoor equipment, in-line skates, and accessories for mountain bikes. 360-377-0668. MTSHOPPE@MOUNTAINSHOPPE.com

**O.H. Mullen Sales Inc.,** 9928 Rd. 171, Oakwood, OH 45873: Free information ◆ Clothing and rainwear. 800-258-6625.

**New Balance Athletic Shoe Inc.,** 61 N. Deacon St., Boston, MA 02134: Free list of retail sources ◆ Exercise suits, leotards, workout and hiking shoes, shorts and singlets for men and women, and warm-up suits. 800-622-1218. www.newbalance.com

**Nike Footwear Inc.,** One Bowerman Dr., Beaverton, OR 97005: Free list of retail sources ◆ Climbing shoes. 800-344-6453. www.nike.com

**North by Northeast,** 181 Conant St., Pawtucket, RI 02860: Free information ◆ Clothing and rainwear. 800-556-7262.

**North Face,** 2013 Farallon Dr., San Leandro, CA 94577: Free list of retail sources ◆ Clothing and rainwear. 800-447-2333.

**Northern Outfitters,** 14072 Pony Express Rd., Draper, UT 84020: Catalog $2 ◆ Clothing, sleeping bags, and accessories. 800-944-9276; 801-571-9979 (in UT). www.gorp.com/northern

**One Sport Outdoor Footwear,** 1003 6th Ave. South, Seattle WA 98134: Free list of retail sources ◆ Outdoor footwear. 206-621-9303.

**Only the Lightest Camping Equipment,** P.O. Box 266, Troutdale, OR 97060: Catalog $1 ◆ Lightweight clothing and camping equipment. 503-666-9365.

**Orvis Manchester,** 1711 Blue Hills Dr., P.O. Box 12000, Roanoke, VA 24022: Free catalog ◆ Outdoor clothing and equipment. 800-541-3541. www.orvis.com

**Pachmayr Ltd.,** 1875 S. Mountain Ave., Monrovia, CA 91016: Free catalog ◆ Shooting and hunting accessories, clothing, camping equipment, books, and videos. 800-423-9704.

**Patagonia,** 8550 White Fir St., Reno, NV 89523: Free catalog ◆ Outdoor clothing for children and adults. 800-638-6464. www.patagonia.com

**R.U. Outside Inc.,** 455 S. Main, Driggs, ID 83422: Free catalog ◆ Clothing and sports gear. 800-279-7123. www.ruoutside.com

**Raichle Molitor USA,** Geneva Rd., Brewster, NY 10509: Free list of retail sources ◆ Climbing and hiking boots. 800-431-2204. raichleus@aol.com

**Rainshed Outdoor Fabrics,** 707 NW 11th, Corvallis, OR 97330: Catalog $1 ◆ Outdoor fabrics, hardware, webbing, patterns, and supplies. 541-753-8900.

**Ramsey Outdoor Store,** 226 N. Rt. 17, P.O. Box 1689, Paramus, NJ 07653: Free catalog ◆ Outdoor apparel and equipment. 201-261-5000.

**REI Recreational Equipment Company,** Sumner, WA 98352: Free catalog ◆ Outdoor equipment and clothing, exercise and walking shoes, rainwear, packs that convert to tents, ski equipment, knives, cooking utensils, sunglasses, and foods. 800-426-4840. www.rei.com

**Rocky Shoes & Boots Inc.,** 294 Harper St., Nelsonville, OH 45764: Free list of retail sources ◆ Outdoor shoes and boots. 614-753-1951.

**The Royal Robbins Company,** 1314 Coldwell Ave., Modesto, CA 95350: Free information ◆ Outdoor clothing. 800-587-9044.

**Salomon/North America,** 400 E. Main St., Georgetown, MA 01833: Free list of retail sources ◆ Outdoor shoes and boots. 800-225-6850. www.salomonsports.com

**Sierra Trading Post,** 5025 Campstool Rd., Cheyenne, WY 82007: Free catalog ◆ Outdoor clothing and equipment. 800-713-4534. www.sierra-trading.com

**Solstice,** 2120 NE Oregon St., Portland, OR 97232: Free list of retail sources ◆ Outdoor clothing. 800-878-5733. www.solsticegear.com

**Sportif USA,** 1415 Greg St., Sparks, NV 89431: Free information ◆ Comfortable clothing for active and casual lifestyles. 800-776-7843. www.sportif.com

**Tecnica,** 19 Technology Dr., West Lebanon, NH 03784: Free list of retail sources ◆ Outdoor footwear. 800-258-3897. www.technicausa.com

**Thousand Mile Outdoor Wear,** 1894 Alta Vista Dr., Vista, CA 92084: Free catalog ◆ Men and women's outdoor clothing. 800-786-7577; 760-945-1609 (in CA).

**Vasque Boots,** 314 Main St., Red Wing, MN 55066: Free list of retail sources ◆ Hiking and climbing boots. 800-224-4453. www.vasque.com

**Jack Wolfskin,** 1326 Willow Rd., Sturtevant, WI 53177: Free list of retail sources ◆ Outerwear, backpacks, sleeping bags, tents, travel luggage, and outdoor equipment. 800-847-1460. www.jwa.com

**Wyoming River Raiders,** P.O. Box 50490, Casper, WY 82605: Free catalog ◆ Outdoor clothing, camping and river expedition equipment, fishing, hiking equipment, books, and supplies. 800-247-6068. www.riverraiders.com

## Equipment

**ActionDirect,** P.O. Box 830760, Miami, FL 33283: Free catalog ◆ Gear and clothing for outdoor activities. 800-667-4191. www.action-direct.com

**Adirondack Outfitters,** P.O. Box 431, Massena, NY 13662: Free information ◆ Rock and ice climbing, camping, and outdoor photography equipment. 888-315-0747.

**Alpine Adventures,** 7012 S. 300 East, Midvale, UT 84047: Free catalog ◆ Outdoor apparel and camping gear. 801-561-1592. rich@alpine-adventures.com

**Appalachian Mountain Supply,** 731 Highland Ave. NE, Studio C, Atlanta, GA 30312: Free brochure ◆ Self-inflating sleeping pads, hydration systems, and accessories. 800-569-4110. www.amsgear.com

**B-West Outdoor Specialties,** 2425 N. Huachuca, Tucson, AZ 85745: Free catalog ◆ Backpacks, shoes and boots, and outdoor accessories. 800-293-7855; 520-628-1990 (in AZ).

**Backcountry Equipment USA,** 214 Southill, San Antonio, TX 78201: Free information ◆ Tents, sleeping bags, and other gear. 888-779-5075. questions@backcountry-equipment.com

**Bass Pro Shops,** 1935 S. Campbell, Springfield, MO 65898: Free information ◆ Camping and backpacking equipment. 800-227-7776. www.basspro.com

**Bay Archery Sales,** 2713 W. Center Ave., Essexville, MI 48732: Free catalog ◆ Camping, backpacking, and outdoor survival supplies.

**L.L. Bean,** Casco St., Freeport, ME 04032: Free catalog ◆ Tents, backpacks, bicycles, boats, and outdoor equipment. 800-221-4221. www.llbean.com

**Bear Archery Inc.,** 4600 SW 41st Blvd., Gainesville, FL 32608: Free information ◆ Backpacks, eating utensils, knives, camping tools, lanterns and flashlights, and other equipment. 800-874-4603; 352-376-2327 (in FL). www.thebowman.com

**The Boundary Waters Catalog,** 105 N. Central Ave., Ely, MN 55731: Free catalog ◆ Canoeing, skiing, camping, and winter gear. 800-223-6565. www.piragis.com

**Brule Mountain Gear,** 1385 Klock Rd., Aylmer, Quebec, Canada J9H 5E1: Free brochure ◆ Bicycles and backpacks. 819-685-9163. www.panpack.com

**Brunton,** 620 E. Monroe, Riverton, WY 82501: Free brochure ◆ Pocket transits, compasses and accessories, binoculars, pocket field vests, and handcrafted knives. 800-443-4871. www.brunton.com

**Buck Knives,** P.O. Box 1267, El Cajon, CA 92022: Free list of retail sources ◆ Knives. 800-215-2825. www.knifecenter.com

**Buy The World,** 3944 Mountain View Dr., Boise, ID 83704: Free information ◆ Camping, backpacking, and other outdoor equipment. 800-636-7881. www.buytheworld.com/norest/westmoun

**Cabela's,** One Cabela Dr., Sidney, ME 69160: Free catalog ◆ Tents, sleeping bags, outdoor clothing, footwear, and hunting equipment. 800-237-4444. www.cabelas.com

**Camel Outdoor Products,** P.O. Box 7225, Norcross, GA 30091: Free list of retail sources ◆ Camping equipment and easy-to-set-up dome tents. 770-449-4687.

**Camp Trails,** 1326 Willow Rd., Sturtevant, WI 53177: Free list of retail sources ◆ Backpacks, eating utensils, sleeping bags, and equipment. 888-245-4985. www.jwa.com

**Camper's Choice,** 502 4th St. NW, P.O. Box 1546, Red Bay, AL 35582: Free catalog ◆ Trailer accessories and equipment for outdoor activities and camping. 800-833-6713. www.camperschoice.com

**Camping World,** P.O. Box 90017, Bowling Green, KY 42102: Free information ◆ Accessories and supplies for recreational vehicles. 800-626-6189. www.campingworld.com

**Campmor,** P.O. Box 700, Saddle River, NJ 07458: Free catalog ◆ Clothing and equipment for climbing, camping, hiking, backpacking, and biking. 800-226-7667. www.campmore.com

**Caribou Mountaineering,** 400 Commerce Rd., Alice, TX 78332: Free catalog ◆ Backpacks, sleeping and shoulder bags, tents, travel packs, and soft luggage. 800-824-4153. www.caribou.com

**Cheaper than Dirt,** 2536 NE Loop 820, Fort Worth, TX 76106: Free catalog ◆ Holsters and cases, scopes, survival supplies, gun smithing and cleaning supplies, clothing, hunting and camping gear, and archery, crossbow, and shotgun equipment. 888-625-3848. www.cheaperthandirt.com

**Climb High Inc.,** 1861 Shelburne Rd., Shelburne, VT 05482: Free catalog ◆ Boots and clothing, carabineers, ropes, backpacks, sleeping bags, and equipment. 802-985-5056. www.climbhigh.com

**CMI Outdoor Equipment,** P.O. Box 535, Franklin, WV 26807: Free catalog ◆ Outdoor, camping, and mountaineering equipment. 800-247-5901. www.cmi-gear.com

**Coghlan's, The Outdoor Accessory People,** 121 Irene St., Winnipeg, Manitoba, Canada R3T 4C7: Free information ◆ Camping, fishing, hunting, backpacking, trailering, and boating equipment. 204-284-9550.

**Coleman Outdoor Products Inc.,** P.O. Box 2931, Wichita, KS 67201: Free catalog ◆ Backpacks, dining utensils, knives, camping tools, lanterns and flashlights, sleeping bags, and equipment. 800-835-3278. www.coleman.com

**Colorado Saddlery Company,** 1631 15th St., Denver, CO 80202: Free catalog ◆ Tents and accessories, sleeping bags, stoves, tack and pack equipment, and supplies. 800-521-2465; 303-572-8350 (in CO).

**Colorado Tent Company,** 2228 Blake St., Denver, CO 80205: Free information ◆ Tents and sleeping bags. 800-354-TENT.

**Comtrad Industries,** 2820 Waterford Lake Dr., Ste. 102, Midlothian, VA 23113: Free information ◆ Portable refrigerator with optional built-in food warmer. 800-992-2966. www.comtrad.com

**Crazy Creek Products Inc.,** P.O. Box 1050, 1401 S. Broadway, Red Lodge, MT 59068: Free list of retail sources ◆ Folding transportable chairs for backpacking, mountaineering, and outdoor activities. 800-331-0304.

**Dana Designs,** 333 Simmental Way, Bozeman, MT 59715: Free list of retail sources ◆ Backpacks and external frames for men and women. 888-357-3262.

**Design Salt,** P.O. Box 1220, Redway, CA 95560: Free catalog ◆ Sleeping bags. 800-254-7258. www.designsalt.com

**Diamond Brand Canvas Products,** P.O. Box 249, Naples, NC 28760: Free information ◆ Two and four-person tents. Also camping accessories, backpacks, and duffels. 800-258-9811. www.diamondbrand.com/canvasproducts.htm

**Eagle Creek,** 1740 La Costa Meadows Dr., San Marcos, CA 92069: Free list of retail sources ◆ Backpacks. 800-874-9925. www.eaglecreek.com

**Early Winters,** P.O. Box 4333, Portland, OR 97208: Free catalog ◆ Camping and backpacking clothing and equipment. 800-458-4438. www.normthompson.com

**Eastern Mountain Sports Inc.,** One Vose Farm Rd., Peterborough, NH 03458: Free information ◆ Camping equipment and outdoor clothing. 888-463-6367. www.emsonline.com

**Eastpak,** 50 Rogers Rd., P.O. Box 8232, Ward Hill, MA 01835: Free list of retail sources ◆ Backpacks that convert to a suitcase. 978-373-1581.

**Ensign Mountaineering,** 1405 N. 600 West, Orem, UT 84057: Free catalog ◆ Backpacks. 800-560-7529.

**Enviro Ltd.,** 127 Elm St., Cortland, NY 13045: Free catalog ◆ All-weather and all-terrain sleeping enclosures. 607-753-8801.

**Eureka Tents,** 1326 Willow Rd., Sturtevant, WI 53177: Free list of retail sources ◆ Backpacks and self-supporting tents. 888-245-4984. www.jwa.com

**Feathered Friends Mail Order,** 1415 10th Ave., Seattle, WA 98122: Free information ◆ Sleeping bags in short, regular, and long sizes. Options include Gore-Tex, down collar, overfill, and underfill. 206-328-0887. www.halcyon.com/feathered

**Fieldline,** 1919 Vineburn Ave., Los Angeles, CA 90032: Free brochure ◆ Backpacks. 213-226-0830.

**Fiskars Incorporated,** Gerber Legendary Blades Division, Customer Service, P.O. Box 23088, Portland, OR 97281: Free catalog ◆ Outdoor recreational equipment, knives, sheaths, pocket tools, and accessories. 503-655-6004.

**Flaghouse Camping Equipment,** 601 Flaghouse Dr., Hasbrouck Heights, NJ 07604: Free catalog ◆ Outdoor equipment. 800-221-5185. www.flaghouse.com

**Four Seasons Tentmasters,** 4221 Livesay Rd., Sand Creek, MI 49279: Catalog $2 ◆ Tipis, wall and wege tents, marquees, and camping equipment. 517-436-6246.

**Fox Ridge Outfitters Inc.,** 400 N. Main St., P.O. Box 1700, Rochester, NH 03866: Free catalog ◆ Clothing, solid pine carvings, cookware, knives and cutlery, equipment and supplies for outdoor sportsmen, and guns. 800-243-4570. www.foxridgeoutfitters.com/fro.htm

**Frank's Center Inc.,** RR 1, Box 45, Nevada, MO 64772: Catalog $2 ◆ Backpacking, camping, rescue/repelling equipment, and sportshooting guns. 417-667-9190. www.frankscenterinc.com

**Gander Mountain (Cabela's),** One Cabela Dr., Sidney, ME 69160: Free catalog ◆ Camping and outdoor equipment, boats, archery supplies, knives, rifle reloading equipment and scopes, and hunting and fishing videos. 800-237-4444. www.cabelas.com

**Garmont USA Inc.,** Adams Park, 75 Boyer Circle, Williston, VT 05495: Free information ◆ Boots, backpacks, and hiking poles. 800-343-5200.

**Garuda Mountaineering,** 333 Simmental Way, Bozeman, MT 59715: Free catalog ◆ One, two, and three-person tents. 406-587-4153.

**Don Gleason's Camping Supply Inc.,** 9 Pearl St., Northampton, MA 01060: Free catalog ◆ Camping and backpacking equipment. 413-584-4895. www.gleasoncamping.com

**Gorilla & Sons,** P.O. Box 2309, Bellingham, WA 98227: Free catalog ◆ Outdoor apparel and equipment. 800-246-7455.

**Gregory Mountain Products,** 100 Calle Cortez, Temecula, CA 92390: Free list of retail sources ◆ Backpacks. 800-477-3420.

**Henderson Camp Products Inc.,** P.O. Box 867, Henderson, NC 27536: Free information ◆ Tents and sleeping bags. 800-547-4605; 919-492-6061 (in NC).

**High Sierra,** H. Bernbaum Import Export, 880 Corporate Woods, Vernon Hills, IL 60061: Free information ◆ Backpacks, dining utensils, sleeping bags, and equipment. 800-323-9590; 847-913-1100 (in IL).

**Hilton's Tent City,** 272 Friend St., Boston, MA 02114: Free catalog ◆ Tents and back country equipment. 617-227-9242.

**Integral Designs,** 5516 3rd St., Calgary, Alberta, Canada T2H 1J9: Free catalog ◆ Sleeping bags, tents, and outerwear. 403-640-1445. www.integraldesigns.com

**James Kits,** P.O. Box 933, 164 E. Deloney, Jackson, WY 83001: Free information ◆ Pocket survival kits. 800-396-KITS.

**JanSport Inc.,** P.O. Box 1817, Appleton, WI 54913: Free list of retail sources ◆ Backpacks and sleeping bags. 800-552-6776. www.jansport.com

**Jordan's Wilderness Shop & Outfitters,** 7940 Hawthorne Pl., Dyer, IN 46311: Free catalog ◆ Ultra lightweight camping equipment and supplies. 800-644-9955.

**Kelty Packs Inc.,** 6235 Lookout Rd., Boulder, CO 80301: Free list of retail sources ◆ Tents, sleeping bags, and backpacks that convert to luggage. 800-423-2320. www.kelty.com

**Lafuma Camping Equipment,** 16745 Saticoy St., Unit 112, Van Nuys, CA 91406: Free information ◆ Sleeping bags, backpacks, and two, three, and four-person tents. 800-514-4807.

**Leatherman Tool Group Inc.,** P.O. Box 20595, Portland, OR 97220: Free information ◆ Compact folding multi-purpose tools for campers. 503-253-7826. www.leatherman.com

**Leisure Outlet,** 953 Towes Pl., Santa Cruz, CA 95062: Free catalog ◆ Camping equipment and clothing. 800-322-1460. duraprod@aol.com

**Leisure Pro,** 42 W. 18th St., 3rd Floor, New York, NY 10011: Catalog $5 ◆ Expedition and day packs, tents, sleeping bags, and accessories. Also scuba and tennis equipment. 212-645-1234. www.leisure-pro.com

**Leki USA,** 356 Sonwil Dr., Buffalo, NY 14225: Free catalog ◆ Hiking and trekking poles. 800-255-0082; 716-683-1022 (in NY). custservice@leki.com

**Liberty Mountain Sports,** 4875 W. 1980 South, Salt Lake City, UT 84104: Free list of retail sources ◆ Sleeping bags. 800-366-2666.

**Lowe Alpine,** P.O. Box 1449, Broomfield, CO 80038: Free list of retail sources ◆ Outdoor clothing, mountaineering fleecewear, and backpacks. 303-465-0522. www.lowealpine.com

**Madden Mountaineering,** 2400 Central Ave., Boulder, CO 80301: Free catalog ◆ Backpacks and equipment. 303-442-5828. www.maddenusa.com

**Mark One Distributors,** 627 N. Morton, Bloomington, IN 47404: Free catalog ◆ Camping equipment, sporting goods, hardware and outdoor maintenance equipment, and safety aids. 800-869-9058.

**Marmot Mountain Works,** 827 Bellevue Way NE, Bellevue, WA 98004: Free catalog ◆ Sleeping bags. 800-254-6246. www.premier1.net/~marmot

**McHale & Company,** 29 Dravus St., Seattle, WA 98109: Catalog $2 ◆ Backpacks. 206-281-7861. www.aa.net/mchalepacks

**Moonstone Mountaineering,** 5350 Ericson Way, Arcata, CA 95521: Free information ◆ Clothing, sleeping bags, and accessories. 800-822-2985. www.moonstone.com

**Moss Tents Inc.,** P.O. Box 577, Camden, ME 04843: Free list of retail sources ◆ One, two, three, and four-person tents. 800-859-5322.

**Mountain Equipment Inc.,** 4776 E. Jensen, Fresno, CA 93725: Free list of retail sources ◆ Adjustable backpacks. 209-486-8211.

**Mountain Hardware,** 950 Gilman St., Berkeley, CA 94710: Free list of retail sources ◆ Sleeping bags. 510-559-6700. joeweb@mtnhdw.com

**Mountainsmith,** 18301 W. Colfax Ave., Heritage Square, Bldg. P, Golden, CO 80401: Free list of retail sources ◆ Backpacks, external frames, and two, four, and eight-person tents. 800-426-4075. mountsmith@aol.com

**O.H. Mullen Sales Inc.,** 9928 Rd. 171, Oakwood, OH 45873: Free information ◆ Backpacks, dining utensils, knives, camping tools, sleeping bags, and equipment. 800-258-6625.

**Natural Balance,** 503 S. Main, Fairfield, IA 52556: Catalog $2 ◆ Internal frame backpacks. 515-472-7918. Fun@KDSI.net

**Nexco,** Box 13081, Ogden, UT 84412: Free catalog ◆ Backpacking equipment. 800-597-4743.

**Noall Tents,** 59530 Devils Ladder Rd., Mountain Center, CA 92561: Free catalog ◆ Tents. 909-659-4219.

**Norland Trading Company,** Box 10, Norland, Ontario, Canada K0M 2L0: Video catalog $5 (refundable) ◆ Hunting, fishing, and outdoor equipment. 800-318-0717. ntc@cancom.net

**North Face,** 2013 Farallon Dr., San Leandro, CA 94577: Free list of retail sources ◆ Backpacks, camping equipment, and sleeping bags. 800-447-2333.

**Northern Outfitters,** 14072 Pony Express Rd., Draper, UT 84020: Catalog $2 ◆ Clothing, sleeping bags, and accessories. 800-944-9276; 801-571-9979 (in UT). www.gorp.com/northern

**Northwest River Supplies Inc.,** 2009 S. Main, Moscow, ID 83843: Free catalog ◆ Backpacks and equipment. 800-635-5202. nrs@moscow.com

**Only the Lightest Camping Equipment,** P.O. Box 266, Troutdale, OR 97060: Catalog $1 ◆ Lightweight clothing and camping equipment. 503-666-9365.

**The Original I. Goldberg,** 902 Chestnut St., Philadelphia, PA 19107: Free catalog ◆ Military surplus merchandise, footwear, clothing, and camping equipment. 215-925-9393.

**Osprey Packs,** P.O. Box 539, Dolores, CO 81323: Free list of retail sources ◆ External frame backpacks. 970-882-2221. ospreypack@aol.com

**Outdoor Outlet,** 1062 E. Tabernacle, St. George, UT 84770: Free catalog ◆ Tents, backpacks, and sleeping bags. 800-726-8106. www.outdooroutlet.com

**Outdoor Research,** 2203 1st Ave. South, Seattle, WA 98134: Free information ◆ Outdoor first aid kits, sleeping bags, and accessories. 888-467-4327. www.orgear.com

**Outfitters Pack Station,** 2070 W. Broadway, Idaho Falls, ID 83402: Free catalog ◆ Riding accessories, tack, and camping gear. 800-657-2644; 208-522-3446 (in ID). www.scenic-idaho.com/outfitterspackstation

**Overland Equipment,** 2145 Park Ave., Ste. 4, Chico, CA 95928: Free catalog ◆ Frame and saddle bags and backpacks. 800-487-8851.

**Pachmayr Ltd.,** 1875 S. Mountain Ave., Monrovia, CA 91016: Free catalog ◆ Shooting and hunting accessories, clothing, camping equipment, books, and videos. 800-423-9704. www.pachmayr.com

**Peak 1,** P.O. Box 2931, Wichita, KS 67201: Free catalog ◆ Backpacks and tents. 800-835-3278. www.coleman.com

**Premier International Inc.,** 901 N. Stuart St., Ste. 804, Arlington, VA 22203: Free catalog ◆ Backpacks with built-in rain covers. 800-354-5420.

**Pyromid Outdoor Cooking Systems,** American Innovation Marketing Inc., 3292 S. Hwy. 97, Redmond, OR 96656: Free brochure ◆ Outdoor cooking systems. 800-824-4288. EFW3@aol.com

**R.U. Outside Inc.,** 455 S. Main, Driggs, ID 83422: Free catalog ◆ Clothing and sports gear. 800-279-7123. www.ruoutside.com

**Ramsey Outdoor Store,** 226 N. Rt. 17, P.O. Box 1689, Paramus, NJ 07653: Free catalog ◆ Camping and backpacking equipment. 201-261-5000.

**Red Hawk Trading,** 224 Sand Ridge Rd., Malad, ID 83252: Catalog $2 ◆ Tipis, mountain man style tents, and mountain man gear. 208-766-2960. www.cyberhighway.net/~redhawk

**REI Recreational Equipment Company,** Sumner, WA 98352: Free catalog ◆ Exercise and walking shoes, Gore-Tex rainwear , day packs that convert to tents, ski equipment, gifts, knives and utensils, sunglasses, and camping foods. 800-426-4840. www.rei.com

**Rocky Mountain Connection,** P.O. Box 2800, Estes Park, CO 80517: Catalog $1 (specify type of items wanted) ◆ Outdoor and western-style clothing, Boy Scouts clothing and outdoor gear, hiking staffs, backpacks, and more. 800-679-3600. www.RMConnection.com

**A.G. Russell Knives,** 1705 Hwy. 71 B North, Springdale, AR 72764: Free catalog ◆ Knives and cutlery. 800-255-9034. www.agrussell.com

**Siemens Solar Industries,** P.O. Box 6032, Camarillo, CA 93120: Free information ◆ Rechargeable solar-operated lantern. 800-272-6765. www.siemenssolar.com

**Sierra Designs,** 1255 Powell St., Emeryville, CA 94608: Free list of retail sources ◆ Light-weight two-person free-standing tent. 800-635-0461.

**Sierra Trading Post,** 5025 Campstool Rd., Cheyenne, WY 82007: Free catalog ◆ Outdoor clothing and equipment. 800-713-4534. www.sierra-trading.com

**Sims Stoves,** P.O. Box 21405, Billings, MT 59104: Free information ◆ Folding camp stoves, tents, pack saddles, books, and equipment. 800-736-5259. www.imox.com/simsstove/index.htm

**Slumberjack Inc.,** P.O. Box 7048, St. Louis, MO 63177: Free information ◆ Insulated sleeping bags. 800-233-6283. www.slumberjack.com

**The Sportsman's Guide,** 411 Farwell Ave., South St. Paul, MN 55075: Free catalog ◆ Camping equipment. 800-888-3006. www.sportsmansguide.com

**SunDog,** 6700 S. Glacier St., Seattle, WA 98188: Free catalog ◆ Packs, bags, and cases for sports, travel, and photography. 800-742-2623. www.sun-dog.com

**Swallow's Nest,** 2308 6th Ave., Seattle, WA 98121: Free catalog ◆ Backpacking, climbing, and mountaineering equipment. 800-676-4041; 206-441-4100 (in WA). www.swallowsnest.com

**Tents & Trails,** 21 Park Pl., New York, NY 10007: Free information ◆ Camping and mountaineering equipment and clothing. 888-227-1760; 212-227-1760 (in NY). www.tenttrails.com

**Texsport,** P.O. Box 55326, Houston, TX 77255: Free list of retail sources ◆ Backpacks, dining utensils, knives, camping tools, lanterns and flashlights, sleeping bags, and equipment. 800-231-1402; 713-464-5551 (in TX). www.broadway.ipresent.com/texsport/product.htm

**Tough Traveler,** 1012 State St., Schenectady, NY 12307: Free catalog ◆ Backpacks. 800-468-6844. www.toughtraveler.com/tt

**Trail Ridge Traders,** 334 E. Mountain, Fort Collins, CO 80524: Free catalog ◆ New and used camping equipment. 970-484-8895.

**Traveling Light/Cascade Designs,** 4000 1st Ave. South, Seattle, WA 98134: Free list of retail sources ◆ Fuel-efficient compact oven for outdoor use. 800-527-1527. www.cascadedesigns.com

**Variety International,** 1977 O'Toole Ave., San Jose, CA 95131: Free information ◆ Camping furniture. 800-700-1666.

**VauDe Sports Inc.,** P.O. Box 3413, Mammoth Lakes, CA 93546: Free catalog ◆ Backpacks. 800-447-1539. www.vaude.com

**Volcano Corp.,** 3450 W. 8550 South, West Jordan, UT 84084: Free information ◆ All-purpose outdoor cook stove. 800-454-8304; 801-566-5496 (in UT).

**Walrus Inc.,** P.O. Box 81227, Seattle, WA 98108: Free information ◆ One, two, three, and four-person tents. 800-550-8368. www.lowealpine.com

**Wenzel,** 1224 Fern Ridge Pkwy., St. Louis, MO 63141: Free list of retail sources ◆ Padded shoulder strap-adjustable frame back pack, sleeping bags, tents, and accessories. 800-325-4121.

**Wiggy's Inc.,** P.O. Box 2124, Grand Junction, CO 81502: Free information ◆ Sleeping bags and insulated clothing. 970-241-6465. www.wiggys.com

**Wild Country,** 60 Northside Dr., Shelburne, VT 05482: Free catalog ◆ Two, three, and four-person tents. 802-985-5056. www.climbhigh.com

**Wild Things,** P.O. Box 400, North Conway, NH 03800: Free catalog ◆ Backpacks. 603-356-6907. wildthings@landmarknet.net

**Jack Wolfskin,** 1326 Willow Rd., Sturtevant, WI 53177: Free list of retail sources ◆ Outerwear, backpacks, sleeping bags, tents, travel luggage, and outdoor equipment. 800-847-1460. www.jwa.com

**Wyoming River Raiders,** P.O. Box 50490, Casper, WY 82605: Free catalog ◆ Outdoor clothing, camping and river expedition equipment, fishing gear, hiking equipment, books, and supplies. 800-247-6068. www.riverraiders.com

**ZZ Manufacturing Inc.,** 1520A Industrial Park, Covina, CA 91722: Free information ◆ Woodburning backpacker stoves. 800-594-9046; 818-332-5906 (in CA). www.gorp.com/zzstove/default.htm

## Trail Foods

**Adventure Foods,** 481 Banjo Ln., Whittier, NC 28789: Free brochure ◆ Freeze-dried and dehydrated entree specialties. Also individual food items in bulk and vegetarian packaging. 828-497-4113. www.adventurefoods.com

**AlpineAire,** P.O. Box 926, Nevada City, CA 95959: Free information ◆ Freeze-dried and concentrated foods. 800-322-6325. www.alpineairefoods.com

**Clearwater Trader,** 637 Fairview Dr., Wood-land, CA 95695: Free information ◆ Backpacking and emergency preparation foods. 800-440-9904.

**Hardee,** 579 Speers Rd., Oakville, Ontario, Canada L6K 2G4: Free price list ◆ Freeze-dried foods. 905-844-1471.

**L.D.P. Foods,** 1101 NW Evangeline, Lafayette, LA 70501: Free price list ◆ Freeze-dried foods. 800-826-5767. www.ldpcamingfoo0ds.com

**Myers Meats,** Rt. 1, Box 132, Parshall, ND 58770: Free information ◆ Original or peppered beef jerky and beef stick. 800-635-3759; 701-743-4451 (in ND). www.tradecorridor.com/myersmeats

**Nitro-Pak Preparedness Center,** 151 N. Main St., Heber City, UT 84032: Catalog $3 ◆ Survival equipment and supplies, freeze-dried and dehydrated foods, books, and videos. 800-866-4876. www.nitro-pak.com

**Oregon Freeze Dry Inc.,** P.O. Box 1048, 525 25th Ave. SW, Albany, OR 97321: Free brochure ◆ Freeze dried foods. 541-926-6001. www.ofd.com

**Piragis Northwoods Company,** 105 N. Central Ave., Ely, MN 55731: Catalog $2 ◆ Canoes, boating gear, boats, videos, and trail foods. 800-223-6565. www.piragis.com

**REI Recreational Equipment Company,** Sumner, WA 98352: Free catalog ◆ Exercise and walking shoes, Gore-Tex rain gear, day packs that convert to tents, shoes, ski equipment, gifts, knives, and utensils, sunglasses, and camping foods. 800-426-4840. www.rei.com

**Richmoor Corp.,** P.O. Box 8092, Van Nuys, CA 91409: Free information ◆ Freeze-dried and concentrated foods. 800-423-3170; 818-787-2510 (in CA). www2.richmoor.com/richmoor

**Trail Foods Company,** 12455 Branford St., Arleta, CA 91331: Free catalog ◆ Two and four-person meal pouches and other foods. 800-304-4370; 818-897-4370 (in CA).

## CANDLES, CANDLE MAKING, & CANDLE HOLDERS

**All Aglow Candles,** P.O. Box 1200, Germantown, MD 20875: Free information ◆ Scented beeswax candles in a choice of colors and sizes. 800-279-9483.

**Angel's Earth,** 1633 Scheffer Ave., St. Paul, MN 55116: Catalog $2 ◆ Soaps, candles, cosmetics, incense, skin care preparations, essential oils, and aromatherapy items. 612-698-3601.

**Angelic Candles,** 1818 Avenue M, Lubbock, TX 79401: Free catalog ◆ Candles that burn with a long-lasting fragrance. 800-687-7646; 806-785-6777 (in TX). www.angeliccandles.com

**Barker Enterprises Inc.,** 15106 10th Ave. SW, Seattle, WA 98166: Catalog $2 ◆ Candle-making supplies and molds. 800-543-0601. www.barkerco.com

**Bee Services,** 2211 Boman Ave., Mesquite, TX 75150: Free brochure ◆ Molds and equipment for making candles. 972-270-0683.

**Brian's Crafts Unlimited,** P.O. Box 731046, Ormond Beach, FL 32173: Catalog $1 (refundable) ◆ Candle-making supplies. 904-672-2726.

**The Candle Company,** P.O. Box 3190, Nashua, NH 03061: Free catalog ◆ Votive and contemporary candles in square flat top jars, with a choice of sizes and fragrances. 603-578-9392.

**Candlechem Products,** 32 Thayer Circle, P.O. Box 705, Randolph, MA 02368: Catalog $1 ◆ Oils, perfume oils, dyes, and scents for making candles and perfumery items. 781-963-4161. www.alcasoft.com/candlechem

**Christy's Country Candles,** 2631 Michigan Rd., Madison, IN 47250: Free brochure ◆ Fragrant scented country candles and wax potpourri pieces. 800-940-3031; 812-273-3072 (in IN). www.seidata.com/~cbrogan

**Gardens Past,** P.O. Box 1846, Estes Park, CO 80517: Catalog $1 ◆ Soaps and soap-making supplies, dried flowers, potpourri, herbs, candles, and aromatherapy items. 970-823-5565.

**Krafty Creations,** 13501 100th Ave. NE, Ste. 5091, Kirkland, CA 98034: Free information ◆ Hand-rolled honeycomb beeswax candles. 425-487-4834.

**Lava Enterprises Inc.,** 3979 Lockridge St., San Diego, CA 92102: Free information ◆ Decorative candles and holders. 800-622-6353. www.lavacandles.com

**Mangelsen's Craft Supplies,** P.O. Box 3314, Omaha, NE 68103: Free information ◆ Supplies for general crafts, candle-making, and leather-working. 800-228-2601; 402-339-3922 (in NE).

**Mann Lake Supply,** 501 S. 1st St., Hackensack, MN 56452: Free catalog ◆ Beekeeping and honey production equipment, protective clothing, candle molds and kits, and how-to books. 800-233-6663. www.mannlakeltd.com

**Maple Shade Crafts,** Catalog Department, RR 1, Box 186, Pulaski, VA 24301: Catalog $4 (refundable) ◆ Craft supplies, sewing notions, Victorian jewelry, scented candles, cameos, and potpourri. 800-986-9674. www.swva.net/mapleshade

**Mid-Continent Agrimarketing Inc.,** 1465 N. Winchester, Overland Park, KS 66061: Free catalog ◆ Beekeeping and candle-making supplies. 800-547-1392; 913-768-8967 (in KS).

**MoonAcre IronWorks,** 62 Chambersburg St., Gettysburg, PA 17325: Catalog $2 ◆ Simulated pewter candleholders. 800-966-4766. moonacre@cvn.net

**Nasco,** 901 Janesville Ave., Fort Atkinson, WI 53538: Free catalog ◆ Candle-making supplies. 800-558-9595. www.nascofa.com

**North Country Crafts,** 5247 Central Ave. NE, Minneapolis, MN 55421: Brochure $1 ◆ Fragrant candles in decorative tin holders. 612-571-3636.

**Olympia Potters & Artists Supply Inc.,** 1822 Harrison Ave. NW, Olympia, WA 98502: Free information ◆ Ukranian egg decorating and candle-making supplies. 888-943-5332; 360-943-5332 (in WA). www.webdb.com/opas

**Pot o' Gold Honey Company,** P.O. Box 1200, Hemingway, SC 29554: Free brochure ◆ Beeswax candles. 805-558-9598. PotGold@aol.com

**Pourette Manufacturing,** P.O. Box 17056, Seattle, WA 98107: Catalog $2 ◆ Ready-to-use candles and soap and candle-making supplies. 800-888-9425. www.pourette.com

**Red Door Ceramics,** 888 W. North St., Decatur, IL 62522: Brochure $2 ◆ Ceramic crock candleholders with a country motif. 800-537-4376.

**A.I. Root Company,** P.O. Box 706, Medina, OH 44258: Free catalog ◆ Candle-making supplies and how-to videos. 800-289-7668. www.airoot.com

**Stax of Wax,** 371 Congress Ave., Waterbury, CT 06708: Free brochure ◆ Scented candles, potpourri canisters, herbal baths, and other fragrant products. www.stax-of-wax.com

**Village Candle Factory,** P.O. Box 509, Clemmons, NC 27012: Free brochure ◆ Hand-poured long-burning jar and other candles. 800-487-1180. www.alcandle.com

**Waage Electric Company,** 820 Colfax Ave., P.O. Box 337, Kenilworth NJ 07033: Free catalog ◆ Wax melting pots. Features a choice of sizes. 908-245-9363. www.waageele.com

**Waxman Candles,** 609 Massachusetts, Lawrence, KS 66044: Free catalog ◆ Out of the ordinary candles. 913-843-8593. www.waxmancandles.com

**Yankee Candle Company,** Catalog Sales, P.O. Box 110, South Deerfield, MA 01373: Free brochure ◆ Scented candles, featuring a choice of styles and fragrances. 800-243-1776. www.yankeecandle.com

**Ye Olde Candle Shoppe,** 6525 Washington St., Yountville, CA 94599: Free brochure ◆ Handcrafted candles. 707-944-5633. www.communitynet.net

## CANDY MAKING & CAKE DECORATING

**Assouline & Ting Inc.,** 314 Brown St., Philadelphia, PA 19123: Free information ◆ Cocoa powder and chocolate couverture. 800-521-4491; 215-627-3000 (in PA). www.caviarassouline.com

**Creative Treets,** 475 Sinclair Frontage Rd., Milpitas, CA 95035: Catalog $3 ◆ Candy-making supplies. 408-946-1612. www.creativetreets.com

**Holcraft Collection,** 211 El Cajon Ave., P.O. Box 792, Davis, CA 95616: Catalog $2 ◆ Molds for making chocolate candy. 916-756-3023. www.holcraft.com

**Kitchen Krafts,** P.O. Box 442, Waukon, IA 52172: Free catalog ◆ Cake decorating, candy-making, and bread and pastry baking supplies. 800-776-0575; 319-535-8000 (in IA). www.kitchenkrafts.com

**Log Cabin Crafts,** P.O. Box 1702, Goldsboro, NC 27533: Catalog $2 (refundable) ◆ Lollipop molds and supplies. 800-630-POPS. www.logcc.com

**Lorann Oils,** 4518 Aurelius Rd., Lansing, MI 48910: Catalog $2 ◆ Flavoring oils for making hard candies. 800-248-1302. www.lorannoils.com

**Meadow's Chocolate & Cake Supplies,** 11016 Liberty Ave., Jamaica, NY 11419: Catalog $2 ◆ Candy-making and cake-decorating supplies. 718-835-3600.

**Paradigm Foodworks,** 5775 SW Jean Rd., Ste. 106A, Lake Oswego, OR 97035: Catalog $1 (refundable) ◆ Chocolate for bakers and candy makers. 800-234-0250.

**Parrish's Cake Decorating,** 225 W. 146th St., Gardena, CA 90248: Tools and equipment catalog $3, cake novelties and wedding decorations catalog $3, candy mold catalog $1 ◆ Cake decorating and candy-making supplies. 310-924-2253.

**Schroeder's Bakeries,** 212 Forest Ave., P.O. Box 183, Buffalo, NY 14213: Free catalog ◆ Cake-making kits and decorating supplies. 800-850-7763. bakery@schroedersbakery.com

**Sue Bear's,** 1297 Krumroy Rd., Akron, OH 44306: Catalog $2 ◆ Cake decorating and candy-making supplies. 330-784-1712.

**Albert Uster Imports Inc.,** 9211 Gaither Rd., Gaithersburg, MD 20877: Free catalog ◆ Chocolate couverture, cocoa powder, disposable pastry bags, and candy boxes. 800-231-8154; 301-258-7350 (in MD). swissavi@erols.com

**Wilton Enterprise Inc.,** 2240 W. 75th St., Woodbridge, IL 60517: Catalog $6 (refundable) ◆ Supplies for making candy, cookies, and cakes. 630-963-7100.

## CANES, WALKERS, & HIKING STICKS

**American Walker Inc.,** 900 Market St., Oregon, WI 53575: Free information ◆ Wheeled walkers and walk-a-cycles. 800-828-6808.

**Otto Bock Orthopedic Industry Inc.,** 3000 Xenium Ln. North, Minneapolis, MN 55441: Free information ◆ Durable, functional, and growth-adjustable walkers for children. 800-984-8901. www.ottobock.com

**Cascade Designs Inc.,** 4000 1st Ave. South, Seattle, WA 98134: Free information ◆ Adjustable walking staffs. 800-531-9531. www.cascadedesigns.com

**Garmont USA Inc.,** Adams Park, 75 Boyer Circle, Williston, VT 05495: Free information ◆ Boots, backpacks, and hiking poles. 800-343-5200.

**Guardian Products Inc.,** 4175 Guardian St., Simi Valley, CA 93063: Free catalog ◆ Walkers, crutches, canes, home activity aids, beds, lifters, ramps, and transporting equipment. 800-255-5022.

**Health Products Express Inc.,** P.O. Box 8, Winthrop, MA 02152: Free catalog ◆ Canes, crutches, and walkers with optional accessories and replacement parts. 800-617-5525; 617-846-8924 (in MA).

**House of Canes,** P.O. Box 574, Wilderville, OR 97543: Catalog $1 ◆ Walking sticks and staffs in wrist, elbow, and shoulder lengths. 800-458-5920.

**Miles Kimball Company,** 41 W. 8th Ave., Oshkosh, WI 54906: Free catalog ◆ Canes and aids for people with physical disabilities. 800-546-2255. www.mileskimball.com

**Leki USA,** 356 Sonwil Dr., Buffalo, NY 14225: Free catalog ◆ Hiking and trekking poles. 800-255-0082; 716-683-1022 (in NY). custservice@leki.com

**Lighthouse Enterprises,** 36-20 Northern Blvd., Long Island City, NY 11101: Free catalog ◆ Assistive aids for visually impaired persons. 800-829-0500.

**Momentum,** Medical Corp., 79 W. 4500 South, Ste. 18, Salt Lake City, UT 84107: Free information ◆ Canes and quads with extra-leverage handles for easier standing up from a seated position. 800-644-2263.

**NobleMotion Inc.,** P.O. Box 5366, Pittsburgh, PA 15206: Free information ◆ Products for walking in the face of physical challenge. 800-234-9255. www.noblemotion.com

**Parkview Pharmacy & Home Health Care Inc.,** 8283 Grove Ave., Ste. 105, Rancho Cucamonga, PA 01730: Free catalog ◆ Canes, walkers, wheelchairs, accessories, and other home health care aids. 800-605-0166. www.parkviewrx.com

**Rocky Mountain Connection,** P.O. Box 2800, Estes Park, CO 80517: Catalog $1 (specify type of items wanted) ◆ Outdoor and western-style clothing, Boy Scouts clothing and outdoor gear, hiking staffs, backpacks, and more. 800-679-3600. www.RMConnection.com

**Thompson Pharmacy & Medical,** 324 S. Union St., Traverse City, MI 49684: Free catalog ◆ Diabetes, health maintenance, home diagnostic, ostomy, and health and pain management aids. Also canes and other mobility equipment. 616-947-4212. thompson@carecenter.com

**TR Group Inc.,** 903 Wedel Ln., Glenview, IL 60025: Free information ◆ Rolling walker with back-supported seat and removable basket. 800-752-6900.

**Tracks Walking Staffs,** 4000 1st Ave. South, Seattle, WA 98134: Free information ◆ Telescoping walking staffs. 800-527-1527. www.cascadedesigns.com

**Uncle Sam Umbrella Shop,** 161 W. 57th St., New York, NY 10019: Free catalog ◆ Umbrellas, canes, and walking sticks. 212-247-7163.

**Walk Easy Inc.,** 2915 S. Congress Ave., Delray Beach, FL 33445: Free brochure ◆ Crutches, walkers, commode chairs, and regular, tripod, and quad canes. 800-441-2904. www.walkeasy.com

**Wheelchair House,** 1831 E. Mulberry St., Fort Collins, CO 80524: Free information ◆ Custom wheelchair and seating systems, strollers, scooters, bathing and toileting aids, walkers and walking aids, and more. 800-466-7015; 970-482-7116 (in CO).

**Whistle Creek,** P.O. Box 580, Monument, CO 89132: Free information ◆ Handcrafted hardwood hiking and walking sticks. 719-488-1999.

## CANNING & PRESERVING

**Alltrista Corp.,** P.O. Box 2005, Muncie, IN 47307: Free catalog ◆ Home canning and easy-to-make jams and jellies supplies and kits. 800-240-3340.

**Berry-Hill Limited,** 75 Burwell Rd., St. Thomas, Ontario, Canada N5P 3R5: Catalog $2 ◆ Canning supplies, weather vanes, cider press, and garden tools. 519-631-0480.

**Farmer Seed & Nursery Company,** 818 NW 4th St., Faribault, MN 55021: Free catalog ◆ Canning supplies. 507-334-1623.

**Gardener's Kitchen,** Box 322, Monument Beach, MA 02555: Free information ◆ Canning lids in bulk.

**Gardener's Supply Company,** 128 Intervale Rd., Burlington, VT 05401: Free catalog ◆ Garden carts, composters, sprayers, watering systems, weeding and cultivating tools, organic fertilizers and chemical preparations, leaf mulchers, canning and preserving supplies, and furniture. 800-876-5520. www.gardeners.com

**Gurney Seed & Nursery Company,** 110 Capitol St., Yankton, SD 57079: Free catalog ◆ Canning supplies. 605-665-1671.

**Home Canning Supply,** P.O. Box 1158, Ramona, CA 92065: Catalog $1 ◆ Canning supplies and equipment.

**Kitchen Krafts,** P.O. Box 442, Waukon, IA 52172: Free catalog ◆ Canning and food preservation supplies. 800-776-0575; 319-535-8000 (in IA). www.kitchenkrafts.com

**Lids R Us,** RR 1, Box 1945, Friendsville, PA 18818: Free information ◆ Lids for all size jars.

**Earl May Seeds & Nursery Company,** 208 N. Elm St., Shenandoah, IA 51603: Free catalog ◆ Canning supplies. 712-246-1020.

**Mellinger's,** 2310 W. South Range Rd., North Lima, OH 44452: Free catalog ◆ Canning supplies. 330-549-9861. www.mellingers.com

**Modern Homesteader,** 1825 Big Horn Ave., Cody, WY 82414: Free catalog ◆ Canning supplies. 800-443-4934; 307-587-5946 (in WY). www.modfarm.com

## CARBON MONOXIDE DETECTORS

**Advanced AirCare Inc.,** 281 Delsea Dr., Sewell, NJ 08080: Free brochure ◆ Carbon monoxide detectors. 800-304-9301. advanced@jersey.net

**Coleman Safety & Security Products,** 2820 Thatcher Rd., Downer's Grove, IL 60515: Free list of retail sources ◆ Carbon monoxide alarm. 800-972-2212.

**First Alert,** 780 McClure Rd., Aurora, IL 60404: Free information ◆ Carbon monoxide detectors. 800-323-9005.

**Walter Kidde,** Division Kidde Inc., 1394 S. 3rd St., Mebane, NC 27302: Free information ◆ Carbon monoxide detectors.

**Quantum Group Inc.,** 11211 Sorrento Valley Rd., San Diego, CA 92121: Free information ◆ Carbon monoxide detectors. 800-432-5599.

## CARNIVAL SUPPLIES

**Allen-Lewis Manufacturing Company,** P.O. Box 16546, Denver, CO 80216: Free catalog ◆ Souvenirs, carnival and party supplies, fund-raising merchandise, toys and games, T-shirts and sweatshirts, and craft supplies. 800-525-6658.

**Oriental Trading Company Inc.,** P.O. Box 3407, Omaha, NE 68103: Free catalog ◆ Toys, gifts, novelties, fund raisers, holiday and seasonal items, and carnival supplies. 800-228-0475. www.oriental.com

**B. Palmer Sales Company Inc.,** 3510 Hyw. 80 East, P.O. Box 850247, Mesquite, TX 75185: Free catalog ◆ Carnival, fund-raising, and party supplies. 800-888-3087; 214-288-1026 (in TX).

**U.S. Toy Company Inc.,** 13201 Arrington Rd., Grandview, MO 64030: Catalog $3 ◆ Carnival supplies, prizes, and games. 800-448-7830. www.const/play.com

## CAROUSEL FIGURES & ART

**Americana Antiques,** Rusty & Emmy Donohue, P.O. Box 650, Oxford, MD 21654: Catalog $7.50 ◆ Antique wood carousel horses and menagerie figures. 443-226-5677.

**Americana Carousel Collection,** 3645 NW 67th St., Miami, FL 33147: Catalog $5 ◆ Authentic reproductions of carousel horses, from 1915 to 1927. 800-852-0494.

**The Carousel Catalog,** Chuck Kaparich, 503 Connell Ave., Missoula, MT 59801: Free catalog ◆ Original carved carousel horses. 406-549-9711.

**Carousel Creations,** Hwy. 63, P.O. Box 56, Barronett, WI 54813: Free information ◆ Cigar store Indians, carousel animals, and other wood carvings. 715-822-4189.

**The Carousel Lady,** 1350 Vista Way, Red Bluff, CA 96080: Brochure $3 (refundable) ◆ Carousel posters. 916-347-6985.

**Carousel Magic,** P.O. Box 1466, Mansfield, OH 44901: Catalog $3 ◆ Handcarved carousel horses, menagerie figures, carving kits, and accessories. 888-213-2829; 419-526-4009 (in OH). www.carouselmagic.com

**Carousel Resource Catalog,** P.O. Box 6459, Santa Fe, NM 87502: Catalog $2.50 ◆ Sources for carousel figures, books, events, and organizations. 505-995-0102. zon@nets.com

**Carousel Workshop,** 218 S. High St., DeLand, FL 32720: Catalog $3 ◆ Reproduction and antique carousel collectibles. 904-738-4229. www.carousel.net/workshop

**Corinna's Carousels,** 404 S. Jefferson, La Harpe, KS 66751: Free brochure ◆ Full-size carousel horses. 316-96-2682.

**The Extraordinaire Plaza,** 125 S. Battin, Wichita, KS 67218: Free catalog ◆ Collectible carousel horses. 800-896-9661; 316-685-6602 (in KS).

**J & M Carousel,** Jack & Meg Hurt, 1711 Calavaras Dr., Santa Rosa, CA 95405: Free list with long SASE ◆ Restoration supplies. 800-789-1026.

**Layton Studios,** Joyce A. Hughes, 115 N. Marsh Rd., Savannah, GA 31410: Free information ◆ Restored carousel horses. 912-897-1901.

**Merry-Go-Art,** 2606 Jefferson, Joplin, MO 64804: Free list with long SASE ◆ Antique and restored carousel figures. 417-624-7281.

**Merry-Go-Round Antiques,** Al Rappaport, 29541 Roan Dr., Warren, MI 48093: Free information with long SASE ◆ Antique carousel figures. 810-751-8078.

**Metropolitan Artifacts Inc.,** 4783 Peachtree Rd., Atlanta, GA 30341: Free brochure ◆ Carousel animals of American and European origin. Also reproduction fiberglass and aluminum animals. 770-986-0007.

**Miniature Carousel Components,** 8 N. Munroe Terrace, Dorchester, MA 02122: Free brochure with long SASE ◆ Drive mechanisms and parts. 617-265-6132.

**Robocast American Carousel,** 3645 NW 67th, Miami, FL 33147: Information $5 (refundable) ◆ Handpainted reproduction carousel horses with brass hardware. 305-673-0494.

**Willitts Designs,** 1129 Industrial Ave., Petaluma, CA 94952: Free information ◆ Carousel figures inspired by turn-of-the-century master carvers. 800-358-9184. www.willitts.com

**Wonder Products Inc.,** 12700 S. Figueroa St., Gardena. CA 90248: Free catalog ◆ Unpainted carousel and western-style horses for crafters.

**Zon International Publishing Company,** P.O. Box 6459, Santa Fe, NM 87502: Catalog $2.50 ◆ Blueprints for carving your own carousel figures. 800-266-5767.

## CARRIAGES & BUGGIES (HORSE-DRAWN)

**Cumberland General Store,** #1 Hwy. 68, Crossville, TN 38555: Catalog $4 ◆ Blacksmithing equipment, hand pumps, windmills, wood cooking ranges, gardening tools, cast-iron wares, farm bells, buggies, harnesses, and other equipment. 800-334-4640. www.cumberlandgeneral.com

**Justin Carriage Works,** P.O. Box 336, Nashville, MI 49073: Brochure $5 ◆ Custom-crafted carriages. 517-852-9743. www.buggy.com

## CASINO SUPPLIES

**Casino Productions,** 36 Williams Dr., Prospect, CT 06712: Free information ◆ Casino and gaming equipment. 860-525-3423; 203-758-4538 (in CT).

**Dealer's Choice Gift Shop,** 8025 Black Horse Pike, #470, West Atlantic City, NJ 08232: Free catalog ◆ Gaming gifts. 800-969-0711. www.casinocenter.com

**Marion & Company,** 147 W. 26th St., New York, NY 10001: Free information ◆ Casino equipment and supplies. 800-232-CHIP.

**The Poker Chip Company Ltd.,** 22908 Orefon Ct., Ste. I-11, Torrance, CA 90503: Free information ◆ Casino-style poker chips. 800-722-8742; 310-320-9815 (in CA).

## CDS, CASSETTES, & RECORDS

### Archival Supplies & Record Keeping

**Andy's Record Supplies,** 48 Colonial Rd., Providence, RI 02906: Free information with two 1st class stamps ◆ Album cardboard jackets, blister packs, storage boxes, record sleeves, and other archival supplies. 401-421-9453.

**Bags Unlimited Inc.,** 7 Canal St., Rochester, NY 14608: Free information ◆ Record storage and protection poly bags, cardboard backings, storage and display boxes, and other archival supplies. 800-767-BAGS. www.frontiernet.net/~bags

**House of Collectibles,** P.O. Box 3580, Wallingford, CT 06494: Free information ◆ Software for tracking and managing record collections. 800-800-1462.

**PSG-Homecraft Software,** P.O. Box 974, Tualatin, OR 97062: Free information ◆ Software for music reference and inventory cataloging. 503-692-3732. www.homecraft.com

**Something Special Enterprises,** P.O. Box 74, Allison Park, PA 15101: Free information ◆ Archival supplies. 412-487-2626.

### Children's Recordings

**Music for Little People,** P.O. Box 1460, Redway, CA 95560: Free catalog ◆ Famous stories, favorite songs, lullabies, nature stories, folk music, classical music, and other children's music cassettes and videos. 800-346-4445.

### Collectible Recordings

**American Pie,** P.O. Box 57347, Van Nuys, CA 91413: Free catalog ◆ Hard-to-find hits of the past fifty years on 45s and CDs. 818-786-5788. www.ampie.com

**Benedikt & Salmon Record Rarities,** 3020 Meade Ave., San Diego, CA 92116: Free catalogs (indicate choice of (1) classical (2) jazz, big-bands, and blues (3) personalities, soundtracks, and country music) ◆ Hard-to-find rare records from 1890 to date, early phonographs, cylinders, autographed memorabilia, and rare books on music and the performing arts. 619-281-3345. rarerecords@groupweb.com

**Brandenburg Historical,** P.O. Box 1574, Rutherford, NJ 07070: Catalog $2 ◆ German military collectibles, from 1900 to the present. Also books and German military music CDs.

**C.D.I. Imports,** P.O. Box 471, Lincoln, MA 01773: Catalog $5 ◆ Concert and rare studio CDs and videos from all countries. 781-259-4371.

**California Albums,** P.O. Box 3426, Hollywood, CA 90078: Free information ◆ Collectible recordings. 213-461-9806. home.earthlink.net/~calalbums/index.htm

**CDCellar,** P.O. Box 340324, Dayton, OH 45434: Catalog $2 ◆ Rare CDs, LPs, and VHS tapes from the United States, United Kingdom, Japan, and Germany.

**Collectables Records,** Box 35, Narberth, PA 19072: Free catalog ◆ Rhythm and blues records from the 1970s. 800-446-8426; 610-649-7650 (in PA).

**Coronet Books, CDs & Cassettes,** 311 Bainbridge St., Philadelphia, PA 19147: Catalog $2 ◆ Rhythm, classical, blues, big-band, soundtracks, Broadway musicals, rock, and other recordings. 215-925-5083.

**Dan's Old Record Shelf,** P.O. Box 734, Lake Elsinore, CA 92531: Free information with long SASE (enclose want list) ◆ Jazz, rock and roll, and blues albums. Also 45s, 78s, and tapes from the 1920s to 1980s. 909-674-2794.

**Don Records,** 341 Wisconsin Ave., Massapequa, NY 11758: Catalog $2 ◆ Current and hard-to-find 45rpm records. 516-752-1770.

**Encore Records,** P.O. Box 410126, St. Louis, MO 63141: Catalog $1 (refundable) ◆ 45 rpm records. 314-434-4121.

**Flipside II Records,** 120 Wanaque Ave., Pompton Lakes, NJ 07442: Free information ◆ Punk rock, imports, and other recordings. 973-835-8448.

**Fox Music,** 127 N. Main St., Oconomowoc, WI 53066: Free information ◆ Rare and collectible LPs and 45s. Also new and used domestic and imported CDs. 414-567-0679.

**Frontier Records/Tapes Inc.,** Box 157, Jenks, OK 74037: Catalog $2 ◆ Western swing, singing cowboys, gospel, dobro, big bands, country, and other LPs, cassettes, and CDs. 918-743-3559 (Friday and Saturdays).

**Bob Getreuer,** P.O. Box 582, Nanuet, NY 10954: Catalog $1 ◆ LPs, 45s, CDs, and tapes, from the 1940s to the 1980s. 914-352-5259.

**Graceland Records,** 2036 Dixie Garden Loop, Holiday, FL 34690: Free price list with long SASE ◆ Records, tapes, CDs, and memorabilia. 813-942-1935.

**Harvard Square Records Inc.,** P.O. Box 381975, Cambridge, MA 02238: Free catalog ◆ Cassettes, sealed vinyl records, and other recordings. Includes rare and out-of-print issues. 617-868-3385. hsrecord@userl.channel1.com

**Bob Iuliucci,** One Surrey Ln., Allendale, NJ 07401: Free list ◆ Out-of-print laser discs, rare promotional import CDs, rare vinyl 45s and LPs, promotional posters, rare concert tickets, and other theatrical memorabilia. 201-236-9107.

**The Jazz Store,** 91 Edgemont Rd., Upper Montclair, NJ 07043: Annual guide $3 ◆ Jazz videos and CDs, T-shirts, and posters. 201-509-8834.

**Rick Jorgensen,** 18021 150th Ave. East, Orthing, WA 98360: General catalog $7; country music catalog $6 ◆ Original music recordings on cassettes, from 1886 to 1960.

**Loran Records,** P.O. Box 1604, Florissant, MO 63031: Free information ◆ Collectible record albums. 314-837-2649.

**Mainly Music,** 36 Main St., Brattleboro, VT 05301: Catalog $3 (refundable) ◆ CDs, tapes and new, used, and rare records. Also vintage sheet music and other memorabilia. 802-257-0881.

**Manchester/Manchester,** 1711 S. Willow St., Manchester, NH 03103: Catalog $2 ◆ Out-of-print and used records, CDs, and tapes. 603-644-0199.

**Memory Lane Records,** 1321 Grand Ave., North Baldwin, NY 11510: Catalog $7 ◆ LPs, 45s, and other recordings, from the 1950s to the 1980s. 516-623-2247.

**Metro Music,** P.O. Box 10004, Silver Spring, MD 20904: Catalog $1 ◆ Vinyl records and CDs, from the 1960s, 10670s, and 1980s. Also rock-and-roll recordings from the 1990s. 301-622-2473. www.metro-music.com

**Moviecraft Inc.,** P.O. Box 438, Orland Park, IL 60462: Catalog $1 ◆ Video films. 708-460-9082.

**Music Books Plus,** 23 Hannover Dr., #7, St. Catharines, Ontario, Canada L2W 2A3: Free catalog ◆ Books, instructional videos, audio cassettes, CD-ROMs, computer software, and other music-related items. 800-265-8481.

**Nauck's Vintage Records,** 6323 Inway Dr., Spring, TX 77389: Catalog $3 ◆ Cylinder and 78 rpm records. Also turntables, books, antique phonographs, music boxes, and more. 281-370-7899. www.78rpm.com

**Richard Newman,** 222-A Purchase St., #321, Rye, NY 10580: Free catalog ◆ Rare videos and CDs from the 1960s to the 1990s.

**Oldies Unlimited,** 4667 Turney Rd., Cleveland, OH 44125: Free information ◆ Records, CDs, 45s, LPs, and other recordings from the 1950s to 1980s. 440-441-3361.

**Opera World,** Box 800, Concord, MA 01742: Free catalog ◆ Videos, laser discs, CDs, and books on the opera. 800-99-OPERA. www.operaworld.com

**Pack Central Inc.,** 6745 Denny Ave., North Hollywood, CA 91606: Catalog $2 ◆ Records and cassettes from the 1950s, 1960s, 1970s, and 1980s. 818-760-2828.

**Paradise City Music & Collectibles,** 1558 S. King St., Honolulu, HI 96826: Free information ◆ Rare, out-of-print, and hard-to-find imports, CDs, tapes, videos, records, and other recordings. 808-946-7625.

**Park Avenue Record Planet,** 532 Queen Anne Ave. North, Seattle, WA 98109: Free information ◆ Out-of-print records, rare LPs, CDs, and imports. 206-284-2390.

**The Record Groove,** 203 Skyland Dr., Staunton, VA 24401: Catalog $5 ◆ Collectible phonograph records and related materials. 540-885-6614. trgroove@juno.com

**Roanoke's Record Room,** P.O. Box 2445, Roanoke, VA 24010: Free price list ◆ Out-of-print 10 and 12-inch rock and pop LPs, from 1949 to 1992. 540-343-9570 WWW.SWIFTSITE.com/USEDLPs

**Rock Classics,** 1511 E. Babydoll Rd., Port Orchard, WA 98366: Catalog $1 ◆ Rock classics on CDs, from the 1950s, 1960s, and 1970s. 360-769-0456.

**Rock Island,** 13162 N. Dale Mabry Island, Tampa, FL 33619: Free information ◆ Collectible recordings. 813-933-2823. www.musicparadise.com

**Rockaway Records,** 2395 Glendale Blvd., Los Angeles, CA 90039: Free information ◆ Posters, photographs, other memorabilia, LPs, and 45s. 213-664-3232.

**Serendipity Recordings,** 4775 Durham Rd., Rt. 77, Guilford, CT 06437: Catalog $2 ◆ Big bands, easy-listening, great American popular singers and vocal groups, cabaret, jazz, nostalgia of the 1940s and 1950s, and more. 203-457-1039.

**The Soar Corp.,** P.O. Box 8606, Albuquerque, NM 87198: Free catalog ◆ Contemporary and traditional Native American music. 505-268-6110.

**Jim Spotts, Rare Serials,** Rt. 422 East, Penn Run, PA 15765: Free information ◆ Amos 'N Andy shows recorded on video tapes. 412-349-4455.

**John Tefteller,** P.O. Box 1727, Grants Pass, OR 97526: Free information ◆ Rhythm and blues, rock-a-billy, rock-and-roll, country music. and other rare 45s, 78s, and a few LPs. 541-476-1326.

**Time Machine Music & Video,** P.O. Box 6961, Metairie, LA 70009: Catalog $3 ◆ Hard-to-find music and video recordings.

## Current Recordings

**Ace Video & Music,** 285 Caillavet St., Biloxi, MS 39530: Catalog $5 ◆ Vinyl recordings in all categories. 601-374-0777.

**Acorn Music,** P.O. Box 9453, Berkeley, CA 94709: Free brochure ◆ Appalachian dance, folk, rock, traditional carols, and melodies from around the world on CDs and cassettes. 800-742-2676. www.acornmusic.com

**Acoustic Sounds,** P.O. Box 1905, Salina, KS 67402: Catalog $3 ◆ Classical, waltzes, rhythm, Latin American, and other recordings. Includes CDs. 800-525-1630; 913-825-8609 (in KS).

**Alligator Records,** P.O. Box 60234, Chicago, IL 60660: Free catalog ◆ Blues and rock CDs, cassettes, and LPs. 800-344-5609.

**AMI Music,** P.O. Box 72124, Marietta, GA 30007: Free catalog (specify interest) ◆ (1) Traditional jazz blues and big band hits prior to 1980; (2) new age, jazz fusion, smooth jazz, and others. 770-977-4172.

**Andy's Front Hall,** P.O. Box 307, Wormer Rd., Voorheesville, NY 12186: Free catalog ◆ Domestic and imported cassettes and CDs. 800-759-1775; 518-765-4193 (in NY). members.aol.com/fronthal

**Arhoolie Records,** 10341 San Pablo Ave., El Cerrito, CA 94530: Catalog $3 ◆ Old-time folk, blues, country, cajun, and other music. 510-525-7471. www.arhoolie.com

**Audio-Forum,** 96 Broad St., Guilford, CT 06437: Free catalog ◆ Full-length courses for teaching yourself a foreign language. 800-448-7671; 203-453-9794 (in CT). 74537.550@compuserve.com

**Audio House,** 8105 Hawkcrest Dr., Grand Blanc, MI 48439: Catalog $3 ◆ Used CDs. 810-695-3415. www.audiohousecd.com

**Barnes & Noble,** 126 5th Ave., New York, NY 10011: Free catalog ◆ Records, cassettes, and books. 800-242-6657. www.barnesandnoble.com

**The Beautiful Music Company,** 320 Main St., Northport, NY 11768: Free catalog ◆ Bluegrass and country, marches, instrumentals, jazz, gospel, big bands and favorite artists, classics and opera, and barbershop quartet recordings on cassettes, records, and CDs.

**Blind Pig Records,** P.O. Box 2344, San Francisco, CA 94126: Free catalog ◆ Blues records, CDs, and cassettes. 415-550-6484.

**Boogie Music,** P.O. Box 2054, San Mateo, CA 94401: Free list ◆ LPs and 45s from 1950 to 1990. 415-348-5422.

**Bop Shop Records,** 274 N. Goodman St., Rochester, NY 14607: Free catalog ◆ LP sets in sealed or mint condition. 716-271-3354.

**C.D.I. Imports,** P.O. Box 471, Lincoln, MA 01773: Catalog $5 ◆ Concert and rare studio CDs and videos from all countries. 781-259-4371.

**Catalog Music Company,** P.O. Box 159297, Nashville, TN 37215: Free information ◆ Country music recordings. 800-992-4487.

**CD Research,** Mail Order Dept., 407 G St., Davis, CA 95616: Catalog $3 ◆ New and used CDs. 916-756-0499.

**Coast Records Inc.,** P.O. Box 82040, Las Vegas, NV 89180: Free list ◆ Vocal group records. 702-255-6601.

**Coin Machine Trader,** P.O. Box 602, Huron, SD 57350: Information $4 ◆ 45 rpm records for most jukeboxes. 605-352-7590.

**Collectors' Choice Music,** P.O. Box 838, Itasca, IL 60143: Free catalog ◆ Popular and hard-to-find music recordings. 800-494-2211.

**Concord Records Inc.,** P.O. Box 845, Concord, CA 94522: Free catalog ◆ Classical recordings on CDs. 800-551-5299.

**Cornerstone Music,** 2119 Missouri Blvd., Jefferson City, MO 65109: Free catalog ◆ Vinyl 45s, LPs, and other recordings, from the 1950s to 1990s. 573-636-9166.

**Coronet Books, CDs & Cassettes,** 311 Bainbridge St., Philadelphia, PA 19147: Catalog $2 ◆ CDs and cassettes. 215-925-5083.

**Country Music Hall of Fame,** 4 Music Square East, Nashville, TN 37203: Catalog $2 ◆ Cajun, bluegrass, old-time and early country classics, country fiddling, western swing and cowboy, Elvis Presley and rock, gospel, and Christmas albums, cassettes, CDs, books about country music, and song books. 800-255-2357; 615-256-1639 (in TN).

**Ken Crane's Laser Discs,** 15251 Beach Blvd., Westminster, CA 92683: Free catalog ◆ Laser disks. 800-624-3078; 714-892-2283 (in CA). www.kencranes.com

**Critics' Choice Video,** P.O. Box 749, Itasca, IL 60143: Free catalog ◆ Records, tapes, videos, and books. 800-544-9852. www.ccvideo.com

**DA Music,** P.O. Box 3, Little Silver, NJ 07739: Free catalog ◆ Contemporary, traditional, smooth, and European jazz. Also historic blues, new age, new instrumental, pop, and other music. 800-219-5140.

**Diamond Needle Enterprises,** 3550 Wilshire Blvd., Ste. 1500, Los Angeles, CA 90010: Free catalog ◆ Audiophiles, imports, and domestic recordings. 800-296-DISC.

**Double-Time Jazz,** Jamey & Julia Aebersold, P.O. Box 1244, New Albany, IN 47151: Free catalog ◆ Jazz records and videos. 800-293-8528. www.doubletimejazz.com

**Earwig Music Company Inc.,** 1818 W. Pratt Blvd., Chicago, IL 60626: Catalog $1 ◆ Traditional and modern blues recordings. 773-262-0278.

**Edirol,** P.O. Box 4919, Blaine, WA 98231: Free catalog ◆ Keyboards, electronics, software, and recordings. 800-380-2580. www.edirol.com

**Effective Learning Systems Inc.,** 5255 Edina Industrial Blvd., Edina, MN 55439: Free catalog ◆ Self-improvement tapes. 800-966-5683.

**Evidence Music Inc.,** 1100 E. Hector St., Ste. 392, Conshohocken, PA 19428: Free catalog ◆ Blues and jazz CDs. 610-832-0844.

**Explorations,** 360 Interlocken Blvd., Ste. 300, Broomfield, CO 80021: Free catalog ◆ Videos, audio recordings, and other products on yoga, meditation, magnetic response, world knowledge, human relations, and more. 800-720-2114.

**Express Trax Accompaniment Tapes,** P.O. Box 681945, Franklin, TN 37068: Free catalog ◆ Sound-alike sing-along professional accompaniment cassettes. 800-844-8273.

**Facets Video,** 1517 W. Fullerton Ave., Chicago, IL 60614: Free catalog ◆ Thousands of foreign, classic American, silent, documentary, experimental, cult, music, fine art and children's videos, laser discs, and CDs. 800-331-6197. sales@facets.org

**FarPointer Sports Corp.,** P.O. Box 702618, Tulsa, OK 74170: Free information ◆ Books, videos, audio tapes, and software covering training, coaching, and motivational and skills improvement. Also sports-related items. 918-587-6477.

**Flipside Records,** 940 Hermitage Rd., Hermitage, PA 16148: Free record list ◆ New, old, and rare records. 412-342-0824. www.burghnet.com

**Floyd's Record Shop,** P.O. Drawer 10, Ville Platte, LA 70586: Catalog $1 (refundable) ◆ Cajun and Creole music, books, videos, and T-shirts. 318-363-2184. www.floydsrecords.com

**Folk-Legacy Records Inc.,** Box 1148, 85 Sharon Mountain Rd., Sharon, CT 06069: Free information ◆ Country folk music on records, CDs, and cassettes. 800-836-0901; 860-364-5661 (in CT). www.folklegacy.com

**Footlight Records,** 113 E. 12th St., New York, NY 10003: Free information ◆ Cast recordings, soundtracks, and vocals. Also CDs, records, and tapes. 212-533-1572. www.footlight.com

**Fort Brooke Quartermaster,** Brandon B. Barszcz, P.O. Box 1628, Brandon, FL 33509: Catalog $2.50 ◆ Native American, square dancing, and other cassettes and CDs. 813-621-7256.

**Fox Music,** 127 N. Main St., Oconomowoc, WI 53066: Free information ◆ Rare and collectible LPs and 45s. Also new and used domestic and imported CDs. 414-567-0679.

**Full Circle Records,** Gloucester Rd., Blackwood, NJ 08012: Free information ◆ New and used CDs, imported recordings, other records, and videos. 609-227-0662.

**Gambler's Book Shop,** 630 S. 11th, Las Vegas, NV 89101: Free catalog ◆ Cassettes on how to achieve personal success, succeed in the stock market, business, finance, how to win at sports betting, poker, blackjack, keno, baccarat, craps, and roulette. 702-382-7555. www.gamblersbook.com

**Garage A Records,** 11695 N. Pied Piper Pkwy., Cromwell, IN 46732: Free catalog ◆ Phonographs, needles, cartridges, cleaning aids, accessories and rock, blues, rock-a-billy, soul, jazz, country, pop, teen, and other 45s and LPs. 219-856-4868.

**Robert Gentry,** P.O. Box 850, Many, LA 71449: Free list ◆ Country music albums, 78 and 45 rpm records, autographs, movie posters, books and magazines, press kits, and other collectibles. 318-256-2886.

**Golden Gallery,** P.O. Box 267, Strausstown, PA 19559: Free information ◆ Imported and domestic CDs. 215-933-5361.

**Good Music Record Company,** P.O. Box 1935, Ridgely, MD 21681: Free catalog ◆ CDs, cassettes, and videos. 800-538-4200.

**H & B Recordings,** P.O. Box 309, Waterbury Center, VT 05677: Free catalog ◆ Classical and jazz CDs and videos. 800-222-6872. www.hbdirect.com

**Hammer the Jammers,** 7801 Taft St., Merrillville, IN 46410: Catalog $2 ◆ Thousands of LPs and 45s. 219-736-9199.

**Heartland Music,** E. Parham Rd., P.O. Box 85535, Richmond, VA 23285: Free catalog ◆ Big-band, nostalgic, patriotic, romantic, inspirational, gospel, rock-and-roll, country, and easy listening music. 800-788-2400.

**Hepcat Records,** P.O. Box 1108, Orange, CA 92668: Free catalog ◆ Rockability, hillbilly, jump jive, western, swing, and 1950s rock and roll on CDs and LPs. 714-532-2095.

**Homespun Tapes,** Box 694, Woodstock, NY 12498: Free catalog ◆ Blues video and audio cassettes. 800-33-TAPES.

**Hot Platters,** P.O. Box 4213, Thousand Oaks, CA 91359: Free catalog ◆ Thousands of 45s and 78s in all categories. Also sheet music, tapes, and music videos. www.hotplatters.com

**The House of Music,** 2057 W. 95th St., Chicago, IL 60643: Free information ◆ Hard-to-find records, tapes, CDs, and videos. 773-239-4114.

**The House of Musical Traditions,** 7040 Carroll Ave., Takoma Park, MD 20912: Free catalog ◆ Folk music books and recordings. 800-540-3794; 301-270-9090 (in Metro DC area). www.hmtrad.com/index.html

**Jade Hubertz,** 111 N. Sheridan Ave., Indianapolis, IN 46219: Free catalog ◆ CD reissues from all over the world. 317-356-0685.

**Infinity Records Ltd.,** 3852 Sunrise Hwy., Seaford, NY 11783: Free information ◆ Jazz, soul, doo-wop, and other records. 516-221-0634.

**J & R Music World,** 59-50 Queens-Midtown Expwy., Maspeth, NY 11378: Free catalog ◆ Records, cassettes, and videos. 800-221-8180.

**Jay Distributors,** Box 191332, Dallas, TX 75219: Free information ◆ Ballet, tap, and jazz videos and records, tapes, CDs, and cassettes. 800-793-6843. www.flash.net/~jaydist

**Jersey Shore Video,** P.O. Box 293, Whiting, NJ 08759: Free catalog ◆ Verve, Columbia, and Epic jazz. Also RCA living stereo and rock the house pop titles. 908-350-1446.

**Joyce Record Club,** Box 1687, Zephyrhills, FL 33539: Free information ◆ Big band records and CDs. 813-715-7688. dgehr@zephyrnet.com

**KaleiDISCope,** P.O. Box 558, Oakton, VA 22124: Free list ◆ Jazz, soul, R&R, R&B, C&W, vocals, instrumentals, and other records. 707-620-9216.

**Kimbo Educational,** P.O. Box 477, Long Branch, NJ 07740: Free catalog ◆ Cassettes, CDs, records, videos, read-alongs, and filmstrips for children. 800-631-2187. www.kimboed.com

**Ladyslipper Inc.,** P.O. Box 3124-R, Durham, NC 27715: Free catalog ◆ Music by women. 800-634-6044.

**Lark in the Morning,** P.O. Box 1176, Mendocino, CA 95460: Catalog $3 ◆ Hard-to-find musical instruments, books about music, and CDs, cassettes, and videos. 707-964-5569. larkinam@larkinam.com

**Lasertown Video Discs,** 50 School House Rd., Kulpsville, PA 19443: Free catalog ◆ Laser disks, DVDs, players, and accessories. 800-893-0390; 215-721-8688 (in PA). www.lasertown.com

**Last Vestige Music Shop,** 173 Quail St., Albany, NY 12203: Free information ◆ Used, rare, and other hard-to-find out-of-print records, tapes, and CDs. 518-432-7736.

**Lyric Distribution Inc.,** P.O. Box 66, Albertson, NY 11507: Free information ◆ Operatic CDs. 516-484-5100. lyric1@ix.netcom.com

**Maine Record Sales,** P.O. Box 1054, Bangor, ME 04401: Free information (enclose want list) ◆ Rock, country, and soul music cassettes and albums. 207-285-7002.

**Mainly Music,** 36 Main St., Brattleboro, VT 05301: Catalog $3 (refundable) ◆ New, used, and rare records, CDs, and tapes. Also vintage sheet music and other memorabilia. 802-257-0881.

**Metro Music,** P.O. Box 10004, Silver Spring, MD 20904: Catalog $1 ◆ Vinyl records and CDs, from the 1960s, 10670s, and 1980s. Also rock-and-roll recordings from the 1990s. 301-622-2473. www.metro-music.com

**Metropolitan Opera Shop,** Lincoln Center, 135 W. 65th St., New York, NY 10023: Free catalog ◆ Books and classical, concert, operatic, and documentary videos, records, and CDs. 800-453-2258; 212-580-4090 (in NY). www.metguild.com

**Midnight Productions Inc.,** P.O. Box 68, Waldwick, NJ 07463: Free catalog ◆ Theater organ music on cassettes and CDs. 201-670-6660. www.theaterorgan.com

**Midnight Records,** Box 390, Old Chelsea Station, New York, NY 10011: Catalog $1 ◆ Rock and roll, blues, and other hard-to-find records. 212-675-2768. midnight@cerfnet.com

**Craig Moerer Records,** P.O. Box 42546, Portland, OR 97242: Free list (specify interests) ◆ All categories of LPs and 45s. 503-232-1735.

**Mosaic Records,** 35 Melrose Pl., Stamford, CT 06902: Free catalog ◆ Jazz records and CDs. 203-327-7111.

**Music By Mail,** P.O. Box 090424, Fort Hamilton Station, Brooklyn, NY 11209: Catalog $2 ◆ Rock, soul, country, Latin, and other music on cassettes and CDs. 718-921-2182.

**Music Connection,** 430 Market St., Elmwood Park, NJ 07407: Free information ◆ New and used CDs, imported recordings, and videos. 201-797-5212.

**The Music Connection Records,** 1711 S. Willow St., Manchester, NH 03103: Free information ◆ Past and present records, CDs, and tapes. 603-644-0199.

**Thomas Nelson Publishers,** P.O. Box 140300, Nashville, TN 37214: Free catalog ◆ Christian books, bibles, audio cassettes and videos, and music. 800-933-9673. wwwnelsonworddirect.com

**The Noontide Press,** P.O. Box 2719, Newport Beach, CA 92659: Free catalog ◆ Books, audio cassettes, and videos on the social, political, economic, and historical taboos of the modern age. 714-631-1490.

**Opera World,** Box 800, Concord, MA 01742: Free information ◆ Opera videos and laser discs. 800-99-OPERA. www.operaworld.com

**Pack Central Inc.,** 6745 Denny Ave., North Hollywood, CA 91606: Catalog $2 ◆ Records and cassettes from the 1950s, 1960s, 1970s, and 1980s. 818-760-2828.

**Park Avenue Record Planet,** 532 Queen Anne Ave. North, Seattle, WA 98109: Free information ◆ Out-of-print records, rare LPs, CDs, and imports. 206-284-2390.

**Precept Ministries,** P.O. Box 182218, Chattanooga, TN 37422: Free catalog ◆ Religious books, audio cassettes, and videos. 423-894-3277. www.precept.org

**Qualiton Imports Ltd.,** 24-02 40th Ave., Long Island City, NY 11101: Free catalog ◆ Classical CDs. 718-937-8515.

**Razor & Tie Music,** P.O. Box 585, Cooper Station, New York, NY 10276: Free catalog ◆ Re-issues, anthologies, and new recordings. 800-443-3555.

**Rediscover Music Catalogue,** 705 S. Washington St., Naperville, IL 60540: Catalog $3 ◆ Hard-to-find CDs from the 1950s and 1960s. 800-232-7328. www.rediscover.com

**Rego Irish Records & Tapes Inc.,** 64 New Hyde Park Rd., Garden City, NY 11530: Catalog $2 ◆ Irish records and tapes. 800-854-3746; 516-328-7800 (in NY).

**Revolution Records,** 1620 Alton Rd., Miami Beach, FL 33139: Free information (specify items wanted) ◆ New and used CDs and records. 305-673-6464.

**Rhythm Recordings,** P.O. Box 22372, San Francisco, CA 94116: Free catalog ◆ Rare and obscure originals, reproductions, and imports, from the 1940s to the present. 415-753-3480.

**Rick's Music Inc.,** 3791 Mercer University Dr., Macon, GA 31204: Free catalog ◆ Audio and video recordings, memorabilia, posters, and photos. 912-757-9253.

**Roberts Rinehart Publishers,** 6309 Monarch Place Park, Niwot, CO 80503: Free brochure ◆ Videos, CDs, and books about Ireland. 800-352-1985. www.robertsrinehart.com

**Rockin Rudys Record Heaven,** 1710 Brooks St., Missoula, MT 59801: Free information ◆ New and used LPs, 45s, and other collectible records. 406-542-1104.

**Marion Roehl Recordings,** 2208 220th St., Donnellson. IA 52625: Free catalog ◆ Audio cassettes and CDs of antique music machines, carousels, calliopes, player pianos, and music boxes. 319-837-8106. www.mrreecordings.com

**Roots & Rhythm Inc.,** P.O. Box 837, El Cerrito, CA 94530: Catalog $5 (specify blues, country, or vintage rock-and-roll) ◆ Records, tapes, CDs, music books, and videos. 510-525-1494. roots@hooked.net

**Roots CDs & Vinyl,** 118 A E. Main St., Carrboro, NC 27510: Free catalog ◆ New and used CDs and vinyl records. 919-969-8827. www.NUTEKNET.com/ROOTS

**Rose Records,** 214 S. Wabash Ave., Chicago, IL 60604: Free catalog ◆ New releases, imports, and overstocks of classical, folk, blues, pop, jazz, soul, and country music records. 800-955-ROSE.

**Rounder Roundup Records,** 1 Camp St., Cambridge, MA 02140: Catalog $1 ◆ Blues, rock, jazz, and folk CDs, LPs, and cassettes. Includes instrumental and vocal recordings. 617-354-0700.

**Shoji Entertainments Inc.,** Mail Order Department, 2709 State Hwy. 248, Branson, MO 65616: Free brochure ◆ Recordings of the Shoji Tabuchi show on CDs and audio cassettes. 417-334-5974.

**Siren Disc,** 5850 W. 3rd St., Ste. 155, Hollywood, CA 90034: Free information ◆ Imported CDs. 213-935-0578.

**Sonic Recollections,** 2701 SE Belmont St., Portland, OR 97214: Free catalog with long SASE ◆ Specializes in weird and other recordings. 503-236-3050.

**Sounds True Audio,** 413 S. Arthur Ave., Louisville, CO 80027: Free catalog ◆ Audio and video recordings on personal discovery, relationships, sacred music of the world, homeopathy, psychology, health and healing, and other life-related topics. 800-333-9185. info@soundstrue.com

**Special Products Corp.,** 1081 S. Main St., Ste. 186, Cheshire, CT 06410: Free catalog ◆ Instructional, educational, motivational, and inspirational videos and CD-ROMs. 203-271-0470.

**Sports Music Inc.,** Box 769689, Roswell, GA 30076: Free catalog ◆ All styles of music on tapes for walking, running, aerobics, cycles, treadmills, and ski machines. 800-878-4764.

**StageStep,** 2000 Hamilton St., Philadelphia, PA 19130: Free catalog ◆ Dance, theater, film, music, and fitness books. Also videos and CDs. 800-523-0960. www.stagestep.com

**Starship Industries,** 605 Utterback Store Rd., Great Falls, VA 22066: Free catalog ◆ Laser and CD video disks. 703-450-5780.

**Tara Publications,** P.O. Box 707, Owings Mills, MD 21117: Free catalog ◆ Jewish music books, cassettes, CDs, and videos. 800-TARA-400; 410-654-0880 (in MD). www.jewishmusic.com

**Tower Records Mailorder,** 22 E. 4th St., 3rd Floor, New York, NY 10003: Free information ◆ Classical and opera recordings. 800-648-4844. www.towerrecords.com

**VAI Direct,** 109 Wheeler Ave., Pleasantville, NY 10570: Free catalog ◆ Classical music videos and CDs. Includes recordings of historic performances and rare repertoire. 800-477-7146. inquiries@vaimusic.com

**Vinyl Ink,** 955 Bonifant St., Silver Spring, MD 20910: Catalog $1 ◆ New domestic and imported rock, new wave, alternative, punk, jazz, and other recordings, from the 1960s to the 1990s. 301-588-4695.

**Vinyl Vendors,** 1800 S. Robertson Blvd., #279, Los Angeles, CA 90035: Free catalog ◆ Thousands of 7- and 12-inch vinyls, CDs, and LPs. 310-275-1444. www.vinylvendors.com

**Vinylmaniac,** Bill Jurof, 1829 SW 14th St., Miami, FL 33145: Catalog $5 ◆ LPs. 305-854-5903.

**Wagon Wheel Records & Books,** 17191 Corbina Ln., #203, Huntington Beach, CA 92649: Free catalog ◆ Rhythm, movement, and folk records for education and recreation. 714-846-8169.

**Waterloo Records & Video,** 600 N. Lamar Blvd., Austin, TX 78703: Free information ◆ Imports, dance music, and Texas favorites. 512-474-2525.

**The Wireless Music Source,** P.O. Box 64422, St. Paul, MN 55164: Free catalog ◆ Records, CDs, and cassettes. 800-726-8742. www.mpr.org

**Wolftrax Records,** P.O. Box 40007, Houston, TX 77240: Free brochure ◆ Texas music on records and CDs.

**Sylvia Woods Harp Center,** P.O. Box 816, Montrose, CA 91021: Free catalog ◆ Harps and recordings, books, harp-theme jewelry, and other gifts. 800-272-4277; 818-956-1363 (in CA). www.harpcenter.com

**Worldwide CD,** 2501 N. Lincoln Ave., #289, Chicago, IL 60614: Free information ◆ CDs. 773-665-0030.

**The Write Source,** P.O. Box 164, Grand Isle, VT 05458: Free catalog ◆ Rock, pop, folk, comedy, and classical LPs. 514-487-3123.

**Yodelin' Pig CD & Collectables,** 10435 Reistertown Rd., Bldg. 3, Owings Mills, MD 21117: Free information ◆ CDs and other hard-to-find recordings. 410-654-0516.

## Radio Recordings

**Adventures in Cassettes,** 5353 Nathan Ln., Plymouth, MN 55442: Free information ◆ Cassette recordings of old radio shows from the 1930s and 1940s. 800-328-0108. www.aic-radio.com

**Dorothy Radio Classics,** Box 156, Keeler, CA 93530: Catalog $3 ◆ Over 5000 old classic radio selections.

**Erstwhile Radio,** P.O, Box 2284, Peabody, MA 01960: Catalog $2 ◆ Old-time radio broadcasts on cassettes.

**Carl Froelich,** 2 Heritage Farm, New Freedom, PA 17349: Free catalog ◆ Classic broadcasts from America's golden age of radio.

**Charlie Garant,** P.O. Box 331, Greeneville, TN 37744: Free catalog with two 1st class stamps ◆ Comedy, mystery, and drama from radio's golden age.

**Hello Again, Radio,** P.O. Box 6176, Cincinnati, OH 45206: Free catalog ◆ Old-time radio shows on cassettes. 606-282-0333.

**How Well I Remember,** P.O. Box 1069, Richland, WA 99352: Catalog $2 (refundable) ◆ Old radio shows on cassettes and reels.

**Radio Memories,** 1600 Wewoka St., North Little Rock, AR 72116: Free catalog ◆ Tapes of shows from the golden age of radio. 888-35-RA-DIO. www.old-time.com/radiomemories

**Radio Showcase,** P.O. Box 4357, Santa Rose, CA 95402: Catalog $10; free sample list ◆ Audio cassettes of radio programs from the 1930s to 1950s. 800-500-8086. www.sonic.net/~otrsteve/Radio_Showcase_index.html

**Radio Yesteryear,** Box C, Sandy Hook, CT 06482: Free catalog ◆ Old-time radio shows on audio cassettes, CDs, and LPs. 800-243-0987. radio@yesteryear.com

## Soundtracks

**Coronet Books, CDs & Cassettes,** 311 Bainbridge St., Philadelphia, PA 19147: ◆ Rhythm, classical, blues, big-band, soundtracks, Broadway musicals, rock, and other recordings. 215-925-5083.

**Footlight Records,** 113 E. 12th St., New York, NY 10003: Free information ◆ Cast recordings, soundtracks, and vocals. Also CDs, records, and tapes. 212-533-1572. www.footlight.com

**Hollywood Legends,** 6621 Hollywood Blvd., Hollywood, CA 90028: Free information ◆ Theatrical performers memorabilia, press kits, Disney books, autographed photos, and other collectibles. 213-962-7411.

**Jim's TV Collectibles,** P.O. Box 4767, San Diego, CA 92164: Catalog $2 ◆ TV and movie soundtracks, from 1950 to 1990.

**Nathan Muchnick Inc.,** The Audio/Video Store, 1725 Chestnut St., Philadelphia, PA 19103: Free catalog ◆ Original cast soundtracks, nostalgia, and classic jazz and cabaret CDs. 215-564-0209. NMlcd@aol.com

**RTS Video Movies,** Box 93897, Las Vegas, NV 89193: Catalog $1 ◆ Rare soundtracks; movies, from the silents to today's films, Broadway show LPs, and more. 702-896-1300 (after 2 PM). www.rtsvideo.qpg.com

**Sparky's Mail Order,** 3724 N. Page, Chicago, IL 60634: Free information with long SASE ◆ Movie and TV soundtrack records. Also movie and TV paperbacks. 312-625-8732.

**Star Soundtracks,** P.O. Box 487, New Holland, PA 17557: Free catalog ◆ Soundtracks with original casts.

### Storage Cabinets & Supplies

**Allen Products Company,** 1635 E. Burnett St., Signal Hill, CA 90806: Free information ◆ Storage cabinets for CDs and audio and video equipment. 800-4-APC-INC.

**CAN-AM,** 70 Shields Ct., Markham, Ontario, Canada L3R 9T5: Free catalog ◆ Video cassette storage cabinets. 800-387-9790.

**Creative Video Products,** P.O. Box 7032, Endicott, NY 13761: Free information ◆ Video cassette albums. 607-754-6767.

**Leslie Dame Enterprises Ltd.,** 111-20 73rd Ave., Forest Hills, NY 11375: Free information ◆ CD, video cassette, and audio cassette storage cabinets. 718-261-4919.

**Door County Design & Woodworking,** 22 E. Pine St., Sturgeon Bay, WI 54235: Free information ◆ Storage systems. 800-746-0881.

**HY-Q Enterprises,** 14040 Mead St., Longmont, CO 80504: Free information ◆ Storage cabinets for CDs, video cassettes, and audio cassettes. 800-878-7458.

**LDI Inc.,** P.O. Box 277, Lanesboro, MN 55949: Free brochure ◆ Disc, tape, and component storage cabinets. 800-933-0403.

**Lorentz Design Inc.,** P.O. Box 277, Lanesboro, MN 55949: Free catalog ◆ Storage cabinets for CDs, video cassettes, and video game cartridges. 800-933-0403.

**Per Madsen Design,** P.O. Box 882464, San Francisco, CA 94188: Free brochure ◆ Stackable portable units for storing disks, tapes, and components. 415-822-4883.

**Salamander Designs Ltd.,** 32 Hillsboro Dr., West Hartford, CT 06107: Free brochure ◆ Modular shelving and cabinets for equipment and accessories. 800-201-6533.

**Soricé,** P.O. Box 747, Nutley, NJ 07110: Free information ◆ Audio cassette and video storage cabinets. 800-432-8005.

## CERAMICS & POTTERY SUPPLIES

**A.R.T. Studio Clay Company,** 1555 Louis Ave., Elk Grove Village, IL 60007: Catalog $5 ◆ Ceramics supplies. 800-323-0212; 847-593-6060 (in IL).

**Aegean Sponge Company Inc.,** 4722 Memphis Ave., Cleveland, OH 44144: Free catalog ◆ Ceramics supplies. 216-749-1927.

**Africana Colors,** Batavia, OH 45103: Free information ◆ Textured stains. 513-625-9486.

**Aftosa,** 1034 Ohio Ave., Richmond, CA 94804: Free catalog ◆ Pottery-making supplies. 800-231-0397. www.aftosa.com

**Aim Kiln,** 350 SW Wake Robin, Corvallis, OR 97333: Free information ◆ Electric and gas kilns for pottery, ceramics, porcelain, glass, and heat treating. 800-246-5456. www.1kiln.com

**Alberta's Molds Inc.,** P.O. Box 2018, Atascadero, CA 93423: Catalog $6 ◆ Ceramics molds. 805-466-9255.

**AMACO,** 4717 W. 16th St., Indianapolis, IN 46222: Free catalog ◆ Under glaze colors for brush application on bisque or greenware. 800-374-1600; 317-244-6871 (in IN). www.amaco.com

**American Art Clay Company Inc.,** 4717 W. 16th St., Indianapolis, IN 46222: Free catalog ◆ Clays, kilns, pottery-making equipment, glazes, tools, coloring materials, and metal enameling supplies. 800-374-1600; 317-244-6871 (in IN). www.amaco.com

**Art Decal Company,** 1145 Loma Ave., Long Beach, CA 90804: Free information ◆ Ceramics decals. 800-742-0270; 562-434-2711 (in CA).

**Astro Artcraft Supply,** 1026 W. 44th St., Norfolk, VA 23508: Free information ◆ Ceramics supplies. 800-USA-COST; 757-440-1373 (in VA).

**Badger Air-Brush Company,** 9128 W. Belmont Ave., Franklin Park, IL 60131: Brochure $1 ◆ Air brushes. 800-247-2787. www.badger-airbrush.com

**Bailey Pottery Equipment,** Box 1577, Kingston, NY 12401: Free catalog ◆ Ceramics supplies. 800-431-6067.

**Bennett's Pottery & Ceramic Supplies,** 431 Enterprise St., Ocoee, FL 34761: Free information ◆ Kilns, glazes, potter wheels, clay, slip, tools, and supplies for ceramics and pottery. 407-877-6311.

**Blue Diamond Kiln Company,** P.O. Box 172, Metairie, LA 70004: Information $1 ◆ Automatic kilns. 800-USA-KILN; 504-835-2035 (in LA).

**Boothe Mold Company,** 9 Boothe Plaza, Dupo, IL 62239: Catalog $8 ◆ Ceramics molds. 800-782-0512. www.boothemold.com

**Brickyard House of Ceramics,** 4721 W. 16th St., Speedway, IN 46222: Free information ◆ Glazes, stains, under-glazes, brushes, tools, molds, kiln and potter wheel repair parts, and kilns. 800-677-3289.

**Byrne Ceramic Supply Company Inc.,** 95 Bartley Rd., Flanders, NJ 07836: Free information ◆ White and colored, stoneware, and firebird porcelain slips. Also wheel and modeling clays and liquid silk one-coat clear glaze. 201-584-7492.

**C & F Wholesale Ceramics,** 3241 E. 11th Ave., Hialeah, FL 33013: Catalog $4 ◆ Ceramics supplies, stains and glazes, brushes, tools, music boxes, clock works, and airbrushes. 305-835-8200.

**Campbell Pump Company Inc.,** 351 Cromwell, Ste. 105, Fresno, CA 93711: Free information ◆ Slip pump. 800-869-7867.

**Cedar Heights Clay Company Inc.,** P.O. Box 295, Oak Hill, OH 45656: Free information ◆ Foundry and ceramics clay. 614-682-7794.

**Cer Cal Decals Inc.,** 626 N. San Gabriel Ave., Azusa, CA 91702: Free brochure ◆ Ceramics decals. 818-969-1456.

**Cerami Corner,** P.O. Box 1206, Grants Pass, OR 97528: Catalog $8 ◆ Ceramics molds, decals, china paints, and brushes. 800-423-8543.

**Ceramic Supply of NY/NJ,** 7 US Hwy. 46 West, Lodi, NJ 07644: Catalog $4 ◆ Electric and gas kilns, clays, colors, slip casting and sculpting equipment, potter wheels, and glazes. 800-7-CERAMIC; 201-340-3005 (in NJ).

**Ceramichrome,** P.O. Box 327, Stanford, KY 40484: Catalog $6.50 ◆ Ceramics molds, colors, and supplies. 800-544-0764.

**Chaselle Inc.,** 101 Almgren Dr., Agawam, MA 01001: Catalog $4 ◆ Art software and books, brushes and paints, tempera colors, acrylics, pastels, ceramics molds and kilns, sculpture equipment, silk-screening supplies, and other craft supplies. 800-628-8608. www.schoolspecialty.com

**Clay Magic Ceramic Products Inc.,** 21201 Russell Dr., P.O. Box 148, Rockwood, MI 48173: Catalog $8 ◆ Ceramics molds. 313-379-3400.

**Continental Clay Company,** 1101 Stinson Blvd., Minneapolis, MN 55413: Catalog $4 ◆ Ceramics supplies. 800-432-CLAY.

**Creative Hobbies,** 900 Creek Rd., Bellmawr, NJ 08031: Free catalog ◆ Ceramics supplies. 800-THE-KILN; 609-933-2540 (in NJ).

**Cridge Inc.,** Box 210, Morrisville, PA 19067: Catalog $2 ◆ Jewelry supplies for decorating ceramics. 215-295-3667.

**Crusader Kilns,** American Art Clay Company Inc., 4717 W. 16th St., Indianapolis, IN 46222: Free information with long SASE ◆ Energy-saving kilns. 800-374-1600; 317-244-6871 (in IN). www.amaco.com

**Debcor Inc.,** 513 W. Taft Dr., South Holland, IL 60473: Free list of retail sources ◆ Furniture for art and ceramics-working and industrial and graphic arts. 708-333-2191.

**Doc Holliday Molds Inc.,** 125 MacArthur Ct., Nicholasville, KY 40356: Catalog $7.50 ◆ Ceramics molds. 606-887-1427.

**Dona's Molds Inc.,** P.O. Box 145, West Milton, OH 45383: Catalog $7.50 ◆ Ceramics molds and coloring materials. 937-947-1333.

**Dove Brushes,** 280 Terrace Rd., Tarpon Springs, FL 34689: Catalog $2.50 ◆ Brushes. 800-334-3683; 813-934-5283 (in FL). www.dovebrushes.com

**Duncan Enterprises,** 5673 E. Shields Ave., Fresno, CA 93727: Free list of retail sources ◆ Molds, surface-texture products, and supplies. 800-438-6226; 209-291-4444 (in CA). www.duncan-enterprises.com

**Evenheat Kiln Inc.,** 6949 Legion Rd., Caseville, MI 48725: Free information ◆ Kilns. 517-856-2281.

**Ex-Cel Inc.,** 1011 N. Hollywood, Memphis, TN 38108: Free information ◆ Slip for ceramics-casting. 800-238-7270; 901-324-3851 (in TN). www.hocmen.com

**Fash-en-Hues,** 118 Bridge St., Piqua, OH 45356: Free information ◆ Translucent colors for staining ceramics and porcelain crafts. 937-778-8500.

**G & J Enterprises,** 4199 State Rd. 144, Mooresville, IN 46158: Catalog $2 (refundable) ◆ Ceramics and electrical supplies. 317-831-1452.

**Gare Incorporated,** 165 Rosemont St., P.O. Box 1686, Haverhill, MA 01830: Catalog $9 ◆ Ceramics molds, fired colors, stains, stone washed glazes, brushes, tools, and kilns. 978-373-9131.

**Georgies Ceramics & Clay Company,** 756 NE Lombard, Portland, OR 97211: Supplies catalog $5.50, mold catalog $5 ◆ Ceramics supplies and molds. 800-999-2529. www.georgies.com

**Highlands Ceramic Supply,** 4605 Oak Circle, Sebring, FL 33872: Free information ◆ Ceramics molds, kilns and kiln parts, pouring equipment, slip, clay, and greenware. 941-385-6656.

**Hill Decal Company,** 5746 Schutz St., Houston, TX 77032: Catalog $2 ◆ Decals for ceramics or glass. 281-449-1942.

**Holland Mold Inc.,** 1040 Pennsylvania Ave., P.O. Box 5021, Trenton, NJ 08638: Catalog $7 ◆ Ceramics molds. 609-392-7032.

**House of Caron,** 10111 Larrylyn Dr., Whittier, CA 90603: Catalog $3 ◆ Molds and supplies for miniature dolls. 562-947-6753.

**House of Ceramics Inc.,** 1011 N. Hollywood, Memphis, TN 38108: Free catalog ◆ Molds for ceramics and chinaware-crafting. 901-324-3851.

**Iandola Mold Company,** P.O. Box 5507, Trenton, NJ 08638: Catalog $6 ◆ Ceramics molds. 609-396-8832.

**Indiana Hobby Molds,** 3844 Hwy. 62 West, Boonville, IN 47601: Catalog $4 ◆ Ceramics molds. 812-897-4467.

**International Technical Ceramics Inc.,** P.O. Box 1726, Ponte Vedra, FL 32004: Free information ◆ Kilns and repair parts. 904-285-0200.

**Jay-Kay Molds,** P.O. Box 2307, Quinlan, TX 75474: Catalog $5 ◆ Ceramics molds. 903-356-3416.

**Jones Mold Company,** 919 4th Ave. South, Nashville, TN 37210: Ceramics catalog $6.25, doll catalog $6.75 ◆ Molds for ceramics and dolls. 615-251-8989.

**K-Ceramic Imports,** 732 Ballough Rd., Daytona Beach, FL 32114: Catalog $10 ◆ European decals, sponges, and brushes. 904-252-6530.

**Kelly's Ceramics Inc.,** 3016 Union Ave., Merchantville, NJ 08109: Free information ◆ Ceramics supplies and molds. 609-665-4181.

**Kemper Tools & Doll Supplies Inc.,** 13595 12th St., Chino, CA 91710: Free catalog ◆ Pottery, sculpting, craft, and art tools. Also doll-making supplies. 800-388-5367.

**Kerry Specialties,** P.O. Drawer 999, DeLand, FL 32721: Free information ◆ Brushes and cleaning tools. 888-738-0029.

**Kimple Mold Corp.,** P.O. Box 734, Goddard, KS 67052: Catalog $7 (plus $2 shipping/handling) ◆ Ceramics molds. 316-794-8621.

**Lynn Taylor Kingston Pottery,** 1505 Geyers Church Rd., Middletown, PA 17057: Catalog $3 ◆ Classic designed pottery. 717-944-5445.

**L & L Kiln,** Kiln Manufacturing Inc., P.O. Box 2409, Aston, PA 19014: Free information ◆ Kilns. 610-558-3899. www.hotkilns.com

**L & R Specialties,** 202 E. Mount Vernon St., P.O. Box 309, Nixa, MO 65714: Free price list ◆ Basic and moist clays, chemicals, glazes, stains, accessories, and equipment. 417-725-2606.

**Laguna Clay Company,** 14400 Lomitas Ave., City of Industry, CA 91746: Free information ◆ Ceramic clays, glazes, tools, and supplies. 800-452-4862. www.lagunaclay.com

**Lamp Specialties Inc.,** Box 240, Westville, NJ 08093: Catalog $5 (refundable) ◆ Electrical supplies for ceramics-crafting. 800-225-5526.

**Lee's Ceramic Supply,** P.O. Box 63, Mercedes, TX 78570: Catalog $2 (refundable) ◆ Ceramics supplies, molds, decals, and kits. 800-424-LEES.

**Lehman Manufacturing Company Inc.,** P.O. Box 46, Kentland, IN 47951: Free information ◆ Casting and mixing machines, parts, and slip. 800-348-5196. GetLehmans@aol.com

**Lily Pond Products,** 351 W. Cromwell, Ste. 105, Fresno, CA 93711: Free information ◆ Easy-to-store portable drain table. 209-431-5003.

**Little Falls School of Decorative Arts,** 242 Maple Ln., Valatie, NY 12184: Brochure $2 ◆ Ready-to-finish and paint statuary. 518-784-9779.

**Marx Brush Manufacturing Company Inc.,** 130 Beckwith Ave., Paterson, NJ 07503: Catalog $2 ◆ Ceramics adhesive for mending greenware, bisque, fastening greenware to bisque, adding pieces, mending hairline cracks, and repairing broken stilts and hard spots. 800-654-6279. symfau@aol.com

**Mayco Molds,** 4077 Weaver Ct. South, Hilliard, OH 43026: Catalog $6.95 ◆ Ceramics molds, tools, brushes, colors, and supplies. 614-876-1171.

**McRon Ceramic Molds,** 2660 NE 7th Ave., Pompano Beach, FL 33064: Catalog $8 ◆ Ceramics molds. 954-784-7707.

**Med-Mar Metals,** P.O. Box 6453, Anaheim, CA 92816: Free information ◆ Lusters, enamels, and paints. 714-533-6280.

**Miami Clay Company,** 270 NE 183rd St., North Miami, FL 33179: Catalog $2 ◆ Pottery supplies. 305-651-4695.

**Mike's Ceramic Molds Inc.,** 5217 8th Ave. South, St. Petersburg, FL 33707: Catalog $6 ◆ Ceramics molds. 813-321-3725.

**Mile Hi Ceramics Inc.,** 77 Lipan, Denver, CO 80223: Free catalog ◆ Clays and ceramics supplies. 303-825-4570.

**Minnesota Ceramic Supply,** 962 Arcade St., St. Paul, MN 55106: Free catalog ◆ Ceramics molds and supplies. 800-652-9724.

**Minnesota Clay USA,** 8001 Grand Ave. South, Bloomington, MN 55420: Free catalog ◆ Equipment, clays, glazes, tools, and books on ceramics and pottery crafts. 800-252-9872; 612-884-9101 (in MN). mnclayus@mn.com

**Mr. & Mrs. of Dallas,** 1301 Ave. K, Plano, TX 75074: Free catalog ◆ Ceramics and china painting supplies. 972-881-1699.

**Mug Merchant,** 982 N. Batavia St., Ste. B-11, Orange, CA 92667: Free information ◆ Decals for ceramics and glass. 714-532-2298.

**Nasco,** 901 Janesville Ave., Fort Atkinson, WI 53538: Free catalog ◆ Ceramics supplies, potter's tools, glazes, and kilns. 800-558-9595. www.nascofa.com

**National Artcraft Company,** 7996 Darrow Rd., Twinsburg, OH 44087: Catalog $4 ◆ Tools and supplies for floral-crafting, ceramics, and making clocks, lamps, dolls, candles, and jewelry. 800-793-0152. nationalartcraft@worldnet.att.net

**Nowell's Molds,** 1532 Pointer Ridge Pl., Bowie, MD 20716: Catalog $6 ◆ Ceramics molds. 301-249-0846.

**Ohio Ceramic Supply Inc.,** 2881 State Rt. 59, P.O. Box 630, Kent, OH 44240: Free information ◆ Ceramics supplies. 800-899-4627.

**Olympic Enterprises,** P.O. Box 321, Campbell, OH 44405: Catalog $5 ◆ Decals, brushes, tools, and sponges. 330-755-2726.

**Olympic Kilns,** Division Haugen Manufacturing Inc., 6301 Button Gwinnett Dr., Atlanta, GA 30340: Free catalog ◆ Kilns. 770-441-5550.

**Paragon Industries,** 2011 S. Town East Blvd., Mesquite, TX 75149: Free catalog ◆ Kilns. 800-876-4328; 972-288-7557 (in TX). www.paragonweb.com

**Pierce Tools,** 1610 Parkdale Dr., Grants Pass, OR 97527: Free catalog ◆ Ceramics, pottery, doll, and sculpting tools. 541-476-1778.

**Pine Tree Molds,** 225 Leed Rd. 20, Auburn, AL 36830: Catalog $6.50 ◆ Ceramics molds. 800-346-4428.

**The Potters Shop,** 31 Thorpe Rd., Needham Heights, MA 02194: Free brochure ◆ Pottery-making supplies, books, videos, and tools. 781-449-7687.

**Red Barn Ceramics Inc.,** Cortland Rd. South, Cortland, NY 13045: Catalog $3 (refundable) ◆ Ceramics equipment and electrical supplies. 607-756-2039.

**Riverview Molds Inc.,** 2141 P Ave., Williamsburg, IA 52361: Catalog $7 ◆ Ceramics molds. 319-668-9800.

**Heinz Scharff Brushes,** P.O. Box 746, Fayetteville, GA 30214: Free catalog ◆ Brushes for ceramics and tole painting, china decoration, and other decorative crafts. 770-461-2200. www.artbrush.com

**Scioto Ceramic Products Inc.,** 2455 Harrisburg Pike, Grove City, OH 43123: Catalog $5.95 ◆ Ceramics molds. 614-871-0090.

**Scott Publications,** 30595 W. 8 Mile Rd., Livonia, MI 48152: Free catalog ◆ Books for the ceramist, china painter, and doll maker. 800-458-8237; 313-477-6650 (in MI).

**Sheffield Pottery Inc.,** US Rt. 7, P.O. Box 399, Sheffield, MA 01257: Free catalog ◆ Kilns, stains, equipment and supplies, and moist, screened fire, and slip clays. 413-229-7700.

**Skutt Ceramic Products,** 2618 SE Steele St., Portland, OR 97202: Free brochure ◆ Electric kilns. 503-231-7726.

**Southern Oregon Pottery & Supply,** 111 Talent Ave., P.O. Box 158, Talent, OR 97540: Catalog $4 ◆ Manual, automatic, and electronic 110 and 240-volt kilns. Also tools, plasters, glazes, clays, books, and supplies. 503-535-6700.

**Star Stilts,** P.O. Box 367, Feasterville, PA 19053: Free catalog ◆ Stilts and supports. 215-357-1893.

**Stewart's of California Inc.,** 16055 Heron Ave., La Mirada, CA 90638: Catalog $2 ◆ Ceramics supplies. 800-252-2603; 714-523-2603 (in CA).

**Streamers Country Ceramics,** 1 Hazelwood Dr., Baltic, CT 06330: Free catalog ◆ Clocks, lamp parts, music boxes, Christmas items, tools and brushes, special touches, ready-to-finish pieces, and ceramics-making accessories. 860-822-0151. www.streamers.com

**Sugar Creek Industries Inc.,** P.O. Box 354, Linden, IN 47955: Free catalog ◆ Ceramics equipment. 317-339-4641.

**Tampa Bay Mold Company,** 2724 22nd St. North, St. Petersburg, FL 33713: Catalog $5 ◆ Ceramics molds. 800-359-0534.

**Tari Tan Ceramic & Craft Supply,** 3919 N. Greenbrooke SE, Grand Rapids, MI 49512: Free information ◆ Ceramics molds and supplies. 616-698-2460.

**Truebite Inc.,** 2590 Glenwood Rd., Vestal, NY 13850: Free catalog ◆ Cutting, grinding, drilling, and clean-up aids for porcelain and ceramics. 800-676-8907.

**V.I.P. Molds Inc.,** 6717 Townsend Dr., Erie, PA 16505: Catalog $8 ◆ Ceramics molds. 814-455-3396.

**Weaver's Ceramic Mold Inc.,** 684 W. Main St., New Holland, PA 17557: Catalog $2 ◆ Ceramics molds. 717-354-4491.

**Weidlich Ceramics Inc.,** 2230 Camplain Rd., Somerville, NJ 08876: Free information ◆ Greenware, kilns, and fired and non-fired colors. 908-725-8554.

**Wise Screenprint Inc.,** 1011 Valley St., Dayton, OH 45404: Free information ◆ Decals for ceramics and glass. 937-223-1573.

**The Wishing Well,** 221 W. 8th, Box 226, Cozad, NE 69130: Free information ◆ Liquid suede kits and non-toxic water soluble ceramics paints. 308-784-3100.

**Jonathan & Jan Wright,** 40 Beltrees Rd., Elsah, IL 62028: Free information ◆ Traditional Early American folk pottery. 800-683-1804.

**Yozie Molds Inc.,** 124 College Ave., Dunbar, PA 15431: Catalog $12 ◆ Ceramics molds. 724-628-3693.

## CHAIR CANING

**A & H Brass & Supply,** 126 W. Main St., Johnson City, TN 37604: Catalog $2 ◆ Chair-caning restoration materials. 800-638-4252; 423-928-8220 (in TN).

**Alcon Braid,** P.O. Box 429, Hickory, NC 28603: Free catalog ◆ Macrame, chair-weaving, and crochet supplies. 800-523-4371. sandra@griffinshine.com

**Bamboo & Rattan Works Inc.,** 470 Oberlin Ave. South, Lakewood, NJ 08701: Free information ◆ Rattan, cords, chair canes, matting, and bamboo, flat, and round reeds. 800-4-BAMBOO.

**Cane & Basket Supply Company,** 1283 S. Cochran, Los Angeles, CA 90019: Catalog $2 ◆ Reeds, fiber and rush, Danish seat cord, raffia, rattan sea grass, and caning and basket-making accessories. 800-468-3966.

**Caning Shop,** 926 Gilman St., Berkeley, CA 94710: Catalog $2 (refundable) ◆ Caning and basket-making supplies and tools. 800-544-3373.

**Connecticut Cane & Reed Company,** P.O. Box 762, Manchester, CT 06040: Catalog 50¢ ◆ Caning and basket-making supplies. 860-646-6586.

**Country Seat,** 1013 Old Philly Pike, Kempton, PA 19529: Free catalog with long SASE and three 1st class stamps ◆ How-to books and basket-making and chair-caning supplies. 610-756-6124. www.countryseat.com

**Earth Guild,** 33 Haywood St., Asheville, NC 28801: Catalog $3 ◆ Basket-making, weaving, spinning, dyeing, pottery, woodcarving, hand and machine knitting, rug-making, netting, and chair-caning supplies. 800-327-8448. www.earthguild.com

**Frank's Cane & Rush Supply,** 7252 Heil Ave., Huntington Beach, CA 92647: Free information ◆ Cane, rush, basket-making supplies, and wood parts. 714-847-0707.

**Gundula's & Peerless Rattan & Reed,** 624 S. Burnett Rd., Springfield, OH 45505: Catalog $1.50 ◆ Caning supplies. 937-323-7353. www.weavenet.com

**Michigan Cane Supply,** 5348 N. Riverview Dr., Kalamazoo, MI 49004: List $1 ◆ Chair cane, rush, and basket-weaving supplies. 616-282-5461.

**Ozark Basketry Supply,** P.O. Box 599, Fayetteville, AR 72702: Catalog $1 ◆ Books, basket-making kits, chair cane, dyes, hoops, and handles. 501-442-9292.

**P.L. Butte Baskets,** 44 W. Park Ave., Long Beach, NY 11561: Free t list of retail sources ◆ Basket-making and caning supplies. 800-289-1049. www.PLButte.com

**Peerless Rattan at the Wrap n Post,** 624 S. Burnett Rd., Springfield, OH 45505: Free information ◆ Chair caning and basket weaving supplies. 937-323-7353. www.weavenet.com

**H.H. Perkins Company,** 10 S. Bradley Rd., Woodbridge, CT 06525: Free catalog ◆ Seat-weaving and basket-making supplies, macrame supplies, and how-to books. 800-462-6660.

**Plymouth Reed & Cane,** 1200 W. Ann Arbor Rd., Plymouth, MI 48170: Brochure $1 ◆ Reed, cane, fiber rush, handles, hoops, kits, dyes, tools, books, and other basket-making and chair-caning materials. 734-455-2150.

**Royalwood Ltd.,** 517 Woodville Rd., Mansfield, OH 44907: Catalog $1 ◆ Caning and basket-making supplies, tools, kits, and dyes. 800-526-1630; 419-526-1630 (in OH). www.bright.net/~roylwood

**Snapvent Company,** 147 W. Baxter Ave., Knoxville, TN 37917: Free price list with long SASE ◆ Basket and chair-caning supplies. 423-523-6784.

**V.I. Reed & Cane,** Rt. 5, Box 632, Rogers, AR 72756: Free catalog ◆ Flat and round reeds, smoked reed, cane, hoops, handles, raffia, dyes, and basket-weaving kits. 800-852-0025. www.basketweaving.com

**Veterans Caning Shop,** 442 10th Ave., New York, NY 10001: Free catalog ◆ Caning supplies. 212-868-3244.

## CHECKS

**Artistic Checks,** P.O. Box 1556, Elmira, NY 14902: Free information ◆ Personalized top-tear or side-tear checks with original designs. 800-362-5718.

**Business Envelopes,** P.O. Box 517, Thorofare, NJ 08086: Free catalog ◆ Business envelopes, checks, pens, and office supplies. 800-275-4400.

**Checks in the Mail,** 2435 Goodwin Ln., New Braunfels, TX 78135: Free brochure ◆ Personalized desk and business checks with optional designs and colors. 800-733-4443.

**Current Checks Inc.,** Express Processing Center, Colorado Springs, CO 80941: Free catalog ◆ Personalized checks with optional designs and colors, greeting cards, stationery, gift wrapping, holiday and special occasion decorations, toys, calendars, and gifts. 800-848-2848. www.currentchecks.com

**Identity Check Printers,** Box 818, Park Ridge, IL 60068: Free information ◆ Personalized checks that reflect an individual's interest. Choose from trains, planes, automobiles, birds, and other designs. 800-874-5910.

**Kansas Bank Note Company,** P.O. Box 360, Fredonia, KS 66736: Free brochure ◆ Specialty personalized and business checks, memo pads, and gift certificates. 316-378-3026.

**Message Products,** P.O. Box 64800, St. Paul, MN 55164: Free information ◆ Sierra Club checks. 800-243-2565.

**NEBS Inc.,** 500 Main St., Groton, MA 01471: Free catalog ◆ Computerized and manual business forms, stationery, labels, checks, business cards, and supplies. 800-367-6327. www.nebs.com

**Salt & Light Scripture Checks,** P.O. Box 7276, Wilmington, NC 28406: Free information ◆ Custom-made religious theme checks. 910-343-0551.

**The Styles Company,** P.O. Box 5000, Lake Forest, CA 92630: Free information ◆ Custom checks and easy-to-use peel and stick address labels.

**Viking Office Products,** 13809 S. Figueroa St., P.O. Box 61144, Los Angeles, CA 90061: Free catalog ◆ Personalized checks and office supplies. 800-421-1222. www.VikingOP.com

## CHEERLEADING

**A+ Uniforms Inc.,** Box 1149, Walker, LA 70785: Free information ◆ Cheerleader uniforms. 800-775-2075.

**American Cheerleader Specialists Inc.,** 32 Farm St., Medfield, MA 02052: Free catalog ◆ Skirts, sweaters, chenille letters, and fabric. 888-827-9300.

**Betlin Manufacturing,** 1445 Marion Rd., Columbus, OH 43207: Free information ◆ Jackets, skirts, and uniforms. 614-443-0248.

**Butwin Sportwear Company,** 3401 Spring St. NE, Minneapolis, MN 55413: Free information ◆ Jackets. 800-328-1445.

**CAMBER Universal Sportswear,** 2 Dekalb, Norristown, PA 19401: Free information ◆ Jackets, skirts, and uniforms. 800-345-7518.

**Cheertime U.S.A.,** P.O. Box 2844, Edmond, OK 73083: Free brochure ◆ How-to books, cassettes, and videos on cheerleading. 405-359-1231.

**Colorifics,** 8325 Green Meadows Dr. North, Westerville, OH 43081: Free information ◆ Women's costumes for color guards, drill teams, dance lines, majorettes, and cheerleaders. 800-322-1961.

**The Competitor,** 2200 Sunset Blvd., Jesup, GA 31545: Catalog $5 ◆ Women's costumes for dance and kicklines, drill teams, pom pom squads, flag teams, baton twirlers, and others. 912-530-6726.

**Danskin,** 111 W. 40th St., 18th Floor, New York, NY 10018: Free information ◆ Uniforms. 212-764-4630.

**Dodger Industries,** 1702 21st St., Eldora, IA 50627: Free information ◆ Sweaters. 800-247-7879; 515-858-5464 (in IA).

**Elaine's Cheerleading Supply,** Attention: Lynda Haller, 111 Jordan Rd., Rockaway, NJ 07886: Free information ◆ Cheerleader apparel. 201-625-4830.

**Fancy Pants,** 2500 Hoover Ave., Ste. J, National City, CA 91950: Free information ◆ Skirts and uniforms. 800-755-9565. fancy@adnc.com

**Wm. Getz Corp.,** 1024 S. Linwood Ave., Santa Ana, CA 92705: Free information ◆ Pom poms and megaphones. 800-854-7447; 714-835-0100 (in CA).

**Hatchers Manufacturing Inc.,** 130 Condor St., Box 424, East Boston, MA 02128: Free information ◆ Megaphones, pom poms, and sweaters. 800-225-6842; 617-568-1262 (in MA).

**Let's Cheer Inc.,** 529 S. Washington Hwy., Ashland, VA 23005: Free information ◆ Sweats, jewelry, gifts, T-shirts, shorts, and more for cheerleaders in youth and adult sizes. 800-223-2266; 804-798-7293 (in VA).

**Markwort Sporting Goods,** 4300 Forest Park Ave., St. Louis, MO 63108: Catalog $8 (request list of retail sources) ◆ Pom poms. 800-669-6626; 314-652-3757 (in MO).

**Dick Martin Sports Inc.,** 181 E. Union Ave., P.O. Box 7381, East Rutherford, NJ 07073: Free information ◆ Megaphones. 800-221-1993; 201-438-5255 (in NJ).

**Pepco Poms,** 9611 Hwy. 60 South, Lane City, TX 77453: Free information ◆ Megaphones and pom poms. 800-527-1150.

**Recreonics Corp.,** 4200 Schmitt Ave., Louisville KY 40213: Free information ◆ Megaphones. 800-428-3254. www.recreonics.com

**Satin Stitches,** 11894 Reisling Blvd. NW, Minneapolis, MN 55433: Free information ◆ Custom clothing for performance teams. 800-48-SATIN.

**Shaffer Sportswear,** 224 N. Washington, Neosho, MO 64850: Free information ◆ Jackets and uniforms. 417-451-9444.

**Spiritwear,** P.O. Box 114, State Road 9 South, Alexandria, IN 46001: Free catalog ◆ Uniforms and other team-wear clothing for men and women. 800-531-4656.

**Sportime,** Customer Service, 1 Sporting Way, Atlanta, GA 30340: Free information ◆ Megaphones. 800-444-5700; 770-449-5700 (in GA).

**Team Cheer,** By Swain Ski & Sport, 131 Main St., Geneseo, NY 14454: Free catalog ◆ Warm-ups, cheerleader outfits, camp wear, other clothing, and accessories. 800-350-1562.

## CHEESE MAKING

**Caprine Supply Company,** P.O. Box Y, De Soto, KS 66018: Catalog $3 ◆ Mesophilic culture for making cheese. Also supplies for goats (raising or producing milk and meat). 913-585-1191.

**Cheesemaking Supply Outlet,** 9155 Madison Rd., Montville, OH 44064: Catalog $1 ◆ Cheese-making supplies. 410-968-3770.

**K & G Cork'n Keg,** P.O. Box 85745, Tucson, AZ 85754: Free catalog ◆ Beer, wine, and cheese-making kits. 800-743-9970. KGCORKNKEG@AOL.com

**Lehman Hardware & Appliances Inc.,** P.O. Box 41, Kidron, OH 44636: Catalog $2 ◆ Vegetable rennet and mesophilic culture for making cheese. 330-857-5757. GetLehmans@aol.com

**New England Cheesemaking Supply Company,** P.O. Box 85, Ashfield, MA 01330: Catalog $1 ◆ Supplies and how-to books for making and using cheese, butter, yogurt, and buttermilk. 413-628-3808. www.cheesemaking.com

## CHESS

**Always Something Different,** 5502 Pebble Springs Dr., Houston, TX 77066: Free information ◆ Custom made over-size collector chess sets and boards. 713-440-5943.

**Bookup Inc.,** 2763 Kensington Pl. West, Columbus, OH 43202: Free information ◆ Lessons by Bobby Fischer on how to play chess on a Windows CD-ROM. 800-949-5445; 614-263-1434 (in OH).

**The Chessworks Studio,** David Weinstock, 6253 36th Ave. NE, Seattle, WA 98115: Free catalog ◆ Chess accessories, software, contemporary chess books, and rare and hard-to-find chess books. 206-526-8116. www.chessmate.com

**Expert Software,** 800 Douglas Rd., Executive Tower, 7th Floor, Coral Cables, FL 33134: Free information ◆ Windows how-to play chess software. 800-759-2562; 305-567-9990 (in FL). www.expertsoftware.com

**International Chess Enterprises Inc.,** P.O. Box 19457, Seattle, WA 98109: Free information ◆ Chess games on CD-ROMs, magazines, and books. 800-26-CHESS. www.insidechess.com

**Nomi Klein Design Inc.,** 9682 Claiborne Square, La Jolla, CA 92037: Free brochure ◆ Custom-made and life-size handpainted chess sets. 619-457-2825.

**Legend Products,** 15 NW Bella Vista, Gresham, OR 97030: Catalog $8 ◆ Chess sets and handcrafted solid wood folding or one-piece chessboards with storage bag. 800-650-8813.

**U.S. Chess Federation,** 3054 NYS Rt. 9W, New Windsor, NY 12553: Free catalog ◆ Conventional and computer chess sets, books, timers, and competition supplies. 800-388-KING. www.uschess.org

## CHINA PAINTING & METAL ENAMELING

**Allcraft Tool & Supply Company,** 666 Pacific St., Brooklyn, NY 11207: Catalog $5 ◆ Metal enameling tools and supplies. 800-645-7124; 718-789-2800 (in NY).

**American Art Clay Company Inc.,** 4717 W. 16th St., Indianapolis, IN 46222: Free catalog ◆ Clays, kilns, pottery-making equipment, glazes, tools, coloring materials, and metal enameling supplies. 800-374-1600; 317-244-6871 (in IN). www.amaco.com

**Cerami Corner,** P.O. Box 1206, Grants Pass, OR 97528: Catalog $8 ◆ Ceramics molds, decals, china paints, and brushes. 800-423-8543.

**Charlie's Rock Shop,** P.O. Box 399, Penrose, CO 81240: Catalog $3 (refundable) ◆ Metal enameling tools and supplies. 719-372-0117.

**Chaselle Inc.,** 101 Almgren Dr., Agawam, MA 01001: Catalog $4 ◆ Art software and books, brushes and paints, tempera colors, acrylics and sets, pastels, ceramics molds and kilns, sculpture equipment, and screen-printing supplies. 800-628-8608. www.schoolspecialty.com

**Cridge Inc.,** Box 210, Morrisville, PA 19067: Catalog $2 ◆ Gold and silver settings, bisque and glazed porcelain insets, and china painting supplies. 215-295-3667.

**Evenheat Kiln Inc.,** 6949 Legion Rd., Caseville, MI 48725: Free information ◆ Kilns. 517-856-2281.

**Fire Mountain Gems,** 28195 Redwood Hwy., Cave Junction, OR 97523: Catalog $3 ◆ Metal enameling tools and supplies. 800-423-2319. www.firemtn.com

**T.B. Hagstoz & Son Inc.,** 709 Sansom St., Philadelphia, PA 19106: Catalog $5 (refundable with $25 order) ◆ Metal enameling tools and supplies. 800-922-1006; 215-922-1627 (in PA).

**Maryland China Company,** 54 Main St., Reisterstown, MD 21136: Free catalog ◆ China painting supplies. 800-638-3880. mdchina@worldnet.att.net

**Mr. & Mrs. of Dallas,** 1301 Ave. K, Plano, TX 75074: Free catalog ◆ Ceramics and china painting supplies. 972-881-1699.

**Nasco,** 901 Janesville Ave., Fort Atkinson, WI 53538: Free catalog ◆ Metal enameling supplies. 800-558-9595. www.nascofa.com

**National Artcraft Company,** 7996 Darrow Rd., Twinsburg, OH 44087 Catalog $4 ◆ Tiles, china, paints and coloring preparations, and brushes. 800-793-0152. nationalartcraft@worldnet.att.net

**Paragon Industries,** 2011 S. Town East Blvd., Mesquite, TX 75149: Free catalog ◆ Kilns. 800-876-4328; 972-288-7557 (in TX). www.paragonweb.com

**Rynne China Company,** 222 W. 8 Mile Rd., Hazel Park, MI 48030: Free information ◆ Decals, books, china and glass paints, overglaze, kilns, brushes, and supplies. 800-468-1987.

**Southern Oregon Pottery & Supply,** 111 Talent Ave., Box 158, Talent, OR 97540: Catalog $4 ◆ Manual, automatic, and electronic 110- and 240-volt kilns and supplies. 503-535-6700.

## CHINA, POTTERY, & STONEWARE

**Alice's Past & Presents Replacements,** P.O. Box 465, Merrick, NY 11566: Free information ◆ Replacement crystal, china, and flatware. 516-737-5223. ALICECHINA@AOL.com

**Ann Arbor Dinner Exchange,** P.O. Box 6054, Ann Arbor, MI 48106: Free information ◆ China and crystal. 888-244-6239.

**William Ashley,** 50 Boor St. West, Toronto, Ontario, Canada M4W 3L8: Free information ◆ China, crystal, and silver. 800-268-1122.

**Atlantic Silver & China,** 7471 NW 57th St., Tamarac, FL 33319: Free price list ◆ Sterling flatware, hollowware, and china. 800-288-6665. www.atlanticsilver.com

**Baccarat,** 625 Madison Ave., New York, NY 10022: Brochure $3 ◆ Crystal and china Baccarat. 800-777-0100.

**Barrons,** P.O. Box 994, Novi, MI 48376: Free information ◆ China, crystal, and silver. 800-538-6340.

**Barton-Sharpe Ltd.,** 119 Spring St., New York, NY 10012: Free information ◆ Reproduction 18th and 19th-century furniture, lighting, bedding, stoneware, and decorative items. 212-925-9562.

**David Baruch,** 36-42 W. 47th St., New York, NY 10036: Free information ◆ China, crystal, and sterling. 800-338-6961.

**Bennington Potters,** P.O. Box 199, Bennington, VT 05257: Free catalog ◆ Pottery. 802-447-7531.

**Cee Cee China,** 3904 Parsons, Chevy Chase, MD 20815: Free information ◆ Discontinued china. 800-619-6226.

**The China Cabinet (South Carolina),** P.O. Box 426, Clearwater, SC 29822: Free information with long SASE ◆ China and crystal. 803-593-9655.

**The China Connection,** Box 972, Pineville, NC 28134: Free information ◆ Inactive fine and everyday china. 800-421-9719; 704-889-8198 (in NC).

**China, Crystal & Flatware Replacements,** P.O. Box 508, High Ridge, MO 63049: Free information ◆ China, crystal, and flatware. 800-562-2655.

**China Finders,** 1-B South Holly, Highland Springs, VA 23075: Free information ◆ China and crystal replacements. 888-244-6239; 804-328-2897 (in VA).

**The China Hutch,** 1333 Ivey Dr., Charlotte, NC 28205: Free information ◆ Discontinued china. 800-524-4397.

**China Replacements,** P.O. Box 508, High Ridge, MO 63049: Free information with long SASE ◆ Discontinued china and crystal. 800-562-2655. www.IAdm.com/chinarep

**Circa 1820,** RR 1, Box 4040, Vassalboro, ME 04989: Catalog $5 (refundable) ◆ Reproduction Shaker and country furniture, redware, pewter, and tin lighting. 207-877-9863.

**Clay Craftsman,** Willis & Denise Myers, 686 Barts Church Rd., Hanover, PA 17331: Brochure $1 ◆ Handmade pottery. 717-359-9458.

**Clay in Motion Inc.,** Regional Airport Bldg. 202, Walla Walla, WA 99362: Free brochure ◆ Handmade dinnerware. 509-529-6146.

**Clintsman International,** 20855 Watertown Rd., Waukesha, WI 53186: Free information ◆ Discontinued china, crystal, and flatware. 800-781-8900.

**Collectibles Outlet Inc.,** 6925 Oakland Mills Rd., Columbia, MD 21045: Free price guide with long SASE ◆ China and accessories. 800-555-6022.

**The Collector's Teapot,** P.O. Box 1193, Kingston, NY 12401: Catalog $2 ◆ English eccentric teapots, handmade cozies, tea accessories, miniature tea sets, and gourmet teas. 800-724-3306.

**Crystal Lalique,** 680 Madison Ave., New York, NY 10021: Free information ◆ Crystal and china Lalique. 800-214-2738; 212-355-6550 (in NY).

**Dansk International Design,** 108 Corporate Park Dr., White Plains, NY 10604: Free list of retail sources ◆ Dinnerware, stemware, flatware, kitchenware, and serving pieces. 914-697-6400. www.danskfurnishings.com

**Designs in the Home,** 417-B W. Foothill Blvd., #525, Glendora, CA 91741: Brochure $2 ◆ Hand-decorated oven-proof stoneware. 818-334-3438.

**Dishes from the Past,** 3701 Lovell, Fort Worth, TX 76107: Free information ◆ Discontinued patterns. 800-984-8801.

**Eldreth Pottery,** 902 Hart Rd., Oxford, PA 19363: Catalog $2 ◆ Salt-glazed stoneware and Pennsylvania redware. 717-529-6241.

**Felissimo Gifts,** 10 W. 56th South, New York, NY 10019: Free catalog ◆ Porcelain dinnerware, handcrafted silver serving pieces, and accessories. 800-565-6785. www.felissimo.com

**Michael C. Fina,** 580 5th Ave., New York, NY 10036: Free catalog ◆ Sterling serving pieces, tea sets, crystal stemware, bone china, and pewter. 800-BUY-FINA; 718-937-8484 (in NY).

**Fitz & Floyd Consumer Relations,** P.O. Box 516125, Dallas, TX 75251: Free list of retail sources ◆ China.

**The Five Seasons Corp.,** 1901 Rt. 332, Canandaigua, NY 14425: Free information ◆ Handpainted personalized stoneware crocks. 800-724-4064; 716-396-2021 (in NY).

**Flat Earth Clay Works Inc.,** 5760 N. Broadway, Wichita, KS 67219: Brochure $2 ◆ Lead-free microwave and oven-safe earthenware pottery. 800-654-8695.

**Fortunoff Fine Jewelry,** P.O. Box 1550, Westbury, NY 11590: Free catalog ◆ China, silver plate and stainless steel serving pieces, and sterling flatware. 800-937-4376. service@fortunoff.com

**Golden Gift Company,** 304 New St., Philadelphia, PA 19106: Free information ◆ Handcrafted European vases, bowls, stemware, baskets, and figurines. 800-GOLD-171.

**Gorham,** 100 Lenox Dr., Lawrenceville, NJ 08648: Free list of retail sources ◆ Fine china dinnerware, crystal, and silver. 800-635-3669.

**Granite Lake Pottery Inc.,** Rt. 9, P.O. Box 236, Munsonville, NH 03457: Free catalog ◆ Handcrafted oven, microwave, and dishwasher-safe stoneware. 800-443-9908.

**Grace Graves Haviland Matching Service,** 219 N. Milwaukee St., Milwaukee, WI 53202: Free information ◆ Haviland matching services. Includes single pieces, complete sets, and collector items. 414-291-9111.

**Hartstone Inc.,** P.O. Box 2626, Zanesville, OH 43702: Free information ◆ Hand-decorated dinnerware and accessories. 614-452-9992.

**Holy Mountain Trading Company,** P.O. Box 457, Fairfax, CA 94978: Free catalog ◆ Asian ceramic bowls and cups. 888-832-8008. www.holymtn.com

**Jacquelynn's China Matching Service,** 219 N. Milwaukee St., Milwaukee, WI 53202: Free information with long SASE ◆ Discontinued American and English china. 800-4UA-TCUP. www.jacquelynnschina.com

**Jepson Studios Inc.,** RR 1, Box 69, Harveyville, KS 66431: Brochure $2 (refundable) ◆ Country ceramics. 913-589-2481.

**Kitchen Etc.,** 32 Industrial Dr., Exeter, NH 03833: Catalog $2 ◆ Cookware, cutlery, flatware, crystal, and dinnerware. 800-232-4070. www.kitchenetc.com

**Lanac Sales,** 500 Driggs Ave., Brooklyn, NY 11211: Free catalog ◆ China, crystal, sterling, and gifts. 800-522-0047; 718-782-7200 (in NY).

**Le Fanion,** 299 W. 4th St., New York, NY 10014: Free catalog ◆ French country antique and contemporary pottery. 212-463-8760.

**Lenox Collections,** P.O. Box 519, Langhorne, PA 19047: Free catalog ◆ China, crystal, and porcelain sculptures. 800-225-1779. www.lenoxcollections.com

**Lesley's Lenox,** 24438 SE 46th Pl., Issaquah, WA 98029: Free information ◆ Lenox china and crystal replacements. 800-553-6693.

**Locators Inc.,** 2217 Cottondale Ln., Little Rock, AR 72202: Free information ◆ Discontinued china, crystal, and silver. 800-367-9690.

**Marks China, Crystal & Silverware,** 315 Franklin Ave., Wyckoff, NJ 07481: Free information ◆ China, stainless, crystal, and silverware. 800-862-7578.

**Martin's Herend Imports Inc.,** P.O. Box 1178, Sterling, VA 20167: Free list of retail sources ◆ Handpainted porcelain decorative pieces and dinner service. 800-643-7363; 703-450-1601 (in VA).

**Mikasa,** P.O. Box 1549, Secaucus, NJ 07096: Free catalog ◆ Designer china, stoneware, crystal, and flatware. 800-833-4681; 201-867-9210 (in NJ).

**Mountain Meadows Pottery,** P.O. Box 163, South Ryegate, VT 05069: Free catalog ◆ Functional stoneware and humorous and sentimental plaques. 800-639-6790.

**MS China,** 2020 Sunset Dr., Pacific Grove, CA 93950: Free information ◆ Newly discontinued and pre-war Noritake patterns. 800-688-6807.

**Teresita Naranjo,** Santa Clara Pueblo, Rt. 1, Box 455, Espanola, NM 87532: Free information with long SASE ◆ Ceremonial and melon bowls, wedding vases, and traditional Santa Clara black and red pottery. 505-753-9655.

**Noël Pie Plate Company,** 771 Hwy 7, Tonasket, WA 98855: Free information ◆ Personalized platters, bowls, canister sets, and pottery accessories for the kitchen. 509-486-4372.

**Noritake China Replacements,** 2635 Clearbrook Dr., Arlington Heights, IL 60005: Free information ◆ Noritake china replacements. 888-NORITAKE. www.noritake.com

**The Old Sturbridge Village Museum Gift Shop,** 1 Old Sturbridge Village Rd., Sturbridge, MA 01566: Catalog $1 (refundable) ◆ Reproduction redware and other crafts. 508-347-3362.

**Olympus Cove Antiques,** 179 E. 300 South, Salt Lake City, UT 84111: Free information ◆ Discontinued china. 800-564-8253. www.olympuscove.com

**Pfaltzgraff Factory Outlet,** 2900 Whiteford Rd., York, PA 17402: Catalog $1 (refundable) ◆ Dinnerware, baking and serving pieces, decorative accessories, and stoneware irregulars. 800-999-2811; 717-757-2200 (in PA).

**The Potter's House,** Rt. 133, RR 3, Box 4040, Winthrop, ME 04364: Free brochure ◆ Microwave, oven, and dishwasher-safe pottery. 800-572-8782; 207-377-4290 (in ME).

**Replacement Service,** P.O. Box 508, High Ridge, MO 63049: Free information ◆ China, crystal, and flatware. 800-562-0873.

**Replacements Ltd.,** P.O. Box 26029, Greensboro, NC 27420: Free information with long SASE ◆ Discontinued china, earthenware, and crystal. 800-737-5223. www.replacements.com

**Rogers & Rosenthal,** 22 W. 48th St., Room 1102, New York, NY 10036: Free information with long SASE ◆ China, crystal, and stainless steel. 212-827-0115.

**Ross-Simons Jewelers,** 9 Ross-Simons Dr., Cranston, RI 02920: Free information ◆ Sterling and china. 800-521-7677; 401-463-3100 (in RI). www.ross-simons.com

**Rowe Pottery Works,** 217 W. Main St., Cambridge, WI 53523: Free catalog ◆ Salt-glazed stoneware in early authentic folk designs. 800-356-5003.

**Royal Worcester,** The Royal China & Porcelain Companies Inc., 1265 Glen Ave., Moorestown, NJ 08057: Free list of retail sources ◆ Place settings, cookware, glasses and goblets, and accessories. 609-866-2900.

**Rudi's Pottery, Silver & China,** 180 N. State Rt. 17, Paramus, NJ 07652: Free information with long SASE ◆ Glass stemware, china, and gifts. 201-265-6096.

**Nat Schwartz & Company,** 549 Broadway, Bayonne, NJ 07002: Free catalog ◆ Crystal, sterling, and china. 800-526-1440; 201-437-4443 (in NJ).

**Greg & Mary Shooner Pottery,** 1772 Jeffery Rd., Oregonia, OH 45054: Free brochure ◆ Redware reproductions. 800-452-7058.

**Silver Lane,** P.O. Box 322, San Leandro, CA 94577: Free information ◆ Discontinued crystal and china. Also current and obsolete silver. 510-483-0632.

**Smiling Cat Tea Merchants,** 407 N. 5th Ave., Ann Arbor, MI 48104: Free brochure ◆ Gourmet and imported loose teas and tea bags, tisanes, pristine tea pots, and tea-making accessories. 800-440-TEAS. www.smilingcatteas.com

**Spode,** The Royal China & Porcelain Companies Inc., 1265 Glen Ave., Moorestown, NJ 08057: Free list of retail sources ◆ China and accessories Spode. 800-257-7189.

**Stebner Pottery,** 500 W. Exchange St., Akron, OH 44302: Catalog $2 ◆ Salt-glazed stoneware. 330-374-1965.

**Stegall's Stoneware,** 379 Chandler Cove, Erwin, TN 37650: Free information ◆ Stoneware mugs for grandparents and pottery for baking, serving, and organizing in the kitchen. 800-788-POTS; 423-743-3227 (in TN). www.StegallPOTS.com

**Thurber's,** 2256 Dabney Rd., Richmond, VA 23230: Free information ◆ China and sterling. 800-848-7237.

**Van Ness China Company,** 1124 Fairway Dr., Waynesboro, VA 22980: Free information ◆ Discontinued and current English bone china. 540-942-2827.

**Waterford Crystal Inc.,** 713 Madison Ave., New York, NY 10010: Brochure $2 ◆ Fine china serving pieces, dinnerware, crystal, and gifts. 800-677-7860.

**Wedgwood,** 713 Madison Ave., New York, NY 10010: Brochure $2 ◆ Fine china serving pieces, dinnerware, and gifts. 800-677-7860.

**White's Collectables & Fine China,** P.O. Box 680, Newberg, OR 97132: Free information ◆ Collectible plates and new and discontinued china patterns. 800-618-2782.

**Wisconsin Pottery,** W3199 County Rd. 16, Columbus, WI 53925: Free catalog ◆ Handcrafted and hand-decorated salt-glazed stoneware and redware pottery. 800-669-5196.

**Workshops of David T. Smith,** 3600 Shawhan Rd., Morrow, OH 45152: Catalog $5 ◆ Reproduction furniture, pottery, lamps, and chandeliers. 513-932-2472. www.davidtsmith.com

## CHOIR GOWNS

**Cokesbury,** Division United Methodist Publishing House, 201 8th Ave. South, P.O. Box 801, Nashville, TN 37202: Free information ◆ Bibles and bible reference books, bible study and Christian education books, fund-raising programs, gifts and casual clothing, choir apparel, church and clergy supplies, and church furniture. 800-672-1789. webservant@umph.org

**Lyric Choir Gown Company,** P.O. Box 16954, Jacksonville, FL 32245: Free catalog ◆ Professionally tailored choir gowns. 904-725-7977.

**Murphy Cap & Gown Company,** 4299 31st St. North, St. Petersburg, FL 33714: Free catalog ◆ Choral attire for men and women. 800-237-8951; 813-527-0696 (in FL).

**Regency Cap & Gown Company,** P.O. Box 8988, Jacksonville, FL 32239: Free catalog ◆ Choir robes. 800-826-8612.

## CHRISTMAS DECORATIONS & OTHER ORNAMENTS

**Jean E. Bales,** P.O. Box 193, Cookson, OK 74427: Free information with long SASE ◆ Prints, cards, art, Christmas ornaments, miniatures, sculptures, and carvings. 918-457-4003.

**D. Blümchen & Company Inc.,** P.O. Box 1210, Ridgewood, NJ 07450: Free catalog ◆ Christmas ornaments and decorative items. 201-652-5595.

**Bronner's Christmas Wonderland,** 25 Christmas Ln., P.O. Box 176, Frankenmuth, MI 48734: Free catalog ◆ Ornaments, decorations, and other all-time Christmas favorites. 800-361-6736. www.bronners.com

**Brownell Holly Farms,** P.O. Box 22025, Milwaukee, OR 97269: Free brochure ◆ Christmas holly decorations. 503-631-7475.

**Christmas Bazaar,** P.O. Box 96, Exeter, NH 03833: Catalog $3 ◆ Ornaments and decorations for Christmas, Halloween, Easter, and other occasions. 603-772-1457.

**The Cookie Tree,** 271 Western Ave., Lynn, MA 01904: Free catalog ◆ Handcrafted non-edible dough ornaments. 781-593-3746.

**The Cracker Box,** P.O. Box 413, Solebury, PA 18963: Catalog $4.50 ◆ Christmas ornament kits. 215-862-2100.

**European Imports & Gifts,** Oak Mill Mall, 7900 N. Milwaukee Ave., Niles, IL 60648: Free information ◆ Art collectibles, porcelain, Christmas ornaments, pewter, and gifts. 847-967-5253.

**The Faith Mountain Company,** P.O. Box 199, Sperryville, VA 22740: Free catalog ◆ Kitchen utensils, folk art reproductions, toys and dolls, handmade Appalachian baskets, and Christmas decorations. 800-588-2548. 800-822-7238. www.FaithMountain.com

**Fingerhut,** 11 McLeland Rd., St. Cloud, MN 56395: Free catalog ◆ Greeting cards, gift wrappings, stationery, holiday decorations, organizers, and gifts. 800-233-3588. www.fingerhut.com

**Friends,** 109 Shawnee, Eldridge, IA 52748: Brochure $2 ◆ Country-style Christmas decorative accessories. 319-285-7354.

**Hand & Hammer Silversmiths,** 2610 Morse Ln., Woodbridge, VA 22192: Free information ◆ Handcrafted sterling silver and vermeil jewelry. Also Christmas ornaments. 800-SILVERY.

**Holiday Collectibles of Yesteryear,** P.O. Box 25752, Rochester, NY 14625: Catalog $3 ◆ Christmas decorations and ornaments. 716-787-0299.

**Holiday Treasures Catalog,** P.O. Box 53, Dewitt, NY 13214: Catalog $3 ◆ Collectible holiday decorative items and reproduction antique ornaments.

**The Incredible Christmas Place,** 2470 Parkway, P.O. Box 958, Pigeon Forge, TN 37868: Free catalog ◆ Toys and trains, dolls, Christmas ornaments, and other gifts and collectibles. 800-357-2682. www.christmasplace.com

**Laura Louise Leverich "Skybear",** 9811 NE 90th Ave., Vancouver, WA 98662: Free information with long SASE ◆ Beadwork, children's items, Christmas ornaments, clothing, moccasins, headdresses, and jewelry. 360-254-3227.

**Mad Hatter's Tea Party,** 154 Washington St., Marblehead, MA 01945: Catalog $3 ◆ Handmade, individually blown, molded, and decorated German old world Christmas ornaments. 781-639-9536.

**Nagle Forge & Foundry,** 2 Farvue Rd., Novato, CA 94947: Catalog $2 ◆ Cast pewter Victorian-style Christmas ornaments. 415-897-1732.

**New Candid Calendars,** 10498 Loveland-Madeira Rd., Loveland, OH 45140: Free brochure ◆ Personalized photo calendars, T-shirts and other clothes, ornaments, and more. 800-328-8415; 513-583-0883 (in OH).

**Meg Orr,** P.O. Box 4188, Omac, WA 98841: Free catalog ◆ Cards, prints, art, baskets, beadwork, books, music, educational materials, boxes, children's items, Christmas ornaments, clothing, moccasins, headdresses, dolls, drums, pipes, tomahawks, miniatures, sculptures, and carvings. 509-826-0904.

**Roger & Sharon Perdasofpy,** P.O. Box 682, Zuni, NM 87327: Free information with long SASE ◆ Beadwork, Christmas ornaments, drums, pipes, headdresses, and jewelry. 405-357-1882.

**R & T Distributors,** 6208 Summer Place Dr. North, Mobile, AL 36618: Catalogs $5 ◆ Christmas ornaments and collectibles, fine jewelry, and gifts for all-occasions. 888-343-GIFT; 334-4124-2796 (in AL). www.zebra.net/~Alicia

**Redbox Arts & Crafts,** Mikhail Dmitriev, 1020 View St., Ste. 506, Victoria, British Columbia, Canada V8V 4Y4: Free catalog ◆ Traditional Russian Christmas figurines and tree ornaments. 250-389-0021.

**Roman Inc.,** 555 Lawrence Ave., Roselle, IL 60172: Free catalog ◆ Christmas tree lights and pre-lighted trees. 517-835-6674.

**Select Artificials Inc.,** 701 N. 15th St., St. Louis, MO 63103: Catalog $10 (refundable) ◆ Silk flowers, large plants, and Christmas decorative items. 800-666-6999; 314-621-3050 (in MO).

**Sterling Collectables,** P.O. Box 2098, Mansfield, OH 44905: Free brochure with long SASE ◆ Current and obsolete sterling silver patterns, stainless, serving pieces, and collectible Christmas ornaments. 800-636-4756.

**Truly Victorian Mercantile,** P.O. Box 88231, Black Forest, CO 88231: Catalog $3 ◆ Hard-to-find Victorian-style Christmas decorations. 719-495-2651.

**Williams Nursery & The Gift House,** 524 Springfield Ave., Westfield, NJ 07090: Catalog $15 ◆ Over 700 original Christopher Radko high-style Christmas ornaments and other decorative accessories. 888-887-2356. www.radkoshop.com

**Wooden Soldier,** P.O. Box 800, North Conway, NH 03860: Free catalog ◆ Christmas decorations and ornaments and designer clothing for children. 800-375-6002.

## CHURCH, SYNAGOGUE, & CLERGY SUPPLIES

**Ascalon Studios,** 115 Atlantic Ave., Berlin, NJ 08009: Free brochure ◆ Synagogue art. 609-768-3779.

**W. & E. Baum Bronze Tablet Corp.,** 200 60th St., Brooklyn, NY 11220: Free catalog ◆ Donor walls, trees of life, yahrzeit tablets, plaques and awards, and Judaic tablets. 800-922-7377; 718-439-3311 (in NY).

**Cokesbury,** Division United Methodist Publishing House, 201 8th Ave. South, P.O. Box 801, Nashville, TN 37202: Free information ◆ Bibles and bible reference books, bible study and Christian education books, fund-raising programs, gifts and casual clothing, choir apparel, church and clergy supplies, and church furniture. 800-672-1789. webservant@umph.org

**The Cooper Shop at The Jewish Museum,** 1109 5th Ave., New York, NY 10128: Free information ◆ Judaic gifts. 212-423-3211.

**The Jewish Bride..& More,** P.O. Box 26341, Tamarac, FL 33320: Free catalog ◆ Jewish products and gifts for weddings, bar/bat mitzvah, anniversaries, birthdays, and other occasions. Also printed yarmulkas and assorted tallisim, benchers, and ketuboth. 954-721-5660.

**J. Lowy Company,** 940 E. 19th St., Brooklyn, NY 11230: Free information ◆ Suede and leather yamulkas with optional imprinting. 800-547-7688; 718-338-7324 (in NY). www.kipot.com

**Midwest Church Furnishings,** P.O. Box 380, Carroll, OH 43112: Free information ◆ Church pew padding, cushions, replacement pads for kneelers, and upholstered solid oak and metal chairs. 800-827-1482.

**Emanuel Milstein,** Synagogue Art, 29 Wyncrest Rd., Marlboro, NJ 07746: Free information ◆ Synagogue memorials, sculptures, trees of life, and interior design art. 732-946-8604.

**Presentations Gallery,** 200 Lexington Ave., New York, NY 10016: Free information ◆ Contemporary synagogue art, furniture, memorial renditions, and recognition gifts. 212-481-8181.

**Sanctuary Design Corp.,** 14 Broadway, Malverne, NY 11565: Free information ◆ Eternal lights, holocaust memorials, memorial systems, Torah ornaments, bimahs, and sanctuary design components. 516-599-3173.

**The Source for Everything Jewish,** P.O. Box 48836, Niles, IL 60714: Free catalog ◆ Ritual and ceremonial objects, books, fine art, Kosher gourmet food, and audio and video cassettes. 800-426-2567.

**David Strauss Designs Inc.,** 16 Braeland Ave., Newton Centre, MA 02159: Free information ◆ Synagogue art and furnishings. 617-527-0010.

**U.S. Bronze Sign Company,** 811 2nd Ave., New Hyde Park, NY 11040: Free catalog ◆ Donor recognition signs. 800-872-5155; 516-352-5155 (in NY).

## CIGAR STORE INDIANS

**Carousel Creations,** Hwy. 63, P.O. Box 56, Barronett, WI 54813: Free information ◆ Cigar store Indians, carousel animals, and other wood carvings. 715-822-4189.

**Sedler's Antiques Marketing,** P.O. Box 788, West Newbury, MA 01985: Free information with long SASE ◆ Antique and reproduction cigar store Indians. 978-363-8889. www.cigarindian.com

**Wood Carvings by Hannah,** HCR 62, Box 93, Bomoseen, VT 05732: Free information with long SASE ◆ Handcarved cigar store Indians. 802-273-2783. dhannah@sover.net

**Wood Classic Carvings Ltd.,** P.O. Box 5, Newark, DE 19715: Free information with long SASE ◆ Wood cigar store Indians and other wood carvings. 302-738-9244.

## CLOCKS & CLOCK MAKING

**Alpha Supply,** P.O. Box 2133, Bremerton, WA 98310: Catalog $7 ◆ Clocks, clock movements, parts, and engraving tools. 800-257-4211; 360-373-3302 (in WA).

**Armor Crafts,** P.O. Box 445, East Northport, NY 11731: Free catalog ◆ Replacement movements for mantel, banjo, and grandfather clocks. 800-292-8296.

**B & J Rock Shop,** 14744 Manchester Rd., Ballwin, MO 63011: Catalog $3 ◆ Quartz clock movements and kits. 314-394-4567.

**Bradco Enterprises,** 4242 31st St. North, St. Petersburg, FL 33714: Free catalog ◆ Components, tools, and accessories for custom clock-designing. 888-236-8263. www.bradcoent.com

**Charlie's Rock Shop,** P.O. Box 399, Penrose, CO 81240: Catalog $3 (refundable) ◆ Clocks, movements and parts, beads, display boxes, jewelry-making supplies, and faceted gemstones. 719-372-0117.

**Clock Repair Center,** 33 Boyd Dr., Westbury, NY 11590: Catalog $5.95 ◆ Clock movements, repair parts, supplies, and tools. 516-997-4810.

**Clocks Etc.,** 3401 Mt. Diablo Blvd., Lafayette, CA 94549: Brochure $1 ◆ Old and new clocks, antique furniture, and gifts. 510-284-4720.

**Colonial Times,** 564 Weber St. N., Unit 2, Waterloo, Ontario, Canada N2L 5C6: Free catalog ◆ Clock kits, cuckoo clocks, German clock movements, dials and pendulums, and plans. 519-884-2511.

**Gordon S. Converse & Company,** Spread Eagle Village, 503 W. Lancaster Ave., Stratford, PA 19087: Catalog subscription $25 ◆ Antique clocks. 800-789-1001. www.pond.com/~gfc

**Ebersole Lapidary Supply,** 11417 West Hwy. 54, Wichita, KS 67209: Catalog $5 ◆ Clocks, clock-making parts, tools, findings and mountings, cabochons and rocks, and jewelry kits. 316-722-4771.

**Ed's House of Gems,** 7712 NE Sandy Blvd., Portland, OR 97211: Free information with long SASE ◆ Clocks, clock-making parts, crystals, minerals, gemstones, and lapidary equipment. 503-284-8990.

**Eloxite Corp.,** P.O. Box 729, Wheatland, WY 82201: Catalog $1 ◆ Clock-making parts, tools, gemstones, belt buckles, mountings, equipment for rock hounds, and craft supplies. 307-322-3050. www.eloxite.com

**Emperor Clock LLC,** Emperor Industrial Park, P.O. Box 1089, Fairhope, AL 36533: Catalog $1 ◆ Grandfather clocks, kits, and parts. 800-642-0011; 334-928-2316 (in AL). www.emperorclock.com

**R. Engels & Company,** 4031 Chicago Dr., P.O. Box 235, Grandville, MI 49418: Catalog $5 ◆ Wall, mantel, and grandfather clocks. 800-637-1118.

**Gallery of Time,** P.O. Box 1030, South Orleans, MA 02662: Free information ◆ Grandfather, wall, mantel, and table clocks. 800-325-6259.

**House of Tyrol,** P.O. Box 909, 66 E. Kytle St., Cleveland, GA 30528: Free catalog ◆ Musical cuckoo clocks. 800-241-5404.

**Innovation Clock-Making Specialties,** 11869 Teale St., Culver City, CA 90230: Free catalog ◆ Clock-making components and weather instruments. 800-421-4445; 562-398-8116 (in CA). www.clockparts.com

**Instrument Services Inc.,** 11765 Main St., Roscoe, IL 61073: Free information ◆ Build-it-yourself electric and quartz clock kits. 800-558-2674.

**It's About Time,** 7151 Ortonville Rd., Clarkston, MI 48016: Catalog $5 (refundable) ◆ Grandfather, wall, self-chiming, and other clocks. 800-423-4225.

**Klockit,** P.O. Box 636, Lake Geneva, WI 53147: Free catalog ◆ Grandfather and other clock kits, quartz and mechanical movements, parts, wood-finishing supplies, and tools. 800-556-2548. www.klockit.com

**Kuempel Chime Clock,** Box 462, 21195 Minnetonka Blvd., Excelsior, MN 55331: Free catalog ◆ Kits and plans for grandfather clocks with bells or chimes, handpainted moon wheels, and handcrafted pendulums. 800-328-6445. www.kuempelchimeclock.com

**Lamps by Gramps,** P.O. Box 116, Hygiene, CO 80533: Free information ◆ Pre-designed and custom western-style lamps, clocks, and signs.

**S. LaRose Inc.,** P.O. Box 21208, Greensboro, NC 27420: Catalog $2.50 ◆ Watch and clock replacement movements, motors, parts, and tools. 336-621-1936. SLAROSE@worldnet.att.net

**Little Big Horn Replica Company,** P.O. Box 415, Crow Agency, MT 59022: Brochure $2 ◆ Wagon wheel clocks and chandeliers. 406-638-4458.

**Live Oaks of Savannah,** P.O. Box 16194, Savannah, GA 31416: Free catalog ◆ Victorian-style furniture, lamps, clocks, and accessories. 800-467-5539.

**Merritt's Antiques Inc.,** P.O. Box 277, Douglassville, PA 19518: Catalog $3 ◆ Clock repair supplies and reproduction antique grandfather, wall, and shelf clocks. 610-689-9541.

**Howard Miller Clock Company,** 860 E. Main St., Zeeland, MI 49464: Catalog $5 ◆ Parts for building and repairing clocks. 616-772-9131. www.howardmiller.com

**Murray Clock Craft Ltd.,** 512 McNicoll Ave., Willowdale, Ontario, Canada M2H 2E1: Catalog $3 ◆ Clock case kits, clock movements, dials and plans, wood moldings, case hardware, and more. 800-268-3181.

**Neon Clock,** 246 W. 3rd Ave., New Lenox, IL 60451: Free information ◆ Antique neon clocks. 815-485-5573.

**Oregon Scientific,** 18383 SW Boones Ferry Rd., Portland, OR 97224: Free brochure ◆ Liquid crystal display clocks. 800-869-7779.

**Precision Movements,** P.O. Box 689, Emmaus, PA 18049: Free catalog ◆ Clock kits, quartz movements, and parts. 610-967-3156.

**Richardson's Recreational Ranch Ltd.,** Gateway Route Box 440, Madras, OR 97741: Free information ◆ Clocks, parts, movements, and rock specimens from worldwide sources. 800-433-2680.

**Signature Stationers,** 1800 Mass. Ave., Lexington, MA 02173: Free information ◆ English brass quartz clocks. 800-322-5031.

**Simply Country Furniture,** Box 133, Rover, AR 72860: Brochure $3 ◆ Grandfather clocks. 501-272-4794.

**Steebar,** P.O. Box 980, Andover, NJ 07821: Catalog $3 ◆ Clock kits, quartz clock and music box movements, and parts. 201-383-1026.

**Terry Clocks,** Patrick J. Terry, 2669 N. Lakeview Dr., Warsaw, IN 46580: Free brochure with long SASE ◆ Shelf clocks with a 19th-century-style. 219-858-2404.

**Time & Tide,** 56 Byram Rd., P.O. Box 156, Point Pleasant, PA 18950: Free information ◆ Imported French antique furniture and clocks. 215-297-5854.

**Time Gallery,** 3121 Battleground Ave., Greensboro, NC 28603: Free information ◆ Grandfather clocks. 336-282-5132.

**Timesavers,** 7745 E. Redfield, #500, Scottsdale, AZ 85260: Catalog $3 ◆ Parts, tools, cleaning materials, books, and batteries for restoration and repair of clocks. 602-483-3711.

**Turncraft Clocks Inc.,** P.O. Box 100, Mound, MN 55364: Catalog $2 ◆ Clock kits and parts. 800-544-1711; 612-471-9573 (in MN). www.nonni.com/woodhobby

**Van Dommelen Clocks,** 145 Witherspoon St., Princeton, NJ 08542: Catalog $1 ◆ Imported European clocks. 800-334-0334.

**Warner-Crivellaro,** 1855 Weaversville Rd., Allentown, PA 18103: Free information ◆ Stained glass, jewelry-making, kaleidoscope, and clock kits. Also other craft supplies, and how-to books. 800-523-4242; 610-264-1100 (in PA). www.warner-criv.com

**Whippoorwill Crafts,** 126 S. Market St., Boston, MA 02109: Free information ◆ Kaleidoscopes, wood boxes and chests, chimes, toys and games, clocks, and other crafts. 800-860-9551; 617-523-5149 (in MA).

## CLOSETS & STORAGE SYSTEMS

**California Closets,** 1700 Montgomery St., Ste. 249, San Francisco, CA 94111: Free list of retail sources ◆ Closet storage accessories. 415-433-9999.

**Closet Design Group,** 1000 Clint Moore Rd., Ste. 101, Boca Raton, FL 33487: Free list of retail sources ◆ Closet storage accessories. 800-440-1445.

**Closetmaid,** P.O. Box 4400, Ocala, FL 34478: Free information ◆ Wire basket caddies and other closet storage accessories. 800-227-8319.

**Consolidated Plastics Company Inc.,** 8181 Darrow Rd., Twinsburg, OH 44087: Free information ◆ Closet and storage room accessories. 800-362-1000.

**The Container Store,** 2000 Valwood Pkwy., Dallas, TX 75234: Free catalog ◆ Closet storage accessories. 800-733-3532.

**Elfa Closet Storage Accessories,** 300-3 Rt. 17 South, Lodi, NJ 07644: Free information ◆ Epoxy-covered steel shelves, bins, and accessories for storage rooms and closets. 201-777-1554.

**Hirsh Company,** 8051 Central Ave., Skokie, IL 60076: Free information ◆ Easy-to-install closet organizers and shelf units. 847-673-6610.

**Journeyman Products Ltd.,** 303 Najoles Rd., Millersville, MD 21108: Free information ◆ Stackable tray and box storage system. 800-248-8707.

**Knape & Vogt,** 2700 Oak Industrial Dr. NE, Grand Rapids, MI 49505: Free catalog ◆ Shelving, storage, and work systems. Also drawer slides. 616-459-3311.

**Laminations Inc.,** 3311 Windquest Dr., Holland, MI 49424: Free information ◆ Easy-to-install storage units, shelves, and rods. 800-562-4257.

**Lean-2 Racks,** Jack Murray Company, P.O. Box 298, Penn Valley, CA 95946: Free brochure with long SASE ◆ Sport and home utility storage racks for bicycles, skis, fishing poles, garden pots, books, multi-media, quilts, collectible plates, stereo components, closet and shoe racks, wine, and wine glasses. 530-755-4532. www.lean-2.com

**Lifestyle Systems,** P.O. Box 5031, Huntington Beach, CA 92615: Free information with long SASE ◆ Easy-to-assemble any-size drawer compartment organizers. 800-955-3383; 714-964-3383 (in CA). neatstyle@aol.com

**Material Control Inc.,** 338 Sullivan Rd. East, Aurora, IL 60504: Free catalog ◆ Industrial storage bins and accessories for home use. 800-926-0376; 630-892-4274 (in IL).

**Rubbermaid,** 1147 Akron Rd., Wooster, OH 44691: Free information ◆ Closet and storage room accessories. 330-264-6464. www.rubbermaid.com

**Rutt Custom Cabinetry,** P.O. Box 129, Goodville, PA 17528: Catalog $7 (request list of retail sources) ◆ Storage room and closet cabinets. 800-420-7888. www.rutt1.com

**Schulte Corp.,** 12115 Ellington Ct., Cincinnati, OH 45249: Free information ◆ Closet and room storage organizers. 800-669-3225.

**The SICO Room Makers,** Room Makers Division, 7525 Cahill Rd., P.O. Box 1169, Minneapolis, MN 55440: Free information ◆ Wall beds, home office furniture, and wall systems. 800-328-6138.

**White Home Products,** 2204 Morris Ave., Ste. 203, Union, NJ 07083: Free information ◆ Automatic revolving carousels for closets. 800-200-9272.

## CLOTHING & ACCESSORIES

### Bridal Fashions

**Country Elegance,** 7353 Greenbush Ave., North Hollywood, CA 91605: Catalog $4.50 ◆ Bridal fashions and accessories. 818-765-1551.

**Henri's Full Figure Boutique,** 1419 Krameria St., Denver CO 80220: Free information ◆ Clothing for full-figured women. Includes bridal fashions and accessories. 303-355-1811.

**Hollydays Inc.,** Rt. 2, Box 70-21, Lake Providence, LA 71254: Catalog $5 ◆ Flower girl dresses and wedding accessories. 800-256-9792.

**Jessica McClintock Bridal,** Mail Order Dept., 1400 16th St., San Francisco, CA 94103: Catalog $6 ◆ Bridal fashions and bridesmaid dresses. 415-495-3030.

**P.C. Mary's Inc.,** 10520 Kinghurst Dr., Houston, TX 77099: Free catalog ◆ Wedding gowns. 281-933-9678.

**JCPenney Catalog,** P.O. Box 675, Milwaukee, WI 53201: Free information ◆ Fashions and accessories for the bride and attendants. Includes petite and misses clothing. www.jcpenney.com/shopping

### Children's Clothing

**After the Stork,** 4311 Fulcrum Way, Rio Rancho, NM 87124: Free catalog ◆ Natural fiber clothing for infants and children up to age 7. 800-333-5437.

**Airshop,** 604 E. 11th St., New York, NY 10009: Free catalog ◆ Clothing for young girls. 888-247-0312. www.air-shop.com

**Alloy Children's Clothing,** P.O. Box 182217, Chattanooga, TN 37422: Free catalog ◆ Outdoor and keep-warm clothing. 888-45-ALLOY. www.alloyonline.com

**American Made Leather,** RD 3, Box 379, Cameron, WV 26033: Free catalog ◆ Leather clothing for men, women, and children. 800-584-5184. www.greenepa.net/~anna/aml

**Hanna Andersson,** 1010 NW Flanders, Portland, OR 97209: Free catalog ◆ Children's clothing. 800-222-0544. www.hannaAndersson.com

**Baby Clothes Wholesale,** 60 Ethel Rd. West, Piscataway, NJ 08854: Catalog $3 (3 issues) ◆ Clothing for babies and children. 732-572-9520.

**L.L. Bean,** Casco St., Freeport, ME 04032: Free catalog ◆ Outerwear, footwear, and other clothing for boys and girls. 800-221-4221.

**Bemidji Woolen Mills,** P.O. Box 277, Bemidji, MN 56601: Free brochure ◆ Woolen outerwear for men, women, and children. 218-751-5166.

**Big Dog Sportswear,** Mail Order Dept., 121 Gray Ave., Santa Barbara, CA 93101: Free catalog ◆ T-shirts and clothing for children. 800-642-3647. www.BIGDOGS.com

**Biobottoms,** 617-C 2nd St., Petaluma, CA 94952: Free catalog ◆ Cotton outerwear and dress-up clothing for infants, toddlers, and older children. 800-766-1254; 707-778-7152 (in CA). www.biobottoms.com

**Cherry Tree Clothing,** 166 Valley St., Providence, RI 02909: Free information ◆ Children's outerwear. 800-869-7742.

**Childcraft,** 250 College Park, P.O. Box 1811, Peoria, IL 61656: Free catalog ◆ Play clothes for boys, sizes 4 to 16 and girls, sizes 4 to 6X and 7 to 14. 800-631-5657.

**Children's Wear Digest,** 3607 Mayland Ct., Richmond, VA 23233: Free catalog ◆ Children's clothing for school, playtime, dressing-up, and keeping warm. 800-242-5437.

**Citikids,** 152 Clement St., San Francisco, CA 94118: Free information ◆ Children's furniture, car seats, strollers, carriers, clothing, and baby care items. 415-752-3837.

**The Cotton Fields Company,** P.O. Box 742, Ellendale, TN 38029: Free brochure ◆ One-hundred percent cotton clothing for children, men, and women. 800-883-6336; 901-388-9157 (in TN). cottonfields@worldnet.att.net

**Country Baby of Maine,** 41 Shaker Rd., Rt. 26, New Gloucester, ME 04260: Free information ◆ Handmade clothing and accessories for children, infants, and preemies. 207-657-5443.

**Cowboy Shopper,** P.O. Box 6459, Santa Fe, NM 87502: Free catalog with SASE ◆ Source for antique cowboy gear, books, events, and organizations. 505-995-0102. **zon@nets.com**

**Cry Baby Ranch,** 1422 Larimer Square, Denver, CO 80202: Catalog $2 ◆ Cow-kid furniture, cowboy clothing, and cowgirl gifts. 888-CRY-BABY. www.crybabyranch.com

**Cyclone Apparel,** 10965 SW Commerce Circle, Ste. C, Wilsonville, OR 97070: Free information ◆ Children's clothing.

**Drysdales,** 1555 N. 107th East Ave., Tulsa, OK 74116: Free catalog ◆ Western-style clothing, boots, and gifts for children of all ages. 800-444-6481. www.drysdales.com

**Earthwear,** 1007 Swallow Ln., Chattanooga, TN 37421: Free catalog ◆ Organic clothing for infants and children. 423-894-3674.

**Ecobaby,** 1475 N. Cuyamaca, El Cajon, CA 92020: Free catalog ◆ Organic and natural fiber clothes, bedding, toys, and diapering products. 888-ECOBABY; 619-596-7450 (in CA). www.ecobaby.com

**Eskimo Joes's Clothes,** P.O. Box 729, Stillwater, OK 74076: Free catalog ◆ Fun and relaxed wear clothing for men, women, and children. 800-256-5637. www.eskimojoes.com

**Esprit Outlet,** 499 Illinois St., San Francisco, CA 94107: Free catalog ◆ Clothing for children and their mothers. 415-957-2550. sanfrancisco.sidewalk.com/link/19351

**G-Y-M-B-O-R-E-E,** 2299 Kidds Way, Dixon, CA 95620: Free catalog ◆ Infant and toddler's clothing. 800-990-5060.

**Garnet Hill,** 231 Main St., Franconia, NH 03580: Free catalog ◆ Adult sleepwear, maternity clothing, natural fiber underwear. Also children's sleepwear and outerwear. 800-622-6216.

**Hot off the Ice,** P.O. Box 1620, Secaucus, NJ 07096: Free catalog ◆ Informal, back-to-school, and casual clothing with a hockey theme for teens and young adults. 800-446-85423. www.shop.nhl.com

**Kid Natural & Creation Cottons,** 4302 224th Pl. SW, Mountlake Terrace, WA 98043: Free catalog ◆ Handmade cotton clothing. 206-778-0418.

**Kid Sport,** 122 E. Meadow Dr., Vail, CO 81657: Free catalog ◆ Winterwear and skiwear for children, from newborn through young adult. 800-833-1729; 970-476-1666 (in CO). www.vail.net/internetworks

**Le Petite Baby,** 12105 Leeward Walk Circle, Alpharetta, GA 30202: Free brochure ◆ Premature infant clothes, especially for babies under 7 pounds. 770-475-3247.

**Little Prince and Princess Infants and Toddlers,** 18025 Palm Breeze Dr., Tampa, FL 33647: Free catalog ◆ Infant and toddler's clothing. 813-991-5914.

**Maternity Blues,** 920 S. Olive St., Los Angeles, CA 90015: Free information ◆ Linen sportswear. 800-608-2229; 213-624-6488 (in CA).

**Mothertime,** 4245 Kanox Ave., Chicago, IL 60641: Free list of retail sources ◆ Maternity, newborn, and infant apparel. 800-888-8281.

**The Natural Baby Company,** 7835 Freedom Ave. NW, North Canton, OH 44720: Free information ◆ Children's clothing. 800-388-BABY.

**Oshkosh Direct,** Division Oshkosh B'Gosh Inc., P.O. Box 300, Monroe, WI 54902: Free catalog ◆ Oshkosh clothing for babies and older children. 800-MY-BGOSH. www.oshkoshbgosh.com

**Patagonia,** 8550 White Fir St., Reno, NV 89523: Free catalog ◆ Outdoor clothing for children and adults. 800-638-6464. www.patagonia.com

**JCPenney Catalog,** P.O. Box 675, Milwaukee, WI 53201: Free information ◆ Free information ◆ Children's clothing in large sizes. 800-222-6161. www.jcpenney.com/shopping

**Playclothes,** P.O. Box 44321, Rio Rancho, NM 87174: Free catalog ◆ Playwear, dressing up, matching outfits, and other clothing for boys and girls. 800-926-7118; 800-505-1095 (hearing impaired). www.playclothes.com

**Pleasant Company,** P.O. Box 620190, Middleton, WI 53562: Free catalog ◆ Classic clothing for little girls. 800-845-0005. www.americangirl.com

**The Preemie Store...and More,** 17195 Newhope St., Ste. 105, Fountain Valley, CA 92708: Free information ◆ Caps and clothing for babies. 800-676-8469.

**Premierwear,** 3037 Grass Valley Hwy, #8200, Auburn, CA 95602: Free catalog ◆ Clothing for premature and low birth weight babies. 800-992-TINY.

**Rubens & Marble Inc.,** P.O. Box 14900, Chicago, IL 60614: Free brochure with long SASE ◆ Clothing and bedding for infants. 773-348-6200.

**SEATcovers,** 676 Schoolhouse Ln., Toms River, NJ 08753: Free catalog ◆ Embroidered children's apparel. 908-506-6534.

**Simply Divine-All Cotton Clothing,** 1606 S. Congress, Austin, TX 78704: Catalog $1 ◆ All-cotton clothing for women, infants, and children. 512-444-5546.

**Special Clothes Inc.,** P.O. Box 333, East Harwich, MA 02645: Catalog $1 ◆ Adaptive clothing for children with disabilities. Includes undergarments, casual clothing, sleepwear, footwear, accessories, ponchos, and jackets for wheelchair use. 508-896-7939. www.Special-Clothes.com

**Spencer's Inc.,** P.O. Box 988, Mt. Airy, NC 27030: Free information ◆ Infant and children's clothing. 800-633-9111.

**Spiegel,** P.O. Box 182563, Columbus, OH 43218: Free catalog ◆ Children's clothing, shoes, and toys. 800-345-4500. www.spiegel.com

**Storybook Heirlooms,** 333 Hatch Dr., Foster City, CA 94404: Free catalog ◆ Children's clothing and gifts. 800-825-6565.

**Talbots for Kids,** 175 Beal St., Hingham, MA 02043: Free catalog ◆ Clothing for boys, sizes 4 to 12 and sizes 4 to 14 for girls. 800-543-7123.

**Twincerely Yours,** 748 Lake Ave., Clermont, FL 34711: Free catalog with long SASE ◆ Gifts, novelties, and T-shirts for twins and their families. 352-394-5493.

**Wooden Soldier,** P.O. Box 800, North Conway, NH 03860: Free catalog ◆ Children's designer clothing. 800-375-6002.

**Yellow Turtle,** Mt. Road, Stowe, VT 05672: Free catalog ◆ Clothing, skiwear, and accessories for children. 800-439-4435; 802-253-4434 (in VT).

## Exercise Clothing

**Ace Sports Inc.,** 15889-B Crabbs Branch Way, 2nd Floor, Rockville, MD 20855: Free information ◆ Football, basketball, tennis, hockey, baseball, and other sports apparel. 800-232-4ACE; 301-258-9396 (in MD).

**Adidas USA,** 5675 N. Blackstock Rd., Spartanburg, SC 29303: Free list of retail sources ◆ Men and women's shorts and singlets, aerobic and workout shoes, socks, and warm-up suits. 800-423-4327. www.adidas.com

**Austad's,** Hanover Direct Pennsylvania Inc., Hanover, PA 17333-0001: Free catalog ◆ Sports equipment and accessories. 717-633-3333.

**Body Wrappers,** Attitudes in Dressing Inc., 1350 Broadway, Ste. 304, New York, NY 10018: Free information ◆ Exercise suits, leotards, headbands, leg warmers, women's shorts, and warm-up suits. 800-323-0786; 212-279-3492 (in NY).

**California Best,** 970 Broadway, Ste. 104, Chula Vista, CA 91911: Free catalog ◆ Men and women's exercise and fitness clothing. 800-438-9327.

**Champion Products Inc.,** 475 Corporate Square Dr., Winston-Salem, NC 27105: Free information ◆ Exercise clothing, leotards, shorts, and singlets for men and women.

**Danmar Products Inc.,** 221 Jackson Industrial Dr., Ann Arbor, MI 48103: Free catalog ◆ Hydro-fitness equipment and soft swim boots for sensitive feet. 800-783-1998; 313-761-1990 (in MI).

**Danskin,** 111 W. 40th St., 18th Floor, New York, NY 10018: Free information ◆ Exercise suits, headbands, leg warmers, leotards, singlets for women, warm-up suits, and wrist bands. 212-764-4630.

**Enell Inc.,** P.O. Box 808, 317 Second St., Havre, MT 59501: Free information ◆ Women's sports bras. 800-828-7661; 406-265-825 (in MT). www.gomontana.com/Business/Enell

**The Finals Inc.,** 21 Minisink Ave., Port Jervis, NY 12771: Free catalog ◆ Bicycling, aerobic, swimming, running, and exercise clothing. 800-345-3485. www.thefinals.com

**Freed of London Inc.,** 922 7th Ave., New York, NY 10019: Free price list ◆ Exercise clothing, gym shoes, and footwear for women and men. 212-489-1055.

**Gold's Gym,** 360 Hampton Dr., Venice, CA 90291: Free information ◆ Gloves, headbands, leotards, aerobic and workout shoes, shorts, singlets, and warm-up suits. 800-457-5375; 213-392-6004 (in CA). www.goldsonline.com

**HARDGEAR Incorporated,** 17A Chittick Ave., Dartmouth, Nova Scotia, Canada B2Y 3J7: Free information ◆ Custom made workout clothing for men. 902-463-4669.

**Hind Sportswear,** P.O. Box 12609, San Luis Obispo, CA 93406: Free information ◆ Exercise suits, gloves, leotards, shorts, socks, and singlets for men and women. 800-426-4463.

**Jazzertogs,** 1050 Joshua Way, Vista, CA 92083: Free catalog ◆ Exercise clothing. 800-FIT-ISIT.

**Leo's Dancewear Inc.,** 1900 N. Narragansett Ave., Chicago, IL 60639: Free catalog with request on school stationery ◆ Leg warmers, leotards, workout shoes, and headbands. 312-889-7700. Leos@IX.Netcom.com

**Gilda Marx Industries,** 5340 172 Plummer Rd., Sidman, PA 15955: Free information ◆ Exercise suits, leotards, headbands, leg warmers, shorts, and warm-up suits. 800-876-6279.

**New Balance Athletic Shoe Inc.,** 61 N. Deacon St., Boston, MA 02134: Free information ◆ Exercise suits, leotards, workout shoes, shorts and singlets for men and women, and warm-up suits. 800-622-1218. www.newbalance.com

**Pony Sports & Leisure,** 2801 Red Dog Dr., Knoxville, TN 37914: Free information ◆ Exercise suits, headbands, leotards, aerobic and workout shoes, shorts, singlets, and warm-up suits. 423-546-4703.

**Puma USA Inc.,** 147 Centre St., Brockton, MA 02403: Free information with long SASE ◆ Exercise suits, headbands, leg warmers, leotards, shorts, socks, aerobic and workout shoes, singlets, and warm-up suits. 800-662-7862. www.puma.com

**R.U. Outside Inc.,** 455 S. Main, Driggs, ID 83422: Free catalog ◆ Clothing, boots, socks, gloves, protective and head gear, goggles, and more for outdoor activities. 800-279-7123. www.ruoutside.com

**Rebecca's Mom,** 5445 Ben Ave., Valley Village, CA 91607: Free brochure ◆ Gymnastic leotards in all sizes for children and young adults. 888-289-2536. www.leotard.com

**Royal Textile Mills Inc.,** P.O. Box 250, Yanceyville, NC 27379: Free information ◆ Exercise suits, head and wrist bands, leg warmers, leotards, socks, and warm-up suits. 800-334-9361; 336-694-4121 (in NC).

**K. Smith Consulting,** c/o Gorilla Muscle Workout Wear, 4 McLennan Way, Kanata, Ontario, Canada K2L 2M9: Free information ◆ Gymnasium workout apparel.

**Spalding Sports Worldwide,** 425 Meadow St., P.O. Box 901, Chicopee, MA 01201: Free list of retail sources ◆ Exercise suits, headbands, leotards, shorts and singlets for men and women, and warm-up suits. 800-225-6601. www.spalding.com

**Star Struck,** P.O. Box 308, Bethel, CT 06801: Free catalog ◆ Fitted caps and jerseys for college wear. 800-908-4637; 877-THE-GAME (in CT). www.starstruck.com

## Full-Figured Women & Misses Clothing

**Sue Brett,** P.O. Box 8384, Indianapolis, IN 46283: Free catalog ◆ Women's clothing in sizes 8 to 24, in petite and tall sizes. 800-784-8001.

**Brownstone Woman,** P.O. Box 25367, Shawnee Mission, KS 66225: Free catalog ◆ Women's clothing, sizes 14W to 28W. 800-322-2991.

**Lane Bryant,** P.O. Box 8301, Indianapolis, IN 46283: Free catalog ◆ Misses clothing in size 14 to 20, half sizes 12½ to 34½, and size 36 to 60. Also shoes, size 6 to 12, AA to EEE. 800-477-7030.

**Daphne Clothing,** 467 Amsterdam Ave., New York, NY 10024: Free information ◆ One of a kind made-to-order clothing for full-figured women. 212-877-5073.

**Laura Dion-Jones,** P.O. Box 10876, Chicago IL 60610: Free catalog ◆ Clothing for full-figured women. 312-243-4333.

**Elliot-Brown Boutique,** P.O. Box 49338, Los Angeles, CA 90049: Free catalog ◆ Full-figure special occasion fashions for women, sizes 1X to 3X.

**Henri's Full Figure Boutique,** 1419 Krameria St., Denver CO 80220: Free information ◆ Clothing for full-figured women. Includes bridal fashions and accessories. 303-355-1811.

**J. Jill,** P.O. Box 3006, One Winterbrook Way, Meredith, NH 03253: Free catalog ◆ Women's fashions in misses, petite, and other sizes. 800-642-9989.

**Just My Size,** P.O. Box 748, Rural Hall, NC 27098: Free catalog ◆ Lingerie for full-figured women, size 14 and up. 800-522-9567. www.justmysizebras.com

**Just Right Clothing,** 30 Tozer Rd., Beverly, MA 01915: Free catalog ◆ Clothing, size 14 and up. 800-767-6666.

**Lerner New York,** Midwest Distribution Center, P.O. Box 8380, Indianapolis, IN 46283: Free catalog ◆ Clothing in half sizes, 12½ to 34½; women's sizes 34 to 54; misses sizes 12 to 24. Also shoes, size 6 to 12, AA to EEE. 800-288-4009.

**Peggy Lutz,** 6784 Depot St., Sebastopol, CA 95472: Catalog $2 ◆ Women's full-figured clothing. 800-498-3294. www.plus-size.com

**Making It Big,** 501 Aaron St., Cotati, CA 94931: Free catalog ◆ Natural fiber clothing for large and supersize women. 707-795-1995. www.bigwomen.com

**Old Pueblo Traders,** Palo Verde at 34th, P.O. Box 27800, Tucson, AZ 85726: Free catalog ◆ Women's clothing in misses, full-figured, and half sizes. 520-748-8600.

**JCPenney Catalog,** P.O. Box 675, Milwaukee, WI 53201: Free information ◆ Clothing for full-figured and tall women, in sizes up to 32W. 800-222-6161. www.jcpenney.com/shopping

**Plus Size Designer Outlet,** 6784 Depot St., Sebastopol, CA 95472: Free catalog ◆ Women's fashions, size 14 and larger. 800-498-3294; 707-824-1634 (in CA).

**Plus Woman,** 85 Laurel Haven, Fairview, NC 28730: Free catalog ◆ Super size ladies clothing. Also large petitie and tall sizes. 800-628-5525. www.pluswoman.com

**Ulla Popken Clothing,** 12201 Long Green Pike, Glen Arm, MD 21057: Free catalog ◆ Style-conscious clothing for women, sizes 12 through 30. Includes some items in petite sizes. 800-245-8552. www.ullapopken.com

**Regalia,** Palo Verde at 34th, P.O. Box 27800, Tucson, AZ 85726: Free catalog ◆ Fashions and intimate apparel in large sizes. Also shoes in hard-to-find sizes and narrow to wide-wide widths. 520-747-5000.

**Roaman's,** P.O. Box 8360, Indianapolis, IN 46283: Free catalog ◆ Clothing for full-figured women. Includes sizes 12 to 26 for misses, 34 to 56 for full-figured women, and half sizes. Also shoes and boots in hard-to-fit sizes. 800-436-0800.

**Silhouettes,** Hanover Direct Pennsylvania, Hanover, PA 17333-0069: Free catalog ◆ Women's sportswear and casual clothing, size 14W to 26W. 800-704-3322. www.silhouettes.com

**Spiegel,** P.O. Box 182563, Columbus, OH 43218: Free catalog ◆ Sportswear and casual clothing in large sizes. 800-345-4500. www.spiegel.com

**Nicole Summers,** One Winterbrook Way, P.O. 3003, Meredith, NH 03253: Free catalog ◆ Clothing for women, sizes 10 to 20. 800-642-6786.

**Tweeds,** Hanover Direct Pennsylvania Inc., Hanover, PA 17333-0001: Free catalog ◆ Trendy fashions for misses, sizes 4 to 16. 717-633-3333.

## Lingerie & Underwear

**Al Fancy Dress,** 6245 Bristol Pkwy., Culver City, CA 90230: Free information ◆ Unusual wraps, gifts, hats, robes, house coats, negligees, and more. 213-292-7418.

**Alexi's Lingerie Boutique,** 1041 Honey Creek Rd., Ste. 291, Conyers, GA 30208: Catalog $3 (refundable) ◆ Lingerie in regular and plus sizes.

**B & G Lingerie Direct,** P.O. Box 2235, Ocean, NJ 07712: Free catalog ◆ Intimate apparel and undergarments. 800-447-1082.

**Beauty by Spector Inc.,** One Spector Pl., McKeesport, PA 15134: Catalog $5 ◆ Women's wigs and hairpieces, men's toupees, jewelry, and exotic lingerie. 412-673-3259.

**Sue Brett,** P.O. Box 8384, Indianapolis, IN 46283: Free catalog ◆ Women's lingerie and nighttime wear. 800-784-8001.

**Lane Bryant,** P.O. Box 8301, Indianapolis, IN 46283: Free catalog ◆ Intimate clothing, outerwear, dresses, blouses, coordinates, sweaters, and footwear. 800-477-7030.

**Byrd's Nest,** 1828 Utica Square, Tulsa, OK 74114: Free information ◆ Lingerie, nightshirts and pajamas, sleepwear, loungewear, and unusual gifts. 918-747-4231.

**Celestial Silks,** P.O. Box 824, Fairfield, IA 52556: Free information ◆ In-stock and custom-made silk sheets, pillowcases, and silk-filled comforters. Also silk lingerie. 515-472-9062.

**Chock Catalog Corp.,** 74 Orchard St., New York, NY 10002: Catalog $2 ◆ Lingerie, hosiery, and sleep wear for women, men, and children. 800-222-0020.

**Damart,** 3 Front St., Rollinsford, NH 03805: Free information ◆ Thermal underwear for men and women. 800-258-7300. www.damartusa.com

**De'An Drew Designs,** 8884 Warner Ave., Ste. 172, Fountain Valley, CA 92708: Catalog $2 ◆ Women's stockings, lingerie, and accessories. 714-969-2586. www.deandrewdesigns.com

**Decent Exposures,** P.O. Box 27206, Seattle, WA 98125: Free information ◆ Women's underwear in 100 percent cotton. 800-524-4949; 206-364-4540 (in WA). requests@decentexposures.com

**Frederick's of Hollywood,** P.O. Box 229, Hollywood, CA 90099: Free catalog ◆ Intimate clothing and lingerie, casual clothing, swimwear, jewelry, and shoes. 800-323-9525. www.fredericks.com

**Genie Products,** 843 W. Adams St., Chicago, IL 60607: Free brochure ◆ Slimming lingerie and underwear for men and women. 312-829-1801.

**Gohn Brothers,** 105 S. Main, P.O. Box 111, Middlebury, IN 46540: Free information with long SASE ◆ Men and women's Amish clothing, underwear, and hosiery. 219-825-2400.

**Intimate Appeal,** Palo Verde at 34th, P.O. Box 27800, Tucson, AZ 85726: Free catalog ◆ Intimate clothing for women who have had mastectomies. 520-748-8600.

**JasMar Fashion Designs Inc.,** P.O. Box 4401, Edmonton, Alberta, Canada T6E 4T5: Free brochure ◆ Men and women's underwear and lingerie, T-shirts, and swimwear. 403-413-9867. jasmar@jasmar.com

**Johnson Woolen Mills Inc.,** P.O. Box 12, Johnson, VT 05656: Free brochure ◆ Woolen outerwear for men, women, and children. Also blankets, underwear, and sweaters. 802-635-2271.

**Just My Size,** P.O. Box 748, Rural Hall, NC 27098: Free catalog ◆ Lingerie for full-figured women, size 14 and up. 800-522-9567. www.justmysizebras.com

**L'eggs Brands Inc.,** Outlet Catalog, P.O. Box 748, Rural Hall, NC 27098: Free catalog ◆ L'eggs, Hanes, Bali, and Playtex lingerie and hosiery. 800-522-1151. www.onehanesplace.com

**Lady Grace Stores,** P.O. Box 128, Malden, MA 02148: Free catalog ◆ Intimate apparel for everyday wear, nursing and maternity, and post-breast surgery. 800-922-0504. www.ladygrace.com

**I.C. London,** The Shoppes at Twin Oaks, 1419 E. Boulevard, Charlotte, NC 28203: Free information ◆ Sleepwear, loungewear, and lingerie. 888-ICLondon; 703-377-7955 (in NC).

**Manshape,** P.O. Box 453, Mill Valley, CA 94942: Free brochure ◆ Men's support underwear and tank shirts. 888-626-7427. www.manshape.com

**Midnight Classics Lingerie Boutique,** 2215 South Main St., Elkhart, IN 46517: Free information ◆ Lingerie for petite to full-figured women. 888-BUSTIER; 219-294-1693 (in IN).

**National Wholesale Company Inc.,** 400 National Blvd., Lexington, NC 27294: Free catalog ◆ Hosiery and lingerie. 336-249-4202.

**Newport News Fashions,** Avon Ln., Hampton, VA 23630: Free catalog ◆ Daytime and nighttime intimate clothing. 800-688-2830.

**One Hanes Place,** Outlet Catalog, P.O. Box 748, Rural Hall, NC 27098: Free catalog ◆ Hosiery, lingerie, and women's clothing. 800-522-1151. www.onehanesplace.com

**Petticoat Junction,** 1500 Hudson St., Hoboken, NJ 07030: Free information ◆ Lingerie. 201-798-9077.

**Regalia,** Palo Verde at 34th, P.O. Box 27800, Tucson, AZ 85726: Free catalog ◆ Fashions and intimate apparel in large sizes. Also shoes in hard-to-find sizes and narrow to wide-wide widths. 520-747-5000.

**Roby's Intimates,** 505 Cedar Ln., Teaneck, NJ 07666: Catalog $1 ◆ Bras, lingerie, and hosiery. 800-8788-BRA; 201-836-0630 (in NJ).

**Solace Marbled Silk Clothing & Lingerie,** P.O. Box 295, Penn Laird, VA 22846: Free brochure ◆ Custom-made lingerie and marbled clothing. 540-289-5964. home.rica.net/solace

**Undergear,** Order Processing Center, Hanover, PA 17333: Free catalog ◆ Men's clothing and underwear. 800-853-8555.

**Victoria's Secret,** North American Office, P.O. Box 16589, Columbus, OH 43216: Free catalog ◆ Women's lingerie, intimate wear, formal and casual clothing, and outerwear. 800-888-8200.

## Maternity Clothing

**Abracadabra Maternity,** 4411 San Mateo Blvd. NE, Ste. J, Albuquerque, NM 87109: Free information ◆ Maternity clothing and accessories for new mothers and new mothers-to-be. Includes casual to professional, swimsuits, exercise wear, nursing tops, pajamas, and other fashions. Also nursing accessories and baby care items. 505-881-6820.

**Baby Becoming,** 10 Nate Whipple Hwy., Mich Bldg., Cumberland, RI 02864: Free catalog ◆ Clothing for full-figured, pregnant, and nursing women. 401-658-0688.

**Basics Direct, Maternity & Nursing,** 14 Highview Dr., Uxbridge, MA 01569: Free catalog ◆ Maternity clothing and lingerie, abdominal and lower back supports, breast pumps and accessories, and other nursing aids. 800-954-MOMS.

**Bosom Buddies,** P.O. Box 1250, Port Ewen, NY 12466: Free catalog ◆ Maternity bras, clothing, and accessories for fashion-conscious women. 888-860-0041. www.bosombuddies.com

**Bravado Designs,** 705 Pape Ave., Toronto, Ontario, Canada M4K 3S6: Free information ◆ Maternity and nursing bra. 800-590-7802.

**Caring Products International Inc.,** 200 1st Ave. West, Ste. 200, Seattle, WA 98119: Free information ◆ Incontinence supplies and maternity and special-needs clothing. 800-333-5379; 206-282-6040 (in WA). www.caringproducts.com

**Dax & Coe,** 935 El Camino Real, Menlo Park, CA 94025: Free information ◆ Maternity clothing in all-natural washable fabrics. 415-327-4373.

**Decent Exposures,** P.O. Box 27206, Seattle, WA 98125: Free information ◆ Pregnancy and nursing bras. 800-524-4949; 206-364-4540 (in WA). requests@decentexposures.com

**5 Generations Inc.,** P.O. Box 1056, Craig, CO 81626: Catalog $2 (refundable) ◆ Shirts and jeans in a variety of styles, sizes, and colors. 970-824-7311.

**Garnet Hill,** 231 Main St., Franconia, NH 03580: Free catalog ◆ Natural fiber maternity clothing, sleepwear, underwear, and outerwear for adults and children. 800-622-6216.

**Dan Howard's Maternity Factory Outlet,** 4245 N. Knox Ave., Chicago, IL 60641: Free catalog ◆ Sportswear, casual and informal fashions, career wear, coordinates, sweaters, intimate wear, and maternity fashions. 800-9-MONTHS.

**International Medical Supplies,** 1475 Terminal Way, Ste. E, Reno, NV 89502: Free information ◆ Adjustable maternity bra for use during and after pregnancy. 800-944-4006.

**Jaggar Maternity Clothing,** 55 1st St., Hoboken, NJ 07030: Free information ◆ Jeans for pregnant women. 888-87JAGGAR; 201-792-6070. www.earthlink.net/~jaggar/jaggar.htm

**Japanese Weekend Inc.,** 222 Dore St., San Francisco, CA 94103: Free catalog ◆ Fashionable and relaxed wear maternity fashions. 800-808-0555. www.japaneseweekend.com

**Lady Grace Stores,** P.O. Box 128, Malden, MA 02148: Free catalog ◆ Intimate apparel for everyday wear, nursing and maternity, and post-breast surgery. 800-922-0504. www.ladygrace.com

**Maternal Instincts Inc.,** 439 Shaker Ridge Dr., Canaan, NY 12029: Free brochure ◆ Maternity clothing for active women. 800-579-6464. www.maternal-instincts.com

**Maternity Blues,** 920 S. Olive St., Los Angeles, CA 90015: Free information ◆ Linen sportswear. 800-608-2229; 213-624-6488 (in CA).

**Mother's Place,** P.O. Box 94512, Cleveland, OH 44101: Free catalog ◆ Casual, active, dress-up, and sleepwear for mothers-to-be. 800-829-0080; 216-826-1712 (in OH).

**Motherhood Maternity,** 456 N 5th St., Philadelphia, PA 19123: Free catalog ◆ Maternity clothing. 215-625-9259.

**Mothertime,** 4245 Kanox Ave., Chicago, IL 60641: Free list of retail sources ◆ Maternity, newborn, and infant apparel. 800-888-8281.

**Motherwear Clothing,** 320 Riverside Dr., Northampton, MA 01060: Free catalog ◆ Easy access clothing for nursing mothers. 800-633-0303.

**JCPenney Catalog,** P.O. Box 675, Milwaukee, WI 53201: Free information *: Free information ◆ Career and casual maternity clothing in petite, misses, tall, and regular sizes. www.jcpenney.com/shopping

**Special Addition,** 3005 S. Lamar, Ste. D-112, The Corners Shopping Center, Austin, TX 78704: Free information ◆ Maternity and nursing apparel and accessories for mothers and the mother-to-be. 512-326-9308.

## Men's & Women's Clothing

**Alloy Men & Women's Clothing,** P.O. Box 182217, Chattanooga, TN 37422: Free catalog ◆ Sportswear clothing and gifts for men and women. 888-45-ALLOY. www.alloyonline.com

**Alpha Industries Inc.,** 1600 Spring Hill Rd., Ste. 220, Vienna, VA 22182: Free list of retail sources ◆ Military flight and field-style cold weather apparel for today's casual lifestyles. 615-573-8335.

**American Made Leather,** RD 3, Box 379, Cameron, WV 26033: Free catalog ◆ Leather clothing for men, women, and children. 800-584-5184. www.greenepa.net/~anna/aml

**Ameriwear Apparel,** 222 Industrial Ave., Hohenwald, TN. 38462: Free information ◆ Adult sportswear jackets. 800-244-0863.

**Andover Shop,** 127 Main St., P.O. Box 5127, Andover, MA 01810: Free catalog ◆ Silk ties and clothing for men. 978-475-2252.

**Angels Afoot,** P.O. Box 176, Saginaw, MO 64864: Free information ◆ Clothing and note cards with a catalog motif. 417-623-2073.

**Appleseed's,** 30 Tozer Rd., P.O. Box 1020, Beverly, MA 01915: Free catalog ◆ Clothing for women, size 4 to 18. 800-767-6666.

**Athletic Supply,** 10812 Alder Circle, Dallas, TX 75238: Free catalog ◆ Men and women's sportswear, jackets, T-shirts, memorabilia, figurines, and gifts. 800-627-9843.

**Atlantis,** 30 Barnet Blvd., New Bedford, MA 02745: Free catalog ◆ Foul weather gear and clothing for yachtsmen and fishermen. 508-995-7000.

**Australian Connection,** 1716 E. Brundage Ln., Sheridan, WY 82801: Free information ◆ Outback coats for men and women. 800-248-8355.

**Avirex Aviator's Club,** 33-00 47th Ave., Long Island City, NY 11101: Catalog $2 ◆ Aviation apparel and accessories. Also gifts. 800-272-9464. www.avirex.com

**Bachrach Clothing Catalog,** P.O. Box 8740, Decatur, IL 62524: Free catalog ◆ Men's clothing. 800-637-5840.

**Eddie Bauer,** P.O. Box 182639, Columbus, OH 43218: Free catalog ◆ Active and casual clothing for men and women. 800-426-8020. www.ebauer.com

**L.L. Bean,** Casco St., Freeport, ME 04032: Free catalog ◆ Outdoor clothing, footwear, and sporting accessories for men and women. 800-221-4221. www.llbean.com

**Beau Ties Ltd. of Vermont,** 19 Gorham Ln., Middlebury, VT 05753: Free catalog ◆ Hand-stitched 100 percent silk free-style bow ties. 800-488-8437. beauties@together.net

**Bedford Fair,** 421 Landmark Dr., Wilmington, NC 28410: Free catalog ◆ Women's casual and career clothing and swimwear. 800-964-9030.

**Belldini,** 1428 Maple Ave, Los Angeles, CA 90015: Free information ◆ Women's suits and sweaters. 800-557-5237; 213-748-4442 (in CA).

**Bemidji Woolen Mills,** P.O. Box 277, Bemidji, MN 56601: Free brochure ◆ Woolen outerwear for men, women, and children. 218-751-5166.

**Bertrand Virtual,** P.O. Box 20669, Oakland, CA 94620: Free price list ◆ Scarves by the French Haute Couture. 510-832-1452.

**Atelier Biamón,** P.O. Box 55-7848, Miami, FL 33255: Catalog $4 ◆ Designer haute couture clothing, sizes 6 to 14. 305-663-1577.

**Big Dog Sportswear,** Mail Order Dept., 121 Gray Ave., Santa Barbara, CA 93101: Free catalog ◆ Lounge wear for women, boxer shorts for men, and men and women's outerwear, T-shirts, and sweatshirts. 800-642-3647. www.BIGDOGS.com

**Bila of California,** 320 W. Venice Blvd., Los Angeles, CA 90015: Free catalog ◆ Women's casual clothing and jewelry. 800-824-3541.

**Bills Khakis,** 529 Court St., Reading, PA 19601: Free catalog ◆ Men's khaki clothing. 800-43-KHAKI. www.billskhakis.com

**Blair Menswear,** 220 Hickory St., Warren, PA 16366: Free catalog ◆ Men's clothing. 800-458-2000. blair@blair.com/blair.com

**Blair Womens Wear,** 220 Hickory St., Warren, PA 16366: Free catalog ◆ Women's coordinates, sportswear, and other fashions. 800-458-2000. blair@blair.com/blair.com

**The Blanket Brigade,** Dale & Dona Harrison, P.O. Box 534, Kunkleton, PA 18058: Catalog $2 ◆ Men and women's leather and cloth clothing. Also imported Witney blankets from England. 610-381-4400. www.blanketbrigade.com

**Boathouse Custom Made,** 4700 Wissahickon Ave., Philadelphia, PA 19144: Free catalog ◆ Keep warm clothing for outdoor sports and other activities. 800-875-1883: 215-848-1855 (in PA).

**Boston Proper,** 6500 Park of Commerce Blvd. NW, P.O. Box 3048, Boca Raton, FL 33431: Free catalog ◆ Designer women's sportswear. 800-243-4300.

**The Bow Tie Club,** P.O. Box 20420, Baltimore, MD 21284: Free catalog ◆ Handmade English, Italian, and American silk bow ties. 888-269-8437. www.bowtieclub.com

**Sue Brett,** P.O. Box 8384, Indianapolis, IN 46283: Free catalog ◆ Women's clothing in sizes 8 to 24. Also petite and tall sizes. 800-784-8001.

**Brooks Brothers,** 350 Campus Plaza, P.O. Box 4016, Edison, NJ 08818: Free catalog ◆ Men and women's sportswear, casual clothing, and shoes. 800-274-1815.

**Brownstone Studio,** P.O. Box 25367, Shawnee Mission, KS 66225: Free catalog ◆ Women's sportswear, lounging attire, casual and career clothing, and sleepwear. 800-322-2991.

**Lane Bryant,** P.O. Box 8301, Indianapolis, IN 46283: Free catalog ◆ Women's outerwear, dresses and blouses, sweaters, intimate clothing, and footwear. 800-477-7030.

**Bud's Men's Shop,** 2811 50th St., Lubbock TX 79413: Free information ◆ Clothing for big and tall men in regular, long, extra-long, short, and portly sizes. 888-800-2837.

**Bullock & Jones,** P.O. Box 883124, San Francisco, CA 94188: Free catalog ◆ Men and women's clothing. 800-358-5832. www.bullock-jones.com

**Byrd's Nest,** 1828 Utica Square, Tulsa, OK 74114: Free information ◆ Lingerie, sleepwear, loungewear, and unusual gifts. 918-747-4231.

**Cable Car Clothiers,** 441 Sutter St., San Francisco, CA 94108: Catalog $3 ◆ Men's clothing. 415-397-4740. www.cablecarclothiers.com

**Cahall's Brown Duck,** P.O. Box 450, Mount Orab, OH 45154: Free catalog ◆ Outdoor work and sports clothing. 800-445-9675.

**California Muscle,** 11718 Montana Ave., Ste. 7, Los Angeles, CA 90049: Free information ◆ Men's active and after dark wear. 310-826-7171. www.californiamuscle.com

**Canari Cycle Wear,** 10025 Huennekens St., San Diego, CA 92121: Free information ◆ Winter apparel for bikers. 800-929-2925; 619-455-8245 (in CA). www.sportsx.com/canari/7161.html

**Carabella Collection,** 17662 Armstrong Ave., Irvine, CA 92614: Catalog $3 ◆ Women's swimwear, evening and career wear, party dresses, and other clothing. 800-117-2235.

**Carushka Inc.,** 7716 Kester Ave., Van Nuys, CA 91405: Catalog $3 ◆ Women's sportswear, bodywear, leotards, tank tops, trunks, and bike tights. 800-247-5113; 818-904-0574 (in CA). www.carushka.com

**Cashmeres Etc.,** 1160 Kane Concourse, Bay Harbour, FL 33154: Free catalog ◆ Men and women's cashmere, silk, and cotton clothing. 800-441-7743.

**Chadwick's of Boston,** One Chadwick Pl., Box 1600, Brockton, MA 02403: Free catalog ◆ Casual and career clothing for women. 800-525-4420.

**City Spirit,** 8920 Pershall Rd., St. Louis, MO 63042: Free catalog ◆ Women's clothing. 800-443-1516; 314-521-6178 (in St. Louis).

**The Classic Outfitters,** 1880 Mountain Rd., Stowe, VT 05672: Free catalog ◆ Outdoor clothing. 800-353-3963.

**Clifford & Wills,** One Clifford Way, Asheville, NC 28810: Free catalog ◆ Career and casual clothing for women. 800-922-0114.

**The Cockpit,** 595 Broadway, New York, NY 10310: Free catalog ◆ Leather bombers, motorcycle jackets, varsities, jeans, and accessories. 212-925-5455.

**Columbia Sportswear Company,** 6600 N. Baltimore, Portland, OR 97203: Free list of retail sources ◆ Men's sportswear for fishing and outdoor activities. 800-MA-BOYLE. www.columbia.com

**Joan Cook,** 119 Foster St., P.O. Box 6008, Peabody, MA 01961: Free catalog ◆ Women's classic clothing. 800-935-0971.

**The Cotton Fields,** Company, P.O. Box 742, Ellendale, TN 38029: Free brochure ◆ One-hundred percent cotton clothing for children, men, and women. 800-883-6336. cottonfields@worldnet.att.net

**Creative Designs,** 3704 Carlisle Ct., Modesto, CA 95356: Free information ◆ Change-a-robe, a unisex, hooded robe designed to allow user to change clothes while wearing. 800-335-4852; 209-523-3166. Robes4you@aol.com

**J. Crew Outfitters,** One Ivy Crescent, Lynchburg, VA 24513: Free catalog ◆ Casual clothing for men and women. 800-932-0043. www.jcrew.com

**Betty David,** 105 S. Main St., #325, Seattle, WA 98104: Catalog information online ◆ Native-made shearling coats for women handpainted in the Northwest Coast Indian style. 805-682-5175.

**De Soto Sport,** 5262 Eastgate Mall, San Diego, CA 92121: Free brochure ◆ Clothing for outdoor activities and swim wear for men and women. 800-453-6673; 619-453-6672 (in CA). www.desotosport.com

**Deerskin,** 119 Foster St., Peabody, MA 01960: Free catalog: ◆ Leather clothing. 978-532-2810. www.deerskin.com

**Details Direct,** 502 Water St., Eau Claire, WI 54703: Free information ◆ Classic and casual clothing for women. 800-464-1946. www.detailsdirect.com

**DEVA Lifewear Inc.,** P.O. Box 266, Westhope, ND 58793: Free catalog ◆ Cotton clothing for men and women. 800-222-8024. www.devaLifeWEAR.com

**Draper's & Damon's,** 17911 Mitchell Ave. South, Irvine, CA 92714: Free catalog ◆ Women's fashions for misses, petites, and regular sizes. 800-843-1174. www.Drapers.com

**Dress Fore the 9's,** 613 1st St., Ste. 19, Brentwood, CA 94513: Free catalog ◆ Sportswear, mix-and-match active wear for women, shoes, and jewelry. 800-306-FORE.

**Early Winters,** P.O. Box 4333, Portland, OR 97208: Free catalog ◆ Ski clothing, leisure separates, and outdoor clothing for men and women. 800-458-4438. www.normthompson.com

**Ebbets Field Flannels,** Box 19865, Seattle, WA 98109: Free catalog ◆ Historic jackets, caps, and jerseys of minor, Latin, and African-American baseball teams. 800-377-9777.

**Eskimo Joes's Clothes,** P.O. Box 729, Stillwater, OK 74076: Free catalog ◆ Fun and relaxed wear clothing for men, women, and children. 800-256-5637. www.eskimojoes.com

**Extrasport Inc.,** 5305 NW 35th Ct., Miami, FL 33142: Free catalog ◆ All-terrain clothing and sportswear. 800-633-0837.

**Fisher Henney Naturals,** 1301 Lincoln Ave., Alameda, CA 94501: Free information ◆ Pesticide and herbicide-free women's cotton clothing. 800-3-HENNEY. www.fhnaturals.com/fhnaturals

**Freda's Originals Inc.,** 86 Bathurst St., Toronto, Ontario, Canada M5V 2P5: Free information ◆ Women's fashions. 888-373-3271.

**Habari Gani,** African-American Crafts, P.O. Box 468, 132-05 Merrick Blvd., Jamaica, NY 11434: Catalog $1 ◆ Handcarved items from Kenya, Kente cloth from the Ivory Coast, clothing, accessories, craft kits, books, music, videos, beads, feathers, and supplies. 718-978-7110.

**Garnet Hill,** 231 Main St., Franconia, NH 03580: Free catalog ◆ Natural fiber adult sleepwear, maternity clothing, and underwear. Also sleepwear and outerwear for children. 800-622-6216.

**The Gentlemen's Store,** Jim Tatum, 5318 Normandy Blvd., P.O. Box 37559, Jacksonville, FL 32205: Free brochure ◆ Men's clothing. 800-874-5200.

**Gerry Sportswear,** 1051 1st Ave. South, Seattle, WA 98134: Free information ◆ Men and women's outerwear. 800-934-3779.

**Gohn Brothers,** 105 S. Main, P.O. Box 111, Middlebury, IN 46540: Free information with long SASE ◆ Men and women's Amish clothing, underwear, and hosiery. 219-825-2400.

**Gorsuch Ltd.,** 263 E. Gore Creek Dr., Vail, Colorado 81657: Free catalog ◆ Outdoor clothing for men, women, and children. 800-525-9808. www.gorsuchltd.com

**Grass Court Collection,** P.O. Box 972, Hanover, NH 03755: Free information ◆ Tailored 1940s style tennis, croquet, cricket, lawn-bowling, and sailing apparel for men. 800-829-3412.

**Green Mountain Mercantile,** P.O. Box 3100, Manchester Center, VT 05255: Free catalog ◆ Men and women's clothing. 802-362-4647.

**Haband for Her,** 100 Fairview Ave., Prospect Park, NJ 07530: Free information ◆ Women's fashions. 800-742-2263. www.haband.com

**Haband for Men,** 100 Fairview Ave., Prospect Park, NJ 07530: Free information ◆ Men's shoes and wash-and-wear clothing. 800-742-2263. www.haband.com

**Harold's Stores,** 765 Asp Ave., Norman, OK 73069: Free catalog ◆ Men and women's clothing and accessories. 800-676-5373. www.harolds.net

**Graham Harris Trading Company,** 1520 School House Ln., Ambler, PA 19002: Free catalog ◆ Outdoor clothing for bad and good weather. 800-469-4563.

**Heart & Sew,** P.O. Box 421, Kennebunk, ME 04043: Free information ◆ Custom made bow ties and suspenders.

**High Seas Foul Weather Gear,** 880 Corporate Woods Pkwy., Vernon Hills, IL 60061: Free list of retail sources ◆ Clothing for the outdoors. 847-913-1100. smartgear@hssc.com

**The Horchow Collection,** P.O. Box 620048, Dallas, TX 75262: Free catalog ◆ Women's casual clothing. 800-395-5397. www.neimanmarcus.com

**Hot off the Ice,** P.O. Box 1620, Secaucus, NJ 07096: Free catalog ◆ Informal, back-to-school, and casual clothing with a hockey theme for teens and young adults. 800-446-85423. www.shop.nhl.com

**Huntington Clothiers,** 1285 Alum Creek Dr., Columbus, OH 43209: Free catalog ◆ Traditional fashions for men and women. 800-848-6203. shirts@hclothiers.com

**International Male,** Hanover Direct Pennsylvania Inc., Hanover, PA 17333-0001: Free catalog ◆ Men's clothing. 800-728-8777. www.intmale.com

**J. Jill,** P.O. Box 3006, One Winterbrook Way, Meredith, NH 03253: Free catalog ◆ Women's fashions in misses, petite, and other sizes. 800-642-9989.

**Jim's Formal Wear,** One Tuxedo Park, P.O. Box 125, Trenton, IL 62293: Free list of retail sources ◆ Tuxedo fashions for men. 888-438-8893; 618-224-9211 (in IL).

**Johnson Woolen Mills Inc.,** P.O. Box 12, Johnson, VT 05656: Free brochure ◆ Woolen outerwear for men, women, and children. Also blankets, underwear, and sweaters. 802-635-2271.

**Johnston & Murphy,** Mail Order Shop, 1415 Murfreesboro Rd., Ste. 190, Nashville, TN 37217: Free catalog ◆ Men's shoes, socks, belts, and accessories. 800-424-2853. www.johnstonmurphy.com

**Junonia Women's Clothing,** 800 Transfer Rd., #8, St. Paul, MN 55114: Free catalog ◆ Active and casual women's clothing, size 14 and up. 800-586-6642; 612-647-9100 (in MN). www.JUNONIA.com

**Charles Keath Ltd.,** P.O. Box 48800, Atlanta, GA 30362: Free catalog ◆ Women's casual clothing and jewelry. 800-388-6565; 770-449-3100 (in GA).

**Ruth Kishline's Country Clothes,** 9201 Old Petersburgh Rd., Evansville, IN 47711: Catalog $3 ◆ Women's clothing. 800-343-3062.

**Knights Ltd. Catalog,** 8920 Pershall Dr., Attention: Mailroom, Hazelwood, MO 63042: Free catalog ◆ Women's casual and formal fashions and shoes. 800-240-7052.

**La Costa Products International,** 2875 Laker Ave. East, Carlsbad, CA 92009: Free catalog ◆ Men and women's clothing and spa essentials. 800-308-0358.

**A.B. Lambdin,** US Hwy. 19N, Americus, GA 31710: Free catalog ◆ Women's clothing and shoes. 800-924-8800. www.ablambdin.com

**Landau Woolens,** 102 Nassau St., Princeton, NJ 08542: Free catalog ◆ Hand-knitted sweaters, Icelandic wool coats and jackets, blanket throws, sportswear, cotton knits, sleepwear, and shirts. 800-257-9445.

**The Last Best Place,** Catalog Company, 3650 Milwaukee St., Madison, WI 53779: Free catalog ◆ Men and women's clothing with a western theme. 800-252-4766.

**Lee-McClain Company Inc.,** 2043 Lagrange Rd., Shelbyville, KY 40065: Free brochure ◆ Men's suits, jackets, coats, and blazers. 502-633-3823.

**Lerner New York,** Midwest Distribution Center, P.O. Box 8380, Indianapolis, IN 46283: Free catalog ◆ Women's sportswear, casual clothing, sweaters, lingerie, jewelry, shoes and boots, and outerwear. 800-288-4009.

**Lewis Creek Company,** 1 Pine Haven Shore, Shelburne, VT 05482: Free information ◆ Outerwear. 800-336-4884.

**Lion's Pride Catalog,** P.O. Box 342, Little Chute, WI 54140: Free catalog ◆ Denim shirts, cotton knit sweaters, robes, and other clothing for men and women. 414-731-4242.

**Loftin & Young,** 67 Liberty Church Rd., Carrollton, GA 30116: Free catalog ◆ Business apparel for men (blazers, pants, shirts, and accessories) and women (blazers, blouses, pants, shorts, skirts, vests, and accessories). 800-563-8864.

**I.C. London,** The Shoppes at Twin Oaks, 1419 E. Boulevard, Charlotte, NC 28203: Free information ◆ Sleepwear, loungewear, and lingerie. 888-ICLondon; 703-377-7955 (in NC).

**Lew Magram,** 414 Alfred Ave., P.O. Box 7696, Teaneck, NJ 07666: Free catalog ◆ Casual, career, coordinates, and formal fashions for women. 201-833-8500.

**Mary Orvis Marbury,** 1711 Blue Hills Dr., P.O. Box 12000, Roanoke, VA 24022: Free catalog ◆ Women's career, casual, and evening wear. 800-541-3541. www.orvis.com

**Mark, Fore & Strike,** 6500 Park of Commerce Blvd. NW, P.O. Box 5056, Boca Raton, FL 33431: Free catalog ◆ Classic, casual, and sportswear for men and women. 800-327-3627.

**Mast General Store,** Hwy. 194, Valle Crucis, NC 28691: Free information ◆ Hammocks and porch swings, housewares, boots, and traditional clothing. 704-963-6511.

**Men's Collections,** P.O. Box 882883, San Francisco, CA 94188: Free catalog ◆ Men's casual sportswear and shoes. 800-248-2299.

**Midwestern Sports Togs,** P.O. Box 230, Berlin, WI 54923: Free catalog ◆ Deerskin gloves, jackets and coats for men and women, footwear, handbags, and accessories. 414-361-5050.

**David Morgan,** 11812 Northcreek Pkwy., Ste. 103, Bothell, WA 98011: Free catalog ◆ Hand-braided belts, fur hats, and wool and sheepskin clothing. 800-324-4934. www.davidmorgan.com

**Muldoon's Men's Wear Inc.,** 1506 S. Hastings Way, Eau Claire, WI 54701: Free brochure ◆ Clothing in regular, big, tall, short, and small sizes. 800-942-0783.

**National Distribution Inc.,** 810 Philip Dr., Unit #1, Waukesha, WI 53186: Free catalog ◆ Clothing for relaxed wearing, leather goods, caps and hats, glassware, coffee mugs, black powder arms, knives, and collectibles. 800-962-COLT.

**National Wholesale Company Inc.,** 400 National Blvd., Lexington, NC 27294: Free catalog ◆ Women's hosiery, panty hose, lingerie, sleepwear, and gowns. 336-249-4202.

**Newport News Fashions,** Avon Ln., Hampton, VA 23630: Free catalog ◆ Women's swimwear, casual coordinates, shoes, lingerie, sweaters, and sportswear. 800-688-2830.

**North Beach Leather,** 1714 Stockton St., #400, San Francisco, CA 94133: Catalog $3 ◆ Men and women's leather clothing.

**Olive Bette's,** 155 W. 72nd St., Ste. 406, New York, NY 10023: Free catalog ◆ Women's clothing and accessories for relaxed wearing and other occasions. 888-767-8475.

**Olsen's Mill Direct,** 1641 S. Main St., Oshkosh, WI 54901: Catalog $2 ◆ Clothing for men, women, and children. 800-537-4979.

**1-800-Pro Team,** 100 Plaza Dr., Secaucus, NJ 07094: Free catalog ◆ T-shirts, jackets, polos, sweats, authentic licensed teamwear, and more. 800-PRO-TEAM. www.proteam.com

**The Original I. Goldberg,** 902 Chestnut St., Philadelphia, PA 19107: Free catalog ◆ Military surplus merchandise, footwear, clothing, and camping equipment. 215-925-9393.

**Orvis Manchester,** 1711 Blue Hills Dr., P.O. Box 12000, Roanoke, VA 24022: Free catalog ◆ Outdoor clothing, sportswear, lingerie, sweaters, and shoes. 800-541-3541. www.orvis.com

**Orvis Travel,** 1711 Blue Hills Dr., P.O. Box 12000, Roanoke, VA 24022: Free catalog ◆ Luggage, travel accessories, and men and women's clothing. 800-541-3541. www.orvis.com

**Otsuka,** 122 Kentucky St., Petaluma, CA 94952: Free catalog ◆ Classic silk blouses for women. 800-769-4260.

**Barrie Pace Ltd.,** 100 Enterprise Pl., P.O. Box 7020, Dover, DE 19903: Free catalog ◆ Women's fashions. 800-441-6011.

**Pampas by Mail,** 13440 The Square, Poway, CA 92064: Free catalog ◆ Leather vests and jackets for men and women. Also leather skirts for women and belts, eyeglass holders, and other items. 800-722-0094. www.soho.ios.com/~blue1/107

**Pant Warehouse,** 6230 N. Oracle Rd., Tucson, AZ 85704: Catalog $1 (refundable) ◆ Jeans and shirts. 520-797-1455.

**Papillon,** 2025 Concourse Dr., St. Louis, MO 63146: Free catalog ◆ Sportswear and coordinates for women. 800-336-5112.

**PAR FORE,** P.O. Box 502, East Brunswick, NJ 08816: Free catalog ◆ Golf shirts in 100 percent cotton. 908-238-4071.

**Paradise on a Hanger,** 4389 F Rd., Crawford, CO 81415: Free catalog ◆ Hawaiian-style shirts, skirts, shorts, sarongs, and hair schrunchies. 800-921-3050. www.hotshirts.com

**Passport International Ltd.,** 1007 Johhnie Dodds Blvd., Mt. Pleasant, SC 29464: Free catalog ◆ Men and women's clothing and accessories. 800-533-6904.

**Pearl Izumi,** 620 Compton St., Brownfield, CO 80020: Free information ◆ Wind-resistant tights and jerseys with zippers for easy removal of the front panel. 800-877-7080. www.pearlizumi.com

**JCPenney Catalog,** P.O. Box 675, Milwaukee, WI 53201: Free information ◆ Women's work clothing and casual fashions in full-figured and extra-tall sizes. www.jcpenney.com/shopping

**Perlis Clothing,** 6070 Magazine St., New Orleans, LA 70118: Free brochure ◆ Sport shirts, short-sleeve knits, T-shirts, pants and shorts, hats, boxers, beachwear, belts, ties, and clothing. 800-725-6070; 504-895-8661 (in LA). www.perlis.com

**J. Peterman Company,** 1318 Russell Cave Rd., Lexington, KY 40505: Free catalog ◆ Men and women's apparel, accessories, home furnishings, garden items, gifts, footwear, and luggage. 800-231-7341. www.jpeterman.com

**Physique Bodyware,** 16 Birch Hill Dr., Poughkeepsie, NY 12603: Free brochure ◆ Casual style clothing for men and women. 914-471-5227. www.rsn.vh.net/wayneswear

**Porto Banus,** P.O. Box 182209, Chattanooga, TN 37422: Free catalog ◆ All-occasion clothing for women. 800-335-9440.

**Premier Formal Wear,** 8780 Cedar Mills Circle, Memphis, TN 38018: Free information ◆ Men's tuxedos and other formal wear, shirts, jewelry, and accessories. 800-909-9190.

**Quang's Custom Tailoring,** 232 E. Santa Clara St., San Jose, CA 95113: Free information ◆ Custom made tuxedos and other formal wear, suits, jackets, pants, and shirts for men. 408-279-0499.

**Rackes Direct,** 2930 Devine St., Columbia, SC 29205: Free catalog ◆ Women's custom-designed knit and woven career clothing. 800-765-8642; 803-799-8642 (in SC). www.rackes.com

**Anthony Richards,** 6836 Engle Rd., P.O. Box 94503, Cleveland, OH 44101: Free catalog ◆ Women's fashions. 216-826-1712.

**Roadgear Inc.,** 206 W. Elgin Dr., Pueblo West, CO 81007: Catalog $2 ◆ Leather jackets and clothing. 800-854-4327. www.roadgear.com

**Roaman's,** P.O. Box 8360, Indianapolis, IN 46283: Free catalog ◆ Women's casual and career clothing, intimate wear, knits, shoes and boots, sleepwear, and coordinates. 800-436-0800.

**Samuel Robert Direct,** 414 River St., Haverhill, MA 01832: Free catalog ◆ Women's ultrasuede fashions. 800-288-2556.

**Rocky Mountain Connection,** P.O. Box 2800, Estes Park, CO 80517: Catalog $1 (specify type of items wanted) ◆ Outdoor and western-style clothing, Boy Scouts clothing and outdoor gear, hiking staffs, backpacks, and more. 800-679-3600. www.RMConnection.com

**Saddle USA Inc.,** 49 W. 37th St., New York, NY 10018: Free brochure ◆ Authentic-style leather flight jackets. 212-768-8683.

**Saint Laurie Ltd.,** 895 Broadway, New York, NY 10003: Catalog $2 ◆ Hand-tailored clothing. 212-473-0100.

**Scott-Wynne Outfitters,** 10000 Research Blvd., Ste. 127, Austin, TX 78759: Free catalog ◆ Outdoor and casual clothing, luggage, hunting and fishing accessories, and Native American jewelry. 800-232-2783. www.outfits.com

**Scotland by the Yard,** Rt. 4, Quechee, VT 05059: Free brochure ◆ Classic clothing, sweaters, gifts and jewelry, ties, and scarves from Scotland. 802-295-5351.

**Serengeti,** P.O. Box 3349, Serengeti Park, Chelmsford, MA 01824: Free catalog ◆ Wildlife-theme apparel and gifts. 800-426-2852.

**The Short Shop,** 49 Kearny St., San Francisco, CA 94108: Free brochure ◆ Suits, sport coats, slacks, sport shirts, dress shirts, casual pants and jeans, sweaters, jackets, pajamas, robes, ties, socks, and tuxedos and tux shirts in extra-short, 34 to 46; portly extra-short, 40 to 46; short, 35 to 48; and portly short, 42 to 52. 800-233-9522; 415-296-9744 (in CA). www.shortshop.com

**Sickafus Sheepskins,** Rt. 78 & 183, Strausstown, PA 19559: Free catalog ◆ Sheepskin clothing. 610-488-1782.

**Siegel's Clothing Superstore,** 2366 Mission St., San Francisco, CA 94110: Free information ◆ Suits, shirts, slacks, jeans, leather jackets, casual jackets, tuxedos, topcoats, work boots, sport coats, work clothes, socks, underwear, and men's and boy's accessories, in sizes from toddler 2 to men's size 62 long. 800-408-8933; 415-824-7729 (in CA). www.zootsuitstore.com

**Ben Silver,** 149 King St., Charleston, SC 29401: Free catalog ◆ Blazer buttons with school designs and monograms, cuff links, suspenders, breast patches, blazers, cotton sweats, neckties, shirts, and trousers. 800-849-0973. www.bensilver.com

**Joshua Simon Women's Clothing,** 3915 24th St., San Francisco CA 94114: Free catalog ◆ Loose-fitting clothing. 415-821-1068.

**Simply Divine-All Cotton Clothing,** 1606 S. Congress, Austin, TX 78704: Catalog $1 ◆ All-cotton clothing for women, infants, and children. 512-444-5546.

**Simply Tops,** 7 Avery Row, Roanoke, VA 24012: Free catalog ◆ Tops, casuals, sweaters, jackets, evening attire, lingerie, and other women's fashions. 800-624-5636.

**Smith & Hawken,** P.O. Box 6907, Florence, KY 41022: Free catalog ◆ Casual clothing for men and women. 800-776-3336. www.smith-hawken.com

**Special Clothes Inc.,** P.O. Box 333, East Harwich, MA 02645: Catalog $1 ◆ Undergarments and sleepwear for adults. 508-896-7939. www.Special-Clothes.com

**Spiegel,** P.O. Box 182563, Columbus, OH 43218: Free catalog ◆ Fashions for African-American women. 800-345-4500. www.spiegel.com

**Spike Nashbar Outlet Store,** 4111 Simon Rd., Youngstown, OH 44512: Free catalog ◆ Sports clothing and equipment, bags, books and videos, and protective wear. 800-774-5348. www.nashbar.com

**George Stafford & Sons,** P.O. Box 2055, Thomasville, GA 31799: Free catalog ◆ Men and women's sportswear, casual fashions, and shoes. 800-826-0948.

**Stocks Clothing,** 2736 Erie Ave., Cincinnati, OH 45208: Free information ◆ Custom to casual clothing for men. 513-321-8776.

**Stonewear Designs,** 2697 S. Deframe Circle, Lakewood, CO 80228: Free catalog ◆ Tops, bottoms and tops, and activewear for women. 303-989-2082.

**Swim 'n Sport,** 2396 NW 96th Ave., Miami, FL 33172: Free catalog ◆ Swim wear for women. 800-497-2111.

**Talbots,** 175 Beal St., Hingham, MA 02043: Free catalog ◆ Women's clothing and coordinates. 800-825-2687.

**Ann Taylor,** P.O. Box 1304, New Haven, CT 06505: Free catalog ◆ Women's career, casual, and dress-up fashions. 800-825-6250.

**Team Cheer,** By Swain Ski & Sport, 131 Main St., Geneseo, NY 14454: Free catalog ◆ Warm-ups, cheerleader outfits, camp wear, clothing, and accessories. 800-350-1562.

**Thai Silks,** 252 State St., Los Altos, CA 94022: Free brochure ◆ Silk clothing and fabrics. 800-722-SILK; 800-722-SILK; 650-948-8611 (in CA). www.thaisilks.com

**Norm Thompson,** P.O. Box 3999, Portland, OR 97208: Free catalog ◆ Men and women's clothing and gifts. 800-821-1287. www.normthompson.com

**Thousand Mile Outdoor Wear,** 1894 Alta Vista Dr., Vista, CA 92084: Free catalog ◆ Men and women's outdoor clothing. 800-786-7577; 760-945-1609 (in CA).

**Tiburon,** P.O. Box 737, Naugatuck, CT 06770: Free catalog ◆ Pre-shrunk and washable fashions for women. 800-279-2917. tiburon@goldmtn.com

**Tilley Endurables,** 300 Lagner Rd., West Seneca, NY 14224: Free catalog ◆ Clothing for travelers with security and secret pockets for theft protection. 800-884-3086. www.tilley.com

**Title 9 Sports,** 5743 Landregan St., Emeryville, CA 94608: Free catalog ◆ Women's clothing created by and for women. 510-655-5999. thefolks@title9sports.com

**The Tog Shop,** Lester Square, Americus, GA 31710: Free catalog ◆ Women's jump suits, shirts, outerwear, skirts and blouses, sleepwear, swimwear, and shoes and sandals. 800-342-6789.

**Touch of Class Catalog,** 1905 N. Van Buren St., Huntingburg, IN 47542: Free catalog ◆ Bathroom accessories, comforters, pillows, shams, window treatments, towels, rugs, and sleepwear for men, women, and children. 800-457-7456.

**Trifles,** P.O. Box 620048, Dallas, TX 75262: Free catalog ◆ Clothing and jewelry for men, women, and children. 800-456-7019.

**Tuttle Golf Collection,** P.O. Box 888, Wallingford, CT 06492: Free catalog ◆ Sportswear for men and women. 800-882-7511.

**2BU Wear USA,** 395 S. Van Ness, San Francisco, CA 04103: Free catalog ◆ Leather jackets and button fly trousers. 415-864-2203.

**Jennifer Tyler Cashmeres Etc.,** 1160 Kane Concourse, Ste. 305, Bay Harbor Islands, FL 33154: Free catalog ◆ Classic, tailored, and hand-knitted cashmeres. Also home accessories and gifts. 800-441-7743.

**The Ujena Company,** 235 W. Evelyn Ave., Mountain View, CA 94041: Catalog $2 ◆ Women's swimwear and sportswear. 800-256-8347. www.ujena.com

**The Ultimate Outlet,** P.O. Box 6105, Rapid City, SD 57709: Free catalog ◆ Women's fashions, home furnishings, and accessories. 800-332-6000.

**Undergear,** Order Processing Center, Hanover, PA 17333: Free catalog ◆ Men's clothing and underwear. 800-853-8555.

**Urban Safari Wear,** 12021 Wilshire Blvd., Ste. 792, Los Angeles, CA 90025: Free catalog ◆ Safari/adventure wear and travel accessories for men and women. 800-217-3321; 310-828-3321 (in CA). www.urbansafariwear.com

**US ABE,** 807 E. Carson St., Pittsburgh, PA 15203: Free catalog ◆ Work and casual clothing, boots, shoes, and athletic footwear. 412-431-8861.

**US Authentic Mfg. Company,** P.O. Box 51, Goldens Bridge, NY 10526: Free information ◆ Authentic leather flight jackets with army and navy specifications. 888-777-5433. www.usauthentic.com

**USA FOXX & Furs,** 29 W. Superior St., Duluth, MN 55802: Free catalog ◆ Custom-made fur hats, blankets, mittens, jackets, belts and more. 800-USA-FOXX; 218-722-7742 (in MN). www.usafoxx.com

**The Very Thing,** One Winterbrook Way, P.O. Box 3005, Meredith, NH 03253: Free catalog ◆ Women's clothing. 800-642-0001.

**Victoria's Secret,** North American Office, P.O. Box 16589, Columbus, OH 43216: Free catalog ◆ Women's clothing, lingerie, sleepwear, slippers, and gifts. 800-888-8200.

**Visabella,** P.O. Box 526139, Salt Lake City, UT 84152: Free catalog ◆ Silk and velvet clothing in timeless styles for men and women. 800-474-9567.

**Walrus Inc.,** P.O. Box 81227, Seattle, WA 98108: Free information ◆ Outerwear. 800-550-8368. www.lowealpine.com

**Watkins Aviation Inc.,** 15770 Midway Rd., Hanger #6, Dallas, TX 75244: Free information ◆ United States military and civilian flight clothing. 972-934-0033.

**WearGuard Corp.,** 141 Longwater Dr., Norwell, MA 02061: Free catalog ◆ Clothing for the working man and woman. 800-388-3300.

**What on Earth,** 2451 Enterprise East Pkwy., Twinsburg, OH 44087: Free catalog ◆ Silk-screened T-shirts, casual apparel, and gifts. 800-945-2552.

**Whipp Trading Company,** RR 1, Arrasmith Trail, Ames, IA 50010: Free catalog ◆ Sheepskin rugs, slippers, mittens, and hats. 800-533-9447.

**Wild Man Crowley,** 151 Main St., Danielson, CT 06239: Free catalog ◆ Outdoor and casual clothing for men and women. 800-860-1707.

**Willis & Geiger Outfitters,** 1902 Explorers Trail, Reedsburg, WI 53959: Free catalog ◆ Outdoor clothing and field gear for men. 800-223-1408.

**Willow Ridge,** 421 Landmark Dr., Wilmington, NC 28410: Free catalog ◆ Women's career, dress-up, and casual clothing. 800-388-2012.

**Windjammer,** 525 N. Main St., Bangor, PA 18013: Free information ◆ Jackets, shirts, T-shirts, sweat suits, and sportswear. 800-441-6958; 610-588-0626 (in PA).

**Wintergreen North Woods Apparel,** 205 E. Sheridan, Ely, MN 55731: Free catalog ◆ Outdoor winter clothing for men, women, and children. 800-584-9425. www.wintergreen.org

**WinterSilks,** 2700 Laura Ln., P.O. Box 620130, Middleton, WI 53562: Free catalog ◆ Silk turtlenecks, socks, glove liners, long johns, and ski clothing. 800-621-3229. www.wintersilks.com

**Wissota Trader,** 1313 1st Ave., Chippewa Falls, WI 54729: Free catalog ◆ Women and men's clothing and shoes in hard-to-fit sizes. 800-833-6421.

**WorkAbles for Women,** 96 Combs Rd., Clinton, PA 15026: Free catalog ◆ Gloves, hats, T-shirts, socks, outdoor clothing, rain gear, and personal safety items for women. 800-862-9317.

**Worldwide Aquatics,** 10500 University Center Dr., Tampa, FL 33612: Free catalog ◆ Swimwear and accessories for men and women. 800-726-1530.

## Natural Fiber Clothing

**Garnet Hill,** 231 Main St., Franconia, NH 03580: Free catalog ◆ Clothing, bed linens, comforters, blankets, pillows, pillow shams, and towels. 800-622-6216.

**JANICE Corp.,** 198 Hwy. 46, Budd Lake, NJ 07828: Free catalog ◆ Allergy-free clothing, exercise wear, sleepwear, robes, towels, bath and personal grooming aids, and mattresses, pads, quilts, and linens. 800-JANICES.

**Making It Big,** 501 Aaron St., Cotati, CA 94931: Free catalog ◆ Natural fiber clothing for large and supersize women. 707-795-1995. www.bigwomen.com

**Natural Lifestyle,** 16 Lookout Dr., Asheville, NC 28804: Free catalog ◆ Water filters, organic foods, macrobiotic specialties, cookware, organic cotton clothes, earth care products, and cookbooks. 704-254-9606.

**Red Rose Collection,** P.O. Box 280140, San Francisco, CA 94128: Free catalog ◆ Natural fiber clothing, books and tapes, art works, jewelry, tools, games, decorative accessories, and toiletries. 800-374-5505.

**Vermont Country Store,** Mail Order Office, P.O. Box 3000, Manchester Center, VT 05255: Free catalog ◆ Clothing and household items. 802-362-4667.

**Wildrose Farm,** HCR 2, Box 33, Breezy Point, MN 56472: Free catalog ◆ Natural fiber clothing in hand-dyed colors. 218-562-4864. www.uslink.net/~knierim

## Petite Fashions

**Sue Brett,** P.O. Box 8384, Indianapolis, IN 46283: Free catalog ◆ Women's clothing in sizes 8 to 24. Also petite and tall sizes. 800-784-8001.

**Draper's & Damon's,** 17911 Mitchell Ave. South, Irvine, CA 92714: Free catalog ◆ Women's fashions for misses, petites, and regular sizes. 800-843-1174. www.Drapers.com

**Jean Grayson's Brownstone Studio Collection,** P.O. Box 25367, Shawnee Mission, KS 66225: Free catalog ◆ Fashions for misses and petites. 800-322-2991.

**The Horchow Collection,** P.O. Box 620048, Dallas, TX 75262: Free catalog ◆ Petite women's clothing. 800-395-5397. www.neimanmarcus.com

**J. Jill,** P.O. Box 3006, One Winterbrook Way, Meredith, NH 03253: Free catalog ◆ Women's fashions in misses, petite, and other sizes. 800-642-9989.

**Old Pueblo Traders,** Palo Verde at 34th, P.O. Box 27800, Tucson, AZ 85726: Free catalog ◆ Dresses, casual fashions, coordinates, outerwear, shoes, lingerie, and sweaters in petite sizes. 520-748-8600.

**Papillon,** 2025 Concourse Dr., St. Louis, MO 63146: Free catalog ◆ Sportswear and coordinates for misses and petites. 800-336-5112.

**JCPenney Catalog,** P.O. Box 675, Milwaukee, WI 53201: Free information ◆ Sportswear, casual fashions, and petite and misses clothing for brides and attendants. 800-222-6161. www.jcpenney.com/shopping

**Petite Ms,** 555 Perkins Extd., Memphis, TN 38117: Catalog $2 ◆ Clothing for women 5'4" and under, sizes 2 to 16. 901-767-3183.

**Plus Size Designer Outlet,** 6784 Depot St., Sebastopol, CA 95472: Free catalog ◆ Women's fashions for petites. 800-498-3294; 707-824-1634 (in CA).

**Plus Woman,** 85 Laurel Haven, Fairview, NC 28730: Free catalog ◆ Super size ladies clothing. Also large petite and tall sizes. 800-628-5525. www.pluswoman.com

**Ulla Popken Clothing,** 12201 Long Green Pike, Glen Arm, MD 21057: Free catalog ◆ Style-conscious clothing for women, sizes 12 through 30. Includes some items in petite sizes. 800-245-8552. www.ullapopken.com

**Spiegel,** P.O. Box 182563, Columbus, OH 43218: Free catalog ◆ Career and weekend fashions for women under 5'4". 800-345-4500. www.spiegel.com

**Talbots,** 175 Beal St., Hingham, MA 02043: Free catalog ◆ Clothing for petite women. 800-825-2687.

**Unique Petite,** Palo Verde at 34th, P.O. Box 27800, Tucson, AZ 85726: Free catalog ◆ Sweaters, jeans, swimwear, and fashions for women 5'4" and under. Also shoes in hard-to-fit sizes. 520-748-8600.

## Scarves & Capes

**Alberene Scottish Cashmeres,** 435 5th Ave., New York, NY 10016: Free catalog ◆ Sweaters, capes, and scarves in 100 percent Scottish cashmere. 800-566-6817. www.scottishcashmere.com

**Casco Bay Fine Woolens,** 34 Danforth St., Portland, ME 04101: Free brochure ◆ Handcrafted wool capes. 800-788-9842. www.cascobaywoolworks.com

**Scotland by the Yard,** Rt. 4, Quechee, VT 05059: Free brochure ◆ Classic clothing, sweaters, gifts and jewelry, ties, and scarves from Scotland. 802-295-5351.

## Shirts

**Ascot Chang,** A Gentlemen's Shirtmaker, 7 W. 57th St., New York, NY 10019: Free information ◆ Custom-made shirts. 800-486-9966.

**Burberry's Limited,** 9 E. 57th St., New York, NY 10022: Free list of retail sources ◆ Burberry's classic cotton shirts. 212-371-5010.

**The Custom Shop,** 402-412 Rt. 23, Franklin, NJ 07416: Free list of retail sources ◆ Handcrafted custom-made shirts for men.

**Paul Frederick Shirt Company,** 223 W. Poplar St., Fleetwood, PA 19522: Free catalog ◆ Men's shirts with French cut, button-down, tab or straight collars, and French or button cuffs. 800-247-8162. www.menstyle.com

**Huntington Clothiers,** 1285 Alum Creek Dr., Columbus, OH 43209: Free catalog ◆ Men's shirts with optional monograms. 800-848-6203. shirts@hclothiers.com

**JCPenney Catalog,** P.O. Box 675, Milwaukee, WI 53201: Free information ◆ Shirts for men in regular, extra tall, and large sizes. Also ties and accessories. 800-222-6161. www.jcpenney.com/shopping

**The Queensboro Shirt Company,** 1400 Marstellar St., Wilmington, NC 28401: Free brochure ◆ Custom-embroidered clothing in 100 percent cotton. 800-847-4478; 910-251-1251 (in NC).

**Tilley Endurables,** 300 Lagner Rd., West Seneca, NY 14224: Free catalog ◆ Cotton hooded shirts. 800-884-3086. www.tilley.com

**Treadwell Shirt Company,** P.O. Box 667, Hartwell, GA 30643: Free brochure ◆ Cotton shirts for men. 800-367-7158.

## Short Men

**Bills Khakis,** 529 Court St., Reading, PA 19601: Free catalog ◆ Khaki clothing for short men. 800-43-KHAKI. www.billskhakis.com

**Muldoon's Men's Wear Inc.,** 1506 S. Hastings Way, Eau Claire, WI 54701: Free brochure ◆ Clothing in regular, big, tall, short, and small sizes. 800-942-0783.

**The Short Shop,** 49 Kearny St., San Francisco, CA 94108: Free information ◆ Suits, sport coats, slacks, sport shirts, dress shirts, casual pants and jeans, sweaters, jackets, pajamas, robes, ties, socks, and tuxedos and tux shirts in extra-short, 34 to 46; portly extra-short, 40 to 46; short, 35 to 48; and portly short, 42 to 52. 800-233-9522; 415-296-9744 (in CA). www.shortshop.com

**Bob Stern's Short Sizes Inc.,** 5385 Warrensville Center Rd., Cleveland, OH 44137: Free information ◆ Clothing for men under 5'8" 216-475-2515. www.shortsizesinc.com

## Special-Needs Clothing

**Caring Concepts,** 315 Tucapau Rd., Duncan, SC 29334: Free catalog ◆ Clothing for persons that need assistive care. 800-500-0260. www.caringconcepts.com

**Creative Designs,** 3704 Carlisle Ct., Modesto, CA 95356: Free brochure ◆ Specially designed robe for wheelchair users and others with physical disabilities. 800-355-4852; 209-523-3166 (in CA). www.sonnet.com/dws/handi.html

**Danmar Products Inc.,** 221 Jackson Industrial Dr., Ann Arbor, MI 48103: Free catalog ◆ Special-needs clothing. 800-783-1998; 313-761-1990 (in MI).

**Fashion Ease,** Division M & M Health Care, 1541 60th St., Brooklyn, NY 11219: Free catalog ◆ Special-needs clothing and accessories. 800-221-8929; 718-871-8188 (in NY). www.fashionease.com

**Just For You Fashions,** 810 Busch St., Columbus, OH 43229: Free catalog ◆ Men and women's special-needs clothing and accessories for walkers and wheelchairs. 800-445-8474; 614-846-6133 (in OH).

**Mamie's Gracious Living Apparel,** 1313 E. Duke St., Ste. C, Sutherlin, OR 97479: Free catalog ◆ Special clothes for special people. 888-92-MAMIES.

**Rolli-Moden Designs,** 12225 World Trade Dr., San Diego, CA 92128: Free catalog ◆ Contemporary fashions for people in wheelchairs. 800-707-2395. www.rolli-moden.com

**Specially for You,** P.O. Box 272, Willlow Lake, SD 57278: Free catalog ◆ Clothing for the physically challenged. 605-625-3765.

**Support Plus,** Box 500, Medfield, MA 02052: Free catalog ◆ Medically acceptable support hosiery, personal hygiene and home health care aids, bath safety accessories, and walking shoes. 800-229-2910.

**U.S.A. Jeans,** 1422 N. Utica, Tulsa, OK 74110: Free brochure ◆ Heavy weight soft denim jeans for men and women in wheelchairs. 800-935-5170. www.usajeans.net

**Wardrobe Wagon,** Special Needs Clothing Store, 555 Valley Rd., West Orange, NJ 07052: Free catalog ◆ Special-needs clothing. 800-992-2737.

**Worldwide Home Health Center Inc.,** 926 E. Tallmadge Ave., Akron, OH 44310: Free catalog ◆ Ostomy appliances, mastectomy breast forms, special-needs clothing, and skin care products. 800-223-5938; 330-633-0366 (in OH).

## Suspenders, Belts, & Buckles

**Buckles Unlimited,** Box 196, Winthrop, AR 71866: Free catalog ◆ Belt buckles, belts, money clips, key chains, hat tacks, tie bars, and other coin jewelry. 501-381-7891.

**Caballo,** 727 Canyon Rd., Santa Fe, NM 87501: Catalog $1 (refundable) ◆ Handmade leather belts. 800-359-4174.

**Comstock Silversmiths,** 2300 Lockheed Way, Carson City, NV 89706: Free list of retail sources ◆ Silver belt buckles, pins, and jewelry. 702-882-8500.

**Drysdales,** 1555 N. 107th East Ave., Tulsa, OK 74116: Free catalog ◆ Western-style belts and buckles for adults and children. 800-444-6481. www.drysdales.com

**L.M. Easterling Custom Boots,** 215 W. Maine St., Fredericksburg, TX 78624: Catalog $1 ◆ Handmade boots and belts. 888-811-8980.

**Eloxite Corp.,** P.O. Box 729, Wheatland, WY 82201: Catalog $1 ◆ Belt buckles, tools, gemstones, jewelry mountings, and clock-making, rockhounding, and jewelry-making supplies. 307-322-3050. www.eloxite.com

**Hay Charlie,** 541 Historic Main St., Park City, UT 84060: Free information ◆ Handcrafted western-style boots, buckles and belts, hats, jewelry, clothing, and accessories.

**Heart & Sew,** P.O. Box 421, Kennebunk, ME 04043: Free information ◆ Custom made bow ties and suspenders.

**Jesser's Classic Keys,** 26 West St., Akron, OH 44303: Free information ◆ Western style 18k gold plated belt buckles with a choice of 100 different emblems to match cars, trucks, or motorcycles. 330-376-8181.

**Johnston & Murphy,** Mail Order Shop, 1415 Murfreesboro Rd., Ste. 190, Nashville, TN 37217: Free catalog ◆ Men's shoes, socks, belts, and accessories. 800-424-2854. www.johnstonmurphy.com

**Lifton Studio Inc.,** 121 S. 6th St., Stillwater, MN 55082: Catalog $5 ◆ Buckles, leather belts, trophy buckles, and reproductions of Old West badges in sterling silver. 612-439-7208.

**David Morgan,** 11812 Northcreek Pkwy., Ste. 103, Bothell, WA 98011: Free catalog ◆ Hand-braided belts, wool and sheepskin clothing, and hats. 800-324-4934. www.davidmorgan.com

**Bernard Myles Jewelry,** 1605 S. 7th St., Terre Haute, IN 47802: Catalog $1 ◆ Coin jewelry, belt buckles, tie-tacks, key chains, bolo ties, money clips, and other items. 812-232-4405.

**Naples Creek Leather,** 188 S. Main St., Naples, NY 14512: Free catalog ◆ Leather moccasins, slippers, belts, gloves, casual footwear, and deerskin handbags. 800-836-0616.

**R.T's Custom Leather & Silver,** Box 1, Raymond, CA 93653: Catalog $3 ◆ Hand-tooled cowboy belts with optional personalization. 209-675-9518.

**Wage's Silversmiths,** 1598-C S. Anaheim Blvd., Anaheim, CA 92805: Free list of retail sources ◆ Silver belt buckles, money clips, saddle trim, card cases, bracelets, and other accessories. 800-621-8077; 800-327-2214 (in CA).

## Sweaters

**Henri Bendel,** 712 5th Ave., New York, NY 10019: Free information ◆ Casual, outdoor, and dress sweaters for women. 212-247-1100.

**BJ & Friends,** Susan K. Stone, 2061 St. Andrews Dr., Berwyn, PA 19312: Free brochure ◆ Handcrafted sweaters for children, dolls, and dogs. 610-640-0479.

**J. Crew Outfitters,** One Ivy Crescent, Lynchburg, VA 24513: Free catalog ◆ Mock turtlenecks, cardigans, button-down, and other sweaters for men and women. 800-932-0043. www.jcrew.com

**Garnet Hill,** 231 Main St., Franconia, NH 03580: Free catalog ◆ Cashmere sweaters. 800-622-6216.

**Johnson Woolen Mills Inc.,** P.O. Box 12, Johnson, VT 05656: Free brochure ◆ Woolen outerwear for men, women, and children. Also blankets, underwear, and sweaters. 802-635-2271.

**Landau Woolens,** 102 Nassau St., Princeton, NJ 08542: Free catalog ◆ Men and women's hand-knitted wool sweaters, Icelandic wool coats and jackets, blanket throws, wool sportswear, shirts, and cotton knits. 800-257-9445.

**Lion's Pride Catalog,** P.O. Box 342, Little Chute, WI 54140: Free catalog ◆ Cotton knit sweaters and clothing for big and tall men. 414-731-4242.

**The Nordic Shop,** 201 Centerplace Pavilion, Rochester, MN 55904: Free brochure ◆ Sweaters and Scandinavian gifts. 800-282-NORD. TNordShop@aol.com

**Scotland by the Yard,** Rt. 4, Quechee, VT 05059: Free brochure ◆ Classic clothing, sweaters, gifts and jewelry, ties, and scarves from Scotland. 802-295-5351.

**Jennifer Tyler Cashmeres Etc.,** 1160 Kane Concourse, Ste. 305, Bay Harbor Islands, FL 33154: Free catalog ◆ Cashmere sweaters for men and women. 800-441-7743.

**Wanderings Inc.,** P.O. Box 4344, Warren, NJ 07059: Free catalog ◆ Hand-knitted wool sweaters and special occasion gifts. 800-456-KNIT.

**Winona,** P.O. Box 5400, 1200 Storr's Pond Rd., Winona, MN 55987: Free catalog ◆ Sweaters for men and women. 800-994-6662. www.winona.com

**WinterSilks,** 2700 Laura Ln., P.O. Box 620130, Middleton, WI 53562: Free catalog ◆ Turtlenecks, sweaters, silk long johns, and other fashions. 800-621-3229. www.wintersilks.com

## Tall & Big Men's Clothing

**L.L. Bean,** Casco St., Freeport, ME 04032: Free catalog ◆ Outdoor clothing and sportswear for tall men. 800-221-4221. www.llbean.com

**Bud's Men's Shop,** 2811 50th St., Lubbock TX 79413: Free information ◆ Clothing for big and tall men in regular, long, extra-long, short, and portly sizes. 888-800-2837.

**Casual Male Big & Tall,** P.O. Box 709, Addison, IL 60101: Free list of retail sources ◆ Clothing for big and tall men. 800-THINK-BIG.

**Congress Men's Shop,** 2400 Massachusetts Ave., Cambridge, MA 02140: Free information ◆ Clothing for big and tall men, with emphasis on larger sizes. 617-547-3775.

**Drysdales,** 1555 N. 107th East Ave., Tulsa, OK 74116: Free catalog ◆ Outerwear and western-style shirts, in sizes medium to 6XL and XLT to 3XLT. 800-444-6481. www.drysdales.com

**King Size Company,** P.O. Box 8385, Indianapolis, IN 46283: Free catalog ◆ Tall and big men's clothing. 800-846-1600. www.kingsizemen.com

**Lion's Pride Catalog,** P.O. Box 342, Little Chute, WI 54140: Free catalog ◆ Recycled cotton knit sweaters and clothing for big and tall men. 414-731-4242.

**JCPenney Catalog,** P.O. Box 675, Milwaukee, WI 53201: Free information ◆ Shirts, pants, and clothing. 800-222-6161. www.jcpenney.com/shopping

**Muldoon's Men's Wear Inc.,** 1506 S. Hastings Way, Eau Claire, WI 54701: Free brochure ◆ Clothing in regular, big, tall, short, and small sizes. 800-942-0783.

**Repp Big & Tall,** 1492 Bluegrass Lakes Pkwy., Alpharetta, GA 30004: Free catalog ◆ Tall and big men's clothing. 800-690-7377. www.reppltd.com

**Rochester Big & Tall,** 1301 Ave. of Americas, New York, NY 10019: Free catalog ◆ Tall and big men's clothing. 800-282-8200.

**Sheplers,** P.O. Box 7702, Wichita, KS 67277: Free catalog ◆ Western clothing for tall men. 800-242-6540.

**I. Spiewak & Sons Inc.,** 469 7th Ave., 10th Floor, New York, NY 10018: Free brochure ◆ Outerwear for men, sizes 6X to XXXXLT. 800-223-6850; 212-695-1620 (in NY). www.spiewak.com

**US ABE Clothing,** 807 E. Carson St., Pittsburgh, PA 15203: Free catalog ◆ Uniforms, work attire, and casual clothing for big and tall men. 412-431-8861.

## Tall Women's Clothing

**L.L. Bean,** Casco St., Freeport, ME 04032: Free catalog ◆ Outdoor clothing and sportswear for tall women. 800-221-4221. www.llbean.com

**Sue Brett,** P.O. Box 8384, Indianapolis, IN 46283: Free catalog ◆ Women's clothing in sizes 8 to 24, petite and tall sizes. 800-784-8001.

**Lane Bryant,** P.O. Box 8301, Indianapolis, IN 46283: Free catalog ◆ Clothing for tall women. 800-477-7030.

**Gander Mountain (Cabela's),** One Cabela Dr., Sidney, ME 69160: Free catalog ◆ Clothing for tall women. 800-237-4444. www.cabelas.com

**Long Elegant Legs,** 5 Homestead Rd., Ste. 9, Belle Mead, NJ 08502: Free brochure ◆ Fashionable clothing for tall women. 800-344-2235.

**Newport News Fashions,** Avon Ln., Hampton, VA 23630: Free catalog ◆ Fashions for tall women. 800-688-2830.

**Old Pueblo Traders,** Palo Verde at 34th, P.O. Box 27800, Tucson, AZ 85726: Free catalog ◆ Fashions for women, 5'7" and taller. 520-748-8600.

**JCPenney Catalog,** P.O. Box 675, Milwaukee, WI 53201: Free information ◆ Sportswear and casual fashions. 800-222-6161. www.jcpenney.com/shopping

**Plus Size Designer Outlet,** 6784 Depot St., Sebastopol, CA 95472: Free catalog ◆ Tall women's fashions. 800-498-3294; 707-824-1634 (in CA).

**Plus Woman,** 85 Laurel Haven, Fairview, NC 28730: Free catalog ◆ Super size ladies clothing. Also large petitie and tall sizes. 800-628-5525. www.pluswoman.com

**Spiegel,** P.O. Box 182563, Columbus, OH 43218: Free catalog ◆ Clothing for tall women. 800-345-4500. www.spiegel.com

**Statuesque,** 2225 S. University Dr., Davie, FL 33324: Free catalog ◆ Fashion footwear in sizes 9½ to 14. Also tall fashions. 800-367-7167.

**Tallclassics,** 12680 Shawnee Mission Pkwy., Shawnee Mission, KS 66216: Free catalog ◆ Clothing for women 5'10" and taller. 800-345-1958. www.tallclassics.com

## T-Shirts & Sweatshirts

**Allen-Lewis Manufacturing Company,** P.O. Box 16546, Denver, CO 80216: Free catalog ◆ Souvenirs, carnival and party supplies, fund-raising merchandise, toys and games, T-shirts and sweatshirts, and craft supplies. 800-525-6658.

**Ande Inc.,** 1310 53rd St., West Palm Beach, FL 33407: Free brochure ◆ T-shirts for fishing enthusiasts. 561-842-2474.

**Art-Wear,** P.O. Box 691, New Cumberland, PA 17070: Free brochure ◆ Comical T-shirts and sweatshirts. 800-543-0431; 717-774-7080 (in PA).

**Artrock Posters,** 1153 Mission St., San Francisco, CA 94103: Free catalog ◆ T-shirts, embroidered shirts, one-size hats for all heads, and belt buckles. 415-255-7390.

**Aussie Connection,** 135 NE 3rd Ave., Hillsboro, OR 97124: Free catalog ◆ "Down Under" T-shirts in medium, large, extra-large, and extra-extra-large. 800-950-2668. aussco@teleport.com

**Big Dog Sportswear,** Mail Order Dept., 121 Gray Ave., Santa Barbara, CA 93101: Free catalog ◆ Lounge wear for women, boxer shorts for men, and men and women's outerwear, T-shirts, and sweatshirts. 800-642-3647. www.BIGDOGS.com

**Caledonian Graphics,** 1516 Sydney Hill Rd., Plant City, FL 33567: Free catalog ◆ Skydiving-theme T-shirts. 813-752-0300.

**California T's,** 1611 University, Lubbock, TX 79401: Free information ◆ T-shirts with unique sayings. 800-658-6697.

**CCS Skateboards,** 2701 McMillan Ave., San Luis Obispo, CA 93401: Free catalog ◆ T-shirts, shoes, stickers, skateboards and parts, and safety gear. 800-477-9283.

**Christian Book Distributors,** P.O. Box 7000, Peabody, MA 01961: Free catalog ◆ Religious-theme T-shirts in small, medium, large, extra-large, and extra-extra-large. 978-977-5050. www.chrbook.com

**Christian T-Shirts,** Ally & Sons Inc., 1101 NW 17th St., Fort Lauderdale, FL 33311: Free information ◆ Religious T-shirts. 954-584-2708.

**Computer Gear,** 4028 148th Ave. NE, Redmond, WA 98052: Free catalog ◆ T-shirts and other gifts with a computer theme and graphics. 800-373-6353. www.computergear.com

**CongoGear,** P.O. Box 6433, Springfield, VA 22150: Free information ◆ Full-size pre-shrunk 100 percent cotton T-shirts, sweatshirts, and caps with original designs. 703-690-7312.

**Dallas Alice,** 8001 Cessna Ave., Ste. 203, Gaithersburg, MD 20879: Free catalog ◆ Silk-screened T-shirts. 301-948-0400.

**Daydreams Stencil Company,** P.O. Box 65, Oregon, WI 53575: Catalog $3 ◆ Heavyweight T-shirts with a choice of folk-art designs. 608-873-3399.

**007 Internet Services,** 832 NE 206 St., North Miami Beach, FL 33179: Free information ◆ T-shirts with vibrant pictures and slogans. 305-654-1399.

**EarthSHIRTZ,** Box 827, Shady Cove, OR 97539: Free catalog ◆ Original T-shirts for adults and youths. 800-845-3469. mind.net/darnell

**Eastern Emblem,** Box 828, Union City, NJ 07087: Free catalog ◆ T-shirts, jackets, patches, cloisonne pins, decals, and stickers. 800-344-5112.

**Floyd's Record Shop,** P.O. Drawer 10, Ville Platte, LA 70586: Catalog $1 (refundable) ◆ Cajun and Creole music, books, videos, and T-shirts. 318-363-2184. www.floydsrecords.com

**Frosty Little,** 222 E. 8th St., Burley, ID 83318: Free information ◆ Sweatshirts, T-shirts, pins, and patches with clown graphics. 208-678-0005.

**FTC Ski & Sports,** 1586 Bush St., San Francisco, CA 94109: Free catalog ◆ Skateboards and parts, snowboards, T-shirts, and clothing. 415-673-8363.

**Genius T-Shirts,** America's T-Shirt Catalog, 546 S. Meridian St., Ste. 205, Indianapolis, IN 46225: Free information ◆ Artistic and scholarly T-shirts and sweatshirts, painted with historical and enigmatic quotations. 800-259-SAVE; 317-321-9999 (in IN).

**Goose & Gander Country Gift Shop,** 6483 E. Seneca Tnpk., Jamesville, NY 13078: Free information ◆ Women's Battenburg-inlay and collar T-shirts, applique sweatshirts, and Battenburg lace collar cardigans. 315-492-1266.

**Hard Times Cafe,** 310 Commerce St., Alexandria, VA 22314: Free brochure ◆ Aprons, T-shirts, and sweatshirts. 703-836-7449. www.hardtimes.com

**Hound Dog Fashions,** Box 2525, Winnipeg, Manitoba, Canada R3C 4AZ: Free catalog ◆ T-shirts and sweatshirts featuring 70 different breeds of dogs and cats. 800-667-4957.

**Hugger-Mugger Yoga Products,** 31 W. Gregson Ave., Salt Lake City, UT 84115: Free catalog ◆ Yoga-inspired T-shirts and sweatshirts in medium, large, and extra-large. 800-473-4888; 801-487-4888 (in CA).

**JasMar Fashion Designs Inc.,** P.O. Box 4401, Edmonton, Alberta, Canada T6E 4T5: Free brochure ◆ Men and women's underwear and lingerie, T-shirts, and swimwear. 403-413-9867. jasmar@jasmar.com

**Katie's Kid's Gear,** c/o Aquarian Resources, P.O. Box 9341, Tyler, TX 75711: Free information ◆ Hand-embroidered and appliqued T-shirts for children.

**Kountry Kloset T-shirts,** 676 State Rd., Plymouth, MA 02860: Free information ◆ T-shirts with Christmas, winter, teddy bear, teacher, garden, and herbal designs. 508-224-4463.

**Little Green Man,** P.O. Box 20904, Oakland, CA 94620: Catalog $1 ◆ Humorous and thought-provoking T-shirts featuring attitudes, philosophies, brains, cats, and in-your-face witticisms. 800-931-2332. www.sirius.com/~torch

**Martyr Apparel,** 1134 N. 22nd, #3, Billings, MT 59101: Free brochure ◆ T-shirts with silk-screened novelty graphics. 800-305-0210; 408-245-5589 (in MT).

**Rebecca Mims,** 4620 Tradewinds Ave. West, Lauderdale-By The Sea, FL 33308: Free information ◆ T-shirts for adults and children with whimsical animal, famous people, and custom portraits. 954-771-9978.

**Moonlighting,** 337 W. Benson St., Cincinnati, OH 45215: Free information ◆ Custom screen-printed and embroidered sportswear. Includes T-shirts, sweatshirts, caps, aprons, and jackets. 800-829-TEES; 513-821-8585 (in OH).

**Jim Morris Environmental T-Shirts,** P.O. Box 18270, Boulder, CO 80308: Free catalog ◆ T-shirts and sweatshirts with environmental and nature graphics. 800-788-5411. www.jimmorris.com

**The Nature Company,** Catalog Division, P.O. Box 188, Florence, KY 41022: Free catalog ◆ T-shirts with pictures of African animals. 800-227-1114. www.natureco.com

**New Candid Calendars,** 10498 Loveland-Madeira Rd., Loveland, OH 45140: Free brochure ◆ Personalized photo calendars, T-shirts, other clothes, ornaments, and more. 800-328-8415; 513-583-0883 (in OH).

**1-800-Pro Team,** 100 Plaza Dr., Secaucus, NJ 07094: Free catalog ◆ T-shirts, jackets, polos, sweats, authentic licensed teamwear, and more. 800-PRO-TEAM. www.proteam.com

**Original Face T-shirts,** P.O. Box 10276, Phoenix, AZ 85064: Free brochure ◆ Enlightened (Eastern wisdom designs) T-shirts. 800-895-1587.

**Pendleton Cowgirl Company,** P.O. Box 19474, Portland, OR 97280: Catalog $2 ◆ Classic western theme T-shirts, lithographs, note cards, and calendars. 503-977-0292.

**Primalink Originals Inc.,** 11401 Fairoak Dr., Silver Spring, MD 20902: Free brochure ◆ Plain and tie-dyed T-shirts with original nature-inspired art. 800-754-3660; 301-754-3757 (in MD).

**Rockabilia Inc.,** P.O. Box 4206, Hopkins, MN 55343: Free catalog ◆ T-shirts, backstage passes, promotional glossy photographs, imported rare posters from around the world, and concert collectibles. 612-942-7895.

**SDISLE T-Shirts,** P.O. Box 501424, Indianapolis, IN 46250: Free brochure ◆ Cotton basketball theme T-shirts. 888-999-4753; 317-823-4263 (in IN).

**Soho Design,** 10 Main St., P.O. Box 418, Dobbs Ferry, NY 10522: Free catalog ◆ Sweatshirts with a choice of graphics and designs. 800-933-8649. sohodes@westnet.com

**Stand Out Designs,** 9323 Activity Rd., Ste. A, San Diego, CA 92126: Free information ◆ T-shirts with wildlife, reptile, and floral designs. 800-331-1914; 619-536-8744 (in CA).

**John Tackett Galleries,** 1616 Holt St., Fort Worth, TX 76103: Free catalog ◆ Aviation art prints, T-shirts, and computer screen savers with over 25 full-color images for Windows. 800-243-1661.

**Teacher Smith,** Division SMARTWORKS Inc., P.O. Box 1588, San Marcos, TX 78667: Free information ◆ T-shirts with educational-related graphics. 512-392-9677.

**USA SportWear,** 4901 W. Van Buren, Ste. 1, Phoenix, AZ 85043: Catalog $2 ◆ Motorcycle art T-shirts. 800-323-7734. bebent@aol.com

**V1-Rotate,** P.O. Box 51354, Phoenix, AZ 85076: Free information ◆ T-shirts and caps with a choice of photos or drawings. 602-893-3579.

**Warner Brothers Catalog,** P.O. Box 60048, Tampa, FL 33660: Catalog $3 ◆ Bugs Bunny, Looney Tunes, and other T-shirts and sweatshirts for children and adults. Also movie-theme gifts. 800-223-6524. www.warnerbros.com

**Wireless,** Minnesota Public Radio, P.O. Box 64422, St. Paul, MN 55164: Free catalog ◆ T-shirts and sweatshirts, old time radio broadcasts, toy banks, coffee mugs, Disney cartoons on videos, books, wind chimes, and electronics. 800-570-5003. www.mpr.org

**WorkAbles for Women,** 96 Combs Rd., Clinton, PA 15026: Free catalog ◆ Gloves, hats, T-shirts, socks, outdoor clothing, rain gear, and personal safety items for women. 800-862-9317.

## Uniforms & Professional Clothing

**Aureus International Inc.,** South Circle Dr., Colorado Springs, CO 80906: Free information ◆ Fire retardant clothing, specializing in flight suits, coveralls, and uniforms. 800-448-9034; 719-540-9077 (in CO).

**Chefwear USA,** 833 N. Orleans, 4th Floor, Chicago, IL 60610: Free catalog ◆ Chef's clothing for men and women. 800-568-2433. www.chefwearusa.com

**Commodore Uniform & Nautical Supplies,** 335 Lower County Rd., Harwichport, MA 02646: Free information ◆ Boating uniforms, insignia, and flags. 800-438-8643; 508-430-7877 (in MA). www.capecod.com/allenharbor

**Culinary Classics,** 1626 S. Prairie Ave., Chicago, IL 60616: Free catalog ◆ Chef's clothing for men and women. 800-373-2963. www.culinaryclassics.com

**Dornan Uniforms,** 653 11th Ave., New York, NY 10036: Free catalog ◆ Work uniforms and embroidery screen printing. 800-223-0363. www.dornanuniforms.com

**Industrial Uniforms,** 906 E. Waterman, Wichita, KS 67202: Catalog $1.50 ◆ Uniforms and work clothing for men and women. 800-333-3666; 316-264-2871 (in KS).

**JCPenney Catalog,** P.O. Box 675, Milwaukee, WI 53201: Free information ◆ Women's clothing for health care personnel, in petite, misses, tall, and regular sizes. 800-222-6161. www.jcpenney.com/shopping

**Red the Uniform Tailor,** 2161 Whitesville Rd., Toms River, NJ 08755: Free catalog ◆ Uniforms and other work clothing. 800-272-7337.

**Sears Uniforms,** P.O. Box 7308, Rutherford, NJ 07073: Free catalog ◆ Uniforms for women and men nurses. 800-542-4380.

**Smallwoods Yachtwear,** 1001 SE 17th St., Fort Lauderdale, FL 33316: Free catalog ◆ Uniforms for boating and casual sportswear. 800-771-2283. www.smallwoods.com

**Tafford Manufacturing Inc.,** P.O. Box 1006, Montgomeryville, PA 18936: Free catalog ◆ Nurse uniforms. 800-283-0065.

**Todd Uniform Inc.,** P.O. Box 29107, St. Louis, MO 63126: Free catalog ◆ Work clothing and uniforms. 800-458-3402.

**Uniforms To You Corporate Headquarters,** 5600 W. 73rd St., Chicago, IL 60638: Free catalog ◆ Professional attire, food service apparel, and housekeeping workwear. 708-563-8929.

**US ABE Clothing,** 807 E. Carson St., Pittsburgh, PA 15203: Free catalog ◆ Uniforms, work, and casual clothing for big and tall men. 412-431-8861.

**Wasserman Uniform Company,** 1082 W. Mound St., Columbus, OH 43223: Free catalog ◆ Uniforms and shoes for men and women. 800-848-3576. www.wassermanuniform.com

## Western Clothing

**America's Western Stores,** 2816 S. Ingram Mill Rd., Springfield, MO 65804: Free catalog ◆ Western-style clothing, shoes and boots, and gifts. 800-284-8191.

**Back at the Ranch,** 235 Don Gaspar, Santa Fe, NM 87501: Free information ◆ Vintage western clothing, boots, and hats. 505-989-8110.

**Buckaroo Bobbins,** P.O. Box 95314, Las Vegas, NV 89193: Catalog $1 ◆ Authentic vintage western clothing sewing patterns. 801-865-7922.

**CaLyCo Crossing,** 407 Main St., Laurel, MD 20707: Free catalog ◆ Square dance and western-style clothing. 800-627-0412. calycocrossing@calyco.com

**Cattle Kate,** Box 572, Wilson, WY 83014: Catalog $3 ◆ Contemporary western-style clothing for men, women, and children. 307-733-7414.

**Cheyenne Outfitters,** P.O. Box 12013, Cheyenne, WY 82003: Free catalog ◆ Western-style clothing, jewelry, and gifts. 800-234-0432. www.chey-outfit.com

**Coldwater Creek,** One Coldwater Dr., Sandpoint, ID 83864: Free catalog ◆ Western-style women's fashions, jewelry, and accessories. 800-262-0040. www.coldwater-creek.com

**The Cowboy's Closet,** P.O. Box 16186, Lubbock, TX 79490: Free catalog ◆ Western apparel and accessories. 800-687-4357.

**Creations in Leather,** 1212 Sheridan Ave., Cody, WY 82414: Brochure $5 ◆ Leather coats, shirts, vests, chaps, chinks, and jackets. 307-587-6461.

**Drysdales,** 1555 N. 107th East Ave., Tulsa, OK 74116: Free catalog ◆ Western-style clothing, hats, and boots for children and adults. 800-444-6481. www.drysdales.com

**GJ's Wild West,** P.O. Box 6202, San Carlos St., Carmel, CA 93921: Free catalog ◆ Contemporary western apparel. 800-613-2762.

**Hay Charlie,** 541 Historic Main St., Park City, UT 84060: Free information ◆ Handcrafted western-style boots, buckles and belts, hats, jewelry, clothing, and accessories.

**Hobby Horse Clothing Company Inc.,** 13775 Stockton Ave., Chino, CA 91710: Catalog $2 ◆ Western clothing and tack, show apparel, and accessories for horseback riders. 800-569-5885. www.hobbyhorseinc.com

**The Last Best Place,** Catalog Company, 3650 Milwaukee St., Madison, WI 53779: Free catalog ◆ Men and women's western-style clothing and accessories. 800-252-4766.

**Luskey/Ryon's Western Stores Inc.,** 2601 N. Main, Fort Worth, TX 76106: Free catalog ◆ Western fashions, boots, and hats. 800-725-7966.

**Main-ly Country Western Wear,** 166 Yarmouth Rd., Gray, ME 04039: Catalog $1 (refundable) ◆ Western-style clothing for men and women. 207-657-3412. afoster1@maine.com

**Maverick Fine Western Wear,** 100 E. Exchange in the Stockyards, Fort Worth, TX 76106: Video catalog $5 ◆ Western apparel, accessories, and gifts. 800-282-1315.

**Miller-Stockman Western Wear,** P.O. Box 5127, Denver, CO 80217: Free catalog ◆ Men and women's western wear. 800-688-9888. www.millerstockman.com

**The Old Frontier Clothing Company,** 7412 Fulton Ave., North Hollywood, CA 91605: Catalog $3 ◆ Men and women's western clothing. 818-764-7787.

**Rocky Mountain Connection,** P.O. Box 2800, Estes Park, CO 80517: Catalog $1 (specify type of items wanted) ◆ Outdoor and western-style clothing, Boy Scouts clothing and outdoor gear, hiking staffs, backpacks, and more. 800-679-3600. www.RMConnection.com

**Rod's Western Palace,** 3099 Silver Dr., Columbus, OH 43224: Free catalog ◆ Western-style clothing and tack. 800-325-8508. www.rods.com

**Roemers,** 1920 N. Broadway, Santa Maria, CA 93455: Free catalog ◆ Western-style clothing and gifts for men and women. 800-242-1890.

**Ryon's Saddle & Ranch Supplies,** 2601 N. Main, Fort Worth, TX 76106: Free catalog ◆ Western-style clothing and boots for men, women, and children. Also saddles and tack. 800-725-7966. www.luskey.com

**Denny Sergeant's Western World,** 4905 South Cooper St., Arlington, TX 76017: Free catalog ◆ Show clothing, saddles, and other western gear. 800-383-3669. www.sergeantswestern.com

**Sheplers,** P.O. Box 7702, Wichita, KS 67277: Free catalog ◆ Western clothing. 800-242-6540.

**Soda Creek Western Outfitters,** P.O. Box 4343, Steamboat Springs, CO 80477: Free catalog ◆ Western clothing, hats, and dusters for men and women. 800-824-8426. www.soda-creek.com

**The Territory Ahead,** PFI Western Stores, 2816 S. Ingram Mill Rd., Springfield, MO 65804: Free catalog ◆ Men and women's western-style clothing. 800-686-8178. www.territoryahead.com

**Wild Bills Originals,** P.O. Box 13037, Burton, WA 98013: Catalog/poster $10 ◆ Original and authentic frontier leather goods and historical western items. 206-463-5738.

**Wild West Mercantile,** 5130 N. 19th Ave., Phoenix, AZ 85015: Catalog $3 ◆ Original and authentic traditional cowboy clothing. 800-596-0444.

## CLOWN SUPPLIES

**Abracadabra Magic Shop,** 125 Lincoln Blvd., Middlesex, NJ 08846: Catalog $5 ◆ Magic and juggling equipment, balloons, clown props, costumes, and make-up. 732-805-0200. umsi@erols.com

**Apples & Company,** 414 Conant Ave., Union, NJ 07083: Free information ◆ Clown-white make-up. 908-353-2193.

**Aunt Clowney's Warehouse,** P.O. Box 1444, Corona, CA 91718: Free catalog with two 1st class stamps ◆ Books on clowning. 909-273-0900. auntc@empirenet.com

**Axtell Expressions,** 230 Glencrest Circle, Ventura, CA 93003: Catalog $2 ◆ Clown supplies. 805-642-7282. www.axtell.com

**Bigfoot Stilt Company,** 7111 Gardner St., #7, Winter Park, FL 32792: Free information ◆ Custom stilts. 407-677-5900. www.h2orocket.com/company.html

**Bubba's Clown Supplies,** P.O. Box 2939, Orange Park, FL 32067: Catalog $2.50 ◆ Clown supplies. 904-272-5878. members.aol.com/jtbubba2/clownsupplies.htm

**Burpo the Clown,** P.O. Box 299, McMinnville, OR 97128: Free information ◆ Face-painting rubber stamps and supplies. 503-434-1243.

**Brad Burt's Magic Shop,** 4204 Convoy St., Ste. 103, San Diego, CA 92111: Free catalog ◆ Magic for amateur and professional magicians, how-to-do-magic video cassettes, gag items, and clown supplies. 615-571-4749. bb@magicshop.com

**Chazpro Magic Company,** P.O. Box 41415, Eugene, OR 97404: Catalog $3 ◆ Juggling and clown props, books, jokes, and novelties. 541-689-6919. www.chazpro.com

**Cheri-Oats & Company,** P.O. Box 367, Destrahan, LA 70047: Free information ◆ Wigs, stickers, puppets, and face painting supplies. 504-764-0080. www.mooseburger.com/cheri.htm

**Circus Clowns,** 3556 Nicollet Ave., Minneapolis, MN 55408: Catalog $3 ◆ Clown costumes and props. 612-822-4243.

**Clarkson Studio,** 401 N. Hoback St., Helena, MT 59601: Free brochure ◆ Gag items, magic tricks, make-up, and other clown supplies. 406-442-2046.

**Clown-So-Port,** 405 Forest St., Oconomowoc, WI 53066: Free brochure ◆ Clown shoes and other clown-related accessories. 800-679-7463. www.clownsoport.com

**Clown City,** 6 Salem Market Pl., Salem, CT 06420: Catalog $2 ◆ Balloons and clown supplies. 203-889-1000.

**The Clown Factory,** 5724 N. Meridian, Wichita, KS 67204: Catalog $1 (refundable) ◆ Balloons, magic, and clown comedy props, gags, and supplies. 316-838-0818.

**Clown Heaven,** 4792 Old State Rd. 37 South, Martinsville, IN 46152: Catalog $3 ◆ Balloons, make-up, puppets, wigs, ministry and gospel items, novelties, magic, clown props, and books. 317-342-6888.

**Clown Supplies Inc.,** The Castles Rt. 101, Brentwood, NH 03833: Free catalog ◆ Clown supplies. 603-679-3311. www.clownsupplies.com

**Comanche Clown Shoes Mfg.,** P.O. Box 551, Mountain View, OK 73062: Free information ◆ Clown shoes. 800-832-3424; 405-347-2817 (in OK).

**Costumes by Betty,** 2181 Edgerton St., St. Paul, MN 55117: Catalog $5 (refundable) ◆ Clown costumes, make-up, wigs, and shoes. 612-771-8734. www.clowncostumes.com

**Steve Dawson's Magic Touch Catalog,** 144 N. Milpitas Blvd., Milpitas, CA 95035: Catalog $3 ◆ Magic effects, books, videos, accessories, clown and juggling supplies, and make-up. 408-263-9404.

**The Designer of Smiles,** Gary & Nicki Zwerin, 4125 Stagwood Dr., Raleigh, NC 27613: Free information ◆ Wigs, custom-made hats, make-up, and other supplies. 919-782-8841.

**Dewey's Good News Balloons,** 1202 Wildwood, Deer Park, TX 77536: Free catalog ◆ Gospel clown supplies and balloons. 281-479-2759. balloonz@flash.net

**Eddie's Trick Shop,** 70 S. Park Square, Marietta, GA 30060: Free information ◆ Magic and clown supplies. 800-429-4314. www.eddiestricks.com

**Frankel's Costume Company Inc.,** 4815 Fannin St., Houston, TX 77004: Free brochure ◆ Snap-over teeth for special effects. 888-33-FAIRY; 713-528-6036 (in TX). www.frankelcostume.com

**Freckles Clown Supplies,** 5509 Roosevelt Blvd., Jacksonville, FL 32244: Catalog $6 ◆ Costumes, make-up, clown supplies, puppets, how-to books on clowning and ballooning, and theatrical supplies. 904-388-5541. www.freckles1.com/index.html

**Fun Technicians Inc.,** P.O. Box 160, Syracuse, NY 13215: Free information ◆ Clown props. 315-492-4523. lafmaker@aol.com

**Funny Feet Fashions,** c/o George Kondiles, 5047 W. Chase Ave., Skokie, IL 60077: Free brochure ◆ Clown shoes. 847-251-4545. www.idt.net/~fufefa9

**David Ginn Magic,** 4387 St. Michaels Dr., Lilburn, GA 30247: Catalog $10 ◆ Books, props, and how-to-do magic on videos for magicians and clowns. 770-923-1899.

**Graftobian Ltd.,** 510 Tasman St., Madison, WI 53714: Free information ◆ Face-painting supplies. 800-255-0584. www.graftobian.com

**La Rock's Fun & Magic Outlet,** 3847 Rosehaven Dr., Charlotte, NC 28205: Catalog $3 ◆ Clown and balloon how-to books, balloon sculpture kits, and magic equipment. 704-563-9300. larocks1@aol.com

**Laflin's Magic & Silks,** P.O. Box 228, Sterling, CO 80751: Free information ◆ Entertaining and educational magic on videos for clowns and magicians. 970-522-2589.

**Lynch's Clown Supplies,** 939 Howard, Dearborn, MI 48124: Catalog $5 ◆ Wigs, shoes, noses, novelty items, make-up, and costume accessories. 800-24-LYNCH. www.lynchs.com

**Magic & Fun Shop,** 16872 Hwy. 3, Webster, TX 77598: Free catalog ◆ Jokes, gags, novelties, clown supplies, make-up, magic tricks, and puzzles. 281-332-8142. www.fun-shop.com

**The Magic Corner & Costume Shop,** 1213 Hillsborough St., Raleigh, NC 27603: Free catalog ◆ Magic and books, costumes, and clown supplies. 919-834-0925.

**Mecca Magic Inc.,** 49 Dodd St., Bloomfield, NJ 07003: Catalog $10 ◆ Clown equipment, make-up, balloons, magic, costumes and wigs, puppets, ventriloquism and clown props, and juggling supplies. 201-429-7597. meccamagic@meccamagic.com

**Pricilla Mooseburger Originals,** P.O. Box 700, Maple Lake, MN 55358: Catalog $2 ◆ Clown hats and clothing. 800-973-6277. www.mooseburger.com

**Morris Costumes,** 3108 Monroe Rd., Charlotte, NC 28205: Catalog $20 ◆ Costumes, clown props, masks, joke items, magic and special effects, novelties, balloons, and books. 704-332-3304.

**T. Myers Magic Inc.,** 6513 Thomas Springs Rd., Austin, TX 78736: Free catalog ◆ Magic and other supplies for balloon twisters, face painters, clowns, and magicians. 800-288-7925; 512-288-7925 (in TX). www.tmyers.com

**Novelties Unlimited,** 410 W. 21st St., Norfolk, VA 23517: Catalog $5 ◆ Clown supplies, props and gags, magic, balloons, make-up, and party decorations. 757-622-0344.

**Ben Nye Makeup,** 5935 Bowcroft St., Los Angeles, CA 90016: Catalog $2.50 ◆ Clown make-up. 310-839-1984.

**Potsy & Blimpo Clown Supplies,** P.O. Box 2075, Huntington Beach, CA 92647: Free catalog ◆ Clown make-up, wigs, and supplies. 800-897-0749; 714-897-0749 (in CA). potsyblimpo@earthlink.net

**Sparkle's Entertainment Express,** Jan Lovell, 152 N. Water St., Gallatin, TN 37066: Product list $1 ◆ Make-up, costumes and clown shoes, balloons, juggling and magic equipment, puppets, books, and supplies. 615-452-9755.

**Spear's Specialty Shoe Company,** 12 Orlando St., Springfield, MA 01108: Brochure $2 ◆ Clown shoes. 413-739-5693. www.ourworld.compuserve.com/homepages/SpearShoes

**Under the Big Top,** P.O. Box 807, Placentia, CA 92670: Catalog $4 ◆ Clown props, costumes, make-up, juggling equipment, balloons, and party supplies. 800-995-7727.

**Up, Up & Away,** P.O. Box 159, Beallsville, PA 15313: Catalog $3 ◆ Clown make-up and props. 412-769-5447. peacheyk@usaor.net

**World Clown Association,** P.O. Box 1413, Corona, CA 91718: Free catalog ◆ T-shirts, pins, decals, and buttons. 800-336-7922

**Wyco Props,** 8344 Yecker Ave., Kansas City, KS 66109: Free catalog ◆ Make-up, face paint, costumes, and other clown props. 913-788-9338. www.wycoprops.com

## COFFEE & ESPRESSO MAKERS

**Ako-Ismet Electrical,** P.O. Box 1303, Franklin, TN 37065: Free information ◆ Double carafe coffee maker. 800-996-6466.

**Chef's Catalog,** P.O. Box 620048, Dallas, TX 75262: Free catalog ◆ Calphalon cookware, Cuisinart accessories, Henckels cutlery, coffee-making equipment, and professional restaurant equipment for the home chef. 800-338-3232. www.chefscatalog.com

**Enzos Gourmet Coffee,** 215 N. Federal Hwy., Hallandale, FL 33009: Free brochure ◆ Espresso and cappuccino machines. 954-455-0611.

**Estro Espresso,** 451-A1 Defense Hwy., Annapolis, MD 21401: Free information ◆ Self-grinding espresso machines. 410-573-0562.

**Gensaco Inc.,** P.O. Box 1399, 153 E. 43rd St., New York, NY 10163: Free brochure ◆ Automatic and semi-automatic professional and for home-use espresso machines. 800-732-1555; 212-697-3708 (in NY).

**Mazzoli Coffee Inc.,** 236 Ave. U, Brooklyn, NY 11223: Catalog 50¢ ◆ Coffee brewers and grinders. 718-449-0909.

**Pannikin Mail Order,** 1205 J St., San Diego, CA 92101: Free brochure ◆ Gourmet spices, tea, hot chocolate, espresso machines, and coffee makers. 800-232-6482.

**World Java House,** P.O. Box 347, Monrovia, CA 91017: Free catalog ◆ Espresso machines, coffee presses and grinders, coffee makers, mugs, flavoring syrups, accessories, and imported coffees from worldwide sources. 800-528-3833. www.worldjava.com

**Zabar's & Company,** 2245 Broadway, New York, NY 10024: Free catalog ◆ Coffee makers, cookware, food processors, microwave ovens, kitchen tools, gourmet foods, and gift baskets. 800-697-6301; 212-496-1234 (in NY).

## COIN-OPERATED MACHINES

**Amusementica Americana,** 414 N. Prospect Manor Ave., Mt. Prospect, IL 60056: Free list with seven 1st class stamps ◆ Old saloon artifacts, coin-operated machines, advertising collectibles, paper memorabilia, and antique artifacts. 847-253-0791.

**Antique Slot Machine Part Company,** 140 N. Western Ave., Carpentersville, IL 60110: Free catalog ◆ Books and manuals, slot stands and pads, and parts for slot machines, jukeboxes, and pinballs. 847-428-8476.

**L.M. Becker & Company Inc.,** P.O. Drawer 1459, Appleton, WI 54913: Free catalog ◆ Bulk vending products and equipment. 414-739-5269.

**Durham's Antiques,** 909 26th St. NW, Washington, DC 20037: Catalog $5 ◆ Antique coin-operated vending and arcade machines, pinballs, counter-top games, and books. 202-338-1342.

**Fabulous Fantasies,** 12602 Ventura Blvd., Studio City, CA 91604: Free price list ◆ Pinball machines, arcade games, jukeboxes, and game room furnishings. 800-5-PINBALL.

**Howard J. Fink,** 174 Main St., Acton, MA 01720: Free information ◆ Vintage pinball and slot machines. 978-263-6480.

**The Game Gallery,** 7941 N. Armenia Ave., Tampa, FL 33604: Free catalog ◆ Coin-operated amusement and vending equipment. 800-966-9873.

**Game Room Warehouse,** 826 W. Douglas Ave., Wichita, KS 67203: Free information ◆ New and used coin-operated games and machines. Includes juke boxes, pinball machines, pachinkos, slot machines, bowling machines, pool tables, and arcade games. 316-263-1848.

**Illinois Antique Slot Machine Company,** P.O. Box 542, Westmont, IL 60559: Free information ◆ Wurlitzer jukeboxes, slot machines, nickelodeons, music boxes, and coin-operated devices. 630-985-2742. zygmunt@mcs.net

**International Amusement Distributors,** 1 Park Ave., Derby, CT 06418: Free list ◆ Pinball and video games.

**Norman Johnson,** 13820 County Home Rd., Bowling Green, OH 43402: Free list with long SASE ◆ Antique coin-operated machines before the 1950s. 419-352-3041.

**Jukebox City,** 1950 1st Ave. South, Seattle, WA 98134: Free photos with long SASE ◆ Jukeboxes and coin-operated machines. 206-625-1950.

**Jukebox Classics & Vintage Slot Machines Inc.,** 6742 5th Ave., Brooklyn, NY 11220: Free information ◆ Antique coin-operated machines and jukeboxes. 718-833-8455.

**Lazarus Auto Collection,** P.O. Box 6732, Rockford, IL 61125: Free information ◆ Jukeboxes and arcade machines. 815-229-1258.

**Marco Specialties,** 5290 Platt Springs, Lexington, SC 29073: Catalog $2 ◆ Pinball machines, parts, and books. 803-957-5500.

**National Jukebox Exchange,** 121 Lakeside Dr., Mayfield, NY 12117: Free catalog ◆ Antique jukeboxes, slot machines, arcade machines, and parts. 888-321-PAPA.

**Bob Nelson's Game Room Warehouse,** 826 W. Douglas, Wichita, KS 67203: Free information ◆ Antique coin-operated machines and parts. 316-263-1848. www.gameroomw@aol.com

**Orange Trading Company,** 57 S. Main St., Orange, MA 01364: Free list with long SASE ◆ Antique jukeboxes, pinballs, and coin-operated machines. 978-544-6683.

**R & J Amusement,** 249 Blue Ridge Dr., Orange, VA 22960: Free list ◆ Used slot machines. 540-672-4500.

**Remember When Collectibles,** 6570 Memorial Dr., Stone Mountain, GA 30083: Free brochure ◆ Vintage Coca-Cola machines and jukeboxes. 770-879-7878. www.fiftiescollectibles.com/

**Royal Bell Ltd.,** 5815 W 52nd Ave., Denver, CO 80212: Catalog $5 ◆ Slot machines and mechanical memorabilia. 303-431-9266. www.royalbell.com

**St. Louis Slot Machine Company,** 9400 Manchester Rd., St. Louis, MO 63119: Catalog $3 ◆ Common to rare Coca Cola and coin-operated machines. 314-961-4612.

**Ted Salveson,** P.O. Box 602, Huron, SD 57350: Free catalog ◆ Coin-operated machines. 605-352-3870.

**U.S. Slot Machine Dist. Company,** P.O. Box 1691, Bemidji, MN 56601: Free information ◆ Slot machines. 800-USA-SLOT.

**Zielbauer,** 2210 Miramonte, Tucson, AZ 85713: Free list ◆ Slot machines.

**Zygmunt & Associates,** P.O. Box 542, Westmont, IL 60559: Free brochure ◆ Jukeboxes and slot machines. 630-985-2742. zygmunt@mcs.net

## COMIC BOOKS & ARCHIVAL SUPPLIES

**Bags Unlimited Inc.,** 7 Canal St., Rochester, NY 14608: Free information ◆ Comic book storage and archival supplies. 800-767-BAGS. www.frontiernet.net/~bags

**Bill Cole Enterprises Inc.,** P.O. Box 60, Randolph, MA 02368: Free information ◆ Comic book archival supplies. 781-986-2653.

**Comic Conservation Company,** P.O. Box 44803, Madison, WI 53744: Free information ◆ Archival supplies. 608-277-8750.

**Gary Dolgoff Comics,** Brooklyn Navy Yard, Bldg. 280, Ste. 608/609, Brooklyn, NY 11205: Catalog $1 ◆ Collector comic books. 718-596-5719.

**Dover Cards & Comics,** 11 Main St., Dover, NH 03820: Free catalog ◆ Gold and Silver Age comic books. 603-749-6862.

**Fantasy Distribution Company,** 2831 Miller St., San Leandro, CA 94577: Free information ◆ Back issue comic books. 510-352-5832.

**A Good Time Charlie's,** 114 W. Knox, Ennis, TX 75119: Free information with long SASE (specify items wanted) ◆ New and back issue comic books. 972-875-9737.

**Will Gorges Civil War Antiques,** 2100 Trent Blvd., New Bern, NC 28560: Catalog $10 ◆ Authentic Civil War uniforms, weapons, photographs, and pre-1964 comic books. 919-636-3039. www.collectorsnet.com/gorges

**John M. Hauser,** 15225 W. Lynwood Ct., New Berlin, WI 53151: Price list $1 ◆ Comic books for collectors. 414-784-0332.

**High-Quality Comics,** 1603 Calavo Rd., Fallbrook, CA 92028: Catalog $1 ◆ Hard-to-find comic books. 619-723-7269.

**Gregory Johnson/Game Traders,** 1327 Andover Dr., Aurora, IL 60504: Free catalog ◆ Comics. 630-585-5245.

**Joseph Koch,** 76 Carroll St., Brooklyn, NY 11231: Catalog $3 ◆ Old and new comic books. 718-834-0398.

**Metropolis,** 873 Broadway, Ste. 201, New York, NY 10003: Free information ◆ Vintage comic books and movie posters. 212-260-4147. comicbooks@earthlink.net

**Mint Condition Comic Books & Baseball Cards Inc.,** 664 Port Washington Blvd., Port Washington, NY 11050: Free information with long SASE ◆ Current and back issue comic books and sports cards. 516-883-0631.

**Moondog's Comicland,** Randburst Shopping Center, Mt. Prospect, IL 60056: Free information ◆ Comic books and archival supplies. 847-577-8668.

**Movie Gallery,** 111 E. 3rd, Sedalia, MO 65301: Catalog $5 ◆ Plates, comics, posters, and other new and old collectibles. 816-826-3834.

**New England Comics,** P.O. Box 310, Quincy, MA 02269: Catalog $1 ◆ Subscription service and collectible comics. 617-774-1745. www.necomics.com

**The Nostalgia Zone,** P.O. Box 6106, Minneapolis, MN 55406: Free catalog ◆ Collectible comic books. 612-822-2806. nostzone@spacestar.net

**Paul & Judy's Coins & Cards,** P.O. Box 409, Arthur, IL 61911: Free information ◆ Collectible comic books. 217-543-3366. sales@pjcc.com

**Bud Plant Comic Art,** P.O. Box 1689, Grass Valley, CA 95945: Catalog $3 ◆ Comic books, comic strip collections, books about the history of comics and their creators, limited edition books, and prints. 916-273-2166. www.budplant.com

**Stand-Up Comics,** 10020 San Pablo Ave., El Cerrito, CA 94530: Free information with long SASE (specify items wanted) ◆ Collectible comic books. 510-525-3223.

**Tomorrow Is Yesterday,** 5600 N. 2nd St., Rockford, IL 61111: Free information with long SASE ◆ New and back issue comic books, games, and collectibles. 815-633-0330.

**Unique Dist.,** 110 Denton Ave., New Hyde Park, NY 11040: Free information ◆ Sports and non-sports cards and comics. 800-294-5901; 516-294-5900 (in NY). www.uniquedist.com

**Westfield Comics,** 8608 University Green, P.O. Box 620470, Middleton, WI 53562: Free catalog ◆ Comics and collectibles. 800-WESTFIELD. www.westfield.com

## COMPASSES

**Edmund Scientific Company,** Edscorp Bldg., Barrington, NJ 08007: Free catalog ◆ Compasses, binoculars, telescopes, and educational and science equipment. 609-547-8880. www.edsci.com

**Goldbergs' Marine,** 201 Meadow Rd., Edison, NJ 08818: Free catalog ◆ Compasses and power and sail boat equipment. 800-BOA-TING.

**Haverhills,** Customer Service, 185 Berry St., San Francisco, CA 94107: Free information ◆ Digital electronic car compass. 800-797-7367.

**Magellan's,** Box 5485, Santa Barbara, CA 93150: Free catalog ◆ Compasses and other travel aids and gifts. 800-962-4943. sales@magellans.com

**The Map Shack,** 959 Main St., Winchester, MA 01890: Free catalog ◆ Maps for recreational activities, hiking and biking books and guides, software, atlases, and compasses. 800-617-MAPS; 781-721-4943 (in MA). http://maps.bx.com

**Skipper Marine Electronics Inc.,** 1511 Reidel Dr., Mundelein, IL 60060: Free catalog ◆ Compasses and marine electronics. 800-SKIPPER; 847-566-1800 (in IL).

**Sporty's Preferred Living Catalog,** Clermont Airport, Batavia, OH 45103: Free catalog ◆ Compasses. 800-543-8633. www.sportys-catalogs.com

**Stocker & Yale Inc.,** 32 Hampshire Rd., Salem, NH 03079: Free brochure ◆ Compasses and authentic United States Army watches. 800-843-8011; 603-893-8778 (in NH).

**Suunto USA,** 2151 Las Palmas Dr., Carlsbad, CA 92009: Free list of retail sources ◆ Easy-to-attach and demount illuminated compasses. 800-543-9124, ext. 228. www.suuntousa.com

# COMPUTERS

## Accessories

**Acecad,** P.O. Box 431, Monterey, CA 93942: Free information ◆ Stylus and touch-sensitive input screen. 800-676-4ACE.

**Agfa Computers,** Bayer Industries, 200 Ballardvale St., Wilmington, MA 01887: Free list of retail sources ◆ Scanners, accessories, and software. 800-685-4271. www.agfahome.com

**Alltech Electronics Company Inc.,** 2618 Temple Heights, Oceanside, CA 92056: Free catalog ◆ Computer components and surplus electronics. 619-724-2404. www.allelec.com

**Altra,** 520 W. Cedar St., Rawlins, WY 82301: Free brochure ◆ Maintenance and cleaning-free optical-tracking mouse. 800-445-6778.

**American Power Conversion,** 132 Fairgrounds Rd. West, Kingston, RI 02852: Free information ◆ Power backup and surge protectors for PCS. 800-788-2208.

**Apple Computer Inc.,** 1 Infinite Loop, Cupertino, CA 95014: Free information ◆ Flatbed scanner. 800-776-2333. www.powermacintosh.apple.com

**Associates Computer Supply,** 275 W. 231st St., Riverdale, NY 10463: Free information ◆ Cases, video cards, hard drives, motherboards, keyboards, CD-ROMs, memory accessories, and more. 718-543-8686.

**ATI Technologies,** 33 Commerce Valley Dr. East, Thornhill, Ontario, Canada L3T 7N6: Free catalog ◆ Graphics and multimedia upgrades, accelerators, TV and VCR import accessories, and more. www.atitech.ca

**AverMedia Technologies Inc.,** 47923A Warm Springs Blvd., Fremont, CA 94539: Free information ◆ Add-on TV and video phone adapter for PCS. 510-770-9899.

**Best Power Technology Inc.,** P.O. Box 280, Necedah, WI 54646: Free information ◆ Uninterruptible power systems. 800-356-5794.

**BISME Computers Inc.,** 1443 Angie Ave., Modesto, CA 95351: Free information ◆ Computer components and accessories. 800-899-6430.

**Bottom Line Distribution,** 4544 S. Lamar Blvd., Ste. 100, Austin, TX 78745: Free information ◆ Macintosh storage devices, disk drives, scanners, modems, and peripherals. 800-990-5795.

**Brother International Corp.,** 200 Cottontail Ln., Somerset, NJ 08875: Free information ◆ Laser printers. 908-356-8880. www.brother.com

**Canon Computer Systems,** P.O. Box 3900, Peoria, IL 61612: Free list of retail sources ◆ Laser, bubble jet, and portable printers. 800-848-4123.

**CCS International Headquarters,** 360 Madison Ave., New York, NY 10017: Free information ◆ On-line monitor system that provides constant supervision and recordkeeping. Prevents computer theft when in and away from the office. 800-685-6374; 212-557-3040 (in NY). ccsnychq@aol.com

**CH Products,** 970 Park Center Dr., Vista, CA 92083: Free brochure ◆ Easy-to-use joysticks, flight yokes, gamepads, rudder pedals, trackballs, and throttles. 619-598-2524.

**CMS Enhancements,** 3095 Redhill Ave., Costa Mesa, CA 92626: Free information ◆ Mass storage accessories for network servers, workstations, and portable computers. 714-424-5520. www.cmsperipheralsinc.com

**CNF Inc.,** 15345 Calle Enrique, Morgan Hill, CA 95037: Free information ◆ Peripherals for portable computers. 800-8326-3642; 408-778-1160 (in CA).

**Computer Products Corp.,** 1431 S. Cherryvale Rd., Boulder, CO 80303: Free information ◆ Multi-media equipment, modems, accessories, and hard, tape, and CD-ROM drives. 800-338-4273.

**Corporate Systems Center,** 3310 Woodward Ave., Santa Clara, CA 95054: Free catalog ◆ Add-on cards, hard drives, disk arrays, controllers, CD-ROMs, tape backups, other tools, and utilities. 408-588-1110. www.corpsys.com

**Creative Labs Inc.,** 1901 McCarthy Blvd., Milpitas, CA 95035: Free catalog ◆ Sound cards, multi-media kits, video equipment, and accessories for PCS. 800-998-1000. www.soundblaster.com

**Crucial Technology,** 8000 S. Federal Way, P.O. Box 6, Boise, ID 83707: Free brochure ◆ Memory upgrades for PCs. 888-363-2561.

**Dirt Cheap Drives,** 3716 Timber Dr., Dickinson, TX 77539: Free information ◆ Disk, tape, and CD-ROM drives. Also controllers and optical devices. 800-637-4743; 281-534-6292 (in TX). www.dirtcheapdrives.com

**Epson America Inc.,** Corporate Information Center, 20770 Madrona Ave., P.O. Box 2842, Torrance, CA 90509: Free catalog ◆ Ink-jet, laser, and dot matrix printers. Also flat bed scanners, photo PC color digital camera, data/video projection system, and accessories. 800-442-1977. www.epson.com

**Fujitsu Microelectronics Inc.,** 3545 N. 1st St., San Jose, CA 95134: Free list of retail sources ◆ PC cards for portable computers. 888-FMI-GO-PC.

**Ganson Engineering Inc.,** 18678 142nd Ave. NE, Woodinville, WA 98072: Free information ◆ Laser and matrix impact printers, supplies, and parts. 425-489-2090. www.ganson.com

**Genovation Inc.,** 17741 Mitchell North, Irvine, CA 92714: Free information ◆ DOS and Windows compatible keypad for portable computers. 800-822-4333; 714-833-3355 (in CA).

**Glyph Technologies Inc.,** 735 W. Clinton, Ithaca, NY 14850: Free information ◆ Dual-speed CD-ROM drive with optional multi-media capability and CD audio playback. 800-335-0345.

**Hello Direct,** 5893 Rue Ferrari Dr., San Jose, CA 95138: Free catalog ◆ Modems, telephones, and accessories. 800-444-3556. www.hello-direct.com

**Hewlett-Packard Company,** Direct Marketing Organization, 5301 Stevens Creek Blvd., P.O. Box 58059, MS 51LSJ, Santa Clara, CA 95052: Free information ◆ PC portables, laser and ink-jet printers, and accessories. 800-752-0900. www.hp.com

**Industrial Computer Source,** P.O. Box 910557, San Diego, CA 92191: Free catalog ◆ Computers and accessories for industrial applications. 800-459-7442. www.indcompsrc.com

**Infogrip Inc.,** 1141 E. Main St., Ventura, CA 93001: Free information ◆ Ergonomic keyboards for Macintosh and PC computers. 800-397-0921.

**Intelligent Electronic Solutions Inc.,** 179 E. Main St., Sandy, UT 84070: Free brochure ◆ Electronic networking, hook-up, and control distribution equipment. 800-903-4237; 801-566-8892 (in UT).

**The Iomega Corp.,** P.O. Box 208, Roy, UT 84067: Free information ◆ Hard drives for PCs and the Macintosh. 800-456-5522; 801-778-3450 (in UT). www.iomega.com

**JAMECO Electronic and Computer Products,** 1355 Shoreway Rd., Belmont, CA 94002: Free information ◆ Electronic and computer components. 800-831-4242. www.jameco.com

**Kingston Technology Company,** 17600 Newhope St., Fountain Valley, CA 92708: Free information ◆ Memory add-ons, networking and PC enhancement products, and mass storage accessories. 800-337-8410. www.kingston.com

**Krex Computers,** 9320-22 Waukegan Rd., Morton Grove, IL 60053: Free information ◆ Networking and multi-media kits. 800-377-KREX; 847-967-0200 (in IL).

**La Paz Electronics International,** P.O. Box 261095, San Diego, CA 92196: Free information ◆ Computer parts and accessories. 619-586-7610. lapazusa@pobox.com

**Lexmark International,** 740 New Circle Rd. NW, Lexington, KY 40511: Free list of retail sources ◆ Laser, ink-jet, and color printers. Also plain paper fax, scanner, and copier. 800-358-5835. www.lexmark.com

**Matrox Graphics Inc.,** 1025 St-Regis Blvd., Dorval, QC, Canada H9P 2T4: Free list of retail sources ◆ Video upgrades and controller displays, graphics boards, accelerators, and other state-of-the-art add-ons. 800-844-8302. www.matrox.com

**Maxtor Corp.,** 510 Cottonwood Dr., Milpitas, CA 95035: Free list of retail sources ◆ Hard drives. 408-432-1700.

**MegaHaus,** 2201 Pine Dr., Dickinson, TX 77539: Free information ◆ Removable and portable hard drives, CD-ROMs and recorders, optical drives, and accessories. 800-786-1191. www.megahaus.com

**Memory Plus Inc.,** 22 Water St., Westborough, MA 01581: Free information ◆ PC and Macintosh upgrade components. 800-388-7587; 508-366-2240 (in MA).

**Micro Design International Inc.,** 6985 University Blvd., Winter Park, FL 32792: Free information ◆ Quad-speed CD-ROM drive for PCs. 407-677-8333.

**Micro Sense Inc.,** 370 Andrew Ave., Leucadia, CA 92024: Free information ◆ Do-it-yourself notebook hard drive upgrades. 800-544-4252; 760-632-8621 (in CA).

**MicroBiz,** 777 Corporate Dr., Mahwah, NJ 07430: Free brochure ◆ Business software and accessories. 800-637-8268. www.microbiz.com

**Micropolis Inc.,** 21211 Nordhoff St., Chatsworth, CA 91311: Free list of retail sources ◆ Hard drives. 818-709-3300.

**Microtek Lab Inc.,** 3715 Doolittle Dr., Redondo Beach, CA 90278: Free information ◆ Scanners, software, and accessories. 310-297-5000. www.microtekusa.com

**Midwest Computer Works,** 600 Bunker Ct., Vernon Hills 60061: Free catalog ◆ PC portables, desktop systems, peripherals, and upgrade accessories. 800-659-5400. www.mcworks.com

**Mobile Office Outfitter,** 1048 Serpentine Ln., #308, Pleasanton, CA 94566: Free catalog ◆ Mobile car desks, laptop accessories, cellular phone accessories, office supplies, and more. 800-426-3453. www.mobilegear.com

**Mobile Planet,** 21228 Vanowen St., Canoga Park, CA 91303: Free catalog ◆ Computer accessories and hardware. 1-800-MPLANET.

**Motherboard Discount Center,** 670 N. Arizona Ave., Ste. 11, Chandler, AZ 85224: Free information ◆ Motherboards. 800-4486-2026.

**Motor City Micro,** 889 Sumpter Rd., Belleville, MI 48111: Free information ◆ Motherboards, CD-ROMs, hard and floppy drives, controller cards, sound cards and speakers, fax/modems, mouse devices and trackballs, RAM add-ons, and keyboards. 313-697-7292.

**NEC Computer Systems Division,** Packard Bell NEC Inc., 1414 Massachusetts Ave., Boxboro, MA 01719: Free information ◆ Laser printers. 888-8-NEC-NOW. www.necnow.com

**NETIS Technology Inc.,** 1606 Centre Point Dr., Milpitas, CA 95035: Free information ◆ Computer components, add-on cards, multi-media products, software, custom-configured and barebone PC systems, and network stations. 408-263-0368.

**New Media Corp.,** One Technology, Bldg. A, Irvine, CA 92718: Free brochure ◆ Fax/modems, stereo sound cards, and accessories. 800-CARDS-4-U; 714-453-0100 (in CA). www.newmediacorp.com

**New MMI Corp.,** 2400 Reach Rd., Williamsport, PA 17701: Free catalog ◆ Desktop and portable PCs, printers, multi-media upgrades, scanners, and accessories. 800-221-4283.

**Okidata,** 532 Fellowship Rd., Mt. Laurel, NJ 08054: Free information ◆ Laser and color ink-jet printers. 800-OKIDATA.

**1-800-Batteries,** 2301 Robb Dr., Reno, NV 89523: Free catalog ◆ Batteries, tools, and accessories for portable computers. 800-228-8374. www.1800Batteries.com

**P.C. Age,** 3329 S. Memorial Dr., Greenville, NC 27834: Free catalog ◆ Hardware, software, and technical products. 800-637-0979.

**Pentax Technologies,** 100 Technology Dr., Broomfield, CO 80021: Free information ◆ Portable printers. 303-460-1600. www.pentax.com

**Philips Laser Magnetic Storage,** 4425 Arrows West Dr., Colorado Springs, CO 80907: Free information ◆ Quad-speed CD-ROM drive for PCs. 719-593-7900.

**Play Incorporated,** 2890 Kilgore Rd., Rancho Cordova, CA 95670: Free information ◆ Video screen image-capture aid for PCs. 916-851-0800.

**Procom Technology Inc.,** P.O. Box 8975, Newport Beach, CA 92658: Free brochure ◆ Tape backup and recovery systems. 800-800-8600. www.procom.com/jetstream

**Proxima Multimedia Projectors,** 9440 Carroll Park Dr., San Diego, CA 92121: Free information ◆ Lightweight and portable multi-media projectors for notebook computers. 800-447-7692; 619-457-5500 (in CA). www.proxima.com

**QMS Inc.,** One Magnum Pass, Mobile, AL 36618: Free information ◆ Color laser printers. 800-392-7559.

**Safe Computing,** 2059 Camden Ave., Ste. 285, San Jose, CA 95124: Free brochure ◆ Voice recognition systems for DOS and Windows. Also ergonomic accessories. 408-269-5430.

**Seagate Technology,** 920 Disc Dr., Scotts Valley, CA 95066: Free list of retail sources ◆ Hard drives. 408-438-6550.

**Smart Modular Technologies,** 4305 Cushing Pkwy., Fremont, CA 94538: Free information ◆ Fax-modem for mobile computers. 510-623-1231.

**Star Micronics America Inc.,** 70-D Ethel Rd. West, Piscataway, NJ 08854: Free information ◆ Laser printers. 908-572-5550.

**Surplus Direct,** P.O. Box 2000, Hood River, OR 97031: Free catalog ◆ Computers, accessories, peripherals, and software. 800-753-7877.

**Thrustmaster,** 7175 NW Evergreen Pkwy., #400, Hillsboro, OR 97124: Free catalog ◆ Game controllers and add-on cards. 503-615-3200.

**Tiger Software,** 8700 W. Flagler St., 4th Floor, Miami, FL 33174: Free catalog ◆ Software, CD-ROMs, other software, and accessories for PCs and the Macintosh. 800-888-4437. www.tigerdirect.com

**Turtle Beach Systems,** Turtle Beach Systems, 5 Odell Plaza, Yonkers, NY 10701: Free information ◆ Multi-media upgrade kit. 800-645-5640. www.tbeach.com

**UMAX Technologies,** 47470 Seabridge Dr., Fremont, CA 94538: Free information ◆ Sheet-fed color scanner with detachable head. 888-289-8629. www.umaxpc.com

**Unisys Direct,** 1100 Corporate Dr., Farmington, NY 14425: Free catalog ◆ Printers, power protection products, terminals, desktop accessories and data collection devices, printing and cleaning supplies, cables and connectors, and more. 800-448-1424; 800-387-6127 (in Canada).

**USA Flex Inc.,** 471 Brighton Dr., Bloomingdale, IL 60108: Free catalog ◆ Computer components, PC desktops and portables, upgrade kits, and peripherals. 800-872-3539. www.USAFLEX.com

**Western Digital Corp.,** 8105 Irvine Center Dr., Irvine, CA 92718: Free list of retail sources ◆ Hard drives and multi-media, and battery management accessories. 714-932-4900. www.wdc.com

## Dust Covers & Cases

**Cases By Bea Maurer,** 113 Executive Dr., Dulles, VA 20166: Free information ◆ Soft and made-to-order hard cases with optional wheels and extension handles. 800-969-8527; 703-709-8118 (in VA).

**Co-Du-Co Computer Dust Covers,** 4802 W. Wisconsin Ave., Milwaukee, WI 53208: Free catalog ◆ Dust covers. 800-735-1584.

**Epson America Inc.,** Corporate Information Center, 20770 Madrona Ave., P.O. Box 2842, Torrance, CA 90509: Free catalog ◆ Dust covers for Epson printers. 800-442-1977. www.epson.com

**NougaCase,** 5681 West Cleveland Rd., South Bend, IN 46628: Free list of retail sources ◆ Full-grain custom Naugahyde laptop cases for computers and other equipment. 800-426-9887.

**Targus Inc.,** 6180 Valley View, Buena Park, CA 90620: Free catalog ◆ Carrying cases for computers and scientific equipment. 800-400-1011. www.targus.com

**Tenba Quality Cases Ltd.,** 503 Broadway, New York, NY 10012: Free list of retail sources ◆ Computer cases. 800-328-3622; 212-966-1013 (in NY). www.tenba.com

**Zero Halliburton,** 500 W. 200 North, North Salt Lake City, UT 84054: Free list of retail sources ◆ Aluminum compartmentized laptop cases with combination locks. 800-728-2511; 801-299-7355 (in UT).

## Education & Training

**Allegro New Media,** 16 Passaic Ave., Fairfield, NJ 07004: Free information ◆ Interactive tutorial for Windows 95. 800-424-1992.

**Class Act Multi-media,** 1121 S. Orem Blvd., Orem, UT 84058: Free information ◆ Interactive Windows software training CD-ROMs. 800-CD-LEARN.

**The Economics Press Inc.,** 12 Daniel Rd., Fairfield, NJ 07004: Free information ◆ Windows training CD-ROMs. 800-526-2554.

**KeyStone Learning Systems,** 2241 Larsen Pkwy., Provo, UT 84606 Free catalog ◆ Training videos for Windows software. 800-647-2368; 801-375-8680 (in UT). www.klscorp.com/cat

**LearnKey Inc.,** 1845 W. Sunset Blvd., St. George, UT 84770: Free catalog ◆ Computer training videos and CD-ROMs. 800-865-0165.

**WEKA Publishing Inc.,** 1077 Bridgeport Ave., P.O. Box 886, Shelton, CT 06484: Free information ◆ Easy-to-follow references and hardware questions for PCs on disks. 800-222-WEKA.

## Furniture

**Anthro Corp.,** 10450 SW Manhasset Dr., Tualatin, OR 97062: Free catalog ◆ Computer furniture. 800-325-3841. www.anthro.com

**Factory Direct.Furniture,** P.O. Box 92967, Milwaukee, WI 53202: Free catalog ◆ Office and computer furniture. 800-972-6570; 289-9770 (in Milwaukee). www.furniture2u.com

**Global Computer Supplies,** 1050 Northbrook Pkwy., Suwanee, GA 30174: Free catalog ◆ Furniture and work stations, hardware, software, peripherals, and printing supplies. 800-227-1246. www.globalcomputer.com

**Innovative Office Products Inc.,** 2100 Liberty St., Easton, PA 18042: Free brochure ◆ Ergonomic space saving computer furniture and accessories. 610-253-9554.

**ScanCo,** P.O. Box 3217, Redmond, WA 98073: Free catalog ◆ Computer furniture. 800-722-6263.

**Wright-Line,** 160 Gold Star Blvd., Worcester, MA 01606: Free brochure ◆ Modular furniture. 508-852-4300.

## Manufacturers (Macintosh)

**Apple Computer Inc.,** 1 Infinite Loop, Cupertino, CA 95014: Free information ◆ Macintosh desktops and portables, printers, and peripherals. 800-776-2333. www.powermacintosh.apple.com

## Manufacturers (Macintosh Compatibles)

**APS Technologies,** 6131 Deramus, P.O. Box 4987, Kansas City, MO 64120: Free catalog ◆ Macintosh compatible desktop systems, drives, supplies, and accessories. 800-233-7550. www.apstech.com

**UMAX Technologies,** 47470 Seabridge Dr., Fremont, CA 94538: Free information ◆ Macintosh compatible desktop systems. 888-289-8629. www.umaxpc.com

## Manufacturers (PCs)

**ABS Computer Technologies Inc.,** 9997 Rose Hills Rd., Whittier, CA 90601: Free information ◆ PC systems and upgrades. 800-876-8088. www.abscomputer.com

**Acer America Corp.,** 2641 Orchard Pkwy., San Jose, CA 95134: Free information ◆ PC desktops and portables. 800-558-ACER. www.acer.com

**Advanced Logic Research Inc.,** 9401 Jeronimo, Irvine, CA 92718: Free information ◆ PC desktops and portables. 800-444-4ALR; 714-581-6770 (in CA).

**Altima Systems Inc.,** 2440 Stanwell Dr., Ste. 1050, Concord, CA 94520: Free information ◆ PC portables. 800-356-9990.

**American Research Corp.,** 602 Monterey Pass Rd., Monterey Park, CA 91754: Free information ◆ PC portables. 800-346-3272; 408-265-0835 (in CA).

**Amrel Technology Inc.,** 11801 Goldring Rd., Arcadia, CA 91006: Free information ◆ PC portables. 800-882-6735.

**APS Technologies,** 6131 Deramus, P.O. Box 4987, Kansas City, MO 64120: Free catalog ◆ Computer systems, drives, supplies, and accessories. 800-233-7550. www.apstech.com

**Ashtek Computers Corp.,** 14712 Franklin Ave., Tustin, CA 92780: Free information ◆ PC desktop systems. 714-505-3157. Ashtek.orders@Juno.com

**AST Research Inc.,** 16215 Alton Pkwy., Irvine, CA 92713: Free information ◆ PC desktops and portables. 800-876-4278. www.ast.com

**AT&T Capital Corp.,** 1830 W. Airfield Dr., P.O. Box 619260, DFW Airport, TX 75261: Free information ◆ PC desktops and portables. 800-874-7123.

**ATD-American Company,** 135 Greenwood Rd., Wyncote, PA 19095: Free catalog ◆ Office and computer furniture, storage and filing cabinets, and display cases. 800-523-2300; 576-1000 (in area code 215).

**Austin Computer Systems,** 603 W. 13th St., Austin, TX 78701: Free catalog ◆ PC portables and desktops. 512-339-4161. www.goaustin.com

**Autotech Corp.,** 343 St. Paul Blvd., Carol Stream, IL 60188: Free information ◆ PC portables. 800-527-2841; 630-668-3900 (in IL).

**Canon Computer Systems,** P.O. Box 3900, Peoria, IL 61612: Free list of retail sources ◆ PC portables. 800-848-4123.

**Chem USA Corp.,** 8445 Central Ave., Newark, CA 94560: Free brochure ◆ Multimedia PC portables. 510-608-8818.

**Commax Technologies,** 2031 Concourse Dr., San Jose, CA 95131: Free information ◆ PC portables. 800-526-6629; 408-435-5000 (in CA).

**Compaq Computer Corp.,** P.O. Box 692000, Houston, TX 77269: Free information ◆ PC desktops and portables. 800-345-1518. www.compaq.com

**Compass Computer Products Corp.,** 17 Harrison Ave., Garfield, NJ 07026: Free information ◆ PC desktops. 973-340-8855.

**Compulink Research Inc.,** 3949 Commerce Pkwy., Miramar, FL 33025: Free information ◆ PC desktop systems. 800-611-1555.

**CTX Computers,** 20470 Walnut Dr., Walnut, CA 91789: Free information ◆ Notebook computers. 909-595-6146.

**Creative Vision Technologies Inc.,** 4113 Sunset Dr., Spring Park, MN 55384: Free information ◆ PC desktop systems. 888-770-0500.

**Data General Corp.,** 4400 Computer Dr., Westborough, MA 01580: Free information ◆ PC portables and dot matrix printers. 800-328-2436; 508-898-5000 (in MA).

**Dell Computer Corp.,** One Dell Way, Round Rock, TX 78682: Free catalog ◆ PC desktops and portables. 800-879-3355. www.dell.com

**Digital Equipment Corp.,** Personal Computer Group, 100 Nagog Rd., Acton, MA 01720: Free information ◆ Personal PCs including handhold portables. 800-722-9332. www.windows.digital.com

**EPS Technologies,** 8877 S. 137th Circle, Omaha, NE 68138: Free information ◆ Notebook computers and PC systems with optional configurations. 800-447-0921. sales@epstech.com

**Everex Systems Inc.,** 5020 Brandin Ct., Fremont, CA 94538: Free information ◆ PC desktops. 800-821-0806.

**Falcon Northwest Computer Systems,** 263 S. Bayshore Dr., Coos Bay, OR 97420: Free information ◆ PC desktops. 800-258-6778; 541-269-0775 (in OR).

**FOSA Computer Inc.,** 120 Corporate Blvd., South Plainfield, NJ 07080: Free brochure ◆ PC portable computers. 908-753-6100. www.fosa.com

**Fujitsu Personal Systems,** 5200 Patrick Henry Dr., Santa Clara, CA 95054: Free information ◆ PC portables. 800-831-3183. www.fpsi.fujitsu.com

**FutureTech Systems Inc.,** 6 Bridge St., Hackensack, NJ 07601: Free information ◆ PC desktops and portables. 201-488-4414.

**Gateway 2000 Computers,** 610 Gateway, North Sioux City, SD 57049: Free information ◆ PC desktops and portables. 800-846-2059; 605-232-2000 (in SD). www.gateway.com

**Goldstar,** 1000 Sylvan Ave., Englewood, NJ 07632: Free information ◆ Portables and PC desktops. 201-816-2000.

**Hewlett-Packard Company,** Direct Marketing Organization, 5301 Stevens Creek Blvd., P.O. Box 58059, MS 51LSJ, Santa Clara, CA 95052: Free information ◆ PC portables, laser and ink-jet printers, and accessories. 800-752-0900. www.hp.com

**HyperData,** 809 S. Lemon Ave., Walnut, CA 91789: Free information ◆ PC portables. 800-786-3343; 909-468-2955 (in CA). www.hyperdatadirect.com

**IBM-PC Direct Marketing,** 3039 Cornwalis Rd., Bldg. 203, Research Triangle Park, NC 27709: Free information ◆ IBM desktops and portables, dot matrix and laser printers, and accessories. 800-426-3333. www.us.pc.ibm.com

**Infostar Inc.,** 165 Main St., Mount Kisco, NY 10549: Free information ◆ PC desktops. 914-666-2358.

**Keydata International,** 111 Corporate Blvd., South Plainfield, NJ 07080: Free information ◆ PC portables. 888-586-5800. sales@keydata-pc.com

**Kingdom Computers,** Lambs Creek Rd., P.O. Box 506, Mansfield, PA 16933: Free information ◆ PC desktop systems and portables. 800-385-3436. www.kingdomcomputers.com

**Long Island Power Computers,** 665 Jericho Tnpk., St. James, NY 11780: Free information ◆ PC desktop systems. 516-265-4525.

**Mega Computer Systems,** 10840 Thornmint Rd., Ste. 118, San Diego, CA 92127: Free information ◆ PC desktops. 619-618-1612.

**Micro Express,** 1811 Kaiser Ave., Irvine, CA 92713: Free information ◆ PC desktops, portables, and multi-media upgrade kits. 800-989-9900.

**Micron Electronics Inc.,** 900 E. Karcher Rd., Nampa, ID 83687: Free information ◆ Notebook computers and PC systems with optional configurations and upgrade accessories. 800-707-2329. www.micronpc.com

**Midern Computer Inc.,** 18005 Courtney Ct., City of Industry, CA 91748: Free information ◆ PC portables. 800-669-1624; 818-964-8682 (in CA).

**Midwest Micro,** 6910 US Rt. 36 East, Fletcher, OH 45326: Free information ◆ PCs, power protection equipment, and peripherals. 800-203-2079. www.mwmicro.com

**Mikon Inc./Mikon Computers,** 13604 Merriman Rd., Livonia, MI 48150: Free information ◆ Portable computers. 800-216-4566.

**Mitsuba Computers,** 1925 Wright Ave., La Verne, CA 91750: Free information ◆ PC portables. 800-648-7822; 909-392-2000 (in CA).

**National MicroComputers Inc.,** 5544 Green St., Murray, UT 84123: Free information ◆ PC desktop systems. 801-265-3700.

**NEC Computer Systems Division,** Packard Bell NEC Inc., 1414 Massachusetts Ave., Boxboro, MA 01719: Free information ◆ PC desktops, portables, and printers. 888-8-NEC-NOW. www.necnow.com

**New World Technologies Inc.,** 110 Greene St., Ste. 5100, New York, NY 10012: Free brochure ◆ Handhold computers with optional modems and other accessories. Also software for business and travel planning, language translation, general information, money management, and games. 212-941-4633. www.nwt.com

**Nimantics Inc.,** 2913 El Camino Real, Ste. 411, Tustin, CA 92782: Free information ◆ Notebook computers. 714-440-8160.

**Olivetti North America Inc.,** 22425 E. Appleway Ave., Liberty Lake, WA 99019: Free information ◆ PC desktops and portables. 800-633-9909; 509-927-5600 (in WA).

**Packard Bell,** One Packard Bell Way, Sacramento, CA 95828: Free information ◆ PC desktops and portables. 888-474-6772. www.packardbell.com

**Panasonic,** Panasonic Way, Secaucus, NJ 07094: Free list of retail sources ◆ PC desktops and portables. 201-348-7000. www.panasonic.com

**Polywell Computers Inc.,** 1461 San Mateo Ave., South San Francisco, CA 94080: Free information ◆ PC desktops. 415-583-7222.

**Premio Computer Inc.,** 1306 John Reed Ct., City of Industry, CA 91745: Free information ◆ PC desktop systems. 800-677-6477.

**Professional Technologies,** 21038 Commerce Pointe Dr., Walnut, CA 91789: Free information ◆ PC desktops. 800-949-5018. www.professionalpc.com

**Prolinear Corp.,** 150 N. Santa Anita Ave., Ste. 300, Arcadia, CA 91006: Free information ◆ Lightweight handhold computer. 800-830-5977; 818-821-1881 (in CA).

**ProStar Company Inc.,** 1128 Coiner Ct., City of Industry, CA 91748: Free information ◆ Notebook computers, memory upgrades, and accessories. 800-576-1134; 626-854-3428 (in CA). www.pro-star.com

**SAG Electronics,** 451 Andover St., North Andover, MA 01845: Free information ◆ Notebook and PC computers with custom configured systems. 800-989-3475.

**Sager Computers,** 18005 Cortney Ct., City of Industry, CA 91748: Free information ◆ Notebook computers with optional configurations. 800-669-1624. www.sager-midern.com

**Samsung Opto-Electronics,** 40 Seaview Dr., Secaucus, NJ 07094: Free information ◆ PC portables. 800-762-7746. www.simplyamazing.com

**Seanix Technology Inc.,** 1501 Zenith Dr., Sioux City, IA 51103: Free information ◆ PC desktops. 888-252-1192.

**Sharp Electronics,** Sharp Plaza, Mahwah, NJ 07496: Free information ◆ PC desktops and portables. 800-BE-SHARP. www.sharp-usa.com

**Swan Technologies,** 313 Boston Post Rd., Ste. 200, Marlborough, MA 01752: Free information ◆ PC desktops and portables. 800-645-7789.

**TC Computers,** 5005 Bloomfield St., Jefferson, LA 70121: Free information ◆ PC computers with custom configured systems. 800-723-8282. www.tccomputers.com

**Tempest Micro,** 18760 E. Amar Rd., Walnut, CA 91789: Free information ◆ PC desktops. 800-818-5163.

**Toshiba America,** P.O. Box 19724, Irvine, CA 92713: Free information ◆ PC portables. 800-457-7777. www.toshiba.com

**Tri-Star Computer Corp.,** 2424 W. 14th St., Tempe, AZ 95281: Free information ◆ PC desktops. 800-800-1929.

**Twinhead Corp.,** 48295 Fremont Blvd., Fremont, CA 94538: Free information ◆ PC portables. 800-995-8946; 510-492-0828 (in CA). www.twinhead.com

**U.S. Robotics,** 8100 N. McCormick Blvd., Skokie, IL 60076: Free information ◆ PC desktops, portables, and handhold notebooks. 800-881-PALM. www.3com.com

**WinBook Computer Corp.,** 1160 Steelwood Rd., Columbus, OH 43212: Free information ◆ PC portables and accessories. 800-468-7502. www.winbook.com

**Zenith Data Systems Direct,** 313 Boston Post Rd., Ste. 200, Marlborough, MA 01752: Free information ◆ PC desktops, portables, and monitors. 800-645-7789. www.zds.com

## Retailers

**Arlington Computer Products Inc.,** 851 Commerce Ct., Buffalo Grove, IL 60089: Free information ◆ Computer systems, peripherals, and software. 800-548-5105; 847-541-6333 (in IL). www.arlingtoncp.com

**Barnett's Computer,** 417 5th Ave., New York, NY 10016: Free information ◆ Desktop systems, portables, and accessories. 800-931-7070; 212-252-0979 (in NY). www.barnettscomputer.com

**BayTech,** Data Communications Products Division, 200 N. 2nd St., P.O. Box 387, Bay St. Louis, MS 38520: Free information ◆ Printer sharing equipment. 800-523-2702; 601-467-8231 (in MS).

**Big City Express,** 96 Hobart St., Hackensack, NJ 07601: Free catalog ◆ Portable and desktop computer systems, accessories, software, and other equipment. 888-252-CITY. www.bigcityexpress.com

**Blitz Computer,** 313 S. 2nd St., Laramie, WY 82070: Free information ◆ PC computers, printers, and peripherals. 800-332-1100.

**Broadway Computer & Video,** 1619 Broadway, New York, NY 10019: Free information ◆ Desktop systems, portables, and accessories. 212-307-6260.

**Business Technology,** 4100 N. Powerline Rd., Pompano Beach, FL 33073: Free information ◆ Portable and desktop computer systems, accessories, software, and other equipment. 800-677-1822. www.anotebook.com

**CDW Computer Centers Inc.,** 200 N. Milwaukee Ave., Vernon Hills, IL 60061: Free information ◆ Hardware, software, and peripherals. 800-434-4239. www.cdw.com

**Chinon America Inc.,** 1065 Bristol Rd., Mountainside, NJ 07092: Free information ◆ CD-ROM drives for the Macintosh. 908-654-0404.

**Club Mac,** 7 Hammond Dr., Irvine, CA 92618: Free catalog ◆ Macintosh and UMAX systems (Macintosh compatibles), peripherals, accessories, and software. 800-258-2622. www.club-mac.com

**Club PC,** 7 Hammond Dr., Irvine, CA 92618: Free catalog ◆ PC systems, peripherals, accessories, and software. 800-258-2622. www.club-mac.com

**CMO Corp.,** 2400 Reach Rd., Williamsport, PA 17701: Free information ◆ Computer systems, peripherals, and software. 800-233-8950.

**Compu-D International Inc.,** 6741 Van Nuys Blvd., Van Nuys, CA 91405: Free catalog ◆ Notebook and desktop computers, printers, scanners, monitors, and accessories. 800-929-9333.

**CompUSA Direct,** 34 St. Martin Dr., Marlborough, MA 01752: Free catalog ◆ Computer equipment, accessories, software, books, and more. 888-421-9005. www.compusa.com

**ComputAbility Consumer Electronics,** P.O. Box 17882, Milwaukee, WI 53217: Free information ◆ Computer systems, peripherals, electronics, and software. 800-558-0003. www.computability.com/csh.html

**Computer Friends Inc.,** 14250 NW Science Park Dr., Portland, OR 97229: Free information ◆ Ribbon inkers and inks. 800-547-3303. www.cfriends.com

**Creative Computers,** Attention: Order Dept., 2645 Maricopa St., Torrance, CA 90503: Free catalog ◆ Desktop PCs, portables, accessories, and supplies. 800-555-6255.

**Dalco Electronics,** 425 S. Pioneer Blvd., Springboro, OH 45066: Free catalog ◆ Computer equipment, tools, and accessories. 800-449-8487. www.dalco.com

**Dartek Computer Supply Group,** 175 Ambassador Dr., Naperville, IL 60540: Free catalog ◆ Hardware, software, peripherals, printing supplies, and more. 800-832-7835; 630-355-3335 (in IL). www.dartek.com

**Data Cal Corp.,** 531 E. Elliot Rd., Chandler, AZ 85225: Free catalog ◆ Computer productivity enhancements, software, keyboard overlays, and templates. 800-223-0123. www.datacal.com

**DataCom Mall Order Department,** 2645 Maricopa St., Torrance, CA 90503: Free catalog ◆ Networking accessories and supplies. 800-560-6800. www.datacom.com

**Data Comm Warehouse,** 1720 Oak St., P.O. Box 301, Lakewood, NJ 08701: Free information ◆ Networking products. 800-328-2261.

**Data Vision,** 445 5th Ave., New York, NY 10016: Free information ◆ Computers and accessories. 888-888-2087; 212-689-1111 (in NY). www.datavis.com

**Daystar Digital,** 5556 Atlanta Hwy., Flowery Branch, GA 30542: Free brochure ◆ Peripheral upgrades for the Macintosh. 800-942-2077.

**DigiCore Inc.,** 15500 Erwin St., Van Nuys, CA 91411: Free information ◆ Macintosh hardware, add-on accessories, software, and peripherals. 800-858-4622.

**Digital Vision Inc.,** 270 Bridge St., Dedham, MA 02026: Free information ◆ Video equipment for PC desktops and the Macintosh. 781-329-5400.

**DirectTech Systems Inc.,** 7615 Golden Triangle Dr., Eden Prairie, MN 55344: Free information ◆ Hard drives, tape backups, and optical drives for the Macintosh. 612-941-2616.

**Dirt Cheap Drives,** 3716 Timber Dr., Dickinson, TX 77539: Free information ◆ Disk, tape, and CD-ROM drives. Also controllers and optical devices. 800-637-4743; 281-534-6292 (in TX). www.dirtcheapdrives.com

**DTPdirect,** 5198 W. 76th St., Edina, MN 55439: Free catalog ◆ Portable and desktop computer systems, accessories, software, and other equipment. 800-759-2133.

**Eastern Camera & Computer Company,** 425 Madison Ave., New York, NY 10017: Free information ◆ Desktop PCs, portables, accessories, and supplies. 888-818-0099; 212-838-1450 (in NY).

**Eastern Computer & Notebook Company,** 425 Madison Ave., New York, NY 10017: Free information ◆ PC and Macintosh desktop computers, portables, and accessories. 888-818-0099; 212-838-1450 (in NY).

**Educational Resources,** 1550 Executive Dr., P.O. Box 1900, Elgin, IL 60121: Free catalog ◆ Software, disks, peripherals, and other equipment. 800-624-2926. Custserv@edresources.com

**Envisions,** 3485 Kifer Rd., Santa Clara, CA 95051: Free information ◆ Scanners. 800-365-7226. www.envisions.com

**Express Direct,** 2720 N. Paulina, Chicago, IL 60614: Free information ◆ Macintosh systems and peripherals. 800-535-3252.

**First Source International,** 7 Journey, Aliso Viejo, CA 92656: Free information ◆ Portable and desktop computer systems, accessories, software, and other equipment. 800-509-9866.

**Future Computing Solutions Inc.,** 23800 Via Del Rio, Yorba Linda, CA 92887: Free information ◆ Portable and desktop computer systems, accessories, software, and other equipment. 714-692-9120.

**GCC Technologies,** 209 Burlington Rd., Bedford, MA 01730: Free catalog ◆ Computer peripherals. 800-422-7777.

**Global Computer Supplies,** 1050 Northbrook Pkwy., Suwanee, GA 30174: Free catalog ◆ Furniture and work stations, hardware, software, peripherals, and printer supplies. 800-227-1246. www.globalcomputer.com

**Harmony Computers,** 1801 Flatbush Ave., Brooklyn, NY 11210: Free information ◆ Computer systems, portables, peripherals, and software. 800-441-1144; 718-692-3232 (in NY). www.shopharmony.com

**Hartford Computer Group Inc.,** 1610 Colonial, Pkwy., Inverness, IL 60067: Free catalog ◆ Portable and desktop computers, accessories, carrying cases, memory upgrades, monitors, printers, input devices, scanners, hard drives, networking accessories, power protection aids, and software. 800-424-8715.

**Hi-Tech USA,** 1582 Centre Pointe Dr., Milpitas, CA 95035: Free information ◆ PCs and add-on components, monitors, VGA cards, modems/faxes, and other peripherals. 800-818-5163.

**Insight Computers,** 6820 S. Harl Ave., Tempe, AZ 85283: Free information ◆ Computers, hardware, and software. 800-467-4448; 602-333-3330 (in AZ). www.insight.com

**The Iomega Corp.,** P.O. Box 208, Roy, UT 84067: Free information ◆ Hard drives for PCs and the Macintosh. 800-456-5522; 801-778-3450 (in UT). www.iomega.com

**K-12 MicroMedia Publishing,** 16 McKee Dr., Mahwah, NJ 07430: Free catalog ◆ Teaching aids, software, and accessories for PC desktops and the Macintosh. 800-292-1997.

**Kenosha Computer Center,** 2133 91st St., Kenosha, WI 53140: Free information ◆ Computers, cards, peripherals, and software. 800-255-2989. www.kcc-online.com

**Lyben Computer Systems,** 5545 Bridgewood, P.O. Box 130, Sterling Heights, MI 48311: Free catalog ◆ Computer supplies and accessories. 800-493-5777. www.lyben.com

**Mac Bargains,** 707 S. Grady Way, Renton, WA 98055: Free information ◆ Macintosh hardware, add-on accessories, software, and peripherals. 800-619-9091.

**Mac Warehouse,** P.O. Box 3031, Lakewood, NJ 08701: Free information ◆ Macintosh accessories and software. 800-367-0440.

**MacConnection,** 528 Rt. 13, Milford, NH 03055: Free information ◆ Macintosh accessories and software. 800-800-3333. www.macconnection.com

**MacMall Order Department,** 2555 W. 190th St., Torrance, CA 90504: Free catalog ◆ Macintosh hardware, add-on accessories, software, and peripherals. 800-222-2808. www.macmall.com

**Macronix Inc.,** 1338 Ridder Park Dr., San Jose, CA 95131: Free information ◆ Voice and fax mail box accessories. 800-858-5311.

**Magellan's,** 110 W. Sola St., Santa Barbara, CA 93101: Free catalog ◆ Compasses, travel aids, and gifts. 800-962-4943. www.magellans.com

**Marine Park Camera & Video Inc.,** 3126 Avenue U, Brooklyn, NY 11229: Free information ◆ Desktop PCs and portables. 800-360-1722; 718-891-1878 (in NY).

**MicroSYSTEMS Warehouse,** 1720 Oak St., P.O. Box 3014, Lakewood, NJ 08701: Free catalog ◆ PCs, peripherals, software, and supplies. 800-660-3222.

**Midland Computers,** 5699 W. Howard, Niles, IL 60714: Free information ◆ PCs and add-on components, plotters, digitizers, and other peripherals. 800-407-0700; 847-588-2130 (in IL).

**MobilePlanet,** 445 5th Ave., New York, NY 10016: Free information ◆ Portable and desktop computer systems, accessories, software, and other equipment. 818-888-7267.

**NETIS Technology Inc.,** 1606 Centre Point Dr., Milpitas, CA 95035: Free information ◆ Computer components, add-on cards, multi-media products, software, bare-bone systems, network stations, and custom-configured PCs. 408-263-0368.

**Network Express,** 1611 1720 Oak St., P.O. Box 301, Lakewood, NJ 08701: Free information ◆ Computer systems, portables, software, peripherals, and CD-ROMs. 800-333-9899.

**New MMI Corp.,** 2400 Reach Rd., Williamsport, PA 17701: Free catalog ◆ Desktop and portable PCs, printers, multi-media equipment, scanners, and accessories. 800-221-4283.

**New World Computers Direct,** 120 McGaw Dr., Edison, NJ 08837: Free catalog ◆ Notebook and desktop computers, printers, scanners, monitors, and accessories. 800-922-6923.

**Newtech Video & Computers,** 350 7th Ave., New York, NY 10001: Free information ◆ Video equipment, computers and peripherals, software, cellular phones, fax machines, and office equipment. 800-554-9747.

**Olivetti North America Inc.,** 22425 E. Appleway Ave., Liberty Lake, WA 99019: Free information ◆ Scanners and dot matrix printers. 800-633-9909; 509-927-5600 (in WA).

**Panasonic,** Panasonic Way, Seacaucus, NJ 07094: Free list of retail sources ◆ Monitors and printers. 201-348-7000. www.panasonic.com

**Para Systems Inc.,** 1455 LeMay Dr., Carrollton, TX 75007: Free information ◆ Un-interruptible power supplies. 800-238-7272.

**PC Computer Solutions,** 130 W. 32nd St., New York, NY 10001: Free information ◆ Portable and desktop computer systems, accessories, software, and other equipment. 800-573-6245. www.pccomputersolution.com

**PC Mall Order Department,** 2645 Maricopa St., Torrance, CA 90503: Free catalog ◆ Hardware, add-on accessories, software, and peripherals for PCs. 800-560-6800. www.macmall.com

**PC Universe Inc.,** 2302 North Dixie Hwy., Boca Raton, FL 33431: Free catalog ◆ PC desktops, portables, accessories, multimedia upgrades, software, and more. 800-728-6483. www.pcuniverse.com

**The PC Zone,** 707 S. Grady Way, Renton, WA 98055: Free catalog ◆ Computer systems, furniture, disks, networking and communications equipment, and software. 800-258-2088. www.pczone.com

**PCS Compleat,** 34 St. Martin Dr., Marlborough, MA 01752: Free catalog ◆ Portable computers and accessories, desktop systems, multi-media equipment, scanners, printers, other peripherals, and software. 800-700-5898. www.PCscompleat.com

**Pinnacle Micro,** 19 Technology Dr., Irvine, CA 92718: Free information ◆ Recordable CD-ROM, optical drives, optical library systems, and more. 800-553-7070. www.pinnaclemicro.com

**Power Up,** 8700 W. Flagler St., 4th Floor, Miami, FL 33174: Free catalog ◆ Portable and desktop computer systems, accessories, software, supplies, and other equipment. 800-335-4055. www.tigerdirect.com

**Publishing Perfection,** P.O. Box 307, Menomonee Falls, WI 53052: Free catalog ◆ Publishing, graphics, and video computer accessories. 800-808-5288. www.publishingperfection.com

**Quill Computers,** 100 Schelter Rd., Lincolnshire, IL 60197: Free catalog ◆ Calculators, computers and accessories, and office supplies. 800-789-1331. www.quillcorp.com

**Radio Shack,** Division Tandy Corp., One Tandy Center, Fort Worth, TX 76102: Free information ◆ PC desktops, portables, monitors, dot matrix and laser printers, and supplies. 817-390-3011. www.radioshack.com

**Rose Electronics,** P.O. Box 742571, Houston, TX 77274: Free information ◆ Printer-sharing control units. 800-333-9343.

**Seiko Instruments USA Inc.,** Graphic Devices and Systems Division, 1130 Ringwood Ct., San Jose, CA 95131: Free information ◆ Thermal-transfer printer. 800-888-0817. www.seiko.com

**Software House International,** 2 Riverview Dr., Somerset, NJ 08873: Free information ◆ Software and peripherals for PC desktops. 800-777-5014.

**Sun Remarketing,** P.O. Box 4059, Logan, UT 84323: Free catalog ◆ PC desktops and Macintosh computers, portables, printers, accessories, books, and software. 800-821-3221. www.sunrem.com

**Sunshine Video & Computers,** 1172 Coney Island Ave., Brooklyn, NY 11230: Free information ◆ Computers, memory upgrades, fax modems, carrying cases, mouse devices, batteries, and other electronics. 800-331-6251; 718-434-1500 (in NY).

**Supra Corp.,** 312 SE Stonemill Dr., Ste. 150, Vancouver, WA 98684: Free information ◆ FAX-modem, disk and hard drives, RAM expansion cards, and accessories. 360-604-1400.

**Tatung Company of America Inc.,** 2850 El Presidio St., Long Beach, CA 90810: Free information ◆ Monitors. 800-829-2850.

**Tri-State Computer,** 650 6th Ave., New York, NY 10011: Free information ◆ Computers, monitors, expansion systems, drives, peripherals, and software. 800-433-5199; 212-633-2530 (in NY). tscamvid@aol.com

**United CD Rom,** 800 United CD Rom Dr., Champaign-Urbana, IL 61802: Free catalog ◆ Computers and accessories, printers, other peripherals, and CD-Roms and software for PCs and the Macintosh. 800-864-8334. www.unitedCDROM.com

**United Computer Warehouse,** 7909 3rd Ave., Brooklyn, NY 11209: Free information ◆ Portable and desktop computer systems, accessories, software, and other equipment. 800-727-8786.

**USA Flex Inc.,** 471 Brighton Dr., Bloomingdale, IL 60108: Free catalog ◆ Components, PC desktops and portables, upgrade kits, and accessories. 800-872-3539. www.USAFLEX.com

## Software (Public Domain & Shareware)

**CompuServe,** P.O. Box 20212, Columbus, OH 43220: Free information ◆ Public domain software and shareware for PCs. 800-848-8990.

**Crazy Bob's Software,** 50 New Salem St., Wakefield, MA 01880: Free information ◆ Public domain software, shareware, and CD-ROMs for PCs. 800-776-5865.

**Data Mate,** Box 2811, Ronkonkoma, NY 11779: Free catalog ◆ Over 3000 shareware programs.

**Donnux Shareware,** P.O. Box 410, Milford, VA 22514: Free catalog ◆ Shareware for the Macintosh and PCS. 800-352-3878.

**Educorp Computer Services,** 7434 Trade St., San Diego, CA 92121: Free information ◆ Public domain software and multi-media CD-ROMs for the Macintosh and PCs. 800-843-9497; 619-536-9999 (in CA).

**IBM Shareware,** Box 2424, Scottsdale, AZ 85252: Free catalog ◆ Shareware for PCs. 602-496-6547.

**Reasonable Solutions,** 1221 Disk Dr., Medford, OR 97501: Free information ◆ User-supported software for PCs. 800-876-3475.

**Walnut Creek Software,** 4041 Pike Ln., Ste. D, Concord, CA 94520: Free information ◆ Music education for PCS on CD-ROMs that includes how-to create, play, mix, and change music. Also CD-ROMs and public domain software and shareware for PCS. 800-786-9907.

## Software Publishers (Disks & CD-ROMs)

**The following are examples of some of the publishers that one can choose from to find software. They are intended only to illustrate the many types and formats of software available.**

**Aatrix Software,** P.O. Box 5359, Grand Forks, ND 58201: Free information ◆ Business and home management software for the Macintosh. 800-426-0854.

**Abacus Software,** 5370 52nd St. SE, Grand Rapids, MI 49512: Free information ◆ Home and business applications and utilities for PCS. 800-451-4319.

**Abracadata,** P.O. Box 2440, Eugene, OR 97402: Free catalog ◆ Graphics software for PCS and the Macintosh. 800-451-4871. 800-451-4871; 541-342-3030 (in OR). www.abracadata.com

**Acceleration Software International Corp.,** 699 3rd Ave., Ste. 3800, Seattle, WA 98104: Free information ◆ Acceleration software for the Macintosh, DOS, and Windows 3.1 and 95. 800-754-1128.

**Access Software Inc.,** 4750 Wiley Post Way, Bldg. 1, Ste. 200, Salt Lake City, UT 84116: Free information ◆ Games and adventure software for PCS and the Macintosh. 800-800-4880.

**Accolade Inc.,** 5300 Stevens Creek Blvd., San Jose, CA 95128: Free information ◆ Software for PCs and the Macintosh. 800-245-7744. www.accolade.com

**Active Arts,** 610 SW Broadway, Ste. 500, Portland, OR 97205: Free information ◆ Educational software on CD-ROMs. 503-228-8000.

**Adobe Systems Inc.,** P.O. Box 1034, Buffalo, NY 14240: Free information ◆ Desktop publishing and graphics software for PCS. Desktop publishing, graphics, home and business applications, and productivity software for the Macintosh. 800-685-4586. www.adobe.com

**Adventures In Ancestry,** 10714 Hepburn Circle, Culver City, CA 90232: Free brochure ◆ Genealogy software for checking background information. 310-842-7442.

**AEC Software Inc.,** 22611 Markey Ct., Bldg. 113, Sterling, VA 20166: Free information ◆ Scheduling software for the Macintosh. 703-450-1980.

**Agfa Computers,** Bayer Industries, 200 Ballardvale St., Wilmington, MA 01887: Free list of retail sources ◆ Scanners, scanning and color management software, typeface packs, and font management software for PCs. 800-685-4271. www.agfahome.com

**Aladdin Systems,** P.O. Box 629000, El Dorado Hills, CA 95762: Free brochure ◆ Spell checker, data compression, disk-cleaning, clip art, and other Macintosh software. 800-242-1550.

**Alpha Software Corp.,** 168 Middlesex Tnpk., Burlington, MA 01803: Free brochure ◆ DOS and Windows database software. 800-858-4411.

**American Business Information,** 5711 S. 86th Circle, P.O. Box 27347, Omaha, NE 68127: Free information ◆ Windows CD-ROM telephone directories. 800-555-5666.

**American Megatrends,** 6145-F Northbelt Pkwy., Norcross, GA 30071: Free information ◆ Diagnostic software for PCS. 800-828-9264.

**American Microsystems Inc.,** 2190 Regal Pkwy., Euless, TX 76040: Free information ◆ Windows label designing and bar coding software. 800-648-4452.

**Apple Computer Inc.,** 1 Infinite Loop, Cupertino, CA 95014: Free information ◆ Software for the Macintosh. 800-776-2333. www.powermacintosh.apple.com

**Argos Gameware,** 25 E. Spring Valley Ave., Maywood, NJ 07067: Free brochure ◆ CD-ROM games for PCs. 800-327-3713.

**AskSam Systems,** 119 S. Washington St., P.O. Box 1428, Perry, FL 32347: Free information ◆ PC information manager programs that include word processing, text retrieval, and a database. 800-800-1997.

**Athnena Design,** 132 Berkeley St., Boston, MA 02116: Free information ◆ OS/2 spreadsheet software. 617-262-1604.

**Avalan Technology Inc.,** P.O. Box 6888, Holliston, MA 01746: Free information ◆ Windows remote communications software for PCS. 800-441-2281.

**Avery Dennison,** 20955 Pathfinder Rd., Diamond Bar, CA 91765: Free catalog ◆ Laser and ink-jet printer labels, label-printing software, and other related products. 800-252-8379. www.avery.com

**Axiom Research Inc.,** 2450 E. Speedway, Ste. 3, Tucson, AZ 85719: Free information ◆ Astronomy image-processing software. 520-791-2864.

**Baler Software Corp.,** 1400 Hicks Rd., Rolling Meadows, IL 60008: Free information ◆ Spreadsheet software for PCs. 800-327-6108.

**Bandai Digital Entertainment,** 5551 Katella Ave., Cypress, CA 90630: Free information ◆ Windows and Macintosh adventure, action games, and lifestyle software. 714-816-9700.

**Berkeley Systems,** 2095 Rose St., Berkeley, CA 94709: Free information ◆ Entertainment and games software for PCS and the Macintosh. 510-540-5535.

**Best Ware,** 300 Roundill Dr., Rockaway, NJ 07866: Free information ◆ Windows bookkeeping and accounting software for PCS. 800-322-6962.

**Bethesda Softworks,** 1370 Piccard Dr., Ste. 120, Rockville, MD 20850: Free brochure ◆ Windows 95 games software. 800-677-0700; 301-963-2000 (in MD).

**Bible Research Systems,** 2013 Wells Branch Pkwy., Ste. 304, Austin, TX 78728: Free brochure ◆ Bible education software for PCs and the Macintosh. 800-423-1228. www.brs-inc.com/bible

**BibleSoft,** 22014 7th Ave. South, Seattle, WA 98198: Free information ◆ Windows and DOS bible-study software. 800-995-9058.

**Bitstream Inc.,** 215 1st St., Cambridge, MA 02142: Free information ◆ Windows fonts and font management software for PCS. 800-522-3668.

**Block Financial Software,** 55 Walls Dr., P.O. Box 912, Fairfield, CT 06430: Free information ◆ DOS and Windows financial management and tax preparation software for PCS. 800-288-6322.

**Blue Byte Software Inc.,** 870 Higgins Rd., Ste. 143, Schaumburg, IL 60173: Free catalog ◆ Games software for PCS. 800-933-2983. www.bluebyte.com

**Borland International,** 100 Borland Way, Scotts Valley, CA 95066: Free information ◆ Debugger and assembly software for PCS. Database, desktop publishing, education, programming tools, and utilities software for the Macintosh. 800-645-4559. www.borland.com

**Brainstorm Concepts,** 2609 Windmere Dr., Norcross, GA 30071: Free information ◆ DOS integrated accounting system for PCS. 800-240-6257.

**The Bridge World,** 717 White Plains Rd., Ste. 106, Scarsdale, NY 10583: Free catalog ◆ Bridge books, magazines, computer software for Windows, games, and accessories. 914-725-6712. www.bridgeworld.com

**Broderbund Software,** P.O. Box 6125, Novato, CA 94948: Free catalog ◆ Entertainment and games software and CD-ROMs for PCs and the Macintosh. 800-521-6263. www.broderbund.com

**Bureau of Electronic Publishing,** 141 New Rd., Parsippany, NJ 07054: Free information ◆ Education, Windows, and DOS multi-media CD-ROMs for PCs and the Macintosh. 800-828-4766.

**BytePro Corp.,** 2192 Martin, Ste. 220, Irvine, CA 92612: Free brochure ◆ Integrated client information, scheduling, billing, and accounts payable and receivable software. 800-713-5322.

**Caere Corp.,** 100 Cooper St., Los Gantos, CA 95030: Free brochure ◆ Windows forms management and design software. 800-535-SCAN.

**Cakewalk Music Software,** P.O. Box 760, Watertown, MA 02272: Free brochure ◆ Integrated, multi-track MIDI, and digital audio editing programs for recordings. 888-CAKEWALK.

**Canon Computer Systems,** P.O. Box 3900, Peoria, IL 61612: Free list of retail sources ◆ Creative graphics CD-ROM for making stickers, labels, photo collages and layouts, greeting cards, stationery, and other projects. 800-848-4123.

**Cardiff Software Inc.,** 1782 La Costa Meadows Dr., San Marcos, CA 92069: Free brochure ◆ Data collection and management software for PCS. 800-659-8755.

**Carlisle Development Corp.,** P.O. Box 291, Carlisle, MA 01741: Free information ◆ Windows inventory control system for coin collectors. 800-219-0257.

**Cartesia Software,** 80 Lambert Ln., P.O. Box 757, Lambertville, NJ 08530: Free brochure ◆ Digital data-created mapping CD-ROMs for Windows and the Macintosh. 609-397-1611. www.map-art.com

**Casady & Greene Inc.,** 22734 Portola Dr., Salinas, CA 93908: Free brochure ◆ Business and entertainment software for PCS and the Macintosh. 800-339-4920; 408-484-9228 (in CA).

**CE Software Inc.,** P.O. Box 65580, West Des Moines, IA 50265: Free information ◆ Macintosh communications, graphics, home and business applications, and utilities software. 800-523-7638.

**Charles River Media,** P.O. Box 417, 403 VFW Dr., Rockland, MA 02370: Free catalog ◆ Web page construction and other Internet software. 800-382-8505.

**Cheyenne Software, A Division of Computer Associates,** P.O. Box 1624, Buffalo, NY 14240: Free brochure ◆ Anti-virus software for Windows 95. 888-216-9278.

**The Church of Jesus Christ of Latter-day Saints,** Salt Lake Distribution Center, 1999 W. 1700 South, Salt Lake City, UT 84104: Free information ◆ Macintosh and PC genealogy software. 800-537-5950; 801-240-2584 (in UT).

**Claris Corp.,** 5201 Patrick Henry Dr., P.O. Box 58168, Santa Clara, CA 95052: Free information ◆ Software for Macintosh computers. 800-331-6187. www.claris.com

**Clear Software Inc.,** 199 Wells Ave., Newton, MA 02159: Free information ◆ Flow charting software. 800-338-1759.

**Cliff's Notes Inc.,** P.O. Box 80728, Lincoln, NE 68501: Free information ◆ SAT study guide software for the Macintosh. 800-228-4078; 402-423-5050 (in NE).

**Computer Support Corp.,** 15926 Midway Rd., Dallas, TX 75244: Free information ◆ Windows drawing program for PCS. 972-661-8960.

**CompTutor Software, LLC,** 8174 S. Holly St., #199, Littleton, CO 80122: Free catalog ◆ Educational and language software for the Macintosh and PC computers. 800-654-2328.

**ConnectSoft Inc.,** 11130 NE 33rd Pl., Ste. 250, Bellevue, WA 98004: Free information ◆ Windows e-mail software. 800-234-9497.

**Corel Corp.,** 1600 Carling Ave., Ottawa, Ontario, Canada K1Z 8R7: Free information ◆ Graphics, drawing, and image-editing software for PCs and the Macintosh. 613-728-8200. www.corel.com

**Corex Technologies,** 130 Prospect St., Ste. 201, Cambridge, MA 02139: Free information ◆ Easy-to-use database for business location and organization. 617-492-4200.

**COSMI Corp.,** 2600 Homestead Pl., Rancho Dominguez, CA 90220: Free information ◆ Screen saver for Windows. Also fonts, forms-maker, spreadsheet, word processor, and other programs for PCS. 310-833-2000.

**Cougar Mountain Software,** 7180 Potomac Dr., Boise, ID 83704: Free information ◆ Accounting, business, and financial management software. 800-388-3038. www.cougarmtn.com

**Creative Wonders,** P.O. Box 7532, San Mateo, CA 94403: Free information ◆ Educational alphabet-learning software for children, ages 3 to 6. 800-245-4525; 650-573-7111 (in CA).

**CyberMedia,** 3000 Ocean Park Blvd., Ste. 2001, Santa Monica, CA 90405: Free brochure ◆ Software for diagnosing and correcting Windows problems. Also uninstall and privacy protection software. 800-721-7824. www.cybermedia.com

**DacEasy Inc.,** 17950 Preston Rd., Ste. 800, Dallas, TX 75252: Free information ◆ Windows business and financial management software for PCs. 800-322-3279.

**Data Pro Accounting Software Inc.,** 5439 Beaumont Center Blvd., Ste. 1050, Tampa, FL 33634: Free information ◆ Financial management software for PCS. 800-237-6377.

**DataViz Inc.,** 55 Corporate Dr., Trumbull, CT 06611: Free information ◆ Software for converting PC files for use with the Macintosh, and Macintosh to PC format. 800-270-0030. www.dataviz.com

**Davidson & Associates,** P.O. Box 2961, Torrance, CA 90509: Free catalog ◆ Education software for PCS and the Macintosh. 800-545-7677. www.davd.com

**Davka Corp.,** 7074 N. Western Ave., Chicago, IL 60645: Free information ◆ Hebrew and Judaic software for PCs and the Macintosh. 800-621-8227; 773-465-4070 (in IL).

**Decathlon Corp.,** 4100 Executive Dr., #16, Cincinnati, OH 45241: Free information ◆ Logo design software for PCs and the Macintosh. 800-648-5646; 513-421-1938 (in OH).

**Deep River Publishing Inc.,** 565 Congress St., Portland, ME 04101: Free brochure ◆ DOS and Windows travel guides and where-to-eat, what-to-see, house designing, and fractal patterns software on CD-ROMs. 800-643-5630; 207-871-1684 (in ME).

**DeLorme Mapping,** P.O. Box 298, 2 DeLorme Dr., Yarmouth, ME 04096: Free information ◆ Windows atlas information and telephone number software. Also maps, gazetteers, and atlases in print form. 800-452-5931. www.delorme.com

**DeltaPoint,** 22 Lower Ragsdale Dr., Monterey, CA 93940: Free information ◆ Word processing software for PCs and charting software for PCS and the Macintosh. 408-648-4000. www.deltapoint.com

**Deneba Software,** 7400 SW 87th Ave., Miami, FL 33173: Free information ◆ Macintosh productivity, utilities, and graphics software. Graphics software for PCs. 305-273-9877. www.deneba.com

**Digital Directory Assistance,** 6931 Arlington Rd., Ste. 405, Bethesda, MD 20814: Free information ◆ Windows CD-ROM telephone directory. 800-284-8353; 301-639-2900 (in MD).

**Digital Impact,** 6506 S. Lewis, Ste. 250, Tulsa, OK 74136: Free brochure ◆ Software libraries on CD-ROMs. 800-775-4232.

**Disney Interactive,** 500 S. Buena Vista St., Burbank, CA 91521: Free information ◆ Entertainment, games, and educational software for PCS. 800-228-0988. www.disneyinteractive.com

**DK Publishing Inc.,** 95 Madison Ave., New York, NY 10016: Free catalog ◆ Muilti-media CD-ROM software for Windows and the Macintosh. 800-DKMM-575. www.dk.com

**DogByte Developments,** 612 Moulton Ave., Ste. 7, Los Angeles, CA 90031: Free information ◆ Graphics and designing software for picture framing, card-making, photo album designing, and creating scrapbook pages. 800-936-4298. www.dogbyte.com

**Dor L'Dor Software,** 7103 Mill Run Dr., Rockville, MD 20855: Free brochure ◆ Interactive Judaic learning software for PCS and the Macintosh. 301-963-9303.

**Dow Jones & Company Inc.,** US Hwy. 1, Princeton, NJ 08541: Free information ◆ Stock and investment management programs for PCS. 609-520-5111.

**Dream Maker Software,** 925 W. Kenyon Ave., Ste. 16, Englewood, CO 80110: Free information ◆ Clip-art for PCs and the Macintosh. 303-762-1001.

**Edmark Software,** P.O. Box 97021, Redmond, WA 98073: Free information ◆ Educational software for young children, ages 2 to 14. 425-556-8400. www.edmark.com

**EKEBA Software,** P.O. Box 15131, Columbus, OH 43215: Free brochure ◆ Event management software for Windows 3.x, 95/98, or NT. 800-847-4561. www.ekeba.com

**Electronic Arts,** 1450 Fashion Island Blvd., San Mateo, CA 94404: Free information ◆ Arcade, sports, flight simulation, and other software for PCS and the Macintosh. 800-245-4525; 415-573-7111 (in CA).

**Executive Software,** 701 N. Brand Blvd., 6th Floor, Glendale, CA 91203: Free brochure ◆ Defragmenter software for Windows NT. 800-829-6468. www.diskeeper.com

**Expert Software Inc.,** 800 Douglas Rd., Executive Tower, 7th Floor, Coral Gables, FL 33134: Free information ◆ Clip art, educational astronomy, creating legal documents, games, entertainment, fonts, art and drawing, home design, and other software for PCs. 800-759-2562; 305-567-9990 (in FL). www.expertsoftware.com

**Falcon Software Inc.,** 1 Hollis St., Wellesley, MA 02181: Free catalog ◆ Environmental science, general and organic chemistry, and electronics simulator software. 617-235-1767.

**Fineware Systems,** P.O. Box 75776, Oklahoma City, OK 73147: Free information ◆ Windows disk manager software for PCs. 800-544-1740.

**1st Desk Systems Inc.,** 7 Industrial Park Rd., Medway, MA 02053: Free information ◆ Database software for the Macintosh. 800-522-2286.

**Flix Productions Animated Educational Software,** 601 Ranch Rd., DelValle, TX 78617: Free information ◆ Windows 3.1 and 95 educational programs.

**FontHaus Inc.,** 1375 Kings Hwy. East, Fairfield, CT 06430: Free information ◆ Font software for PCs. 800-942-9110.

**FontShop USA Inc.,** 47 W. Polk St., #100-310, Chicago, IL 60605: Free information ◆ Font software for PCs. 800-897-3872.

**ForeFront Direct,** 25400 US Hwy. 19 North, Clearwater, FL 34623: Free information ◆ Diagnostic, data recovery, computer training, and Internet software. 800-475-5831; 813-724-8994 (in FL).

**Frame Technology Corp.,** 333 W. San Carlos, San Jose, CA 95110: Free information ◆ Desktop publishing software for PCs. 408-975-6000.

**Fujitsu Networks Industry Inc.,** 1266 E. Main St., Stamford, CT 06902: Free information ◆ Windows communications program. 800-446-4736.

**Fusion Software,** 9039 Katy Fwy., Houston, TX 77024: Free information ◆ Inventory management control and consumer-oriented software for PCs. 800-856-8566; 713-465-6363 (in TX).

**G & A Imaging,** 975 St. Joseph Blvd., Hull, Quebec, Canada J8Z 1W8: Free list of retail sources ◆ Management software for displaying, searching, inputting into computers from external sources, and enhancing photographs. 888-772-7601.

**Global Village Communications Inc.,** 1144 E. Arques Ave., Sunnyvale, CA 94086: Free information ◆ DOS and Windows fax software. 800-FAX-WORK; 408-523-1000 (in CA).

**Globalink Inc.,** 9302 Lee Hwy., 12th Floor, Fairfax, VA 22031: Free information ◆ DOS and Windows foreign language translation programs for PCs. 800-255-5660.

**The Gold Bug,** P.O. Box 588, Alamo, CA 94507: Free brochure ◆ United States historical and site finder Windows software. 888-653-6277. www.goldbug.com

**Golfstats,** Box 366, Long Valley, NJ 07853: Free information ◆ Windows and DOS golf score-keeping software. 908-850-5252.

**Great Games Products,** 8804 Chalon Dr., Bethesda, MD 20817: Free brochure ◆ Mouse-supported computer bridge games for DOS 2.0 or higher, Windows, and the Macintosh. 800-GAMES-4-U.

**Grolier Electronic Publishing Inc.,** 90 Sherman Tnpk., Danbury, CT 06816: Free information ◆ The New Grolier multi-media encyclopedia for PCs. 800-285-4534. www.grolier.com

**GT Interactive Software,** 16 E. 40th St., New York, NY 10016: Free information ◆ PC games software. 212-726-6500. www.gtineractive.com

**Harmonic Vision,** 906 University Pl., Evanston, IL 60201: Free information ◆ Music education software for PCs. 800-644-4994. www.harmonicvision.com

**Hayes Microcomputer Products Inc.,** 5835 Peachtree Corners East, Norcross, GA 30092: Free information ◆ Communications software for PCs and the Macintosh. 770-840-9200.

**HobbyWare,** P.O. Box 501996, Indianapolis, IN 46250: Free brochure ◆ Pattern maker software for cross-stitching. 800-768-6257.

**Horse Feathers Graphics,** N. 27310 Short Rd., Deer Park, WA 99006: Free information ◆ Western computer graphics for PCs and the Macintosh. 509-276-6928. www.horse-feathers.com

**Houghton-Mifflin,** 120 Beacon St., Somervlle, MA 02143: Free catalog ◆ Interactive software for building children's scientific skills. 800-829-7962. www.hminet.com

**Humongous Entertainment,** 13110 NE 177th Pl., Ste. B101, Box 180, Woodinville, WA 98072: Free catalog ◆ Windows and Macintosh CD-ROM problem-solving and educational games. 800-499-8386. www.humongous.com

**Imaja Software,** P.O. Box 6386, Albarry, CA 94706: Free brochure ◆ Music, history, and interactive animated painting educational software. 510-526-4621.

**IMC Software,** 7318 Harrison St., Omaha, NE 68128: Free information ◆ Account management and scheduling system for PCs. 800-704-9009.

**Impresario Software,** 1705 S. Pearl St., Denver, CO 80210: Free information ◆ Hand and machine-knitting software for PCs and the Macintosh. 303-698-9233.

**Impressions Software,** 222 3rd St., Ste. 0234, Cambridge, MA 92142: Free information ◆ Games software for PCs. 800-545-7677.

**IMSI Software,** 1895 Francisco Blvd. East, San Rafael, CA 94901: Free brochure ◆ Office automation and project management, lifestyles and learning, computer aided design, and desktop publishing software for PCs. 800-833-4674; 415-257-3000 (in CA).

**Informix Software Inc.,** 4100 Bohannan Dr., Menlo Park, CA 94025: Free information ◆ Spreadsheet software for the Macintosh. 800-331-1763.

**Innovation Advertising & Design,** 41 Mansfield Ave., Essex Junction, VT 05452: Free information ◆ PC and Macintosh clip-art. 800-255-0562.

**Inset Systems Inc.,** 71 Commerce Rd., Brookfield, CT 06804: Free information ◆ DOS graphics capture and conversion utility for PCS. 800-374-6738.

**Interactive Image Technologies Ltd.,** 908 Niagara Falls Blvd., North Tonawanda, NY 14120: Free information ◆ Electronic circuit and layout design software. 800-263-5552. www.interactiv.com

**International Chess Enterprises Inc.,** P.O. Box 19457, Seattle, WA 98109: Free information ◆ Chess games on CD-ROMs, magazines, and books. 800-26-CHESS. www.insidechess.com

**Intuit,** 2650 E. Elvira Rd., Ste. 100, Tucson, AZ 85706: Free information ◆ Home and business applications and tax preparation software for PCS and the Macintosh. 800-544-1365. www.intuit.com

**IVI Publishing,** 7500 Flying Cloud Dr., Eden Prairie, MN 55344: Free information ◆ Windows human anatomy on CD-ROMs. 800-432-1332; 612-996-6000 (in MN).

**Jeppesen,** 55 Inverness Dr. East, Englewood, CO 80112: Free information ◆ Flight planning and training, logging and record-keeping, moving map software, and marine navigation software. 800-628-4640. www.jeppesen.com

**JetForm Corp.,** 800 South St., Ste. 305, Waltham, MA 02154: Free information ◆ Windows forms design program. 800-FORM-DSK.

**Jewish Software Center,** 15466 Los Gatos Blvd., Ste. 109-106, Los Gatos, CA 95032: Free information ◆ Software programs for all aspects of Jewish life. 408-395-6457.

**Jian Software,** 1975 W. El Camino Real, Ste. 301, Mountain View, CA 94040: Free brochure ◆ Software on how to start, build, and run a business. 415-254-5600.

**Knowledge Adventure Inc.,** 4502 Dyer St., La Crescenta, CA 81214: Free information ◆ United States geography, other educational, and multi-media programs for PCS. 800-542-4240; 626-542-4200 (in CA).

**Dave Koch Sports,** P.O. Box 656, Stevens Point, WI 54481: Free information ◆ PC football. 715-344-2480.

**Landmark Research International Corp.,** 5770 Roosevelt Blvd., Clearwater, FL 34615: Free information ◆ Windows compression software. 800-683-6696.

**Laureate Learning Systems,** 110 E. Spring St., Winooski, VT 05404: Free information ◆ Talking software programs for children 6 months to 8 years of age. Includes language intervention, cognitive processing, reading, and instructional games. 802-655-4755. www.llsys.com

**The Learning Company,** 1 Athenaeum St., Cambridge, MA 02142: Free information ◆ Education software and games for PCS and the Macintosh. 617-494-5700. www.learningco.com

**Leister Productions,** P.O. Box 289, Mechanicsburg, PA 17055: Free information ◆ Genealogy family tree software for the Macintosh. 717-697-1378. info@LeisterPro.com

**Letraset USA,** 40 Eisenhower Dr., Paramus, NJ 07653: Free information ◆ Font software for PCS. 800-343-8973.

**LEV Software,** 693 Racquet Club Rd., #2, Fort Lauderdale, FL 33326: Free information ◆ Interactive software for learning how to speak Hebrew. 800-776-6538. www.levsoftware.com

**Linotype-Hell Company,** 425 Oser Ave., Hauppauge, NY 11788: Free information ◆ Fonts for PCs. 800-633-1900 (in USA); 800-366-3735 (in Canada).

**Lionheart Press Inc.,** P.O. Box 20756, Mesa, AZ 85277: Free information ◆ Macintosh home and business applications, productivity, and database management software. 602-396-0899.

**Lotus Development Corp.,** P.O. Box 31755, Salt Lake City, UT 84131: Free information ◆ Communications, desktop publishing, education, graphics, home and business applications, productivity, utilities, and word processing software for PCs. 800-346-4010.

**LucasArts Entertinment Company**, P.O. Box 1567, Orem, UT 84059: Free catalog ◆ Windows 95 and Macintosh games and entertainment software. 888-538-7529. www.lucasarts.com

**Lyriq International Corp.,** 1701 Highland Ave., Cheshire, CT 06410: Free information ◆ Golf games software on CD-ROMs for PCs. 203-250-2070.

**MacMillan Digital Publishing,** 201 W. 103rd St., Indianapolis, IN 46290: Free catalog ◆ DOS and Windows software. 800-545-5914; 317-581-5801 (in IN). www.superlibrary.com

**Manhattan Analytics Inc.,** 912 Manhattan Ave., 2nd Floor, Manhattan Beach, CA 90266: Free information ◆ Mutual funds management system. 800-251-3863.

**Maxis Software,** Electronic Arts, 1450 Fashion Island Blvd., San Mateo, CA 94404: Free information ◆ DOS games for PCs. Also astronomy software. 800-245-4525; 415-573-7111 (in CA). www.maxis.com

**MECC Software,** 6160 Summit Dr. North, Minneapolis, MN 55430: Free information ◆ Education software for PCs. 800-685-6322.

**Media Cybernetics L.P.,** 8484 Georgia Ave., Ste. 200, Silver Spring, MD 20910: Free information ◆ Windows desktop imaging utility for adding graphics to documents. 800-992-4256.

**Merriam-Webster Inc.,** P.O. Box 281, Springfield, MA 01102: Free brochure ◆ Word games, reference materials, and learning tools. 800-201-5029. www.m-w.com

**MetaCreations Corp.,** P.O. Box 724, Pleasant Grove, UT 84062: Free catalog ◆ Animation and graphics software for Windows and Macintosh computers. 800-846-0111. www.metacreations.com

**Metro ImageBase Inc.,** 18623 Ventura Blvd., Ste. 210, Tarzana, CA 91356: Free information ◆ Disk and CD-ROM clip-art for PCs and the Macintosh. 800-525-1552.

**MiBAC Music Software,** P.O. Box 468, Northfield, MN 55057: Free information ◆ How to read and understand music software for PCS. 800-645-3945.

**Micro 2000 Inc.,** 1100 E. Broadway, Ste. 301, Glendale, CA 91205: Free information ◆ DOS data recovery program for PCS. 800-864-8008.

**Micro Vision Software Inc.,** 140 Fell Ct., Hauppage, NY 11788: Free information ◆ DOS and Windows tax preparation and other DOS software for PCs. 800-829-7353; 516-232-1040 (in NY). www.mvsinc.com

**MicroBiz,** 777 Corporate Dr., Mahwah, NJ 07430: Free brochure ◆ Business software and accessories. 800-637-8268. www.microbiz.com

**MicroCode Engineering,** 573 W. 1830 N., Ste. 4, Orem, UT 84057: Free information ◆ Software for designing electronic circuits. 800-419-4242.

**Microforum,** 1 Woodborough Ave., Toronto, Ontario, Canada M6M 5A1: Free information ◆ Voice-operated Windows game on CD-ROMs. 800-465-2323.

**MicroLogic Software,** 1351 Ocean Ave., Emeryville, CA 94608: Free information ◆ Windows and DOS true-type fonts. 800-888-9078.

**Microsoft Corp.,** One Microsoft Way, Redmond, WA 98052: Free information ◆ Productivity software for the Macintosh and PCs. Database, entertainment, games, graphics, home and business applications, productivity and programming tools, and spreadsheet software for the Macintosh. 800-426-9400; 425-882-8080 (in WA). www.microsoft.com

**Mindscape Inc.,** 88 Rowland Way, Novato, CA 94945: Free information ◆ Windows and DOS programs. 415-897-9900. www.mindscape.com

**MKS Inc.,** 35 King St. North, Waterloo, Ontario, Canada N2J 2W9: Free information ◆ Software programs for PCs. 800-884-8861.

**ModelOffice,** 4815 W. Braker Ln., #502-332, Austin, TX 78759: Free brochure ◆ Business, personal letters, speech-writing, how-to make toasts, and sales letters software for PCs. 800-801-3880; 512-302-3888 (in TX).

**Monotype Typography Inc.,** 985 Busse Rd., Elk Grove Village, IL 60007: Free information ◆ Font software for PCs. 800-666-6897; 847-718-0400 (in IL). www.monotype.com

**Multicom Publishing,** 188 Embarcadero, 5th Floor, San Fransisco, CA 94105: Free brochure ◆ Home improvement, food and wine, travel, special events, just for kids, gardening, travel, sports, and special interest CD-ROMs. www.multicom.com

**Nautical Software,** 14657 SW Teal Blvd., Beaverton, OR 97007: Free information ◆ Windows tides and currents software for PCs. 503-579-1414. www.tides.com

**Neosoft Corp.,** 354 NE Greenwood Ave., Ste. 108, Bend, OR 97701: Free information ◆ Easy-to-use publishing software. 541-389-5489. admin@neosoftware.com

**New World Technologies Inc.,** 110 Greene St., Ste. 5100, New York, NY 10012: Free brochure ◆ Handheld computers with optional modems and other accessories. Also software for business and travel planning, language translation, general information, money management, and games. 212-941-4633. www.nwt.com

**Nolo Press,** 950 Parker St., Berkeley, CA 94710: Free catalog ◆ Home, business, and productivity software for PCs and the Macintosh. 800-992-6656. www.nolo.com

**North Systems,** 6821 Lemongrass Loop SE, Salem, OR 97306: Free information ◆ Investment indicator software for PCs. 503-364-3829.

**Nova Development Corp.,** 23801 Calabasa Rd., Ste. 2005, Calabasas, CA 91302: Free brochure ◆ Clip-art and other software for Windows 3.1 and 95. 800-395-NOVA.

**Odyssey Development,** The Denver Technology Center, 8775 E. Orchard Rd., Ste. B11, Englewood, CO 80111: Free information ◆ Windows and DOS information retrieval software for WordPerfect and word processing programs. 800-992-4797.

**Omega Research,** 9200 Sunset Dr., Miami, FL 33173: Free information ◆ Windows stock charting software for investors. 800-422-3410.

**Open Systems Computing Corp.,** 45 Whitney Rd., Ste. B8, Mahwah, NJ 07430: Free information ◆ DOS word processing program and database for PCs. 800-445-9292.

**Optelec,** 6 Lyberty Way, Westford, MA 01886: Free catalog ◆ Low-vision aids for visually impaired people. Includes software for magnifying text to large print and an add-on color magnifier for PCs. 800-828-1056; 978-392-0707 (in MA).

**Orange Cherry,** New Media Schoolhouse, Box 390, Pound Ridge, NY 10576: Free catalog ◆ Educational software on disks and CD-ROMs for the Macintosh and PCs. 800-672-6002.

**Origin Systems Inc.,** 5918 W. Courtyard Dr., Austin, TX 78730: Free information ◆ Entertainment and games for PCs. 800-245-4525; 512-434-4263 (in TX).

**Papyrus Design Group,** 35 Medford St., Ste. 305, Somerville, MA 02143: Free information ◆ Simulated Indianapolis car racing software for PCs. 617-868-5440.

**Parsons Technology,** P.O. Box 100, Hiawatha, IA 52233: Free information ◆ Virus-detection, business and financial-management, entertainment, games, educational software, health, and other software. 800-779-6000. www.parsonstech.com

**Peachtree Software,** 1505 Pavilion Pl., Norcross, GA 30093: Free information ◆ Windows business and financial management software for PCs. 800-247-3224.

**Penelope Craft Programs Inc.,** P.O. Box 1204, Maywood, NJ 07607: Free information ◆ PC and Macintosh software for knitters. 201-368-8379.

**Pinnacle Webworks,** P.O. Box 4620, Seattle, WA 98104: Free information ◆ Windows graphics, charts, and presentation software. 800-231-1293. www.thewebworkz.com

**PKWARE Inc.,** 9025 N. Deerwood Dr., Brown Deer, WI 53223: Free brochure ◆ Data compression software for Windows, MS-DOS and DOS 32, OS/2, and UNIX. 414-354-8699.

**Raima Corp.,** 701 5th Ave., Ste. 4800, Seattle, WA 98104: Free information ◆ Database program for PCs. 800-327-2462. www.raima.com

**Rand McNally New Media,** 8255 N. Central Park Ave., Skokie, IL 60076: Free catalog ◆ Street-finding, travel-planning, and general reference software. 800-671-5006. www.randmcnally.com

**Relay Technology Inc.,** 1604 Spring Hill Rd., Ste. 400, Vienna, VA 22182: Free information ◆ General-purpose Windows and DOS relay operating and control program for PCs. 800-795-8674.

**Resolution Mapping Inc.,** One Riverside Dr., Andover, MA 01810: Free information ◆ Nautical mapping and charting software for PCS. 978-933-3000. www.maptech.com

**RMS Technology Inc.,** 124 Berkley, P.O. Box 249, Molalla, OR 97038: Free information ◆ Flight planning and moving map software programs. 800-533-3211. www.RMSTek.com

**Rockware Inc.,** The Rockware Bldg., 2221 East St., Ste. 101, Golden, CO 80401: Free catalog ◆ Earth science software. 800-775-6745; 303-278-534 (in CO). www.rockware.com

**RT Computer Graphics Inc.,** P.O. Box 45300, Rio Rancho, NM 87174: Free information ◆ Native America, southwest-style, and wild west clip-art for PCs and the Macintosh. 505-891-1600. www.rtcomputer.com

**Rupp Technology Corp.,** 2240 N.Scottsdale Rd., Tempe, AZ 85281: Free information ◆ Hard drive locking program for PCs. 800-852-7877. www.rupp.com

**Scholastic Software,** 555 Broadway, New York, NY 10012: Free information ◆ Education, utilities, programming tools, and word processing software for PCs and the Macintosh. 212-343-6100.

**Serif Inc.,** P.O. Box 803, Nashua, NH 03061: Free information ◆ Windows desktop publishing and graphic design software. 800-55-SERIF.

**Sierra Direct,** 7100 W. Center Rd., Ste. 301, Omaha, NE 68106: Free information ◆ Software for PCS and Macintosh computers. 800-757-7707. www.sierra.com

**Sir-Tech Software,** P.O. Box 245, Ogdensburg, NY 13669: Free information ◆ Games software for PCs. 315-393-6633.

**Tom Snyder Productions,** 80 Coolidge Rd., Watertown, MA 02172: Free information ◆ Education software for PCs and Macintosh computers. 800-342-0236.

**Softdisk Publishing,** P.O. Box 30008, Shreveport, LA 71130: Free catalog ◆ Software for PCs and Macintosh computers. 800-831-2694.

**SoftKey International Inc.,** 1 Athenaeum St., Cambridge, MA 023142: Free information ◆ Windows CD-ROM road atlas and street map, label-making, and graphics-photograph manipulation software. 617-494-5700. www.learningco.com

**Software Studios,** 52 E. Main St., #2, American Fork, UT 84003: Free information ◆ Easy-to-use address book software for WordPerfect. 800-700-0545.

**Software Systems for Golf,** Attention: Chuck Fain, 1512 Seabrook Ave., Cary, NC 27511: Free information ◆ Handicap system, tournament manager, foursome generator, and league manager software for PCs. 919-460-7424. www.golfsoftware.com

**Solution Technology,** 1101 S. Rogers Circle, Bldg. 14, Boca Raton, FL 33487: Free information ◆ OS/2 graphics for PCs. 407-241-3210.

**Soundtrek,** 3408 Howell St., Ste. F, Duluth, GA 30136: Free information ◆ Windows song writing software. 770-623-0879.

**Spectrum Holobyte,** 2490 Mariner Square Loop, Alameda, CA 94501: Free information ◆ Software for PCs and Macintosh computers. 510-522-3584.

**Spellex Development Inc.,** P.O. Box 271264, Tampa, FL 33688: Free information ◆ Legal and medical dictionary modules for WordPerfect, Microsoft, or Lotus. Also spelling checkers. 813-933-7394.

**Spinnaker Software Corp.,** 201 Broadway, 6th Floor, Cambridge, MA 02139: Free catalog ◆ Software for PCs and the Macintosh. 617-494-1200.

**SportsProducts.com,** P.O. Box 702618, Tulsa, OK 74170: Free information ◆ Sports instructional videos, books, and software for professional and amateur youth coaches and players. 800-926-5892. www.sportsproducts.com

**SPSS Software Inc.,** 444 N. Michigan Ave., Chicago, IL 60611: Free information ◆ Spreadsheet software with statistics, graphs, and report-writing capability. 800-543-5837.

**Starboard Software,** Box 1462, Royal Oak, MI 48068: Free information ◆ Boating navigation software for PCs and the Macintosh. 248-545-9928.

**Strata Inc.,** 37 E. St. George, St. George, UT 84770: Free information ◆ Graphics modeling and animation software for the Macintosh. 801-628-9512.

**Strategic Simulations Inc.,** c/o Electronic Arts, 1450 Fashion Island Blvd., San Mateo, CA 94404: Free information ◆ Entertainment and games software for PCs. 800-245-4525.

**Streetwise Software,** 2116 Wilshire Blvd., Ste. 230, Santa Monica, CA 90403: Free brochure ◆ Add-on modules for WordPerfect and MS-Word desktop publishing programs. 800-743-6765. www.swsoftware.com

**Success Learning Systems,** P.O. Box 1536, Mukilteo, WA 98275: Free catalog ◆ Early-learning language arts, mathematics, science, social studies, general reference, and foreign language CD-ROMs for Macintosh computers and Windows. 800-990-6674.

**Sumeria Inc.,** 329 Bryant St., Ste. 3D, San Francisco, CA 94107: Free information ◆ Educational information CD-ROMs for PCs. 800-478-6374.

**Surado Solutions Inc.,** 1960 Chicago Ave., Ste. D9, Riverside, CA 92507: Free information ◆ Home manager software for PCs. 800-478-7236; 909-682-4895 (in CA). www.surado.com

**Symantec Corp.,** 10201 Torre Ave., Cupertino, CA 95014: Free information ◆ Graphics, productivity, communications, virus-protection, and utilities software for the Macintosh and PCs. 800-441-7234. www.symantec.com

**TechPool Studios,** 1463 Warrensville Rd., Cleveland, OH 44121: Free catalog ◆ Anatomy, dental, and emergency medical clip-art for the Macintosh and PCs. 800-543-3278.

**Terrapin Software,** Division Harvard Associates Inc., 10 Holworthy St., Cambridge, MA 02138: Free catalog ◆ Macintosh, Windows, and DOS software. 800-972-8200. info@terrapinlogo.com

**Theatrix Interactive,** 1250 45th St., Emeryville, CA 94608: Free brochure ◆ Windows and Macintosh CD-ROM interactive science, math, writing and creativity, and music software for children. 800-955-TRIX.

**TikSoft Inc.,** 803 East St., Frederick, MD 21701: Free information ◆ Macintosh speed doubler, ram doubler, clip-art, and uninstall software. 888-890-3982.

**Torah Educational Software,** 21 Main St., Monsey, NY 10952: Free information ◆ Judaic educational software on CD-ROMs for PCs and Macintosh computers. 914-356-1485. www.jewishsoftware.com

**Totem Graphics Inc.,** 6200 Capitol Blvd., Ste F, Tumwater, WA 98501: Free information ◆ Clip-art for PCs and the Macintosh. 360-352-1851. gototem@orcalink.com

**TouchStone Software,** 2124 Main St., Huntington Beach, CA 92648: Free information ◆ Windows trouble-shooting, file transfer and synchronization, and anti-virus software. 800-932-5566; 714-969-7746 (in CA). www.touchstonesoftware.com

**Transparent Language Inc.,** P.O. Box 575, Hollis, NH 03049: Free brochure ◆ Spanish, French, German, Italian, Russian, and Latin language-learning disks and CD-ROMs for Windows and the Macintosh. 800-332-8851.

**Transparent Software Systems,** 2639 N. Adoline Ave., Fresno, CA 93705: Free information ◆ DOS and Windows Judaic organization management software. 209-226-5147.

**TRIUS Software,** 231 Sutton St., P.O. Box 249, North Andover, MA 01845: Free information ◆ Spreadsheet programs for PCs. 800-468-7487.

**Tropich Software Inc.,** 529 Central Ave., Scarsdale, NY 10583: Free information ◆ Windows filing system for photographs. 914-472-0278.

**Trove Software,** P.O. Box 218, Olathe, KS 66051: Free information ◆ Windows, DOS, and Macintosh inventory control software for coin collectors. 800-548-8901.

**True BASIC Inc.,** 12 Commerce Ave., West Lebanon, NH 03784: Free information ◆ Communications, desktop publishing, education, graphics, programming tools, and productivity software for the Macintosh. 800-436-2111.

**Twelve Tone Systems,** P.O. Box 760, Watertown, MA 02272: Free information ◆ Easy-to-use Windows music software for PCs. 800-234-1171.

**Ulead Systems,** 970 W. 190th St., Ste. 520, Torrance, CA 90502: Free brochure ◆ Multi-media editing and information-management software for PCs. 800-858-5323.

**Unicorn Software Company,** 6000 S. Eastern Ave., Bldg. 9, Ste. A, Las Vegas, NV 89119: Free information ◆ Education software for PCs and the Macintosh. Entertainment and games for the Macintosh. 702-597-0818.

**Unitype Software,** 3023 80th Ave. SE, Ste. 200, Mercer Island, WA 98040: Free information ◆ Windows multi-lingual word processing programs. 206-230-4911. info@unitype.com

**ViaGrafix,** One American Way, Pryor, OK 74361: Free catalog ◆ Computer training, graphics, and other designing software. 800-842-4723; 918-825-6700 (in OK). www.viagrafix.com

**Virtual Entertainment,** 200 Highland Ave., Needham, MA 02194: Free information ◆ Entertainment and educational software for PCS. 781-449-7567.

**Voice Pad Software,** 11236 Aurora Ave., Urbandale, IA 50322: Free brochure ◆ Voice recognition software. Create documents hands-free, simply by speaking to your PC and without using a keyboard. 888-256-5441.

**Walnut Creek Software,** 4041 Pike Ln., Ste. D, Concord, CA 94520: Free information ◆ Music education for PCs on CD-ROMs that includes how to create, play, mix, and change music. Also CD-ROMs and public domain software and shareware for PCs. 800-786-9907.

**Wheeler Arts,** 66 Lake Park, Champaign, IL 61821: Free information ◆ Re-sizable black-and-white drawings and cartoons for the Macintosh, DOS, and Windows. Available on CD-ROMs and disks. 217-359-6816.

**Wizard Games of Scotland Ltd.,** P.O. Box 498, Wilmington, MA 01887: Free information ◆ Sports management, software simulations, and software games. 800-ITS-GOAL.

**Worden Brothers,** 4905 Pine Cone Dr., Ste. 12, Durham, NC 27707: Free information ◆ Stock and mutual fund analysis system for PCs. 800-776-4940.

**WordPerfect,** Division Corel Corp., 1600 Carling Ave., Ottawa, Ontario, Canada K1Z 8R7: Free information ◆ Word processing software. 613-728-8200. www.corel.com

**World Book Educational Products,** 525 W. Monroe St., 20th Floor, Chicago, IL 60661: Free information ◆ World Book multi-media encyclopedia on Windows CD-ROMs. 312-876-2200. www.worldbook.com/company/html/company.htm

**World Software Corp.,** 124 Prospect St., Ridgewood, NJ 07450: Free brochure ◆ Windows document profiling and retrieval system for PCS. 201-444-3228.

**WritePro,** 43 S. Highland, Ossining, NY 10562: Free information ◆ Writer's software. 800-755-1124.

**Zedcor Publishing,** 3420 Dodge Blvd., Tucson, AZ 85716: Free information ◆ Clip art for PCs. 520-881-8101.

## Software & CD-ROM Retailers

**CCV Software,** P.O. Box 6724, Charleston, WV 25362: Free catalog ◆ Educational software and multimedia products. 800-680-7707.

**The Chessworks Studio,** David Weinstock, 6253 36th Ave. NE, Seattle, WA 98115: Free catalog ◆ Chess accessories, software, contemporary chess books, and rare and hard-to-find chess books. 206-526-8116. www.chessmate.com

**Christian Book Distributors,** P.O. Box 7000, Peabody, MA 01961: Free catalog ◆ Windows, DOS, and Macintosh religious computer software. Also CD-ROMs. 978-977-5050. www.chrbook.com

**ComputAbility Consumer Electronics,** P.O. Box 17882, Milwaukee, WI 53217: Free information ◆ Software on CD-ROMs and disks. 800-558-0003. www.computability.com/csh.html

**Computer Express,** 31 Union Ave., Sudbury, MA 01776: Free information ◆ Sports, entertainment, and games software for PCs. 800-228-7449.

**Data Cal Corp.,** 531 E. Elliot Rd., Chandler, AZ 85225: Free catalog ◆ Computer productivity enhancements and software. 800-223-0123. www.datacal.com

**Dell Computer Corp.,** One Dell Way, Round Rock, TX 78682: Free catalog *PC desktops, portables, software, and accessories. 800-879-3355. www.dell.com

**Educational Resources,** 1550 Executive Dr., P.O. Box 1900, Elgin, IL 60121: Free catalog ◆ Software, disks, peripherals, and computers. 800-624-2926. Custserv@edresources.com

**The Edutainment Catalog,** P.O. Box 21210, Boulder, CO 80308: Free catalog ◆ Games and learning software for the entire family. 800-338-3844. www.edutainco.com

**Egghead Software,** 22705 E. Mission, Liberty Lake, WA 99019: Free catalog ◆ DOS, Windows, and Macintosh software on disks and CD-ROMs. 800-EGGHEAD. www.egghead.com

**Gamer's Gold,** 1008 W. 41st St., Sioux Falls, SD 57105: Free price list ◆ Used games and hint books for PCS. 800-377-8578.

**Global Computer Supplies,** 1050 Northbrook Pkwy., Suwanee, GA 30174: Free catalog ◆ Work stations and furniture, hardware, software, peripherals, and printing supplies. 800-227-1246. www.globalcomputer.com

**Great Christian Books,** 229 S. Bridge St., P.O. Box 8000, Elkton, MD 21922: Free catalog ◆ Bible study software. 800-775-5422.

**Hearlihy & Company,** 714 W. Columbia St., Springfield, OH 45504: Free catalog ◆ Software for education, computer-aided designing, and drawing and drafting. Also drafting and graphics equipment, instructional aids and how-to information, plotters, furniture, supplies, and accessories. 800-622-1000. www.hearlihy.com

**Kidsoft,** Attn. Order Processing, 10275 N. DeAnza Blvd., Cupertino, CA 95014: Free catalog ◆ Windows and Macintosh educational games, fun, and other software for children. 800-354-6150; 408-255-3434 (in CA).

**Mac Warehouse,** P.O. Box 3013, Lakewood, NJ 08701: Free catalog ◆ Macintosh software. 800-367-0440.

**The Mac Zone,** 707 S. Grady Way, Renton, WA 98055: Free information ◆ Macintosh software. 800-248-0800.

**MacConnection,** 528 Rt. 13, Milford, NH 03055: Free information ◆ Macintosh accessories and software. 800-800-3333. www.macconnection.com

**National CD-ROM,** 11005 Indian Trail, Ste. 101-A, Dallas, TX 75229: Free information ◆ CD-ROMs. 800-237-6613.

**Newtech Video & Computers,** 350 7th Ave., New York, NY 10001: Free information ◆ Video equipment, computers and peripherals, software, cellular phones, fax machines, and office equipment. 800-554-9747.

**PC Connection,** 6 Mill St., Marlow, NH 03456: Free information ◆ Software for PCs. 800-800-5555. www.pcconnection.com

**Peripherals Plus,** 5016 Rt. 9 South, Howell, NJ 07731: Free information ◆ Software for PCS and the Macintosh. 800-444-7369.

**Precision Type,** 47 Mall Dr., Commack, NY 11725: Free information ◆ Software fonts for PCs. 800-248-3668.

**The Programmer's Shop,** 33 Riverside Dr., Hingham, MA 02043: Free information ◆ Software for PCs. 781-740-0120.

**Queue Software Inc.,** 338 Commerce Dr., Fairfield, CT 06432: Free catalog ◆ Educational CD-ROMs and software for DOS, Windows, and the Macintosh. 800-232-2224; 203-335-0906 (in CT).

**Schoolmasters Science,** 745 State Circle, Box 1941, Ann Arbor, MI 48106: Catalog $2 ◆ Interactive CD-ROMs on science. 800-521-2832. www.schoolmasters.com

**Software Clearance Outlet,** 3501 W. Moore, #C, Santa Ana, CA 92704: Free catalog ◆ Software from auctions, liquidation, and close-outs. 800-230-SOFT. www.SOFTWAREOUTLET.com

**Software House International,** 2 Riverview Dr., Somerset, NJ 08873: Free information ◆ Software and peripherals for PCs. 800-777-5014.

**Surplus Software Inc.,** 489 N. 8th St., Hood River, OR 97031: Free information ◆ Clearinghouse specials of overstocked, over-produced, and distressed software inventories. 800-753-7877; 503-386-1375 (in OR).

**Tiger Software,** 8700 W. Flagler St., 4th Floor, Miami, FL 33174: Free catalog ◆ Accessories and software on CD-ROMs and disks for PCs and the Macintosh. 800-888-4437. www.tigerdirect.com

**Titan Games,** 1 W. Seminary St., Brandon, VT 05733: Free catalog ◆ Games on disks and CD-ROMs for PCs. 800-247-5447.

**United CD Rom,** 800 United CD Rom Dr., Champaigne-Urbana, IL 61802: Free catalog ◆ Computers and accessories, printers, other peripherals, and CD-ROMs and software for PCS and the Macintosh. 800-864-8334. www.unitedCDROM.com

**Water Fountain Software Inc.,** 13 E. 17th St., New York, NY 10003: Free information ◆ Pattern printing software in custom-fitted full sizes for men and women. 800-605-7460.

**Wright-Line,** 160 Gold Star Blvd., Worcester, MA 01606: Free brochure ◆ CD-ROMs for the Macintosh. 508-852-4300.

**WWW.UNITED CD.ROM,** 800 United CD-ROM Dr., Urbana, IL 61802: Free catalog ◆ CD-ROMs for PCs and the Macintosh computer. 800-864-8334. www.unitedCDROM.com

### Supplies

**Action Office Supplies,** P.O. Box 277, Adelphia, NJ 07710: Free catalog ◆ Hewlett-Packard supplies and accessories. 800-298-1000. www.actoff.com

**American Ribbon Company,** 2895 W. Prospect Rd., Fort Lauderdale, FL 33309: Free information ◆ Printer ribbons, laser toner cartridges, and ink-jet refills. 800-327-1013. www.icanet.net/arctoner

**Chenesko Products Inc.,** 2221 5th Ave., Ste. 4, Ronkonkoma, NY 11779: Free catalog ◆ Recharging kits for laser printer and copier toner cartridges. 800-221-3516; 516-467-3205 (in NY). www.chenesko.com

**Columbia Omnicorp,** 14 W. 33rd St., New York, NY 10001: Free catalog ◆ Office and computer supplies, furniture, and artist materials. 212-279-6161.

**Dayton Computer Supply,** 6501 State Rt. 123 North, Franklin, OH 45005: Free information ◆ Printer ribbons. 800-735-3272.

**Function One,** 13641 John Glenn Rd., Apple Valley, CA 92307: Free information ◆ Printer ribbons, ink-jet refills, and formatted disks. 760-247-4755.

**Global Computer Supplies,** 1050 Northbrook Pkwy., Suwanee, GA 30174: Free catalog ◆ Work stations and furniture, hardware, software, peripherals, and printing supplies. 800-227-1246. www.globalcomputer.com

**Idea Art,** 2603 Elm Hill Pike, Ste. P, Nashville, TN 37229: Free catalog ◆ Pre-designed paper and supplies for desktop publishing. 800-433-2278; 615-889-4989 (in TN). www.ideaart.com

**Image Papers by Data Cal,** 531 E. Elliot Rd., Chandler, AZ 85225: Free catalog ◆ Paper for flyers, greeting cards, professional brochures, and letterheads. 800-223-0123. www.datacal.com

**International Ribbons,** 7707 E. Acoma Dr., Scottsdale, AZ 85260: Free information ◆ Printer ribbons. 800-292-6272.

**Island Computer Supply,** 305 Grand Blvd., Massapequa Park, NY 11762: Catalog $2 (refundable) ◆ Printer ribbons and disks. 516-798-6500.

**MEI/Micro Center,** 1100 Steelwood Rd., Columbus, OH 43212: Free information ◆ Disks, disk cases, ribbons, surge protectors, and accessories. 800-634-3478.

**MIS Associates Inc.,** 282 Kirksway Ct., Lake Orion, MI 48362: Free information ◆ Refill kits for ink-jet printers, re-manufactured laser toner cartridges, and high-resolution ink-jet papers. 800-445-8296.

**Omnicorp,** 14 W. 33rd St., New York, NY 10001: Free catalog ◆ Art supplies, drafting materials, ink jet and toner cartridges, and more. 212-279-6161. www.columbiaomni.com

**Paper Access,** 23 W. 18th St., New York, NY 10011: Free information ◆ Over 500 choices of paper for laser printers. 800-PAPER-01.

**Paper Direct Inc.,** 100 Plaza Dr., Secaucus, NJ 07094: Free catalog ◆ Pre-designed paper and supplies for enhancing printed projects. 800-272-7377. www.paperdirect.com

**RAMCO Computer Supplies,** P.O. Box 475, Manteno, IL 60950: Free information ◆ Printer and heat transfer ribbons, printer paper, and supplies. 800-522-6922.

**Visible,** Subsidiary Wallace Computer Services Inc., 1750 Wallace Ave., St. Charles, IL 60174: Free catalog ◆ Computer and office supplies. 800-323-0628.

## COOKIE CUTTERS

**The Basket Case,** P.O. Box 3230, Hayden Lake, ID 83835: Catalog $1 ◆ Cookie cutters. 208-664-1261.

**Bayberry Farm Peddlers,** P.O. Box 447, Perkasie, PA 18944: Catalog $2 ◆ Cookie cutters.

**Cookie Craft,** P.O. Box 295, Hope, NJ 07844: Free catalog ◆ Cookie cutters. 800-272-3822; 908-459-4220 (in NJ).

**Cookie Cutter Cupboard,** 1305 Kearney, Laramie, WY 82070: Free catalog ◆ Cookie cutters and sets.

**D.D. Dillon,** 850 Meadow Ln., Camp Hill, PA 17011: Free information ◆ Handcarved cookie and shortbread molds. 717-761-6895.

**The-House-on-the-Hill,** P.O. Box 7003, Villa Park, IL 60181: Brochure $2 (refundable) ◆ Replicas of antique European cookie molds. Also Springerle molds. 630-969-2624.

**Kitchen Collectibles,** Attn: Order Processing, 5062 S. 108th St., Ste. 184, Omaha, NE 68137: Free price list ◆ Solid copper cookie cutters, available individually or in sets. 888-593-2436; 402-597-0980 (in NE). www.kitchengifts.com

**The Little Fox Factory,** 931 Marion Rd., Bucyrus, OH 44820: Brochure $1 ◆ Handcrafted cookie cutters. 419-562-5420.

**Sur La Table,** Catalog Division, 1765 6th Ave., Seattle, WA 98134: Free information ◆ Handcarved thistle-pattern wood shortbread molds and cooking and baking equipment. 800-243-0852.

**Wilton Enterprise Inc.,** 2240 W. 75th St., Woodridge, IL 60517: Catalog $6 (refundable) ◆ Cookie cutters and supplies for making and decorating cookies, candies, and cakes. 630-963-7100.

## COPIERS & FAX MACHINES

**AV Distributors,** 10765 Kingspoint, Houston, TX 77075: Free information ◆ Fax machines and audio, video, stereo, and TV equipment. 800-843-3697.

**Computability Consumer Electronics,** P.O. Box 17882, Milwaukee, WI 53217: Free catalog ◆ Fax machines and copiers. 800-558-0003. www.computability.com/csh.html

**Crutchfield,** 1 Crutchfield Park, Charlottesville, VA 22906: Free catalog ◆ Fax machines, telephones and answering machines, word processors, personal copiers, and software. 800-955-9009. www.crutchfield.com

**Newtech Video & Computers,** 350 7th Ave., New York, NY 10001: Free information ◆ Video equipment, computers and peripherals, software, cellular phones, fax machines, and office equipment. 800-554-9747.

**Olden Video,** 1265 Broadway, New York, NY 10001: Free information ◆ Telephones, copiers, and photographic equipment. 212-226-3727.

**Reliable Home Office,** P.O. Box 1502, Ottawa, IL 61350: Catalog $2 ◆ Computer accessories and furniture, filing and storage systems, and fax machines. 800-326-6230.

**Sound City,** 45 Indian Lane East, Towaco, NJ 07082: Free information ◆ Audio and video equipment, cassette and CD players, camcorders, TVS, word processors, fax machines, telephones, and electronics. 800-432-0007; 973-263-6060 (in NJ). www.soundcity.com

**Staples Inc.,** P.O. Box 5173, Westborough, MA 01581: Free catalog ◆ Fax machines, typewriters, word processors, office supplies and furniture, computer supplies, and drafting equipment. 800-333-3330. www.staples.com

**Tri-State Camera,** 650 6th Ave., New York, NY 10011: Free information ◆ Fax machines, copiers, audio and video equipment, camcorders, and photography equipment. 800-221-1926; 212-633-2290 (in NY). tscamvid@aol.com

## COSMETICS & SKIN CARE

**All Natural Botanicals,** 112001 44th St. North, Clearwater, FL 33762: Free catalog ◆ Fragrance and essential oils, bath and body preparations, potpourri, incense, diffusers, and more. 813-572-7800. allnatbo@aol.com

**Angel's Earth,** 1633 Scheffer Ave., St. Paul, MN 55116: Catalog $2 ◆ Soaps, candles, cosmetics, incense, skin care preparations, essential oils, and aromatherapy items. 612-698-3601.

**Arizona-Sun Products Inc.,** P.O. Box 1786, Scottsdale, AZ 85252: Catalog $2 ◆ PABA-free lotions and oil-free sun screens. 800-442-4786. www.arizonasun.com

**Aveda Cosmetics,** 4000 Pheasant Ridge Dr., Minneapolis, MN 55434: Catalog $3.95 ◆ Plant-based cosmetics and skin care products. 800-328-0849. www.aveda.com

**Avon Beauty & Fashion by Mail,** One Pine St., Ridgely, MD 21685: Free catalog ◆ Moisturizers, sun protection and special treatments, bath preparations, fragrances, cosmetics, and skin care aids. 800-500-2866. www.avon.com

**Barth's,** P.O. Box 50289, Pompano Beach, FL 33074: Free catalog ◆ Natural vitamin and mineral supplements, cosmetics, health foods, and home health aids. 800-645-2328.

**Baudelaire Fine Imported Cosmetics Inc.,** 160 Emerald St., Keene, NH 03431: Free information ◆ Imported European therapeutic bath oils rich in herbal extracts and essential oils. 603-352-9234.

**Beautiful Visions,** 1233 Montauk Hwy., P.O. Box 9000, Oakdale, NY 11769: Free catalog ◆ Women and men's nationally advertised cosmetics and toiletries. 800-645-1030.

**Beauty Boutique,** 6836 Engle Rd., P.O. Box 94520, Cleveland, OH 44101: Free catalog ◆ Cosmetics, toiletries, skin care items, costume jewelry, and women's fashions. 440-826-1712.

**Beehive Botanicals Inc.,** Rt. 8, Box 8257, Hayward, WI 54843: Free brochure ◆ Skin care products made with natural ingredients and propolis produced by honeybees. 800-283-4483. www.beehive-botanicals.com

**Bioenergy Nutrients,** 6565 Odell Pl., Boulder, CO 80301: Catalog $1 ◆ Nutritional supplements, homeopathic medicines, antioxidants, and all-natural skin care products. 800-627-7775. www.amiron.com

**The Body Shop Inc.,** Attention: Catalog Dept., 45 Horsehill Rd., Cedar Knolls, NJ 07927: Free catalog ◆ Toiletries, cosmetics, and hair care products. 800-426-3922.

**Brookside Soap Company,** P.O. Box 55638, Seattle, WA 98155: Free catalog ◆ Natural body care products. 425-742-2265. BrooksideSoap@msn.com

**Caswell-Massey Company Ltd.,** Catalog Division, 100 Enterprise Pl., Dover, DE 19901: Catalog $1 ◆ Toiletries, cosmetics, and personal care products. 800-326-0500. caswell@maui.net

**Mary Chess Inc.,** P.O. Box 754, FDR Station, New York, NY 10150: Free information ◆ Skin care and fragrance toiletries. 800-225-3235.

**Churchill Herbs,** 608 Chimborazo Blvd., Richmond, VA 23223: Free catalog ◆ Potpourri, potpourri supplies, essential and fragrance oils, and homemade soaps.

**Classique Perfumes Inc.,** 139-01 Archer Ave., Jamaica, NY 11435: Free catalog ◆ Designer fragrances for women and men. 718-657-8200.

**Common Scents,** 3920 24th St., San Francisco, CA 94114: Free catalog ◆ Bath and skin care products and essential oils. 800-850-6519.

**Crabtree & Evelyn Limited,** P.O. Box 167, Woodstock Hill, CT 06281: Catalog $3.50 ◆ Soaps and shampoos, bath gels and oils, colognes and toilet waters, creams, lotions, talcum powders, sponges, brushes, and combs from England, France, and Switzerland. 800-624-5211. www.crabtree-evelyn.com

**Dry Creek Herb Farm,** 13935 Dry Creek Rd., Auburn, CA 95602: Free information ◆ Skin care products and herbal teas. 916-878-2441.

**East End Import Company,** 1699 Roosevelt Ave., Bohemia, NY 11716: Free brochure with long SASE ◆ Essential oils, absolutes, concretes, creams, lotions, and floral waters. 516-562-2436.

**Essential Products Company Inc.,** 90 Water St., New York, NY 10005: Free catalog ◆ Copies of fragrances for men and women. 212-344-4288.

**Famous Smoke Shop Inc.,** 55 W. 39th St., New York, NY 10018: Free catalog ◆ Women and men's cosmetic fragrances. 800-672-5544.

**Floris of London,** 703 Madison Ave., New York, NY 10021: Free catalog ◆ English perfumes and toiletries for men and women. 800-5-FLORIS; 212-935-9100 (in NY).

**Fragrance International,** 398 East Raven Ave., Youngstown, OH 44505: Free price list ◆ Body lotions, dusting powders, perfumes and colognes, soap and bath products, and health and beauty items. 216-747-3341.

**FragranceNet,** 2070 Deer Park Ave., Deer Park, NY 11729: Free catalog ◆ Over 1200 name brand fragrances for men and women. 800-987-3738; 516-242-3205 (in NY). www.fragrancenet.com

**Frontier Cooperative Herbs,** P.O. Box 299, Norway, IA 52318: Free information ◆ Essential and fragrance oils and herbal extracts. 800-786-1388. www.frontierherb.com

**Fredericksburg Herb Farm,** P.O. Drawer 927, Fredericksburg, TX 78624: Catalog $2 ◆ Herb plants, seeds, flowers, toiletries, oils, and seasonings. 800-259-4372. www.fredericksburgherbfarm.com

**Gold Medal Hair Products Inc.,** 1 Bennington Ave., Freeport, Long Island, NY 11520: Free catalog ◆ Wigs for African American men and women, hair and beauty preparations, hair styling supplies, eye glasses, and jewelry. 800-535-8101. www.catalogmall.com

**Green Cedar Needle Sachets,** Box 551, State Rd. 165, Placitas, NM 87043: Free brochure ◆ Sachets, incense cones, and fragrance toiletries. 800-557-3463.

**Heartfelt Creations,** P.O. Box 3063, 4237 S. Adrian Hwy., Adrian, MI 49221: Free brochure ◆ All-natural bath and body products. 517-265-5041.

**Ole Henriksen of Denmark,** 8601 W. Sunset Blvd., Los Angeles, CA 90069: Free information ◆ Face and body care treatments. 800-327-0331; 310-854-7700 (in CA).

**Herb & Spice Collection,** P.O. Box 299, Norway, IA 52318: Free catalog ◆ Natural herbal body care toiletries, potpourris, culinary herbs and spices, other herbs, and teas. 800-786-1388. www.frontierherb.com

**Herbal Accents,** P.O. Box 12303, El Cajon, CA 92022: Catalog $1 ◆ Aromatherapy skin care toiletries. 619-440-4380.

**Herbs for Healthful Living,** 25236 Dibble Hill Rd., Saegertown, PA 16433: Catalog $2 ◆ Skin care and bath toiletries and herbal soaps. 814-763-2309.

**Holbrook Wholesalers,** 255 5th Ave., 3rd Floor, New York, NY 10016: Free information ◆ Designer perfumes. 212-889-8681.

**Holzman & Stephanie Perfumes Inc.,** P.O. Box 921, Lake Forest, IL 60045: Catalog $4.50 (refundable) ◆ Copies of world-famous perfumes. 847-234-7667.

**Honeybee Gardens,** 141 Heather Ln., Wyomissing, PA 19610: Free catalog ◆ Natural herbal bath and body care products. 888-478-9090.

**Indiana Botanic Gardens,** P.O. Box 5, Hobart, IN 46342: Catalog $1 ◆ Vitamins, herbs, spices, and personal care toiletries. 800-644-8327. www.botanichealth.com

**Island Tan,** 125A Maunalua Ave., Honolulu, HI 96821: Free information ◆ Sunscreens, fragrances, and skin care toiletries with natural ingredients. 800-926-5800.

**Key West Aloe Inc.,** P.O. Box 1079, Key West, FL 33041: Free catalog ◆ Men's personal care toiletries. Also cosmetics and skin care toiletries for women. 800-445-2563. www.keywestaloe.com

**La Costa Products International,** 2875 Laker Ave. East, Carlsbad, CA 92009: Free catalog ◆ Hair, skin, and body care toiletries for men and women. 800-308-0358.

**Le Village,** P.O. Box 20669, Oakland, CA 94620: Free catalog ◆ Bath and skin care products. 415-861-2196. www.levillage.com

**Legacy Herbs,** Sue Lukens Herbalist/Potter, HC 70, Box 442, Mountain View, AR 72560: Catalog 50¢ ◆ Herbs, wildflowers, perennial plants, soaps, bath and body care products, oils and fragrance, incense, potpourri, herbal food products, and other scented items. 870-269-4051.

**Lite-Cosmetics,** 4061 Oceanside Blvd., Ste. M, Oceanside, CA 92056: Free catalog ◆ Skin care products for damaged, extra-sensitive, allergic, and senior skin. 760-630-8888. www.litecosmetics.com

**Lucky Heart Cosmetics,** 138 Huling Ave., Memphis, TN 38103: Free catalog ◆ Cosmetics and skin care toiletries. 800-526-5825.

**Maui Amenities Inc.,** P.O. Box 1243, Lahaina, Maui, HI 96767: Free brochure ◆ Cosmetics, bath toiletries, hair products, and other formulas made from Hawaiian fruits. 800-393-MAUI. www.planet-hawaii.com/~amen

**Miracle of Aloe,** 802 Rosita St., P.O. Box 5230, Pagosa Springs, CO 81147: Free information ◆ Aloe skin treatments and insect repellants. Also foot care, relief from muscle pain, hair and scalp, and health care products. 800-966-2563. www.miracleofaloe.com

**The Natural Body Bar Inc.,** P.O. Box 28, Lincolnville Beach, ME 04849: Free catalog ◆ Botanically formulated hair and skin care products. 800-913-9421. www.bodybar.com

**NaturElle Cosmetics,** P.O. Box 9, Pine, CO 80470: Free catalog ◆ All-natural cosmetics. 800-442-3936. www.naturalbeauty.com

**New Life Systems,** 2853 Hedberg Dr., Minneapolis, MN 55305: Catalog $3 ◆ Health and wellness products. Includes massage, salon, and spa supplies and equipment and air purifiers. 800-852-3082.

**Nutrition Headquarters,** One Nutrition Plaza, Carbondale, IL 62901: Free catalog ◆ Vitamins and mineral supplements, health and beauty aids, and herbal formulas.

**Oleda & Company Inc.,** 6467 Southwest Blvd., Fort Worth, TX 76132: Free catalog ◆ Nutrition, health, and beauty aids. 817-731-1147.

**Operose Herbals,** 9305 Miami Shelby West, Piqua, OH 45356: Brochure $1 ◆ Skin care products made from organically grown herbs. 937-778-3059.

**Perfect Skin by Buddy Maurice,** 3100 NW Boca Raton Blvd. #217, Boca Raton, FL 33431: Brochure $2 ◆ Skin care products. 800-642-7546; 561-367-0881 (in FL).

**Perfumes for Less,** 476 E. South Temple, Ste. 167, Salt Lake City, UT 84111: Free catalog ◆ Men and women's original designer perfumes. 800-374-LESS.

**Planet Natural,** P.O. Box 3146, Bozeman, MT 59772: Free catalog ◆ Beneficial insects, garden seeds, composting equipment, organic fertilizers and pest controls, garden supplies, and pet and body care products. 800-289-6656. www.planetnatural.com

**Planta Dei Medicinal Herb Farm,** Millville, New Brunswick, Canada E0H 1M0: Catalog $2 (refundable) ◆ Biologically grown teas, medicinal herbs, healing tea mixtures, cosmetics, natural ointments, and massage oils. 506-463-8169.

**Puritan's Pride,** 1233 Montauk Hwy., P.O. Box 9001, Oakdale, NY 11769: Free catalog ◆ Natural vitamins and health and beauty aids. 800-645-1030. www.puritan.com

**Scentimental Journey,** 3809 Rose Canyon Dr., North Las Vegas, NV 89030: List $1.25 ◆ Perfumes and other fragrances. 702-460-2207.

**Sharper Image SPA,** 650 Davis St., San Francisco, CA 94111: Free catalog ◆ Skin care products, SPA essentials, and health aids. 800-344-3440. www.sharperimage.com

**Simmons Natural Bodycare,** 42295 Hwy. 36, Bridgeville, CA 95526: Catalog $1 ◆ Natural products for home and personal care. 800-428-0412; 707-777-1920 (in CA). www.akamaiddesign.com/Simmons

**Syd Simons Cosmetics,** 2 E. Oak St., Chicago, IL 60611: Free price list ◆ Women's cosmetics and make-up. 312-943-2333.

**Smith & Hawken,** P.O. Box 6907, Florence, KY 41022: Free catalog ◆ Skin care preparations derived from herbs, flowers, and plants. 800-776-3336. www.smith-hawken.com

**The Soap Opera,** 319 State St., Madison, WI 55703: Free price list ◆ Cruelty-free, 100 percent safe private label bodycare products and aromatics. 608-251-SOAP. www.thesoapopera.com

**Star Pharmaceuticals/Puritan's Pride,** 1500 New Horizons Blvd., Amityville, NY 11701: Free catalog ◆ Vitamin products, nutritional supplements, toiletries, health care products, and pet supplies. 800-274-6400. www.puritan.com

**Stax of Wax,** 371 Congress Ave., Waterbury, CT 06708: Free brochure ◆ Scented candles, potpourri canisters, herbal baths, and other scented products. www.stax-of-wax.com

**Sugar Plum Sundries,** 5152 Fair Forest Dr., Stone Mountain, GA 30088: Free catalog ◆ Natural handmade soaps, soap-making supplies, and bath items. 404-297-0158. www.mindspring.com/~sugarplum

**Sun Feather Herbal Soap,** 1551 State Hwy. 72, Potsdam, NY 13676: Catalog $2 ◆ Herbal soaps, shampoos, candles, how-to soap-making books, videos, kits, molds, and supplies. 315-265-3648. www.electronicottage.com/sunfeathersoaps

**Sunburst Biorganics,** 832 Merrick Rd., Baldwin, NY 11510: Free catalog ◆ Nutritional supplements and toiletries. 800-645-8448; 516-623-8478 (in NY). www.sunburstbiorganics.com

**Torling Fragrance Products,** 8320 Cutler Way, Sacramento, CA 95828: Catalog $2 (refundable off $10 order) ◆ Essential, perfume, and designer oils. Also scented and unscented skin and bath care products. 916-682-1334.

**The Uncommon Herb,** P.O. Box 2980, Seal Beach, CA 90740: Catalog $1 ◆ Essential oils, handmade soaps, skin care products, teas, and seasonings. 800-308-6284.

**A Vermont Store,** 27 Catherine Dr., Rutland, VT 05701: Free brochure ◆ Old-fashioned handmade natural soaps. 888-265-6250. www.avermontstore.com

**The Vitamin Shoppe,** 4700 Westside Ave., North Bergen, NJ 07047: Free catalog ◆ Vitamins, herbs, homeopathic medicines, and natural cosmetics. 800-223-1216. www.vitaminshoppe.com

**Watkins Inc.,** 150 Liberty St., P.O. Box 5570, Winona, MN 55987: Free catalog ◆ Personal care products and toiletries. 800-247-5907.

**Wynnewood Pharmacy,** 50 E. Wynnewood Rd., Wynnewood, PA 19096: Free catalog ◆ Perfumes and colognes. 800-966-9999; 610-642-9091 (in PA).

**ZIA Cosmetics,** 410 Townsend Pl., San Francisco, CA 94107: Free brochure ◆ Skin care cosmetics. 800-334-7546.

## COSTUMES & VINTAGE CLOTHING

**Abracadabra Magic Shop,** 125 Lincoln Blvd., Middlesex, NJ 08846: Catalog $5 ◆ Close-up and stage magic, juggling equipment, balloons, clown props, costumes, and theatrical supplies. 732-805-0200. umsi@erols.com

**Alter Years,** 3749 E. Colorado Blvd., Pasadena, CA 91107: Catalog $5 ◆ Underpinnings and accessories, costume-making supplies, over 1000 costume reference books, and patterns. 818-585-2994.

**Arts of Avalon,** P.O. Box 366, Davenport, CA 95017: Free brochure ◆ Children's imagination dress-up clothing and costumes. 408-459-9499.

**Caped Crusaders,** 1309 Village Meadows, Lompoc, CA 93436: Free information ◆ Children's costumes and dress-up clothes. 805-740-1228.

**Cattle Kate,** Box 572, Wilson, WY 83014: Catalog $3 ◆ Contemporary western-style clothing for men, women, and children. 307-733-7414.

**Chivalry Sports,** P.O. Box 18904, Tucson, AZ 85731: Free catalog ◆ Medieval, renaissance, and fantasy costumes. Also gifts and books. 800-730-5464. www.RenStore.com

**Circus Clowns,** 3556 Nicollet Ave., Minneapolis, MN 55408: Catalog $3 ◆ Clown costumes and props. 612-822-4243.

**Clown Heaven,** 4792 Old State Rd. 37 South, Martinsville, IN 46152: Catalog $3 ◆ Balloons, make-up, puppets, wigs, ministry and gospel items, novelties, magic, clown props, and books. 317-342-6888.

**Confederate Yankee,** P.O. Box 192, Guilford, CT 06437: Catalog $3 ◆ Men, women, and children's reproduction Revolutionary to Civil War clothing. 203-453-9900.

**The Costume Connection,** P.O. Box 4518, Falls Church, VA 22044: Free catalog ◆ Character costumes. 703-237-1373.

**Costumers Quarterly,** 2400 E. Colonial Dr., Orlando, FL 32803: Catalog $2 ◆ Costume-making supplies. 407-898-3646.

**Costumes by Betty,** 2181 Edgerton St., St. Paul, MN 55117: Catalog $5 (refundable) ◆ Clown costumes, make-up, wigs, and shoes. 612-771-8734. www.clowncostumes.com

**Country Hearts Boutique,** P.O. Box 793, Delta, UT 84624: Free information ◆ Handmade costumes for children. 801-864-4219.

**Creations by Lauren,** 921 Rosilee Ln., Rapid City, SD 57701: Catalog $2 (refundable) ◆ Custom handmade beaded clothing and accessories in traditional Native American style. Also moccasins, knife cases, war shirts, dresses, and other crafts.

**D-C Theatricks,** 747 Main St., Buffalo, NY 14203: Free information ◆ Costumes and uniforms for professional theaters. 716-847-0180. www.costume.com

**Doering Designs,** 68935 233rd St., Dassel, MN 55325: Catalog $2 ◆ Old country costumes and multi-size costumes for boys, girls, and dolls.

**Eastern Costume Company,** 510 N. Elm St., Greensboro, NC 27401: Free information ◆ Theatrical and masquerade costumes and make-up. 800-968-8461; 336-379-1026 (in NC).

**Harriet A. Engler,** P.O. Box 1363, Winchester, VA 22604: Adult catalog $7, children's catalog $3 ◆ Military and civilian reproduction costumes, uniforms, patterns, and crinolines. 540-667-2541.

**Freckles Clown Supplies,** 5509 Roosevelt Blvd., Jacksonville, FL 32244: Catalog $6 ◆ Costumes, make-up, clown supplies, puppets, clowning and ballooning how-to books, and theatrical supplies. 904-388-5541.

**Golden Age Productions,** 3130 Castle Cove Ct., Kissimmee, FL 34746: Free information ◆ Hard-to-find props and costume accessories. 800-671-4867.

**Grand Illusions,** 7704 Fair Oaks Blvd., Carmichael, CA 95608: Free catalog ◆ Magic, costumes, and juggling equipment. 916-944-2970. www.grandillusions.com

**Harriet's TCS,** P.O. Box 1363, Winchester, VA 22604: Catalog $12 ◆ Kits, supplies, hoops and parasols, lace, and more for then and now clothing. 540-662-5157. www.harriets.com

**The Heirloom Shoppe,** 6334 Waltway, Houston, TX 77008: Free catalog ◆ Handmade children's costumes for fantasy and dress-up play. 713-861-0477.

**The House of Times Past,** 634 W. Darby Rd., Greenville, SC 29609: Catalog $2 ◆ Authentic reproduction clothing and accessories from Colonial America, 1750 to 1790; the transitional period, 1790 to 1814; the mountain man and exploration period, 1804 to 1840; and the Civil War era, 1859 to 1865. 864-834-0061.

**K & P Weaver,** P.O. Box 1131, Orange, CT 06477: Catalog $1 ◆ Historically accurate custom made reproductions of military and civilian Civil War era clothing.

**Lacey Costume Wig,** 505 8th Ave., 11th Floor, New York, NY 10018: Free catalog ◆ Wigs, mustaches, beards, and supplies. 800-562-9911.

**Lynch's Clown Supplies,** 939 Howard, Dearborn, MI 48124: Catalog $5 ◆ Clown wigs, shoes, noses, novelties, make-up, and costumes. 800-24-LYNCH. www.lynchs.com

**Magic Makers Costumes Inc.,** 940 4th Ave., Ste. 360, Huntington, WV 25701: Free catalog ◆ Costumes, accessories, theatrical props, and special stage effects. 800-233-5810. www.magicmakers.com

**Mary Ellen & Company,** 100 N. Main St., North Liberty, IN 46554: Catalog $3 ◆ Victorian-style clothing, lace-up shoes, hats, fans, parasols, books, and patterns. 800-669-1860.

**Mecca Magic Inc.,** 49 Dodd St., Bloomfield, NJ 07003: Catalog $10 ◆ Costumes, wigs, and make-up. 201-429-7597. meccamagic@meccamagic.com

**Morris Costumes,** 3108 Monroe Rd., Charlotte, NC 28205: Catalog $20 ◆ Costumes, clown props, masks, joke items, magic tricks and special effects, novelties, and books. 704-332-3304.

**New York Theatrical Supply,** 263 W. 38th St., New York, NY 10018: Free information ◆ Costume-making fabrics, notions and accessories, and other supplies. 212-840-3120.

**The 1909 Company,** 63 Thompson St., New York, NY 10012: Catalog $2 ◆ Reproduction vintage clothing. 800-331-1909.

**The Old Frontier Clothing Company,** 7412 Fulton Ave., North Hollywood, CA 91605: Catalog $3 ◆ Men and women's western clothing. 818-764-7787.

**Past Patterns,** 217 S. 5th St., Richmond, IN 47374: Catalog $4 ◆ Patterns for historically authentic clothing for men, women, and children. 317-962-3333.

**Pierre's Costumes,** 7882 Browning Rd., Pennsauken, NJ 08109: Free information ◆ Costume rentals and sales. 888-PIERRE-1. www.costumers.com

**Premier Designs Historic Clothing,** 15512 State Rt. 613, Van Buren, OH 45889: Catalog $4 ◆ Men and women's historic clothing, from Victorian styles to the 1930s. 800-427-0907. www.bright.net/~premier

**Quartermaster Shop,** Jeff O'Donnell, 5565 Griswold Rd., Kimball, MI 48074: Catalog $5 ◆ Reproduction Union, Confederate, and civilian Civil War-period clothing. 810-367-6702.

**Raiments,** P.O. Box 93095, Pasadena, CA 91109: Catalog $5 ◆ Books, under pinnings, and patterns for historical costumes, from the middle ages to the 1950s. 818-797-2723.

**Reflections of the Past,** P.O. Box 40361, Bay Village, OH 44140: Catalog $5 ◆ Men, women, and children's American and European fashions, from the 17th to 19th-century. 216-835-6924.

**Ronjo's Magic & Costumes Inc.,** 4600 Nesconset Hwy., Unit 4, Port Jefferson Station, NY 11776: Catalog $9.95 (receive $25 in coupons)* Magic for amateur and professional magicians, costumes, make-up, and theatrical effects. 516-928-5005. www.ronjo.com

**Murielle Roy & Company,** 67 Plain Mill Rd., Naugatuck, CT 06770: Catalog $4 ◆ Fabric and trim for costumes. 203-729-0480.

**Rubie's Costume Company**, National Sales Office, 999 Gould St., New Hyde Park, NY 11040: Free information ◆ Costumes, make-up, hair goods, and special effects. 516-326-1500.

**Salt Lake Costume Company,** 1701 S. 1100 East, Salt Lake City, UT 84105: Free catalog ◆ Historical costumes and make-up. 801-467-9494.

**Servant & Company,** Centennial General Store, 230 Steinwehr Ave., Gettysburg, PA 17325: Catalog $6 ◆ Civil War uniforms and accouterments, lady's clothing and accessories, and clothing patterns. 717-334-9712. www.servantandco.com

**Star Styled Dancewear,** P.O. Box 119029, Hialeah, FL 33011: Free information ◆ Bodywear, shoes, and costumes for dancers. 800-532-6237. www.starstyled.com

**Stitches In Time,** Shirley & Jim Wolf, 61 Trux St., Plymouth, OH 44865: Free information ◆ Vintage-style clothing. 419-687-2061.

**James Townsend & Son Inc.,** 133 N. 1st St., P.O. Box 415, Pierceton, IN 46562: Catalog $2 ◆ Historical clothing, hats, lanterns, tomahawks, knives, tents, guns, and blankets. 800-338-1665.

**Tracy Theatre Originals,** 70 High St., Hampton, NH 03842: Free information ◆ Theatrical costumes, props, and make-up. 800-926-8351; 603-926-8315 (in NH). Crfts4stge@aol.com

**Under the Big Top,** P.O. Box 807, Placentia, CA 92670: Catalog $4 ◆ Costumes, clown props, make-up, juggling equipment, and party supplies. 800-995-7727.

**The Victorian Lady,** P.O. Box 424, 102 S. Main, Waxhaw, NC 28173: Catalog $5 (refundable) ◆ Antique Victorian fashions and accessories. 800-786-1886.

**Del & Jean Warren,** P.O. Box 364, Liberty, MO 64068: Catalog $6 ◆ Civil War era historic books and patterns, jewelry and accessories, underpinnings, uniforms and accouterments, black powder rifles, and shooting supplies. 816-781-9473. Jamescntry@aol.com

## COUNTRY CRAFTS

**A & P Craft Supply,** 850 W. 200 South, Lindon, UT 84042: Catalog $2 ◆ Wood crafts and accessories. 800-748-5090; 801-785-1770 (in UT). www.craft.com

**Adirondack Store & Gallery,** 109 Saranac Ave., Lake Placid, NY 12946: Free information ◆ Country-style twig furniture, stoneware and pottery, rugs, fire boards, outdoor lawn and wood furniture, baskets, and pillows. 518-523-2646.

**Alaska Wilderness Woodworking,** 11941 Mary Ave., Anchorage, AK 99515: Free information ◆ Rustic wood birdhouses, hanging birdhouse-theme clocks, and other crafts. 907-522-9663.

**Amish Country Collection,** Sunset Valley Rd., RD 5, Box 271, New Castle, PA 16105: Catalog $5 ◆ Amish-style pillows, quilts, wall hangings, rugs, cribs and beds, and household items. 412-458-4811.

**Dennis & CeCe Bork,** 715 Genesee St., Delafield, WI 53018: Catalog $5 ◆ Custom furniture, folk art, period lighting, Colonial Williamsburg reproductions, Windsor chairs and settees, and accessories. 414-646-4911.

**Brown's Country Creations,** Rt. 1, Box 1228, Dunnegan, MO 65640: Catalog $2.50 ◆ Handcrafted bathroom ensembles and hanging towel and matching table sets. 800-338-7696; 417-326-4880 (in MO).

**Brush Strokes,** 19312 Haviland Dr., South Bend, IN 46637: Brochure $3 ◆ Signed and numbered limited edition prints reproduced from original oil paintings with a choice of mats and frames. 219-277-5414.

**Chriswill Forge,** 2255 Manchester Rd., North Lawrence, OH 44666: Catalog $2 ◆ Country-style floor lamps with a heavy-duty steel plate base and a choice of designs for the top. 330-832-9136.

**Classics by Simply Country,** P.O. Drawer 656, Wytheville, VA 24382: Brochure $2 (refundable) ◆ Wall hangings, throws, pillows, clothing, and afghans. 800-537-8911.

**Colonial Casting Company Inc.,** 68 Liberty St., Haverhill, MA 01832: Catalog $3 ◆ Handcrafted lead-free pewter miniature castings. 978-374-8783.

**Colonial Collections of New England Inc.,** 202 Idlewood Dr., Stamford, CT 06905: Catalog $2 ◆ Weather vanes, cupolas, sundials, mailboxes, door knockers, personalized and date plaques, lanterns, and home and garden decorative items. 203-322-0078.

**Conewago Junction,** 1255 Oxford Rd., New Oxford, PA 17350: Catalog $2 ◆ Colonial chests, cupboards, wood buckets, tools, afghans, tinware, and household items. 717-624-4786.

**The Cotton Gin Inc.,** Deep Creek Farm, P.O. Box 414, Jarvisburg, NC 27947: Free catalog ◆ Country collectibles, women's clothing, and antiques. 800-637-2446.

**Country Accents,** P.O. Box 437, Montoursville, PA 17754: Catalog $5 ◆ Museum tin replicas and accent pieces. 717-478-4127.

**Country Store Crafts,** 5925 Country Ln., P.O. Box 990, Greendale, WI 53129: Free catalog ◆ Country gifts for men, women, and children. 800-558-1013.

**The Country Store of Geneva,** 28 James St., Geneva, IL 60134: Catalog $3 ◆ Punched tin and turned wood chandeliers, ceiling lights, outlet covers, country-style decorative accessories, braided rugs, and stoneware. 630-879-0098.

**Crafts by Pat,** 194 Grove St., Reading, MA 01867: Free catalog ◆ Afghans, dressed teddy bears, all-occasion wreaths, baskets, and other crafts. 781-944-1294.

**Gregan T. Crawford,** Cabinetmaker, 295 RR 2, Oakland, MD 21550: Catalog $2 ◆ Shaker-inspired furniture and home accessories. 800-531-4109.

**Creative Crafts,** 308 S. Todd, McComb, OH 45858: Brochure $2 ◆ Handcrafted earthenware pottery. 419-293-3838.

**Darowood Farms,** 4614 School Rd., P.O. Box 470, Egg Harbor, WI 54209: Brochure $2 ◆ Handcrafted country wood items. 800-228-3908.

**Dee's Country Craft Barn,** 17588 E. 3200 North Rd., Blackstone, IL 61313: Free catalog ◆ Handpainted country wood crafts. 815-586-4344.

**D.D. Dillon,** 850 Meadow Ln., Camp Hill, PA 17011: Free information ◆ Wall hangings and handcarved cookie and shortbread molds. 717-761-6895.

**Everything Ewenique,** RR 1, Box 73, Mt. Pleasant Mills, PA 17853: Free catalog ◆ Country accents for the home. 800-800-4846.

**Fair Oak Workshops,** P.O. Box 5578, River Forest, IL 60305: Free brochure ◆ Handcrafted arts and crafts style reproductions. 800-341-0597.

**The Faith Mountain Company,** P.O. Box 199, Sperryville, VA 22740: Free catalog ◆ Kitchen utensils, country-style gifts, folk art reproductions, toys and dolls, handmade Appalachian baskets, and Christmas decorations. 800-588-2548. 800-822-7238. www.FaithMountain.com

**Friends,** 109 Shawnee, Eldridge, IA 52748: Brochure $2 ◆ Country-style Christmas decorative accessories. 319-285-7354.

**Frye's Measure Mill,** 12 Frye Mill Rd., Wilton, NH 03086: Catalog $3.75 ◆ Early American woodenware. 603-654-6581.

**Gard Woodworking,** 121 N. Walnut, Colfax, IA 50054: Brochure $1 ◆ Wood country crafts and decorative accessories. 515-674-3060.

**Grandpa's Crafts,** 577 Hwy. 70 West, Havelock, NC 28532: Brochure $1 ◆ Country craft decorative accessories. 800-344-4602; 252-444-1603 (in NC). www.grandpascrafts.com

**Green Mountain Studios,** Rt. 10 North, Box 158, Lyme, NH 03768: Catalog $2 ◆ Country crafts. 603-795-4398.

**Handcrafted Wood Products,** 11280 US Hwy. 90, Daphne, AL 36526: Free information ◆ Wood-crafted spool and bobbin organizer and wall rack for serger cones. 334-633-4570.

**The Harp & Dragon,** 25 Madison St., Cortland, NY 13045: Free catalog with two 1st class stamps ◆ Celtic theme crafts. 607-756-7372. www.HarpAndDragon.com

**Heart of the Woods Inc.,** P.O. Box 210, Ely, MN 55731: Catalog $1 (refundable) ◆ Wood country-style decorative accessories. 800-852-2075.

**Independence Forge,** 309 W. Nash St., Whitakers, NC 27891: Brochure $1 ◆ Furniture, chandeliers, floor lamps, table and wall lamps, and country-style handcrafted iron pieces. 919-437-1452.

**Jepson Studios Inc.,** RR 1, Box 69, Harveyville, KS 66431: Brochure $2 (refundable) ◆ Country ceramics. 913-589-2481.

**Lambs Farm,** P.O. Box 520, Jct. I-94 & Rt. 176, Libertyville, IL 60048: Free catalog ◆ Country crafts, specialty foods, nuts, candies, and gifts for pets. 800-52-LAMBS. www.LAMBSFARM.ORG

**Loose Ends,** P.O. Box 20310, Salem, OR 97307: Catalog $5 (refundable) ◆ Country crafts and craft-related gifts. 503-390-7457. www.4looseends.com

**McVay's Old Wood Creations,** P.O. Box 553, Leslie, MI 49251: Brochure $2 ◆ Wall accents, game boards, weather vanes, handcrafted household items, and gifts. 517-589-5312.

**MoonAcre IronWorks,** 62 Chambersburg St., Gettysburg, PA 17325: Catalog $2 ◆ Country-style iron trellises for climbing plants. 800-966-4766. moonacre@cvn.net

**North Country Crafts,** 5247 Central Ave. NE, Minneapolis, MN 55421: Brochure $1 ◆ Country-style upholstered storage ottomans and accessories. 612-571-3636.

**Orleans Carpenters,** P.O. Box 217, Orleans, MA 02653: Catalog $3 ◆ Shaker-style oval bentwood boxes and small wood crafts. 508-255-2646.

**Plain Folk,** 21 School St., Box 265, Riverton, CT 06065: Free catalog ◆ Early New England wrought-iron, tinware, pottery, and folk art. 860-379-0492.

**Charles Putt,** Box 144, Robesonia, PA 19551: Catalog $2 ◆ Authentic reproductions, folk art paintings, and woodwork in an 18th and 19th-century style. 610-488-0543.

**Raindrops on Roses Rubber Stamps,** 4808 Winterwood Dr., Raleigh, NC 27613: Catalog $3 ◆ Country-style rubber stamp sets with brush markers. 800-245-8617; 919-846-8617 (in NC).

**Redwood Unlimited,** P.O. Box 2344, Valley Center, CA 92082: Brochure $2 ◆ Wall and post-mounted mailboxes with ornamental scrolls, posts, and weather vanes. 800-283-1717.

**The Rocking Horse Country Store,** Rt. 4, Rutland, VT 05701: Free brochure ◆ Vermont maple syrup, cheese, crafts, and country collectibles. 802-773-7882.

**Shaker Shops West,** P.O. Box 487, Inverness, CA 94937: Catalog $3 ◆ Reproductions of traditional music boxes, country-style furniture, candles, accessories for the home, teas and herbs, and books on the lifestyles, traditions, and history of the Shakers. 415-669-7256. www.shakershops.com

**Simply Country Furniture,** Box 133, Rover, AR 72860: Brochure $2 ◆ Grandfather clocks. 501-272-4794.

**Studio Workshop Inc.,** 2808 Tucker St., Omaha, NE 68112: Catalog $2 ◆ Country-style bathroom accessories, oak shelves, shadow boxes, and furniture. 800-383-7072.

**Sutter Creek Antiques,** 28 Main St., Box 699, Sutter Creek, CA 95685: Free brochure with long SASE ◆ Antique country-style lamps, pottery, and carved wood items. 209-267-5574.

**The Symmetree Company,** P.O. Drawer E, West Rockport, ME 04865: Free brochure ◆ Country crafts, decorative accessories, and country-style gifts. 800-824-2402.

**Three Rivers Pottery Productions Inc.,** 1436 S. 6th St., Coshocton, OH 43812: Free information ◆ Oven, microwave, and dishwasher-safe pottery. 614-622-4154.

**Tidy's Storehouse,** 1102 Hopewell Rd., Oxford, PA 19363: Catalog $3 ◆ Books and reproduction 18th-century pottery, glass, tinware, clothing, patterns, and shoes. 610-932-8441.

**Tin Bin,** 20 Valley Rd., Neffsville, PA 17601: Catalog $2.50 ◆ Country crafts and 18th-century lighting. 717-569-6210. TheTinBin@aol.com

**Valerie's Hattery Inc.,** 13535 S. Cedar Rd., Cedar, MI 49621: Free information ◆ Rose-scented potpourri bonnets, teddy bear door knob covers, dolls, storage bags, and other original crafts. 616-228-4562.

**Vermont FurnitureWorks,** P.O. Box 1496, Stowe, VT 05672: Free catalog ◆ Handcrafted 18th and 19th-century reproduction New England furniture, traditional folk art, and Americana accessories. 802-253-5094.

**Western Woodworks,** 1142 Olive Branch Ln., San Jose, CA 95120: Free catalog ◆ Hurricane lamps and accessories, designer bud vases, painted pens and accessories, decorative bottle stoppers, and other crafts. 408-997-2356. www.craftnet.org/westwood

**Westwinds Trading Company,** 3540 76th St. SE, Caledonia, MI 49316: Free brochure ◆ Weather vanes, signs, sundials, and birdbaths. 800-635-5262.

**Wink's Woods,** 1225 US Hwy. 2 South, Crystal Falls, MI 49920: Free information with long SASE ◆ Country-style wood decorative accessories. 906-875-3750.

**Zimmerman Handcrafts,** 254 E. Main St., Leola, PA 17540: Brochure $1 ◆ Country-style decorative items and traditional crafts. 800-267-5689.

## CRAFT SUPPLIES

**A & P Craft Supply,** 850 W. 200 South, Lindon, UT 84042: Catalog $2 (refundable) ◆ Over 1200 woodcraft projects. 800-748-5090; 801-785-1770 (in UT). www.craft.com

**ADCO Inc.,** P.O. Box 814745, Dallas, TX 75381: Free catalog ◆ Gluesticks, glue guns, and glitter sticks. 800-486-4583. www.gluestick.com

**Adhesive Technologies,** 3 Merrill Industrial Dr., Hampton, NH 03842: Free information ◆ Glue guns and glue sticks. 603-926-1616.

**Allen-Lewis Manufacturing Company,** P.O. Box 16546, Denver, CO 80216: Free catalog ◆ Souvenirs, carnival and party supplies, fund-raising merchandise, toys and games, T-shirts and sweatshirts, and craft supplies. 800-525-6658.

**American Crafters,** 29722 Merjanian Rd., Menifee, CA 92584: Free catalog ◆ Craft supplies. 800-326-5223. www.procrafter.com/ac.htm

**Art N' Craft Supply,** P.O. Box 5070, Slidell, LA 70469: Free catalog ◆ Craft supplies. 800-642-1062; 504-641-2545 (in LA). www.craftmaker.com

**The Art Store,** 935 Erie Blvd. East, Syracuse, NY 13210: Price list $3 ◆ Supplies for fabric dyeing, screen-printing, marbling, and other art decor. 800-669-2787.

**Atlas Art & Stained Glass,** P.O. Box 76084, Oklahoma City, OK 73147: Catalog $3 ◆ Kaleidoscopes, frames, lamp bases, and craft, stained glass, jewelry-making, and foil-crafting supplies. 405-946-1230.

**Bovis Bead Company,** P.O. Box 13345, Tucson, AZ 85732: Catalog $5 ◆ French glass beads and Native American craft supplies. 520-318-9512.

**Brian's Crafts Unlimited,** P.O. Box 731046, Ormond Beach, FL 32173: Catalog $1 (refundable) ◆ Craft supplies. 904-672-2726.

**Cabin Craft Southwest,** 1500 Westpack Way, Euless, TX 76040: Catalog $4 ◆ Tole and decorative painting supplies and other craft materials. 800-877-1515. www.flash.net/~cabin

**Caldwell Craft Supply,** Hwy. 21 East, Caldwell, TX 77836: Free catalog ◆ Craft supplies. 409-567-7590.

**Carolan Craft Supplies,** P.O. Box 42129, Cleveland, OH 44142: Catalog $3 ◆ Beads, plastic canvas, craft books, stencils, basket-making supplies, jewelry, quilts and needle crafts, pom poms, bears, dolls, and wire crafts. 216-362-7900.

**Chaselle Inc.,** 101 Almgren Dr., Agawam, MA 01001: Catalog $4 ◆ Ceramics and pottery-making equipment, and supplies for art, sculpting, stained glass, weaving, leather-crafting, etching, and other crafts. 800-628-8608. www.schoolspecialty.com

**Circle Craft Supply,** P.O. Box 3000, Dover, FL 33527: Catalog $1 ◆ Craft supplies. 813-659-0992.

**Columbia Arts,** 1515 E. Burnside St., Portland, OR 97214: Free information ◆ Craft supplies. 800-547-9750.

**Craft Catalog,** P.O. Box 1069, Reynoldsburg, OH 43068: Catalog $2 ◆ Wood and wire, acrylic paints, brushes, paper mache, mini brass stencils, needlework supplies, laces and trim, terra cotta molds, and other craft supplies. 800-777-1442; 614-863-4004 (in OH). www.craftcatalog.com

**Craft King Mail Order Catalog,** P.O. Box 90637, Lakeland, FL 33804: Free catalog ◆ Craft, needlework, and macrame supplies. 888-CRAFTY-1. www.weshop.com/craftking

**Craft Kits,** 936 E. Green St., Ste. 113, Pasadena, CA 91106: Free information ◆ Educational and cultural craft kits. 818-568-0400.

**Craft Makers,** 3958 Linden Ave., Dayton, OH 45432: Catalog $2 ◆ Craft supplies. 800-CRAFTS-5.

**The Craft Market,** 401 5th Ave., Fairbanks, AK 99701: Jewelry supply catalog $2.95; tool catalog $5.95 ◆ Jewelry-making supplies and tools. Also other crafting tools. 907-452-5495.

**Craft Resources Inc.,** Box 828, Fairfield, CT 06430: Catalog $1 ◆ String art, basket-making, metal and wood-crafting, stained glass, and craft supplies. Also needlework kits for latch hooking, needlepoint, cross-stitching, and crewel. 800-243-2874; 203-254-7702 (in CT).

**Craftime Inc.,** P.O. Box 93706, Atlanta, GA 30377: Catalog $5 (refundable) ◆ Craft supplies. 404-873-2028. www.craftimeinc.com

**Crafts by Pat,** 194 Grove St., Reading, MA 01867: Free catalog ◆ Craft kits for bears, baskets, all-occasion wreaths, and ornaments. 781-944-1294.

**Crafty's Featherworks,** P.O. Box 370, Overton, NV 89040: Free information ◆ Feathers for floral arrangements, Native American and other crafts, millinery, fly-tying, and accent pieces. 702-397-8211.

**Create-Your-Own Inc.,** 12531 Old Snohomish-Monroe Rd., Snohomish, WA 98290: Free information ◆ Blank paper for crafting. Available in assorted colors and sizes. 360-794-0671.

**Creative Craft House,** Box 2567, Bullhead City, AZ 86430: Catalog $2 (refundable) ◆ Seashells, pine cones, and craft supplies.

**Creative Hands,** P.O. Box 2217, Eugene, OR 97402: Catalog $2 ◆ Natural fiber dolls, crafts, kits, and supplies. 541-343-1562.

**Creative Kids,** 8124 W. 4th Pl., Highland, IN 46322: Free catalog with long SASE ◆ Craft kits for children, ages 3 to 12. 219-838-0465.

**Crysbi Crafts Inc.,** 17514 South Ave. 4 E, Yuma, AZ 85365: Catalog $2 ◆ Craft supplies and accessories. 520-317-1508.

**Lou Davis Ceramics & Crafts,** P.O. Box 21, N3211 County Rd. H., Lake Geneva, WI 53147: Free catalog ◆ Craft supplies. 800-748-7991.

**Discount Bead House,** P.O. Box 186, The Plains, OH 45780: Catalog $5 ◆ Leather, seed beads, findings, wood items, tools, and modeling supplies. 800-793-7592.

**Eagle Feather Trading Post,** 168 W. 12th St., Ogden, UT 84404: Catalog $3.50 ◆ Beads, bead crafting accessories, kits, books, and Native American craft supplies. 801-393-3991.

**Earth Guild,** 33 Haywood St., Asheville, NC 28801: Catalog $3 ◆ Basket-making, weaving, spinning, dyeing, pottery, woodcarving, hand and machine knitting, rug-making, netting, and chair-caning supplies. 800-327-8448. www.earthguild.com

**Eastern Art Glass,** P.O. Box 9, Wyckoff, NJ 07481: Catalog $2 (refundable) ◆ Stained glass kits, glass-etching equipment, glass coloring materials, fabric dyes, mirror-removing and woodburning supplies, and how-to videos. 800-872-3458. www.etchworld.com

**Enterprise Art,** P.O. Box 2918, Largo, FL 33779: Free catalog ◆ Beads from around the world, bead and jewelry-making kits, and craft and jewelry-making supplies. 800-366-2218. www.enterpriseart.com

**Evening Star Designs,** 69 Coolidge Ave., Haverhill, MA 01832: Catalog $3 ◆ Craft and jewelry-making supplies. 800-666-3562.

**Factory Direct Craft Supplies,** P.O. Box 16, Franklin, OH 45005: Catalog $2 ◆ Craft supplies. 800-252-5223; 937-743-5855 (in OH). www.crafts2urdoor.com

**Fairfield Processing Corp.,** P.O. Box 1130, Danbury, CT 06813: Free information ◆ Fiberfill and batting products. 800-980-8000; 203-371-1901 (in CT). www.poly-fil.com

**Freudenberg/Pellon,** 1040 Avenue of Americas, New York, NY 10018: Free information ◆ Supplies for bonding fabrics to fabric, card-board, wood, and porous surfaces. 800-223-5275; 212-391-6300 (in NY).

**G & J Enterprises,** 4199 State Rd. 144, Moorseville, IN 46158: Catalog $2 (refundable) ◆ Craft and electrical supplies. 317-831-1452.

**Habari Gani,** African-American Crafts, P.O. Box 468, 132-05 Merrick Blvd., Jamaica, NY 11434: Catalog $1 ◆ Handcarved items from Kenya, Kente cloth from the Ivory Coast, clothing, accessories, craft kits, books, music, videos, beads, feathers, and supplies. 718-978-7110.

**Rolf Gille Import Ltd.,** P.O. Box 747, San Francisco, CA 94101: Free catalog ◆ Craft supplies from nature. 800-448-9988.

**Green Mountain Studios,** Rt. 10 North, Box 158, Lyme, NH 03768: Catalog $2 ◆ Craft supplies. 603-795-4398.

**Guildcraft Company,** 100 Firetower Dr., Tonawanda, NY 14150: Free catalog ◆ Supplies for fabric dyeing and foil, chair-caning, basket-making, plaster, candle, wood, leather, and egg-crafting. 716-743-8336.

**House of White Birches,** 306 E. Parr Rd., Berne, IN 46711: Free catalog ◆ Plastic canvas kits and plans.

**Houston Art Inc.,** 10770 Moss Ridge Rd., Houston, TX 77043: Free catalog ◆ Art and craft supplies and accessories. 800-272-3804. www.houstonart.com

**J & R Industries,** P.O. Box 4221, Shawnee Mission, KS 66204: Catalog $3 (refundable) ◆ Art and craft supplies. 800-999-9513.

**JoyFul Art,** P.O. Box 60206, King of Prussia, PA 19406: Free catalog ◆ Craft kits. 800-358-4581.

**Kieffer's Craft Supplies,** 51 Ferry St., P.O. Box 7500, Jersey City, NJ 07307: Catalog $2 ◆ Craft supplies, books, and kits. 201-798-2266.

**Kirchen Brothers,** Box 1016, Skokie, IL 60076: Catalog $2 ◆ Craft supplies. 847-647-6747.

**Lace & Things,** Hwy. 441, Whittier, NC 28789: Free price list ◆ Native American craft supplies and jewelry. 704-586-9500.

**Lark Books,** P.O. Box 2580, Asheville, NC 28802: Free catalog ◆ Kits, books, and gifts. 800-284-3388. www.larkbooks.com

**Mangelsen's Craft Supplies,** P.O. Box 3314, Omaha, NE 68103: Free information ◆ Supplies for general crafts, candle-making, and leather-working. 800-228-2601; 402-339-3922 (in NE).

**Maple Shade Crafts,** Catalog Department, RR 1, Box 186, Pulaski, VA 24301: Catalog $4 (refundable) ◆ Craft supplies, sewing notions, Victorian jewelry, scented candles, cameos, and potpourri. 800-986-9674. www.swva.net/mapleshade

**Maplewood Crafts,** Humboldt Industrial Park, 1 Maplewood Dr., Hazleton, PA 18201: Free catalog ◆ Beading and needlecraft supplies, craft materials, kits, tools, and books. 800-899-0134.

**The Mercantile Company,** 2016 N. 4th St., Flagstaff, AZ 86004: Free catalog (specify supplies and findings or finished products) ◆ Sterling silver jewelry supplies, Native American arts and crafts, feathers, and leather supplies. 800-413-CHUCK.

**Mountain Ridge Training,** Box 1702, Red Lodge, MT 59068: Catalog $1 ◆ Nature's craft supplies. 406-446-2740.

**MPR Associates,** A Specialty Ribbon Company, P.O. Box 7343, High Point, NC 27264: Free catalog ◆ Paper ribbons, twists, kits, and finishing products. 800-454-3331.

**Nasco,** 901 Janesville Ave., Fort Atkinson, WI 53538: Free catalog ◆ Supplies for art projects, calligraphy, leather-crafting, metal enameling, ceramics, photography, and needle crafts. 800-558-9595. www.nascofa.com

**National Artcraft Company,** 7996 Darrow Rd., Twinsburg, OH 44087: Catalog $4 ◆ Tools and supplies for floral-crafting, ceramics, and making clocks, lamps, dolls, candles, and jewelry. 800-793-0152. nationalartcraft@worldnet.att.net

**National Supply Inc.,** 9666 Olive Blvd., Ste. 145, St. Louis, MO 63132: Catalog $4 (refundable) ◆ Beads, jewelry findings, tools, crafts, and supplies. 800-221-9032; 314-567-1928 (in MO). www.nationalsupply.com

**Noc Bay Trading Company,** P.O. Box 295, Escanaba, MI 49829: Catalog $3 (refundable) ◆ Craft supplies. 800-652-7192. NocGay@aol.com

**Oppenheim's,** P.O. Box 29, North Manchester, IN 46962: Catalog $1 ◆ Sewing notions, fabrics, and craft supplies. 800-461-6728.

**Oriental Trading Company Inc.,** P.O. Box 3407, Omaha, NE 68103: Free catalog ◆ Craft supplies and kits. 800-228-0475. www.oriental.com

**Oxmoor House,** P.O. Box 2463, Birmingham, AL 35282: Free catalog ◆ Creative craft glues and how-to information. 205-877-6000.

**Painted Dreams,** 4835 S. 102nd St., Omaha, NE 68127: Catalog $1 ◆ Craft supplies. 402-339-5744.

**Cliff C. Paulsen,** P.O. Box 19146, Sacramento, CA 95819: Catalog $1 ◆ Indian (Native American) beads, bells, feathers, and other craft supplies. 916-485-9838.

**Pepperell Braiding Company,** Craft Products Division, P.O. Box 1487, Pepperell, MA 01463: Free information ◆ Braiding cord. 800-343-8114. www.pepperell.com

**A Real Doll & Company,** P.O. Box 1044, Sebastopol, CA 95473: Free catalog ◆ Natural fiber doll and craft-making supplies. 707-829-7265.

**Red Hill Corp.,** P.O. Box 4234, Gettysburg, PA 17325: Free catalog ◆ Hot melt glue sticks, glue guns, and sandpaper belts, sheets, and disks. 800-822-4003. www.supergrit.com

**Sax Arts & Crafts,** P.O. Box 51710, New Berlin, WI 51710: Free catalog ◆ Craft supplies. 800-323-0388. www.saxarts.com

**Scrapbooks 'n More,** 5769 Westcreek Dr., Fort Worth, TX 76133: Catalog 25¢ with long SASE ◆ Scrapbook-making kits and supplies.888-312-4449; 817-294-4600 (in TX). www.scrapbooksnmore.com

**Stormcloud Trading,** 725 Snelling Ave. North, St. Paul, MN 55104: Free information ◆ Native American arts and crafts supplies. 612-645-0343.

**Suncoast Discount Arts & Crafts Warehouse,** 10601 47th St. North, Clearwater, FL 34622: Catalog $2 ◆ Craft supplies. 813-572-1600.

**Sunshine Discount Crafts,** 12335 62nd St. North, Largo, FL 33773: Free catalog ◆ Modeling clays and accessories, art supplies, beads, tole and decorative painting supplies, and more. 800-720-2878. www.sunshinecrafts.com

**Taylor's Cutaways & Stuff,** 2802 E. Washington St., Urbana, IL 61801: Brochure $1 ◆ Satins, lace, velvet, cottons, felt, calico, trim, polyester squares, sewing notions, craft supplies, soft toy and crochet patterns, and books. home.sprynet.com/sprynet/tcutaway

**United Art & Education,** P.O. Box 9219, Fort Wayne, IN 46899: Free catalog ◆ Craft supplies, books, and tools. 800-322-3247.

**Vanguard Crafts Inc.,** P.O. Box 340170, Brooklyn, NY 11234: Free catalog ◆ Craft supplies. 800-662-7238; 718-377-5188 (in NY).

**Wakeda Trading Post,** P.O. Box 19146, Sacramento, CA 95819: Catalog $2 ◆ Craft supplies, books, sound recordings, botanicals, and more. 916-485-9838. wakeda@pacbell.net

**The Wandering Bull,** 247 S. Main St., Attleboro, MA 02703: Free catalog ◆ Craft supplies. 800-430-2855. www.wanderingbull.com

**Warner-Crivellaro,** 1855 Weaversville Rd., Allentown, PA 18103: Free information ◆ Stained glass, jewelry-making, kaleidoscope and clock kits, other supplies, and how-to books. 800-523-4242; 610-264-1100 (in PA). www.warner-criv.com

**Weaving Works,** 4717 Brooklyn Ave. NE, Seattle, WA 98105: Catalog $4.50 ◆ Supplies for making baskets, dyeing, weaving, spinning, and knitting. 206-524-1221.

**West Mountain Gourd Farm,** Rt. 1, Box 853, Gilmer, TX 75644: Information $2 ◆ Ready-to-paint gourds. 903-734-5204. www.texaseast.com/westmountain

**Willow Woods,** 4365 Willow Ave., Medina, IN 55340: Free catalog ◆ Kits and craft supplies. 800-376-7856. www.willowwoods.com

**Wood-N-Crafts Inc.,** P.O. Box 140, Lakeview, MI 48850: Catalog $2 ◆ Craft and woodworking supplies. 800-444-8075; 517-352-8075 (in MI). www.wood-n-crafts.com

**Wooden Penny Trading Post,** 105 Vois D'Arc, Lake Jackson, TX 77566: Catalog $2 ◆ American Indian (Native American) craft supplies. 409-297-8953.

**Zim's,** 4370 S. 3rd West, Salt Lake City, UT 84107: Catalog $10 (refundable) ◆ Craft and painting supplies. 801-268-2505.

## CRICKET

**General Sportcraft Company,** 140 Woodbine Rd., Bergenfield, NJ 07621: Free information ◆ Bats, balls, and gloves. 201-384-4242.

**Genesport Industries Ltd.,** Hokkaido Karate Equipment Manufacturing Company, 150 King St., Montreal, Quebec, Canada H3C 2P3: Free information ◆ Bats, balls, and gloves. 514-861-1856.

**Grass Court Collection,** P.O. Box 972, Hanover, NH 03755: Free catalog ◆ Custom men's clothing for tennis, croquet, lawn bowling, cricket, and squash. 800-829-3412.

**Don Jagoda Associates Inc.,** 100 Marcus Dr., Melville, NY 11747: Free information ◆ Bats, balls, and gloves. 516-454-1800.

## CROQUET

**American Croquet Enterprises,** Bill Hoy, 743 Hollonville Rd., Williamson, GA 30292: Free information ◆ Mallets, wickets, deadness boards, and other equipment. 770-884-5432.

**Bauer Sports,** 150 Ocean Rd., Greenland, NH 03840: Free list of retail sources ◆ Croquet sets. 800-362-3146.

**Clarkpoint Croquet Company,** P.O. Box 457, Southwest Harbor, ME 04679: Free information with long SASE ◆ Croquet sets and mallets. 207-244-9284.

**Croquet International Ltd.,** 7100 Fairway Dr., Palm Beach Gardens, FL 33418: Free catalog ◆ Croquet and tennis sets. 800-533-9061; 561-627-4009 (in FL).

**The Croquet People,** Fred & Jackie Jones, 1626 Liscourt Dr., Venice, FL 34292: Free information ◆ Mallets, balls, boards, wickets, stakes, clips, and gifts. 941-484-3206.

**Escalade Sports,** P.O. Box 889, Evansville, IN 47706: Free information ◆ Croquet accessories. 800-457-3373; 812-467-1200 (in IN).

**Indian Industries Inc.,** P.O. Box 889, Evansville, IN 47706: Free catalog ◆ Croquet sets. 800-457-3373; 812-467-1200 (in IN).

**Kentucky Croquet Equipment,** Archie Burchfield, 328 Locust Fork Rd., Stamping Ground, KY 40379: Free information ◆ Wickets. 502-535-6167.

**Oakley Woods,** Don Oakley, P.O. Box 3045, Brighton, Ontario, Canada K0K 1H0: Free information ◆ Mallets, wickets, balls, deadness boards, and flags. 613-475-3541.

**Olympia Sports,** P.O. Box 1941, Ann Arbor, MI 48106: Free information ◆ Croquet sets. 800-521-2832. www.wolverinesports.com

**Porter Athletic Equipment Company,** 2500 S. 25th Ave., Broadview, IL 60153: Free information ◆ Croquet sets. 630-338-2000.

**Wayne Rodoni,** 1435 Kalmia St., San Mateo, CA 94402: Free information ◆ Wickets, wicket clamps, and clips. 415-349-7913.

**Russell Corp.,** Russell Athletic Division, P.O. Box 272, Alexander City, AL 35010: Free information ◆ Croquet sets. 256-329-4000.

**Spalding Sports Worldwide,** 425 Meadow St., P.O. Box 901, Chicopee, MA 01201: Free list of retail sources ◆ Croquet accessories. 800-225-6601. www.spalding.com

**Sportime,** Customer Service, 1 Sporting Way, Atlanta, GA 30340: Free information ◆ Croquet accessories. 800-444-5700; 770-449-5700 (in GA).

## CRYSTAL & GLASSWARE

**Alice's Past & Presents Replacements,** P.O. Box 465, Merrick, NY 11566: Free information ◆ Replacement crystal, china, and flatware. 516-379-1352. ALICECHINA@AOL.com

**Ann Arbor Dinner Exchange,** P.O. Box 6054, Ann Arbor, MI 48106: Free information ◆ China and crystal. 888-244-6239.

**Baccarat,** 625 Madison Ave., New York, NY 10022: Brochure $3 ◆ Crystal and china Baccarat. 800-777-0100.

**Barrons,** P.O. Box 994, Novi, MI 48376: Free information ◆ China, crystal, and silver. 800-538-6340.

**David Baruch,** 36-42 W. 47th St., New York, NY 10036: Free information ◆ China, crystal, and sterling. 800-338-6961.

**The China Cabinet (South Carolina),** P.O. Box 426, Clearwater, SC 29822: Free information with long SASE ◆ China and crystal. 803-593-9655.

**China, Crystal & Flatware Replacements,** P.O. Box 508, High Ridge, MO 63049: Free information ◆ China, crystal, and flatware. 800-562-2655.

**China Finders,** 1-B South Holly, Highland Springs, VA 23075: Free information ◆ China and crystal replacements. 888-244-6239; 804-328-2897 (in VA).

**China Replacements,** P.O. Box 508, High Ridge, MO 63049: Free information with long SASE ◆ Discontinued china and crystal. 800-562-2655. www.IAdm.com/chinarep

**Clintsman International,** 20855 Watertown Rd., Waukesha, WI 53186: Free information ◆ Discontinued china, crystal, and flatware. 800-781-8900.

**Custom Glass Etching,** 1139 E. Las Tunas Dr., San Gabriel, CA 91776: Free catalog ◆ Personalized crystal glass awards, gifts, wedding gifts, and promotional products. 626-287-3775.

**Dansk International Design,** 108 Corporate Park Dr., White Plains, NY 10604: Free list of retail sources ◆ Dinnerware, stemware, flatware, kitchenware, and serving pieces. 914-697-6400. www.danskfurnishings.com

**Fellowship Foundry Pewtersmiths,** 1605 Abram Ct., San Leandro, CA 94577: Free catalog ◆ Goblets, sculptures, switch plates, jewelry, cups and steins, glassware and crystal, and other pewter gifts. 510-352-0935.

**Golden Gift Company,** 304 New St., Philadelphia, PA 19106: Free information ◆ Handcrafted European vases, bowls, stemware, baskets, and figurines. 800-GOLD-171.

**Gorham,** 100 Lenox Dr., Lawrenceville, NJ 08648: Free list of retail sources ◆ Fine china dinnerware, crystal, and silver. 800-635-3669.

**Irish Crystal Company,** 102 W. Washington St., P.O. Box 2134, Middleburg, VA 20118: Free brochure ◆ Waterford crystal. 540-687-3422.

**Kitchen Etc.,** 32 Industrial Dr., Exeter, NH 03833: Catalog $2 ◆ Cookware, cutlery, flatware, crystal, and dinnerware. 800-232-4070. www.kitchenetc.com

**Lanac Sales,** 500 Driggs Ave., Brooklyn, NY 11211: Free catalog ◆ China, crystal, sterling, and gifts. 800-522-0047; 718-782-7200 (in NY).

**Lenox Collections,** P.O. Box 519, Langhorne, PA 19047: Free catalog ◆ China, crystal, and porcelain sculptures. 800-225-1779. www.lenoxcollections.com

**Locators Inc.,** 2217 Cottondale Ln., Little Rock, AR 72202: Free information ◆ Discontinued china, crystal, and silver. 800-367-9690.

**Marks China, Crystal & Silverware,** 315 Franklin Ave., Wyckoff, NJ 07481: Free information ◆ China, stainless, crystal, and silverware. 800-862-7578.

**Mikasa,** P.O. Box 1549, Secaucus, NJ 07096: Free catalog ◆ China, stoneware, crystal, and flatware. 800-833-4681; 201-867-9210 (in NJ).

**Miki's Crystal Registry,** 100 W. Bridge Ave., P.O. Box 320, Delano, MN 55328: Free information ◆ Fostoria crystal matching service. 800-628-9394.

**Orrefors Kosta Boda USA,** 58 E. 57th St., New York, NY 10022: Free information ◆ Orrefors crystal. 800-351-9842; 212-753-3442 (in NY).

**Jeffrey F. Purtell,** P.O. Box 28, Amherst, NH 03031: Free information with long SASE ◆ Steuben crystal. 800-973-4331.

**Replacements Ltd.,** P.O. Box 26029, Greensboro, NC 27420: Free information with long SASE ◆ Discontinued bone china, earthenware, and crystal. 800-737-5223. www.replacements.com

**Rogers & Rosenthal,** 22 W. 48th St., Room 1102, New York, NY 10036: Free information with long SASE ◆ Crystal, china, silver, silver plate, and stainless steel. 212-827-0115.

**Royal Mail,** 435 5th Ave., New York, NY 10016: Free information ◆ Thistle crystal, Fraser minatures, andother gifts. 800-843-9078.

**Royal Worcester,** The Royal China & Porcelain Companies Inc., 1265 Glen Ave., Moorestown, NJ 08057: Free list of retail sources ◆ Place settings, cookware, glasses and goblets, and accessories. 609-866-2900.

**Rudi's Pottery, Silver & China,** 180 N. State Rt. 17, Paramus, NJ 07652: Free information with long SASE ◆ Glass stemware, china, and gifts. 201-265-6096.

**Steuben Glass,** Customer Relations, Corning Glass Center, Corning, NY 14831: Catalog $8 ◆ Steuben crystal and gifts. 800-424-4240.

**Waterford Crystal Inc.,** 713 Madison Ave., New York, NY 10010: Brochure $2 ◆ Fine china serving pieces, dinnerware, crystal, and gifts. 800-677-7860.

**Zucker's Fine Gifts,** 151 W. 26th St., New York, NY 10001: Free catalog ◆ Hummel, Swarovski silver and crystal, Waterford crystal, Lladro porcelain, and other gifts. 212-989-1450.

## CURTAINS, DRAPES, & BLINDS

### Accessories & Controls

**Connecticut Curtain Company,** Commerce Plaza, RR 6, Danbury, CT 06810: Catalog $2 ◆ Drapery hardware. 800-732-4549; 203-798-1850 (in CT).

**DrapeBoss,** 3135 Osgood Ct., Fremont, CA 94539: Free information ◆ Automatic drapery and vertical blind opener. 800-318-7307.

**Makita USA Inc.,** Drapery Opener Division, 14930 Northam St., La Mirada, CA 90638: Free information ◆ Motorized drapery system. 800-462-5482. MAKITAAPD@AOL.com

**Old Smithy Shop,** 195 Rt. 13, Brookline, NH 03055: Catalog $3 ◆ Hand-forged reproduction colonial hardware, fireplace equipment, curtain accessories, and bathroom fixtures. 603-672-4113.

**SMAutomatic,** 10301 Jefferson Blvd., Culver City, CA 90232: Free list of retail sources ◆ Motor and remote controls for draperies, blinds, and window coverings. 310-559-6405.

**Steptoe & Wife Antiques Ltd.,** 322 Geary Ave., Toronto, Ontario, Canada M6H 2C7: Catalog $3 ◆ Decorative drapery accessories. 416-530-4200. www.terraport.net/steptoe

### Blinds & Window Shades

**American Blind, Wallpaper & Carpet Factory,** 909 N. Sheldon Rd., Plymouth, MI 48170: Free information ◆ Wood, micro, mini, and vertical blinds. Also roller and pleated shades, wallpaper, and carpet. 800-889-2631 (for blinds and wallpaper); 800-346-0608 (for carpet). www.abwf.com

**Blind Center USA,** 7013 3rd Ave., Brooklyn, NY 11209: Free information ◆ Vertical, mini, micro, duettes, and wood blinds. 800-676-5029.

**Colorel Blinds,** 8200 E. Park Meadows Dr., Littleton, CO 80124: Free information ◆ Window treatments. 800-877-4800.

**Devenco Products Inc.,** Box 700, Decatur, GA 30031: Free brochure ◆ Period reproductions of wood blinds and plantation-style, traditional, and movable shutters. Also exterior shutters. 800-888-4597; 404-378-4597 (in GA).

**Global Wallcoverings & Blinds,** 4125 W. Main St., Skokie, IL 60076: Free information ◆ Wallcoverings and blinds. 800-220-7610. www.globalwcb.com

**Headquarters Windows & Walls,** 82 Speedwell Ave., Morristown, NJ 07960: Free information ◆ Wall coverings and micro, mini, verticals, and pleated blinds. 800-338-4882.

**Hunter Douglas Window Fashions,** 1 Duette Way, Broomfield, CO 80020: Free information ◆ Window coverings. 800-22-STYLE. www.hunterdouglas.com

**Kestrel Manufacturing,** 9 E. Race St., Stowe, PA 19464: Information $2 ◆ Knock-down and ready-to-hang folding screens and interior and exterior shutters. Also available as kits. 800-494-4321; 610-326-6679 (in PA). www.diyshutters.com

**MDC Direct Inc.,** P.O. Box 569, Marietta, GA 30061: Free information ◆ Wood blinds, cellular shades, and area rugs. 800-892-2083.

**National Blind & Wallpaper Factory,** 400 Galleria, Southfield, MI 48034: Free information ◆ Window blinds. 800-477-8000.

**Picture Perfect Window Coverings,** 111 W. Frankford, #105, Carrollton, TX 75007: Free brochure ◆ Vertical blinds with optional track systems. 972-492-8535.

**Premier Blind Factory,** 23000 West 8 Mile Rd., Southfield, MI 48034: Free information ◆ Custom blinds, shades, and drapery. 888-254-6373. www.premierblinds.com

**The Shutter Depot,** 437 LaGrange, Greenville, GA 30222: Free brochure ◆ Interior and exterior raised panel and fixed louver shutters. 706-672-1214. www.shutterdepot.com

**Shuttercraft,** 282 Stepstone Hill Rd., Guilford, CT 06437: Free brochure ◆ Moveable door fixed louver and raised panel shutters. 203-453-1973.

**Smith & Noble,** P.O. Box 1838, Corona, CA 91718: Free catalog ◆ Window shades and blinds. 800-248-8888.

**3 Day Blinds,** Attention: Mail Order, 2220 E. Cerritos Ave., Anaheim, CA 92806: Free information ◆ Pleated shades and vertical, mini, and wood blinds. 800-966-3DAY.

**USA Blind Factory,** 1312 Live Oak, Houston, TX 77003: Free information ◆ Vertical, pleated, mini, micro, and wood blinds. 800-275-9416.

**Wallpaper & Blinds Connection,** P.O. Box 492, Budd Lake, NJ 07828: Free information ◆ Wallpaper, fabrics, and blinds. 800-488-WALL. blindscom@aol.com

**Wells Interiors,** 7171 Amador Valley Plaza Rd., Dublin, CA 95468: Free catalog ◆ Kits for energy-efficient Roman shades or adding fabric to existing decorative arrangements and mini, wood, vertical, pleated, and woven wood blinds. 800-547-8982.

### Curtains & Drapes

**Bucks Trading Post,** 930 Old Bethlehem Pike, Sellersville, PA 18960: Catalog $2 ◆ European lace curtains and matching tablecloths and doilies. 800-242-0738; 610-453-0623 (in PA).

**Caroline's Country Ruffles,** 420 W. Franklin Blvd., Gastona, NC 28052: Catalog $2 ◆ Curtains. 800-426-1039.

**Country Curtains,** Red Lion Inn, Stockbridge, MA 01262: Free catalog ◆ Cotton muslin and permanent-press country-style curtains.800-456-0321. www.countrycurtains.com

**Curtains Up,** 2709 S. Park Rd., Louisville, KY 40219: Free information ◆ Drapery accessories. 502-969-1464.

**Dianthus Ltd.,** P.O. Box 870, Plymouth, MA 02362: Catalog $6 ◆ Curtains with a country look. 508-747-4179.

**Dimestore Cowboys,** 407 2nd St. SW, Albuquerque, NM 87102: Catalog $7 ◆ Door sets, cabinet pulls, shutters, bathroom accessories, curtain rods and rings, and handcrafted hardware. 505-244-1493.

**Dorothy's Ruffled Originals Inc.,** 6721 Market St., Wilmington, NC 28405: Catalog $4 ◆ Ruffled curtains and window treatments. 800-367-6849.

**Especially Lace,** 202 5th St., West Des Moines, IA 50265: Catalog $4.50 ◆ European lace curtains and ready-to-hang valances. 515-277-8778.

**Virginia Goodwin,** 1363 Big Hill Rd., Boone, NC 28607: Information $1 ◆ Window valances, hand-tied fishnet bed canopies, dust ruffles, and bedspreads. 800-735-5191.

**Harding's Custom Sheers,** 807 S. Auburn, Grass Valley, CA 95945: Free brochure ◆ Pleated seamless sheers. 800-228-0825.

**Heritage Lace,** 309 South St., P.O. Box 328, Pella, IA 50219: Free brochure ◆ Lace curtains. 800-354-0668.

**Lifespace Interiors International,** 3946 S. Magnolia Way, Denver, CO 80237: Catalog $4 ◆ Slipcovers, table and other furniture cover-ups, shower curtains, window treatments, and more. 303-759-3024. www.dimensional.com/lifespace-interiors

**Linen & Lace,** 4 Lafayette, Washington, MO 63090: Catalog $2 ◆ Linen and imported Bavarian lace curtains, runners, and accent pillows. 800-332-5223.

**Marje Lomoriello,** 799 Broadway, Ulster Park, NY 12487: Brochure with cotton and linen swatches $8.50 ◆ Historical replica window and bed hangings.

**London Lace,** 215 Newbury St., Boston, MA 02116: Catalog $2.50 ◆ Lace window coverings. 800-926-LACE.

**Marlborough Country Barn,** N. Main St., Marlborough, CT 06447: Catalog $3 ◆ Handcrafted curtains and decorative accessories. 800-852-8993.

**Rue de France,** 78 Thames St., Newport, RI 02840: Catalog $3 ◆ Lace curtains, tablecloths, runners, and pillows. 800-777-0998.

**The Seraph,** P.O. Box 500, 420 Main St., Sturbridge, MA 01566: Catalog $6 ◆ Bed hangings and window treatments with coordinating rugs and accessories. 508-347-2241.

**Spring Lace,** 221 Morris Ave., Spring Lake, NJ 07762: Free brochure ◆ Lace curtains. 232-449-0021.

**Straw and Feathers,** A Creative Company, 4911 W. Clay St., Richmond, VA 23230: Catalog $5 ◆ Ruffled curtains, in-stock and made-to-order drapes, bedspreads, pillow shams, and accessories. 800-933-0455; 804-359-0455 (in VA).

**Vintage Valances,** P.O. Box 43326, Cincinnati, OH 45243: Catalog $12 ◆ Ready-to-hang period-style drapes, bed hangings, and window shades, from 1800 to 1930. 513-561-8665.

**Ann Wallace & Friends,** 767 Linwood Ave., St. Paul, MN 55105: Catalog $8 (refundable) ◆ Natural fiber curtains. 612-228-9611.

**Window Quilts,** P.O..Box 975, Brattleboro, VT 05301: Information $1 ◆ Insulating window shades. 800-257-4501.

## DANCING

### Ballet Barres

**Ballet Barres Inc.,** 5705 W. Sligh Ave., Tampa, FL 33634: Free catalog ◆ Dance shoes, bodywear, legwear, and ballet barres. 813-884-9203.

**Panache,** P.O. Box 5332, Chesapeake, VA 23324: Free brochure ◆ Free-standing ballet barres. 888-663-2623.

**Victoria's Dance-Theatrical Supply,** 1331 Lincoln Ave., San Jose, CA 95125: Catalog $2 ◆ Wall-mounted ballet barres, dance shoes, dancewear, costume accessories, and make-up. 800-626-9258; 408-295-9317 (in CA).

### Clothing & Costumes

**Algy Dancewear,** 440 NE 1st Ave., P.O. Box 090490, Hallandale, FL 33008: Free catalog ◆ Costumes and uniforms for dancers. 800-458-ALGY.

**Apparel Warehouse,** 6010 Yolanda St., Tarzana CA 91356: Free catalog ◆ Briefs, leotards, leg warmer socks, and spandex tights. 800-245-8434; 818-344-3224 (in CA).

**Back Bay Dancewear,** 181 Mass Ave., Boston, MA 02115: Free catalog ◆ Dancewear. 800-554-2340.

**Ballet Barres Inc.,** 5705 W. Sligh Ave., Tampa, FL 33634: Free catalog ◆ Dance shoes, bodywear, legwear, and ballet barres. 813-884-9203.

**Ballet Etc.,** 5205 Simpson Ferry Rd., Mechanicsburg, PA 17055: Free information ◆ Dance and gymnastic wear, shoes, and clothing for ice skaters. 800-DANCE-25.

**Mary Barstow's Expressions Inc.,** 30-04 Warwick Rd., P.O. Box 502, Winchester, NH 03470: Free catalog with request on school stationery ◆ Dancewear and activewear. 800-253-2623.

**Baum's Inc.,** 106 S. 11th St., Philadelphia, PA 19107: Free catalog with request on school stationery ◆ Costumes, leotards, shoes, fabrics, and majorette items. 215-923-2244.

**Carushka Inc.,** 7716 Kester Ave., Van Nuys, CA 91405: Catalog $3 ◆ Women's sportswear, bodywear, leotards, tank tops, trunks, and bike tights. 800-247-5113; 818-904-0574 (in CA). www.carushka.com

**Chatila Dance & Gymnastic Fashions,** P.O. Box 508, Staten Island, NY 10304: Free catalog with request on school stationery ◆ Bodywear, lyrical dresses, and tap, ballet, and jazz shoes. 718-720-3632.

**Clingons Activewear,** P.O. Box 721, Millersville, MD 21108: Free information ◆ Activewear for dancers. 410-987-2724.

**Colorifics,** 8325 Green Meadows Dr. North, Westerville, OH 43081: Free information ◆ Women's costumes for color guards, drill teams, dance lines, majorettes, and cheerleaders. 800-322-1961.

**The Competitor,** 2200 Sunset Blvd., Jesup, GA 31545: Catalog $5 ◆ Women's costumes for dance and kicklines, drill teams, pom pom squads, flag teams, baton twirlers, and others. 912-530-6726.

**Costume Gallery,** 1604 South Rt. 130, Burlington, NJ 08016: Free catalog with request on school stationery ◆ Costumes and dancewear. 609-386-6501.

**The Costume Shop,** 253 Broad St., P.O. Box 1497, Manchester, CT 06045: Free catalog with request on school stationery ◆ Dance costumes. 860-646-5758.

**Creations by Lauren,** 921 Rosilee Ln., Rapid City, SD 57701: Catalog $2 (refundable) ◆ Custom handmade beaded clothing and accessories in traditional Native American style. Also moccasins, knife cases, war shirts, dresses, and other crafts.

**Curtain Call Costumes,** 333 E. 7th Ave., P.O. Box 709, York, PA 17405: Free catalog with request on school stationery ◆ Dancing attire. 717-852-6910.

**Dance Shop,** 2485 Forest Park Blvd., Fort Worth, TX 76110: Free catalog ◆ Shoes and bodywear. 800-22-DANCE.

**Dance Supplies Etc.,** 474-D Ritchie Hwy., Severna Park, MD 21146: Free catalog ◆ Clothing and shoes for adults and children. www.dancesupply.com

**Dance Vision,** 8933 W. Sahara Ave., Ste. 101, Las Vegas, NV 89117: Catalog $5 ◆ Clothing, jewelry, fabrics, instructional books, dance shoes, CDs, and videos. 800-851-2813; 702-256-3830 (in NV). www.dancevision.com

**Dansant Boutique,** 1020 S. Wabash Ave., Ste. 5D, Chicago, IL 60605: Free catalog ◆ Dancewear, leotards, tights, and shoes. 800-DANSANT; 312-922-6186 (in IL).

**Danskin,** 111 W. 40th St., 18th Floor, New York, NY 10018: Free information ◆ Leotards, tights, costumes, ballet shoes, swimsuits, lingerie, and hosiery. 212-764-4630.

**Discount Dance Supply,** 1401 Village Way, Santa Ana, CA 92705: Free catalog ◆ Clothing, leotards, tights, and shoes. 800-328-7107. www.discdance.com

**Freed of London Inc.,** 922 7th Ave., New York, NY 10019: Free price list ◆ Soft ballet slippers, leotards and ballroom attire, exercise wear, and pointe, jazz, character, and gym shoes. 212-489-1055.

**Hoctor Products,** P.O. Box 38, Waldwick, NJ 07463: Free catalog ◆ Costumes, records, dance routines, videos, cassettes, phonographs and cassette players, and video recorders. 800-HOCTOR-9.

**Illinois Theatrical,** P.O. Box 34284, Chicago, IL 60634: Free catalog with request on school stationery ◆ Costumes. 800-745-3777.

**Instructor's Choice,** Oakbrook Sales Corp., 5020 Sunrise Hwy., Ste. 3, Massapequa Park, NY 11762: Free information ◆ Tights, leotards, and other attire. 800-622-7667.

**Kling's Theatrical Shoe Company,** 218 S. Wabash Ave., Chicago, IL 60604: Catalog 50¢ ◆ Shoes and dancewear. 312-427-2028.

**Lebo's of Charlotte Inc.,** 4118 E. Independence Blvd., Charlotte, NC 28205: Free catalog with request on school stationery ◆ Costumes, footwear, leotards, tights, fabrics, record players, tapes, and records. 704-535-5000.

**Leo's Dancewear Inc.,** 1900 N. Narragansett Ave., Chicago, IL 60639: Free catalog with request on school stationery ◆ Dance costumes. 312-889-7700. Leos@IX.Netcom.com

**Loshin's Dancewear,** 5141 Kennedy Ave., Cincinnati, OH 45213: Free catalog with request on school stationery ◆ Costumes, leotards, tights, sequin trimmings, tiaras, hats, and shoes. 513-531-5800.

**Lynch's Clown Supplies,** 939 Howard, Dearborn, MI 48124: Catalog $5 ◆ Dancewear, shoes, super tone taps, sequin appliques and fabrics, trim, rhinestones, hats, and make-up. 800-24-LYNCH. www.lynchs.com

**Marcéa,** 1374 S. Flower, Los Angeles, CA 90015: Free information ◆ Clothing for dancers. 800-821-7737.

**New York Dancewear Company,** 188-06 Union Tnpk., Flushing, NY 11366: Free catalog ◆ Dancewear and clothing for theatrical productions. 800-775-3262. www.nydancewear.com

**Pep Threads,** 1141 W. Katella Ave., Orange, CA 92867: Free catalog with request on school stationery (request list of retail sources)* Dance clothing and accessories. 800-367-8195.

**Sadé Bodywear,** 516 W. 34th St., New York, NY 10001: Free information ◆ Dancer's clothing. 800-563-9384; 212-563-9383 (in NY).

**Satin Stitches,** 11894 Reisling Blvd. NW, Minneapolis, MN 55433: Free information ◆ Custom clothing for performance teams. 800-48-SATIN.

**H.W. Shaw Inc.,** P.O. Box 4034, Hollywood, FL 33083: Free catalog ◆ Dancewear. 800-327-9548; 954-989-1300 (in FL).

**Star Styled Dancewear,** P.O. Box 119029, Hialeah, FL 33011: Free information ◆ Bodywear, shoes, and costumes for dancers. 800-532-6237. www.starstyled.com

**Art Stone Dancewear,** 1795 Express Dr. North, Smithtown, NY 11787: Free catalog with request on school stationery ◆ Bodywear and footwear for dancers. 516-582-9500.

**Victoria's Dance-Theatrical Supply,** 1331 Lincoln Ave., San Jose, CA 95125: Catalog $2 ◆ Wall-mounted ballet barres, dance shoes, dancewear, costume accessories, and make-up. 800-626-9258; 408-295-9317 (in CA).

**Weissman's Designs for Dance,** 1600 Macklind Ave., St. Louis, MO 63110: Free catalog with request on school stationery ◆ Dancewear and footwear. 800-477-5410.

**R.B. Williams Company Inc.,** 157 6th Ave. NE, St. Petersburg, FL 33701: Free information ◆ Sweat pants in small, medium, and large. 800-843-7346. www.trim-ez.com

## Music

**Dance Vision,** 8933 W. Sahara Ave., Ste. 101, Las Vegas, NV 89117: Catalog $5 ◆ Clothing, jewelry, fabrics, instructional books, dance shoes, CDs, and videos. 800-851-2813; 702-256-3830 (in NV). www.dancevision.com

**Hoctor Products,** P.O. Box 38, Waldwick, NJ 07463: Free catalog ◆ Records, cassettes, dance routines, cassette players, video recorders, phonographs, and books. 800-HOCTOR-9.

**Jay Distributors,** Box 191332, Dallas, TX 75219: Free information ◆ Ballet, tap, and jazz videos and records, tapes, CDs, and cassettes. 800-793-6843. www.flash.net/~jaydist

**Lebo's of Charlotte Inc.,** 4118 E. Independence Blvd., Charlotte, NC 28205: Free catalog with request on school stationery ◆ Costumes, dancewear, footwear, leotards and tights, fabrics, record players, tapes, and records. 704-535-5000.

**Patzius Performing Arts,** 754 New Ballas Rd., Creve Coeur, MO 63141: Free brochure ◆ Instrumental music for tap, ballet, jazz, modern, and ballroom dancing. 314-432-3890.

**Roper Records,** 45-15 21st St., Long Island City, NY 11101: Free catalog ◆ Ballet and ballroom dance music. 718-786-2401.

### Shoes

**Ballet Barres Inc.,** 5705 W. Sligh Ave., Tampa, FL 33634: Free catalog ◆ Dance shoes, bodywear, legwear, and ballet barres. 813-884-9203.

**Capezio/Ballet Makers Inc.,** 1776 Broadway, 2nd Floor, New York, NY 10019: Free information with long SASE ◆ Shoes. 800-234-4858; 212-586-5140 (in NY). www.capezio.com

**Chatila Dance & Gymnastic Fashions,** P.O. Box 508, Staten Island, NY 10304: Free catalog with request on school stationery ◆ Bodywear, lyrical dresses, and tap, ballet, and jazz shoes. 718-720-3632.

**Coast Shoes Inc.,** 13401 Saticoy, North Hollywood, CA 91605: Free list of retail sources ◆ Tap, jazz, ballet, and character dance shoes. 800-262-7851.

**Dance Shop,** 2485 Forest Park Blvd., Fort Worth, TX 76110: Free catalog ◆ Shoes and bodywear. 800-22-DANCE.

**Dance Vision,** 8933 W. Sahara Ave., Ste. 101, Las Vegas, NV 89117: Catalog $5 ◆ Clothing, jewelry, fabrics, instructional books, dance shoes, CDs, and videos. 800-851-2813; 702-256-3830 (in NV). www.dancevision.com

**Danskin,** 111 W. 40th St., 18th Floor, New York, NY 10018: Free information ◆ Ballet shoes, costumes, leotards, tights, swimsuits, lingerie, and hosiery. 212-764-4630.

**Freed of London Inc.,** 922 7th Ave., New York, NY 10019: Free price list ◆ Pointe shoes, soft ballet slippers, jazz and character shoes, ballet accessories, and leotards. 212-489-1055.

**Gaynor Minden,** 140 W. 16th St., New York, NY 10011: Free brochure ◆ Ballet shoes. 212-929-0087.

**Grishko,** 1655 Mt. Pleasant Rd., Villanova, PA 19085: Free information ◆ Dancing shoes. 610-527-9553.

**Kling's Theatrical Shoe Company,** 218 S. Wabash Ave., Chicago, IL 60604: Catalog 50c ◆ Shoes and dancewear. 312-427-2028.

**La Mendola,** 1795 Express Dr. North, Smithtown, NY 11787: Free list of retail sources ◆ Lyrical/ballet shoes and dance sneakers for jazz, hip-hop, street dance, and kicklines. 800-645-5115; 516-582-3230 (in NY).

**La Ray,** 633 Alacci Way, River Vale, NJ 07675: Free information ◆ Toe shoes and ballet slippers. 201-664-5882.

**Loshin's Dancewear,** 5141 Kennedy Ave., Cincinnati, OH 45213: Free catalog with request on school stationery ◆ Costumes, leotards, tights, sequin trimmings, tiaras, hats, and shoes. 513-531-5800.

**Lynch's Clown Supplies,** 939 Howard, Dearborn, MI 48124: Catalog $5 ◆ Dancewear, shoes, super tone taps, sequin appliques and fabrics, trim, rhinestones, hats, and make-up. 313-565-3425. www.lynchs.com

**Sansha USA Company,** 1733 Broadway, New York, NY 10019: Free information ◆ Shoes for dancers. 800-398-9562; 212-246-6212 (in NY).

**Soloist Corp.,** 95 Horatio St., Ste. 2S, New York, NY 10014: Free information ◆ Pointe shoes. 212-645-5858.

**Star Styled Dancewear,** P.O. Box 119029, Hialeah, FL 33011: Free information ◆ Bodywear, shoes, and costumes for dancers. 800-532-6237. www.starstyled.com

**Art Stone Dancewear,** 1795 Express Dr. North, Smithtown, NY 11787: Free catalog with request on school stationery ◆ Bodywear and footwear for dancers. 516-582-9500.

**Victoria's Dance-Theatrical Supply,** 1331 Lincoln Ave., San Jose, CA 95125: Catalog $2 ◆ Portable wall-mounted ballet barres, dance shoes, dancewear, costume accessories, and make-up. 800-626-9258; 408-295-9317 (in CA).

**Weissman's Designs for Dance,** 1600 Macklind Ave., St. Louis, MO 63110: Free catalog with request on school stationery ◆ Dancewear and footwear. 800-477-5410.

## DARTS

**Accudart,** 163 E. Union Ave., East Rutherford, NJ 07073: Free catalog ◆ Darts and dart boards. 800-526-0451; 201-896-3200 (in NJ).

**Bottelsen Dart Company Inc.,** 945 W. McCoy Ln., Santa Maria, CA 93455: Free list of retail sources ◆ Darts and accessories. 805-922-4519.

**Buck Knives,** P.O. Box 1267, El Cajon, CA 92022: Free list of retail sources ◆ Darts and dart boards. 800-215-2825. www.knifecenter.com

**Compleat Gamester,** 350 Moody St., Waltham, MA 02154: Free information ◆ Juggling, dart, and billiard supplies. 800-698-9505. www.compgames.com

**Dart Mart Inc.,** 2255 Computer Ave., Willow Grove, PA 19090: Free information ◆ Dart boards, cabinets, dart-making supplies, and sets. 800-423-3220; 215-830-0501 (in PA).

**Dart World Inc.,** P.O. Box 845, Lynn, MA 01904: Free information ◆ Dart boards, cabinets, dart-making supplies, and sets. 800-225-2558; 781-581-6035 (in MA).

**Darts Unlimited,** 282 N. Henry St., Brooklyn, NY 11222: Free information ◆ Dart boards, cabinets, dart-making supplies, and sets. 718-389-7755.

**Escalade Sports,** P.O. Box 889, Evansville, IN 47706: Free catalog ◆ Dart boards, darts, and cabinets. 800-457-3373; 812-467-1200 (in IN).

**Franklin Sports Industries Inc.,** 17 Campanelli Pkwy., P.O. Box 508, Stoughton, MA 02072: Free information ◆ Dart boards, cabinets, and sets. 800-426-7700. www.eisnerbros.com

**General Sportcraft Company,** 140 Woodbine Rd., Bergenfield, NJ 07621: Free information ◆ Dart boards, cabinets, dart-making supplies, and sets. 201-384-4242.

**Great Lakes Dart Distributors Inc.,** S84W 19093 Enterprise Dr., Muskego, WI 52150: Free information ◆ Darts. 800-225-7593.

**Horizon Dart Supply,** 2415 S. 50th St., Kansas City, KS 66106: Free information ◆ Darts and dart boards. 800-732-7864.

**Indian Industries Inc.,** P.O. Box 889, Evansville, IN 47706: Free catalog ◆ Dart boards, cabinets, dart-making supplies, and sets. 800-457-3373; 812-467-1200 (in IN).

**Don Jagoda Associates Inc.,** 100 Marcus Dr., Melville, NY 11747: Free information ◆ Boards, cases, darts, and dart-making supplies. 516-454-1800.

**Marksman Products,** 5482 Argosy Dr., Huntington Beach, CA 92649: Free information ◆ Dart boards, cabinets, dart-making supplies, and sets. 714-898-7535.

**Mueller Sporting Goods Inc.,** 4825 S. 16th, Lincoln, NE 68512: Free catalog ◆ Billiards and dart supplies. 800-925-7665. www.Mueller-Sporting-Goods.com

**Orion Dart Products,** P.O. Box 13346, Fairlaw, OH 44333: Free brochure ◆ Darts, flights, and shafts. 330-867-0330.

**Owl Darts,** 1001 SW Adams, Peoria, IL 61602: Free catalog ◆ Billiards supplies and darts. 800-832-7871.

**Pennray Billiard & Recreational Products,** 7847 N. Calswell Ave., Niles, IL 60714: Free catalog ◆ Darts, billiards, and soccer equipment. 800-523-8934. www.wicothesource.com

**Saunier-Wilhem Company,** 3216 5th Ave., Pittsburgh, PA 15213: Free catalog ◆ Board games and equipment for bowling, billiards, darts, table tennis, and shuffleboard. 412-621-4350.

**Spalding Sports Worldwide,** 425 Meadow St., P.O. Box 901, Chicopee, MA 01021: Free list of retail sources ◆ Dart boards, cabinets, dart-making supplies, and sets. 800-225-6601. www.spalding.com

**Sportime,** Customer Service, 1 Sportime Way, Atlanta, GA 30340: Free information ◆ Darts and dart boards. 800-444-5700; 770-449-5700 (in GA).

**Tide-Rider Inc.,** P.O. Box 429, Oakdale, CA 95361: Free information ◆ Dart boards, cabinets, dart-making supplies, and sets. 209-848-4420.

**Valley Recreation Products Inc.,** P.O. Box 656, Bay City, MI 48707: Free information ◆ Dart boards, cabinets, dart-making supplies, and sets. 800-248-2837; 517-892-4536 (in MI).

## DECALS, EMBLEMS, & PATCHES

**AB Emblems & Caps,** P.O. Box 695, Weaverville, NC 28787: Free catalog ◆ Embroidered emblems and caps. 704-645-3015.

**Adhatters,** Box 667, Effingham, IL 62401: Free information ◆ Patches, pins, and decals. 800-225-7642.

**Bee Hive,** 12413 Tomanet, Austin, TX 78758: Catalog $2 (refundable) ◆ Iron-on transfer printing. 512-836-4424.

**Chimneyville Hobbies,** 233 Penner Dr., Pearl, MS 39208: Free list of retail sources with long SASE ◆ All types of law enforcement and fire apparatus decals. 601-932-6165.

**Decals For Fun,** P.O. Box 890305, Houston, TX 77289: Catalog $2 ◆ Decals for fun and decoration. 888-338-3750. Decals@phoenix.net

**Decorcal Inc.,** 165 Marine St., Farmingdale, NY 11735: Free catalog ◆ Decorative, stained glass, letter and number, sports, and wildlife decals. 800-645-9868; 516-752-0076 (in NY).

**Eastern Emblem,** Box 828, Union City, NJ 07087: Free catalog ◆ Patches, cloisonne pins, decals, stickers, T-shirts, caps, and jackets. 800-344-5112.

**Frosty Little,** 222 E. 8th St., Burley, ID 83318: Free information ◆ Sweatshirts, T-shirts, pins, and patches with clown graphics. 208-678-0005.

**A Graphic Edge,** 1313 Simpson Way, Ste. F, Escondido, CA 92029: Free brochure ◆ Dimensional signs, bumper stickers, and decals. 760-735-8494.

**Hoover's Manufacturing Company,** P.O. Box 547, Peru, IL 61354: Free catalog ◆ Dog tag key rings, beer and coffee mugs, belt buckles, patches, flags, and Vietnam, Korea, and World War II hat pins. 815-223-1159.

**HSU Patches,** P.O. Box 700310, San Jose, CA 95170: Free information ◆ Custom embroidered patches. 408-996-8989.

**Instar Enterprises International,** P.O. Box 6609, East Brunswick, NJ 08816: Free catalog ◆ Open stock and custom designed decals, both for vitrifiable and cold application. 732-238-4100. instar@instar-usa.com

**Lane 4 Awards,** P.O. Box 451591, Sunrise, FL 33345: Free catalog ◆ Embroidered emblems, medals, pins, ribbons, and trophies. 954-742-8609. lane4@interpoint.net

**McGrogan's Military Patches,** P.O. Box 502, Orofino, ID 83544: Free information ◆ Military patches. 800-861-9398.

**Microscale Industries Inc.,** P.O. Box 11950, Costa Mesa, CA 92627: Catalog $4 ◆ Micro-scale decals for decorating miniatures. 714-434-8995.

**Recco Maid Embroidery Company,** 4626 W. Cornelia Ave., Chicago, IL 60641: Free catalog ◆ Embroidered emblems. 800-345-3458; 773-286-6333 (in IL).

**Southern Emblem,** P.O. Box 8, Toast, NC 27049: Free catalog ◆ Embroidered emblems, emblematic jewelry, badges, flags, and screen-printing supplies. 800-522-8518.

**Stadri Emblems,** 71 Tinker St., Woodstock, NY 12498: Free catalog ◆ Embroidered emblems, pins, and decals. 914-679-6600.

**United Stitch Associates,** 807 Turnbull, Canyon Rd., Hacienda Heights, CA 91745: Free information ◆ Custom designed and in-stock martial arts patches and pins. 800-842-6294.

## DECORATIVE ITEMS & MISCELLANEOUS ACCESSORIES

**AC Originals,** Rt. 2, Box 478, Claremore, OK 74017: Free information ◆ Country-style pine bookcases, plate racks, and baker's rack with a choice of finishes. 918-341-1604.

**Cristina Acosta Design Art Studio,** P.O. Box 923, Bend, OR 97709: Free brochure ◆ Custom handpainted tiles. 541-388-5157. www.cristina-acosta.com

**Amish Country Collection,** Sunset Valley Rd., RD 5, Box 271, New Castle, PA 16105: Catalog $5 ◆ Amish-style pillows, quilts, wall hangings, rugs, beds and cribs, and crafts. 412-458-4811.

**Anichini Accessories,** Rt. 110, Tunbridge, VT 05077: Free list of retail sources ◆ Accessories for the home. 800-553-5309.

**Artisans,** The Mail Order Folk Art Gallery, P.O. Box 256, Mentone, AL 35984: Free information ◆ Folk art, quilts, and unusual antiques. 256-634-4037. www.folkartisans.com

**Baldwin Hardware Corp.,** P.O. Box 15048, Reading, PA 19612: Bathroom accessories brochure 75¢, light fixtures brochure $3, door hardware brochure 75¢, hardware brochure 75¢ ◆ Brass dead bolts and door hardware, bathroom accessories, and light fixtures. 800-566-1986.

**Ballard Designs,** 1670 DeFoor Ave. NE, Atlanta, GA 30318: Catalog $3 ◆ Furniture, pillows, prints, and accessories for indoor room arrangements and outdoor landscaping. 800-367-2810. www.ballard-designs.com

**Betsy's Place,** 323 Arch St., Philadelphia, PA 19106: Free information ◆ Sundials and stands, trivets, brass reproduction door knockers, banners and flags, and other decorative accessories. 800-452-3524; 215-922-3536 (in PA).

**Bregstone Associates Inc.,** 500 S. Wabash, Chicago, IL 60605: Free catalog ◆ Indoor and outdoor all-seasons decorative accessories. 312-939-5130.

**By Good Hands,** P.O. Box 4104, Portsmouth, NH 03801: Catalog $5 ◆ Iron, lighting, pottery, decoys, mirrors, paintings, assorted wood items, and accessories to enhance colonial settings. 603-547-2011.

**C & E Cottage Enterprises,** P.O. Box 221, Wheaton, MD 20693: Catalog $2 ((refundable) ◆ Handcrafted decorative accessories. 301-609-4540.

**Carol's Creative Ceramics,** P.O. Box 5406, San Mateo, CA 94402: Free brochure ◆ Ceramic decor accessories. 800-594-9620. www.creativeceramics.com

**Cassandra's Artist Direct,** 12628 Woodland Trail, Parker, CO 80134: Catalog $2 ◆ Handpainted candle holders, bowls, trays, boxes, and more. 303-805-7078.

**Chelsea House,** Box 399, Gastonia, NC 28053: Free list of retail sources ◆ Accessories for the home. 704-867-5926.

**The Craft Room,** 584 W. Girard Rd., Union City, MI 49094: Catalog $3 ◆ Original pictures framed in oak or barn wood. 517-741-5511.

**Creative Country Products,** P.O. Box 132, Neche, ND 58265: Brochure $2 (refundable) ◆ Authentic horseshoes welded together to make unusual gifts, household items, and decorative accessories. 800-257-6422.

**Decorator & Craft Corp.,** 428 S. Zelta, Wichita, KS 67207: Free catalog ◆ Paper mache decorator items. 800-835-3013.

**Deena'd Li'l Country Nook,** 6922 Liverpool Ct. NE, Bremerton, WA 98311: Brochure $1 (refundable) ◆ Decorative country-style wall accessories. 360-698-0803.

**Design Toscano,** 17 E. Campbell St., Arlington Heights, IL 60005: Catalog $4 ◆ Historical European reproductions for the home and garden. 800-525-1233. www.aaweb.com/toscano/

**Domain,** 110 Gough St., San Francisco, CA 94102: Free list of retail sources ◆ Accessories for the home. 415-431-4254.

**Everything Ewenique,** RR 1, Box 73, Mt. Pleasant Mills, PA 17853: Free catalog ◆ Country accents for the home. 800-800-4846.

**Fabric Hutch,** Main St., Box 201, Croghan, NY 13327: Free price list ◆ Napkins, place mats, pads for chairs, appliance covers, towels, and fabric accessories. 315-346-6360.

**Fire & Shadow Creations,** 6021 Redondo Ct. NW, Albuquerque, NM 87107: Brochure $3 ◆ Antique rust-finished and copper-plated Southwestern art. 505-343-9639.

**The Fountain Source,** 30799 Pinetree Rd., Pepper Pike, OH 44124: Free information ◆ Fountains for homes and gardens. 216-247-2843.

**Frontier Classix,** P.O. Box 1865, Magnolia, AR 71753: Free catalog ◆ Old west pistols, sculptures, bronzes, signs, badges, hand and leg-cuffs, jailer's keys, and realistic western collectibles.

**Garbe's,** 4137 S. 72nd East Ave., Tulsa, OK 74145: Free catalog ◆ Home and office accessories. 800-735-2241; 918-627-0284 (in OK). www.garbes.com

**Gift & Wicker Import Inc.,** 12770 Moore St., Cerritos, CA 90701: Catalog $5 ◆ Wickerware, hobby craft supplies, basket planters, home decorative accessories, and furniture. 800-622-6209; 310-407-3319 (in CA).

**Good Catalog Company,** 5484 SE International Way, Portland, OR 97222: Catalog $5 ◆ Kitchen gadgets and dining, gardening, and decorative accessories. 800-225-3870.

**Grandpa's Crafts,** 577 Hwy. 70 West, Havelock, NC 28532: Brochure $1 ◆ Country craft decorative accessories. 919-444-1603.

**Great American Log,** Box 3360, Ketchum, ID 83340: Catalog $4 ◆ Western-style decorative items for the home. 800-624-5779.

**Great City Traders,** 537 Stevenson St., San Francisco, CA 94103: Free list of retail sources ◆ Decorative accessories and gifts for the home.

**Guildmaster Imports,** Box 10725, Springfield, MO 65808: Free list of retail sources ◆ Accessories for the home. 417-869-3600.

**Harmony Hollow,** Box 1303, Ann Arbor, MI 48106: Free catalog ◆ Bells, musical chimes, mobiles, garment hangers, other interior and garden accents, and ornaments. 800-468-2355. www.harmonyhollow.com

**Heath Sedgwick,** P.O. Box 1305, Stony Brook, NY 11790: Catalog $4 ◆ Decorative accessories. 516-751-1129. www.heathsedgwick.com

**Here's My Heart,** 53 Kings Hwy. East, Haddonfield, NJ 08033: Free brochure ◆ Country-style decorative accessories. 609-354-2064.

**Historic Housefitters Company,** Farm to Market Rd., Brewster, NY 10509: Catalog $3 ◆ Hand-forged iron hardware, interior and exterior handmade light, brass and porcelain knobs, and more. 914-278-2427.

**Home Decorators Collection,** 8920 Pershall Rd., Hazelwood, MO 63042: Free catalog ◆ Hardware, switch plates, mail boxes, weather vanes, plant stands, furniture, clocks, fixtures, chandeliers, bathroom accessories, and wicker items. 800-240-6047.

**Hoyt & Hallowell,** HC63, Box 40, Rt. 153, East Madison, NH 03849: Free brochure ◆ Decorative iron accessories. 603-367-4794. ironworks@landmarketnet.net

**Images In Steel,** P.O. Box 288, Clyde Park, MT 59018: Catalog $2 (refundable) ◆ Weather vanes, fireplace screens, furniture, custom designed art, and western art handcrafted from plate steel. 800-511-1324; 406-686-4166 (in MT).

**Inter-Tribal Traders,** 3207 E. Washington St., Phoenix, AZ 85034: Free information ◆ Western and Native American-style decorative accessories. 800-766-4431.

**Interiors,** 320 Washington St., Mt. Vernon, NY 10553: Free catalog ◆ Art and furnishings for the home. 800-228-5215.

**Jay "Bird" Jones,** 520 Pine Oaks Rd., #4, Colorado Springs, CO 80926: Catalog $10 (refundable); brochure $1 ◆ Antler chairs, lamps, chandeliers, and carvings. 719-527-1845.

**Just Between Us,** 41 W. 8th Ave., Oshkosh, WI 54906: Free catalog ◆ Decorative accessories for the home. 800-258-3750. www.mileskimball.com

**Just Quackers,** 840 F Ave., Plano, TX 75074: Brochure $2 with long SASE ◆ Wood-framed stained glass art pictures for window treatments. 800-437-3147; 972-0423-2736 (in TX). www.metroplex.com/JustQuackers

**Lifespace Interiors International,** 3946 S. Magnolia Way, Denver, CO 80237: Catalog $4 ◆ Slipcovers, table and other furniture cover-ups, shower curtains, and more. 303-759-3024. www.dimensional.com/lifespace-interiors

**Marble Arch,** Box 833, High Point, NC 27261: Catalog $4 ◆ Brass and crystal finials and accessories. 800-723-1328.

**Marlborough Country Barn,** N. Main St., Marlborough, CT 06447: Catalog $3 ◆ Handcrafted curtains and decorative accessories. 800-852-8993.

**McJenn Gifts,** 8619 Hutch Ln., Columbia, IL 62236: Free brochure ◆ Floral settings and accessories for decorative arrangements. 618-939-8701.

**Memory Quilts & Accessories,** 49 Long Bow Dr., Sewell, NJ 08080: Free brochure ◆ Personalized quilts and other accessories made by transfer of photos, invitations, announcements, or notes. 800-582-1530.

**Metropolitan Artifacts Inc.,** 4783 Peachtree Rd., Atlanta, GA 30341: Free brochure ◆ Architectural decor and antiques for residential, commercial, and theatrical settings. 770-986-0007.

**J. Michael's Catalog Company,** 152 E. Main St., Rigby, ID 83442: Free catalog ◆ Home decorative and gift items. 208-523-0011.

**Mills River Industries,** 824 Locust St., Hendersonville, NC 28792: Catalog $1 ◆ Butter churns and decorative accents for the home. 704-697-9778.

**A.J. Munzinger & Company,** 2010 S. Shady Hill Rd., Springfield, MO 65809: Brochure $1 ◆ Antique housewares from the late 19th and early 20th-century. 417-886-9184.

**Museum Collections,** 340 Poplar St., Bldg. 20, Hanover, PA 17333: Free catalog ◆ Decorative glass accessories. 800-442-2460.

**Museum of Modern Art New York,** Mail Order Dept., 11 W. 53rd St., New York, NY 10019: Free catalog ◆ Contemporary items for homes, offices, or gifts. 800-447-6662. www.moma.org

**Nature's Gifts Wreath Company,** HC 35, Box 1044, St. George, ME 04857: Free catalog ◆ Decorated balsam fir wreaths for beautifying office and home interiors and exteriors. 800-348-0824.

**Old West Charm,** P.O. Box 311, Mountain Center, CA 92561: Brochure $6 (refundable) ◆ Handcrafted wood wagon wheel furnishings, lamps, wall hangings, and decorative items.

**The Old Wicker Garden,** 6606 Snider Plaza, Dallas, TX 75225: Photos $5 (refundable) ◆ Antique wicker furniture, brass and iron beds, hooked rugs and quilts, folk art, and decorative accessories. 972-373-8241.

**Panther Primitives,** P.O. Box 32, Normantown, WV 25267: Catalog $2 (refundable) ◆ Early American items. 304-462-7718.

**Simon Pearce,** 170 Main St., Westport, CT 06880: Free list of retail sources ◆ Accessories for the home. 203-226-2353.

**A Penchant for Primitive,** P.O. Box 806, Yarmouth, ME 04096: Catalog $3.50 ◆ 17th and 18th-century reproductions. 207-865-2293.

**Pierced Tin,** Country Accents, P.O. Box 437, Montoursville, PA 17754: Catalog $5 ◆ Handcrafted and make-them-yourself kits for pierced decorative tin items with optional finishes and designs. 717-478-4127.

**Precious Impressions,** P.O. Box 50536, Provo, UT 84605: Free information ◆ Kits for making personalized 3-dimensional replicas or statuettes of a baby's hand or foot. 888-758-4611.

**Ragged Mountain Antlers,** P.O. Box 1164, Hamilton, MT 59840: Free brochure ◆ Western-style home decorative items. 406-961-2400. www.bittersweet.net/antler/artist

**Reed Brothers,** 5000 Turner Rd., Sebastopol, CA 95472: Catalog $15 ◆ Wall plaques. 707-795-6261.

**The Renovator's Supply,** P.O. Box 2515, Conway, NH 03818: Free catalog ◆ Reproduction antique hardware, lighting and plumbing fixtures, curtains, and accessories. 800-659-0203.

**Rockin' H Designs,** P.O. Box 1072, Sandpoint, ID 83864: Free catalog ◆ Custom iron designs and artwork. 208-265-4050.

**N. Schumann Publisher Inc.,** P.O. Box 504, East Boothbay, ME 04544: Free information ◆ Original poster calendars and prints and note cards adapted from past calendars. Also children's posters for classroom and home use. 888-383-6027. www.nikkischumann.com

**Seay Marketing Inc.,** 1325 Tarman Circle, Norman, OK 73071: Free information ◆ Reproduction beverage company signs. 800-729-7086; 405-321-8681 (in OK). www.seaymarketing.com

**Southwest Decor & More,** 7820 Bayview St., Port Richey, FL 34668: Free catalog ◆ Southwest style lamps, chandeliers, figurines, and pottery. 800-250-9964. www.shopbasket.com

**Steel Silhouettes,** 2319 N. 60th St., Seattle, WA 98103: Free catalog ◆ Cut metal art, crafts, and lighting for decorative settings. 206-525-2205. www.eskimo.com/~steelsil

**Sycamore Creek,** P.O. Box 16, Ancram, NY 12502: Free brochure ◆ Copper trellises, arbors, and handcrafted garden and home furnishings. 518-398-6393. sycamorecreek@taconic.net

**Texas Basket Company,** P.O. Box 1110, Jacksonville, TX 75766: Free catalog ◆ Wall baskets and raffia, other baskets, cedar buckets, barrels, paper mache fruits and vegetables, and other decor accessories. 903-586-8014.

**Touch of Class Catalog,** 1905 N. Van Buren St., Huntingburg, IN 47542: Free catalog ◆ Bedroom furnishings, bathroom accessories, and draperies. 800-457-7456.

**Trumble Greetings,** P.O. Box 9800, Boulder, CO 80301: Catalog $1 ◆ Western-style decorative items for the home. 800-525-0656.

**Uwchlan Farm,** 303 Greenridge Rd., Glenmoore, PA 19343: Free catalog ◆ Wrought-iron accessories for the home and garden. 800-900-IRON.

**Vietri Accessories,** 343 Elizabeth Brady Rd., Hillsborough, NC 27278: Free list of retail sources ◆ Accessories for the home. 800-677-7860.

**Wild Wings,** P.O. Box 451, Lake City, MN 55041: Free catalog ◆ Home furnishings and accessories with a wildlife theme. 800-445-4833.

**Wood Wizard Works,** N. 1302 Cty. Road Y, Wautoma, WI 54982: Catalog $3 ◆ Decorative accessories for the home and office. 888-618-WOOD.

**Yield House,** P.O. Box 2525, Conway, NH 03818: Free catalog ◆ Furniture and accessories in a Shaker tradition. 800-659-0206.

**Jacqueline Zanca,** 140 E. 28th St., New York, NY 10016: Free information ◆ Victorian table accessories, decorative porcelains, and ceramics. 212-686-1719.

**Zimmerman Handcrafts,** 254 E. Main St., Leola, PA 17540: Brochure $1 ◆ Country-style accessories. 800-267-5689.

**Zona,** 97 Green St., New York, NY 10012: Free list of retail sources ◆ Accessories for the home. 212-925-6750.

## DECOUPAGE

**Fascinating Folds,** P.O. Box 10070, Glendale, AZ 85318: Catalog $1 ◆ Supplies, kits, and how-to books on decoupage. 800-968-2418. www.fascinating-folds.com

**Gemé Art Inc.,** 209 W. 6th St., Vancouver, WA 98660: Free information ◆ Paper tole (dimensional decoupage) kits, and supplies. 360-693-7772.

**Nautilus Arts & Crafts Inc.,** 6075 Kingston Rd., Fundry Plaza, Scarborough, Ontario, Canada M1C 1K5: Free catalog ◆ Decoupage prints and supplies. 800-472-2275.

## DECOYS & WOOD CARVINGS

**Beaver Dam Decoys,** 3311 State Rt. 305, P.O. Box 40, Cortland, OH 44410: Catalog $2 ◆ Decoys and carving supplies. 330-637-4007.

**Birds in Wood,** P.O. Box 2649, Meriden, CT 06450: Catalog $2 (refundable) ◆ Decoy carving kits. 203-634-1953.

**Blue Ribbon Bases,** 100-K Knickerbocker Ave., Bohemia, NY 11716: Free catalog with long SASE ◆ Walnut and hardwood bases and plaques for mounting projects. 516-589-0707. 888-692-5257.

**By Good Hands,** P.O. Box 4104, Portsmouth, NH 03801: Catalog $5 ◆ Iron, lighting, pottery, decoys, mirrors, paintings, assorted wood items, and accessories to enhance colonial settings. 603-547-2011.

**Carousel Creations,** Hwy. 63, P.O. Box 56, Barronett, WI 54813: Free information ◆ Cigar store Indians, carousel animals, and other wood carvings. 715-822-4189.

**The Decoy,** P.O. Box 3652, Carmel, CA 93921: Free brochure ◆ Handcarved wood birds, antique decoys, limited edition prints, and original art. 800-332-6988. decoy1881.aol.com

**Decoy Den Galleries,** P.O. Box 412, Columbia, IL 62236: Free brochure ◆ Handcarved wood geese, ducks, swans, shorebirds, and other decoys. 800-255-0551.

**Dux' Dekes Decoy Company,** RD 2, Box 66, Greenwich, NY 12834: Free information ◆ Goose, duck, loon, shorebird decoys and carving blanks. 800-553-4725; 518-692-7703 (in NY).

**Herter's,** 2800 Southcross Dr. West, P.O. Box 1819, Burnsville, MN 55337: Free information ◆ Flexible plastic or mahogany decoys. Available mounted on steel stakes for easy penetration in frozen ground. 800-654-3825. www.herters.com

**Jennings Decoy Company,** 601 Franklin Ave. NE, St. Cloud, MN 56304: Catalog $1 ◆ Decoy and carving supplies, finished decoys, and figurines. 800-331-5613.

**Will Kirkpatrick Decoys,** 124 Forest Ave., Hudson, MA 01749: Catalog $3 ◆ Handcarved and handpainted shorebird decoy reproductions. 800-505-7841. www.kirkpatrickdecoy.com

**Penn's Woods Products Inc.,** P.O. Box 306, Delmont, PA 15626: Free information ◆ Decoys. 412-468-8311.

**Wonderduck Decoys,** 505 N. Price St., Marshall, TX 75670: Free information ◆ Moving decoys. 800-876-1697.

**Wing Supply,** P.O. Box 367, Greenville, KY 42345: Free catalog ◆ Camouflage clothing, boots, blinds, decoys, treestands, calls, and more.

**The Wood Age,** 5690 Shady Ln., Florence, OR 97439: Free information ◆ Totem poles, custom plaques, and wildlife carvings. 888-4-TOTEMS. woodage@presys.com

## DEPARTMENT & GENERAL MERCHANDISE STORES

**The department stores listed below publish special edition, general merchandise, and seasonal specialty catalogs. In some instances there may be a small charge for these catalogs. However, the price may be waived or refunded if you satisfy minimum purchase requirements. For information on how to obtain these catalogs, write or call the stores directly.**

**Bennett Brothers Inc.,** 30 E. Adams St., Chicago, IL 60603. 800-621-2626. www.bennettbros.com

**Bergdorf Goodman,** 754 5th Ave., New York, NY 10019. 800-662-5455.

**Bloomingdales's by Mail Ltd.,** 475 Knotter Dr., Cheshire, CT 06410. 800-777-0000. www.bloomingdales.com

**Burdines,** T.O.B. Office, 7303 SW 88th St., Miami, FL 33156. 305-577-2311.

**Filene's,** 426 Washington St., Boston, MA 02101. 800-345-3637. www.maycompany.com

**Hecht's,** 685 N. Glebe Rd., Arlington, VA 22203. 703-558-1200. www.maycompany.com

**Lord & Taylor,** 424 5th Ave., New York, NY 10018. 800-223-7440. www.maycompany.com

**Macy's,** Herald Square, New York, NY 10001. 212-695-4400. www.macys.com

**Neiman-Marcus,** 221 E. Walnut Hill Ln., Irving, TX 75039. 800-825-8000. www.neimanmarcus.com

**Nordstrom Mail Order,** P.O. Box 91018, Seattle, WA 98111. 800-285-5800. www.nordstrom-pta.com

**JCPenney Catalog,** P.O. Box 675, Milwaukee, WI 53201. www.jcpenney.com/shopping

**Saks Fifth Ave.,** Folio Collections Inc., 500 Hickory Dr., Aberdeen, MD 21001. 800-345-3454.

**Service Merchandise Catalog,** Mail Order, P.O. Box 25130, Nashville, TN 37202. 800-251-1212. www.servicemerchandise.com

**Spiegel,** P.O. Box 182563, Columbus, OH 43218. 800-345-4500. www.spiegel.com

## DIABETIC SUPPLIES

**AD-RX Pharmacy,** 6256 Wilshire Blvd., Los Angeles, CA 90048: Free information ◆ Diabetic supplies. 800-435-1992.

**American Diabetes Association,** Order Fulfillment Dept., P.O. Box 930850, Atlanta, GA 31193: Free information ◆ Recipe and general diabetes information books for diabetics and professionals. 800-232-6733. www.diabetes.org

**Anything Diabetic,** 7124 N. University Dr., #267, Tamarac, FL 33321: Free catalog ◆ Supplies for diabetic and visually impaired persons. 800-644-7444.

**Atwater-Carey Ltd.,** 2986 Grove St., Denver, CO 80211: Free information *Purse-size and belt-pack carryall cases for diabetic supplies. 800-976-6664; 303-477-9689 (in CO). www.omnibus.com/atwatercarey

**Bayer Corp.,** Diagnostics Division, P.O. Box 2009, Mishawaka, IN 46546: Free information ◆ Glucometer blood glucose monitoring system. 800-445-5901.

**Boehringer Mannheim Corp.,** Patient Care Systems, 9115 Hague Rd., P.O. Box 50100, Indianapolis, IN 46250: Free information ◆ Glucose monitoring system. 800-858-8072.

**Bruce Medical Supply,** 411 Waverly Oaks Rd., P.O. Box 9166, Waltham, MA 02154: Free catalog ◆ Health supplies for diabetics, ostomy patients, sick rooms, and first aid. 800-225-8446.

**Cascade Medical Inc.,** 10180 Viking Dr., Eden Prairie, MN 55344: Free information ◆ Blood glucose test strips and monitoring system. 800-525-6718.

**Cases Plus,** 7757 Bell Rd., Windsor, CA 95492: Free information ◆ Organizer cases for diabetic supplies. 800-982-1880.

**Diabetic Express,** 31128 Vine St., Willowick, OH 44095: Free information ◆ Insulin, blood glucose monitoring equipment, test strips, and health care supplies. 800-338-4656. diabetcare@worldnet.att.net

**Diabetic Promotions,** P.O. Box 5400, Willowick, OH 44095: Free catalog ◆ Insulin, blood glucose monitoring equipment, test strips, and health care supplies. 800-433-1477; 216-943-6185 (in OH). diabpro@en.com

**Disetronic Medical Systems Inc.,** 5201 E. River Rd., Ste. 312, Minneapolis, MN 55421: Free information ◆ Insulin pumps. 800-280-7801.

**Edwards Healthcare Services,** P.O. Box 309, Hudson, OH 44236: Free information ◆ Diabetic supplies. 800-353-7318.

**Gainor Medical U.S.A. Inc.,** P.O. Box 353, McDonough, GA 30253: Free information ◆ Easy-to-use lancets that provide protection from accidental puncture and risks associated with cross-infection of blood-borne illnesses. 800-825-8282; 770-474-0474 (in GA). www.gainor.com

**GEM Diabetic Supplies Inc.,** P.O. Box 1148, Twinsburg, OH 44087: Free information ◆ Diabetic supplies. 800-793-1995.

**Generation Software Corp.,** P.O. Box 363, Bloomingdale, IL 60108: Free information ◆ Window diabetes tracking and data management software. 800-455-4GSC.

**H-S Medical Supplies,** P.O. Box 42, Whitehall, PA 18052: Free information ◆ Blood glucose meters, test strips, and other supplies for diabetics. 800-344-7633. www.hartzells.com

**Hospital Center Pharmacy,** 433 Brookline Ave., Boston, MA 02215: Free information ◆ Insulin, blood glucose monitoring equipment, test strips, and health care supplies. 800-824-2401.

**Liberty Medical Supply,** P.O. Box 1966, Palm City, FL 34990: Free information ◆ Blood glucose meters, test strips, lancets, monolets, and diabetic supplies. 800-762-8026. www.oldlibmed.com

**Medi-Ject,** 161 Cheshire Ln. North, Ste. 100, Minneapolis, MN 55441: Free information ◆ Medi-Jector EZ needle-free insulin injection system. 800-328-3074; 612-475-7700 (in MN). www.mediject.com

**Medical Home Supply,** 1853 W. 52nd Ave., Denver, CO 80221: Free catalog ◆ Blood glucose monitors and test strips, syringes, lancets, insulin, and health care supplies. 800-748-1909.

**Medicool Inc.,** 23520 Telo Ave., Torrance, CA 90505: Free information ◆ Insulin protector for use while traveling. 800-342-8483. www.medicool.com

**MediSense Inc.,** 4A Crosby Dr., Bedford, MA 01730: Free information ◆ Blood glucose monitoring systems. 800-316-7952.

**Medport Inc.,** 23 Acorn St., Providence, RI 02903: Free information ◆ Combination separate cool-storage and room-temperature carry-all cases for insulin and diabetic equipment. 800-368-7248.

**MiniMed Technologies,** 12744 San Fernando Rd., Sylmar, CA 91342: Free information ◆ MiniMed pumps for insulin therapy control. 800-933-3322. www.minimed.com

**Moms Mail Order Medical Supply,** 24700 Avenue Rockefeller, Valencia, CA 91355: Free catalog ◆ Medical supplies for incontinence, urological and ostomy needs, aids for daily living, wound and skin care, and diabetes. 800-232-7443. www.momsup.com

**National Diabetic Pharmacies,** 2157 Apperson Dr., Salem, VA 24513: Free information ◆ Diabetic supplies. 800-467-8546; 540-776-5572 (in VA).

**Owen-Mumford Inc.,** 849 Pickens Industrial Dr., Ste. 14, Marietta, GA 30062: Free information ◆ Easy-to-use mini lancing devices. 800-421-6936. www.owenmumford.com

**Preferred Rx of Ohio,** 34208 Aurora Rd., Ste. 132, Solon, OH 44139: Free information ◆ Diabetic supplies. 800-843-7038. www.preferredrx.com

**Suncoast Pharmacy & Surgical Supplies,** 9060 Kimberly Blvd., Boca Raton, FL 33434: Free information ◆ Diabetic supplies. 800-799-1991.

**Terumo Medical Corp.,** Consumer Products Division, 2100 Cottontail Ln., Somerset, NJ 08873: Free information ◆ Insulin syringes. 800-252-6782.

**Thompson Pharmacy & Medical,** 324 S. Union St., Traverse City, MI 49684: Free catalog ◆ Diabetes, health maintenance, home diagnostic, ostomy, and health and pain management aids. Also canes and other mobility equipment. 616-947-4212. thompson@carecenter.com

**Ulster Scientific Inc.,** P.O. Box 819, New Paltz, NY 12561: Free information ◆ Autojector which inserts the needle and injects insulin automatically and almost without pain. 800-431-8233.

**Vitajet Corp.,** 27075 Cabot Rd., #102, Laguna Hills, CA 92653: Free information ◆ Needle-free injector. 800-848-2538.

## DISABILITY-RELATED PRODUCTS

**A-Med Health Care Center,** 21572 Surveyor Circle, Huntington Beach, CA 92646: Free catalog ◆ Medical supplies for the physically challenged. 800-289-5476. www.a-med.com

**Abilitations,** One Sportime Way, Atlanta, GA 30340: Free catalog ◆ Equipment for developing and restoring physical and mental ability in children and adults through movement. 800-850-8603. www.abilitations.com

**Access to Recreation Inc.,** 8 Sandra Ct., Newbury Park, CA 91320: Free catalog ◆ Adaptive recreation equipment for people with physical disabilities. 800-634-4351.

**Access with Ease Inc.,** P.O. Box 1150, Chino Valley, AZ 86323: Catalog $2 (refundable) ◆ Self-help products for people with physical disabilities. 800-531-9479. kmjc@northlink.com

**AdaptAbility,** P.O. Box 515, Colchester, CT 06415: Free catalog ◆ Mobility, grooming, dressing, bathing, eating and cooking aids, exercise and therapy games, and adaptive home products for independent living. 800-288-9941. service@snswwide.com

**The Adaptive Design Shop,** 12847 Point Pleasant Dr., Fairfax, VA 22033: Free brochure ◆ Toilet supports and combination bath and shower chairs for children and adults. 800-351-2327.

**Altimate Medical Inc.,** P.O. Box 180, 262 W. 1st St., Morton, MN 56270: Free brochure ◆ Standing-seating support and mobility systems. 800-342-8968; 507-697-6393 (in MN). www.easystand.com

**American Printing House for the Blind,** 1839 Frankfort Ave., P.O. Box 6085, Louisville, KY 40206: Free catalog ◆ Braille writing and embossing equipment, electronic devices, reading readiness products, and educational aids and accessories for people with visual handicaps. 800-223-1839; 502-895-2405 (in KY). www.aph.org

**American Standard Inc.,** P.O. Box 6820, Piscataway, NJ 08855: Free information ◆ Assistive aids for use in the bathroom. 800-524-9797.

**Associated Handicapable Vans,** 12117 Riverwood Dr., Burnsville, MN 55337: Free information ◆ Used vans converted for wheelchair use. 800-956-6668. www.rollxvans.com

**Attainment Company Inc.,** P.O. Box 930160, Verona, WI 53593: Free catalog ◆ Special needs products (books, games, toys, adaptive equipment) for children and adults. 800-327-4269. www.attainment-inc.com

**Axiom Industries Inc.,** Prime Engineering, 4838 W. Jacquelyn, Ste. 105, Fresno, CA 93722: Free information ◆ Standing system and other standing aids that enable independent user mobility. 800-82-STAND. www.primeng.com

**Barrier Free Lifts Inc.,** 9230 Prince William St., Manassas, VA 20110: Free information ◆ Battery-operated multi-directional barrier-free ceiling lift. 800-582-8732; 703-361-6531 (in VA). www.bfl-inc.com

**Bathroom Access,** P.O. Box 342, Cathedral Station, New York, NY 10025: Free catalog ◆ Products that enhance bathroom access for persons with disabilities. 800-791-6426.

**Otto Bock Orthopedic Industry Inc.,** 3000 Xenium Ln. North, Minneapolis, MN 55441: Free information ◆ Durable, functional, and growth-adjustable walkers for children. 800-984-8901. www.ottobock.com

**The Braun Corp.,** P.O. Box 310, Winamac, IN 46996: Free information ◆ Van conversion and driving accessories and wheelchair lifts. 800-THE-LIFT; 219-946-6153 (in IN).

**Bruno Independent Living Aids,** 1780 Executive Dr., P.O. Box 84, Oconomowoc, WI 53066: Free information ◆ Wheelchair and scooter lifts. 800-882-8183. www.bruno.com

**Caring Products International Inc.,** 200 1st Ave. West, Ste. 200, Seattle, WA 98119: Free information ◆ Incontinence supplies and maternity and special-needs clothing. 800-333-5379; 206-282-6040 (in WA). www.caringproducts.com

**Clarion Bathware,** 205 Amsler Ave., Shippenville, PA 16254: Free information ◆ Fiberglass and acrylic shower stall or tub/shower unit for residential and institutional use for individuals who require assistive care. 800-576-9228. www.cfmcorp.com

**Clarke Health Care,** 1003 International Dr., Oakdale, PA 15071: Free information ◆ Bathlifts for transfer in and out of bathtubs. 412-695-2122. www.weir.net/clarke

**Columbia Medical Manufacturing Corp.,** P.O. Box 633, Pacific Palisades, CA 90272: Free catalog ◆ Car seats, bath and toilet supports, commodes, exercise equipment, and rehabilitation products for children and adults with disabilities. 800-454-6612; 310-454-6612 (in CA). www.columbiamedical.com

**Columbus McKinnon Corp.,** Medical Products Division, 140 John James Audubon Pkwy., Amherst, NY 14228: Free information ◆ Easy-to-operate mobility and lift system. 800-888-0985. www.cmworks.com

**Consumer Care Products Inc.,** P.O. Box 684, Sheboygan, WI 53082: Free catalog ◆ Wheelchair trays and positioning, communication, and mobility aids. 414-459-8353.

**Creative Designs,** 3704 Carlisle Ct., Modesto, CA 95356: Free brochure ◆ Specially designed robe for wheelchair users and others with physical disabilities. 800-355-4852; 209-523-3166 (in CA). www.sonnet.com/dws/handi.html

**Crestwood Company,** 6625 N. Sidney Pl., Milwaukee, WI 53209: Free catalog ◆ Communication aids for children and adults, including talking aids, switches, and adapted toys. 414-352-5678. www.communicationaids.com

**Crow River Industries,** 2800 Northwest Blvd., Minneapolis, MN 55441: Free list of retail sources ◆ Wheelchair lifts for recreational vehicles. 800-488-7688.

**Danmar Products Inc.,** 221 Jackson Industrial Dr., Ann Arbor, MI 48103: Free catalog ◆ Easy-to-hold utensil handles and other assistive aids for people with arthritis. 800-783-1998; 313-761-1990 (in MI).

**Enabling Devices,** Division Toys for Special Children, 385 Warburton Ave., Hastings-on-Hudson, NY 10706: Free catalog ◆ Assistive devices for people with physical disabilities. 800-832-8697.

**Equipment Shop,** P.O. Box 33, Bedford, MA 01730: Free catalog ◆ Adaptive equipment. 781-275-7681.

**Flaghouse Sports Equipment,** 601 Flaghouse Dr., Hasbrouck Heights, NJ 07604: Free catalog ◆ Physical education, recreation, sports and play, and rehabilitation equipment. 800-793-7900. www.flaghouse.com

**Freedom Motors USA,** 5633 King Hwy., Kalamazoo, MI 49001: Free information ◆ Power-operated rear entry systems for vans. 888-625-6335; 616-343-9464 (in MI). www.freedommotors.com

**GPK Exerciser,** P.O. Box 2636, 9380 Bond Ave., Ste. B, El Cajon, CA 92021: Free brochure ◆ Upper body exerciser for quads. 619-390-5884. www.gpk.com

**Grant Waterx Corp.,** 144 Prospect St., Stamford, CT 06901: Free information ◆ Pivoting bathtub lift that operates with household water pressure. 800-243-5237. grantairmass@aol.com

**Guardian Products Inc.,** 4175 Guardian St., Simi Valley, CA 93063: Free catalog ◆ Walkers, crutches, canes, home activity aids, beds, lifts, ramps, and assistive transport equipment. 800-255-5022.

**Handi-Ramp Inc.,** 1414 Armour Blvd., Mundelein, IL 60060: Free catalog ◆ Fixed-in-place and portable ramps for vans and homes. 800-876-RAMP. www.marketzone.com/Handi-Ramp

**Haverich Ortho-Sport Inc.,** 67 Emerald St., Keene, NH 03431: Free information ◆ Specialized bicycles, tricycles, and tandems with specially designed accessories to meet most needs. 603-358-0438.

**T.F. Herceg Inc.,** 982 Pine Island Tnpk., Pine Island, NY 10969: Free information ◆ Remote hand-controlled overhead track and free-standing lifts. 800-724-5305.

**Homecare Assistive Products,** Assistive Rehabilitation Equipment, 2808 Water Oaks Dr., West Bloomfield, MI 48324: Free information ◆ Quick-installation and electrical-free standard and mobile power-operated toilet aid complete with plumbing. 800-727-8483; 810-360-2818 (in MI). www.mobileaid.com

**Homecare Products Inc.,** 15824 SE 296th St., Kent, WA 98042: Free information ◆ Portable mobility ramps for wheelchairs and scooters. 800-451-1903; 253-631-4633 (in WA).

**Imaginart Communication Products,** 307 Arizona St., Bisbee, AZ 85603: Free catalog ◆ Speech, language, and learning materials for special education, speech and language pathology, occupational therapy, geriatric rehabilitation, and early childhood education. 800-828-1376.

**Independence Providers Inc.,** P.O. Box 172, Thornwood, NY 10594: Free information ◆ Power-assisted combination standing aid and wheelchair. 888-542-6608. StandUSA@AOL.com

**Independent Living Aids/Can-Do Products,** 27 East Mall, Plainview, NY 11803: Free catalog ◆ Self-help products for individuals with visual impairments and physical disabilities. 800-537-2118; 516-752-8080 (in NY). www.independentliving.com

**Independent Mobility Systems,** 4100 W. Piedras, Farmington, NM 87401: Free information ◆ Automatic door ramp for automotive vehicles. 800-IMS-VANS. www.ims-vans.com

**JoAnne's Bed & Back Shops,** 5640 Sunnyside Ave., Unit G, Beltsville, MD 20705: Free catalog ◆ Ergonomic chairs, sofas, beds, and accessories for back and neck support. 800-767-2225; 301-220-0800 (in MD).

**Judson Enterprises,** P.O. Box 1069, Johnston, CO 80534: Free information ◆ Easy-installation automotive portable hand controls. Also a portable shower chair. 800-587-5212. www.blvd.com/judson/index.html

**Kaye Products Inc.,** 535 Dimmocks Hill Rd., Hillsborough, NC 27278: Free information ◆ Children's adaptive equipment and therapy aids. 919-732-6444.

**Miles Kimball Company,** 41 W. 8th Ave., Oshkosh, WI 54906: Free catalog ◆ Bathroom and kitchen accessories, arthritis aids, clothing, canes, and personal care items for people with disabilities. 800-546-2255. www.mileskimball.com

**Kohler Company,** 444 Highland Dr., Kohler, WI 53044: Catalog $3 ◆ Low threshold shower stalls for wheelchair accessibility. 800-220-2291. www.kohlerco.com

**Laureate Learning Systems,** 110 E. Spring St., Winooski, VT 05404: Free information ◆ Talking software programs for children 6 months to 8 years of age. Includes language intervention, cognitive processing, reading, and instructional games. 802-655-4755. www.llsys.com

**Leckey Support Furniture,** 360 Merrimac, Bldg. 5, Lawrence, MA 01843: Free information ◆ Adjustable bath chair. 800-LECKEY-0. info@leckey.com

**Lifestand,** Independence Providers, P.O. Box 172, Thornwood, NY 10594: Free information ◆ Combination power-assisted standing aid and wheelchair. 800-782-6324. StandUSA@AOL.com

**Lighthouse Enterprises,** 36-20 Northern Blvd., Long Island City, NY 11101: Free catalog ◆ Assistive aids for people with visual impairments. 800-829-0500.

**Lindustries,** P.O. Box 66295, Auburndale, MA 02166: Free information ◆ Lever convertible adapters for making doors easy to open. 617-237-8177.

**Lubidet USA Inc.,** 1980 S. Quebec St., Ste. 4, Denver, CO 80231: Free information ◆ Personal cleansing accessory that attaches to most toilets. 800-582-4338. www.lubidet.com

**Maddak Inc.,** 6 Industrial Rd., Pequannock, NJ 07440: Free catalog ◆ Products for independent living. 973-628-7600. www.maddak.com

**Maxi-Aids,** P.O. Box 3209, Farmingdale, NY 11735: Free catalog ◆ Communications devices, eating and kitchen aids, dressing aids, wheelchair accessories, and more. 800-522-6294. sales@maxiaids.com

**Mobilitis Corp.,** 6809 N. 56th Ave., Glendale, AZ 85301: Free information ◆ Three-wheel multiple-speed control bicycle with a built-in seat. 800-266-2454.

**Mobility Products & Design,** 2800 North West Blvd., Minneapolis, MN 55441: Free information ◆ Hand controls for automotive vehicles. 800-488-7688. www.nellcorpb.com

**Mulholland Positioning Systems Inc.,** P.O. Box 391, 215 N. 12th St., Santa Paula, CA 93061: Free video ◆ Positioning aids that help in the development of children's functional skills. 800-543-4769; 805-525-7165 (in CA).

**NCM Consumer Products Division,** P.O. Box 6070, San Jose, CA 95150: Free catalog ◆ Functional aids for independent living. 800-235-7054.

**Open Sesame,** 1933 Davis St., #279, San Leandro, CA 94577: Free information ◆ Remote-controlled door systems that open and close automatically from wheelchairs. 800-673-6911.

**Parisi Enterprises Inc.,** 23 Southward Ave., Congers, NY 10920: Free brochure ◆ Automated sliding door opener. 914-268-5982.

**PDLX Company Inc.,** P.O. Box 129, Shelton, WA 98584: Free information ◆ Motor-equipped exercise machine for people with physical disabilities. 800-314-4851. pdlxco@aol.com

**Power Access Corp.,** P.O. Box 235, Collinsville, CT 06022: Free brochure ◆ Easily attached remote or manually operated door opener. 800-344-0088; 860-693-0751 (in CT).

**Prentke Romich Company,** 1022 Heyl Rd., Wooster, OH 44691: Free catalog ◆ Communication devices for people who can't use their voice. Also computer access products. 800-262-1984. www.prentrom.com

**R.D. Equipment Inc.,** 230 Percival Dr., West Barnstable, MA 02668: Free information ◆ Tub-slide shower chair for easy accessibility. 508-362-7498. www.capecod.net/rdequip

**Relaxo-Back Inc.,** P.O. Box 2613, Anderson, IN 46018: Free information ◆ Form-fitting auxiliary seat that can be used to relieve lower back pain. 800-527-5496.

**Rock N' Roll Cycles,** P.O. Box 1558, Levelland, TX 79336: Free information ◆ Single riders, tandems, and hand and foot-powered cycles with optional seat configurations and custom fitting for individual needs. 800-654-9664. www.rocknrollcycles.com

**S & S Opportunities,** P.O. Box 513, Colchester, CT 06415: Free catalog ◆ Products for occupational therapy, sensory stimulation, recreation therapy, special education, physical therapy, and communication. 800-266-8856.

**Sammons-Preston Inc.,** P.O. Box 5071, Bolingbrook, IL 60440: Free catalog ◆ Rehabilitation aids and equipment for children and young adults with special needs. 800-323-5547. www.sammonpreston.com

**Silcraft Corp.,** 528 Hughes Dr., Traverse City, MI 49686: Free information ◆ Barrier-free roll-in showers, shower and bath accessories, lifts, and transporters. 616-946-4221.

**Sinties Scientific Inc.,** 5616A S. 122nd East Ave., Tulsa, OK 74146: Free information ◆ Folding and adjustable power trainer for arms or legs. 800-852-6869; 918-254-7395 (in OK). www.theshowplace.com/sinties

**Space Tables Inc.,** P.O. Box 32082, Minneapolis, MN 55432: Free catalog ◆ Adjustable tables for wheelchairs. 800-328-2580.

**Special Clothes Inc.,** P.O. Box 333, East Harwich, MA 02645: Catalog $1 ◆ Adaptive clothing for children with disabilities. Includes undergarments, casual clothing, sleepwear, footwear, accessories, ponchos, and jackets. 508-896-7939. www.Special-Clothes.com

**Special Designs Inc.,** P.O. Box 130, Gillette, NJ 07933: Free catalog ◆ Custom equipment for children with special needs. 908-464-8825.

**Special Needs Project World Wide,** 3463 State St., #282, Santa Barbara, CA 93105: Free catalog ◆ Books, periodicals, audiotapes, videos, and other special-needs disability information resources. 800-333-6867.

**Stand-Aid of Iowa Inc.,** Box 386, Sheldon, IA 51201: Free information ◆ Equipment to assist in standing and turning a manual wheelchair into a power-operated chair. 800-831-8580; 712-324-2153 (in IA). standaid@rconnect.com

**Step 'n Go Cycles,** Field's Farm Rd., Charlotte, VT 05445: Free information ◆ Functional cycles for physical therapy and therapeutic recreation. 800-648-7335.

**SureHands International,** 982 Rt. 1, Pine Island, NY 10969: Free information ◆ Remote overhead track or free-standing movable lift. 800-724-5305. www.surehand.com

**Swift Medical International,** 364 W. Fallbrook Ave., Ste. 101, Fresno, CA 93711: Free information ◆ Urological supplies, ramps, manual and power-operated wheelchairs, bathroom equipment, cushions, and more. 800-659-9207. www.swiftmedical.com

**Talk-A-Phone,** 5013 N. Kedzie Ave., Chicago, IL 60625: Free brochure ◆ Compliant emergency hands-free telephones. 773-539-1100.

**Thoele Manufacturing,** 849 US Rt. 40, Montrose, IL 62445: Free information ◆ Pedal-in-place exerciser. 217-924-4553.

**Toys for Special Children,** 385 Warburton Ave., Hastings-on-Hudson, NY 10706: Free catalog ◆ Toys and self-help and special devices for children with disabilities. 914-478-0960.

**Ultimate Home Care Company,** 3250 E. 19th St., Long Beach, CA 90804: Free information ◆ Portable threshold and folding ramps. Also power-assisted lift commodes. 800-475-8122.

**Vantage Mini Vans,** 5214 S. 30th St., Phoenix, AZ 85040: Free catalog ◆ Mini-van conversions for the physically challenged. 800-348-8267. www.vantageminivans.com

**Venture Products Inc.,** P.O. Box 148, Orrville, OH 44667: Free brochure ◆ Wheelchair accessible mobile riding garden equipment. 330-683-0075. www.venturepro.com

**Viewpoint Mfg. Inc.,** P.O. Box 108, Spanish Fork, UT 84660: Free information ◆ Therapeutic tricycle for children with special needs. 800-798-2430.

**Walk Easy Inc.,** 2915 S. Congress Ave., Delray Beach, FL 33445: Free brochure ◆ Crutches, walkers, commode chairs, and regular, tripod, and quad canes. 800-441-2904. www.walkeasy.com

**Walton Way Medical,** 948 Walton Way, Augusta, GA 30901: Free catalog ◆ Medical supplies and rehabilitation equipment. 800-241-4636.

**Wheelchair House,** 1831 E. Mulberry St., Fort Collins, CO 80524: Free information ◆ Custom wheelchair and seating systems, strollers, scooters, bathing and toileting aids, walkers and walking aids, and more. 800-466-7015; 970-482-7116 (in CO).

**Wheelchairs of Kansas,** P.O. Box 320, 204 W. 2nd St., Ellis, KS 67637: Free catalog ◆ Easy-on and easy-off clothing and accessories. Also medical products for bariatric (obese) persons. 800-537-6454.

## DISPLAY FIXTURES & PORTABLE EXHIBITS

**Aftosa,** 1034 Ohio Ave., Richmond, CA 94804: Free catalog ◆ Clear acrylic plate stands and bowl holders. 800-231-0397. www.aftosa.com

**Armstrong Products Inc.,** P.O. Box 979, Guthrie, OK 73044: Free catalog ◆ Portable display system with interchangeable panels. 800-278-4279; 405-282-7584 (in OK).

**Art Wire Works Company,** 5401 W. 65th St., Chicago, IL 60638: Free catalog ◆ Wire display racks and accessories. 800-336-0097; 708-458-3993 (in IL).

**Bluegrass Case Company,** 272 Airport Rd., Box 386, Stanton, KY 40380: Free information ◆ Collector and display frames. 606-663-9871.

**Cabinets by Vector,** 64956 Lutz Rd., Constantine, MI 49092: Free catalog ◆ Specimen storage cabinets. 616-651-3823.

**Dave Cohen & Associates Inc.,** P.O. Box 6517, Freehold, NJ 07728: Free information ◆ Showcases, shelving, and custom woodwork. 732-727-1800.

**Collector Case Company,** P.O. Box 126, Jeffersonville, KY 40337: Free information ◆ Display cases. 800-553-5294; 606-873-3569 (in KY).

**Collectors House,** 1739 Hwy. 9 N, Howell, NJ 07751: Free information ◆ Showcases, jewelry displays, butterfly boxes, and accessories. 800-448-9298. collectorshouse@iop.com

**Columbus Show Case Company,** 850 5th Ave., Columbus, OH 43212: Free information ◆ Display fixtures. 800-848-3573; 614-299-3161 (in OH).

**D & M Woodcrafts Display Case Company,** 5363 Oakwood Dr., North Tonawonda, NY 14120: Brochure $2 ◆ Hardwood display cases. 800-498-7820. www.localnet.com/~dmgerber.

**Designs Plus,** P.O. Box 1927, Santa Rosa, CA 95402: Free brochure ◆ Stack storage system for flat files and art. 800-253-7224.

**Display Fixtures Company,** P.O. Box 7245, Charlotte, NC 28241: Free catalog ◆ Display fixtures. 800-737-0880; 704-588-0880 (in NC).

**Emerson Wood Works Inc.,** 2640 E. 43rd Ave., Denver, CO 80216: Free brochure ◆ Drawers and cases for collectors. 303-295-1360.

**ESV Lighting Inc.,** 525 Court St., Pekin, IL 61554: Free information ◆ Lighting systems for displays. 800-225-5378.

**The Fixture Factory,** 835 NE 8th St., Gresham, OR 97030: Free information ◆ Display fixtures. 503-661-6525.

**Franklin Fixtures Inc.,** 59 Commerce Park Rd., Brewster, MA 02631: Free catalog ◆ Display fixtures. 508-896-3713.

**Global Fixtures Inc.,** 4121 Rushton St., Florence, AL 35631: Free catalog ◆ Display fixtures. 256-767-5200.

**Graphic Display Systems,** 308 S. 1st St., Lebanon, PA 17042: Free information ◆ Easy-to-set-up lightweight display system. Comes with base, leg adjusters, and clips. 800-848-3020.

**Handy Store Fixtures,** 337 Sherman Ave., Newark, NJ 07114: Free catalog ◆ Display fixtures. 888-HANDYSF.

**JAMAR Company,** 5015 State Rd., Medina, OH 44256: Information $2 (refundable) ◆ Acrylic display cases. 330-239-2889.

**Medals of America,** 1929 Fairview Rd., Fountain Inn, SC 29644: Catalog $2 ◆ Display cases for military awards. 864-862-6425.

**Pennzoni Wood Products,** 1182 White St., Sturgis, MI 49091: Free information ◆ Display showcases and wood and acrylic forming. 800-206-6852; 616-659-1093 (in MI). www.displayco.com

**Personal Treasures,** 4980 Oak Dale Rd., Smyrna, GA 30080: Free price list with long SASE ◆ Display cases. 770-431-1689.

**Raynabows,** 385 Gilston Ct., Lake Mary, FL 32746: Free brochure ◆ Life-size display dolls, sized to children ages newborn through 6 years. 407-333-1775. www.Raynabows.com

**Melvi-S. Roos & Company Inc.,** 4465 Commerce Dr. SW, Atlanta, GA 30336: Free information ◆ Display fixtures. 800-241-6897; 404-691-4234 (in GA).

**Ruddles Mills Products,** 19 S. Main St., Cynthiana, KY 41031: Free information ◆ Handcrafted hardwood display cases. 800-825-6951; 606-234-9224 (in KY).

**Sankey Design Group,** P.O. Box 295, Avon Lake, OH 44012: Free brochure ◆ Decorative Shaker, Normandy, Legacy, and Grenadier-style easels and accessories. 888-213-2735.

**Showbest Fixture Corp.,** P.O. Box 25336, Richmond, VA 23260: Free catalog ◆ Display fixtures. 804-643-3600.

**Showcase Sales Gallery,** P.O. Box 312, Otego, NY 13825: Free information ◆ Display cases. 800-246-2940. monique@norwich.net

**Siegel Display Products,** P.O. Box 95, Minneapolis, MN 55440: Free catalog ◆ Display racks. 612-340-9235.

**Venus Displays,** 10713 Ashby Ave., Los Angeles, CA 90064: Free information ◆ Blocks, platforms, easels, and boxes; stands for minerals, shells, and crystals; and jewelry and counter displays. 800-870-5633; 310-836-3177 (in CA).

## DOG SLEDDING

**Alyeska Sled Dog Products,** Chris & Diane Flaten, P.O. Box 627, Hovland, MN 55606: Free catalog ◆ Handcrafted sleds and accessories for professional and recreational mushers. 218-475-2649.

**Nordkyn Outfitters,** Rip & Jane Riffle, P.O. Box 1023, Graham, WA 98338: Free catalog ◆ Harnesses, collars, packs, ganglines, leads, books, and other accessories. 253-847-4128. www.nordkyn.com

## DOLLHOUSES & MINIATURES

**A-C's Emporium of Miniatures,** 100 E. McMurray Rd., McMurray, PA 15317: Catalog $15 ◆ Handcrafted miniatures and dollhouses. 412-942-4120.

**Acquisto Silver Company,** 8901 Osuna Rd. NE, Albuquerque, NM 87111: Free brochure with long SASE ◆ Sterling silver miniatures. 505-292-0910.

**Angel Children,** 4977 Sparr Rd., Gaylord, MI 49735: Catalog $2 ◆ Miniature porcelain dolls. 517-732-1931. www.angelfire.com/mi/angelchildren

**Angela's Miniature World,** 2237 Ventura Blvd., Camarillo, CA 93010: Free information with long SASE ◆ Miniatures, dollhouses, building materials, and collectibles. 805-482-2219.

**Archangel,** 7060 Garden Grove Blvd., Westminster, CA 92683: Catalog $25 plus UPS shipping ◆ Electrical supplies, dolls, furniture and other miniatures, and accessories. 310-596-0660.

**B.H. Miniatures,** 1831 Rose Garden Ln., Ste. 1, Phoenix, AZ 85027: Catalog $3 with long SASE ◆ Pre-pasted wallpaper, coordinated print and solid color fabrics, velvet carpeting, and furniture in kits or assembled. 602-582-3385.

**Bauder-Pine Ltd.,** P.O. Box 518, Langhorne, PA 19047: Catalog $5 ◆ Furniture and kits. 215-355-2033. www.bauderpine.com

**Cecil Boyd's Miniatures,** 16007 Scenic Oak Tr., Buda, TX 78610: Free information with long SASE and two 1st class stamps ◆ Realistic human figures with a choice of scale. 512-295-2294.

**Brodnax Printing Company Inc.,** 2338 Reagan St., Dallas, TX 75219: Catalog $1 ◆ Wallpapers for dollhouses. 214-528-2622.

**C & J Gallery,** 109 S. Elmwood, Ste. 18, Oak Park, IL 60302: Catalog $2 ◆ Museum-quality miniature art. 708-383-3634.

**Cape May Miniatures,** 219 Jackson St., Cape May, NJ 08204: Catalog $27 ◆ Dollhouses, furniture and accessories, lighting, and building supplies. 800-544-8777; 609-884-7999 (in NJ).

**Cardinal Incorporated,** 400 Markley St., Port Reading, NJ 07064: Catalog $7.50 (refundable) ◆ Miniature dollhouse furniture and porcelain collectible dolls. 800-888-0936.

**Castle Antiques & Reproductions,** 515 Welwood Ave., Hawley, PA 18428: Free information ◆ Doll-size antique and reproduction furniture. 717-226-8550.

**Cir-Kit Concepts Inc.,** 32 Woodlake Dr. SE, Rochester, MN 55904: Catalog $4 ◆ Electrical miniatures and wiring kits for dollhouses. 800-676-4252. www.cir-kitconcepts.com

**Corona Concepts,** 10 Depot St., Schenevus, NY 12155: Free brochure ◆ Pre-cut all-wood dollhouse kits. 800-253-7150.

**Country House Collection,** P.O. Box 5022, Manchester, NH 03108: Free catalog ◆ Dollhouses, barns, churches, schoolhouses, stables, and other buildings in 1- and ½- inch scale. Available assembled or in kit form. 800-292-7905.

**Country Store Miniatures,** 813 Main, Vancouver, WA 98660: Catalog $26 ◆ Dollhouses and miniatures. 800-295-1425.

**Crystal Brook Gift & Miniature Shop,** Rt. 20, P.O. Box 354, Brimfield, MA 01010: Free information ◆ Furniture, doll houses, log cabins, accessories and kits, books, and building materials. 413-245-7647.

**DD's Dollhouse,** 1527 Upper Ottawa St., Hamilton, Ontario, Canada L8V 3J4: Catalog $10 ◆ Dollhouses and accessories. 905-574-2942.

**Diamond M Brand Mold Company,** 15W081 91st St., Hinsdale, IL 60521: Catalog $3 ◆ Molds for making miniatures. 847-323-5691.

**DMJ Nick Nacks,** 743 E. Bell Rd., Ste. 2-105, Phoenix, AZ 85022: Free brochure ◆ Dollhouse furnishings and accessories.

**Doll Faire Miniatures,** 3183 Wayside Plaza, Walnut Creek, CA 94596: Catalog $4 ◆ Miniature Victorian trim and lace. 510-680-1993.

**The Doll Lady,** 247 N. Sycamore St., Newtown, PA 18940: Free information with long SASE ◆ Miniatures, collectibles, dollhouses, furniture, miniature dolls, gifts, and accessories. 215-504-5588.

**The Dollhouse,** 6107 N. Scottsdale Rd., Scottsdale, AZ 85253: Free information with long SASE ◆ Miniatures and dollhouses. 800-398-3981.

**The Dollhouse Factory,** 157 Main St., P.O. Box 456, Lebanon, NJ 08833: Catalog $5.50 ◆ Dollhouses, miniatures, tools, books, and plans. 908-236-6404.

**Dollhouses & Miniatures of Myrtle Beach,** 10824 Shoppers Walk, The Colonial Shops, Myrtle Beach, SC 29572: Free information with long SASE ◆ Dollhouses, furnishings, and other miniatures. 803-497-9722.

**Dollhouses+,** 33 Clearwater/Largo Rd., Largo, FL 33770: Free information ◆ Dollhouse kits and in-stock ready-to-use or custom models, furniture, lighting, and accessories. 813-581-8626.

**Dwyer's Doll House,** 1944 Warwick Ave., Warwick, RI 02889: Catalog $25 ◆ Dollhouses, building supplies, and miniatures. 401-738-3248.

**Elena's Dollhouses & Miniatures,** 5565 Schueller Crescent, Burlington, Ontario, Canada L7L 3T1: Free information ◆ Dollhouses and miniatures. 905-333-3402.

**Enchanted Doll House,** Rt. 7A, RR 1, Box 2535, Manchester Center, VT 05255: Catalog $2 ◆ Dollhouses and kits, furniture, dolls, stuffed animals, and toys. 802-362-1327.

**England Things,** 15 Sullivan Farm, New Milford, CT 06776: Catalog $20 (refundable) ◆ Miniatures by English artisans. 800-350-4565.

**Favorite Things,** York & Monton Rd., Hereford, MD 21111: Catalog $1 ◆ Alexander dolls and dollhouse miniatures. 800-343-0407.

**Fred's Dollhouse & Miniature Center,** Rt. 7, Pittsford, VT 05763: Catalog $5 ◆ Dollhouses and kits, building supplies, and furniture. 802-483-6362.

**Grandt Line Products,** 1040 Shary Ct., Concord, CA 94518: Catalog $4.75 ◆ Small scale structural items and accessories. 510-671-0143.

**Greenhouse Miniature Shop,** 6616 Monroe St., Sylvania, OH 43560: Catalog $3 ◆ Miniatures. 419-882-8259.

**Handcraft Designs Inc.,** 63 E. Broad St., Hatfield, PA 19440: Free information with long SASE ◆ Miniature upholstered furniture. 800-523-2430; 215-855-3022 (in PA). hdclays@aol.com

**Happy House Miniatures,** 135 N. Main St., Mocksville, NC 27028: Catalog $5 (refundable) ◆ Dollhouses and accessories. 704-634-1424.

**Haslam's Doll Houses,** 7208 S. Tamiami Trail, Sarasota, FL 34231: Free information with long SASE ◆ Dollhouses, miniatures, and building supplies. 941-922-8337.

**Hearth Song,** Mail Processing Center, 6519 N. Galena Rd., P.O. Box 1773, Peoria, IL 61656: Free catalog ◆ Dollhouse miniatures, books for children, toiletries for babies, cuddly dolls, party decorations, art supplies, and games. 800-325-2502.

**Heritage Miniatures,** 44 Mountain Base Rd., Goffstown, NH 03045: Catalog $5 ◆ Authentic 18th and 19th-century English kitchenware and porcelains.

**Hobby Craft,** 6632 Odama Rd., Madison, WI 53719: Free information (specify item wanted) ◆ Dollhouses, furniture and furniture kits, wallpaper, lighting, and building materials. 608-833-4944.

**Hobby World Miniatures,** 5450 Sherbrooke St. West, Montreal, Quebec, Canada H4A 1V9: Catalog $5 ◆ Dollhouses and miniatures. 514-481-5434.

**House of Caron,** 10111 Larrylyn Dr., Whittier, CA 90603: Price list $3 ◆ Molds and supplies for making miniature dolls. 310-947-6753.

**Houseworks,** 2388 Pleasantdale Rd., Atlanta, GA 30340: Catalog $4 (request list of retail sources) ◆ Dollhouse building components, hardware, lighting, flooring, and furniture. 404-448-6596.

**Innovative Photography,** 1724 NW 36th, Lincoln City, OR 97367: Catalog $3 ◆ Miniature photographs and framed Victorian-style prints, from the 1920s to 1930s. 541-994-9421.

**Jackie & Pat's Dollhouses Inc.,** 3050 Wade Hampton Blvd., Taylors, SC 29687: Catalog $30 ◆ Dollhouses, building materials, accessories, and furniture. 864-292-2877.

**Jan's Dollhouse,** 6600 Dixie Hwy., Diplomat Village, Fairfield, OH 45014: Catalog $18.95 ◆ Miniatures, dolls, bears, and dollhouses. 800-528-9135.

**Jeepers Miniatures,** 1315 S. Rangeline Rd., Carmel, IN 46032: Catalog $21 ◆ Miniatures and finished or ready-to-wire and paint dollhouses. 317-846-6708.

**Janna Joseph,** 2465 Northside Dr., Clearwater, FL 34621: Catalog $5 ◆ Miniature doll molds. 813-784-1877.

**Karen's Miniatures,** 6020 Doniphan, Ste. B1, El Paso, TX 79932: Catalog $4 ◆ Architectural moldings and cast metal miniature kits. 505-532-0939.

**The Lawbre Company,** 888 Tower Rd., Mundelein, IL 60060: Catalog $4 ◆ Reproduction period-designed dollhouses and miniatures. 800-253-0491.

**Lilliput Land,** 89 Lisa Dr., Northport, NY 11768: Brochure $8 ◆ English, French, and American handcrafted miniatures. 516-754-5511.

**A Little Something for Everyone,** 6203 S. Dover St., Littleton, CO 80123: Catalog $2 ◆ Kits and accessories.

**Littlethings,** 129 Main St., Irvington, NY 10533: Free list with long SASE ◆ Miniature paintings, dollhouses, furniture, bears, and collectibles. 914-591-9150.

**Lolly's,** 1054 Dundee Ave., Elgin, IL 60120: Catalog $21.50 (refundable with $50 order) ◆ Dollhouses and miniatures. 630-697-4040.

**Lookingglass Miniatures,** 635 NE Chestnut, Roseburg, OR 97470: Catalog $4 ◆ Miniature furniture kits. 541-673-5445.

**MacDoc Designs,** 405 Tarrytown Rd., White Plains, NY 10607: Free list of retail sources ◆ Miniature rugs. 914-376-2156.

**Maison des Maisons,** 460 S. Marion Pkwy., Denver, CO 80209: Price list $5 ◆ Southwest Indian-style furniture and miniatures. 303-871-0731.

**Microscale Industries Inc.,** P.O. Box 11950, Costa Mesa, CA 92627: Catalog $4 ◆ Micro-scale decals for decorating miniatures and trains. 714-434-8995.

**Mini Splendid Things,** 626 Main St., Covington, KY 41011: Catalog $25 ◆ Dollhouses and miniatures. 606-261-5500. www.minisplendid.com

**Mini Temptations,** 3633 W. 95th, Overland Park, KS 66206: Catalog $10 ◆ Dollhouse accessories, miniatures, and collectibles. 800-878-8469; 913-648-2050 (in KS).

**Miniature Makers' Workshop,** 4515 N. Woodward Ave., Royal Oak, MI 48073: Catalog $10 ◆ Furniture, dolls, and dollhouses. 248-549-0633.

**Miniature Village,** 1725 50th St., Kenosha, WI 53140: Catalog $35 (refundable with $100 order) ◆ Dollhouses, furniture, and electrical accessories. 800-383-0188.

**Miniatures Plus,** P.O. Box 160, Place Bonaventure, Montreal, Quebec, Canada H5A 1A7: Catalog $1.50 ◆ Dollhouse furniture and accessories. 514-393-8742.

**Mott Miniatures & Doll House Shop,** 7942 La Palma Ave., Buena Park, CA 90621: Catalog $30 ◆ Furniture, dolls, dollhouses and kits, and building materials. 800-874-6222. www.mottsminis.com

**My Dollhouse,** 7 S. Broadway, Nyack, NY 10960: Free information with long SASE ◆ Dolls, dollhouses, and miniatures. 914-358-4185.

**My Sister's Shoppe Inc.,** 1671 Penfield Rd., Rochester, NY 14625: Catalog $3 (refundable) ◆ Victorian furniture miniatures. 800-821-0097.

**Nola's Miniature Shop,** 2351 A Rosewall Crescent, Courtenay, British Columbia, Canada V9N 8R9: Catalog $5 ◆ Furniture, books, supplies, collectibles, and other handcrafted accessories. 604-338-8700.

**North Country Gardens,** P.O. Box 277, Northport, MI 49670: Catalog $20 ◆ Museum-quality miniature replicas. 800-551-5031.

**Northeastern Scale Models Inc.,** P.O. Box 727, Methuen, MA 01844: Catalog $1 ◆ Materials for constructing dollhouses. 978-688-6019.

**The Oakridge Corp.,** P.O. Box 247, Lemont, IL 60439: Free catalog price information (specify ¼-, ½-, or 1-inch scale) ◆ Dollhouse kits, building supplies, and furniture. 708-739-4554.

**Old World Craftsmen Dollhouses Inc.,** 643 Industrial Dr., Hartland, WI 53029: Brochure $2 ◆ Custom-made or in-stock dollhouses. 800-234-4748; 414-367-2753 (in WI).

**Once Upon A Time,** 120 Church St. NE, Vienna, VA 22180: Free information ◆ Miniature wire wicker furniture. 703-255-3285.

**Pat's Miniatures,** 515 Highland Ave., Carrollton, KY 41008: Catalog $30 ◆ Miniatures and dollhouse accessories. 800-644-6857; 502-732-6440 (in KY).

**Peg's Dollhouse,** 4019 Sebastopol Rd., Santa Rosa, CA 95407: Information $1 ◆ Miniatures and dollhouses. 707-546-6137.

**Petite Innovations,** 243 High St., Burlington, NJ 08016: Catalog $25 (refundable) ◆ Dollhouses and furnishings, lighting supplies, building materials, and miniatures. 609-386-7476.

**Pinocchio's Miniatures,** 465 S. Main St., Frankenmuth, MI 48734: Catalog $22.50 ◆ Handmade miniatures. 517-652-2751.

**PJ's Miniatures,** 5818 Hwy. 74 West, Monroe, NC 28110: Catalog $14.95 ◆ Miniatures. 704-821-9144.

**Precious Little Things,** The Fieldwood Company, P.O. Box 6, Chester, VT 05143: Catalog $3.50 ◆ Handcrafted miniature furnishings. 802-875-4127.

**R & N Miniatures,** 458 Wythe Creek Rd., Poquoson, VA 23662: Price list $2 ◆ Everything to finish and furnish dollhouses. 757-868-7103.

**Real Good Toys,** 10 Quarry Hill, Barre, VT 05641: Catalog $3 (request list of retail sources) ◆ Dollhouse kits with easy-to-follow instructions. 802-479-2217.

**Rose's Doll House Store,** 6572 Lover's Ln., Milwaukee, WI 53132: Free catalog ◆ Bears, dolls, and dollhouse furnishings and miniatures. 800-926-9093; 414-529-3020 (in WI).

**Scientific Models Inc.,** 340 Snyder Ave., Berkeley Heights, NJ 07922: Catalog $1 ◆ Easy-to-assemble museum-quality dollhouse furniture. 908-464-7070.

**Shaker Workshops,** Box 8001, Ashburnham, MA 01430: Catalog $1 ◆ Furniture and dolls and Shaker furniture in kits or assembled. 800-840-9121.

**Skycrest Ceramics,** 149 W. Oak, Ste. 8, Fort Collins, CO 80524: Free information ◆ Ceramics miniatures. 970-493-8075.

**Small Houses,** 8064 Columbia Rd., Olmsted Falls, OH 44138: Catalog $6 ◆ Dollhouse kits, furniture, wallpaper, and building supplies. 216-235-5051.

**Treasures by Paula K,** Village Plaza, Rt. 202 & Lovell St., Lincolndale, NY 10540: Catalog $12 (refundable) ◆ Everything to fully furnish a dollhouse from start to finish. 914-248-7262.

**Vicki's Miniatures,** P.O. Box 142407, Anchorage, AK 99514: Free information: Brochure $1 ◆ Handcrafted detailed miniature gym equipment. 907-333-5470.

**Jeffrey W. Vigeant,** P.O. Box 414, Williamsburg, VA 23187: Brochure $4 ◆ Miniature Victorian lamps. 757-258-0425.

**Walmer Doll Houses,** 2100 Jefferson Davis Hwy., Alexandria, VA 22301: Catalog $3 (refundable) ◆ Dollhouses. 800-336-0285.

**Donna Wolf,** 1200 E. 21st, Hutchinson, KS 67502: Information $1 with long SASE ◆ Handcrafted counted cross-stitch samplers, pillows, quilts, table runners, and comforter sets.

## DOLL MAKING & DOLL CLOTHING

**All About Dolls,** 72 Lakeside Blvd., Hopatcong, NJ 07843: Catalog $3 ◆ Porcelain for making dolls, kilns, eyes, wigs, and other supplies. 201-770-3228.

**Apple Valley Doll Works,** P.O. Box 170, Midland, MI 48640: Free information ◆ Vinyl doll kits. 800-635-7933. www.applevalleydolls.com

**The Baby Makers,** P.O. Box 295, Aitkin, MN 56431: Free information ◆ Vinyl doll kits. 800-517-3367.

**BBDS Inc.,** 7800 Mockingbird Ln., North Richland Hills, TX 76180: Catalog $5 ◆ Everything to start, make, and finish a doll. 800-227-3655; 817-656-3378 (in TX).

**Bell Ceramics,** P.O. Box 120127, Clermont, FL 34712: Catalog $8 (request list of retail sources) ◆ Antique reproduction and modern doll molds and supplies. 800-874-9025; 352-394-2175 (in FL).

**Gina C. Bellows Creations,** 8006 Chase Ave., Los Angeles, CA 90045: Catalog $3 with long SASE and two 1st class stamps ◆ Molds, porcelain blanks, and doll kits. 310-645-8288.

**Broadview Dolls,** 5247 State Rd., Parma, OH 44134: Catalog $4 ◆ Doll bisque kits and doll-making supplies. 216-661-4856.

**Brown House Dolls,** 3200 N. Sand Lake Rd., Allen, MI 49227: Catalog $2 ◆ Easy-to-sew patterns for doll clothing. 517-869-2833.

**Carolee Creations,** 787 Industrial Dr., Elmhurst, IL 60126: Free catalog ◆ Cloth doll making supplies. 630-530-7175.

**Collectible Doll Company,** 4216 6th NW, Seattle, WA 98107: Catalog $9 ◆ Fashions, accessories, molds, and doll-making supplies. 800-566-6646; 206-781-1963 (in WA).

**CR's Crafts,** Box 8, Leland, IA 50453: Catalog $2 ◆ Doll and bear-making supplies, kits, and patterns for jointed bears. 515-567-3652. www.crscrafts.com

**Creative Paperclay Company,** 1800 S. Robertson Blvd., Ste. 907, Los Angeles, CA 90035: Free information ◆ Air-hardening sculpting material for doll artists. 800-899-5952; 213-839-0466 (in CA).

**D & L Doll Supply,** 224-228 Admiral St., Providence, RI 02908: Free information ◆ Soft-fired greenware, wigs, eyes, shoes, patterns, and supplies. 401-421-7558.

**Marl Davidson,** 10301 Braden Run, Bradenton, FL 34202: Catalog $7.95 ◆ Barbie doll fashions and dolls, from 1959 to the present. 941-751-6275. auntie.com/marl

**Lou Davis Doll Supply,** P.O. Box 21, N3211 County Rd. H., Lake Geneva, WI 53147: Free catalog ◆ Doll-making supplies. 800-748-7991.

**Dee's Place of Dolls,** 140 E. College St., Covina, CA 91723: Free information ◆ Doll-making supplies and dolls. 626-915-1005.

**Doll Gallery Supplies,** 7822 4th St. NW, Albuquerque, NM 87107: Free information with long SASE ◆ Doll-making supplies. 505-898-4883.

**Doll Stuff,** 7018 W. 85th St., Los Angeles, CA 90045: Free brochure with long SASE ◆ Handmade clothes, hand-crocheted afghans, and accessories for 18-inch dolls.

**Doll Supplies Warehouse,** 6154 126th Ave. North, Kargo, FL 33771: Free information ◆ Doll-making supplies, molds, and tools. 813-535-3655.

**Doll Works Etc.,** 1915 Peters Rd., Ste. 201, Irving, TX 75061: Free price list with long SASE ◆ Doll-making supplies. 972-721-0819.

**Dollmasters,** P.O. Box 2319, Annapolis, MD 21404: Catalog $5 ◆ Nostalgic gifts and collectibles that celebrate yesterday's childhood. Also doll clothing and reference books. 800-966-3655; 410-224-4386 (in MD). www.ea.net/dollmasters

**Dolls Delight Inc.,** P.O. Box 3226, Alexandria, VA 22302: Brochure $2 ◆ Clothing for 18-inch dolls. 800-257-6301.

**Dollspart Supply Company,** 8000 Cooper Ave., Bldg. 28, Glendale, NY 11385: Free catalog ◆ Anything and everything for dolls. Includes wigs, shoes, books and patterns, doll bodies, kits, and supplies. 800-336-3655.

**Nancy Eichenberger,** P.O. Box 1552, Westport, WA 98595: Catalog $2 (refundable) ◆ Cloth doll patterns. 360-268-9759.

**Fancy Frocks,** 2373 NW 185th, Ste. 141, Hillsboro, OR 97124: Catalog $4 ◆ Custom doll costume patterns. 888-648-5289; 503-648-8420 (in OR). www.FancyFrocks.com

**Fashion Doll Originals,** 5704 N. 81st St., Scottsdale, AZ 85250: Free information ◆ Easy-to-sew doll clothing patterns.

**Fun Stuf,** P.O. Box 999, Yuma, AZ 85366: List $1 ◆ Artist vinyl and porcelain doll kits and supplies. 520-783-7470.

**Global Dolls Corp.,** 1903 Aviation Blvd., Lincoln, CA 95648: Catalog $5 ◆ Doll wigs. 916-645-3000.

**Happy Apple Doll Company,** 70 W. Highland Ave., Atlantic Highlands, NJ 07716: Catalog $6.50 ◆ Doll-making supplies, clothing, and patterns. 908-435-0014.

**Heavenly Made Seasons,** 614 E. 8th St., Cheyenne, WY 82007: Brochure $3 (refundable) ◆ Cloth healing and era dolls, limited patterns, and decorative painted wood and metal accessories. 800-484-9606

**Hello Dolly,** 6550 Mobile Hwy., Pensacola, FL 32526: Catalog $5 ◆ Doll-making supplies. 800-438-7227.

**Herb's Porcelain Doll Studio,** 1208 E. 15th St., Plano, TX 75074: Price list $2 (refundable) ◆ Bisque kits for making dolls. 800-628-4696; 972-578-1128 (in TX).

**Heritage Miniatures,** 44 Mountain Base Rd., Goffstown, NH 03045: Catalog $5 ◆ European lace and trim for doll clothing.

**Hickory Dickory Dolls,** 124 E. Aurora Rd., Northfield, OH 44067: Free price list ◆ Dolls, clothing, and shoes. 800-468-2085.

**House of Caron,** 10111 Larrylyn Dr., Whittier, CA 90603: Catalog $3 ◆ Miniature doll molds and doll-making supplies. 562-947-6753.

**House of White Birches,** 306 E. Parr Rd., Berne, IN 46711: Free catalog ◆ Doll-making kits.

**Huston Dolls,** 7960 US Rt. 23, Chillicothe, OH 45601: Catalog $2 ◆ Handmade porcelain dolls and make-them-yourself kits. 614-663-2881.

**Jennell's Doll House,** Rt. 9, Box 939, Hwy. 274, Tool, TX 75143: Catalog $4 ◆ Doll kits, supplies, pre-sewn bodies, and clothes. 903-432-4894.

**Jo's Dolls-N-Fine Porcelain,** 7508 SW 12th, Des Moines, IA 50315: Catalog $7.95 ◆ Doll-making supplies. 800-323-4689.

**Jomac Dolls & Supplies,** 702 Crenshaw, Pasadena, TX 77504: Free information ◆ Doll-making supplies, bisque and wax kits, and greenware. 713-944-8221.

**Jones Mold Company,** 919 4th Ave. South, Nashville, TN 37210: Ceramics catalog $6.25; doll catalog $6.75 ◆ Molds for making ceramics and dolls. 615-251-8989.

**Janna Joseph,** 2465 Northside Dr., Clearwater, FL 34621: Catalog $5 ◆ Miniature doll molds. 813-784-1877.

**Judi's Dolls,** P.O. Box 6165, Aloha, OR 97007: Catalog $2.50 ◆ Patterns and supplies for cloth dolls. 503-848-8361. www.thedollnet.com/judi

**Kemper Tools & Doll Supplies Inc.,** 13595 12th St., Chino, CA 91710: Free catalog ◆ Pottery and sculpting crafting tools. Also doll-making supplies. 800-388-5367.

**The Kezi Works,** P.O. Box 17631, Portland, OR 97217: Free catalog ◆ Cloth doll patterns. 503-286-9385.

**Kirchen Brothers,** Box 1016, Skokie, IL 60076: Catalog $2 ◆ Doll-making supplies and kits, ready-to-wear and ready-to-sew clothing, shoes and socks, and craft supplies. 847-647-6747.

**La Petite Galerie,** 111 Columbus Circle, Longwood, FL 32750: Catalog $3.50 ◆ Doll dresses. 407-339-8833.

**Ledgewood Studio,** 6000 Ledgewood Dr., Forest Park, GA 30050: Catalog $2 with long SASE and three 1st class stamps ◆ Dress patterns, period clothing, fabrics, supplies for antique dolls, and sewing notions. 404-361-6098.

**Victor H. Levy Inc.,** 1355 S. Flower St., Los Angeles, CA 90015: Catalog $5 ◆ Doll and jewelry-making supplies. 800-421-8021; 213-749-8247 (in CA).

**Magic Cabin Dolls,** P.O. Box 1996, Prairie Edge Rd., Peoria, IL 61656: Free information ◆ Doll-making supplies, kits and patterns, cotton knits, yarns, and handmade dolls. 888-623-3655.

**Maybelle's Doll Works,** 140 Space Park Dr., Nashville, TN 37211: Catalog $6 ◆ Doll-making supplies and molds. 615-831-0661.

**Mini World Doll Supplies,** 11917 E. 83rd St., Raytown, MO 64138: Catalog $3 ◆ Doll-making supplies. 816-353-5988.

**Minnie's Doll House,** Knight Rd., Rt. 3, Box 527, Lake Providence, LA 71254: Catalog $3 ◆ Original doll clothes. 318-559-2857.

**Monique Trading Corp.,** 270 Oyster Point Blvd., South San Francisco, CA 94080: Catalog $3 ◆ Doll wigs and accessories. 800-621-4338; 415-266-6863 (in CA).

**Mystic Mold Company,** Rt. 2, Box 241, DeKalb, TX 75559: Catalog $7.50 ◆ Doll molds. 903-667-5659.

**National Artcraft Company,** 7996 Darrow Rd., Twinsburg, OH 44087: Catalog $4 ◆ Tools and supplies for floral-crafting, ceramics, and making clocks, lamps, dolls, candles, and jewelry. 800-793-0152. nationalartcraft@worldnet.att.net

**Needleworks by Nancy,** 417 Kenwood Ct., Raleigh, NC 27609: Free brochure with long SASE ◆ Doll clothing patterns for 18-inch dolls. 919-571-1872.

**One & Only Creations,** P.O. Box 2730, Napa, CA 94558: Free catalog ◆ Doll making supplies. 800-262-6768.

**Originals By Elaine Inc.,** 901 Oak Hollow Pl., Brandon, FL 33510: Catalog $6 ◆ Molds for miniature dolls. 813-654-0335.

**The Parchment Press,** 55 Grandview St., Tolland, CT 06084: Brochure $2 ◆ Doll-making patterns. 860-872-3977. gopatterns@aol.com

**Pierce Tools,** 1610 Parkdale Dr., Grants Pass, OR 97527: Free catalog ◆ Tools for the dollmaker, ceramist, potter, and sculptor. 541-476-1778.

**Platypus,** Box 396, Planetarium Station, New York, NY 10024: Free information ◆ Stuffed toy and doll patterns.

**Porcelain by Marilyn,** 3687 W. US 40, Greenfield, IN 46140: Free list with long SASE and two 1st class stamps ◆ Porcelain doll kits. 317-462-5063.

**R & A Mold Shop,** 2416 Amsler St., Torrance, CA 90505: Free information ◆ Custom made molds. 310-326-9982.

**Mary Radbill Doll Supplies,** 4512 Eden St., Philadelphia, PA 19114: Catalog $3 ◆ Doll-making supplies. 215-632-4606.

**A Real Doll & Company,** P.O. Box 1044, Sebastopol, CA 95473: Free catalog ◆ Natural fiber doll and craft-making supplies. 707-829-7265.

**Thelma Resch,** 89 Purple Martin Dr., Murrells Inlet, SC 29576: Brochure $2 ◆ Original doll molds. 803-651-0596.

**Rivendell Inc.,** 125 North Lake Rd., Madison, OH 44057: Pattern catalog $4; general merchandise catalog $6 ◆ Supplies for porcelain dolls. 216-428-0042.

**Sandcastle Creations,** 255 SW 9th St., Newport, OR 97365: Free information ◆ Wig-making supplies and kits, doll dresses, and accessories. 541-574-1901. sandcastle@fbo.com

**Seeley's Modern Doll Art Company,** 9 River St., Oneonta, NY 13820: Free catalog ◆ Doll-making supplies. 800-871-3655.

**Sew Sweet Dolls,** 787 Industrial Dr., Elmhurst, IL 60126: Catalog $2 ◆ Paper patterns for cloth dolls and accessories, hair materials, yarns, books, and supplies. 630-530-7175.

**Sharon's Designs,** 1390 N. McDowell, Petaluma, CA 94954: Free list with long SASE ◆ Custom made doll clothes. 707-769-9329.

**Doreen Sinnett,** Box 789, Paso Robles, CA 93447: Catalog $4.50 ◆ Molds for miniature dolls. 805-239-2048.

**Standard Doll Company,** 23-83 31st St., Long Island City, NY 11105: Catalog $3 ◆ Supplies for making and repairing dolls, clothing, doll stands, shoes and socks, buttons, wigs, books, and sewing notions. 800-543-6557.

**Sterling Mold Company,** 351 Magnolia Pl., Debary, FL 32713: Catalog $7 ◆ Antique reproductions and artist doll molds. 407-668-8379.

**Sugar Creek Industries Inc.,** P.O. Box 354, Linden, IN 47955: Free catalog ◆ Porcelain pouring equipment and supplies. 317-339-4641.

**T & M Ceramics,** 654 Page Ave., Jackson, MI 49203: Catalog $7.50 ◆ Doll-making supplies and molds. 517-783-4419.

**Tallina's Doll Supplies Inc.,** 15791 Southeast Hwy. 224, Clackamas, OR 97015: Catalog $2 ◆ Doll-making supplies. 503-658-6148.

**TDI Dolls,** P.O. Box 690, Cave Creek, AZ 85331: Catalog $1 ◆ Porcelain doll kits, porcelain doll heads, stands, wigs, and patterns.

**Tender Heart Treasures Ltd.,** 10525 J St., Omaha, NE 68127: Free catalog ◆ Clothing and accessories for bears and dolls. 800-443-1367. www.tenderheart.com

**Theriault's the Dollmaster,** P.O. Box 151, Annapolis, MD 21404: Free information ◆ Antique, collectible, and other dolls. 410-224-3655. www.ea.net/theriaults

**Timberpond Press,** 1133 W. Broad St., Williamstown, PA 17098: Catalog $5 ◆ Doll-making supplies, books, and vintage-style clothing patterns. 717-647-7463.

**TLC Doll,** Mail Order Department, P.O. Box 2383, Brentwood, TN 37024: Catalog $4 ◆ Over 200 patterns for 18-inch dolls. 615-661-5454.

**Unicorn Studios,** 424 Blount Ave., Knoxville, TN 37920: Catalog $1 ◆ Easy-to-install windup and electronic music box movements, winking light units, and voices for dolls and bears. 423-573-1863. www.imox.com/unicorn

**Kate Webster Company,** 83 Granite St., Rockport, MA 01966: Catalog $3 ◆ Doll costuming supplies and jewelry. 978-546-6462.

**Wilder's Doll Center,** 3345 Dixie Hwy., Waterford, MI 48328: Catalog $5 ◆ Porcelain dolls, clothes, patterns, supplies, and more. 246-618-9506.

**Wishing-U-Well Doll & Ceramic Studio,** 323 Norton Rd., Columbus, OH 43228: Free information ◆ Everything needed to start, finish, dress, and display dolls. 614-878-5466.

## DOLLS

**All God's Children Collectors Club,** P.O. Box 5038, Glencoe, AL 35905: Free list of retail sources ◆ Historical-theme dolls. 205-492-0221.

**Angel Children,** 4977 Sparr Rd., Gaylord, MI 49735: Catalog $2 ◆ Miniature porcelain dolls. 517-732-1931. www.angelfire.com/mi/angelchildren

**Annette & Friends,** 13238 Springdale St., Westminister, CA 92683: Free newsletter ◆ Collectible dolls. 714-897-5937. www.afdoll.com

**Anything Goes Inc.,** 9801 Gulf Dr., Anna Maria, FL 34216: Quarterly newsletter $2 ◆ Current Barbie, other artist, and collectible dolls. 800-780-2327; 813-778-4456 (in FL).

**The Ashton-Drake Galleries,** 9200 N. Maryland, Niles, IL 60714: Free catalog ◆ Collectible dolls. 800-346-2460. www.ashtondrake.com

**Aurelia's World of Dolls Inc.,** 2025 Merrick Rd., Merrick, NY 11566: Free newsletter ◆ United States and international artist dolls. 516-378-3556.

**Baby Me,** 730 Boston Rd., Rt. 3A, Billerica, MA 01821: Free information ◆ Dolls. 978-667-1187.

**Barbara's Dolls,** Barbara Spears, P.O. Box 126095, Fort Worth, TX 76126: Free list with long SASE and three 1st class stamps (specify interest) ◆ Barbie, antique, or collectible dolls. 817-738-0771.

**Bears 'n Wares,** 312 Bridge St., New Cumberland, PA 17070: Brochure $2 ◆ Artist and other dolls. 717-774-1261.

**Bébé House of Dolls,** 282 3rd Ave., Chula Vista, CA 91910: Free information with long SASE ◆ Dolls. 619-476-0680.

**Dee Benisek Studio,** 2210 Williamsburg, Arlington Heights, IL 60004: Catalog $2 ◆ Antique reproduction dolls. 847-394-8910.

**Best of Everything,** 199 Main St., Hackettstown, NJ 07840: Free information ◆ Dolls. 908-850-4858.

**Biggs Limited Editions,** 5517 Lakeside Ave., Richmond, VA 23228: Free information with long SASE ◆ Limited edition artist and other dolls. 800-637-0704. www.biggsltd.com

**Joe Blitman Dolls,** 5163 Franklin Ave., Los Angeles, CA 90027: Sample list $5; 4-issue subscription $13 ◆ Barbie dolls, clothing, and accessories. 213-953-0888.

**Bodzer's Collectibles,** White Marsh Mall, Baltimore, MD 21236: Free catalog ◆ Ashton-Drake and collectible dolls. 410-931-9222.

**Browns Gallery,** 12585 10th Line, Stouffville, Ontario, Canada L4A 7X3: Free information ◆ Collectible dolls. 905-642-3606.

**Cardinal Incorporated,** 400 Markley St., Port Reading, NJ 07064: Catalog $7.50 (refundable) ◆ Miniature dollhouse furniture and porcelain collectible dolls. 800-888-0936.

**Celia's & Susan's Dolls & Collectibles,** 800 E. Hallandale Beach Blvd., Hallandale, FL 33009: Catalog $5 ◆ Dolls. 954-458-0661.

**CJ's Dolls & Dreams,** 5 Plaistow Rd., Rt. 125, Plaistow, NH 03865: Free information ◆ Artist dolls. 603-382-3449.

**Classic Toys,** 112 Southgate Plaza, Sarasota, FL 34239: Free list with long SASE and two 1st class stamps ◆ Barbie dolls and collectibles, Star Trek and Star Wars classic collectibles, Patsy dolls, figurines, and ornaments. 941-365-1121.

**Collectibles Etc.,** 105 N. Main St., Boaz, AL 35957: Free information ◆ Barbie dolls and collector books featuring Barbie dolls. 205-593-7270.

**Collector's Gallery of Dolls,** 647 Delaware Ave., Marion, OH 43302: Free list: Free catalog ◆ Collectible dolls. 614-387-0602.

**Corbett's Collectable Dolls,** 120 E. Kings Hwy., Maple Shade, NJ 08052: Catalog $5 ◆ Artist and other dolls. 609-866-9787.

**Country Loft Doll Haus,** 204 N. Minnesota St., New Ulm, MN 56073: Free information ◆ Collectible dolls. 507-354-8493.

**Creative Hands,** P.O. Box 2217, Eugene, OR 97402: Catalog $2 ◆ Natural fiber dolls, crafts, kits, and supplies. 541-343-1562.

**Marl Davidson,** 10301 Braden Run, Bradenton, FL 34202: Catalog $7.50 ◆ Barbie doll fashions and dolls, from 1959 to the present. 941-751-6275. www.auntie.com/marl

**Doll Centre,** 665 Placerville Dr., Placerville, CA 95667: Free catalog ◆ Limited edition dolls. 916-621-2889.

**Doll City USA,** 2080 S. Harbor Blvd., Anaheim, CA 92802: Price list $2 ◆ Dolls. 714-750-3585.

**Doll Gallery Supplies,** 7822 4th St. NW, Albuquerque, NM 87107: Free information with long SASE ◆ Dolls. 505-898-4883.

**The Doll House,** 18 S. Broadway, Edmond, OK 73034: Free information ◆ Collectible dolls. 405-348-9895.

**The Doll Lady,** 247 N. Sycamore St., Newtown, PA 18940: Free information with long SASE ◆ Miniatures, collectibles, dollhouses, furniture, miniature dolls, gifts, and accessories. 215-504-5588.

**Doll Parlor,** 7 Church St., Allentown, NJ 08501: Free information with long SASE ◆ Dolls. 609-259-8118.

**Doll Showcase,** 104 Front St., Marietta, OH 45750: Free price list with long SASE ◆ Artist and other dolls. 800-933-6557

**dolls 'n bearland,** 15001 N. Hayden Rd., Ste. 104, Scottsdale, AZ 85260: Free catalog with two 1st class stamps ◆ Collectible dolls and teddy bears. 800-359-9541. www.dollsnbearland.com

**Dollsville Dolls & Bearsville Bears,** 292 N. Palm Canyon Dr., Palm Springs, CA 92262: Catalog $2 ◆ Dolls. 800-225-2327. www.dollsville.com

**Dwyer's Doll House,** 1944 Warwick Ave., Warwick, RI 02889: Catalog $25 ◆ Dolls, dollhouses, miniatures, and dollhouse building supplies. 401-738-3248.

**Dynasty Doll Collection,** 1 Newbold Rd., P.O. Box 36, Fairless Hills, PA 19030: Catalog $7.50 ◆ Limited edition storybook and other collectible dolls. 215-428-9100.

**Enchanted Doll House,** Rt. 7A, RR 1, Box 2535, Manchester Center, VT 05255: Catalog $2 ◆ Dolls, miniatures, bears, stuffed animals, and toys. 802-362-1327.

**Enesco Corp.,** 1 Enesco Plaza, Elk Grove Village, IL 60007: Free list of retail sources ◆ Figurines, sculptures, ornaments, Barbie dolls, and gifts. www.enesco.com

**Ernie's Toyland,** 1012 6th St., Ste. 120, Yuba City, CA 95901: Free information ◆ Barbies and other dolls. 800-367-1233. www.erniestoyland.com

**For The Love Of Dolls,** 4359 Lovers Ln., Dallas, TX 75225: Catalog $2 ◆ Artist and other dolls. 972-528-5683.

**Gepetto's Dolls N' More,** P.O. Box 524, Hwy. 441 North, Cherokee, NC 28719: Free information with long SASE ◆ Collector dolls. 704-497-7995.

**GiGi's Dolls & Sherry's Teddy Bears Inc.,** 6029 N. Northwest Hwy., Chicago, IL 60631: Free catalog ◆ Bears, dolls, plush toys, and miniatures. 773-594-1540.

**Global Friends,** 100 Plaza Dr., Secaucus, NJ 07094: Free catalog ◆ Dolls and accessories with an international theme. 800-393-5421. www.globalfriends.com

**Grandma's Attic,** Joyce Kekatos, 3144 Ampere Ave., Bronx, NY 10465: Free information with long SASE ◆ French nd German bisque dolls. 718-863-0373.

**Jan Hagara Collectors Club,** 40114 Industrial Park North, Georgetown, TX 78626: Free information ◆ Jan Hagara porcelain dolls. 512-863-9499.

**Hello Dollies,** Donna Catellan, 2564 Wigwam Pkwy., Ste. 206, Henderson, NV 89014: Free list with 6x9-inch envelope and three 1st class stamps ◆ Barbie dolls, wardrobe accessories, and Tammy and Dawn collectibles. 702-897-7624.

**Hickory Dickory Dolls,** 124 E. Aurora Rd., Northfield, OH 44067: Free price list with long SASE ◆ Dolls, clothing, and shoes. 800-468-2085.

**Hidden Treasures,** 1509 Huron Avery Rd., Huron, OH 44839: Free list ◆ Artist dolls. 800-265-3802.

**The Hobby Gallery Miniature Loft,** 1810 Meriden Rd., Wolcott, CT 06716: Free information with long SASE ◆ Dolls, dollhouses, miniatures, and plush animals. 203-879-2316.

**The Incredible Christmas Place,** 2470 Parkway, P.O. Box 958, Pigeon Forge, TN 37868: Free catalog ◆ Toys and trains, dolls, Christmas ornaments, and other gifts and collectibles. 800-357-2682. www.christmasplace.com

**Integrity Toys,** 39 Jewett Ave., #2, Jersey City, NJ 07304: Free brochure ◆ Dolls with original clothing and accessories. 770-808-1549.

**Irma's Gallery Dolls,** P.O. Box 1167, Boring, OR 97009: Catalog $5 (refundable) ◆ Rag dolls. 503-663-4122.

**Iron Horse Gifts,** 608 New London Rd., Latham, NY 12110: Free information ◆ Designer dolls. 800-237-3735.

**JoNans Dolls,** 79 Scioto St., Ashville, OH 43103: Free brochure ◆ One-of-a-kind handcrafted soft sculpture dolls of the medieval and renaissance ages.

**Kathy Library,** 43 DeKoven Ct., Brooklyn, NY 11230: Catalog $3 (refundable) ◆ Antique French and German dolls in antique clothes, dating from the 1870s to 1930s. 718-859-0901.

**Kish & Company,** 11632 Busy St., Richmond, VA 23236: Free catalog ◆ Collectible dolls. 804-379-4362.

**Lane's Toyland & Gifts,** 720 Realtor Ave., Texarkana, TX 75502: Free catalog ◆ Barbies and other dolls. 800-421-8697.

**Lanell's Dolls,** 2760 Wears Valley Rd., Sevierville, TN 37862: Free information ◆ Collectible dolls. 941-792-8487.

**Le Allala's Doll Shop,** 88 N. Paint St., Chillicothe, OH 45601: Catalog $3 ◆ Collector dolls. 800-577-3655; 614-775-5960 (in OH).

**Lee's Collectibles,** P.O. Box 19133, Sacramento, CA 95819: Free information with long SASE ◆ Wood, cloth, and contemporary artist dolls. 916-457-4308.

**Li'l Bit O'Heaven Inc.,** 1143 Columbia Ave., Franklin, TN 37064: Free information ◆ Artist dolls. 800-591-1868; 615-790-3790 (in TN).

**Little Shoppe of Dolls & Things,** 138 Main St., Milford, MA 01757: Free information ◆ Collectible dolls. 800-473-6867.

**Lynn's Lil' Darlings,** 209 N. 13th St., Griffin, GA 30223: Free list with long SASE ◆ New and old Barbie dolls. 770-228-5918.

**Magic Cabin Dolls,** Prairie Edge Rd., P.O. Box 1996, Peoria, IL 61656: Free catalog ◆ Handcrafted natural fiber dolls, kits, supplies, and accessories. 888-623-3655.

**Seymour Mann,** 225 5th Ave., New York, NY 10010: Catalog $7.50 ◆ Dolls. 212-683-7262.

**Marj's Doll Sanctuary,** 5238 Plainfield Ave. NE, Grand Rapids, MI 49505: Catalog $1 ◆ Dolls and bears. 616-361-0054. marjsdolls@compuserve.com

**Mary Ann's Doll Boutique,** Ron & Mary Morales, 192 Franciscan Dr., Daly City, CA 94014: Free list with long SASE and two 1st class stamps ◆ Barbie dolls. 415-755-1587.

**Mary D's Dolls & Bears & Such,** 423-431 3rd St., Osseo, MN 55369: Catalog $2 ◆ Dolls. 612-424-4375.

**Matrix Dolls,** P.O. Box 1410, New York, NY 10023: Free list with long SASE ◆ Antique dolls. 212-787-7279.

**Melton's Antique Dolls,** 4201 Indian River Rd., Chesapeake, VA 23325: Free information with long SASE ◆ Antique dolls. 757-420-9226.

**Monarch Collectibles,** 2012 NW Military Hwy., San Antonio, TX 78213: Free information ◆ Dolls. 800-648-3655. www.dollsdolls.com

**My Favorite Doll,** 1771 Poets Walk, Mississauga, Ontario, Canada L5M 4M4: Free information ◆ Barbie collectibles. 905-819-8326.

**Not Just Dolls,** 2447 Gus Thomasson Rd., Dallas, TX 75228: Price list $2 ◆ Artist and other dolls. 972-321-0412.

**Originals By Elaine Inc.,** 901 Oak Hollow Pl., Brandon, FL 33510: Catalog $6 ◆ Molds for miniature dolls. 813-654-0335.

**The Paper Place & Doll Place,** 212 S. River, Holland, MI 49423: Catalog $3 (refundable) ◆ Collectible bears and dolls. 616-392-7776.

**Patt & Billy's Dolls & Collectibles,** 3045 N. Federal Hwy., Fort Lauderdale, FL 33306: Free catalog ◆ Collectible dolls. Includes many closed editions. 954-568-9066.

**Pewter Classics,** 3635 28th St. SE, Eastbrook Mall, Grand Rapids, MI 49512: Catalog $2 ◆ Dolls, bears, and collectibles. 800-833-3655.

**A Piece of My Heart,** 2201 1st Ave. East, Williston, ND 58801: Free information ◆ Primitive doll patterns and finished dolls. 701-572-2374.

**Playhouse,** Mary Radbill, 4512 Eden St., Philadelphia, PA 19114: Free catalog ◆ Artist dolls, bears, and accessories. 215-632-4606.

**Pleasant Company,** P.O. Box 620190, Middleton, WI 53562: Free catalog ◆ Dolls with an American theme. 800-845-0005. www.americangirl.com

**Porter Emporium,** P.O. Box 5, Rt. 25, Porter, ME 04068: Free list with long SASE ◆ Barbie dolls. 207-625-8989.

**Rainbow Factory,** 131 W. Vienna St., Clio, MI 48420: Free information with long SASE ◆ Dolls, miniatures, carrousels, music boxes, and bears. 810-687-1351.

**Rose's Doll House Store,** 6572 Lover's Ln., Milwaukee, WI 53132: Free catalog ◆ Bears, dolls, and dollhouse furnishings and miniatures. 800-926-9093; 414-529-3020 (in WI).

**Samurai Antiques,** 229 Santa Ynez Ct., Santa Barbara, CA 93103: Price list $1 with long SASE ◆ Japanese antique dolls by Samurai, Emperor, and Empress. 805-965-9688.

**Sandy's Dolls & Collectables Inc.,** 7221 W. College Dr., Palos Heights, IL 60463: Price list $1 ◆ Artist and limited edition dolls. 708-423-0070.

**Sandy's Dream Dolls,** 7154 N. 58th Dr., Glendale, AZ 85301: Free list ◆ Barbie and other dolls. 602-931-1579.

**Shirley's Doll House,** 971 N. Milwaukee Ave., Wheeling, IL 60090: Free information with long SASE ◆ Dolls, bears, antiques, doll house furniture, wigs, clothing, and shoes. 847-537-1632.

**Simply Lovely Gift Shoppe,** 572 New Brunswick Ave., Fords, NJ 08863: Free price list with long SASE ◆ Dolls. 732-738-4181.

**Society's Child,** 28686 W. Northwest Hwy., Barrington, IL 60010: Free information with long SASE ◆ Artist and limited edition dolls. 847-381-9559.

**Sophia's Heritage Collection,** 8 Shepherd Rd., Malvern PA 19355: Free brochure ◆ German, Irish, and English immigrant dolls, clothing, furniture, and accessories. 610-647-2118.

**Mary Stolz Doll Shop,** RR 6, Box 6767, East Stroudsburg, PA 18301: Free catalog ◆ Barbies and collectible dolls. 717-588-7566.

**Sutter Street Emporium,** 731 Sutter St., Folsom, CA 95630: Free information ◆ Limited edition original artist and other dolls. 916-985-4647.

**Tide-Rider Inc.,** P.O. Box 429, Oakdale, CA 95361: Free information ◆ Handcrafted felt dolls with detailed facial features and costuming. 209-848-4420.

**Today's Treasures,** 655 73rd St., Niagara Falls, NY 14304: Catalog $3 (refundable) ◆ Collector dolls and bears. 716-283-1726.

**Toni Ann's Doll House,** 213 S. Caroline St., Herkimer, NY 13350: Free catalog ◆ Collectible dolls. 800-445-3655; 315-866-3655 (in NY).

**Toy Shoppe,** 11632 Busy St., Richmond, VA 23236: Free information ◆ Collectible dolls and bears. 800-447-7995.

**Toy Village,** 3105 W. Saginaw, Lansing, MI 48917: Free information ◆ Toys, dolls, bears, and collectibles. 517-323-1145.

**The Treasure Trove,** P.O. Box 416, Fisherville, VA 22939: Free catalog with long SASE ◆ Rare dolls. 540-949-5378.

**Ryan Twist Gallery,** 430 Teaneck Rd., Ridgefield Park, NJ 07660: Free information with long SASE ◆ Dolls. 800-421-0171.

**Your Old Friends Doll Shop,** 21 5th St. SW, Mason City, IA 50401: Catalog $3 ◆ Barbie dolls, clothing, and accessories. 515-424-0984. www.radiopark.com/yofds.html

**Donna Zielgler,** 408 Tenburg Ct., Allen, TX 75002: Brochure $2 ◆ Original one-of-a-kind handpainted cloth clowns and Mardi Gras, cowboy, ballerina, bride and groom, and other dolls. 972-396-0631.

## DRAFTING SUPPLIES

**Alvin & Company Inc.,** P.O. Box 188, Windsor, CT 06095: Free catalog ◆ Drafting, engineering, and graphic art supplies. 800-444-2584. www.alvinco.com

**Dick Blick Company,** P.O. Box 1267, Galesburg, IL 61402: Catalog $1 ◆ Books, videos, airbrushes, printing and drafting equipment, and commercial art supplies. 800-447-8192. www.artmaterials.com/

**Fairgate Rule Company Inc.,** 22 Adams Ave., P.O. Box 278, Cold Spring, NY 10516: Free catalog ◆ Rulers, other measuring devices, stencils, and drawing aids. 800-431-2180; 914-265-3677 (in NY).

**Hearlihy & Company,** 714 W. Columbia St., Springfield, OH 45504: Free catalog ◆ Drafting and graphics equipment, software for education and computer-aided designing, drawing and drafting aids, videos, plotters, and furniture. 800-622-1000. www.hearlihy.com

**Nasco,** 901 Janesville Ave., Fort Atkinson, WI 53538: Free catalog ◆ Drawing and drafting supplies. 800-558-9595. www.nascofa.com

**Office Depot Inc.,** 2200 Old Germantown Rd., Delray Beach, FL 33445: Free catalog ◆ Drafting equipment, office supplies, and accessories. 800-685-8800. www.officedepot.com

**Omnicorp,** 14 W. 33rd St., New York, NY 10001: Free catalog ◆ Art supplies, drafting materials, ink jet and toner cartridges, and more. 212-279-6161. www.columbiaomni.com

**Daniel Smith Art Supplies,** 4150 1st Ave. South, Seattle, WA 98134: Catalog $5 (refundable) ◆ Art and framing supplies, books, studio and drafting equipment, and furniture. 800-426-6740. www.danielsmith.com

**Staples Inc.,** P.O. Box 5173, Westborough, MA 01581: Free catalog ◆ Office and computer supplies, drafting equipment, furniture, fax machines, and typewriters. 800-333-3330. www.staples.com

## DUMBWAITERS & ELEVATORS

**Aid-O-Maid Company,** P.O. Box 3, Waco, TX 76703: Free information ◆ Residential dumbwaiters. 817-752-8702.

**Econol Lift Corp.,** 2513 Center St., Box 854, Cedar Falls, IA 50613: Free information ◆ Dumbwaiters and residential elevators. Also vertical, wheelchair, and stair-riding lifts. 319-277-4777.

**W. Bruce Fowler Industries Inc.,** 292 Queen, Lennoxville, Quebec City, Canada J1M 1K6: Free information ◆ Built-in electric-operated lift for moving wood from cellars to wood stoves or fireplaces. 819-562-8510.

**Inclinator Company of America,** P.O. Box 1557, Harrisburg, PA 17105: Free information ◆ Dumbwaiters. 800-456-1329.

**Miller Manufacturing Inc.,** 165 Cascade Ct., Rohnert Park, CA 94928: Free information ◆ Commercial and residential manual-operated dumbwaiters. 800-232-2177. www.silentservant.com

**Powerlift,** P.O. Box 4390, Georgetown, CA 95634: Free brochure ◆ Dumbwaiters, wheelchair and stairway lifts, and elevators. 800-409-LIFT. www.dumbwaiters.com

**Whitco/Vincent Whitney Company,** 60 Liberty Ship Way, Sausalito, CA 94966: Free information ◆ Residential and commercial hand-operated dumbwaiters. 800-332-3286.

## EDUCATIONAL/TEACHING RESOURCES

**Allied Video Corp.,** P.O. Box 702618, Tulsa, OK 74170: Free information ◆ Educational videos and software. 800-926-5892; 918-587-6477 (in OK). www.alliedvd.com

**Bemiss-Jason Corp.,** P.O. Box 699, Neenah, WI 54956: Free list of retail sources ◆ Tools for creative learning, instructional materials, craft supplies, creative and colorful papers, and more. 414-722-9000. www.bemiss-jason.com

**Different Roads to Learning,** 12 W. 18th St., New York, NY 10011: Free catalog ◆ Learning materials and educational playthings for children with learning challenges. 800-853-1057. www.difflearn.com

**DK Family Learning,** 7800 Southland Blvd., Ste. 200, Orlando, FL 32809: Free catalog ◆ Learning-books, CDs, and videos for children and adults. 800-DK-BOOK-1.

**Educational Resources,** 1550 Executive Dr., P.O. Box 1900, Elgin, IL 60121: Free catalog ◆ Software, disks, peripherals, and other educational resources. 800-624-2926. Custserv@edresources.com

**Educorp CD-ROMs,** 12 B West Main St., Elmsford, NY 10523: Free catalog ◆ Educational and how-to CD-ROMs for the Macintosh and Windows. 800-943-8487. www.educorp.com

**Gamble Music Company,** 312 S. Wabash Ave., Chicago, IL 60604: Free catalog ◆ Music supplies for schools and churches. Also everything for musical programs. 800-621-4290. www.gamblemusic.com

**The Home School,** P.O. Box 308, North Chelmsford, MA 01863: Free catalog ◆ Curriculum and other educational materials for home schools. 800-788-1221.

**Judy/Instructo,** Division Frank Schaffer Publications, 23740 Hawthorne Blvd., Torrance, CA 90509: Free catalog ◆ Classroom teaching aids and resources. 800-421-5565.

**Kimbo Educational,** P.O. Box 477, Long Branch, NJ 07740: Free catalog ◆ Educational cassettes, CDS, records, videos, read-alongs, and filmstrips for children. 800-631-2187. www.kimboed.com

**Learning How,** 8895 McGaw Rd., Ste. 200, Columbia, MD 21045: Free catalog ◆ Teaching resources, arts and crafts supplies, workbooks, classroom furniture, teacher's gifts, specialty toys, and supplies for early childhood, middle, and upper grades. 800-675-7627; 410-381-0828 (in MD).

**Fred Levine Productions,** P.O. Box 4010, Portsmouth, NH 03802: Free catalog ◆ Educational videos, toys, books, and CD-ROM software. 800-843-3686.

**Music World,** P.O. Box 352, Midlothian, VA 23115: Free catalog ◆ Music educational resources for teachers. 800-414-8003; 804-272-4250 (in VA).

**Queue Software Inc.,** 338 Commerce Dr., Fairfield, CT 06432: Free catalog ◆ Educational CD-ROMs and software for DOS, Windows, and the Macintosh. 800-232-2224; 203-335-0906 (in CT).

**Redleaf Press,** 450 N. Syndicate, Ste. 5, St. Paul, MN 55104: Free catalog ◆ Resources for early childhood professionals. 800-423-8309.

**Rex Games Inc.,** 530 Howard St., Ste. 100, San Francisco, CA 94105: Free brochure ◆ Games, puzzles, and toys that teach and entertain. 800-542-6375; 415-777-2900 (in CA). www.rexgames.com

**Special Products Corp.,** 1081 S. Main St., Ste. 186, Cheshire, CT 06410: Free catalog ◆ Instructional, educational, motivational, and inspirational videos and CD-ROMs. 203-271-0470.

**Sybervision,** One Sanson St., Ste. 810, San Francisco, CA 94104: Free information ◆ Foreign language learning programs on cassettes. 800-777-8077. www.sybervision.com

**ZPG Population Education Program,** 1400 16th St. NW, Ste. 320, Washington, DC 20036: Free brochure ◆ Environmental curriculum resources for science, social studies, and math. 800-POP-1956; 202-332-2200 (in DC metro area).

## EGG CRAFTING

**Brownie's Bazaar,** Karen Bennett, P.O. Box 485, Fraser, MI 48026: Free brochure ◆ Ukrainian Easter egg dyes, crafted Easter eggs, and supplies. 810-415-8820. pages.prodigy.com/esuark/pysanky.htm

**Eggs by Byrd,** Rt. 2, Box 2030, Wappapello, MO 63966: Catalog $4.50 ◆ Egg decorating supplies. 800-235-3447.

**Metzer Farms,** 26000 Old Stage Rd., Gonzales, CA 93926: Free information ◆ Blown goose and duck eggs. 408-679-2355. metzer@metzerfarms.com

**Olympia Potters & Artists Supply Inc.,** 1822 Harrison Ave. NW, Olympia, WA 98502: Free information ◆ Ukrainian egg decorating and candle-making supplies. 888-943-5332; 360-943-5332 (in WA). webdb.com/opas

**Schiltz Goose Farm,** 7 Oak St. West, P.O. Box 267, Sisseton, SD 57262: Free information ◆ Decorating supplies, tools, egg stands, and blown goose eggs in jumbo, X-large, large, and regular sizes. 605-698-7651. www.schiltzfoods.com

**Surma Egg Crafting,** 11 E. 7th St., New York, NY 10003: Free catalog ◆ Dyes, tools, supplies, and kits for Ukrainian Easter egg decorating. 212-477-0729. www.brama.com/SURMA

## ELECTRIC GENERATORS & ENGINES

**Apollo Diesel Generators,** 833 W. 17th St., #3, Costa Mesa, CA 92627: Free information ◆ Lightweight high-performance diesel generators. 714-650-1240.

**China Diesel Imports,** 15749 Lyons Valley Rd., Jamul, CA 92035: Free catalog ◆ Diesel generators and parts for an economical power source. 619-699-1995.

**Engine Mart,** 2642 Newfound, Merritt Island, FL 32952: Catalog $2 ◆ Engines.

**Generac Corp.,** Box 8, Waukesha, WI 53187: Free information ◆ Emergency electricity-generating source. 414-968-2561.

**Kohler Company,** 444 Highland Dr., Kohler, WI 53044: Catalog $3 (request list of retail sources) ◆ Automatic standby generators. 800-220-2291. www.kohlerco.com

**MTS Power Products,** 4501 NW 27th Ave., Miami, FL 33142: Free information ◆ Ready-to-work diesel generators. 800-541-7677.

**Northern Hydraulics,** P.O. Box 1219, Burnsville, MN 55337: Free catalog ◆ Electric generators and gas engines. 800-533-5545. www.northern-online.com

**Smith's Engines,** Rt. 1, Box 153, Clifton, TX 76634: Catalog $2 ◆ Small engine parts.

## ELECTRICAL SUPPLIES

**Barnett Inc.,** 333 Lenox Ave., Jacksonville, FL 32254: Free catalog ◆ Plumbing, HVAC, hardware, and electrical products. 904-384-6530. www.bntt.com

**Dale Electric Supply,** P.O. Box 305, Glen Falls, NY 12801: Free catalog ◆ Electrical equipment, supplies, and tools. 800-833-8788; 800-462-7733 (in NY); 518-793-4927 (local).

**Ericson Manufacturing Company,** 4215 Hamann Pkwy., P.O. Box 800, Willoughby, OH 44094: Free list of retail sources ◆ Safety electrical specialties. 800-ERICSON.

**Marlin P. Jones & Associates,** P.O. Box 12685, Lake Park, FL 33403: Free catalog ◆ Electrical and electronics components. 407-848-8236. www.electricnet.com/cofolder/mpjones.htm

**Wiremold Company,** 60 Woodlawn St., West Hartford, CT 06110: Free information ◆ Fixtures, switches, controls, and grounding outlets for installation without having to break into walls or ceilings. 800-621-0049.

## ELECTRONICS EQUIPMENT

### Components & Equipment

**Abacom Technologies,** 32 Blair Athol Crescent, Etobicoke, Ontario, Canada M9A 1X5: Free catalog ◆ Radio data modules. Includes transmitters, receivers, and transceivers. 416-236 3858.

**Ace Communications,** 7399 N. Shadeland Rd., Indianapolis, IN 46266: Free information ◆ Electronics equipment. 800-445-7717. 207.221.37.99/1order.htm

**All Electronics Corp.,** P.O. Box 567, Van Nuys, CA 91408: Free catalog ◆ New and surplus electronics parts and supplies. 800-826-5432; 818-904-0524 (in CA). www.allcorp.com

**Allied Electronics,** 7134 Columbia Gateway Dr., Ste. 200, Columbia, MD 21046: Free catalog ◆ Electronics parts, tools, and books. 800-433-5700. www.allied.avnet.com

**Alltech Electronics Company Inc.,** 2618 Temple Heights, Oceanside, CA 92056: Free catalog ◆ Computer components and surplus electronics. 619-724-2404. www.allelec.com

**Alltronics,** 2300 Zanker Rd., San Jose, CA 95131: Catalog $3 ◆ Electronics components and test equipment. 408-943-9773. www.alltronics.com

**American Electronics Inc.,** 164 Southpark Blvd., P.O. Box 301, Greenwood, IN 46142: Free information ◆ Electronics components. 800-872-1373.

**ARS Electronics,** 7110 de Celis Pl., Van Nuys, CA 91409: Catalog $2.50 ◆ Electronics equipment and tubes. 800-422-4250.

**Brigar Electronics,** 7-9 Alice St., Binghamton, NY 13904: Free information ◆ Electronics parts. 607-723-3111. members./aol.com/brigar2/brigar.html

**Calcera,** P.O. Box 489, Belmont, CA 94002: Free information ◆ Surplus electronics components. 800-257-5549.

**Capital Electronics Inc.,** 303 Sherman St., Ackley, IA 50601: Free information ◆ Printed circuit boards and other parts. 515-847-3888. www.capital-elec.com

**Circuit Specialists Inc.,** 220 S. Country Club Dr., Mesa, AZ 85210: Free catalog ◆ Electronics equipment. 800-528-1417. www.cir.com

**Communications Electronics Inc.,** P.O. Box 1045, Ann Arbor, MI 48106: Free information ◆ Scanners, transceivers, and emergency broadcast, weather station, monitoring, and other electronics. 800-USA-SCAN. www.usascan.com

**Consolidated Electronics Inc.,** 705 Watervliet Ave., P.O. Box 2, Dayton, OH 45420: Catalog $5 ◆ Semi-conductors, tools, soldering and testing equipment, and other electronics. 800-543-3568.

**Contact East,** 335 Willow St. South, North Andover, MA 01845: Free catalog ◆ Tools and equipment for testing, repairing, and assembling electronics equipment. 800-225-5334; 978-682-2000 (in MA). www.contact-east.com

**Dalbani Electronics,** 4225 NW 72nd Ave., Miami, FL 33166: Free catalog ◆ Electronics components. 800-325-2264; 305-716-1016 (in FL).

**Debco Electronics,** 4025 Edwards Rd., Cincinnati, OH 45209: Free information ◆ Components and tools. 800-423-4499.

**Derf Electronics,** 1 Biehn St., New Rochelle, NY 10801: Free catalog ◆ Surplus electronics components. 800-431-2912; 914-235-4600 (in NY). www.derf.com

**Digi-Key Corp.,** 701 Brooks Ave. South, P.O. Box 677, Thief River Falls, MN 56701: Free catalog ◆ Electronics components. 800-344-4539. www.digikey.com

**The Electronic Goldmine,** P.O. Box 5408, Scottsdale, AZ 85261: Free catalog ◆ Electronics components, kits, and accessories. 800-445-0697; 602-451-7454 (in AZ). www.goldmine-elec.com

**Electronix Express,** 365 Blair Rd., Avenel, NJ 07001: Free catalog ◆ Electronic equipment, tools, and components. 800-872-2225; 908-381-8020 (in NJ). www.elexp.com

**Fair Radio Sales Company Inc.,** P.O. Box 1105, Lima, OH 45802: Free information ◆ Surplus electronics parts. 419-227-657. alpha.wcoll.com/~fairadio

**Gateway Electronics,** 8123 Page Blvd., St. Louis, MO 63130: Free information ◆ New and surplus electronics equipment. 314-427-6116. www.gatewayelex.com

**Halted Electronic Supply,** 3500 Ryder St., Santa Clara, CA 95051: Catalog $1 ◆ Electronics equipment. 800-442-5833. www.halted.com

**Haltek Electronics,** 1062 Linda Vista Ave., Mountain View, CA 94043: Free information ◆ New, used, and surplus electronics equipment. 415-969-0510.

**Hosfelt Electronics Inc.,** 2700 Sunset Blvd., Steubenville, OH 43952: Free catalog ◆ Electronics components. 800-524-6464; 614-264-6464 (in OH).

**JAMECO Electronic and Computer Products,** 1355 Shoreway Rd., Belmont, CA 94002: Free information ◆ Electronic and computer components. 800-831-4242. www.jameco.com

**Jan Crystals,** P.O. Box 60017, Fort Myers, FL 33906: Free catalog ◆ Crystals for radio operation and experimenters. 800-JAN-XTAL; 941-936-2397 (in FL).

**Javanco,** 501 12th Ave. South, Nashville, TN 37203: Free catalog ◆ Electronics components and equipment. 615-244-4444. www.javanco.com

**JDR Microdevices,** 1850 S. 10th St., San Jose, CA 95112: Free information ◆ Electronics components, micro-devices, tools, chips, and computer equipment. 800-538-5000. www.jdr.com

**Marlin P. Jones & Associates,** P.O. Box 12685, Lake Park, FL 33403: Free catalog ◆ Electrical and electronics components. 407-848-8236. www.electricnet.com/cofolder/mpjones.htm

**Joseph Electronics,** 8830 N. Milwaukee Ave., Niles, IL 60648: Free catalog ◆ Electronics components, test instruments, tools, and soldering equipment. 800-323-5925; 847-297-4200 (in IL).

**K & F Electronics Inc.,** 33041 Groesbeck, Fraser, MI 48026: Free information ◆ Printed circuit boards. 810-294-8720. www.circuitboards.com

**K & K Electronics,** 109 W. 23rd St., Alliance, OH 44601: Free information ◆ Printed circuit boards. 800-356-6238.

**The M.O.O. Corp.,** 809 W. Estes, Schaumberg, IL 60193: Free catalog ◆ Surplus electronic components. 800-323-8962.

**MCM Electronics,** 650 E. Congress Park Dr., Centerville, OH 45459: Free catalog ◆ Test equipment, computer and telephone accessories, TV and electronics components, and speakers. 800-543-4330. www.mcmelectronics.com

**Mendelson Electronics Company Inc.,** 340 E. 1st St., Dayton, OH 45402: Free catalog ◆ Electronics components. 800-422-3525; 937-461-3525 (in OH).

**MFJ Enterprises,** P.O. Box 494, Mississippi State, MS 39762: Free catalog ◆ Equipment for electronics experimenters and amateur radio operators. 800-647-1800. www.mfjenterprises.com

**Mouser Electronics,** P.O. Box 699, Mansfield, TX 76063: Free catalog ◆ Electronics components. 800-992-9943. www.mouser.com

**New England Circuit Sales,** 4 Technology Dr., Peabody, MA 01960: Free information ◆ Surplus electronics components. 800-922-NECS.

**Ocean Electronics,** P.O. Box 90, Buford, GA 30518: Free catalog ◆ Equipment and accessories. 800-373-9758; 770-271-5753 (in GA). www.randomc.com/~oceanel

**Ocean State Electronics,** P.O. Box 1458, Westerly, RI 02891: Free catalog ◆ Electronics components, kits, test equipment, and books. 800-866-6626.

**Parts Express,** 340 E. 1st St., Dayton, OH 45042: Free catalog ◆ Parts for electronics projects, repair, experimentation, and research. 800-338-0531; 937-222-0173 (in OH). www.parts-express.com

**PCBoards,** 2110 14th Ave. South, Birmingham, AL 35205: Free information ◆ Printed circuit design software and supplies. 800-473-7227; 205-933-1122 (in AL).

**PolyPhaser Corp.,** P.O. Box 9000, 2225 Park Pl., Minden, NV 89423: Free information ◆ Grounding and lightning protection equipment. 800-325-7170; 702-782-2511 (in NV).

**Prime Electronic Components Inc.,** 150 W. Industry Ct., Deer Park, NY 11729: Free information ◆ Electronics components. 516-254-0101. www.primelec.com

**R.A. Enterprises,** 2260 De La Cruz Blvd., Santa Clara, CA 95050: Free information ◆ Surplus and new test equipment, electrical-mechanical devices, and other electronics. 408-986-8286.

**Radio Shack,** Division Tandy Corp., One Tandy Center, Fort Worth, TX 76102: Free information ◆ Electronics components, science kits, computers, stereo equipment, toys, and games. 817-390-3011. www.radioshack.com

**RF Parts,** 435 S. Pacific St., San Marcos, CA 92069: Free information ◆ Power transistors and parts for amateur, marine, and commercial radio operation. 760-744-0700. rfp@rfparts.com

**Scanner World USA,** 10 New Scotland Ave., Albany, NY 12208: Free information ◆ Scanners. 518-436-9606. www.scannerworld.com

**Sescom Inc.,** 2100 Ward Dr., Henderson, NV 89015: Free information ◆ Sheet metal boxes for electronics construction. 702-565-3400. www.sescom.com

**3M Electronic Products Division,** P.O. Box 3064, Cedar Rapids, IA 52406: Free information ◆ Solder-less breadboards. 800-328-0016.

**Tucker Electronics,** P.O. Box 551419, Dallas, TX 75355: Free information ◆ Surplus electronics equipment. 800-527-4642; 972-348-8800 (in TX). www.tucker.com

**Unicorn Electronics,** 1142 State Rt. 18, Aliquippa, PA 15001: Free information ◆ Electronics components, tools and vises, soldering products, batteries, robotic kits, and fiber optics training aids. 800-824-3432. unielect@aol.com

**Visitect Inc.,** P.O. Box 14156, Fremont, CA 94539: Free information ◆ Miniature transmitters and receivers. 510-651-1425.

## Kits & Plans

**Almost All Digital Electronics,** 1412 Elm St. SE, Auburn, WA 98902: Free information ◆ Electronic kits. 253-351-9316. www.aade.com

**Amazing Concepts,** Box 716, Amherst, NH 03031: Catalog $1 ◆ Easy-to-assemble sub-miniature FM transmitters for voice transmission over telephones. 603-673-4730. www.amazing1.com

**Berger's Equipment,** P.O. Box 271031, Concord, CA 94527: Free catalog ◆ Educational electronic kits. 800-588-KITS.

**Black Feather Electronics,** 10841 Noel St., Ste. 106, Los Alamitos, CA 90720: Free information ◆ Electronics kits, security cameras, parts, and components. 714-236-1776. www.blackfeather.com

**Cal West Supply Inc.,** 31320 Via Colinas, #105, Westlake Village, CA 91362: Free information ◆ Electronics kits. 800-892-8000.

**Carl's Electronics,** P.O. Box 722, Leominster, MA 01453: Free catalog ◆ Electronic kits and plans. 978-840-8834. www.electronickits.com

**Centerpointe Electronics Inc.,** 5241 Lincoln Ave., Cypress, CA 90630: Free catalog ◆ Educational electronic kits. 800-272-2737; 714-821-1100 (in CA). www.cpcares.com

**Consumertronics,** P.O. Box 23097, Albuquerque, NM 87192: Catalog $2 ◆ Electronics kits and parts. 505-237-2073. www.tsc-global.com

**Dan's Small Parts & Kits,** Box 3634, Missoula, MT 59806: Free information ◆ Electronic kits and parts for amateur radio in small quantities. 406-258-2782. www.fix.net/dans.html

**DC Electronics,** 2334 N. Scottsdale Rd., Scottsdale, AZ 85257: Free information ◆ Electronics kits. 602-945-7736.

**Edlie Electronics,** 2700 Hempstead Tnpk., Levittown, NY 11756: Free catalog ◆ Electronics kits, parts, and test equipment. 516-735-3330.

**The Electronic Goldmine,** P.O. Box 5408, Scottsdale, AZ 85261: Free catalog ◆ Electronics components, kits, and accessories. 800-445-0697; 602-451-7454 (in AZ). www.goldmine-elec.com

**Electronic Rainbow,** 6227 Coffman Rd., Indianapolis, IN 46268: Free information ◆ Easy-to-assemble kits. 317-291-7262. www.rainbowkits.com

**Elekit Company,** 1160 Mahalo Pl., Ste. B, Rancho Dominguez, CA 90220: Free information ◆ Educational electronic robot and science kits. 310-638-7970.

**GO-4-KITS,** 292 Queen St., Kingston, Ontario, Canada K7K 1B8: Free information ◆ Electronic project kits. 888-GO-4-KITS. www.qkits.com

**Graymark,** P.O. Box 2015, Tustin, CA 92681: Free catalog ◆ Easy-to-build robot kits. 800-854-7393. www.labvolt.com

**Heathkit Educational Systems,** 455 Riverview Dr., Benton Harbor, MI 49022: Free catalog ◆ Electronics kits. 800-253-0570. www.heathkit.com

**IEC Electronic Kits,** P.O. Box 52347, Knoxville, TN 37950: Free catalog with long SASE ◆ PC micro controller and surveillance kits. 800-417-6689. www.irmicrolink.com

**Images Company,** P.O. Box 140742, Staten Island, NY 10314: Free information ◆ Science and electronic supplies. 718-698-8305.

**Information Unlimited,** P.O. Box 716, Amherst, NH 03031: Catalog $1 ◆ Lasers, communication equipment, Tesla coils and experiments, mini radios, rocket equipment, flying saucers, and other kits. 603-673-4730. www.amazing1.com

**Lynxmotion,** 104 Patridge Rd., Pekin, IL 61554: Free catalog ◆ Robotic kits. 309-382-1816. www.lynxmotion.com

**Mark V Electronics Inc.,** 8019 E. Slauson Ave., Montebello, CA 90640: Free catalog ◆ Electronics kits for beginning, intermediate, and advanced experimenters. 213-888-8988. www.mark5co.com

**Meredith Instruments,** P.O. Box 1724, Glendale, AZ 85301: Free catalog ◆ Lasers and optical equipment, parts, and accessories. 602-934-9387. www.mi-lasers.com

**Micro Kits,** 177 Telegraph Rd., Ste. 680, Bellingham, WA 98226: Free information ◆ Educational kits. 800-474-7644.

**Midwest Laser Products,** P.O. Box 262, Frankfort, IL 60423: Free catalog ◆ Laser equipment. 815-464-0085. www.midwest-laser.com

**Mondo-tronics,** 4286 Redwood Hwy., #226, San Rafael, CA 94903: Free brochure ◆ Miniature robot kits, books, parts, and more. 800-374-5764; 415-491-4600 (in CA). www.RobotStore.com

**MWK Industries,** 1269 W. Pomona Rd., Bldg. 112, Corona, CA 91720: Free catalog ◆ Laser equipment, power supplies, optics and light shows, and books. 909-278-0563. www.mwkindustries.com

**Ocean State Electronics,** P.O. Box 1458, Westerly, RI 02891: Free catalog ◆ Electronics components, kits, test equipment, and books. 800-866-6626.

**Radio Adventures Inc.,** Main St., Seneca, PA 16346: Free information ◆ Classic radio accessories, transmitter and test equipment kits, and high-frequency receivers. 814-677-7221.

**Radio Shack,** Division Tandy Corp., One Tandy Center, Fort Worth, TX 76102: Free information ◆ Electronics components, science kits, computers, stereo equipment, toys, and games. 817-390-3011. www.radioshack.com

**Ramsey Electronics Inc.,** 793 Canning Pkwy., Victor, NY 14564: Free information ◆ Test equipment and easy-to-assemble electronics kits. 716-924-4560. www.ramseyelectronics.com

**Robot Store,** Mondo-tronics Inc., 4286 Redwood Hwy., #226, San Rafael, CA 94903: Free catalog ◆ Robot kits, parts, videos, and supplies. 800-374-5764; 415-491-4600 (in CA). info@mondo.com

**Silicon Valley Surplus,** 1273 Industrial Pkwy. West, Bldg. 460, P.O. Box 55125, Hayward, CA 94545: Free information ◆ Light and motion projects, laser applications, computer interface equipment, and other kits. 510-582-6602.

**Solarbotics,** 179 Harvest Glen Way NE, Calgary, Alberta, Canada T3K 3J4: Free brochure ◆ Easy-to-build robotic kits and equipment. 403-818-3374. www.solarbotics.com

**Unicorn Electronics,** 1142 State Rt. 18, Aliquippa, PA 15001: Free information ◆ Electronics components, tools and vises, soldering products, batteries, robotic kits, and fiber optics training aids. 800-824-3432. unielect@aol.com

**Weeder Technologies,** P.O. Box 2426, Fort Walton Beach, FL 32549: Free information ◆ Kits for electronics hobbyists. 850-863-5723.

**Xandi Electronics,** P.O. Box 25647, Tempe, AZ 85285: Catalog $2 ◆ Satellite TV receivers, voice disguisers, FM bugs, telephone transmitters, phone snoops, and other easy-to-build kits. 800-336-7389.

## Test Equipment

**ABC Electronics,** 315 7th Ave. N., Minneapolis, MN 55401: Free information ◆ Test equipment and components. 612-332-2378. SURP1@VISI.COM

**Advantage Instruments Corp.,** P.O. Box 20235, Beaumont, TX 77720: Free catalog ◆ Test equipment. 409-842-0300. www.advantage-instruments.com

**Alfa Electronics,** P.O. Box 8089, Princeton, NJ 08543: Free information ◆ Test and measuring equipment, power supplies, and other electronics. 800-526-2532. www.alfaelectronics.com

**Wm. B. Allen Supply Company,** 300 N. Rampart St., New Orleans, LA 70112: Free information ◆ Multi-purpose test equipment, replacement probes, and electronics components. 800-535-9593.

**Alltronics,** 2300 Zanker Rd., San Jose, CA 95131: Catalog $3 ◆ Test equipment and electronics components. 408-943-9773. www.alltronics.com

**AT&T Capital Corp.,** 1830 W. Airfield Dr., P.O. Box 619260, DFW Airport, TX 75261: Free information ◆ Test and measuring instruments. 800-874-7123.

**B.C. Electronics,** P.O. Box 744, Lake Forest, CA 94630: Free catalog ◆ Test equipment. 800-532-3221.

**Bell Electronics,** P.O. Box 1762, San Mateo, CA 94401: Free information ◆ Reconditioned electronic test equipment. 415-579-1711. www.bellelect.com

**C & H Sales Company,** 2176 E. Colorado Blvd., Pasadena, CA 91107: Free catalog ◆ Test equipment. 800-325-9465. www.candhsales.com

**C & S Sales Inc.,** 150 W. Carpenter Ave., Wheeling, IL 60090: Free catalog ◆ Test equipment. 800-292-7711; 847-541-0710 (in IL). www.elenco.com/cs_sales

**Contact East,** 335 Willow St. South, North Andover, MA 01845: Free catalog ◆ Tools for testing, repairing, and assembling electronics equipment. 800-225-5334; 978-682-2000 (in MA). www.contact-east.com

**Danbar Sales Company,** 14455 N. 79th St., Scottsdale, AZ 85260: Free catalog ◆ Test equipment. 602-483-6202.

**Davilyn Corp.,** 13406 Saticoy St., North Hollywood, CA 91605: Free information ◆ Test equipment. 800-235-6222; 818-787-3334 (in CA). www.Davilyn.com/Electronics

**Electro Tool Inc.,** 9103 Gillman, Livonia, MI 48150: Free information ◆ Tools and electronics test equipment. 313-422-1221.

**Electronix Express,** 365 Blair Rd., Avenel, NJ 07001: Free information ◆ Parts, test equipment, and tools. 800-972-2225; 908-381-8020 (in NJ). www.elexp.com

**Fotronic Corp.,** P.O. Box 708, Medford, MA 02155: Free information ◆ New and pre-owned test equipment. 800-996-3837.

**Global Specialties,** 70 Fulton Terrace, New Haven, CT 06512: Free information ◆ Compact multi-meters that measure AC and DC voltage, current, resistance, and check diodes and continuity. 800-572-1028. www.globalspecialties.com

**GoldStar Precision,** 13013 E. 166th St., Cerritos, CA 90701: Free information ◆ Test equipment. 310-404-0101.

**Helps Instruments,** 2631 Hillside Ave., Narc, CA 91760: Free information ◆ Used test equipment. 909-279-7347.

**JDR Microdevices,** 1850 S. 10th St., San Jose, CA 95112: Free information ◆ Multi-purpose test equipment. 800-538-5000. www.jdr.com

**Joseph Electronics,** 8830 N. Milwaukee Ave., Niles, IL 60648: Free catalog ◆ Multi-purpose test equipment. 800-323-5925; 847-297-4200 (in IL).

**MCM Electronics,** 650 E. Congress Park Dr., Centerville, OH 45459: Free catalog ◆ Test equipment, computer and telephone accessories, speakers, and parts. 800-543-4330. www.mcmelectronics.com

**Metric Equipment Sales Inc.,** 351 Foster City Blvd., Foster City, CA 94404: Free information ◆ Refurbished test and measuring equipment. 800-432-3424. www.metricsales.com

**Ocean State Electronics,** P.O. Box 1458, Westerly, RI 02891: Free catalog ◆ Electronics components, kits, test equipment, and books. 800-866-6626.

**R & S Surplus,** 1050 E. Cypress St., Covina, CA 91724: Free information ◆ Surplus test equipment. 626-967-0846. www.rssurplus.com

**Specialized Products Company,** 1100 S. Kimball Ave., Southlake, TX 76092: Free catalog ◆ Diagnostic test equipment, tools, and supplies. 800-866-5353; 817-329-6647 (in TX). www.specializedproducts.com

**Sun Equipment Corp.,** P.O. Box 97903, Raleigh, NC 27624: Free catalog ◆ Test equipment. 800-870-1955; 919-870-1955 (in NC). sunequipco@lpass.net

**Tech Systems Electronics Inc.,** 1309 Hwy. 71, Ballmer, NJ 07719: Free information ◆ Reconditioned test equipment. 800-435-1516. www.tec-systems.com

**Techni-Tool,** P.O. Box 368, 5 Apollo Rd., Plymouth Meeting, PA 19462: Free catalog of retail sources ◆ Hand tools, production aids, test instruments, safety aids, and other equipment. 800-832-4860; 610-941-2400 (in PA). www.techni-tool.com

**Test Equipment Depot,** P.O. Box 708, Medford, MA 02155: Free information ◆ New and pre-owned test equipment. 800-996-3837. afoti@fotronic.com

**Test Equipment Plus,** 3331 W. Bright Terrace, Tucson, AZ 85741: Free information ◆ Used test equipment. 520-575-6967.

**Test Equipment Sales,** 66 Chase Rd., Londonberry, NH 03053: Free list ◆ New and surplus test equipment. 603-434-2544. www.tesales.com

**Test Lab Company,** 1066 Linda Vista Ave., Mountain View, CA 94043: Free information ◆ Test equipment. 800-442-5835; 415-969-1142 (in CA). www.testlabco.com

**Toronto Surplus & Scientific,** 608 Gordon Baker Rd., Willowdale, Ontario, Canada M2H 3B4: Free information ◆ Test equipment, experimental accessories, and electronics. 416-490-8865.

**Wavetek Corp.,** 9045 Balboa Ave., San Diego, CA 92123: Free information ◆ Handheld digital multi-meters. 619-279-2200.

**Western Test Systems,** 530 Compton St., Unit C, Broomfield, CO 80020: Free information ◆ New and used test equipment. 303-438-9662.

### Tools & Accessories

**Electro Tool Inc.,** 9103 Gillman, Livonia, MI 48150: Free information ◆ Tools and electronics test equipment. 313-422-1221.

**Electronix Express,** 365 Blair Rd., Avenel, NJ 07001: Free information ◆ Parts, test equipment, and tools. 800-972-2225; 908-381-8020 (in NJ). www.elexp.com

**W.S. Jenks & Son,** 1933 Montana Ave. NE, Washington, DC 20002: Free catalog ◆ Hand and power tools for electronics. 202-529-6020. www.wsjenks.com

**Jensen Tools Inc.,** 7815 S. 46th St., Phoenix, AZ 85044: Free catalog ◆ Precision tools for electronics. 800-426-1194; 602-968-6231 (in AZ). www.jensentools.com

**Joseph Electronics,** 8830 N. Milwaukee Ave., Niles, IL 60648: Free catalog ◆ Electronics components, test instruments, tools, and soldering equipment. 800-323-5925; 847-297-4200 (in IL).

**Specialized Products Company,** 1100 S. Kimball Ave., Southlake, TX 76092: Free catalog ◆ Diagnostic test equipment, tools, and supplies. 800-866-5353; 817-329-6647 (in TX). www.specializedproducts.com

**Technic-Tool,** P.O. Box 368, 5 Apollo Rd., Plymouth Meeting, PA 19462: Free list of retail sources ◆ Hand tools, production aids, test instruments, safety aids, and other equipment. 800-832-4860; 610-941-2400 (in PA). www.techni-tool.com

## ELECTROPLATING

**Caswell Electroplating in Miniature,** 4336 Rt. 31, Palmyra, NY 14522: Free information ◆ Electroplating kits for nickel, chrome, and copper. 315-597-5140. www.caswellplating.com

**Dalmar,** 11759 S. Cleveland Ave., Ste. 28, Fort Myers, FL 33907: Free information ◆ Brush or tank electroplating kits for chrome, gold, nickel, copper, or silver. 941-275-6540. www.dalmarplating.com

**Eastwood Company,** 580 Lancaster Ave., Box 3014, Malvern, PA 19355: Free catalog ◆ Electroplating kits. 800-343-9353. www.ewab.com

**Edmund Scientific Company,** Edscorp Bldg., Barrington, NJ 08007: Free catalog ◆ Electroplating kits. 609-547-8880. www.edsci.com

**Estes-Simmons Silverplating Ltd.,** 1050 Northside Dr. NW, Atlanta, GA 30318: Free brochure ◆ Silver repair and plating. 800-645-4193. info@estes-simmons.com

**New England International Gems,** 188 Pollard St., Billerica, MA 01862: Free catalog ◆ Casting and plating equipment. 978-863-8331.

**Strassen Plating Company,** 3619 Walton Ave., Cleveland, OH 44113: Free information ◆ Metal polishing and brass, nickel, and chrome plating. 216-961-1525.

## ENERGY CONSERVATION

**Energy Savers,** Solar Components Corp., 121 Valley St., Manchester, NH 03103: Catalog $2 ◆ Energy-saving products. 603-668-8186.

**Real Goods,** 555 Leslie St., Ukiah, CA 95482: Free catalog ◆ Solar-operated tank-less water heater, water-saving appliances, composting toilets, gas appliances, and recycled paper products. 800-762-7325. www.realgoods.com

## ENGRAVING, ETCHING, & SANDBLASTING

**Alpha Supply,** P.O. Box 2133, Bremerton, WA 98310: Catalog $7 ◆ Engraving and jewelry-making tools and supplies, and casting, faceting, and lapidary equipment. 800-257-4211; 360-373-3302 (in WA).

**B. Rush Apple Company,** 3855 W. Kennedy Blvd., Tampa, FL 33609: Free price list ◆ Engraving tools. 813-870-3180.

**Auto-Etch,** 325 Cherry St., Rear, Philadelphia, PA 19106: Information $2 ◆ Benchtop auto-etching system.

**B & B Etching Products Inc.,** 18700 N. 107th Ave., Sun City, AZ 85373: Free catalog ◆ Etching creme and supplies for glass and mirrors. 888-ETCHALL. www.etchall.com

**B & B Products Inc.,** 18700 N. 107th Ave., #13, Sun City, AZ 85373: Free information ◆ Glass and mirror etching supplies. 888-ETCHALL. www.etchall.com

**Ken Brown Studio,** P.O. Box 22, McKinney, TX 75069: Catalog $1 ◆ Calligraphy supplies and engraving equipment . 800-654-6100. www.kenbrownink.com

**Brownells Inc.,** 200 S. Front St., Montezuma, IA 50171: Free catalog ◆ Engraving tools. 515-623-5401. brownells.com/brownells

**Crystal Blanc,** 225 Gap Way, Erlanger, KY 41018: Free catalog ◆ Glass blanks for engraving. 800-806-4808.

**Eastern Art Glass,** P.O. Box 9, Wyckoff, NJ 07481: Catalog $2 (refundable) ◆ Stained glass kits and glass etching, engraving, and crafting supplies. 800-872-3458. www.etchworld.com

**Gamblin,** P.O. Box 625, Portland, OR 97207: Free brochure of retail sources ◆ Oil paints, oil painting mediums, and etching inks. 503-228-9763. www.gamblincolors.com

**Glendo Corporation,** 900 Overlander Rd., P.O. Box 1153, Emporia, KS 66801: Free catalog ◆ Multi-purpose equipment for jewelry-making, diamond setters, engravers, and others. 800-835-3519. www.glendo.com

**Graphic Chemical & Ink Company,** P.O. Box 27, Villa Park, IL 60181: Free catalog ◆ Print-making supplies for etching, block printing, lithography, and other reproduction processes. 630-832-6004.

**GRS Tools,** 900 Overlander Rd., P.O. Box 1153, Emporia, KS 66801: Free catalog ◆ Engraving tools. 800-835-3519.

**H & L Products,** 1410 S. Bentley, #206, Los Angeles, CA 90025: Free information ◆ Electric engraver for plastics, wood, metals, and glass.

**Indian Jewelers Supply Company,** P.O. Box 1774, Gallup, NM 87305: Catalog $6 ◆ Precious and base metals, findings, metal-working equipment, lapidary and engraving tools and supplies, semiprecious stones, shells, and coral. 505-722-4451.

**Ken Jantz Supply,** P.O. Box 584, Davis, OK 73030: Catalog $5 ◆ Engraving tools. 580-369-2315. www.jantzsupply.com

**Marking Methods Inc.,** 301 S. Raymond Ave., Alhambra, CA 91803: Free information ◆ Acid-free electro-chemical etching-marking kit. 818-282-8823.

**Neycraft,** Division of Ney, Ney Industrial Park, Bloomfield, CT 06002: Free information ◆ Engraving tools. 800-538-4593.

**Rayzist Photomask Inc.,** 955 Park Center Dr., Vista, CA 92083: Free catalog ◆ Sand carving equipment, glass and crystal blanks, and other supplies. 800-729-9478; 760-727-8185 (in CA). www.rayzist.com

**SCM Sandblasting,** W140 N5946 Lilly Rd., Menomonee Falls, WI 53051: Free information ◆ Easy-to-use, no experience necessary engraving tool. 800-755-0261. www17.scmsysteminc.com/scm/default.html

**Technical Papers Corp.,** P.O. Box 546, Dedham, MA 02027: Free catalog ◆ Sheets and rolls of handmade rice paper in prints, solid, and multi-colors for all types of artistic and block printing, etching, lithography, and silk screening. 781-461-1111. www.technicalpapers.com

**Viramontez Engraving,** 601 Springfield Dr., Albany, GA 31707: Free catalog ◆ Engraving tools. 912-432-9683. sgtvira@aol.com

## EXERCISE EQUIPMENT

**Access to Recreation Inc.,** 8 Sandra Ct., Newbury Park, CA 91320: Free catalog ◆ Adaptive exercise equipment for the disabled. 800-634-4351.

**Ajay Leisure Products Inc.,** 1501 E. Wisconsin St., Delavan, WI 53115: Free list of retail sources ◆ Monitoring aids and weight training, body building, and exercise equipment. 800-558-3276; 414-728-5521 (in WI).

**All Pro Exercise Products,** 135 Hazelwood Dr., Jericho, NY 11753: Free list of retail sources ◆ Home exercise equipment. 800-735-9287; 516-938-9287 (in NY).

**American Athletic Inc.,** 200 American Ave., Jefferson, IA 50129: Free information ◆ Monitoring aids, home gymnasiums, and weight training, body building, and exercise equipment. 800-247-3978; 515-386-3125 (in IA). www.americanathletic.com

**Austin Athletic Equipment Corp.,** 705 Bedford Ave., Box 423, Bellmore, NY 11710: Free information ◆ Monitoring aids, home gymnasiums, and weight training, body building, and exercise equipment. 516-785-0100.

**The Baby Jogger Company,** P.O. Box 2189, Yakima, WA 98902: Free brochure ◆ Baby Joggers for exercise fun. 800-241-1848; 509-457-0925 (in WA). www.babyjogger.com

**Bauer Sports,** 150 Ocean Rd., Greenland, NH 03840: Free list of retail sources ◆ Monitoring aids, trampolines, weight lifting and exercise equipment, and home gymnasiums. 800-362-3146. www.bauer.com

**Better Health Fitness,** 5302 New Utrecht Ave., Brooklyn, NY 11219: Free information with long SASE ◆ Home gymnasium, exercise and weight lifting equipment, and other body building systems. 718-436-4693.

**BioTech Corp.,** P.O. Box 949, Rocky Hill, CT 06067: Free information ◆ Home fitness equipment. 800-774-3664.

**Body Masters,** P.O. Box 259, Rayne, LA 70578: Free information ◆ Home exercise equipment. 800-325-8964. www.body-masters.com

**BodyBridge,** 6281 S. Park Ave., Tucson, AZ 85706: Free information ◆ Stretching equipment for relaxation and back pain elimination. 800-326-2724. www.bodybridge.com

**Bollinger Industries,** 602 Fountain Pkwy., Grand Prairie, TX 75050: Free information ◆ Home gymnasiums, trampolines, monitoring aids, and other weight training and body building equipment. 800-527-1166. www.bollinger.com

**BSN Sports,** P.O. Box 7726, Dallas, TX 75209: Free information ◆ Equipment for archery, aquatic fitness, baseball, basketball, boxing, field hockey, football, weight lifting, and other sports. 800-527-7510; 972-484-9484 (in TX). www.bsnsports.com

**California Gym Equipment Company,** 14829 Salt Lake Ave., City of Industry, CA 91748: Free list of retail sources ◆ Home gymnasiums, monitoring aids, and weight training, body building, and exercise equipment. 800-824-5210; 818-961-6564 (in CA).

**Concept II Inc.,** 105 Industrial Park Dr., Morrisville, VT 05661: Free list of retail sources ◆ Total body exercise machine. 800-245-5676. www.concept2.com

**Country Technology Inc.,** P.O. Box 87, Gays Mills, WI 54631: Free information ◆ Rehabilitation, sports, and physical fitness products. 608-735-4718.

**Creative Health Products Inc.,** 5148 Saddle Ridge Rd., Plymouth, MI 48170: Free catalog ◆ Exercise bicycles, rowing machines, stethoscopes, thermometers, digital blood pressure units, scales, lung capacity testers, and pulse monitors. 800-742-4478.

**Diamondback Exercise Equipment,** 4030 Via Pescador, Camarillo, CA 93012: Free list of retail sources ◆ Easy-to-operate exercise and stamina-training equipment. www.diamondback.com

**Dynamic Classics Ltd.,** 58 2nd Ave., Brooklyn, NY 11215: Free information ◆ Gymnastic bars, home gymnasiums, and weight training, body building, and exercise equipment. 718-369-4167.

**Escalade Sports,** P.O. Box 889, Evansville, IN 47706: Free catalog ◆ Home fitness equipment. 800-457-3373; 812-467-1200 (in IN).

**Everlast Sports Manufacturing Corp.,** 750 E. 132nd St., Bronx, NY 10454: Free information ◆ Home exercise equipment. 800-221-8777; 718-993-0100 (in NY).

**ExerSpa,** 4216 6th Ave. South, Seattle, WA 98108: Free brochure ◆ Above-ground pool water fitness exerciser, books, videos, and other equipment. 888-EXERSPA.

**Fitness Factory Outlet,** 2875 S. 25th Ave., Broadview, IL 60135: Free catalog ◆ Aerobic and strength training equipment. 800-383-9300. www.fitnessfactory.com

**Fitness To Go Inc.,** 4251 NE Port Dr., Lee Summit, MO 64064: Free information ◆ Motorized and mechanical isokinetic treadmills. 800-821-3126.

**Flaghouse Sports Equipment,** 601 Flaghouse Dr., Hasbrouck Heights, NJ 07604: Free catalog ◆ Physical fitness and gymnastic equipment. Also equipment for camping, playgrounds, and other outdoor activities. 800-793-7900. www.flaghouse.com

**GameTime,** P.O. Box 121, Fort Payne, AL 35967: Free information ◆ Playground and backyard play systems and outdoor fitness equipment. 800-235-2440. www.gametime.com

**Gold's Gym,** 360 Hampton Dr., Venice, CA 90291: Free information ◆ Home exercise equipment. 800-457-5375; 213-392-6004 (in CA). www.goldsonline.com

**GPK Exerciser,** P.O. Box 2636, 9380 Bond Ave., Ste. B, El Cajon, CA 92021: Free brochure ◆ Upper body exerciser for quads. 619-390-5884. www.gpk.com

**Gravity Plus,** P.O. Box 1166, La Jolla, CA 92038: Free catalog ◆ Inversion equipment, books, tables, swings, and other equipment. 800-383-8056; 619-456-0926 (in CA). gravity@san.rr.com

**The Gym,** 591 Camino de la Reina, #709, San Diego, CA 92108: Free information ◆ Fitness equipment. 800-980-2225.

**Heart-Rate Inc.,** 3188 Airway Ave., Ste. E, Costa Mesa, CA 92626: Free brochure ◆ Total body aerobic exercise machine. 800-237-2271. www.heartrateinc.com

**Herb Industries,** 10243 CR 2121, Tyler, TX 75707: Free list of retail sources ◆ Treadmills that include an optional folding model. 903-534-3832.

**Hoist Fitness Systems,** 9990 Empire St., Ste. 130, San Diego, CA 92126: Free list of retail sources ◆ Home exercise equipment. 800-548-5438; 619-578-7676 (in CA).

**Holabird Sports Discounters,** 9220 Pulaski Hwy., Baltimore, MD 21220: Free catalog ◆ Exercise equipment and clothing for basketball, tennis, running and jogging, golf, racquetball, and other sports. 410-687-6400. www.holabirdsports.com

**Holl Meditronics,** 4 Marconi Ct., Bolton, Ontario, Canada L7E-1E7: Free brochure ◆ Motor driven or muscular force-operated exercise equipment for wheelchair users, other disabled persons, and the elderly. 905-857-6867. hollmedi@netcom.ca

**Icon Health & Fitness Inc.,** P.O. Box 313, Logan, UT 84323: Free brochure ◆ Total body low-impact exercise machine with display that shows speed, time, distance, and calories burned. 800-727-9777. www.iconfitness.com

**Ivanko Barbell Company,** P.O. Box 1470, San Pedro, CA 90731: Free list of retail sources ◆ Weight lifting equipment. 800-247-9044; 310-514-1155 (in CA). www.advmax.com/ivanko

**Jayfro Corp.,** Unified Sports Inc., 976 Hartford Tnpk., P.O. Box 400, Waterford, CT 06385: Free catalog ◆ Wall-mounted gyms and physical fitness and exercise equipment. 860-447-3001.

**M.W. Kasch Company,** 5401 W. Donges Bay Rd., Mequon, WI 53092: Free information ◆ Home gymnasiums and weight training, body building, and exercise equipment. 414-242-5000.

**Landice,** 111 Canfield Ave., Randolph, NJ 07869: Free list of retail sources ◆ Treadmills with state-of-the-art programmability. 800-LANDICE. www.landice.com

**LifeFitness Inc.,** 10601 W. Belmont Ave., Franklin Park, IL 60131: Free list of retail sources ◆ Home fitness equipment. 800-877-3867. lifefitness.com

**Lifegear Inc.,** 300 Round Hill Dr., Rockaway, NJ 07876: Free brochure ◆ Home exercise equipment. 800-882-1113; 201-627-3065 (in NJ).

**Mongoose Bicycles,** 3400 Kashiwa St., Torrance, CA 90505: Catalog $3 ◆ Lightweight fitness exercise bicycles. 562-539-8860. www.mongoose.com

**Nautilus Direct,** 709 Powerhouse Rd., Independence, VA 24348: Free information ◆ Multi-station gym and exercise machines. 800-628-8458. www.affnet.com/nautilus

**New York Barbells,** P.O. Box 3473, Elmira, NY 14905: Free information ◆ Home gymnasium and exercise equipment. 800-446-1833; 607-733-8038 (in NY). www.newyorkbarbells.com

**NordicTrack,** 104 Peavey Rd., Chaska, MN 55318: Free brochure ◆ Total body exercisers and other equipment. 800-441-7512. www.nordictrack.com

**Olympia Sports,** P.O. Box 1941, Ann Arbor, MI 48106: Free information ◆ Home exercise equipment. 800-521-2832. www.wolverinesports.com

**PDLX Company Inc.,** P.O. Box 129, Shelton, WA 98584: Free information ◆ Motor-equipped exercise machine for physically disabled individuals. 800-314-4851. pdlxco@aol.com

**JCPenney Catalog,** P.O. Box 675, Milwaukee, WI 53201: Free information ◆ Athletic clothing and equipment. 800-222-6161. www.jcpenney.com/shopping

**Power Systems,** P.O. Box 12620, Knoxville, TN 37912: Free catalog ◆ Physical fitness and exercise equipment. 800-321-6975. www.power-systems.com

**Precor USA,** 20001 North Creek Pkwy., Bothell, WA 98011: Free list of retail sources ◆ Off-snow cross-country skier exercise machine. 800-477-3267. www.precor.com

**Pro-Form,** Icon Health & Fitness Inc., P.O. Box 313, Logan, UT 84323: Free brochure ◆ Walking exerciser with easy-to-read motivational electrics for constant feedback. 800-514-4554. www.iconfitness.com

**Professional Gym Inc.,** P.O. Box 188, Marshall, MO 65340: Free brochure ◆ Weight training, body building, and exercise equipment. 800-821-7665.

**Ross Bicycles USA,** 51 Executive Blvd., Farmingdale, NY 11735: Free information ◆ Home exercise equipment. 800-338-7677; 516-249-6000 (in NY).

**Saratoga Access & Fitness Inc.,** P.O. Box 1427, Fort Collins, CO 80522: Free brochure ◆ Bicycle exercise machines. 970-484-4010.

**Savage Accessories,** 15 Macarthur Dr., Millbury, MA 01527: Free brochure ◆ Accessory holders and adapters, reading racks, and mats for weights, treadmills, and other exercise equipment. 800-682-8416; 508-797-3772 (in MA). www.savagefitness.com

**Sharper Image SPA,** 650 Davis St., San Francisco, CA 94120: Free catalog ◆ Aerobic non-impact fitness machines, treadmills, massagers, and other equipment. 800-344-3440. www.sharperimage.com

**Soloflex Inc.,** Hawthorn Farm Park, 570 NE 53rd Ave., Hillsboro, OR 97124: Free catalog ◆ Machine exercise equipment that duplicates the squat and lunge. 800-547-8802. www.soloflex.com

**Spalding Sports Worldwide,** 425 Meadow St., P.O. Box 901, Chicopee, MA 01021: Free list of retail sources ◆ Home gymnasiums, trampolines, monitoring aids, and weight training, body building, and exercise equipment. 800-225-6601. www.spalding.com

**Sports Play,** 5642 Natural Bridge, St. Louis, MO 63120: Free information ◆ Gymnastic bars and floor equipment. 800-727-8180.

**SPRI Products Inc.,** 1026 Campus Dr., Mundelein, IL 60060: Free catalog ◆ Rubber resistance fitness equipment and accessories. 800-222-7774. www.fitnessonline.com

**StairMaster Sports/Medical Products Inc.,** 12421 Willows Rd. NE, Ste. 100, Kirkland, WA 98034: Free information ◆ Exercise equipment. 800-666-9936.

**Task Industries,** 1325 E. Franklin Ave., Pomona, CA 91766: Free catalog ◆ Exercise and body building equipment. 909-629-1600.

**Tectrix,** 68 Fairbanks, Irvine, CA 92718: Free catalog ◆ Exercise equipment and cardiac rate monitors. 800-767-8082; 714-380-8082 (in CA). www.tectrix.com

**Trek Bicycle Corp.,** 801 W. Madison St., P.O. Box 183, Waterloo, WI 53594: Free list of retail sources ◆ Exercise bicycles with control and programmable options. 800-369-8735. www.trekbikes.com

**True Fitness Technology Inc.,** 865 Hoff Rd., O'Fallon, MO 63366: Free list of retail sources ◆ Home fitness equipment. 800-426-6570. www.truefitness.com

**Vectra Fitness Inc.,** 15135 NE 90th St., Edmond, WA 98052: Free list of retail sources ◆ Home gymnasium equipment. 800-2-VECTRA; 206-867-1500 (in WA). www.vectrafitness.com

**WaterRower Inc.,** 453 Cottage St., Pawtucket, RI 02861: Free list of retail sources ◆ Water resistance-operated exercise rowing machine. 401-728-1966. www.waterrower.co.uk

## FABRIC PAINTING, DYEING, & OTHER DECORATING

**Advanced Color & Chemical,** 4800 Littletown St., Baldwin Park, CA 91706: Free information ◆ Pigments and dyes for textiles, graphic arts, hand printing, and more. 616-960-6656. www.acolor.com

**Aljo Dyes,** 81 Franklin St., New York, NY 10013: Free catalog ◆ Fabric dyes. 212-226-2878.

**Alpine Imports,** 7106 N. Alpine Rd., Rockford, IL 61111: Free information ◆ Craft and fabric painting supplies. 800-654-6114.

**The Art Store,** 935 Erie Blvd. East, Syracuse, NY 13210: Price list $3 ◆ Supplies for fabric dyeing, screen-printing, marbling, and other art decor. 800-669-2787.

**Atelier De Paris,** 1543 S. Robertson Blvd., Los Angeles, CA 90035: Free information ◆ Silk painting and fabric decorating supplies. 213-553-6636.

**Badger Air-Brush Company,** 9128 W. Belmont Ave., Franklin Park, IL 60131: Brochure $1 ◆ Airbrushes and fabric paints. 800-247-2787. www.badger-airbrush.com

**Blueprint-Printables,** 1400-A Marsten Rd., Burlingame, CA 94010: Catalog $3 ◆ Fabrics, T-shirts, and blueprinting kits. 800-356-0445.

**Createx Colors,** 14 Airport Park Rd., East Granby, CT 06026: Free list of retail sources ◆ Fabric dyes. 800-243-2712. www.easelart.com

**Creative Wholesale,** 4739 Jonesboro Rd., Forest Park, GA 30050: Free information ◆ Craft and fabric painting supplies. 800-347-0930.

**Decart Inc.,** P.O. Box 309, Morrisville, VT 05661: Free list of retail sources ◆ Permanent machine-washable and dry-cleanable fabric paints, airbrushing paints, and water-based enamels. 802-888-4217.

**DecoArt,** P.O. Box 370, Stanford, KY 40484: Free list of retail sources ◆ Easy-to-apply acrylics for fabric decorating. 606-365-3193. www.decoart.com

**Dharma Trading Company,** P.O. Box 150916, San Rafael, CA 94902: Free catalog ◆ Dyes and fabric paints. 800-542-5227. www.dharmatrading.com

**Drake Distributing,** Rt. 4, Box 298-B, P.O. Box 69, Cottondale, AL 35453: Free information ◆ Craft and fabric painting supplies. 800-888-8653; 205-556-8082 (in AL).

**Duncan Enterprises,** 5673 E. Shields Ave., Fresno, CA 93727: Free list of retail sources ◆ Easy-to-apply iron-on-patterns, foil transfers, and glitter. 800-438-6226; 209-291-4444 (in CA). www.duncan-enterprises.com

**Eastern Art Glass,** P.O. Box 9, Wyckoff, NJ 07481: Catalog $2 (refundable) ◆ Fabric painting kits and supplies. 800-872-3458. www.etchworld.com

**G & S Dye,** 250 Dundas Street West, #8, Toronto, Ontario, Canada M5T 2Z5: Free brochure ◆ Natural fabrics and textile design supplies. 416-596-0550. gsdye@interlog.com

**Nasco,** 901 Janesville Ave., Fort Atkinson, WI 53538: Free catalog ◆ Fabric paints, silk painting supplies, and textile dyes. 800-558-9595. www.nascofa.com

**PRO Chemical & Dye Inc.,** P.O. Box 14, Somerset, MA 02726: Free information ◆ Fabric dyes, textile inks and pigments, and other supplies. 888-2-BUY-DYE. PRO-CHEMICAL@worldnet.att.net

**Qualin International,** P.O. Box 31145, San Francisco, CA 94131: Free catalog with long SASE and two 1st class stamps ◆ Silk fabrics, scarf blanks, and silk painting supplies. 415-333-8500.

**Rupert, Gibbon & Spider Inc.,** P.O. Box 425, Healdsburg, CA 95448: Free catalog ◆ Textile dyes and paints, brushes, resists, and silk and cotton fabrics for printing and dyeing. 800-442-0455. nature@microweb.com

**Silkpaint Corp.,** P.O. Box 18, Waldron, MO 64092: Free information ◆ Fabric dyes. 816-891-7774.

**Soho South,** P.O. Box 1324, Cullman, AL 35056: Catalog $2.50 (refundable) ◆ Beads and findings, fabric dyes and paints, silk scarves, other fabrics, and marbling supplies. 256-739-6114. soho@airnet.net

**Texicolor Corp.,** Eric Hoyer, 444 Castro St., Ste. 425, Mountain View, CA 94041: Free information ◆ Water-based textile screen-printing inks and fabric paints. 650-968-8183.

**Tole Americana,** P.O. Box 20236, Portland, OR 97230: Free information ◆ Craft and fabric painting supplies. 503-287-6878.

## FABRICS & TRIM

### Fabrics

**ABC Decorative Fabrics,** 29909 US 19 North, Clearwater, FL 33761: Free information ◆ Decorator fabrics. 800-500-9022.

**AK Sew & Serge,** 1602 6th St. SE, Winter Haven FL 33880: Catalog $5 ◆ Designer and other fabrics, smocking, Battenberg lace, and sewing notions. 800-299-8096; 813-299-3080 (in FL).

**Alexandra's Homespun Textile & Seraph Textile Collection,** P.O. Box 500, Sturbridge, MA 01566: Catalog $2 ◆ Hand-woven homespun and reproduction museum fabrics for household furnishings and upholstery. 508-347-2241.

**Apple Annie Fabrics,** 566 Wilbur Ave., Swansea, MA 02777: Free information ◆ Fabrics. 508-678-5187. aafabrics@aol.com

**Baer Fabrics,** 515 E. Market St., Louisville, KY 40202: Catalog $3 ◆ Sewing notions, trim, and fabrics. 800-769-7778.

**Baltazor Fabrics,** 3262 Severen Ave., Metairie, LA 70002: Catalog $3 ◆ Lace and lace-making supplies, fabrics, smocking, and bridal fashion-making supplies. 800-532-5223. www.baltazor.com

**Barbeau Fine Fabrics,** 2201 S. Lemay Ave., Apt. 150, Fort Collins, CO 80525: Information $12 ◆ Silks, wools, cottons, and other fabrics.

**Beacon Fabric & Notions,** 6801 Gulfport Blvd. South, South Pasadena, FL 33707: Free catalog ◆ Active wear, outdoor clothing, flag and banner fabrics, machine embroidery and other threads, and sewing supplies. 800-713-8157; 813-345-6994 (in FL). www.beaconfabric.com

**Philips Boyne Corp.,** 135 Rome St., Farmingdale, NY 11735: Information $3 ◆ Imported and domestic cotton fabrics. 800-292-2830.

**Bridals International,** 45 Albany St., Cazenovia, NY 13035: Catalog $9.50 ◆ Imported fabrics and lace for bridal fashions. 800-752-1171.

**Buttons 'n' Bows,** 14086 Memorial, Houston, TX 77079: Catalog $2 (refundable) ◆ Fabrics and smocking and heirloom sewing supplies. 281-496-0170.

**Calico Corners,** 203 Gale Ln., Kennett Square, PA 19348: Free catalog ◆ Decorative fabrics and custom furniture. 800-213-6366. www.calicocorners.com

**California Bridal Fabrics,** Hyman Hendler & Sons Inc., 729 E. Temple St., Los Angeles, CA 90012: Catalog $10 ◆ Satin, taffeta, lace, and metallic fabrics. 800-421-8963.

**Carolina Mills Factory Outlet,** Hwy. 76 West, Box V, Branson, MO 65615: Free brochure ◆ Designer fabrics. 417-334-2291.

**Central Shippee Inc.,** 46 Star Lake Rd., Bloomingdale, NJ 07403: Free brochure ◆ Protective packaging, wool felts, velvets and suedes, Velcro, and cotton, metallic, satin, and burlap fabrics. 201-838-1100. felt@webspan.net

**Cherrywood Fabrics Inc.,** P.O. Box 486, Brainerd, MN 56401: Information $7 ◆ Solid color gradations and suede look-alike fabrics. 218-829-0967.

**Classic Cloth,** 34930 US 19 North, Fountain Shopping Center, Palm Harbor, FL 34684: Swatches $5 ◆ Cotton fabrics. 800-237-7739; 813-785-6593 (in FL).

**Clearbrook Woolen Shop,** P.O. Box 8, Clearbrook, VA 22624: Free information with long SASE ◆ Wool fabrics. 703-662-3442.

**D'Anton Leathers,** 5530 Vincent Ave. NE, West Branch, IA 52358: Catalog $1 ◆ Garment leathers and suede. 319-643-2568.

**Delectable Mountain Cloth,** 125 Main St., Brattleboro, VT 05301: Brochure $1 with long SASE ◆ Buttons and natural fabrics from worldwide sources.

**Denham Fabrics,** P.O. Box 241275, Memphis, TN 38124: Fabric portfolio $8 ◆ Polyester and cotton fabrics. 901-683-4574.

**Designer Home Fabrics,** 5018 France Ave. South, Edina, MN 56410: Catalog $2 (refundable) ◆ Traditional and contemporary cotton prints, chintzes, damasks, tapestries, solids, and other fabrics. 800-666-4202.

**Dharma Trading Company,** P.O. Box 150916, San Rafael, CA 94902: Free catalog ◆ Clothing blanks and silk, cotton, and rayon fabrics. 800-542-5227. www.dharmatrading.com

**DK Sports,** Division Daisy Kingdom, 134 NW 8th St., Portland, OR 97209: Free information ◆ Rainwear and outerwear fabrics and sewing notions. 800-234-6688.

**Elna,** 1032-C 4th Ave. SE, Decatur, AL 35601: Free information ◆ Smocking and heirloom sewing supplies and fabrics. 256-351-6196.

**Exotic Silks,** 1959 Leghorn St., Mountain View, CA 94043: Brochure 25¢ ◆ Natural silks and scarves in white, solid colors, and patterns. 800-845-SILK; 415-965-7760 (in CA).

**Fabric Center,** P.O. Box 8212, Fitchburg, MA 01420: Catalog $2 ◆ Decorator fabrics. 978-343-4402.

**Fabric Depot,** 700 SE 122nd Ave., Portland, OR 97233: Free information ◆ Fabrics, notions, thread and zippers, and sewing supplies. 800-392-3376.

**Fabric Direct,** P.O. Box 194, Mt. Marion, NY 12456: Free information ◆ Apparel fabrics and cotton prints. 800-529-1684. www.woodstockweb.com/fabricdirect

**Fabric Gallery,** 146 W. Grand River, Williamston, MI 48895: Information $4 ◆ Imported and domestic silks, wools, cottons, blends, and synthetics. 517-655-4573.

**The Fabric Outlet,** 30 Airport Rd., West Lebanon, NH 03784: Free information ◆ Decorator fabrics. 800-635-9715.

**Fabrics For The Great Outdoors,** 60 Bristol Rd. East, #9, Mississauga, Ontario Canada L4Z 3K8: Free catalog ◆ Fabrics for the outdoors. 800-798-5885. www.fabrics-outdoors.ca

**Fabrics Unlimited,** 5015 Columbia Pike, Arlington, VA 22204: Free information ◆ Fabrics from designer cutting rooms, ultrasuede, and imported silks, wools, and cottons. 703-671-0324.

**Felt People,** Box 135, Bloomingdale, NJ 07403: Information $2 (refundable) ◆ Wool felt. 800-631-8968; 201-838-1100 (in NJ). www.centralshippee.com

**Fine Line Fabrics,** 1153 El Camino Real, Menlo Park, CA 94025: Free information ◆ Silk, linen, rayon, cotton, wool and other fabrics, Also designer ends and pieces, buttons, notions, and trim. 650-322-8775. www.finelinefabrics.com

**Fishman's Fabrics,** 1101-43 S. Desplaines St., Chicago, IL 60607: Free information ◆ Designer wool, silk, cotton, and linen fabrics in three weights and over 60 colors. 800-648-5161.

**G & S Dye,** 250 Dundas Street West, #8, Toronto, Ontario, Canada M5T 2Z5: Free brochure ◆ Natural fabrics and textile design supplies. 416-596-0550. gsdye@interlog.com

**G Street Fabrics,** Mail Order Service, 12240 Wilkins Ave., Rockville, MD 20852: Free catalog ◆ Decorator, clothing, and drapery fabrics. 800-333-9191.

**Green Pepper,** 1285 River Rd., Eugene, OR 97404: Catalog $2 ◆ Rainwear and outerwear fabrics, spandex fabrics, sewing notions, and patterns. 541-689-3292.

**Gutcheon Patchworks Inc.,** 917 Pacific Ave., #305, Tacoma, WA 98402: Information and fabric samples $3 ◆ Coordinating plain color fabrics and 100 percent cotton prints. 206-383-3047.

**Hambrick's Fabrics,** 820 Regal Dr., Huntsville, AL 35801: Information $3 ◆ Fabrics. 256-534-4704.

**Hancock Fabrics,** 3841 Hinkleville Rd., Paducah, KY 42001: Free information ◆ Quilting supplies, fabrics, and sewing notions. 800-845-8723.

**Heirloom Creations,** 431 Rena Dr., Lafayette, LA 70503: Free information ◆ Swiss and silk batiste, linen, velveteen, cotton corduroy, and lace. 318-984-8949.

**Home Fabric Mills Inc.,** 882 S. Main St., Cheshire, CT 06410: Free brochure ◆ Velvets, upholstery and drapery fabrics, prints, sheers, antique satins, and thermal fabrics. 203-272-3529.

**Homespun Fabrics & Draperies,** P.O. Box 4315, Thousand Oaks, CA 91359: Catalog $2 ◆ Washable, 10-foot wide and seamless cotton fabrics. 888-543-2998. members.aol.com/widefabric

**Homespun Weavers,** 55 S. 7th St., Emmaus, PA 18049: Brochure 50¢ ◆ Cotton fabrics. 800-290-4550; 610-967-4550 (in PA).

**House of Laird,** Box 246, Wilson, NC 37893: Free information ◆ Silk and blends, wool, and rayon suiting. 800-338-4618. www.houseoflaird.com

**International Fabric Collection,** 3445 W. Lake Rd., Erie, PA 16505: Catalog $3 ◆ Fabrics from Italy, India, Japan, Holland, Africa, and other worldwide sources. Also quilting and embroidery books. 800-462-3891; 814-838-0740 (in PA). www.intfab.com

**Jehlor Fantasy Fabrics,** 730 Andover Park West, Seattle, WA 98188: Catalog $5 ◆ Bridal fabrics, appliques, trims, and jewelry sew-on notions. 206-575-8250.

**Judy's Heirloom Sewing,** 13650 E. Zayante Rd., Felton, CA 95018: Catalog $6.50 ◆ Sewing and smocking supplies, fabrics, lace, ribbons, and yarns. 408-335-1050.

**Kiyo Design Inc.,** 11 Annapolis St., Annapolis, MD 21041: Catalog $15 ◆ Notions, fabrics, lace, beads, and more. 410-280-1942. www.kiyoinc.com/fabric.html

**Kunin Felt,** P.O. Box 5000, Hampton, NH 03842: Free information ◆ Felt. 800-292-7900.

**Laces 'N Rags,** 714 Mall Blvd., Savannah, GA 31406: Free information ◆ Fabrics, lace, and smocking and sewing supplies. 912-354-8863.

**Landau Woolen Company Inc.,** 561 7th Ave., New York, NY 10018: Free information ◆ Worsted wools, merino jerseys, luxury fibers, rayons, and cottons. 800-553-2292; 212-391-8371 (in NY).

**Laube's Stretch & Sew Fabrics,** 609 W. 98th St., Bloomington, MN 55420: Catalog $1 with long SASE ◆ Stretch-and-sew fabrics. 612-884-7321.

**Lauratex Fabrics Inc.,** 153 W. 27th St., New York, NY 10001: Free information ◆ Sateen, ottoman, batiste, canvas, polished cotton, and 100 percent cotton fabrics. 212-645-7800.

**Leandro Fabrics,** 6538 E. Tanque Verde, Tucson, AZ 85715: Free information ◆ Silks, cottons, woolens, rayons, linens, and silk lining. 888-LEANDRO.

**Ledgewood Studio,** 6000 Ledgewood Dr., Forest Park, GA 30050: Catalog $2 with long SASE and three 1st class stamps ◆ Dress patterns for antique dolls, supplies for recreating period costumes, braids, French lace, silk ribbons and taffeta, China silk, Swiss batiste, trims, and notions. 404-361-6098.

**Donna Lee's Sewing Center,** 25234 Pacific Hwy. South, Kent, WA 98032: Catalog $4 ◆ Swiss and imperial batiste, China silk, silk charmeuse, French val lace, English lace, Swiss embroideries, trims and yardage, ribbons, smocking, doll patterns, books, and sewing notions. 206-941-9466.

**Samuel Lehrer & Company Inc.,** 7 Depinedo Ave., Stamford, CT 06902: Free information ◆ Wool flannels, gabardines, linen blends, pinstripes, and plaids for men and women's clothing. 800-221-2433.

**Les Fabriques,** 1422 Seminole Trail, Charlottesville, VA 22901: Catalog and swatch selection $5 ◆ Imported and domestic fabrics. 804-975-0710. lfabriques@aol.com

**Linen & Lace,** 4 Lafayette, Washington, MO 63090: Catalog $2 ◆ Linen and lace fabrics. 800-332-5223.

**The Linen Fabric World,** 1246 Bird Rd., Miami, FL 33146: Information $5 ◆ Imported linen fabrics. 305-663-1577.

**Marine Sewing,** 6801 Gulfport Blvd., South Pasadena, FL 33707: Catalog $3 with long SASE ◆ Canvas, vinyl, and notions for boaters, campers, and outdoor enthusiasts. 800-713-8157.

**Mill End Store,** 9701 SE McLoughlin, Milwaukie, OR 97222: Free information ◆ Silk fabrics from designer back rooms. 503-786-1234.

**Monterey Outlet Store,** 1725 E. Delavan Dr., Janesville, WI 53546: Brochure $4 ◆ Deep pile fabrics (fake furs). 800-432-9959; 608-754-8309 (in WI). www.montereyoutlet.com

**Nancy's Notions,** P.O. Box 683, Beaver Dam, WI 53916: Free catalog ◆ Sewing notions, threads, books, patterns, how-to videos, and interlock knits, fleece, gabardines, sweater knits, challis, and other fabrics. 800-245-5116. www.nancysnotions.com

**Needle & Thread,** 2215 Fairfield Rd., Gettysburg, PA 17325: Free information ◆ Wool, cotton, linen, silk, and other fabrics. Also historical folkwear and past clothing patterns. 717-334-4011.

**Needles & Pins,** 3019 SW Martin Downs Blvd., Palm City, FL 34990: Free information ◆ Smocking supplies, quilting and other fabrics, imported lace, buttons, and notions. 561-220-9198.

**Oppenheim's,** P.O. Box 29, North Manchester, IN 46962: Catalog $1 ◆ Sewing notions, fabrics, and craft supplies. 800-461-6728.

**Outdoor Wilderness Fabrics,** 16415 Midland Blvd., Nampa, ID 83687: Free price list ◆ Coated and non-coated nylon fabrics, fleece and blends in coat weights, waterproof fabrics, webbing, patterns, and sewing notions. 208-466-1602. 800-093-7467. www.owfinc.com

**The Patchworks,** 6676 Amsterdam Rd., Manhattan, MT 59741: Catalog $1 ◆ Reproduction cotton fabrics for quilts and clothing. 800-426-3126. www.patchworks.com

**Martha Pullen Company Inc.,** 518 Madison St., Huntsville, AL 35801: Catalog $2 ◆ Fabrics and trims. 800-547-4176. www.marthapullenco.com

**Qualin International,** P.O. Box 31145, San Francisco, CA 94131: Free catalog with long SASE and two 1st class stamps ◆ Silk fabrics, scarf blanks, and silk painting supplies. 415-333-8500.

**Rainshed Outdoor Fabrics,** 707 NW 11th, Corvallis, OR 97330: Catalog $1 ◆ Outdoor fabrics, hardware, webbing, and patterns. 541-753-8900.

**Murielle Roy & Company,** 67 Plain Mill Rd., Naugatuck, CT 06770: Catalog $4 ◆ Fabrics and trim. 203-729-0480.

**S & S Sewing Machine Company Inc.,** 900 Bob Wallace Ave., #105-B, Huntsville, AL 35801: Free information ◆ Notions, fabrics, sewing machines, and accessories. 800-SEW-ELNA.

**Donna Salyers' Fabulous-Furs,** 700 Madison Ave., Covington, KY 41011: Catalog $1 ◆ Alternatives to natural furs and leather, kits, and patterns. 800-848-4650.

**Sawyer Brook Fabrics,** P.O. Box 1800, Clinton, MA 01510: Catalog $15 (3 issues) ◆ Natural fiber fabrics, polyesters and blends, wools, silks, and cotton prints. 800-290-2739. SBDF@ultranet.com

**Seattle Fabrics,** 8702 Aurora North, Seattle, WA 98103: Price list $3 (refundable) ◆ Outdoor and recreational fabrics, notions, and hardware for outdoor enthusiasts. 206-525-0670. www.seattlefabrics.com

**The Seraph,** P.O. Box 500, 420 Main St., Sturbridge, MA 01566: Catalog $6 ◆ Fabrics. 508-347-2241.

**Sew Fancy,** Unit 23, RR 1, Beeton, Ontario, Canada L0G 1A0: Catalog $5 ◆ Fabrics, notions, needle art patterns, and supplies for heirloom sewing, smocking, and quilting. 800-SEW-FNCY. www.sewfancy.com

**Sew Natural Fabrics,** 21780 N. Essex Dr., Lexington Park, MD 20653: Catalog $4 ◆ Twill, denim, French terry, interlock jersey, and other cotton fabrics.

**Sew Quick,** 2688 Coolidge Hwy., Berkley, MI 48072: Free information ◆ Fabrics, silk ribbon, and smocking and heirloom supplies. 810-542-7174.

**Sew Sassy Lingerie,** 900 Bob Wallace Ave. SW, Huntsville, AL 35801: Catalog $2 (refundable) ◆ Lingerie fabrics and supplies. 256-536-4405. webmail@sewsassy.com

**The Sew Shoppe,** 3220 Lithia-Pinecrest Rd., Valrico, FL 33594: Catalog $2 ◆ Denim fabrics. 888-685-6760; 813-685-6760 (in FL).

**Sew So Fancy,** 914 Queen City Ave., Tuscaloosa, AL 35401: Free information with long SASE ◆ Lace, mother of pearl buttons, Swiss embroideries, fabrics, and supplies. 800-821-0607.

**Sew Special,** 777 E. Vista Way, Ste. 20, Vista, CA 92084: Catalog $2 ◆ Fabrics and lace. 760-940-0365. sewspeci@mailhost2.csusm.edu

**Sew Unique,** 626 15th St. East, Tuscaloosa, AL 35401: Free brochure with long SASE ◆ Fabrics and lace, smocking and embroidery supplies, and ready-to-smock kits. 800-837-8799.

**Shama Imports,** P.O. Box 2900, Farmington Hills, MI 48018: Free brochure ◆ Hand-embroidered crewel fabrics. 248-478-7740.

**Smock & Sew,** 2211 21st Ave. South, Nashville, TN 37212: Free information ◆ Fabrics, smocking supplies, notions, silk ribbon, and accessories. 615-269-5177.

**Smocking Bonnet,** 1341 W. Liberty Rd., Lisbon, MD 21765: Catalog $3 ◆ English smocking, French hand sewing, fabrics, and lace. 800-524-1678; 410-489-7110 (in MD).

**Soho South,** P.O. Box 1324, Cullman, AL 35056: Catalog $2.50 (refundable) ◆ Beads and findings, fabric dyes and paints, silk scarves, other fabrics, and marbling supplies. 256-739-6114. soho@airnet.net

**Stretch & Sew,** 8697 La Mesa Blvd., La Mesa, CA 91941: Catalog $3 ◆ Fabrics, patterns, and notions. 800-547-7717. www.stretch-and-sew.com

**Super Silk,** P.O. Box 527596, Flushing, NY 11352: Free brochure ◆ Silk fabrics. 800-432-7455; 718-886-2606 (in NY).

**Sure Fit,** Division Fieldcrest Cannon Inc., 939 Marcon Blvd., Allentown, PA 18103: Free catalog ◆ Slipcovers, matching draperies, and fabrics. 888-754-7166.

**Taylor's Cutaways & Stuff,** 2802 E. Washington St., Urbana, IL 61801: Brochure $1 ◆ Satins, lace, velvet, cottons, felt, calico, trims, polyester squares, sewing notions, craft supplies, books, and patterns. home.sprynet.com/sprynet/tcutaway

**Testfabrics Inc.,** P.O. Box 420, Middlesex, NJ 08846: Free catalog ◆ Cotton, linen, silk, wool, blends, synthetics, muslin, satin, twill, and other fabrics. 908-469-6446. testfabric@aol.com

**Thai Silks,** 252 State St., Los Altos, CA 94022: Free brochure ◆ Silk clothing and imported silk fabrics. Also velvets, chiffons, satins, and more. 800-722-SILK; 800-722-SILK; 650-948-8611 (in CA). www.thaisilks.com

**Thoburn's,** P.O. Box 231, Londonderry, NH 03053: Brochure and swatches $6 ◆ Fleece in prints and solids, sewing patterns, and notions. 603-437-4924.

**Threads at Gingerbread Hill,** 356 E. Garfield, Aurora, OH 44202: Information and samples $10 ◆ Imported and domestic silks, wools, cottons, synthetics, and other fabrics. 330-562-7100.

**L.P. Thur Discount Fabrics,** 126 W. 23rd St., New York, NY 10011: Free information ◆ Costume, designer, craft, theatrical, and other fabrics. 212-243-4913.

**Tioga Mill Outlet,** 200 S. Hartman St., York, PA 17403: Free brochure ◆ Upholstery and drapery fabrics. 717-843-5139.

**Treadle Yard Goods,** 1338 Grand Ave., St. Paul, MN 55105: Free information ◆ Natural fiber fabrics. 612-698-9690.

**Treasured Heirlooms,** 13507 Candlewood Ct., Moorpark, CA 93021: Free newsletter with long SASE ◆ Fabrics, lace, embroideries, needlework supplies, notions, and more. 805-523-2520.

**Ultramouse Ltd.,** 3433 Bennington Ct., Bloomfield Hills, MI 48301: Catalog $2 ◆ Sewing notions, ultrasuede, and fabric scraps. 800-225-1887.

**Utex Trading,** 710 9th St., Ste. 5, Niagara Falls, NY 14301: Free brochure with long SASE ◆ Imported silk fabrics and sewing supplies. 716-282-8211.

**With Heart And Hand,** 541 South St., Wrentham, MA 02093: Brochure and samples $10 ◆ Hard-to-find hand-woven and authentically reproduced fabrics for quilting, sewing, and home decorating. 508-384-6568.

### Lace & Ribbon

**Baltazor Fabrics,** 3262 Severen Ave., Metairie, LA 70002: Catalog $3 ◆ Lace and lace-making supplies, fabrics, smocking, and bridal fashion-making supplies. 800-532-5223. www.baltazor.com

**Beggars' Lace,** P.O. Box 481223, Denver, CO 80248: Catalog $2 (refundable) ◆ Lace-making materials and kits. 303-233-2600.

**Cache Junction,** 2701 W. 1800 South, Logan, UT 84321: Brochure $2 ◆ Iron-on lace. 800-999-1989.

**Denham Fabrics,** P.O. Box 241275, Memphis, TN 38124: Fabric portfolio $8 ◆ Lace. 901-683-4574.

**Fabric Barn,** 3123 E. Anaheim St., Long Beach, CA 90804: Free catalog ◆ Ribbon and lace. 800-544-9374; 310-498-0285 (in CA).

**Ginsco Trims,** 242 W. 38th, New York, NY 10018: Catalog $6 (refundable) ◆ Fashion trims and braids. 800-929-2529; 212-719-4871 (in NY). www.ginstrim.com

**Glimakra Looms & Yarns Inc.,** 1338 Ross St., Petaluma, CA 94954: Catalog $2.50 ◆ Weaving equipment, looms, yarns, and lace-making equipment. 800-289-9276; 707-762-3362 (in CA).

**Heirloom Creations,** 431 Rena Dr., Lafayette, LA 70503: Free information ◆ Lace, Swiss and silk batiste, linen, velveteen, and cotton corduroy. 318-984-8949.

**Heritage Miniatures,** 44 Mountain Base Rd., Goffstown, NH 03045: Catalog $5 ◆ European lace and trim for miniature doll dressmakers.

**Judy's Heirloom Sewing,** 13650 E. Zayante Rd., Felton, CA 95018: Catalog $6.50 ◆ Sewing and smocking supplies, fabrics, lace, ribbons, and yarns. 408-335-1050.

**Kiyo Design Inc.,** 11 Annapolis St., Annapolis, MD 21041: Catalog $15 ◆ Notions, fabrics, lace, beads, and more. 410-280-1942. www.kiyoinc.com/fabric.html

**Lace Corner,** Box 1224, Weaverville, CA 96093: Catalog $3 (refundable with $25 order) ◆ Ruffled flat lace, ribbons, and appliques. 530-623-3586.

**Lacis,** 3163 Adeline St., Berkeley, CA 94703: Catalog $5 ◆ Hairpin lace looms. 510-843-7178. www.lacis.com

**Mimi's Fabrications,** 77 Howell St., Waynesville, NC 28786: Catalog $3 ◆ Silk ribbon and embroidery supplies. 800-948-3455. www.mimisbymail.com

**Needles & Pins,** 3019 SW Martin Downs Blvd., Palm City, FL 34990: Free information ◆ Smocking supplies, fabrics, imported lace and buttons, quilting fabrics, and supplies. 561-220-9198.

**New Scotland Lace Company,** P.O. Box 181, Dartmouth, Nova Scotia, Canada B2Y 3Y3: Catalog $3 (refundable) ◆ Scottish Victorian lace window panels and yardage. 902-462-4212.

**The Ribbon Factory Outlet,** P.O. Box 405, Titusville, PA 16354: Catalog $2 ◆ Ribbons. 814-827-6431.

**Murielle Roy & Company,** 67 Plain Mill Rd., Naugatuck, CT 06770: Catalog $4 ◆ Fabrics and trim. 203-729-0480.

**Sand Dollar,** 1740 E. Pass Rd., Gulfport, MS 39507: Free information ◆ Smocking and heirloom sewing supplies. Also ribbons. 800-230-3995; 601-896-3995 (in MS).

**Sew 'n Sew,** 1111 N. Main St., Summerville, NC 29483: Free information ◆ Smocking and heirloom sewing supplies, English and French lace, fabrics, and knitting aids. 803-871-7822.

**Sew Fine,** 18399 Ventura Blvd., Tarzana, CA 91356: Free information with long SASE ◆ Smocking and sewing supplies, French and English lace, buttons, ribbons, and Swiss embroideries. 818-886-1108.

**Sew Quick,** 2688 Coolidge Hwy., Berkley, MI 48072: Free information ◆ Fabrics, silk ribbon, and smocking and heirloom supplies. 810-542-7174.

**Sew So Fancy,** 914 Queen City Ave., Tuscaloosa, AL 35401: Free information with long SASE ◆ Lace, mother of pearl buttons, Swiss embroideries, fabrics, and supplies. 800-821-0607.

**Sew Special,** 777 E. Vista Way, Ste. 20, Vista, CA 92084: Catalog $2 ◆ Fabrics and lace. 760-940-0365. sewspeci@mailhost2.csusm.edu

**Sew Unique,** 626 15th St. East, Tuscaloosa, AL 35401: Free brochure with long SASE ◆ Fabrics and lace, smocking and embroidery supplies, ready-to-smock kits, and supplies. 800-837-8799.

**Smock & Sew,** 2211 21st Ave. South, Nashville, TN 37212: Free information ◆ Fabrics, smocking supplies, notions, silk ribbon, and accessories. 615-269-5177.

**Treasured Heirlooms,** 13507 Candlewood Ct., Moorpark, CA 93021: Free newsletter with long SASE ◆ Fabrics, lace, pleaters, notions, and supplies. 805-523-2520.

**Van Sciver Bobbin Lace,** 130 Cascadilla Park, Ithaca, NY 14850: Catalog $2 ◆ Lace-making supplies. 607-277-0498. vsblace@mail.claityconnect.com

**Wimpole Street Creations,** P.O. Box 585, North Salt Lake, UT 84054: Free information ◆ Battenburg and cutwork lace. 801-294-0700.

**Wooded Hamlet Designs,** 4044 Coseytown Rd., Greencastle, PA 17225: Catalog $1 ◆ Wool, linen, and cotton-woven trims; webbing and braids; and military lace. 717-597-1782.

**YLI Corp.,** 161 W. Main St., Rock Hill, SC 29730: Catalog $2.50 ◆ Silk, spark organdy, synthetic silk, ribbons, silk thread, and craft supplies. 800-854-1932.

## FANS

**A to Z Vac-Fan Showroom,** 300 E. Oakland Park Blvd., Fort Lauderdale, FL 33334: Free catalog ◆ Ceiling, wall, and floor-mounted fans. Also light kits and accessories.

**Casablanca Fan Company,** 761 Carpointe Center Dr., Pomona, CA 91768: Free information ◆ Ceiling fans and replacement parts. 818-369-6441.

**Fan Fair,** 2251 Wisconsin Ave. NW, Washington, DC 20007: Free catalog ◆ Casablanca and Hunter ceiling fans and unusual table and floor lamps. 202-342-6290.

**The Fan Man Inc.,** 1914 Abrams Pkwy., Dallas, TX 75214: Brochure $2 ◆ Fans from the 1890s to 1990s. 214-826-7700.

**The Fan Man (Oklahoma City),** 2721 NW 109th Terrace, Oklahoma City, OK 73120: Free information ◆ New and restored antique fans. 405-751-0933.

**Hunter Fan Company,** 2500 Fisco Ave., Memphis, TN 38114: Catalog $1 ◆ Ceiling fans, remote control units, fixtures, and electronic thermostats. 901-745-9222. www.hunterfan.com

**Lamp Warehouse,** 1073 39th St., Brooklyn, NY 11219: Free information with long SASE ◆ Ceiling fans and fixtures. 800-52-LITES; 718-436-8500 (in NY).

## FAUCETS & PLUMBING FIXTURES

**Barnett Inc.,** 333 Lenox Ave., Jacksonville, FL 32254: Free catalog ◆ Plumbing, HVAC, hardware, and electrical products. 904-384-6530. www.bntt.com

**Chicago Faucet Company,** 2100 S. Clearwater Dr., Des Plaines, IL 60018: Free list of retail sources ◆ Bathroom plumbing fixtures. 847-803-5000.

**Delta Faucet Company,** 55 E. 111th St., Indianapolis, IN 46280: Free information ◆ Solid brass plumbing fixtures. 800-345-3358.

**Elkay Manufacturing Company,** 2222 Camden Ct., Oak Brook, IL 60521: Free information ◆ Faucets with retractable nozzles. 847-574-8484. www.elkay.com

**The Fixture Exchange,** P.O. Box 307, Bainbridge, GA 31717: Catalog $5 ◆ Plumbing fixtures and faucets, lighting, kitchen appliances, and more. 800-326-2694.

**Faucet Outlet,** P.O. Box 547, Middletown, NY 10940: Free catalog ◆ Bathroom and kitchen faucets, sinks, and other accessories. 800-444-5783. www.faucet.com

**Grohe America Inc.,** 241 Covington Dr., Bloomingdale, IL 60108: Information $3 ◆ Kitchen faucets and attachments. 847-582-7711. www.grohe.com

**Kohler Company,** 444 Highland Dr., Kohler, WI 53044: Catalog $3 ◆ Solid brass faucets and plumbing fixtures. 800-220-2291. www.kohlerco.com

**MAC the Antique Plumber,** 6325 Elvas Ave., Sacramento, CA 95819: Catalog $6 (refundable) ◆ Plumbing fixtures in a 1900s style. 916-454-4507.

**Moen Inc.,** 25300 Al Moen Dr., North Olmsted, OH 44070: Free information ◆ Single and double-handle faucets for bathrooms and kitchens. 800-533-6636.

**The Renovator's Supply,** P.O. Box 2515, Conway, NH 03818: Free catalog ◆ Plumbing fixtures and hardware. 800-659-0203.

**Ultraflo,** P.O. Box 2294, 310 Industrial Ln., Sandusky, OH 44870: Free brochure ◆ Push-button temperature-controlled plumbing systems. 419-626-8182. www.ultraflo.com

## FEATHERS

**Crafty's Featherworks,** P.O. Box 370, Overton, NV 89040: Free information ◆ Feathers for making floral arrangements, Native American crafts, millinery, fly-tying, and accent pieces. 702-397-8211.

**Feathermakers,** Jerry & Karen Snyder, 1090 Kitt Narcisse Rd., Colville, WA 99114: Catalog $2 ◆ Handpainted and custom made reproduction eagle tail feathers. Also beadwork, bonnets, bustles, and more. 509-684-3210.

**Gettinger Feather Corp.,** 16 W. 36th St., New York, NY 10033: Price list $2 ◆ Raw or dyed ostrich, marabou, or turkey feathers and feathers from other birds. 212-695-9470.

**The Mercantile Company,** 2016 N. 4th St., Flagstaff, AZ 86004: Free catalog (specify supplies and findings or finished products) ◆ Sterling silver jewelry supplies, Native American arts and crafts, feathers, and leather supplies. 800-413-CHUCK.

**Cliff C. Paulsen,** P.O. Box 19146, Sacramento, CA 95819: Catalog $1 ◆ Indian (Native American) beads, bells, feathers, and other craft supplies. 916-485-9838.

**The White Buffalo Stores Inc.,** 418 E. Beale, Kingman, AZ 86401: Catalog $1 (refundable) ◆ Exotic feathers. 520-753-7800. www.ctaz.com/~whitbuflo

## FENCES & GATES

**Abode Lumber Corp.,** 4872 Topanga Canyon Blvd., #410, Woodland Hills, CA 91364: Free list of retail sources ◆ Polyethylene coated wood fences. 800-521-3633. www.wood-guard.com

**Architectural Iron Company,** 104 Ironwood Ct., Milford, PA 18337: Catalog $4 ◆ Reproduction cast-iron 18th and 19th-century gates, fences, and fountains. 800-442-4766.

**Bamboo & Rattan Works Inc.,** 470 Oberlin Ave. South, Lakewood, NJ 08701: Free information ◆ Custom bamboo fences. 800-4-BAMBOO.

**Bamboo Fencer,** 179 Boyston St., Jamaica Plain, MA 02130: Catalog $3 ◆ Fences, gates, and construction materials. 617-524-6137.

**Beaver Industries of Baldwin,** 1950 8th Ave., Baldwin, WI 54002: Free brochure ◆ Never-needs-painting, easy-to-install all-vinyl fences. 800-828-2947.

**Benner's Gardens,** P.O. Box 875, Bala Cynwyd, PA 19004: Free information ◆ Easily attached mesh barrier for garden and property protection. 800-753-4660. www.bennersgardens.com

**Bufftech Inc.,** 2525 Walden Ave., Cheektowaga, NY 14225: Free brochure ◆ Maintenance-free vinyl fence. 716-685-1600. www.bufftech.com

**California Redwood Association,** 405 Enfrente Dr., Ste. 200, Novato, CA 94949: Free information with long SASE ◆ Redwood fences. 415-382-0662. www.calredwood.org

**Centaur HTP Fencing Systems,** 2802 E. Avalon Dr., Muscle Shoals, AL 35661: Free information ◆ Flexible fences with rails that return to their original shape after being struck. 800-368-7635.

**Central Tractor Farm & Family Center,** P.O. Box 3330, Des Moines, IA 50316: Free catalog ◆ Fence supplies. 800-247-1760; 515-266-3101 (in IA).

**Color Guard Fence Company,** P.O. Box 28, Sheboygan Falls, WI 53085: Free information ◆ Vinyl fences. 800-832-8914.

**Comtrad Industries,** 2820 Waterford Lake Dr., Ste. 102, Midlothian, VA 23113: Free information ◆ Electric invisible pet containment systems. 800-992-2966. www.comtrad.com

**Custom Ironwork Inc.,** P.O. Box 180, Union, KY 41091: Catalog $2 ◆ Reproduction cast and wrought iron fences in Victorian and other styles. 606-384-4122.

**Delgard Fence,** 8600 River Rd., Delair, NJ 08110: Free information ◆ Weather-resistant aluminum fences. 800-235-0185.

**Elite Aluminum Fence Products,** 6675 Burroughs, Sterling Heights, MI 48314: Free information ◆ Aluminum fences with a baked-on enamel finish. 810-731-1331.

**Furman Lumber Inc.,** P.O. Box 130, Nutting Lake, MA 01865: Free information ◆ Factory-assembled picket fences. 800-843-9663. www.furmanlumber.com

**Gardner Fence Systems,** 5525 34th Ave. North, Minneapolis, MN 55422: Free information ◆ Maintenance free vinyl fencing. 800-788-3461; 612-531-3910 (in MN). www.gardnerfence.com

**Genova Products,** 7034 E. Court St., Box 309, Davison, MI 48423: Free brochure ◆ Easy installation solid vinyl fencing products. 810-744-3130. www.genovaproducts.com

**Heritage Fence Company,** P.O. Box 121, Skippack, PA 19464: Catalog $2 ◆ Reproduction wood colonial and Victorian-style fences. 610-584-6710.

**Innotek Pet Products Inc.,** One Innoway Dr., Garrett, IN 46738: Free list of retail sources ◆ Pet containment system and remote training equipment. 800-826-5527. www.pet-products.com

**Invisible Fence Company Inc.,** 355 Phoenixville Pike, Malvern, PA 19355: Free information ◆ Invisible electronic pet containment fence. 800-538-DOGS. www.ifco.com

**Jerith Manufacturing Company Inc.,** 3901 G St., Philadelphia, PA 19124: Free brochure ◆ Rust-proof high-strength aluminum alloy fences with a baked on enamel finish. 800-344-2242.

**Moultrie Manufacturing,** P.O. Drawer 1179, Moultrie, GA 31776: Catalog $3 ◆ Reproduction "Old South" gates and fences. 800-841-8674.

**OuterSpace Landscape Furnishings Inc.,** 7533 Draper Ave., La Jolla, CA 92037: Free information ◆ Steel fences, gates, and modular components for trellis and garden structures. 800-338-2499.

**Pool Fence Company,** 1791-907 Blount Rd., Pompano Beach, FL 33069: Free brochure ◆ Protection-against entry fences for swimming pools. 800-992-2206. www.protectachild.com

**Premier Fence Systems,** 2031 300th St., Washington, IA 52353: Free catalog ◆ Animal and rodent control fences. 800-282-6631.

**Radio Fence,** 230 E. Russell St., Fayetteville, NC 28301: Free information ◆ Easy-to-install electronic invisible pet containment systems. 800-775-8404.

**Southeastern Wood Products Company,** P.O. Box 113, Griffin, GA 30224: Free brochure ◆ Wire and wood fences, plant supports, and cold frames. 800-722-7486; 770-227-7486 (in GA).

**Stewart Iron Works Company,** P.O. Box 2612, Covington, KY 41012: Catalog $3 ◆ Victorian-style fences and gates. 606-431-1985.

**Texas Standard Picket Company,** P.O. Box 12345, Austin, TX 78711: Free brochure ◆ Reproduction Victorian-style fence pickets. 512-472-1101.

**Triple Crown Fence,** P.O. Box 2000, Milford, IN 46542: Free list of retail sources ◆ Vinyl fences. 800-365-3625; 219-658-9442 (in IN).

**UltraGuard Fence,** P.O. Box 2010, Akron, OH 44309: Free information ◆ Vinyl post and rail fences. 800-457-4342. www.ultraguardvinylfence.com

**West Virginia Fence Corp.,** RR 81, Box 3, Lindside, WV 24951: Free catalog ◆ Permanent and portable electric pet containment fences. 800-356-5458; 304-753-4387 (in WV).

## FENCING

**American Fencers Supply Company,** 1180 Folsom St., San Francisco, CA 94103: Free information ◆ Gloves, masks, shoes, uniforms, blades, epees, foils, rapiers, and sabers. 415-863-7911. www.amfence.com

**Blade Fencing Equipment Inc.,** 212 W. 15th St., New York, NY 10011: Free information ◆ Gloves, masks, shoes, uniforms, blades, epees, foils, rapiers, and sabers. 212-620-0114. www.blade-fencing.com

**The Fencing Post,** 1004 Bird Ave., San Jose, CA 05125: Free catalog ◆ Fencing equipment. 408-297-4448.

**Genesport Industries Ltd.,** Hokkaido Karate Equipment Manufacturing Company, 150 King St., Montreal, Quebec, Canada H3C 2P3: Free information ◆ Gloves, masks, uniforms, blades, and sabers. 514-861-1856.

**The Knife Center,** P.O. Box 902, 11263 Somerset Ave., Beltsville, MD 20705: Free catalog ◆ Knives, cases, accessories, fencing swords, and martial arts weapons. 800-338-6799.

**M.A.S. Weapons,** 5600 E. 36th St. North, Tulsa, OK 74115: Free catalog ◆ Fencing equipment. 918-835-0467.

**Sportime,** Customer Service, 1 Sportime Way, Atlanta, GA 30340: Free information ◆ Fencing equipment. 800-444-5700; 770-449-5700 (in GA).

## FIRE FIGHTING & POLICE ITEMS

**The Baird Company,** P.O. Box 7240, Moreno Valley, CA 92552: Free catalog ◆ Police insignia and other collectibles. Also books on law enforcement, crime, and the military. 909-943-4180. bairdco@aol.com

**Chimneyville Hobbies,** 233 Penner Dr., Pearl, MS 39208: Free list of retail sources with long SASE ◆ Law enforcement and fire apparatus decals. 601-932-6165.

**CIAssociates,** 2801 Shelterwood, Arlington, TX 76016: Catalog $5 ◆ Investigative aids and accessories.

**Darrell's Automotive & Restorations,** 2639 N. Tripp Ave., Odessa, TX 79763: Free information ◆ Restored fire-fighting equipment. 915-381-7713.

**Firefighters Bookstore,** 18281 Gothard St., #105, Huntington Beach, CA 92648: Free catalog ◆ Books, software, and videos for firefighters. 714-375-4888. www.firebooks.com

**Frontier Lassix,** P.O. Drawer 1865, Magnolia, AR 71753: Free information ◆ Reproduction silver-plated badges worn by Old West lawmen. 501-234-7402.

**Mountain Sales,** 163 E. Main St., Little Falls, NJ 07424: Free brochure ◆ Audiocassettes on fire fighting activities. 800-575-1075. www.hicom.net/~mountainsales

**NIC Law Enforcement Supply,** 500 Flournoy Lucas Rd., Bldg. 3, P.O. Box 5950, Shreveport, LA 71135: Free catalog ◆ Law enforcement supplies. 888-642-0007. alanh@nic-inc.com

**REFUNDABLE Instruments Inc.,** 535 W. Iron Ave., #125, Mesa, AZ 85210: Free catalog ◆ Systems and equipment for law enforcement and security. 800-216-2531.

## FIRE SAFETY

### Books & Educational Materials

**National Fire Protection Association,** 1 Batterymarch Park, P.O. Box 9101, Quincy, MA 02269: Free catalog ◆ Fire safety books, products, and services. 800-344-3555. www.nfpa.org

### Escape Ladders

**Jomy Safety Ladder Company,** 6255 Longbow Dr., Boulder, CO 80301: Free information ◆ Collapsible fire escape ladder. 800-255-2591. www.jomy.com

**Walter Kidde,** Division Kidde Inc., 1394 S. 3rd St., Mebane, NC 27302: Free information ◆ Escape ladders, smoke and fire alarms, and fire extinguishers.

**Ladder Man Inc.,** 3025 Silver Dr., Columbus, OH 43224: Free catalog ◆ Safety, attic, and other fire escape equipment. Also specialty, articulating, and stairwell ladders. 800-783-8887.

### Fire Extinguishers

**Black & Decker,** 6 Armstrong Rd., Shelton, CT 06484: Free information ◆ Fire extinguishers. 800-544-6986. www.blackandecker.com

**Fireboy/Xintex,** P.O. Box 152, Grand Rapids, MI 49502: Free information ◆ Fire extinguishers for boats. 616-454-8337. www.fireboy-xintex.com

**First Alert,** 780 McClure Rd., Aurora, IL 60404: Free information ◆ Fire extinguishers. 800-323-9005.

**Walter Kidde,** Division Kidde Inc., 1394 S. 3rd St., Mebane, NC 27302: Free information ◆ Escape ladders, smoke and fire alarms, and fire extinguishers.

### Smoke Detectors

**Black & Decker,** 6 Armstrong Rd., Shelton, CT 06484: Free information ◆ Smoke alarms. 800-544-6986. www.blackandecker.com

**First Alert,** 780 McClure Rd., Aurora, IL 60404: Free information ◆ Smoke alarms. 800-323-9005.

**Walter Kidde,** Division Kidde Inc., 1394 S. 3rd St., Mebane, NC 27302: Free information ◆ Escape ladders, smoke and fire alarms, and fire extinguishers.

**Radio Shack,** Division Tandy Corp., One Tandy Center, Fort Worth, TX 76102: Free information ◆ Smoke alarms. 817-390-3011. www.radioshack.com

**Sanyo Fisher Service Corp.,** 1411 W. 190th St., Ste. 800, Gardena, CA 90248: Free information with a long SASE ◆ Electrostatic air cleaner/ionizer with a smoke sensor.

### Sprinkler Systems

**Central Fire Sprinkler Corp.,** 451 N. Cannon Ave., Lansdale, PA 19446: Free information ◆ Residential sprinkler systems. 215-362-0700.

**The Reliable Automatic Sprinkler Company,** 103 Fairview Park Dr., Elmsford, NY 10523: Free information ◆ Residential sprinkler systems. 800-431-1588.

## FIREPLACES

### Accessories & Tools

**The Adams Company,** P.O. Box 268, Dubuque, IA 52004: Free list of retail sources ◆ Solid brass and black cast-iron fireplace tool sets, baskets, screens, firebacks, lighters, and fenders. 800-553-3012.

**Alco-Brite,** P.O. Box 840926, Hildale, UT 84784: Free information ◆ Canned jelled fire starter with dampered snap-on stoves for emergency preparedness and outdoor activities. 800-473-0717. www.alco-brite.com

**Art Marble & Stone,** 5862 Peachtree Industrial Blvd., Atlanta, GA 30341: Free brochure ◆ Glass doors, tools, mantels, and gas logs with glowing embers for natural or LP gas. 800-476-0298.

**Bona Decorative Hardware,** 3073 Madison Rd., Cincinnati, OH 45209: Price list $2 ◆ Solid brass hardware for fireplaces, bathrooms, doors, cabinets, furniture, and kitchens. 513-321-7877.

**Chadds Ford Fireside Shop,** 103 Wilmington, Chadds Ford, PA 19317: Free information ◆ Custom mantels, reproduction firebacks, realistic gas logs, screens, bellows, and accessories. 610-358-9355.

**Coppersmiths,** Custom Copper & Brass Works, P.O. Box 2675, Oakhurst, CA 93644: Free brochure ◆ Fireplace hoods, cupolas, mailboxes, and dormers. 209-658-8909.

**Country Iron Foundry,** P.O. Box 600, Paoli, PA 19301: Catalog $2 ◆ Handcrafted colonial-style and other firebacks. 610-353-5542.

**EP Importers,** P.O. Box 80250, Portland, OR 97280: Information $5 (refundable) ◆ Gas fire units for conventional fireplaces. 503-246-8031. www.gasfires.com

**Fireside Distributors Inc.,** 4013 Atlantic Ave., Raleigh, NC 27604: Free information ◆ Fireplace accessories. 800-333-3473; 919-872-4434 (in NC).

**The Fireside Shop,** 5862 Peachtree Industrial Blvd., Atlanta, GA 30341: Free brochure ◆ Gas logs and fireplace accessories. 800-827-3897; 770-458-2331 (in GA). www.fireside.com

**Grate Fires,** P.O. Box 351, Athens, GA 30603: Free brochure ◆ Authentic English gas-coal fires. 706-353-8281.

**Halides America Inc.,** P.O. Box 731, Sparta, NJ 07871: Free information ◆ Fireplace accessories, handcarved mantels, and wood moldings. 973-729-8876.

**Hargrove Manufacturing Corp.,** 207 Wellston Park Rd., Sand Springs, OK 74063: Free information ◆ Gas log sets. 800-725-4166.

**High Country Antler Art,** 210 E. Creek, Fredericksburg, TX 78624: Catalog $5 ◆ Custom designed internally wired chandeliers, candelabras, lamps, and fireplace tools. 210-997-2263.

**Images In Steel,** P.O. Box 288, Clyde Park, MT 59018: Catalog $2 (refundable) ◆ Weather vanes, fireplace screens, furniture, custom designed art, and functional western pieces handcrafted from plate steel. 800-511-1324; 406-686-4166 (in MT).

**Iron Craft,** Old Rt. 28, P.O. Box 351, Ossipee, NH 03864: Free catalog ◆ Kettles and grates, enameled cookware, butcher aprons, bellows, heating systems for fireplaces, weather vanes, signs, cast-iron items, and gifts. 603-539-6159.

**Kayne & Son Custom Hardware,** 100 Daniel Ridge Rd., Candler, NC 28715: Catalog $4.50 ◆ Fireplace tools and hand-forged hardware. 704-667-8868.

**Lemee's Fireplace Equipment,** 815 Bedford St., Bridgewater, MA 02324: Catalog $2 ◆ Fireplace equipment. 508-697-2672.

**Jim Leonard Antique Hardware,** 509 Tangle Dr., Jamestown, NC 27282: Catalog $3 ◆ Wrought-iron 18th and 19th-century fireplace equipment. 910-454-3583.

**New England Fire-backs,** 161 Main St., P.O. Box 268, Woodbury, CT 06798: Free brochure ◆ Reproduction antique firebacks. 203-263-5737.

**Old Smithy Shop,** 195 Rt. 13, Brookline, NH 03055: Catalog $3 ◆ Hand-forged reproduction colonial hardware, fireplace equipment, curtain accessories, and bathroom fixtures. 603-672-4113.

**Plow & Hearth,** P.O. Box 5000, Madison, VA 22727: Free catalog ◆ Gardening tools, birdhouses and feeders, porch and lawn furniture, fireplace accessories, and gifts for pets. 800-627-1712. peggy@plowhearth.com

**Portland Willamette,** Byers Industries Inc., 6800 NE 59th Pl., Portland, OR 97213: Free list of retail sources ◆ Fireplace screens and radiant heat ceramic gas logs. 503-288-7511.

**Prestons Household Accessories,** P.O. Box 369, Ossipee, NH 03864: Catalog $3 ◆ Stove and fireplace accessories and cast-iron cookware. 603-539-4114.

**Seymour Manufacturing Company Inc.,** 500 N. Broadway, P.O. Box 248, Seymour, IN 47274: Free list of retail sources ◆ Fireplace tools, stove and fireplace repair accessories, brooms, bellows, and fire-starting supplies. 812-522-2900.

## Fireplaces (Indoor/Outdoor) & Fireplace Kits

**Aladdin Steel Products Inc.,** 401 N. Wynne St., Colville, WA 99114: Free list of retail sources ◆ Wood, pellet, and gas-burning stoves. Also fireplace inserts. 800-234-2508.

**Alco-Brite,** P.O. Box 840926, Hildale, UT 84784: Free information ◆ Canned-jelled firestarter and other accessories. 800-473-0717. www.alco-brite.com

**Century Fireplace Furnishings Inc.,** 1606 E. 20th St., Joplin, MO 64804: Free information ◆ Fireplace furnaces. 800-284-4328.

**Charmaster Products Inc.,** 2307 Hwy. 2 West, Grand Rapids, MN 55744: Free brochure ◆ Fireplaces and wood-burning, wood-gas, and wood-oil furnaces and conversion units. 218-326-6786.

**Coleman Outdoor Products Inc.,** P.O. Box 2931, Wichita, KS 67201: Free catalog ◆ Portable outdoor patio fireplace. Uses firewood or pressed-wood logs. 800-835-3278. www.coleman.com

**Country Stoves Inc.,** P.O. Box 987, Auburn, WA 98071: Free information ◆ Wood and gas stoves, fireplaces, and inserts. 206-735-1100.

**Dietmeyer,** Ward & Stroud Inc., P.O. Box 323, Vashon Island, WA 98070: Free information ◆ Wood-burning radiant heat fireplaces. 800-325-3629.

**Empire Control Systems,** 1918 Freeburg Ave., Belleville, IL 62222: Free brochure ◆ Room heaters, floor furnaces, commercial/industrial unit heaters and duct furnaces, fireplace products, free-standing and semi-enclosed gas stoves, chicken and turkey fryers, and accessories. 800-851-3153; 618-233-7420 (in IL). www.empirecomfort.com

**Grate Fires,** P.O. Box 351, Athens, GA 30603: Free brochure ◆ Authentic English gas-coal fireplace unit. 706-353-8281.

**Heat-N-Glo,** 6665 W. Hwy. 13, Savage, MN 55378: Free brochure ◆ Fireplaces and accessories. 800-669-4328. www.heatnglo.com

**Heatilator Inc.,** 1915 W. Saunders St., Mt. Pleasant, IA 52641: Free information ◆ Wood-burning stoves and fireplace inserts. 800-926-4356. www.heatilator.com

**Jotul USA,** 400 Riverside St., Portland, ME 04104: Free list of retail sources ◆ Wood and gas cast iron stoves and fireplace inserts. 800-797-5912.

**Lopi International Ltd.,** Travis Industries, 10850 117th Pl. NE, Kirkland, WA 98033: Free information ◆ Fireplace inserts. 800-654-1177.

**Majestic Fireplaces,** 1000 E. Market St., Huntington, IN 46750: Free information ◆ Fireplaces and accessories. 800-525-1898. www.majesticproducts.com

**Napoleon Fireplaces,** RR 1, Barrie, Ontario, Canada L4M 4Y8: Free information ◆ Gas and wood-fired fireplaces. 705-721-1212.

**Quartermoon International,** 3785 Myers Ln., St. James City, FL 33956: Free brochure ◆ No-assembly portable outdoor fireplaces. 941-283-1931.

**Rais & Wittus Inc.,** 23 Hack Green Rd., Pound Ridge, NY 10576: Free catalog ◆ Fireplace stoves for heating and cooking. 914-764-5679.

**Rüegg Fireplaces,** 216 US Hwy. 206, Ste. 12, Somerville, NJ 08876: Free information ◆ Fireplaces. 800-347-3843.

**Superior Fireplace,** 4325 Artesia Ave., Fullerton, CA 92633: Free information ◆ Fireplaces and accessories. 714-521-7302.

**Vermont Castings Inc.,** Rt. 107, P.O. Box 501, Bethel, VT 05032: Free information ◆ Easy-to-install energy-efficient fireplaces. 800-227-8683.

**Wilkening Fireplace Company,** P.O. Box 366, Walter, MN 56484: Free brochure ◆ Fireplace units, new and replacement doors, and inserts. 800-367-7976.

## Mantels

**A.D.I. Corp.,** 5000 Nicholson Ct., North Bethesda, MD 20895: Free information ◆ Wood mantels. 301-564-1550.

**Architectural Paneling Inc.,** 979 3rd Ave., New York, NY 10022: Catalog $10 (refundable) ◆ Handcarved wood mantels and moldings. 212-371-9632.

**Art Di Rico,** 4109 E. Parkway, Gatlinburg, TN 37738: Free information ◆ Custom-sculpted oak and mahogany wood doors and mantels. 800-434-5427.

**Bryant Stove Inc.,** Box 2048, Thorndike, ME 04986: Free brochure ◆ Wood mantels and ornamental trim. 207-568-3665.

**By-Gone Days Antiques Inc.,** 3100 South Blvd., Charlotte, NC 28209: Free information ◆ Mantels, restored door hardware, and architectural antiques. 704-527-8717.

**Chadds Ford Fireside Shop,** 103 Wilmington, Chadds Ford, PA 19317: Free information ◆ Custom mantels, reproduction firebacks, realistic gas logs, screens, bellows, and accessories. 610-358-9355.

**Decorators Supply Corp.,** 3610 S. Morgan St., Chicago, IL 60609: Free list of retail sources ◆ Wood mantels and other detailed replicas of hand carvings. 773-847-6300.

**Driwood Ornamental Wood Moulding,** P.O. Box 1729, Florence, SC 29503: Catalog $6 (refundable) ◆ Mantels, embossed wood molding, raised paneling, curved stairs, and doors. 803-669-2478.

**Halides America Inc.,** P.O. Box 731, Sparta, NJ 07871: Free information ◆ Fireplace accessories, handcarved mantels, and wood moldings. 973-729-8876.

**Heritage Mantels Inc.,** P.O. Box 240, Bridgeport, CT 06490: Catalog $3 ◆ Reproduction antique marble composition mantels. 203-335-0552.

**House of Moulding,** 15202 Oxnard St., Van Nuys, CA 91411: Catalog $5 ◆ Fireplaces, mantels, wood moldings and trim, and ceiling medallions. 800-327-4186.

**C. Larkin Company,** 510 E. Barnard St., West Chester, PA 19382: Catalog $8 (refundable) ◆ Handcrafted mantels, wainscoting, and moldings. 610-696-9096.

**The Maizefield Company,** P.O. Box 336, Port Townsend, WA 98368: Free brochure ◆ Mantels, turnings, staircases, and moldings. 360-385-6789.

**Mantels of Yesteryear Inc.,** P.O. Box 908, 70 W. Tennessee Ave., McCaysville, GA 30555: Free information ◆ Custom and restored antique mantels. 706-492-5534. www.mantelsofyesteryear.com

**Piedmont Mantel & Millwork,** 4320 Interstate Dr., Macon, GA 31210: Catalog $3 ◆ Colonial-style mantels and salvaged heart-pine flooring. 912-477-7536.

**Readybuilt Products Company,** 1701 McHenry St., Baltimore, MD 21223: Catalog $2 ◆ Handcarved wood mantels in American and English-styles, electric/gas fireplace logs, facings, and fireplaces. 410-233-5833. www.readybuilt.com

**Stone Magic,** 301 Pleasant Dr., Dallas, TX 75217: Free brochure ◆ Classic to contemporary cast stone mantels. Also interior and exterior cast stone for other building projects. 800-597-3606. www.stonelegends.com

**Urban Artifacts,** 4700 Wissahickon Ave., Philadelphia, PA 19144: Free information ◆ Carved antique wood and marble mantels. 800-621-1962.

**Vintage Pine Company,** P.O. Box 85, Prospect, VA 23960: Free information ◆ Custom heart-pine flooring, cabinets, doors, mantels, moldings, and other architectural accouterments. 804-248-9102.

**Westfire Manufacturing,** 19322 SW Mohave Ct., Tualatin, OR 97062: Free catalog ◆ Handcrafted fireplace mantels. Includes direct vent cabinet and corner designs. 503-692-8105.

**The Wood Factory,** 111 Railroad St., Navasota, TX 77868: Catalog $2 ◆ Ornamental trim, mantels, doors, and reproduction millwork. 409-825-7233.

## FIREWORKS

**Because regulations governing the purchase and use of fireworks vary from state to state, consumers should read applicable regulations before ordering them from the companies listed below. Consumers should also make certain that they buy fireworks only from licensed or certified vendors who meet the requirements governing their sale and manufacture. Using fireworks illegally can result in substantial fines and possible jail sentences.**

### "Backyard" Fireworks

**Bethany Sales Company,** P.O. Box 248, Bethany, IL 61914: Catalog $10 ◆ Class C "backyard" fireworks. 217-665-3395.

**Golden Gate Fireworks Inc.,** 360 Post St., Ste. 705, San Francisco, CA 94108: Free catalog ◆ Class C "backyard" fireworks.

**Neptune Fireworks Company Inc.,** 768 E. Dania Beach Blvd., P.O. Box 398, Dania, FL 33004: Free catalog ◆ Class C "backyard" fireworks. 800-456-2264; 954-920-6770 (in FL). www.neptunefireworks.com

**Phantom Fireworks,** P.O. Box 66, Columbiana, OH 44408: Free information ◆ Class C "backyard" fireworks. 800-777-1699. www.fireworks.com

### Fireworks Display Specialists

**Fireworks by Grucci,** One Grucci Ln., Brookhaven, NY 11719: Free information ◆ Class B display fireworks. 800-227-0088; 516-286-0088 (in NY). fireworksbygrucci@worldnet.att.net

**Zambelli Internationale,** P.O. Box 1463, New Castle, PA 16103: Free information ◆ Class B display fireworks. 800-245-0397.

### Fireworks Memorabilia

**American Fireworks News,** HC67, Box 30, Dingmans Ferry, PA 18328: Free brochure ◆ Books, manuals, and information for people who collect and research fireworks and fireworks memorabilia. 717-828-8417. www.98.net/afn

**Dennis C. Manochio, Curator,** 4th of July Americana & Fireworks Museum, P.O. Box 2010, Saratoga, CA 95070: Free information ◆ Old fireworks catalogs, literature, toys, and fireworks memorabilia. 408-996-1963.

## FISHING & FLY-TYING

### Equipment & Supplies

**Abby Precision Manufacturing,** 70 Industrial Dr., Cloverdale, CA 95425: Free list of retail sources ◆ Fly-tying vises and accessories. 800-DYNA-KING; 707-894-5566 (in CA).

**Abel Reels,** 165 Aviador St., Camarillo, CA 93010: Free information ◆ Precision-engineered fly reels. 800-848-7335.

**Access to Recreation Inc.,** 8 Sandra Ct., Newbury Park, CA 91320: Free catalog ◆ Adaptive fishing equipment for the disabled. 800-634-4351.

**Adams Reels,** P.O. Box 104, Shushan, NY 12874: Free information ◆ Reels. 518-677-2276.

**American Angling Supplies,** 23 Main St., Salem, NH 03079: Free information ◆ Fly-fishing equipment and supplies. 603-893-3333.

**Ande Inc.,** 1310 53rd St., West Palm Beach, FL 33407: Free brochure ◆ Monofilament fishing line, T-shirts, bags, hats, and accessories. 561-842-2474.

**Angler's Workshop,** P.O. Box 1010, Woodland, WA 98674: Free catalog ◆ Fishing and hunting videos and rods, tackle, reels, and other equipment. 360-225-9445. www.anglersworkshop.com

**Area Rule Engineering,** 931 Calle Negocio, San Clemente, CA 92673: Free information ◆ Big-game fishing tackle and accessories. 714-366-1333. www.area-rule.com

**Atlantis,** 30 Barnet Blvd., New Bedford, MA 02745: Free catalog ◆ Foul weather gear and clothing for yachtsmen and fishermen. 508-995-7000.

**B'n'M Pole Company,** Box 231, West Point, MS 39773: Free information ◆ Graphite and fiberglass poles and rods for crappie fishing. 800-647-6363; 601-494-5092 (in MS).

**Bagley Baits,** P.O. Box 810, Winter Haven, FL 33880: Free information ◆ Lures. 941-294-4271.

**Dan Bailey's Fly Shop,** P.O. Box 1019, Livingston, MT 59047: Free catalog ◆ Tackle, fly-tying supplies, and fishing and hunting videos. 800-356-4052.

**Barlow's Tackle Shop,** Box 830369, Richardson, TX 75083: Free catalog ◆ Tackle and rod-building supplies, lure components, plastic lures, and fishing and hunting videos. 972-231-5982.

**The Bass Pond,** 5211 S. Santa Fe Dr., Littleton, CO 80120: Catalog $1 ◆ Flies, fly-tying components, fly rods, reels, lines, leaders, floats, and clothing. 303-795-8956.

**Bass Pro Shops,** 1935 S. Campbell, Springfield, MO 65898: Free information ◆ Float fishing and outdoor equipment. 800-227-7776. www.basspro.com

**Bead Tackle,** 600 Main St., Monroe, CT 06468: Catalog $1 ◆ Rod caddies, swivels, bait and eel rigs, sinkers, jigs, and lures. 203-459-1213.

**L.L. Bean,** Casco St., Freeport, ME 04032: Free catalog ◆ Fly-tying supplies, fishing and hunting videos, and fly, bass, and saltwater fishing equipment. 800-221-4221. www.llbean.com

**Berkeley Inc.,** 1900 18th St., Spirit Lake, IA 51360: Free catalog ◆ Fishing and fly lines, fly leaders, and spinning, plug and bait casting, and saltwater rods. 800-237-5539; 712-336-1520 (in IA).

**Best American Duffel,** 2601 Elliot Ave., Ste. 4317, Seattle, WA 98121: Free information ◆ Tackle bags. 800-424-BAGS.

**Blue Ribbon Flies,** Box 1037, West Yellowstone, MT 59758: Free catalog ◆ Flies and fly-tying materials. 406-646-7642. brflies@alpinet.net

**J.A. Bradford Company,** 3700 Lawndale, Fort Worth, TX 76133: Free information ◆ Handmade split bamboo rods. 817-292-3324.

**Braid Products Inc.,** 616 E. Avenue P, Palmdale, CA 93550: Free information ◆ Trolling lures. 805-266-9791.

**Charlie Brewer's Slider Company,** P.O. Box 130, Lawrenceburg, TN 38464: Free information ◆ Soft plastic crawfish lures. 800-762-4701; 615-762-4700 (in TN).

**Browning Company,** Dept. C006, One Browning Pl., Morgan, UT 84050: Catalog $2 ◆ Saltwater spinning reels, spinning rods, and plug and bait casting reels and rods. 800-333-3288. www.browning.com

**Bud Lilly's Trout Shop,** P.O. Box 530, West Yellowstone, MT 59758: Catalog $2 ◆ Rods, reels, flies, and fly-fishing tackle. 800-854-9559. info@budlillys.com

**Cabela's,** One Cabela Dr., Sidney, NE 69160: Free catalog ◆ Float fishing supplies and hunting and outdoor equipment. 800-237-4444. www.cabelas.com

**Capt. Harry's Fishing Supplies,** 100 NE 11th St., Miami, FL 33132: Catalog $3 ◆ Fly and saltwater fishing, bass fishing, and fly-tying supplies. 800-327-4088; 305-374-4661 (in FL). www.captharry.com

**Centennial Classic Sales,** 256 Nashua Ct., Grand Junction, CO 81503: Free catalog ◆ Fly-fishing equipment and accessories. 970-243-8780. spurr@kingfisher.com

**Dale Clemens Custom Tackle,** 444 Schantz Spring Rd., Allentown, PA 18104: Catalog $2 ◆ Rod-building and fly-tying materials and tools. 610-395-5119. www.clemenstackle.com

**Clouser's Fly Shop,** 101 Ulrich St., Middletown, PA 17057: Catalog $1 ◆ Flies and fly-tying supplies. 717-944-6541.

**Cold Spring Anglers,** P.O. Box 129, Carlisle, PA 17013: Catalog $3 ◆ Flies, tackle, and fly-tying supplies. 717-245-2646. www.coldspringanglers.com

**Compleat Angler Inc.,** 1320 Marshall Ln., Helena, MT 59601: Free information ◆ Fly-fishing accessories. 406-442-1973.

**Cortland Line Company,** P.O. Box 5588, Cortland, NY 13045: Free information ◆ Fly reels, lines, and leaders. 607-756-2851. www.cortlandline.com

**Cougar Claw-Zetabait,** 9559 Hickory St. South, Foley, AL 36535: Free information ◆ Tree stands and plastic fishing lures. 334-943-1902.

**Dan Craft Enterprises,** 88354 Westoak Rd., Westfir, OR 97492: Free catalog ◆ Flies and custom, handmade fly rods. 541-782-4404. www.dancraftent.com

**Creme Lure Company,** P.O. Box 6162, Tyler, TX 75711: Free information ◆ Lures. 903-561-0522.

**D & T Enterprises,** 20518 Meadow Lake Rd., Snohomish, WA 98290: Free information ◆ Fly-fishing products. 360-805-9231. www.freightrain.com

**Daiwa Corp.,** 12851 Midway Pl., Cerritos, CA 90703: Catalog $1 ◆ Plug and bait casting reels and rods, saltwater reels and rods, and spin casting reels. 562-802-9589. www.daiwa.com

**Atelier De Pêche,** Richard Verret, 104 Proulx Ave., Vanier, Québec, Canada G1M 1W4: Free catalog ◆ Fly-tying supplies and equipment. 418-688-7590.

**Defender Industries Inc.,** 42 Great Neck Rd., Waterford, CT 06385: Free catalog ◆ Fishing and tackle equipment. 800-435-7180; 860-701-3415 (in CT). defenderus@aol.com

**Diamondback,** Rt. 100 South, P.O. Box 308, Stowe, VT 05672: Free catalog ◆ Fishing rods. 800-626-2970.

**Discount Flies & Tackle,** 7425 E. Peakview Ave., Englewood, CO 80110: Free catalog ◆ Fishing flies, tackle, float tubes and pontoons, and clothing. 888-483-5437. www.crccnet.com/flyfishing

**Dr. Slick Tools,** 114 S. Pacific, Dillon, MT 59725: Free catalog ◆ Surgical-quality scissors, clamps, pliers, accessories for fly-tying, and kits for beginners. 406-683-6489. www.drslick.com

**Eagle Claw Fishing Tackle,** P.O. Box 16011, Denver, CO 80216: Catalog 50¢ ◆ Reels, rods, and fishing hooks. 303-321-1481.

**Eagle River Fly Shop,** P.O. Box 12859, Rochester, NY 14580: Free catalog ◆ Fly-fishing equipment. 716-265-3593.

**EdgeWater Fishing Products,** 35 N. 1000 West, Clearfield, UT 84015: Catalog $5 ◆ Handmade flies and fly-tying supplies. 800-584-7647. www.FishtheEdge.com

**Egger's,** P.O. Box 1344, Cumming, GA 30130: Free catalog ◆ Fly-tying supplies, tools, and kits.

**English Angling Trappings,** P.O. Box 8885, Danbury, CT 06812: Catalog $1 (refundable) ◆ Fly-tying materials, tools, and accessories. 203-746-4121.

**Eppinger Manufacturing Company,** 6340 Schaefer Hwy., Dearborn, MI 48126: Free brochure ◆ Fishing lures. 313-582-3205.

**Feather-Craft Fly-fishing,** 8307 Manchester Rd., P.O. Box 19904, St. Louis, MO 63144: Free catalog ◆ Fly-tying supplies and accessories. 800-659-1707.

**Fenwick Corp.,** 1900 18th St., Spirit Lake, IA 51360: Catalog $1 ◆ Saltwater spinning reels and spinning, plug and bait casting, and fly rods. 800-642-7637. www.fenwickfishing.com

**Fly & Field,** 560 Crescent Blvd., Glen Ellyn, IL 60137: Catalog $2 ◆ Fly-tying accessories and videos. 800-328-9753. Flyfield@Flyfield.com

**The Fly Box,** 1293 NE 3rd St., Bend, OR 97701: Catalog $1 ◆ Rods and blanks, reels, rod-building components, fly-lines, cases, wading boots and clothing, float tubes and pontoon boats, custom-tied flies, fishing accessories, and books. 541-388-3330. flybox@empnet.com

**The Fly Shop,** 4140 Churn Creek Rd., Redding, CA 96002: Free information ◆ Fly-fishing supplies, tackle, and fishing and hunting videos. 800-669-3474. www.theflyshop.com

**The Fly Tyers,** 3020 Secor Ave., Bozeman, MT 59715: Free catalog ◆ Fly-tying materials. 888-243-3597.

**Freddie Bear Sports,** 17250 S. Oak Park, Tinley Park, IL 60477: Free information ◆ Hunting and fishing equipment. 708-532-4133. www.bowhunting.net/fbs

**Frontier Anglers,** 680 N. Montana St., Dillon, MT 59725: Free catalog ◆ Fly-fishing equipment and supplies. 800-228-5263.

**Gander Mountain (Cabela's),** One Cabela Dr., Sidney, ME 69160: Free catalog ◆ Outdoor sports equipment and clothing for fishing, hunting, and camping. 800-237-4444. www.cabelas.com

**J. Garman,** 316 Hartford Rd., Manchester, CT 06040: Free information ◆ Flies, fly-tying tools, and equipment. 203-643-2401.

**The Global Flyfisher,** 2849 W. Dundee Rd., Ste. 132, Northbrook, IL 60062: Catalog $2 ◆ Fly-fishing equipment. 800-531-1106.

**The Golden Hackle Fly Shop,** 329 Crescent Pl., Flushing, MI 48433: Catalog $2 (refundable) ◆ Fly-tying tools, supplies, hooks, flies, and accessories. 810-659-0018.

**Gone Fishin' Ent. Inc.,** P.O. Box 466, Custer, WA 98240: Free information ◆ Fly-tying materials. 360-366-5894.

**Green River Rodmakers,** Box 817, Green River, VT 05301: Free list of retail sources ◆ Bamboo and graphite fly rods. 802-257-4553. www.flyrods.com

**Griffin Enterprises Inc.,** P.O. Box 754, Bonner, MT 59823: Free list of retail sources ◆ Fly-tying tools and vises. 406-244-5407.

**Griffin Rod Company,** 1512 Yanovsky St., Kodiak, AK 99615: Free information ◆ Custom-built fly rods. 907-486-1439. www.griffinrods.com

**Phil Griffiths Fishing Tackle,** 1190 Genella, Waterford, MI 48328: Free list of retail sources ◆ Fly-tying materials and equipment. 810-673-7701.

**Gorilla & Sons,** P.O. Box 2309, Bellingham, WA 98227: Free catalog ◆ Fishing equipment. 800-246-7455.

**Hagen's Fishing Tackle,** 3150 W. Havens, Mitchell, SD 57301: Free catalog ◆ Tackle components. 800-541-4586.

**Harrison-Hoge Industries Inc.,** 19 N. Columbia St., Port Jefferson Station, NY 11776: Free catalog ◆ Fishing lures. 800-852-0925. www.panther-martinc.com

**Hart Tackle Company Inc.,** P.O. Box 898, 300 W. Main St., Stratford, OK 74872: Free information ◆ Bass lures. 580-759-2391. www.harttackle.com

**Phil Heck,** P.O. Box 425, Hartland, MI 48353: Free list ◆ Bamboo rods and accessories. 810-887-1458.

**High Mountain Rod Company,** 175 Tamboer Dr., North Haledon, NJ 07508: Free brochure ◆ Custom graphite rods. 201-4233-4500.

**Hodgson Hook Company,** 7116 W. Rowland Ave., Littleton, CO 80123: Free catalog ◆ Hooks.

**Hook & Hackle Company,** 7 Kaycee Loop Rd., Plattsburgh, NY 12901: Free catalog ◆ Fly-fishing tackle, fly-tying and fly rod-building supplies, hand-tied flies, clothing, and wading boots. 518-561-5893. bob@hookhack.com

**Hopkins Fishing Tackle,** 1130 Boissevan Ave., Norfolk, VA 23507: Free information ◆ Saltwater lures. 757-622-0977.

**House of Hardy (USA) Inc.,** 10 Godwin Plaza, Midland Park, NJ 07432: Free information ◆ Fly reels. 201-481-7557.

**Hunters North Country Outfitters,** 2 Central Square, Box 300, New Boston, NH 03070: Catalog $3 ◆ Fly-fishing, bass and saltwater fishing, and fly-tying supplies. 800-331-8558; 603-487-3388 (in NH).

**Islander Reels,** 6771 Kirkpatrick Crescent, Saanichton, British Columbia, Canada V8M 1Z8: Free information ◆ Direct drive and anti-reverse reels. 250-544-1440. www.info@islander.com

**Jann's Netcraft,** P.O. Box 89, Maumee, OH 43537: Free catalog ◆ Lures, rods, and fly-tying supplies. 800-346-6590; 419-868-8288 (in OH). www.jannsnetcraft.com

**The C.W. Jenkins Fly Rod,** 5735 S. Jericho Way, Aurora, CO 80015: Brochure $1 ◆ Fishing rods. 303-699-9128.

**Johnson Fishing Inc.,** 1531 E. Madison Ave., Mankato, MN 56002: Free information ◆ Lures for large and small mouth bass. 507-345-4623.

**Just Reels,** P.O. Box 493, Big Bend, WI 53103: Free information ◆ Fly reels and cases. 414-662-3626.

**K & K Flyfishers' Supply,** 8643 Grant, Overland Park, KS 66212: Free catalog ◆ Fly-fishing equipment. 800-795-8118. www.kkflyfisher.com

**Kane Klassics,** P.O. Box 8124, Fremont, CA 94537: Free information ◆ Bamboo and graphite fly rods. 800-337-5200.

**Kaufmann's Streamborn,** P.O. Box 23032, Portland, OR 97281: Free catalog ◆ Fly and bass fishing, saltwater fishing, and fly-tying supplies. 800-442-4359. www.kman.com

**Kelly's Boulder Enterprises,** 1705 14th St., Unit 301, Boulder, CO 80302: Free catalog ◆ Fly-tying tools and vises, supplies, weights, and accessories. 303-415-1100. KBEFLIES@AOL.COM

**King Sports Inc.,** 1230 Johnson Ferry Rd., Ste. J-60, Marietta, GA 30068: Free information ◆ Fishing, golf, and baseball equipment. 800-344-1480.

**G. Loomis Company,** 1359 Down River Dr., Woodland, WA 98674: Catalog $1 ◆ Spinning, fly, and plug and bait casting rods. 800-662-8818; 360-225-6516 (in WA). www.gloomis.com

**Loon Outdoors,** 7737 W. Mossy Cup St., Boise, ID 83709: Free brochure ◆ Rod-building components, fly-fishing accessories, fly-tying supplies, and fly-dressing caddies. 800-580-3811.

**Lure-Craft Industries Inc.,** 7129 E. 46th St., Indianapolis, IN 46226: Catalog $2 ◆ Plastic worm and lure-making components. 800-925-9088; 317-357-7555 (in IN).

**Maxwell MacPherson Jr.,** P.O. Box 141, Bristol, NH 03222: Free brochure ◆ Salmon flies. 603-744-3313.

**Madison River Fishing Company,** Box 627, Ennis, MT 59729: Free catalog ◆ Fly-fishing and tying accessories, rod-building supplies, and books. 800-227-7127. www.mrfc.com

**Manhattan Custom Tackle Ltd.,** 913 Broadway, New York, NY 10010: Catalog $2 (refundable) ◆ Hard-to-find rod-building components. 212-505-6690. www.fishdoc.com

**Mann's Bait Company,** 1111 State Docks Rd., Eufaula, AL 36027: Free information ◆ Lures. 800-841-8435.

**Marriott's Fly Fishing Store,** 2700 W. Orangethorpe, Fullerton, CA 92633: Catalog $3 ◆ Fly-tying and fly, bass, and saltwater fishing supplies. 800-535-6633. www.bobmarriotts.com

**Mason Tackle Company,** 11273 Center St., P.O. Box 56, Otisville, MI 48463: Free list of retail sources ◆ Fishing lines. 810-631-4571.

**Merco Products,** 1525 Norland Dr., Sunnyvale, CA 94087: Free catalog ◆ Fly-tying cord and thread. 408-245-7803.

**Midland Tackle Company,** 66 Rt. 17, Sloatsburg, NY 10974: Free catalog ◆ Molds, lures, and rod-building materials. 800-521-0146.

**Mikes Fly Desk,** 2395 S. 150 East, Bountiful, UT 84010: Free catalog ◆ Float tube fly fishing products. 801-292-4736.

**Mister Twister Inc.,** P.O. Drawer 1152, Minden, LA 71058: Free information ◆ Lures. 318-377-8818. www.mistertwister.com

**Mudhole Custom Tackle,** 813 Ensign Dr., Forked River, NJ 08731: Free catalog ◆ Fishing tackle, books, and do-it-yourself components. 609-242-1414. mudhole@vitinc.com

**Netcraft Company,** P.O. Box 5510, Toledo, OH 43613: Free catalog ◆ Rods, reels, marine electronics, rod and lure building components, and fly-tying supplies. 419-472-9826.

**New England Angler,** P.O. Box 105, Steuben, ME 04680: Free catalog ◆ Fly-tying materials and fishing equipment. 207-546-2018.

**Norland Trading Company,** Box 10, Norland, Ontario, Canada K0M 2L0: Video catalog $5 (refundable) ◆ Hunting, fishing, and outdoor products. 800-318-0717. ntc@cancom.net

**The Norlander Company,** P.O. Box 926, Kelso, WA 98626: Free information ◆ Rotary vises and tools for fly-tying. 360-636-2525.

**Normark,** 10395 Yellow Circle Dr., Minneapolis, MN 55343: Free information ◆ Lures, knives, and accessories. 612-933-7060.

**North Country Outfitters,** 2 Central Square, Box 300, New Boston, NH 03070: Free catalog ◆ Fly-tying supplies. 800-331-8558; 603-487-3388 (in NH).

**On the Fly,** 3628 Sage Dr., Rockford, IL 61111: Free catalog ◆ Fly-fishing and fly-tying supplies. 815-877-0090.

**Orvis Manchester,** 1711 Blue Hills Dr., P.O. Box 12000, Roanoke, VA 24022: Free catalog ◆ Fly-fishing rods, reels, leaders, neoprene waders, tackle boxes, and lures. 800-541-3541. www.orvis.com

**Pamola Fly Tool Company,** Box 435, Upton, MA 01568: Free brochure ◆ Multi-position fly lathe. 508-529-6086.

**Parker Rods,** P.O. Box 1379, Saratoga, WY 82331: Free brochure ◆ Hand-planed split bamboo fly rods.

**Patrick's Fly Shop,** 2237 Eastlake Ave., Seattle, WA 98102: Free information ◆ Fly rod-building supplies. 800-398-7693.

**Peerless Reel Company,** 427-3 Amherst St., Ste. 177, Nashua, NH 03063: Free information ◆ Fishing reels. 603-595-2458.

**Penn Fishing Tackle,** 3028 W. Hunting Park Ave., Philadelphia, PA 19132: Catalog $2 ◆ Saltwater spinning reels, spinning rods, and plug and bait casting reels. 215-229-9415. www.pennreels.com

**Phone Flies,** 90 Broad St., Red Bank, NJ 07701: Free catalog ◆ Fishing flies. 800-367-3543. phone-flies@netlabs.net

**Powell Rod Company,** P.O. Box 4000, Chico, CA 95927: Free brochure ◆ Fishing rods. 800-228-0615. www.powellrod.com

**PRADCO,** P.O. Box 1587, Fort Smith, AR 72902: Free information ◆ Fishing line, lures, and fish attractants. 800-422-FISH.

**R.J. Tackle Inc.,** 5719 Corp. Circle, Unit 1, Fort Meyers, FL 33905: Free information ◆ Lures. 941-693-7070.

**Rainy's Flies & Supplies,** 690 N. 100 East, Logan, UT 84321: Free information ◆ Fly-tying supplies. 801-753-6766.

**Ramsey Outdoor Store,** 226 N. Rt. 17, P.O. Box 1689, Paramus, NJ 07653: Free catalog ◆ Fly-tying and fishing equipment and fishing and hunting videos. 201-261-5000.

**Rangeley Rod Company,** P.O. Box 1270, Rangeley, ME 04970: Free information ◆ Hand-planed fly rods. 207-864-3898.

**Redington Fly Rods,** 906 S. Dixie Hwy., Stuart, FL 34994: Free information ◆ Fly rods and reels. 561-223-1342. www.redington.com

**Regal Engineering Inc.,** RFD 2, Tully Rd., Orange, MA 01364: Free brochure ◆ Big game fly reels, fly-tying vises, and accessories. 978-575-0488.

**Renzetti Inc.,** 6080 Grisson Pkwy., Titusville, FL 32780: Free list of retail sources ◆ Fly-tying tools and vises. 407-267-7705.

**RIO Products,** P.O. Box 684, Blackfoot, ID 83221: Free information ◆ Saltwater tapered leaders, hand-tied leaders, and supplies. 208-785-1244.

**Riverside Sports,** P.O. Box 241, Post Falls, ID 83854: Free list ◆ Reels, lines, and flies. 208-777-7527.

**George Roberts,** 4801 Tholozan, St. Louis, MO 63116: Free catalog ◆ Fly-making table. 800-747-1897; 314-351-8988 (in MO).

**Robichaud Reels,** P.O. Box 119, Hudson, NH 03051: Free information ◆ Fishing reels. 603-880-6484.

**Ross Reels,** One Ponderosa Ct., Montrose, CO 81401: Free information ◆ Fully machined, saltwater approved, disc drag system reels. 800-336-1050. www.ross-reels.com

**Roth Angling,** Box 602, Manitou Springs, CO 80829: Free catalog ◆ Custom tied flies. 719-685-0316.

**Round Rocks Fly Fishing,** P.O. Box 4059, Logan, UT 84323: Free catalog ◆ Fly fishing supplies and equipment. 800-992-8774. www.roundrocks.com

**Ryobi America Corp.,** P.O. Box 1207, Anderson, SC 29622: Free information ◆ Plug and bait casting reels and rods, saltwater reels and rods, and spin casting reels. 800-525-2579. www.ryobi.com

**Sadu Blue Water Inc.,** 4660 122nd Dr. North, West Palm Beach, FL 33411: Free information ◆ Trolling lures. 561-795-9516.

**The Saltwater Angler,** Capt. Jeffrey Cardenas, 219 Simonton, Key West, FL 33040: Free catalog ◆ Saltwater fly rods. 800-223-1629.

**Scientific Anglers,** 3M Center, St. Paul, MN 55144: Free information ◆ Reels, fly lines, fishing accessories, and how-to cassettes on bass and fly-fishing and deer, waterfowl, and turkey hunting. 800-430-5000. www.3m.com/front/angler

**Scott-Wynne Outfitters,** 10000 Research Blvd., Ste. 127, Austin, TX 78759: Free catalog ◆ Outdoor and casual clothing, luggage, hunting and fishing accessories, and Native American jewelry. 800-232-2783. www.outfits.com

**Senco Inc.,** 520 8th St., Gwinn, MI 49841: Free information ◆ Recreational shelters, portable hunting blinds, ice fishing houses, and green-houses. 906-346-4116.

**Sheldon's Inc.,** 626 Center St., Antigo, WI 54409: Free information ◆ Freshwater lures. 715-623-2382. www.mistertwister.com

**Shimano American Corp.,** P.O. Box 19615, Irvine, CA 92713: Catalog $1 ◆ Plug and bait casting reels and rods, saltwater reels and rods, and accessories. 714-951-5003. www.shimano.com/fishing/rods

**Shoff's Custom Tackle,** P.O. Box 1227, Kent, WA 98035: Catalog $1 ◆ Rod-building supplies. 206-852-4760. www.shofftackle.com

**Silstar America Corp.,** P.O. Box 6505, West Columbia, SC 29171: Catalog $2 ◆ Saltwater spinning reels and rods, plug and bait casting reels and rods, and accessories. 803-794-8521.

**Snag Proof,** 11387 Deerfield Rd., Cincinnati, OH 45232: Free information ◆ Bass and pike lures. 800-762-4773. www.snagproof.com

**South Bend Sporting Goods,** 1950 Stanley St., Northbrook, IL 60062: Catalog $2 ◆ Rods, reels, and tackle. 847-564-1900.

**South Creek Ltd.,** P.O. Box 981, Lyons, CO 80540: Catalog $1 ◆ Fishing accessories and one, two, and three-piece bamboo rods. 800-354-5050.

**STH Reels USA Inc.,** 3736 Kellogg Rd., Cortland, NY 13045: Free information ◆ Quick-change reels. 607-756-2851. www.cortlandline.com

**Storm Manufacturing Company,** Box 720265, Norman, OK 73070: Free information ◆ Lures. 405-329-5894.

**Stren Fishing Lines,** Division Remington Arms Company, 870 Remington Dr., Madison, NC 27025: Free information ◆ Fishing lines. 910-548-8700. www.remington.com/stren.htm

**Tackle Craft,** P.O. Box 280, Chippewa Falls, WI 54729: Free catalog ◆ Fly and jig-tying supplies, spinner-making tools, and fishing aids. 715-723-3645.

**Teton Fly Reels,** 924 Church Hill Rd., San Andreas, CA 95249: Free list of retail sources ◆ Fly-fishing reels. 800-831-0855.

**Thomas & Thomas,** 2 Avenue A, Turner Falls, MA 01376: Catalog $3 (request list of retail sources) ◆ Fly-tying equipment and rods. 413-863-9727. info@thomasandthomas.com

**D.H. Thompson Inc.,** 200 Industrial Dr., Hampshire, IL 60140: Free information ◆ Docking station for fly-tying tools and supplies. 847-683-0051.

**Tournament Tackle Inc.,** P.O. Box 372820, Satellite Beach, FL 32937: Free information ◆ Trolling lures. 407-259-1903.

**Triple Fish Fishing Line,** 321 Enterprise Dr., Ocoee, FL 34761: Free information ◆ Fishing line. 407-656-7834.

**Umpqua Feather Merchants,** P.O. Box 700, Glide, OR 97443: Free list of retail sources ◆ Fly-fishing hooks. 800-322-3218. www.umpqua.com

**Universal Vise Corp.,** 16 Union Ave., Westfield, MA 01085: Free list of retail sources) ◆ Fly-tying kits. 413-568-0964.

**Urban Angler,** 118 E. 25th St., New York, NY 10010: Catalog $4 ◆ Fly-fishing equipment. 800-255-5488; 212-979-7600 (in NY). urbang@panix.com

**Versitex of America Ltd.,** 3545 Schuylkill Rd., Spring City, PA 19475: Free catalog ◆ Fresh and saltwater fly rods and braided fishing line. 610-948-4442. www.vitinc.com/versitex/versi11.html

**Wapsi Fly Inc.,** 27 County Rd. 458, Mountain Home, AR 72653: Free list of retail sources ◆ Fly-tying supplies. 501-425-9500.

**Westbank Anglers,** P.O. Box 523, Teton Village, WY 83025: Free catalog ◆ Fly-fishing supplies. 800-922-3474.

**Whitetail Fly Tieing Supplies,** 7060 Whitetail Ct., Toledo, OH 43613: Catalog $2 (refundable) ◆ Fly-tying supplies, videos, books, tools, and more. 419-843-2106.

**Willow Creek Outfitters,** 424 E. 12300 South, Draper, UT 84020: Free catalog ◆ Flies, clothing, rods and reels, and accessories. 801-576-1946.

**R.L. Winston Rod Company,** 500 S. Main St., Drawer T, Twin Bridges, MT 59754: Free list of retail sources ◆ Salt water salmon rods and handcrafted bamboo, glass, and graphite fly rods. 406-684-5674. www.winstonrods.com/winston.html

**Wyoming River Raiders,** P.O. Box 50490, Casper, WY 82605: Free catalog ◆ Outdoor clothing, books, fishing gear, and camping, river expedition, and hiking equipment. 800-247-6068. www.riverraiders.com

**Yakima Bait Company,** P.O. Box 310, Granger, WA 98932: Free information ◆ Freshwater lures including spinners, spoons, crankbaits, plugs, and more. 509-854-1311. www.yakimabait.com/

### Fish-Finding Electronics

**Apelco Marine Electronics,** 676 Island Pond Rd., Manchester, NH 03109: Free information ◆ Electronic fish-finding equipment. 800-539-5539. www.raytheon.com

**Bottom Line/Computrol,** 499 E. Corporate Dr., Meridian, ID 83642: Free information ◆ Electronic fish-finding equipment. 800-456-5432. www.computrol.com

**Defender Industries Inc.,** 42 Great Neck Rd., Waterford, CT 06385: Free catalog ◆ Electronic fish-finding equipment. 800-435-7180; 860-701-3415 (in CT). defenderus@aol.com

**Eagle Electronics Inc.,** P.O. Box 669, Catoosa, OK 74015: Free information ◆ Electronic fish-finding equipment. 800-324-1354. www.eaglesonar.com

**Furuno USA,** 271 Harbor Way, South San Francisco, CA 94083: Free information ◆ Electronic fish-finding equipment. 415-873-9393. www.FurunoUSA.com

**Garmin,** 1200 E. 151st St., Olathe, KS 66062: Free list of retail sources ◆ Electronic fish-finding equipment. 800-800-1020; 913-397-8200 (in KS).

**Humminburd,** No. 3 Humminburd Ln., Eufaula, AL 36027: Free information ◆ Electronic fish-finding equipment. 334-687-6613. www.humminbird.com

**Interphase Technologies Inc.,** 2880 Research Park Dr., Ste. 140, Soquel, CA 95073: Free information ◆ Electronic fish-finding equipment. 408-477-4944. www.interphase-tech.com

**Lowrance Electronics,** 12000 E. Skelly Dr., Tulsa, OK 74128: Free list of retail sources ◆ Electronic fish-finding equipment. 800-324-4737. www.lowrance.com

**Magellan Systems Corp.,** 960 Overland Ct., San Dimas, CA 91773: Free list of retail sources ◆ Electronic fish-finding equipment. 800-669-4477. www.magellangps.com

**Si-Tex Marine Electronics,** 11001 Roosevelt Blvd., St. Petersburg, FL 34716: Free information ◆ Electronic fish-finding equipment. 813-576-5734. www.si-tex.com

**Skipper Marine Electronics Inc.,** 1511 Reidel Dr., Mundelein, IL 60060: Free catalog ◆ Electronic fish-finding equipment. 800-SKIP-PER; 847-566-1800 (in IL).

**Techsonic Industries Inc.,** 1 Hummingbird Ln., Eufaula, AL 36027: Free information ◆ Electronic fish-finding equipment. 334-687-6613.

**Vexilar,** 200 W. 88th St., Minneapolis, MN 55420: Free information ◆ Electronic fish-finding equipment. 612-884-5291. www.vexilar.com

**Zercom,** 1865 Old Hudson Rd., Ste. 201, St. Paul, MN 55119: Free information ◆ Electronic fish-finding equipment. 800-952-9122. www.nortechsys.com/Zercom/Marineproducts.htm

## FLAGS & FLAG POLES

**American Flag & Gift,** 737 Manuela Way, Arroyo Grande, CA 93420: Catalog $2 ◆ Flags, banners, bunting, and flag poles. 800-448-3524; 805-473-0395 (in CA). www.anyflag.com

**American Flagpoles & Flags,** 109 Lumber Ln., Goose Creek, SC 29445: Free catalog ◆ Flagpoles and United States, state, international, nautical, and historical flags. 800-777-1706.

**Banner Fabric,** Kite Studio, 5555 Hamilton Blvd., Wescosville, PA 18106: Catalog $1 ◆ Fabrics, notions, and hardware for kites, flags, banners, and windsocks. 800-KITE-991; 610-395-3560 (in PA).

**Banner Ideas,** 1811 Huguenot Rd., Ste. 101, Midlothian, VA 23113: Catalog $2 (refundable) ◆ Special occasion flags and banners. 804-366-3524.

**Banners & Flags,** 1379 Economou Rd., P.O. Box 33, Huntington, VT 05462: Free information ◆ Custom crafted banners and flags. 802-434-3410.

**Carrot-Top Industries Inc.,** P.O. Box 820, Hillsborough, NC 27278: Free catalog ◆ Ready-made and made-to-order flags, banners, and decorations. 800-628-3524.

**Classic Memorials Inc.,** P.O. Box 4843, Fort Walton Beach, FL 32549: Free information ◆ Memorial flag cases. Available in mahogany, cherry, walnut, and traditional or pickled oak. 800-752-0503.

**Flag America Company,** 2708 Long Beach Blvd., Ship Bottom, NJ 08008: Free information ◆ Flags, banners, windsocks, and flag poles. 609-494-2626.

**Flag Fables Inc.,** 113 Vermont St., Springfield, MA 01108: Free catalog ◆ All-occasion decorative flags. 800-257-1025. www.flagfables.com

**Flagship Distributors,** 3746 6th Ave., San Diego, CA 92103: Free catalog ◆ Flags and accessories for land and sea. 800-25-FLAGS; 619-491-0424 (in CA). www.electriciti.com/~flagship

**Frenchtown Flags Inc.,** 700 N. 5th St., St. Charles, MO 63301: Free brochure with long SASE ◆ Decorative double-appliqued, weather-proof nylon garden flags. 314-724-0404.

**Frontier Flags,** 1761 Owl Creek Rt., Thermopolis, WY 82443: Catalog $3 ◆ Hand-sewn historic flag reproductions from all eras and accessories. 888-432-4324.

**Hennessy House,** P.O. Box 57, Sierra City, CA 96125: Free brochure ◆ Handmade wood flag poles and flags. 800-285-2122. www.woodenflagpoles.com

**House of Flags,** P.O. Box 4707, East Providence, RI 02916: Catalog $4 ◆ Flagpoles, weather vanes, eagles, and United States, historical, state, foreign, holiday, seasonal, nautical, and other flags. 800-45-FLAGS.

**Hudson Valley Flags & Banners,** 282 Grand Ave., Englewood, NJ 07631: Free catalog ◆ Festive flags and banners. 800-349-3524.

**Lighten Up,** 283 96th St., Stone Harbor, NJ 08247: Free catalog ◆ Decorative, United States, state, and garden flags. Also flagpoles. 800-679-5747.

**Martin's Flag Company,** P.O. Box 1118, Fort Dodge, IA 50501: Free catalog ◆ Flags and accessories. 800-992-3524; 800-248-3524 (in IA). 800-992-3524. www.dodgenet.com/~pages/martins/home.htm

**Marvin Display,** 322 Boston Post Rd., Milford, CT 06460: Free information ◆ Flagpoles, hardware, and United States, historical, state, foreign, nautical, and fun flags. 800-322-8587.

**Montpelier Stove Works,** 178 River St., Montpelier, VT 05601: Free information ◆ Flags for civic, business, religious, and social ceremonies. 800-287-0150.

**Patriots Plus,** Box 35414, Canton, OH 44735: Catalog $2 ◆ United States, other countries, historic, celebrations, and custom flags. Also flagpoles. 330-493-4030.

**Piedmont Flag Company,** P.O. Box 685, Maiden, NC 28650: Free information ◆ Custom 100 percent cotton historical standards and colors of the United States and Confederate States of America. 800-467-0082.

**Chris Reid Company Inc.,** P.O. Box 1827, Midlothian, VA 23113: Free catalog ◆ Ethnic, special occasion, state, country, religious, decorative, and other flags. Also flag poles and accessories. 804-744-5862.

**Safety Flag Company of America,** P.O. Box 1088, Pawtucket, RI 02862: Free catalog ◆ Flags and safety equipment for boats. 401-722-0900.

**Vaughn Display & Flag,** 7951 Computer Ave., Edina, MN 55435: Free catalog ◆ Flagpoles, floor stands, holders, brackets, bunting, pennants, banners, and religious, United States, foreign, state, territorial, and other flags. 612-832-3200. www.vaughn.com

## FLASHLIGHTS

**Bright Star,** 380 Stewart Rd., Wilkes-Barre, PA 18706: Free list of retail sources ◆ Aluminum, plastic, and rubber waterproof flashlights. 717-825-1900. www.flashlight.com

**Flashlights Inc.,** 12220 Five Mile Rd., Fredericksburg, VA 22407: Free brochure ◆ Conventional and hands-free rechargeable, pocket, and other flashlights. 888-LIGHTS-1. www.flashlights.com

**Fulton Industries,** 135 E. Linfoot, Wauseon, OH 43567: Free information ◆ Waterproof and floating flashlights. 800-537-5012; sales@fultonindoh.com

**Lamp Technology Inc.,** 1645 Sycamore Ave., Bohemia, NY 11716: Free brochure ◆ Conventional, hands-free, convertible to head-mounting, rechargeable, and other flashlights. 800-533-7548; 516-567-1800 (in NY.

## FLOWERS & PLANTS

### Artificial Flowers

**Billiann's Bridal,** P.O. Box 35, Atlanta, IN 46031: Catalog $4 ◆ Bridal flowers, other floral arrangements, jewelry, and arranging supplies. 765-292-6388.

**Fine Design,** P.O. Box 310704, New Braunfels, TX 78131: Free information ◆ Silk rose arrangements. 800-200-2224.

**May Silk,** 16202 Distribution Way, Cerritos, CA 90703: Free catalog ◆ Silk plants, trees, and flowers. 800-282-7455.

**Petals,** 1 Aqueduct Rd., White Plains, NY 10606: Free catalog ◆ Silk floral arrangements, flowers, plants, and trees. 800-738-2570. www.petals.com

**Select Artificials Inc.,** 701 N. 15th St., St. Louis, MO 63103: Catalog $10 (refundable) ◆ Silk flowers, large plants, and Christmas decorative items. 800-666-6999; 314-621-3050 (in MO).

### Dried Flowers

**Caswell-Massey Company Ltd.,** Catalog Division, 100 Enterprise Pl., Dover, DE 19901: Catalog $1 ◆ Potpourri and pomander mixes, dried flowers, herb plants, essential oils, and perfumery supplies. 800-326-0500. caswell@maui.net

**Chalmers-Gabrych Plantasia,** 3282 Constitution Dr., Yuba City, CA 95933: Free information ◆ Preserved pest-free miniature show roses. 916-673-8494.

**Chelsea Farms,** 18222 Plantation Rd., Onancock, VA 23417: Free price list ◆ Dried flowers. 757-787-4410. www.chelseafarms.com

**Doering Company,** 3531 Niles Rd., St. Joseph, MI 49085: Catalog $3 ◆ Dried floral products, floral arranging supplies, basketry materials, and how-to videos. 616-429-3961.

**The Galveston Wreath Company,** 1124 25th St., Galveston, TX 77550: Free price list ◆ Dried flowers and wreath frames. 409-765-8597.

**Gardens Past,** P.O. Box 1846, Estes Park, CO 80517: Catalog $1 ◆ Soaps and soap-making supplies, potpourri, dried flowers, herbs, candles, and aromatherapy items. 970-823-5565.

**Goodwin Creek Gardens,** P.O. Box 83, Williams, OR 97544: Catalog $1 ◆ Dried floral arrangements, seeds and plants, trees, shrubs, and perennial flowers. 541-846-7357.

**Hartman's Herb Farm,** 1026 Old Dana Rd., Barre, MA 01005: Catalog $2 ◆ Herbs and herb products, dried flowers and potpourri, and essential oils. 978-355-2015.

**Herbs-Licious,** 1702 S. 6th St., Marshalltown, IA 50158: Catalog $2 (refundable) ◆ Dried flowers, herbs and spices, oils and fragrances, and potpourri.

**Leaves an Impression,** P.O. Box 2068, New London, NH 03257: Free catalog ◆ Freeze-dried flowers, fruits, and vegetables. 603-526-2876.

**Lilac Rose,** 1117 E. Van Owen Ave., Orange, CA 92867: Free brochure ◆ Preserved dried and pressed flowers. 714-744-5906. Lilacrose2@aol.com

**Meadow Everlastings,** 16464 Shabbona Rd., Malta, IL 60150: Catalog $2 (refundable) ◆ Dried flowers, wreath kits, and potpourri.

**Meadows Direct,** 13805 Hwy. 136, Onslow, IA 52321: Free list ◆ Dried and preserved leaves and flowers. 800-542-9771.

**Mills Floral Company,** 4550 Peachtree Lakes Dr., Duluth, GA 30096: Catalog $4 (refundable) ◆ Dried floral products. 800-762-7939; 770-729-8995 (in GA). www.abci.com/millsfloral

**Mountain Valley Farms,** 158 W. Hills Way, Hamilton, MT 59840: Free brochure ◆ Dried flowers, preserved floral products, and wreaths. 800-225-2543; 406-363-7566 (in MT). www.montananet.com/mvf/statice.htm

**Naturally Yours,** P.O. Box 2896, Santa Maria, CA 93457: Free price list ◆ Freeze-dried flowers. 805-934-8189. www.naturally-yours.com

**J. Page Basketry,** 820 Albee Rd. West, Nokomis, FL 34275: Catalog $2 (refundable) ◆ Dried flowers and herbs, books, and pine needle, wheat weaving, and basket-making supplies and tools. 941-485-6730.

**Riverside Gardens,** 300 E. Riverside, Timberville, VA 22853: Free price list ◆ Dried flowers and plants. 800-847-6449; 540-896-9859 (in VA).

**The Scented Room,** 108 Mashapaug Rd., Holland, MA 01521: Information $1 ◆ Dried flowers, wreaths, other floral products, and do-it-yourself kits.

**Shady Acres Herb Farm,** 7815 Hwy. 212, Chaska, MN 55318: Free list with long SASE ◆ Dried plants. 612-466-3391.

**Something's Blooming,** Hwy. 17, Alba, TX 75410: Free price list ◆ Organically grown and air-dried everlasting herbs and flowers. 903-765-2132.

**Southwest Decor,** 409 Indian Creek, Comanche, TX 76442: Catalog $4 (refundable) ◆ Dried flowers. 800-733-5969.

**Tom Thumb Workshops,** Rt. 13, P.O. Box 357, Mappsville, VA 23407: Catalog $1 ◆ Potpourri, herbs, spices, essential oils, dried flowers, and craft supplies. 757-824-3507.

**Well-Sweep Herb Farm,** 205 Mt. Bethel Rd., Port Murray, NJ 07865: Catalog $2 ◆ Potpourri and pomander mixes, dried flowers, and herbs. 908-852-5390.

## FOIL CRAFTS

**Atlas Art & Stained Glass,** P.O. Box 76084, Oklahoma City, OK 73147: Catalog $3 ◆ Kaleidoscopes, frames, lamp bases, and craft, stained glass, jewelry-making, and foil-crafting supplies. 405-946-1230.

**Bare-Metal Foil Company,** P.O. Box 82, Farmington, MI 48332: Catalog $2.50 ◆ Adhesive-backed chrome, black chrome, gold, matte aluminum, and real copper foil sheets. Also quick-setting molding materials. 248-477-0813.

**Guildcraft Company,** 100 Firetower Dr., Tonawanda, NY 14150: Free catalog ◆ Colored metal foils and supplies. 716-743-8336.

**Veach Foil Accessories,** 37007 S. Oak St., Kennewick, WA 99337: Free information ◆ Gold stamping machines, pens, photo button machines, accessories, and supplies. 800-523-9944. www.veachco.com

## FOOD PROCESSORS & DRYERS

**American Harvest,** 4064 Peavey Rd., Chaska, MN 55318: Free information ◆ Food dehydrators. 800-288-4545.

**A Cook's Wares,** 211 37th St., Beaver's Falls, PA 15010: Catalog $2 ◆ Food processors, cutlery, bake-ware, porcelain, French copper pans, and kitchen aids. 412-846-9490.

**Environmental Solar Systems,** 119 West St., Methuen, MA 01844: Free information ◆ Solar food dryers. 800-934-3848.

**Excalibur Dehydrator,** 6083 Power Inn Rd., Sacramento, CA 95824: Free information ◆ Food dehydrator. 800-875-4254. www.kctc.net/life/excalho.cgi

**Kitchen Krafts,** P.O. Box 442, Waukon, IA 52172: Free catalog ◆ Food dryers and preservation supplies. 800-776-0575; 319-535-8000 (in IA). www.kitchenkrafts.com

**Oreck Corp.,** 100 Plantation Rd., New Orleans, LA 70123: Free catalog ◆ Small kitchen appliances and food processors. 800-989-4200. www.oreck.com

**Vita-Mix Corp.,** 8615 Usher Rd., Cleveland, OH 44138: Free information ◆ Vita-Mix food processor. 800-848-2649. www.vita-mix.com

**Zabar's & Company,** 2245 Broadway, New York, NY 10024: Free catalog ◆ Cookware, food processors, microwave ovens, kitchen tools, and coffee makers. 800-697-6301; 212-496-1234 (in NY).

# FOODS

## Apple Cider

**Berry-Hill Limited,** 75 Burwell Rd., St. Thomas, Ontario, Canada N5P 3R5: Catalog $2 ◆ Cider press, canning equipment, weather vanes, and garden equipment. 519-631-0480.

**Happy Valley Ranch,** 16577 W. 327th, Paola, KS 66071: Catalog $1 ◆ Cider and wine presses. 913-849-3103. www.happyvalleyranch.com

**Stout's Cider Mill,** P.O. Box 1100, Wilcox, AZ 85644: Free brochure ◆ Apple cider, cider specialties, mulling spices, gift foods, and more. 520-384-5557. www.cidermill.com

## Beverages

**Blenheim Bottlers,** Box 452, Hamer, SC 29547: Free information ◆ Old-fashioned ginger ale. Available hot, mild, or mixed to individual taste. 800-270-9344.

**Bounty Hunter Rare Wine & Provisions,** 101 S. Coombs, #5, Napa, CA 94559: Catalog $2 ◆ Wines and related life style products. 800-943-9463. www.bountyhunterwine.com

**Corti Brothers,** 5810 Folsom Blvd., Sacramento, CA 95819: Free newsletter ◆ Chinese teas, regional olive oils, vintage cognac, and other food and drink specialties. 916-736-3800.

**Martinelli's Gold Medal,** Box 1868, Watsonville, CA 95077: Free information ◆ Sparkling cider.

**Sam's Wines & Spirits,** 1720 N. Marcey St., Chicago, IL 60614: Free catalog ◆ Imported and domestic wines, spirits, and other beverages. 800-777-9137; 312-664-4394 (in IL).

**Windsor Vineyards,** P.O. Box 368, Windsor, CA 95492: Free catalog ◆ Personalized holiday labels on favorite wines. Also food and wine gifts. 800-333-9987. www.windsorvineyards.com

## Breads & Rolls

**Bagel Oasis,** 183-12 Horace Harding Expwy., Fresh Meadows, NY 11365: Free brochure ◆ Overnight door-to-door delivery of bagels, bialys, mini bagels, and twists. 800-BA-GELS-61. www.bageloasis.com

**Bagelicious,** 1864 Front St., East Meadow, NY 11554: Free information ◆ Fresh-baked bagels and gift packages. 800-55-BAGEL; 516-794-0552 (in NY).

**Balducci's,** Shop from Home Service, 42-26 13th St., Long Island City, NY 11101: Catalog $3 ◆ Bread and food specialties. 800-225-3822. www.balducci.com

**Baldwin Hill Bakery,** 15 Baldwin Hill Rd., Phillipston, MA 01331: Free brochure ◆ Organic sourdough bread. 978-249-4691. www.baldwinhill.com

**Barn Stream Natural Foods,** P.O. Box 760, Walpole, NH 03608: Free brochure ◆ Handmade low-fat and additive-, preservative-, and cholesterol-free Yankee sourdough, salt-free garlic whole wheat, and hearty multi-grain breads. 800-654-2882.

**Boudin Gifts,** P.O. Box 885421, San Francisco, CA 94188: Free information ◆ San Francisco sourdough French bread. 800-992-1855.

**Bread Alone,** Rt. 28, Boiceville, NY 12412: Free information ◆ Hearth-baked bread made with organic grains. 914-657-3328.

**Burnt Cabins Grist Mill,** Cowans Gap Rd., Burnt Cabins, PA 17215: Free brochure ◆ Old-fashioned buckwheat and wheat flour, roasted and regular cornmeal, and pancake and muffin mixes. 717-987-3244.

**C'est Croissant Inc.,** 22138 S. Vermont Ave., Unit A, Torrance, CA 90502: Free brochure ◆ Plain, fluffy French almond, chocolate, and all-butter croissants. 800-633-2767.

**Critter Spreads Inc.,** 1746 Academy Rd., Bellingham, WA 98226: Free brochure ◆ Fruit spreads and muffin mixes. 800-447-5847. www.critterspreads.com

**Dean & DeLuca Mail-Order,** Attention: Catalog Dept., 560 Broadway, New York, NY 10012: Free information ◆ Bread. 800-221-7714. www.dean-deluca.com

**DiCamillo Bakery,** 811 Linwood Ave., Niagara Falls, NY 14305: Free catalog ◆ Italian bread and specialties. 800-634-4363; 716-282-2341 (in NY).

**French Meadow Bakery,** 2610 Lyndale Ave. South, Minneapolis, MN 55408: Free information ◆ Yeast and wheat-free organic sourdough bread. 612-870-4740.

**Genie's Kitchen,** 150 Magic Ln., Box 456, Wibaux, MT 59353: Free information ◆ Low-fat and no cholesterol muffin mixes. 800-276-5259.

**The Gluten-Free Pantry,** P.O. Box 849, Glastonbury, CT 06033: Free catalog ◆ Easy-to-make wheat and gluten-free bread and cake mixes. 800-291-8386. www.glutenfree.com

**H & H Bagels,** 2239 Broadway, New York, NY 10024: Free catalog ◆ Bagels. 800-NY-BAGEL.

**HeartyMix Company,** 1231 Madison Hill Rd., Rahway, NJ 07065: Free catalog ◆ Mixes for bread machines. 732-382-3010.

**The J.B. Dough Company,** 5600 E. Napier, Benton Harbor, MI 49022: Free price list ◆ Mixes for automatic bread machines. 800-528-6222. jbdough@jbdough.com

**The King Arthur Flour Baker's Catalog,** P.O. Box 876, Norwich, VT 05055: Free information ◆ Pizza dough and sourdough starter for bread, pancakes, biscuits, and cakes. 800-827-6836. www.kingarthurflour.com

**Moishe's Homemade Kosher Bakery,** 181 E. Houston St., New York, NY 10002: Free information ◆ Corn bread, challah, and bagels. 212-475-9624.

**R.F. Nature Farm Foods Inc.,** 925 S St., Lincoln, NE 68508: Free list of retail sources ◆ All-natural mixes for bread machines and oven-baking. 800-222-FARM; 402-474-7576 (in NE).

**Rubschlager Baking Corp.,** 3320 W. Grand Ave., Chicago, IL 60651: Free information ◆ European-style whole rye and stone-ground wheat bread. 773-826-1245.

**Sherwood Brands Inc.,** 6110 Executive Blvd., Ste. 1080, Rockville, MD 20852: Free list of retail sources ◆ Kosher, all-natural, and cholesterol-free bagel chips. 301-881-9340. www.sherwoodbrands.com

**Sunrise Gourmet Foods & Gifts,** 1813 3rd Ave. East, Hibbing, MN 55746: Free information ◆ Bread and specialties. 800-782-6736.

**Wanda's Nature Farm Foods,** 925 S St., Lincoln, NE 68508: Free catalog ◆ All-natural bread, muffin, pancake, waffle, and double-chocolate cake mixes. 800-222-FARM. naturefarmfood@aol.com

**Whistling Wings Farms,** 427 West St., Biddeford, ME 04005: Free brochure ◆ Low calorie spreadable fruits, syrups, and sauces; vinegars; and muffin mixes and other food products that are naturally fat-free and contain no preservatives or cholesterol. 800-765-8989; 207-282-1146 (in ME). www.wwfarm.com

**Wolferman's,** One Muffin Ln., P.O. Box 15913, Lenexa, KS 66215: Free catalog ◆ English muffins, crumpets, scones, and bagels. 800-999-0169. www.wolfermans.com

**Ye Olde Sweet Shoppe Bakery,** P.O. Box 1672, Shepherdstown, WV 25443: Free information ◆ Home-baked bread, strudels, German stollen, and specialties. 800-922-5379.

## Breakfast Favorites

**American Spoon Foods,** P.O. Box 566, Petoskey, MI 49770: Free information ◆ Pancake and waffle mix made with organic-grown Indian blue corn. Also wild rice, berry preserves, and pecans. 800-222-5886. www.spoon.com

**Best Products Company,** 3806 Fond Du Lac Dr., Richfield, WI 53076: Free catalog ◆ Fat-free whipped honey spreads and mixes for muffins, pancakes, and scones. 414-644-6239.

**Bette's Oceanview Diner,** 1807 4th St., Berkeley, CA 94710: Free information ◆ Scone and pancake mixes. 510-601-6980.

**Burnt Cabins Grist Mill,** Cowans Gap Rd., Burnt Cabins, PA 17215: Free brochure ◆ Old-fashioned buckwheat and wheat flour, roasted and regular cornmeal, and pancake and muffin mixes. 717-987-3244.

**Da Vinci Gourmet,** 823 Yale Ave., Ste. E, Seattle, WA 98109: Free information ◆ Syrups for baked goods, beverages, desserts, and pancake toppings. 800-640-6779; 206-682-4682 (in WA).

**Fiddler's Green Farm,** P.O. Box 254, Belfast, ME 04915: Free information ◆ Certified organic pancake and baking mixes, cereals, jams, syrups, honey, coffee, teas, and gift packages. 800-729-7935.

**Green Mountain Sugar House,** Rt. 100N, Box 820, Ludlow, VT 05149: Free catalog ◆ Maple syrup, maple sugar candy, nut brittle, cheese, smoked slab bacon, candy and fudge, pancake mix, mincemeat, homemade jams, and other Vermont specialties. 800-643-9338; 802-228-7151 (in VT). gmsh@ludl.tds.net

**Harman's Cheese & Country Store,** Sugar Hill, NH 03585: Free catalog ◆ Cheddar cheese, maple syrup, fruit preserves, salad dressings, plain and smoked salmon, crab meat, honey, smoked herring fillets, pancake mixes, maple butter, and candy. 603-823-8000.

**The House of Webster,** P.O. Box 9610, Rogers, AR 72757: Catalog $2 ◆ Preserves and jellies, cheese, country cured and smoked bacon, biscuit and pancake mixes, candy, syrups, wild honey, and country sorghum. 501-636-4640. www.houseofwebster.com

**The King Arthur Flour Baker's Catalog,** P.O. Box 876, Norwich, VT 05055: Free information ◆ Pizza dough and sourdough starter for bread, pancakes, biscuits, and cakes. 800-827-6836. www.kingarthurflour.com

**Maverick Sugarbush Inc.,** P.O. Box 99, Sharon, VT 05065: Free brochure ◆ Certified organic Vermont maple syrup, organic cornmeal, and multi-grain pancake mixes. 802-763-8680.

**Morgan's Mills,** RD 2, Box 4602, Union, ME 04862: Free information ◆ Salt-free mixes for pancakes, waffles, and bran muffins. 800-373-2756.

**Napa Valley Pantry,** P.O. Box 50, Oakville, CA 94892: Free information ◆ Waffle mixes and syrups. 414-679-7207.

**Pepperidge Farm,** P.O. Box 917, Clinton, CT 06413: Free catalog ◆ Soups, cookies and other pastries, crackers, candy, cheese, sausage, popcorn, and breakfast mixes. 800-243-9314.

**Wanda's Nature Farm Foods,** 925 S St., Lincoln, NE 68508: Free catalog ◆ All-natural bread, muffin, pancake, waffle, and double-chocolate cake mixes. 800-222-FARM. naturefarmfood@aol.com

## Cakes, Cookies, & Pies

**An American Kitchen,** P.O. Box 418, Flourtown, PA 19031: Free catalog ◆ Cookies, brownies, and decadent brownie truffles. 800-428-8879. www.americankitchen.com

**The Antique Mall & Crown Restaurant,** P.O. Box 540, Indianola, MS 38751: Free information ◆ Catfish paté and pie mixes. 800-833-7731; 601-887-2522 (in MS).

**Ariola Foods Inc.,** 218-35 98th Ave., Queens Village, NY 11429: Free information ◆ Cannoli shells, cheesecakes, and Italian pastries. 800-443-0777. HJFM@JUNO.COM

**The Artful Cookie,** 318 Ontario St., St. Catharines, Ontario, Canada L2R 5L8: Free brochure ◆ Cookie gift packages for special occasions. 905-688-0400.

**The Baker's Catalogue,** P.O. Box 876, Norwich, VT 05055: Free catalog ◆ Baking equipment and recipe ingredients. 800-827-6836.

**Best Products Company,** 3806 Fond Du Lac Dr., Richfield, WI 53076: Free catalog ◆ Fat-free whipped honey spreads and mixes for muffins, pancakes, and scones. 414-644-6239.

**Beth's Fine Desserts,** 1201 Andersen Dr., San Rafael, CA 94901: Free information ◆ Gourmet cookies. 800-425-BETH.

**Bette's Oceanview Diner,** 1807 4th St., Berkeley, CA 94710: Free information ◆ Scone and pancake mixes. 510-601-6980.

**Bob's Brownstone Brownies,** 276 6th Ave., Brooklyn, NY 11215: Free brochure ◆ Over 20 varieties of brownies, cookies, dessert pizzas, and other specialties. 718-369-2627.

**Boca Bons Inc.,** 10720 Wiles Rd., Pompano Beach, FL 33076: Free list of retail sources ◆ Handmade truffles, fudge, and brownies. 800-314-2835; 964-346-0494 (in FL).

**Boston Coffee Cake Company,** 4 Henshaw St., Woburn, MA 01801: Free information ◆ Coffee cakes. 800-434-0500.

**Brass Ladle Products,** 1406-D Olde Ridge Village, Chadds Ford, PA 19317: Free list of retail sources ◆ Gourmet cake mixes. 610-558-4171. www.brassladle.com

**Brent & Sam's Handmade Cookies,** P.O. Box 2098, Little Rock, AR 72203: Free brochure ◆ Chocolate chip-pecan, oatmeal raisin-pecan, extra-chocolate with no nuts, white chocolate with macadamia nuts, and key lime with white chocolate cookies. 800-825-1613; 501-562-4300 (in AR). www.perfectcookie.com

**Brigitte's Brownies,** 120 Doyle St., Doylestown, PA 18901: Free catalog ◆ Gourmet brownies. 888-340-2040; 215-340-1000 (in PA). www.brigittesbrownie.com

**Byrd Cookie Company,** P.O. Box 13086, Savannah, GA 31406: Free brochure ◆ Preservative-free Southern-style cookies and confections by Savannah's cookie maker, Benjamin "Cookie" Byrd. 800-291-2973.

**Cafe Beaujolais,** Box 730, Mendocino, CA 95460: Free catalog ◆ Pastries and desserts, candy assortments, hot chocolate mix, and other specialties. 800-930-0443.

**Celebration Specialties,** 17 S. Greenbush Rd., Orangeburg, NY 10962: Free list of retail sources ◆ All-natural bittersweet chocolate truffle cakes, tarts, and other pastries. 888-313-2253. www.celebrationspecialty.com

**Celia's Sweets Inc.,** P.O. Box 424, Grand Ledge, MI 48837: Free brochure ◆ Italian wafer cookies and candy. 517-627-1910.

**Cereal Bowl,** RD 1, Box 199, Kittanning, PA 16201: Free information with long SASE ◆ Sugar and preservative-free high-fiber muffin mixes. 888-747-2467. CEREAL@NB.NET

**Charleston Cake Lady,** 774 Woodward Rd., Charleston, SC 29407: Free catalog ◆ Cakes made with fresh and natural ingredients. 800-488-0830.

**Cheesecake Royale,** 9016 Garland Rd., Dallas, TX 75218: Free information with long SASE ◆ Cheesecakes. 800-328-9102; 214-328-9102 (in TX).

**Collin Street Bakery,** P.O. Box 79, Corsicana, TX 75151: Free brochure ◆ Fruitcakes, cheesecakes, pecan pies, and other bakery favorites. 800-248-3366. www.collinstreetbakery.com

**Cookie Bouquets Inc.,** 6665-H Huntley Rd., Columbus, OH 43229: Free catalog ◆ Edible cookie bouquet-style gift arrangements. 800-233-2171; 614-846-2171 (in OH). www.cookiebouquets.com

**The Cookie Garden,** 1508 Miner St., Des Plaines, IL 60016: Free catalog ◆ Gift bouquets made with cookies. 800-582-9191. www.cookiegarden.com

**Cougar Mountain Baking Company,** 1200 6th Avenue South, Seattle, WA 98134: Free information ◆ Gourmet cookies. 206-467-0448. www.cmbc.com

**Crabtree & Evelyn Limited,** P.O. Box 167, Woodstock Hill, CT 06281: Catalog $3.50 ◆ English biscuits and cookies, gingerbread, ginger and butter-ginger cookies, Scottish shortbread, Belgian chocolates, cheese wafers and biscuits from Holland, Italian biscuits, preserves, marmalades, jellies, honey, English sauces, spices and condiments, herbs, tea, and candy. 800-624-5211. www.crabtree-evelyn.com

**Cryer Creek Kitchens,** P.O. Box 9003, Corsicana, TX 75151: Free catalog ◆ Homemade cakes, pies, and cookies. 800-353-7437. www.cryercreekkitchens.com

**Delancey Dessert Company,** 573 Grand St., New York, NY 10002: Free information ◆ All-natural Kosher rugelach and other baked goods. 800-254-5254; 212-254-5254 (in NY).

**Delectable Edibles,** Easy Video Plaza, 335 Rt. 9 South, Manlapan, NJ 07726: Free brochure ◆ Cookie gift baskets for all occasions. 908-462-5808. www.delectableedible.com

**Desserts by David Glass,** 140-150 Huyshope Ave., Hartford, CT 06106: Free catalog ◆ Desserts made with all-natural ingredients. 800-DAVID-99. www.davidglass.com

**DFP International Inc.,** Delizioso Food Products, 331 Corporate Cl., Golden, CO 80401: Free information ◆ Italian pizzelle cookies in five flavors and tiramisu. 800-749-3553; 303-278-8289 (in CO).

**DiCamillo Bakery,** 811 Linwood Ave., Niagara Falls, NY 14305: Free catalog ◆ Almond macaroons, sesame-coated red wine and finger biscuits, butter cookies, cakes, and bread. 800-634-4363; 716-282-2341 (in NY).

**Divine Delights,** 24 Digital Dr., Ste. 10, Novato, CA 94949: Free information ◆ Triple-chocolate petit fours and fudge brownies, cakes, truffles, and tea cakes. 800-4-HEAVEN.

**Duo Delights,** 1515 S. Fairgrounds Rd., Midland, TX 79705: Free information ◆ Lemon crunch cookies and other favorites. 915-684-6166.

**Eilenberger's Bakery,** P.O. Box 710, 512 N. John, Palestine, TX 75802: Free brochure ◆ Cakes, brownies, cookies, and other pastries. 800-788-2996; 903-729-2253 (in TX). www.eilenberger.com

**Elegant Sweets,** 11836 NE 112th Ave., Kirkland, WA 98033: Free list of retail sources ◆ Biscotti, chocolates, toffee, gourmet-flavored white barks, and specialties. 425-814-2500.

**Erica's Rugelach & Baking Company Inc.,** 265 5th Ave., Brooklyn, NY 11215: Free list of retail sources ◆ Certified Kosher bakery specialties. 718-449-0445.

**The Estee Corp.,** 169 Lackawanna Ave., Parsippany, NJ 07054: Free catalog ◆ Sugarless candy and cookies. 800-34-ESTEE.

**Fairytale Brownies,** 2724 N. 68th St., Ste. 1, Scottsdale, AZ 85257: Free brochure ◆ Certified kosher gourmet brownies. 800-324-1982. www.brownies.com

**The Famous Pacific Dessert Company,** 2414 SW Andover St., Seattle, WA 98106: Free information ◆ Tortes, cheesecakes, and baked goods. 800-666-1950; 206-935-1999 (in WA).

**Fancy Fortune Cookies,** 6265 Coffman Rd., Indianapolis, IN 46268: Free information ◆ Fortune cookies in twelve flavors and brilliant colors. Individually wrapped and with custom messages, they are available in tins or loose by the case. 317-299-8900. www.fortunecookiesonline.com

**Fanny's Fat Free Foods,** Pompano Business Park, 1405 SW 6th Ct., Pompano Beach, FL 33069: Free catalog ◆ Fat and sugar-free prepared cakes, mixes, and batters. 800-989-0152; 954-783-0506 (in FL). www.fannysfatfree.com

**FortuneGram,** 2873 Fox Tail Dr., Montrose, CO 81401: Free brochure ◆ Giant fortune cookies for celebrations and other occasions. 800-377-8476; 970-252-1391 (in CO). www.fortunegram.com/index.html

**Four Oaks Farm Inc.,** P.O. Box 987, Lexington, SC 29071: Free brochure ◆ Country-style ham and bacon, jams, jellies, pickles, relishes, salad dressings, cakes, and other favorites. 800-858-5006; 803-356-3194 (in SC). fouroaks@scsn.net

**Fralinger's Inc.,** 1325 Boardwalk, Atlantic City, NJ 08401: Free brochure ◆ Saltwater taffy, sugar-free low-sodium salt water taffy, fudge, almond and coconut macaroons, chocolates, and other candy. 609-345-2177.

**Gloria's Kitchen,** P.O. Box 1415, Guilford, CT 06437: Free price list ◆ Almond marzipan tea cake mixes. 800-680-9944.

**The Gluten-Free Pantry,** P.O. Box 840, Glastonbury, CT 06033: Free catalog ◆ Easy-to-make wheat and gluten-free bread and cake mixes. 800-291-8386. www.glutenfree.com

**Godiva Direct,** P.O. Box 945, Clinton, CT 06413: Free catalog ◆ Cakes, pastries, and chocolate candy. 800-946-3482. www.godiva.com

**Golden Walnut Specialty Foods,** 3200 16th St., Zion, IL 60099: Free catalog ◆ Packaged all-Kosher cookies, cakes, and candies. 800-445-3957.

**Good Fortunes,** 6754 Eton Ave., Canoga Park, CA 91303: Free information ◆ Gourmet chocolate or caramel-dipped giant-size fortune cookies with personalized messages. 800-644-9474.

**Grandma's Fruit Cake,** Division Metz Baking Company, Box 457, Beatrice, NE 68310: Free brochure ◆ Fruitcake. 800-228-4030; 402-223-2358 (in NE).

**William Greenberg Desserts Inc.,** 1100 Madison Ave., New York, NY 10028: Free catalog ◆ Brownies, butter cookies, cheese straws, pound cake, schnecken, Danish pastries, kugelhopf, coffee and chocolate yeast loaves, muffins, pecan rings, and angel food and carrot cakes. 800-255-8278.

**Harry & David,** P.O. Box 712, Medford, OR 97501: Free catalog ◆ Cakes, baklava, cinnamon pastries, tortes, candy, preserves, fresh and dried fruits, and specialties. 800-345-5655. www.harryanddavid.com

**HeartyMix Company,** 1231 Madison Hill Rd., Rahway, NJ 07065: Free catalog ◆ Salt-free bread, wheat-free products, and preservative-, cholesterol-, and saturated fat-free baking mixes for cookies and cakes. 732-382-3010.

**Hermitage Bakery,** Immaculate Heart Hermitage, Big Sur, CA 93920: Free brochure ◆ Date-nut cake and fruitcakes. 408-667-2456. NCamaldoli@aol.com

**Holy Cross Abbey,** RR 2, Box 3870, Berryville, VA 22611: Free information ◆ Traditional fruitcakes, with a choice of fruits and nut meats, in a brandy-laced batter.

**Home Baked Group Inc.,** 1084 S. Rogers Circle, Boca Raton, FL 33487: Free list of retail sources ◆ Kosher fat-free and low-fat brownies. 800-683-3467; 561-995-0767 (in FL).

**Hunt Country Foods Inc.,** P.O. Box 876, Middleburg, VA 22117: Free information ◆ Shortbread cookies. 540-364-2622.

**Indian Hill Farms,** 213 Old Indian Rd., Milton, NY 12547: Free catalog ◆ Smoked whole turkey and turkey breast, Kosher turkey, smoked ham, Norwegian smoked salmon, and brandied fruitcake. 914-795-2700.

**International Brownie,** 602 Middle St., Weymouth, MA 02189: Free brochure ◆ Fudge brownie gift assortments. 800-230-1588; 781-340-1588 (in MA). www.internationalbrownie.com

**Jubilations Cheesecakes,** 1536 Gardner Blvd., Bldg. 7, Columbus, MS 39702: Free brochure ◆ Over 35 varieties of cheesecakes. 800-530-7808; 601-328-9210 (in MS). jubilations@tile.com

**Junior's Cheesecake,** 386 Flatbush Ave. Extension, Brooklyn, NY 11201: Free brochure ◆ Plain, chocolate swirl, black forest, pumpkin New York style gourmet, and fat-free cheesecakes. 800-958-6467.

**Koinonia Partners Inc.,** 1324 Georgia Hwy. 49 South, Americus, GA 31709: Free catalog ◆ Pecan and peanut candy, baked goods, shelled pecan halves, pecans in the shell, and raw-shelled peanuts. 800-569-4128.

**Laura's Classic Cheesecakes,** 109 N. Madison, Mt. Pleasant, TX 75455: Free information ◆ Cheesecakes with chocolate chips blended with creamy caramel and blueberries. 800-252-8727; 903-577-8177 (in TX).

**Linn's Fruit Bin,** 2485 Village Ln., Cambria, CA 93428: Free catalog ◆ Homestyle preserves and bakery specialties. 800-676-1670.

**MacNab's Teas,** P.O. Box 206, Back River Rd., Boothbay, ME 04537: Catalog $2 ◆ MacNab's black teas, Scots tea, tea from Maine, and other favorites. Also shortbread and scone mixes. 800-884-7222.

**Magic Seasonings Mail Order,** P.O. Box 23342, New Orleans, LA 70183: Free catalog ◆ New Orleans cinnamon-flavored coffee cake and sweet potato pecan pie. 800-457-2857. www.chefpaul.com

**Marriott Specialty Foods,** P.O. Box 3005, Humble, TX 77347: Free catalog ◆ Cheesecakes and other desserts. 800-29-CAKES; 281-540-1249 (in TX).

**Mary of Puddin Hill,** P.O. Box 241, Greenville, TX 75403: Free catalog ◆ Fruitcakes, other cakes, pies, and candy. 800-545-8889. www.puddinhill.com

**Matthews 1812 House,** 250 Kent Rd., P.O. Box 15, Cornwall Bridge, CT 06754: Free brochure ◆ Original fruit, holiday, and special occasion cakes. 800-662-1812. matthews@mohawk.net

**Michael's Bakery,** P.O. Box 7, Millville, CA 96062: Free brochure ◆ Applesauce, zucchini-oatmeal, and carrot cakes. Also cookies and chewy brownies. 800-449-CAKE. www.michaelsbakery.com

**Mom's Apple Pie Company,** 296 Sunset Park, Herndon, VA 22070: Free brochure ◆ Low-sugar fruit pies. 800-221-3897.

**Mother Myrick's Confectionary,** P.O. Box 1142, Manchester Center, VT 05255: Free brochure ◆ Hot fudge sauce, maple cheesecake, linzer torte, stollen, fudge, butter crunch, truffles, and caramels. 802-362-1560.

**Mrs. Hanes' Moravian Cookies,** Moravian Sugar Crisp Company, 4643 Friedberg Church Rd., Clemmons, NC 27012: Free brochure ◆ Moravian butterscotch cookies and sugar, lemon, and chocolate crisp. 888-764-1402; 336-764-1402 (in NC). www.hanescookies.com

**Mrs. Morrison's Shortbread,** 4061-C Oceanside Blvd., Oceanside, CA 92056: Free information ◆ Shortbread specialties, shortbread baking molds, jams and jellies, and fruit-flavored teas. 760-414-1218. www.shortbread.com

**Muffins Galore & More Inc.,** 220 Campbell St., Geneva, IL 60134: Free information ◆ Sixty flavors of muffins, from all-time classics to ones that are decadent in taste. 800-619-6190; 630-208-4848 (in IL).

**My Grandma's of New England Coffee Cake,** 231 Bussey St., Dedham, MA 02026: Free brochure ◆ Regular and low-fat coffee cakes. 800-847-2636.

**Nanco,** P.O. Box 100549, Terra Bedlla, CA 93270: Free list of retail sources ◆ Roasted pistachios and shortbread cookies. 209-535-1030.

**New York's Turf Cheesecakes,** 47 Halstead Ave., Ste. 204, Harrison, NY 10528: Free information ◆ Gourmet cheesecakes. 800-221-8873. www.turfcc.com

**No Pudge! Foods Inc.,** P.O. Box 215, Elkins, NH 03233: Free brochure ◆ All-natural fat-free brownie mixes. 800-730-7547. www.nopudge.com

**Northwest Specialty Baking Mixes,** P.O. Box 25240, Portland, OR 97225: Free information ◆ Baking mixes. 800-666-1727.

**One Cookie Place,** P.O. Box 160756, Altamonte Springs, FL 32716: Free brochure ◆ Chocolate and white-chocolate chip, peanut butter, oatmeal raisin, chocolate crunch, and raspberry white cookies. 800-992-6654; 407-774-9433 (in FL). www.selmas.com

**Paradigm Foodworks,** 5775 SW Jean Rd., Ste. 106A, Lake Oswego, OR 97035: Catalog $1 (refundable) ◆ Scone and Belgian waffle mixes, fruit spreads, and dessert sauces. 800-234-0250.

**Racine Danish Kringles,** 2529 Golf Ave., Racine, WI 53404: Free brochure ◆ Danish pastries. 800-4-DANISH. www.kringle.com

**Real Cookies Inc.,** 2123 Wantagh Ave., Wantagh, NY 11793: Free list of retail sources ◆ Cookie mixes. 800-822-5113. www.realcookies.com

**Rhino Foods Inc.,** 79 Industrial Pkwy., Burlington, VT 05401: Free information ◆ Creamy cheesecakes and cheesecake cookies. 800-639-3350; 802-862-0252 (in VT).

**Rowena's,** 758 W. 22nd, Norfolk, VA 23517: Free information ◆ Cakes, preserves and jams, and cooking sauces. 800-627-8699. www.rowenas.com

**Santa Fe Cookie Company,** 3905 San Mateo NE, Albuquerque, NM 87110: Free brochure ◆ Sugar-free cookies, spicy snacks, pretzels, crackers, and nut mixes. 800-873-5589.

**Schroeder's Bakeries,** 212 Forest Ave., P.O. Box 183, Buffalo, NY 14213: Free catalog ◆ Cake-making kits and decorating supplies. 800-850-7763. bakery@schroedersbakery.com

**Steve's Mom Inc.,** 113 16th St., Brooklyn, NY 11215: Free list of retail sources ◆ Kosher strudel, rugelach, and bakery specialties. 718-832-6300.

**The Sundial Gardens & Tea Room,** 59 Hidden Lake Rd., Higganum, CT 06441: Free catalog ◆ Teas, herbal tisanes, and mixes for easy-to-make toasted hazelnut, cranberry, and traditional English currant scones. 203-345-4290.

**Sweet Street Desserts,** 722 Hiesters Ln., Reading, PA 19605: Free catalog ◆ Fruit crisp, pies and crumbles, cakes, and other pastries. 610-921-8113. www.sweetstreet.com

**Swiss Connection,** 501 1st St., Orlando, FL 32824: Free catalog ◆ Swiss chocolates and candies, traditional Italian cakes, and novelties. 800-LE-SWISS. www.swissconnection.com

**Turf Cheesecake Corp.,** 499 Veteran Dr., Burlington, NJ 08016: Free information ◆ Cheesecakes. 800-565-9437.

**Albert Uster Imports Inc.,** 9211 Gaither Rd., Gaithersburg, MD 20877: Free catalog ◆ Ready-to-serve petite-size pastries. 800-231-8154; 301-258-7350 (in MD). swissavi@erols.com

**Walkers Shortbread Ltd.,** 170 Commerce Dr., Hauppauge, NY 11788: Free list of retail sources ◆ Shortbread cookies, Scottish biscuits, fruit cakes, and dessert meringues. 800-521-0141; 516-273-0011 (in NY).

**Ye Olde Sweet Shoppe Bakery,** P.O. Box 1672, Shepherdstown, WV 25443: Free information ◆ Home-baked bread, strudels, German stollen, and specialties. 800-922-5379.

**YZ Enterprises Inc.,** 1930 Indian Wood Circle, Maumee, OH 43537: Free information ◆ Parve Kosher cookies. 800-736-8779.

## Candy & Dessert Sauces

**Angell & Phelps,** 154 S. Beach St., Daytona Beach, FL 32114: Free brochure ◆ Handmade chocolate candy. 800-969-2634.

**Aplets & Cotlets Factory,** P.O. Box 179, Cashmere, WA 98815: Free catalog ◆ Aplets and Cotlets, Washington's famous fruit and nut confection. 800-888-5696. www.libertyorchards.com

**Arkansas Blue Heron Farms,** Rt. 2, Box 323, Lowell, AR 72745: Free catalog ◆ Blueberry jam and marmalades, Amaretto dessert sauce, and specialties. 800-225-6849.

**Aunt Leah's Fudge,** P.O. Box 981, Nantucket, MA 02554: Free brochure ◆ Homemade fudge and other candy. 800-824-6330.

**Karl Bissinger's French Confections,** 3983 Gratiot, St. Louis, MO 63110: Free catalog ◆ Chocolates, fruit and nut bars, jellies, jams, cheese, meat, and tea. 800-325-8881.

**Black Hound New York,** 149 1st Ave., New York, NY 10003: Free information ◆ Belgian chocolate truffles and other favorites. 212-979-9505.

**Boca Bons Inc.,** 10720 Wiles Rd., Pompano, FL 33076: Free list of retail sources ◆ Handmade truffles, fudge, and brownies. 800-314-2835; 964-346-0494 (in FL).

**Andre Bollier Ltd.,** 5018 Main St., Kansas City, MO 64112: Free brochure ◆ Chocolate candy and gift packages. 800-892-1234. www.andreschocolates.com

**C & C Candies,** 1305 Long Run Rd., Friedensburg, PA 17933: Free brochure ◆ Chocolate candy for all occasions. 800-567-2462; 717-739-2963 (in PA). www.cccandies.com

**Cafe Beaujolais,** Box 730, Mendocino, CA 95460: Free catalog ◆ Pastries and desserts, candy assortments, hot chocolate mix, and other specialties. 800-930-0443.

**The Candy Store,** 8 E. Main St., Bozeman, MT 59715: Free list ◆ Homemade fudge and chocolates. 800-682-2639; 406-585-9737 (in MT). www.montana.avicom.net/candystore

**Carp River Trading Company,** 6005 E. Traverse Hwy., Traverse City, MI 49864: Free catalog ◆ Sugar-free hot fudge, other dessert sauces, preserves, and condiments. 800-526-9876.

**Casa de Fruta,** 6680 Pacheco Pass Hwy., Holister, CA 95023: Free brochure ◆ Candy, dried fruit, and gift nut assortments. 800-543-1702. www.casadefruta.com

**Chapin's Fudge & Chocolates,** 1924 NE 181st Ave., Portland, OR 97230: Free brochure ◆ Assorted chocolate covered fudge. 503-588-3200.

**Choco-Logo,** 459 Broadway, Buffalo, NY 14201: Free information ◆ Molded chocolate specialties. 716-855-3500.

**Chocoholics Divine Desserts,** 3765 N. Wilcox Rd., Stockton, CA 95215: Catalog $5 ◆ Semi-sweet chocolate, fat-free and reduced calorie semi-sweet, and fruit-source sweetened chocolate syrups. 800-760-CHOC.

**The Chocolate Barn,** Historic Rt. 7A, Shaftsbury, VT 05262: Free information ◆ Hand-dipped chocolates, fudge, molded solid chocolate, and other favorites. 802-375-6928.

**Chocolate Emporium,** 14439 Cedar Rd., South Euclid, OH 44121: Free brochure *Certified kosher and pareve, gourmet hand-dipped chocolates. 888-CHOCLAT; 216-382-0140 (in OH). www.choclat.com

**Chocolate Factory,** 118 N. Main St., P.O. Box 567, Trumbauersville, PA 18970: Free brochure ◆ Molded chocolate novelties for weddings, birthdays, anniversaries, and other occasions. 800-779-7004; 215-536-7004 (in PA).

**The Chocolate Gallery,** 5705 Calle Real, Goleta, CA 93117: Free brochure ◆ Chocolate novelties. 800-426-4796. www.chocolategallery.com

**Chocolates to Die For,** 6320 Far Hills Ave., Centerville, OH 45459: Free catalog ◆ Fresh Belgian chocolates, chocolate fondue, and special gift packaging. 888-BELCHOC. www.chocolatestodiefor.com

**Chukar Cherries,** P.O. Box 510, Prosser, WA 99350: Free catalog ◆ Cherry preserves and chocolate candy. 800-624-9544.

**Clearbrook Farms,** 5514 Fair Ln., Fairfax, OH 45227: Free brochure ◆ Semi-sweet chocolate sauces, marmalades, and preserves. 800-222-9966; 513-271-2053 (in OH).

**Cocoa-Mill Chocolate Company,** 15 W. Nelson St., Lexington, VA 24450: Catalog $1 ◆ Truffles, turtles, and other favorites. 800-421-6220; 540-464-8400 (in VA).

**Community Products Inc.,** RD 2, Box 1950, Montpelier, VT 05602: Free list of retail sources ◆ Dairy-free chocolate bars. 800-927-2695; 802-229-5702 (in VT).

**Da Vinci Gourmet,** 823 Yale Ave., Ste. E, Seattle, WA 98109: Free information ◆ Syrups for baked goods, beverages, desserts, and pancake toppings. 800-640-6779; 206-682-4682 (in WA).

**Daskalides U.S.A.,** 860 Sand Pine Dr. NE, St. Petersburg, FL 33703: Free brochure ◆ Candy made with Belgian chocolate. 800-625-7177; 813-521-3008 (in FL). www.daskalides.com

**Donells Candies,** 201 E. 2nd St., Ste. 2, Casper, WY 82601: Free information ◆ Hand-dipped homemade creams and nuts. 888-412-3786. sweet1@caspers.net

**Richard H. Donnelly Fine Chocolates,** 1509 Mission St., Santa Cruz, CA 95060: Free information ◆ Chocolate candy specialties. 408-458-4214.

**Double Springs Homebrew Supply,** 4697 Double Springs Rd., Valley Springs, CA 95252: Free catalog ◆ Syrups for sodas, Italian ices, mixing with coffee and tea, and serving over ice cream. 209-754-4888. www.doublesprings.com

**Elegant Sweets,** 11836 NE 112th Ave., Kirkland, WA 98033: Free list of retail sources ◆ Biscotti, chocolates, toffee, gourmet-flavored white barks, and specialties. 425-814-2500.

**Enclosures Chocolate,** 9211 Gaither Rd., Gaithersburg, MD 20877: Free catalog ◆ Milk chocolate specialties. 800-231-8154.

**Enstrom Candies,** P.O. Box 1088, Grand Junction, CO 81502: Free brochure ◆ Almond toffee. 800-367-8766. www.enstrom.com

**Essentially Chocolate,** 15737 Crabbs Branch Way, Rockville, MD 20855: Free information ◆ Chocolate candy and brownies. 301-770-5660.

**The Estee Corp.,** 169 Lackawanna Ave., Parsippany, NJ 07054: Free catalog ◆ Sugarless candy and cookies. 800-34-ESTEE.

**Ethel-M Chocolates Mail-order,** P.O. Box 98505, Las Vegas, NV 89193: Free catalog ◆ Milk and dark chocolate truffles, butter creams, nuts, and other candy. 800-4-ETHEL-M. www.ethelm.com

**Evans Creole Candy Company,** 848 Decatur St., New Orleans, LA 70116: Free information ◆ Nut clusters, turtles, Creole hash, and old-fashioned favorites. 800-637-6675; 504-522-7111 (in LA).

**Fannie May Candies,** Attention: Mail Order Dept., P.O. Box 6939, Chicago, IL 60607: Free brochure ◆ Chocolates, nuts and nut candy, hard candy, and other favorites. 800-333-3629. www.fanniemaycandies.com

**Figi's,** 3200 S. Maple, Marshfield, WI 54404: Free catalog ◆ Candy and specialties. 715-341-1363.

**Fralinger's Inc.,** 1325 Boardwalk, Atlantic City, NJ 08401: Free brochure ◆ Saltwater taffy, sugar-free low-sodium salt water taffy, fudge, almond and coconut macaroons, chocolates, and other candy. 609-345-2177.

**Fran's Chocolates,** 1300 E. Pike St., Seattle, WA 98122: Free information ◆ Handmade and handwrapped chocolates. 800-422-FRAN. www.franschocolates.com

**Ghirardelli Chocolate,** 1111 139th Ave., San Leandro, CA 94578: Free brochure ◆ Chocolate specialties. 888-402-6262. www.ghirardellisq.com

**Godiva Direct,** P.O. Box 945, Clinton, CT 06413: Free catalog ◆ Chocolate candy and pastries. 800-946-3482. www.godiva.com

**Golden Walnut Specialty Foods,** 3200 16th St., Zion, IL 60099: Free catalog ◆ Packaged all-Kosher cookies, cakes, and candies. 800-445-3957.

**Gourmet Chocolate Inc.,** P.O. Box 208, Halstead, KS 67056: Free catalog ◆ European-style chocolate candy and nuts, from novelties to boxed assortments. 800-835-2040. www.gourmetchocolate.com

**Green Mountain Chocolate Company,** RR 2, Box 1447, Waterbury, VT 05676: Free brochure ◆ Handmade truffles. 800-686-8783.

**Hammond's Candy,** 2550 W. 29th Ave., Denver, CO 80211: Free brochure ◆ Seasonal, holiday, and other traditional handmade candies. 888-CANDY-99; 303-455-2320 (in CO).

**Harbor Candy Shop,** P.O. Box 2064, Ogunquit, ME 03907: Free catalog ◆ Chocolate-covered fruit and dark or milk-chocolate pecan or cashew-caramel turtles. 800-331-5856.

**Harbor Sweets Inc.,** Palmer Cove, 85 Leavitt St., Salem, MA 01970: Free catalog ◆ Handmade chocolates, sugar-free candy, seasonal favorites, gift assortments, chunks for ice-cream, and selections for special-occasions, weddings, and stocking stuffers. 800-243-2115. www.harbor-sweets.com

**Harry & David,** P.O. Box 712, Medford, OR 97501: Free catalog ◆ Candy, cakes, baklava, cinnamon pastries, tortes, preserves, fresh and dried fruits, and specialties. 800-345-5655. www.harryanddavid.com

**Haven's Candies,** 87 County Rd., Westbrook, ME 04092: Free brochure ◆ Chocolates, fudge, nuts, salt water taffy, and novelties. 800-639-6309. www.havens-candies.com

**Hershey's Mailorder,** P.O. Box 801, Hershey, PA 17033: Free catalog ◆ Hershey specialties and novelties. 800-544-1347. www.hersheys.com/~hershey

**Hoffman's Chocolate Shoppes,** 5190 Lake Worth Rd., Greenacres, FL 33463: Free brochure ◆ Nuts, fruits, cherry cordials, truffles, and chocolate-covered candy favorites. 888-281-8800. www.hoffmans.com

**How Sweet It Is,** P.O. Box 376, Jenkintown, PA 19046: Free information ◆ Low-fat and salt or sugar-free candy. 215-784-9980. www.howsweet.com

**Jinil Au Chocolat,** 414 Central Ave., Cedarhurst, NY 11516: Free information ◆ Custom-molded chocolate and gift baskets. 800-64-JINIL; 516-295-2550 (in NY). www.jinil.com

**Jo's Candies,** 2530 W. 237th St., Torrance, CA 90505: Free brochure ◆ Hand-dipped premium chocolates. 800-770-1946; 310-257-0260 (in CA). www.joscandies.com

**Kailua Candy Company,** P.O. Box 2761, Kailua-Kona, HI 96745: Free brochure ◆ Handmade chocolate candies. 800-622-2462. www.kailua-candy.com

**Knudsen's Candy & Nut Company,** 25067 Viking St., Hayward, CA 94545: Free catalog ◆ Butter cream caramels, triple-chocolate truffles, and dessert sauces. 800-736-6887; 510-293-6887 (in CA).

**Koinonia Partners Inc.,** 1324 Georgia Hwy. 49 South, Americus, GA 31709: Free catalog ◆ Pecan and peanut candy, baked goods, shelled pecan halves, pecans in the shell, and raw-shelled peanuts. 800-569-4128.

**Koppers Chocolate Specialty Company Inc.,** 39 Clarkson St., New York, NY 10014: Free list of retail sources ◆ Cordials, chocolate-covered fruits and nuts, and candy. 800-325-0026; 212-243-0220 (in NY).

**La Maison du Chocolat,** 25 E. 73rd St., New York, NY 10021: Free information ◆ Imported chocolates from Paris, France. 212-744-7117.

**Lake Champlain Chocolates,** 431 Pine St., Burlington, VT 05401: Free brochure ◆ Chocolate candy made with natural ingredients. 800-465-5909.

**Lammes Candy,** P.O. Box 1885, Austin, TX 78767: Free catalog ◆ Pecan pralines. 800-252-1885; 512-248-3465 (in TX). www.lammes.com

**Liberty Orchards,** P.O. Box 179, Cashmere, WA 98815: Free catalog ◆ Aplets and Cotlets, all-natural candy, and fruit specialties. 800-888-5696. www.libertyorchards.com

**Long Grove Confectionery Company,** 333 Lexington Dr., Buffalo, IL 60089: Free catalog ◆ Chocolate candies. Includes seasonal specialties. 800-373-3102. www.longgrove.com

**Maggie Lyon Chocolatiers,** 6000 Peachtree Industrial Blvd., Norcross, GA 30071: Free list of retail sources) ◆ Regular and sugar-free truffles. 800-969-3500.

**Margaret's Superior Desserts,** P.O. Box 908, Marquette, MI 49855: Free information ◆ Truffles and truffle cake, baklava, and cheesecakes. 906-226-9001.

**Marshall's Fudge Shops,** 308 E. Central Ave., Mackinaw City, MI 49701: Free catalog ◆ Preservative-free fudge, homemade candy, and nuts. 800-343-8343. www.marshallsfudge.com

**Mary of Puddin Hill,** P.O. Box 241, Greenville, TX 75403: Free catalog ◆ Candy, fruitcakes, pies, and other baked goods. 800-545-8889. www.puddinhill.com

**Matthews 1812 House,** 250 Kent Rd., P.O. Box 15, Cornwall Bridge, CT 06754: Free brochure ◆ Candy, dessert sauces, maple syrup, nuts and snacks, and other specialties. 800-662-1812. matthews@mohawk.net

**Monin Syrups Inc.,** 2100 Range Rd., Clearwater, FL 34625: Free information ◆ Concentrated syrups made from fruit, sugar, and water. 800-966-5225.

**Moonstruck Chocolatier,** 6663 SW Beaverton Hillsdale Hwy., Ste. 194, Portland, OR 97225: Free information ◆ Gourmet chocolate specialties. 800-557-6666.

**Moore's Candies Inc.,** 3004 Pinewood Ave., Baltimore, MD 21214: Free brochure ◆ Homemade candy. 410-426-2705.

**Mother Myrick's Confectionary,** P.O. Box 1142, Manchester Center, VT 05255: Free brochure ◆ Hot fudge sauce, maple cheesecake, linzer torte, stollen, fudge, butter crunch, truffles, and caramels. 802-362-1560.

**Mrs. Nelson's Candy House,** 292 Chelmsford St., Chelmsford, MA 01824: Free brochure ◆ Candy favorites. 978-256-4061.

**Neuhaus USA Inc.,** 2 Secatoag Ave., Port Washington, NY 11050: Free list of retail sources ◆ Belgium chocolates. 516-883-7400.

**New Canaan Farms,** P.O. Box 386, Dripping Springs, TX 78620: Free brochure ◆ Ice cream toppings, jellies, and mustard. 800-727-5267.

**New Orleans Snow Balls,** 11 Carriage Square, Boone, NC 28607: Free information ◆ Snowball syrups. 704-262-3952.

**Nunes Farms Almonds,** 73 Alder Ave., San Anselmo, CA 94960: Free information ◆ Almond candy, English toffee, and fresh, roasted and salted, honey-glazed, and Cheddar cheese almonds. 800-255-1641.

**Old Kentucky Candies,** P.O. Box 4245, Lexington, KY 40544: Free brochure ◆ Chocolate nuts, assorted soft cream centers, pecan logs, peanut brittle, and other candies. 800-786-0579; 606-278-4444 (in KY). www.oldkycandy.com

**C.J. Olson Cherries,** Rt. 1, Box 140, El Camino Real, Sunnyvale, CA 94087: Free brochure ◆ Dried fruit packs, chocolate covered fruits and nuts, and gift assortments. 800-738-2464. www.olsonscherries.com

**Palais du Chocolat,** 3309 Connecticut Ave. NW, Washington, DC 20008: Free information ◆ Gourmet candy inspired by French and Belgian favorites. 202-363-2462.

**Paradigm Foodworks,** 5775 SW Jean Rd., Ste. 106A, Lake Oswego, OR 97035: Catalog $1 (refundable) ◆ Scone and Belgian waffle mixes, fruit spreads, and dessert sauces. 800-234-0250.

**Pecan Producers International,** 2131 East Hwy. 31, Corsicana, TX 75110: Free information ◆ Chocolate covered pecans. 800-732-2648.

**Perugina Chocolates,** 299 Market St., Saddle Brook, NJ 07663: Free information ◆ Chocolate candy specialties. 201-587-8080.

**Plimoth Lollipop Company,** 286 Court St., Plymouth, MA 02360: Free information ◆ Old-fashioned hand-poured lollipops. 800-777-0115.

**Esther Price Candies,** 1709 Wayne Ave., Dayton, OH 45410: Free catalog ◆ Chocolates for everyone and all occasions. 800-782-0326; 937-253-2121 (in OH). www.estherprice.com

**Ann Raskas Candies,** P.O. Box 13367, Kansas City, KS 66113: Free information ◆ Candy for dieters. 913-422-7230.

**Rising Moon Grassroots Gourmet,** 1432 Williamette St., Eugene, OR 97401: Free brochure ◆ Dessert sauces. 541-684-8977.

**Rocky Mountain Chocolate Factory,** 547 Cannery Row, Monterey, CA 93940: Free brochure ◆ Handmade chocolates, popcorn, caramel and chocolate coated apples, and other favorites. 800-658-2020.

**Rogers' Chocolates Ltd.,** 913 Government St., Victoria, British Columbia, Canada V8W 1X5: Free brochure ◆ Handmade chocolates packaged in classic boxes. 250-384-7021. www.rogerschocolates.com

**The San Francisco Chocolate Factory,** P.O. Bo 2666, San Francisco, CA 94126: Free information ◆ White, milk, and dark chocolate bars. Also other chocolate specialties. 888-732-4626.

**Sarris Candies,** 511 Adams Ave., Canonsburg, PA 15317: Free catalog ◆ Candy made with all-natural ingredients. 800-255-7771.

**See's Candies,** P.O. Box S, Culver City, CA 90231: Free catalog ◆ Chocolate candy, seasonal and holiday specialties, lollipops, and assortments. 800-347-7337.

**Señor Murphy, Candymaker,** P.O. Box 2505, Santa Fe, NM 87504: Free catalog ◆ Sugar-free and other gourmet chocolate favorites. 505-988-4311.

**Seroogy's Chocolates,** P.O. Box 143, De Pere, WI 54115: Free catalog ◆ Candy and nut assortments. 800-776-0377; 414-336-1383 (in WI).

**Society Hill Snacks,** 2121 Gillingham St., Philadelphia, PA 19124: Free list of retail sources ◆ Chocolate confections. 800-595-0050; 215-288-2888 (in PA).

**Splurge Inc.,** 207 E. 74th St., New York, NY 10021: Free information ◆ Low-calorie specialties. 212-439-6181.

**Standard Candy Company,** Mail Order Service, P.O. Box 697, Eastman, GA 31023: Free catalog ◆ Goo Goo Clusters, an original combination of chewy caramel, creamy marshmallow, roasted peanuts, and milk chocolate. Also old-fashioned stick candy and southern-style foods. 800-231-3402. www.googoo.com

**C.S. Steen Syrup Mill Inc.,** 119 N. Main St., P.O. Box 339, Abbeville, LA 70510: Free brochure ◆ Pure cane syrup and natural light and dark molasses. 800-725-1654.

**Stirling Foods,** Box 582, Renton, WA 98057: Free information ◆ Gourmet syrups. 800-332-1714.

**Swiss Connection,** 501 1st St., Orlando, FL 32824: Free catalog ◆ Swiss chocolates and candies, traditional Italian cakes, and novelties. 800-LE-SWISS. www.swissconnection.com

**Teuscher Chocolates of Switzerland,** 620 5th Ave. at Rockefeller Center, New York, NY 10020: Free catalog ◆ Assorted pralines, truffles, chocolate fantasies, and other Swiss specialties. 800-554-0924; 212-246-4416 (in NY). www.teuscher.com

**Three Georges Southern Chocolates,** 226 Dauphin St., Mobile, AL 36602: Free brochure ◆ Heavenly hash, pralines, pecan and cashew candies, and other southern-style specialties. 800-669-5175.

**Top Hat Company,** Box 66, Wilmette, IL 60091: Free brochure ◆ Dessert sauces. 847-256-6565.

**Trappistine Creamy Caramels,** 8325 Abbey Hill Rd., Dubuque, IA 52003: Free brochure ◆ Caramels and creamy mints. 319-556-6330.

**Vermont Confectionery,** Historic Rt. 7A at the Iron Kettle, Shaftsbury, VT 05262: Free information with long SASE ◆ Chocolates, handmade lollipops, novelty chocolates, and other confections. 802-447-2610.

**Carol Wayne Homemade Chocolates,** 123 Ritter Rd., Mt. Nebo, Sewickley, PA 15143: Free brochure ◆ Chocolate candies, novelties, and other specialties. 412-741-7777.

**Wertz Candies,** 718 Cumberland St., Lebanon, PA 17042: Free brochure ◆ Hand-dipped milk and semi-sweet chocolates. 717-627-0114. www.wertzcandy.com

**World of Chantilly,** 4302 Farragut Rd., Brooklyn, NY 11203: Free list of retail sources ◆ Certified Kosher French pastries. Also chocolate candy and gift baskets. 718-859-1110.

**Young Pecans,** c/o Pecan Plantations, P.O. Drawer 6709, Florence, SC 29502: Free catalog ◆ Butter-roasted and salted pecans and cashews, double-dipped chocolate pecan halves, butter-toffee pecan popcorn, and pecan divinity logs. Also praline, sugar and orange, sugar and spiced, and Cheddar cheese pecans. 800-729-8004.

**Yummies Candy & Nuts,** Rt. 1, Kittery, ME 03904: Free catalog ◆ Candy and nut favorites. 800-638-9377. www.yummies.com

## Caviar

**Assouline & Ting Inc.,** 314 Brown St., Philadelphia, PA 19123: Free information ◆ Imported and domestic caviar, smoked fish, snails, and other specialties. 800-521-4491; 215-627-3000 (in PA). www.caviarassouline.com

**Caspian Star Caviar Inc.,** 46 Washington Ave., Brooklyn, NY 11205: Free brochure ◆ Fresh Malossol caviar from Russia and domestic varieties. Also pre-sliced Scottish and Norwegian smoked salmon. 610-617-9646.

**Caviamur,** 613 W. 47th St., Chicago, IL 60609: Free information ◆ Malossol caviar from Far East Russia. 800-228-4268.

**Caviarteria Inc.,** 502 Park Ave., New York, NY 10022: Free catalog ◆ Smoked fish and American whitefish, sturgeon, salmon, Beluga, and Sevruga caviar. Also French foie gras. 800-422-8427; 212-759-7410 (in NY). www.caviarteria.com

**Hansen Caviar Company,** 93D S. Railroad Ave., Bergenfield, NJ 07621: Free information ◆ American sturgeon and Russian Beluga caviar. 888-BELUGA-1.

**Poriloff Caviar,** 47-39 49th St., Woodside, NY 11377: Free information ◆ American sturgeon and Russian Beluga caviar. 718-784-3344.

**Tsar Nicoulai Caviar,** California Sunshine Fine Foods Inc., 144 King St., San Francisco, CA 94107: Free brochure ◆ Beluga, Osetra, Sevruga, American sturgeon, and other caviars. 415-543-3007.

## Cheese

**Bandon Cheese Inc.,** P.O. Box 1668, Bandon, OR 97411: Free brochure ◆ Jalapeno and Monterey Jack, medium and aged sharp Baja; sharp, garlic, onion Cheddar; and Cajun Cheddar cheese. 800-548-8961.

**Bel Canto Fancy Foods Ltd.,** 555 2nd Ave., New York, NY 10016: Free list of retail sources ◆ Italian sheep's milk cheese. 212-689-4433.

**Blaser's Premium Cheese,** P.O. Box 36, Comstock, WI 54826: Free price list ◆ Cheddar, Colby, Havarti, Monterey Jack, Muenster, and other Wisconsin cheeses. 715-822-2437.

**The British Gourmet Chandlers,** 45 Wall St., Madison, CT 06443: Free catalog ◆ Traditional British foods and cheeses. 203-245-4521.

**The British Shoppe,** 45 Wall St., Madison, CT 06443: Free catalog ◆ Traditional British foods and cheese. 800-842-6674; 203-245-4521 (in CT). www.thebritishshoppe.com

**Cabot Creamery,** P.O. Box 128, Cabot, VT 05647: Free information ◆ All-natural cheese with half the fat and cholesterol and 33 percent fewer calories than Cheddar. 800-639-3198. www.cabotcheese.com

**Calef's Country Store,** P.O. Box 57, Barrington, NH 03825: Free brochure ◆ Homemade cheese, maple syrup, and candy. 800-462-2118.

**Carr Valley Cheese,** S. 3797 County G, La Valle, WI 53941: Free information ◆ Aged sharp Cheddar cheeses. 800-462-7258; 608-986-2781 (in WI).

**The Cheese Box,** 801 Wells St., Lake Geneva, WI 53147: Free catalog ◆ Cheese, wine, and other Wisconsin favorites. 800-345-6105; 414-248-3440 (in WI). www.cheesebox.com

**Chicory Farm,** P.O. Box 25, Mount Hermon, LA 70450: Free information ◆ European-style goat, cow, and sheep's milk cheese. 504-877-4550.

**Coach Dairy Goat Farm,** 105 Mill Hill Rd., Pine Plains, NY 12567: Free list of retail sources ◆ Goat cheese and yogurt. 518-398-5325.

**Crowley Cheese,** Healdville Rd., Healdville VT 05758: Free brochure ◆ Mild, medium, and sharp cheese. Also smoked or spiced with garlic, hot pepper, caraway, or dill varieties. 800-683-2606.

**Di Bruno Bros. House of Cheese,** 930 S. 9th St., Philadelphia, PA 19147: Free brochure ◆ Homemade cheese spreads, Italian cheeses, and other specialties. 888-322-4337. www.dibruno.com

**Durrett Cheese Sales,** P.O. Box 4191, 2641 Stephenson Dr., Murfreesboro, TN 37133: Free information ◆ Mild, medium, and aged sharp Cheddar cheese. Also Monterey Jack, Colby, and other specialty cheeses. 615-896-5378.

**Egg Farm Dairy,** 2 John Walsh Blvd., Peekskill, NY 10566: Free brochure ◆ Cultured butter and churned buttermilk, clabbered cream, and Mascarpone wild-ripened cheeses. 800-CREAMERY. www.creamery.com

**Eichten's Hidden Acres Cheese and Bison Farm,** 16705 310th St., Center City, MN 55012: Free catalog ◆ Artificial flavor, color, and preservative-free Dutch Gouda cheeses. 800-657-6752.

**Fennimore Cheese,** 1675 Lincoln Ave., Fennimore, WI 53809: Free brochure ◆ Gift boxes and bulk cheeses in one pound packages. 608-822-3777. wischeese@hotmail.com

**Figi's,** 3200 S. Maple, Marshfield, WI 54404: Free catalog ◆ Gourmet cheese. 715-341-1363.

**Formagg,** Galaxy Foods, 2441 Viscount Row, Orlando, FL 32809: Free list of retail sources ◆ Low-fat and low-cholesterol cheese. 800-441-9419. www.galaxyfoods.com

**Fortuna's Sausage Company,** 975 Greenville Ave., Greenville, RI 02828: Free catalog ◆ All-natural dry cured Italian sausages, sausage-making kit, pasta, imported Italian cheese, gift baskets, and natural New England specialties. 800-42-SOUPY. SOUPY@Edgenet.net

**Fruit Ranch-West,** 6301 W. Bluemound Rd., Milwaukee, WI 53213: Free catalog ◆ Fruit gift baskets, assorted nuts, and Wisconsin cheese variety packages. 800-433-3289. www.choicemall.com/fruitranch

**G & G Foods,** 1012 Revere St., San Francisco, CA 94124: Free list of retail sources ◆ Cheese spreads. 415-715-2250.

**Gibbsville Cheese Sales,** W2663 CTH OO, Sheboygan Falls, WI 53085: Free price list ◆ Natural rindless and flavored processed cheese. Also cheese spreads in bulk and gift assortments. 920-564-3242.

**Gourm-E-Co Imports,** 405 Glenn Dr., Sterling, VA 20164: Free information ◆ Imported cheese. 800-899-5616.

**Grafton Village Cheese Company,** P.O. Box 87, Grafton, VT 05146: Free brochure ◆ Cheddar cheese. 800-472-3866. www.graftonvillagecheese.com/company.htm

**The Granville Country Store,** P.O. Box 141, Granville, MA 01034: Free information ◆ Aged Cheddar cheese. 800-356-3141.

**Harlow's Sugar House,** RD 1, Box 395, Putney, VT 05346: Free brochure ◆ Maple syrup and specialties, jams, jellies, and Vermont cheese. 802-387-5852.

**Hawkeye Dairy,** 118 S Fourth St., Abbotsford, WI 54405: Free information ◆ Wisconsin cheeses. 715-223-6358.

**Heluva Good Cheese Inc.,** 6152 Barclay Rd., P.O. Box C, Sodus, NY 14551: Free catalog ◆ Cheese specialties. 800-445-0269.

**Hickory Farms,** P.O. Box 75, Maumee, OH 43537: Free brochure ◆ Cheese, smoked meat, and specialties. 800-222-4438. www.hickoryfarms.com

**Ideal Cheese Shop,** 1205 2nd Ave., New York, NY 10021: Catalog $2 ◆ Imported and domestic cheese. 800-382-0109.

**Imperia Foods,** 234 St. Nicholas Ave., South Plainfield, NJ 07080: Free list of retail sources ◆ Imported regular, reduced fat, and low-cholesterol grated Romano and Parmesan cheese. 908-756-7333.

**Lioni Famous Mozzarella Company,** 7803 15th Ave., Brooklyn, NY 11228: Free catalog ◆ Mozzarella cheese and other Italian favorites. 800-86-LIONI. www.lioni.com

**Lynn Dairy Inc.,** W1929 US Hwy. 10, Granton, WI 54436: Free catalog ◆ Gourmet cheese. 715-238-7129.

**Mahogany Smoked Meats,** P.O. Box 1387, Bishop, CA 93515: Free brochure ◆ Smoked jerky, Cheddar cheese, chileno peppers, stuffed olives, smoked trout, and specialties. 888-624-6426.

**Maytag Dairy Farms Inc.,** P.O. Box 806, Newton, IA 50208: Free catalog ◆ Cheddar cheese spreads, blue cheese, natural white Cheddar, brick, baby Swiss, Edam, and other cheeses. 800-247-2458; 515-792-1133 (in IA).

**Mozzarella Company,** 2944 Elm St., Dallas, TX 75226: Free brochure ◆ Queso fresco, a crumbly cheese that resembles farmer's cheese. Also rindless crescenza, semisoft herb-like caciotta, creamy Mascarpone, and cheeses made from cow, goat, and sheep's milk. 972-741-4072.

**Plymouth Cheese Corp.,** P.O. Box 1, Plymouth, VT 05056: Free catalog ◆ Mild or medium-sharp sage, garlic, and caraway cheese. Also aged and naturally cured Vermont granular curd cheese. 802-672-3650.

**Renard's Cheese,** 248 Country Hwy. S, Algoma, WI 54201: Free brochure ◆ Assorted Wisconsin natural cheese. 414-743-6626. www.renards.com

**Rock Cheese Company,** 110 Elm St., Madison, WI 53705: Free brochure ◆ Cheese favorites, honey products, seasonings, and condiments. Also gift assortments. 608-233-7681.

**The Rocking Horse Country Store,** Rt. 4, Rutland, VT 05701: Free brochure ◆ Vermont maple syrup, cheese, crafts, and country collectibles. 802-773-7882.

**Smith's Country Cheese,** 20 Otter River Rd., Winchendon, MA 01475: Free information ◆ Gouda and Cheddar cheese. 978-939-5738.

**Sonoma Cheese Factory,** 2 W. Spain St., Sonoma, CA 95476: Free brochure ◆ Light garlic, hot pepper, and Jack cheese with reduced fat, cholesterol, calories, and salt. 800-535-2855.

**Soyco Foods,** Galaxy Foods, 2441 Viscount Row, Orlando, FL 32809: Free list of retail sources ◆ Casein-free cheese alternative. 800-441-9419. www.soyco.com

**Specialty Cheese Company Inc.,** P.O. Box 425, 455 S. River St., Lowell, WI 53557: Free information ◆ Hispanic and other ethnic natural cheeses. 414-927-3888.

**Split Creek Farm,** 3806 Centerville Rd., Anderson, SC 29625: Free information ◆ Fresh goat cheese. 864-287-3921.

**Sugarbush Farm,** RR 1, Box 568, Woodstock, VT 05091: Free information with long SASE ◆ Maple syrup and cheese. 802-457-1757.

**Sweet Home Farm,** 27107 Schoen Rd., Elberta, AL 36530: Free information ◆ Fresh and aged goat and cow's milk cheese. 334-986-5663.

**Swiss Colony,** Catalog Request Dept., P.O. Box 8994, Madison, WI 53794: Free catalog ◆ Cheese, meat, sausage, pastries, nuts, candy, snacks, and gift assortments. 608-324-4000. www.swisscolony.com

**Vermont Butter & Cheese Company,** P.O. Box 95, Websterville, VT 05678: Free catalog ◆ Chèvre (goat cheese), cow's milk cheese, cultured cream, and butter. 800-884-6287.

**Washington State University Creamery,** 101 Food Quality Bldg., Pullman, WA 99164: Free brochure ◆ Cougar Gold, American, smoky Cheddar, sweet basil, dill garlic, hot pepper, and other cheese. 800-457-5442.

**Westby Cooperative Creamery,** 401 S. Main, Westby, WI 54667: Free brochure ◆ Pre-packaged gift boxes and individual cheeses. 800-634-3183.

**Westfield Farm Inc.,** 28 Worcester Rd., Hubbardton, MA 01452: Free brochure ◆ Natural goat and cow's milk cheese. 978-928-5110.

**Wisconsin Cheeseman,** P.O. Box 1, Madison, WI 53701: Free catalog ◆ Aged Wisconsin natural cheese, sausage, cookies and pastries, fruits, nuts, and specialties. 608-837-4100.

## Creole & Cajun

**Cajun Country Classics,** P.O. Box 1631, Eunice, LA 70535: Free information ◆ Cajun food specialties. 800-780-3708. www.cajuncountry.com

**Tony Chachere's Creole Foods,** P.O. Box 1687, Opelousas, LA 70571: Free catalog ◆ Creole specialties. 800-551-9066. www.cajunspice.com/index.html

**Comeaux's Grocery & Market,** 118 Canaan Dr., Lafayette, LA 70508: Free information ◆ Andouille, boudin (regular, crawfish, and seafood), tasso, and Cajun specialties. 800-323-2492; 318-989-1528 (in LA). www.comeaux.com

**Creole Delicacies,** 533 Saint Ann St., New Orleans, LA 70116: Free brochure ◆ Pecan pralines, remoulade sauce, hot pepper jellies, Creole seasonings, and specialties from Brennan's restaurant. 800-523-6425.

**Maison Louisianne Creole Products,** 2212 19th St., San Francisco, CA 94107: Free information ◆ Creole mustard, spice, marinade, and pepper sauce. 415-285-7731. www.shutmymouth.com

**Pure Cajun Products,** P.O. Box 1485, Lake Charles, LA 70602: Free price list ◆ Cajun, Creole, and other authentic Louisiana specialties. 800-259-3263. www.purecajun.com

## Ethnic

**All Cajun Food Company,** 1019 Delcambre Rd., Breaux Bridge, LA 70503: Free information ◆ Barbecue sauce, Cajun cayenne juice, chow chow, Cajun powder, and other condiments. 800-467-3613.

**The Amishman,** P.O. Box 128, Mount Holly Springs, PA 17065: Free brochure ◆ Candy, apple butter, chow chow, nuts, pretzels, and other snacks. 800-233-7082.

**Amore Gourmet Foods,** P.O. Box 4456, Waterbury, CT 06704: Free catalog ◆ Italian specialty foods. 888-292-6673. www.amorefoods.com

**B & L Specialty Foods Inc.,** P.O. Box 80068, Seattle, WA 98108: Free catalog ◆ Imported pasta, oils, and Italian specialties. 800-EAT-PASTA.

**Bangkok Produce,** 966 San Julian St., Los Angeles, CA 90015: Free information ◆ Oriental fruits and vegetables. 213-689-7933.

**Birky Cafe,** 205 S. Main, Box 318, Kouts, IN 46347: Free information ◆ Amish foods. 219-766-3851. www.birkycafe.com

**Tony Chachere's Creole Foods,** P.O. Box 1687, Opelousas, LA 70570: Free catalog ◆ Creole and Cajun seasonings, crawfish and crab boil, rice mixes, Etouffee sauce, and other cooking specialties. 800-551-9066. www.cajunspice.com/index.html

**Chile La Isla,** P.O. Box 1379, Fabens, TX 79838: Free information ◆ Roasted and individually quick-frozen chili peppers. 800-895-4603.

**CMC Company,** P.O. Box 322, Avalon, NJ 08202: Free catalog ◆ Mexican, Thai-Indonesian, and Szechuan-Chinese cooking ingredients. 800-CMC-2780.

**Corti Brothers,** 5810 Folsom Blvd., Sacramento, CA 95819: Free newsletter ◆ Single garden Chinese teas, regional olive oils, vintage cognac, and food and drink specialties. 916-736-3800.

**Coyote Cafe General Store,** 132 W. Water St., Santa Fe, NM 87501: Free catalog ◆ Hot sauces, salsa, sweet and spicy products, coffee and teas, and gift baskets. 800-866-HOWL.

**Delancey Dessert Company,** 573 Grand St., New York, NY 10002: Free information ◆ All-natural Kosher rugelach and other baked goods. 800-254-5254; 212-254-5254 (in NY).

**El Paso Chili Company,** 909 Texas Ave., El Paso, TX 79901: Free information ◆ Medium-hot cactus salsa made from vine-ripened tomatillos, onions, fresh cilantro, mild chilies, fiery Jalapeno, vinegar, spices, and nopalitos. 915-544-3434. 800-27-IS-HOT. www.elpasochile.com

**Epicurean International,** P.O. Box 13242, Berkeley, CA 94701: Free information ◆ Authentic Thai food specialties. 510-268-0209.

**Erica's Rugelach & Baking Company Inc.,** 265 5th Ave., Brooklyn, NY 11215: Free list of retail sources ◆ Certified Kosher bakery specialties. 718-449-0445.

**Ferrara Foods & Confections Inc.,** 195 Grand St., New York, NY 10013: Free brochure ◆ Coffee, candy, syrups, sauces, bread sticks, vegetables, pasta, baked goods, and Italian specialties. 212-226-6150.

**Fortuna's Sausage Company,** 975 Greenville Ave., Greenville, RI 02828: Free catalog ◆ All-natural dry cured Italian sausages, sausage-making kit, pasta, imported Italian cheese, gift baskets, and natural New England specialties. 800-42-SOUPY. SOUPY@Edgenet.net

**Frieda's by Mail,** P.O. Box 58488, Los Angeles, CA 90058: Free catalog ◆ Habaneras and fresh and dried chilies. 800-241-1771; 714-826-6100 (in CA). www.friedas.com

**GNS Spices,** P.O. Box 90, Walnut, CA 91788: Free information ◆ Dried, flaked, pureed, brined, ground, and fresh Habaneras. 909-594-9505.

**The Great Valley Mills,** 1774 County Line Rd., Barto, PA 19504: Free brochure ◆ Family farm grown and produced foods. Gift packs available. 800-688-6455.

**Hard Times Chili,** 310 Commerce St., Alexandria, VA 22314: Free brochure ◆ Texas Roadhouse and Cincinnati Chili mixes. 703-836-7449. www.hardtimes.com

**Hellas International Inc.,** 35 Congress St., Salem, MA 01970: Free information ◆ Foods from Greece. 800-274-1233.

**Home Baked Group Inc.,** 1084 S. Rogers Circle, Boca Raton, FL 33487: Free list of retail sources ◆ Kosher fat-free and low-fat brownies. 800-683-3467; 561-995-0767 (in FL).

**House of Fire,** 1108 Spruce St., Boulder, CO 80302: Free information ◆ Hot and spicy foods from around the world. 800-717-5787; 303-440-0929 (in CO). www.houseoffire.com

**Jardine's Texas Foods,** 1 Chisholm Trail, Buda, TX 78610: Free catalog ◆ Chili fixings, salsa, hand-stuffed olives, and spicy Bloody Mary mix. 888-544-0110; 512-295-4600 (in TX). www.jardinefoods.com

**Katagiri & Company,** 224 E. 59th St., New York, NY 10022: Free information ◆ Japanese foods, sundries, and magazines. 212-755-3566.

**KDI Specialty Foods Inc.,** 15 W. Jefryn Blvd., Deer Park, NY 11729: Free list of retail sources ◆ Salsa. 516-595-2525.

**Kosher Cornucopia,** Beechwoods Rd., Jeffersonville, NY 12748: Free catalog ◆ Kosher gifts and baskets for any occasion. 800-756-7437. www.koshercornucopia.com

**Lanvino,** P.O. Box 6724, Whitneyville, CT 06517: Free list of retail sources ◆ All-natural sauces and pesto for pasta, seafood, meat, and poultry. 203-230-9362.

**Lioni Bufala Corp.,** 78-19 15th Ave., Brooklyn, NY 11228: Free information ◆ Italian specialty products. 718-234-3373.

**Locus Foods Inc.,** P.O. Box 1531, Findlay, OH 45840: Free information ◆ Caribbean black bean soup, Italian beans and pasta, Senate soup mix, New Orleans beans and rice, and other all-bean mixes. 800-MR-BEANS; 419-425-1118 (in OH).

**Manganaro Foods,** 488 9th Ave., New York, NY 10018: Free information ◆ Italian salami, prosciutto ham, cheese, panettone, amaretto, colomba, torrone desserts, and specialties. 800-472-5264.

**Millie's Pierogi,** 129 Broadway, Chicopee Falls, MA 01020: Free information ◆ Cabbage, potato and cheese, farmer's cheese, and prune-filled pierogi. 800-743-7641.

**Old Southwest Trading Company,** P.O. Box 7545, Albuquerque, NM 87194: Free catalog ◆ Habanera, exotic, and domestic chilies. 505-836-0168.

**The Oriental Pantry,** 423 Great Rd., Acton, MA 01720: Free catalog ◆ Oriental foods, exotic spices, sauces, and specialties. 800-828-0368; 978-264-4576 (in MA). www.orientalpantry.com

**Pasta Mama's,** 1270 Lee Blvd., Richland, WA 99352: Free list of retail sources ◆ Kosher parve egg and cholesterol-free pasta and low-fat sauces. 800-456-4045; 509-946-8282 (in WA).

**Patsy's Italian Restaurant,** 236 W. 56th St., New York, NY 10019: Free information ◆ Marinara sauce. 800-3-PATSYS; 212-247-3491 (in NY).

**Pedro's Tamales Inc.,** 8207 Hwy. 87, P.O. Box 3571, Lubbock, TX 79452: Free brochure ◆ Shredded sirloin and pork hand-wrapped tamales in stone-ground corn masa inside genuine corn shucks. Shipped frozen. 800-522-9531. www.tamale.com

**Pendery's Inc.,** 1221 Manufacturing St., Dallas, TX 75207: Catalog $2 ◆ Mexican spices, seasonings, flavorings, and specialties. 800-533-1870; 972-741-1870 (in TX).

**Petra Foods International Inc.,** 1350 Beverly Rd., McLean, VA 22101: Free information ◆ All-natural imported Japanese, Kosher, Middle East, Greek, and other international foods. 800-356-1807.

**Salumeria Italiana,** 151 Richmond St., Boston, MA 02109: Free brochure ◆ Aged balsamic vinegar and other Italian specialties. 800-400-5916.

**Schaller & Weber Inc.,** 22-35 46th St., Long Island City, NY 11105: Free catalog ◆ Sausage, liverwurst, cold cuts, salami and cervelats, Westphalian-style smoked ham, roast beef, bacon, and other meat. 800-847-4115.

**2nd Avenue Deli,** 156 2nd Ave., New York, NY 10003: Free catalog ◆ Delicatessen favorites and baked goods. 800-692-3354. www.2ndAveDeli.com

**Sinai Kosher Foods Corp.,** 1000 W. Pershing Rd., Chicago, IL 60609: Free information ◆ Kosher beef, lamb, veal, roasts, steaks, chops, and ground beef. 800-823-7746; 770-650-6330 (in IL).

**Start Fresh Weight Control Program,** 4813 12th Ave., Brooklyn, NY 11219: Free catalog ◆ Prepared Kosher meals for weight loss. 800-226-5000.

**Sultan's Delight Inc.,** 59 88th St., Brooklyn, NY 11209: Free catalog ◆ Mid-east specialties, grains and beans, spices, flower water, Turkish coffee and tea, olives and specialty oils, cheese, and foods from all over the world. 718-745-2121.

**Taos Mesa Gourmet,** 2400 Rio Grande Blvd. NW, Ste. 234, Albuquerque, NM 87104: Free information ◆ Blue corn bread and pancakes, bean dip, salsa, soups, chile jam, beer bread, and other foods from the southwest. 800-494-0069.

**Teitel Brothers,** 2372 Arthur Ave., Bronx, NY 10458: Free catalog ◆ Aged cheese, extra virgin cold pressed olive oil, porcini mushrooms, pasta, and Italian specialties. 800-850-7055.

**3E Market,** 6753 Jones Mill Ct., Ste. A, Norcross, GA 30092: Free catalog ◆ Oils and dressings, antipasto vegetables, pasta, bread sticks and crackers, canned foods and soups, and other Italian specialties. 800-333-5548. www.3emarket.com

**To Life Food & Herbs,** P.O. Box 711385, Houston, TX 77271: Free catalog ◆ Vegetarian and kosher health foods. 800-317-3449; 713-771-5366 (in TX). www.flash.net/~tolife

**Tryson House,** 15635 Alton Pkwy., Ste. 260, Irvine, CA 92718: Free list of retail sources ◆ Preservative-free, low-fat parve, and Kosher seasoning sprays. 800-672-7929; 714-453-8820 (in CA).

**VIVANDE'S Italian Pantry,** 2125 Fillmore St., San Francisco, CA 94115: Free information ◆ Extra virgin olive oils, vinegars, flours, grains, legumes, condiments, honey, dolci, and other specialties. 415-346-4430.

**Volpi Foods,** 5250 Daggett Ave., St. Louis, MO 63110: Free information ◆ Sliced prosciutto and filsette, sopressata, calabrese, and napoli salami. Includes gift assortments. 800-288-3439.

**Wagner Gourmet Foods,** 900 Jacksonville Rd., Ivyland, PA 18974: Free brochure ◆ Soups and chili, spices and spicy specialties, Mexican specialties, salsa, and barbecue and pasta sauces. 800-392-2041. www.wagner-gourmet.com

**World of Chantilly,** 4302 Farragut Rd., Brooklyn, NY 11203: Free list of retail sources ◆ Certified Kosher French pastries, chocolate candy, and gift baskets. 718-859-1110.

**Wolsk's Gourmet Confections,** 81 Ludlow St., New York, NY 10002: Free information ◆ Biscuits, confections, dried fruits, nuts, coffee and tea, and other international specialties. 800-692-6887.

**YZ Enterprises Inc.,** 1930 Indian Wood Circle, Maumee, OH 43537: Free information ◆ Kosher parve cookies. 800-736-8779.

## Fruits & Vegetables

**Apricot Farm Inc.,** 2620 Buena Vista Rd., Hollister, CA 95023: Free catalog ◆ Dried fruit. 800-233-4413.

**Atkinson's Vidalia Onions,** Box 121, Garfield, GA 30425: Free information ◆ Vidalia onions. 800-241-3408; 912-763-2149 (in GA).

**Bangkok Produce,** 966 San Julian St., Los Angeles, CA 90015: Free information ◆ Oriental fruits and vegetables. 213-689-7933.

**Bess' Beans,** 461 Fleming Rd., Charleston, SC 29412: Free brochure with long SASE ◆ Bean soups and other Southern favorites. 803-795-0249.

**Bilgore Groves,** 807 Court St., P.O. Box 1958, Clearwater, FL 34616: Free catalog ◆ Fruit gift assortments and specialties. 813-442-2171.

**Bland Farms,** P.O. Box 506, Glennville, GA 30427: Free catalog ◆ Vidalia onions, marinated mushrooms, relishes, sauces, pickled items, salad dressings, meat, peanuts, nut candy and fudge, and pecans. 800-843-2542. www.blandfarms.com

**Blood's Hammock Groves,** 4549 Linton Blvd., Delray Beach, FL 33445: Free catalog ◆ Florida oranges, grapefruit, mixed fruit assortments, gift baskets, and other specialty foods. 800-255-5188; 561-498-3400 (in FL). www.bhgcitrus.com

**Blue Heron Fruit Shippers,** P.O. Box 936, Sarasota, FL 34234: Free brochure ◆ Tree-ripened citrus fruit, candy, marmalades, pecans, Southern foods, stone crab claws, and honey. 800-237-3920; 941-954-1605 (in FL). blueheron1@compuserve.com

**Chile La Isla,** P.O. Box 1379, Fabens, TX 79838: Free information ◆ Roasted and individually quick-frozen chili peppers. 800-895-4603.

**Chukar Cherries,** P.O. Box 510, Prosser, WA 99350: Free catalog ◆ Preservative and sulfite-free dried cherries and cherry specialties. 800-624-9544.

**Crayton Cove Gourmet Shop Inc.,** 800 12th Ave. South, Naples, FL 34102: Free brochure ◆ Florida fruit assortments. 800-678-4362; 941-262-4362 (in FL).

**Crockett Farms,** P.O. Box 1150, Harlingen, TX 78551: Free catalog ◆ Ruby red grapefruit and sun-ripened oranges. 800-580-1900.

**Cushman's,** 3325 Forest Hill Blvd., West Palm Beach, FL 33406: Free catalog ◆ Florida-fresh citrus fruits. 561-965-3535.

**Delegeane Garlic Farms,** P.O. Box 2561, Yountville, Napa Valley, CA 94599: Free brochure ◆ Fresh garlic, chili ristras, salt-free herb seasonings, wildflower honey, berry jams, dessert sauces, and specialties. 800-726-6692.

**Delftree Farm,** 234 Union St., North Adams, MA 01247: Free price list ◆ Fresh and wild dried mushrooms, books, soups, sauces, and other specialties. 800-243-3742.

**Dundee Orchards,** P.O. Box 327, Dundee, OR 97115: Free information ◆ Oregon hazelnut butter, other hazelnut products, and Oregon cherries. 503-538-8105.

**Fruit Ranch-West,** 6301 W. Bluemound Rd., Milwaukee, WI 53213: Free catalog ◆ Fruit gift baskets, assorted nuts, and Wisconsin cheese variety packages. 800-433-3289. www.choicemall.com/fruitranch

**Georgia "Sweets" Brand Inc.,** 1606 W. North St., Vidalia, GA 30474: Free information ◆ Jumbo and sandwich-size Vidalia onions. 800-552-9902.

**Jim & Megan Gerritsen,** WoodPrarie Farm, 4952 Kinney Rd., Bridgewater, ME 04735: Free catalog ◆ Certified organic potatoes. 800-829-9765.

**Giant Artichoke Company,** 11241 Merritt St., Castroville, CA 95012: Free price list ◆ Fresh artichokes and artichoke specialties. 831-633-2778. RAXBEI@AOL.COM

**Gracewood Fruit Company,** 9075 17th Pl., P.O. Box 2590, Vero Beach, FL 32961: Free information ◆ Navel oranges and ruby red grapefruit. 800-678-1154.

**Susan Green's California Cuisine,** Catalog Order Center, P.O. Box 596, Maumee, OH 43537: Free catalog ◆ Dried and fresh fruit, nuts, delicatessen favorites, baked goods, ham, and candy. 800-753-8558. www.california-cuisine.com

**Hadley Fruit Orchards,** P.O. Box 246, Cabazon, CA 92230: Free catalog ◆ Dried fruit, nuts, candy, honey, and jellies. 800-854-5655.

**Harry & David,** P.O. Box 712, Medford, OR 97501: Free catalog ◆ Oregold peaches, Alphonse LaValle grapes, Royal Riviera pears, Crisp Mountain apples, other fruits, and gift assortments. 800-345-5655. www.harryanddavid.com

**Harry's Crestview Groves,** 9030 17th Pl., Vero Beach, FL 32966: Free catalog ◆ Tree-ripened ruby red grapefruit, oranges, and gifts. 800-285-8488.

**Harvey's Groves,** P.O. Box 560700, Rockledge, FL 32956: Free catalog ◆ Fresh and dried fruits. 800-327-9312; 407-636-6072 (in FL).

**Hendrix Farm,** P.O. Box 175, Metter, GA 30439: Free information ◆ Vidalia onions. 800-221-5050.

**Indian River Groves,** P.O. Box 3689, Seminole, FL 34645: Free brochure ◆ Valencia oranges and ruby red grapefruit from Florida. 800-940-3344; 813-399-8500 (in FL). www.floridafruit.com

**Jaffe Brothers Natural Foods,** P.O. Box 636, Valley Center, CA 92082: Free catalog ◆ Organically grown foods. 760-749-1133.

**Kelly & Sons,** 3086 Co. Rte. 176, Oswego, NY 13126: Free brochure ◆ Braided onions and shallots. 800-496-3363; 315-343-3610 (in NY). www.onionsusa.com

**Frank Lewis' Alamo Fruit,** 100 N. Tower Rd., Alamo, TX 78516: Free brochure ◆ Farm-fresh tomatoes, tangelos, apples, persimmons, cheesecake, smoked turkey breast, and other specialties. 800-477-4773.

**Mariani Nut Company,** 709 Dutton St., P.O. Box 808, Winters, CA 95694: Free information ◆ Almonds, pistachios, walnuts, and dried tomatoes. 916-795-3311.

**Melissa's By Mail,** P.O. Box 21127, Los Angeles, CA 90021: Free catalog ◆ Exotic mushrooms, dandelion greens, peppers and squashes, dates, fresh herbs, and other vegetables. 800-588-0151. www.melissas.com

**Metz & Waite Farm,** Rt. 3, Box 124, Mission, TX 78572: Free brochure ◆ Texas-grown red grapefruit and juicy sweet oranges. 800-811-3276. www.atexstore.com/citrus

**Mission Orchards,** Mail Processing Center, P.O. Box 546, Maumee, OH 43537: Free catalog ◆ Comice pears, red dessert grapes, navel oranges, red grapefruit, cherries, plums, tangelos, pineapples, kiwi fruit, cheese, candy, dried fruit, nuts, truffles, fruit cakes and pastries, and smoked meat and seafood. 419-893-5149. www.mission-orchards.com

**Mister Spear Inc.,** P.O. Box 178, Stockton, CA 95201: Free catalog ◆ Garden-fresh California vegetables. 800-677-7327; 209-464-5365 (in CA). www.misterspear.com

**Mulrennan Groves,** 4209 Durant Rd., Valrico, FL 33594: Free brochure ◆ Navel oranges, grapefruits, and tangerines. 800-662-8357; 813-689-4792 (in FL). www.thefrontpage.com/MULGROVE

**Mushroom Man,** Box 321, Eugene, OR 97140: Free information ◆ Italian dried porcini mushrooms and exotic wild mushroom cooking powders. 800-945-3404. webmaster@mushroomman.com

**Neill's Farm,** 2722 S. Jenkins Rd., Fort Pierce, FL 34981: Free catalog ◆ Fresh-picked tomatoes. 800-441-6740.

**New Penny Farm,** P.O. Box 448, Presque Isle, ME 04769: Free catalog ◆ Organic-grown potatoes. 800-827-7551.

**Newbern Groves Gift Shop,** 15315 N. Nebraska Ave., Tampa, FL 33682: Free information ◆ Navel oranges, tangelos, and sweet red grapefruit. 800-486-0441; 813-0440 (in Tampa).

**Oasis Date Gardens,** P.O. Box 757, Thermal, CA 92274: Free information ◆ Medjool and Noor dates, dried figs, and candied apricots. 800-827-8017. www.oasisdate.com

**Old Southwest Trading Company,** P.O. Box 7545, Albuquerque, NM 87194: Free catalog ◆ Habanera, exotic, and domestic chilies. 505-836-0168.

**Phillips Exotic Mushrooms,** 909 E. Baltimore Pike, Kennet Square, PA 19348: Free catalog ◆ Crimini, shitake, oyster, and portabella mushrooms. 800-243-8644.

**Poinsettia Groves,** P.O. Box 1388, Vero Beach, FL 32961: Free brochure ◆ Oranges and grapefruits, fruit candies, jellies, and marmalades. 800-327-8624. www.pgroves.com

**Riverside Gardens,** 300 E. Riverside, Timberville, VA 22853: Free price list ◆ Dried fruit slices. 800-847-6449; 540-896-9859 (in VA).

**Smith's Farm Restaurant,** P.O. Box 189, Blaine, ME 04734: Free information ◆ Potatoes for baking, casseroles, soups, and salads. 800-294-6868.

**Sphinx Date Ranch,** 3039 N. Scottsdale Rd., Scottsdale, AZ 85251: Free brochure ◆ Date-pecan loaves, trail mixes, fruit cakes, jellies, nuts, and Medjool dates pitted and hand-dipped in creamy milk chocolate, stuffed with walnuts, rolled in powdered sugar, or for cooking. 800-482-3283; 602-941-2261 (in AZ).

**Spyke's Grove,** 7250 Griffin Rd., Davie, FL 33314: Free catalog ◆ Florida oranges, mangos, avocados, and grapefruit. 800-327-9713; 954-583-0426 (in FL).

**Sullivan Victory Groves,** P.O. Box 10, Cocoa, FL 32923: Free brochure ◆ Indian River citrus fruits. 800-672-6431. www.flafruit.com

**Sweet Energy,** 4 Acorn Ln., Colchester, VT 05446: Free brochure ◆ Apricots and other high-fiber fruit. 800-9-SWEETO.

**Timber Crest Farms,** 4791 Dry Creek Rd., Healdsburg, CA 95448: Free catalog ◆ Dried fruit, dried tomato products, fruit butters, nuts, and trail mixes. 707-433-8251.

**Todaro Brothers,** 555 2nd Ave., New York, NY 10016: Catalog $1 ◆ Cheese, pasta, dried mushrooms, olives and olive oil, legumes, truffles and porcini, grains, vinegars, and other specialties. 212-532-0633.

**Tom Vorbeck,** AppleSource, 1716 Apples Rd., Chapin, IL 62628: Free brochure ◆ Over 100 varieties of apples. 800-588-3854. www.applesource.com

**Walla Walla Gardener's Association,** 210 N. 11th Ave., Walla Walla, WA 99362: Free information ◆ Sweet Walla Walla onions. 800-553-5014; 509-525-7070 (in WA).

**Wicklund's Farms,** 3959 Maple Island Farm Rd., Springfield, OR 97477: Free price list ◆ Spiced green beans. 541-747-5998.

## Gift Assortments & Gourmet Specialties

**Ace Specialty Foods,** Catalog Order Center, P.O. Box 1013, Maumee, OH 43537: Free catalog ◆ Cakes, fruit gifts, candy, and nuts. 800-323-9754; 419-893-5149 (in OH). www.ace-specialty.com

**The Antique Mall & Crown Restaurant,** P.O. Box 540, Indianola, MS 38751: Free information ◆ Smoked catfish specialties and other favorites. 800-833-7731; 601-887-2522 (in MS).

**Ash Enterprises Inc.,** P.O. Box 40113, Tucson, AZ 85717: Free information ◆ Gift assortments. 800-597-8259.

**Australian Catalogue Company,** 7605 Welborn St., Raleigh, NC 27615: Free catalog ◆ Australian cakes, puddings, chocolates, and biscuits. 800-808-0938. www.aussiecatalog.com

**Balducci's,** Shop from Home Service, 42-26 13th St., Long Island City, NY 11101: Catalog $3 ◆ Bread and food specialties. 800-225-3822. www.balducci.com

**Baskets Everywhere,** 4658 Airport Blvd., Mobile, AL 36608: Free catalog ◆ Gift baskets, old-fashioned chocolates, baker goods, fresh seafood, and other gourmet specialties. 888-882-2753. www.baskets.com

**Baskets Galore,** P.O. Box 7292, Aloha, OR 97007: Free brochure ◆ Fruit and specialty gift baskets. 503-591-7170.

**Basse's Choice Plantation,** P.O. Box 1, Smithfield, VA 23431: Free information ◆ Virginia gourmet foods from the coast, Piedmont, and the mountains. 800-292-2773. www.smithfieldhams.com

**Beauhouse Gifts & Baskets,** 2024 Perkins Rd., Baton Rouge, LA 70808: Free brochure ◆ Gift baskets. 504-383-8851.

**Bertrand Virtual,** P.O. Box 20669, Oakland, CA 94620: Free price list ◆ Sausages, mushrooms, vegetables, nuts, spices, and other French specialties. 510-832-1452.

**Black Shield Inc.,** 5356 Pan American Freeway NE, Albuquerque, NM 87109: Free information ◆ Gourmet flavored popcorn. 800-653-9357. www.crownjewels.com

**Bland Farms,** P.O. Box 506, Glennville, GA 30427: Free catalog ◆ Vidalia onions, marinated mushrooms, relishes, sauces, pickled items, salad dressings, meat, peanuts, nut candy, fudge, and Georgia pecans. 800-843-2542. www.blandfarms.com

**Blooming Candies,** 1402 Corinth St., Ste. 211, Dallas, TX 75215: Free brochure ◆ Candy-flowers in bouquet-style gift baskets. Includes sugar-free assortments. 800-242-1005. www.marketnet.com/bloom

**Blue Heron Fruit Shippers,** P.O. Box 936, Sarasota, FL 34234: Free brochure ◆ Tree-ripened citrus fruit, candy, marmalades, pecans, Southern foods, stone crab claws, and honey. 800-237-3920; 941-954-1605 (in FL). blueheron1@compuserve.com

**Bogland Inc.,** 300 Oak St., Pembroke, MA 02359: Free information ◆ Cranberry salsa, grilling sauce, catsup, and specialties. 800-BOGLAND.

**Bounty Hunter Rare Wine & Provisions,** 101 S. Coombs, #5, Napa, CA 94559: Catalog $2 ◆ Wines and related life style products. 800-943-9463. www.bountyhunterwine.com

**The British Express,** P.O. Box 3190, Nashua, NH 03061: Free catalog ◆ Foods with a taste of a British accent. 603-578-9392. www.britishexpress.com

**The British Gourmet Chandlers,** 45 Wall St., Madison, CT 06443: Free catalog ◆ Traditional and other British foods and cheeses. 203-245-4521.

**The British Shoppe,** 45 Wall St., Madison, CT 06443: Free catalog ◆ Traditional British foods and cheese. 800-842-6674; 203-245-4521 (in CT). www.thebritishshoppe.com

**Brittigan's Specialty Soups,** 74 Tracey Rd., Huntington Valley, PA 19006: Free brochure ◆ Gourmet clam chowder, mushroom soup, bean and leek soup, and soup sampler packages. 215-830-0942.

**Burberry's Limited,** 9 E. 57th St., New York, NY 10022: Free list of retail sources ◆ International tea, preserves and marmalades, chutney, mustards, horseradish sauces, cakes, and shortbread biscuits. 212-371-5010.

**Burnt Cabins Grist Mill,** Cowans Gap Rd., Burnt Cabins, PA 17215: Free brochure ◆ Old-fashioned buckwheat and wheat flour, roasted and regular cornmeal, and pancake and muffin mixes. 717-987-3244.

**Callaway Gardens Country Store,** US Hwy. 27 South, Pine Mountain, GA 31822: Free catalog ◆ Southern-style bacon, ham, other meat, and jellies. 800-225-5292.

**Caribbean Island Imports Inc.,** 4253 Park Place, Crown Point, IN 46307: Free catalog ◆ Imported foods and gifts. 800-246-4639; 219-663-0025 (in IN). caribisi@pla-net.net

**Cavanaugh Lakeview Farms Ltd.,** 2000 Thorn Apple Valley Dr., Ponca City, OK 74601: Free information ◆ Honey-cured and smoked poultry, smoked ham and bacon, fresh-frozen poultry, steaks, game, smoked seafood, desserts, and popcorn. 800-243-4438.

**Cesta Gift Baskets,** 5042 Wilshire Blvd., Ste. 576, Los Angeles, CA 90036: Catalog $1 ◆ Custom gift assortments including kosher specialties. Also baskets for Christmas, Hanukkah, and other holidays. 800-236-3806. www.cesta.net

**Chalet Suzanne Foods,** 3800 Chalet Suzanne Dr., Lake Wales, FL 33853: Free brochure ◆ Gourmet soups and sauces. 800-433-6011. www.chaletsuzanne.com

**The Cheese Box,** 801 Wells St., Lake Geneva, WI 53147: Free catalog ◆ Cheese, wine, and other Wisconsin favorites. 800-345-6105; 414-248-3440 (in WI). www.cheesebox.com

**Cheese Straws & More,** 3126 Hwy. 594, Monroe, LA 71203: Free information ◆ Cheese straws, gourmet cookies, spices, pickles, and gift baskets. 800-997-1921.

**The Chef's Store,** 836 Traction Ave., Los Angeles, CA 90013: Free catalog ◆ Chefware, tools, other equipment, supplies, specialty foods, and how-to-ideas for gourmet chefs and home cooks. 888-334-CHEF; 213-680-0418 (in CA). www.chefstore.com

**Cherchies Ltd.,** One South Bacton Hill Rd., Malvern, PA 19355: Free brochure ◆ Gourmet foods and gifts. 800-644-1980; 610-640-9440 (in PA).

**Chukar Cherries,** P.O. Box 510, Prosser, WA 99350: Free catalog ◆ Cherry trail mixes. 800-624-9544.

**Cold Hollow Cider Mill,** P.O. Box 430, Waterbury Center, VT 05677: Free information ◆ Vermont foods, apple cider, and gifts. 802-244-8771.

**Colonial Williamsburg Dining,** P.O. Box 1776, Williamsburg, VA 23187: Free information ◆ Traditional favorites served in Williamsburg's colonial museum restaurants and taverns. 804-220-7503.

**Colorado Creations,** 20419 Pahgre Rd., Montrose, CO 81401: Free catalog ◆ Soup mixes, seasonings, flapjack and scone mixes, chili and dip mixes, jams and jellies, and more Colorado favorites. 888-249-9793; 970-249-9793 (in CO).

**Corti Brothers,** 5810 Folsom Blvd., Sacramento, CA 95819: Free newsletter ◆ Chinese teas, regional olive oils, vintage cognac, and other food and drink specialties. 916-736-3800.

**Coyote Moon,** 1709 So. Braddock Ave., Pittsburgh, PA 15218: Free brochure ◆ Spicy foods and gifts. 415-594-4830. www.coyote-moon.com

**Dakin Farm,** Rt. 7, Ferrisburg, VT 05456: Free catalog ◆ Vermont smoked ham and bacon, maple syrup, and aged Cheddar cheese. 800-993-2546. www.dakinfarm.com

**Delegeane Garlic Farms,** P.O. Box 2561, Yountville, Napa Valley, CA 94599: Free brochure ◆ Fresh garlic, chili ristras, salt-free herb seasonings, wildflower honeys, berry jams, dessert sauces, and specialties. 800-726-6692.

**Deli Direct,** 416 Diens, Wheeling, IL 60090: Free brochure ◆ Delicatessen meat, aged Wisconsin cheese spreads, barbecue sauce, and condiments. 800-321-3354.

**Double D Industries,** 10911 State Rd., Dittmer, MO 63023: Free catalog ◆ Meat products, candy, hot chocolate, teas, and other specialties. 800-823-4996. www.marketplaza.com/doubled

**Dufour Pastry Kitchens Inc.,** 25 9th Ave., New York, NY 10014: Free information ◆ Hors d'oeuvres. 212-929-2800. www.newyork.digitalcity.com/nyeats/dufour.dci

**Dunderbak's Market Gourmet,** Lehigh Valley Mall, Whitehall, PA 18052: Free brochure ◆ Baskets and other gift assortments. 610-264-4963. www.dunberbak.com

**Dusty's Cellar,** 1839 W. Grand River, Okemos, MI 48864: Free brochure ◆ Gift baskets. 517-349-5150.

**S. Wallace Edwards & Sons Inc.,** P.O. Box 25, Surry, VA 23883: Free catalog ◆ Virginia meat, seafood selections, candy and nuts, and baked specialties. 800-222-4267. www.virginiatraditions.com

**Essentially Chocolate,** 15737 Crabbs Branch Way, Rockville, MD 20855: Free information ◆ Chocolate candy and food gifts. 301-770-5660.

**Everything Garlic,** P.O. Box 91104, West Vancouver, British Columbia, Canada V7N 3N3: Free catalog ◆ Specialty garlic foods and other items. 800-668-6299.

**Fancy Foods Gourmet Club,** 330-E N. Stonestreet Ave., Rockville, MD 20850: Free information ◆ Foods and gift assortments. 800-576-3548. www.ffgc.com

**Figi's,** 3200 S. Maple, Marshfield, WI 54404: Free catalog ◆ Baked goods, meat, cheese, candy, jams and jellies, and nuts. 715-341-1363.

**Fin 'n Feather,** P.O. Box 487, Smithfield, VA 23430: Free catalog ◆ Smoked meat, poultry, pastries, candy, and regional specialties. 800-628-2242. www.smithfieldcompanies.com

**Fortuna's Sausage Company,** 975 Greenville Ave., Greenville, RI 02828: Free catalog ◆ All-natural dry cured Italian sausages, sausage-making kit, pasta, imported Italian cheese, gift baskets, and natural New England specialties. 800-42-SOUPY. SOUPY@Edgenet.net

**Frieda's By Mail,** P.O. Box 58488, Los Angeles, CA 90058: Free catalog ◆ Gift baskets of exotic fruits and vegetables. 800-241-1771; 714-826-6100 (in CA). www.friedas.com

**Gazin's Cajun Creole Foods,** 2910 Toulouse St., P.O. Box 19221, New Orleans, LA 70179: Catalog $2 ◆ Specialties from New Orleans. 800-262-6410; 504-482-0302 (in LA). gazins@aol.com

**Gift Baskets International,** 37 W. 20th St., 6th Floor, New York, NY 10011: Free brochure ◆ Gift baskets for every occasion. 212-604-9022. www.gift-baskets.com

**Maggie Gin's Inc.,** 127 10th Ave., San Francisco, CA 94118: Free list of retail sources ◆ Stir-fry sauces. 415-221-6080.

**Good Wives Inc.,** 86 Sanderson Ave., Lynn, MA 01902: Free list of retail sources ◆ Overnight shipment of frozen hors d'oeuvres. 781-596-0070.

**Goodies from Goodman,** 11390 Grissom Ln., Dallas, TX 75229: Free catalog ◆ Fruit, cheese, nuts, candy, popcorn specialties, and smoked meat and fish. 800-535-3136; 972-484-3236 (in TX). www.goodiesgifts.com

**The Gourmets Pantry,** P.O. Box 702618, Tulsa, OK 74170: Free information ◆ Gourmet, specialty, ethnic, and regional foods. Also seasonings and accessories. 918-587-6477. www.gourmetspantry.com

**Great Food Online,** 2030 1st Ave., 3rd Floor, Seattle, WA 98121: Free catalog ◆ Coffees, hors d'oeuvres and accompaniments, olive oils, vinegars, sauces, relishes, meats, seafood, snacks, desserts, and more. 800-841-5984. www.greatfood.com

**The Great Valley Mills,** 1774 County Line Rd., Barto, PA 19504: Free brochure ◆ Family farm grown and produced foods. Gift packs available. 800-688-6455.

**Green Bay Basket Company,** P.O. Box 8281, Green Bay, WI 54308: Free brochure ◆ Gift assortments. 888-476-2293.

**Susan Green's California Cuisine,** Catalog Order Center, P.O. Box 596, Maumee, OH 43537: Free catalog ◆ Candy, dried fruits, sourdough bread, nuts, seasonings and condiments, farm-fresh crops, cheese, meat, seafood, and pastries. 800-753-8558. www.california-cuisine.com

**Hagensborg Foods U.S.A. Inc.,** P.O. Box 6058, Kent, WA 98064: Free information ◆ Smoked salmon, shrimp, and ready-to-spread salmon and shrimp pates. 800-851-1771; 253-395-9373 (in WA).

**Hard Times Cafe,** 310 Commerce St., Alexandria, VA 22314: Free brochure ◆ Chili spice mixes. 703-836-7449. www.hardtimes.com

**Harman's Cheese & Country Store,** Sugar Hill, NH 03585: Free catalog ◆ Cheddar cheese, maple syrup, fruit preserves, salad dressings, plain and smoked salmon, crab meat, honey, smoked herring fillets, pancake mixes, maple butter, and candy. 603-823-8000.

**Harrington Ham Company,** Main St., Richmond, VT 05477: Free information ◆ Spiral-sliced and cob-smoked maple-glazed ham and smoked bacon, turkey breast, pheasant, cheese, maple syrup, pastries, plum pudding, fruitcakes, and dried fruit. 802-434-4444.

**Harrington's of Vermont,** Shelburne, Rt. 7, Shelburne, VT 05482: Free information ◆ Ham and specialty foods from Vermont. 802-985-2000.

**Harry & David,** P.O. Box 712, Medford, OR 97501: Free catalog ◆ Fruit, cakes, baklava, cinnamon pastries, tortes, candy, preserves, and gift assortments. 800-345-5655. www.harryanddavid.com

**Hasty-Bake,** P.O. Box 471285, Tulsa, OK 74147: Free catalog ◆ Gourmet foods, charcoal ovens, and grilling accessories. 800-426-6836.

**Hickory Farms,** P.O. Box 75, Maumee, OH 43537: Free brochure ◆ Cheese, meat, candy, pastries, deli specialties, seafood, nuts, truffles, fruit and liqueur cakes, tea and coffee, dried fruit, jellies and preserves, fresh fruit, and popcorn. 800-222-4438. www.hickoryfarms.com

**The HoneyBaked Ham Company,** P.O. Box 965, Holland, OH 43528: Free catalog ◆ Hams, cheeses, nuts, desserts and baked goods, and entrees. 800-892-4267. www.honeybaked.com

**Hors D'Oeuvres Unlimited,** 4209 Dell Ave., P.O. Box 31, North Bergen, NJ 07047: Free brochure ◆ Gourmet hors d'oeuvres. 800-648-3787; 201-865-4545 (in NJ).

**The House of Webster,** P.O. Box 9610, Rogers, AR 72757: Catalog $2 ◆ Preserves and jellies, cheese, country cured and smoked bacon, biscuit and pancake mixes, candy, syrups, wild honey, and country sorghum. 501-636-4640. www.houseofwebster.com

**Hybird Vigor Kitchen,** P.O. Box 245, Georgetown, IL 61846: Free catalog ◆ Polenta and cornbread mixes, herb meat rubs, vinegars, and garlic sauces. 217-662-2799.

**Indian Harvest Specialtifoods Inc.,** P.O. Box 428, Bemidji, MN 56619: Free catalog ◆ Rice, grain, and bean specialties for healthier living. 800-294-2433. www.indianharvest.com

**Karen James Ltd.,** 896 S. Broadway, Hicksville, NY 11801: Free catalog ◆ Gift baskets for special people on special occasions. 800-870-2969. www.karenjamesltd.com

**Jasper's Sugar Bush,** 1867 County Rd. 374, Carney, MI 49812: Free information ◆ Maple syrup, maple cream, maple sugar candy, chocolate maple cream, and gift baskets. 800-646-2753.

**Knott's Berry Farm,** P.O. Box 1989, Placentia, CA 92670: Free catalog ◆ Jellies and preserves, cheese, sausage, candy, cakes, cookies, and dried fruit. 800-877-6887.

**Kozlowski Farms,** 5566 Gravenstein Hwy. North, Forestville, CA 95436: Free brochure ◆ Marmalades, jams, preserves, honey, mustards, barbecue sauce, fruit butters, sugar-free berry vinegars, conserves, and chutney. 707-887-1587.

**Kuhn's Delicatessen & Liquors of Des Plaines,** 749 West Golf Rd., Des Plaines, IL 60016: Free catalog ◆ Gourmet foods that include 150 German style or imported sausages and smoked meats; 85 cheeses from Germany, France, Italy, Holland, Norway, Sweden, Switzerland, and Denmark; 50 domestic and imported rye breads; 60 herring and fish specialties; and more. 800-522-9019; 847-640-0222 (in IL).

**Lambs Farm,** P.O. Box 520, Jct. I-94 & Rt. 176, Libertyville, IL 60048: Free catalog ◆ Country crafts, specialty foods, nuts, candy, and gifts for pets. 800-52-LAMBS. WWW.LAMBSFARM.ORG

**Le Village,** P.O. Box 20669, Oakland, CA 94620: Free catalog ◆ Meats, candies, cheeses, and other specialties. 415-861-2196. www.levillage.com

**Stew Leonard's,** 55 Westport Ave., Norwalk, CT 06851: Free catalog ◆ Fruit, cakes and cookies, cheese, breads, candy, nuts, and meat. 800-SAY-STEW. www.stew-leonards.com

**Les Trois Petits Cochons Company,** 453 Greenwich St., New York, NY 10013: Free information ◆ Terrines, pates, and mousses. 800-LES-PATES; 212-219-1230 (in NY).

**Mackinlay Teas,** P.O. Box 6, Saline, MI 48176: Catalog $1 ◆ Teas, premium rice, lentils, beans, soup mixes, and Italian syrups. 313-482-4600.

**Majestic Choices,** 10332 Federal Blvd., Ste. 331, Denver. CO 80221: Free catalog ◆ Gift baskets and specialty foods with an international flair. www.majestic-choices.com

**Manitok Wild Rice,** Box 97, Callaway, MN 56521: Free brochure ◆ Hand-harvested organic wild rice, syrups, honey, pancake mix, jellies, sauces, and spices. www.manitok.com

**Matthews 1812 House,** 250 Kent Rd., P.O. Box 15, Cornwall Bridge, CT 06754: Free brochure ◆ Cakes, nuts, chocolates, jams, tea, condiments, and smoked meat. 800-662-1812. matthews@mohawk.net

**Mikdash Foods Inc.,** 75 St. Alphonsus St., Ste. D, Roxbury MA 02120: Free list of retail sources ◆ Certified Kosher and all-natural international foods. 800-645-3274.

**Mountain Man Nut & Fruit Company,** Branson Meadows, 4210 Gretna Rd., Branson, MO 65616: Free catalog ◆ Gift baskets for any occasion, regular and sugar-free candies, nuts, homemade jams, dried fruits, trail mixes, and coffees. 800-336-6203.

**Nabisco Direct,** P.O. Box 7106, Dover, DE 19903: Free catalog ◆ Gift packages of cookies, candy, and peanut favorites. Also non-food gifts with the Nabisco logo. 800-738-6720. www.nabisco.com

**Nauvoo Mill & Bakery,** 1530 Mulholland, Nauvoo, IL 62354: Free brochure ◆ Food gift assortments. 217-453-6734.

**The New Mexican Connection,** 2833 Rhode Island NE, Albuquerque, NM 87110: Free catalog ◆ Salsa, beef jerky, coffee, jams, and other Southwestern food items. 800-933-2736. www.rtis.com/nmchile

**The New Orleans School of Cooking and Louisiana General Store,** The Jackson Brewery, 620 Decatur St., New Orleans, LA 70130: Free catalog ◆ New Orleans specialties and cookbooks. 800-237-4841. www.nosoc.com

**Northern Lakes Wild Rice Company,** P.O. Box 988, Winter Park, CO 80482: Free information ◆ Certified hand-harvested wild rice. 970-726-2002.

**OH'Brines Pickling Inc.,** 4103 E. Mission Ave., Spokane, WA 99202: Free request list of retail sources ◆ Pickled vegetables. 800-264-1264; 509-534-7255 (in WA).

**Oregon Cupboard,** P.O. Box 30895, Portland, OR 97294: Free brochure ◆ Salmon fillets, salmon jerky, salmon pate, sturgeon and other smoked seafood specialties, jams and other fruit spreadables, pie fillings, syrups, and fat-free peanut brittle. 800-442-3653. www.oregoncupboard.com

**The Peanut Shop of Williamsburg,** P.O. Box GN, Williamsburg, VA 23187: Free brochure ◆ Peanut specialties, Virginia country ham, Williamsburg soups, salad dressings, sauces, and other foods. 800-637-3268.

**Pearl's Pantry,** P.O. Box 4055, Vail, CO 81658: Free price list ◆ Kitchen accessories, cooking aids, and foods. 800-544-9714.

**Pepperidge Farm,** P.O. Box 917, Clinton, CT 06413: Free catalog ◆ Soups, cookies and other pastries, crackers, candy, cheese, sausage, popcorn, and breakfast mixes. 800-243-9314.

**Pfaelzer Brothers,** Catalog Order Dept., P.O. Box 1015, Maumee, OH 43537: Free catalog ◆ Food specialties and gift baskets. 800-621-0226. www.pfaelzer-brothers.com

**Pine River Pre-Pack,** 10134 Pine River Rd., Newton, WI 53063: Free catalog ◆ Cheese spreads, confections and other old-fashioned chocolates, sausage, and more. 414-726-4216. www.pineriver.com

**The Pleasure Gifters,** 23011 Alcade Dr., Unit-D, Laguna Hills, CA 92653: Free brochure ◆ Custom created gift assortments for all occasions. 888-443-8480. www.pleasuregifters.com

**Pride of Oklahoma,** 216 Randolph, Enid, OK 73701: Free brochure ◆ Vegetable and fruit dips and spreads; barbecue sauces, seasonings, and rubs; and beverages. 800-259-0926. www.prideok.com

**Pueblo to People,** 2105 Silber Rd., Houston, TX 77065: Free catalog ◆ Nuts, dried fruit, ceramics, jewelry, coffee, and gift baskets. 800-843-5257.

**Purely American,** 1060 W. 35th St., Norfolk, VA 23508: Free list of retail sources ◆ Gift packaged food mixes. 800-359-7873.

**Quintessence,** 301 N. Cañon Dr., Beverly Hills, CA 90210: Free catalog ◆ Custom gift baskets. 310-858-7450.

**Rena Chocolations,** 13190 Telfair Ave., Sylmar, CA 91342: Free brochure ◆ Gift baskets and assortments, handcrafted chocolate specialties, and novelties. 800-364-8300. www.cocolates.ala.carte.com

**Rocky Top Farms,** RR 1, Box 163, Ellsworth, MI 49729: Free brochure ◆ Custom gifts made from fruit products. 800-862-9303.

**Rossi Pasta,** P.O. Box 759, Marietta, OH 45750: Free brochure ◆ Black olive, linguine, garlic fettuccini, saffron linguine, and other pasta. 800-227-6774.

**San Antonio River Mill,** 205 E. Gunther, San Antonio, TX 78204: Free catalog ◆ Chili, biscuit and other baking mixes; preserves and jellies; and cooking equipment. 800-235-8186. donna@guntherhouse.com

**Santa Fe Select,** 410 Old Santa Fe Trail, Santa Fe, NM 87501: Free information ◆ Southwest salsa, hot chiles, soups, breads, and cookies. Also gift baskets. 800-243-0353; 505-986-0454 (in NM). www.santafeselect.com

**Seyco Fine Foods,** 970 E. Santa Clara St., Ventura, CA 93001: Catalog $2 ◆ Old-fashioned pure American food specialties. 800-423-2942. www.seycoff.com

**Snookies Cookies,** 1753 Victory Blvd., Glendale, CA 91201: Free catalog ◆ All-occasion gift baskets, decorated gift tin assortments, and other specialties. 800-927-3747. www.snookies.com

**Splurge Inc.,** 207 E. 74th St., New York, NY 10021: Free information ◆ Low-fat and no-guilt snacks and confections. 212-439-6181.

**The Squire's Choice,** Mail Order Dept., 2250 W. Cabot Blvd., Langhorne, PA 19047: Free catalog ◆ Food gifts. 800-523-6163.

**Standard Candy Company,** Mail Order Service, P.O. Box 697, Eastman, GA 31023: Free catalog ◆ Goo Goo Clusters, an original combination of chewy caramel, creamy marshmallow, roasted peanuts, and milk chocolate. Also old-fashioned stick candy and southern-style foods. 800-231-3402. www.googoo.com

**Sunnyland Farms Inc.,** P.O. Box 8200, Albany, GA 31706: Free catalog ◆ Pecans, nuts, candy, baked specialties, dried fruits, maple syrup, honey, jellies, and gift assortments. 800-999-2488; 912-883-3085 (in GA). www.sunnylandfarms.com

**Sutton Place Gourmet,** 10323 Old Georgetown Rd., Bethesda, MD 20814: Free catalog ◆ International and domestic seafood, coffee and tea, fruit, caviar, foie gras, champagnes, nuts, wild rices, condiments, meat, dried fruit, cheese, deli specialties, sauces, candy, and wines. 800-346-8763. www.suttongourmet.com

**Swiss Colony,** Catalog Request Dept., P.O. Box 8994, Madison, WI 53794: Free catalog ◆ Cheese, meat, sausage, pastries, nuts, candy, snacks, and gift assortments. 608-324-4000. www.swisscolony.com

**Texas Treats,** P.O. Box 861298, Plano, TX 75074: Free brochure ◆ Personalized gifts. 800-561-3280; 972-516-3280 (in TX). www.texastreats.com

**Norm Thompson,** P.O. Box 3999, Portland, OR 97208: Free catalog ◆ Food and floral gifts. 800-821-1287. www.normthompson.com

**Tillamook Cheese,** P.O. Box 313, Tillamook, OR 97141: Free catalog ◆ Cheese, exotic delicacies, candy, meat and fowl, smoked fish, jellies, and preserves. 800-542-7290.

**Todaro Brothers,** 555 2nd Ave., New York, NY 10016: Catalog $1 ◆ Cheese, pasta, dried mushrooms, olives and olive oil, legumes, truffles, grains, vinegars, and other specialties. 212-532-0633.

**Traphagen Honey,** Rt. HCR 1, Box 36, Hunter, NY 12442: Free brochure ◆ Honey spreads, baked goods, candy, preserves and jams, and condiments. 800-838-9194.

**Twin Peaks Gourmet Trading Post,** 725 Burnett Ave., #6, San Francisco, CA 94131: Free catalog ◆ Sauces, condiments, Creole and Cajun specialties, Caribbean Island imports, flavored olive oils, and more. 888-4-TPEAKS. www.tpeaks.com

**Virginia Traditions,** P.O. Box 25, Surry, VA 23883: Free catalog ◆ Southern smoked meats, seafood, and dessert specialties. 800-222-4267. www.virginiatraditions.com

**Whitley's Peanut Factory,** P.O. Box 647, Hayes, VA 23072: Free catalog ◆ Peanuts, peanut candy and soup, peanut-carrot cake, peanut butter cookie mixes, and other peanut products. Also cured uncooked country ham and gift assortments. 800-470-2244. www.whitleyspeanut.com

**Wild Game Inc.,** 2315 W. Huron, Chicago, IL 60612: Free information ◆ Venison, buffalo, boar, and other exotic meat. Also turkey breast, pates, terrines, mushrooms and truffles, smoked seafood, cheese, and other foods. 773-278-1661.

**Wileswood Country Store,** Mail Order Dept., P.O. Box 328, Huron, OH 44839: Free brochure ◆ Old-fashioned candy, popcorn and popping oil, cooking accessories, gifts, and gadgets. 419-433-4244.

**Windsor Vineyards,** P.O. Box 368, Windsor, CA 95492: Free catalog ◆ Personalized holiday labels on favorite wines. Also food and wine gifts. 800-333-9987.

**Wolsk's Gourmet Confections,** 81 Ludlow St., New York, NY 10002: Free information ◆ Low-calorie sugar-free Kosher cookies. Also crackers, biscuits, confections, dried fruits, nuts, coffee and tea, and other international specialties. 800-692-6887.

**World of Chantilly,** 4302 Farragut Rd., Brooklyn, NY 11203: Free list of retail sources ◆ Certified Kosher French pastries. Also chocolate candy and gift baskets. 718-859-1110.

**Yoders Country Market,** P.O. Box 249, Grantsville, MD 21536: catalog $1 ◆ Food specialties, seasonings and spices, candy, popcorn, baked goods, breads, and favorites. 800-321-5148. www.yodermarket.com

**Zabar's & Company,** 2245 Broadway, New York, NY 10024: Free catalog ◆ Smoked fish, condiments and spices, candy, crackers, and specialties. Also cookware, food processors, microwave ovens, kitchen tools, and coffee makers. 800-697-6301; 212-496-1234 (in NY).

**Zingerman's Delicatessen,** 422 Detroit St., Ann Arbor, MI 48104: Free catalog ◆ Domestic and imported cheese, ethnic and low-fat specialties, condiments, baked goods, pasta, and traditional Jewish foods. 888-636-8162. zing@chamber.ann-arbor.mi.us

## Gingerbread Houses

**Creative Cakes,** 8814 Brookville Rd., Silver Spring, MD 20910: Free information ◆ Gingerbread house kits. 301-587-1599.

## Health, Natural, & Organic

**Akin's Natural Foods Market,** 7807 E. 51st St., Tulsa, OK 74145: Free catalog ◆ Wheat-free groceries, vitamins, and nutritional supplements. 800-800-3133; 918-663-4137 (in OK). www.akins.com

**Allergy Resources Inc.,** 557 Burbank St., Ste. K, Broomfield, CO 80020: Free catalog ◆ Alternative foods, air purifiers, cosmetics, bedding, cleaning products, and other supplies. 888-308-4826; 303-438-0600 (in CO). AllergyRe@aol.com

**The Alternative Food Cooperative,** 3362 Kingston Rd., West Kingston, RI 02892: Free information ◆ Organic fruits and vegetables, spices, and herbs. 401-789-2240.

**Always Natural Foods,** 3323 E. Patterson Rd., Beavercreek, OH 45430: Free price list ◆ Celiac prue and gluten-free natural foods.

**American Spoon Foods,** P.O. Box 566, Petoskey, MI 49770: Free information ◆ Pancake and waffle mix made with organic-grown Indian blue corn. Also wild rice, wild berry preserves, and wild pecans. 800-222-5886. www.spoon.com

**Barn Stream Natural Foods,** P.O. Box 760, Walpole, NH 03608: Free brochure ◆ Additive, preservative, and cholesterol-free Yankee sourdough, salt-free garlic whole wheat, and hearty multi-grain breads. 800-654-2882.

**Blue Heron Farm,** P.O. Box 68, Rumsey, CA 95679: Free information ◆ Oranges, other citrus fruits, and nuts. 916-796-3799.

**Brownville Mills,** Box 145, Brownville, NE 68321: Free price list ◆ Fresh natural foods and vitamins. 800-305-7990; 402-825-4131 (in NE). www.skyport.com/brownvillemills

**Cabot Creamery,** P.O. Box 128, Cabot, VT 05647: Free information ◆ All-natural cheese with half the fat and cholesterol and 33 percent fewer calories than Cheddar. 800-639-3198. www.cabotcheese.com

**Cascadian Farm,** 719 Metcalf St., Sedro Wooley, WA 98284: Free information ◆ Canned fruit juices, vegetables, and other foods. 360-855-0100.

**Cereal Bowl,** RD 1, Box 199, Kittanning, PA 16201: Free information with long SASE ◆ Sugar and preservative-free high-fiber muffin mixes. 888-747-2467. CEREAL@NB.NET

**Community Products Inc.,** RD 2, Box 1950, Montpelier, VT 05602: Free list of retail sources ◆ Dairy-free chocolate bars. 800-927-2695; 802-229-5702 (in VT).

**Deer Valley Farm,** 202 County Rt. 37, Guilford, NY 13780: Catalog 50¢ ◆ Natural and organic foods. 607-764-8556.

**Diamond Organics,** P.O. Box 2159, Freedom, CA 95019: Free information ◆ Lettuce, greens, roots, herbs, and fruits. 888-674-2642. www.diamondorganics.com

**Eden Foods,** 701 Tecumseh Rd., Clinton, MI 49236: Free information ◆ Organic foods. 800-424-EDEN.

**Elderflower Farm,** 501 Callahan Rd., Roseburg, OR 97470: Free brochure ◆ Organically-grown herbs. 541-672-9803. eff@rosenet.net

**Elena's by Houlihan's,** Culinary Traditions Ltd., 70 S. Squirrel Rd., Ste. H, Auburn Hills, MI 48326: Free list of retail sources ◆ Low-fat pasta sauces. 800-72-ELENA.

**Fiddler's Green Farm,** P.O. Box 254, Belfast, ME 04915: Free information ◆ Certified organic pancake and baking mixes, cereals, jams, syrups, honey, coffee, teas, and gift packages. 800-729-7935.

**G! Foods,** 3536 17th St., San Francisco, CA 94110: Free catalog ◆ Wheat and gluten-free foods. 415-255-2139. www.g-foods.com

**Garden Spot Distributor,** 438 White Oak Rd., New Holland, PA 17557: Free information ◆ Apples, apple cider vinegar, and apple juice. 800-829-5100.

**The Gluten-Free Pantry,** P.O. Box 840, Glastonbury, CT 06033: Free catalog ◆ Easy-to-make wheat and gluten-free bread, cake mixes, and specialties. 800-291-8386. www.glutenfree.com

**Gold Mine Natural Food Company,** 3419 Hancock St., San Diego, CA 92110: Free information ◆ Organic brown rice and beans. 800-475-FOOD.

**Gluten-Free Pantry,** P.O. Box 840, Glastonbury, CT 06033: Free information ◆ Gluten-free baking mixes. 800-291-8386. www.glutenfree.com

**Granola Sales & Marketing Company,** P.O. Box 756, Amherst, MA 01004: Free brochure ◆ Sweetened and unsweetened, dairy and wheat-free, low-fat or fat-free, and salt-free foods. 800-472-6652. www.800granola.com

**Harvest Direct Inc.,** P.O. Box 988, Knoxville, TN 37901: Free catalog ◆ All-natural products for vegetarians. 800-835-2867. harvest@slip.net

**The Healthy Trader,** 31921 Camino Capistrano, #411, San Juan Capistrano, CA 92675: Free catalog ◆ Health foods and gift baskets for all appetites. 800-636-2584. www.healthytrader.com

**Indian Harvest Specialtifoods Inc.,** P.O. Box 428, Bemidji, MN 56619: Free catalog ◆ Rice, grain, and bean specialties for healthier living. 800-294-2433. www.indianharvest.com

**Jaffe Brothers Natural Foods,** P.O. Box 636, Valley Center, CA 92082: Free catalog ◆ Preservative and chemical additive-free dried foods. 760-749-1133.

**Kitchen Kneads,** 725 W. Riverdale Rd., Ogden, UT 84405: Free catalog ◆ Kitchen equipment and accessories for healthy cooking, foods, and herbs. 800-658-8521; 801-399-3221 (in UT).

**Living Farms,** Box 50, Tracey, MN 56175: Free information ◆ Grains, beans, rice, wheat, sunflower, and alfalfa, clover, and radish sprouting seeds. 800-533-5320.

**Living Tree Community Foods,** P.O. Box 10082, Berkeley, CA 94709: Free catalog ◆ Organic almonds, almond butter, and dried fruit. 860-260-5534. organic87@aol.com

**Lumen Foods,** 409 Scott St., Lake Charles, LA 70601: Free catalog ◆ Meatless meats, jerky, and other vegetarian snacks. 318-436-6748. www.lumenfds.com

**The Mail Order Catalog,** Box 180, Summertown, TN 38483: Free catalog ◆ Regular, beef-style, and organic textured vegetable protein products and books. 800-695-2241; 615-964-2241 (in TN). www.healthy-eating.com

**Marscell's Organic Gourmet,** P.O. Box 15214, San Luis Obispo, CA 93406: Free information ◆ Freshly-made and frozen vegetarian entrees, natural pastries, and other specialties. 888-754-2813.

**Maverick Sugarbush Inc.,** P.O. Box 99, Sharon, VT 05065: Free brochure ◆ Certified organic Vermont maple syrup, organic cornmeal, and multi-grain pancake mixes. 802-763-8680.

**Miss Roben's,** P.O. Box 1434, Frederick, MD 21702: Free catalog ◆ Gluten and wheat-free mixes for breads, cakes, cookies, and pizza and pie crusts. Also baking supplies for cooking from scratch. 800-891-0083. www.jagunet.com/~msrobens/

**Morgan's Mills,** RD 2, Box 4602, Union, ME 04862: Free information ◆ Salt-free mixes for pancakes, waffles, and bran muffins. 800-373-2756.

**Mountain Ark Trading Company,** P.O. Box 3170, Fayetteville, AR 72702: Free information ◆ Vegetables, miso, seasonings, rice, pasta, fruit, spreads, oils, beans, and soups. 800-643-8909.

**Natural Lifestyle,** 16 Lookout Dr., Asheville, NC 28804: Free catalog ◆ Water filters, organic foods, macrobiotic specialties, cookware, organic cotton clothes, earth care products, and cookbooks. 704-254-9606.

**Natural Resources Mail Order,** 6680 Harvard Dr., Sebastopol, CA 95472: Free information ◆ All-natural and dairy-free chocolate candy and chocolate chips, organic chocolate bars, and other natural foods. 800-747-0390; 707-823-4340 (in CA).

**Southern Brown Rice,** P.O. Box 185, Weiner, AR 72479: Free catalog ◆ Rice products fresh from the farm. 800-421-7423.

**Soyco Foods,** Galaxy Foods, 2441 Viscount Row, Orlando, Fl 32809: Free list of retail sources ◆ Casein-free cheese alternative. 800-441-9419. www.soyco.com

**Timber Crest Farms,** 4791 Dry Creek Rd., Healdsburg, CA 95448: Free catalog ◆ Dried fruit, dried tomato products, fruit butters, nuts, and trail mixes. 707-433-8251.

**To Life Food & Herbs,** P.O. Box 711385, Houston, TX 77271: Free catalog ◆ Vegetarian and kosher health foods. 800-317-3449; 713-771-5366 (in TX). www.flash.net/~tolife

**Transpacific Health Products,** 3924 Central Ave., St. Petersburg, FL 33711: Free catalog ◆ Herb teas for health-related conditions. 800-336-9636.

**Walnut Acres Organic Farms,** Penns Creek, PA 17862: Free catalog ◆ Fresh and canned vegetables, canned and dried fruit, grains, baked goods, natural cheese, fruit and vegetable juices, nuts, jams, preserves, and other specialties. 800-433-3998.

**Wanda's Nature Farm Foods,** 925 S St., Lincoln, NE 68508: Free catalog ◆ All-natural bread, muffin, pancake, waffle, and double-chocolate cake mixes. 800-222-FARM. naturefarmfood@aol.com

**War Eagle Mill,** Rt. 5, Box 411, Rogers, AR 72756: Free catalog ◆ Whole grain meals and flours. 501-789-5343.

**Wax Orchards,** 22744 Wax Orchards Rd. SW, Vashon, WA 98070: Free list of retail sources ◆ Conserves, fruit butters and syrups, dessert toppings, and other food products sweetened with concentrated natural fruit juices. 800-634-6132.

## Maple Syrup

**Auger Sugarmill Farm,** Rt. 16, Box 26, Barton, VT 05822: Free catalog ◆ Vermont maple syrup. 800-688-7978.

**Bascom Maple Farms Inc.,** RR 1, Box 137, Alstead, NH 03602: Free brochure ◆ Maple syrup and candy. 800-835-6361; 603-835-2135 (in NH).

**Bragg Farm,** Rt. 14 North, East Montpelier, VT 05651: Free brochure ◆ Maple syrup. 800-376-5757; 802-223-5757 (in VT).

**Butternut Mountain Farm,** P.O. Box 381, Johnson, VT 05656: Free information ◆ Maple syrup and sugar. 800-828-2376.

**Clear's Maple Products,** 574, Notre-Dame Nord, C.P. 74, Robertsonville, Quebec, Canada G0N 1L0; Free brochure ◆ Pure maple syrup, maple syrup candies, maple sugar, and novelties. 800-461-8872.

**Couture's Maple Shop,** RR 1, Box 47, Rt. 100, Westfield, VT 05874: Free catalog ◆ Maple syrup, maple leaf candies, maple cream, maple French salad dressing, maple lollipops, and maple granulated sugar. 800-845-2733.

**Danforth's Sugarhouse,** US Rt. 2, East Montpelier, VT 05651: Free information ◆ Maple syrup. 802-229-9536.

**Grafton Village Apple Company,** 703 Main St., Weston, VT 05161: Free catalog ◆ Maple syrup and sugar. 800-843-4822.

**Green Mountain Sugar House,** Rt. 100N, Box 820, Ludlow, VT 05149: Free catalog ◆ Maple syrup, maple sugar candy, nut brittle, cheese, smoked slab bacon, candy and fudge, pancake mix, mincemeat, homemade jams, and other Vermont specialties. 800-643-9338; 802-228-7151 (in VT). gmsh@ludl.tds.net

**Harlow's Sugar House,** RD 1, Box 395, Putney, VT 05346: Free brochure ◆ Maple syrup and specialties, jams, jellies, and Vermont cheese. 802-387-5852.

**Jasper's Sugar Bush,** 1867 County Rd. 374, Carney, MI 49812: Free information ◆ Maple syrup, maple cream, maple sugar candy, chocolate maple cream, and gift baskets. 800-646-2753.

**Maverick Sugarbush Inc.,** P.O. Box 99, Sharon, VT 05065: Free brochure ◆ Certified organic Vermont maple syrup, organic cornmeal, and multi-grain pancake mixes. 802-763-8680.

**Morse Farm,** County Rd., HCR 32, Box 870, Montpelier, VT 05602: Free information ◆ Maple syrup and specialties. 800-223-2740.

**New England Maple Museum,** Gift Shop, P.O. Box 1615, Rutland, VT 05701: Free brochure ◆ Maple syrup and specialties. 802-483-9414.

**The Rocking Horse Country Store,** Rt. 4, Rutland, VT 05701: Free brochure ◆ Vermont maple syrup, cheese, crafts, and country collectibles. 802-773-7882.

**Spring Tree Corp.,** P.O. Box 1160, Brattleboro, VT 05302: Free list of retail sources ◆ Additive and preservative-free, 100 percent pure maple syrup. 802-254-8784.

**Sugarbush Farm,** RR 1, Box 568, Woodstock, VT 05091: Free information with long SASE ◆ Maple syrup and cheese. 802-457-1757.

**Titcomb Hill Maple Products,** RR 1, Box 1019, Farmington, ME 04938: Free information ◆ Pure maple syrup, honey, jellies, jams, maple candy, and gift packages. 800-451-7390.

**The Vermont Maple Syrup Company,** Michael Elliot Enterprises Inc., Mr. Michael Char, 107 Gair St., Piermont, NY 10968: Free information ◆ All-natural maple syrup. 914-398-0574.

**A Vermont Store,** 27 Catherine Dr., Rutland, VT 05701: Free brochure ◆ Pure maple syrup, maple sugar candy, Cabot cheese, Vermont common crackers, mustards, honey, pancake mixes, preserves, and other Vermont specialty foods. 888-265-6250. www.avermontstore.com

**Wood's Cider Mill,** RFD 2, Box 477, Springfield, VT 05156: Free catalog with long SASE ◆ Maple syrup, cider jelly and syrup, and boiled cider. 802-263-5547.

## Meats

**Aidells Sausage Company,** Mail Order Dept., 1625 Alvarado St., San Leandro, CA 94577: Free catalog ◆ Filler-, MSG-, and binder-free sausage. 800-546-5795.

**Allen Brothers,** 3737 S. Halsted St., Chicago, IL 60609: Free catalog ◆ Steakhouse steaks, veal, and lamb chops. 800-957-0111. www.allenbrothers.com

**Amana Meat Shop & Smokehouse,** P.O. Box 158, Amana, IA 52203: Free brochure ◆ Ham, bacon, sausage, cheese, and specialties. 800-373-MEAT; 319-622-3113 (in IA).

**Basse's Choice Plantation,** P.O. Box 1, Smithfield, VA 23431: Free information ◆ Cured, smoked, aged, low-salt, country, and honey-cured ham. 800-292-2773. www.smithfieldhams.com

**W.A. Bean & Sons Inc.,** 229 Bomarc Rd., P.O. Box 1446, Bangor, ME 04401: Free brochure ◆ Frankfurters, premium hams, and sausages. 800-649-1958; 207-947-0364 (in ME). www.mint.net/beans

**Boyles Famous K.C. Steaks,** 1638 St. Louis: Free brochure ◆ Filets, rib-eyes, and T-bones, and other steaks. 800-821-3626. www.boylesteaks.com

**Broadbent's Foods & Gifts,** 5695 Hopkinsville Rd., Cadiz, KY 42211: Free catalog ◆ Jams, jellies, cheese, smoked and hand-cured country ham, bacon, and sausage. 800-841-2202; 502-522-6674 (in KY).

**Broadleaf Venison USA,** 3050 E. 11th St., Sun Valley, CA 91352: Free information ◆ Farm-raised venison, buffalo, lamb, and pheasant. 800-336-3844.

**Broken Arrow Ranch,** P.O. Box 530, Ingram, TX 78025: Free brochure ◆ Venison, smoked wild boar, antelope, emu, and other exotic meat. 800-962-4263.

**B3R Country Meats Inc.,** 2100 W. Hwy. 287, P.O. Box 374, Childress, TX 79201: Free information ◆ All-natural premium beef. 940-937-8870.

**Burgers' Ozark Country Cured Hams Inc.,** Rt. 3, Box 3248, California, MO 65018: Free catalog ◆ Barbecued chickens, sausage, cheese, and hickory-smoked and sugar-cured ham, ham steaks, bacon, and turkey. 800-624-5426; 573-796-4111 (in MO).

**Cavanaugh Lakeview Farms Ltd.,** 2000 Thorn Apple Valley Dr., Ponca City, OK 74601: Free information ◆ Honey-cured and smoked poultry, smoked ham and bacon, fresh-frozen poultry, steaks, game, and smoked seafood. 800-243-4438.

**Chickasaw Trading Company,** 821 N. Avenue B, Denver City, TX 78323: Free catalog ◆ Lean beef jerky and turkey. 800-848-3515.

**Classic Steaks,** 4430 S. 110th St., Omaha, NE 68137: Free catalog ◆ USDA choice steaks. 800-288-2783. www.classicsteaks.com

**Clifty Farm,** P.O. Box 1146, Paris, TN 38242: Free brochure ◆ Country-cooked hams, baby back pork ribs, slab bacon, hickory-smoked turkey, and gift packages. 800-486-HAMS.

**Colonel Bill Newsom's Hams,** Newsom's Old Mill Store, 208 E. Main St., Princeton, KY 42445: Free information ◆ Vidalia onion salad dressing, corn relish, mild or hot chow chow, preserves, and hickory-smoked ham, sorghum, and other smoked meats. 502-365-2482.

**Critchfield Meat,** 2254 Zandale Center, Lexington, KY 40503: Free catalog ◆ Old-fashioned sugar-cured country ham and other meat. 800-86-MEATS; 606-276-4965 (in KY).

**Custom Ribs Company,** 7800 Metro Pkwy., Ste. 300, Minneapolis, MN 55425: Free brochure ◆ Ready-to-serve loin back ribs with or without sauce. 800-314-7427; 612-858-9666 (in MN).

**D'Artagnan,** 399 St. Paul Ave., Jersey City, NJ 07306: Free catalog ◆ Foie gras, pates, Muscovy duck, fresh game, and organic poultry. 800-DARTAGN.

**Dakin Farm,** Rt. 7, Ferrisburg, VT 05456: Free catalog ◆ Smoked ham and bacon, maple syrup, and Cheddar cheese. 800-993-2546. www.dakinfarm.com

**Denver Buffalo Company,** 1120 Lincoln St., Ste. 905, Denver, CO 80203: Free catalog ◆ All-natural buffalo meat and smoked sausage. 888-336-2833. www.denverbuffalo.com

**Early's Honey Stand,** 5087 Colombia Pike, Springhill, TN 37174: Free catalog ◆ Honey-glazed hams, whole smoked turkey, country favorites, and gift assortments. 800-523-2015.

**Edes Custom Meats Inc.,** 6700 W. McCormick Rd., Amarillo, TX 79118: Free information with long SASE ◆ Sausage, ham, bacon, beef jerky, grain fed and aged USA choice beef, lamb, and turkey. 800-537-5902; 806-622-0205 (in TX).

**S. Wallace Edwards & Sons Inc.,** P.O. Box 25, Surry, VA 23883: Free catalog ◆ Preserves from the Blue Ridge Mountains, seafood from the Eastern Shore, and hickory-smoked Virginia ham, bacon, and sausage. 800-222-4267. www.virginiatraditions.com

**Eichten's Hidden Acres Cheese and Bison Farm,** 16705 310th St., Center City, MN 55012: Free catalog ◆ Farm-raised buffalo meat free of growth additives, hormones, or other drugs. 800-657-6752.

**FatBoys BBQ,** 4280 S. Washington Ave., Titusville, FL 32780: Free information ◆ Ribs, chopped beef and pork in barbecue sauce, barbecued beans, and barbecue sauce. 888-880-7427; 407-267-3468 (in FL).

**Fiddler's Creek Farm Inc.,** RD 2, Box 188, Hunter Rd., Titusville, NJ 08560: Free brochure ◆ Country smoked turkeys, turkey breast, pork tenderloin, bacon, and chicken breast. 609-737-0685.

**Fiddler's Green Farm,** P.O. Box 254, Belfast, ME 04915: Free information ◆ Certified organic pancake and baking mixes, cereals, jams, syrups. Honey, coffee, teas, and gift packages. 800-729-7935.

**Folk's Folly Prime Cut Shoppe,** 551 S. Mendenhall, Memphis, TN 38117: Free catalog ◆ Prime veal, lamb loin chops, steaks, and other meat. 800-467-0245. www.memphistravelfolksfolly.com

**Fortuna's Sausage Company,** 975 Greenville Ave., Greenville, RI 02828: Free catalog ◆ Fresh and dry-cured sausage and Italian specialties. 800-42-SOUPY. SOUPY@Edgenet.net

**Four Oaks Farm Inc.,** P.O. Box 987, Lexington, SC 29071: Free brochure ◆ Country-style ham and bacon, jams, jellies, pickles, relishes, salad dressings, cakes, and other favorites. 800-858-5006; 803-356-3194 (in SC). fouroaks@scsn.net

**Gaspar's Sausage Company,** 384 Faunce Corner Rd., North Dartmouth, MA 02747: Free information ◆ Hot and mild Portuguese-style sausage, sweet breads, and sliced meat. 800-542-2038; 508-998-2012 (in MA).

**Gerhard's Sausage,** 901 Enterprise Way, Napa, CA 94558: Free list of retail sources ◆ MSG and filler-free smoked and fresh sausage. 707-252-4116.

**Giuseppe's Original Sausage Company,** 181 Cumberland, Memphis, TN 38112: Free brochure ◆ Lean and natural handmade fresh sausage. Includes chicken, lamb, turkey, and pork. 800-893-3497.

**Golden Trophy,** 1101 Perimeter Dr., Ste. 210, Schaumberg, IL 60173: Free catalog ◆ Fully aged and hand-trimmed beef. 800-835-6607.

**Great Plains Meats,** P.O. Box 630, Wisner, NE 8791: Free information ◆ Aged steaks. 800-871-6328.

**The Great Valley Mills,** 1774 County Line Rd., Barto, PA 19504: Free brochure ◆ Family farm grown and produced foods. Gift packs available. 800-688-6455.

**Greenberg Smoked Turkey Inc.,** P.O. Box 4818, Tyler, TX 75712: Free information ◆ Smoked turkey. 903-595-0725.

**Harrington Ham Company,** Main St., Richmond, VT 05477: Free information ◆ Spiral-sliced and cob-smoked maple-glazed ham and smoked bacon, turkey breast, pheasant, cheese, maple syrup, pastries, plum pudding, fruitcakes, and dried fruit. 802-434-4444.

**Harrington's of Vermont,** Shelburne, Rt. 7, Shelburne, VT 05482: Free information ◆ Ham and Vermont specialty foods. 802-985-2000.

**Hawaii's Jungle Jerky,** P.O. Box 31062, Honolulu, HI 96820: Free brochure ◆ Low-sodium beef jungle jerky. 800-872-5642. www.junglejerky.com

**Hoffman's Quality Meats,** 13225 Cearfoss Pike, Hagerstown, MD 21740: Free brochure ◆ Country ham and bacon, Delmonico and boneless New York strip steaks, and country sausage. 800-356-3193.

**Hot Bites LLC,** P.O. Box 223, South Milwaukee, WI 52172: Free information ◆ Hot-smoked, fresh, and medium hot with garlic Italian sausage. 888-HOT-BITES.

**Howie G's,** 4002 Deerwood Trail, Egan, MN 55122: Free brochure ◆ USDA choice top sirloin, T-bone, ribeye, NY strip, bacon-wrapped sirloin, and other steaks. 800-446-9434; 612-452-3363 (in MN).

**The Ideal Sausage Company,** 245 W. 38th St., New York, NY 10018: Free catalog ◆ Low-fat spicy poultry sausage. 212-719-0850.

**Indian Hill Farms,** 213 Old Indian Rd., Milton, NY 12547: Free catalog ◆ Smoked whole turkey and turkey breast, Kosher turkey, smoked ham, Norwegian smoked salmon, and brandied fruitcake. 914-795-2700.

**International Home Cooking,** 305 Mallory St., Rocky Mount, NC 27801: Free catalog ◆ Exotic fresh meats. 919-972-7423.

**Jackson Hole Buffalo Meat,** P.O. Box 2100, Jackson, WY 83001: Free catalog ◆ Low-fat, low-cholesterol, and hormone-free steaks, jerky, and salami from ranch-raised buffalo meat. Includes gift packages. 800-543-6328.

**Jamison Farm,** 171 Jamison Ln., Latrobe, PA 15650: Free brochure ◆ Lamb products. 800-237-5262. www.jamisonfarm.com

**Jones Dairy Farm,** P.O. Box 808, Fort Atkinson, WI 53538: Free brochure ◆ Hams, sausage, and smoked bacon. 800-635-6637. www.jonessausage.com/ham

**Kansas City Steak Company,** 2501 Guinotte, P.O. Box 33442, Kansas City, MO 64120: Free catalog ◆ Corn-fed aged beef. 800-987-8325.

**Klement Sausage Company,** 207 E. Lincoln Ave., Milwaukee, WI 53207: Free catalog ◆ Gourmet sausage and other gifts from Milwaukee. 800-553-6368; 414-744-5554 (in WI).

**Koenemann Sausage Company Inc.,** 27090 Volo Village Rd., Volo, IL 60073: Free brochure ◆ German-style sausages. 800-662-5584. www.marketplaza.com/koenemann/sausage.html

**Frank Lewis' Alamo Fruit,** 100 N. Tower Rd., Alamo, TX 78516: Free brochure ◆ Farm-fresh tomatoes, tangelos, apples, persimmons, cheesecake, smoked turkey breast, and other specialties. 800-477-4773.

**Butch Long's Steaks of Nebraska,** P.O. Box 2166, Omaha, NE 68103: Free information ◆ Gourmet meats. 800-579-0333.

**M & S Buffalo Specialty,** Hwy. 93 South, Rollins, MT 59931: Free brochure ◆ Honey-cured hams, bacon, and buffalo meat sausage and jerky. 800-454-3414; 406-844-3414 (in MT).

**Mahogany Smoked Meats,** P.O. Box 1387, Bishop, CA 93515: Free brochure ◆ Smoked jerky, Cheddar cheese, chileno peppers and stuffed olives, smoked trout, and other specialties. 888-624-6426.

**Jody Maroni's Sausage Kingdom,** 2011 Ocean Front Walk, Venice, CA 90291: Free information ◆ Low fat and nitrate, MSG, and preservative-free all-natural sausage. 800-HAUTDOG. www.maroni.com

**Maurice's Gourmet BBQ,** P.O. Box 6847, West Columbia, SC 29171: Free catalog ◆ Chopped ham BBQ, racks of ribs, turkeys, pigs, BBQ hams, and 5 flavors of BBQ sauce. 800-628-7423. www.mauricesbbq.com

**Maverick Ranch Specialty Meats,** 5360 N. Franklin St., Denver, CO 80216: Free catalog ◆ Lean and lite buffalo, lamb, and ostrich meats. 800-497-2624.

**Meadow Farms Country Smokehouse,** 2345 N. Sierra Hwy., P.O. Box 1387, Bishop, CA 93515: Free brochure ◆ Peppered, teriyaki, Indian, sweet and spicy, and other beef jerky. 888-624-6426; 760-873-8761 (in CA).

**Myers Meats,** Rt. 1, Box 132, Parshall, ND 58770: Free information ◆ Country-style sausage, beef jerky, country-cured dried beef, beef sticks, and other specialties. 800-635-3759; 701-743-4451 (in ND). www.tradecorridor.com/myersmeats

**New Braunfels Smokehouse,** P.O. Box 311159, New Braunfels, TX 78131: Free catalog ◆ Bin-cured and hickory-smoked turkey, ham, sausage, bacon, chicken, and beef. 800-537-6932. www.nbsmokehouse.com

**New Skete Farms,** P.O. Box 128, Cambridge, NY 12816: Catalog $1 ◆ Smoked whole ducks and chickens, turkey and chicken breasts, bacon, ham, sausage, Cheddar cheese, and cheese spreads. 518-677-3928.

**Noble Farms Inc.,** P.O. Box 1612, Sedalia, MO 65301: Free information ◆ Smoked whole pheasant and smoked pheasant breast. 800-827-5907.

**North Country Smokehouse,** P.O. Box 1415, Claremont, NH 03743: Free brochure ◆ All-natural old-fashioned cob-smoked meat. Also ham, slab and Canadian bacon, pork chops, sausage, spareribs, boneless lamb, whole turkey and turkey breasts, duck, pheasant, and sharp Vermont and mozzarella cheese. 800-258-4304. www.ncsmokehouse.com

**Nueske's Hillcrest Farm Meats,** RR 2, Wittenberg, WI 54499: Free brochure ◆ Smoked ham, sausage, bacon, smoked shanks, pork loins, pork chops, duck, turkey and turkey breasts, chicken and chicken breasts, and Cornish game hens. 800-382-2266.

**The O.K. Market,** 542 N. Linden St., Wahoo, NE 68066: Free information ◆ Polish sausage, bologna, beef jerky, wieners, and other meat products. 800-847-6328; 402-443-3015 (in NE).

**Oak Grove Smokehouse Inc.,** 17618 Old Jefferson Hwy., Prairieville, LA 70769: Free catalog ◆ Specialty smoked meats and dried Cajun spice mixes. 225-673-6857.

**Oakridge Smokehouse Restaurant,** P.O. Box 146, Schulenburg, TX 78956: Free information ◆ Peppered beef tenderloins, smoked pork tenderloins, and smoked baby-back pork spare ribs. 800-548-6325.

**Omaha Steaks,** P.O. Box 3300, Omaha, NE 68103: Free catalog ◆ Aged steaks and beef. 800-228-9055. www.omahasteaks.com

**Pfaelzer Brothers,** Catalog Order Dept., P.O. Box 1015, Maumee, OH 43537: Free catalog ◆ Meat, fruit and gift baskets, desserts, and other specialties. 800-621-0226. www.pfaelzer-brothers.com

**Pigman's Barbeque,** 1606 S. Croatan Hwy., Kill Devil Hills, NC 27948: Free brochure ◆ Ready-to-cook hickory-smoked and salted Virginia country hams. Also cooked, boned, and trimmed hams and other family favorites. 800-442-5207; 919-441-6803 (in NC). www.pigman.com

**Prime Access,** P.O. Box 8187, White Plains, NY 10602: Free information ◆ Gourmet meats. 800-314-2875.

**The Sausage Maker Inc.,** 1500 Clinton St., Bldg. 123, Buffalo, NY 14206: Free catalog ◆ Sausage-making and meat curing equipment and supplies. 716-824-6510.

**Sayersbrook Bison Ranch,** 6286 Spencer Rd., Bonne Terre, MO 63628: Free catalog ◆ Low-calorie and cholesterol bison meats. 888-472-9377. www.sayersbrook.com

**Schaller & Weber Inc.,** 22-35 46th St., Long Island City, NY 11105: Free catalog ◆ Sausage, liverwurst, cold cuts, salami and cervelats, Westphalian-style smoked ham, roast beef, bacon, and other meat. 800-847-4115.

**Schiltz Goose Farm,** 7 Oak St. West, P.O. Box 267, Sisseton, SD 57262: Free information ◆ Geese, shipped early October through the holidays, packaged for the freezer. Also goose eggs. 605-698-7651. www.schiltzfoods.com

**Scott Hams,** 1301 Scott Rd., Greenville, KY 42345: Free information ◆ Hickory-smoked country-cured ham, bacon, and sausage. 502-338-3402.

**Semplex of USA,** P.O. Box 11476, Minneapolis, MN 55411: Free catalog ◆ Sausage-making equipment and ingredients. 888-255-7997.

**Sinai Kosher Foods Corp.,** 1000 W. Pershing Rd., Chicago, IL 60609: Free information ◆ Kosher beef, lamb, veal, roasts, steaks, chops, and ground beef. 800-823-7746; 770-650-6330 (in IL).

**Smithfield Direct Marketing,** One Monette Pkwy., Smithfield, VA 23430: Free catalog ◆ Uncooked or fully cooked and ready-to-serve ham and bacon. 800-926-8448. www.smithfieldhams.com

**SmokeShack BBQ,** 134 Brooklyn Ave., Laurel, DE 19956: Free brochure ◆ Hickory smoked ham, beef, and pork. 888-767-4227. www.smokeshackbbq.com

**Sonny Bryan's Smokehouse,** 2625 Seelco St., Dallas, TX 75235: Free catalog ◆ Fully-cooked barbecued beef brisket, pork ribs, and sausage. 800-5-SONNYS.

**Sunday House Foods Inc.,** P.O. Box 818, Fredericksburg, TX 78624: Free brochure ◆ Hickory smoked turkey Cajun style and baked with honey. Also hickory smoked, lemon-peppered, and Cajun style smoked chickens. 800-541-3934.

**Summerfield Farm,** 10044 James Monroe Hwy., Culpeper, VA 22701: Free brochure ◆ Veal, venison, lamb, sausage, prime beef, game birds, and smoked salmon halves. 540-547-9600.

**Texas Wild Game Cooperative,** P.O. Box 530, Ingram, TX 78025: Free catalog ◆ Venison, antelope, wild boar, and other exotic meat. 800-962-4263.

**Thundering Herd Buffalo Products,** P.O. Box 1051, Reno, NV 89504: Free catalog ◆ Ranch-raised buffalo meat. 800-525-9730.

**Usinger's Famous Sausage,** 1030 N. Old World 3rd St., Milwaukee, WI 53203: Free catalog ◆ Sausage, ham, steaks, and Wisconsin cheese. Includes gift packages. 800-558-9997. www.usinger.com

**Virginia Diner,** P.O. Box 1030, Rt. 460, Wakefield, VA 23888: Free catalog ◆ Virginia bacon and ham, fudge, homemade jellies and jams, peanuts, and peanut specialties. 800-642-6887. www.vadiner.com

**Volpi Foods,** 5250 Daggett Ave., St. Louis, MO 63110: Free information ◆ Sliced prosciutto and filsette, sopressata, calabrese, and napoli salami. Includes gift assortments. 800-288-3439.

**The Daniel Weaver Company,** P.O. Box 525, Lebanon, PA 17042: Free catalog ◆ Lebanon bologna, smoked meat, and specialties. 800-932-8377; 717-274-6100 (in PA).

**Wild Game Inc.,** 2315 W. Huron, Chicago, IL 60612: Free information ◆ Venison, buffalo, boar and other exotic meat. Also turkey breast, pates, terrines, mushrooms and truffles, smoked seafood, cheese, and other foods. 773-278-1661.

**Wimmer's Meat Products,** 126 W. Grant, West Point, NE 68788: Free catalog ◆ Ham, sausage, bacon, and meat cured using old-world spice recipes. 800-358-0761.

**Wolfe's Neck Farm,** 10 Burnett Rd., Freeport, ME 04032: Free catalog ◆ All-natural Angus beef. 207-865-4469.

## Nuts

**A & B Milling Company Inc.,** P.O. Box 327, Enfield, NC 27823: Free information ◆ Shelled and fried peanuts, chocolate peanut clusters, redskins, and other peanut favorites. 800-843-0105. www.auntrubyspeanuts.com

**Ace Pecan Company,** P.O. Box 1013, Maumee, OH 43537: Free catalog ◆ Pecans and pecan candy. 800-323-9754.

**Almond Plaza,** Catalog Order Center, P.O. Box 426, Maumee, OH 43537: Free catalog ◆ Almonds, candy, and herbs. 800-225-6887. www.almond-plaza.com

**America's Best Pecan Company,** 1125 Foster Rd., Las Cruces, NM 88001: Free information ◆ Natural or roasted, buttered, and salted shelled pecan halves. 800-756-6929. www.wwmalls.com/nm/pecan

**Assouline & Ting Inc.,** 314 Brown St., Philadelphia, PA 19123: Free information ◆ Nut specialties. 800-521-4491; 215-627-3000 (in PA). www.caviarassouline.com

**Aunt Ruby's Peanuts,** 200 Halifax St., P.O. Box 327, Enfield, NC 27823: Free catalog ◆ Peanut and peanut specialties in gift packages. 800-843-0105. www.auntrubyspeanuts.com

**Azar Nut Company,** 1800 Northwestern Dr., El Paso, TX 79912: Free information ◆ Mixed nuts, jumbo and honey-roasted cashews and peanuts, pistachios, roasted pecans, and macadamias. 800-351-8178; 915-877-4079 (in TX).

**Bates Nut Farm Inc.,** 15954 Woods Valley Rd., Valley Center, CA 92082: Free price list ◆ Walnuts, pecans, cashews, macadamias, pistachios, fresh apricots, prunes, dates, candy, granola, dried fruit, preserves, and honey. 800-642-0348; 760-749-3333 (in CA).

**Buchanan Hollow Nut Company,** 6510 Minturn, Le Grand, CA 95333: Free information ◆ Fresh-roasted pistachios. 800-532-1500; 209-389-4594 (in CA). www.bhnc.com

**CityFarm,** 1545 Clay St., Detroit, MI 48211: Free information ◆ Peanuts, cashews, pistachios, and other nuts. 800-437-6825; 313-871-5100 (in MI). www.city-farm.com/nuts

**Country Estate Pecans,** P.O. Box 7, Sahuarita, AZ 85629: Free information ◆ Pecans. 800-327-3226.

**Dundee Orchards,** P.O. Box 327, Dundee, OR 97115: Free information ◆ Oregon hazelnut butter, other hazelnut products, and Oregon cherries. 503-538-8105.

**Durey-Libby Nuts Inc.,** P.O. Box 345, Carlstadt, NJ 07072: Free brochure ◆ Walnuts, cashews, pecans, macadamias, almonds, and pistachios. 201-939-2775.

**Fran's Pecans,** 4733 Dwight Evans Rd., Charlotte, NC 28217: Free brochure ◆ Honey-roasted and cinnamon-sugar pecan specialties, pralines, and roasted and salted pecan halves. 800-476-6887. www.FransPecans.com

**Fruit Ranch-West,** 6301 W. Bluemound Rd., Milwaukee, WI 53213: Free catalog ◆ Fruit gift baskets, assorted nuts, and Wisconsin cheese variety packages. 800-433-3289. www.choicemall.com/fruitranch.

**Golden Kernel Pecan Company Inc.,** Box 613, Cameron, SC 29030: Free brochure ◆ Roasted pecans, pecan candies, and other specialties. 800-845-2448; 803-823-2311 (in SC). www.goldenkernel.com

**House of Almonds,** 5634 River Rd., Oakdale, CA 95361: Free catalog ◆ Chocolate almonds, English toffee, chocolate cherries, pistachios, cashews, and other specialties. 800-225-6663. www.houseofalmonds.com

**Hubbard Peanut Company,** P.O. Box 94, Sedley, VA 23878: Free brochure ◆ Home-cooked peanuts. 800-889-7688; 757-562-4081 (in VA). www.hubspeanuts.com

**Huntley-Moore Farms,** 5910 N. Monroe, Fresno, CA 93722: Free catalog ◆ Pistachios, macadamias, nut candy, and other specialties. 800-700-5779; 209-275-9381 (in CA.

**International Nut Company,** 5 South St., Box 540, Walpole, MA 02081: Free price list ◆ Imported nuts and snacks. 800-710-9380.

**Krema Nut Company,** 1000 W. Goodale Blvd., Columbus, OH 43212: Free brochure ◆ All-time favorites and seasonal nut assortments. 800-222-4132. www.krema.com

**Mariani Nut Company,** 709 Dutton St., P.O. Box 808, Winters, CA 95694: Free information ◆ Almonds, pistachios, walnuts, and dried tomatoes. 916-795-3311.

**Mashuga Nuts Inc.,** 169 Paulin Dr., San Rafael, CA 94903: Free list of retail sources ◆ Thai-flavored hot and sweet-spiced pecans. 800-Mashuga.

**Missouri Dandy Pantry,** P.O. Box A, Stockton, MO 65785: Free brochure ◆ Cashews, pistachios, black walnuts, other nuts, and candy. 800-872-6879. www.marketplaza.com/walnuts

**Nanco,** P.O. Box 100549, Terra Bedlla, CA 93270: Free list of retail sources ◆ Pistachios and hand-dipped pistachio/milk chocolate/caramel candy. 209-535-1030.

**Nick's Nuts,** 2691-B Peachtree Square, Atlanta, GA 30360: Free brochure ◆ Nuts, nut-candies, and other favorites. 770-445-4442. www.nicksnuts.com

**Nunes Farms Almonds,** 73 Alder Ave., San Anselmo, CA 94960: Free information ◆ Fresh, roasted and salted, honey-glazed, and Cheddar cheese almonds. 800-255-1641.

**Nuts 4U,** P.O. Box 1864, Sugar Land, TX 77487: Free brochure ◆ Nuts, fruit and nut mixes, dried fruit, and other snacks. 281-242-2794. www.nuts4u.com/nut

**Peanut Patch Inc.,** P.O. Box 186, Courtland, VA 23837: Free brochure ◆ Peanuts, peanut candy assortments, and raw peanuts in bulk. 800-544-0896. www.peanutpatch.com

**The Peanut Shop of Williamsburg,** P.O. Box GN, Williamsburg, VA 23187: Free brochure ◆ Peanut specialties, Virginia country ham, Williamsburg soups, salad dressings, sauces, and other foods. 800-637-3268.

**Pecan Producers International,** 2131 East Hwy. 31, Corsicana, TX 75110: Free information ◆ Pecans and pecan candy. 800-732-2648.

**Priester's Pecans,** 227 Old Fort Dr., Fort Deposit, AL 36032: Free catalog ◆ Nut brittle, pecan candy, pecan brownies and pie, sugar-free pecan clusters, and roasted, salted, and salt-free pecans. 800-277-3226. www.priester.com

**Pueblo to People,** 2105 Silber Rd., Houston, TX 77065: Free catalog ◆ Nuts, dried fruit, gift baskets, and coffees. Also ceramics, jewelry, and gifts. 800-843-5257.

**Ross-Smith Pecan Company Inc.,** 700 Oak St., McRae, GA 31055: Free brochure ◆ Pecans. 800-841-5503; 912-868-5693 (in GA).

**Santa Fe Cookie Company,** 3905 San Mateo NE, Albuquerque, NM 87110: Free brochure ◆ Sugar-free cookies, spicy snacks, pretzels, crackers, and nut mixes. 800-873-5589.

**J.H. Sherard,** P.O. Box 75, Sherard, MS 38669: Free brochure ◆ Shelled and unshelled pecans, pistachios, and other nuts. 800-647-5518; 205-627-7211 (in MS).

**Society Hill Snacks,** 2121 Gillingham St., Philadelphia, PA 19124: Free list of retail sources ◆ Butter-toasted pecans, cashews, almonds, peanuts, mixed nuts, and pistachios. 800-595-0050; 215-288-2888 (in PA).

**The Squire's Choice,** Mail Order Dept., 2250 W. Cabot Blvd., Langhorne, PA 19047: Free catalog ◆ Nuts, coffee, and other specialties. 800-523-6163.

**Sun River Packing Company,** P.O. Box 10, Waterford, CA 95386: Free information ◆ Fresh, blanched, and hickory-smoked almonds. 800-334-NUTS.

**Sunnyland Farms Inc.,** P.O. Box 8200, Albany, GA 31706: Free catalog ◆ Pecans, other nuts, candy, baked specialties, dried fruits, maple syrup, honey, jellies, and gift assortments. 800-999-2488; 912-883-3085 (in GA). www.sunnylandfarms.com

**Tanner Pecan Company,** 10 Springdale Blvd., Mobile, AL 36606: Free catalog ◆ Pecans and pecan confections. 800-635-3651.

**H.M. Thames Pecan Company,** P.O. Box 2206, Mobile, AL 36652: Free catalog ◆ Nuts and nut specialties, pralines, candy, baked goods, and fruitcake. 800-633-1306. www.3georges.com

**Virginia Diner,** P.O. Box 1030, Rt. 460, Wakefield, VA 23888: Free catalog ◆ Peanuts, peanut specialties and pie, homemade jellies and jams, Virginia bacon and ham, and fudge. 800-642-6887. www.vadiner.com

**Wakefield Peanut Company,** P.O. Box 538, Wakefield, VA 23888: Free catalog ◆ Extra-large cocktail, roasted in the shell, and raw peanuts. Also chocolate covered seasonal favorites, sampler boxes, and peanut candies. 800-803-1309.

**Young Pecans,** c/o Pecan Plantations, P.O. Drawer 6709, Florence, SC 29502: Free catalog ◆ Butter-roasted and salted pecans and cashews, double-dipped chocolate pecan halves, butter-toffee pecan popcorn, and pecan divinity logs. Also praline, sugar and orange, sugar and spiced, and Cheddar cheese pecans. 800-729-8004.

**Yummies Candy & Nuts,** Rt. 1, Kittery, ME 03904: Free catalog ◆ Candy and nut favorites. 800-638-9377. www.yummies.com

**Waterford Nut Company,** P.O. Box 37, Waterford, CA 95386: Free information ◆ Natural fresh shelled almonds and almond butter. 209-874-2317.

**Whitley's Peanut Factory,** P.O. Box 647, Hayes, VA 23072: Free catalog ◆ Peanuts, peanut candy and soup, peanut-carrot cake, peanut butter cookie mixes, other peanut products, cured uncooked country ham, and gift assortments. 800-470-2244. www.whitleyspeanut.com

**Joe C. Williams,** P.O. Box 640, Camden, AL 36726: Free brochure ◆ Fresh-shelled pecans. 800-967-3226. joepecan@mont.mindspring.com

## Pasta & Sauces

**B & L Specialty Foods Inc.,** P.O. Box 80068, Seattle, WA 98108: Free catalog ◆ Imported pasta, oils, and Italian specialties. 800-EAT-PASTA.

**Cuisine Perel,** 3100 Kerner Blvd., San Rafael, CA 94901: Free catalog ◆ Flavored and colored pasta. 800-88-PEREL; 415-456-4406 (in CA).

**DeCio Pasta Inc.,** P.O. Box 4391, Cave Creek, AZ 85331: Free catalog ◆ Herbs, spices, and vegetable purees for pasta recipes. 800-97-0770.

**Elena's by Houlihan's,** Culinary Traditions Ltd., 70 S. Squirrel Rd., Ste. H, Auburn Hills, MI 48326: Free list of retail sources ◆ Low-fat pasta sauces. 800-72-ELENA.

**Ferrara Foods & Confections Inc.,** 195 Grand St., New York, NY 10013: Free brochure ◆ Coffee, candy, syrups, sauces, bread sticks, vegetables, pasta, baked goods, and Italian specialties. 212-226-6150.

**Flying Noodle Pasta,** 1 Arrowhead Rd., Duxbury, MA 02332: Free brochure ◆ Pasta specialties. 800-566-0599. www.flyingnoodle.com

**Fortuna's Sausage Company,** 975 Greenville Ave., Greenville, RI 02828: Free catalog ◆ All-natural dry cured Italian sausages, sausage-making kit, pasta, imported Italian cheese, gift baskets, and natural New England specialties. 800-42-SOUPY. SOUPY@Edgenet.net

**Lanvino,** P.O. Box 6724, Whitneyville, CT 06517: Free list of retail sources ◆ All-natural sauces and pesto for pasta, seafood, meat, and poultry. 203-230-9362.

**Locus Foods Inc.,** P.O. Box 1531, Findlay, OH 45840: Free information ◆ Caribbean black bean soup, Italian beans and pasta, Senate soup mix, New Orleans beans and rice, and other all-bean mixes. 800-MR-BEANS; 419-425-1118 (in OH).

**Morisi's Pasta,** 186 8th St., Brooklyn, NY 11215: Catalog $2.50 (refundable) ◆ All-natural pasta. 800-253-6044. moripasta@aol.com

**Mountain Ark Trading Company,** P.O. Box 3170, Fayetteville, AR 72702: Free information ◆ Vegetables, miso, seasonings, rice, pasta, fruit, spreads, oils, beans, and soups. 800-643-8909.

**Pasta Fresca,** P.O. Box 243, 112 S. Main St., New Lexington, OH 43764: Free list of retail sources ◆ Flavored dried pasta in a variety of shapes. 800-343-5266.

**Pasta Mama's,** 1270 Lee Blvd., Richland, WA 99352: Free list of retail sources ◆ Kosher parve egg and cholesterol-free pasta and low-fat sauces. 800-456-4045; 509-946-8282 (in WA).

**Premier Pasta,** 1817 S. Holladay Dr., Seaside, OR 97138: Free brochure ◆ Pasta and sauce mixes. 503-738-3692.

**Rossi Pasta,** P.O. Box 759, Marietta, OH 45750: Free brochure ◆ Black olive, linguine, garlic fettuccini, saffron linguine, and other pasta. 800-227-6774.

**Savoia Foods Inc.,** 85 Independence Way, Chicago Heights, IL 60411: Free catalog ◆ Fresh homemade pastas. 800-867-2782.

**Todaro Brothers,** 555 2nd Ave., New York, NY 10016: Catalog $1 ◆ Cheese, pasta, dried mushrooms, olives and olive oil, legumes, truffles and porcini, grains, vinegars, and other specialties. 212-532-0633.

**Teitel Brothers,** 2372 Arthur Ave., Bronx, NY 10458: Free catalog ◆ Aged cheese, extra virgin cold pressed olive oil, porcini mushrooms, pasta, and Italian specialties. 800-850-7055.

**Wagner Gourmet Foods,** 900 Jacksonville Rd., Ivyland, PA 18974: Free brochure ◆ Soups and chili, spices and spicy specialties, Mexican specialties, salsa, and barbecue and pasta sauces. 800-392-2041. www.wagner-gourmet.com

**Zingerman's Delicatessen,** 422 Detroit St., Ann Arbor, MI 48104: Free catalog ◆ Domestic and imported cheese, ethnic and low-fat specialties, condiments, baked goods, pasta, and traditional Jewish foods. 888-636-8162. zing@chamber.ann-arbor.mi.us

## Popcorn

**Black Shield Inc.,** 5356 Pan American Freeway NE, Albuquerque, NM 87109: Free information ◆ Gourmet flavored popcorn. 800-653-9357. www.crownjewels.com

**Fisher's Popcorn,** 200 South Boardwalk, Ocean City, MD 21842: Free brochure ◆ Caramel popcorn. 410-289-5638.

**Garrett Popcorn Shops,** Mail Order Division, Box 11342, Chicago, IL 60611: Free brochure ◆ Caramel-flavored popcorn specialties. 888-476-7267; 311-944-4730 (in IL). www.garrettpopcorn.com

**Karmelkorn,** 320 Northtown Dr., Blaine, MN 55434: Free information ◆ Flavored popcorn packed in decorative gift canisters. 612-780-2807. www.3lefties/com/karmelkorn.html.

**Myers Gourmet Popcorn,** 8025 W. Hwy. 24, Cascade, CO 80809: Free brochure ◆ Gourmet popcorn. 800-684-1155. www.users.aol.com/mgp

**Popcorn Factory,** Mail Order Dept., P.O. Box 4530, Lake Bluff, IL 60044: Free catalog ◆ Butter-flavored, Cheddar cheese, homemade caramel, and other popcorn favorites. 800-541-2676. www.thepopcornfactory.com

**Popcorn World Inc.,** 2303 Princeton Rd., P.O. Box 507, Trenton, MO 64683: Free brochure ◆ Butter, caramel, cheese, cinnamon, cinnamon with almonds and pecans, vanilla-butter with almonds, and popcorn with pecans. 800-443-8226.

**Rural Route 1 Popcorn,** RR 1, Hwy. 80, Livingston, WI 53554: Free brochure ◆ Popcorn gifts and snacks. 800-828-8115; 608-943-8283 (in WI). www.ruralroute1.com

## Preserves, Jellies, & Honey

**American Spoon Foods,** P.O. Box 566, Petoskey, MI 49770: Free information ◆ Fruit preserves and jellies, pumpkin butter, rhubarb marmalade, and fruit conserves. 800-222-5886. www.spoon.com

**Arkansas Blue Heron Farms,** Rt. 2, Box 323, Lowell, AR 72745: Free catalog ◆ Blueberry jam and marmalades and Amaretto dessert sauce. 800-225-6849.

**Best Products Company,** 3806 Fond Du Lac Dr., Richfield, WI 53076: Free catalog ◆ Fat-free whipped honey spreads and mixes for muffins, pancakes, and scones. 414-644-6239.

**Beth's Farm Kitchen,** P.O. Box 113, Stuyvesant Falls, NY 12174: Free catalog ◆ Jams, preserves, spreads, chutneys, mustards, and vinegars. 800-331-JAMS. beth4jam@aol.com

**Blackberry Patch,** Rt. 7, Box 918C, Tallahassee, FL 32308: Free list of retail sources ◆ Jellies, fresh fruit jams, syrups, honey, and salad dressings. 800-8-JELLY-8; 850-893-3183 (in FL).

**Carp River Trading Company,** 6005 E. Traverse Hwy., Traverse City, MI 49864: Free catalog ◆ Fruit preserves. 800-526-9876.

**Cascade Conserves Inc.,** P.O. Box 8306, Portland, OR 97207: Free brochure ◆ All-natural low-sugar conserves and fruit syrups. 800-846-7396; 503-243-3608 (in OR).

**Cheri's Desert Harvest,** 1840 E. Winsett St., Tucson, AZ 85719: Free information ◆ Cholesterol and fat-free all-natural Southwestern preserves and syrups. 800-743-1141; 520-623-4141 (in AZ).

**Chukar Cherries,** P.O. Box 510, Prosser, WA 99350: Free catalog ◆ Cherry preserves and sauces. 800-624-9544.

**Clearbrook Farms,** 5514 Fair Ln., Fairfax, OH 45227: Free brochure ◆ Semi-sweet chocolate sauce, fruit sauces, and marmalades. 800-222-9966; 513-271-2053 (in OH).

**Colonel Bill Newsom's Hams,** Newsom's Old Mill Store, 208 E. Main St., Princeton, KY 42445: Free information ◆ Fruit preserves, fruit-sweetened spreads, relishes, sorghum, hickory-smoked ham, and other meats. 502-365-2482.

**Crabtree & Evelyn Limited,** P.O. Box 167, Woodstock Hill, CT 06281: Catalog $3.50 ◆ English biscuits and cookies, gingerbread, ginger and butter-ginger cookies, Scottish shortbread, Belgian chocolates, cheese wafers and biscuits from Holland, Italian biscuits, preserves, marmalades, jellies, honey, English sauces, spices and condiments, herbs, tea, and candy. 800-624-5211. www.crabtree-evelyn.com

**Critter Spreads Inc.,** 1746 Academy Rd., Bellingham, WA 98226: Free brochure ◆ Fruit spreads and muffin mixes. 800-447-5847. www.critterspreads.com

**Dutch Gold Honey Inc.,** 2220 Dutch Gold Dr., Lancaster, PA 17601: Free list of retail sources ◆ All-natural honey spreads. 717-393-1716.

**Four Oaks Farm Inc.,** P.O. Box 987, Lexington, SC 29071: Free brochure ◆ Country-style ham and bacon, jams, jellies, pickles, relishes, salad dressings, cakes, and other favorites. 800-858-5006; 803-356-3194 (in SC). fouroaks@scsn.net

**Glorybee Honey & Supplies,** P.O. Box 2744, Eugene, OR 97402: Catalog 50¢ ◆ Beekeeping and honey processing supplies, honey, honey-prepared foods, and gift assortments. 800-456-7923; 541-689-0913 (in OR).

**Grandma's Spice Shop,** Spice Valley Way, Upper Tract, WV 26866: Free catalog ◆ Teas, coffees, cocoa, spices, and herbs. 304-358-2345.

**Hadley Fruit Orchards,** P.O. Box 246, Cabazon, CA 92230: Free catalog ◆ Jams and jellies, dried fruits, nuts, candy, and honey. 800-854-5655.

**Harlow's Sugar House,** RD 1, Box 395, Putney, VT 05346: Free brochure ◆ Maple syrup and specialties, jams, jellies, and Vermont cheese. 802-387-5852.

**Harry & David,** P.O. Box 712, Medford, OR 97501: Free catalog ◆ Fruit preserves, fruits, baked specialties, desserts, and gift assortments. 800-345-5655. www.harryanddavid.com

**Honey Acres,** Hwy. 67 North, Ashippun, WI 53003: Free information ◆ Honey, honey-fruit spreads, candy, beeswax candles, mustards, gifts, and cookbooks. 800-558-7745.

**Jan's Sweetness & Light Shop,** Pot o' Gold Honey Company, P.O. Box 1200, Hemingway, SC 29554: Free brochure ◆ Honey specialties and gift assortments. 803-558-9598. www.users.aol.com/SweetnessL/sweetlit.htm

**Knott's Berry Farm,** P.O. Box 1989, Placentia, CA 92670: Free catalog ◆ Jellies and preserves, cheese, sausage, candy, cakes, cookies, and dried fruit. 800-877-6887.

**Kozlowski Farms,** 5566 Gravenstein Hwy. North, Forestville, CA 95436: Free brochure ◆ Marmalades, jams, preserves, honey, mustards, barbecue sauce, fruit butters, sugar-free berry vinegars, conserves, and chutney. 707-887-1587.

**Limited Edition Presents,** 604 S. Marienfeld, Midland, TX 79701: Free list of retail sources ◆ Honey butters. 800-926-8188; 915-686-2008 (in TX).

**Linn's Fruit Bin,** 2485 Village Ln., Cambria, CA 93428: Free catalog ◆ Low-sugar preserves and sugar-free fruit spreads. 800-676-1670.

**Lollipop Tree Inc.,** 319 Vaughan St., Portsmouth, NH 03801: Free list of retail sources ◆ All-natural preserves, condiments, and baking mixes. 800-842-6691.

**Maury Island Farm,** P.O. Box L, Vashon, WA 98070: Free brochure ◆ Preserves. 800-356-5880.

**The Mayhaw Tree,** P.O. Box 3430, Peachtree City, GA 30269: Free information ◆ Sauces, mustard, preserves, and Mayhaw berry jelly, sauce, and syrup. 800-262-9429.

**McCutcheon Apple Products Inc.,** P.O. Box 243, Frederick, MD 21705: Free information ◆ Apple butter, preserves, relishes, dessert toppings, salad dressings, honey, hot sauces, and specialties. 800-875-3451. www.mccutcheons.com

**Midway Plantation,** HC-62, Box 77, Waterproof, LA 71375: Free information ◆ Country-fresh jams and jellies. 800-336-JAMS.

**Millicent's Preserves,** 2028 Primrose Ave., South Pasadena, CA 91030: Free list of retail sources ◆ All-natural jams, jellies, marmalades, and butters. 626-682-1233.

**Moon Shine Trading Company,** 1250A Harter Ave., Woodland, CA 95694: Free catalog ◆ California honey apricot spread and other tangy fruit spreads. Varietal honeys from across the United States, and nut butters. 800-678-1226; 916-753-0601 (in CA). www.moonshinetrading.com

**New Canaan Farms,** P.O. Box 386, Dripping Springs, TX 78620: Free brochure ◆ Ice cream toppings, jellies and jams, mustard, and specialties. 800-727-5267.

**Oregon Apiaries,** P.O. Box 1078, Newberg, OR 97132: Free information ◆ Honey, honey cream spreads, and fruit-honey syrups. 800-676-1078.

**Oregon Hill Farms Inc.,** 32861 Pittsburgh Rd., St. Helens, OR 97051: Free information ◆ Naturally sweetened fruit spreads. 800-243-4541.

**Pan Handler Products Inc.,** 1799 Mountain Rd., Stowe, VT 05672: Free brochure ◆ Conserves, jams, and jellies. 800-338-5354.

**Penelope's of Evergreen Ltd.,** P.O. Box 2863, Evergreen, CO 80439: Free list of retail sources ◆ Artificial color and additive-free wine jellies and sauces. 800-748-3443.

**Rock Cheese Company,** 110 Elm St., Madison, WI 53705: Free brochure ◆ Cheese favorites, honey products, seasonings, and condiments. Also gift assortments. 608-233-7681.

**Rocky Top Farms,** RR 1, Box 163, Ellsworth, MI 49729: Free information ◆ All-natural additive-free preserves and fruit butters. 800-862-9303.

**Rowena's,** 758 W. 22nd, Norfolk, VA 23517: Free information ◆ Cakes, preserves and jams, and cooking sauces. 800-627-8699. www.rowenas.com

**St. Dalfour Conserves,** 2180 Oakdale Dr., Philadelphia, PA 19125: Free information ◆ No-sugar added, all-natural conserves imported from France. 800-523-3811.

**Sarabeth's Kitchen,** 2291 2nd Ave., New York, NY 10035: Free brochure ◆ Marmalades, preserves, additive and preservative-free fruit butters, chunky apple butter, and cranberry relish. 800-552-JAMS.

**Traphagen Honey,** HCR 1, Box 36, Hunter, NY 12442: Free brochure ◆ Honey spreads, baked goods, candy, preserves and jams, and condiments. 800-838-9194.

**Trillium International,** 310 Willow Ln., New Holland, PA 17557: Free information ◆ Specialty honeys and honey products. 717-354-4503.

**Virginia Diner,** P.O. Box 1030, Rt. 460, Wakefield, VA 23888: Free catalog ◆ Homemade jellies and jams, Virginia bacon and ham, fudge, peanuts, and peanut specialties. 800-642-6887. www.vadiner.com

**Whistling Wings Farms,** 427 West St., Biddeford, ME 04005: Free brochure ◆ Low calorie spreadable fruits, syrups, and sauces; vinegars; and muffin mixes and other food products that are naturally fat-free and contain no preservatives or cholesterol. 800-765-8989; 207-282-1146 (in ME). www.wwfarm.com

**Wood's Cider Mill,** RFD 2, Box 477, Springfield, VT 05156: Free catalog with long SASE ◆ Maple syrup, cider jelly and syrup, and boiled cider. 802-263-5547.

**Zimmerman Foods,** 1980 New Danville Pike, Lancaster, PA 17603: Free catalog ◆ All-natural jams, jellies, and relishes. 717-393-4240.

## Salt-free & Low-salt

**Ener-G Foods,** P.O. Box 84487, Seattle, WA 98124: Free information ◆ Low-sodium, gluten-free, low-protein, and non-allergenic foods. 800-331-5222. www.ener-g.com

**HeartyMix Company,** 1231 Madison Hill Rd., Rahway, NJ 07065: Free catalog ◆ Salt-free bread, wheat-free products, and preservative-, cholesterol-, and saturated fat-free baking mixes for cookies and cakes. 732-382-3010.

**How Sweet It Is,** P.O. Box 376, Jenkintown, PA 19046: Free information ◆ Low-fat and salt or sugar-free candy. 215-784-9980. www.howsweet.com

## Seafood

**Alaskan Harvest Seafood,** P.O. Box 31179, Seattle, WA 98103: Free catalog ◆ Crab, salmon, halibut, scallops, shrimp, and smoked fish. 800-824-6389. www.alaskanharvest.com

**Annapolis Seafood Market,** 1300 Forest Dr., Annapolis, MD 21403: Free information ◆ Next-day air shipment of soft-shell crabs. 410-263-7787.

**The Antique Mall & Crown Restaurant,** P.O. Box 540, Indianola, MS 38751: Free information ◆ Catfish paté and pie mixes. 800-833-7731; 601-887-2522 (in MS).

**Assouline & Ting Inc.,** 314 Brown St., Philadelphia, PA 19123: Free information ◆ Imported and domestic caviar, smoked fish, snails, and specialties. 800-521-4491; 215-627-3000 (in PA). www.caviarassouline.com

**Baycliff Company Inc.,** 242 E. 72nd St., New York, NY 10021: Free information ◆ Sushi-making products and equipment. 212-772-6078.

**Bayley's Lobster Pound,** P.O. Box 304, Scarborough, ME 04074: Free information ◆ Live and cooked lobsters, lobster meat, shrimp, scallops, and Maine crabmeat. 800-932-6456; 207-883-4571 (in ME). www.bayleys.com

**Beach Seafood Market,** 1100 Shrimpboat Ln., P.O. Box 2490, Fort Myers Beach, FL 33932: Free catalog ◆ Fresh-frozen shrimp, crab, and spiny lobster. 800-771-5050.

**Blue Heron Fruit Shippers,** P.O. Box 936, Sarasota, FL 34234: Free brochure ◆ Tree-ripened citrus fruit, candy, marmalades, pecans, Southern foods, stone crab claws, and honey. 800-237-3920; 941-954-1605 (in FL). blueheron1@compuserve.com

**Carolina Blue Smoked Fish,** 1378 Deck Rd., Deck, NC 27949: Free brochure ◆ Natural-smoked seafood from North Carolina's Outer Banks. 800-589-1690.

**Carolina Mountain,** 9 Industrial Park Blvd., Andrews, NC 28901: Free information ◆ Fresh and smoked salmon and trout. 800-722-9477.

**Carolina Smoked Specialties Inc.,** 215 S. Mullins St., Mullins, SC 29574: Free information ◆ Oak-apple-smoked trout fillets. 803-464-4627.

**Caviar House Inc.,** 687 NE 79th St., Miami, FL 33138: Free catalog ◆ Imported fresh Russian caviar, smoked Scottish salmon, foie gras, and truffles. 800-522-8427.

**Chesapeake Bay Gourmet,** 3916 Old North Point Rd., Baltimore, MD 21222: Free information ◆ Crab cakes, crab imperial, crab quiche, crab soup, and other seafood specialties. 800-432-CRAB; 410-477-8790 (in MD). www.cbgourmet.com

**Chesapeake Express,** 1129 Hope Rd., Centreville, MD 21617: Free brochure ◆ Maryland's Eastern Shore backfin meat crab cakes, oysters, and soft shell crabs. Delivered ready to heat and serve. 800-282-CRAB.

**Clambake Celebrations,** 9 West Rd., Skaket Corners, Orleans, MA 02653: Free information ◆ Cape Cod seafood dinners with live lobsters, shellfish, and fresh corn. Ready to cook, they are shipped air direct to your door. 800-423-4038. www.netplaza.com/clambake

**Cotuit Oyster Company,** P.O. Box 563, Little River Rd., Cotuit, MA 02635: Free catalog ◆ New England oysters and cherrystone clams. 508-428-6747.

**Down East Direct,** 77 Atlantic Ave., Boothbay Harbor, ME 04538: Free information ◆ Fresh live lobsters shipped overnight. 800-972-1454.

**Ducktrap River Fish Farm Inc.,** RR 2, Box 378, Lincolnville, ME 04849: Free brochure ◆ Naturally smoked seafood from Maine. 800-828-3825.

**S. Wallace Edwards & Sons Inc.,** P.O. Box 25, Surry, VA 23883: Free catalog ◆ Preserves from the Blue Ridge Mountains, seafood from the Eastern Shore, and hickory-smoked Virginia ham, bacon, and sausage. 800-222-4267. www.virginiatraditions.com

**Fisherman's Fleet,** 689 Salem, Malden, MA 02148: Free information ◆ Overnight delivery of Maine lobsters, other shellfish, fresh and frozen fish, lobster bisque, clam chowder, and more. 888-376-6732; 781-322-5200 (in MA). www.freshfish.net

**The Fishermen's Net,** 849 Forest Ave., Portland, ME 04103: Free brochure ◆ Fresh Maine lobsters shipped direct. 800-556-2783; 772-9056 (in ME).

**Francesca's Favorites,** Mail Order Dept., 2046 McKinley St., Hollywood, FL 33020: Free catalog ◆ Florida-fresh stone crabs and other seafood. 800-865-2722.

**Gerard & Dominique Seafood,** P.O. Box 1845, Bothell, WA 98041: Free brochure ◆ Smoked salmon. 800-858-0449.

**Gourmet Snail Ranch Ltd.,** P.O. Box 202, Hathaway Pines, CA 95223: Free brochure ◆ Fresh, frozen, or blanched custom grown escargot. www.goldrush.net/gsr

**Graffam Brothers,** Box 340, Rockport, ME 04856: Free information ◆ Live Maine lobsters. 207-236-8391.

**Green Turtle Cannery,** P.O. Box 585, Islamorada, Florida Keys 33036: Free information ◆ Turtle and conch chowder, spicy soup stocks, and other seafood. 305-664-4918.

**Grossman's Seafood Inc.,** P.O. Box 205, West Mystic, CT 06388: Free information ◆ Steamers, mussels, shelled sea scallops, oysters in the shell. Also seafood dinners and clambakes. Features next day shipping. 800-742-5511. www.lobster2go.com

**Hagensborg Foods U.S.A. Inc.,** P.O. Box 6058, Kent, WA 98064: Free information ◆ Smoked salmon, shrimp, and ready-to-spread salmon and shrimp pates. 800-851-1771; 253-395-9373 (in WA).

**Handy Softshell Crawfish,** P.O. Box 309, Crisfield, MD 21817: Free brochure ◆ Softshell crabs and crawfish. 800-426-3977.

**Hegg & Hegg,** 801 Marine Dr., Port Angeles, WA 98363: Free information ◆ Pacific Northwest smoked salmon, nova smoked salmon, Puget Sound red sockeye salmon steaks, sturgeon, shrimp, baby clams, tuna, smoked shad, and dungeness crab meat seafood. 800-435-3474; 360-457-3344 (in WA).

**Homarus Inc.,** 76 Kisco Ave., Mount Kisco, NY 10549: Free brochure ◆ Cured salmon smoked in pastrami spices, smoked trout, and Norwegian smoked salmon. 800-666-8992.

**Horton's Seafood,** 809 Broadway, East Providence, RI 02914: Free catalog ◆ Naturally smoked Maine salmon, mussels, trout, shrimp, mackerel, and blue fish. 401-434-3116.

**Houston Seafood Corp.,** 6115 Skyline, Houston, TX 77257: Free information ◆ Seafood specialties from around the world. 800-953-1472.

**Indian Hill Farms,** 213 Old Indian Rd., Milton, NY 12547: Free catalog ◆ Smoked whole turkey and turkey breast, Kosher turkey, smoked ham, Norwegian smoked salmon, and brandied fruitcake. 914-795-2700.

**Josephson's Smokehouse,** 106 Marine Dr., Astoria, OR 97103: Free catalog ◆ Preservative-free smoked salmon and oysters, scallops, boneless trout and sturgeon, salmon steaks, and sturgeon caviar. 800-772-3474.

**Katch Seafoods,** P.O. Box 2677, Homer, AK 99603: Free information ◆ Halibut and red salmon steaks. 800-368-7400; 907-7953 (in AK).

**Kirkland Custom Seafood,** P.O. Box 2040, Kirkland, WA 98083: Free brochure ◆ Smoked and canned salmon, oysters, sturgeon, trout, and pates. 800-321-3474.

**Legal Sea Foods,** 33 Everett St., Boston, MA 02134: Free brochure ◆ Overnight shipment of fresh seafood. 800-343-5804. www.lsf.com

**The Lobster Net,** P.O. Box 146, Beverly, MA 01915: Free information ◆ Shrimp, clams, live lobsters, and other seafood. 978-631-7728. www.pactive.com/lobsters

**Mahogany Smoked Meats,** P.O. Box 1387, Bishop, CA 93515: Free brochure ◆ Smoked jerky, Cheddar cheese, chileno peppers and stuffed olives, smoked trout, and other specialties. 888-624-6426.

**Maine Lobster Direct,** 48 Union Wharf, Portland, ME 04101: Free brochure ◆ Hardshell Maine lobsters, lobster with optional steamer clams dinners, gift baskets, lobster tails, and more. 800-556-2783.

**The Marketplace Food Store,** 521 W. Diversey, Chicago, IL 60614: Free information ◆ Overnight delivery of crab favorites. 800-998-2271.

**Nelson Crab Inc.,** 3088 Kindred Ave., P.O. Box 520, Tokeland, WA 98590: Free brochure ◆ Dungeness crab, smoked sturgeon and shad, albacore tuna, chinook and blueback salmon, minced razor clams, and Pacific shrimp. 800-262-0069; 360-267-2911 (in WA).

**Northern Discovery Seafoods Inc.,** P.O. Box 310, Grapeview, WA 98546: Free catalog ◆ Smoked salmon and other seafood products from Pacific Northwest waters. 800-843-6921; 360-275-7246 (in WA).

**Oregon Cupboard,** P.O. Box 30895, Portland, OR 97294: Free brochure ◆ Salmon fillets, salmon jerky, salmon pate, sturgeon and other smoked seafood specialties, jams and other fruit spreadables, pie fillings, syrups, and fat-free peanut brittle. 800-442-3653. www.oregoncupboard.com

**Port Chatham Smoked Seafood,** 632 NW 46th St., Seattle, WA 98107: Free brochure ◆ Hand-packed smoked Sockeye, Coho, and kipper-smoked salmon, salmon pate, smoked rainbow trout and rainbow trout pate, smoked sturgeon, Pacific Northwest oysters, and Dungeness crab. 800-872-5666; 206-783-8200 (in WA).

**Rent Mother Nature,** P.O. Box 193, 52 New St., Cambridge, MA 02238: Free catalog ◆ Clam, lobster, mussels, cod, onion, and potato seafood dinners for two and four persons in a reusable enameled pot. Includes corn, when in season. 800-232-4048.

**Salsa Vita,** 600 E. Northern Lights Blvd., Anchorage, AK 99503: Free information ◆ Skinless and boneless canned salmon packaged with jalapenos. 907-274-5830.

**Scottish Crown Ltd.,** 1704 Thomasville Rd., Ste. 115, Tallahassee, FL 32303: Free information ◆ Scottish smoked salmon. 800-331-3001.

**SeaBear,** 605 30th St., P.O. Box 591, Anacortes, WA 98221: Free catalog ◆ Alderwood-smoked Pacific Northwest sockeye salmon and oysters. 800-645-3474. www.seabear.com

**Seafood Direct,** P.O. Box 1836, Woodinville, WA 98072: Free brochure ◆ Canned fresh sockeye salmon, kippered salmon, trout pate, smoked trout and oysters, and salmon pate. 800-732-1836.

**Shore to Door Seafood,** 5151 NW 17th St., Margate, FL 33063: Free brochure ◆ Next-day shipping of seafood. 800-218-8147. www.shoretodoor.com

**Silver Lining Seafood,** Box 6092, Ketchikan, AK 99901: Free brochure ◆ Smoked salmon and other seafood specialties. 907-225-6664.

**Simply Shrimp,** 7794 NW 44th St., Fort Lauderdale, FL 33351: Free information ◆ Seafood from the Gulf and around the world. Also Florida stone-crab claws (when in season). 800-833-0888.

**Smokehouse,** 1906 Pike Place Market, Seattle, WA 98101: Free brochure ◆ Alderwood-smoked red sockeye salmon and other seafood. 800-972-5666.

**Stacey's Foods Inc.,** 1757 E. Bayshore Rd., Redwood City, CA 94063: Free catalog ◆ Assorted all-natural seafood patties. 800-782-2395.

**Sullivan Harbor Farms,** Rt. 1, P.O. Box 96, Sullivan Harbor, ME 04664: Free information ◆ Maine smoked salmon. 207-422-3735.

**Summerfield Farm,** 10044 James Monroe Hwy., Culpeper, VA 22701: Free brochure ◆ Veal, venison, lamb, sausage, prime beef, game birds, and smoked salmon halves. 540-547-9600.

**10th & M Seafoods,** 1020 M St., Anchorage, AK 99501: Free catalog ◆ Prawns, scallops, lox, king crab, halibut, shrimp, smoked and fresh salmon, and seafood. 907-272-3474.

**Villa Tatra Colorado,** 729 Pinewood Dr., Lyons, CO 80540: Free information ◆ Preservative-free all-natural smoked salmon, trout, and sausage. 800-430-4003.

**Weathervane Seafood,** Public Landing, Belfast, ME 04915: Free information ◆ Maine lobsters, steaming clams, fantail shrimp, scallops, and other seafood specialties. 800-914-1774.

**Wisconsin Fishing Company,** P.O. Box 965, Green Bay, WI 54305: Free catalog ◆ Shrimp, lobster, crab, herring, smoked fish, and other seafood. 800-527-3590.

## Seasonings, Condiments, & Oils

**Alabama Sunshine,** P.O. Box 263, Fayette, AL 35555: Free catalog ◆ Jalapeno hot sauce, Tabasco pepper sauce, and other seasonings and condiments. 205-932-3933.

**Alfa Casa Company,** 1925 Borneman St., Elkhart, IN 46517: Free list of retail sources ◆ Dressings and marinades for fish, poultry, beef, and pork. 800-293-5070.

**Almond Plaza,** Catalog Order Center, P.O. Box 426, Maumee, OH 43537: Free catalog ◆ Herbs, almonds, and candy. 800-225-6887. www.almond-plaza.com

**The Alternative Food Cooperative,** 3362 Kingston Rd., West Kinston, RI 02892: Free information ◆ Organic fruits and vegetables, spices, and herbs. 401-789-2240.

**Anjo's Imports,** P.O. Box 4031, Cerritos, CA 90703: Free information ◆ All-natural, MSG and preservative-free sauces and seasonings. 562-865-9544.

**Arden's Gardens,** 4603 Berkshire, Detroit, MI 48224: Free catalog ◆ Vinegars, mustards, salsa, herb blends, and specialties. 810-882-2222.

**Ashman Manufacturing & Distributing Company,** P.O. Box 1068, Sea Pines Station, Virginia Beach, VA 23451: Free list of retail sources ◆ Marinades for fresh vegetables, beef, and fresh tuna steaks. 800-641-9924; 757-428-6734 (in VA).

**Assouline & Ting Inc.,** 314 Brown St., Philadelphia, PA 19123: Free information ◆ Fruit and nut extracts, vinegars, and olive, nut, and specialty oils. 800-521-4491; 215-627-3000 (in PA). www.caviarassouline.com

**Atlantic Spice Company,** P.O. Box 205, North Truro, MA 02652: Free information ◆ Bulk herbs and spices. 800-316-7965. www.atlanticspice.com

**Aussom Aussie Products,** 730 Carraige Rd., Ste. 1B, Pittsburgh, PA 15220: Free brochure ◆ Hot pepper seasoning blends, barbecue seasonings and sauces, and more. 888-742-6283. www.AussieQ.com

**Bachri's Chili & Spice Gourmet,** 5617 Villa Haven, Pittsburgh, PA 15236: Free brochure ◆ Indonesian sauces and spices.

**Charles Baldwin & Sons,** 1 Center St., West Stockbridge, MA 01266: Free price list with long SASE ◆ Pure vanilla extract, imitation vanilla, other flavors and extracts, spices, Dutch process cocoa, and walnut pieces. 413-232-7785.

**Beth's Farm Kitchen,** P.O. Box 113, Stuyvesant Falls, NY 12174: Free catalog ◆ Jams, preserves, spreads, chutneys, mustards, and vinegars. 800-331-JAMS. beth4jam@aol.com

**Bickford Flavors,** 19007 St. Clair Ave., Cleveland, OH 44117: Free list ◆ Flavorings, extracts, oils, and syrups. 800-283-8322; 440-531-6006 (in OH).

**Big Dix,** 2674 Broadwater Dr., Gulfport, MS 39507: Free information ◆ Mild, medium, and hot all-natural preservative and cholesterol-free, with no sugar added sauces. 800-366-0824.

**Blackberry Patch,** Rt. 7, Box 918C, Tallahassee, FL 32308: Free list of retail sources ◆ Jellies, fresh fruit jams, syrups, honey, and salad dressings. 800-8-JELLY-8; 850-893-3183 (in FL).

**Blanchard & Blanchard Ltd.,** P.O. Box 1080, Norwich, VT 05055: Free information ◆ Preservative-free natural salad dressings, dessert sauces, mustards, glazes, and marinades. 802-295-9200.

**Blue Sky Farm,** P.O. Box 1178, Wells, ME 04090: Free catalog ◆ Seasonings, vinegars, and condiments blended from organically grown herbs. 800-7BLU-SKY.

**Boetje's Foods Inc.,** 2736 12th St., Rock Island, IL 61201: Free information ◆ Stone-ground Dutch mustard. 309-788-4352.

**Cactus Concoctions,** P.O. Box 274, Burnt Hills, NY 12027: Free catalog ◆ Spiced Cajun, Habaneras, salsa, mustard, herb and spice combinations, and other hot sauces. 888-468-8371; 518-384-1979 (in NY).

**California-Antilles Trading,** 3735 Adams Ave., San Diego, CA 92116: Free information ◆ Hot sauces, salsas, cookbooks. Bodycare products from the Caribbean and Mexico. 619-283-4834.

**Campagna Distinctive Flavors,** 40759 McDowell Creek Dr., Lebanon, OR 97355: Free information ◆ Herb and pepper jellies and chive, dill, and peppercorn vinegars. 800-959-4372; 541-258-6806 (in OR).

**Canterbury's Crack & Peel Inc.,** 109½ Pleasant St., Claremont, NH 03743: Free information ◆ Fresh garlic dressings and marinades made with natural ingredients. 888-705-4779.

**Caribbean Spice Company,** 8 S. Church St., Fairhope, AL 36532: Free catalog ◆ Hot sauces and condiments from around the world. 800-990-6088.

**Carp River Trading Company,** 6005 E. Traverse Hwy., Traverse City, MI 49864: Free catalog ◆ Vegetable dips, salsa, vinaigrettes, mustards, and other condiments. 800-526-9876.

**Century Sauce Kitchens,** P.O. Box 4057, Copley, OH 44321: Free information ◆ Habanera and Thai pepper sauces with fresh garlic, herbs, and spices. 800-831-4687; 330-666-2578 (in OH).

**Chile La Isla,** P.O. Box 1379, Fabena, TX 79838: Free information ◆ Quick-frozen chile peppers. 800-895-4603.

**Chukar Cherries,** P.O. Box 510, Prosser, WA 99350: Free catalog ◆ Cherry sauces, salsa, and relishes. 800-624-9544.

**Classic KC BBQ Sauces,** 6105 Manning, Raytown, MO 64133: Free brochure ◆ Barbecue sauces from Kansas City's famous barbecue restaurants. 816-356-9278. www.worldmall.com/bbq

**Colonel Bill Newsom's Hams,** Newsom's Old Mill Store, 208 E. Main St., Princeton, KY 42445: Free information ◆ Vidalia onion salad dressing, corn relish, mild or hot chow chow, preserves, and hickory-smoked ham, sorghum, and other smoked meats. 502-365-2482.

**Corti Brothers,** 5810 Folsom Blvd., Sacramento, CA 95819: Free newsletter ◆ Chinese teas, regional olive oils, vintage cognac, and other food and drink specialties. 916-736-3800.

**Crabtree & Evelyn Limited,** P.O. Box 167, Woodstock Hill, CT 06281: Catalog $3.50 ◆ English mustards and chutney, herbs and spices, French mustard and mustard sauces, oils and vinegars, fruit vinegars and syrups, preserves, biscuits and cookies, and candy. 800-624-5211. www.crabtree-evelyn.com

**Crazy Cajun Enterprises Inc.,** P.O. Box 804, Cobb, CA 95426: Free information ◆ Authentic Cajun sauces.

**Dat'l Do-It World Headquarters,** 3255 Parker Dr., St. Augustine, FL 32095: Free catalog ◆ Hot sauces. 800-468-3285.

**Dave's Gourmet,** 1255 Montgomery Ave., San Bruno, CA 94066: Free information ◆ Sauces, salsa, and other condiments. 800-758-0372. www.davesgourmet.com

**Delegeane Garlic Farms,** P.O. Box 2561, Yountville, Napa Valley, CA 94599: Free brochure ◆ Fresh garlic, chili ristras, salt-free herb seasonings, and California wildflower honey. 800-726-6692.

**Desert Rose Foods Inc.,** P.O. Box 5391, Tucson, AZ 85703: Free brochure ◆ Salsa, spicy mesquite honey-based barbecue sauce, spicy Italian peppers, and tortilla chips. 800-937-2572. www.desertrosefoods.com

**East Earth Trade Winds,** P.O. Box 493151, 1620 E. Cypress Ave., Ste. 8, Redding, CA 96049: Catalog $1 ◆ Traditional Chinese herbs and herb products. 800-258-6878. www.snowcrest.net/eetw

**Eden Foods,** 701 Tecumseh Rd., Clinton, MI 49236: Free information ◆ Organic foods. 800-424-EDEN.

**El Paso Chile Company,** 909 Texas Ave., El Paso, TX 79901: Free information ◆ Chili and spice blends. 800-27-IS-HOT. www.elpasochile.com

**Elderflower Farm,** 501 Callahan Rd., Roseburg, OR 97470: Free brochure ◆ Organically-grown herbs. 541-672-9803. eff@rosenet.net

**Farmers Pick,** 10400 Overland Rd., #393, Boise, ID 83709: Catalog $1 (refundable) ◆ Short and long garlic braids, braids with culinary herbs, wreaths, elephant garlic, and other varieties. 208-333-0066. www.farmerspick.com

**Fire & Spice,** 757 Hwy. 97E, #14-246, Destin, FL 32541: Free information ◆ Mild to very hot sauces, marinades, snacks, and spice specialties. 888-933-FIRE. www.fire-spice.com

**Fitzgerald Fairfield Inc.,** P.O. Box 3151, Palm Beach, FL 33480: Free information ◆ Herb blends and seasonings. 800-955-4372.

**Four Oaks Farm Inc.,** P.O. Box 987, Lexington, SC 29071: Free brochure ◆ Country-style ham and bacon, jams, jellies, pickles, relishes, salad dressings, cakes, and other favorites. 800-858-5006; 803-356-3194 (in SC). fouroaks@scsn.net

**Fox's Fine Foods,** 750 W. 16th St., Bldg. J, Costa Mesa, CA 92627: Free list of retail sources ◆ Relishes and sauces with no added fat or preservatives. 714-722-6651.

**Fox Hollow Farm,** 10 Old Lyme Rd., Hanover, NH 03755: Free information ◆ Gourmet mustard. 603-643-6002.

**Fredericksburg Herb Farm,** P.O. Drawer 927, Fredericksburg, TX 78624: Catalog $2 ◆ Herb seeds, flowers, toiletries, oils, and seasonings. 800-259-4372. www.fredericksburgherbfarm.com

**Garden Medicinals & Culinaries,** P.O. Box 320, Earlysville, VA 22936: Catalog $2 ◆ Herb seeds, roots, and tubers. Also books, tinctures, extracts, supplies for herb growers. 804-973-4703. herbs@gardenmedicinals.com

**Gardner Resources Inc.,** P.O. Box 363, Highlands, NJ 07732: Free information ◆ All-natural jalapeno and hemp, garlic, tomato-basil, roasted pepper, and other hot sauces. 800-98-BLAIR. www.deathsauce.com

**Garlic Survival Company,** 1094 Revere Ave., San Francisco, CA 94124: Free information ◆ All-natural garlic sauces and spices. 800-955-4372.

**F.P. Garrettson Inc.,** 230 Main St., Chatham, NJ 07928: Free brochure ◆ Rare teas, coffees, cocoa, spices, and legumes. 800-821-2549; 201-635-7264 (in NJ).

**Get Sauced,** P.O. Box 426, Manteo, NC 27954: Free catalog ◆ Mild, zesty, sweet, tangy, and spicy sauces and condiments. 800-948-0274; 919-473-2036 (in NC). www.getsauced.com

**GNS Spices,** P.O. Box 90, Walnut, CA 91788: Free information ◆ Dried, flaked, pureed, brined, ground, and fresh Habaneras. 909-594-9505.

**Gourmet Gallery,** 1071 Avenida Acaso, Unit E, Camarillo, CA 93012: Free brochure ◆ Hot sauces, seasonings, and flavor-adding specialties. 800-888-3484; 805-389-4787 (in CA).

**Grandma's Spice Shop,** Spice Valley Way, Upper Tract, WV 26866: Free catalog ◆ Teas, coffees, cocoa, spices, and herbs. 304-358-2345.

**Great Southern Sauce Company,** 5705 Kavanaugh, Little Rock, AR 72207: Free information ◆ Sauces, salsa, marinades, and other specialties. 800-437-2823.

**Gunpowder Foods,** 4514 E. Desert Trumpet Rd., Phoenix, AZ 85044: Free list of retail sources ◆ Chili mix, seasonings, and spices. 800-PEPPERS. www.bigbruce.com

**Carol Hall,** 330 N. Main St., Fort Bragg, CA 95437: Free list of retail sources ◆ Jams, pepper jellies, syrups, chutneys, mustards, salsa, and other favorites. 800-892-4823.

**Helen's Tropical Exotics,** 1017 Lees Mill Rd., College Park, GA 30349: Free brochure ◆ Dips, marinades, sauces, Jamaican pimentos, tropical spices, and hot peppers. 800-544-JERK.

**Herb & Spice Collection,** P.O. Box 299, Norway, IA 52318: Free catalog ◆ Culinary herbs and spices, herbs and tea, natural herbal body care products, and potpourris. 800-786-1388. www.frontierherb.com

**Herbs-Licious,** 1702 S. 6th St., Marshalltown, IA 50158: Catalog $2 (refundable) ◆ Herb plants, dried herbs, spices, and oils.

**Hosgood's Culinary Delights,** P.O. Box 1265, Stafford, TX 77497: Free brochure ◆ Garlic seasonings and other specialties. 800-4-GAR-LIC. www.4garlic.com

**The Hot Shop,** P.O. Box 7917, North Augusta, SC 29861: Free catalog ◆ Hot and spicy sauces, salsa, peppered pickles, and other condiments. 888-850-4688; 803-202-0395 (in SC). www.hotstuff4u.com

**House of Fire,** 1108 Spruce St., Boulder, CO 80302: Free catalog ◆ Hot sauces, salsa, barbecue sauces, spices, and other specialties from worldwide sources. 800-717-5787; 303-440-0929 (in CO). www.houseoffire.com

**Hybird Vigor Kitchen,** P.O. Box 245, Georgetown, IL 61846: Free catalog ◆ Polenta and cornbread mixes, herb meat rubs, vinegars, and garlic sauces. 217-662-2799.

**Jo B's Sauces Inc.,** Box 316, Warren, VT 05674: Free information ◆ All-natural hot sauces. 800-496-7889.

**Jones Barbecue Sauce Inc.,** P.O. Box 331220, Coconut Grove, FL 33233: Free list of retail sources ◆ Hot and spicy or mildly-sweetened barbecue sauces that are fat-free and low in sodium and calories. 800-DJ-SAUCE; 305-445-1814 (in FL).

**Joy's Jams Inc.,** 187 Redman Ln., Durango, CO 81301: Free information ◆ Mild to hot chile jams, sweet and spicy grilling and dipping sauce, meat soak, salsa mix, and other specialties. 800-831-5697.

**Kelchner's Horseradish Products,** Box 245, Dublin, PA 18917: Free information ◆ Horseradish, cocktail sauce, hot horseradish mustard, and other specialties. 800-424-1952; 215-249-3439 (in PA).

**Kim's Gourmet Products Inc.,** 7433 Temby Ct., Castle Rock, CO 80104: Free list of retail sources ◆ Low-fat and low-sodium sauces for use in stir-frying, as dipping sauces, or salad dressings. 800-7-SAUCES.

**Kozlowski Farms,** 5566 Gravenstein Hwy. North, Forestville, CA 95436: Free brochure ◆ Condiments and mustards, sugar-free berry vinegars, barbecue sauce, conserves, chutney, jams, marmalades, honey, and salad dressings. 707-887-1587.

**Le Saucier,** Faneuil Hall Marketplace, Boston, MA 02109: Free catalog ◆ Sauces from around the world. 617-227-9649.

**Legacy Herbs,** Sue Lukens Herbalist/Potter, HC 70, Box 442, Mountain View, AR 72560: Catalog 50¢ ◆ Herbs, wildflowers, perennial plants, soaps, bath and body care products, oils and fragrance, incense, potpourri, herbal food products, and other scented items. 870-269-4051.

**The Magic of Chef Paul Prudhomme,** P.O. Box 23342, New Orleans, LA 70183: Free catalog ◆ All-natural MSG and preservative-free Habanera and cayenne pepper sauces and other seasonings. 800-457-2857. www.chefpaul.com

**Mahogany Smoked Meats,** P.O. Box 1387, Bishop, CA 93515: Free brochure ◆ Smoked jerky, Cheddar cheese, chileno peppers and stuffed olives, smoked trout, and other specialties. 888-624-6426.

**Mannon's Foods,** 5580 S. Nogales Hwy., #140, Tucson, AZ 85706: Free information ◆ Herb and spice blends and specialty products. 800-622-7178; 520-889-4598 (in AZ).

**Maui Jelly Factory,** 1464 Lower Main St., Wailuku, Maui, HI 96793: Free information ◆ Onion jelly, mustard, and other food products. 800-803-8343.

**The Mayhaw Tree,** P.O. Box 3430, Peachtree City, GA 30269: Free information ◆ Sauces, mustard, preserves, and Mayhaw berry jelly, sauce, and syrup. 800-262-9429.

**McCutcheon Apple Products Inc.,** P.O. Box 243, Frederick, MD 21705: Free information ◆ Apple butter, preserves, relishes, salad dressings, honey, hot sauces, and specialties. 800-875-3451. www.mccutcheons.com

**McIlhenny Company,** Tabasco Country Store, Avery Island, LA 70513: Free information ◆ Tabasco and barbecue sauces and other Louisiana seasonings and spices. 800-634-9599.

**Mendocino Mustard,** 1260 N. Main, Fort Bragg, CA 95437: Free brochure ◆ Gourmet, sodium-free mustard. Also seeds and spicy, seeded beer mustard. 800-964-2270; 707-964-2250 (in CA).

**Midwest Pepper Trading Company,** 3 Swannanoa, Rochester, IL 62563: Free catalog ◆ Hot sauces and salsa. 217-498-9233. www.midwestpepper.com

**Mo Hotta-Mo Betta,** P.O. Box 4136, San Luis Obispo, CA 93403: Free catalog ◆ Chili pepper and hot pepper sauces, pickled products, spicy condiments, barbecue sauces, seasonings and spices to shake on, curries and chutney, soups, dried chilies, cooking sauces and pastes, and snacks. 800-462-3220. www.mohotta.com

**Morris Farms,** Rt. 1, Hwy. 56 East, Uvalda, GA 30473: Free catalog ◆ Vidalia onion relish, relish with mustard, barbecue sauce, onion pickles, and sweet onion vinaigrette. 800-447-9338. www.sweetonion.com

**Mount Horeb Mustard Museum,** 109 E. Main St., P.O. Box 468, Mount Horeb, WI 53572: Free catalog ◆ Mustards from around the world. 800-438-6878. www.mustardweb.com

**Mushroom Man,** Box 321, Eugene, OR 97140: Free information ◆ Dried Italian porcini mushrooms and exotic wild mushroom cooking powders. 800-945-3404. webmaster@mushroomman.com

**Myron's Fine Foods Inc.,** P.O. Box 862, Wendell, MA 01379: Free list of retail sources ◆ All-natural, reduced sodium, and MSG-free Asian cooking sauces. 978-544-2086.

**Nantucket Off-Shore Seasonings Inc.,** P.O. Box 1437, Nantucket, MA 02554: Free information ◆ Salt and preservative-free seasonings for grilled or broiled fish, meat, and poultry. 508-228-9292.

**Napa Valley Kitchens,** 910 Enterprise Way, Napa, CA 94558: Free list of retail sources ◆ Seasoning vinegars, mustards, flavored olive oils and vinaigrettes, garlic and pepper spreads, and other specialties. 800-288-1089; 707-967-1107 (in CA).

**New Canaan Farms,** P.O. Box 386, Dripping Springs, TX 78620: Free brochure ◆ Ice cream toppings, jellies and jams, mustard, and other specialties. 800-727-5267.

**Old Southwest Trading Company,** P.O. Box 7545, Albuquerque, NM 87194: Free catalog ◆ Habanera, exotic, and domestic chilies. 505-836-0168.

**The Tony Packo Food Company,** 1902 Front St., Toledo, OH 43605: Free catalog ◆ Pickles, relishes, salsa, sauces, and other condiments. 800-366-4218. www.tonypacko.com

**Panola Pepper Corp.,** Rt. 2, Box 148, Lake Province, LA 71254: Free price list ◆ Pepper sauces, stuffed olives, green Tabasco peppers, other hot sauces, and boil for crab, shrimp, and crawfish. 800-256-3013; 318-559-1774 (in LA).

**Pendery's Inc.,** 1221 Manufacturing St., Dallas, TX 75207: Catalog $2 ◆ Spices, seasonings, and flavorings for Mexican cooking. 800-533-1870; 972-741-1870 (in TX).

**Penzey's Spice House,** P.O. Box 933, Muskego, WI 53150: Free information ◆ Fresh-ground spices. 414-679-7207.

**Pepper Island Beach,** P.O. Box 484, Lawrence, PA 15055: Free catalog ◆ All-natural hot sauces. 724-746-2401. www.pepperisland.com

**The Pepper Plant,** P.O. Box 1119, Atascadero, CA 93423: Free brochure ◆ Spices, hot pepper sauce with garlic, barbecue sauces, and other seasonings. 800-541-4355.

**Peppers Catalog,** 2009 Hwy. One at Saulsbury St., Dewey Beach, DE 19971: Free catalog ◆ Hot sauces and other specialties. 800-998-3473; 302-227-4608 (in FL). www.peppers.com

**Phamous Phloyd's Inc.,** 2998 S. Steele St., Denver, CO 80210: Free information ◆ Barbecue sauce, marinade, and dry rub-on condiments. 800-497-3281; 303-757-9285 (in CO). www.epol.com/phloyds

**Pikled Garlik Company,** P.O. Box 846, Pacific Grove, CA 93950: Free information ◆ Jalapeno, red chili, lemon dill, smoke-flavored, and mild marinated garlic specialties. 800-775-9788. www.pikledgarlik.com

**Poblanos to Serranos,** P.O. Box 691902, San Antonio, TX 78269: Free catalog ◆ Spices, salsa, and smoke for grilling or as an accompaniment for beef, poultry, pork, or seafood. 800-723-1005.

**Porter's Pick-A-Dilly,** P.O. Box 1166, Quechee, VT 05059: Free list of retail sources ◆ Oil, preservative, and additive-free pickles. 802-295-1888.

**Rafal Spice Company,** 2521 Russell, Detroit, MI 48207: Free catalog ◆ Bulk spices, herbs, teas, coffees, and exotic food specialties. 800-228-4276; 313-259-6373 (in MI).

**Rapazzini Winery,** P.O. Box 247, Gilroy, CA 95021: Free information ◆ Mustard and spices, cooking wines, bordelaise sauce, olives, and garlic-flavored specialties. 800-842-MAMA; 408-842-5649 (in CA).

**Raven's Nest Herbals,** P.O. Box 370, Duluth, GA 30136: Catalog $1.50 ◆ Herbs, spices, oils, incense, potpourri, and other herbal products. 770-242-3901.

**Rex Pure Foods Inc.,** 4200 Poche Court West, New Orleans, LA 70129: Free list of retail sources ◆ Spices, seasoning blends, Creole mustards, sauces, crab boil, olives, vinegars, and fish fry. 504-254-9903.

**Rock Cheese Company,** 110 Elm St., Madison, WI 53705: Free brochure ◆ Cheese favorites, honey products, seasonings, and condiments. Also gift assortments. 608-233-7681.

**The Rosemary House,** 120 S. Market St., Mechanicsburg, PA 17055: Catalog $2 ◆ Spices. 717-697-5111.

**Rowena's,** 758 W. 22nd, Norfolk, VA 23517: Free information ◆ Cakes, preserves and jams, and cooking sauces. 800-627-8699. www.rowenas.com

**Salumeria Italiana,** 151 Richmond St., Boston, MA 02109: Free brochure ◆ Aged balsamic vinegar and other Italian specialties. 800-400-5916.

**San Francisco Herb Company,** 250 14th St., San Francisco, CA 94103: Free catalog ◆ Herbs and spices for cooking. 800-227-4530; 415-861-7174 (in CA). www.sfherb.com

**San Francisco Mustard Company,** 4049 Petaluma Blvd. North, Petaluma, CA 94952: Free information ◆ All-natural salt-free whole seed mustards. 707-769-0866.

**Santa Barbara Olive Company,** P.O. Box 1570, Santa Ynez, CA 93460: Free information ◆ Estate grown, low-sodium, and certified kosher olives and related products. 800-4-SB-OLIV. www.sbolive.com

**Sassy Sauces,** 430 Quintana Rd., #138, Morro Bay, CA 93442: Free information ◆ Fruit sauces for barbecuing. 888-767-2770.

**Sauces & Salsa Ltd.,** 1892 Oakland Park Ave., Columbus, OH 43224: Free brochure ◆ Hot sauces. 614-268-7330.

**Scott's Food Products,** 122 S. Guadalupe Ave., Ste. 4, Redondo Beach, CA 90277: Free list of retail sources ◆ Sauces, marinades, and spice blends. 800-376-6995; 310-376-6995 (in CA).

**The Screaming Habanera,** 238 M. Kentucky Ave., Lakeland, FL 33801: Free brochure ◆ Barbecue, wing, and other hot sauces. 800-810-0989. thescreaminghabanero@juno.com

**Shady Acres Herb Farm,** 7815 Hwy. 212, Chaska, MN 55318: Free list with long SASE ◆ Dried plants and herbal vinegars. 612-466-3391.

**Smith & Smith,** P.O. Box 1950, Ventura, CA 93002: Free catalog ◆ Certified kosher hot horseradish, chili hot sauce, and other fiery foods. 800-567-7541. www.smithandsmith.com

**Sotto Voce Samplers,** 211 171st St. South, Spanaway, WA 98387: Free brochure ◆ Herb vinegars, spiced olive oils, garlic pasta, spicy seafood marinade, and other specialties. 800-487-0730. www.sottovoce.com

**Southwest Specialty Food Inc.,** 5805 W. McLellan, Glendale, AZ 85301: Free catalog ◆ Horseradish, roasted garlic, Cajun, and other original Habanera pepper sauces. 800-536-3131.

**Specialty Sauces,** 444 Lake Cook Rd., Ste. 2, Deerfield, IL 60015: Free brochure ◆ Salsa and barbecue sauces. 800-SAUCES-1.

**Spice Merchant,** P.O. Box 524, Jackson Hole, WY 83001: Free catalog ◆ Spices, herbs, and flavoring condiments from China, Japan, Indonesia, Thailand, and other countries. Also kitchen accessories for Oriental cooking. 800-551-5999. www.emall.com/spice

**Spices Etc,** P.O. Box 5266, Charlottesville, VA 22905: Free catalog ◆ Herbs and spices, seasoning blends, flavors and extracts, grinders, and gifts. 800-827-6373. spices@spicesetc.com

**Stonewall Chili Pepper Company,** Hwy. 290 East, Stonewall, TX 78671: Free price list ◆ Chili pepper specialties. 800-232-2995.

**Stonewall Kitchen,** 469 US Rt. 1, York, ME 03909: Free brochure ◆ Mustard, country style marinade, horseradish sauce, and other condiments. 800-207-JAMS.

**Suzie Hot Sauce,** 129 S. Main St., New Hope, PA 18938: Free catalog ◆ Gourmet hot sauces. 800-60-SAUCE. www.suziehotsauce.com

**Talk O'Texas,** 1610 Roosevelt St., San Angelo, TX 76905: Free information ◆ Hot and mild crisp okra pickles. 800-749-6572.

**U-Brew,** 1207 Hwy. 17 South, North Myrtle Beach, SC 29582: Free catalog ◆ Hot sauces, salsa, barbecue and wing sauces, marinades, dried chiles and seasonings, and snacks. 800-845-4441. www.ubrewit.com

**The Uncommon Herb,** P.O. Box 2980, Seal Beach, CA 90740: Catalog $1 ◆ Essential oils, handmade soaps, skin care products, teas, and seasonings. 800-308-6284.

**Watkins Inc.,** 150 Liberty St., P.O. Box 5570, Winona, MN 55987: Free catalog ◆ Extracts, flavors, and spices. 800-247-5907.

**Whistling Wings Farms,** 427 West St., Biddeford, ME 04005: Free brochure ◆ Low calorie spreadable fruits, syrups, and sauces; vinegars; and muffin mixes and other food products that are naturally fat-free and contain no preservatives or cholesterol. 800-765-8989; 207-282-1146 (in ME). www.wwfarm.com

**Wild Thymes Farm,** Rt. 351, Medussa, NY 12120: Free information ◆ Herb, berry, and other vinegars; herb, fruit, spice mustards, and virgin olive oils; and other all-natural condiments. 800-724-2877.

**Wisconsin Wilderness Food Products,** 101 W. Capitol Dr., Milwaukee, WI 53212: Free catalog ◆ Cranberry mustards, preserves, and chutney. 800-359-3039.

**World Variety Produce Inc.,** Customer Service, P.O. Box 21127, Los Angeles, CA 90021: Free catalog ◆ Herbs, spices, and exotic produce from around the world. 800-588-0151. www.melissa.com

**Zimmerman Foods,** 1980 New Danville Pike, Lancaster, PA 17603: Free catalog ◆ All-natural jams, jellies, and relishes. 717-393-4240.

## Snacks

**The Amishman,** P.O. Box 128, Mount Holly Springs, PA 17065: Free brochure ◆ Candy, apple butter, chow chow, nuts, pretzels, and other snacks. 800-233-7082.

**Benzel's Pretzels,** 5200 6th Ave., Altoona, PA 16602: Free brochure ◆ Assorted pretzels in decorated gift tins and special occasion variety packs. 800-344-4438; 814-942-5062 (in PA). www.benzel.com

**Chickasaw Trading Company,** 821 N. Avenue B, Denver City, TX 78323: Free catalog ◆ Lean beef jerky and turkey. 800-848-3515.

**Chile Today,** 919 Hwy. 33, Ste. 47, Freehold, NJ 07728: Free information ◆ Hot Habanera, medium Chipotte, and mild flavored sourdough pretzels. 800-468-7377.

**Colorado Jerky Company,** 9901 Garland Ct., Westminster, CO 80021: Free brochure ◆ Ready-to-eat and make-them-at-home beef and turkey jerky kits. 800-741-1547.

**Fatwise,** 1130 E. Linden Ave., Colina, NJ 07036: Free catalog ◆ Fat-free foods and snacks. 908-862-3886.

**Fire & Spice,** 757 Hwy. 97E, #14-246, Destin, FL 32541: Free information ◆ Mild to very hot sauces, marinades, snacks, and spice specialties. 888-933-FIRE. www.fire-spice.com

**Humpty Dumpty Potato Chips,** P.O. Box 2247, South Portland, ME 04116: Free brochure ◆ Original and ripple style, barbecue, cheese and onion, sour cream and clam, and other potato chips. 800-274-2447; 207-883-8422 (in ME). www.humptydumpty.com

**International Nut Company,** 5 South St., Box 540, Walpole, MA 02081: Free price list ◆ Imported nuts and snacks. 800-710-9380.

**Harry London Candies Inc.,** 1281 S. Main St., North Canton, OH 44720: Free list of retail sources ◆ Milk chocolate specialties, mocha confections, fondue dessert and dipping sauce, confection snacks, and candy. 800-321-0444.

**Matthews 1812 House,** 250 Kent Rd., P.O. Box 15, Cornwall Bridge, CT 06754: Free brochure ◆ Candy, dessert sauces, maple syrup, nuts and snacks, and other specialties. 800-662-1812. matthews@mohawk.net

**Mo Hotta-Mo Betta,** P.O. Box 4136, San Luis Obispo, CA 93403: Free catalog ◆ Chili pepper and hot pepper sauces, pickled products, spicy condiments, barbecue sauces, seasonings and spices to shake, curries and chutney, soups, dried chilies, cooking sauces and pastes, and snacks. 800-462-3220. www.mohotta.com

**Mountain Man Nut & Fruit Company,** Branson Meadows, 4210 Gretna Rd., Branson, MO 65616: Free catalog ◆ Gift baskets for any occasion, regular and sugar-free candies, nuts, homemade jams, dried fruits, trail mixes, and coffees. 800-336-6203.

**Nuts 4U,** P.O. Box 1864, Sugar Land, TX 77487: Free brochure ◆ Nuts, fruit and nut mixes, dried fruit, and other snacks. 281-242-2794. www.nuts4u.com/nut

**Reyna Foods Inc.,** 388-390 Butler St., Etna, PA 15223: Free information ◆ Blue, white, red, and yellow corn and garbanzo bean tortilla chips. 800-33-REYNA; 412-261-2606 (in PA).

**Salsa Express,** P.O. Box 3985, Albuquerque, NM 87190: Free catalog ◆ Salsa, dips, condiments, nuts, snack foods, chili peppers, and spicy food specialties. 800-437-2572. www.salsaexpress.com

**Santa Fe Cookie Company,** 3905 San Mateo NE, Albuquerque, NM 87110: Free brochure ◆ Sugar-free cookies, spicy snacks, pretzels, crackers, and nut mixes. 800-873-5589.

**Splurge Inc.,** 207 E. 74th St., New York, NY 10021: Free information ◆ Low-fat and no-guilt snacks and confections. 212-439-6181.

**Swiss Colony,** Catalog Request Department, P.O. Box 8994, Madison, WI 53794: Free catalog ◆ Cheese, meat, sausage, pastries, nuts, candy, and snacks. 608-324-5050.

**Taylor Country Farms,** P.O. Box 432, Hubbard, OR 07032: Free information ◆ Beef jerky snacks. 800-321-8808. www.tcfarm.com

## Sugar-free & Dietetic

**Bob's Candies Inc.,** P.O. Box 3170, Albany, GA 31706: Free catalog ◆ Sugar-free candy. 800-569-4033; 912-430-8384 (in GA). www.bobscandies.com

**The Estee Corp.,** 169 Lackawanna Ave., Parsippany, NJ 07054: Free catalog ◆ Sugarless candy and cookies. 800-34-ESTEE.

**HeartyMix Company,** 1231 Madison Hill Rd., Rahway, NJ 07065: Free catalog ◆ Preservative, cholesterol, and saturated fat-free baking mixes for cookies, cakes, and other pastries. Also salt-free bread and wheat-free items. 732-382-3010.

**How Sweet It Is,** P.O. Box 376, Jenkintown, PA 19046: Free information ◆ Low-fat and salt or sugar-free candy. 215-784-9980. www.howsweet.com

**Mountain Man Nut & Fruit Company,** Branson Meadows, 4210 Gretna Rd., Branson, MO 65616: Free catalog ◆ Gift baskets for any occasion, regular and sugar-free candies, nuts, homemade jams, dried fruits, trail mixes, and coffees. 800-336-6203.

**1-Stop Sugarless Shop,** 700 Merritt Blvd., Baltimore, MD 21222: Free catalog ◆ Sugar-free and other sugar-less products. Also diabetic-friendly specialties. 800-898-7571. www.sugarlessshop.com

**Ann Raskas Candies,** P.O. Box 13367, Kansas City, KS 66113: Free information ◆ Candy for dieters. 913-422-7230.

**Señor Murphy, Candymaker,** P.O. Box 2505, Santa Fe, NM 87504: Free catalog ◆ Sugar-free and other chocolates. 505-988-4311.

**Thee Diet Shop,** Calco Company, 3540 W. Jarvis, Skokie, IL 60076: Free catalog ◆ Low-fat and sugar-free dietetic foods and candies. 800-325-5409. www.diet-shoppe.com

## Tea, Coffee, & Cocoa

**Amazon Gourmet Coffee,** Division Amazon's Gourmet Foods, P.O. Box 530156, Miami Shores, FL 33153: Free information ◆ Fresh-roasted coffees from around the world. 800-335-JAVA.

**American Coffee Company,** French Market, 800 Magazine St., New Orleans, LA 70130: Free catalog ◆ Gourmet coffees. 800-554-7234.

**Armeno Coffee Roasters Ltd.,** 75 Otis St., Northborough, MA 01532: Free brochure ◆ Gourmet coffees. 800-ARMENO-1; 508-393-2821 (in MA).

**Assouline & Ting Inc.,** 314 Brown St., Philadelphia, PA 19123: Free information ◆ Whole bean coffees. 800-521-4491; 215-627-3000 (in PA). www.caviarassouline.com

**Atlanta Coffee Roastery Inc.,** P.O. Box 1638, Woodstock, GA 30188: Free list of retail sources ◆ Instant cocoa mixes. 800-929-7035.

**B & D Gourmet Coffees,** 21 River Dr., Crane, MO 65633: Free information ◆ Coffees and teas. 417-369-6265.

**Baltimore Coffee,** 9 W. Aylesbury Rd., Timonium, MD 21093: Free brochure ◆ Freshly roasted whole bean coffee, water-decaffeinated coffee, and teas from worldwide sources. 800-823-1408. www.baltcoffee.com

**Baronet Gourmet Coffee,** 77 Weston St., Hartford, CT 06120: Free catalog ◆ Coffee and brewing equipment. 860-527-7253.

**Bean Bag,** 10400 Old Georgetown Rd., Bethesda, MD 20814: Free catalog ◆ Exotic blends of coffee and tea. 301-530-8090.

**Boyd Coffee Company,** P.O. Box 20547, Portland, OR 97220: Free catalog ◆ Gourmet coffees. 800-221-8211. www.boyds.com/info/index.htm

**Brothers Coffee,** 101 Western Ave., Watertown, WI 53094: Free catalog ◆ Flavored and non-flavored caffeinated and decaffeinated coffees. Also espresso makers, grinders, filters, thermal carafes, and gift baskets. 800-284-5776.

**Brothers Gourmet Coffees,** P.O. Box 812124, Boca Raton, FL 33481: Free information ◆ Whole bean, roasts, blends, decaffeinated, flavored, and other coffees. 800-284-5776. www.pwr.com/bean

**Cafe Anatole,** 13440 The Square, Poway, CA 92064: Free catalog ◆ Whole bean and ground specialty coffees. 619-673-7587. 800-722-0094. www.soho.ios.com/~blue1/café

**Cafe Beaujolais,** Box 730, Mendocino, CA 95460: Free catalog ◆ Pastries and desserts, candy assortments, hot chocolate mix, and other specialties. 800-930-0443.

**Café La Semeuse,** 55 Nassau Ave., Brooklyn, NY 11222: Free brochure ◆ Regular and water-processed whole bean decaffeinated coffee. 718-387-9696.

**Caffeinds,** 6990-D Peachtree Industrial Blvd., Norcross, GA 30071: Free information ◆ Varietal, estate, blended, and flavored coffees; blended, scented, imported, herbal, and fruit teas; fruit tisanes; and chocolate and other syrups. 800-803-7774. www.caffeinds.com

**Cappucine Inc.,** 1285 Vazdivia Way, Palm Springs, CA 92262: Free brochure ◆ Instant cappucine coffee mixes. 800-511-3127. www.cappucine.com

**Chado Tea Room,** 8422½ W. 3rd St., Los Angeles, CA 90048: Catalog $3 ◆ Over 200 varieties of tea. Also tea-making accessories. 213-655-2056.

**Cocoa Beach Coffee,** P.O. Box 112516, Tacoma, WA 98141: Free catalog ◆ Gourmet coffees. 800-755-9497.

**Coffee Caboodle,** 525 Maple Ave. West, Vienna, VA 22180: Free price list ◆ Coffee and tea from worldwide sources. 800-541-2469; 703-281-5599 (in VA). J.Beamer@cais.com

**Coffee Odyssey,** P.O. Box 39074, Minneapolis, MN 55439: Free catalog ◆ Micro-roasted coffee beans. 888-207-9647.

**The Collector's Teapot,** P.O. Box 1193, Kingston, NY 12401: Catalog $2 ◆ English teapots, handmade cozies, tea accessories, miniature tea sets, and teas. 800-724-3306.

**Country Coffee Company Inc.,** 13081 State Hwy. 64 West, Tyler, TX 75704: Free list of retail sources ◆ Old-fashioned cocoa mixes. 903-592-9771.

**Dean & DeLuca Mail-Order,** Attention: Catalog Dept., 560 Broadway, New York, NY 10012: Free information ◆ Bensdorp and Droste cocoa for chocolate and dessert creations. 800-221-7714. www.dean-deluca.com

**Door County Coffees,** P.O. Box 638, Sturgeon Bay, WI 54235: Free catalog ◆ Freshly roasted varietals and coffee blends from worldwide sources. 800-856-6613.

**Double Springs Homebrew Supply,** 4697 Double Springs Rd., Valley Springs, CA 95252: Free catalog ◆ Imported caffeinated and decaffeinated coffees. Also an easy-to-use kit for home coffee roasting. 209-754-4888. www.doublesprings.com

**Dry Creek Herb Farm,** 13935 Dry Creek Rd., Auburn, CA 95602: Free information ◆ Skin care products and herbal teas. 916-878-2441.

**Fireside Coffee Company,** 3239 S. Elms Rd., Swartz Creek, MI 48473: Free information ◆ Cinnamon chocolate, chocolate raspberry, orange-spice mocha, butter rum, and gourmet flavored coffees. 800-344-5282.

**First Colony Coffee & Tea Company,** P.O. Box 11005, Norfolk, VA 23517: Free catalog ◆ Coffees, fruit-flavored teas, and hot chocolate. 800-523-1983. www.firstcolony.com

**F.P. Garrettson Inc.,** 230 Main St., Chatham, NJ 07928: Free brochure ◆ Teas, coffees, cocoa, spices, and legumes. 800-821-2549; 201-635-7264 (in NJ).

**Gevalia Kaffe,** P.O. Box 11424, Des Moines, IA 50336: Free catalog ◆ Coffees from around the world. 800-678-2687. www.gevalia.com

**Gilette's Coffee,** 9885 Georgetown Pike, Great Falls, VA 22066: Free information ◆ Imported coffees and teas from worldwide sources. 800-221-3030.

**Gillies Coffee Company,** 150 19th St., Brooklyn, NY 11232: Free brochure ◆ Imported coffee and tea from around the world. 800-344-5526.

**The Gilway Company Ltd.,** 17 Arcadian Ave., Paramus, NJ 07652: Free list of retail sources ◆ Decaffeinated herbal and fruit teas. 201-843-8152.

**Golden Walnut Specialty Foods,** 3200 16th St., Zion, IL 60099: Free catalog ◆ Packaged all-Kosher cookies, cakes, and candies. 800-445-3957.

**Grace Tea Company,** 50 W. 17th St., New York, NY 10011: Free information ◆ Traditional loose teas from Asia. 212-255-2935.

**Grandma's Spice Shop,** Spice Valley Way, Upper Tract, WV 26866: Free catalog ◆ Teas, coffees, cocoa, spices, and herbs. 304-358-2345.

**Green Mountain Coffee Roasters,** 33 Coffee Ln., Waterbury, VT 05676: Free catalog ◆ Fresh-roasted Colombian coffee. 800-223-6768.

**Greene Brothers,** 313 High St., Hackettstown, NJ 07840: Free information ◆ Imported specialty coffees. 888-MOKA-MAN.

**Harney & Sons Tea Company,** P.O. Box 676, Salisbury, CT 06068: Free price list ◆ Features tea in bulk, in bags, gift canisters, and hotel-style packaging. 800-TEA-TIME; 860-435-9218 (in CT). www.harney.com

**Hawaiian Isles Kona Coffee Company,** 2839 Mokumoa St., Honolulu, HI 96819: Free brochure ◆ Kona bean coffees from Hawaii. www.hawaii-coffee.com

**The Herb Patch Ltd.,** P.O. Box 1111, 471 South St., Middletown Springs, VT 05757: Free brochure ◆ All-natural cocoa in several flavors. 800-235-2466.

**High Tea,** Center Village, Box 902, Harrisville, NH 03450: Free catalog ◆ British teas, teapots, and accessories. 800-547-9595. www.alberene.com

**Himalayan Tea Garden,** 6325-9 Falls of the Neuse, #345, Raleigh, NC 27615: Free catalog ◆ Imported, blends, aromatic, herb and fruit, and estate teas. 800-832-8732.

**Holy Mountain Trading Company,** P.O. Box 457, Fairfax, CA 94978: Free catalog ◆ Hand-picked rare and exotic teas in blended and unblended full-leaf varieties. Also Asian teapots and tea-making accessories. 888-832-8008. www.holymtm.com

**The Honorable Jane Company,** Fine Teas & Teawares, Box 35, Potter Valley, CA 95469: Free catalog ◆ Single-estate and blended teas. 888-743-1966. www.honorablejane.com

**Huxdotter Specialty Coffee Inc.,** P.O. Box 553, North Bend, WA 98045: Free information ◆ Flavored hand-roasted coffee blends. 888-HUX-JAVA.

**JBR Inc.,** 1933 Davis St., Ste. 308, San Leandro, CA 94577: Free catalog ◆ Premium arabica coffees and flavored teas. 800-732-2948.

**Kobricks Coffee Company,** 693 Henderson St., Jersey City, NJ 07302: Free catalog ◆ Flavored specialty and espresso coffees. 201-656-6313.

**Liberty Richter,** 400 Lyster Ave., Saddle Brook, NJ 07662: Free list of retail sources ◆ Unsweetened and caffeine-free packets of ready-to-use cappuccino. 201-843-8900.

**Lion Coffee,** 831 Queen St., Honolulu, HI 96813: Free catalog ◆ Gourmet coffees. 800-338-8353. www.lioncoffee.com

**Mackinlay Teas,** P.O. Box 6, Saline, MI 48176: Catalog $1 ◆ Teas, premium rice, lentils, beans, soup mixes, and Italian syrups. 313-482-4600.

**MacNab's Teas,** P.O. Box 206, Back River Rd., Boothbay, ME 04537: Catalog $2 ◆ NacNabs black teas, Scots tea, tea from Maine, and other favorites. Also shortbread and scone mixes. 800-884-7222.

**McNultys Tea & Coffee Company,** 109 Christopher St., New York, NY 10014: Free brochure ◆ Imported tea and coffee from around the world and brewing equipment. 800-356-5200; 212-242-5351 (in NY).

**Mountain Chai Company,** 2525 Arapahoe Ave., Boulder, CO 80302: Free information ◆ Robust and exotic blends of Assam black tea, natural sweeteners, and premium spices from around the world. 800-498-4986.

**Northwestern Coffee Mills,** Middle Rd., Box 370, La Pointe, WI 54850: Free brochure ◆ Imported and domestic coffee and tea, herbal teas, and coffee syrup. 800-243-5283.

**O'Mona International Tea Company,** 6 S. Main St., Port Chester, NY 10573: Catalog $1 ◆ Tea from worldwide sources.

**Orleans Coffee Exchange,** 712 Orleans St., New Orleans, LA 70116: Free catalog ◆ Estate and organic coffees from over 30 countries in American and French-style roasts. 800-737-5464. www.orleanscoffee.com

**Pannikin Mail Order,** 1205 J St., San Diego, CA 92101: Free brochure ◆ Spices, tea, hot chocolate, espresso machines, and coffee makers. 800-232-6482.

**Pele Plantation,** P.O. Box 809, Honaunau, HI 96726: Free information ◆ Estate grown Kona-flavored coffees, chocolate covered Kona beans, and plain and chocolate covered macadamia nuts. 800-366-0487.

**N.M. Pinon Coffee,** 1470A Bosque Farms Blvd., Bosque Farms, NM 87068: Free brochure ◆ Coffee with New Mexico pinon nuts. 800-572-0624; 505-869-3101 (in NM). www.nmpinoncoffee.com

**Rafal Spice Company,** 2521 Russell, Detroit, MI 48207: Free catalog ◆ Bulk spices, herbs, teas, coffees, and exotic food specialties. 800-228-4276; 313-259-6373 (in MI).

**The Roasterie,** 2601 Madison, Kansas City, MO 64108: Free information ◆ Custom blends, roasts, and origin coffees. 800-376-0245.

**Sattwa Enterprises,** P.O. Box 805, Newberg, OR 97132: Free information ◆ Concentrated and loose Chai tea. 888-841-CHAI.

**Shock Coffee,** P.O. Box 2545, Redwood City, CA 94064: Free information ◆ Hyper-caffeinated coffee. 888-89-SHOCK.

**Simpson & Vail,** P.O. Box 765, 3 Quarry Rd., Brookfield, CT 06804: Free catalog ◆ Teas, coffees, gift baskets, tea-making accessories, books, and more. 800-282-TEAS; 203-775-0240 (in CT). www.SVTEA.com

**Smiling Catalog Tea Merchants,** 407 N. 5th Ave., Ann Arbor, MI 48104: Free brochure ◆ Imported loose teas and tea bags, tisanes, pristine tea pots, and tea-making accessories. 800-440-TEAS. www.smilingcatteas.com

**The Squire's Tea Pub,** 1928 Walnut St., Allentown, PA 18104: Free information ◆ Decaffeinated, estate, imported, and domestic teas. 800-836-0209.

**Starbucks Coffee,** P.O. Box 34067, Seattle, WA 98124: Free catalog ◆ Coffees, coffee-making equipment and accessories, and gifts. 800-STARBUC. sbux@aol.com

**Stash Tea,** P.O. Box 910, Portland, OR 97207: Free catalog ◆ Traditional, rare and exotic, herb, decaffeinated, and spiced teas. Also teapots, accessories, and gifts. 800-697-8274. www.stashtea.com

**The Sundial Gardens & Tea Room,** 59 Hidden Lake Rd., Higganum, CT 06441: Free catalog ◆ Teas, herbal tisanes, and mixes for easy-to-make toasted hazelnut, cranberry, and traditional English currant scones. 203-345-4290.

**Tea Traders of Mount Vernon,** 4202 Mount Vernon Hwy., Alexandria, VA 22309: Free price list ◆ Flavored gourmet and other coffee blends. Also flavored, decaffeinated, regular, standard black, single estate, and other teas. 800-846-1947.

**Teaism,** 2009 R St. NW, Washington, DC 2009: Free catalog ◆ Loose tea leaf blends. Also Chinese and Japanese tea accouterments. 202-667-3827.

**Todd & Holland Tea Merchants,** 7577 Lake St., River Forest, IL 60305: Free catalog ◆ Choice rare loose-leaf teas from worldwide sources. 800-747-8327. www.Todd-Holland.com

**Torrefazione Italia Inc.,** 1321 2nd Ave., Ste. 200, Seattle, WA 98101: Free information ◆ Coffee. 800-827-2333.

**The Uncommon Herb,** P.O. Box 2980, Seal Beach, CA 90740: Catalog $1 ◆ Essential oils, handmade soaps, skin care products, teas, and seasonings. 800-308-6284.

**Upton Tea Imports,** P.O. Box 159, Upton, MA 01568: Free information ◆ Over 120 varieties of garden-fresh loose teas. 800-234-8327.

**Mark T. Wendell,** P.O. Box 1312, West Concord, MA 01742: Free information ◆ Regular and decaffeinated imported teas and coffees. 978-369-3709.

**The White Coffee Corp.,** 18-35 Steinway Pl., Long Island City, NY 11105: Free list of retail sources ◆ Flavored and decaffeinated green teas. 800-221-0140; 718-204-7900 (in NY).

**Williams-Sonoma,** Mail Order Dept., P.O. Box 7456, San Francisco, CA 94120: Free catalog ◆ Pernigotti and Dark Jersey cocoa for chocolate and dessert creations. 800-541-1262.

**Williamsburg Coffee & Tea Company,** 5251-27 John Tyler Hwy., Williamsburg VA 23185: Free catalog ◆ Freshly roasted Coffees and teas from around the world. 888-565-1400. www.wcoffee.com

**Willoughby's Coffee,** 550 E. Main St., Branford, CT 06405: Free catalog ◆ Gourmet coffees. 800-388-8400. www.willoughbyscoffee.com

**World Java House,** P.O. Box 347, Monrovia, CA 91017: Free catalog ◆ Espresso machines, coffee presses and grinders, coffee makers, mugs, flavoring syrups, accessories, and imported coffees from worldwide sources. 800-528-3833. www.worldjava.com

## FOODS, RECIPE MANAGEMENT, & COOKBOOK SOFTWARE

**Books-On-Disk,** 311 Harvard St., Brookline, MA 02146: Free information ◆ Windows and Macintosh cookbooks. 800-717-4478; 617-734-9700 (in MA).

**East Hampton Industries Inc.,** P.O. Box 5069, East Hampton, NY 11937: Free brochure ◆ Software for recipe-collecting, cookbook organizing, and meal planning. Also kitchen gadgets. 800-645-1188; 516-324-2224 (in NY).

**Lifestyle Software Group,** 2155 Old Moultrie Rd., St. Augustine, FL 32086: Free information ◆ Windows Betty Crocker's cookbook on CD-ROMs. 800-289-1157; 904-825-0220 (in FL). www.lifeware.com

**Microsoft Corp.**, One Microsoft Way, Redmond, WA 98052: Free information ◆ Julia Child's Home Cooking with Master Chefs on Windows CD-ROMs. 800-426-9400; 425-882-8080 (in WA). www.microsoft.com

**Multicom Publishing,** 188 Embarcadero, 5th Floor, San Francisco, CA 94105: Free brochure ◆ Home improvement and food and wine CD-ROMs. www.multicom.com

**Odyssey Computing,** 1515 S. Melrose Dr., Ste. 90, Vista, CA 92083: Free brochure ◆ Windows software for recipe, cookbook, and meal planning. 619-599-0823.

**Pinpoint Publishing,** P.O. Box 7329, Santa Rosa, CA 95407: Free information ◆ Cooking and recipe management software for the PC. 800-788-5236.

**Sierra Direct,** 7100 W. Center Rd., Ste. 301, Omaha, NE 68106: Free information ◆ Windows and Macintosh recipe storage and meal-management software. 800-757-7707. www.sierra.com

# FOOTBALL

## Clothing

**Betlin Manufacturing,** 1445 Marion Rd., Columbus, OH 43207: Free information ◆ Clothing for players and coaches. 614-443-0248.

**Bomark Sportswear,** P.O. Box 2068, Belair, TX 77402: Free information ◆ Clothing for players and coaches. 800-231-3351.

**Bristol Athletic,** 700-726 Shelby St., Bristol, TN 37621: Free information ◆ Basketball, baseball and softball, football, track, volleyball, and lacrosse uniforms for men, women, and youths. 800-336-8775; 615-968-4140 (in TN).

**DeLong,** 733 Broad St., P.O. Box 189, Grinnell, IA 50112: Free information ◆ Clothing for players and coaches. 800-733-5664; 515-236-3106 (in IA).

**Empire Sporting Goods Manufacturing Company,** 443 Broadway, New York, NY 10013: Free information ◆ Clothing for players and coaches. 800-221-3455; 212-966-0880 (in NY).

**Fab Knit Manufacturing,** Division Anderson Industries, 1415 N. 4th St., Waco, TX 76707: Free information ◆ Clothing for players and coaches. 800-333-4111; 817-752-2511 (in TX).

**JCPenney Catalog,** P.O. Box 675, Milwaukee, WI 53201: Free information ◆ Athletic clothing and accessories. 800-222-6161. www.jcpenney.com/shopping

**Shaffer Sportswear,** 224 N. Washington, Neosho, MO 64850: Free information ◆ Jackets, pants, and uniforms. 417-451-9444.

**Southland Athletic,** P.O. Box 280, Terrell, TX 75160: Free list of retail sources ◆ Jackets and uniforms. 800-527-7637; 972-563-3321 (in TX).

**Venus Knitting Mills Inc.,** 140 Spring St., Murray Hill, NJ 07974: Free information ◆ Clothing for players and coaches. 800-955-4200; 908-464-2400 (in NJ).

**Wilson Sporting Goods,** 8700 Bryn Mawr, Chicago, IL 60631: Free information ◆ Clothing for players and coaches. 800-946-6060; 773-714-6400 (in IL). www.wilsonsports.com

## Equipment

**Adams USA,** P.O. Box 489, Cookeville, TN 38501: Free information ◆ Protective gear. 800-251-6857; 615-526-2109 (in TN).

**Ampac Enterprises Inc.,** All Star Division, Box 1356, Shirley, MA 01464: Free information ◆ Field and playing equipment and protective gear. 800-777-3810; 978-425-6266 (in MA).

**The Athletic Connection,** 1901 Diplomat, Dallas, TX 75234: Free information ◆ Footballs, goal posts, kicking tees, and equipment. 800-527-0871; 972-243-1446 (in TX).

**Austin Athletic Equipment Corp.,** 705 Bedford Ave., Box 423, Bellmore, NY 11710: Free information ◆ Goal posts, markers, and marking machines. 516-785-0100.

**Baden Sports Inc.,** 34114 21st Ave. South, Federal Way, WA 98003: Free information ◆ Leather, rubber-covered, synthetic, and juvenile footballs. 800-544-2998; 206-925-0500 (in WA).

**Ballwall,** 5 Flint Ave., Larchmont, NY 10538: Free brochure ◆ Indoor and outdoor backstop training wall for sports that use a ball. 800-966-1190; 914-833-0390 (in NY).

**Bauer Sports**, 150 Ocean Rd., Greenland, NH 03840: Free list of retail sources ◆ Protective gear. 800-362-3146. www.bauer.com

**Beacon Ballfields,** P.O. Box 45557, Madison, WI 53744: Free catalog ◆ Baseball, football, and soccer field equipment. 800-747-5985; 608-274-5985 (in WI).

**Bike Athletic Company,** P.O. Box 666, Knoxville, TN 37901: Free information ◆ Protective gear. 800-251-9230. www.bike-athletic.com

**Body Glove International,** 530 6th St., Hermosa Beach, CA 90254: Free information ◆ Protective gear. 800-678-7873; 310-374-4074 (in CA). www.bodyglove.com

**H.D. Brown Enterprise Ltd.,** 23 Beverly St. East, St. George, Ontario, Canada N0E 1N0: Free information ◆ Footballs. 519-448-1381.

**BSN Sports,** P.O. Box 7726, Dallas, TX 75209: Free information ◆ Equipment for archery, aquatic fitness, baseball, basketball, boxing, field hockey, football, weight lifting, and other sports. 800-527-7510; 972-484-9484 (in TX). www.bsnsports.com

**Carron Net Company,** 1623 17th St., P.O. Box 177, Two Rivers, WI 54241: Free information ◆ Archery, baseball, basketball, gymnasium and climbing, football, racquetball, soccer, tennis, and volleyball equipment. 800-558-7768; 414-793-2217 (in WI). sales@carronnet.com

**Gerry Cosby & Company,** 3 Pennsylvania Plaza, New York, NY 10001: Free information ◆ Protective gear. 800-548-4003; 212-563-6464 (in NY).

**Cougar Sports,** 6667 W. Old Shakopee Rd., Wilmington, MN 55438: Free information ◆ Protective gear. 800-445-2664.

**Cramer Products Inc.,** P.O. Box 1001, Gardner, KS 66030: Free information ◆ Protective gear. 800-345-2231; 913-884-7511 (in KS).

**Flaghouse Sports Equipment,** 601 Flaghouse Dr., Hasbrouck Heights, NJ 07604: Free catalog ◆ Football equipment. 800-793-7900. www.flaghouse.com

**Franklin Sports Industries Inc.,** 17 Campanelli Pkwy., P.O. Box 508, Stoughton, MA 02072: Free information ◆ Leather, rubber-covered, synthetic, and juvenile footballs. 800-426-7700. www.eisnerbros.com

**Gared Sports Inc.,** 1107 Mullanphy St., St. Louis, MO 63106: Free information ◆ Goal posts, markers, and marking machines. 800-325-2682.

**GeorGI-Sports,** P.O. Box 1107, Lancaster, PA 17603: Free information ◆ Leather, rubber-covered, synthetic, and juvenile footballs. Also protective gear. 800-338-2527; 717-291-8924 (in PA).

**Marty Gilman Inc.,** P.O. Box 97, Gilman, CT 06336: Free information ◆ Blockers and chargers, charging and blocking sleds, kicking cages, and tackling dummies. 800-243-0398; 203-889-7334 (in CT). gilmangear.com

**Gopher Sport,** 2929 Park Dr., Owatonna, MN 55060: Free information ◆ Equipment and accessories for basketball, football, soccer, track and field, and other net games. 800-533-0446; 507-451-7470 (in MN).

**Grid Inc.,** NDL Products, 4031 NE 12th Terrace, Oakland Park, FL 33334: Free information ◆ Protective gear. 800-843-3021.

**Jayfro Corp.,** Unified Sports Inc., 976 Hartford Tnpk., P.O. Box 400, Waterford, CT 06385: Free catalog ◆ Goals, training equipment, and field markers. 860-447-3001.

**Leisure Marketing Inc.,** 2204 Morris Ave., Ste. 202, Union, NJ 07083: Free information ◆ Leather, rubber-covered, synthetic, and juvenile footballs. 908-851-9494.

**Markwort Sporting Goods,** 4300 Forest Park Ave., St. Louis, MO 63108: Catalog $8 (request list of retail sources) ◆ Footballs, face masks, gloves, helmets, and shoulder guards. 800-669-6626; 314-652-3757 (in MO).

**Dick Martin Sports Inc.,** 181 E. Union Ave., P.O. Box 7384, East Rutherford, NJ 07073: Free information ◆ Footballs. 800-221-1993; 201-438-5255 (in NJ).

**Mueller Sports Medicine Inc.,** One Quench Dr., Prairie du Sac, WI 53578: Free information ◆ Protective gear. 800-356-9522; 608-643-8530 (in WI).

**New South Athletic Company Inc.,** 301 E. Main, P.O. Box 604, Dallas, NC 28034: Free information ◆ Protective gear. 800-438-9934; 704-922-1557 (in NC).

**Nocona Athletic Goods Company,** P.O. Box 329, Nocona, TX 76255: Free catalog ◆ Football equipment. 817-825-3326.

**Olympia Sports,** P.O. Box 1941, Ann Arbor, MI 48106: Free information ◆ Blockers and chargers, charging and blocking sleds, kicking cages, and tackling dummies. 800-521-2832. www.wolverinesports.com

**Rawlings Sporting Goods,** 1859 Impertech Dr., Fenton, MO 63026: Free list of retail sources ◆ Leather, rubber-covered, synthetic, and juvenile footballs, and protective gear. 800-426-3334. www.rawlings.com

**Reda Sports Express,** P.O. Box 68, Easton, PA 18044: Free information ◆ Footballs and protective equipment. 800-444-REDA; 610-258-5271 (in PA).

**Riddell Inc.,** 3670 N. Milwaukee Ave., Chicago, IL 60641: Free information ◆ Helmets, kicking tees, protective gear, footballs, and equipment. 800-445-7344; 773-794-1994 (in IL).

**Royal Textile Mills Inc.,** P.O. Box 250, Yanceyville, NC 27379: Free information ◆ Protective gear. 800-334-9361; 336-694-4121 (in NC).

**Spalding Sports Worldwide,** 425 Meadow St., P.O. Box 901, Chicopee, MA 01021: Free list of retail sources ◆ Leather, rubber-covered, synthetic, and juvenile footballs. 800-225-6601. www.spalding.com

**The Training Camp,** c/o Genesis Direct, 100 Plaza Dr., Secaucus, NJ 07094: Free catalog ◆ Basketball, football, golf, hockey, and soccer training aids for children. 800-ATHLETE. care@GenesisDirect.com

**Venus Knitting Mills Inc.,** 140 Spring St., Murray Hill, NJ 07974: Free information ◆ Clothing for players and coaches. Also protective gear. 800-955-4200; 908-464-2400 (in NJ).

**Wilson Sporting Goods,** 8700 Bryn Mawr, Chicago, IL 60631: Free information ◆ Clothing for players and coaches and leather, rubber-covered, synthetic, and juvenile footballs. 800-946-6060; 773-714-6400 (in IL). www.wilsonsports.com

**Wolvering Sports,** P.O. Box 1941, Ann Arbor, MI 48106: Catalog $1 ◆ Baseball, basketball, field hockey, soccer, football, other athletic, and recreation equipment. 313-761-5691.

## FOUNTAINS

**The BB Brass,** 10151 Pacific Mesa Blvd., San Diego, CA 92121: Free catalog ◆ Brass fountains and sculptures. 800-536-0987.

**Cast Aluminum Reproductions,** P.O. Box 1060, San Elzario, TX 79849: Catalog $2 ◆ Cast-aluminum and brass furniture, street lights, outdoor furniture, fountains, mail boxes, and plant stands. 915-764-3793.

**Robert Compton Ltd.,** 3600 Rt. 116, Bristol, VT 05443: Brochure $2 ◆ Original stone fountains. 802-453-3778.

**Florentine Craftsmen,** 46-24 28th St., Long Island City, NY 11101: Catalog $5 ◆ Ornamental sculptures, fountains, birdbaths, and outdoor furniture. 718-937-7632. www.florentinecraftsmen.com

**The Fountain Source,** 30799 Pinetree Rd., Pepper Pike, OH 44124: Free information ◆ Fountains for homes and gardens. 216-247-2843.

**Hermitage Gardens,** P.O. Box 361, Canastota, NY 13032: Catalog $1 ◆ Fiberglass rocks and waterfalls, redwood water wheels, wood bridges, garden pools, and bubbling fantasias. 315-697-9093.

**Hines Pottery,** 6747 Signat Dr., Houston, TX 77041: Free information ◆ Miniature fountains and decorative garden accessories. 800-231-0875. www.rampages.omramp.net/~asd

**Holy Mountain Trading Company,** P.O. Box 457, Fairfax, CA 94978: Free catalog ◆ Ceramic fountains and water fountain accessories. 888-832-8008. www.holymtm.com/watercat.htm

**Moultrie Manufacturing,** P.O. Drawer 1179, Moultrie, GA 31776: Catalog $3 ◆ Cast-aluminum tables, chairs, settees, planters, urns, fountains, chaises, and fixtures. 800-841-8674.

**Stone Forest,** P.O. Box 2840, Santa Fe, NM 87504: Catalog $3 ◆ Fountains, lanterns, water basins, birdbaths, pedestals, and handcarved granite statuary. 505-986-8883.

**Strassacker Bronze America Inc.,** P.O. Box 931, Spartanburg, SC 29304: Catalog $15 ◆ Contemporary and abstract bronze sculptures, fountains, and lighting equipment. 864-579-2579.

## FRAMES, FRAMING SUPPLIES, & SHRINK WRAPPING SYSTEMS

**American Frame Corp.,** 400 Tomahawk Dr., Maumee, OH 43537: Free information ◆ Metal and wood frames, mat boards, and other supplies. 800-537-0944. www.Americanframe.com

**Artistic Wood Carving Inc.,** 630 Broadway, Brooklyn, NY 11206: Free catalog ◆ Custom picture frames. 800-829-2462; 718-384-1088 (in NY).

**Atlas Art & Stained Glass,** P.O. Box 76084, Oklahoma City, OK 73147: Catalog $3 ◆ Kaleidoscopes, frames, lamp bases, and craft, stained glass, jewelry-making, and foil-crafting supplies. 405-946-1230.

**AWC Masterworks,** 630 Broadway, Brooklyn, NY 11206: Free catalog ◆ French, Italian, Spanish, or English-style handcarved traditional frames with a choice of finish. 800-829-2462.

**California Frame Company,** 494 W. Calle Primera, Ste. 913, San Ysidro, CA 92173: Free catalog ◆ Frames. 619-662-1264.

**Colorado Frame Manufacturing,** 1230 Blue Spruce Dr., Fort Collins, CO 80524: Free information ◆ Wholesale supplier of frames and framing materials. 970-493-5966. www.coloradoframe.com

**Contemporary Frame Company,** 346 Scott Swamp Rd., P.O. Box 514, Farmington, CT 06032: Free information ◆ Aluminum section frames. 800-243-0386; 860-677-7787 (in CT). conframe@aol.com

**Crown Art Products,** 90 Dayton Ave., Passaic, NJ 07055: Free catalog ◆ Metal section frames and framing supplies. 201-777-6010.

**Cupid's Bow,** Box 489, Saline, MI 48176: Catalog $3 (refundable) ◆ Antique replica picture frames. 313-429-7894.

**DAB Studio,** P.O. Box 57, 11 Kent Pl., Pompton Plains, NJ 07444: Free catalog ◆ Stained glass picture frames. 973-616-7676.

**William L. Day Companies Inc.,** 1237 Shipp St., Hendersonville, NC 28791: Free catalog ◆ Frames and framing supplies. 800-334-9060; 704-693-1333 (in NC). www.FramingSupplies.com

**Decor Frame Company,** 4307 Metzger Rd., Fort Pierce, FL 34947: Free catalog ◆ Aluminum section frames with hardware, optional springs, and hangers. 800-826-7969.

**Discount Framesource USA Inc.,** Graphik Dimensions Ltd., 2103 Brentwood St., High Point, NC 27263: Free information ◆ Frames. 800-221-0262.

**Documounts,** P.O. Box 26239, Eugene, OR 97402: Free information ◆ Wood picture frames and beveled edge mats. 800-769-5639. www.documounts.com

**Exposures,** 1 Memory Ln., P.O. Box 3615, Oshkosh, WI 54903: Free catalog ◆ Albums and frames. 800-572-5750. www.mileskimballco.com

**Fine Art Packaging Company,** P.O. Box 625, Bethany, OK 73008: Free information ◆ Shrink wrapping supplies. 888-232-0892.

**Fletcher-Terry Company,** 65 Spring Ln., Farmington, CT 06032: Free information ◆ Easy-to-use picture framing tool that won't tear or dent backing materials or cause frames to split. 800-THE-FTCO; 203-677-7331 (in CT).

**Frame Factory,** 1909 W. Diversey Pkwy., Chicago, IL 60614: Free catalog ◆ Frames and framing supplies. 800-621-6570.

**Frame Fit Company,** P.O. Box 8926, Philadelphia, PA 19135: Free information ◆ Aluminum picture frames and hangers. 800-523-3693. www.netaxs.com/~framefit

**Frames By Mail,** 11551 Adie Rd., St. Louis, MO 63043: Free catalog ◆ Wood and metal picture frames and mat board. 800-332-2467.

**Franken Frames,** 609 W. Walnut, Johnson City, TN 37604: Free catalog ◆ Frames and moldings. 800-322-5899.

**G-M Marketing,** 960 Melaleuca Ave., Carlsbad, CA 92009: Brochure $1 ◆ Reproduction museum-quality gold leaf baroque-style antique frames. 619-929-9164.

**Gold Leaf Studios,** P.O. Box 50156, Washington, DC 20091: Free brochure with long SASE ◆ Frames. 202-638-4660.

**Graphik Dimensions Ltd.,** 2103 Brentwood St., High Point, NC 27263: Free information ◆ Frames and framing supplies. 800-221-0262. www.graphikdimensions.com

**Hardwood Frames of America,** P.O. Box 2426, Cleveland, TN 37320: Free information ◆ Frames. 800-426-1933; 423-472-9593 (in TN).

**Russell Harrington Cutlery Inc.,** 44 Green River St., Southbridge, MA 01550: Free information ◆ Mat cutters. 508-765-0201. www.russell-harrington.com

**C.H. Hinds Company,** 125 John Roberts Rd., South Portland, ME 04106: Free brochure ◆ Custom cut and joined octagonal wood frames. 800-377-9727.

**Holton Furniture & Frame,** 5515 Doyle St., Ste. 2, Emeryville, CA 94608: Catalog $8 ◆ Arts and Crafts era picture frames and mirrors, in quartersawn white oak and other hardwoods. 800-250-5277. holton@lmi.net

**Lee House,** P.O. Box 35148, Charlotte, NC 28235: Free information ◆ Framing supplies. 800-532-0461; 704-375-0644 (in NC).

**Light Impressions,** 439 Monroe Ave., P.O. Box 940, Rochester, NY 14607: Free catalog ◆ Custom-cut frames. 800-828-6216. www.lightimpressionsdirect.com

**M & M Distributors,** Rt. 522, P.O. Box 189, Tennent, NJ 07763: Free catalog ◆ Glass and framing products. 800-526-2302. MMFRAM@aol.com

**Magnetic Imaginations,** 5122 Romohr Rd., Cincinnati, OH 45208: Free brochure ◆ Magnetic picture frames. 513-248-2268.

**The Mettle Company,** P.O. Box 525, Fanwood, NJ 07023: Free information ◆ Aluminum frames. 800-621-1329.

**Abe Munn Picture Frames Inc.,** 51-02 21st St., Long Island City, NY 11101: Free list of retail sources ◆ Antique reproduction picture frames. 800-847-4026.

**Pictureframe Products Inc.,** 34 Hamilton Rd., Arlington, MA 02174: Free information ◆ Shrink package system for artists. 800-221-0530.

**Plaid Enterprises,** P.O. Box 7600, Norcross, GA 30091: Free information ◆ Frame-making supplies and accessories. 770-923-8200.

**Pootatuck,** P.O. Box 24, Windsor, VT 05089: Free information ◆ Framing accessories. 802-674-5984.

**Press-On-Products,** 1020 S. Westgate, Addison, IL 60101: Free catalog ◆ Framing accessories and mat boards. 800-323-1745. presoncorp@aol.com

**Putnum Distributors,** P.O. Box 477, Westfield, NJ 07091: Free catalog ◆ Frames. 800-631-7330; 908-232-9200 (in NJ).

**Sawdust & Stitches,** 9 Timber Ln., New Cumberland, PA 17070: Free information ◆ Shadowbox frames and display cases. 717-774-3893.

**Daniel Smith Art Supplies,** 4150 1st Ave. South, Seattle, WA 98134: Catalog $5 (refundable) ◆ Framing supplies. 800-426-6740. www.danielsmith.com

**Stu-Art Supplies,** 2045 Grand Ave., Baldwin, NY 11510: Free catalog ◆ Mats, plastic and glass, pre-assembled frames, aluminum and wood frame-making components, shrink wrap, plastic picture saver panels, and framing supplies. 516-546-5151.

**Summit Stained Glass,** 657 SW 2nd St., Lee's Summit, MO 64063: Free brochure ◆ Hardwood framing stock. 888-270-0037; 816-525-0037 (in MO).

**United Mfrs. Supplies Inc.,** 80 Gordon Dr., Syosset, NY 11791: Free catalog ◆ Frames and framing supplies. 800-645-7260.

**Vintage Photo & Frameworks,** 8523 Park Dr., Omaha, NE 68127: Catalog $1 ◆ Reproduction and antique photo frames. 888-723-7263.

**Wayne Frame Products Inc.,** 5832 Lakeside Ave., Toledo, OH 43611: Free information ◆ Horizontal and vertical-style frames. 800-331-5265; 419-729-4006 (in OH).

**Mary Webster Frames,** 12 Edwards St., Binghamton, NY 13905: Free information ◆ Antique picture frames. 607-722-1483.

**Wholesale Frame Service-USA,** P.O. Box 49067, Greensboro, NC 27419: Free catalog ◆ Wood frames in colorful rustics, traditional wood tones, weathered driftwood, gold, and silver. 800-522-3726. www.pictureframe-usa.com

## FRISBEES

**The Wright Life,** 200 Linden, Fort Collins, CO 80524: Free catalog ◆ Frisbees (flying discs), skateboards, snowboards, in-line skates, boomerangs, stunt kites, juggling equipment, and more. 800-321-8833. www.wrightlife.com

## FUND-RAISING

**Accents,** 215 Moody Rd., Enfield, CT 06083: Free catalog ◆ Fund-raising with greeting cards, calendars, and gifts. 800-357-1000. www.accentsosi.com

**Ace Pecan Company,** P.O. Box 1013, Maumee, OH 43537: Free catalog ◆ Fund-raising programs selling nuts and nut specialties. 800-323-9754.

**Allen-Lewis Manufacturing Company,** P.O. Box 16546, Denver, CO 80216: Free catalog ◆ Souvenirs, carnival and party supplies, fund-raising merchandise, toys and games, T-shirts and sweatshirts, and craft supplies. 800-525-6658.

**America's Best,** P.O. Box 6380, Montgomery, AL 36106: Free information ◆ Fund-raising products and how-to guide. 800-633-6750.

**Burger Marketing,** 1212 Red Hill Vly Rd. SE, Cleveland, TN 37323: Free information ◆ Fund-raising programs selling coffee, tea, and hot chocolate mix. 800-319-6817; 423-559-1620 (in TN).

**Calico Kitchen Press,** 142 Athens St., Hartwell, GA 30643: Free information ◆ Fund-raising cookbook plan. 706-376-5711.

**Classic American Fund Raisers,** Cookbook Plan, 10800 Lakeview Ave., Lenexa, KS 66219: Free information ◆ Custom cookbooks for fund-raising. 800-821-5745. www.cookbookpublishers.com

**Cokesbury,** Division United Methodist Publishing House, 201 8th Ave. South, P.O. Box 801, Nashville, TN 37202: Free information ◆ Bibles and bible reference books, bible study and Christian education books, fund-raising programs, gifts and casual clothing, choir apparel, church and clergy supplies, and church furniture. 800-672-1789. webservant@umph.org

**Cookbooks by Morris Press,** 3212 E. Hwy. 30, Kearney, NE 68848: Free information ◆ Custom cookbooks for fund-raising. 800-445-6621. www.morriscookbooks.com

**Crunch Time,** 137A Sutherland Rd., Boston, MA 02146: Free brochure ◆ Environmental education fund raisers. 800-2-CRUNCH.

**Designs by Lucinda,** 19 Rigby Rd., Scarborough, ME 04704: Free brochure ◆ Fund-raising with jewelry. 207-885-0200. www.lucinda.com

**Fancy Fortune Cookies,** 6265 Coffman Rd., Indianapolis, IN 46268: Free information ◆ Individually wrapped fortune cookies in twelve flavors and brilliant colors. Enclosed messages can be customized for the occasion. 317-299-8900. www.svr.com/cookies

**Fundcraft,** P.O. Box 340, Collierville, TN 38027: Free information ◆ Fund-raising programs. 800-853-1364; 901-853-7070 (in TN). www.fundcraft.com/funcrft.htm

**G & R Publishing Company,** 507 Industrial St., Waverly, IA 50677: Free information ◆ Custom cookbooks for churches, schools, groups, and individuals. 800-383-1679. gandr@gandrpublishing.com

**Genevieve's Gift Wrap Sales,** P.O. Box 147, West Springfield, MA 01090: Free catalog ◆ Fund-raising programs with distinctive gift wraps, gifts, and food products. 800-842-6656. dac@mclaughlin-paper.com

**Hale Indian River Groves,** Indian River Plaza, P.O. Box 217, Wabasso, FL 32970: Free catalog ◆ Fund-raising program with oranges and grapefruit. 800-289-4253.

**Krum's Chocolatier,** 4 Dexter Plaza, Pearl River, NY 10965: Free catalog ◆ Fund-raising program with Kosher chocolates. 800-ME-CANDY.

**Logo USA,** P.O. Box 2070, Cottonwood, CA 96022: Free information ◆ Customized logo watches, both casual and corporate. Also logo desk and wall clocks. 800-655-3364; 530-347-9178 (in CA). www.logousa.com

**Mascot Pecan Company,** P.O. Box 765, Glennville, GA 30427: Free information ◆ Fund-raising program with pecans and pecan candy. 800-841-3985; 912-654-2195 (in GA).

**My Rules Fund-Raising,** 17 Saw Mill River Rd., Ste. 43, Hawthorne, NY 10532: Free catalog ◆ Fund-raising with sportswear for children and adults. 914-742-2702. www.myrules.com

**Nagle Forge & Foundry,** 2 Farvue Rd., Novato, CA 94947: Catalog $2 ◆ Jewelry fund-raising program. 415-897-1732.

**Nestle-Beich,** P.O. Box 2914, Bloomington, IL 61702: Free information ◆ Fund-raising program with boxed chocolates and candy. 800-431-1248.

**Oriental Trading Company Inc.,** P.O. Box 3407, Omaha, NE 68103: Free catalog ◆ Fund-raising merchandise, toys, gifts, novelties, carnival supplies, and holiday and seasonal items. 800-228-0475. www.oriental.com

**B. Palmer Sales Company Inc.,** 3510 Hwy. 80 East, P.O. Box 850247, Mesquite, TX 75185: Free catalog ◆ Carnival, fund-raising, and party supplies. 800-888-3087; 214-288-1026 (in TX).

**The Peanut Shop of Williamsburg,** P.O. Box GN, Williamsburg, VA 23187: Free brochure ◆ Peanut specialties, Virginia country ham, Williamsburg soups, salad dressings, sauces, and other foods for fund-raising programs. 800-637-3268.

**Revere Company,** P.O. Box 751, Montgomery, AL 36101: Free catalog ◆ Fund-raising merchandise. 800-876-9967.

**Riversweet Fund Raising Citrus,** 11350 66th St., Ste. 102, Largo, FL 33773: Free catalog ◆ Fund-raising programs with gift boxes of citrus fruit. 800-741-0004; 813-545-0002 (in FL). www.riversweet.com

**Spirit of America Fund Raisers,** P.O. Box 709, Montgomery, AL 36101: Sample $2 ◆ Fund-raising program featuring daily planners with memo pads. 800-628-3671.

**Treasure Chest Fund Raising,** Division Enesco Corp., P.O. Box 295, Elk Grove Village, IL 60009: Free catalog ◆ Fund-raising programs. 800-438-3203. www.enesco.com

**U.S. Pen Fund Raising Company,** P.O. Box 1027, Montgomery, AL 36101: Free information ◆ Fund-raising programs for schools, churches, and organizations selling home, office, and school products. 800-633-8738.

**Walter's Cookbooks,** 215 5th Ave. SE, P.O. Box 1469, Waseca, MN 56093: Free information ◆ Custom cookbooks for fund-raising. 800-447-3274. www.custom-cookbooks.com

## FURNACES, HEATING SYSTEMS, & CONTROLS

**AGA Cookers,** Classic Cookers, RD 3, Box 180-6176, Montpelier, VT 05602: Brochure $2 ◆ Radiant heating systems. 800-633-9200. www.agacooker.com

**Carrier Corp.,** Box 408, Syracuse, NY 13221: Free information ◆ Combination gas and electric heating and cooling system, gas and electric furnaces, heat pumps, and air conditioners. 800-227-7437. www.carrier.com

**Central Boiler Inc.,** Rt. 1, Box 220, Greenbrush, MN 56726: Free brochure ◆ Outdoor wood furnaces. 800-248-4681. www.centralboiler.com

**Charmaster Products Inc.,** 2307 Hwy. 2 West, Grand Rapids, MN 55744: Free brochure ◆ Forced air and hot water wood-burning furnaces. 218-326-6786.

**Domo Teck,** 176 Abbeywood Circle, Ste. 100, Streamwood, IL 60107: Free information ◆ House current-operated low-temperature floor warming systems. 800-875-5285,

**Edwards Engineering Corp.,** 101 Alexander Ave., Pompton Plains, NJ 07444: Free information ◆ Blower and fan-free hydronic cooling and heating system. 800-526-5201; 201-835-2800 (in NJ).

**Empire Control Systems,** 1918 Freeburg Ave., Belleville, IL 62222: Free brochure ◆ Room heaters, floor furnaces, commercial/industrial unit heaters and duct furnaces, fireplace products, free-standing and semi-enclosed gas stoves, chicken and turkey fryers, and accessories. 800-851-3153; 618-233-7420 (in IL). www.empirecomfort.com

**Enerzone Systems Corp.,** 4103 Pecan Orchard, Parker, TX 75002: Free information ◆ Heating and air conditioning controls. 888-782-8638. www.enerzone.com

**G.E. Appliances,** General Electric Company, Appliance Park, Louisville, KY 40225: Free information ◆ Air conditioners and heat pumps. 800-626-2000. www.ge.com

**HAI Home Automation Inc.,** 5725 Powell St., Ste. A, New Orleans, LA 70123: Free brochure ◆ Programmable thermostats. 800-229-7256. www.homeauto.com

**Heatway Radiant Floors & Snowmelting,** 3131 W. Chestnut Expwy., Springfield, MO 65802: Free information ◆ Heating systems for installation under frame or slab floors. 800-255-1996.

**Hunter Fan Company,** 2500 Fisco Ave., Memphis, TN 38114: Catalog $1 ◆ Electronic-programmable thermostats, ceiling fans, fixtures, air conditioners, and dehumidifiers. 901-745-9222. www.hunterfan.com

**Hydrol-Sil,** P.O. Box 662, Fort Mill, SC 29715: Free information ◆ Electric-operated zone heating system units. 800-627-9276.

**Maxxon Corp.,** 920 Hamel Rd., Hamel, MN 55340: Free list of retail sources ◆ In-floor hot water and electric radiant heating systems. Includes do-it-yourself floor warming kits. 612-478-9600.

**Orbit Manufacturing Company,** 1507 Park Ave., Perkasie, PA 18944: Free information ◆ Residential electric heating equipment. 215-257-0727.

**Panelectric,** 1010 Winchester Rd., Irvine, KY 40336: Free information ◆ In-ceiling radiant heating systems. 800-228-9022.

**Radiant Technology Inc.,** 11 Farber Dr., Bellport, NY 11713: Free list of retail sources ◆ Hot water baseboard heating equipment. 516-286-0900.

**Radiantec,** Box 1111, Lyndonville, VT 05851: Free information ◆ Under-the-floor heating systems. 800-451-7593; 802-626-8045 (in VT).

**Rinnai,** 1662 Lukken Industrial Dr., West LaGrange, GA 30240: Free information ◆ Energy-saving gas furnaces. 800-621-9419.

**Solid State Heating,** 146 Elm St., P.O. Box 769, Old Saybrook, CT 06475: Free information ◆ Easy-to-install high-tech heating system for new and remodeled homes. 800-544-5182.

**Stadler Corp.,** 3 Alfred Circle, Bedford, MA 01730: Free information ◆ Radiant floor heating systems. 800-370-3122.

**Sunquest Inc.,** 1555 N. Rankin Ave., Newton, NC 28658: Free information ◆ Solar energy and radiant floor heating systems. 704-465-6805.

**Taylor Manufacturing,** P.O. Box 518, Elizabethtown, NC 28337: Free information ◆ Outdoor wood heating systems. 800-545-2293.

**TEMP-CAST Enviroheat Ltd.,** 3332 Yonge St., P.O. Box 94059, Toronto, Ontario, Canada M4N 3R1: Free brochure ◆ Gas/propane or wood-fired masonry heaters. 800-561-8594.

**Wirsbo Floor Heating,** 5925 148th St. West, Apple Valley, MN 55124: Free information ◆ Radiant floor heating systems. 800-321-4739.

## FURNITURE

### Beds

**American Starbuck,** P.O. Box 15376, Lenexa, KS 66215: Free catalog ◆ Pencil-post beds and bedroom furniture. 800-245-7188.

**American Waterbed Wholesalers,** 10 Stage Door Rd., Fishkill, NY 12524: Free catalog ◆ Waterbeds with optional heaters, other bedroom furniture, mattress pads, non-electric heating systems, and sheets. 800-233-7191.

**Amish Country Collection,** Sunset Valley Rd., RD 5, Box 271, New Castle, PA 16105: Catalog $5 ◆ Early American rustic bedroom furniture. 412-458-4811.

**Bartley Collection Ltd.,** 65 Engerman Ave., Denton, MD 21629: Free catalog ◆ Antique reproduction furniture kits. 800-787-2800.

**The Bed Factory,** P.O. Box 791, Westerville, OH 43086: Catalog $5 ◆ Heirloom wood, iron, and brass beds. Also juvenile beds and mattresses. 614-470-0146.

**Bedlam Brass,** 530 River Dr., Garfield, NJ 07026: Free catalog ◆ Brass beds and mirrors, tables, and racks for coats, quilts and blankets. 973-546-5000.

**Brass Bed Shoppe,** 12421 Cedar Rd., Cleveland, OH 44106: Catalog $1 ◆ Solid brass and iron beds. 216-379-0400.

**Carpenter's Brothers Furniture,** Box 425, Sunderland, MA 01375: Free information ◆ Desks, dressers, bookcases, furniture, and bunk, twin, full, and queen-size beds. 800-777-BUNK.

**Cohasset Colonials,** 10 Churchill Rd., Hingham, MA 02043: Catalog $3 ◆ Kits for Early American, Shaker, Queen Anne, and Chippendale beds and other furniture. 800-288-2389.

**Country Bed Shop,** 328 Richardson Rd., Ashby, MA 01431: Catalog $4 ◆ Handcrafted reproductions of 17th and 18th-century American beds, chairs, tables, and other furniture. 978-386-7550.

**Create-A-Bed,** 5100 Preston Hwy., Louisville, KY 40213: Catalog $2 ◆ Easy-to-install wallbeds. 502-966-3852. www.wallbed.com

**Dreambeds,** P.O. Box 205, Rockport, MA 01966: Free information ◆ Pencil post canopy bed frames, netted canopies, and bed curtains. 978-546-5808.

**Ecologic Inc.,** 1140 Elizabeth Ave., Waukegan, IL 60085: Free brochure ◆ Bedroom and outdoor furniture made from recycled harder-than-oak materials. 800-899-8004; 847-244-4466 (in IL).

**Hollingsworth Furniture,** 3306 E. Ash St., Goldsboro, NC 27534: Free brochure ◆ Handpainted, stained, or unfinished American country-style reproduction pencil post and sleigh beds and other furniture. 919-778-9721.

**Iron Design Center,** 83 Yesler Way, Seattle, WA 98104: Catalog $5 ◆ Metal beds and accessories. 800-971-IRON.

**Leonard's Antiques,** 600 Taunton Creek, Seekonk, MA 02771: Catalog $4 ◆ Original and reproduction antique beds. 508-336-8585.

**Mountain Woodworking,** 483 Mountain Rd., High Falls, NY 12240: Free brochure ◆ Easy-to-assemble pencil post beds. 914-687-4892.

**Murphy Bed Company Inc.,** 42 Central Ave., Farmingdale, NY 11735: Free information ◆ Wall beds. 800-845-2337.

**The Old Wicker Garden,** 6606 Snider Plaza, Dallas, TX 75225: Photos $5 (refundable) ◆ Antique wicker furniture, brass and iron beds, hooked rugs and quilts, folk art, and decorative accessories. 972-373-8241.

**Osborne Wood Products,** 8116 Hwy. 123 North, Toccoa, GA 30577: Free information ◆ Easy-to-assemble pencil-post beds. 800-849-8876; 706-886-1065 (in GA).

**Charles P. Rogers Beds,** 899 1st Ave., New York, NY 10022: Catalog $1 ◆ Original 19th and 20th-century brass and iron beds, headboards, canopy beds, and daybeds. 800-272-7726; 212-935-6900 (in NY).

**Room & Board,** 4600 Olson Memorial Hwy., Minneapolis, MN 55422: Free information ◆ Handcrafted steel beds and tables. 800-486-6554.

**The SICO Room Makers,** Room Makers Division, 7525 Cahill Rd., P.O. Box 1169, Minneapolis, MN 55440: Free information ◆ Wall beds, home office furniture, and wall systems. 800-328-6138.

**Thomasville Furniture,** P.O. Box 339, Thomasville, NC 27360: Catalog $3.50 ◆ Early American-style beds and other furniture. 800-225-0265. www.thomasville.com

**A Touch of Brass,** 9052 Chevrolet Dr., Ellicott City, MD 21042: Catalog $3 ◆ Reproduction iron and solid brass beds. 800-272-7734.

**Lisa Victoria Brass Beds,** 17106 S. Crater Rd., Petersburg, VA 23805: Catalog $4 ◆ Brass beds. 804-862-1491.

## Beds, Adjustable & Mattresses

**Advanced Comfort,** 10 Stage Door Rd., Fishkill, NY 12524: Free catalog ◆ Airbeds, foam mattresses, and waterbeds. 800-896-1552.

**Craftmatic Beds,** 2500 Interplex Dr., Trevose, PA 19047: Free information ◆ Adjustable beds with electric hand controls. 800-677-8200.

**Electric Mobility Corp.,** 1 Mobility Plaza, P.O. Box 156, Sewell, NJ 08080: Free brochure ◆ Adjustable beds with electric hand controls. 800-662-4548. www.electricmobility.com

**Flex-A-Bed,** P.O. Box 568, Lafayette, GA 30728: Free information ◆ Electrically-adjustable bed. 800-787-1337.

**Natural Form 2000,** P.O. Box 146, Hoosick Falls, NY 12090: Free brochure ◆ Mattresses. 800-882-4767.

**Select Comfort,** 6105 Trenton North, Minneapolis, MN 55442: Free information ◆ Adjustable mattress for individual body support and comfort selection. 800-831-1211.

**TEMPUR-Pedic Mattress,** 848G Nandino Blvd., Lexington, KY 40511: Free video ◆ Mattress and pillows that mold and respond to a person's need for comfort to help relieve suffering from back pain, arthritis, or sleeplessness. 800-886-6466. www.tempurpedic.com

**Ultimate Home Care Company,** 3250 E. 19th St., Long Beach, CA 90804: Free information ◆ Regular and adjustable beds for unassisted transfers from wheel chairs. 800-475-8122.

## Children's Furniture

**Child Craft,** P.O. Box 444, 501 E. Market St., Salem, IN 47167: Free list of retail sources ◆ Nursery and other children's furniture. 812-883-3111.

**Citikids,** 152 Clement St., San Francisco, CA 94118: Free information ◆ Children's furniture, car seats, strollers, clothing, and baby care items. 415-752-3837.

**Cry Baby Ranch,** 1422 Larimer Square, Denver, CO 80202: Catalog $2 ◆ Children's cowboy-style furniture and clothing. 888-CRY-BABY. www.crybabyranch.com

**KinderKraft,** 8150 W. 30th Ct., Hialeah, FL 33016: Free brochure ◆ Crib to toddler bed convertibles, dresser-to-desks, and other children's furniture. 800-822-6748.

**Little Colorado Inc.,** 4450 Lipan St., Denver, CO 80211: Catalog $2 ◆ Handcrafted children's furniture and accessories. 303-964-3212. sales@littlecolorado.com

**Reed Brothers,** 5000 Turner Rd., Sebastopol, CA 95472: Catalog $15 ◆ Children's furniture. 707-795-6261.

**The Uptown Nursery,** 1601 Mt. Rushmore Dr., Rapid City, SD 57701: Free catalog ◆ Heirloom round crib bedding, cribs, and accessories. 888-545-2742.

## Furniture Kits

**Adams Wood Products Inc.,** 974 Forest Dr., Morristown, TN 37814: Free catalog ◆ Ready-to-assemble furniture. 615-587-2942.

**Andover Wood Products,** P.O. Box 38, Andover, ME 04216: Free information ◆ Ready-to-assemble Windsor and Shaker-style chairs. 207-392-2101.

**Available Plastic Inc.,** P.O. Box 924, Huntsville, AL 35804: Free price list ◆ PVC components for making your own furniture. 800-633-7212.

**Bartley Collection Ltd.,** 65 Engerman Ave., Denton, MD 21629: Free catalog ◆ Antique reproduction furniture kits. 800-787-2800.

**Cohasset Colonials,** 10 Churchill Rd., Hingham, MA 02043: Catalog $3 ◆ Kits for Early American, Shaker, Queen Anne, and Chippendale beds and other furniture. 800-288-2389.

**Emperor Clock LLC,** Emperor Industrial Park, P.O. Box 1089, Fairhope, AL 36533: Catalog $1 ◆ Build-it-yourself grandfather clocks and furniture kits. 800-642-0011; 334-928-2316 (in AL). www.emperorclock.com

**K. Kraft Furniture,** 617 Lynne Ave., Ypsilanti, MI 48198: Free information ◆ Ready-to-assemble contemporary-style country furniture. 313-484-0830.

**Shaker Workshops,** Box 8001, Ashburnham, MA 01430: Catalog $1 ◆ Shaker furniture in kits or assembled, needle crafts, dolls, and dollhouse furniture. 800-840-9121. www.shakerworkshops.com

**Yield House,** P.O. Box 2525, Conway, NH 03818: Free catalog ◆ Pre-sanded furniture kits. 800-659-0206.

## Home Furnishings

**Stephen Adams, Furnituremaker,** P.O. Box 130, Rt. 160, Denmark, ME 04022: Catalog $5 ◆ Period furniture reproductions. 207-452-2378.

**Adriance Furniture Makers,** 288 Gulf Rd., South Dartmouth, MA 02748: Catalog $3 ◆ Classic New England designed furniture. 508-993-4800.

**Alcyon Woodworks,** P.O. Box 11165, Portland, ME 04104: Free information ◆ Traditional custom made American-style furniture for the home and office. 207-657-3356.

**American Furniture Galleries,** P.O. Box 60, Montgomery, AL 36101: Brochure $1 ◆ Handcrafted reproduction Victorian-style furniture. 800-547-5240.

**American Log Furniture Designs,** 163 N. Woodward Ave., Birmingham, MI 48660: Free information ◆ Bedroom, family room, and dining room contemporary log furniture. 800-435-LOGS.

**American Reproductions,** Atrium Mall, 4th Floor, 430 S. Main St., High Point, NC 27260: Free information ◆ Entertainment centers with storage areas. Also wine serving carts. 336-889-8305.

**Americana Logworks,** 241 Addison Square, Kalispell, MT 59901: Free information ◆ Custom log furniture. 406-257-4161. amicana@digisys.net

**Amish Country Collection,** Sunset Valley Rd., RD 5, Box 271, New Castle, PA 16105: Catalog $5 ◆ Amish-style oak and hickory twig furniture, rugs, quilts, and wall hangings. 412-458-4811.

**Angel House Designs,** RFD 1 Box 1, Rt. 148, Brookfield, MA 01506: Information $3 ◆ Dress-up and country-style furniture. 508-867-2517.

**Antiquarian Traders,** 399 LaFayette St., New York, NY 10003: Catalog $25 ◆ American Renaissance, revival Victorian, American oak, country French, English-style, and other furniture. 212-260-1200.

**Antiquity,** 719 Genesee St., Delafield, WI 53018: Catalog $5 ◆ Handcrafted reproduction 18th-century furniture. 414-646-4911.

**Arts By Alexander,** 701 Greensboro Rd., High Point, NC 27260: Free information ◆ Home furnishings. 336-884-8062.

**V. Michael Ashford,** 6543 Alpine Dr. SW, Olympia, WA 98512: Brochure $1 ◆ Reproduction furniture and lighting. 360-352-0694.

**The Atrium,** 430 S. Main St., High Point, NC 27260: Free information ◆ Home furnishings in wood. 800-527-2570.

**Back Country Western Design,** 708 S. Daisy St., Salmon, ID 83467: Free information ◆ Log furniture. 208-756-4951. www.wolfpk.com/backcountry

**Backwoods Furnishings,** Box 161, Indian Lake, NY 12842: Free brochure ◆ Rustic-style tables and chairs, rocking chairs, four-poster beds, and desks. 518-251-3327.

**Badlands Outpost,** P.O. Box 3768, Ogden, UT 84409: Catalog $4 ◆ Custom log and western-style furniture for the home or office. 800-457-3922; 801-732-1100 (in UT).

**Bargain John's Antiques,** 700 S. Washington, P.O. Box 705, Lexington, NE 68850: Free information ◆ Antique furniture.

**Barn Again Furniture Company,** 835 Fairfax St., Altoona, WI 54720: Free information ◆ Country-style furniture.

**Barnes & Barnes Fine Furniture,** 190 Commerce Ave., Southern Pines, NC 28387: Free brochure ◆ Home furnishings. 800-334-8174.

**Barton-Sharpe Ltd.,** 119 Spring St., New York, NY 10012: Free information ◆ Reproduction 18th and 19th-century furniture, lighting, bedding, stoneware, and decorative items. 212-925-9562.

**C.H. Becksvoort,** Box 12, New Gloucester, ME 04260: Catalog $5 ◆ Cherry furniture and accessories. 207-926-4608.

**Bentwood Building,** 241 Addison Square, Kalispell, MT 59901: Catalog $4 ◆ Log spiral stairways and furniture. 406-257-4161.

**Berkeley Mills,** 2830 7th St., Berkeley, CA 94710: Free catalog ◆ In-stock and custom furniture and accessories. 510-549-2854.

**Bisciotti Design,** 1914 S. Raymond Ave., Loft A, Los Angeles, CA 90007: Catalog $6 ◆ Contemporary home furnishings and functional art pieces. 213-734-2391. www.bisciotti.com

**Blackwelder's,** 294 Turnersburg Hwy., Statesville, NC 28677: Free information with long SASE ◆ Home furnishings. 800-438-0201. www.blackwelder.com

**Blake Industries,** P.O. Box 155, Abington, MA 02351: Free information ◆ Outdoor and indoor teak furniture, ornamental cast-iron pole lights, and fixtures. 781-337-8772.

**Blue Ridge Log Works,** 3910 Lynda Ln., Fort Collins, CO 80526: Free brochure ◆ Handcrafted log furniture and hand railings. 800-313-0431.

**Bonita Furniture Galleries,** P.O. Box 9143, Hickory, NC 28603: Free information with long SASE ◆ Home furnishings. 704-324-1992.

**BookHut,** 33 Chester Ct., Peekskill, NY 10566: Free information ◆ Custom solid hardwood bookcases crafted for the home, school, office, and library. 800-295-2488. sales@bookhut.com

**Dennis & CeCe Bork,** 715 Genesee St., Delafield, WI 53018: Catalog $5 ◆ Custom furniture, folk art, period lighting, Colonial Williamsburg reproductions, Windsor chairs and settees, and accessories. 414-646-4911.

**Brentwood Manor Furnishings,** 316 Virginia Ave., Clarksville, VA 23927: Free brochure ◆ Home furnishings, clocks, draperies, and mirrors. 800-225-6105.

**Curtis Buchanan, Windsor Chairmaker,** 208 E. Main St., Jonesborough, TN 37659: Brochure $2 with long SASE ◆ Windsor chairs. 423-753-5160.

**Cabin Outfitters,** P.O. Box 20359, Billings, MT 59104: Free brochure ◆ Handcrafted log furniture. 800-661-6407.

**Calico Corners,** 203 Gale Ln., Kennett Square, PA 19348: Free catalog ◆ Decorative fabrics and custom furniture. 800-213-6366. www.calicocorners.com

**Michael Camp,** Cabinetmaker, 495 Amelia, Plymouth, MI 48170: Catalog $4 ◆ Reproduction 18th and 19th-century furniture. 313-459-1190.

**Candlertown Chairworks,** 14 Boylston Hwy., Mills River, NC 28742: Catalog $2 ◆ Handbuilt country-style adult and children's chairs, benches, bar stools, and other furniture. 800-282-0406. www.chairworks.com

**Carolina Interiors,** 115 Oak Ave., Kannapolis, NC 28081: Free brochure ◆ Home furnishings. 704-933-2261.

**Carpenter's Brothers Furniture,** Box 425, Sunderland, MA 01375: Free information ◆ Desks, dressers, bookcases, other furniture, and bunk, twin, full, and queen-size beds. 800-777-BUNK.

**Cast Aluminum Reproductions,** P.O. Box 1060, San Elzario, TX 79849: Catalog $2 ◆ Cast-aluminum and brass furniture, street lights, outdoor furniture, fountains, mail boxes, and plant stands. 915-764-3793.

**CCSI Furniture,** 13509 Method St., Dallas, TX 75243: Free information with long SASE ◆ Deacon's benches and rustic country-style furniture. 214-231-7178.

**Cedar Rock Furniture,** P.O. Box 515, Hudson, NC 28638: Free information ◆ Home furnishings. 704-396-2361.

**Chapman Manufacturing,** 481 W. Main St., Avon, MA 02322: Brochure $4 (request list of retail sources) ◆ Lighting, furniture, and accessories. 508-588-3200.

**Cherry Hill Furniture,** Box 7405, Furnitureland Station, High Point, NC 27264: Free brochures ◆ Home furnishings. 800-666-0933. www.cherryhillfurn.com

**Cherry Pond Designs,** P.O. Box 6, Jefferson, NH 03583: Catalog $10 ◆ Shaker furniture. 800-643-7384; 603-586-7795 (in NH).

**Chestnut Hill Furniture,** 511 W. King St., East Berlin, PA 17316: Free information ◆ Upholstered home furnishings. 717-259-7502.

**Circa 1820,** RR 1, Box 4040, Vassalboro, ME 04989: Catalog $5 (refundable) ◆ Reproduction Shaker and country furniture, redware, pewter, and tin lighting. 207-877-9863.

**Clear Lake Furniture,** 322 Rt. 100 North, Ludlow, VT 05149: Free information ◆ Handcrafted furniture. 800-758-8767.

**Coffey Furniture Galleries,** Box 141, Granite Falls, NC 28630: Free information ◆ Home furnishings. 704-396-4999.

**Cohasset Colonials,** 10 Churchill Rd., Hingham, MA 02043: Catalog $3 ◆ Reproduction furniture in kits or assembled, fabrics, paints and stains, brass and pewter items, and fixtures. 800-288-2389.

**Cole's Appliance & Furniture Company,** 4026 Lincoln Ave., Chicago, IL 60618: Free information with long SASE ◆ Home furnishings, audio and video equipment, TVs, and kitchen appliances. 773-525-1797.

**Colonial Williamsburg Furniture,** P.O. Box 1776, Williamsburg, VA 23187: Catalog $14.65 ◆ Reproduction colonial furnishings and decorative accessories. 804-220-7503.

**Conrad Furniture,** P.O. Box 1411, Wausau, WI 54402: Free information ◆ Assembled and ready-to-finish solid oak paddle back side chairs. 715-842-8022.

**Country Bed Shop,** 328 Richardson Rd., Ashby, MA 01431: Catalog $4 ◆ Handcrafted reproductions of 17th and 18th-century American beds, chairs, and tables. 978-386-7550.

**Gregan T. Crawford,** Cabinet Maker, 374 Landon's Dam Rd., Oakland, MD 21550: Catalog $2 ◆ Shaker inspired furniture and home accessories. 800-531-4109.

**Gerald Curry, Cabinetmaker,** Pound Hill Rd., Union, ME 04862: Free brochure ◆ Traditional American furniture with emphasis on Shaker styling. 207-785-4633.

**Danish Country Antique Furniture,** 138 Charles St., Boston, MA 02114: Free information ◆ Danish farm furniture from the 18th and 19th-century. 617-227-1804.

**Davis Cabinet Company,** 505 Crutcher St., Nashville, TN 37213: Free information ◆ Bedroom and custom-built furniture. 615-244-7100.

**The Deep River Trading Company,** 2436 Willard Rd., High Point, NC 27265: Free information ◆ Reproduction 18th-century furniture. 336-885-2436.

**Door Creek Forge,** 2562 Door Creek Rd., Stoughton, WI 53589: Catalog $2 ◆ Hand-forged wrought iron furniture and accessories. 608-877-1247.

**Dovetail Wood Works,** 116 W. Boylston St., Worcester, MA 01606: Catalog $3 (refundable) ◆ Handcrafted hardwood furniture. 508-853-3151.

**Dubrow Antiques,** P.O. Box 128, Bayside, NY 11361: Free information ◆ American-style 19th-century furniture. 718-767-9758.

**Frederick Duckloe & Bros. Inc.,** P.O. Box 427, Portland, PA 18351: Catalog $6 ◆ Handcrafted Windsor chairs, rockers, benches, and bar stools. 717-897-6172.

**Charles Durfee Cabinetmaker,** RD 1, Box 1132, Woolwich, ME 04579: Brochure $1 ◆ Shaker and Early American-style solid wood furniture. 207-442-7049.

**E.P. Woodworks,** Lance & Vicki Munn, P.O. Box 271, Bloomfield, IN 47424: Free information with long SASE ◆ Handcrafted hardwood furniture in red oak, black walnut, and wild cherry. 812-384-4806.

**European Furniture Importers,** 2145 W. Grand Ave., Chicago, IL 60612: Catalog $3 ◆ Imported European furniture. 800-283-1955; 312-243-1955 (in IL). www.eurofurniture.com

**William Evans Furniture,** P.O. Box 757, Waldoboro, ME 04572: Catalog $5 ◆ Handmade period reproduction furniture. 207-432-4175.

**Farm River Antiques,** 26 Broadway, North Haven, CT 06473: Free brochure ◆ Original high-style 19th-century American furniture. 203-239-2434.

**Fireside Reproductions,** 4727 Winterset Dr., Columbus, OH 43220: Catalog $10 ◆ Handcrafted reproduction American country and 18th and early 19th-century furniture. 614-451-7695.

**Foreign Objects,** 2721 W. 81st St., Hialeah, FL 33016: Free brochure ◆ Handmade rustic pine and custom or standard wrought iron furniture. Also decorative accessories. 305-558-7212.

**Frontier Furniture,** 815 Montana Hwy. 82, Somers, MT 59932: Catalog $4 ◆ Handcrafted log furniture. 406-857-3525. www.frontierlog.com

**Full Upright Position,** 1101 NW Glisan, Portland, OR 97209: Free catalog ◆ Modern furniture. 800-431-5134. www.f-u-p.com

**The Furniture Patch of Calabash Inc.,** P.O. Box 4970, Calabash, NC 28467: Free brochure ◆ Home furnishings. 910-579-2001.

**Genada Imports,** P.O. Box 204, Teaneck, NJ 07666: Catalog $1 ◆ Danish-style furniture. 201-790-7522.

**Gertz Seating & Upholstery,** 642 State St. Rear, New Albany, IN 47150: Free catalog ◆ Upholstered headboards, cedar storage chests, and bedroom accessories. 800-652-6233.

**Great American Log,** Box 3360, Ketchum, ID 83340: Catalog $4 ◆ Handcrafted log furniture. 800-624-5779.

**Great Meadows Joinery,** 234 Boston Post Rd., Rt. 20, Wayland, MA 01778: Catalog $4 ◆ Handmade reproduction Shaker-style furniture. 508-358-4370.

**Green Design Furniture Company,** 267 Commercial St., Portland, ME 04101: Free brochure ◆ Original designs in custom built home furnishings. 800-853-4234. www.greendesigns.com

**Jeffrey P. Greene, Furniture Maker,** 1 W. Main St., Wickford, RI 02852: Catalog $5 ◆ Handcrafted 18th-century style furniture. 401-295-1200.

**Habersham Plantation,** P.O. Box 1209, Toccoa, GA 30577: Catalog $12 ◆ Reproduction 17th and 18th-century country and contemporary furniture. 800-241-0716.

**Hamilton's Furniture,** 506 Live Oak St., Beaufort, NC 28516: Free information ◆ Home furnishings and accessories. 800-488-4720.

**Handcrafted Log Furnishings,** 11372 Ave. 272, Visalia, CA 93278: Information package $10 ◆ Custom log furniture and railings. 209-687-0744.

**Harden Furniture,** Mill Pond Way, McConnellsville, NY 13401: Free brochure ◆ Handcrafted chairs and upholstered and solid wood furniture.

**Heirloom Reproductions,** 1834 W. 5th St., Montgomery, AL 36106: Catalog $3 ◆ Victorian and French-style period furniture reproductions. 800-288-1513. www.angelfire.com/ok/furnitureman/index.html

**Hendricks Furniture Inc.,** P.O. Box 828, Mocksville, NC 27028: Free information ◆ Home furnishings. 336-998-7712.

**Hickory Furniture Mart,** 2220 Hwy. 70 SE, Hickory, NC 28602: Free information ◆ Traditional and contemporary furniture. 800-462-MART.

**Warren Hile Studio,** 310 N. Sunnyside Ave., Sierra Madre, CA 91024: Catalog $1 ◆ Handcrafted mission-style furniture. 818-355-3943.

**Historic Charleston Reproductions,** 105 Broad St., P.O. Box 622, Charleston, SC 29402: Catalog $10 ◆ Reproduction furniture. 803-723-8292.

**Holiday Patio Showcase,** P.O. Box 727, Hudson, NC 28638: Free catalog ◆ Outdoor and indoor furnishings. 704-728-2664.

**Hollingsworth Furniture,** 3306 E. Ash St., Goldsboro, NC 27534: Free brochure ◆ Handpainted, stained, or unfinished American country-style reproduction pencil post and sleigh beds and other furniture. 919-778-9721.

**Martha M. House,** 1022 S. Decatur St., Montgomery, AL 36104: Catalog $3 ◆ Custom French and Victorian reproductions available in many fabrics and finishes. 800-255-4195; 334-264-3558 (in AL). www.marthahouse.com

**House Dressing Furniture,** 3608 W. Wendover, Greensboro, NC 27407: Free information ◆ Home furnishings. 800-322-5850. www.housedressing.com

**Hudson's Discount Furniture,** P.O. Box 2547, Hickory, NC 28603: Free information ◆ Home furnishings. 704-322-4996.

**Hunt Galleries Inc.,** P.O. Box 2324, Hickory, NC 28603: Catalog $5 ◆ Sofas, upholstered chairs, ottomans, benches, lounges, headboards, and other furniture. 800-248-3876.

**Images In Steel,** P.O. Box 288, Clyde Park, MT 59018: Catalog $2 (refundable) ◆ Weather vanes, fireplace screens, furniture, custom designed art, and functional western pieces handcrafted from plate steel. 800-511-1324; 406-686-4166 (in MT).

**Imelda,** 16960 S.R. 12 East., Findlay, OH 45840: Free catalog ◆ Antiques, Victorian furniture, and cast aluminum lighting. 800-483-7105; 419-424-1722 (in OH).

**Ian Ingersoll, Cabinetmakers,** 136 Town St., West Cornwall, CT 06796: Brochure $3 ◆ Reproduction Shaker furniture and chairs. 800-237-4926.

**Interior Furnishings Ltd.,** P.O. Box 1644, Hickory, NC 28603: Free brochure ◆ Home furnishings. 704-328-5683.

**Irion Company Furniture Makers,** 1 S. Bridge St., Christiana, PA 17509: Free brochure ◆ Custom-made 18th-century furniture reproductions. 610-593-2153.

**Iverson Snowshoe Company,** Maple St., P.O. Box 85, Shingleton, MI 49884: Free information ◆ Handcrafted white ash furniture. 906-452-6370.

**Jackson's Cabinet Shop,** 2879 Wildwood Rd. Extension, Allison Park, PA 15101: Free brochure ◆ Reproduction period furniture of the 18th and early 19th-century. 412-487-1291.

**Jennifer's Trunk Antiques & General Store,** 201 N. Riverside, Dr., St. Clair, MI 48079: Free brochure ◆ Victorian-style antique furniture, books, jewelry, lamps and shades, and gifts. 810-329-2032.

**JoAnne's Bed & Back Shops,** 5640 Sunnyside Ave., Unit G, Beltsville, MD 20705: Free catalog ◆ Ergonomic chairs, sofas, beds, and accessories for proper back and neck support. 800-767-2225; 301-220-0800 (in MD).

**Jay "Bird" Jones,** 520 Pine Oaks Rd., #4, Colorado Springs, CO 80926: Catalog $10 (refundable); brochure $1 ◆ Antler chairs, lamps, chandeliers, and carvings. 719-527-1845.

**Jungle Zoo Furniture,** P.O. Box 809, Tucson, AZ 85702: Free information ◆ Indoor and outdoor furniture with a Mexican and southwestern theme. 800-99-JUNGLE; 520-887-8645 (in AZ).

**The Karges Furniture Company Inc.,** P.O. Box 6517, Evansville, IN 47719: Brochure $10 ◆ Home furnishings. 800-252-7437.

**Kauffman Wood Products,** P.O. Box 143, Kerby, OR 97531: Free information ◆ Indoor and outdoor country style classic log furniture. 800-867-8585; 541-592-2568 (in OR). www.kauffmanwood.com

**The Keeping Room Furniture,** 8405 Richmond Hwy., Alexandria, VA 22309: Catalog $5 ◆ Classic furniture. 703-360-6399.

**Kestrel Manufacturing,** 9 E. Race St., Stowe, PA 19464: Information $2 ◆ Knock-down and ready-to-hang folding screens and interior and exterior shutters. Also available as kits. 800-494-4321; 610-326-6679 (in PA). www.diyshutters.com

**Klein Design Inc.,** 99 Sadler St., Gloucester, MA 01930: Free brochure ◆ Rockers, chairs, love-seats, sofas, and side tables. 800-451-7247. www.kleindesign.com

**Knight Galleries,** P.O. Box 1254, Lenoir, NC 28645: Free information ◆ Home furnishings. 800-334-4721.

**Kozmiuk Cabinetry & Fine Woodworking,** 301 E. Main St., Harrisville, MI 48740: Free information ◆ Custom museum-quality antique furniture reproductions. 517-724-6541.

**Lanier Furniture Company,** P.O. Box 3576, Wilmington, NC 28406: Catalog $3 ◆ Handcrafted reproduction Shaker furniture. 800-453-1362.

**Leather Interiors,** Box 9305, Hickory, NC 28603: Free information ◆ Traditional and contemporary leather furniture. 800-627-4526.

**Levenger,** P.O. Box 1256, Delray Beach, FL 33447: Free catalog ◆ Books, furniture, pens, briefcases, and other gifts for serious readers. 800-545-0242. www.levenger.com

**Lexington Furniture,** 1117 Winchester Rd., Lexington, KY 40505: Free information ◆ Leather and 18th-century mahogany and cherry reproduction furniture. 606-254-5362. www.lexfurniture.com

**Live Oaks of Savannah,** P.O. Box 16194, Savannah, GA 31416: Free catalog ◆ Victorian-style furniture, lamps, clocks, and accessories. 800-467-5539.

**Loftin-Black Furniture Company,** 111 Sedgehill Dr., Thomasville, NC 27360: Free catalog ◆ Home furnishings. 800-334-7398; 336-472-4711 (in NC).

**Log Cabin Rustic Furniture,** 158 Partridgeville Rd., Templeton, MA 01468: Brochure $2 ◆ Log furniture and accessories.

**Russ Loomis Master Furniture Maker,** 1413 West Rd., Williamsburg MA 01096: Catalog $3 ◆ Classic home furnishings. 413-628-3813.

**Louisiana Furniture Gallery,** 495 SW Railroad Ave., Ponchatoula, LA 70754: Free brochure ◆ Handcrafted Louisiana-style furniture from salvaged and antique woods. 504-386-0471.

**Mack & Rodel Cabinet Makers,** 44 Leighton Rd., Pownal, ME 04069: Catalog $5 ◆ Home furnishings. 207-688-4483.

**MacPhail's Studio,** 1417 N. Kickapoo, Ste. 4, Lincoln, IL 62656: Free information ◆ Antler chandeliers, lamps, and chairs. 217-732-7538.

**Magnolia Hall,** 726 Andover, Atlanta, GA 30327: Catalog $3 ◆ Carved furniture. 404-351-1910.

**Maine Cottage Furniture Inc.,** P.O. Box 935, Yarmouth, ME 04096: Free brochure ◆ Custom-finished furniture in a choice of 22 colors. 207-846-1430.

**Mallory's Furniture,** P.O. Box 1150, Jacksonville, NC 28546: Free brochure ◆ Home furnishings. 910-353-1828. mallorys@mallorys.com

**Marlborough Country Barn,** N. Main St., Marlborough, CT 06447: Catalog $3 ◆ Handcrafted reproduction furniture. 800-852-8993.

**Mayfield Leather,** 340 9th St. SE, Hickory, NC 28603: Free brochure ◆ Heirloom and classic reproductions in leather. 800-342-7729.

**Maynard House Antiques,** 11 Maynard St., Westborough, MA 01581: Brochure $2 ◆ Handcrafted American country sofas and wing chairs, from the 1780s to 1820s. 508-366-2073.

**Mill Creek Antiques,** 109 Newbury, Paxico, KS 66526: Free information ◆ Antique furniture, lighting, and stoves. 913-636-5520.

**P.J. Milligan & Company,** P.O. Box 4069, Santa Barbara, CA 93140: Free information ◆ Handmade pine furniture. 805-963-4038.

**Modern Classics,** P.O. Box 20023, New York, NY 10021: Free catalog ◆ Classic, modern, and other styles of wood and leather furniture. 800-853-2030.

**Mom's Place,** Karen & Tom Sauer, 227 Main, Kalispell, MT 59901: Free information ◆ Unfinished log furniture. 406-257-4333.

**Monaghan Log Furniture,** 3487 North M18, Gladwin, MI 48624: Information $2 ◆ Handmade log furniture. 517-426-5962.

**Montana Woodworks,** 250 Whitetail Dr., Rexford, MT 59930: Brochure $2 ◆ Log furnishings, outdoor furniture, and deck railings. 406-889-3728.

**Alex Moore Furniture,** 6448 N. Aspen St., Lincolnton, NC 28092: Catalog $5 ◆ Custom upholstered furniture. 704-732-7553.

**MOR Design,** 351 Pleasant St., Box 161, Northampton, MA 01060: Free information ◆ Baltic birch snack and beverage tables with a choice of light honey or dark cherry finish. 800-585-5002.

**Thos. Moser Cabinetmakers,** 72 Wright's Landing, Auburn, ME 04211: Catalog $10 ◆ Handcrafted furniture for homes and offices. 800-708-9703. www.thosmoser.com

**Moultrie Manufacturing,** P.O. Drawer 1179, Moultrie, GA 31776: Catalog $3 ◆ Southern-style furniture reproductions for homes and gardens. 800-841-8674.

**Mountain Timber Decor,** 122 Mason Ln., Laramie, WY 82070: Free information ◆ Home furnishings, specializing in handcrafted log glider rockers. 307-742-8826. www.mountaintimber.com

**Mountainman Woodshop,** Rt. 2, Box 37A, Eagle Rock, VA 24085: Free brochure ◆ Handcrafted traditional Appalachian slot-back chairs and wood farming tools. 540-884-2197.

**Murrow Furniture Galleries,** P.O. Box 4337, Wilmington, NC 28406: Free information ◆ Home furnishings and accessories. 910-799-4010.

**Lawrence P. Neal,** 212 Old Hebron Rd., Colchester, CT 06415: Catalog $5 (refundable) ◆ Shaker reproductions. 860-537-4007.

**North Carolina Furniture Showrooms,** 12 W. 21st St., 5th Floor, New York, NY 10010: Free catalog (specify items wanted and manufacturer) ◆ Home furnishings and accessories. 800-627-3503; 212-645-2524 (in NY).

**North Country Crafts,** 5247 Central Ave. NE, Minneapolis, MN 55421: Brochure $1 ◆ Country-style upholstered storage ottomans and other accessories. 612-571-3636.

**North Woods Chair Shop,** 237 Old Tilton Rd., Canterbury, NH 03224: Catalog $3 ◆ Handcrafted Shaker furniture. 603-783-4595.

**Old Wagon Factory,** P.O. Box 1427, Clarksville, VA 23927: Catalog $2 ◆ Chippendale furniture, Victorian-style railings and brackets, and Victorian-style and Chippendale storm screen doors. 804-374-5717. 800-874-9358. www.wagonfactory.com

**Old West Charm,** P.O. Box 311, Mountain Center, CA 92561: Brochure $6 (refundable) ◆ Handcrafted wood wagon wheel furnishings, lamps, wall hangings, and decorative items.

**Orleans Carpenters,** P.O. Box 217, Orleans, MA 02653: Catalog $3 ◆ Shaker and colonial furniture reproductions. 508-255-2646.

**Osceola Antiques,** 117 Cascade St., P.O. Box 297, Osceola, WI 54020: Free information ◆ Antique furniture. 715-294-2886. oscantiq@centuryinter.net

**Darrell Peart FurnitureMaker,** 3401 17th Ave. West, Ste. E, Seattle, WA 98119: Free information ◆ Furniture influenced by the American arts and crafts movement. 206-935-2874. www.furnituremaker.com

**The Pine-Tique Furniture Company,** 6022 Culligan Way, Minnetonka, MN 55345: Free brochure ◆ Handcrafted furniture with a blend of American styling. 612-935-9595. www.furniture.com/pinetique

**Plexi-Craft Quality Products,** 514 W. 24th St., New York, NY 10011: Catalog $2 ◆ Lucite and Plexiglas furniture. 800-24-PLEXI; 212-924-3244 (in NY). www.escape.com/~plexi

**Priba Furniture Sales & Interiors,** P.O. Box 13295, Greensboro, NC 27415: Free information ◆ Home furnishings. 336-855-9034. www.pribafurniture.com

**Rhoney Furniture House,** 2401 Hwy. 70 SW, Hickory, NC 28602: Free information ◆ Traditional and contemporary furniture. 704-328-2034.

**Richmond's Woodworks Inc.,** 1577 SR 39 NE, New Philadelphia, OH 44663: Free information ◆ Amish-style furniture. 330-343-8184.

**Dana Robes Wood Craftsmen,** Lower Shaker Village, P.O. Box 707, Enfield, NH 03748: Catalog $5 ◆ Shaker reproduction furniture. 800-722-5036.

**Rocky Mountain Lodgepole Furniture Company,** P.O. Box 2656, Evanston, WY 82931: Free brochure ◆ Log beds, footboards, wall mirrors, chests, tables, chairs and swings, and other furniture. 800-827-9042; 307-789-9042 (in WY). treasure@webcom.com

**Rocky Mountain Log Furniture Inc.,** P.O. Box 3124, 1502 Miner St., Idaho Springs, CO 80452: Brochure $2 ◆ Handcrafted log furniture and wagon wheel chandeliers. 800-305-6030; 303-567-0480 (in CO). treasure@webcom.com

**Rocky Top Furniture,** 131 W. Main St., P.O. Box 500, Burgin, KY 40310: Free information ◆ Handcrafted Northern white pine furniture. 800-332-1143.

**Rose Furniture Company,** 916 Finch Ave., P.O. Box 1829, High Point, NC 27261: Free information ◆ Home furnishings. 336-886-6050. www.rosefurniture.com

**Rustic Designs,** P.O. Box 176, Montague, MA 01376: Free brochure ◆ Handmade rustic-style furniture. 508-544-8513.

**David Sawyer,** RD 1, East Calais, VT 05650: Brochure $1 ◆ Windsor chairs. 802-456-8836.

**The Seraph,** P.O. Box 500, 420 Main St., Sturbridge, MA 01566: Catalog $6 ◆ 18th-century-style home furnishings and accessories. 508-347-2241.

**Shaker Workshops,** Box 8001, Ashburnham, MA 01430: Catalog $1 ◆ Shaker furniture in kits or assembled, needle crafts, dolls, and dollhouse furniture. 800-840-9121. www.shakerworkshops.com

**Shakerpine Furniture,** 222 Hwy. 96, Douglas, WY 82633: Free information ◆ Shaker-inspired furniture. 307-358-3909.

**Sharper Image Home Collection,** 650 Davis St., San Francisco, CA 94120: Free catalog ◆ Furniture and accessories from the Hearst Castle collection. 800-448-8444. www.sharperimage.com

**Shaw Furniture Galleries,** 131 W. Academy St., P.O. Box 1328, Randleman, NC 27317: Free brochure ◆ Home furnishings. 336-498-2628. Shawfurniture.com

**The Shop Woodcrafters Inc.,** P.O. Box 1450, Quitman, TX 75783: Catalog $4 ◆ Stained white pine furniture. 903-763-5704.

**The SICO Room Makers,** Room Makers Division, 7525 Cahill Rd., P.O. Box 1169, Minneapolis, MN 55440: Free information ◆ Wall beds, home office furniture, and wall systems. 800-328-6138.

**Silver Creek Antler Company,** P.O. Box 3463, Glenwood Springs, CO 81602: Free brochure ◆ Chandeliers and furnishings made from antlers. 970-945-0507.

**Simply Country Furniture,** Box 133, Rover, AR 72860: Brochure $3 ◆ Country-style furniture. 501-272-4794.

**Simply Together Furniture,** 701 W. Ward Ave., High Point, NC 27260: Free catalog ◆ Easy-to-assemble modular furniture units into upholstered furniture of choice. 800-424-1304. www.simplytogether.com

**George Smith Sofas & Chairs Inc.,** 73 Spring St., New York, NY 10012: Catalog $5 ◆ Traditionally-made English furniture, fabrics, and kilims. 212-226-4747.

**Sobol House of Furnishings,** 141 Richardson Blvd., Black Mountain, NC 28711: Free brochure ◆ Home and office furnishings. 704-669-8031.

**Southampton Antiques,** 172 College Way, Rt. 10, Southampton, MA 01073: Video catalog $25 ◆ Antique American oak and Victorian-style furniture. 413-527-1022.

**Southwest Designs,** 18352 Gothard St., Huntington Beach, CA 92648: Free information ◆ Rustic to Southwestern-style log furnishings. 888-LODGPOL. www.southwestdesigns.com

**Spirit of the West,** Tomoka Center, 1095 N. US Hwy. 1, Ormond Beach, FL 32174: Free information with long SASE ◆ Southwest furniture, art, and decorative accessories. 800-831-9663; 904-673-9402 (in FL). www.volusia.com

**M. Star Antler Designs,** P.O. Box 3093, Lake Isabella, CA 93240: Catalog $5 ◆ Antler-designed chandeliers, lamps, furniture, mirrors, and accessories. 619-379-5777.

**Stevens Furniture,** 1258 Hickory Blvd. SW, P.O. Box 270, Lenoir, NC 28645: Free information ◆ Home furnishings. 704-728-5511.

**Stickley Furniture,** Stickley Dr., P.O. Box 480, Manlius, NY 13104: Catalog $5 (request list of retail sources) ◆ Cherry and mahogany 18th-century furniture. 315-682-5500.

**Stuckey Brothers Furniture,** Box 527, Stuckey, SC 29554: Free information with long SASE ◆ Indoor and outdoor furniture. 803-558-2591.

**Sutton-Council Furniture,** 421 S. College Rd., Wilmington, NC 28406: Free catalog (specify items) ◆ Home furnishings. 910-799-9000.

**Swartzendruber Hardwood Creations,** 4 Longview Dr., Bacova, VA 24412: Free catalog ◆ Handcrafted prairie-theme and arts and crafts style furniture. 800-953-2502. www.swartzendruber.com

**T-M Cowboy Classics,** 463 Main St., Longmont, CO 80501: Brochure $3 ◆ Western-style furniture. 303-776-3394.

**Taylor Made Saddles,** P.O. Box 141, Barksdale, TX 78828: Free information ◆ Hand-tooled saddles. Also wood, metal, and leather furniture and gifts. 830-234-3322.

**Ernest Thompson,** 4531 Osuna NE, Albuquerque, NM 87109: Catalog $8 ◆ Home furnishings. 800-568-2344.

**Tiger Mountain Woodworks,** P.O. Box 1088, Highlands, NC 28741: Free information ◆ Rustic-style handcrafted furniture. 704-526-5577.

**S. Timberlake Company,** 13 Fore Rd., Eliot, ME 03903: Free catalog ◆ Shaker reproduction furniture. 207-438-9706. www.stimberlake.com

**Timberline Furniture,** 4040 Heeb Rd., Manhattan, MT 59741: Brochure $3 ◆ Rustic-looking log furniture. 406-282-7152.

**Time & Tide,** 56 Byram Rd., P.O. Box 156, Point Pleasant, PA 18950: Free information ◆ Imported French antique furniture and clocks. 215-297-5854.

**Marion Travis,** P.O. Box 1041, Statesville, NC 28677: Catalog $1 ◆ Hand-woven fiber rush seats on native hardwood chairs. 800-806-2398.

**Marty Travis,** RR 1, Box 96, Fairbury, IL 61739: Catalog $3 ◆ Shaker furniture and woodenware reproductions. 815-692-3336.

**Triad Furniture Discounters,** P.O. Box 7505, Myrtle Beach, SC 29577: Catalog $12 ◆ Furniture and accessories. 800-497-6400.

**Valley Furniture Shop,** 20 Stirling Rd., Watchung, NJ 07060: Catalog $5 ◆ Reproduction 18th-century furniture. 908-756-7623.

**Van Campen's,** Noone Falls, Rt. 202 South, Peterborough, NH 03458: Free information ◆ Furniture, lighting, and other 18th-century reproductions. 603-924-4225.

**Vermont FurnitureWorks,** P.O. Box 1496, Stowe, VT 05672: Free catalog ◆ Handcrafted 18th and 19th-century reproduction New England furniture, traditional folk art, and Americana accessories. 802-253-5094.

**Victorian Replicas,** P.O. Box 866, Menlo Park, CA 94026: Catalog $10 ◆ Mahogany chair frames and other furniture. 415-552-6367.

**Village Furniture House,** 146 West Ave., Kannapolis, NC 28081: Free brochure ◆ Home furnishings. 704-938-9171.

**Walpole Woodworkers,** 767 East St., Walpole, MA 02081: Catalog $6 ◆ Handcrafted natural cedar New England-style furniture. 800-343-6948.

**Watauga Creek,** 232 NE Main St., Franklin, NC 28734: Free information ◆ Custom upholstered western style leather furniture. 800-443-1131.

**Wellington's Furniture,** P.O. Box 1849, Blowing Rock, NC 28605: Free catalog ◆ Traditional, transitional, Southwestern, contemporary, office, and occasional seating leather furniture. 800-262-1049. www.fineleatherfurniture.com

**Eldred Wheeler,** 60 Sharp St., Hingham, MA 02043: Catalog $5 ◆ Reproduction 18th-century furniture. 781-337-5311.

**Wild West Log Furniture,** 213 W. Appleway, Coeur d'Alene, ID 83814: Brochure $2 ◆ Rustic lodgepole pine furniture. 208-664-8502. www.dmi.net/log-furniture

**Randy Wilkinson,** 69 Bushnell Hollow Rd., Baltic, CT 06330: Free brochure ◆ American-style furniture. 860-822-6790.

**Willsboro Wood Products,** P.O. Box 509, Keeseville, NY 12944: Free brochure ◆ Folding Adirondack chairs, rocking chairs, and country-style furniture. 800-342-3373.

**Wood-Armfield Furniture Company,** P.O. Box C, High Point, NC 27261: Free brochure ◆ Home furnishings. 336-889-6522.

**Workshops of David T. Smith,** 3600 Shawhan Rd., Morrow, OH 45152: Catalog $5 ◆ Reproduction furniture, pottery, lamps, and chandeliers. 513-932-2472. www.davidtsmith.com

**York Leather Collection of Hickory,** P.O. Box 785, Hickory, NC 28603: Catalog $5 (refundable) ◆ Handcrafted leather furniture. 704-459-2879.

## Lift Chairs

**Ortho-Kinetics,** The Independence Company, 1 Mobility Centre, P.O. Box 1647, Waukesha, WI 53187: Free information ◆ Combination power recliner/lounger/lift chair. 800-446-4522.

**Uplift Seat Assist,** Daylight Technologies Inc., 100 Walnut St., Champlain, NY 12919: Free information ◆ Aid for converting armchairs into automatic lifting chairs. 800-387-0896.

**Whitakers,** 1 Odell Plaza, Yonkers, NY 10703: Free catalog ◆ Lifts for transporting people with physical disabilities up and down and into the bathtub. 800-44-LIFTS; 800-924-LIFT (in NY).

## Office Furniture

**Alcyon Woodworks,** P.O. Box 11165, Portland, ME 04104: Free information ◆ Traditional custom made American-style furniture for homes and offices. 207-657-3356.

**Alfax Wholesale Furniture,** 370 7th Ave., Ste. 1101, New York, NY 10001: Free catalog ◆ Office furniture. 800-221-5710; 212-947-9560 (in NY).

**American Security Products Company,** 11925 Pacific Ave., Fontana, CA 92335: Free information ◆ Gun and other safes for homes and offices. 800-421-6142. qsd@amersecurity.com

**Arrow Star,** 3-1 Park Plaza, Glen Head, NY 11546: Free catalog ◆ Storage and shelving, tables, chairs, desks, filing cabinets, lockers, and accessories. 800-645-2833; 516-484-3100 (in NY).

**ATD-American Company,** 135 Greenwood Rd., Wyncote, PA 19095: Free catalog ◆ Office and computer furniture, storage and filing cabinets, and display cases. 800-523-2300; 576-1000 (in area code 215).

**Basil & Jones Cabinetmakers,** 2712 36th St. NW, Washington, DC 20007: Free brochure ◆ Wood and leather-finished stand-up desks in period and contemporary styles. 202-337-4369.

**Bevis Furniture,** P.O. Box 2280, Florence, AL 35630: Free catalog ◆ Bookcases, tables, chairs, panel dividers, and custom furniture. 256-766-6497. www.bevis.com

**Business & Institutional Furniture Company,** P.O. Box 92039, Milwaukee, WI 53202: Free catalog ◆ Office and institutional furniture. 800-558-8662.

**ChairNet Inc.,** 1933 Dina Ct., Powell, OH 43065: Free catalog ◆ Chairs, desks, conference tables, and other office furnishings. 614-792-9674.

**W.A. Charnstrom Company,** 5391 12th Ave. East, Shakopee, MN 55379: Free catalog ◆ Office and mail center furnishings and accessories. 800-328-2962; 612-403-0303 (in MN). www.charnstrom.com

**Columbia Omnicorp,** 14 W. 33rd St., New York, NY 10001: Free catalog ◆ Office and computer supplies, furniture, and artist materials. 212-279-6161.

**Frank Eastern Company,** 599 Broadway, New York, NY 10012: Catalog $1 ◆ Office furniture. 800-221-4914; 212-219-0007 (in NY).

**Factory Direct Furniture,** P.O. Box 92967, Milwaukee, WI 53202: Free catalog ◆ Office and computer furniture. 800-972-6570; 289-9770 (in Milwaukee). www.furniture2u.com

**Furniture Express,** P.O. Box 270461, San Diego, CA 92198: Free catalog ◆ Modular office furniture for residential or commercial application. 800-838-0803; 619-487-8260 (in CA). www.f-ex.com

**Lyon Metal Products Inc.,** P.O. Box 671, Aurora, IL 60507: Free catalog ◆ Shelving, cabinets, racks, lockers, and shop furniture. 800-323-0096.

**Office Depot Inc.,** 2200 Old Germantown Rd., Delray Beach, FL 33445: Free catalog ◆ Office supplies and furniture. 800-685-8800. www.officedepot.com

**Office Images Inc.,** P.O. Box 6724, High Point, NC 27262: Free information ◆ Functional office furniture. 336-841-6665. www.officeimages.com

**Office Zone,** 461 W. 200 North, P.O. Box 808, Bountiful, UT 84011: Free catalog ◆ Desks for homes and offices, library supplies, binding equipment, folders, labels and labeling tapes, and other supplies and equipment. 800-543-5454; 801-298-3839 (in UT).

**PAR Seating Specialists,** 310 Main St., New Rochelle, NY 10802: Free catalog ◆ Office chairs and automotive seats. 800-367-7270.

**Reliable Home Office,** P.O. Box 1501, Ottawa, IL 61350: Catalog $2 ◆ Office furniture. 800-326-6230.

**Repo Depo,** 1669 Old Bayshore Hwy., Burlingame, CA 94010: Free catalog ◆ New and used office furniture. 415-692-5000. www.repodepo.com

**Safe Specialties Inc.,** 10932 Murdock Rd., Knoxville, TN 37932: Catalog $2 ◆ Office and home safes. 800-695-2815. www.imagesbuilder.com/safespec.1.html

**The Stand-Up Desk Company,** 5207 Baltimore Ave., Bethesda, MD 20816: Free brochure ◆ Handcrafted stand-up desks and stools. 301-657-3630.

**Staples Inc.,** P.O. Box 5173, Westborough, MA 01581: Free catalog ◆ Office furniture, drafting equipment, fax machines, typewriters, and supplies. 800-333-3330. www.staples.com/

**Stuart-Townsend-Carr Furniture,** P.O. Box 373, Limington, ME 04049: Free information ◆ Classic furniture for offices and dens. 800-637-2344.

## Outdoor Furniture

**Adirondack Designs,** 350 Cypress St., Fort Bragg, CA 95437: Free catalog ◆ Redwood chairs, love seats, swings, and tables. 800-222-0343. www.adirondackdesign.com

**Adirondack Store & Gallery,** 109 Saranac Ave., Lake Placid, NY 12946: Free information ◆ Oak and maple outdoor furniture. 518-523-2646.

**AK Exteriors,** 101 Montoya Rd., El Paso, TX 79932: Catalog $4 ◆ Cast-aluminum furniture, light fixtures, and mail boxes. 800-253-9837.

**Amish Country Collection,** Sunset Valley Rd., RD 5, Box 271, New Castle, PA 16105: Catalog $5 ◆ Amish-style twig furniture, rugs, quilts, and wall hangings. 412-458-4811.

**Barlow Tyrie,** 1263 Glen Ave., Ste. 230, Moorestown, NJ 08057: Free brochure and list of retail sources ◆ English-style teak outdoor furniture. 609-273-7878.

**The BenchSmith,** P.O. Box 86, Warrington, PA 18976: Free catalog ◆ Benches, rockers, tables, and planters. 800-482-3327.

**Blake Industries,** P.O. Box 155, Abington, MA 02351: Free information ◆ Outdoor and indoor teak furniture, ornamental cast-iron pole lights, and fixtures. 781-337-8772.

**Brown-Jordan,** P.O. Box 5688, El Monte, CA 91734: Free information ◆ Aluminum furniture. 818-443-8971.

**Carolina Patio Warehouse,** 54 Largo Dr., Stamford, CT 06907: Free catalog ◆ Patio and garden furniture. 800-672-8466. www.carolinapatio.com

**Charleston Battery Bench,** 191 King St., Charleston, SC 29401: Catalog $1 ◆ Reproduction cast-iron and cypress benches from the 1880s. 803-722-3842.

**Charleston Gardens,** 61 Queen St., Charleston, SC 29401: Catalog $3 ◆ Outdoor furniture and garden furnishings. 803-723-0252.

**Clapper's,** P.O. Box 2278, West Newton, MA 02165: Free catalog ◆ Teak furniture for gardens, patios, and breezeways. 617-244-7900.

**Columbia Cascade,** 1975 SW 5th Ave., Portland, OR 97201: Free catalog ◆ Outdoor furniture. 800-547-1940.

**Coppa Woodworking Inc.,** 1231 Paraiso Ave., San Pedro, CA 90731: Catalog $1 ◆ Adirondack chairs, screen doors, and furniture. 310-548-5332.

**Country Casual,** 17317 Germantown Rd., Germantown, MD 20874: Catalog $5 ◆ Teak benches, swings, chairs, tables, and planters. 301-540-0040.

**Diversified Overseas Marketing,** 200 Main St., Coraopolis, PA 15108: Free information ◆ Cast-aluminum furniture with all-weather cushions. 412-269-2690.

**Dovetail Woodworks of North Carolina,** 1877 Niagra Rd., Carthage, NC 28327: Free catalog ◆ Outdoor furniture. 910-949-2963.

**DuMor Inc.,** P.O. Box 142, Mifflintown, PA 17059: Free catalog ◆ Outdoor furniture. 800-598-4018.

**Ecologic Inc.,** 1140 Elizabeth Ave., Waukegan, IL 60085: Free brochure ◆ Bedroom and outdoor furniture made from recycled harder-than-oak materials. 800-899-8004; 847-244-4466 (in IL).

**Fib-Con Corp.,** Box 3387, Silver Spring, MD 20918: Free catalog ◆ Reinforced fiberglass planters, benches, waste receptacles, and patio furniture. 301-572-5333.

**Flanders Industries Inc.,** P.O. Box 1788, Fort Smith, AR 72902: Free brochure ◆ Casual and outdoor pool furniture. 800-843-7532.

**Green Enterprises,** 43 S. Rogers St., Hamilton, VA 22068: Brochure $1 ◆ Swings, gliders, tables, and benches. 540-338-3606.

**The Hammock Company,** P.O. Box 7295, Hilton Head, SC 29938: Free brochure ◆ Hammocks, swings, and other outdoor furnishings. 800-344-4264. www.hhisc.com/hammock

**Holiday Patio Showcase,** P.O. Box 727, Hudson, NC 28638: Free catalog ◆ Outdoor and indoor furnishings. 704-728-2664.

**Kingsley-Bate Ltd.,** 5587 Guinea Rd., Fairfax, VA 22032: Catalog $2 ◆ Teak planters, window boxes, and garden furniture. 703-978-7200.

**Kloter Farms Inc.,** 216 West Rd., Ellington, CT 06029: Brochure $3 (request list of retail sources) ◆ Sheds, gazebos, playscapes, and lawn furniture. 800-289-3463; 203-871-1048 (in CT). www.kloterfarms.com

**Kramer Brothers,** P.O. Box 255, Dayton, OH 45404: Free catalog ◆ Garden furniture and ornaments. 937-228-4194.

**Landscape Forms Inc.,** 431 Lawndale Ave., Kalamazoo, MI 49001: Free information ◆ Outdoor furniture and garden planters. 800-521-2546; 616-381-0396 (in MI). www.landscapeforms.com

**Kenneth Lynch & Sons,** 84 Danbury Rd., Wilton, CT 06897: Catalog $4 ◆ Outdoor benches, gates, fountains, and pools. 203-762-8363.

**MacMillan-Bloedel,** 5895 Windward Pkwy., Ste. 200, Alpharetta, GA 30201: Free information ◆ Unfinished Western red cedar outdoor furniture. 800-432-6226.

**Mel-Nor Industries,** 303 Gulf Bank, Houston, TX 77037: Information $1 ◆ Hanging lawn and porch swings, park benches, and old-time lamp posts. 281-445-3485.

**Moultrie Manufacturing,** P.O. Drawer 1179, Moultrie, GA 31776: Catalog $3 ◆ Indoor and outdoor aluminum furniture. 800-841-8674.

**Nebraska Plastics Inc.,** P.O. Box 45, Cozad, NE 69130: Free information ◆ Rose trellises, garden arbors, picnic tables, outdoor furniture, and accessories. 800-445-2887. www.countryestate.com

**Old Hickory Furniture Company,** 403 S. Noble St., Shelbyville, IN 46176: Free list of retail sources ◆ Casual and outdoor furniture. 800-232-2275.

**Parents & Friends Inc.,** P.O. Box 656, 350 Cypress St., Fort Bragg, CA 95437: Free brochure ◆ Outdoor furniture and accessories. 800-222-0343.

**The Patio,** P.O. Box 1042, Murrieta, CA 92564: Catalog $2 ◆ Outdoor patio furniture. 800-81-PATIO.

**Plow & Hearth,** P.O. Box 5000, Madison, VA 22727: Free catalog ◆ Gardening tools, birdhouses and feeders, porch and lawn furniture, fireplace accessories, and gifts for pets. 800-627-1712. peggy@plowhearth.com

**Pompeian Studios,** 90 Rockledge Rd., Bronxville, NY 10708: Catalog $10 ◆ Original sculptures, ornaments, and forged furniture for patios and gardens. 800-457-5595.

**Reed Brothers,** 5000 Turner Rd., Sebastopol, CA 95472: Catalog $15 ◆ Handcarved wood furniture for the home and garden. 707-795-6261.

**Roberts Furniture,** 65 Commerce Rd., Stamford, CT 06902: Free catalog ◆ Brown Jordan, Tropitone, Barlow Tyrie, and Lloyd Flanders furniture. 800-899-4610.

**Robinson Iron Corp.,** P.O. Box 1119, Alexander City, AL 35010: Catalog $5 ◆ Cast-iron benches. 256-329-8486.

**Sittin' Easy,** 284 Eagle Springs Rd., Eagle Springs, NC 27242: Free catalog ◆ Appalachian white oak outdoor furniture. 910-673-0033.

**Smith & Hawken,** P.O. Box 6907, Florence, KY 41022: Free catalog ◆ Garden furniture. 800-776-3336. www.smith-hawken.com

**Southerlands for Leisure Living,** 15 Biltmore Ave., Asheville, NC 28801: Free catalog ◆ Outdoor furniture and garden accessories. 800-968-5596.

**Stuckey Brothers Furniture,** Box 527, Stuckey, SC 29554: Free information with long SASE ◆ Indoor and outdoor furniture. 803-558-2591.

**Sun Designs,** P.O. Box 6, Oconomowoc, WI 53066: Plan book $9.95 plus $3.95 postage ◆ Gazebos and garden structures. 414-567-4255.

**Telescope Casual Furniture,** P.O. Box 299, Granville, NY 12832: Free information ◆ Outdoor furniture. 518-642-1100. www.telescopecasual.com

**Tidewater Workshop,** P.O. Box 456, Oceanville, NJ 08231: Free information ◆ Outdoor furniture. 800-666-TIDE. www.tidewaterworkshop.com

**Vermont Outdoor Furniture,** East Barre, VT 05649: Free catalog ◆ Outdoor furniture in white cedar. 800-588-8834. www.vermontoutdoorfurnitur.com

**Walpole Woodworkers,** 767 East St., Walpole, MA 02081: Catalog $6 ◆ Porch and children's swings and handcrafted lawn and garden cedar furniture. 800-343-6948.

**Wicker Works,** 7021 Market St., Wilmington, NC 28405: Free information ◆ Wicker and rattan outdoor furniture. 888-255-0590; 910-686-0844 (in NC). www.wicker1.com

### Shoji Screens

**Cherry Tree,** Light Division, 34154 E. Frontage Rd., Bozeman, MT 59715: Catalog $15 ◆ Traditional handcrafted lamps and shoji screens. 800-634-3268. www.cherrytreedesign.com

**Miya Shoji & Interiors Inc.,** 109 W. 17th St., New York, NY 10011: Free brochure ◆ Japanese shoji screens. 212-243-6774.

### Wicker & Rattan

**Catherine Ann Furnishings,** 615 Loudonville Rd., Latham, NY 12110: Free brochure ◆ Indoor and outdoor wicker furniture. 518-785-4175.

**Deutsch Inc.,** 31 E. 32nd St., New York, NY 10016: Catalog $3 ◆ Rattan furniture. 800-223-4550; 212-683-8746 (in NY).

**Dovetail Antiques,** 474 White Pine Rd., Columbus, NJ 08022: Catalog $5 ◆ Antique wicker furniture. 609-298-5245.

**Ellenburg's Furniture,** P.O. Box 5638, Statesville, NC 28687: Catalog $6 ◆ Wicker and rattan furniture with optional upholstered cushions, padding, and covers. 800-841-1420. www.ellenburgs.com

**Fran's Wicker & Rattan Furniture,** 295 Rt. 10, Succasunna, NJ 07876: Catalog $3 (refundable) ◆ Wicker and rattan furniture. 800-531-1511.

**Gift & Wicker Import Inc.,** 12770 Moore St., Cerritos, CA 90701: Catalog $5 ◆ Wickerware, hobby craft supplies, basket planters, home decorative accessories, and furniture. 800-622-6209; 310-407-3319 (in CA).

**Masterworks Rustic Furniture,** 354 Kenesaw Ave., Marietta, GA 30060: Catalog $2.50 ◆ Indoor, outdoor, children's, and bent-willow furniture. 770-423-9000.

**The Old Wicker Garden,** 6606 Snider Plaza, Dallas, TX 75225: Photos $5 (refundable) ◆ Antique wicker furniture, brass and iron beds, hooked rugs and quilts, folk art, and decorative accessories. 972-373-8241.

**Wicker Warehouse Inc.,** 195 S. River St., Hackensack, NJ 07601: Catalog $5 (refundable) ◆ Wicker and rattan furniture. 800-989-4253. www.WickerWarehouse.com

**Wicker Works,** 7021 Market St., Wilmington, NC 28405: Free information ◆ Wicker and rattan outdoor furniture. 888-255-0590; 910-686-0844 (in NC). www.wicker1.com

**Yesteryear Wicker,** 7616 Investment Ct., Owings, MD 20736: Brochure $3.50 (refundable) ◆ Reproduction porch groupings, rockers, dinettes, daybeds, dressers, and other furniture. 410-257-9387.

## GARAGE DOORS & OPENERS

**Clopay Building Products Company,** Consumer Affairs Dept., 312 Walnut St., Ste. 1600, Cincinnati, OH 45202: Free information ◆ Garage doors with raised panels. 800-225-6729.

**Designer Doors Inc.,** 283 Troy St., River Falls, WI 54022: Free information ◆ Custom vintage garage doors. 800-241-0525.

**Overhead Door,** P.O. Box 809046, Dallas, TX 75380: Free information ◆ Insulated steel overhead garage doors and opener with a microprocessor controller program to detect obstructions. 800-543-2269.

**Raynor Garage Doors,** P.O. Box 448, Dixon, IL 61021: Free information ◆ Steel garage doors. 800-4-RAYNOR. www.Raynor.com

**Ridge Doors,** 335 New Rd., Monmouth, NJ 08852: Free information ◆ Solid wood garage doors with carved or plain panels and optional trim and glass. 800-631-5656; 800-872-4980 (in NJ).

**Schweiss Doors,** Box 220, Fairfax, MN 55332: Free information ◆ Bi-fold doors. 507-426-8273.

**Stanley Door Systems,** 1225 E. Maple Ave., Troy, MI 48083: Free information ◆ Garage door opener transmitter. 800-521-2752.

**Wayne-Dalton Corp.,** 1 Door Dr., Mount Hope, OH 44660: Free information ◆ Insulated steel garage doors. 800-827-3667.

## GARDENING EQUIPMENT & SUPPLIES

### Beneficial Insects, Organisms, & Pest Controls

**Arbico Environmentals,** P.O. Box 4247, Tucson, AZ 85738: Free catalog ◆ Beneficial insects. 800-827-2847; 520-825-9785 (in AZ). www.usit.net.BICONET

**Bozeman Bio-Tech,** P.O. Box 3146, 1612 Gold Ave., Bozeman, MT 59772: Free catalog ◆ Beneficial insects and pest controls. 800-289-6656.

**W. Atlee Burpee & Company,** 300 Park Ave., Warminster, PA 18974: Free catalog ◆ Beneficial insects. 800-888-1447. www.burpee.com

**Cape Cod Worm Farm,** 30 Center Ave., Buzzards Bay, MA 02532: Free information ◆ Red worms for soil improvement and composting. 508-759-5664.

**M & R Durango Inc.,** P.O. Box 886, Bayfield, CO 81122: Free catalog ◆ Beneficial insects. 800-526-4075; 303-259-3521 (in CO). sales@goodbug.com

**Farmer Seed & Nursery Company,** 818 NW 4th St., Faribault, MN 55021: Free catalog ◆ Beneficial organisms. 507-334-1623.

**Henry Field's Seed & Nursery,** 415 N. Burnett, Shenandoah, IA 51602: Free catalog ◆ Beneficial organisms. 605-665-4491.

**Gardener's Supply Company,** 128 Intervale Rd., Burlington, VT 05401: Free catalog ◆ Beneficial insects. 800-876-5520. www.gardeners.com

**Gardens Alive,** 5100 Schenley Pl., Lawrenceburg, IN 47025: Free catalog ◆ Beneficial insects and organisms. 812-537-8650.

**The Green Spot Ltd.,** 93 Priest Rd., Barrington, NH 03825: Catalog $4 ◆ Beneficial insects and other pest controls. 603-942-8925.

**Harmony Farm Supply & Nursery,** 3244 Hwy. 116, No. A, Sebastopol, CA 95472: Catalog $2 (refundable) ◆ Beneficial insects. 707-823-9125.

**IPM Laboratories,** P.O. Box 300, Locke, NY 13092: Free catalog ◆ Beneficial insects. 315-497-3129.

**Haney Johnson,** Rt. 2, Box 2175, Gresham, SC 29546: Free information ◆ Redworms.

**Mellinger's,** 2310 W. South Range Rd., North Lima, OH 44452: Free catalog ◆ Beneficial organisms. 330-549-9861. www.mellingers.com

**Natural Gardening Company,** 217 San Anselmo Ave., San Anselmo, CA 94960: Free catalog ◆ Beneficial insects, organic gardening supplies, pest controls, drip irrigation equipment, and wildflower seeds. 415-456-5060.

**Nature's Control,** P.O. Box 35, Medford, OR 97501: Free catalog ◆ Beneficial insects and organisms. 541-899-8318.

**Necessary Trading Company,** One Natures Way, New Castle, VA 24127: Catalog $2 ◆ Beneficial insects. 800-447-5354.

**Peaceful Valley Farm Supply,** P.O. Box 2209, Grass Valley, CA 95945: Catalog $2 (refundable) ◆ Beneficial organisms. 916-272-4769.

**Planet Natural,** P.O. Box 3146, Bozeman, MT 59772: Free catalog ◆ Beneficial insects, garden seeds, composting equipment, organic fertilizers, pest controls, garden supplies, and pet and body care products. 800-289-6656. www.planetnatural.com

**Rincon-Vitova Insectaries Inc.,** P.O. Box 1555, Ventura, CA 93002: Free catalog ◆ Beneficial insects. 800-643-5407.

**Season Extenders,** 971 Nichols Ave., Stratford, CT 06497: Free catalog ◆ Propagation supplies, pots and baskets, lights, greenhouses, pest controls, hydroponic growing aids, fertilizers, and tools. 203-375-1317.

**Silver Creek Supply,** RR 1, Box 70, Port Treverton, PA 17864: Free catalog ◆ Regular and king-size plant protectors, ball weeders, mulch film, and growing aids. 717-374-8010.

**Territorial Seed Company,** P.O. Box 157, Cottage Grove, OR 97424: Free catalog ◆ Organic fertilizers, natural insecticides, biological pest controls, and vegetable, herb, and flower seeds. 541-942-9547. www.territorial-seed.com

## Carts & Wheelbarrows

**Ames Lawn & Garden Tools,** P.O. Box 14854, Mansfield, OH 44901: Free information ◆ Easy-to-roll lawn cart.

**BCS America,** 13601 Providence Rd., Matthews, NC 28105: Free catalog ◆ Garden carts, chippers and shredders, tillers, sprayers, mowers, and tractors. 800-227-8791.

**Carts Vermont,** 1890 Airport Pkwy., South Burlington, VT 05403: Free information ◆ Garden carts. 800-732-7417.

**Country Manufacturing,** P.O. Box 104, Fredericktown, OH 43019: Free catalog ◆ Quick-dump carts, lawn brooms, pressure sprayers, turf spreaders, wagons, and trailers. 704-694-9926. www.countrymfg.com

**Garden Way,** 1 Garden Way, Troy, NY 12179: Free information ◆ Carts, tillers, clippers, sickle bar mowers, garden composters, and other equipment. 800-446-4991.

**Gardener's Supply Company,** 128 Intervale Rd., Burlington, VT 05401: Free catalog ◆ Garden carts, composters, sprayers, watering systems, weeding and cultivating tools, organic fertilizers and chemical preparations, leaf mulchers, and canning and preserving supplies. 800-876-5520. www.gardeners.com

**Homestead Carts,** 2396 Perkins St. NE, Salem, OR 97303: Free brochure ◆ Garden carts and composters. 800-825-1925; 503-393-3973 (in OR).

**Misty Parker Gifts,** 67 S. River Rd., Bedford, NH 03110: Free brochure ◆ Amish-built wood wheelbarrows. 603-464-4839.

**Norway Industries,** E. 9237 Cty. Rd. O, Sauk City, WI 53583: Free brochure ◆ Garden carts. 608-544-5000.

**True Engineering Inc.,** 999 Roosevelt Trail, Windham, ME 04962: Free list of retail sources ◆ Utility garden cart with snap-out container. 800-366-6026.

**WheelAround Corp.,** 243 Grandview Ave., Bellevue, KY 41073: Free brochure ◆ Lawn and garden cart. 800-335-CART.

## Chippers & Shredders

**Amerind MacKissic Inc.,** P.O. Box 111, Parker Ford, PA 19457: Free information ◆ Gasoline-operated chipper-shredder. 610-495-7181.

**Flowtron Outdoor Products,** 2 Main St., Melrose, MA 02176: Free information ◆ Electric chipper-shredder. 781-321-2300.

**Garden Way,** 1 Garden Way, Troy, NY 12179: Free information ◆ Compact chipper-shredder. 800-446-4991.

**Gardener's Supply Company,** 128 Intervale Rd., Burlington, VT 05401: Free catalog ◆ Gasoline- powered chipper-shredder. 800-876-5520. www.gardeners.com

**The Kinsman Company,** River Rd., Point Pleasant, PA 18950: Free catalog ◆ Electric chipper-shredder. 800-733-4146.

**Mantis Manufacturing Company,** 1028 Street Rd., Southampton, PA 18966: Free information ◆ Gasoline and electric-powered chipper-shredders. 800-366-6268.

**Mighty Mac,** Mackissic Inc., P.O. Box 111, Parker Ford, PA 19457: Free information ◆ Chippers, tillers, blowers, and sprayers. 610-495-7181.

**The Patriot Company,** 944 N. 45th St., Milwaukee, WI 53208: Free information ◆ Compact chipper-shredder vacuum. 800-798-CHIP.

**Snapper Power Equipment,** P.O. Box 777, McDonough, GA 30253: Free list of retail sources ◆ Shredder. 770-954-2500.

## Farm Equipment & Supplies

**Sutton Agriculture Enterprise,** 746 Vertin Ave., Salinas, CA 93901: Free brochure ◆ Seed planters, measuring devices, field supplies, and bird control products. 831-422-9693.

## Plant Food

**Bozeman Bio-Tech,** P.O. Box 3146, 1612 Gold Ave., Bozeman, MT 59772: Free catalog ◆ Organic fertilizers, weed and plant disease control aids, and pesticides. 800-289-6656.

**Garden City Seeds,** 778 Hwy. 93 North, Hamilton, MT 59840: Free catalog ◆ Fertilizers, pest controls, and seeds for short growing seasons. 406-961-4837. seeds@juno.com

**Gardener's Supply Company,** 128 Intervale Rd., Burlington, VT 05401: Free catalog ◆ Garden carts, composters, sprayers, watering systems, weeding and cultivating tools, organic fertilizers and chemical preparations, leaf mulchers, and canning and preserving supplies. 800-876-5520. www.gardeners.com

**Harmony Farm Supply & Nursery,** 3244 Hwy. 116, No. A, Sebastopol, CA 95472: Catalog $2 (refundable). ◆ Organic fertilizers. 707-823-9125.

**North Country Organics,** P.O. Box 372, Bradford, VT 05033: Free catalog ◆ All-natural land care supplies. 802-222-4277. www.norganics.com

**Ohio Earth Food,** 5488 Swamp St. SE, Hartville, OH 44362: Free information ◆ Organic fertilizers and natural farming and gardening products. 330-877-9356.

**Planet Natural,** P.O. Box 3146, Bozeman, MT 59772: Free catalog ◆ Beneficial insects, garden seeds, composting equipment, organic fertilizers, pest controls, garden supplies, and pet and body care products. 800-289-6656. www.planetnatural.com

**Primary Products for Serious Gardeners,** 175-R New Boston St., Woburn, MA 01801: Free brochure ◆ Fertilizers, plant stimulants, sprays, and other supplies. 800-841-6630. PrimaryP@AOL.com

**Ringer,** 9555 James Ave. South, Ste. 200, Bloomington, MN 55431: Free catalog ◆ Chemical treatments and fertilizers, tools, growing and propagation aids, and pest controls,. 800-654-1047.

**Rush Industries Inc.,** 75 Albertson Ave., Albertson, NY 11507: Catalog $2 ◆ Plant growth hormone and other gardening supplies and equipment. 516-741-0345. www.rushindustries.com

**Season Extenders,** 971 Nichols Ave., Stratford, CT 06497: Free catalog ◆ Propagation supplies, pots and baskets, lights, greenhouses, pest controls, hydroponic growing aids, fertilizers, and tools. 203-375-1317.

**Territorial Seed Company,** P.O. Box 157, Cottage Grove, OR 97424: Free catalog ◆ Organic fertilizers, natural insecticides, biological pest controls, and vegetable, herb, and flower seeds. 541-942-9547. www.territorial-seed.com

## Greenhouses & Window Gardens

**Cascade Greenhouse Supply,** 2626 15th Ave. West, Seattle, WA 98199: Free catalog ◆ Hobby greenhouses and fans, heaters, misting, other equipment, and other equipment. 800-353-0264.

**Charlottesville Glass & Mirror Corp.,** 1428 E. High St., Charlottesville, VA 22902: Free catalog ◆ Easy-to-assemble greenhouses. 804-293-9188.

**Cropking Inc.,** 5050 Greenwich Rd., Seville, OH 44273: Catalog $3 ◆ Greenhouses. 800-321-5656.

**Dixie Greenhouse Manufacturing Company,** Rt. 1, Box 558, Alapaha, GA 31622: Free information ◆ Build-it-yourself greenhouse kits. 800-346-9902; 912-532-4600 (in GA).

**Elite Greenhouses Ltd.,** P.O. Box 22960, Rochester, NY 14962: Free information ◆ Aluminum frame greenhouses. 800-514-4441. www.trine.com/gardennet/harrisseeds

**Farm Wholesale Inc.,** 2396 Perkins St. NE, Salem, OR 97303: Free catalog ◆ Easy-to-assemble greenhouses. 800-825-1925.

**Fiberlux,** 3010 Westchester Ave., Purchase, NY 10577: Free information ◆ Garden greenhouse windows. 914-253-6400.

**Florian Greenhouses,** 64 Airport Rd., West Milford, NJ 07480: Catalog $5 ◆ Greenhouses. 800-FLORIAN. www.florian-greenhouse.com

**Florist Products Inc.,** P.O. Box 3190, Barrington, IL 60011: Catalog $3 ◆ Greenhouse equipment and supplies. 800-828-2242.

**Four Seasons Sunrooms,** 5005 Veterans Memorial Hwy., Holbrook, NY 11741: Free information ◆ Greenhouses. 800-FOURSEASONS; 516-563-4000 (in NY). www.four-seasons-sunrooms.com

**Gardener's Greenhouse,** A PBM Group Product, 160 Koser Rd., Lititz, PA 17543: Free information ◆ Indoor, outdoor, and mini greenhouses. 800-429-5005.

**Gardener's Supply Company,** 128 Intervale Rd., Burlington, VT 05401: Free catalog ◆ Greenhouses. 800-876-5520. www.gardeners.com

**GardenStyles,** 10740 Lyndale Ave. South, Bloomington, MN 55420: Free brochure ◆ Greenhouses. 800-203-6409.

**Gothic Arch Greenhouses,** P.O. Box 1564, Mobile, AL 36633: Free brochure ◆ Redwood fiberglass greenhouse kits. 800-531-GROW. www.ZEBRA.NET/~Gothic

**GreenTech,** 1201 Minters Chapel Rd., Grapevine, TX 76051: Free information ◆ Indoor greenhouses. 800-844-3665.

**Grow-It Instant Greenhouses,** P.O. Box 26037, West Haven CT 06515: Free brochure ◆ Greenhouse kits. 800-932-9344.

**Hoophouse,** 1358 Rt. 28, South Yarmouth, MA 02664: Free brochure ◆ Greenhouse kits. 800-760-5192.

**Jacobs Greenhouse Manufacturing,** 371 Talbot Rd., Delhi, Ontario, Canada N4B 2A1: Catalog $2 ◆ Greenhouses with tempered glass and automatic roof vents. 519-582-2880.

**Janco Greenhouses,** 9390 Davis Ave., Laurel, MD 20707: Brochure $5 ◆ Greenhouses. 800-323-6933.

**Lindal Cedar Homes,** P.O. Box 24426, Seattle, WA 98124: Catalog $15 ◆ Greenhouses and sun rooms. 800-426-0536. www.lindal.com

**Mellinger's,** 2310 W. South Range Rd., North Lima, OH 44452: Free catalog ◆ Greenhouses for the backyard gardener and commercial grower. 330-549-9861. www.mellingers.com

**Powell & Powell Supply Company,** 1206 Broad St., Fuquay-Varina, NC 27526: Free brochure ◆ Greenhouses. 919-552-9708.

**Private Garden Greenhouses,** 10 Allen St., Box 403, Hampden, MA 01036: Free brochure ◆ Greenhouses. 800-287-4769; 413-566-0277 (in MA).

**Rain or Shine,** 13126 NE Airport Way, Portland, OR 97230: Free catalog ◆ Hobby greenhouses and supplies. 800-248-1981.

**Santa Barbara Greenhouses,** 721 Richmond Ave., Oxnard, CA 93030: Free catalog ◆ Redwood greenhouses. 800-544-5276.

**Season Extenders,** 971 Nichols Ave., Stratford, CT 06497: Free catalog ◆ Propagation supplies, pots and baskets, lights, greenhouses, pest controls, hydroponic growing aids, fertilizers, and tools. 203-375-1317.

**Senco Inc.,** 520 8th St., Gwinn, MI 49841: Free information ◆ Recreational shelters, portable hunting blinds, fishing houses, and greenhouses. 906-346-4116.

**Simpson Strong-Tie Company Inc.,** Box 10789, Pleasanton, CA 94588: Free list of retail sources ◆ Easy-to-assemble greenhouse kits. 800-937-7922.

**Solar Components Corp.,** 121 Valley St., Manchester, NH 03103: Brochure $1 ◆ Lean-to and free-standing build-it-yourself greenhouse kits and solar energy equipment. 603-668-8186.

**Southeastern Insulated Glass,** 6477 Peachtree Industrial Blvd., Atlanta, GA 30360: Free information ◆ Greenhouse and sun room kits, sliding glass doors, and skylights. 800-841-9842; 770-455-8838 (in GA).

**SSHC Inc.,** P.O. Box 769, Old Saybrook, CT 06475: Free information ◆ Easy-to-install radiant heating systems for greenhouses. 800-544-0525.

**Sturdi-Built Manufacturing Company,** 11304 SW Boones Ferry Rd., Portland, OR 97219: Free catalog ◆ Greenhouses, cold frames, and sun rooms. 800-722-4115; 503-244-4100 (in OR).

**Sun 'N Rain Greenhouses,** 45 Dixon Ave., Amityville, NY 11701: Free information ◆ Easy-to-assemble greenhouses. 800-999-9459.

**Sun-Porch Division,** Vegetable Factory Inc., P.O. Box 368, Westport, CT 06881: Catalog $3 ◆ Solar greenhouses. 203-324-0010.

**Sundance Supply,** 1678 Shattuck Ave., Ste. 173, Berkeley, CA 94709: Catalog $2 ◆ Building components for greenhouses, sun rooms, pool enclosures, and skylights. 800-776-2534. www.sundancesupply.com

**Sunglo Solar Greenhouses,** 2626 15th Ave. West, Seattle, WA 98119: Free brochure ◆ Solar greenhouses and solariums. 800-647-0606; 206-284-8900 (in WA).

**Texas Greenhouse Company,** 2524 White Settlement Rd., Fort Worth, TX 76107: Catalog $4 ◆ Greenhouse kits. 800-227-5447.

**Troy-Bilt Manufacturing Company,** 1 Garden Way, Troy, NY 12179: Free information ◆ Greenhouses. 800-446-4991.

**Turner Greenhouses,** P.O. Box 1260, Goldsboro, NC 27533: Free catalog ◆ Free-standing and lean-to greenhouses. Also equipment and accessories. 800-672-4770. www.turnergreenhouses.com

**Under Glass Manufacturing Corp.,** P.O. Box 798, Lake Katrine, NY 12449: Catalog $3 ◆ Indoor window greenhouses, other greenhouses, and solariums. 914-298-0645.

## Hydroponic Gardening Supplies

**Albuquerque Hydroponics & Lighting,** 1051 San Mateo SE, Albuquerque, NM 87108: Free catalog ◆ Hydroponic supplies and lighting equipment. 800-753-4617; 505-255-3677 (in NM). www.ahl-hydroponics.com

**Alternative Garden Supply Inc.,** P.O. Box 662, Cary, IL 60113: Free catalog ◆ Hydroponic supplies. 800-444-2837.

**American Agriculture,** 9220 SE Stark, Portland, OR 97216: Free catalog ◆ Indoor garden supplies,hydroponics, and, lighting. 800-433-6805. www.AmericanAG.com

**American Hydroponics,** 286 South G St., Arcata, CA 95521: Free brochure ◆ Hydroponic supplies and kits for beginners. 800-458-6543.

**Aqua Culture Inc.,** 700 1st St., Tempe, AZ 85281: Free catalog ◆ Hydroponic systems, lights, and plant food. 800-633-2137.

**Aqua-Ponics Brew & Grow,** 2535 West Coast Hwy., Newport Beach, CA 92663: Free catalog ◆ Hydroponic supplies. 800-426-1261; 714-642-7776 (in CA).

**Bloomington Wholesale Garden Supply,** 7854 N. Hwy. 37, Bloomington, IN 47404: Free information ◆ Hydroponic systems, growing supplies, equipment, and books. 800-316-1306. www.wormsway.com

**Brew & Grow,** 1824 N. Besly Ct., Chicago, IL 60622: Free information ◆ Home brewing supplies for making beer and hydroponic gardening equipment. 312-395-1500.

**Brite-Lite,** 1991 Francis Hugues, Laval, Quebec, Canada H7S 2G2: Free catalog ◆ Hydroponic supplies and equipment. 514-669-3903.

**Cropking Inc.,** 5050 Greenwich Rd., Seville, OH 44273: Catalog $3 ◆ Hydroponic supplies. 800-321-5656.

**Diamond Lights,** 628 Lindaro St., San Rafael, CA 94901: Free catalog ◆ Hydroponic nutrients, supplies, and lighting. 800-331-3994.

**Discount Garden Supply Inc.,** 14109 E. Sprague, Spokane, WA 99216: Free catalog ◆ Hydroponic systems, lights, nutrients and fertilizers, and propagation aids. 509-924-8333.

**East Coast Hydroponics,** 439 Castleton Ave., Staten Island, NY 10301: Free catalog ◆ Hydroponic and outdoor gardening supplies. 718-727-9300.

**Eco Enterprises,** 1240 NE 175th St., Shoreline, WA 98155: Free catalog ◆ Hydroponic equipment. 800-426-6937. www.ecogrow.com

**Foothill Hydroponics,** 10705 Burbank Blvd., North Hollywood, CA 91601: Free catalog ◆ Nutrients, grow-lights, climate controls, testing and irrigation equipment, rock wool, and other supplies. 818-760-0688.

**Frank's Magic Crops Inc.,** 480 Guelph Line, Burlington, Ontario, Ontario, Canada L7R 3M1: Free catalog ◆ Light, growing systems, and other hydroponic equipment. 905-333-3282.

**General Hydroponics,** P.O. Box 1576, Sebastopol, CA 95473: Free catalog ◆ Hydroponic equipment and supplies for homes, educational and commercial farming, and research. 800-374-9376; 707-824-9376 (in CA).

**Gold Coast Greenhouse,** 7390 Bird Rd., Miami, FL 33155: Free information ◆ Hydroponic supplies and lighting equipment. 800-780-6805.

**Green Gardens,** 12748 Bel-Red Rd., Bellevue, WA 98005: Free catalog ◆ Hydroponic and indoor garden supplies. 800-214-6851.

**GreenFire,** P.O. Box 3442, Chico, CA 959267: Free brochure ◆ Natural liquid fertilizers and hydroponic equipment. 916-895-8301.

**The Growing Experience,** 1901 NW 18th St., Bldg. E, Pompano Beach, FL 33069: Free information ◆ Hydroponic supplies and equipment. 800-273-6092; 954-960-0822 (in FL).

**Hamilton Technology Corp.,** 14902 S. Figueroa St., Gardena, CA 90248: Free catalog ◆ Lights, hydroponic systems, and gardening supplies. 800-458-7474.

**Harvest Moon Hydroponics Inc.,** Airport Plaza, 4214 Union Rd., Cheektowaga, NY 14225: Free catalog ◆ Hydroponic supplies. 800-635-1383.

**Higher Yield,** 29211 NE Wylie Rd., Camas, WA 98607: Free catalog ◆ Lights, growing equipment, and supplies. 800-451-1952; 360-834-6962 (in WA).

**Homegrown Hydroponics Inc.,** 15 McCulloch Ave., #3, Rexdale, Ontario, Canada M9W 4M5: Free information ◆ Hydroponic supplies, lighting equipment, reflectors, nutrients, flood trays, and accessories. 416-242-4769.

**Hydroasis,** 7961 Melrose Ave., Los Angeles, CA 90046: Free information (enclose want list) ◆ Hydroponic systems, supplies, and equipment. 888-355-GROW.

**Hydrofarm,** 1455 East Francisco Blvd., San Rafael, CA 94901: Free catalog ◆ Lights and hydroponic supplies. 800-634-9999; 415-459-6095 (in CA).

**Indoor/Outdoor Gardener,** 8225 5th Ave., Brooklyn, NY 11209: Free information ◆ Supplies, equipment, lights, growing media, and accessories for hydroponic gardening.

**Light Manufacturing Company,** 1634 SE Brooklyn, Portland, OR 97202: Free catalog ◆ Hydroponic systems, lights, and nutrient controls. 800-NOW-LITE.

**MAH Hydroponics,** 175 Commerce Dr., Hauppage, NY 11788: Free information ◆ Hydroponic equipment. 516-434-6872.

**Mrs. Greenjeans Hydroponic & Garden Supplies,** 5020 S. Federal, Englewood, CO 80110: Free catalog ◆ Hydroponic and garden supplies. 800-469-2550.

**New Earth Hydroponics & Homebrewing,** 9810 Taylorsville Rd., Louisville, KY 40299: Free catalog ◆ Hydroponic and outdoor gardening supplies. 800-462-5953; 502-261-0005 (in KY).

**Perfect World Hydroponics Inc.,** P.O. Box 662, Rocky Hill, NJ 08553: Free information ◆ Indoor and outdoor hydroponic growing systems. 908-422-9429.

**Sea of Green Hydroponics,** Urban Garden Supplies Center, 1828 E. University, Ste. 3, Tempe, AZ 85281: Free information ◆ Hydroponic systems and supplies. 602-829-6100.

**SHIVA Environmental Systems,** P.O. Box 1287, Keene, NH 03431: Free information ◆ All-in-one indoor climate controller for temperature, humidity, and carbon dioxide. 800-507-8587.

**Simply Hydroponics,** 1795 Starkey Rd., Largo, FL 34641: Free catalog ◆ Do-it-yourself hydroponic kits and supplies. 813-531-5355.

**Superior Growers Supply,** 4870 Dawn Ave., East Lansing, MI 48823: Free catalog ◆ Hydroponic supplies. 800-227-0027.

**Virginia Hydroponics,** 368 Newtown Rd., Ste. 105, Virginia Beach, VA 23462: Free information ◆ Hydroponic supplies. 800-490-5425.

**Worm's Way,** 7850 N. State Rd. 37, Bloomington, IN 47404: Free catalog ◆ Hydroponic and organic gardening supplies. 800-274-9676. www.wormsway.com

## Indoor Gardening Supplies

**Alternative Garden Supply Inc.,** P.O. Box 662, Cary, IL 60113: Free catalog ◆ Indoor lighting systems, growing kits, and biological pest controls. 800-444-2837.

**Floralight,** 6-620 Supertest Rd., North York, Ontario, Canada M3J 2M5: Free information ◆ Indoor lights and garden supplies. 416-665-4000.

**Florist Products Inc.,** P.O. Box 3190, Barrington, IL 60011: Catalog $3 ◆ Greenhouse equipment and supplies. 800-828-2242.

**Indoor Gardening Supplies,** P.O. Box 40567, Detroit, MI 48240: Free catalog ◆ Indoor gardening supplies, stands, lights, and books. 810-426-9080.

**Plant Collectibles,** 103 Kenview Ave., Buffalo, NY 14217: Free catalog with two 1st class stamps ◆ Garden and greenhouse supplies and light stands. 716-875-1221.

## Landscaping Stone & Other Supplies

**Allan Block,** 7400 Metro Blvd., Ste. 185, Edina, MN 55435: Free list of retail sources ◆ Mortar-less concrete blocks for retaining walls, curves, corners, stairways, and terraces. 800-899-5309; 612-835-5309 (in MN).

**Eurocobble,** 4265 Lemp Ave., Studio City, CA 91604: Free information ◆ Cobblestone in modules and sets. 818-877-5012.

**Proline Edging,** 13505 Barry St., Holland, MI 49424: Free catalog ◆ Easy-to-install aluminum landscape edging. 800-356-9660.

**Stone Company Inc.,** W4520 Lime Rd., Eden, WI 53019: Free information ◆ Natural building and landscaping cobblers, granite boulders, and stone for building walls, steppers, and flagstone walks. 920-477-2521.

**Urdl's Waterfall Creations Inc.,** 2010 NW 1st St., Delray Beach, FL 33445: Free information ◆ Manufactured hollow concrete rocks for landscaping and waterfall settings. 561-278-3320.

## Lawn Ornaments & Statues

**Amdega & Machin Conservatories,** 3515 Lakeshore Dr., St. Joseph, MI 49085: Catalog $10 ◆ English-style conservatories constructed in western red cedar or aluminum. Also garden ornaments. 800-922-0110.

**Armchair Shopper,** P.O. Box 419464, Kansas City, MO 64141: Free catalog ◆ Classic old world-style sundials, wind chimes, and lawn ornaments. 816-767-3200.

**Ballard Designs,** 1670 DeFoor Ave. NE, Atlanta, GA 30318: Catalog $3 ◆ Castings for indoor and outdoor settings, furniture, lamps, fireplace accessories, pillows, and art prints. 800-367-2810. www.ballard-designs.com

**The BB Brass,** 10151 Pacific Mesa Blvd., San Diego, CA 92121: Free catalog ◆ Brass fountains and sculptures. 800-536-0987.

**BowBends,** P.O. Box 900, Bolton, MA 01740: Catalog $3 ◆ Arbors, bridges, gazebos, and other garden structures. 800-518-6471.

**Carruth Studio Inc.,** 1178 Farnsworth Rd., Waterville, OH 43566: Free catalog ◆ Hand-cast limestone garden art. 800-225-1178. www.carruthstudio.com

**Cherry Blossom Gardens,** 15709 N. Lund Rd., Eden Prairie, MN 55346: Free catalog ◆ Cast stone Japanese ornaments and garden accents, bamboo accessories, and Oriental granite sculptures. 612-975-0976. www.garden-gifts.com

**Chestnut Knob,** Box 4882, Martinsville, VA 24115: Free catalog ◆ Garden furnishings and accessories. 800-266-3035.

**Robert Compton Ltd.,** 3600 Rt. 116, Bristol, VT 05443: Brochure $2 ◆ Stone fountains and water sculptures. 802-453-3778.

**Country Casual,** 17317 Germantown Rd., Germantown, MD 20874: Catalog $5 ◆ Garden furnishings. 301-540-0040.

**Cross Vinyl Lattice,** 3174 Marjan Dr., Atlanta, GA 30340: Free information ◆ Trellises, arbors, and fencing. 800-521-9878.

**Design Toscano,** 17 E. Campbell St., Arlington Heights, IL 60005: Catalog $4 ◆ European reproductions for homes and gardens. 800-525-1233. www.aaweb.com/toscano

**Excel Bridge Manufacturer,** 12001 Shoemaker Ave., Santa Fe Springs, CA 90670: Free information ◆ Easy-to-install pre-fabricated bridges. 800-548-0054; 310-944-0701 (in CA).

**Flora Fauna,** P.O. Box 578, Gualala, CA 95445: Free information ◆ Lattice panels, columns, arches, and sundials. 800-358-9120. flora@mcn.org

**Florentine Craftsmen,** 46-24 28th St., Long Island City, NY 11101: Catalog $5 ◆ Sculptures, fountains, birdbaths, and furniture. 718-937-7632. www.florentinecraftsmen.com

**Brian Foster's Garden Architecture,** 719 S. 17th St., Philadelphia, PA 19146: Free information ◆ Garden architecture. 215-545-5442. www.brianfoster.com

**FrenchWyres,** P.O. Box 131655, Tyler, TX 75713: Catalog $3 ◆ Trellises, topiary frames, urns, plant stands, cache pots, window boxes, and arches. 903-597-8322.

**Garden Accents,** 4 Union Hill Rd., West Conshohocken, PA 19428: Video catalog $15 ◆ Antique and contemporary garden sculptures and ornaments. 610-825-5525.

**Garden Arches by Anderson Design,** P.O. Box 4057, Bellingham, WA 98227: Brochure $2 (refundable) ◆ Arbors and trellises in cedar, iron, and copper. 800-947-7697; 360-650-0733 (in WA). www.gardenarches.com

**Garden Architecture,** 719 S. 17th St., Philadelphia, PA 19146: Free catalog ◆ Easy-to-assemble trellis structures. 215-545-5442.

**Garden Concepts Collection,** 6621 Poplar Woods Circle South, Germantown, TN 38138: Catalog $5 ◆ Handcrafted furniture and trellises. 901-756-1649.

**The Garden Gate,** 5122 Morningside Dr., Houston, TX 77005: Catalog $10 ◆ Imported classical English cast-stone statuary. 713-528-2654. www.gardengate.com

**Garden Highlights,** P.O. Box 48, Cozad, NE 69130: Free catalog ◆ Polyvinyl garden and landscaping accessories. 800-691-6221. www.countryestate.com

**Garden Trellises,** P.O. Box 105, LaFayette, NY 13084: Free catalog ◆ Galvanized steel or copper trellises, arbors, and other supports. 800-498-0584. www.Gardentrellises.com

**Good Catalog Company,** 5484 SE International Way, Portland, OR 97222: Catalog $5 ◆ Kitchen, dining, gardening, and decorative accessories. 800-225-3870.

**Haddonstone (USA) Ltd.,** 201 Heller Pl., Bellmawr, NJ 08031: Catalog $10 ◆ English garden ornaments and architectural stonework. 609-931-7011.

**Hen-Feathers & Company Inc.,** 250 King Manor Dr., King of Prussia, PA 19406: Free catalog ◆ Hand-cast architectural and garden accents. 800-282-1910.

**Hines Pottery,** 6747 Signat Dr., Houston, TX 77041: Free information ◆ Miniature fountains and decorative garden accessories. 800-231-0875. www.rampages.omramp.net/~asd

**Ironwood,** 3435 Junction Rd., Egg Harbor, WI 54209: Free catalog ◆ Handcrafted metal items and original sculptures. 800-823-4769.

**Kestrel Manufacturing,** 9 E. Race St., Stowe, PA 19464: Information $2 ◆ American and English garden accessories. 800-494-4321; 610-326-6679 (in PA). www.diyshutters.com

**Kramer Brothers,** P.O. Box 255, Dayton, OH 45404: Free catalog ◆ Garden furniture and ornaments. 937-228-4194.

**Nebraska Plastics Inc.,** P.O. Box 45, Cozad, NE 69130: Free information ◆ Rose trellises, garden arbors, picnic tables, outdoor furniture, and accessories. 800-445-2887. www.countryestate.com

**New England Garden Ornaments,** P.O. Box 235, North Brookfield, MA 01535: Free catalog ◆ Garden ornaments and furniture. 508-867-4474. www.negardenornaments.com

**OuterSpace Landscape Furnishings Inc.,** 7533 Draper Ave., La Jolla, CA 92037: Free information ◆ Steel fences, gates, and modular components for trellises and garden structures. 800-338-2499.

**Park Place,** 2251 Wisconsin Ave. NW, Washington, DC 20007: Free catalog ◆ Classic outdoor furniture in wood, metal, and wicker, and architectural products. 202-342-6294.

**Pompeian Studios,** 90 Rockledge Rd., Bronxville, NY 10708: Catalog $10 ◆ Original sculptures, ornaments, and forged furniture for patios and gardens. 800-457-5595.

**Gary Price Studio,** 1307 E. 1200 South, Springville, UT 84663: Free information with long SASE ◆ Garden sculptures. 801-489-1110.

**Rivertown Products,** 1919 Garfield Ave., St. Joseph, MO 64503: Brochure $1 ◆ Handcrafted arbors and outdoor products. 816-232-8822.

**Sculpture Placement Ltd.,** P.O. Box 9709, Washington, DC 20016: Free catalog ◆ Bronze life-size sculptures. 202-362-9310.

**Somerset,** 5456 SE International Way, Portland, OR 97222: Catalog $5 (refundable) ◆ Garden landscaping furniture and accessories. 800-225-3870.

**Southerlands for Leisure Living,** 15 Biltmore Ave., Asheville, NC 28801: Free catalog ◆ Outdoor furniture and garden accessories. 800-968-5596.

**Stone Forest,** P.O. Box 2840, Santa Fe, NM 87504: Catalog $3 ◆ Fountains, lanterns, water basins, birdbaths, pedestals, and handcarved granite statuary. 505-986-8883.

**Strassacker Bronze America Inc.,** P.O. Box 931, Spartanburg, SC 29304: Catalog $15 ◆ Contemporary and abstract bronze sculptures, fountains, and lighting equipment. 864-579-2579.

**Studio Gerald Corbeil,** 704 Lytle St., West Palm Beach, FL 33405: Free brochure ◆ Handcarved featherlight lava rock Japanese lanterns and water basins. 561-586-4398.

**Sun Garden Specialties,** P.O. Box 52382, Tulsa, OK 74152: Free information ◆ Wood landscaping items for gardens. 800-468-1638.

**Sycamore Creek,** P.O. Box 16, Ancrâm, NY 12502: Free brochure ◆ Copper trellises and arbors. Also handcrafted copper garden and home furnishings. 518-398-6393. sycamorecreek@taconic.net

**Tom Torrens Sculpture Design Inc.,** P.O. Box 1876, Gig Harbor, WA 98335: Catalog $2 ◆ Sculptures, fountains, birdbaths, and other accessories for the home and garden. 253-265-8811.

**Toscano Design,** 17 E. Campbell St., Arlington Heights, IL 60005: Catalog $5 ◆ Hand-cast replica artifacts and sculptures. 800-525-1733.

**Trellis Structures,** P.O. Box 380, Beverly, MA 01915: Catalog $2 ◆ Trellis sculptures and furniture. 978-921-1235.

**Unit Structures,** 5724 McCrimmon Pkwy., Morrisville, NC 27560: Free information ◆ Easy-to-assemble prefabricated pedestrian and vehicular shelters and bridges. 800-777-UNIT.

**Uwchlan Farm,** 303 Greenridge Rd., Glenmoore, PA 19343: Free catalog ◆ Wrought-iron accessories for the home and garden. 800-900-IRON.

**Samuel Welch Sculpture Inc.,** P.O. Box 55, Cincinnati, OH 45201: Catalog $10 ◆ Large-scale sculptures in bronze, aluminum, steel, concrete, marble, and granite. 513-321-8882. WelchHome@aol.com

**Wind & Weather,** P.O. Box 2320, Mendocino, CA 95460: Free catalog ◆ Garden ornaments. 800-922-9463. weather@men.org

## Markers

**Eon Industries,** P.O. Box 11, Liberty Center, OH 43532: Free brochure ◆ Metal flower and garden markers.

**Evergreen Garden Plant Labels,** P.O. Box 922, Cloverdale, CA 95425: Free brochure with first class stamp ◆ Engraved name plates, metal plant markers, and holders.

**Paw Paw Everlast Label Company,** P.O. Box 93, Paw Paw, MI 49079: Free information with long SASE ◆ Permanent metal garden labels.

**Vermont Natural Stoneworks,** Depot St., Box 275, Fair Haven, VT 05743: Free list of retail sources ◆ Tile products that include floors, pet memorials and urns, entryway systems, house and garden markers, instant patios and walkways, and gas stove mats. 802-265-2200. www.sover.net/~stone

## Mowers, Trimmers, & Blowers

**Agri-Fab Inc.,** 303 W. Raymond St., Sullivan, IL 61951: Free list of retail sources ◆ Walk-behind mowers, spreaders, sprayers, rollers, and other equipment. 217-728-8388. www.agri-fab.com

**American Lawn Mower Company,** P.O. Box 369, Shelbyville, IN 46176: Free information ◆ Push-type lawn mowers. 800-633-1501.

**Ariens Company,** 655 W. Ryan St., P.O. Box 157, Brillion, WI 54110: Free information ◆ Self-propelled and riding mowers with electric start engines. 414-756-2141.

**BCS America,** 13601 Providence Rd., Matthews, NC 28105: Free catalog ◆ Garden carts, chippers and shredders, tillers, sprayers, lawn and garden tractors, and mowers. 800-227-8791.

**Black & Decker Garden Tools,** Consumer Services, P.O. Box 618, Hampstead, MD 21074: Free information ◆ Portable vacuums and blowers in gasoline-powered and cordless electric models, electric hedge trimmers, and lawn mowers. 800-762-6672. www.blackandecker.com

**Country Home Products,** Meigs Rd., Box 25, Vergennes, VT 05491: Free information ◆ Power trimmer on wheels. 800-635-4848.

**Dixon Industries Inc.,** P.O. Box 1569, Coffeyville, KS 67337: Free information ◆ Riding mowers. 316-251-2000.

**Echo Inc.,** 400 Oakwood Rd., Lake Zurich, IL 60047: Free catalog ◆ Trimmers, blowers, hedge clippers, sprayers, chain saws, and shredders. 800-432-3246.

**Excel Industries Inc.,** P.O. Box 7000, Hesston, KS 67062: Free information ◆ Riding mowers that mow, shred, edge, and vacuum. 800-395-4757. www.excelhustler.com

**Garden Way,** 1 Garden Way, Troy, NY 12179: Free information ◆ Carts, tillers, clippers, sickle bar mowers, garden composter, and other equipment. 800-446-4991.

**The Grasshopper Company,** P.O. Box 637, Moundridge, KS 67107: Free list of retail sources ◆ Riding mowers. 316-345-8621.

**Homelite Sales,** Box 7047, Charlotte, NC 28241: Free information with long SASE ◆ Push and riding mowers, lawn tractors, electric and gasoline-operated trimmers, gasoline-powered blowers, vacuums, sprayers, cut-off saws, and snow removal equipment. 800-242-4672.

**Husqvarna Power Products,** 9006 Perimeter Woods Dr., Charlotte, NC 28216: Free information ◆ Walk-behind and riding mowers. 800-438-7297.

**Kubota Tractor Corp.,** P.O. Box 2992, Torrance, CA 90509: Free information ◆ Walk-behind mowers. 562-370-3370.

**Lawn-Boy,** 8111 Lyndale Ave. South, Bloomington, MN 55420: Free information ◆ Walk-behind and riding mowers, lawn and garden tractors, and power-operated tillers. 800-526-6937. www.toro.com

**Mainline of North America,** P.O. Box 526, London, OH 43140: Free information ◆ All-gear driven tiller with optional sickle bar and no belts or chains, hydraulic log splitters, carts, and snow throwers. 800-837-2097.

**MTD Products Inc.,** P.O. Box 360900, Cleveland, OH 44136: Free information ◆ Walk-behind and riding mowers with optional mulching and bagging attachments. 800-800-7310. www.mtdproducts.com

**Poulan,** 5020 Flournoy-Lucas Rd., Shreveport, LA 71129: Free information ◆ Handheld gasoline-powered blowers and lawn trimmers. 318-683-3546. www.poulan.com/poulan.html

**Ryobi America Corp.,** P.O. Box 1207, Anderson, SC 29622: Free information ◆ Combination self-propelled mower and mulcher. 800-525-2579. www.ryobi.com

**Simplicity Manufacturing Inc.,** P.O. Box 997, Port Washington, WI 53074: Free information ◆ Walk-behind and riding mowers. 800-945-0235.

**Snapper Power Equipment,** P.O. Box 777, McDonough, GA 30253: Free list of retail sources ◆ Walk-behind and riding mowers. 770-954-2500.

**Steiner Turf Equipment Inc.,** 289 N. Kurzen Rd., P.O. Box 504, Dalton, OH 44618: Free list of retail sources ◆ Powered mowers with optional power blower, slip scoop, chipper/shredder, and other attachments. 330-828-0200.

**Toro Company,** 8111 Lyndale Ave., Bloomington, MN 55420: Free information ◆ Riding trimmers and other home yard care, golf course management, and grounds care management equipment. 800-526-6937. www.toro.com

**Walker Manufacturing Company,** 5925 E. Harmony Rd., Fort Collins, CO 80525: Free information ◆ Riding mowers with a vacuum collection system. 800-279-8537.

## Organic Gardening Supplies

**Bountiful Gardens,** 18001 Shafer Ranch Rd., Willits, CA 95490: Free catalog ◆ Seeds for vegetables, compost crops, herbs, and flowers. Also books and organic gardening supplies. 707-459-6410. www.bountifulgardens.com

**Brown's Edgewood Gardens,** 2611 Corrine Dr., Orlando, FL 32803: Catalog $3 ◆ Butterfly-attracting plants, herbs, and organic gardening products. 407-896-3203.

**Gardens Alive,** 5100 Schenley Price list., Lawrenceburg, IN 47025: Free catalog ◆ Organic gardening supplies. 812-537-8650.

**Green Earth Organics,** c/o Soil Conditioning, P.O. Box 206, 90 W. 1st St., Zillah, WA 98953: Free information ◆ Environmentally-safe fertilizers and nutrients for grasses, shrubs, flowers, and vegetables. 509-829-5733. sci1954@wolfener.com

**Harmony Farm Supply & Nursery,** 3244 Hwy. 116, No. A, Sebastopol, CA 95472: Catalog $2 (refundable) ◆ Organic fertilizers. 707-823-9125.

**High Country Gardens,** 2902 Rufina St., Santa Fe, NM 87505: Free catalog ◆ Organic gardening products and flowering plants. 800-925-9387.

**Koos Inc.,** 4500 13th Ct., Kenosha, WI 53140: Free information ◆ Fertilizers, herbicides, insecticides, and organic plant foods. 800-558-5667; 414-654-5301 (in WI).

**Natural Gardening Company,** 217 San Anselmo Ave., San Anselmo, CA 94960: Free catalog ◆ Beneficial insects, organic gardening supplies, pest controls, drip irrigation equipment, and wildflower seeds. 415-456-5060.

**Nitron Industries Inc.,** P.O. Box 1447, Fayetteville, AR 72702: Free catalog ◆ Organic fertilizers, enzyme soil conditioners, natural pest controls, and pet care products. 800-835-0123. www.nitron.com

**Peaceful Valley Farm Supply,** P.O. Box 2209, Grass Valley, CA 95945: Catalog $2 (refundable) ◆ Organic gardening supplies. 916-272-4769.

**Raintree Nursery,** 393 Butts Rd., Morton, WA 98356: Free information ◆ Organic gardening supplies. 360-496-6400.

**Saltwater Farms,** P.O. Box 740, South Freeport, ME 04078: Free information ◆ Seaweed-based products for lawns and gardens. 800-293-KELP. saltwater@maine.com

**Season Extenders,** 971 Nichols Ave., Stratford, CT 06497: Free catalog ◆ Propagation supplies, pots and baskets, lights, greenhouses, pest controls, hydroponic growing aids, fertilizers, and tools. 203-375-1317.

## Pots & Planters

**Cambridge Designs,** Rt. 4, Box 188, Greenville, AL 36077: Catalog $3 ◆ Landscaping benches, planters, receptacles, fountains, and pedestrian control screens. 800-477-7320.

**The Carpenter's Shop,** 1573 Princeton, Berley, MI 48072: Brochure $1 ◆ Handcrafted redwood boxes for homes, decks, patios, or gardens. 248-414-9060.

**Cast Aluminum Reproductions,** P.O. Box 1060, San Elzario, TX 79849: Catalog $2 ◆ Cast-aluminum and brass furniture, street lights, fountains, mail boxes, and plant stands. 915-764-3793.

**Claycraft,** 807 Avenue of Americas, New York, NY 10001: Catalog $2 ◆ Indoor and outdoor fiberglass planters. 212-242-2903.

**Flower Framers,** 671 Wilmer Ave., Cincinnati, OH 45226: Free brochure ◆ Portable or permanent indoor and outdoor flowerbeds. 800-315-1805; 513-321-7001 (in OH).

**Gift & Wicker Import Inc.,** 12770 Moore St., Cerritos, CA 90701: Catalog $5 ◆ Wickerware, hobby craft supplies, basket planters, home decorative accessories, and furniture. 800-622-6209; 310-407-3319 (in CA).

**Kingsley-Bate Ltd.,** 5587 Guinea Rd., Fairfax, VA 22032: Catalog $2 ◆ Handcarved and traditional teak planters, window boxes, and garden furniture. 703-978-7200.

**Landscape Forms Inc.,** 431 Lawndale Ave., Kalamazoo, MI 49001: Free information ◆ Outdoor furniture and garden planters. 800-521-2546; 616-381-0396 (in MI). www.landscapeforms.com

**Malley Supply,** P.O. Box 96, Idyllwild, CA 92549: Catalog $1 (refundable) ◆ Plastic pots and growing containers.

**MoonAcre IronWorks,** 62 Chambersburg St., Gettysburg, PA 17325: Catalog $2 ◆ Country-style iron trellises for climbing plants. 800-966-4766. moonacre@cvn.net

**Plant Collectibles,** 103 Kenview Ave., Buffalo, NY 14217: Free catalog with two 1st class stamps ◆ Plastic pots, hanging baskets, starter trays, watering equipment, plant foods, insecticide sprays, and light units. 716-875-1221.

**Season Extenders,** 971 Nichols Ave., Stratford, CT 06497: Free catalog ◆ Propagation supplies, pots and baskets, lights, greenhouses, pest controls, hydroponic growing aids, fertilizers, and tools. 203-375-1317.

**Seibert & Rice,** P.O. Box 365, Short Hills, NJ 07078: Catalog $2 ◆ Terra cotta planters. 201-467-8266.

**The Village Wrought Iron Inc.,** 7756 Main St., Fabius, NY 13063: Brochure $2 (refundable) ◆ Hand-forged planters. 315-683-5589. villagewroughtiron.com

**Violet House,** P.O. Box 1274, Gainesville, FL 32601: Free catalog ◆ Indoor and outdoor plastic pots, hanging baskets, African violet seeds, insecticides, potting soils, fertilizers, perlite, vermiculite, books, and trays. 352-377-8465.

**Water-Well Planters,** 41 Alpha Park, Highland Heights, OH 44143: Free information ◆ Easy-to-use, no assembly self-watering planters. 800-341-2673; 216-461-4252 (in OH). www.water-well.com

## Software

**Abracadata,** P.O. Box 2440, Eugene, OR 97402: Free catalog ◆ Gardening DOS, Windows, and Macintosh gardening software. 800-451-4871; 541-342-3030 (in OR). www.abracadata.com

**Expert Software,** 800 Douglas Rd., Executive Tower, 7th Floor, Coral Gables, FL 33134: Free information ◆ Landscaping design software. 800-759-2562; 305-567-9990 (in FL).

**Multicom Publishing,** 188 Embarcadero, 5th Floor, San Francisco, CA 94105: Free brochure ◆ Home improvement and gardening CD-ROMs. www.multicom.com

## Soil Testing

**Cook's Consulting,** RD 2, Box 13, Lowville, NY 13367: Free information ◆ Soil testing services. 315-376-3002.

**Green Gems,** P.O. Box 6007, Healdsburg, CA 95448: Free information ◆ Soil testing services. 800-431-SOIL.

**Necessary Trading Company,** One Natures Way, New Castle, VA 24127: Catalog $2 ◆ Soil and garden testing services, testing supplies and equipment, plant nutrients, fertilizers, and pest controls,. 800-447-5354.

## Tillers

**Ariens Company,** 655 W. Ryan St., P.O. Box 157, Brillon, WI 54110: Free information ◆ Power-operated tillers. 414-756-2141.

**BCS America,** 13601 Providence Rd., Matthews, NC 28105: Free catalog ◆ Garden carts, chippers and shredders, tillers, sprayers, lawn and garden tractors, and mowers. 800-227-8791.

**Black & Decker Garden Tools,** Consumer Services, P.O. Box 618, Hampstead, MD 21074: Free information ◆ Power-operated tillers. 800-762-6672. www.blackandecker.com

**Garden Way,** 1 Garden Way, Troy, NY 12179: Free information ◆ Power-operated tiller and composter for small gardens. 800-446-4991.

**Hoffco,** 358 NW F St., Richmond, IN 47374: Free information ◆ Mini tillers. 800-999-8161.

**Husqvarna Power Products,** 9006 Perimeter Woods Dr., Charlotte, NC 28216: Free information ◆ Power-operated tillers. 800-438-7297.

**Kubota Tractor Corp.,** P.O. Box 2992, Torrance, CA 90509: Free information ◆ Power-operated tillers. 310-370-3370.

**Lawn-Boy,** 8111 Lyndale Ave. South, Bloomington, MN 55420: Free information ◆ Walk-behind and riding mowers, lawn and garden tractors, and power-operated tillers. 800-526-6937. www.toro.com

**Mainline of North America,** P.O. Box 526, London, OH 43140: Free information ◆ All-gear driven tiller with optional sickle bar and no belts or chains, hydraulic log splitters, carts, and snow throwers. 800-837-2097.

**Mantis Manufacturing Company,** 1028 Street Rd., Southampton, PA 18966: Free information ◆ Electric-powered tiller with optional border edger, planter furrower, lawn aerator, and thatch remover. 800-366-6268.

**Mighty Mac,** Mackissic Inc., P.O. Box 111, Parker Ford, PA 19457: Free information ◆ Chippers, tillers, blowers, and sprayers. 610-495-7181.

**New Holland North America Inc.,** P.O. Box 1895, New Holland, PA 17557: Free list of retail sources ◆ Lawn and garden tractors with optional attachments. 717-355-1121.

**Poulan,** 5020 Flournoy-Lucas Rd., Shreveport, LA 71129: Free information ◆ Handheld gasoline-powered blowers and lawn trimmers. 318-683-3546. www.poulan.com/poulan.html

## Tools & Sprayers

**Alsto Company,** P.O. Box 1267, Galesburg, IL 61401: Catalog $1 ◆ Tools, pet products, kitchen aids, and convenience items. 800-447-0048.

**American Arborist Supplies Inc.,** 882 S. Matlack St., West Chester, PA 19382: Catalog $4 ◆ Supplies for tree care needs and landscaping. 800-441-8381.

**Amerind MacKissic Inc.,** P.O. Box 111, Parker Ford, PA 19457: Free information ◆ Sprayers for fruit trees, shrubs, gardens, and lawns. 610-495-7181.

**Ames Lawn & Garden Tools,** P.O. Box 14854, Mansfield, OH 44901: Free information ◆ Garden tools. 800-624-2654.

**Brookstone Company,** Order Processing Center, 1655 Bassford Dr., Mexico, MO 65265: Free catalog ◆ House and garden tools. 800-926-7000.

**W. Atlee Burpee & Company,** 300 Park Ave., Warminster, PA 18974: Free catalog ◆ Tools, equipment, and growing aids. 800-888-1447. www.burpee.com

**Carts Vermont,** 1890 Airport Pkwy., South Burlington, VT 05403: Free information ◆ Garden carts. 800-732-7417.

**Charley's Greenhouse Supply,** 1569 Memorial Hwy., Mt. Vernon, WA 98273: Catalog $2 ◆ Shading materials, fans, watering and misting equipment, and propagating aids. 800-322-4707.

**Chestnut Knob,** Box 4482, Martinsville, VA 24115: Free catalog ◆ Potting benches, garden furnishings, and accessories. 800-266-3035.

**Clapper's,** P.O. Box 2278, West Newton, MA 02165: Free catalog ◆ Spreaders, sprayers, sprinkling and full-flow watering systems, outdoor furniture, landscaping ornaments, and outdoor lighting. 617-244-7900.

**ComposTumbler,** 160 Koser Rd., Lititz, PA 17543: Free information ◆ Easy-to-use fast-working compost-maker. 800-880-2345.

**Creative Enterprises Inc.,** P.O. Box 3452, Idaho Falls, ID 83403: Free information ◆ Weeding tools and all-season plant protectors. 208-523-0526. wweeder@srv.net

**Crown Botanicals,** 1036 Fairview Dr., Reading, PA 19605: Free information ◆ Tools, rare plants, gifts, and a lightweight, portable, and expandable garden workshop center. 888-384-2427.

**Denman & Company,** 1202 E. Pine St., Placentia, CA 92870: Free information ◆ Pruning and other gardening tools. 714-524-0668.

**Duraco Products,** 1109 E. Lake St., Streamwood, IL 60107: Free information ◆ Garden accessories. 800-888-POTS.

**Echo Inc.,** 400 Oakwood Rd., Lake Zurich, IL 60047: Free list of retail sources ◆ Power blowers. 800-432-3246.

**Environmental Concepts,** 710 NW 57th St., Fort Lauderdale, FL 33309: Free brochure ◆ Meters that measure soil temperature, pH, light intensity, and the need for fertilizer. 954-491-4490.

**Florian Gardening Tools,** 157 Water St., Southington, CT 06489: Free information ◆ Ratchet-cut pruning tools. 800-275-3618.

**Four Seasons Nursery,** 1706 Morrisey Dr., Bloomington, IL 61704: Free catalog ◆ Tools, plants, seeds, and growing stock. 309-663-9551.

**Gardener's Supply Company,** 128 Intervale Rd., Burlington, VT 05401: Free catalog ◆ Composter, pest control sprayers, watering systems and controls, weeding and cultivating tools, organic fertilizers, garden carts, leaf mulchers, canning and preserving supplies, and furniture. 800-876-5520. www.gardeners.com

**Gardeners Eden,** P.O. Box 7307, San Francisco, CA 94133: Free catalog ◆ Tools, landscaping accessories, growing and transplanting aids, and furniture. 800-822-1214.

**E.C. Geiger,** P.O. Box 285, Harleysville, PA 19438: Free catalog ◆ Greenhouses, gardening supplies, and tools. 800-4-GEIGER.

**Harmony Farm Supply & Nursery,** 3244 Hwy. 116, No. A, Sebastopol, CA 95472: Catalog $2 (refundable). ◆ Tools and horticultural supplies. 707-823-9125.

**Harris Seeds Inc.,** P.O. Box 22960, Rochester, NY 14692: Free catalog ◆ Gardening equipment, seeds, and plants. 800-514-4441. www.trine.com/gardennet/harrisseeds

**Indoor Gardening Supplies,** P.O. Box 40567, Detroit, MI 48240: Free catalog ◆ Supplies, lights, and books. 810-426-9080.

**Johnny's Selected Seeds,** Foss Hill Rd., Albion, ME 04910: Free catalog ◆ Tools, growing aids, and gardening supplies. 207-437-4301. www.johnnyseeds.com

**K & G Manufacturing Inc.,** P.O. Box 350, Duke, OK 73532: Free catalog ◆ Easy-to-use on-wheels lawn and garden power sprayer. 405-679-3955.

**The Kinsman Company,** River Rd., Point Pleasant, PA 18950: Free catalog ◆ Composters, compost bins, chipper-shredders, rose arbors, garden arches, plant supports, and tools. 800-733-4146.

**Lee Valley Tools Inc.,** P.O. Box 1780, Ogdensburg, NY 13669: Free catalog ◆ Garden tools and other work-saving aids. 800-871-8158. www.leevalley.com

**Leichtung Workshops,** 1108 N. Glenn Rd., Casper, WY 82601: Free catalog ◆ Tools and accessories for gardeners, woodworkers, and hobby do-it-yourselfers. 800-321-6840.

**A.M. Leonard Inc.,** P.O. Box 816, Piqua, OH 45356: Free catalog ◆ Tools, sprayers, and gardening supplies. 800-543-8955.

**MacKenzie Nursery Supply Inc.,** P.O. Box 322, Perry, OH 44081: Free brochure ◆ Tools and supplies. 800-777-5030.

**Mainline of North America,** P.O. Box 526, London, OH 43140: Free information ◆ All-gear driven tiller with optional sickle bar and no belts or chains, hydraulic log splitters, carts, and snow throwers. 800-837-2097.

**Mantis Manufacturing Company,** 1028 Street Rd., Southampton, PA 18966: Free information ◆ Portable sprayer for gardens, washing windows and outside walls, and other uses. 800-366-6268.

**Mellinger's,** 2310 W. South Range Rd., North Lima, OH 44452: Free catalog ◆ Tools, plants and seeds, and growing aids. 330-549-9861. www.mellingers.com

**Mighty Mac,** Mackissic Inc., P.O. Box 111, Parker Ford, PA 19457: Free information ◆ Chippers, tillers, blowers, and sprayers. 610-495-7181.

**Modern Homesteader,** 1825 Big Horn Ave., Cody, WY 82414: Free catalog ◆ Gardening equipment, clothing and hats, tools, truck and automotive accessories, and canning equipment. 800-443-4934; 307-587-5946 (in WY). www.modfarm.com

**Mountainman Woodshop,** Rt. 2, Box 37A, Eagle Rock, VA 24085: Free brochure ◆ Handcrafted traditional Appalachian slot-back chairs and wood farming tools. 540-884-2197.

**Natural Gardening Company,** 217 San Anselmo Ave., San Anselmo, CA 94960: Free catalog ◆ Tools, seeds, fertilizers, pest controls, birdhouses, and books. 415-456-5060.

**Nature's Backyard Inc.,** 585 State Rd., North Dartmouth, MA 02747: Free brochure ◆ Easy-to-assemble and use composter. Also other garden products made from recycled plastic. 800-853-2525. www.naturesbackyard.com

**Walt Nicke Company,** P.O. Box 433, Topsfield, MA 01983: Free information ◆ Garden tools. 978-887-3388.

**L.L. Olds Seed Company,** P.O. Box 7790, Madison, WI 53707: Catalog $2.50 ◆ Tools, growing aids, seeds, and plants. 608-249-9291.

**Park Seed Company,** 1 Parkron Ave., Greenwood, SC 29648: Free catalog ◆ Tools, plants and seeds, and growing aids. 800-845-3369. www.parkseed.com

**PeCo Inc.,** P.O. Box 1197, Arden, NC 28704: Free information ◆ Battery-powered sprayer with charger and wand. 800-438-5823; 704-684-1234 (in NC).

**Pinetree Garden Seeds,** Box 300, New Gloucester, ME 04260: Free catalog ◆ Sprayers. 207-926-3400. www.maine.com/seeds

**Planet Natural,** P.O. Box 3146, Bozeman, MT 59772: Free catalog ◆ Beneficial insects, garden seeds, composting equipment, organic fertilizers, pest controls, garden supplies, and pet and body care products. 800-289-6656. www.planetnatural.com

**Plastopan North America Inc.,** 812 E. 59th St., Los Angeles, CA 90001: Free brochure ◆ Backyard composter. 800-416-6005.

**Plow & Hearth,** P.O. Box 5000, Madison, VA 22727: Free catalog ◆ Tools, outdoor furniture, bird houses and feeders, and birdbaths. 800-627-1712. peggy@plowhearth.com

**Poulan,** 5020 Flournoy-Lucas Rd., Shreveport, LA 71129: Free information ◆ Gasoline-powered handheld blowers and lawn trimmer. 318-683-3546. www.poulan.com/poulan.html

**Ringer,** 9555 James Ave. South, Ste. 200, Bloomington, MN 55431: Free catalog ◆ Tools, chemical treatments and fertilizers, growing aids, propagation aids, compost-making equipment, lawn care supplies, and planters. 800-654-1047.

**S.A.N. Associates Inc.,** P.O. Box 88, Greendell, NJ 07839: Free information ◆ Rolling tool carrier. 201-852-4612.

**Season Extenders,** 971 Nichols Ave., Stratford, CT 06497: Free catalog ◆ Propagation supplies, pots and baskets, lights, greenhouses, pest controls, hydroponic growing aids, fertilizers, and tools. 203-375-1317.

**Shape Plastics Corp.,** 1110 N. Old World 3rd St., Milwaukee, WI 53203: Free information ◆ Easy-to-use backyard composter.

**Smith & Hawken,** P.O. Box 6907, Florence, KY 41022: Free catalog ◆ Tools, sprayers, and greenhouse supplies. 800-776-3336. www.smith-hawken.com

**Stillbrook Horticultural Supplies,** P.O. Box 600, Bantam, CT 06750: Free information ◆ Garden tools and accessories. 800-414-4468.

**Stokes Seeds Inc.,** Box 548, Buffalo, NY 14240: Free catalog ◆ Greenhouse tools and supplies. 716-695-6980.

**Techni-Tool,** P.O. Box 368, 5 Apollo Rd., Plymouth Meeting, PA 19462: Free list of retail sources ◆ Easy-to-use gasoline-powered telescoping pruner. 800-832-4860; 610-941-2400 (in PA). www.techni-tool.com

**Tote Tree,** P.O. Box 1133, Hudson, NH 03051: Free brochure ◆ Garden tool organizer and transporter.

**V & B Manufacturing,** P.O. Box 268, Walnut Ridge, AR 72476: Free information ◆ Landscaping tools. 800-443-1987. www.hammernet.com

**Vermont Garden Shed,** RR 2, Box 180, East St., Wallingford, VT 05773: Free catalog ◆ Garden tools, supplies, and home accents. 800-288-SHED.

**Yazoo Manufacturing Company,** 3650 Bay St., Jackson, MS 39213: Free information ◆ Lawn care equipment. 800-354-6562.

## Topiary Frames & Supplies

**By The Vine,** 3140 Clay St., #3, San Francisco, CA 94115: Free catalog ◆ Topiaries, frames, and supplies. 800-298-4384.

**Devrou & Company,** P.O. Box 228, Jamestown, MI 49427: Free brochure ◆ Custom topiary frames. 616-892-7544.

**FrenchWyres,** P.O. Box 131655, Tyler, TX 75713: Catalog $3 ◆ Trellises, topiary frames, urns, plant stands, cache pots, window boxes, and arches. 903-597-8322.

**The Kinsman Company,** River Rd., Point Pleasant, PA 18950: Free catalog ◆ Topiary forms. 800-733-4146.

**Rabbit Shadow Farm,** 2880 E. Hwy. 402, Loveland, CO 80537: Free information ◆ Herbs, roses, topiary supplies, and scented geraniums. 970-667-5531.

**Topiary Inc.,** 4520 Watrous Ave., Tampa, FL 33629: Free brochure ◆ Geometric and animal topiary shapes. 813-286-8626. www.topiaryinc.com

## Tractors

**Ariens Company,** 655 W. Ryan St., P.O. Box 157, Brillion, WI 54110: Free information ◆ Lawn and garden tractors. 414-756-2141.

**BCS America,** 13601 Providence Rd., Matthews, NC 28105: Free catalog ◆ Garden carts, chippers and shredders, tillers, sprayers, mowers, and tractors. 800-227-8791.

**Cub Cadet Lawn Equipment,** 1145 Cleveland Ave., Ashland, OH 44805: Free information ◆ Easy-to-operate tractor with optional snow thrower and bagging attachment. 419-289-3610.

**Garden Way,** 1 Garden Way, Troy, NY 12179: Free information ◆ Carts, tillers, clippers, sickle bar mowers, garden composter, tractors, and other equipment. 800-446-4991.

**Husqvarna Power Products,** 9006 Perimeter Woods Dr., Charlotte, NC 28216: Free information ◆ Lawn and garden tractors. 800-438-7297.

**Kubota Tractor Corp.,** P.O. Box 2992, Torrance, CA 90509: Free information ◆ Lawn and garden tractors. 562-370-3370.

**Lawn-Boy,** 8111 Lyndale Ave. South, Bloomington, MN 55420: Free information ◆ Walk-behind and riding mowers, lawn and garden tractors, and power-operated tillers. 800-526-6937. www.toro.com

**Poulan,** 5020 Flournoy-Lucas Rd., Shreveport, LA 71129: Free information ◆ Handheld gasoline-powered blowers and lawn trimmers. 318-683-3546. www.poulan.com/poulan.html

**Power-King,** 1100 Green Valley Rd., Beaver Dam, WI 53916: Free list of retail sources ◆ Garden and lawn tractors with optional custom attachments. 800-262-1191.

**Simplicity Manufacturing Inc.,** P.O. Box 997, Port Washington, WI 53074: Free information ◆ Lawn and garden tractors. 800-945-0235.

**Snapper Power Equipment,** P.O. Box 777, McDonough, GA 30253: Free list of retail sources ◆ Lawn and garden tractors. 770-954-2500.

**Yamaha Outdoor Power Equipment Division,** 6555 Katella Ave., Cypress, CA 90630: Free list of retail sources ◆ Lawn and garden tractors. www.yamaha-motor.com

## Water Gardening Supplies

**Aquatics & Exotics,** P.O. Box 693, Indian Rocks Beach, FL 34635: Free price list ◆ Waterlilies. Also lotus and bog plants. 813-595-3075.

**Bamboo Gardens of Washington,** 5016 192nd Pl. NE, Redmond,WA 98053: Catalog $4 ◆ Bamboo and waterlilies. 206-868-5166.

**Beckett Corp.,** 2521 Willowbrook Rd., Dallas, TX 75220: Free list of retail sources ◆ Water gardening accessories. 972-357-6421.

**Cambridge Designs,** Rt. 4, Box 188, Greenville, AL 36077: Free catalog ◆ Landscaping benches, planters, receptacles, fountains, and pedestrian control screens. 800-477-7320.

**Crystal Palace Perennials,** P.O. Box 154, St. John, IN 46373: Catalog $3 (refundable) ◆ Water garden plants. 219-374-9052.

**Daydreamer Perennial Gardens,** Route 1, Box 438, Belpre OH 45714: Catalog $3 (refundable) ◆ Tropical water lilies, bog and lotus plants, perennials, pond liners, and pumps. 800-741-3867.

**Dolphin Inc.,** Dolphin Pet Village, 90 N. San Tomas Aquino Rd., Campbell, CA 95008: Free brochure with long SASE ◆ Fiberglass ponds for water gardens. Also filters, plants, and fish.

**Eastern Nishikigoi,** 14382 Hoover St., Ste. A-7, Westminster, CA 92683: Free catalog ◆ Japanese koi, water gardening supplies, and accessories. 714-890-1989.

**Green & Hagstrom Inc.,** P.O. Box 658, Fairview, TN 37062: Free list ◆ Water plants and koi. 615-799-0708.

**Grovhac Inc.,** 4310 N. 126th St., Brookfield, WI 53005: Free information ◆ Power-operated aerating equipment. 414-781-5020.

**Hardwicke Gardens,** 254-A Turnpike Rd., Westborough, MA 01581: Catalog $2 ◆ Water garden essentials. 508-366-5478.

**Hemlock Hollow Nursery & Folk Art,** P.O. Box 125, Sandy Hook, KY 41171: Free catalog ◆ Water lilies and lotus plants. 606-738-6285.

**Japonica,** 36484 Camp Creek Rd., Springfield, OR 97478: Free list with long SASE ◆ Waterlilies. Also lotus and bog plants.

**Lily Blooms,** The Water Garden Store, 932 S. Main St., North Canton, OH 44720: Free catalog ◆ Water garden products, fish, aquatic plants, ponds, and accessories. 800-921-0005. www.lilyblooms.com

**Lilypons Water Gardens,** P.O. Box 10, Buckeystown, MD 21717: Catalog $5 ◆ Aquatic garden supplies. 800-999-5459. www.lilypons.com

**Maryland Aquatic Nurseries,** 3427 N. Furnace Rd., Jarrettsville, MD 21084: Catalog $5 (refundable) ◆ Water garden plants, ornamental grasses, and Japanese irises. 410-557-7615.

**Paradise Water Gardens,** 14 May St., Whitman, MA 02382: Catalog $3 (refundable) ◆ Fountains, pools, pumps, goldfish, aquatic plants, and books. 781-447-4711.

**Patio Garden Ponds**, 2500 N. Moore Ave., Moore, OK 73160: Catalog $3 ◆ Water garden supplies and accessories. Includes water lilies, nitrifying aids, and bacteria. 405-793-7661. www.patio-garden-ponds.com

**Perry's Water Gardens,** 1831 Leatherman Gap Rd., Franklin, NC 28734: Catalog $1 ◆ Fish, water lilies, and water garden supplies. 704-524-3264. www.dnet.net/perrywat

**Pet Solutions,** 802 N. Orchard Ln., Beavercreek, OH 45434: Free catalog ◆ Tropical fish and pond supplies. 800-737-3868. www.petsolutions.com

**Pond Doctor,** HC 65, Box 265, Kingston, AZ 72742: Catalog $2 ◆ Water lilies and aquatic plants. 501-665-2232.

**PONDFiltration Inc.,** 11551 Rupp Dr., Burnsville, MN 55337: Free information ◆ Pumping filter systems and accessories. 888-766-3128; 612-890-1840 (in MN). www.pondfiltration.com

**Resource Conservation Technology,** 2633 N. Calvert St., Baltimore, MD 21218: Free information ◆ Rubber liners for garden ponds. 800-477-7724.

**S. Scherer & Sons,** 104 Waterside Rd., Northport, NY 11768: Free price list ◆ Aquatic plants, pools, pumps, waterfalls, and fish. 516-261-7432

**Shady Lakes Water Lily Gardens,** 11033 Hwy. 85 NW, Alameda, NM 87114: Free catalog ◆ Aquatic plants and garden pond supplies. 505-898-2565.

**Slocum Water Gardens,** 1101 Cypress Gardens Rd., Winter Haven, FL 33884 Catalog $3 ◆ Water garden supplies. 941-293-7151.

**Stigall Water Gardens,** 7306 Main, Kansas City, MO 64114: Free catalog ◆ Water gardening supplies. 816-822-1256.

**Urdl's Waterfall Creations Inc.,** 2010 NW 1st St., Delray Beach, FL 33445: Free information ◆ Manufactured hollow concrete rocks for landscaping and waterfall settings. 561-278-3320.

**Van Ness Water Gardens,** 2460 N. Euclid, Upland, CA 91786: Catalog $1 ◆ Water lilies, other aquatic plants, waterfalls, and other eco-system supplies. 800-205-2425. www.vnwg.com

**Waterford Gardens,** 74 E. Allendale Rd., Saddle River, NJ 07458: Catalog $5 ◆ Water lilies, lotus and bog plants, pools, and fish. 201-327-0721. www.waterford-gardens.com

**Wildlife Nurseries,** P.O. Box 2724, Oshkosh, WI 54903: Catalog $3 ◆ Upland game birdseed combinations and gardening supplies. 414-231-3780.

**Windy Oaks,** W377 S10677 Betts Rd., Eagle, WI 53119: Catalog $2 ◆ Water garden supplies. 414-594-280.

### Watering & Irrigation Equipment

**Acu-Drip Water System,** Wade Manufacturing Company, P.O. Box 23666, Portland, OR 97281: Free brochure ◆ Easy-to-install drip watering systems. 800-222-7246.

**Drip Rite Irrigation Products,** Division Strong Enterprises, 4235 Pacific St., Ste. H, Rocklin, CA 95677: Free information ◆ Drip irrigation equipment. 916-652-1008. www.DripIrr.com

**DripWorks,** 231 E. San Francisco St., Willits, CA 95490: Free catalog ◆ Drip and micro irrigation equipment. 800-522-3747. www.dripworksusa.com

**Harmony Farm Supply & Nursery,** 3244 Hwy. 116, No. A, Sebastopol, CA 95472: Catalog $2 (refundable) ◆ Watering system kits, outdoor drip and sprinkler irrigation equipment, and soaker hoses. 707-823-9125.

**Hunter Industries,** 1940 Diamond St., San Marcos, CA 92069: Catalog $1.70 ◆ Automatic sprinkler systems for homes and businesses. Also valves, controllers, sprinklers, and more. 760-744-5240. www.Hunterindustries.com

**International Irrigation Systems (Irrigo),** P.O. Box 360, Niagara Falls, NY 14304: Catalog $1 ◆ Micro-porous irrigation systems for home gardeners and commercial growers. 716-688-4090. www.irrigo.com

**International Irrigation Systems (Oxyflo),** P.O. Box 360, Niagara Falls, NY 14304: Catalog $1 ◆ Micro-porous irrigation systems for fish farming and general aeration applications. 716-688-4090. www.irrigo.com

**Jamar Distributing,** 1292 Montclair Dr., Pasadena, MD 21122: Catalog $3 ◆ Garden watering systems, pop-up sprinklers, and other equipment. 800-477-4181.

**Mel-Nor Industries,** 303 Gulf Bank, Houston, TX 77037: Information $1 ◆ Time controlled sprinklers, hose reel carts, hanging lawn and porch swings, park benches, and old-time lamp posts. 281-445-3485.

**Natural Gardening Company,** 217 San Anselmo Ave., San Anselmo, CA 94960: Free catalog ◆ Beneficial insects, organic gardening supplies, pest controls, drip irrigation equipment, and wildflower seeds. 415-456-5060.

**Rain Bird,** 7590 Britannia Ct., San Diego, CA 92173: Free catalog ◆ Drip irrigation equipment and conventional do-it-yourself watering systems. 619-661-4200.

**Rain Control,** P.O. Box 662, Adrian, MI 49221: Free brochure ◆ Easy-to-install watering systems. Available as kits. 800-536-RAIN.

**Raindrip Inc.,** Box 510, Simi Valley, CA 93062: Free catalog ◆ Watering system kits, outdoor irrigation supplies, and soaker hoses. 888-923-3747. www.raindrip.com

**Ramsey Irrigation Systems,** 7711 Knoxville Dr., Lubbock, TX 79423: Free information ◆ Drip irrigation equipment. 800-477-2347.

**Salco Products Inc.,** 4463 W. Rosecrans Ave., Hawthorne, CA 90250: Free information ◆ Drip irrigation equipment. 310-973-2400

**Submatic Irrigation Systems,** P.O. Box 3965, Lubbock, TX 79452: Free catalog ◆ Irrigation systems. 800-692-4100.

**Urban Farmer Store,** 2833 Vicente St., San Francisco, CA 94116: Catalog $1 ◆ Low-voltage outdoor lighting. 800-753-3747; 415-661-2204 (in CA).

**Weiss Brothers Nursery,** 11690 Colfax Hwy., Grass Valley, CA 95945: Free catalog ◆ Drip irrigation supplies. 916-272-7657.

## GARDENING - PLANTS & SEEDS

### African Violets & Gesneriads

**Alice's Violet Room,** 129 Zeigenbein Rd., Waynesville, MO 65583: Catalog $1 (refundable) ◆ African violets. 314-336-4763.

**Florals of Fredericks,** 155 Spartan Dr., Maitland, FL 32751: Catalog $2 ◆ African violets and growing supplies. 800-771-0899.

**JoS Violets,** 2205 College Dr., Victoria, TX 77901: Free list ◆ Standard and miniature African violets. 800-295-1344; 512-575-1344 (in TX).

**Judy's Violets,** 12047 State Hwy. 104, Fairhope, AL 36532: Catalog $1 ◆ African violets. 334-928-9932.

**Kartuz Greenhouses,** 1408 Sunset Dr., Vista, CA 92083: Catalog $2 ◆ Gesneriads, begonias, miniature terrariums, and unusual tropical plants. 760-941-3613.

**Lauray of Salisbury,** 432 Undermountain Rd., Salisbury, CT 06068: Catalog $2 ◆ Gesneriads, begonias, orchids, cacti and succulents, and other plants. 203-435-2263.

**Lyndon Lyon Greenhouses Inc.,** 14 Mutchler St., Dolgeville, NY 13329: African violets and exotic house plants. 315-429-8291. www.lyndonlyon.com

**Louisiana Nursery,** 8680 Perkins Rd., Baton Rouge, LA 70810: Catalog $4 ◆ Gesneriads. 504-272-9795.

**Richters,** 357 Hwy. 47, Goodwood, Ontario, Canada L0C 1A0: Catalog $2 ◆ Gesneriads.

**Tinari Greenhouses,** 2325 Valley Rd., Huntingdon Valley, PA 19006: Catalog $1 ◆ Standard, miniature, trailer, and variegated African violets. 215-947-0144.

**Twombly Nursery,** 163 Barn Hill Rd., Monroe, CT 06790: Catalog $4 ◆ Gesneriads.

**Violets by Appointment,** Bill & Kathryn Paauwe, 45 3rd St., West Sayville, NY 11796: List $1.50 (refundable) ◆ African violets. 516-589-2724.

**Volkmann Bros. Greenhouses,** 2714 Minert St., Dallas, TX 75219: Catalog $1 ◆ African violets. 972-526-3484.

## Aquatic Plants

**Kester's Wild Game Food Nursery,** P.O. Box 516, Omro, WI 54963: Catalog $3 ◆ Aquatic plants. 800-558-8815; 920-685-2929 (in WI). www.kesternursery.com

**Maryland Aquatic Nurseries,** 3427 N. Furnace Rd., Jarrettsville, MD 21084: Catalog $5 (refundable) ◆ Marginal and bog plants for aquatic gardens. 410-557-7615.

**Meadow View Farms,** 3360 N. Pacific Hwy., Medford, OR 97501 Catalog $3 ◆ Perennials, grasses, herbs, vines, and aquatic plants.

**Nursery & Water Garden Supply,** 7767 Fernvale Rd., P.O. Box 658, Fairview, TN 37062: Free information ◆ Aquatic plants. 615-799-0708. www.greenandhagstrom.com

**S. Scherer & Sons,** 104 Waterside Rd., Northport, NY 11768: Free price list ◆ Aquatic plants, pools, pumps, waterfalls, and fish. 516-261-7432

**William Tricker Inc.,** 7125 Tanglewood Dr., Independence, OH 44131: Catalog $2 ◆ Water lilies, other aquatic plants, exotic fish for indoor and outdoor gardens, pumps, pool liners, and supplies. 800-524-3492. www.tricker.com

**Waterford Gardens,** 74 E. Allendale Rd., Saddle River, NJ 07458: Catalog $5 ◆ Water lilies, lotus and bog plants, and pools. 201-327-0721. www.waterford-gardens.com

**Wicklein's Aquatic Farm & Nursery Inc.,** 1820 Cromwell Bridge Rd., Baltimore, MD 21234: Catalog $1 ◆ Water lilies, aquatic plants, and perennials. 410-823-1335.

## Azaleas & Rhododendrons

**Carlson's Gardens,** Box 305, South Salem, NY 10590: Catalog $3 ◆ Dwarf rhododendrons and landscape-size azaleas. 914-763-5958

**Crownsville Nursery,** P.O. Box 797, Crownsville, MD 21032: Catalog $2: Ferns, wildflowers, azaleas, ornamental grasses, and perennials. 410-849-2212.

**Flora Lan Nursery,** 7940 NW Kansas City Rd., Forest Grove, OR 97116:Free catalog ◆ Azaleas and rhododendron hybrids. 503-357-8386.

**Girard Nurseries,** P.O. Box 428, Geneva, OH 44041:Free catalog ◆ Azaleas and rhododendrons. 440-466-2881.

**Greer Gardens,** 1280 Goodpasture Island Rd., Eugene, OR 97401: Catalog $3 ◆ Azaleas and rhododendrons. 800-548-0111.

**Kelleygreen Nursery,** P.O. Box 1130, Drain, OR 97435: Free catalog ◆ Rhododendrons. 800-477-5676.

**Pen Y Bryn,** RR 1, Box 1313, Forksville, PA 18616: Catalog $2 ◆ Azaleas. 717-924-3377.

**Roslyn Nursery,** 211 Burrs Ln., Dix Hills, NY 11746: Catalog $3 ◆ Rhododendrons, shrubs, trees, and perennials. 516-643-9347. www.cris.com/~Roslyn

**Shepherd Hill Farm,** 200 Peekskill Hollow Rd., Putnam Valley, NY 10579: Free catalog ◆ Azaleas, rhododendrons, and dwarf conifers. 914-528-5917.

## Bamboo

**A Bamboo Shoot Nursery,** P.O. Box 121, Potter Valley, CA 95469: Free information ◆ Bamboo for indoor and outdoor growing. 707-743-1710.

**Bamboo Sourcery,** 666 Wagnon Rd., Sebastopol, CA 95472: Catalog $2 ◆ Bamboo plants. 707-823-5866.

**Kurt Bluemel Inc.,** 2740 Greene Ln., Baldwin, MD 21013: Catalog $3 ◆ Bamboo plants, perennials, ferns, and ornamental grasses. 410-557-7229.

**Burt Associates Bamboo,** P.O. Box 719, Westford, MA 01886: Catalog $2 (refundable) ◆ Bamboo plants. 978-692-3240. bamboo@bamboos.com

**Colvos Creek Nursery,** P.O. Box 1512, Vashon Island, WA 98070: Catalog $3 ◆ Trees, shrubs, rare and unusual plants, and bamboo plants. 206-749-9508. colvoscreek@juno.com

**Endangered Species,** P.O. Box 1830, Tustin, CA 92681: Catalog $6 ◆ Giant, medium-size, dwarf-green, and variegated bamboo and other rare plants. 714-544-9505. nursery@endangeredspecies.com

**Floribunda Palms,** Box 635, Mt. View, HI 96771: Free information with long SASE ◆ Bamboo plants.

**Fruitland Nursery,** 12571 Red Hill Ave., Tustin, CA 92680: Catalog $1 with long SASE ◆ Bamboo.

**Gardens of the Blue Ridge,** P.O. Box 10, Pineola, NC 28662: Catalog $3 (refundable) ◆ Bamboo plants. 704-733-2417.

**Live Oak Gardens,** Box 284, New Iberia, LA 70560: Catalog $1 with long SASE ◆ Bamboo.

**Louisiana Nursery,** 8680 Perkins Rd., Baton Rouge, LA 70810: Catalog $4 ◆ Bamboo and other rare, unusual, and hard-to-find plants. 504-272-9795.

**New England Bamboo Company,** 5 Granite, Rockport, MA 01966: Catalog $2 ◆ Bamboo plants. 978-546-3581. www.newengbamboo.com

**Pen Y Bryn,** RR 1, Box 1313, Forksville, PA 18616: Catalog $2 ◆ Bamboo plants. 717-924-3377.

**Steve Ray's Bamboo Gardens,** 909 79th Place South, Birmingham, AL 35206: Catalog $3 ◆ Bamboo plants. 205-833-3052

**Tornello Landscape Corp.,** P.O. Box 788, Ruskin, FL 33570: Free information ◆ Bamboo plants. 813-645-5445.

**Tradewinds Bamboo Nursery,** 28446 Hunter Creek Loop, Gold Beach, OR 97444: Catalog $2 ◆ Bamboo plants and books. 541-247-0835

**Tripple Brook Farm,** 37 Middle Rd., Southampton, MA 01073: Catalog 50¢ ◆ Bamboo plants, exotic fruits, trees, perennials, and shrubs. 413-527-4626.

**Upper Bank Nurseries,** P.O. Box 486, Media, PA 19063: Free list with long SASE ◆ Bamboo. 215-566-0679.

## Banana Plants

**Banana Tree,** 715 Northampton St., Easton, PA 18042: Catalog $3 ◆ Banana and tropical plants and seeds. 610-253-9589.

**Going Bananas,** 24401 SW 197th Ave., Homestead, FL 33031: Catalog $1 ◆ Banana plants and corms. 305-247-0397. goingbananas@bellsouth.net

## Begonias

**Antonelli Brothers,** 2545 Capitola Rd., Santa Cruz, CA 95062: Catalog $1 ◆ Tuberous and miniature begonias. 408-475-5222.

**Davidson-Wilson Greenhouses,** Rt. 2, Box 168, Dept. 38, Crawfordsville, IN 47933: Catalog $3.75 ◆ Geraniums, house plants, begonias, impatiens, herbs, and succulents. 765-364-0556. www.davidson-wilson.com

**Glasshouse Works Greenhouses,** P.O. Box 97, Stewart, OH 45778: Catalog $3 ◆ Citrus and exotic fruits. 614-662-2142. www.glasshouseworks.com

**Kartuz Greenhouses,** 1408 Sunset Dr., Vista, CA 92083: Catalog $2 ◆ Gesneriads, begonias, miniature terrariums, and unusual tropical plants. 760-941-3613.

**Lauray of Salisbury,** 432 Undermountain Rd., Salisbury, CT 06068: Catalog $2 ◆ Gesneriads, begonias, orchids, cacti and succulents, and other plants. 203-435-2263.

**Palos Verdes Begonia Farm,** 4111 W. 242nd St., Torrance, CA 90505: Free information ◆ Begonia tubers. 800-349-9299.

## Berry Plants

**Allen Plant Company,** P.O. Box 310,
**Enoch's Berry Farm,** Rt. 2, Box 227, Fouke, AR 71837: Free price list ◆ Blackberry plants and root cuttings. 870-653-2806.

**Farmer Seed & Nursery Company,** 818 NW 4th St., Faribault, MN 55021: Free catalog ◆ Vegetable seeds, flowering bulbs, fruit and shade trees, ornamental shrubs and hedges, berry plants, and roses. 507-334-1623.

**Henry Field's Seed & Nursery,** 415 N. Burnett, Shenandoah, IA 51602: Free catalog ◆ Strawberry and other berry plants. 605-665-4491.

**Fig Tree Nursery,** P.O. Box 124, Gulf Hammock, FL 32639: Catalog $1 ◆ Berry plants, ornamentals, and grapes for southern climates. 904-486-2930.

**Finch Blueberry Nursery,** P.O. Box 699, Bailey, NC 27807: Free information with long SASE ◆ Blueberry cultivars. 919-235-4662.

**Harris Seeds Inc.,** P.O. Box 22960, Rochester, NY 14692: Free catalog ◆ Berry plants and seeds. 800-514-4441. www.trine.com/gardennet/harrisseeds

**Hartmann's Plantation,** P.O. Box E, Grand Junction, MI 49056: Catalog $2.25 (refundable) ◆ Blueberry plants. 616-253-4281

**Highlander Nursery,** P.O. Box 177, Pettigrew, AR 72752:Free catalog ◆ Hardy low-chill blueberry plants. 501-677-2300.

**Indiana Berry & Plant Company,** 5218 W. 500 South, Huntingburg, IN 47542: Free catalog ◆ Raspberries, blueberries, and blackberries. Also books, tools, and equipment. 800-295-2226; 812-683-3055 (in IN).

**Ison's Nursery,** P.O. Box 190, Brooks, GA 30205: Free catalog ◆ Muscadine grapevines, fruit and nut trees, and berry plants. 800-733-0324.

**Johnny's Selected Seeds,** Foss Hill Rd., Albion, ME 04910: Free catalog ◆ Strawberry plants, flower and vegetable seeds for northern climates, tools, and growing supplies. 207-437-4301. www.johnnyseeds.com

**Johnson Nursery,** Rt. 5, Box 29-J, Ellijay, GA 30540: Free catalog ◆ Strawberry plants, grapevines, and apple, plum, pear, cherry, apricot, walnut, and almond trees. Also orchard supplies, tools and accessories, and books. 888-276-3187. www.johnsonnursery.com

**Kelly Nurseries,** 1708 Morrissey Dr., Bloomington, IL 61704: Free catalog ◆ Heavily rooted fruit and nut trees, landscaping trees, shrubs, ornamentals, berry plants, grapevines, and flowers. 309-334-1623.

**Krohne Plant Farms,** 65295 CR 342, Hartford, MI 49057: Free information ◆ Strawberry plants and asparagus crowns. 616-424-5423.

**Lewis Strawberry Nursery Inc.,** P.O. Box 24, Rocky Point, NC 28457: Free catalog ◆ Strawberry plants. 800-453-5346.

**Earl May Seeds & Nursery Company,** 208 N. Elm St., Shenandoah, IA 51603: Free catalog ◆ Grapevines, berry plants, roses, flowering shrubs, gardening supplies, and fruit, nut, shade, and ornamental trees. 712-246-1020.

**Mellinger's,** 2310 W. South Range Rd., North Lima, OH 44452: Free catalog ◆ Fruit, nut, shade, and ornamental trees. Also berry plants, gladioli, flowering shrubs, hedges, irises, wildflowers, and gardening equipment. 330-549-9861. www.mellingers.com

**J.E. Miller Nurseries,** 5060 W. Lake Rd., Canandaigua, NY 14424: Free catalog ◆ Grapevines, berry plants, and fruit trees. 800-836-9630.

**Nichols Garden Nursery,** 1194 Pacific, Albany, OR 97321: Free catalog ◆ Vegetable seeds, herb seeds and plants, saffron crocus, garlic and shallots, and strawberry plants. 541-928-9280.

**Nourse Farms,** 41 River Rd., South Deerfield, MA 01373:Free information ◆ Raspberry, strawberry, asparagus, and rhubarb plants. 413-665-2568. www.noursefarms.com

**The Nursery,** Hwy. 82, P.O. Box 130, Ty Ty, GA 31795: Free catalog ◆ Fruits, nuts, berries, bulbs, trees, and shrubs. 800-972-2101.

**Park Seed Company,** 1 Parkron Ave., Greenwood, SC 29648: Free catalog ◆ Vines, strawberry plants, seeds, bulbs, and gardening tools. 800-845-3369. www.parkseed.com

**Patrick's Nursery,** P.O. Box 130, Ty Ty, GA 31795: Free catalog ◆ Perennials, vegetables, fruit and nut trees, berry plants, and grapevines. 800-972-2101.

**Peaceful Valley Farm Supply,** P.O. Box 2209, Grass Valley, CA 95945: Catalog $2 (refundable) ◆ Berry plants. 916-272-4769.

**Pense Nursery,** 16518 Marie Ln., Mountainburg, AR 72946: Free information ◆ Blackberry, raspberry, blueberry, strawberry, asparagus, and grape growing stock. 501-369-2494. www.alcasoft.com/Pense

**Raintree Nursery,** 393 Butts Rd., Morton, WA 98356: Free information ◆ Berry plants. 360-496-6400.

**R.H. Shumway Seedsman,** P.O. Box 1, Graniteville, SC 29829: Free catalog ◆ Roses, berry plants, fruit trees, seeds and bulbs, ornamental shrubs and plants, and gardening supplies. 803-737-0399.

**Stark Brothers,** Nurseries & Orchards Company, P.O. Box 10, Louisiana, MO 63353: Free catalog ◆ Fruit trees, berry and landscaping plants, and garden supplies. 800-775-6415.

**Thompson & Morgan Inc.,** P.O. Box 1308, Jackson, NJ 08527: Free catalog ◆ Strawberry plants. 800-274-7333.

**Bob Wells Nursery,** P.O. Box 606, Lindale, TX 75771: Free catalog ◆ Fruit, nut, and shade trees. Also berries, grapes, muscadines, roses, ornamentals, and flowering shrubs. 903-882-3550.

**White Flower Farm,** Catalog Services, 30 Irene St., Torrington, CT 06790: Free catalog ◆ Bulbs, perennials, shrubs, strawberry plants, seeds and plants, books, tools, and gardening supplies. 800-475-0148.

## Bonsai

**Artistic Plants,** 608 Holly Dr., Burleson, TX 76028: Catalog $2 ◆ Bonsai. 817-295-0802.

**Avid Gardener,** Box 200, Hamburg, IL 62045: Catalog $3 ◆ Dwarf conifers, companion shrubs, ground covers, and potential bonsai. 618-232-1108.

**The Big Creek Company,** 1130 SE Howard Rd., Corbett, OR 97019: Free catalog ◆ Bonsai and related plant materials. 503-695-5766.

**Bonsai Boy of New York,** 7 Format Ln., Smithtown, NY 11787: Free catalog ◆ Bonsai trees. 800-790-2793. www.bonsaiboy.com

**Bonsai by the Monastery,** 2625 Hwy. 212 SW, Conyers, GA 30208: Catalog $5 ◆ Japanese and Chinese pots, tools, wire, books, videos, and clay figurines. 770-918-9661.

**Bonsai Farm,** P.O. Box 130, Lavernia, TX 78121: Catalog $1 ◆ Bonsai trees, indoor and outdoor bonsai plants, books, tools, and pots. 210-649-2109.

**Bonsai of Brooklyn,** 2443 McDonald Ave., Brooklyn, NY 11223: Free price list ◆ Potted and established bonsai, trained and semi-trained pre-bonsai stock, tools, books, pottery, and supplies. 800-8-BONSAI; 718-339-8252 (in NY).

**The Bonsai Shop,** P.O. Box 76, Nesconsett, NY 11767: Catalog $3 ◆ Bonsai, growing supplies, tools, and books.

**Bonsai West,** P.O. Box 1291, Littleton, MA 01460: Catalog $2 ◆ Bonsai. 978-486-4066.

**Brussel's Bonsai Nursery,** 8365 Center Hill Rd., Olive Branch, MS 38654: Catalog $2 ◆ Finished bonsai. 601-895-7457.

**Byles Nursery,** P.O. Box 7705, Olympia, WA 98507: Catalog $1.80 ◆ Related maples. Includes rare, unusual, and dwarfs for containers, patios, and landscapes. 360-352-4725. Byles@JUNO.COM

**Dallas Bonsai Garden,** P.O. Box 551087, Dallas, TX 75355: Free catalog ◆ Bonsai and supplies. 800-982-1223. www.dallasbonsai.com

**Evergreen Gardenworks,** P.O. Box 1357, Ukiah, CA 95482: Free catalog ◆ Bonsai stock, rock garden plants, alpines, and ornamentals. 707-462-8909.

**Flowertown Bonsai,** 207 E. Luke St., Summerville, SC 29483: Free price list ◆ Bonsai and pottery. 800-774-0003.

**Forestfarm,** 990 Tetherow Rd., Williams, OR 97544: Catalog $3 ◆ Plants, ornamental trees, shrubs, and perennials for bonsai. 541-846-7269.

**Gardenworks,** 430 North Oak St., P.O. Box 1357, Ukiah, CA 95482: Catalog $2 ◆ Bonsai and rock garden plants. 707-462-8909.

**Girard Nurseries,** P.O. Box 428, Geneva, OH 44041: Free catalog ◆ Bonsai and ornamental trees, shrubs, and evergreen seeds and trees. 440-466-2881.

**Granite State Bonsai,** P.O. Box 4122, Windham, NH 03087: Free catalog ◆ Bonsai supplies. 603-894-6832. www.gsbonsai.com

**Greer Gardens,** 1280 Goodpasture Island Rd., Eugene, OR 97401: Catalog $3 ◆ Bonsai, azaleas and rhododendrons, trees, shrubs, Japanese maples, and succulents. 800-548-0111.

**Hortica Gardens,** Box 308, Placerville, CA 95667: Free information ◆ Bonsai plants.

**Jope's Bonsai Nursery,** P.O. Box 594, Wenham, MA 01984: Catalog $2 ◆ Japanese maples, five-needle pines, pre-bonsai, imported and domestic bonsai, tools, pots, books and supplies. 978-468-2249.

**Marrs Tree Farm,** P.O. Box 375, Puyallup, WA 98371: Catalog $1 (refundable) ◆ Uncommon trees for bonsai. 253-848-5755. members.aol.com/marrstree

**Miniature Plant Kingdom,** 4125 Harrison Grade Rd., Sebastopol, CA 95472: Catalog $2.50 ◆ Japanese maples, conifers, other bonsai plants, and miniature roses. 707-874-2233.

**Mt. Si Bonsai,** 43321 SE Mt. Si Rd., North Bend, WA 98045: Catalog $1 ◆ Indoor and outdoor bonsai, pots, tools, and bonsai starters. 425-888-0350.

**Mountain Maples,** P.O. Box 1329, Laytonville, CA 95454: Catalog $2 ◆ Japanese maples for bonsai. 707-984-6522.

**Nature's Way Nursery,** 1451 Pleasant Hill Rd., Harrisburg, PA 17112: Free information ◆ Japanese maples, conifers, and bonsai.

**New England Bonsai,** 914 S. Main St., Bellingham, MA 02019: Free information ◆ Tropical, sub-tropical, and juniper bonsai in ceramic bonsai pots. Also tools and supplies. 800-457-5445.

**Northland Gardens,** 315 West Mountain Rd., Queensbury, NY 12804: Information $2 ◆ Bonsai, starter stock, books, pottery, tools, and growing aids. 800-4-BONSAI.

**Northridge Gardens Nursery,** 9821 White Oak Ave., Northridge, CA 91325: Catalog $1 (refundable) ◆ Cacti, bonsai, and rare and unusual plants. 818-349-9798.

**Pen Y Bryn,** RR 1, Box 1313, Forksville, PA 18616: Catalog $2 ◆ Pre-bonsai trees and growing supplies. 717-924-3377.

**Pine Garden Bonsai,** 20331 SR 530 NE, Arlington, WA 98223: Catalog $2 ◆ Stoneware bonsai containers and finished bonsai. 360-435-5995. bonsai@premier1.net

**Roots 'N All Bonsai Gardens,** RR 1, Box 586, Warner, NH 03278: Free information ◆ Bonsai.

**Shanti Bithi,** 3047 High Ridge Rd., Stamford, CT 06903: Catalog $2 ◆ Bonsai. 203-329-0768.

**Spring Hill Nurseries,** 6523 N. Galena Rd., P.O. Box 1758, Peoria, IL 61632: Free catalog ◆ Bonsai, perennials, roses, annuals, ground covers, small fruits, house plants, seeds and plants, and gardening supplies. 800-582-8527. www.springhillnursery.com

**Wildwood Gardens,** 14488 Rock Creek Rd., Chardon, OH 44024: Catalog $1 ◆ Imported and domestic bonsai, pre-bonsai plants, and tools. 216-286-3714.

## Bromeliads

**Bird Rock Tropicals,** 6523 El Camino Real, Carlsbad, CA 92009: Free catalog with long SASE ◆ Bromeliads, specializing in Tillandsia.

**Cornelison Bromeliads,** 225 San Bernardino, North Fort Myers, FL 33903: Free list with long SASE ◆ Bromeliads.

**Tropiflora,** 3530 Tallevast Rd., Sarasota, FL 34243: Free information ◆ Tillandsia. 800-613-7520.

## Cacti & Succulents

**Abbey Garden Cactus,** P.O. Box 2249, La Habra, CA 90632: Catalog $2 (refundable) ◆ Cacti and succulents. 562-905-3520.

**Aztekakti Seeds,** 11306 Gateway East, El Paso, TX 79927: Catalog $1 ◆ Seeds for cacti and succulents. 915-838-1130.

**Betsy's Briar Patch,** 1610 Ellis Hollow Rd., Ithaca, NY 14850: Free catalog with long SASE ◆ Cacti and succulents. 607-273-6266.

**Cactus by Mueller,** 10411 Rosedale Hwy., Bakersfield, CA 93312: Catalog $2 ◆ Cacti and succulents. 805-589-2674.

**Christa's Cactus,** 529 W. Pima, Coolidge, AZ 85228: Catalog $1 ◆ Cacti, succulents, desert trees, and shrubs. 602-723-4185.

**Crown Botanicals,** 1036 Fairview Dr., Reading, PA 19605: Free catalog ◆ Rare and easy-to-care euphorbias, pachypodiums, hoyas, stapleliads, and other varieties. 888-384-2427.

**Desert Nursery,** 1301 S. Copper, Deming, NM 88030: Free list ◆ Winter-hardy, semi-hardy, and greenhouse cacti and succulents. 505-546-6264.

**Epi World,** 10607 Glenview Ave., Cupertino, CA 95014: Catalog $2 ◆ Orchid cacti. 408-865-0566.

**Gray-Davis Epiphylliums,** Box 710443, Santee, CA 92072: Catalog $2 ◆ Orchid cacti.

**Grigsby Cactus Gardens,** 2354 Bella Vista, Vista, CA 92084: Catalog $2 ◆ Rare cacti and succulents. 760-727-1323.

**Henrietta's Nursery,** 1345 N. Brawley, Fresno, CA 93722: Catalog 50¢ ◆ Cacti and succulents. 209-275-2166.

**Highland Succulents,** 1446 Bear Run Rd., Gallipolis, OH 45631: Catalog $2 ◆ Succulents. 614-256-1428.

**Intermountain Cactus,** 1478 N. 750 East, Kaysville, UT 84037: Price list $1 ◆ Winter-hardy cacti. 801-546-2006.

**K & L Cactus/Succulent Nursery,** 9500 Brook Branch Rd. East, Ione, CA 95640: Catalog $3 (refundable) ◆ Cacti and succulents. 209-274-0360. kandlcactus@hotmail.com

**Lauray of Salisbury,** 432 Undermountain Rd., Salisbury, CT 06068: Catalog $2 ◆ Cacti and succulents, begonias, gesneriads, and orchids. 860-435-2263.

**Loehman's Cactus,** Box 871, Paramount, CA 90723: List $1 (refundable) ◆ Rare, unusual, and common cacti and succulent plants. 562-428-4501.

**Mesa Garden,** Box 72, Belen, NM 87002: Free catalog with two 1st class stamps ◆ Cacti and succulent seeds and plants. 505-864-3131. www.cactus-mall.com

**Northridge Gardens Nursery,** 9821 White Oak Ave., Northridge, CA 91325: Catalog $1 (refundable) ◆ Cacti, bonsai, and rare and unusual plants. 818-349-9798.

**Rainbow Gardens Bookshop,** 1444 E. Taylor St., Vista, CA 92084: Catalog $2 ◆ Cacti, hoyas, and books on cacti. 760-758-4290. www.cactus-mall.com/rainbow_bookshop

**Shein's Cactus,** 3360 Drew St., Marina, CA 93933: Catalog $1 ◆ Rare cacti and succulents. 831-384-7765.

**Strong's Alpine Succulents,** P.O. Box 50115, Parks, AZ 86018: Catalog $2 (refundable) ◆ Alpine succulents and books. 520-635-1127. www.com/~amdigest/strongs.htm

**Succulents,** P.O. Box 480325, Los Angeles, CA 90048: Catalog $1 ◆ Rare and unusual cacti and succulents. 213-933-8676.

**Tropiflora,** 3530 Tallevast Rd., Sarasota, FL 34243: Free information ◆ Rare succulents, caudiciforms, and other unusual exotic flora. 800-613-7520.

## Carnivorous Plants

**Black Copper Kits,** 111 Rigwood Ave., Pompton Lakes, NJ 07442: Catalog 50¢ ◆ Carnivorous plants and supplies.

**Carolina Exotic Gardens,** Rt. 5, Box 283-A, Greenville, NC 27834: Catalog $1 ◆ Carnivorous plants and seeds and terrarium plant groupings. 919-758-2600.

**Lee's Botanical Gardens,** P.O. Box 669, LaBelle, FL 33975: Free catalog ◆ Carnivorous plants, orchids, and ferns. 813-675-8728.

**Orgel's Orchids,** 18950 SW 136th St., Miami, FL 33196: Free catalog ◆ Carnivorous plants and orchids. 305-233-7168.

**Peter Pauls Nurseries,** 4665 Chapin Rd., Canandaigua, NY 14424: Free catalog ◆ Carnivorous and woodland terrarium plants. 716-394-7397. www.peterpauls.com

## Chrysanthemums

**Dooley Mum Gardens,** 210 N. High St., Hutchinson, MN 55350: Free catalog ◆ New and old chrysanthemums. 320-587-3050.

**King's Chrysanthemums,** P.O. Box 368, Clements, CA 94227: Catalog $2 (refundable) ◆ Rooted cuttings. 209-759-3571.

## Citrus & Exotic Fruits

**Alberts & Merkel Brothers Inc.,** 2210 S. Federal Hwy., Boynton Beach, FL 33435: Catalog $1 ◆ Citrus and exotic fruits. 407-732-2071.

**Aloha Tropicals,** 1247 Browning Ct., Vista, CA 92083: Catalog $2 ◆ Heliconias, gingers, bananas, plumeria, and other plants. 760-941-0920. www.alohatropicals.com

**The Banana Tree,** 715 Northampton St., Easton, PA 18042: Catalog $3 ◆ Citrus and exotic fruits. 610-253-9589.

**W. Atlee Burpee & Company,** 300 Park Ave., Warminster, PA 18974: Free catalog ◆ Exotic fruits. 800-888-1447. www.burpee.com

**Crockett's Tropical Plants,** P.O. Box 1150, Harlingen, TX 78551: Catalog $3 ◆ Container-grown ornamentals, citrus plants, and palms. 800-580-1747.

**Edible Landscaping,** P.O. Box 77, Afton, VA 22920: Catalog $1 ◆ Exotic fruits. 800-524-4156; 804-361-9134 (in VA). www.EAT-IT.com

**Henry Field's Seed & Nursery,** 415 N. Burnett, Shenandoah, IA 51602: Free catalog ◆ Exotic fruits. 605-665-4491.

**Fig Tree Nursery,** P.O. Box 124, Gulf Hammock, FL 32639: Catalog $1 ◆ Exotic fruits. 904-486-2930.

**Four Seasons Nursery,** 1706 Morrisey Dr., Bloomington, IL 61704: Free catalog ◆ Citrus and exotic fruits. 309-663-9551.

**Garden of Delights,** 14560 SW 14th St., Davie, FL 33325: Catalog $2 (refundable) ◆ Fruiting plants and trees, dwarf citrus, and more. 954-370-9004.

**Glasshouse Works Greenhouses,** P.O. Box 97, Stewart, OH 45778: Catalog $3 ◆ Citrus and exotic fruits. 614-662-2142. www.glasshouseworks.com

**Gurney Seed & Nursery Company,** 110 Capitol St., Yankton, SD 57079: Free catalog ◆ Citrus and exotic fruits. 605-665-1671.

**Kartuz Greenhouses,** 1408 Sunset Dr., Vista, CA 92083: Catalog $2 ◆ Citrus and exotic fruits. 760-941-3613.

**Logee's Greenhouses,** 141 North St., Danielson, CT 06239: Catalog $3 (refundable) ◆ Citrus and exotic fruits. 860-774-8038.

**Mellinger's,** 2310 W. South Range Rd., North Lima, OH 44452: Free catalog ◆ Citrus and exotic fruits. 330-549-9861. www.mellingers.com

**Northwoods Retail Nursery,** 27635 S. Oglesby Rd., Canby, OR 97013: Free catalog ◆ Citrus and exotic fruits. 503-266-5432.

**Pacific Tree Farms,** 4301 Lynnwood Dr., Chula Vista, CA 92010: Catalog $2 ◆ Citrus and exotic fruits. 619-422-2400.

**Peaceful Valley Farm Supply,** P.O. Box 2209, Grass Valley, CA 95945: Catalog $2 (refundable) ◆ Citrus fruits. 916-272-4769.

**Raintree Nursery,** 393 Butts Rd., Morton, WA 98356: Free information ◆ Citrus and exotic fruits. 360-496-6400.

**Tripple Brook Farm,** 37 Middle Rd., Southampton, MA 01073: Catalog 50¢ ◆ Bamboo plants, exotic fruits, trees, perennials, and shrubs. 413-527-4626.

## Daffodils

**Bonnie Brae Gardens,** 1105 SE Christensen Rd., Corbett, OR 97019: Free catalog with long SASE ◆ Novelty daffodils. 503-695-5190.

**Breck's Dutch Bulbs,** Mail Order Reservation Center, 6523 N. Galena Rd., Peoria, IL 61632: Free catalog ◆ Daffodil bulbs. 800-722-9069. www.brecks.com

**Cascade Daffodils,** 1790 Richard Circle, St. Paul, MN 55118: Catalog $2 ◆ Standard, miniature, and show daffodils. 612-426-9616.

**The Daffodil Mart,** 30 Irene St., Torrington, CT 06790: Free catalog ◆ Novelty, miniature, hybridized, and species daffodils. 800-255-2852.

**Mad River Imports,** P.O. Box 1685, Moretown, VT 05660: Free catalog ◆ Daffodil bulbs. 802-496-3004.

**McClure & Zimmerman,** P.O. Box 368, Friesland, WI 53935: Free catalog ◆ Daffodil bulbs. 800-692-5864; 414-326-4220 (in WI).

**Messelaar Bulb Company,** 150 County Rd., Ipswich, MA 01938: Free catalog ◆ Daffodil bulbs. 978-356-3737.

**Grant Mitsch Novelty Daffodils,** P.O. Box 218, Hubbard, OR 97032: Catalog $3 (refundable) ◆ Exhibition and garden varieties of pink and hybrid daffodils. 503-651-2742.

**Oakwood Daffodils,** 2330 W. Bertrand Rd., Niles, MI 49120: Free catalog ◆ Daffodils.

**Oregon Trail Daffodils,** 41905 SE Louden, Corbett, OR 97019: Free catalog ◆ Daffodils for show and garden-growing. 503-695-5513.

**Quality Dutch Bulbs,** P.O. Box 434, Stockertown, PA 18083: Free catalog ◆ 18083: Free catalog ◆ Daffodils, irises, tulips, and other bulbs. 800-755-2852.

**Van Dyck's Flower Farms,** P.O. Box 430, Brightwater, NY 11718: Free catalog ◆ Daffodil bulbs. 800-248-2852.

**Veldheer Tulip Gardens,** 12755 Quincy St., Holland, MI 49424: Free catalog ◆ Daffodil bulbs. 616-399-1900.

## Dahlias

**BJ's Dahlias,** 130 Taylor Loop Rd., Selah, WA 98942: Free catalog with two 1st class stamps ◆ Dahlias. 509-697-6089.

**Connell's,** 10616 Waller Rd. East, Tacoma, WA 98446: Catalog $2 ◆ Exhibition and garden varieties of dahlias from worldwide sources. 800-673-5139.

**Dan's Dahlias,** 994 South Bank Rd., Oakville, WA 98568: Free price list ◆ Dahlias. 360-482-2607.

**Dick's Flower** Farm, 30656 North US Rt. 12, Volo, IL 60073: Free information ◆ Dahlias, gladioli, hybrid lilies, and summer bulbs. 815-385-3162.

**Ferncliff Gardens,** Box 66, Sumas, WA 98295: Free catalog ◆ Dahlias. 604-826-2447.

**Garden Valley Dahlias,** 406 Lower Garden Valley, Roseburg, OR 97470: Free catalog ◆ Dahlias. 541-673-8521.

**Homestead Gardens,** 125 Homestead Rd., Kalispell, MT 59901: Free catalog ◆ Dahlias. 406-756-6631.

**Swan Island Dahlias,** P.O. Box 700, Canby, OR 97013: Catalog $3 (refundable) ◆ Dahlias. 503-266-7711. www.dahlias.com

## Ferns

**Kurt Bluemel Inc.,** 2740 Greene Ln., Baldwin, MD 21013: Catalog $3 ◆ Ferns, perennials, bamboo plants, and ornamental grasses. 410-557-7229.

**Busse Gardens,** 5873 Oliver Ave. SW, Cokato, MN 55321: Catalog $2 ◆ Ferns, seeds and plants, and Siberian irises. 800-544-3192.

**Crownsville Nursery,** P.O. Box 797, Crownsville, MD 21032: Catalog $2 (minimum order $25) ◆ Ferns, wildflowers, azaleas, ornamental grasses, and perennials. 410-923-2212.

**Foliage Gardens,** 2003 128th Ave. SE, Bellevue, WA 98005: Catalog $2 ◆ Indoor and outdoor ferns. 206-747-2998.

**Gardens of the Blue Ridge,** P.O. Box 10, Pineola, NC 28662: Catalog $3 (refundable) ◆ Wildflower seeds, ferns, trees, plants, shrubs, and bulbs. 704-733-2417.

**Gilson Gardens Inc.,** 3059 US Rt. 20, P.O. Box 277, Perry, OH 44081: Free catalog ◆ Ground covers, perennials, and ferns. 216-259-5252.

**Jerry Horne Rare Plants,** 10195 SW 70th St., Miami, FL 33173: Free list with long SASE ◆ Ferns, platyceriums, palms and cycads, and rare and unusual plants. 305-270-1235.

**Lee's Botanical Gardens,** P.O. Box 669, LaBelle, FL 33975: Free catalog ◆ Carnivorous plants, orchids, and ferns. 813-675-8728.

**Limerock Ornamental Grasses Inc.,** RD 1, Box 111, Port Matilda, PA 16870: Catalog $3 ◆ Ornamental and native grasses, companion perennials, and nursery-grown hardy ferns. 814-692-2272.

**Oakridge Nurseries,** P.O. Box 182, East Kingston, NH 03827: Catalog $1 (refundable) ◆ Ferns and native wildflowers. 603-642-8227.

**Pen Y Bryn,** RR 1, Box 1313, Forksville, PA 18616: Catalog $2 ◆ Ferns. 717-924-3377.

**Ridge Road Gardens,** 15948 SE Division, Portland, OR 97236: Catalog $1 ◆ Ferns.

**Sandy Mush Herb Nursery,** 316 Surrett Cove Rd., Leicester, NC 28748: Catalog $4 ◆ Herbs, flowering perennials, geraniums, ferns, ivies, and other growing stock. 828-683-2014.

**Shady Oaks Nursery,** P.O. Box 708, Waseca, MN 56093: Free list ◆ Ferns, shrubs, perennials, and wildflowers. 800-504-8006. www.shadyoaks.com

**Squaw Mountain Gardens,** P.O. Box 946, Estacada, OR 97023: Catalog $2 (refundable) ◆ Ferns and companion rock garden plants. 503-630-5458. www.squawmountaingardens.com

**Sunlight Gardens,** 174 Golden Ln., Andersonville, TN 37705: Catalog $3 ◆ Hardy ferns and perennials. 615-494-8237.

**T.D. Field Ferns & Wildflowers,** 395 Newington Rd., Newington, NH 03801: Free catalog ◆ Wildflowers and hardy ferns. 603-436-0457.

**Varga's Nursery,** 2631 Pickertown Rd., Warrington, PA 18976: Price list $1 ◆ Ferns. 215-343-0646.

**Wild Earth Nursery,** 49 Mead Ave., Freehold, NJ 07728: Catalog $2 (refundable) ◆ Propagated wildflowers, ferns, and grasses. 908-308-9777.

**Wildflower Nursery,** 1680 Hwy. 25-70, Marshall, NC 28753: Free catalog ◆ Ferns. 704-656-2723.

## Geraniums

**Davidson-Wilson Greenhouses,** Rt. 2, Box 168, Dept. 38, Crawfordsville, IN 47933: Catalog $3.75 ◆ Geraniums, house plants, begonias, impatiens, herbs, and succulents. 765-364-0556. www.davidson-wilson.com

**Good Hollow Greenhouse & Herbarium,** 50 Slaterock Mill Rd., Taft, TN 38488: Catalog $1 ◆ Herb plants and dried herbs, perennials, wildflowers, scented geraniums, essential oils and potpourris, teas, and spices. 615-433-7640.

**Lily of the Valley Herb Farm,** 3969 Fox Ave., Minerva, OH 44657: Price list $1 (refundable) ◆ Herbs and herbal products, everlastings, perennials, and scented geranium plants. 330-862-3920.

**Rabbit Shadow Farm,** 2880 E. Hwy. 402, Loveland, CO 80537: Free information ◆ Herbs, roses, topiary supplies, and scented geraniums. 970-667-5531.

**Sandy Mush Herb Nursery,** 316 Surrett Cove Rd., Leicester, NC 28748: Catalog $4 ◆ Geraniums. 828-683-2014.

**Sunnybrook Farms Nursery,** P.O. Box 6, Chesterland, OH 44026: Catalog $1 (refundable) ◆ Hostas, herb plants, scented geraniums, perennials, and ivies. 216-729-7232.

**Well-Sweep Herb Farm,** 205 Mt. Bethel Rd., Port Murray, NJ 07865: Catalog $2 ◆ Geraniums. 908-852-5390.

**Wheeler Farm Gardens,** 171 Bartlett St., Portland, CT 06480: Free brochure ◆ New and old ivy geraniums. 888-437-2648; 860-342-2374 (in CT).

## Ginseng

**Anker Enterprises,** 221 N. 152nd Ave., Marathon, WI 54448: Free information ◆ Stratified ginseng seed.

**John Batz,** RR 2, Box 261, Pittsfield, IL 62363: Free information ◆ Stratified seed and dry roots. 217-285-6022.

**Buckhorn Ginseng,** Richland Center, WI 53581: Free information with long SASE ◆ Ginseng seed.

**Ginseng,** Flag Pond, TN 37657: Information $1 ◆ Stratified seed and 1st year roots.

**Heartland Herbs,** 113 Whiteside, Columbia, IL 62236: Free information ◆ Stratified ginseng seed. 618-281-4537.

**The Homestead,** 72799 Old 21 Rd., Kimbolton, OH 43749: Free information ◆ Ginseng planting stock.

**HSU's Ginseng Enterprises Inc.,** P.O. Box 509, Wausau, WI 54402: Free information ◆ American and Canadian stratified ginseng seed, rootlets, and ginseng health products and extracts. 800-826-1577; 715-675-2325 (in WI).

**Roots "O" Gold,** Box 92, LeCenter, MN 56057: Free information ◆ Seed, roots, books, and ginseng products. 507-665-6310.

**Schumaker Enterprises Inc.,** 1006 Hickory St., Marathon, WI 54448: Free price list ◆ Stratified seed for spring planting. 715-443-2393.

**The Thyme Garden,** 20546 Alsea Hwy., Alsea, OR 97324: Catalog $2 (refundable) ◆ Herb seeds, plants, hops, ginseng, dried herbs, and teas. 541-487-8671. www.proaxis.com/~thymegarden

**Yellow Dragon Ginseng,** P.O. Box 201, Hadley, MA 01035: Free information ◆ Pre-sprouted ginseng seed.

## Gladioli

**Blooming Prairie Gardens,** 10061 89th Ave. SE, Blooming Prairie, MN 55917: Free catalog ◆ World's finest gladiolus bulbs and flowers. Time-tested, all-American varieties. 507-583-2648; 612-985-5692.

**Connell's,** 10616 Waller Rd. East, Tacoma, WA 98446: Catalog $2 ◆ Gladioli bulbs. 800-673-5139.

**Dick's Flower Farm,** 30656 North US Rt. 12, Volo, IL 60073: Free information ◆ Dahlias, gladioli, hybrid lilies, and summer bulbs. 815-385-3162.

**Jasperson's Hersey Nursery,** 2915 74th Ave., Wilson, WI 54027: Free information with long SASE and three 1st class stamps ◆ Irises, gladioli, and daylilies.

**Kingfisher Glads,** 11734 Road 33½, Madera, CA 93638: Free catalog ◆ New gladioli and older cultivars. 209-645-5329.

**Mellinger's,** 2310 W. South Range Rd., North Lima, OH 44452: Free catalog ◆ Fruit, nut, shade, and ornamental trees. Also gladioli, flowering shrubs, hedges, irises, wildflowers, and gardening equipment. 330-549-9861. www.mellingers.com

**Skolaski's Glads & Flowers,** 4821 County Trunk Hwy. Q, Waunakee, WI 53597: Catalog $1 ◆ Gladioli bulbs, lilies, and perennials. 608-836-4822.

**Waushara Gardens,** 5491 5th Dr., Plainfield, WI 54966: Catalog $1 ◆ Gladioli. 715-335-4462. waugardn@uniontel.net

## Gourds

**Alfrey Seeds,** P.O. Box 415, Knoxville, TN 37901: List $3 ◆ Gourds and seeds for chili peppers and vegetables.

**J.L. Hudson, Seedsman,** Box 1058, Redwood City, CA 94064: Catalog $1 ◆ Gourd seeds.

**Nichols Garden Nursery,** 1194 Pacific, Albany, OR 97321: Free catalog ◆ Gourd seeds. 541-928-9280.

**West Mountain Gourd Farm,** Rt. 1, Box 853, Gilmer, TX 75644: Information $2 ◆ Ready-to-paint gourds in all shapes and sizes. 903-734-5204. www.texaseast.com/westmountain

## Grapes

**Concord Nurseries Inc.,** 10175 Mile Block Rd., North Collins, NY 14111: Catalog $1 ◆ Grapevines.

**Fig Tree Nursery,** P.O. Box 124, Gulf Hammock, FL 32639: Catalog $1 ◆ Berry plants, ornamentals, and grapes for southern climates. 904-486-2930.

**Ison's Nursery,** P.O. Box 190, Brooks, GA 30205: Free catalog ◆ Muscadine grapevines, fruit and nut trees, and berry plants. 800-733-0324.

**Earl May Seeds & Nursery Company,** 208 N. Elm St., Shenandoah, IA 51603: Free catalog ◆ Grapevines, berry plants, roses, flowering shrubs, gardening supplies, and fruit, nut, shade, and ornamental trees. 712-246-1020.

**J.E. Miller Nurseries,** 5060 W. Lake Rd., Canandaigua, NY 14424: Free catalog ◆ Grapevines, berry plants, and fruit trees. 800-836-9630.

**W.K. Morss & Son,** RFD 2, Boxford, MA 01921: Free brochure ◆ Grapevines and rhubarb, strawberry, and raspberry plants. 978-352-2633.

**The Nursery,** Hwy. 82, P.O. Box 130, Ty Ty, GA 31795: Free catalog ◆ Fruits, nuts, berries, bulbs, trees, and shrubs. 800-972-2101.

**Patrick's Nursery,** P.O. Box 130, Ty Ty, GA 31795: Free catalog ◆ Grapevines, vegetable seeds, berry plants, and fruit and nut trees. 800-972-2101.

**Pense Nursery,** 16518 Marie Ln., Mountainburg, AR 72946: Free information ◆ Blackberry, raspberry, blueberry, strawberry, asparagus, and grape growing stock. 501-369-2494. www.alcasoft.com/Pense

**Lon J. Rombough,** P.O. Box 365, Aurora, OR 97002: Free catalog with long SASE ◆ Grapevine cuttings. 503-678-1410. www.hevanet.com/lonrom

**Bob Wells Nursery,** P.O. Box 606, Lindale, TX 75771: Free catalog ◆ Fruit, nut, and shade trees. Also berries, grapes, muscadines, roses, ornamentals, and flowering shrubs. 903-882-3550.

## Grasses & Ground Covers

**Ambergate Gardens,** 8730 County Rd. 43, Chaska, MN 55318: Catalog $2 ◆ Grasses and perennial flowers. 612-443-2248.

**Avid Gardener,** Box 200, Hamburg, IL 62045: Catalog $3 ◆ Dwarf conifers, companion shrubs, ground covers, and potential bonsai. 618-232-1108.

**The Bethlehem Seed Company,** P.O. Box 1351, Bethlehem, PA 18018: Free information ◆ Bulbs and seed for vegetables, grass, and flowers. 610-691-6697.

**Bishop Seeds Ltd.,** Box 338, Belleville, Ontario, Canada K8N 5A5: Free catalog ◆ Turf grasses. 613-968-5533.

**Kurt Bluemel Inc.,** 2740 Greene Ln., Baldwin, MD 21013: Catalog $3 ◆ Ornamental grasses, water garden plants, and perennials. 410-557-7229.

**Bluestone Perennials,** 7211 Middle Ridge Rd., Madison, OH 44057: Free catalog ◆ Ground covers. 800-852-5243.

**W. Atlee Burpee & Company,** 300 Park Ave., Warminster, PA 18974: Free catalog ◆ Ornamental grasses. 800-888-1447. www.burpee.com

**Classic Groundcovers Inc.,** 405 Belmont Rd., Athens, GA 30605: Free catalog ◆ Ground covers. 800-248-8424; 503-640-1179 (in GA).

**Comstock Seed,** 8520 West 4th St., Reno, NV 89523: Free catalog ◆ Native grasses. 702-746-3681.

**Crownsville Nursery,** P.O. Box 797, Crownsville, MD 21032: Catalog $2 (minimum order $25) ◆ Ferns, wildflowers, azaleas, ornamental grasses, and perennials. 410-923-2212.

**Digging Dog Nursery,** P.O. Box 471, Albion, CA 95410: Catalog $3 ◆ Grasses, vines, trees, perennials, and shrubs. 707-937-1130.

**Evergreen Nursery,** 1220 Dowdy Rd., Athens, GA 30606: Free catalog ◆ Bare root and potted ground covers. 800-521-7267; 706-548-7781 (in GA).

**Fieldstone Gardens Inc.,** 620 Quaker Ln., Vassalboro, ME 04989: Catalog $2 ◆ Mature plants for sun, shade, rock gardens, and ground covers. 207-923-3836.

**Gilson Gardens Inc.,** 3059 US Rt. 20, P.O. Box 277, Perry, OH 44081: Free catalog ◆ Ground covers, perennials, and ferns. 216-259-5252.

**Greenlee Nursery,** 257 E. Franklin Ave., Pomona, CA 91766: Catalog $5 ◆ Ornamental grasses. 909-629-9045.

**Heyne Custom Seed Service,** RR 1, Box 78, Walnut, IA 51577: Free information ◆ Native grasses. Will custom blend. 800-784-3454.

**Hobbs & Hopkins,** 1712 SE Ankeny, Portland, OR 97214: Free catalog ◆ Flowering lawn mix. 503-239-7518.

**Limerock Ornamental Grasses Inc.,** RD 1, Box 111, Port Matilda, PA 16870: Catalog $3 ◆ Ornamental and native grasses, companion perennials, and nursery-grown hardy ferns. 814-692-2272.

**Maryland Aquatic Nurseries,** 3427 N. Furnace Rd., Jarrettsville, MD 21084: Catalog $5 (refundable) ◆ Water garden plants, ornamental grasses, and Louisiana and Japanese irises. 410-557-7615.

**Meadow View Farms,** 3360 N. Pacific Hwy., Medford, OR 97501: Catalog $3 ◆ Perennials, grasses, herbs, vines, and aquatic plants.

**J.E. Miller Nurseries,** 5060 W. Lake Rd., Canandaigua, NY 14424: Free catalog ◆ Fruit and nut trees, vines, ornamentals, and ground covers. 800-836-9630.

**Park Seed Company,** 1 Parkron Ave., Greenwood, SC 29648: Free catalog ◆ Ornamental grasses. 800-845-3369. www.parkseed.com

**Peekskill Nurseries,** P.O. Box 428, Shrub Oak, NY 10588: Free catalog ◆ Ground covers. 914-245-5595.

**Plants of the Southwest,** Rt. 6, Box 11A, Santa Fe, NM 87501: Catalog $3.50 ◆ Native trees, grasses, wildflowers, shrubs, and plants. 800-788-7333; 505-438-8888 (in NM). www.plantsofthesouthwest.com

**Prairie State Commodities,** P.O. Box 6, Trilla, IL 62469: Catalog $1 ◆ Seeds for annuals, perennial rye grass and Park Kentucky bluegrass, corn, clover, and alfalfa. 217-235-4322.

**Southern Perennials & Herbs,** 98 Bridges Rd., Tylertown, MS 39667: Free catalog ◆ Perennials, gingers, herbs, grasses, and vines for the south. 800-774-0079. www.s-p-h.com

**Stock Seed Farm,** 28008 Mill Rd., Murdock, NE 68407: Free catalog ◆ Native prairie grasses. 800-759-1520. www.stockseed.com

**Stoecklein Nursery,** 135 Critchow Rd., Renfrew, PA 16053: Catalog $1 ◆ Ground covers. 412-586-7882.

**Thompson & Morgan Inc.,** P.O. Box 1308, Jackson, NJ 08527: Free catalog ◆ Ornamental grasses. 800-274-7333.

**Wild Earth Nursery,** 49 Mead Ave., Freehold, NJ 07728: Catalog $2 (refundable) ◆ Propagated wildflowers, ferns, and grasses. 908-308-9777.

**Zoysia Farm Nurseries,** General Offices & Store, 3617 Old Taneytown Rd., Taneytown, MD 21787: Free information ◆ Zoysia plugs. 410-756-2311.

## Herb Plants

**Aphrodesia Products,** 62 Kent St., Brooklyn, NY 11222: Catalog $3 ◆ Dried herbs, herb products, and books. 800-221-6898.

**Bountiful Gardens,** 18001 Shafer Ranch Rd., Willits, CA 95490: Free catalog ◆ Seeds for vegetables, compost crops, herbs, and flowers. Also books and organic gardening supplies. 707-459-6410. www.bountifulgardens.com

**Brown's Edgewood Gardens,** 2611 Corrine Dr., Orlando, FL 32803: Catalog $3 ◆ Butterfly-attracting plants, herbs, and organic gardening products. 407-896-3203.

**Companion Plants,** 7247 N. Coolville Ridge, Athens, OH 45701: Catalog $3 ◆ Seeds for exotic, herb, and native plants. 614-592-4643.

**Comstock, Ferre & Company,** 263 Main St., Wethersfield, CT 06109: Catalog $2 ◆ Vegetable, flower, and herb seeds. 860-571-6590.

**Davidson-Wilson Greenhouses,** Rt. 2, Box 168, Dept. 38, Crawfordsville, IN 47933: Catalog $3.75 ◆ Geraniums, house plants, begonias, impatiens, herbs, and succulents. 765-364-0556. www.davidson-wilson.com

**The Flowery Branch Seed Company,** P.O. Box 1330, Flowery Branch, GA 30542: Catalog $4 (refundable) ◆ Heirloom flowers, edible and medicinal herbs, and annuals and perennials from worldwide sources. 770-536-8380. www.flowerybranchseeds.com

**Garden Medicinals & Culinaries,** P.O. Box 320, Earlysville, VA 22936: Catalog $2 ◆ Herb seeds, roots, and tubers. Also books, tinctures, extracts, supplies for herb growers. 804-973-4703. herbs@gardenmedicinals.com

**Good Hollow Greenhouse & Herbarium,** 50 Slaterock Mill Rd., Taft, TN 38488: Catalog $1 ◆ Herb plants and dried herbs, perennials, wildflowers, scented geraniums, essential oils and potpourris, teas, and spices. 615-433-7640.

**Goodwin Creek Gardens,** P.O. Box 83, Williams, OR 97544: Catalog $1 ◆ Dried floral arrangements, herb plants, container-grown native American trees, shrubs, and perennial flowers. 541-846-7357.

**The Gourmet Gardener,** 8650 College Blvd., Overland Park, KS 66210: Catalog $2 ◆ Herb, vegetable, and edible flower seeds from around the world. 913-345-0490. www.gourmetgardener.com

**Greenfield Herb Garden,** P.O. Box 9, Shipshewana, IN 46565: Catalog $1.50 ◆ Herb books and plants. 800-831-0504.

**Hartman's Herb Farm,** 1026 Old Dana Rd., Barre, MA 01005: Catalog $2 ◆ Herbs and herb products, potpourris, essential oils, and wreaths. 978-355-2015.

**Harvest Health Inc.,** 1944 Eastern Ave. SE, Grand Rapids, MI 49507: Free catalog ◆ Herbs, spices, and essential and perfume oils. 616-245-6268.

**Herb Products Company,** P.O. Box 898, 11012 Magnolia Blvd., North Hollywood, CA 91603: Free price list ◆ Botanicals, oils and fragrances, extracts and tinctures, and books. 818-761-0351. www.herbproducts.com

**Herban Garden,** 5002 2nd St., Rainbow, CA 92028: Catalog $1 ◆ Herbs, vegetables, and everlastings. 619-723-2967.

**The Herbfarm,** 32804 Issaquah-Fall City Rd., Fall City, WA 98024: Information $1 ◆ Herb plants, seed, and herbal items. 800-866-4372.

**Herbs-Liscious,** 1702 S. 6th St., Marshalltown, IA 50158: Catalog $2 (refundable) ◆ Herb plants, dried herbs, spices, and oils.

**Hillary's Garden,** P.O. Box 430, Warwick, NY 10990: Catalog $2 ◆ Perennials and organically grown herbs. 914-987-1175.

**Indiana Botanic Gardens,** P.O. Box 5, Hobart, IN 46342: Catalog $1 ◆ Herbs, herb seeds, and essential oils. 800-644-8327. www.botanichealth.com

**Le Jardin du Gourmet,** P.O. Box 75, St. Johnsbury Center, VT 05863: Catalog $1 ◆ Herb plants and seeds and vegetable seeds. 802-748-1446.

**Lily of the Valley Herb Farm,** 3969 Fox Ave., Minerva, OH 44657: Price list $1 (refundable) ◆ Herb plants, everlastings, perennials, scented geraniums, and herbal products. 330-862-3920.

**Meadow View Farms,** 3360 N. Pacific Hwy., Medford, OR 97501: Catalog $3 ◆ Perennials, grasses, herbs, vines, and aquatic plants.

**Nichols Garden Nursery,** 1194 Pacific, Albany, OR 97321: Free catalog ◆ Seeds, plants, and herbal products. 541-928-9280.

**Perennial Pleasures Nursery,** P.O. Box 147, East Hardwick, VT 05836: Catalog $3 ◆ Heirloom herbs and flowers. 802-472-5104.

**Planta Dei Medicinal Herb Farm,** Millville, New Brunswick, Canada E0H 1M0: Catalog $2 (refundable) ◆ Biologically grown teas, medicinal herbs, healing tea mixtures, cosmetics, natural ointments, and massage oils. 506-463-8169.

**Redwood City Seed Company,** P.O. Box 361, Redwood City, CA 94064: Catalog $1 ◆ Herb and vegetable seeds from worldwide sources. 650-325-7333. www.ecoseeds.com

**Richters,** 357 Hwy. 47, Goodwood, Ontario, Canada L0C 1A0: Catalog $2 ◆ Seeds and growing stock for allium shade plants, herbs, and other garden varieties. 905-640-6677. www.richters.com

**The Rosemary House,** 120 S. Market St., Mechanicsburg, PA 17055: Catalog $2 ◆ Plants, seeds, herb products, and books. 717-697-5111.

**Sandy Mush Herb Nursery,** 316 Surrett Cove Rd., Leicester, NC 28748: Catalog $4 ◆ Culinary and tea herbs, other herbs, scented geraniums, and flowering perennials. 828-683-2014.

**Seeds of Change,** Box 15700, Santa Fe, NM 87506: Free information ◆ Organic and open-pollinated hard-to-find vegetable, herb, and flower seeds. 800-957-3337. www.seedsofchange.com

**Shady Acres Herb Farm,** 7815 Hwy. 212, Chaska, MN 55318: Free list with long SASE ◆ Herbs, wildflowers, everlastings, and vegetables. 612-466-3391.

**Southern Perennials & Herbs,** 98 Bridges Rd., Tylertown, MS 39667: Free catalog ◆ Perennials, gingers, herbs, grasses, and vines for the south. 800-774-0079. www.s-p-h.com

**Spice Discounters,** P.O. Box 2263, Napa, CA 94558: Free catalog ◆ Herbs, spices, oils, extracts, and vitamins. 800-610-5950. www.spicediscounters.com

**Sunnybrook Farms Nursery,** P.O. Box 6, Chesterland, OH 44026: Catalog $1 (refundable) ◆ Hostas, herb plants, scented geraniums, perennials, and ivies. 216-729-7232.

**The Thyme Garden,** 20546 Alsea Hwy., Alsea, OR 97324: Catalog $2 (refundable) ◆ Herb seeds, plants, hops, ginseng, dried herbs, and teas. 541-487-8671. www.proaxis.com/~thymegarden

**Tinmouth Channel Farm,** Box 428B, Tinmouth, VT 05773: Catalog $2 ◆ Vermont-certified organic plants and seeds. 802-446-2812.

**Vermont Bean Seed Company,** 95 Garden Ln., Fair Haven, VT 05743: Free catalog ◆ Bean seeds, heirloom plants, and herbs. 802-273-3400.

**Well-Sweep Herb Farm,** 205 Mt. Bethel Rd., Port Murray, NJ 07865: Catalog $2 ◆ Seeds for herbs, plants, and perennials. 908-852-5390.

**Westview Herb Farm,** P.O. Box 3462, Poughkeepsie, NY 12603: Free catalog ◆ Herb and wildflower seeds. 914-462-3534.

**Woodside Gardens,** 1191 Egg & I Rd., Chimacum, WA 98325: Catalog $2 ◆ Perennials and herb plants. 360-732-4754.

## Hostas

**American Daylily & Perennials,** P.O. Box 210, Grain Valley, MO 64029: Catalog $3 (refundable) ◆ Daylilies,lantanas, and cannas. 816-224-2852. www.americandaylily.com

**Brookwood Gardens Inc.,** 303 Fir St., Michigan City, IN 46360: Catalog $2.98 ◆ Daylilies and hostas. 219-873-0198.

**Caprice Farm Nursery,** 15425 SW Pleasant Hill Rd., Sherwood, OR 97140: Catalog $2 ◆ Peonies, irises, daylilies, and hostas. 503-625-7241.

**Carroll Gardens,** 444 E. Main St., P.O. Box 310, Westminster, MD 21157: Catalog $3 (refundable) ◆ Hostas plants and cultivars. 800-638-6334.

**Crownsville Nursery,** P.O. Box 797, Crownsville, MD 21032: Catalog $2 (minimum order $25) ◆ Hosta plants and cultivars. 410-849-2212.

**Good's Nursery,** 51225 Ann Arbor Rd., Canton, MI 48187: List $2 with long SASE ◆ Hostas. 313-453-2126.

**Homestead Farms,** 3701 Hwy. EE, Owensville, MO 65066: Free catalog ◆ Daylilies, hostas, peonies, irises, and more. 573-437-4277.

**Klehm Nursery,** 4210 N. Duncan Rd., Champaign, IL, 61821: Catalog $4 ◆ Peonies, irises, daylilies, hostas, and perennials. 800-553-3715.

**Pine Ridge Gardens,** 832 Sycamore Rd., London, AR 72847: Catalog $1 ◆ Nursery-propagated wildflowers, hostas, and unusual ornamentals. 501-293-4359.

**Plant Delights Nursery,** 9241 Sauls Rd., Raleigh, NC 27603: Catalog $2 ◆ Rare and other hard-to-find plants. Specializes in hostas. 919-772-4794. www.plantdel.com

**Savory's Gardens Inc.,** 5300 Whiting Ave., Edina, MN 55439: Catalog $2 ◆ Hostas. 612-941-8755.

**Shady Oaks Nursery,** P.O. Box 708, Waseca, MN 56093: Free list ◆ Ferns, shrubs, perennials, and wildflowers. 800-504-8006. www.shadyoaks.com

**Sunnybrook Farms Nursery,** P.O. Box 6, Chesterland, OH 44026: Catalog $1 (refundable) ◆ Hostas, herb plants, scented geraniums, perennials, and ivies. 216-729-7232.

**Andre Viette Nurseries,** Rt. 1, Box 16, Fishersville, VA 22929: Catalog $3 ◆ Hosta plants and cultivars. 540-942-2118.

**Wayside Gardens,** 1 Garden Ln., Hodges, SC 29695: Free catalog ◆ Hosta plants and cultivars. 800-845-1124. www.waysidegardens.com

## House Plants & Indoor Gardens

**Appalachian Gardens,** Box 82, Waynesboro, PA 17268: Free catalog ◆ Hardy native plants, old favorites, and rare and unusual plants. 717-762-4312.

**Avid Gardener,** Box 200, Hamburg, IL 62045: Catalog $3 ◆ Dwarf conifers, companion shrubs, ground covers, and potential bonsai. 618-232-1108.

**Belisle's Violet House,** P.O. Box 111, Radisson, WI 54867: Catalog $2 ◆ Miniature sinninglas tubers and plants. 715-945-2687.

**The Compleat Garden Clematis Nursery,** 217 Argilla Rd., Ipswich, MA 01938: Descriptive listing $3 ◆ Unusual and hard-to-find flowering clematis varieties in small and large pots.

**Crockett's Tropical Plants,** P.O. Box 1150, Harlingen, TX 78551: Catalog $3 ◆ Container-grown ornamentals, citrus plants, and palms. 800-580-1747.

**Davidson-Wilson Greenhouses,** Rt. 2, Box 168, Dept. 38, Crawfordsville, IN 47933: Catalog $3.75 ◆ Geraniums, house plants, begonias, impatiens, herbs, and succulents. 765-364-0556. www.davidson-wilson.com

**Gardeners' Choice,** 81961 Country Rd. 687, P.O. Box 8000, Hartford, MI 49057: Free catalog ◆ House plants, vegetables, flowers, and trees. 800-274-4096.

**Glasshouse Works Greenhouses,** P.O. Box 97, Stewart, OH 45778: Catalog $3 ◆ Windowsill jasmine plants. 614-662-2142. www.glasshouseworks.com

**Golden Lake Greenhouses,** 10782 Citrus Dr., Moorpark, CA 93021: Catalog $2 ◆ Bromeliads, tillandsias, ephylliums, hoyas, and other plants.

**Holladay Jungle,** P.O. Box 5727, Fresno, CA 93755: Free information ◆ Tillandsias. 209-229-7371.

**Lauray of Salisbury,** 432 Undermountain Rd., Rt. 41, Salisbury, CT 06068: Catalog $2 ◆ Begonias, orchids, cacti, and succulents. 203-435-2263.

**Logee's Greenhouses,** 141 North St., Danielson, CT 06239: Catalog $3 (refundable) ◆ Begonias, geraniums, exotics, herbs, and other house plants. 860-774-8038.

**Lyndon Lyon Greenhouses Inc.,** 14 Mutchler St., Dolgeville, NY 13329: Catalog $3 ◆ African violets and exotic house plants. 315-429-8291. www.lyndonlyon.com

**Merry Gardens,** P.O. Box 595, Camden, ME 04843: Catalog $2 ◆ House and flowering plants, herbs, ivies, gesneriads, ferns and mosses, impatiens, jasmines, and geraniums. 207-236-9064.

**Michael's Bromeliads,** 1365 Canterbury Rd. North, St. Petersburg, FL 33710: Free catalog ◆ Species and hybrid bromeliads. 813-347-0349.

**Oak Hill Gardens,** P.O. Box 25, West Dundee, IL 60118: Catalog $1 ◆ Orchids, bromeliads, and tropical house plants. 847-428-8500.

**The Plumeria People,** 1846 Eagle Falls Dr., Houston, TX 77077: Catalog $3 (refundable) ◆ Flowering tropical house plants. 281-496-2352.

**Spring Hill Nurseries,** 6523 N. Galena Rd., P.O. Box 1758, Peoria, IL 61632: Free catalog ◆ House plants, perennials, roses, annuals, ground covers, and bonsai. 800-582-8527. www.springhillnursery.com

**Teas Nursery Company,** P.O. Box 1603, Bellaire, TX 77401: Catalog $1 (refundable) ◆ Orchid and exotic plant supplies. 800-446-7723.

**Trans-Pacific Nursery,** 16065 Oldsville Rd., McMinnville, OR 97128: Catalog $2 (refundable) ◆ Rare, unique, and unusual plants. 503-472-6215.

**Well-Sweep Herb Farm,** 205 Mt. Bethel Rd., Port Murray, NJ 07865: Catalog $2 ◆ Windowsill jasmine plants. 908-852-5390.

## Hoyas

**Golden Lake Greenhouses,** 10782 Citrus Dr., Moorpark, CA 93021: Catalog $2 ◆ Bromeliads, tillandsias, ephylliums, and hoyas.

**Rainbow Gardens Bookshop,** 1444 E. Taylor St., Vista, CA 92084: Catalog $2 ◆ Cacti, hoyas, and books on cacti. 760-758-4290. www.cactus-mall.com/rainbow_bookshop

## Hydrangeas

**Bell Family Nursery,** 6543 S. Zimmerman Rd., Aurora, OR 97002: Catalog $3.50 (refundable) ◆ Rare and unusual hydrangeas. 503-651-2887.

**Wilkerson Mill Gardens,** 9595 Wilkerson Mill Rd., Palmetto, GA 30268: Catalog $2 (refundable) ◆ Hydrangea species and cultivars.

## Ivies & Vines

**Bluestone Perennials,** 7211 Middle Ridge Rd., Madison, OH 44057: Free catalog ◆ Ivies and vines, perennial flowers, and ground covers. 800-852-5243.

**Burnt Ridge Nursery & Orchards,** 432 Burnt Ridge Rd., Onalaska, WA 98570: Free brochure with long SASE ◆ Disease-resistant fruit and nut trees and native plants. 360-985-2873. www.carow-ww.com/brnursery

**Meadow View Farms,** 3360 N. Pacific Hwy., Medford, OR 97501: Catalog $3 ◆ Perennials, grasses, herbs, vines, and aquatic plants.

**Park Seed Company,** 1 Parkron Ave., Greenwood, SC 29648: Free catalog ◆ Vines, strawberry plants, seeds, bulbs, and gardening tools. 800-845-3369. www.parkseed.com

**Sandy Mush Herb Nursery,** 316 Surrett Cove Rd., Leicester, NC 28748: Catalog $4 ◆ Herbs, flowering perennials, geraniums, ferns, ivies, and other growing stock. 828-683-2014.

**Southern Perennials & Herbs,** 98 Bridges Rd., Tylertown, MS 39667: Free catalog ◆ Perennials, gingers, herbs, grasses, and vines for the south. 800-774-0079. www.s-p-h.com

**Sunnybrook Farms Nursery,** P.O. Box 6, Chesterland, OH 44026: Catalog $1 (refundable) ◆ Hostas, herb plants, scented geraniums, perennials, and ivies. 216-729-7232.

## Lilacs

**Heard Gardens,** 5355 Merle Hay Rd., Johnston, IA 50131: Catalog $2 ◆ Lilacs. 515-276-4533.

**Wildflower Nursery,** 1680 Hwy. 25-70, Marshall, NC 28753: Free catalog ◆ Vines. 704-656-2723.

## Marigolds

**W. Atlee Burpee & Company,** 300 Park Ave., Warminster, PA 18974: Free catalog ◆ Marigolds. 800-888-1447. www.burpee.com

**Park Seed Company,** 1 Parkron Ave., Greenwood, SC 29648: Free catalog ◆ Marigolds. 800-845-3369. www.parkseed.com

**Stokes Seeds Inc.,** Box 548, Buffalo, NY 14240: Free catalog ◆ Marigolds. 716-695-6980.

**Thompson & Morgan Inc.,** P.O. Box 1308, Jackson, NJ 08527: Free catalog ◆ Marigolds. 800-274-7333.

## Mushrooms

**Field & Forest Products Inc.,** N3296 Kozuzek Rd., Peshtigo, WI 54157: Catalog $2 (refundable) ◆ Mushroom-growing supplies. 800-792-6220; 715-582-4997 (in WI).

**Fungi Perfecti,** P.O. Box 7634, Olympia, WA 98507: Catalog $4.50 ◆ Mushroom-growing supplies, kits, and spawn. 800-780-9126. www.fungi.com

**Fungus Among Us,** P.O. Box 352, Snohomish, WA 98291: Free brochure ◆ Home-growing kits. 360-568-3403.

**Fungus Foods Inc.,** P.O. Box 6035, St. Louis, MO 63139: Free brochure ◆ Shiitake, portabella, oyster, and reishi mushroom-growing terrarium for the home. 800-299-1352. www.fungusfoods.com

**Gourmet Mushrooms,** P.O. Box 515, Graton, CA 95444: Free information ◆ Organic mushroom growing kits for home and garden. Includes morel, shiitake, and oyster mushrooms. 800-789-9121; 707-829-7301 (in CA). www.gmushrooms.com

**Hardscrabble Enterprises Inc.,** P.O. Box 1124, Franklin, WV 26807: Catalog $4 ◆ Grow-your-own Shiitake mushroom kits, other mushroom-growing supplies, and spawn. 304-358-2921.

**Lost Creek Mushroom Farm,** P.O. Box 520, Perkins, OR 74059: Free brochure ◆ Shiitake mushroom-growing supplies. 800-792-0053. www.cowboy/net/~lcmf

**Mushroom Kingdom,** P.O. Box 901, Elkin, NC 28621: Catalog $2 ◆ Spawn culture, books, and supplies for growing mushrooms. 704-297-4725.

**MushroomPeople,** P.O. Box 220, 560 Farm Rd., Summertown TN 38483: Free catalog ◆ Mushroom-growing kits, spawn, supplies, and how-to books. 800-FUNGI-95. mushroom@thefarm.org

**Sohn's Oak Forest Mushrooms,** 617 S. Main St., Westfield, WI 53964: Free brochure ◆ Shiitake and oyster spawn, inoculation supplies, and books. 608-296-2456.

**Western Biologicals,** Box 283, Aldergrove, British Columbia, Canada V0X 1AO: Catalog $3 ◆ Spawn, cultures, kits, books, and cultivation supplies. 604-856-3339.

## Nurseries

**The companies in this section are representative of those that offer a wide variety of seeds and plants, gardening supplies, tools, and equipment.**

**W. Atlee Burpee & Company,** 300 Park Ave., Warminster, PA 18974: Free catalog. 800-888-1447. www.burpee.com

**Ferry-Morse Seed Company,** P.O. Box 488, Fulton, KY 42041: Free catalog. 800-283-3400.

**Henry Field's Seed & Nursery,** 415 N. Burnett, Shenandoah, IA 51602: Free catalog ◆ 605-665-4491.

**Harmony Farm Supply & Nursery,** 3244 Hwy. 116, No. A, Sebastopol, CA 95472: Catalog $2 (refundable). 707-823-9125.

**Harris Seeds Inc.,** P.O. Box 22960, Rochester, NY 14692: Free catalog ◆ 800-514-4441. www.trine.com/gardennet/harrisseeds

**J.W. Jung Seed Company,** 335 High St., Randolph, WI 53957: Free catalog ◆ 414-326-4100.

**Earl May Seeds & Nursery Company,** 208 N. Elm St., Shenandoah, IA 51603: Free catalog ◆ 712-246-1020.

**Mellinger's,** 2310 W. South Range Rd., North Lima, OH 44452: Free catalog ◆ 330-549-9861. www.mellingers.com

**Miles Estate Herb & Berry Farm,** 4309 Marthaler Rd. NE, Woodburn, OR 97071: Free catalog ◆ Custom grower of herbs, spices, flowers, berries, exotics, and aromatics. 503-792-3898. 888-810-0196. www.herbs-spices-flowers.com

**Miller Nurseries,** 5060 W. Lake Rd., Canandaigua, NY 14424: Free catalog. 800-836-9630.

**Nichols Garden Nursery,** 1194 Pacific, Albany, OR 97321: Free catalog ◆ 541-928-9280.

**L.L. Olds Seed Company,** P.O. Box 7790, Madison, WI 53707: Catalog $2.50 ◆ 608-249-9291.

**Richard Owen Nursery,** 2300 E. Lincoln St., Bloomington, IL 61701: Free catalog. 309-663-9551.

**Park Seed Company,** 1 Parkron Ave., Greenwood, SC 29648: Free catalog. 800-845-3369. www.parkseed.com

**Shady Oaks Nursery,** P.O. Box 708, Waseca, MN 56093: Free list. 800-504-8006. www.shadyoaks.com

**R.H. Shumway Seedsman,** P.O. Box 1, Graniteville, SC 29829: Free catalog. 803-737-0399.

**Stark Brothers,** Nurseries & Orchards Company, P.O. Box 10, Louisiana, MO 63353: Free catalog ◆ 800-775-6415.

**Otis Twilley Seed Company,** P.O. Box 65, Trevose, PA 19047: Catalog $1 ◆ 800-622-7333.

## Orchids

**Alberts & Merkel Brothers Inc.,** 2210 S. Federal Hwy., Boynton Beach, FL 33435: Catalog $1 ◆ Orchid plants and growing supplies. 407-732-2071.

**Carter & Holmes Inc.,** P.O. Box 668, Newberry, SC 29108: Catalog $1.50 (refundable) ◆ New and unusual orchid hybrids and clones. Also growing supplies. 803-276-0579. orchids@carterandholmes.com

**Clargreen Gardens,** 814 Southdown Rd., Mississauga, Ontario, Canada L5J 2Y4: Catalog $2 (refundable) ◆ Orchids.

**Epi World,** 10607 Glenview Ave., Cupertino, CA 95014: Catalog $2 ◆ Orchid cactus starter collections and hybrids. 408-865-0566.

**John Ewing Orchids Inc.,** 487 White Rd., Watsonville, CA 95076: Catalog 50¢ ◆ Easy-to-grow Phalaenopsis seedlings and plants. 408-684-1111.

**Fox Valley Orchids,** 1980 Old Willow Rd., Northbrook, IL 60062: Free information ◆ New hybrids and other orchid species. 847-205-9660. www.fvo.com

**G & B Orchid Laboratory & Nursery,** 2426 Cherimoya Dr., Vista, CA 92084: Free catalog ◆ Growing supplies, flasking media, chemical supplies, laboratory glassware, fertilizers, seedlings, and orchid species. 760-727-2611.

**J & L Orchids,** 20 Sherwood Rd., Easton, CT 06612: Catalog $1 ◆ Hybrid orchids, rare and unusual species, and easy-to-grow miniatures. 203-261-3772.

**Kensington Orchids,** 3301 Plyers Mill Rd., Kensington, MD 20895: Price list $1 (refundable) ◆ Orchid plants. 301-933-0036.

**Krull-Smith Orchids,** 2800 W. Ponkan Rd., Apopka, FL 32712: Free catalog ◆ Easy-to-grow orchids. 407-886-0915.

**Lauray of Salisbury,** 432 Undermountain Rd., Salisbury, CT 06068: Catalog $2 ◆ Orchids, begonias, gesneriads, cacti, and succulents. 203-435-2263.

**Lee's Botanical Gardens,** P.O. Box 669, LaBelle, FL 33975: Free catalog ◆ Carnivorous plants, orchids, and ferns. 813-675-8728.

**Lenette Greenhouses,** 1440 Pom Orchid Ln., Kannapolis, NC 28081: Free catalog ◆ Orchids, hybridizers, and growing supplies. 704-938-2042.

**Lion's Den Orchids,** 275 Olive Hill Ln., Woodside, CA 94062: Free brochure ◆ Orchid plants. 415-851-3303.

**Majestic Orchids,** 11701 SW 80th Rd., Miami, FL 33156: Free list ◆ Orchid plants. 305-233-7270.

**Makai Farms Orchids,** P.O. Box 93, Kilauea, HI 96754: Free price list ◆ Orchid plants.

**Rod McLellan Company,** 1450 El Camino Real, South San Francisco, CA 94080: Catalog $2 ◆ Orchid plants and growing supplies. 415-871-5655.

**Mellinger's,** 2310 W. South Range Rd., North Lima, OH 44452: Free catalog ◆ Fruit, nut, shade, and ornamental trees. Also gladioli, flowering shrubs, hedges, irises, wildflowers, and gardening equipment. 330-549-9861. www.mellingers.com

**Oak Hill Gardens,** P.O. Box 25, West Dundee, IL 60118: Catalog $1 ◆ Orchids, bromeliads, and tropical house plants. 847-428-8500.

**Odom's Orchids,** 1611 S. Jenkins Rd., Fort Pierce, FL 34947: Catalog $5 ◆ Orchids, specializing in cattleyas, phalaenopsis, oncidiums, dendrobiums, and vandas. 561-467-1386. www.odoms.com

**The Orchid Club,** P.O. Box 40, Walanae, HI 96792: Free brochure ◆ Each month club members receive a different plant flown overnight from Hawaii with instructions for care. 800-822-9411.

**The Orchid House,** 1699 Sage Ave., Los Osos, CA 93402: Cultural bulletin and lists $5 ◆ Orchids. 800-235-4139; 805-528-1417 (in CA).

**Orgel's Orchids,** 18950 SW 136th St., Miami, FL 33196: Free catalog ◆ Orchids and carnivorous plants. 305-233-7168.

**River Valley Orchids,** 3015 Shoemaker Rd., Lebanon, OH 45036: Free brochure ◆ Orchid seedlings. 513-934-3046.

**Stewart Orchids,** P.O. Box 550, Carpinteria, CA 93014: Free catalog ◆ Orchid-growing supplies. 800-621-2450.

**Sunswept Laboratories,** P.O. Box 1913, Studio City, CA 91614: Catalog $2 ◆ Rare and endangered orchid species. 818-506-7271.

**Teas Nursery Company,** P.O. Box 1603, Bellaire, TX 77401: Catalog $1 (refundable) ◆ Orchid and exotic plant supplies. 800-446-7723.

## Palms

**Crockett's Tropical Plants,** P.O. Box 1150, Harlingen, TX 78551: Catalog $3 ◆ Container-grown ornamentals, citrus plants, and palms. 800-580-1747.

**Floribunda Palms,** Box 635, Mt. View, HI 96771: Free information with long SASE ◆ Barefoot seedlings from worldwide locations.

**The Green Escape,** P.O. Box 1417, Palm Harbor, FL 34682: Catalog $6 (refundable) ◆ Indoor, cold-hardy, and tropical palm species. 813-784-1991.

**Jerry Horne Rare Plants,** 10195 SW 70th St., Miami, FL 33173: Free list with long SASE ◆ Ferns, platyceriums, palms and cycads, and rare and unusual plants. 305-270-1235.

**Pen Y Bryn,** RR 1, Box 1313, Forksville, PA 18616: Catalog $2 ◆ Palm trees. 717-924-3377.

**Rhapis Gardens,** P.O. Drawer 287, Gregory, TX 78359: Catalog $2 ◆ Green, variegated, and other dwarf indoor rhapis excella plants. 512-643-2061. www.rarepalms.com

## Peonies, Irises, & Daylilies

**Aitken's Salmon Creek Garden,** 608 NW 119th St., Vancouver, WA 98685: Catalog $2 ◆ Tall-bearded, medians, Japanese, Siberian, and other irises. 360-573-4472.

**Amberway Gardens,** 5803 Amberway Dr., St. Louis, MO 63128: Catalog $1 (refundable) ◆ Bearded and beardless irises and reblooming iris. 314-842-6103.

**American Daylily & Perennials,** P.O. Box 210, Grain Valley, MO 64029: Catalog $5 (refundable) ◆ Daylilies, hostas, and dwarf cannas. 800-770-2777.

**Anderson Iris Gardens,** 22179 Keather Ave. North, Forest Lake, MN 55025: Catalog $1 ◆ Peonies, daylilies, and irises. 612-433-5268.

**B & D Lilies,** 330 P St., Port Townsend, WA 98368: Catalog $3 ◆ Species and hybrid lilies and special heirloom collections. 360-385-1738.

**Big Tree Daylily Garden,** 777 General Hutchinson Pkwy., Longwood, FL 32750: Catalog $1 ◆ Daylilies. 407-831-5430.

**Borbeleta Gardens,** 15980 Canby Ave., Faribault, MN 55021: Catalog $3 ◆ Hardy lilies, daylilies, Siberian irises, and peonies. 507-334-2807. campbell@means.net

**Brookwood Gardens Inc.,** 303 Fir St., Michigan City, IN 46360: Catalog $2.98 ◆ Daylilies and hostas. 219-873-0198.

**The Bulb Crate,** 2560 Deerfield Rd., Riverwoods, IL 60015: Catalog $1 (refundable) ◆ Peonies, daylilies, and irises. 847-317-1414.

**Busse Gardens,** 5873 Oliver Ave. SW, Cokato, MN 55321: Catalog $2 ◆ Ferns, seeds and plants, and Siberian irises. 800-544-3192.

**Cape Iris Gardens,** 822 Rodney Vista Blvd., Cape Giradeau, MO 63701: Catalog $1 ◆ Bearded, median, spuria, and species irises. 314-334-3383.

**Caprice Farm Nursery,** 15425 SW Pleasant Hill Rd., Sherwood, OR 97140: Catalog $2 ◆ Peonies, irises, daylilies, and hostas. 503-625-7241.

**Comache Acres Iris Gardens,** Rt. 1, Box 258, Gower, MO 64454: Catalog $3 ◆ Bearded, Louisiana, and other irises. 816-424-6436.

**Contemporary Gardens of Perry Dyer,** Box 534, Blanchard, OK 73010: Catalog $1 ◆ Daylilies and bearded and Louisiana irises. 405-485-3302.

**Cooley's Gardens,** 11553 Silverton Rd. NE, P.O. Box 126, Silverton, OR 97381: Catalog $5 (refundable) ◆ Irises. 800-225-5391.

**Cordon Bleu Daylilies,** P.O. Box 2033, San Marcos, CA 92067: Catalog $2 ◆ Large flowered, double, mini and spider form daylilies. 760-744-8367.

**Cricket Hill Garden,** 670 Walnut Hill Rd., Thomaston, CT 06787: Free catalog ◆ Chinese tree peonies. 860-283-1042. www.treepeony.com

**Daylily Discounters,** One Daylily Plaza, Alachua, FL 32615: Catalog $2 ◆ Award winning daylilies. 904-462-1539. www.daylily-discounters.com

**Daylily World,** P.O. Box 1612, Sanford, FL 32772: Catalog $5 (refundable) ◆ Daylilies. 407-322-4034. www.daylilyworld.com

**Dick's Flower Farm,** 30656 North US Rt. 12, Volo, IL 60073: Free information ◆ Dahlias, gladioli, hybrid lilies, and summer bulbs. 815-385-3162.

**Ensata Gardens,** 9823 E. Michigan Ave., Galesburg, MI 49053: Catalog $2 ◆ Japanese irises. 616-665-7500.

**Greenwood Daylily & Iris Gardens,** 5595 E 7th St., #490, Long Beach, CA 90804: Free brochure ◆ Re-blooming irises and daylilies. 310-494-8944.

**Homestead Farms,** 3701 Hwy. EE, Owensville, MO 65066: Free catalog ◆ Daylilies, hostas, peonies, irises, and more. 573-437-4277.

**Jasperson's Hersey Nursery,** 2915 74th Ave., Wilson, WI 54027: Free information with long SASE and three 1st class stamps ◆ Irises, gladioli, and daylilies.

**Johnson Daylily Garden,** 70 Lark Ave., Brooksville, FL 34601: Free price list with 1st class stamp ◆ Daylilies. 352-544-0330. gjohnson@atlantic.net

**Kirkland Daylilies,** Union Springs Rd., P.O. Box 176, Newville, AL 36353: Free catalog ◆ Daylilies and hybrid amaryllis. 205-889-3313.

**Klehm Nursery,** 4210 N. Duncan Rd., Champaign, IL, 61821: Catalog $4 ◆ Peonies, irises, hostas, daylilies, and perennials. 800-553-3715.

**Long's Gardens,** P.O. Box 19, Boulder, CO 80306: Free catalog ◆ Tall, intermediate, and dwarf irises. 303-442-2535.

**Louisiana Nursery,** 8680 Perkins Rd., Baton Rouge, LA 70810: Catalog $4 ◆ Daylily and iris cultivars. 504-272-9795.

**Marietta Gardens,** NC 904 Hwy., Fairmont, NC 28340: Catalog $1 ◆ Daylilies. 910-628-8425.

**Maryland Aquatic Nurseries,** 3427 N. Furnace Rd., Jarrettsville, MD 21084: Catalog $5 (refundable) ◆ Water garden plants, ornamental grasses, and Louisiana and Japanese irises. 410-557-7615.

**Mellinger's,** 2310 W. South Range Rd., North Lima, OH 44452: Free catalog ◆ Fruit, nut, shade, and ornamental trees. Also gladioli, flowering shrubs, hedges, irises, wildflowers, and gardening equipment. 330-549-9861. www.mellingers.com

**Oakes Daylilies,** 8204 Monday Rd., Corryton, TN 37721: Free catalog ◆ Hybrid daylilies. 800-532-9545. www.oakesdaylilies.com

**Quality Dutch Bulbs,** P.O. Box 434, Stockertown, PA 18083: Free catalog ◆ 18083: Free catalog ◆ Daffodils, irises, tulips, and other bulbs. 800-755-2852.

**Roycroft Daylily Nursery,** 942 White Hall Ave., Georgetown, SC 29440: Catalog $3 ◆ Award-winning daylilies. 800-950-5459. www.roycroftdaylilies.com

**Schreiner's Gardens,** 3642 Quinaby Rd. NE, Salem, OR 97303: Catalog $4 ◆ Dwarf and tall-bearded irises. 800-525-2367.

**Serendipity Gardens,** 3210 Upper Bellbrook Rd., Bellbrook, OH 45305: Free catalog ◆ Daylilies. 513-426-6596.

**Skolaski's Glads & Flowers,** 4821 County Trunk Hwy. Q, Waunakee, WI 53597: Catalog $1 ◆ Gladioli bulbs, lilies, and perennials. 608-836-4822.

**Snow Creek Nursery,** 330 P St., Port Townsend, WA 98368: Catalog $2 ◆ Daylilies.

**Spring Creek Daylily Garden,** 25150 Gosling, Spring, TX 77389: Free catalog ◆ All sizes, types, and colors of daylilies. 281-351-8827.

**Tranquil Lake Nursery,** 45 River St., Rehoboth, MA 02769: Catalog $1 ◆ Daylilies, Siberian irises, and Japanese irises. 508-252-4002. www.tranquil-lake.com

**Van Bourgondien Bros.,** P.O. Box 1000, Babylon, NY 11702: Free catalog ◆ Lilies. 800-622-9959. blooms@dutchbulbs.com

**Wayside Gardens,** 1 Garden Ln., Hodges, SC 29695: Free catalog ◆ Siberian irises. 800-845-1124. www.waysidegardens.com

**White Flower Farm,** Catalog Services, 30 Irene St., Torrington, CT 06790: Free catalog ◆ Daylilies. 800-475-0148.

**Gilbert H. Wild & Son Inc.,** P.O. Box 338, Sarcoxie, MO 64862: Catalog $3 (refundable) ◆ Peonies, irises, and daylilies. 417-548-3514.

**Windmill Gardens,** P.O. Box 351, Luverne, AL 36049: Catalog $2 ◆ Daylilies. 334-335-5568.

## Perennials & Ornamentals

**Ambergate Gardens,** 8730 County Rd. 43, Chaska, MN 55318: Catalog $2 ◆ Perennial flowers and grasses. 612-443-2248.

**Autumn Glade Botanical,** 46857 Ann Arbor Trail, Plymouth, MI 48170: Free catalog ◆ Perennials and bulbs. 800-331-7969.

**Blossom Creek Greenhouse,** P.O. Box 598, North Plain, OR 97133: Free information ◆ Flowering jungle plants. 503-647-0915.

**Kurt Bluemel Inc.,** 2740 Greene Ln., Baldwin, MD 21013: Catalog $3 ◆ Perennials, ferns, bamboo plants, and ornamental grasses. 410-557-7229.

**Bluestone Perennials,** 7211 Middle Ridge Rd., Madison, OH 44057: Free catalog ◆ Perennial flowers, ground covers, ivies, and vines. 800-852-5243.

**Brickman's Botanical Gardens,** RR 1, Sebringville, Ontario, Canada N0K 1X0: Catalog $2 (refundable) ◆ Over 3000 perennial varieties.

**Busse Gardens,** 5873 Oliver Ave. SW, Cokato, MN 55321: Catalog $2 ◆ Cold-hardy and native perennials. 800-544-3192.

**Canyon Creek Nursery,** 3527 Dry Creek Rd., Oroville, CA 95965: Catalog $2 ◆ Perennials. 916-533-2166.

**Cattail Meadows Ltd.,** P.O. Box 39391, Solon, OH 44139: Catalog $1 ◆ Nursery-propagated wildflowers and companion perennials.

**Crown Botanicals,** 1036 Fairview Dr., Reading, PA 19605: Free information ◆ Tools, rare plants, gifts, and a lightweight, portable, and expandable garden workshop center. 888-384-2427.

**Crownsville Nursery,** P.O. Box 797, Crownsville, MD 21032: Catalog $2 (minimum order $25) ◆ Ferns, wildflowers, azaleas, ornamental grasses, and perennials. 410-923-2212.

**Daisy Fields,** 12635 SW Brighton Ln., Hillsboro, OR 97123: Catalog $2 ◆ Old-fashioned perennials.

**Digging Dog Nursery,** P.O. Box 471, Albion, CA 95410: Catalog $3 ◆ Grasses, vines, trees, perennials, and shrubs. 707-937-1130.

**Evergreen Gardenworks,** P.O. Box 1357, Ukiah, CA 95482: Free catalog ◆ Bonsai stock, rock garden plants, alpines, and ornamentals. 707-462-8909.

**Exotics Hawaii Ltd.,** 1344 Hoakoa Pl., Honolulu, HI 96821: Free list with long SASE ◆ Orchids, tropical plants, and seeds.

**Exotree,** 3010 Sparks Ave., Nampa, ID 83686: Free catalog ◆ Acacias and tropicals.

**Fieldstone Gardens Inc.,** 620 Quaker Ln., Vassalboro, ME 04989: Catalog $2 ◆ Nursery-propagated perennials. 207-923-3836.

**Flower Scent Gardens,** 14820 Moine Rd., Daylestown, OH 44230: Catalog $2 (refundable) ◆ Perennials and shrubs. 330-658-5946.

**Garden Place,** 6842 Heisley Rd., Mentor, OH 44060: Catalog $1 ◆ Perennials. 216-255-3705.

**Gilson Gardens Inc.,** 3059 US Rt. 20, P.O. Box 277, Perry, OH 44081: Free catalog ◆ Ground covers, perennials, and ferns. 216-259-5252.

**Good Hollow Greenhouse & Herbarium,** 50 Slaterock Mill Rd., Taft, TN 38488: Catalog $1 ◆ Herb plants and dried herbs, perennials, wildflowers, scented geraniums, essential oils and potpourris, teas, and spices. 615-433-7640.

**The Gourmet Gardener,** 8650 College Blvd., Overland Park, KS 66210: Catalog $2 ◆ Herb, vegetable, and edible flower seeds from around the world. 913-345-0490. www.gourmetgardener.com

**Heronswood Nursery,** 7530 NE 288th St., Kingston, WA 98346: Catalog $4 ◆ Perennials.

**High Country Gardens,** 2902 Rufina St., Santa Fe, NM 87505: Free catalog ◆ Perennials. 800-925-9387.

**Highfield Garden,** 4704 NE Cedar Creek Rd., Woodland, WA 98674: Catalog $1 ◆ Unique perennials.

**Hillary's Garden,** P.O. Box 430, Warwick, NY 10990: Catalog $2 ◆ Perennials and organically grown herbs. 914-987-1175.

**Jerry Horne Rare Plants,** 10195 SW 70th St., Miami, FL 33173: Free list with long SASE ◆ Ferns, platyceriums, palms and cycads, and rare and unusual plants. 305-270-1235.

**Joy Creek Nursery,** 20300 NW Watson Rd., Scappoose, OR 97056: Catalog $2 (refundable) ◆ Unique and unusual perennials and native plants.

**Klehm Nursery,** 4210 N. Duncan Rd., Champaign, IL, 61821: Catalog $4 ◆ Peonies, irises, daylilies, hostas, and perennials. 800-553-3715.

**Lily of the Valley Herb Farm,** 3969 Fox Ave., Minerva, OH 44657: Price list $1 (refundable) ◆ Herb, everlasting, perennial, and scented geranium plants. 330-862-3920.

**Limerock Ornamental Grasses Inc.,** RD 1, Box 111, Port Matilda, PA 16870: Catalog $3 ◆ Ornamental and native grasses, companion perennials, and nursery-grown hardy ferns. 814-692-2272.

**Meadow View Farms,** 3360 N. Pacific Hwy., Medford, OR 97501: Catalog $3 ◆ Perennials, grasses, herbs, vines, and aquatic plants.

**Mellinger's,** 2310 W. South Range Rd., North Lima, OH 44452: Free catalog ◆ Fruit, nut, shade, and ornamental trees. Also gladioli, flowering shrubs, hedges, irises, wildflowers, and gardening equipment. 330-549-9861. www.mellingers.com

**Milaeger's Gardens,** 4838 Douglas Ave., Racine, WI 53402: Catalog $1 ◆ Perennials. 800-669-9956.

**J.E. Miller Nurseries,** 5060 W. Lake Rd., Canandaigua, NY 14424: Free catalog ◆ Fruit and nut trees, vines, ornamentals, and ground covers. 800-836-9630.

**Niche Gardens,** 1111 Dawson Rd., Chapel Hill, NC 27516: Catalog $3 ◆ Nursery-propagated wildflowers, perennials, trees, and shrubs. 919-967-0078. www.nichegdn.com

**Patrick's Nursery,** P.O. Box 130, Ty Ty, GA 31795: Free catalog ◆ Perennials, vegetables, fruit and nut trees, berry plants, and grapevines. 800-972-2101.

**Pen Y Bryn,** RR 1, Box 1313, Forksville, PA 18616: Catalog $2 ◆ Oriental plants. 717-924-3377.

**Perennial Pleasures Nursery,** P.O. Box 147, East Hardwock, VT 05836: Catalog $3 ◆ Heirloom herbs and flowers. 802-472-5104.

**Pine Ridge Gardens,** 832 Sycamore Rd., London, AR 72847: Catalog $1 ◆ Nursery-propagated wildflowers, hostas, and unusual ornamentals. 501-293-4359.

**Plant Delights Nursery,** 9241 Sauls Rd., Raleigh, NC 27603: Catalog $2 ◆ Rare and other hard-to-find plants. Specializes in hostas. 919-772-4794. www.plantdel.com

**Plantation Bulb Company,** P.O. Box 159, Ty Ty, GA 31795: Free catalog ◆ Bulbs and perennials. 800-972-2101.

**The Plumeria People,** 1846 Eagle Falls Dr., Houston, TX 77077: Catalog $3 (refundable) ◆ Easy-to-grow flowering, fragrant, and unusual tropical plants. 281-496-2352.

**Roslyn Nursery,** 211 Burrs Ln., Dix Hills, NY 11746: Catalog $3 ◆ Rhododendrons, hardy shrubs, trees, and perennials. 516-643-9347. www.cris.com/~Roslyn

**Sandy Mush Herb Nursery,** 316 Surrett Cove Rd., Leicester, NC 28748: Catalog $4 ◆ Herbs, flowering perennials, geraniums, ferns, ivies, and other growing stock. 828-683-2014.

**Shady Oaks Nursery,** P.O. Box 708, Waseca, MN 56093: Free list ◆ Ferns, shrubs, perennials, and wildflowers. 800-504-8006. www.shadyoaks.com

**Skolaski's Glads & Flowers,** 4821 County Trunk Hwy. Q, Waunakee, WI 53597: Catalog $1 ◆ Gladioli bulbs, lilies, and perennials. 608-836-4822.

**Southern Perennials & Herbs,** 98 Bridges Rd., Tylertown, MS 39667: Free catalog ◆ Perennials, gingers, herbs, grasses, and vines for the south. 800-774-0079. www.s-p-h.com

**Spring Hill Nurseries,** 6523 N. Galena Rd., P.O. Box 1758, Peoria, IL 61632: Free catalog ◆ Perennials, roses, annuals, ground covers, bonsai, and house plants. 800-582-8527. www.springhillnursery.com

**Stokes Tropicals,** P.O. Box 9868, New Iberia, LA 70562: Catalog $4 ◆ Ginger plants, fertilizer, and ginger-growing kits. Also banana, bromeliads, heliconias, plumerias, and other plants. 800-624-9706; 318-365-6998 (in LA). www.stokestropicals.com

**Sunlight Gardens,** 174 Golden Ln., Andersonville, TN 37705: Catalog $3 ◆ Hardy ferns and perennials. 615-494-8237.

**Sunnybrook Farms Nursery,** P.O. Box 6, Chesterland, OH 44026: Catalog $1 (refundable) ◆ Hostas, herb plants, scented geraniums, perennials, and ivies. 216-729-7232.

**Surry Gardens,** P.O. Box 145, Surry, ME 04684: Free information ◆ Border, wild garden, and rock garden perennials. 207-667-4493.

**Twombly Nursery,** 163 Barn Hill Rd., Monroe, CT 06468: Catalog $4 ◆ Dwarf conifer miniatures, rare and unusual plants, and trees. 203-261-2133.

**Van Bourgondien Bros.,** P.O. Box 1000, Babylon, NY 11702: Free catalog ◆ Perennials. 800-622-9959. blooms@dutchbulbs.com

**Vandenberg Bulb Company,** 1 Black Meadow Rd., Chester, NY 10918: Free catalog ◆ Perennials, hybrid lilies, seeds, and bulbs. 800-221-6017.

**Andre Viette Nurseries,** Rt. 1, Box 16, Fishersville, VA 22939: Catalog $3 ◆ Flowering and rock garden perennials, woodland plants, and daylilies. 540-942-2118.

**Wayside Gardens,** 1 Garden Ln., Hodges, SC 29695: Free catalog ◆ Perennials, trees, shrubs, ground covers, and gardening supplies. 800-845-1124. www.waysidegardens.com

**Weiss Brothers Nursery,** 11690 Colfax Hwy., Grass Valley, CA 95945: Free catalog ◆ Perennials and drip irrigation supplies. 916-272-7657.

**Wildflower Nursery,** 1680 Hwy. 25-70, Marshall, NC 28753: Free catalog ◆ Perennials. 704-656-2723.

**Woodside Gardens,** 1191 Egg & I Rd., Chimacum, WA 98325: Catalog $2 ◆ Perennials and herb plants. 360-732-4754.

## Rock Gardens

**Carroll Gardens,** 444 E. Main St., P.O. Box 310, Westminster, MD 21157: Catalog $3 (refundable) ◆ Rock garden and alpine plants. 800-638-6334.

**Endangered Species,** P.O. Box 1830, Tustin, CA 92681: Catalog $6 ◆ Rare and unusual rock garden plants. 714-544-9505. nursery@endangeredspecies.com

**Evergreen Gardenworks,** P.O. Box 1357, Ukiah, CA 95482: Free catalog ◆ Bonsai stock, rock garden plants, alpines, and ornamentals. 707-462-8909.

**Fieldstone Gardens Inc.,** 620 Quaker Ln., Vassalboro, ME 04989: Catalog $2 ◆ Mature plants for sun, shade, rock gardens, and ground covers. 207-923-3836.

**The Primrose Path,** RD 2, Box 110, Scottdale, PA 15683: Catalog $2 ◆ Rock garden plants. 412-887-6756.

**Squaw Mountain Gardens,** P.O. Box 946, Estacada, OR 97023: Catalog $2 (refundable) ◆ Ferns and companion rock garden plants. 503-630-5458. www.squawmountaingardens.com

**Twombly Nursery,** 163 Barn Hill Rd., Monroe, CT 06468: Catalog $4 ◆ Dwarf conifer miniatures, rare and unusual plants, and trees for water gardens. 203-261-2133.

## Roses

**Antique Rose Emporium,** Rt. 5, Box 143, Brenham, TX 77833: Catalog $5 ◆ Antique roses for southern climates. 800-441-0002.

**Bridges Roses,** 2734 Toney Rd., Lawndale, NC 28090: Free catalog ◆ Miniature roses. 704-538-9412.

**Butner's Old Mill Nursery,** 806 S. Belt., St. Joseph, MO 64507: Free catalog ◆ Bare root roses. 800-344-8107.

**Edmunds Roses,** 6235 SW Kahle Rd., Wilsonville, OR 97070: Free catalog ◆ Exhibition and European roses. 888-481-7673. www.edmundsroses.com

**Garden Valley Ranch,** 498 Pepper Rd., Petaluma, CA 94952: Free catalog ◆ Modern, climbers and ramblers, miniatures, heirlooms, and tree roses. 707-795-0919. bareroot@gardenvalley.com

**Heirloom Old Garden Roses,** 24062 NE Riverside Dr., St. Paul, OR 97137: Catalog $5 ◆ Old garden, English, and winter-hardy roses. 503-538-1576.

**Jackson & Perkins,** P.O. Box 1028, Medford, OR 97501: Free catalog ◆ Roses. 800-872-7673. www.jackson-perkins.com

**Earl May Seeds & Nursery Company,** 208 N. Elm St., Shenandoah, IA 51603: Free catalog ◆ Roses, shade and ornamental trees, flowering shrubs, vegetable and flower seeds, bulbs, and gardening supplies. 712-246-1020.

**The Mini Rose Garden,** P.O. Box 203, Cross Hill, SC 29332: Free catalog ◆ Miniature roses. 864-998-4331.

**Miniature Plant Kingdom,** 4125 Harrison Grade Rd., Sebastopol, CA 95472: Catalog $2.50 ◆ Miniature roses, Japanese maples, conifers, and bonsai plants. 707-874-2233.

**Nor'East Miniature Roses Inc.,** P.O. Box 307, Rowley, MA 01969: Free catalog ◆ Miniature roses. 978-948-7964.

**Oregon Miniature Roses,** 8285 SW 185th Ave., Beaverton, OR 97007: Catalog $1 ◆ Micro-mini, climbing miniature, and miniature tree roses. 503-649-4482.

**Rabbit Shadow Farm,** 2880 E. Hwy. 402, Loveland, CO 80537: Free information ◆ Herbs, roses, topiary supplies, and scented geraniums. 970-667-5531.

**Rosehill Farm,** P.O. Box 188, Galena, MD 21635: Free catalog ◆ Roses. 410-648-5538.

**Roses of Yesterday & Today,** 803 Brown's Valley Rd., Watsonville, CA 95076: Catalog $3 ◆ Old, rare, and unusual roses. 408-724-3537.

**Roses Unlimited,** Rt. 1, Box 587, Laurens, SC 29360: Free list with long SASE ◆ Hybrid tea, old garden, climbers, shrubs, English, and buck roses. 864-682-7673. members.aol.com/rosesunlmt/index.html

**Royall River Roses,** 70 New Gloucester Rd., North Yarmouth, ME 04097: Catalog $2 ◆ Old-fashioned, uncommon, and hardy roses. Also shrub and hybrid tea roses and floribunda. 207-829-5830.

**Savage Farms Nursery,** 6255 Beersheba Hwy., McMinnville, TN 37110: Free catalog ◆ Flowering trees and shrubs, roses, evergreens, berry plants, and gardening supplies. Also fruit and shade trees. 615-668-8902.

**R.H. Shumway Seedsman,** P.O. Box 1, Graniteville, SC 29829: Free catalog ◆ Roses, berry plants, fruit trees, seeds and bulbs, ornamental shrubs and plants, and gardening supplies. 803-737-0399.

**Spring Hill Nurseries,** 6523 N. Galena Rd., P.O. Box 1758, Peoria, IL 61632: Free catalog ◆ Perennials and annuals, trees, shrubs, ground covers, bonsai, house plants, and old, miniature, and other roses. 800-582-8527. www.springhillnursery.com

**Vintage Gardens,** 2833 Gravenstein Hwy. South, Sebastopol, CA 95472: Catalog $4 ◆ Antique and extraordinary roses. 707-829-2035.

**Bob Wells Nursery,** P.O. Box 606, Lindale, TX 75771: Free catalog ◆ Fruit, nut, and shade trees. Also berries, grapes, muscadines, roses, ornamentals, and flowering shrubs. 903-882-3550.

**Womack's Nursery Company,** Rt. 1, Box 80, De Leon, TX 76444: Free catalog ◆ Roses and fruit, nut, shade, and flowering trees. (Note: Nursery stock is adapted for planting in southern states.) 817-893-6497.

## Sassafras

**Vernon Barnes & Son Nursery,** P.O. Box 250, McMinnville, TN 37110: Free catalog ◆ Vines, wildflowers, hedges and shrubs, berry plants, and shade, sassafras, flowering, fruit, and nut trees. 615-668-8576.

**Forestfarm,** 990 Tetherow Rd., Williams, OR 97544: Catalog $3 ◆ Sassafras trees. 541-846-7269.

**Louisiana Nursery,** 8680 Perkins Rd., Baton Rouge, LA 70810: Catalog $4 ◆ Sassafras trees and rare, unusual, and hard-to-find plants. 504-272-9795.

## Seeds & Bulbs

**Abundant Life Seed Foundation,** P.O. Box 772, Port Townsend, WA 98368: Catalog $2 ◆ Organic and untreated vegetable, grain, herb, wildflower, and other seeds. 360-385-5660.

**Alfrey Seeds,** P.O. Box 415, Knoxville, TN 37901: List $3 ◆ Seeds for chili peppers, vegetables, and gourds.

**Jacques Amand,** P.O. Box 59001, Potomac, MD 20859: Free catalog ◆ Imported rare and unusual bulbs from England. 800-452-5414.

**Amaryllis Incorporated,** P.O. Box 318, Baton Rouge, LA 70821: Catalog $1 ◆ Imported hybrid and species amaryllis from Holland and India. 504-924-5560.

**American Horticultural Society,** 7931 East Blvd. Dr., Alexandria, VA 22308: Free list for members ◆ Heirloom and hard-to-find seeds. 703-768-5700.

**Archia's Floral & Plants,** 712 S. Ohio, Sedalia, MO 65301: Free catalog ◆ Vegetable and flower seeds, gardening supplies, nursery stock, and beekeeping equipment. 816-826-4000.

**Autumn Glade Botanical,** 46857 Ann Arbor Trail, Plymouth, MI 48170: Free catalog ◆ Perennials and bulbs. 800-331-7969.

**The Banana Tree,** 715 Northampton St., Easton, PA 18042: Catalog $3 ◆ Seeds from temperate and tropical climates. 610-253-9589.

**The Bethlehem Seed Company,** P.O. Box 1351, Bethlehem, PA 18018: Free information ◆ Bulbs and seed for vegetables, grass, and flowers. 610-691-6697.

**Bountiful Gardens,** 18001 Shafer Ranch Rd., Willits, CA 95490: Free catalog ◆ Seeds for vegetables, compost crops, herbs, and flowers. Also books and organic gardening supplies. 707-459-6410. www.bountifulgardens.com

**Breck's Dutch Bulbs,** Mail Order Reservation Center, 6523 N. Galena Rd., Peoria, IL 61632: Free catalog ◆ Spring flowering bulbs. 800-722-9069. www.brecks.com

**Brent & Becky's Bulbs,** 7463 North Trail, Gloucester, VA 23061: Free catalog ◆ Flowering bulbs. 804-693-3966. www.BrentandBeckysbulbs.com

**Burgess Seed & Plant Company,** 905 Four Seasons Rd., Bloomington, IL 61701: Free catalog ◆ Seeds.

**W. Atlee Burpee & Company,** 300 Park Ave., Warminster, PA 18974: Free catalog ◆ Seeds and bulbs. 800-888-1447. www.burpee.com

**D.V. Burrell Seed Company,** P.O. Box 150, Rocky Ford, CO 81067: Free catalog ◆ Seeds, gardening supplies, and tools. 719-254-3318.

**Butterbrooke Farm,** 78 Barry Rd., Oxford, CT 06478: Free catalog ◆ Chemically untreated and open-pollinated rapidly maturing vegetable seeds. 203-888-2000.

**Caladium World,** P.O. Drawer 629, Sebring, FL 33872: Free catalog ◆ Caladium bulbs. 941-385-7661. www.caladium.com

**Carolina Seeds,** P.O. Box 2658, Boone, NC 28607: Free information ◆ Flower and vegetable seeds. 800-825-5477. www.carolinaseeds.com

**Cascade Bulb & Seed,** P.O. Box 271, Scotts Mills, OR 97375: Free information ◆ Daylilies, lilies, irises, and alliums.

**Comstock, Ferre & Company,** 263 Main St., Wethersfield, CT 06109: Catalog $2 ◆ Vegetable, flower, and herb seeds. 860-571-6590.

**The Cook's Garden,** P.O. Box 535, Londonberry, VT 05148: Catalog $1 ◆ Seeds for flowers and vegetables. 802-824-3400. www.cooksgarden.com

**Cruickshank's,** 1015 Mount Pleasant Rd., Toronto, Ontario, Canada M4P 2M1: Catalog $3 ◆ Tulip bulbs.

**The Daffodil Mart,** Rt. 3, Box 794, Gloucester, VA 23061: Free catalog ◆ Daffodils, tulips, autumn flowering and forcing bulbs, other bulbs, and growing supplies. 800-255-2852.

**Dan's Garden Shop,** 5821 Woodwinds Circle, Frederick, MD 21701: Free catalog ◆ Seeds for annuals, perennials, and vegetables. 301-695-5966.

**DeGiorgi Seed Company Inc.,** 6011 N St., Omaha, NE 68117: Catalog $2 ◆ Seeds. 800-858-2580.

**Peter de Jager Bulb Company,** 188 Asbury St., South Hamilton, MA 01982: Free catalog ◆ Dutch bulbs. 978-468-4707.

**Dutch Gardens Inc.,** P.O. Box 200, Adelphia, NJ 07710: Free information ◆ Tulip, hyacinth, crocus, iris, amaryllis, and other bulbs. 800-775-2852. www.dutchgardens.nl

**Evergreen Y.H. Enterprises,** P.O. Box 17538, Anaheim, CA 92817: Catalog $2 (refundable) ◆ Gardening tools, cookbooks, and vegetable seeds from China, Japan, and other countries. 714-637-5769. EESeeds@aol.com

**Fancy Plants Farms,** P.O. Box 989, Lake Placid, FL 33862: Free information ◆ Caladium bulbs. 800-869-0953.

**Farmer Seed & Nursery Company,** 818 NW 4th St., Faribault, MN 55021: Free catalog ◆ Vegetable seeds, flowering bulbs, fruit and shade trees, ornamental shrubs and hedges, berry plants, and roses. 507-334-1623.

**Henry Field's Seed & Nursery,** 415 N. Burnett, Shenandoah, IA 51602: Free catalog ◆ Strawberry and other berry plants, vegetable and flower seeds, hedges, ornamental shrubs, roses, and fruit, nut, and shade trees. 605-665-4491.

**Fisher's Garden Store,** P.O. Box 236, Belgrade, MT 59714: Free catalog ◆ Vegetable and flower seeds for high altitude gardening and short growing seasons. 406-388-6052.

**The Flowery Branch Seed Company,** P.O. Box 1330, Flowery Branch, GA 30542: Catalog $4 (refundable) ◆ Heirloom flowers, edible and medicinal herbs, and annuals and perennials from worldwide sources. 770-536-8380. www.flowerybranchseeds.com

**Four Seasons Nursery,** 1706 Morrisey Dr., Bloomington, IL 61704: Free catalog ◆ Citrus and exotic fruits. 309-663-9551.

**The Fragrant Path,** P.O. Box 328, Fort Calhoun, NE 68023: Catalog $2 ◆ Seeds for prairie wildflowers. Also grasses, ferns, trees, shrubs, and climbing plants.

**French's Bulb Importer,** P.O. Box 565, Pittsfield, VT 05762: Free information ◆ Unusual bulb species. 802-746-8148.

**Garden City Seeds,** 778 Hwy. 93 North, Hamilton, MT 59840: Free catalog ◆ Fertilizers, pest controls, and seeds for short growing seasons. 406-961-4837.

**Gardeners' Choice,** 81961 Country Rd. 687, P.O. Box 8000, Hartford, MI 49057: Free catalog ◆ Seeds for house plants, vegetables, flowers, and trees. 800-274-4096.

**Gladside Gardens,** 61 Main St., Northfield, MA 01360: Price list $1 ◆ Gladioli, dahlias, cannas, and unusual bulbs.

**Gurney Seed & Nursery Company,** 110 Capitol St., Yankton, SD 57079: Free catalog ◆ Seeds, bulbs, and semi-dwarf and standard varieties of apple trees. 605-665-1671.

**Happiness Farms,** Fancy Leaf Caladiums, 705 Country Rd East, Lake Placid, FL 33852: Free catalog ◆ Caladium bulbs. 941-465-0044.

**Harris Seeds Inc.,** P.O. Box 22960, Rochester, NY 14692: Free catalog ◆ Seeds and gardening supplies. 800-514-4441. www.trine.com/gardennet/harrisseeds

**Heirloom Gardens,** P.O. Box 138, Guerneville, CA 95446: Free catalog ◆ Unusual seed varieties for easy growing.

**Holland Bulb Farms,** P.O. Box 220, Tatamy, PA 18085: Free catalog ◆ Imported bulbs from Holland. 800-283-5082. www.hollandbulbs.com

**J.L. Hudson, Seedsman,** Box 1058, Redwood City, CA 94064: Catalog $1 ◆ Seeds from around the world.

**Ed Hume Seeds Inc.,** P.O. Box 1450, Kent, WA 98035: Catalog $1 ◆ Herb, flower, and vegetable seeds.

**Imported Dutch Bulbs,** P.O. Box 32, Cavendish, VT 05142: Free catalog ◆ Daffodils, tulips, and other bulbs. 802-226-7653.

**Jackson & Perkins,** P.O. Box 1028, Medford, OR 97501: Free catalog ◆ Seeds, plants, and roses. 800-872-7673. www.jackson-perkins.com

**Johnny's Selected Seeds,** Foss Hill Rd., Albion, ME 04910: Free catalog ◆ Strawberry plants and flower and vegetable seeds for cool northern climates. 207-437-4301. www.johnnyseeds.com

**J.W. Jung Seed Company,** 335 High St., Randolph, WI 53957: Free catalog ◆ Seeds and gardening supplies. 414-326-4100.

**Kitazawa Seed Company,** 1111 Chapman St., San Jose, CA 95126: Free price list ◆ Chinese and Japanese vegetable seeds. 408-243-1330.

**D. Landreth Seed Company,** P.O. Box 6398, Baltimore, MD 21230: Catalog $2 ◆ Vegetable and flower seeds. 800-654-2407.

**Le Jardin du Gourmet,** P.O. Box 75, St. Johnsbury Center, VT 05863: Catalog $1 ◆ Seeds for vegetables and herb plants. 802-748-1446.

**Liberty Seed Company,** P.O. Box 806, New Philadelphia, OH 44663: Free catalog ◆ Flower and vegetable seeds. 800-541-6022. www.libertyseed.com

**The Lily Nook,** Box 846, Neepawa, Mannitoba, Canada R0J 1H0: Catalog $2 ◆ One thousand varieties of bulbs. Includes exclusive and original varieties.

**Lindenberg Seeds Ltd.,** 803 Princess Ave., Brandon, Manitoba, Canada R7A 0P5: Catalog $1 ◆ Vegetable and flower seeds and gardening supplies. 204-727-0575.

**Earl May Seeds & Nursery Company,** 208 N. Elm St., Shenandoah, IA 51603: Free catalog ◆ Vegetable and flower seeds, bulbs, fruit and nut trees, roses, grapes, and flowering shrubs. 712-246-1020.

**McClure & Zimmerman,** P.O. Box 368, Friesland, WI 53935: Free catalog ◆ Tulip bulbs. 800-692-5864; 414-326-4220 (in WI).

**Mellinger's,** 2310 W. South Range Rd., North Lima, OH 44452: Free catalog ◆ Fruit, nut, shade, and ornamental trees. Also gladioli, flowering shrubs, hedges, irises, wildflowers, and gardening equipment. 330-549-9861. www.mellingers.com

**Michigan Bulb Company,** 1950 Waldorf NW, Grand Rapids, MI 49550: Free catalog ◆ Bulbs, perennials, foliage plants, trees, shrubs, exotic house plants, hedges and climbers, and roses. 616-771-9500.

**Moon Mountain Wildflowers,** P.O. Box 725, Carpinteria, CA 93014: Catalog $3 ◆ Wildflower seeds. 805-684-2565. ssseeds@silcom.com

**Charles H. Mueller Company,** 7091 N. River Rd., New Hope, PA 18938: Free catalog ◆ Old favorites and new bulbs. 215-862-2033.

**Netherland Bulb Company,** 13 McFadden Rd., Easton, PA 18045: Free catalog ◆ Imported Holland bulbs. 800-755-2852.

**Nichols Garden Nursery,** 1194 Pacific, Albany, OR 97321: Free catalog ◆ Vegetable seeds, herb seeds and plants, saffron crocus, garlic and shallots, and strawberry plants. 541-928-9280.

**Old House Gardens,** 536 THIRD St., Ann Arbor, MI 48103: Catalog $1 ◆ Specializes in heirloom bulbs. Includes colonial daffodils, Victorian tulips, jazz age dahlias, and more. 734-995-1486. www.oldhousegardens.com

**The Old Sturbridge Village Museum Gift Shop,** 1 Old Sturbridge Village Rd., Sturbridge, MA 01566: Catalog $1 (refundable) ◆ 19th-century varieties of flower and vegetable seeds. 508-347-3362.

**L.L. Olds Seed Company,** P.O. Box 7790, Madison, WI 53707: Catalog $2.50 ◆ Vegetable, herb, and flower seeds. 608-249-9291.

**P & P Seed Company,** 14050 Rt. 62, Collins, NY 14034: Free information ◆ Seed for growing giant-size pumpkins, tomatoes, and sunflowers. 800-449-5681; 716-532-5995 (in NY).

**Park Seed Company,** 1 Parkron Ave., Greenwood, SC 29648: Free catalog ◆ Bulbs, vegetable and flower seeds, gardening tools, and supplies. 800-845-3369. www.parkseed.com

**Patrick's Nursery,** P.O. Box 130, Ty Ty, GA 31795: Free catalog ◆ Vegetable and flower seeds, fruit and nut trees, berry plants, and grapevines. 800-972-2101.

**Pepper Gal,** P.O. Box 23006, Fort Lauderdale, FL 33307: Price list $1 ◆ Seeds for peppers. 954-537-5540.

**Pinetree Garden Seeds,** Box 300, New Gloucester, ME 04260: Free catalog ◆ Seeds for vegetables, herbs, flowers, house plants, and perennials. 207-926-3400. www.maine.com/seeds

**Planet Natural,** P.O. Box 3146, Bozeman, MT 59772: Free catalog ◆ Beneficial insects, garden seeds, composting equipment, organic fertilizers, pest controls, garden supplies, and pet and body care products. 800-289-6656. www.planetnatural.com

**Plantation Bulb Company,** P.O. Box 159, Ty Ty, GA 31795: Free catalog ◆ Bulbs and perennials. 800-972-2101.

**Pleasant Valley Glads,** P.O. Box 494, Agawam, MA 01001: Free catalog ◆ Gladioli bulbs. 413-789-0307.

**Quality Dutch Bulbs,** P.O. Box 434, Stockertown, PA 18083: Free catalog ◆ 18083: Free catalog ◆ Daffodils, irises, tulips, and other bulbs. 800-755-2852.

**Richters,** 357 Hwy. 47, Goodwood, Ontario, Canada L0C 1A0: Catalog $2 ◆ Seeds and growing stock for Allium shade plants, herbs, and other garden varieties. 905-640-6677. www.richters.com

**John Scheepers Inc.,** 23 Tulip Dr., Bantam, CT 06750: Free catalog ◆ Flowering bulbs. 860-567-0838. www.johnscheepers.com

**Schipper & Company USA,** P.O. Box 7584, Greenwich, CT 06836: Catalog $1 ◆ Tulip bulbs. 800-877-8637. www.colorblends.com

**F.W. Schumacher Company,** 36 Spring Hill Rd., Sandwich, MA 02563: Free catalog ◆ Seeds for nurserymen, foresters, and horticulturists. 508-888-0659.

**Seeds Blüm,** HC 33, Idaho City Stage, Boise, ID 83706: Catalog $3 ◆ Hybrid and heirloom vegetable seeds. 800-528-3658.

**Seeds of Change,** Box 15700, Santa Fe, NM 87506: Free information ◆ Organic and open-pollinated hard-to-find vegetable, herb, and flower seeds. 800-957-3337. www.seedsofchange.com

**Seeds of Distinction,** P.O. Box 86, Station A, Toronto, Ontario, Canada M9C 4V2: Free catalog ◆ Hard-to-find seeds from worldwide sources. 416-255-3060.

**Seeds Trust, High Altitudes Gardens,** P.O. Box 1048, Hailey, ID 83333: Free catalog ◆ Open-pollinated vegetable, native wildflower, native grass, and medicinal herb seeds for cold climates and short growing seasons. 208-788-4363. www.seedsave.org

**Seedway Inc.,** 1225 Zeager Rd., Elizabethtown, PA 17022: Free catalog ◆ Vegetable seeds. 800-952-7333. www.seedway.com

**Select Seeds,** 180 Stickney Rd., Union, CT 06076: Catalog $3 ◆ Seeds for foxgloves, mignonetta, balloon flowers, hollyhocks, sweet peas, nicotiana, and other old-fashioned flowers. 860-684-9310. www.selectseeds.com

**Shepherd's Garden Seeds,** 30 Irene St., Torrington, CT 06790: Catalog $1 ◆ Seeds for baby, Mexican, Italian, Oriental, and French vegetables. 860-482-3638. garden@shepherdseeds.com

**Seymour's Selected Seeds,** P.O. Box 1346, Sussex, VA 23884: Free catalog ◆ Rare and other flower seeds. Includes many imported from England. 804-663-9771.

**R.H. Shumway Seedsman,** P.O. Box 1, Graniteville, SC 29829: Free catalog ◆ Seeds and bulbs, berry plants, fruit trees, roses, ornamental shrubs and plants, and gardening supplies. 803-737-0399.

**Southern Exposure Seed Exchange,** P.O. Box 170, Earlysville, VA 22936: Catalog $2 (refundable) ◆ Seeds for vegetables, flowers, herbs, and plants. 804-973-4703. www.southernexposure.com

**Southern Oregon Organics,** 1130 Tetherow Rd., Williams, OR 97544: Free catalog ◆ Organic garden seeds. 541-846-7173.

**Southern Seeds,** P.O. Box 2091, Melbourne, FL 32902: Catalog $1 ◆ Seeds for bananas, passion fruit, papaya, and other edible exotics. 407-727-3662.

**Stark Brothers,** Nurseries & Orchards Company, P.O. Box 10, Louisiana, MO 63353: Free catalog ◆ Fruit trees, berry and landscaping plants, and garden supplies. 800-775-6415.

**Stokes Seeds Inc.,** Box 548, Buffalo, NY 14240: Free catalog ◆ Vegetable and flower seeds. 716-695-6980.

**Terra Time & Tide,** 590 E. 59th St., Jacksonville, FL 32208: Free catalog ◆ Seeds for flowers, vegetables, potpourri plants, medicinal herbs and healing plants, exotic and unusual vines, ornamental grasses, and more. 904-764-0376.

**Territorial Seed Company,** P.O. Box 157, Cottage Grove, OR 97424: Free catalog ◆ Organic fertilizers, natural insecticides, biological pest controls, and vegetable, herb, and flower seeds. 541-942-9547. www.terrirorial-seed.com

**Thompson & Morgan Inc.,** P.O. Box 1308, Jackson, NJ 08527: Free catalog ◆ Vegetable and flower seeds. 800-274-7333.

**Otis Twilley Seed Company,** P.O. Box 65, Trevose, PA 19047: Catalog $1 ◆ Seeds for fruits, vegetables, and flowers. 800-622-7333.

**Van Bourgondien Bros.,** P.O. Box 1000, Babylon, NY 11702: Free catalog ◆ Holland flower bulbs. 800-622-9959. blooms@dutchbulbs.com

**Van Engelen Inc.,** 23 Tulip Dr., Bantam, CT 06750: Free catalog ◆ Tulips, daffodils, narcissi, crocuses, hyacinths, irises, muscari, and other imported Dutch bulbs. 860-567-8734. www.vanengelen.com

**Mary Mattison Van Schaik,** P.O. Box 32, Cavendish, VT 05142: Catalog $1 ◆ Novelty and miniature tulip, daffodil, and hyacinth bulbs. 802-226-7653.

**Vandenberg Bulb Company,** 1 Black Meadow Rd., Chester, NY 10918: Free catalog ◆ Perennials, hybrid lilies, seeds, and imported bulbs. 800-221-6017.

**Vermont Bean Seed Company,** 95 Garden Ln., Fair Haven, VT 05743: Free catalog ◆ Bean seeds, heirloom plants, and herbs. 802-273-3400.

**Vesey Seeds Ltd.,** P.O. Box 9000, Charlottetown, Prince Edward Island, Canada C0A 1P0: Free catalog ◆ Early maturing vegetable and flower seeds.

**Dirk Visser & Company,** P.O. Box 295, 201 High St., Ipswich, MA 01938: Free catalog ◆ Imported Holland bulbs. 978-356-3632. www.dutchbulb.com

**Wayside Gardens,** 1 Garden Ln., Hodges, SC 29695: Free catalog ◆ Bulbs. 800-845-1124. www.waysidegardens.com

**White Flower Farm,** Catalog Services, 30 Irene St., Torrington, CT 06790: Free catalog ◆ Bulbs, perennials, shrubs, strawberry plants, seeds and plants, books, tools, and gardening supplies. 800-475-0148.

**Willhite Seed Company,** P.O. Box 23, Poolville, TX 76076: Free catalog ◆ Seeds. 800-8328-1840. www.willhiteseed.com

**Wooden Shoe Bulb Company,** P.O. Box 127, Mt. Angel, OR 97362: Free catalog ◆ Tulips, daffodils, and other bulbs. 800-711-2006; 503-634-2243 (in OR).

**Wyatt-Quarles Seed Company,** P.O. Box 739, Garner, NC 27529: Free catalog ◆ Seeds. 919-772-4243.

## Shrubs

**Appalachian Gardens,** Box 82, Waynesboro, PA 17268: Free catalog ◆ Trees, shrubs, and rare to unusual plants. 717-762-4312.

**Arborvillage Farm Nursery,** P.O. Box 227, Holt, MO 64048: Catalog $1 ◆ Trees and shrubs. 816-264-3911.

**Vernon Barnes & Son Nursery,** P.O. Box 250, McMinnville, TN 37110: Free catalog ◆ Wildflowers, hedges and shrubs, vines, berry plants, and sassafras. Also flowering, shade, fruit, and nut trees. 615-668-8576.

**Colvos Creek Nursery,** P.O. Box 1512, Vashon Island, WA 98070: Catalog $3 ◆ Trees, shrubs, bamboo, and rare and unusual plants. 206-749-9508. colvoscreek@juno.com

**Emlong Nurseries,** 2671 Marquette Woods Rd., Stevensville, MI 49127: Free catalog ◆ Thornless blackberries, other berry plants, shrubs, flowers, landscaping plants, roses, and dwarf and standard fruit, nut, and ornamental trees. 616-429-3431.

**Farmer Seed & Nursery Company,** 818 NW 4th St., Faribault, MN 55021: Free catalog ◆ Ornamental shrubs and hedges, vegetable seeds, flowering bulbs, fruit and shade trees, berry plants, and roses. 507-334-1623.

**Henry Field's Seed & Nursery,** 415 N. Burnett, Shenandoah, IA 51602: Free catalog ◆ Strawberry and other berry plants, vegetable and flower seeds, hedges, ornamental shrubs, roses, and fruit, nut, and shade trees. 605-665-4491.

**Flower Scent Gardens,** 14820 Moine Rd., Daylestown, OH 44230: Catalog $2 (refundable) ◆ Perennials and shrubs. 330-658-5946.

**Girard Nurseries,** P.O. Box 428, Geneva, OH 44041: Free catalog ◆ Baby evergreen seeds and seedlings, shade trees, and flowering shrubs. 440-466-2881.

**Goodwin Creek Gardens,** P.O. Box 83, Williams, OR 97544: Catalog $1 ◆ Container-grown native American trees, shrubs, and perennial flowers. 541-846-7357.

**Gossler Farms Nursery,** 1200 Weaver Rd., Springfield, OR 97478: Catalog $2 ◆ Magnolias and new, rare, and unusual trees and shrubs that include maples, stewartias, and styrax. 541-746-3922.

**Greer Gardens,** 1280 Goodpasture Island Rd., Eugene, OR 97401: Catalog $3 ◆ Azaleas and rhododendrons, trees, shrubs, Japanese maples, and bonsai. 800-548-0111.

**Kelly Nurseries,** 1708 Morrissey Dr., Bloomington, IL 61704: Free catalog ◆ Heavily rooted fruit and nut trees, landscaping trees, shrubs, ornamentals, berry plants, grapevines, and flowers. 309-334-1623.

**Mellinger's,** 2310 W. South Range Rd., North Lima, OH 44452: Free catalog ◆ Fruit, nut, shade, and ornamental trees. Also gladioli, flowering shrubs, hedges, irises, wildflowers, and gardening equipment. 330-549-9861. www.mellingers.com

**Musser Forests,** P.O. Box 340, Indiana, PA 15701: Free catalog ◆ Evergreen hardwood seedlings and transplants, other trees and shrubs, and ground covers. 800-643-8319.

**National Arbor Day Foundation,** 100 Arbor Ave., Nebraska City, NE 68410: Free catalog ◆ Berry plants, flowering shrubs and trees, evergreens, nut and standard and dwarf fruit trees, and flowering bulbs. (Note: This is an optional membership organization that offers savings to its members.) 402-474-5655.

**Niche Gardens,** 1111 Dawson Rd., Chapel Hill, NC 27516: Catalog $3 ◆ Nursery-propagated wildflowers, trees, shrubs, and perennials. 919-967-0078. www.nichegdn.com

**Northwoods Retail Nursery,** 27635 S. Oglesvy Rd., Canby, OR 97013: Free catalog ◆ Shrubs, vines, and ornamental trees. 503-651-5432.

**The Nursery,** Hwy. 82, P.O. Box 130, Ty Ty, GA 31795: Free catalog ◆ Fruits, nuts, berries, bulbs, trees, and shrubs. 800-972-2101.

**Roslyn Nursery,** 211 Burrs Ln., Dix Hills, NY 11746: Catalog $3 ◆ Rhododendrons, hardy shrubs, trees, and perennials. 516-643-9347. www.cris.com/~Roslyn

**Savage Farms Nursery,** 6255 Beersheba Hwy., McMinnville, TN 37110: Free catalog ◆ Flowering trees and shrubs, roses, evergreens, berry plants, and gardening supplies. Also fruit and shade trees. 615-668-8902.

**R.H. Shumway Seedsman,** P.O. Box 1, Graniteville, SC 29829: Free catalog ◆ Ornamental shrubs and plants, berry plants, fruit trees, roses, seeds and bulbs, and gardening supplies. 803-737-0399.

**Stark Brothers,** Nurseries & Orchards Company, P.O. Box 10, Louisiana, MO 63353: Free catalog ◆ Fruit trees, berry and landscaping plants, shrubs, and garden supplies. 800-775-6415.

**Tripple Brook Farm,** 37 Middle Rd., Southampton, MA 01073: Catalog 50¢ ◆ Bamboo plants, exotic fruits, trees, perennials, and shrubs. 413-527-4626.

**Wildflower Nursery,** 1680 Hwy. 25-70, Marshall, NC 28753: Free catalog ◆ Shrubs. 704-656-2723.

## Terrariums

**Carolina Exotic Gardens,** Rt. 5, Box 283-A, Greenville, NC 27834: Catalog $1 ◆ Carnivorous plants, seeds, terrarium plants, and soil. 919-758-2600.

**Kartuz Greenhouses,** 1408 Sunset Dr., Vista, CA 92083: Catalog $2 ◆ Gesneriads, begonias, miniature terrariums, and unusual tropical plants. 760-941-3613.

**Peter Pauls Nurseries,** 4665 Chapin Rd., Canandaigua, NY 14424: Free catalog ◆ Woodland terrarium and carnivorous plants. 716-394-7397. www.peterpauls.com

## Trees

**Ames Orchard & Nursery,** 18292 Wildlife Rd., Rt. 5, Box 194, Fayetteville, AR 72701: Free information ◆ Apple, pear, and peach trees. 800-443-0283.

**Appalachian Gardens,** Box 82, Waynesboro, PA 17268: Free catalog ◆ Trees, shrubs, and rare to unusual plants. 717-762-4312.

**Arborvillage Farm Nursery,** P.O. Box 227, Holt, MO 64048: Catalog $1 ◆ Trees and shrubs. 816-264-3911.

**Vernon Barnes & Son Nursery,** P.O. Box 250, McMinnville, TN 37110: Free catalog ◆ Wildflowers, hedges and shrubs, vines, berry plants, and sassafras, flowering, shade, fruit, and nut trees. 615-668-8576.

**Bear Creek Nursery,** P.O. Box 41175, Northport, WA 99157: Catalog $1 ◆ Fruits, nuts, and old apples. 509-732-6219.

**Boston Mountain Nurseries,** 20189 N. Hwy. 71, Mountainburg, AR 72946: Catalog 50¢ ◆ Berry plants, grapevines, and fruit trees. 501-369-2007.

**Burford Brothers,** Rt. 1, Nursery, Monroe, VA 24574: Catalog $2 ◆ Modern and antique apples. 804-929-4950.

**Burnt Ridge Nursery & Orchards,** 432 Burnt Ridge Rd., Onalaska, WA 98570: Free brochure with long SASE ◆ Disease-resistant fruit and nut trees and native plants. 360-985-2873. www.carow-ww.com/brnursery

**C & O Nursery,** P.O. Box 116, Wenatchee, WA 98807: Free catalog ◆ Apple, peach, apricot, cherry, and pear trees. 800-232-2636; 509-662-7164 (in WA). www.c-onursery.com

**Carino Nurseries,** P.O. Box 538, Indiana, PA 15701: Free catalog ◆ Christmas trees, seedlings, and transplants. 800-223-7075. www.carinonurseries.com

**Classical Fruit,** 8831 AL Hwy. 157, Moulton, AL 35650: Free catalog ◆ Antique and new varieties of fruit trees from local and worldwide sources. 256-974-8813.

**Colvos Creek Nursery,** P.O. Box 1512, Vashon Island, WA 98070: Catalog $3 ◆ Trees, shrubs, bamboo, and rare and unusual plants. 206-749-9508. colvoscreek@juno.com

**Cumberland Valley Nurseries Inc.,** P.O. Box 471, McMinnville, TN 37110: Free catalog ◆ Fruit trees. 800-492-0022; 615-668-4153 (in TN).

**Datil Mountain Evergreen,** White House Canyon, Datil, NM 87821: Free information ◆ Supplies for sprouting, growing, and transplanting trees. 800-343-2313.

**Digging Dog Nursery,** P.O. Box 471, Albion, CA 95410: Catalog $3 ◆ Grasses, vines, trees, perennials, and shrubs. 707-937-1130.

**Edible Landscaping,** P.O. Box 77, Afton, VA 22920: Catalog $1 ◆ Dwarf citrus trees. 800-524-4156; 804-361-9134 (in VA). www.EAT-IT.com

**Emlong Nurseries,** 2671 Marquette Woods Rd., Stevensville, MI 49127: Free catalog ◆ Thornless blackberries and other berry plants. Also shrubs, flowers, landscaping plants, roses, and dwarf and standard fruit, nut, and ornamental trees. 616-429-3431.

**Fairweather Gardens,** Box 330, Greenwich, NJ 08323: Catalog $3 ◆ Trees and shrubs. 609-451-6261.

**Famous & Historic Trees,** 8701 Old Kings Rd., Jacksonville, FL 32219: Free information ◆ Tree seedlings from historic sites. 800-320-TREE; 904-765-0727 (in FL). www.amfor.org/fht

**Farmer Seed & Nursery Company,** 818 NW 4th St., Faribault, MN 55021: Free catalog ◆ Fruit and shade trees, vegetable seeds, flowering bulbs, ornamental shrubs and hedges, berry plants, and roses. 507-334-1623.

**Henry Field's Seed & Nursery,** 415 N. Burnett, Shenandoah, IA 51602: Free catalog ◆ Berry plants, hedges, ornamental shrubs, and roses. Also dwarf, standard, and seedling apple trees and fruit, nut, and shade trees. 605-665-4491.

**Flickingers' Nursery,** P.O. Box 245, Sagamore, PA 16250: Free catalog ◆ Seedlings and transplants. 800-368-7381.

**Frysville Farms,** 300 Frysville Rd., Ephrata, PA 17522: Free catalog ◆ Trees. 800-422-FRYS.

**Gleckler Seedmen,** 104 Meadows Ln., Metamora, OH 43540: Free catalog ◆ Unusual seed varieties. 419-644-2211.

**Gurney Seed & Nursery Company,** 110 Capitol St., Yankton, SD 57079: Free catalog ◆ Seeds, bulbs, and semi-dwarf and standard varieties of apple trees. 605-665-1671.

**Girard Nurseries,** P.O. Box 428, Geneva, OH 44041: Free catalog ◆ Baby evergreen seeds and seedlings, shade trees, and flowering shrubs. 440-466-2881.

**Goodwin Creek Gardens,** P.O. Box 83, Williams, OR 97544: Catalog $1 ◆ Container-grown native American trees, shrubs, and perennial flowers. 541-846-7357.

**Gossler Farms Nursery,** 1200 Weaver Rd., Springfield, OR 97478: Catalog $2 ◆ Magnolias and new, rare, and unusual trees and shrubs that include maples, stewartias, and styrax. 541-746-3922.

**Greer Gardens,** 1280 Goodpasture Island Rd., Eugene, OR 97401: Catalog $3 ◆ Azaleas and rhododendrons, trees, shrubs, Japanese maples, and bonsai. 800-548-0111.

**Grimo Nut Nursery,** RR 3, Niagara-on-the-Lake, Ontario, Canada L0S 1J0: Catalog $2 (refundable) ◆ Grafted and seed varieties of nut trees. 905-935-6887.

**Gurney Seed & Nursery Company,** 110 Capitol St., Yankton, SD 57079: Free catalog ◆ Semi-dwarf and standard varieties of apple trees. 605-665-1671.

**Harmony Farm Supply & Nursery,** 3244 Hwy. 116, No. A, Sebastopol, CA 95472: Catalog $2 (refundable) ◆ Miniature and standard size fruit and nut trees. 707-823-9125.

**Hollydale Nursery,** P.O. Box 69, Pelham, TN 37366: Free list ◆ Fruit trees. 800-222-3026; 615-467-3600 (in TN).

**Ison's Nursery,** P.O. Box 190, Brooks, GA 30205: Free catalog ◆ Muscadine grapevines, berry plants, and apple, pear, fig, peach, walnut and pecan trees. 800-733-0324.

**Johnson Nursery,** Rt. 5, Box 29-J, Ellijay, GA 30540: Free catalog ◆ Strawberry plants, grapevines, and apple, plum, pear, cherry, apricot, walnut, and almond trees. Also orchard supplies, tools and accessories, and books. 888-276-3187. www.johnsonnursery.com

**Kelly Nurseries,** 1708 Morrissey Dr., Bloomington, IL 61704: Free catalog ◆ Heavily rooted fruit and nut trees, landscaping trees, shrubs, ornamentals, berry plants, grapevines, and flowers. 309-334-1623.

**Lawson's Nursery,** 2730 Yellow Creek Rd., Ball Ground, GA 30107: Free list ◆ Antique apple trees. 770-893-2141.

**Henry Leuthardt Nurseries,** Box 666, East Moriches, NY 11940: Free catalog ◆ Dwarf fruit trees that grow full-size fruit. 516-878-1387.

**Lychee Woods,** 721 SE 9th St., Fort Lauderdale, FL 33316: Free catalog ◆ Rare tropical fruits for backyard growing. 954-728-8089.

**Earl May Seeds & Nursery Company,** 208 N. Elm St., Shenandoah, IA 51603: Free catalog ◆ Flowering shrubs, berry plants, roses, and seeds for vegetables and fruit. Also fruit, nut, shade, and ornamental trees. 712-246-1020.

**Mellinger's,** 2310 W. South Range Rd., North Lima, OH 44452: Free catalog ◆ Fruit, nut, shade, and ornamental trees. Also gladioli, flowering shrubs, hedges, irises, wildflowers, and gardening equipment. 330-549-9861. www.mellingers.com

**J.E. Miller Nurseries,** 5060 W. Lake Rd., Canandaigua, NY 14424: Free catalog ◆ Berry plants, grapevines, spring and fall varieties of semi-dwarf hybrid antique apples, and other fruit and nut trees. 800-836-9630.

**Musser Forests,** P.O. Box 340, Indiana, PA 15701: Free catalog ◆ Evergreen hardwood seedlings and transplants, other trees and shrubs, and ground covers. 800-643-8319.

**National Arbor Day Foundation,** 100 Arbor Ave., Nebraska City, NE 68410: Free catalog ◆ Flowering trees and shrubs, shade and ornamental trees, evergreens, and fruit trees. (Note: This is an optional membership organization that offers savings to its members.) 402-474-5655.

**Niche Gardens,** 1111 Dawson Rd., Chapel Hill, NC 27516: Catalog $3 ◆ Nursery-propagated wildflowers, trees, shrubs, and perennials. 919-967-0078. www.nichegdn.com

**Nolin River Nut Tree Nursery,** 797 Port Wooden Rd., Upton, KY 42784: Free price list ◆ Grafted or budded walnut, pecan, chestnut, heartnut, and butternut trees. 502-369-8551.

**Northwoods Retail Nursery,** 27635 S. Oglesby Rd., Canby, OR 97013: Free catalog ◆ Growing stock for figs, persimmons, kiwis, Asian pears, passion fruit, and pomegranates. 503-651-5432.

**The Nursery,** Hwy. 82, P.O. Box 130, Ty Ty, GA 31795: Free catalog ◆ Fruits, nuts, berries, bulbs, trees, and shrubs. 800-972-2101.

**Oikos Tree Crops,** P.O. Box 19425, Kalamazoo, MI 49019: Free information ◆ Trees and growing stock for nuts and native fruits and exotic plants. 616-624-6233.

**Pacific Tree Farms,** 4301 Lynnwood Dr., Chula Vista, CA 92010: Catalog $2 ◆ Miniature trees, genetic dwarf avocados, and exotic ornamentals. 619-402-2400.

**Patrick's Nursery,** P.O. Box 130, Ty Ty, GA 31795: Free catalog ◆ Vegetable seeds, fruit and nut trees, berry plants, and grapevines. 800-972-2101.

**Peaceful Valley Farm Supply,** P.O. Box 2209, Grass Valley, CA 95945: Catalog $2 (refundable) ◆ Miniature fruit and nut trees, tools, propagation supplies, seeds, and farming equipment. 916-272-4769.

**Pikes Peak Nurseries,** Box 75, Penn Run, PA 15765: Free catalog ◆ Evergreen and deciduous seedlings, transplants, and nut trees. 412-463-7747.

**Raintree Nursery,** 393 Butts Rd., Morton, WA 98356: Free information ◆ Asian pear trees. 360-496-6400.

**Rocky Meadow Nursery,** 360 Rocky Meadow Rd., New Salisbury, IN 47161: Catalog $1 ◆ Pear, plum, and dwarf and semi-dwarf apple trees. Also grafting supplies. 812-347-2213.

**Savage Farms Nursery,** 6255 Beersheba Hwy., McMinnville, TN 37110: Free catalog ◆ Flowering trees and shrubs, roses, evergreens, berry plants, gardening supplies, and fruit and shade trees. 615-668-8902.

**Shady Oaks Nursery,** P.O. Box 708, Waseca, MN 56093: Free list ◆ Ferns, shrubs, perennials, and wildflowers. 800-504-8006. www.shadyoaks.com

**Sonoma Antique Apple Nursery,** 4395 Westside Rd., Healdsburg, CA 95448: Catalog $2 ◆ Old-time apple and pear trees on semi-dwarf root stocks. 707-433-6420.

**Southmeadow Fruit Gardens,** 10603 Cleveland Ave., P.O. Box 211, Baroda, MI 49101: Free information ◆ Apples, rare grapes and gooseberries, mediars, nectarines, pears, peaches, cherries, plums, apricots, currants, quince, other trees, and shrubs. 616-422-2411. SMFRUIT@AOL.COM

**Spring Valley Nursery,** 11096 Spring Valley Ln., Delaplane, VA 22025: Free catalog ◆ Antique apple trees. 540-364-3160.

**Stark Brothers,** Nurseries & Orchards Company, P.O. Box 10, Louisiana, MO 63353: Free catalog ◆ Fruit trees, berry and landscaping plants, and garden supplies. 800-775-6415.

**TEC Trees,** P.O. Box 539, Osseo, MN 55369: Free catalog ◆ Seedlings and transplants.

**Trees on the Move Inc.,** P.O. Box 462, Cranbury, NJ 08512: Free information ◆ Rare, unusual, native, and exotic trees and shrubs. 609-395-1366.

**Tripple Brook Farm,** 37 Middle Rd., Southampton, MA 01073: Catalog 50¢ ◆ Bamboo plants, exotic fruits, trees, perennials, and shrubs. 413-527-4626.

**Twombly Nursery,** 163 Barn Hill Rd., Monroe, CT 06468: Catalog $4 ◆ Dwarf conifer miniatures, rare and unusual plants, and trees. 203-261-2133.

**Waynesboro Nurseries,** P.O. Box 987, Waynesboro, VA 22980: Free list of retail sources ◆ Ornamentals and dwarf and standard antique apple, fruit and nut, flowering, and shade trees. 800-868-8676; 540-946-3814 (in VA). www.waynesboronurseries.com

**Wayside Gardens,** 1 Garden Ln., Hodges, SC 29695: Free catalog ◆ Container-grown trees ready for transplanting. 800-845-1124. www.waysidegardens.com

**Bob Wells Nursery,** P.O. Box 606, Lindale, TX 75771: Free catalog ◆ Fruit, nut, and shade trees. Also berries, grapes, muscadines, roses, ornamentals, and flowering shrubs. 903-882-3550.

**Western Maine Nurseries,** One Evergreen Dr., Fryeburg, ME 04037: Free catalog ◆ Evergreen trees. 800-447-4745; 207-935-2161 (in ME).

**Wildflower Nursery,** 1680 Hwy. 25-70, Marshall, NC 28753: Free catalog ◆ Evergreens. 704-656-2723.

**Womack's Nursery Company,** Rt. 1, Box 80, De Leon, TX 76444: Free catalog ◆ Fruit, nut, and shade and flowering trees. Also roses and other nursery stock. (Note: Nursery stock is adapted for planting in southern states.) 817-893-6497.

## Vegetable Plants & Seeds

**Alfrey Seeds,** P.O. Box 415, Knoxville, TN 37901: List $3 ◆ Pepper seeds.

**The Bethlehem Seed Company,** P.O. Box 1351, Bethlehem, PA 18018: Free information ◆ Bulbs and seed for vegetables, grass, and flowers. 610-691-6697.

**Brown's Omaha Plant Farms Inc.,** P.O. Box 787, Omaha, TX 75571: Catalog 25¢ ◆ Onion, cauliflower, cabbage, broccoli, and brussels sprouts plants. 903-884-2421.

**W. Atlee Burpee & Company,** 300 Park Ave., Warminster, PA 18974: Free catalog ◆ Sweet potato slips. 800-888-1447. www.burpee.com

**Cross Country Nurseries,** P.O. Box 170, Rosemont, NJ 08556: Free information ◆ Chile pepper plants. 908-996-4646. www.chileplants.com

**Delegeane Garlic Farms,** P.O. Box 2561, Yountville, Napa Valley, CA 94599: Free brochure ◆ Garlic cloves for planting. 800-726-6692.

**Dixondale Farms,** P.O. Box 127, Carrizo Springs, TX 78834: Free information ◆ Onion plants. 830-876-2430.

**Evergreen Y.H. Enterprises,** P.O. Box 17538, Anaheim, CA 92817: Catalog $2 (refundable) ◆ Oriental vegetable seeds. 714-637-5769. EESeeds@aol.com

**Fedco Seeds,** P.O. Box 520, Waterville, ME 04903: Catalog $2 ◆ Heirloom hybrid vegetable and herb seeds. 207-873-7333.

**Filaree Farm,** 182 Conconully Hwy., Okanogan, WA 98840: Catalog $2 ◆ Over 100 strains of certified organic seed garlic. 509-422-6940. www.quikpage/F/filaree

**Fisher's Garden Store,** P.O. Box 236, Belgrade, MT 59714: Free catalog ◆ Vegetable and flower seeds for high altitude gardening and short growing seasons. 406-388-6052.

**Fred's Plant Farm,** 4589 Ralston Rd., Martin, TN 38237: Free information ◆ Sweet potato seeds and plants. 800-550-2575.

**The Gourmet Gardener,** 8650 College Blvd., Overland Park, KS 66210: Catalog $2 ◆ Herb, vegetable, and edible flower seeds from around the world. 913-345-0490. www.gourmetgardener.com

**Gurney Seed & Nursery Company,** 110 Capitol St., Yankton, SD 57079: Free catalog ◆ Sweet potato slips and ginger rhizomes. 605-665-1671.

**Hardscrabble Enterprises Inc.,** P.O. Box 1124, Franklin, WV 26807: Catalog $4 ◆ Grow-your-own Shiitake mushroom kits, other mushroom-growing supplies, and spawn. 304-358-2921.

**Herban Garden,** 5002 2nd St., Rainbow, CA 92028: Catalog $1 ◆ Herbs, vegetables, and everlastings. 619-723-2967.

**Illinois Foundation Seeds,** Box 722, Champaign, IL 61824: Free price list ◆ Seeds for sweet corn. 217-485-6260.

**J.W. Jung Seed Company,** 335 High St., Randolph, WI 53957: Free catalog ◆ Sweet potato slips. 414-326-4100.

**Lockhart Seeds Inc.,** P.O. Box 1361, Stockton, CA 92505: Free catalog ◆ Asparagus cultivars and hybrids and vegetables. 209-466-4401.

**Omaha Plant Farms,** Box 787, Omaha, TX 75571: Free information ◆ Sweet Texas onion plants. 903-884-2421.

**Piedmont Plant Company,** P.O. Box 424, Albany, GA 31703: Free catalog ◆ Field-grown vegetable plants. 800-541-5185. piedmont@surfsouth.com

**Redwood City Seed Company,** P.O. Box 361, Redwood City, CA 94064: Catalog $1 ◆ Herb and vegetable seeds from worldwide sources. 650-325-7333. www.ecoseeds.com

**Ronniger's Seed & Potato Company,** Box 1838, Orting, WA 98360: Catalog $1 ◆ Traditional, heirloom, European strains, and hard-to-find seed potatoes. 360-893-8782.

**Roswell Seed Company Inc.,** P.O. Box 725, Roswell, NM 88202: Free price list with long SASE ◆ Chili pepper seed. 505-622-7701.

**Seeds Blüm,** HC 33, Idaho City Stage, Boise, ID 83706: Catalog $3 ◆ Seed potatoes. 800-528-3658.

**Seedway Inc.,** 1225 Zeager Rd., Elizabethtown, PA 17022: Free catalog ◆ Vegetable seeds. 800-952-7333. www.seedway.com

**Shady Acres Herb Farm,** 7815 Hwy. 212, Chaska, MN 55318: Free list with long SASE ◆ Seeds for herbs, wildflowers, everlastings, and vegetables. 612-466-3391.

**R.H. Shumway Seedsman,** P.O. Box 1, Graniteville, SC 29829: Free catalog ◆ Non-hybrid vegetable seeds and sweet potato slips. 803-737-0399.

**South Carolina Foundation Seed Association,** 1162 Cherry Rd., Clemson University, Clemson, SC 29634: List $1 (refundable) ◆ Sweet potato plants and seed for growing vegetables. 864-656-2520.

**Steele Plant Company,** Gleason, TN 38229: Free catalog with two 1st class stamps ◆ Sweet potato, brussels sprouts, onion, cabbage, cauliflower, and broccoli plants. 901-648-5476.

**Stokes Tropicals,** P.O. Box 9868, New Iberia, LA 70562: Catalog $4 ◆ Ginger plants, fertilizer, and ginger-growing kits. Also banana, bromeliads, heliconias, plumerias, and other plants. 800-624-9706; 318-365-6998 (in LA). www.stokestropicals.com

**Sunrise Enterprises-Oriental Seed Catalog,** P.O. Box 1960, Chesterfield, VA 23832: Catalog $2 ◆ Oriental vegetable seeds. 804-796-6735.

**Thogmartin Farm,** 8830 Reche Canyon Rd., Colton, CA 92324: Free information ◆ Garlic for planting.

**Tomato Growers Supply Company,** P.O. Box 2237, Fort Myers, FL 33902: Free catalog ◆ Seeds for growing tomatoes and peppers. Also books and other gardening supplies. 941-768-1119. www.tomatogrowers.com

**Totally Tomatoes,** P.O. Box 1626, Augusta, GA 30903: Free catalog ◆ Tomato seeds. 706-663-0016.

**Otis Twilley Seed Company,** P.O. Box 65, Trevose, PA 19055: catalog $1 ◆ Vegetable and flower seeds. 800-622-7333.

## Wildflowers & Native Plants

**Vernon Barnes & Son Nursery,** P.O. Box 250, McMinnville, TN 37110: Free catalog ◆ Wildflowers, nut and sassafras trees, hedges, vines, and berry plants. 615-668-8576.

**Blossom Farm,** Johnny Cake Ln., Greenville, NY 12083: Free information ◆ Assorted wildflower seeds and individual seed packets. 518-966-5722.

**Boothe Hill Wildflowers,** 23 B Boothe Hill, Chapel Hill, NC 27514: Catalog $1 ◆ Wildflower seeds and plants. 919-967-4091.

**Cattail Meadows Ltd.,** P.O. Box 39391, Solon, OH 44139: Catalog $1 ◆ Nursery-propagated wildflowers and companion perennials.

**Crownsville Nursery,** P.O. Box 797, Crownsville, MD 21032: Catalog $2 (minimum order $25) ◆ Ferns, wildflowers, azaleas, ornamental grasses, and perennials. 410-923-2212.

**Earthly Goods Ltd.,** P.O. Box 614, Albany, IN 47151: Free catalog ◆ Wildflower seeds and mixtures. Also grass seeds. 812-944-2903. www.earthlygoods.com

**Forestfarm,** 990 Tetherow Rd., Williams, OR 97544: Catalog $3 ◆ Native and unusual ornamental American plants, shrubs, and trees. 541-846-7269.

**The Fragrant Path,** P.O. Box 328, Fort Calhoun, NE 68023: Catalog $2 ◆ Seeds for prairie wildflowers. Also grasses, ferns, trees, shrubs, and climbing plants.

**Gardens of the Blue Ridge,** P.O. Box 10, Pineola, NC 28662: Catalog $3 (refundable) ◆ Wildflower seeds, ferns, trees, plants, shrubs, and bulbs. 704-733-2417.

**Good Hollow Greenhouse & Herbarium,** 50 Slaterock Mill Rd., Taft, TN 38488: Catalog $1 ◆ Herb plants and dried herbs, perennials, wildflowers, scented geraniums, essential oils and potpourris, teas, and spices. 615-433-7640.

**Green Horizons,** 145 Scenic Hill Rd., Kerrville, TX 78028: Free brochure ◆ Texas wildflower seeds and books. 210-257-5141.

**Ion Exchange,** 1878 Old Mission Dr., Harpers Ferry, IA 52146: Free brochure ◆ Wildflower seeds. 800-291-2143; 319-535-7231 (in IA).

**Las Pilitas Nursery,** Las Pilitas Rd., Santa Margarita, CA 93453: Catalog $6 ◆ Native plants and seeds from California. 805-438-5992.

**Mellinger's,** 2310 W. South Range Rd., North Lima, OH 44452: Free catalog ◆ Fruit, nut, shade, and ornamental trees. Also gladioli, flowering shrubs, hedges, irises, wildflowers, and gardening equipment. 330-549-9861. www.mellingers.com

**Midwest Wildflowers,** P.O. Box 64, Rockton, IL 61072: Catalog $1 ◆ Woodland wildflowers.

**Moon Mountain Wildflowers,** P.O. Box 725, Carpinteria, CA 93014: Catalog $3 ◆ Wildflower seeds. 805-684-2565. ssseeds@silcom.com

**Native Gardens,** 5737 Fisher Ln., Greenback, TN 37742: Catalog $2 ◆ Native wildflowers, shrubs, vines, and trees of the Eastern United States. 423-856-0220.

**Natural Gardening Company,** 217 San Anselmo Ave., San Anselmo, CA 94960: Free catalog ◆ Beneficial insects, organic gardening supplies, pest controls, drip irrigation equipment, and wildflower seeds. 415-456-5060.

**New England Wildflower Society,** 180 Hemenway Rd., Framingham, MA 01701: Free catalog with long SASE and two 1st class stamps ◆ Wildflower seeds native to New England. 508-877-7630.

**Niche Gardens,** 1111 Dawson Rd., Chapel Hill, NC 27516: Catalog $3 ◆ Nursery-propagated wildflowers, perennials, trees, and shrubs. 919-967-0078. www.nichegdn.com

**Oakridge Nurseries,** P.O. Box 182, East Kingston, NH 03827: Catalog $1 (refundable) ◆ Ferns and native wildflowers. 603-642-8227.

**Pine Ridge Gardens,** 832 Sycamore Rd., London, AR 72847: Catalog $1 ◆ Nursery-propagated wildflowers, hostas, and unusual ornamentals. 501-293-4359.

**Plants of the Southwest,** Rt. 6, Box 11A, Santa Fe, NM 87501: Catalog $3.50 ◆ Wildflowers and native plants from the southwest. 800-788-7333; 505-438-8888 (in NM). www.plantsofthesouthwest.com

**Prairie Moon Nursery,** Rt. 3, Box 163, Winona, MN 55987: Catalog $2 ◆ Plants and seeds for prairie wildflowers and grasses. 507-452-1362.

**Prairie Nursery,** P.O. Box 306, Westfield, WI 53964: Catalog $3 ◆ Plants and seeds for prairie wildflowers and grasses. 608-296-3679.

**The Primrose Path,** RD 2, Box 110, Scottdale, PA 15683: Catalog $2 ◆ Alpine and woodland plants. 412-887-6756.

**Putney Nursery Inc.,** Rt. 5, Putney, VT 05346: Catalog $1 (refundable) ◆ Wildflowers, ferns, herbs, perennials, orchids, and gardening supplies. 802-387-5577.

**Clyde Robin Seed Catalog,** 3670 Enterprise Ave., Hayward, CA 94545: Catalog $2 ◆ Wildflower seeds, trees, and shrubs. 510-785-0425.

**Shady Acres Herb Farm,** 7815 Hwy. 212, Chaska, MN 55318: Free list with long SASE ◆ Herbs, wildflowers, everlastings, and vegetables. 612-466-3391.

**Shady Oaks Nursery,** P.O. Box 708, Waseca, MN 56093: Free list ◆ Ferns, shrubs, perennials, and wildflowers. 800-504-8006. www.shadyoaks.com

**Sunlight Gardens,** 174 Golden Ln., Andersonville, TN 37705: Catalog $3 ◆ Nursery-grown wildflowers for the north and south, planting in the sun or shade, or for wet and dry locations. 615-494-8237.

**T.D. Field Ferns & Wildflowers,** 395 Newington Rd., Newington, NH 03801: Free catalog ◆ Wildflowers, hardy ferns, native lilies, bulbs, and perennials. 603-436-0457.

**Vermont Wildflower Farm,** Ferry Road Business Center, Charlotte, VT 05445: Free catalog ◆ Seeds for wildflowers, annuals, and perennial flowers. 802-424-1165.

**Westview Herb Farm,** P.O. Box 3462, Poughkeepsie, NY 12603: Free catalog ◆ Herb and wildflower seeds. 914-462-3534.

**Wild Earth Nursery,** 49 Mead Ave., Freehold, NJ 07728: Catalog $2 (refundable) ◆ Propagated wildflowers, ferns, and grasses. 908-308-9777.

**Wildflower Nursery,** 1680 Hwy. 25-70, Marshall, NC 28753: Free catalog ◆ Wild native flowering plants. 704-656-2723.

**Wildseed Farms,** P.O. Box 3000, 425 Wildflower Hills, Fredericksburg, TX 78624: Catalog $2 ◆ Wildflower seeds. 800-848-0078. www.wildseedfarms.com

**Woodlanders Inc.,** 1128 Collerton Ave., Aiken, SC 29801: Catalog $2 ◆ Native and wildlife-attracting plants. 803-648-7522.

## GAZEBOS & OTHER GARDEN STRUCTURES

**Apollo Plastics,** 4006 Meridian St., Bellingham, WA 98226: Free brochure ◆ Hot tubs, jet baths, and gazebos. 360-738-1748.

**BowBends,** P.O. Box 900, Bolton, MA 01740: Brochure $3 ◆ Easy-to-assemble gazebos, bridges, and arbors. 800-518-6471.

**Caldera Spas,** 1080 W. Bradley Ave., El Cajon, CA 92020: Free information ◆ Build-it-yourself gazebo kits. 800-669-1881.

**California Redwood Association,** 405 Enfrente Dr., Ste. 200, Novato, CA 94949: Free information with long SASE ◆ Easy-to-build redwood gazebos. 415-382-0662. www.calredwood.org

**City Visions Inc.,** 311 Seymour St., Lansing, MI 48933: Catalog $3 ◆ Classical and Victorian-style garden houses. 517-372-3385.

**Cumberland Woodcraft Company Inc.,** P.O. Drawer 609, Carlisle, PA 17013: Catalog $5 ◆ Gazebo kits in 10-, 12-, and 16-foot diameters. 717-243-0063. www.pa.net/cwc

**Dalton Pavilions Inc.,** 20 Commerce Dr., Telford, PA 18969: Catalog $5 ◆ Prefabricated cedar gazebos and pavilions. 800-532-5866; 215-721-1492 (in PA).

**Gazebo Woodcrafters,** P.O. Box 187, Bellingham, WA 98227: Free brochure ◆ Easy-to-assemble gazebo kits. 800-634-0463.

**Gazebos Ltd.,** 140 W. Summit St., Milford, MI 48381: Free information ◆ Build-it-yourself gazebo and outdoor enclosure kits. 800-701-6767.

**Hand-y Home Products,** 6400 E. 11 Mile Rd., Warren, MI 48091: Free information ◆ Build-it-yourself gazebo kits. 800-221-1849.

**Kloter Farms Inc.,** 216 West Rd., Ellington, CT 06029: Brochure $3 (request list of retail sources) ◆ Sheds, gazebos, playscapes, and lawn furniture. 800-289-3463; 860-871-1048 (in CT). www.kloterfarms.com

**Leisure Woods Inc.,** P.O. Box 177, Genoa, IL 60135: Free information ◆ Colonial and Victorian-style gazebos. 815-784-2497.

**Litchfield Industries Inc.,** 4 Industrial Dr., Litchfield, MI 49252: Free catalog ◆ Garden shelters. 800-542-5282.

**Old World Gazebos,** 41 N. Business Park, 1033 E. Mt. Pleasant Rd., Evansville, IN 47711: Free catalog ◆ Build-it-yourself gazebo kits. 800-877-3622. www.gazebos.com

**Sun Designs,** P.O. Box 6, Oconomowoc, WI 53066: Plan book $9.95 plus $3.95 postage ◆ Gazebos and garden structures. 414-567-4255.

**Thaxted Cottage,** Gardener, 121 Driscoll Way, Gaithersburg, MD 20878: Catalog $2 ◆ Redwood cottage with trellis sides and built-in seat, Amish-style wheelbarrows, and porch swings. 301-330-6211.

**Vintage Wood Works,** Hwy. 34, Box R, Quinlan, TX 75474: Catalog $2 ◆ Pre-assembled gazebos with bolt-together solid wood panels. 903-356-2158. www.vintagewoodworks.com

**Vixen Hill,** Main St., P.O. Box 389, Elverson, PA 19520: Catalog $4 ◆ Pre-engineered gazebos for easy assembly by non-carpenters. 800-423-2766. www.vixenhill.com

## GENEALOGY

### State Offices & Genealogical Associations

#### ALABAMA

**State of Alabama Archives & History,** 624 Washington Ave., Montgomery, AL 36130. 205-242-4435.

**State of Alabama Genealogical Society,** Samford University Library, American Genealogical Society Depository & Headquarters, 800 Lakeshore Dr., Birmingham, AL 35229. 205-870-2749.

**State of Alabama Historical Association,** P.O. Box 870380, Tuscaloosa, AL 35487.

#### ALASKA

**State of Alaska Archives & Records Management,** Division of Libraries & Archives, Dept. of Education, 141 Willoughby, Juneau, AK 99801. 907-465-2275.

**State of Alaska Genealogical Society,** 7030 Dickerson Dr., Anchorage, AK 99504.

**State of Alaska Historical Society,** P.O. Box 100299, Anchorage, AK 99510. 907-276-1596.

#### ARIZONA

**Arizona Archives & Public Records,** Arizona Library Dept., State Capitol, 1700 W. Washington, Phoenix, AZ 85007. 602-542-3942.

**State of Arizona Genealogical Society,** P.O. Box 42075, Tucson, AZ 85733.

**State of Arizona Historical Society,** 949 E. 2nd St., Tucson, AZ 85719. 520-628-5774.

#### ARKANSAS

**History Commission of Arkansas,** 1 Capitol Mall, Little Rock, AR 72201. 501-682-6900.

**State of Arkansas Genealogical Society,** P.O. Box 908, Hot Springs, AR 71902.

**State of Arkansas Historical Society,** University of Arkansas, Dept. of History, Old Main 416, Fayetteville, AR 72701. 501-575-5884.

#### CALIFORNIA

**State Library of California,** California Section, P.O. Box 942837, Sacramento, CA 94237. 916-654-0176.

**State of California Archives,** Office of the Secretary of State, 1020 O St., Room. 130, Sacramento, CA 95814.

**State of California Genealogical Society,** P.O. Box 77105, San Francisco, CA 94107. 415-777-9936.

**State of California Historical Society,** 2099 Pacific Ave., San Francisco, CA 94109. 415-567-1848.

#### COLORADO

**Colorado Division of Archives & Public Records,** Dept. of Administration, 1313 Sherman St., Denver, CO 80203. 303-866-2358.

**State Library of Colorado,** 201 E. Colfax Ave., Denver, CO 80203. 303-866-6728.

**State of Colorado Genealogical Society,** P.O. Box 9218, Denver, CO 80209.

**State of Colorado Historical Society,** Stephen H. Hart Library, 1300 Broadway, Denver, CO 80203. 303-866-2305.

#### CONNECTICUT

**Connecticut State Archives,** 231 Capitol Ave., Hartford, CT 06106. 860-566-5650.

**State Library of Connecticut,** History & Genealogy Unit, 231 Capitol Ave., Hartford, CT 06106. 302-566-3690.

**State of Connecticut Historical Society,** 1 Elizabeth St., Hartford, CT 06105. 203-236-5621.

**State of Connecticut Society of Genealogists,** P.O. Box 435, Glastonbury, CT 06433. 203-569-0002.

## DELAWARE

**Delaware Historical Society**, 505 Market St., Wilmington, DE 19801. 302-655-7161.

**Delaware State Genealogical Society,** 505 Market St., Wilmington, DE 19801.

**State of Delaware Archives,** Hall of Records, Dover, DE 19901. 302-739-5318.

## DISTRICT OF COLUMBIA

**The Columbia Historical Society,** 1307 New Hampshire Ave. NW, Washington, DC 20036. 202-785-2068.

**District of Columbia Archives,** 1300 Naylor Ct. NW, Washington, DC 20001. 202-727-2054.

## FLORIDA

**Florida Genealogical Society,** P.O. Box 18624, Tampa, FL 33679.

**State Archives of Florida,** Bureau of Archives & Records Management, Division of Library & Information Services, Public Services Section, R.A. Gray Bldg., 500 S. Bronough St., Tallahassee, FL 32399. 904-487-2073.

**State of Florida Genealogical Society,** P.O. Box 10249, Tallahassee, FL 32302.

**State of Florida Historical Society,** University of South Florida Library, P.O. Box 3645, University Station, Gainesville, FL 32601. 813-974-3815.

## GEORGIA

**Georgia Dept. of Archives & History,** Secretary of State, 330 Capitol Ave. SE, Atlanta, GA 30334. 404-656-2350.

**State of Georgia Genealogical Society,** P.O. Box 54575, Atlanta, GA 30308. 404-475-4404.

**State of Georgia Historical Society,** 501 Whittaker St., Savannah, GA 31499. 912-651-2128.

## HAWAII

**Sandwich Islands Genealogy Society,** Hawaii State Library, 478 S. King St., Honolulu, HI 96813.

**State of Hawaii Archives,** Dept. of Accounting & General Services, Iolani Palace Grounds, 478 S. King St., Honolulu, HI 96813. 808-586-0329.

**State of Hawaii Historical Society,** 560 Kawaiahao St., Honolulu, HI 96813. 808-537-6271.

## IDAHO

**State of Idaho Genealogical Society,** 4620 Overland Rd., Boise, ID 83705. 208-384-0542.

**State of Idaho Historical Society,** Library and Archives Division, 450 N. 4th St., Boise, ID 83702. 208-334-2305.

**State of Idaho Historical Society,** Genealogical Library, 450 N. 4th St., Boise, ID 83702. 208-334-2441.

## ILLINOIS

**State of Illinois Archives Division,** Secretary of State, Archives Bldg., Capitol Complex, Springfield, IL 62756. 217-782-4682.

**State of Illinois Genealogical Society,** P.O. Box 2225, Springfield, IL 62791. 217-789-1968.

**State of Illinois Historical Society,** Illinois State Historical Library, Old State Capitol, Springfield, IL 62701. 217-782-4836.

## INDIANA

**State of Indiana Archives,** 140 N. Senate Ave., Indianapolis, IN 46204.

**State of Indiana Genealogical Society,** P.O. Box 10507, Fort Wayne, IN 46852.

**State of Indiana Historical Society**, Indiana State Library & Historical Bldg., P.O. Box 88255, Indianapolis, IN 46202. 317-232-1879.

**State of Indiana Library,** Indiana Division, 140 N. Senate Ave., Indianapolis, IN 46204. 317-232-2537.

## IOWA

**Historical Iowa State Society,** Library-Archives Bureau, Iowa State Historical Bldg., 600 E. Locust, Des Moines, IA 50319. 515-281-3007.

**State of Iowa Archives,** Iowa Historical Bldg., 600 E. Locust, Capitol Complex, Des Moines, IA 50319. 515-281-3007.

**State of Iowa Genealogical Society,** P.O. Box 7735, Des Moines, IA 50322.

## KANSAS

**Kansas State Genealogical Society,** P.O. Box 103, Dodge City, KS 67801. 316-225-1951.

**Kansas State Historical Society,** Reference 6425 SW 6th Ave., Topeka, KS 66615. 913-272-8681.

**State Library of Kansas,** Statehouse, 3rd Floor, Topeka, KS 66612. 913-296-3296.

## KENTUCKY

**Kentucky Historical Society,** 300 Broadway, P.O. Box H, Frankfort, KY 40602. 502-564-3016.

**State Archives of Kentucky,** Kentucky Dept. of Archives & Library, Division of Public Records, 300 Coffee Tree Rd., P.O. Box 537, Frankfort, KY 40602. 502-875-7000.

**State of Kentucky Genealogical Society,** P.O. Box 153, Frankfort, KY 40602. 502-875-4452.

## LOUISIANA

**Genealogical & Historical Society of Louisiana,** P.O. Box 3454, Baton Rouge, LA 70821.

**Le Comité des Archives de la Louisiane,** P.O. Box 44370, Capitol Station, Baton Rouge, LA 70804. 504-355-9906.

**State of Louisiana Archives & Records,** Office of the Secretary of State, P.O. Box 94125, Baton Rouge, LA 70804. 504-922-1206.

## MAINE

**Historical Society of Maine,** L.M.A. Bldg., 485 Congress St., No. 84, Portland, ME 04111. 207-774-1822.

**Maine State Archives,** State House Station, Augusta, ME 04333. 207-289-5795.

**State of Maine Genealogical Society,** P.O. Box 221, Farmington, ME 04938.

## MARYLAND

**Maryland Historical Society,** 201 W. Monument St., Baltimore, MD 21201. 410-685-3750.

**Maryland State Genealogy Society,** 201 W. Monument St., Baltimore, MD 21201. 410-685-3750.

**State Archives of Maryland,** Hall of Records Bldg., 350 Rowe Blvd., Annapolis, MD 21401. 410-974-3914.

## MASSACHUSETTS

**Commonwealth of Massachusetts Archives,** Reference Desk, 220 Morrissey Blvd., Boston, MA 02125. 617-727-2816.

**The Massachusetts Society of Genealogists,** P.O. Box 215, Ashland, MA 01721.

**State of Massachusetts Historical Society,** 1154 Boylston St., Boston, MA 02215. 617-536-1608.

## MICHIGAN

**Michigan Genealogical Council,** P.O. Box 80953, Lansing, MI 48908.

**Michigan Historical Society,** 2117 Washtenaw Ave., Ann Arbor, MI 48104. 313-769-1828.

**Michigan State Archives**, Bureau of History, State Dept., 717 W. Allegan, Lansing, MI 48918. 517-373-1408.

## MINNESOTA

**Minnesota Historical Society Research Center,** 345 Kellogg Blvd. West, St. Paul, MN 55102. 612-296-2143.

**State of Minnesota Historical Society,** 345 Kellogg Blvd. West, St. Paul, MN 55102. 612-296-2143.

**State of Minnesota Genealogical Society,** P.O. Box 16069, St. Paul, MN 55116. 612-645-3671.

## MISSISSIPPI

**Genealogical Society of Mississippi,** P.O. Box 5301, Jackson, MS 39296.

**Mississippi Archives & History Department,** Archives & Library Division, P.O. Box 571, Jackson, MS 39205. 601-359-6876.

**Mississippi History and Genealogy Association,** 618 Avalon Rd., Jackson, MS 39206. 601-362-3079.

## MISSOURI

**Historical Society of Missouri,** 1020 Lowry St., Columbia, MO 65201. 314-882-7083.

**Missouri State Archives,** P.O. Box 778, Jefferson City, MO 65102. 314-751-3280.

**Missouri State Genealogical Association,** P.O. Box 833, Columbia, MO 65205.

## MONTANA

**Genealogical Society of Montana,** P.O. Box 555, Chester, MT 59522.

**Montana Historical Society,** Memorial Bldg., 225 N. Roberts St., Helena, MT 59620. 406-444-2716.

**State Library of Montana,** 1515 E. 6th Ave., Helena, MT 59620. 406-444-3004.

**State of Montana Archives,** Montana Historical Society, Memorial Bldg., 225 N. Roberts St., Helena, MT 59620.

## NEBRASKA

**Nebraska State Genealogical Society,** P.O. Box 5608, Lincoln, NE 68505. 402-266-8881.

**State Historical Society of Nebraska,** Archives Division, P.O. Box 82554, Lincoln, NE 68501. 402-471-4771.

## NEVADA

**Nevada Genealogical State Society,** P.O. Box 20666, Reno, NV 89515.

**State of Nevada Historical Society,** 1650 N. Virginia St., Reno, NV 89503. 702-688-1190.

**State of Nevada Library & Archives,** Archives & Records Division, 100 Stewart St., Carson City, NV 89710. 702-687-5210.

## NEW HAMPSHIRE

**New Hampshire Division of Records Management & Archives,** New Hampshire Dept. of State, 71 S. Fruit St., Concord, NH 03301. 603-271-2236.

**New Hampshire Historical Society,** 30 Park St., Concord, NH 03301. 603-225-3381.

**New Hampshire Society of Genealogists,** P.O. Box 633, Exeter, NH 03833. 603-432-8137.

## NEW JERSEY

**New Jersey Genealogical Society,** P.O. Box 1291, New Brunswick, NJ 08903. 201-356-6920.

**New Jersey State Department of Archives,** CN 307, Trenton, NJ 08625. 609-292-6260.

**New Jersey State Library,** Genealogy Section, CN 520, Trenton, NJ 08625. 609-292-6274.

## NEW MEXICO

**New Mexico Archives & Records Center,** 404 Montezuma St., Santa Fe, NM 87501. 505-827-7332.

**New Mexico Historical Society,** P.O. Box 1912, Santa Fe, NM 87504.

**New Mexico State Genealogical Society,** P.O. Box 8283, Albuquerque, NM 87198. 505-256-3217.

## NEW YORK

**New York State Archives,** Dept. of Education, Cultural Education Center, Room 11D40, Albany, NY 12230. 518-474-8955.

**State of New York Genealogical & Biographical Society,** 122 E. 58th St., New York, NY 10022. 212-755-8532.

**State of New York Historical Association,** Fenimore House, West Lake Rd., P.O. Box 800, Cooperstown, NY 13326. 607-547-2533.

## NORTH CAROLINA

**Federation of North Carolina Historical Society,** 109 E. Jones St., Raleigh, NC 27601. 919-733-7305.

**North Carolina State Archives,** Dept. of Cultural Resources, Archives & History Division, State Library Bldg., 109 E. Jones St., Raleigh, NC 27601. 919-733-3952.

**State of North Carolina Genealogical Society,** P.O. Box 1492, Raleigh, NC 27602.

## NORTH DAKOTA

**North Dakota State Historical Society,** State Archives & Historical Research Library, North Dakota Heritage Center, 612 E. Boulevard Ave., Bismarck, ND 58505. 701-224-2091.

**State Library of North Dakota,** Liberty Memorial Bldg., Capital Grounds, Bismarck, ND 58505. 701-224-2091.

## OHIO

**Ohio Historical Society,** Archives & Library Division, Interstate Rt. 71 & 17th Ave., 1982 Velma Ave., Columbus, OH 43211. 614-297-2510.

**State Genealogical Society of Ohio,** Library Section, P.O. Box 2625, Mansfield, OH 44906. 419-522-9077.

**State Library of Ohio,** 65 S. Front St., Columbus, OH 43266. 614-644-6966.

## OKLAHOMA

**Federation of Oklahoma Genealogical Societies,** P.O. Box 26151, Oklahoma City, OK 73157.

**Oklahoma Department of Libraries,** Office of Archives & Records, 200 NE 18th St., Oklahoma City, OK 73105. 405-521-2502.

**Oklahoma Historical Society,** Division of Library Resources, Wiley Post Historical Bldg., 2100 N. Lincoln Blvd., Oklahoma City, OK 73105. 405-521-2491.

## OREGON

**Archives Division of Oregon,** Secretary of State, 800 Summer St. NE, Salem, OR 97310. 503-373-0701.

**Genealogical Forum of Oregon,** Headquarters & Library, 1410 SW Morrison St., Room 812, Portland, OR 97205. 503-227-2398.

**Oregon Historical Society,** 1230 SW Park Ave., Portland, OR 97205. 503-222-1741.

## PENNSYLVANIA

**Pennsylvania Heritage Society,** P.O. Box 146, Laughlintown, PA 15655.

**Pennsylvania Historical & Genealogy Society,** 1300 Locust St., Philadelphia, PA 19107. 215-545-0391.

**Pennsylvania State Archives,** Reference Division, P.O. Box 1206, Harrisburg, PA 17108. 717-783-3281.

## RHODE ISLAND

**Rhode Island State Archives,** 337 Westminster St., Providence, RI 02903. 401-277-2353.

**Rhode Island State Genealogical Society,** 13 Countryside Dr., Cumberland, RI 02864.

**State of Rhode Island Historical Society,** 110 Benevolent St., Providence, RI 02906. 401-331-8575.

## SOUTH CAROLINA

**South Carolina Department of Archives & History,** P.O. Box 11669, Columbia, SC 29211. 803-734-8577.

**South Carolina Historical Society,** 100 Meeting St., Charleston, SC 29401. 803-723-3225.

**State of South Carolina Genealogy Society,** P.O. Box 16355, Greenville, SC 29606.

## SOUTH DAKOTA

**South Dakota Archives,** Cultural Heritage Center, 900 Governors Dr., Pierre, SD 57501. 605-773-3804.

**South Dakota Genealogical Society,** Rt. 2, Box 10, Burke, SD 57523. 605-835-9364.

**State of South Dakota Historical Society,** Cultural Heritage Center, South Dakota Archives, 900 Governors Dr., Pierre, SD 57501. 605-773-3804.

## TENNESSEE

**Tennessee Genealogical Society,** P.O. Box 111249, Memphis, TN 38111. 901-327-3273.

**Tennessee Historical Commission,** Dept. of Environment & Conservation, 701 Broadway, B-30, Nashville, TN 37243. 615-532-1550.

**Tennessee State Archives & Library,** 403 7th Ave. North, Nashville, TN 37243. 615-741-2764.

## TEXAS

**Historical Association of Texas,** 2.306 SRH, University Station, Austin, TX 78712. 512-471-1525.

**State of Texas Genealogy Society,** 2507 Tannehill, Houston, TX 77008. 713-864-6862.

**Texas State Library,** P.O. Box 12927, Capital Station, Austin, TX 78711. 512-463-5463.

### UTAH

**Family History Library of The Church of Jesus Christ of Latter-day Saints,** Genealogical Society of Utah, 35 N. West Temple, Salt Lake City, UT 84150. 801-240-2331.

**Utah Archives & Record Services,** Archives Bldg., State Capitol, Salt Lake City, UT 84114. 801-538-3013.

**Utah Genealogical Association,** P.O. Box 1144, Salt Lake City, UT 84110. 801-262-7263.

**Utah State Historical Society,** 300 Rio Grande, Salt Lake City, UT 84101. 801-533-5808.

### VERMONT

**Genealogy Society of Vermont,** P.O. Box 422, Pittsford, VT 05763. 802-483-2957.

**Historical Society of Vermont,** Pavilion Office Bldg., 109 State St., Montpelier, VT 05609. 802-828-2291.

**State of Vermont Archives,** Office of the Secretary of State, 26 Terrace St., Redstone Bldg., Montpelier, VT 05609. 802-828-2308.

### VIRGINIA

**Historical Society of Virginia,** P.O. Box 7311, Richmond, VA 23211. 804-342-9677.

**Virginia Genealogical Society,** 5001 W. Broad St., Ste. 115, Richmond, VA 23230. 804-285-8954.

**Virginia State Library & Archives,** Genealogy & Archives Section, 11th Street at Capitol Square, Richmond, VA 23219. 804-786-2306.

### WASHINGTON

**State of Washington Historical Society,** Special Collections Division, 315 N. Stadium Way, Tacoma, WA 98403. 206-593-2830.

**Washington State Archives,** Main Office, Division of Archives & Records Management, Office of the Secretary of State, State Archives & Records Center Bldg., 1120 Washington St SE, EA-11, Olympia, WA 98504. 360-586-1492.

**Washington State Genealogical Society,** P.O. Box 1422, Olympia, WA 98507. 360-352-0595.

### WEST VIRGINIA

**Archives & History Division of West Virginia,** The Cultural Center, Capitol Complex, Charleston, WV 25305. 304-348-2277.

**State of West Virginia Genealogy Society,** P.O. Box 249, Elkview, WV 25071.

**West Virginia Genealogical Society,** 5238 Elk River Rd. North, P.O. Box 249, Elkview, WV 25071.

### WISCONSIN

**Genealogy Society of Wisconsin,** P.O. Box 5106, Madison, WI 53705. 378-3006-9405.

**Wisconsin State Historical Society,** 816 State St., Madison, WI 53706. 608-264-6535.

### WYOMING

**Wyoming State Archives,** Research Division, Barrett State Office Bldg., 2301 Capitol Ave., Cheyenne, WY 82002. 307-777-7826.

**Wyoming State Library,** Supreme Court Bldg., 2301 Capitol Ave., Cheyenne, WY 82002. 307-777-7281.

## Retail Sources & Publishers

**Blazon Art Creation,** 3116 N. Federal Hwy., Pompano Beach, FL 33064: Free brochure ◆ Reproduction coats of arms.

**Family Coats of Arms,** Petersen Village, 1576 Mission Dr., Solvang, CA 93463: Free brochure ◆ Handpainted coats of arms, life-size shields, authentic detailed armor, hand-sewn embroideries, and other genealogical remembrances. 805-688-3040.

**French Creek Trading Post,** P.O. Box 822, Kimberton, PA 19442: Free brochure ◆ Gifts and research tools for the genealogist. 610-942-0137.

**Genealogical Publishing Company Inc.,** 1001 N. Calvert St., Baltimore, MD 21202: Free catalog ◆ General reference and how-to books, manuals, directories and finding aids, and state guides. 800-296-6687. www.genealogical.com

**The Genealogical Research Library,** 100 Adelaide St. West, 5th Floor, Toronto, Ontario, Canada M5H 1S3: Free catalog ◆ Reference books, family tree kits, and other information resources about Canadians. 416-360-3929.

**Heritage Books Inc.,** 1540 E. Pointer Ridge Pl., Ste. 207, Bowie, MD 20716: Free catalog ◆ Books on history, genealogy, and Early American life. 301-390-7709. www.heritagebooks.com

**Higginson Books,** 14 Derby Square, Salem, MA 01970: Catalog $3 ◆ Genealogies, how-to guides, and local histories. 978-745-7170.

**HRC Family Coats-of-Arms,** 5577 N. Moccasin Trail, Tucson, AZ 85750: Catalog $1 ◆ Heraldic giftware. 520-529-6899. www.hrc-crest.com

**David Morgan,** 11812 Northcreek Pkwy., Ste. 103, Bothell, WA 98011: Free catalog ◆ Maps of Great Britain for travel or genealogy research. 800-324-4934. www.davidmorgan.com

**National Archives & Records Administration,** Publications Distribution, 7th & Pennsylvania Ave. NW, Washington, DC 20408: Free publications ◆ Aids for Genealogical Research; Using Records in the National Archives for Genealogical Research; Military Service Records in the National Archives of the United States; Select List of Publications; and the National Archives Catalog of Publications. 800-234-8861; 202-501-5235 (in DC area).

**New England Historic Genealogical Society,** The Sales Department, 160 N. Washington St., Boston, MA 02114: Free catalog ◆ Genealogies, histories, reference works, vital records, software, and CD-ROMs. 888-296-3447; 617-624-0341 (in MA). sales@nehgs.org

**Palladium Interactive,** 900 Larkspur Landing Circle, Ste. 295, Larkspur, CA 94939: Free brochure ◆ Genealogy software for making family trees. www.uftree.com

**The Ships Chandler,** Wilmington, VT 05363: Free catalog ◆ Thousands of names from 32 countries in report form, genealogical paintings, plaques, coats of arms, and needlepoints. 802-375-9469. www.coatsofarms.com

**Tuttle Antiquarian Books Inc.,** 28 S. Main St., Rutland, VT 05701: Free catalog ◆ Books on family histories and other miscellany. 802-773-8229. tuttbook@interloc.com

**John F. Walter,** 79-13 67th Dr., Middle Village, NY 11379: Free information ◆ Histories of Union and Confederate Civil War units.

## Software

**Adventures In Ancestry,** 10714 Hepburn Circle, Culver City, CA 90232: Free brochure ◆ Genealogy software for checking background information. 310-842-7442.

**Broderbund Software,** P.O. Box 6125, Novato, CA 94948: Free information ◆ Windows 3.1 and Windows 95 genealogy family tree-maker software. 800-521-6263. www.broderbund.com

**The Church of Jesus Christ of Latter-day Saints,** Salt Lake Distribution Center, 1999 W. 1700 South, Salt Lake City, UT 84104: Free information ◆ DOS and Macintosh and PC genealogy software. 800-537-5950; 801-240-2584 (in UT).

**Expert Software,** 800 Douglas Rd., Executive Tower, 7th Floor, Coral Cables, FL 33134: Free information ◆ DOS and Windows genealogy software. 800-759-2562; 305-567-9990 (in FL).

**Family History Library,** 35 NW Temple St., Salt Lake City, UT 84150: Free information ◆ DOS personal ancestral file software. 800-346-6044; 801-240-2584 (in UT).

**Individual Software Inc.,** 5870 Stoneridge Dr., #1, Pleasanton, CA 94588: Free information ◆ Windows family organizer software. 800-822-3522; 510-734-6767 (in CA).

**Leister Productions,** P.O. Box 289, Mechanicsburg, PA 17055: Free information ◆ Genealogy family tree software for the Macintosh. 717-697-1378. info@LeisterPro.com

**Parsons Technology,** P.O. Box 100, Hiawatha, IA 52233: Free information ◆ Windows family origins software. 800-779-6000. www.parsonstech.com

# GIFTS & GENERAL MERCHANDISE

## Children's Gifts

**Cry Baby Ranch,** 1422 Larimer Square, Denver, CO 80202: Catalog $2 ◆ Children's cowboy-style furniture and clothing. 888-CRY-BABY. www.crybabyranch.com

**Daisy Kingdom Inc.,** 134 NW 8th St., Portland, OR 97210: Catalog $2 ◆ Apparel, bedding, and ready-to-wear clothing or sew-it-yourself kits. 800-234-6688.

**Gifts for Grandkids,** c/o Genesis Direct, Customer Care, 100 Plaza Dr., Secaucus, NJ 07094: Free catalog ◆ Gifts for grandparents to buy grandchildren. 800-873-8263. care@GenesisDirect.com

**Hand in Hand,** Catalogue Center, 100 Plaza Dr., Secaucus, NJ 07094: Free catalog ◆ Teaching toys, travel items, videos, and nursery room furniture that helps nurture, teach, and protect children. 800-872-9745. hihcatalog@aol.com

**Hearth Song,** Mail Processing Center, 6519 N. Galena Rd., P.O. Box 1773, Peoria, IL 61656: Free catalog ◆ Books for children, dollhouse miniatures, toiletries for babies, dolls, party decorations, backyard play structures, art supplies, kites, games, and musical instruments. 800-325-2502.

**Just Pretend,** P.O. Box 887, Naugatuck, CT 06770: Free catalog ◆ Make-believe gifts for children. 800-286-7166.

**Lilly's Kids,** Lillian Corp., Virginia Beach, VA 23479: Free catalog ◆ Games, science sets, art, backyard and outdoor toys, dolls, animal toys, and fun things to do on rainy days and while traveling. 800-285-5555. LVCcustsrv@aol.com

**Metropolitan Museum of Art,** Special Service Office, Middle Village, NY 11381: Free catalog ◆ Books, cassettes, records, cards, games, and toys. 800-662-3397. www.metmuseum.org

**Music in Motion,** P.O. Box 83314, Richardson, TX 75083: Free catalog ◆ Music education and gift catalog for all ages. 800-445-0649. www.music-in-motion.com

**Out of the Woodwork,** 437 Robert E. Lee Dr., Wilmington, NC 28412: Free brochure ◆ Personalized educational gifts for children. 910-792-6882.

**Right Start Catalog,** Right Start Plaza, 5334 Sterling Center Dr., Westlake Village, CA 91361: Catalog $2 ◆ Music and videos, strollers and car seats, swings, crib sets, personal care aids, clothing, bathtime aids, highchairs, and infant, toddler, and pre-school toys and games. 800-548-8531.

**Storybook Heirlooms,** 333 Hatch Dr., Foster City, CA 94404: Free catalog ◆ Clothing and gifts. 800-825-6565.

**Twincerely Yours,** 748 Lake Ave., Clermont, FL 34711: Free catalog with long SASE ◆ Gifts, novelties, and T-shirts for twins and their families. 352-394-5493.

## Miscellaneous Gifts

**ABC Distributing Inc.,** 14445 NE 20th Ln., North Miami, FL 33181: Free catalog ◆ Gifts for men, women, and children. 305-944-3291.

**Accents,** 215 Moody Rd., Enfield, CT 06083: Free catalog ◆ Greeting cards, calendars, and gifts. 800-357-1000.

**Ace Luggage & Gifts,** 2122 Avenue U, Brooklyn, NY 11229: Catalog $2 ◆ Desk sets, leather attaché cases, luggage, wallets, handbags, and other gifts. 800-342-5223; 718-891-9713 (in NY).

**Alfa Color Labs,** 535 W. 135th St., Gardena, CA 90248: Free information ◆ Handcrafted wood music boxes with inlaid ceramic tile and glaze-mounted personalized portraits. 310-532-2532.

**Amazon Drygoods,** 2218 E. 11th St., Davenport, IA 52803: Catalog $7 ◆ Victorian-style clothing, toiletries, books, toys, hats, fans, and garden and home accessories. 800-798-7979. www.amazondrygoods.com

**America's Western Stores,** 2816 S. Ingram Mill Rd., Springfield, MO 65804: Free catalog ◆ Western-style clothing, shoes and boots, and gifts. 800-284-8191.

**American National Parks,** 1100 Hector St., Ste. 105, Conshohocken, PA 19428: Free catalog ◆ Gifts that commemorate American history. 800-821-2903.

**Amish House,** 6420 Rockmeadows, Rockford, MI 49341: Free catalog ◆ Amish-crafted gifts and home furnishings. 616-866-8361.

**Amplestuff,** P.O. Box 116, Bearsville, NY 12409: Free catalog ◆ New and unusual gifts and accessories for full-figured persons. 914-679-3316. amplestuff@aolo.com

**Linda Anderson,** 211 Fairview St., Longmont, CO 80504: Free catalog ◆ Gifts and casual apparel. 800-437-1500.

**Angler's Catalog Company,** P.O. Box 161, Twin Falls, ID 83303: Free catalog ◆ Gifts for the fly fisherman. 800-657-8040; 208-735-8755 (in ID). anglecat@micron.net

**Anheuser-Busch Inc.,** P.O. Box 503015, St. Louis, MO 63150: Free catalog ◆ Heirloom Budweiser and other collectible plates and steins and gifts for men and women. 800-325-9665. www.Budshop.com

**Anticipations by Ross Simons,** 9 Ross Simons Dr., Cranston, RI 02920: Free catalog ◆ Decorative accessories, jewelry, rugs, sterling silver flatware, crystal, furniture, artwork, china, gifts for babies, quilts, and porcelain dinnerware. 800-556-7376; 401-463-3100 (in RI).

**Anyone Can Whistle,** P.O. Box 4407, Kingston, NY 12401: Free catalog ◆ Bird feeders, wind chimes, and musical gifts. 800-435-8863. anyonecan@chimes.com

**Apple Basket Antiques & Gifts,** 867 N. Hanover St., Pottstown, PA 19464: Free catalog ◆ Wrought iron gifts. 800-546-4766; 610-326-7937 (in PA).

**The Arabesque Collection,** P.O. Box 6009, Buffalo Grove, IL 60089: Catalog $1 ◆ Handpainted ceramic vases, silk scarves, pictures, and other Middle-Eastern items. 800-884-1996.

**Armchair Shopper,** P.O. Box 419464, Kansas City, MO 64141: Free catalog ◆ Classic old world-style sundials, wind chimes, and lawn ornaments. 816-767-3200.

**Art & Artifact,** 2451 E. Enterprise Pkwy., P.O. Box 8021, Twinsburg, OH 44087: Free catalog ◆ Oriental amenities, exotic luxuries, Celtic inspirations, contemporary accessories, crafts, comfort items for the home, products from foreign countries, impressionist objects, and gifts. 800-950-9540.

**Art Institute of Chicago,** Fulfillment Center, 125 Armstrong Rd., Des Plaines, IL 60019: Free catalog ◆ Museum reproductions and publications that relate to the Institute's collections. 800-637-9110.

**Artistic Greetings Catalog,** P.O. Box 1050, Elmira, NY 14902: Catalog $2 ◆ Personalized stationery, memo and informal note cards, toys and puzzles, kitchen accessories, and gifts for pets. 800-733-6313. www.artisticgreetings.com

**Athletic Supply,** 10850 Sanden Dr., Dallas, TX 75238: Free catalog ◆ Men and women's sportswear, jackets, T-shirts, memorabilia, and figurines. 800-627-9843.

**Australian Catalogue Company,** 7605 Welborn St., Raleigh, NC 27615: Free catalog ◆ Memorabilia, stationery, books and travel videos, crafts, gifts from Australia, and glass, stoneware, and pewter collectibles. 800-808-0938. www.aussiecatalog.com

**Auto Motif Inc.,** 2968 Atlanta Rd., Smyrna, GA 30080: Catalog $3 ◆ Car models, gifts and collectibles with an automotive-theme, books, prints, puzzles, office accessories, lamps, original art, and posters. 800-367-1161.

**Aviation Book Company,** 7201 Perimeter Rd. S, Ste. C, Seattle, WA 98108: Free catalog ◆ Books, videos, pilot supplies, clothing, and gifts. 800-423-2708. www.aviationbook.com

**Avirex Aviator's Club,** 33-00 47th Ave., Long Island City, NY 11101: Catalog $2 ◆ Aviation apparel and accessories. Also gifts. 800-272-9464. www.avirex.com

**William Barthman Jewelers,** 174 Broadway, New York, NY 10038: Free information ◆ Jewelry, watches, porcelain, crystal, and sterling. 800-727-9782; 212-227-3524 (in NY).

**Bennett Brothers Inc.,** 30 E. Adams St., Chicago, IL 60603: Free catalog ◆ Rings, pins and bracelets, pearls, semi-precious and precious stones, lockets, charms, electronics gifts, toys, cameras, and leather goods. 800-621-2626. www.bennettbros.com

**Bentley's Luggage Corp.,** National Distribution Center, 3353 NW 74th Ave., Miami, FL 33122: Free catalog ◆ Luggage and gifts. 800-330-0050. bentley@gate.net

**Jody Bergsma Galleries Inc.,** 1 Bell's Fair Pkwy., Bellingham, WA 98226: Catalog $4 ◆ Statuary and figurines, plates and porcelain collectibles, dolls, and gifts. 800-237-4762; 360-733-2037 (in WA).

**Better Living,** 411 Waverly Oaks Rd., P.O. Box 9199, Waltham, MA 02254: Free catalog ◆ Gifts that provide a better living theme. 800-424-6848.

**Biesanz Woodworks,** 1940 NW 82nd Ave., Miami, FL 33126: Free brochure ◆ Handcrafted wooden gifts. 506-228-1811.

**Big Dog Sportswear,** Mail Order Dept., 121 Gray Ave., Santa Barbara, CA 93101: Free catalog ◆ Gifts for pets and their owners. 800-642-3647. www.BIGDOGS.com

**Biggs Limited Editions,** 5517 Lakeside Ave., Richmond, VA 23228: Free information with long SASE ◆ Statuary and figurines, plates, dolls, and other porcelain collectibles. 800-637-0704. www.biggsltd.com

**Biltmore Estate Direct Inc.,** One N. Pack Square, Attention: Mail Order, Asheville, NC 28801: Free catalog ◆ Reproduction and exclusive items from George Vanderbilt's original collection. 800-968-0558.

**Bits & Pieces,** 1 Puzzle Pl., Stevens Point, WI 54481-7199: Free catalog ◆ Jigsaw puzzles, books, games, and gifts for adults and children. 800-884-2637.

**Blair Shoppe,** 220 Hickory St., Warren, PA 16366: Free catalog ◆ Gifts for everyone and the home. 800-458-2000. blair@blair.com/blair.com

**The Blarney Gift Catalogue,** Blarney Woollen Mills Inc., 373D Rt. 46 West, Fairfield, NJ 07004: Free catalog ◆ Waterford crystal, Belleek china, jewelry, and Irish gifts. 800-451-8720.

**The Blue Buffalo Gallery,** 1750 30th St., #352, Boulder, CO 80301: Free catalog ◆ Arts and crafts from artists of the southwest. 800-868-7808.

**Bruce Bolind,** P.O. Box 9751, Boulder, CO 80301: Free catalog ◆ Novelty and gift merchandise for adults, children, and pets. 303-443-9688.

**Booker's Specialty Gifts,** 2111 Sterne Ave., Palestine, TX 75801: Free catalog ◆ Gifts for the holidays and other occasions. 903-729-3766.

**Holland Boone Polished Pewter,** 7125 E. Sahuaro Dr., Scottsdale, AZ 85254: Brochure $2 ◆ Polished pewter items, handcrafted jewelry boxes, candlesticks, picture frames, serving trays, and other gifts. 800-973-9837.

**The Boone Trading Company Inc.,** 562 Coyote Rd., Brinnon, WA 98230: Free catalog ◆ Natural history specimens, primitive artifacts, antiques, curios, and unusual art. 800-423-1945.

**Brainstorms,** Division Anatomical Chart Company, 8221 Kimball, Skokie, IL 60076: Catalog $3 ◆ Mind-boggling and creative gift ideas and fun items. 800-621-7500; 847-679-4700 (in IL).

**Brielle Galleries,** P.O. Box 475, Brielle, NJ 08730: Free catalog ◆ Watches, jewelry, paperweights, and crystal, silver, bronze, pewter, and porcelain gifts. 800-542-7435.

**Bright-Life,** Box 3703, Hicksville, NY 11855: Free catalog ◆ Gifts, toys, and accessories for everyone. 516-334-1356.

**Brookstone Company,** Order Processing Center, 1655 Bassford Dr., Mexico, MO 65265: Free catalog ◆ Homewares, tools, travel aids, and gifts. 800-926-7000.

**Budget Europe Travel Service,** 2557 Meade Ct., Ann Arbor, MI 48105: Free information ◆ Eurail passes and other passes for Europe, money belts, travel bags, foreign exchange calculators, and more. 800-441-2387; 734-668-0529 (in MI).

**Buffalo Bill Historical Center,** Museum Selections Gift Shop, P.O. Box 2630, Cody, WY 82414: Free catalog ◆ Western frontier-style decorative accessories. 800-533-3838.

**Burberry's Limited,** 9 E. 57th St., New York, NY 10022: Free list of retail sources ◆ Clothing, handbags, luggage, silk scarves and shawls, belts, hats, shoes, and toiletries. 212-371-5010.

**By Nature,** 3930 NE 2nd Ave., Ste. 208, Miami, FL 33137: Free catalog ◆ Gifts made using wildlife and natural products. 888-938-8811. www.bynature.com

**Camellia & Main,** P.O. Box 1709, Fort Valley, GA 31030: Free catalog ◆ All-occasion gifts and room accessories. 800-920-9494.

**Carousel of Gifts,** 307 McClintock St., Longwood, FL 32750: Free catalog ◆ All-occasion gifts for everyone.

**Harriet Carter,** Dept. 37, North Wales, PA 19455: Free catalog ◆ Distinctive gifts. 800-377-7878; 215-361-5122 (in PA).

**Cash's of Ireland,** Mail Order Courier Center, P.O. Box 158, Plainview, NY 11803: Catalog $3 ◆ China, crystal, walking sticks, wool stoles and cardigans, pottery, frames, serving pieces, lamps and chandeliers, and gifts from Ireland. 800-223-8100.

**The Castriota Collection,** P.O. Box 12631, Pittsburgh, PA 15241: Free catalog ◆ Gifts, prizes, and mementos for golfers. 800-344-8640.

**Casual Collections,** P.O. Box 61160, Seattle, WA 98121: Free catalog ◆ All-occasion gifts. 800-886-6878.

**Casual Living,** 5401 Hangar Ct., P.O. Box 31273, Tampa, FL 33631: Free catalog ◆ Toys, books, furniture, watches and clocks, puzzles, kitchen accessories, handpainted portraits made from photographs, lamps, mailboxes, music boxes, model construction kits, and computer games. 800-843-1881.

**Cat Claws,** 1004 W. Broadway, P.O. Box 1001, Morrilton, AR 72110: Free catalog ◆ Gifts, supplies, and other accessories for cats. 800-783-0977. www.catclaws.com

**Cats, Cats & More Cats,** Rt. 17M, P.O. Box 270, Monroe, NY 10950: Free catalog ◆ Gifts for Catalog lovers. 914-782-4141. cats@catscats.com

**The Celebration Fantastic,** 104 Challenger Dr., Portland, TN 37148: Free catalog ◆ Romantic, whimsical, and imaginative gifts for special occasions. 800-235-3272.

**Ann Chapman,** 246 N. Main St., Galena, IL 61036: Free catalog ◆ Equestrian gifts. 815-777-3322.

**Atelier Bernard Chaudron Inc.,** 2449 Chemin de l'ile, Val-David, Quebec, Canada J0T 2N0: Free catalog ◆ Functional and artistic pewterware, lamps, trophies, medals, sculptures, murals, and commissioned work. 819-322-3944.

**Chivalry Sports,** P.O. Box 18904, Tucson, AZ 85731: Free catalog ◆ Medieval, renaissance, and fantasy costumes. Also gifts and books. 800-730-5464. www.RenStore.com

**Clocks Etc.,** 3401 Mt. Diablo Blvd., Lafayette, CA 94549: Brochure $1 ◆ Old and new clocks, antique furniture, and gifts. 510-284-4720.

**Coach Leatherware Company,** 410 Commerce Blvd., Carlstadt, NJ 07072: Free catalog ◆ Leather bags, belts, wallets, briefcases, and accessories. 201-804-8200. www.coach.com

**The Coca-Cola Catalog,** 2515 E. 43rd St., P.O. Box 182264, Chattanooga, TN 37422: Free catalog ◆ Coca-Cola-theme gifts for men, women, and children. 800-872-6531.

**Cokesbury,** Division United Methodist Publishing House, 201 8th Ave. South, P.O. Box 801, Nashville, TN 37202: Free information ◆ Bibles and bible reference books, bible study and Christian education books, fund-raising programs, gifts and casual wear, choir apparel, church and clergy supplies, and church furniture. 800-672-1789. webservant@umph.org

**Cold Hollow Cider Mill,** P.O. Box 430, Waterbury Center, VT 05677: Free information ◆ Vermont foods, apple cider, and gifts. 802-244-8771.

**Coldwater Creek,** One Coldwater Creek Dr., Sandpoint, ID 83864: Free catalog ◆ Nature-related and Native American jewelry, clothing, decorative accessories, art, pottery, wind chimes, and gifts. 800-262-0040. www.coldwater-creek.com

**Collector's Armoury,** 800 Slaters Ln., P.O. Box 59, Alexandria, VA 22313: Free catalog ◆ Western and Civil War collectibles and gifts. 800-544-3456.

**Colonial Casting Company Inc.,** 68 Liberty St., Haverhill, MA 01832: Catalog $3 ◆ Handcrafted lead-free pewter miniature castings. 978-374-8783.

**Colonial Williamsburg Furniture,** P.O. Box 1776, Williamsburg, VA 23187: Catalog $14.65 ◆ Reproduction colonial furnishings and decorative accessories. 804-220-7503.

**Colorful Images,** 2910 Colorful Ave., Longmont, CO 80504: Free catalog ◆ Decorative accessories, watches and jewelry, pens, note cards, cookie jars, wind chimes, desk accessories, novelty telephones, fancy kitchen mugs, calculators, and paperweights. 800-458-7999.

**Computer Gear,** 4028 148th Ave. NE, Redmond, WA 98052: Free catalog ◆ T-shirts and other gifts with a computer theme. 800-373-6353. www.computergear.com

**The Cotton Gin Inc.,** Deep Creek Farm, P.O. Box 414, Jarvisburg, NC 27947: Free catalog ◆ Country collectibles, women's clothing, and antiques. 800-637-2446.

**The Country House,** 805 E. Main St., Salisbury, MD 21804: Catalog $3 ◆ Antique reproductions and other gifts. 800-331-3602. www.thecountryhouse.com

**Country Store Gifts,** 5925 Country Ln., P.O. Box 990, Greendale, WI 53129: Free catalog ◆ Country-style gifts and crafts. 800-558-1013.

**Coyote Catalogue Sales,** P.O. Box 1879, Rosamond, CA 93560: Catalog $7 ($8 refundable) ◆ Religious, spun glass and crystal, Native American heritage, porcelain, art and cloisonné, doll house furnishings, photo frames, and other gifts. 800-647-5699.

**Crate & Barrel,** P.O. Box 9059, Wheeling, IL 60090: Free catalog ◆ Personalized stationery, kitchen aids, storage systems, sound equipment, and decorative accessories. 800-323-5461.

**Creative Bird Accessories,** P.O. Box 2157, Darien, CT 06820: Free catalog ◆ Apparel and jewelry, home accessories, posters for bird lovers, toys, and food for birds. 800-765-2325. www.creativebird.com

**Creative Country Products,** P.O. Box 132, Neche, ND 58265: Brochure $2 (refundable) ◆ Authentic horseshoes welded together to make unusual gifts and decorative items. 800-257-6422.

**Creative Reflections,** 114 Stuart Rd., Ste. 144, Cleveland, TN 37312: Free brochure ◆ Jewelry, art, and collectibles. 800-363-8684.

**The Crow's Nest Birding Shop,** Cornell Laboratory of Ornithology, 159 Sapsucker Woods Rd., Ithaca, NY 14850: Free catalog ◆ Books and gifts for bird enthusiasts. 607-254-2400.

**The CSA Galleries Gifts,** 2150 Northwoods Blvd., North Charleston, SC 29406: Catalog $5 (refundable) ◆ Civil War Confederate-related gifts. 800-256-1861; 803-818-2009 (in SC). www.csagalleries.com

**Cumberland General Store,** #1 Hwy. 68, Crossville, TN 38555: Catalog $4 ◆ Cooking ranges, gardening tools, cast-iron ware, farm bells, buggies, blacksmithing equipment, harnesses, and old-fashioned gifts. 800-334-4640. www.cumberlandgeneral.com

**Custom Glass Etching,** 1139 E. Las Tunas Dr., San Gabriel, CA 91776: Free catalog ◆ Personalized crystal glass awards, gifts for weddings and other occasions, and promotional products. 626-287-3775.

**D.L. Accents Inc.,** P.O. Box 401493, Redford, MI 48240: Free brochure ◆ Photography-related decorative items and gifts. 800-467-1911.

**D-Mail,** 91 Market St., Wappinger Falls, NY 12590: Free catalog ◆ Holiday and other all-occasion gifts and novelties. 800-686-1727. www.d-mail.com

**The Daily Planet,** P.O. Box 64411, St. Paul, MN 55164: Free catalog ◆ Novelties, gifts, stationery, musical instruments, T-shirts, jewelry, reproduction memorabilia from the past, toys, and items from worldwide locations. 800-324-5950.

**Dancing Dragon,** 5670 West End Rd., #4, P.O. Box 1106, Arcata, CA 95518: Free catalog ◆ Dragon-theme decorative items and gifts. 800-322-6040. www.dancing-dragon.com

**Dealer's Choice Gift Shop,** 8025 Black Horse Pike, #470, West Atlantic City, NJ 08232: Free catalog ◆ Gaming gifts. 800-969-0711. www.casinocenter.com

**Discovery Channel,** P.O. Box 788, Florence, KY 41022: Free catalog ◆ Exclusive gifts for men, women, and children. 800-938-0333. www.discovery.com

**The Disney Catalog,** P.O. Box 29144, Shawnee Mission, KS 66201: Free catalog ◆ Disney-theme gifts, collectibles, home furnishings, and clothing for men, women, and children. 800-247-8996. www.disneystore.com

**Dollmasters,** P.O. Box 2319, Annapolis, MD 21404: Catalog $5 ◆ Nostalgic gifts and collectibles that celebrate yesterday's childhood. Also doll clothing and reference books. 800-966-3655; 410-224-4386 (in MD). www.ea.net/dollmasters

**Down East Books & Gifts,** P.O. Box 679, Camden, ME 04843: Free catalog ◆ Calendars, books, and crafts from Maine and New England. 800-766-1670.

**Walter Drake & Sons,** Drake Bldg., Colorado Springs, CO 80940: Free catalog ◆ Personalized stationery, toys, household items, clothing, decorative and office accessories, and other items. 800-525-9291. amyconnors@wdrake.com

**Early Winters,** P.O. Box 4333, Portland, OR 97208: Free catalog ◆ Men and women's outdoor equipment, ski wear and accessories, other clothing, and gifts. 800-458-4438. www.normthompson.com

**Earth Care,** 555 Leslie St., Ukiah, CA 95482: Free catalog ◆ Recycled paper products, environmental gifts, and household goods. 800-992-7747.

**Earthmade Products,** P.O. Box 609, Jasper, IN 47547: Free catalog ◆ Gifts for the gardener that enhance garden decor and backyard living. 800-843-1819.

**The Edge Company,** P.O. Box 826, Brattleboro, VT 05302: Free catalog ◆ Electronics, other hi-tech gifts, toys, fun things, optics, watches, and more. 800-732-9976. www.edgeco.com

**Emporium of the Rockies,** 306 W. Adams, Pueblo, CO 81004: Free catalog ◆ Decorative accessories, jewelry and watches, cloisonné, dollhouse furnishings, music boxes, and other all-occasion gifts. 719-583-1268.

**Enesco Corp.,** 1 Enesco Plaza, Elk Grove Village, IL 60007: Free list of retail sources ◆ Figurines, sculptures, ornaments, Barbie dolls, and gifts. www.enesco.com

**European Imports & Gifts,** Oak Mill Mall, 7900 N. Milwaukee Ave., Niles, IL 60714: Free catalog ◆ Imported and other gifts and collectibles. 847-967-5253.

**The Executive Gallery,** 814 W. 3rd Ave., Columbus, OH 43212: Free catalog ◆ Self-organizational, travel, and executive accessories. Also other gifts and awards. 800-848-2618.

**Eximious,** 201 Northfield Rd., Northfield, IL 60093: Free catalog ◆ Travel aids, desk and office accessories, garden aids, and American crafts. 800-446-9454. eximious@aol.com

**Expressions from Potpourri,** 120 N. Meadows Rd., Medfield, MA 02052: Free catalog ◆ Toys and puzzles for children and adults, jewelry and watches, note cards and stationery, and decorative accessories. 800-688-8051.

**The Faith Mountain Company,** P.O. Box 199, Sperryville, VA 22740: Free catalog ◆ Herbs and flowers, clothing, home furnishings, garden accessories, and American crafts. 800-588-2548. 800-822-7238. www.FaithMountain.com

**Falcon,** P.O. Box 1718, Helena, MT 59624: Free catalog ◆ Outdoor gifts, books, and gear. 800-582-2665.

**Fantastic Glass,** 909 Walnut St., Emporia, KS 66801: Free catalog ◆ Carved glass awards and specialty gifts. 316-343-4877. www.Fantasticglass.com

**Felissimo Gifts,** 10 W. 56th South, New York, NY 10019: Free catalog ◆ Turn-of-the-century style gifts and other special-occasion selections. 800-565-6785. www.felissimo.com

**Fellowship Foundry Pewtersmiths,** 1605 Abram Ct., San Leandro, CA 94577: Free catalog ◆ Goblets, sculptures, switch plates, jewelry, cups and steins, glassware and crystal, and other pewter gifts. 510-352-0935.

**Fingerhut,** 11 McLeland Rd., St. Cloud, MN 56395: Free catalog ◆ Greeting cards, gift wraps, stationery, holiday decorations, organizers, and gifts. 800-233-3588. www.fingerhut.com

**Flax Art & Design,** P.O. Box 7216, San Francisco, CA 94120: Free catalog ◆ All-occasion gifts for everyone. 800-547-7778. www.flaxart.com

**Flibbertigibbet,** 6 Home Croft Ct., Durham, NC 27703: Free catalog ◆ Antique miniatures, porcelain sculptures, statuary, tools, music boxes, toys, miniature furniture, wall masks, jewelry, and other gifts. 919-598-0858.

**Flights of Fantasy,** 1832 9th St., #2, Hempstead, TX 77445: Free catalog ◆ Gifts for holiday giving, graduations, weddings, anniversaries, and other occasions. 409-826-4623. www.io.com/~fantasy.

**Fox Ridge Outfitters Inc.,** 400 N. Main St., P.O. Box 1700, Rochester, NH 03866: Free catalog ◆ Clothing, guns, solid pine carvings, cookware, knives and cutlery, and equipment and supplies for outdoor sportsmen. 800-243-4570. www.foxridgeoutfitters.com/fro.htm

**The Franklin Mint,** Franklin Center, PA 19092: Free catalog ◆ Distinctive gifts for family and friends. 800-843-6468.

**Frontgate,** 2800 Henkle Dr., Lebanon, OH 45036: Free catalog ◆ Housewares, bathroom and kitchen accessories, games, automobile gadgets, outdoor equipment, and other gifts. 800-626-6488. www.frontgate.com

**G & R Publishing Company,** 507 Industrial St., Waverly, IA 50677: Free catalog ◆ Perpetual calendars, miniature cookbooks, memory journals, and inspirational gift items. 800-383-1679. www.cookbookprinting.com

**Garage Company,** 13211 Washington Blvd., Los Angeles, CA 90066: Free catalog ◆ Motorcycle books, videos, T-shirts, magazines, gifts, and memorabilia. 800-39-DESMO.

**J. Gates,** 1026 Stanton Rd., P.O. Box 2492, Daphne, AL 36526: Free catalog ◆ Special gifts for family and friends. 888-595-7258. smartmale@msn.com

**Geary's,** 437 N. Beverly Dr., Beverly Hills, CA 90210: Free catalog ◆ Silver sculptures, Lladro porcelain, Christofle French silver plate, Halcyon enamels, tapestries, dinnerware, desk accessories, and Waterford, Baccarat and Lalique crystal. 800-243-2797; 310-273-4741 (in CA).

**Gift Gallery Catalog,** 5955 Phelan, Beaumont, TX 77706: Catalog $3 ◆ Custom art and museum-quality recreated artifacts. 409-866-4451.

**Gift World,** 2392 Locust St., Portage, IN 46368: Free brochure ◆ Wholesale supplier of cloth dolls, miniatures, florals, and other gifts. 800-847-4450; 219-763-2408 (in IN).

**Gifts & Novelties,** P.O. Box 8953, Mandeville, LA 70470: Free catalog ◆ All-occasion gifts. 504-727-3459.

**Gimbel & Sons Country Store,** 14/16 Commercial St., P.O. Box 57, Boothbay Harbor, ME 04538: Free catalog ◆ Thimbles, collectible crafted porcelains and miniatures, and other gifts. 207-633-5088.

**Glass House,** 3584 Kennebec Dr., Eagan, MN 55122: Free catalog ◆ Stained glass gifts. 800-283-4309; 612 405-0653 (in MN).

**Gnome Cottage Gifts,** 53500 N. Foster Rd., Chesterfield, MI 48051: Free catalog ◆ Gifts with fantasy and Victorian elegance themes. 800-992-2202. www.gnomecottage.com

**Good Catalog Company,** 5484 SE International Way, Portland, OR 97222: Catalog $5 ◆ All-occasion gifts. 800-225-3870.

**Graceland Gifts Mail Order,** 3734 Elvis Presley Blvd., Memphis, TN 38116: Free catalog ◆ Elvis Presley-theme gifts. 800-238-2000. www.elvis-presley.com

**Great Gifts & Collectibles,** 1101 E. Hallendale Beach Blvd., Hallandale, FL 33009: Free brochure ◆ Collectible figurines. 800-445-9911; 954-454-9911 (in FL). www.agreatgift.com

**Guide Dog Foundation for the Blind,** 371 E. Jericho Tnpk., Smithtown, NY 11787: Free catalog ◆ Limited edition guide dog-theme prints, holiday cards, mugs, mats, key rings, stationery, pet accessories, and gifts. 800-443-8372.

**Gumps by Mail,** P.O. Box 489, New Oxford, PA 17350: Free catalog ◆ Rare, unique, and imaginative gifts. 800-284-8677. www.gumps.com

**H & L Productions Inc.,** 1425 Oakbrook Dr., Ste. 100, Norcross, GA 30093: Free catalog ◆ NASCAR wearables, collectibles, and gifts.

**Hahn Enterprises,** P.O. Box 191296, Little Rock, AR 72219: Free information ◆ Shirts, prints, stationery, and other gift items. 800-822-3257. www.hahnenterprises.com

**Haitian Art Company,** 600 Frances St., Key West, FL 33040: Free information with long SASE ◆ Paintings, wood sculptures, steel cut-outs, paper maché crafts, and gifts. 305-296-8932. www.haitian-art-co.com

**Hallmark Gifts,** P.O. Box 10300, Canoga Park, CA 91309: Free catalog ◆ Gifts for special relationships and occasions. 800-983-4663. www.hallmark.com

**Hammacher Schlemmer,** Operations Center, 180 LeSaint Dr., Fairfield, OH 45014: Free catalog ◆ Gifts for the entire family. 800-227-3528. America Online keyword: Hammacher

**Handsome Rewards,** 19465 Brennan Ave., Perris, CA 92599: Free catalog ◆ Household accessories, tools, games, and all-occasion gifts. 909-943-2023.

**Hanover House,** Hanover Direct Pennsylvania Inc., Hanover, PA 17333-0001: Free catalog ◆ Clothing, gardening supplies, household aids, jewelry, and novelties. 717-633-3333.

**Hansen Planetarium,** 1845 S. 300 West, Salt Lake City, UT 84115: Catalog $1 ◆ Gifts for astronomy buffs. 801-483-5400.

**The Harp & Dragon,** 25 Madison St., Cortland, NY 13045: Free catalog with two 1st class stamps ◆ Celtic theme gifts. 607-756-7372. www.HarpAndDragon.com

**Heartland America,** 6978 Shady Oak Rd., Eden Prairie, MN 55344: Free catalog ◆ High-tech electronics, household accessories, telephones, computers, tools, leather goods and luggage, games, office and home furniture, and audio and stereo, optical and astronomy, and exercise equipment. 800-229-2901.

**Herrington,** 3 Symmes Dr., Londonderry, NH 03053: Free catalog ◆ Automotive gadgets and tools, photographic and video equipment, CD-ROMs, disk and cassette storage cabinets, gifts for music lovers, and astronomy equipment. 800-903-2878.

**Hitching Post Supply,** 10312 210th St. SE, Snohomish, WA 98296: Free catalog ◆ Gifts for horse owners. 800-689-9971; 360-668-2349 (in WA). www.hitchingpostsupply.com

**The Horchow Collection,** P.O. Box 620048, Dallas, TX 72262: Free catalog ◆ Home furnishings and accessories, dishes and serving pieces, rugs, bedroom linens, and lamps. 800-395-5397. www.neimanmarcus.com

**House of Tyrol,** P.O. Box 909, 66 E. Kytle St., Cleveland, GA 30528: Free catalog ◆ Musical cuckoo clocks, crystal, porcelain, lamps, music boxes, pillows, knitted items, decorative accessories, bar accessories, collector plates, pewter, tapestries, cards, Alpine hat pins, Christmas decorations, and folk music videos. 800-241-5404. www.tyrolinternational.com

**Hubbardton Forge & Wood Corp.,** P.O. Box 827, Rt. 30, Castleton, VT 05735: Catalog $3 ◆ Wrought-iron and brass chandeliers, other hand-forged lighting accessories, hanging pan racks, bathroom and home accessories, plant hangers, and table, wall, and candlestick lamps. 802-468-3090.

**Impressions,** 16 S. Jackson St., Greencastle, IN 46135: Free catalog ◆ Gifts for journalists. 765-653-3333. www.spj.org

**The Incredible Christmas Place,** 2470 Parkway, P.O. Box 958, Pigeon Forge, TN 37868: Free catalog ◆ Toys and trains, dolls, Christmas ornaments, other gifts, and collectibles. 800-357-2682. www.christmasplace.com

**Irvin's,** RD 1, Box 73, Mt. Pleasant Mills, PA 17853: Free catalog ◆ Handcrafted colonial tinware gifts and lighting. 717-539-8200.

**ISLA Gifts,** P.O. Box 9112, San Juan, PR 00908: Free catalog ◆ Music, books, foods, and other gifts from Puerto Rico. 800-575-4752. www.latino.com/isla

**James II Galleries Inc.,** 11 E. 57th St., New York, NY 10022: Free information ◆ Corporate and personal gifts with optional engraving. 212-355-7040.

**Jasper Publications Inc.,** P.O. Box 725, Rhinebeck, NY 12572: Free catalog ◆ Pet-oriented calendars, note and postcards, jewelry, T-shirts, clocks, stencils, and more. 914-876-2643. www.jack-russell.com

**Thomas Jefferson Memorial Foundation Inc.,** Monticello Catalog, P.O. Box 318, Charlottesville, VA 22902: Free catalog ◆ Gifts and other items that reflect Thomas Jefferson's varied interests and intellectual thinking. 800-243-0743.

**Jennifer's Trunk Antiques & General Store,** 201 N. Riverside, Dr., St. Clair, MI 48079: Free brochure ◆ Victorian-style antique furniture, books, jewelry, lamps and shades, and gifts. 810-329-2032.

**The Jewish Bride...& More,** P.O. Box 26341, Tamarac, FL 33320: Free catalog ◆ Jewish gifts for weddings, bar/bat mitzvah, anniversaries, birthdays, and other occasions. Also printed yarmulke and assorted tallisim, benchers, and ketuboth. 954-721-5660.

**Just Between Us,** 41 W. 8th Ave., Oshkosh, WI 54906: Free catalog ◆ Decorative items for the home and gifts for family members and friends. 800-258-3750. www.mileskimball.com

**Kansas Industries for the Blind,** 425 SW MacVicar Ave., Topeka, KS 66606: Free price list ◆ Blind and handicapped person-made products. 913-296-3211.

**Charles Keath Ltd.,** P.O. Box 48800, Atlanta, GA 30362: Free catalog ◆ Women's clothing, jewelry, watches, decorative and fireplace accessories, luggage, and purses. 800-388-6565; 770-449-3100 (in GA).

**Miles Kimball Company,** 41 W. 8th Ave., Oshkosh, WI 54906: Free catalog ◆ Gifts and gadgets from around the world. 800-546-2255. www.mileskimball.com

**Lakeside Products Company,** 6646 N. Western Ave., Chicago, IL 60645: Catalog $1 (refundable) ◆ Housewares, novelties, and gifts. 773-761-5495.

**Lane Luggage,** 1146 Connecticut Ave. NW, Washington, DC 20036: Free catalog ◆ Luggage, toys and games, desk and decorative accessories, and electronic gadgets. 202-452-1146.

**The Last Best Place,** Catalog Company, 3650 Milwaukee St., Madison, WI 53779: Free catalog ◆ Gifts for all-occasions. 800-252-4766.

**Lefthanders International,** P.O. Box 8249, Topeka, KS 66608: Catalog $2 ◆ Items for lefties. 913-234-2177.

**Lehman Hardware & Appliances Inc.,** P.O. Box 41, Kidron, OH 44636: Catalog $2 ◆ Kitchen accessories, housewares, stoves for heating and cooking, farming and homesteading equipment, non-electric appliances, woodworking and log-smithing tools, and old-time gifts. 330-857-5757. GetLehmans@aol.com

**The William Leigh Company,** 255 Rt. 12, Ste. 776, Groton, CT 06340: Free catalog ◆ Unusual gifts for the entire family. 860-464-1696.

**Leisure Living Stores,** 415 Pottsville-Minersville Hwy., Minersville, PA 17954: Free catalog ◆ Household accessories, tools, games, all-occasion gifts, and other aids. 800-441-7789. www.leisureliving.com

**Levenger,** P.O. Box 1256, Delray Beach, FL 33447: Free catalog ◆ Books, furniture, pens, briefcases, and gifts for serious readers. 800-545-0242. www.levenger.com

**Lifestyle Fascination Gifts,** 1935 Swarthmore Ave., CN 3023, Lakewood, NJ 08701: Free catalog ◆ High-tech and unusual gifts. 800-669-8875.

**Lifton Studio Inc.,** 121 S. 6th St., Stillwater, MN 55082: Catalog $5 ◆ Harley Davidson-theme money clips, belt buckles, badges, desk accessories, and gifts. 612-439-7208.

**Lighter Side Company,** 4514 19th St. Court East, P.O. Box 25600, Bradenton, FL 34206: Free catalog ◆ Lighthearted surprises and all-occasion gifts. 941-747-6645.

**Lighthouse Depot,** P.O. Box 427, Wells, ME 04090: Free catalog ◆ Lighthouse memorabilia and other maritime gifts. 800-758-1444. www.lhdigest.com

**The Limited of Michigan Ltd.,** 10861 Paw Paw Dr., Holland, MI 49424: Free catalog ◆ Old and new Hummel figurines, back-issue plates, bells, and gifts. 800-355-6363.

**Literary Calligraphy,** 5326 White House Rd., Moneta, VA 24121: Catalog $2 ◆ Literary calligraphy gifts. 800-261-6325. susanloy@rev.net

**Loose Ends,** P.O. Box 20310, Salem, OR 97307: Catalog $5 (refundable) ◆ Country crafts and craft-related gifts. 503-390-7457. www.4looseends.com

**Lynchburg Hardware & General Store,** Public Square, Lynchburg, TN 37352: Catalog $1 ◆ Gifts, novelty items, housewares, tools, and gardening supplies. 615-759-4200.

**MacBirdie Golf Gifts,** 5250 W. 73rd St., Minneapolis, MN 55439: Free catalog ◆ Gifts for golfers. 800-343-1033. www.macbirdie.com

**Made in Colorado,** 4840 W. 29th Ave., Denver, CO 80212: Free brochure ◆ Finely crafted gifts that reflect the tradition and unique heritage of Colorado from the past to present. 800-272-1046; 303-480-9050 (in CO). www.madeincolorado.com

**Magellan's,** 110 W. Sola St., Santa Barbara, CA 93101: Free catalog ◆ Travel supplies and aids. 800-962-4943. www.magellans.com

**Maplewood Crafts,** Humboldt Industrial Park, 1 Maplewood Dr., Hazleton, PA 18201: Free catalog ◆ Decorative accessories, mini models, embroidery and needle crafts, craft supplies and kits, candy molds, and family fun items. 800-899-0134.

**J. Marco Galleries,** 758 Medina Rd., Medina, OH 44256: Free catalog ◆ Handmade pottery, jewelry, and gifts that reflect Native American culture. 800-948-3100. www.jmarco.com

**The Maritime Store,** 2905 Hyde St. Pier, San Francisco, CA 94109: Free catalog ◆ Maritime maps, greeting cards, boat models, children's and maritime books, and gifts. 415-775-BOOK.

**Marlborough Country Barn,** N. Main St., Marlborough, CT 06447: Catalog $3 ◆ Handcrafted curtains, decorative accessories, country crafts, and gifts. 800-852-8993.

**Mathews Wire,** 654 W. Morrison, Frankfort, IN 46041: Catalog $2 ◆ Wire-formed giftwares for the home. 800-826-9650. www.mathewswire.com

**May Silk,** 16202 Distribution Way, Cerritos, CA 90703: Free catalog ◆ Silk plants, gifts, housewares, and jewelry. 800-282-7455.

**Metropolitan Museum of Art,** Special Service Office, Middle Village, NY 11381: Free catalog ◆ Greeting and note cards, ornaments, books, jewelry, ties, frames, calendars, and reproductions from museum collections. 800-662-3397. www.metmuseum.org

**J. Michael's Catalog Company,** 152 E. Main St., Rigby, ID 83442: Free catalog ◆ Home decorative gifts. 208-523-0011.

**Danna Michaels Gifts,** 3123 Commerce Pkwy., Miramar, FL 33025: Free catalog ◆ All-occasion gifts for everyone. 800-944-4384.

**The Mind's Eye,** P.O. Box 6547, Chelmsford, MA 01824: Free catalog ◆ Imaginative gifts for men, women, and children. 800-949-3333.

**Moby Dick Marine Specialties,** 21 William St., New Bedford, MA 02740: Catalog $5 ◆ Nautical gifts, decorative accessories, and scrimshaw. 800-343-8044.

**Modern Farm,** 963 Big Horn Ave., Cody, WY 82414: Free catalog ◆ Field and farm items, home and family products, auto accessories and tools, and clothing. 800-443-4934.

**Montgomery Ward Direct,** Order Processing Dept., 6700 Shady Oak Rd., Eden Prairie, MN 55344: Free catalog ◆ Household and kitchen accessories, furniture, bedding, decorative items, audio and TV equipment, rugs and curtains, and all-occasion gifts. 800-852-2711.

**Claire Murray Inc.,** P.O. Box 390, Ascutney, VT 05030: Catalog $5 ◆ Handpainted ceramics, quilts, and hand-hooked rugs. 800-252-4733. www.clairemurray.com

**Museum Collections,** 340 Poplar St., Bldg. 20, Hanover, PA 17333: Free catalog ◆ Museum replicas and gifts. 800-442-2460.

**Museum of Fine Arts, Boston,** Catalog Sales Dept., P.O. Box 244, Avon, MA 02322: Free catalog ◆ Museum replicas. 800-225-5592. customerservice@mfa.org

**Museum of Modern Art New York,** Mail Order Dept., 11 W. 53rd St., New York, NY 10019: Free catalog ◆ Museum replicas. 800-447-6662. www.moma.org

**Museum Replicas Limited,** P.O. Box 840, Conyers, GA 30207: Catalog $1 (refundable) ◆ Reproductions of historic weapons and period battle wear. 800-883-8838. www.museumreplicas.com

**Music in Motion,** P.O. Box 83314, Richardson, TX 75083: Free catalog ◆ Music education accessories and gifts for all ages. 800-445-0649.

**Music Stand,** 1 Music Stand Plaza, 66 Benning St., West Lebanon, OH 03784: Free catalog ◆ Gifts with a music theme, candy, gift baskets, trophies, plaques, and certificates. 800-717-7010. www.musicstand.com

**Nabisco Direct,** P.O. Box 7106, Dover, DE 19903: Free catalog ◆ Gift packages of cookies, candy, and peanut favorites. Also non-food gifts with the Nabisco logo. 800-738-6720. www.nabisco.com

**National Distribution Inc.,** 810 Philip Dr., Unit #1, Waukesha, WI 53186: Free catalog ◆ Clothing for relaxed wearing, leather goods, caps and hats, glassware, coffee mugs, black powder arms, knives, and collectibles. 800-962-COLT.

**National Geographic Society,** 1145 17th St. NW, Washington, DC 20036: Free catalog ◆ Books, games, videos, maps and globes, travel aids, and magazine subscriptions. 800-225-5647. www.nationalgeographic.com/main.html

**The National Museum of Women in the Arts,** 1250 New York Ave. NW, Washington, DC 20005: Free catalog ◆ All-occasion gifts by and about women. 202-783-5000. www.nmwa.org

**The Nature Company,** Catalog Division, P.O. Box 188, Florence, KY 41022: Free catalog ◆ Jewelry made from natural materials, high-tech devices, science gadgets, T-shirts, books, sculptures, optics, clocks, garden accessories, puzzles and toys, and archaeological reproductions. 800-227-1114. www.natureco.com

**Naval Academy Gift Shop,** Halsey Field House, Annapolis, MD 21402: Free catalog ◆ Gifts from the United States Naval Academy. 410-268-3355.

**The New England Trader,** 336 Lordship Rd., Stratford, CT 06497: Free catalog ◆ Distinctive gifts, jewelry, and household accessories. 203-375-6639.

**The Nordic Shop,** 201 Centerplace Pavilion, Rochester, MN 55904: Free brochure ◆ Sweaters and Scandinavian gifts. 800-282-NORD. TNordShop@aol.com

**Northstyle Gifts,** P.O. Box 6529, Chelmsford, MA 01824: Free catalog ◆ Gifts with a Native American and western-theme. 800-336-5666. www.netplaza.com/northstyle

**Northwest Passages,** By Harry & David, P.O. Box 1548, Medford, OR 97501: Free catalog ◆ Gifts and clothing for men, women, and pets. 800-727-7243. www.northwestexpress.com

**Northwest's Best Ltd.,** 598 Mason Way, Medford, OR 97501: Free catalog ◆ Handcrafted arts, crafts, and gifts by artisans of the Northwest. 800-692-3781. www.nwbest.com

**The Nostalgic Aviator,** 1012 Hollywood Way, Burbank, CA 91505: Free catalog ◆ One-of-a-kind aviation memorabilia. 818-558-7870.

**O'Grady Presents,** 150 E. Huron St., Ste. 1200, Chicago, IL 60611: Free catalog ◆ Gifts for the holidays, young at heart, and adults. 800-548-5759; 312-642-2000 (in IL).

**The Oakridge Corp.,** P.O. Box 247, Lemont, IL 60439: Free catalog price information ◆ Gifts, crafts, and collectibles. 708-739-4554.

**The Old Sturbridge Village Museum Gift Shop,** 1 Old Sturbridge Village Rd., Sturbridge, MA 01566: Catalog $1 (refundable) ◆ Reproduction redware and crafts. 508-347-3362.

**1-800-FLOWERS,** 1600 Stewart Ave., Westbury, NY 11590: Free catalog ◆ Flower and fruit gift assortments and baskets. 800-356-9377.

**Orchids etc!,** 1 Orchid Ln., Medford, OR 97501: Free catalog ◆ Plants, fresh flowers, and floral gifts. 800-525-7510.

**Oriental Trading Company Inc.,** P.O. Box 3407, Omaha, NE 68103: Free catalog ◆ Toys, gifts, novelties, carnival supplies, and holiday and seasonal items. 800-228-0475. www.oriental.com

**Orvis Manchester,** 1711 Blue Hills Dr., P.O. Box 12000, Roanoke, VA 24022: Free catalog ◆ Men and women's clothing, country gifts, rugs, fireplace and kitchen accessories, gifts for pets, luggage, lamps, and fishing equipment. 800-541-3541. www.orvis.com

**Orvis Travel,** 1711 Blue Hills Dr., P.O. Box 12000, Roanoke, VA 24022: Free catalog ◆ Men and women's clothing, outerwear, luggage, and accessories for travelers. 800-541-3541. www.orvis.com

**Our Designs Inc.,** P.O. Box 17404, Covington, KY 41017: Free catalog ◆ Special gifts for men, women, children, and the home. 800-382-5252. sales@ourdesigns.com

**Out of the Woodwork,** 437 Robert E. Lee Dr., Wilmington, NC 28412: Free brochure ◆ Personalized educational gifts for children. 910-792-6882.

**The Outhouse,** 2853 Lincoln Hwy. East, Ronks, PA 17572: Free catalog ◆ Gifts and unusual items. 800-346-7678; 717-687-9580 (in PA).

**The Paragon Gifts,** 89 Tom Harvey Rd., Westerly, RI 02891: Free catalog ◆ Casual clothing, housewares, decorative accessories, games and toys, and bathroom items. 800-343-3095.

**Past Times,** 280 Summer St., Boston, MA 02210: Free catalog ◆ Gifts from Great Britain inspired by the past. 800-242-1020.

**Peak Ski & Sport,** 230 S. Hale Ave., Ste. 200, Escondiso, CA 92029: Free catalog ◆ Gifts, clothing, ski gear, and travel accessories. 800-550-7669. peakski@ix.netcom.com

**Personal Creations,** 145 Tower Dr., Burr Ridge, IL 60521: Free catalog ◆ Frames, office and desk accessories, leather goods, and personalized gifts for weddings, birthdays, other occasions, and the home. 800-326-6626; 630-655-3200 (in IL). www.personalize.com

**Pet Classics Ltd.,** 2326 E. Baltimore St., Ste. 100, Baltimore, MD 21224: Free catalog ◆ Accessories and gifts for pet owners and animal lovers. 888-263-9253. PetClassic@aol.com

**Petals,** 1 Aqueduct Rd., White Plains, NY 10606: Free catalog ◆ All-occasion floral arrangements and gifts. 800-738-2570. www.petals.com

**J. Peterman Company,** 1318 Russell Cave Rd., Lexington, KY 40505: Free catalog ◆ Men and women's apparel, accessories, home furnishings, garden items, gifts, footwear, and luggage. 800-231-7341. www.jpeterman.com

**Pety4s,** 6501 Vegas Dr., Apt. 1043, Las Vegas, NV 89108: Free brochure ◆ Personalized gifts with pictures of pets for pets and their owners. 702-880-7136.

**Playboy,** P.O. Box 809, Itasca, IL 60143: Free catalog ◆ Gifts for men and women. 800-423-9494.

**Plow & Hearth,** P.O. Box 5000, Madison, VA 22727: Free catalog ◆ Gardening tools, birdhouses and feeders, porch and lawn furniture, fireplace accessories, and gifts for pets. 800-627-1712. peggy@plowhearth.com

**Plummer-McCutcheon,** A Hammacher Schlemmer Company, Operations Center, 180 LeSaint Dr., Fairfield, OH 45014: Free catalog ◆ Distinctive and unusual gifts. 800-227-3528. America Online keyword: Hammacher

**Post Scripts from Joan Cook,** 119 Foster St., P.O. Box 6008, Peabody, MA 01961: Free catalog ◆ Women and children's clothing, toys, home accessories, luggage, personal care items, and electronic gadgets. 978-532-4040.

**Potpourri,** 120 N. Meadows Rd., Medfield, MA 02052: Free catalog ◆ Jewelry, clothing, party items, games, and decorative accessories. 800-688-8051.

**Pottery Barn,** Mail Order Dept., P.O. Box 7044, San Francisco, CA 94120: Free catalog ◆ Gifts for the home. 800-922-5507.

**Precious Impressions,** P.O. Box 50536, Provo, UT 84605: Free information ◆ Kits for making personalized 3-dimensional replicas or statuettes of a baby's hand or foot. 888-758-4611.

**Preferred Living,** A Catalog from Sporty's, Clermont Century Airport, Batavia, OH 45103: Free catalog ◆ Household accessories, tools, games, and all-occasion gifts. 800-543-8633. www.sportys-catalogs.com

**Pueblo to People,** 2105 Silber Rd., Houston, TX 77065: Free catalog ◆ Nuts, dried fruit, ceramics, jewelry, coffee, and gift baskets. 800-843-5257.

**The Pyramid Collection,** Altid Park, P.O. Box 3333, Chelmsford, MA 01824: Free catalog ◆ Jewelry, home decorative items, games, figurines, clothing, and other museum-theme reproductions. 800-333-4220. www.netplaza.com/pyramid

**R & T Distributors,** 6208 Summer Place Dr. North, Mobile, AL 36618: Catalog $5 ◆ Christmas ornaments and collectibles, jewelry, and gifts for special and other occasions. 888-343-GIFT; 334-4124-2796 (in AL). www.zebra.net/~Alicia

**Rand McNally & Company,** Catalog Operations Center, 2515 E. 43rd St., P.O. Box 182257, Chattanooga, TN 37422: Free catalog ◆ Gifts for sports enthusiasts, health and exercise equipment, maps, world globes, books, videos, clocks, prints, travel aids, and watches. 800-234-0679. www.randmcnallystore.com

**Raycon Enterprises,** 2778 Sweetwater Springs Blvd., Ste. 326, Spring Valley, CA 91977: Free catalog ◆ Specialty gifts, cookware and accessories, tools and items for the home and office, and self-help books and videos. 619-670-9863.

**Real Goods,** 555 Leslie St., Ukiah, CA 95482: Free catalog ◆ Solar energy components and educational toys, environmental books and games, and alternative energy-related gifts. 800-762-7325. www.realgoods.com

**Red Cross Gifts,** 122 Walnut St., Spooner, WI 54801: Free information ◆ Collectible plates, Ashton-Drake dolls, gifts, and collectibles. 800-344-9958.

**Red Rose Collection,** P.O. Box 280140, San Francisco, CA 94128: Free catalog ◆ Books and tapes, art works, jewelry, tools, games, natural fiber clothing, decorative accessories, and toiletries. 800-374-5505.

**Redbox Arts & Crafts,** Mikhail Dmitriev, 1020 View St., Ste. 506, Victoria, British Columbia, Canada V8V 4Y4: Free catalog ◆ Traditional Russian lacquer boxes, miniatures, and watches. 250-389-0021.

**Redline,** P.O. Box 1629, Secaucus, NJ 07096: Free catalog ◆ Nascar clothing and collectibles. 800-GO-NASCAR. www.nascar.com

**Remarkable Moments,** 946 Calle Amanecer, Ste. P, San Clemente, CA 92673: Free brochure ◆ Printed images with authentic audio to honor great moments in sports, history, and entertainment. 800-MOMENT-5.

**Rent Mother Nature,** P.O. Box 193, 52 New St., Cambridge, MA 02238: Free catalog ◆ Food-related gifts. 800-232-4048.

**Rodco Products,** 2565 16th Ave., Columbus, NE 68601: Catalog 50¢ ◆ High-tech equipment for the home and office. 800-323-2799.

**The Rosemary House,** 120 S. Market St., Mechanicsburg, PA 17055: Catalog $2 ◆ Herbs, oils, spices, candles, soaps, teas, books, potpourris, and gifts. 717-697-5111.

**RoughOut,** Box 2667, Missoula, MT 59806: Free catalog ◆ Riding equipment, clothing, and gifts. 800-428-1098.

**Royal Mail,** P.O. Box 902, Harrisville, NH 03450: Free catalog ◆ Scottish products: books, videos, tartan scarves and ties, thistle crystal. 800-843-9078. www.alberene.com

**Leonard Rue Enterprises,** 138 Millbrook Rd., Blairstown, NJ 07825: Free catalog ◆ Books, videos, and equipment and gifts for photographers and outdoor enthusiasts. 908-362-6616.

**Running Delights,** P.O. Box 94, Wheat Ridge, CO 80034: Free catalog ◆ Greeting cards and novelty gifts for runners. 888-786-3587; 303-232-1308 (in CO).

**Russian Collection,** Rt. 16A, Box 5, Intervale, NH 03845: Free catalog ◆ Russian lacquer boxes, artistic nesting dolls, and gifts. 603-356-7832.

**The Scandinavian Country Shop,** Warm Brook Rd., Arlington, VT 05250: Free information with long SASE ◆ Scandinavian gifts and handcrafts. 802-375-6666.

**Schrader's Railroad Catalog,** 230 S. Abbe Rd., Fairview, MI 48621: Catalog $1 ◆ Gifts for the railroad enthusiast. 517-848-2225.

**Scintilla,** P.O. Box 78982, Atlanta, GA 30357: Free catalog ◆ Jewelry, lighting, and accessories. 800-975-0191.

**Scotland by the Yard,** Rt. 4, Quechee, VT 05059: Free brochure ◆ Classic clothing, sweaters, gifts and jewelry, and ties and scarves from Scotland. 802-295-5351.

**Scottish Lion Import Shop,** P.O. Box 1700, Rt. 16, North Conway, NH 03860: Free catalog ◆ Imported gifts from Scotland. 800-355-SCOT.

**Scotty's Gifts & Accessories,** 3802 Ivey Ln., Lilburn, GA 30047: Free catalog ◆ Jewelry, art, collectibles, clothing, stationery, and gifts. 800-638-2338. www.scottysgifts.com

**Scully & Scully Inc.,** 504 Park Ave., New York, NY 10126: Free catalog ◆ Handcrafted reproductions of 18th-century enamels by English artisans, figurines, furniture, books and games, men's clothing, crystal, and home office aids. 800-223-3717; 212-755-2590 (in NY).

**Seacraft Classics,** 7850 E. Evans Rd., Ste. 109, Scottsdale, AZ 85260: Free catalog ◆ Handmade detailed models of 19th-century ships and boats with hardwood display stands and brass name plates. 800-356-1987; 602-998-4988 (in AZ).

**Seagull Pewter,** P.O. Box 370, Pugwash, Nova Scotia, Canada B0K 1L0: Free information ◆ Pewter giftwares, holiday and home decorative merchandise, and jewelry. 902-243-2526.

**Seasons,** P.O. Box 64545, St. Paul, MN 55164: Free catalog ◆ All-occasion gifts. 800-776-9677.

**Serengeti,** P.O. Box 3349, Serengeti Park, Chelmsford, MA 01824: Free catalog ◆ Wildlife apparel and gifts. 800-426-2852.

**Service Merchandise Catalog,** Mail Order, P.O. Box 25130, Nashville, TN 37202: Free catalog ◆ Homewares, toys and games, hobby supplies, and jewelry. 800-251-1212. www.servicemerchandise.com

**Sharmbã LLC,** The African Hut, 17 Bridge St., Ste. 132, Stamford, CT 06905: Free catalog ◆ Gifts that reflect the essence of Africa and Native America. 203-961-9459.

**Sharper Image,** 650 Davis St., San Francisco, CA 94111: Free catalog ◆ Health and exercise equipment, toys, watches and clocks, pet products, calculators, telephones, sunglasses, electronics, and other gifts. 800-344-5555. www.sharperimage.com

**Ship's Hatch,** 10376 Main St., Fairfax, VA 22030: Brochure $1 ◆ Military patches, pins and insignia, official USN ship ball caps, ship's clocks, hatch cover tables, nautical and military gifts, jewelry, lamps and lanterns, ship's wheels, and gifts. 703-691-1670.

**Shirley Pewter Shops,** P.O. Box 553, Williamsburg, VA 23187: Free catalog ◆ Pewter serving pieces, other gifts, and decorative accessories. 800-550-5356.

**Shop at Home,** 200 N. Martingale Rd., Schaumburg, IL 60173: Free catalog ◆ Over 350,000 products featured in a shopping and buying service. 888-291-8572.

**Shoppers Advantage,** P.O. Box 1016, Trumbull, CT 06611: Free catalog ◆ Gourmet foods and gift baskets, video games, dinnerware and crystal, toys, jewelry and watches, and other gifts. 800-562-8888.

**A Shoppers Dream,** 6011 NW 42nd Way, Coconut Creek, FL 33073: Free catalog ◆ Religious, hand-spun glass, African American figurines and other statuary, sculptures, carousel horses, collector items, and other gifts. 800-848-8853; 954-426-6101 (in FL). www.ashoppersdream.com

**Signals Catalog,** P.O. Box 10299, Des Moines, IA 50336: Free catalog ◆ Books, T-shirts and sweat shirts, videos and audio cassettes, and other gifts for fans and friends of public television. 800-669-9696.

**Signatures,** 19465 Brennan Ave., Perris, CA 92599: Free catalog ◆ All-occasion gifts. 909-943-2021.

**Ben Silver,** 149 King St., Charleston, SC 29401: Free catalog ◆ Seasonal and graduation gifts for men. 800-849-0973. www.bensilver.com

**Silver of Westport Inc.,** 404 Post Rd. East, Compo Shopping Center, Westport, CT 06880: Free catalog ◆ Luggage, leather goods, challenging games, high-tech electronics, and other gifts and aids for travelers. 203-226-0761; 800-894-5268 (in CT).

**Annette Skoff Studios,** 267 Forsythe Rd., Mars, PA 16046: Free brochure ◆ Personalized watercolor and pen-and-ink portraits. 412-625-3335.

**Smithsonian Catalogue,** 3900 Stonecroft Blvd., Chantilly, VA 20151: Catalog $1 ◆ Gifts, toys, games, books, puzzles, and replicas from the Smithsonian Institution's collections. 800-521-5330. www.si.edu

**Soccer International Inc.,** P.O. Box 7222, Arlington, VA 22207: Catalog $1 ◆ Gifts and novelties with a soccer motif. 703-524-4333. www.soccerinternational.com

**Solutions,** P.O. Box 6878, Portland, OR 97228: Free catalog ◆ Home accessories, tableware, jewelry, exercise equipment, and travel aids. 800-342-9988.

**Southwest Indian Foundation,** P.O. Box 86, Gallup, NM 87302: Free catalog ◆ Native American (Navajo, Zuni, and Laguna) crafts and gifts. 505-726-8329.

**Sovietski Collection,** P.O. Box 81347, San Diego, CA 92138: Free catalog ◆ Exciting, unusual, and distinctive timepieces, optics, and historical collectibles from bygone eras of the Soviet Union and Eastern Europe. 800-442-0002. www.sovietski.com

**Speak To Me Catalog,** 17913 108th Ave. SE, #155, Renton, VA 98055: Free catalog ◆ Unusual and innovative talking gifts. 800-248-9965. www.clickshop.com/speak

**Spilsbury Puzzle Company,** 3650 Milwaukee St., P.O. Box 8922, Madison, WI 53708: Free catalog ◆ Puzzles, games, and gifts. 800-772-1760.

**Sportsman's Guide,** 411 Farwell Ave., South St. Paul, MN 55075: Free catalog ◆ Gifts for sports enthusiasts. 800-888-3006. www.sportsmansguide.com

**Sporty's Preferred Living Catalog,** Clermont Airport, Batavia, OH 45103: Free catalog ◆ Garden aids, outdoor furniture, sundials, mailboxes, gourmet meat smokers, portable refrigerators, kitchen aids and cutlery, embroidered shirts, automotive aids, sports equipment, games and toys, optics, gifts for pets, and weather forecasting equipment. 800-543-8633. www.sportys-catalogs.com

**Staffords,** P.O. Box 2055, Thomasville, GA 31799: Free catalog ◆ Jewelry, luggage, books on the outdoors, mugs and dishes, men and women's clothing, and shoes. 800-826-0948. www.stafford-catalog.com

**Steed Limited,** 4455 Torrance Blvd., #781, Torrance, CA 90503: Free catalog ◆ Equestrian gifts. 310379-7533. www.gifthorses.com

**Stik-EES,** 1165 Joshua Way, P.O. Box 9630, Vista, CA 92085: Free catalog ◆ Re-usable static cling pre-cut vinyl stickers for decorating gifts, windows, and other surfaces. 800-2-STIKEE; 760-727-7011 (in CA). www.stikees.com

**Store of Knowledge,** 2695 E. Dominguez St., P.O. Box 10, Long Beach, CA 90801: Free catalog ◆ Family gifts that entertain, enlighten, and inspire. 800-746-7765.

**Drew Strouble's Cat-A-Log,** 539 Avenida Del Norte, Sarasota, FL 34242: Free information ◆ Art for cat lovers. 800-349-MEOW. www.catmandrew.com

**Sturbridge Yankee Workshop,** P.O. Box 9797, Portland, ME 04104: Free catalog ◆ Home furnishings, Victorian and Shaker-style items, kitchen and bathroom accessories, and country crafts. 800-343-1144.

**Sugar Hill,** P.O. Box 1300, Columbus, GA 31902: Free catalog ◆ Bedroom linens, furniture, mirrors, lamps, and gifts. 800-344-6125.

**Sundance Catalog,** 3865 W. 2400 South, Salt Lake City, UT 84120: Free catalog ◆ Sculptures, lamps, stoneware, jewelry, decorative accessories, and western and Native American gifts. 800-422-2770. service@sundance.net

**Sunset Catalog,** Good Catalog Company, 5484 SE International Way, Portland, OR 97222: Catalog $5 ◆ Gifts and decorative items. 800-225-3870.

**Tender Heart Treasures Ltd.,** 10525 J St., Omaha, NE 68127: Free catalog ◆ Gifts for homes, offices, friends, and family. 800-443-1367. www.tenderheart.com

**Terry's Village,** P.O. Box 2309, Omaha, NE 68103: Free catalog ◆ Gifts, decorative items, and home accessories. 800-200-4400. www.terrysvillage.com

**Norm Thompson,** P.O. Box 3999, Portland, OR 97208: Free catalog ◆ Kitchen and bathroom aids, automotive accessories, storage and closet organizers, clothing, shoes and boots, and high-tech gadgets. 800-821-1287. www.normthompson.com

**Thompson Cigar Company,** P.O. Box 31274, Tampa, FL 33633: Free catalog ◆ Gifts for smokers. 800-435-0467. www.thompsoncigar.com

**Thoroughbred Racing Catalog,** P.O. Box 610, Warsaw, VA 22572: Free catalog ◆ Calendars and limited edition prints with pictures of famous racing horses and horse-decorated mailboxes, doormats, sweatshirts and T-shirts, mugs and glasses, jewelry, and wall clocks. 800-777-RACE. www.thoroughbred-racing.com

**Tidewater Specialties,** Box 158, Wye Mills, MD 21679: Free catalog ◆ Gifts for wildlife enthusiasts, dog owners and trainers, golfers, and other outdoor sports persons. 800-535-1314.

**Tiffany & Company,** Customer Service, 801 Jefferson Rd., P.O. Box 5477, Parsippany, NJ 07054: Catalog $1 ◆ Jewelry, crystal, watches, cultured pearls and settings, serving pieces, pens and pencils, and desk accessories. 800-452-9146.

**TimesPast,** P.O. Box 1, Osceola, WI 54020: Free catalog ◆ Nostalgic books, collectibles, and other presents from the past. 800-826-6600. www.motorbooks.com

**Touch Consumer Products,** 3107 S. Academy Blvd., #240, Colorado Springs, CO 80916: Catalog $3 ($5 refundable) ◆ Giftwares, jewelry, electronics, toys, seasonal and holiday items, figurines, and more. 719-392-0311.

**Touchstone,** Order Processing Center, 10 Georgian Ct., Ridgely, MD 21605: Free catalog ◆ Decorative and desk accessories, furniture and lamps, and traditional American-style gifts. 800-962-6890.

**Trifles,** P.O. Box 620048, Dallas, TX 75262: Free catalog ◆ Jewelry, coffee and tea service sets, stationery, porcelain and bone china, linens, toys, fireplace accessories, crystal, luggage, furniture, and clothing for men, women, and children. 800-456-7019.

**Troll Family Gift Catalog,** 100 Corporate Dr., Mahwah, NJ 07430: Free catalog ◆ Clocks, electronic baby sitters, photo albums, stationery, kitchen gadgets, toys, books, cassettes, and gifts. 800-247-6106.

**TYROL International,** P.O. Box 909, 66 E. Kytle St., Cleveland, GA 30528: Free catalog ◆ Figurines and limited edition collectibles, gifts for holidays, steins, bears, dolls, music videos, CDs, audio cassettes, and items from worldwide sources. 800-241-5404. www.tyrolinternational.com

**Unicef,** P.O. Box 182233, Chattanooga, TN 37422: Free catalog ◆ Greeting and note cards, toys, limited edition plates, postcards, and gifts. 800-553-1200. www.unicefusa.org

**Velo,** 1830 N. 55th St., Boulder, CO 80301: Free catalog ◆ Gifts for bicycle riders. 303-440-0601. www.VeloNews.com

**Vermont Country Store,** Mail Order Office, P.O. Box 3000, Manchester Center, VT 05255: Free catalog ◆ Clothing, shoes, purses, watches, pillows and linens, bed coverings, travel aids, throw rugs, stove top potpourris, cleaning aids, kitchen accessories, and gifts from New England. 802-362-4667.

**Vermont Industries,** P.O. Box 301, Rt. 103, Cuttingsville, VT 05738: Catalog $3 ◆ Hand-forged Vermont wrought-iron gifts and home accessories. 800-639-1715; 802-492-3451 (in VT).

**Lillian Vernon,** Virginia Beach, VA 23479: Free catalog ◆ Holiday specialties, clothing, electronic gadgets, jewelry, closet organizers, toys, baby care items, kitchen and cooking accessories, luggage, and leather accessories. 800-285-5555. LVCcustsrv@aol.com

**Walkabout Travel Gear,** P.O. Box 1115, Moab, UT 84532: Free catalog ◆ Gifts and essential gear for travelers. 800-852-7085. www.walkabouttravelgear.com

**Wanderings Inc.,** P.O. Box 4344, Warren, NJ 07059: Free catalog ◆ Hand-knitted wool sweaters and special occasion gifts. 800-456-KNIT.

**Wanderlust,** 8457 NW 66th St., Miami, FL 33166: Free catalog ◆ Handmade jade, silver, and wood jewelry. Also other gifts. 888-WANDER-1. www.towander.com

**War Eagle Mill,** Rt. 5, Box 411, Rogers, AR 72756: Free catalog ◆ Arts and crafts, enamelware dishes, foods, specialty items, and gifts. 501-789-5343.

**Warner Brothers Catalog,** P.O. Box 60048, Tampa, FL 33660: Catalog $3 ◆ Bugs Bunny, Looney Tunes, and other T-shirts and sweatshirts for children and adults. Also movie-theme gifts. 800-223-6524. www.warnerbros.com

**The Westbury Collection**, Good Catalog Company, 5484 SE International Way, Portland, OR 97222: Catalog $5 ◆ All-occasion gifts. 800-225-3870.

**Weston Bowl Mill,** P.O. Box 218, Weston, VT 05161: Catalog $1 ◆ Wood bowls, crafts, and kitchen and dining room accessories. 800-824-6219.

**Westview Herb Farm,** P.O. Box 3462, Poughkeepsie, NY 12603: Free catalog ◆ Unusual gifts, garden tools, baskets, pottery, books, potpourri, medicinal products, and herbal teas. 914-462-3534.

**What on Earth,** 2451 Enterprise East Pkwy., Twinsburg, OH 44087: Free catalog ◆ Silk-screened T-shirts, casual apparel, and gifts. 800-945-2552.

**Wild Wings,** P.O. Box 451, Lake City, MN 55041: Free catalog ◆ Art prints, gun cabinets, solid oak wall clocks, gifts for fishermen and animal lovers, and note cards. 800-445-4833.

**Williams-Sonoma,** Mail Order Dept., P.O. Box 7456, San Francisco, CA 94120: Free catalog ◆ Kitchenware, gourmet foods, and gifts. 800-541-1262.

**Winterthur Museum & Gardens,** Kennett Pike, Winterthur, DE 19810: Free catalog ◆ American art, jewelry, playing cards, lamps, dinnerware, clocks, planters, wind chimes, garden sculptures, and reproductions from the Henry Francis du Pont Winterthur Museum. 800-448-3883.

**Wireless,** Minnesota Public Radio, P.O. Box 64422, St. Paul, MN 55164: Free catalog ◆ T-shirts and sweat shirts, old time radio broadcasts, toy banks, coffee mugs, Disney cartoons on videos, books, wind chimes, and electronics. 800-570-5003. www.mpr.org

**Woodbury Pewterers Inc.,** 860 Main St. South, P.O. Box 482, Woodbury, CT 06798: Free catalog ◆ Handmade pewter gifts. 800-648-2014.

**Worldwide Collectibles & Gifts,** P.O. Box 158, 2 Lakeside Ave., Berwyn, PA 19312: Free catalog ◆ Gifts and jewelry, porcelain collectibles, crystal, and items by famous artists. 800-644-2442. www.worldwidecollectibles.com

**Carol Wright Gifts,** P.O. Box 83409, Lincoln, NE 68501: Free catalog ◆ Gifts for homes, offices, friends, and family. 402-437-2201.

**Write Touch,** The Rytex Company, P.O. Box 68188, Indianapolis, IN 46268: Free catalog ◆ Stationery, writing aids, and gifts. 800-288-6824.

**Yankee Barn Catalog,** 1120 W. Maple, Hartville, OH 44632: Free catalog ◆ Decorative pieces, exclusive designer apparel, and handcrafted items. 800-794-8394.

**The Yankee Catalog,** Good Catalog Company, 5484 SE International Way, Portland, OR 97222: Catalog $5 ◆ Unique gifts and decorative items. 800-828-1334.

**Zucker's Fine Gifts,** 151 W. 26th St., New York, NY 10001: Free catalog ◆ Hummel items, Swarovski silver and crystal, Waterford crystal, Lladro porcelain, and gifts. 212-989-1450.

### Religious Gifts

**Abbey Press,** 1384 Hill Dr., St. Meinrad, IN 47577: Free catalog ◆ Religious gifts for people of Christian faith. 800-962-4760.

**Augsburg Fortress Publishers,** 426 S. 5th St., Minneapolis, MN 55415: Free catalog ◆ Books, educational materials, music, gifts, audiovisuals, and ecclesiastical arts items. 800-328-4648; 612-330-3341 (in MN). www.augusburgfortress.org

**California Stitchery,** P.O. Box 2007, Van Nuys, CA 91404: Free catalog ◆ Judaic design and other needlepoint, embroidery, and latch-hook kits. 800-345-3332.

**Ergo Media,** P.O. Box 2037, Teaneck, NJ 07666: Free catalog ◆ Entertaining and informative programs on different aspects of Jewish life. 800-695-3746. www.jewishvideo.com

**Galerie Robin,** P.O. Box 42275, Cincinnati, OH 45242: Free information ◆ Judaic art, graphics, and handcrafted gifts. 800-635-8279. www.judaica-online.com

**Hamakor Judaica Inc.,** Mail Order Dept., P.O. Box 48836, Niles, IL 60714: Free catalog ◆ Kosher foods, kitchen accessories, Jewish art, watches and pendants, Seder dishes, mezuzahs, candelabras, and other items. 800-426-2567. www.jewishsource.com

**Judaica Occasions,** 5 Ronan Blvd., Monsey, NY 10952: Free catalog ◆ Gifts for Bar and Bat Mitzvahs, weddings, and other occasions. 800-336-2291. www.monseyny.com/judacai

**Leaflet Missal Company,** 976 W. Minnehaha Ave., St. Paul, MN 55104: Free catalog ◆ Christian religious gifts. 800-328-9582; 487-2816 (in St. Paul/Minneapolis area).

**Museum of Tolerance,** 9786 W. Pico Blvd., Los Angeles, CA 90035: Free catalog ◆ Judaic theme gifts. 800-553-4474.

**NightinGale Resources, Judacai Gifts,** P.O. Box 322, Cold Spring, NY 10516: Catalog $3 ◆ Judacai gifts for children and adults. 914-753-5383.

**Presentations Gallery,** 200 Lexington Ave., New York, NY 10016: Free information ◆ Contemporary synagogue art, furniture, memorial renditions, and recognition gifts. 212-481-8181.

**Red Rose Collection,** P.O. Box 280140, San Francisco, CA 94128: Free catalog ◆ Religious gifts. 800-374-5505.

**Shasta Abbey Buddhist Supplies,** 3724 Summit Dr., Mt. Shasta, CA 96067: Catalog $2 ◆ Buddhist meditation supplies and gifts. 800-653-3315. www.obcon.org

**Simcha Designs,** P.O. Box 6562, Fresh Meadows Station, Flushing, NY 11365: Free catalog ◆ Judaic artware and jewelry. 718-776-6688.

**The Source for Everything Jewish,** P.O. Box 48836, Niles, IL 60714: Free catalog ◆ Ritual and ceremonial objects, books, art, Kosher gourmet food, and audio cassettes and videos. 800-426-2567.

**Ufaratzta Judacai Center,** 8971 W. Price Blvd., Los Angeles, CA 90035: Free catalog ◆ Judacai-related items and resources for adults and children of all ages. 310-858-3897.

**Whole Life Products,** 1334 Pacific Ave., Forest Grove, OR 97116: Free catalog ◆ Yoga and religious-inspired gifts. 800-634-9056.

## GLASS COLLECTIBLES & DESIGNER ITEMS

**Blenko Glass Company Inc.,** P.O. Box 67, Milton, WV 25541: Free catalog ◆ Hand-blown and finished decorative glass designer items. 304-743-9081.

**Historic Glasshouse,** 200 Mile Common Rd., Easton, CT 06612: Free information ◆ Collectible bottles and glass items. 203-254-2183. www.erols.com/hglass

**Renaissance Marketing,** 24181 S. Tamiani Trail, Bonita Springs, FL 34134: Free catalog ◆ Bronze sculptures and collectible art glass. 941-495-6033.

**Sweetwater Glass,** RD 1, Box 88, De Lancey, NY 13752: Free information ◆ Hand-blown 18th and 19th-century classical designs in glass. 914-676-4622.

## GLOBES

**George F. Cram Company Inc.,** 301 S. LaSalle St., Indianapolis, IN 46201: Free catalog ◆ Maps, atlases, globes, and charts. 800-227-4199; 317-635-5564 (in IN).

**Creative Imaginations,** 10879 Portal Dr., Los Alamitos, CA 90720: Free information ◆ Inflatable globes. 800-942-6487.

**First State Map & Globe,** 12 Mary Ella Dr., Wilmington, DE 19805: Free catalog ◆ Globes and map-related items. 800-327-7992.

**National Geographic Society,** 1145 17th St. NW, Washington, DC 20036: Free catalog ◆ Books, games, videos, maps and globes, travel aids, and magazine subscriptions. 800-225-5647. www.nationalgeographic.com/main.html

**Omni Resources,** 1004 S. Mebane St., P.O. Box 2096, Burlington, NC 27216: Free catalog ◆ Fossils, rocks, hiking and topography maps, and globes. 800-742-2677. custserv@omnimap.com

**Rand McNally & Company,** Catalog Operations Center, 2515 E. 43rd St., P.O. Box 182257, Chattanooga, TN 37422: Free catalog ◆ Gifts for sports enthusiasts, health and exercise equipment, maps, world globes, books, videos, clocks, prints, travel aids, and watches. 800-234-0679. www.randmcnallystore.com

**Replogle Globes Inc.,** 2801 S. 25th Ave., Broadview, IL 60153: Free catalog ◆ Earth and space globes in desk and floor models. 708-343-0900.

**Trippensee Transparent Globes,** 301 Cass St., Saginaw, MI 48602: Free catalog ◆ World globes in desk and floor models. 517-799-8102.

## GO KARTS & MINICARS

**American Power Sports,** 12300 Kinsman Rd., Newbury, OH 44065: Catalog $5 ◆ Go-kart parts, kits, and engines. 216-564-7254.

**K & P Manufacturing,** 950 W. Foothill Blvd., Box 987, Azusa, CA 91702: Free brochure ◆ Go-kart parts, tools, how-to books, and frames. 818-334-0334.

**Kart World,** 1488 Mentor Ave., Painesville, OH 44077: Catalog $3 ◆ Go-karts and minicars, engines, kits, and parts. 440-357-5569.

**S & M Kart Supply Inc.,** 313 Bruns Ln., Springfield, IL 62702: Free catalog ◆ Performance parts, frames, and accessories for go-karts. 217-546-9120.

**SGD Company Inc.,** P.O. Box 8410, Akron, OH 44320: Free information ◆ Go-kart supplies. 216-239-2828. www.sgdgolf.com

## GOLF

### Clothing

**A.B. Emblem Corp.,** P.O. Box 695, Weaverville, NC 28787: Free information ◆ Caps, hats, shirts, and sweaters. 800-438-4285; 704-645-3015 (in NC).

**Tommy Armour Golf Company,** 8350 N. Lehigh Ave., Morton Grove, IL 60053: Free information ◆ Gloves, shirts, skirts, slacks, sweaters, and visors. 800-723-4653. www.armourgolf.com

**Austad's Golf,** Hanover Direct Pennsylvania Inc., Hanover, PA 17333-0001: Free catalog ◆ Golf, other sports equipment, and clothing. 717-633-3333.

**Back 9 Inc.,** 14 Woodbury Ln., Rockport, MA 01966: Free brochure ◆ Golf shoes. 888-GO-BACK-9; 978-546-7600 (in MA).

**Bogner of America,** Bogner Dr., Newport, VT 05855: Free information ◆ Caps, hats, gloves, jackets, shirts, skirts, slacks, sweaters, and visors. 800-451-4417; 802-334-6507 (in VT). www.bogner.com

**Broder Brothers,** 4555 Port St., Plymouth, MI 48170: Free information ◆ Jackets, shirts, sweaters, and visors. 800-521-0850.

**Competitive Edge Golf,** 526 W. 26th St., 10th Floor, New York, NY 10001: Free catalog ◆ Golf equipment, bags, gloves, clothing, and accessories. 800-344-8586. www.golfedge.com

**Elandale,** 7750 E. Redfield Rd., Ste. 101, Scottsdale, AZ 85260: Free catalog (request list of retail sources) ◆ Clothing for women. 800-532-4808; 602-905-8598 (in AZ).

**The Golf Shop,** 2070 Attic Pkwy. SW, Ste. 204, Kennesaw, GA 30152: Free brochure ◆ Shirts. 800-292-8918.

**M. Handelsman Company,** 1323 S. Michigan Ave., Chicago, IL 60605: Free information ◆ Caps, hats, shirts, socks, sweaters, and visors. 800-621-4454; 312-427-0784 (in IL). www.mogar.com

**HJ Glove of America,** 31364 Via Collins, Ste. 105, Westlake Village, CA 91362: Free information ◆ Gloves for women. 800-426-3509.

**King Louie International,** 13500 15th St., Grandview, MO 64030: Free information ◆ Caps, hats, jackets, shirts, sweaters, and visors. 800-521-5212; 816-765-5212 (in MO).

**Lady Fairway,** 3803 Corporex Park Dr., Ste. 400, Tampa, FL 33619: Free information ◆ Golf shoes for women. 800-770-5239; 813-246-4414 (in CA).

**Le Coq Sportif,** 5675 N. Blackstock Rd., Spartanburg, SC 29303: Free information ◆ Caps, hats, shoes, shirts, skirts, slacks, socks, and sweaters. 800-524-2377.

**Lily's of Beverly Hills,** 4910 W. Rosecrans Ave., Hawthorne, CA 90250: Free information ◆ Caps, hats, shoes, shirts, skirts, slacks, socks, sweaters, and visors. 800-421-4474.

**MacGregor Golf Clubs,** 1601 S. Slappey Blvd., Albany, GA 31708: Free information ◆ Caps, hats, shoes, gloves, shirts, skirts, slacks, socks, sweaters, and visors. 800-841-4358; 912-888-0001 (in GA).

**Odyssey Golf,** 1969 Kellog Ave., Carlsbad, CA 92008: Free brochure ◆ Bags, hats, shirts, and left-handed putters. 800-991-1788. www.odysseygolf.com

**Planet Golf,** 1800 Abbot Kinney Blvd., Ste. D, Venice, CA 90291: Free catalog ◆ Clothing for golfers. 310-8232-5936.

**Sandbaggers Enterprises Inc.,** P.O. Box 2404, Lewiston, ME 04241: Free brochure ◆ Spiked or spikeless golf sandals for women. 800-659-9607.

**Spalding Sports Worldwide,** 425 Meadow St., P.O. Box 901, Chicopee, MA 01021: Free list of retail sources ◆ Caps, hats, gloves, jackets, shirts, skirts, slacks, socks, sweaters, and vests. 800-225-6601. www.spalding.com

**Sunderland of Scotland,** 20844 Plummer St., Chatsworth, CA 91311: Free information ◆ Rainwear for women. 800-999-6599. www.sunderlandgolf.com

**T-Shirt City,** 4501 W. Mitchell Ave., Cincinnati, OH 45232: Free information ◆ Caps, hats, jackets, shirts, sweaters, socks, and visors. 800-543-7230.

**Tuttle Golf Collection,** P.O. Box 888, Wallingford, CT 06492: Free catalog ◆ Sportswear for men and women. 800-882-7511.

**The Women's Golf Catalog,** P.O. Box 1249, Sagamore Beach, MA 02562: Free catalog ◆ Accessories, jewelry, footwear, gift and novelty items, and equipment. 800-984-7324. www.womensgolf.com

### Equipment Manufacturers

**Access to Recreation Inc.,** 8 Sandra Ct., Newbury Park, CA 91320: Free catalog ◆ Adaptive golf equipment for the disabled. 800-634-4351.

**Accuform Golf Clubs,** 6380 Viscount Rd., Mississaugua, Toronto, Ontario, Canada L4B 1H3: Free information. 800-668-7873.

**Alien Sport Inc.,** 2085 Landing Dr., Mountain View, CA 94043: Free information ◆ Matched clubs. 800-972-6900.

**Tommy Armour Golf Company,** 8350 N. Lehigh Ave., Morton Grove, IL 60053: Free information. 800-723-4653. www.armourgolf.com

**Bridgestone Sport GDS Manufacturing,** 15320 Industrial Park Blvd. NE, Covington, GA 30209: Free information. 800-358-6310; 770-787-7400 (in GA). www.preceptgolf.com

**Browning Golf Clubs,** 3123 MacArthur Blvd., Santa Ana, CA 92704: Free information. 800-666-6033.

**Callaway Golf Clubs,** 2285 Rutherford Rd., Carlsbad, CA 92008: Free information. 800-228-2767; 619-931-1771 (in CA). www.callawaygolf.com

**Cobra Golf,** 1818 Aston Ave., Carlsbad, CA 92008: Free information. 800-BAFFLER; 619-929-0377 (in CA). www.cobragolf.com/ns

**Components Plus,** 7550 Sterns Rd., Ottawa Lake, MI 49267: Free catalog ◆ Woods, irons, putters, putter shafts, graphite components, and assembled irons. 800-242-1977. www.golfcompplus.com

**Continental Golf Warehouse,** 31093 Schoolcraft, Livonia, MI 48150: Free information ◆ Golf clubs and equipment. 313-422-4300.

**Jan Craig Headcovers,** 1000 N. Milwaukee, Ste. 203, Chicago, IL 60622: Free information ◆ Headcovers. 312-278-8366.

**Cubic Balance Golf Technology,** 30231 Tomas Rd., Rancho Santa Margarita, CA 92688: Free information. 888-77-CUBIC. www.cubicbalance.com

**Daiwa Corp.,** 12851 Midway Pl., Cerritos, CA 90703: Catalog $1. 562-802-9589. www.daiwa.com

**Dalee Imports,** P.O. Box 2075, Revelstroke, British Columbia, Canada V0E 2S0: Free information ◆ Electronic golf score calculator. 800-705-9991.

**Duffix Golf Products,** 5340 South Ave., Youngstown, OH 44512: Free brochure ◆ A swing trainer that teaches how to eliminate slice and hooking problems. 800-972-2947.

**Dynacraft Golf Products,** 71 Maholm St., Newark, OH 43055: Free information. 800-321-4833. www.dynacraftgolf.com

**Echelon Golf,** 1016 Lawson St., City of Industry, CA 91748: Free brochure (request list of retail sources) ◆ State-of-the-art golf clubs. 800-964-4899; 818-964-4799 (in CA). www.echelongolf.com

**Golden Shine Inc.,** 4075 E. La Palma Ave., Ste. Q, Anaheim, CA 92807: Free information ◆ Practice net, ball holder, and spectator seats. 800-852-8525.

**Goldentouch Golf Inc.,** 1116 E. Valencia Dr., Fullerton, CA 92631: Free information. 800-423-2220. www.crtvsprts@aol.com

**Goldwin Golf Inc.,** 2460 Impala Dr., Carlsbad, CA 92008: Free information ◆ Milled metal-wood clubs. 800-609-4653. www.goldwin.com

**Golf Design Inc.,** 12200 28th St. North, St. Petersburg, FL 33716: Free brochure ◆ Bobby Grace engraved mallet putters. 813-573-1945.

**Hillerich & Bradsby Company Inc.,** P.O. Box 35700, Louisville, KY 40232: Free list of retail sources. 800-282-2287.

**House of Tees,** P.O. Box 5000, Dover, NJ 07801: Free information ◆ Personalized golf tees. 800-832-5457.

**Hurricane Sports Inc.,** 1130 Commerce Blvd. North, Sarasota, FL 34243: Free information. 800-749-8848.

**International Golf Outlet,** 6005 Median Rd., Austin, TX 78734: Free catalog ◆ Golf equipment, bags, and accessories. 800-444-3173.

**La Jolla Golf Club Company,** 2440 La Mirada Dr., Ste. A, Vista, CA 92083: Free brochure ◆ Golf clubs for children and adults. 800-468-7700; 619-599-9400 (in CA).

**Lynx Golf Clubs,** 16017 E. Valley Blvd., City of Industry, CA 91749: Free information. 800-233-5969; 818-961-0222 (in CA). www.lynxgolf.com

**MacGregor Golf Clubs,** 1601 S. Slappey Blvd., Albany, GA 31708: Free information. 800-841-4358; 912-888-0001 (in GA).

**Makser,** 848 Brickell Ave., Miami, FL 33131: Free information ◆ Putters and metal-wood drivers. 800-925-0477.

**Memphis Net & Twine Company Inc.,** 2481 Matthews Ave., P.O. Box 80331, Memphis, TN 38108: Free catalog ◆ Cages and backstops, soccer nets, tennis windscreens, pitching machines, protector and miscellaneous nets for other sports, and other sports accessories. 800-238-6380. memnet@netten.net

**Mizuno Corp.,** 1 Jack Curran Way, Norcross, GA 30071: Free information. 800-966-1211. www.mizunogolf.com

**Tad Moore Golf,** 1710 Shorewood Dr., LaGrange, GA 30240: Free brochure ◆ Golf clubs and accessories. 888-236-6673. www.tadmoorw@mindspring.com

**Odyssey Golf,** 1969 Kellog Ave., Carlsbad, CA 92008: Free brochure ◆ Bags, hats, shirts, and left-handed putters. 800-991-1788. www.odysseygolf.com

**Par Golf Supply Inc.,** 550 Pratt Ave., Schaumberg, IL 60193: Free brochure ◆ Imprinted logo golf balls and golf gift packages. 800-572-4824. www.pargolf.com

**PING Golf,** Karsten Manufacturing Corp., P.O. Box 9990, Phoenix, AZ 85068: Free information ◆ Putters, irons, and metal-wood drivers. 800-474-6434. www.pinggolf.com

**Pinseeker Golf Clubs,** 1956 E. McFadden Ave., Santa Ana, CA 92705: Free information. 714-835-1935.

**Prosimmon Golf Equipment,** 3749 Middleburg Rd., Union Bridge, MD 21791: Free brochure ◆ Left and right-handed irons and woods for men and women. 410-751-6481.

**Ram Golf Clubs,** 2020 Indian Boundary Dr., Melrose Park, IL 60160: Free information. 800-TEE-GOLF. www.ramgolf.com

**Ryobi-Toski Golf Clubs,** 160 Essex St., Box 576, Newark, OH 43055: Free information. 800-848-2075.

**Kenneth Smith Golf Clubs,** 12931 W. 71st St., Shawnee, KS 66216: Free catalog ◆ Custom handmade golf clubs. 800-234-8968. www.kennethsmithgolf.com

**Spalding Sports Worldwide,** 425 Meadow St., P.O. Box 901, Chicopee, MA 01021: Free list of retail sources. 800-225-6601. www.spalding.com

**Sportek,** 7801 E. Gray Rd., Ste. 7, Scottsdale, AZ 85260: Free catalog ◆ Starter sets, woods, irons, putters, shafts, grips, and more. 800-234-4653.

**Stephs Golf,** 29120 N. 68th St., Cave Creek, AZ 85331: Free catalog ◆ Used golf balls and custom clubs. 888-55-BALLS.

**Sweet Spot International,** 1090 Avon Rd., Rochester Hills, MI 48307: Free brochure ◆ Custom men and women's right and left-handed putters. 800-876-7178.

**Taylor Made Golf Clubs,** 2271 Cosmos Ct., Carlsbad, CA 92009: Free information. 800-888-CLUB. www.taylormadegolf.com

**Titleist Golf Equipment,** 12 Laguna Circle, Wylie, TX 75098: Free list of retail sources. 972-442-5081. www.titleist.com

**Traxx Golf Company,** 2701 Fondren St., Ste. 114, Dallas, TX 75206: Free information ◆ Putters. 214-373-6576. www.traxxgolf.com

**Yamaha Sporting Goods,** 6600 Orangethorpe Ave., Buena Park, CA 90620: Free list of retail sources. 800-541-6514; 714-522-9011 (in CA). www.yamaha-motor.com

**Yonex Corp.,** 3520 Challenger St., Torrance, CA 90503: Free list of retail sources. 800-44-YONEX.

**Zevo Inc.,** 42000 Zevo Dr., Temecula, CA 92590: Free brochure ◆ Custom fitted golf clubs. 800-599-4653; 909-699-1771 (in CA). www.zevo.com

## Equipment Retailers

**Austad's Golf,** Hanover Direct Pennsylvania Inc., Hanover, PA 17333-0001: Free catalog ◆ Golf, other sports equipment, and clothing. 717-633-3333.

**Ballwall,** 5 Flint Ave., Larchmont, NY 10538: Free brochure ◆ Indoor and outdoor backstop training wall for sports that use a ball. 800-966-1190; 914-833-0390 (in NY).

**Cayman Golf Company Inc.,** P.O. Box 5287, Albany, GA 31706: Free information ◆ Golf balls. 800-344-0220. www.surfsouth.com/~cayman

**Clarke Distributing Company,** 9233 Bryant St., Houston, TX 77075: Catalog $2 ◆ Tennis, golf, soccer equipment, novelties, and gifts. 800-777-3444.

**Competitive Edge Golf,** 526 W. 26th St., 10th Floor, New York, NY 10001: Free catalog ◆ Golf equipment, bags, gloves, clothing, and accessories. 800-344-8588. www.golfedge.com

**Custom Golf Clubs Inc.,** 11000 N. Interstate Hwy. 35, Austin, TX 78753: Free catalog ◆ Repair supplies, clothing, gloves, bags, and other equipment. 800-456-3344; 512-837-4810 (in TX).

**D.B. Enterprises,** 425 Maplewood Dr., Norristown, PA 19401: Free information ◆ Indoor and outdoor golf net kits. 610-272-1228.

**Dimmock Hill Golf Course,** 279 Dimmock Hill Rd., Binghamton, NY 13905: Free information ◆ Golf equipment and accessories. 800-727-5511.

**Dorson Sports Inc.,** 1 Roebling Ct., Ronkonkona, NY 51779: Free information ◆ Bags and bag covers, grips, head covers, tubes, and other equipment. 800-645-7215; 516-585-5400 (in NY).

**Dynacraft Golf Products,** 71 Maholm St., Newark, OH 43055: Free information ◆ Club heads, shafts, and other components for custom club building. 800-321-4833. www.dynacraftgolf.com

**Essex Manufacturing,** 330 5th Ave., New York, NY 10001: Free information ◆ Golf umbrellas. 800-648-6010; 212-239-0080 (in NY).

**Global Golf,** 59 S. State St., Westerville, OH 43081: Free catalog ◆ Heads, shafts, grips, and other golf club components. 614-523-7402.

**Golf Day,** 135 American Legion Hwy., Revere, MA 02151: Free catalog ◆ Bags and bag covers, clubs, shoes, gloves, clothing, grips, head covers, tubes, and other equipment. 800-669-8600.

**Golf Haus,** 700 N. Pennsylvania, Lansing, MI 48854: Free catalog ◆ Clubs, bags, clothing, umbrellas, and score keepers. 517-482-8842.

**Golfsmith,** 11000 N. Interstate Hwy. 35, Austin, TX 78753: Free catalog ◆ Golf club-making supplies. 800-925-7709. www.golfsmith.com

**Harris International Inc.,** 9999 NE Glisan St., Portland, OR 97220: Free information ◆ Head covers, clubs, bags, bag covers, and other equipment. 800-547-2880; 503-256-2302 (in OR).

**Hill Billy USA,** 9 E. Pueblo St., Santa Barbara, CA 93105: Free brochure ◆ Lighweight and folding battery-powered golf club trolley. 888-682-7757. www.hillbillyusa.com

**Holabird Sports Discounters,** 9220 Pulaski Hwy., Baltimore, MD 21220: Free catalog ◆ Equipment and clothing for golf, basketball, tennis, running and jogging, racquetball, and other sports. 410-687-6400. www.holabirdsports.com

**Jayfro Corp.,** Unified Sports Inc., 976 Hartford Tnpk., P.O. Box 400, Waterford, CT 06385: Free catalog ◆ Outdoor practice cages, chipping and driving mats, and target baffles. 860-447-3001.

**JOMC Enterprises,** 914 9th St., Lakeview, IA 51450: Free brochure ◆ Used golf balls. 800-238-8679; 712-657-2393 (in IA).

**Kangaroo Products Company,** P.O. Box 607, Columbus, NC 28722: Free information ◆ Motorized caddies for golf bags. 800-438-3011; 704-894-8241 (in NC). www.kangaroogolf.com

**King Sports Inc.,** 1230 Johnson Ferry Rd., Ste. J-60, Marietta, GA 30068: Free information ◆ Fishing, golf, and baseball equipment. 800-344-1480.

**Las Vegas Discount Golf & Tennis,** 5325 S. Valley View Blvd., Ste. 10, Las Vegas, NV 89118: Free catalog ◆ Equipment, clothing, and shoes for golf, tennis, racquetball, walking and jogging, and other sports. 702-798-5500. www.lvgolf.com

**Ralph Maltby's Golfworks,** P.O. Box 3008, Newark, OH 43055: Free catalog ◆ Golf supplies for repair shops, club makers, manufacturers, and do-it-yourselfers. Also how-to books, videos, and audiocassettes. 800-562-5829. www.golfworks.com

**Marvelous Golf Products,** 121 Torrey Pines Dr., New Orleans, LA 70128: Free information ◆ Golf balls, shirts, irons, woods, and other accessories. 504-441-1090.

**Masters Golf,** 521 Main St., Islip, NY 11751: Free catalog ◆ Golf clubs, other equipment, and shoes. 800-825-9025.

**McCann Precision Golf Inc.,** 6511 Proprietors Rd., Worthington, OH 43085: Free catalog ◆ Heads, shafts, grips, and components. 800-969-2525.

**MegCor Golf,** 3525 Lackey St., Lumberton, NC 28358: Free catalog ◆ Golf equipment and accessories. 800-230-GOLF.

**Richard Metz Golf Studio Inc.,** 425 Madison Ave., New York, NY 10017: Free information ◆ Golf equipment, antique and collectible clubs, videos, and books. 212-759-6940.

**Mizuno Corp.,** 1 Jack Curran Way, Norcross, GA 30071: Free information ◆ Clubs and lightweight waterproof full-grain leather golf shoes. 800-966-1211. www.mizunogolf.com

**New York Golf Center,** 131 W. 35th St., New York, NY 10001: Free information ◆ Golf equipment. 212-564-2255.

**Outbound Golf Inc.,** 12305 W. Maple Rd., Omaha, NE 68164: Free catalog ◆ Golf clubs and accessories, club-making supplies, shoes, carts, and AccuSYSTEM golf products. 800-913-4653.

**Polar Golf,** 3877 Pacific Hwy., San Diego, CA 92110: Free information ◆ Golf equipment and accessories. 800-334-7741.

**Prima,** 5375 Procyon St., Ste. 101, Las Vegas, NV 89118: Free information ◆ Golf clubs for women. 800-932-1622.

**Professional Golf & Tennis Suppliers,** 7825 Hollywood Blvd., Pembroke Pines, FL 33024: Free catalog with long SASE ◆ Golf, tennis, and racquetball equipment. 305-981-7283.

**SGD Company Inc.,** P.O. Box 8410, Akron, OH 44320: Free information ◆ Golf balls, ball retrievers, ball washers, and golf course equipment. 330-239-2828. www.sgdgolf.com

**Southeast Discount Golf,** 1900 N. Kings Hwy., Girardeau, MO 63701: Free information ◆ Golf equipment and accessories. 800-462-4516.

**Sports Express,** 5050 F.M. West, Houston, TX 77069: Free information ◆ Golf equipment. 800-533-6321.

**Steph's Golf,** 29120 N. 68th St., Cave Creek, AZ 85331: Free catalog ◆ Used golf balls and custom clubs. 888-55-BALLS.

**Taylor Made Golf Clubs,** 2271 Cosmos Ct., Carlsbad, CA 92009: Free information ◆ Leather and all-weather gloves, ultra-lightweight bags, and golf clubs. 800-888-CLUB. www.taylormadegolf.com

**Telepro Golf Shops,** 17642 Armstrong Ave., Irvine, CA 92714: Free information ◆ Golf clubs, shoes, carts, and equipment. 800-333-9903.

**The Training Camp,** c/o Genesis Direct, 100 Plaza Dr., Secaucus, NJ 07094: Free catalog ◆ Basketball, football, golf, hockey, and soccer training aids for children. 800-873-8263. care@GenesisDirect.com

**UT Golf,** 3123 MacArthur Blvd., Santa Ana, CA 92704: Free information ◆ Golf club components. 800-800-666-6033.

**Wa-Mac Inc.,** P.O. Box 128, Carlstadt, NJ 07410: Free information ◆ Golf balls, ball washers, and golf course equipment. 800-447-5673; 201-438-7200 (in NJ).

**Edwin Watts Golf Shops,** 20 Hill Ave., Walton Beach, FL 32548: Free catalog ◆ Golf clubs, carts, bags, and equipment. 800-874-0146. www.edwinwatts.com

**Tom Wells Golf Company,** 7806 Aurora Ave. North, Seattle, WA 98103: Free catalog ◆ Custom-made computer-fitted clubs and components. 800-800-5417.

**Wittek Golf Supply Company Inc.,** 3650 N. Avondale, Chicago, IL 60618: Free information ◆ Golf course equipment, grips, head covers, tubes, clubs, bags, and bag covers. 773-463-2636.

**The Women's Golf Catalog,** P.O. Box 1249, Sagamore Beach, MA 02562: Free catalog ◆ Accessories, jewelry, footwear, gift and novelty items, and equipment. 800-984-7324. www.womensgolf.com

**The World of Golf,** 147 E. 47th St., New York, NY 10017: Free catalog ◆ Equipment for men and women. 800-818-5840. www.theworldofgolf.com

**World of Golf Equipment,** 8130 N. Lincoln Ave., Skokie, IL 60077: Free information ◆ Equipment for men, women, and juniors. 800-323-4047; 847-675-5286 (in IL). proshopwog@aol.com

### Left-handed Equipment

**Lefties Only,** 1972 Williston Rd., South Burlington, VT 05403: Free price list ◆ Golf equipment for left-handed persons. 800-533-8437.

**Odyssey Golf,** 1969 Kellog Ave., Carlsbad, CA 92008: Free brochure ◆ Bags, hats, shirts, and left-handed putters. 800-991-1788. www.odysseygolf.com

**Prosimmon Golf Equipment,** 3749 Middleburg Rd., Union Bridge, MD 21791: Free brochure ◆ Left and right-handed irons and woods for men and women. 410-751-6481.

**Sweet Spot International,** 1090 Avon Rd., Rochester Hills, MI 48307: Free brochure ◆ Custom men and women's right and left-handed putters. 800-876-7178.

## GREETING CARDS & GIFT WRAPPING

**Accents,** 215 Moody Rd., Enfield, CT 06083: Free catalog ◆ Greeting cards, calendars, and gifts. 800-357-1000.

**Associated Photo Company,** 7103 Turfway Rd., Florence, KY 41022: Free information ◆ Imprinted photo Christmas cards. 800-727-2580; 606-282-0011 (in KY).

**Auto Cards Inc.,** P.O. Box 452, Stuart, FL 34996: Brochure $2 ◆ All-occasion and Christmas cards for auto enthusiasts. 561-287-6970.

**BowMasters,** 17 Wapping Rd., Kingston, MA 02364: Free information ◆ Bow-making kit. 800-335-8312.

**Car Collectables,** 32 White Birch Rd., Madison, CT 06443: Free brochure ◆ Christmas cards, note cards, and gifts with an automotive theme. 203-245-7299.

**Currênt Inc.,** Express Processing Center, Colorado Springs, CO 80941: Free catalog ◆ Greeting cards, stationery, gift wrapping, decorations, toys, calendars, and gifts. 800-848-2848.

**Diebold Designs,** P.O. Box 236, Lyme, NH 03769: Free catalog (specify area of interest) ◆ Holiday greeting cards. 603-795-4422. www.cardmakers.com

**Walter Drake & Sons,** Drake Bldg., Colorado Springs, CO 80940: Free catalog ◆ Christmas cards. 800-525-9291. amyconnors@wdrake.com

**Kristin Elliott Inc.,** 6 Opportunity Way, Newburyport, MA 01950: Free catalog ◆ Boxed notes, gift enclosures, Christmas and other greeting cards, desk memos, memo pads, postcards, correspondence cards, and gift wrapping. 800-922-1899; 978-465-1899 (in MA).

**Embellishments,** P.O. Box 1506, Cleveland, MS 38732: Free brochure ◆ Gift packaging and presentation supplies for the home gourmet. 800-600-6885. embell@info.com

**Enfield Stationers,** Olympia Sales, 215 Moody Rd., Enfield, CT 06082: Free catalog ◆ Greeting cards, calendars, and gifts. 860-749-0751.

**Evergreen Bag Company,** 22 Ash St., East Hartford, CT 06108: Free catalog ◆ Gift, clothing, and jewelry boxes. Also ribbons, bows, tissue paper, bags, and more. 800-775-3595. sales@everbag.com

**Faded Rose,** P.O. Box 19575, Portland, OR 97219: Brochure $1 ◆ Recycled paper greeting cards. 503-245-2694.

**Fingerhut,** 11 McLeland Rd., St. Cloud, MN 56395: Free catalog ◆ Greeting cards, gift wraps, stationery, holiday decorations, organizers, and gifts. 800-233-3588. www.fingerhut.com

**G & K Enterprises,** 1408 Glenwood Ave., Greensboro, NC 27403: Free information ◆ Calendars and all-occasion and Christmas cards with a western-theme. 910-275-0049.

**Guide Dog Foundation for the Blind,** 371 E. Jericho Tnpk., Smithtown, NY 11787: Free catalog ◆ Limited edition guide dog-theme prints, holiday cards, mugs, mats, key rings, stationery, pet accessories, and gifts. 800-443-8372.

**H & F Announcements,** 9219 Quivira Rd., Overland Park, KS 66215: Free catalog ◆ Birth announcements and children's party invitations. 800-289-1560.

**Handshake Greeting Cards,** P.O. Box 9027, Columbus, GA 31908: Free catalog ◆ Personalized greeting cards. 800-634-2134.

**Heirloom Editions,** Box 520-B, Rt. 4, Carthage, MO 64836: Catalog $4 ◆ Lithographs, greeting cards, stickers, miniatures, stationery, framed prints, turn-of-the-century art, and paper collectibles. 800-725-0725.

**House-Mouse Designs,** P.O. Box 48, Williston, VT 05495: Free catalog ◆ Christmas cards, note and recipe cards, magnets, and stickers. 800-242-6423. www.house-mouse.com

**Keepsake Creations,** 407 Lyme St., Bellevue, OH 44811: Free catalog ◆ Note and greeting cards for all occasions. 419-483-7189.

**Miles Kimball Company,** 41 W. 8th Ave., Oshkosh, WI 54906: Free catalog ◆ Christmas cards with optional personalization. 800-546-2255. www.mileskimball.com

**Kimmeric Studio,** P.O. Box 10749, Lake Tahoe, CA 96158: Catalog $2 ◆ Craft hang tags. 530-573-1616.

**Lang Companies,** P.O. Box 55, Delafield, WI 53018: Catalog $1 ◆ Country-style calendars, boxed note cards, and greeting cards. 800-967-3399. www.lang.com

**Literary Calligraphy,** 5326 White House Rd., Moneta, VA 24121: Catalog $2 ◆ Literary calligraphy gifts. 800-261-6325. susanloy@rev.net

**Main Street Press,** P.O. Box 126, Delafield, WI 53018: Catalog $1 ◆ Wall calendars, boxed greeting cards, note cards and pads, and stationery. 414-646-8511.

**The Maritime Store,** 2905 Hyde St. Pier, San Francisco, CA 94109: Free catalog ◆ Maritime maps, greeting cards, boat models, children's and maritime books, and gifts. 415-775-BOOK.

**Naptime Productions,** 525 Highland Dr., Rossford, OH 43460: Free information ◆ Baby announcements, shower invitations, Christmas cards, and baby items. 419-666-3742. wwwmembers.aol.com/naptimeTwo

**Nasco,** 901 Janesville Ave., Fort Atkinson, WI 53538: Free catalog ◆ Calligraphy supplies and greeting cards. 800-558-9595. www.nascofa.com

**National Wildlife Federation,** P.O. Box 9004, Winchester, VA 22604: Free catalog ◆ Books, holiday cards, and gifts. 800-477-5560. www.nwf.org

**Novagraphics,** P.O. Box 37197, Tucson, AZ 85740: Catalog $3 ◆ Astronomy and space-decorative artwork and greeting cards. 800-727-6682. www.novaspace.com

**Posty Cards,** 1600 Olive St., Kansas City, MO 64127: Free catalog ◆ Calendars and greeting and birthday cards. 800-554-5018. www.postycards.com

**The Printery House,** Conception Abbey, Conception, MO 64433: Free information ◆ Folk art and religious greeting cards. 800-322-2737.

**Prudent Publishing,** 65 Challenger Rd., Ridgefield Park, NJ 07660: Free brochure ◆ Special occasion greeting cards for business and personal use. 201-641-8996.

**R & M Retail Merchandising Products,** 12342 Bell Ranch Dr., Santa Fe Springs, CA 90670: Free catalog (minimum order $20) ◆ Pricing cards, promotional signs, gift wrapping supplies and boxes, realistic props, other merchandising aids, and more. 800-231-9600; 562-946-6900 (in CA).

**Renaissance Greeting Cards Inc.,** P.O. Box 845, Springvale, ME 04083: Catalog $1 ◆ Greeting cards. 800-688-9998.

**Running Delights,** P.O. Box 94, Wheat Ridge, CO 80034: Free catalog ◆ Greeting cards and novelty gifts for runners. 888-786-3587; 303-232-1308 (in CO).

**Stik-EES,** 1165 Joshua Way, P.O. Box 9630, Vista, CA 92085: Free catalog ◆ Re-usable static cling pre-cut vinyl stickers for decorating gifts, windows, and other surfaces. 800-2-STIKEE; 760-727-7011 (in CA). www.stikees.com

**Trumble Greetings,** P.O. Box 9800, Boulder, CO 80301: Catalog $1 ◆ Greeting cards with country and wildlife scenes that depict America's heritage. 800-525-0656.

**Unicef,** P.O. Box 182233, Chattanooga, TN 37422: Free catalog ◆ Greeting and note cards, toys, limited edition plates, gifts, and postcards. 800-553-1200. www.unicefusa.org

**Victorian Papers,** P.O. Box 411332, Kansas City, MO 61141: Catalog $2 ◆ Greeting and note cards for birthdays, holidays, graduation, and other occasions. 800-800-6647.

## GUM BALL MACHINES

**Norman & Mary Johnson,** 13820 County Home Rd., Bowling Green, OH 43402: Free information with long SASE ◆ Slot machines, old arcade games, peanut and gumball machines, mechanical and still banks, and other coin-operated machines. 419-352-3041.

**KAPS Vending,** 593 Lavina Ct., Helmet, CA 92544: Free price list with long SASE ◆ Antique gumball machines, globes, parts, decals, gumballs, candy, and toys. 909-658-4620.

## GUNS & AMMUNITION

### Air Guns & Supplies

**Armsport Inc.,** 3950 NW 49th St., Miami, FL 33142: Free information ◆ Air rifles and pistols, scopes, pellets and bb ammunition, and targets. 305-635-7850.

**Beeman Precision Arms Inc.,** 5454 Argosy Dr., Huntington Beach, CA 92649: Catalog $2 ◆ Air rifles and pistols, scopes, pellets and bb ammunition, and targets. 800-822-8005. www.beeman.com

**Benjamin/Sheridan Company,** Rt. 5 & 20, East Bloomfield, NY 14443: Free catalog ◆ Single shot and repeater air rifles, pistols, scopes, pellets and bb ammunition, and targets. 716-657-6161.

**Century International Arms,** P.O. Box 714, St. Albans, VT 05478: Free information ◆ Air rifles and pistols. 800-258-8879. www.centuryarms.com

**Compasseco Inc.,** 151 Atkinson Hill, Bardstown, KY 40004: Free information ◆ Air rifles and ammunition. 800-726-1696. www.compasseco.com

**Crosman Air Guns,** Rt. 5 & 20, East Bloomfield, NY 14443: Free information ◆ Air rifles and pistols, scopes, pellets and bb ammunition, and targets. 800-7AIR-GUN. www.crosman.com

**Daisy Manufacturing Company Inc.,** P.O. Box 220, Rogers, AR 72757: Free information ◆ Air rifles and pistols, pellets and bb ammunition, scopes, and targets. 501-636-1200. www.daisy.com

**Dixie Gun Works Inc.,** P.O. Box 130, Union City, TN 38261: Catalog $5 ◆ Air rifles and pistols. 800-238-6785.

**Mandall Shooting Supplies,** 3616 N. Scottsdale Rd., Scottsdale, AZ 85251: Free information ◆ Air guns, scopes, other equipment, and ammunition. 602-945-2553.

## Ammunition & Ammunition-Loading Equipment

**Accurate Arms Company,** 5891 Hwy. 230 West, McEwen, TN 37101: Free information ◆ Black powder cartridges. 800-416-3006.

**Alpine Range Supply,** 5482 Shelby, Fort Worth, TX 76140: Free information ◆ Reloading equipment. 817-572-1242.

**Ammo Depot,** 7325 Ingham Ln., Godfrey, IL 62035: Catalog $1.50 ◆ Rifle and pistol ammunition, powder handling equipment, and reloading supplies. 618-466-2666.

**Badger Shooter's Supply Inc.,** 202 N. Harding, Owen, WI 54460: Free catalog ◆ Sporting firearms and ammunition. 800-424-9069.

**Ballistic Products Inc.,** 20015 75th Ave. North, Corcoran, MN 55340: Catalog $1 ◆ Ammunition supplies. 612-494-9237.

**Blount Inc.,** 605 Oro Dam Blvd., Oroville, CA 95965: Free information ◆ Big game hunting bullets and ammunition for rifles and handguns. 800-627-3640.

**Buffalo Bullet Company,** 12637 Los Nietos Rd., Unit A, Santa Fe Springs, CA 90670: Free brochure ◆ Bullets for muzzle-loaders and other ammunition. 562-944-0322.

**Century International Arms,** P.O. Box 714, St. Albans, VT 05478: Free information ◆ Ammunition supplies. 800-258-8879. www.centuryarms.com

**Cheap Shot,** 950 S. Central Ave., Canonsburg, PA 15317: Free catalog ◆ Ammunition. 412-745-2658.

**Dillon Precision Products Inc.,** 8009 E. Dillon's Way, Scottsdale, AZ 85260: Free catalog ◆ Reloading equipment. 800-223-4570; 602-948-8009 (in AZ). www.dillonprecision.com

**Federal Cartridge Company,** 900 Ehlen Dr., Anoka, MN 55303: Free information ◆ Ammunition supplies. 800-322-2342. www.federalcartridge.com

**Gander Mountain (Cabela's),** One Cabela Dr., Sidney, NE 69160: Free catalog ◆ Reloading supplies. 800-237-4444. www.cabelas.com

**Graf & Sons,** 4050 S. Clark, Mexico, MO 65265: Free information ◆ Hunting accessories, scopes, and reloading equipment. 800-531-2666.

**Art Green,** 485 S. Robertson Blvd., Beverly Hills, CA 90211: Catalog $2 ◆ Bullet casting metals. 310-274-1283.

**Hercules Incorporated,** Hercules Plaza, Wilmington, DE 19894: Free information ◆ Propellants for handguns, rifles, and shotguns. 302-594-5000.

**HKS Products Inc.,** 7841 Foundation Dr., Florence, KY 41042: Free information ◆ Revolver and magazine speed loaders. 606-342-7841.

**Hornady Manufacturing Company,** P.O. Box 1848, Grand Island, NE 68802: Catalog $2 ◆ Ammunition supplies and loading equipment. 800-338-3220. www.hornady.com

**Huntington,** P.O. Box 991, 601 Oro Dam Blvd., Oroville, CA 95965: Free catalog ◆ Standard and hard-to-find reloading products. 916-534-1210.

**K & T Company,** Division T & S Industries Inc., 1027 Skyview Dr., West Carrollton, OH 45449: Free information ◆ Rust-inhibiting snap caps for shotguns and gun lubricants and grease. 937-859-8414.

**Lee Precision Inc.,** 4275 Hwy. U, Hartford, WI 53027: Catalog $1 ◆ Reloading equipment and supplies. 414-673-3075.

**Mayville Engineering Company Inc.,** 715 South St., Mayville, WI 53050: Free brochure ◆ Shotgun shell reloading equipment. 920-387-4500. www.mayvl.com

**Michaels of Oregon Company,** P.O. Box 1690, Oregon City, OR 97045: Free information ◆ Ammunition supplies. 503-655-7964. www.uncle-mikes.com

**Midway Arms Inc.,** P.O. Box 718, Columbia, MO 65205: Free catalog ◆ Reloading equipment and ammunition. 800-243-3220.

**National Bullet Company,** 1585 E. 361st St., Eastlake, OH 44095: Free catalog ◆ Cast lead bullets and ammunition. 216-951-1854. www.nationalbullet.com

**Nosler Bullets Inc.,** P.O. Box 671, Bend, OR 97709: Free catalog ◆ Hunting bullets. 800-285-3701. www.nosler.com

**Ponsness/Warren,** P.O. Box 8, Rathdrum, ID 83858: Free catalog ◆ Reloading equipment and supplies. 208-687-2231. www.reloader.com

**Precision Reloading Inc.,** P.O. Box 122, Stafford Springs, CT 06076: Free information ◆ Reloading components and accessories. 860-684-5680. www.precisionreloading.com

**Rapine Bullet Manufacturing Company,** P.O. Box 1119, RD 1, East Greenville, PA 18041: Catalog $2 ◆ Bullet molds. 215-679-5413.

**Remington Arms,** 870 Remington Dr., Madison, NC 27025: Free information ◆ Ammunition supplies. 910-548-8700. www.remington.com

**Speer Products,** Blount Sporting Equipment Division, 2299 Snake River Ave., Lewiston, ID 83501: Free information ◆ Hunting bullets and other ammunition. 208-746-2351. www.blount.com/operations.html

**Widener's Reloading & Shooting Supply Inc.,** P.O. Box 3009, Johnson City, TN 37602: Free catalog ◆ Reloading supplies. 800-615-3006. www.wideners.com

**WilsonTrace Distribution,** 1808 Sportsman Ln., Huntsville, AL 35816: Free catalog ◆ Reloading equipment, scopes, sportshooting rifles, binoculars, and accessories. 800-494-5397. www.wileyoutdoorsports.com

## Antique, Muzzle Loading, & Replica Guns

**Armoury Inc.,** Rt. 202, Box 2340, New Preston, CT 06777: Free information ◆ Black powder handguns and rifles, black powder, kits, and replica guns. 860-868-0001.

**Armsport Inc.,** 3950 NW 49th St., Miami, FL 33142: Free information ◆ Antique handguns, rifles, and kits. 305-635-7850.

**Buffalo Arms Company,** 99 Raven Ridge, Sandpoint, ID 83864: Catalog $2 ◆ Black powder cartridge rifles, target barrels and sights, lead and tin, and other supplies. 208-263-6953. www.buffaloarms.com

**Cabin Creek Gun Shop,** 25 S. Broad St., Hellam, PA 17406: Catalog $2 ◆ Handmade reproduction 18th century rifles, pistols, and fowling pieces. 717-757-5841.

**Douglas R. Carlson,** Antique American Firearms, P.O. Box 71035, Des Moines, IA 50325: Catalog $20 (annual subscription) ◆ Antique firearms. 515-224-6552.

**Cash Manufacturing Company Inc.,** P.O. Box 130, Waunakee, WI 53507: Free catalog ◆ Muzzle-loading equipment. 608-849-5664.

**Cimarron,** P.O. Box 906, Fredericksburg, TX 78624: Free information ◆ Replica cowboy guns. 830-997-9090.

**Collector's Armoury,** 800 Slaters Ln., P.O. Box 59, Alexandria, VA 22313: Free catalog ◆ Replica and antique guns. 800-544-3456.

**Daisy Manufacturing Company Inc.,** P.O. Box 220, Rogers, AR 72757: Free information ◆ Replica guns. 501-636-1200. www.daisy.com

**Dixie Gun Works Inc.,** P.O. Box 130, Union City, TN 38261: Catalog $5 ◆ Antique and replica black powder handguns and rifles. Also black powder. 800-238-6785.

**EMF Company,** 1900 E. Warner Ave., Santa Ana, CA 92705: Catalog $1 ◆ Replica United States Cavalry and artillery revolvers. 714-261-6611.

**Euroarms of America Inc.,** 208 E. Piccadilly St., P.O. Box 3277, Winchester, VA 22601: Catalog $3 ◆ Black powder rifles and handguns, replica guns, and kits. 540-662-1863.

**N. Flayderman & Company Inc.,** P.O. Box 2446, Fort Lauderdale, FL 33303: Catalog $10 ◆ Antique guns, swords, knives, and western, nautical, and military collectibles. 305-761-8855.

**Golden Age Arms Company,** 115 High St., Box 366, Ashley, OH 43003: Catalog $4 ◆ Muzzle-loading guns, parts, and books. 614-747-2488.

**Hansen Cartridge Company,** 244 Old Post Rd., Southport, CT 06490: Free information ◆ Replica and antique guns. 203-259-5424.

**Kahnke Gunworks,** 206 W. 11th St., Redwood Falls, MN 56283: Free information ◆ Muzzle-loading handguns. 507-637-2901. www.powderandbow.com/kahnke

**Little Bat's Trading Post,** 123 Main St., Crawford, NE 69339: Catalog $10 ◆ Antique firearms, Old West collectibles, and militaria. 308-665-1900.

**Lyman Products Corp.,** 475 Smith St., Middletown, CT 06457: Catalog $2 ◆ Black powder rifles and handguns. Also kits. 800-22-LYMAN. www.lymanproducts.com

**Miltech,** P.O. Box 322, Los Altos, CA 94023: Catalog $1 ◆ Hand-restored original vintage firearms. 415-948-3500.

**Walt Moreau,** P.O. Box 14764, San Francisco, CA 94114: Catalog $7 ◆ Fine, rare, and unusual classic antique arms and Plains Indian (Native American) art. 415-861-8319. www.moreau.com

**Mountain State Muzzleloading Supplies Inc.,** Rt. 2, Box 154-1, Williamstown, WV 26187: Catalog $4 ◆ Black powder rifles, handguns, and kits. 304-375-7842. www.msmfg.com

**Mowrey Gun Works,** P.O. Box 246, Waldron, IN 46182: Catalog $2 ◆ Handmade rifles, shotguns, and muzzle-loaders. 317-525-6181.

**Muzzle Loaders Etcetera Inc.,** 9901 Lyndale Ave. South, Bloomington, MN 55420: Free information ◆ Black powder and muzzle-loading guns. 612-884-1161.

**Navy Arms Company,** 689 Bergen Blvd., Ridgefield, NJ 07657: Catalog $2 ◆ Black powder rifles and handguns, replica guns, kits, and black powder. 201-945-2500.

**October Country,** P.O. Box 969, Hayden Lake, ID 83835: Catalog $3 (refundable) ◆ Muzzle-loading equipment. 208-772-2068. www.oct-country.com

**Mark Odle,** Rt. 1, Box 40, Reedy, WV 25270: Free brochure with long SASE ◆ Handcrafted colonial and early American-style powderhorns, hunting bags, and shooting accessories. 304-927-4988.

**Ogan Antiques Ltd.,** P.O. Box 14831, North Palm Beach, FL 33408: Catalog $10 ◆ Antique firearms. 407-844-2434.

**S & S Firearms,** 7411 Myrtle Ave., Glendale, NY 11385: Free information ◆ Antique guns. 718-497-1100. www.ssfirearms.com

**Shiloh Rifle Manufacturing Company Inc.,** P.O. Box 279, Big Timber, MT 59011: Free information ◆ Black powder and muzzle-loading guns. 406-932-4270.

**Simmons Gun Specialties Inc.,** 20241 W. 207th, Spring Hill, KS 66083: Free information ◆ Black powder rifles and handguns, kits, and black powder. 800-444-0220.

**South Bend Replicas Inc.,** 61650 Oak Rd., South Bend, IN 46614: Catalog $7 ◆ Replica and antique guns. 219-289-4500. www.specialtymile.com/southbendreplicas

**Springfield Sporters Inc.,** RD 1, Penn Ruth, PA 15765: Catalog $2 ◆ Replica and antique guns. 412-254-2626.

**Taylor's & Company Inc.,** 304 Lenoir Dr., Winchester, VA 22603: Catalog $3 ◆ Black powder guns and accessories. 540-722-2017.

**Tennessee Valley Manufacturing,** Rt. 8, Box 440, Corinth, MS 38834: Catalog $3 ◆ Custom muzzleloading rifles, parts, and accouterments. 601-286-5014. tvm@avsiA.com

**Thompson/Center Arms,** P.O. Box 5002, Rochester, NH 03866: Free catalog ◆ Muzzle-loading rifles, handguns, kits, and black powder. 603-332-2333. www.tcarms.com

**Traditions Inc.,** P.O. Box 776, Old Saybrook, CT 06476: Free information ◆ Black powder rifles and handguns, kits, and replica guns. 860-388-4656.

**Del & Jean Warren,** P.O. Box 364, Liberty, MO 64068: Catalog $6 ◆ Civil War era historic books and patterns, jewelry and accessories, underpinnings, uniforms and accouterments, black powder rifles, and shooting supplies. 816-781-9473. Jamescntry@aol.com

**Warren Muzzle Loading Company Inc.,** P.O. Box 100, Ozone, AR 72854: Catalog $2 ◆ Pistol and rifle bullets and muzzle-loading supplies. 800-874-3810.

**The Winchester Sutler Inc.,** 270 Shadow Brook Ln., Winchester, VA 22603: Catalog $4 ◆ Reproduction Civil War muskets and carbines. 540-888-3595.

## Racks, Cases, & Holsters

**Bob Allen Sportswear,** Box 477, Des Moines, IA 50302: Free catalog ◆ Carrying cases, holsters, and racks. 515-283-2191.

**American Import Company,** 1453 Mission St., San Francisco, CA 94103: Free information ◆ Gun racks, soft cases, and slings. 415-863-1506.

**American Sales & Manufacturing,** Box 677, Laredo, TX 78042: Catalog $3 ◆ Handcrafted gun belts and holsters. 210-723-6893.

**American Security Products Company,** 11925 Pacific Ave., Fontana, CA 92335: Free information ◆ Gun and other safes for home and office security. 800-421-6142. qsd@amersecurity.com

**Americase,** Box 271, Waxahachie, TX 75165: Free information ◆ Carrying cases. 800-880-3629.

**API Outdoors Inc.,** P.O. Box 1432, Tallulah, LA 71282: Free information ◆ Gun racks. 800-228-4846; 318-574-4903 (in (LA).

**Beeman Precision Arms Inc.,** 5454 Argosy Dr., Huntington Beach, CA 92649: Catalog $2 ◆ Holsters, slings, and soft cases. 800-822-8005. www.beeman.com

**Brauer Brothers Manufacturing Company,** 2020 Delmar Blvd., St. Louis, MO 63112: Free information ◆ Soft cases, cabinets, slings, and holsters. 314-231-2864.

**Browning Company,** Dept. C006, One Browning Pl., Morgan, UT 84050: Catalog $2 ◆ Hard and soft cases, holsters, and slings. 800-333-3288. www.browning.com

**Cheyenne Saddle Company,** 308 Strathmore Rd., Lexington, KY 40505: Catalog $2 ◆ Authentic Old West holsters and leather gear.

**Coronado Leather,** 120 C Ave., Coronado, CA 92118: Free information ◆ Dual-ply leather holsters. 800-283-9509. www.coronadoleather.com

**Vee Dennis Manufacturing Company,** 620 Park Rd., Cherry Hill, NJ 08034: Free brochure ◆ Gun rests. 609-428-7676.

**DeSantis Holster & Leather Company,** P.O. Box 2039, New Hyde Park, NY 11040: Free information ◆ Gun holsters. 516-354-8000. www.desantisholster.com

**A.G. English Inc.,** 708 S. 12th St., Broken Arrow, OK 74012: Free information ◆ Gun safes. 800-222-7233.

**Fort Knox Security Products,** 993 N. Industrial Park Rd., Orem, UT 84057: Free information ◆ Burglar-proof gun safes. 800-821-5216. www.ftknox.com

**Hawks,** P.O. Box 207, Blytheville, AR 72316: Free catalog ◆ Hunting clothing and footwear, knives, gun safes, guns, and more.

**Hilsport by Hilco Inc.,** 2102 Fair Park Blvd., Harlingen, TX 78550: Free brochure ◆ Luggage and gun cases. 956-423-1885. 800-451-9236.

**Don Hume Leathergoods,** Box 351, Miami, OK 74355: Catalog $1 ◆ Holsters. 800-331-2686; 918-542-6604 (in OK). don_humw@edumaster.net

**Hunter Company Inc.,** P.O. Box 467, Westminster, CO 80030: Catalog $1 ◆ Holsters, slings, scabbards, and other leather goods. 800-676-HUNT. www.huntercompany.com

**Richard Kirkland,** Leather Artisan, 4020 NE 81st Ave., Portland, OR 97213: Catalog $3 ◆ Authentic hand-stitched and handcrafted leather Cheyenne-style holsters. 503-335-0713.

**Liberty Safe,** 1060 N. Spring Creek Pl., Springville, UT 84663: Free brochure ◆ Gun safes. 800-247-5625.

**National Security Safe Company,** 12757 East Fwy., Houston, TX 77015: Free brochure ◆ Gun safes with double steel walls. 800-574-7924. safe@net1.net

**Penguin Industries Inc.,** Airport Industrial Mall, Coatesville, PA 19320: Free information ◆ Gun cases and cabinets. 610-384-6000.

**Pleasant Valley Saddle Shop,** 1220 S. County Rd. 21, Loveland, CO 80537: Information $2 ◆ Handcrafted leather cowboy-style holsters of the 1950s. 970-669-1588. www.info2000.net/~pvsaddle

**Pullman Saddle Company,** P.O. Box 567, New Palestine, IN 46163: Free information ◆ Hand-built saddles and gun holsters. 800-783-7996; 317-861-6871 (in IN0. www.harpdepot.com/pullman

**Quality Arms Inc.,** Box 19477, Houston, TX 77224: Free information ◆ Gun cases. 713-870-8377.

**Rhino Guns,** 4340 SE 53rd Ave., Ocala, FL 34480: Free information ◆ Aluminum gun cases and ported chokes. 800-226-3613. www.rhinoguns.com

**Safariland Leather Products,** 3120 E. Mission Blvd., P.O. Box 51478, Ontario, CA 91761: Free information ◆ Gun holsters. 800-347-1200. www.safariland.com

**Shooting Systems,** 1075 Headquarters Park, Fenton, MO 63026: Free information ◆ Canvas carrying and gun storage cases, holsters, and slings. 800-325-3049; 314-343-3575 (in MO). www.shootingsystems.com

**Southern Security Safes,** 1700 Oak Hills Dr., Kingston, TN 37763: Free information ◆ Gun safes with protective bolt-locking systems. 800-251-9992.

**Sun Welding Safe Company,** 290 Easy St., Ste. 3, Simi Valley, CA 93065: Free brochure ◆ Gun safes. 800-729-7233.

**Tombstone Leather Company,** P.O. Box 262220, San Diego, CA 92196: Catalog $5 ◆ Handcrafted gun belts and holsters.

**Treadlok,** 1764 Granby St. NE, Roanoke, VA 24012: Free catalog ◆ Safes for guns and valuables. 800-729-8732. www.billsgs.com/safes

**Versatile Rack Company,** 5761 Anderson St., Vernon, CA 90058: Free brochure ◆ Portable gun racks and accessories. 213-588-0137.

**Wild Bills Originals,** P.O. Box 13037, Burton, WA 98013: Catalog/poster $10 ◆ Authentic reproduction holsters, gun belts, and accessories. 206-463-5738.

**Wilson Case Company,** P.O. Box 1106, Hastings, NE 68902: Free information ◆ Gun cases. 800-322-5493. www.wilsoncase.com

**Wolf Ears Equipment,** 702 S. Pine St., Laramie, WY 82070: Catalog $2 ◆ Cartridge belts and boxes, United States prairie belts, and 1800s-style holsters. 307-745-7135.

## Scopes, Mounts, & Sights

**Aimpoint,** 420 W. Main St., Geneseo, IL 61254: Free brochure ◆ Lightweight red dot sights. 309-944-1702. www.aimpointusa.com

**American Import Company,** 1453 Mission St., San Francisco, CA 94103: Free information ◆ Scopes, mounts, and storage racks. 415-863-1506.

**B-Square Company,** P.O. Box 11281, Fort Worth, TX 76110: Free catalog ◆ Scope mounts for handguns, rifles, and shotguns. 800-433-2909.

**Ball Photo Supply Company,** 85 Tunnel Rd., Asheville, NC 28805: Free information ◆ Telescopes, spotting scopes, camera equipment, binoculars, eyepieces, and accessories. 704-252-2443.

**Bausch & Lomb,** 9200 Cody, Overland Park, KS 66214: Free list of retail sources ◆ Spotting scopes, night vision viewers, and mounts. 800-423-3537. www.bushnell.com

**Binocular City,** 811 Hwy. 13, Diamond Jims Mall, Mendola Heights, MN 55118: Free information ◆ Binoculars, spotting and rifle scopes, and accessories. 800-473-1621.

**Maynard P. Buehler,** 17 Orinda Way, Orinda, CA 94563: Free catalog ◆ Mounting bases and rings for rifle and handgun scopes. 510-254-3201.

**Burris Company Inc.,** P.O. Box 1747, Greeley, CO 80632: Free catalog ◆ Mounts and spotting scopes. 888-228-7747. www.burrisoptics.com

**Camera Bug Ltd.,** 1799 Briarcliff Rd., Atlanta, GA 30306: Free information ◆ Telescopes, binoculars, spotting scopes, and accessories. 404-873-4513. www.cam bug@msn.com

**Conetrol Scope Mounts,** 10225 S. Hwy. 123, Sequin, TX 78155: Free information ◆ Split-ring scope mounting systems. 800-CONETROL. www.conetrol.com

**Europtik Ltd.,** P.O. Box 319, Dunmore, PA 18509: Free information ◆ Binoculars and rifle scopes. 717-347-6049. www.europtik.com

**Internet Telescope Exchange,** 7151 Market St., Wilmington, NC 28405: Free catalog ◆ Night vision scopes, goggles, binoculars, and accessories. 416-663-6963. www.europtik.com

**Keng's Firearms Specialty Inc.,** 875 Wharton Dr. SW, Atlanta, GA 30336: Free information ◆ Scope mounts. 800-848-4671.

**Kowa Optimed Inc.,** 20001 S. Vermont Ave., Torrance, CA 90502: Free information ◆ Spotting scopes. 800-966-5692.

**Leupold & Stevens Inc.,** P.O. Box 688, Beaverton, OR 97075: Free catalog (request list of retail sources) ◆ Low-light rifle scope with variable power settings. 800-929-4949. www.leupstv.com/gidealer.html

**Millett Sights,** 7275 Murdy Circle, Huntington Beach, CA 92647: Catalog $2 ◆ Gun sights. 800-645-5388; 714-842-5575 (in CA). www.millettsights.com

**Night Vision Headquarters,** 90 S. Spruce, South San Francisco, CA 94080: Free catalog ◆ Night vision scopes. 415-588-3075.

**Quarton USA,** 7042 Alamo Downs Pkwy., San Antonio, TX 78238: Free information ◆ Laser sighting systems and accessories. 800-520-8435; 210-520-8430 (in TX). www.quarton.com

**Simmons Outdoor Company,** 201 Plantation Oak, Thomasville, GA 31792: Catalog $2 ◆ Rifle scopes. 912-227-9053.

**Tasco Sales Inc.,** Box 520080, Miami, FL 33152: Free information ◆ Gun scopes. 305-591-3670.

**Warne Manufacturing Company,** 9039 SE Jannsen Rd., Clackamas, OR 97015: Free information ◆ Easy-to-install detachable rifle scope mounts. 503-657-5590.

**Williams Gun Sight Company,** 7389 Lapeer Rd., P.O. Box 329, Davison, MI 48423: Free information ◆ Scope mounts for rifles, shotguns, and black powder guns. 800-530-9028. www.williamsgunsight.com

**WilsonTrace Distribution,** 1808 Sportsman Ln., Huntsville, AL 35816: Free catalog ◆ Reloading equipment, scopes, sportshooting rifles, binoculars, and accessories. 800-494-5397. www.wileyoutdoorsports.com

## Sportshooting Rifles, Handguns, & Shotguns

**Access to Recreation Inc.,** 8 Sandra Ct., Newbury Park, CA 91320: Free catalog ◆ Adaptive shooting equipment for the disabled. 800-634-4351.

**Accupro USA,** Box 2270, 936 Peace Portal Dr., Blaine, WA 98231: Free catalog ◆ Gun cleaning system and supplies. 800-822-1366. www.accupro.com

**American Derringer Corp.,** 127 N. Lacy Dr., Waco, TX 76705: Free information ◆ Sport-shooting automatic pistols, derringers, and revolvers. 800-642-7817. www.amderringer.com

**Armoury Inc.,** Rt. 202, Box 2340, New Preston, CT 06777: Free information ◆ Guns for sport-shooting. 860-868-0001.

**Badger Shooter's Supply Inc.,** 202 N. Harding, Owen, WI 54460: Free catalog ◆ Sporting firearms and ammunition. 800-424-9069.

**Beretta U.S.A.,** 17601 Beretta Dr., Accokeek, MD 20607: Free information ◆ Shotguns and other guns. 800-528-7453.

**Billingsley & Brownell Rifle Metalsmith,** Box 25, Dayton, WY 82836: Brochure $2 ◆ Rifle accessories. 307-655-9344.

**Brownells Inc.,** 200 S. Front St., Montezuma, IA 50171: Free catalog ◆ Gunsmithing supplies and tools. 515-623-5401. www.brownells.com/brownells

**Browning Company,** Dept. C006, One Browning Pl., Morgan, UT 84050: Catalog $2 ◆ Bolt-and-lever action guns, semi-automatics and single shot rifles, and over and under, side-by-side, and single barrel shotguns. 800-333-3288. www.browning.com

**Century International Arms,** P.O. Box 714, St. Albans, VT 05478: Free information ◆ Bolt-and-lever action guns, semi-automatic rifles, and single shot rifles. 800-258-8879. www.centuryarms.com

**Cheaper than Dirt,** 2536 NE Loop 820, Fort Worth, TX 76106: Free catalog ◆ Accessories, holsters and cases, scopes, survival supplies, gunsmith and cleaning supplies, clothing, hunting and camping gear, archery and crossbow equipment, and shotgun equipment. 888-625-3848. www.cheaperthandirt.com

**Clark Custom Guns Inc.,** 336 Shootout Ln., Princeton, LA 71067: Catalog $3 ◆ Custom handguns. 318-949-9884.

**Denny's Shooters Supply Inc.,** P.O. Box 402, Cedar Falls, IA 50613: Free catalog ◆ Handgun accessories. 800-747-3845.

**Douglas Barrels Inc.,** 5504 Big Tyler Rd., Charleston, WV 25313: Free information ◆ Rifle barrels. 304-776-1341.

**Dunn's Supply Catalog,** P.O. Box 509, Grand Junction, TN 38039: Free catalog ◆ Camouflage and insulated clothing, outerwear, shoes and boots, hunting equipment, day and belt packs, gun care kits, sunglasses, game calls, decoys, and supplies. 800-427-6572. www.dunnscatalog.com

**Eagle Arms Inc.,** 5701 N. Mio Ed., Rose City, MI 48654: Free information ◆ Parts and complete rifles. 517-685-2286.

**EMF Company,** 1900 E. Warner Ave., Santa Ana, CA 92705: Catalog $1 ◆ United States and foreign revolvers, rifles, pistols, and shotguns. Includes reproduction single-action revolvers. 714-261-6611.

**Frank's Center Inc.,** RR 1, Box 45, Nevada, MO 64772: Catalog $2 ◆ Sportshooting guns and backpacking, camping, and rescue/rappelling equipment. 417-667-9190. www.frankscenterinc.com

**Galati International,** P.O. Box 10, Wesco, MO 65586: Free catalog ◆ Accessories and supplies. 800-444-2550. galati@usmo.com

**Gun Parts Corp.,** Williams Ln., West Hurley, NY 12491: Catalog $7.95 ◆ Commercial, military, antique, and foreign gun parts. 914-679-2417.

**Gil Hebard Guns,** 125 Public Square, Knoxville, IL 61448: Free catalog ◆ Handguns. 309-289-2700.

**Hi-Grade Shooter's Supply,** Box 448, Jacktown, PA 15642: Free information ◆ Guns and accessories. 800-245-6824; 412-863-8200 (in AK & HI).

**Interarms,** P.O. Box 208, Alexandria, VA 22313: Catalog $2 ◆ Bolt-and-lever action, target, semi-automatic, and single-shot rifles. 703-548-1400. www.interarms.com

**Harry Lawson Company,** 3328 N. Richey Blvd., Tucson, AZ 85716: Catalog $1 ◆ Rifles. 520-326-1117.

**Liberty Mountain Sports,** 4875 W. 1980 South, Salt Lake City, UT 84104: Free list of retail sources ◆ Automatic and blank pistols, derringers, revolvers and auto-loading, automatic, over and under, semi-automatic, side-by-side, and single barrel shotguns. 800-366-2666.

**Marlin Firearms Company,** 100 Kenna Dr., North Haven CT 06473: Catalog $1 ◆ Automatic and blank pistols, derringers, revolvers and auto-loading, automatic, over and under, semi-automatic, side-by-side, and single barrel shotguns. 203-239-5621. www.MarlinFirearms.com

**O.F. Mossberg & Sons Inc.,** 7 Grasso Ave., P.O. Box 497, North Haven, CT 06473: Free information ◆ Shotguns. 203-288-6491. www.mossberg.com

**Mowrey Gun Works,** P.O. Box 246, Waldron, IN 46182: Catalog $2 ◆ Handmade rifles, shotguns, and muzzle-loaders. 317-525-6181.

**Murray's Gunshop Inc.,** 208 Madison St., The Dalles, OR 97058: Free information ◆ Custom gun stocks and gunsmithing and blueing supplies. 541-298-1220.

**Navy Arms Company,** 689 Bergen Blvd., Ridgefield, NJ 07657: Catalog $2 ◆ Automatic pistols, blank guns, revolvers, and target, bolt-and-lever action, semi-automatic, and single shot rifles. 201-945-2500.

**Pachmayr Ltd.,** 1875 S. Mountain Ave., Monrovia, CA 91016: Free catalog ◆ Shooting and hunting accessories, other guns, clay-target shooting equipment, and supplies. 800-423-9704. www.pachmayr.com

**Perazzi USA Inc.,** 1207 S. Shamrock Ave., Monrovia, CA 91016: Free information ◆ Combination, single, sporting, skeet, and trap shotguns. 626-303-0068. www.perazzi.com

**Remington Arms,** 870 Remington Dr., Madison, NC 27025: Free information ◆ Auto-loading, automatic, over and under, and semi-automatic shotguns. 910-548-8700. www.remington.com

**Savage Arms,** 100 Springdale Rd., Westfield, MA 01085: Free information ◆ Sporting firearms for deer hunting. 413-568-7001. www.savagearms.com

**Sherwood,** 14830 Alondra Blvd., La Mirada, CA 90638: Free information ◆ Parts for guns. 800-962-3203.

**Shooters Emporium,** 606 SE 162nd, Portland, OR 97233: Free information ◆ Custom stocks. 800-323-7940.

**Simmons Gun Specialties Inc.,** 20241 W. 207th, Spring Hill, KS 66083: Free information ◆ Automatic pistols, revolvers, derringers, and target, bolt-and-lever action, semi-automatic, and single shot rifles. 800-444-0220.

**Smith & Wesson,** 2100 Roosevelt Ave., Springfield, MA 01102: Free information ◆ Firearms. 800-331-0852. www.smith-wesson.com

**Southwest Shooter's Supply,** P.O. Box 9987, Phoenix, AZ 85068: Free information ◆ Guns and accessories. 602-943-8595. www.southwest-shooters.com

**Springfield Armory,** 420 W. Main St., Geneseo, IL 61254: Catalog $3 ◆ Pistols, handguns, and rifles. 309-944-5631. www.springfield-armory.com

**Sturm, Ruger & Company Inc.,** 10 Lacey Pl., Southport, CT 06490: Free catalog ◆ Semi-automatic and single shot, bolt-and-lever action, and target rifles. 203-259-7843. www.ruger-firearms.com

**TAPCO,** P.O. Box 2408, Kennesaw, GA 30144: Free catalog ◆ Military, shooting, and outdoor gear. 800-554-1445.

**Tar-Hunt Rifles Inc.,** RR 3, Box 572, Bloomsburg, PA 17815: Free information ◆ Left and right-handed sport-shooting slug guns. 717-784-6368.

**U.S. Repeating Arms Company,** 275 Winchester Ave., New Haven, CT 06511: Free information ◆ Firearms. 203-789-5000.

**Ultra Light Arms Inc.,** P.O. Box 1270, Granville, WV 26534: Free information ◆ Sporting firearms for deer hunting. 304-599-5687.

**Weatherby Inc.,** 3100 El Camino Real, Atascadero, CA 93422: Free information ◆ Sporting firearms. 805-466-1767.

**WilsonTrace Distribution,** 1808 Sportsman Ln., Huntsville, AL 35816: Free catalog ◆ Reloading equipment, scopes, sportshooting rifles, binoculars, and accessories. 800-494-5397. www.wileyoutdoorsports.com

### Targets & Range Supplies

**Beeman Precision Arms Inc.,** 5454 Argosy Dr., Huntington Beach, CA 92649: Catalog $2 ◆ Targets and range equipment. 800-822-8005. www.beeman.com

**Birchwood Laboratories Inc.,** 7900 Fuller Rd., Eden Prairie, MN 55344: Free catalog ◆ Spinning, swinging, and action targets. 800-328-6156.

**Buckhorn Outdoor Sports,** 14714 Park Almeda Dr., Houston, TX 77047: Free information ◆ Natural-looking targets with optional replacement cores. 888-BUCKHORN.

**Caswell International Corp.,** 1215 Marshall St. NE, Minneapolis, MN 55413: Free information ◆ Range supplies and target carriers. 612-379-2000.

**Crosman Air Guns,** Rt. 5 & 20, East Bloomfield, NY 14443: Free information ◆ Targets and range equipment. 800-7AIR-GUN. www.crosman.com

**Daisy Manufacturing Company Inc.,** P.O. Box 220, Rogers, AR 72757: Free information ◆ Targets and range equipment. 501-636-1200. www.daisy.com

**Marksman Products,** 5482 Argosy Dr., Huntington Beach, CA 92649: Free information ◆ Targets and range equipment. 714-898-7535.

**National Target Company,** 4960 Wyaconda Rd., Rockville, MD 20852: Free information ◆ Paper and cardboard targets for rifle and pistol shooting. 800-827-7060; 301-770-7060 (in MD).

**NRA Store,** 11250 Waples Mill Rd., Fairfax, VA 22030: Free information ◆ Life-size game targets. 800-336-7402. www.nra.org

**Outers Laboratories Inc.,** Division Blount, N-5549-CTH-Z, Onalaska, WI 54650: Free information ◆ Targets and range equipment. 608-781-5800. www.blount.com/operations.html

### Trap & Clay Target Shooting

**Ballistic Products Inc.,** 20015 75th Ave. North, Corcoran, MN 55340: Catalog $1 ◆ Targets and traps. 612-494-9237.

**Beeman Precision Arms Inc.,** 5454 Argosy Dr., Huntington Beach, CA 92649: Catalog $2 ◆ Targets and traps. 800-822-8005. www.beeman.com

**Briley,** 1230 Lumpkin, Houston, TX 77043: Free information ◆ Replacement chokes. 800-331-5718; 713-932-6995 (in TX).

**Gamaliel Shooting Supply Inc.,** 1525 Ft. Run Rd., P.O. Box 156, Gamaliel, KY 42140: Free information ◆ Shooting supplies. 502-457-2825.

**The Hunters Pointe,** 14264 SW 50th St., Benton, KS 67017: Free information ◆ Manual and automatic traps for clay targets. 316-778-1122.

**Kolar Arms,** 1925 Roosevelt Ave., Racine, WI 53406: Free information ◆ Small gauge sporting clays and shooting supplies. 414-554-0800.

**Monterey Sporting Clays,** 2726 134th Ave., Hopkins, MI 49328: Free information ◆ Lightweight hand-manageable sporting clays. 616-793-7400.

**Omark Industries,** Blount Sporting Equipment Division, 2299 Snake River Ave., Lewiston, ID 83501: Free information ◆ Launchers, traps, and targets. 208-746-2351. www.blount.com/operations.html

**Rhino Guns,** 4340 SE 53rd Ave., Ocala, FL 34480: Free information ◆ Aluminum gun cases and ported chokes. 800-226-3613. www.rhinoguns.com

**Shydas Shoe & Clothing Barn,** 1635 S. Lincoln Ave., Lebanon, PA 17042: Free catalog ◆ Clay pigeon traps and trap shooting equipment. 717-274-2551.

**Simmons Gun Specialties Inc.,** 20241 W. 207th, Spring Hill, KS 66083: Free information ◆ Traps, launchers, and targets. 800-444-0220.

**Trius Inc.,** P.O. Box 25, Cleves, OH 45002: Free catalog ◆ Portable traps and range equipment. 513-941-5682.

**Wings & Clays,** P.O. Box 410, Birmingham, MI 48012: Free information ◆ Shotguns, clothing, and accessories.

## GYMNASTICS, GYMNASIUM & CLIMBING EQUIPMENT

**Ballet Etc.,** 5205 Simpson Ferry Rd., Mechanicsburg, PA 17055: Free information ◆ Dance and gymnastic wear, shoes, and clothing for ice skaters. 800-DANCE-25.

**Carron Net Company,** 1623 17th St., P.O. Box 177, Two Rivers, WI 54241: Free information ◆ Archery, baseball, basketball, gymnasium and climbing, football, racquetball, soccer, tennis, and volleyball accessories. 800-558-7768; 414-793-2217 (in WI). sales@carronnet.com

**Flaghouse Sports Equipment,** 601 Flaghouse Dr., Hasbrouck Heights, NJ 07604: Free catalog ◆ Gymnastics equipment. 800-793-7900. www.flaghouse.com

**JCPenney Catalog,** P.O. Box 675, Milwaukee, WI 53201: Free information: ◆ Athletic clothing and gymnastic equipment. 800-222-6161. www.jcpenney.com/shopping

**Quest & Sons Inc.,** 222 E. 3rd St., Lubbock, TX 79404: Free catalog ◆ Pole vault and high-jump pits, folding and hanging wall mats, landing cushions, exercise mats, volleyball pads, bags, banners, and other equipment. 800-456-4040; 806-744-2351 (in TX). www.hub.ofthe.net/quest

**TUMBL TRAK,** P.O. Box 312, 206 N. Court St., Mt. Pleasant, MI 48804: Free catalog ◆ Gymnastics training and competition equipment. 800-331-4362. tumbl800@aol.com

## HAMMOCKS & SWINGS

**Adirondack Store & Gallery,** 109 Saranac Ave., Lake Placid, NY 12946: Free information ◆ Oak and maple porch swings, lawn furniture, and picnic table sets. 518-523-2646.

**Barrier Bay Industries,** P.O. Box 975, Brattleboro, VT 05302: Free information ◆ Adjustable hammocks with optional canopy and mosquito netting. 800-877-1820.

**Brushy Mountain Bee Farm,** P.O. Box 135, Moravian Falls, NC 28654: Free catalog ◆ Porch swings, birdhouses and feeders, and beekeeping supplies. 800-BEESWAX.

**Country Casual,** 17317 Germantown Rd., Germantown, MD 20874: Catalog $3 ◆ Porch swings and classic British-style solid teak garden seats. 301-540-0040.

**Denyll Enterprises,** P.O. Box 199, Pembina, ND 58271: Information $2 ◆ Old-fashioned cedar garden swings, porch and platform glider swings, and indoor/outdoor glider chairs. 800-255-7119.

**Gazebo & Porchworks,** 728 9th Ave. SW, Puyallup, WA 98371: Catalog $2 ◆ Outdoor swings and backyard play structures. 253-848-0502.

**Grand ERA Reproductions,** P.O. Box 1026, Lapeer, MI 48446: Catalog $2 ◆ Porch swings. 810-664-1756.

**Green Enterprises,** 43 S. Rogers St., Hamilton, VA 22068: Brochure $1 ◆ Swings, gliders, tables, and benches. 540-338-3606.

**The Hammock Company,** P.O. Box 7295, Hilton Head, SC 29938: Free brochure ◆ Hammocks, swings, and other outdoor furnishings. 800-344-4264. www.hhisc.com/hammock

**The Hammock Source,** P.O. Box 1602, Greenville, SC 27835: Free list of retail sources ◆ Classic and innovative hammocks, accessories, and other outdoor leisure products. 800-334-1078; 919-758-0641 (in SC).

**Hangouts Handwoven Hammocks,** 1328 Pearl St., Boulder, CO 80302: Free brochure ◆ Hand-woven hammocks with optional stand for indoor or outdoor use. 800-426-4688. www.hangouts.com

**Mast General Store,** Hwy. 194, Valle Crucis, NC 28691: Free information ◆ Hammocks and porch swings, housewares, boots, and clothing. 704-963-6511.

**Mel-Nor Industries,** 303 Gulf Bank, Houston, TX 77037: Information $1 ◆ Hanging lawn and porch swings, park benches, and old-time lamp posts. 281-445-3485.

**O'Connor's Cypress Woodworks,** 1259 Lions Club Rd., Scott, LA 70583: Brochure $2 ◆ Porch swings. 800-786-1051.

**Quality Swings Inc.,** P.O. Box 813, State College, PA 16801: Free information ◆ Easy-to-assemble wood swing kits. 800-952-6713.

**Sun Designs,** 173 E. Wisconsin Ave., Oconomowoc, WI 53066: Plan book $9.95 plus $3.95 postage ◆ Plans for gazebos, bridges, doghouses, arbors, lawn furniture, swings, outdoor play structures, and birdhouses. 414-567-4255.

**Thaxted Cottage,** Gardener, 121 Driscoll Way, Gaithersburg, MD 20878: Catalog $2 ◆ Redwood cottage with trellis sides and built-in seat, Amish-style wheelbarrows, and porch swings. 301-330-6211.

**Marion Travis,** P.O. Box 1041, Statesville, NC 28677: Catalog $1 ◆ Wood porch swings. 800-806-2398.

**Twin Oaks Hammocks,** 138 Twin Oaks Rd., Louisa, VA 23093: Free brochure ◆ Woven rope hammocks and chairs. 800-688-8946. www.twinoaks.org/hammocks.htm

**Unique Simplicities,** 93 Anderson Rd., Gardiner, NY 12525: Free catalog ◆ Easy-to-install hammocks. 800-845-1119.

**Walpole Woodworkers,** 767 East St., Walpole, MA 02081: Catalog $6 ◆ Porch and covered swings, swing sets for children, chairs, tables, and picnic table sets. 800-343-6948.

## HANDBALL

**Adidas USA,** 5675 N. Blackstock Rd., Spartanburg, SC 29303: Free list of retail sources ◆ Balls. 800-423-4327. www.adidas.com

**Baden Sports Inc.,** 34114 21st Ave. South, Federal Way, WA 98003: Free information ◆ Balls. 800-544-2998; 206-925-0500 (in WA).

**Canstar Sports,** 150 Ocean Rd., Greenland, NH 03840: Free list of retail sources ◆ Balls and eye guards. 800-362-3146.

**Ektelon,** Prince Sports Group, 1 Sportsystem Plaza, Bordentown, NJ 08505: Free information ◆ Eye guards and gloves. 800-283-2635. www.princetennis.com

**Professional Gym Inc.,** P.O. Box 188, Marshall, MO 65340: Free brochure ◆ Eye guards. 800-821-7665.

**Spalding Sports Worldwide,** 425 Meadow St., P.O. Box 901, Chicopee, MA 01021: Free list of retail sources ◆ Balls. 800-225-6601. www.spalding.com

**Unique Sports Products Inc.,** 840 McFarland Rd., Alpharetta, GA 30201: Free information ◆ Eye guards and gloves. 800-554-3707; 770-442-1977 (in GA).

**Wa-Mac Inc.,** P.O. Box 128, Carlstadt, NJ 07410: Free information ◆ Balls and gloves. 800-447-5673; 201-438-7200 (in NJ).

## HARDWARE

**A & H Brass & Supply,** 126 W. Main St., Johnson City, TN 37604: Catalog $2 ◆ Restoration furniture hardware. 800-638-4252; 423-928-8220 (in TN).

**Acorn Manufacturing Company Inc.,** 457 School St., P.O. Box 31, Mansfield, MA 02048: Catalog $6 (request list of retail sources) ◆ Reproduction colonial hardware, sconces, hurricane lamps, fireplace tools, and bathroom accessories. 800-835-0121; 508-339-4500 (in MA).

**Addkison Hardware Company Inc.,** 126 E. Amite St., P.O. Box 102, Jackson, MS 39205: Free information ◆ Decorative cabinet and other hardware. 800-821-2750. www.addkison.com

**American Home Supply,** 191 Lost Lake Ln., Campbell, CA 95009: Catalog $2 ◆ Victorian and contemporary-style knobs, cabinet hardware and locks, faucets and bathroom hardware, grills and registers, and restoration items. 408-246-1962.

**Antique Brass Works,** 290 Port Richmond Ave., Staten Island, NY 10302: Free brochure ◆ Restored brass, hardware, and other metal fixtures. 718-273-6030.

**Antique Treasures,** 19 Buckingham Plantation Dr., Bluffton, SC 29910: Catalog $3 (request list of retail sources) ◆ Wholesale supplier of home accents in the antique style for dealers only. 800-422-9982. www.antiquehardware.com

**Antique Trunk Supply Company,** 360 Kenilworth Rd., Bay Village, OH 44140: Catalog $1 ◆ Trunk repair parts and accessories. 440-808-8085.

**Armor Crafts,** P.O. Box 445, East Northport, NY 11731: Free catalog ◆ Hardware, lamp parts, wood turnings and parts for toys and crafts, and replacement movements for mantel, banjo, and grandfather clocks. 800-292-8296.

**Arrow Components & Fasteners,** 31012 Huntwood Ave., Hayward, CA 94544: Free catalog ◆ Anchors, panel fasteners, cap screws and bolts, machine screws, nuts, washers, and other electro-mechanical components. 800-227-2901. www.arrow.com

**Baldwin Hardware Corp.,** P.O. Box 15048, Reading, PA 19612: Bathroom accessories brochure 75¢, light fixtures brochure $3, door hardware brochure 75¢, hardware brochure 75¢ ◆ Brass dead bolts and door hardware, bathroom accessories, and light fixtures. 800-566-1986.

**Ball & Ball,** 463 W. Lincoln Hwy., Exton, PA 19341: Catalog $7 (refundable) ◆ Brass and wrought-iron reproductions of American hardware, from 1680 to 1900. 610-363-7330. www.ballandball-us.com

**Barnett Inc.,** 333 Lenox Ave., Jacksonville, FL 32254: Free catalog ◆ Plumbing, HVAC, hardware, and electrical products. 904-384-6530. www.bntt.com

**Bathroom Machineries,** 495 Main St., Murphys, CA 95247: Catalog $3 ◆ Solid brass reproduction Victorian door and cabinet hardware. 209-728-2031. www.deabath.com

**The Bed Rizer,** 736 Federal St., Davenport, IA 52803: Free information ◆ Bed elevating legs, bed ruffles, and matching accessories. 800-321-9447. www.bedrizer.com

**Beech River Mill Company,** Old Rt. 16, Box 236, Centre Ossipee, NH 03814: Brochure $5 ◆ Custom-louvered and paneled products and period shutters. Also blinds hardware. 603-539-2636.

**Blaine Window Hardware,** 17319 Blaine Dr., Hagerstown, MD 21740: Free catalog ◆ Current, obsolete, and hard-to-find window and door hardware. 800-678-1919. www.blainewindow.com

**Bona Decorative Hardware,** 3073 Madison Rd., Cincinnati, OH 45209: Price list $2 ◆ Solid brass hardware for bathrooms, doors, cabinets, furniture, kitchens, and fireplaces. 513-321-7877.

**Brandywine Valley Forge,** P.O. Box 1129, Valley Forge, PA 19482: Catalog $2 ◆ Custom period hardware. 610-948-5116.

**Brass Menagerie,** 524 St. Louis St., New Orleans, LA 70130: Free information with long SASE (specify items wanted) ◆ Hardware, fixtures, and plumbing. 504-524-0921.

**Brassworks Hardware,** P.O. Box 22, Colfax, WA 99111: Free information ◆ Renovation and miscellaneous hardware. Also furniture. 800-842-4640. www.brassworks-sbh.com

**The Broadway Collection,** 1010 W. Santa Fe, Olathe, KS 66061: Free list of retail sources ◆ Plumbing fittings, brass bowls and bar sinks, grab bars, switch plates, and cabinet hardware. 800-766-1966.

**By-Gone Days Antiques Inc.,** 3100 South Blvd., Charlotte, NC 28209: Free information ◆ Mantels, restored door hardware, and architectural antiques. 704-527-8717.

**Camelot Enterprises,** Box 65, Bristol, WI 53104: Catalog $2 (refundable) ◆ Bolts, screws, and tools. 414-857-2695.

**A Carolina Craftsman,** 975 S. Avocado St., Anaheim, CA 92805: Catalog $5 ◆ Hard-to-find replacement hardware for houses and furniture. 714-776-7877.

**Cirecast Inc.,** 380 7th St., San Francisco, CA 94103: Brochure $2.50 ◆ Reproduction, custom decorative, and functional hardware. 415-863-8319.

**Clement Hardware,** 500 Ritchie Hwy., Severna Park, MD 21146: Free information ◆ Designer hardware. 410-647-4611.

**Cobblestone & Vine,** 5100 Kavanaugh Blvd., Little Rock, AR 72207: Free information ◆ Decorative drawer and cabinet pulls. 501-664-4249.

**The Coldren Company,** 100 Race St., P.O. Box 668, North East, MD 21901: Catalog $3 ◆ Reproduction 18th and 19th-century hardware. 410-287-2082.

**Colonial Bronze Company,** P.O. Box 207, Torrington, CT 06790: Free list of retail sources ◆ Brass hardware. 860-489-9233.

**Constantine,** 2050 Eastchester Rd., Bronx, NY 10461: Catalog $1 ◆ Cabinet and furniture wood, hardware, veneers, plans and how-to books, carving tools, chisels, and inlay designs. 800-223-8087; 718-792-1600 (in NY). www.constantines.com

**Craftsmen in Wood,** 5441 W. Hadley St., Phoenix, AZ 85043: Catalog $8 ◆ Door pulls, levers, knobs, and cabinet hardware. 602-278-8054.

**Crown City Hardware,** 1047 N. Allen Ave., Pasadena, CA 91104: Catalog $6.50 ◆ Restoration and decorative hardware. 626-794-1188. CrownCity1@aol.com

**Decorum Inc.,** 231 Commercial St., Portland, ME 04101: Free information ◆ Decorative hardware, custom lighting, old-style bathroom fixtures, and accessories. 207-775-3346.

**Dimestore Cowboys,** 407 2nd St. SW, Albuquerque, NM 87102: Catalog $7 ◆ Door sets, cabinet pulls, shutters, bathroom accessories, curtain rods and rings, and handcrafted hardware. 505-244-1493.

**Ed Donaldson Hardware Reproductions,** 1488 York Rd., Carlisle, PA 17013: Free brochure ◆ Restoration hardware. 717-249-3624.

**18th Century Hardware Company,** 131 E. 3rd St., Derry, PA 15627: Catalog $3 ◆ Early American and Victorian-style hardware in black iron, porcelain, and brass. 412-694-2708.

**Equiparts,** 817 Main St., Pittsburgh, PA 15215: Free information ◆ Vintage plumbing, heating, and electrical parts. 800-442-6622.

**Eugenia's,** 5370 Peachtree Rd., Chamblee, GA 30341: Catalog $1 ◆ Hard-to-find antique hardware. 800-337-1677; 770-458-1677 (in GA).

**Fagan's Forge,** P.O. Box 964, Dayville, CT 06241: Free brochure ◆ Hand-forged hardware.

**Faneuil Furniture Hardware Company Inc.,** 163 Main St., Salem, NH 03079: Catalog $5 ◆ Reproduction brass hardware for cabinets and furniture. 603-898-7733.

**Charolette Ford Trunks,** P.O. Box 536, Spearman, TX 79081: Catalog $2.75 ◆ Supplies and tools for restoring trunks. 806-659-3027. www.charolettefordtrunks.com

**Gainsborough Hardware,** 1255 Oakbrook Dr., Norcross, GA 30093: Free catalog ◆ Door hardware, key locks, passage sets, and accessories. 800-845-5662.

**GRANTCO,** 349 Peel St., New Hamburg, Ontario, Canada N0B 2G0: Free brochure ◆ Reproduction Victorian window and door hardware. 519-662-2892.

**Hardware, Bath & More,** 20830 Coolidge Hwy., Oak Park, MI 48237: Free information ◆ Decorative hardware, plumbing, and lighting fixtures. 800-760-3278. www.h-b-m.com

**Horton Brasses,** Nooks Hill Rd., P.O. Box 120, Cromwell, CT 06416: Catalog $4 ◆ Reproduction Chippendale, Queen Anne, Hepplewhite, Sheraton, Victorian, and early 1900s knobs, drawer pulls, and hardware. 860-635-4400. www.horton-brasses.com

**Kayne & Son Custom Hardware,** 100 Daniel Ridge Rd., Candler, NC 28715: Catalog $4.50 ◆ Fireplace tools and hand-forged hardware. 704-667-8868.

**Phyllis Kennedy Restoration Hardware,** 10655 Andrade Sr., Zionsville, IN 46077: Catalog $3 ◆ Antique trunk hardware. 317-873-1316. www.kennedyhardware.com

**Klockit,** P.O. Box 636, Lake Geneva, WI 53147: Free catalog ◆ Hardware, Swiss music box movements, clock-building components, and music box and clock kits. 800-556-2548. www.klockit.com

**Liz's Antique Hardware,** 453 S. La Brea, Los Angeles, CA 90036: Catalog $5 ◆ Vintage and contemporary hardware. 800-939-9003.

**Meisel Hardware Specialties,** P.O. Box 70, Mound, MN 55364: Catalog $2 ◆ Plans for over 1000 woodworking projects for the home hobbyist.612-471-8550. www.nonni.com/woodhobby

**Merit Metal Products Corp.,** 242 Valley Rd., Warrington, PA 18976: Catalog $10 ◆ Brass locks, hinges, and other hardware for doors, furniture, and cabinets. 215-343-2500.

**Nexton Industries Inc.,** 51 S. 1st St., Brooklyn, NY 11211: Free information ◆ Brass hardware and bath accessories. 718-599-3837.

**Nostalgic Warehouse,** 701 E. Kingsley Rd., Garland, TX 75041: Catalog $5 ◆ Period, restoration colonial, Victorian, nouveau, and decorative hardware. 800-522-7336.

**Notting Hill Decorative Hardware,** P.O. Box 1376, Lake Geneva, WI 53147: Free information ◆ Decorative hardware. 414-248-8890. www.nottinghill-usa.com

**Old Smithy Shop,** 195 Rt. 13, Brookline, NH 03055: Catalog $3 ◆ Hand-forged reproduction colonial hardware, fireplace equipment, curtain accessories, and bathroom fixtures. 603-672-4113.

**Omnia,** Box 330, Cedar Grove, NJ 07009: Free list of retail sources ◆ Lock sets and architectural hardware. 201-239-7272.

**Paxton Hardware Ltd.,** P.O. Box 256, Upper Falls, MD 21156: Catalog $4 ◆ Cabinet hardware, hinges, lamp shades, pulls, locks, and more. 800-241-9741. www.PaxtonHardware.com

**Professional Hardware & Supply Company,** P.O. Box 11800, Casa Grande, AZ 85230: Catalog $3 ◆ Hardware and supplies. 800-248-1919. www.profhdwr.com

**The Renovator's Supply,** P.O. Box 2515, Conway, NH 03818: Free catalog ◆ Old-style hardware, plumbing, fixtures, and accessories. 800-659-0203.

**Restoration Works Inc.,** P.O. Box 486, Buffalo, NY 14205: Catalog $3 ◆ Hardware, ceiling medallions and trims, plumbing fixtures, and bathroom accessories. 716-856-6400.

**Wm. J. Rigby Company,** 73 Elm St., Cooperstown, NY 13326: Catalog $7 ◆ Antique hardware. 607-547-1900.

**Rusty Bolt Screw Company,** P.O. Box 708, North Attleboro, MA 02761: Free information ◆ Screws, nuts, washers, and stainless steel fasteners.

**Stock Drive Products,** 2101 Jeritho Tnpk., New Hyde Park, NY 11042: Catalog $5.95 ◆ Over 62,000 off-the-shelf mechanical drive components. 516-328-3300. www.sdp-si.com

**Van Dyke's Restorers,** P.O. Box 178, Woonsocket, SD 57385: Free catalog ◆ Brass, glass, and wood hardware. 800-843-3320.

**Garrett Wade Company,** 161 6th Ave., New York, NY 10013: Catalog $4 ◆ English-made solid brass hardware with many patterns similar to those of 100 years ago. 800-221-2942. www.garrettwade.com

**Wayne's Woods Inc.,** 39 N. Plains Industrial Rd., Wallingford, CT 06492: Catalog $2 (refundable) ◆ Refinishing supplies and brass and wood reproduction hardware. 800-793-6208.

**Williamsburg Blacksmiths Inc.,** P.O. Box 1776, Williamsburg, MA 01096: Catalog $5 ◆ Reproduction Early American hardware and wrought-iron furniture. 800-248-1776.

**Windy Hill Forge,** 3824 Schroeder Ave., Perry Hall, MD 21128: Catalog $3 (refundable) ◆ Custom-made and restored hardware. 410-256-5890.

**Wise Company,** 6503 St. Claude Ave., P.O. Box 118, Arabi, LA 70032: Catalog $4 ◆ Antique restoration materials, hardware, and furniture refinishing supplies. 504-277-7551.

**Woodbury Blacksmith & Forge Company,** P.O. Box 268, Woodbury, CT 06798: Catalog $3 ◆ Hand-forged Early American wrought-iron hardware. 203-263-5737.

**Woodworker's Emporium,** 5461 S. Arville, Las Vegas, NV 89118: Catalog $3 ◆ Polished iron and brass pull knobs and keyholes. 800-779-7458.

**The Woodworkers' Store,** 4365 Willow Dr., Medina, MN 55340: Free catalog ◆ Tools and hardware, woodworking, and finishing supplies. 800-279-4441. www.woodworkerstore.com

## HATS

**Az-Tex Hat Company,** 15044 N. Cave Creek Rd., Phoenix, AZ 85032: Free brochure ◆ Traditionally styled hats with an American southwest style. 800-972-2095.

**Back at the Ranch,** 235 Don Gaspar, Santa Fe, NM 87501: Free information ◆ Vintage western clothing, boots, and hats. 505-989-8110.

**BC Hats,** P.O. Box 602, St. Augustine, FL 32085: Free information ◆ Western-style leather hats from Australia. Also straw, canvas, felt, and oilskin hats. 800-922-4288. www.BCHATS.com

**Caledonia Hats,** 300 Chestnut Hill Rd., Stevens, PA 17578: Free information ◆ Western-style hats. 800-338-2410.

**Catalena Hatters,** 203 N. Main, Bryan, TX 77803: Free information ◆ Custom western hats. 800-976-7816. www.texascowboy.com

**Custom Cowboy Shop,** 350 N. Main, Sheridan, WY 82801: Free information ◆ Cowboy hats. 800-487-2692.

**D Bar J Hat Company,** 3873 Spring Mt. Rd., Las Vegas, NV 89102: Free information ◆ Panama straw and dress hats. 800-654-1137; 702-362-4287 (in NV).

**D.L. Designs,** P.O. Box 1382, Studio City, CA 91604: Catalog $1 (refundable) ◆ Modern and historical hat patterns for men and women. www.home.earthlink.net/~dlhp

**Drysdales,** 1555 N. 107th East Ave., Tulsa, OK 74116: Free catalog ◆ Fur and straw western-style hats by Stetson, MHT, and Wrangler. Also care, storage, and transport products for hats. 800-444-6481. www.drysdales.com

**Manny Gammage's Texas Hatters,** P.O. Box 100, 5003 Overpass Rd., Buda, TX 78610: Free brochure ◆ Texas-style hats for men and women. 800-421-4287; 512-295-4287 (in TX). www.texashatters.com

**Grady's Western Store & Hatters,** 1125 S. Summit, Arkansas City, KS 67005: Free information ◆ Cowboy hat renovation. 316-442-7871.

**The Hat Store,** 5587 Richmond, Houston, TX 77056: Catalog $2 ◆ Western-style hats. 713-780-2480.

**Tom Hirt Custom Hats,** Box 31751, Tucson, AZ 85751: Free information ◆ Made to order cowboy hats. 520-749-5221.

**Luskey/Ryon's Western Stores Inc.,** 2601 N. Main, Fort Worth, TX 76106: Free catalog ◆ Hats and boots in a western tradition for the entire family. 800-725-7966.

**Mackey Custom Hats,** 1485 Ward Rd., Bozeman, MT 59715: Free brochure ◆ Handcrafted western hats. 406-586-4993.

**Malcom Designs Ltd.,** P.O. Box 2613, Nantucket Island, MA 02584: Free brochure ◆ Stovepipe hats for the winter. 508-325-4373. www.malcolmdesigns.com

**David Morgan,** 11812 Northcreek Pkwy., Ste. 103, Bothell, WA 98011: Free catalog ◆ Hand-braided belts, fur hats, and wool and sheepskin clothing. 800-324-4934. www.davidmorgan.com

**Rainbow Road,** 12 Via Calandria, San Clemente, CA 92672: Free catalog ◆ Original hats and accessories for women. 714-492-3235. www.rainbowroad.com

**Stark & Legum Inc.,** 739 Granby St., Norfolk, VA 23510: Free catalog ◆ Dressy felts, light-weight straws, and sporty head gear for men and hats for women. 800-357-HATS; 804-627-1018 (in VA).

**Andrew Thompson Company,** 843 Arden Way, Signal Mountain, TN 37377: Free information ◆ Multi-sizing airflow and dermatologist-recommended sun hats. 615-886-5189.

**Tonto Rim Trading Company,** 5028 N. US Hwy. 31, Seymour, IN 47274: Free catalog ◆ Western boots and hats. 800-242-4287.

**Weather Hat Company,** 211 W. Main, Lead, SD 57754: Brochure $1 ◆ Cowboy-style and other hats. 605-584-1664.

**Wheeling Western Wear,** 642 S. Milwaukee Ave., Wheeling, IL 60090: Free information ◆ Handmade western hats. 800-850-0383.

**Whipp Trading Company,** RR 1, Arrasmith Trail, Ames, IA 50010: Free catalog ◆ Sheepskin rugs, slippers, mittens, and hats. 800-533-9447.

## HEALTH CARE SUPPLIES & AIDS

### General

**AARP Pharmacy Service Center Catalog,** P.O. Box 13671, Richmond, VA 23225: Free catalog for American Association Retired Persons members ◆ Over-the-counter medications, cosmetics, vitamins, dental needs, sick room and other health care supplies, and personal care items. 800-456-2277.

**Adventure Medical Kits,** Campmore Inc., P.O. Box 700-M, Upper Saddle River, NJ 07458: Free catalog ◆ Compact sport-specific medical kits. 800-525-4784. customer-service@campmor.com

**Allergy Control Products,** 96 Danbury Rd., Ridgefield, CT 06877: Free catalog ◆ Air filters, mattress and pillow covers, face masks, dehumidifiers, and books. 800-422-3878; 203-438-9580 (in CT). www.allergycontrol.com

**Allergy Resources Inc.,** 557 Burbank St., Ste. K, Broomfield, CO 80020: Free catalog ◆ Alternative foods, air purifiers, cosmetics, bedding, cleaning products, and other supplies. 888-308-4826; 303-438-0600 (in CO). AllergyRe@aol.com

**Atwater-Carey Ltd.,** 2986 Grove St., Denver, CO 80211: Free information ◆ First aid kits. 800-976-6664; 303-477-9689 (in CO). www.omnibus.com/atwatercarey

**BackSaver,** 53 Jeffrey Ave., Holliston, MA 01746: Free catalog ◆ Aids for prevention and relief of pain to the back, neck, shoulders, wrists, and arms. 800-251-2225. www.backsaver.com

**Best Buy Medical,** 21572 Surveyor Circle, Huntington Beach, CA 92646: Free catalog ◆ Incontinent, urological, ostomy, wound care, and other medical supplies. 800-289-5476. www.a-med.com

**Biodex Medical Systems,** 20 Ramsay Rd., Shirley, NY 11967: Free catalog ◆ Nuclear medicine supplies and accessories. 800-224-6339; 516-924-9000 (in NY). www.biodex.com

**Bioenergy Nutrients,** 6565 Odell Pl., Boulder, CO 80301: Catalog $1 ◆ Nutritional supplements, homeopathic medicines, antioxidants, and all-natural skin care products. 800-627-7775. www.amiron.com

**Bosom Buddy Breast Forms,** 2417 Bank Dr., P.O. Box 5731, Boise, ID 83705: Free information ◆ All-fabric, weight adjustable external breast prosthesis. 800-262-2789. www.bosombuddy.com

**Bruce Medical Supply,** 411 Waverly Oaks Rd., P.O. Box 9166, Waltham, MA 02154: Free catalog ◆ Health care supplies for ostomy patients, diabetics, sick rooms, post hospital care, and first aid. 800-225-8446.

**Care Catalog Services,** 1877 NE 7th Ave., Portland, OR 97212: Free catalog ◆ Wheelchairs, wheelchair ramps and parts, urological supplies, and other health care aids. 503-288-8174.

**Chinook Medical Gear Inc.,** P.O. Box 1736, Edwards, CO 81632: Catalog $1 (refundable) ◆ Emergency medical and first aid equipment. Also survival kits. 800-766-1365. chinook@vail.net

**Comfort House,** 189 Frelinghuysen Ave., Newark, NJ 07114: Free catalog ◆ Aids and accessories that make daily activities easier. 800-359-7701. www.comforthouse.com

**Dr. Clayton's Herbs,** Division American Herbal Science Inc., 2717 7th Ave. South, Birmingham, AL 35233: Free catalog ◆ All-natural health care products. 800-633-6286. www.drclayton.com

**Dr. Leonard's Health Care Catalog,** 42 Mayfield Ave., P.O. Box 7821, Edison, NJ 08818: Free catalog ◆ Health care supplies. 800-785-0880. www.drleonards.com

**DS Medical,** 1725 Breckinridge Pkwy., Ste. 500, Duluth, GA 30136: Free information ◆ Wheelchair parts and urological, ostomy, wound care, and other health care products. 800-722-2604. www.dsmedical.com

**Dyna-Med,** 6300 Yarrow Dr., Carlsbad, CA 92009: Free catalog ◆ Emergency care products. 800-334-8211.

**East Earth Trade Winds,** P.O. Box 493151, 1620 E. Cypress Ave., Ste. 8, Redding, CA 96049: Catalog $1 ◆ Traditional Chinese herbs and herb products. 800-258-6878. www.snowcrest.net/eetw

**Enrichments,** P.O. Box 5071, Bolingbrook, IL 60440: Free information ◆ Health care products, personal care needs, and dressing and comfort aids. 800-323-5547. www.sammonspreston.com

**Express Medical Supply Inc.,** P.O. Box 1164, Fenton, MO 63026: Free catalog ◆ Urological, ostomy, incontinence, and skin care products. 800-633-2139. www.exmed.net

**Fashion Ease,** Division M & M Health Care, 1541 60th St., Brooklyn, NY 11219: Free catalog ◆ Clothing with Velcro closures, wheelchair accessories, and incontinence supplies. 800-221-8929; 718-871-8188 (in NY). www.fashionease.com

**The Feelgood Catalog,** 2895 W. Oxford Ave., Ste. 1, Englewood, CO 80110: Free catalog ◆ Pain-relief accessories for backs, knee pain, wrist and elbow tendinitis, weak ankles, shoulder pain, and sore muscles. Also magnetic therapy aids. 800-997-6789. www.feelgoodcatalog.com

**Frohock-Stewart Inc.,** P.O. Box 330, Northborough, MA 01532: Free information ◆ Clamp-on bathtub bench and grip for bathing comfort and safety. 800-343-6059.

**Gaia Garden Herbal Apothecary,** 2672 W. Broadway, Vancouver, British Columbia, Canada V6K 2G3: Catalog $2 ◆ Herbal, aromatherapy, and related products. 604-734-4372.

**Guardian Products Inc.,** 4175 Guardian St., Simi Valley, CA 93063: Free catalog ◆ One-piece, assembly-not-required, height-adjustable shower and commode chair. 800-255-5022.

**Health Center for Better Living,** 1414 Rosemary Ln., Naples, FL 33940: Free catalog ◆ Herbal health care products. 800-544-4225.

**Health Products Express Inc.,** P.O. Box 8, Winthrop, MA 02152: Free catalog ◆ Products for treatment, comfort, and personal care. 800-617-5525; 617-846-8924 (in MA).

**Healthhouse USA,** Box 9036, Jericho, NY 11753: Free catalog ◆ Emergency medical and first aid equipment and other supplies. 516-334-2099.

**Healthy Living,** 6836 Engle Rd., P.O. Box 94512, Cleveland, OH 44101: Free catalog ◆ Aids, appliances, and supplies for health and comfort. 800-800-0100.

**Home Health Products,** 949 Seahawk Circle, Virginia Beach, VA 23452: Free catalog ◆ Natural health care products and supplies, skin care preparations, and herbal medications. 800-284-9123.

**House Calls,** P.O. Box 331148, Fort Worth, TX 76163: Free catalog ◆ Health care supplies and equipment for the home. 800-460-7282.

**Hyland's Standard Homeopathic Company,** 154 W. 131st St., Los Angeles, CA 90061: Free information ◆ Homeopathic medicines. 800-624-9659; 213-321-4284 (in CA).

**Independent Living Aids/Can-Do Products,** 27 East Mall, Plainview, NY 11803: Free catalog ◆ Health care supplies. 800-537-2118; 516-752-8080 (in NY). www.independentliving.com

**Intimate Appeal,** Palo Verde at 34th, P.O. Box 27800, Tucson, AZ 85726: Free catalog ◆ Intimate clothing for women who have had mastectomies. 520-748-8600.

**Just My Size,** P.O. Box 748, Rural Hall, NC 27098: Free catalog ◆ Aids for better living, elastic supports, foot care items, and home health care products. 800-522-9567. www.justmysizebras.com

**Miles Kimball Company,** 41 W. 8th Ave., Oshkosh, WI 54906: Free catalog ◆ Bathroom and kitchen accessories, arthritis aids, clothing, canes, and personal care items for people with disabilities. 800-546-2255. www.mileskimball.com

**L & H Vitamins Inc.,** 32-33 47th Ave., Long Island City, NY 11101: Free catalog ◆ Vitamins and nutritional supplements, homeopathic medicines, aromatherapy products, and natural health care products. 800-221-1152; 618-937-7400 (in NY). www.lhvitamins.com

**Lady Grace Stores,** P.O. Box 128, Malden, MA 02148: Free catalog ◆ Intimate apparel for everyday wear, nursing and maternity, and post-breast surgery. 800-922-0504. www.ladygrace.com

**Lady's Choice-Donna Mello,** 114 Tawney View, Hamilton, MT 59840: Free brochure ◆ Mastectomy breast forms. 800-775-3251.

**Masuen First Aid & Safety,** P.O. Box 901, Tonawanda, NY 14151: Free catalog ◆ First aid remedies and kits. Also health care and medical supplies. 800-831-0894.

**Medship Direct,** P.O. Box 956848, Duluth, GA 30095: Free catalog ◆ Urological, wound care, ostomy, incontinence, and aids to daily living. Also wheelchair parts. 800-633-1565. www.medshipdirect.com

**MOMS Mail Order Medical Supply,** 24700 Avenue Rockefeller, Valencia, CA 91355: Free catalog ◆ Medical supplies and aids for incontinence, urological and ostomy conditions, daily living, wound and skin care, and diabetes. 800-232-7443. www.momsup.com

**Mountain View Medical Supply Inc.,** Mountain View Medical Supply, P.O. Box 117, Broomfield, CO 80038: Free catalog ◆ Health care supplies. 800-873-7121. www.mvms.com

**Nitro-Pak Preparedness Center,** 151 N. Main St., Heber City, UT 84032: Catalog $3 ◆ Survival equipment and supplies, freeze-dried and dehydrated foods, books, and videos. 800-866-4876. www.nitro-pak.com

**Oregon Scientific,** 18383 SW Boones Ferry Rd., Portland, OR 97224: Free brochure ◆ Digital blood pressure meter. 800-869-7779.

**Out N Back,** 1797 S. State St., Orem, UT 84058: Free catalog ◆ Survival equipment for outdoor recreational activities. 800-533-7415.

**Outdoor Research,** 2203 1st Ave. South, Seattle, WA 98134: Free information ◆ Outdoor first aid kits. 888-467-4327. www.orgear.com

**Parkview Pharmacy & Home Health Care Inc.,** 8283 Grove Ave., Ste. 105, Rancho Cucamonga, CA 91730: Free catalog ◆ Ostomy, wound care, incontinence, and other home health care aids. 800-605-0166. www.parkviewrx.com

**Planta Dei Medicinal Herb Farm,** Millville, New Brunswick, Canada E0H 1M0: Catalog $2 (refundable) ◆ Biologically grown teas, medicinal herbs, healing tea mixtures, cosmetics, natural ointments, and massage oils. 506-463-8169.

**PolyMedica Healthcare Inc.,** 581 Conference Pl., Golden, CO 80401: Free list of retail sources ◆ Self-adhesive and water-based resistant dressings for blisters and abrasions. 303-271-0300.

**J.A. Preston Corp.,** P.O. Box 89, Jackson, MI 49204: Free catalog ◆ Exercise equipment, walkers, crutches, mats, positioning aids, perceptual motor accessories, self-help aids, and professional equipment for the doctor's office. 800-631-7277.

**Radio Shack,** Division Tandy Corp., One Tandy Center, Fort Worth, TX 76102: Free information ◆ Health care supplies. 817-390-3011. www.radioshack.com

**St. Louis Medical Supply,** 10821 Manchester Rd., Kirkwood, MO 63122: Free catalog ◆ Health care and medical supplies. 800-950-6020.

**Sarjenco Home Medical Supply,** 428 2nd Ave., East Northport, NY 11731: Free catalog ◆ Products for treatment, comfort, and personal care. 800-785-8775; 516-368-1630 (in NY). sarjenco@aol.com

**Sears Home Healthcare,** 9804 Chartwell, Dallas, TX 75238: Free catalog ◆ Products for health maintenance and rehabilitation. 800-326-1750; 800-733-7249 (for the hearing impaired).

**SelfCare Catalog,** 104 Challenger Dr., Portland, TN 37148: Free catalog ◆ Health care supplies and accessories. 800-345-3371. SlfCare@aol.com

**Shield Healthcare Centers,** 4340 Viewridge Ave., San Diego, CA 92123: Free catalog ◆ Ostomy, urological, skin care, and home diagnostic products. 800-675-8845.

**Slide Zone,** P.O. Box 781572, San Antonio, TX 78278: Free information ◆ First-aid kits for disinfecting and treating wounds, repelling insects, and relieving discomfiture. 800-754-3305.

**Support Plus,** Box 500, Medfield, MA 02052: Free catalog ◆ Support hosiery, personal hygiene and home health care aids, bath safety products, and walking shoes. 800-229-2910.

**The Survival Center,** P.O. Box 234, McKenna, WA 98558: Catalog $2 ◆ Survival equipment for outdoor activities. 800-321-2900; 360-458-6778 (in WA). www.survivalcenter.com

**Thompson Pharmacy & Medical,** 324 S. Union St., Traverse City, MI 49684: Free catalog ◆ Diabetes, health maintenance, home diagnostic, ostomy, and health and pain management aids. Also canes and other mobility equipment. 616-947-4212. thompson@carecenter.com

**The Vitamin Shoppe,** 4700 Westside Ave., North Bergen, NJ 07047: Free catalog ◆ Vitamins, herbs, homeopathic medicines, and natural cosmetics. 800-223-1216. www.vitaminshoppe.com

**W.R. Medical Electronics Company,** 123 N. 2nd St., Stillwater, MN 55082: Free information ◆ Drug-free paraffin-heat therapy system for arthritis pain relief, joint stiffness, inflammation, and muscle spasms. 800-321-6387. www.wrmed.com

**Walton Way Medical,** 948 Walton Way, Augusta, GA 30901: Free catalog ◆ Health care supplies and rehabilitation equipment. 800-241-4636.

**Wheelchair Warehouse,** 100 E. Sierra, #3309, Fresno, CA 93710: Free information ◆ Ostomy appliances, incontinence supplies, mastectomy breast forms, skin care products, and health care aids. 800-829-0202; 209-436-6147 (in OH).

**Worldwide Home Health Center Inc.,** 926 E. Tallmadge Ave., Akron, OH 44310: Free catalog ◆ Ostomy appliances, incontinence supplies, mastectomy breast forms, skin care products, and health care aids. 800-223-5938; 330-633-0366 (in OH).

### Software

**IVI Publishing,** 7500 Flying Cloud Dr., Minneapolis, MN 55344: Free information ◆ Windows and Macintosh Mayo Clinic family health and medication management software on CD-ROMs. 800-952-4773; 612-996-6000 (in MN).

**Lifestyle Software Group,** 2155 Old Moultrie Rd., St. Augustine, FL 32086: Free information ◆ Information software for managing personal health care programs. 800-289-1157; 904-825-0220 (in FL). www.lifeware.com

**LivingSoft Inc.,** 40 S. Lassen St., Box 189, Susanville, CA 96130: Free information ◆ DOS dieting software. 888-626-1262. www.livingsoft.com

**SoftKey International Inc.,** 1 Athenaeum St., Cambridge, MA 02142: Free information ◆ Windows drug information software on CD-ROMs. 617-494-5700. www.learningco.com

## HEARING & COMMUNICATION AIDS

**Ameriphone,** 12082 Western Ave., Garden Grove, CA 92841: Free list of retail sources ◆ Remote controlled speaker telephone with voice-activated answering. 800-874-3005. www.ameriphoneinc.com

**Audiological Engineering Corp.,** 35 Medford St., Somerville, MA 02143: Free information ◆ Infrared and loop hearing systems and other assistive aids for the hearing impaired. 800-283-4601.

**G & R Publishing Company,** 507 Industrial St., Waverly, IA 50677: Free information ◆ Sign language workbooks. 800-383-1679. www.cookbookprinting.com

**General Technologies,** 7415 Winding Way, Fair Oaks, CA 95628: Free catalog ◆ Assistive listening devices. 800-328-6684.

**Harris Communications,** 15159 Technology Dr., Eden Prairie, MN 55344: Free catalog ◆ Closed caption and cable-ready decoder, TDDs, signalers, clocks, other devices, and publications for deaf and hearing impaired individuals. 800-825-6758 (voice); 800-825-9187 (TDD). www.harriscom.com

**Hear You Are Inc.,** 4 Musconetcong Ave., Stanhope, NJ 07874: Free catalog ◆ Doorbell signal, telephone aids, visual and smoke alarms, and assistive listening devices. 201-347-7662 (voice/TTY).

**Hello Direct,** 5893 Rue Ferrari Dr., San Jose, CA 95138: Free catalog ◆ Amplification aids, cellular and paging accessories, telephones and answering machines, and other telephone productivity tools. 800-444-3556. www.hello-direct.com

**Hitec Group International,** 8160 Madison, Burr Ridge, IL 60521: Free catalog ◆ Assistive devices for people with hearing impairments. 800-288-8303.

**Independent Living Aids/Can-Do Products,** 27 East Mall, Plainview, NY 11803: Free catalog ◆ Writing, low-vision, Braille, and communication aids. 800-537-2118; 516-752-8080 (in NY). www.independentliving.com

**Maxi-Aids,** P.O. Box 3209, Farmingdale, NY 11735: Free catalog ◆ Communication devices, eating and kitchen aids, dressing aids, wheelchair accessories, and more. 800-522-6294. sales@maxiaids.com

**Nationwide Flashing Signal Systems Inc.,** 8120 Fenton St., Silver Spring, MD 20910: Free catalog ◆ Visual alerting devices and TDDs. 888-589-6671. www.nfss.com

**Phone-TTY Inc.,** 202 Lexington Ave., Hackensack, NJ 07601: Free information ◆ Modems and software for using computers to talk with TDDs. 201-489-7889; 201-489-7890(TDD).

**Phonic Ear Inc.,** 3880 Cypress Dr., Petaluma, CA 94954: Free catalog ◆ Sound enhancers for use in group settings and Phonic Ear personal FM systems. 800-227-0735; 707-769-1110 (in CA).

**Potomac Technology,** One Church St., Ste. 101, Rockville, MD 20850: Free information ◆ Assistive devices for people with hearing impairments. 800-433-2838 (voice/TTY). info@potomactech.com

**Radio Shack,** Division Tandy Corp., One Tandy Center, Fort Worth, TX 76102: Free information ◆ Assistive devices.817-390-3011. www.radioshack.com

**Science Products,** Box 888, Southeastern, PA 19399: Free catalog ◆ Voice sensory aids and electronics for people with hearing or visual impairments. 800-888-7400; 610-296-2111 (in PA).

**Sennheiser Electronics,** P.O. Box 987, Old Lyme, CT 06371: Free information ◆ Easy-to-use transmitters and receivers with 16 selectable frequencies, infrared add-on systems, and assistive devices for people with hearing impairments. 860-434-9190 (voice/TDD). www.sennheiserusa.com/2

**Siemans Hearing Instruments Inc.,** 16 E. Piper Ln., Ste. 128, Prospect Heights, IL 60070: Free information ◆ Easy-to-install infrared in-home TV listening system. 800-333-9083.

**Silver Creek Industries,** P.O. Box 1988, Manitowoc, WI 54221: Free information ◆ Sound amplifying devices. 800-533-3277. members.lsol.net/sci

**Temasek Telephone Inc.,** 21 Airport Rd., South San Francisco, CA 94080: Free information ◆ Voice-activated telephones. 800-647-8887.

**Ultratec,** 450 Science Dr., Madison, WI 53711: Free catalog ◆ All-in-one phone for people with different hearing abilities. 800-482-2424 (voice/TTY).

**Weitbrecht Communications Inc.,** 2656 29th St., Ste. 205, Santa Monica, CA 90405: Free catalog ◆ Assistive listening devices and portable TDDs. 800-233-9130; 310-452-8613 (voice, in CA); 310-452-5460 (TTY). www.weitbrechtcom.com

## HEAT EXCHANGERS

**Gaylord Industries Inc.,** P.O. Box 1149, Tualatin, OR 97062: Free information ◆ Air-to-air heat exchangers. 800-547-9696.

## HOCKEY, FIELD

**Action Sport Systems Inc.,** P.O. Box 1442, Morganton, NC 28680: Free information ◆ Uniforms, balls, nets, cages, and leg guards. 800-631-1091; 704-584-8000 (in NC).

**Austin Athletic Equipment Corp.,** 705 Bedford Ave., Box 423, Bellmore, NY 11710: Free information ◆ Nets and cages. 516-785-0100.

**BSN Sports,** P.O. Box 7726, Dallas, TX 75209: Free information ◆ Equipment for archery, hockey, aquatic fitness, baseball, basketball, boxing, field hockey, football, weight lifting, and other sports. 800-527-7510; 972-484-9484 (in TX). www.bsnsports.com

**Doss Shoes,** Soccer Sport Supply Company, 1745 1st Ave., New York, NY 10128: Free information ◆ Uniforms, balls, nets, cages, leg guards, shoes, and sticks. 800-223-1010; 212-427-6050 (in NY).

**E.Z. Enterprises,** 205 D Exeter Rd., London, Ontario, Canada N6L 1A4: Free information ◆ Lightweight portable and collapsible goals. 519-472-5261.

**Goal Sporting Goods Inc.,** 37 Industrial Park Rd., P.O. Box 236, Essex, CT 06426: Free catalog ◆ Telescoping, folding, and adjustable goals and nets. 800-334-GOAL. www.goalsports.com

**Hot Off The Ice,** P.O. Box 1620, Secaucus, NJ 07096: Free catalog ◆ Equipment and clothing. 800-446-8423. www.shop.nhl.com

**JMP Enterprises,** 652 Retriever Dr., Hampstead, MD 21074: Free catalog ◆ Skateboards, roller skates, in-line skates, and hockey equipment. 410-239-5081.

**Olympia Sports,** P.O. Box 1941, Ann Arbor, MI 48106: Free information ◆ Balls, nets, cages, leg guards, and sticks. 800-521-2832. www.wolverinesports.com

**Sportime,** Customer Service, 1 Sportime Way, Atlanta, GA 30340: Free information ◆ Balls, nets, cages, leg guards, and sticks. 800-444-5700; 770-449-5700 (in GA).

**TC Sports,** 7251 Ford Hwy., Tecumseh, MI 49286: Free information ◆ Balls, nets, and cages. 800-523-1498; 517-451-5221 (in MI).

**Wolvering Sports,** P.O. Box 1941, Ann Arbor, MI 48106: Catalog $1 ◆ Baseball, basketball, field hockey, soccer, football, other athletic, and recreation equipment. 313-761-5691.

# HOCKEY, ICE

## Clothing

**Austin Sportsgear,** 621 Liberty St., Jackson, MI 49203: Free information ◆ Uniforms. 800-999-7543; 517-784-1120 (in MI).

**Betlin Manufacturing,** 1445 Marion Rd., Columbus, OH 43207: Free information ◆ Uniforms. 614-443-0248.

**Hot Off The Ice,** P.O. Box 1620, Secaucus, NJ 07096: Free catalog ◆ Equipment and clothing. 800-446-8423. www.shop.nhl.com

**Cliff Keen Athletic,** 1235 Rosewood, P.O. Box 1447, Ann Arbor, MI 48106: Free information ◆ Uniforms. 800-992-0799. www.cliffkeen.com

**Majestic Athletic Wear,** 636 Pen Argyl St., Pen Argyl, PA 18072: Free information ◆ Uniforms and sportswear. 800-955-8555; 610-863-6161 (in PA).

**Star Struck,** P.O. Box 308, Bethel, CT 06801: Free catalog ◆ Fitted caps and jerseys. 800-908-4637; 877-THE-GAME (in CT). www.starstruck.com

**Venus Knitting Mills Inc.,** 140 Spring St., Murray Hill, NJ 07974: Free information ◆ Uniforms, clothing for ice skaters, and sportswear. 800-955-4200; 908-464-2400 (in NJ).

## Equipment

**Bauer Precision In-Line Skates,** 150 Ocean Rd., Greenland, NH 03840: Free information ◆ Gloves, nets, cages, protective gear, helmets, pucks, sticks, and skates. 800-622-2189.

**Boni Goalie Trainers Inc.,** 558 Scarlett, Weston, Ontario, Canada M9P 2S2: Free brochure ◆ Puck shooting machines for goalie training. 416-241-0030.

**Canstar Sports,** 150 Ocean Rd., Greenland, NH 03840: Free list of retail sources ◆ Figure and hockey ice skates and blade sharpeners. 800-362-3146.

**Cooper International Inc.,** 501 Alliance Ave., Toronto, Ontario, Canada M6N 2J3: Free information ◆ Guards and pads, helmets, masks, mouth guards, pucks, nets, cages, sticks, figure and hockey ice skates, and blade protectors. 416-763-3801.

**E.Z. Enterprises,** 205 D Exeter Rd., London, Ontario, Canada N6L 1A4: Free information ◆ Lightweight portable and collapsible goals. 519-472-5261.

**Goal Sporting Goods Inc.,** 37 Industrial Park Rd., P.O. Box 236, Essex, CT 06426: Free catalog ◆ Telescoping, folding, and adjustable goals and nets. 800-334-GOAL. www.goalsports.com

**Gould Goalie Equipment Inc.,** 848 Dodge Ave., Ste. 371, Evanston, IL 60202: Free catalog ◆ Custom goalie equipment. 888-462-5723; 847-864-5784 (in IL).

**Great Skate Hockey Supply Company,** 3395 Sheridan Dr., Amherst, NY 14226: Free information ◆ Ice skating and hockey equipment. 800-828-7496; 716-838-5100 (in NY).

**Hot Off The Ice,** P.O. Box 1620, Secaucus, NJ 07096: Free catalog ◆ Equipment and clothing. 800-446-8423. www.shop.nhl.com

**Irwin Sports,** 43 Hanna Ave., Toronto, Ontario, Canada M6K 1X6: Free information ◆ Gloves, nets, cages, protective gear, pucks, and skates. 800-268-1732.

**Maska USA Inc.,** 139 Harvest Ln., Williston, VT 05495: Free information ◆ Guards and pads, helmets, masks, pucks, and figure and hockey ice skates. 800-451-4600. www.ccmsports.com

**Mylec Inc.,** Mill Circle Rd., Winchendon Springs, MA 01477: Free list of retail sources ◆ Hockey sticks, goals, pucks, protective and goalie gear, and more. 978-297-0089.

**National Sporting Goods Corp.,** 25 Brighton Ave., Passaic, NJ 07055: Free information ◆ Figure and hockey ice skates, blade protectors, and sharpeners. 201-779-2323.

**Ocean Hockey Supply Company,** 197 Chambers Bridge Rd., Bricktown, NJ 08723: Free catalog ◆ Hockey equipment. 800-631-2159; 732-477-4411 (in NJ). www.oceanhockey.com

**Rawlings Sporting Goods,** 1859 Impertech Dr., Fenton, MO 63026: Free list of retail sources ◆ Guards and pads, nets, cages, sticks, and skates. 800-426-3334. www.rawlings.com

**Riedell Shoes Inc.,** P.O. Box 21, Red Wing, MN 55066: Free information ◆ Blade sharpeners, protectors, and figure, racing, and hockey skates. 612-388-8251.

**The Training Camp,** c/o Genesis Direct, 100 Plaza Dr., Secaucus, NJ 07094: Free catalog ◆ Basketball, football, golf, hockey, and soccer training aids for children. 800-873-8263. care@GenesisDirect.com

# HOME BUILDING & IMPROVEMENT

## Ceilings

**AA-Abbingdon Affiliates,** 2149 Utica Ave., Brooklyn, NY 11234: Brochure $1 ◆ Tin ceiling cornice moldings. 718-258-8333.

**Chelsea Decorative Metal Company,** 9603 Moonlight Dr., Houston, TX 77096: Catalog $2 ◆ Embossed art decorative tin for ceilings and walls. 713-721-9200. www.telluscom.com/chelsea

**Classic Ceilings,** 902 E. Commonwealth Ave., Fullerton, CA 92831: Free catalog ◆ Authentic decorative metal walls and ceilings. 800-992-8700; 714-526-8062 (in CA). www.classicceilings.com

**W.F. Norman Corp.,** P.O. Box 323, Nevada, MO 64772: Catalog $3 ◆ Cornices and sheet metal ornaments for ceilings. Also wallcoverings, corner and border trims, and filler plates. 800-641-4038. suev241845@aol.com

**Snelling's Thermo-Vac,** P.O. Box 210, Blanchard, LA 71009: Free information ◆ Replica tin ceilings in high-impact plastic. 318-929-7398.

## Cupolas

**Accent Millworks,** 285 N. Amboy Rd., Conneaut, OH 44030: Free information ◆ Easy-to-install cupolas. 440-593-6775.

**Allen Cupolas,** 2242 Bethel Rd., Lansdale, PA 19446: Free information ◆ Wood and metal cupolas. 215-699-8100.

**C & R Inquiries,** P.O. Box 1874, Stillwater, OK 74076: Free catalog ◆ Weather vanes, sundials, bird baths, and cupolas. 800-248-5445. www.crhooks.com

**Cape Cod Cupola Company Inc.,** 78 State Rd., North Dartmouth, MA 02747: Catalog $2 (refundable) ◆ Early American-style weather vanes and cupolas. 508-994-1956.

**Colonial Cupolas,** P.O. Box 38, 1816 Nemoke Trail, Haslett, MI 48840: Brochure $3 ◆ Wood cupolas and aluminum or copper weather vanes. Includes build-it-yourself kits. 800-678-1965.

**Coppersmiths,** Custom Copper & Brass Works, P.O. Box 2675, Oakhurst, CA 93644: Free brochure ◆ Fireplace hoods, cupolas, mailboxes, and dormers. 209-658-8909.

**Country Cupolas,** P.O. Box 400, East Conway, NH 03813: Free information ◆ Country-style cupolas assembled or ready-to-build kits. 603-939-2698.

**Crosswinds Gallery,** 29 Buttonwood St., Bristol, RI 02809: Free catalog ◆ Cupolas with copper roofs and weather vanes. 800-638-8263. www.crosswinds-gallery.com

**Denninger Weathervanes & Finials,** 77 Whipple Rd., Middletown, NY 10940: Catalog $4 ◆ Redwood cupolas with copper roofs and weather vanes. 914-343-2229. www.denninger.com

**The Outhouse,** 2853 Lincoln Hwy. East, Ronks, PA 17572: Free catalog ◆ Cupolas and copper, iron, and aluminum weather vanes. 800-346-7678; 717-687-9580 (in PA).

**Sun Designs,** 173 E. Wisconsin Ave., Oconomowoc, WI 53066: Plan book $9.95 plus $3.95 postage ◆ Plans for gazebos, bridges, cupolas, and structures. 414-567-4255.

## Door Chimes

**Caradon Friedland,** 255 Quaker Ln., Ste. 100, West Warwick, RI 02893: Free information ◆ Door chimes and push buttons. 800-767-1837.

**Hear You Are Inc.,** 4 Musconetcong Ave., Stanhope, NJ 07874: Free catalog ◆ Doorbell signals, telephone aids, visual and smoke alarms, and assistive listening devices for hearing-impaired persons. 201-347-7662 (voice/TTY).

## Doors & Door Surrounds

**Andersen Windows,** P.O. Box 203070, Austin, TX 78720: Free information ◆ Energy-efficient windows and patio doors. 800-426-4261. www.andersenwindows.com

**Architectural Components,** 26 N. Leverett Rd., Montague, MA 01351: Brochure $5 ◆ Reproduction doors from the 18th and 19th centuries, windows, window frames, and moldings. 413-367-9441.

**Arctic Glass & Window Outlet,** 565 County Rd. T, Hammond, WI 54015: Catalog $4 ◆ Windows, entryway and patio doors, skylights, and sun rooms. 800-428-9276.

**Benchmark Doors,** P.O. Box 7387, Fredericksburg, VA 22408: Free information ◆ Steel doors with a wood-grain finish. 800-755-3667. www.benchmark.hw.net

**Beveled Glass Works,** 23852 Pacific Coast Hwy., Malibu, CA 90265: Free information ◆ Wood doors with sidelights and beveled glass. 888-421-0518. www.beveledglassworks.com

**The Bilco Company,** P.O. Box 1203, New Haven, CT 06505: Free information ◆ All-steel outside basement doors. 203-934-6363. www.bilco.com

**Ciro Coppa Doors,** 1231 Paraiso Ave., San Pedro, CA 90731: Free catalog ◆ Wood screen doors and Adirondack chairs. 562-548-4142.

**Combination Door Company,** P.O. Box 1076, Fond du Lac, WI 54936: Free list of retail sources ◆ Wood combination windows and storm and screen doors. 920-922-2050.

**Craftsmen in Wood,** 5441 W. Hadley St., Phoenix, AZ 85043: Catalog $8 ◆ Distinctive doors and hardware. 602-278-8054.

**Creative Openings,** P.O. Box 4204, Bellingham, WA 98225: Catalog $4 ◆ Historical, traditional screen, and other doors. 360-671-6420.

**Crestline,** 888 Southview Dr., Mosinee, WI 54455: Free information ◆ French doors with optional glass panels and transoms. 800-552-4111. www.crestlineonline.com

**Driwood Ornamental Wood Moulding,** P.O. Box 1729, Florence, SC 29503: Catalog $6 (refundable) ◆ Doors, embossed wood molding, raised paneling, mantels, and curved stairs. 803-669-2478.

**Drums Sash-Door Company,** P.O. Box 207, Drums, PA 18222: Free catalog ◆ Window sashes, thresholds, risers, screen and storm doors, double-hung windows, and trim. 717-788-1145.

**Entrances Inc.,** 164 Poocham Rd., Westmoreland, NH 03467: Catalog $2 ◆ Interior and exterior insulated wood doors with optional beveled and stained glass. 603-399-7723.

**Entry Systems,** 911 E. Jefferson, Pittsburg, KS 66762: Free information ◆ Steel doors with a choice of transom designs. 800-835-0364.

**Fineman Doors Inc.,** 16020 Valley Wood Rd., Sherman Oaks, CA 91403: Information $2 ◆ Handcrafted solid hardwood entry and interior doors. 818-990-3667.

**Georgia-Pacific,** P.O. Box 2808, Norcross, GA 30091: Free information ◆ Doors and windows. 770-662-0512. www.gp.com

**Grand ERA Reproductions,** P.O. Box 1026, Lapeer, MI 48446: Catalog $2 ◆ Easy-to-assemble screen and storm door kits. 810-664-1756.

**Hendricks Woodworking,** P.O. Box 139, Kempton, PA 19529: Free brochure ◆ Authentically styled reproduction doors. 610-756-6187. historic@ot.com

**Hess Manufacturing Company,** Box 127, Quincy, PA 17247: Free information ◆ Insulated aluminum doors and windows. 800-541-6666; 717-749-3141 (in PA). www.armaclad.com

**Hurd Millwork Company,** 575 S. Whelen Ave., Medford, WI 54451: Free information ◆ Windows and hinged, sliding wood, and insulated aluminum patio doors. 800-223-4873; 715-748-2011 (in WI). www.hurd.com

**Iberia Millwork,** P.O. Box 12139, New Iberia, LA 70562: Free information ◆ French doors, interior and exterior shutters, and cabinets. 318-365-8129.

**International Wood Products,** 7312 Convoy Ct., San Diego, CA 92111: Free information ◆ Single and double wood doors with a choice of transom designs and sidelights. 800-468-3667. www.iwpdoor.com

**Jeld-Wen,** 3303 Lake Port Blvd., Klamath Falls, OR 97601: Free information ◆ Pre-finished or ready for finishing provincial and colonial-style bi-fold interior doors. 800-877-9482. www.jeld-wen.com

**L.E. Johnson Products Inc.,** 2100 Sterling Ave., Elkhart, IN 46516: Free brochure ◆ Sliding pocket door frame kit and folding door hardware. 800-837-5664. www.johnsonhardware.com

**Joinery Company,** P.O. Box 518, Tarboro, NC 27886: Catalog $5 ◆ Reproduction antique entryways and doors. 800-726-7463. www.joinery.com

**Kenmore Industries,** One Thompson Square, Boston, MA 02129: Catalog $3 ◆ Federal, Georgian, and Revival-style carved historical entries. 617-242-1711.

**Kolbe & Kolbe Millwork Company,** 1323 S. 11th Ave., Wassau, WI 54401: Free catalog ◆ Wood windows and doors. 800-955-8177. www.kolbe-kolbe.com

**Lamson-Taylor Custom Doors,** 5 Tucker Rd., South Acworth, NH 03607: Catalog $2 ◆ Energy-efficient doors. 603-835-2992.

**Ledco Inc.,** 801 Commerce Circle, Shelbyville, KY 40065: Free list of retail sources ◆ Bi-fold glass and mirror doors in pine and oak. 805-626-6367.

**Mad River Woodworks,** P.O. Box 1067, Blue Lake, CA 95525: Catalog $3 ◆ Reproduction doors from the mid-1800s ready for painting or staining. 800-446-6580; 707-668-5671 (in CA). mrww@reninet.com

**Marvin Windows,** P.O. Box 100, Warroad, MN 56763: Free information ◆ Windows and doors with divided and insulated storm windows and transoms. 800-346-5128. www.marvin.com

**Maurer & Shepherd Joyners Inc.,** 122 Naubuc Ave., Glastonbury, CT 06033: Brochure $2.25 ◆ Windows, doors, entryways, and authentic colonial woodworking. 203-633-2383.

**Morgan Manufacturing,** P.O. Box 2446, Oshkosh, WI 54903: Free list of retail sources ◆ Paneled and carved wood, sliding glass, and hinged patio doors. 920-235-7170.

**Old Wagon Factory,** P.O. Box 1427, Clarksville, VA 23927: Catalog $2 ◆ Victorian and Chippendale-style storm screen doors and furniture. 800-874-9358. www.wagonfactory.com

**Oregon Wooden Screen Door Company,** 2767 Harris St., Eugene, OR 97405: Catalog $3 (refundable) ◆ Screen and energy-efficient storm doors. 541-485-0279.

**Pacific Mutual Door Company,** 1525 W. 31st St., Kansas City, MO 64108: Free list of retail sources ◆ Doors. 816-531-0161.

**Peachtree Windows & Doors,** P.O. Box 5700, Norcross, GA 30091: Free information ◆ Steel, wood, glass, and aluminum doors and windows. 800-732-2499

**Pease Industries Inc.,** 7100 Dixie Hwy., Fairfield, OH 45014: Information $1 ◆ Hi-strength doors and entry ways with optional trim and glass. 800-883-6677. www.peasedoor.com

**Ricketson Sash & Door Company,** 100 Bidwell Rd., South Windsor, CT 06074: Free brochure ◆ Windows and doors for homes. 860-289-1222.

**Scherr's Cabinet & Doors,** 5315 Burdick Expwy. East, RR 5, Box 12, Minot, ND 58701: Brochure $2 ◆ Raised panel doors for cabinets, drawer fronts, and dovetail drawers. 701-839-3384. www.scherrs.com

**Cole Sewell Corp.,** 2288 University Ave., St. Paul, MN 55114: Free information ◆ Reinforced wood storm doors with optional security protection. 800-328-6596.

**Silverton Victorian Millworks,** P.O. Box 2987, Durango, CO 81302: Catalog $4 ◆ Doors with stained glass or etched glass inserts. 970-259-5915. www.themillworks.com

**Simpson Door Company,** P.O. Box 210, McCleary, WA 98557: Free brochure ◆ Paneled, carved, and standard wood doors. 800-952-4057; 206-495-3291 (in WA).

**Southeastern Insulated Glass,** 6477-B Peachtree Industrial Blvd., Atlanta, GA 30360: Free information ◆ Greenhouse and sun room kits, sliding glass doors, and skylights with optional tempered insulated glass. 800-841-9842; 770-455-8838 (in GA).

**Specialty Woodworks,** P.O. Box 1450, Hamilton, MT 59840: Catalog $7 ◆ Doors and cabinets. 406-363-6353. www.montana.com/specialtywoodworks

**Superior Hardwoods,** P.O. Box 4731, Missoula, MT 59806: Information $3 ◆ Fir, larch, and pine flooring. Also paneling, doors, and molding. 800-572-9601; 406-251-2272 (in MT).

**Taylor Brothers,** P.O. Box 11198, Lynchburg, VA 24506: Catalog $2 ◆ Handcrafted storm screen doors. 800-288-6767. www.taylorbrothers.com

**Touchstone Woodworks,** P.O. Box 112, Ravenna, OH 44266: Catalog $2 ◆ Authentic Victorian-style screen doors, moldings, porch parts, and ornamental trim. 330-297-1313.

**Vermont Natural Stoneworks,** Depot St., Box 275, Fair Haven, VT 05743: Free list of retail sources ◆ Tile products that include floors, pet memorials and urns, entryway systems, house and garden markers, instant patios and walkways, and gas stove mats. 802-265-2200. www.sover.net/~stone

**Victoriana East,** 2635 Center St., Merchantville, NJ 08109: Free information ◆ Victorian storm doors. 609-662-8480.

**Vintage Pine Company,** P.O. Box 85, Prospect, VA 23960: Free information ◆ Custom heart-pine flooring, cabinets, doors, mantels, moldings, and other architectural accouterments. 804-248-9102.

**Jack Wallis Door Emporium,** 2985 Butterworth Rd., Murray, KY 42071: Catalog $4 ◆ Handcrafted doors with optional stained glass. 502-489-2613.

**Weather Shield Mfg. Inc.,** One Weather Shield Plaza, Medford, WI 54451: Free information ◆ Wood windows, patio doors, and steel entryways. 800-222-2995; 715-748-2100 (in WI). www.weathershield.com

**Wing Industries,** 6202 Industrial Dr., Greenville, TX 75042: Free information ◆ Bi-fold French doors for interiors. 800-699-9464.

**The Wood Factory,** 111 Railroad St., Navasota, TX 77868: Catalog $2 ◆ Ornamental trim, mantels, screen doors, and millwork. 409-825-7233.

**Woodfold-Marco Mfg. Inc.,** Box 346, Forest Grove, OR 97116: Free catalog ◆ Custom accordion doors. 503-357-7181.

**Woodstone Company,** P.O. Box 223, Westminster, VT 05158: Brochure $4 ◆ Insulated solid wood doors and single, double, or triple-glazed windows with palladians and straight and fanned transoms. 802-722-9217. www.woodstone.com

## Flooring

**Aged Woods,** 2331 E. Market St., York, PA 17402: Free brochure ◆ Re-milled flooring from antique boards and beams. 800-233-9307; 717-840-0330 (in PA).

**Albany Woodworks,** P.O. Box 729, Albany, LA 70711: Free brochure ◆ Antique heart pine and American hardwood flooring. 504-567-1155. woods@i-55.com

**Authentic Pine Floors Inc.,** 4042 Hwy. 42, P.O. Box 206, Locust Grove, GA 30248: Free information ◆ Wide plank pine flooring. 800-283-6038. www.authentic-pine-floors.com

**Bamboo Flooring International Corp.,** 20950 Currier Rd., Walnut, CA 91789: Free brochure ◆ Three-layer, all bamboo tongue-and-groove cross-laminated plank flooring. 800-827-9261; 909-594-4189 (in CA). www.bamboo-flooring.com

**Carlisle Restoration Lumber,** HCR 32, Box 556C, Stoddard, NH 03464: Free information ◆ Wide pine flooring and paneling. 603-446-3937. carlisle@wideplankflooring.com

**Carpet Express,** 915 Market St., Dalton, GA 30720: Free information ◆ Carpet, oriental rugs, vinyl, and hardwood flooring. 800-922-5582.

**Goodwin Lumber,** Rt. 2, Box 119, Micanopy, FL 32667: Free information ◆ Heart pine and red cypress flooring, paneling, and beams. 800-336-3118. www.heartpine.com

**Granville Manufacturing Company Inc.,** P.O. Box 15, Rt. 100, Granville, VT 05747: Free brochure ◆ Quarter-sawn clapboard siding, wide pine and hardwood flooring, and building materials. 802-767-4747. www.woodsiding.com

**Hartco Flooring Company,** P.O. Box 4009, Oneida, TN 37841: Catalog $1 (request list of retail sources) ◆ Oak flooring in parquet, combination, parallel, herringbone, and basket-weave patterns. 800-769-8526. www.hartcoflooring.com

**Historic Floors of Oshkosh Inc.,** 911 E Main St., Winneconne, WI 54986: Free list of retail sources ◆ Hardwood reproduction borders and patterned flooring. 920-582-9977.

**Johnsonius Precision Millworks,** P.O. Box 275, McKenzie, TN 38201: Free information ◆ Solid hardwood and cypress lumber and siding, plank flooring and paneling, standard and custom molding, and accessories. 901-352-5656.

**Joinery Company,** P.O. Box 518, Tarboro, NC 27886: Catalog $5 ◆ Antique heart pine tongue-and-groove flooring, paneling, and trim from authentic colonial buildings. 800-726-7463. www.joinery.com

**Kentucky Wood Floors,** P.O. Box 33276, Louisville, KY 40232: Catalog $2 ◆ Walnut, oak, cherry, and ash borders ready for glue-down installation. 502-451-6024. www.kentuckywood.com

**Launstein Hardwoods,** 384 S. Every Rd., Mason, MI 48854: Free information ◆ Easy-to-install and finish pre-sanded hardwood flooring. 517-676-1133. www.launstein.com

**Lee's Carpet Showcase,** 3068 N. Dug Gap Rd., Dalton, GA 30720: Free information ◆ Carpet and Oriental rugs, vinyl and wood flooring, and accessories. 800-433-8479. hfnet.com/lees.html

**Memphis Hardwood Flooring Company,** 1551 Thomas St., Memphis, TN 38107: Free information ◆ Unfinished and finished oak flooring. 800-346-3010; 901-526-7306 (in TN). www.chickasawflooring.com

**Northfields Restorations,** 10 Kensington Rd., Hampton Falls, NH 03844: Free brochure ◆ Antique flooring. 603-926-5383.

**Piedmont Mantel & Millwork,** 4320 Interstate Dr., Macon, GA 31210: Catalog $3 ◆ Salvaged heart-pine flooring and colonial-style mantels in a choice of woods. 912-477-7536.

**J.L. Powell & Company Inc.,** 600 S. Madison St., Whiteville, NC 28472: Free information ◆ Antique heart pine flooring. 800-227-2007; 910-642-8989 (in NC).

**Quality Woods Ltd.,** 63 Flanders Bartley Rd., Flanders, NJ 07836: Free brochure ◆ Teak, plywood, teak and Asian rosewood parquet, tongue-and-groove planks, and strip flooring. 201-584-7554.

**Rare Earth Hardwoods,** 6778 E. Traverse Hwy., Traverse City, MI 49684: Free information ◆ Hardwood, other lumber, flooring, and decking. 800-968-0074. www.rare-earth-hardwoods.com

**Sheoga Hardwood Flooring & Paneling Inc.,** 15320 Burton Windsor Rd., Middlefield, OH 44062: Free list of retail sources ◆ Unfinished, pre-sanded, and milled tongue-and-groove flooring. 216-834-1710.

**Superior Hardwoods,** P.O. Box 4731, Missoula, MT 59806: Information $3 ◆ Fir, larch, and pine flooring. Also paneling, doors, and molding. 800-572-9601; 406-251-2272 (in MT).

**Vermont Natural Stoneworks,** Depot St., Box 275, Fair Haven, VT 05743: Free list of retail sources ◆ Tile products that include floors, pet memorials and urns, entryway systems, house and garden markers, instant patios and walkways, and gas stove mats. 802-265-2200. www.sover.net/~stone

**Vintage Lumber Company,** 1 Council Dr., Woodsboro, MD 21798: Free information ◆ Remilled antique heart pine, oak, chestnut, oak, cherry, walnut, and poplar flooring. 800-499-7859. www.vintagelumber.com

**Vintage Pine Company,** P.O. Box 85, Prospect, VA 23960: Free information ◆ Custom heart-pine flooring, cabinets, doors, mantels, moldings, and other architectural accouterments. 804-248-9102.

**Woodmill,** Box 146, East Livermore, ME 04228: Free information ◆ Cherry, oak, maple, ash, wide pine, walnut, and birch flooring. 207-897-5211.

**Woodstone Company,** P.O. Box 223, Westminster, VT 05158: Brochure $4 ◆ Antique wide and new plank flooring. 802-722-9217. www.woodstone.com

## Frames & Beams

**Bear Creek Lumber,** P.O. Box 669, Winthrop, WA 98862: Brochure $4 ◆ Western red cedar building supplies. 800-597-7191. www.bearcreeklumber.com/welcome.html

**E.F. Bufton & Son, Builders Inc.,** P.O. Box 164, Princeton, MA 01541: Brochure $5 ◆ Oak post-and-beam frames. 978-464-5418.

**Goodwin Lumber,** Rt. 2, Box 119, Micanopy, FL 32667: Free information ◆ Heart pine lumber and red cypress flooring, paneling, and beams. 800-336-3118. www.heartpine.com

**Vermont Frames,** P.O. Box 100, Hinesburg, VT 05461: Free brochure ◆ Post-and-beam frames. 802-453-3727. foamlam@sover.net

## Keys & Locks

**American Home Supply,** 191 Lost Lake Ln., Campbell, CA 95009: Catalog $2 ◆ Victorian and contemporary-style knobs, cabinet hardware and locks, faucets and bathroom hardware, grills and registers, and restoration items. 408-246-1962.

**Gainsborough Hardware,** 1255 Oakbrook Dr., Norcross, GA 30093: Free catalog ◆ Door hardware, key locks, passage sets, and accessories. 800-845-5662.

**Merit Metal Products Corp.,** 240 Valley Rd., Warrington, PA 18976: Catalog $10 ◆ Brass locks, hinges, and other hardware for doors, furniture, and cabinets. 215-343-2500.

## Paint & Refinishing Supplies

**H. Behlen & Bro.,** Division Mohawk Finishing Products Inc., 4715 State Hwy. 30, Amsterdam, NY 12010: Free information ◆ Dry-stain powders. 800-545-0047.

**Burr Tavern,** Rt. 1, Box 474, East Meredith, NY 13757: Free information ◆ Reproduction 18th and 19th-century paints, brushes, and materials. 800-664-6293.

**Gryphin,** P.O. Box 5910, Philadelphia, PA 19137: Catalog $3 ◆ Oil, acrylic, and milk paints. 800-482-1886.

**Janovic/Plaza Inc.,** 30-35 Thomson Ave., Long Island City, NY 11101: Catalog $4.95 ◆ Hard-to-find tools and finishes for painting and dyeing. 800-772-4381. www.janovic.com

**Johnson Paint Company Inc.,** 355 Newbury St., Boston, MA 02115: Catalog $1 ◆ Painting supplies, brushes, and tools. 617-536-4838.

**W.D. Lockwood & Company,** 81-83 Franklin St., New York, NY 10013: Free information ◆ Water, alcohol, and oil-soluble stain powders. 212-966-4046.

**The Old Fashioned Milk Paint Company,** P.O. Box 222, Groton, MA 01450: Free information ◆ Authentic colonial and Shaker milk paint in several colors. 978-448-6336.

**Primrose Distributing,** 54445 Rose Rd., South Bend, IN 46628: Information $3 ◆ Original oil base and acrylic paints for authentic restoration of historic architecture. 800-222-3092.

**Stulb Colour Craftsmen,** P.O. Box 1030, Fort Washington, PA 19034: Catalog $3 ◆ Natural earth pigment paints for authentic color decoration, restoration, and preservation. 215-654-1770.

**Sinopia,** 229 Valencia St., San Francisco, CA 94103: Free catalog ◆ Pigments and other materials for restoration, interior design, and fine arts. 415-621-2898. www.sinopia.com

**Target Enterprises,** P.O. Box 1582, Rutherford, NJ 07070: Free information ◆ Water topcoat finishes and stains. 800-752-9922.

## Paneling

**AFCO Industries Inc.,** 615 E. 40th St., Holland, MI 49423: Free information ◆ Scratch-resistant waterproof hardwood panels. 800-253-4644.

**California Redwood Association,** 405 Enfrente Dr., Ste. 200, Novato, CA 94949: Free information with long SASE ◆ Redwood paneling. 415-382-0662. www.calredwood.org

**Driwood Ornamental Wood Moulding,** P.O. Box 1729, Florence, SC 29503: Catalog $6 (refundable) ◆ Embossed wood molding and raised paneling, mantels, curved stairs, and doors. 803-669-2478.

**Georgia-Pacific,** P.O. Box 2808, Norcross, GA 30091: Free information ◆ Wall paneling and pre-hung wallpaper on plywood panels. 770-662-0512. www.gp.com

**Goodwin Lumber,** Rt. 2, Box 119, Micanopy, FL 32667: Free information ◆ Heart pine and red cypress flooring, paneling, and beams. 800-336-3118. www.heartpine.com

**Griffis Lumber & Sawmill,** 9333 NW 13th St., Gainesville, FL 32653: Free information ◆ Cypress shingles and custom kiln-dried cypress siding and paneling. 352-372-9965.

**Johnsonius Precision Millworks,** P.O. Box 275, McKenzie, TN 38201: Free information ◆ Solid hardwood and cypress lumber and siding, plank flooring and paneling, standard and custom molding, and accessories. 901-352-5656.

**Maple Grove Restorations,** P.O. Box 9194, Bolton, CT 06043: Brochure $2 ◆ Interior raised panel shutters and wainscoting. 203-742-5432.

**Masonite Corp.,** 1 S. Wacker Dr., Chicago, IL 60606: Free information ◆ Hardboard paneling. 800-446-1649.

**Simpson Timber,** Box 1169, Arcata, CA 95518: Free information ◆ Redwood paneling. 800-637-7077; 707-822-0371 (in CA).

**Superior Hardwoods,** P.O. Box 4731, Missoula, MT 59806: Information $3 ◆ Fir, larch, and pine flooring. Also paneling, doors, and molding. 800-572-9601; 406-251-2272 (in MT).

## Radiator Enclosures & Registers

**All American Wood Register Company,** 239 E. Main St., Cary, IL 60013: Free brochure ◆ Surface, flush, and baseboard solid wood registers with or without adjustable dampers. 847-639-0393.

**Arsco Manufacturing Company Inc.,** 3564 Blue Rock Rd., Cincinnati, OH 45247: Free information ◆ Radiator covers and enclosures for steam and hot water heating systems. 800-543-7040; 513-385-0555 (in OH). www.arsco.com

**Barker Metalcraft,** 1701 W. Belmont, Chicago, IL 60657: Free catalog ◆ Drop-in and flat grills, grills with borders, convector grills, and other radiator covers and registers. 800-397-0129.

**Grate Vents,** 9502 Linder Ave., Crystal Lake, IL 60014: Catalog $2 ◆ Unfinished and finished wood floor and baseboard grates. 815-459-4306.

**Hinges & Handles,** 100 Lincoln Way East, Osceola, IN 46561: Free catalog ◆ Solid brass registers. 800-533-4782.

**Monarch Radiator Enclosures,** 2744 Arkansas Dr., Brooklyn, NY 11234: Brochure $1 (refundable) ◆ Easy-to-assemble all-steel radiator enclosures. 201-796-4117.

**Walter Norman & Company,** P.O. Box 148037, Chicago, IL 60614: Free information ◆ Ready-to- assemble Prairie and Shaker-style radiator cabinets. 312-281-1088.

**RadCo Woodworks,** 580 Mountain Ave., North Caldwell, NJ 07006: Free information ◆ Traditional and ultra-contemporary wood radiator enclosures. 201-226-2236.

**The Reggio Register,** P.O. Box 511, Ayer, MA 01432: Catalog $1 ◆ Solid brass and cast-iron registers and grills. 978-772-3493.

**A Touch of Brass,** 9052 Chevrolet Dr., Ellicott City, MD 21042: Catalog $3 ◆ Polished stamped and cast-brass registers. 800-272-7734.

**The Wooden Radiator Cabinet Company,** P.O. Box 148037, Chicago, IL 60614: Free information ◆ Handcrafted Prairie and Shaker-style wood radiator cabinets. 800-817-9110.

## Rain Gutters

**Genova Products,** 7034 E. Court St., Box 309, Davison, MI 48423: Free brochure ◆ Vinyl gutters and downspout systems. 810-744-3130. www.genovaproducts.com

**Plastmo Inc.,** 8246 Sandy Ct., Jessup, MD 20794: Free catalog ◆ Easy-installation rain gutters. 800-899-0992. plastmo@erols.com

## Restoration Materials & Equipment

**A & H Brass & Supply,** 126 W. Main St., Johnson City, TN 37604: Catalog $2 ◆ Wood ornaments, moldings, and veneers. 800-638-4252; 423-928-8220 (in TN).

**Abatron,** 5501 95th Ave., Kenosha, WI 53144: Free information ◆ Concrete restoration materials. 800-445-1754; 414-653-2000 (in WI). www.abatron.com

**Adkins Architectural Antiques,** 3515 Fannin, Houston, TX 77004: Free brochure ◆ Salvaged architectural antiques. 713-522-6547.

**American Wood Column Corp.,** 913 Grand St., Brooklyn, NY 11211: Free brochure ◆ Locked-joint staved columns for exterior and interior use. 718-782-3163.

**Architectural Antiquities,** Harborside, ME 04642: Free brochure ◆ Victorian supplies from the 18th and 19th-century for home building and restoration. 207-326-4938.

**Architectural Components Inc.,** 26 N. Leverett Rd., Montague, MA 01351: Free brochure ◆ Reproduction and custom windows, doors, and architectural millwork. 413-367-9441.

**Architectural Iron Company,** 104 Ironwood Ct., Milford, PA 18337: Catalog $4 ◆ Reproduction 18th and 19th-century castings and wrought-iron accessories. 800-442-4766.

**The Bank Architectural Antiques,** 1824 Felicity St., New Orleans, LA 70113: Free brochure ◆ Reproduction and repaired New Orleans-style shutters, doors, hardware, and architectural supplies. 800-274-8883.

**Bendix Moldings Inc.,** 37 Ramland Rd. South, Orangeburg, NY 10962: Catalog $3 ◆ Decorative wood moldings and ornaments. 800-526-0240; 914-365-1111 (in NY).

**Campbellsville Industries Inc.,** P.O. Box 278. Campbellsville, KY 42718: Free catalog ◆ Aluminum cornices, louvers, cupolas, columns, balustrades, and shutters with an optional baked-on finish. 502-465-8135.

**A Carolina Craftsman,** 975 S. Avocado St., Anaheim, CA 92805: Catalog $5 (refundable) ◆ Hard-to-find antique replacement parts for houses and furniture. 714-776-7877.

**Cathedral Stone Products Inc.,** 8332 Bristol Ct., Ste. 107, Jessup, MD 20749: Free information ◆ Acrylic and latex-free bonding agents and restoration mortars. 301-317-4670.

**Chadsworth Incorporated,** P.O. Box 53268, Atlanta, GA 30355: Catalog $5 (refundable ◆ Columns and replacement components in wood and fiberglass. 800-265-8667.

**Donald Durham Company,** 59 Forest Ave., Des Moines, IA 50314: Free list of retail sources ◆ Self-hardening water putty for many kinds of repairs. 515-243-0491. www.waterputty.com

**Epoxy Technology Inc.,** 14 Fortune Dr., Billerica, MA 01821: Free information ◆ Epoxy adhesives for artifact restoration. 800-227-2201; 978-667-3805 (in MA). www.epotek.com

**Hardware Plus,** 701 E. Kingsley Rd., Garland, TX 75041: Catalog $5 ◆ Supplies for restoring old houses and furniture. 800-522-7336.

**Hartman-Sanders,** 4340 Bankers Circle, Atlanta, GA 30360: Free brochure ◆ Authentic architectural columns. 800-241-4303; 770-449-1561 (in GA).

**Improvements,** Hanover Direct Pennsylvania Inc., Hanover, PA 17333-0084: Free catalog ◆ Products that improve your home and security. 800-642-2112. www.improvementscatalog.com

**Janovic/Plaza Inc.,** 30-35 Thomson Ave., Long Island City, NY 11101: Catalog $4.95 ◆ Restoration supplies, hard-to-find tools, and finishes for painting and dyeing. 800-772-4381. www.janovic.com

**Kentucky Millwork,** 4200 Reservoir Ave., Louisville, KY 40213: Free catalog ◆ Architectural millwork, store fronts and fixtures, and more. 502-451-3456. www.kentuckywood.com

**Outwater Plastic Industries Inc.,** 4 Passaic St., P.O. Drawer 403, Wood-Ridge, NJ 07075: Free catalog ◆ Building components, other parts, millwork, brass hardware, and more. 800-631-8375. www.outwater.com/outwater.html

**Park Place,** 2251 Wisconsin Ave. NW, Washington, DC 20007: Catalog $2 ◆ Classic outdoor furnishings and architectural products. 202-342-6294.

**A.F. Schwerd Manufacturing Company,** 3215 McClure Ave., Pittsburgh, PA 15212: Free brochure ◆ Wood columns in seasoned northern white pine with matching pilasters and aluminum bases. 412-766-6322.

**Tremont Nail Company,** P.O. Box 111, Wareham, MA 02571: Free catalog ◆ Old-fashioned cut nails. 800-842-0560.

**Tuff-Kote Company Inc.,** 210 N. Seminary Ave., Woodstock, IL 60098: Free information ◆ Filler for wall and ceiling cracks. 815-338-2006.

**The Wood Factory,** 111 Railroad St., Navasota, TX 77868: Catalog $2 ◆ Victorian-style moldings, screen doors, porch parts, ornamental trim, and other woodwork. 409-825-7233.

## Roofing Materials & Roof Ornaments

**C & H Roofing,** P.O. Box 2105, Lake City, FL 32056: Free information ◆ Red cedar shingles with a thatched look and historical roofing restoration supplies. 800-327-8115.

**Cedar Valley Shingle Systems,** 943 San Felipe Rd., Hollister, CA 95023: Free brochure ◆ Cedar shingle panels in regular or rough-sawn textures. 800-521-9523.

**Celadon,** P.O. Box 860, Valley Forge, PA 19482: Free brochure ◆ Slate-looking fired ceramic roofing material. 800-CEL-SLATE.

**CertainTeed,** P.O. Box 860, Valley Forge, PA 19482: Free information ◆ Asphalt-based roof shingles that resemble wood shakes. 800-782-8777. www.certainteed.com

**Conklin Metal Industries,** P.O. Box 1858, Atlanta, GA 30301: Brochure $3 ◆ Roofing shingles in galvanized steel, copper, and other materials. 404-688-4510.

**Elcor Corp.,** Wellington Centre, Ste 1000, 14643 Dallas Pkwy., Dallas, TX 75240: Free list of retail sources ◆ Wind resistant and Class A fire rated shingles. 972-851-0500. info@elcor.com

**Georgia-Pacific,** P.O. Box 2808, Norcross, GA 30091: Free information ◆ Easy-to-install shingles with a textured look of cedar. 770-662-0512. www.gp.com

**Griffis Lumber & Sawmill,** 9333 NW 13th St., Gainesville, FL 32653: Free information ◆ Cypress shingles and custom kiln-dried cypress siding and paneling. 352-372-9965.

**Liberty Cedar,** 535 Liberty Ln., West Kingston, RI 02892: Free information ◆ Wood roofing. 800-88-CEDAR; 401-789-6626 (in RI).

**Ludowici Roof Tile,** 4757 Tile Plant Rd., P.O. Box 69, New Lexington, OH 43764: Free brochure ◆ Clay roof tiles. 800-945-TILE. www.ludowici.com

**Masonite Corp.,** 1 S. Wacker Dr., Chicago, IL 60606: Free information ◆ Wood-fiber shingles with an authentic shake look. 800-446-1649.

**The New England Slate Company,** Burr Pond Rd., Sudbury, VT 05733: Free brochure ◆ New and salvaged roofing slate. 802-247-8809.

**Preservation Products,** 221 Brooke St., Media, PA 19063: Free brochure ◆ Acrylic roof-coating system. 800-553-0523.

**Revere Copper Products Inc.,** P.O. Box 300, Rome, NY 13442: Free information ◆ Copper shingles. 800-490-1776. www.borg.com/~reverecp

**The Roof Tile & Slate Company,** 1290 Carroll St., Carrolton, TX 75006: Free information ◆ Restored roof tiles from salvaged buildings. 800-446-0220; 972-446-0005 (in TX). www.RTSC.com

**ShakerTown Corp.,** 1400 Kerron St., Winlock, WA 98596: Free catalog ◆ Cedar shingles. 800-426-8970.

**Shingle Mill Inc.,** 73 Stuart St., Gardner, MA 01440: Free catalog ◆ Wood shingles for roofing and exterior siding. 978-632-3015.

**The Tile Man Inc.,** Rt. 6, Box 494, Louisburg, NC 27549: Free information ◆ Matching clay and slate roofing materials. 919-853-6923.

**Tile Roofs Inc.,** P.O. Box 177, Mokena, IL 60448: Free brochure ◆ New and used slate and tile roofing materials. 708-479-4366. www.tileroofs.com/slate.htm

**Vulcan Supply Corp.,** P.O. Box 100, Westford, VT 05494: Catalog $3 (refundable) ◆ Copper roof ornaments. 802-878-4103.

## Salvaged Building Materials

**Aged Woods,** 2331 E. Market St., York, PA 17402: Free brochure ◆ Re-milled flooring from antique boards and beams. 800-233-9307; 717-840-0330 (in PA).

**Albany Woodworks,** P.O. Box 729, Albany, LA 70711: Free brochure ◆ Reclaimed antique building materials. 504-567-1155. woods@i-55.com

**Architectural Antiques,** 801 Washington Ave. North, Minneapolis, MN 55401: Free information ◆ Architectural elements and ecclesiastical artifacts. 612-332-8344.

**Architectural Antiques Exchange,** 715 N. 2nd St., Philadelphia, PA 19123: Free brochure ◆ Salvaged building components and trim. 215-922-3669.

**Architectural Antiquities,** Harborside, ME 04642: Free brochure ◆ Brass light fixtures and hardware, Victorian plumbing fixtures, fireplace mantels, doors, windows, stained glass, and architectural antiquities. 207-326-4938.

**Architectural Artifacts Inc.,** 4325 N. Ravenswood, Chicago, IL 60613: Free information ◆ American and European antiques with an emphasis on architectural ornaments. 312-348-0622.

**Architectural Salvage Warehouse,** 212 Battery St., Burlington, VT 05401: Free information ◆ Hardware, doors, stained glass, woodwork, mantels, fixtures, columns, and architectural antiques. 802-658-5011.

**The Bank Architectural Antiques,** 1824 Felicity St., New Orleans, LA 70113: Free brochure ◆ Salvaged building components. 800-274-8883.

**Sylvan Brandt,** 653 Main St., Lititz, PA 17543: Free information ◆ Salvaged materials from 18th and 19th-century houses, grist mills, and barns. 717-626-4520.

**The Brass Knob,** 2311 18th St. NW, Washington, DC 20009: Free information ◆ Hardware, garden ornaments, bathroom accessories, fireplace equipment, and antique lighting, from 1870 to 1930. 202-332-3370.

**By-Gone Days Antiques Inc.,** 3100 South Blvd., Charlotte, NC 28209: Free information ◆ Mantels, restored door hardware, and architectural antiques. 704-527-8717.

**Conner's Architectural Antiques,** 701 P St., Lincoln, NE 68508: Free information ◆ Interior and exterior architectural antiques. 402-435-3338.

**Coronado Wrecking & Salvage,** 4200 Broadway SE, Albuquerque, NM 87105: Free information ◆ Architectural salvage. 505-877-2821.

**The Emporium,** 1800 Westheimer, Houston, TX 77098: Catalog $3 ◆ Plumbing, furniture, garden accessories, mantels, and architectural antiques. 713-528-3808.

**Florida Victorian Architectural Antiques,** 112 W. Georgia Ave., DeLand, FL 32720: Free brochure ◆ Authentic salvaged Victorian-style structural building components. 904-734-9300.

**Governor's Antiques & Architectural Materials Ltd.,** 6240 Meadowbridge Rd., Mechanicsville, VA 23111: Free catalog ◆ Original and reproduction 18th and 19th-century furnishings, authentic antiques, and architectural antique building materials. 804-746-1030.

**Great Gatsby's,** 5070 Peachtree Industrial Blvd., Atlanta, GA 30341: Free brochure ◆ Architectural antiquities and ornamental trim. 800-428-7297. Greatgatsbys@mindspring.com

**Historic York Architectural Warehouse,** 224 N. George St., York, PA 17401: Free information ◆ Architectural salvage. 717-843-0320.

**Horsefeathers Architectural Antiques,** 346 Connecticut St., Buffalo, NY 14213: Free information ◆ Salvaged doors, mantels, lighting, furniture, and other architectural items. 716-882-1581.

**Ken Hunt Building Supply & Salvage,** 2050 SE Army Post Rd., Des Moines, IA 50320: Free information ◆ Architectural salvage. 515-287-0007.

**Materials Unlimited,** 2 W. Michigan Ave., Ypsilanti, MI 48197: Free information ◆ Architectural salvage. 800-299-9462. www.mat-unl.com

**Off the Wall,** Box 4561, Carmel-by-the-Sea, CA 93921: Free information ◆ Architectural antiques. 408-624-6165. www.imperialearth.com/~OTW

**Olde Bostonian Salvage,** 66 Von Hillern St., Dorchester, MA 02125: Free information ◆ Architectural salvage. 617-282-9300.

**Omega Too,** 2204 San Pablo Ave., Berkeley, CA 94702: Free information ◆ Architectural ornamentation for houses and gardens. 510-843-3636.

**The Original Cast Lighting,** 6120 Delmar Blvd., St. Louis, MO 63112: Catalog $2 ◆ Restored antique fixtures. 314-863-1895.

**Pittsburgh Antique Company,** 143 West College St., Canonsburg, PA 15317: Free brochure ◆ Gas fixtures, early electric chandeliers, other period lighting, mantels, doors, hardware, newel posts, columns, ornamental iron, and other architectural antiques. 412-222-8586. PPAC@city-net.com

**Queen City Architectural Salvage,** 4750 Brighton Blvd., Denver, CO 80216: Free information ◆ Architectural salvage. 303-296-0925.

**The Restoration Source,** 3512 N. Southport, Chicago, IL 60657: Free information ◆ Architectural salvage. 773-327-1250.

**Salvage One,** 1524 S. Sangamon St., Chicago, IL 60608: Free brochure ◆ Salvaged building components. 312-733-0098. www.salvageone.com

**United House Wrecking Inc.,** 535 Hope St., Stamford, CT 06906: Free brochure ◆ Doors, mantels, beveled glass, Victorian gingerbread, paneling, fixtures, dividers, screens, and salvaged architectural building components and trim. 203-348-5371.

**Urban Archaeology,** 143 Franklin St., New York, NY 10013: Catalog $8.66 ◆ Staircases, balconies, plaster moldings, windows and skylights, doors, and entryways. Also Victorian and architectural antiques and accessories. 212-431-4646.

**Wooden Nickel Architectural Antiques,** 1400-1414 Central Pkwy., Cincinnati, OH 45210: Free information ◆ Salvaged building components and trims. 513-241-2985.

## Shutters

**Alside Corp.,** P.O. Box 2010, Akron, OH 44309: Free list of retail sources ◆ Shutter sets. 330-929-1811.

**Beech River Mill Company,** Old Rt. 16, Box 236, Centre Ossipee, NH 03814: Brochure $5 ◆ Custom-louvered and paneled products. Also period shutter and blinds hardware. 603-539-2636.

**Devenco Products Inc.,** Box 700, Decatur, GA 30031: Free brochure ◆ Period reproduction wood blinds and plantation-style, traditional, and movable shutters. Also exterior shutters. 800-888-4597; 404-378-4597 (in GA).

**Historic Windows,** P.O. Box 1172, Harrisonburg, VA 22801: Catalog $3 ◆ Handcrafted Victorian-style hardwood shutters. 540-434-5855.

**Iberia Millwork,** P.O. Box 12139, New Iberia, LA 70562: Free information ◆ Interior and exterior shutters, cabinets, and French doors. 318-365-8129.

**Inter Trade Inc.,** 3175 Fujita St., Torrance, CA 90505: Free information ◆ Roll shutters that provide security and protection from heat, sun, cold, rain, and noise. 310-515-7177.

**Kestrel Manufacturing,** 9 E. Race St., Stowe, PA 19464: Catalog $5 (refundable) ◆ Knock-down and ready-to-hang folding screens and interior and exterior shutters. Also available as kits. 800-494-4321; 610-326-6679 (in PA). www.diyshutters.com

**Maple Grove Restorations,** P.O. Box 9194, Bolton, CT 06043: Brochure $2 ◆ Interior raised panel shutters, panel walls, and wainscoting. 203-742-5432.

**Perkowitz Window Fashions Inc.,** 135 Green Bay Rd., Wilmette, IL 60091: Catalog $1 ◆ Moveable louvered and interior shutters, window shades, and blinds. 847-251-7700.

**The Shutter Depot,** 437 LaGrange, Greenville, GA 30222: Free brochure ◆ Shutter kits and pre-finished and unfinished interior and exterior shutters. 706-672-1214. www.shutterdepot.com

**Shutter Shop,** P.O. Box 11882, Charlotte, NC 28220: Catalog $3 ◆ Interior and exterior shutters. 704-334-8031.

**Shuttercraft,** 282 Stepstone Hill Rd., Guilford, CT 06437: Free brochure ◆ Unfinished or primed and painted western white pine shutters with movable or fixed louvers. 203-453-1973.

**Timberlane Woodcrafters Inc.,** 197 Wissahickon Ave., North Wales, PA 19454: Free catalog ◆ Shutters. 800-250-2221. www.timberlane-wood.com

**Vixen Hill,** Main St., P.O. Box 389, Elverson, PA 19520: Catalog $4 ◆ Wood shutters. 800-423-2766. www.vixenhill.com

## Siding

**California Redwood Association,** 405 Enfrente Dr., Ste. 200, Novato, CA 94949: Free information with long SASE ◆ Redwood siding. 415-382-0662. www.calredwood.org

**Cedar Valley Shingle Systems,** 943 San Felipe Rd., Hollister, CA 95023: Free brochure ◆ Red cedar shingle panels. 800-521-9523.

**Dryvit Systems Inc.,** 1 Energy Way, West Warwick, RI 02893: Free information ◆ Siding that looks like stucco. 401-822-4100. www.dryvit.com

**Georgia-Pacific,** P.O. Box 2808, Norcross, GA 30091: Free information ◆ Hardboard siding with a colonial wood-grain texture. 770-662-0512. www.gp.com

**Granville Manufacturing Company Inc.,** P.O. Box 15, Rt. 100, Granville, VT 05747: Free brochure ◆ Quarter-sawn clapboard siding, wide pine and hardwood flooring, and other building materials. 802-767-4747. www.woodsiding.com

**Griffis Lumber & Sawmill,** 9333 NW 13th St., Gainesville, FL 32653: Free information ◆ Cypress shingles and custom kiln-dried cypress siding and paneling. 352-372-9965.

**Louisiana-Pacific Corp.,** P.O. Box 10266, Portland, OR 97210: Free information ◆ Treated and weatherized wood siding. 800-299-0028.

**Shingle Mill Inc.,** 73 Stuart St., Gardner, MA 01440: Free catalog ◆ Wood shingles for roofing and exterior siding. 978-632-3015.

**VIPCO,** P.O. Box 1058, Columbus, OH 43216: Free information ◆ Solid-vinyl exterior siding with a look of carved wood clapboard. 800-366-8472. www.crane-plastics.com

**Ward Clapboard Mill Inc.,** P.O. Box 1030, Waitsfield, VT 05673: Free information ◆ Spruce quarter-sawn clapboard siding. 802-496-3581.

## Stairways

**A.J. Stairs Inc.,** 1095 Towbin Ave., Lakewood, NJ 08701: Brochure $1 ◆ Easy-to-assemble spiral and curved stairways. 800-425-7824.

**American Ornamental Metal,** 5013 Kelley St., P.O. Box 21548, Houston, TX 77026: Free catalog ◆ Iron and wood spiral staircases. 800-231-3693.

**Atlantic Stairworks Inc.,** P.O. Box 244, Newburyport, MA 01950: Free catalog ◆ Free-standing staircases. 978-462-7502.

**Bentwood Building,** 241 Addison Square, Kalispell, MT 59901: Catalog $4 ◆ Log spiral stairways and furniture. 406-257-4161.

**Curvoflite,** 205 Spencer Ave., Chelsea, MA 02150: Free information ◆ Spiral and circular oak staircases, paneling, moldings, cabinets, and millwork. 617-889-0007. www.curvoflite.com

**Driwood Ornamental Wood Moulding,** P.O. Box 1729, Florence, SC 29503: Catalog $6 (refundable) ◆ Curved stairs, embossed wood molding, raised paneling, mantels, and doors. 803-669-2478.

**Duvinage Corp.,** 60 W. Oakridge Dr., Hagerstown, MD 21740: Free catalog ◆ Spiral and circular stairways. 800-541-2645.

**Goddard Spiral Stairs,** Box 502, Logan, KS 67646: Free information ◆ Wood and wrought-iron spiral staircases. 800-536-4341. www.adnetmk.com/goddard

**The Iron Shop,** 400 Reed Rd., P.O. Box 547, Broomall, PA 19008: Free brochure ◆ Iron circular stairway kits. 800-523-7427. www.theironshop.com

**The Maizefield Company,** P.O. Box 336, Port Townsend, WA 98368: Free brochure ◆ Mantels, staircases, and moldings. 360-385-6789.

**Mylen Industries,** 650 Washington St., Peekskill, NY 10566: Free brochure ◆ Easy-to-install space-saving indoor and outdoor spiral stairs. 800-431-2155; 914-739-8486 (in NY). www.mylen.com

**Piedmont Home Products Inc.,** P.O. Box 269, Ruckersville, VA 22968: Free brochure ◆ Handcrafted spiral stairs, rails, balusters, and newel posts. 800-622-3399. www.piedmontstairs.com

**Safeway Stair Inc.,** 30 Pine St., Stoneham, MA 02180: Free information ◆ Handcrafted oak spiral staircases. 781-438-4286. info@safew.com

**Salter Industries,** P.O. Box 183, Eagleville, PA 19408: Free brochure ◆ Easy-to-install spiral stairs. 800-368-8280.

**Spiral Manufacturing Inc.,** 17251 Jefferson Hwy., Baton Rouge, LA 70817: Free brochure ◆ Wood spiral and curved stairway kits. 800-535-9956. www.spiralstair.com

**Spiral Stairs of America,** 1700 Spiral Ct., Erie, PA 16510: Free brochure ◆ Spiral stairways. 800-422-3700. spiralstairs-america@mail.com

**SpiralStairs,** Box 1220, Benton Rd., Albion, ME 04910: Free brochure ◆ Assembled wood spiral, straight, or combination straight and curved stairs. 800-924-2985; 207-437-2415 (in ME).

**Stair Systems Inc.,** 1480 E. 6th St., Sandwich, IL 60548: Free information ◆ Easy-to-assemble staircases with factory pre-assembled sections. 800-962-4299.

**Stairways Inc.,** 4166 Pinemont, Houston, TX 77018: Free brochure ◆ Wood and metal stairways. 800-231-0793. www.stairwaysinc.com

**Steptoe & Wife Antiques Ltd.,** 322 Geary Ave., Toronto, Ontario, Canada M6H 2C7: Catalog $3 ◆ Easy-to-assemble Victorian interior and exterior cast-iron spiral and straight staircases. 416-530-4200. www.terraport.net/steptoe

## Stucco, Bricks, & Stones

**Keystone Retaining Wall Systems,** 4444 W. 78th St., Minneapolis, MN 55435: Free information ◆ Modular retaining wall systems. 800-891-9791. keystone@keystonewalls.com

**Old Carolina Brick Company,** 475 Majolica Rd., Salisbury, NC 28147: Free brochure ◆ Authentic handmade brick. 704-636-8850.

**Stone Company Inc.,** W4520 Lime Rd., Eden, WI 53019: Free information ◆ Natural building and landscape cobblers, granite boulders, wall stone, steppers, and flagstone. 920-477-2521.

**Stone Legends,** 301 Pleasant Dr., Dallas, TX 75217: Free information ◆ Manufactured stone. 972-398-1199.

**Stone Magic,** 301 Pleasant Dr., Dallas, TX 75217: Free brochure ◆ Interior and exterior cast-stone and classic to contemporary cast-stone mantels. 800-597-3606. www.stonelegends.com

## Switch Plates

**Classic Accents Inc.,** P.O. Box 1181, Southgate, MI 48195: Catalog $1.50 ◆ Switch cover plates, push-button light switches, and solid brass cover plates. 313-282-5525.

**The Country Store of Geneva,** 28 James St., Geneva, IL 60134: Catalog $3 ◆ Pewter-finished, punched tin switch plate covers. 630-879-0098.

**Derk's Switchplates,** 4176 S. Luce Ave., Fremont, MI 49412: Free information ◆ Handcarved wood switch plates. 616-924-3382.

## Tile & Linoleum

**American Olean Tile Company,** 1000 Cannon Ave., Lansdale, PA 19446: Free information ◆ Easy-to-install ceramic mosaic tiles. 215-855-1111. www.aotile.com

**Amsterdam Corp.,** 150 E. 58th St., 9th Floor, New York, NY 10155: Catalog $3 ◆ Authentic Dutch handpainted tiles. 212-644-1350.

**Armstrong World Industries,** P.O. Box 3233, Lancaster, PA 17604: Free information ◆ Tile, linoleum, and other floor coverings with an optional no-wax surface. 800-232-4832. www.armstrong.com

**Carpet Express,** 915 Market St., Dalton, GA 30720: Free information ◆ Carpet and vinyl. 800-922-5582.

**Country Floors Inc.,** 15 E. 16th St., New York, NY 10003: Catalog $6 ◆ Hand-molded and painted ceramic tiles. 212-627-8300. www.countryfloors.com

**Designs in Tile,** P.O. Box 358, Mt. Shasta, CA 96067: Brochure $3 ◆ Historic reproductions, contemporary and traditional patterns, other ceramic tiles, murals, corner blocks, and coordinated borders. 916-926-2629. www.designsintile.com/angjap.html

**Epro Tiles Inc.,** 156 E. Broadway, Westerville, OH 43081: Free information ◆ Sandstone collection of handmade tiles. 614-882-6990.

**Interceramic USA,** 2333 S. Jupiter Rd., Garland, TX 75041: Free list of retail sources ◆ Floor tile. 800-496-TILE. www.interceramicusa.com/feedback.htm

**Italian Tile Center,** 499 Park Ave., New York, NY 10022: Free information ◆ Italian tiles with flowers, fruit, and other patterns. 212-980-1500.

**Sun House Tiles,** 9986 Happy Acres West, Bozeman, MT 59715: Free information ◆ Handmade reproduction period tiles. 406-587-3651.

**Tile Restoration Center,** 3511 Interlake North, Seattle, WA 98103: Brochure $10 (check only) ◆ Tile reproduction and restoration. 206-633-4866. www.aimnet.com/~tcolson/pages/trc/trc.htm

**Victorian Collectibles,** 845 E. Glenbrook Rd., Milwaukee, WI 53217: Catalog $5 ◆ Tiles and matching wallpaper duplicated from 19th-century patterns. 414-352-6971.

## Trim & Ornamental Woodwork

**A & M Victorian Decorations,** 2411 Chico Ave., El Monte, CA 91733: Free brochure ◆ Custom architectural trim. 818-575-0693.

**American Custom-Millwork Inc.,** 3904 Newton Rd., P.O. Box 3608, Albany, GA 31706: Catalog $5 ◆ Embossed and plain architectural moldings and millwork. 912-888-3303.

**Anderson-McQuaid Company Inc.,** 170 Fawcett St., Cambridge, MA 02138: Free price list ◆ Custom and restored moldings, flooring, paneling, and hardwood lumber. 800-640-3050.

**Anthony Wood Products Inc.,** P.O. Box 1081, Hillsboro, TX 76645: Catalog $3 ◆ Handcrafted Victorian gingerbread. 800-969-2181.

**Architectural Components,** 26 N. Leverett Rd., Montague, MA 01351: Brochure $5 ◆ Custom and reproduction 18th and 19th-century doors, windows, window frames, moldings, and French doors. 413-367-9441.

**Architectural Sculpture Ltd.,** 242 Lafayette St., New York, NY 10012: Free information ◆ Turn-of-the-century plaster ornaments, plaques, sculptures, and building and remodeling accouterments. 212-431-5873.

**Aristocrat,** 8215 Roswell Rd., Bldg. 600, Atlanta, GA 30350: Free brochure; catalog $10 ◆ Moldings, mantels, niches, brackets, and medallions. 770-913-1272.

**Arvid's Woods,** 2500 Hewitt Ave., Everett, WA 98201: Catalog $6 ◆ Interior and exterior historical moldings and accessories. 800-627-8437.

**The Balmer Studios Inc.,** 9 Codeco Ct., Don Mills, Ontario, Canada M3A 1B6: Catalog $25 ◆ Interior plaster molding patterns. 416-449-2155.

**Bendix Moldings Inc.,** 37 Ramland Rd. South, Orangeburg, NY 10962: Catalog $3 ◆ Wood moldings and ornaments. 800-526-0240; 914-365-1111 (in NY).

**Boston Turning Works,** 42 Plympton St., Boston, MA 02118: Brochure $1 ◆ Finials for gates, fence posts, and balustrades. 617-482-9085.

**Bryant Stove Inc.,** Box 2048, Thorndike, ME 04986: Free brochure ◆ Wood mantels and ornamental trim. 207-568-3665.

**Campbellsville Industries Inc.,** P.O. Box 278, Campbellsville, KY 42718: Free catalog ◆ Aluminum cornices, louvers, cupolas, columns, balustrades, and shutters. 502-465-8135.

**Chadsworth Incorporated,** P.O. Box 53268, Atlanta, GA 30355: Catalog $5 (refundable ◆ Columns and replacement components in wood, fiberglass, and other materials. 800-265-8667.

**CinderWhit & Company,** 733 11th Ave. South, Wahpeton, ND 58075: Catalog $3 ◆ Custom and in-stock wood turnings. 800-527-9064.

**Classic Architectural Specialties,** 3223 Canton St., Dallas, TX 75226: Catalog $6 ◆ Architectural embellishments. 800-662-1221; 214-748-1113 (in TX). www.casdesign.com

**Copper Beech Millwork,** 30 Industrial Dr., P.O. Box 718, Northampton, MA 01061: Free catalog ◆ Architectural moldings and trim. 800-532-9110; 413-584-3003 (in MA). www.copperbeech.com/retail.htm

**Cross Vinyl Lattice,** 3174 Marjan Dr., Atlanta, GA 30340: Free information ◆ Vinyl lattice panels with diagonal or rectangular patterns. 800-521-9878.

**Cumberland Woodcraft Company Inc.,** P.O. Drawer 609, Carlisle, PA 17013: Catalog $5 ◆ Ceiling treatments, corbels, brackets, molding, grilles, and Victorian architectural millwork, carvings, and trims. 717-243-0063. www.pa.net/cwc

**Custom Woodturnings,** 4000 Telephone Rd., Houston, TX 77087: Catalog $3 ◆ Reproduction Victorian millwork. 713-641-6254.

**Decorators Supply Corp.,** 3610 S. Morgan St., Chicago, IL 60609: Free list of retail sources ◆ Detailed replicas of hand carvings. 773-847-6300.

**Design Toscano,** 17 E. Campbell St., Arlington Heights, IL 60005: Catalog $5 ◆ Replica gargoyles and goddesses, classical columns, capitals, table bases, brackets, urns, wall friezes, and other decorative objects. 800-525-1233. www.aaweb.com/toscano

**Driwood Ornamental Wood Moulding,** P.O. Box 1729, Florence, SC 29503: Catalog $6 (refundable) ◆ Embossed wood molding, raised paneling, mantels, curved stairs, and doors. 803-669-2478.

**Drummond Woodworks,** 327 Bay St. South, Hamilton, Ontario, Canada L8P 3J7: Free brochure ◆ Reproduction ornamental woodcarvings. 800-263-2543.

**Empire Woodworks,** P.O. Box 717, Blanco, TX 78606: Catalog $3 ◆ Country-style and Victorian trim. 800-360-2119.

**Raymond Enkeboll,** 16506 Avalon Blvd., Carson, CA 90746: Free brochure; catalog $20 ◆ Architectural woodcarvings. 310-532-1400. www.enkeboll.com

**Erb Lumber Company,** 1210 Morse Ave., Royal Oak, MI 48067: Free brochure ◆ Architectural millwork. 800-686-5317; 810-543-9100 (in MI).

**Falcon Products Inc.,** 8858 SW 129th St., Miami, FL 33176: Free brochure ◆ Lightweight, easy-to-cut and install decorative trim and molding. 305-255-6555.

**Federal Cabinet Company Inc.,** 409 Highland Ave., Middletown, NY 10940: Free brochure ◆ Architectural wood curved rails and balustrade systems. 800-342-1514.

**Felber Ornamental Plastering Corp.,** 1000 W. Washington St., P.O. Box 57, Norristown, PA 19404: Catalog $3 ◆ Period-style and plaster cornices, medallions, sculptures, niches, capitals, brackets, and domes. 800-392-6896; 610-275-4713 (in PA). www.felbert.net

**Fischer & Jirouch Company,** 4821 Superior Ave., Cleveland, OH 44103: Catalog $15 ◆ Architectural plaster ornaments. 440-361-3840.

**Florida Wood Moulding & Trim,** 10780 47th St. North, Clearwater, FL 34622: Catalog $5 ◆ Hardwood moldings. 813-572-1983.

**Focal Point Inc.,** P.O. Box 93327, Atlanta, GA 30377: Free information ◆ Ceiling medallions, cornice moldings, niche caps, and doorway treatments. 800-662-5550.

**Forester Moulding & Lumber Inc.,** 152 Hamilton St., Leominster, MA 01453: Free catalog ◆ Hardwood and softwood molding. 800-649-9734; 840-3100 (in Leominster). www.forestermoulding.com

**Fox Woodcraft,** P.O. Box 846, Sutter Creek, CA 95685: Catalog $2 ◆ Custom gingerbread decorative trim. 209-267-0774.

**Fypon Molded Millwork,** 22 W. Pennsylvania Ave., Stewartstown, PA 17363: Free catalog ◆ Architectural trim and other building components. 800-537-5349. www.fypon.com

**Gazebo & Porchworks,** 728 9th Ave. SW, Puyallup, WA 98371: Catalog $2 ◆ Wood trims, ornamental items, outdoor swings, and backyard play structures. 253-848-0502.

**The Gingerbread Man,** 327-3 Industrial Dr., Placerville, CA 95667: Catalog $3 ◆ Victorian-style trim and ornamental woodwork. 916-644-0440.

**Hallidays America Inc.,** P.O. Box 731, Sparta, NJ 07871: Free information ◆ Fireplace accessories, handcarved mantels, and wood moldings. 973-729-8876.

**Heritage Woodcraft,** 1230 Oakland St., Hendersonville, NC 28739: Catalog $2 ◆ Corbels, brackets, finials, scrolls, headers, trim, and balusters. 704-692-8542.

**House of Moulding,** 15202 Oxnard St., Van Nuys, CA 91411: Catalog $5 ◆ Wood moldings and trim, ceiling medallions, fireplaces, and mantels. 800-327-4186.

**J.S. Keller & Associates,** P.O. Box 270359, St. Louis, MO 63127: Catalog $10 (refundable) ◆ Reproduction paneling, moldings, and trim. 314-843-1199.

**Dimitrios Klitsas,** Wood Sculptor, 378 North Rd., Hampden, MA 01036: Free information ◆ Wood carvings for decorating. 413-566-5301.

**Mad River Woodworks,** P.O. Box 1067, Blue Lake, CA 95525: Catalog $3 ◆ Corbels, balusters, trims, brackets, spandrels, wood gutters, and railings. 800-446-6580; 707-668-5671 (in CA). mrww@reninet.com

**The Maizefield Company,** P.O. Box 336, Port Townsend, WA 98368: Free brochure ◆ Mantels, turnings, staircases, and moldings. 360-385-6789.

**Melkton Classics Inc.,** P.O. Box 465020, Lawrenceville, GA 30246: Free catalog ◆ Classic columns. 800-963-3060.

**Old World Moulding & Finishing Inc.,** 115 Allen Blvd., Farmingdale, NY 11735: Catalog $3 ◆ Wood moldings. 516-293-1789.

**Omega Too,** 2204 San Pablo Ave., Berkeley, CA 94702: Free information ◆ Architectural embellishments for houses and gardens. 510-843-3636.

**Ornamental Mouldings,** 3804 Comanche Rd., Archdale, NC 27263: Free brochure ◆ Hardwood molding and accessories. 910-431-9120.

**Pagliacco Turning & Milling,** P.O. Box 225, Woodacre, CA 94973: Catalog $6 ◆ Wood balusters, newel and porch posts, railings, columns, and custom-turning. 415-488-4333.

**Perkins Architectural Millwork & Hardwood Mouldings,** Rt. 5, Box 264, Longview, TX 75605: Catalog $5 ◆ Moldings, staircases, interior and exterior doors, windows, shutters, mantels, and trim. 903-663-3036.

**The Porch Factory,** P.O. Box 231, White House, TN 37188: Catalog $2 ◆ Victorian country trim and other ornamental woodwork. 615-672-0998.

**Richards Studio,** Rt. 3, Box 848, Spicewood, TX 78669: Catalog $2.50 ◆ Decorative architectural accessories. 512-264-2007.

**River Bend Turnings,** 3730 Vandermark Rd., Scio, NY 14880: Free brochure ◆ Porch turnings, table and chair legs, newel posts, balusters, and finials. 716-593-3495.

**A.F. Schwerd Manufacturing Company,** 3215 McClure Ave., Pittsburgh, PA 15212: Free brochure ◆ Standard and detailed wood columns in seasoned northern white pine with matching pilasters and aluminum bases. 412-766-6322.

**Sepp Leaf Products Inc.,** 381 Park Ave. South, New York, NY 10016: Free information ◆ Gold and palladium metal leaf, tools, and kits. 800-971-7377. www.seppleaf.com

**Silverton Victorian Millworks,** P.O. Box 2987, Durango, CO 81302: Catalog $4 ◆ Castings, crowns, corner blocks, doors, bases, wainscot, architectural accouterments, and Victorian moldings and millwork. 970-259-5915. www.themillworks.com

**Style-Mark,** 960 W. Barre Rd., Archbold, OH 43502: Free catalog ◆ Arches, brackets, trim, louvers, window heads, moldings, entryways, millwork, and architectural accents. 800-446-3040.

**Superior Hardwoods,** P.O. Box 4731, Missoula, MT 59806: Information $3 ◆ Fir, larch, and pine flooring. Also paneling, doors, and molding. 800-572-9601; 406-251-2272 (in MT).

**M. Swift & Sons Inc.,** 10 Love Ln., Hartford, CT 06141: Free information ◆ Gold, silver, palladium, aluminum, and composite leaf for decorating and restoring interiors and exteriors of buildings, domes, walls, ceilings, furniture, and works of art. 800-628-0380.

**Uncle John's Gingerbread House Trim,** 5229 Choupique Rd., Sulphur, LA 70663: Catalog $2 ◆ Brackets, pendants, and gables in matched sets. 318-527-9696.

**Victorian Interiors,** 575 Hayes St., San Francisco, CA 94102: Catalog $10 ◆ Victorian trim and ornamental woodwork. 415-431-7191.

**Victorian Millworks Company,** 5709A E. Hanna Ave., Tampa, FL 33610: Catalog $2 ◆ Fretwork, brackets, balusters, gables, spandrels, and other woodwork. 813-622-7299. info@victorianmillworks.com

**Vintage Pine Company,** P.O. Box 85, Prospect, VA 23960: Free information ◆ Custom heart-pine flooring, cabinets, doors, mantels, moldings, and other architectural accouterments. 804-248-9102.

**Vintage Wood Works,** Hwy. 34, Box R, Quinlan, TX 75474: Catalog $2 ◆ Spandrels and shelves, fans, porch posts, balusters, brackets, signs, corbels, headers, gazebos, and handcrafted Victorian gingerbread. 903-356-2158. www.vintagewoodworks.com

**Weaver Company,** 941 Air Way, Glendale, CA 91201: Brochure $7 ◆ Ornaments for decorating mantels, doors, furniture, walls, and ceilings. 818-500-1740.

**The Wood Factory,** 111 Railroad St., Navasota, TX 77868: Catalog $2 ◆ Authentic Victorian-style moldings, screen doors, porch parts, ornamental trim, and custom woodwork. 409-825-7233.

**The Woodworkers' Store,** 4365 Willow Dr., Medina, MN 55340: Free catalog ◆ Tools and hardware, woodworking, and finishing supplies. 800-279-4441. www.woodworkerstore.com

**Worthington,** P.O. Box 868, Troy, AL 36081: Free catalog ◆ Architecturally detailed building materials. 800-872-1608. www.architectural-details.com

## Wallcoverings

**American Blind, Wallpaper & Carpet Factory,** 909 N. Sheldon Rd., Plymouth, MI 48170: Free information ◆ Wood, micro, mini, and vertical blinds; roller and pleated shades; and wallpaper and carpet. 800-889-2631 (for blinds and wallpaper); 800-346-0608 (for carpet). www.abwf.com

**American Wallcovering Distributors,** 2260 Rt. 22, Union, NJ 07083: Free information ◆ Wallpaper and fabrics. 800-843-6567.

**Benington's,** 1271 Manheim Pike, Lancaster, PA 17601: Catalog $5 ◆ Wallpaper and rugs. 800-252-5060. www.beningtons.com

**Bentley Brothers,** 2709 Southpark Rd., Louisville, KY 40219: Free information ◆ Embossed wallcoverings with an ornate look of detailed plasterwork. 800-824-4777.

**BMI Home Decorating,** 5976 E. Slauson Ave., Commerce, CA 90040: Free information ◆ Decorator fabrics and wallcoverings. 800-537-4374.

**Bradbury & Bradbury Wallpapers,** P.O. Box 155, Benicia, CA 94510: Catalog $10 ◆ Victorian-style wallpapers, hand-printed borders, friezes, ceiling papers, and coordinated wall frills. 707-746-1900. www.bradbury.com

**J.R. Burrows & Company,** P.O. Box 522, Rockland, MA 02370: Catalog $5 ◆ Artistic wallpaper, fabrics, and period carpet reproductions by special order. 800-347-1795. www.burrows.com/index.html

**Carter & Company/Mt. Diablo Handprints,** 451 Ryder St., Vallejo, CA 94590: Free information ◆ Hand-printed reproduction historic wallpaper. 707-554-2682.

**East Carolina Wallpaper Market,** 1165 Hwy. 11/55, Kinston, NC 28504: Free information ◆ Wallpaper, fabrics, and borders. 800-848-7283. www.ecwallpaper.com

**Eisenhart Wallcoverings Company,** 1649 Broadway, Hanover, PA 17331: Free list of retail sources ◆ Wallcoverings and coordinated fabrics. 800-726-3267. www.eisenwalls.com

**Georgia-Pacific,** P.O. Box 2808, Norcross, GA 30091: Free information ◆ Wall paneling and pre-hung wallpaper on plywood panels. 770-662-0512. www.gp.com

**Global Wallcoverings & Blinds,** 4125 W. Main St., Skokie, IL 60076: Free information ◆ Wallcoverings and blinds. 800-220-7610. www.globalwcb.com

**Harmony Supply Company Inc.,** P.O. Box 313, Medford, MA 02155: Free information (specify book and manufacturer's name, pattern number or style and color number, and number of rolls wanted with exact measurements) ◆ Wallpaper and fabrics for coordinating wall and window treatments. 781-395-2600.

**Motif Designs,** 20 Jones St., New Rochelle, NY 10802: Free list of retail sources ◆ Wallcoverings and fabrics. 800-431-2424.

**Nation Wide Outlet,** P.O. Box 135, Flanders, NJ 07836: Free information ◆ Wallcoverings and blinds. 800-537-WALL.

**Number One Wallpaper,** 2914 Long Beach Rd., Oceanside, NY 11572: Free information ◆ Wallpaper. 800-423-0084; 516-678-4445 (in NY).

**Robinson's Wallcoverings,** 225 W. Spring St., Titusville, PA 16354: Catalog $2 (refundable) ◆ Wallcoverings and decorator fabrics. 800-458-2426. rwallcover@mail.usachoice.net

**Charles Rupert, The Shop,** 2004 Oak Bay Ave., Victoria, British Columbia, Canada V8R 1E4: Catalog $6 ◆ Wallpapers and fabrics for traditional homes. 250-592-4916.

**Singer Wallcoverings,** Box 300, Kings Island, OH 45034: Free information ◆ Vinyl wallcoverings. 800-543-0412; 513-398-1611 (in OH).

**U.S.A. Express,** Rt. 22 East, Union, NJ 07083: Free information ◆ Wallpaper and fabrics. 800-965-5678.

**Victorian Collectibles,** 845 E. Glenbrook Rd., Milwaukee, WI 53217: Catalog $5 ◆ Wallpaper in 19th-century patterns with matching tiles. 414-352-6971.

**Wallpaper & Blinds Connection,** P.O. Box 492, Budd Lake, NJ 07828: Free information ◆ Wallpaper, fabrics, and blinds. 800-488-WALL. blindscom@aol.com

**The Warner Company,** 108 S. Desplaines St., Chicago, IL 60661: Free list of retail sources ◆ Wallcoverings, fabrics, and borders. 800-685-8822. www.thewarnerco.com/Warner.htm

**Yield House,** P.O. Box 2525, Conway, NH 03818: Free catalog ◆ Wallcoverings. 800-659-0206.

## Window Coverings & Screens

**Petit Industries Inc.,** P.O. Box 1156, Saco, ME 04072: Free information ◆ Roll-up, single-door, and double-door hide-away screens. 207-283-1900.

**Screen Tight Porch Screening System,** 407 St. James St., Georgetown, SC 29440: Free information ◆ Easy-to-do porch-screening system. 800-768-7325. www.lowes.com

**Shade & Comfort Company,** P.O. Box 1808, Centralia, IL 62801: Free information ◆ Patio covers, window awnings, porch curtains, and other coverings. 800-442-7423.

## Windows & Skylights

**Allied Window Inc.,** 2724 W. McMicken Ave., Cincinnati, OH 45214: Free information ◆ Interior and exterior windows. 800-445-5411. www.invisiblestorm.com

**Alside Corp.,** P.O. Box 2010, Akron, OH 44309: Free list of retail sources ◆ Outdoor windows with vinyl trim and insulating glass. 330-929-1811.

**The Alternative Window Company,** 11-D Herman Dr., Simsbury, CT 06070: Catalog $5 (refundable) ◆ Glass interior storm windows. 800-743-6207; 860-651-3951 (in CT).

**Andersen Windows,** P.O. Box 203070, Austin, TX 78720: Free information ◆ Energy-efficient windows, roof windows, and patio doors. 800-426-4261. www.andersenwindows.com

**Arctic Glass & Window Outlet,** 565 County Rd. T, Hammond, WI 54015: Catalog $4 ◆ Windows, entryway and patio doors, skylights, and sun rooms. 800-428-9276.

**Art Glass Studio,** 543 Union St., Brooklyn, NY 11215: Free brochure ◆ Custom-made and restoration of leaded and stained glass windows. 718-596-4353.

**Bristolite Skylights,** 401 E. Goetz Ave., P.O. Box 2515, Santa Ana, CA 92707: Free catalog ◆ Fixed residential skylights or with electric and manual openers. 800-854-8618.

**Combination Door Company,** P.O. Box 1076, Fond du Lac, WI 54936: Free list of retail sources ◆ Wood combination windows and storm and screen doors. 920-922-2050.

**DAB Studio,** P.O. Box 57, 11 Kent Pl., Pompton Plains, NJ 07444: Free catalog ◆ Stained glass windows and decorative accessories. 973-616-7676.

**Drums Sash-Door Company,** P.O. Box 207, Drums, PA 18222: Free catalog ◆ Window sashes, thresholds, risers, screen and storm doors, double-hung windows, and trim. 717-788-1145.

**Fox Lite,** 8300 Dayton Rd., Fairborn, OH 45324: Free information ◆ Skylights that can be converted from closed to opening units. 800-233-FOXX. www.foxlite.com

**Georgia-Pacific,** P.O. Box 2808, Norcross, GA 30091: Free information ◆ Doors and windows. 770-662-0512. www.gp.com

**Great Lakes Windows,** P.O. Box 1896, Toledo, OH 43603: Free information ◆ Windows. 800-666-0000.

**Kolbe & Kolbe Millwork Company,** 1323 S. 11th Ave., Wassau, WI 54401: Free catalog ◆ Wood windows and doors. 800-955-8177. www.kolbe-kolbe.com

**Louisiana-Pacific Corp.,** P.O. Box 10266, Portland, OR 97210: Free information ◆ Windows. 800-299-0028.

**Marvin Windows,** P.O. Box 100, Warroad, MN 56763: Free information ◆ Divided and insulated storm windows and transoms. 800-346-5128. www.marvin.com

**Maurer & Shepherd Joyners Inc.,** 122 Naubuc Ave., Glastonbury, CT 06033: Brochure $2.25 ◆ Windows, doors, entryways, and authentic colonial woodworking. 203-633-2383.

**Midwest Architectural Wood Products,** 300 Trails Rd., Eldridge, IA 52748: Catalog $2.50 ◆ Divided insulated storm windows. 319-285-8000.

**Pella Windows & Doors,** 100 Main St., Pella, IA 50219: Free list of retail sources ◆ Custom windows. 800-54-PELLA. www.pella.com

**Perkasie Industries Corp.,** 50 E. Spruce St., Perkasie, PA 18944: Free information ◆ Storm window kits for the do-it-yourselfer. 800-523-6747.

**Petit Industries Inc.,** P.O. Box 1156, Saco, ME 04072: Free information ◆ Custom-made magnetic interior storm windows for installation over existing windows. Available in kits or assembled. 207-283-1900.

**Pozzi Wood Windows,** P.O. Box 5249, Bend, OR 97708: Free information ◆ Divided windows. 800-257-9663. www.pozzi.com

**Ricketson Sash & Door Company,** 100 Bidwell Rd., South Windsor, CT 06074: Free brochure ◆ Windows and doors for homes. 860-289-1222.

**Rollamatic Roofs Incorporated,** P.O. Box 24087, San Francisco, CA 94124: Free brochure ◆ Electrically controlled retractable skylights. 800-345-7392; 415-822-5655 (in CA).

**Roto Frank of America,** Research Park, Chester, CT 06412: Free list of retail sources ◆ Roof windows. 800-243-0893.

**Southeastern Insulated Glass,** 6477-B Peachtree Industrial Blvd., Atlanta, GA 30360: Free information ◆ Greenhouse and sun room kits and sliding glass doors. Also skylights with optional tempered insulated glass. 800-841-9842; 770-455-8838 (in GA).

**Sundance Supply,** 1678 Shattuck Ave., Ste. 173, Berkeley, CA 94709: Catalog $2 ◆ Building components for greenhouses, sun roofs, pool enclosures, and skylights. 800-776-2534. www.sundancesupply.com

**Thermo-Press/Norvell Corp.,** 1735 Arlington Rd., Richmond, VA 23230: Information $1 ◆ Storm windows. 804-355-9147.

**Velux-America Inc.,** P.O. Box 5001, Greenwood, SC 29648: Free brochure ◆ Weather-tight roof windows and skylights. 800-283-2831.

**Walsh Screen & Window Inc.,** 555 E. 3rd St., Mount Vernon, NY 10553: Free information ◆ Screens, windows, storm windows, and doors. 914-668-7811.

**Weather Shield Mfg. Inc.,** One Weather Shield Plaza, Medford, WI 54451: Free information ◆ Wood windows, patio doors, and steel entryways. 800-222-2995; 715-748-2100 (in WI). www.weathershield.com

**Window Creations,** P.O. Box 127, Scott, OH 45886: Free brochure ◆ Stained glass window restoration. 419-622-3210.

**Window Saver Company,** 177 E. Riding Dr., Carlisle, MA 01741: Free information ◆ Storm window kits for do-it-yourselfers. 800-321-WARM.

**Woodstone Company,** P.O. Box 223, Westminster, VT 05158: Brochure $4 ◆ Insulated solid wood doors and single, or triple-glazed, windows, with palladians and straight and fanned transoms. 802-722-9217. www.woodstone.com

## HOMES & PREFABS

### Building Supplies

**Cedar Log & Lumber Company,** 6019 S. Millersburg Rd., P.O. Box 155, Millersburg, MI 49759: Free information ◆ Dock and deck materials, kiln-dried lumber, tongue and groove cabin logs, panel siding, and Northern Michigan white cedar. 517-733-2676.

**Schroeder Log Home Supply Inc.,** P.O. Box 864, Grand Rapids, MN 55744: Catalog $2 ◆ Tools, preservatives, stains, chinking, hardware, fasteners, and other supplies. 800-359-6614. www.loghelp.com

### Conventional & Timber Frame Homes

**Classic Colonial Homes,** P.O. Box 31, Historic Old Deerfield, MA 01342: Study folio $14 ◆ Saltboxes, capes, colonials, gambrels, and carriage sheds. Features classic exteriors and modern interiors. 800-413-9111.

**Deltec Homes,** 604 College St., Asheville, NC 28801: Planning portfolio $12 ◆ Pre-engineered panel kits for circular homes. 800-642-2508. www.deltechomes.com

**Honest Abe Timber Frame Homes Inc.,** 3855 Clay County Hwy., Moss, TN 38575: Brochure $10 ◆ Timber frame homes. 800-231-3695. www.honestabe.com

**Lindal Cedar Homes,** P.O. Box 24426, Seattle, WA 98178: Catalog $15 ◆ Plans for custom sizing or building a new home. 800-426-0536. www.lindal.com

**Pan Abode Inc.,** 4350 Lake Washington Blvd. North, Renton, WA 98056: Catalog $18 ◆ Post and beam and timberwall constructed homes. 800-782-2633; 425-255-8261 (in WA). www.PanAbodeWorldwide.com

**Post & Beam Homes,** 21 Elm St., South Deerfield, MA 01373: Information $5 ◆ Timber frame homes. 800-992-0121.

**Riverbend Timber Framing Inc.,** P.O. Box 26, Blissfield, MI 49228: Catalog $20 ◆ Timber frame home plans. 517-486-4355.

**Sunset Structures Ltd.,** 390 Sunset Dr., Elkview, WV 25071: Portfolio $15; free brochure ◆ Kiln-dried oak timber frames. 304-965-6831.

**Thistlewood Timber Frame Homes,** RR 6, Markdale, Ontario, Canada N0C 1H0: Free brochure ◆ Timber frame homes. 519-986-3280.

**Timber Craft,** 85 Martin Rd., Port Townsend, WA 98368: Brochure $10 ◆ Timber frame homes and commercial structures. 360-385-3051.

**Vermont Timber Frames,** 130 Bowen Rd., P.O. Box 410, Bennington, VT 05201: Free information ◆ Timber frame homes. 802-447-8860.

### Domes

**American Ingenuity,** 8777-E Holiday Springs Rd., Rockledge, FL 32955: Catalog $2 (refundable) ◆ Easy-to-build concrete and steel geodesic dome from kit of pre-finished panels.

**GeoDomes WoodWorks,** Bldg. C, Box 4141, Riverside, CA 92514: Catalog $15 ◆ Pre-cut ready-to-assemble dome kits. 909-787-8800.

**Monolithic Constructors Inc.,** P.O. Box 479, Italy, TX 76651: Free brochure ◆ Concrete dome kit. 800-608-0001. www.monolithicdome.com

**Oregon Dome Inc.,** 3215 Meadow Ln., Eugene, OR 97402: Catalog $12 ◆ Energy-efficient domes. 800-572-8943; 541-689-3443 (in OR). www.domes.com

**Timberline Geodesics,** 2015 Blake St., Berkeley, CA 94704: Catalog $12 ◆ Easy-to-assemble pre-cut geodesic dome homes kits. Also plans. 800-DOME-HOME. www.domehome.com

### Log Homes

**Air-Lock Log Homes,** P.O. Box 2506, Las Vegas, NM 87701: Catalog of plans $7 ◆ Log homes. 800-786-0525; 505-425-8888 (in NM). www.air-lock.com

**Alta Log Homes,** P.O. Box 88, Halcottsville, NY 12438: Catalog $5 ◆ Log homes. 800-926-2582. www.altahome.com

**American Southwest Log Homes,** P.O. Box 1360, Pagosa Springs, CO 81147: Design book $8 ◆ Rustic log homes. 800-999-0832.

**AmerLink Log Homes,** P.O. Box 669, Battleboro, NC 27809: Planning guide and construction video $19.95 ◆ Log homes. 800-872-4254. www.amerlinkloghomes.com

**L.C. Andrew Maine Cedar Log Homes,** 35 Main St., Windham, ME 04062: Catalog $5 ◆ Log homes. 800-427-5647; 207-892-8561 (in ME).

**Anthony Log Homes,** P.O. Box 787, Mountain Home, NC 28758: Plan book $8 ◆ Log homes. 800-837-8786. www.anthonyforest.com

**Appalachian Log Homes,** 11312 Station West, Knoxville, TN 37922: Catalog $8 ◆ Log homes in chinked and log-on-log styles. 423-966-6440.

**Appalachian Log Structures,** P.O. Box 614, Ripley, WV 25271: Catalog $10; Free brochure ◆ Log homes. 800-458-9990.

**Asperline Log Homes,** Rt. 150, Box 240, Lock Haven, PA 17745: Plan book $12.50 (request list of retail sources) ◆ Easy-to-construct log homes. 800-428-4663. asperlin@oak.kcsd.k12.pa.us

**Jim Barna Log Systems,** P.O. Box 4529, Oneida, TN 37841: Catalog $7 ◆ Log homes. 800-962-4734. www.logcabins.com

**Beaver Log Homes,** P.O. Box 236, Beloit, WI 53512: Catalog $6 ◆ Pre-cut log home kits. 608-365-6833.

**Centennial Log Homes,** P.O. Box 5100, Kalispell, MT 59903: Free information ◆ Handcrafted log homes. 800-456-5647; 406-756-6502 (in MT). www.cenlog.com

**Century Cedar Log Homes,** P.O. Box 746, Running Springs, CA 92382: Free brochure ◆ Log homes. 800-383-5648.

**Conestoga Log Cabins,** 987 Valley View Rd., New Holland, PA 17557: Catalog $10 ◆ One and two-room log cabin kits. 800-914-4606. www.campnetAmerica.com

**Confederation Log Homes,** 14200 El Camino Ln., Lenoir City, TN 37771: Catalog $10 ◆ Log homes. 800-298-1867.

**Country Log Homes,** 79 Clayton Rd., Ashley Falls, MA 01222: Catalog $10 ◆ Log homes. 413-229-8084.

**Coventry Log Homes,** 161 Central St., Woodsville, NH 03785: Free information ◆ Outdoor cabins and ranch log homes. 800-308-7505. LogHomes@connriver.net

**Four Seasons Log Homes,** P.O. Box 631, Parry Sound, Ontario, Canada P2Z 2Z1: Catalog $10 ◆ Log homes. 705-342-5211.

**Garland Homes,** 2172 Hwy. 93 North, Victor, MT 59875: Catalog $15 ◆ Log homes. 800-642-3837.

**Gastineau Log Homes Inc.,** 10423 Old Hwy. 54 Dept., New Bloomfield, MO 65063: Planning kit $8 ◆ Log homes. 800-654-9253; 973-896-5122 (in MO).

**Greatwood Log Homes,** P.O. Box 707, Elkhart, WI 53020: Planning guide $9.50 ◆ Log homes. 800-558-5812. www.greatwood.com

**Hearthstone Log Homes,** 1630 East Hwy., Dandrige, TN 37725: Plan book $15 ◆ Log homes. 800-247-4442. www.hearthstonehomes.com

**Heritage Log Homes,** P.O. Box 610, Gatlinburg, TN 37738: Catalog $12 ◆ Log homes. 800-456-4663. www.heritagelog.com

**Hiawatha Log Homes,** P.O. Box 8, Munising, MI 49862: Plan book $6 ◆ Log homes. 800-876-8100. www.hiawatha.com

**Holland Log Homes,** 13352 Van Buren, Holland, MI 49424: Plan book $8.95 ◆ Pre-cut log homes. 800-968-7564. hlh@novagate.com

**Homestead Log Homes,** 6301 Crater Lake Hwy., Medford, OR 97502: Catalog $10 ◆ Pre-cut kits or on-site factory built log homes. 541-826-6888.

**Honest Abe Log Homes Inc.,** 3855 Clay County Hwy., Moss, TN 38575: Brochure $10 ◆ Log homes. 800-231-3695. www.honestabe.com

**Honka Log Homes,** 7465 Crosswood Blvd., Knoxville, TN 37924: Free information ◆ Log homes. 888-HONKA-SE. www.honka.com

**Katahdin Forest Products,** P.O. Box 145, Oakfield, ME 04763: Video catalog $14.95 ◆ Log homes. 800-845-4533.

**Kuhns Brothers Log Homes,** RD 2, Box 406A, Lewisburg, PA 17837: Catalog and video package $15 ◆ Log homes. 800-326-9614.

**Lodge Logs,** 3200 Gowen Rd., Boise, ID 83705: Catalog $8 ◆ Log homes. 800-533-2450; 208-336-2450 (in ID). www.cyberhighway.net/~lodgelog

**Log & Timber Homes Inc.,** P.O. Box 448, St. Ignatius, MT 59865: Information packet $7 ◆ Log and timber-constructed homes. 800-735-4425; 406-745-3482 (in MT).

**Log Knowledge,** P.O. Box 1025, LaPorte, CO 80535: Plan booklet $12 ◆ Log homes. 800-348-9910.

**Lok-N-Logs,** P.O. Box 677, Sherburne, NY 13460: Catalog $7.50 ◆ Log homes. 800-343-8928; 607-674-4447 (in NY).

**Maple Island Log Homes,** Traverse City Office, 5046 S. West Bayshore Dr., Ste. A, Suttons Bay, MI 49682: Plan packet $12 ◆ Log homes. 616-271-4042.

**Mountaineer Log Homes Inc.,** P.O. Box 248, Morgantown, PA 19543: Catalog $8 ◆ Log homes. 610-286-2005.

**Neville Log Homes,** 2036 Hwy. 93, Victor, MT 59875: Catalog $10 ◆ Log homes. 800-635-7911. www.nevilog.com

**Northeastern Log Homes,** P.O. Box 7966, Louisville, KY 40257: Brochure $5 ◆ Log homes. 800-451-2724.

**Northern Land & Lumber Company,** 7000 P Rd., Gladstone, MI 49837: Free information ◆ Kiln-dried pine and cedar log home kits. 800-338-2994. nlandl@up.net

**Northern Log Homes,** 300 Bomarc Rd., Bangor, ME 04401: Home planning kit $6; free brochure ◆ Log homes. 800-553-7311. www.mainerec.com/loghomes

**Old Style Log Works,** P.O. Box 255, Kalispell, MT 59903: Planning guide $10 ◆ Full scribe and chink-style log homes. 888-850-4665. www.loghomes1.com/oldstyle

**The Original Lincoln Logs,** Riverside Dr., Box 135, Chestertown, NY 12817: Plans portfolio $12.50 (request list of retail sources) ◆ Log homes. 800-833-2461.

**The Original Log Cabin Homes Ltd.,** P.O. Drawer 1457, 410 N. Pearl St., Rocky Mount, NC 27802: Planning guide $15.95 ◆ Log homes. 800-56-CABIN; 919-977-7785 (in NC). www.logcabinhomes.com

**Original Log Homes,** P.O. Box 1301, 100 Mile House, British Columbia, Canada V0K 2E0: Plan book $5 ◆ Log homes. 800-664-9344. www.sni.net/loginfo

**Otsego Cedar Log Homes,** P.O. Box 127, Waters, MI 49797: Catalog $6 ◆ Post-and-beam log homes. 517-732-6268.

**Pacific Log Homes Ltd.,** P.O. Box 80868, Vancouver, British Columbia, Canada V5H 3Y1: Free brochure ◆ Log homes. 800-663-1577. pacific@lightspeed.bc.ca

**Pioneer Log Systems Inc.,** P.O. Box 226, Kingston Springs, TN 37082: Catalog $10 ◆ Log and post-and-beam homes. 615-952-5647.

**Precision Craft Log Structures,** 711 E. Broadway Ave., Meridian, ID 83642: Planning package $14.95 ◆ Log homes. 208-887-1020. www.precisioncraft.com

**Rapid River Rustic Inc.,** P.O. Box 10, Rapid River, MI 49878: Planning guide $10 ◆ Log homes. 800-422-3327. www.visit-usa.com/loghome

**Real Log Homes,** P.O. Box 202, Hartland, VT 05048: Catalog $15 ◆ Log homes with optional full basements, garages, slabs, crawl spaces, and piers. 800-732-5564. www.realloghomes.com

**Rocky Mountain Log Homes,** 1883 Hwy. 93 South, Hamilton, MT 59840: Catalog $14 ◆ Log homes. 406-363-5680. www.rocky-mtn-log-homes.com

**Satterwhite Log Homes,** Rt. 2, Box 256, Longview, TX 75605: Planning guide $5 ◆ Log homes. 800-777-7288. www.dfw.net/~loghome

**Snake River Log Homes,** 4220 E. 653 North, Rigby, ID 83442: Free information ◆ Log homes with optional add-ons. 208-745-6396. loghomes@srv.net

**Southern Cypress Log Homes Inc.,** P.O. Box 209, Crystal River, FL 32629: Plan book $4.95 ◆ Log homes. 352-795-0777.

**Southland Log Homes,** 7521 Broad River Rd., P.O. Box 1668, Irmo, SC 29063: Planning guide $7.50 ◆ Log homes. 800-845-3555.

**Stone Mill Log Homes,** 7015 Stonemill Rd., Knoxville, TN 37919: Catalog $6 ◆ Log homes with a choice of hand-hewn or hand-planed finish. 800-438-8274; 423-693-4833 (in TN). www.stonemill.com

**Tennessee Log Homes,** P.O. Box 865, Athens, TN 37371: Planning guide $8 ◆ Log homes. 800-251-9218. www.tnloghomes.com/tnlog

**Timber Log Building Systems,** 639 Old Hartford Rd., Colchester, CT 06415: Planning portfolio $10 ◆ Log homes. 800-533-5906.

**Tomahawk Log & Country Homes Inc.,** 2285 Bus. 51 Cty. L, Tomahawk, WI 54487: Floor plans $13 ◆ Log homes. 800-544-0636; 715-453-3265 (in WI).

**Town & Country Cedar Homes,** 4772 US 131 South, Petoskey, MI 49770: Plan book $6 ◆ Log homes. 800-968-3178; 616-347-4360 (in MI). www.cedarhomes.com

**Traverse Bay Log Homes,** 6446 M-72 West, Traverse City, MI 49684: Planning guide $12 ◆ Log homes. 616-947-1881.

**Ward Log Homes,** P.O. Box 72, Houlton, ME 04730: Planning guide $8 ◆ Log homes. 800-341-1566. www.loghome.net/ward

**Wilderness Building Systems,** 3015 S. 460 West, Salt Lake City, UT 84115: Catalog $8 ◆ Log homes. 801-972-6084. www.dolog.com

**Wilderness Log Homes,** P.O. Box 902, Plymouth, WI 53073: Planning guide $15 ◆ Log homes. 800-237-8564.

**Wisconsin Log Homes Inc.,** P.O. Box 11005, Green Bay, WI 54307: Plan book $14.95 ◆ Log homes. 800-844-7972.

### Post & Beam Homes

**Classic Post & Beam,** P.O. Box 546, York, ME 03909: Catalog $6 ◆ Post-and-beam homes. 800-872-2326.

**Country Carpenters,** 5 Webster Ln., Bolton, CT 06043: Catalog $3 ◆ Pre-cut post and beam buildings. 860-649-0822.

**Deck House,** 930 Main St., Acton, MA 01720: Information $20 ◆ Post-and-beam homes. 800-727-3325. www.deckhouse.com

**Habitat Post & Beam Homes,** 21 Elm St., South Deerfield, MA 01373: Brochure $12 ◆ Homes with natural wood posts, beams, and interiors. 800-992-0121.

**Linwood Homes,** 8250 River Rd., Delta, British Columbia, Canada V4G 1B5: Plan book $12 ◆ Post-and-beam and truss kits. 888-546-9663.

**New Dimension Homes Inc.,** RFD 3, Box 1452, Skowhegan, ME 04976: Free information ◆ Post and beam homes. 207-474-5376.

**Oak Post & Beam,** P.O. Box 164, Princeton, MA 01541: Brochure $3 ◆ Oak post and beam homes with mortise and tennon joinery. 978-464-8464.

**Timberpeg,** Box 1500, Claremont, NH 03743: Information $15 ◆ Post-and-beam single and multi-level homes. 603-542-7762.

**Woodhouse Post & Beam Inc.,** P.O. Box 219, Mansfield, PA 16933: Catalog $10 ◆ Post-and-beam homes. 800-227-4311; 717-549-6232 (in PA).

## HORSE & STABLE EQUIPMENT

### Health Care & Stable Supplies

**Bargain Corral,** P.O. Box 856, Allan, TX 75002: Free information with long SASE ◆ Saddles, stirrups and straps, blankets, spurs, halters, pads, bits, bridles and breast collars, boots, dusters, rain slickers, and supplies. 800-955-5616.

**Chick's Harness & Supply,** P.O. Box 59, Harrington, DE 19952: Free catalog ◆ Horse equipment. 800-444-2441; 302-398-4630 (in DE). www.chicksaddlery.com

**Classic Corrals Inc.,** 1025 Center Dr., Bismarck, MO 63624: Free catalog ◆ Stall fronts and partitions, custom stalls, round pen and arenas, stall flooring, and multiple barn accessories. 800-444-7430. www.classiccorals.com

**Colorado Saddlery Company,** 1631 15th St., Denver, CO 80202: Free catalog ◆ Grooming supplies. 800-521-2465; 303-572-8350 (in CO). 800-247-5901. gobus@earthlink.net

**Country Manufacturing,** P.O. Box 104, Fredericktown, OH 43019: Free catalog ◆ Easy-to-install and use accessories and equipment for horse stalls. 704-694-9926. www.countrymfg.com

**Cowboy Shopper,** P.O Box 6459, Santa Fe, NM 87502: Free catalog with SASE ◆ Antique cowboy gear, books, events, and organizations. 505-995-0102. zon@nets.com

**Drs. Foster & Smith Inc.,** 2253 Air Park Rd., P.O. Box 100, Rhinelander, WI 54501: Free catalog ◆ Pet and equine products and health care supplies. 800-826-7206. www.drsfosterandsmith.com

**Eisers,** 360 Kiwanis Blvd., P.O. Box 159, Hazleton, PA 18201: Free list of retail sources ◆ Health care supplies, saddles, tack, stable needs, books, and clothing for men and women. 800-526-6987. www.eisers.com

**Farnam Companies Inc.,** Horse Products Division, P.O. Box 34820, Phoenix, AZ 85013: Free list of retail sources ◆ Equine health care products. 800-234-2269. www.farnam.com

**Fuerst Brothers,** Division Alamo Group Company, 1020 S. Sangamon Ave., Gibson City, IL 60936: Free information ◆ Maintenance equipment for arenas, rings, pastures, tracks, and other areas. 800-435-9630.

**Happy Jack Inc.,** Box 475, Snow Hill, NC 28580: Free catalog ◆ Animal health care products. 800-326-5225. www.happyjackinc.com

**Horsemen's General Store,** 1001 Shiloh Springs Rd., Dayton, OH 45415: Catalog $3 ◆ Everything for horse owners, trainers, breeders, riders, and horses. 800-343-4987; 937-278-2380 (in OH).

**Pony Express Horsemen's Supply,** P.O. Box 505, Santa Ynez, CA 93460: Free information ◆ Grooming supplies. 805-688-3624.

**Priefert Manufacturing Company,** P.O. Box 1540, Mt. Pleasant, TX 75456: Free information ◆ Horse-safe round pens and arenas, box and stall fronts, box stalls and feeders, and more. 800-527-8616. www.priefert.com

**Red River Portable Arenas,** P.O. Box 549, Carbon, TX 76435: Free list of retail sources ◆ Portable enclosures for roping, riding and training, and team penning. 800-343-1026.

**Joe Roberts Welding,** P.O. Box 777, Ringling, OK 73456: Free information ◆ Portable roping arenas. 800-654-4584; 405-662-2071 (in OK).

**Texas Outfitters Supply Inc.,** Rt. 6, Box 25, Sulphur Springs, TX 75482: Catalog $2 (refundable) ◆ Wall tents, folding stoves, panning equipment, saddles, team and driving harnesses, and pack equipment for horses and mules. 800-551-3534.

**Valley Vet Supply,** P.O. Box 504, Marysville, KS 66508: Free catalog ◆ Equine health products, roping gear, pack equipment, horse blankets, and English, Western, and Arabian tack. 800-835-2978. www.valleyvet.com

**Wiese Equine Supply,** 1989 Transit Way, Brockport, NY 14420: Free catalog ◆ Equine equipment, health care products, accessories, and clothing. 800-869-4373.

### Horse Trailers

**Charmac Trailers,** Box 205, Twin Falls, ID 83303: Free information ◆ Horse trailers. 208-733-5241.

**Circle J Trailers,** 2646 Greens Rd., Houston, TX 77032: Free information ◆ Horse trailers. 800-247-2535; 281-449-8989 (in TX).

**Diamond D Trailer Manufacturing,** 1000 N. Hwy. 48, Box 339, Shenandoah, IA 51601: Free information ◆ Horse trailers. 712-246-5375.

**Exxiss Aluminum Trailers,** 2613 Hwy 30, Box 634, Soda Springs, ID 83276: Free information ◆ Horse trailers. 800-733-0322.

**Featherlite Inc.,** P.O. Box 320, Cresco, IA 52136: Free list of retail sources ◆ Horse trailers. 800-800-1230; 319-547-6000 (in IA). www.featherliteinc.com

**4-Star Trailers Inc.,** 10000 Northwest 10th, Oklahoma City, OK 73128: Free information ◆ Horse trailers. 405-324-7827. www.4startrailers.com

**Hillsboro Industries Inc.,** 220 Industrial Rd., Hillsboro, KS 67063: Free information ◆ Horse trailers. 800-835-0209; 316-947-3127 (in KS).

**Kiefer Built,** P.O. Box 88, Kanawha, IA 50447: Free information ◆ All-aluminum horse trailers. 515-762-3201.

**Logan Coach,** P.O. Box 746, Logan, UT 84323: Free information ◆ Horse trailers. 800-752-3737.

**Pierce Sales,** Rt. 1, Box 3A, Henrietta, TX 76365: Catalog $1 ◆ Cargo carriers, runabouts, horse trailers, and truck beds. 940-538-5646.

**S & H Trailer Manufacturing Company,** 800 Industrial Dr., Madill, OK 73446: Free information ◆ Recreational vehicles and horse, cargo, equipment, stock, RV, utility, and carryall trailers with optional features. 405-795-5577.

**Silverado Trailers,** 632 Shelley St., Springfield, OR 97477: Free list of retail sources ◆ Combination living quarters and horse transportation trailers. 800-644-7155. www.silveradotrailers.com

**Sooner Trailers,** 1515 McCurdy, Duncan, OK 73533: Free information ◆ Horse trailers. 405-255-6979. www.soonertrailers.com

**Sundowner Trailer Inc.,** HC 61, Box 27, Coleman, OK 73432: Free information ◆ Horse trailers. 800-438-4294.

**Trails West Manufacturing of Idaho Inc.,** Box 67, Preston, ID 83263: Free information ◆ Horse trailers. 208-852-2200.

**Turnbow Trailers Inc.,** P.O. Box 300, Oilton, OK 74052: Free information ◆ Horse trailers. 918-862-3233. www.turnbowtrailers.com

**W-W Trailer,** Box 807, Hwy. 177 West, Madill, OK 73446: Free information ◆ Horse trailers. 405-795-5571.

### Saddles, Tack, & Cowboy Equipment

**The Australian Stock Saddle Company,** P.O. Box 987, Malibu, CA 90265: Catalog $6 ◆ Fleece-lined Aussie saddles. 562-889-6988. tassc@aol.com

**Bargain Corral,** P.O. Box 856, Allan, TX 75002: Free information with long SASE ◆ Saddles, stirrups and straps, blankets, spurs, halters, pads, bits, bridles and breast collars, boots, dusters, rain slickers, and supplies. 800-955-5616.

**Bridger Creek Outfitters,** P.O. Box 126, Alder, MT 59710: Catalog $3 ◆ Western gear for people and horses. 406-842-5044.

**J.M. Capriola Company,** 500 Commercial St., Elko, NV 89801: Catalog $5 ◆ Authentic western equipment and tack. 702-738-5816. www.cattle-log.com

**Circle R Boot & Saddle,** 909 W. 8th St., Okumulgee, OK 74447: Free information ◆ Custom boots and saddles. 918-756-3090.

**Colorado Saddlery Company,** 1631 15th St., Denver, CO 80202: Free catalog ◆ Tents and accessories, sleeping bags, stoves, tack and pack equipment, and supplies. 800-521-2465; 303-572-8350 (in CO). gobus@earthlink.net

**Country Supply,** 12627 River Rd., Ottumwa, IA 52501: Free catalog ◆ Saddles, pads, harnesses, books and videos, and tack. 800-637-6721.

**Courbette Saddlery Company,** 585 Industrial Pkwy., P.O. Box 2131, Heath, OH 43056: Free information ◆ Handmade saddles with anatomically shaped front and thigh rolls. 614-522-1555.

**The Cowboy Tack Catalog Company,** P.O. Box 945, Brockport, NY 14420: Free catalog ◆ Cowboy-designed horse equipment and tack. 800-807-7391.

**Crooked Pine Saddle Shop,** 662 Dry Gulch Rd., Stevensville, MT 59870: Catalog $4 (refundable) ◆ Custom saddles and pack equipment. 406-777-3108. www.CrookedPine.com

**Down Under Saddle Supply,** 5470 E. Evans Ave., Denver, CO 80222: Catalog $4 ◆ Australian saddles and tack. 303-753-6737. www.downunderweb.com

**Eisers,** 360 Kiwanis Blvd., P.O. Box 158, Hazleton, PA 18201: Free list of retail sources ◆ Health care supplies, saddles, tack, stable needs, books, and clothing for men and women. 800-526-6987. www.eisers.com

**John M. Fallis Custom Saddles,** P.O. Box 50, 540 Country Rd. 42, Wyarno, WY 82845: Catalog $4 ◆ Custom-built saddles. 307-737-2264.

**Heisler Saddle Shop,** 211 S. Main St., South Hutchinson, KS 67505: Free information ◆ Handmade saddles. 800-663-6541; 316-663-6241 (in KS).

**Hitching Post Supply,** 10312 210th St. SE, Snohomish, WA 98296: Free catalog ◆ Handmade saddles and horseback riding accessories. 800-689-9971; 360-668-2349 (in WA). www.hitchingpostsupply.com

**Hobby Horse Clothing Company Inc.,** 13775 Stockton Ave., Chino, CA 91710: Catalog $2 ◆ Western clothing and tack, show apparel, and accessories for horseback riders. 800-569-5885. www.hobbyhorseinc.com

**The Horse of Course,** 6395 Gunpark Dr., Boulder, CO 80301: Free catalog ◆ Saddle packing gear and horse blankets. 800-569-1880.

**Horseman's Corral,** 906 N. Carpenter Rd., Modesto, CA 95351: Free information ◆ Saddles. 209-571-2863.

**Horsemen's General Store,** 1001 Shiloh Springs Rd., Dayton, OH 45415: Catalog $3 ◆ Everything for horse owners, trainers, breeders, riders, and horses. 800-343-4987; 937-278-2380 (in OH).

**Ronnie Jones Leather Crafts,** Box 283, Hooker, OK 73945: Brochure $1 ◆ Handmade spurs, bits, and other leather crafts. 405-652-3295.

**K & B Saddlery,** 11003 192nd St., Council Bluffs, IA 51503: Catalog $1 ◆ Western saddles. 712-366-1026.

**K\J Leather Company,** P.O. Box 38, Branson, CO 81027: Free brochure ◆ Custom chaps, chinks, cowboy gear, and hitched horsehair items. 719-946-5252.

**Kate's Saddle Supply,** 3551 S. Monaco Pkwy., Denver, CO 80237: Free information ◆ General purpose and Australian-style saddles. 800-395-TACK.

**King's Saddlery,** 184 N. Main, Sheridan, WY 92801: Free catalog ◆ Ropes, saddlery, and other cowboy gear. 800-443-8919; 307-672-2702 (in WY).

**Richard Kirkland,** Leather Artisan, 4020 NE 81st Ave., Portland, OR 97213: Catalog $3 ◆ Saddle bags, holsters, pommel bags, rifle scabbards, and other leather cowboy items. 503-335-0713.

**Libertyville Saddle Shop Inc.,** P.O. Box M, Libertyville, IL 60048: Catalog $3 ◆ Saddles and clothing. 800-872-3353.

**Mary's Tack & Feed,** 3675 Via De La Valle, Del Mar, CA 92014: Free catalog ◆ Saddles and pads, bridles, books, and tack. 800-551-6279. marystack@aol.com

**Out West Designs,** 2679 Midland Dr., Ogden, UT 84401: Free catalog ◆ Horse blankets, saddle and pack bags, wall tents, and other equipment. 801-393-6839. outwestpro@aol.com

**Outfitters Pack Station,** 2070 W. Broadway, Idaho Falls, ID 83402: Free catalog ◆ Riding accessories, tack, and camping gear. 800-657-2644; 208-522-3446 (in ID). www.scenic-idaho.com/outfitterspackstation

**Performance Saddlery Inc.,** 420 Sheffield Rd., Ithaca, NY 14850: Free list of retail sources ◆ Saddles, bridles and whips, and wraps. 800-258-0006; 607-277-3541 (in NY). www.saddlefit.com/selecta.htm

**Platte Valley Saddle Shop Inc.,** P.O. Box 1683, Kearney, NE 68848: Catalog $5 ◆ Custom-made saddles and cowboy saddle bags. 308-234-4015.

**Professional's Choice Sports Medicine Inc.,** 2709 Via Orange Way, Spring Valley, CA 91978: Free list of retail sources ◆ Saddle pads. 800-670-7170. info@profchoice.com

**Pullman Saddle Company,** P.O. Box 567, New Palestine, IN 46163: Free information ◆ Hand-built saddles and gun holsters. 800-783-7996; 317-861-6871 (in IN). www.harpdepot.com/pullman

**Rod's Western Palace,** 3099 Silver Dr., Columbus, OH 43224: Free catalog ◆ Western wear and tack. 800-325-8508. rods@www.rods.com

**RoughOut,** Box 2667, Missoula, MT 59806: Free catalog ◆ Riding equipment, clothing, and gifts. 800-428-1098.

**Ryon's Saddle & Ranch Supplies,** 2601 N. Main, Fort Worth, TX 76106: Free catalog ◆ Saddles, tack, and Western-style clothing and boots for men, women, and children. 800-725-7966. www.luskey.com

**Sawtooth Saddle Company,** 14340 W. Dry Fork Cnyn., Vernal, UT 84078: Catalog $5 ◆ Custom handmade saddles and gear. 435-789-5400. www.sawtoothsaddle.com

**Denny Sergeant's Western World,** 4905 South Cooper St., Arlington, TX 76017: Free catalog ◆ Show clothing, saddles, and other western gear. 800-383-3669. www.sergeantswestern.com

**Sherer Custom Saddles Inc.,** P.O. Box 385, Franktown, CO 80116: Catalog $5 (refundable) ◆ Handmade saddles.

**Sports Medicine Products,** 2709 Via Orange Way, Spring Valley, CA 91978: Free information ◆ Lightweight orthopedic saddle pad. 800-331-9421. www.pcsmp.com

**State Line Tack Inc.,** P.O. Box 935, Brockport, NY 14420: Free catalog ◆ English and western riding tack and clothing. 800-228-9208. www.statelinetack.com

**Stelzig's Western Store,** 3123 Post Oak Rd., Houston, TX 77056: Free catalog ◆ Saddles and other leather goods for horsemen. 713-629-7779.

**Taylor Made Saddles,** P.O. Box 141, Barksdale, TX 78828: Free information ◆ Hand-tooled saddles. Also wood, metal, and leather furniture and gifts. 830-234-3322.

**Thornhill Enterprises,** P.O. Box 3643, Wilmington, DE 19807: Free information ◆ Saddles and tack. 610-444-3998.

**Top Tack Inc.,** 802 Hillman Rd., Yakima, WA 98908: Free information ◆ Training tack and apparel. 800-419-1392; 509-966-2090 (in WA).

**Tortuga Forge Inc.,** 720 N. Golden Key St., Ste. B5, Gilbert, AZ 85233: Free information ◆ Saddle stand. 602-813-9611.

**Valley Vet Supply,** P.O. Box 504, Marysville, KS 66508: Free catalog ◆ Equine health products, roping gear, pack equipment, horse blankets, and English, Western, and Arabian tack. 800-835-2978. www.valleyvet.com

**Wiese Equine Supply**, 1989 Transit Way, Brockport, NY 14420: Free catalog ◆ Equine equipment, health care products, accessories, and clothing. 800-869-4373.

## HORSESHOES (FOR HORSES)

**Farrier's Choice Horseshoes,** 915 S. Cocalico Rd., Denver, PA 17517: Free information ◆ Horseshoes, sizes 00 to 2 in front and hind patterns. 800-746-3766.

**NC Tool Company,** 6568 Hunt Rd., Pleasant Garden, NC 27313: Free information ◆ Horseshoe supplies. 800-446-6498.

**Slypner Athletic Horseshoes,** 150 Sullivan St., Claremont, NH 03743: Free catalog ◆ Horseshoes for different terrain conditions, tack, and other supplies. 800-759-7637.

**Wagon Mound Ranch Supply,** Box 218, Wagon Mound, NM 87752: Free catalog ◆ Horseshoe supplies. 800-666-2489.

## HORSESHOES (PITCHING)

**Franklin Sports Industries Inc.,** 17 Campanelli Pkwy., P.O. Box 508, Stoughton, MA 02072: Free information ◆ Horseshoes. 800-426-7700. www.eisnerbros.com

**General Sportcraft Company,** 140 Woodbine Rd., Bergenfield, NJ 07621: Free information ◆ Horseshoes. 201-384-4242.

**N.H.P.A. Game Sales,** Dennis R. Ohms, 777 W. Midvalley Rd., Cedar City, UT 84720: Free price list ◆ Professional horseshoe pitching equipment. 801-586-9352.

**The Queen City Forging Company,** 235 Tennyson St., Cincinnati, OH 45226: Free brochure ◆ Multi-grip pitching horseshoes.

**Spalding Sports Worldwide,** 425 Meadow St., P.O. Box 901, Chicopee, MA 01021: Free list of retail sources ◆ Horseshoes. 800-225-6601. www.spalding.com

**Sport Fun Inc.,** 4621 Sperry St., Los Angeles, CA 90039: Free information ◆ Horseshoes. 800-423-2597; 213-245-7530 (in CA).

**White Distributors,** P.O. Box 3652, Erie, PA 16508: Free catalog ◆ Professional horseshoe pitching equipment and accessories. 800-841-4685. home.att.net/~rwhite1639

**Worldwide Games,** P.O. Box 517, Colchester, CT 06415: Free catalog ◆ Equipment for badminton, horseshoes, and boccie. 800-888-0987. www.worldwidegames.com

## HOT TUBS, WHIRLPOOLS, & SAUNAS

**Almost Heaven Ltd.,** Rt. 219 North, Renick, WV 24966: Free catalog ◆ Hot tubs, spas, saunas, and whirlpools. 304-497-3163. www.almostheaven.net

**Amerec Sauna & Steam,** P.O. Box 40569, Bellevue, WA 98004: Free information ◆ Pre-assembled and easy-to-install free-standing modular saunas and controls. 800-331-0349; 425-643-7500 (in WA). www.amerec.com

**American Bath Factory,** 376 American Circle, Corona, CA 91720: Free list of retail sources ◆ Victorian-style clawfoot tub with concealed whirlpool action. 800-422-2284.

**Americh,** 13208 Saticoy St., North Hollywood, CA 91605: Free list of retail sources ◆ Whirlpool tubs and accessories. 800-453-1463; 818-982-1711 (in CA).

**Apollo Plastics,** 4006 Meridian St., Bellingham, WA 98226: Free brochure ◆ Hot tubs, jet baths, and gazebos. 360-738-1748.

**Aqua Glass Corp.,** P.O. Box 412, Industrial Park, Adamsville, TN 38310: Free list of retail sources ◆ Whirlpool baths, combination steam showers, lavatories, wall surrounds, and shower floors. 800-238-3940; 901-632-0911 (in TN). www.aquaglass.com

**Bruce Manufacturing Inc.,** 5203 North US 45, Bruce Crossing, MI 49912: Free brochure ◆ Wood, gas, and electric sauna heaters. 906-827-3906. www.Nippa.com

**Coleman Spas Inc.,** 25605 S. Arizona, Chandler, AZ 85248: Free information ◆ Spas and hot tubs. 800-926-5362.

**Grohe America Inc.,** 241 Covington Dr., Bloomingdale, IL 60108: Information $3 ◆ Thermostat-controlled water valves. 847-582-7711. www.grohe.com

**Hot Spring Portable Spas,** 76 N. 625 West, Bountiful, UT 84010: Free catalog ◆ Easy-to-use portable spas. 801-298-7665.

**Jacuzzi Whirlpool Bath,** 2121 N. California Blvd., Walnut Creek, CA 94596: Free catalog ◆ Whirlpool spas, baths, and towers with hydro-massage control. 800-678-6889. www.jacuzzi.com

**Lyons Industries,** P.O. Box 88, Dowagiac, MI 49047: Free information ◆ Whirlpools for space-saving corner installation with optional walls and shatter-proof folding shower stall doors. 800-458-9036.

**Northstar Acrylic Designs,** P.O. Box 370350, Denver, CO 80237: Catalog $15 ◆ Victorian and contemporary whirlpool bathtubs. Other Victorian-style products include acrylic drop-in sinks, shower and lavatory faucets, and acrylic shower bases. 888-225-8827; 303-337-0688 (in CO). www.northstarcrylics.com

**Plastic Creations,** 1023 S. Hamilton St., Dalton, GA 30720: Free brochure ◆ Acrylic whirlpool baths. 800-868-0254.

**Snorkel Stove Company,** 4216 6th Avenue, Seattle, WA 98108: Free information ◆ Wood-fired hot tubs. 800-962-6208. www.snorkel.com

**Sonoma Spas,** 406 Railroad St., P.O. Box 1409, Yelm, WA 98597: Free list of retail sources ◆ Hot tubs. 888-998-1772; 360-458-1371 (in WA).

**Southland Spa,** Box 638, Ray Farm Rd., Haleyville, AL 35565: Free information ◆ Spas, whirlpool baths, and saunas. 205-486-7919.

**Steam-Whirl,** 3251 Corte Malpaso, Unit 502, Camarillo, CA 93010: Free brochure ◆ Personal steambaths and accessories. 805-987-7957.

**Sundance Spas,** P.O. Box 2900, 13051 Monte Vista Ave., Chino, CA 91708: Free list of retail sources ◆ Hydrotherapy spas and accessories. 909-591-9977.

**Sussman Automatic,** 43-20 34th St., Long Island City, NY 11101: Free information ◆ Equipment to convert shower stalls into steam rooms. 800-238-3535.

**Swirl-way,** 1505 Industrial Dr., Henderson, TX 76563: Free list of retail sources ◆ Acrylic whirlpool tubs. 903-657-1436.

**Universal Rundle,** 303 North St., P.O. Box 29, New Castle, PA 16103: Free information ◆ Portable spa that operates by plugging into a standard grounded outlet. 800-965-2284.

**Watkins Manufacturing Spas,** 1280 Park Center Dr., Vista, CA 92083: Free information ◆ Portable spas. 800-999-4688.

## HOT WATER HEATERS

**BSAR Solar,** 980 Santa Estella, Solana, Beach, CA 92075: Free information ◆ Solar system for making hot and distilled water. 714-993-5890.

**Kansas Wind Power,** 13569 214th Rd., Holton, KS 66436: Catalog $4 ◆ Sun ovens, wind generators, composting toilets, tank-free water heaters, air coolers, and other solar energy equipment. 913-364-4407.

**Refrigeration Research Inc.,** P.O. Box 869, Brighton, MI 48116: Free information ◆ Solar water heating systems for homes. 810-227-1151.

**Solar Depot,** 61 Paul Dr., San Rafael, CA 94903: Catalog $5 ◆ Solar electric power systems, water heaters, electric and thermal systems, and other equipment. 415-499-1333. www.solardepot.com

**Sunelco,** P.O. Box 1499, Hamilton, MT 59840: Catalog $4.95 ◆ Solar modules, controllers, batteries, inverters, water pumps, propane-operated appliances, and power and heating systems for recreational vehicles and cabins. 800-338-6844.

**Thermo Dynamics Ltd.,** 81 Thornhill Dr., Darmouth, Nova Scotia, Canada B3B 1R9: Free information ◆ Solar hot water system. 902-468-1001.

## HOURGLASSES

**The Hourglass Connection,** 320 Heather Dr., Stanfield, OR 97875: Catalog $2.50 ◆ Handcrafted and imported custom made hourglasses. 888-777-7027. www.hourglasses.com

## HOUSEWARES & CLEANING PRODUCTS

**Able Service & Supply,** 7323 North Monticello, Skokie, IL 60076: Free information ◆ Cleaning supplies. 888-289-2253. www.ablesupply.com

**Agelong Catalog,** P.O. Box 411068, Kansas City, MO 64141: Free catalog ◆ Home and garden products, cleaning aids, and more. 800-892-8022.

**Betty Crocker Making A Home,** P.O. Box 5372, Minneapolis, MN 55460: Free catalog ◆ Housewares and kitchen accessories. 800-432-4959. www.bettycrocker.com

**Brookstone Company,** Order Processing Center, 1655 Bassford Dr., Mexico, MO 65265: Free catalog ◆ Housewares and tools. 800-926-7000.

**Chef's Catalog,** P.O. Box 620048, Dallas, TX 75262: Free catalog ◆ Professional restaurant equipment for the home chef. 800-338-3232. www.chefscatalog.com

**Colonial Garden Kitchens,** Hanover Direct Pennsylvania Inc., Hanover, PA 17333-0001: Free catalog ◆ Housewares, storage and bathroom accessories, cleaning and cooking needs, furniture, and laundry room aids. 800-245-3333.

**Joan Cook,** 119 Foster St., P.O. Box 6008, Peabody, MA 01961: Free catalog ◆ Housewares for cooking and home care. 800-935-0971.

**Hold Everything,** Mail Order Dept., P.O. Box 7807, San Francisco, CA 94120: Free catalog ◆ Clothing and closet organizers, garment protectors, kitchen and laundry aids, bathroom space makers, and bedroom furnishings. 800-421-2285.

**Home Trends,** 1450 Lyell Ave., Rochester, NY 14606: Free catalog ◆ Cleaning supplies, energy-saving devices, lighting equipment, pest controls, brushes, vacuums and accessories, and more. 716-254-6520. home@eznet.net

**Lakeside Products Company,** 6646 N. Western Ave., Chicago, IL 60645: Catalog $1 (refundable) ◆ Housewares, novelties, and gifts. 312-761-5495.

**Stone Care International,** P.O. Box 703, Owings Mills, MD 21117: Free brochure ◆ Kitchen and bathroom care kits for marble and granite. 800-839-1654; 410-363-8788 (in MD). www.stonecare.com

## HUMIDIFIERS

**Broan Manufacturing Company,** 926 W. State St., Hartford, WI 53027: Free information ◆ Humidifiers. 800-558-1711.

**Carrier Corp.,** Box 408, Syracuse, NY 13221: Free information ◆ Humidifiers. 800-227-7437. www.carrier.com

**Herrmidifier Company,** Tion Inc., 101 McNeill Rd., Sanford, NC, 27331: Free list of retail sources ◆ Residential humidifiers. 800-884-0002. www.herrmidifier.com

**Hunter Fan Company,** 2500 Fisco Ave., Memphis, TN 38114: Catalog $1 ◆ Electronic-programmable thermostats. 901-745-9222. www.hunterfan.com

**Nortec Industries,** Box 698, Ogdensburg, NY 13669: Free information ◆ Humidifiers. 315-425-1255.

**Whirlpool Corp.,** 2000 M63 North, Benton Harbor, MI 49022: Free information ◆ Humidifiers. 800-253-1301. www.whirlpool.com

## HUNTING

### Clothing & Equipment

**Advantage Camouflage,** 1390 Box Circle, Columbus, GA 21907: Free information ◆ Camouflage clothing. 706-569-9101.

**Ambusher,** 2007 W. 7th St., Texarkana, TX 75501: Free information ◆ Portable climbing ladders. 800-332-HUNT. www.ambusher.com

**American Camper,** 14760 Santa Fe Trail Dr., Lenexa, KS 66215: Free list of retail sources ◆ Camouflage clothing and backpacks. 800-315-2267. www.americancamper.com

**API Outdoors Inc.,** P.O. Box 1432, Tallulah, LA 71282: Catalog $2 ◆ Tree stands. 800-228-4846; 318-574-4903 (in (LA).

**Avid Outdoor,** 1120 W. 149th St., P.O. Box 578, Olathe, KS 66051: Free list of retail sources ◆ Camouflage patterned clothing. 913-780-2843.

**L.L. Bean,** Casco St., Freeport, ME 04032: Free catalog ◆ Outdoor clothing. 800-221-4221. www.llbean.com

**Bear River Industries Inc.,** 3110 Ranchview Ln., Minneapolis, MN 55447: Free information ◆ Portable tree stands and hunting supplies. 800-536-3337; 612-559-1092 (in MN).

**Big Buck Treestands,** 855 Chicago Rd., Quincy, MI 49082: Free information ◆ Tree stands. 517-639-3815.

**Black Hole Blinds,** P.O. Box 177, West Point, IA 52656: Free information ◆ Small and lightweight for transporting, easy-to-assemble total concealment blinds. 319-837-6942.

**Bowhunters Discount Warehouse Inc.,** P.O. Box 158, Wellsville, PA 17365: Free catalog ◆ Rifles, game calls, targets, camouflage clothing, and hunting, bow-hunting, archery, and camping equipment. 800-735-BOWS. www.bowhunterswarehouse.com

**Brigade Quartermasters Inc.,** 1025 Cobb International Blvd., Kenesaw, GA 30144: Free catalog ◆ Camouflage clothing. 800-338-4327. www.actiongear.com

**Browning Company,** Dept. C006, One Browning Pl., Morgan, UT 84050: Catalog $2 ◆ Camouflage clothing. 800-333-3288. www.browning.com

**Bruin Industries Inc.,** 1840 County Line Rd., Unit 203, Huntingdon Valley, PA 19006: Free brochure ◆ Tree stands. 800-779-6010.

**Cabela's,** One Cabela Dr., Sidney, NE 69160: Free catalog ◆ Hunting, fishing, and outdoor equipment. 800-237-4444. www.cabelas.com

**Cheaper than Dirt,** 2536 NE Loop 820, Fort Worth, TX 76106: Free catalog ◆ Holsters and cases, scopes, survival supplies, gunsmith and cleaning supplies, clothing, hunting and camping gear, and archery, crossbow, and shotgun equipment. 888-625-3848. www.cheaperthandirt.com

**Cougar Claw-Zetabait,** 9559 Hickory St. South, Foley, AL 36535: Free information ◆ Tree stands and plastic fishing lures. 334-943-1902.

**Day One Camouflage,** 3300 S. Knox Ct., Denver, CO 80110: Free information ◆ Camouflage clothing. 800-347-2979.

**Delta Decoys,** 117 E. Kenwood St., Reinbeck, IA 50669: Free information ◆ Life-size ultra-light and collapsible deer decoys. 319-345-6476.

**Double/Triple Trading,** P.O. Box 5425, Buena Park, CA 90022: Free information ◆ Hunting accessories. 800-949-8546.

**Dunn Manufacturing Company,** P.O. Drawer E, Mineral Wells, TX 76068: Free information ◆ Tree stands. 817-325-2402.

**Dunn's Supply Catalog,** P.O. Box 509, Grand Junction, TN 38039: Free catalog ◆ Camouflage and insulated clothing, outerwear, shoes and boots, hunting equipment, day and belt packs, gun care kits, sunglasses, game calls, decoys, and supplies. 800-427-6572. www.dunnscatalog.com

**Fieldline,** 1919 Vineburn Ave., Los Angeles, CA 90032: Free brochure ◆ Fleece packs, pouches, and gaiters for hunters. 213-226-0830.

**Flambeau Products Corp.,** 15981 Valplast Rd., Middlefield, OH 44062: Free information ◆ Realistic deer decoys. 800-232-3474.

**Flint River Outdoor Wear Inc.,** 5731 Miller Ct., Columbus, GA 31909: Free list of retail sources ◆ Briar-proof, waterproof, and snake proof chaps. Also other clothing and accessories. 800-241-8801.

**Freddie Bear Sports,** 17250 S. Oak Park, Tinley Park, IL 60477: Free information ◆ Hunting and fishing equipment. 708-532-4133. www.bowhunting.net/fbs

**Gander Mountain (Cabela's),** One Cabela Dr., Sidney, NE 69160: Free catalog ◆ Camping equipment, boats, archery supplies, knives, rifle scopes, and hunting videos. 800-237-4444. www.cabelas.com

**Graf & Sons,** 4050 S. Clark, Mexico, MO 65265: Free information ◆ Hunting accessories, scopes, and reloading equipment. 800-531-2666.

**Haas Outdoors Inc.,** P.O. Box 757, West Point, MS 39773: Free information ◆ Camouflage supplies. 800-331-5624. www.mossyoak.com

**Hawks,** P.O. Box 207, Blytheville, AR 72316: Free catalog ◆ Hunting clothing and footwear, knives, gun safes, guns, and more.

**Loggy Bayou Tree Stands,** P.O. Box 1209, Natchitoches, LA 71458: Free information ◆ Climbing and hang-on tree stands. 800-544-8733.

**Lone Wolf Tree Stands,** 3308 E. Grange Ave., Cudahy, WI 53110: Free information ◆ Tree stands. 414-744-4984.

**Mossy Oak,** P.O. Box 757, West Point, MS 39773: Free information ◆ Hunting apparel, casual clothes, outdoor wear, and golf attire. 800-331-5624. www.mossyoak.com

**Natgear Camouflage,** 4209 S. Shackleford Rd., Ste. D, Little Rock, AR 72204: Free list of retail sources ◆ Camouflage accessories. 501-228-5590.

**Nature's Edge Camouflage,** P.O. Box 194, Columbus, GA 31902: Free information ◆ Camouflage patterns.

**Nite Lite Company,** P.O. Box 8300, Little Rock, AR 72221: Free catalog ◆ Kennel, training, and hunting supplies for dogs. Clothing and accessories for the hunter. 800-648-5483.

**Norland Trading Company,** Box 10, Norland, Ontario, Canada K0M 2L0: Video catalog $5 (refundable) ◆ Hunting, fishing, and outdoor products. 800-318-0717. ntc@cancom.net

**RealBark Hunting Systems,** P.O. Box 2078, Henderson, TX 75653: Free brochure ◆ Blinds, seat tripods, platforms, and game feeders. 800-256-4465.

**Realtree Camouflage,** P.O. Box 9638, Columbus, GA 21907: Free information ◆ Camouflage clothing. 706-569-9101.

**Redhead,** 1935 S. Campbell, Springfield, MO 65898: Free catalog ◆ Equipment and clothing for hunters. 800-227-7776.

**Scott-Wynne Outfitters,** 10000 Research Blvd., Ste. 127, Austin, TX 78759: Free catalog ◆ Outdoor and casual clothing, luggage, hunting and fishing accessories, and Native American jewelry. 800-232-2783. www.outfits.com

**Senco Inc.,** 520 8th St., Gwinn, MI 49841: Free information ◆ Recreational shelters, portable hunting blinds, ice fishing houses, and greenhouses. 906-346-4116.

**Shelter-Pro,** Hwy 92, Stearns, KY 42647: Free catalog ◆ Portable hunting blinds. 888-376-2004.

**Shydas Shoe & Clothing Barn,** 1635 S. Lincoln Ave., Lebanon, PA 17042: Free catalog ◆ Hunting and outerwear clothing. 717-274-2551.

**Skyline Camo,** 184 Ellicott Rd., West Falls, NY 14170: Free brochure ◆ Camouflage supplies. 716-655-0230.

**Sport Climbers,** 2926 75th St., Kenosha, WI 53143: Free catalog ◆ Tree-climbing spikes. 800-877-7025.

**Summit Specialties Inc.,** P.O. Box 786, Decatur, AL 35602: Brochure $1 ◆ Climbing tree stands. 256-353-0634.

**TAPCO,** P.O. Box 2408, Kennesaw, GA 30144: Free catalog ◆ Military, shooting, and outdoor gear. 800-554-1445.

**10X Products,** 2915 LBJ Fwy., Dallas, TX 75243: Free information ◆ Camouflage clothing. 972-243-4016.

**Trax America,** Box 898, Forrest City, AR 72335: Free information ◆ Tree stands. 800-232-2327. www.traxamerica.com

**Trebark Camouflage,** 3434 Buck Mountain Rd., Roanoke, VA 24014: Free catalog ◆ Camouflage gear for hunters. 800-843-2266; 540-774-9248 (in VA).

**Trophy Whitetail Products,** 329 E. Shockley Ferry Rd., Anderson, SC 29624: Free information ◆ Tree stands. 864-231-9506.

**Underbrush Concealment Shelter,** Shelter-Pro, Highway 92 A, Stearns, KY 42647: Free catalog ◆ Compact and easy-to-setup hunting blinds. 888-376-2004.

**Walls Industries,** P.O. Box 98, Cleburne, TX 76031: Free information ◆ Camouflage clothing. 800-447-WEAR.

**Warren & Sweat Manufacturing Company,** Box 350440, Grand Island, FL 32735: Free information ◆ Portable and semi-permanent ladders. 352-669-3166.

**Whitewater Outdoors Inc.,** W4118 Church St., Highdam, WI 53031: Free information ◆ Camouflage clothing. 800-666-2674.

**Wiley Outdoor Sports,** 1808 Sportsman Ln., Huntsville, AL 35816: Free catalog ◆ Hunting equipment. 800-494-5397. www.wileyoutdoorsports.com

**Wing Supply,** P.O. Box 367, Greenville, KY 42345: Free catalog ◆ Camouflage clothing, boots, blinds, decoys, tree stands, calls, and accessories.

**Woodstream Corp.,** P.O. Box 327, Lititz, PA 17543: Free catalog ◆ Hunting and shooting equipment. 800-800-1819; 717-626-2125 (in PA).

**Woolrich,** Mill St., Woolrich, PA 17779: Free information ◆ Camouflage clothing. 800-995-1299. www.woolrich.com

## Game Calls, Lures, & Scents

**Abe & Son Natural Elk Sounds,** 880 Sunshine Ln., Coos Bay, OR 97420: Free information ◆ Game calls. 800-426-2417.

**Big River Game Calls,** P.O. Box 388, Dunlap, IL 61525: Free information ◆ Game calls. 309-243-7515.

**Buck Stop Lure Company Inc.,** P.O. Box 636, Stanton, MI 48888: Free information ◆ Scents and lures. 800-477-2368; 517-762-5091 (in MI).

**Burnham Game Calls,** P.O. Box 1018, Marble Falls, TX 78654: Free information ◆ Game calls. 210-693-3112.

**Calls-M-All,** Rt. 2, Box 246A, Walla Walla, WA 99362: Free information ◆ Wildlife game calls. 509-522-0964. www.Archery-innovations.com/hancocks.html

**Chestnut Ridge,** P.O. Box 546, Kent, OH 44240: Free information ◆ Wild turkey calls. 330-947-0330. www.WildTurkeyCalls.com

**Cover Up Products,** Rt. 1, Box 66, Hill City, KS 67642: Free information ◆ Deer scents. 913-674-5503.

**Dunn's Supply Catalog,** P.O. Box 509, Grand Junction, TN 38039: Free catalog ◆ Camouflage and insulated clothing, outerwear, shoes and boots, hunting equipment, day and belt packs, gun care kits, sunglasses, game calls, decoys, and supplies. 800-427-6572. www.dunnscatalog.com

**Faulk's Game Call Company,** 616 18th St., Lake Charles, LA 70601: Free information ◆ Game calls. 318-436-9726.

**Haydel's Game Calls Inc.,** 5018 Hazel Jones Rd., Bossier City, LA 71111: Free information ◆ Game calls. 318-746-3586.

**Hulme,** P.O. Box 670, Hwy. 641 South, Paris, TN 38242: Free catalog ◆ Game calls and scents. 901-642-6400.

**Hunter's Specialties Inc.,** 6000 Huntington Ct. NE, Cedar Rapids, IA 52402: Free list of retail sources ◆ Game calls, decoys, lures, and scents. 319-395-0321.

**J.R. & Sons,** P.O. Box 603, Monroeville, OH 44847: Catalog $1 (refundable) ◆ Lures, scents, baits, essences, and lure-making ingredients.

**James Valley Scents,** Box 47, Mellette, SD 57461: Free catalog ◆ Gel and liquid animal scents. 605-887-3125.

**Knight & Hale Game Calls,** Drawer 670, Cadiz, KY 42211: Free information ◆ Game calls. 800-500-9357.

**Lohman Manufacturing Company,** Box 220, Neosho, MO 64850: Free information ◆ Game calls. 417-451-4438.

**Mad Calls,** 1595 County Rd. 256, Columbia, MO 65201: Free information ◆ Turkey, deer, and elk calls. 888-TEAM-MAD.

**Mike Marsyada,** 722 North St., West Hazleton, PA 18201: Catalog $1 (refundable) ◆ Hunting scents.

**Midwest Turkey Call Supply,** RR 3, Box 354, Sullivan, IL 61951: Free information ◆ Calls and decoys. 800-541-1638.

**Nature's Essence,** 6950 Rawson Rd., Coba, NY 14727: Free brochure ◆ Spray-on and wash-off scent eliminating products for hunters. 716-968-3338. home.eznet.net/~natsess

**Perfection Turkey Calls,** Box 164, Stephenson, VA 22656: Free information ◆ Turkey calls. 800-422-9357.

**Primos Inc.,** Box 12785, Jackson, MS 39236: Information $2 (request list of retail sources) ◆ Turkey, deer, elk, waterfowl, and other calls. 800-523-2395. www.predatorcalls.com

**Quaker Boy Inc.,** 5455 Webster Rd., Orchard Park, NY 14127: Free information ◆ Turkey calls. 800-544-1600; 716-662-3979 (in NY).

**Pete Rickard Inc.,** RD 1, Box 292, Cobleskill, NY 12043: Free information ◆ Animal scents for deer. 800-282-5663.

**Ridge Runner Turkey Calls,** P.O. Box 6893, Maryville, TN 37802: Free brochure ◆ Hand-made turkey calls. 800-593-9357.

**Robinson Laboratories,** 293 Commercial St., St. Paul, MN 55106: Free information ◆ Deer lure gel. 800-397-1927; 612-224-1927 (in MN).

**Rose's Animal Lures,** 2879 10 Mile Rd. NE, Rockford, MI 49341: Free catalog ◆ Animal lures. 616-866-4341.

**Simmons Gun Specialties Inc.,** 20241 W. 207th, Spring Hill, KS 66083: Free information ◆ Game calls, decoys, lures, and scents. 800-444-0220.

**Southland Callers,** 2031 Horns Lake Rd., Talladega, AL 35160: Free information ◆ Game calls. 256-362-7418.

**Johnny Stewart Wildlife Calls,** 5100 Fort Ave., Waco, TX 76714: Free list of retail sources ◆ Game calls. 800-537-0652.

**Sullivan's Scents & Supplies,** 429A Upper Twin, Blue Creek, OH 45616: Free information ◆ Animal scents.

**Sure-Shot Game Calls Inc.,** Box 816, Groves, TX 77619: Free information ◆ Game calls. 409-962-1636.

**Thunder Dome Game Calls,** 4500 Doniphan Dr., P.O. Box 220, Neosho, MO 64850: Free catalog ◆ Deer, elk, turkey, predator, and other game calls. 417-451-4438.

**Tink's Safariland Hunting Corp.,** P.O. Box 244, Madison, GA 30650: Free information ◆ Game calls, decoys, lures, and scents. 800-221-5054; 706-342-1916 (in GA).

**Triple S Trapping Supply,** 166 Warren Cemetery Rd., Sandy Hook, MS 39478: Free catalog ◆ Deer scents. 601-736-1789.

**Wellington Leisure Products,** P.O. Box 244, Madison, GA 30650: Free information ◆ Game calls. 706-342-4915.

**Wilderness Sound Productions Ltd.,** 4015 Main St., Springfield, OR 97478: Free brochure ◆ Game calls. 800-437-0006.

**Wildlife Research Center,** 1050 McKinley St., Anoka, MN 55303: Free catalog ◆ Human scent eliminators, attractor and masking scents, and scent dispensers. 800-USE-LURE; 612-427-3350 (in MN).

**Wing Supply,** P.O. Box 367, Greenville, KY 42345: Free catalog ◆ Camouflage clothing, boots, blinds, decoys, tree stands, calls, and accessories.

**Woods Wise Callmasters,** P.O. Box 681552, Franklin, TN 37068: Free catalog ◆ Deer, elk, squirrel, turkey, and waterfowl game calls. 800-735-8182.

## ICE-CREAM MACHINES

**Chef's Catalog,** P.O. Box 620048, Dallas, TX 75262:Free catalog ◆ Manual and electric-operated self-chilling ice-cream makers. 800-338-3232. www.chefscatalog.com

**Lello Appliances Corp.,** 355 Murray Hill Pkwy., East Rutherford, NJ 07073: Free information ◆ Electric-powered ice-cream maker. 800-527-4336.

**Sun Appliances,** 4554 E. Princess Anne Rd., Norfolk, VA 23502: Free information ◆ Electric-operated salt and ice ice-cream maker. 800-347-4197.

**White Mountain Freezer Inc.,** 217 E. 16th St., Sedalia, MO 65301: Free information ◆ Old-fashioned rock salt and ice electric-operated ice-cream maker. 800-343-0065. www.rivco.com

**Williams-Sonoma,** Mail Order Dept., P.O. Box 7456, San Francisco, CA 94120: Free catalog ◆ Hand-cranked ice-cream machine. 800-541-1262.

**Zabar's & Company,** 2245 Broadway, New York, NY 10024: Free catalog ◆ Hand-cranked ice-cream maker. 800-697-6301; 212-496-1234 (in NY).

## ICE SKATING & RINKS

**Backyard Rinks,** 29 Sinclair Ct., Barrie, Ontario, Canada L4N 5YI: Free brochure ◆ Easy-to-assemble rinks for use in the backyard. 705-739-0925.

**Canstar Sports,** 150 Ocean Rd., Greenland, NH 03840: Free information ◆ Figure and hockey skates and blade sharpeners. 800-362-3146.

**Chisco Sports Accessories,** 2424 S. 2570 West, Salt Lake City, UT 84119: Free information ◆ Skates. 800-825-4555.

**Cooper International Inc.,** 501 Alliance Ave., Toronto, Ontario, Canada M6N 2J3: Free information ◆ Figure and hockey skates and blade protectors. 416-763-3801.

**Great Skate Hockey Supply Company,** 3395 Sheridan Dr., Amherst, NY 14226: Free information ◆ Ice skating and hockey equipment. 800-828-7496; 716-838-5100 (in NY).

**Maska USA Inc.,** 139 Harvest Ln., Williston, VT 05495: Free information ◆ Figure and hockey skates. 800-451-4600. www.ccmsports.com

**National Sporting Goods Corp.,** 25 Brighton Ave., Passaic, NJ 07055: Free information ◆ Figure and hockey skates, blade protectors, and sharpeners. 201-779-2323.

**NiceRink,** P.O. Box 310, Genoa City, WI 53128: Free catalog ◆ Easy-to-set up and maintain outdoor ice rinks for backyards and play-grounds. 888-NICERINK.

**Oberhamer USA,** 4775 Dakota St. SE, Prior Lake, MN 55372: Free catalog ◆ Skating attire and skates for men and women. 800-207-OBER.

**Riedell Shoes Inc.,** P.O. Box 21, Red Wing, MN 55066: Free information ◆ Blade protectors, sharpeners, and figure, racing, and hockey skates. 612-388-8251.

**Roller Derby Skate Company,** Box 930, Litchfield, IL 62056: Free information ◆ Skates. 217-324-3961.

**Seneca Sports Inc.,** 75 Fortune Blvd., P.O. Box 719, Milford, MA 01757: Free information ◆ Skates and blade protectors. 800-861-7867; 508-634-3616 (in MA).

## INCENSE & HOLDERS

**All Natural Botanicals,** 112001 44th St. North, Clearwater, FL 33762: Free catalog ◆ Fragrance and essential oils, bath and body preparations, potpourri, incense, diffusers, and more. 813-572-7800. allnatbo@aol.com

**Angel's Earth,** 1633 Scheffer Ave., St. Paul, MN 55116: Catalog $2 ◆ Soaps, candles, cosmetics, incense, skin care preparations, essential oils, and aromatherapy items. 612-698-3601.

**Angels & Us-Angel Gallery,** 3257 SE Hawthorne Blvd., Portland, OR 97214: Free information ◆ Incense holders. 503-239-5330.

**Bear Essentials,** P.O. Box 154, Madison, NJ 07940: Free catalog ◆ Incense and oils. 800-834-BEAR.

**Cambridge Zen Center,** 199 Auburn St., Cambridge, MA 02139: Catalog $2 ◆ Pants, mats, incense, Buddha figurines, malas, benches, and books. 617-576-3229.

**Changes in Artitude,** 10460 Roosevelt Blvd., #210, St. Petersburg, FL 33716: Free information ◆ Incense.

**Dharma Crafts,** 405 Waltham St., Ste. 234, Lexington, MA 02173: Catalog $2 ◆ Statues, cushions, ritual objects, benches, books, incense, and meditation supplies. 781-862-9211.

**The Essential Oil Company,** P.O. Box 206, Lake Oswego, OR 97034: Free catalog ◆ Aromatherapy supplies and essential oils, soap molds and supplies, potpourri and fragrance oils, and incense. 800-729-5912.

**The Excelsior Incense Works,** 1413 Van Dyke, San Francisco, CA 94124: Catalog $1 ◆ How-to books and incense-making supplies, and incense sticks, cones, and coils. 415-822-9124.

**Green Cedar Needle Sachets,** Box 551, State Rd. 165, Placitas, NM 87043: Free brochure ◆ Sachets, incense cones, and other fragrance products. 800-557-3463.

**Legacy Herbs,** Sue Lukens Herbalist/Potter, HC 70, Box 442, Mountain View, AR 72560: Catalog 50¢ ◆ Herbs, wildflowers, perennial plants, soaps, bath and body care products, oils and fragrance, incense, potpourri, herbal food products, and other scented items. 870-269-4051.

**Raven's Nest Herbals,** P.O. Box 370, Duluth, GA 30136: Catalog $1.50 ◆ Herbs, spices, oils, incense, potpourri, and other herbal products. 770-242-3901.

**Scentsational Scents,** P.O. Box 818, Roseburg, OR 97470: Free information ◆ Charcoal, incense, and burners. 541-672-3676.

**Surya Trading Company,** 724 Peaceful Valley, Lyons, CO 80540: Free brochure ◆ Hand-rolled all-natural incense sticks from India. 303-747-2989. www.suryatrading.com

## INCONTINENCE SUPPLIES

**AC Medical Supplies,** P.O. Box 29011, Westmount Mall, London, Ontario, Canada N6K 1M0: Free catalog ◆ Hygienic waterproof pants for disabled adults. 519-471-8049.

**Access Medical Supply,** 2300 Edison Blvd., Cleveland, OH 44087: Free catalog ◆ Incontinence shields, pads, undergarments, and other supplies for men, women, and children. 800-242-2460.

**Aplus Medical,** 16 Alden Pl., Newton, MA 02165: Free information ◆ Female urinal system that works in any position. 888-843-3334; 617-964-7412 (in MA). aplusmedical@earthlink.net

**ARC Home Health Products,** 3 Bronwne St., Oneonta, NY 13820: Free catalog ◆ Incontinence care products. 800-278-8595.

**Bruce Medical Supply,** 411 Waverly Oaks Rd., P.O. Box 9166, Waltham, MA 02254: Free catalog ◆ Health equipment for disabled and incontinent persons. 800-225-8446.

**Caring Products International Inc.,** 200 1st Ave. West, Ste. 200, Seattle, WA 98119: Free information ◆ Incontinence supplies and maternity and special-needs clothing. 800-333-5379; 206-282-6040 (in WA). www.caringproducts.com

**Comco Inc.,** P.O. Box 9039, North St. Paul, MN 55109: Free information ◆ Reusable incontinence products. 800-348-8375.

**Duraline Medical Products,** P.O. Box 67, Leipsic, OH 45856: Free catalog ◆ Incontinence aids and other health care items for children and adults. 800-654-3376. www.dmponline.com

**Express Medical Supply Inc.,** P.O. Box 1164, Fenton, MO 63026: Free catalog ◆ Urological, ostomy, incontinence, and skin care products. 800-633-2139. www.exmed.net

**Fashion Ease,** Division M and M Health Care, 1541 60th St., Brooklyn, NY 11219: Free catalog ◆ Incontinence supplies, wheelchair accessories, health care aids, and clothing with Velcro closures for arthritic, elderly, and handicapped persons. 800-221-8929; 718-871-8188 (in NY). www.fashionease.com

**Home Delivery Incontinent Supplies Company,** 1215 Dielman Industrial Ct., Olivette, MO 63132: Free catalog ◆ Briefs, undergarments, shields, underpads, catheters, and skin care products. 800-2MY-HOME. www.hdisnet.com

**L.L. Medico Inc.,** 1512 West Chester Pike, #255, West Chester, PA 19382: Free information ◆ Pants, in a choice of sizes and styles, for incontinent men and women. 610-436-8831.

**LDB Medical Inc.,** 2909 Langford Rd., Ste. 500-B, Norcross, GA 30071: Free catalog ◆ Ostomy and incontinence supplies, urological products, and skin care items. 800-243-2554. ldb@baiusa.com

**MOMS Mail Order Medical Supply,** 24700 Avenue Rockefeller, Valencia, CA 91355: Free catalog ◆ Urological, ostomy, incontinence, skin and wound care, daily living, diabetic, and home diagnostic aids. 800-232-7443. www.momsup.com

**Parkview Pharmacy & Home Health Care Inc.,** 8283 Grove Ave., Ste. 105, Rancho Cucamonga, CA 91730: Free catalog ◆ Ostomy, wound care, incontinence, and other home health care aids. 800-605-0166. www.parkviewrx.com

**Shield Healthcare Centers,** 4340 Viewrige Ave., San Diego, CA 92123: Free catalog ◆ Ostomy, urological, skin care, and home diagnostic products. 800-675-8845.

**Wearever Health Care Products,** 202 Red Mountain Rd., Rougemont, NC 27572: Free information ◆ Washable and re-usable absorbent briefs for men, women, and children with bladder control problems. 800-307-4968.

**Woodbury Products Inc.,** 4410 Austin Blvd., Island Park, NY 11558: Free information ◆ Disposable diapers. 800-777-1111.

## INDIAN (NATIVE AMERICAN) ARTS & CRAFTS

### Alabama

**American Indian Books & Relics,** P.O. Box 16175, Huntsville, AL 35802: Free information with long SASE ◆ American Indian relics. 256-881-6727.

### Alaska

**Chilkat Valley Arts,** Box 145, Haines, AK 99827: Free price list with long SASE ◆ Northwest Coast Tlingit Native American silver jewelry. 907-766-2990.

**Musk Ox Producers Cooperative,** 604 H St., Anchorage, AK 99501: Free information with long SASE ◆ Hand-knitted Qiviut scarves, caps, tunics, and clothing. 907-272-9225. www.qiviut.com

**Savoonga Native Store,** P.O. Box 100, Savoonga, AK 99769: Free price list with long SASE ◆ Figurines, scrimshaw, ivory carvings, jewelry, and other crafts.

**Amos Wallace,** P.O. Box 478, Juneau, AK 99802: Free information with long SASE ◆ Carved silver and gold bracelets and earrings. 907-586-9000.

### Arizona

**Arlene's Southwest Trading Company,** P.O. Box 340, Tombstone, AZ 85638: Free information ◆ Cards, prints, other art, baskets, kachinas, knives, jewelry, miniatures, rugs, weavings, wall hangings, sculptures, carvings, and other Native American crafts. 520-457-3344.

**Boucher Boys & the Indian,** 5230 Via Buena Vista, Paradise Valley, AZ 85253: Free information ◆ Native American blankets, pillows, and wall hangings. 602-948-2423.

**Bovis Bead Company,** P.O. Box 13345, Tucson, AZ 85732: Catalog $5 ◆ French glass beads and Native American craft supplies. 520-318-9512.

**John Christensen,** 2438 E. Fairmount, Phoenix, AZ 85016: Free information with long SASE ◆ Jewelry. 602-955-4722.

**Dancing Horses,** P.O. Box 30357, Mesa, AZ 85275: Catalog with 2 first class stamps ◆ Authentic hand-crafted American Indian collectibles, from dream catchers to tomahawks. 602-924-3226. www.galaxymall.com/shops/dancing_horses.html

**Honani Crafts Gallery,** P.O. Box 221, Second Mesa, AZ 86043: Free information with long SASE ◆ Honani silver jewelry, pottery, paintings, and baskets; Navajo rugs; and Zuni, Navajo, and Santa Domingo jewelry. 602-734-2238.

**Jay's of Tucson Inc.,** 4621 E. Speedway Blvd., Tucson, AZ 85712: Catalog $5 (refundable) ◆ Navajo, Hopi, and Zuni jewelry; southwestern gifts; Navajo rugs; Taos moccasins; drums and paintings; and Czech seed, pony, Peruvian, and other beads and findings. 602-294-3397.

**The Mercantile Company,** 2016 N. 4th St., Flagstaff, AZ 86004: Free catalog (specify supplies and findings or finished products) ◆ Sterling silver jewelry supplies, Native American arts and crafts, feathers, and leather supplies. 800-413-CHUCK.

**Skystone Creations,** 833 E. Broadway, Mesa, AZ 85204: Free catalog ◆ Authentic Native American jewelry. 602-964-1922.

**Teec Nos Pos Arts & Crafts,** Box 113, Teec Nos Pos, AZ 86514: Free catalog ◆ Baskets, beadwork, boxes, Christmas ornaments, dolls, jewelry, rugs, weavings, wall hangings, sandpaintings, sculptures, carvings, and other Native American crafts. 520-656-3228.

**The White Buffalo Stores Inc.,** 418 E. Beale, Kingman, AZ 86401: Catalog $1 (refundable) ◆ Arts and crafts, jewelry, kachinas, feathers, moccasins, music, books, craft supplies, and gifts. 520-753-7800. www.ctaz.com/~whitbuflo

## Arkansas

**Caddo Trading,** Box 669, Murfreesboro, AR 71958: Free list ◆ Native American artifacts, minerals, and fossils.

## California

**American Indian Art & Gift Shop,** 241 F St., Eureka, CA 95501: Free information ◆ Cards, prints, other art, baskets, beadwork, boxes, dolls, fetishes, jewelry, clothing, moccasins, head-dresses, dolls, miniatures, pottery, rugs, weavings, sculptures, carvings, sandpaintings, and other Native American crafts. 707-871-1858.

**Autry Museum of Western Heritage,** 4700 Western Heritage Way, Los Angeles, CA 90027: Free information ◆ Cards, prints, other art, baskets, beadwork, boxes, dolls, fetishes, jewelry, miniatures, pottery, rugs, weavings, sculptures, carvings, and other Native American crafts. 323-667-2000. www.autry-museum.org

**Black Eagle,** P.O. Box 621, Copperopolis, CA 95228: Free information with long SASE ◆ Cards, prints, other art, beadwork, clothing, moccasins, headdresses, drums, pipes, toma-hawks, jewelry, knives, and miniatures. 209-785-5259.

**De Luna Jewelers,** 521 2nd St., Davis, CA 95616: Free information with long SASE ◆ Pottery, Navajo rugs, jewelry, baskets, paintings, carvings, and beadwork. 916-753-3351.

**Eagle Wing Indian Art,** P.O. Box 1741, San Juan Capistrano, CA 92693: Free information ◆ Kachina dolls, pottery, jewelry, and other Native American art. 714-493-5760.

**Going-to-the-Sun Studio,** 1063 Hillendale Ct., Walnut Creek, CA 94596: Free information with long SASE ◆ Paintings, bas relief sculptures, tapestries, block-printed fabrics, drums, parfleche containers, dolls, beadwork, ribbon shirts, and shawls. 510-939-8803.

**Jamboree Jewelry,** 1501 E. Chapman, Ste. 245, Fullerton, CA 92631: Free catalog ◆ Contempo-rary handcrafted American Indian (Native American) jewelry. 714-996-5005.

**Karok Originals by Vit,** P.O. Box 3317, Eureka, CA 95502: Free information with long SASE ◆ Jewelry and wall hangings. 707-442-8800.

**Matoska Trading Company,** P.O. Box 2004, Yorba Linda, CA 92885: Catalog $3 ◆ Native American crafts and supplies, books, music, botanicals, flutes, ceremonial recordings, and more. 800-926-6286. sales@atoska.com

**Walt Moreau,** P.O. Box 14764, San Francisco, CA 94114: Catalog $7 ◆ Fine, rare, and unusual classic antique arms and Plains Indian (Native American) art. 415-861-8319. www.moreau.com

## Colorado

**Ben Nighthorse Campbell,** P.O. Box 639, Ignacio, CO 81137: Free information with long SASE ◆ Contemporary silver, gold, and silver jewelry inlaid with copper, brass, and German silver. 970-563-4623.

**Cliff Dweller,** P.O. Box 9, Cortez, CO 81321: Free catalog ◆ Cards, prints, other art, baskets, beadwork, children's items, clothing and moccasins, headdresses, dolls, jewelry, miniatures, sculptures, carvings, jewelry findings, and other Native American crafts. 303-565-3424.

**Steve Eagles,** Native American Regalia, 12335 Oregon Wagon Trail, Elbert, CO 80106: Catalog $3 ◆ Native American regalia, crafts, musical instruments, souvenirs, and more. 719-495-0798. Seagles254@aol.com

**Mesa Verde Pottery,** P.O. Box 9, Cortez, CO 81321: Free catalog ◆ Cards, prints, other art, baskets, beadwork, children's items, clothing and moccasins, headdresses, dolls, jewelry, miniatures, sculptures, carvings, pottery, storytellers, rugs, weavings, wall hangings, and other Native American crafts. 800-441-9908; 303-565-4492 (in CO).

**Navajo Manufacturing Company,** 5330 Fox St., Denver, CO 80216: Catalog $2 ◆ Handmade Navajo and Zuni jewelry. 800-625-5097. www.noblemotion.com

**Squash Blossom Colorado Springs,** 2531 W. Colorado, Colorado Springs, CO 80904: Free catalog ◆ Cards, prints, other art, baskets, beadwork, drums, pipes, tomahawks, fetishes, heishi, sandpaintings, kachinas, pottery, storytellers, rugs, weavings, wall hangings, jewelry, jewelry findings, miniatures, sculptures, carvings, and other Native American crafts. 719-632-1899.

**Squash Blossom Vail,** 198 Gore Creek Dr., Vail, CO 81657: Free catalog ◆ Cards, prints, other art, baskets, beadwork, children's items, clothing and moccasins, headdresses, drums, pipes, tomahawks, kachinas, pottery, storytellers, rugs, weavings, wall hangings, jewelry, miniatures, sculptures, carvings, and other Native American crafts. 303-476-3129.

**Toh-Atin Gallery,** P.O. Box 2329, Durango, CO 81301: Free catalog ◆ Cards, prints, other art, baskets, beadwork, books, boxes, children's items, Christmas ornaments, drums, pipes, tomahawks, fetishes, heishi, sandpaintings, kachinas, pottery, storytellers, rugs, weavings, wall hangings, jewelry, miniatures, sculptures, carvings, and other Native American crafts. 800-525-0384; 970-247-8277 (in CO).

## Florida

**Aboriginals: Art of the First Person,** 2340 Periwinkle Way, Sanibel, FL 33957: Free information ◆ Cards, prints, other art, baskets, beadwork, boxes, dolls, fetishes, jewelry, miniatures, pottery, rugs, weavings, sculptures, carvings, and other Native American crafts. 941-395-2200.

**Plains Indian Metalwork,** 2609 Mango Tree Dr., Edgewater, FL 32141: Free information ◆ Traditional, contemporary, and custom Plains Indian (Native American) metalwork. 904-428-8347.

**This N' That,** 204 Brevard Ave., Cocoa Village, FL 32922: Free information with long SASE ◆ Beadwork, jewelry, pottery, carvings, fetishes, baskets, moccasins, dolls, and Navajo rugs. 407-631-6609.

## Idaho

**The Dream Catcher of Idaho,** P.O. Box 6586, Ketchum, ID 83340: Free catalog ◆ Cards, prints, other art, baskets, beadwork, children's items, clothing and moccasins, headdresses, dolls, jewelry, miniatures, sculptures, carvings, jewelry findings, pottery, story tellers, and other Native American crafts. 208-726-1305.

**Kaibab Traditionals,** P.O. Box 955, Marsing, ID 83639: Free catalog ◆ Suede or smooth cowhide moccasins with bleached rawhide soles, clothing, jewelry, leather goods, and gifts. 888-524-2227.

## Illinois

**Bill & Kathy Brewer,** 203 Asbury Ave., Greenville, IL 62246: Price list $2 ◆ Reproduc-tions and restoration of Plains Indian (Native American) art. 618-664-3384.

**Native American Art Gallery Ltd.,** 810 W. Dempster, Evanston, IL 60202: Free catalog ◆ Cards, prints, other art, baskets, beadwork, clothing, moccasins, headdresses, dolls, jewelry, miniatures, sculptures, carvings, pottery, storytellers, and other Native American crafts. 708-864-0400.

**Two Bears Trading,** P.O. Box 347, Wonder Lake, IL 60097: Catalog $2 ◆ Native American arts and crafts, artifacts, gifts, and beadwork. 815-653-1045. www.twobearz.com

## Maine

**Basket Bank,** Aroostook Micmac Council Inc., 8 Church St., Presque Isle, ME 04769: Free brochure with long SASE ◆ Potato, pack, clothes, fishing, decorative, shopping, cradle, and sewing baskets. 207-764-1972.

**The Center of Native Art,** Rt. 1, Woolwich, ME 04579: Free catalog ◆ Cards, prints, other art, baskets, beadwork, children's items, clothing and moccasins, headdresses, dolls, jewelry, miniatures, sculptures, carvings, jewelry findings, rugs and weavings, and other Native American crafts. 602-688-2603.

**Wabanaki Arts,** RR 2, Box 3390, Dexter, ME 04930: Free price list with long SASE ◆ Carved Penobscot canes, war clubs, totem poles, stone tomahawks, baskets, beadwork, and quill work. 207-278-3584.

**Wilderness Crafts,** 3 Andrews Rd., Bath, ME 04530: Price list $1 ◆ Drums, sage, beads, and other Native American crafts and supplies. 207-442-8447.

## Maryland

**Jewelry by Avery,** 5134 Chalk Point Rd., West River, MD 20778: Free information with long SASE ◆ Kachinas, Native American art, precious and semi-precious gemstones, mineral specimens, and handcrafted Zuni, Navajo, and Hopi turquoise jewelry. 410-867-4752.

## Massachusetts

**Firehawk Native American Studio,** P.O. Box 60337, Florence, MA 01060: Free catalog ◆ Beadwork, clothing, moccasins, headdresses, drums, pipes, tomahawks, jewelry, knives, pottery, storytellers, and other Native American gifts. 413-586-5131.

**The Wandering Bull,** 247 S. Main St., Attleboro, MA 02703: Free catalog ◆ Leather goods, art prints, musical instruments, jewelry, beads and beading supplies, pipes and tomahawks, and gifts. 800-430-2855. www.wanderingbull.com

## Minnesota

**Karen Floan,** 1535 Willard Ave., Detroit Lakes, MN 56501: Free catalog ◆ Beadwork, clothing, moccasins, and headdresses. 218-846-9911.

**Gems by Jak,** 113 Sherman St., Ihlen, MN 56140: Free catalog ◆ Plains Indian (Native American) peace pipes and other gifts. 507-348-8617.

**Lady Slipper Designs,** RR 3, Box 556, Bemidji, MN 56601: Free information with long SASE ◆ Beaded charms, moccasins, birch bark birdhouses, crafts, and birch bark, willow, and black ash baskets. 800-950-5903.

**Manitok Food & Gifts,** P.O. Box 97, Callaway, MN 56521: Free brochure ◆ Gift assortments of chokeberry syrup, jellies, wild rice, pancake mix jelly, and other specialties in birch bark baskets. 800-726-1863.

**Stormcloud Trading,** 725 Snelling Ave. North, St. Paul, MN 55104: Free catalog ◆ Native American arts and crafts supplies. 612-645-0343.

## Mississippi

**Choctaw Museum,** P.O. Box 6010, Philadelphia, MS 39350: Free brochure ◆ Books, videos, and cassette tapes about the Choctaw Indians (Native American) for adults and children. Also Choctaw cane baskets, beaded crafts, handmade dolls, and souvenirs. 601-650-1685.

## Missouri

**Navajo Trading Company,** 3562 Shepherd of the Hills Expwy., Branson, MO 65616: Free information ◆ Native American crafts and jewelry. 17-339-3601.

## Montana

**Doug Allard's Trading Post & Museum,** P.O. Box 460, St. Ignatius, MT 59865: Free catalog ◆ Cards, prints, other art, baskets, beadwork, children's items, clothing and moccasins, headdresses, dolls, jewelry, miniatures, sculptures, carvings, jewelry findings, and other Native American crafts. 406-745-2951.

**Bruce P. Contway,** P.O. Box 920, Whitehall, MT 59759: Free catalog ◆ Drums, pipes, tomahawks, jewelry, miniatures, pottery, story tellers, nativity sets, jewelry supplies and findings, stones, and shells. 406-287-5122.

**Jay Contway,** 434 McIver Rd., Great Falls, MT 59404: Free catalog ◆ Cards, prints, other art, jewelry, rugs, weavings, wall hangings, sculptures, and carvings. 406-452-7647.

**Four Winds Indian Trading Post,** P.O. Box 580, St. Ignatius, MT 59865: Catalog $3 ◆ American Indian (Native American) artifacts. 406-745-4336.

**K & M Creations,** P.O. Box 521, St. Ignatius, MT 59865: Brochure $3 ◆ Beadwork and quill work. 405-745-4186. www.montana.com/k&m

**Harvey Rattey,** P.O. Box 1184, Glendive, MT 59330: Free catalog ◆ Miniatures, sculptures, and carvings. 406-365-8505.

## Nevada

**Arnold Aragon Sculpture & Illustration,** Box 64, Schurz, NV 89427: Free information with long SASE ◆ Stone sculptures, drawings, and paintings. 702-773-2542.

## New Jersey

**Adobe East Gallery,** 445 Springfield Ave., Summit, NJ 07901: Free information ◆ Cards, prints, other art, baskets, kachinas, knives, jewelry, miniatures, rugs, weavings, wall hangings, sculptures, carvings, and other Native American crafts. 908-277-1483.

## New Mexico

**Andy & Robert Abeita,** 12 Chaparral Ln., Peralta, NM 87042: Free catalog ◆ Drums, pipes, tomahawks, fetishes, jewelry, sculptures and carvings, and knives. 505-869-8148.

**Adla Southwest,** P.O. Box 82130, Albuquerque, NM 87108: Free catalog ◆ Jewelry. 505-254-1157.

**AI-SE-TE-WA Traders,** P.O. Box 652, Zuni, NM 87327: Free information ◆ Fetishes, jewelry, sculptures, and carvings. 505-870-7108.

**Ancient Mesas Gifts Southwestern,** P.O. Box 220, Grants, NM 87020: Free information ◆ Cards, prints, other art, baskets, kachinas, knives, jewelry, miniatures, rugs, weavings, wall hangings, sculptures, carvings, and other Native American crafts.

**Arroyo Trading Company,** 2111 W. Apache St., Farmington, NM 87401: Free catalog ◆ Cards, prints, other art, beadwork, pottery, storytellers, and sandpaintings. 505-326-7427.

**Atkinson Trading Company,** P.O. Box 566, Gallup, NM 87305: Free information ◆ Drums, pipes, tomahawks, jewelry, knives, pottery, storytellers, rugs, weavings, and wall hangings. 505-722-4435.

**Carolyn Bobelue,** 731 Krevin Ct., Gallup, NM 87301: Free information with long SASE ◆ Jewelry. 505-722-4939.

**Foutz Trading Company,** P.O. Box 1894, Shiprock, NM 97420: Free catalog ◆ Baskets, beadwork, children's items, Christmas ornaments, dolls, sandpaintings, and other Native American crafts. 800-383-0615; 505-368-5790 (in NM).

**Cliff Fragua,** P.O. Box 250, Jemez Pueblo, NM 87024: Free catalog ◆ Pottery, storytellers, nativity sets, sculptures, and carvings. 505-892-6516.

**Gowen Arts Galore,** 303 Romero NW, Ste. 205, Albuquerque, NM 87104: Free catalog ◆ Baskets, beadwork, children's items, clothing and moccasins, headdresses, dolls, jewelry, miniatures, sculptures, carvings, sandpaintings, and other Native American crafts. 505-242-4113.

**Grandfather Eagle,** 202-A San Felipe NW, Albuquerque, NM 87104: Free catalog ◆ Baskets, beadwork, children's items, knives, pottery, rugs and weavings, wall hangings, jewelry, miniatures, sculptures, carvings, sandpaintings, and other Native American crafts. 505-242-5376.

**Brad Hawiyeh-ehi,** Cherokee Artist/Craftsman, 33 Calle Cintmoon, Edgewood, NM 87015: Information $2 ◆ Painted gourds with ancient cultural designs. Includes Woodland Plains and Pueblo motifs. 505-286-4159. Hawiyehehi@aol.com

**Nussie & Ronnie Henry,** P.O. Box 496, Crownpoint, NM 87313: Free information with long SASE ◆ Jewelry. 505-786-5678.

**Many Nations,** 46 Burnham St., Silver City, NM 88061: Catalog $5 (refundable) ◆ Cards, prints, other art, beadwork, sculptures, carvings, jewelry, miniatures, pottery, storytellers, rugs, weavings, wall hangings, and other Native American crafts. 800-420-1233; 505-638-2471 (in NM).

**Mary Laura's,** 3636 San Mateo Blvd. NE, Albuquerque, NM 87110: Catalog $2 ◆ Native American jewelry from the Zuni Pueblo. 800-662-4848.

**Teresita Naranjo,** Santa Clara Pueblo, Rt. 1, Box 455, Espanola, NM 87532: Free information with long SASE ◆ Santa Clara black and red pottery. 505-753-9655.

**Oke Oweenge Arts & Crafts,** P.O. Box 1095, San Juan Pueblo, NM 87566: Catalog $3 ◆ Wall hangings, pillows, pottery, dolls, beadwork, silver jewelry, baskets, paintings, and ceremonial mantas, shirts, sashes, vests, and blouses. 505-852-2372.

**Roger & Sharon Perdasofpy,** P.O. Box 682, Zuni, NM 87327: Free information with long SASE ◆ Beadwork, Christmas ornaments, drums, pipes, headdresses, and jewelry. 405-357-1882.

**Pueblo of Zuni Arts & Crafts,** P.O. Box 425, Zuni, NM 87327: Free catalog ◆ Cards, prints, other art, baskets, beadwork, children's items, clothing and moccasins, headdresses, dolls, jewelry, miniatures, sculptures, carvings, jewelry findings, and other Native American crafts. 505-782-5531.

**Pueblo Pottery,** P.O. Box 366, San Fidel, NM 87049: Free catalog ◆ Cards, prints, other art, Christmas ornaments, baskets, beadwork, clothing and moccasins, headdresses, jewelry, miniatures, sculptures, carvings, fetishes, kachinas, pottery, storytellers, rugs, weavings, wall hangings, and other Native American crafts.

**Silver Nugget,** 416 Juan Tabo NE, Albuquerque, NM 87123: Catalog $2 ◆ Native American jewelry. 800-343-9380. www.silver-nugget.com

**Southwest Indian Foundation,** P.O. Box 86, Gallup, NM 87302: Free catalog ◆ Navajo, Zuni, and Laguna crafts and gifts. 505-726-8329.

**Tecolote Tiles & Gallery Ltd.,** 303 Romero NW, Albuquerque, NM 87104: Free catalog ◆ Native American arts and crafts. 505-243-3403.

**Towa Arts & Crafts-Pueblo of Jemez,** P.O. Box 100, Jemez Pueblo, NM 87024: Free catalog ◆ Cards, prints, other art, books, Christmas ornaments, dolls, rugs, weavings, wall hangings, and other Native American crafts. 505-834-7235.

**Ray Tracey,** P.O. Box 443, Gallup, NM 87305: Free catalog ◆ Jewelry. 505-883-8868.

**Trade Roots,** 411 Paseo de Peralta, Santa Fe, NM 87501: Free catalog ◆ Fetishes, jewelry, miniatures, sculptures, carvings, jewelry findings, and other Native American crafts. 505-982-8168.

**Ron Upshaw,** 4113 Hermosa NE, Albuquerque, NM 87110: Free information with long SASE ◆ Fetishes, clothing, moccasins, headdresses, knives, miniatures, sculptures, and carvings. 505-884-6476.

**Virginia Yazzie-Ballenger,** P.O. Box 1282, Gallup, NM 87305: Free catalog ◆ Children's items, clothing, moccasins, and headdresses. 800-377-6837.

**Zuni Craftsmen Cooperative Association,** P.O. Box 426, Zuni, NM 87327: Information $2 with long SASE ◆ Zuni silver and turquoise jewelry, beadwork, fetishes, pottery, and paintings. 505-782-4425.

## New York

**Grey Owl Indian Craft Sales Corp.,** P.O. Box 468, 132-05 Merrick Blvd., Jamaica, NY 11434: Catalog $3 ◆ Native American craft supplies. 718-341-4000.

**Seneca-Iroquois National Museum Gift Shop,** Broad St., Salamanca, NY 14779: Free price list with long SASE ◆ Iroquois beadwork, baskets, false face masks, cornhusk masks and dolls, rattles, wampum and scrimshaw jewelry, leather crafts, ribbon shirts, and pottery. 716-945-1738.

**Tuskewe Krafts,** 2089 Upper Mountain Rd., Sanborn, NY 14132: Free brochure with long SASE ◆ Women and men's field and box lacrosse sticks. 716-297-1821.

## North Carolina

**Haliwa-Saponi Tribal Pottery & Arts,** P.O. Box 99, Hollister, NC 27844: Free price list with long SASE ◆ Pottery, quilts, beadwork, woodwork, and stonework. 919-586-4017.

**Lace & Things,** Hwy. 441, Whittier, NC 28789: Free price list ◆ Native American craft supplies and jewelry. 704-586-9500.

**Qualla Arts & Crafts,** Box 310, Cherokee, NC 28719: Free brochure with long SASE ◆ Animal figurines, wood carvings, masks, beadwork, pottery, dolls, metalwork, and river cane, oak splint, storytellers, sculptures, carvings, and baskets. 704-497-3103.

## Ohio

**American Indian Arts & Crafts,** 3547 Raymar Dr., Cincinnati, OH 45208: Free information ◆ Cards, prints, other art, baskets, beadwork, children's items, clothing and moccasins, headdresses, dolls, jewelry, miniatures, sculptures, carvings, jewelry findings, and other Native American crafts. 513-871-1858.

**American Silver from the Southwest,** 5700 Frederick Rd., Dayton, OH 45414: Free information ◆ Native American and contemporary jewelry, pottery, and kachinas. 937-890-0138.

## Oklahoma

**Jean E. Bales,** P.O. Box 193, Cookson, OK 74427: Free information with long SASE ◆ Prints, cards, other art, Christmas ornaments, miniatures, sculptures, and carvings. 918-457-4003.

**Buffalo Sun,** 122 N. Main St., Miami, OK 74354: Free information with long SASE ◆ Native American blouses, skirts, ribbon shirts, dresses, jackets, vests, coats, moccasins, belts, shawls, and jewelry. 918-542-8870.

**Cherokee National Museum Gift Shop,** P.O. Box 515, TSA-LA-GI, Tahlequah, OK 74464: Free price list with long SASE ◆ Baskets, weapons, paintings, prints, and sculptures. 918-456-6007.

**Gilcrease Museum Shop,** 1400 Gilcrease Museum Rd., Tulsa, OK 74127: Free catalog ◆ Baskets, beadwork, children's items, clothing and moccasins, headdresses, dolls, jewelry, miniatures, sculptures, carvings, sandpaintings, and other Native American crafts.

**Greg Gray,** P.O. Box 818, Bartlesville, OK 74005: Free catalog ◆ Books, music, educational materials, and jewelry. 918-336-0049.

**Enoch Kelley Haney Art Gallery,** P.O. Box 72, Seminole, OK 74868: Free brochure with long SASE ◆ Original paintings and prints, sculptures, and carvings. 405-382-3369.

**Robert Kaniatobe,** 431 W. Tennessee St., Durant, OK 74701: Free information with long SASE ◆ Beadwork, fetishes, jewelry, pottery, storytellers, sculptures, and carvings.

**Ted Miller Custom Knives,** Rt. 2, Box 242, Vinita, OK 74301: Free catalog ◆ Wood and horn carvings, deer horn pipes, elk horn belt buckles, bolos, and knives with hand-tooled steel blades in elk, stag horn, or bone handles. 800-984-0337; 918-782-4312 (in OK).

**Mister Indian's Cowboy Store,** 1000 S. Main, Sapulpa, OK 74066: Free information with long SASE ◆ Moccasins, fans, shawls, beadwork, ribbon shirts, rugs, pottery, purses, cradle boards, drums, dolls, silver and turquoise jewelry, and paintings. 918-224-6511.

**The Swimmer Collection of American Indian Art,** 1560 E. 21st St., Tulsa, OK 74114: Free information ◆ Limited edition American Indian (Native American) arts and crafts. 800-926-5892. www.swimmercollection.com

**Tah-Mels,** P.O. Box 1123, Tahlequah, OK 74465: Free information with long SASE ◆ Dolls, beadwork, baskets, quilts, and Oochelata pink mussel shell, silver, and gold jewelry. Also oil and watercolor paintings and wood carvings. 918-456-5451.

**Tiger Art Gallery,** 2110 E. Shawnee St., Muskogee, OK 74403: Free information with long SASE ◆ Paintings and sculptures. 918-687-7006.

**Touching Leaves Indian Crafts,** 927 Portland Ave., Dewey, OK 74029: Catalog $1 ◆ Beadwork, German silver jewelry, and leather crafts. 918-534-2859.

## Oregon

**Jim Bond Native American Music,** 35113 Brewster Rd., Lebanon, OR 97355: Catalog $1 ◆ Native American flute music and ceremonial supplies. 541-258-3645.

**Ed's House of Gems,** 7712 NE Sandy Blvd., Portland, OR 97211: Free information with long SASE ◆ Clocks, clock-making parts, minerals, gemstones, lapidary equipment, mountings, shells, jewelry, and Native American relics. 503-284-8990.

**Quintana's Gallery of Indian & Western Art,** 501 SW Broadway, Portland, OR 97205: Free information with long SASE ◆ Northwest Coast art, contemporary western paintings, bronze sculptures, and antique and contemporary Native American art from over 300 tribes. 503-223-1729.

**Spotted Horse Tribal Gifts,** Diane McAlister, P.O. Box 869, Oakridge, OR 97463: Catalog $2 ◆ Native American craft-making kits, tools, patterns, cassette tapes, books, and crafts.

**Nadine Van Mechelen,** Rt. 1, Box 270, Pendleton, OR 97801: Free information with long SASE ◆ Handmade dolls in authentic Native American costumes. 541-276-2566.

## Pennsylvania

**Southwest Visions,** 36 W. Mechanic St., New Hope, PA 18938: Free catalog ◆ Cards, prints, other art, baskets, beadwork, children's items, clothing and moccasins, headdresses, children's items, drums, pipes, tomahawks, kachinas, pottery, storytellers, rugs, weavings, wall hangings, jewelry, miniatures, sculptures, carvings, and other Native American crafts. 215-862-0323.

## South Carolina

**Canyon Road,** 1314 Celebrity Circle, Myrtle Beach, SC 29577: Free catalog ◆ Cards, prints, other art, beadwork, baskets, dolls, drums, pipes, tomahawks, jewelry, pottery, sculptures, carvings, sandpaintings, and other Native American crafts. 800-622-8202; 803-448-4880 (in SC).

**Western Visions,** 4728 C Hwy. 17 South, North Myrtle Beach, SC 29582: Free catalog ◆ Cards, prints, other art, baskets, beadwork, books, music, educational materials, boxes, children's items, Christmas ornaments, clothing, moccasins, sandpaintings, headdresses, dolls, drums, pipes, tomahawks, sculptures, carvings, and other Native American crafts. 800-745-5691; 803-272-2698 (in SC).

**Wolf Creek Gallery,** 1315 Celebrity Circle, Myrtle Beach, SC 29577: Free catalog ◆ Cards, prints, other art, baskets, beadwork, books, music, educational materials, boxes, children's items, Christmas ornaments, clothing, moccasins, headdresses, dolls, drums, pipes, tomahawks, sculptures, carvings, and other Native American crafts. 800-664-0484; 803-448-4780 (in SC).

## South Dakota

**Creations by Lauren,** 921 Rosilee Ln., Rapid City, SD 57701: Catalog $2 (refundable) ◆ Custom handmade beaded clothing and accessories in traditional Native American style. Also moccasins, knife cases, war shirts, dresses, and other crafts.

**The Lakota Fund,** P.O. Box 340, Kyle, SD 57752: Free information ◆ Baskets, beadwork, children's items, clothing and moccasins, headdresses, dolls, jewelry, miniatures, sculptures, carvings, sandpaintings, and other Native American crafts. 605-455-2555.

**Prairie Edge,** P.O. Box 8303, Rapid City, SD 57709: Catalog $5 ◆ Native American artifacts and collectibles. 605-341-4525.

**Rings 'N' Things,** P.O. Box 360, Mission, SD 57555: Free information with long SASE ◆ Silver gifts, quill work, and beadwork. 605-856-4548.

**Sioux Pottery & Crafts,** 2209 Hwy. 79 South, Rapid City, SD 57701: Free catalog ◆ Beadwork, Christmas ornaments, clothing, moccasins, headdresses, dolls, drums, pipes, tomahawks, jewelry, knives, pottery, storytellers, sculptures, carvings, and other Native American crafts. 800-657-4366; 605-341-3657 (in SD).

**Sioux Trading Post Inc.,** 415 6th St., Rapid City, SD 57701: Catalog $2 ◆ Craft supplies, beads and beadwork, quill work, T-shirts and sweatshirts, books, tapes and CDs, botanicals, moccasins, and crafts. 800-456-3394. www.prairieedge.com

## Texas

**Crazy Crow Trading Post,** P.O. Box 847, Pottsboro, TX 75076; Catalog $2 ◆ Silver items, moccasins, beadwork, and reproduction eagle feather war bonnets. 800-786-6210; 903-786-2287 (in TX). www.texoma.com/cctp

**Eagle Dancer,** 159 Gulf Freeway South, League City, TX 77573: Free information with long SASE ◆ Leather work, paintings, wood carvings, sculptures, jewelry, pottery, rugs, dolls, and other crafts. 281-332-6028.

**Gift Gallery Catalog,** 5955 Phelan, Beaumont, TX 77706: Catalog $3 ◆ Native America style art and museum-quality recreated artifacts. 409-866-4451.

**Donald E. Greenwood,** c/o Fetch & Send, 10414 Autumn Meadow Ln., Houston, TX 77064: Free catalog ◆ Jewelry.

**Scott-Wynne Outfitters,** 10000 Research Blvd., Ste. 127, Austin, TX 78759: Free catalog ◆ Outdoor and casual clothing, luggage, hunting and fishing accessories, and Native American jewelry. 800-232-2783. www.outfits.com

## Utah

**Eagle Feather Trading Post,** 168 W. 12th St., Ogden, UT 84404: Catalog $3.50 ◆ Native American craft supplies, beads and bead-stringing kits, and how-to beading and craft books. 801-393-3991.

**Victor Ha Reece,** 3183 Hammonton Circle, Apt. B, West Valley City, UT 84119: Free information with long SASE ◆ Carvings. 801-975-7533.

## Washington

**Betty David,** 105 S. Main St., #325, Seattle, WA 98104: Catalog information online ◆ Native-made shearling coats for women handpainted in the Northwest Coast Indian style. 805-682-5175.

**Troy De Roche,** P.O. Box 490, Chimacum, WA 98325: Free catalog ◆ Books, music, flutes, and Native American artifacts and reproductions. 360-732-4279.

**Feathermakers,** Jerry & Karen Snyder, 1090 Kitt Narcisse Rd., Colville, WA 99114: Catalog $2 ◆ Handpainted and custom made reproduction eagle tail feathers. Also beadwork, bonnets, bustles, and more. 509-684-3210.

**Laura Louise Leverich "Skybear",** 9811 NE 90th Ave., Vancouver, WA 98662: Free information with long SASE ◆ Beadwork, children's items, Christmas ornaments, clothing, moccasins, headdresses, and jewelry. 360-254-3227.

**Makah Cultural Research Center,** P.O. Box 160, Neah Bay, WA 98357: Free price list with long SASE ◆ Woven baskets, replicas of archaeological artifacts, carved wood masks, totem poles, rattles and bowls, shell jewelry, engraved silver bracelets, miniature basket earrings, painted drums, beadwork, and original serigraphs. 360-645-2711.

**Meg Orr,** P.O. Box 4188, Omac, WA 98841: Free catalog ◆ Cards, prints, other art, baskets, beadwork, books, music, educational materials, boxes, children's items, Christmas ornaments, clothing, moccasins, headdresses, dolls, drums, pipes, tomahawks, miniatures, sculptures, and carvings. 509-826-0904.

**Suquamish Museum,** P.O. Box 498, Suquamish, WA 98392: Free information with long SASE ◆ Suquamish/Puget Sound Salish clam baskets, dolls, whistles, museum replicas, wood bowls, spoons, canoe bailers, and wood carvings. 360-598-3311.

## Wisconsin

**American Indian Gift Store,** 132 Main St., Box 73, Hayward, WI 54843: Free information ◆ Baskets, beadwork, children's items, clothing and moccasins, headdresses, dolls, jewelry, miniatures, sculptures, carvings, jewelry findings, and other Native American crafts. 715-634-2655.

**Reflection of Culture,** P.O. Box 104, 145 W. Main St., Cambridge, WI 53523: Free catalog ◆ Cards, prints, other art, baskets, beadwork, books, music, educational materials, boxes, children's items, Christmas ornaments, clothing, moccasins, headdresses, dolls, drums, pipes, tomahawks, miniatures, sculptures, and carvings.

**Wa-Swa-Gon Arts & Crafts,** P.O. Box 477, Lac du Flambeau, WI 54538: Free information with long SASE ◆ Beadwork, birch bark items, moccasins, finger weavings, traditional and ceremonial clothes, and carvings. 715-588-7636.

**Winnebago Indian Museum,** P.O. Box 441, Wisconsin Dells, WI 53965: Price list $1 ◆ Winnebago baskets, beadwork, deerskin products, pottery, Navajo rugs, and silver items. 608-254-2268.

## Wyoming

**La Ray Turquoise Company,** P.O. Box 83, Cody, WY 82414: Free information with long SASE ◆ Navajo rugs, Ojibwa beadwork, and Navajo, Zuni, Chippewa, and Hopi silver items. 307-587-9564.

**Tecumseh's Frontier Trading Post,** 140 W. Yellowstone Ave., Cody, WY 82414: Catalog $4 ◆ Handmade Native American and cowboy frontiersman's buckskin clothing, moccasins, ceremonial items, headdresses, and more. 307-587-5362.

**Warbonnet,** P.O. Box 3494, Jackson, WY 83001: Free catalog ◆ Cards, prints, other art, baskets, beadwork, books, music, educational materials, boxes, children's items, Christmas ornaments, clothing, moccasins, headdresses, dolls, drums, pipes, tomahawks, miniatures, sculptures, and carvings. 800-950-0154; 307-733-6158 (in WY).

### Canada

**Guy Du Sault,** 630 Atrironta, Wendake, Quebec, Canada G0A 4V0: Free catalog ◆ Clothing, moccasins, and headdresses. 418-847-3332.

**Turtle Island Trading Company,** 3516-114 St., Edmonton, Alberta, Canada T6J 1L7: Free catalog ◆ Cards, prints, other art, baskets, beadwork, clothing, moccasins, headdresses, boxes, knives, rugs, weavings, wall hangings, drums, pipes, tomahawks, miniatures, sculptures, and carvings. 403-488-9103.

## INTERCOMS

**Doorking,** 120 Glasgow Ave., Inglewood, CA 90301: Free information ◆ Telephone entry and access control systems. 800-826-7493. www.doorking.com

**Interactive Technologies Inc.,** 2266 N. 2nd St., St. Paul, MN 55109: Free information ◆ Telephone-based home security systems. 612-777-2690.

**JDS Technologies,** 16750 W. Bernardo Dr., San Diego, CA 92127: Free information ◆ Telephone-based home security systems and remote controls for computers, lights, and other devices. 800-983-5537; 619-487-8787 (in CA). www.jdstechnologies.com/index.html

**M & S Systems Inc.,** 2861 Congressman Ln., Dallas, TX 75220: Free information ◆ Intercom with door chimes and release. 800-877-6631.

**NuTone Inc.,** P.O. Box 1580, Cincinnati, OH 45201: Catalog $3 ◆ Video door-answering system with voice transmission over telephones and a wireless security system that can be zone programmed. 800-543-8687. www.nutone.com

**Paladin Electronics,** 19425 Soledad Cyn Rd., Ste. 333, Canyon Country, CA 91351: Free information ◆ Talking security systems. 805-251-8725.

**Siedle Communication System,** 750 Parkway, Broomall, PA 19008: Free information ◆ Video intercom systems. 800-874-3353.

**Talk-A-Phone,** 5013 N. Kedzie Ave., Chicago, IL 60625: Free information ◆ Intercoms for two-way conversation with optional integration with a master system. 773-539-1100. www.talkaphone.com

## JAPANESE LANTERNS

**Japanese Lanterns,** P.O. Box 2791, Tupelo, MS 38803: Free information ◆ Weatherproof Japanese lantern kits.

**Studio Gerald Corbeil,** 704 Lytle St., West Palm Beach, FL 33405: Free brochure ◆ Handcarved featherlight lava rock Japanese lanterns and water basins. 561-586-4398.

## JET SKIS (PERSONAL WATERCRAFT) & TRAILERS

**Arizona Jet Ski Center,** 2430 E. Danbury, Phoenix, AZ 85032: Free information ◆ Jet skis. 800-245-3875.

**Bert's Wholesale,** 900 W. Foothill Blvd., Azusa, CA 91702: Free catalog ◆ Personal watercraft accessories. 800-367-9464; 800-237-8159 (in CA).

**Butch's Jet Ski,** 7357 Expressway Ct., Ste. A, Grand Rapids, MI 49548: Free information ◆ Jet skis. 800-54-BUTCH.

**Castaic Ski and Sport,** 32203 Castaic Rd., Castaic, CA 91384: Free catalog ◆ Personal watercraft and accessories. 805-257-3033.

**Competition Accessories Inc.,** 345 W. Leffel Ln., Springfield, OH 45506: Catalog $5 ◆ Personal watercraft accessories. 800-543-4709.

**Davit Master,** 5560 Ulmerton Rd., Clearwater, FL 34620: Free information ◆ Personal watercraft lift systems. 800-878-5560.

**DCT Sports,** 4060 Palm, Ste. 602, Fullerton, CA 92635: Free information with long SASE ◆ Personal watercraft. 714-526-8415.

**DG Performance Specialties Inc.,** 1230 La Loma Circle, Anaheim, CA 92806: Free catalog ◆ Performance parts and accessories for all-terrain vehicles and personal watercraft. 800-854-9134; 714-630-5471 (in CA).

**Follansbee Dock Systems,** P.O. Box 640, Follansbee, WV 26037: Free information ◆ Personal watercraft lifts in easy-to-assemble kits. Also floating and stationary docks, building components, and accessories. 800-223-3444; 304-527-4500 (in WV). www.foldocks.lbcorp.com

**Intraser Inc.,** 428 N. La Cienega Blvd., Los Angeles, CA 90048: Free information ◆ New and pre-owned motorcycles, ATVs, snowmobiles, trailers, personal water vehicles, and small boats. 213-652-6966.

**Jet-Dolly Inc.,** 4208 Gravois Ave., St. Louis, MO 63116: Free information ◆ Dollies for personal watercraft. 800-564-2929.

**Jet Express,** 111 W. C St., Encinata, CA 92024: Free catalog ◆ Personal watercraft accessories. 800-538-3977.

**Jetinetics Jet Ski,** 357 S. Acacia Ave., Fullerton, CA 92631: Free catalog ◆ Personal watercraft, parts, and tools. 714-525-9930. www.jetinetics.com

**Kawasaki Motors Corp.,** 9950 Jeronimo Rd., Irvine, CA 92619: Free list of retail sources ◆ One and two-person jet skis. 714-770-0400. www.kawasaki.com

**KG Industries,** 140 Pacific Dr., Quakertown, PA 18951: Free information ◆ Personal watercraft. 800-531-4252. www.kwikgoal.com

**Dennis Kirk Inc.,** 955 Southfield Ave., Rush City, MN 55069: Free catalog ◆ Personal watercraft. 800-328-9280.

**Polaris Industries,** 1225 Hwy. 169 North, Minneapolis, MN 55441: Free list of retail sources ◆ Personal watercraft and wetsuits. 800-POLARIS; 612-542-0500 (in MN). www.polarisusa.com

**Porta Dock Inc.,** 175 3rd St., P.O. Box 409, Dassel, MN 55325: Information $1 ◆ Single and double personal watercraft and boat lifts. 320-275-3304.

**PSI Performance,** P.O. Box 72, Wild Rose, WI 54984: Catalog $4 ◆ Personal watercraft engines, specialty kits, and sand painting accessories. 414-622-4555.

**Recreation Unlimited,** 1021 W. Taft Ave., Orange, CA 92665: Free information ◆ Personal watercraft accessories. 800-472-3754.

**Riva-Yamaha,** 3801 N. Dixie Hwy., Pompano Beach, FL 33064: Free catalog ◆ Yamaha watercraft and parts. 800-241-4544.

**Rossier Engineering,** 1340 Okray Ave., Plover, WI 54467: Free information ◆ Personal watercraft and accessories. 715-341-9919.

**Sea-Doo,** Bombardier Motor Corp. Of America, 7575 Bombardier, Wausau, WI 54402: Free information ◆ Personal watercraft. 800-882-2900. Sea-Doo@Sea-Doo.com

**Shorelander,** Division Midwest Industries Inc., P.O. Box 235, Ida Grove, IA 51445: Free information ◆ Personal watercraft trailers. 712-364-3365.

**Solas USA Inc.,** 15998 NW 49th Ave., Miami, FL 33014: Free information ◆ Personal watercraft. 305-625-4389.

**Tigershark Watercraft,** South Brooks Ave., Thief River Falls, MN 56701: Free information ◆ Personal watercraft and wetsuits. 218-681-4999. www.arctic-cat.com

**Top Gun Racing,** Rt. 122 South, P.O. Box 429, Wirtz, VA 24184: Free information ◆ Jet ski parts. 540-721-4900.

**Bob Traceys World of Cycles,** 604 Narrows Run Rd., Moon Township, PA 15108: Free information ◆ Parts for Suzuki dirt and street bikes, ATVs, and watercraft. 800-860-0686. www.partswarehouse.com

**VM Custom Boat Trailers,** 5200 S. Peach Ave., Fresno, CA 93725: Free information ◆ Jet ski trailers. 209-486-0410.

**Warner's Dock Inc.,** 928 N. Knowles Ave., New Richmond, WI 54017: Free information ◆ Personal watercraft gear and parts. 800-292-1760.

**WetJet International Ltd.,** 100 Cherokee Cove, Venore, TN 37885: Free information ◆ Personal watercraft and clothing. 800-2-WETJET.

**Yamaha Motor Corp.,** P.O. Box 6555, Cypress, CA 90630: Free list of retail sources ◆ One and two-person jet skis. 800-526-6650. www.yamahausa.com

## JEWELRY

**A.R.C. Traders Inc.,** Box 3429, Scottsdale, AZ 85257: Free information ◆ Findings, chains, earrings, jewelry, and sterling silver, gold-filled, and 14k gold beads. 800-528-2374; 602-945-0769 (in AZ).

**American Pearl,** 25 W. 47th St., New York, NY 10036: Free catalog ◆ Imported cultured and South Sea pearls. 800-84-PEARL.

**American Silver from the Southwest,** 5700 Frederick Rd., Dayton, OH 45414: Free information ◆ Native American and contemporary jewelry, pottery, and kachinas. 937-890-0138.

**Antiquewear,** 82 Front St., Marblehead, MA 01945: Free brochure ◆ Jewelry fashioned from original antique buttons of the 1800s. 781-639-0070. www.shore.net/~antiquew

**Arizona Traders,** 1104 E. San Antonio, El Paso, TX 79901: Free price list ◆ Native American mandellas and handmade turquoise and silver jewelry. 800-351-1674; 915-544-7692 (in AZ).

**Arrow Gems & Minerals Inc.,** 9827 Cave Creek Rd., Phoenix, AZ 85020: Free catalog ◆ Pewter figurines, pendants, buckles, beads and findings, mineral specimens, and faceted gemstones. 602-997-6373.

**Art de Corps,** 6018 NE Bothell Way, Ste. 173, Seattle, WA 98155: Free brochure ◆ Original classic-styled bead and pearl jewelry and eyeglass holders. 206-361-1498.

**Gary Arthur Accessories Inc.,** P.O. Box 1655, Attleboro, MA 02703: Free catalog ◆ Sterling silver and 14k gold jewelry. 800-675-9762.

**Artistic Judaic Promotions,** 4990 S. Lafayette Ln., Englewood, CO 80110: Free information ◆ Handmade jewelry, Judaica, art, and ketubot. 303-789-3879. ajpi@ixnetcom.com

**Atocha Treasure Company,** 20710 Persimmon Pl., Estero, FL 33928: Free brochure ◆ Reproduction shipwreck coins in jewelry settings. 800-650-9030; 941-936-2884 (in FL). www.netcom.com/~coinkeny/atocha.html

**James Avery Craftsman,** P.O. Box 1367, Kerrville, TX 78029: Free catalog ◆ Men and women's handcrafted gold and silver jewelry. 800-283-1770.

**Babette's Treasures,** 8013 Merry Oaks Ct., Vienna, VA 22182: Free catalog ◆ Unique and custom jewelry. Includes custom jewelry for bridesmaids. 703-734-9819. www.erols.com/lewistm/babette.htm

**Maurice Badler Jewelry,** 578 5th Ave., New York, NY 10036: Catalog $3 ◆ Men and women's jewelry. 800-M-BADLER; 212-575-9632 (in NY).

**Marilyn Barnes Jewelry,** 3512 S. Fort, Springfield, MO 65807: Brochure $1 ◆ Original Victorian-style jewelry. 417-887-1608.

**Beaded Fashions by Shayla Arrasmith,** P.O. Box 7996, Riverside, CA 92513: Brochure $2 ◆ Handmade earrings and necklaces. 909-359-7119.

**Beauty by Spector Inc.,** One Spector Pl., McKeesport, PA 15134: Catalog $5 ◆ Women's wigs and hairpieces, men's toupees, jewelry, and exotic lingerie. 412-673-3259.

**J.H. Breakell & Company,** 132 Spring St., Newport, RI 02840: Catalog $2 ◆ Handcrafted sterling silver and gold jewelry. 800-767-6411. www.breakell.com

**Broadway Jewelry Ent.,** 287 Broadway, Brooklyn, NY 11211: Free brochure ◆ Women's high-fashion jewelry. 800-933-6465; 718-782-7088 (in NY).

**Buckles Unlimited,** Box 196, Winthrop, AR 71866: Free catalog ◆ Belt buckles, belts, money clips, key chains, hat tacks, tie bars, and other coin jewelry. 501-381-7891.

**Caribone Designs,** Box 2128, Schefferville, P.Q., Canada G0G 2T0: Free catalog ◆ Original, handcrafted jewelry bone and stone jewelry. 418-585-3808.

**The Cedar Chest Fine Jewelry,** 1987 Periwinkle Way, Sanibel Island, FL 33957: Free catalog ◆ Handcrafted nautical jewelry in 18k gold. 800-749-1987; 941-472-2876 (in FL).

**Christian Dior,** 417 5th Ave., New York, NY 10016: Free catalog ◆ Fashionable jewelry for most occasions. 800-456-9444.

**Comstock Silversmiths,** 2300 Lockheed Way, Carson City, NV 89706: Free list of retail sources ◆ Silver belt buckles, pins, and other accessories. 702-882-8500.

**Creative Reflections,** 114 Stuart Rd., Ste. 144, Cleveland, TN 37312: Free brochure ◆ Jewelry, art, and collectibles. 800-363-8684.

**Creative Sports Jewelry,** 19744 Beach Blvd., #244, Huntington Beach, CA 92646: Free brochure ◆ Sterling silver and 14k gold jewelry with a sports theme. 800-606-8887; 714-960-0982 (in CA). www.ontherun.com/sportsjewelry

**Cross Jewelers,** 570 Congress St., Portland, ME 04101: Free catalog ◆ Original jewelry. 800-433-2988.

**Crown Galleries,** Division Platron Inc., 1706 Morrissey Dr., Bloomington, IL 61704: Free catalog ◆ Fashionable jewelry for women. 800-544-8200.

**Desert Jewels,** 2377 Squaw Creek Rd., Lander, WY 82520: Free brochure ◆ Black Hills gold jewelry.

**Diamond Essence Company,** 6 Saddle Rd., Cedar Knolls, NJ 07927: Free catalog ◆ Men and women's jewelry with simulated diamonds. 973-267-7370.

**Discoveries,** 526 N. Fayette St., Alexandria, VA 22314: Free information ◆ Handmade pendants, rings, bracelets, earrings, and personalized cartouche jewelry. 800-237-3358.

**DoPaso Jewelry,** P.O. Box 35430, Albuquerque, NM 87176: Catalog $7 ◆ Southwestern-style turquoise and sterling silver pins. 800-992-5234.

**Ed's House of Gems,** 7712 NE Sandy Blvd., Portland, OR 97211: Free information with long SASE ◆ Clocks, clock-making parts, minerals, gemstones, lapidary equipment, mountings, shells, jewelry, and Native American relics. 503-284-8990.

**Exclusive Sports Jewelry,** 124 N. Cardinal Dr., Ste. 101, Wilmington, NC 28405: Free catalog ◆ Golf-related jewelry. 800-533-3653.

**Foley's Rings,** P.O. Box 546, Skaneateles, NY 13153: Free information ◆ Men and women's military rings with a gold or silver finish. Also sterling silver and solid gold rings. 800-334-2908.

**Fortunoff Fine Jewelry,** P.O. Box 1550, Westbury, NY 11590: Free catalog ◆ Jewelry for men and women. 800-937-4376. service@fortunoff.com

**Foster Distributing Company,** P.O. Box 3601, Lawrence, KS 66046: Free catalog ◆ Charms, chains, bracelets, and earrings. 913-749-4857.

**Gold Moon Jewelry,** 3055 Talon Circle, Lake Orion, MI 48360: Free catalog ◆ Contemporary deco, nouveau, and antique precious metal and gemstone jewelry. 800-478-6018.

**Goldware Medical Jewelry,** P.O. Box 22335, San Diego, CA 92192: Free brochure ◆ Medical identification jewelry in 14k gold and sterling silver. 800-669-7311. www.medical-ID.net

**Grafstein & Company,** Division Capetown Diamonds, 3340 Peachtree Rd. NE, Atlanta, GA 30326: Free brochure ◆ Jewelry and watches. 800-442-7866; 404-365-9503 (in GA). www.capetowncorp.com

**Gray & Sons,** 2998 McFarlane Rd., Coconut Grove, FL 33133: Catalog $10 ◆ Pre-owned and restored fine watches. 800-654-0756.

**H & A Enterprises Inc.,** P.O. Box 570489, Whitestone, NY 11357: Free catalog ◆ Women's jewelry. 800-327-3427.

**Hand & Hammer Silversmiths,** 2610 Morse Ln., Woodbridge, VA 22192: Free information ◆ Handcrafted sterling silver and vermeil jewelry. Also Christmas ornaments. 800-SILVERY.

**Harmon's Agate & Silver Shop,** Box 94, Crane, MT 59217: Free catalog ◆ Montana agate slabs, cabochons, carvings, designer jewelry, and more. 406-482-2534. www.harmons.net

**Hay Charlie,** 541 Historic Main St., Park City, UT 84060: Free information ◆ Handcrafted western-style boots, buckles and belts, hats, jewelry, and clothing.

**Heaven & Earth,** RR 1, Box 25, Marshfield, VT 05658: Free catalog ◆ Jewelry, gemstones, and minerals. 800-348-5155; 802-426-3440 (in VT).

**Heavenly Treasures,** 321 Main St, Allenhurst, NJ 07711: Free catalog ◆ Women's gold and silver jewelry. Some with pearls, diamonds, and other gemstones. 800-269-4637. www.heavenlytreasurers.com

**Heirloom Pearl Company,** 28555 Balmoral Way, Farmington Hills, MI 48334: Free catalog ◆ Hand-forged sterling silver and fresh water pearls jewelry. 810-615-6960.

**Heraldica Imports,** 21 W. 46th St., New York, NY 10036: Free brochure ◆ Engraved family crest rings and jewelry. 212-719-4204.

**Highglow Jewelry,** 18618 Pioneer Blvd., Artesia, CA 90701: Free catalog ◆ Handcrafted 22k gold and diamond jewelry. 562-860-2706.

**Horsemen's General Store,** 1001 Shiloh Springs Rd., Dayton, OH 45415: Catalog $3 ◆ Western-style jewelry. 800-343-4987; 937-278-2380 (in OH).

**International Jewelers,** 6407 Mill Rd., Egg Harbor Twp., NJ 08234: Free information ◆ Judaic jewelry and Hebraic names in block or script with or without diamonds. 888-927-9511; 609-927-9511 (in NJ).

**Jaeger-LeCoultre,** P.O. Box 1608, Winchester, VA 22604: Free list of retail sources ◆ Jaeger-LeCoultre watches. 800-JLC-TIME.

**Jamboree Jewelry,** 1501 E. Chapman, Ste. 245, Fullerton, CA 92631: Free catalog ◆ Contemporary handcrafted American Indian (Native American) jewelry. 714-996-5005.

**Jewelry by Avery,** 5134 Chalk Point Rd., West River, MD 20778: Free information with long SASE ◆ Kachinas, Native American art, precious and semi-precious gemstones, mineral specimens, and handcrafted Zuni, Navajo, and Hopi turquoise jewelry. 410-867-4752.

**Jewelry Company,** P.O. Box 551, Park Rapids, MN 56470: Free brochure ◆ Military rings in yellow or white 10k or 14k solid gold. Also birthstones and gemstone and diamond rings. 800-544-9706; 602-982-2273 (in AZ).

**Sharon E. Johnson Jewelry,** 6 Murray Ct., Rockville Centre, NY 11570: Free brochure ◆ Wire-wrapped gold and gemstone jewelry. 800-304-1282.

**Karat Patch Jewelry Inc.,** 300 Charlotte Merchandise Mart, 2500 E. Independence Blvd., Charlotte, NC 28205: Free catalog ◆ Women's gold, platinum, and other rare metal jewelry with optional gemstones. 800-768-0457; 704-334-3188 (in NC). www.karatpatch.com

**The Kenya Gem Company,** 6504 Ventnor Ave., Ventnor, NJ 08406: Catalog $5 ◆ Men and women's jewelry with simulated diamonds. 800-523-0158.

**Richard L. Kollinger Company Inc.,** 5952 Royal Ln., Ste. 103, Dallas, TX 75230: Free catalog ◆ Polished diamond-cut cubic zirconia jewelry with 14k gold mountings. 800-527-6983. members.aol.com/nkcoinc/rlk.html

**Lace & Things,** Hwy. 441, Whittier, NC 28789: Free price list ◆ Native American craft supplies and jewelry. 704-586-9500.

**Lenox Jewelers,** 2379 Black Rock Tnpk., Fairfield, CT 06430: Free catalog ◆ Watches, figurines, jewelry, porcelain, china, and crystal. 800-243-4473; 203-374-6157 (in CT).

**Lonnie's Inc.,** 7155 E. Main St., Mesa, AZ 85207: Free findings catalog; tool catalog $5; silver jewelry catalog $5 ◆ Silver jewelry and supplies for jewelers, casters, silversmiths, and lapidarists. 602-832-2641.

**Lorent Fine Coins & Precious Metals,** 215 S. Broadway, #177, Salem, NH 03079: Free catalog ◆ Custom designed medallions, rare collectibles, coin jewelry, and ornaments. 603-599-1174.

**Lovell Designs,** P.O. Box 7130, Portland, ME 04112: Free catalog ◆ Pendants, pins, earrings, and jewelry in pewter, sterling silver, and gold plate. 800-533-9685.

**Maple Shade Crafts,** Catalog Department, RR 1, Box 186, Pulaski, VA 24301: Catalog $4 (refundable) ◆ Craft supplies, sewing notions, Victorian jewelry, scented candles, cameos, and potpourri. 800-986-9674. www.swva.net/mapleshade

**Alan Marcus & Company,** 815 Connecticut Ave. NW, Washington, DC 20006: Free catalog ◆ Jewelry and Rolex, Patek, Phillippe, Audemars Piguet, Baume Mercier, and Cartier watches. 800-654-7184; 202-331-0671 (in Metro DC).

**Mark Steel Jewelry,** Rachael M. Roberts, 35 N. Main St., Spring City, UT 84662: Free catalog ◆ Handcrafted jewelry. 800-765-4667.

**Mary Laura's,** 3636 San Mateo Blvd. NE, Albuquerque, NM 87110: Catalog $2 ◆ Native American jewelry from the Zuni Pueblo. 800-662-4848.

**Merlite Industries Inc.,** 114 5th Ave., New York, NY 10011: Free catalog ◆ Contemporary and classic jewelry for men and women. 212-924-3500.

**Mignon Faget Jewelry,** 710 Dublin St., New Orleans, LA 70118: Catalog $3 ◆ Handcrafted gold and sterling silver jewelry. 800-375-7557.

**Museum of Jewelry,** 3000 Larkin St., San Francisco, CA 94109: Free catalog ◆ Handcrafted reproductions of historic jewelry originals. 800-258-0888.

**Bernard Myles Jewelry,** 1605 S. 7th St., Terre Haute, IN 47802: Catalog $1 ◆ Coin jewelry, belt buckles, tie-tacks, key chains, bolo ties, money clips, and other items. 812-232-4405.

**The Mystic Trader,** 1334 Pacific Ave., Forest Grove, OR 97116: Free catalog ◆ Gemstone jewelry and other gifts with a religious theme. 800-634-9057.

**Nature's Jewelry,** 222 Mill Rd., Chelmsford, MA 01824: Free catalog ◆ Leaves, shells, and other natural objects transformed into jewelry by preservation in precious metals. 800-333-3235.

**Navajo Manufacturing Company,** 5330 Fox St., Denver, CO 80216: Catalog $2 ◆ Turquoise and sterling silver jewelry, novelties and crafts, and sunglasses. 800-625-5097. www.noblemotion.com

**Nigro's Western Store,** 3320 Merriam Ln., Kansas City, KS 66106: Free information ◆ Western-style jewelry. 800-521-3330; 913-262-1709 (in KS).

**Olympia Gold,** 11540 Wiles Rd., Coral Springs, FL 33076: Free catalog ◆ Necklaces, bracelets, diamond charms, filigree rings, and Austrian crystal chain. 800-395-7774.

**Open Circle Distributors,** 1750 E. Hill Rd., Willits, CA 95490: Free catalog ◆ Symbolic design jewelry and medallions. 707-459-2418.

**Oriental Crest Inc.,** 6161 Savoy Dr., Houston, TX 77036: Free information ◆ Semi-precious gemstone and other jewelry, bead-stringing supplies, pendant carvings, and earring jackets. 800-367-3954; 713-780-2425 (in TX).

**Pacific Basin Exports Company,** 92-973 Makakilo Dr., #16, Makakilo, HI 96707: Free brochure ◆ Stylish butterflies, hummingbirds, bees, and other motion jewelry. 800-290-8056; 808-672-3466 (in HI).

**Palancar Jewelers,** 1156 E. Alosta Ave., Glendora, CA 91740: Free catalog ◆ Diver's jewelry in 14k gold and sterling. 800-467-9067; 626-963-9660 (in CA).

**Palm Beach International,** 6400 E. Rogers Circle, Boca Raton, FL 33499: Free catalog ◆ Earrings and jewelry for men and women. 800-954-7753.

**S.A. Peck & Company,** 55 E. Washington St., Chicago, IL 60602: Free catalog ◆ Diamonds and jewelry. 800-922-0090. sapeck.com

**Barbra Pehrson Jewelry,** 1435 Quebec St., Denver, CO 80220: Free information ◆ Custom-designed costume jewelry. 303-322-7576.

**Pididdly Links Ltd.,** P.O. Box 1728, Kingston, NY 12402: Catalog $1 ◆ Antique reproduction Edwardian, Victorian, and art nouveau costume jewelry. 800-933-9383. www.Dididdlylinks.com

**R.E. Piland Goldsmiths,** P.O. Box 607, Haymarket, VA 20168: Free catalog ◆ Original Celtic designed jewelry. 703-754-8403.

**Q-C Turquoise,** 3340 E. Washington, Phoenix, AZ 85034: Free information ◆ Turquoise nugget jewelry, nuggets by the strand or pound, and cutting material or blocks. 602-267-1164.

**R & T Distributors,** 6208 Summer Place Dr. North, Mobile, AL 36618: Catalogs $5 ◆ Christmas ornaments and collectibles, jewelry, and gifts for all-occasions. 888-343-GIFT; 334-4124-2796 (in AL). www.zebra.net/~Alicia

**Rex's Astro Stuff,** 63 Observatory Ln., Dover, AR 72837: Free catalog ◆ Telescopes, binoculars, and accessories. Includes new and used equipment, books, posters, star charts, meteorites, and meteorite jewelry. 501-331-3773.

**Rose Petal Jewelry of Cape Cod,** P.O. Box 742, Marston Mills, MA 02648: Free catalog ◆ Nautical and floral jewelry and gifts in 14k gold, sterling silver, and vermeil. 617-698-5091. www.nvi.com/rosepetal

**Ross-Simons Jewelers,** 9 Ross-Simons Dr., Cranston, RI 02920: Free catalog ◆ China, crystal, flatware, silver, watches, figurines, and diamond, gold, pearl, and gemstone jewelry. 800-521-7677; 401-463-3100 (in RI). www.ross-simons.com

**Roussels,** P.O. Box 476, Arlington, MA 02174: Catalog $1 ◆ Jewelry-making supplies and ready-to-wear jewelry. 781-443-8888.

**Richard Sabol,** 1 Pisacatqua Rd., Dover, NH 03820: Free brochure with long SASE and two 1st class stamps ◆ Cross-stitch kits, rubber stamps, and jewelry. 603-742-6324.

**Sadigh Gallery of Ancient Art,** 303 5th Ave., Ste. 1603, New York, NY 10016: Free catalog ◆ Authentic ancient art and jewelry. 800-426-2007; 212-725-7537 (in NY).

**Scintilla,** P.O. Box 78982, Atlanta, GA 30357: Free catalog ◆ Jewelry, lighting, and accessories. 800-975-0191.

**Scott-Wynne Outfitters,** 10000 Research Blvd., Ste. 127, Austin, TX 78759: Free catalog ◆ Outdoor and casual clothing, luggage, hunting and fishing accessories, and Native American jewelry. 800-232-2783. www.outfits.com

**Second Look,** c/o Silver Works Inc., 3234 Kirkwood Hwy., Wilmington, DE 19808: Free catalog ◆ Silver and turquoise earrings, bracelets, necklaces, watch bands, and jewelry by Southwest artisans. 800-544-8200.

**Silver Nugget,** 416 Juan Tabo NE, Albuquerque, NM 87123: Catalog $2 ◆ Native American jewelry. 800-343-9380. www.silver-nugget.com

**Simcha Designs,** P.O. Box 6562, Fresh Meadows Station, Flushing, NY 11365: Free catalog ◆ Judaic artware and jewelry. 718-776-6688.

**Simply Whispers,** 430 Court St., Plymouth, MA 02362: Free catalog ◆ Hypo-allergenic earrings and jewelry. 800-451-5700.

**Wm. Spear Designs,** 227 7th St., Juneau, AK 99801: Catalog $3 ◆ Talismans, amulets, and charms. 907-586-2209. www.wmspear.com

**Tener's Western Outfitters,** 4320 W. Reno Ave., Oklahoma City, OK 73107: Free catalog ◆ Western-style jewelry. 800-654-6715; 405-946-5500 (in OK).

**Tiffany & Company,** Customer Service, 801 Jefferson Rd., P.O. Box 5477, Parsippany, NJ 07054: Catalog $1 ◆ Jewelry, silver, china, crystal, watches and clocks, and other gifts. 800-452-9146.

**TopGallant Merchants,** 648-E Dauphine Ct., Elk Grove Village, IL 60007: Free brochure ◆ Handcrafted coin jewelry and embroidered gifts. 800-544-8194; 847-981-1121 (in IL).

**Vanity Fair,** S.A. Peck & Company, 55 E. Washington St., Chicago, IL 60602: Free catalog ◆ Diamond jewelry. 800-922-0090. www.sapeck.com

**Wage's Silversmiths,** 1598-C S. Anaheim Blvd., Anaheim, CA 92805: Free list of retail sources ◆ Silver belt buckles, money clips, saddle trim, card cases, bracelets, and other accessories. 800-621-8077; 800-327-2214 (in CA).

**Wanderlust,** 8457 NW 66th St., Miami, FL 33166: Free catalog ◆ Handmade jade, silver, and wood jewelry. Also other gifts. 888-WANDER-1. www.towander.com

**Wayfarer Trading Company,** 2094 343rd St., Vail, IA 51465: Free brochure ◆ Sterling silver and 18k gold Egyptian cartouche pendants and jewelry. 800-432-1892.

**Kate Webster Company,** 83 Granite St., Rockport, MA 01966: Catalog $3 ◆ Doll costuming supplies and jewelry. 978-546-6462.

**What on Earth Naturally,** 6250 Busch Blvd., Columbus, OH 43229: Free information ◆ Minerals, fossils, jewelry, gemstones, and shells. 614-436-1458.

**Wild Spirit Jewelry,** Sequoia Enterprises Ltd., P.O. Box 129, Nodal, NM 88341: Free catalog ◆ Jewelry with a Greek revival, fossil replicas, nautical, Native American, and other themes. 505-354-2229.

**Williamsburg Merchants,** 223 Parkway Dr., Williamsburg, VA 23185: Catalog $2 ◆ Sterling silver jewelry. 800-545-4556.

**Windsor Collection,** 6836 Engle Rd., P.O. Box 94549, Cleveland, OH 44101: Free catalog ◆ Men and women's fashion watches and jewelry. 216-826-1712.

**Zales By Mail,** 6301 New Loop 410, San Antonio, TX 78238: Free catalog ◆ Jewelry for anniversaries, weddings, birthdays, holidays, and other special occasions. 210-681-6510. www.amn-mall.com/national/zaljew

**Zina Jewelry & Gifts,** 470 S. Beverly Dr., Beverly Hills, CA 90212: Free list of retail sources ◆ Sterling silver jewelry and other gifts. 800-336-3822; 310-286-2206 (in CA).

## JEWELRY MAKING SUPPLIES & TOOLS

**A & A Jewelry Tools & Findings,** 319 W. 6th St., Los Angeles, CA 90014: Free catalog ◆ Jewelry-making tools and accessories. 213-627-8004.

**A & B Jewels & Tools,** 350 W. Grand River, Williamston, MI 48895: Catalog $2 ◆ Jewelry-making tools and supplies. 517-655-4664.

**A & D Jewelry,** P.O. Box 951, West Sacramento, CA 95691: Free catalog ◆ Supplies, findings, and enhancements for making jewelry. 800-466-4453.

**A.R.C. Traders Inc.,** Box 3429, Scottsdale, AZ 85257: Free information ◆ Findings, chains, earrings, jewelry, and sterling silver, gold-filled, and 14k gold beads. 800-528-2374; 602-945-0769 (in AZ).

**Ackley's Rocks & Stamps,** 3230 N. Stone Ave., Colorado Springs, CO 80907: Catalog $1 ◆ Lapidary and silversmithing supplies, mountings, and findings. 719-633-1153.

**Aleta's Rock Shop,** 1515 Plainfield NE, Grand Rapids, MI 49505: Catalog $1.50 ◆ Jewelry-making supplies, tumblers, lapidary equipment, findings, silicon carbide grits, diamond material, and rocks for cutting, tumbling, and polishing. 616-363-5394.

**Allcraft Tool & Supply Company,** 666 Pacific St., Brooklyn, NY 11207: Catalog $5 ◆ Lapidary tools and supplies. 800-645-7124; 718-789-2800 (in NY).

**Alpha Supply,** P.O. Box 2133, Bremerton, WA 98310: Catalog $7 ◆ Casting and faceting equipment, jewelry-making tools, silver rings, wax models, lapidary tools, and clock movements and parts. 800-257-4211; 360-373-3302 (in WA).

**Amazon Imports,** P.O. Box 58, Williston Park, NY 11596: Free price list ◆ Amethyst, aquamarine, emerald, garnet, kunzite, blue topaz, imperial topaz, and tourmaline from Brazil. 800-888-GEMS; 516-621-7481 (in NY).

**Amber Treasure,** P.O. Box 99103, Emeryville, CA 94662: Catalog $2 ◆ Calibrated and free-form cabochons, amber spheres and beads, polished amber stones, Baltic amber rough, and finished jewelry. 510-547-8660.

**Ambush Wholesale Beads & Findings,** P.O. Box 144, Worcester, MA 01613: Catalog $1 ◆ Charms, beads, findings, and jewelry-making supplies.

**Amulet,** P.O. Box 2089, Sonoma, CA 95476: Free catalog ◆ Platinum, gold, and sterling custom mountings and loose gemstones, gifts, tools, and books. 800-777-9940. www.gemstones.com

**APL Trader,** P.O. Box 1900, New York, NY 10185: Catalog $1 ◆ Precious and semi-precious gemstones, cabachons, carvings, and beads. 718-454-2954.

**B. Rush Apple Company,** 3855 W. Kennedy Blvd., Tampa, FL 33609: Free price list ◆ Jeweler's tools and supplies, casting equipment, and findings. 813-870-3180.

**ARE Inc.,** Rt. 16, Box 8, Greensboro Bend, VT 05842: Catalog $3 ◆ Silver, gold, pewter, base metals, tools, findings, chains, other jewelry-making supplies, and semi-precious stones. 800-736-4273.

**Arizona Gems & Crystals,** 1705 W. 14th Dr., Safford, AZ 85546: Free catalog ◆ Arizona fire agate, beads, cabochons, findings, silver, jewelry kits, rough and slabs, and other supplies. 800-657-6263.

**Arizona Gems & Minerals Inc.,** 6370 East Hwy. 69, Prescott Valley, AZ 86314: Catalog $4 ◆ Chip beads, other beads and findings, silversmithing and lapidary tools, jewelry-making supplies, and mineral specimens. 602-772-6443.

**Arjan Enterprises Inc.,** 43 Bethune Blvd., Spring Valley, NY 10977: Free information ◆ Mini-rolling mill and jewelry-making tools. 800-221-4812.

**Art to Wear,** 5 Crescent Pl., St. Petersburg, FL 33711: Catalog $1 ◆ Bead-stringing supplies, tools, and jewelry-making kits. 272-867-3711.

**Aurora Gems,** Box 40, Anola, Manitoba, Canada R0E 0A0: Free price list ◆ Phenomenon stones and gems from around the world. 204-866-3784.

**B & J Rock Shop,** 14744 Manchester Rd., Ballwin, MO 63011: Catalog $3 ◆ Jewelry-making supplies, beads and bead-stringing supplies, quartz clock movements and crystals, clock-building kits, amethyst crystal clusters, Brazilian agate nodules, geodes, and imported and domestic gemstones. 314-394-4567.

**Bead Bazaar,** 1001 Harris Ave., Bellingham, WA 98225: Catalog $2.50 ◆ Jewelry-making supplies. 800-671-5655.

**Bead Boppers,** 11224 S. Meridian, Puyallup, WA 98373: Catalog $2.50 (refundable) ◆ Beads and findings, tools, charms, seed beads, leather, supplies, and books. 206-848-3880. www.ibrowse.com/boppers

**Bead Warehouse,** 4 Meadowlake Dr., Mendon, VT 05701: Free catalog ◆ Beads, books, tools, clay, necklace and earring kits, and other craft items. 800-736-0781.

**Beada Beada,** 4262 N. Woodward Ave., Royal Oak, MI 48073: Free catalog ◆ Semi-precious beads, cabochons, cultured and freshwater pearls, and 14k gold, gold-filled, and sterling findings. 248-549-1005.

**Beadbox Inc.,** 10135 E. Via Linda, Scottsdale, AZ 85258: Catalog $5 ◆ Ready-to-assemble jewelry kits and beads from worldwide sources. 800-232-3269.

**Beadworks,** 149 Water St., Norwalk, CT 06854: Catalog $7.95 ◆ Glass, ceramic, porcelain, pearl, stone, and other beads. 800-232-3761. www.beadworks.com

**Big Stone Beads & Findings Inc.,** 6222 Richmond Ave., Houston, TX 77057: Free information ◆ Beads, cabochons, and findings. 800-733-1313.

**Bourget Bros.,** 1636 11th St., Santa Monica, CA 90404: Catalog $5 ◆ Jewelry-making and lapidary tools, gemstones, cabochons, wax patterns, beads, bead-stringing supplies, and sterling silver and gold-filled chains. 800-828-3024. www.bourgetbros.com

**Brown Brothers Lapidary,** 2248 S. 1st Ave., Safford, AZ 85546: Catalog $1 (refundable) ◆ Gemstones. 520-428-6433.

**Bucks County Classic,** 73 Coventry Ln., Langhorne, PA 19047: Catalog $2 ◆ Fresh water pearls, Chinese cloisonne, cabachons, findings, and gemstone, metal, Austrian crystal, and stone accent beads. 800-942-4367. www.xmission.com/~arts

**California Bolas,** 5090 10th Ave. SW, Naples, FL 34116: Free information ◆ Jewelry findings. 941-352-8457.

**Castaldo,** 120 Constitution Blvd., Franklin, MA 02038: Free information ◆ Jewelry molding rubber. 508-520-1666.

**CGM Inc.,** 19562 Ventura Blvd., Tarzana, CA 91356: Free catalog ◆ Precious and semi-precious gemstones and 14k gold, gold-filled, and sterling silver findings. 818-609-7088.

**Charlie's Rock Shop,** P.O. Box 399, Penrose, CO 81240: Catalog $3 (refundable) ◆ Clocks, clock movements and parts, beads, jewelry-making supplies, and faceted gemstones. 719-372-0117.

**Comstock Creations,** P.O. Box 2715, Durango, CO 81302: Free information ◆ Cut and polished Brazilian agate and geodes. 800-844-9000; 970-247-3836 (in CO).

**Contempo Lapidary,** 12257 Foothill Blvd., Sylmar, CA 91342: Catalog $3 ◆ Lapidary equipment and supplies. 800-358-2441; 818-899-1973 (in CA). www.paleoart.com/contempo.htm

**Covington Engineering Corp.,** P.O. Box 35, Redlands, CA 92373: Free catalog ◆ Lapidary equipment. 909-793-6636. www.catalogcity.com/mm/covington

**Craft Harbor,** 1320 Heather Ridge Blvd., Dunedin, FL 34698: Free catalog ◆ Jewelry-making supplies. 813-736-6187.

**The Craft Market,** 401 5th Ave., Fairbanks, AK 99701: Jewelry supply catalog $2.95; tool catalog $5.95 ◆ Jewelry-making supplies and tools. Also other crafting tools. 907-452-5495.

**Creative Beginnings,** 475 Morro Bay Blvd., Morro Bay, CA 93442: Free brochure ◆ Kits, findings, books, brass-plated and silver charms, and ornaments for jewelry-making. 800-367-1739.

**Creative Castle,** 2321 Michael Dr., Newbury Park, CA 91320: Free catalog ◆ Bead-making jewelry kits. 805-499-1377. www.creativecastle.com

**Cridge Inc.,** Box 210, Morrisville, PA 19067: Catalog $2 ◆ Jewelry findings and supplies. 215-295-3667.

**Crystalite Corp.,** 8400 Green Meadows Dr., Westerville, OH 43081: Free list of retail sources ◆ Lapidary and glass-working equipment and supplies. 800-777-2894.

**Cupboard Distributing,** P.O. Box 148, Urbana, OH 43078: Catalog $2 ◆ Unfinished wood parts for jewelry-making, miniatures, toys, tole and decorative painting, and woodworking crafts. 937-652-3338. cupboard@foryou.net

**Custom Technology Ltd.,** 407-411 W. Main St., New London, IA 52645: Free list of retail sources ◆ Easy loading and unloading tumblers for finishing and burnishing gemstones. Also gem materials, minerals, and cut and tumbled stones from around the world. 800-YTUMBLE.

**Dad's Rock Shop,** P.O. Box 169, 112 E. Cherry Ave., Arroyo Grande, CA 93421: Free catalog ◆ Lapidary equipment, gems, minerals, fossils, metal detectors, prospecting equipment, and supplies. 805-489-2470.

**Dawn's Hide & Bead Away,** 521 E. Washington St., Iowa City, IA 52240: Free catalog ◆ Tools, jewelry wire, necklace findings, gemstones, beads, and accessories. 319-338-1566.

**Diamond Pacific Tool Corp.,** P.O. Box 1180, Barstow, CA 92312: Free catalog ◆ Lapidary, rockhounding, and jewelry-making supplies. 800-253-2954. www.diamondpacific.com

**Dikra Gem Inc.,** 56 W. 45th St., Ste. 1005, New York, NY 10036: Free information ◆ Semi-precious gemstones. 800-873-4572; 212-869-6332 (in NY).

**Discount Agate House,** 3401 N. Dodge Blvd., Tucson, AZ 85716: Free information ◆ Rocks and minerals from around the world, lapidary equipment, sterling silver and metalsmithing supplies, and findings. 520-323-0781.

**Discount Bead House,** P.O. Box 186, The Plains, OH 45780: Catalog $5 ◆ Seed beads, findings, and tools. 800-793-7592.

**Dremel Moto-Tool,** P.O. Box 468, Racine, WI 53406: Free information ◆ Tools for grinding, sawing, drilling, carving, shaping, and polishing gemstones. 414-554-1390. www.dremel.com

**Dyer's Jewelers' Tools & Supplies,** 4525 Guadelupe St., Austin, TX 78751: Tool catalog $4; findings catalog $3; wax pattern catalog $4 ◆ Tools, findings, wax and wax patterns, gemstones and rocks, rubber molds, lost wax steam casting kit for making jewelry, and other supplies. 800-683-1631.

**E & W Imports Inc.,** P.O. Box 15703, Tampa, FL 33684: Price list $3.50 ◆ Gemstone, cloisonne, and Austrian crystal beads and 14k findings. 813-885-1138. www.wp.com/E&WImports

**Eastern Findings Corp.,** 19 W. 34th St., New York, NY 10001: Free information ◆ Findings. 800-EFC-6640; 212-695-6640 (in NY). www.easternfindings.com

**Ebersole Lapidary Supply Inc.,** 11417 West Hwy. 54, Wichita, KS 67209: Catalog $5 ◆ Tools, findings, mountings, cabochons and rocks, jewelry-making kits, petrified wood, clocks and clock-making parts, beads, and bead-stringing supplies. 316-722-4771.

**Ed's House of Gems,** 7712 NE Sandy Blvd., Portland, OR 97213: Free information with long SASE ◆ Clocks, clock-making parts, minerals, gemstones, lapidary equipment, mountings, shells, jewelry, and Native American relics. 503-284-8990.

**Eloxite Corp.,** P.O. Box 729, Wheatland, WY 82201: Catalog $1 ◆ Clock-making supplies, tools, gemstones, belt buckles, jewelry mountings, and rockhounding and jewelry do-it-yourself equipment. 307-322-3050. www.eloxite.com

**Enterprise Art,** P.O. Box 2918, Largo, FL 33779: Free catalog ◆ Beads from around the world, bead and jewelry-making kits, and supplies. 800-366-2218. www.enterpriseart.com

**Euro Tool,** 11449 Randall Dr., Lenexa, KS 66215: Free list of retail sources ◆ Tools for cutting and finishing diamonds. 800-552-3131.

**Evening Star Designs,** 69 Coolidge Ave., Haverhill, MA 01832: Catalog $3 ◆ Craft and jewelry-making supplies. 800-666-3562.

**Fac-Ette Manufacturing Inc.,** P.O. Box 550, Wrightsville Beach, NC 28480: Free information ◆ Gem-cutting equipment. 910-256-9248.

**Fancifuls,** P.O. Box 76, Killawog, NY 13794: Catalog $3.50 ◆ Brass charms and other jewelry-making embellishments. 607-849-6870. www.fancifulsinc.com

**David H. Fell & Company Inc.,** 6009 Bandini Blvd., City of Commerce, CA 90040: Catalog $5 ◆ Precious metals for craft-making and photo-etched sheets. 800-822-1996; 213-722-9992 (in CA). www.MJSA.Polygon.net/~10204

**Fire Mountain Gems,** 28195 Redwood Hwy., Cave Junction, OR 97523: Catalog $3 ◆ Beads, gems, and jewelry-making supplies and tools. 800-423-2319. www.firemtn.com

**Foredom Electric Company,** 16 Stony Hill Rd., Bethel, CT 06801: Free information ◆ Tools for grinding, sawing, drilling, carving, shaping, and polishing gemstones. 203-792-8622.

**Gem Center U.S.A. Inc.,** 4100 Alameda Ave., El Paso, TX 79905: Free price list ◆ Geodes and nodules. 915-533-7153.

**Gem-Fare,** P.O. Box 213, Pittstown, NJ 08867: Price list 50¢ ◆ Rare and unusual gemstones and crystals. 732-806-3339. abeada@aol.com

**Gem-O-Rama Inc.,** 150 Recreation Park Dr., Hingham, MA 02043: Free catalog ◆ Gemstones, beading supplies, and 14k gold, gold-filled, and sterling silver beads. 781-749-8250. www.Gemorama.Com

**Gemstone Equipment Manufacturing Company,** 750 Easy St., Simi Valley, CA 93065: Free information ◆ Vibratory tumblers and lapidary equipment. 800-235-3375; 805-527-6990 in CA).

**Gilman's Lapidary Supply,** Durham St., P.O. Box M, Hellertown, PA 18055: Free information ◆ Lapidary equipment, findings and mountings, silver and gold metal crafting supplies, and genuine and synthetic gemstones. 610-838-8767.

**Kenneth Glasser,** P.O. Box 28048, Las Vegas, NV 89126: Catalog $10 ◆ Cut and polished diamonds and other precious and semi-precious stones. 702-880-9044. www.diamondrough.com

**Glendo Corporation,** 900 Overlander Rd., P.O. Box 1153, Emporia, KS 66801: Free catalog ◆ Multi-purpose equipment for jewelry-making, diamond setters, engravers, and others. 800-835-3519. www.glendo.com

**A. Goodman Video Tapes,** P.O. Box 667, Beaumont, CA 92223: Free information ◆ How-to videos on jewelry-making. 800-382-3237.

**Goodnow's,** 3415 S. Hayden St., Amarillo, TX 79109: Free list with long SASE ◆ Gem roughs for faceting, cabbing, and tumbling. 806-352-0725.

**Graves Company,** 1800 Andrews Ave., Pompano Beach, FL 33069: Free catalog ◆ Lapidary equipment. 800-327-9103. www.rockhounds.com/graves

**Griffith Distributors,** Box 662, Louisville, CO 80027: Free information ◆ Jewelry-making chemicals. 303-442-8284.

**T.B. Hagstoz & Son Inc.,** 709 Sansom St., Philadelphia, PA 19106: Catalog $5 (refundable with $25 order) ◆ Metal findings, jeweler's tools, casting equipment, gold and silver solders, and gold, silver, gold-filled, copper, bronze, brass-nickel, silver, and pewter metals. 800-922-1006; 215-922-1627 (in PA).

**Handy & Harman,** 1907 W. Historic Rt. 66, Gallup, NM 87301: Free information ◆ Trim saws, diamond blades, other lapidary equipment, and rough and cut stones. 505-722-4323.

**Hanneman Gemological Instruments,** P.O. Box 942, Poulsbo, WA 98370: Catalog $2 (refundable) ◆ Gemological instruments and tools.

**Hardies,** P.O. Box 1920, Quartzsite, AZ 85346: Catalog $3 (refundable) ◆ Beads, findings, buckles, bolas, Native American jewelry, gems, rocks, and books. 800-962-2775; 520-927-6381 (in AZ). Ahardies@aol.com

**Harmon's Agate & Silver Shop,** Box 94, Crane, MT 59217: Free catalog ◆ Montana agate slabs, cabochons, carvings, designer jewelry, and more. 406-482-2534. www.harmons.net

**Heaven & Earth,** RR 1, Box 25, Marshfield, VT 05658: Free catalog ◆ Jewelry, gemstones, and minerals. 800-348-5155; 802-426-3440 (in VT).

**HHH Enterprises,** P.O. Box 390, Abilene, TX 79604: Catalog $2 ◆ Jewelry components and make-your-own jewelry kits. 800-777-0218.

**Hong Kong Lapidary Supplies,** 2801 University Dr., Coral Springs, FL 33065: Catalog $3 ◆ Semi-precious gemstones and beads. 954-755-8777.

**House of India,** World Trade Center, P.O. Box 58316, Dallas, TX 75258: Free information ◆ Accessories and supplies for making designer watches. 800-527-7139; 214-741-6133 (in TX).

**House of Onyx,** P.O. Box 261, 120 N. Main St., Greenville, KY 42345: Free catalog ◆ Jewelry, gemstones, and jewelry-making supplies. 800-844-3100; 502-338-2363 (in KY). www.houseofonyx.com

**Indian Jewelers Supply Company,** 601 E. Coal Ave., Gallup, NM 87301: Catalog $6 ◆ Precious and base metals, findings, metalsmithing and lapidary equipment, semi-precious gemstones, shells, and coral. 505-722-4451.

**International Gem Merchants Inc.,** 4168 Oxford Ave., Jacksonville, FL 32210: Free information ◆ Gemstones, pearls, and synthetic gemstones. 800-633-3653; 904-388-5130 (in FL). igminc@bellsouth.net

**Jarvi Tool Company,** 780 E. Debra Ln., Anaheim, CA 92805: Free information ◆ Lapidary equipment, faceting machines, and tools. 714-774-9104.

**Jems Inc.,** 2293 Aurora Rd., Melbourne, FL 32935: Free price list ◆ Gem trees, wire-crafting supplies, tumbled gemstones, figurines, and jewelry-making supplies. 407-254-5600.

**Jewelry Plus,** P.O. Box 10036, Prescott, AZ 86304: Catalog $3 (refundable) ◆ Silver and pewter figures and shapes for jewelry-making. 520-717-2084.

**Johnson Brothers Inc.,** 18434 Oxnard St., Unit G, Tarzana, CA 91356: Free request list of retail sources ◆ Combination lapidary machine complete with blade, wheel, polishing head, discs, and felt. 818-705-7400.

**KERR Jewelry & Specialty Products,** 1717 W. Collins Ave., Orange, CA 92867: Free catalog ◆ Jewelry-making supplies, casting materials, and equipment. 714-516-7650.

**Kingsley North Inc.,** 910 Brown St., Norway, MI 49870: Free catalog ◆ Jewelry-making tools and supplies, metal casting and lapidary equipment, and rough, cut, and calibrated opals. 800-338-9280. www.kingsleynorth.com

**Knight's,** P.O. Box 411, Waitsfield, VT 05673: Free catalog ◆ Cut and rough gemstones. 802-496-3707. Knights@MadRiver.com

**Krona Gem Merchants,** Box 9968, Colorado Springs, CO 80932: Free price list ◆ Faceted and rare gemstones. 719-597-8779.

**RM Lambert Gemstones,** 450 Riverdale Dr., Merritt Island, FL 32953: Free brochure ◆ Diamond powder, lapidary supplies, gemstones, jewelry, and gem rough. 407-452-2023. www.rmi-gemstones.com/index.html

**Lapcraft Company Inc.,** 195 W. Olentangy St., P.O. Box 389, Powell, OH 43065: Free information ◆ Lapidary equipment. 208-764-8993.

**Lee Lapidaries Inc.,** 3425 W. 117th St., Cleveland, OH 44111: Free information ◆ Faceting equipment. 440-941-7458.

**Lentz Lapidary Inc.,** 11760 S. Oliver, Rt. 2, Box 134, Mulvane, KS 67110: Catalog $2 ◆ Jewelry, mountings, clocks and parts, rough rock specimens and cabochons, and rockhounding and lapidary equipment. 316-777-1372.

**Victor H. Levy Inc.,** 1355 S. Flower St., Los Angeles, CA 90015: Catalog $5 ◆ Findings, rhinestones, gemstones, braids, and jewelry-making supplies. 800-421-8021; 213-749-8247 (in CA).

**Lochs,** P.O. Box 58, Emmaus, PA 18049: Catalog $4 ◆ Faceted and polished gemstones, 14k gold findings, and biron-created emeralds. 610-965-7833.

**Lonnie's Inc.,** 7155 E. Main St., Mesa, AZ 85207: Free findings catalog; tool catalog $5; silver jewelry catalog $5 ◆ Silver jewelry and supplies for jewelers, casters, silversmiths, and lapidarists. 602-832-2641.

**Lortone Inc.,** 2856 NW Market St., Seattle, WA 98107: Free catalog with long SASE ◆ Lapidary equipment. 206-789-3100. equipment@lortone.com

**W.L. Maison Opals Inc.,** 394 Mesa Rd., Salinas, CA 93908: Free price list ◆ Rough opals, triplets, and crystal triplet tops. 408-455-1765.

**Maxant Industries Inc.,** P.O. Box 454, Ayer, MA 01432: Catalog $1 ◆ Lapidary equipment. 978-772-0576.

**MDR Manufacturing Inc.,** P.O. Box 6951, Kingwood, TX 77325: Free price list ◆ Faceting equipment. 281-358-3027.

**Melanie Collection,** 12105 Bermuda NE, Albuquerque, NM 87111: Charm catalog $6; button catalog $2 ◆ Silver and bronze replicas of old, new, ancient, and ethnic artifacts. 505-298-7036.

**The Mercantile Company,** 2016 N. 4th St., Flagstaff, AZ 86004: Free catalog (specify supplies and findings or finished products) ◆ Sterling silver jewelry supplies, Native American arts and crafts, feathers, and leather supplies. 800-413-CHUCK.

**Metalliferous,** 34 W. 46th St., New York, NY 10036: Catalog $5 ◆ Metals, tools, and supplies for jewelry-making and metal crafting. 212-944-0909.

**Microstamp Tools,** 2770 E. Walnut St., Pasadena, CA 91107: Free brochure ◆ Jewelry marking tools. 800-243-3543; 818-793-9489 (in CA).

**MIMports,** 590 Silverado Dr., Lafayette, CA 94549: Free list ◆ Synthetic stones. Available faceted. 510-284-4196.

**Minnesota Lapidary Supply Corp.,** 2825 Dupont Ave. South, Minneapolis, MN 55408: Free catalog ◆ Lapidary equipment and supplies. 612-872-7211.

**Morning Light Emporium,** Roxy Grinnell, P.O. Box 1155, Paronia, CO 81428: Free catalog ◆ Beads and jewelry-making supplies. 800-392-0365. www.wic.net/mle/mle.htm

**Otto H. Mueller,** 444 Wellington Ave., Cranston, RI 02910: Free information ◆ Jewelry findings. 401-467-7910.

**Nasco,** 901 Janesville Ave., Fort Atkinson, WI 53538: Free catalog ◆ Jewelry-making supplies and tools. 800-558-9595. www.nascofa.com

**National Supply Inc.,** 9666 Olive Blvd., Ste. 145, St. Louis, MO 63132: Catalog $4 (refundable) ◆ Beads, jewelry findings, tools, crafts, and supplies. 800-221-9032; 314-567-1928 (in MO). www.nationalsupply.com

**New England International Gems,** 188 Pollard St., Billerica, MA 01862: Free catalog ◆ Brazilian quartz, rocks from India, beads, jewelry-making supplies, tools, and findings. 978-863-8331.

**New Era Gems,** 14923 Rattlesnake Rd., Grass Valley, CA 95945: Catalog $5 ◆ Gemstones from worldwide locations. 800-752-2057.

**Neycraft,** Division of Ney, Ney Industrial Park, Bloomfield, CT 06002: Free information ◆ Benchtop furnaces, ultrasonic cleaners, centrifugal casting machine, and air-driven and electric tools for jewelry-making. 800-538-4593.

**The NgraveR Company,** 67 Wawecus Hill Rd., Bozrah, CT 06334: Catalog $1 (refundable) ◆ Easy-to-use engraving tools and jewelry-making equipment. 860-823-1533.

**Nonferrous Metals,** P.O. Box 2595, Waterbury, CT 06723: Catalog $3 (refundable) ◆ Plain and ornamental brass, copper, bronze, and nickel-silver wire. 203-264-7255.

**M. Nowotny & Company,** 8823 Callahan Rd., San Antonio, TX 78230: Free information ◆ Gemstones and fossils from worldwide sources, jewelry, pewter figurines, key chains, scarabs, obsidian eggs, and peacock feathers. 800-950-8276; 210-342-2512 (in TX).

**H. Obodda Mineral Specimens,** P.O. Box 51, Short Hills, NJ 07078: Free list ◆ Rare and semi-precious gemstones. 973-467-0212.

**Olympic Mountain Gems,** 3664 Briarwood Dr. SE, Port Orchard, WA 98366: Free catalog ◆ Lapidary equipment, jewelery-making tools, gemstones, and supplies. 360-895-9344. www.omgems.com

**Optional Extras,** P.O. Box 8550, Burlington, VT 05402: Catalog $2 ◆ Jewelry findings and beads from worldwide sources. 800-736-0781.

**Oriental Crest Inc.,** 6161 Savoy Dr., Houston, TX 77036: Free information ◆ Semi-precious gemstone jewelry, gemstones and findings, bead-stringing supplies, pendant carvings, and earring jackets. 800-367-3954; 713-780-2425 (in TX).

**Ornamental Resources Inc.,** P.O. Box 3010, Idaho Springs, CO 80452: Catalog $15 ◆ Glass beads, pendants, stones and buttons, metal charms and stampings, rhinestones, findings and tools. 800-876-6762. www.ornabead.com

**Out On A Whim,** 121 E. Cotati Ave., Cotati, CA 94931: Free information ◆ Glass beads, semi-precious stones, jewelry findings and supplies, and beading accessories. 707-664-8343.

**Pioneer Gem Corp.,** P.O. Box 1513, Auburn, WA 98071: Catalog $5 (6 issues) ◆ Unset gemstones for jewelers, hobbyists, and collectors. 253-833-2760. www.pioneergem.com

**Prospectors Pouch Inc.,** P.O. Box 112, Kennesaw, GA 30144: Free information ◆ Rocks, gemstones, and jewelry-making supplies. 770-427-6481.

**Q-C Turquoise,** 3340 E. Washington, Phoenix, AZ 85034: Free information ◆ Turquoise nugget jewelry, nuggets by the strand or pound, and cutting material or blocks. 602-267-1164.

**Raytech,** 475 Smith St., Middletown, CT 06457: Free information ◆ Lapidary and ultraviolet lighting equipment. 860-632-2020.

**Richardson's Recreational Ranch Ltd.,** Gateway Route Box 440, Madras, OR 97741: Free information ◆ Rocks and gemstones from worldwide locations, lapidary equipment, and clocks, clock movements, and parts. 800-433-2680.

**Rings & Things,** P.O. Box 450, Spokane, WA 99210: Catalog $2 (refundable) ◆ Earring findings, chains, clasps, polymer clay, beads, charms, and other jewelry-making supplies. 800-366-2156. www.rings-things.com

**Rio Grande Tools & Equipment,** 7500 Bluewater Rd. NW, Albuquerque, NM 87121: Free catalog ◆ Jewelry findings and tools for grinding and sanding metal and gemstones. 800-545-6566.

**Robins Mining Company,** P.O. Box 236, Mt. Ida, AR 71957: Free information ◆ Quartz crystals, other gems, and minerals. 501-867-2530.

**The Rock Barrell,** 13650 Floyd Rd., Dallas, TX 75243: Free catalog ◆ Findings and settings for jewelry design. 972-231-4809.

**The Rock Peddler,** 5561 S. Stockwell Rd., Tucson, AZ 85746: Free catalog ◆ Lapidary equipment. 800-416-4348. www.donriddle.com/pedl/contents.htm

**Rockhound Shop,** 5348 N. Riverview Dr., Kalamazoo, MI 49004: Catalog $2 ◆ Lapidary equipment, rock tumblers, rocks, and supplies. 616-382-5461

**Ross Metals,** 54 W. 47th St., New York, NY 10036: Free information ◆ Findings, gold and silver wire, and spooled chains. 800-654-ROSS; 212-869-3993 (in NY).

**Roussels,** P.O. Box 476, Arlington, MA 02174: Catalog $1 ◆ Jewelry-making supplies and ready-to-wear jewelry. 781-443-8888.

**Russell's Rock Shop,** 27911 North St., North Liberty, IN 46554: Free information ◆ Gem trees and supplies, bookends, agate slabs, amethyst, cabs, findings, and lucite stands. 219-289-7446.

**Marvin Schwab,** 2740 Garfield Ave., Silver Spring, MD 20910: Catalog $3.50 (refundable) ◆ Beads and gems, jewelry, findings, and supplies. 301-565-0487. beadware@erols.com

**South Pacific Wholesale Company,** Rt. 2, P.O. Box 249, East Montpelier, VT 05651: Free price list ◆ Beads, findings, semi-precious gemstone settings, gold and silver bracelets, necklaces, and earrings. 800-338-2162. sopacvt@aol.com

**Star Diamond Industries West,** 17022 Montanero Ave., Carson, CA 90746: Free list of retail sources ◆ Slab and trim saws, grinders, sanders, and polishers. 310-325-9696.

**Stone Age Industries Inc.,** P.O. Box 383, Powell, WY 82435: Catalog $1.50 ◆ Rough gemstones, slabs, cutting and polishing equipment, and lapidary supplies. 800-751-4681.

**Swest Inc.,** Catalog Dept., 11090 N. Stemmons Freeway, Dallas, TX 75229: Free information ◆ Jeweler's tools, wax patterns, findings, gemstones, and supplies. 800-527-5057.

**Tagit,** P.O. Box 1534, San Juan Capistrano, CA 92675: Free list of retail sources ◆ Equipment and supplies for jewelry finishing and lapidary crafting. 714-949-8380.

**Thunderbird Supply Company,** 1907 W. 66th Ave., Gallup, NM 87301: Free catalog ◆ Metals, findings, and jewelry-making supplies. 800-545-7968.

**Tierracast,** 3177 Guerneville Rd., Santa Rosa, CA 95401: Free catalog ◆ Jewelry-making findings. 800-222-9939; 707-545-5787 (in CA).

**Myron Toback Inc.,** 25 W. 47th St., New York, NY 10036: Free information ◆ Tools for jewelry-making and silversmithing. 800-223-7550; 212-398-8300 (in NY).

**Tripp's Manufacturing,** P.O. Box 1369, Socorro, NM 87801: Free catalog ◆ Pre-notched mounts. 800-545-7962; 505-835-2461 (in NM).

**Tru-Square Metal Products,** P.O. Box 585, Auburn, WA 98071: Free brochure ◆ Tumblers and other rock polishing equipment. 800-225-1017.

**TSI Jewelry Supply,** 101 Nickerson St., Seattle, WA 98109: Free catalog ◆ Jewelry-making tools and supplies. 800-426-9984. www.Tsijeweltools.com

**Tumblecraft,** 5401 James Ave., Minneapolis, MN 55430: Free catalog ◆ Rockhounding supplies, polished agate, opals, and mineral specimens. 612-560-0736.

**Ultra Tec,** 1025 E. Chestnut, Santa Ana, CA 92701: Free brochure ◆ Lapidary equipment. 714-542-0608. ultratec@primenet.com

**Veon Creations,** 3565 State Rd. V, De Soto, MO 63020: Catalog $4 ◆ Beads, gemstones, pearls, findings, and jewelry-making supplies. 314-586-5377.

**Vibra-Tek Company,** 1844 Arroya Rd., Colorado Springs, CO 80906: Free information ◆ Rock polishers. 800-634-8611.

## JOKES & NOVELTIES

**Pete Best's Discount Magic Warehouse,** The Best Bldg., P.O. Box 285063, Boston, MA 02128: Free catalog ◆ Novelty and professional magic, books, and jokes. 800-438-7236. www.pbdm.com

**Brad Burt's Magic Shop,** 4204 Convoy St., Ste. 103, San Diego, CA 92111: Free catalog ◆ Magic for amateur and professional magicians, how-to-do magic video cassettes, gag items, and clown supplies. 615-571-4749. bb@magicshop.com

**Chazpro Magic Company,** P.O. Box 41415, Eugene, OR 97404: Catalog $3 ◆ Clown props, books, juggling equipment, jokes, and novelties. 541-689-6919. www.chazpro.com

**Clarkson Studio,** 401 N. Hoback St., Helena, MT 59601: Free brochure ◆ Gag items, magic tricks, make-up, and other clown supplies. 406-442-2046.

**Conleys House of Magic,** 4910-A Hwy. 17 South, North Myrtle Beach, SC 29582: Free catalog ◆ Jokes, novelties, and magic. 803-272-4227. trirmagic@aol.com

**Elmwood Magic & Novelty,** 507 Elmwood Ave., Buffalo, NY 14222: Free catalog ◆ Magic, jokes, and novelties. 800-764-2372. members@aol.com/elmmagic

**Fun Magic Tricks,** 520 Broadway, San Antonio, TX 78215: Catalog $1 (refundable) ◆ Magic tricks, books, gags, juggling equipment, puzzles, and collectibles.

**Funny Side Up,** P.O. Box 2800, 425 Stump Rd., North Whales, PA 19454: Free catalog ◆ Gag gifts, practical jokes, and entertaining thing-a-ma-jigs. 800-247-3747.

**Global Shakeup,** 235 East Colorado Blvd., Ste. 178, Pasadena, CA 91101: Catalog $2 (refundable with $25 order) ◆ Snowdomes, snowglobes, waterbells, and more. 213-259-8988. www.snowdomes.com

**Klutz Press,** 2121 Staunton Ct., Palo Alto, CA 94306: Free information ◆ Novelty and fun merchandise, juggling equipment, and books. 650-424-0739. www.klutz.com

**Lighter Side Company,** 4514 19th St. Court East, P.O. Box 25600, Bradenton, FL 34206: Free catalog ◆ Jokes and novelties, tricks, science and sports equipment, and hobby supplies. 941-747-6645.

**Magic & Fun Shop,** 16872 Hwy. 3, Webster, TX 77598: Free catalog ◆ Jokes, gags, novelties, clown supplies, make-up, magic tricks, and puzzles. 281-332-8142. www.fun-shop.com

**Archie McPhee & Company**, Box 30852, Seattle, WA 98103: Free catalog ◆ Voodoo dolls to fashion items, party supplies to flamingos, science things, footwear, T-shirts, outdoor lawn art, exotica, clocks, and exclusive gifts. 206-745-0711. www.halcyon.com/mcphee.welcome.html.

**Things You Never Knew Existed,**c/o Johnson Smith Company, 4514 19th St. Court East, Bradenton, FL 34203: Free catalog ◆ Novelties, tricks, hobby supplies, and other unusual things. 941-747-6645.

## JUGGLING

**Abracadabra Magic Shop,** 125 Lincoln Blvd., Middlesex, NJ 08846: Catalog $5 ◆ Close-up and stage magic, clown props, juggling equipment, balloons, costumes, and theatrical make-up. 732-805-0200. umsi@erols.com

**Aunt Clowney's Warehouse,** P.O. Box 1444, Corona, CA 91718: Free catalog ◆ Books on juggling and clowning. 909-273-0900. auntc@empirenet.com

**Browser's Den of Magic,** 875 Eglinton Ave. W., #13, Toronto, Ontario, Canada M6C 3Z9: Free catalog ◆ Magic for amateurs and professionals, juggling equipment, and ventriloquist dolls. 416-783-7022. www.websmart.com/browsers

**Chazpro Magic Company,** P.O. Box 41415, Eugene, OR 97404: Catalog $3 *Juggling and clown supplies, books, jokes, and novelties. 541-689-6919. www.chazpro.com

**Compleat Gamester,** 350 Moody St., Waltham, MA 02154: Free information ◆ Juggling, dart, and billiard supplies. 800-698-9505. www.compgames.com

**Steve Dawson's Magic Touch Catalog,** 144 N. Milpitas Blvd., Milpitas, CA 95035: Catalog $3 ◆ Magic effects, books, videos, accessories, clown and juggling supplies, and make-up. 408-263-9404.

**Dekker Service Inc.,** 5433 116th Ave. SE, Bellevue, WA 98006: Free brochure ◆ Pashley mountain unicycles. 425-641-9639. www.eskimo.com/~mdekker

**Brian Dube Inc.,** 520 Broadway, 3rd Floor, New York, NY 10012: Free catalog ◆ Juggling equipment, boomerangs, yo-yo's, and books. 212-941-0060. www.dube.com

**Florida Magic Company,** P.O. Box 290781, Fort Lauderdale, FL 33329: Free information ◆ Puppets, magic tricks, and juggling supplies. 954-473-1902. FlaMagicCo@aol.com

**Fun Magic Tricks,** 520 Broadway, San Antonio, TX 78215: Catalog $1 (refundable) ◆ Magic tricks, books, gags, juggling equipment, puzzles, and collectibles.

**Grand Illusions,** 7704 Fair Oaks Blvd., Carmichael, CA 95608: Free catalog ◆ Magic, costumes, and juggling equipment. 916-944-2970. www.grandillusions.com

**Infinite Illusions,** P.O. Box 2584, Tallahassee, FL 32316: Free information ◆ Juggling supplies, boomerangs, and yo-yo's. 800-548-6724; 904-385-6463 (in FL). www.yoyoguy.com

**Juggling Arts,** 5535 N. 11th St., Phoenix, AZ 85014: Catalog $1 ◆ Juggling props. 602-266-4391.

**Juggling Capitol,** The Old Post Office Pavilion, 1100 Pennsylvania Ave. NW, Washington, DC 20004: Free catalog ◆ Juggling props and books. 888-584-4536. www.jugglingcapitol.com/

**Klutz Press,** 2121 Staunton Ct., Palo Alto, CA 94306: Free information ◆ Novelty and fun merchandise, juggling equipment, and books. 650-424-0739. www.klutz.com

**La Rock's Fun & Magic Outlet,** 3847 Rosehaven Dr., Charlotte, NC 28205: Catalog $3 ◆ Clown and balloon how-to books, balloons, balloon sculpture kits, juggling supplies, and magic equipment. 704-563-9300. larocks1@aol.com

**Mecca Magic Inc.,** 49 Dodd St., Bloomfield, NJ 07003: Catalog $10 ◆ Juggling equipment, theatrical make-up, clown props, balloons, magic, costumes and wigs, puppets, and ventriloquism dummies. 201-429-7597. meccamagic@meccamagic.com

**T. Myers Magic Inc.,** 6513 Thomas Springs Rd., Austin, TX 78736: Free catalog ◆ Magic and other supplies for balloon twisters, jugglers, facepainters, clowns, and magicians. 800-288-7925; 512-288-7925 (in TX). www.tmyers.com

**Renegade Juggling Equipment,** P.O. Box 406, Santa Cruz, CA 95061: Free catalog ◆ Juggling equipment. 831-426-7343. www.renegadejuggling.com

**Todd Smith Products,** 13401 Lakeshore Blvd., Cleveland, OH 44110: Free information ◆ Juggling equipment. 216-761-6388. www.toddsmith.com

**Sparkle's Entertainment Express,** Jan Lovell, 152 N. Water St., Gallatin, TN 37066: Product list $1 ◆ Make-up, costumes and clown shoes, balloons, juggling and magic equipment, puppets, books, and supplies. 615-452-9755.

**Teresa & Sem Unicycles,** P.O. Box 40353, Redford, MI 48240: Free brochure ◆ Unicycles and other juggling accessories. 313-537-8175. members.aol.com/semcycle

**Under the Big Top,** P.O. Box 807, Placentia, CA 92670: Catalog $4 ◆ Juggling equipment, clown props, costumes, make-up, balloons, and party supplies. 800-995-7727.

**The Wright Life,** 200 Linden, Fort Collins, CO 80524: Free catalog ◆ Frisbees (flying discs), skateboards, snowboards, in-line skates, boomerangs, stunt kites, juggling equipment, and more. 800-321-8833. www.wrightlife.com

## JUKEBOXES

**Antique Slot Machine Part Company,** 140 N. Western Ave., Carpentersville, IL 60110: Free catalog ◆ Books and manuals, slot stands and pads, and parts for slot machines, jukeboxes, and pinballs. 847-428-8476.

**Back Pages Antiques,** 125 Greene St., New York, NY 10012: Free information ◆ Collector jukeboxes. 212-460-5998.

**Coin Machine Trader,** P.O. Box 602, Huron, SD 57350: Information $4 ◆ Manuals for most jukeboxes and slot machines. 605-352-7590.

**Fabulous Fantasies,** 12602 Ventura Blvd., Studio City, CA 91604: Free price list ◆ Pinball machines, arcade games, jukeboxes, and gameroom furnishings. 800-5-PINBALL.

**Illinois Antique Slot Machine Company,** P.O. Box 542, Westmont, IL 60559: Free information ◆ Antique Wurlitzer jukeboxes, nickelodeons, music boxes, and slot and other coin-operated machines. 630-985-2742. zygmunt@mcs.net

**Jukebox City,** 1950 1st Ave. South, Seattle, WA 98134: Free photos with long SASE ◆ Jukeboxes and coin-operated machines. 206-625-1950.

**Jukebox Classics & Vintage Slot Machines Inc.,** 6742 5th Ave., Brooklyn, NY 11220: Free information ◆ Antique jukeboxes and coin-operated machines. 718-833-8455.

**Jukebox Junction,** 203 4th, Cumming, IA 50061: Catalog $2.50 ◆ Antique jukeboxes. 515-981-4019.

**Lazarus Auto Collection,** P.O. Box 6732, Rockford, IL 61125: Free information ◆ Jukeboxes and arcade machines. 815-229-1258.

**National Jukebox Exchange,** 121 Lakeside Dr., Mayfield, NY 12117: Free catalog ◆ Antique jukeboxes, slot and other arcade machines, and parts. 888-321-PAPA.

**New England Jukebox,** 77 Tolland Tnpk., Manchester, CT 06040: Free list with long SASE and two 1st class stamps ◆ Jukeboxes and accessories. 860-646-1533.

**Nostalgic Music Company,** 58 Union Ave., New Providence, NJ 07974: Free information ◆ Restored jukeboxes, from the 1940s and 1950s. 908-464-5538.

**Remember When Collectibles,** 6570 Memorial Dr., Stone Mountain, GA 30083: Free brochure ◆ Vintage Coca-Cola machines and jukeboxes. 770-879-7878. www.fiftiescollectibles.com

**Row/AMI Jukeboxes,** 1500 Union Ave. SE, Grand Rapids, MI 49507: Free request list of retail sources ◆ Jukeboxes. 800-636-2787. www.roweami.com

**Zygmunt & Associates,** P.O. Box 542, Westmont, IL 60559: Free brochure ◆ Jukeboxes and slot machines. 630-985-2742. zygmunt@mcs.net

## KALEIDOSCOPES

**Atlas Art & Stained Glass,** P.O. Box 76084, Oklahoma City, OK 73147: Catalog $3 ◆ Kaleidoscopes, frames, lamp bases, and art and craft, stained glass, jewelry-making, and foil-crafting supplies. 405-946-1230.

**Gemini Kaleidoscopes,** 203 Lindsay Rd., Zelienople, PA 16063: Free information ◆ Handcrafted kaleidoscopes. 412-452-8700.

**Bensley Enterprises,** 1116 Madison Ave., Charleston, IL 61920: Free brochure ◆ Brass and stained glass kaleidoscopes with optional colors and glass patterns. 217-348-0855. csbdb@ux1.cts.eiu.edu

**Van Cort Instruments Inc.,** 29 Industrial Dr., Northampton, MA 01060: Free list of retail sources ◆ Kaleidoscopes and optical equipment. 413-586-9800.

**Warner-Crivellaro,** 1855 Weaversville Rd., Allentown, PA 18103: Free information ◆ Stained glass, jewelry-making, kaleidoscope, clock kits, and other supplies. Also how-to books. 800-523-4242; 610-264-1100 (in PA). www.warner-criv.com

**Whippoorwill Crafts,** 126 S. Market St., Boston, MA 02109: Free information ◆ Kaleidoscopes, wood boxes and chests, instrumentalist chimes, toys and games, clocks, and imaginative crafts. 800-860-9551; 617-523-5149 (in MA).

## KARAOKE MUSIC

**Karaoke Direct,** 4425 Fitch Ave., #122, Baltimore, MD 21236: Free catalog ◆ Karaoke compact discs and playing equipment. 800-879-7664. www.KARAOKE.com

**Karaoke WOW,** P.O. Box 12781, Scottsdale, AZ 85267: Free catalog ◆ Equipment, software, videos, CDs, laser discs, audio cassettes, and more. 800-293-7464.

## KITCHEN UTENSILS & COOKWARE

**Alsto Company,** P.O. Box 1267, Galesburg, IL 61401: Catalog $1 ◆ Tools, pet products, and kitchen aids. 800-447-0048.

**American Harvest,** 4064 Peavey Rd., Chaska, MN 55318: Free information ◆ Food dehydrator and bread machine. 800-288-4545.

**B-West Outdoor Specialties,** 2425 N. Huachuca, Tucson, AZ 85745: Free information ◆ Outdoor cookware. 800-293-7855; 520-628-1990 (in AZ).

**The Baker's Catalogue,** P.O. Box 876, Norwich, VT 05055: Free catalog ◆ Baking equipment and recipe ingredients. 800-827-6836.

**Bourgeat Cookware,** Au Service De La Grande Cuisine, 20 Fernwood Rd., Boston, MA 02132: Catalog $1 ◆ Copper, aluminum, and stainless-steel kitchen accessories. 617-469-0189.

**Bridge Kitchenware Corp.,** 214 E. 52nd St., New York, NY 10022: Catalog $3 ◆ Imported cooking utensils. 212-838-1901.

**Brookstone Company,** Order Processing Center, 1655 Bassford Dr., Mexico, MO 65265: Free catalog ◆ Professional restaurant equipment for home chefs. 800-926-7000.

**Chef's Catalog,** P.O. Box 620048, Dallas, TX 75262: Free catalog ◆ Instant-reading cooking thermometers. 800-338-3232. www.chefscatalog.com

**The Chef's Store,** 836 Traction Ave., Los Angeles, CA 90013: Free catalog ◆ Chefware, tools, equipment, supplies, specialty foods, and how-to-ideas for professional chefs and home cooks. 888-334-CHEF; 213-680-0418 (in CA). www.chefstore.com

**Colonial Garden Kitchens,** Hanover Direct Pennsylvania Inc., Hanover, PA 17333-0001: Free catalog ◆ Cookware and accessories. 800-245-3333.

**Commercial Aluminum Cookware Company,** P.O. Box 583, Toledo, OH 43697: Free information ◆ Calphalon cookware. 419-666-8700.

**A Cook's Wares,** 211 37th St., Beaver's Falls, PA 15010: Catalog $2 ◆ Cookware, cutlery, bakeware, French copper pans, and food processors. 412-846-9490.

**Crate & Barrel,** P.O. Box 9059, Wheeling, IL 60090: Free catalog ◆ Gourmet cooking equipment and appliances. 800-323-5461.

**Cris Enterprises Inc.,** P.O. Box 10654, Daytona Beach, FL 32120: Free brochure ◆ An easy-to-assemble motorized mill for use in the home that grinds or flakes whole-grain kernels into flour, coarse meal, or anything in between. 904-238-7572.

**Cutco Cutlery,** P.O. Box 1230, Olean, NY 14760: Catalog $1 ◆ Cutlery, knives, and kitchen accessories. 800-828-0448. www.xnet.com/~usable/CUTCO/Cutco.html

**Dansk International Design,** 108 Corporate Park Dr., White Plains, NY 10604: Free list of retail sources ◆ Dinnerware, stemware, flatware, kitchenware, and serving pieces. 800-293-2675; 914-697-6400 (in NY). www.danskfurnishings.com

**East Hampton Industries Inc.,** P.O. Box 5069, East Hampton, NY 11937: Free brochure ◆ Software for recipe-collecting, cookbook organizing, and meal planning. Also kitchen gadgets. 800-645-1188; 516-324-2224 (in NY).

**EdgeCraft Corp.,** 825 Southwood Rd., Avondale, PA 19311: Free list of retail sources ◆ Professional style food slicer for the home. 800-342-3255.

**The Faith Mountain Company,** P.O. Box 199, Sperryville, VA 22740: Free catalog ◆ Kitchen utensils, country-style gifts, folk art reproductions, toys and dolls, handmade Appalachian baskets, and Christmas decorations. 800-822-7238. 800-822-7238. www.FaithMountain.com

**Good Catalog Company,** 5484 SE International Way, Portland, OR 97222: Catalog $5 ◆ Kitchen gadgets and dining, gardening, and decorative accessories. 800-225-3870.

**Iron Craft,** Old Rt. 28, P.O. Box 351, Ossipee, NH 03864: Catalog $2 ◆ Kettles and grates, enamel cookware, butcher aprons, bellows, heating systems for fireplaces, weather vanes, signs, gifts, and cast-iron items. 603-539-6159.

**K-Tec,** 420 N. Geneva Rd., Lindon, UT 84042: Free information ◆ Multi-function food preparation machine. 800-748-5400.

**Kamper's Kettle,** 2165 Bruneau Dr., Boise, ID 83709: Free catalog ◆ Outdoor cooking tables, ovens, cast-iron accessories, Dutch ovens, other cookware and accessories, and books and videos on cooking with Dutch ovens. 800-860-1100; 208-377-0344 (in ID). Kampers@RMC.NET

**King Arthur Flour Baker's Catalog,** P.O. Box 876, Norwich, VT 05055: Free catalog ◆ Baking, bread-making, and pasta equipment. 800-827-6836. www.kingarthurflour.com

**Kitchen & Home,** Hanover Direct Pennsylvania Inc., Hanover, PA 17333-0001: Free catalog ◆ Culinary tools, appliances, and gadgets. 717-633-3333.

**Kitchen Etc.,** 32 Industrial Dr., Exeter, NH 03833: Catalog $2 ◆ Cookware, cutlery, flatware, crystal, and dinnerware. 800-232-4070. www.kitchenetc.com

**Kitchen Kneads,** 725 W. Riverdale Rd., Ogden, UT 84405: Free catalog ◆ Kitchen equipment and accessories for healthy cooking. Also foods and herbs. 800-658-8521; 801-399-3221 (in UT).

**Kitchen Krafts,** P.O. Box 442, Waukon, IA 52172: Free catalog ◆ Food crafting equipment, cake decorating accessories, and supplies. 800-776-0575; 319-535-8000 (in IA). www.kitchenkrafts.com

**Lamson & Goodnow Manufacturing Company,** P.O. Box 128, Shelburne Falls, MA 01370: Free brochure ◆ Handcrafted kitchen cutlery. 800-872-6564; 413-625-6331 (in MA).

**Lehman Hardware & Appliances Inc.,** P.O. Box 41, Kidron, OH 44636: Catalog $2 ◆ Kitchen accessories, housewares, stoves for heating and cooking, farming and homesteading items, non-electric appliances, woodworking and log-smithing tools, and other old-time general store items. 330-857-5757. GetLehmans@aol.com

**Natural Lifestyle,** 16 Lookout Dr., Asheville, NC 28804: Free catalog ◆ Water filters, organic foods, macrobiotic specialties, cookware, organic cotton clothes, earth care products, and cookbooks. 704-254-9606.

**Pearl's Pantry,** P.O. Box 4055, Vail, CO 81658: Free price list ◆ Kitchen accessories, cooking aids, and gourmet foods. 800-544-9714.

**Pepperidge Farm,** P.O. Box 917, Clinton, CT 06413: Free catalog ◆ Specialty and microwave cookware, tools, kitchen gadgets, glassware, silverware, cookbooks, and gourmet foods. 800-243-9314.

**Plastaket Manufacturing Company,** 6220 E. Hwy. 12, Lodi, CA 95240: Free information ◆ Easy-to-use juicer and homogenizer. 209-369-2154.

**Polder Thermometers,** 8 Slater St., Port Chester, NY 10573: Free information ◆ Instant-reading cooking thermometers. 914-937-8200.

**Professional Cutlery Direct,** 170 Boston Post Rd., Ste. 135, Madison, CT 06443: Free catalog ◆ Easy-to-read cooking thermometers with an LCD display, professional cutlery, and kitchen tools. 800-859-6994. SV85@cutlery.com

**Prestons Household Accessories,** P.O. Box 369, Ossipee, NH 03864: Catalog $3 ◆ Stove and fireplace accessories and cast iron cookware. 603-539-4114.

**Spice Merchant,** P.O. Box 524, Jackson Hole, WY 83001: Free catalog ◆ Spices, herbs, and flavoring condiments from China, Japan, Indonesia, Thailand, and other countries. Also kitchen accessories for Oriental cooking. 800-551-5999. www.emall.com/spice

**The Spanish Table,** 1427 Western Ave., Seattle, WA 98101: Free information ◆ Paella pans and other kitchen accessories. 206-682-2827.

**Sur La Table,** Catalog Division, 1765 6th Ave., Seattle, WA 98134: Free information ◆ Handcarved thistle-pattern wood shortbread molds and cooking and baking equipment. 800-243-0852.

**Taylor Thermometers,** P.O. Box 1349, Fletcher, NC 28732: Free information ◆ Instant-reading cooking thermometers. 704-684-5178.

**21st Century Quality Cookware,** 20006 44th St., North Bergen, NJ 07047: Free catalog ◆ Imported cookware, cutlery, and kitchen accessories. 800-405-0334.

**Vermont Country Store,** Mail Order Office, P.O. Box 3000, Manchester Center, VT 05255: Free catalog ◆ Cookware and home accessories. 802-362-4667.

**Lillian Vernon Kitchen,** Virginia Beach, VA 23479: Free catalog ◆ Kitchen accessories, serving pieces, dinnerware, and outdoor cooking aids. 800-285-5555. LVCcustsrv@aol.com

**Williams-Sonoma,** Mail Order Department, P.O. Box 7456, San Francisco, CA 94120: Free catalog ◆ Cookware for home chefs, serving pieces, household accessories, books, and gourmet foods. 800-541-1262.

**Wilton Enterprise Inc.,** 2240 W. 75th St., Woodridge, IL 60517: Catalog $6 (refundable) ◆ Supplies for making cookies, cakes, and candy. 630-963-7100.

**Winterthur Museum & Gardens,** Kennett Pike, Winterthur, DE 19810: Free catalog ◆ Cookware. 800-448-3883.

**Zabar's & Company,** 2245 Broadway, New York, NY 10024: Free catalog ◆ Cookware, food processors, microwave ovens, kitchen tools, coffee makers, and gourmet foods. 800-697-6301; 212-496-1234 (in NY).

## KITES & WINDSOCKS

**Aerie Kiteworks,** 200 Prairie St., Rockford, IL 61107: Free information ◆ Competition kites. 815-962-9680.

**Aerodrome Sport Kites**, 399 Church St., Wood River Junction, RI 02894: Free information ◆ Self-adjusting sail kites. 401-364-8989.

**Banner Fabric,** Kite Studio, 5555 Hamilton Blvd., Wescosville, PA 18106: Catalog $1 ◆ Fabrics, notions, and hardware for kites, flags, banners, and windsocks. 800-KITE-991; 610-395-3560 (in PA).

**Becky's Performance Kites,** 3530 Woodbine Ave., Lincoln, NE 68506: Free catalog ◆ Kites, kits and accessories, wind toys, flags, and windsocks. 800-BECKYS-4; 402-489-4902 (in NE). www.4W.com/beckys

**BFK Kite Store,** 3111 S. Valley View, A-116, Las Vegas, NV 89102: Free catalog ◆ Accessories and single, dual, and quad-line kites. 800-638-5483; 702-220-4340 (in NV). www.kitestore.com

**Big Wind Kite Factory,** 120 Maunaloa Hwy., P.O. Box 10, Maunaloa, Molokai, HI 96770: Free information ◆ Handmade kites that fold for easy transporting. 808-552-2364.

**Caribbean Kite Company,** 1096 NE 45th St., Fort Lauderdale, FL 33334: Catalog $1 ◆ Stunt, sport, and single-line kites. 954-776-5433. www.caribbean-kite.com

**Catch the Wind,** 266 SE Hwy. 101, Lincoln City, OR 97367 ◆ A complete collection of kites, windsocks, banners, and toys from around the world. 800-227-7878. www.catchthewind.com

**Colors in Flight,** 3169 E. Maplewood Ave., Littleton, CO 80121: Catalog $5 ◆ Banners, party pennants, flags and windsocks, and hardware. 303-794-1095.

**The Crystal Kite Company,** 1320 Lakeview Dr., La Habra, CA 90631: Free information ◆ Competition stunt kites. 714-870-4546.

**Delta Breeze Kites,** 304 Marble Dr., Antioch, CA 94509: Free information ◆ Soft quad kite systems. 510-754-3091.

**Dyna-Kite Corp.,** P.O. Box 24, Three Rivers, MA 01080: Free information ◆ Kites. 413-283-2555.

**Force 10 Foils,** 10920 N. Port Washington Rd., Mequon, WI 53092: Free list of retail sources ◆ Easy-to-fly foil kites. 414-241-8862. www.execpc.com/~force10attila

**The Gasworks Park Kite Shop,** 333 Wallingford North, Seattle, WA 98003: Free catalog ◆ Kite-making supplies. 206-633-4780.

**Gone with the Wind Kites,** 1601 Industrial Way, Ste. 100, Belmont, CA 94002: Free catalog ◆ Kites and accessories. 415-594-1055. www.gwtw-kites.com

**Great Winds Kites,** 402 Occidental Ave. South, Seattle, WA 98104: Free catalog ◆ Kites. 206-624-6886.

**Grizzly Peak Kiteworks,** 1305 Alvarado Rd., Berkeley, CA 94705: Free catalog ◆ Kites and kite-making materials. 510-644-2981.

**Hang-Em High Fabrics,** 1420 Yale Ave., Richmond, VA 23224: Free information ◆ Kite-making supplies. 804-233-6155.

**Hearth Song,** Mail Processing Center, 6519 N. Galena Rd., P.O. Box 1773, Peoria, IL 61656: Free catalog ◆ Kites, books, dollhouse miniatures, dolls, and art supplies. 800-325-2502.

**Hyperkites,** 2979 A St., San Diego, CA 92102: Free catalog ◆ High-performance kites. 619-702-7061.

**Into the Wind/Kites,** 1408 Pearl St., Boulder, CO 80302: Free catalog ◆ Kites, windsocks, flags, and flying toys. 800-204-5483. www.intothewind.com

**KiteCo,** Division North Cloth/North Sails, 189 Pepe's Farm Rd., Milford, CT 06460: Free price list ◆ Ripstop fabric for kites and sails. 203-877-7638. Brenda@ncloth.northsails.com

**Kite Studio,** 5555 Hamilton Blvd., Wescosville, PA 18106: Catalog $2 ◆ Kite-building supplies. 800-KITE-991; 610-395-3560 (in PA).

**Kites & Fun Things,** 1049 S. Main, Plymouth, MI 48170: Free information ◆ Kite-building supplies. 313-454-3760.

**Klig's Kites,** 811 Seaboard St., Myrtle Beach, SC 29577: Free catalog ◆ Stunt kites, single-line kites, windsocks, banners, and flags. 800-333-5944. www.kligs.com

**Krazy Kites,** 8445 International Dr., Orlando, FL 32819: Free catalog ◆ Stunt and single-line kites, windsocks, and banners. 800-982-2635.

**MacKinaw Kite Company,** 116 Washington St., Grand Haven, MI 49417: Free catalog ◆ Stunt kites. 800-622-4655.

**New Tech Kites,** 7208 McNeil Dr., Ste. 207, Austin, TX 78729: Free information ◆ Stunt and high-flying kites. 800-325-4768.

**Ocean Kites,** P.O. Box 1287, Long Beach, WA 98631: Free catalog ◆ Kites and accessories, windsocks, and flags. 360-642-2299.

**Sky Delight Kites,** P.O. Box 1989, Kingsland, TX 78639: Free information ◆ Single-line stunt kites that collapse for portability. 915-388-9288. jkscholz@tstar.net

**Spectra Star Kites,** 350 E. 18th St., Yuma, AZ 85364: Free information ◆ Competition kites. 520-782-2541.

**Squadron Kites,** 15953 Minnesota Ave., Paramount, CA 90723: Free information ◆ Kites. 800-735-4837. www.squadronkites.com

**Trlby Kites,** 65 New Litchfield St., Torrington, CT 06790: Free information ◆ Stunt kites. 800-328-7529.

**What's Up Kites,** 4500 Chagrin River Rd., Chagrin Falls, OH 44022: Free list of retail sources ◆ Ultra-light, stunt, and airfoil kites. 216-247-4222.

**Wind Related Inc.,** 109 4th St., Hamilton, MT 59840: Free information ◆ Windsocks, windcircles, and wind-banners. 800-735-1885. www.bitterroot.net/wind/index.html

**The Wright Life,** 200 Linden, Fort Collins, CO 80524: Free catalog ◆ Frisbees (flying discs), skateboards, snowboards, in-line skates, boomerangs, stunt kites, juggling equipment, and more. 800-321-8833. www.wrightlife.com

# KNITTING

## Knitting Machines

**All Brands Sewing Machines,** 9789 Florida Blvd., Baton Rouge, LA 70815: Free brochure (specify type of machine) ◆ Knitting, serger, and sewing machines and accessories. 800-739-7374. sewserg@aol.com

**Brother International Corp.,** 200 Cottontail Ln., Somerset, NJ 08875: Free information ◆ Knitting machines. 908-356-8880. www.brother.com

**Fiber Studio,** 9 Foster Hill Rd., Box 637, Henniker, NH 03242: Spinning fibers catalog $1; yarn samples $4; equipment catalog $1 ◆ Spinning, weaving, and knitting equipment. Also cotton, mohair, wool, alpaca, silk, linen yarn, and spinning fibers. 603-428-7830.

**Knit 'N Needle,** 722 W. Center, Duncanville, TX 75116: Free information ◆ Hand and machine yarns, books, and knitting machines. 972-296-4008.

**Knitpicky Knitting Machines,** 1505 Mayfair, Champaign, IL 61821: Free information ◆ New and used knitting machines and computer interface programs. 217-355-5400.

**Krh Knits,** P.O. Box 1587, Avon, CT 06001: Catalog $5 ◆ Knitting machines, accessories, how-to information, yarn winders, yarns, fabric paints, finishing tools, crochet accessories, elastic thread, patterns, and notions. 800-248-KNIT.

**Mary Lue's Knitting World,** 101 W. Broadway, St. Peter, MN 56082: Free information ◆ Refurbished and used Brother knitting machines. 507-931-3734.

**Piney Mountain Cottage,** 466 Mill Creek Rd., Sunset, SC 29685: Free catalog ◆ Knitting machines, accessories, yarns, and patterns. 864-878-5839.

**Sew-Knit Distributors,** 9789 Florida Blvd., Baton Rouge, LA 70815: Free catalog ◆ Sewing and knitting machines. 800-739-7374. serg@aol.com

**Threads Etc.,** 61568 Eastlake Dr., Bend, OR 97702: Catalog $2 (refundable) ◆ Knitting machines and accessories, yarns, books, patterns, and kits. 800-208-2046; 541-388-2046 (in OR).

**Weaving Works,** 4717 Brooklyn Ave. NE, Seattle, WA 98105: Catalog $4.50 ◆ Looms, spinning wheels, hand and machine knitting supplies, traditional and fashion yarns, and books. 206-524-1221.

## Patterns, Kits, & Accessories

**Allegro Yarns,** 3535 Pierce St. NE, Minneapolis, MN 55418: Catalog $3 ◆ Yarns, needles, patterns, and kits. 800-547-3808 (evenings).

**Aura Yarns,** Box 602, Derby Line, VT 05830: Free information ◆ Icelandic wool sweater kits and alpaca, cashmere, mohair, merino, shetland, silk, and cotton yarns. 802-876-2998.

**Bette Bornside Company,** 2733 Dauphine St., New Orleans, LA 70117: Catalog $4 ◆ Yarns, patterns, books, and needles. 800-221-9276.

**Samuel Charis Knits,** 372 Florin Rd., Ste. 312, Sacramento, CA 95831: Free catalog ◆ Sweater kits. 800-321-KNIT; 916-392-8213 (in CA).

**Cotton Clouds,** 5175 S. 14th Ave., Safford, AZ 85546: Catalog $6.50 ◆ Cotton yarns, spinning fibers, tools, books, looms, kits, and patterns. 800-322-7888; 520-428-5885 (in AZ). www.cottonclouds.com

**Dollettes-N-Things,** P.O. Box 1005, Herndon, VA 20172: Free catalog ◆ Knitting patterns for 3-dimensionals. 800-547-2994.

**Earth Guild,** 33 Haywood St., Asheville, NC 28801: Catalog $3 ◆ Basket-making, weaving, spinning, dyeing, pottery, woodcarving, hand and machine knitting, rug-making, netting, and chair-caning supplies. 800-327-8448. www.earthguild.com

**Martha Hall,** 20 Bartol Island Rd., Freeport, ME 04032: Catalog $2 ◆ Easy-to-knit wool sweater kits and hand-dyed silk, mohair, linen, cotton, cashmere, and alpaca yarn. 800-643-4566.

**Herrschners Inc.,** 2800 Hoover Rd., Stevens Point, WI 54492: Free catalog ◆ Yarns, knitting accessories, and needle craft, crochet, and hooking kits. 800-441-0838. www.herrschners.com

**Knitting Traditions,** P.O. Box 421, Delta, PA 17314: Catalog $5 ◆ Kits for making socks, sweaters, and mittens. Also patterns, knitting tools, books, and more. 717-456-7950. members.aol.com/KnitTradit

**Betty Lampen,** 2930 Jackson St., San Francisco, CA 94115: Free information ◆ Knitting pattern books. www.bettylampenknitbooks.com

**Carolin Lowy Needlecraft,** 630 Sun Meadows Dr., Kernersville, NC 27284: Price list $2 ◆ Needlepoint, knitting, embroidery, and counted cross- stitching patterns. 336-784-7576. www.kernersville.com/lowy

**Mary Maxim Inc.,** 2001 Holland Ave., P.O. Box 5019, Port Huron, MI 48061: Free catalog ◆ Needle craft kits, yarn, and other supplies. 800-962-9504.

**Moonrise,** 2804 Fretz Valley Rd., Perkasie, PA 18944: Free catalog ◆ Books, yarn, thread, and lace-knitting supplies. 215-795-0345.

**Patternworks,** P.O. Box 1690, Poughkeepsie, NY 12601: Catalog $3 ◆ Knitting supplies and accessories. 800-438-5464; 914-462-8000 (in NY). www.patternworks.com

**P.G. Roberts Company,** P.O. Box 2468, Loves Park, IL 61132: Free information ◆ Interchangeable knitting needle sets.

**Sew 'n Sew,** 1111 N. Main St., Summerville, NC 29483: Free information ◆ Smocking and heirloom sewing supplies, English and French lace, fabrics, and knitting aids. 803-871-7822.

**Stitches East,** 55 E. 52nd St., New York, NY 10022: Free information ◆ Knitting and needlepoint supplies, yarns, patterns, needles, and canvases. 212-421-0112.

**Swedish Yarn Imports,** P.O. Box 2069, Jamestown, NC 37282: Free information ◆ Patterns.

**Thumbelina Needlework Shop,** P.O. Box 1065, Solvang, CA 93464: Information $1.75 ◆ Books, fabrics, threads, yarns, kits, and other supplies. 800-789-4136. www.thumbelina.com

**The Weaver's Loft,** 308 S. Pennsylvania Ave., Centre Hall, PA 16828: Free information ◆ Yarns and knitting, weaving and spinning supplies, and equipment. 800-693-7242; 814-364-1433 (in PA). www.knitters-underground.com

**Web-sters Handspinners, Weavers & Knitters,** 11 N. Main St., Ashland, OR 97520: Free catalog ◆ Designer yarns, books, and tools. 800-482-9801.

**Woodland Woolworks,** 262 S. Maple St., P.O. Box 400, Yamhill, OR 97148: Catalog $3 ◆ Yarns, equipment, and supplies. 800-547-3725.

**Wooly Knits,** 6728 Lowell Ave., McLean, VA 22101: Catalog $5 (12 issues) ◆ Designer yarns, unusual buttons, needle craft kits, how-to knitting books, and needlework supplies. 703-448-9665. www.woolyknits.com

### Software

**Cochenille Design Studio,** P.O. Box 4276, Ecinas, CA 92023: Catalog $1 ◆ Garment styler for Windows and the Macintosh. 619-259-1698. www.cochenille.com

**Impresario Software,** 1705 S. Pearl St., Denver, CO 80210: Free information ◆ Hand-knitting software for PCs and machine-knitting software for PCs and the Macintosh. 303-698-9233.

**M & R Technologies Inc.,** P.O. Box 9403, Wright Brothers Branch, Dayton, OH 45409: Free information ◆ Windows software for cross-stitch pattern design. 800-800-8517.

**Oxford Craft Software,** P.O. Box 208, Bonsall, CA 92003: Free information with long SASE ◆ Cross-stitch designer software for Macintosh, DOS, and Windows computers. 800-995-0420.

**Penelope Craft Programs Inc.,** P.O. Box 1204, Maywood, NJ 07607: Free information ◆ PC and Macintosh software for knitters. 201-368-8379.

## KNIVES & KNIFE MAKING

### Knives & Knife Making Supplies

**Americana Ltd.,** 219 Stucker Ln., Smithfield, KY 40068: Catalog $3 ◆ Supplies for knife makers and finished blades. 502-845-2222.

**Arizona Custom Knives,** 8617 E. Clysdale, Scottsdale, AZ 85258: Price list $3 ◆ Handmade knives. 602-951-0699.

**Atlanta Cutlery,** Box 839, Conyers, GA 30207: Catalog $1 ◆ Knife-making supplies. 800-883-0300.

**Barrett-Smythe,** 30 E. 81st St., #GF-1, New York, NY 10021: Free photos ◆ One-of-a-kind folding knives. 212-249-5500.

**L.L. Bean,** Casco St., Freeport, ME 04032: Free catalog ◆ Knives for hunters, fishermen, and campers. 800-221-4221. www.llbean.com

**Beck's Cutlery Specialties,** 748 E. Chatham St., Cary, NC 27511: Price list $2 ◆ Custom knives. 919-460-0203.

**Benchmade Knife Company Inc.,** 300 Beavercreek Rd., Oregon City, OR 97045: Brochure $2 ◆ Folding knives. 503-655-6004.

**Beretta U.S.A.,** 17601 Beretta Dr., Accokeek, MD 20607: Free information ◆ Lightweight, standard, serrated, and other knives. 800-528-7453.

**Berkshire Mountain Trading,** 92 Bridges Rd., Williamstown, MA 01267: Catalog $2 (refundable) ◆ Knives and cutlery. 413-458-8669.

**Blue Mountain Turquoise,** P.O. Box 112, Quemado, NM 87829: Catalog $4 (refundable) ◆ Handmade knife handles. 505-773-4767.

**Boker Knives,** 1550 Balsam St., Lakewood, CO 80215: Free catalog ◆ Knives and sheaths. 800-992-6537.

**Steve Brooks,** Box 105, Big Timber, MT 59011: Catalog $2 ◆ Custom hand-forged, hunting, utility, and one-of-a-kind collectible knives. 406-932-5114.

**Bud K Worldwide,**P.O. Box 2768, Moultrie, GA 31776: Free catalog ◆ Hunting and throwing knives, survival tools, medieval swords, and self-defense products. 800-543-5061. www.budkww.com

**C.C. Knife Products**, 754 Nicola St., Kamloops, British Columbia, Canada V2C 2R4: Catalog $2 ◆ Knife-making tools and supplies. 250-374-0473.

**W.R. Case & Sons Cutlery Company,** Owens Way, Bradford, PA 16701: Catalog $2 ◆ Handcrafted knives. 814-368-4123.

**Chef's Catalog,** P.O. Box 620048, Dallas, TX 75262: Free catalog ◆ Professional kitchen knives by Henckels and Sabatier. 800-338-3232. www.chefscatalog.com

**Classic Cutlery,** 39 Roosevelt Ave., Hudson, NH 03051: Catalog $5 ◆ Custom and commemorative, pocket, tactical and military, law enforcement, sporting, and other knives. Also cutlery and sharpeners. 603-883-1199.

**Cold Steel,** 2128 Knoll Dr., Ventura, CA 93003: Free catalog ◆ Limited edition, specialty, and closeout knives. 800-255-4716.

**Pat Crawford,** 205 N. Center, West Memphis, AR 73201: Catalog $1 ◆ Custom knives. 501-735-4632.

**Cutlery Shoppe,** P.O. Box 610, Meridian, ID 83680: Free catalog ◆ Knives and sheaths. 800-231-1272.

**Dixie Gun Works Inc.,** P.O. Box 130, Union City, TN 38261: Catalog $5 ◆ Knife-making supplies. 800-238-6785.

**Doc Hagen Custom Knives,** P.O. Box 58, Pelican Rapids, MN 56572: Catalog $2 ◆ Handmade knives and folders. 218-863-8503. www.dochagen.com

**The Edge Company,** P.O. Box 826, Brattleboro, VT 05302: Free catalog ◆ Knives and tools. 800-732-9976. www.edgeco.com

**Fowler Custom Knives,** Rt. 4, Box 83-B, Richton, MS 39476: Brochure $2 ◆ Custom handmade knives and sheaths. 601-989-2553.

**Frost Cutlery,** P.O. Box 22636, Chattanooga, TN 37422: Free information ◆ Knives. 800-251-7768; 423-894-6079 (in TN). frostcutlery@mindspring.com

**Gallagher & Forsythe Ltd.,** 714 Main St., Bldg. 704, Yarmouth Port, MA 02675: Free catalog ◆ Swiss Army knives. 508-362-1366.

**Gaston Knives,** 330 Gaston Dr., Woodruff, SC 29388: Catalog $3 ◆ Knives. 864-433-0807.

**Golden Edge Cutlery,** P.O. Box 1279, Golden, CO 80402: Free catalog ◆ Knives and natural and man-made sharpening stones. 800-828-1925.

**Hawks,** P.O. Box 207, Blytheville, AR 72316: Free catalog ◆ Hunting clothing and footwear, knives, gun safes, guns, and more.

**Ironstone Distinctive Bladewear,** P.O. Box 1279, Golden, CO 80402: Free catalog ◆ Sport and culinary knives, sharpeners, and accessories. 800-828-1925. www.fe3stone.com

**Ken Jantz Supply,** P.O. Box 584, Davis, OK 73030: Catalog $5 ◆ Knife-making supplies and kits. 580-369-2315. www.jantzsupply.com

**Katz Knives Inc.,** P.O. Box 730, Chandler, AZ 85224: Catalog $2 ◆ Fixed blade knives, pocket knives, belt buckles, and sharpening stones. 800-848-7084.

**Terry Kerwin,** 4017 Keene St., Martinez, GA 30907: Brochure $1 ◆ Handmade custom knives. 706-860-2985.

**Knife & Cutlery Products Inc.,** 4122 N. Troost Ave., Kansas City, MO 64116: Catalog $2 ◆ Knife-making supplies. 800-659-2712.

**Knife & Gun Finishing Supplies,** P.O. Box 458, Lakeside, AZ 85929: Catalog $3 ◆ Metal-finishing supplies for making knives. 602-537-8877.

**The Knife Center,** P.O. Box 902, 11263 Somerset Ave., Beltsville, MD 20705: Free catalog ◆ Knives, cases, accessories, fencing swords, and martial arts weapons. 800-338-6799.

**R.C. Knipstein,** 731 N. Fielder Rd., Arlington, TX 76012: Brochure $2 ◆ Custom knives. 817-265-2021.

**Koval Knives,** P.O. Box 492, New Albany, OH 43054: Catalog $4 ◆ Knife-making supplies and equipment. 800-556-4837; 614-855-0777 (in OH).

**Alexander Kozlow,** 153 Priscilla St., Bridgeport, CT 06610: Catalog $2 ◆ Sheaths and scabbards in Plains Indian (Native American) styles. 203-374-5214 (after 6 PM).

**Jarrell Lambert,** Rt. 1, Box 67, Ganado, TX 77962: Free information ◆ Knives. 512-771-3744.

**Lile Handmade Knives,** 2721 S. Arkansas Ave., Russellville, AR 72801: Free information ◆ Handmade knives. 501-968-2011.

**Magnum USA,** 1550 Balsam St., Lakewood, CO 80215: Free catalog ◆ Knives. 800-835-6433.

**Masecraft Supply Company,** 170 Research Pkwy., P.O. Box 423, Meriden, CT 06450: Free information ◆ Stag, pearl, horn, bone, mammoth ivory, and other knife handle materials. 800-682-5489.

**Sean McWilliams Knives,** P.O. Box 3897, Durango, CO 81302: Catalog $3 ◆ Hand-forged knives. 970-884-9854.

**Myerchin Knife,** P.O. Box 911, Rialto, CA 92376: Free catalog ◆ Knives. 909-875-3592.

**Nordic Knives,** 1634 Copenhagen Dr., Solvang, CA 93463: Catalog $4 ◆ Custom and Randall knives. 805-688-3612.

**Northwest Knife Supply,** 621 Fawn Ridge Dr., Oakland, OR 97462: Catalog $2 ◆ Knife-making supplies. 541-459-2216.

**Ontario Knife Company,** 26 Empire St., Franklinville, NY 14737: Free information ◆ Folding and fixed blade knives. 800-222-5233; 716-676-5527 (in NY).

**Parkers' Knife Collector Service,** 6715 Heritage Business Ct., P.O. Box 23522, Chattanooga, TN 37422: Free catalog ◆ Knives. 800-247-0599; 423-892-0448 (in TN).

**Pioneer Millworks,** 1755 Pioneer Rd., Shortsville, NY 14548: Free information ◆ Reproduction period flooring from reclaimed timbers, trim, lumber, and board stock. 716-289-3090.

**Darrel Ralph Bladesmith,** 7032 E. Livingstone Ave., Reynoldsburg, OH 43068: Catalog $4 ◆ Custom knives. 614-577-1040.

**Randall-Made Knives,** P.O. Box 1988, Orlando, FL 32802: Catalog $2 ◆ Knives. 407-855-8075. www.randallknives.com

**Jim Ray,** 756 Camp Branch Rd., Waynesville, NC 28786: Free information ◆ Custom and production knives. 704-926-1626 (daytime); 704-452-4158 (evening).

**A.G. Russell Knives,** 1705 Hwy. 71 B North, Springdale, AR 72764: Free catalog ◆ Knives and cutlery. 800-255-9034. www.agrussell.com

**Scott Sawby Custom Knives,** 400 W. Center Valley Rd., Sandpoint, ID 83864: Brochure $1 ◆ Custom knives, specializing in folders. 208-263-4171.

**Schrade Corp.,** 7 Schrade Ct., Ellenville, NY 12428: Free information ◆ Knives and accessory carrying system for outdoor people.

**Schroen Knives,** Karl Schroen, 4042 Bones Rd., Sebastopol, CA 95472: Free information ◆ Hand-forged kitchen cutlery, paring knives to cleavers, and other knives. 707-823-4057.

**Sheffield Knifemakers Supply,** P.O. Box 141, Deland, FL 32721: Catalog $5 ◆ Knife-making supplies. 904-775-6453.

**Cleston R. Sinyard,** Nimo Forge, 27522 Burkhardt Dr., Elberta, AL 36530: Free information ◆ Damascus blade knives. 334-987-1361.

**Jim Siska Knives,** 6 Highland Ave., Westfield, MA 01085: Free brochure ◆ Knives. 413-568-9787.

**Skylands Cutlery,** P.O. Box 87, Ringwood, NJ 07456: Catalog $1 ◆ Factory and custom knives. 201-962-6143.

**Smoky Mountain Knife Works,** P.O. Box 4430, Sevierville, TN 37864: Free catalog ◆ Hunting, work, and survival knives. 800-251-9306.

**SOG Specialty Knives & Tools Inc.,** 6521 212th St. SW, Lynwood, WA 98036: Free brochure ◆ Pocket tool knives. 817-595-2485. www.remtek.com/cfi/sog/sog.htm

**Spyderco Inc.,** P.O. Box 800, Golden, CO 80402: Free information ◆ Pocket folding and kitchen knives. Also accessories. 800-525-7770. www.spyderco.com

**Star Sales Company Inc.,** 1803 N. Central St., P.O. Box 1503, Knoxville, TN 37901: Catalog $3 ◆ Knives. 800-745-6433.

**Sunshine Knife Outlet,** 2509 Sunset Dr., Kissimmee, FL 34746: Catalog $4 ◆ Throwing knives, tomahawks, and security products. 888-556-2572.

**Swiss Armory,** 2838 Juniper St., San Diego, CA 92104: Free catalog ◆ Swiss army knives. 800-437-5423.

**Texas Knifemakers Supply,** P.O. Box 79402, Houston, TX 77279: Catalog $3 ◆ Knife-making supplies. 713-461-8632.

**Brian Tighe Knifemaker,** RR 1, Ridgefield, Ontario, Canada L0S 1M0: Free information ◆ Custom knives. 905-892-2734.

**Treestump Leather,** 18 State St., Ellsworth, ME 04605: Brochure $2 ◆ Leather sheaths. 207-667-8756.

**United Cutlery,** 1425 United Blvd., Sevierville, TN 37876: Free list of retail sources ◆ Knives. 800-548-0835.

### Sharpeners & Other Tools

**Classic Cutlery,** 39 Roosevelt Ave., Hudson, NH 03051: Catalog $5 ◆ Custom and commemorative, pocket, tactical and military, law enforcement, sporting, other knives and cutlery, and sharpeners. 603-883-1199.

**Edge Pro Knife Sharpeners,** P.O. Box 95, Hood River, OR 97031: Free brochure ◆ Bench-mounted knife sharpeners with quick-change water stones. 541-387-2222.

**Golden Edge Cutlery,** P.O. Box 1279, Golden, CO 80402: Free catalog ◆ Knives and natural and man-made sharpening stones. 800-828-1925.

**The Great American Tool Company,** P.O. Box 600, Getzville, NY 14066: Free information ◆ Easy-to-use sharpening tools. 800-LIV-SHARP.

**Harper Manufacturing,** Stamp & Dies, 3050 Westwood Dr., Las Vegas, NV 89109: Brochure $1 ◆ Custom steel stamps for marking knives. 800-776-8407; 702-735-8467 (in NV).

**Ironstone Distinctive Bladewear,** P.O. Box 1279, Golden, CO 80402: Free catalog ◆ Sport and culinary knives, sharpeners, and accessories. 800-828-1925. www.fe3stone.com

**K & G Finishing Supplies,** P.O. Box 980, Lakeside, AZ 85929: Catalog $3 ◆ Belts, buffers and buffing compounds, grinders, knife blanks and cases, sharpeners, steels, and other supplies. 520-537-8877.

**L.S. Lansky Sharpeners,** P.O. Box 800, Buffalo, NY 14231: Free catalog ◆ Knife and tool sharpeners. 716-877-7511. www.customcpu.com/alaskaknife/lansky.htm

**Marking Methods Inc.,** 301 S. Raymond Ave., Alhambra, CA 91803: Free information ◆ Acid-free electro-chemical etching-marking kit. 818-282-8823.

**Razor Edge Systems Inc.,** 303 N. 17th St., Ely, MN 55731: Free catalog ◆ Sharpening equipment. 800-541-1458.

**Tru-Grit,** 760 E. Frances St., Ontario, CA 91761: Free information ◆ Knife-making machines and accessories. 800-532-3336; 909-923-4116 (in CA).

## LABORATORY & SCIENCE EQUIPMENT

**Advance Scientific,** 2345 SW 34th St., Fort Lauderdale, FL 33312: Catalog $3 ◆ Laboratory chemicals, glassware, instrumentation, and supplies. 305-327-0900.

**American Science & Surplus,** 3605 Howard St., Skokie, IL 60076: Catalog $1 ◆ Surplus science and electro-mechanical supplies, other equipment, and kits. 847-982-0870. www.sciplus.com

**Analytical Scientific,** 11049 Bandera, San Antonio, TX 78250: Catalog $3 (refundable) ◆ Laboratory glassware, chemicals, equipment, books, and charts. 830-684-7373. analyticalscientific@compuserve.com

**Anatomical Chart Company,** 8221 N. Kimball, Skokie, IL 60076: Catalog $2 ◆ Educational anatomical products on health, human anatomy, and other sciences. 800-621-7500; 847-679-4700 (in IL).

**ASC Scientific,** 2075 Corte del Nogal, Carlsbad, CA 92009: Free catalog ◆ Pocket transit for geologists, handheld satellite navigator, and earth science equipment. 800-272-4327.

**Bunting Magnetics Company,** 500 S. Spencer Rd., Newton, KS 67114: Free catalog ◆ Magnets. 800-835-2526; 316-284-2020 (in KS). www.bunting-magnetics.com

**Chem-Lab,** 1060 Ortega Way, Placentia, CA 92670: Catalog $5 ◆ Chemicals, glassware, scales, microscopes, and other equipment. 714-630-7902. www.CHEMLAB.COM

**Dino Productions,** P.O. Box 3004, Englewood, CO 80155: Free catalog ◆ Fossils, rocks and minerals, ecology and oceanography equipment, and chemistry, general science, astronomy, and biology supplies. 303-741-1587. www.dinoproductions.com

**Edmund Scientific Company,** Edscorp Bldg., Barrington, NJ 08007: Free catalog ◆ Microscopes, magnifiers, weather forecasting instruments, magnets, telescopes, binoculars and optical accessories, laser, and other science equipment. 609-547-8880. www.edsci.com

**The Electronic Goldmine,** P.O. Box 5408, Scottsdale, AZ 85261: Free catalog ◆ Science kits. 800-445-0697; 602-451-7454 (in AZ). www.goldmine-elec.com

**J.L. Hammett Company,** P.O. Box 9057, Braintree, MA 02184: Free catalog ◆ Science kits, microscopes, laboratory apparatus, rock collections, magnets, astronomy charts, and anatomical models. 781-848-1000.

**Hubbard Scientific Company,** American Educational Products, 1120 Halbleib Rd., Chippewa Falls, WI 54729: Free catalog ◆ Hands-on educational manipulative activities and relief maps for the world, United States, international regional areas, and more. 800-323-8368; 715-723-4427 (in WI). www.amep.com

**Magnet Sales & Manufacturing Company,** 11248 Playa Ct., Culver City, CA 90230: Free brochure ◆ Flexible strip, flex-dot, button, and bar magnets. 800-421-6692; 310-391-7213 (in CA).

**Merrell Scientific/World of Science,** 900 Jefferson Rd., Bldg. 4, Rochester, NY 14623: Catalog $2 ◆ Chemicals, glassware, and equipment for biology, nature, physical and earth science, rocket, and astronomy experiments. 716-475-0100. www.roccplex.com/wos

**Nasco,** 901 Janesville Ave., Fort Atkinson, WI 53538: Free catalog ◆ Science and ultraviolet lighting equipment, kits, microscopes and dissection kits, rock collections, magnets, electric motors, astronomy charts and star maps, anatomical models, and other supplies. 800-558-9595. www.nascofa.com

**The Nature Company,** Catalog Division, P.O. Box 188, Florence, KY 41022: Free catalog ◆ Science supplies, kits, books, toys, novelties, and gifts. 800-227-1114. www.natureco.com

**Omni Resources,** 1004 S. Mebane St., P.O. Box 2096, Burlington, NC 27216: Free catalog ◆ Earth science and laboratory equipment. 800-742-2677. custserv@omnimap.com

**Pyrotek,** P.O. Box 300, Sweet Valley, PA 18656: Catalog $2 ◆ Laboratory chemicals, glassware, books and manuals, and other supplies. 717-256-3087.

**Schoolmasters Science,** P.O. Box 1941, Ann Arbor, MI 48106: Catalog $2 ◆ Laboratory science equipment and kits for schools, hobbyist laboratories, and home science fair projects. 800-521-2832. www.schoolmasters.com

**Southern Oregon Scientific,** 1000 SE M St., Unit A, Grants Pass, OR 97526: Catalog $2 ◆ Laboratory glassware and chemicals. 541-955-8073.

**United Laboratory Plastics,** P.O. Box 8585, St. Louis, MO 63126: Free catalog ◆ Plastic supplies and accessories. 800-722-2499; 314-343-2202 (in MO).

**Unitron Inc.,** 170 Wilbur Pl., P.O. Box 469, Bohemia, NY 11716: Free catalog ◆ Stereo microscopes and optical and scientific equipment. 516-589-6666.

**Ward's Natural Science,** P.O. Box 92912, 5100 W. Henrietta Rd., Rochester, NY 14692: Earth science catalog $10; biology catalog $15; middle school catalog $10 ◆ Science equipment and supplies. 800-962-2660. www.wardsci.com

**Whatman LabSales,** P.O. Box 1359, Hillsboro, OR 97123: Free catalog ◆ Laboratory science equipment. 800-Whatman.

## LACROSSE

**AZRU Sports,** P.O. Box 166, Glenelg, MD 21737: Free brochure ◆ Lacrosse equipment, clothing, instructional and training aids, goals, and accessories. 800-320-3028.

**Ballwall,** 5 Flint Ave., Larchmont, NY 10538: Free brochure ◆ Indoor and outdoor backstop training wall for sports that use a ball. 800-966-1190; 914-833-0390 (in NY).

**Brine Inc.,** 47 Sumner St., Milford, MA 01757: Free information ◆ Balls, gloves, goals, protective equipment, sticks, and uniforms. 800-227-2722; 508-478-3250 (in MA).

**Bristol Athletic,** 700-726 Shelby St., Bristol, TN 37621: Free information ◆ Basketball, baseball and softball, football, track, volleyball, and lacrosse uniforms for men, women, and youths. 800-336-8775; 615-968-4140 (in TN).

**Wm. T. Burnett & Company Inc.,** 1500 Bush St., Baltimore, MD 21230: Free information ◆ Balls and gloves, goals, protective gear, and sticks. 800-368-2250.

**Jayfro Corp.,** Unified Sports Inc., 976 Hartford Tnpk., P.O. Box 400, Waterford, CT 06385: Free catalog ◆ Lacrosse and field hockey goals, nets, and other equipment. 860-447-3001.

**Lacrosse Unlimited,** 365 Nesconset Hwy., Hauppauge, NY 11788: Free catalog ◆ Lacrosse equipment. 800-366-LAXX. www.LACROSSEUNLTD.COM

**LAX World,** 9505 Deereco Rd., Timonium, MD 21093: Free brochure ◆ Lacrosse equipment and clothing. 800-PLAY-LAX.

**Olympia Sports,** 745 State Cir., Ann Arbor, MI 48106: Free information ◆ Goal nets, balls, and sticks. 800-521-2832. www.wolverinesports.com

**Queen City Lacrosse Equipment,** 1320 Manor Dr., Pittsburgh, PA 15241: Free catalog ◆ Men and women's lacrosse equipment and clothing. 800-240-0178; 412-831-8364 (in PA). www.qclax.com

**Reda Sports Express,** P.O. Box 68, Easton, PA 18044: Free information ◆ Balls, protective gear, helmets, and sticks. 800-444-REDA; 610-258-5271 (in PA).

**Riddell Inc.,** 3670 N. Milwaukee Ave., Chicago, IL 60641: Free information ◆ Helmets. 800-445-7344; 773-794-1994 (in IL).

**Seneca Sports Inc.,** 75 Fortune Blvd., P.O. Box 719, Milford, MA 01757: Free information ◆ Sticks and balls. 800-861-7867; 508-634-3616 (in MA).

**STX Inc.,** 1500 Bush St., Baltimore, MD 21230: Free information ◆ Goal nets, protective gear, gloves, balls, and sticks. 800-368-2250; 410-837-2022 (in MD).

**Title 9 Sports,** 5743 Landregan St., Emeryville, CA 94608: Free catalog ◆ Women's clothing created by and for women. 510-655-5999. thefolks@title9sports.com

**Tuskewe Krafts,** 2089 Upper Mountain Rd., Sanborn, NY 14132: Free brochure with long SASE ◆ Women and men's field and box lacrosse sticks. 716-297-1821.

# LADDERS

**Jomy Safety Ladder Company,** 6255 Longbow Dr., Boulder, CO 80301: Free information ◆ Collapsible fire escape ladder. 800-255-2591. www.jomy.com

**Walter Kidde,** Division Kidde, 1394 S. 3rd, Mebane St., NC 27302: Free information ◆ Escape ladders.

**Ladder Man Inc.,** 3025 Silver Dr., Columbus, OH 43224: Free catalog ◆ Safety equipment, attic and fire escape equipment, and specialty, articulating, stairway, and stairwell ladders. 800-783-8887.

**Lynn Ladder & Scaffolding & Company,** 220 S. Common St., Lynn, MA 01905: Free list of retail sources ◆ Wood, aluminum, and fiberglass ladders. 800-225-2510.

**The New Rebel Workshop,** Robert & Sandy Little, P.O. Box 658, Franklin, TX 77856: Brochure $2 ◆ Chair step that converts to a stepladder. Also other craft items. 409-828-3849.

**Pro Ladder Supply,** 440 Pershing Ave., Pocatello, ID 83201: Free brochure ◆ Portable and safe-to-use ladders. 800-735-8281; 208-234-0543 (in ID).

**Putnam Rolling Ladder Company Inc.,** 32 Howard St., New York, NY 10013: Catalog $1 ◆ Ladders, library carts, and furniture. 212-226-5147.

# LAMPS & LIGHTING

## Chandeliers

**A.J.P. Coppersmith & Company,** 20 Industrial Pkwy., Woburn, MA 01801: Catalog $3 ◆ Chandeliers, sconces, cupolas, weather vanes, and handcrafted copper, tin, and brass reproduction colonial lanterns. 800-545-1776.

**American Light Source,** 5211D W. Market St., Ste. 803, Greensboro, NC 27265: Free catalog ◆ Chandeliers. 800-741-0571.

**Antique Treasures,** 19 Buckingham Plantation Dr., Bluffton, SC 29910: Catalog $3 (request list of retail sources) ◆ Wholesale supplier of home accents in the antique style for dealers only. 800-422-9982. www.antiquehardware.com

**Antler Art Inc.,** P.O. Box 2006, Grand Junction, CO 81502: Free catalog ◆ Chandeliers and lamps made from antlers. 970-243-5114.

**Antler Design,** P.O. Box 2367, Idaho Falls, ID 83403: Free catalog ◆ Custom antler chandeliers and hardware. 800-221-5715.

**Architectural Emporium,** 207 Adams Ave., Canonsburg, PA 15317: Free information ◆ Antiques, specializing in restored lighting, chandeliers, and sconces. 724-222-8586. www.architectural-emporium.com

**V. Michael Ashford,** 6543 Alpine Dr. SW, Olympia, WA 98512: Brochure $1 ◆ Hand-hammered copper and mica table. Also floor lamps, sconces, and chandeliers. 360-352-0694.

**Authentic Designs,** The Mill Rd., West Rupert, VT 05776: Catalog $3 ◆ Handcrafted reproduction 18th-century Early American light fixtures and chandeliers in brass, copper, and tin. 802-394-7713.

**Ball & Ball,** 463 W. Lincoln Hwy., Exton, PA 19341: Catalog $7 (refundable) ◆ Reproduction antique light fixtures and chandeliers. 610-363-7330. www.ballandball-us.com

**Brass Light Gallery,** 131 S. 1st St., Milwaukee, WI 53204: Catalog $5 ◆ Solid brass chandeliers with glass shades, from the early 1900s. 800-243-9595.

**Brass Reproductions,** 9711 Canoga Ave., Chatsworth, CA 91311: Catalog $8 ◆ Solid brass Victorian and traditional chandeliers, floor and table lamps, and sconces. 818-709-7844.

**Classic Illumination,** 2743 9th St., Berkeley, CA 94710: Free information ◆ Chandeliers and wall sconces. 510-849-1842.

**Collector's Gallery,** 300 E. Market St., Hallam, PA 17406: Free catalog ◆ Western-style hand-forged and custom-made lamps, sconces, and chandeliers. 800-800-6989.

**The Coppersmith,** Rt. 20, P.O. Box 755, Sturbridge, MA 01566: Catalog $3 ◆ Handcrafted reproduction chandeliers, lanterns, and sconces. 508-347-7038.

**Roc Corbett Custom Lighting,** P.O. Box 339, Bigfork, MT 59911: Catalog $10 (refundable) ◆ Elk, deer, moose, and caribou antler-crafted wagon wheel chandeliers. 406-837-5823.

**The Country Store of Geneva,** 28 James St., Geneva, IL 60134: Catalog $3 ◆ Punched tin and turned wood chandeliers, ceiling lights, outlet covers, country-style decorative accessories, and braided rugs. 630-879-0098.

**Crystal Clear Chandelier Care,** 9602 W. 156th St., Overland Park, KS 66221: Free information ◆ Replacement parts for antique light fixtures and chandeliers. 913-681-6700.

**Eagle Emporium,** P.O. Box 282, Rt. 100, Eagle, PA 19480: Brochure $2 ◆ Amish-crafted iron chandeliers. 610-458-7188.

**Gaslight Time,** 5 Plaza St. West, Brooklyn, NY 11217: Catalog $4 ◆ Restored antique gas, early electric chandeliers, and wall sconces, from 1850 to 1925. 718-789-7185.

**Georgia Lighting Supply Company Inc.,** 530 14th St. NW, Atlanta, GA 30318: Catalog $12 ◆ Light fixtures in iron, brass, and bronze from European and American artisans. 800-282-0220.

**Golden Valley Lighting,** 274 Eastchester Dr., Ste. 117A, High Point, NC 27262: Catalog $5 (refundable) ◆ Light fixtures and lamps. 800-735-3377; 919-882-7330 (in NC). www.gvlight.com

**Greene's Lighting Fixtures,** 1059 3rd Ave., New York, NY 10021: Catalog $10 (refundable) ◆ Custom-made chandeliers. 212-753-2507.

**Hammerworks,** 6 Fremont St., Worcester, MA 01603: Catalog $3 ◆ Handmade reproductions of copper, brass, iron, and tin colonial post and wall lanterns, chandeliers, and sconces. 508-755-3434. www.hammerworks.com

**Hardware, Bath & More,** 20830 Coolidge Hwy., Oak Park, MI 48237: Free information ◆ Decorative hardware, plumbing, and light fixtures. 800-760-3278. www.h-b-m.com

**Heritage Lanterns,** 70-A Main St., Yarmouth, ME 04096: Catalog $5 ◆ Colonial-style chandeliers. 800-648-4449.

**High Country Antler Art,** 210 E. Creek, Fredericksburg, TX 78624: Catalog $5 ◆ Custom-designed and wired chandeliers, candelabras, lamps, and fireplace tools. 210-997-2263.

**Historic Lighting Restoration,** 10341 Jewell Lake Ct., Fenton, MI 48430: Free brochure with long SASE ◆ Electric-operated reproduction kerosene chandeliers. 810-629-4934.

**Howard's Antique Lighting,** Rt. 23 West, P.O. Box 472, South Egremont, MA 01258: Free information ◆ Floor lamps, sconces, and electric, gas, and kerosene chandeliers. 413-528-1232.

**Hubbardton Forge & Wood Corp.,** P.O. Box 827, Rt. 30, Castleton, VT 05735: Catalog $3 ◆ Wrought-iron and brass chandeliers, other hand-forged lighting accessories, hanging pan racks, bathroom and home accessories, plant hangers, and table, wall, and candlestick lamps. 802-468-3090.

**Hurley Patentee Lighting,** 464 Old Rt. 209, Hurley, NY 12443: Catalog $3 ◆ Handcrafted replicas of Early American chandeliers, sconces, lanterns, and other lamps. 914-331-5414.

**Iron Apple Forge,** P.O. Box 724, Buckingham, PA 18912: Catalog $4 ◆ Traditional wrought-iron chandeliers. 215-794-7351.

**Irvin's,** RD 1, Box 73, Mt. Pleasant Mills, PA 17853: Free catalog ◆ Handcrafted colonial tinware and light fixtures. 717-539-8200.

**Jay "Bird" Jones,** 520 Pine Oaks Rd., #4, Colorado Springs, CO 80926: Catalog $10 (refundable); brochure $1 ◆ Antler-crafted chairs, lamps, chandeliers, and carvings. 719-527-1845.

**King's Chandelier Company,** P.O. Box 667, Eden, NC 27289: Catalog $5 ◆ Chandeliers, candelabras, and crystal sconces. 336-623-6188. www.chandelier.com

**Lamp Warehouse,** 1073 39th St., Brooklyn, NY 11219: Free information with long SASE ◆ Ceiling fans and light fixtures. 800-52-LITES; 718-436-8500 (in NY).

**Little Big Horn Replica Company,** P.O. Box 415, Crow Agency, MT 59022: Brochure $2 ◆ Wagon wheel clocks and chandeliers. 406-638-4458.

**Lt. Moses Willard Inc.,** 1156 US 50, Milford, OH 45150: Catalog $8.50 (request list of retail sources) ◆ Reproduction chandeliers, wall sconces, exterior light units, candle holders, lanterns, and wall and table lamps, from the 1700s. 937-248-5500.

**MacPhail's Studio,** 1417 N. Kickapoo, Ste. 4, Lincoln, IL 62656: Free information ◆ Antler chandeliers, lamps, and chairs. 217-732-7538.

**Marlborough Country Barn,** N. Main St., Marlborough, CT 06447: Catalog $3 ◆ Reproduction lighting for log homes. 800-852-8993.

**Nowell's Inc.,** 490 Gate 5 Rd., P.O. Box 295, Sausalito, CA 94966: Catalog $5 ◆ Reproduction and restored antique chandeliers and other light fixtures. 415-332-4933.

**The Original Cast Lighting,** 6120 Delmar Blvd., St. Louis, MO 63112: Catalog $2 ◆ Light fixtures and reproduction and restored antique units. 314-863-1895.

**Period Lighting Fixtures,** 167 River Rd., P.O. Box 26017, Clarksburg, MA 01247: Free catalog ◆ Early American light fixtures, chandeliers, lanterns, and sconces. 800-828-6990.

**Pittsburgh Antique Company,** 143 West College St., Canonsburg, PA 15317: Free brochure ◆ Gas fixtures, early electric chandeliers, and other period lighting. Also mantels, doors, hardware, newel posts, columns, ornamental iron, and other architectural antiques. 412-222-8586. PPAC@city-net.com

**Ragged Mountain Antlers,** P.O. Box 1164, Hamilton, MT 59840: Free brochure ◆ Traditional and asymmetrical lighting centerpieces and chandeliers made from antlers. 406-961-2400.

**The Renovator's Supply,** P.O. Box 2515, Conway, NH 03818: Free catalog ◆ Solid brass chandeliers. 800-659-0303.

**Rocky Mountain Log Furniture Inc.,** P.O. Box 3124, 1502 Miner St., Idaho Springs, CO 80452: Brochure $2 ◆ Handcrafted log furniture and wagon wheel chandeliers. 800-305-6030; 303-567-0480 (in CO). treasure@webcom.com

**Roy Electric Company,** 22 Elm St., Westfield, NJ 07090: Free catalog ◆ Victorian-style and turn-of-the-century chandeliers, sconces, and light fixtures. 800-366-3347; 908-317-4665 (in NJ).

**Saltbox Inc.,** 3004 Columbia Ave., Lancaster, PA 17603: Catalog $2.50 ◆ Handcrafted brass, copper, and tin colonial-style chandeliers, post lights, lanterns, and foyer lights. 717-392-5649.

**Silver Creek Antler Company,** P.O. Box 3463, Glenwood Springs, CO 81602: Free brochure ◆ Chandeliers and furnishings made from antlers. 970-945-0507.

**Stanley Galleries,** 2118 N. Clark St., Chicago, IL 60614: Free information ◆ Antique American chandeliers and light fixtures. 312-281-1614.

**M. Star Antler Designs,** P.O. Box 3093, Lake Isabella, CA 93240: Catalog $5 ◆ Antler chandeliers, lamps, furniture, mirrors, and decorative accessories. 619-379-5777.

**The Stone House,** 28 E. Market St., Middleburg, PA 17842: Free catalog ◆ Colonial period light fixtures. 800-923-2260.

**Studio Steel,** 159 New Milford Tnpk., New Preston, CT 06777: Catalog $2 ◆ Lamps, chandeliers, sconces, mirrors, and hand-wrought metalwork. 800-800-5712.

**Sugar Hill,** P.O. Box 1300, Columbus, GA 31902: Free catalog ◆ Handpainted decorative tin chandeliers. 800-344-6125.

**Tin Bin,** 20 Valley Rd., Neffsville, PA 17601: Catalog $2.50 ◆ Country crafts and 18th-century lighting. 717-569-6210. TheTinBin@aol.com

**Vermont Industries,** P.O. Box 301, Rt. 103, Cuttingsville, VT 05738: Catalog $3 ◆ Wrought-iron and solid brass chandeliers, floor and table lamps, and wall fixtures. 800-639-1715; 802-492-3451 (in VT).

**Victorian Lighting Works,** 251 S. Pennsylvania Ave., P.O. Box 469, Centre Hall, PA 16328: Catalog $5 (refundable) ◆ Victorian-style wall sconces and chandeliers. 814-364-9577.

**Workshops of David T. Smith,** 3600 Shawhan Rd., Morrow, OH 45152: Catalog $5 ◆ Reproduction furniture, pottery, lamps, and chandeliers. 513-932-2472. www.davidtsmith.com

## Lamps & Fixtures

**A.J.P. Coppersmith & Company,** 20 Industrial Pkwy., Woburn, MA 01801: Catalog $3 ◆ Handcrafted copper, tin, and brass reproduction colonial lanterns, chandeliers, sconces, cupolas, and weather vanes. 800-545-1776.

**Aladdin Industries Inc.,** Lamp Division, P.O. Box 100255, Nashville, TN 37224: Free catalog ◆ Lamps, lamp shades, and replacement parts. 800-456-1233.

**American Home Supply,** P.O. Box 697, Campbell, CA 95009: Catalog $2 ◆ Reproduction heritage light fixtures. 408-246-1962.

**American Period Showcase,** 3004 Columbia Ave., Lancaster, PA 17603: Catalog $2.50 ◆ Handcrafted lanterns, table lamps, chandeliers, and post lamps. 717-392-5649.

**Antique Treasures,** 19 Buckingham Plantation Dr., Bluffton, SC 29910: Catalog $3 (request list of retail sources) ◆ Wholesale supplier of home accents in the antique style for dealers only. 800-422-9982. www.antiquehardware.com

**Antler Art Inc.,** P.O. Box 2006, Grand Junction, CO 81502: Free catalog ◆ Chandeliers and lamps made from antlers. 970-243-5114.

**Architectural Emporium,** 207 Adams Ave., Canonsburg, PA 15317: Free information ◆ Antiques, specializing in restored lighting, chandeliers, and sconces. 724-222-8586. www.architectural-emporium.com

**Arroyo Craftsman,** 4509 Little John St., Baldwin Park, CA 91706: Catalog $5 (request list of retail sources) ◆ Original indoor and outdoor brass light fixtures. 800-400-ARROYO.

**V. Michael Ashford,** 6543 Alpine Dr. SW, Olympia, WA 98512: Brochure $1 ◆ Hand-hammered copper and mica table. Also floor lamps, sconces, and chandeliers. 360-352-0694.

**Aunt Sylvia's Victorian Lamps,** P.O. Box 67364, Chestnut Hill, MA 02167: Catalog $3 ◆ Traditional and reproduction Victorian-style lamps. 800-231-6644.

**Authentic Designs,** The Mill Rd., West Rupert, VT 05776: Catalog $3 ◆ Handcrafted reproduction of early 18th-century brass, copper, and tin American light fixtures and chandeliers. 802-394-7713.

**Baldwin Hardware Corp.,** P.O. Box 15048, Reading, PA 19612: Bathroom accessories brochure 75¢, light fixtures brochure $3, door hardware brochure 75¢, decorative hardware brochure 75¢ ◆ Brass dead bolts and door hardware, bathroom accessories, and light fixtures. 800-566-1986.

**Ball & Ball,** 463 W. Lincoln Hwy., Exton, PA 19341: Catalog $7 (refundable) ◆ Reproduction light fixtures and chandeliers. 610-363-7330. www.ballandball-us.com

**Barton-Sharpe Ltd.,** 119 Spring St., New York, NY 10012: Free information ◆ Reproduction 18th and 19th-century furniture, lighting, bedding, stoneware, and decorative items. 212-925-9562.

**Dennis & CeCe Bork,** 715 Genesee St., Delafield, WI 53018: Catalog $5 ◆ Custom furniture, folk art, period lighting, Colonial Williamsburg reproductions, Windsor chairs and settees, and decorative items. 414-646-4911.

**Brandon Industries,** 1601 W. Wilmeth Rd., McKinney, TX 75069: Free catalog ◆ Wall sconces, aluminum lamp posts, planters, and mailboxes. 972-542-3000. www.brandonmail.com

**The Brass Knob,** 2311 18th St. NW, Washington, DC 20009: Free information ◆ Antique light fixtures, from 1870 to 1930. 202-332-3370.

**Brass Menagerie,** 524 St. Louis St., New Orleans, LA 70130: Free information with long SASE (specify items wanted) ◆ Light fixtures, plumbing, and hardware. 504-524-0921.

**Brass Reproductions,** 9711 Canoga Ave., Chatsworth, CA 91311: Catalog $8 ◆ Solid brass Victorian and traditional chandeliers, floor and table lamps, and sconces. 818-709-7844.

**Brass Works Lighting,** 292 Main St., Nyack, NY 10960: Catalog $5 ◆ Ceiling, wall, and table lighting in antique and polished brass, chrome, pewter, and combinations. 800-358-5843.

**Brooke-Grove Antique & Custom Lighting,** 21412 Laytonsville Rd., Laytonsville, MD 20882: Free information ◆ Custom and restored antique lighting. 301-948-0392.

**Brubaker Metalcrafts,** 209 N. Franklin St., Eaton, OH 45320: Catalog $2 ◆ Reproduction 18th-century tin and brass chandeliers, wall sconces, Paul Revere lanterns, and other fixtures. 937-456-5834.

**Century Studio,** 200 3rd Ave. North, Minneapolis, MN 55401: Brochure $10 (refundable) ◆ Reproduction Tiffany lamps. 612-339-0239.

**Chapman Manufacturing,** 481 W. Main St., Avon, MA 02322: Brochure $4 (request list of retail sources) ◆ Light fixtures, furniture, and accessories. 508-588-3200.

**Cherry Tree,** Light Division, 34154 E. Frontage Rd., Bozeman, MT 59715: Catalog $15 ◆ Traditional handcrafted lamps and shoji screens. 800-634-3268. www.cherrytreedesign.com

**Circa 1820,** RR 1, Box 4040, Vassalboro, ME 04989: Catalog $5 (refundable) ◆ Reproduction Shaker and country furniture, redware, pewter, and tin lighting. 207-877-9863.

**City Lights,** 2226 Massachusetts Ave., Cambridge, MA 02140: Free information (specify items wanted) ◆ Restored one-of-a-kind antique light fixtures. 617-547-1490.

**Classic Illumination,** 2743 9th St., Berkeley, CA 94710: Free information ◆ Chandeliers and wall sconces. 510-849-1842.

**Collector's Gallery,** 300 E. Market St., Hallam, PA 17406: Free catalog ◆ Western-style hand-forged custom lamps, sconces, and chandeliers. 800-800-6989.

**Conant Custom Brass,** 270 Pine St., Burlington, VT 05401: Free catalog ◆ Restored antique lighting. 800-832-4482.

**The Coppersmith,** Rt. 20, P.O. Box 755, Sturbridge, MA 01566: Catalog $3 ◆ Handcrafted reproduction colonial lanterns, sconces, and chandeliers. 508-347-7038.

**Crystal Clear Chandelier Care,** 9602 W. 156th St., Overland Park, KS 66221: Free information ◆ Replacement parts for antique light fixtures and chandeliers. 913-681-6700.

**D.F. Metalworks,** Daniel Joseph, 31921 Camino Capistrano, #347, San Juan Capistrano, CA 92675: Free information ◆ Recreated Old West lamps with electric bulbs instead of kerosene. 714-841-6200.

**D'Lights,** 533 W. Windsor Rd., Glendale, CA 91204: Catalog $3 ◆ Traditional and Victorian-style solid brass light fixtures and lamps. 818-956-5656.

**Early American Lighting,** 10 Mabel Terrace, Queensbury, NY 12804: Catalog $3 ◆ Reproduction electric or cordless Early American light fixtures. 518-745-1334.

**Elcanco Ltd.,** P.O. Box 682, Westford, MA 01886: Brochure $1 ◆ Handcrafted electric wax candles with flame-like bulbs. 978-392-0830.

**Everything Ewenique,** RR 1, Box 73, Mt. Pleasant Mills, PA 17853: Free catalog ◆ Tinware interior and exterior lighting, sconces, table lamps, potpourri tart warmers, and other units. 800-800-4846.

**Fabby,** 450 S. La Brea Ave., Los Angeles, CA 90036: Catalog $3 ◆ Ceramic wall sconces and handmade indoor and outdoor light fixtures. 213-939-1388.

**Faire Harbour Ltd.,** 44 Captain Pierce Rd., Scituate, MA 02066: Catalog $2 ◆ One-of-a-kind antique lamps, parts, and oil, early gas, electric, and kerosene lamps. 781-545-2465.

**Gaslight Time,** 5 Plaza St. West, Brooklyn, NY 11217: Catalog $4 ◆ Restored antique gas, combination, and early electric chandeliers and wall sconces, from 1850 to 1925. 718-789-7185.

**Genie House,** P.O. Box 2478, Vincentown, NJ 08088: Catalog $5 ◆ Handcrafted copper, tin, and brass 17th and 18th-century reproduction light fixtures. 800-634-3643.

**Georgia Lighting Supply Company Inc.,** 530 14th St. NW, Atlanta, GA 30318: Catalog $12 ◆ Light fixtures in iron, brass, and bronze from European and American artisans. 800-282-0220.

**Halcyon Times Ltd.,** 267 Kentlands Blvd., #505, Gaithersburg, MD 20878: Free information ◆ Cordless picture lamps. 800-711-1573.

**Hammerworks,** 6 Fremont St., Worcester, MA 01603: Catalog $3 ◆ Handmade reproductions of copper, brass, iron, and tin colonial post and wall lanterns, chandeliers, and sconces. 508-755-3434. www.hammerworks.com

**Hardware, Bath & More,** 20830 Coolidge Hwy., Oak Park, MI 48237: Free information ◆ Decorative hardware, plumbing, and light fixtures. 800-760-3278. www.h-b-m.com

**Heirloom Reproductions,** 1834 W. 5th St., Montgomery, AL 36106: Catalog $3 ◆ Reproduction French and Victorian lamps and furniture. 800-288-1513. www.angelfire.com/ok/furnitureman/index.html

**Heritage Lanterns,** 70-A Main St., Yarmouth, ME 04096: Catalog $5 ◆ Colonial-style wall and ceiling lights and sconces. 800-648-4449.

**High Country Antler Art,** 210 E. Creek, Fredericksburg, TX 78624: Catalog $5 ◆ Custom-designed and wired chandeliers, candelabras, lamps, and fireplace tools. 210-997-2263.

**Home Decorators Collection,** 8920 Pershall Rd., Hazelwood, MO 63042: Free catalog ◆ Lamp shades and contemporary, traditional, floor, table, halogen lamps, and light fixtures for the bathroom, ceiling, wall, and outdoors. 800-240-6047.

**Home Trends,** 1450 Lyell Ave., Rochester, NY 14606: Free catalog ◆ Cleaning supplies, energy-saving devices, lighting equipment, pest controls, brushes, vacuums and accessories, and more. 716-254-6520. home@eznet.net

**Howard's Antique Lighting,** Rt. 23 West, P.O. Box 472, South Egremont, MA 01258: Free information ◆ Floor lamps, sconces, and electric, gas, and kerosene chandeliers. 413-528-1232.

**Hurley Patentee Lighting,** 464 Old Rt. 209, Hurley, NY 12443: Catalog $3 ◆ Handcrafted replica Early American chandeliers, sconces, lanterns, and other lamps. 914-331-5414.

**Independence Forge,** 309 W. Nash St., Whitakers, NC 27891: Brochure $1 ◆ Handcrafted country-style iron furniture, chandeliers, and floor, table, and wall lamps. 919-437-1452.

**Irish Crystal Company,** 102 W. Washington St., P.O. Box 2134, Middleburg, VA 20118: Free brochure ◆ Waterford crystal lamps. 540-687-3422.

**Irvin's,** RD 1, Box 73, Mt. Pleasant Mills, PA 17853: Free catalog ◆ Handcrafted colonial tinware and lighting. 717-539-8200.

**Jay "Bird" Jones,** 520 Pine Oaks Rd., #4, Colorado Springs, CO 80926: Catalog $10 (refundable); brochure $1 ◆ Antler chairs, lamps, chandeliers, and carvings. 719-527-1845.

**Daniel Joseph Historic Styled Lighting,** 31921 Camino Capistrano, #347, San Juan Capistrano, CA 92675: Free brochure ◆ Historic-styled light fixtures. 800-548-6984; 714-841-6200 (in CA).

**Juno Lighting Inc.,** P.O. Box 5065, Des Plaines, IL 60017: Free information ◆ Indoor and outdoor light fixtures. 800-323-5068.

**Lamp Shop,** P.O. Box 3606, Concord, NH 03302: Catalog $2.50 ◆ Chandeliers and sconces. 603-224-1603.

**Lamps by Gramps,** P.O. Box 116, Hygiene, CO 80533: Free information ◆ Pre-designed and custom western-style lamps, clocks, and signs.

**Lamps by Lynne,** P.O. Box 190, Pipersville, PA 18947: Free information ◆ Lamps and lamp shades. 215-766-7615.

**Levenger,** P.O. Box 1256, Delray Beach, FL 33447: Free catalog ◆ Reproduction brass-shade desk lamps. 800-545-0242. www.levenger.com

**Leviton Manufacturing Company,** 59-25 Little Neck Pkwy., Little Neck, NY 11362: Free information ◆ Indoor and outdoor light fixtures. 800-323-8920.

**Lighting by Gregory,** 158 Bowery, New York, NY 10012: Free catalog ◆ Fixtures and accessories that enable design of lighting to accommodate individual desires and activities. 800-796-1965; 212-226-1276 (in NY).

**Lightolier,** 7151 Columbia Gateway Dr., Ste. A, Columbia, MD 21046: Free information ◆ Indoor and outdoor light fixtures. 410-995-6395.

**Live Oaks of Savannah,** P.O. Box 16194, Savannah, GA 31416: Free catalog ◆ Victorian-style furniture, lamps, clocks, and accessories. 800-467-5539.

**Lt. Moses Willard Inc.,** 1156 US 50, Milford, OH 45150: Catalog $8.50 (request list of retail sources) ◆ Chandeliers, wall sconces, exterior lighting units, candle holders and lanterns, wall lamps, table lamps, and reproduction light fixtures from styles of the 1700s. 937-248-5500.

**Lucid Lighting,** 287 S. Main St., Lamberville, NJ 08530: Catalog $5 ◆ Custom-made historic-style light fixtures. 609-397-9581.

**MacPhail's Studio,** 1417 N. Kickapoo, Ste. 4, Lincoln, IL 62656: Free information ◆ Antler chandeliers, lamps, and chairs. 217-732-7538.

**Marlborough Country Barn,** N. Main St., Marlborough, CT 06447: Catalog $3 ◆ Reproduction lighting for log homes. 800-852-8993.

**Meyda Tiffany,** 55 Oriskany Blvd., Yorkville, NY 13495: Catalog $5 ◆ Victorian light fixtures. Also beaded and Tiffany lamps. 800-222-4009.

**Mica Lamp Company,** 517 State St., Glendale, CA 91203: Free brochure ◆ Handcrafted turn-of-the-century copper light fixtures. 800-90-LAMPS.

**Mill Creek Antiques,** 109 Newbury, Paxico, KS 66526: Free information ◆ Antique furniture, lighting, and stoves. 913-636-5520.

**Gates Moore Lighting,** River Rd., Norwalk, CT 06580: Catalog $2 ◆ Early American chandeliers, copper lanterns, and wall sconces. 203-847-3231.

**Moultrie Manufacturing,** P.O. Drawer 1179, Moultrie, GA 31776: Catalog $3 ◆ Colonial lanterns and "Old South" reproductions for the home. 800-841-8674.

**The Nauset Lantern Shop,** 169 Rt. 6A, P.O. Box 1198, Orleans, MA 02653: Catalog $4 (refundable) ◆ Handcrafted reproduction colonial and Early American light fixtures. 800-899-2660; 508-255-1009 (in MA).

**C. Neri Antiques,** 313 South St., Philadelphia, PA 19147: Catalog $5 ◆ Antique light fixtures. 215-923-6669. Havoc@snet.net

**New England Stained Glass,** 5 Center St., West Stockbridge, MA 01266: Brochure $5 (refundable) ◆ Tiffany reproductions. 413-232-7181.

**Newstamp Lighting Company,** 227 Bay Rd., P.O. Box 189, North Easton, MA 02356: Catalog $2 ◆ Handmade replica Early American lamps for indoors and outdoors, sconces, chandeliers, and other light fixtures. 508-238-7071.

**Old West Charm,** P.O. Box 311, Mountain Center, CA 92561: Brochure $6 (refundable) ◆ Handcrafted wood wagon wheel furnishings, lamps, wall hangings, and decorative items.

**The Original Cast Lighting,** 6120 Delmar Blvd., St. Louis, MO 63112: Catalog $2 ◆ Light fixtures and reproduction and restored antique units. 314-863-1895.

**Period Lighting Fixtures,** 167 River Rd., P.O. Box 26017, Clarksburg, MA 01247: Free catalog ◆ Early American light fixtures, chandeliers, lanterns, and sconces. 800-828-6990.

**Rejuvenation Lamp & Fixture Company,** 1100 SE Grand Ave., Portland, OR 97214: Free catalog ◆ Reproduction gas-style, gas and electric, early electric, 20th-century, colonial revival, and other chandeliers, sconces, and lamps. 503-231-1900. www.rejuvenation.com

**The Renovator's Supply,** P.O. Box 2515, Conway, NH 03818: Free catalog ◆ Replacement glass shades and ceiling light fixtures and hanging, table, floor, and wall lamps. 800-659-0203.

**Roy Electric Company,** 22 Elm St., Westfield, NJ 07090: Free catalog ◆ Victorian-style and turn-of-the-century chandeliers, sconces, and other light fixtures. 800-366-3347; 908-317-4665 (in NJ).

**St. Louis Antique Lighting Company Inc.,** 801 N. Skinker, St. Louis, MO 63130: Catalog $3 ◆ Handcrafted antique brass reproduction ceiling fixtures, lamps, and sconces. 314-863-1414.

**Saltbox Inc.,** 3004 Columbia Ave., Lancaster, PA 17603: Catalog $2.50 ◆ Handcrafted brass, copper, and tin colonial-style post lights, chandeliers, lanterns, and foyer lights. 717-392-5649.

**Scintilla,** P.O. Box 78982, Atlanta, GA 30357: Free catalog ◆ Jewelry, lighting, and accessories. 800-975-0191.

**Asher Shahar,** P.O. Box 640684, North Miami, FL 33164: Catalog $3 ◆ Reproduction Tiffany lamps.

**Shelburne Lighting & Metal Crafts,** 1012 State Rt. 2, Shelburne, NH 03581: Free information ◆ Reproduction colonial-style light fixtures. 603-466-2971.

**Stanley Galleries,** 2118 N. Clark St., Chicago, IL 60614: Free information ◆ Antique American chandeliers and light fixtures. 312-281-1614.

**M. Star Antler Designs,** P.O. Box 3093, Lake Isabella, CA 93240: Catalog $5 ◆ Antler chandeliers, lamps, furniture, mirrors, and decorative accessories. 619-379-5777.

**The Stone House,** 28 E. Market St., Middleburg, PA 17842: Free catalog ◆ Colonial period light fixtures. 800-923-2260.

**Studio Steel,** 159 New Milford Tnpk., New Preston, CT 06777: Catalog $2 ◆ Lamps, chandeliers, sconces, mirrors, and hand-wrought metalwork. 800-800-5712.

**Task Lighting Corp.,** P.O. Box 1090, Kearney, NE 68848: Free information ◆ Indoor light fixtures. 800-445-6404.

**Urban Archaeology,** 143 Franklin St., New York, NY 10013: Catalog $8.66 ◆ Reproduction lighting, bathroom and kitchen accessories, and more. 212-431-4646.

**Van Campen's,** Noone Falls, Rt. 202 South, Peterborough, NH 03458: Free information ◆ Furniture, lighting, and other 18th-century reproductions. 603-924-4225.

**Vermont Industries,** P.O. Box 301, Rt. 103, Cuttingsville, VT 05738: Catalog $3 ◆ Wrought-iron and solid brass chandeliers, floor and table lamps, and wall fixtures. 800-639-1715; 802-492-3451 (in VT).

**Victorian Lampshades,** Nadja Rider, 3440 Essex Ct., Craig, CO 81625: Catalog $4 (refundable) ◆ Handcrafted Victorian lamps. 970-824-9333.

**Victorian Lightcrafters Ltd.,** P.O. Box 350, Slate Hill, NY 10973: Catalog $3 (refundable) ◆ Handcrafted Victorian-style light fixtures. 914-355-1300. www.lightcrafters.qpg.com

**Victorian Lighting Works,** 251 S. Pennsylvania Ave., P.O. Box 469, Centre Hall, PA 16828: Catalog $5 (refundable) ◆ Victorian-style light fixtures. 814-364-9577.

**Workshops of David T. Smith,** 3600 Shawhan Rd., Morrow, OH 45152: Catalog $5 ◆ Reproduction lamps and chandeliers, furniture, and pottery. 513-932-2472. www.davidtsmith.com

## Lamp Shades

**Aladdin Industries Inc.,** Lamp Division, P.O. Box 100255, Nashville, TN 37224: Free catalog ◆ Lamps, lamp shades, and replacement parts. 800-456-1233.

**Alfa Lite,** 380 E. 1700 South, Salt Lake City, UT 84115: Free information ◆ Reproduction and restoration of antique lamps and shades. 800-388-5456.

**Art Wire Works Company,** 5401 W. 65th St., Chicago, IL 60638: Free catalog ◆ Lampshade components. 800-336-0097; 708-458-3993 (in IL).

**Birds of Paradise Lampshades,** 114 Sherbourne St., Toronto, Ontario, Canada M5A 2R2: Free information ◆ Custom silk, parchment, and mica lampshades. 416-366-4067.

**Brass Light Gallery,** 131 S. 1st St., Milwaukee, WI 53204: Catalog $5 ◆ Replacement glass shades and lamps. 800-243-9595.

**Burdoch Victorian Lamp Company,** 757 N. Twin Oaks Valley Rd., San Marcos, CA 92069: Catalog $5 ◆ Reproduction Victorian lighting. 800-783-8738.

**Fantasy Lighting,** 7126 Melrose Ave., Los Angeles, CA 90046: Brochure $4 ◆ Victorian shades and lamp bases. 213-933-7244.

**Garber's Crafted Lighting,** P.O. Box 140, Mammoth Spring, AR 72554: Catalog $4 ◆ Punched pewter-tin Tiffany shades. 501-966-4996.

**Heart Enterprise/Victorian Lamp Shades,** 101 Sharon Way, Roseville, CA 95678: Catalog $5 ◆ Victorian-style lamp shade kits and supplies. 800-398-4981. www.galaxymall.com/product/lampshade

**Herr's & Bernat,** 70 Eastgate Dr., P.O. Box 630, Danville, IL 61834: Free information ◆ Latch-hook kits and lampshade making supplies. 800-637-2647.

**Indulgence Lampshade Supplies,** P.O. Box 8180, Bend, OR 97701: Free catalog ◆ Frames, beaded fringes, lace, bases, and lamp supplies. 541-317-1900.

**Kiti Inc.,** P.O. Box 368, Woodstock, IL 60098: Catalog $4 ◆ Easy-to-follow patterns for hand-sewn Victorian lamp shades. 815-338-7970.

**Lamp Glass,** P.O. Box 791, Cambridge, MA 02140: Catalog $1 ◆ Replacement glass lamp shades and parts. 617-497-0770.

**Lamp Shop,** P.O. Box 3606, Concord, NH 03302: Catalog $2.50 ◆ Lampshade crafting supplies. 603-224-1603.

**Lamps by Lynne,** P.O. Box 190, Pipersville, PA 18947: Free information ◆ Lamps and lamp shades. 215-766-7615.

**Lampshades of Antique,** P.O. Box 2, Medford, OR 97501: Catalog $5 ◆ Victorian-style lamp shades. 800-928-7613; 541-826-9737 (in OR). www.internetcds.com/Business/Shades

**Mainly Shades,** One Hundred Gray Rd., Falmouth, ME 04105: Catalog $3 ◆ Lampshade-making supplies and how-to books. 800-624-6359. www.maineguide.com/maineshade

**Oriental Lamp Shade Company,** 816 Lexington Ave., New York, NY 10021: Free information ◆ In-stock silk and custom hand-sewn lampshades. 212-832-8190.

**The Renovator's Supply,** P.O. Box 2515, Conway, NH 03818: Free catalog ◆ Replacement glass shades, ceiling fixtures, and hanging, table, floor, and wall lamps. 800-659-0203.

**Shades of Antique,** P.O. Box 1507, Medford, OR 97501: Catalog $4 ◆ In-stock and custom-made antique style lampshades. 541-826-9737.

**Shady Lady Handmade Lampshades,** 5020 W. Eisenhower, Loveland, CO 80537: Catalog $3.50 ◆ Lamp shades. 970-669-1080.

**Turn of the Century Lampshades,** P.O. Box 6599, Bend, OR 97708: Brochure $5 ◆ Victorian-style lampshades. 541-382-1802.

**Victorian Classics Lampshades,** 4128 NE Sandy Blvd., Ste. C, Portland, OR 97212: Catalog $3 ◆ Handcrafted Victorian-style lampshade-making supplies and parts. 503-282-7055.

**Victorian Lampshades,** Nadja Rider, 3440 Essex Ct., Craig, CO 81625: Catalog $4 (refundable) ◆ Victorian-style fabric lampshades and bases. 970-824-9333.

**Yestershades,** 4327 SE Hawthorne, Portland, OR 97214: Catalog $3.50 ◆ Victorian-style lamp shades. 503-235-5645.

## Outdoor Lighting

**AK Exteriors,** 101 Montoya Rd., El Paso, TX 79932: Catalog $4 ◆ Cast-aluminum furniture, light fixtures, and mail boxes. 800-253-9837.

**Ameron Pole Products Division,** 1020 B St., Fillmore, CA 93015: Free information ◆ Traditional light poles that complement period and modern architectural styles. 800-552-6376.

**Authentic Designs,** The Mill Rd., West Rupert, VT 05776: Catalog $3 ◆ Outdoor post lighting units and handcrafted reproduction 18th-century Early American light fixtures in brass, copper, or tin. 802-394-7713.

**Brandon Industries,** 1601 W. Wilmeth Rd., McKinney, TX 75069: Free catalog ◆ Cast-aluminum street lamps and old-fashioned pedestal mail boxes with solid brass letter slot and cylinder key lock. 972-542-3000. www.brandonmail.com

**Cast Aluminum Reproductions,** P.O. Box 1060, San Elzario, TX 79849: Catalog $2 ◆ Cast-aluminum and brass furniture, street lights, outdoor furniture, fountains, mail boxes, and plant stands. 915-764-3793.

**Classic Lamp Posts,** 3645 NW 67th St., Miami, FL 33147: Free catalog ◆ Colonial and Victorian-style lamp posts with single or multiple plastic globes. 800-654-5852.

**Copper Craft Lighting Inc.,** 5100 Clayton Rd., Ste. 291, Concord, CA 94521: Free information ◆ Handmade copper landscape lights. 510-672-4337.

**Copper House,** RFD 1, Box 4, Epsom, NH 03234: Catalog $3 ◆ Indoor and outdoor light fixtures and hand-hammered copper weather vanes. 800-281-9798.

**Josiah R. Coppersmythe,** 80 Stiles Rd., Boylston, MA 01505: Catalog $3 ◆ Handcrafted brass or copper Early American indoor and outdoor light fixtures. 508-869-2769.

**Doner Design Inc.,** 2175 Beaver Valley Pike, New Providence, PA 17560: Free brochure ◆ Copper landscape lights. 717-786-8891.

**Genie House,** P.O. Box 2478, Vincentown, NJ 08088: Catalog $5 ◆ Indoor and outdoor reproduction light fixtures. 800-634-3643.

**Great Plains Polymers,** 3385 N. 88th Plaza, Omaha, NE 68134: Free brochure ◆ Steel light poles for residential and courtyard lighting. 800-677-1131.

**Hanover Lantern,** 470 High St., Hanover, PA 17331: Free information ◆ Heavy duty cast-aluminum landscape light fixtures. 717-632-6464.

**Heathkit Educational Systems,** 455 Riverview Dr., Benton Harbor, MI 49022: Free catalog ◆ Automatic turn-on and turn-off lighting controls. 800-253-0570. www.heathkit.com

**Heritage Lanterns,** 70-A Main St., Yarmouth, ME 04096: Catalog $5 ◆ Colonial-style outdoor light fixtures. 800-648-4449.

**Herwig Lighting,** P.O. Box 768, Russellville, AR 72801: Free brochure ◆ Light fixtures, bollards, street furniture, antique fence posts, street clocks, and post lanterns. 800-643-9523. www.herwig.com

**Honeywell Inc.,** Customer Assistance Center, P.O. Box 524, Minneapolis, MN 55440: Free information ◆ Motion activated lighting controls. 800-345-6770. www.honeywell.com

**Hubbell Lighting,** 2000 Electric Way, Christiansburg, VA 24073: Catalog $5 ◆ Low-voltage outdoor lighting systems. 800-270-3737.

**Imelda,** 16960 S.R. 12 East., Findlay, OH 45840: Free catalog ◆ Antiques, Victorian furniture, and cast-aluminum lighting. 800-483-7105; 419-424-1722 (in OH).

**Intermatic Lighting Inc.,** Intermatic Plaza, Spring Grove, IL 60081: Free information ◆ Low-voltage outdoor lighting systems. 815-675-2321.

**Juno Lighting Inc.,** P.O. Box 5065, Des Plaines, IL 60017: Free information ◆ Indoor and outdoor light fixtures. 800-323-5068.

**KIM Lighting,** 16555 E. Gale Ave., P.O. Box 60080, City of Industry, CA 91716: Free information ◆ Landscape lighting equipment. 818-968-5666.

**Lamplighter Corner Inc.,** P.O. Box 235, Edgartown, MA 02539: Free brochure ◆ Handmade solid brass and copper lanterns. 508-627-4656.

**Leviton Manufacturing Company,** 59-25 Little Neck Pkwy., Little Neck, NY 11362: Free information ◆ Indoor and outdoor light fixtures. 800-323-8920.

**Lightolier,** 7151 Columbia Gateway Dr., Ste. A, Columbia, MD 21046: Free information ◆ Indoor and outdoor light fixtures. 410-995-6395.

**Mel-Nor Industries,** 303 Gulf Bank, Houston, TX 77037: Information $1 ◆ Park benches, old-time lamp posts, and lawn and hanging porch swings. 281-445-3485.

**Moultrie Manufacturing,** P.O. Drawer 1179, Moultrie, GA 31776: Catalog $3 ◆ Cast-aluminum indoor and outdoor light fixtures, tables, chairs, settees, planters, urns, fountains, and chaises. 800-841-8674.

**Rejuvenation Lamp & Fixture Company,** 1100 SE Grand Ave., Portland, OR 97214: Free catalog ◆ Reproduction gas-style, gas and electric, early electric, 20th-century, colonial revival, and other chandeliers, sconces, and lamps. 503-231-1900.

**Robbins Lighting Inc.,** 124 E. 2nd St., P.O. Box 440, Maryville, MO 56648: Free information ◆ Weather vanes and residential and commercial light protection systems. 800-426-3792. www.robbinslightning.thomasregister.com

**Sentry Electric Corp.,** 185 Buffalo Ave., Freeport, NY 11520: Free information ◆ Colonial and early 1900s-style cast-aluminum lamp posts, area light fixtures, and accessories. 516-379-4660.

**Spring City Electrical Manufacturing Company,** P.O. Box 19, Spring City, PA 19475: Free catalog ◆ Heavy-duty cast-iron ornamental lamp posts. 610-948-4000.

**Task Lighting Corp.,** P.O. Box 1090, Kearney, NE 68848: Free information ◆ Indoor light fixtures. 800-445-6404.

**Toro Company,** 8111 Lyndale Ave., Bloomington, MN 55420: Free information ◆ Outdoor lighting units for landscape and security settings with optional power packs and photo sensors. 800-526-6937. www.toro.com

**Tower Lighting Center,** P.O. Box 1043, North Adams, MA 01247: Catalog $3 ◆ Hand-wrought copper lanterns. 413-663-7681.

**Urban Farmer Store,** 2833 Vicente St., San Francisco, CA 94116: Catalog $1 ◆ Low-voltage outdoor lighting. 800-753-3747; 415-661-2204 (in CA).

**U.S. Gaslight Company,** 4658 S. Old Peachtree Rd., Norcross, GA 30071: Free information ◆ Lighting standards. 800-241-4317.

### Ultraviolet Light

**Alpha Supply,** P.O. Box 2133, Bremerton, WA 98310: Catalog $7 ◆ Ultraviolet lighting, jewelry-making, prospecting, and rockhounding equipment. 800-257-4211; 360-373-3302 (in WA).

**Bourget Bros.,** 1636 11th St., Santa Monica, CA 90404: Catalog $3 ◆ Ultraviolet lighting and rock-polishing equipment, jewelry-making tools, and supplies. 800-828-3024. www.bourgetbros.com

**Cal-Gold,** 2569 E. Colorado Blvd., Pasadena, CA 91107: Free catalog ◆ Ultraviolet lighting equipment, metal detectors, supplies for miners and geologists, maps, and books. 626-792-6161. calgold@earthlink.net

**Diamond Pacific Tool Corp.,** P.O. Box 1180, Barstow, CA 92312: Free catalog ◆ Ultraviolet lighting equipment. 800-253-2954. www.diamondpacific.com

**Ebersole Lapidary Supply Inc.,** 11417 West Hwy. 54, Wichita, KS 67209: Catalog $5 ◆ Ultraviolet lighting equipment and jewelry-making, rockhounding, and bead-stringing supplies. 316-722-4771.

**Gemstone Equipment Manufacturing Company,** 750 Easy St., Simi Valley, CA 93065: Free information ◆ Ultraviolet lighting and lapidary equipment. 800-235-3375; 805-527-6990 (in CA).

**Graves Company,** 1800 Andrews Ave., Pompano Beach, FL 33069: Free catalog ◆ Ultraviolet lighting, rockhounding, and lapidary equipment. 800-327-9103. www.rockhounds.com/graves

**Jeanne's Rock & Jewelry,** 5420 Bissonet, Bellaire, TX 77401: Price list $1 ◆ Ultraviolet lighting equipment. 713-664-2988.

**Raytech,** 475 Smith St., Middletown, CT 06457: Free information ◆ Cabochon machines, trim and slab saws, faceting machines, and ultraviolet lighting and other equipment. 860-632-2020.

**Riviera Lapidary Supply,** 50898 7th St., Box 40, Riviera, TX 78379: Catalog $3 ◆ Ultraviolet lighting equipment. 512-296-3958.

**Taiclet Enterprises,** Margie Taiclet, 440 Los Encinos Ave., San Jose, CA 95110: Free information ◆ Portable long-wave ultraviolet blacklight. 408-954-8556.

**UV Systems Inc.,** 16605 127th Ave. SE, Renton, WA 98058: Free information ◆ Ultraviolet and black lighting equipment, replacement bulbs, and ultraviolet glass filters. 888-228-9988. www.uvsystems.com

**UVP Inc.,** 2066 W. 11th St., Upland, CA 91786: Free information ◆ Short-wave, long-wave, and short/long-wave ultraviolet lighting equipment. 800-452-6788.

**Wright's Rock Shop,** 3612 Albert Pike, Hot Springs, AR 71913: Catalog $3 ◆ Ultraviolet lighting equipment. 501-767-4800.

## LANGUAGE TRANSLATORS & SPELLING AIDS

**American Consumer Group,** 125 Armstrong Rd., Des Plaines, IL 60018: Free information ◆ Electronic spelling dictionary. 800-671-2958.

**Bengold Associates Inc.,** P.O. Box 3608, Cherry Hill, NJ 08034: Free information ◆ Portable light-weight electronic English-Hebrew and Hebrew-English dictionary. Optional installable extension cards for medical, legal, technical/ professional, and business/office terminology available. 800-783-7417; 609-779-7841 (in NJ).

**Linguistic Products Inc.,** P.O. Box 8263, The Woodlands, TX 77387: Free information ◆ PC translators for language translation. 713-298-2565.

## LAWN BOWLING

**Grass Court Collection,** P.O. Box 972, Hanover, NH 03755: Free catalog ◆ Custom men's clothing for tennis, croquet, lawn bowling, cricket, and squash. 800-829-3412.

## LEAD TESTING

**Innovative Synthesis,** 2143 Commonwealth Ave., Newton, MA 02166: Free brochure ◆ An easy-to-use at-home test for lead paint. 617-965-5653.

**The Lead Tester,** 2115 Parkway Dr., Reno, NV 89205: Free information ◆ Lead testing kit. 800-896-5323.

**Priorities,** 70 Walnut St., Wellesley, MA 02181: Free catalog ◆ Easy-to-use swab test to check for lead. 800-553-5398. getrelief@priorities.com

## LEATHER CRAFTING

**Appalachian Leather Works & Trading Company,** 2230 High Point Ln., Slatington, PA 18080: Catalog $2 (refundable) ◆ Handcrafted leather products. 610-767-8368.

**Bead Boppers,** 3924 S. Meridian, Puyallup, WA 98373: Catalog $2.50 (refundable) ◆ Beads and findings, tools, charms, seed beads, leather, supplies, and books. 888-848-3880. www.ibrowse.com/boppers

**Berman Leathercraft,** 229 A St., S. Boston, MA 02210: Catalog $3 (refundable) ◆ Chamois, suede, and leather for crafting. 617-426-0870.

**Leather Unlimited,** 7155 Hwy. B, Belgium, WI 53004: Catalog $2 (refundable) ◆ Leather-crafting supplies and kits. 414-999-9464. leather@execpc.com

**Mangelsen's Craft Supplies,** P.O. Box 3314, Omaha, NE 68103: Free information ◆ Supplies for general crafts, candle-making, and leather-working. 800-228-2601; 402-339-3922 (in NE).

**Muir & McDonald Company,** P.O. Box 136, Dallas, OR 97338: Free brochure ◆ Vegetable tanned leather. 800-547-1299.

**Nasco,** 901 Janesville Ave., Fort Atkinson, WI 53538: Free catalog ◆ Leather-crafting supplies, tools, and kits. 800-558-9595. www.nascofa.com

**Siegel of California,** Box 595, Santa Ynez, CA 93460: Catalog $5 ◆ Leather crafting supplies and tools. 800-862-8956; 805-686-2700 (in CA).

**Stillson Leather,** Rt. 1, Box 88-A, Prague, OK 74864: Free information ◆ Handcrafted leather products. 405-567-3927.

**Tandy Leather Company,** P.O. Box 791, Fort Worth, TX 76101: Catalog $3 (refundable) ◆ Leather-crafting kits, tools, books, patterns, sewing notions, and how-to videos. 800-555-3130. www.tandyleather.com

## LEFT-HANDED MERCHANDISE

**Left Hand Center,** 210 W. Grant, Unit 215, Minneapolis, MN 55403: Catalog $2 ◆ Gifts for left-handed persons. 612-375-0319.

**Left Hand Supply Company,** P.O. Box 20188, Oakland, CA 94620: Free catalog ◆ Left-handed products. 510-658-5338.

**The Lefthand,** P.O. Box 3263, Bethlehem, PA 18020: Catalog $2 ◆ Stationery and office supplies, computer accessories, gifts, tools, kitchen aids, books, and other items for left-handed persons. 800-462-5338. rightstuff@thelefthand.com

**Lefthanders International,** P.O. Box 8249, Topeka, KS 66608: Catalog $2 ◆ Items for lefties. 913-234-2177.

**Lefties Only,** 1972 Williston Rd., South Burlington, VT 05403: Free price list ◆ Golf equipment for left-handed persons. 800-533-8437.

**Odyssey Golf,** 1969 Kellog Ave., Carlsbad, CA 92008: Free brochure ◆ Bags, hats, shirts, and left-handed putters. 800-991-1788. www.odysseygolf.com

**Southpaw Enterprises,** Box 835, Nelson, British Columbia, Canada V1L 5S9: Free catalog ◆ Left-handed scissors, pinking shears, kitchen aids and measuring devices, and more. 800-818-9616.

**The Southpaw Shoppe,** Catalog Dept., P.O. Box 2870, San Diego, CA 92112: Free catalog ◆ Products for the left-handed person. 619-239-1731.

## LIBRARY SUPPLIES

**Office Zone,** 461 W. 200 North, P.O. Box 808, Bountiful, UT 84011: Free catalog ◆ Desks for homes and offices, library supplies, binding equipment, folders, labels and labeling tapes, and other supplies. 800-543-5454; 801-298-3839 (in UT).

**Vernon Library Supplies,** 2851 Cole Ct., Norcross, GA 30071: Free catalog ◆ Library supplies and equipment. 800-878-0253; 770-446-1128 (in GA). www.vernlib.com

## LIGHT BULBS

**Associated Photo Company,** 7103 Turfway Rd., Florence, KY 41022: Free information ◆ Replacement bulbs for photography, medical and dental, video, stage and studio, and other needs. 800-727-2580; 606-282-0011 (in KY).

**Bulbman,** P.O. Box 12280, Reno, NV 89510: Free information ◆ Replacement bulbs for theatrical lighting equipment, darkrooms, studio lights, flash-heads, and modeling. 800-648-1163.

**Firestone Electric,** P.O. Box 616, Salem, OH 44460: Free information ◆ Sun-like full-spectrum 60-, 100-, and 150-watt light bulbs.

**Gray Supply Company,** 5204 Indianapolis Blvd., East Chicago, IN 46312: Free catalog ◆ Replacement projection, medical, and specialty light bulbs and accessories. 800-867-2852. www.topbulb.com

## LIGHTHOUSES

**Lighthouse Depot,** P.O. Box 427, Wells, ME 04090: Free catalog ◆ Lighthouse memorabilia. 800-758-1444. www.lhdigest.com

**PuzzleKing,** P.O. Box 128, Brewster, MA 02631: Free brochure ◆ Nostalgic architectural landmarks featuring famous American lighthouses. 800-750-4552. www.capecod.net/puzzleking

## LOG SPLITTERS & SAW MILLS

**Bailey's,** P.O. Box 550, Laytonville, CA 95454: Free catalog ◆ Chain saws, bars, files, protective gear, forestry supplies, log splitters, books, other woodsman supplies, and gifts. 707-984-6133. www.bbaileys.com/bbaileys/west.htm

**Better Built Corp.,** 845 Woburn St., Wilmington, MA 01887: Free brochure ◆ One-man portable sawmills. 978-657-5636.

**Mainline of North America,** P.O. Box 526, London, OH 43140: Free information ◆ Hydraulic log splitter, carts, snow throwers, and all-gear driven tiller with optional sickle bar and no belts or chains. 800-837-2097.

**Mighty Mite Sawmill,** 3931 NE Columbia Blvd., Portland, OR 97211: Free information ◆ Transportable sawmill. 503-288-5923.

**Mobile Manufacturing Company,** P.O. Box 250, Troutdale, OR 97060: Free brochure ◆ Portable electric or gasoline-powered saw for cutting logs. 503-666-5593.

**Northern Hydraulics,** P.O. Box 1219, Burnsville, MN 55337: Free catalog ◆ Log splitters, gas engines, trailer parts, and tools. 800-533-5545. www.northern-online.com

**Norwood Sawmills,** 90 Curtwright Dr., Unit 3, Amherst, NY 14221: Free information ◆ Sawmills. 800-661-7746.

**Silvacraft Sawmills,** 90 Curtwright Dr., Unit 3, Amherst, NY 14221: Free information ◆ Sawmills. 800-661-7746. www.norwoodindustries.com

**Timberking Inc.,** P.O. Box 34284, Kansas City, MO 64120: Free information ◆ Portable one-man saw mill. 800-942-4406.

**Wood-Mizer,** 8180 W. 10th St., Indianapolis, IN 46214: Catalog $2 ◆ Portable sawmills and tools. 800-553-0219. www.woodmizer.com

## LUGGAGE, LUGGAGE-CARRIERS, & BRIEFCASES

**A to Z Luggage,** 4627 New Utrecht Ave., Brooklyn, NY 11219: Free catalog ◆ Luggage and small leather goods. 800-342-5011; 718-435-6330 (in NY).

**Ace Luggage & Gifts,** 2122 Avenue U, Brooklyn, NY 11229: Catalog $2 ◆ Desk sets, leather attache cases, luggage, wallets, handbags, and other gifts. 800-342-5223; 718-891-9713 (in NY).

**Al's Luggage,** 2134 Larimer St., Denver, CO 80205: Catalog $2 (refundable) ◆ Luggage carts and luggage. 303-295-9009.

**Altman Luggage,** 135 Orchard St., New York, NY 10001: Free information ◆ Luggage, leather goods, pens, and pencils. 800-372-3377.

**American Executive,** Kittery Business Center, 72 Dow Hwy., Kittery, ME 03904: Catalog $2 ◆ Writing portfolios, travel cases, day planners, wallets, briefcases, backpacks, and other leather essentials. 800-804-0825.

**ASU Incorporated,** 5725 Paradise Dr., Ste. 800, Corte Madera, CA 94925: Free catalog ◆ Traditional luggage, casual bags, accessories, and business cases. 800-756-1444.

**Bally of Switzerland,** 628 Madison Ave., New York, NY 10153: Free information ◆ Men's and women's shoes and clothing. Also luggage and other small leather goods. 212-751-2163.

**Bentley's Luggage Corp.,** National Distribution Center, 3353 NW 74th Ave., Miami, FL 33122: Free catalog ◆ Luggage and gifts. 800-330-0050. bentley@gate.net

**Bondy Export Corp.,** 40 Canal St., New York, NY 10002: Free information with long SASE ◆ Luggage and accessories, appliances, typewriters, cameras, TVs, and video equipment. 212-925-7785.

**Border Leather,** 3800 Main St., Chula Vista, CA 91911: Free catalog ◆ Leather and textile goods. 800-732-6936.

**Bottega Veneta,** 635 Madison Ave., New York, NY 10022: Free catalog ◆ Wallets, purses and handbags, luggage, and small leather goods. 212-371-5511.

**Coach Leatherware Company,** 410 Commerce Blvd., Carlstadt, NJ 07072: Free catalog ◆ Leather handbags, gloves, belts, wallets, and briefcases. 201-804-8200. www.coach.com

**The Complete Traveler of Overland Park,** 7321 W. 80th St., Overland Park, KS 66204: Free catalog ◆ Maps, travel books, travel accessories, and luggage. 888-862-0888. www.completetrav.com

**Copper Star Cattle & Trading Company,** 2000 W. 3rd St., Amarillo, TX 79106: Catalog $2 ◆ Cowhide purses, wallets, satchels and bags, and accessories. 800-828-0442.

**Crouch & Fitzgerald,** 400 Madison Ave., New York, NY 10017: Free information ◆ Leather goods with optional monogramming. 800-6-CROUCH; 212-755-5888 (in NY).

**Dare Classics,** P.O. Box 1834, Elk Grove, CA 95759: Free information ◆ Reproduction and custom-fitted luggage for antique and classic automobiles. 916-687-6018.

**Dooney & Bourke Inc.,** 759 Madison Ave., New York, NY 10021: Free catalog ◆ Leather goods and accessories. 800-226-9046. www.Dooney.com

**Duluth Pack,** 357 Canal Park Dr., Duluth, MN 55802: Free catalog ◆ Traditional canvas canoe packs and luggage. 800-849-4489. www.duluthpacks.com

**Dunn's Supply Catalog,** P.O. Box 509, Grand Junction, TN 38039: Free catalog ◆ Camouflage and insulated clothing, outerwear, shoes and boots, hunting equipment, day and belt packs, leather goods, gun care kits, sunglasses, game calls, decoys, and supplies. 800-427-6572. www.dunnscatalog.com

**Eagle Creek,** 1740 La Costa Meadows Dr., San Marcos, CA 92069: Free list of retail sources ◆ Luggage. 800-874-9925. www.eaglecreek.com

**Charolette Ford Trunks,** P.O. Box 536, Spearman, TX 79081: Catalog $2.75 ◆ Supplies and tools for restoring trunks. 806-659-3027. www.charolettefordtrunks.com

**Hilsport by Hilco Inc.,** 2102 Fair Park Blvd., Harlingen, TX 78550: Free brochure ◆ Luggage and gun cases. 800-451-9236.

**Innovation Luggage,** 20 Enterprise Ave., Secaucus, NJ 07094: Free list of retail sources ◆ Luggage, briefcases, portfolios, attaché cases, and handbags. 800-722-1800.

**Jet-Eze Travelmaxx Luggage,** 2150 Dodd Rd., Mendota Heights, MN 55120: Free brochure ◆ Roll-on luggage with retractable wheel mechanisms. 800-274-4597.

**Kart-A-Bag,** Division of Remin, 510 Manhattan Rd., Joliet, IL 60433: Free list of retail sources ◆ Telescoping easy-to-store luggage transporter. 800-423-9328; 815-723-1940 (in IL). www.kart-a-bag.com

**Kelty Packs Inc.,** 6235 Lookout Rd., Boulder, CO 80301: Free list of retail sources ◆ Cordura nylon backpacks that convert to luggage. 800-423-2320. www.kelty.com

**Lodis Corp.,** 2261 S. Carme Lina Ave., Los Angeles, CA 90064: Free catalog ◆ Leather luggage, shaving and toilet kits, briefcases, note pads, wallets, and management systems. 800-421-8674; 310-207-6841 (in CA).

**The Luggage Center,** 960 Remillard St., San Jose, CA 95122: Free information with long SASE ◆ Luggage and accessories. 800-626-6789.

**Madden Mountaineering,** 2400 Central Ave., Boulder, CO 80301: Free catalog ◆ Carryalls, tote bags, duffles, and shoulder bags. 303-442-5828. www.maddenusa.com

**Mascot Metropolitan Inc.,** 380 Swift Ave., Unit 18, South San Francisco, CA 94080: Free brochure ◆ Luggage and computer equipment carriers. Also luggage on wheels and other carry-all styles. 800-949-1288. www.tutto.com

**Charles Miller Designs,** 521 Truett Dr., Tallahassee, FL 32303: Free brochure ◆ Soft leather bags for carrying or wearing on the back. 800-624-4443.

**North Beach Leather,** 1714 Stockton St., #400, San Francisco, CA 94133: Catalog $3 ◆ Men and women's leather clothing.

**North Face,** 2013 Farallon Dr., San Leandro, CA 94577: Free list of retail sources ◆ Carryalls, tote bags, duffels, and shoulder bags. 800-447-2333.

**Orvis Travel,** 1711 Blue Hills Dr., P.O. Box 12000, Roanoke, VA 24022: Free catalog ◆ Luggage, travel accessories, and men and women's clothing. 800-541-3541. www.orvis.com

**Port Canvas Inc.,** P.O. Box H, Kennebunkport, ME 04046: Free brochure ◆ Canvas duffels, handbags, briefcases, luggage and accessories, totes, and stroller and sports bags. 800-333-6788. www.portcanvas.com

**Rock N' Roller,** M.J. Corp., 99 Tulip Ave., Floral Park, NY 11001: Free information ◆ Luggage carrier that converts from a two-wheel hand truck to a variable length hi-stacker, platform truck, or mobile workstation. 800-431-6699.

**Scott-Wynne Outfitters,** 10000 Research Blvd., Ste. 127, Austin, TX 78759: Free catalog ◆ Outdoor and casual clothing, luggage, hunting and fishing accessories, and Native American jewelry. 800-232-2783. www.outfits.com

**Simonds Photographic,** 88 Thomas St., East Hartford, CT 06108: Free information ◆ Folding-flat cart for carrying equipment and luggage. 800-992-0607.

**Wildwest Travel Inc.,** 1101 Main St., Evanston, WY 82930: Free brochure ◆ Rolling luggage, attachable add-ons, and accessories. 307-789-5750.

## LUMBER

**A & M Wood Specialty Inc.,** 358 Eagle St. North, Box 32040, Cambridge, Ontario, Canada N3H 5M2: Free catalog ◆ Hardwoods and veneers. 519-653-9322.

**Adams Wood Products Inc.,** 974 Forest Dr., Morristown, TN 37814: Free catalog ◆ Kiln-dried oak, Honduras mahogany, walnut, cherry, maple, pine turning squares, and carving blanks. 615-587-2942.

**Albany Woodworks,** P.O. Box 729, Albany, LA 70711: Free brochure ◆ Antique pine lumber. 504-567-1155. woods@i-55.com

**Alva Hardwoods,** 7307 Rt. 80, Alva, FL 33920: Free information ◆ Domestic hardwoods. 941-728-2484.

**Anderson-McQuaid Company Inc.,** 170 Fawcett St., Cambridge, MA 02138: Free price list ◆ Custom and restoration molding, flooring, and paneling. 800-640-3250.

**Architectural Timber & Millwork,** 35 Mount Warner Rd., P.O. Box 719, Hadley, MA 01035: Free information ◆ Antique flooring, new wide plank flooring, and antique and reproduction beams and timber frames. 413-586-3045.

**Barber Lumber Sales Inc.,** P.O. Box 263, Alachua, FL 32615: Free information ◆ Heart cypress, pine, and other softwood. 904-462-3772.

**Berea Hardwoods Company,** 125 Jacqueline Dr., Berea, OH 44017: Free information ◆ Exotic hardwoods, figured woods, other lumber, and squares, planks, and burls. 440-243-4452.

**Blue Ox Lumber,** 2050 Elmwood Ave., Buffalo, NY 14207: Free information ◆ Optional wide and thick hardwoods. 800-758-0950.

**Boulter Plywood Corp.,** 24 Broadway, Somerville, MA 02145: Free catalog ◆ Domestic and exotic hardwood, other lumber, and marine plywood. 617-666-1340.

**Bristol Valley Hardwoods,** 4054 Rt. 64 at Rt. 20A, Canandaigua, NY 14424: Catalog $1 ◆ Cherry, poplar, red oak, and hard maple. 800-724-0132.

**Broad-Axe Beam Company,** RD 2, Box 417, West Brattleboro, VT 05301: Price list $2 ◆ Wide pine flooring and beaded edge paneling. 802-257-0064.

**California Walnut Designs,** 12681 Wolf Rd., Grass Valley, CA 95949: Free information ◆ Walnut slabs, planks, and blocks. 916-268-0203.

**Certainly Wood,** 11753 Big Tree Rd., East Aurora, NY 14052: Free catalog ◆ Veneers and plywood. 716-655-0206.

**Cirtain Plywood Inc.,** 677 Galloway Ave., Memphis, TN 38105: Free information ◆ Exotic and domestic premium hardwoods, abrasives, glues, and veneer. 800-593-3304.

**Colonial Hardwoods Inc.,** 7953 Cameron Brown Ct., Springfield, VA 22158: Free information ◆ Hardwood and moldings. 800-466-5451.

**Maurice L. Condon Company,** 252 Ferris Ave., White Plains, NY 10603: Catalog $2 ◆ Exotic woods and plywood. 914-946-4111.

**Constantines,** 2050 Eastchester Rd., Bronx, NY 10461: Catalog $1 ◆ Cabinet and furniture wood, veneers, plans, hardware, how-to books, carving tools, chisels, inlay designs, and supplies. 800-223-8087; 718-792-1600 (in NY). www.constantines.com

**Craftsman Lumber Company,** 436 Main St., Groton, MA 01450: Information $2 ◆ Oak and pine flooring and paneling in widths up to 30 inches. 978-448-5621.

**Diener Woodworks,** 3955 Mt. Pisgah Rd., York, PA 17402: Free information ◆ Kiln-dried rough red and white oak, basswood, birch, walnut, cherry, sassafras, polar, maple, and ash. 888-243-WOOD.

**Donnell's Clapboard Mill,** Country Rd., RR Box 1560, Sedgwick, ME 04676: Free information ◆ Quarter-sawn clapboard. 207-359-2036.

**Downes & Reader Hardwood Company Inc.,** Box 456, Stoughton, MA 02072: Free information ◆ Hardwoods, softwoods, and plywood. 800-788-5568; 781-442-8050 (in MA).

**Duluth Timber Company,** P.O. Box 16717, Duluth, MN 55816: Free information ◆ Beams, millwork, paneling, and flooring from recycled old-growth timbers from bridges and buildings. 218-727-2145. www.duluthtimber.com

**Gilmer Wood Company,** 2211 NW St. Helens Rd., Portland, OR 97210: Free information ◆ Exotic wood logs, planks, and squares. 503-274-1271.

**Goby Walnut Products,** 5016 Palestine Rd., Albany, or 97321: Free information ◆ Oregon black walnut turning squares, carving blocks, lumber, and highly-figured wide boards. 541-926-7516.

**Good Hope Hardwoods,** 1627 New London Rd., Landenberg, PA 19350: Free information ◆ Exotic and domestic hardwoods. 610-274-8842.

**Granville Manufacturing Company Inc.,** P.O. Box 15, Rt. 100, Granville, VT 05747: Free brochure ◆ Quarter-sawn clapboard siding. 802-767-4747. www.woodsiding.com

**Groff & Hearne Lumber,** 858 Scotland Rd., Quarryville, PA 17566: Free information ◆ Walnut, cherry, and other woods. 800-342-0001; 717-284-0001 (in PA).

**The Harbor Sales Company Inc.,** 1401 Russell St., Baltimore, MD 21230: Information $1 ◆ Exotic woods. 800-345-1712.

**The Hardwood Store,** 1695 Dalton Dr., New Carlisle, OH 45344: Free catalog ◆ Lumber, plywood, and veneers. 800-849-9174.

**Hochstetler Lumber,** 77 W. C.R. 113, Bellefontaine, OH 43311: Free information ◆ Kiln dried lumber. 513-468-2482.

**Johnsonius Precision Millworks,** P.O. Box 275, McKenzie, TN 38201: Free information ◆ Solid hardwood and cypress lumber and siding, plank flooring and paneling, and standard and custom molding. 901-352-5656.

**Joinery Company,** P.O. Box 518, Tarboro, NC 27886: Catalog $5 ◆ Reproduction flooring, millwork, cabinets, furniture, and timber frames in antique heart pine. 800-726-7463. www.joinery.com

**Michigan Woodworkers & Supply,** 4133 S. Dort Hwy., Burton, MI 48529: Free catalog ◆ Power tools and accessories, veneers, plywood, and hard, soft, and exotic woods. 800-433-9663.

**Mountain Lumber,** P.O. Box 289, Ruckersville, VA 22968: Free information ◆ Recycled antique heart pine from pre-1900 buildings and antique American oak from century-old Appalachian barns. 800-445-2671.

**Niagara Lumber & Wood Products Inc.,** 47 Elm St., East Aurora, NY 14052: Free information ◆ Northern Appalachian hardwood. 800-274-0397.

**Oakwood Veneer Company,** 3642 W. 11 Mile Rd., Berkley, MI 48072: Free catalog ◆ Flexible paper-backed veneer. Also exotic and burl woods. 800-426-6018.

**Pioneer Millworks,** 1755 Pioneer Rd., Shortsville, NY 14548: Free information ◆ Reproduction period flooring from reclaimed timbers, trim, lumber, and board stock. 716-289-3090.

**Precision Woodworks,** 507 E. Jackson St., Burnet, TX 78611: Free information ◆ Antique white pine, fir, and native Texas hardwoods. 512-756-6950.

**Rare Earth Hardwoods,** 6778 E. Traverse Hwy., Traverse City, MI 49684: Free information ◆ Exotic hardwoods, other lumber, flooring, and decking. 800-968-0074. www.rare-earth-hardwoods.com

**Randle Woods,** P.O. Box 96, Randle, WA 98377: Free information ◆ Custom-cut wood from the northwest. 800-845-8042; 360-497-2071 (in WA). www.randlewoods.com

**Sandy Pond Hardwoods,** 921-A Lancaster Pike, Quarryville, PA 17566: Free information ◆ Exotic and domestic hardwoods. 800-546-9663; 717-284-5030 (in PA). www.figuredhardwoods.com

**Specialty Lumber Inc.,** 6412 Yelton Rd., Appling, GA 30802: Free information ◆ Antique heart pine and lumber. 706-541-9231.

**Superior Hardwoods,** P.O. Box 4731, Missoula, MT 59806: Information $3 ◆ New and antique flooring, paneling, and molding. 800-572-9601; 406-251-2272 (in MT).

**Talarico Hardwoods,** RD 3, Box 3268, Mohnton, PA 19540: Free catalog ◆ Quarter-sawn white oak, red oak, and figured lumber. 610-775-0400. tpics@ptd.net

**Tradewinds,** HCR Box 64, Grafton, VT 05146: Free information ◆ Hardwoods. 802-843-2594.

**Tropical Exotic Hardwoods,** Box 1806, Carlsbad, CA 92018: Free information with long SASE ◆ Ebony, cocobolo, satinwood, and other exotic species. 619-434-3030.

**Steve Wall Lumber Company,** Box 287, Mayodan, NC 27027: Catalog $1 ◆ Hardwoods and woodworking machinery. 800-633-4062; 910-427-0637 (in NC). www.walllumber.com

**West Wind Hardwood Inc.,** P.O. Box 2205, Sidney, British Columbia, Canada V8L 3S8: Free catalog ◆ Hardwoods, softwoods, marine grade and other plywood, and boat lumber. 800-667-2275.

**Wood-Ply Lumber Corp.,** 100 Bennington Ave., Freeport, NY 11520: Free price list ◆ Domestic and exotic hardwoods. 800-354-9002.

**Woodhouse Antique Flooring,** P.O. Box 7336, Rocky Mount, NC 27804: Free brochure; sample kit $15 ◆ Antique flooring, molding, parts for stair, and new wood. 919-977-7336.

**The Woods Company,** 2357 Boteler Rd., Brownsville, MD 21715: Free information ◆ Antique lumber, custom flooring, and interior millwork. 301-432-8419.

**Woodworker's Dream,** Division Martin Guitar Company, 510 Sycamore St., Nazareth, PA 18064: Free information ◆ Exotic and domestic hardwoods and musical instrument woods. 800-345-3103.

**Woodworkers Source,** 5402 S. 40th St., Phoenix, AZ 85040: Free information ◆ Exotic and domestic lumber, plywood, veneers, turning squares, and blanks. 800-423-2450.

**World Timber Corp. Inc.,** 2906 William Penn Hwy., Easton, PA 18045: Free information ◆ Foreign and domestic hardwoods. 610-515-0658.

## MACRAMÉ

**Alcon Braid,** P.O. Box 429, Hickory, NC 28603: Free catalog ◆ Macramé, chair-weaving, and crochet supplies. 800-523-4371. sandra@griffinshine.com

**Craft King Mail Order Catalog,** P.O. Box 90637, Lakeland, FL 33804: Free catalog ◆ Craft, needlework, and macramé supplies. 888-CRAFTY-1. www.weshop.com/craftking

**Frederick J. Fawcett Inc.,** 1338 Ross St., Petaluma, CA 94954: Free information ◆ Looms, linen embroidery fabrics, macramé supplies, linen/cotton and wool yarns, and fibers. 800-289-9276.

**King's Kountry,** Macramé Wholesale Warehouse, 112 Main St., Yale, MI 48097: Free catalog ◆ Macramé and chair weaving supplies. 810-387-9122.

**H.H. Perkins Company,** 10 S. Bradley Rd., Woodbridge, CT 06525: Free catalog ◆ Seat weaving and basket-making supplies, macramé supplies, and how-to books. 800-462-6660.

## MAGIC TRICKS & VENTRILOQUISM

**Abbott's Magic Company,** 124 St. Joseph, Colon, MI 49040: Catalog $12.50 ◆ Props, close-up, and stage magic for amateur and professional magicians. 616-432-3235. GBord98968@aol.com

**Abracadabra Magic Shop,** 125 Lincoln Blvd., Middlesex, NJ 08846: Catalog $5 ◆ Magician's props, close-up, and stage magic. Also juggling equipment, balloons, clown accessories, costumes, and make-up. 732-805-0200. umsi@erols.com

**Axtell Expressions,** 230 Glencrest Circle, Ventura, CA 93003: Catalog $2 ◆ Magic for amateur and professional magicians. 805-642-7282. www.axtell.com

**Aunt Clowney's Warehouse,** P.O. Box 1444, Corona, CA 91718: Free catalog with two 1st class stamps ◆ Books and novelties for clowns, magicians, puppeteers, face painters, and balloon artists. 909-273-0900. auntc@empirenet.com

**Pete Best's Discount Magic Warehouse,** The Best Bldg., P.O. Box 285063, Boston, MA 02128: Free catalog ◆ Novelty and professional magic, books, and jokes. 800-438-7236. www.pbdm.com

**Black Diamond Entertainment Company,** P.O. Box 42, Summit Hill, PA 18250: Free catalog ◆ Close-up, beginner's, and stage magic. 717-645-3634. members.tripod.com/~DiamondCutter

**Mike Bornstein Clowns,** 319 W. 48th St., New York, NY 10036: Free information with long SASE ◆ Magic for amateur and professional magicians.

**Brad Burt's Magic Shop,** 4204 Convoy St., Ste. 103, San Diego, CA 92111: Free catalog ◆ Magic for amateur and professional magicians, how-to-do-magic videos, gag items, and clown supplies. 615-571-4749. bburt@magicshop.com

**Browser's Den of Magic,** 875 Eglinton Ave. W., #13, Toronto, Ontario, Canada M6C 3Z9: Free catalog ◆ Magic, juggling equipment, and ventriloquist dolls for amateurs and professionals. 416-783-7022. www.websmart.com/browsers

**C & M Productions,** 5601 Bridgeport Way, Ste. A, University Place, WA 98467: Free information ◆ Magic for amateur and professional magicians. 253-564-5416. www.home.earthlink.net/~royal/cmprod

**California Magic & Novelty Company,** 1930 Oak Park Blvd., Pleasant Hill, CA 94523: Video catalogs $7.50 each (specify interest) ◆ Card magic, close-up and pocket tricks, and stage magic. 510-939-6420. www.calmagic.com

**Captain Dick's Dummy Depot,** 2631 NW 95th St., Seattle, WA 98117: Information $3 with long SASE ◆ New and used ventriloquist figures and books. 206-784-0883.

**Chazpro Magic Company,** P.O. Box 41415, Eugene, OR 97404: Catalog $3 ◆ Magic for amateur and professional magicians. 541-689-6919. www.chazpro.com

**Conleys House of Magic,** 4910-A Hwy. 17 South, North Myrtle Beach, SC 29582: Free catalog ◆ Jokes, novelties, and magic. 803-272-4227. trirmagic@aol.com

**Steve Dawson's Magic Touch Catalog,** 144 N. Milpitas Blvd., Milpitas, CA 95035: Catalog $3 ◆ Magic effects, books, videos, accessories, clown and juggling supplies, and make-up. 408-263-9404.

**Daytona Magic,** Harry Allen & Irv Cook, 136 S. Beach St., Daytona, FL 32114: Catalog $10 ◆ Props, close-up, and stage magic for amateur and professional magicians. 904-252-6767. www.daytonamagic.com

**Diamond Magic,** P.O. Box 3335, Peabody, MA 01961: Free catalog ◆ Magic for amateur and professional magicians. 800-330-2713; 978-535-8950 (in MA). www.diamondsmagic.com

**Eddie's Trick Shop,** 70 S. Park Square, Marietta, GA 30060: Free information ◆ Magic and clown supplies. 800-429-4314. www.eddiestricks.com

**The Electronic Magic Store,** Library Services Inc., 1498-M Reistertown Rd., #337, Baltimore, MD 21208: Free catalog ◆ New and used magic books and videos. 888-622-7376; 410-358-8889 (in MD). emagic@universe.digex.net

**Elmwood Magic & Novelty,** 507 Elmwood Ave., Buffalo, NY 14222: Free catalog ◆ Magic, jokes, and novelties. 800-764-2372. members.aol.com/elmmagic

**Empire Magic,** 99 Stratford Ln., Rochester, NY 14612: Free catalog ◆ Magic for amateur and professional magicians. 716-227-2981. empirema@frintiernet.net

**Alan Ende,** 40 Morrow Ave., Scarsdale, NY 10583: List $3 ◆ Ventriloquist figures, accessories, and vintage magic books. 914-961-7066.

**Fearson's Magic,** 3700 E. Stewart, #348, Las Vegas, NV 89110: Catalog $1 ◆ Original magic. home.navisoft.com/magicbymax/fearsons/tricks.html

**FishNet Magic,** 70100 E. Hwy. 26, #13, Welches, OR 97067: Free price list ◆ Gospel-related magic supplies. 503-622-4016. members.aol.com/rhodoxx

**Flora & Company Productions,** P.O. Box 8263, Albuquerque, NM 87198: Free catalog ◆ Multi-media equipment and illusions for magicians. 505-255-9988. postmaster@floraco.com

**Florida Magic Company,** P.O. Box 290781, Fort Lauderdale, FL 33329: Free information ◆ Puppets, magic tricks, and juggling supplies. 954-473-1902. FlaMagicCo@aol.com

**Fun Magic Tricks,** 520 Broadway, San Antonio, TX 78215: Catalog $1 (refundable) ◆ Magic tricks, books, gags, juggling equipment, puzzles, and collectibles.

**Fun Technicians Inc.,** P.O. Box 160, Syracuse, NY 13215: Free brochure ◆ Magic for children's shows. 315-492-4523. lafmaker@aol.com

**General Grant,** 1 Oxford St., Natick, MA 01760: Free price list ◆ Magic for amateur and professional magicians. GGMagic@aol.com

**David Ginn Magic,** 4387 St. Michaels Dr., Lilburn, GA 30247: Catalog $10 ◆ Props, books, and how-to-do magic on video tapes for magicians and clowns. 770-923-1899.

**Grand Illusions,** 7704 Fair Oaks Blvd., Carmichael, CA 95608: Free catalog ◆ Magic, costumes, and juggling equipment. 916-944-2970. www.grandillusions.com

**Bob James Magic Shop,** 131 W. 1st St., Elmhurst, IL 60126: Catalog $5 ◆ Magic for amateur and professional magicians. 630-833-8749. BOBMAGCSHP@aol.com

**Jesters Magic Workshop,** 1070 Bank St., Painesville, OH 44077: Free information ◆ Magic and props for amateur and professional magicians. 440-354-8749.

**Klamm Magic,** 1412 Appleton, Independence, MO 64052: Small props catalog $2; illusions catalog $3 ◆ Magic equipment for amateur and professional magicians. 816-461-4595. klamm@micro.com

**La Rock's Fun & Magic Outlet,** 3847 Rosehaven Dr., Charlotte, NC 28205: Catalog $3 ◆ Clown and balloon how-to books, balloons, balloon sculpture kits, juggling supplies, and magic equipment. 704-563-9300. larocks1@aol.com

**Laflin's Magic & Silks,** P.O. Box 228, Sterling, CO 80751: Free information ◆ Entertaining and educational magic on video tapes for clowns and magicians. 970-522-2589.

**Hank Lee's Magic Factory,** Mail Order Division, P.O. Box 789, Medford, MA 02155: Catalog $4.50 ◆ Magic tricks and illusions, books, props, jokes, and novelties. 781-482-8749. www.hanklee.com

**Magic & Fun Shop,** 16872 Hwy. 3, Webster, TX 77598: Free catalog ◆ Jokes, gags, novelties, clown supplies, make-up, magic tricks, and puzzles. 281-332-8142. www.fun-shop.com

**The Magic Corner & Costume Shop,** 1213 Hillsborough St., Raleigh, NC 27603: Free catalog ◆ Magic and books, costumes, and clown supplies. 919-834-0925.

**The Magic Shop,** 1501 Pike Pl., #427, Seattle, WA 98101: Free catalog ◆ Magic for amateur and professional magicians. 206-MAGIC-71.

**Magic World Inc.,** 10122 Topanga Cyn Blvd., Chatsworth, CA 91311: Free catalog ◆ Magic and juggling supplies for amateur and professional magicians. 818-700-8100.

**Maher Studios,** P.O. Box 420, Littleton, CO 80160: Free catalog ◆ Ventriloquist dummies, scripts and dialogues, puppets, and how-to books. 303-798-6830. www.maherstudios.com

**Mamma Mia Magic,** P.O. Box 7117, Thousand Oaks, CA 91359: Free catalog ◆ Books, videos, and close-up and other magic. 805-499-3161. www.mammamiamagic.com

**Mastercraft Puppets,** P.O. Box 2002, Branson, MO 65615: Catalog $2 ◆ Puppets, clown supplies, and ventriloquist dummies. 417-561-8100. www.devoted.to/puppets

**Mecca Magic Inc.,** 49 Dodd St., Bloomfield, NJ 07003: Catalog $10 ◆ Magic and ventriloquism accessories, juggling supplies, make-up, clown equipment, balloons, costumes and wigs, puppets, and props. 201-429-7597. meccamagic@meccamagic.com

**Steven Meltzer,** 670 San Juan, Venice, CA 90291: Free list with long SASE ◆ Marionettes, puppets, and ventriloquist dummies. 310-396-6007.

**More Than Balloons Inc.,** 2409 Ravendale Ct., Kissimmee, FL 34758: Free information ◆ Regular balloons and accessories, balloons for making sculptures, how-to books, and magic. 800-BALUNES.

**Morris Costumes,** 3108 Monroe Rd., Charlotte, NC 28205: Catalog $20 ◆ Magic tricks and special effects, costumes, clown props, masks, jokes, novelties, balloons, and books. 704-332-3304.

**T. Myers Magic Inc.,** 6513 Thomas Springs Rd., Austin, TX 78736: Free catalog ◆ Magic and other supplies for balloon twisters, face painters, clowns, and magicians. 800-288-7925; 512-288-7925 (in TX). www.tmyers.com

**Nielsen Magic,** P.O. Box 34300, Las Vegas, NV 89133: Catalog $1 ◆ Magic for amateur and professional magicians. 702-656-7674. www.nnmagic.com

**One Way Street Inc.,** P.O. Box 5077, Englewood, CO 80155: Free catalog ◆ Ventriloquism resources. 800-569-4537. www.onewaystreet.com

**Palmer Magic,** 23 Duane, #6, Redwood City, CA 94062: Free brochure ◆ Original and other magic and accessories. 415-365-3818.

**Matthew Roddy,** 3283 Belvedere, Riverside, CA 92507: Free catalog ◆ Magic for amateur and professional magicians. 909-369-9704.

**Ronjo's Magic & Costumes Inc.,** 4600 Nesconset Hwy., Unit 4, Port Jefferson Station, NY 11776: Catalog $9.95 (receive $25 in coupons) ◆ Magic for amateur and professional magicians, costumes, make-up, and theatrical effects. 516-928-5005. www.ronjo.com

**St. Croix Studios,** P.O. Box 6662, Fullerton, CA 92834: Catalog $3 ◆ Custom magic. 714-773-0556. members.aol.com/stcroixmgc/shop.htm

**Samuel Patrick Smith,** P.O. Box 787, Eustis, FL 32727: Free catalog ◆ Pocket and stage magic. 800-810-0722. spspub@aol.com

**Sparkle's Entertainment Express,** Jan Lovell, 152 N. Water St., Gallatin, TN 37066: Product list $1 ◆ Make-up, costumes and clown shoes, balloons, juggling and magic equipment, puppets, books, and supplies. 615-452-9755.

**Stevens Magic Emporium,** 2520 E. Douglas, Wichita, KS 67208: Catalog $7.50 ◆ Professional magic and books. 316-683-9582. www.uelectric.com/stevensmagic

**Tannen's Magic,** 24 W. 25th St., New York, NY 10010: Catalog $15 ◆ Close-up and parlor magic, illusions, books, and props for amateurs and professionals. 212-929-4500. www.tannenmagic.com

**Douglas L. Tilford,** 1 Ocean West Blvd., Daytona Beach Shores, FL 32118: Catalog $10 ◆ Magic for amateur and professional magicians. 800-537-5381. www.tilfordmagic.com

**U.S. Toy Company Inc.,** 122713201 Arrington Rd., Grandview, MO 64030: Catalog $3 ◆ Parlor magic, illusions, and props for magicians. 800-448-7830. www.const/play.com

**Viking Magic Company,** P.O. Box 1778, McAllen, TX 78502: Free catalog ◆ Custom magic. 956-380-3929. www.vikingmagic.com

**Meir Yedid Magic,** P.O. Box 2566, Fair Lawn, NJ 07410: Catalog $2 ◆ Magic equipment for amateur and professional magicians. 201-703-1171. www.mymagic.com/atoz.htm

## MAGNETS

**A-L-L Magnetics Inc.,** 930 S. Placentia, Placentia, CA 92670: Free brochure ◆ Magnets for ceramics, hold-everything magnets, magnetic wands, and more. 800-262-4638; 714-632-1754 (in CA).

**Bunting Magnetics Company,** 500 S. Spencer Rd., Newton, KS 67114: Free catalog ◆ Magnets. 800-835-2526; 316-284-2020 (in KS). www.bunting-magnetics.com

**Edmund Scientific Company,** Edscorp Bldg., Barrington, NJ 08007: Free catalog ◆ Magnets, binoculars, telescopes, and educational and science equipment. 609-547-8880. www.edsci.com

**LPS Photo Svc. Inc.,** 46-21 70th St., Woodside, NY 11377: Free information ◆ Photo magnets made from your personal negatives or slides. 800-786-6106.

**Magnet Sales & Manufacturing Company,** 11248 Playa Ct., Culver City, CA 90230: Free brochure ◆ Flexible strip, flex-dot, button, and bar magnets. 800-421-6692; 310-391-7213 (in CA).

**The Magnet Source,** 607 S. Gilbert, Castle Rock, CO 80104: Free catalog ◆ Magnets for arts and crafts projects. 303-688-3966.

**Marla Trading Company,** 466 77th St., Brooklyn, NY 11209: Sample magnet and brochure $4 ◆ Custom magnets made from antique postcards, labels, or photographs.

**Master Magnetics Inc.,** 607 S. Gilbert, Castle Rock, CO 80104: Free brochure ◆ Magnets for ceramics, hold-everything magnets, magnetic wands, and more. 800-525-3536; 303-688-3966 (in CO).

**Miami Magnet Company,** 6073 NW 167th St., Ste. C26, Miami, FL 33015: Free brochure ◆ Magnets for ceramics, hold-everything magnets, magnetic wands, and more. 800-222-7846; 305-823-0641 (in FL).

**Nasco,** 901 Janesville Ave., Fort Atkinson, WI 53538: Free catalog ◆ Science equipment, kits, microscopes and dissection kits, rock collections, magnets, electric motors, ultraviolet lighting equipment, astronomy charts and star maps, and anatomical models. 800-558-9595. www.nascofa.com

**S & S Arts & Crafts,** P.O. Box 513, Colchester, CT 06415: Free catalog ◆ Magnets, educational games, puzzles, arts and crafts projects, and supplies. 800-937-3482. www.snswide.com

**Schoolmasters Science,** 745 State Circle, Box 1941, Ann Arbor, MI 48106: Catalog $2 ◆ Bar, horseshoe, floating, strips, and other magnets and accessories. Also a magnet kit with more than 34 experiments. 800-521-2832. www.schoolmasters.com

**Southpaw Enterprises,** Box 835, Nelson, British Columbia, Canada V1L 5S9: Free catalog ◆ Refrigerator magnets, other novelties, and aids for left-handed persons. 800-818-9616.

**Totem Graphics Inc.,** 6200 Capitol Blvd., Ste F, Tumwater, WA 98501: Free information ◆ Refrigerator magnets. 360-352-1851. gototem@orcalink.com

## MAGNIFYING GLASSES

**Bestwell Optical & Instrument Corp.,** P.O. Box 396, Merrick, NY 11566: Free information ◆ Focusing magnifiers, photographic enlarger focusing aid, loupes, and other equipment. 516-379-2280.

**Walter Drake & Sons,** Drake Bldg., Colorado Springs, CO 80940: Free catalog ◆ Magnifying glasses. 800-525-9291. amyconnors@wdrake.com

**Edmund Scientific Company,** Edscorp Bldg., Barrington, NJ 08007: Free catalog ◆ Magnifying glasses, binoculars, telescopes, and educational and science equipment. 609-547-8880. www.edsci.com

**Harrison Astronomy,** 2574 Granville St., Vancouver, British Columbia, Canada V6H 3C8: Free information ◆ Telescopes and accessories, binoculars, microscopes, magnifiers, meteorological instruments, and books. 604-737-4303.

**MagEyes,** 222 Sidney Baker South, Ste 202, Kerrville, TX 78028: Free brochure ◆ Hands-free head-mounted magnifiers. 210-896-6060. sales@mageyes.com

**Schoolmasters Science,** 745 State Circle, Box 1941, Ann Arbor, MI 48106: Catalog $2 ◆ Hand and page magnifiers. 800-521-2832. www.schoolmasters.com

## MAH-JONGG

**The Dragon Lady,** P.O. Box 1075, West Palm Beach, FL 33402: Free information ◆ Custom mah-jongg sets with optional engraved personalization.

## MAILBOXES

**Acorn Manufacturing Company Inc.,** 457 School St., P.O. Box 31, Mansfield, MA 02048: Catalog $6 (request list of retail sources) ◆ Locking forged iron mailboxes in vertical and horizontal styles. 800-835-0121; 508-339-4500 (in MA).

**AK Exteriors,** 101 Montoya Rd., El Paso, TX 79932: Catalog $4 ◆ Cast-aluminum furniture, light fixtures, and mail boxes. 800-253-9837.

**Brandon Industries,** 1601 W. Wilmeth Rd., McKinney, TX 75069: Free catalog ◆ Old-fashioned cast-aluminum pedestal mailboxes with solid brass letter slots and cylinder key locks. 972-542-3000. www.brandonmail.com

**Cast Aluminum Reproductions,** P.O. Box 1060, San Elzario, TX 79849: Catalog $2 ◆ Cast-aluminum and brass street lights, outdoor furniture, fountains, mail boxes, and plant stands. 915-764-3793.

**Coppersmiths,** Custom Copper & Brass Works, P.O. Box 2675, Oakhurst, CA 93644: Free brochure ◆ Fireplace hoods, cupolas, mailboxes, and dormers. 209-658-8909.

**The Edisonville Woodshop,** 1916 Edisonville Rd., Strasburg, PA 17579: Brochure $1 ◆ Handcrafted all-wood mailboxes. 717-687-0116.

**Frank's Country Store,** 162 Washington Ave., North Haven, CT 96473: Free brochure ◆ Handcrafted mailboxes with cedar shingle roofs. 800-875-1960.

**Home Decorators Collection,** 8920 Pershall Rd., Hazelwood, MO 63042: Free catalog ◆ Mailboxes in contemporary and other styles. 800-240-6047. 800-240-6047.

**Mel-Nor Industries,** 303 Gulf Bank, Houston, TX 77037: Information $1 ◆ Mailboxes, park benches, swings, lights, and landscaping items. 281-445-3485.

**Redwood Unlimited,** P.O. Box 2344, Valley Center, CA 92082: Brochure $2 ◆ Wall and post-mounted mail boxes and weather vanes. 800-283-1717.

**Reed Brothers,** 5000 Turner Rd., Sebastopol, CA 95472: Catalog $15 ◆ Mail boxes. 707-795-6261.

**The Renovator's Supply,** P.O. Box 2515, Conway, NH 03818: Free catalog ◆ Victorian-style solid brass mailboxes, decorative accessories, and gifts. 800-659-0203.

## MAILING LISTS

**Advon,** Drawer B, Shelley, ID 83274: Free information ◆ Mixed states mailing lists with adhesive labels. 800-992-3866.

**American List Counsel Inc.,** 88 Orchard Rd., CN 5219, Princeton, NJ 08543: Free catalog ◆ Mailing and telemarketing lists and special high interest databases. 800-ALC-LIST.

**Cahners Direct Marketing,** 1350 E. Toughy Ave., Des Plaines, IL 60018: Free information ◆ Mailing lists. 800-537-7930.

**Database America,** 100 Paragon Dr., Montvale, NJ 07645: Free catalog ◆ Lists for direct mail. 800-551-1533.

**List Associates,** 116 Kellogg Ave., Ames, IA 50010: Free information ◆ Zip-code sorted mailing lists on self-adhesive labels, magnetic tape, or disk. 800-359-2621.

**List-Masters,** Box 425, Mt. Sinai, NY 11766: Free information ◆ Mailing lists on adhesive labels. 800-356-8664.

**Mascor Lists,** P.O. Box 110, Laurel, MD 20725: Free information ◆ Mailing lists. 800-568-6127. www.mascorpub.com

**Quality Lists,** P.O. Box 6060, Miller Place, NY 11764: Free information ◆ United States and Canadian mailing lists. 516-744-7289.

## MAPS & INFORMATION NAVIGATORS

**Adventure Cycling Association,** P.O. Box 8308, 150 E. Pine St., Missoula, MT 59807: Free catalog ◆ Maps and gear for cyclists. 800-721-8719. www.adv-cycling.org

**Adventurous Traveler Bookstore,** P.O. Box 64769, Burlington, VT 05406: Free catalog ◆ Books and maps for hiking, climbing, kayaking, diving, and travel. 800-282-3963; 802-860-6776 (in VT). www.atb-rarebooks.com

**American Map Corp.,** 46-35 54th Rd., Maspeth, NY 11378: Free information ◆ Maps, travel guides, and atlases. 718-784-0055.

**Big Ten Inc.,** P.O. Box 321231, Cocoa Beach, FL 32932: Free information with long SASE ◆ Geological maps that locate gold-mining sites in California, Alabama, Virginia, and the Carolinas. 407-783-4595. www.megabits.net/gold

**Bikecentennial,** P.O. Box 8308, Missoula, MT 59802: Free catalog ◆ Maps, books, and gear for the adventure cyclist. 800-721-8719. www.adv-cycling.org

**The Complete Traveler of Overland Park,** 7321 W. 80th St., Overland Park, KS 66204: Free catalog ◆ Maps, travel books, travel accessories, and luggage. 888-862-0888. www.completetrav.com

**George F. Cram Company Inc.,** 301 S. LaSalle St., Indianapolis, IN 46201: Free catalog ◆ Maps, atlases, globes, and charts. 800-227-4199; 317-635-5564 (in IN).

**DeLorme Mapping,** P.O. Box 298, 2 DeLorme Dr., Yarmouth, ME 04096: Free information ◆ Windows atlas information and telephone number software. Also maps, gazetteers, and atlases in print form. 800-452-5931. www.delorme.com

**Eagle Electronics,** P.O. Box 669, Catoosa, OK 74015: Free list of retail sources ◆ Handheld global positioning navigation aid. 800-324-1354. www.eaglesonar.com

**First State Map & Globe,** 12 Mary Ella Dr., Wilmington, DE 19805: Free information ◆ USA and world wall maps. 800-327-7992.

**Richard Fitch Maps,** 2324 Calle Halcon, Santa Fe, NM 87505: Catalog $6 ◆ Antiquarian maps and prints prior to 1900. 505-982-2939. oldmaps@swcp.com

**Forsythe Travel Library Inc.,** P.O. Box 2975, Shawnee Mission, KS 66201: Free brochure ◆ Travel books, maps, and other publications. 800-367-7984; 913-384-3440 (in KS). www.raileurope.com

**Garmin,** 1200 E. 151st St., Olathe, KS 66062: Free list of retail sources ◆ Handheld global positioning navigation aid. 800-800-1020; 913-397-8200 (in KS).

**The Globe Corner Bookstore,** 28 Church St., Cambridge, MA 02138: Free information ◆ Books and maps for the traveler. 800-358-6013. info@gcb.com

**The Gold Bug,** P.O. Box 588, Alamo, CA 94507: Free brochure ◆ Historical map reproductions. 888-653-6277. www.goldbug.com

**GORP,** P.O. Box 3016, Everett, WA 98206: Free catalog ◆ Over 3000 maps, guidebooks, handbooks, videos, CD-ROMs, and more on the outdoors. 888-994-4677. www.gorp.com

**Grace Galleries Inc.,** Box 2488, Brunswick, ME 04011: Free information (specify items wanted) ◆ Original antique maps, prints, sea charts, and cartographic books. 207-729-1329.

**Hammond Incorporated,** 515 Valley St., Maplewood, NJ 07040: Free information ◆ Maps and prints, travel guides, road atlases, adult and juvenile references, and books on business. 201-763-6000. www.hammondmap.com

**Hays Electronics,** P.O. Box 26848, Prescott Valley, AZ 86312: Free catalog ◆ Metal detectors, maps, electronic prospecting tools and accessories, and books on prospecting, mining, and relic hunting. 800-699-2624.

**Heritage Map Museum,** P.O. Box 412, Lititz, PA 17543: Free information ◆ Antique maps and books. 800-432-8183; 717-626-5002 (in PA). www.carto.com

**High-Grade Publications,** P.O. Box 20904, Cheyenne, WY 82003: Catalog $1 ◆ Books and maps on treasure hunting, gold locations, lost mines, ghost towns, gems and minerals, and geology. 307-634-8835.

**Historical Ink,** RR 1, Secret Lake, Phillipston, MA 01331: Catalog $2 ◆ New England town map reproductions and other items of historical interest.

**Hubbard Scientific Company,** American Educational Products, 1120 Halbleib Rd., Chippewa Falls, WI 54729: Free catalog ◆ Hands-on educational manipulative activities and relief maps for the world, United States, international regional areas, and more. 800-323-8368; 715-723-4427 (in WI). www.amep.com

**Lowrance Electronics,** 12000 E. Skelly Dr., Tulsa, OK 74070: Free list of retail sources ◆ Handheld electronic global positioning system with on-screen mapping. 800-324-4737. www.lowrance.com

**Magellan Systems Corp.,** 960 Overland Ct., San Dimas, CA 91773: Free list of retail sources ◆ Handheld global positioning navigation aid. 800-669-4477. www.magellangps.com

**Map Express,** P.O. Box 280445, Lakewood, CO 80228: Free catalog ◆ Maps and photographs from the United States Geological Service. 800-MAP-0039; 303-989-0003 (in CO). www.mapexp.com

**The Map Shack,** 959 Main St., Winchester, MA 01890: Free catalog ◆ Maps for recreational activities, hiking and biking books and guides, software, atlases, and compasses. 800-617-MAPS; 781-721-4943 (in MA). http://maps.bx.com

**MapLink,** 30 S. La Paterna Ln., Goleta, CA 93117: Free catalog ◆ Topographic, regional, county, state, city, country, world, and trail maps. 805-965-4402.

**The Maritime Store,** 2905 Hyde St. Pier, San Francisco, CA 94109: Free catalog ◆ Maritime maps, greeting cards, boat models, children's and maritime books, and gifts. 415-775-BOOK.

**David Morgan,** 11812 Northcreek Pkwy., Ste. 103, Bothell, WA 98011: Free catalog ◆ Maps of Great Britain for travel or genealogy research. 800-324-4934. www.davidmorgan.com

**National Geographic Society,** 1145 17th St. NW, Washington, DC 20036: Free catalog ◆ Books, games, videos, maps and globes, travel aids, and magazine subscriptions. 800-225-5647. www.nationalgeographic.com/main.html

**Northern Map Company,** Box 129, Dunnellon, FL 34430: Catalog $5 ◆ Maps from the Civil War, Canadian maps, map kits, and old state, city, railroad, and county maps, from 70 to 120 years old. 800-314-2474. www.losttreasure.com/northernmap

**The Old Print Gallery,** 1220 31st St. NW, Washington, DC 20007: Catalog $3 ◆ Prints and original antique maps from around the world. American maps range from pre-colonial times to 1880. 202-965-1818.

**Old World Heritage Maps,** P.O. Box 6094, Annapolis, MD 21401: Free brochure ◆ Family village and town plans from Eastern Europe.

**Omni Resources,** 1004 S. Mebane St., P.O. Box 2096, Burlington, NC 27216: Free catalog ◆ Fossils, rocks, hiking and topography maps, and globes. 800-742-2677. custserv@omnimap.com

**Alfred B. Patton Inc.,** 64 Swamp Rd., Doylestown, PA 18901: Free brochure ◆ Maps, mapping accessories, compasses, atlases, posters, software, and other map-related supplies. 215-345-0700.

**Philadelphia Print Shop Ltd.,** 8441 Germantown Ave., Philadelphia, PA 19118: Catalog $4 ◆ Antique maps, prints, and books. 215-242-4750.

**Rand McNally & Company,** Catalog Operations Center, 2515 E. 43rd St., P.O. Box 182257, Chattanooga, TN 37422: Free catalog ◆ Gifts for sports enthusiasts, health and exercise equipment, maps, world globes, books, videos, clocks, prints, travel aids, and watches. 800-234-0679. **www.randmcnallystore.com**

**Rand McNally New Media,** 8255 N. Central Park Ave., Skokie, IL 60076: Free catalog ◆ Maps, travel guides, and other references. 800-671-5006. www.randmcnally.com

**Raven Maps & Images,** Box 850, Medford, OR 97501: Free catalog ◆ Mounted and framed maps. 800-237-0798. www.ravenmaps.com

**Silva US Marine Inc.,** 333 Falkenburg Rd., B-221, Tampa, FL 33619: Free list of retail sources ◆ Handheld global positioning navigation aid. 800-237-4582.

**K.B. Slocum Books,** P.O. Box 10998, Austin, TX 78766: Free catalog ◆ Books on treasure hunting and old city, county, state, and military maps. 800-521-4451.

**Trails Illustrated,** P.O. Box 4357, Evergreen, CO 80439: Free information ◆ Maps of the National Parks and other areas in the United States. 800-962-1643.

**Travelers Bookstore,** 22 W. 52nd St., New York, NY 10019: Catalog $2 ◆ Maps and books on travel. 800-755-8728; 212-664-0995 (in NY).

**Trimble Navigation,** 645 N. Mary Ave., Sunnyvale, CA 94086: Free information ◆ Handheld global positioning navigation aid. 800-827-2424; 408-481-8000 (in CA). www.trimble.com

**United Nations Publications,** 820 2nd Ave., New York, NY 10017: Free information ◆ Maps and other United Nations publications. 212-963-1234.

**Universal Map,** 201 Tech Dr., Sanford, FL 32771: Free catalog ◆ United States state and city maps. 800-359-6277; 407-324-4401 (in FL). www.universalmap.com/html

**Wilderness Press,** 2440 Bancroft Way, Berkeley, CA 94704: Free catalog ◆ Outdoor books and maps. 800-443-7227. www.wildernesspress.com

## MARBLES

**Bertram M. Cohen,** 169 Marlborough St., Boston, MA 02116: Free information ◆ Collectible marbles and books on marbles. 617-247-4754.

**Heartbreak Ridge,** 108 Public Square, Lebanon, TN 37087: Video catalog $20 ◆ Marbles, teddy bears, antiques, and other gifts. 615-449-5993. www.shootinmarbles.com

**J. Fine Glass Marbles,** 2547 8th St., #25, Berkeley, CA 94710: Free information ◆ Marbles for collectors and shooters. 510-845-4270.

**Running Rabbit Video Auctions,** P.O. Box 701, Waverly, TN 37185: Free information ◆ Antique and contemporary marbles. 615-296-3600.

**Vitro Agate Corp.,** Division JABO Inc., P.O. Box 242, Parkersburg, WV 26102: Free list ◆ Classic, decorative, and Chinese checkers marbles. 800-338-9578.

## MARTIAL ARTS

**Academy of Karate Martial Arts Supplies,** 405 Black Horse Pike, Haddon Heights, NJ 08035: Free catalog ◆ Martial arts supplies. 609-547-5445.

**Artistic Video,** 87 Tyler Ave., Sound Beach, NY 11789: Free brochure ◆ Martial arts training videos. 888-982-4244; 516-744-5999 (in NY). www.nsws.com/TAI-CHI

**Asian World of Martial Arts,** 11601 Caroline Rd., Philadelphia, PA 19154: Catalog $5 ◆ Training and protective equipment, weapons, uniforms, belts, books, and videos. 800-345-2962. www.awma.com

**Black Belt Magazine Video,** P.O. Box 918, Santa Clarita, CA 91380: Catalog $2 ◆ Martial arts weapons, books and videos, and accessories. 800-423-2874.

**BLT Supplies Inc.,** Mail Order Dept., 35-01 Queens Blvd., Long Island City, NY 11101: Free information ◆ Asian martial arts films. 800-322-2860.

**The Brute Group,** 2126 Spring St., P.O. Box 2788, Reading, PA 19609: Free information ◆ Training equipment. 800-486-2788; 610-678-4050 (in PA).

**Bud K Worldwide Inc.,** P.O. Box 2768, Moultrie, GA 31776: Free catalog ◆ Knives, swords, and self-defense items. 800-543-5061. www.budkww.com

**CD-Mart International,** P.O. Box 16194, San Francisco, CA 94116: Free information ◆ Uniforms and equipment. 415-759-8640.

**Century Martial Art Supply Inc.,** 1705 National Blvd., Midwest City, OK 73110: Free information ◆ Sparring gear, belts, and clothing. 800-626-2787. www.centuryma.com

**Crown Trophy,** 1 Odell Plaza, Yonkers, NY 10701: Free information ◆ Martial arts awards. 800-227-1557; 914-963-0005 (in NY). www.crowntrophy.com

**Discount Martial Art Supply Inc.,** 7657 Winnetka Ave., #227, Winnetka, CA 91306: Free catalog ◆ Martial arts equipment. 800-341-8741.

**Dolan's Sports Inc.,** 26 Hwy. 547, P.O. Box 26, Farmingdale, NJ 07727: Free catalog ◆ Training and safety equipment, uniforms, shoes, Samurai swords, and books. 908-938-6656.

**Edges Inc.,** 6609 Oliver St., Riverdale, MD 20737: Free catalog ◆ Handmade training knives and swords. 301-306-0194.

**ESPY-TV,** 611 Broadway, New York, NY 10012: Free information ◆ Martial arts training videos. 800-735-6521. www.ESPY.com

**Extreme Sport Karate,** 9650 Dice Ln., Lenexa, KS 66215: Free catalog ◆ Martial arts equipment and clothing. 800-KARATE-1; 913-888-1719 (in KS).

**Genesport Industries Ltd.,** Hokkaido Karate Equipment Manufacturing Company, 150 King St., Montreal, Quebec, Canada H3C 2P3: Free information ◆ Belts, clothing, and equipment. 514-861-1856.

**High View Publications,** P.O. Box 51967, Pacific Grove, CA 93950: Free catalog ◆ Chinese martial arts books and videos. 408-622-0789.

**Honda Martial Arts Supply,** 120 W. 30th St., New York, NY 10001: Free information ◆ Clothing, protective and safety equipment, shoes, books, and training gear. 212-620-4050. www.hondamartialarts.com

**Carson Hurley Enterprises Inc.,** 2945 Orange Ave. NE, Roanoke, VA 24012: Free information ◆ Stretching racks. 540-342-7550.

**Jonie Collection,** 2409 25th Ave., San Francisco, CA 94116: Free information ◆ Martial arts clothing. 415-566-5566.

**K.P. Sporting Goods,** 4141 Business Center Dr., Fremont, CA 94538: Free information ◆ Chop gloves, protective equipment, and kicking targets. 800-227-0500. kpacific@packbell.net

**Karate Martial Arts Supply,** 405 Black Horse Pike, Haddon Heights, NJ 08035: Free catalog ◆ Martial arts equipment and clothing. 609-547-5445.

**Kens Trading Company Inc.,** 13832 Magnolia Ave., Chino, CA 91710: Free information ◆ Martial arts equipment. 800-331-KENS.

**Kim Pacific Trading Corp. Inc.,** 4141 Business Center Dr., Fremont, CA 94538: Catalog $2 ◆ Uniforms, shoes, and protective gear. 510-490-0300. www.kimpacific.com

**The Kiyota Company,** 2326 N. Charles St., Baltimore, MD 21218: Free information ◆ Budo supplies, specializing in Japanese-made uniforms and equipment. 410-366-8275.

**The Knife Center,** P.O. Box 902, 11263 Somerset Ave., Beltsville, MD 20705: Free catalog ◆ Knives, cases, accessories, fencing swords, and martial arts weapons. 800-338-6799.

**Kris Cutlery,** P.O. Box 133, Pinole, CA 94564: Catalog $1 ◆ High carbon steel bladed weapons and swords. 510-758-9912.

**Kwon Martial Arts,** 3755 Broadmoor, Grand Rapids, MI 49512: Free catalog ◆ Martial arts equipment. 616-940-8889.

**Lionheart Enterprises,** P.O. Box 207, North Windham, CT 06256: Free brochure ◆ Lightweight full-size training dummy. 860-456-3621.

**Macho Products Inc.,** 10045 102nd Terrace, Sebastian, FL 32958: Free catalog ◆ Training equipment, belts, and clothing. 800-327-6812; 561-388-9892 (in FL).

**Marco Lala Karate Academy,** P.O. Box 979, Yonkers, NY 10704: Free information ◆ Martial arts instructional videos. 800-573-7655.

**The Martial Artist,** 9 Franklin Blvd., Philadelphia, PA 19154: Free information ◆ Martial arts equipment. 800-726-0438.

**9-90 Variety Inc.,** 5290 Kuhl Rd., Erie, PA 16510: Free information ◆ Sparring gear. 800-891-5220.

**Ohara Publications Inc.,** P.O. Box 918, Santa Clarita, CA 91380: Free information ◆ Books on martial arts. 800-423-2874. www.blackbeltmag.com/email

**Otomix,** 3691 Lenawee Ave., Los Angeles, CA 90016: Free information ◆ Fitness shoes and martial arts equipment. 800-701-7867. www.otomix.com

**Panther Productions,** 1010 Calle Negocio, San Clemente, CA 92672: Free catalog ◆ Training videos for beginners and advanced students. 800-332-4442.

**PFS Video Inc.,** P.O. Box 50, Oley, PA 19547: Free information ◆ Martial arts videos on defense techniques. 610-689-5871.

**RevGear Sports Company,** 1015 N. Lake Ave., Ste. 204, Pasadena, CA 91104: Free information ◆ Kick and punch shields and other protection equipment. 800-767-8288.

**RheeMax,** 9000 Mendenhall Ct., Columbia, MD 21045: Free catalog ◆ Uniforms, competition equipment, protective gear, and exercisers. 800-247-2467; 410-381-2900 (in MD).

**Royal Martial Art Supplies,** 2605 Peach St., Erie, PA 16508: Catalog $1 ◆ Martial arts supplies. 814-454-2774.

**Ryukyu Imports Inc.,** 5005 Merriam Dr., Olathe, KS 66203: Free price list ◆ Books on martial arts. 913-782-3920. www.ryukyu.com

**Springtime Martial Arts Products Inc.,** P.O. Box 13031, Gainesville, FL 32604: Free information ◆ Wood dummies, dragon poles, swords, and other supplies. 352-376-0349. www.springtimemartialarts.com

**Stretch Rite Corp.,** 4205 E. Carlisle Ave., Spokane, WA 99207: Free information ◆ Leg stretching machine. 800-787-6332.

**Pil Sung Martial Arts Supply,** 6300 Ridglea Pl., #1008, Fort Worth, TX 76116: Free brochure ◆ Martial arts protective gear, clothing, and accessories. 800-992-0388; 817-738-5408 (in TX). www.pil-sung.com

**TKD Enterprises Inc.,** 1423 18th St., Bettendorf, IA 52722: Free information ◆ Martial arts books, videos, and shoes. 800-388-5966.

**Turtle Press,** P.O. Box 290206, Wethersfield, CT 06129: Free catalog ◆ Books on martial arts. 800-77-TURTL. www.turtlepress.com/

**Unique Publications,** 4201 W. Vanowen Pl., Burbank, CA 91505: Free information ◆ Martial arts videos. 800-332-3330.

**United Stitch Associates,** 807 Turnbull Canyon Rd., Hacienda Heights, CA 91745: Free information ◆ Custom and in-stock martial arts patches and pins. 800-842-6294.

**Wandix International Inc.,** 17 Dicarolis St., Hackensack, NJ 07601: Free brochure ◆ Portable and water-proof interlockable sports mat. 800-385-6855; 201-385-6855 (in NJ).

**Wing Lam Enterprises Inc.,** 1155 Reed Ave., Ste. 5, Sunnyvale, CA 94086: Free information ◆ Martial arts equipment, books and videotapes, uniforms, and collectibles. 800-700-3698.

**YMAA Publication Center,** 38 Hyde Park Ave., Jamaica Plain, MA 02130: Free catalog ◆ Martial arts books, videos, clothing, and music. 800-669-8892. www.ymaa.com/pubcenter.html

## MASSAGE, SALON, & SPA EQUIPMENT

**Golden Ratio Bodyworks,** P.O. Box 297, Emigrant, MT 59027: Free catalog ◆ Massage tables, chairs, equipment, and related accessories. 800-345-1129. www.goldenratio.com

**Golden Ratio Woodworks,** Hwy. 89, Seven Point Ranch, Emigrant, MT 59027: Free catalog ◆ Bodywork and therapy tables.

**New Life Systems,** 2853 Hedberg Dr., Minneapolis, MN 55305: Catalog $3 ◆ Massage, salon, and spa supplies and equipment. 800-852-3082.

**Oakworks,** P.O. Box 99, 34 Main St., Glen Rock, PA 17327: Free catalog ◆ Massage therapy equipment and supplies. 800-558-8850; 717-235-6807 (in PA).

**Planta Dei Medicinal Herb Farm,** Millville, New Brunswick, Canada E0H 1M0: Catalog $2 (refundable) ◆ Biologically grown teas, medicinal herbs, healing tea mixtures, cosmetics, natural ointments, and massage oils. 506-463-8169.

**Sharper Image SPA,** 650 Davis St., San Francisco, CA 94120: Free catalog ◆ Aerobic non-impact fitness machines, treadmills, massagers, and equipment. 800-448-8444. www.sharperimage.com

## MATCHBOOK COVERS

**Remember These,** P.O. Box 736, Meadows of Dan, VA 24120: Free information (send want list) ◆ Matchbook covers and postcards from the United States and Canada. 540-952-1211. wmankins@swva.net

**Write Touch,** The Rytex Company, P.O. Box 68188, Indianapolis, IN 46268: Free information ◆ Loose-leaf matchbook cover albums with padded covers of leather-grained vinyl. 800-288-6824.

## MEMORABILIA & COLLECTIBLES (MISCELLANEOUS)

**A & K Sports Collectibles,** 106 Galway Tr., Moore, SC 29369: Free list ◆ Autographed and other sports collectibles. 864-576-1942.

**Jon Wm. Aldrich,** Airport Box 706, Groveland, CA 95321: Catalog $5 ◆ Aviation memorabilia. 209-962-6121.

**American Pie Collectibles,** 29 Sullivan Rd., Peru, NY 12972: Free list ◆ Movie, TV, and promotional memorabilia; books and magazines; sheet music, LPs and 45s, sports cards, and other collectibles. 888-458-2200; 518-643-0993 (in NY). www.serftech.com/apc

**Amusementica Americana,** 414 N. Prospect Manor Ave., Mt. Prospect, IL 60056: Free list with seven 1st class stamps ◆ Old saloon artifacts, coin-operated machines, advertising collectibles, paper memorabilia, and other antique artifacts. 847-253-0791.

**Asahi Japan Collectibles,** 141 Wilbur Cross Hwy., Ste. 182, Kensington, CT 06037: Free information ◆ Kimonos, dolls, swords, and other collectibles from Japan. 888-272-4452.

**Aviators World,** 1434 Flightline, #13, Mojave, CA 93501: Catalog subscription $5 (6 issues) ◆ Air combat, military, civil aeronautics, space plane, and pilot collectibles. 805-824-2424.

**Back to the 50's,** 6870 S. Paradise Rd., Las Vegas, NV 89119: Free catalog ◆ Collectibles and memorabilia from the 1950s, 1960s, and 1970s. 800-224-1950.

**Beverage Containers Museum,** 1055 Ridgecrest Dr., Millersville, TN 37072: Free catalog ◆ Beer and soda cans, signs, trays, glasses, steins, bottle caps, advertising memorabilia, and other nostalgic and reproduction collectibles. 615-859-5236. www.gono.com

**BOJO,** P.O. Box 1403, Cranberry Twp., PA 16066: Catalog $2 ◆ Beatles memorabilia. 412-776-0621.

**Camden Marketing Group,** P.O. Box 22395, Minneapolis, MN 55422: Free catalog ◆ Licensed sports merchandise and collectibles.

**Cowboy Collectibles,** 85418 N. 7th St., Phoenix, AZ 85020: Catalog $2 ◆ Old west collectibles. 800-300-8334.

**Eagle Editions,** P.O. Box 580, Hamilton, MT 59840: Free brochure ◆ Historical fine art, limited edition prints, bronzes, books, western collectibles, posters, and more. 800-255-1830; 406-363-5415 (in MT). www.eagle-editions.com

**4x1 Imports Inc.,** 5873 Day Rd., Cincinnati, OH 45251: Catalog $4 ◆ Nostalgic tin advertising signs and other collectibles. 513-385-8185.

**HCB Sports-Collectibles,** 1858 Pleasantville Rd., Ste. 335, Briarcliff Manor, NY 10510: Free catalog ◆ Vintage memorabilia, including sports legends collectibles and presidential, political, and celebrity related items. 914-773-0499.

**Hoop Heaven,** P.O. Box 398, Bloomfield, CT 06002: Free catalog ◆ Posters, general books and encyclopedias, team yearbooks, trading cards, and other basketball collectibles. 860-286-8664.

**The Humane Society of the United States,** P.O. Box 1519, Elmira, NY 14902: Free information ◆ Clothing, greeting cards, and miscellaneous collectibles with a pet theme. 800-486-2630.

**Ivy Creek Recordings,** P.O. Box 220822, Charlotte, NC 28222: Free brochure ◆ Collectible railroadiana. Includes music, sounds, books, software, and amusements. 800-338-9918. ivycreek@mindspring.com

**Kohl's Celebrity Gallery,** 1840 N. Federal Hwy., Boynton Beach, FL 33435: Catalog $5 ◆ Autographs and vintage sports memorabilia. 800-344-9103; 561-364-0453 (in FL).

**Lighthouse Depot,** P.O. Box 427, Wells, ME 04090: Free catalog ◆ Lighthouse memorabilia and other maritime gifts. 800-758-1444. www.lhdigest.com

**The Limited of Michigan Ltd.,** 10861 Paw Paw Dr., Holland, MI 49424: Free catalog ◆ Hard-to-find Disney wood carvings and collectibles. 800-355-6363.

**Little Bat's Trading Post,** 123 Main St., Crawford, NE 69339: Catalog $10 ◆ Antique firearms, old west collectibles, and militaria. 308-665-1900.

**Moody's Collectibles,** 319 Wake Forest Dr., Warner Robins, GA 31093: Free catalog ◆ Auto racing, baseball, basketball, boxing, football, golf, hockey, Olympics, and other collectibles. 800-779-4024.

**Movie Gallery,** 111 E. 3rd, Sedalia, MO 65301: Catalog $5 ◆ Plates, comics, posters, and other new and old collectibles. 816-826-3834.

**Norma's Jeans,** 3511 Turner Ln., Chevy Chase, MD 20815: Catalog $2 ◆ Movie star memorabilia, costumes, autographs, personal belongings, historical artifacts, and other collectibles. 301-652-4644.

**The Old West Shop,** P.O. Box 5232, Vienna, WV 26105: Catalog $6 ◆ Replica old west collectibles. 304-295-3143. www.oldwestshop.com

**The Opera Box,** P.O. Box 994, Teaneck, NJ 07666: Free catalog ◆ Rare books, magazines, autograph material, and other opera collectibles. 201-833-4176.

**Opera World Inc.,** Box 800, Concord, MA 01742: Free catalog ◆ Opera videos, laser discs, CDs, and books. 800-99-OPERA. www.operaworld.com

**The Owl's Nest,** P.O. Box 990, Depoe Bay, OR 97341: Free catalog ◆ Owl collectibles. 888-345-6957; 541-765-2473 (in OR).

**Photo Antiquities,** 531 E. Ohio St., Pittsburgh, PA 15212: Free information ◆ Vintage photography collectibles. 800-474-6862.

**Rex Stark-Americana,** P.O. Box 1029, Gardner, MA 01440: Catalog $5 ◆ Historical Americana collectibles. 978-630-3237.

**Rockabilia Inc.,** P.O. Box 4206, Hopkins, MN 55343: Free catalog ◆ T-shirts, backstage passes, promotional glossy photographs, imported rare posters from around the world, and other concert collectibles and investment memorabilia. 612-942-7895.

**SR Collectibles,** P.O. Box 340658, Brooklyn, NY 11234: Free catalog ◆ Disney, Beatles, movie stars, tobacco, postcards, premiums, and other collectibles. 718-951-3629.

**Trendco Inc.,** 4723 W. Atlantic Ave., Delray Beach, FL 33445: Free catalog ◆ Figurines, plates, bobbing heads, and hand-signed memorabilia. 800-881-0181.

**Tribute International Corporation,** 2800 SW 4th Ave., Ste. 11, Fort Lauderdale, FL 33315: Catalog $2 ◆ Sports and entertainment collectibles. Also gifts. 800-310-9428. www.moments.com

**Voyager Western Reproductions,** P.O. Box 30414, Albuquerque, NM 87110: Catalog $3 ◆ Authentic Western reproductions. 505-256-0258. www.voyagerartifacts.com

## METAL CRAFTING & SILVERSMITHING

**Ackley's Rock & Stamps,** 3230 N. Stone Ave., Colorado Springs, CO 80907: Catalog $1 (refundable) ◆ Silversmithing supplies. 719-633-1153.

**Allcraft Tool & Supply Company,** 666 Pacific St., Brooklyn, NY 11207: Catalog $5 ◆ Tools and supplies for jewelry-making, metal-crafting and casting, and silversmithing. 800-645-7124; 718-789-2800 (in NY).

**American Art Clay Company Inc.,** 4717 W. 16th St., Indianapolis, IN 46222: Free catalog ◆ Ceramics and metal enameling supplies, pottery-making equipment, tools, kilns, and coloring materials. 800-374-1600; 317-244-6871 (in IN). www.amaco.com

**ARE Inc.,** Rt. 16, Box 8, Greensboro Bend, VT 05842: Catalog $3 ◆ Silver, gold, pewter, base metals, tools, findings, chains, other jewelry-making supplies, and semi-precious stones. 800-736-4273.

**Atlas Metal Sales,** 1401 Umatilla St., Denver, CO 80204: Free brochure ◆ Specialty metals. Includes aluminum, brass, bronze, lead, nickel, pewter, tin, and zinc. 800-662-0143; 303-623-0143 (in CO).

**Automatic Tubing Corp.,** 888 Lorimer St., Brooklyn, NY 11222: Free information ◆ Custom brass tubing. 800-527-3091; 718-383-0100 (in NY).

**Bourget Bros.,** 1636 11th St., Santa Monica, CA 90404: Catalog $3 ◆ Silversmithing supplies and copper, gold, and silver wire and sheet. 800-828-3024. www.bourgetbros.com

**Campbell Tools Company,** 2100 Selma Rd., Springfield, OH 45505: Catalog $2 ◆ Tools, supplies, and brass, aluminum, steel, and other metals. 937-322-8562.

**Cardinal Engineering Inc.,** 2211-C 155th St., Cameron, IL 61423: Catalog $2 ◆ Brass, aluminum, stainless, and tool steel. Also tools and other shop supplies. 309-342-7474.

**Country Accents,** P.O. Box 437, Montoursville, PA 17754: Catalog $5 ◆ Handcrafted metal panels, pierced metal kits, patterns, and tools. 717-478-4127.

**Discount Agate House,** 3401 N. Dodge Blvd., Tucson, AZ 85716: Free information ◆ Rocks and minerals from around the world, lapidary equipment, sterling silver and metalsmithing supplies, and findings. 520-323-0781.

**East West DyeCom,** 5238 Peters Creek Rd., Bldg. B, Roanoke, VA 24019: Catalog $5 (refundable) ◆ Pre-anodized aluminum sheets and colored tubing, dyes, kits, books, and other supplies. 800-407-6371. www.eastwestdye.com

**Ebersole Lapidary Supply Inc.,** 11417 West Hwy. 54, Wichita, KS 67209: Catalog $5 ◆ Gold and silver sheet and wire. Also silversmithing supplies. 316-722-4771.

**Enco Manufacturing Company,** 5000 W. Bloomingdale Ave., Chicago, IL 60639: Free catalog ◆ Metal-working tools, machinery, and accessories. 800-860-3400; 773-745-1520 (in IL).

**David H. Fell & Company,** 6009 Bandini Blvd., Los Angeles, CA 90040: Catalog $5 ◆ Precious metals for craft-making and photo-etched sheets. 800-822-1996; 213-722-9992 (in CA). www.MJSA.Polygon.net/~10204

**T.B. Hagstoz & Son Inc.,** 709 Sansom St., Philadelphia, PA 19106: Catalog $5 (refundable with $25 order) ◆ Metal findings, jeweler's tools, casting equipment, gold and silver solders, and gold, silver, gold-filled metals, copper, bronze, brass nickel, silver, and pewter. 800-922-1006; 215-922-1627 (in PA).

**Indian Jewelers Supply Company,** 601 E. Coal Ave., Gallup, NM 87301: Catalog $6 ◆ Copper and silver wire and sheet, silversmithing supplies, precious and base metal findings, tools and supplies, and semi-precious stones, shells, and coral. 505-722-4451.

**K & S Engineering,** 6917 W. 59th St., Chicago, IL 60638: Catalog $1 ◆ Aluminum and other metal tubing, rods, and sheets. 312-586-8503.

**Kingsley North Inc.,** 910 Brown St., Norway, MI 49870: Free catalog ◆ Silversmithing supplies, tools, and casting, lapidary, and glass polishing equipment. 800-338-9280. www.kingsleynorth.com

**Laney Company,** 6449 S. 209 East Ave., Broken Arrow, OK 74014: Free information ◆ German silver and gold wire, fancy strip, sheet, and findings for silver and goldsmithing. Also letters and numbers for trophies, buckles, and other projects. 918-355-1955.

**Lewis Brass & Copper Company,** Box 67, 69-61 78th St., Middle Village, NY 11379: Free information ◆ Brass and copper tubing, sheets, round and square rods, plates, channels, pipes, and other shapes. 800-221-5579; 718-894-1442 (in NY).

**Lonnie's Inc.,** 7155 E. Apache Trail, Mesa, AZ 85207: Free findings catalog; tool catalog $5; silver jewelry catalog $5 ◆ Tools, equipment, and supplies for jewelers, casters, silversmiths, and lapidarists. 602-832-2641.

**MBM Sales Ltd.,** West 229 North 2464, Joseph Rd., Waukesha, WI 53186: Catalog $2 ◆ Hard-to-find metals and fasteners in small quantities. 800-657-0721. www.metalmart.com

**Metal Buyers Mart,** N15 W22218, Watertown Rd., Waukesha, WI 53186: Free information ◆ Specializes in metals in small quantities. 800-657-0721; 414-547-3606 (in WI).

**Metalliferous,** 34 W. 46th St., New York, NY 10036: Catalog $5 ◆ Metals, tools, and supplies for jewelry-making and metal crafting. 212-944-0909.

**The NgraveR Company,** 67 Wawecus Hill Rd., Bozrah, CT 06334: Catalog $1 (refundable) ◆ Easy-to-use engraving tools and jewelry-making equipment. 860-823-1533.

**Nonferrous Metals,** P.O. Box 2595, Waterbury, CT 06723: Catalog $3 (refundable) ◆ Plain and ornamental brass, copper, bronze, and nickel-silver wire. 203-264-7255.

**Shapiro Supply Company,** 5617 Natural Bridge Rd., St. Louis, MO 63120: Catalog $2 ◆ Aluminum, brass, and stainless supplies. 800-833-1259; 314-382-7000 (in MO).

**Myron Toback Inc.,** 25 W. 47th St., New York, NY 10036: Free information ◆ Tools for metal crafting and silversmithing. 800-223-7550; 212-398-8300 (in NY).

**Unique Tool,** P.O. Box 34, Miami, NM 87729: Catalog $3 ◆ Silversmithing stamps and tools. 505-483-2940.

## METAL DETECTORS

**Alpha Supply,** P.O. Box 2133, Bremerton, WA 98310: Catalog $7 ◆ Metal detectors, prospecting and gem-finishing equipment, and jewelry-making tools. 800-257-4211; 360-373-3302 (in WA).

**American Detector Distributors,** 626 Grapevine Hwy., Hurst, TX 76054: Free information ◆ Metal detecting equipment and accessories. 800-933-BUYS; 817-498-7100 (in TX).

**Arizona Al's Discount,** 4238 W. Northern Ave., Phoenix, AZ 85051: Free information ◆ Metal detectors and prospecting equipment. 602-930-1755. www.arizonaals.com

**Armadillo Mining Shop,** 2041 NW Vine, Grants Pass, OR 97526: Free information ◆ Metal detectors and mining supplies. 541-476-6316.

**Barnes Enterprises,** 254 Kent Ave. NE, Hartville, OH 44632: Free information ◆ Metal detectors. 800-559-5449.

**Cal-Gold,** 2569 E. Colorado Blvd., Pasadena, CA 91107: Free catalog ◆ Metal detectors, supplies for miners and geologists, maps, and books. 626-792-6161. calgold@earthlink.net

**Clevenger Metal Detector Sales,** 8206 N. Oak, Kansas City, MO 64118: Free information ◆ New and used detectors. 800-999-9147.

**Cochran & Associates Inc.,** 808 Newberry St., Bowling Green, KY 42103: Catalog $10 ◆ Long-range treasure locating equipment. 502-843-0706. www.premiernet.net/~detectors

**D & K Detector Sales,** 13809 Southeast Division, Portland, OR 97236: Catalog $2 ◆ Metal detectors and prospecting equipment. 800-542-GOLD; 503-761-1521 (in OR). sales@dk-Nugget.com

**Detector Distribution Center,** 11900 Montana Ave., El Paso, TX 79936: Free list of retail sources ◆ Metal detectors. 915-855-4206.

**Detector Electronics Corp.,** 419 Worcester Rd., P.O. Box 2132, Framingham, MA 01703: Free brochure ◆ Metal detectors. 800-446-0244. www.metaldetector.com

**Discovery Electronics Inc.,** 1415 Poplar St., Sweet Home, OR 97386: Free list of retail sources ◆ Metal detectors. 800-337-4815; 541-367-2585 (in OR).

**Down Under Treasures,** P.O. Box 92080, Henderson, NV 89009: Free list of retail sources ◆ Metal detectors. 702-565-1353.

**East Coast Prospecting & Mining Supplies,** Rt. 3, Box 321J, Ellijay, GA 30540: Catalog $3 ◆ Metal detectors and accessories. 706-276-4433.

**Falcon Prospecting Equipment,** 6529 E. Fairbrook St., Mesa, AZ 85205: Free information ◆ Placer gold probe for prospecting. 602-854-0324.

**Fisher Research Laboratory,** 200 W. Wilmott Rd., Los Banos, CA 93635: Free information ◆ Metal detectors. 209-826-3292. www.fisherlab.com

**JW Fishers Manufacturing Inc.,** 65 Anthony St., Berkley, MA 02779: Free information ◆ Underwater metal detectors. 800-822-4744; 508-822-7330 (in MA). www.treasurenet.com/jwfishers

**49'er Metal Detectors,** 14093 Irishtown Rd., Pine Grove, CA 95665: Free information ◆ Metal detectors. 800-538-7501; 209-296-3544 (in CA).

**Garrett Metal Detectors,** 1881 W. State St., Garland, TX 75042: Free buyer's guide ◆ Metal detectors. 800-527-4011; 972-278-6151 (in TX). email@gmdi.com

**Gettysburg Electronics,** 24 Chambersburg St., Gettysburg, PA 17325: Free information ◆ Metal detectors. 717-334-8634.

**The Golddigger,** 253 N. Main, Moab, UT 84532: Catalog $3 ◆ Metal detectors. 801-259-5150.

**Hays Electronics,** P.O. Box 26848, Prescott Valley, AZ 86312: Free catalog ◆ Metal detectors, maps, electronic prospecting tools and accessories, and books on prospecting, mining, and relic hunting. 800-699-2624.

**House of Treasure Hunters,** 5714 El Cajon Blvd., San Diego, CA 92115: Free information ◆ Metal detectors and gold prospecting equipment. 619-286-2600.

**Kansas/Texas Metal Detectors,** P.O. Box 1500, Dept. C, Colleyville, TX 76034: Free information ◆ Low-cost metal detectors for treasure, hobby, professional, and security use. 800-876-3463; 817-498-2228 (in TX).

**Kellyco Detector Distributors,** 1085 Belle Ave., Winter Springs, FL 32708: Free catalog ◆ Metal detectors. 407-699-8700. www.kellycodetectors.com

**Metal Detectors of Minneapolis,** 3746 Cedar Ave. South, Minneapolis, MN 55407: Free information ◆ Metal detectors, maps, books, accessories, and recovery tools. 800-876-8377; 612-721-1901 (in MN). trovers@webtv.net

**Mid-West Metal Detectors,** 8338 Pillsbury Ave. South, Bloomington, MN 55420: Free information ◆ Metal detectors and books. 612-881-5254.

**The Midas Touch,** 15 Thorncliffe Park Dr., Ste. 412, Toronto, Ontario, Canada M4H 1H6: Catalog $6 ◆ Metal detectors and accessories, prospecting tools, water hunting equipment, and books on treasure hunting. 416-467-6016.

**Northwest Treasure Supply,** P.O. Box 6986, Bellevue, WA 98008: Free information ◆ Metal detectors. 800-845-5258. www.treasurenet.com/nwts

**Panna's Electronics,** Box 167, Geneva, NY 14456: Free information ◆ Metal detectors. 315-539-8645.

**Patrick Electronics,** P.O. Box 760, West Elizabeth, PA 15088: Free brochure ◆ Metal detectors and accessories. 412-384-2742. dtekt@aol.com

**Pedersen's Metal Detectors,** 2521 N. Grand Ave., Santa Ana, CA 92705: Free information ◆ Walk-through and handheld detectors. Also gold and treasure-finding supplies. 800-953-3832.

**Pioneer Mining Supplies,** 943 Lincoln Way, Auburn, CA 95603: Free information ◆ Mining equipment and metal detectors. 530-885-1801.

**Pot of Gold,** 2616 Griffin Rd., Fort Lauderdale, FL 33312: Free catalog ◆ Metal detectors, books, and prospecting equipment. 954-987-2888.

**Reilly's Treasured Gold Inc.,** P.O. Box 2975, Pompano Beach, FL 33072: Free information ◆ Metal detecting equipment and accessories. 954-971-6102. www.rtgstore.com

**Jimmy Sierra Products,** 3095 Kerner Blvd., Ste. H, San Rafael, CA 94901: Free information ◆ Metal detectors, treasure hunting, prospecting equipment, and accessories. 415-456-0891. jsierra@nbm.com

**Simmons Scientific Inc.,** P.O. Box 10057, Wilmington, NC 28405: Free brochure ◆ Directional locating equipment.

**Tesoro Electronics,** 715 White Spar Rd., Prescott, AZ 86303: Free list of retail sources ◆ Easy-to-use lightweight metal detectors with high gain sensitivity. 800-528-3352. www.tesoro.com

**Treasure Center,** 534 W. Liberty St., Hubbard, OH 44425: Free catalog ◆ Metal detectors. 800-767-2646.

**White's Electronics,** 1011 Pleasant Valley Rd., Sweet Home, OR 97386: Free list of retail sources ◆ Metal detectors. 800-547-6911. www.whitescatalog.com

## MICROSCOPES

**Chem-Lab,** 1060 Ortega Way, Placentia, CA 92670: Catalog $5 ◆ Chemicals, glassware, scales, microscopes, and other science equipment. 714-630-7902. www.chemlab.com

**Collector's Optics & Supplies,** P.O. Box 281, Elk Grove Village, IL 60009: Free information ◆ Stereo and pocket microscopes. 847-439-8266.

**Edmund Scientific Company,** Edscorp Bldg., Barrington, NJ 08007: Free catalog ◆ Microscopes, magnifiers, weather forecasting instruments, magnets, telescopes, binoculars, lasers, and other science equipment. 609-547-8880. www.edsci.com

**J.L. Hammett Company,** P.O. Box 9057, Braintree, MA 02184: Free catalog ◆ Science kits, microscopes, laboratory apparatus, rock collections, magnets, astronomy charts, and anatomical models. 781-848-1000.

**Harrison Astronomy,** 2574 Granville St., Vancouver, British Columbia, Canada V6H 3C8: Free information ◆ Telescopes and accessories, binoculars, microscopes, magnifiers, meteorological instruments, and books. 604-737-4303.

**Mineralogical Research Company,** 15840 E. Alta Vista Way, San Jose, CA 95127: Free list with long SASE and two 1st class stamps ◆ Microscopes, rare mineral specimens, meteorites, micro-mounts, specimen boxes, and other science equipment. 408-923-6800.

**Nurnberg Scientific,** 6310 SW Virginia Ave., Portland, OR 97201: Free information ◆ Microscopes. 503-246-8297.

**Seabird Technical,** 3580 Haven Ave., Redwood City, CA 94063: Free catalog ◆ Stereo microscopes. 650-367-8320. jlittle@netwizards.net

**Unitron Inc.,** 170 Wilbur Pl., P.O. Box 469, Bohemia, NY 11716: Free catalog ◆ Stereo microscopes. Also other optical and scientific equipment. 516-589-6666.

**White Nights Company,** 420 Oceanview Dr., Anchorage, AL 99515: Free brochure ◆ Mineral collections, individual specimens, collecting materials, and mineralogical microscopes. 907-345-5531.

## MILITARY MEMORABILIA

### General Memorabilia

**Dale C. Anderson Company,** 4 W. Confederate Ave., Gettysburg, PA 17325: Catalog $12 (6 issues) ◆ Civil War, Indian War, and other militaria.

**Arms & Armor,** 1101 Stinson Blvd. NE, Minneapolis, MN 55413: Catalog $2 ◆ Reproduction weapons and armor. 612-331-6473.

**BattleZone Ltd.,** P.O. Box 266, Towaco, NJ 07082: Free information ◆ Military memorabilia. www.military-patches.com

**Brandenburg Historical,** P.O. Box 1574, Rutherford, NJ 07070: Catalog $2 ◆ German military collectibles, from 1900 to the present. Also books and German military music on CDs.

**British Collectibles Ltd.,** 1727 Wilshire Blvd., Santa Monica, CA 90403: Catalog $15 ◆ British military collectibles, from the 1800s to World War II. 310-453-3322.

**British Regalia Imports,** P.O. Box 37, Palm Harbor, FL 34683: Catalog $6 ◆ British armed forces insignia.

**BRS Militaria,** 1950-5 Bush River Rd., Ste. 31, Columbia, SC 29210: Catalog $10 (4 issues) ◆ WWI and WWII, German, and United States military collectibles.

**C & D Jarnagin Company,** P.O. Box 1860, Corinth, MS 38834: Civil War catalog $3, 18th-century (1750 to 1815) catalog $3 ◆ Military and historical memorabilia. 601-287-4977. www.jarnaginco.com

**Collector of Antique Militaria,** Thomas F. Whitman, P.O. Box 350, Moorestown, NJ 08057: Catalog subscription $45 (2 copies) ◆ Militaria, specializing in Imperial and 3rd Reich edged weapons. Also medals and badges, art, headgear, and more. members.aol.com/Twittm350

**Collector's Armoury,** 800 Slaters Ln., P.O. Box 59, Alexandria, VA 22313: Free catalog ◆ Replica model guns, medals, armor, swords, helmets, and other military collectibles. 800-544-3456.

**The Collector's Guild,** P.O. Box 1255, Postal Station A, Fredericton, N.B., Canada E3B 5C8: Free catalog ◆ Military collectibles. 506-450-9405.

**Dan Farek,** Box 1212, Bellaire, TX 77402: Free list ◆ Medals from worldwide sources, military autographs, photographs, and other militaria.

**N. Flayderman & Company Inc.,** P.O. Box 2446, Fort Lauderdale, FL 33303: Catalog $10 ◆ Antique guns, swords, knives, and nautical, western, and military collectibles from the Civil War through World War II. 305-761-8855.

**James E. Garcia,** 9 Autumnwood Ct., Tieras, NM 87059: Catalog $3 ◆ Vintage aviation collectibles. Includes many one-of-a-kind rare items. 505-286-1771.

**Great War Militaria,** P.O. Box 552, Chambersburg, PA 17201: Catalog subscription $10 ◆ United States and foreign military collectibles and war relics. 717-264-6834.

**Hutchinson House,** Box 41021, Chicago, IL 60641: Catalog $2 ◆ Full-size, made from the originals, World War I and Civil War reproduction war mementos and medals.

**Jacques Noel Jacobsen,** 60 Manor Rd., Ste. 300, Staten Island, NY 10310: Catalog $10 ◆ Antiques and military collectibles, insignia, weapons, photos and paintings, band instruments, and Native American and western items. 718-981-0973.

**Steve Johnson,** P.O. Box 4706, Aurora, IL 60507: Catalog $2 ◆ Medals and militaria. 708-851-0744.

**Lancer Militaria,** P.O. Box 886, Mt. Ida, AR 71957: Catalog $2 ◆ Military and police insignia. 501-867-2232. www.warbooks.com

**Legendary Arms Inc.,** P.O. Box 479, Three Bridges, NJ 08887: Free information ◆ Reproduction military period knives and swords. 800-528-2767; 908-788-7330 (in NJ).

**Little Bat's Trading Post,** 123 Main St., Crawford, NE 69339: Catalog $10 ◆ Antique firearms, old west collectibles, and other militaria. 308-665-1900.

**Lodgewood Mfg.,** William H. Osborne, P.O. Box 611, Whitewater, WI 53190: Catalog $5 ◆ Civil War guns, parts, and United States martial arms, from 1780 to 1898. 414-473-5444.

**Fred Lohman Company,** 3405 NE Broadway, Portland, OR 97232: Catalog $5 ◆ Japanese sword-making supplies, scabbards, polishing aids, and other accessories.

**Manion's,** P.O. Box 12214, Kansas City, KS 66112: Catalog subscription $10 (6 issues) ◆ Militaria. 913-299-6692.

**McGrogan's Military Patches,** P.O. Box 502, Orofino, ID 83544: Free information ◆ Military patches. 800-861-9398.

**Medals of America,** 1929 Fairview Rd., Fountain Inn, SC 29644: Catalog $2 ◆ Full-size medals, miniatures and badges, ribbons and patches, display cases, flag cases and flags, ship photos and histories, and other memorabilia. 864-862-6425. www.usmedals.com

**Medieval Replicas,** 6444 E. Spring St., #207, Long Beach, CA 90815: Free catalog with 1st class stamp ◆ Replica medieval weapons and armor.

**Mid-Missouri Surplus,** Russ Hinnard, 780 W. Boyd St., Marshall, MO 65340: Free catalog ◆ Soviet military collectibles. 816-886-3585.

**Military Antiques & Museum Shop,** 260 Petaluma Blvd. North, Petaluma, CA 94952: Free list ◆ War souvenirs, military relics and insignia, and war trophies from the Civil War, Indian Wars, World War I and II, Viet Nam, and the Gulf War. 707-763-2220. www.sonic.net/~warstuff

**Military Art China Company Inc.,** P.O. Box 406, Westford, MA 01886: Catalog $3 ◆ Handcrafted coffee mugs and steins with military crests. 978-392-0751.

**The Military Collection,** 13059 SW 133rd Ct., Miami, FL 33186: Catalog $8 ◆ Aviation and war relics. 305-253-9138.

**Igor Moiseyev,** Atlantic Crossroad Inc., P.O. Box 290715, Brooklyn, NY 11229: Catalog $1 ◆ Russian medals and militaria. 718-891-4595.

**Museum Replicas Limited,** P.O. Box 840, Conyers, GA 30207: Catalog $1 (refundable) ◆ Authentic museum quality historical replicas of weapons and period battle wear. 800-883-8838. www.museumreplicas.com

**The Noble Collection,** P.O. Box 1476, Sterling, VA 20167: Free catalog ◆ Swords, armor, shields, helmets, sidearms, miniatures, and military collectibles. 800-866-2538.

**Hayes Otoupalik,** P.O. Box 8423, Missoula, MT 59807: Catalog $5 ◆ United States militaria, from 1833 to 1945. 406-549-4817.

**Terry Patton-Numismatist,** Box 441175, Kennesaw, GA 30152: Catalog $5 ◆ Coins, medals, documents, autographs, swords, daggers, uniforms, hats, flags, and other historical militaria. 770-419-7897.

**Pieces of History,** P.O. Box 4470, Cave Creek, AZ 85331: Catalog $2 ◆ Medals from around the world. 602-488-1377.

**Red Lancer,** P.O. Box 8056, Mesa, AZ 85214: Catalog $12 ◆ Original 19th-century military art, rare books, campaign medals, helmets, and toy soldiers. 602-964-9667.

**Rocky Mountain Rarities,** P.O. Box 303, Bountiful, UT 84011: Free list ◆ World War II collectibles. 801-296-6276.

**TAPCO,** P.O. Box 2408, Kennesaw, GA 30144: Free catalog ◆ Military, shooting, and outdoor gear. 800-554-1445.

**United States Marine Corps Collectables,** James A. Johnson, 25 Northwood Dr., Laredo, TX 78041: Free information ◆ United States Marine Corps collectibles. 210-717-0166.

**Vasily's Souvenir Shop,** 427 Main St., Highland Falls, NY 10928: Catalog $2 (refundable) ◆ United States West Point Military Academy-related clothing, glassware, hats, and other gift items. 800-238-9969.

**World Wide Militaria,** P.O. Box 522, Germantown, MD 20875: Catalog $3 ◆ Uniforms, insignia, and field gear from all countries and periods.

## Civil War Collectibles

**Dale C. Anderson Company,** 4 W. Confederate Ave., Gettysburg, PA 17325: Catalog $12 (6 issues) ◆ Civil War, Indian War, and other militaria.

**Battleground Antiques Inc.,** 3910 US Hwy. 70 East, New Bern, NC 28560: Catalog $10 (annual subscription) ◆ Authentic Civil War weapons, uniforms, photographs, and more. 252-636-3039. www.civilwarantiques.com

**Broadfoot Publishing Company,** 1907 Buena Vista Circle, Wilmington, NC 28405: Free catalog ◆ Old and new books about the Civil War. 910-686-4816. www.broadfoot.wilmington.net

**C & D Jarnagin Company,** P.O. Box 1860, Corinth, MS 38834: Civil War catalog $3, 18th-century (1750 to 1815) catalog $3 ◆ Military and historical memorabilia. 601-287-4977. www.jarnaginco.com

**Cedar Creek Relic Shop,** P.O. Box 232, Middletown, VA 22645: Catalog $6 ◆ Civil War relics, weapons and firearms, and collectibles. 540-869-5207.

**Civil War Antiquities,** P.O. Box 1411, Delaware, OH 43015: Free catalog ◆ Civil War collectibles. 740-363-1862. www.civilwarantiquities.com

**Collector's Armoury,** 800 Slaters Ln., P.O. Box 59, Alexandria, VA 22313: Free catalog ◆ Civil War memorabilia, World War II medals, Samurai swords, flags, and replica model guns. 800-544-3456.

**Country Mercantile,** 111 N. Main, Liberty, MO 64068: Catalog $6 ◆ Weapons, accouterments, clothing, and patterns. 816-781-9473. JAMESCNTRY@aol.com

**Dixie Fashions,** 11300 Cedar Hill Ct., Richmond, VA 23233: Catalog $3 (refundable) ◆ Reproduction Confederate and Union uniforms. Also Civil War period leather accessories and civilian clothing. 804-527-2028.

**Fair Oaks Sutler Inc.,** 9905 Kershaw Ct., Spotsylvania, VA 22553: Free catalog with two 1st class stamps ◆ Reproduction Civil War military collectibles. 540-972-7744. www.fairoakssutler.com

**Farnsworth Military Gallery,** 401 Baltimore St., Gettysburg, PA 17325: Free information ◆ Art prints and new, used, and rare books on the Civil War. 717-334-8838.

**Fields of Glory,** 55 York St., Gettysburg, PA 17325: Catalog subscription $10 (12 issues) ◆ Civil War memorabilia. 800-517-3382. www.collectorsnet.com

**Will Gorges Civil War Antiques,** 2100 Trent Blvd., New Bern, NC 28560: Catalog $10 ◆ Authentic Civil War uniforms, weapons, photographs, and pre-1964 comic books. 919-636-3039. www.collectorsnet.com/gorges

**Grand Illusions Clothing,** 705 Interchange Blvd., Newark, DE 19711: Catalog $3 ◆ Civil War uniforms and clothing for men, women, and children. 302-366-0300.

**Brian & Maria Green,** P.O. Box 1816, Kernersville, NC 27285: Free price list ◆ Civil War autographs, letters, diaries, stamps, and currency. 336-993-5100. www.collectorsnet.com/bmg

**Horner Enterprises,** 20 Horner Rd., Gettysburg, PA 17325: Free information ◆ Civil War collectibles. 717-334-8916. jhorner@mail.cvn.net

**The Horse Soldier,** 777 Baltimore St., Gettysburg, PA 17325: Catalog $5 each (specify interest) ◆ Guns, swords, uniforms, books, relics, buttons, and bullets. 717-334-0347. hsoldier@pa.net

**Lawrence of Dalton,** 4773 Tammy Dr. NE, Dalton, GA 30721: List $4 ◆ Civil War relics. 800-336-8894; 706-226-8894 (in GA).

**Bill Mason Books,** 104 N. 7th St., Morehead City, NC 28557: Free catalog ◆ Rare, new, and used books. Also prints, and Civil War, Western Americana, military, and nautical collectibles. 919-247-6161. bmasonbks@collectorsnet.com

**NMC Enterprises,** 913 18th St., Ste. 2, Santa Monica, CA 90403: Free catalog ◆ Civil War and old west style handcrafted leather holsters, gun belts, and cavalry accessories. 310-582-1937.

**Northern Map Company,** Box 129, Dunnellon, FL 34430: Catalog $5 ◆ Maps from the Civil War, Canadian maps, map kits, and old state, city, railroad, and county maps, from 70 to 120 years old. 800-314-2474. www.losttreasure.com/northernmap

**Old Sutler John,** P.O. Box 174, Westview Station, Binghamton, NY 13905: Catalog $3 ◆ Reproduction Civil War guns, bayonets, swords, uniforms, leather items, and other collectibles. 607-775-4434.

**Olde Soldier Books Inc.,** 18779 N. Frederick Ave., Gaithersburg, MD 20879: Free information ◆ Civil War books, documents, autographs, prints, and Americana. 301-963-2929. Warbooks@erols.com

**Panther Primitives,** P.O. Box 32, Normantown, WV 25267: Catalog $2 (refundable) ◆ Historical re-enactment Civil War items. 304-462-7718.

**Charles T. Phillips,** 3863 Old Shell Rd., Mobile, AL 36608: Free catalog ◆ Reproductions of Civil War photographs. 334-633-4685.

**Rapine Bullet Manufacturing Company,** P.O. Box 1119, RD 1, East Greenville, PA 18041: Catalog $2 ◆ Civil War bullet molds. 215-679-5413.

**Reb Acres,** Bill & Sue Coleman, Rt. 2, Box 314, Raphine, VA 24472: Free catalog with three 1st class stamps ◆ Civil War memorabilia. 540-377-2057. rebacres@cfw.com

**The Regimental Quartermaster,** P.O. Box 553, Hatboro, PA 19040: Catalog $2 ◆ Civil War reproductions. 215-672-6891. members.aol.com/regtqm

**Len Rosa Military Collectibles,** P.O. Box 3965, Gettysburg, PA 17325: Catalog subscription $10 ◆ Union and Confederate Civil War memorabilia and artifacts. 717-337-2853.

**Scotty's Scale Soldiers,** 1008 Adams St., Bay City, MI 48708: Small scale catalog $6; large scale catalog $5; both catalogs $10 ◆ Miniatures, 6mm to 30mm and 54mm to 120mm. 517-892-6177.

**Steen Cannons,** 10730 Midland Trail Rd., Cannonsburg, KY 41102: Catalog $5 ◆ Authentic and full-scale reproduction cannons. 606-329-2477. www.wwd.net/steen

**The Union Drummer Boy,** 34 York St., Gettysburg, PA 17325: Free information ◆ Authentic Civil War artifacts. 717-334-2350. www.uniondb.com

**Upper Mississippi Valley Mercantile Company,** 1607 Washington St., Davenport, IA 52804: Catalog $3 ◆ Reproduction Civil War memorabilia. 319-322-0896.

**James Townsend & Son Inc.,** 133 N. 1st St., P.O. Box 415, Pierceton, IN 46562: Catalog $2 ◆ Historical clothing, hats, lanterns, tomahawks, knives, tents, guns, and blankets. 800-338-1665.

**Del & Jean Warren,** P.O. Box 364, Liberty, MO 64068: Catalog $6 ◆ Civil War era historic books and patterns, jewelry and accessories, underpinnings, uniforms and accouterments, black powder rifles, and shooting supplies. 816-781-9473. Jamescntry@aol.com

**The Winchester Sutler Inc.,** 270 Shadow Brook Ln., Winchester, VA 22603: Catalog $4 ◆ Civil War reproductions. 540-888-3595.

### War Medals & Souvenirs

**Call To Colors,** Box 5403, Towson, MD 21204: Catalog $2 ◆ Full-size and miniature medals, insignia, and badges. Also cases for awards.

**Collector's Armoury,** 800 Slaters Ln., P.O. Box 59, Alexandria, VA 22313: Free catalog ◆ Collectible World War II medals, Samurai swords, flags, Civil War memorabilia, and replica model guns. 800-544-3456.

**Dan Farek,** Box 1212, Bellaire, TX 77402: Free list ◆ Medals from worldwide sources, military autographs, photographs, and other militaria.

**R. Andrew Fuller Company,** Box 2071, Pawtucket, RI 02861: Free catalog ◆ Medals, ribbons, and display cases.

**Great War Militaria,** P.O. Box 552, Chambersburg, PA 17201: Catalog subscription $10 ◆ United States and foreign military medals, insignia, and other decorations. 717-264-6834.

**W.D. Grissom,** P.O. Box 59, Cabot, AR 72023: Free catalog ◆ Military medals and antiques.

**Hoover's Manufacturing Company,** P.O. Box 547, Peru, IL 61354: Free catalog ◆ Dog tag key rings, beer and coffee mugs, belt buckles, patches, flags, and Vietnam, Korea, and World War II hat pins. 815-223-1159.

**Steve Johnson,** P.O. Box 4706, Aurora, IL 60507: Catalog $2 ◆ Medals and militaria. 708-851-0744.

**Medals of America,** 1929 Fairview Rd., Fountain Inn, SC 29644: Catalog $2 ◆ Full-size medals, miniatures and badges, ribbons and patches, display cases, flag cases and flags, ship photos and histories, and other memorabilia. 864-862-6425. www.usmedals.com

**Igor Moiseyev,** Atlantic Crossroad Inc., P.O. Box 290715, Brooklyn, NY 11229: List $1 ◆ Russian medals and militaria. 718-332-5889.

**H.J. Saunders/Military Insignia,** Box 3133, Naples, FL 33939: Catalog $3 ◆ Collectible United States military insignia, books, and other reference material. 941-775-2100. www.SaundersInsignia.com

**Sydney B. Vernon,** Box 890280, Temecula, CA 92589: Catalog $8 (10 issues) ◆ Military medals and related collectibles. 909-698-1646. home.earthlink/~svernon

## MIRRORS

**Atlantic Glass & Mirror Works,** 437 N. 63rd St., Philadelphia, PA 19151: Free information ◆ Antique mirrors and restoration of antique frames. 215-747-6866.

**European Tradition,** P.O. Box 01-0055, Miami, FL 33101: Catalog $5 (refundable) ◆ Victorian-style paintings, prints, and mirrors. 305-371-4474.

**Hansgrohe Inc.,** 1465 Ventura Dr., Cumming, GA 30130: Catalog $3 ◆ Faucets, massaging and handheld showers, make-up and shaving mirrors, and other accessories. 770-844-7414.

**Holton Furniture & Frame,** 5515 Doyle St., Emeryville, CA 94608: Brochure $3 ◆ Classic frames and mirrors. 510-450-0350.

**La Barge Mirrors,** P.O. Box 1769, Holland, MI 49422: Catalog $7 ◆ Handcrafted mirrors with optional decorative complements. 616-392-1473.

**Ledco Inc.,** 801 Commerce Circle, Shelbyville, KY 40065: Free list of retail sources ◆ Bi-fold glass and mirror doors in pine and oak. 805-626-6367.

**The Masters' Collection,** 40 Scitico Rd., Somersville, CT 06072: Catalog $5 ◆ Custom mirrors and oil reproductions on canvas. 800-222-6827. www.MastersCollection.com

**Robern Inc.,** 7 Wood Ave., Bristol, PA 19007: Free list of retail sources ◆ Bathroom mirrors and cabinets. 215-826-9800.

**Studio Steel,** 159 New Milford Tnpk., New Preston, CT 06777: Catalog $2 ◆ Lamps, chandeliers, sconces, mirrors, and hand-wrought metalwork. 800-800-5712.

**Williams Cabinetry,** P.O. Box 39, Sullivan, ME 04664: Free information ◆ Country and Victorian-style wall mirrors. 207-422-9532.

## MODELS & MODEL BUILDING

### Aircraft Models

**Ace R/C,** 116 W. 19th St., P.O. Box 472, Higginsville, MO 64037: Catalog $2 ◆ R/C gliders. 816-584-7121.

**The Airplane Shop,** 18 Passaic Ave., Unit #6, Fairfield, NJ 07004: Free catalog ◆ Models and collectibles. 800-752-6346.

**Airtronics Inc.,** 15311 Barranca Pkwy., Irvine, CA 92618: Free information ◆ Helicopter models and electric sailplane with folding propeller and removable plug-in wing tips. 714-727-1474.

**Altech Marketing,** P.O. Box 7182, Edison, NJ 08818: Free information ◆ Ready-to-fly models. 908-248-8738.

**America's Hobby Center Inc.,** P.O. Box 829, North Bergen, NJ 07047: Catalog $3 ◆ Models, R/C equipment, and tools. 201-662-2800.

**Anderson Enterprises,** 405 Osage Dr., Derby, KS 67037: Free information ◆ Handcarved solid mahogany models. 800-732-6875.

**Aristo-Craft,** Polk's Model Craft Hobbies Inc., 346 Bergen Ave., Jersey City, NJ 07304: Catalog $2 ◆ R/C models. 201-332-8100. www.aristocraft.com/aristo

**Astro Flight Inc.,** 13311 Beach Ave., Marina Del Ray, CA 90292: Free information ◆ Electric-powered airplanes and engines. 310-821-6242.

**Aveox Electric Flight Systems,** 31324 Via Colinas, #103, Westlake Village, CA 91362: Free catalog ◆ Electric powered model airplanes. 818-597-8915. www.aveox.com

**Aviation Models,** P.O. Box 4078, College Point, NY 11356: Free catalog ◆ Classic and historical aviation and space replicas. 800-591-4823. www.aviation-models.com

**Bob & Di-Versions,** P.O. Box 2115, Broken Arrow, OK 74013: Free list with long SASE ◆ Die-cast models. 918-455-5037.

**Bob's Hobby Center,** 7333 Lake Underhill Rd., Orlando, FL 32822: Free information ◆ R/C airplanes, helicopters, boats, and cars. 407-277-1248.

**Bridi Aircraft Designs Inc.,** 640 Flint Ave., Wilmington, CA 90744: Free information ◆ R/C airplane kits and gliders. 310-549-8264.

**Brison Aircraft Engines,** 12075 Denton Dr., Dallas, TX 75234: Free information ◆ Custom aircraft engines. 972-241-9152. rampages.onramp.net/~brison

**Brodak's,** 100 Park Ave., Carmichaels, PA 15320: Catalog $3 ◆ Control-line airplanes. 416-966-5178.

**Bruckner Hobbies Inc.,** 2908 Bruckner Blvd., Bronx, NY 10465: Free information ◆ Airplane and automobile kits, R/C equipment, and building supplies. 800-288-8185.

**Byron Originals Inc.,** P.O. Box 279, Ida Grove, IA 51445: Catalog $4 ◆ Easy-to-assemble models and jet engines. 712-364-3165.

**Cactus Aviation Models,** 10380 E. Heritage, Tucson, AZ 85730: Free information ◆ Acrobatic aircraft models. 520-721-0087. www.pclink.com/cactus

**Century Helicopter Products,** 521 Sinclair Frontage Rd., Milpitas, CA 95035: Free information ◆ R/C helicopters. 408-942-9525.

**Century Jet Models Inc.,** 11216 Bluegrass Pkwy., Louisville, KY 40299: Catalog $3 ◆ R/C jet airplane kits, large scale models, and accessories. 502-266-9234.

**Cermark Electronic & Model Supply,** 107 Edward Ave., Fullerton, CA 92633: Free information ◆ Ready-to-fly R/C airplanes. 714-680-5888.

**Classic Aircraft Collections,** 3321 Suffolk Ct. West, Ste. 105, Fort Worth, TX 76133: Free brochure ◆ World War II and postwar aircraft recognition models. 800-289-3167.

**Cleveland Model & Supply Company,** P.O. Box 55962, Cleveland, OH 46205: Catalog $2 ◆ Airplane models. 440-681-1444.

**Colpar Hobbies,** 804 S. Havana St., Aurora, CO 80012: Free newsletter with long SASE ◆ Airplanes, armor, automobiles, ships, R/C equipment, parts, and accessories. 800-876-0414. www.colpar.com

**Combat Models Inc.,** 8535 Arjons Dr., San Diego, CA 92126: Free information ◆ R/C gliders and almost ready-to-fly R/C models. 619-536-9922.

**Cox Hobbies Inc.,** 1925 H St., Penrose, CO 81240: Free list of retail sources ◆ R/C model airplanes and cars. 719-372-6565.

**Danielle's R/C Specialists,** 3141 Ambrose Ave., Nashville, TN 37207: Free information ◆ R/C planes, helicopters, and equipment. 800-235-6253

**Dean's Hobby Shop,** 214 E. Main St., Flushing, MI 48433: Free list (specify cars or military models) with long SASE and two 1st class stamps ◆ Hard-to-find old and collectible model kits. 810-659-2137.

**Don's Hobby Shop Inc.,** 1819 S. Broadway, Salina, KS 67401: Free information ◆ Scale and large aircraft models, engines, and supplies.

**Dream Catcher Hobby Inc.,** P.O. Box 77, Bristol, IN 46507: Catalog 60¢ ◆ Glider kits. 219-848-1427. www.dchobby.com

**Dynaflite,** Great Planes, P.O. Box 9021, Champaign, IL 61826: Free list of retail sources ◆ R/C sailplanes, other R/C planes, launching systems, and accessories. 800-682-8948. www.dynaflite.com

**Easy Built Models,** Box 425, Lockport, NY 14095: Free catalog with long SASE ◆ Easy-to-build airplane kits. 716-438-0545.

**Evers Toy Store,** 204 1st Ave. East, Dyersville, IA 52040: Free information with long SASE ◆ Airplane models and miniature die-cast automobiles. 800-962-9481.

**G & P Sales,** 455 Sunset Dr., Angwin, CA 94508: Information $3 ◆ R/C model airplane kits. 707-965-1216.

**Global Hobby Distributors,** 10725 Ellis Ave., Fountain Valley, CA 92728: Free information ◆ R/C model airplane kits and gliders. 714-963-0133.

**Great Planes,** P.O. Box 9021, Champaign, IL 61826: Free list of retail sources ◆ R/C models.

**Helicopter World Inc.,** 521 Sinclair Frontage Rd., Milpitas, CA 95035: Catalog $5 ◆ Helicopter models, accessories, parts, and R/C equipment. 408-942-9521.

**Helicopters Unlimited,** P.O. Box 726, Avon, CT 06001: Free information ◆ Helicopters, accessories, R/C equipment, and tools. 860-677-7278.

**Herr Engineering Corp.,** 1431 Chaffee Dr., Ste. 3, Titusville, FL 32780: Catalog $2 ◆ Rubber-powered model airplane kits. 407-264-2488.

**Hobbico,** Great Planes Distributors Company, P.O. Box 9021, Champaign, IL 61826: Free list of retail sources ◆ R/C model airplanes, and accessories. www.hobbico.com

**Hobby Barn,** P.O. Box 17856, Tucson, AZ 85731: Free catalog ◆ Airplane and boat models. 520-747-3792.

**Hobby Hangar,** 1862 Petersburg Rd., Hebron, KY 41048: Catalog $2 ◆ R/C airplanes and accessories. Also helicopters, boats, and cars. 800-611-3860. www.hobbyhangar.com

**Hobby Horse Planes,** 1769 Thierer Rd., Madison, WI 53704: Free information ◆ R/C equipment and accessories, engines, building supplies, and models. 800-604-6229.

**Hobby Lobby International Inc.,** 5614 Franklin Pike Circle, Brentwood, TN 37027: Catalog $2.50 ◆ Airplane models. 615-373-1444. 74164.2423@Compuserve.com

**Hobby Shack,** 18480 Bandilier Circle, Fountain Valley, CA 92728: Free catalog ◆ R/C systems and ready-to assemble airplanes and automobiles. 800-854-8471. www.hobbyshack.com

**Hobby Surplus Sales,** P.O. Box 2170, New Britain, CT 06050: Catalog $4 ◆ Airplanes, cars, ships, trains, armor, R/C equipment, and craft supplies. 800-233-0872.

**Hobby World,** 523 Sinclair Frontage Rd., Milpitas, CA 95035: Free information ◆ Airplane kits, engines, and R/C equipment. 408-946-7201.

**Hobby World Ltd. of Montreal,** 5450 Sherbrooke St. West, Montreal, Quebec, Canada H4A 1V9: Catalog $5 ◆ Airplanes, helicopters, cars and trucks, ships, military vehicles, and science models. 514-481-5434.

**Hobbycraft Canada,** 140 Applewood Crescent, Concord, Ontario, Canada L4K 4E2: Free information ◆ Scale models from the first World War to the Gulf War. 905-738-6556.

**Bob Holman Plans,** P.O. Box 741, San Bernardino, CA 92402: Catalog $5 ◆ R/C model airplane kits. 714-885-3959.

**Ikon N'wst,** P.O. Box 306, Post Falls, ID 83854: Catalog $4 ◆ Giant scale and R/C model airplane kits. 800-327-7198; 208-773-9001 (in ID).

**Indy R/C Sales Inc.,** 10620 N. College Ave., Indianapolis, IN 46280: Free information ◆ Pre-assembled airplane models, engines, and R/C equipment. 800-338-4639.

**International Hobby Corp.,** 413 E. Allegheny Ave., Philadelphia, PA 19134: Catalog $4.98 ◆ Battery-powered tools, model airplanes, railroad accessories, and military miniatures. 800-875-1600.

**J'Tec,** 164 School St., Daly City, CA 94014: Free catalog with long SASE ◆ Model engine mounts, mufflers, engine test stands, and accessories. 415-756-3400.

**J-Bar Hobbies,** 117 E. Chicago, Tecumseh, MI 49286: Free information ◆ Plastic models. 517-423-3684.

**Jr. Custom Products,** 140 S. Camino Seco, Unit 415, Tucson, AZ 85710: Free information ◆ Models of famous aircraft. 520-886-3678. members.aol.com/jrcustomindex.html

**K & B Manufacturing Inc.,** 2100 College Dr., Lake Havasu City, AZ 86403: Free information ◆ Airplane and marine engines. 520-453-3030. k&b@inknet.com

**Kress Jets Inc.,** 800 Ulster Landing Rd., Saugerties, NY 12477: Free information ◆ Jet engine and prop propulsion systems. 914-336-8149.

**Kyosho Models,** Great Planes Distributors Company, P.O. Box 9021, Champaign, IL 61826: Free list of retail sources ◆ Boats, cars, airplanes, and helicopters. 800-682-8948. www.hobbies.net/kyosho

**Lanier RC,** P.O. Box 458, Oakwood, GA 30566: Free catalog with long SASE ◆ R/C models, almost ready-to-fly models, and free-flight and R/C gliders. 770-532-6401. www.lanierrc.com

**Lencraft,** P.O. Box 770, Springville, CA 93265: Free list with long SASE ◆ New and out-of-production hard-to-find aircraft kits, decals, and accessories.

**Lite Machines 100+,** 1291 Cumberland Ave., West Lafayette, IN 47906: Free brochure ◆ Easy-to-fly, maintain, and control helicopters. 317-463-0959.

**Major Hobby,** 1520 Corona Dr., Lake Havasu City, AZ 86403: Free information ◆ R/C sailplanes, other aircraft, engines, R/C systems, accessories, and building components. 520-855-7901. www.majorhobby.com

**Megatech,** America's Hobby Center, P.O. Box 32, North Bergen, NJ 07047: Free information ◆ Ready-to-fly 3-channel electric R/C airplanes. www.megatechrc.com

**Micro-X Incorporated,** P.O. Box 1063, Lorain, OH 44055: Catalog $2 ◆ R/C and rubber-powered indoor models. 216-282-8354.

**Midwest Products Company Inc.,** P.O. Box 564, Hobart, IN 46342: Free list of retail sources ◆ Giant scale models and building supplies. 800-348-3497.

**Minimax Enterprise,** P.O. Box 2374, Chelan, WA 98816: Free information ◆ Model gliders. 509-683-1288. minimax@nwi.net

**Model Expo Inc.,** P.O. Box 229140, Hollywood, FL 33022: Catalog $5 (refundable) ◆ Airplane models, automobile and boat kits, wood and plastic ship models, trains, and tools. 800-222-387. www.modelexpoinc.com

**Morris Hobbies,** 4200 Leghorn Dr., Louisville, KY 40218: Free information ◆ R/C acrobatic model aircraft. 800-826-6054. www.morrishobbies.com

**MRC Models,** Model Rectifier Corp., 80 Newfield Ave., Edison, NJ 08837: Free information ◆ Helicopter kits, airplanes, and automobiles. 732-225-2100.

**National Hobby Supply**, 353 Pat Mell Rd., Marietta, GA 30060: Free information ◆ Models and accessories. 800-437-2736.

**O.S. Engines,** Great Planes Distributors Company, P.O. Box 9021, Champaign, IL 61826: Free list of retail sources ◆ Fuel-powered engines. www.osengines.

**OmniModels,** P.O. Box 708, Mahomet, IL 61853: Free information ◆ Airplane models, R/C equipment, engines, accessories, and building supplies. 800-342-6464; 217-398-7738 (in IL).

**Pacific Aeromodel Mfg. Inc.,** 15437 Proctor Ave., City of Industry, CA 91745: Free information ◆ Aircraft model kits and parts. 626-961-6199. www.pacaeromodel.com

**Pacific Aircraft,** 14255 N. 79th St., Scottsdale Airpark, AZ 85260: Free catalog ◆ Handcarved solid mahogany models. 800-950-9944. www.warplanes.com

**Peck-Polymers,** Box 710399, Santee, CA 92072: Catalog $4 ◆ Kits and accessories for rubber-powered flying models. 619-448-1818. www.peck-polymers.com

**Phoenix Model Company,** P.O. Box 15390, Brooksville, FL 34609: Catalog $3 ◆ Aircraft, motorcycles, automobiles, boats, and other models. 352-754-8522.

**Pirate Models,** 13907 Hirschfield, Unit L, Tomball, TX 77375: Free information ◆ Giant scale and jig-built ready-to-assemble kits. 281-351-6617.

**Polk's Model-Craft Hobbies Inc.,** 346 Bergen Ave., Jersey City, NJ 07304: Catalog $2 ◆ Tools, R/C equipment, building supplies, and airplane, car, and boat models. 201-332-8100.

**Proctor Enterprises,** 25450 NE Eilers Rd., Aurora, OR 97002: Catalog $5 (refundable) ◆ R/C model airplane kits and hardware. 503-678-1300.

**Replicas by Tyson,** P.O. Box 159, Covington, OH 45318: Free catalog ◆ Miniature aircraft, ships, rockets, vehicles, and figurines. 937-473-5726. www.replicasbytyson.com

**Rosemont Hobby Shop,** P.O. Box 996, Fogelsville, PA 18051: Free information with long SASE ◆ Scale aircraft models. 610-398-0210.

**Sheldon's Hobbies,** 2135 Old Oakland Rd., San Jose, CA 95131: Free catalog ◆ Airplane models and R/C equipment, engines, accessories, and building supplies. 800-822-1688.

**Showcase Model Company,** P.O. Box 129, Covington, OH 45318: Catalog $5 ◆ Pre-built display aviation, space craft, and ship models. 937-473-5725.

**SIG Manufacturing Company Inc.,** 401 S. Front St., Montezuma, IA 50171: Catalog $3 ◆ R/C, control line, and rubber-powered airplanes. 515-623-5154. www.netins.net/showcase/sig

**Sky Master Industries,** 2440 Colonial Pkwy., Fort Worth, TX 76109: Free catalog with long SASE ◆ Custom handcrafted kits. 817-924-9737.

**Squadron Mail Order,** 1115 Crowley Dr., Carrollton, TX 75011: Catalog $4.50 ◆ Aircraft, ships, and military models. 972-242-8663.

**Standard Hobby Supply,** P.O. Box 801, Mahwah, NJ 07430: Catalog $2 ◆ Ready-to-fly airplanes, off-road buggies, racing cars, other models, and parts. 201-825-2211.

**Technopower II Inc.,** 610 North St., Chagrin Falls, OH 44022: Catalog $3 ◆ Radial gas engines. 216-564-9787. www.technopower.com

**Glen Torrance Models,** 1258 Dogwood Rd., Snellville, GA 30278: Free information ◆ Scale replica models of historical aircraft. 919-846-4816. www.gtmodels.com

**Tower Hobbies,** P.O. Box 9078, Champaign, IL 61826: Catalog $3 ◆ Model airplanes, cars, and boats. Also R/C equipment, engines, and building supplies. 800-637-6050. www.towerhobbies.com

**Vailly Aviation,** 18 Oakdale Ave., Farmingville, NY 11738: Catalog $1 ◆ R/C model airplane kits. 516-732-4715.

**VLS Mail Order,** Lone Star Industrial Park, 811 Lone Star Dr., O'Fallon, MO 63366: Catalog $6 ◆ Aircraft and car models, other models, and military miniatures. 314-281-5700. www.vls-vp.com

**Windsor Propeller Company,** 3219 Monier Circle, Rancho Cordova, CA 95742: Free information ◆ Propellers and electric flight accessories. 916-631-8385. 72673.110@compuserve.com

**Wing Manufacturing,** 306 E. Simmons, Galesburg, IL 61401: Free information ◆ R/C model airplane kits and building materials. 309-342-3009.

**Wings America,** P.O. Box 4701, Carmel, CA 93921: Free catalog ◆ Handmade and finished mahogany aircraft sculptures on desk stands. 800-946-4711.

## Armor & Military Models

**Colpar Hobbies,** 804 S. Havana St., Aurora, CO 80012: Free newsletter with long SASE ◆ Airplanes, armor, automobiles, ships, R/C equipment, parts, and accessories. 800-876-0414. www.colpar.com/
**Dean's Hobby Shop,** 131 E. Main St., Flushing, MI 48433: Free list with long SASE (specify cars, planes, or military models) ◆ Old and collectible model kits. 810-659-2137.

**Hobby Surplus Sales,** P.O. Box 2170, New Britain, CT 06050: Catalog $4 ◆ Aircraft and armor models. 800-233-0872.

**International Hobby Supply,** P.O. Box 426, Woodland Hills. CA 91365: Automotive catalog $3; military catalog $4; science fiction catalog $3 ◆ Plastic model kits, accessories, books, decals, and collectibles. 818-886-0423.

**The Kit Bunker,** 2905 Spring Park Rd., Jacksonville, FL 32207: Catalog $2 with long SASE and 75¢ postage ◆ Out-of-production and current military model kits. 904-399-1911.

**Land, Sea, Air Hobbies,** 30683 Dequindre, Madison Heights, MI 48071: Free information ◆ Military models. 810-585-8011.

**M & Models,** P.O. Box 434, Oak Lawn, IL 60454: Catalog $3 ◆ Military and armor models. 708-423-7202.

**Monsters In Motion,** 330 E. Orangethorpe Ave., #H, Placentia, CA 92870: Catalog $5 ◆ Sci-fi and fantasy movie collectibles, figurines, models, videos, and soundtracks. Also hobby supplies. 714-577-8863. www.monstersinmotion.com

**Pony Toy Go-Round,** 714 Ducommun St., Los Angeles, CA 90012: Free brochure ◆ Comic and science fiction character statuettes and mini-bust models. 213-617-0058.

**SCI-Space Craft International,** P.O. Box 61027, Catalina Station, Pasadena, CA 91116: Free brochure ◆ Easy-to-assemble scale model space craft kits. 800-4-SCI-KITS; 818-793-4233 (in CA). www.scikits.com

**Squadron Mail Order,** 1115 Crowley Dr., Carrollton, TX 75011: Catalog $4.50 ◆ Aircraft, ships, and military models. 972-242-8663.

**Stuempfle's Military Miniatures,** 13190 Scott Rd., Waynesboro, PA 17268: Catalog $4 ◆ Military miniatures. 717-765-0201.

**Triceratops Hill Ranch,** 7868 S. Magnolia Way, Englewood, CO 80112: Free catalog with long SASE ◆ Science fiction, horror, and dinosaur models.

**VLS Mail Order,** Lone Star Industrial Park, 811 Lone Star Dr., O'Fallon, MO 63366: Catalog $6 ◆ Military and aircraft models and miniature military figures. 314-281-5700. www.vls-vp.com

## Automobile & Motorcycle Models

**Accent Models Inc.,** P.O. Box 295, Denville, NJ 07834: Catalog $2 ◆ Collectible car models. 973-887-8403.

**All American Models,** 22 S. 16th St., Lafayette, IN 47905: Free list with long SASE ◆ Resin cast kits and conversions. 765-423-4565.

**America's Hobby Center Inc.,** P.O. Box 829, North Bergen, NJ 07047: Catalog $3 ◆ Car model kits. 201-662-2800.

**American Classics Unlimited,** Frank Troll, President, P.O. Box 192, Oak Lawn, IL 60454: Catalog $1 ◆ Promotional model cars and banks, collectible automobilia, other cars, and kits. 708-424-9223.

**Asheville Diecast,** 1434 Brevard Rd., Asheville, NC 28806: Free information ◆ Die-cast collectible banks, signs and vehicle replicas. 800-343-4685. www.asheville-diecast.com

**Auto Motif Inc.,** 2968 Atlanta Rd., Smyrna, GA 30080: Catalog $3 ◆ Car models, gifts and collectibles with an automotive theme, books, prints, puzzles, office accessories, lamps, original art, and posters. 800-367-1161.

**Auto Toys,** P.O. Box 81385, Bakersfield, CA 93380: Free price list with long SASE ◆ Die-cast racing collectibles, scale car models, and automobilia. 805-588-2277.

**Autofanatics Ltd.,** P.O. Box 55158, Sherman Oaks, CA 91413: List $2 ◆ Scale model automobiles in kits or assembled. 818-788-5440.

**Automobilia,** Division Lustron Industries, 18 Windgate Dr., New City, NY 10956: Free catalog ◆ 1:43 scale die-cast auto models of historic European racecars and classics. 914-639-6806. Lustron@worldnet.att.net

**Benjy's Trains & Toys,** 8715 N. 40th St., Tampa, FL 33604: Free price list with long SASE ◆ Slot cars and accessories, trains, and toys. 813-980-3790.

**Bill & Sharon's Collectables,** 110 S. Main St., Randleman, NC 27317: Free price list with long SASE ◆ Die-cast models. 336-498-8244.

**Bob's Hobby & Collector's Shop,** 115 N. Main St., P.O. Box 796, Watervliet, MI 49098: Catalog $2 (refundable) ◆ Model kits. 616-463-7452.

**Bob's Hobby Center,** 7333 Lake Underhill Rd., Orlando, FL 32822: Free information ◆ R/C airplanes, helicopters, boats, and cars. 407-277-1248.

**Bolink R/C Cars Inc.,** 420 Hosea Rd., Lawrenceville, GA 30245: Catalog $3 ◆ R/C cars, hardware, and parts. 770-963-0252.

**Bruckner Hobbies Inc.,** 2908 Bruckner Blvd., Bronx, NY 10465: Free information ◆ Automobile and airplane kits, R/C equipment, and building supplies. 800-288-8185.

**BSR Replicas & Finishes,** 101 Rainbow Way, Fayetteville, GA 30214: Catalog $1 ◆ NASCAR modeling supplies, kits and resin bodies, and decals. 770-719-8195.

**Cars & Parts Collectibles,** 911 Vandemark Rd., P.O. Box 482, Sidney, OH 45365: Free information ◆ Scale car models. 800-448-3611; 800-327-1259 (in OH).

**CH Racing Enterprises,** P.O. Box 663, Hamburg, NY 14075: Free brochure ◆ Die-cast model NASCAR cars in 1/24 and 1/64 scale, officially licensed NASCAR shirts and other apparel, photos, and books. 716-649-6753. CHRaceEnt@aol.com

**Charles & Son Ltd. Collectibles,** P.O. Box 267, Greenlawn, NY 11740: List $1 ◆ Hot Wheels and Matchbox collectibles. 800-699-8374; 516-261-1523 (in NY).

**Coker Tires,** 1317 Chestnut St., Chattanooga, TN 37402: Free information ◆ Collectible toy trucks. 800-251-6336; 423-265-6368 (in TN). www.coker.com

**Collectible Toy Mart,** 10737 University Ave. NE, Blaine, MN 55434: Free price list ◆ Die-cast auto-related collectibles. 800-325-8481; 612-757-3036 (in MN).

**Colpar Hobbies,** 804 S. Havana St., Aurora, CO 80012: Free newsletter with long SASE ◆ Airplanes, armor, automobiles, ships, R/C equipment, parts, and accessories. 800-876-0414. www.colpar.com

**Cox Hobbies Inc.,** 1925 H St., Penrose, CO 81240: Free list of retail sources ◆ R/C model airplanes and cars. 714-372-6565.

**Dahm's Automobiles,** P.O. Box 360, Cotati, CA 94931: Catalog $4 ◆ Bodies for R/C cars and trucks. 707-792-1316.

**Dave's Die Cast Collectibles,** 15721 Simonds St., Granada Hills, CA 91344: Free list ◆ Die-cast car models. 888-722-3334. www.racing-collectibles.com

**Dean's Hobby Shop,** 214 E. Main St., Flushing, MI 48433: Free list (specify cars or military models) with long SASE and two 1st class stamps ◆ Hard-to-find old and collectible model kits. 810-659-2137.

**Detail Master,** P.O. Box 1465-A, Sterling, VA 20167: Catalog $2 (refundable) ◆ Precision scale model car accessories.

**Direct Hobby Supply Center,** P.O. Box 743, Nashville, NC 27856: Catalog $3 ◆ Plastic automobile kits, airbrushes, resin bodies, tools, decals, and supplies. 919-937-1014.

**Eastwood Automobilia,** 580 Lancaster Ave., P.O. Box 3014, Malvern, PA 19355: Free catalog ◆ Transportation collectibles. 800-343-9353. www.ewab.com

**Evers Toy Store,** 204 1st Ave. East, Dyersville, IA 52040: Free information with long SASE ◆ Model cars and airplanes. 800-962-9481.

**EWA & Miniature Cars USA,** 205 US Hwy. 22, Green Brook, NJ 08812: Catalog $6 ◆ Die-cast models, metal and plastic kits, other model cars, books and magazines, videos, and collectibles. 800-392-4454. www.ewacars.com

**Exoticar Model Company,** 2 New York Ave., Framingham, MA 01701: Free catalog ◆ Die-cast model cars. 800-348-9159.

**Fantastic Plastics,** 1933 Hay Terrace, Easton, PA 18042: Catalog $2 (refundable) ◆ New, current, discontinued, and other kits. 610-923-7534.

**The Good Stuff,** P.O. Box 131351, Roseville, MN 55113: Free catalog with long SASE ◆ Resin bodies and parts. 612-566-9540.

**Hobby Heaven,** P.O. Box 3229, Grand Rapids, MI 49501: Free catalog with long SASE and $1.01 postage ◆ Ready-to-build model automobiles, from the 1950s, 1960s, and 1970s. 616-453-1094.

**Hobby House Inc.,** 30991 Five Mile Rd., Livonia, MI 48154: Free information ◆ Model cars and supplies. 313-425-9720.

**Hobby Shack,** 18480 Bandilier Circle, Fountain Valley, CA 92728: Free catalog ◆ R/C equipment and ready-to-assemble airplanes and automobiles. 800-854-8471. www.hobbyshack.com

**Hobby Surplus Sales,** P.O. Box 2170, New Britain, CT 06050: Catalog $4 ◆ Planes, cars, ships, model trains, R/C models, and craft supplies. 800-233-0872.

**Hobby Warehouse of Sacramento,** 8950 Osage Ave., Sacramento, CA 95828: Free information ◆ R/C automobiles and kits. 916-381-7588.

**International Hobby Supply,** P.O. Box 426, Woodland Hills. CA 91365: Automotive catalog $3; military catalog $4; science fiction catalog $3 ◆ Plastic model kits, accessories, books, decals, and collectibles. 818-886-0423.

**Kyosho Models,** Great Planes Distributors Company, P.O. Box 9021, Champaign, IL 61826: Free list of retail sources ◆ Boats, cars, airplanes, and helicopters. 800-682-8948. www.hobbies.net/kyosho

**Long Island Train & Hobby Center,** 192 Jericho Tnpk., Mineola, NY 11501: Price list $3 ◆ Car models. 516-742-5621.

**Merkel Model Car Company,** 9564 W. Grand Ave., Franklin Park, IL 60131: Catalog $2.95 each (specify type of car model) ◆ Collectible and current car model kits, promotional and pre-assembled cars, die-cast models, and building supplies. 847-455-1495.

**Mill City Replicas,** P.O. Box 40, Carver, MN 55315: Free catalog with two 1st class stamps ◆ Hand-cast resin conversions for existing kits.

**Miniatures of the World Inc.,** 104 May Dr., Harrison, OH 45030: Catalog $3 ◆ Trucks, motorcycles, fire trucks, farm and construction equipment, collectibles, and racing, performance, exotic, and sports cars. 513-367-1746.

**The Model Car Garage,** 2908 SE Bella Rd., Port St. Lucie, FL 34984: Catalog $2 with long SASE and two 1st class stamps ◆ Automotive modeling detailing accessories. 561-343-0494.

**Model Empire,** 7116 W. Greenfield Ave., West Allis, WI 53214: Catalog $3 (refundable with $20 order) ◆ Cars, trucks, figures, racers, space and military models, boats, airplanes, and die-cast models. 414-453-4610.

**Model Expo Inc.,** P.O. Box 229140, Hollywood, FL 33022: Catalog $5 (refundable) ◆ Scale models of legendary automobiles in kits or assembled. 800-222-387. www.modelexpoinc.com

**Model Kit Hobbies,** P.O. Box 1012, Clearfield, PA 16830: Catalog $2 ◆ Kits, decals, paints, tools, and supplies. 888-MODEL-KT; 814-768-7899(in PA).

**The Model Shop,** P.O. Box 68, Onalaska, WI 54650: Catalog $3 ◆ Model cars, trucks, and hobby supplies. 608-781-1864.

**Motor City U.S.A.,** 13400 Satcoy St., #12, North Hollywood, CA 91605: Free brochure ◆ Scale model automobiles. 818-503-4835.

**Motorhead Art & Collectibles,** 1917 Dumas Circle NE, Tacoma, WA 98422: Catalog $5 ◆ Scale models and kits, art prints, and collectibles. 800-859-0164.

**Mountain State Hobby Supply,** P.O. Box 356, Teays, WV 25569: Catalog $3 ◆ Model car kits and supplies. 304-757-3242.

**MRC Models,** Model Rectifier Corp., 80 Newfield Ave., Edison, NJ 08837: Free information ◆ Helicopter kits, airplanes, and automobiles. 732-225-2100.

**Munchkin Motors,** P.O. Box 266, Eastford, CT 06242: Catalog $3 ◆ Collectible miniature cars. 860-974-2545.

**North Coast Miniature Motors,** 3724 W. 32nd St., Erie, PA 16506: Free information ◆ Antique, classic, racing, promotional models, die-cast, and handbuilt automotive miniatures. 814-838-1921.

**North Coast Racing,** 7280 Noble Rd., Windsor, OH 44099: Free price list ◆ Die-cast models. 216-272-5541.

**Novak Electronics Inc.,** 18910 Teller Ave., Irvine, CA 92715: Free list of retail sources ◆ One-touch set-up speed controls. 714-833-8873.

**Past-Time Hobbies Inc.,** 9311 Ogden Ave., Brookfield, IL 60513: Free information with long SASE ◆ American model cars. 708-485-4544.

**Performance Miniatures,** 118 N. Black Horse Pike, Bellmawr, NJ 08031: Free catalog ◆ Die-cast cars. 800-931-1227.

**Phoenix Model Company,** P.O. Box 15390, Brooksville, FL 34609: Catalog $3 ◆ Aircraft, motorcycles, automobiles, boats, and other models. 352-754-8522.

**Photorific,** 10815 SW 57th Ave., Portland, OR 97219: Free catalog ◆ Racing car models. 503-245-7194.

**Pit Stop Racing Collectibles,** 415 N. Main St., Ste. 106, Euless, TX 76039: Free list ◆ Collectible die-cast model cars and banks. 817-354-7657. www.pitstopracing.com

**Polk's Model-Craft Hobbies Inc.,** 346 Bergen Ave., Jersey City, NJ 07304: Catalog $2 ◆ Tools, R/C equipment, and airplane, car, and boat models. 201-332-8100.

**Neal Pope Inc.,** 4420 Buford Hwy. NE, Atlanta, GA 30341: Free information ◆ Die-cast models. 770-455-7673.

**Quality Steins & Collectibles,** Box 762, Bowling Green, OH 43402: Free catalog ◆ Collectible automotive models. 419-353-6847.

**Ranch Pit Shop,** 1655 E. Mission Blvd., Pomona, CA 91766: Free catalog ◆ Automobiles and accessories. 909-623-1506.

**Replicarz,** 99 State St., Rutland, VT 05701: Free catalog ◆ Die-cast and plastic scale models of racing and street cars. 802-747-7151.

**Sentinel Miniatures,** 4 Broadway, Valhalla, NY 10595: Catalog $9 ◆ Military, historical, fantasy figure kits, and die-cast cars. Also HO and N scale trains. 914-682-3932.

**Sheldon's Hobbies,** 2135 Old Oakland Rd., San Jose, CA 95131: Free catalog ◆ Automobiles and accessories. 800-822-1688.

**Sinclair's Auto Miniatures,** P.O. Box 8403, Erie, PA 16505: Catalog $2 ◆ Die-cast and handcrafted miniature cars. 814-838-2274.

**Southside Hobbys,** 1950 E. Springhill Dr., Terre Haute, IN 47802: Catalog $4 ◆ Model car kits and supplies. 800-782-4164.

**Specialty Diecast Company,** 370 Miller Rd., Medford, NJ 08055: Free information ◆ Die-cast models. 800-432-1933.

**Standard Hobby Supply,** P.O. Box 801, Mahwah, NJ 07430: Catalog $2 ◆ Ready-to-fly airplanes, off-road buggies and cars, racing cars, and parts. 201-825-2211.

**Stormer Racing,** P.O. Box 126, Glasgow, MT 59230: Free information ◆ Kits and parts for R/C automobiles. 800-255-7223.

**Tower Hobbies,** P.O. Box 9078, Champaign, IL 61826: Catalog $3 ◆ Model airplanes, cars, and boats. Also R/C equipment, engines, and building supplies. 800-637-6050. www.towerhobbies.com

**The Upper Groove,** 2490 Black Rock Tnpk., #419, Fairfield, CT 06430: Catalog $4 ◆ Car model kits. 203-384-1008.

**Valley Plaza Hobbies,** 3633 Research Way, Unit 104, Carson City, NV 89706: Catalog $6 ◆ Miniature car models. 702-887-1131.

**Wheel to Wheel Hobbies,** 508 Loch Alsh Ave., Ambler, PA 19002: Catalog $2 (refundable) ◆ Models, decals, tools, parts, and accessories. 215-643-3398.

## Dioramas

**Armand P. Bayardi-Model Maker,** P.O. Box 50, Penns Park, PA 18943: Catalog $3 ◆ Diorama accessories and architectural components. 215-598-8102.

**Hansa Plastics,** 8 Meadow Glen Rd., Kings Park, NY 11754: Catalog $5 (refundable) ◆ Scale building components. 516-269-9050.

**Scale Equipment Ltd.,** P.O. Box 20715, Bradenton, FL 34203: Catalog $5 (refundable) ◆ Diorama-making supplies and scale model kits for doll houses and automotive and railroad projects. 941-751-6584. seltd1@aol.com

## Flying Saucers

**Information Unlimited,** P.O. Box 716, Amherst, NH 03031: Catalog $1 ◆ Lasers, communication equipment, Tesla coils and experiments, mini radios, rocket equipment, flying saucers, and other kits. 603-673-4730. www.amazing1.com

## Radio Control Equipment

**Ace R/C,** 116 W. 19th St., P.O. Box 472, Higginsville, MO 64037: Catalog $2 ◆ R/C model airplane equipment. 816-584-7121.

**America's Hobby Center Inc.,** P.O. Box 829, North Bergen, NJ 07047: Catalog $3 ◆ Model airplanes, R/C equipment, and tools. 201-662-2800.

**Balsa USA,** P.O. Box 164, Marinette, WI 54143: Catalog $1 ◆ Balsa wood, tools, and R/C models. 800-225-7287; 906-863-6421 (in WI). www.balsausa.com

**Bruckner Hobbies Inc.,** 2908 Bruckner Blvd., Bronx, NY 10465: Free information ◆ Airplane and automobile kits, R/C equipment, and building supplies. 800-288-8185.

**Colpar Hobbies,** 804 S. Havana St., Aurora, CO 80012: Free newsletter with long SASE ◆ Airplanes, armor, automobiles, ships, R/C equipment, parts, and accessories. 800-876-0414. www.colpar.com

**Custom Electronics,** RR 1, Box 123B, Higginsville, MO 64037: Free information ◆ Electronic support equipment for R/C systems. 816-584-6284.

**Danielle's R/C Specialists,** 3141 Ambrose Ave., Nashville, TN 37207: Free information ◆ R/C planes, helicopters, and equipment. 800-235-6253.

**Draganfly Innovations Inc.,** 1206 Coy Ave., Saskatoon, Sask., Canada S7M 0H1: Free brochure ◆ Remote R/C flying saucers. 306-931-0055. www.draganfly.com

**Futaba Corp. of America,** P.O. Box 19767, Irvine, CA 92723: Free information ◆ R/C systems for cars, trucks, and buggies. 714-455-9888.

**Hitec,** 10729 Wheatlands Ave., Santee, CA 92071: Free list of retail sources ◆ R/C systems. 619-258-4940. www.hitecrcd.com

**Hobby Shack,** 18480 Bandilier Circle, Fountain Valley, CA 92708: Free catalog ◆ R/C equipment. 800-854-8471. www.hobbyshack.com

**Hobby World,** 523 Sinclair Frontage Rd., Milpitas, CA 95035: Free information ◆ Airplane kits, engines, and R/C equipment. 408-946-7201.

**Horizon Hobby Distributors,** 4105 Fieldstone Rd., Champaign, IL 61821: Free information ◆ R/C systems. 217-355-9511. www.horizonhobby.com

**McDaniel R.C. Inc.,** 1654 Crofton Blvd., Ste. 4, Crofton, MD 21114: Free information ◆ Accessories for R/C systems. 410-721-6303.

**MTA Hobbies,** 2341 W. 205th St., Ste. 115, Torrance, CA 90501: Free information ◆ Helicopters and R/C equipment. 800-952-2143.

**Northeast Sailplane Products,** 16 Kirby Ln., Williston, VT 05495: Catalog $7 ◆ R/C and electric flight sailplanes and accessories. 802-658-9482. salnsp@together.net

**Ohio R/C Models,** 30 W. Lincoln Ave., Miamisburg, OH 45342: Free catalog ◆ R/C models, parts, and accessories. 937-859-1660. ohiorcmds@aol.com

**SR Batteries Inc.,** Box 287, Bellport, NY 11713: Information $3 ◆ Batteries. 516-286-0079.

**Jack Stafford Models,** 383 Chicago Rd., Coldwater, MI 49036: Catalog $2 ◆ Scale R/C airplane kits. 517-279-9380.

**Jim Walston,** Retrieval Systems, 725 Cooper Lake Rd., South East Smyrna, GA 30082: Free catalog ◆ Retrieval systems. 800-657-4672; 770-434-4905 (in GA).

## Rocket Models

**Apogee Components Inc.,** 1431 Territory Trail, Colorado Springs, CO 80919: Catalog $2 ◆ Model rocket components, kits, design software, and supplies. 719-548-5075. www.Apogeerockets.com

**Commonwealth Displays,** 12649 Dix-Toledo Rd., Southgate, MI 48195: Catalog $2 ◆ Rocketry supplies. 313-282-1055.

**Countdown Hobbies,** 3 P.T. Barnum Square, Bethel, CT 06801: Catalog $2.50 ◆ Rocket and space flight equipment. 203-790-9010.

**Merrell Scientific/World of Science,** 900 Jefferson Rd., Bldg. 4, Rochester, NY 14623: Catalog $2 ◆ Rockets, engines, and igniters. Also chemicals, laboratory glassware, and equipment for biology, chemistry, physical and earth science, and astronomy experiments. 716-475-0100. www.roccplex.com/wos

**Public Missiles Ltd.,** 349 Cass Ave., Mt. Clemens, MI 48043: Catalog $3 ◆ Rocket kits, accessories, and modeling supplies. 810-468-1748. www.publicmissiles.com

**Vaughn Brothers Rocketry,** 4575 Ross Dr., Paso Robles, CA 93446: Catalog $1 ◆ Rocket kits and accessories. 805-239-3818.

## Ship Models

**AC Model Boats,** P.O. Box 23041, Plaza 33 Postal Outlet, Kelowna, British Columbia, Canada V1X 7K7: Price list $2 ◆ Catamarans, hydrofoils, and tunnel and vee hulls. 250-765-7730.

**America's Hobby Center Inc.,** P.O. Box 829, North Bergen, NJ 07047: Catalog $3 ◆ Ship building kits. 201-662-2800.

**American Marine Model Gallery,** 12 Derby Square, Salem, MA 01970: Catalog $10 ◆ One-of-a-kind rare antique ship models. 978-745-5777.

**Bluejacket Ship Crafters,** P.O. Box 425, Stockton Springs, ME 04981: Catalog $2 (refundable) ◆ Kits, fittings, supplies, and tools. 800-448-5567.

**Bob's Hobby Center,** 7333 Lake Underhill Rd., Orlando, FL 32822: Free information ◆ R/C airplanes, helicopters, boats, and cars. 407-277-1248.

**Colpar Hobbies,** 804 S. Havana St., Aurora, CO 80012: Free newsletter with long SASE ◆ Airplanes, armor, automobiles, ships, R/C equipment, parts, and accessories. 800-876-0414. www.colpar.com

**The Dromedary,** Ship Modeler's Center, 6324 Belton Dr., El Paso, TX 79912: Catalog $6 ◆ Working or static ship models, fittings, and supplies for most types of ships and boats. 915-584-2445.

**Dumas Boats,** 909 E. 17th St., Tucson, AZ 85719: Free catalog ◆ R/C models. 800-458-2828.

**The Floating Drydock,** c/o General Delivery, Kresgeville, PA 18333: Free catalog ◆ Plans, kits, books, fittings, and other supplies. www.usbusiness.com/drydock

**Hobby Barn,** P.O. Box 17856, Tucson, AZ 85731: Free catalog ◆ Boat and airplane models. 520-747-3792.

**Hobby House Inc.,** 30991 Five Mile Rd., Livonia, MI 48154: Free information ◆ Model boats, fittings, supplies, and tools. 313-425-9720.

**Hobby Surplus Sales,** P.O. Box 2170, New Britain, CT 06050: Catalog $4 ◆ Planes, cars, ships, trains, and R/C models. 800-233-0872.

**Hobby World Ltd. of Montreal,** 5450 Sherbrooke St. West, Montreal, Quebec, Canada H4A 1V9: Catalog $5 ◆ Airplanes, helicopters, cars and trucks, ships, military vehicles, and science models. 514-481-5434.

**International Marine Exchange,** 37 Addington Dr., Feasterville, PA 19053: Catalog $5 ◆ Model ships, fittings, and more. 215-322-4773.

**K & B Manufacturing Inc.,** 2100 College Dr., Lake Havasu City, AZ 86403: Free information ◆ Airplane and marine engines. 520-453-3030. k&b@inknet.com

**Kyosho Models,** Great Planes Distributors Company, P.O. Box 9021, Champaign, IL 61826: Free list of retail sources ◆ Boats, cars, airplanes, and helicopters. 800-682-8948. www.hobbies.net/kyosho

**The Maritime Store,** 2905 Hyde St. Pier, San Francisco, CA 94109: Free catalog ◆ Maritime maps and books, greeting cards, boat models, children's books, and gifts. 415-775-BOOK.

**Model Boats Unlimited,** P.O. Box 1135, Haddonfield, NJ 08033: Catalog $11 ◆ R/C and other boats, electric and sailboat accessories, fittings, and supplies. 609-783-9163.

**Model Expo Inc.,** P.O. Box 229140, Hollywood, FL 33022: Catalog $5 (refundable) ◆ Airplane models, automobile and boat kits, wood and plastic ship models, trains, and tools. 800-222-387. www.modelexpoinc.com

**Nature Coast Hobby Shop,** 6773 S. Hancock Rd., Homosassa, FL 34448: Free information ◆ Wood and plastic ship model kits, books, tools, and supplies. 800-714-9478; 352-628-3990 (in FL). www.naturecoast.com/hobby

**The Naval Base,** P.O. Box 207, Cedarhurst, NY 11516: Catalog $4 ◆ Plastic ships. 718-471-3226.

**Octura Models Inc.,** 7351 N. Hamlin Ave., Skokie, IL 60076: Free information with long SASE ◆ R/C boats. 847-674-7351.

**Phoenix Model Company,** P.O. Box 15390, Brooksville, FL 34609: Catalog $3 ◆ Aircraft, motorcycles, automobiles, boats, and other models. 352-754-8522.

**Polk's Model-Craft Hobbies Inc.,** 346 Bergen Ave., Jersey City, NJ 07304: Catalog $2 ◆ Tools, R/C equipment, building supplies, and airplane, car, and boat models. 201-332-8100.

**Prather Products Inc.,** 1660 Ravenna Ave., Wilmington, CA 90744: Catalog $2 ◆ High-performance epoxy glass boats. 562-835-4764.

**Preston's,** Main Street Wharf, Greenport, NY 11944: Free catalog ◆ Ship models. 800-836-1165.

**Seacraft Classics,** 7850 E. Evans Rd., Ste. 109, Scottsdale, AZ 85260: Free catalog ◆ Handmade detailed models of 19th-century ships and boats with hardwood display stands and brass name plates. 800-356-1987; 602-998-4988 (in AZ).

**Seaworthy Small Ships,** P.O. Box 2863, Prince Frederick, MD 20678: Catalog $1 ◆ Wooden model boat kits with pre-cut and pre-drilled parts. 410-586-2700. www.azinet.com/seaw.html

**Ships N' Things,** P.O. Box 605, Somerville, NJ 08876: Catalog $5 (refundable with $25 order) ◆ Competition boats and hardware. 908-722-0075.

**Shoreline Design Racing Team,** 6864 SW 114th Pl., Bldg. F, Miami, FL 33173: Free brochure ◆ Easy-to-control racing boats. 305-252-8414.

**Squadron Mail Order,** 1115 Crowley Dr., Carrollton, TX 75011: Catalog $4.50 ◆ Aircraft, ships, and military models. 972-242-8663.

**Swampworks Mfg.,** 1810 N. Farm Rd. 197, Springfield, MO 65802: Video catalog $6 ◆ Warship kits, drive gear, bilge pumps, BB cannons, and carbon dioxide delivery systems for R/C models. 417-831-2309.

**Tower Hobbies,** P.O. Box 9078, Champaign, IL 61826: Catalog $3 ◆ Model airplanes, cars, and boats. Also R/C equipment, engines, and building supplies. 800-637-6050. www.towerhobbies.com

**Toys for Big Boys,** 2358 E. Orangethorpe Ave., Anaheim, CA 92806: Catalog $4.50 ◆ High-performance R/C boats, hardware, engines, and racing accessories. 714-449-2242. www.toys4BigBoys.com

**Trinity Products Inc.,** 1901 E. Linden Ave., Linden, NJ 07036: Free catalog with long SASE ◆ Electric motors and cooling units for model boats. 908-862-1705.

**Victor Model Products,** 12260 Woodruff Ave., Downey, CA 90241: Free brochure with long SASE ◆ R/C sailing yachts. 562-803-1897.

**Warehouse Hobbies,** 1180 C.R. 621 East, Lake Placid, FL 33852: Catalog $2 ◆ Ready-to-run gasoline-powered model boats. 941-699-1231.

## Steam-Operated Models & Engine Kits

**Allen Models,** 5994 Cuesta Verde, Goleta, CA 93117: Catalog $4 ◆ Steam-operated locomotives. 805-967-2095.

**Coles' Power Models Inc.,** P.O. Box 788, 839 E. Front St., Ventura, CA 93001: Catalog $5 ◆ Steam and gas engine castings and fittings, tools, metals, books, and model engineering supplies. 805-643-7065.

**Diamond Enterprises,** Box 537, Alexandria Bay, NY 13607: Catalog $6.95 (refundable) ◆ Kits or assembled live steam models. 800-481-1353.

**Graham Industries,** P.O. Box 15230, Rio Rancho, NM 87174: Free brochure ◆ Twin cylinder vertical reversing steam engine kit.

**Hartland Scale Models,** Box 120, New Norway, AB, Canada T0B 3L0: Catalog $4 ◆ Steam traction engines and other models. 403-855-3921.

**The Locomotive Works,** 131 La Grande Ave., Moss Beach, CA 94038: Catalog $8.50 ◆ Steam-operated model locomotives and accessories. 650-728-1852.

**M.T.H. Electric Trains,** 9693 Gerwig Ln., Columbia, MD 21046: Free list of retail sources ◆ Live steam, ready-to-run, trains and kits. 800-640-3700.

**Power Model Supply Company,** 13260 Summit Dr., De Soto, MO 63020: Catalog $5 ◆ Steam engines, parts, and accessories. 314-586-6466.

**Sulphur Springs Steam Models Ltd.,** P.O. Box 6165, Chesterfield, MO 63006: Catalog $3 ◆ Engineering supplies for steam-operated models. 314-527-8326. www.steamup.com/sulphur

**Superscale Locomotive Company,** 367-A Beckett Pl., Grover Beach, CA 93433: Catalog $9 ◆ Accessories for steam models.

**Tiny Power,** Steam Engines & Supplies, P.O. Box 1605, Branson, MO 65615: Catalog $5 ◆ Steam engines and pumps. 417-334-2655.

**Yesteryear Toys & Books Inc.,** Box 537, Alexandria Bay, NY 13607: Catalog $6.95 (refundable) ◆ Working steam engine models. Available assembled or as kits. 800-481-1353. www.yesteryeartoys.com

## Supplies, Hardware, & Plans

**Autogyro Company of Arizona,** 3307 W. Renee Dr., Phoenix, AZ 85027: Free information with long SASE ◆ Plans for scale R/C autogyros. 602-582-9428. giroman@prodigy.net

**Balsa USA,** P.O. Box 164, Marinette, WI 54143: Free information ◆ Balsa wood, tools, and R/C models. 800-225-7287; 906-863-6421 (in WI). www.balsausa.com

**Dave Brown Products,** 4560 Layhigh Rd., Hamilton, OH 45013: Free information ◆ R/C airplane equipment and building materials. 513-738-1576. www.dbproducts.com

**Bruckner Hobbies Inc.,** 2908 Bruckner Blvd., Bronx, NY 10465: Free information ◆ Airplane and automobile kits, R/C equipment, and building supplies. 800-288-8185.

**Direct Hobby Supply Center,** P.O. Box 743, Nashville, NC 27856: Catalog $3 ◆ Plastic automobile kits, airbrushes, resin bodies, tools, decals, and supplies. 919-937-1014.

**Du-Bro Products,** 480 Bonner Rd., P.O. Box 815, Wauconda, IL 60084: Free information ◆ Hardware, tools, and building supplies. 800-848-9411.

**F & M Enterprises,** 22522 Auburn Dale Dr., El Toro, CA 92630: Information $1 ◆ Easy-to-apply covering. 714-583-1455. www.stits.com

**Gallant Models Inc.,** P.O. Box 2459, Capistrano Beach, CA 92624: Catalog $2 ◆ Model building plans. 714-496-5411.

**Hobby Shack,** 18480 Bandilier Circle, Fountain Valley, CA 92728: Free catalog ◆ Model-making supplies and tools. 800-854-8471. www.hobbyshack.com

**Wendell Hostetler Plans,** 1041 Heatherwood, Orrville, OH 44667: Free information with long SASE ◆ Giant scale plans. 330-682-8896. www.aero-sports.com/whplans

**K & S Engineering,** 6917 W. 59th St., Chicago, IL 60638: Catalog $1 ◆ Aluminum and other metal tubes, rods, and sheets for model building. 312-586-8503.

**Kress Jets Inc.,** 800 Ulster Landing Rd., Saugerties, NY 12477: Free information ◆ Scale model aircraft plans. 914-336-8149.

**Lone Star Models,** Rt. 9, Box 437, Lubbock, TX 79423: Catalog $1 ◆ Balsa wood, plywood, basswood, model airplanes, and accessories. 806-745-6394.

**MCW Automotive Finishes,** Box 518, Burlington, NC 27216: Information $1 with long SASE ◆ Authentic model paints for American cars, from the 1930s to the 1990s.

**Midwest Products Company Inc.,** P.O. Box 564, Hobart, IN 46342: Free list of retail sources ◆ Giant scale model airplanes and building supplies. 800-348-3497.

**Miniatronics,** 561 Acorn St., Deer Park, NY 11729: Free catalog with long SASE ◆ Miniature electrical supplies for the hobbyist. 800-942-9439.

**Model Electronics Corp.,** 14550 20th Ave. NE, Seattle, WA 98155: Catalog $3 ◆ Electric-powered flight motors. 206-440-5772.

**Northeastern Scale Models Inc.,** P.O. Box 727, Methuen, MA 01844: Catalog $1 ◆ Basswood and supplies for building models and doll houses. 978-688-6019.

**Palmer Plans,** 6047 Pomegranate Ln., Woodland Hills, CA 91367: Catalog $2 with long SASE ◆ Precision scale aircraft plans. 818-348-0879. www.mag-web.com/rc-modeler/palmer

**Plastruct,** 1020 S. Wallace Pl., City of Industry, CA 91748: Catalog $2 ◆ Scratch-building model parts and kits.

**Preston's Car Parts,** 7221 White Eagle Dr., Fort Wayne, IN 46815: Catalog $1 ◆ Scale model accessories. 219-493-2032.

**Proctor Enterprises,** 25450 NE Eilers Rd., Aurora, OR 97002: Catalog $5 (refundable) ◆ R/C model airplane kits and hardware. 503-678-1300.

**Robart Manufacturing,** P.O. Box 1247, St. Charles, IL 60174: Free catalog with long SASE ◆ Model airplane accessories and tools. 630-584-7616.

**SIG Manufacturing Company Inc.,** 401 S. Front St., Montezuma, IA 50171: Catalog $3 ◆ Balsa wood. 515-623-5154. www.netins.net/showcase/sig

**Special Shapes Company,** P.O. Box 7487, Romeoville, IL 60446: Catalog $2 ◆ Structural brass shapes for model building. 630-759-1970.

**Superior Balsa & Hobby Supply,** 12020 Centralia, Hawaiian Gardens, CA 90716: Free catalog with long SASE ◆ Balsa wood, birch, plywood, and other building materials. 800-488-9525.

**Nick Ziroli Plans,** 29 Edgar Dr., Smithtown, NY 11787: Catalog $2 ◆ Giant scale model airplane plans and accessories. 516-467-4765.

## Tools

**Badger Air-Brush Company,** 9128 W. Belmont, Franklin Park, IL 60131: Brochure $1 ◆ Tools and supplies for building models. 800-247-2787. www.badger-airbrush.com

**Campbell Tools Company,** 2100 Selma Rd., Springfield, OH 45505: Catalog $2 ◆ Lathes, mills, taps, dies, micrometers, cutting tools, miniature screws, and brass, aluminum, steel, and other supplies. 937-322-8562.

**Dremel Moto-Tool,** P.O. Box 468, Racine, WI 53406: Free information ◆ Power tools for modelers. 414-554-1390. www.dremel.com

**Du-Bro Products,** 480 Bonner Rd., P.O. Box 815, Wauconda, IL 60084: Free information ◆ Hardware, tools, and building supplies. 800-848-9411.

**Griffin Manufacturing Company Inc.,** 1656 Ridge Rd. East, P.O. Box 308, Webster, NY 14580: Free catalog ◆ Cutters, knives, blades, and tools. 716-265-1991.

**Hobby Hangar,** 1862 Petersburg Rd., Hebron, KY 41048: Catalog $2 ◆ Precision power tools for model building. 800-611-3860. www.hobbyhangar.com

**In Scale,** P.O. Box 5267, Eureka, CA 95502: Catalog $1 ◆ Hobby supplies, kits, miniature jewelers and scratch-building tools, and accessories. 707-445-9435.

**International Hobby Corp.,** 413 E. Allegheny Ave., Philadelphia, PA 19134: Catalog $4.98 ◆ Battery-powered tools, model airplanes, railroading accessories, and military miniatures. 800-875-1600.

**K & S Engineering,** 6917 W. 59th St., Chicago, IL 60638: Catalog $1 ◆ Precision tools. 312-586-8503.

**Mascot Precision Tools,** 750 Washington Ave., Carlstadt, NJ 07072: Free catalog ◆ Precision tools for the hobbyist and craftsman. 800-847-4188. www.w-s-o.com/MascotPrecisionTools/index.htm

**Micro-Mark,** 340 Snyder Ave., Berkeley Heights, NJ 07922: Catalog $1 ◆ Miniature and standard size tools. 800-225-1066. www.micromark.com

**Model Expo Inc.,** P.O. Box 229140, Hollywood, FL 33022: Catalog $5 (refundable) ◆ Airplane models, automobile and boat kits, wood and plastic ship models, trains, and tools. 800-222-387. www.modelexpoinc.com

**Polk's Model-Craft Hobbies Inc.,** 346 Bergen Ave., Jersey City, NJ 07304: Catalog $2 ◆ Modeling tools and supplies, R/C equipment, and airplanes, cars, and boats. 201-332-8100.

**Robart Manufacturing,** P.O. Box 1247, St. Charles, IL 60174: Free catalog with long SASE ◆ Model airplane accessories and tools. 630-584-7616.

**Sherline Products Inc.,** 170 Navajo St., San Marcos, CA 92069: Free catalog ◆ Precision-made miniature power-operated tools. 800-541-0735.

**Warehouse Hobbies,** 1180 C.R. 621 East, Lake Placid, FL 33852: Catalog $2 ◆ Three-in-one milling, drilling, and lathe machine shop for model builders. 941-699-1231.

**Xuron Corp.,** 60 Industrial Park Rd., Saco, ME 04072: Free catalog ◆ Precision cutting tools and construction aids. 207-283-1401.

## Train Models

**Accurate Dimensions,** 4185 S. Fox St., Englewood, CO 80110: Free brochure with long SASE ◆ Z, N, HO, O, and S scale trees for scenery settings. 303-762-0460.

**Allied Model Trains,** 4411 S. Sepulveda Blvd., Culver City, CA 90230: Catalog $1 ◆ Brass HO and N equipment, detail parts, tools, and supplies. 310-313-9353.

**America's Hobby Center Inc.,** P.O. Box 829, North Bergen, NJ 07047: Catalog $3 ◆ Kits and equipment for building train layouts. 201-662-2800.

**Amro Ltd.,** 121 Lincolnway West, New Oxford, PA 17350: Catalog $3 ◆ Foreign railway models. 717-624-8920.

**Aristo-Craft,** Polk's Model Craft Hobbies Inc., 346 Bergen Ave., Jersey City, NJ 07304: Catalog $2 ◆ Scale trestle sets, water towers, bridges, and more. 201-332-8100. www.aristocraft.com/aristo

**Artista Accessories,** 1616 S. Franklin St., Philadelphia, PA 19148: Free information with long SASE ◆ O and O27-gauge metal figures and accessories. 800-316-2493; 215-467-2493 (in PA).

**Benjy's Trains & Toys,** 8715 N. 40th St., Tampa, FL 33604: Free price list with long SASE ◆ Slot cars and accessories, trains, and toys. 813-980-3790.

**Myron J. Biggar Group,** P.O. Box 239, 65 S. Broad St., Nazareth, PA 18064: Free brochure ◆ O gauge easy-to-build kits for customizing layouts. 610-759-0406. members.aol.com/Ogaugerwy/OGR.html

**Blackstone Valley Railway,** 54 Juniper Rd., Tomah, WI 54660: Free information ◆ Custom built wood bridges in HO, S, and O scales. 608-372-7467.

**Bookbinder's Trains Unlimited,** P.O. Box 660086, Flushing, NY 11366: Catalog $5 ◆ Lionel standard and O-gauge trains. 718-657-2224.

**British Trains,** 1070 Thornwood Ln., Dacula, GA 30211: HO/OO scale catalog $3; N scale catalog $2 ◆ British trains and accessories. 770-995-5720.

**The Building & Structure Company,** Box 1296, Fenton, MO 63026: Free brochure ◆ S, HO, and O scale structure kits. Also rolling stock parts and accessories. 618-624-6909.

**Caboose Hobbies,** 500 S. Broadway, Denver, CO 80209: Free information ◆ Z and G scale model trains and books. 303-777-6766. www.caboosehobbies.com

**The Candy Store,** 8 E. Main St., Bozeman, MT 59715: Free list ◆ Train models and sets. 800-682-2639; 406-585-9737 (in MT). www.Montana.avicom.net/candystore

**Cannonball Ltd.,** 211 NE 38th St., Oklahoma City, OK 73105: Catalog $7 ◆ Large scale trains. 405-524-4400.

**Champion Decal Company,** P.O. Box 1178, Minot, ND 58702: Catalog $5 ◆ HO and O scale model railroad decals. 701-852-4938. www.minot.com/~champ

**City Streets,** P.O. Box 269, Ridgewood, NJ 07451: Catalog sheets with long SASE and $1 ◆ HO scale recreations of vintage period signs.

**Colibri's,** 5600 W. Lovers Ln., Ste. 139, Dallas, TX 75209: Free information ◆ Trains and accessories. 972-352-3394.

**Dallee Electronics,** 10 Witmer Rd., Lancaster, PA 17602: Catalog $6.50 ◆ Electronic control equipment for model railroads. 717-392-1705.

**Davis Electronics' Electric Trains,** 217 Main St., Milford, OH 45150: Free price list ◆ Trains and accessories. 800-663-4680.

**Daylight Distributors,** 4411 Sepulveda Blvd., Culver City, CA 90230: HO gauge catalog $10; N gauge catalog $8; both catalogs $15 ◆ HO and N scale 2-rail systems. 310-313-9370.

**Decho Scale Models,** 1559 Portsmouth Ave., Westchester, IL 60154: Catalog $5 ◆ Large-scale ready-to-run freight cars and diesel locomotives. Also available as kits. 708-865-0132.

**Details West,** P.O. Box 61, Corona, CA 91718: Catalog $2 ◆ Rolling stock and parts.

**Anthony F. Dudynski Supply Company,** 2036 Story Ave., Bronx, NY 10473: Free information with long SASE ◆ Trains and scenic accessories. 718-863-9422.

**Express Station Hobbies Inc.,** 640 Strander Blvd., Tukwila, WA 98188: Free information ◆ HO rolling stock, books, and scenery for train layouts. 800-237-5139.

**F & H Enterprises,** 7501 McFaddon Ave., Huntington Beach, CA 92647: Free flyer with long SASE ◆ N gauge trackage.

**GarGraves Trackage Corp.,** 8967 Ridge Rd., North Rose, NY 14516: Free information ◆ Track for model railroad layouts. 315-483-6577.

**Gene's Trains,** 1905 State Hwy. 88 East, Brick Town, NJ 08724: Free list with long SASE ◆ Engines and sets, rolling stock, and accessories. 732-840-9728.

**Grand Central Ltd.,** P.O. Box 29109, Lincoln, NE 68529: Free information with long SASE ◆ Lionel classics and new equipment, operating and layout accessories, and large gauge items. 402-467-3738.

**Great Traditions Toy Trains,** 11706 Bustleton Ave., Philadelphia, PA 19116: Free information ◆ Rolling stock, kits, parts, and accessories. 215-698-1993.

**Great West Models,** P.O. Box 224, Franktown, CO 80116: Catalog $1 ◆ Model buildings for scenery settings. 303-840-0872.

**Joseph A. Grzyboski Jr.,** P.O. Box 3475, Scranton, PA 18505: Free information ◆ Limited edition and classic trains. 717-347-3315.

**H & R Trains,** 6901 US 19 North, Pinellas Park, FL 33781: Free information ◆ Lionel, LGB, and Marklin trains and accessories. 813-526-4682.

**Hansel Hardware,** 13320 W. Warren, Dearborn, MI 48126: Free information ◆ New and used trains. 800-LIONEL-1. d00222a@acehardware.com

**Hobby Gallery Miniature Loft,** 1810 Meriden Rd., Wolcott, CT 06716: Free information with long SASE ◆ Trains, accessories, and other supplies. 203-879-2316.

**Hobby Surplus Sales,** P.O. Box 2170, New Britain, CT 06050: Catalog $4 ◆ Tools, scenery, hobby and craft supplies, and Lionel, American Flyer, and HO and N-gauge accessories. 800-233-0872.

**Hobbyland,** 1810 E. 12th St., Mishawaka, IN 46544: Catalog $2 ◆ Trains and scenic accessories. 800-225-6509.

**The Incredible Christmas Place,** 2470 Parkway, P.O. Box 958, Pigeon Forge, TN 37868: Free catalog ◆ Toys and trains, dolls, Christmas ornaments, other gifts, and collectibles. 800-357-2682. www.christmasplace.com

**International Hobby Corp.,** 413 E. Allegheny Ave., Philadelphia, PA 19134: Catalog $4.98 ◆ Trains and scenic accessories. 800-875-1600.

**The Iron Pony,** 12630 Hoover St., Garden Grove, CA 92841: Free information ◆ Large scale locomotives and passenger cars. 714-893-3119.

**Isabel Central Enterprises,** P.O. Box 771407, Wichita, KS 67277: Price list $2 with long SASE ◆ Railway modular roadbeds for permanent or temporary indoor and outdoor layouts. 316-942-3413. www2.southwind.net/~ice

**J & B Models,** 1508 Ralston Dr., Mt. Laurel, NJ 08054: Free catalog with long SASE ◆ Model railroad supplies and accessories.

**K & S Scenery Products,** P.O. Box 117824, Carrollton, TX 75011: Free brochure with long SASE ◆ Foreground and background trees for scenery arrangements.

**K-Line Electric Trains Inc.,** P.O. Box 2831, Chapel Hill, NC 27515: Free catalog ◆ Electric trains. 800-866-9986. www.k-linetrains.com

**Ken's Trains,** P.O. Box 636, Sudbury, MA 01776: Free catalog ◆ Rolling stock and accessories. 978-443-6883.

**Klamath Machine & Locomotive Works,** P.O. Box 350, Calpella, CA 95418: Catalog $7 ◆ Large scale locomotives. 707-485-8634.

**Lark Spur Line Ltd.,** Box 416, 230 St. Lawrence St., Merrickville, Ontario, Canada K0G 1N0: Catalog $5 ◆ HO equipment and accessories. 613-269-3600.

**Legacy Station,** 251 Hurricane Shoals Rd., Lawrenceville, GA 30245: Free information with long SASE ◆ N and HO-gauge, American Flyer, Lionel, and other trains. 800-282-9311; 770-339-7780 (in GA). www.trainworks.com

**Leventon's Hobby Supply,** P.O. Box 1525, Chehalis, WA 98532: Free train list with long SASE, parts catalog $2 ◆ Standard, HO, S, and O-gauge parts and rolling stock. 360-748-3643.

**Mainline Hobby Supply,** 15066 Buchanan Trl. E., Blue Ridge Summit, PA 17214: Free newsletter with long SASE ◆ Books, videos, locomotives, rolling stock, parts, tools, scenery, and other accessories. 717-794-2860.

**Donald B. Manlick,** 2127 S. 11th St., Manitowoc, WI 54220: Free information with long SASE and two 1st class stamps ◆ Custom decals for HO, N, O, and S scale railroads.

**Miami Trains,** 7448 SW 48th St., Miami, FL 33155: Catalog $2 ◆ All makes and scales of European trains. 305-666-6555.

**Miami Valley Products Company,** P.O. Box 144, Morrow, OH 45152: Free information with long SASE ◆ HO, O, and G-gauge bridge and trestle kits. 513-899-9904.

**Mike's Train House,** 9693 Gerwig Ln., Columbia, MD 21046: Catalog $2 ◆ Locomotives, cars, Lionel and Williams rolling stock, and accessories. 410-381-2580.

**Mike's Trains & Hobbies,** 104 W. Ocean Ave., Lompoc, CA 93436: Catalog $2 (refundable) ◆ New, used, and reproduction Lionel parts. 805-736-6747.

**Model Expo Inc.,** P.O. Box 229140, Hollywood, FL 33022: Catalog $5 (refundable) ◆ Airplane models, automobile and boat kits, wood and plastic ship models, trains, and tools. 800-222-387. www.modelexpoinc.com

**Model Railway Post Office,** Box 426, Hewitt, NJ 07421: Free price list ◆ Trains, kits, and accessories. 973-728-7595.

**Model Rectifier Corp.,** 80 Newfield Ave., Edison, NJ 08837: Free information ◆ Power control units. 732-225-2100.

**Model Train Works,** 2934 Cedarhurst Rd., Finksburg, MD 21048: Free information ◆ Engines, rolling stock, accessories, and scenery building supplies. 800-852-2441; 410-526-0018 (in MD).

**Mountain Car Company,** P.O. Box 1073, Salem, VA 24153: Free catalog ◆ Kits and partially assembled railroad rolling stock and accessories. 540-387-0124.

**Mountain State Hobby Supply,** P.O. Box 356, Teays, WV 25569: Catalog $3 ◆ Scenery building kits, trains, and accessories. 304-757-3242.

**The Oakridge Corp.,** P.O. Box 247, Lemont, IL 60439: Free catalog price information ◆ Model miniature railroad accessories. 708-739-4554.

**One Stop Hobbies,** 110 Hublard Dr., Vernon, CT 06066: Railroad catalog $12.95; decal catalog $8; both catalogs $15.95 ◆ Engines, rolling stock, accessories, and decals.

**Orange Blossom Hobbies,** 1975 NW 36th St., Miami, FL 33142: Free list with long SASE ◆ New and used HO equipment. 305-633-1517.

**P & P Lines,** P.O. Box 102, Easton, CT 06612: Catalog $2 ◆ Scenic-making supplies. 203-268-3243.

**Perry's Hobbies,** 114 Vernon Ave., Morgan, MN 56266: Free information with long SASE (specify N, O, HO, or book and video list) ◆ Books and videos on trains, brass, and accessories. 507-249-3173.

**Plastruct,** 1020 S. Wallace Pl., City of Industry, CA 91748: Catalog $2 ◆ Scratch-building model parts and kits.

**Precision Scale Company,** P.O. Box 288, Stevensville, MT 59870: Free list with long SASE ◆ Detailed parts. 406-777-5071.

**Railroad Hobbies,** 119 Vernon St., Roseville, CA 95678: Free list with long SASE ◆ Railroad brass. 916-782-6067.

**Red Caboose,** 23 W. 45th St. (basement), New York, NY 10036: Free information ◆ European scale, American Flyer, and Lionel trains, Also HO, N, and O-gauge equipment. 212-354-7349.

**Charles Ro Supply Company,** 662 Cross St., P.O. Box 100, Malden, MA 02148: Catalog 50¢ ◆ Lionel and LGB trains, HO rolling stock, and other equipment. 781-321-0090.

**Roundhouse South,** 4611 Ridgewood Ave., Port Orange, FL 32127: Free information with long SASE ◆ Lionel, LGB, and Weaver trains. 904-304-7002.

**Rudy's Choo Choo,** P.O. Box 291, Chester Heights, PA 19017: Free information with long SASE ◆ Toy trains, parts, and books. 610-558-5699. www.ufsi.com/rudyschoochoo

**San Antonio Hobby Shop,** 2550 W. El Camino, Mountain View, CA 94040: Free information ◆ Scratch-building and brass supplies, books, and Lionel, LGB, HO, N, O, Z, and other narrow gauge equipment. 650-941-1278.

**Scenery Unlimited,** 7236 W. Madison, Forest Park, IL 60130: Catalog $7.95 ◆ Locomotives and rolling stock, tools, and scenery supplies. 708-366-7763.

**Sentinel Miniatures,** 4 Broadway, Valhalla, NY 10595: Catalog $9 ◆ Military, historical, and fantasy figure kits. Also HO and N scale trains and die-cast cars. 914-682-3932.

**Shepaug Railroad Company,** 24 Columbia St., Leominster, MA 01453: Free information ◆ Model trains, layout accessories, and more. 978-537-2277. shepaugrr@aol.com

**Charles Siegel's Train City,** 3133 Zuck Rd., Erie, PA 16506: Price list $3 ◆ American Flyer, Lionel, MPC, Marx, and other trains. 814-833-8313.

**Nicholas Smith Trains,** 2343 W. Chester Pike, Broomall, PA 19008: Free information with long SASE ◆ Pola, LGB, and other equipment. 610-353-8585.

**Standard Hobby Supply,** P.O. Box 801, Mahwah, NJ 07430: Catalog $2 ◆ Model railroad equipment. 201-825-2211.

**T-Reproductions,** 227 W. Main St., Johnson City, TN 37603: Catalog $3 (refundable) ◆ Buddy "L" railroad reproductions. 800-825-4287.

**Todd's Train Depot,** 404 W. Wilson Ave., P.O. Box 849, Wendell, NC 27591: Free price list ◆ Trains, engines, accessories, and supplies. 919-365-5006.

**A Toy Train Depot,** 681 4th St., Oakland, CA 94607: Free information ◆ Trains, engines, accessories, and supplies. 510-444-8724.

**Toy Train Heaven,** P.O. Box 332, Montoursville, PA 17754: Price list $1 ◆ HO and N scale engines, HO rolling stock, and accessories. 717-368-5045.

**Toy Trains of Yesteryear,** 65 Bethany Circle, Closter, NJ 07624: Free information with long SASE ◆ Pre- and post-war trains and accessories. 201-768-5931.

**Train Express,** 4310 W. 96th St., Indianapolis, IN 46268: Free information with long SASE ◆ Lionel train sets, American Flyer equipment, rolling stock, operating cars, accessories, kits, and track. 800-428-6177.

**The Train Factory,** Box 394, Irwin, PA 15642: Free brochure ◆ Z and N gauge Lilliputian layouts. 412-863-7909.

**The Train Station,** 12 Romaine Rd., P.O. Box 381, Mountain Lakes, NJ 07046: Free information ◆ Classic trains and accessories. 201-263-1979. www.train-station.com

**Trainworld,** 751 McDonald Ave., Brooklyn, NY 11218: Catalog $2 ◆ Engines, rolling stock, and accessories. 718-436-7072.

**Twin Whistle Sign & Kit Company,** 60 Silk St., Arlington, MA 02174: Catalog $2 ◆ Scenery accessories in O, S, and HO scale. 781-646-1132.

**Uncle Dave's,** 1035 Rt. 46 East, Clifton, NJ 07013: Free list with long SASE and two 1st class stamps ◆ New and used HO brass. 201-471-3607.

**Owen Upp Railroader's Supply Company,** 11300 W. Greenfield Ave., West Allis, WI 53214: Free list with 1st class stamp ◆ Lionel, K-Line, and Williams equipment. Also Gargraves track, books, and videos. 414-771-2353.

**Warren's Model Trains,** 20520 Lorain Rd., Fairview Park, OH 44126: Price list $2 ◆ Lionel parts. 216-331-2900.

**Watts' Train Shop,** 9180 Hunt Club Rd., Zionsville, IN 46077: Free information ◆ Trains and scenic accessories. 800-542-7652.

**Willard Animations,** 96 Greenwich Dr., Mt. Holly, NJ 08060: Video catalog $5 (refundable) ◆ Custom O gauge animations. 609-265-0321.

**Williams Electric Trains,** 8835 Columbia 100 Pkwy., Columbia, MD 21045: Free information ◆ Railroad classics, track, and accessories. 410-997-7766.

**Charles C. Wood,** P.O. Box 179, Hartford, OH 44424: Catalog $2 ◆ Standard gauge electric trains. 330-772-5177.

**Woodland Scenics,** P.O. Box 98, Linn Creek, MO 65052: Catalog $1.50 ◆ Trees, turf, foliage, ballast, other scenery supplies, and kits. 573-346-5555.

**World of Trains,** 105-18 Metropolitan Ave., Forest Hills, NY 11375: Free information ◆ Engines, rolling stock, and accessories. 718-520-9700.

# MOTORCYCLES & MOTOR BIKES

## Clothing & Helmets

**Arai Helmets Ltd.,** P.O. Box 9485, Daytona, FL 32120: Brochure $3 ◆ Helmets. 800-766-ARAI.

**Bates Leathers,** 3700 N. Industry Ave., Ste. 102, Lakewood, CA 90712: Free information ◆ Leather riding suits. 760-426-8668.

**Bell Safety Gear,** 2675 Industrial Dr., Ogden, UT 84401: Free information ◆ Helmets. 801-627-2355.

**Brockton Cycle Center,** 2020 Main St., Brockton, MA 02401: Catalog $1 ◆ Clothing and helmets. Also parts and accessories for Kawasaki and Yamaha motorcycles. 508-584-1451.

**Buell American Motorcycles,** 3700 W. Juneau Ave., P.O. Box 653, Milwaukee, WI 53201: Free list of retail sources ◆ Motorcycle apparel. 414-343-8400.

**Chaparral,** 555 S. H St., San Bernardino, CA 92410: Free catalog ◆ Clothing, boots, goggles, and soft luggage. 800-841-2960; 909-889-2761 (in CA).

**Comp-A Motorcycle Store,** 345 W. Leffel Ln., Springfield, OH 45506: Free information ◆ Motorcycles, parts and accessories, helmets, shoes and boots, and clothing. 800-543-5139; 937-323-0513 (in OH).

**Helimot European Accessories,** 1141 Old Bayshore Hwy., San Jose, CA 95112: Free information ◆ Motorcycle riding apparel and accessories. 408-298-9608.

**Langlitz Leathers,** 2443 Southeast Division, Portland, OR 97202: Catalog $1 ◆ Leather clothing. 503-235-0959.

**Lockhart-Phillips,** P.O. Box 4802, San Clemente, CA 92672: Catalog $5 ◆ Leather jackets in small to extra-large. 800-221-7291; 714-498-9090 (in CA).

**Motoport USA,** 6110 Yarrow Dr., Carlsbad, CA 92009: Free information ◆ Men and women's touring and biker clothing and accessories. 800-777-6499.

**Rider Wearhouse,** 8 S. 18th Ave., Duluth, MN 55805: Free catalog ◆ Weatherproof motorcycle clothing. 800-222-1994.

**Roadgear Inc.,** 206 W. Elgin Dr., Pueblo West, CO 81007: Catalog $2 ◆ Leather jackets and other clothing. 800-854-4327. www.roadgear.com

**Specialty Sports Limited,** 532 Wolverine St., Rockford, MI 49341: Free list of retail sources ◆ Leather clothing, boots, gloves, and accessories. 616-866-3722.

**StarCycle Motorcycle Accessories Inc.,** 31581 Castaic Rd., Castaic, CA 91384: Catalog $2 ◆ Clothing, helmets, and parts. 800-990-2453. www.starcycle.com

**Tour Master Riding Gear,** 26855 Malibu Hills Rd., Calabasas, CA 91301: Free catalog ◆ Sport, Spandex finger-less, knit and leather finger-less summer, and gauntlet gloves. Also tail and tank bags, clothing, rain suits and boots, and dry-knit socks. 800-421-7247; 805-373-6868 (in CA).

**Vanson Leathers Inc.,** 213 Turnpike St., Stoughton, MA 02072: Catalog $8 ◆ Leather clothing. 781-344-5444.

**Z Custom Leathers,** 5445 Oceanus Dr., Ste 107, Huntington Beach, CA 92649: Free information ◆ Leather clothing. 714-890-5721. www.zcustom.com

## Parts & Accessories

**A & J Cycle Salvage,** 10 Industrial Hwy., Lester, PA 19113: Free information ◆ New and used parts for Japanese motorcycles. 610-521-6700.

**A-1 Used Cycle Parts Inc.,** 106 E. Arlington, St. Paul, MN 55117: Free information ◆ Honda, Suzuki, Yamaha, and Kawasaki used parts. 800-522-7891.

**AA Cycles,** 4701 Belle Grove Rd., Baltimore, MD 21225: Free information ◆ Used parts for Honda, Kawasaki, Yamaha, Suzuki, and street bikes. 800-278-7099.

**Alfa Heaven Inc.,** 2698 Nolan Rd., Aniwa, WI 54408: Free information ◆ Parts for Japanese motorcycles, from the 1960s and 1970s. 715-449-2141.

**American Jawa Ltd.,** 185 Express St., Plainview, NY 11803: Free brochure ◆ Motorcycle side cars. 516-938-3210.

**Aritronix Ltd.,** 6000 Cornell Rd., Cincinnati, OH 45242: Free information ◆ Easy-to-install motorcycle security alarms. 800-428-0440.

**Autoxtra California,** 1624 Wilshire Blvd., Santa Monica, CA 90403: Free information ◆ Covers for most makes and models. 800-221-9872. autoxtra@earthlink.NET

**Avon Innovation,** P.O. Box 336, Edmonds, WA 98020: Free information ◆ Motorcycle tires. 800-624-7470.

**Ron Ayers Motorsports,** 1918 N. Memorial Dr., Hwy. 11 North, Greenville, NC 27834: Free information ◆ Honda, Suzuki, and Kawasaki parts and accessories. 800-888-3084.

**Baltimore Cycle Salvage Inc.,** 1629 Warner St., Baltimore, MD 21230: Free information ◆ Used parts for Japanese motorcycles. 410-962-1335.

**Banzai Parts,** 611 N. Milwaukee Ave., Libertyville, IL 60048: Free information ◆ Honda, Suzuki, Kawasaki, and Yamaha parts and accessories. 800-405-7283; 847-362-7146 (in IL).

**Baxter Cycle,** Box 85, Marne, IA 51552: Free information ◆ Parts for Triumph, Moto Guzzo, and other British motorcycles, from 1950 and later. 712-781-2351.

**Blue Moon Cycle,** 752 W. Peachtree St., Norcross, GA 30071: Free catalog ◆ Sidecars and BMW parts. 770-447-6945.

**Brickhouse Cycles,** 7819 N. Military Hwy., Norfolk, VA 23518: Free information ◆ Used parts for late model Japanese bikes. 800-877-4804; 804-480-4800 (in VA).

**Britalia Motors,** 1027 Rosedale, Capitola, CA 95010: Catalog $8 ◆ Triumph, BSA, Norton, Matchless, Ducati, Cagiva, Moto Guzzi, and Italjet parts. 408-476-3663.

**British Cycle Supply Company,** P.O. Box 119, Wolfville, Nova Scotia, Canada B0P 1X0: Free information ◆ Parts and accessories for Triumph, BSA, and Norton motorcycles. 902-542-7478.

**British Marketing,** 27324 Camino Capistrano, Laguna Niguel, CA 92677: Free information ◆ Norton and Triumph factory replacement parts. 714-582-2902.

**British Only Motorcycles & Parts Inc.,** 32451 Park Ln., Garden City, MI 48135: Free information ◆ Reproduction parts for British motorcycles. 800-278-6659; 734-421-0303 (in MI). www.british-only.com

**Brockton Cycle Center,** 2020 Main St., Brockton, MA 02401: Catalog $1 ◆ Clothing and helmets. Also parts and accessories for Kawasaki and Yamaha motorcycles. 508-584-1451.

**Buell American Motorcycles,** 3700 W. Juneau Ave., P.O. Box 653, Milwaukee, WI 53201: Free list of retail sources ◆ Motorcycle accessories. 414-343-8400.

**California Side Car,** 15641 Computer Ln., Huntington Beach, CA 92649: Free information ◆ Motorcycle side cars. 800-824-1523; 714-891-1033 (in CA).

**Dennis Carpenter Cushman Reproductions,** P.O. Box 26398, Charlotte, NC 28221: Catalog $4 ◆ Cushman motor scooter parts. 704-782-1237.

**CC Products BMW Performance Center,** 1886 W. San Carlos St., San Jose, CA 95128: Free catalog ◆ Performance accessories, BMW gifts, and other items. 408-295-0208.

**Chaparral,** 555 S. H St., San Bernardino, CA 92410: Free catalog ◆ Clothing, boots, goggles, soft luggage, and Dunlop, Metzeler, Michelin, Continental, Bridgestone, Cheng Shin, and other tires. 800-841-2960; 909-889-2761 (in CA).

**Charleston Custom Cycle,** 211 Washington, Charleston, IL 61920: Free information ◆ NOS parts for Harley-Davidson Lightweights and other motorcycles, from 1948 to 1978. 217-345-2577.

**Clubman Racing Accessories,** P.O. Box 59, Fairfield, CT 06430: Catalog $3 ◆ Standard parts and cafe and racing equipment for Norton, Triumph, Triton, and Ducati motorcycles. 203-256-1224.

**Cobra Engineering Inc.,** 4915 E. Hunter St., Anaheim, CA 92807: Free information ◆ Motorcycle customizing parts and accessories. 714-779-7798.

**Comp-A Motorcycle Store,** 345 W. Leffel Ln., Springfield, OH 45506: Free information ◆ Motorcycles, parts and accessories, helmets, shoes and boots, and clothing. 800-543-5139; 937-323-0513 (in OH).

**Competition Accessories Inc.,** 345 W. Leffel Ln., Springfield, OH 45506: Catalog $5 ◆ BMW, Moto Guzzi, Triumph, Yamaha, and Ducati accessories. 800-543-4709.

**Competition Werkes,** P.O. Box 5233, Rosebud, OR 97470: Free brochure ◆ Motorcycle parts. 800-736-2114.

**Cosmopolitan Motors Inc.,** 301 Jacksonville Rd., Hatboro, PA 19040: Free information ◆ Bicycle locks, packs and bags, tires, and other accessories for bicycles and mopeds. 800-523-2522; 215-672-9100 (in PA). www.full-motion-net.com/cosmo

**Cover-Up Enterprises,** 1444 Manor Ln., Blue Bell, PA 19422: Free information ◆ Covers for most cars, trucks, vans, and motorcycles. 800-268-3757.

**Cycle Outlet,** 12104 Bedford Rd., Cumberland, MD 21502: Free information (enclose want list) ◆ Used parts and motorcycles. 301-724-6923.

**Cycle Re-Cycle,** 2233 E. 10th St., Indianapolis, IN 46201: Free information ◆ Honda, Kawasaki, Suzuki, and Yamaha parts. 317-634-7550.

**Cycle Recyclers,** 1538 Park Ave., Chico, CA 95928: Free information ◆ Used motorcycle parts. 800-356-4735.

**Cycle Salvage Fontana,** 14550 Arrow, Fontana, CA 92335: Free information ◆ Used parts. 800-659-6524; 909-355-3427 (in CA).

**Cycle Stowage Systems,** 1335 Claude Ave., Salisbury, NC 28147: Free brochure ◆ Sport-bike tail trunks with keys, turn signals, and tag lights. 704-636-3056.

**D & M Sportbike,** 2520 Cass St., Fort Wayne, IN 46808: Free information ◆ Used Honda, Yamaha, Kawasaki, and Suzuki parts. 219-483-6833.

**Donelson Cycles Inc.,** 9851 St. Charles Rock Rd., St. Ann, MO 63074: Free information ◆ Clothing, helmets, boots, rain suits, saddlebags, and BMW, Triumph, Norton, and Yamaha parts. 800-325-4144.

**Dow Canvas Products Inc.,** 4230 Clipper Dr., Manitowoc, WI 54220: Free list of retail sources ◆ Vented water-repellant motorcycle cover. 800-558-7755.

**Dunlop Tire Corp.,** P.O. Box 1109, Buffalo, NY 14240: Free catalog ◆ Motorcycle tires. 800-548-4714.

**Eastland Motorcycle,** 5760 Albemarle Rd., Charlotte, NC 28212: Free information ◆ Salvaged motorcycle parts. 704-532-2282.

**Eric's Motorcycle Company,** 1361 E. Walnut St., Pasadena, CA 91106: Free information ◆ Current and vintage dirt bike and motorcycle parts and accessories. 818-449-3742.

**Exigent Inc.,** Box 157, Mt. Holly Springs, PA 17065: Free information ◆ Bike covers. 717-486-3238.

**Fairing Screens Gustafson,** P.O. Box 3567, St. Augustine, FL 32085: Free catalog ◆ Standard and customized motorcycle fairing screens. 904-824-2119.

**Freedom Cycles,** 12505 S. 71 Hwy., Grandview, MO 64030: Free information ◆ Kawasaki, Honda, Suzuki, Yamaha, KTM, Ducati, Cagiva, and parts for other motorcycles. 800-438-0316.

**Gorilla Products,** 2141 E. 51st St., Los Angeles, CA 90058: Free list of retail sources ◆ Cycle alarm for protection against theft or tampering. 800-262-6267.

**Harbor Vintage Motor Company,** Rt. 2, Box 248, Jonesville, VT 05466: Catalog $2 ◆ Parts for 1916 to 1994 motorcycles. 802-434-4040.

**Harper's MotoGuzzi,** 32401 Stringtown Rd., Greenwood, MO 64034: Free information (specify parts wanted) ◆ New, used, and hard-to-find MotoGuzzi parts, bikes, and after-market accessories. 800-752-9735.

**Honda-Suzuki of Greenville,** 1918 N. Memorial Dr., Greenville, NC 27834: Free information ◆ Motorcycle parts. 800-888-3084.

**Hymer Manufacturing,** 315 N. Silver St., Lexington, NC 27292: Free information ◆ Easy-to-install automobile bike rider. 704-869-4998.

**Hyperformance Accessories,** 15131 Triton, #122, Huntington Beach, CA 92648: Catalog $2 ◆ Machined parts, fasteners, and apparel accessories for competition and sport. 714-893-0030. www.hyperprod.com

**Indian Motorcycle Supply Inc.,** P.O. Box 207, Sugar Grove, IL 60554: Free information ◆ New parts for Indian Chief, Four Sport Scout, Arrow, VT Scout, and Warrior motorcycles. 630-466-4601.

**Intraser Inc.,** 428 N. La Cienega Blvd., Los Angeles, CA 90048: Free information ◆ New and pre-owned motorcycles, ATVs, snowmobiles, trailers, personal water vehicles, and small boats. 213-652-6966.

**Jack's Cycle Salvage,** 225 Kell Rd., Tifton, GA 31794: Free information ◆ Used motorcycle parts. 800-210-0435.

**Kart World,** 1488 Mentor Ave., Painesville, OH 44077: Catalog $3 ◆ Parts, engines, and accessories for mini-cars and bikes. 440-357-5569.

**Kerkmer Exhaust Products,** 4540 W. 160th St., Cleveland, OH 44135: Free information ◆ Exhaust systems. 216-265-8400.

**Dennis Kirk Inc.,** 955 Southfield Ave., Rush City, MN 55069: Free information ◆ Motorcycle tires and tubes, accessories, gloves, helmets, luggage racks, carryall bags, and boots. 800-328-9280.

**Klempf's British Parts Warehouse,** RR 1, Box 85, Dodge Center, MN 55927: Free catalog ◆ Triumph, BSA, and Norton parts, from the 1960s to the present. 507-374-2222.

**KTM Sportmotorcycle,** 930 Fesler St., El Cajon, CA 92020: Free information ◆ Dirt bikes, parts, and accessories. 619-246-6301.

**Limelite Electric Arts Inc.,** P.O. Box 11183, Fort Wayne, IN 46856: Free catalog ◆ High-intensity neon lighting for motorcycles, Honda accessories, and more. 800-860-4950.

**Lockhart-Phillips,** P.O. Box 4802, San Clemente, CA 92672: Catalog $4 ◆ Motorcycle accessories and windscreens. 800-822-221-7291; 714-498-9090 (in CA).

**M.A.P. Cycle Enterprises,** 7165 30th Ave. North, St. Petersburg, FL 33710: Catalog $3 ◆ New, used, stock, and NOS parts for BSA motorcycles. 813-381-1151.

**Mac's Motor Sports,** P.O. Box 7190, Wesley Chapel, FL 33544: Free information ◆ Motorized scooters, bicycles, and folding bikes. 813-973-7108.

**MAI Motor Bike,** Terratran Manufacturing, 1819 Timberlake Dr., Delaware, OH 43015: Free information ◆ Folding motor bike. 614-548-5561.

**Marbel Associates Inc.,** 1819 Timberlake Dr., Delaware, OH 43015: Free information ◆ Folding motor bikes. 614-548-5561.

**Marsee Luggage,** P.O. Box 2588, Temecula, CA 92583: Free information ◆ Motorcycle expandable tank, magnetic tank, seats, and saddle bags. 909-694-9742.

**Midwest Action Cycle,** 251 Host Dr., Lake Geneva, WI 53147: Free information ◆ Suzuki, Kawasaki, and Honda parts. 800-343-9065; 414-249-0600 (in WI).

**Mike's Cycle Parts,** 3511 Boone Rd. SE, Salem, OR 97301: Free information ◆ Used Japanese motorcycle parts. 800-327-7304.

**Moores Cycle Supply,** 49 Custer St., West Hartford, CT 06110: Catalog $4 ◆ Triumph and BSA parts. 860-953-1689.

**Moto Race,** P.O. Box 861, Wilbraham, MA 01095: Free information ◆ Tires, brakes, accessories, and clothing. 800-628-4040. motorace@motorace.com

**Motofixx,** 277 Main Ave., Norwalk, CT 06851: Free catalog ◆ Ducati parts. 800-8-DUCATI.

**Motorcycle Accessory Warehouse,** 3620 Jeannine Dr., Colorado Springs, CO 80917: Free information ◆ Tires, helmets, batteries, seats, saddlebags, and sportswear. 800-241-2222. maw@iex.net

**Motorcycle Salvage Company Inc.,** 3008 W. Mercury Blvd., Hampton, VA 23666: Free information ◆ Parts for Japanese street bikes. 800-346-4424.

**Motoxtra,** 1624 Wilshire Blvd., Santa Monica, CA 90403: Free information ◆ Motorcycle covers. 800-221-9872.

**MR Cycles Inc.,** 774 Hendersonville Rd., Asheville, NC 28803: Free information ◆ Honda, Kawasaki, Suzuki, and Yamaha parts. 800-359-0567. www.mrcycles.com

**National Cycle Inc.,** P.O. Box 158, Maywood, IL 60153: Free list of retail sources ◆ Motorcycle windshields. 708-343-0400.

**Performance Machine Inc.,** P.O. Box 1739, 15535 Garfield Ave., Paramount, CA 90723: Free information ◆ Racing and street-style spun aluminum wheels. 310-634-6532.

**Pine Ridge Enterprise,** 13165 Center Rd., Bath, MI 48808: Free brochure ◆ Easy-to-use dust-free car and motorcycle covers. 800-522-7224.

**Pingel Enterprise Inc.,** 2076C 11th Ave., Adams, WI 53910: Catalog $5 ◆ Street and drag performance products. 608-339-7999.

**Pit Pages,** 1417 Wellington Pl., Aberdeen, NJ 07747: Free catalog ◆ Professional tools, equipment, and other accessories. 908-290-2693.

**Point Cycle,** 11 Brilliant Ave., Pittsburgh, PA 15215: Free information ◆ Kawasaki parts and accessories. 800-448-8611; 412-782-2453 (in PA).

**Rick's Motorcycle Enterprises Inc.,** 33 Newton Rd., Plastow, NH 03865: Free information ◆ Used parts. 800-423-1320; 603-382-5299 (in NH).

**Rifle Fairings,** 3140 El Camino Real, Atascadero, CA 93422: Free information ◆ Rifle windshields for all popular sport bikes. 800-262-1237. www.rifle.com

**RKA Accessories,** 2175 Bluebell Dr., Ste. B, San Rosa, CA 95403: Free information ◆ Soft luggage for motorcycles. 800-349-1752.

**Sam's Motorcycles,** 605 Silver, Houston, TX 77007: Free information ◆ Used parts for most motorcycles. 713-862-4026.

**Samson Motorcycle Products Inc.,** 220 S. Loara St., Anaheim, CA 92802: Catalog $3 ◆ Motorcycle exhaust systems. 888-5-SAMSON; 714-518-2482 (in CA).

**David Sarafan Inc.,** 374 2nd Crown Point Rd., Rochester, NH 03867: Free information ◆ Parts for Harley-Davidson civilian and military motorcycles. 603-332-4280.

**Sky Cycle Inc.,** Rt. 13, Lunenburg, MA 01462: Free information ◆ Used Honda, KAW, Suzuki, and Yamaha parts. 800-345-6115; 978-345-4647 (in MA).

**Spec II,** 8927 Lankershim Blvd., Sun Valley, CA 91352: Catalog $3 ◆ High-performance parts and fairings. 818-504-6364.

**StarCycle Motorcycle Accessories Inc.,** 31581 Castaic Rd., Castaic, CA 91384: Catalog $2 ◆ Clothing, helmets, and parts. 800-990-2453. www.starcycle.com

**Steve's Cycle,** Rt. 5, Box 109, Tifton, GA 31794: Free information ◆ Used parts. 800-622-9253; 912-386-8666 (in GA).

**Storz Performance,** 239 S. Olive St., Ventura, CA 93001: Catalog $4 ◆ Performance motorcycle accessories. 805-641-9540.

**Rich Suski,** 7061 County Rd. 108, Town Creek, AL 35672: Free catalog ◆ Cushman parts for vintage motorbikes and scooters. 256-685-2510.

**Suzuki Parts Warehouse,** Bob Tracey's World of Cycles, 604 Narrows Run Rd., Moon Township, PA 15108: Free information ◆ Suzuki parts and accessories. 800-860-0686. www.partswarehouse.com

**Targa Accessories Inc.,** 21 Journey, Aliso Viejo, CA 92656: Catalog $5 ◆ Motorcycles and parts. 800-521-7845.

**Bob Traceys World of Cycles,** 604 Narrows Run Rd., Moon Township, PA 15108: Free information ◆ Suzuki parts for dirt and street bikes, ATVs, and watercraft. 800-860-0686. www.partswarehouse.com

**Travelcade,** 6325 Alondra Blvd., Paramount, CA 90723: Free brochure ◆ Touring and custom saddles. 800-397-7709.

**Vance & Hines Motorcycle Center,** 14010 Marquardt Ave., Santa Fe Springs, CA 90670: Catalog $3 ◆ Performance accessories. 562-921-7461. www.vanceandhines.com

**Western Manufacturing Corp.,** Box 130, Marshalltown, IA 50158: Free information ◆ Air-operated motorcycle lift. Available in an electric version. 800-247-7594.

**J.C. Whitney & Company,** 1 JC Whitney Way, P.O. Box 3000, Chicago, IL 61301: Free catalog ◆ Hard-to-find items and custom-fit accessories. 312-431-6102. www.jcwhitneyusa.com

**World of Cycles,** 604 Narrows Run Rd., Moon Township, PA 15108: Free information ◆ Yamaha parts. 800-860-0686. www.partswarehouse.com

**WWC Wholesale Parts,** Rt. 1, Box 216, Waynesville, NC 28786: Free information ◆ Honda, Kawasaki, Suzuki, and Yamaha parts and accessories. 800-438-7921.

**Yamaha Parts Warehouse,** 604 Narrows Run Rd., Moon Township, PA 15108: Free information ◆ Yamaha parts. 800-860-0686. www.partswarehouse.com

## MOUNTAIN, ROCK, ICE, & WALL CLIMBING

**Adirondack Outfitters,** P.O. Box 431, Massena, NY 13662: Free information ◆ Rock and ice climbing, camping, and outdoor photography equipment. 888-315-0747.

**Black Diamond Equipment,** 2084 E. 3900 South, Salt Lake City, UT 84124: Free information ◆ Mountain boots, backpacks, and other equipment. 801-278-5533.

**W. Born & Associates,** 2438 Blacklick-Eastern Rd., Millersport, OH 43046: Free information with long SASE ◆ Equipment and supplies for mountain climbing and rescue activities. 614-467-2676.

**Climb Axe Ltd.,** 3341 SE Hawthorne Blvd., Portland, OR 97214: Free information ◆ Mountain climbing ropes and hardware. 503-797-1991. climbaxe@aracnet.com

**Climb High Inc.,** 135 Northside Dr., Shelburne, VT 05482: Free catalog ◆ Boots and clothing, carabiners, ropes, backpacks, and other equipment. 802-985-5056. www.climbhigh.com

**CMI Outdoor Equipment,** P.O. Box 535, 1 Mill Rd., Franklin, WV 26807: Free catalog ◆ Camping and mountaineering equipment. 800-247-5901. www.cmi-gear.com

**Franklin Climbing Equipment,** Box 7465, Bend, OR 97708: Free information ◆ Climbing equipment. 541-317-5716.

**Garuda Mountaineering,** 333 Simmental Way, Bozeman, MT 59715: Free catalog ◆ Tents. 406-587-4153.

**Gregory Mountain Products,** 100 Calle Cortez, Temecula, CA 92590: Free list of retail sources ◆ Back packs and equipment for mountain climbers. 800-477-3420.

**LaSportiva,** 3245 Prairie Ave., Boulder, CO 80301: Free list of retail sources ◆ Climbing footwear. 303-443-8710.

**Lowe Alpine,** P.O. Box 1449, Broomfield, CO 80038: Free list of retail sources ◆ Mountain climbing boots and clothing, backpacks, ropes, and other equipment. 303-465-0522. www.lowealpine.com

**Misty Mountain Threadworks,** 718 Burma Rd., Banner Elk, NC 28604: Free list of retail sources ◆ Harnesses and other climbing equipment. 704-963-6688.

**Moab Adventure Outfitters,** 550 N. Main, Moab, UT 84532: Free catalog ◆ Climbing equipment. 801-259-2725.

**Mountain Dreams International Inc.,** 1121 Bower Hill Rd., Pittsburgh, PA 15243: Free information ◆ Rock climbing shoes. 412-276-8660.

**Mountain Gear,** 730 N. Hamilton St., Spokane, WA 99202: Free information ◆ Mountaineering equipment, clothing, shoes and boots, and clothing. 800-829-2009.

**Mountain Hardware,** 950 Gilman St., Berkeley, CA 94710: Free list of retail sources ◆ Fast-setting-up tent. 510-559-6700. joeweb@mtnhdw.com

**Mountain High Ltd.,** 123 Diamond Peak Ave., Ridgecrest, CA 93555: Free catalog ◆ Climbing gear. 760-375-2612.

**Mountain Safety Research,** P.O. Box 24547, Seattle, WA 98124: Free list of retail sources ◆ Mountaineering equipment. 800-877-9677; 206-624-8573 (in WA).

**Mountain Sports,** 821 Pearl St., Boulder, CO 80302: Free catalog ◆ Outdoor and climbing gear. 800-558-6770; 303-443-6770 (in CO).

**Mountain Tools Catalog & Equipment Guide,** P.O. Box 22788, Carmel, CA 93922: Catalog $3 ◆ Equipment and soft goods for mountain and ice climbing. 800-510-2514.

**New England Ropes,** 848 Airport Rd., Fall River, MA 02720: Free information ◆ Climbing ropes. 800-333-6679; 508-678-8200 (in MA). www.neropes.com

**Nicros,** 519 Payne Ave., St. Paul, MN 55101: Free information ◆ Climbing handholds. 800-699-1975; 612-7789-1975 (in MN). www.nicros.com

**Omega Pacific Inc.,** P.O. Box 1780, Airway Heights, WA 99001: Free information ◆ Climbing gear. 509-244-0949.

**Pagan Mountaineering,** Outack Plaza, 2615 Capital Mall Dr. SW, Olympia, WA 98502: Free information ◆ Mountaineering equipment. 360-956-0360.

**PMI Petzal Distribution Inc.,** P.O. Box 803, LaFayette, GA 30728: Free list of retail sources ◆ Belay devices, harnesses, and equipment. 800-282-7673.

**Ragged Mountain Equipment,** Box 130, Rt. 16, Intervale, NH 03845: Free price list ◆ Mountaineering equipment, shoes and boots, and clothing. 603-356-3042.

**Shoreline Mountain Products,** 11 Navajo Ln., Corte Madera, CA 94925: Free information ◆ Mountaineering equipment. 800-381-2733.

**Sterling Rope Company,** 300 Cummings Center, Beverly, MA 01915: Free information ◆ Climbing ropes. 978-921-5500.

**Stone Age Climbing Implements,** 2238 Brittan Ave., San Carlos, CA 94070: Free brochure ◆ Rock climbing aids. 415-595-2527.

**Summit Canyon Mountaineering,** 549 Main St., Grand Junction, CO 81501: Free price list ◆ Mountaineering equipment. 800-254-6248.

**Sunrise Mountain Sports,** 490 Ygnacio Valley Rd., Walnut Creek, CA 94596: Free catalog ◆ Mountain climbing gear. 800-910-ROCK.

**Swallow's Nest,** 2308 6th Ave., Seattle, WA 98121: Free catalog ◆ Backpacking and mountaineering equipment. 800-676-4041; 206-441-4100 (in WA). www.swallowsnest.com

**Tents & Trails,** 21 Park Pl., New York, NY 10007: Free information ◆ Camping and mountaineering equipment and clothing. 888-227-1760; 212-227-1760 (in NY). www.tenttrails.com

**Terramar Sports Ltd.,** 10 Midland Ave., Port Chester, NY 10573: Free information ◆ Insulated outdoor clothing. 800-468-7455.

**Title 9 Sports,** 5743 Landregan St., Emeryville, CA 94608: Free catalog ◆ Women's clothing created by and for women. 510-655-5999. thefolks@title9sports.com

**Trango USA,** 4439 N. Broadway, Boulder, CO 80304: Free list of retail sources ◆ Crampons. 800-860-3653.

**Troll Harnesses,** 759 N. 3rd St., Laramie, WY 82070: Free information ◆ Climbing harnesses. 307-745-5893.

**VauDe Sports Inc.,** P.O. Box 3413, Mammoth Lakes, CA 93546: Free information ◆ Mountaineering equipment. 800-447-1539. www.vaude.com

**J.E. Weinel Inc.,** P.O. Box 213, Valencia, PA 16059: Free information with long SASE ◆ Equipment and supplies for caving, climbing, and rappelling. 800-346-7673; 412-898-2335 (in PA).

**Wild Things,** P.O. Box 400, North Conway, NH 03860: Free catalog ◆ Clothing and equipment. 603-356-6907. wildthings@landmarknet.net

## MOVIE & THEATRICAL MEMORABILIA

**American Pie Collectibles,** 29 Sullivan Rd., Peru, NY 12972: Free list ◆ Movie, TV, and promotional memorabilia. Also books and magazines, sheet music, LPs and 45s, sports cards, and other collectibles. 888-458-2200; 518-643-0993 (in NY). www.serftech.com/apc

**Art & Music Collectibles,** 3633 E. 15th St., Long Beach, CA 90804: Free catalog ◆ Original concert posters. 562-498-0641.

**Artrock Posters,** 1155 Mission St., San Francisco, CA 94103: Free catalog ◆ Original rock concert posters, T-shirts, books, and other memorabilia. 415-255-7390.

**Pamela Banner,** 3409 Lake Montebello Dr., Baltimore, MD 21218: Catalog $3 ◆ Foreign and domestic posters, lobby cards, press books, and stills. 410-235-7427.

**Captain Bijou,** P.O. Box 87, Toney, AL 35773: Catalog $4 ◆ Original movie posters, from 1930 to the present. 205-852-0198.

**Celluloid Dreams,** 4309 Radford Ave., Studio City, CA 91604: Free information ◆ Posters and lobby cards. 818-763-8465. celluloid@juno.com

**Cinema City,** Box 1012, Muskegon, MI 49443: Catalog $3 ◆ Movie posters, photos, autographs, and scripts. 616-739-8303.

**Cinema Collectors,** 1507 Wilcox Ave., Hollywood, CA 90028: Free catalog ◆ Movie posters, star photos, and books. 213-461-6516.

**Cinema Graphics,** 1640 E. Evans Ave., Denver, CO 80210: Catalog $5 ◆ Original movie posters and lobby cards, from 1918 to the 1980s. 303-744-3855.

**Cinemonde,** 1932 Polk St., San Francisco, CA 94109: Free information ◆ Rare movie posters, lobby cards, and books. 415-776-9988.

**Classic Legends,** P.O. Box 600233, San Diego, CA 92160: Free catalog ◆ Original concert posters. 619-295-4669.

**Dwight Cleveland,** P.O. Box 10922, Chicago, IL 60614: Free information ◆ Lobby cards, one-sheets, window cards, glass slides, motion picture heralds, exhibitor's books, and studio annuals. 312-525-9152.

**Daniel Cohen,** 24 The Links Rd. #120, Willowdale, Ontario, Canada M2P 1T6: Free catalog ◆ Autographs and Hollywood television and music memorabilia. 416-222-0232. www.danielcohen.com

**Collectors Warehouse Inc.,** 5437 Pearl Rd., Cleveland, OH 44129: Catalog $2 ◆ Rare movie posters, stills, scripts, sports and non-sports cards, games, toys, and more. 440-842-2896. www.collectorswarehouse.com

**Design Evolution,** P.O. Box 341, Boulder, CO 80306: Free information ◆ Original vintage movie posters from the 1930s, 1940s, and 1950s. 888-779-3337.

**800-TREKKER,** P.O. Box 13131, Reading, PA 19612: Free information ◆ Star Trek collectibles. 800-TREKKER.

**Euro Posters,** 531 Clayton, Denver, CO 80206: Catalog $1 ◆ European and United States movie posters and lobbies. 303-329-0707.

**Filmart's Cartoon World,** 362 New York Ave., Huntington, Long Island, NY 11743: Free catalog ◆ Contemporary and vintage animation art from most major studios. 800-ART-CELS. celworld@aol.com

Bill Fisher, How Sweet It Was, 16104 Dezaire Lnd. Rd., Philadelphia, PA 19114: Free catalog ◆ Posters, lobby cards, and other movie memorabilia. 888-3-POSTER.

**Scott Ford's Drive-In-Graphics,** 7050 Tulane Ave., 2nd Floor, St. Louis, MO 63130: Catalog $2 ◆ Original movie memorabilia. 314-726-3208.

**Gifted Images Gallery,** P.O. Box 34, Baldwin, NY 11510: Free catalog ◆ Cels, drawings, backgrounds, and animation art. 800-726-6708; 516-536-6886 (in NY).

**Gone Hollywood,** 172 Bella Vista Ave., Belvedere, CA 94920: Free information ◆ Vintage movie posters. 415-435-1929.

**Joel F. Goodman,** 872 Jenkintown Rd., Elkins Park, PA 19027: Free information ◆ Collectible rock and roll art from the 1960s, 1970s, and 1980s. 215-881-7707. JGOOD8848@aol.com

**John Hazelton Posters,** P.O. Box 119, Huntington, NY 11743: Catalog $10 ◆ Movie posters, from Hollywood classics to other eras. 516-421-7203. www.filmposters.com

**Bruce Hershenson,** 1 Court Square Dock, P.O. Box 874, West Plains, MO 65775: List $3 ◆ Movie posters. 417-256-9616.

**Hollywood Collectibles,** P.O. Box 4035, Sedona, AZ 96339: Catalog $2 ◆ Movie posters, lobby cards, and glossies. 520-204-1965.

**Hollywood Legends,** 6621 Hollywood Blvd., Hollywood, CA 90028: Free information ◆ Theatrical performers memorabilia, press kits, Disney books, autographed photos, and other collectibles. 213-962-7411.

**Hollywood North,** 4510 Excelsior Blvd., #102, St. Louis Park, MN 55416: Free catalog ◆ Lobby cards, stills, press books, movie sheet music, soundtracks, and miscellaneous movie collectibles. 612-925-8695.

**Hollywood Toy & Poster Company,** 1001 Banning St., Winnipeg, Manitoba, Canada R3E 2J1: Free catalog ◆ Press kits, lobby cards, standees, buttons, celebrity photo, stills, and scripts. 204-783-3717. www.hollywoodposter.com

**Hummerdude's,** P.O. Box 4348, Dunellan, NJ 08812: Catalog $4 ◆ Celebrity photos, posters, and autographs. 732-424-9367.

**Intergalactic Trading Company,** P.O. Box 521516, Longwood, FL 32752: Free catalog ◆ Movie posters and related material. 800-383-0727. sales@intergalactictrading.com

**Bob Iuliucci,** One Surrey Ln., Allendale, NJ 07401: Free list ◆ Out-of-print laser discs, rare promotional import CDs, rare vinyl 45s and LPs, promotional posters, rare concert tickets, and other theatrical memorabilia. 201-236-9107.

**Jim's TV Collectibles,** P.O. Box 4767, San Diego, CA 92164: Catalog TV collectibles $2, TV photos $2 ◆ Television and theatrical collectibles, from the 1950s through 1990s. Also TV star photos.

**John's Collectible Toys & Gifts,** 57 Bay View Dr., Shrewsbury, MA 01545: Catalog $2 ◆ Character toys and movie and TV collectibles. 508-797-0023. www.ewtech.com/Johns

**Richard Kohl,** 1848 N. Federal Hwy., Boynton Beach, FL 33435: Free information ◆ Vintage movie posters. 800-344-9103. www.strikezone.com

**Mark Kotasek,** 111 Adams Dr., Binghamton, NY 13905: List $3 (refundable) ◆ Original one-sheets and lobby cards, from the 1950s to 1990s. 607-723-7724.

**La Belle Epoque,** 11661 San Vincente Blvd., Ste. 304, Los Angeles, CA 90024: Free information ◆ Rare prints and lithographs. Includes deco, nouveau, vanity fair, and movie, travel, and sport posters. 310-442-0054.

**Last Moving Picture Company,** 2044 Euclid Ave., Cleveland, OH 44115: Free information with long SASE ◆ Window and lobby cards, inserts, one-sheets, stills, and posters. 216-781-1821.

**Werner H. Lehmann,** Euro Posters, 531 Clayton St., Denver, CO 80206: Catalog $1 ◆ European and United States movie posters and lobbies. 303-329-0707.

**LeMay Movie Posters,** P.O. Box 480879, Los Angeles, CA 90048: Catalog $5 ◆ Movie posters, lobby cards, and other memorabilia. 800-565-3629. www.csmonline.com/lemay

**Alan Levine Movie & Book Collectibles,** P.O. Box 1577, Bloomfield, NJ 07003: Catalog $5 ◆ Movie magazines from 1915 to 1970, movie posters, lobby cards, and celebrity autographs. 973-743-5288.

**Rick Lipp,** 427 Broadway, Jackson, CA 95642: Free information with long SASE ◆ Stills, lobby sets, inserts, posters, and press kits. 209-296-4754. ricklipp@goldrush.com

**Luton's Memorabilia,** P.O. Box 752302, Memphis, TN 38175: Free catalog ◆ Movie posters.

**Memory Lane Records,** 1321 Grand Ave., North Baldwin, NY 11510: Catalog $7 ◆ Records from the 1950s to the 1980s. Also photos, movie prints, and nostalgia. 516-623-2247.

**Metropolis,** 873 Broadway, Ste. 201, New York, NY 10003: Free information ◆ Vintage comic books and movie posters. 212-260-4147. comicbooks@earthlink.net

**Mile High Comics,** 2151 W. 56th Ave., Denver, CO 80221: Catalog $1 ◆ Original and re-issued movie posters. 303-455-2659.

**Miscellaneous Man,** George Theofiles, Box 1000, New Freedom, PA 17349: Catalogs $5 each (specify type of poster wanted, or request free list of current catalogs) ◆ Rare posters and vintage graphics.

**Motion Picture Arts Gallery,** 133 E. 58th St., New York, NY 10022: Free information ◆ Vintage movie posters. 212-223-1009.

**Movie Market,** P.O. Box 3900, Dana Point, CA 92629: Catalog $5 ◆ Movie star photos, posters, and collectibles. 714-488-8444.

**Movie Memorabilia,** Richard A. Lessard, 35 Broad St., East Hartford, CT 06118: Catalog $3 ◆ Foreign and domestic movie posters, half sheets, one sheets, and inserts. 860-568-3212.

**Movie Poster Place Inc.,** P.O. Box 128, Lansdowne, PA 19050: Catalog $1 (refundable) ◆ Movie posters, stills, press books, trailers, and other related memorabilia. 610-622-6062.

**Movie Poster Shop,** 1314 S. Grand Blvd., Ste. 2-156, Spokane, WA 99202: Free catalog ◆ Posters, photos, and prints. Movie stars, celebrities, and more. 403-250-7588. www.movieapostershop.com

**Movie Press Kits,** P.O. Box 1911, Whittier, CA 90609: Catalog $2 with long SASE ◆ Movie press kits, from 1980 to 1995.

**Movie Star News,** 134 W. 18th St., New York, NY 10011: Brochure $5 ◆ Movie photos and posters. 212-620-8160.

**New Eye Studio,** P.O. Box 632, Willimantic, CT 06226: Catalog $2 ◆ Star Trek, Star Wars, X-File, and other action figure collectibles.

**Odyssey Auctions Inc.,** 510-A South Corona Mall, Corona, CA 91719: Catalog $20 ◆ Movie memorabilia and autographed letters, manuscripts, photographs, and documents from the arts and sciences to politics and entertainment. 800-996-3977. OdysGroup@aol.com

**Jerry Ohlinger's Movie Material Store Inc.,** 242 W. 14th St., New York, NY 10011: Free catalog ◆ Stills, movie posters, star photos, magazines, and books. 212-989-0869.

**One Shubert Alley,** 346 W. 44th St., New York, NY 10036: Free information ◆ T-shirts, posters, mugs, jewelry from old and new Broadway shows, and other theatrical memorabilia. 800-223-1320; 212-586-7610 (in NY). www.playbill.com

**Paper Chase,** 23253 Lake Park Dr., Albany, GA 31707: Free information ◆ Movie posters, used videos, baseball cards, and comics. 912-439-0310.

**Photoworld II,** P.O. Box 20747, Houston, TX 77225: Free list with long SASE (enclose want list) ◆ Celebrity photo posters and TV, music, country, and soap collectibles.

**Poster Source,** P.O. Box 31107, Flagstaff, AZ 86003: Catalog $1 ◆ Movie and music posters. 888-527-6876; 520-527-6876 (in AZ). www.infomagic.com/~psource

**Posteritati,** 241 Centre St., Ste. 5F, New York, NY 10013: Free information ◆ Vintage movie posters and lobby cards. 212-226-2207. www.posterltail.com

**Reel Memories,** 3101 N. Rock Rd., Ste. 120, Wichita, KS 67226: Catalog $5 ◆ Original movie posters. Also reprints and custom framing. 316-636-5340.

**Remember Marilyn,** P.O. Box 4796, San Diego, CA 92164: Catalog $2 ◆ Marilyn Monroe magazines, movie posters, soundtracks, paperbacks, and other collectibles. 619-469-8790. www.remembermarilyn.com

**Deke Richards,** 648 W. Lake Samish Dr., Bellingham, WA 98226: Catalog $5 ◆ Foreign and American movie posters. 360-671-4490.

**Rick's Movie Posters,** P.O. Box 23709, Gainesville, FL 32602: Catalog $3 ◆ Original movie posters and photos, from the 1950s to the present. Includes many classic reproductions from earlier years. 800-252-0425; 352-373-7202 (in FL). www.ricksmovie.com

**Rockabilia Inc.,** P.O. Box 4206, Hopkins, MN 55343: Free catalog ◆ T-shirts, backstage passes, promotional glossy photographs, imported rare posters from around the world, and other concert collectibles. 612-942-7895.

**Rockaway Records,** 2395 Glendale Blvd., Los Angeles, CA 90039: Free information ◆ Posters, photographs, other memorabilia, LPs, and 45s. 213-664-3232.

**Rogofsky Movie Collectibles,** Box 107, Glen Oaks, NY 11004: Catalog $3 ◆ TV and movie magazines, photos, and collectibles. 718-723-0954.

**S & P Parker's Movie Market,** P.O. Box 3900, Dana Point, CA 92629: Catalog $5 ◆ Movie, TV, and rock star photos. 714-488-8444.

**Salzer's,** 5801 Valentine Rd., Ventura, CA 93003: Free information ◆ Vintage concert posters. 805-639-2169.

**Soitenly Stooges,** P.O. Box 63, Highland Park, IL 60035: Catalog $2 ◆ Three Stooges-related T-shirts, hats, videos, books, watches, and other collectibles. 847-432-9270.

**Starland Collector's Gallery,** P.O. Box 622, Los Olivos, CA 93441: Catalog $2.50 ◆ Sports cards, movie posters, comic art, and hard-to-find movies. 805-688-8300.

**Toy Scouts Inc.,** 137 Casterton Ave., Akron, OH 44303: Catalog $5 ◆ Movie posters, Disney collectibles, and movie memorabilia. 330-836-0668.

**Triton Gallery,** 323 W. 45th St., New York, NY 10036: Catalog 50¢ ◆ Current and rare theatrical posters with optional frames. 212-765-2472.

**Truly Unique Collectibles,** P.O. Box 29, Suffern, NY 10901: Free catalog ◆ Hand-signed color photos, framed photos, movie one-sheet posters, classic TV and movie toys, figures, other Americana, and more. 888-725-7614. www.uniquecollectibles.com

**S. Wallach,** 1875 Leslie St., Unit 17, North York, Ontario, Canada M3B 2M5: Catalog $2 ◆ Vintage and current movie posters, lobbies, stills, and trailers. 416-391-0133.

**Wex Rex Records & Collectibles,** 280 Worcester Rd., Framingham, MA 01701: Catalog $3 ◆ Movie and theatrical memorabilia, movie and TV show character toys, and other collectibles. 508-620-6181.

**Yesterday,** 1143 W. Addison St., Chicago, IL 60613: Free information with long SASE ◆ Original stills, lobby cards, posters, press books, magazines, and newspapers. 773-248-8087.

**Gabriel Zeldin,** Box 5163, Fort Lauderdale, FL 33310: Free list ◆ Posters, magazines, photos, records, and foreign movie memorabilia. gabriel.zeldin@worldnet.att.net

## MOVIE, STAGE, & TV SCRIPTS

**Book City of Burbank,** 308 N. San Fernando, Burbank, CA 91502: Catalog $2.50 ◆ Movie and TV scripts. 818-848-4417.

**Broadway Play Publishing Inc.,** 56 E. 81st St., New York, NY 10028: Free catalog ◆ Full-length, contemporary American plays. Also some musicals and one-act plays. 212-772-8334. www.BroadwayPlayPubl.com

**Cinema City,** Box 1012, Muskegon, MI 49443: Catalog $3 ◆ Movie scripts, posters, photos, and autographs. 616-739-8303.

**Hollywood Scripts,** 11288 Ventura Blvd., #431, Studio City, CA 91604: Free information ◆ Thousands of film and TV scripts. 818-980-3545.

**Bea Kalisch,** 27675 Chatsworth Rd., Farmington Hills, MI 48334: Free price list with long SASE: Original Movie and television scripts. 248-932-3130. BooksMana@aol.com

**Mysteries by Moushey,** P.O. Box 3593, Kent, OH 44240: Free information ◆ Audience-participation mystery scripts and production packages. 330-678-3893. members.aol.com/mystmoush

## MOVIE & VIDEO PROJECTION EQUIPMENT

**Chambless Cine Equipment,** Rt. 1, Box 1595, Hwy. 2, Ellijay, GA 30540: Free information ◆ New and used professional motion picture equipment. 706-636-5210.

**DA-LITE Screen Company,** 3100 N. Detroit St., P.O. Box 137, Warsaw, IN 46581: Free information ◆ Movie projection screens. 800-622-3737; 219-267-8101 (in IN).

**Irv Higdon,** 16454 Tulsa St., Granada Hills, CA 91344: Free information ◆ Sound cameras and editors. 818-360-7955.

**International Cinema Equipment Company,** 100 NE 39th St., Miami, FL 33137: Free information ◆ Audiovisual and cinema sound equipment, cameras, sound projectors, and film editing equipment. 305-573-7339.

**NVIEW Corp.,** 860 Omni Blvd., Newport News, VA 23606: Free information ◆ LCD video projection equipment. 800-775-7575.

**Polaroid Imaging Systems,** P.O. Box 100, Penfield, NY 14526: Free information ◆ Electronic imaging systems. 800-816-2611.

**Stewart Filmscreen Corp.,** 1161 W. Sepulveda Blvd., Torrance, CA 90502: Free list of retail sources ◆ Movie projection screens. 310-784-5300.

**Urbanski Film & Equipment,** P.O. Box 438, Orland Park, IL 60462: Free list with 1st class stamp ◆ Reels, equipment, and reconditioned 16 and 35mm projectors. Also TV shows, films, and other media presentations. 708-460-9082.

## MOVIES (FILMS)

**Dennis Atnip,** 7284 Menge, Center Line, MI 48015: Free list ◆ 35mm trailers. 810-756-9545.

**Ray Beam's Video Dreams,** 2209 S. Webster St., Kokomo, IN 46902: Free catalog ◆ Serials and B-movies on videos. 765-455-1958.

**Belle & Blade,** 124 Penn Ave., Dover, NJ 07801: Catalog $3 ◆ Classic western films on video cassettes.

**Canyon Cinema,** 2325 3rd St., Ste. 338, San Francisco, CA 94107: Catalog $20 ◆ Slides and documentary movies. 415-626-2255.

**Captioned Films/Videos Program,** National Association of the Deaf, 1447 E. Main St., Spartanburg, SC 29307: Free information ◆ Free loan service of over 4000 films and videos for persons with a hearing loss. 800-237-6213 (voice); 800-237-6819 (TTY). www.cfv.org

**Classic Cinema,** P.O. Box 18932, Encino, CA 91416: Catalog $5 ◆ Westerns, mysteries, comedies, and drama on video cassettes. 800-94-MOVIE.

**Dorothy Movie Classics,** Box 156, Keeler, CA 93530: Catalog $5 ◆ Silent and sound old movie classics, from the 1920s to 1950s.

**Euro Posters,** 531 Clayton, Denver, CO 80206: Catalog $1 ◆ Foreign films. 303-329-0707.

**Festival Films,** 6115 Chestnut Terrace, Shorewood, MN 55331: Free catalog ◆ United States and foreign films on video cassettes. Includes the silent era, early feature films, and other classics. 612-470-2172.

**Foothill Video,** 42257 6th St. West, Bldg. 306, Lancaster, CA 93534: Catalog $5 ◆ Westerns, feature films, serials, and foreign classics on video cassettes. 805-726-7533.

**Home Film Festival,** P.O. Box 2032, Scranton, PA 18501: Catalog $15 ◆ Hard-to-find films on video cassettes. 800-258-3456. www.homefilmfestival.com

**Kino Video,** 333 W. 39th St., Ste. 503, New York, NY 10018: Free catalog ◆ International and classic movies from Hollywood's golden era on video cassettes. 800-562-3330; 212-629-6880 (in NY). www.kino.com

**Meridian Video Corp.,** 1575 Westwood Blvd., Ste. 305, Los Angeles, CA 90024: Free catalog ◆ Foreign films. 800-529-2300.

**Moviecraft Inc.,** P.O. Box 438, Orland Park, IL 60462: Catalog $1 ◆ Video films. 708-460-9082.

**National Cinema Service,** 12022 Laurel Terrace Dr., Studio City, CA 91604: Free list ◆ New and used 16mm full-length features, shorts, and cartoons. 818-753-9770. NatCinServ@aol.com

**Pyramid Media,** P.O. Box 1048, Santa Monica, CA 90406: Free information ◆ Educational and entertainment films and videos. 800-421-2304. www.pyramidmedia.com

**Richard Semowich,** Upper Front, Binghamton, NY 13901: Free information ◆ 16mm films. 607-648-4025.

**Sinister Cinema,** P.O. Box 4369, Medford, OR 97501: Free information ◆ Science fiction, horror, mystery, suspense, fantasy, and other films on video cassettes. 541-773-6860. www.cinemaweb.com/sinister

**Something Weird Video,** P.O. Box 33664, Seattle, WA 98133: Catalog $5 ◆ Rare vintage feature films, shorts, movie trailers, and classic TV commercials, from the 1930s to 1970s. 206-361-3759.

**Jim Spotts,** Rt. 422 East, Penn Run, PA 15765: Free information ◆ Rare movie serials. 412-349-4458.

**Starland Collector's Gallery,** P.O. Box 622, Los Olivos, CA 93441: Catalog $2.50 ◆ Sports cards, movie posters, comic art, and hard-to-find movies. 805-688-8300.

**Thornhill Entertainment,** P.O. Box 577, Woodleaf, NC 27054: Catalog $5 ◆ 16mm films. 704-636-1116.

**Urbanski Film & Equipment,** P.O. Box 438, Orland Park, IL 60462: Free list with 1st class stamp ◆ Reels, equipment, and reconditioned 16 and 35mm projectors, and TV shows, films, and other media presentations. 708-460-9082.

**The Video Beat,** 351 Kiely Rd., Ste. 301, San Jose, CA 95129: Free catalog with long SASE ◆ Trailers, shorts, commercials, and movies from the 1950s and 1960s. 408-260-0266.

## MUSIC BOOKS & SHEET MUSIC

**Alcazar Records,** P.O. Box 429, Waterbury, VT 05676: Free information ◆ Children's, folk, Celtic, blues, Cajun, bluegrass, world music, and other hard-to-find music. 800-541-9904.

**Andy's Front Hall,** P.O. Box 307, Wormer Rd., Voorheesville, NY 12186: Free catalog ◆ Books and music for and about folk, traditional, and acoustic arrangements. 800-759-1775; 518-765-4193 (in NY). members.aol.com/fronthal

**Augsburg Fortress Publishers,** 426 S. 5th St., Minneapolis, MN 55415: Free catalog ◆ Books, curriculum materials, music, gifts, audiovisuals, and ecclesiastical arts items. 800-328-4648; 612-330-3341 (in MN). www.augsburgfortress.org

**Jim Bond Native American Music,** 35113 Brewster Rd., Lebanon, OR 97355: Catalog $1 ◆ Native American flute music and ceremonial supplies. 541-258-3645.

**Boston Music Company,** 172 Tremont St., Boston, MA 02111: Free catalog ◆ Sheet music. 617-426-5100.

**Captain Fiddle Publications,** 4 Elm Ct., Newmarket, NH 03857: Free brochure ◆ Music for folk instruments and country dancing. 603-659-2658.

**Chinaberry Book Service,** 2780 Via Orange Way, Ste. B, Spring Valley, CA 91978: Free catalog ◆ Books and music for children and adults. 800-776-2242.

**Flute World,** P.O. Box 250248, Franklin, MI 48025: Free catalog ◆ Professional and student flutes and piccolos, accessories, recorders, and recordings. 248-855-0410.

**Four Winds Trading Company,** 635 S. Broadway, Ste. E, Boulder, CO 80303: Free catalog ◆ Traditional and contemporary Native American music and books. 800-456-5444; 303-499-4484 (in CO). www.Fourwinds-Trading.com

**Fun Publishing Company,** 3322 Erie Ave., Cincinnati, OH 45208: Free information ◆ Teach-yourself books for the portable keyboard, piano, and xylophone. 513-533-3636.

**Hickey's Music Center,** 104 Adams St., Ithaca, NY 14850: Free catalog ◆ Print music, CDs, and trombone accessories. 800-442-5397; 607-272-8262 (in NY).

**Hollywood Legends,** 6621 Hollywood Blvd., Hollywood, CA 90028: Free information ◆ Theatrical performers memorabilia, press kits, Disney books, autographed photos, and other collectibles. 213-962-7411.

**Hollywood North,** 4510 Excelsior Blvd., #102, St. Louis Park, MN 55416: Free catalog ◆ Lobby cards, stills, press books, movie sheet music, soundtracks, and miscellaneous movie collectibles. 612-925-8695.

**Hollywood Sheet Music,** Beverly A. Hamer, Box 75, East Derry, NH 03041: Free information with long SASE ◆ Collectible movie sheet music. 603-432-3528.

**Indian House,** P.O. Box 472, Taos, NM 87571: Free catalog ◆ Traditional Native American music. 505-776-2953. www.indianhouse.com

**Luthier Music Corp.,** 341 W. 44th St., New York, NY 10036: Free information ◆ Classical and flamenco guitars and sheet music, CDs, videos, nylon strings, and accessories. 212-397-6038. www.luthiermusic.com

**Mainly Music,** 32 Main St., Brattleboro, VT 05301: Catalog $3 (refundable) ◆ New, used, and rare records, CDs, and tapes. Also vintage sheet music and collectibles. 802-257-0881.

**Mel Bay Publications Inc.,** 4 Industrial Dr., Pacific, MO 63069: Free catalog ◆ How-to-play and other music books. 800-8-MELBAY.

**Melody's Traditional Music & Harp Shoppe,** 9410 FM 1960 W, Houston, TX 77070: Free catalog ◆ Harps, dulcimers, whistles, flutes, recorders, music, and instruction books. 800-893-4277; 281-890-4500 (in TX). www.folkharp.com

**Midnight Productions,** P.O. Box 68, Waldwick, NJ 07463: Free catalog ◆ Theater organ music. 201-670-6660. www.theaterorgan.com

**Thomas Nelson Publishers,** P.O. Box 140300, Nashville, TN 37214: Free catalog ◆ Christian books, bibles, audio and video recordings, and music. 800-933-9673. www.nelsonworddirect.com

**Player Piano Company,** 704 E. Douglas, Wichita, KS 67202: Free catalog ◆ Player piano music rolls, piano parts, and accessories. 316-263-3241.

**Paul A. Riseman,** 2205 S. Park Ave., Springfield, IL 62704: Free information (enclose want list) ◆ Sheet music. 217-787-2634. riseman@riseman.com

**Southwest Strings,** 1050 S. Park Ave., Tucson, AZ 85719: Free catalog ◆ Sheet music for professionals, teachers, and students. 800-528-3430. www.swstrings.com

**Tara Publications,** P.O. Box 707, Owings Mills, MD 21117: Free catalog ◆ Jewish music. 800-827-4000; 410-654-0880 (in MD). www.jewishmusic.com

**Willis Music Company,** 7380 Industrial Rd., Florence, KY 41022: Free catalog ◆ Sheet music, educational audio cassettes, and accessories. 800-354-9799.

**World Around Songs Inc.,** 20 Colberts Creek Rd., Burnsville, NC 28714: Free catalog ◆ American and international folk, country, party, and religious music song books. 704-675-5343.

## MUSIC BOXES

**Alfa Color Labs,** 535 W. 135th St., Gardena, CA 90248: Free information ◆ Handcrafted wood music boxes with inlaid ceramic tile and glaze-mounted personalized portraits. 310-532-2532.

**Anyone Can Whistle,** 323 Wall St., Kingston, NY 12401: Free catalog ◆ Musical instruments, music boxes, wind chimes, whistles, and musical-sounding toys. 800-435-8863. anyonecan@chimes.com

**Emporium of the Rockies,** 306 W. Adams, Pueblo, CO 81004: Free catalog ◆ Decorative accessories, jewelry and watches, cloisonné, dollhouse furnishings, music boxes, and all-occasion gifts. 719-583-1268.

**Klockit,** P.O. Box 636, Lake Geneva, WI 53147: Free catalog ◆ Clock-building parts, music box kits, and Swiss music box movements in 144-, 72-, 50-, 36-, and 18-notes. 800-556-2548. www.klockit.com

**Rocking B Mfg.,** The West Coast Music Box Company, 3924 Camphor Ave., Newbury Park, CA 91320: Free catalog ◆ Children's, Christmas, and popular tunes for music boxes. 805-499-9336.

**San Francisco Music Box Company,** Mail Order Dept., P.O. Box 7817, San Francisco, CA 94120: Free catalog ◆ Reproduction antique and other music boxes. 800-227-2190.

**Shaker Shops West,** P.O. Box 487, Inverness, CA 94937: Catalog $3 ◆ Reproduction Shaker music boxes and country crafts. 415-669-7256. www.shakershops.com

**Smocking Bonnet,** 1341 W. Liberty Rd., Lisbon, MD 21765: Catalog $3 ◆ Music box movements. 800-524-1678; 410-489-7110 (in MD).

**Unicorn Studios,** 424 Blount Ave., Knoxville, TN 37920: Catalog $1 ◆ Windup and electronic music box movements, winking light units, and voice boxes for talking dolls and bears. 423-573-1863. www.imox.com/unicorn

## MUSICAL INSTRUMENTS

### General

**Alden Lee Company,** P.O. Box 7627, Menlo Park, CA 94026: Free information ◆ Music stands, sheet music cabinets, instrument racks, musician's tables, and other classic music furniture. 800-324-5200. aldenlee@aol.com

**Alto Music,** 680 Rt. 211 East, Middletown, NY 10940: Free information ◆ New and used guitars, recording and professional sound equipment, keyboards, amplifiers, keyboards, and drums. 914-692-6922.

**American Musical Supply,** 600 Industrial Ave., Paramus, NJ 07652: Free catalog ◆ Musical instruments. 800-458-4076. www.americanmusical.com

**Anyone Can Whistle,** 323 Wall St., Kingston, NY 12401: Free catalog ◆ Musical instruments, music boxes, wind chimes, whistles, and musical-sounding toys. 800-435-8863. anyonecan@chimes.com

**Ash Music Corp.,** 401 Old Country Rd., Carle Place, NY 11514: Free information with long SASE ◆ Musical instruments. 800-4-SAMASH; 516-333-8700 (in NY).

**Boosey Hawkes Musical Instruments Inc.,** 1925 Enterprise Ct., P.O. Box 130, Libertyville, IL 60048: Free catalog ◆ Musical instruments. 708-816-2500. www.boosey.com/mi

**Elderly Instruments,** 1100 N. Washington, Lansing, MI 48906: Free catalog ◆ Musical instruments, strings, straps, pickups, records, and books. 517-377-7890. www.elderly.com

**Factory Music,** 962 Washington St., Hanover, MA 02339: Free catalog ◆ Musical instruments and accessories. 781-829-0004.

**Freeport Music,** 41 Shore Dr., Huntington Bay, NY 11743: Free catalog ◆ Musical instruments and electronics. 888-549-4108; 516-549-4108 (in NY). www.freeportmusic.com

**Gamble Music Company,** 312 S. Wabash Ave., Chicago, IL 60604: Free catalog ◆ Music supplies for schools and churches. Also everything for musical programs. 800-621-4290. www.gamblemusic.com

**Gear By Mail,** P.O. Box 1018, Salem, NH 03079: Free information ◆ Used musical equipment. 603-894-6492.

**Giardinelli Band Instrument Company Inc.,** 7845 Maltlage Dr., Liverpool, NY 13090: Free catalog ◆ Guitars and amplifiers, percussion, orchestral, electronic portable keyboard, other musical instruments, and accessories. 800-288-2334; 315-652-4792 (in NY). www.giardinelli.com

**The House of Musical Traditions,** 7040 Carroll Ave., Takoma Park, MD 20912: Free catalog ◆ Bagpipes, flutes, and other percussion, string, and wind instruments. 800-540-3794; 301-270-9090 (in Metro DC area). www.hmtrad.com/index.html

**Interstate Musician Supply,** P.O. Box 510865, 13819 W. National Ave., New Berlin, WI 53151: Free catalog ◆ Musical instruments. 800-IN-A-BAND. musician@execpc.com

**Interworld Music & DJ Supply,** 270 Lafayette S., Ste. 1510, New York, NY 10012: Free catalog ◆ Musical equipment and DJ's supplies. Includes guitars, cases, pianos, and more. 800-394-6971.

**Kennelly Keys Music Inc.,** 20505 Hwy. 99, Lynnwood, WA 98036: Free catalog ◆ Musical instruments. 206-771-7020.

**L & M Music,** 6228 Airpark Dr., Chattanooga, TN 37421: Free information ◆ Musical instruments. 800-876-8638.

**Lark in the Morning,** P.O. Box 1176, Mendocino, CA 95460: Catalog $3 ◆ Hard-to-find musical instruments, books about music, CDs and cassettes, and videos. 707-964-5569. larkinam@larkinam.com

**Victor Litz Music Center,** 305 N. Frederick Ave., Gaithersburg, MD 20877: Free catalog ◆ Musical instruments. 301-948-7478. www.his.com/~vlitz

**Manny's Musical Instruments & Accessories Inc.,** 156 W. 48th St., New York, NY 10036: Free catalog ◆ Musical instruments. 212-869-5172.

**Musician's Friend,** P.O. Box 4520, Medford, OR 97501: Free catalog ◆ Musical instruments, recording equipment, and accessories. 800-776-5173. www.musiciansfriend.com

**National Educational Music Company Inc.,** 1181 Rt. 22, Box 130, Mountainside, NJ 07092: Free catalog ◆ Musical instruments, recorders, and accessories. 800-526-4593.

**New York Music,** 7144 Market St., Boardman, OH 44512: Free information ◆ Musical instruments and accessories. 800-241-6330; 216-758-9432 (in OH).

**Rhythm Band Instruments,** P.O. Box 126, Fort Worth, TX 76101: Free catalog ◆ Musical instruments and accessories for children and adults. 800-424-47244. www.rhythband.com

**Rock 'n Rhythm,** 19880 State Line Rd., South Bend, IN 46637: Free catalog ◆ Guitars, keyboards, and professional audio equipment. 888-472-7625.

**Used Gear by Mail,** Division Daddy's Junky Music Stores Inc., 1015 Candia Rd., Manchester, NH 03109: Free catalog ◆ Vintage, rare, and collectible used musical equipment. 603-623-4751. www.daddys.com

**West Manor Music,** 831 E. Gun Hill Rd., Bronx, NY 10467: Free price list ◆ Brass, woodwind, string, and percussion instruments. 718-655-5400.

**Whippoorwill Crafts,** 126 S. Market St., Boston, MA 02109: Free information ◆ Kaleidoscopes, wood boxes and chests, instrumentalist chimes, toys and games, clocks, and imaginative crafts. 800-860-9551; 617-523-5149 (in MA).

**Wichita Band Instrument Company,** 2525 E. Douglas, Wichita, KS 67211: Free catalog ◆ New and used brass and woodwind instruments of professional quality. 800-835-3006; 316-684-0291 (in KS). www.wichitaband.com

**The Willis Music Company,** 7380 Industrial Rd., Florence, KY 41022: Free catalog ◆ Keyboard, guitar, instrumental music, and accessories. 800-354-9799.

**Workshop Records,** Box 49507, Austin, TX 78765: Free catalog ◆ Instruments, recorders, amplifiers, videos, cassettes, and books. 800-543-6125. www.jumpnet.com/~musicianworkshop

**E.U. Wurlitzer Music & Sound,** Mail Order Division, 25 Bryant Ave., Milton, MA 02186: Free catalog ◆ Guitars, bases, drums, keyboards, recorders, mixers, and other used equipment. 617-696-2006. www.wurlitzer.com/maillist.html

**Yamaha Corp. of America,** Professional Audio Dept., P.O. Box 6600, Buena Park, CA 90622: Free list of retail sources ◆ Band instrument equipment and audio accessories. 800-937-7171. www.yamaha.com

## Accordions

**Castiglione Accordion,** 13300 E. 11 Mile, Warren, MI 48089: Catalog $5 ◆ New and used accordions, concertinas, and button boxes. 800-325-1832.

**Tessar Accordions,** 91 Winslow St., Riverside, RI 02915: Free catalog ◆ Accordions. 401-437-0235.

## Electronic Instruments & Equipment

**Pro-Sing Karaoke,** 7457 S. Sayre Ave., Bedford Park, IL 60638: Free information ◆ Karaoke hardware, software, and K-Tel and classical music. 708-594-1155. www.prosing.com

**Rich Music,** 264 South I-35, Denton, TX 76205: Free information ◆ Keyboards, recording equipment, synthesizers, drum machines, mixers and amplifiers, special effects, software, and accessories. 800-795-8493. www.richmusic.com

**Sweetwater Sound Inc.,** 5335 Bass Rd., Fort Wayne, IN 46808: Free information ◆ Keyboards, audio equipment and accessories, consoles, stands, monitors, mixers, and other equipment. 800-222-4700. www.sweetwater.com

**Synthony Music,** 3939 E. Campbell, Phoenix, AZ 85018: Free information ◆ Electronic music instruments, midi peripherals, and other equipment. 800-221-KEYS; 602-955-3590 (in AZ). www.synthony.com

**Thoroughbred Music,** 5511 Pioneer Park Blvd., Tampa, FL 33634: Free information ◆ Keyboards, electronics, drum machines, guitars, and accessories. 800-800-4654. www.tbred-music.com

## Folk & Traditional Instruments

**Cedar Creek Dulcimers Inc.,** 408 River Bluff Dr., Branson, MO 65616: Free brochure ◆ Dulcimers, cases, picks, and music books. 417-334-1395.

**Douglas Harp Company,** Arsalaan Fay-Harpbuilder, 44 White Pl., Brookline, MA 02146: Free brochure ◆ Celtic harps. 617-566-8644.

**The Early Music Shop,** 59-65 Boylston St., Brookline, MA 02146: Free information ◆ Spinets, harpsichords, clavichords, naker drums, lutes, organs, other reproduction historical instruments, do-it-yourself kits, and accessories. 617-277-8690. www.world.std.com/~vonhuene

**Earthshaking Music,** P.O. Box 18372, Atlanta, GA 30316: Free catalog ◆ Authentic instruments from Africa, Morocco, China, and other worldwide sources. 800-646-6795.

**Folk Mote Music,** 1034 Santa Barbara St., Santa Barbara, CA 93101: Free catalog ◆ Folk harps, banjos, music books, cassettes, CDs, and harp accessories. 805-962-0830. www.folkmote.com

**Folkcraft Instruments,** P.O. Box 807, Winsted, CT 06098: Catalog $1 ◆ Mountain and hammered dulcimers, folk harps, psalteries, books, and recordings. 800-433-3655; 860-379-9857 (in CT). www.folkcraft.com

**The Harp & Dragon,** 25 Madison St., Cortland, NY 13045: Free catalog with 1st class stamp ◆ Celtic musical instruments. 607-756-7372. www.HarpAndDragon.com

**Hobgoblin-Stoney End Music Company,** 34000 205th Ave., Red Wing, MN 55066: Free catalog ◆ Harps and cases, dulcimers, bodhran drums, flutes and fifes, other instruments, and accessories. 612-923-4709. www.stoneyend.com

**Hughes Dulcimer Company,** 4419 W. Colfax, Denver, CO 80204: Free catalog ◆ Kits for Appalachian and hammered dulcimers, banjos, mandolins, harps, and harpsichords. 303-572-3753.

**The Instrument Workshop,** 7793 Hwy. 66, P.O. Box 1060, Ashland, OR 97520: Free catalog ◆ Accessories and supplies for building early keyboard instruments, hammered dulcimers, psalteries, harps, and other instruments of the sirar family. 541-488-4671. www.fortepiano.com

**Ledford's Musical Instruments,** 125 Sunset Heights, Winchester, KY 40391: Free information ◆ Handmade dulcimers. 606-744-3974.

**Melody's Traditional Music Harp Shoppe,** 9410 FM 1960 W, Houston, TX 77070: Free catalog ◆ Harps, dulcimers, whistles, flutes, recorders, and music and instruction books. 800-893-4277; 281-890-4500 (in TX). www.folkharp.com

**Mid-East Manufacturing,** 7694 Progress Circle, West Melbourne, FL 32904: Free catalog ◆ Folk musical instruments. 407-724-1477. www.mid-east.com

**Musicmaker Kits,** P.O. Box 2117, Stillwater, MN 55082: Free catalog ◆ Build-them-yourself musical instrument kits. 800-432-5487; 651-439-9120 (in MN). www.musikit.com

**Red Dragon Music Den,** P.O. Box 1776, Martinsburg, WV 25401: Free catalog ◆ Fifes, rope tension drums, bagpipes, dulcimers, other traditional musical instruments, books, tapes, and CDs.

**Rocky Mountain Highland Supply,** 4421 Serra Pl., Lincoln, NE 68516: Free brochure ◆ Bagpipes, music, clothing, and accessories. 800-282-9351; 402-421-8202 (in NE). www.rmhs.com

## Guitars & Other Stringed Instruments

**Acacia Instruments,** 2091 Pottstown Pike, Pottstown, PA 19465: Free brochure ◆ Custom high-tech guitars with optional electronics. 610-469-3820. acacia@prolog.net

**Allen Guitars,** P.O. Box 1883, Colfax, CA 95713: Free brochure ◆ Handmade guitars, mandolins, and resophonic guitars. 916-346-6590. www.allenguitar.com

**Bell Brass Guitars,** 2901 N. Monroe, Spokane, WA 99205: Free information ◆ Resonator guitars. 509-448-7777.

**Bernunzio Vintage Instruments,** 875 East Ave., Rochester, NY 14607: Free catalog ◆ Banjos, mandolins, ukuleles, and guitars. 716-473-6140. bvi@servtech.com

**R.E. Bruné, Luthier,** 800 Greenwood St., Evanston, IL 60201: Free catalog ◆ Handmade harpsichords, lutes, and classical and baroque guitars. 847-864-7730. www.rebrune.com

**Calton Cases of Canada,** 4027 7th St. SE, Calgary, Alberta, Canada T2G 2Y9: Free information ◆ Cases for most stringed instruments. 403-243-4099.

**Caruso Music,** 94 State St., New London, CT 06320: Free information ◆ Keyboard and recording equipment for guitarists. 860-442-9600. www.caruso.net

**Carter Steel Guitars,** 617 W. Kearney St., Ste. 101, Mesquite, TX 75149: Free information ◆ Carter Pedal Steel guitars. 972-288-9100. www.steelguitar.com

**Carvin,** 12340 World Trade Dr., San Diego, CA 92128: Free catalog ◆ Guitars, amplifiers, recording mixers, equalizers, crossovers, speakers, microphones, and other equipment. 800-854-2235. www.carvin.com

**Casa Del Sol Violins Ltd.,** 4302 E. 62nd St., Indianapolis, IN 46220: Free price list ◆ Violins and cases. 800-423-0236. www.violincasa.com

**Celestial Wind,** 5221 SE 171st St., Hawthorne, FL 32640: Free brochure ◆ Handcrafted harps. 352-481-5856. 888-481-5856. www.oldcity.com/harps

**Chanterelle Banjo Shop,** Rt. 2, Box 564B, Appomattox, VA 24522: Free information ◆ Custom open-back banjos. 804-248-9234.

**Charley's Guitar Shop,** 2720 Royal Ln., Dallas, TX 75229: Free information ◆ New, used, and vintage guitars. 972-243-4187.

**Daddy's Junky Music,** 1015 Candia Rd., Manchester, NH 03109: Free catalog ◆ Used and new guitars, amplifiers and professional audio equipment, drums, keyboards, other instruments, accessories, and special effects. 603-623-4751. www.daddys.com

**Dave's Guitar Shop,** 1227 S. 3rd St., La Crosse, WI 54601: Free list ◆ New and used guitars. 608-785-7704. davesgtr@aol.com

**Discount Music Supply,** 41 Vreeland Ave., Totowa, NJ 07512: Free catalog ◆ Guitars and electronics equipment. 973-942-9411.

**Fender Guitar Strings,** 7975 N. Hayden Rd., Scottsdale, AZ 85258: Information $3 ◆ Guitar strings and picks. www.fender.com

**Fret 'N Fiddle,** 809 Pennsylvania Ave., St. Albans, WV 25177: Free list ◆ Vintage guitars. 304-722-5212.

**Garrett Park Guitars,** 150 E. Jennifer Rd., Annapolis, MD 21401: Free information ◆ New, used, and vintage guitars, amplifiers, and special effects equipment. 410-573-0500.

**Gibson Guitar Corp.,** 641 Massman Dr., Nashville, TN 37210: Free catalog ◆ Gibson guitars. 800-4-GIBSON. www.gibson.com

**Gruhn Guitars Inc.,** 400 Broadway, Nashville, TN 37203: Free list ◆ Vintage, used, and new electric and acoustic guitars, banjos, mandolins, and violins. 615-256-2033. www.gruhn.com

**Guitar Emporium,** 1610 Bardstown Rd., Louisville, KY 40205: Free list ◆ Vintage, new, and used guitars. 502-459-4153.

**Guitarmaker's Connection,** Martin Guitar Company, P.O. Box 329, Nazareth, PA 18064: Catalog $2 ◆ Guitar kits, parts, and exotic and domestic hardwoods. 800-633-2060. www.mguitar.com

**Guitars Unlimited,** 3255 Fairfield Ave., Bridgeport, CT 06605: Free information ◆ Vintage, new, and used guitars; mandolins and banjos; and amplifiers. 203-331-0040.

**Gulfcoast Guitars,** 1927 Beach Rd., Englewood, FL 34223: Free list ◆ Vintage and rare guitars. 941-474-1214.

**House of Strings,** 3411 Ray St., San Diego, CA 92104: Free list ◆ Guitars, mandolins, banjos, hammer and fretted dulcimers, psalteries, harps, and strings. 800-9-GUITAR. www.ally.ios.com/~hofstr19

**Intermountain Guitar & Banjo,** 712 E. 100 South, Salt Lake City, UT 84102: Free information ◆ New, used, and vintage banjos, mandolins, and guitars. 801-322-4682.

**International Luthiers Supply,** Box 580397, Tulsa, OK 74158: Catalog $1 ◆ Violin, banjo, and mandolin-making supplies and books. 918-835-4181.

**International Violin Company,** 1421 Clarkview Rd., Ste. 118, Baltimore, MD 21209: Free catalog ◆ European violins and bows, strings, tone wood, tools, varnishes, cases, and parts. 800-542-3538. www.Internationalviolin.com

**Ithaca Guitar Works,** 215 N. Cayuga St., Ithaca, NY 14850: Free information ◆ Handcrafted acoustic-electric guitars and new and vintage instruments. 607-272-2602. www.guitarworks.com

**Klein Electric Guitars,** 2560 Knob Hill Rd., Sonoma, CA 95476: Information $2 ◆ Electric guitars. 707-938-4189. klein@genesisnetwork.net

**Lark Street Music,** 227 Lark St., Albany, NY 12210: Price list $1 ◆ Rare, vintage, and used guitars. 518-463-6033. www.larkstreet.com

**Bernard E. Lehmann Stringed Instruments,** 34 Elton St., Rochester, NY 14607: Free information ◆ Handmade and vintage guitars, basses, banjos, mandolins, and violins. 716-461-2117.

**Local Music,** 774 E. 800 South, Salt Lake City, UT 84102: Free information ◆ Handcrafted guitars. 801-539-1439.

**J.K. Lutherie Guitars,** 11115 Sand Run, Harrison, OH 45030: Free catalog ◆ Vintage guitar parts, new and vintage accessories, catalogs and literature, guitar magazines, and out-of-print guitar books. 800-344-8880; 513-353-3320 (in OH). www.jklutherie.com

**Luthier Music Corp.,** 341 W. 44th St., New York, NY 10036: Free information ◆ Classical and flamenco guitars and sheet music, CDs, videos, nylon strings, and accessories. 212-397-6038. www.luthiermusic.com

**Luthiers Mercantile,** P.O. Box 774, Healdsburg, CA 95448: Catalog $10 ◆ Banjo and guitar kits. 800-477-4437; 707-433-1823 (in CA). www.lmi.com/~lmi

**Mandolin Brothers,** 629 Forest Ave., Staten Island, NY 10310: Free catalog ◆ Electronic and acoustic mandolins, guitars, autoharps, and banjos. 718-981-3226. www.mandoweb.com

**Matt's Music,** 778 Washington St., Hanover, MA 02339: Free catalog ◆ Free catalog ◆ Guitars and accessories. 781-829-0111.

**Metropolitan Music Store,** P.O. Box 1415, Mountain Rd., Stowe, VT 05672: Catalog $1.25 ◆ Violins, violas, cellos, luthier supplies, tools, and wood. 802-253-4814.

**Monster Strings,** P.O. Box 39551, Fort Lauderdale, FL 33339: Free brochure ◆ Acoustic instrument strings. 800-750-9946. www.monsterstrings.com

**National Resophonic Guitars,** 871 Via Esteban, San Luisa Obispo, CA 93401: Free information ◆ Resonator guitars. 805-546-8442. www.nationalguitars.com

**Ovation Instruments,** P.O. Box 597, Bloomfield, CT 06002: Free information ◆ Finger-style guitars.

**Rhoads Music,** 9 N. Market St., Elizabethtown, PA 17022: List $1 ◆ New and used guitars, amplifiers, and special effects equipment. 717-361-9272.

**Rhythm City,** 1485 NE Expressway, Atlanta, GA 30329: Free information ◆ Guitars, amplifiers, special effects and recording equipment, keyboards, drums, and accessories. 404-320-7253.

**Ribbecke Guitars,** P.O. Box 1581, Santa Rosa, CA 95402: Free information ◆ Handcrafted acoustic archtops and flattop guitars. 707-433-3778. www.ribbecke.com

**Robinson's Harp Shop,** P.O. Box 161, 33908 Mount Laguna Dr., Mount Laguna, CA 91948: Free catalog ◆ Harp-making parts, plans, strings, hardware, and books. 619-473-8556.

**S.I.T. Strings Company,** 815 S. Broadway, Akron, OH 44311: Free catalog ◆ Strings. 800-258-2211.

**Smith Music Products,** 9175 Butte Rd., Sweet, ID 83670: Free information ◆ Enhancers for any style acoustic guitar. 800-942-6509.

**Southwest Strings,** 1050 S. Park Ave., Tucson, AZ 85719: Free catalog ◆ Violins, other string instruments, strings, and accessories. 800-528-3430. www.swstrings.com

**Stewart-MacDonalds Guitar Shop Supply,** P.O. Box 900, Athens, OH 45701: Free catalog ◆ Parts, tools, and supplies for building and repairing guitars, violins, banjos, dulcimers, and mandolins. 800-848-2273; 614-592-3021 (in OH). www.stewmac.com

**Stringed Instrument Division,** 123 W. Alder, Missoula, MT 59802: Catalog $15 (annual subscription) ◆ New and vintage banjos, mandolins, acoustic guitars, and electric instruments. 406-549-1502. sid@netguitar.com

**Matt Umanov,** 273 Bleecker St., New York, NY 10014: Free list ◆ Used and vintage guitars. 212-675-2157.

**Weinkrantz Musical Supply Company,** 870 Market St., Ste. 1265, San Francisco, CA 94102: Free catalog ◆ Violins, violas, and cellos. 800-736-8742.

**West L.A. Music,** 11345 Santa Monica Blvd., West Los Angeles, CA 90025: Free information ◆ New and vintage guitars. Also sound systems, keyboards, recording equipment, and accessories. 310-477-1945. www.westlamusic.com

**Sylvia Woods Harp Center,** P.O. Box 816, Montrose, CA 91021: Free catalog ◆ Harps, recordings, books, jewelry, and gifts. 800-272-4277; 818-956-1363 (in CA). www.harpcenter.com

**Yamaha Music Corp.,** P.O. Box 6600, Buena Park, CA 90622: Free list of retail sources ◆ Handcrafted guitars, keyboards, and audio equipment. 714-522-9011. www.yamaha-motor.com

**Zeta Music,** 2230 Livingston Ave., Oakland, CA 94606: Catalog $5 ◆ Electronic guitars, violins, and controllers. 800-622-6434. www.zetamusic.com

## Harmonicas

**Kevins Harps,** 210 Farnsworth Ave., Bordentown, NJ 08505: Catalog $2 ◆ Harmonicas and how-to videos and audio cassettes. 800-274-2776; 609-298-2202 (in NJ). www.kharps.com

**Klutz Press,** 2121 Staunton Ct., Palo Alto, CA 94306: Free information ◆ Harmonicas and how-to books. 650-424-0739. www.klutz.com

**Melody By Mail,** P.O. Box 830, Glen Allen, VA 23060: Free information ◆ Harmonicas and how-to-play instruction package.

## Keyboard Instruments

**Altenburg Piano House Inc.,** 1150 E. Jersey St., Elizabeth, NJ 07201: Free catalog ◆ Organs (including church organs) and pianos. 800-526-6979.

**Bedient,** 4221 NW 37th St., Lincoln, NE 68524: Free brochure ◆ Pipe organs. 402-470-3675.

**Edirol,** P.O. Box 4919, Blaine, WA 98231: Free catalog ◆ Keyboards, electronics, software, and recordings. 800-380-2580. www.edirol.com

**Johnson Music Company,** P.O. Box 615, Mt. Airy, NC 27030: Brochure $2 ◆ Antique pump organ parts. 919-320-2212.

**Keyboard Outlet,** 14235 Inwood, Dallas, TX 75244: Free information with long SASE ◆ New and used keyboards. 972-490-5397. koutlet@gte.net

**Keyboards Today,** 21110 Nordhoff St., Unit L, Chatsworth, CA 01311: Free brochure ◆ Casio keyboard accessories. 800-266-2159. www.casiomusic.com

**Player Piano Company,** 704 E. Douglas, Wichita, KS 67202: Free catalog ◆ Player piano restoration supplies and music rolls. 316-263-3241.

**Ragtime Automated Music,** 4218 Jessup Rd., Ceres, CA 95307: Catalog $10 ◆ Calliopes, band organs, nickelodeons, player pianos, other Victorian musical instruments, and kits to convert regular pianos to player-pianos. 209-667-5525.

**Speir Music,** 510 S. Garland Ave., Garland, TX 75040: Free information ◆ New and used keyboards, other instruments, and accessories. 800-219-3281.

**Valiant Industries Inc.,** 2110 Nordhoff St., Unit L, Chatsworth, CA 91311: Free brochure ◆ Casio keyboard accessories. 800-266-2159. www.casiokeyboards.com

**Yamaha Music Corp.,** P.O. Box 6600, Buena Park, CA 90622: Free list of retail sources ◆ Handcrafted guitars, keyboards, and audio equipment. 714-522-9011. www.yamaha-motor.com

## Percussion Instruments

**Aquarian Accessories,** 1140 N. Tustin Ave., Anaheim, CA 92807: Free information ◆ Drumheads and accessories. 800-473-0231. aquarian98@aol.com

**Fork's Drum Closet,** 2707 12th Ave. South, Nashville, TN 37204: Free information ◆ Drum sets, cymbals, drumsticks, drumheads, and hardware. 800-55-FORKS. www.forksdrumcloset.com

**HQ Percussion Products,** P.O. Box 430065, St. Louis, MO 63143: Free information ◆ Cymbals, hi-hats, drum set silencers, and percussion accessories. 314-647-9009. www.hqpercussion.com

**Lone Star Percussion,** 10611 Control Pl., Dallas, TX 75238: Free catalog ◆ Percussion instruments. 214-340-0835. www.lonestarpercussion.com

**Pro-Mark Corp.,** 10707 Craighead Dr., Houston, TX 77025: Free information ◆ Drumsticks and percussion accessories. 800-233-5250. www.promark-stix.com

**Vintage Drum Center,** 2243 Ivory Dr., Libertyville, IA 52567: Free catalog ◆ Vintage drum sets and singles. 800-729-3111. www.vintagedrum.com/

**Waddell's Drum Center,** 6433 Leechburg Rd., Leechburg, PA 15656: Free catalog ◆ Drums and accessories. 800-933-DRUM. www.waddellsdrums.com

## Wind Instruments

**Charles Double Reed Company,** P.O. Box 2610, 30 Pleasant St., Conway, NH 03818: Free catalog ◆ Reeds and accessories. 800-REED-TIP. www.charlesmusic.com

**Coyote Flutes,** 2942 41st Ave. SE, Albany, OR 97321: Free information ◆ Native American flutes. 541-928-2097.

**Discount Reed Company,** 24307 Magic Mountain Pkwy., Ste. 181, Valencia, CA 91355: Free catalog ◆ Reeds for clarinets, saxophones, bassoons, oboes, and other instruments. 800-428-5993. www.discountreed.com

**Flute World,** P.O. Box 250248, Franklin, MI 48025: Free catalog ◆ Professional and student flutes and piccolos, music accessories, recorders, and recordings. 248-855-0410.

**Hickey's Music Center,** 104 Adams St., Ithaca, NY 14850: Free catalog ◆ Print music, compact discs, and trombone accessories. 800-442-5397; 607-272-8262 (in NY). www.hickeys.com/newsite

**Oregon Flute Store,** 29765 Gimpl Way, Eugene, OR 97402: Free brochure ◆ Handmade flutes. 888-88-FLUTE. www.teleport.com/~orflute

**The Saxophone Shop,** 2834 Central St., Evanston, IL 60201: Free information ◆ New and used saxophones, reeds, and mouthpieces. 847-328-5711. www.saxshop.com

**Schilke Music Inc.,** 4520 James Pl., Melrose Park, IL 60160: Free list of retail sources, specify instruments or mouthpieces ◆ Trumpets and mouthpieces. 708-343-8858.

**The White Buffalo Stores Inc.,** 416 E. Beale St., Kingman, AZ 86401: Catalog $2 (refundable) ◆ Handmade flutes. 520-753-7800. www.ctaz.com/~whitbuflo

**The Woodwind & the Brasswind,** 19880 State Line Rd., South Bend, IN 46637: Free catalog (specify wood or brass) ◆ Musical instruments. 219-272-8266. www.wwandbw.com

## NAMEPLATES

**John Hinds & Company,** 81 Greenridge Dr. West, Elmira, NY 14905: Free brochure ◆ Cast plaques and nameplates for homes, offices, buildings, parks, historic areas, and other uses. 607-733-6712.

**Newman Brothers Inc.,** 5609 Center Hill Ave., Cincinnati, OH 45216: Free information ◆ Standard and custom cast bronze and aluminum plaques. 800-447-1072.

**Smith-Cornell Inc.,** 1545 Holland Rd., Maumee, OH 43537: Free brochure ◆ Brass and aluminum historic markers. 800-325-0248; 419-891-4335 (in OH).

## NEEDLECRAFTS

**Alcon Braid,** P.O. Box 429, Hickory, NC 28603: Free catalog ◆ Macramé, chair-weaving, and crochet supplies. 800-523-4371. sandra@griffinshine.com

**American Needlewomen,** P.O. Box 6472, Fort Worth, TX 76140: Catalog $1 ◆ Needlecraft kits and supplies from Europe and the United States. 800-433-2231.

**Ann's Needlework Shop,** P.O. Box 3766, Springfield, IL 62708: Free price list ◆ Needlepoint and cross-stitch supplies. 800-553-0040. www.webmarketing.com/anns

**Annie's Attic,** 1 Annie Ln., Big Sandy, TX 75755: Catalog $2 ◆ Sewing and needlecraft patterns. 800-282-6643.

**Artisan Design,** 808 S. 9th St., Broken Arrow, OK 74012: Free information ◆ Floor stand, ultra-compact tabletop or lap stand, and scroll frame for needlecrafting. 800-747-8263; 918-251-9795 (in OK).

**Artistic Needle,** 6241 Kevin Ct., Brighton, MI 48116: Free brochure ◆ Needlework kits. 313-229-2309.

**Arts 'N Crafts 'N Things,** 2260 N. Orange Mall, Orange, CA 92665: Free brochure ◆ Needlework supplies. 714-637-6292.

**Barkim Ltd.,** 47 W. Polk St., Ste. 100, Chicago, IL 60653: Catalog and yarn samples $4 ◆ Sweater kits, books, patterns, and yarns. 888-548-2211. www.barkim.com

**Beacon Fabric & Notions,** 6801 Gulfport Blvd. South, Ste. 10, South Pasadena, FL 33707: Free brochure ◆ Machine embroidery thread and supplies. 800-713-8157; 813-345-6994 (in FL).

**Debra R. Bergmann,** 172 Cardinal Rd., Chalfont, PA 18914: Free brochure ◆ Counted cross-stitch kits for clergy-related stoles. 215-822-3835.

**Braid-Aid,** 466 Washington St., Pembroke, MA 02359: Catalog $4 ◆ Braided rug kits and braiding accessories, wool by the pound or yard, and hooking, basket-making, shirret, spinning, and weaving supplies. 781-826-2560.

**Brittany,** P.O. Box 130, Elk, CA 95432: Free information ◆ How-to crochet books and wood knitting needles. 888-488-9669.

**Cactus Punch Embroidery Digitizing,** 12995 N. Oracle Rd., #147-327, Tucson, AZ 85739: Free catalog ◆ Macintosh and PC digitized designs for disk-based embroidery machines. 800-487-6972. www.cactus-punch.com

**California Stitchery,** P.O. Box 2007, Van Nuys, CA 91404: Free catalog ◆ Judaic design and other needlepoint, embroidery, and latch-hook kits. 800-345-3332.

**Camus International,** 740 Conlon Rd., Lansing, NY 14882: Price list $2 ◆ Tartan point pillow, cross-stitch, and needlepoint kits. 800-38-CAMUS.

**Carolina Country House Inc.,** 10326 Hollybrook Dr., Charlotte, NC 28227: Free brochure ◆ Counted cross-stitch kits. 704-364-1414.

**Samuel Charis Knits,** 372 Florin Rd., Ste. 312, Sacramento, CA 95831: Free catalog ◆ Sweater-making kits. 800-321-KNIT; 916-392-8213 (in CA).

**Cottage Creek Cross-stitch,** 13327 187th Ct. NE, Woodinville, WA 98072: Free information ◆ Counted needlework patterns made from personal photographs. 800-963-3357.

**The Cotton Patch,** 3405 Hall Ln., Lafayette, CA 94549: Catalog $8 ($5 refundable) ◆ Quilting books, fabric swatches, silk wire ribbon, hand-dyed fabrics, knitting needles, and other supplies. 800-835-4418. CottonPa@aol.com

**Count Your Blessings,** 8301 Philadelphia Rd., Baltimore, MD 21237: Free brochure ◆ Cross-stitching supplies. 410-686-2655. www.count-your-blessings.com

**The Counted Thread,** 200 Turner Rd., Richmond, VA 23225: Free price list ◆ Needlework kits. 800-390-0035; 804-276-5434 (in VA).

**The Country Quayle,** 1090 W. 2700 South, Perry, UT 84302: Free brochure ◆ Needlecraft patterns. 801-723-6580.

**Kirsten Cowan Needleworks,** 72 Earl Grey Rd., Toronto, Ontario, Canada M4J 3L5: Free catalog ◆ Needlepoint sweater kits. 800-203-7985; 416-778-8283 (in Toronto). www.interlog.com/~kcowan

**Craft King Mail Order Catalog,** P.O. Box 90637, Lakeland, FL 33804: Free catalog ◆ Needlecraft, art and craft, and macramé supplies. 888-CRAFTY-1. www.weshop.com/craftking

**Craft Resources Inc.,** P.O. Box 828, Fairfield, CT 06430: Catalog $1 ◆ Latch-hooking, needlepoint, crewel, and cross-stitching kits. Also supplies for string art, basket-making, metal and wood crafts, stained glass, and other crafts. 800-243-2874; 203-254-7702 (in CT).

**Crafts by Donna,** P.O. Box 1456, Costa Mesa, CA 92626: Catalog $2 ◆ Threads, craft supplies, and how-to books for Brazilian embroidery. 714-545-8567. donnaf2@juno.com

**Crafty Lady,** 15401 Hall Rd., Macomb, MI 48044: Free information ◆ Exotic and natural fibers, counted cross-stitch and needlepoint supplies, and knit-wear kits. 800-455-YARN.

**Crafty Needle,** Division California Stitchery, 6015 Sunnyslope Ave., Van Nuys, CA 91401: Free catalog ◆ Needlecraft kits and supplies. 800-345-3332.

**Creative Keepsakes,** P.O. Box 7651, Monroe, LA 71203: Free catalog ◆ Samplers and counted cross-stitch kits. 800-227-7996. www.creativekeepsakes.com

**Creative Stitches,** P.O. Box 89, Bountiful, UT 84011: Free information ◆ Machine embroidery supplies. 800-748-5144.

**Dyed in the Wool,** P.O. Box 498, Crowley, LA 70527: Free list of retail sources with long SASE ◆ Needlecraft kits and yarns. 800-426-3393. www.dyedinthewool.com

**Ehrman Tapestries,** 5300 Dorsey Hall Dr., Ste. 110, Ellicott City, MD 21042: Catalog $5 (refundable) ◆ Needlepoint kits with gardening and floral themes. 888-826-8600. www.ehrmantapestry.com

**Ernel Yarns,** 1419 Burlingame, Burlingame, CA 94010: Free information ◆ Yarns and kits. 800-343-4874.

**The Essamplaire,** 4126 44th St., Red Deer, Alberta, Canada T4N 1H2: Catalog $3 ◆ Counted thread sampler kits and chart packs. Includes authorized reproductions from Canadian and European museums and private collections. 403-347-3574.

**Fingerlakes Yarns,** 1193 Stewarts Corners Rd., Genoa, NY 13071: Yarn samples $3 (request list of retail sources) ◆ Sweater kits and merino, angora, and silk yarns. 800-441-9665.

**Fireside Stitchery,** The Frazer Shopping Center, 490 Lancaster Pike, Frazer, PA 19355: Catalog $4 ◆ Handpainted canvases, threads, handcrafted wood frames, and other supplies. 800-531-2607.

**5T's Embroidery Supply,** P.O. Box 484, Macedon, NY 14502: Free catalog ◆ Machine embroidery supplies. 315-986-8434.

**Four Corners Designs Inc.,** 910 Vinecrest, Richardson, TX 75080: Free brochure ◆ Needlecraft patterns. 800-573-3687; 972-758-9248 (in TX).

**Friendstitch Ltd.,** Savage Mill Box 2037, 8600 Foundry St., Savage, MD 20763: Catalog $2 ◆ Needlecraft supplies and yarns. 301-317-9965. www.stitching.com/friendstitch

**Ginger & Spice Needlework Designs,** P.O. Box 303, Reading, PA 19607: Free catalog ◆ Needlecraft designs. 800-543-1359.

**Green Apple Inc.,** 4537 Hwy. 17 S. Bypass, Myrtle Beach, SC 29577: Free catalog ◆ Samplers and other needlecraft projects. 800-745-0641; 803-293-4424 (in SC). www.stitching.com/greenapple

**Halcyon Yarn,** 12 School St., Bath, ME 04530: Free information ◆ Yarn and knitting accessories. 800-341-0282. www.halcyonyarn.com

**Martha Hall,** 20 Bartol Island Rd., Freeport, ME 04032: Catalog $2 ◆ Easy-to-knit wool sweater kits and hand-dyed silk, mohair, linen, cotton, cashmere, and alpaca yarn. 800-643-4566.

**Hands to Work, Hearts to God,** P.O. Box 263, Cottage Grove, OR 97424: Catalog 50¢ ◆ Patterns and kits featuring cross-stitching, ribbon embroidery, hemstitching, and open work. 541-942-4227. www.handstowork.com

**Heartland-House-Designs,** 741 N. Oak Park Ave., Oak Park, IL 60302: Free brochure ◆ Cross-stitch and needlepoint designs available as kits or chart packs. 888-875-3980.

**Hedgehog Handworks,** P.O. Box 45384, Westchester, CA 90045: Catalog $5 ◆ Semi-precious beads and attachments, sewing notions, gold and silver threads, needlecraft and embroidery supplies, and accessories. 888-670-6040; 310-670-6040 (in CA).

**Herr's & Bernat,** 70 Eastgate Dr., P.O. Box 630, Danville, IL 61834: Free information ◆ Latch-hook kits and lampshade making supplies. 800-637-2647.

**Herrschners Inc.,** 2800 Hoover Rd., Stevens Point, WI 54492: Free catalog ◆ Needlecraft supplies, kits, and yarns. 800-441-0838. www.herrschners.com

**HH Designs,** 170 Boston Post Rd., Madison, CT 06443: Catalog $2 ◆ Needlecraft candlewick pillow kits. 800-309-5348.

**The Hill Knittery,** 10720 Yonge St., Richmond Hill, Ontario, Canada L4C 3C9: Free information ◆ Yarns, kits, books, and how-to videos. 800-551-KNIT.

**Homestead Needle Arts,** 12235 S. Saginaw St., Grand Blanc, MI 48439: Catalog $3 (refundable) ◆ Threads, charts, handpainted canvases, books, and accessories. 800-365-1462.

**House of White Birches,** 306 E. Parr Rd., Berne, IN 46711: Free catalog ◆ Crochet kits and patterns.

**Imagiknit Ltd.,** 2586 Yonge St., Toronto, Ontario, Canada M4P 2J3: Catalog $4.50 ◆ Yarns, how-to books, and kits. 800-318-9426.

**Just CrossStitch,** 405 Riverhills Business Park, Birmingham, AL 35242: Free information ◆ Counted cross-stitch kits. 800-768-5878.

**Just Needlin',** 611 NE Woods Chapel Rd., Lee's Summit, MO 64064: Catalog $3 (refundable) ◆ Cross-stitch kits and supplies. 816-246-5102.

**Keepsake Quilting,** Rt. 25B, P.O. Box 1618, Centre Harbor, NH 03226: Free catalog ◆ Quilting books and accessories, patterns, notions, fabrics, scrap bags, and batting. 800-865-9458. www.keepsakequilting.com

**Ladybug Creations,** P.O. Box 30694, Middleburg Heights, OH 44130: Free catalog with long SASE ◆ Brazilian embroidery kits.

**Carolin Lowy Needlecraft,** 630 Sun Meadows Dr., Kernersville, NC 27284: Price list $2 ◆ Needlepoint, knitting, embroidery, and counted cross-stitch patterns. 336-784-7576. www.kernersville.com/lowy

**Mary Maxim Inc.,** 2001 Holland Ave., P.O. Box 5019, Port Huron, MI 48061: Free catalog ◆ Needlecraft kits, yarn, and accessories. 800-962-9504.

**Mimi's Fabrications,** 77 Howell St., Waynesville, NC 28786: Catalog $3 ◆ Silk ribbon and embroidery supplies. 800-948-3455. www.mimisbymail.com

**Moss Yarns Needlearts,** 225 Pinewood, Hot Springs National Park, AR 71913: Catalog $3 ◆ Needlecraft supplies and imported and domestic yarns. 501-623-5106.

**Claire Murray Inc.,** P.O. Box 390, Ascutney, VT 05030: Catalog $5 ◆ Hand-hooked rugs and kits. 800-252-4733. www.clairemurray.com

**Nasco,** 901 Janesville Ave., Fort Atkinson, WI 53538: Free catalog ◆ Weaving supplies, looms, tools, yarn, and needlecraft accessories. 800-558-9595. www.nascofa.com

**Needle Magic Inc.,** 2815 Orchard Rd., Dandridge, TN 37725: Free catalog ◆ Cross-stitch kits. 423-397-9423.

**The Needlecraft Shop,** 23 Old Pecan Rd., Big Sandy, TX 75755: Free catalog ◆ Plastic canvas supplies and patterns. 903-636-4000.

**Needlecraft Shop,** 23 Old Pecan Rd., Big Sandy, TX 75755: Free catalog ◆ Needlecraft kits and supplies. 903-636-4000.

**Needlepoint Inc.,** Catalog & Mail Order Division, 420 Sutter St., San Francisco, CA 94108: Free catalog ◆ Exclusive needlepoint designs. 800-616-1622.

**Nordic Needle,** 1314 Gateway Dr., Fargo, ND 58103: Free catalog ◆ Needlework projects, supplies, and books. 800-433-4321; 701-235-5231 (in ND). www.nordicneedle.com

**Northwest Peddlers,** P.O. Box 70779, Eugene, OR 97401: Free information ◆ Yarns, needlecraft kits, and supplies. 800-764-9276; 541-465-9003 (in OR).

**Patterncrafts,** 3919 Van Teylingen, Colorado Springs, CO 80917: Catalog $2 ◆ Quilt patterns and hoops, counted cross-stitch and sewing projects, stencils, country crafts, wall hangings, needlecrafts, dolls, and stuffed animals. 800-414-3888.

**Patternworks,** P.O. Box 1690, Poughkeepsie, NY 12601: Catalog $3 ◆ Knitting supplies and kits. 800-438-5464; 914-462-8000 (in NY). www.patternworks.com

**Peacock Alley Needlepoint Crafts,** 650 Croswell SE, Grand Rapids, MI 49506: Catalog $2 ◆ Needlecraft kits, supplies, and canvasses. 616-454-9898.

**Personal Threads Boutique,** 8025 W. Dodge Rd., Omaha, NE 68114: Free information ◆ Yarns and needlecraft supplies. 800-306-7733.

**Anne Powell Ltd.,** P.O. Box 3060, Stuart, FL 34995: Catalog $5 ◆ Needlework supplies and one-of-a-kind antique sewing tools. 407-287-3007. www.annepowellltd.com

**Pretty Punch,** P.O. Box 13087, Scottsdale, AZ 85267: Free catalog ◆ Punch embroidery supplies. 800-486-1234. www.ascotchase.com

**Ragtime Crochet,** 12105 W. Center Rd., Ste. 286, Omaha, NE 68144: Catalog $2 (refundable) ◆ Rag crochet fabrics and supplies. 800-228-6633.

**Catherine Reurs Needlepoint,** 50 Marion Rd., Watertown, MA 02172: Catalog $1 ◆ Needlepoint kits. 800-743-0675.

**Robin's Nest Designs,** 6303 Craig Rd., Durham, NC 27712: Free brochure ◆ Specializes in personalized and exclusive cross-stitch and needlepoint designs from photographs, artwork, or pictures. 919-471-6576.

**The Royal Gallery,** 5518 Cathedral Oaks, Santa Barbara, CA 93111: Free catalog ◆ Tapestry kits. 805-964-8899.

**Richard Sabol,** 1 Pisacatqua Rd., Dover, NH 03820: Free brochure with long SASE and two 1st class stamps ◆ Cross-stitch kits, rubber stamps, and jewelry. 603-742-6324.

**The Scarlet Letter,** P.O. Box 397, Sullivan, WI 53178: Catalog $4 ◆ Museum reproduction counted thread sampler kits, hand-woven linens and silks, sewing notions, books, and frames. 414-593-8470.

**Schoolhouse Press,** 6899 Cary Bluff, Pittsville, WI 54466: Catalog $3 ◆ Knitting books, kits, and supplies. 715-884-2799.

**Sew Fancy,** Unit 23, RR 1, Beeton, Ontario, Canada L0G 1A0: Catalog $5 ◆ Fabrics, notions, needle art patterns, and supplies for heirloom sewing, smocking, and quilting. 800-SEW-FNCY. www.sewfancy.com

**Sew Unique,** 626 15th St. East, Tuscaloosa, AL 35401: Free brochure with long SASE ◆ Fabrics and laces, smocking and embroidery supplies, ready to smock kits, and other supplies. 800-837-8799.

**Sheep Dreams,** Box 103, Prattsburgh, NY 14873: Free catalog ◆ Needlepunch hooking kits. 607-522-4305.

**Shillcraft,** 8899 Kelso Dr., Baltimore, MD 21221: Catalog $2 ◆ Needlecraft supplies and latch-hook kits for rugs, wall hangings, and other crafts. 410-682-3060.

**Southwest Decoratives,** 191 Bighorn Ridge NE, Albuquerque, NM 87122: Catalog $3 ◆ Quilt patterns and kits, applique patterns and kits, cross-stitch charts and kits, and stenciling supplies. 505-856-9585. www.swdecoratives.com

**The Spinning Wheel,** Martha Hauschka, 2 Ridge St., Dover, NH 03820: Free information ◆ Needlecraft supplies, yarns, and natural fibers. Also cross-stitch, crewel, candle-wicking, and other needlecrafts. 603-749-4246.

**The Stitchery,** 120 N. Meadows Rd., Medfield, MA 02052: Free catalog ◆ Needlecraft kits. 800-225-4127.

**Stitches East,** 55 E. 52nd St., New York, NY 10022: Free information ◆ Knitting and needlecraft supplies. 212-421-0112.

**Things Japanese,** 9805 NE 116th St., Ste. 7160, Kirkland, WA 98034: Catalog $1 ◆ Brocade threads and yarns, silk-blend and metallic threads, needlework kits, silk ribbons, and embroidery and other supplies. 425-821-2287.

**Three Kittens Yarn Shoppe,** 805 Sibley Memorial Hwy., St. Paul, MN 55118: Free catalog ◆ Needlecraft supplies. 800-489-4969; 612-457-4969 (in MN).

**Thumbelina Needlework Shop,** P.O. Box 1065, Solvang, CA 93464: Information $1.75 ◆ Books, fabrics, threads, yarns, and kits. 800-789-4136. www.thumbelina.com

**Tomorrow's Treasures,** 19722 144th Ave. NE, Woodinville, WA 98072: Free brochure ◆ Needlework frames for the lap and floor. 800-882-8932; 425-487-2636 (in WA).

**The Tracery,** P.O. Box 340, Oriental, NC 28571: Free catalog ◆ Needlepoint kits and accessories. 800-797-9025. www.tracery.com

**Treasured Heirlooms,** 13507 Candlewood Ct., Moorpark, CA 93021: Free newsletter with long SASE ◆ Fabrics, lace, embroideries, needlework supplies, notions, and more. 805-523-2520.

**Susan Vale Sweaters,** Denver International Airport, Denver, CO 80249: Free information ◆ Mohair sweaters and jackets in knit-yourself kits. 303-342-8485.

**The Weaver's Loft,** 308 S. Pennsylvania Ave., Centre Hall, PA 16828: Free information ◆ Knitting, weaving, and spinning supplies and yarn. 800-693-7242; 814-364-1433 (in PA). www.knitters-underground.com

**The Weaver's Place,** 75 Mellor Ave., Baltimore, MD 21228: Free information ◆ Japanese braiding equipment and books. 410-788-7262.

**Web of Thread,** 1410 Broadway, Paducah, KY 42001: Catalog $3 ◆ Supplies for serging and embroidery. Also metallic, rayon, and silk threads for hand and machine embroidery. 800-955-8185; 502-575-9700 (in KY). www.webofthread.com

**Erica Wilson Needle Works,** 717 Madison Ave., New York, NY 10021: Free brochure ◆ Needlepoint, cross-stitch, and crewel projects. Also how-to books, handpainted canvasses, and embroidery frames. 800-973-7422.

**The Woolery,** RD 1, Genoa, NY 13071: Catalog $2 ◆ Books and spinning, weaving, and knitting supplies. 315-497-1542. jive@woolery.com

**Woolgathering,** 750 Calico Ct., Waukesha, WI 53186: Free price list ◆ Rowan yarns, needlepoint kits, buttons, books, magazines, and sewing notions. 888-248-3225.

**Wooly Knits,** 6728 Lowell Ave., McLean, VA 22101: Catalog $5 (12 issues) ◆ Designer yarns, unusual buttons, needlecraft kits, how-to knitting books, and needlework supplies. 703-448-9665. www.woolyknits.com

**Yarn Shop,** 20 Suomi Rd., Hyannis, MA 02601: Free brochure ◆ Fashion kits for children and adults. Also supplies. 508-775-2241.

**Your Accents,** 4502 Troon Tr., Dayton, OH 45429: Free catalog ◆ Greek fraternity and sorority cross-stitch and needlepoint kits. 937-298-9905.

## NEWSPAPERS & MAGAZINES

**American Family Publishers,** P.O. Box 62000, Tampa, FL 33662: Free information ◆ Magazine subscriptions. 800-237-2400.

**Below Wholesale Magazines,** 1909 Prosperity St., Reno, NV 89502: Free catalog ◆ Magazine subscriptions. 800-800-0062. www.magazinediscounts.com

**Box Seat Collectibles,** P.O. Box 2013, Halesite, NY 11743: Catalog $5 ◆ Sports collectibles, historical newspapers from the 19th to 20th century, and other memorabilia. 516-423-1025.

**Stephen A. Goldman Historical Newspapers,** P.O. Box 359, Parkton, MD 21120: Catalog $2 ◆ Historical newspapers. 410-357-8204. www.historicalnews.com

**Historic Newspaper Archives,** 1582 Hart St., Rahway, NJ 07065: Free catalog ◆ Newspapers for the day on which you were born. 800-221-3221; 908-381-2332 (in NJ).

**Hughes Newspapers,** Box 3636, Williamsport, PA 17701: Catalog $1 ◆ Rare and historic newspapers, from the 1600s through the 1880s. 717-326-1045.

**Alan Levine Movie & Book Collectibles,** P.O. Box 1577, Bloomfield, NJ 07003: Catalog $5 ◆ Books on collecting, old-time movie posters and lobby cards, and radio, television, and movie magazines. 973-743-5288.

**J.K. Lutherie Guitars,** 11115 Sand Run, Harrison, OH 45030: Free catalog ◆ Vintage and new guitar parts, catalogs and other literature, guitar magazines, and out-of-print guitar books. 800-344-8880; 513-353-3320 (in OH). www.jklutherie.com

**Jim Lyons,** 970 Terra Bella Ave., Mountain View, CA 94043: Free information ◆ Historic newspapers, from the 1600s to the 1970s. 415-969-6612.

**Robert A. Madle,** 4406 Bestor Dr., Rockville, MD 20853: Catalog $3 ◆ Science fiction and fantasy magazines and books, from 1900 to present. 301-460-4712.

**MultiNewspapers,** Box 866, Dana Point, CA 92629: Free brochure ◆ English language magazines and newspapers from over 60 countries. 949-499-6207. multinewspapers@compuserve.com

**The Opera Box,** P.O. Box 994, Teaneck, NJ 07666: Free catalog ◆ Rare books, magazines, autograph material, and other opera collectibles. 201-833-4176.

**The Overlook Connection,** P.O. Box 526, Woodstock, GA 30188: Catalog $1 ◆ Books, audio cassettes, and magazines on horror, science fiction, fantasy, and mystery. 770-926-1762. www.overlookconnection.com

**Steven S. Raab,** P.O. Box 471, Ardmore, PA 19003: Catalog $5 ◆ Autographs, signed books and photos, historic newspapers, World War I posters, and other memorabilia. 610-446-6193. www.raabautographs.com

**Rogofsky Movie Collectibles,** Box 107, Glen Oaks, NY 11004: Catalog $3 ◆ TV and movie magazines, photos, and other collectibles. 718-723-0954.

**Sparky's Mail Order,** 3724 N. Page, Chicago, IL 60634: Free information with long SASE ◆ Movie and TV soundtrack records on vinyl. Also movie and TV paperbacks. 312-625-8732.

**Richard W. Spellman,** 610 Monticello Dr., Bricktown, NJ 08723: Catalog $1 ◆ Old and rare historical newspapers, from the 1600s to 1800s.

**Vintage Newspapers,** P.O. Box 48621, Los Angeles, CA 90048: Free catalog ◆ Authentic newspapers and magazines, from 1880 to the present. 800-235-1919.

**Yesterday,** 1143 W. Addison St., Chicago, IL 60613: Free information with long SASE ◆ Original stills, lobby cards, posters, press books, magazines, and newspapers. 773-248-8087.

## NURSING SUPPLIES

**Abracadabra Maternity,** 4411 San Mateo Blvd. NE, Ste. J, Albuquerque, NM 87109: Free information ◆ Maternity clothing and accessories for new mothers and mothers-to-be. Includes casual to professional, swimsuits, exercise wear, nursing tops, pajamas, other fashions, nursing accessories, and baby care items. 505-881-6820.

**Basics Direct, Maternity & Nursing,** 14 Highview Dr., Uxbridge, MA 01569: Free catalog ◆ Maternity clothing and lingerie, abdominal and lower back supports, breast-pumps and accessories, and other nursing aids. 800-954-MOMS.

**Born To Love,** 5775 Yonge St., 8th Floor, North York, Ontario, Canada M2M 4J1: Free catalog ◆ Natural baby care products for nursing mothers. 416-226-9520. born2luv@idirect.com

**Bravado Designs,** 705 Pape Ave., Toronto, Ontario, Canada M4K 3S6: Free information ◆ Maternity and nursing bras. 800-590-7802.

**Breast is Best,** 110 Milverton Blvd., Toronto, Ontario, Canada M4J 1T9: Free catalog ◆ Clothing for nursing mothers. 416-461-3890.

**C.D.M. Nursingwear,** P.O. Box 5191, San Clemente, CA 92674: Free catalog ◆ Clothes for nursing mothers, nighttime wear, breast pumps, milk storage aids, over-the-shoulder baby holder, and more. 800-637-9246.

**Decent Exposures,** P.O. Box 27206, Seattle, WA 98125: Free information ◆ Pregnancy and nursing bras. 800-505-4949; 206-364-4540 (in WA). requests@decentexposures.com

**L.A. Nursingwear,** 3337 Stevens St., La Crescenta, CA 91214: Free brochure ◆ Breast feeding fashions.

**Lady Grace Stores,** P.O. Box 128, Malden, MA 02148: Free catalog ◆ Intimate apparel for everyday wear, nursing and maternity, and post-breast surgery. 800-922-0504. www.ladygrace.com

**Little Koala,** 614 Bellefonte St., Shadyside, PA 15232: Free catalog ◆ Clothing, nursing aids, everything for the breast-feeding mother, and other alternative products for mother and baby. 800-950-1239.

**Maturna,** P.O. Box 3500, Milford, CT 06460: Free information ◆ Adjustable maternity bra for use during and after pregnancy. 800-944-4006.

**Mommy's Little Helpers,** 9250 Watson Rd., St. Louis, MO 63126: Free catalog ◆ Sling carriers, breast-feeding apparel and supplies, diapers, and accessories.

**Motherwear Diapers,** 320 Riverside Dr., Northampton, MA 01061: Free brochure ◆ Contour-shaped diapers, covers, and easy-access clothing for nursing mothers. 800-633-0303.

**The Zaks Company,** 12905 Alderleaf Dr., Germantown, MD 20874: Free information ◆ Nursing tops, jogging sets, and jumpers. 301-972-5669.

## OFFICE & BUSINESS SUPPLIES

### Business Forms & Booklets

**Adams Business Forms,** P.O. Box 91, Topeka, KS 66601: Free information ◆ Manifold books, guest checks, and forms. 800-444-3508.

**Business Forms by Carlson Craft,** P.O. Box 8700, North Mankato, MN 56002: Free information ◆ Business forms. 800-292-9207.

**Caprock Business Forms Inc.,** 1211 Ave. F, Lubbock, TX 79401: Free information ◆ Continuous computer forms, letterheads and envelopes, snap-apart sets, manifold books, and scratch pads. 800-666-3322.

**CFO Forms,** 2205 Forsyth Rd., Unit L, Orlando, FL 32807: Free price list ◆ Carbonless business forms. 800-451-3676.

**Champion Industries Inc.,** 2450 1st Ave., P.O. Box 2968, Huntington, WV 25728: Free information ◆ Continuous and snap-out forms. 800-624-3431; 304-528-2791 (in WV).

**Champion Printing Company,** 3250 Spring Grove Ave., Cincinnati, OH 45225: Free information ◆ Self-mailers and bind-ins. 800-543-1957.

**Colonial Business Forms Inc.,** 355 Sackett Point Rd., North Haven, CT 06473: Free price list ◆ Snap-out forms. 800-562-4790.

**Columbus Bookbinders & Printers Inc.,** 3908 Hamilton Rd., Columbus, GA 31904: Free information ◆ Brochures, printed and bound books, and newsletters. 706-323-9313.

**The Drawing Board,** P.O. Box 2995, Hartford, CT 06104: Free catalog ◆ Business forms, envelopes and stationery, labels, receipt books, and other supplies. 800-527-9530.

**Economy Printing Company,** 5067 W. 12th St., Jacksonville, FL 32205: Free information ◆ Business forms and booklets. 800-423-1475; 904-786-4070 (in FL).

**Grand Forms & Systems Inc.,** 211 S. Arlington Heights, Arlington Heights, IL 60005: Free information ◆ Business forms. 800-682-1924; 847-259-4600 (in IL).

**Greater American Business Products,** 6701 Concord Park Dr., Houston, TX 77040: Free catalog ◆ Business forms, stationery, and signs. 800-231-0329; 713-329-9400 (in TX). www.gabp.com

**HG Professional Forms Company,** 2000 California St., Omaha, NE 68102: Free catalog ◆ Pre-printed forms, accounting supplies, computer paper, record-keeping systems, binders, report covers, and envelopes. 800-228-1493. www.hgproforms.com

**Mattick Business Forms Inc.,** 333 W. Hintz Rd., Wheeling, IL 60090: Free catalog ◆ Stationery, office and business forms, and labels. 847-541-7345.

**Moore Business Products,** Catalog Division, P.O. Box 1448, Lincolnshire, IL 60069: Free catalog ◆ Business forms, typewriter and printer ribbons, print wheels, copier supplies, laser printer paper and toner cartridges, fax paper, computer accessories, and supplies. 800-323-6230. www.moorebp.com

**Morgan Printing Company,** 2365 Wyandotte Rd., Willow Grove, PA 19090: Free information ◆ Continuous letterheads, labels, and business forms. 800-435-3892.

**NEBS Inc.,** 500 Main St., Groton, MA 01471: Free catalog ◆ Computerized and manual business forms, stationery, labels, checks, business cards, and supplies. 800-367-6327. www.nebs.com

**News Printing Company Inc.,** 819 E. Main St., P.O. Box 190, Roaring Spring, PA 16673: Free information ◆ Volume printing and bindery services with on-site mailing. 814-224-2176. www.newsprinting.com

**Rapidforms Inc.,** 301 Grove Rd., Thorofare, NJ 08086: Free catalog ◆ Business forms and labels. 800-257-8354. www.rapidforms.com

**Shipman Printing Industries,** P.O. Box 157, Niagara Falls, NY 14302: Free information ◆ Business forms, letterheads, padded forms, and window-style and other envelopes. 800-462-2114.

**Stationery House,** 1000 Florida Ave., Hagerstown, MD 21740: Free catalog ◆ Business stationery and forms, supplies, and gifts. 301-739-4487.

**Triangle Printing Company,** 325 Hill Ave., Nashville, TN 37210: Free information ◆ Booklets. 800-843-9529.

### General Office Supplies & Equipment

**Accountants Supply House,** 301 Grove Rd., Thorofare, NJ 08086: Free catalog ◆ Stationery and envelopes, forms and labels, adding machines, shipping materials, disk storage cabinets, typewriter and data processing ribbons, furniture, and supplies. 800-342-5274.

**Action Office Supplies,** P.O. Box 277, Adelphia, NJ 07710: Free catalog ◆ Office supplies, attache and business cases, computer accessories, presentation aids, mailroom equipment, and more. 800-298-1000. www.actoff.com

**Ad Lib Advertising,** P.O. Box 531, North Bellmore, NY 11710: Free information ◆ Custom Post-It Notes. 800-622-3542.

**Alfax Wholesale Furniture,** 370 7th Ave., Ste. 1101, New York, NY 10001: Free catalog ◆ General office equipment, furniture, and supplies. 800-221-5710; 212-947-9560 (in NY).

**American Loose Leaf Business Products,** 4015 Papin, St. Louis, MO 63110: Free catalog ◆ Binders, folders, and indexes. 800-467-7000.

**American Thermoplastic Company,** 106 Gamma Dr., Pittsburgh, PA 15238: Free catalog ◆ Binders, index sets, sheet protectors, clipboards, report and presentation folders, data processing and catalog binders, and cassette albums. 800-245-6600. www.binders.com

**Arrow Star,** 3-1 Park Plaza, Glen Head, NY 11546: Free catalog ◆ Office equipment and supplies. 800-645-2833; 516-484-3100 (in NY).

**Artgrafix Warehouse,** 15 Tech Circle, Natick, MA 01760: Free catalog ◆ Office supplies. 800-443-4421.

**Artistic Greetings Catalog,** P.O. Box 1050, Elmira, NY 14902: Catalog $2 ◆ Business cards, memo and informal note cards, and personalized stationery. 800-733-6313. www.artisticgreetings.com

**Avery Dennison,** 20955 Pathfinder Rd., Diamond Bar, CA 91765: Free catalog ◆ Laser and ink-jet printer labels, label-printing software, and other related products. 800-252-8379. www.avery.com

**Bangor Cork Company Inc.,** William & D Streets, Pen Argyl, PA 18072: Free catalog ◆ Cork bulletin, marker, and chalkboards. 610-863-9041.

**Blue Dolphin,** 1920 Abrams Pkwy., #416, Dallas, TX 75214: Free catalog ◆ Recycled paper and re-engineered toner cartridges for copiers, laser printers, and plain paper fax machines. 800-932-7715.

**Browncor International,** 400 S. 5th St., Milwaukee, WI 53204: Free catalog ◆ Mailing and shipping supplies. 800-874-1475.

**The Business Book,** P.O. Box 1393, Hagerstown, MD 21741: Free catalog ◆ Pressure sensitive labels, stampers, personalized business envelopes and stationery, speed letters, memo pads, business cards and forms, greeting cards, books, and other office supplies. 800-558-0220.

**Carlson Craft,** 1625 Roe Crest Dr., P.O. Box 8625, North Mankato, MN 56002: Free information ◆ Custom Post-It notes. 800-292-9207.

**Chenesko Products Inc.,** 2221 5th Ave., Ste. 4, Ronkonkoma, NY 11779: Free catalog ◆ Recharge kits for laser printer and copier toner cartridges. 800-221-3516; 516-467-3205 (in NY). www.chenesko.com

**Columbia Omnicorp,** 14 W. 33rd St., New York, NY 10001: Free catalog ◆ Office and computer supplies, furniture, and artist materials. 212-279-6161.

**Colwell Systems,** P.O. Box 9024, Champaign, IL 61826: Free catalog ◆ Office supplies. 800-637-1140.

**Day-Timers,** One Day-Timer Plaza, Allentown, PA 18195: Free catalog ◆ Stationery and business cards. 800-225-5005. www.daytimer.com

**Frank Eastern Company,** 599 Broadway, New York, NY 10012: Catalog $1 ◆ Office equipment and supplies, furniture, and shipping materials. 800-221-4914; 212-219-0007 (in NY).

**Fidelity Products,** P.O. Box 155, Minneapolis, MN 55440: Free catalog ◆ Office equipment and supplies. 800-328-3034; 612-526-6500 (in MN).

**Grayarc,** P.O. Box 2944, Hartford, CT 06104: Free catalog ◆ Office equipment and supplies. 800-562-5468.

**HG Professional Forms Company,** 2000 California St., Omaha, NE 68102: Free catalog ◆ Pre-printed forms, computer paper, record-keeping systems, binders, report covers, and envelopes. 800-228-1493. www.hgproforms.com

**Idea Art,** 2603 Elm Hill Pike, Ste. P, Nashville, TN 37229: Free catalog ◆ Pre-designed paper and supplies for desktop publishing. 800-433-2278; 615-889-4989 (in TN). www.ideaart.com

**Robert James Company Inc.,** P.O. Box 520, Moody, AL 35004: Free information with long SASE ◆ Office supplies. 800-633-8296; 205-640-7081 (in AL).

**Memindex Inc.,** 149 Carter St., P.O. Box 20566, Rochester, NY 14602: Free catalog ◆ Organizational tools for scheduling, planning, and controlling time. 716-342-7740.

**Mobile Office Outfitter,** 1048 Serpentine Ln., #308, Pleasanton, CA 94566: Free catalog ◆ Mobile car desks, laptop accessories, cellular phone accessories, office supplies, and more. 800-426-3453. www.mobilegear.com

**Moore Business Products,** Catalog Division, P.O. Box 1448, Lincolnshire, IL 60069: Free catalog ◆ Business forms, typewriter and printer ribbons, print wheels, copier supplies, laser printer paper and toner cartridges, fax and computer paper, and binders. 800-323-6230. www.moorebp.com

**Office Depot Inc.,** 2200 Old Germantown Rd., Delray Beach, FL 33445: Free catalog ◆ Office supplies and equipment. 800-685-8800. www.officedepot.com

**The Office Mates,** P.O. Box 306, W227 N6370 Sussex Rd., Sussex, WI 53089: Free brochure ◆ Vinyl envelopes and related products. 800-238-3957.

**Office Zone,** 461 W. 200 North, P.O. Box 808, Bountiful, UT 84011: Free catalog ◆ Desks for homes and offices, library supplies, binding equipment, folders, labels and labeling tapes, and other supplies and equipment. 800-543-5454; 801-298-3839 (in UT).

**Paper Direct Inc.,** 100 Plaza Dr., Secaucus, NJ 07094: Free catalog ◆ Pre-designed paper and supplies for enhancing printed projects. 800-272-7377. www.paperdirect.com

**Paper Showcase,** P.O. Box 8465, Mankato, MN 56002: Free catalog ◆ Laser-compatible paper. 800-287-8163.

**Quill Office Supplies,** 100 Schelter Rd., Lincolnshire, IL 60197: Free catalog ◆ Office supplies. 800-789-8965. www.quillcorp.com

**C.E. Sanders Company,** P.O. Box 597, 400 N. Cherry St., Bunnell, FL 32110: Free brochure ◆ Desk organizers, message and note holders, privacy locks, and other original desk accessories. 888-228-1985.

**Staples Inc.,** P.O. Box 5173, Westborough, MA 01581: Free catalog ◆ Office supplies, furniture, computer supplies and paper, drafting equipment, fax machines, and typewriters. 800-333-3330. www.staples.com

**The Staplex Company,** 777 5th Ave., Brooklyn, NY 11232: Free catalog ◆ Electric staplers. 800-221-0822. www.staplex.com

**Viking Office Products,** 13809 S. Figueroa St., P.O. Box 61144, Los Angeles, CA 90061: Free catalog ◆ Office supplies. 800-421-1222. www.VikingOP.com

**Visible,** Subsidiary Wallace Computer Services Inc., 1750 Wallace Ave., St. Charles, IL 60174: Free catalog ◆ Computer and office supplies. 800-323-0628.

**Vulcan Binder & Cover,** 1 Looseleaf Ln., Vincent, AL 35178: Free catalog ◆ Ring binders. 800-633-4526. www.vulcanbinder.com

## Labels & Tags

**Artistic Greetings Catalog,** P.O. Box 1050, Elmira, NY 14925: Catalog $2 ◆ Personalized designer labels. 800-330-5531. www.artisticgreetings.com

**Colorful Images,** 2910 Colorful Ave., Longmont, CO 80504: Free catalog ◆ Personal labels with hundreds of art options and styles. 800-458-7999.

**Continental Data Forms,** 69 Veronica Ave., Somerset, NJ 08873: Free information ◆ Pinfeed pressure-sensitive labels. 800-947-8020.

**Data Label Inc.,** 1000 Spruce St., Terre Haute, IN 47807: Free information ◆ Labels. 800-457-0676.

**DAYDOTS Label Company Inc.,** 2501 Ludelle St., Fort Worth, TX 76105: Free catalog ◆ Easy-to-remove labels. 800-321-3687.

**The Drawing Board,** P.O. Box 2995, Hartford, CT 06104: Free catalog ◆ Business forms, envelopes and stationery, labels, receipt books, and other supplies. 800-527-9530.

**Ennis Express Label Service,** Tag & Label Division, P.O. Box D, Wolfe City, TX 75496: Free information ◆ Labels. 800-527-1008; 903-496-2244 (in TX). www.ennis.com

**Five Star Publications,** P.O. Box 6698, Chandler, AZ 85246: Free catalog ◆ Custom-printed labels. 602-940-8182. www.fivestarsupport.com

**C.J. Fox Company,** P.O. Box 6186, Providence, RI 02940: Free information ◆ Labels. 800-556-6868. cjfoxco@worldnet.att.net

**GraphComm Services,** P.O. Box 220, Freeland, WA 98249: Free catalog ◆ Labels. 800-488-7436.

**Graphic Impressions,** 8538 W. Grand Ave., River Grove, IL 60171: Free information ◆ Pressure-sensitive labels. 800-451-6658.

**Grayarc,** P.O. Box 2944, Hartford, CT 06104: Free catalog ◆ Stationery, business cards, forms, labels, envelopes, and supplies. 800-562-5468.

**Hawks Tag Service,** 3959 Fulton Grove, Cincinnati, OH 45245: Free price list ◆ Tags in short run orders. 800-752-5765.

**Jet Labels,** 3875 S. Blue Star Dr., Traverse City, MI 49684: Free catalog ◆ Labels. 800-622-3883.

**Kay Toledo Tag,** P.O. Box 5038, Toledo, OH 43611: Free brochure ◆ Tags in fluorescent, cloth, vinyl, and other materials. 800-822-8247.

**Lancer Label,** 301 S. 74th St., Omaha, NE 68114: Free catalog ◆ Bumper stickers and labels in rolls, sheets, and pinfeed. 800-228-7074.

**Lixx Labelsz,** 2619 14th St. SW, P.O. Box 32055, Calgary, Alberta, Canada T2T 5X0: Catalog $4 ◆ Labels and bookmarks that combine wildlife designs, calligraphy, eco-action, and recycling. 403-245-2331.

**Morgan Printing Company,** 2365 Wyandotte Rd., Willow Grove, PA 19090: Free information ◆ Continuous letterheads, labels, and business forms. 800-435-3892.

**NEBS Inc.,** 500 Main St., Groton, MA 01471: Free catalog ◆ Computerized and manual business forms, stationery, labels, checks, business cards, and supplies. 800-367-6327. www.nebs.com

**New York Label,** 50 Oval Dr., Central Islip, NY 11722: Free catalog ◆ Self-adhesive labels in singles, rolls, or sheets. 800-257-2300.

**PrintProd Inc.,** 419 Bainbridge St., Dayton, OH 45410: Free information ◆ Multi-color tags. 800-322-TAGS; 937-228-2181 (in OH).

**Seton Identification Products,** 20 Thompson Rd., Branford, CT 06405: Free catalog ◆ Heavy duty paper tags, write-on and bar code labels, and other identification supplies. 800-243-6624; 203-488-8059 (in CT). www.seton.com

**Short Run Labels,** 1681 Industrial Rd., San Carlos, CA 94070: Free catalog ◆ Self-adhesive labels in small orders. 800-522-3583; 415-592-7683 (in CA).

**The Styles Company,** P.O. Box 5000, Lake Forest, CA 92630: Free information ◆ Custom checks and easy-to-use peel and stick address labels.

**Superfast Label Service,** 300 E. 4th St., Safford, AZ 85546: Free information ◆ Labels. 800-767-8566. sfaz1@aol.com

**U.S. Tag & Label Corp.,** 2217 Robb St., Baltimore, MD 21218: Free catalog ◆ Tags and labels. 800-638-1018; 410-467-2633 (in MD).

**Write Touch,** The Rytex Company, P.O. Box 68188, Indianapolis, IN 46268: Free information ◆ Stationery and envelopes, note cards, memo pads, and labels. 800-288-6824.

### Receipt Books

**Cook Receipt Book Manufacturing Company,** Box 2005, Dothan, AL 36302: Free catalog ◆ Receipt books. 800-842-0444.

**The Drawing Board,** P.O. Box 2995, Hartford, CT 06104: Free catalog ◆ Business forms, envelopes and stationery, labels, receipt books, and other supplies. 800-527-9530.

**Herald Multiforms Inc.,** P.O. Box 1288, Dillon, SC 29536: Free information ◆ Continuous forms, checks, and snap-out receipt books. 800-845-5050; 803-774-9051 (in SC).

**Rapidforms Inc.,** 301 Grove Rd., Thorofare, NJ 08086: Free catalog ◆ Labels and business forms. 800-257-8354. www.rapidforms.com

**Rush Receipt Book Company,** 457 Houston South, Mobile, AL 36606: Free price list ◆ Receipt books. 800-654-4237.

**Superior Receipt Book Company,** 215 S. Clark St., P.O. Box 326, Centreville, MI 49032: Free information ◆ Receipt books. 800-624-2887; 616-467-8265 (in MI).

### Shipping & Packaging Supplies

**Action Bag Company,** 501 N. Edgewood Ave., Wood Dale, IL 60191: Free catalog ◆ Bags, packaging accessories, bubble-cushioned mailers, display accessories, and other merchandising aids. 630-766-2881. actionbg@ix.netcom.com

**Beaver Prints,** 305 Main St., Bellwood, PA 16617: Free catalog ◆ Custom printing for mailing services that includes addressing, inserting, sorting, and postal barcoding. 814-742-6070.

**Cases by Masco,** 1121 S. Placentia Ave., Fullerton, CA 92831: Free brochure ◆ Reusable shipping containers, cases, and packaging. 800-772-1960; 714-680-9180 (in CA).

**Chiswick Trading Inc.,** 33 Union Ave., Sudbury, MA 01776: Free catalog ◆ Shipping and packaging supplies. 800-225-8708.

**Consolidated Plastics Company,** 8181 Darrow Rd., Twinsburg, OH 44087: Free catalog ◆ Bags, packaging, and shipping supplies. 800-362-1000.

**Cornell Paper & Box Company Inc.,** 168 Van Dyke St., Brooklyn, NY 11231: Free catalog ◆ Packaging supplies. 718-875-3202.

**Evergreen Bag Company,** 22 Ash St., East Hartford, CT 06108: Free catalog ◆ Shipping and retail packaging supplies. Also poly bags and gift wrapping. 800-775-3595. sales@everbag.com

**Fidelity Products,** P.O. Box 155, Minneapolis, MN 55440: Free catalog ◆ Office equipment and supplies. 800-328-3034; 612-526-6500 (in MN).

**Freund Can Company,** 155 W. 84th St., Chicago, IL 60620: Free catalog ◆ Shipping cartons and stock boxes, cans and paint pails, mailers, and other packaging supplies. 773-224-4230. www.freundcan.com

**Jones West Packaging Products,** P.O. Box 1084, Rohnert Park, CA 94927: Free catalog ◆ Packaging products. 707-795-8552.

**Kole Industries,** P.O. Box 020152, Miami, FL 33102: Free catalog ◆ Shipping, storing, and organizing supplies. 800-327-6085. www.koleindustries.com

**National Bag Company Inc.,** 2233 Old Mill Rd., Hudson, OH 44236: Free catalog ◆ Bags and wrapping, packaging, and shipping supplies. 800-247-6000.

**U.S. Box Corp.,** 1296 McCarter Hwy., Newark, NJ 07104: Catalog $3 ◆ Boxes and other containers. 201-481-2000.

**Volk Corp.,** 23936 Industrial Park Dr., Farmington Hills, MI 48335: Free information ◆ Marking devices, packaging supplies, and shipping room equipment. 800-521-6799; 248-477-6700 (in MI).

**YAZOO Mills Inc.,** P.O. Box 369, New Oxford, PA 17350: Free information ◆ Mailing tubes. 800-242-5216. www.thomasregister.com/yazoo

## ORIGAMI (PAPER FOLDING)

**Fascinating Folds,** P.O. Box 10070, Glendale, AZ 85318: Catalog $1 ◆ Origami supplies, kits, how-to books, and videos. 800-968-2418. www.fascinating-folds.com

**Origami USA,** 15 W. 77th St., New York, NY 10024: Free information with long SASE and two 1st class stamps ◆ Books, origami paper, and supplies. 212-769-5635. www.origami-usa.org

## OSTOMY SUPPLIES

**A-Z Ostomy Supply,** 321 W. Main, Marshall, MN 56258: Free catalog ◆ Ostomy supplies. 800-345-7850; 507-532-5754 (in MN).

**AARP Ostomy Care Center,** 5050 E. Belknap, Fort Worth, TX 76117: Free catalog ◆ Ostomy supplies. 800-284-4788.

**American B & K Prescriptions,** 601 E. Iron, Salina, KS 67104: Free information ◆ Ostomy supplies. 800-831-5219.

**Blanchard Ostomy Products,** 1510 Raymond Ave., Glendale, CA 91201: Free information ◆ Products for ileostomies, urostomies, and wet colostomies. 626-242-6789.

**Bruce Medical Supply,** 411 Waverly Oaks Rd., P.O. Box 9166, Waltham, MA 02154: Free catalog ◆ Ostomy supplies. 800-225-8446.

**Coloplast Inc.,** 1955 W. Oak Circle, Marietta, GA 30062: Free information ◆ Conseal Colostomy System. 800-237-4555.

**Doubek Pharmacy Inc.,** 3846 W. 63rd St., Chicago, IL 60629: Free information ◆ Ostomy supplies. 800-DOUBLERS; 773-581-1122 (in IL).

**DS Medical,** 1725 Breckinridge Pkwy., Ste. 500, Duluth, GA 30136: Free information ◆ Wheelchair parts and urological, ostomy, and wound care products. 800-722-2604. www.dsmedical.com

**Edgepark Surgical Inc.,** 1810 Summit Commerce Park, Twinsburg, OH 44087: Free catalog ◆ Ostomy supplies. 800-321-0591.

**Express Medical Supply Inc.,** P.O. Box 1164, Fenton, MO 63026: Free catalog ◆ Urological, ostomy, incontinence, and skin care products. 800-633-2139. www.exmed.net

**Georgetown Health Care Center,** 9338 W. 75th St., Shawnee Mission, KS 66204: Free information ◆ Ostomy supplies. 800-279-3026; 913-262-0313 (in KS).

**Hammer Medical Supply,** 523 E. Grand Ave., Des Moines, IA 50309: Free information ◆ Ostomy supplies. 800-388-1187; 515-243-2886 (in IA). www.iowahealth.net/hammerrx

**Hollister,** 2000 Hollister Dr., Libertyville, IL 60048: Free information ◆ Men and women's ostomy pouches. 800-323-4060.

**Home Health Express,** 8400 Baymeadows Way, Ste. 3, Jacksonville, FL 32256: Free information ◆ Ostomy supplies. 800-828-7123.

**Home Medical Center Hospital Supplies,** 7173 W. Cermack, Irwin, IL 60402: Free information ◆ Ostomy supplies. 800-323-2828.

**Hospital Drug Store,** 200 Loyola, New Orleans, LA 70112: Free information ◆ Ostomy supplies. 800-256-2007; 504-524-2254 (in LA).

**King Ostomy Products,** 431 W. 13th Ave., Ste. 4, Eugene, OR 97401: Free information ◆ Ostomy health care products. 503-345-0391.

**LDB Medical Inc.,** 2909 Langford Rd., Ste. 500-B, Norcross, GA 30071: Free catalog ◆ Ostomy, incontinence, urological, and skin care supplies. 800-243-2554. ldb@baiusa.com

**Marlen Manufacturing & Development Company,** 5150 Richmond Rd., Bedford, OH 44146: Free information ◆ Protective adhesive skin barriers for ileostomies, colostomies, and urostomies. 216-292-7060.

**Mason Laboratories Inc.,** P.O. Box 334, Horsham, PA 19044: Free information ◆ Ostomy pouches, pouch odor deodorant, and supplies. 800-523-2302; 215-675-6044 (in PA).

**Medic Pharmacy & Surgical,** 5100 W. Commercial Blvd., Fort Lauderdale, FL 33319: Free information ◆ Ostomy and medical supplies. 800-888-9417.

**Medical Care Products,** P.O. Box 10239, Jacksonville, FL 32247: Free information ◆ Ostomy supplies. 800-741-0110.

**Medical Home Supply,** 1853 W. 52nd Ave., Denver, CO 80221: Free catalog ◆ Ostomy supplies. 800-748-1909.

**Medship Direct,** P.O. Box 956848, Duluth, GA 30095: Free catalog ◆ Urological, wound care, ostomy, incontinence, aids to daily living, and wheelchair parts. 800-633-1565. www.medshipdirect.com

**MOMS Mail Order Medical Supply,** 24700 Avenue Rockefeller, Valencia, CA 91355: Free catalog ◆ Urological, ostomy, incontinence, skin and wound care, daily living, diabetic, and home diagnostic aids. 800-232-7443. www.momsup.com

**Nihan & Martin Pharmacy,** 1417 Myott Ave., Rockford, IL 60619: Free catalog ◆ Ostomy appliances. 815-963-8594.

**Nu-Hope Laboratories Inc.,** P.O. Box 331150, Pacoima, CA 91333: Free information ◆ Urostomy pouches. 818-899-7711.

**Ostomed Healthcare,** 3116 S. Oak Park Ave., Berwyn, IL 60402: Free information ◆ Ostomy supplies. 800-323-1353; 708-795-7979 (in IL).

**Palisades Pharmaceuticals Inc.,** 64 N. Summit St., Tenafly, NJ 07670: Free information ◆ Internal deodorant for patients with colostomies, ileostomies, and incontinence. 800-237-9083.

**Parkview Pharmacy & Home Health Care Inc.,** 8283 Grove Ave., Ste. 105, Rancho Cucamonga, CA 91730: Free catalog ◆ Ostomy, wound care, incontinence, and other home health care aids. 800-605-0166. www.parkviewrx.com

**The Perma-Type Company Inc.,** 83 Northwest Dr., Plainville, CT 06062: Free catalog ◆ Ileostomy, colostomy, wet colostomy, ileal bladder, and ureterostomy appliances. 800-243-4234; 860-676-8787 (in CT).

**Salk Company Inc.,** 119 Braintree St., Allston, MA 02134: Free information ◆ Natural-looking undergarments for active ostomates. 800-343-4497; 617-782-4030 (in MA).

**Shield Healthcare Centers,** 4340 Viewrige Ave., San Diego, CA 92123: Free catalog ◆ Ostomy, urological, skin care, and home diagnostic products. 800-675-8845.

**Tennessee Home Medical,** 2005 Memorial Blvd., Springfield, TN 37172: Free information ◆ Ostomy supplies. 800-966-6093; 615-384-6093 (in TN).

**Thompson Pharmacy & Medical,** 324 S. Union St., Traverse City, MI 49684: Free catalog ◆ Diabetes, health maintenance, home diagnostic, ostomy, and health and pain management aids. Also canes and other mobility equipment. 616-947-4212. thompson@carecenter.com

**Torbot Group Inc.,** Ostomy Specialists, 1185 Jefferson Blvd., Warwick, RI 02886: Free brochure ◆ Ostomy appliances. 800-545-4254.

**VPI,** A Cook Group Company, 127 S. Main St., P.O. Box 266, Spencer, IN 47460: Free information ◆ Non-adhesive systems for colostomy, urostomy, and ileostomy patients. 800-843-4851; 812-829-4891 (in IN).

**Worldwide Home Health Center Inc.,** 926 E. Tallmadge Ave., Akron, OH 44310: Free catalog ◆ Ostomy and incontinence supplies, mastectomy breast forms, and clothing. 800-223-5938; 330-633-0366 (in OH).

## PADDLEBALL

**Cannon Sports,** P.O. Box 797, Greenland, NH 03840: Free list of retail sources ◆ Paddles and balls. 800-362-3146.

**Century Sports Inc.,** Lakewood Industrial Park, 1995 Rutgers University Blvd., Box 2035, Lakewood, NJ 08701: Free information ◆ Balls and paddles. 800-526-7548; 732-905-4422 (in NJ).

**Spalding Sports Worldwide,** 425 Meadow St., P.O. Box 901, Chicopee, MA 01021: Free list of retail sources ◆ Paddles and balls. 800-225-6601. www.spalding.com

**Sportime,** Customer Service, 1 Sportime Way, Atlanta, GA 30340: Free information ◆ Balls and paddles. 800-444-5700; 770-449-5700 (in GA).

**Wa-Mac Inc.,** P.O. Box 128, Carlstadt, NJ 07410: Free information ◆ Paddles and balls. 800-447-5673; 201-438-7200 (in NJ).

## PAGERS

**Everything Wireless,** 3380 N, 28th Terrace, Hollywood, FL 33020: Free catalog ◆ Cellular telephones, pagers, and accessories. 888-383-7999. www.everythingwireless.com

**Hello Direct,** 5893 Rue Ferrari Dr., San Jose, CA 95138: Free catalog ◆ Amplification aids, cellular and paging accessories, telephones and answering machines, and other telephone productivity tools. 800-444-3556. www.hello-direct.com

**Socket Communications,** 37400 Central Ct., Newark, CA 94560: Free information ◆ Wireless Windows message system for use with computers and as a stand-alone pager. 510-744-2700.

## PAINTBALL

**National Paintball Supply,** 1200 Woodruff Rd., Unit C-5, Greenville, SC 29607: Free information ◆ Equipment and supplies. 864-458-7221.

**Paintball Games of Dallas,** 3305 E. John Carpenter Freeway, Irving, TX 75062: Free catalog ◆ Equipment and supplies. 888-55-SPLAT; 972-554-1937.

**Point Blank Paintball Inc.,** 1457 Riverdale St., West Springfield, MA 01089: Free information ◆ Equipment and supplies. 413-788-7352.

## PAPER COLLECTIBLES

**Amusementica Americana,** 414 N. Prospect Manor Ave., Mt. Prospect, IL 60056: Free list with seven 1st class stamps ◆ Old saloon artifacts, coin-operated machines, advertising collectibles, paper memorabilia, and other antique artifacts. 847-253-0791.

**Barbara's Papertiques,** P.O. Box 317, Port Jervis, NY 12771: Free information with long SASE ◆ Postcards and paper collectibles. 914-856-8572.

**Box Seat Collectibles,** P.O. Box 2013, Halesite, NY 11743: Catalog $5 ◆ Sports collectibles, historical newspapers from the 19th to 20th century, and other memorabilia. 516-423-1025.

**Buck Hill Associates,** P.O. Box 4736, Queensbury, NY 12804: Free catalog ◆ Posters, handbills, historical documents, Americana from America's past, and other paper collectibles.

**Cal National Coin Exchange,** P.O. Box 1334, Roseville, CA 95678: Free information (specify items wanted) ◆ Americana and paper collectibles. 916-781-2991.

**The Cartophilians,** 430 Highland Ave., Cheshire, CT 06410: Free information with long SASE ◆ Collectible postcards, trading cards, and paper memorabilia. 203-272-1143.

**Cerebro,** Box 327, Prospect, PA 17317: Catalog $5 ◆ Cigar bands and box, fruit crate, and can labels. 800-69-LABEL.

**Cobweb Collectibles,** 9 Walnut Ave., Cranford, NJ 07016: Free information with long SASE ◆ Postcards, autographs, other paper collectibles, political memorabilia, and more. 908-272-5777. cobwebcol@aol.com

**D & D Scripophily,** Box 580063, Flushing, NY 11358: Free information with long SASE ◆ Railroad stock certificates.

**The Evergreen Press,** 9 Camino Arroyo Pl., Palm Desert, CA 92260: Free information with long SASE ◆ Adult and children's books, greeting cards, book marks and bookplates, wedding certificates, calendars, ornaments, paper dolls, postcards, and 19th and early 20th-century paper memorabilia. 213-510-1700.

**Harper's Landing,** 109 E. Hopkins, San Marcos, TX 78666: Free information ◆ Postcards and paper collectibles. 512-754-7182.

**Hi-De-Ho Collectibles,** P.O. Box 2841, Gaithersburg, MD 20886: Catalog $2.50 ◆ Antique movie posters and lobby cards, cartoon memorabilia, TV toys, games, puzzles, and dolls, advertising collectibles, and nostalgia. 301-926-4438.

**Clinton Hollins,** 9215 Setter Pl., Springfield, VA 22153: Free list with long SASE: Free information ◆ Old stock certificates. 703-644-0933.

**Richard T. Hoober Jr.,** P.O. Box 3116, Key Largo, FL 33037: Free list with long SASE ◆ Bank and other financial paper collectibles.

**New York Gift Exchange,** P.O. Box 1441, New York, NY 10156: Free catalog ◆ Stock and bond certificates and other script collectibles. 212-889-6448. www.nyge.com

**The Old Print Gallery,** 1220 31st St. NW, Washington, DC 20007: Catalog $3 ◆ Paper collectibles. 202-965-1818.

**Old Print Shop,** 150 Lexington Ave., New York, NY 10016: Free information ◆ Paper collectibles. 212-683-3950.

**Olde Soldier Books Inc.,** 18779 N. Frederick Ave., Gaithersburg, MD 20879: Free information ◆ Civil War books, documents, autographs, prints, manuscripts, photographs, and Americana. 301-963-2929. Warbooks@erols.com

**The Paperpreneur Inc.,** P.O. Box 819, Concrete, WA 98237: List 55¢ ◆ Engravings, historical collectibles, and other paper Americana. 360-853-8228.

**William Petersen,** 322 Scott St., San Marcos, TX 78666: Free information with long SASE ◆ Postcards and other paper collectibles. 512-353-7574. www.web-pac.com/mall

**Lee Poleske,** Box 871, Seward, AK 99664: Free list with long SASE ◆ Bank and other financial paper collectibles. 907-224-5525.

**Ken Prag,** P.O. Box 14817, San Francisco, CA 04114: Free information ◆ Old postcards, stocks and bonds, passes, time tables, and other paper Americana. 415-586-9386.

**Steven S. Raab,** P.O. Box 471, Ardmore, PA 19003: Catalog $5 ◆ Autographs, signed books and photos, historic newspapers, World War I posters, and other historic paper memorabilia. 610-446-6193. www.raabautographs.com

**Russell's Paper Collectibles,** 2404 W. 111th St., Chicago, IL 60655: List $5 (specify interests) ◆ Thousands of stocks and bonds.

**R.M. Smythe,** 26 Broadway, New York, NY 10004: Catalog $15 ◆ Obsolete stocks and bonds, bank notes, and autographs. 800-622-1880; 212-943-1880 (in NY).

**Mark Vardakis Autographs,** Box 1430, Coventry, RI 02816: Catalog $2 ◆ Autographs, paper Americana, other collectibles, and financial memorabilia that includes pre-1900 stocks, bonds, and checks. 800-342-0301; 401-823-8440 (in RI). sigking@aol.com

## PAPER CRAFTING, MAKING & SCULPTING

**Aiko's Art Materials Import,** 3347 N. Clark St., Chicago, IL 60657: Catalog $1.50 ◆ Japanese handmade paper, Oriental and art supplies, and fabric dyes. 312-404-5600.

**American Art Clay Company Inc.,** 4717 W. 16th St., Indianapolis, IN 46222: Free catalog ◆ Modeling and self-hardening clay, paper mache, casting compounds, mold-making materials, acrylics, fabric dyes, fillers and patching compounds, wood stains, and metallic finishes. 800-374-1600; 317-244-6871 (in IN). www.amaco.com

**Christy Crafts,** P.O. Box 492, Hinsdale, IL 60521: Brochure $1 ◆ Snipping designs, other paper crafting projects, and kits. 630-323-6505.

**Collage Studio,** P.O. Box 3455, Sunriver, OR 97707: Free price list ◆ Paper-making and molding supplies. 541-593-6041. PaperFiber@aol.com

**Cotton Press,** 11187 Tamarack Dr., Highland, UT 84003: Free brochure ◆ Paper supplies. Also mold-making and paper-crafting kits. 801-756-1712.

**Create-Your-Own Inc.,** 12531 Old Snohomish-Monroe Rd., Snohomish, WA 98290: Free information ◆ Paper for crafting in assorted colors and sizes. 360-794-0671.

**Essex House,** P.O. Box 8684, Prairie Village, KS 66208: Free information ◆ Paper-making kits. 800-581-0949. www.i-netmall.com/shops/essex

**Fascinating Folds,** P.O. Box 2820-235, Torrance, CA 90509: Catalog $1 ◆ Supplies, kits, and how-to books on paper crafting and making. 800-968-2418. www.fascinating-folds.com

**Fiskars Corp.,** 7811 W. Stewart Ave., Wausau, WI 54401: Free list of retail sources ◆ Paper crafting project books and supplies. 715-842-2091. www.fiskars.com

**Gerlachs of Lecha,** P.O. Box 213, Emmaus, PA 18049: Catalog $2.25 ◆ Paper-sculpting kits. 610-965-9181.

**Gold's Artworks Inc.,** 2100 N. Pine St., Lumberton, NC 28358: Free catalog with long SASE ◆ Paper-making pigments and chemicals, pulp materials, kits, and supplies. 800-356-2306; 910-739-9605 (in NC).

**Green EN,** 2 Hanover Rd., Ste. 1913, Brampton, Ontario, Canada L6S 4H9: Samples and price list $10 ◆ Handmade paper and wedding invitations. 905-789-0313. kant@usa.net

**Holcraft Collection,** 211 El Cajon Ave., P.O. Box 792, Davis, CA 95616: Catalog $2 ◆ Molds for paper mache and craft supplies. 916-756-3023. www.holcraft.com

**Lake City Crafts,** P.O. Box 2009, Nixa, MO 65714: Catalog $2 ◆ Supplies for paper-quilling, crafting, and filigree projects. 417-725-8444. www.quilling.com

**Carol Menninga,** 14044 Ridgemont, Gregory, MI 48137: Free information ◆ Folk-art hand-cut paper patterns. 402-330-6186.

**Nasco,** 901 Janesville Ave., Fort Atkinson, WI 53538: Free catalog ◆ Paper-making and sculpting supplies. 800-558-9595. www.nascofa.com

**Paper Pieces,** P.O. Box 2931, Redmond, WA 98703: Free information ◆ Precut paper shapes for quilling. 800-337-1537.

**Papercuttings by Alison,** P.O. Box 2771, Sarasota, FL 34236: Catalog $2.50 ◆ Paper-cutting patterns and supplies. 941-957-0328.

**Pequeno Press,** P.O. Box 1711, Bisbee, AZ 85603: Catalog $2 ◆ Cast paper and handmade paper-covered basketry vessels. 520-432-5924.

**Quill-It,** P.O. Box 1304, Elmhurst, IL 60126: Catalog $1 (refundable) ◆ Quilling papers, paper-snipping supplies, kits, books, tools, plaques, frames, and fringes. 888-9-ALBUMS.

**Solvang Papirklip,** P.O. Box 612, Solvang, CA 93464: Brochure $2 (refundable) ◆ Paper cuttings that express home and family histories. 805-688-3059.

**Twinrocker Papermaking Supplies,** P.O. Box 413, Brookston, IN 47923: Free catalog ◆ Paper-making supplies and ready-to-use handmade paper. 800-757-8946; 765-563-3119 (in IN). www.twinrocker.com

**Yuemei Paper,** 1033 Farmington Ave., Farmington, CT 06032: Free catalog ◆ Handmade papers and silk for fine art and desk top projects, Chinese art supplies, and stationery. 860-674-0128.

## PAPERWEIGHTS

**Brielle Galleries,** P.O. Box 475, Brielle, NJ 08730: Free catalog ◆ Watches, jewelry, paperweights, and crystal, silver, bronze, pewter, and porcelain items. 800-542-7435.

**The Paperweight Shoppe,** 2507 Newport Dr., Bloomington, IL 61704: Video catalog $8 (refundable) ◆ Contemporary and antique glass paperweights. 309-662-1956. Paperwgt1@aol.com

**L.H. Selman Ltd.,** 761 Chestnut St., Santa Cruz, CA 95060: Free catalog ◆ Antique, modern, and contemporary paperweights. 800-538-0766; 408-427-1177 (in CA).

## PARTY DECORATIONS

**Allen-Lewis Manufacturing Company,** P.O. Box 16546, Denver, CO 80216: Free catalog ◆ Souvenirs, carnival and party supplies, fund-raising merchandise, toys and games, T-shirts and sweatshirts, and craft supplies. 800-525-6658.

**Celebrations,** 14704 100th Ave. NE, Bothell, WA 98011: Free catalog ◆ Party supplies. 888-577-2789; 425-806-8182 (in WA). www.party-supply.com

**Colors in Flight,** 3169 E. Maplewood Ave., Littleton, CO 80121: Catalog $5 ◆ Banners, party pennants, flags, windsocks, and hardware. 303-794-1095.

**The Cracker Box,** P.O. Box 413, Solebury, PA 18963: Catalog $4.50 ◆ Ornament kits. 215-862-2100.

**Hearth Song,** Mail Processing Center, 6519 N. Galena Rd., P.O. Box 1773, Peoria, IL 61656: Free catalog ◆ Party decorations, children's books, dollhouse miniatures, art supplies, kites, and games. 800-325-2502.

**Novelties Unlimited,** 410 W. 21st St., Norfolk, VA 23517: Catalog $5 ◆ Magic, balloons, make-up, party decorations, and clown supplies, props, and gags. 757-622-0344.

**B. Palmer Sales Company Inc.,** 3510 Hyw. 80 East, P.O. Box 850247, Mesquite, TX 75185: Free catalog ◆ Carnival, fund-raising, and party supplies. 800-888-3087; 214-288-1026 (in TX).

**Paradise Products,** P.O. Box 568, El Cerrito, CA 94530: Catalog $2 ◆ Party decorations and supplies. 510-524-8300.

**Party Planners Plus,** P.O. Box 771, Cicero, IN 46034: Free catalog ◆ Plates, cups, napkins, punch and serving bowls, special occasion items, other party products, and catering supplies. 317-984-2704.

**Sally Distributors,** 4100 Quebec Ave. North, Minneapolis, MN 55427: Free information ◆ Party supplies and decorations. Includes holiday theme items, balloons, gift wrap, toys, novelty items, children's activities and games, headwear, and tissue bells. 800-472-5597; 612-533-7100 (in MN).

**U.S. Toy Company Inc.,** 13201 Arrington Rd., Grandview, MO 64030: Catalog $3 ◆ Magic equipment and novelties, carnival supplies, and decorations and supplies for holidays, parties, and other celebrations. 800-448-7830. www.const/play.com

**Under the Big Top,** P.O. Box 807, Placentia, CA 92670: Catalog $4 ◆ Party supplies, costumes, clown props, and balloons. 800-995-7727.

## PATIOS & WALKWAYS

**Stone Company Inc.,** W4520 Lime Rd., Eden, WI 53019: Free information ◆ Natural building and landscape cobblers, granite boulders, wall stone, steppers, and flagstone. 920-477-2521.

## PEDAL CARS

**AutoBike Creations,** 1464 Madera Rd., Ste. N-160, Simi Valley, CA 93065: Free information ◆ Pedal cars for adults with optional gas motors. 805-527-5850.

**C & N Reproductions Inc.,** 1341 Ashover Ct., Bloomfield Hills, MI 48304: Catalog $4 ◆ Pedal planes, plans, parts, and kits. 248-852-1998.

**J & S Pedalin,** Jim & Sandy Kay, 2536 Willow Dr., Arnold, MO 63010: Catalog $4 ◆ Pedal car parts. 314-296-5908.

**Juvenile Automobiles,** P.O. Box 221, Sheldonville, MA 02070: Catalog $4.50 ◆ Pedal cars and parts. 401-766-9661.

**Mobileation,** 445 E. 87th St., Ste 4, New York, NY 10128: Free catalog ◆ Mobile interactive riding toys for children. Includes electric and gasoline-engine cars, battery operated and pedal driven vehicles, ride-on toys for toddlers and infants, tricycles, bikes, scooters, seesaws, build-them-yourself pedal car kits, and handcrafted rocking horses. 888-88-MOBILE; 212-426-8074 (in NY). service@mobileation.com

**Texas Pedal Car Peddler Inc.,** 213 Stone Dr., Fort Worth, TX 76108: Catalog and reference book $5 plus $2 shipping and handling ◆ Pedal car parts. 817-238-8363.

**Matthew Vaznaian,** 101 Main St., Woonsocket, RI 02895: Catalog $5 ◆ Pedal car parts. 401-762-9661.

**Allen Wilson,** 1709 St. Cecelia, Kingsville, TX 78363: Catalog $5 ◆ Pedal car parts. 512-595-1015.

## PENS, PENCILS, & DESK SETS

**Ace Luggage & Gifts,** 2122 Avenue U, Brooklyn, NY 11229: Catalog $2 ◆ Desk sets, leather attach cases, luggage, wallets, handbags, and other gifts. 800-342-5223; 718-891-9713 (in NY).

**Altman Luggage,** 135 Orchard St., New York, NY 10001: Free information ◆ Writing instruments, luggage, and leather goods. 800-372-3377.

**Arthur Brown & Bros. Inc.,** 2 W. 46th St., New York, NY 10036: Free catalog ◆ New and contemporary-style fine writing instruments. 800-772-7367. www.artbrown.com

**Brugmansia Writing Instruments,** P.O. Box 30003, Palm Beach Gardens, FL 33420: Free information ◆ Pen and desk sets and other writing aids. 888-966-3736.

**Fahrney Pens Inc.,** 8329 Old Marlboro Pike, Upper Marlboro, MD 20772: Catalog $2 ◆ Writing instruments. 800-624-7367.

**Fountain Pen Hospital,** 10 Warren St., New York, NY 10007: Free information ◆ Fountain pens, pencils, and other writing accessories. 800-253-PENS; 212-964-0580 (in NY). www.fountainpenhospital.com

**The Fountain Pen Shop,** 510 W. 6th St., Ste. 1032, Los Angeles, CA 90014: Catalog $4 ◆ Pens, pencils, desk sets, and other writing accessories. 213-891-1581.

**Gabriel Da Silva & Ariel Crespo,** 1212 Forest Rd., New Haven, CT 06515: Free information ◆ Handcrafted sculptured pens. 203-387-9701.

**Hunt Manufacturing Company,** 2005 Market St., Philadelphia, PA 19103: Free information ◆ Calligraphy papers, markers, kits and supplies, fountain pens, pen sets, nibs, inks, acrylics, oil paints, and water colors. 800-765-5669.

**Levenger,** P.O. Box 1256, Delray Beach, FL 33447: Free catalog ◆ Books, furniture, pens, briefcases, and gifts for serious readers. 800-545-0242. www.levenger.com

**Mackin & Company Inc.,** 2632 S. 24th St., Ste. A, Phoenix, AZ 85034: Free brochure ◆ Pens in various finishes. Includes conventional writing instruments and letter opener, pointers, and caliper pens. 800-280-PENS.

**Menash Signatures Inc.,** 743 Madison Ave., New York, NY 10021: Free catalog ◆ Writing instruments and refills. 800-PEN-SHOP. www.pensandthings.com

**Office Depot Inc.,** 2200 Old Germantown Rd., Delray Beach, FL 33445: Free catalog ◆ Pens, pencils, desk sets, and office supplies and equipment. 800-685-8800. www.officedepot.com

**Silver Eagle,** 617 Airport Rd., Fall River, MA 02720: Free brochure ◆ Fine writing ballpoint or fountain pens. 508-677-0047.

**Staples Inc.,** P.O. Box 5173, Westborough, MA 01581: Free catalog ◆ Pens, pencils, desk sets, and office supplies and equipment. 800-333-3330. www.staples.com

**Viking Office Products,** 13809 S. Figueroa St., P.O. Box 61144, Los Angeles, CA 90061: Free catalog ◆ Pens, pencils, desk sets, and office supplies and equipment. 800-421-1222. www.VikingOP.com

**WoodWrite Handcrafted Pens,** 216 Lemmon Dr., #373, Reno, NV 89506: Free brochure ◆ Precision turned writing instruments in a variety of hardwoods. 702-677-8581. www.woodwriteltd.com

## PERFUMERY & AROMATHERAPY SUPPLIES

**All Natural Botanicals,** 12001 44th St. North, Clearwater, FL 33762: Free catalog ◆ Fragrance and essential oils, bath and body preparations, potpourri, incense, diffusers, and more. 800-377-4850. allnatbo@aol.com

**Angel's Earth,** 1633 Scheffer Ave., St. Paul, MN 55116: Catalog $3 ◆ Natural ingredients and supplies for making soaps, candles, toiletries, and other fragrance items. Also labels, containers, molds, kits, and how-to books. 612-698-3601.

**Aphrodesia Products,** 62 Kent St., Brooklyn, NY 11222: Catalog $3 ◆ Herbs, essential oils, and perfumery supplies. 800-221-6898.

**Aroma Therapy International,** 300 N. 5th Ave., Ste. 210, Ann Arbor, MI 48104: Free information ◆ Essential oils. 313-741-1617.

**The Aromatherapy Catalog,** P.O. Box 824, Rogers, AR 72757: Free catalog ◆ Essential oils, aromatic gifts, and personal care items. 501-636-0579. www.AccessNewAge.com/aroma

**Candlechem Products,** 32 Thayer Circle, P.O. Box 705, Randolph, MA 02368: Catalog $1 ◆ Essential oils, dyes, and scenting materials for use in making candles and perfumes. 781-963-4161. www.alcasoft.com/candlechem

**Caswell-Massey Company Ltd.,** Catalog Division, 100 Enterprise Pl., Dover, DE 19901: Catalog $1 ◆ Herbs, essential oils, and perfumery supplies. 800-326-0500. caswell@maui.net

**Churchill Herbs,** 608 Chimborazo Blvd., Richmond, VA 23223: Free catalog ◆ Potpourri, potpourri-making supplies, essential and fragrance oils, and homemade soaps.

**Common Scents,** 3920 24th St., San Francisco, CA 94114: Free catalog ◆ Bath and skin care products and essential oils. 800-850-6519.

**Doering Company,** 3531 Niles Rd., St. Joseph, MI 49085: Catalog $3 ◆ Essential oils, other perfumery supplies, books and videos, glassware, aromatherapy lamps, and blank incense sticks. 616-429-3961.

**East End Import Company,** 1699 Roosevelt Ave., Bohemia, NY 11716: Free brochure with long SASE ◆ Essential oils, absolutes, concretes, creams, lotions, and floral waters. 516-562-2436.

**Essential Aromatics,** 205 N. Signal St., Ojai, CA 93023: Catalog $3 ◆ Premium-quality pure essential oils, carriers, blends, diffusers, supplies, and books. 800-211-1313; 805-640-1300 (in CA).

**The Essential Oil Company,** P.O. Box 206, Lake Oswego, OR 97034: Free catalog ◆ Essential oils, soap-making molds and supplies, incense materials, potpourri, and aromatherapy items. 800-729-5912.

**Fairewood Botanicals,** Box 1273, Freeland, WA 98249: Free catalog ◆ Hand-harvested and cold-processed fresh herbals. 360-579-8963.

**The Faith Mountain Company,** P.O. Box 199, Sperryville, VA 22740: Free catalog ◆ Herbs, essential oils, and perfumery supplies. 800-822-7238. www.FaithMountain.com

**Flossy Eddy,** 153 Sundance Dr., Grand Junction, CO 81503: Free catalog ◆ Essential oils. 800-763-9963.

**Frog Pond Organic Farm,** 5300 Stoney Ridge Rd., Campbell, NY 14821: Free catalog with long SASE ◆ Organically grown floral and other herb plants. 607-537-3308.

**Frontier Cooperative Herbs,** P.O. Box 299, Norway, IA 52318: Free information ◆ Essential and fragrance oils and herbal extracts. 800-786-1388. www.frontierherb.com

**Gaia Garden Herbal Apothecary,** 2672 W. Broadway, Vancouver, British Columbia, Canada V6K 2G3: Catalog $2 ◆ Herbal, aromatherapy, and perfumery products. 604-734-4372.

**Good Hollow Greenhouse & Herbarium,** 50 Slaterock Mill Rd., Taft, TN 38488: Catalog $1 ◆ Herb plants and dried herbs, perennials, wildflowers, scented geraniums, essential oils and potpourris, teas, and spices. 615-433-7640.

**Grandma's Spice Shop,** Spice Valley Way, Upper Tract, WV 26866: Catalog $1 ◆ Essential oils and herbal potpourris. 304-358-2346.

**Hartman's Herb Farm,** 1026 Old Dana Rd., Barre, MA 01005: Catalog $2 ◆ Herbs and herb products, potpourris, and essential oils. 978-355-2015.

**Harvest Health Inc.,** 1944 Eastern Ave. SE, Grand Rapids, MI 49507: Free catalog ◆ Herbs, spices, and essential and perfume oils. 616-245-6268.

**The Herb Lady,** P.O. Box 2129, Shepherdstown, WV 25443: Free catalog ◆ Essential oils, potpourris, sachets, and aromatic blends to simmer on the stove top. 800-537-1846.

**Herb Products Company,** P.O. Box 898, 11012 Magnolia Blvd., North Hollywood, CA 91603: Free price list ◆ Botanicals, oils and fragrances, extracts, tinctures, and books. 818-761-0351. www.herbproducts.com

**Herbal Accents,** P.O. Box 12303, El Cajon, CA 92022: Catalog $1 ◆ Aromatherapy skin care products. 619-440-4380.

**Indiana Botanic Gardens,** P.O. Box 5, Hammond, IN 46325: Catalog $1 ◆ Herbs, fragrances, and essential oils. 800-644-8327. www.botanichealth.com

**Joint Adventure,** Aromatherapy Catalog, P.O. Box 824, Rogers, AR 72757: Free catalog ◆ Essential oils and aromatherapy supplies. 800-898-PURE.

**Lavender Lane,** 7337 Roseville Rd., Sacramento, CA 95842: Catalog $2 ◆ Essential and alcohol-free perfume oils, perfumery supplies, and equipment. 916-334-4400. www.choicemall.com/lavender/donna@ricp.com

**Legacy Herbs,** Sue Lukens Herbalist/Potter, HC 70, Box 442, Mountain View, AR 72560: Catalog 50¢ ◆ Herbs, wildflowers, perennial plants, soaps, bath and body care products, oils and fragrance, incense, potpourri, herbal food products, and other scented items. 870-269-4051.

**Nature's Finest,** 3323 Lee Hwy., Bristol, VA 24202: Catalog $2.50 (refundable) ◆ Dried flowers, herbs, spices, oils, fixatives, bottles, books, and potpourri supplies. 540-669-5553.

**OlFactorium,** 401 Euclid Ave., Ste. 155, Cleveland, OH 44114: Free information ◆ Botanical essential and carrier oils. 216-566-8234. sunymed@en.com

**Oshadhi Aromatherapy,** P.O. Box 824, Rodgers, AR 72757: Free catalog ◆ Oils and aromatherapy products. 501-636-0579.

**Raven's Nest Herbals,** P.O. Box 370, Duluth, GA 30136: Catalog $1.50 ◆ Herbs, spices, oils, incense, potpourri, and other herbal products. 770-242-3901.

**The Rosemary House,** 120 S. Market St., Mechanicsburg, PA 17055: Catalog $2 ◆ Herbs, oils, and spices. Also candles, soaps, teas, books, and potpourris. 717-697-5111.

**The Soap Opera,** 319 State St., Madison, WI 55703: Free price list ◆ Cruelty-free, 100 percent safe private label bodycare products and aromatics. 608-251-SOAP. www.thesoapopera.com

**Spice Discounters,** P.O. Box 2263, Napa, CA 94558: Free catalog ◆ Herbs, spices, oils, extracts, and vitamins. 800-610-5950. www.spicediscounters.com

**Tom Thumb Workshops,** Rt. 13, P.O. Box 357, Mappsville, VA 23407: Catalog $1 ◆ Potpourri, herbs and spices, essential oils, and dried flowers. 757-824-3507.

**Torling Fragrance Products,** 8320 Cutler Way, Sacramento, CA 95828: Catalog $2 (refundable off $10 order) ◆ Essential, perfume, and designer type oils. Also scented and unscented skin and bath care products. 916-682-1334.

**The Uncommon Herb,** P.O. Box 2980, Seal Beach, CA 90740: Free catalog ◆ Aromatherapy products and guide to essential oils. Also diffusers and earth-friendly natural products. 800-308-6284.

## PERSONALIZED & PROMOTIONAL PRODUCTS

**Advertising Ideas Company,** 833 Wooster Rd. North, Barberton, OH 44203: Free catalog ◆ Luggage, desk accessories, caps, T-shirts, badges and holders, toys, and other advertising and promotional novelties. 800-848-8851.

**Alfa Color Labs,** 535 W. 135th St., Gardena, CA 90248: Free information ◆ Handcrafted wood music boxes with inlaid ceramic tile and glaze-mounted personalized portraits. 310-532-2532.

**Amsterdam Printing & Litho Corp.,** 55 Wallins Corners Rd., Amsterdam, NY 12010: Free catalog ◆ Advertising novelties. 800-543-6882.

**Atlas Pen & Pencil Corp.,** 3040 N. 9th Ave., Hollywood, FL 33022: Free catalog ◆ Custom imprinted advertising specialties. 800-327-3232.

**Award Pros,** 4175 US Rt. 1 South, Monmouth Junction, NJ 08852: Free catalog ◆ Trophies, plaques, advertising specialties, and imprinted activewear. 908-274-2255.

**Balloon Printing Company,** P.O. Box 150, Rankin, PA 15104: Free information ◆ Imprinted balloons. 800-533-5221.

**Best Impressions Company,** P.O. Box 802, LaSalle, IL 61301: Free catalog ◆ Advertising specialties for promotional, incentive, and gift-giving programs. 800-635-2378. www.bestimpressions.com

**Born Enterprises,** 10932 E. Sahuaro Dr., Scottsdale, AZ 85259: Free catalog ◆ Promotional and incentive merchandise, corporate gifts, and premiums. 800-745-7530; 602-370-1922 (in AZ).

**Candid Calendars,** 10498 Loveland-Madeira Rd., Loveland, OH 45140; Free information ◆ Personalized photo calendars, puzzles, coasters, hats, mouse pads, neckties, aprons, and more. 800-328-8415; 513-583-0883 (in OH). www.candidcalendars.com

**CHS Inc.,** 5055 NE 13th Ave., Fort Lauderdale FL 33334: Free information ◆ Advertising specialties. 800-872-5329.

**Collmer Etched Glass,** 16431 S. Front Ave., Oregon City, OR 97045: Free brochure ◆ Custom designed sandcarved mugs, steins, stemware, and beveled glass pieces. 800-655-0893.

**Custom Glass Etching,** 1139 E. Las Tunas Dr., San Gabriel, CA 91776: Free catalog ◆ Personalized crystal glass awards, wedding and other gifts, and promotional products. 626-287-3775.

**Desperate Enterprises Inc.,** 620 E. Smith Rd., Medina, OH 44256: Free catalog ◆ Advertising collectibles. 800-732-4859. questions@desperate.com

**Fancy Fortune Cookies,** 6265 Coffman Rd., Indianapolis, IN 46268: Free information ◆ Gourmet fortune cookies in twelve flavors and brilliant colors. Individually wrapped and with custom messages, they are available in tins or loose by the case. 317-299-8900. www.fortunecookiesonline.com

**Logo USA,** P.O. Box 2070, Cottonwood, CA 96022: Free information ◆ Customized logo watches, both casual and corporate. Also logo desk and wall clocks. 800-655-3364; 530-347-9178 (in CA). www.logousa.com

**Marco Promotional Supplies,** 4211 Elmerton Ave., Harrisburg, PA 17109: Free catalog ◆ Convention, meeting, trade show, and promotional supplies. 800-232-1121.

**Multi Visual Products Inc.,** 28991 Front St., Ste. 205, Temecula, CA 92590: Free information ◆ Personalized photo trading cards. 800-293-9055.

**Neil Enterprises Inc.,** 450 E. Bunker Ct., Vernon Hills, IL 60061: Free catalog ◆ Photo novelties. 800-621-5584; 847-549-7627 (in IL).

**Nelson Marketing,** P.O. Box 320, Oshkosh, WI 54902: Free catalog ◆ Imprinted promotional products. 800-546-7746. www.nelsonmarketing.com

**Prestige Promotions,** 4875 White Bear Pkwy., White Bear Lake, MN 55110: Free information ◆ Pens, coffee mugs, calendars, and bumper stickers. 800-328-9351.

**Royal Graphics Inc.,** 3117 N. Front St., Philadelphia, PA 19133: Free information ◆ Posters, show cards, and bumper stickers. 215-739-8282.

**Sales Guides Inc.,** 4937 Otter Lake Rd., St. Paul, MN 55110: Free catalog ◆ Pens and pencils, key fobs, memo cubes, desk items, food and candy, games, and gifts. 800-654-6666.

**Scratch-It Promotions Inc.,** 1763 Barnum Ave., Bridgeport, CT 06610: Free information ◆ Scratch-off, pull tabs, and fragrance promotional products. 800-966-9467; 203-367-5377 (in CT).

**Shazzam Advertising Specialties,** 14792 Alder Creek Rd., Truckee, CA 96161: Free information ◆ Promotional advertising specialties. 800-999-8907. shazzam@telis.org

**N.G. Slater Corp.,** 220 W. 19th St., New York, NY 10011: Free catalog ◆ T-shirts, tote bags, pins, bumper stickers, jewelry, button-making supplies, and other advertising novelties. 800-848-4621. www.ngslater.com

**Spartan Products Inc.,** 12427 Foothill Blvd., Sylmar, CA 91342: Free catalog ◆ Equipment and supplies for making souvenir, identification, and promotional photo buttons. 800-288-3948; 818-899-2626 (in CA).

**Successful Events,** P.O. Box 64784, St. Paul, MN 55164: Free catalog ◆ Custom imprinted products for meetings, conventions, and trade shows. 800-896-9221.

**J.T. Townes Inc.,** P.O. Box 760, Danville, VA 24543: Free information ◆ Scratch pads. 800-437-PADS; 804-792-3711 (in VA).

**WesCat Inc.,** 8601 Meadow Brook Dr., Largo, FL 33777: Free brochure ◆ T-shirts, bumper stickers, and coffee mugs. 813-393-0454. www.bossbasher.com

**Windsor Vineyards,** P.O. Box 778, Marlboro, NY 12542: Free catalog ◆ Personalized holiday labels on favorite wines and gourmet gift baskets. 800-333-9987. www.windsorvineyards.com

## PEST, INSECT, & BIRD CONTROL

**Bird-X,** 300 N. Elizabeth St., Chicago, IL 60607: Free information ◆ Bird repellant products. 800-662-5021.

**Bird Barrier America Inc.,** 300 Calvert Ave., Alexandria, VA 22301: Free information ◆ Bird control systems. 800-NO-BIRDS; 703-299-8855 (in VA). www.birdbarrier.com

**Bug Baffler,** P.O. Box 444, Goffstown, NH 03045: Free information ◆ Protective clothing. 800-662-8411.

**Home Trends,** 1450 Lyell Ave., Rochester, NY 14606: Free catalog ◆ Cleaning supplies, energy-saving devices, lighting equipment, pest controls, brushes, vacuums and accessories, and more. 716-254-6520. home@eznet.net

**Nixalite of America,** 1025 16th Ave., P.O. Box 727, East Moline, IL 61244: Free information ◆ Humane bird control products. 800-624-1189. www.nixalite.com

**Planet Natural,** P.O. Box 3146, Bozeman, MT 59772: Free catalog ◆ Beneficial insects, garden seeds, composting equipment, organic fertilizers and pest controls, other garden supplies, and pet care, home, and body products. 800-289-6656. www.planetnatural.com

**Sutton Agriculture Enterprises,** 746 Vertin Ave., Salinas, CA 93901: Free brochure ◆ Bird control products, seed planters, measuring devices, and field supplies. 831-422-9693.

## PETS

### Bird Supplies

**About Birds,** P.O. Box 387, Hebron, IL 60034: Free catalog ◆ Bird food, toys, and other supplies. 800-724-7370; 815-648-4078 (in IL).

**Adams Associates,** P.O. Box 162071, Altamonte Springs, FL 32716: Free brochure ◆ Parrot perches. 407-862-0716. www.uran.net/fbn/adams

**American Pet Supplies,** P.O. Box 251231, West Bloomfield, MI 48325: Free information ◆ Bird cages and supplies for birds, dogs and cats, tropical fish, and other small animals. 800-255-0919; 810-681-2860 (in MI). www.amercanpet.com

**Animal Environments,** 1954 Kellogg Ave., Carlsbad, CA 92008: Free brochure ◆ Bird cages, safety toys, and accessories. 619-438-4442. www.animalenvironments.com

**Arbico Environmentals,** P.O. Box 4247, Tucson, AZ 85738: Free catalog ◆ Live and dried feeder insects. 800-827-2847; 520-825-9785 (in AZ). www.usit.net.BICONET

**Avian Accents,** P.O. Box 109, Troy, IL 62294: Free information ◆ Double-wide cages for finches to hyacinth macaws. 618-667-2243.

**Avitech Exotic Birds,** P.O. Box 329, Frazier Park, CA 93225: Free information ◆ Brooders, heat sources, breeding supplies, and feed products. 800-646-2473. www.avitec.com

**Bassetts Cricket Ranch Inc.,** 365 S. Mariposa, Visalia, CA 93292: Free information ◆ Crickets and king meal worms for reptiles, birds, fish, hamsters, and other animals. 800-634-2445.

**Bird City USA,** 14715 Live Oak Dr., Panama City Beach, FL 32413: Free information ◆ Wrought iron and regular exotic bird cages, toys, and toy parts. 850-233-3006. www.birdcity.com

**The Birdie Boutique Direct,** 4502-B Bennett Memorial Rd., Durham, NC 27715: Free catalog ◆ Bird care products, supplies, and toys. 888-442-8426; 919-383-8878 (in NC). birdvet@mindspring.com

**C & R Inquiries,** P.O. Box 1874, Stillwater, OK 74076: Free catalog ◆ Weather vanes, sundials, bird baths, and cupolas. 800-248-5445. www.crhooks.com

**C & S Products Company Inc.,** Box 848, Fort Dodge, IA 50501: Free catalog ◆ Wild bird suet products and suet-related feeders. 515-955-5605.

**Bill Chandler Farms,** RR 2, Box 105, Noble, IL 62868: Free price list ◆ Wild bird food. 800-752-2473.

**Clear Flite Inc.,** P.O. Box 478, Elyria, OH 44036: Free catalog ◆ Bird cages and accessories. 800-497-8263.

**Creative Bird Accessories,** P.O. Box 2157, Darien, CT 06820: Free catalog ◆ Apparel and jewelry, home accessories, posters for bird lovers, and toys and food for birds. 800-765-2325. www.creativebird.com

**Dakota Quality Bird Food,** Box 3084, Fargo, ND 58108: Free catalog ◆ Niger thistle, small sunflower seeds, royal finch mix, safflower seed, and mixes for wild birds. 800-356-9220.

**Duncraft,** 102 Fisherville Rd., Concord, NH 03303: Free catalog ◆ Wild bird supplies, squirrel-proof feeders, birdhouses, bird baths, and books. 800-763-7878. www.duncraft.com

**James J. Durant,** P.O. Box 7278, Newport Beach, CA 92660: Information $5 ◆ Handcrafted solid brass aviaries. 714-673-5625.

**Feather Fantasy,** P.O. Box 730, Chicago, CA 95712: Catalog $2 (refundable) ◆ Bird supplies. 530-274-7090. www.featherfan.com

**The Feather Farm,** 1181 4th Ave., Napa, CA 94559: Free catalog ◆ Breeding cages. 707-255-8833. www.featherfarm.com

**Joe Freed's Petiatric Supply Inc.,** 3030 Mascot St., Wichita, KS 67204: Free catalog ◆ Portable brooders, hand feeding supplies, baby and egg scales, and other egg hatching accessories.

**Hornbeck's,** 7088 Lyndon St., Rosemont, IL 60018: Free catalog ◆ Hard-to-find supplies, custom-blended foods, and other specialty bird items. 888-224-3247. www.hornbecks.com

**Hyde Bird Feeder Company,** 56 Felton St., P.O. Box 168, Waltham, MA 02254: Free catalog ◆ Bird feeders and wild bird food. 781-893-6780.

**Morton Jones Company,** P.O. Box 123, Ramona, CA 92065: Free information ◆ Bird supplies. Also cages, walk-in aviaries, and breeders. 800-443-5769.

**Jungle Talk International,** P.O. Box 111, Lafayette, CO 80026: Free information ◆ Bird toys. 800-247-3869.

**Kester's Wild Game Food Nursery,** P.O. Box 516, Omro, WI 54963: Catalog $3 ◆ Seed mixes for cockatiels, lovebirds, parakeets, parrots, canaries, and finches. 800-558-8815; 920-685-2929 (in WI). www.kesternursery.com

**King's Cages,** 145 Sherwood Ave., Farmingdale, NY 11735: Free information ◆ Parrot cages. 516-777-7300.

**L/M Animal Farms,** 10279 State Rt. 132, Pleasant Plain, OH 45162: Free information ◆ Bird food and treats. 800-332-5623; 513-877-2131 (in OH).

**LA Jolla Group Inc.,** 107 E. Vallette, Elmhurst, IL 60126: Free information ◆ Bird toys, playpens, pet landscape furniture, cages, bird food, and treats. 800-647-PETS.

**Lafeber Company,** 24981 N. 1400 East Rd., Cornell, IL 61319: Free information ◆ Nutritional products for birds. 800-842-6445. www.lafeber.com

**Master Animal Care,** 12 Maplewood Dr., Hazleton, PA 18201: Free catalog ◆ Dog and cat grooming and health care supplies, bird supplies, professional care pet products, toys, books, and gifts. 800-346-0749.

**Mellinger's,** 2310 W. South Range Rd., North Lima, OH 44452: Free catalog ◆ Thistle, safflower, finch mix, and sunflower birdseed. 330-549-9861. www.mellingers.com

**Pacific Cage & Furniture Corp.,** 3110 S. Main St., Los Angeles, CA 90007: Free catalog ◆ Animal and bird cages and accessories. 213-231-9232.

**Palace Cages,** 63 Prospect Ave., Danielson, CT 06239: Information $2 ◆ All-metal cages with cups, perches, and optional accessories. 860-774-2664.

**Parrot Paradise,** 22701 Wood St., St. Clair Shores, MI 48080: Free brochure ◆ Wrought iron cages and other supplies for parrots. 800-472-7768; 810-776-3595 (in MI).

**Pet Bird Express,** 42307 Osgood Rd., Fremont, CA 94539: Free catalog ◆ Products and supplies for pet birds and their handlers. 800-729-7734.

**Pet Warehouse,** 8177 Washington Church Rd., Dayton, OH 45458: Free catalog ◆ Bird, tropical fish, dog, and cat supplies. 800-443-1160. www.petwhse.com

**Playbird Gyms,** P.O. Box 126, 84 Hwy. 105, Palmer Lake, CO 80133: Free brochure ◆ Hard maple play gyms with replaceable parts to custom change the configuration. 719-597-3937.

**Polly's Pet Products Inc.,** 122 Julee Emilyn Dr., Bonaire, GA 31005: Free information ◆ Therapeutic perches for trimming bird's nails, swings and balancing wheels, toys for trimming beaks, and small and large stands. 888-765-5971.

**Poozleanimus,** Division of Poozle Press, 39120 Argonaut Way, Fremont, CA 94538: Free information ◆ Cages, perches, UV lighting, toys, swings, nutrition and health aids, and other accessories. 501-794-7650. www.poozleanimus.com

**RR Manufacturing Company,** P.O. Box 1415, Buffalo, MO 65622: Free catalog ◆ Exotic bird incubator, water brooders, feeders, and thermometers. 417-345-2200.

**Saltwater Farms,** P.O. Box 740, South Freeport, ME 04078: Free information ◆ Kelp meal for birds. 800-293-KELP. saltwater@maine.com

**Star Pet Supply,** 1500 New Horizons Blvd., Amityville, NY 11701: Free catalog ◆ Supplies and grooming aids for dogs, cats, birds, and other pets. 800-274-6400.

**Sundown Avery,** 871 E. Lodi Ave., P.O. Box 1406, Lodi, CA 95241: Free catalog ◆ Breeding supplies, toys, cages and accessories, and more. 800-655-7679. www.sundownaviary.com

**Sunshine Bird Supplies,** 8535 NW 56th St., Miami, FL 33166: Catalog $1.50 ◆ Bird food, medications, breeding cages, spray millet, and other supplies. 800-878-2666.

**Swelland's Cage & Supply Company,** P.O. Box 1619, Ramona, CA 92065: Free catalog information ◆ Cage supplies, wire, nesting boxes, and other bird supplies. 619-789-3572. swelland@keyinfo.com

**That Pet Place,** 237 Centerville Rd., Lancaster, PA 17603: Free catalog (specify catalog wanted) ◆ Supplies for birds, dogs, cats, reptiles, and other small animals. 800-733-3829. www.thatpetplace.com

**UPCO,** P.O. Box 969, St. Joseph, MO 64502: Free catalog ◆ Cages, birdseed, supplies, books, toys, and remedies for birds. 800-444-8651. www.upco.com

**Vann's of LA,** P.O. Box 1501, Slidell, LA 70459: Free information ◆ Custom fabric bird cage covers. 504-649-1416.

**Volkman Seed Company,** P.O. Box 96, Ceres, CA 96307: Free information ◆ Premium birdseed and cuttlebone.

**Web Cage Inc.,** 1250 Greenleaf Ave., Elk Grove Village, IL 60007: Free information ◆ Stainless steel cages for amazons and standard and large macaws. 847-228-1403. www.webcage.com

**The Whole Pet, Naturally Inc.,** 44 Coachlight Square, Montrose, NY 10548: Free catalog ◆ Health foods, herbs, vitamins and minerals, homeopathic remedies, and other holistic products for pets. 800-965-PETS; 914-739-3276 (in NY).

**Wild Bird Supplies,** 4815 Oak St., Crystal Lake, IL 60012: Free catalog ◆ Feeders, bird houses, bird baths, birdseed mixes, and books on bird care. 815-455-4020.

**Wildlife Nurseries,** P.O. Box 2724, Oshkosh, WI 54903: Catalog $3 ◆ Upland game birdseed combinations and water gardening supplies. 414-231-3780.

## Dog & Cat Supplies

**AAC Litter Box Liners,** 9 Ivy Place, Howell, NJ 07731: Free information with long SASE and two 1st class stamps ◆ Litter box liners. 800-208-9048. www.njplaza.com/AAC

**All American Pet Products,** P.O. Box 3178, North Hollywood, CA 91609: Free information ◆ Anti-jump training harness for dogs. 800-349-7333. www.ameripet.com

**Alsto Company,** P.O. Box 1267, Galesburg, IL 61401: Catalog $1 ◆ Tools, pet products, kitchen aids, and convenience items. 800-447-0048.

**American Pet Supplies,** P.O. Box 251231, West Bloomfield, MI 48325: Free information ◆ Bird cages and supplies for birds, dogs and cats, tropical fish, and other small animals. 800-255-0919; 810-681-2860 (in MI). www.amercanpet.com

**Angelical Cat Company,** 9311 NW 26th Pl., Sunrise, FL 33322: Free information ◆ Cat furniture, trees, play pieces, scratching accessories, and more. 954-747-3629. www.angelicalcat.com

**Canine Cookie Company,** 21527 Paine Ave., Lago Vista, TX 78645: Free catalog ◆ Meat byproduct and preservative-free dog treats. 512-267-9729. www.canine-cookie.com

**Care-A-Lot,** 1617 Diamond Springs Rd., Virginia Beach, VA 23455: Free catalog ◆ Dog and cat supplies, cages, crates, treats, books, and more. 800-343-7680; 757-460-9771 (in VA). www.cyberfocus.net/80schica/Care-a-Lot

**Cat Claws,** 1004 W. Broadway, P.O. Box 1001. Morrilton, AR 72110: Free catalog ◆ Gifts, supplies, and other accessories for cats. 800-783-0977. www.catclaws.com

**Cat Faeries,** 584 Castro St., San Francisco, CA 94114: Free catalog ◆ Toys, grow-your-own indoor grass, and other healthy things for cats. 415-585-6400. www.catfaeries.com

**Cathy's Cat Country,** P.O. Box 86181, Madeira Beach, FL 33738: Free catalog ◆ Chemical-free veterinarian tested cat supplies. 813-327-5054. cathycat@gate.net

**Cornucopia Express,** 229 Wall St., Huntington, NY 11743: Free brochure ◆ Natural health food for dogs, cats, and horses. Also herbal flea collars, cat and critter litter, catnip, natural jerky treats for dogs, and other supplies. 800-PET-8280; 516-427-7479 (in NY).

**The Dog's Outfitter,** Division Humboldt Industries Inc., Humboldt Industrial Park, 1 Maplewood Dr., Hazleton, PA 18201: Free catalog ◆ Dog grooming, training, and general pet care accessories. 800-FOR-DOGS.

**Dr. Goodpet,** P.O. Box 4547, Inglewood, CA 90309: Free catalog ◆ Natural vitamin and mineral supplements and other medications. 800-222-9932. www.goodpet.com

**Drs. Foster & Smith Inc.,** 2253 Air Park Rd., P.O. Box 100, Rhinelander, WI 54501: Free catalog ◆ Pet and equine products and health care supplies. 800-826-7206. www.drsfosterandsmith.com

**Duke's Dog Fashions Inc.,** 10950 SW 5th St., Ste. 145, Beaverton, OR 97005: Free list of retail sources ◆ Dog fashions, leads, and collars. 800-880-8969. dukesdog@teleport.com

**Feline Tested (Owner Approved),** P.O. Box 2433, Dale City, VA 22193: Free catalog ◆ Owner-approved, hard-to-find Catalog toys. 203-492-9246. www.erols.com/jrdixon

**Flexi-Mat Corp.,** 2244 South Western Ave., Chicago, IL 60608: Free list of retail sources ◆ Combination window perch cat bed. 773-376-5500. info@leisure-time.com

**For Your Dog Only,** 4131 Business Center Dr., Fremont, CA 94538: Free information ◆ Dog beds and futons with washable furniture-grade fabrics. 888-413-0290. beds4dogs@aol.com

**George Pet Gifts,** 375 Alabama St., Ste. 400, San Francisco, CA 94110: Free catalog ◆ Gifts and supplies for cats and dogs. 415-922-9111.

**Hulme,** P.O. Box 670, Hwy. 641 South, Paris, TN 38242: Free catalog ◆ Pet supplies, medications, flea control products, and training aids. 901-642-6400.

**J-B Wholesale Pet Supplies,** P.O. Box 948, West Plains, MO 65775: Free catalog ◆ Supplies for cats and dogs. 800-JEFFERS. www.1800jeffers.com/default.htm

**JD Enterprises,** P.O. Box 2433, Dale City, VA 22193: Free catalog ◆ Cat toys. jrdixon@erols.com

**Jeffers Vet Supply,** P.O. Box 948, West Plains, MO 65775: Free catalog ◆ Books, medications, and pet supplies. 800-JEFFERS. www.1800jeffers.com/default.htm

**Kayla's Kritters,** P.O. Box 7623, La Verne, CA 91750: Free catalog ◆ Dog squeak toys in original breed designs. www.home.earthlink.net/~jmo

**Kennel Vet Corp.,** P.O. Box 523, Laurel, DE 19956: Free catalog ◆ Grooming and health supplies and kennels. 800-782-0627. www.petmarket.com

**Kitty Wanna Catnip,** 324 N. 80th St., Seattle, WA 98103: Free information ◆ Catnip in designer tins. 206-706-8791.

**Leather Brothers Inc.,** P.O. Box 700, Conway, AR 72033: Free catalog ◆ Leather and nylon collars and leads, wire muzzles, dog harnesses, name tags, and training leads. 800-442-5522.

**Leatherrite Manufacturing Inc.,** 251 2nd St. SW, Carmel, IN 46032: Free catalog ◆ Leather, nylon, and vinyl leads. Also collars and harnesses. 800-722-5222; 317-844-7241 (in IN). lnmfg@induweb.net

**Leerburg Video Productions,** P.O. Box 218, Menomonie, WI 54751: Free catalog ◆ Dog training videos. 715-235-6502. Frawley@win.bright.net

**Master Animal Care,** 12 Maplewood Dr., Hazleton, PA 18201: Free catalog ◆ Dog and cat grooming and health care supplies, bird supplies, professional care pet products, toys, books, and gifts. 800-346-0749.

**Michael J. Fashions,** Box 400, Solebury, PA 18963: Free catalog ◆ Outerwear and beds for dogs. 215-297-5332. www.michaeljfashions.com

**Mountain Lion Catnip,** P.O. Box 120, Forest Hill, WV 24935: Catalog $1 ◆ Catnip, beds, and toys for cats. 800-390-5588. www.mtlioncatnip.com

**The Natural Pet Care Company,** 2713 E. Madison, Seattle, WA 98112: Free catalog ◆ Natural pet care products. 800-962-8266; 206-329-1417 (in WA).

**NDR Tattoo Equipment,** P.O. Box 116, Woodstock, NY 12498: Free information ◆ New and used tattoo equipment and supplies for pet identification. 800-637-3647. www.natidogregistry.com

**Nite Lite Company,** P.O. Box 8300, Little Rock, AR 72221: Free catalog ◆ Kennel, training, and hunting supplies for dogs. Also clothing and accessories for the hunter. 800-648-5483.

**Nitron Industries Inc.,** P.O. Box 1447, Fayetteville, AR 72702: Free catalog ◆ Organic fertilizers, enzyme soil conditioners, natural pest controls, and pet care products. 800-835-0123. www.nitron.com

**Omaha Vaccine Company Inc.,** 3030 L St., P.O. Box 7228, Omaha, NE 68107: Free catalog ◆ Health, grooming, and training supplies for dogs, cats, other house pets, and horses. 800-367-4444. www.omahavaccine.com/divov.htm

**PawsXpress,** P.O. Box 528, Wainscott, NY 11975: Free catalog ◆ Dog and cat products. 888-808-7297. www.pawsxpress.com

**Pendleton Catalog Furniture,** 1273 Dawnridge Ave., El Cajon, CA 92021: Free information ◆ Cat furniture and other accessories. 619-443-2006. www.pendletoncatfurniture.com

**Pet Pouch,** P.O. Box 797144, Dallas, TX 75379: Free information ◆ Hands-free pet carrier. 972-931-6534. www.connect.net/petpouch

**Pet Warehouse,** 8177 Washington Church Rd., Dayton, OH 45458: Free catalog ◆ Bird, tropical fish, dog, and cat supplies. 800-443-1160. www.petwhse.com

**PetSolutions,** 802 Orchard Ln., Beavercreek, OH 45434: Free catalog ◆ Toys, treats, bedding, and grooming, training, and healthcare products for dogs. 800-737-3868.

**Planet Natural,** P.O. Box 3146, Bozeman, MT 59772: Free catalog ◆ Beneficial insects, garden seeds, composting equipment, organic fertilizers and pest controls, other garden supplies, and pet care, home, and body products. 800-289-6656. www.planetnatural.com

**Pooch! Emporium for Dogs & Cats,** 2817 E. 3rd Ave., Denver, CO 80206: Free catalog ◆ Whimsical and practical products for dogs and cats. 800-95-POOCH.

**Pupular Show Products,** 5301-43 Ave., Beaumont, Alberta, Canada T4X 1C5: Free catalog ◆ Dog grooming and hair care products, leads, doggy treats, toys and dishes, and more. 403-929-5089. www.telusplanet.net/public/silkyd

**PurePet,** 4435 1st St., Ste. 353, Livermore, CA 94550: Free information ◆ Natural salon-quality shampoos, conditioners, sprays, powders, and other grooming aids for dogs and cats. 800-288-2275. www.purepet.com

**R.C. Steele Dog Equipment,** 1989 Transit Way, Box 910, Brockport, NY 14420: Free catalog ◆ Dog and kennel supplies. 800-872-3773. www.rcsteele.com

**That Pet Place,** 237 Centerville Rd., Lancaster, PA 17603: Free catalog (specify catalog wanted) ◆ Supplies for birds, dogs, cats, reptiles, and other small animals. 800-733-3829. www.thatpetplace.com

**United Pharmacal Company Inc.,** P.O. Box 969, St. Joseph, MO 64502: Free catalog ◆ Health and medical supplies for dogs, cats, and horses. 816-233-8809. www.upco.com

**UPCO,** P.O. Box 969, St. Joseph, MO 64502: Free catalog ◆ Dog and cat supplies. 800-444-8651. www.upco.com

**Valley Vet Supply,** P.O. Box 504, Marysville, KS 66508: Free catalog ◆ Grooming and health aids, collars, toys, kennel and training equipment, leashes, carriers, and other supplies for dogs. 800-835-2978. www.valleyvet.com

**Vermont Natural Stoneworks,** Depot St., Box 275, Fair Haven, VT 05743: Free list of retail sources ◆ Tile products that include floors, pet memorials and urns, entryway systems, house and garden markers, instant patios and walkways, and gas stove mats. 802-265-2200. www.sover.net/~stone

**Virtual Vet,** PO Box 20107, Bloomington, MN 55420: Free information ◆ Breath aids for dogs and cats. 888-414-7387. global1@macconnect.com

**Wahl Clipper Corp.,** 2900 Locust St., Sterling, IL 61081: Free information ◆ Animal grooming accessories. 800-435-7748. user5@wahlclipper.com

**The Whole Pet, Naturally Inc.,** 44 Coachlight Square, Montrose, NY 10548: Free catalog ◆ Health foods, herbs, vitamins and minerals, homeopathic remedies, and other holistic products for pets. 800-965-PETS; 914-739-3276 (in NY).

**Wow - Bow Distributors Ltd.,** 13 Lucon Dr., Deer Park, NY 11729: Free catalog ◆ Health food for pets. 800-326-0230; 516-254-6064 (in NY).

## Tropical Fish Supplies

**All-Glass Aquarium Company Inc.,** 9675 S. 60th St., Franklin, WI 53132: Free catalog ◆ Aquariums and accessories. 414-421-9670. www2.all-glass.com/allglass

**American Pet Supplies,** P.O. Box 251231, West Bloomfield, MI 48325: Free information ◆ Bird cages and supplies for birds, dogs, cats, tropical fish, and other small animals. 800-255-0919; 810-681-2860 (in MI). www.amercanpet.com

**Anchor Bay Aquarium Inc.,** 36457 Alfred St., New Baltimore, MI 48047: Catalog $2 ◆ Rare cichlids, catfish, exotic tropical fish, books, supplies, and live plants. 810-725-1383. www.anchorbayaquarium.com

**Angels Plus,** P.O. Box 886, Olean, NY 14760: Free catalog ◆ Angel fish, fish food, medications, and general supplies. 716-372-5273. www.angelsplus.com

**Aquacon,** 10211 Pines Blvd., Ste. 120, Pembroke Pines, FL 33026: Free catalog ◆ Marine specimens and aquarium accessories. 800-798-7625; 954-441-5999 (in FL). www.aquacon.com

**Aquanetics Systems Inc.,** 5251 Lovelock St., San Diego, CA 92110: Free list of retail sources ◆ Easy-to-install and no-tools-needed for maintenance filtration system. 619-291-8444. www.aquanetics.com

**Aquarium Concepts,** 933 C St., Hayward, CA 94541: Free catalog ◆ Exotic and tropical fish, aquarium supplies and equipment, books, and other aids. 510-583-9029.

**The Aquarium Mail Order,** 933 S. Orange Blossom Trail, Apopka, FL 32703: Free information ◆ Tropical fish and reptile supplies. 800-258-8444. www.aquariummo.com

**Aquarium Products,** 180 Penrod Ct., Glen Burnie, MD 21061: Free information ◆ Medications and water conditioners for tropical fish. 410-761-2100.

**Aquarium Systems,** 8141 Tyler Blvd., Mentor, OH 44060: Free information ◆ Saltwater aquarium test kits. 800-822-1100; 440-255-1997 (in OH). info@aquariumsystems.com

**Aquatic Specialists,** 3721 N. Broadway, Knoxville, TN 37940: Catalog $5 (refundable) ◆ Net-caught marine fish, marine invertebrates, macro algae, and cured live rock. 423-687-2704.

**Aquatic Warehouse,** 5466 Complex Dr., #204, San Diego, CA 92123: Free information ◆ Filtration systems, skimmers, and other aquarium accessories. 800-557-8118. www.aquaticwarehouse.com

**Bassetts Cricket Ranch Inc.,** 365 S. Mariposa, Visalia, CA 93292: Free information ◆ Crickets and king meal worms for reptiles, birds, fish, hamsters, and other animals. 800-634-2445.

**Buckaroo Marine,** 1319 N. Main, Tucson, AZ 85705: Free brochure ◆ Saltwater fish and invertebrates. 800-927-1050.

**J.P. Burleson Inc.,** P.O. Box 32, Frederick, MD 21701: Catalog $3 ◆ Aquarium testing kits, cleansing solutions, water stabilization products, filter media, water conditioners, and conductivity meters. 301-846-4800. www.jpburleson.com

**By-Rite Pet Supplies,** 23450 Kidder St., Hayward, CA 94545: Catalog $2 ◆ Aquarium supplies. 800-321-3448.

**California Aquarium Supply Company,** Attention: Catalog Department, 17719 Valley View St., Cerritos, CA 90701: Catalog $5 ◆ Acrylic aquariums, filters, and accessories. 714-522-8373.

**Champion Lighting & Supply,** 570 Bethlehem Pike, Fort Washington, PA 19034: Free information ◆ Aquarium supplies, test kits, lights, and other accessories. 800-673-7822; 215-283-9400 (in PA). www.championlighting.com

**Champion Supply Company,** 570 Bethlehem Pike, Fort Washington, PA 19034: Free information ◆ Automatic water changing and evaporation control pumps. 800-673-7822; 215-283-9400 (in PA). www.championlighting.com

**Daleco Master Breeder Products,** 3556 N. 400 East, Warsaw, IN 46580: Catalog $6 ◆ Tropical fish supplies, live food cultures, power filters, purification equipment, medications, light and temperature controls, fresh and salt water support systems, and aquariums. 219-268-6300. daleco@kconline.com

**Debron Aquatics,** 1800 W. Oxford Ave., Englewood, CO 80110: Free catalog ◆ Tropical fish equipment and supplies. 800-249-4375.

**The Discus Place,** 5617 Oakmeadow Dr., Fort Worth, TX 76132: Free information ◆ Parent-raised tropical and exotic fish. 817-346-0384. discusplaz@aol.com

**Enviro-Lite Industries,** 22126 S. Vermont Ave., Torrance, CA 90502: Free information ◆ Aquarium lighting systems. 310-787-0541.

**Exotic Aquaria Inc.,** 1672 NE 205th Terrace, North Miami Beach, FL 33179: Free information ◆ Tropical fish, algae, and corals. 305-654-1171. www.exoticaquaria.com

**Exotic Fish,** 406 Northside Dr., Valdosta, GA 31602: Catalog $3 ◆ Tropical fish supplies and aquarium accessories. 800-736-0473.

**Filtronics,** 4000 E. Leaverton Ct., Anaheim, CA 92807: Free information ◆ Semi-submersible aquarium testers. 714-630-5040.

**Hamilton Technology Corp.,** 14902 S. Figueroa St., Gardena, CA 90248: Free catalog ◆ Reef tank lights, digital electronic pH meter, and other aquarium equipment. 800-458-7474.

**Hawaiian Marine Imports Inc.,** 1234 N. Post Oak Rd., Houston, TX 77055: Free information ◆ Filters and hoses. 713-680-2227. www.eheim.com

**Hikari Sales USA Inc.,** 2804 McCone Ave., Hayward, CA 94545: Free information ◆ Algae wafers, micro pellets, sinking wafers, food sticks, and other tropical fish food. 800-621-5619. www.hikariusa.com

**Dale Jordan,** 76 Tanya Crescent, Winnipeg, Manitoba, Canada R2G 2Z8: Free information ◆ Tropical fish. 204-668-9780.

**Kent Marine,** 2123 Corporate Dr., Marietta, GA 30067: Free information ◆ Saltwater aquarium supplies. 770-955-7750. www.kentmarine.com

**Kordon,** Division Novalek Inc., 2242 Davis Ct., Hayward, CA 94545: Free information ◆ Live and frozen brine shrimp, brine shrimp eggs, and a salt water mix. 510-782-4058. KORDON@prado.com

**Leisure Time Pet Center,** 43041 W. Seven Mile Rd., Northville, MI 48167: Free price list ◆ Aquatic plants and supplies. 810-380-5051.

**Lifereef Filter Systems,** 4628 S. Ward Way, Morrison, CO 80465: Free catalog ◆ Aquarium filter systems, skimmers, controllers, air dryers, light fixtures, chillers, and water pumps. 303-978-0940. www.lifereef.com/home.html

**Mac's Discus,** 20103 174th Ave. NE, Woodinville, WA 98072: Free information ◆ Discus fish. 206-483-3729.

**Mail Order Pet Shop,** 250 W. Executive Dr., Edgewood, NY 11717: Free catalog ◆ Filters, heaters, medications, marine supplies, plastic plants, air pumps, water conditioners for tropical fish, and supplies for dogs, cats, birds, and hamsters. 800-366-7387; 516-595-1717 (in NY). www.mopetshop.com

**Majestic Pet Supply,** 1550 N. Northwest Hwy., Park Ridge, IL 60068: Catalog $2.50 ◆ Tropical fish supplies. 847-635-7711. www.miraclemile.com/majesticpet

**Marine Technologies,** 30100 Town Center Dr., Laguna Niguel, CA 92677: Free information ◆ Aquariums, tropical fish supplies, and accessories. 714-363-9560.

**Marine World Warehouse,** P.O. Box 522881, Miami, FL 33152: Free price list ◆ Exotic and tropical fish, corals, inverts, and supplies. 305-228-0029.

**Natural Aquarium & Terrarium,** 2906 Ossenfort Rd., Glencoe, MO 63038: Free catalog ◆ Potted live aquarium plants. 800-423-4717.

**Nature's Way,** 4023 Sawyer Ct., Sarasota, FL 34233: Free information ◆ Aquarium filters, pumps, and water purification equipment. 800-780-2320. www.rosystems.com

**Nippon Pet Food,** 1327 Post Ave., Torrance, CA 90501: Free information ◆ Tropical fish food for cichlids, goldfish, and koi. 310-787-8706.

**O.S.I. Marine Lab Inc.,** 3550 Arden Rd., Hayward, CA 94545: Free information ◆ Tropical fish food. 510-670-0888. www.osimarinelabs.com

**Pet Solutions,** 802 N. Orchard Ln., Beavercreek, OH 45434: Free catalog ◆ Tropical fish and pond supplies. 800-737-3868. www.petsolutions.com

**Pet Warehouse,** 8177 Washington Church Rd., Dayton, OH 45458: Free catalog ◆ Bird, tropical fish, dog, and cat supplies. 800-443-1160. www.petwhse.com

**M. Reed Enterprises,** P.O. Box 1930, Sutter Creek, CA 95685: Free brochure ◆ Frozen fish food shipped direct to the hobbyist. 209-267-1175. lakemarie@depot.net

**Reef Displays,** 10925 Overseas Hwy., Marathon, FL 33050: Free catalog ◆ Net-caught Atlantic fish and invertebrates, macro algae, algae snails, Caribbean live rock, and fresh and cured reef rock. 305-743-0070.

**Reef Life Inc.,** 5925 Ravenswood Rd., Fort Lauderdale, FL 33312: Free information ◆ Live rock and sand. 800-903-3474; 954-983-2663 (in FL).

**Reef Tech,** 4550 Wadsworth, Ste. 179, Wheatridge, CO 80033: Free information ◆ Aquariums, filters, canopies, and stands. 303-422-3882.

**San Francisco Bay Brand Inc.,** 8239 Enterprise Dr., Newark, CA 94560: Free brochure ◆ Frozen and packaged tropical fish foods. 510-792-7200. www.sfbb.com

**Sanders Brine Shrimp Company,** 3850 S. 540 West, Ogden, UT 84405: Free price list ◆ Brine shrimp eggs. 801-393-5027.

**Scientific Corals,** 850 Dogwood Rd., Lawrenceville, GA 30244: Free price list ◆ Tank-raised corals. 770-736-9220. www.scientificcorals.home.mindspring.com

**Sea-Aquatic International,** 1631 S. Dixie Hwy., Pompano Beach, FL 33060: Free price list ◆ Tropical fish, invertebrates, live rock, and supplies. 954-784-9278.

**Sea & Sea,** 5116 Bissonette, Bellaire, TX 77401: Free information ◆ Live rock and sand. 713-869-0017.

**South Pacific Imports,** 563 5th St., Struthers, OH 44471: Free brochure ◆ Coral and shells. 216-755-0522.

**Spectacular Sea Systems,** 4169 N. Dixie Hwy., Pompano Beach, FL 33064: Free information ◆ Aquarium systems. 954-941-3792. www.spectacularsea.com

**SpectraPure,** 738 S. Perry Ln., Tempe, AZ 85281: Free information ◆ Aquarium water purification systems. 800-685-2783. spectra@syspac.com

**R.C. Steele Tropical Fish,** 1989 Transit Way, Box 910, Brockport, NY 14420: Free information ◆ Aquarium supplies. 800-872-3773. www.rcsteele.com

**Sub-Sea Specialties,** 13051 Center Ave., Largo, FL 34643: Free list ◆ Caribbean marine life. 813-584-3950.

**That Fish Place,** 237 Centerville Rd., Lancaster, PA 17603: Free catalog ◆ Aquarium supplies. 800-733-3829. www.thatpetplace.com

**Total Marine Aquaria,** 615-A North Ave., New Rochelle, NY 10801: Free information ◆ Live corals and inverts. 914-632-0889.

**Ultra Pure Water Systems,** 539 Diana Ave., Morgan Hill, CA 95037: Free information ◆ Reverse osmosis filtration systems. 800-407-8734; 408-779-8482 (in CA).

**Village Wholesale,** 704 New Loudon Rd., Latham, NY 12110: Free catalog ◆ Tropical fish and supplies. 518-783-6878.

**Kent Webster,** 6 Coach Rd., Rancho Palos Verdes, CA 90275: Free list with long SASE ◆ Rare angels and other fish. 310-831-5695.

**Marc Weiss Companies Inc.,** 5935 Ravenswood Rd., Fort Lauderdale, FL 33312: Free information ◆ Discus, angel fish, and fish care products. 954-894-9222.

**Won Brothers Pet Supply,** P.O. Box 1844, Rockville, MD 20849: Free information ◆ Aquarium equipment and supplies. 888-417-6969.

**World of Aquatics,** 525 Jubilee St., Emmaus, PA 18049: Catalog $2 ◆ Live rock and sand, corals, saltwater fish, and invertebrates. 610-967-1456.

## Carriers

**DAFCO,** 2411 Grear St., Salem, OR 97301: Free brochure ◆ Lightweight collapsible dog carrier. 800-458-1562.

## Kennels & Enclosures

**Animal Environments,** 2201 Camino Vida Roble, Carlsbad, CA 92009: Free information ◆ Animal cages. 619-438-4442. www.animalenvironments.com

**Cal-Formed Plastics Company,** 2050 E. 48th St., Los Angeles, CA 90058: Free information ◆ Easy-to-clean interlocking two-piece dog house with 5-way flow-through ventilation. 800-772-7723.

**Central Metal Products Inc.,** North State Rt. 213, North Edge, Windfall, IN 46076: Free catalog ◆ Wire cages for dogs. 800-874-3647; 317-945-7677 (in IN).

**Comtrad Industries,** 2820 Waterford Lake Dr., Ste. 102, Midlothian, VA 23113: Free information ◆ Electric invisible pet containment systems. 800-992-2966. www.comtrad.com

**Innotek Pet Products Inc.,** One Innoway Dr., Garrett, IN 46738: Free list of retail sources ◆ Pet containment system and products for behavior problem solutions. 800-826-5527. www.pet-products.com

**Invisible Fence Company Inc.,** 355 Phoenixville Pike, Malvern, PA 19355: Free information ◆ Invisible electronic pet containment fence. 800-538-DOGS. www.ifco.com

**Kennel-Aire Manufacturing Company,** 3580 Holly Ln. North, Plymouth, MN 55447: Free catalog ◆ Wire animal enclosures. 800-346-0134.

**Mason Company,** 260 Depot St., Box 365, Leesburg, OH 45135: Free catalog ◆ Kennels and cages for dogs. 800-543-5567.

**Pacific Cage & Furniture Corp.,** 3110 S. Main St., Los Angeles, CA 90007: Free catalog ◆ Animal and bird cages and accessories. 213-231-9232.

**Radio Fence,** 230 E. Russell St., Fayetteville, NC 28301: Free information ◆ Easy-to-install electronic invisible pet containment systems. 800-775-8404.

**West Virginia Fence Corp.,** RR 81, Box 3, Lindside, WV 24951: Free catalog ◆ Permanent and portable electric pet containment fences. 800-356-5458; 304-753-4387 (in WV).

## Pet Doors

**Borwick Innovations,** P.O. Box 30345, Santa Barbara, CA 93130: Free information ◆ Easy-to-install screen door that snaps into any screen door. 800-365-5657. ewinters@silcom.com

**Hale Security Pet Door,** 5622 N. 52nd Ave., Glendale, AZ 85301: Free information ◆ Pet doors for walls and wood doors. 800-646-4773. halepet@ix.netcom.com

**Patio Pacific Inc.,** 1931-C N. Gaffey St., San Pedro, CA 90731: Free catalog ◆ Pet door panels for sliding glass doors. 800-826-2871. www.petdoors.com

**Petdoors U.S.A.,** 4523 30th St. West, Bradenton, FL 34207: Free brochure ◆ Easy-to-install and self-closing, energy-efficient doors with a security locked see-through panel. 800-749-9609. www.petdoor.com

## Reptiles & Amphibians

**Al Reptiles,** P.O. Box 452, Bainbridge, OH 45612: Free information ◆ Captive-bred reptiles. 614-493-0029. www.a1reptiles.com

**All-Glass Aquarium Company Inc.,** 9675 S. 60th St., Franklin, WI 53132: Free catalog ◆ Reptile cages and tanks for turtles and amphibians. 414-421-9670.

**The Aquarium Mail Order,** 933 S. Orange Blossom Trail, Apopka, FL 32703: Free information ◆ Tropical fish and reptile supplies. 800-258-8444.

**Armstrong's Cricket Farm,** P.O. Box 125, West Monroe, LA 71294: Free information ◆ Crickets, superworms, giant mealworms, mealworms, waxworms, and accessories. 800-345-8778.

**Bassetts Cricket Ranch Inc.,** 365 S. Mariposa, Visalia, CA 93292: Free information ◆ Crickets and king meal worms for reptiles, birds, fish, hamsters, and other animals. 800-634-2445.

**The Bean Farm,** 32514 NE 77th St., Carnation, WA 98014: Free catalog ◆ Herpetological and small animal supplies. 425-861-7964. www.beanfarm.com

**Big Apple Herpetological,** 18 East Mall, Plainview, NY 11803: Free catalog ◆ Reptile and amphibian supplies, cages, care products, and books. 800-92-APPLE. www.bigappleherp.com

**Black Jungle Terrarium Supply,** P.O. Box 93895, Las Vegas, NV 89195: Catalog $1 (refundable) ◆ Terrarium supplies. 800-268-1813. www.blackjungle.com

**Randall Burkey Company Inc.,** P.O. Box 1090, Boerne, TX 78006: Free catalog ◆ Incubators and incubating supplies. 800-531-1097. www.randallburkey.com

**Bush Herpetological Supply,** P.O. Box 539, Neodesha, KS 66757: Free information ◆ Custom and standard cages and herpetological supplies. 800-451-6178. www.pythons.com/bush/bush.html

**Central Florida Reptile Farm,** 4800 Kumquat St., Cocoa, FL 32926: Free information ◆ Captive-born turtles and tortoises. 407-639-3325. cfrf@herp.com

**Bob Clark,** 12316 Val Verde Dr., Oklahoma City, OK 73142: Free information ◆ Captive-bred pythons. 405-722-5017. www.bobclark.com/

**Critters Ltd.,** Bill & Philip Harris, 6 Project 32 Rd., Accord, NY 12404: Free information ◆ Imported and captive-bred reptiles. Also live and frozen rodents. 914-626-8620.

**Custom Cages,** 14 Dry Run Rd., River Falls, WI 54022: Free catalog ◆ Custom cages for reptiles. 800-766-6354; 715-425-8888 (in WI).

**Enviro-Lite Industries,** 22126 S. Vermont Ave., Torrance, CA 90502: Free information ◆ Reptile enclosure lighting and accessories. 310-787-0541.

**Fluker Farms,** 1333 Plantation Rd., Port Allen, LA 70767: Free information ◆ P.O. Box 378, Baton Rouge, LA 70821: Free information ◆ Feeder insects. 800-735-8537. www.flukerfarms.com

**Freedom Breeder,** 38 Beta Ct., San Ramon, CA 94583: Free information ◆ Reptile and rodent breeding racks. 510-838-2331. freedom@herp.com

**Ghann's Cricket Farm Inc.,** P.O. Box 211840, Augusta, GA 30917: Free information ◆ Live crickets and mealworms for reptiles and amphibians. 800-476-2248. www.ghann.com

**Glades Herp Inc.,** P.O. Box 50911, Fort Myers, FL 33905: Free information ◆ Captive-bred herps. 941-693-1077.

**Grubco,** Box 15001, Hamilton, OH 45015: Free brochure ◆ Live pet food for reptiles, amphibians, birds, and small animals. 800-222-3563. www.herp.com/grubco

**L/M Animal Farms,** 10279 State Rt. 132, Pleasant Plain, OH 45162: Free information ◆ Reptile food and supplements. 800-332-5623; 513-877-2131 (in OH).

**Live Cargo Inc.,** 6886 NW 82nd Terrace, Parkland, FL 33067: Stock list $5 (annual subscription) ◆ Geckos, turtles, and tortoises. 954-753-2869.

**Lyon Electric Company,** 2765 Main St., Chula Vista, CA 91911: Free information ◆ Reptile incubation system. 619-585-9900. lyon@herp.com

**Mail Order Pet Shop,** 250 W. Executive Dr., Edgewood, NY 11717: Free catalog ◆ Supplies for herpetoculturists. 800-366-7387; 516-595-1717 (in NY). www.mopetshop.com

**Manimal Brand Products,** 12602 Daryl Hill Rd., Jacksonville, FL 32218: Free catalog ◆ Custom reptile enclosures. 904-751-0849. manimal@jax-inter.net

**Maryland Reptile Farm,** 109 W. Cherry Hill Rd., Reistertown, MD 21136: Free catalog with long SASE ◆ Books and related herp supplies. 410-526-4184.

**Mice Unlimited,** P.O. Box 71142, Project City, CA 96079: Free information ◆ Live and frozen feeder mice. 800-MICE-4-YOU. www.snowcrest.net/mice/mice.htm

**Midwest Custom Products Inc.,** 14505 S. Harris, Greenwood, MO 64034: Free information ◆ Professional animal handling equipment. 816-861-3351. www.tongs.com

**Nekton USA Inc.,** 120 S. Ring Ave., Tarpon Springs, FL 34689: Free information ◆ Food supplements for reptiles and amphibians.

**Neodesha Plastics Inc.,** Twin Rivers Industrial Park, P.O. Box 371, Neodesha, KS 66757: Free information ◆ Reptile cages. 316-325-3096.

**Pet Exotic,** Allen Shelton, 1609 Carolyn, Irving, TX 75061: Free price list ◆ Captive-born reptiles. 972-438-8091.

**Pet Food Warehouse,** 777 N. Quentin Rd., Palatine, IL 60067: Free stock list ◆ Reptiles, amphibians, arachnids, and supplies. 847-705-7745.

**Port Credit Pet Centre,** 219 Lakeshore Rd. East, Mississauga, Ontario, Canada L5G 1G5: Free information ◆ Captive-bred reptiles, amphibians, and arachnids. Also live and frozen foods. 905-274-8018.

**Prairieland Herpetoculture,** Larry Keller, P.O. Box 267, Sidney, IL 61877: Free price list with long SASE ◆ Captive-bred snakes.

**Python Products Inc.,** 7000 W. Marcia Rd., Milwaukee, WI 53223: Free information ◆ Aquarium maintenance systems for aquatic turtles and herps. 414-355-7000. www.pythonproducts.com

**Rainbow Mealworms & Crickets,** 126 E. Spruce St., P.O. Box 4907, Compton, CA 90224: Free information ◆ Mealworms and crickets for reptiles and amphibians. 800-777-9676.

**Rep-Cal Research Labs.,** P.O. Box 727, Los Gatos, CA 95031: Free information ◆ Calcium supplement for reptiles and amphibians. 408-356-4289. www.repcal.com

**Reptile Specialties,** 7473 Foothill Blvd., P.O. Box 31, Tujunga, CA 91042: Free information ◆ Farm-raised imports and captive-bred chameleons. Also custom cages and terrariums. 818-352-1796.

**Reptiles & Beyond,** 809 Southbridge St., Auburn, MA 01501: Free information ◆ Reptiles and live and frozen rodents. 508-832-5113.

**S.O.S. Rodent Express,** 54 Club Rd., Oley, PA 19547: Free price list with long SASE ◆ Live or frozen mice, rats, hamsters, guinea pigs, and rabbits. 610-689-4770.

**San Diego Reptile Breeders,** P.O. Box 556, Campo, CA 91906: Information $3 with long SASE ◆ Captive-bred boas, pythons, and other snakes. 619-478-5794.

**Southeast Reptile Exchange Inc.,** 4805 N. Westshore Blvd., Tampa, FL 33614: Free price list ◆ Captive-born and hand-picked imported reptiles from around the world. 800-881-3126.

**Street Reptiles & Rodents,** Joe & Karen Street, 1302 N. Capitol Ave., Indianapolis, IN 46202: Free information ◆ Captive-produced snakes. Also live or frozen mice and rats. 317-254-8520.

**That Pet Place,** 237 Centerville Rd., Lancaster, PA 17603: Free catalog (specify catalog wanted) ◆ Supplies for birds, dogs, cats, reptiles, and other small animals. 800-733-3829. www.thatpetplace.com

**Top Hat Cricket Farm Inc.,** 1919 Forest Dr., Kalamazoo, MI 49002: Free information ◆ Live crickets. 800-638-2555. www.tophatcrickets.com

**V.P.I. Reptiles,** P.O. Box 300, Boerne, TX 78006: Price list $2 ◆ Captive-hatched pythons. 210-537-5000.

**Valentine Inc.,** 4259 S. Western Blvd., Chicago, IL 60609: Free catalog ◆ Supplies for the care and breeding of reptiles and amphibians. 800-GET-STUF.

**Weis Reptiles,** Rt. 4, Box 468, Tallahassee, FL 32304: Free price list with long SASE ◆ Captive-born lizards. 904-574-1037. weisrep@herp.com

**Zeigler Brothers Inc.,** P.O. Box 387, Hebron, IL 60034: Free price list with long SASE ◆ Reptile food. 800-724-7370.

## PEZ COLLECTIBLES

**David Welch,** P.O. Box 714, Murphysboro, IL 62966: Free list with long SASE ◆ PEZ related collectibles and books. 618-687-2282. PEZDUDE1@aol.com

## PHONE CARDS

**Acme Telecards,** P.O. Box 450957, Sunrise, FL 33345: Free information ◆ Corporate promotional and other phone cards. 800-405-2263. www.acmetel.com

**Asia Telecard,** P.O. Box 938, San Jacinto, CA 92581: Free information ◆ Japanese phone cards.

**Blue Ribbon Phone Cards,** 79 W. High St., Somerville, NJ 08876: Free information ◆ Collectible phone cards. 908-725-4645.

**Buffalo Bill Telecard Gallery,** 1980 Cliff Dr., Ste. 130, Santa Barbara, CA 93109: Free catalog ◆ Low mintage United States cards. 805-564-1473.

**Fiedler & Associates,** P.O. Box 2382, Redondo Beach, CA 90278: Free information ◆ Collectible phone cards featuring licensed art work. 310-376-4078.

**Freedman Collectibles Inc.,** P.O. Box 125, Newtonville, MA 02160: Free price list ◆ Major and minor United States telecards. 617-965-7635.

**Global Telecard Company,** 1133 Dobbs Ferry Rd., White Plains, NY 10607: Free list with long SASE ◆ Limited issue and other collectible phone cards. 914-674-0408.

**JR's Telecards,** 206 Cooper Dr., Aiken, SC 29803: Free information ◆ Promotional and hard-to-find low-mintage phone cards. 803-652-7485.

**KARS Unlimited,** P.O. Box 1385, Ormond Beach, FL 32175: Free information ◆ Phone and money cards from worldwide sources. 800-750-3506; 904-441-1101 (in FL).

**Powell Associates,** 1270 Avenue of Americas, Ste. 212, New York, NY 10020: Free information ◆ Corporate and other collectible phone cards. 800-528-8819.

**Sears Phone Card Department,** 3111 E. Colonial Dr., Orlando, FL 32894: Free list ◆ United States and topical foreign phone cards. 407-898-7778.

**TW Phonecards,** P.O. Box 551, Augusta, KS 67010: Free price list ◆ Collection-building phone cards. 316-965-7635.

**United America Cards,** P.O. Box 966, Menomonee Falls, WI 53052: Free catalog ◆ Corporate, promotional, and other phone cards. 414-353-3024.

**Wesberg Telecom Systems,** P.O. Box 127, Kasson, MN 55944: Free information ◆ Private issue and corporation phone cards. 507-634-6050.

## PHONOGRAPHS

**John Andolina Jr.,** The Early Sound Man, 28 Glen Oaks Dr., Rochester, NY 14624: Free information ◆ Antique phonographs. 716-247-3056.

**Antique Phonograph,** 19 Cliff, Johnsbury, VT 05819: Free catalog ◆ Antique phonographs, parts, and springs. 800-239-4188.

**Benedikt & Salmon Record Rarities,** 3020 Meade Ave., San Diego, CA 92116: Free catalogs: indicate choice of (1) autographs and rare books, (2) classical, (3) jazz, big bands, and blues, and (4) personalities, soundtracks, and country music ◆ Early phonographs and cylinders, autographed memorabilia and rare books in music and the performing arts, and hard-to-find phonograph recordings from 1890 to date. 619-281-3345. rarerecords@groupweb.com

**Garage A Records,** 11695 N. Pied Piper Pkwy., Cromwell, IN 46732: Free catalog ◆ Phonographs, needles, cartridges, cleaning aids, accessories and rock, blues, rock-a-billy, soul, jazz, country, pop, teen, and other 45s and LPs. 219-856-4868.

**Hoctor Products,** P.O. Box 38, Waldwick, NJ 07463: Free catalog ◆ Costumes, records, dance routines, videos, cassettes, phonographs and cassette players, and video recorders. 800-HOCTOR-9.

**K-A-B Electro-Acoustics,** P.O. Box 2922, Plainfield, NJ 07062: Free information ◆ Phono cartridges, needles, 2 and 3-speed turntables, record cleaners, sound enhancers, audio components, archival supplies, and other accessories. 908-754-1479.

## PHOTOGRAPHY

### Albums, Scrapbooks, & Photo Mounts

**Albums Inc.,** 6549 Eastland Rd., Brook Park, OH 44142: Free catalog ◆ Wedding albums, photo mounts, plaques, and frames. 800-662-1000. www.AlbumsInc.com

**AlbumX Corp.,** 5 Grace Church St., Port Chester, NY 10578: Free list of retail sources ◆ Professional albums. 914-939-6878. www.bridalalbum.com

**Art 'Z' Cards,** P.O. Box 6568, Bozeman, MT 59771: Free information ◆ Archival photo cards and albums. 800-789-6503.

**Arts 'N Crafts 'N Things,** 2260 N. Orange Mall, Orange, CA 92665: Free brochure ◆ Scrapbook-making supplies. 714-637-6292.

**Camille Company Inc.,** 828 Bergen St., Brooklyn, NY 11238: Free list of retail sources ◆ Photo albums. 800-528-8855.

**Chadwicks Photo Specialties,** P.O. Box 2370, Chatsworth, CA 91313: Free catalog ◆ Photo albums, scrapbooks, and specialty items. 818-882-8776.

**Clear-File (USA) Inc.,** 7549 Brokerage Dr., Orlando, FL 32809: Free brochure ◆ Presentation and storage supplies. 407-851-5966.

**Crown Products,** 2180 Superior Ave., Cleveland, OH 44114: Free information ◆ Albums, folios, and photo mounts. 800-827-0363.

**DoRose Albums,** 5904 Ditmas Ave., Brooklyn, NY 11203: Free information ◆ Traditional handcrafted wedding albums. 718-451-3088.

**Exposures,** 1 Memory Ln., P.O. Box 3615, Oshkosh, WI 54903: Free catalog ◆ Photo mounting supplies, albums, and frames. 800-572-5750. www.mileskimballco.com

**J.G.S. Productions,** J & T Scrapbook Design, P.O. Box 7000-108, Corona, CA 91718: Free catalog ◆ Scrapbook-making and archival supplies. 800-972-0490.

**Kambara USA,** 18355 SW Teton Ave., Tualatin, OR 97062: Free list of retail sources ◆ Handcrafted and embossed padded library-bound covers and companion albums. 800-662-6650.

**Keeping Memories Alive,** P.O. Box 728, 260 N. Main, Spanish Fork, UT 84660: Free brochure ◆ Scrapbook-making supplies. 800-419-4949; 801-798-3471 (in UT).

**Michel Company,** 4664 N. Pulaski, Chicago, IL 60630: Free catalog ◆ Albums, photo mounts, and frames. 800-621-6649.

**Pebbles in My Pocket,** P.O. Box 1506, Orem, UT 84059: Free catalog ◆ Scrapbook-making supplies. www.pebblesinmypocket.com

**Pierce Company,** 9801 Nicollet, Minneapolis, MN 55420: Catalog $1 (refundable) ◆ Handpainted backgrounds for portrait photography, mounts, albums, drapes, and printed forms. 612-884-1991.

**Reel 3-D Enterprises Inc.,** P.O. Box 2368, Culver City, CA 90231: Free information ◆ Stereo and cardboard slip-in slide mounts and 3-D supplies. 562-837-2368.

**Scrapbooks 'n More,** 5769 Westcreek Dr., Fort Worth, TX 76133: Catalog 25¢ with long SASE ◆ Scrapbook- making kits and supplies.888-312-4449; 817-294-4600 (in TX). www.scrapbooksnmore.com

**Signature Stationers,** 1800 Mass. Ave., Lexington, MA 02173: Free information ◆ Handmade European photo albums. 800-322-5031.

**Dave Sirken Distributors Inc.,** 1550 Wentzel St., Rochester, IN 46975: Free information ◆ Frames, folders, and albums. 800-348-2510.

**Skolnick Photo Frames Inc.,** 29245 Dequindre, Madison Heights, MI 48071: Free catalog ◆ Frames, proof books, albums, folios, photo mounts, and supplies. 800-972-5286. www.2frameit.com

**Wooden Nickel Albums Inc.,** 900 US Hwy. 68, Benton, KY 42025: Free information ◆ Wedding albums and inserts, proof books, folios, and other presentation supplies. 800-325-5179.

## Backgrounds

**Backdrop Outlet,** 2215 S. Michigan Ave., Chicago, IL 60615: Free catalog ◆ Handpainted backgrounds. 800-466-1755. backdrop@jubo.com

**Backgrounds by David Maheu,** 483 Steere Farm Rd., Harrisville, RI 02830: Free catalog ◆ Canvas and muslin backgrounds. 800-237-1883; 401-568-8469 (in RI).

**James Bright Backgrounds,** 460 Elder Ave., Sand City, CA 93955: Free information ◆ Fine art backgrounds and motorized roller systems. 800-821-5796; 408-899-5011 (in CA).

**Calumet Photographic,** 890 Supreme Dr., Bensenville, IL 60106: Free list of retail sources ◆ Translucent backgrounds. 800-CALUMET. www.calumetphoto.com

**Dancing Light Photographic Backdrops,** 1419 Clearlake Rd., Cocoa, FL 32922: Free brochure ◆ Professional canvas and muslin backdrops. 888-355-8941. www.dancinglight.com

**Denny Manufacturing Company Inc.,** P.O. Box 7200, Mobile, AL 36670: Free catalog ◆ Background scenes and professional backdrops. 800-844-5616.

**Steve Kaeser,** 1333 Tower Square, Ste. 4, Ventura, CA 93003: Free information ◆ Backgrounds and accessories. 800-495-8148.

**Owen's Original Backgrounds,** 211½ C St., Washington, KS 66968: Free brochure ◆ Handpainted backgrounds on heavy duty canvas or muslin. 800-767-3122.

**Photek Backgrounds,** 549 Howe Rd., Shelton, CT 06484: Free information ◆ Featherlite, reversible, and washable backgrounds and support systems. 800-648-8868.

**Photo-Tech Inc.,** P.O. Box 9326, North St. Paul, MN 55109: Free information ◆ Easy-to-use background system. 612-771-4438.

**Photographers Specialized Services,** 650 Amour Rd., P.O. Box 46, Oconomowoc, WI 53066: Catalog $8 ◆ Free-standing and folding background screens. Also professional and amateur accessories. 800-558-0114.

**Pierce Company,** 9801 Nicollet, Minneapolis, MN 55420: Catalog $1 (refundable) ◆ Handpainted backgrounds for portrait photography, photo supplies, mounts, albums, drapes, and printed forms. 612-884-1991.

**Studio Dynamics,** 2400 Gundry Ave., Long Beach, CA 90806: Free catalog ◆ Backdrops. 800-595-4273. www.studiodynamics.com

**Superior Specialties Inc.,** 3013 Gilroy St., Los Angeles, CA 90039: Free list of retail sources ◆ Seamless background papers. 800-354-3049; 213-662-3031 (in CA). lastudio02@sprynet.com

**Unique Backgrounds,** 9021 Pleasant Ln., Ooltewah, TN 37363: Free brochure ◆ Standard designs or create your own backgrounds. 423-238-6255.

**F.J. Westcott Company,** P.O. Box 1596, Toledo, OH 43603: Free information ◆ Reflectors and backgrounds. 419-243-7311.

## Bags & Camera Cases

**Charles Beseler Company,** 1600 Lower Rd., Linden, NJ 07036: Free brochure ◆ Bags for cameras, video equipment, and camcorders. 800-678-8324. www.beseler-photo.com

**Coast Manufacturing Company,** P.O. Box 67, Old Bethpage, NY 11804: Free information ◆ Camera bags. 516-822-3101.

**Domke,** Division Saunders Group, 21 Jet View Dr., Rochester, NY 14624: Free information ◆ Camera bags and photo equipment. 800-394-3686. www.saundersphoto.com

**GMI/Division Omega,** 191 Shaeffer Ave., Westminster, MD 21158: Free information ◆ Camera bags and equipment cases. 800-777-6634. www.omega.satter.com

**Leica Camera Inc.,** 156 Ludlow Ave., Northvale, NJ 07647: Free information ◆ Handcrafted bags for cameras, lenses, binoculars, and accessories. 800-222-0118. www.leica-camera-usa.com

**Lightware,** 1329 W. Byers Pl., Denver, CO 80223: Free catalog ◆ Camera cases. Includes lightweight airline shippable cases. 303-744-0202.

**LowePro,** P.O. Box 6189, Santa Rosa, CA 95406: Free information ◆ Camera bags. 707-575-4363. www.lowepro.com

**Pelican Products Inc.,** 23215 Early Ave., Torrance, CA 90505: Free information ◆ Watertight and unbreakable corrosion-proof cases. 800-4-PELICAN. www.pelican.com

**Photoflex,** 333 Encinal St., Santa Cruz, CA 95060: Free information ◆ Camera bags, studio lights, and accessories. 800-486-2674. www.photoflex.com

**SunDog,** 6700 S. Glacier St., Seattle, WA 98188: Free catalog ◆ Packs, bags, and cases for sports, travel, and photography equipment. 800-742-2623. www.sun-dog.com

**Tamrac,** 9240 Jordan Ave., Chatsworth, CA 91311: Free catalog ◆ Camera and video bags. 800-662-0717.

**Tenba Quality Cases Ltd.,** 503 Broadway, New York, NY 10012: Free list of retail sources ◆ Camera equipment bags. 800-328-3622; 212-966-1013 (in NY). www.tenba.com

**ToCad America Inc.,** 300 Webro Rd., Parsippany, NJ 07054: Free information ◆ Protective camera cases. 973-428-9800. www.tocad.com

**Tundra Camjacket,** Satter Inc., 4100 Dahlia St., Denver, CO 80207: Free information ◆ Camera bags. 800-525-0196. www.omega.satter.com

## Books

**Harry N. Abrams Inc.,** 100 5th Ave., New York, NY 10011: Free information ◆ Books on photography. 212-206-7715. www.abramsbooks.com

**Aperture Foundation,** 20 E. 23rd St., New York, NY 10010: Free information ◆ Fine art photography books. 800-929-2323; 212-505-5555 (in NY).

**John S. Craig,** P.O. Box 1637, Torrington, CT 06790: Free information ◆ Hard-to-find instruction books for photography equipment. Also other photographic literature. 860-496-9791. john@craigcamera.com

**Eastman Kodak Company,** Information Center, 343 State St., Rochester, NY 14650: Free information ◆ Books and other publications on photography. 800-242-2424. www.kodak.com

**Hudson Hills Press,** 230 5th Ave., Ste. 1308, New York, NY 10001: Free information ◆ Books on photography and art. 212-889-3090.

**Light Impressions,** 439 Monroe Ave., P.O. Box 940, Rochester, NY 14607: Free catalog ◆ Books on photography and supplies for archival storage of negatives and prints. 800-828-6216. www.lightimpressionsdirect.com

**A Photographer's Place,** P.O. Box 274, Prince St., New York, NY 10012: Free information ◆ Books on photography. 212-431-9358.

**Leonard Rue Enterprises,** 138 Millbrook Rd., Blairstown, NJ 07825: Free catalog ◆ How-to photography books. 908-362-6616.

**Shutterbug Store,** 5211 S. Washington Ave., Titusville, FL 32780: Free information ◆ Books on photography. 800-677-5212. www.shutterbug.net

## Camera Making Kits

**Bender Photographic,** 19691 Beaver Valley Rd., Leavenworth, WA 98826: Free information ◆ Build-it-yourself camera kit. 800-776-3199. 509-763-2626 (in WA). www.benderphoto.com

## Cameras (Optical Systems) & Equipment

**Ansco PhotoOptical,** 1801 Touhy Ave., Elk Grove Village, IL 60007: Free information ◆ Cameras. 800-323-6697. www.anscophoto.com

**Argus Camera,** 2121 Oxford Rd., Des Plaines, IL 60018: Free information ◆ Cameras. 847-297-8900. www.Arguscamera.com

**Bronica,** Tamron Industries Inc., 125 Schmitt Blvd., Farmingdale, NY 11735: Free information ◆ Cameras and lenses. 516-694-8700. www.tamron.com

**Calumet Photographic,** 890 Supreme Dr., Bensenville, IL 60106: Free list of retail sources ◆ Lenses. 800-CALUMET. www.calumetphoto.com

**Camerama Corp.,** 131 Newton St., Weston, MA 02193: Free information ◆ Panoramic cameras. 800-274-5722.

**Canon,** One Canon Plaza, Lake Success, NY 11042: Free list of retail sources ◆ Cameras and lenses. 516-488-6700. www.usa.canon.com

**Chinon America Inc.,** 1065 Bristol Rd., Mountainside, NJ 07092: Free information ◆ Lenses. 908-654-0404.

**Contax,** 100 Randolph Rd., Box 6802, Somerset, NJ 08875: Free information ◆ Cameras. 800-526-0266. www.yashica.com

**Eastman Kodak Company,** Information Center, 343 State St., Rochester, NY 14650: Free information ◆ Cameras. 800-242-2424. www.kodak.com

**Fuji Photo Film USA Inc.,** Attention: Consumer Service, 400 Commerce Blvd., Carlstadt, NJ 07072: Free information ◆ Cameras. 800-800-3854. www.fujifilm.com

**Peter Gowland Cameras,** 609 Hightree Rd., Santa Monica, CA 90402: Free information ◆ Cameras. 310-454-7867.

**Victor Hasselblad Inc.,** 10 Madison Rd., Fairfield, NJ 07004: Free brochure ◆ Cameras and lenses. 800-338-6477. www.hasselblad.com

**Jim Kendrick Studio,** 2775 Dundas St. West, Toronto, Ontario, Canada M6P 1Y4: Free information ◆ Heating system for telescopes, binoculars, and cameras. 416-762-7946. www.kendrick-studio.com

**Keystone Cameras,** Concord Corp., 35 Mileed Way, Avenel, NJ 07001: Free information ◆ Cameras. 908-499-8280.

**Kirk Enterprises,** 107 Lange Ln., Angola, IN 46703: Free catalog ◆ Tripods and other camera mounts for accessories. 800-626-5074. www.kirkphoto.com

**Konica USA Inc.,** 440 Sylvan Ave., Englewood Cliffs, NJ 07632: Free information ◆ Cameras and lenses. 201-568-3100. www.konica.com

**Leica Camera Inc.,** 156 Ludlow Ave., Northvale, NJ 07647: Free information ◆ Cameras and lenses. 800-222-0118. www.leica-camera-usa.com

**Leland Limited Inc.,** Box 466, South Plainfield, NJ 07080: Free list of retail sources ◆ Easy-to-use cleaning tool for camera equipment. 800-984-9793.

**Mamiya America Corp.,** 8 Westchester Plaza, Elmsford, NY 10523: Free information ◆ Cameras and lenses. 914-347-3300. www.mamiya.com

**Minolta,** 101 Williams Dr., Ramsey, NJ 07446: Free information ◆ Cameras and lenses. 201-825-4000. www.minolta.com

**Minox,** HP Marketing Corp., 16 Chapin Rd., Pine Brook, NJ 07058: Free information ◆ Cameras and accessories for miniature picture taking. 201-808-9010. www.minox.com

**Nikon Photo,** 1300 Walt Whitman Rd., Melville, NY 11747: Free brochure ◆ Cameras and lenses. 516-547-4200. www.nikonusa.com

**Nikonos Cameras,** 1300 Walt Whitman Rd., Melville, NY 11747: Free brochure ◆ Cameras and lenses. 516-547-4200. www.nikonusa.com

**Olympus Corp.,** 2 Corporate Center Dr., Melville, NY 11747: Free information ◆ Cameras and lenses. 800-221-3000. www.olympusamerica.com

**Pentax Corp.,** 35 Inverness Dr. East, Englewood, CO 80112: Free brochure ◆ Cameras and lenses. 303-799-8000. www.pentax.com

**Phoenix Corp.,** 112 Mott St., Oceanside, NY 11572: Free information ◆ Zoom, macro-zoom, and wide-angle zoom lenses. 516-764-5890.

**Polaroid Corp.,** Customer Care Center, 201 Burlington Rd., Bedford, MA 01730: Free information ◆ Cameras. 800-343-5000. www.polaroid.com

**Ricoh Consumer Products Group,** 475 Lillard, Sparks, NV 89434: Free brochure ◆ Lenses. 800-225-1899. www.ricohcpg.com

**Ritz Cameras,** 6711 Ritzway, Beltsville, MD 20705: Free catalog ◆ Lenses. 301-419-0000.

**Rollei Fototechnic,** 40 Seaview Dr., Secaucus, NJ 07094: Free brochure ◆ Cameras. 800-762-7746. www.rolleifoto.com

**Samsung Optical America Inc.,** 40 Seaview Dr., Secaucus, NJ 07094: Free information ◆ Cameras and lenses. 800-762-7746. www.simplyamazing.com

**Sigma Corp. of America,** 15 Fleetwood Ct., Ronkonkoma, NY 11779: Brochure $1 ◆ Lenses. 516-585-1144.

**Tamron Industries Inc.,** 125 Schmitt Blvd., Farmingdale, NY 11735: Free brochure ◆ Lenses. 516-694-8700. www.tamron.com

**Tokina Optical Corp.,** 1512 Kona Dr., Rancho Dominguez, CA 90220: Free information ◆ Lenses. 800-421-1141. www.thkphoto.com

**Universal Bellows Company Inc.,** 25 Hans Ave., Freeport, NY 11520: Free information ◆ Standard or custom replacement bellows. 516-378-1264.

**Vivitar Corp.,** 1280 Rancho Conejo Blvd., Newbury Park, CA 91320: Free brochure ◆ Cameras and lenses. 805-498-7008. www.vivitarcorp.com

**Wisner Large Format Cameras,** Wisner Classic Manufacturing Company Inc., P.O. Box 21, Marion, MA 02738: Free information ◆ Large format cameras. 800-848-0448. www.wisner.com

**WISTA Large Format Cameras,** Foto-Care Ltd., 132 W. 21st St., New York, NY 10011: Free information ◆ Large format cameras. 212-741-2990.

**Yashica Inc.,** 100 Randolph Rd., P.O. Box 6802, Somerset, NJ 08875: Free information ◆ Cameras and lenses. 800-526-0266. www.yashica.com

## Cameras, Digital Systems

**Adobe Systems Inc.,** P.O. Box 1034, Buffalo, NY 14240: Free information ◆ Photo-editing equipment. 800-685-4586. www.adobe.com

**Agfa Division,** Bayer Industries, 100 Challenger Rd., Ridgefield Park, NJ 07660: Free information ◆ Professional-level digital cameras, scanners, and printers. 201-440-2500. www.agfahome.com

**Canon,** One Canon Plaza, Lake Success, NY 11042: Free information ◆ Professional-level digital cameras and accessories. 516-488-6700. www.usa.canon.com

**Casio,** P.O. Box 7000, Dover, NJ 07801: Free information ◆ Digital cameras. 201-361-5400. www.usa.canon.com

**Chinon America Inc.,** 1065 Bristol Rd., Mountainside, NJ 07092: Free information ◆ Digital cameras. 908-654-0404.

**Digital Solution Corp.,** 5361 NW 170th Terr., Miami, FL 33055: Free catalog ◆ Digital cameras and accessories. 305-623-4438.

**Eastman Kodak Company,** Information Center, 343 State St., Rochester, NY 14650: Free information ◆ Digital cameras and scanners. 800-242-2424. www.kodak.com

**Epson America Inc.,** 20770 Madrona Ave., P.O. Box 2903, Torrance, CA 90509: Free information ◆ Digital cameras and print-making accessories. 800-873-7766. www.epson.com

**Fargo Electronics Inc.,** 7901 Flying Cloud Dr., Eden Prairie, MN 55344: Free information ◆ Print-making equipment. 800-327-4622. www.fargo.com

**Fuji Photo Film USA Inc.,** Attention: Consumer Service, 400 Commerce Blvd., Carlstadt, NJ 07072: Free information ◆ Amateur and professional level digital cameras. Also imaging and print-making equipment. 800-800-3854. www.fujifilm.com

**Minolta,** 101 Williams Dr., Ramsey, NJ 07446: Free information ◆ Digital cameras for amateurs and professionals. 201-825-4000. www.minolta.com

**Nikon Photo,** 1300 Walt Whitman Rd., Melville, NY 11747: Free brochure ◆ Professional-level and compact digital cameras, accessories, and print and slide scanners. 516-547-4200. www.nikonusa.com

**Olympus Corp.,** 145 Crossways Park, Woodbury, NY 11797: Free information ◆ Professional-level digital cameras and image storage equipment. 800-221-3000. www.olympusamerica.com

**Polaroid Corp.,** Customer Care Center, 201 Burlington Rd., Bedford, MA 01730: Free information ◆ Digital cameras and slide-negative scanners. 800-343-5000. www.polaroid.com

**Sony Consumer Products,** 1 Sony Dr., Park Ridge, NJ 07656: Free information ◆ Digital cameras, recordable CD drive, and computer monitors. 201-930-1000. www.sony.com

**Storm Software,** 1861 Landings Dr., Mountain View, CA 94043: Free information ◆ Scanners. 800-275-5734.

**Tamron Industries Inc.,** 125 Schmitt Blvd., Farmingdale, NY 11735: Free brochure ◆ Scanners. 516-694-8700. www.tamron.com

**Yashica Inc.,** 100 Randolph Rd., P.O. Box 6802, Somerset, NJ 08875: Free information ◆ Digital cameras, ultra-compact storage disk system, and accessories. 800-526-0266. www.yashica.com

## Darkroom Equipment & Supplies

**Alta Photographic Inc.,** 1421 International Dr., Bartlesville, OK 74006: Free information ◆ Darkroom chemicals. 800-688-8688.

**Bencher Inc.,** 831 N. Central Ave., Wood Dale, IL 60191: Free information ◆ Enlargers, copystands, and darkroom equipment. 773-282-8787. www.bencher.com

**Berg Color Tone,** 72 Ward Rd., Lancaster, NY 14086: Free information ◆ Color toners and retouching supplies. 716-681-2696.

**Bestwell Optical & Instrument Corp.,** P.O. Box 396, Merrick, NY 11566: Free information ◆ Focusing magnifiers, photographic enlarger focusing aid, loupes, and other equipment. 516-379-2280.

**Bogen Photo Corp.,** 565 E. Crescent Ave., P.O. Box 506, Ramsey, NJ 07446: Free information ◆ Dry-mount presses. 201-818-9500. www.bogenphoto.com

**Bostick & Sullivan,** P.O. Box 16639, Santa Fe, NM 87506: Free information ◆ Chemicals and paper for platinum and palladian printing. 505-474-0890. www.bostick-sullivan.com

**Bryant Laboratory Inc.,** 1101 5th St., Berkeley, CA 94710: Free information ◆ Photographic chemicals. 800-367-3141; 510-526-3141 (in CA).

**Cachet Photo Paper,** 3701 W. Moore Ave., Santa Ana, CA 92704: Sample pack $14.95 plus $2 shipping ◆ Fine art photographic papers. 714-432-7070. www.onecachet.com

**California Stainless Manufacturing,** 32 N. Wood Rd., Camarillo, CA 93010: Free catalog ◆ Stainless sinks, film dryers, and accessories. 805-484-1038.

**Darkroom Aids Company,** 10 S. Wacker Dr., Chicago, IL 60657: Free information ◆ Used darkroom equipment. 773-248-4301.

**Darkroom Innovations,** P.O. Box 3620, Carefree, AZ 85377: Free information ◆ Darkroom equipment and accessories. 602-488-8012. www.darkroom-innovations.com

**Darkroom Photographic Products Ltd.,** 2955 11th St., Rockford, IL 61109: Free catalog ◆ Photography kits and accessories. 800-322-8365.

**Daylab,** 400 E. Main, Ontario, CA 91761: Free catalog ◆ All-in-one, self-contained color enlarger with exposure meter, timer, and developing system. 800-678-3669. www.daylab.com

**Delta 1,** CPM Inc., 10830 Sanden Dr., Dallas, TX 75238: Free catalog ◆ Temperature-regulated sinks and darkroom equipment. 800-627-0252.

**Dimco-Gray,** 8200 S. Suburban Rd., Centerville, OH 45459: Free brochure ◆ Darkroom timers. 937-433-7600. www.dimco-gray.com

**Doran Enterprises,** 2779 S. 34th St., Milwaukee, WI 53215: Free catalog ◆ Color print processors. 414-645-0109.

**Durst,** 10 County Line Rd., Ste. 29, Branchburg, NJ 08876: Free information ◆ Easy-to-operate continuous paper processor and enlarger system. 800-463-8778.

**Freestyle,** 5124 Sunset Blvd., Los Angeles, CA 90027: Free information ◆ Darkroom supplies and equipment. 800-292-6137. www.freestylesalesco.com

**Helix,** 310 S. Racine Ave., Chicago, IL 60607: Free catalog ◆ Cameras and accessories, darkroom equipment and supplies, and video and underwater photo equipment. 800-33-HE-LIX; 312-421-6000 (in IL). helixuw@aol.com

**Jobo Fototechnic Inc.,** P.O. Box 3721, Ann Arbor, MI 48106: Free information ◆ Photo processing chemicals, color retouching dyes for color and black-and-white photography, and processing equipment. 800-828-9859. www.jobo-usa.com

**KingConcept,** Division Omega, 191 Shaeffer Ave., Westminster, MD 21157: Free information ◆ Automatic rotary tube film and print processor. 800-777-6634. www.omega.satter.com

**Leedal Inc.,** 1918 S. Prairie Ave., Chicago, IL 60616: Free brochure ◆ Stainless steel darkroom sinks with plumbing and back splash, stands, and shelves. 312-842-6588.

**Luminos,** P.O. Box 158, Yonkers, NY 10705: Free information ◆ Processing chemicals and paper. 800-LUMINOS. www.luminos.com/

**The Maine Photographic Resource,** 2 Central St., Rockport, ME 04856: Free catalog ◆ Photography and darkroom equipment. 800-227-1541; 207-236-4788 (in ME).

**Omega,** 191 Schaeffer Ave., Westminster, MD 21157: Free information ◆ Darkroom equipment and enlargers. 410-857-6353. www.omega.satter.com

**The Palladio Company,** P.O. Box 28, Cambridge, MA 02140: Free information ◆ Platinum and palladium printing papers. 617-393-0814.

**Photo-Therm,** 110 Sewell Ave., Trenton, NJ 08610: Free catalog ◆ Automatic film processor/dryer for slides, black-and-white film, and color negatives. 609-396-1456.

**Porter's Camera Store Inc.,** Box 628, Cedar Falls, IA 50613: Free catalog ◆ Picture-taking equipment, darkroom supplies, photography novelties, and accessories. 800-553-2001. www.porters.com

**Seal Products,** 550 Spring St., Naugatuck, CT 06770: Free information ◆ Mounting, laminating, and texturizing products. 203-729-5201.

**Solar Cine Products Inc.,** 4247 S. Kedzie Ave., Chicago, IL 60632: Free catalog ◆ Darkroom and other photographic equipment and supplies. 800-621-8796; 773-254-8310 (in IL).

**Zone VI Studios Inc.,** Division Calumet Photographic Inc., 890 Supreme Dr., Bensenville, IL 60106: Free catalog ◆ Picture-taking and darkroom equipment. 800-CALUMET. www.calumetphoto.com

## Enlargers

**Bencher Inc.,** 831 N. Central Ave., Wood Dale, IL 60191: Free information ◆ Enlargers and darkroom equipment. 773-282-8787. www.bencher.com

**Charles Beseler Company,** 1600 Lower Rd., Linden, NJ 07036: Free brochure ◆ Enlargers, color heads and electronic controls, modular units for color or black-and-white enlarging, and other equipment. 800-678-8324. www.beseler-photo.com

**Doran Enterprises,** 2779 S. 34th St., Milwaukee, WI 53215: Free catalog ◆ Color print processors. 414-645-0109.

**Durst,** 10 County Line Rd., Ste. 29, Branchburg, NJ 08876: Free information ◆ Easy-to-operate continuous paper processor and enlarger system. 800-463-8778.

**Omega,** 191 Schaeffer Ave., Westminster, MD 21157: Free information ◆ Darkroom accessories and enlargers. 410-857-6353. www.omega.satter.com

**Paterson,** Division Saunders Group, 21 Jet View Dr., Rochester, NY 14624: Free catalog ◆ Darkroom equipment and enlargers. 800-394-3686. www.saundersphoto.com

**The Saunders Group,** 21 Jet View Dr., Rochester, NY 14624: Free catalog ◆ Exposure and flash meters, medium format dichroic enlargers and equipment, strobe brackets, tripods, and other equipment. 800-394-3686. www.saundersphoto.com

**Testrite Instrument Company Inc.,** 135 Monroe St., Newark, NJ 07105: Free catalog ◆ Enlargers and other equipment. 973-589-6767. www.testrite.com

## Equipment Carriers

**Kart-A-Bag,** Division of Remin, 510 Manhattan Rd., Joliet, IL 60433: Free list of retail sources ◆ Folding rolling cart. 800-423-9328; 815-723-1940 (in IL). www.kart-a-bag.com

**Porter Case Inc.,** 3718 W. Western Ave., South Bend, IN 46619: Free information ◆ Wheeled carry-on case with a built-in carrying cart. 800-356-8348. www.portercase.com

**Rock N' Roller,** M.J. Corp., 99 Tulip Ave., Floral Park, NY 11001: Free information ◆ Luggage carrier that converts from a two-wheel hand truck to a variable length hi-stacker, platform truck, or mobile workstation. 800-431-6699.

**Simonds Photographic,** 88 Thomas St., East Hartford, CT 06108: Free information ◆ Folding-flat cart for carrying equipment and luggage. 800-992-0607.

## Exposure Meters & Guides

**Bogen Photo Corp.,** 565 E. Crescent Ave., Ramsey, NJ 07446: Free information ◆ Multi-purpose exposure meters, tripods, enlargers, and other equipment. 201-818-9500. www.bogenphoto.com

**Harris Photoguides,** 83 Rock Beach Rd., Rochester, NY 14617: Free information ◆ Easy-to-use handheld exposure calculators. 716-342-3691.

**Lattin Photography,** 3508 Terrace Dr., Cedar Falls, IA 50613: Free information ◆ Exposure guides and equipment. 800-728-7676.

**Minolta,** 101 Williams Dr., Ramsey, NJ 07446: Free information ◆ Exposure meters. 201-825-4000. www.minolta.com

**Pentax Corp.,** 35 Inverness Dr. East, Englewood, CO 80112: Free brochure ◆ Exposure meters. 303-799-8000. www.pentax.com

**The Saunders Group,** 21 Jet View Dr., Rochester, NY 14624: Free catalog ◆ Exposure and flash meters, medium format dichroic enlargers, strobe brackets, tripods, and other equipment. 800-394-3686. www.saundersphoto.com

**Sekonic,** Mamiya America Corp., 8 Westchester Plaza, Elmsford, NY 10523: Free list of retail sources ◆ Exposure meters, flash guns, and tripod studio ball heads. 914-347-3300. www.sekonic.com

**Shepherd Meters,** Division Saunders Group, 21 Jet View Dr., Rochester, NY 14624: Free catalog ◆ Exposure meters. 800-394-3686. www.saundersphoto.com

**Sinar Bron,** 17 Progress St., Edison, NJ 08820: Free information ◆ Three-in-one meter that measures color temperature for flash, continuous light sources and flash-duration, and lux. 800-456-0203. www.sinarbron.com

**Smith-Victor,** 301 N. Colfax St., Griffith, IN 46319: Free information ◆ Light meters and lighting equipment. 800-348-9862.

## Film Manufacturers & Distributors

**Agfa Division,** Bayer Industries, 100 Challenger Rd., Ridgefield Park, NJ 07660: Free information ◆ Color slide, color print, and black-and-white film. 201-440-2500. www.agfahome.com

**Eastman Kodak Company,** Information Center, 343 State St., Rochester, NY 14650: Free information ◆ Color slide, color print, black-and-white, infrared, and special process films. 800-242-2424. www.kodak.com

**The Film Shop,** 140 58th St., Ste. 4E, Brooklyn, NY 11220: Free information ◆ Full line of film, cameras, accessories, video cassettes, and more. 888-345-6746. www.filmshop.com

**Freestyle,** 5124 Sunset Blvd., Los Angeles, CA 90027: Free information ◆ Film and paper. 800-292-6137. www.freestylesalesco.com

**Fuji Photo Film USA Inc.,** Attention: Consumer Service, 400 Commerce Blvd., Carlstadt, NJ 07072: Free information ◆ Color slide, color print, and black-and-white film. 800-800-3854. www.fujifilm.com

**Ilford Photo Corp.,** W. 70 Century Rd., Paramus, NJ 07653: Free information ◆ Chromogenic black-and-white film. 800-631-2522. www.ilford.com

**Imation Film,** Photo Color Systems, 1 Imation Pl., Oakdale, MN 55128: Free information ◆ Color slide and print film. 800-695-FILM. www.imation.com

**Konica USA Inc.,** 440 Sylvan Ave., Englewood Cliffs, NJ 07632: Free information ◆ Color slide and print film. 201-568-3100. www.konica.com

**Polaroid Corp.,** Customer Care Center, 201 Burlington Rd., Bedford, MA 01730: Free information ◆ Color slide, black-and-white slide, color print pack, and black-and-white pack film. 800-343-5000. www.polaroid.com

**Universal Distributors Corp.,** 677 8th St., Lakewood, NJ 08701: Free information ◆ Fuji, Kodak, Polaroid, Agfa, and Konica film. Also Kodak and Fuji disposable cameras. 800-872-FILM; 908-364-0802 (in NJ).

## Filters

**Calumet Photographic,** 890 Supreme Dr., Bensenville, IL 60106: Free list of retail sources: Free information ◆ Gelatin, resin, and polyester color correction, conversion, neutral density, and black-and-white filters. 800-CALUMET. www.calumetphoto.com

**Cambridge Camera Exchange,** 119 W. 17th St., New York, NY 10011: Free information ◆ Cambron filters. 800-221-2253; 212-675-8600 (in NY). www.cambridge.com

**Cokin Creative Filter System,** Minolta Corp., 101 Williams Dr., Ramsey, NJ 07446: Free information ◆ Filters. 201-825-4000. www.minolta.com

**Contax,** 100 Randolph Rd., Box 6802, Somerset, NJ 08875: Free information ◆ Filters for the Contax camera. 800-526-0266. www.yashica.com

**Eastman Kodak Company,** Information Center, 343 State St., Rochester, NY 14650: Free information ◆ Wratten filters. 800-242-2424. www.kodak.com

**Harrison & Harrison Filters,** P.O. Box 1797, Porterville, CA 93258: Free information ◆ Screw-on and slip-on filters, bayonet-style holders, other filters, and accessories. 209-782-0121.

**Victor Hasselblad Inc.,** 10 Madison Rd., Fairfield, NJ 07004: Free brochure ◆ Filters for Hasselblad cameras. 800-338-6477. www.hasselblad.com

**Lee Filters,** 2301 W. Victory Blvd., Burbank, CA 91506: Free information ◆ Filters and filter holders. 800-576-5055.

**Pro4 Imaging Inc.,** 21 Spragg Cir., Markham, Ontario, Canada L3P 5W1: Free information ◆ Filter systems for 35mm, medium, and large-format cameras. 800-636-0844.

**Schneider Corp.,** 285 Oser Ave., Hauppage, NY 11788: Free information ◆ Filters for black-and-white photography, neutral density filters, star and diffraction filters, lens shades, masks for matte boxes, lens reversal rings, tele-converters, and auto-extension tubes. 516-761-5000. www.schneideroptics.com

**Singh-Ray Corp.,** 153 Progress Circle, Venice, FL 34292: Free information ◆ Neutral density graduated filters. 800-486-5501.

**THK Photo Products Inc.,** 1512 Kona Dr., Rancho Dominguez, CA 90220: Free information ◆ Tokina, Hoya, and Kenko filters. 800-421-1141. www.thkphoto.com

**Tiffen Manufacturing,** 90 Oser Ave., Hauppage, NY 11788: Free information ◆ Filters. 800-645-2522. www.tiffen.com

## Flash Units & Lighting

**American Photographic Instrument Company Inc.,** P.O. Box 322, 12 Lincoln Blvd., Emerson, NJ 07630: Free information ◆ Light stands, tripod accessories, and monopods. 800-600-1147. apic@earthlink.net

**APV Inc.,** 1689 Production Circle, Riverside, CA 92509: Free information ◆ Remote flash trigger. 800-959-8083.

**Bogen Photo Corp.,** 565 E. Crescent Ave., Ramsey, NJ 07446: Free information ◆ Compact studio electronic flash systems and Metz Mecablitz flash units with a choice of power sources and system accessories. 201-818-9500. www.bogenphoto.com

**Brandess-Kalt-Aetna,** 701 Corporate Woods Pkwy., Vernon Hills, IL 67061: Free list of retail sources ◆ Easy-to-use professional portrait lighting kit.

**Britek Inc.,** 12704 Marquardt Ave., Santa Fe Springs, CA 90670: Free information ◆ Professional studio flash and lighting equipment. 800-925-6258.

**Paul C. Buff Inc.,** 2725 Bransford Ave., Nashville, TN 37204: Free information ◆ Compact lightweight studio flash equipment. 800-443-5542; 615-383-3982 (in TN). www.white-lightning.com

**Canon,** One Canon Plaza, Lake Success, NY 11042: Free list of retail sources ◆ Flash units for the Canon and other cameras. 516-488-6700. www.usa.canon.com

**Chimera,** 1812 Valtec Ln., Boulder, CO 80301: Free catalog ◆ Portable lighting units and accessories. 800-424-4075. www.chimeralighting.com

**Courtenay Solaflash,** Division Saunders Group, 21 Jet View Dr., Rochester, NY 14624: Free catalog ◆ Professional studio light equipment. 800-394-3686. www.saundersphoto.com

**Creative Light Works,** 4633 Mill Rd., Red Wing, MN 55066: Free information ◆ Adjustable light booms and flexible light systems. 612-388-5444.

**Delta 1,** CPM Inc., 10830 Sanden Dr., Dallas, TX 75238: Free catalog ◆ Studio lighting and special effects equipment. 800-627-0252.

**Dyna-Lite,** 311-319 Long Ave., Hillside, NJ 07205: Free information ◆ Professional studio flash and other light equipment. 800-722-6638. flash@dynalite.com

**Konica USA Inc.,** 440 Sylvan Ave., Englewood Cliffs, NJ 07632: Free brochure ◆ Konica flash equipment and accessories. 201-568-3100. www.konica.com

**Larson Enterprises Inc.,** 365 S. Mountainway Dr., P.O. Box 2150, Orem, UT 84058: Free information ◆ Compact lighting equipment and soft box systems. 800-227-5533.

**Lowel-Light Manufacturing Inc.,** 140 58th St., Brooklyn, NY 11220: Free information ◆ Quick and easy-to-setup lighting equipment. 718-921-0600.

**Lumedyne Lighting,** 6010 Wall St., Port Richey, FL 34668: Free information ◆ Light systems. 813-847-5394. www.lumedyne.com

**Lumiquest,** P.O. Box 310248, New Braunfels, TX 78131: Free information ◆ Tabletop lighting accessories, reflectors, and other lighting equipment. 830-438-4646. www.lumiquest.com

**Minolta,** 101 Williams Dr., Ramsey, NJ 07446: Free information ◆ Flash units for Minolta cameras. 201-825-4000. www.minolta.com

**The Morris Company,** 1205 W. Jackson Blvd., Chicago, IL 60607: Free information ◆ Light-weight and portable slave kits. 312-421-5739.

**Nikon Photo,** 1300 Walt Whitman Rd., Melville, NY 11747: Free brochure ◆ Flash units and accessories. 516-547-4200. www.nikonusa.com

**Nikonos Cameras,** 1300 Walt Whitman Rd., Melville, NY 11747: Free brochure ◆ Electronic flash systems for general and under water use. 516-547-4200. www.nikonusa.com

**Norman Enterprises Inc.,** 2601 Empire Ave., Burbank, CA 91504: Free list of retail sources ◆ Lighting accessories. 818-843-6811.

**Novatron of Dallas Inc.,** 8230 Moberly Ln., Dallas, TX 75227: Free catalog ◆ Studio flash equipment. 800-527-1595.

**Olympus Corp.,** 2 Corporate Center Dr., Melville, NY 11747: Free information ◆ Flash systems for use with Olympus cameras. 800-221-3000. www.olympusamerica.com

**Pentax Corp.,** 35 Inverness Dr. East, Englewood, CO 80112: Free brochure ◆ Electronic flash units for Pentax cameras. 303-799-8000. www.pentax.com

**Phoenix Corp.,** 112 Mott St., Oceanside, NY 11572: Free information ◆ Flash equipment. 516-764-5890.

**Photoflex,** 333 Encinal St., Santa Cruz, CA 95060: Free information ◆ Camera bags, studio lights, and accessories. 800-486-2674. www.photoflex.com

**Photogenic Machine Company,** P.O. Box 3365, Youngstown, OH 44513: Free brochure ◆ Soft lighting equipment for use with studio or small battery-operated strobes. 800-682-7668.

**Photographer's Warehouse,** P.O. Box 3365, Boardman, OH 44513: Free information ◆ Electronic flash systems. 800-521-4311.

**Quantum Instruments Inc.,** 1075 Stewart Ave., Garden City, NY 11530: Free information ◆ Portable studio-style flash units. 516-222-0611. www.qtm.com

**Ricoh Consumer Products Group,** 475 Lillard Dr., Sparks, NV 89434: Free brochure ◆ Flash equipment for Ricoh cameras. 800-225-1899. www.ricohcpg.com

**Satter Distributing,** 4100 Dahlia, Denver, CO 80207: Free information ◆ Electronic flash systems. 800-525-0196. www.omega.satter.com

**The Saunders Group,** 21 Jet View Dr., Rochester, NY 14624: Free catalog ◆ Bounce lighting equipment. 800-394-3686. www.saundersphoto.com

**Sekonic,** Mamiya America Corp., 8 Westchester Plaza, Elmsford, NY 10523: Free list of retail sources ◆ Exposure meters, flash guns, and tripod studio ball heads. 914-347-3300. www.sekonic.com

**Sigma Corp. of America,** 15 Fleetwood Ct., Ronkonkoma, NY 11779: Brochure $1 ◆ Flash equipment. 516-585-1144.

**Sinar Bron,** 17 Progress St., Edison, NJ 08820: Free information ◆ Three-in-one meter that measures color temperature for flash, continuous light sources and flash-duration, and lux. 800-456-0203. www.sinarbron.com

**Smith-Victor,** 301 N. Colfax St., Griffith, IN 46319: Free information ◆ Light meters and lighting equipment. 800-348-9862.

**Speedotron Corp.,** 310 S. Racine Ave., Chicago, IL 60607: Free information ◆ Electronic flash equipment. 312-421-4050.

**Sto-Fen Products,** P.O. Box 7609, Santa Cruz, CA 95061: Free information ◆ Custom all-directional bounce attachments for strobes. 800-538-0730.

**Studiomate,** 12704 Marquardt Ave., Santa Fe Springs, CA 90670: Free information ◆ Studio lighting equipment. 800-283-8346.

**Sunpak Division of ToCad America,** 300 Webrow Rd., Parsippany, NJ 07054: Free information ◆ Electronic flash equipment. 973-428-9800. www.tocad.com

**Testrite Instrument Company Inc.,** 135 Monroe St., Newark, NJ 07105: Free catalog ◆ Portable light box systems, lightweight aluminum and chrome easels, opaque projectors, and darkroom equipment. 973-589-6767. www.testrite.com

**TriStar Photo Industrial Inc.,** 9960 Indiana Ave., Riverside, CA 92503: Free catalog ◆ Studio lighting equipment, backgrounds, light stands, brackets and holders, soft boxes, umbrellas, video camera supports, and other equipment. 800-424-8801.

**Vivitar Corp.,** 1280 Rancho Conejo Blvd., Newbury Park, CA 91320: Free brochure ◆ Electronic flash equipment, cameras, and lenses. 805-498-7008. www.vivitarcorp.com

**Wein Products Inc.,** The Saunders Group, 21 Jet View Dr., Rochester, NY 14624: Free information ◆ Sound and light-operated wireless meter and switches. 800-394-3686. www.saundersphoto.com

**Woods Electronics Inc.,** 14781 Pomerado Rd., Poway, CA 92064: Free information ◆ Sound and infrared-operated remote flash triggering devices. 619-486-0806.

**Zone VI Studios Inc.,** Division Calumet Photographic Inc., 890 Supreme Dr., Bensenville, IL 60106: Free catalog ◆ Picture-taking and darkroom equipment. 800-CALUMET. www.calumetphoto.com

## Photo Processing

**Associated Photo Company,** 7103 Turfway Rd., Florence, KY 41022: Free information ◆ Photo Christmas cards with name imprint. 800-727-2580; 606-282-0011 (in KY).

**Black and White Connection,** 904 E. 12th St., Austin, TX 78703: Free information ◆ Full-service black-and-white photo processing. 800-472-2972; 512-472-29782 (in TX). www.citysearch.com/aus/bwc

**Dale Laboratories,** 2960 Simms St., Hollywood, FL 33020: Free information ◆ Processes slides, prints, and negatives from Kodacolor film. 800-327-1776. www.dalelabs.com

**Darkroom Unlimited,** 7855 McKern Rd., Rome, NY 13440: Free catalog ◆ Full-service photo processing. 800-566-9504; 315-336-9152 (in NY). www.borg.com/~photo

**El-Co Color Labs Inc.,** 290 Gordons Corner Rd., Manalapan, NJ 07726: Free information ◆ Quantity prints and enlargements from the same negative. 800-446-ELCO. www.elcocolor.com

**The Enlargement Works Inc.,** 316 N. Milwaukee St., Ste. 406, Milwaukee, WI 53202: Free information ◆ Handmade color enlargements from slides or negatives. 414-278-1210.

**Film Processing Ltd.,** 1314 W. Church St., Champaign, IL 61821: Free brochure ◆ Full-service photo processing lab. 217-359-5953. flp@c-u.net

**Flair Pro Color Lab,** P.O. Box 140240, Gainesville, FL 32614: Free price list ◆ Fuji photo processing. 800-741-6004.

**Foto Fabric Images,** 10 Bonnie Dr., Northport, NY 11768: Free information ◆ Image transfer services onto a variety of surfaces. 800-745-8735.

**G-B Color Lab,** P.O. Box 562, Hawthorne, NJ 07507: Free brochure ◆ Ilfochrome color prints from slides. 973-427-0460.

**Gemini Print Lab.,** P.O. Box 1777, Las Vegas, NM 87701: Free information ◆ C-41 film processing with custom hand-printed color enlargements. 800-779-4484. www.geminilab.com

**General Color Corp.,** 604 Brevard Ave., P.O. Box 70, Cocoa, FL 32923: Free brochure ◆ Photo and print processing with enlargements up to 24 x 30 inches. 800-321-1602.

**Golden Color Engineering,** 271 S. Beverly Dr., Beverly Hills, CA 90212: Free information ◆ Color-corrected enlargements. 310-274-3445.

**Holland Photo,** 1221 S. Lamar, Austin, TX 78704: Free information ◆ Ilfochrome prints from slides or transparencies. 800-477-4024.

**Images Photo Processing,** P.O. Box 32590, Tucson, AZ 85751: Free information ◆ Black-and-white photo processing. 800-337-5631.

**Kelly Color,** Box 576, Morganton, NC 28680: Free information ◆ Proofing, candid and portrait photos, package assortments, copy and restoration services, montages and composites, and display transparencies for light boxes. 704-433-0934.

**Lear-Tech,** P.O. Box 522, Fayetteville, NY 13066: Free information ◆ Custom enlargements. 315-637-2245.

**Lightworks Custom B & W Lab,** P.O. Box 37, Goose Creek, SC 29445: Free catalog ◆ Black-and-white enlargements and archival film processing. 803-797-5760.

**Lustre-Color,** 540 Turnpike St., Canton, MA 02021: Free information ◆ Full-service photo processing lab. www.lustrecolor.com

**Minox Processing Laboratories,** 250 Meacham Ave., Elmont, NY 11003: Free information ◆ Sub-miniature film processing. 516-437-6245.

**Modernage Photographic Services,** 1150 Avenue of Americas, New York, NY 10036: Free information with long SASE ◆ Photo restoration, custom color and black-and-white processing, exhibition prints, stills from black-and-white movies, and other services. 800-997-2510.

**Mystic Color Lab,** P.O. Box 144, Mystic, CT 06355: Free information ◆ Processes black-and-white, Kodachrome and Ektachrome slide and movie film, and Kodacolor 35mm, 110, 126, and disc film. 800-367-6061. www.mysticcolorlab.com

**National Color Labs,** 306 W. 1st Ave., Roselle, NJ 07203: Free information ◆ Copy, restoration and retouching, custom processing and finishing services. Also albums, special effects, and business, holiday, and thank-you cards. 800-284-1947; 908-241-1010 (in NJ).

**Owl Photo Corp.,** 701 E. Main St., Weatherford, OK 73096: Free information ◆ Film processing and print-making services. 405-772-3353.

**PFS Photo Finishing,** 1124 Norwood St., Radford, VA 24141: Free information with long SASE ◆ Custom color, black-and-white, and E-6 photo finishing. 540-639-6911. www.pfsphoto.com

**Photo Lab Express,** 560 Main St., Islip, NY 11751: Free information ◆ Photographic images from traditional and digital technologies, ranging from sticker-size to wall murals. 800-647-5850.

**Photosmith,** 263 Central Ave., Dover, NH 03820: Free information ◆ Processes photographs on business cards, refrigerator art, T-shirts, steins, and gifts. 603-742-6659.

**Photosmith Custom Pro-Lab,** 1634 S. Boston, Tulsa, OK 74119: Free information ◆ Color, black-and-white, and other photo processing services. 918-584-6623.

**Phototech,** 109A N. 18th St., Richmond, VA 23223: Free information ◆ Archival printing and reproduction services. 804-648-2012.

**Pro Photo Labs,** 213-219 S. Tyler Ave., P.O. Drawer 777, Lakeland, FL 33802: Free information ◆ Film developing, enlarging, and other services. 800-237-6429.

**Rode's Camera & Photo,** 2204 Roosevelt Rd., Kenosha, WI 53143: Free price list ◆ Black-and-white, color, and enlargement processing. 414-654-2410; 800-252-5269 (in WI).

**S & S Photo Lab.,** 10152 Mission Gorge Rd., Santee, CA 92071: Free information ◆ Photographic sports cards, posters, buttons, hats, T-shirts, and other novelties. 619-448-3424. www.sportsphoto.com

**San Miguel Lab,** Drawer A, Las Vegas, NM 87701: Free information ◆ Black-and-white processing. 800-493-2727. www.bestlab.com

**Seattle Filmworks,** 5624 15th Ave. NW, Seattle, WA 98107: Free information ◆ Color or black-and-white prints, prints and slides (from same roll), slides (from 35mm color film), and pictures on disks. 206-782-3700.

**Shore Color Lab.,** 9378 Calumet Ave., P.O. Box 3229, Munster, IN 46321: Free information ◆ Custom package printing services. 800-422-2575.

**Silver Image Photographics,** 3102 Vestal Pkwy. East, Vestal, NY 13850: Free information ◆ Custom photo cards, color business cards, enlargements and poster prints. 607-797-8795.

**Skrudland Photo,** 5311 Fleming Ct., Austin, TX 78744: Free information ◆ Film and slide processing, print-making, photo greeting cards, and special services. 512-444-0958.

**Skyline Color Lab,** 9016 Prince William St., Manassas, VA 22110: Free information ◆ Full-service color and black-and-white photo processing laboratory. 703-369-1906.

**Mark Sonners Photographic Printer,** 13330 Arminta St., North Hollywood, CA 91605: Free information ◆ Color, black-and-white, and other processing services. 800-806-4345.

**Technilab Inc.,** P.O. Box 857, 53 S. Main, New City, NY 10956: Free information ◆ Black-and-white film processing. 888-888-6220. www.technilab.com

**UCL Photo,** 812 S. La Brea Ave., Los Angeles, CA 90036: Free information ◆ Custom processing, slide duplication, and prints from slides. 800-933-2977.

**Westside Processing Inc.,** 1523 26th St., Santa Monica, CA 90404: Free information ◆ Film processing. 310-4828-6850.

## Photo Restoration

**B & L Photo Lab Inc.,** 3486 N. Oakland Ave., Milwaukee, WI 53211: Free information ◆ Copy and restoration processing and electronic imaging services. 800-289-9435; 414-964-6626 (in WI).

**Elbinger Laboratories Inc.,** P.O. Box 23128, Lansing, MI 48909: Free information ◆ Archival reproduction of photographs in sepia, oil coloring, and black-and-white. Also professional black-and-white processing. 800-332-0302; 317-267-9000 (in MI). www.elbinger.com

**Kelly Color,** Box 576, Morganton, NC 28655: Free information ◆ Restoration and copy services, proofing, portraits and machine-processed candid photos, package assortments, montages and composites, and display transparencies for light boxes. 704-433-0934.

**Modernage Photographic Services,** 1150 Avenue of Americas, New York, NY 10036: Free information with long SASE ◆ Photo restoration services. 800-997-2510.

## Retail Suppliers

**A.C. Photographic,** 611 Broadway, Ste. 210, New York, NY 10012: Free information ◆ New and used photography equipment, cameras, and accessories.

**AAA Camera Exchange Inc.,** 113 W. 17th St., New York, NY 10011: Free catalog ◆ Cameras and darkroom equipment. 800-221-9521; 212-242-5800 (in NY). www.aaacamera.com

**Abbey Camera Inc.,** 1417-25 Melon St., Philadelphia, PA 19130: Free information ◆ Photographic accessories, studio equipment, and darkroom supplies. 800-25-ABBEY; 215-236-1200 (in PA). www.abbeycamera.com

**Abe's of Maine Camera & Electronics,** 1957 Coney Island Ave., Brooklyn, NY 11223: Free information ◆ Photography equipment. 800-531-2237. ABEMAINE@aol.com

**Adirondack Outfitters,** P.O. Box 431, Massena, NY 13662: Free information ◆ Rock and ice climbing, camping, and outdoor photography equipment. 888-315-0747.

**Adorama,** 42 W. 18th St., New York, NY 10011: Catalog $3 ◆ Photography, darkroom, and underwater photo equipment. 212-741-0466. goadorama@aol.com

**All Seasons Camera,** 5 Harvard Ln., Box 111, Hastings On Hudson, NY 10706: Free information ◆ Photography equipment, cameras, and accessories. 914-478-0931. www.allcamera.com

**Alt Camera Exchange,** 69 Queen St. East, Toronto, Ontario, Canada M5C 1R8: Free information ◆ New and used photographic equipment. 800-387-9891.

**Stan Amarkin & Company,** 198 Amity Rd., Woodbridge, CT 06525: Free information ◆ New and used equipment and photographic accessories. 800-289-5342; 203-397-7766 (in CT).

**B & H Photo-Video,** 420 9th Ave., New York, NY 10001: Catalog $3.95 ◆ Photographic and video equipment and camcorders. 800-947-9903; 212-444-5001 (in NY). www.bhphotovideo.com

**Ball Photo Supply Company,** 85 Tunnel Rd., Asheville, NC 28805: Free information ◆ Telescopes, spotting scopes, camera equipment, binoculars, eyepieces, and accessories. 704-252-2443.

**Beach Camera,** 203 Rt. 22 East, Greenbrook, NJ 08812: Free information ◆ Photography equipment, binoculars, radar detectors, and video equipment. 800-634-1811. www.beachcamera.com

**Beach Photo & Video Inc.,** 604 Main St., Daytona Beach, FL 32118: Free information ◆ Photography equipment and supplies. 904-252-0577. www.beachphoto.com

**Bel Air Camera & Video,** 1025 Westwood Blvd., Los Angeles, CA 90024: Free information ◆ Photographic equipment and video cameras. 800-200-4999.

**Bergen County Camera,** 270 Westwood Ave., Westwood, NJ 07675: Free information ◆ Photography equipment. 800-262-5425; 201-664-4113 (in NJ). www.bergencountycamera.com

**Berger Brothers Camera Exchange,** 209 Broadway, Amityville, NY 11701: Free information ◆ Photography equipment, camcorders, and accessories. 800-262-4160; 516-264-4160 (in NY). www.berger-bros.com

**Bill's Camera Classics,** 4183 Dundee Rd., Northbrook, IL 60062: Free information ◆ Cameras and accessories. 800-755-5342.

**Dan Black,** Box 2072, Bala Cynwyd, PA 19004: Free information ◆ Leica equipment. 610-664-7345. mrdblack@aol.com

**Bromwell Marketing,** 3 Alleghany Center, Pittsburgh, PA 15212: Free catalog ◆ Large-format view cameras, lenses, and tripods. 412-321-4118.

**Brooklyn Camera Exchange,** 488 Sunrise Hwy., Rockville Centre, NY 11570: Free information ◆ New and used cameras and supplies. 516-678-5333.

**Cambridge Camera Exchange,** 119 W. 17th St., New York, NY 10011: Free information ◆ Photography equipment. 800-221-2253; 212-675-8600 (in NY). www.cambridge.com

**Camera Care,** 906 Arch St., Philadelphia, PA 19107: Free information ◆ Photographic equipment. 800-845-4696. CAMCARE@AOL.COM

**Camera City Inc.,** 342 Kings Hwy., Brooklyn, NY 11223: Free information ◆ Photographic equipment and accessories. 800-896-2626.

**Camera Corner of Iowa,** 3523 Eastern Ave., Davenport, IA 52807: Free information ◆ Camera equipment and binoculars. 800-762-4282.

**Camera Outlet Dallas,** KEH Camera Outlet, 3767 Forest Ln., Ste. 126, Dallas, TX 75234: Free information ◆ Used cameras. 972-620-9800.

**Camera Sound of Pennsylvania,** 1104 Chestnut St., Philadelphia, PA 19107: Free information ◆ Cameras and accessories, camcorders, laser disk players, and portable audio and high-fidelity equipment. 800-477-0022; 215-627-1080 (in PA.

**Camera Traders Ltd.,** 44 W. 17th St., New York, NY 10011: Free information ◆ Cameras, lenses, filters, enlargers and projectors, slide duplicators, tripods, copy equipment, flash and lighting equipment, cases, and books. 212-463-0097. www.cameratradersltd.com

**Camera World,** 1809 Commonwealth Ave., Charlotte, NC 28205: Catalog $1 ◆ Darkroom accessories and equipment for still, movie, video, and underwater photography. 800-868-3686; 704-375-8453 (in NC). www.cameraworld.com

**Camera World of Oregon,** 700 NW 55th Ave., Portland, OR 97213: Free information ◆ Photography equipment, cameras, and accessories. 800-729-8941; 503-227-6008 (in OR). www.cameraworld.com

**Cameras & Electronics of New Jersey & Maine,** 982 River Rd., Edgewater, NJ 07020: Free information ◆ Photography equipment. 201-886-7400.

**Bill Cameta's,** 253 Broadway, Amityville, NY 11701: Free information ◆ Photography equipment, cameras, and accessories. 516-691-1190. www.cameta.com

**Central Camera Company,** 230 S. Wabash Ave., Chicago, IL 60604: Free information ◆ Photography equipment. 800-421-1899; 312-427-5580 (in IL). www.central-camera.com

**Charlotte Camera Brokers Inc.,** 2400 Park Rd., Charlotte, NC 28203: Free information ◆ Photography equipment. 704-339-0084. www.charlottecamera.com

**Don Chatterton of Seattle,** P.O. Box 15150, Seattle, WA 98115: Free information ◆ Photographic equipment. 206-525-1100. www.donchatterton.com

**Clayton Classic Cameras,** 44 N. Central Ave., Clayton, MO 63105: Free catalog ◆ Large and medium format, collectible, and other cameras. www.classiccamera.com

**Coast to Coast,** 2570 86th St., Brooklyn, NY 11214: Free information ◆ Cameras and audio and video equipment. 800-788-5555. www.coasttocoastcamera.com

**Columbus Camera Group Inc.,** 55 E. Blake, Columbus, OH 43202: Free information ◆ Photography equipment. 614-267-0686. www.columbuscamera.com

**Custom Photo Manufacturing,** 10830 Sanden Dr., Dallas, TX 75238: Free catalog ◆ Darkroom and studio equipment for amateurs, professionals, and industrial use. 800-627-0252.

**Del's Camera,** 923 Olive St., 2nd Floor, Santa Barbara, CA 93101: Free information ◆ Photographic equipment. 805-962-7557. DelsCamera@compuserve.com

**The F Stops Here,** 1725 State St., Santa Barbara, CA 93101: Free information ◆ Large-format cameras and accessories. 805-898-8800. thefstop@thefstop.com

**Family Photo & Video,** 1957 Coney Island Ave., Brooklyn, NY 11257: Free information ◆ Cameras, camcorders, video equipment, VCRs, and accessories. 800-405-7468; 718-645-1298 (in NY).

**Focus Camera,** 4419 13th Ave., Brooklyn, NY 11219: Free information ◆ Cameras and darkroom equipment. 718-437-8810. orders@focuscamera.com

**Foto Electric Supply Company,** 31 Essex St., New York, NY 10002: Free information ◆ Cameras, lenses, and darkroom equipment. 212-673-5222. www.fotoelectric.com

**Fotographica,** 27 W. 20th St., New York, NY 10011: Free information ◆ Cameras, lighting equipment, and accessories. 212-929-6080. www.fotografica.com

**Frank's Highland Park Camera,** 5715 N. Figueroa St., Los Angeles, CA 90042: Catalog $3 ◆ Cameras, underwater photography and video, and darkroom equipment. Also books. 800-421-8230; 213-255-0123 (in CA).

**Freestyle,** 5124 Sunset Blvd., Los Angeles, CA 90027: Free information ◆ Photography and darkroom equipment. 800-292-6137. www.freestylesalesco.com

**Genesis Camera Inc.,** 814 W. Lancaster Ave., Bryn Mawr, PA 19010: Free information ◆ Audio, video, and photographic equipment. 800-575-9977; 610-527-5260 (in PA). GENESIS@DVOL.COM

**Ghitelman Cameras Inc.,** 166 5th Ave., New York, NY 10010: Free information ◆ Photographic equipment and video cameras. 212-924-3020. GGCAM@aol.com

**Ken Hansen Photographic,** 509 Madison Ave., New York, NY 10022: Free information ◆ New and used photographic equipment. 212-317-0923.

**Helix,** 310 S. Racine Ave., Chicago, IL 60607: Free catalog ◆ Cameras and accessories, darkroom equipment and supplies, and video and underwater photo equipment. 800-33-HELIX; 312-421-6000 (in IL). helixuw@aol.com

**Hunt's Photo & Video,** 100 Main St., Melrose, MA 02176: Free information ◆ Photography equipment, cameras, and accessories. 800-924-8682. www.wbhunt.com

**Jack's Camera Shop,** 300 E. Main St., Muncie, IN 47305: Free information ◆ Photography equipment, cameras, and accessories. 317-282-0204.

**Jefferson Camera Shop Inc.,** 2009 S. Jefferson Ave., St. Louis, MO 63104: Free information ◆ New and used cameras and other photographic equipment. 314-773-8539.

**KEH Camera Brokers,** 188 14th St., Atlanta, GA 30318: Free catalog ◆ Used cameras and accessories. 800-DIAL-KEH. www.keh.com

**Ken-Mar Camera & Video,** 27 Great Neck Rd., Great Neck, NY 11021: Free information ◆ Camera equipment, binoculars, and video equipment. 516-482-1025. kenmarcam@aol.com

**Khan Scope Center,** 3243 Dufferin St., Toronto, Ontario, Canada M6A 2T2: Free price list ◆ Telescopes, telescope-making supplies, binoculars, audiovisual aids, books, photographic equipment, computers and software, and planetariums. 416-783-4140. www.khanscope.com

**KOH'S Camera Sales & Service Inc.,** 2 Heitz Pl., Hicksville, NY 11801: Free information ◆ Cameras, studio accessories, and optical equipment. 516-933-9790. www.kohscamera.com

**Jim Kuehl & Company,** 8527 University Blvd., Des Moines, IA 50325: Free information ◆ Leica cameras, photographic accessories, and optical equipment. 515-225-0110.

**Lauderdale Camera,** South Harbor Plaza, 1316 SE 17th St., Fort Lauderdale, FL 33316: Free information ◆ Photographic equipment. 800-749-4990; 954-524-9447 (in FL). www.photovillage.com/lauderdale

**Le Camera,** 2930 Brunswick Pike, Lawrenceville, NJ 08648: Free information ◆ Camera equipment. 800-786-3686. www.lecamera.com

**The Lens & Repro Equipment Corp.,** 33 W. 17th St., New York, NY 10011: Free information ◆ Used equipment. 212-675-1900.

**Lincoln Camera & Video Store,** 20001 Delaware Ave., Wilmington, DE 19806: Free information ◆ New and used photographic equipment. 302-654-6241.

**Lindahl Specialties Inc.,** P.O. Box 1365, Elkhart, IN 46515: Free information ◆ Strobe adapters, vignetters, and other special effects accessories. 800-572-2011; 219-296-7823 (in IN). www.lslindahl.com

**M & M Photo Source Limited,** 1135 37th St., Brooklyn, NY 11218: Free information ◆ Cameras, lenses, film, darkroom supplies, lighting and digital imaging equipment, and other accessories. 800-606-6746. www.mmphoto.com

**MAC Camera Inc.,** 321 W. Grand Ave., El Segundo, CA 90245: Free information ◆ Cameras and accessories. 310-322-3433.

**Midwest Photo Exchange,** 3313 N. High St., Columbus, OH 43202: Free information ◆ Camera equipment, darkroom supplies, and lighting accessories. 614-261-1264. www.mpex.com

**Milford Camera Shop,** 9 River St., Milford, CT 06460: Free information ◆ Photographic equipment. 203-878-0156; 800-562-5048 (in CT).

**National Camera Exchange,** 9300 Olson Memorial Hwy., Golden Valley, MN 55427: Free information ◆ Telescopes, audiovisual aids, photographic equipment, charts and star maps, books, and binoculars. 888-873-1979; 612-591-5175 (in MN). usedcameras@natcam.com

**Negri's Camera Shop,** 287 Main St., Farmingdale, NY 11735: Free information ◆ Used equipment. 516-249-1305.

**Olden Camera & Lens Company Inc.,** 1265 Broadway, New York, NY 10001: Free information ◆ Photography and video equipment, darkroom supplies, computers, and electronics. 212-226-3727.

**The Photo Emporium,** 4304½ W. Lawrence Ave., Chicago, IL 60630: Free information ◆ Photography equipment, cameras, and accessories. 312-777-3915. www.info@photoemporium.com

**Photographic Systems,** 412 Central SE, Albuquerque, NM 87102: Free catalog ◆ Used equipment. 505-247-9780.

**PHOTOGraphics,** 515 5th Ave., McKeesport, PA 15132: Free information ◆ Used cameras and accessories. photosupply@worldnet.att.net

**Pittsburgh Camera Exchange,** 529 E. Ohio St., Pittsburgh, PA 15212: Free information ◆ Photography equipment, cameras, and accessories. 412-422-6372. www.pghcamex.com

**Porter's Camera Store Inc.,** Box 628, Cedar Falls, IA 50613: Free catalog ◆ Photography equipment and darkroom supplies. 800-553-2001. www.porters.com

**Profoto,** 128 W. 31st St., New York, NY 10001: Free information ◆ Photographic equipment. 212-239-8689. www.profotonyc.com

**Reimers Photo Materials Company,** 300 E. Bay St., Milwaukee, WI 53207: Free information ◆ Used and new cameras. 800-236-5435; 414-744-4471 (in WI).

**Roberts,** 255 S. Meridian St., Indianapolis, IN 46225: Free information ◆ Used photographic equipment. 800-726-5544; 636-5544 (in IN). www.robertsimaging.com

**Leonard Rue Enterprises,** 138 Millbrook Rd., Blairstown, NJ 07825: Free catalog ◆ Books, video tapes, equipment, and gifts for photographers and outdoor enthusiasts. 908-362-6616.

**Samy's Camera,** 200 S. La Brea, Los Angeles, CA 90036: Free information ◆ Photographic equipment, new and used cameras, and flash accessories. 800-321-4SAM. www.samys.com

**SBI Sales,** 259 A St., Boston, MA 02210: Free information ◆ Used and demonstration equipment and darkroom supplies. 800-234-5724.

**Service Photo,** 2225 N. Charles St., Baltimore, MD 21218: Free information ◆ Photographic equipment and darkroom supplies. 800-344-3PRO; 410-235-6200 (in MD). www.ServicePhoto.com

**Stephen Shuart,** 102 Pine Ave., Kane, PA 16735: Free information ◆ Large-format cameras and accessories. shufly@penn.com

**Shutan Camera & Video,** 312 W. Randolph, Chicago, IL 60606: Free catalog ◆ Cameras and other photography equipment. 800-621-2248; 312-332-2000 (in IL). www.shutan.com

**Silvio's Photoworks,** 3854 Sepulveda Blvd., Torrance, CA 90505: Free information ◆ New and used photographic equipment. 310-791-7100.

**Smile Photo & Video,** 29 W. 35th St., New York, NY 10001: Free information ◆ Photography and video equipment and supplies. 212-967-5900.

**Solar Cine Products Inc.,** 4247 S. Kedzie Ave., Chicago, IL 60632: Free catalog ◆ Darkroom and photographic equipment and supplies. 800-621-8796; 773-254-8310 (in IL).

**Su's Cameras,** 1161 Rt. 27, Highland Park, NJ 08904: Free information ◆ New and used photographic equipment. 908-572-5709.

**Supreme Camera & Video,** 1562 Coney Island Ave., Brooklyn, NY 11234: Free information ◆ Cameras and accessories. 800-332-2661; 718-692-4140 (in NY).

**Tamarkin & Company,** 670 Broadway, #501, New York, NY 10012: Free price list ◆ Photographic equipment, new and used cameras, and flash accessories. 800-289-5342. TamarkinS@aol.com

**Testrite Instrument Company Inc.,** 135 Monroe St., Newark, NJ 07105: Free catalog ◆ Photography equipment for the darkroom and studio. 973-589-6767. www.testrite.com

**Tri-State Camera,** 650 6th Ave., New York, NY 10011: Free information ◆ Photography equipment. 800-221-1926; 212-633-2290 (in NY). tscamvid@aol.com

**Unique Photo,** 11 Vreeland Rd., Florham Park, NJ 07932: Free information ◆ Paper, chemistry, film, accessories, and other supplies. 800-631-0300. info@uniquephoto.com

**George Ury Photographic Equipment,** 801 E. Ogden Ave., Naperville, IL 60563: Free information ◆ Photography equipment, cameras, and accessories. 630-420-2925. GEORGEURY@AOL.Com

**Vistek,** 496 Queen St. East, Toronto, Canada M5A 4G8: Free information ◆ New and used photographic equipment. 800-561-1777. sales@vistek.net

**The Wall Street Camera,** 82 Wall St., New York, NY 10005: Catalog $2.95 (refundable with $50 purchase) ◆ Photography equipment. 212-344-0011. www.WallStreetCamera.com

**Willoughby's Photo,** 136 W. 32nd St., New York, NY 10001: Free information ◆ Photography equipment, cameras, and accessories. 212-564-1600.

**Woodmere Camera Inc.,** 337 Merrick Rd., Ste. 7, Lynbrook, NY 11563: Free information with long SASE ◆ Photography equipment. 516-599-6013. www.woodcam.com

**World Photo & Video,** 225 Liberty St., New York, NY 10281: Free information ◆ New and used photography equipment, binoculars, camcorders, and other electronics. 212-945-7415.

**Worldwide Photo, Video & Electronics,** 203 US Hwy. 22, Greenbrook, NJ 08812: Free information ◆ Cameras, video equipment, camcorders, VCRs, and accessories. 800-617-4686. WWPVE@AOL.Com

**Zeff Photo Supply,** P.O. Box 311, Brighton St., Belmont, MA 02178: Free catalog ◆ Supplies for the professional photographer. 800-343-5055. zeffphoto@aol.com

**Zone VI Studios Inc.,** Division Calumet Photographic Inc., 890 Supreme Dr., Bensenville, IL 60106: Free catalog ◆ Photography and lighting equipment and darkroom supplies. 800-CALUMET. www.calumetphoto.com

## Slides

**The Astronomical Society of the Pacific,** 390 Ashton Ave., San Francisco, CA 94112: Free catalog ◆ Slide sets of the solar system and universe. 800-962-3412. www.aspsky.org/

**Cornell Laboratory of Ornithology,** 159 Sapsucker Woods Rd., Ithaca, NY 14850: Free brochure ◆ Slides of North American birds. 607-254-2450.

**MMI Corp.,** P.O. Box 19907, Baltimore, MD 21211: Catalog $2 ◆ Astronomy 35mm slides. 410-366-1222. members.aol.com/mmicorp

**The Planetary Society,** 65 N. Catalina Ave., Pasadena, CA 91106: Free brochure ◆ Astronomy books, videos, and slide sets. 626-793-1675.

**Worldwide Slides,** 7427 Washburn, Minneapolis, MN 55423: Catalog $1 ◆ Travel slides about the United States, foreign countries, historic and scenic sites, and nature settings. 612-869-6482.

## Storage & Filing Systems

**Clear-File (USA) Inc.,** 7549 Brokerage Dr., Orlando, FL 32809: Free brochure ◆ Presentation and storage supplies. 407-851-5966.

**Get Smart Products,** P.O. Box 522, Manhasset, NY 11030: Free catalog ◆ Archival storage supplies and photographic accessories. 800-827-0673. www.pfile.com

**Icon Distribution,** 3956 Town Center Blvd., Ste. 122, Orlando, FL 32837: Free information ◆ Archival supplies and photographic storage systems. 800-801-2128. www.IconUSA.com

**Light Impressions,** 439 Monroe Ave., P.O. Box 940, Rochester, NY 14607: Free catalog ◆ Books on photography and supplies for archival storage of negatives and prints. 800-828-6216. www.lightimpressionsdirect.com

**Tropich Software Inc.,** 529 Central Ave., Scarsdale, NY 10583: Free information ◆ Windows-based filing system for photographs. 914-472-0278.

**20th Century Plastics Inc.,** P.O. Box 2393, Brea, CA 92622: Free catalog ◆ Plastic pages to protect, organize, and display slides, prints, and negatives. 800-767-0777.

## Tripods, Monopods, & Brackets

**American Photographic Instrument Company Inc.,** P.O. Box 322, 12 Lincoln Blvd., Emerson, NJ 07630: Free information ◆ Light stands, tripod accessories, and monopods. 800-600-1147. apic@earthlink.net

**Benbo Tripods,** Division Saunders Group, 21 Jet View Dr., Rochester, NY 14624: Free catalog ◆ Adjustable tripods. 800-394-3686. www.saundersphoto.com

**Bogen Photo Corp.,** 565 E. Crescent Ave., Ramsey, NJ 07446: Free information ◆ Adjustable tripods for 35mm to medium format cameras. 201-818-9500. www.bogenphoto.com

**Cambridge Camera Exchange,** 119 W. 17th St., New York, NY 10011: Free information ◆ Tripods and monopods in several sizes to accommodate most photographic requirements. 800-221-2253; 212-675-8600 (in NY). www.cambridge.com

**Cascade Designs Inc.,** 4000 1st Ave. South, Seattle, WA 98134: Free information ◆ Walking stick equipped with a universal camera mount that converts to a monopod. 800-527-1527. www.cascadedesigns.com

**Coast Manufacturing Company,** P.O. Box 67, Old Bethpage, NY 11804: Free information ◆ Photo and video luggage and tripods. 516-822-3101.

**Crane Enterprises,** Box 143, Green Forest, AR 72638: Free information ◆ Clip-on quick-release brackets for cameras, strobes, umbrellas, and other equipment. 501-553-2222.

**Cullman Tripods,** Beseler Photo Marketing, 1600 Lower Rd., Linden, NJ 07036: Free brochure ◆ Cullman tripods. 800-678-8324. www.beseler-photo.com

**Davis & Sanford Tripods,** Tiffen Manufacturing, 90 Oser Ave., Hauppage, NY 11788: Free information ◆ Compact and heavy-duty monopods and tripods. 800-645-2522. www.tiffen.com

**Foba Tripods,** Sinar Bron, 17 Progress St., Edison, NJ 08820: Free information ◆ Heavy-duty tripods for large single lens reflex and other medium to large format cameras. 800-456-0203.

**Gitzo Tripods,** Division Bogen Photo Corp., 565 E. Crescent Ave., Ramsey, NJ 07446: Free information ◆ All-purpose tripods. 201-818-9500.

**Kalimar Tripods,** Kalimar Inc., 722 Goddard Ave., Chesterfield, MO 63017: Free information ◆ Tripods for compact and lightweight cameras. Also heavy-duty models for large cameras. 314-532-4511.

**KB Systems,** 10407 62nd Pl. West., Mukilteo, WA 98275: Free information ◆ Wood tripods. 425-355-8740.

**Kirk Enterprises,** 107 Lange Ln., Angola, IN 46703: Free catalog ◆ Tripods and other camera mounts for accessories. 800-626-5074. www.kirkphoto.com

**Linhof Tripods,** HP Marketing Corp., 16 Chapin Rd., Pine Brook, NJ 07058: Free information ◆ General purpose tripods. 201-808-9010.

**Majestic Tripods,** Bencher Inc., 831 N. Central Ave., Wood Dale, IL 60191: Free information ◆ Tripods for heavy-duty cameras and video equipment. 773-282-8787. www.bencher.com

**The Morris Company,** 1205 W. Jackson Blvd., Chicago, IL 60607: Free information ◆ Compact standard and tabletop tripods. 312-421-5739.

**Phoenix Corp.,** 112 Mott St., Oceanside, NY 11572: Free information ◆ Ultra-compact tripods for small single lens reflex and point-and-shoot cameras. 516-764-5890.

**The Saunders Group,** 21 Jet View Dr., Rochester, NY 14624: Free catalog ◆ Tripods, exposure and flash meters, enlargers, strobe brackets, and other equipment. 800-394-3686. www.saundersphoto.com

**Sekonic,** Mamiya America Corp., 8 Westchester Plaza, Elmsford, NY 10523: Free list of retail sources ◆ Exposure meters, flash guns, and tripod studio ball heads. 914-347-3300. www.sekonic.com

**ToCad America,** 300 Webrow Rd., Parsippany, NJ 07054: Free catalog ◆ Adjustable tripods. 973-428-9800. www.tocad.com

**Tracks Walking Staffs,** 4000 1st Ave. South, Seattle, WA 98134: Free information ◆ Telescoping sectioned walking staffs that convert to a camera monopod. 800-527-1527. www.cascadedesigns.com

**Velbon,** 2433 Moreton St., Torrance, CA 90505: Free information ◆ Tripods. 800-423-1623. www.velbon.com

**Vivitar Corp.,** 1280 Rancho Conejo Blvd., Newbury Park, CA 91320: Free brochure ◆ Tripods for photographic and video equipment. 805-498-7008. www.vivitarcorp.com

**Zone VI Studios Inc.,** Division Calumet Photographic Inc., 890 Supreme Dr., Bensenville, IL 60106: Free catalog ◆ Heavy-duty wood tripods for large single lens reflex, view, and video cameras. 800-CALUMET. www.calumetphoto.com

## Underwater Photography Equipment

**Adorama,** 42 W. 18th St., New York, NY 10011: Catalog $3 ◆ Underwater and other photography equipment. 212-741-0466. goadorama@aol.com

**B & H Photo-Video,** 420 9th Ave., New York, NY 10001: Catalog $3.95 ◆ Underwater photography equipment. 800-947-9903 212-444-5001 (in NY). www.bhphotovideo.com

**Berry Scuba Company,** 6674 Northwest Hwy., Chicago, IL 60631: Free catalog ◆ Skin diving, scuba, and underwater camera equipment. Also diving lights. 800-621-6019; 312-763-1626 (in IL).

**Camera World,** 1809 Commonwealth Ave., Charlotte, NC 28205: Catalog $1 ◆ Equipment and supplies for still, movie, video, and underwater photography. 800-868-3686; 704-375-8453 (in NC). www.cameraworld.com

**Frank's Highland Park Camera,** 5715 N. Figueroa St., Los Angeles, CA 90042: Catalog $3 ◆ Cameras, darkroom accessories, and underwater photography equipment. 800-421-8230; 213-255-0123 (in CA).

**Fuji Photo Film USA Inc.,** Attention: Consumer Service, 400 Commerce Blvd., Carlstadt, NJ 07072: Free information ◆ Underwater camera equipment. 800-800-3854. www.fujifilm.com

**GMI/Division Omega,** 191 Shaeffer Ave., Westminster, MD 21158: Free information ◆ Underwater cameras with electronic flash, close-up lenses, automatic film winding and re-winding, and built-in film coding. 800-777-6634. www.omega.satter.com

**Helix,** 310 S. Racine Ave., Chicago, IL 60607: Free catalog ◆ Cameras, underwater photography equipment, darkroom supplies, and video equipment. 800-33-HELIX; 312-421-6000 (in IL). helixuw@aol.com

**Ikelite Underwater Systems,** 50 W. 33rd St., Indianapolis, IN 46208: Catalog $1 ◆ Underwater housings for most cameras. 317-923-4523. www.ikelite.com

**Marine Camera Distributors,** 11717 Sorrento Valley Rd., San Diego, CA 92121: Free information ◆ Cameras and accessories. 619-481-0604.

**Minolta,** 101 Williams Dr., Ramsey, NJ 07446: Free information ◆ Underwater camera equipment. 201-825-4000. www.minolta.com

**Nikon Photo,** 1300 Walt Whitman Rd., Melville, NY 11747: Free brochure ◆ Underwater camera equipment and lenses. 516-547-4200. www.nikonusa.com

**Nikonos Cameras,** 1300 Walt Whitman Rd., Melville, NY 11747: Free brochure ◆ Underwater camera equipment and lenses. 516-547-4200. www.nikonusa.com

**Pioneer Research,** 216 Haddon Ave., Westmont, NJ 08108: Free information ◆ Underwater housings for cameras and video equipment. 800-257-7742; 609-854-2424 (in NJ). www.pioneer-research.com

**The Right Spirit Corp.,** 118 S. Westshore Blvd., Ste. 231, Tampa, FL 33609: Free information ◆ Underwater video camera housings. 800-269-6867.

**Vivitar Corp.,** 1280 Rancho Conejo Blvd., Newbury Park, CA 91320: Free brochure ◆ Underwater camera equipment. 805-498-7008. www.vivitarcorp.com

## PIÑATAS

**La Piñata,** Number 2 Patio Market, Old Town, Albuquerque, NM 87104: Brochure $1 (refundable) ◆ Piñatas. 800-657-6208; 505-242-2400 (in NM).

**Piñata Designs,** 298 Lemon Grove, Irvine, CA 92620: Free brochure ◆ Handcrafted custom piñatas in all sizes, colors, and shapes. 800-975-5597. www.pinatadesign.com

## PINE CONES

**Creative Craft House,** Box 2567, Bullhead City, AZ 86430: Catalog $2 (refundable) ◆ Seashells, pine cones, and craft supplies.

**Nature Crafts,** Rt. 521, Stillwater, NJ 07875: Catalog $2 (refundable) ◆ Pine cone crafting supplies. 201-383-4836.

**J. Page Basketry,** 820 Ablee Rd. West, Nokomis, FL 34275: Catalog $2 (refundable) ◆ Pine needle-crafting and wheat-weaving supplies, dried and preserved flowers and herbs, basket-making and craft materials, tools, and books. 941-485-6730.

**Pine View Farm,** 430 Hutto Pond Rd., Aiken, SC 29801: Free brochure with long SASE ◆ Moss, large pine cones, and long pine needles.

## PINS & PINBACK BUTTONS

**A.T. Patch Company,** Whitefield, NH 03598: Free catalog ◆ Embroidered emblems, decals, and enameled pins. 603-837-3072.

**Adhatters,** Box 667, Effingham, IL 62401: Free information ◆ Patches, pins, and decals. 800-225-7642.

**Bale Company,** 222 Public St., Box 6400, Providence, RI 02940: Free catalog ◆ Athletic, academic, and scholastic medals and pins. Also class and club school rings, novelties, charms, and awards. 800-822-5350. www.bale.com

**Eastern Emblem,** Box 828, Union City, NJ 07087: Free catalog ◆ Patches, cloisonné pins, decals, stickers, T-shirts, caps, and jackets. 800-344-5112.

**Hoover's Manufacturing Company,** P.O. Box 547, Peru, IL 61354: Free catalog ◆ Dog tag key rings, beer and coffee mugs, belt buckles, patches, flags, and Vietnam, Korea, and World War II hat pins. 815-223-1159.

**Frosty Little,** 222 E. 8th St., Burley, ID 83318: Free information ◆ Sweatshirts, T-shirts, pins, and patches with clown graphics. 208-678-0005.

**Stadri Emblems,** 71 Tinker, Woodstock, NY 12498: Free catalog ◆ Embroidered emblems, pins, and decals. 914-679-6600.

**United Stitch Associates,** 807 Turnbull Canyon Rd., Hacienda Heights, CA 91745: Free information ◆ Custom and in-stock martial arts patches and pins. 800-842-6294.

## PLASTICS

**Castcraft,** P.O. Box 17000, Memphis, TN 38187: Free information ◆ How-to information, rubber and plastic materials, and other mold-making and casting supplies. 901-682-0961. www.castcraft.com

**Castolite,** 4915 Dean, Woodstock, IL 60098: Catalog $3 ◆ Casting resins, mold-making supplies, and how-to books. 815-338-4670.

**Synair Corp.,** P.O. Box 5269, Chattanooga, TN 37406: Free information ◆ Urethane casting resin and molding systems. 800-251-7642; 423-698-8801 (in TN).

## PLATES, COLLECTIBLE

**Aftosa,** 1034 Ohio Ave., Richmond, CA 94804: Free catalog ◆ Clear acrylic plate stands and bowl holders. 800-231-0397. www.aftosa.com

**Allen's Porcelains,** 399 S. State St., Westerville, OH 43081: Free information ◆ Plates, Hummels, Precious Moments, Royal Doultons, and other collectibles. 800-848-3966.

**Anheuser-Busch Inc.,** P.O. Box 503015, St. Louis, MO 63150: Free catalog ◆ Heirloom Budweiser and other collectible plates and steins. Also gifts for men and women. 800-325-9665. www.Budshop.com

**Jody Bergsma Galleries Inc.,** Bell's Fair Pkwy., Bellingham, WA 98226: Catalog $4 ◆ Statuary and figurines, plates, dolls, porcelain collectibles, and gifts. 800-237-4762; 360-733-2037 (in WA).

**Biggs Limited Editions,** 5517 Lakeside Ave., Richmond, VA 23228: Free information with long SASE ◆ Statuary and figurines, plates, dolls, other porcelain collectibles, and gifts. 800-637-0704. www.biggsltd.com

**Churchills,** Twelve Oaks Mall, Novi, MI 48377: Free information ◆ Collectible plates. 800-388-1141.

**Dexter & Company,** 53 W. 49th St., New York, NY 10020: Free information ◆ Collectible plates. 800-BUY-DEXT; 212-245-7460 (in NY).

**DR Sports,** 1275 Bloomfield Ave., Bldg. 6, Unit 34, Fairfield, NJ 07004: Free information ◆ Major and minor league baseball card sets. Also other sports cards, figurines, plates, and ceramics and pewter collectibles. 973-227-6547.

**David Epstein Sports Collectibles,** 6 Robin Rd., Edison, NJ 08820: Free information ◆ Figurines, plates, lithographs, and other collectibles. 800-343-1256; 908-549-4648 (in NJ). dmepstein@aol.com

**Gallery 247,** 814 Merrick Rd., Baldwin, NY 11510: Free brochure ◆ Collectible plates and prints. 516-868-4800.

**Gartlan USA Inc.,** 575 Rt. 73N, Ste. A-6, West Berlin, NJ 08091: Free catalog ◆ Autographed limited edition collector plates, figurines, ceramic trading cards, and lithographs featuring athletes and entertainers. 609-753-9280.

**Green Gable Gifts,** Box 2525, Winnipeg, Manitoba, Canada R3C 4A7: Free catalog ◆ Figurines that are certified and authorized by the descendents of Lucy Maud Montgomery. 800-667-4957.

**House of Tyrol,** P.O. Box 909, 66 E. Kytle St., Cleveland, GA 30528: Free catalog ◆ Musical cuckoo clocks, steins, crystal, porcelain, lamps, music boxes, pillows, knitted items, decor accessories, bar equipment, collector plates, pewter, tapestries, cards, Alpine hat pins, Christmas decorations, and folk music videos. 800-241-5404.

**Kaymon Arts & Design,** RR 2, Box 41, Blueback Nanoose Bay, British Columbia, Canada V0R 2R0: Free information ◆ Limited edition china collector plates. 403-986-9891.

**The Limited of Michigan Ltd.,** 10861 Paw Paw Dr., Holland, MI 49424: Free price list ◆ Old, new, club, dated, rare, and back-issue plates and bells and other hard-to-find collectibles. 800-355-6363.

**Movie Gallery,** 111 E. 3rd, Sedalia, MO 65301: Catalog $5 ◆ Plates, comics, posters, and other new and old collectibles. 816-826-3834.

**Quality Collectables,** 71 S. Mast St., Goffstown, NH 03045: Free information ◆ Limited edition figurines and statues, signed plates, lithographs, and sports art. 603-497-4721. mattmo@aol.com

**Red Cross Gifts,** 122 Walnut St., Spooner, WI 54801: Free information ◆ Collectible plates, Ashton-Drake dolls, gifts, and collectibles. 800-344-9958.

**Sports Memorabilia Etc.,** 11841 Ventura Blvd., Studio City, CA 91604: Free information ◆ Autographed lithographs, signed plates, figurines, plaques, baseball cards, and other sports cards. 800-995-0650. sports1@earthlink.net

**Trendco Inc.,** 4723 W. Atlantic Ave., Delray Beach, FL 33445: Free catalog ◆ Figurines, plates, bobbing heads, and signed memorabilia. 800-881-0181.

**Unicef,** P.O. Box 182233, Chattanooga, TN 37422: Free catalog ◆ Stationery, postcards, gifts, and limited edition plates. 800-553-1200. www.unicefusa.org

**The Village Plate Collector,** P.O. Box 1118, Cocoa, FL 32923: Free information ◆ Limited edition plates. 800-752-8371; 407-636-6914 (in FL).

**White's Collectables & Fine China,** P.O. Box 680, Newberg, OR 97132: Free information ◆ Collectible plates and new and discontinued china patterns. 800-618-2782.

**Willitts Designs,** 1129 Industrial Ave., Petaluma, CA 94952: Free information ◆ Amish-influenced collector plates. 800-358-9184. www.willitts.com

**Zaslow's Fine Collectibles,** Strathmore Shopping Center, Rt. 34, Matawan, NJ 07747: Free information ◆ Plates, figurines, and collectibles. 800-526-2355; 908-583-1499 (in NJ).

## PLATFORM TENNIS

**Century Sports Inc.,** Lakewood Industrial Park, 1995 Rutgers University Blvd., Box 2035, Lakewood, NJ 08701: Free information ◆ Balls and paddles. 800-526-7548; 732-905-4422 (in NJ).

**Sportime,** Customer Service, 1 Sportime Way, Atlanta, GA 30340: Free information ◆ Balls and paddles. 800-444-5700; 770-449-5700 (in GA).

## PLAYGROUND EQUIPMENT

**All-American Playground Factory,** 16728 IH-34, Schertz, TX 78154: Free brochure ◆ Playground equipment. 888-484-5668; 218-651-9235 (in TX). www.aapfi.com/order.htm

**American Swing Products,** 2533 N. Carson St., #1062, Carson City, NV 89706: Free catalog ◆ Playground swings and swing set components. 800-433-2573. www.americanswing.com

**Belson Outdoors,** P.O. Box 207, North Aurora, IL 60542: Free catalog ◆ Picnic tables, park benches, bike racks, camp stoves, portable grills and toilets, and grandstands. 800-323-5664; 630-897-8489 (in IL). www.belson.com

**Cedar Works,** P.O. Box 990, Rockport, ME 04856: Free catalog ◆ Wood playsets for backyards and playgrounds. 800-462-3327; 207-236-3183 (in ME). www.cedarworks.com

**ChildLife Inc.,** 55 Whitney St., Holliston, MA 01746: Free list of retail sources ◆ Backyard play systems. 800-462-4445. www.childlife.com

**Dana Playground Equipment Inc.,** 40 E. Southern Ave., Mesa, AZ 85210: Free information ◆ Trampolines and other playground equipment. 800-676-5841. www.danaplayground.com

**Florida Playground & Steel Company,** 4701 S. 50th St., Tampa, FL 33619: Free brochure ◆ Swings and equipment for backyards and playgrounds. 800-444-2655; 813-247-2812 (in FL). www.fla-playground.com

**Fun 'N' Play Inc.,** 607 Industrial Park Dr., Newport News, VA 23608: Free information ◆ Swing and gym set plans. 888-FUNNPLA. www.fun-n-play.com

**GameTime,** P.O. Box 121, Fort Payne, AL 35967: Free information ◆ Playground/backyard play systems and outdoor fitness equipment. 800-235-2440. www.gametime.com

**Gazebo & Porchworks,** 728 9th Ave. SW, Puyallup, WA 98371: Catalog $2 ◆ Swings and backyard play structures. 253-848-0502.

**GYM-N-I Playgrounds Inc.,** 1980 IH 35 North, New Braunfels, TX 78130: Free information ◆ Modular playground structures, swing sets, and other equipment. 800-294-9664.

**Kompan Inc.,** 7717 New Market St., Olympia, WA 98502: Free catalog ◆ Outdoor playground equipment. 800-426-9788; 360-943-6374 (in WA). www.kompan.com

**Miracle Recreation Equipment Company,** P.O. Box 420, Monett, MO 65708: Free catalog ◆ Recreation and playground equipment. 800-523-4202.

**Playkids Playgrounds,** 4281 SW 75th Ave., Miami, FL 33155: Free brochure ◆ Pre-assembled playground equipment and play sets. 800-958-KIDS; 305-267-KIDS (in FL). www.swingset.com

**Playworld Systems,** P.O. Box 505, New Berlin, PA 17855: Free information ◆ Wood and metal play equipment. 800-233-8404; 717-966-1015 (in PA). www.playworldsystems.com

**Recreation Creations Inc.,** 215 W. Mechanic St., Hillsdale, MI 49242: Free list of retail sources ◆ Playground, school, and early childhood equipment. 800-766-9458.

**Schirmer's Casual Furniture & Pool Center,** 2916 Annandale Rd., Falls Church, VA 22042: Free catalog ◆ Backyard play systems. 703-534-1400.

**Sports Play,** 5642 Natural Bridge, St. Louis, MO 63120: Free information ◆ Aluminum playground equipment. 800-727-8180.

**Sun Designs,** P.O. Box 6, Oconomowoc, WI 53066: Plan book $8.95 plus $3.95 postage ◆ Backyard play structures. 414-567-4255.

**Ultra Play Systems Inc.,** 425 Sycamore St., Anderson, IN 46016: Free information ◆ Outdoor gym equipment. 800-458-5872.

## POLITICAL MEMORABILIA

**Cobweb Collectibles,** 9 Walnut Ave., Cranford, NJ 07016: Free information with long SASE ◆ Collectible postcards, autographs, other paper collectibles, political memorabilia, and more. 908-272-5777. cobwebcol@aol.com

**The Nickel Trader,** 3025 Washington Rd., McMurray, PA 15317: Free information with long SASE ◆ Postcards, sports cards, and political items. 412-941-2338. www.nickeltrader.com

**Political Americana,** Mail Order Department, 1456 G St. NW, Washington, DC 20005: Free catalog ◆ Political collectibles. 800-333-4555; 202-547-0500 (in Metro DC area). www.polamericana.com

**The Political Gallery,** 5335 N. Tacoma Ave., Ste. 24, Indianapolis, IN 46220: Free information ◆ Political campaigns and sports memorabilia. 317-257-0863.

**Presidential Coin & Antique Company,** 6550 Little River Tnpk., Alexandria, VA 22312: Free catalog ◆ Political memorabilia, medals, and tokens. Also antiques, coins, and Americana. 703-354-5454.

**Rex Stark-Americana,** P.O. Box 1029, Gardner, MA 01440: Catalog $5 ◆ Political memorabilia, posters, flags, needlework, textiles, china, needlework, folk art, toys, and paintings. 978-630-3237.

## PORCELAIN COLLECTIBLES & FIGURINES

**All God's Children Collectors Club,** P.O. Box 5038, Glencoe, AL 35905: Free list of retail sources ◆ Miss Martha original porcelain dolls. 205-492-0221.

**Allen's Porcelains,** 399 S. State St., Westerville, OH 43081: Free information ◆ Hummels, Precious Moments, Royal Doultons, and other rare and new issues. 800-848-3966.

**AMT Collectibles,** 4411 Sepulveda Blvd., Culver City, CA 90230: Catalog $5 ◆ Department 56 buildings and accessories. 800-433-7856. www.alliedmodeltrains.com

**Jody Bergsma Galleries Inc.,** Bell's Fair Pkwy., Bellingham, WA 98226: Catalog $4 ◆ Statuary and figurines, plates, dolls, other porcelain collectibles, and gifts. 800-237-4762; 360-733-2037 (in WA).

**Biggs Limited Editions,** 5517 Lakeside Ave., Richmond, VA 23228: Free information ◆ Statuary and figurines, plates, dolls, other porcelain collectibles, and gifts. 800-266-7744. www.biggsltd.com

**Callahan's Calabash Nautical City,** 9937 Beach Rd., Calabash, NC 28467: Free information ◆ Statuary and figurines, dolls, other porcelain collectibles, and gifts. 800-344-3816.

**Department 56 Showroom,** 4411 Sepulveda Blvd., Culver City, CA 90230: Catalog $5 ◆ Dickens Village, Department 56 Snow Village, and Heritage Village buildings and accessories. 800-433-7856. www.alliedmodeltrains.com

**David Epstein Sports Collectibles,** 6 Robin Rd., Edison, NJ 08820: Free information ◆ Figurines, plates, lithographs, and other collectibles. 800-343-1256; 908-549-4648 (in NJ). dmepstein@aol.com

**European Imports & Gifts,** Oak Mill Mall, 7900 N. Milwaukee Ave., Niles, IL 60648: Free information ◆ Art and porcelain collectibles, Christmas ornaments, and pewter. 847-967-5253.

**Gartlan USA Inc.,** 575 Rt. 73N, Ste. A-6, West Berlin, NJ 08091: Free catalog ◆ Autographed limited edition collector plates, figurines, ceramic trading cards, and lithographs featuring athletes and entertainers. 609-753-9280. www.gartlanusa.com

**Golden Gift Company,** 304 New St., Philadelphia, PA 19106: Free information ◆ Handcrafted European vases, bowls, stemware, baskets, and figurines. 800-GOLD-171.

**Jan Hagara Collectors Club,** 40114 Industrial Park North, Georgetown, TX 78626: Free information ◆ Jan Hagara porcelain dolls. 512-863-9499.

**Hawthorne,** 9210 N. Maryland Ave., Niles, IL 60714: Free catalog ◆ Collectible cottages and sculptures. 800-772-4277.

**Martin's Herend Imports Inc.,** P.O. Box 1178, Sterling, VA 20167: Free list of retail sources ◆ Handpainted porcelain decorative pieces and dinner service. 800-643-7363; 703-450-1601 (in VA).

**Intrigue Gift Shop,** 112 E. Elkhorn Ave., P.O. Box 2147, Estes Park, CO 80517: Free information ◆ Statuary and figurines, plates, dolls, other porcelain collectibles, and gifts. 800-735-GIFT.

**Just Animals,** 15525 Fitzgerald, Livonia, MI 48154: Free brochure with long SASE ◆ Detailed and handpainted pottery, pine collectibles, and gifts for the animal lover. 313-464-8493.

**Lenox Collections,** P.O. Box 519, Langhorne, PA 19047: Free catalog ◆ Porcelain sculptures, china, and crystal. 800-225-1779. www.lenoxcollections.com

**The Limited Edition,** 2170 Sunrise Hwy., Merrick, NY 11566: Free information ◆ Precious Moments porcelain dolls and statuary. 800-645-2864; 516-623-4400 (in NY).

**The Limited of Michigan Ltd.,** 10861 Paw Paw Dr., Holland, MI 49424: Free price list ◆ Old, new, club, dated, rare, and back-issue plates and bells and other hard-to-find collectibles. 800-355-6363.

**Lladró Society,** 43 W. 57th St., New York, NY 10019: Free list of retail sources ◆ Porcelain collectibles. 800-785-2490. www.lladro.com

**Quality Collectables,** 71 S. Mast St., Goffstown, NH 03045: Free information ◆ Limited edition figurines and statues, signed plates, lithographs, and sports art. 603-497-4721. mattmo@aol.com

**Red Cross Gifts,** 122 Walnut St., Spooner, WI 54801: Free information ◆ Collectible plates, Ashton-Drake dolls, gifts, and collectibles. 800-344-9958.

**Royal Copenhagen Porcelain,** 683 Madison Ave., New York, NY 10021: Free brochure ◆ Danish porcelain statuary, fine china, and crystal. 212-759-6457.

**Seaway China Company,** 135 Broadway, Marine City, MI 48039: Free catalog ◆ Royal Doulton collectibles. 800-968-2424. www.seawaychina.com

**Sports Memorabilia Etc.,** 11841 Ventura Blvd., Studio City, CA 91604: Free information ◆ Autographed lithographs, signed plates, figurines, plaques, baseball cards, and other sports cards. 800-995-0650. sports1@earthlink.net

**Staffordshire Catalog,** P.O. Box 324, Old Westbury, NY 11568: Free brochure ◆ Animals, cottages, and historical figures. 800-294-0324. www.elinorpenna.com

**Trendco Inc.,** 4723 W. Atlantic Ave., Delray Beach, FL 33445: Free catalog ◆ Figurines, plates, bobbing heads, and signed memorabilia. 800-881-0181.

**Willitts Designs,** 1129 Industrial Ave., Petaluma, CA 94952: Free information ◆ Americana dolls and toys inspired by the Amish. 800-358-9184. www.willitts.com

**The Windsor Shoppe,** 117 Washington Ave., North Haven, CT 06473: Free information ◆ Department 56 collectibles. 800-676-4644; 203-239-4644 (in CT).

**Windy Meadows Pottery Ltd.,** 1036 Valley Rd., Knoxville, MD 21758: Free brochure ◆ Handbuilt cottages with optional special treatments and personalization. 800-527-6274.

**Zaslow's Fine Collectibles,** Strathmore Shopping Center, Rt. 34, Matawan, NJ 07747: Free information ◆ Plates, figurines, and gifts. 800-526-2355; 908-583-1499 (in NJ).

**Zucker's Fine Gifts,** 151 W. 26th St., New York, NY 10001: Free catalog ◆ Hummel, Swarovski silver and crystal, Waterford crystal, Lladro porcelain, and gifts. 212-989-1450.

## POSTCARDS

**Bob Abbott Postcards,** 901 S. Superior St., Albion, MI 49224: Free information ◆ German postcards. 517-629-6580.

**Diane Allmen Postcard Sales,** P.O. Box 248, Cohoctah, MI 48816: Free information with long SASE ◆ Collectible postcards. 517-545-7397. dianeall@ismi.net

**Barbara's Papertiques,** P.O. Box 317, Port Jervis, NY 12771: Free information with long SASE ◆ Postcards and paper collectibles. 914-856-8572.

**Ellen Budd Postcards,** 6910 Tenderfoot Ln., Cincinnati, OH 45249: Free information with long SASE ◆ Collectible postcards. 513-489-0518. gusluckey@aol.com

**Bullthistle Postcards,** Suzanne F. Knapp, 14 Locust St., Norwich, NY 13815: Free information (enclose want list) ◆ Collectible postcards.

**The Cartophilians,** 430 Highland Ave., Cheshire, CT 06410: Free information with long SASE ◆ Collectible postcards, trading cards, and paper memorabilia. 203-272-1143.

**Agnes Cavalari,** Old Windsor, 89 Bethlehem Rd., New Windsor, NY 12553: Free information with long SASE ◆ State views, glamour, topicals, foreign, greetings, and other postcards. 914-564-6775.

**Kay Clark Postcards,** 221 E. 8th St., Newton, KS 67114: Free information with long SASE ◆ Collectible postcards. 316-283-7401. akayc@feist.com

**Cobweb Collectibles,** 9 Walnut Ave., Cranford, NJ 07016: Free information with long SASE ◆ Collectible postcards, autographs, other paper collectibles, political memorabilia, and more. 908-272-5777. cobwebcol@aol.com

**Consolidated Markets,** P.O. Box 97024, Tacoma, WA 98497: Free information (enclose want list) ◆ Collectible postcards. 253-581-2494. www.home.earthlink.net/~consmkts

**Courthouse Square Postcards,** 210 S. Washington St., Neosho, MO 64850: Free information with long SASE ◆ Collectible postcards. 417-451-3463. jmtaylor@clandjop.com

**Jack & Susan Davis Postcards,** 501 E. Peach, Bozeman, MT 59715: Free information with long SASE ◆ Antique postcards. 406-587-0937. jdavis@gomontana.com

**S. Dobres Postcards,** P.O. Box 1855, Baltimore, MD 21203: Price list $1.50 ◆ Postcards. 800-342-5983.

**Jeff Eastland Antiques & Collectibles,** P.O. Box 5253, Falmouth, VA 22403: Free information with long SASE ◆ Postcards, sports memorabilia, advertising items, and other collectibles. baberuth@fls.infi.net

**Barbara Eggleson,** 7305 Marsh Terrace, Port St. Lucie, FL 34986: Free information with long SASE ◆ Collectible postcards. 561-466-7305. Beggleson@aol.com

**Glimpse of Time,** Doug Walberg, P.O. Box 589, Bandon, OR 97411: Free information with long SASE ◆ Postcards. 541-347-3881.

**Greg Golden Postcards,** 334 Scott Dr., Silver Spring, MD 20904: Free information with long SASE ◆ Collectible postcards. 301-384-0617. greggolden@delphi.com

**Harper's Landing,** 109 E. Hopkins, San Marcos, TX 78666: Free information ◆ Postcards and paper collectibles. 512-754-7182.

**Mel Harvey Postcards,** P.O. Box 1048, Floral City, FL 34436: Free information (enclose want list) ◆ Collectible postcards. 352-726-6764.

**Roger Harvey Postcards,** 76 W. Dundee Rd., Ste. 405, Buffalo Grove, IL 60089: Free information with long SASE ◆ Collectible postcards. 847-520-8145. www.thepostcard.com

**Hey Enterprises,** 2100 Hwy. 35, Old Mill Plaza, Sea Girt, NJ 08750: Free catalog ◆ Postcards, rare books, and collectibles. 908-974-8855.

**Hobby House Distributors,** P.O. Box 18025, Indianapolis, IN 46218: Free information ◆ Archival protection sleeves. 800-544-6229; 317-547-1306 (in IN).

**Houde's Postcards,** P.O. Box 2577, Missoula, MT 59806: Free information with long SASE ◆ Collectible postcards. 406-549-2115. HOUDE55@aol.com

**Frank E. Howard Postcards,** 856 Charlotte St., Macon, GA 34236: Free information with long SASE ◆ Postcards. 912-788-1514.

**Fred N. Kahn Postcards,** 258 Stratford Rd., Asheville, NC 28804: Free information with long SASE ◆ Postcards. 704-252-6507.

**Hal Lutsky Postcards,** 298 4th Ave., Ste. 475, San Francisco, CA 94118: Free information with long SASE ◆ Postcards. 800-501-5001.

**Sandra Malinas Postcards,** P.O. Box 805, Port Richey, FL 34673: Free information with long SASE ◆ Collectible postcards. 813-846-0017. srm@kcii.com

**Keith Marsh Stamp Center,** 4115 Concord Pike, Wilmington, DE 19803: Free information with long SASE ◆ Collectible postcards. 302-478-8740. www.TheStampCenter.com

**Mary Martin Postcards,** P.O. Box 787, Perryville, MD 21903: Free brochure with long SASE ◆ New, old, and hard-to-find United States views, topicals, greetings, foreign cards, rarities, and other postcards. 410-575-7768. jjad00a@prodigy.com

**Susan Mast Postcards,** 849 Almar Ave., Santa Cruz, CA 95060: Free information with long SASE ◆ Collectible postcards. 800-366-9816. www.cruzio.com/~alohasmc

**Memory Lane Postcards,** P.O. Box 66, Keymar, MD 21757: Free information with long SASE ◆ Postcards and collecting supplies, magazines, comics, sheet music, sports cards, and old newspapers. 410-775-0188.

**Merry's Collectibles,** Box 281, Carleton, MI 48117: Free information with long SASE ◆ Collectible postcards.

**Marty Michaels Postcards,** 1286 Sierra Ct., San Jose, CA 95132: Free information with long SASE ◆ Collectible postcards. 408-729-0608. martylm@aol.com

**The Morgan Company,** 6301 Highbanks Rd., Mascoutah, IL 62258: Free price list ◆ Postcard archival supplies. 800-422-4510.

**Alison & Richard Moulton,** 138 Linden Ave., Victoria, British Columbia, Canada V8V 4E1: Free information (send want list) ◆ Postcards from worldwide locations. 250-381-6198.

**National Postcards,** 780 Baconsfield Dr., Ste. 112, Macon, GA 31211: Free information with long SASE ◆ Foreign postcards, topicals, and postcards from the early 1900s to the present. 912-743-8951. www.nationalpostcards.com

**The Nickel Trader,** 3025 Washington Rd., McMurray, PA 15317: Free information with long SASE ◆ Postcards, sports cards, political items, and supplies. 412-941-2338. www.nickeltrader.com

**NuAce Company,** 131 Main St., Reading, MA 01867: Free information ◆ Albums for postcards and first day covers. 781-944-4960.

**The Paper Lady,** 1850 Folsom St., #209, Boulder, CO 80302: Free information (enclose want list) ◆ Collectible postcards. 303-442-0772.

**William Petersen,** 322 Scott St., San Marcos, TX 78666: Free information with long SASE ◆ Postcards and other paper collectibles. 512-353-7574. www.web-pac.com/mall

**V. Peterson,** 928 Dellapenna Dr., Johnson City, NY 13790: Free information (enclose want list) ◆ Collectible postcards.

**Philatelic Specialties,** 106 Hemlock Rd., Manhasset, NY 11030: Free information with long SASE ◆ Collectible postcards. 516-365-7696. juceаro@ffhsj.com

**Postcard Emporium,** P.O. Box 1518, LaFayette, CA 94549: Free information with long SASE ◆ Collectible postcards. 510-283-4490. postcrdemp@aol.com

**Postcards Etc.,** 2101 L St., Sacramento, CA 95816: Free information with long SASE ◆ Postcards. 916-446-8049.

**Postcards from Paradise,** P.O. Box 265, Goodlettsville, TN 37070: Free information with long SASE (specify items wanted) ◆ Collectible postcards. 615-859-7499. TWODICES2@AOL.COM

**Postcards International,** 2321 Whitney Ave., Ste. 102, Hamden, CT 06518: Free information ◆ Postcards. 203-248-6621. quality@vintagepostcards.com

**Potlatch Traders,** Kent & Sandy Renshaw, P.O. Box 1349, Freeland, WA 98249: Free information with long SASE ◆ Old topical and rare postcards and Victorian collectibles. 360-331-0729. potlatch@whidbey.com

**Ken Prag,** P.O. Box 14817, San Francisco, CA 04114: Free information ◆ Old postcards, stocks and bonds, passes, time tables, and other paper Americana. 415-586-9386.

**Michael G. Price Postcards,** P.O. Box 468, Michigan Center, MI 49254: Free information with long SASE ◆ Postcards. 517-764-4517. mgprice@sojourn.com

**Arlene L. Raskin Postcards,** 2580 Ocean Pkwy., Apt. 2L, Brooklyn, NY 11235: Free information with long SASE ◆ Postcards. 718-998-1910.

**Mike E. Rasmussen Postcards,** P.O. Box 726, Marina, CA 93933: Free information with long SASE ◆ Postcards. 408-759-0259.

**Remember These,** P.O. Box 736, Meadows of Dan, VA 24120: Free information (send want list) ◆ Matchbook covers and postcards from the United States and Canada. 540-952-1211. wmankins@swva.net

**RNProducts,** 39 Monmouth St., Red Bank, NJ 07701: Free catalog with long SASE ◆ Archival supplies for postcards. 908-741-0626.

**Ruggiero's Postcards,** 359 Silver Sands Rd., East Haven, CT 06512: Free information with long SASE (enclose want list) ◆ States, foreign views, holidays, greetings, topicals, and other postcards. 203-469-7083.

**Sally's Vintage Postcards,** 4420 Flintstone Rd., Alexandria, VA 22306: Free information with long SASE ◆ Collectible postcards. 703-765-3819. SalRaynes@aol.com

**The Salty Professor Antiques,** Bob & Myra Siegel, 42 Milk St., Portland, ME 04101: Free information with long SASE ◆ Postcards. 207-772-4640.

**Shiloh Postcards,** P.O. Box 728, Clayton, GA 30525: Catalog $1 ◆ Postcards, collecting supplies, and books. 706-782-4100.

**Mrs. Esther K. Springston,** 1610 Park Ave. West, Mansfield, OH 44906: Free information with long SASE ◆ Postcards. 419-529-3667.

**Mary Twyce Antiques & Books,** 601 E. 5th St., Winona, MN 55987: Free information with long SASE ◆ Postcards. 507-454-4412.

**Van Dolson Postcards,** P.O. Box 5485, Vallejo, CA 94591: Free information with long SASE ◆ Collectible postcards. 707-552-2301. Norbayphil@aol.com

**Stan & Frances Walter,** 1027 Jefferson St., Paducah, KY 42001: Free information with long SASE ◆ Collectible postcards. 502-442-1740. swalter@sunsix.infi.net

**G. Wilson Postcards,** 215 Chestnut St., Florence, MA 01060: Free information with long SASE ◆ Collectible postcards. 413-586-8554. www.valinet.com/~buttons

**Write Touch,** The Rytex Company, P.O. Box 68188, Indianapolis, IN 46268: Free information ◆ Loose-leaf postcard albums with leather-grained vinyl padded covers and optional personalization. 800-288-6824.

## POTPOURRI

**All Natural Botanicals,** 112001 44th St. North, Clearwater, FL 33762: Free catalog ◆ Fragrance and essential oils, bath and body preparations, potpourri, incense, diffusers, and more. 813-572-7800. allnatbo@aol.com

**Angel's Earth,** 1633 Scheffer Ave., St. Paul, MN 55116: Catalog $3 ◆ Natural ingredients and supplies for making soaps, candles, toiletries, and other fragrance items. Also labels, containers, molds, kits, and how-to books. 612-698-3601.

**Caswell-Massey Company Ltd.,** Catalog Division, 100 Enterprise Pl., Dover, DE 19901: Catalog $1 ◆ Potpourri and pomander mixes, dried flowers, and herb plants. 800-326-0500. caswell@maui.net

**Churchill Herbs,** 608 Chimborazo Blvd., Richmond, VA 23223: Free catalog ◆ Potpourri, potpourri supplies, essential and fragrance oils, and homemade soaps.

**The Essential Oil Company,** P.O. Box 206, Lake Oswego, OR 97034: Free catalog ◆ Essential oils, soap-making molds and supplies, incense materials, potpourri, and aromatherapy items. 800-729-5912.

**Floris of London,** 703 Madison Ave., New York, NY 10021: Free catalog ◆ English perfumes and toiletries for men and women. Also room sprays, potpourri, and perfumed candles. 800-5-FLORIS.

**Gardens Past,** P.O. Box 1846, Estes Park, CO 80517: Catalog $1 ◆ Soaps and soap making supplies, potpourri, dried flowers, herbs, candles, and aromatherapy items. 970-823-5565.

**Good Hollow Greenhouse & Herbarium,** 50 Slaterock Mill Rd., Taft, TN 38488: Catalog $1 ◆ Herb plants and dried herbs, perennials, wildflowers, scented geraniums, essential oils and potpourris, teas, and spices. 615-433-7640.

**Grandma's Spice Shop,** Spice Valley Way, Upper Tract, WV 26866: Catalog $1 ◆ Essential oils and herbal potpourris. 304-358-2346.

**Hartman's Herb Farm,** 1026 Old Dana Rd., Barre, MA 01005: Catalog $2 ◆ Potpourris, sachets, bath herbs and oils, herbal pillows, dried flowers, spices, teas, essential oils, and pomander balls. 978-355-2015.

**Herb & Spice Collection,** P.O. Box 299, Norway, IA 52318: Free catalog ◆ Potpourris, culinary herbs and spices, and natural herbal body care products. 800-786-1388. www.frontierherb.com

**The Herb Lady,** P.O. Box 2129, Shepherdstown, WV 25443: Free catalog ◆ Essential oils and potpourris. 800-537-1846.

**Herbs-Licious,** 1702 S. 6th St., Marshalltown, IA 50158: Catalog $2 (refundable) ◆ Dried flowers, herbs and spices, oils and fragrances, and potpourri.

**Legacy Herbs,** Sue Lukens Herbalist/Potter, HC 70, Box 442, Mountain View, AR 72560: Catalog 50¢ ◆ Herbs, wildflowers, perennial plants, soaps, bath and body care products, oils and fragrance, incense, potpourri, herbal food products, and other scented items. 870-269-4051.

**Maple Shade Crafts,** Catalog Department, RR 1, Box 186, Pulaski, VA 24301: Catalog $4 (refundable) ◆ Craft supplies, sewing notions, Victorian jewelry, scented candles, cameos, and potpourri. 800-986-9674. www.swva.net/mapleshade

**Meadow Everlastings,** 16464 Shabbona Rd., Malta, IL 60150: Catalog $2 (refundable) ◆ Dried flowers, wreath kits, and potpourri supplies.

**Milda Jane Fragrances,** 1170 Wells Ave., #4, Reno, NV 89502: Free catalog ◆ All-natural aromatic products from the Sierra Nevada Mountains. 800-275-8553.

**Nature's Finest,** 3323 Lee Hwy., Bristol, VA 24202: Catalog $2.50 (refundable) ◆ Dried flowers, herbs, spices, oils, fixatives, bottles, books, equipment, and potpourri supplies. 540-669-5553.

**Raven's Nest Herbals,** P.O. Box 370, Duluth, GA 30136: Catalog $1.50 ◆ Herbs, spices, oils, incense, potpourri, and other herbal products. 770-242-3901.

**San Francisco Herb Company,** 250 14th St., San Francisco, CA 94103: Free catalog ◆ Potpourri supplies and spices and herbs for cooking. 800-227-4530; 415-861-7174 (in CA). www.sfherb.com

**Scentchips,** 1019 E. Nakoma, Ste. 118, San Antonio, TX 78216: Free brochure ◆ Wax potpourri chips. 800-472-3687. www.scentchips.com

**Stax of Wax,** 371 Congress Ave., Waterbury, CT 06708: Free brochure ◆ Scented candles, potpourri canisters, herbal baths, and other scented products. www.stax-of-wax.com

**Tussie Mussies,** 16001 Water Gap Rd., Williams, OR 97544: Free brochure ◆ Hand-blended potpourris, colognes, and lotions. 800-445-5563.

**Tom Thumb Workshops,** Rt. 13, P.O. Box 357, Mappsville, VA 23407: Catalog $1 ◆ Potpourris, herbs and spices, essential oils, dried flowers, and craft supplies. 757-824-3507.

**Well-Sweep Herb Farm,** 205 Mt. Bethel Rd., Port Murray, NJ 07865: Catalog $2 ◆ Potpourri and pomander mixes, dried flowers, and herb plants. 908-852-5390.

## PRINTING PRESSES & SUPPLIES

**Graphic Chemical & Ink Company,** P.O. Box 27, Villa Park, IL 60181: Free catalog ◆ Printing supplies. 630-832-6004.

**The Printers Shopper,** 111 Press Ln., Chula Vista, CA 91910: Free catalog ◆ Printing and graphic arts supplies. 800-854-2911. www.printersshopper.com

**Quaker City Type,** RD 3, Box 134, Honeybrook, PA 19344: Catalog $2 (refundable) ◆ Type for printing presses and stamps. 610-942-3637.

**Think Ink,** 7526 Olympic View Dr., Edmonds, WA 98026: $2 (refundable) ◆ Multi-color, hand printing press and embossing powders. 800-778-1935; 425-778-1935 (in WA). www.thinkink.net

## PROSPECTING & ROCKHOUNDING

**A & B Prospectors' Supply,** 3929 E. Main, Mesa, AZ 85206: Catalog $1 ◆ Prospecting and metal assay equipment. 602-832-4524.

**Alpha Supply,** P.O. Box 2133, Bremerton, WA 98310: Catalog $3 ◆ Prospecting and rockhounding equipment, jewelry-making tools, gem finishing equipment, and metal detectors. 800-257-4211; 360-373-3302 (in WA).

**Arizona Al's Discount,** 4238 W. Northern Ave., Phoenix, AZ 85051: Free information ◆ Metal detectors and prospecting equipment. 602-930-1755. www.arizonaals.com

**Arizona Gems & Crystals,** 1705 W. 14th Dr., Safford, AZ 85546: Free catalog ◆ Gold mining and rockhounding equipment. 800-657-6263.

**Armadillo Mining Shop,** 2041 NW Vine, Grants Pass, OR 97526: Free information ◆ Metal detectors and mining supplies. 541-476-6316.

**B & J Rock Shop,** 14744 Manchester Rd., Ballwin, MO 63011: Catalog $3 ◆ Rockhounding equipment, quartz crystals, amethyst crystal clusters, Brazilian agate nodules, and imported and domestic stones. 314-394-4567.

**Bourget Bros.,** 1636 11th St., Santa Monica, CA 90404: Catalog $3 ◆ Gemstones and cabochons, wax patterns, beads and bead-stringing supplies, lapidary equipment, and rockhounding, treasure hunting, and prospecting equipment. 800-828-3024. www.bourgetbros.com

**Cal-Gold,** 2569 E. Colorado Blvd., Pasadena, CA 91107: Free catalog ◆ Metal detectors, mining and geology equipment, maps, books, and ultraviolet lighting accessories. 626-792-6161. calgold@earthlink.net

**Covington Engineering Corp.,** P.O. Box 35, Redlands, CA 92373: Free catalog ◆ Gold mining and rockhounding equipment. 909-793-6636. www.catalogcity.com/mm/covington

**D & K Detector Sales,** 13809 Southeast Division, Portland, OR 97236: Catalog $2 ◆ Prospecting equipment and metal detectors. 800-542-GOLD; 503-761-1521 (in OR). sales@dk-Nugget.com

**Dad's Rock Shop,** P.O. Box 169, 112 E. Cherry Ave., Arroyo Grande, CA 93421: Free catalog ◆ Lapidary equipment, gems, minerals, fossils, metal detectors, prospecting equipment, and supplies. 805-489-2470.

**East Coast Prospecting & Mining Supplies,** Rt. 3, Box 321J, Ellijay, GA 30540: Catalog $3 ◆ Mining and prospecting equipment and supplies. 706-276-4433.

**Ebersole Lapidary Supply Inc.,** 11417 West Hwy. 54, Wichita, KS 67209: Catalog $5 ◆ Rockhounding equipment, lapidary and jewelry-making tools, findings, mountings, cabochons, gemstones, and rocks. 316-722-4771.

**Eloxite Corp.,** P.O. Box 729, Wheatland, WY 82201: Catalog $1 ◆ Clock-making supplies, gemstones, beads, cabochons, jewelry mountings, and equipment for rockhounding and jewelry do-it-yourself crafters. 307-322-3050. www.eloxite.com

**Estwing Manufacturing Company,** 2647 8th St., Rockford, IL 61109: Free information ◆ Equipment for geologists and rockhounds. 815-397-9558. www.estwing.com

**Falcon Prospecting Equipment,** 6529 E. Fairbrook St., Mesa, AZ 85205: Free information ◆ Placer gold probe for prospecting. 602-854-0324.

**Fisher Research Laboratory,** 200 W. Wilmott Rd., Los Banos, CA 93635: Free information ◆ Metal detectors. 209-826-3292. www.fisherlab.com

**49'er Metal Detectors,** 14093 Irishtown Rd., Pine Grove, CA 95665: Free information ◆ Prospecting supplies, tools, books, and videos. 800-538-7501; 209-296-3544 (in CA).

**Fortyniner Mining Supply,** 16238 Lakewood Blvd., Bellflower, CA 90706: Free information ◆ Mining and treasure hunting equipment, metal detectors, magazines, and books. 310-925-2271.

**The Golddigger**, 253 N. Main, Moab, UT 84532: Free information ◆ Prospecting supplies and equipment. 801-259-5150.

**Graves Company,** 1800 Andrews Ave., Pompano Beach, FL 33069: Free catalog ◆ Rockhounding and ultraviolet lighting equipment. 800-327-9103. www.rockhounds.com/graves

**Hays Electronics,** P.O. Box 26848, Prescott Valley, AZ 86312: Free catalog ◆ Metal detectors, electronic prospecting tools and accessories, and books. 800-699-2624.

**Herkimer Diamond Mines,** RD 1, P.O. Box 233, Herkimer, NY 13350: Free information ◆ Petrified wood products, rockhounding equipment, minerals and rocks, and quartz crystals. 315-866-2011.

**House of Treasure Hunters,** 5714 El Cajon Blvd., San Diego, CA 92115: Free information ◆ Gold prospecting equipment and metal detectors. 619-286-2600.

**International Resource Development,** 5055 Convair Dr., Carson City, NV 89706: Free information ◆ New and used mining equipment. 702-882-6025.

**Jeanne's Rock & Jewelry,** 5420 Bissonet, Bellaire, TX 77401: Price list $1 ◆ Rockhounding equipment, shells, petrified wood products, beads, and bead-stringing supplies. 713-664-2988.

**Kansas/Texas Metal Detectors,** P.O. Box 1500, Dept. C, Colleyville, TX 76034-1500: Free information ◆ Metal detectors and prospecting equipment for treasure, hobby, professional, and security use. 800-876-3463.

**Keene Engineering Inc.,** 20201 Bahama St., Chatsworth, CA 91311: Free catalog ◆ Portable mining equipment. 800-841-7833; 800-392-4653 (in CA).

**Kingsley North Inc.,** 910 Brown St., Norway, MI 49870: Free catalog ◆ Rockhounding and metal-casting equipment, jewelry-making tools, tumblers, and opals. 800-338-9280. www.kingsleynorth.com

**Lentz Lapidary Inc.,** 11760 S. Oliver, Rt. 2, Box 134, Mulvane, KS 67110: Catalog $2 ◆ Jewelry, mountings, clocks and motors, rough rock specimens, cabochons, and rockhounding and lapidary equipment. 316-777-1372.

**The Midas Touch,** 15 Thorncliffe Park Dr., Ste. 412, Toronto, Ontario, Canada M4H 1H6: Catalog $6 ◆ Metal detectors and accessories, prospecting tools, water hunting equipment, and books on treasure hunting. 416-467-6016.

**Miners Inc.,** P.O. Box 1301, Riggins, ID 83549: Free catalog ◆ Sample bags, instruments, hand tools, leather cases, and books for geologists and prospectors. 800-824-7452; 208-628-3247 (in ID). minerox@rmci.net

**Pedersen's Metal Detectors,** 2521 N. Grand Ave., Santa Ana, CA 92705: Free information ◆ Walk-through and handheld detectors and gold and treasure finding supplies. 800-953-3832.

**Pioneer Mining Supplies,** 943 Lincoln Way., Auburn, CA 95603: Free information ◆ Mining equipment and metal detectors. 530-885-1801.

**Placer Equipment Mfg. Inc.,** 427 N. 1st St., Buckeye, AZ 85326: Catalog $3 (refundable) ◆ Dredges, dry washers, sluice boxes, gold pans, equipment, and prospecting kits for beginners. 602-386-7006.

**Pot of Gold,** 2616 Griffin Rd., Fort Lauderdale, FL 33312: Free catalog ◆ Metal detectors, books, and prospecting equipment. 954-987-2888.

**Pro-Mack South,** 940 W. Apache Trail, Apache Junction, AZ 85220: Catalog $3 ◆ Prospecting supplies and tools. 800-722-6463.

**Jimmy Sierra Products,** 3095 Kerner Blvd., Ste. H, San Rafael, CA 94901: Free information ◆ Metal detectors, treasure hunting, and prospecting equipment and accessories. 415-456-0891. jsierra@nbm.com

**Treasure Coast Scoops,** 119 Melton Ave., Sebastian, FL 32958: Free brochure ◆ Scoops, books, and metal detectors. 888-671-9172.

## PUPPETS & MARIONETTES

**Aunt Clowney's Warehouse,** P.O. Box 1444, Corona, CA 91718: Free catalog with two 1st class stamps ◆ Books and novelties for puppeteers, clowns, magicians, face painters, and balloon artists. 909-273-0900. auntc@empirenet.com

**Axtell Expressions,** 230 Glencrest Circle, Ventura, CA 93003: Catalog $2 ◆ Puppets for professionals. 805-642-7282. www.axtell.com

**Cheri-Oats & Company,** P.O. Box 367, Destrahan, LA 70047: Free information ◆ Wigs, stickers, puppets, and face painting supplies. 504-764-0080. www.mooseburger.com/cheri.htm

**Clown Heaven,** 4792 Old State Rd. 37 South, Martinsville, IN 46152: Catalog $3 ◆ Balloons, make-up, puppets, wigs, ministry and gospel items, novelties, magic, clown props, and books. 317-342-6888.

**Cricket Works,** 625 34th St., Sacramento, CA 95816: Free information ◆ Puppet-making kits. 916-851-0170.

**Florida Magic Company,** P.O. Box 290781, Fort Lauderdale, FL 33329: Free information ◆ Puppets, magic tricks, and juggling supplies. 954-473-1902. FlaMagicCo@aol.com

**Freckles Clown Supplies,** 5509 Roosevelt Blvd., Jacksonville, FL 32244: Catalog $6 ◆ Puppets, make-up, clown supplies, costumes, how-to books on clowning and ballooning, and theatrical supplies. 904-388-5541. www.freckles1.com/index.html

**Maher Studios,** P.O. Box 420, Littleton, CO 80160: Free catalog ◆ Ventriloquist dummies, scripts and dialogues, puppets, and how-to books. 303-798-6830. www.maherstudios.com

**Mastercraft Puppets,** P.O. Box 2002, Branson, MO 65615: Catalog $2 ◆ Puppets, clown supplies, and ventriloquist dummies. 417-561-8100. www.devoted.to/puppets

**Mecca Magic Inc.,** 49 Dodd St., Bloomfield, NJ 07003: Catalog $10 ◆ Puppets, juggling supplies, theatrical make-up, clown equipment, balloons, and magic tricks. 201-429-7597. meccamagic@meccamagic.com

**Steven Meltzer,** 670 San Juan, Venice, CA 90291: Free list with long SASE ◆ Marionettes, puppets, and ventriloquist figures. 310-396-6007.

**One Way Street Inc.,** P.O. box 5077, Englewood, CO 80155: Free catalog ◆ Puppets and accessories with a religious theme. 800-569-4537. www.onewaystreet.com

**Pelham Marionettes,** Doris & Jerry Barrows, 5128 Ridge Rd., Lockport, NY 14094: Free list with long SASE ◆ Marionettes, from the 1960s to 1970s. 716-433-4329.

**Sparkle's Entertainment Express,** Jan Lovell, 152 N. Water St., Gallatin, TN 37066: Product list $1 ◆ Make-up, costumes and clown shoes, balloons, juggling and magic equipment, puppets, books, and other supplies. 615-452-9755.

**Toys by Monica,** Monica Peri, 6424 Louis XIV St., New Orleans, LA 70124: Free information ◆ Handmade original design cloth toys. 504-482-0428. www.craftmall.com/booths/row-h/handmade

## PURSES & WALLETS

**Ace Luggage & Gifts,** 2122 Avenue U, Brooklyn, NY 11229: Catalog $2 ◆ Desk sets, leather attach cases, luggage, purses, wallets, handbags, and other gifts. 800-342-5223; 718-891-9713 (in NY).

**American Executive,** Kittery Business Center, 72 Dow Hwy., Kittery, ME 03904: Catalog $2 ◆ Writing portfolios, travel cases and packs, day planners, wallets, briefcases and backpacks, and other leather essentials. 800-804-0825.

**Arazzo Italy,** 860 N. Lake Shore Dr., Chicago, IL 60611: Free catalog ◆ Tapestry and leather purses, bags, satchels, and accessories. 800-326-8125; 312-943-9872 (in IL).

**Bally of Switzerland,** 628 Madison Ave., New York, NY 10153: Free information ◆ Men's and women's shoes and clothing. Also luggage and other small leather goods. 212-751-2163.

**Bottega Veneta,** 635 Madison Ave., New York, NY 10022: Free catalog ◆ Wallets, purses and handbags, luggage, and other small leather goods. 212-371-5511.

**Burberry's Limited,** 9 E. 57th St., New York, NY 10022: Free list of retail sources ◆ Clothing, handbags, luggage, silk scarves and shawls, belts, hats, shoes, tennis accessories, sports bags, and toiletries. 212-371-5010.

**Coach Leatherware Company,** 410 Commerce Blvd., Carlstadt, NJ 07072: Free catalog ◆ Leather handbags, gloves, belts, wallets, briefcases, and accessories. 201-804-8200. www.coach.com

**Copper Star Cattle & Trading Company,** 2000 W. 3rd St., Amarillo, TX 79106: Catalog $2 ◆ Cowhide purses, wallets, satchels and bags, and accessories. 800-828-0442.

**Deerskin,** 119 Foster St., Peabody, MA 01960: Free catalog ◆ Leather clothing and accessories. 978-532-2810. www.deerskin.com

**Lamb's Baa'tique,** P.O. Box 8, Hopeton, OK 73746: Free information ◆ Tapestry purses and satchels. 580-435-2333.

**Maple Leather Company,** Rt. 519, P.O. Box 319, Rosemont, NJ 08556: Free brochure ◆ Women's leather purses and bags. 800-826-1199; 609-397-1199 (in NJ).

**Mid Western Sport Togs,** P.O. Box 230, Berlin, WI 54923: Free catalog ◆ Deerskin gloves, jackets and coats for men and women, footwear, handbags, and accessories. 414-361-5050.

**Naples Creek Leather,** 188 S. Main St., Naples, NY 14512: Free catalog ◆ Leather moccasins, slippers, belts, gloves, casual footwear, and deerskin handbags. 800-836-0616.

**ROCHE Leather,** 161 Harkins Slough Rd., Watsonville, CA 95076: Free brochure ◆ Bags, cases, and women's purses. 800-ROCHE-90; 408-722-5155 (in CA).

## PUZZLES

**J.C. Ayer,** 6 Ballast Ln., Marblehead, MA 01945: Free catalog ◆ Custom-made hardwood puzzles. 781-639-8162.

**Bits & Pieces,** 1 Puzzle Pl., Stevens Point, WI 54481-7199: Free catalog ◆ Jigsaw puzzles, books, games, and gifts for adults and children. 800-884-2637.

**CalAutoArt,** 1520 S. Lyon St., Santa Ana, CA 92705: Free catalog ◆ Automotive-theme jigsaw puzzles. 714-835-9512.

**Fireside Puzzles of Maine,** Box 1023, Scarborough, ME 04070: Free catalog ◆ Hand-cut wood jigsaw puzzles. 207-782-5298.

**Fun Magic Tricks,** 520 Broadway, San Antonio, TX 78215: Catalog $1 (refundable) ◆ Magic tricks, books, gags, juggling equipment, puzzles, and collectibles.

**Games Direct Inc.,** MS112, 820 MacArthur Blvd., Ste. 10, Coppell, TX 75019: Free catalog ◆ Games and puzzles for teens and grown-ups. 800-344-3328. www.gmsdrct.com

**Kadon Enterprises Inc.,** 1227 Lorene Dr., Ste. 16, Pasadena, MD 21122: Free brochure ◆ Puzzles, challenging and historical games, and abstract strategies. 410-437-2163.

**Livewire Puzzles,** 10552 44th St., Edmonton, Alberta, Canada T6A 1V9: Free brochure ◆ Easy to hard wire puzzles.

**Lucretia's Pieces,** RFD 1, Box 501, Windsor, VT 05089: Free information ◆ Challenging puzzles designed with special shapes and unexpected surprises. 802-436-3006.

**Magic & Fun Shop,** 16872 Hwy. 3, Webster, TX 77598: Free catalog ◆ Jokes, gags, novelties, clown supplies, make-up, magic tricks, and puzzles. 281-332-8142. www.fun-shop.com

**The Old Game Store,** Rt. 11, Manchester, VT 05254: Free information with long SASE ◆ Games, puzzles, collectible teddy bears, and toys. 802-362-2756.

**Out of the Woodwork,** 437 Robert E. Lee Dr., Wilmington, NC 28412: Free brochure ◆ Educational puzzles for children. 910-792-6882.

**Pacific Puzzle Company,** P.O. Box 1001, Anacortes, WA 98221: Free brochure ◆ Hardwood educational and fun wood puzzles. 800-467-0242; 360-293-7034 (in WA).

**Pecos Pine,** 258 A St., Ste. 5, Ashland, OR 97520: Catalog $1 ◆ Handcrafted natural wood toys and puzzles. 541-535-6606.

**Pieceful Solutions Puzzle Company,** P.O. Box 2014, Southeastern, PA 19399: Free catalog ◆ Handcut original wood puzzles. 800-695-9913; 610-640-9913 (in PA).

**PuzzleKing,** P.O. Box 128, Brewster, MA 02631: Free brochure ◆ Nostalgic architectural landmarks featuring famous lighthouses, a part of American history. 800-750-4552. www.capecod.net/puzzleking

**Rainy Lake Puzzles,** 4255 Garfield Ave. South, Minneapolis, MN 55409: Free catalog ◆ Hand-cut wood jigsaw puzzles. 612-827-5757. www.rainylakepuzzles.com

**Rex Games Inc.,** 530 Howard St., Ste. 100, San Francisco, CA 94105: Free brochure ◆ Games, puzzles, and toys that teach and entertain. 800-542-6375; 415-777-2900 (in CA). www.rexgames.com

**Spilsbury Puzzle Company,** 3650 Milwaukee St., P.O. Box 8922, Madison, WI 53708: Free catalog ◆ Puzzles, games, and gifts. 800-772-1760.

**Stave Puzzles,** Box 329, Norwich, VT 05055: Free catalog ◆ Hand-cut jigsaw puzzles. 802-295-5200. www.stave.com

**3 Trolls Games & Puzzles,** P.O. Box 4095, South Chelmsford, MA 01824: Free catalog ◆ Games and puzzles. 800-342-6373.

**Toys from Times Past,** 4299 E. Shearer Rd., Rhodes, MI 48652: Free brochure ◆ Action and skill toys, other toys, tricks, and puzzles. 517-689-4663.

**White Mountain Puzzles,** Jackson Falls Marketplace, P.O. Box 818, Jackson, NH 03846: Free catalog ◆ Challenging 1000-piece jigsaw puzzles. 603-383-4346. www.puzzlemaps.com

**Worldwide Games,** P.O. Box 517, Colchester, CT 06415: Free catalog ◆ Brain teasing games. Also jigsaw and 3-D puzzles. 800-888-0987. www.worldwidegames.com

## QUILTS & QUILTING

**AK Sew & Serge,** 1602 6th St. SE, Winter Haven, FL 33880: Catalog $5 ◆ Supplies for heirloom, fashion sewing, and quilting. 800-299-8096; 813-299-3080 (in FL).

**Brewer Sewing Supplies,** 3800 W. 42nd St., Chicago, IL 60632: Free information ◆ Sewing machines, quilting supplies, batting and stuffing, and notions. 800-621-2501.

**Choices,** 1000 Lake St., Oak Park, IL 60301: Brochure $2 ◆ Hand-quilted 100 percent cotton yarn quilts with bonded cotton batting. Also quilted tote bags and pillow shams. 708-386-6555.

**Connecting Threads,** P.O. Box 8940, Vancouver, WA 98668: Free catalog ◆ Quilting books, patterns, tools, kits, and videos. 800-574-6454.

**The Cotton Patch,** 3405 Hall Ln., Lafayette, CA 94549: Catalog $8 ($5 refundable) ◆ Fabrics, quilting books, and supplies. 800-835-4418. CottonPa@aol.com

**The Creative Needle,** 6905 S. Broadway, Ste. 113, Littleton, CO 80122: Catalog $1 ◆ Heirloom sewing, smocking, stitchery, and quilting supplies. 303-794-7312.

**Gammill Quilting Machine Company,** 1452 W. Gibson St., West Plains, MO 65775: Free information ◆ Quilting machines. 800-659-8224. gammill@townsqr.com

**The Gibbs Company,** 606 6th St., Canton, OH 44702: Free catalog ◆ Quilting and rug-hooking stands. 800-775-4426; 330-455-5344 (in OH).

**Ginger's Needleworks,** P.O. Box 92047, Lafayette, LA 70509: Catalog $2 ◆ Quilting fabrics. 318-232-7847.

**Hancock Fabrics,** 3841 Hinkleville Rd., Paducah, KY 42001: Free information ◆ Quilting supplies, fabrics, and sewing notions. 800-845-8723.

**Hinterberg Design Inc.,** 2805 E. Progress Dr., West Bend, WI 53095: Free information ◆ Quilting frame with adjustable height and tilt, ratchet wheel tensioning, and optional extension or shorter poles. 800-443-5800.

**Homecraft Service,** 340 W. 5th St., Kansas City, MO 64105: Catalog $3 ◆ Pre-cut quilt kits. 816-471-3313.

**House of White Birches,** 306 E. Parr Rd., Berne, IN 46711: Free catalog ◆ Kits and patterns.

**Joanne's Notions,** P.O. Box 44030, Brampton, Ontario, Canada L6V 4H5: Catalog $2 ◆ Sewing, serging, pressing, heirloom, quilting supplies, and notions.

**Keepsake Quilting,** Rt. 25B, P.O. Box 1618, Centre Harbor, NH 03226: Free catalog ◆ Quilting books and accessories, patterns, notions, fabrics, scrap bags, and batting. 800-865-9458. www.keepsakequilting.com

**Missouri Breaks Industries,** Quilt Brochure, HCR 64, Box 52, Timber Lake, SD 57656: Free brochure ◆ Original Sioux Native American star quilt patterns. 605-865-3418.

**Mountain Mist Quilt Center,** The Stearns Technical Textiles Company, 100 Williams St., Cincinnati, OH 45215: Free brochure ◆ Quilting and craft supplies, how-to quilting books, and patterns. 800-543-7173. www.palaver.com/mountainmist

**Claire Murray Inc.,** P.O. Box 390, Ascutney, VT 05030: Catalog $5 ◆ Quilts, handpainted ceramics, and hand-hooked rugs. 800-252-4733. www.clairemurray.com

**Needles & Pins,** 3019 SW Martin Downs Blvd., Palm City, FL 34990: Free information ◆ Smocking supplies, fabrics, imported lace, buttons, quilting fabrics, and other supplies. 561-220-9198.

**Noltings,** Rt. 3, Box 147, Hwy. 52 East, Stover, MO 65078: Free information ◆ Quilting and sewing machines. 573-377-2713.

**Nustyle Quilting Frame Company,** Box 61, Stover, MO 65078: Free information with 1st class stamp ◆ Supplies and long-arm machine for outline quilting. 800-648-2240; 573-377-2244 (in MO).

**The Old Wicker Garden,** 6606 Snider Plaza, Dallas, TX 75225: Photos $5 (refundable) ◆ Antique wicker furniture, brass and iron beds, hooked rugs and quilts, folk art, and other decorative accessories. 972-373-8241.

**Omnigrid Inc.,** 1560 Port Dr., Burlington, WA 98233: Free brochure ◆ Rulers, rotary cutting mats, and accessories. 360-757-4743.

**The Perfect Notion,** Box 521, 7620 Elbow Dr. SW, Calgary, AB, Canada T2V 1K2: Free catalog ◆ Fabrics, quilt batting, books, patterns, notions, sewing and quilting supplies. 888-999-8821. www.perfectnotion.com

**Quilting from the Heartland,** P.O. Box 610, Starbuck, MN 56381: Free catalog ◆ Books, templates, videos, stencils, and more. 800-6737-2541.

**Sew Fancy,** Unit 23, RR 1, Beeton, Ontario, Canada L0G 1A0: Catalog $5 ◆ Fabrics, notions, needle art patterns, and supplies for heirloom sewing, smocking, and quilting. 800-SEW-FNCY. www.sewfancy.com

**Southwest Decoratives,** 191 Bighorn Ridge NE, Albuquerque, NM 87122: Catalog $3 ◆ Quilt patterns and kits, applique patterns and kits, cross-stitch charts and kits, and stenciling supplies. 505-856-9585. www.swdecoratives.com

**Speed Stitch,** 3115 Broadpoint Dr., Harbor Heights, FL 33983: Catalog $3 ◆ Machine arts and quilting supplies. 800-874-4115; 352-629-3199 (in FL).

**That Patchwork Place,** P.O. Box 118, Bothell, WA 95041: Free information ◆ Quilting books and supplies. 800-426-3126. www.patchwork.com

**TreadleArt,** 25834 Narboone Ave., Lomita, CA 90717: Free information ◆ Sewing and quilting supplies. 310-534-5122.

## RACQUETBALL & SQUASH

### Clothing

**Dorson Sports Inc.,** 1 Roebling Ct., Ronkonkona, NY 51779: Free information ◆ Gloves. 800-645-7215; 516-585-5400 (in NY).

**Ektelon,** Prince Sports Group, 1 Sportsystem Plaza, Bordentown, NJ 08505: Free information ◆ Clothing and gloves, socks, sweatbands, bags and balls, racquets, and eye guards. 800-283-2635. www.princetennis.com

**Franklin Sports Industries Inc.,** 17 Campanelli Parkway, P.O. Box 508, Stoughton, MA 02072: Free information ◆ Gloves. 800-426-7700. www.eisnerbros.com

**Grass Court Collection,** P.O. Box 972, Hanover, NH 03755: Free catalog ◆ Custom men's clothing for tennis, croquet, lawn bowling, cricket, and squash. 800-829-3412.

**Holabird Sports Discounters,** 9220 Pulaski Hwy., Baltimore, MD 21220: Free catalog ◆ Clothing and equipment. 410-687-6400. www.holabirdsports.com

**Hunt-Wilde,** 2835 Overpass Rd., Tampa, FL 33619: Free information ◆ Gloves. 800-248-1232.

**Olympia Sports,** P.O. Box 1941, Ann Arbor, MI 48106: Free information ◆ Gloves. 800-521-2832. www.wolverinesports.com

**Pony Sports & Leisure,** 2801 Red Dog Dr., Knoxville, TN 37914: Free information ◆ Shoes, socks, and sweatbands. 423-546-4703.

**Puma USA Inc.,** 147 Centre St., Brockton, MA 02403: Free information with long SASE ◆ Clothing, shoes, socks, and balls. 800-662-7862. www.puma.com

**Reebok International Ltd.,** 100 Technology Center Dr., Stoughton, MA 02072: Free list of retail sources ◆ Clothing, shoes, and socks. 800-843-4444.

**Spalding Sports Worldwide,** 425 Meadow St., P.O. Box 901, Chicopee, MA 01021: Free list of retail sources ◆ Clothing, gloves, shoes, socks, sweatbands, bags, balls, and racquets. 800-225-6601. www.spalding.com

**Wa-Mac Inc.,** P.O. Box 128, Carlstadt, NJ 07410: Free information ◆ Gloves, socks, sweat bands, balls, bags, eye guards, and racquets. 800-447-5673; 201-438-7200 (in NJ).

### Equipment

**Allsop,** P.O. Box 23, Bellingham, WA 98227: Free information ◆ Racquetball equipment. 800-426-4303; 360-734-9090 (in WA).

**Austad's,** Hanover Direct Pennsylvania Inc., Hanover, PA 17333-0001: Free catalog ◆ Racquetball and other sports equipment. 717-633-3333.

**Bauer Sports,** 150 Ocean Rd., Greenland, NH 03840: Free list of retail sources ◆ Balls, racquets, and eye guards. 800-362-3146. www.bauer.com

**Brine Inc.,** 47 Sumner St., Milford, MA 01757: Free information ◆ Bags, balls, and grips. 800-227-2722; 508-478-3250 (in MA).

**H.D. Brown Enterprise Ltd.,** 23 Beverly St. East, St. George, Ontario, Canada N0E 1N0: Free information ◆ Gloves, racquets, and other equipment. 519-448-1381.

**Carron Net Company,** 1623 17th St., P.O. Box 177, Two Rivers, WI 54241: Free information ◆ Archery, baseball, basketball, gymnasium and climbing, football, racquetball, soccer, tennis, and volleyball equipment. 800-558-7768; 414-793-2217 (in WI). sales@carronnet.com

**Century Sports Inc.,** Lakewood Industrial Park, 1995 Rutgers University Blvd., Box 2035, Lakewood, NJ 08701: Free information ◆ Gloves, racquets, and other equipment. 800-526-7548; 732-905-4422 (in NJ).

**Ektelon,** Prince Sports Group, 1 Sportsystem Plaza, Bordentown, NJ 08505: Free information ◆ Bags and balls, racquets, eye guards, thongs, clothing and gloves, socks, and sweatbands. 800-283-2635. www.princetennis.com

**Faber Brothers,** 4141 S. Pulaski Rd., Chicago, IL 60632: Free information ◆ Balls, bags, and racquets. 773-376-9300.

**Grid Inc.,** NDL Products Inc., 4031 NE 12th Terrace, Oakland Park, FL 33334: Free information ◆ Racquetball equipment. 800-843-3021.

**Holabird Sports Discounters,** 9220 Pulaski Hwy., Baltimore, MD 21220: Free catalog ◆ Equipment and clothing for basketball, tennis, running, and jogging, golf, exercising, racquetball, and other sports. 410-687-6400. www.holabirdsports.com

**Charlie Johnson's Tennis & Squash Shop,** 2648 Erie Ave., Cincinnati, OH 45208: Free information ◆ Racquets, shoes, strings, and grips. 800-222-1143. cjtennis@cinti.net

**M.W. Kasch Company,** 5401 W. Donges Bay Rd., Mequon, WI 53092: Free information ◆ Bags, balls, and racquets. 414-242-5000.

**Las Vegas Discount Golf & Tennis,** 5325 S. Valley View Blvd., Ste. 10, Las Vegas, NV 89118: Free catalog ◆ Equipment, shoes, and clothing for tennis, racquetball, golf, running, and jogging. 702-798-5500. www.lvgolf.com

**Leisure Marketing Inc.,** 2204 Morris Ave., Ste. 202, Union, NJ 07083: Free information ◆ Bags and racquets. 908-851-9494.

**Markwort Sporting Goods,** 4300 Forest Park Ave., St. Louis, MO 63108: Catalog $8 (request list of retail sources) ◆ Gloves, racquets, and other equipment. 800-669-6626; 314-652-3757 (in MO).

**New Tech Tennis,** P.O. Box 201896, Austin, TX 78720: Free catalog ◆ Racquetball accessories. 800-577-1916; 512-250-8417 (in TX).

**Penn Racquet Sports,** 306 S. 45th Ave., Phoenix, AZ 85043: Free information ◆ Gloves, racquets, and other equipment. 800-289-7366; 602-269-1492 (in AZ).

**Prince Racquet Sports,** 1 Sport Systems Plaza, Bordentown, NJ 08505: Free information ◆ Gloves, racquets, and other equipment. 800-2-TENNIS; 609-291-5900 (in NJ).

**Professional Golf & Tennis Suppliers,** 7825 Hollywood Blvd., Pembroke Pines, FL 33024: Free catalog with long SASE ◆ Racquetball equipment. 305-981-7283.

**Puma USA Inc.,** 147 Centre St., Brockton, MA 02403: Free information with long SASE ◆ Balls and bags. 800-662-7862. www.puma.com

**Spalding Sports Worldwide,** 425 Meadow St., P.O. Box 901, Chicopee, MA 01021: Free list of retail sources ◆ Bags, balls, and racquets. 800-225-6601. www.spalding.com

**Sportime,** Customer Service, 1 Sportime Way, Atlanta, GA 30340: Free information ◆ Racquets and other equipment. 800-444-5700; 770-449-5700 (in GA).

**Wa-Mac Inc.,** P.O. Box 128, Carlstadt, NJ 07410: Free information ◆ Balls, bags, eye guards, and racquets. 800-447-5673; 201-438-7200 (in NJ).

**Wilson Sporting Goods,** 8700 W. Bryn Mawr, Chicago, IL 60631: Free information ◆ Bags, balls, and racquets. 800-946-6060; 773-714-6400 (in IL). www.wilsonsports.com

# RADIOS

## Amateur Radio Equipment

**Ack Radio Supply Company,** 3101 4th Ave. South, Birmingham, AL 35233: Free information ◆ Amateur radio equipment. 800-338-4218; 205-322-0588 (in AL).

**Advanced Specialties,** 114 Essex St., Lodi, NJ 07644: Free information ◆ Amateur radio equipment, books, and accessories. 201-843-2067.

**Alpha Delta Communications Inc.,** P.O. Box 620, Manchester, KY 40962: Free information ◆ Antennas. 716-598-2029.

**Aluma Tower Company,** P.O. Box 2806, Vero Beach, FL 32961: Free catalog ◆ Telescoping crank-up, guyed stack-up, tilt-over, roof-top, and mobile antenna towers. 561-567-3423. www.alumatower.com

**Amateur & Advanced Communications,** 3208 Concord Pike, Rt. 202, Wilmington, DE 19803: Free information with long SASE ◆ Amateur radio equipment. 302-478-2757.

**Amateur Electronic Supply,** 5710 W. Good Hope Rd., Milwaukee, WI 53223: Free information ◆ Amateur radio equipment. 800-558-0411; 414-358-0333 (in WI). www.aesham.com

**American Radio Relay League,** 225 Main St., Newington, CT 06111: Free information ◆ Books on how to become a HAM radio operator, get a license, learn Morse code, organize equipment, set up a station, and other information. 888-277-5289; 860-594-0250 (in CT). www.arrl.org

**Ameritron,** 116 Willow Rd., Starkville, MS 39759: Free list of retail sources ◆ Radio amateur equipment. 800-647-1800. www.ameritron.com

**Antenna Supermarket,** 138 S. Walnut, Palatine, IL 60067: Free information ◆ Antennas and accessories. 847-359-7092.

**Associated Radio,** Box 4327, Overland Park, KS 66204: Catalog $3 ◆ New and used equipment. 913-381-5900. www.associatedradio.com

**Astron Corp.,** 9 Autry, Irvine, CA 92718: Free information ◆ Power supplies. 714-458-7277.

**Austin Amateur Radio Supply,** 5325 North I-35, Austin, TX 78723: Free information ◆ Amateur radio equipment. 800-423-2604; 512-454-2994 (in TX).

**Barry Electronics Corp.,** 540 Broadway, New York, NY 10012: Free information ◆ Amateur, professional, and commercial electronics equipment. 212-925-7000.

**Base Station Inc.,** 1839 East St., Concord, CA 94520: Free information ◆ Amateur radio equipment. 510-685-7388.

**Bencher Inc.,** 831 N. Central Ave., Wood Dale, IL 60191: Free information ◆ Versatile multi-band vertical antennas. 773-282-8787. www.bencher.com

**Bilal Company,** 137 Manchester Dr., Florissant, CO 80816: Free catalog ◆ Antennas. 719-687-0650.

**Burghardt Amateur Center,** 182 N. Maple, P.O. Box 73, Watertown, SD 57201: Free information ◆ Amateur radio equipment. 800-927-4261; 605-886-7314 (in SD).

**Burk Electronics,** 35 N. Kensington, LaGrange, IL 60525: Free information ◆ Amateur radio equipment. 708-482-9310.

**Wayne Carroll QSL Cards,** P.O. Box 73, Monetta, SC 29105: Free information ◆ QSL cards. 803-685-7117.

**Comm-Pute Inc.,** 7946 S. State St., Midvale, UT 84047: Free information ◆ Amateur radio equipment. 800-942-8873; 801-567-9944 (in UT).

**Communications Electronics Inc.,** P.O. Box 1045, Ann Arbor, MI 48106: Free information ◆ Scanners, transceivers, and emergency broadcast, weather station, monitoring, and other electronics. 800-USA-SCAN. www.usascan.com

**Communication Headquarters Inc.,** 3832 Oleander Dr., Wilmington, NC 28403: Free information ◆ Equipment and accessories. 800-688-0073.

**Copper Electronics Inc.,** 3315 Gilmore Industrial Blvd., Louisville, KY 40213: Free information ◆ Amateur radio equipment. 800-626-6343. www.igla.com/copper

**C. Crane Company,** 558 10th St., Fortuna, CA 95540: Free catalog ◆ Short and long wave radio equipment, scanners, books, weather equipment, and other accessories. 800-522-8863.

**Crystek Corp.,** 2351 Crystal Dr., Fort Myers, FL 33907: Free information ◆ Crystals for radio operation and electronics experimenters. 941-936-2109.

**Cushcraft,** P.O. Box 4680, 48 Perimeter Rd., Manchester, NH 03108: Free list of retail sources ◆ Antennas. 603-627-7877. hamsales@cushcraft.com

**Dan's Small Parts & Kits,** Box 3634, Missoula, MT 59806: Free information ◆ Amateur radio parts and electronic kits. 406-258-2782. www.fix.net/dans.html

**Dentronics,** 6102 Deland Rd., Flushing, MI 48433: Free information ◆ Amateur radio equipment. 810-659-1776.

**Doc's QSL Cards,** 8208 Broken Arrow Trail, Knoxville, TN 37923: Free price list and samples with long SASE ◆ Custom designed QSL cards. 800-430-5046; 423-693-8810 (in TN). user.icx.net/~docs

**Down East Microwave,** 954 Rt. 519, Frenchtown, NJ 08825: Free catalog ◆ Microwave antennas and other equipment. 908-996-3584. www.downeastmicrowave.com

**R.L. Drake Company,** 230 Industrial Dr., Franklin, OH 45005: Free information ◆ World band communications receivers and other shortwave equipment. 800-937-2534. www.rldrake.com

**Electronic Distributors,** 325 Mill St. NE, Vienna, VA 22180: Catalog $2 ◆ Antennas, roof towers, rotators, and other accessories. 703-938-8105.

**Electronix Express,** 365 Blair Rd., Avenel, NJ 07001: Free information ◆ Parts, test equipment, and tools. 800-972-2225; 908-381-8020 (in NJ). www.elexp.com

**Equipment Ltd.,** P.O. Box 9, Oak Lawn, IL 60454: Free catalog ◆ Mobile equipment mounts. 708-423-0605. iix@interaccess.com

**GAP Antenna Products,** 99 N. Willow St., Fellsmere, FL 32948: Free information ◆ Antennas for amateur and commercial use. 561-571-9922. gap@gapantenna.com

**Gateway Electronics,** 8123 Page Blvd., St. Louis, MO 63130: Free information ◆ New and surplus electronics equipment. 314-427-6116. www.gatewayelex.com

**Gilfer Shortwave,** 52 Park Ave., Park Ridge, NJ 07656: Free information ◆ Shortwave radio equipment. 800-GILFER-1; 201-391-7887 (in NJ).

**Grove Enterprises Inc.,** 7540 Hwy. 64 West, Brasstown, NC 28902: Free information ◆ Scanners, shortwave receivers, accessories, monitoring software, antennas, books, and more. 800-438-8155. www.grove-ent.com

**Jo Gunn Enterprises,** Hwy. 82, Box 32-C, Ethelsville, AL 35461: Catalog $2 ◆ Mobile antennas and other electronics equipment. 205-658-2229.

**Ham Radio Outlet,** 933 N. Euclid St., Anaheim, CA 92801: Catalog $1 ◆ Antennas and towers, power supplies, radio amateur communications equipment, books, and other publications. 800-854-6046; 714-533-7373 (in CA). www.hamradio.com

**Ham Radio Toy Store,** 117 W. Wesley St., Wheaton, IL 60187: Free information ◆ Amateur radio equipment. 630-668-9577.

**Ham Station,** 220 N. Fulton Ave., Evansville, IN 47719: Free information with long SASE ◆ New and used amateur radio equipment. 800-729-4373; 812-422-0231 (in IN). www.hamstation.com

**The Ham Store,** 10815 Gulfdale St., San Antonio, TX 78216: Free information ◆ Ham radio equipment. 800-344-3144.

**Hamtronics,** 65 Moul Rd., Hilton, NY 14468: Free catalog ◆ Amateur radio equipment. 716-392-9430. www.hamtronics.com

**Hardin Electronics,** 5635 E. Rosedale St., Fort Worth, TX 76112: Free information ◆ Amateur radio equipment. 800-433-3203; 817-429-9761 (in TX).

**Hatry Electronics,** 500 Ledyard St., Hartford, CT 06114: Free information ◆ Amateur radio equipment. 860-296-1881.

**High Sierra Antennas,** Box 2389, Nevada City, CA 95959: Free information ◆ HF antennas. 916-273-3415. www.hsantennas.com/info

**ICOM America,** 2380 116th Ave. NE, Bellevue, WA 98004: Free list of retail sources ◆ Amateur radio and single-side-band equipment. 800-999-9877. www.icomamerica.com

**Jun's Electronics,** 5563 Sepulveda Blvd., Culver City, CA 90230: Free information ◆ Scanners, amateur and marine radio equipment, and cellular mobile phones. 800-882-1343; 562-390-8003 (in CA). www.juns.com

**Kanga US,** Bill Kelsey N8ET, 3521 Spring Lake Dr., Findlay, OH 45840: Free catalog ◆ Ham equipment kits. 419-423-4604.

**Kantronics,** 1202 E. 23rd St., Lawrence, KS 66046: Free information ◆ Amateur and professional radio equipment. 785-842-7745. www.kantronics.com

**Kenwood,** P.O. Box 22745, Long Beach, CA 90801: Free information ◆ Amateur radio equipment. 310-639-9000. www.kenwood.net

**KLM Antennas Inc.,** 14792 172nd Dr. SE, #1, Monroe, WA 98272: Free catalog ◆ Amateur antennas and accessories. 360-794-2923. www.klm-antennas.com

**Larsen Antennas,** 3611 NE 112th Ave., P.O. Box 1799, Vancouver, WA 98668: Free list of retail sources ◆ High-performance antennas. 800-426-1656; 360-944-7551 (in WA).

**LaRue Electronics,** 1112 Grandview St., Scranton, PA 18509: Free information ◆ Amateur radio equipment. 717-343-2124.

**Lentini Communications Inc.,** 21 Garfield St., Newington, CT 06111: Free information ◆ Shortwave radios, scanners, and other equipment. 800-666-0908; 860-666-6227 (in CT). www.lentinicomm.com

**M2 Enterprises,** 7560 N. Del Mar Ave., Fresno, CA 93711: Free information ◆ Antennas, accessories, and rotators. 209-432-3059. www.minc.com

**Madison Electronics Supply,** 12310 Zavalla St., Houston, TX 77085: Free information ◆ Hard-to-find parts and other equipment for amateur radio operation and electronics hobbyists. 800-231-3057; 713-729-7300 (in TX).

**Maggiore Electronic Lab,** 600 Westtown Rd., West Chester, PA 19382: Free catalog ◆ Amateur and professional radio equipment. 610-436-6051.

**Maryland Radio Center,** 3394 Fort Meade Rd., Laurel, MD 20724: Free information ◆ Amateur radio equipment. 301-725-1212. www.weathernode.com

**Memphis Amateur Electronics,** 1465 Wells Station Rd., Memphis, TN 38108: Free information ◆ Amateur radio equipment. 800-238-6168; 901-683-9125 (in TN).

**MFJ Ham Radio Accessories,** P.O. Box 494, Mississippi State, MS 39762: Free catalog ◆ Ham radio accessories. 800-647-1800. www.mfjenterprises.com

**Michigan Radio,** 23040 Schoenherr, Warren, MI 48089: Free information ◆ Amateur radio base station and other equipment. 800-878-4266; 810-771-4711 (in MI0. www.michiganradio.com

**Mirage Communications Equipment,** 300 Industrial Park Rd., Starkville, MS 39759: Free list of retail sources ◆ Radio amateur equipment. 601-323-8287. www.mirageamp.com

**Mobile Mark Inc.,** 3900 River Rd., Schiller Park, IL 60176: Free information ◆ Easy-to-mount mobile and window antennas. 847-671-6690.

**Mosley Electronics,** 10812 Ambassador Blvd., St. Louis, MO 63132: Free information ◆ HF, VHF, and UHF beam antennas, dipoles, and mobiles. 800-966-7539; 314-994-7872 (in MO). www.mosley-electronics.com

**Oklahoma Comm Center,** 13424 Railway Dr., Oklahoma City, OK 73114: Free information ◆ Amateur radio equipment. 800-765-4267; 405-748-3066 (in OK).

**Omni Electronics,** 1007 San Dario, Laredo, TX 78040: Free information ◆ Amateur radio equipment and antennas. 210-722-5195.

**Palomar,** Box 462222, Escondido, CA 92046: Free catalog ◆ Radio amateur equipment. 760-747-3343. Palomar@compuserve.com

**Portland Radio Supply,** 7276 SW Beaverton Hillsdale, Portland, OR 97225: Free information ◆ New and used amateur radio equipment. 503-233-4904.

**R & L Electronics,** 1315 Maple Ave., Hamilton, OH 45011: Free catalog ◆ Amateur radio equipment and antennas. 800-221-7735; 513-868-6399 (in OH). sales@randl.com

**Radio Adventures Inc.,** Main St., Seneca, PA 16346: Free information ◆ HF receiver and transmitter kits, test equipment kits, and radio accessories. 814-677-7221.

**RF Parts,** 435 S. Pacific St., San Marcos, CA 92069: Free information ◆ Antennas, power transistors, and other parts for amateur, marine, and commercial radio operation. 760-744-0700. rfp@rfparts.com

**Rivendell Electronics,** 8 Londonderry Rd., Derry, NH 03038: Free information ◆ Amateur radio equipment. 603-434-5371.

**Surplus Sales of Nebraska,** 1502 Jones St., Omaha, NE 68102: Catalog $5 ◆ Hard-to-find electronic parts. 402-346-4750. www.surplussales.com

**Telex/Hy-Gain Communications Inc.,** 8601 E. Cornhusker Hwy., Lincoln, NE 68505: Free information ◆ Antennas and rotators. 402-467-5321. www.telex.com

**Ten-Tec Inc.,** 1185 Dolly Parton Pkwy., Sevierville, TN 37862: Free catalog ◆ Ham radio kits. 800-833-7373; 423-453-7172 (in TN). sales@tentec.com

**Texas Towers,** 1108 Summit Ave., Ste. 4, Plano, TX 75074: Free information ◆ Antennas, towers, rotators, and other equipment. 972-422-7306. www.TexasTowers.com

**Tri-Ex Tower Corp.,** 7182 Rasmussen Ave., Visalia, CA 93291: Free information ◆ Antenna towers for amateur radio operation. 209-651-7850. www.tri-ex.com

**Tucker Electronics,** P.O. Box 551419, Dallas, TX 75355: Free information ◆ Shortwave receivers, scanners, antennas, and other electronic equipment. 800-527-4642; 972-348-8800 (in TX). www.tucker.com

**Universal Radio Inc.,** 6830 Americana Pkwy., Reynoldsburg, OH 43068: Free catalog ◆ Equipment for amateur radio operators, shortwave listeners, and scanner enthusiasts. 800-431-3939; 614-866-4267 (in OH). www.universal-radio.com

**Vectronics,** 1007 Hwy. 25 S., Starkville, MS 39759: Free information ◆ Amateur radio equipment. www.vectronics.com

**W & W Associates,** 800 S. Broadway, Hicksville, NY 11801: Free catalog ◆ Batteries and chargers. 800-221-0732; 516-942-0011 (in NY). www.wwassociates.com

**Wilson Antenna Inc.,** 1181 Grier Dr., Ste. A, Las Vegas, NV 89119: Free information ◆ Citizen band and mobile antennas. 800-541-6116.

**Yaesu USA,** 17210 Edwards Rd., Cerritos, CA 90701: Free information ◆ Amateur radio base station equipment. 562-404-2700. www.yaesu.com

**E.H. Yost & Company,** 2211-D Parview Rd., Middleton, WI 53562: Free catalog ◆ Batteries for radios, computers, and other equipment. 608-631-3443. ehyost@midplains.net

### Antique Radios & Repairs

**Alltronics,** 2300 Zanker Rd., San Jose, CA 95131: Catalog $3 ◆ Tubes and other components. 408-943-9773. www.alltronics.com

**Antique Electronic Supply,** 6221 S. Maple St., Tempe, AZ 85238: Catalog $2 ◆ Hard-to-find tubes, parts, and literature for antique radio restoration and repair. 602-820-5411. www.tubesandmore.com

**The Antique Radio Store,** 8376 La Mesa Blvd., La Mesa, CA 91941: Free list with long SASE ◆ Tubes. 619-668-5653.

**ARS Electronics,** 7110 Decelis Pl., Van Nuys, CA 91406: Catalog $2.50 ◆ Electronics equipment and tubes. 800-422-4250.

**Don Diers,** 4276C N. 50th St., Milwaukee, WI 53216: Catalog $3 ◆ Tubes and parts for antique receivers.

**Electron Tube Enterprises,** Box 8311, Essex, VT 05451: Free catalog ◆ Tubes. 802-879-1844.

**Electronics Emporium Inc.,** 107 Trumbull St., Elizabeth, NJ 07206: Free information ◆ Tubes. 800-653-8823.

**The Olde Tyme Radio Company,** 2445 Lyttonsville Rd., Ste. 317, Silver Spring, MD 20910: Free information with long SASE and two 1st class stamps ◆ Antique radios, parts, tubes, and schematics. 301-587-5280.

**Play Things of the Past,** 9511 Sunrise Blvd., Cleveland, OH 44133: Catalog $6 ◆ Antique radio parts, books, and magazines. 216-251-3714.

**Preller TV,** 208 South 2nd St., Augusta, AR 72006: List $1 ◆ Radio and TV tubes, from 1927 to 1977. 501-347-2281.

**PTI Antique Radios,** 7925 Mabelvale Cutoff, Mabelvale, AR 72103: Free information ◆ Antique radio restoration parts. 501-568-1995.

**Radio Electric Supply,** 1298 SE 5th Ave., Melrose, FL 32666: Free price list ◆ Receiving and special purpose tubes. 352-475-1950. www.vacuumtubes.net

**The Radio Man,** P.O. Box 461485, Garland, TX 75046: Free information ◆ Antique radios, tubes, and parts. 972-276-5458.

**Radio-O-Rama,** Mike Stute, 2140 Sequoyah Way, Carrollton, TX 75006: Free catalog ◆ Antique radios and watches from the United States and other worldwide sources. 972-242-1271. www.worldwidewatches.com

**Radiomania Catalog,** Mark V. Stein, 2109 Carterdale Rd., Baltimore, MD 21209: Catalog $5 ◆ Collectible antique radios. 410-466-2814. www.machineage.com/radiomania

**A.G. Tannenbaum,** P.O. Box 386, Ambler, PA 19002: Free catalog ◆ Repair parts. 215-540-8055. www.agtannenbaum.com

### Citizen Band Equipment & Transceivers

**Alinco Electronics Inc.,** 438 Amapola Ave., Torrance, CA 90501: Free information ◆ Handheld transceivers and desktops. 310-618-8616. www.alinco.com

**Cobra,** 6500 W. Cortland St., Chicago, IL 60707: Free information ◆ Fixed-installation and portable citizen band radios. 800-COBRA-22.

**Copper Electronics Inc.,** 3315 Gilmore Industrial Blvd., Louisville, KY 40213: Free catalog ◆ Citizen band radios and accessories. 502-968-8500. www.igla.com/copper

**Firestik Antenna Company,** 2614 E. Adams, Phoenix, AZ 85034: Free catalog ◆ Citizen band antennas and accessories. 602-273-7151. www.firestik.com

**Furuno USA,** 271 Harbor Way, South San Francisco, CA 94083: Free information ◆ Transceivers. 415-873-9393. www.FurunoUSA.com

**Ham Radio Outlet,** 933 N. Euclid St., Anaheim, CA 92801: Catalog $1 ◆ Antennas and towers, power supplies, radio amateur communications equipment, books, and other publications. 800-854-6046; 714-533-7373 (in CA). www.hamradio.com

**ICOM America,** 2380 116th Ave. NE, Bellevue, WA 98004: Free list of retail sources ◆ Handheld transceivers. 206-450-6088. www.icomamerica.com

**Japan Radio Company Ltd.,** 430 Park Ave., 2nd Floor, New York, NY 10022: Free information ◆ Transceivers. 212-355-1180.

**K-40 Electronics,** 1500 Executive Dr., Elgin, IL 60123: Free brochure ◆ Citizen band radios and antennas. 800-323-5608. www.k40.com

**Nady Systems,** 6701 Bay St., Emeryville, CA 94608: Free information ◆ UHF and VHF handheld transceivers. 510-652-2411. www.nadywireless.com

**PageCom,** 11545 Pagemill Rd., Dallas, TX 75243: Free information ◆ Portable outdoor two-way radio. 800-527-1670.

**Radio Shack,** Division Tandy Corp., One Tandy Center, Fort Worth, TX 76102: Free information ◆ Portable and fixed installation citizen band radios, electronics components, science kits, computers and accessories, stereo equipment, and toys and games. 817-390-3011. www.radioshack.com

**Transcrypt International Inc.,** 4800 NW 1st St., Lincoln, NE 68521: Free information ◆ Portable and handheld two-way radios. 800-228-0226. www.transcrypt.com

**Wilson Antenna Inc.,** 1181 Grier Dr., Ste. A, Las Vegas, NV 89119: Free information ◆ Citizen band and mobile antennas. 800-541-6116.

## RADON TESTING

**Air Check Inc.,** Box 2000, Naples, NC 28760: Free brochure ◆ Radon test kits and monitors. 800-247-2435; 704-684-0893 (in NC).

**First Alert,** 780 McClure Rd., Aurora, IL 60404: Free information ◆ Radon detectors. 800-323-9005.

**Heads Up Products,** P.O. Box 8629, St. Louis, MO 63126: Free information ◆ Easy-to-use radon testing accessories. 800-496-2144.

**Priorities,** 70 Walnut St., Wellesley, MA 02181: Free catalog ◆ Radon alarms. 800-553-5398. getrelief@priorities.com

## RAFTING & WHITEWATER RUNNING

**Cascade Outfitters,** P.O. Box 209, Springfield, OR 97477: Free catalog ◆ Rafts, kayaks, touring kayaks, and accessories. 800-223-7238. Casout565@aol.com

**Colorado Kayak,** P.O. Box 1, Nathrop, CO 81236: Free catalog ◆ Paddles, other equipment, and clothing. 888-265-2925. www.coloradokayakusa.com

**Easy Rider Canoe & Kayak Company,** P.O. Box 88108, Seattle, WA 98138: Catalog $5 ◆ Whitewater and sea cruising paddles, single and double-seat kayaks and canoes, and rowing trainers. 206-228-3633.

**Hyside Inflatables,** P.O. Box Z, Kernville, CA 93238: Free information ◆ River running inflatable rafts, self-bailing kayaks, and other equipment. 800-868-5987.

**Mitchell Paddles Inc.,** RD 2, P.O. Box 922, Canaan, NH 03741: Free information ◆ Canoe and kayak paddles, boats, and dry suits. 603-523-7004.

**Nantahala Outdoor Center,** 13077 Hwy. 19 West, Bryson City, NC 28713: Free catalog ◆ Equipment for whitewater paddling. 800-367-3521. www.nocweb.com

**Northwest River Supplies Inc.,** 2009 S. Main, Moscow, ID 83843: Free catalog ◆ Rafts, waterproof bags, paddles, boats, and supplies. 800-635-5202. nrs@moscow.com

**Wyoming River Raiders,** P.O. Box 50490, Casper, WY 82605: Free catalog ◆ Outdoor clothing, camping and river expedition equipment, fishing gear, hiking equipment, books, and other supplies. 800-247-6068. www.riverraiders.com

## RECYCLED & ENVIRONMENTALLY SAFE PRODUCTS

**Atlantic Recycled Paper Company,** 20 Winters Ln., Catonsville, MD 21228: Free catalog ◆ Office and restroom paper supplies. 800-323-2811; 410-747-7314 (in MD).

**Basically Natural,** 109 East G St., Brunswick, MD 21716: Free information ◆ Household cleaners, cosmetics, and pet and personal care products. 800-352-7099. Basnatural@msn.com

**Blue Dolphin,** 1920 Abrams Pkwy., #416, Dallas, TX 75214: Free catalog ◆ Recycled paper and re-engineered toner cartridges for copiers, laser printers, and plain paper fax machines. 800-932-7715.

**Clothcrafters Inc.,** P.O. Box 176, Elkhart Lake, WI 53020: Free catalog ◆ Reusable kitchen supplies and cotton bags, 100 percent cotton diapers, and other environmentally sensitive products. 800-876-2009; 920-876-2112 (in WI). www.clothcrafters.com

**Conservatree Paper Company,** 10 Lombard St., Ste. 200, San Francisco, CA 94111: Free information ◆ Recycled paper products. 415-433-1000.

**Earth Care,** 555 Leslie St., Ukiah, CA 95482: Free catalog ◆ Recycled paper products, environmental gifts, and household goods. 800-992-7747.

**Natural Resources Mail Order,** 6680 Harvard Dr., Sebastopol, CA 95472: Free information ◆ Natural cleansing products. 800-747-0390; 707-823-4340 (in CA).

**Nature's Backyard Inc.,** 585 State Rd., North Dartmouth, MA 02747: Free brochure ◆ Easy-to-assemble and use composter. Also other garden products made from recycled plastic. 800-853-2525. www.naturesbackyard.com

**Seventh Generation,** 1 Mill St., Burlington, VT 05401: Free catalog ◆ Household products and decorative accessories for the environmental enthusiast. 800-456-1177.

**Simmons Natural Bodycare,** 42295 Hwy. 36, Bridgeville, CA 95526: Catalog $1 ◆ Natural products for home and personal care. 800-428-0412; 707-777-1920 (in CA). www.akamaiddesign.com/Simmons

## ROCKS, MINERALS & FOSSILS

### Display Cases, Stands, & Lights

**Cabinets by Vector,** 64956 Lutz Rd., Constantine, MI 49092: Free catalog ◆ Specimen storage cabinets. 616-651-3823.

**Collector Case Company,** P.O. Box 126, Jeffersonville, KY 40337: Free information ◆ Display cases. 800-553-5294; 606-873-3569 (in KY).

**Lustig International,** P.O. Box 2051, San Leandro, CA 94577: Free information ◆ Display stands and mineral specimens. 800-221-4456; 510-351-4444 (in CA).

**National Showcase Company Inc.,** 724 York Rd., Towson, MD 21204: Free catalog ◆ Velvet-lined showcases, with handles and locks. 800-628-2352.

**Sylmar Display Stands,** P.O. Box 362, Youngtown, AZ 85363: Free catalog ◆ Display stands. 602-933-7301.

**Venus Displays,** 10713 Ashby Ave., Los Angeles, CA 90064: Free information ◆ Blocks, platforms, easels, and boxes; stands for minerals, shells, and crystals; and jewelry and counter displays. 800-870-5633; 310-836-3177 (in CA).

### Fossils

**Ackley's Rock & Stamps,** 3230 N. Stone Ave., Colorado Springs, CO 80907: Catalog $1 ◆ Fossils, lapidary and silversmithing supplies, jewelry boxes and trays, mountings, and findings. 719-633-1153.

**Antiquarian Fossils Inc.,** 3217 Patton Way, Bakersfield, CA 93308: Free catalog ◆ Full-size museum-quality fossil skulls, molded directly from originals. 800-249-5512. feedback@fossils.com

**Art By God,** 3705 Biscayne Blvd., Miami, FL 33137: Free information ◆ Rocks, minerals, and fossils. 800-940-4449.

**Hal Bach's Rock Shop,** 137 Marne Rd., Cheektowage, NY 14215: Free information ◆ Fossils, minerals, and rock specimens. 800-568-6888.

**Bitner's,** 42 W. Hatcher, Phoenix, AZ 85021: Free information ◆ Rocks, minerals, and fossils. 800-248-6377; 602-870-0075 (in AZ).

**The Bone Room,** 1569 Solano Ave., Berkeley, CA 94707: Free brochure ◆ Complete animal skeletons, skulls, insects, fossil casts, and animal remnants. 510-526-5252. www.boneroom.com

**Bourget Bros.,** 1636 11th St., Santa Monica, CA 90404: Catalog $3 ◆ Fossils, gemstones, cabochons, wax patterns, beads, and bead-stringing and jewelry-making supplies. 800-828-3024. www.bourgetbros.com

**Caddo Trading,** Box 669, Murfreesboro, AR 71958: Free list ◆ Native American artifacts, minerals, and fossils.

**Dino Productions,** P.O. Box 3004, Englewood, CO 80155: Free catalog ◆ Fossils, rocks and minerals, ecology and oceanography equipment, and supplies for chemistry, general science, astronomy, and biology. 303-741-1587. www.dinoproductions.com

**Discount Agate House,** 3401 N. Dodge, Tucson, AZ 85716: Free information ◆ Rocks, minerals, and fossils. 520-323-0781.

**Earthworks,** P.O. Box 2067, Round Rock, TX 78680: Catalog $1 (refundable) ◆ Minerals, fossils, meteorites, books, supplies, and gifts. 800-255-8121; 512-255-2844 (in TX).

**Ebersole Lapidary Supply Inc.,** 11417 West Hwy. 54, Wichita, KS 67209: Catalog $5 ◆ Fossils, petrified wood and rock specimens, tools, jewelry findings and kits, mountings, and cabochons. 316-722-4771.

**Everything Prehistoric,** 217 Main St., P.O. Box 643, Hill City, SD 57745: Free information ◆ Cretaceous ammonites, eocene fishes, oligocene mammals, dinosaurs, and other fossils. 605-574-4289.

**Extinctions,** P.O. Box 7, Clarita, OK 74535: Free catalog ◆ Trilobites, crinoids, vertebrates, ferns, and other museum and collector fossils. 405-428-3220.

**Geological Enterprises Inc.,** P.O. Box 996, Ardmore, OK 73402: Catalog $5 ◆ Museum-quality specimens. 405-223-8537.

**Jeanne's Rock & Jewelry,** 5420 Bissonet, Bellaire, TX 77401: Price list $1 ◆ Petrified wood products, fossils, seashells, lapidary supplies, and gifts. 713-664-2988.

**Lou-Bon Gems & Rocks,** Lake Barcroft Plaza, 6341 Columbia Pike, Bailey's Crossroads, VA 22041: Free information ◆ Carvings, beads, mineral specimens, fossils, shells, and lapidary and jeweler's equipment. 703-256-1084.

**Minerals Unlimited,** P.O. Box 877, Ridgecrest, CA 93556: Catalog $2 ◆ Rocks, minerals, and fossils. 760-375-5279.

**The Natural Canvas,** 1624 Noe Ave., Ste. 1210, San Mateo, CA 94401: Catalog $3 (refundable) ◆ Unusual and extraordinary fossils. 415-345-3692.

**Omni Resources,** 1004 S. Mebane St., P.O. Box 2096, Burlington, NC 27216: Free catalog ◆ Fossils, rocks, hiking and topography maps, and globes. 800-742-2677. custserv@omnimap.com

**Paleo-Educational Products,** Box 1002, Salmon, ID 83467: Free list ◆ Museum-quality fossils. 208-894-2421.

**PaleoSearch Inc.,** P.O. Box 621, Hays, KS 67601: Catalog $3 ◆ Fossils, educational posters, and rare reproductions. 913-625-2240.

**Potomac Museum Group,** 3730 Toledo Ave. North, Robbinsdale, MN 55422: Free catalog ◆ Rare specimen reproductions. 612-524-0421.

**Second Nature,** P.O. Box 45, New Prague, MN 56071: Information $1 ◆ Museum-quality prehistoric fossil reproductions. 800-815-3466.

**Skullduggery,** 624 South B St., Tustin, CA 92680: Free information ◆ Natural history gifts, fossil replicas, and creative educational kits for home and classroom. 800-336-7745. www.skullduggery.com

**Southeastern Fossil Supply Company,** 1205 N. Eastman Rd., Ste. 209, Kingsport, TN 37664: Free catalog ◆ Fossils, mineral collections, teaching aids, gemstones, artifacts, and antiquities. 800-688-6721.

**StrataGraphics,** 5565 E. Henrietta Rd., Rush, NY 14543: Catalog $1 ◆ Fish, mammals, reptiles, other vertebrates, and petrified wood and plant specimens. 716-533-2301.

**Taylor Studios,** P.O. Box 1063, Mahomet, IL 61853: Catalog $3 ◆ Museum-quality cast reproductions of fossils. 217-586-2047.

**Two Guys Minerals & Fossils,** 1 Lynnes Way, East Bridgewater, MA 02333: Catalog $2 ◆ Rocks, minerals, and fossils. Also fossil reproductions. 800-FOSSILS. www.twoguysfossils.com

**Warfield Fossil Quarries,** HCR 61, P.O. Box 301, Thayne, WY 83127: Catalog $2 ◆ Fish, leaves, turtles, reptiles, trilobites, ammonites, and other fossils. 307-883-2445.

**What on Earth Naturally,** 6250 Busch Blvd., Columbus, OH 43229: Free information ◆ Minerals, fossils, jewelry, gemstones, and shells. 614-436-1458.

## Meteorites

**Bethany Sciences,** P.O. Box 3726, New Haven, CT 06525: Catalog $2 ◆ Stony-iron meteorites, display stands, jewelry, and books. 203-393-3395. bethanysci@aol.com

**Michael Blood,** 6106 Kerch St., San Diego, CA 92115: Free catalog ◆ Meteorites.

**Michael I. Casper,** Meteorites, Drawer J, Ithaca, NY 14851: Free information ◆ Meteorites. www.meteorites.com

**Earthworks,** P.O. Box 2067, Round Rock, TX 78680: Catalog $1 (refundable) ◆ Minerals, fossils, meteorites, books, supplies, and gifts. 800-255-8121; 512-255-2844 (in TX).

**Excalibur-Cureton Company,** Division Excalibur Mineral Company, 1000 N. Division St., Peekskill, NY 10566: Catalog $1 ◆ Meteorites and mineral specimens. 914-739-1134.

**Robert Haag Meteorites,** P.O. Box 27527, Tucson, AZ 85726: Catalog $5 ◆ Meteorites. 520-882-8804.

**Jack L. Martinez Meteorites,** 14700 Sunnybank Ave., Bakersfield, CA 93312: Free list with long SASE ◆ Meteorites.

**Mineralogical Research Company,** 15840 E. Alta Vista Way, San Jose, CA 95127: Free list with long SASE and two 1st class stamps ◆ Meteorites, rare mineral specimens, microscopes, micro-mounts, and specimen boxes. 408-923-6800.

**New England Meteoritical Services,** P.O. Box 440, Mendon, MA 01756: Free list ◆ Meteorites. 508-478-4020.

**Rex's Astro Stuff,** 63 Observatory Ln., Dover, AR 72837: Free catalog ◆ Telescopes, binoculars, and accessories. Includes new and used equipment, books, posters, star charts, meteorites, and meteorite jewelry. 501-331-3773.

**Stewart's Petrified Wood,** P.O. Box 68, Holbrook, AZ 86025: Free information ◆ Slabs and tumbled petrified wood. Also meteorites. 800-414-8533. www.petrifiedwood.com

**Ward's Natural Science,** P.O. Box 92912, 5100 W. Henrietta Rd., Rochester, NY 14692: Earth science catalog $10; biology catalog $15; middle school catalog $10 ◆ Meteorites, telescopes, audio-visual aids, and books. 800-962-2660. www.wardsci.com

## Miscellaneous Varieties & Equipment

**Aleta's Rock Shop,** 1515 Plainfield NE, Grand Rapids, MI 49505: Catalog $1.50 ◆ Mineral specimens, rocks for cutting and tumbling, lapidary equipment, and silversmithing supplies. 616-363-5394.

**Allen's Rocks & Gifts,** 26513 Center Ridge Rd., Cleveland, OH 44145: Free information ◆ Minerals, findings, silversmithing supplies, casting and lapidary equipment, and tools. 216-871-6522.

**Arizona Gems & Minerals Inc.,** 6370 East Hwy. 69, Prescott Valley, AZ 86314: Catalog $4 ◆ Geodes, silversmithing and lapidary tools, jewelry-making supplies, and mineral sets. 520-772-6443.

**Arrow Gems & Minerals Inc.,** 9827 Cave Creek Rd., Phoenix, AZ 85020: Free catalog ◆ Pewter figurines, pendants, buckles, bolas, beads, and findings. Also mineral specimens and faceted stones. 602-997-6373.

**Art by God,** 3705 Biscayne Blvd., Miami, FL 33137: Free information ◆ Rocks, minerals, and fossils. 800-940-4449.

**Aurora Mineral Corp.,** 679 S. Ocean Ave., Freeport, NY 11520: Free information ◆ Amethyst, geodes, fossil fishes, quartz crystals, and mineral specimens from around the world. 516-623-3800.

**Bitner's,** 42 W. Hatcher, Phoenix, AZ 85021: Free information ◆ Rocks, minerals, and fossils. 800-248-6377; 602-870-0075 (in AZ).

**Caddo Trading,** Box 669, Murfreesboro, AR 71958: Free list ◆ Native American artifacts, minerals, and fossils.

**Carousel Gems & Minerals,** 1202 Perion Dr., Belen, NM 87002: Price list $1 ◆ Minerals from worldwide locations. 505-864-2145.

**Charlie's Rock Shop,** P.O. Box 399, Penrose, CO 81240: Catalog $3 (refundable) ◆ Mineral specimens, jewelry supplies and findings, tools, and beads. 719-372-0117.

**Custom Technology Ltd.,** 407-411 W. Main St., New London, IA 52645: Free list of retail sources ◆ Easy loading and unloading tumblers for finishing and burnishing gem stones. Also gem materials, minerals, and cut and tumbled stones from around the world. 800-YTUMBLE.

**Dad's Rock Shop,** P.O. Box 169, 112 E. Cherry Ave., Arroyo Grande, CA 93421: Free catalog ◆ Lapidary equipment, gems, minerals, fossils, metal detectors, prospecting equipment, and supplies. 805-489-2470.

**Dino Productions,** P.O. Box 3004, Englewood, CO 80155: Free catalog ◆ Fossils, rocks and minerals, ecology and oceanography equipment, and supplies for chemistry, general science, astronomy, and biology. 303-741-1587. www.dinoproductions.com

**Discount Agate House,** 3401 N. Dodge, Tucson, AZ 85716: Free information ◆ Rocks, minerals, and fossils. 520-323-0781.

**Dok, Domari Mines & Systems,** 1769 St. Lurent Blvd., #233, Ottawa, Ontario, Canada K1G 5X7: Free price list ◆ Mineral specimens. 613-247-6493.

**Earthworks,** P.O. Box 2067, Round Rock, TX 78680: Catalog $1 (refundable) ◆ Minerals, fossils, meteorites, books, supplies, and gifts. 800-255-8121; 512-255-2844 (in TX).

**Excalibur-Cureton Company,** Division Excalibur Mineral Company, 1000 N. Division St., Peekskill, NY 10566: Catalog $1 ◆ Meteorites and mineral specimens. 914-739-1134.

**Gemco International,** P.O. Box 833, Fayston, VT 05673: Free price list ◆ Faceted rough gemstones and small cut stones. Includes some that are slightly or moderately flawed. 802-496-2770. www.madriver.com/gemco

**Kenneth Glasser,** P.O. Box 28048, Las Vegas, NV 89126: Catalog $10 ◆ Cut and polished diamonds and other precious and semi-precious stones. 702-880-9044. www.diamondrough.com

**Harrison Astronomy,** 2574 Granville St., Vancouver, British Columbia, Canada V6H 3C8: Free information ◆ Telescopes and accessories, binoculars, microscopes, magnifiers, meteorological instruments, and books. 604-737-4303.

**Heaven & Earth,** RR 1, Box 25, Marshfield, VT 05658: Free catalog ◆ Jewelry, gemstones, and minerals. 800-348-5155; 802-426-3440 (in VT).

**Herkimer Diamond Mines,** RD 1, P.O. Box 233, Herkimer, NY 13350: Free information ◆ Petrified wood products, rockhounding equipment, minerals and rocks, and quartz crystals. 315-866-2011.

**Jewelry by Avery,** 5134 Chalk Point Rd., West River, MD 20778: Free information with long SASE ◆ Handcrafted Zuni, Navajo, and Hopi turquoise jewelry, kachinas, Native American art, precious and semi-precious gemstones, and mineral specimens. 410-867-4752.

**Kristalle,** 875 N. Pacific Coast Hwy., Laguna Beach, CA 92651: Free information ◆ Mineral specimens for collectors and museums. 714-494-5155. www.kristalle.com

**Lentz Lapidary Inc.,** 11760 S. Oliver, Rt. 2, Box 134, Mulvane, KS 67110: Catalog $2 ◆ Jewelry, mountings, clocks and motors, rough rock specimens, cabochons, and rockhounding and lapidary equipment. 316-777-1372.

**Lou-Bon Gems & Rocks,** Lake Barcroft Plaza, 6341 Columbia Pike, Bailey's Crossroads, VA 22041: Free information ◆ Carvings, beads, mineral specimens, fossils, shells, and lapidary and jeweler's equipment. 703-256-1084.

**Mineralab,** 695 E. 4th Ave., Durango, CO 81301: Free information ◆ Mineral identification tools. 800-749-3766; 970-247-1022 (in CO). www.mineralab.com

**Mineralogical Research Company,** 15840 E. Alta Vista Way, San Jose, CA 95127: Free list with long SASE and two 1st class stamps ◆ Mineral specimens and meteorites, microscopes, micro-mounts, specimen boxes, and supplies. 408-923-6800.

**Minerals Unlimited,** P.O. Box 877, Ridgecrest, CA 93556: Catalog $2 ◆ Rocks, minerals, and fossils. 760-375-5279.

**Miners Inc.,** P.O. Box 1301, Riggins, ID 83549: Free catalog ◆ Sample bags, instruments, hand tools, leather cases, and books for geologists and prospectors. 800-824-7452; 208-628-3247 (in ID). minerox@rmci.net

**New England International Gems,** 188 Pollard St., Billerica, MA 01862: Free catalog ◆ Brazilian quartz, rocks from India, beads, jewelry-making supplies, tools, and findings. 978-863-8331.

**H. Obodda Mineral Specimens,** P.O. Box 51, Short Hills, NJ 07078: Free list ◆ Afghan and Pakistani pegmatite minerals. 973-467-0212.

**Octahedral Resources,** P.O. Box 1408, Athabasca, Alberta, Canada T9S 2B2: Free price list ◆ Thumbnail to cabinet size mineral specimens.

**Omni Resources,** 1004 S. Mebane St., P.O. Box 2096, Burlington, NC 27216: Free catalog ◆ Fossils, rocks, hiking and topography maps, and globes. 800-742-2677. custserv@omnimap.com

**Parser Mineral Corp.,** P.O. Box 1094, Danbury, CT 06810: Catalog $2 ◆ Mineral and rock specimens. 203-744-6868.

**Pickens Minerals,** 610 N. Martin Ave., Waukegan, IL 60085: Free list with 1st class stamp ◆ Mineral specimens. 847-623-2823. picmin@iconnect.net

**Richardson's Recreational Ranch Ltd.,** Gateway Route Box 440, Madras, OR 97741: Free information ◆ Rock and mineral specimens from all over the world, carving materials, and lapidary equipment. 800-433-2680.

**Robins Mining Company,** P.O. Box 236, Mt. Ida, AR 71957: Free information ◆ Quartz crystals, gemstones, and minerals. 501-867-2530.

**Roth International,** One NE 1st St., Ste. 33, Miami, FL 33132: Free information ◆ Single and multiple quartz crystal clusters from Brazilian mines. 305-372-0630.

**Russell's Rock Shop,** 27911 North St., North Liberty, IN 46554: Free information ◆ Gem trees and supplies, bookends, agate slabs, amethyst, cabs, findings, slabs, and lucite stands. 219-289-7446.

**Rusty's Rock Shop,** 4106 Buckingham Dr., Decatur, IL 62526: Free price list ◆ Fluorite octahedrons, pyrite suns, and other mineral specimens. 217-877-7122.

**Southeastern Fossil Supply Company,** 1205 N. Eastman Rd., Ste. 209, Kingsport, TN 37664: Free catalog ◆ Fossils, mineral collections, teaching aids, gemstones, artifacts, and antiquities. 800-688-6721.

**Two Guys Minerals & Fossils,** 1 Lynnes Way, East Bridgewater, MA 02333: Catalog $2 ◆ Rocks, minerals, and fossils. Also fossil reproductions. 800-FOSSILS. www.twoguysfossils.com

**Rod & Helen Tyson,** 10549 133rd St., Edmonton, Alberta, Canada T5N 2A4: Free information ◆ Mineral specimens. 403-452-5357.

**V-Rock Shop,** 7061 Sunset Strip Ave., North Canton, OH 44720: Free information ◆ Cabochons, beads, pearls, faceted stones, display stands, pyramids, enhydros, citrine, Brazilian agate, amethyst geodes and plates, and quartz specimens. 330-494-1759.

**What on Earth Naturally,** 6250 Busch Blvd., Columbus, OH 43229: Free information ◆ Minerals, fossils, jewelry, gemstones, and shells. 614-436-1458.

**White Nights Company,** 420 Oceanview Dr., Anchorage, AL 99515: Free brochure ◆ Mineral collections, individual specimens, collecting materials, and mineralogical microscopes. 907-345-5531.

**Scott Williams Mineral Company,** P.O. Box 48, Oberlin, KS 67749: Free list ◆ Rare and common minerals from around the world. 913-475-2918.

**Wright's Rock Shop,** 3612 Albert Pike, Hot Springs, AR 71913: Catalog $3 ◆ Quartz, tourmaline, healing crystals, marcasite, minerals and fossils, and lapidary equipment. 501-767-4800.

### Petrified Wood

**Burnett Petrified Wood Inc.,** 37420 Sodaville Cutoff Dr., Lebanon, OR 97355: Free information ◆ Petrified wood. 541-258-3320.

**Ebersole Lapidary Supply Inc.,** 11417 West Hwy. 54, Wichita, KS 67209: Catalog $5 ◆ Tools, findings, mountings, cabochons, rocks, and petrified wood. 316-722-4771.

**Herkimer Diamond Mines,** RD 1, P.O. Box 233, Herkimer, NY 13350: Free information ◆ Petrified wood, mineral and rock specimens, quartz crystals, and gifts. 315-866-2011.

**Jeanne's Rock & Jewelry,** 5420 Bissonet, Bellaire, TX 77401: Price list $1 ◆ Petrified wood, seashells, lapidary supplies, and gifts. 713-664-2988.

**Riviera Lapidary Supply,** 50898 7th St., Box 40, Riviera, TX 78379: Catalog $3 ◆ Petrified wood, cabochons, slabs, cabbing rough, gemstones, crystals, beads, and bead-stringing supplies. 512-296-3958.

**Stewart's Petrified Wood,** P.O. Box 68, Holbrook, AZ 86025: Free information ◆ Slabs and tumbled petrified wood. Also meteorites. 800-414-8533. www.petrifiedwood.com

**StrataGraphics,** 5565 E. Henrietta Rd., Rush, NY 14543: Catalog $1 ◆ Fish, mammals, reptiles, other vertebrates, and petrified wood and plant specimens. 716-533-2301.

## RODEO EQUIPMENT

**Barstow Pro Rodeo Equipment,** P.O. Box 1516, Corsicana, TX 75151: Catalog $2 ◆ Rodeo riding equipment. 903-874-3995.

**Grant Lariat Rope Company,** 9486 Dub Grant Rd., Benton, AR 72015: Free information ◆ Rodeo equipment. 800-223-8478; 501-794-1912 (in AR).

**Top Hand Rodeo Equipment,** 510 S. Main, Farmersville, TX 75442: Catalog $3 ◆ Spurs, rodeo equipment, bullropes, riggings, chaps, and western gifts. 800-959-1245; 972-782-6624 (in TX).

## ROLLER & IN-LINE SKATES

**Dominion Skate Company Ltd.,** 45 Railroad St., Brampton, Ontario, Canada L6X 1G4: Free information ◆ Roller skates and scooters. 416-453-9860.

**Fast Forward Skate Shop,** 4649 Verona Rd., Madison, WI 53711: Free catalog ◆ Skates for speed, hockey, stunts, distance, or recreation. 608-271-6222.

**Grind Zone Skates,** P.O. Box 524, Albertville, AL 35950: Free catalog ◆ In-line skates. 800-322-3851.

**The House,** 300 S. Owasso Blvd., St. Paul, MN 55117: Free catalog ◆ In-line skates and other gear. 800-409-7669. www.the-house.com

**Hyper Wheels,** 3731 W. Warner Center Ave., Santa Ana, CA 92704: Free information ◆ Roller blade skates. 714-950-8800.

**Hypno Inline Skates,** Division Dynastar, P.O. Box 25, Hercules Dr., Colchester, VT 95446: Free list of retail sources ◆ In-line skates. 800-655-2431. www.hypnoskates.com

**JMP Enterprises,** 652 Retriever Dr., Hampstead, MD 21074: Free catalog ◆ Skateboards, roller skates, in-line skates, and hockey equipment. 410-239-5081.

**Kerjean Skate Line,** 2501 NW 72nd Ave., Miami, FL 33122: Free information ◆ In-line skates. 305-499-9952. www.kerjean.com

**Kryptonics Inc.,** 740 S. Pierce Ave., Louisville, CO 80027: Free information ◆ Roller skates and skateboards. 800-766-9146; 303-665-5353 (in CO).

**Labeda & Kuzak,** 181 Lafayette Rd., North Hampton, NH 03862: Free information ◆ In-line skates, replacement wheels, and accessories. Also bicycles and snowboards. 603-964-5581.

**Maska USA Inc.,** 139 Harvest Ln., Williston, VT 05495: Free information ◆ Protective gear and skates. 800-451-4600. www.ccmsports.com

**Mt. Constance Mountain Shoppe,** 1550 NE Riddell Rd., Bremerton, WA 98310: Free catalog ◆ Outdoor equipment, in-line skates, and accessories for mountain bikes. 360-377-8099. MTSHOPPE@MOUNTAINSHOPPE.COM

**National Sporting Goods Corp.,** 25 Brighton Ave., Passaic, NJ 07055: Free information ◆ Roller skates, scooters, skateboards, and protective gear. 201-779-2323.

**Ocean Hockey Supply Company,** 197 Chambers Bridge Rd., Bricktown, NJ 08723: Free catalog ◆ In-line skates and hockey equipment. 800-631-2159; 732-477-4411 (in NJ). www.oceanhockey.com

**Online Sports,** 13692 W. Virginia Dr., Ste. 101, Lakewood, CO 80228: Free information ◆ Skis, snowboards, bindings, clothing, mountain bikes, and roller blades. 303-980-4014.

**Performance Bicycle Shop,** P.O. Box 2741, Chapel Hill, NC 27514: Free catalog ◆ In-line skates and accessories. 800-727-2433.

**Riedell Shoes Inc.,** P.O. Box 21, Red Wing, MN 55066: Free information ◆ Protective gear, skates, and wheels. 612-388-8251.

**Roller Derby Skate Company,** Box 930, Litchfield, IL 62056: Free information ◆ Roller and in-line skates, scooters, skateboards, safety gear, and clothing. 217-324-3961.

**Roller Warehouse,** 4105 Delmar Ave., Bldg. 3, Rocklin, CA 95677: Free catalog ◆ In-line skates, replacement wheels, and protective gear. 800-772-2502. www.rollerwarehouse.com

**Rollerblade Inc.,** 5101 Shady Oak Rd., Minnetonka, MN 55343: Free list of retail sources ◆ Protective gear, skates, and wheels. 800-232-7655.

**Saucony/Hyde,** 13 Centennial Dr., Peabody, MA 01961: Free list of retail sources ◆ Roller skates, scooters, and skateboards. 800-365-7282.

**Seneca Sports Inc.,** 75 Fortune Blvd., Milford, MA 01757: Free information ◆ In-line skates. 800-861-7867; 508-634-3616 (in MA).

**Sportime,** Customer Service, 1 Sportime Way, Atlanta, GA 30340: Free information ◆ Protective gear and skates. 800-444-5700; 770-449-5700 (in GA).

**Sportworks,** 421 SW 2nd Ave., Portland, OR 97204: Free catalog ◆ In-line skates, safety gear, and parts. 800-362-3434. www.sportworks.com

**Team Karim,** 2800 Telegraph Ave., Berkeley, CA 94705: Free information ◆ Speed skates. 510-841-2181.

**Team Paradise,** 16321 Gothard St., Unit D, Huntington Beach, CA 92647: Free catalog ◆ In-line skates, protective gear, clothing, and accessories. 800-756-5629. www.teamparadise.com

**Tecnica,** 19 Technology Dr., West Lebanon, NH 03784: Free list of retail sources ◆ In-line skates. 800-258-3897. www.technicausa.com

**Title 9 Sports,** 5743 Landregan St., Emeryville, CA 94608: Free catalog ◆ Women's clothing created by and for women. 510-655-5999. thefolks@title9sports.com

**UFO Sports Inc.,** 21100 Erwin St., Woodland Hills, CA 91367: Catalog $3 ◆ In-line replacement wheels. 818-701-1521.

**Variflex Inc.,** 5152 N. Commerce Ave., Moorpark, CA 93021: Free information ◆ Roller skates and skateboards. 805-523-0322.

**The Wright Life,** 200 Linden, Fort Collins, CO 80524: Free catalog ◆ Frisbees (flying discs), skateboards, snowboards, in-line skates, boomerangs, stunt kites, juggling equipment, and more. 800-321-8833. www.wrightlife.com

## RUBBER STAMPS & EMBOSSING SUPPLIES

**A La Art Stamp Crafters,** 37500 N. Industrial Pkwy., Willoughby, OH 44094: Catalog $4.50 (refundable) ◆ Rubber stamps. 800-942-7885. www.alaart.com

**Action Office Supplies,** P.O. Box 277, Adelphia, NJ 07710: Free catalog ◆ Custom self-inking and pre-inked rubber stamps. 800-298-1000. www.actoff.com

**Alextamping,** P.O. Box 742, Soulsbyville, CA 95372: Catalog $3.50 ◆ Rubber stamps and accessories. 209-533-1834. alex@mlode.com

**Angel's Attic Rubber Stamps,** P.O. Box 1306, Galesburg, IL 61402: Catalog $5 ◆ Christian theme rubber stamps and accessories. 309-343-1235. www.misslink.net/angelsattic

**Arben Stamp Company,** P.O. Box 353, Evansville, IN 47703: Catalog $2.50 ◆ Rubber stamps. 800-223-3086; 812-423-4269 (in IN).

**Artistic Stamp Exchange,** 5580 Havana, Ste. 3A, Denver, CO 80239: Catalog $5 ◆ Over 1000 rubber stamps. 303-371-1260.

**Bizzaro Rubber Stamps,** 15 Enterprise Ln., Smithfield, RI 02917: Catalog $3 ◆ Artistic rubber stamps and supplies. 401-726-8770.

**Burpo the Clown,** P.O. Box 299, McMinnville, OR 97128: Free information ◆ Face-painting rubber stamps and supplies. 503-434-1243.

**Carousel Collections,** 6-25 Industrial Dr., Elmira, Ontario, Canada N3B 3K3: Catalog $2 (refundable) ◆ Rubber stamps. 800-265-6269.

**Comotion Rubber Stamps Inc.,** 2711 E. Elvira Rd., Tucson, AZ 85706: Catalog $20 ($12 refundable with $20 purchase) ◆ Decorative rubber stamps and accessories. 800-257-1288.

**Country Impressions,** P.O. Box 502, Layton, UT 84041: Catalog $3.50 ◆ Rubber stamps. 801-543-0206.

**Crazy Folks Rubber Stamps,** 855 Jefferson Ave., Livermore, CA 94550: Catalog $2 (refundable) ◆ Rubber stamps. 510-449-6887.

**D.J. Inkers,** P.O. Box 2462, Sandy, UT 84091: Catalog $3 ◆ Rubber art stamps. 800-325-4890.

**DreamInk,** P.O. Box 8028, Woodland, CA 95776: Catalog $2 (refundable with first $10 order) ◆ Rubber stamps. 916-661-1221.

**Embossing Arts Company,** P.O. Box 439, 31961 Rolland Dr., Tangent, OR 97389: Catalog $3 (specify retail) ◆ Rubber stamps, card-making and embossing supplies, and more. 541-928-9898. www.embossingarts.com

**Enchanted Creations,** 347 Fawn Lake Forest, Hawley, PA 18428: Rubber stamps catalog $4.75, accessories catalog $4.75 ◆ Mounted and unmounted rubber stamps and accessories. 717-685-7013.

**Eugenia's Eclectibles,** Eugenia Ahearne, 5800-B Camp Bowie Blvd., Fort Worth, TX 76107: Catalog $2 ◆ Rubber stamps, stamping supplies, stationery, and album-making materials. 817-732-3608.

**Express-It Rubber Stamp,** 1806 Milmont Dr., Ste. 310, Milpitas, CA 95035: Free brochure ◆ Custom and specialty pre-inked and self-inking rubber stamps. 800-667-3374; 408-946-1290 (in CA).

**Five Star Publications,** P.O. Box 6698, Chandler, AZ 85246: Free catalog ◆ Self-inking, pre-inked, and other stock rubber stamps. 602-940-8182. www.fivestarsupport.com

**Good Impressions Rubber Stamps,** P.O. Box 33, Shirley, WV 26434: Catalog $2 ◆ Victorian and Edwardian-style rubber stamps. Also accessories. 800-846-6606.

**Good Stamps-Stamp Goods,** 30901 Timberline Rd., Willits, CA 95490: Catalog $4 ◆ Rubber and make-your-own stamp supplies. 800-637-6401. www.pacific.net/~gssg

**Graphic Rubber Stamp Company,** P.O. Box 255, North Hollywood, CA 91603: Catalog $4 ◆ Rubber stamps. 818-782-9443.

**ImaginAir Designs,** 1007 Woodland NW, Albuquerque, NM 87107: Catalog $2 ◆ Aviation stamps and other designs. 505-345-2308.

**Impress Me Rubber Stamps,** 382 E. 520 North, American Fork, UT 84003: Catalog $3 ◆ Rubber stamps, storage cases, and accessories. 801-756-5447.

**Imprints Graphic Studio Inc.,** P.O. Box 248, Buffalo, NY 14225: Catalog $8 ◆ Rubber stamps and accessories. 716-660-5238.

**Jackson Marketing Products,** Brownsville Rd., Mt. Vernon, IL 62864: Free information ◆ Supplies and equipment for making regular and pre-inked rubber stamps. 800-STAMP-CALL.

**Kidstamps,** P.O. Box 18699, Cleveland Heights, OH 44118: Catalog $3 ◆ Rubber stamps. 800-727-5437. www.kidstamps.com

**Maine Street Stamps,** P.O. Box 14, Kingfield, ME 04947: Catalog $2 (refundable) ◆ Rubber stamps. 207-265-2500. www.mint.net/opdag/ms.html

**Museum of Modern Rubber,** 2457 Hyperion Ave., Los Angeles, CA 90027: Catalog $3 ◆ Rubber stamps. 213-662-1133.

**National Stampagraphic,** P.O. Box 370985, Las Vegas, NV 89137: Single issue $5 ◆ Published quarterly, includes articles and information of interest to rubber stamp users, and advertisements from rubber stamp hobbyists, manufacturers, and distributors. 702-396-2188. www.quikpage.com/A/stampagraphic

**100 Proof Press,** P.O. Box 299, Athens, OH 45701: Catalog $4 (refundable with first $15 order) ◆ Rubber stamps on wood blocks, mounted on self-sticking cushions, or unmounted and untrimmed. 740-594-2315.

**Ornamentum,** 32903 30th Ave. SW, Federal Way, WA 98023: Catalog $3 ◆ Rubber stamps. 206-838-3259.

**Paper Plain,** 849 Almar, C-437, Santa Cruz, CA 95060: Free brochure ◆ Original rubber stamps and creative papers for stamping.

**Pepperell Stamp Works,** 548 High St., Bradford, PA 16701: Free information ◆ Civil War and other rubber stamps. 800-752-4656.

**Posh Impressions,** 4708 Barranca Pkwy., Irvine, CA 92604: Catalog $4 ◆ Original and other rubber stamps from worldwide sources. 800-421-POSH. www.poshimpressions.com

**Purple Wave Stamp Designs,** P.O. Box 5340, Ventura, CA 93005: Catalog $2.50 ◆ Mounted and unmounted rubber stamps. 805-659-0253.

**Raindrops on Roses Rubber Stamps,** 4808 Winterwood Dr., Raleigh, NC 27613: Catalog $3 ◆ Country stamp sets, brush markers, and supplies. 800-245-8617; 919-846-8617 (in NC).

**Rubber Baby Buggy Bumpers,** 1331 W. Mountain Ave., Fort Collins, CO 80521: Catalog $5 ◆ Decorative rubber stamps and accessories. 970-224-3499.

**Rubber Stamps of America,** P.O. Box 567, Warner Center, Saxtons River, VT 05154: Catalog $2.50 (refundable) ◆ Original artist-designed rubber stamps. 800-553-5031.

**Rubber Stamps Unlimited,** 334 S. Harvey, Plymouth, MI 48170: Free brochure ◆ Custom self-inking rubber stamps. 313-451-7300.

**Rubbernecker Stamp Company,** 932 Laroda Ct., Ontario, CA 91762: Catalog $2 ◆ Original rubber stamps. Unmounted stamps available. 909-673-0747.

**The Rubberstampler,** 1945 Wealthy SE, Grand Rapids, MI 49506: Catalog $2.50 (refundable) ◆ Rubber stamps. 800-800-0424; 616-454-0424 (in MI).

**Richard Sabol,** 1 Pisacatqua Rd., Dover, NH 03820: Free brochure with long SASE and two 1st class stamps ◆ Cross-stitch kits, rubber stamps, and jewelry. 603-742-6324.

**Share-A-Stamp,** 210 Southland Sta. Dr., #109, Warner Robins, GA 31088: Catalog $6.50 ◆ Rubber art stamps and accessories.

**Stamp Affair,** P.O. Box 7614, Round Lake, IL 60073: Catalog $5 ◆ Rubber stamps and accessories. 847-740-0967.

**Stamp Arts,** 4201 Picadilly Dr., Fort Collins, CO 80526: Catalog $3 ◆ Rubber stamps and accessories.

**Stamp Francisco Rubber Stamps,** 466 8th St., San Francisco, CA 04103: Catalog $5 ◆ Rubber stamps and accessories. 415-252-5975.

**Stamp Oasis,** 5000 W. Oakey Blvd., #D-14, Las Vegas, NV 89146: Catalog $5 ◆ Fun rubber stamps.800-234-8735. www.stampoasis.com

**STAMPberry Farms,** P.O. Box 370985, Las Vegas, NV 89137: Catalog $2 (refundable) ◆ Rubber stamps. 702-396-2188. natststamp@aol.com

**Stampendous Inc.,** 1357 S. Lewis St., Anaheim, CA 92805: Catalog $3 ◆ Rubber stamps, ink pads, brush markers, and glitter glue. 800-869-0474.

**The Stampin' Place,** P.O. Box 43, Big Lake MN 55309: Catalog $3 (refundable) ◆ Creative rubber stamps. 800-634-3717; 612-263-6646 (in MN).

**Stamps in Motion,** P.O. Box 7150, Van Nuys, CA 91409: Catalog $5 ◆ Over 1300 original rubber stamps. 818-904-0354.

**Stampscapes,** 7451 Warner Ave., Ste. E-124, Huntington Beach, CA 92647: Catalog $2 ◆ Nature-oriented rubber stamps and accessories. www.stampscapes.com

**Stewart-Superior Corp.,** 1800 W. Larchmont Ave., Chicago, IL 60613: Free information ◆ Rubber stamps, inks and ink pads, rollers, cleaners, sponge rubber, cements, and rubber stamp gum. 800-621-1205; 773-935-6025 (in IL).

**Think Ink,** 7526 Olympic View Dr., Edmonds, WA 98026: Catalog $2 (refundable) ◆ Multi-color, hand printing press and embossing powders. 800-778-1935; 425-778-1935 (in WA). www.thinkink.net

**Visual Image,** 1215 N. Grove St., Anaheim, CA 92806: Catalog $3 ◆ Rubber art stamps. 714-632-3491.

**Wood Cellar Graphics,** RR 1, Box 85, Coleridge, NE 68727: Catalog $3 (refundable) ◆ Rubber stamps, ink pads, embossing supplies, and markers. 402-283-4725.

## RUGBY

**Matt Godek Rugby & Soccer Supply,** P.O. Box 565, Merrifield, VA 22116: Free information ◆ Rugby and soccer equipment and clothing. 800-336-3446. www.rugbystore.com

**Mitre Sports,** 690 Genesco Park, Nashville, TN 37202: Free information ◆ Balls and boots. 800-826-7650; 615-367-74754 (in TN).

**Rugby & Soccer Supply,** P.O. Box 565, Merrifield, VA 22116: Free catalog ◆ Balls, boots, jerseys, and shorts. 800-872-7842; 703-280-5540 (in VA).

**Rugby Imports,** 885 Warren Ave., East Providence, RI 02914: Free catalog ◆ Clothing, shoes, and equipment. 800-431-4514; 401-438-2727 (in RI). www.rugbyimports.com

## RUG MAKING

**Braid-Aid,** 466 Washington St., Pembroke, MA 02359: Catalog $4 ◆ Braided rug kits, braiding accessories, wool by the pound or yard, and latch-hooking, weaving, basket-making, shirret, and spinning supplies. 781-826-2560.

**The Dorr Mill Store,** P.O. Box 88, Guild, NH 03754: Free list ◆ Fine wools, fabrics, and hooking supplies. 800-846-DORR; 603-863-1197 (in NH).

**Earth Guild,** 33 Haywood St., Asheville, NC 28801: Catalog $3 ◆ Basket-making, weaving, spinning, dyeing, pottery, woodcarving, hand and machine knitting, rug-making, netting, and chair-caning supplies. 800-327-8448. www.earthguild.com

**Edgemont Yarn Services,** P.O. Box 205, Washington, KY 41086: Free brochure ◆ Weaving and rug-making supplies. 800-446-5977.

**Harry M. Fraser Company,** 433 Duggins Rd., Stoneville, NC 27048: Hooking supplies catalog $2.50; patterns catalog $4.50; both catalogs $6 ◆ Rug-hooking and braiding supplies. Also patterns. 336-573-9830.

**Fredericksburg Rugs,** P.O. Box 649, Fredericksburg, TX 78624: Catalog $4 ◆ Hooking and braiding rug-making supplies and rug-hooking kits. 830-997-6083.

**Great Northern Weaving,** 7653 N. 48th St., Augusta, MI 49012: Catalog $1 ◆ Cotton and wool rags, warp, loopers, fillers, and braiding equipment. 616-731-4487.

**Hooked on Rugs,** P.O. Box 109, Novi, MI 48376: Brochure $3 ◆ Hand-dyed hooked rug kits. 248-344-4367.

**Miller Rug Hooking,** Nancy Miller, 2448 Brentwood, Sacramento, CA 95825: Information $4 ◆ Rug-hooking supplies and kits. 916-482-1234.

**Claire Murray Inc.,** P.O. Box 390, Ascutney, VT 05030: Catalog $5 ◆ Ready-made hand-hooked rugs and kits. 800-252-4733. www.clairemurray.com

**Red Clover Rugs,** 92550 Chardonnay Way, Cheshire, OR 97419: Catalog $4 ◆ Punch-needle and traditional rug hooking kits, yarn, books, and backing. 800-858-9276; 541-998-6610 (in OR).

**Sea Holly Hooked Rugs,** 1906 N. Bayview Dr., Kill Devil Hills, NC 27948: Free information with long SASE ◆ Supplies, equipment, kits, patterns, and hand-dyed wools. 919-441-8961.

**Shillcraft,** 8899 Kelso Dr., Baltimore, MD 21221: Catalog $2 ◆ Latch-hook kits and supplies for rugs and wall hangings. 410-682-3060.

**Shirret,** P.O. Box 1338, Madison, CT 06443: Free brochure ◆ How-to books and equipment for making rugs from fabric scraps.

**Sweet Briar Studio,** Janet Dobson, 866 Main St., Hope Valley, RI 02832: Free catalog ◆ Traditional and primitive rug hooking supplies. 401-539-1009.

## RUG & CARPET RESTORATION

**Restoration by Costikyan Ltd.,** 28-13 14th St., Long Island City, NY 11101: Free information ◆ Carpet re-weaving and restoration services. 718-726-1090.

## RUGS & CARPETS

**Abu Oriental Rugs,** 5626 Riverdale Rd., High Point, NC 27282: Free information ◆ Oriental rugs from Afghanistan, India, Pakistan, and Persia. 336-454-7771.

**Access Carpet,** P.O. Box 1007, Dalton, GA 30722: Free information ◆ Rugs and carpets. 800-848-7747.

**American Blind, Wallpaper & Carpet Factory,** 909 N. Sheldon Rd., Plymouth, MI 48170: Free information ◆ Wood, micro, mini, and vertical blinds. Also roller and pleated shades, wallpaper, and carpet. 800-889-2631 (for blinds and wallpaper); 800-346-0608 (for carpet). www.abwf.com

**American Southern Rug,** 4422 Central Ave., St. Petersburg, FL 33711: Catalog $2 ◆ Authentic American handcrafted braided rugs. 800-541-7847.

**AMS Imports,** 23 Ash Ln., Amherst, MA 01002: Free information ◆ Imported area rugs from Jordan, Tibet, and Egypt. 800-253-2644.

**Armstrong World Industries,** P.O. Box 3233, Lancaster, PA 17604: Free information ◆ Carpet and rugs. 800-232-4832. www.armstrong.com

**The Barn,** Market St., Lehman, PA 18627: Free brochure ◆ Custom-woven rag, hand-stenciled, and hand-woven throw rugs. Also stair carpeting and runners. 717-675-4232.

**Bearden Brothers Carpet,** 4109 S. Dixie Hwy., Dalton, GA 30721: Free catalog ◆ Carpet and other floor coverings. 800-433-0074.

**Bucklers Carpet Inc.,** P.O. Box 9, Dalton, GA 30722: Free information ◆ Rugs and carpets. 800-232-5537.

**J.R. Burrows & Company,** P.O. Box 522, Rockland, MA 02370: Catalog $5 ◆ Period carpet reproductions by special order. Also wallpaper and fabrics. 800-347-1795. www.burrows.com/index.html

**Carousel Carpet Mills Inc.,** One Carousel Ln., Ukiah, CA 95482: Catalog $10 ◆ Natural fiber custom carpets and rugs in cotton, jute, wool, and silk. 707-485-0333.

**Carpet Express,** 915 Market St., Dayton, GA 30720: Free information ◆ Carpet and vinyl. 800-922-5582.

**Carpet Outlet,** Box 417, Miles City, MT 59301: Free information ◆ Carpet and area rugs. 800-225-4351.

**Country Braid House,** 462 Main St., Tilton, NH 03276: Free brochure ◆ Braided wool rugs, kits, and supplies. 603-286-4511.

**Crafts Unlimited,** Julie Topolinski, 2905 West Rd., Mountain Home, AR 72653: Brochure $2 ◆ Kits for making old-fashioned rag rugs in a variety of shapes. 800-792-9080; 870-425-2829 (in AR). www.craftmall.com/booths.row-r/rugs

**Dalton Paradise Carpets,** P.O. Box 1819, Rocky Face, GA 30740: Free information ◆ Carpets, rugs, and other floor coverings. 800-338-7811.

**Elkes Carpet Outlet Inc.,** 1585 Bethel Dr., High Point, NC 27260: Free information with long SASE ◆ First-quality, irregulars, close-outs, and discontinued carpet. 800-727-3553.

**Factory Direct Carpet Outlet,** P.O. Box 417, Miles City, MT 59301: Free brochure ◆ Carpets and vinyl, ceramic, hardwood, and laminated flooring. 800-225-4351.

**Family Heirloom Weavers,** 775 Meadowview Dr., Red Lion, PA 17356: Catalog $4 ◆ All-wool carpets with historic patterns, from the late 18th-century to the early 1920s. 717-246-2431.

**Gazebo of New York,** 114 E. 57th St., New York, NY 10022: Catalog $6 ◆ Handmade braided rugs and quilted pillows. 212-832-7077.

**Heirloom Rugs,** 28 Harlem St., Rumford, RI 02916: Catalog $3.50 ◆ Hand-hooked rugs. 401-438-5672.

**Henderson Creative Carpet Sculpture,** 1655 United Blvd., Coquitlam, British Columbia, Canada V3K 6Y7: Free information ◆ Sheepskin products, custom sisal-look wool rugs, and Northwest Coast native-designed rugs. 888-298-1111. www.creativecarpets.com

**Heritage Rugs,** Street Rd. & Village Ln., Lahaska, PA 18931: Catalog $1 ◆ Custom hand-woven rag wool rugs. 215-794-7229.

**Hooked on Victorian,** 56 Orchard Rd., Patchoque, NY 11772: Catalog $5 ◆ Handmade Victorian wool rugs. 516-654-8139.

**Charles W. Jacobsen Inc.,** 401 N. Salina St., Syracuse, NY 13203: Free brochure ◆ Hand-woven Oriental rugs. 315-422-7832.

**Jax Arts & Crafts Rugs,** 109 Parkway, Berea, KY 40403: Catalog $5 ◆ Rugs in arts and crafts designs. 606-986-5410. www.4berea.com/jaxco

**Johnson's Carpets,** 3610 Corporate Dr., Dalton, GA 30721: Free information ◆ Carpets and rugs. 800-235-1079; 707-277-2775 (in GA).

**Lee's Carpet Showcase,** 3068 N. Dug Gap Rd., Dalton, GA 30720: Free information ◆ Carpet and Oriental rugs, vinyl and wood flooring, and accessories. 800-433-8479. www.hfnet.com/lees.html

**Lizzie & Charlie's Rag Rugs,** 210 E. Bullion Ave., Marysvale, UT 84750: Free brochure ◆ Handmade rag rugs. 801-326-4213.

**Long's Carpet Inc.,** 2625 S. Dixie Hwy., Dalton, GA 30720: Free information ◆ Carpets. 800-545-5664.

**M & M Rag Rug Company,** 11 White Tail Ln., Monterey, CA 93940: Free information ◆ Handcrafted rugs and home accessories. 408-375-6084.

**Marlborough Country Barn,** N. Main St., Marlborough, CT 06447: Catalog $3 ◆ Handcrafted rugs. 800-852-8993.

**MDC Direct Inc.,** P.O. Box 569, Marietta, GA 30061: Free information ◆ Wood blinds, cellular shades, and area rugs. 800-892-2083.

**Michigan Custom Area Rugs,** 1508 Rockwell Dr., Midland, MI 48640: Free brochure ◆ Custom area rugs in any size or shape. 517-839-8230.

**Mills River Industries,** 824 Locust St., Hendersonville, NC 28792: Catalog $1 ◆ Flat-braided oval and round rugs. 704-697-9778.

**Fred Moheban Gallery,** 730 5th Ave., New York, NY 10019: Free information ◆ Rare and unusual decorative Oriental and European carpets and rugs. 212-397-9060.

**Claire Murray Inc.,** P.O. Box 390, Ascutney, VT 05030: Catalog $5 ◆ Hand-hooked rugs and hand-sewn quilts. Available in kits. 800-252-4733. www.clairemurray.com

**Network Floor Covering,** Division Parkers Carpet, 3200 Dug Gap Rd., Dalton, GA 30720: Free brochure ◆ Stain-protected carpets. 800-442-2013.

**The Old Wicker Garden,** 6606 Snider Plaza, Dallas, TX 75225: Photos $5 (refundable) ◆ Antique wicker furniture, brass and iron beds, hooked rugs and quilts, folk art, and other decorative accessories. 972-373-8241.

**Paradise Mills Inc.,** P.O. Box 2488, Dalton, GA 30722: Free information ◆ Rugs and carpets. 800-338-7811.

**Peerless Imported Rugs,** 3033 Lincoln Ave., Chicago, IL 60657: Catalog $1 ◆ Hand and machine-woven Oriental rugs, rag rugs, Navajo rugs, colonial braids, grass rugs, and tapestries from Europe. 800-621-6573.

**Quality Discount Carpet,** 1207 W. Walnut Ave., Dalton, GA 30720: Free brochure ◆ Carpets. 800-233-0993.

**Rave Carpets,** 2875 Cleveland Rd., Dalton, GA 30721: Free information ◆ Residential and commercial carpets. 800-942-6969. www.ravecarpet.com

**S & S Carpet Mills,** 200 Howell Dr., P.O. Box 1568, Dalton, GA 30722: Free brochure ◆ Carpet. 800-363-9034.

**Santa Fe Interiors,** 214 Old Santa Fe Trail, Santa Fe, NM 87501: Portfolio $5 ◆ Handmade 100-percent traditional and contemporary southwestern wool rugs. 505-988-2227.

**Warehouse Carpets Inc.,** P.O. Box 3233, Dalton, GA 30721: Free information ◆ Rugs and carpets. 706-226-2229.

**Whipp Trading Company,** RR 1, Arrasmith Trail, Ames, IA 50010: Free catalog ◆ Sheepskin rugs, slippers, mittens, and hats. 800-533-9447.

**Thomas K. Woodard American Antiques & Quilts,** 506 E. 74th St., 5th Floor, New York, NY 10021: Catalog $6 ◆ Classic American-style room size area rugs and runners. 800-332-7847; 212-988-2906 (in NY).

**Yankee Pride,** 29 Parkside Circle, Braintree, MA 02184: Catalog $3 (refundable) ◆ Handcrafted quilts, Dhurries, comforters and bedspreads, and hand-braided, hooked, and rag rugs. 800-848-7610. www.yankee-pride.com

**York Interiors Inc.,** 2821 E. Prospect Rd., York, PA 17402: Free brochure ◆ Oriental rugs. 800-723-7029.

**Zaki Oriental Rugs,** 600 S. Main St., High Point, NC 27260: Free information ◆ Oriental rugs. 336-884-4407. www.zaki.com

# RUNNING, JOGGING, & WALKING

## Clothing & Shoes

**Adidas USA,** 5675 N. Blackstock Rd., Spartanburg, SC 29303: Free list of retail sources ◆ Shoes, shorts, singlets, socks, sweatbands, and warm-up suits. 800-423-4327. www.adidas.com

**Alpha Shirt Company,** 401 E. Hunting Park Ave., Philadelphia, PA 19124: Free information ◆ Shirts and tops. 800-523-4585; 215-291-0300 (in PA).

**Augusta Sportswear,** Box 14939, Augusta, GA 30919: Free information ◆ Shirts and tops. 800-237-6695; 706-860-4633 (in GA).

**California Best,** 970 Broadway, Ste. 104, Chula Vista, CA 91911: Free catalog ◆ Shoes and clothing. 800-438-9327.

**Champion Products Inc.,** 475 Corporate Square Dr., Winston Salem, NC 27105: Free information ◆ Shorts, singlets, socks, and warm-up suits.

**Converse Inc.,** 1 Fordham Rd., North Reading, MA 01864: Free information ◆ Shoes, shorts, singlets, socks, sweatbands, and warm-up suits. 800-428-2667; 781-664-1100 (in MA).

**Dolfin International Corp.,** P.O. Box 98, Shillington, PA 19607: Free information ◆ Shorts, rainsuits, singlets, and warm-up suits. 800-441-0818; 610-775-5500 (in PA).

**Eastbay,** P.O. Box 8066, Wausau, WI 54402: Free catalog ◆ Shoes and clothing. 800-826-2205. www.eastbay.com

**Empire Sporting Goods Manufacturing Company,** 443 Broadway, New York, NY 10013: Free information ◆ Rainsuits. 800-221-3455; 212-966-0880 (in NY).

**Faber Brothers,** 4141 S. Pulaski Rd., Chicago, IL 60632: Free information ◆ Pedometers, rainsuits, and safety vests. 773-376-9300.

**Gold's Gym,** 360 Hampton Dr., Venice, CA 90291: Free information ◆ Shirts and tops. 800-457-5375; 213-392-6004 (in CA). www.goldsonline.com

**Las Vegas Discount Golf & Tennis,** 5325 S. Valley View Blvd., Ste. 10, Las Vegas, NV 89118: Free catalog ◆ Shoes and clothing. 702-798-5500. www.lvgolf.com

**Movin USA,** 7411 W. Boston, Ste. 1, Chandler, AZ 85225: Free information ◆ Shirts and tops. 800-445-6684.

**New Balance Athletic Shoe Inc.,** 61 N. Deacon St., Boston, MA 02134: Free list of retail sources ◆ Shoes, shorts, singlets, raincoats, sweatbands, and warm-up suits. 800-622-1218. www.newbalance.com

**North Face,** 2013 Farallon Dr., San Leandro, CA 94577: Free list of retail sources ◆ Rainsuits. 800-447-2333.

**Okun Brothers Shoes,** Attention: Mail Order Department, 356 E. South St., Kalamazoo, MI 49007: Free catalog ◆ Shoes for men, women, and children. 800-433-6344.

**Pearl Izumi,** 620 Compton St., Brownfield, CO 80020: Free information ◆ Shirts and tops. 800-877-7080. www.pearlizumi.com

**Puma USA Inc.,** 147 Centre St., Brockton, MA 02403: Free information ◆ Shoes, shorts, singlets, rainsuits, socks, and warm-up suits. 800-662-7862. www.puma.com

**Road Runner Sports,** 6150 Nancy Ridge Dr., San Diego, CA 92121: Free price list ◆ Shoes, other walking accessories, and fitness apparel. 800-551-5558. www.roadrunnersports.com

**The Runners High,** 859 Santa Cruz Ave., Menlo Park, CA 94025: Free brochure ◆ Shoes, clothing, watches, heart monitors, and more for runners, walkers, and racers. 415-325-9432.

**Safesport/Outbound,** 269 Columbia Ave., Chapin, SC 29036: Free list of retail sources ◆ Pedometers, rainsuits, and safety vests. 800-433-6506.

**Shaffer Sportswear,** 224 N. Washington, Neosho, MO 64850: Free information ◆ Shirts and tops. 417-451-9444.

**Spalding Sports Worldwide,** 425 Meadow St., P.O. Box 901, Chicopee, MA 01021: Free list of retail sources ◆ Shoes, shorts, singlets, sweatbands, and warm-up suits. 800-225-6601. www.spalding.com

**Spiegel,** P.O. Box 182563, Columbus, OH 43218: Free catalog ◆ Men and women's walking shoes. 800-345-4500. www.spiegel.com

**Tel-a-Runner,** 80 Speedwell Ave., Morristown, NJ 07960: Free brochure ◆ Shoes for runners. 800-835-2786.

**Terramar Sports Ltd.,** 10 Midland Ave., Port Chester, NY 10573: Free information ◆ Insulated outdoor clothing. 800-468-7455.

**Title 9 Sports,** 5743 Landregan St., Emeryville, CA 94608: Free catalog ◆ Women's clothing created by and for women. 510-655-5999. thefolks@title9sports.com

**Venus Knitting Mills Inc.,** 140 Spring St., Murray Hill, NJ 07974: Free information ◆ Shorts, singlets, sweatbands, and warm-up suits. 800-955-4200; 908-464-2400 (in NJ).

## Pedometers & Stopwatches

**Accusplit,** 2290-A Ringwood Ave., San Jose, CA 95131: Free information ◆ Pedometers and sports watches. 800-935-1996; 408-432-8228 (in CA).

**Aristo Import Company Inc.,** 15 Hunt Rd., Orangeburg, NY 10962: Free information ◆ Pedometers for step counting, walking, or jogging. 800-352-6304; 914-359-0720 (in NY).

**Compass Industries Inc.,** 104 E. 25th St., New York, NY 10010: Free information ◆ Pedometers. 800-221-9904.

**Creative Health Products,** 5148 Saddle Ridge Rd., Plymouth, MI 48170: Free catalog ◆ Pedometers and pulse monitors. 800-742-4478.

**Dynamic Classics Ltd.,** 58 2nd Ave., Brooklyn, NY 11215: Free information ◆ Pedometers. 718-369-4167.

**Faber Brothers,** 4141 S. Pulaski Rd., Chicago, IL 60632: Free information ◆ Pedometers, rainsuits, and safety vests. 773-376-9300.

**General Sportcraft Company,** 140 Woodbine Rd., Bergenfield, NJ 07621: Free information ◆ Pedometers. 201-384-4242.

**Innovative Time Corp.,** 5858 Edison Pl., Carlsbad, CA 92008: Free information ◆ Pedometers. 800-765-0595; 619-438-0595 (in CA).

**Precise International,** 15 Corporate Dr., Orangeburg, NY 10962: Free information ◆ Walking and walking/jogging pedometers. 800-431-2996; 914-365-3500 (in NY).

**The Runners High,** 859 Santa Cruz Ave., Menlo Park, CA 94025: Free brochure ◆ Shoes, clothing, watches, heart monitors, and more for runners, walkers, and racers. 415-325-9432.

**Silva Compass,** P.O. Box 966, Binghamton, NY 13902: Free information ◆ Pedometers. 800-847-1460. www.eureka.com

**Sportline,** 847 S. McGlincey Ln., Campbell, CA 95008: Free information ◆ Pedometers. 408-377-8900.

## SAFES

**American Security Products Company,** 11925 Pacific Ave., Fontana, CA 92335: Free information ◆ Gun and other safes for homes and offices. 800-421-6142. qsd@amersecurity.com

**Boston Lock & Safe Company,** 30 Lincoln St., Brighton, MA 02135: Free information ◆ Alarms, locks, and safes. 617-787-3400.

**Kingsbery Safes,** Kingsbery Mfg. Corp., 715 W. Zavala St., Crystal City, TX 78839: Free brochure ◆ Safes for collectibles and security. 800-445-0763.

**Safe Specialties Inc.,** 10932 Murdock Rd., Knoxville, TN 37932: Catalog $2 ◆ Office and home safes. 800-695-2815. www.imagesbuilder.com/safespec.1.html

**Treadlok,** 1764 Granby St. NE, Roanoke, VA 24012: Free catalog ◆ Safes for guns and valuables. 800-729-8732.

**Value-Tique Inc.,** P.O. Box 67, Leonia, NJ 07605: Free information ◆ Safes. 201-461-6500.

## SAFETY & EMERGENCY EQUIPMENT

**Champion America Inc.,** 1333 Highland Rd., Macedonia, OH 44056: Free catalog ◆ Safety-related products and identification, caution, warning signs, and markers. 800-521-7000. www.champion-america.com

**Conney Safety Products,** 3202 Latham Dr., Madison, WI 53713: Free catalog ◆ First aid supplies, survival equipment, and safety devices. 800-356-9100.

**Consumer Products Group,** P.O. Box 1276, Albrightsville, PA 18210: Free catalog ◆ Personal protection aids. 717-722-2131. members.spree.com/interpro

**Direct Safety Company,** P.O. Box 27648, Tempe, AZ 85258: Free catalog ◆ Safety equipment. 800-528-7405.

**Enviro-Safety Products,** 516 E. Modoc Ave., Visalia, CA 93292: Free information ◆ Safety equipment. 800-637-6606. www.envirosafetyproducts.com

**Keepsake Catalog Company,** 3041 N. Coolidge Ave., Los Angeles, CA 90039: Free catalog ◆ Specialty products that help with the safety and security of family and pets outside and away from the home, for common at-home household concerns, and other needs. 213-666-9172.

**Lab Safety Supply Inc.,** P.O. Box 1368, Janesville, WI 53547: Free information ◆ Dust protection masks. 800-356-0783.

**Moore Medical Corp.,** 389 John Downey Dr., P.O. Box 2740, New Britain, CT 06051: Free catalog ◆ Occupational safety and health accessories. 800-234-1464.

**Nitro-Pak Preparedness Center,** 151 N. Main St., Heber City, UT 84032: Catalog $3 ◆ Survival equipment and supplies, freeze-dried and dehydrated foods, books, and videos. 800-866-4876. www.nitro-pak.com

**Northern Safety Company Inc.,** P.O. Box 4250, Utica, NY 13504: Free information ◆ Dust protection masks, protective clothing, glasses, and more. 800-631-1246. www.northernsafety.com

**Out N Back,** 1797 S. State St., Orem, UT 84058: Free catalog ◆ Survival equipment and supplies for outdoor recreational activities. 800-533-7415.

**Perfectly Safe,** 7835 Freedom Ave. NW, North Canton, OH 44720: Free catalog ◆ Safety items for children age 3 to 6. 800-837-5437.

**Premier Technologies International Inc.,** 7100 N. Broadway, Bldg. 1, Denver, CO 80221: Free brochure ◆ Emergency response dialer which, when pressed, automatically dials 911 to summon emergency aid. 888-373-3911; 303-412-8000 (in CO).

**The Safety Zone,** Hanover Direct Pennsylvania Inc., Hanover, PA 17333-0001: Free catalog ◆ Safety and security products. 717-633-3333.

**Seton Identification Products,** 20 Thompson Rd., Branford, CT 06405: Free catalog ◆ Identification and safety-related products. 800-243-6624; 203-488-8059 (in CT). www.seton.com

**The Survival Center,** P.O. Box 234, McKenna, WA 98558: Catalog $2 ◆ Survival equipment for outdoor activities. 800-321-2900; 360-458-6778 (in WA). www.survivalcenter.com

**Talley Security,** 3900 E. Range Ln., Flagstaff, AZ 86004: Free catalog ◆ Personal security aids. 800-211-0615. www.talleysecurity.com/talley

**United States Survival Society,** 1223 Wilshire Blvd., #492, Santa Monica, CA 90403: Free catalog ◆ Emergency foods, water, solar radios, and survival and emergency equipment. 800-278-7848; 310-652-4777 (in CA).

**WorkAbles for Women,** 96 Combs Rd., Clinton, PA 15026: Free catalog ◆ Gloves, hats, T-shirts, socks, outdoor clothing, rain gear, and personal safety items for women. 800-862-9317.

**Worldwide Outfitters,** 117 Benedict St., Waterbury, CT 06722: Free catalog ◆ Gloves, aprons, safety glasses, hearing protection, disposable clothing, and shoes and boots. 800-243-3570; 800-243-3571 (in CT). Joshterad@wtco.net

## SAILBOARDS (WINDSURFING EQUIPMENT)

**Big Winds,** 505 Cascade St., Hood River, OR 97031: Free catalog ◆ Windsurfing equipment. 888-509-4210; 541-386-6086 (in OR).

**Ezzy Direct USA,** 108 Hwy. 35, Hood River, OR 97031: Free information ◆ Sails. 800-490-7436.

**Front Street Sailboards,** 207 Front St., Hood River, OR 97031: Free catalog ◆ Sailboards. 888-525-6417; 541-386-4044 (in OR).

**HiFly Windsurfing,** 199 Ankeny Hill Rd., Jefferson, OR 97352: Free brochure ◆ Windsurfing boards. 800-424-4359.

**The House,** 300 S. Owasso Blvd., St. Paul, MN 55117: Free catalog ◆ Windsurfing equipment. 800-409-7669. www.the-house.com

**Skip Hutchison,** Rastaboards-Surf-Sail-Snowboards, 4748 NE 11th Ave., Fort Lauderdale, FL 33334: Free information ◆ Sailboards, surfboards, and snowboards. 954-491-7992.

**Isthmus Sailboards,** 5495 Catfish Ct., Waunakee, WI 53597: Free information ◆ Sailboards. 800-473-1153.

**Kinetic Sports Inc.,** 3211 Wood St., Oakland, CA 94608: Free brochure ◆ Sailboards. 510-836-0967.

**Mermaid Stabilizers,** P.O. Box 1072, North Battleford, Sask., Canada S9A 3E6: Free information ◆ Canoe and windsurfing stabilizers and sails. 800-215-5307. www.w2d.com/mermaid

**Murrays WaterSports,** P.O. Box 490, Carpinteria, CA 93014: Free information ◆ Catamaran and windsurfing accessories. 800-788-8964. www.murrays.com

**North Sports,** P.O. Box 1849, White Salmon, WA 98672: Free brochure ◆ Windsurfing boards. 509-493-4938.

**Outside Sports,** P.O. Box 1588, Hood River, OR 97031: Free information ◆ Windsurfing equipment.

**Sailboard Warehouse Inc.,** 300 S. Owasso, St. Paul, MN 55117: Catalog $1.50 ◆ Sailboards, sails and masts, wet suits, roof racks, harnesses, books, and videos. 800-409-7669. www.the-house.com

**Sailways,** 301 Commerce Dr., Fairfield, CT 06432: Free catalog ◆ Windsurfing equipment. 800-544-9463; 203-336-9463 (in CT).

**Santa Fe Windsurfing,** 1086 Siler Rd., Santa Fe, NM 87501: Free information ◆ Windsurfing equipment. 800-825-7755; 505-473-7900 (in NM).

**Waterplay,** 2550 S. Bayshore Dr., Coconut Grove, FL 33133: Free catalog ◆ Windsurfing equipment. 800-841-1225.

**Wind Addiction,** 53 Yonge St., Kingston, Ontario, Canada K7M 1E4: Free catalog ◆ Windsurfing equipment. 800-617-WIND.

## SANDCARVING

**Rayzist Photomask Inc.,** 955 Park Center Dr., Vista, CA 92083: Free catalog ◆ Sandcarving equipment, glass and crystal blanks, and other supplies. 800-729-9478; 760-727-8185 (in CA). www.rayzist.com

## SCIENCE KITS & PROJECTS

**American Science & Surplus,** 3605 Howard St., Skokie, IL 60076: Catalog $1 ◆ Surplus science and electro-mechanical supplies, other equipment, and kits. 847-982-0870. www.sciplus.com

**Edlie Electronics,** 2700 Hempstead Tnpk., Levittown, NY 11756: Free catalog ◆ Electronics kits, parts, and supplies. 516-735-3330.

**Edmund Scientific Company,** Edscorp Bldg., Barrington, NJ 08007: Free catalog ◆ Microscopes, magnifiers, weather forecasting instruments, magnets, telescopes, lasers, and other optical, scientific, and educational items. 609-547-8880. www.edsci.com

**The Electronic Goldmine,** P.O. Box 5408, Scottsdale, AZ 85261: Free catalog ◆ Science kits and supplies. 800-445-0697; 602-451-7454 (in AZ). www.goldmine-elec.com

**Gardens for Growing People,** P.O. Box 630, Point Reyes, CA 94956: Free catalog ◆ Gardening supplies, kits, and other resources for garden-based education. 415-663-9433. growpepl@svn.net

**J.L. Hammett Company,** P.O. Box 9057, Braintree, MA 02184: Free catalog ◆ Science kits and projects, microscopes, laboratory apparatus, rock collections, magnets, astronomy charts, and anatomical models. 781-848-1000.

**Heathkit Educational Systems,** 455 Riverview Dr., Benton Harbor, MI 49022: Free catalog ◆ Computers and robotic projects, TVs, home accessories, and educational and electronic kits. 800-253-0570. www.heathkit.com

**Hobby World Ltd. of Montreal,** 5450 Sherbrooke St. West, Montreal, Quebec, Canada H4A 1V9: Catalog $5 ◆ Airplanes, helicopters, cars and trucks, ships, military vehicles, and science models. 514-481-5434.

**Hubbard Scientific Company,** American Educational Products, 1120 Halbleib Rd., Chippewa Falls, WI 54729: Free catalog ◆ Hands-on educational manipulative activities and relief maps for the world, United States, international regional areas, and more. 800-323-8368; 715-723-4427 (in WI). www.amep.com

**Information Unlimited,** P.O. Box 716, Amherst, NH 03031: Catalog $1 ◆ Lasers, communication equipment, Tesla coils and experiments, mini radios, rocket equipment, flying saucers, and other kits. 603-673-4730. www.amazing1.com

**Merrell Scientific/World of Science,** 900 Jefferson Rd., Bldg. 4, Rochester, NY 14623: Catalog $2 ◆ Chemicals, glassware, and laboratory equipment. Also biology, nature, physical and earth science, astronomy, and model rocketry supplies and equipment. 716-475-0100. www.roccplex.com/wos

**Nasco,** 901 Janesville Ave., Fort Atkinson, WI 53538: Free catalog ◆ Science supplies and kits, microscopes and dissection instruments, rock collections, magnets, electric motors, ultraviolet lighting equipment, astronomy charts and star maps, and anatomical models. 800-558-9595. www.nascofa.com

**The Nature Company,** Catalog Division, P.O. Box 188, Florence, KY 41022: Free catalog ◆ Science supplies, kits, books, toys, novelties, and gifts. 800-227-1114. www.natureco.com

**Radio Shack,** Division Tandy Corp., One Tandy Center, Fort Worth, TX 76102: Free information ◆ Electronic science projects, kits, electronics equipment, and supplies. 817-390-3011. www.radioshack.com

**Silicon Valley Surplus,** 1273 Industrial Pkwy. West, Bldg. 460, P.O. Box 55125, Hayward, CA 94545: Free information ◆ Light and motion projects, laser applications, computer interface equipment, and other kits. 510-582-6602.

**Uptown Sales Inc.,** 33 N. Main St., Chambersburg, PA 17201: Catalog $1 ◆ Science kits for amateur scientists. 800-548-9941.

## SCOOTERS

**Dominion Skate Company Ltd.,** 45 Railroad St., Brampton, Ontario, Canada L6X 1G4: Free information ◆ Roller skates and scooters. 416-453-9860.

**Mac's Motor Sports,** P.O. Box 7190, Wesley Chapel, FL 33544: Free information ◆ Motorized scooters and folding bicycles. 813-973-7108.

**Mark II Enterprises,** 5225 Canyon Quest Dr., Riverside, CA 92507: Free information ◆ Lightweight portable motorized scooters. 909-686-2752.

**Mobileation,** 445 E. 87th St., Ste 4, New York, NY 10128: Free catalog ◆ Mobile interactive riding toys for children. Includes electric and gasoline-engine cars, battery operated and pedal driven vehicles, ride-on toys for toddlers and infants, tricycles, bikes, scooters, seesaws, build-them-yourself pedal car kits, and handcrafted rocking horses. 888-88-MOBILE; 212-426-8074 (in NY). service@mobileation.com

**Motoboard International,** P.O. Box 2224, Los Banos, CA 93635: Information $2 ◆ Motorized scooters. 209-827-1600.

**National Sporting Goods Corp.,** 25 Brighton Ave., Passaic, NJ 07055: Free information ◆ Roller skates, scooters, skateboards, and protective gear. 201-779-2323.

**Roller Derby Skate Company,** Box 930, Litchfield, IL 62056: Free information ◆ Skateboards, roller and in-line skates, and scooters. 217-324-3961.

**Ron's Rad Toys,** 4610 S. 133rd, Ste. 104, Omaha, NE 68137: Free information ◆ Fold-down motorized scooters and accessories. 800-841-3625; 402-333-6950 (in NE).

**Roller Derby Skate Company,** Box 930, Litchfield, IL 62056: Free information ◆ Roller skates, scooters, and skateboards. 217-324-3961.

**Saucony/Hyde,** 13 Centennial Dr., Peabody, MA 01961: Free information ◆ Roller skates, scooters, and skateboards. 800-365-7282.

**Scooterworks USA,** 5709 N. Ravenswood, Chicago, IL 60660: Free information ◆ Scooters, parts, and accessories. 773-271-4242.

**Rich Suski,** 7061 County Road 108, Town Creek, AL 35672: Free catalog ◆ Cushman parts for vintage motorbikes and scooters. 256-685-2510.

## SCOUTING

**Boy Scouts of America,** P.O. Box 909, Pineville, NC 28134: Free catalog ◆ Uniforms and insignia, camping equipment, sportswear, books, and scouting equipment. 800-323-0732.

**Girl Scout Catalog,** 420 5th Ave., New York, NY 10018: Free catalog ◆ Uniforms and insignia, camping equipment, sportswear, books, jewelry, and gifts. 800-221-6707.

**JCPenney Catalog,** P.O. Box 675, Milwaukee, WI 53201: Free information ◆ Boy and girl scout equipment and supplies. 800-222-6161. www.jcpenney.com/shopping

**SEASHE Rocky Mountain Connection,** P.O. Box 2800, Estes Park, CO 80517: Catalog $1 (specify type of items wanted) ◆ Outdoor and western-style clothing, Boy Scouts clothing and outdoor gear, hiking staffs, backpacks, and more. 800-679-3600. www.RMConnection.com

**The Stevensons Scouting Memorabilia,** 316 Sage Ln., Euless, TX 76039: Free list with 1st class stamp ◆ Collectible Boy Scout memorabilia.

## SEASHELLS

**Benjane Arts,** P.O. Box 298, West Hempstead, NY 11552: Catalog $5 ◆ Seashells. 516-483-1330.

**Bourget Bros.,** 1636 11th St., Santa Monica, CA 90404: Catalog $3 ◆ Seashells, jewelry-making tools and supplies, gemstones, beads, and bead-stringing supplies. 800-828-3024. www.bourgetbros.com

**Creative Craft House,** Box 2567, Bullhead City, AZ 86430: Catalog $2 (refundable) ◆ Seashells, pine cones, and craft supplies.

**Ebersole Lapidary Supply Inc.,** 11417 West Hwy. 54, Wichita, KS 67209: Catalog $5 ◆ Shark teeth, cameo shells, murex or fox shells, tiger cowries, mushroom corals, seashells from worldwide sources, and lapidary equipment. 316-722-4771.

**Ed's House of Gems,** 7712 NE Sandy Blvd., Portland, OR 97211: Free information with long SASE ◆ Seashells, crystals, minerals, gemstones, lapidary equipment, mountings, and Native American relics. 503-284-8990.

**Herkimer Diamond Mines,** RD 1, P.O. Box 233, Herkimer, NY 13350: Free information ◆ Petrified wood products, seashells, craft supplies, minerals and rocks, quartz crystals, and gifts. 315-866-2011.

**Indian Jewelers Supply Company,** 601 E. Coal Ave., Gallup, NM 87301: Catalog $6 ◆ Precious and base metals, findings, metalsmithing and lapidary tools and supplies, semi-precious stones, seashells, and coral. 505-722-4451.

**Jeanne's Rock & Jewelry,** 5420 Bissonet, Bellaire, TX 77401: Price list $1 ◆ Seashells, petrified wood products, lapidary supplies, and gifts. 713-664-2988.

**Nature's Jewelry,** 222 Mill Rd., Chelmsford, MA 01824: Free catalog ◆ Leaves, seashells, and other natural objects transformed into jewelry by preservation in precious metals. 800-333-3235.

**Riviera Lapidary Supply,** 50898 7th St., Box 40, Riviera, TX 78379: Catalog $3 ◆ Seashells, beads, cabochons, slabs, cabbing rough gems, and crystals. 512-296-3958.

**Shell-A-Rama,** Box 291327, Fort Lauderdale, FL 33329: Catalog $2 ◆ Seashells for crafts, decorations, and collections. 954-434-2818. www.shellarama.com

**U.S. Shell Inc.,** P.O. Box 1033, Port Isabel, TX 78578: Free catalog ◆ Shells for crafting and making novelties. 956-943-1709.

**What on Earth Naturally,** 6250 Busch Blvd., Columbus, OH 43229: Free information ◆ Minerals, fossils, jewelry, gemstones, and shells. 614-436-1458.

## SEPTIC TANKS

**Krane Products,** P.O. Box 310721, Boca Raton, FL 33431: Free information ◆ Maintenance products for septic tanks. 800-614-0066. www.kraneproducts.com

## SEWING

### Buttons

**Banasch,** 2810 Highland Ave., Cincinnati, OH 45212: Free catalog ◆ Beads, pearls, notions, and buttons. 800-543-0355; 513-731-2040 (in OH).

**The Belt & Button Connection,** 120 Jersey Ave., New Brunswick, NJ 08901: Catalog $1 (refundable) ◆ Custom covered buttons and belts in fabric, suede, or leather. 732-448-0600. www.beltbutton.com

**Button Gallery,** 2283 Business Way, Riverside, CA 92501: Free catalog ◆ Wood, novelty, leather, glass, Victorian fancy, gold, and silver buttons. 800-287-6275. www.procrafter.com/button/bgallery.htm

**The Button Shoppe,** 4744 Oakfield Circle, Carmichael, CA 95608: Catalog $5 ◆ Bold, bulky, tiny, delicate, and other buttons. 916-488-5350.

**Delectable Mountain Cloth,** 125 Main St., Brattleboro, VT 05301: Brochure $1 with long SASE ◆ Buttons and natural fabrics from worldwide sources.

**Dogwood Lane Buttons,** Box 145, Dugger, IN 47848: Catalog $2.50 (refundable) ◆ Handmade porcelain buttons. 800-648-2213.

**Fashion Touches,** 170 Elm St., P.O. Box 804, Bridgeport, CT 06604: Catalog $1 ◆ Covered belts and buttons. 203-333-7738.

**Green Pepper,** 1285 River Rd., Eugene, OR 97404: Catalog $2 ◆ Buckles, Velcro and fasteners, zippers, buttons, notions, and kits for coats and jackets, ski wear, water-repellent clothing, and duffel bags. 541-689-3292.

**Debra J. Rutherford Designs,** P.O. Box 100, Essex, MA 01929: Free information ◆ Handcrafted ceramic buttons and jewelry. 978-927-7012.

**Salem Manufacturing Company,** 170 Braided Blanket Bluff, Alpharetta, GA 30022: Free information ◆ Craft and sewing aids. Also buttons. 770-521-9837. bknezevic@mindspring.com

**Sew Fine,** 18399 Ventura Blvd., Tarzana, CA 91356: Free information with long SASE ◆ Smocking and sewing supplies, French and English lace, buttons, ribbons, and Swiss embroideries. 818-886-1108.

**Ben Silver,** 149 King St., Charleston, SC 29401: Free catalog ◆ College crests, monograms, and blazer buttons. 800-849-0973. www.bensilver.com

**Three Kittens Yarn Shoppe,** 805 Sibley Memorial Hwy., St. Paul, MN 55118: Information $2 ◆ Handpainted porcelain buttons. 800-489-4969; 612-457-4969 (in MN).

**Woolgathering,** 750 Calico Ct., Waukesha, WI 53186: Free price list ◆ Rowan yarns, needle point kits, buttons, books and magazines, and sewing notions. 888-248-3225.

**Wooly Knits,** 6728 Lowell Ave., McLean, VA 22101: Catalog $5 (12 issues) ◆ Designer yarns, unusual buttons, and needlework supplies. 703-448-9665. www.woolyknits.com

### Dress Forms

**Bonfit America Inc.,** 5959 Triumph St., Commerce, CA 90040: Free information ◆ Non-paper pattern-maker that adjusts to different sizes and styles. 800-725-1133.

**CSZ Enterprises Inc.,** 1288 W. 11th St., Ste. 200, Tracy, CA 95376: Free information ◆ Custom-made or make-them-yourself kits for dress and pants forms. 209-832-4324.

**Dress Rite Forms,** 3817 N. Pulaski, Chicago, IL 60641: Free information ◆ Dress-forms in all sizes and shapes. 312-588-5761.

### Notions & Supplies

**Abraham's Lady,** Donna Abraham, 1402 St. Matthew Dr., Verga, NJ 08093: Catalog $1 ◆ Trims, notions, and accessories for Civil War reproduction clothing. 609-853-6882. abraham@comten.com

**AK Sew & Serge,** 1602 6th St. SE, Winter Haven, FL 33880: Catalog $5 ◆ Heirloom and fashion sewing and quilting supplies. 800-299-8096; 813-299-3080 (in FL).

**Alter Years,** 3749 E. Colorado Blvd., Pasadena, CA 91107: Catalog $5 ◆ Underpinnings and accessories, costume-making supplies, over 1000 costume reference books, and patterns. 818-585-2994.

**Atlanta Thread & Supply,** 695 Red Oak Rd., Stockbridge, GA 30281: Catalog $1 ◆ Notions and machines. 800-331-7600.

**Baer Fabrics,** 515 E. Market St., Louisville, KY 40202: Catalog $3 ◆ Sewing notions, trim, and fabrics. 800-769-7778.

**Banasch,** 2810 Highland Ave., Cincinnati, OH 45212: Free catalog ◆ Beads, pearls, notions, and buttons. 800-543-0355; 513-731-2040 (in OH).

**Bay Area Tailoring Supply,** 8000 Capwell Dr., Oakland, CA 94621: Free information ◆ Tailoring supplies. 800-359-0400; 510-635-1100 (in CA).

**Beacon Fabric & Notions,** 6801 Gulfport Blvd. South, South Pasadena, FL 33707: Free catalog ◆ Active wear, outdoor clothing, flag and banner fabrics, machine embroidery and other threads, and sewing supplies. 800-713-8157; 813-345-6994 (in FL). www.beaconfabric.com

**Bee Lee Company,** Box 36108, Dallas, TX 75235: Free catalog ◆ Notions, belt buckles and snaps, trims, zippers, interfacings, threads, and notions. 800-527-5271.

**Britex Fabrics,** 146 Geary St., San Francisco, CA 94108: Free information ◆ Cording, braids, and fabrics. 415-392-2910.

**Buttons 'n' Bows,** 14086 Memorial, Houston, TX 77079: Catalog $2 (refundable) ◆ Fabrics. Also smocking and heirloom sewing supplies. 281-496-0170.

**Clotilde,** B3000, Louisiana, MO 63353: Free catalog ◆ Notions, books, patterns, and videos. 800-772-2891.

**Connecting Threads,** P.O. Box 8940, Vancouver, WA 98668: Free catalog ◆ Sewing supplies and accessories. 800-574-6454.

**The Creative Needle,** 6905 S. Broadway, Ste. 113, Littleton, CO 80122: Catalog $1 ◆ Heirloom sewing, smocking, stitchery, and quilting supplies. 303-794-7312.

**Delectable Mountain Cloth,** 125 Main St., Brattleboro, VT 05301: Brochure $1 with long SASE ◆ Buttons and natural fabrics from worldwide sources.

**Designer Jeans,** P.O. Box 44, Manti, UT 84642: Catalog $2 ◆ Jean-making supplies and ready-to-wear designer jeans. 435-835-0311. www.sisna.com/chaz/dji

**DK Sports,** Division Daisy Kingdom, 134 NW 8th St., Portland, OR 97209: Free information ◆ Rainwear, outerwear fabrics, and notions. 800-234-6688.

**Dritz Corp.,** P.O. Box 5028, Spartanburg, SC 29304: Free information ◆ Marking pens, awls, cutting mats, cutters, scissors, needles, straight and safety pins, zipper glides, craft tape, glue sticks, tape measures, and other notions. 800-845-4948.

**Elna,** 1032-C 4th Ave. SE, Decatur, AL 35601: Free information ◆ Smocking and heirloom sewing supplies and fabrics. 256-351-6196.

**Fabric Depot,** 700 SE 122nd Ave., Portland, OR 97233: Free information ◆ Fabrics, notions, thread, zippers, and other sewing supplies. 800-392-3376.

**Fine Line Fabrics,** 1153 El Camino Real, Menlo Park, CA 94025: Free information ◆ Silk, linen, rayon, cotton, wool and other fabrics, Also designer ends and pieces, buttons, notions, and trim. 650-322-8775. www.finelinefabrics.com

**Fiskars Scissors,** P.O. Box 8027, Wausau, WI 54402: Free information ◆ Safety scissors for children, other scissors, and sharpeners. 715-842-2091.

**Granny's Attic,** 104 N. 3rd St., McCall, ID 83638: Free information ◆ Sewing supplies and accessories. 800-860-5921.

**Green Pepper,** 1285 River Rd., Eugene, OR 97404: Catalog $2 ◆ Buckles, Velcro and fasteners, zippers, buttons, notions, and kits for coats and jackets, ski wear, water-repellent clothing, and duffel bags. 541-689-3292.

**Greenberg & Hammer Inc.,** 24 W. 57th St., New York, NY 10019: Free catalog ◆ Tailoring supplies and notions. 800-955-5135.

**Hancock Fabrics,** 3841 Hinkleville Rd., Paducah, KY 42001: Free information ◆ Quilting supplies, fabrics, and notions. 800-845-8723.

**Handcrafted Wood Products,** 11280 US Hwy. 90, Daphne, AL 36526: Free information ◆ Wood-crafted spool and bobbin organizer and wall rack for serger cones. 334-633-4570.

**Harper House,** P.O. Box 39, Williamstown, PA 17098: Catalog $6 ◆ Historic and ethnic garment patterns, sewing notions, and books. 717-647-7807.

**Hedgehog Handworks,** P.O. Box 45384, Westchester, CA 90045: Catalog $5 ◆ Semi-precious beads, sewing notions, gold and silver threads, and needlecraft and embroidery supplies. 888-670-6040; 310-670-6040 (in CA).

**Home-Sew Inc.,** P.O. Box 4099, Bethlehem, PA 18018: Catalog $1 ◆ Sewing supplies, notions, and craft items. 610-867-3833.

**In The Beginning,** 8201 Lake City Way NE, Seattle, WA 89115: Free information ◆ Sewing supplies and accessories. 206-523-8862.

**Joanne's Notions,** P.O. Box 44030, Brampton, Ontario, Canada L6V 4H5: Catalog $2 ◆ Sewing, serging, pressing, heirloom, quilting supplies, and notions.

**Judy's Heirloom Sewing,** 13650 E. Zayante Rd., Felton, CA 95018: Catalog $6.50 ◆ Sewing and smocking supplies, fabrics, lace, ribbons, and yarns. 408-335-1050.

**Kiyo Design Inc.,** 11 Annapolis St., Annapolis, MD 21041: Catalog $15 ◆ Notions, fabrics, lace, beads, and more. 410-280-1942. www.kiyoinc.com/fabric.html

**Kreinik Manufacturing Company,** 1708 Gihon Rd., P.O. Box 1966, Parkersburg, WV 26102: Free list of retail sources with long SASE ◆ Metallic and decorative threads. 800-311-8061.

**Laces 'N Rags,** 714 Mall Blvd., Savannah, GA 31406: Free information ◆ Fabrics, lace, and smocking and sewing supplies. 912-354-8863.

**Ledgewood Studio,** 6000 Ledgewood Dr., Forest Park, GA 30050: Catalog $2 with long SASE and three 1st class stamps ◆ Dress patterns for antique dolls, supplies for authentic period costumes, notions, and braids, French lace, silk ribbons, silk taffeta, China silk, Swiss batiste, and trim. 404-361-6098.

**Donna Lee's Sewing Center,** 25234 Pacific Hwy. South, Kent, WA 98032: Catalog $4 ◆ Swiss batiste, imperial batiste, China silk, silk charmeuse, French val lace, English lace, Swiss embroidery, trim and yardage fabrics, and silk and embroidered ribbons. 206-941-9466.

**Linda's Silver Needle,** P.O. Box 2167, Naperville, IL 60567: Free information ◆ Sewing and smocking supplies. 800-SMOCK-IT.

**Madeira USA Ltd.,** P.O. Box 6068, Laconia, NH 03246: Free information ◆ Gold and silver metallic thread. 800-225-3001. www.stocko.com/sfg/madeira.html

**Manny's Millinery Supply Center,** 26 W. 38th St., New York, NY 10018: Catalog $3 ◆ Millinery supplies and accessories. 212-840-2235.

**Maple Shade Crafts,** Catalog Department, RR 1, Box 186, Pulaski, VA 24301: Catalog $4 (refundable) ◆ Craft supplies, sewing notions, Victorian jewelry, scented candles, cameos, and potpourri. 800-986-9674. www.swva.net/mapleshade

**Meissner's Sewing,** 2417 Cormorant Way, Sacramento, CA 95815: Free information ◆ Sewing machines and notions. 800-521-2332.

**Mimi's Fabrications,** 77 Howell St., Waynesville, NC 28786: Free information ◆ Sewing supplies and accessories. 800-948-3455. www.mimisbymail.com

**Nancy's Notions,** P.O. Box 683, Beaver Dam, WI 53916: Free catalog ◆ Notions, threads, books, patterns, and interlock knits, fleece, gabardines, sweater knits, challis, and other fabrics. 800-245-5116. www.nancysnotions.com

**National Thread & Supply,** 695 Red Oak Rd., Stockbridge, GA 30281: Free catalog ◆ Cone threads and sewing notions. 800-331-7600.

**Needle Niche,** 518 W. Palmetto St., Florence SC 29501: Free information ◆ Smocking and heirloom sewing supplies. 803-678-9373.

**Needles & Pins,** 3019 SW Martin Downs Blvd., Palm City, FL 34990: Free information ◆ Smocking supplies, fabrics, imported lace and buttons, quilting fabrics, and other supplies. 561-220-9198.

**Newark Dressmaker Supply,** P.O. Box 20730, Lehigh Valley, PA 18002: Free catalog ◆ Supplies for sewing, crafts, and needlework. 800-736-6783.

**Oppenheim's,** P.O. Box 29, North Manchester, IN 46962: Catalog $1 ◆ Sewing notions, fabrics, and craft supplies. 800-461-6728.

**Oregon Tailor Supplies,** P.O. Box 42284, Portland, OR 97242: Free information ◆ Sewing notions. 800-678-2457.

**Ornamental Resources Inc.,** P.O. Box 3010, Idaho Springs, CO 80452: Catalog $15 ◆ Vintage and contemporary glass beads, rhinestones, stones and buttons, and metal charms and stampings. 800-876-6762. www.ornabead.com

**Outdoor Wilderness Fabrics,** 16415 Midland Blvd., Nampa, ID 83687: Free price list ◆ Coated and uncoated nylon fabrics, fleece and blends in coat weights, waterproof fabrics, hardware, webbing, zippers, patterns, and other notions. 800-093-7467. www.owfinc.com

**The Perfect Notion,** Box 521, 7620 Elbow Dr. SW, Calgary, AB, Canada T2V 1K2: Free catalog ◆ Fabrics, quilt batting, books, patterns, sewing and quilting supplies, and notions. 888-999-8821. www.perfectnotion.com

**Rainshed Outdoor Fabrics,** 707 NW 11th, Corvallis, OR 97330: Catalog $1 ◆ Rainwear and outerwear fabrics, notions, webbing, and patterns. 541-753-8900.

**Mary Roehr Books & Videos,** 500 Saddlerock Circle, Sedona, AZ 86336: Free catalog ◆ How-to books, videos, and supplies on sewing and tailoring. 800-291-6764.

**S & S Sewing Machine Company Inc.,** 900 Bob Wallace Ave., #105-B, Huntsville, AL 35801: Free information ◆ Notions, fabrics, sewing machines, and accessories. 800-SEW-ELNA.

**Sand Dollar,** 1740 E. Pass Rd., Gulfport, MS 39507: Free information ◆ Smocking and heirloom sewing supplies. Also ribbons. 800-230-3995; 601-896-3995 (in MS).

**Seattle Fabrics,** 8702 Aurora North, Seattle, WA 98103: Price list $3 (refundable) ◆ Notions and patterns. 206-525-0670. www.seattlefabrics.com

**Sew Fancy,** Unit 23, RR 1, Beeton, Ontario, Canada L0G 1A0: Catalog $5 ◆ Fabrics, notions, needle art patterns, and supplies for heirloom sewing, smocking, and quilting. 800-SEW-FNCY. www.sewfancy.com

**Sew Fine,** 18399 Ventura Blvd., Tarzana, CA 91356: Free information with long SASE ◆ Smocking and sewing supplies, French and English lace, buttons, ribbons, and Swiss embroideries. 818-886-1108.

**Sew 'n Sew,** 1111 N. Main St., Summerville, NC 29483: Free information ◆ Smocking and heirloom sewing supplies, English and French lace, fabrics, and knitting aids. 803-871-7822.

**Sew So Fancy,** 914 Queen City Ave., Tuscaloosa, AL 35401: Free information with long SASE ◆ Lace, mother of pearl buttons, Swiss embroideries, fabrics, and other supplies. 800-821-0607.

**Sew True,** 447 W. 36th St., New York, NY 10018: Free catalog ◆ Notions, thread, lining, patterns, cutting tools, fasteners, and sewing machines. 800-SEW-TRUE.

**Sew Unique,** 626 15th St. East, Tuscaloosa, AL 35401: Free brochure with long SASE ◆ Fabrics and lace, smoking and embroidery supplies, ready to smock kits, and supplies. 800-837-8799.

**Sew-Art International,** P.O. Box 1244, Bountiful, UT 84011: Free information ◆ Sewing supplies and accessories. 800-231-2787.

**Sewin' in Vermont,** 84 Concord Ave., St. Johnsbury, VT 05819: Free information ◆ Sewing machines, sergers, and notions. 800-451-5124.

**The Sewing Place,** 18476 Prospect Rd., Saratoga, CA 95070: Catalog $2 ◆ Sewing supplies and accessories. 800-587-3937. www.thesewingplace.com

**Ben Silver,** 149 King St., Charleston, SC 29401: Free catalog ◆ College crests, monograms, and blazer buttons. 800-849-0973. www.bensilver.com

**Smock & Sew,** 2211 21st Ave. South, Nashville, TN 37212: Free information ◆ Fabrics, smocking supplies, notions, silk ribbon, and accessories. 615-269-5177.

**The Snap Source,** P.O. Box 99733, Troy, MI 48099: Free information ◆ Snaps and snap-attaching tools. 800-725-4600.

**SouthStar Supply Corp.,** P.O. Box 90147, Nashville, TN 37209: Free information ◆ Sewing notions and supplies. 800-288-6739.

**Speed Stitch,** 3115 Broadpoint Dr., Harbor Heights, FL 33983: Catalog $3 ◆ Machine arts and quilting supplies. 800-874-4115; 352-629-3199 (in FL).

**Stonemountain & Daughter Fabrics,** 2518 Shattuck Ave., Berkeley, CA 94704: Free information ◆ Cording and braids. 510-845-6106.

**Stretch & Sew,** 8697 La Mesa Blvd., La Mesa, CA 91941: Catalog $3 ◆ Fabrics, patterns, and notions. 800-547-7717. www.stretch-and-sew.com

**Tandy Leather Company,** P.O. Box 791, Fort Worth, TX 76101: Catalog $3 (refundable) ◆ Leather crafting kits, tools, books, patterns, sewing notions, and how-to videos. 800-555-3130. www.tandyleather.com

**Taylor's Cutaways & Stuff,** 2802 E. Washington St., Urbana, IL 61801: Brochure $1 ◆ Satins, lace, velvet, cottons, felt, calico, trims, polyester squares, sewing notions, craft supplies, books, and soft toy and crochet patterns. www.home.sprynet.com/sprynet/tcutaway

**Things Japanese,** 9805 NE 116th St., Ste. 7160, Kirkland, WA 98034: Catalog $1 ◆ Silk filament sewing thread. 425-821-2287.

**Thoburn's,** P.O. Box 231, Londonderry, NH 03053: Brochure and swatches $6 ◆ Fleece in prints and solids, patterns, and notions. 603-437-4924.

**The Thread Shed,** P.O. Box 898, Horse Shoe, NC 28742: Free catalog with long SASE ◆ Rayon, metallic, cotton, and other embellishing threads. 704-692-5128. www.threadshed.com

**TreadleArt,** 25834 Narboone Ave., Lomita, CA 90717: Free information ◆ Sewing and quilting supplies. 310-534-5122.

**Treasured Heirlooms,** 13507 Candlewood Ct., Moorpark, CA 93021: Free newsletter with long SASE ◆ Fabrics, lace, embroideries, needlework supplies, notions, and more. 805-523-2520.

**Treasures & Keepsakes,** P.O. Box 331825, Fort Worth, TX 76163: Catalog $2 (refundable) ◆ Smocking and heirloom sewing supplies. 817-263-8535.

**Ultramouse Ltd.,** 3433 Bennington Ct., Bloomfield Hills, MI 48301: Catalog $2 ◆ Notions, ultrasuede, and fabric scraps. 800-225-1887.

**Utex Trading,** 710 9th St., Ste. 5, Niagara Falls, NY 14301: Free brochure with long SASE ◆ Sewing supplies and imported silk fabrics. 716-282-8211.

**Wawak Corp.,** 2235 Hammond Dr., Schaumberg, IL 60173: Catalog $4 ◆ Alteration and sewing supplies. 800-654-2235.

**Web of Thread,** 1410 Broadway, Paducah, KY 42001: Catalog $3 ◆ Supplies for serger and embroidery crafts and metallic, rayon, and silk thread for hand and machine embroidery. 800-955-8185; 502-575-9700 (in KY). www.webofthread.com

**Woolgathering,** 750 Calico Ct., Waukesha, WI 53186: Free price list ◆ Rowan yarns, needle point kits, buttons, books and magazines, and sewing notions. 800-248-3225.

**Wooly Knits,** 6728 Lowell Ave., McLean, VA 22101: Catalog $5 (12 issues) ◆ Designer yarns, unusual buttons, and needlework supplies. 703-448-9665. www.woolyknits.com/

## Pattern Making Software

**Cochenille Design Studio,** P.O. Box 4276, Ecinitas, CA 92023: Catalog $1 ◆ Garment styling software for PCs and the Macintosh. 619-259-1698. www.cochenille.com

**LivingSoft Inc.,** 40 S. Lassen St., Box 819, Susanville, CA 96130: Free information ◆ Pattern designing software for Windows 3.1 and 95, DOS, or the Macintosh. 888-626-1262. www.livingsoft.com

**Patternmaking Software,** 2029 144th Ave. SE, Bellevue, WA 98007: Free information ◆ Windows 3.1 and higher pattern-making software for PCs. 425-644-8161. www.eskimo.com/~pmaker

**Water Fountain Software Inc.,** 13 E. 17th St., New York, NY 10003: Free information ◆ Pattern printing software in custom-fitted full sizes for men and women. 800-605-7460.

## Patterns & Kits

**A.C.S.,** 447 W. 36th St., New York, NY 10018: Free catalog ◆ Notions, thread, lining, patterns, cutting tools, fasteners, and sewing machines. 800-SEW-TRUE.

**Alter Years,** 3749 E. Colorado Blvd., Pasadena, CA 91107: Catalog $5 ◆ Underpinnings and accessories, costume-making supplies, over 1000 costume reference books, and patterns. 818-585-2994.

**Amazon Drygoods,** 2218 E. 11th St., Davenport, IA 52803: Catalog $7 ◆ Victorian and Edwardian clothing patterns, from the 1920s and 1930s. 800-798-7979. www.amazondrygoods.com

**Annie's Attic,** 1 Annie Ln., Big Sandy, TX 75755: Catalog $2 ◆ Sewing and needlecraft patterns and supplies. 800-282-6643.

**BottomLine Designs,** 4217 Hildring Dr. West, Fort Worth, TX 76109: Catalog $2 ◆ Clothing patterns. 800-611-7202; 817-926-4863 (in TX).

**Buckaroo Bobbins,** P.O. Box 95314, Las Vegas, NV 89193: Catalog $1 ◆ Authentic vintage western clothing sewing patterns. 801-865-7922

**Butterick Pattern Company,** Consumer Services, 161 6th Ave., New York, NY 10013: Free information ◆ Patterns for clothing. 800-766-2670.

**D.L. Designs,** P.O. Box 1382, Studio City, CA 91604: Catalog $1 (refundable) ◆ Modern and historical hat patterns for men and women. www.home.earthlink.net/~dlhp

**Daisy Kingdom,** 134 NW 8th St., Portland, OR 97209: Catalog $2 ◆ Nursery ensembles and children's ready-made fashions or kits. 800-234-6688.

**Lois Ericson,** Box 5222, Salem, OR 97304: Free information with long SASE ◆ Design and sewing patterns for coats, jackets, vests, and blouses. 503-399-7570.

**Fabricraft,** P.O. Box 962, Cardiff, CA 92007: Catalog $2 ◆ Clothing patterns. 619-436-1281.

**Forever Timeless,** RR 1, Hillsburgh, Ontario, Canada N0B 1Z0: Catalog $6 ◆ Folk wear, historical, period impressions, and other patterns. 519-855-6507.

**Frostline Kits,** 2525 River Rd., Grand Junction, CO 81505: Catalog $2 ◆ Ready-to-sew kits for jackets, vests, comforters, luggage, camping gear, and ski wear. 800-548-7872. www.frostlinekits.com

**Green Pepper,** 1285 River Rd., Eugene, OR 97404: Catalog $2 ◆ Buckles, Velcro fasteners, zippers, buttons, notions, and kits for coats and jackets, ski wear, water-repellent clothing for cold weather, and duffel bags. 541-689-3292.

**Harper House,** P.O. Box 39, Williamstown, PA 17098: Catalog $6 ◆ Historic and ethnic garment patterns, sewing notions, and books. 717-647-7807.

**Kwik-Sew Pattern Company Inc.,** 3000 Washington Ave. North, Minneapolis, MN 55411: Catalog $5 ◆ Patterns and sewing instruction books. 612-521-7651.

**Needle & Thread,** 2215 Fairfield Rd., Gettysburg, PA 17325: Free information ◆ Wool, cotton, linen, silk, and other fabrics. Also historical folkwear and past clothing patterns. 717-334-4011.

**Park Bench Pattern Company,** P.O. Box 837, Longmont, CO 80502: Catalog $3 ◆ Clothing patterns. 303-772-5746. www.SewNet.com/ParkBench

**Past Patterns,** 217 S. 5th St., Richmond, IN 47374: Catalog $4 ◆ Patterns for historically authentic clothing for men, women, and children. 765-962-3333.

**Rainshed Outdoor Fabrics,** 707 NW 11th, Corvallis, OR 97330: Catalog $1 ◆ Rainwear and outerwear fabrics, notions, webbing, and patterns. 541-753-8900.

**Seattle Fabrics,** 8702 Aurora North, Seattle, WA 98103: Price list $3 (refundable) ◆ Notions and patterns. 206-525-0670. www.seattlefabrics.com

**Servant & Company,** Centennial General Store, 230 Steinwehr Ave., Gettysburg, PA 17325: Catalog $6 ◆ Civil War uniforms and accouterments, lady's clothing and accessories, and clothing patterns. 717-334-9712. www.servantandco.com

**Sew/Fit Company,** 5310 W. 66th St., Unit A, Bedford Park, IL 60638: Free catalog ◆ Patterns, books, notions, and supplies. 708-458-5600.

**Sew Special,** 777 E. Vista Way, Ste. 20, Vista, CA 92084: Catalog $2 ◆ Smocking and heirloom sewing supplies. 760-940-0365. sewspeci@mailhost2.csusm.edu

**Stretch & Sew,** 8697 La Mesa Blvd., La Mesa, CA 91941: Catalog $3 ◆ Fabrics, patterns, and notions. 800-547-7717. www.stretch-and-sew.com

**Suitability,** P.O. Box 3244, Chico, CA 95927: Free catalog ◆ Patterns for sew-your-own riding apparel and horse equipment. Includes show clothes, horse clothing, and carry-all bags. 800-207-0256. www.SuitAbility.com

**Thoburn's,** P.O. Box 231, Londonderry, NH 03053: Brochure and swatches $6 ◆ Fleece in prints and solids, patterns, and notions. 603-437-4924.

**Del & Jean Warren,** P.O. Box 364, Liberty, MO 64068: Catalog $6 ◆ Civil War era historic books and patterns, jewelry and accessories, underpinnings, uniforms and accouterments, black powder rifles, and shooting supplies. 816-781-9473. Jamescntry@aol.com

## Sewing Machines, Pleaters, & Sergers

**A.C.S.,** 447 W. 36th St., New York, NY 10018: Free catalog ◆ Notions, thread, lining, patterns, cutting tools, fasteners, sewing machines, and serging accessories. 800-SEW-TRUE.

**All Brands Sewing Machines,** 9789 Florida Blvd., Baton Rouge, LA 70815: Free brochure (specify type of machine) ◆ Knitting, serger, sewing machines, and accessories. 800-739-7374. sewserg@aol.com

**Atlanta Thread & Supply,** 695 Red Oak Rd., Stockbridge, GA 30281: Catalog $1 ◆ Notions and sewing machines. 800-331-7600.

**Bernina,** 3500 Thayer Ct., Aurora, IL 60504: Free information ◆ Sewing machines and sergers. 800-405-2SEW. www.berninausa.com

**Ferdco Sewing Machines,** P.O. Box 261, Harrison, ID 83833: Free information ◆ Heavy-duty sewing machines. 800-645-0197.

**Innovative Sewing Products,** 800 Roswell Ave., #3, Long Beach, CA 90804: Catalog $1 ◆ Sewing machine tools and accessories. 562-986-4343.

**Juki America Inc.,** 14518 Best Ave., Santa Fe Springs, CA 90670: Free information ◆ Sergers. 562-483-5355. murata@juki.com

**Meissner's Sewing,** 2417 Cormorant Way, Sacramento, CA 95815: Free information ◆ Sewing machines and notions. 800-521-2332.

**The New Home Sewing Machine Company,** 10 Industrial St., Mahwah, NJ 07430: Free information ◆ Computerized sewing machines. 800-631-0183.

**Noltings,** Rt. 3, Box 147, Hwy. 52 East, Stover, MO 65078: Free information ◆ Quilting and sewing machines. 573-377-2713.

**Pfaff American Sales Corp.,** 610 Winters Ave., Paramus, NJ 07653: Free list of retail sources ◆ Sewing machines. 800-99-PFAFF. www.pfaff.com

**S & S Sewing Machine Company Inc.,** 900 Bob Wallace Ave., #105-B, Huntsville, AL 35801: Free information ◆ Notions, fabrics, sewing machines, and accessories. 800-SEW-ELNA.

**Sew & Serg Company,** 9789 Florida Blvd., Baton Rouge, LA 70815: Free information ◆ Sewing equipment. 800-739-7374. sewserg@aol.com

**Sew-Knit Distributors,** 9789 Florida Blvd., Baton Rouge, LA 70815: Free catalog ◆ Sewing and knitting machines and supplies. 800-739-7374. serg@aol.com

**Sew Vac City,** 1667 Texas Ave. South, College Station, TX 77840: Brochure $3 ◆ Sewing machines and vacuum cleaners. 800-338-5672.

**Sewin' in Vermont,** 84 Concord Ave., St. Johnsbury, VT 05819: Free information ◆ Sewing machines, sergers, and notions. 800-451-5124.

**Suburban Sew 'N Sweep Inc.,** 8814 Ogden Ave., Brookfield, IL 60513: Free information ◆ Electronic, computerized, and other sewing machines. 800-642-4056.

**Tippman Industrial Products Inc.,** 3518 Adams Center Rd., Fort Wayne, IN 46806: Free information ◆ Manually and air-operated industrial sewing machines and air-powered clicker. 800-533-4831. www.Tippman.com

**Tosca Company,** 13503 Tosca Ln., Ste. 250, Houston, TX 77079: Free information ◆ Pleating machines. 800-290-8327.

**Treasured Heirlooms,** 13507 Candlewood Ct., Moorpark, CA 93021: Free newsletter with long SASE ◆ Fabrics, lace, pleaters, notions, and supplies. 805-523-2520.

**Erica Wilson Needle Works,** 717 Madison Ave., New York, NY 10021: Free brochure ◆ Needlepoint, cross-stitch, and crewel projects. Also how-to books, handpainted canvasses, and embroidery frames. 800-973-7422.

## Stuffing & Fill

**Air-Lite Synthetics Manufacturing,** 342 Irwin St., Pontiac, MI 48341: Free information ◆ Batting, fiber fill, and pillow forms. 800-521-1267.

**Airtex Consumer Products,** P.O. Box 880, Cokato, MN 55321: Free catalog ◆ Free catalog ◆ Unbleached cotton batting. 800-851-8887.

**Brewer Sewing Supplies,** 3800 W. 42nd St., Chicago, IL 60632: Free information ◆ Sewing machines, quilting supplies, batting and stuffing, and notions. 800-621-2501.

**Buffalo Batt & Felt Corp.,** Craft Product Division, 3307 Walden Ave., Depew, NY 14043: Information $1 ◆ Stuffing, polyester fiber fill, and patterns. 716-683-4100.

### Tags & Labels

**Advanced Weaving,** Division Name Maker Inc., 7400 W. Flamingo, Ste. 1003, Las Vegas, NV 89117: Free information ◆ Custom woven and printed labels. 888-460-4623.

**Alpha Impressions Inc.,** P.O. Box 3156, Los Angeles, CA 90051: Free brochure ◆ Woven labels and hang tags. 800-834-8221. AlphaImp@aol.com

**Charm Woven Labels,** 2400 W. Magnolia Blvd., Burbank, CA 91506: Free brochure ◆ Silk, linen, wool, polyester, and cotton labels. 800-843-1111.

**Davies Printing,** P.O. Box 640373, Miami, FL 33164: Free information ◆ Personalized logo labels. 888-4-MY-NAME.

**The Deluxe Woven Label Company,** P.O. Box 229, Altoona, PA 16603: Free information ◆ Iron-on or sew-on personalized woven labels with optional color, lettering, and motif.

**General Label Manufacturing,** P.O. Box 640371, Miami, FL 33164: Free information ◆ Printed fabric labels. 800-944-4696.

**Heirloom Woven Labels,** P.O. Box 428, Moorestown, NJ 08057: Free information ◆ Woven labels. 609-722-1618.

**Ident-ify Label Corp.,** P.O. Box 140204, Brooklyn, NY 11214: Sample kit $1 ◆ Sew-on labels and name tapes. 888-60-LABEL.

**Kimmeric Studio,** P.O. Box 10749, Lake Tahoe, CA 96158: Catalog $2 ◆ Craft hang tags. 530-573-1616.

**Name Maker Inc.,** P.O. Box 43821, Atlanta, GA 30378: Free information ◆ Nylon, taffeta, or satin labels and name tapes with signature, logo, or custom artwork. 800-241-2890.

**Namely Yours,** 4321 Crestfield Rd., Knoxville, TN 37921: Free brochure ◆ Fabric labels with optional personal logos. 423-558-6204.

**Northwest Tag & Label Inc.,** 2435 SE 11th, Portland, OR 97214: Brochure $1 ◆ Nylon, satin, and woven edge iron-on and washable printed fabric tags and labels. 503-423-7914. dpartlow@nwtag.com

**Sterling Name Tape Company,** P.O. Box 939, Winsted, CT 06098: Samples $1 ◆ Printed custom labels. 800-654-5210.

## SHEDS, BARNS, & OTHER BUILDINGS

**A-Cover,** Mark Savran, 965 W. River St., Milford, CT 06460: Free brochure ◆ Easy-to-assemble instant storage and protection shelters. 800-426-8004.

**Barnmaster Inc.,** 10124 Channel Rd., Lakeside, CA 92040: Free list of retail sources ◆ Modular barns for horses. 800-500-2276. www.Barnmaster.com

**Country Designs,** P.O. Box 774, Essex, CT 06426: Catalog $6 ◆ Plans for barns, sheds, and garages. 860-767-1046.

**Hammond Barns,** P.O. Box 584, New Castle, IN 47362: Brochure $2 ◆ Plans for storage and tool sheds, workshops, and other structures. 765-529-7822.

**Handy Home Products,** 6400 E. 11 Mile Rd., Warren, MI 48091: Free information ◆ Easy-to-assemble storage and timber buildings, gazebos, and playhouses. 800-221-1849. www.handyhome.com

**Heritage Garden Houses,** City Visions Inc., 310 Beaver St., Lansing, MI 48906: Catalog $3 ◆ Pool houses, potting and tool storage sheds, hot tub enclosures, colonnades, seats, cabinets, gazebos, and classical, Victorian, Japanese, and other garden retreats. 517-484-3374.

**Homestead Design Inc.,** P.O. Box 2010, Port Townsend, WA 98368: Catalog $3 ◆ Plans for small barns, studios, workshops, garden sheds, and country homes.

**Kloter Farms Inc.,** 216 West Rd., Ellington, CT 06029: Brochure $3 (request list of retail sources) ◆ Sheds, gazebos, playscapes, and lawn furniture. 800-289-3463; 203-871-1048 (in CT). www.kloterfarms.com

**Kwik-Bilt Inc.,** 3114 Benton St., Garland, TX 75042: Free information ◆ Easy-to-assemble galvanized steel buildings. 972-494-1164.

**New England Outbuildings,** 1 Heritage Park Rd., Clinton, CT 06413: Free information ◆ Kits for New England farm structures and outbuildings. 860-669-1776.

**Port-A-Stall,** 213 S. Alma School Rd., Mesa, AZ 85210: Free information ◆ Barns and horse corral panels and accessories. 800-717-7027; 602-649-3997. www.portastall.com

**Porta-Fab Corp.,** P.O. Box 1084, Chesterfield, MO 63006: Free information ◆ Modular buildings for easy expansion. 800-325-3781.

**Quick-Shelter,** P.O. Box 1123, Orange, CT 06477: Free information ◆ Pre-drilled and bolt-together temporary/permanent garages for boats, cars, and other storage. 800-211-3730.

**Senco Inc.,** 520 8th St., Gwinn, MI 49841: Free information ◆ Recreational shelters, portable hunting blinds, ice fishing houses, and greenhouses. 906-346-4116.

**Southeastern Steel Buildings Inc.,** 1023 Laskin Rd., Ste. 109, Virginia Beach, VA 23451: Free information ◆ Easy-to-assemble utility buildings, backyard shops, economical garages, and all-purpose shelters. 800-341-7007.

**Wedgcor Steel Building Systems,** 6800 E. Hampden Ave., Denver, CO 80224: Free brochure ◆ All steel non-combustible and easy-to-maintain steel buildings. 303-759-3200.

**Woodstar Products Inc.,** 916 Industrial Ct., Delavan, WI 53115: Free information ◆ Easy-to-install, carpentry experience not required, horse stalls. 414-728-8460. www.wdstar.com

## SHOES & BOOTS

### Clogs

**Barnum Shoe,** 1436 Barnum Ave., Stratford, CT 06497: Catalog $1 ◆ Medium to extra-wide men and women's clogs. 800-582-7995.

**Birkenstock Express,** 301 SW Madison Ave., Corvallis, OR 97333: Free catalog ◆ Birkenstock sandals, clogs, and walking shoes in sizes for men, women, and children. 800-451-1459. www.birkenstockexpress.com

**Birkenstock Shoes,** 1323 3rd St. Promenade, Santa Monica, CA 90401: Free information ◆ Birkenstock shoes. 310-393-5655. www.birkenstock-shoes.com

**Koson's,** 318 Arricola Ave., #102, St. Augustine, FL 32085: Free brochure ◆ Swedish clogs for men, women, and children. 800-654-0010.

**Swedish Clogs Inc.,** 320 State Rd. 16, St. Augustine, FL 32095: Free price list ◆ Women's clogs. 800-443-8167; 904-824-8844 (in FL).

### Large Sizes

**Church's English Shoes,** 428 Madison Ave., New York, NY 10017: Free brochure ◆ Handcrafted all-leather shoes, sizes 6 to 14, AA-EEE. 800-221-4540; 212-755-4313 (in NY).

**Dalberg's Shoes,** Hwy. 88 East, Laurel Heights Plaza, Brick, NJ 08724: Free information ◆ Wide-width shoes for women and men. Includes dress, casual, bridal, and other styles. 800-886-3668.

**Footprints, The Birkenstock Store,** 1339 Massachusetts, Lawrence KS 66044: Free catalog ◆ Birkenstock sandals and shoes for tall women. 800-827-1339.

**Friedman's Shoes,** 209 Mitchell St., Atlanta, Georgia 30303: Free information ◆ Men's shoes, sizes 7 to 20 in narrow, medium, and wide. 800-886-3668. www.friedmansshoes.com

**King Size Company,** P.O. Box 8385, Indianapolis, IN 46283: Free catalog ◆ Shoes for tall men, sizes 12 to 16. 800-846-1600. www.kingsizemen.com

**Main & Taylor Shoes,** 1614 Main St., Columbia, SC 29201: Free information with long SASE (specify style and shoes wanted) ◆ Hard-to-find small (size 4) up to large (size 12) shoes for women. 888-SHOES-R-US.

**Maryland Square,** 1350 Williams St., Chippewa Falls, WI 54729: Free catalog ◆ Women's footwear, sizes 4 to 14 in AAAA to EE widths. 800-727-3895.

**Regalia,** Palo Verde at 34th, P.O. Box 27800, Tucson, AZ 85726: Free catalog ◆ Fashions and intimate apparel in large sizes. Also shoes in hard-to-find sizes and narrow to wide-wide widths. 520-747-5000.

**Reyers,** Sharon City Centre, Sharon, PA 16146: Free information ◆ Women's shoes, from size 2½ to 14, in widths AAAAAA to EE. 800-245-1550.

**Shoe Express,** 102 Savonne Dr., Scott, LA 70583: Free catalog ◆ Shoes for women in sizes 11-15, all widths, all types of shoes. 800-874-0469. www.shoexpress.com

**Shoecraft Corp.,** 1395 NW 17th Ave., Ste. 102, Delray Beach, FL 33445: Free information ◆ Women's dress shoes, sandals, sport shoes, and flats, sizes 10 to 13. 800-225-5848.

**Standard Shoes,** 48 Main St., Bangor, ME 04401: Free catalog ◆ Arch-supporting shoes for women, sizes 2A to 3A; 6 to 12, A and B; 5 to 12, C and D; 5 to 12, E and EE; and some half sizes. 800-284-8366.

**Statuesque,** 2225 S. University Dr., Davie, FL 33324: Free catalog ◆ Fashion footwear for women in sizes 9½ to 14. Also tall fashions. 800-367-7167.

## Men's & Women's

**Aerosoles Catalog Division,** P.O. Box 1916, Edison, NJ 08818: Free catalog ◆ Fashionable soft-cushioned shoes for casual wearing. 800-79-TWIST.

**Allen-Edmonds Shoe Corp.,** 201 East Seven Hills Road, P.O. Box 998, Port Washington, WI 53074: Free catalog ◆ Men's business, dress, and casual shoes. Also shoe care supplies. 414-284-7158. www.allenedmonds.com

**Appleseed's,** 30 Tozer Rd., P.O. Box 1020, Beverly, MA 01915: Free catalog ◆ Women's leather shoes and boots, size 5-12 in AAAA-EE. 800-767-6666.

**Aussie Connection,** 135 NE Broadway, Hillsboro, OR 97124: Free catalog ◆ Washable Australian sheepskin slippers and boots. 800-950-2668. aussco@teleport.com

**Bally of Switzerland,** 628 Madison Ave., New York, NY 10153: Free information ◆ Men's and women's shoes and clothing. Also luggage, and small leather goods. 212-701-9852.

**L.L. Bean,** Casco St., Freeport, ME 04033: Free catalog ◆ Outdoor footwear for men and women. 800-221-4221. www.llbean.com

**Arthur Beren Shoes,** 111 Maiden Ln., Ste. 402, San Francisco, CA 94108: Free catalog ◆ Women's shoes. 800-886-9797.

**Birkenstock Express,** 301 SW Madison Ave., Corvallis, OR 97333: Free catalog ◆ Birkenstock sandals, clogs, and walking shoes in sizes for men, women, and children. 800-451-1459. www.birkenstockexpress.com

**Birkenstock Shoes,** 1323 3rd St. Promenade, Santa Monica, CA 90401: Free information ◆ Birkenstock shoes. 310-393-5655. www.birkenstock-shoes.com

**Sue Brett,** P.O. Box 8384, Indianapolis, IN 46283: Free catalog ◆ Women's leather and suede shoes and boots. 800-784-8001.

**Lane Bryant,** P.O. Box 8301, Indianapolis, IN 46283: Free catalog ◆ Women's shoes, size 7 to 12. 800-477-7030.

**Church's English Shoes,** 428 Madison Ave., New York, NY 10017: Free brochure ◆ Handcrafted all-leather shoes, sizes 6 to 14, AA-EEE. 800-221-4540; 212-755-4313 (in NY).

**The Comfort Corner,** P.O. Box 649, Nashua, NH 03061: Free catalog ◆ Men's and women's dress and walking shoes, casuals, sandals, and other styles. 800-442-8730.

**The Cordwainer Shop,** 67 Candia Rd., Deerfield, NH 03037: Catalog $3 ◆ Handmade custom footwear. 603-463-7742.

**Coward Shoes,** Palo Verde at 34th, P.O. Box 27800, Tucson, AZ 85726: Free catalog ◆ Leather shoes and boots for men and women. 800-362-8410.

**Tanino Crisci,** 795 Madison Ave., New York, NY 10314: Free catalog ◆ Men's shoes. 212-535-1014.

**Deerskin,** 119 Foster St., Peabody, MA 01960: Free catalog ◆ Leather moccasins, boots, and shoes for men, women, and children. 978-532-2810. www.deerskin.com

**The Dehner Company,** 3614 Martha St., Omaha, NE 68105: Free brochure ◆ Custom leather shoes and boots. 402-342-7788.

**Drew's Boots,** 733 Main St., Klamath Falls, OR 97601: Free list of retail sources ◆ Riding packer boots for men and women. 800-722-0393; 541-884-3121 (in OR). www.198.68.11.3/drews

**Dunn's Supply Catalog,** P.O. Box 509, Grand Junction, TN 38039: Free catalog ◆ Camouflage and insulated clothing, outerwear, shoes and boots. 800-427-6572. www.dunnscatalog.com

**Esprit Outlet,** 499 Illinois St., San Francisco, CA 94107: Free catalog ◆ Leather boots, oxfords, and loafers. 415-957-2550. www.sanfrancisco.sidewalk.com/link/19351

**Executive Shoes,** P.O. Box 9128, Hingham, MA 02043: Free catalog ◆ Business, dress, casual, and walking shoes in hard-to-fit sizes. 800-240-SHOE.

**Fabiano Shoe Company,** 850 Summer St., South Boston, MA 02127: Free information with long SASE ◆ Thinsulate insulated Telemark boots. 617-268-5625. info@fabiano.com

**Friedman's Shoes,** 209 Mitchell St., Atlanta, Georgia 30303: Free information ◆ Men's shoes, sizes 7 to 20 in narrow, medium, and wide. 800-886-3668. www.friedmansshoes.com

**Haband for Men,** 100 Fairview Ave., Prospect Park, NJ 07530: Free information ◆ Men's outdoor insulated boots and wash-and-wear clothing. 800-742-2263. www.haband.com

**Hanover Shoe Company,** 440 Madison St., Hanover, PA 17331: Free catalog ◆ Men's shoes, sizes 6 to 15, AA to EEE. 800-426-3708; 717-632-2444 (in PA).

**Harry's Shoes,** 2299 Broadway & 83rd St., New York, NY 10024: Free catalog ◆ Men and women's shoes with an emphasis on style, size, and width selection. 800-626-5270; 212-874-2035 (in NY). www.harrys-shoes.com

**Hartt Shoes,** 401 York St., Fredericton, New Brunswick, Canada E3B 3P8: Free catalog ◆ All-leather motorcycle and riding boots. Also other shoes for men. 800-268-1433.

**Hitchcock Shoes Inc.,** Hingham, MA 02043: Free catalog ◆ Men's shoes, sizes 5 to 13, EE to EEEEEE. 800-992-WIDE. www.wideshoes.com

**Johansen Bros. Shoe Company,** Hwy. 67 West, Corning, AR 72422: Free catalog ◆ Women's fashion shoes. 800-624-9079.

**Johnston & Murphy,** Mail Order Shop, 1415 Murfreesboro Rd., Ste. 190, Nashville, TN 37217: Free catalog ◆ Men's shoes, socks, belts, and accessories. 800-424-2854. www.johnstonmurphy.com

**Justin Boots,** P.O. Box 548, Fort Worth, TX 76101: Free catalog ◆ Shoes and boots for men and women. 800-3-JUSTIN; 817-332-4385 (in TX). www.justinboots.com

**Knapp Shoes Inc.,** Mail Order Division, One Keuka Business Park, Ste. 300, Penn Yan, NY 14527: Free catalog ◆ Work shoes and boots, hikers, western style boots, dress shoes, casuals, and more. 800-869-9955. www.knappshoes.com

**Main & Taylor Shoes,** 1614 Main St., Columbia, SC 29201: Free information with long SASE (specify style and shoes wanted) ◆ Hard-to-find small (size 4) up to large (size 12) shoes for women. 888-SHOES-R-US.

**Maryland Square,** 1350 Williams St., Chippewa Falls, WI 54729: Free catalog ◆ Women's footwear, sizes 4 to 14 in AAAA to EE widths. 800-727-3895.

**B.A. Mason Footwear,** 1251 1st Ave., Chippewa Falls, WI 54774: Free catalog ◆ Men and women's shoes in regular and large sizes, moccasins, and shoe care supplies. 800-422-1000.

**Masseys,** Direct Footwear Merchants, 601 12th St., Lynchburg, VA 24504: Free catalog ◆ Casual, dress, and athletic shoes. Also boots and slippers. 800-462-7739.

**Stuart McGuire,** 425 Well St., Chippewa Falls, WI 54729: Free catalog ◆ Casual shoes and other styles for men. 800-678-4601.

**Men's Collections,** P.O. Box 882883, San Francisco, CA 94188: Free catalog ◆ Men's casual sportswear and shoes. 800-248-2299.

**Mid Western Sport Togs,** P.O. Box 230, Berlin, WI 54923: Free catalog ◆ Deerskin gloves, footwear, handbags, accessories, jackets, and coats for men and women. 414-361-5050.

**Moonwalker/Sierra Boot Company,** 2001 Chester, Bakersfield, CA 93301: Free catalog ◆ Handmade boots and shoes. 800-93-BOOTS; 805-322-8505 (in CA).

**Naples Creek Leather,** 188 S. Main St., Naples, NY 14512: Free catalog ◆ Leather moccasins, slippers, belts, gloves, casual footwear, and deerskin handbags. 800-836-0616.

**Okun Brothers Shoes,** Attention: Mail Order Department, 356 E. South St., Kalamazoo, MI 49007: Free catalog ◆ Shoes and boots for men, women, and children. 800-433-6344.

**Old Pueblo Traders,** Palo Verde at 34th, P.O. Box 27800, Tucson, AZ 85726: Free catalog ◆ Shoes and boots for women. 520-748-8600.

**The Original I. Goldberg,** 902 Chestnut St., Philadelphia, PA 19107: Free catalog ◆ Military surplus merchandise, footwear, clothing, and camping equipment. 215-925-9393.

**Reyers,** Sharon City Centre, Sharon, PA 16146: Free information ◆ Women's shoes, from size 2½ to 14, in widths AAAAAA to EE. 800-245-1550.

**Richlee Shoe Company,** P.O. Box 3566, Frederick, MD 21701: Free catalog ◆ Elevator shoes for men, sizes 5 to 11, B to EEE. 800-343-3810. www.elevatorshoes.com

**Shoes For Crews Inc.,** 1400 Centrepark Blvd., West Palm Beach, FL 33401: Free catalog ◆ Slip-resistant footwear and floor mats. 800-634-7095. www.shoesforcrews.com

**Standard Shoes,** 48 Main St., Bangor, ME 04401: Free catalog ◆ Arch-supporting shoes for women, sizes 2A to 3A; 6 to 12, A and B; 5 to 12, C and D; 5 to 12, E and EE; and some half sizes. 800-284-8366.

**Talbots,** 175 Beal St., Hingham, MA 02043: Free catalog ◆ Women's shoes in regular, petite, and other sizes. 800-825-2687.

**Norm Thompson,** P.O. Box 3999, Portland, OR 97208: Free catalog ◆ Wood Ducks and casual shoes. 800-821-1287. www.normthompson.com

**Tog Shop,** Lester Square, Americus, GA 31710: Free catalog ◆ Women's footwear in full and half sizes and slim (AAA), narrow (AA), or medium (B) widths. 800-342-6789.

**US ABE Clothing,** 807 E. Carson St., Pittsburgh, PA 15203: Free brochure ◆ Work and casual clothing, boots, shoes, and athletic footwear. 412-431-8861.

**Vasque Boots,** 314 Main St., Red Wing, MN 55066: Free list of retail sources ◆ Hiking boots for men and women. 800-224-4453. www.vasque.com

**White's Boots,** 4002 E. Ferry, Spokane, WA 99202: Free catalog ◆ All-leather boots, boot accessories, and conditioning products. 800-541-3786; 509-535-2422 (in WA).

**Wissota Trader,** 1313 1st Ave., Chippewa Falls, WI 54729: Free catalog ◆ Regular and hard-to-find shoes and clothes for men and women. 800-833-6421.

**Wolverine Boots & Shoes,** 9341 Courtland Dr. NE, Rockford, MI 49351: Free list of retail sources ◆ Footwear for men and women. 800-543-2668.

### Moccasins

**Deerskin,** 119 Foster St., Peabody, MA 01960: Free catalog ◆ Leather moccasins, boots, and shoes for men, women, and children. 978-532-2810. www.deerskin.com

**B.A. Mason Footwear,** 1251 1st Ave., Chippewa Falls, WI 54774: Free catalog ◆ Men and women's shoes in regular and large sizes, moccasins, and shoe care supplies. 800-422-1000.

**Minnetonka Moccasin House,** P.O. Box 16235, St. Paul, MN 55116: Free catalog ◆ Moccasins for men, women, and children. 800-969-6690. www.minnetonkamocc.com

**Moose River Moccasin Company,** 32 Main St., Freeport, ME 04032: Free catalog ◆ Hand-sewn moccasins. 800-851-4449.

**Naples Creek Leather,** 188 S. Main St., Naples, NY 14512: Free catalog ◆ Leather moccasins, slippers, belts, gloves, casual footwear, and deerskin handbags. 800-836-0616.

**World Traders,** Bar Harbor Rd., Box 158, Brewer, ME 04412: Free catalog ◆ Hand-sewn moccasins. 800-603-0003.

### Western Boots

**America's Western Stores,** 2816 S. Ingram Mill Rd., Springfield, MO 65804: Free catalog ◆ Western-style clothing, shoes and boots, and gifts. 800-284-8191.

**Austin-Hall Boot Company,** P.O. Box 220990, El Paso, TX 79905: Catalog $1 ◆ Custom handmade boots. 915-771-6113. AustinHallBoot@juno.com

**Back at the Ranch,** 235 Don Gaspar, Santa Fe, NM 87501: Free information ◆ Vintage western clothing, boots, and hats. 505-989-8110.

**Paul Bond Boot Company,** 915 W. Paul Bond Dr., Nogales, AZ 85621: Free catalog ◆ Made-to-order boots. 520-281-0512.

**Boot Town,** 10838 N. Central Expwy., Dallas, TX 75231: Free catalog ◆ Western boots. 800-222-6687.

**Champion Boot Company,** 505 S. Cotton, El Paso, TX 79901: Catalog $1 ◆ Leather cowboy-style boots. 915-534-7783.

**The Cowhand,** 200 W. Midland Ave., Woodland Park, CO 80863: Free information ◆ Gloves, spurs, bits, belts, buckles, and western-style boots for men, women, and children. 719-687-9688.

**Drysdales,** 1555 N. 107th East Ave., Tulsa, OK 74116: Free catalog ◆ Men, women, and children's western-style boots. 800-444-6481. www.drysdales.com

**L.M. Easterling Custom Boots,** 215 W. Maine St., Fredericksburg, TX 78624: Catalog $1 ◆ Handmade boots and belts. 888-811-8980.

**Tony Lama Boots,** P.O. Box 9518, El Paso, TX 79985: Free list of retail sources ◆ Leather boots for men and women. www.tonylama.com

**Lucchese Boots,** 6601 Montana, El Paso, TX 79925: Free list of retail sources ◆ Handmade boots and shoes. 915-778-8585. www.lucchese.com

**Luskey/Ryon's Western Stores Inc.,** 2601 N. Main, Fort Worth, TX 76106: Free catalog ◆ Western-style clothing, boots, and hats for men, women, and children. 800-725-7966.

**Mercedes Boot Company,** 1009 NE 16th St., Fort Worth, TX 76102: Free information ◆ Custom and in-stock handcrafted boots for cowboys, ranchers, horse trainers, and general wear. 800-552-2668. www.mercedesbootco.com

**Moonwalker/Sierra Boot Company,** 2001 Chester, Bakersfield, CA 93301: Free catalog ◆ Handmade boots and shoes. 800-93-BOOTS; 805-322-8505 (in CA).

**Olathe Boot Company,** 705 S. Kansas, Olathe, KS 66061: Free list of retail sources ◆ Handcrafted cowboy boots, sizes 4 to 15, AAA to EEE. 800-255-6126.

**Ryon's Saddle & Ranch Supplies,** 2601 N. Main, Fort Worth, TX 76106: Free catalog ◆ Saddles, tack, and western-style clothing and boots for men, women, and children. 800-725-7966.

**The Territory Ahead,** PFI Western Stores, 2816 S. Ingram Mill Rd., Springfield, MO 65804: Free catalog ◆ Men and women's western-style clothing. 800-686-8178. www.territoryahead.com

**Tonto Rim Trading Company,** 5028 N. US Hwy. 31, Seymour, IN 47274: Free catalog ◆ Western boots and hats. 800-242-4287.

**West Coast Shoe Company,** P.O. Box 607, Scappoose, OR 97056: Free catalog ◆ Custom boots. 800-326-2711.

**Wilson Boot Company,** 1014 West Park, Livingston, MT 59047: Brochure $1 ◆ Handmade leather boots. 406-222-3842. www.wilsonboots.com

## SHOES FOR BABIES, BRONZING

**American Bronzing Company,** 1313 Alum Creek Dr., Columbus, OH 43209: Free information ◆ Bronzing and antique finish for baby's shoes. 614-252-7388. www.abcbronze.com

**Bron-shoe Company,** American Bronzing Company Division, 1313 Alum Creek Dr., Columbus, OH 43209: Free information ◆ Baby shoe bronzing. 800-345-8112,

**Sentimental Bronzing,** 305 N. Franklin, Spring Hill, KS 66083: Free information ◆ Preservation of baby shoes in bronze, pewter, or gold. 800-679-1914.

## SHUFFLEBOARD

**Allen R. Shuffleboard Company Inc.,** 6585 Seminole Blvd., Seminole, FL 34642: Free information ◆ Cues, disks, and sets. 813-397-0421.

**Champion,** 7100 Burns St., Richland Hills, TX 76118: Free information ◆ Custom stained and finished shuffleboards. 800-826-7856.

**General Sportcraft Company,** 140 Woodbine Rd., Bergenfield, NJ 07621: Free information ◆ Cues, disks, and sets. 201-384-4242.

**International Billiards Inc.,** 2311 Washington Ave., Houston, TX 77007: Free information ◆ Cues, disks, and sets. 800-255-6386; 713-869-3237 (in TX).

**Dick Martin Sports Inc.,** 181 E. Union Ave., P.O. Box 7384, East Rutherford, NJ 07073: Free information ◆ Cues, disks, and sets. 800-221-1993; 201-438-5255 (in NJ).

**Playfair Shuffleboard Company Inc.,** 7021 Bluffton Rd., Fort Wayne, IN 46809: Free information ◆ Shuffleboards and accessories. 800-541-3743.

**Saunier-Wilhem Company,** 3216 5th Ave., Pittsburgh, PA 15213: Free catalog ◆ Equipment and accessories for bowling, billiards, darts, table tennis, shuffleboard, and board games. 412-621-4350.

**SGD Company Inc.,** P.O. Box 8410, Akron, OH 44320: Free information ◆ Cues, disks, and sets. 330-239-2828. www.sgdgolf.com

**Ultra Play Systems Inc.,** 425 Sycamore St., Anderson, IN 46016: Free information ◆ Cues, disks, and sets. 800-458-5872.

## SIGNS, SIGN-MAKING SUPPLIES, & HOUSE NUMBERS

**Americraft Corp.,** 904 4th St. West, Palmetto, FL 34221: Free catalog ◆ Injection molded and formed letters. 800-237-3984; 914-722-6631 (in FL).

**Dick Blick Company,** P.O. Box 1267, Galesburg, IL 61402: Catalog $1 ◆ Sign-making supplies and equipment. 800-447-8192. www.artmaterials.com

**Country Junction,** 9121 Old Hartford Rd., Utica, KY 42376: Brochure $2 ◆ Handpainted country-style wood signs. 800-772-3289.

**Design Workshop,** 66 Winding Ln., Springfield, MA 01118: Free brochure with long SASE ◆ Handcrafted signs with optional goldleaf finish.

**Desperate Enterprises Inc.,** 620 E. Smith Rd., Medina, OH 44256: Free catalog ◆ Nostalgic tin signs and memorabilia. 800-732-4859. questions@desperate.com

**English Country Signs,** 36 Newport Dr., Wayne, PA 19087: Free information ◆ Custom designed hand-cast and painted house signs. 610-296-2839.

**Erie Landmark Company,** 4449 Brookfield Corporate Dr., Chantilly, VA 22021: Free brochure ◆ Outdoor and indoor bronze or redwood markers and signs. 800-874-7848. www.buttons.webrover.com/erielc

**Feather's Plaques & Awards,** P.O. Box 84, 101 Market St., Newburg, WV 26410: Free catalog ◆ Cast-bronze national registers, award plaques, and medallions with a choice of finishes. 304-892-4501.

**4x1 Imports Inc.,** 5873 Day Rd., Cincinnati, OH 45251: Catalog $8 (refundable) ◆ Nostalgic tin advertising signs. 513-385-8185.

**Games People Played,** P.O. Box 1540, 17 James Ln., Pinedale, WY 82941: Catalog $4 ◆ Antique replica game boards and signs. 307-367-2502.

**Gold Leaf & Metallic Powders,** 74 Trinity Pl., Ste. 1200, New York, NY 10006: Catalog $2 ◆ Genuine and composition leaf in rolls, sheets, books, and boxes. Also adhesives, accessories and kits. 800-322-0323; 212-267-4900 (in NY).

**A Graphic Edge,** 1313 Simpson Way, Ste. F, Escondido, CA 92029: Free brochure ◆ Signs, bumper stickers, and decals. 760-735-8494.

**Healy Brothers Foundry,** 60 New River Rd., P.O. Box 4, Manville, RI 02838: Free catalog ◆ Custom cast-bronze and aluminum plaques. 800-626-3229.

**John Hinds & Company,** 81 Greenridge Dr. West, Elmira, NY 14905: Free brochure ◆ Cast plaques and nameplates. 607-733-6712.

**Jewelite Signs,** 106 Reade St., New York, NY 10013: Free catalog ◆ Vinyl letters, graphics, and custom made signs and displays. 212-233-1900.

**La Haye Bronze,** P.O. Box 2319, Corona, CA 91718: Free brochure ◆ Solid cast-bronze signs. 800-523-9544.

**Lake Shore Industries,** P.O. Box 59, Erie, PA 16512: Free information ◆ Cast-aluminum and bronze signs and plaques. 800-458-0463.

**Lamps by Gramps,** P.O. Box 116, Hygiene, CO 80533: Free information ◆ Pre-designed and custom western-style lamps, clocks, and signs.

**Lazer Images,** 33664 5 Mile Rd., Livonia, MI 48154: Free catalog ◆ Easy-to-use sign and banner-making equipment. 313-427-4141.

**Letters Unlimited,** 1010 Morse Ave., Schaumburg, IL 60193: Free catalog ◆ Vinyl letters. 800-422-4231. www.lettersunlimited.com

**Meierjohan-Wengler Inc.,** 10330 Wayne Ave., Cincinnati, OH 45215: Free catalog ◆ Bronze tablets and historic markers. 513-771-6074.

**Earl Mich Company,** 506 N. Peoria St., Chicago, IL 60622: Free information ◆ Vinyl and reflecting letters. 800-MICH-USA; 312-829-1552 (in IL).

**Mossburg's Foam Products,** P.O. Box 340, Chesnee, SC 29323: Free information ◆ Easy-to-install foam, plastic, and vinyl letters. 800-845-6140. monarch@upstate.net

**Mountain Meadows Pottery,** P.O. Box 163, South Ryegate, VT 05069: Free catalog ◆ Stoneware. Also humorous and sentimental plaques. 800-639-6790.

**Nasco,** 901 Janesville Ave., Fort Atkinson, WI 53538: Free catalog ◆ Sign-making supplies. 800-558-9595. www.nascofa.com

**National Banner Company Inc.,** 11938 Harry Hines Blvd., Dallas, TX 75234: Free information ◆ Blank banners hemmed, roped, or grommeted with heavy duty rope sewn on the top and bottom. 800-527-0860.

**National Visual Systems Inc.,** 5482 Oceanus Dr., Unit G, Huntington Beach, CA 92649: Free catalog ◆ Exterior and interior architectural signage, directories, and letters. Also emergency evacuation plan signs that comply with the Americans with Disabilities Act. 800-788-2670; 714-891-2670 (in CA).

**Natural Wood Signs,** John Heimberger, 407 Delannoy Ave., Cocoa, FL 32922: Free brochure ◆ Made-to-order or design your own redwood signs. 800-632-3545.

**Newman Brothers Inc.,** 5609 Center Hill Ave., Cincinnati, OH 45216: Free information ◆ Standard and custom cast bronze and aluminum plaques. 800-447-1072.

**NUDO Products,** 1500 Taylor Ave., Springfield, IL 62703: Free information ◆ Sign-painting boards. 800-826-4132.

**R & J Sign Supply Company,** 4931 Daggett Ave., St. Louis, MO 63110: Free catalog ◆ Sign-making supplies. 314-664-8100.

**R & M Retail Merchandising Products,** 12342 Bell Ranch Dr., Santa Fe Springs, CA 90670: Free catalog ◆ Pricing cards, promotional signs, gift wrapping supplies and boxes, realistic props, other merchandising aids, and more. 800-231-9600; 562-946-6900 (in CA).

**Rayco Paint Company,** 6100 N. Pulaski Rd., Chicago, IL 60646: Free information ◆ Supplies and equipment for sign painters. 800-421-2327.

**Reich Supply Company Inc.,** 811 Broad St., Utica, NY 13501: Free information ◆ Sign-making and screen-printing materials and equipment. 800-338-3322.

**Royal Graphics Inc.,** 3117 N. Front St., Philadelphia, PA 19133: Free information ◆ Posters, show-cards, and bumper stickers. 215-739-8282.

**Ryther-Purdy Lumber Company Inc.,** 174 Elm St., P.O. Box 622, Old Saybrook, CT 06475: Free information ◆ Handcrafted wood signs. 860-388-4405.

**Seay Marketing Inc.,** 1325 Tarman Circle, Norman, OK 73071: Free information ◆ Reproduction beverage company signs. 800-729-7086; 405-321-8681 (in OK). www.seaymarketing.com

**Sepp Leaf Products Inc.,** 381 Park Ave. South, New York, NY 10016: Free information ◆ Gold and palladium leaf, rolled gold, tools, and kits. 800-971-7377. www.seppleaf.com

**Sign-Mart,** 410 W. Fletcher Ave., Orange, CA 92865: Free information ◆ Hemmed banners with grommets. 800-533-9099.

**Signage,** 1545 Saratoga Ave., San Jose, CA 95129: Free information ◆ Banners and magnetic signs. 800-541-SIGN.

**Signs of all Kinds,** 200 W. Main St., Vernon, CT 06066: Free catalog ◆ Hand-cut, sanded, and painted slate signs. Also steel and aluminum signs. 800-214-4449.

**Smith-Cornell Inc.,** 1545 Holland Rd., Maumee, OH 43537: Free brochure ◆ Brass and aluminum historic markers. 800-325-0248; 419-891-4335 (in OH).

**Joseph Struhl Company Inc.,** 195 Atlantic Ave., Garden City Park, NY 11040: Free information ◆ Ready-made window signs for retail stores. 800-552-0023.

**Wensco Sign Supplies,** P.O. Box 1728, Grand Rapids, MI 49501: Catalog $5 ◆ Supplies and equipment for sign painters. 800-253-1569. www.wensco.com

**The Whisperwood Collection,** Box 164, Oxford, MI 48371: Free information ◆ Personalized signs. 800-545-1559.

## SILK-SCREENING

**The Art Store,** 935 Erie Blvd. East, Syracuse, NY 13210: Price list $3 ◆ Supplies for fabric dyeing, screen-printing, marbling, and other art decor. 800-669-2787.

**Chaselle Inc.,** 101 Almgren Dr., Agawam, MA 01001: Catalog $4 ◆ Art software and books, brushes and paints, tempera colors, acrylics, pastels, ceramics molds and kilns, sculpture equipment, and silk-screening supplies. 800-628-8608.

**Crown Art Products,** 90 Dayton Ave., Passaic, NJ 07055: Free catalog ◆ Silk-screening supplies and section frames. 201-777-6010.

**Decart Inc.,** P.O. Box 309, Morrisville, VT 05661: Free list of retail sources ◆ Water-based enamels and paints for transfer techniques, glass-crafting, and silk-screening. 802-888-4217.

**Guildcraft Company,** 100 Firetower Dr., Tonawanda, NY 14150: Free catalog ◆ Supplies for silk-screening, batik, tie-dying, stenciling, block-printing, and foil crafts. 716-743-8336.

**Nasco,** 901 Janesville Ave., Fort Atkinson, WI 53538: Free catalog ◆ Silk-screening and printing supplies. 800-558-9595. www.nascofa.com

**Naz-Dar Company,** 1087 N. North Branch St., Chicago, IL 60622: Free catalog ◆ Silk-screening and graphic arts equipment and supplies. 312-943-8215.

**Reich Supply Company Inc.,** 811 Broad St., Utica, NY 13501: Free information ◆ Sign-making and screen-printing supplies. 800-338-3322.

**Southern Emblem,** P.O. Box 8, Toast, NC 27049: Free catalog ◆ Embroidered emblems, emblematic jewelry, badges, flags, and screen-printing supplies. 800-522-8518.

**Technical Papers Corp.,** P.O. Box 546, Dedham, MA 02027: Free catalog ◆ Sheets and rolls of handmade rice paper in prints and solid and multi-colors for artistic printing. Includes block printing, etching, lithography, silk-screening, and other art forms. 781-461-1111. www.technicalpapers.com

**Welsh Products Inc.,** P.O. Box 845, Benicia, CA 94510: Free catalog ◆ Easy-to-use screen-printing kits. 800-745-3255; 707-645-3252 (in CA).

## SILVER & FLATWARE

**Aaron's,** 76-04 Main St., #113, Flushing, NY 11367: Free information ◆ Active, inactive, and obsolete silverware and flatware. 800-447-5868.

**Alice's Past & Presents Replacements,** P.O. Box 465, Merrick, NY 11566: Free information ◆ Replacement crystal, china, and flatware. 516-379-1352. ALICECHINA@AOL.COM

**As You Like It Silver Shop,** 3025 Magazine St., New Orleans, LA 70115: Free information ◆ Current and obsolete silver flatware and hollowware, flatware sets, serving pieces, trays, and other items. 800-828-2311.

**William Ashley,** 50 Boor St. West, Toronto, Ontario, Canada M4W 3L8: Free information ◆ China, crystal, and silver. 800-268-1122.

**Atlantic Silver & China,** 7471 NW 57th St., Tamarac, FL 33319: Free price list ◆ Sterling flatware, hollowware, and china. 800-288-6665. www.atlanticsilver.com

**Barrons,** P.O. Box 994, Novi, MI 48376: Free information ◆ China, crystal, and silver. 800-538-6340.

**David Baruch,** 36-42 W. 47th St., New York, NY 10036: Free information ◆ China, crystal, and sterling. 800-338-6961.

**Beverly Bremer Silver Shop,** 3164 Peachtree Rd. NE, Atlanta, GA 30305: Free information ◆ New, used, discontinued, and hard-to-find patterns. 404-261-4009.

**Buschemeyer's Silver Exchange,** 515 4th Ave., Louisville, KY 40202: Free information ◆ New and used silver patterns and sterling. 800-626-4555.

**China, Crystal & Flatware Replacements,** P.O. Box 508, High Ridge, MO 63049: Free information ◆ China, crystal, and flatware. 800-562-2655.

**China Cabinet Inc.,** 26 Washington St., Tenafly, NJ 07670: Free information with long SASE ◆ China, crystal, flatware, and gifts. 201-567-2711.

**Clintsman International,** 20855 Watertown Rd., Waukesha, WI 53186: Free information ◆ Discontinued china, crystal, and flatware. 800-781-8900.

**Coinways Antiques,** 475 Central Ave., Cedarhurst, NY 11516: Free information with long SASE ◆ Used and new sterling silver flatware. 800-645-2102; 516-374-1970 (in NY).

**Dansk International Design,** 108 Corporate Park Dr., White Plains, NY 10604: Free list of retail sources ◆ Dinnerware, stemware, flatware, kitchenware, and serving pieces. 914-697-6400. www.danskfurnishings.com

**Felissimo Gifts,** 10 W. 56th S., New York, NY 10019: Free catalog ◆ Porcelain dinnerware and handcrafted silver serving pieces. 800-565-6785. www.felissimo.com

**Fortunoff Fine Jewelry,** P.O. Box 1550, Westbury, NY 11590: Free catalog ◆ Sterling flatware, silverplate and stainless steel serving pieces, and china. 800-937-4376. www.service@fortunoff.com

**Gorham,** 100 Lenox Dr., Lawrenceville, NJ 08648: Free list of retail sources ◆ Fine china dinnerware, crystal gifts, and silver. 800-635-3669.

**Jelly Sandwich,** 940 Royal St., Ste. 252, New Orleans, LA 70116: Free brochure ◆ Dishwasher-safe flatware for adults and infants. 504-522-8752. www.jellysandwich.com

**Kaiser Crow Inc.,** 14998 W. 6th Ave., #500, Golden, CO 80401: Free brochure ◆ Stainless, silver flatware, and other silver patterns. 800-468-2769.

**Kitchen Etc.,** 32 Industrial Dr., Exeter, NH 03833: Catalog $2 ◆ Cookware, cutlery, flatware, crystal, and dinnerware. 800-232-4070. www.kitchenetc.com

**Lanac Sales,** 500 Driggs Ave., Brooklyn, NY 11211: Free catalog ◆ China, crystal, sterling, and gifts. 800-522-0047; 718-782-7200 (in NY).

**Littman's Sterling,** 151 Granby St., Norfolk, VA 23510: Free information ◆ Individual sterling pieces and place settings. 800-368-6348.

**Locators Inc.,** 2217 Cottondale Ln., Little Rock, AR 72202: Free information ◆ Discontinued china, crystal, and silver. 800-367-9690.

**Marks China, Crystal & Silverware,** 315 Franklin Ave., Wyckoff, NJ 07481: Free information ◆ China, stainless, crystal, and silverware. 800-862-7578.

**Michele's Silver Matching Service,** 805 Crystal Mountain Dr., Austin, TX 78733: Free information ◆ Inactive and active silver patterns. 800-332-4693.

**Mikasa,** P.O. Box 1549, Secaucus, NJ 07096: Free catalog ◆ Designer china, stoneware, crystal, and flatware. 800-833-4681; 201-867-9210 (in NJ).

**Replacement Service,** P.O. Box 508, High Ridge, MO 63049: Free information ◆ China, crystal, and flatware. 800-562-0873.

**Replacements Ltd.,** P.O. Box 26029, Greensboro, NC 27420: Free information ◆ Active, inactive, and obsolete sterling and silverplate patterns. 800-525-9291. www.replacements.com

**H.G. Robertson Fine Silver,** 3263 Roswell Rd. NE, Atlanta, GA 30305: Free information ◆ Sterling flatware and hollowware. 800-938-1330; 404-266-1330 (in GA).

**Rogers & Rosenthal,** 22 W. 48th St., Room 1102, New York, NY 10036: Free information with long SASE ◆ Sterling, silverplate, and stainless steel flatware. 212-827-0115.

**Ross-Simons Jewelers,** 9 Ross-Simons Dr., Cranston, RI 02920: Free information ◆ Sterling and china. 800-521-7677; 401-463-3100 (in RI). www.ross-simons.com

**Wilma Saxton Inc.,** P.O. Box 395, Berlin, NJ 08009: Free price list ◆ Sterling silver, silverplate, and stainless matching service. 800-267-8029.

**Nat Schwartz & Company,** 549 Broadway, Bayonne, NJ 07002: Free catalog ◆ Crystal, sterling, and china. 800-526-1440; 201-437-4443 (in NJ).

**Silver Lane,** P.O. Box 322, San Leandro, CA 94577: Free information ◆ Discontinued crystal and china patterns, current and obsolete silver, and serving pieces. 510-483-0632.

**The Silver Queen,** 730 N. Indian Rocks Rd., Belleair Bluffs, FL 34640: Free catalog ◆ New sterling silver and discontinued patterns. Also estate items. 800-262-3134; 813-581-6827 (in FL).

**Silverladies & Nick,** 5650 W. Central Ave., Toledo, OH 43615: Free information ◆ Sterling and silverplate in old, inactive, and obsolete patterns. 800-423-4390.

**Sterling Collectables,** P.O. Box 2098, Mansfield, OH 44905: Free brochure with long SASE ◆ Current and obsolete sterling silver patterns, stainless, serving pieces, and collectible Christmas ornaments. 800-636-4756.

**The Sterling Shop,** P.O. Box 595, Silverton, OR 97381: Free list with long SASE ◆ Inactive and obsolete American-made sterling and discontinued silverplate patterns. 503-873-6315.

**Thurber's,** 2256 Dabney Rd., Richmond, VA 23230: Free information ◆ Sterling and china. 800-848-7237.

**Zucker's Fine Gifts,** 151 W. 26th St., New York, NY 10001: Free catalog ◆ Hummel, Swarovski silver and crystal, Waterford crystal, Lladro porcelain, and gifts. 212-989-1450.

## SKATEBOARDS

**Attitude Skateboards,** 8608 Baltimore Blvd., College Park, MD 20740: Free catalog ◆ Skateboards. 800-786-4973.

**Beer City Skateboards,** P.O. Box 26035, Milwaukee, WI 53226: Free information ◆ Skateboards. 414-257-1511.

**Cali4nia Skate Express,** 4629 N. Blythe, Fresno, CA 93722: Free information ◆ Skateboards, T-shirts, stickers, and shoes. 800-447-8989.

**CCS Skateboards,** 2701 McMillan Ave., San Luis Obispo, CA 93401: Free catalog ◆ T-shirts, shoes, stickers, skateboards, parts, and safety gear. 800-477-9283.

**The Deluxe Store,** 1831 Market St., San Francisco, CA 94103: Free information ◆ Skateboards. 800-275-3359.

**FTC Skateboarding Shop,** 622 Shrader St., San Francisco, CA 94117: Free catalog ◆ Skateboards, parts, snowboards, T-shirts, and clothing. 415-386-6693.

**Intensity Skates,** 11890 Old Baltimore Pike, Beltsville, MD 20705: Free catalog ◆ Skateboards, clothing, accessories, and shoes. 800-965-5050. www.intensity.com

**Jig Enterprises,** P.O. Box 448, Pismo Beach, CA 93448: Free brochure ◆ Engine kits for powering skateboards and bicycles, safety gear, and accessories. 805-473-6997.

**JMP Enterprises,** 652 Retriever Dr., Hampstead, MD 21074: Free catalog ◆ Skateboards, roller skates, in-line skates, and hockey equipment. 410-239-5081.

**Kryptonics Inc.,** 740 S. Pierce Ave., Louisville, CO 80027: Free information ◆ Skateboards and roller skates. 800-766-9146; 303-665-5353 (in CO).

**National Sporting Goods Corp.,** 25 Brighton Ave., Passaic, NJ 07055: Free information ◆ Skateboards, roller skates, and scooters. 201-779-2323.

**Rat City Sports,** 3803 W. Magnolia Blvd., Burbank, CA 91505: Catalog $1 ◆ Skateboards, parts, and clothing. 800-245-2489.

**Roller Derby Skate Company,** Box 930, Litchfield, IL 62056: Free information ◆ Skateboards, roller and in-line skates, and scooters. 217-324-3961.

**Saucony/Hyde,** 13 Centennial Dr., Peabody, MA 01961: Free list of retail sources ◆ Skateboards, roller skates, and scooters. 800-365-7282.

**60/40 Skateboards,** P.O. Box 2067, Freedom, CA 95019: Free information ◆ Skateboards. 408-728-5382.

**Skates on Haight,** 384 Oyster Point Blvd., San Francisco, CA 94080: Free catalog ◆ Skateboards, wheels, shoes, T-shirts, and sweatshirts. 415-244-9800.

**UFO Sports Inc.,** 21100 Erwin St., Woodland Hills, CA 91367: Catalog $3 ◆ Skateboards, wheels, decks, and stickers. 818-701-1521.

**Variflex Inc.,** 5152 N. Commerce Ave., Moorpark, CA 93021: Free information ◆ Skateboards and roller skates. 805-523-0322.

**The Wright Life,** 200 Linden, Fort Collins, CO 80524: Free catalog ◆ Frisbees (flying discs), skateboards, in-line skates, boomerangs, stunt kites, juggling equipment, and more. 800-321-8833. www.wrightlife.com

**Z Products,** P.O. Box 5397, Santa Monica, CA 90409: Free information ◆ Skateboards, trucks, and wheels. 310-476-4857. www.zprod.com

## SKIING

### Clothing

**Eddie Bauer,** P.O. Box 182639, Columbus, OH 43218: Free catalog ◆ Men and women's ski clothing, natural fiber sportswear, down outerwear, footwear, and luggage. 800-426-8020. www.ebauer.com

**L.L. Bean,** Casco St., Freeport, ME 04033: Free catalog ◆ Camping and workout gear. Also men and women's clothing for skiing, backcountry travel, and snowshoeing. 800-221-4221. www.llbean.com

**Big Dog Sportswear,** Mail Order Dept., 121 Gray Ave., Santa Barbara, CA 93101: Free catalog ◆ Insulated outerwear and accessories. 800-642-3647. www.BIGDOGS.com

**Bogner of America,** Bogner Dr., Newport, VT 05855: Free information ◆ Gloves and mittens, hats, parkas, jackets, pants, suits, separates, sweaters, wind shirts, and vests. 800-451-4417; 802-334-6507 (in VT). www.bogner.com

**Columbia Sportswear Company,** 6600 N. Baltimore, Portland, OR 97203: Free list of retail sources ◆ Men, women, and children's hats, gloves, mittens, jackets, pants, suits, parkas, underwear, vests, and wind shirts. 800-MA-BOYLE. www.columbia.com

**Dynastar,** P.O. Box 25, Hercules Dr., Colchester, VT 95446: Free list of retail sources ◆ Ski boots. 800-655-2431. www.dynastar.com

**Eagle River Nordic,** P.O. Box 936, Eagle River, WI 54521: Free catalog ◆ Ski equipment, clothing, boots, gloves, hats, and videos. 800-423-9730; 715-479-7285 (in WI). www.ernordic.com

**Early Winters,** P.O. Box 4333, Portland, OR 97208: Free catalog ◆ Men and women's ski clothing, leisure separates for men and women, gifts, and equipment. 800-458-4438. www.normthompson.com

**Gorsuch Ltd.,** 263 E. Gore Creek Dr., Vail, Colorado 81657: Free catalog ◆ Outdoor clothing for men, women, and children. 800-525-9808. www.gorsuchltd.com

**Kid Sport,** 122 E. Meadow Dr., Vail, CO 81657: Free catalog ◆ Winterwear and skiwear for children, from newborn through young adult. 800-833-1729; 970-476-1666 (in CO). www.vail.net/internetworks

**Ladylike Ski Shop,** 102 N. Ballard, Wylie, TX 75098: Free information ◆ Ski clothing for men, women, and children. 972-442-5842.

**Marker Ltd.,** P.O. Box 26548, Salt Lake City, UT 84119: Free brochure ◆ Men and women's ski clothing. 800-462-7537; 801-972-2100 (in UT).

**Marmot Mountain Works,** 827 Bellevue Way NE, Bellevue, WA 98004: Free catalog ◆ Men and women's ski clothing. 800-254-6246. www.premier1.net/~marmot

**Mt. Constance Mountain Shoppe,** 1550 NE Riddell Rd., Bremerton, WA 98310: Free catalog ◆ Clothing, shoes, safety gear, skis, and snowboards. 360-377-8099. MTSHOPPE@MOUNTAINSHOPPE.COM

**Nordic Sports Catalog,** 643 Upper Glen St., Queensbury, NY 12804: Free information ◆ Skiing equipment and clothing. 800-517-7555; 518-793-6147 (in NY).

**Nordica,** 139 Harvest Ln., P.O. Box 800, Williston, VT 05495: Free information ◆ Caps, gloves, jackets, boots, and pants. 800-343-7800; 802-879-4644 (in VT). www.nordicaskiwear.com

**North Face,** 2013 Farallon Dr., San Leandro, CA 94577: Free list of retail sources ◆ Hats, mittens and gloves, jackets, parkas and suits, underwear, sweaters, vests, and wind shirts. 800-447-2333.

**Northern Outfitters,** 14072 Pony Express Rd., Draper, UT 84020: Catalog $2 ◆ Clothing. 800-944-9276; 801-571-9979 (in UT). www.gorp.com/northern

**Online Sports,** 13692 W. Virginia Dr., Ste. 101, Lakewood, CO 80228: Free information ◆ Skis, snowboards, bindings, clothing, mountain bikes, and roller blades. 303-980-4014.

**Peak Ski & Sport,** 230 S. Hale Ave., Ste. 200, Escondido, CA 92029: Free catalog ◆ Gifts, clothing, and ski and snowboard gear. 800-550-7669. www.peakski.com

**Pearl Izumi,** 620 Compton St., Brownfield, CO 80020: Free information ◆ Caps, jackets, and pants. 800-877-7080. www.pearlizumi.com

**Rossignol Ski Company,** Industrial Ave., P.O. Box 298, Williston, VT 05495: Free information ◆ Alpine skis and bindings, cross-country skis, and alpine boots. 802-863-2511. www.rossignolskico.com

**Scandinavian Ski & Sport Shop,** 40 W. 57th St., New York, NY 10019: Free information ◆ Men and women's ski clothing and equipment. 800-722-6754.

**Sporthill,** 1690 S. Bertelsen Rd., Eugene, OR 97402: Free information ◆ Caps, jackets, and pants. 800-622-8444; 541-345-9623 (in OR).

**Tecnica,** 19 Technology Dr., West Lebanon, NH 03784: Free list of retail sources ◆ Ski boots. 800-258-3897. www.technicausa.com

**Yellow Turtle,** Mt. Road, Stowe, VT 05672: Free catalog ◆ Children's clothing, ski wear, and accessories. 800-439-4435; 802-253-4434 (in VT).

## Equipment & Accessories

**Akers Ski Inc.,** P.O. Box 280, Andover, ME 04216: Free catalog ◆ Cross-country ski equipment. 207-392-4582. www.akers-ski.com

**Allsop,** P.O. Box 23, Bellingham, WA 98227: Free information ◆ Nordic skis and poles, boot trees, and carriers. 800-426-4303; 360-734-9090 (in WA).

**Alpina Sports Corp.,** P.O. Box 23, Hanover, NH 03755: Free list of retail sources ◆ Boot bags, alpine and Nordic boots, and Nordic bindings and skis. 800-4-ALPINA. www.alpinasports.com

**APPEND Multi-Sport Racks,** MascoTech Accessories, 1418 N. Market Blvd., Ste. 500, Sacramento, CA 95834: Free brochure ◆ Bicycle, ski, snowboard, and surf and sailboard carriers for automobiles. 800-527-7363.

**Black Diamond Equipment,** 2084 E. 3900 South, Salt Lake City, UT 84124: Free catalog ◆ Skis. 801-278-5533.

**Backcountry Access,** 4949 N. Broadway, #139, Boulder, CO 80304: Free brochure ◆ Trekking and climbing equipment, country poles, tracker rescue beacon, and accessories. 800-670-TREK.

**The Boundary Waters Catalog,** 105 N. Central Ave., Ely, MN 55731: Free catalog ◆ Canoeing, skiing, camping, and winter gear. 800-223-6565. www.piragis.com

**Chisco Sports Accessories,** 2424 S. 2570 West, Salt Lake City, UT 84119: Free information ◆ Alpine skis. 800-825-4555.

**Climb High Inc.,** 135 Northside Dr., Shelburne, VT 05482: Free catalog ◆ Nordic boots. 802-985-5056. www.climbhigh.com

**Collins Ski Products Inc.,** P.O. Box 11, Bergenfield, NJ 07621: Free brochure ◆ Ski carriers, goggles, ski poles, and locks. 800-526-0369; 201-384-6060 (in NJ).

**Daleboot USA,** 2150 S. 3rd West, Salt Lake City, UT 84115: Free information ◆ Alpine ski poles, boots, and boot bags. 801-487-3649. www.dalebootusa.com

**Eagle River Nordic,** P.O. Box 936, Eagle River, WI 54521: Free catalog ◆ Ski equipment, clothing, boots, gloves, hats, and videos. 800-423-9730; 715-479-7285 (in WI). www.ernordic.com

**Elan-Monark,** 208 Flynn Ave., P.O. Box 4279, Burlington, VT 05401: Free information ◆ Boot and ski bags, alpine ski poles, bindings, boots, and alpine and Nordic skis. 802-863-5593.

**Fabiano Shoe Company,** 850 Summer St., South Boston, MA 02127: Free information with long SASE ◆ Nordic boots, bindings, and après ski boots. 617-268-5625. info@fabiano.com

**Hunt-Wilde,** 2835 Overpass Rd., Tampa, FL 33619: Free information ◆ Nordic ski poles. 800-248-1232.

**Igloo Viksi Inc.,** P.O. Box 180, St. Agathe Des Monts, Quebec, Canada J8C 3A3: Free information ◆ Boot and ski bags, alpine and Nordic ski poles, and Nordic skis, boots, and bindings. 819-326-1662.

**Karhu USA Inc.,** P.O. Box 4249, Burlington, VT 05406: Free list of retail sources ◆ Skis and boots. 800-869-3348.

**Leki USA,** 356 Sonwil Dr., Buffalo, NY 14225: Free catalog ◆ Ski poles. 800-255-0082; 716-683-1022 (in NY). custservice@leki.com

**Marmot Mountain Works,** 827 Bellevue Way NE, Bellevue, WA 98004: Free catalog ◆ Skis, boots, bindings, poles, and accessories. 800-254-6246. www.premier1.net/~marmot

**Maska USA Inc.,** 139 Harvest Ln., Williston, VT 05495: Free information ◆ Nordic skis, poles, and boots. 800-451-4600. www.ccmsports.com

**Mt. Constance Mountain Shoppe,** 1550 NE Riddell Rd., Bremerton, WA 98310: Free catalog ◆ Clothing, shoes, safety gear, skis, and snowboards. 360-377-8099. MTSHOPPE@MOUNTAINSHOPPE.COM

**Nordic Sports Catalog,** 643 Upper Glen St., Queensbury, NY 12804: Free information ◆ Skiing equipment and clothing. 800-517-7555; 518-793-6147 (in NY).

**Nordica,** 139 Harvest Ln., P.O. Box 800, Williston, VT 05495: Free information ◆ Alpine and cross-country skis. 800-343-7800; 802-879-4644 (in VT). www.nordicaskiwear.com

**Online Sports,** 13692 W. Virginia Dr., Ste. 101, Lakewood, CO 80228: Free information ◆ Skis, snowboards, bindings, clothing, mountain bikes, and roller blades. 303-980-4014.

**Peak Ski & Sport,** 230 S. Hale Ave., Ste. 200, Escondido, CA 92029: Free catalog ◆ Ski clothing and ski and snowboard accessories. 800-550-7669. www.peakski.com

**Raichle Molitor USA,** Geneva Rd., Brewster, NY 10509: Free list of retail sources ◆ Alpine and cross-country skis, boots, and poles. 800-431-2204. raichleus@aol.com

**REI Recreational Equipment Company,** Sumner, WA 98352: Free catalog ◆ Exercise and walking shoes, Gore-Tex rain gear, day packs that convert to tents, ski equipment, gifts, knives and utensils, sunglasses, and camping foods. 800-426-4840. www.rei.com

**Reliable Racing Supply Inc.,** 643 Upper Glen St., Queensbury, NY 12804: Free catalog ◆ Ski equipment. 800-223-4448.

**Rossignol Ski Company,** Industrial Ave., P.O. Box 298, Williston, VT 05495: Free information ◆ Alpine skis and bindings, cross-country skis, and alpine boots. 802-863-2511. www.rossignolskico.com

**Salomon/North America,** 400 E. Main St., Georgetown, MA 01833: Free list of retail sources ◆ Alpine and Nordic bindings and boots. 800-225-6850. www.salomonsports.com

**Skis Dynastar Inc.,** Hercules Dr., P.O. Box 25, Colchester, VT 05446: Free information ◆ Alpine and Nordic skis, alpine boots, and boot and ski bags. 802-655-2431. www.dynastar.com

**Spalding Sports Worldwide,** 425 Meadow St., P.O. Box 901, Chicopee, MA 01021: Free list of retail sources ◆ Nordic and alpine skis and poles. 800-225-6601. www.spalding.com

**Sports Express,** 5050 F.M. West, Houston, TX 77069: Free information ◆ Skiing equipment. 800-533-6321.

**Swix Sport USA Inc.,** 261 Ballardvale St., Wilmington, MA 01887: Free information ◆ Boot and ski bags, goggles, alpine and Nordic ski poles, and Nordic bindings and boots. 978-657-4820.

**Yamaha Sporting Goods,** 6600 Orangethorpe Ave., Buena Park, CA 90622: Free list of retail sources ◆ Alpine skis. 800-851-6514; 714-522-9011 (in CA). www.yamaha-motor.com

### Goggles

**Bolle America,** 9500 W. 49th Ave., Ste. B-100, Wheat Ridge, CO 80033: Free information ◆ Ski goggles. 800-554-6686; 303-327-2200 (in CO). www.bolle.com

**Brigade Quartermasters Inc.,** 1025 Cobb International Blvd., Kennesaw, GA 30144: Free catalog ◆ Ski goggles. 800-338-4327. www.actiongear.com

**Collins Ski Products Inc.,** P.O. Box 11, Bergenfield, NJ 07621: Free brochure ◆ Ski carriers, goggles, ski poles, and locks. 800-526-0369; 201-384-6060 (in NJ).

**Gargoyles Performance Eyewear,** 5866 S. 194th St., Kent, WA 98032: Free catalog ◆ Sunglasses and ski goggles. 800-426-6396.

**Martin Sunglasses,** Jack Martin Company Inc., 9830 Baldwin Pl., El Monte, CA 91731: Free information ◆ Ski goggles. 800-767-8555; 213-686-1100 (in CA). martinaccs@aol.com

**Raichle Molitor USA,** Geneva Rd., Brewster, NY 10509: Free list of retail sources ◆ Goggles. 800-431-2204. raichleus@aol.com

**Suunto USA,** 2151 Las Palmas Dr., Carlsbad, CA 92009: Free list of retail sources ◆ Ski goggles. 800-543-9124, ext. 228. www.suuntousa.com

**Swix Sport USA Inc.,** 261 Ballardvale St., Wilmington, MA 01887: Free information ◆ Boot and ski bags, goggles, alpine and Nordic ski poles, and Nordic bindings and boots. 978-657-4820.

## SKIN DIVING & SCUBA EQUIPMENT

**Apollo,** 44 Montgomery St., Ste. 3065, San Francisco, CA 94104: Free information ◆ Skin diving equipment and accessories. 800-231-0909; 415-392-9143 (in CA).

**Aquarius,** 51 Lake St., Nashua, NH 03060: Free information ◆ Skin diving equipment. 800-435-8974; 603-889-4346 (in NH).

**Atlantic Edge Scuba,** 213 Muddy Branch Rd., Gaithersburg, MD 20878: Free catalog ◆ Skin diving equipment. 301-990-0223. www.atlanticedge.com

**Bare Sportswear Corp.,** Box 8110-577, Blaine, WA 98230: Free information ◆ Wet suits and clothing. 360-332-2700.

**Berry Scuba Company,** 6674 N. Northwest Hwy., Chicago, IL 60631: Free catalog ◆ Skin diving and scuba equipment, inflatable boats, and underwater camera equipment. 800-621-6019; 312-763-1626 (in IL).

**Body Glove International,** 530 6th St., Hermosa Beach, CA 90254: Free information ◆ Wet and skin diving suits and equipment. 800-678-7873; 310-374-4074 (in CA). www.bodyglove.com

**Brownie's Third Lung,** 940 NW 1st St., Fort Lauderdale, FL 33311: Free information ◆ Surface air and tank-filling compressors. 800-327-0412.

**Central Skin Divers,** 160-09 Jamaica Ave., Jamaica, NY 11432: Free information ◆ Skin diving equipment and clothing. 718-739-5772.

**Citizen Watch Company of America,** 1200 Wall St. West, Lyndhurst, NJ 07071: Free information ◆ Professional diving watches and sports, flight, yachting, and windsurfer chronographs. 201-438-8150.

**Dacor Corp.,** 161 Northfield Rd., Northfield, IL 60093: Free information ◆ Scuba equipment. 847-446-9555.

**Dive Rite Manufacturing Inc.,** 117 W. Washington St., Lake City, FL 32055: Free information ◆ Lighting equipment for night diving, underwater video-making, or cave and wreck exploration. 904-752-1087.

**Divers Supply,** 5208 Mercer University Dr., Macon, GA 31210: Free catalog ◆ Skin diving equipment and clothing. 800-999-3483.

**Diving Unlimited International,** 1148 Delevan Dr., San Diego, CA 92102: Free list of retail sources ◆ Dry suits, skin diving equipment, and accessories. 800-325-8439.

**Innovative Designs Inc.,** 3785 Alt. 19 North, Ste. C, Palm Harbor, FL 34683: Free information ◆ Compact lightweight air supply equipment. 813-934-4619.

**Ironman Triathlon Wetsuits,** 445 N. Ridge Rd., Ste. B, Richmond, VA 23229: Free brochure ◆ Men and women's wetsuits. 800-897-6464; 804-288-6000 (in VA). ironman-wetsuits@erols.com

**KME Diving Suits Inc.,** 3420 C St. NE, Auburn, WA 98002: Free information ◆ Wet suits. 800-800-8KME.

**Leisure Pro,** 42 W. 18th St., 3rd Floor, New York, NY 10011: Catalog $5 ◆ Scuba and skin diving equipment and clothing. Also tennis and backpacking equipment. 212-645-1234. www.leisure-pro.com

**M & E Marine Supply Company,** P.O. Box 601, Camden, NJ 08101: Catalog $2 ◆ Skin diving equipment. 800-541-6501. www.memarine.com

**Murrays WaterSports,** P.O. Box 490, Carpinteria, CA 93014: Free information ◆ Wet suits. 800-788-8964. www.murrays.com

**Nautica International,** 6135 NW 167th St., Miami, FL 33015: Free information ◆ Compressors. 305-556-5554. www.nauticaintl.com

**Ocean Master,** 1928 Tyler Ave., El Monte, CA 91733: Free information ◆ Diving masks. 800-841-7007.

**Ocean Ray Wet Suits,** 6731-3 Amsterdam Way, Wilmington, NC 28405: Free brochure ◆ Wet suits and skin diving equipment. 800-645-5554. www.oceanray.com

**O'Neill Watersports,** 1071 41st Ave., P.O. Box 6300, Santa Cruz, CA 95062: Free information ◆ Wet suits. 408-475-7500. www.teamoneill.com

**Performance Diver,** P.O. Box 2741, Chapel Hill, NC 27514: Free catalog ◆ Wetsuits, buoyancy control devices, tank holders, boots, gloves, skin diving equipment, goggles, video cameras, and accessories. 800-933-2299. www.performancediver.com

**Sea Quest,** 2151 Las Palmas Dr., Carlsbad, CA 92009: Free information ◆ Scuba equipment. 800-327-7662; 760-438-1101 (in CA).

**Sports Merchandizers,** 1696 Cobb Pkwy. SE, Box 1262, Marietta, GA 30061: Free catalog ◆ Skin diving equipment. 800-241-1856; 770-952-3259 (in GA).

**Submersible Systems,** 18072 Gothard St., Huntington Beach, CA 92648: Free information ◆ Breathing systems. 714-842-6566.

**Sunshine Sports,** 5104 12th Ave., Brooklyn, NY 11219: Free information ◆ Skin diving and scuba equipment. 800-290-5622; 718-437-4257 (in NY). cget@pipeline.com

**Tackle Shack,** 7801 66th St. North, Pinellas Park, FL 33781: Free catalog ◆ Skin diving equipment. 800-537-6099. www.FunOnWater.com

**Tanks D'Art Inc.,** 330 Easy St., Simi Valley, CA 93065: Free information ◆ Diving tanks. 800-635-5815.

**Tektite Manufacturing,** P.O. Box 4209, Trenton, NJ 08610: Free information ◆ Scuba equipment. 609-581-2116.

**3 Little Devils,** S. 5780 A Hwy. 123, Baraboo, WI 53913: Free catalog ◆ Scuba equipment. 800-356-9016.

**U.S. Wet Suits,** P.O. Box 428, Richmond, IL 60071: Free brochure ◆ Wet suits. 800-852-6049. www.uswetsuit.com

**Curt Walker, Optician,** 3434 4th Ave., Ste. 120, San Diego, CA 92103: Free information ◆ Optically corrected dive masks. 800-538-2878; 619-299-2878 (in CA).

**Wenoka Sea Style,** c/o Sea Quest Inc., 2151 Las Palmas Dr., Carlsbad, CA 19009: Catalog $4 ◆ Skin diving equipment. 800-327-7662; 619-438-1101 (in CA).

## SLEDS, SNOWBOARDS, & TOBOGGANS

**APPEND Multi-Sport Racks,** MascoTech Accessories, 1418 N. Market Blvd., Ste. 500, Sacramento, CA 95834: Free brochure ◆ Automobile carriers for bicycles, ski equipment, snowboards, and surfboards. 800-527-7363.

**Dorfman-Pacific,** P.O. Box 213005, Stockton, CA 95213: Free information ◆ Sleds, snowmobile boots, and clothing. 800-367-3626; 209-982-1400 (in CA).

**Faber Brothers,** 4141 S. Pulaski Rd., Chicago, IL 60632: Free information ◆ Sleds. 773-376-9300.

**Flexible Flyer Company,** P.O. Box 1296, West Point, MS 39773: Free information ◆ Sleds. 800-521-6233.

**FTC Ski & Sports,** 1586 Bush St., San Francisco, CA 94109: Free catalog ◆ Skateboards and parts, snowboards, T-shirts, and clothing. 415-673-8363.

**Skip Hutchison,** Rastaboards-Surf-Sail-Snowboards, 4748 NE 11th Ave., Fort Lauderdale, FL 33334: Free information ◆ Sailboards, surfboards, and snowboards. 954-491-7992.

**M.W. Kasch Company,** 5401 W. Donges Bay Rd., Mequon, WI 53092: Free information ◆ Sleds and snowboards. 414-242-5000.

**Mt. Constance Mountain Shoppe,** 1550 NE Riddell Rd., Bremerton, WA 98310: Free catalog ◆ Clothing, shoes, safety gear, skis, and snowboards. 360-377-8099. MTSHOPPE@MOUNTAINSHOPPE.COM

**Murrays WaterSports,** P.O. Box 490, Carpinteria, CA 93014: Free information ◆ Snowboards. 800-788-8964. www.murrays.com

**Online Sports,** 13692 W. Virginia Dr., Ste. 101, Lakewood, CO 80228: Free information ◆ Skis, snowboards, bindings, clothing, mountain bikes, and roller blades. 303-980-4014.

**Paris Company Inc.,** Box 250, South Paris, ME 04281: Free information ◆ Sleds. 207-539-8221.

**Sevylor USA,** 6651 E. 26th St., Los Angeles, CA 90040: Free information ◆ Sleds. 213-727-6013.

**SFO Snowboard Shop,** 618 Shrader St., San Francisco, CA 94117: Free information ◆ Snowboards. 415-386-1666.

**Sportworks,** 421 SW 2nd Ave., Portland, OR 97204: Free catalog ◆ Snowboards, boots, safety gear, goggles, and more. 800-362-3434. www.sportworks.com

**The Wright Life,** 200 Linden, Fort Collins, CO 80524: Free catalog ◆ Frisbees (flying discs), skateboards, in-line skates, boomerangs, stunt kites, juggling equipment, and more. 800-321-8833. www.wrightlife.com

**ZIFFCO,** 18111 S. Santa Fe Ave., Rancho Dominguez, CA 90221: Free information ◆ Toboggans. 800-532-2242.

## SLEEP AIDS

**Audio-Therapy Innovations Inc.,** P.O. Box 550, Colorado Springs, CO 80901: Free information ◆ Rhythmic audio cassette tapes that help relax children and adults and aid in their going to sleep. 719-473-0100.

## SLIPCOVERS & UPHOLSTERY

**AMF Custom Upholstery,** 308 S. Poplar St., Lincolnton, NC 28092: Catalog $10 ◆ Custom upholstery. 704-732-7553.

**Home Fabric Mills Inc.,** 882 S. Main St., Cheshire, CT 06410: Free brochure ◆ Velvets, upholstery, drapery, and thermal fabrics. Also velvets, prints, sheers, and antique satins. 203-272-3529.

**Lifespace Interiors International,** 3946 S. Magnolia Way, Denver, CO 80237: Catalog $4 ◆ Slipcovers, table and other furniture cover-ups, shower curtains, window treatments, and more. 303-759-3024. www.dimensional.com/lifespace-interiors

**Sure Fit,** Division Fieldcrest Cannon Inc., 939 Marcon Blvd., Allentown, PA 18103: Free catalog ◆ Slipcovers, matching draperies, and fabrics. 888-754-7166.

**Tioga Mill Outlet,** 200 S. Hartman St., York, PA 17403: Free brochure ◆ Upholstery and drapery fabrics. 717-843-5139.

## SNOW REMOVAL EQUIPMENT

**Ariens Company,** 655 W. Ryan St., P.O. Box 157, Brillion, WI 54110: Free information ◆ Power-operated snow blowers. 414-756-2141.

**Cub Cadet Lawn Equipment,** 1145 Cleveland Ave., Ashland, OH 44805: Free information ◆ Easy-to-operate tractor with optional snow thrower and bagging attachment. 419-289-3610.

**Homelite Sales,** Box 7047, Charlotte, NC 28241: Free information with long SASE ◆ Push and riding mowers, lawn tractors, electric and gasoline-operated trimmers, gasoline-powered blowers, vacuums, sprayers, cut-off saws, and snow removal equipment. 800-242-4672.

**Mainline of North America,** P.O. Box 526, London, OH 43140: Free information ◆ All-gear driven tiller with optional sickle bar and no belts or chains, hydraulic log splitters, carts, and snow throwers. 800-837-2097.

## SNOWDOMES

**Global Shakeup,** 235 East Colorado Blvd., Ste. 178, Pasadena, CA 91101: Catalog $2 (refundable with $25 order) ◆ Snowdomes, snowglobes, waterbells, and more. 213-259-8988. www.snowdomes.com

## SNOWMOBILES

**Central Snowmobile Salvage,** P.O. Box 13188, Green Bay, WI 54307: Free catalog ◆ Snowmobile parts and accessories. 800-558-6778.

**Hunt-Wilde,** 2835 Overpass Rd., Tampa, FL 33619: Free information ◆ Snowmobiles. 800-248-1232.

**Intraser Inc.,** 428 N. La Cienega Blvd., Los Angeles, CA 90048: Free information ◆ New and pre-owned motorcycles, ATVs, snowmobiles, trailers, personal water vehicles, and small boats. 213-652-6966.

**Dennis Kirk Inc.,** 955 Southfield Ave., Rush City, MN 55069: Free information ◆ Snowmobiles and parts. 800-328-9280.

**Polaris Industries,** 1225 Hwy. 169 North, Minneapolis, MN 55441: Free list of retail sources ◆ Snowmobiles, clothing, and accessories. 800-POLARIS; 612-542-0500 (in MN). www.polarisusa.com

## SNOWSHOES

**Atlas Snow-Shoe Company,** 1830 Harrison St., San Francisco, CA 94103: Free information ◆ Snowshoes. 888-48-ATLAS.

**Good Thunder Snowshoes,** 3404 Lyndale Ave. South, Minneapolis, MN 55408: Free brochure ◆ Light to heavy-duty snowshoes. 612-824-2385.

**Great Bear Enterprises,** P.O. Box 428, Kila, MT 59920: Free brochure ◆ Handcrafted snowshoes. 406-257-6992.

**Havlick Snowshoe Company,** 2513 State Hwy. 30, Drawer QQ, Mayfield, NY 12117: Free brochure with long SASE ◆ Aluminum and wood-framed snowshoes. 800-TOP-SHOE.

**Iverson Snowshoe Company,** Maple St., P.O. Box 85, Shingleton, MI 49884: Free information ◆ Snowshoes and bindings. 906-452-6370.

**Liberty Mountain Sports,** 4875 W. 1980 South, Salt Lake City, UT 84104: Free list of retail sources ◆ Snowshoes and insulated clothing. 800-366-2666.

**Longwood Equipment Company Ltd.,** 1940 Ellesmere Rd., Unit 8, Scarborough, Ontario, Canada M1H 2V7: Free information ◆ Snowshoes. 416-438-3710.

**Northern Lites Snowshoes,** 1300 Cleveland, Wausau, WI 54401: Free list of retail sources ◆ Snowshoes. 800-360-LITE. www.northernlites.com

**Safesport/Outbound,** 269 Columbia Ave., Chapin, SC 29036: Free list of retail sources ◆ Snowshoes and bindings. 800-433-6506.

**Spring Brook Manufacturing Inc.,** 2477 I Rd., Grand Junction, CO 81505: Free brochure ◆ Snowshoes. 800-655-8984; 970-241-8546 (in CO).

**Tubbs Snowshoes,** P.O. Box 1310, Stowe, VT 05672: Free list of retail sources ◆ Snowshoes. 800-882-2748.

## SOAP MAKING

**The Essential Oil Company,** P.O. Box 206, Lake Oswego, OR 97034: Free catalog ◆ Essential oils, soap-making molds and supplies, incense materials, potpourri, and aromatherapy items. 800-729-5912.

**Gardens Past,** P.O. Box 1846, Estes Park, CO 80517: Catalog $1 ◆ Soaps and soap-making supplies, potpourri, dried flowers, herbs, candles, and aromatherapy items. 970-823-5565.

**M.C. Designs,** Kelly Mitchell, P.O. Box 31078, #8-2929 St. Johns St., Port Moody, British Columbia, Canada V3H 4T4: Free information ◆ Vegetable-based soap making kits. 604-469-3379.

**Pourette Manufacturing,** P.O. Box 17056, Seattle, WA 98107: Catalog $2 ◆ Ready-to-use candles and soap. Also candle-making supplies. 800-888-9425. www.pourette.com

**Sugar Plum Sundries,** 5152 Fair Forest Dr., Stone Mountain, GA 30088: Free catalog ◆ Natural handmade soaps, soap-making supplies, and bath items. 404-297-0158. www.mindspring.com/~sugarplum

**Summers Past Farm,** 15602 Old Hwy. 80, El Cajon, CA 92021: Free catalog ◆ Soap-making kit. 800-390-9969. www.soapmaking.com

**Sun Feather Herbal Soap,** 1551 State Hwy. 72, Potsdam, NY 13676: Catalog $2 ◆ Soap-making kits, supplies, and books. 315-265-3648. www.electronicottage.com/sunfeathersoaps

## SOCCER

### Clothing

**Action & Leisure Inc.,** 45 E. 30th St., New York, NY 10016: Free information ◆ Shoes, uniforms, gloves, shorts, shirts, shin guards, and socks. 800-523-8508; 212-684-4470 (in NY).

**Action Sport Systems Inc.,** P.O. Box 1442, Morganton, NC 28680: Free information ◆ Uniforms, shirts, shorts, gloves, and socks. 800-631-1091; 704-584-8000 (in NC).

**Adidas USA,** 5675 N. Blackstock Rd., Spartanburg, SC 29303: Free list of retail sources ◆ Uniforms, shoes, socks, shirts, shorts, and shin guards. 800-423-4327. www.adidas.com

**American Soccer Company Inc.,** 525 Sanford Ave., Wilmington, CA 90744: Free information ◆ Shorts, warm-up clothing, and uniforms. 800-626-7774; 562-834-6576 (in CA).

**Betlin Manufacturing,** 1445 Marion Rd., Columbus, OH 43207: Free information ◆ Shorts, warm-up clothing, and uniforms. 614-443-0248.

**Big Toe Sports,** 5972 Executive Dr., Ste. 200, Madison, WI 53719: Free brochure ◆ Soccer equipment and clothing. 800-244-8637. www.bigtoesports.com

**Bike Athletic Company,** P.O. Box 666, Knoxville, TN 37901: Free information ◆ Shin guards, shirts, shorts, and uniforms. 800-251-9230. www.bike-athletic.com

**Bomark Sportswear,** P.O. Box 2068, Belair, TX 77402: Free information ◆ Uniforms. 800-231-3351.

**Champion Products Inc.,** 475 Corporate Square Dr., Winston Salem, NC 27105: Free information ◆ Uniforms, shoes, socks, and shirts.

**Doss Shoes,** Soccer Sport Supply Company, 1745 1st Ave., New York, NY 10128: Free information ◆ Gloves, shin guards, shirts, shorts, and uniforms. 800-223-1010; 212-427-6050 (in NY).

**Empire Sporting Goods Manufacturing Company,** 443 Broadway, New York, NY 10013: Free information ◆ Shorts and uniforms. 800-221-3455; 212-966-0880 (in NY).

**Genesport Industries Ltd.,** Hokkaido Karate Equipment Manufacturing Company, 150 King St., Montreal, Quebec, Canada H3C 2P3: Free information ◆ Gloves, shin guards, shirts, and shorts. 514-861-1856.

**Holabird Sports Discounters,** 9220 Pulaski Hwy., Baltimore, MD 21220: Free catalog ◆ Soccer and other sports equipment and clothing. 410-687-6400. www.holabirdsports.com

**Lotto Sports,** 1900 Surveyor Blvd., Carrollton, TX 75006: Free information ◆ Soccer shoes. 800-527-5126; 972-416-4003 (in TX).

**Markwort Sporting Goods,** 4300 Forest Park Ave., St. Louis, MO 63108: Catalog $8 (request list of retail sources) ◆ Shorts, warm-up clothing, and uniforms. 800-669-6626; 314-652-3757 (in MO).

**Puma USA Inc.,** 147 Centre St., Brockton, MA 02403: Free information with long SASE ◆ Uniforms, gloves, shorts and shirts, socks, shoes, and shin guards. 800-662-7862. www.puma.com

**Rugby & Soccer Supply,** P.O. Box 565, Merrifield, VA 22116: Free catalog ◆ Balls, boots, jerseys, and shorts. 800-872-7842; 703-280-5540 (in VA).

**Soccer International Inc.,** P.O. Box 7222, Arlington, VA 22207: Catalog $1 ◆ Soccer equipment, uniforms, balls, gifts, T-shirts, and books. 703-524-4333. www.soccerinternational.com

**Soccer Kick,** 9220 SW Barbur Blvd., Portland, OR 97204: Free catalog ◆ Soccer equipment, clothing, shoes, and gifts. 800-288-5425.

**Soccer Madness International,** 5201 NW 108th Ave., Sunrise, FL 33351: Free catalog ◆ Clothing, shoes, and equipment. 800-447-8333. www.soccermadness.com

**Star Struck,** P.O. Box 308, Bethel, CT 06801: Free catalog ◆ Fitted caps and jerseys. 800-908-4637; 877-THE-GAME (in CT). www.starstruck.com

**Title 9 Sports,** 5743 Landregan St., Emeryville, CA 94608: Free catalog ◆ Women's clothing created by and for women. 510-655-5999. thefolks@title9sports.com

**TSI Soccer,** 4324 S. Alston Ave., Durham, NC 27713: Free catalog ◆ Soccer equipment, clothing, and shoes. 800-TSI-1000. www.tsisoccer.com

**Union Jacks,** 3525 Roanoke Rd., Kansas City, MO 64111: Free information ◆ Uniforms, shin guards, shirts, shorts, shoes, and socks. 800-288-5550; 816-561-5550 (in MO).

### Equipment

**Action & Leisure Inc.,** 45 E. 30th St., New York, NY 10016: Free information ◆ Soccer balls, cleats, and wrenches. 800-523-8508; 212-684-4470 (in NY).

**Action Sport Systems Inc.,** P.O. Box 1442, Morganton, NC 28680: Free information ◆ Soccer balls. 800-631-1091; 704-584-8000 (in NC).

**Adidas USA,** 5675 N. Blackstock Rd., Spartanburg, SC 29303: Free list of retail sources ◆ Soccer balls, cleats, and equipment. 800-423-4327. www.adidas.com

**American Soccer Company Inc.,** 525 Sanford Ave., Wilmington, CA 90744: ◆ Balls, goalie gloves, nets, and protective gear. 800-626-7774; 562-834-6576 (in CA).

**The Athletic Connection,** 1901 Diplomat, Dallas, TX 75234: Free information ◆ Balls and nets. 800-527-0871; 972-243-1446 (in TX).

**Ballwall,** 5 Flint Ave., Larchmont, NY 10538: Free brochure ◆ Indoor and outdoor backstop training wall for sports that use a ball. 800-966-1190; 914-833-0390 (in NY).

**Beacon Ballfields,** P.O. Box 45557, Madison, WI 53744: Free catalog ◆ Baseball, football, and soccer field equipment. 800-747-5985; 608-274-5985 (in WI).

**Big Toe Sports,** 5972 Executive Dr., Ste. 200, Madison, WI 53719: Free brochure ◆ Soccer equipment and clothing. 800-244-8637. www.bigtoesports.com

**Brine Inc.,** 47 Sumner St., Milford, MA 01757: Free information ◆ Balls, goalie gloves, nets, and protective gear. 800-227-2722; 508-478-3250 (in MA).

**Carron Net Company,** 1623 17th St., P.O. Box 177, Two Rivers, WI 54241: Free information ◆ Archery, baseball, basketball, gymnasium and climbing, football, racquetball, soccer, tennis, and volleyball equipment. 800-558-7768; 414-793-2217 (in WI). sales@carronnet.com

**Clarke Distributing Company,** 9233 Bryant St., Houston, TX 77075: Catalog $2 ◆ Tennis, golf, soccer equipment, novelties, and gifts. 800-777-3444.

**Doss Shoes,** Soccer Sport Supply Company, 1745 1st Ave., New York, NY 10128: Free information ◆ Goals, nets, and soccer balls. 800-223-1010; 212-427-6050 (in NY).

**E.Z. Enterprises,** 205 D Exeter Rd., London, Ontario, Canada N6L 1A4: Free information ◆ Lightweight portable and collapsible goals. 519-472-5261.

**General Sportcraft Company,** 140 Woodbine Rd., Bergenfield, NJ 07621: Free information ◆ Soccer balls, goals, and nets. 201-384-4242.

**Goal Sporting Goods Inc.,** 37 Industrial Park Rd., P.O. Box 236, Essex, CT 06426: Free catalog ◆ Telescoping, folding, and adjustable goals and nets. 800-334-GOAL. www.goalsports.com

**Matt Godek Rugby & Soccer Supply,** P.O. Box 565, Merrifield, VA 22116: Free information ◆ Rugby and soccer equipment. 800-336-3446. www.rugbystore.com

**Gopher Sport,** 2929 Park Dr., Owatonna, MN 55060: Free information ◆ Equipment for basketball, football, soccer, track and field, and other net games. 800-533-0446; 507-451-7470 (in MN).

**Holabird Sports Discounters,** 9220 Pulaski Hwy., Baltimore, MD 21220: Free catalog ◆ Soccer equipment and clothing. 410-687-6400. www.holabirdsports.com

**Irwin Sports,** 43 Hanna Ave., Toronto, Ontario, Canada M6K 1X6: Free information ◆ Soccer balls, goals, and nets. 800-268-1732.

**Jayfro Corp.,** Unified Sports Inc., 976 Hartford Tnpk., P.O. Box 400, Waterford, CT 06385: Free catalog ◆ Portable goals, nets, and practice equipment. 860-447-3001.

**Kwik Goal,** 140 Pacific Dr., Quakertown, PA 18951: Free information ◆ Soccer balls, goals, nets, wrenches and cleats, training equipment, referee supplies, and video cassettes. 800-531-4252; 215-536-2200 (in PA). www.kwikgoal.com

**Markwort Sporting Goods,** 4300 Forest Park Ave., St. Louis, MO 63108: Catalog $8 (request list of retail sources) ◆ Soccer balls, goals, and nets. 800-669-6626; 314-652-3757 (in MO).

**Memphis Net & Twine Company Inc.,** 2481 Matthews Ave., P.O. Box 80331, Memphis, TN 38108: Free catalog ◆ Cages and backstops, soccer nets, tennis windscreens, pitching machines, protector and miscellaneous nets for other sports, and sports accessories. 800-238-6380. memnet@netten.net

**Pennray Billiard & Recreational Products,** 7847 N. Calswell Ave., Niles, IL 60714: Free catalog ◆ Darts, billiards, and soccer equipment. 800-523-8934. www.wicothesource.com

**Rugby & Soccer Supply,** P.O. Box 565, Merrifield, VA 22116: Free catalog ◆ Balls, boots, jerseys, and shorts. 800-872-7842; 703-280-5540 (in VA).

**Soccer International Inc.,** P.O. Box 7222, Arlington, VA 22207: Catalog $1 ◆ Soccer balls, uniforms, gifts, T-shirts, and books. 703-524-4333. www.soccerinternational.com

**Soccer Kick,** 9220 SW Barbur Blvd., Portland, OR 97204: Free catalog ◆ Soccer equipment, clothing, shoes, and gifts. 800-288-5425.

**Soccer Madness International,** 5201 NW 108th Ave., Sunrise, FL 33351: Free catalog ◆ Clothing, shoes, and equipment. 800-447-8333. www.soccermadness.com

**Spalding Sports Worldwide,** 425 Meadow St., P.O. Box 901, Chicopee, MA 01021: Free list of retail sources ◆ Soccer balls. 800-225-6601. www.spalding.com

**Sportime,** 1 Sportime Way, Atlanta, GA 30340: Free information ◆ Balls and nets. 800-444-5700; 770-449-5700 (in GA).

**Sportline of Hilton Head Ltd.,** Heritage Plaza, Pope Ave., Hilton Head, SC 29928: Free information ◆ Soccer balls. 888-996-8855. www.hiltonhead9.com/sportline

**The Training Camp,** c/o Genesis Direct, 100 Plaza Dr., Secaucus, NJ 07094: Free catalog ◆ Basketball, football, golf, hockey, and soccer training aids. 800-873-8263. care@GenesisDirect.com

**TSI Soccer,** 4324 S. Alston Ave., Durham, NC 27713: Free catalog ◆ Soccer equipment, clothing, and shoes. 800-TSI-1000. www.tsisoccer.com

**Wolvering Sports,** P.O. Box 1941, Ann Arbor, MI 48106: Catalog $1 ◆ Baseball, basketball, field hockey, soccer, football, other athletic, and recreation equipment. 313-761-5691.

## SODA-MAKING (CARBONATING) MACHINES

**Beverage Express,** P.O. Box 720099-179, San Diego, CA 92172: Free information ◆ Easy-to-use portable carbonating appliance. 760-726-9620. www.Beverageexpress.com

## SOLAR, WIND, & OTHER ENERGY SAVING DEVICES

**AAA Solar Supply Inc.,** 2021 Zearing NW, Albuquerque, NM 87104: Free catalog ◆ Do-it-yourself solar systems and parts, wind turbines, heat exchangers, controls and sensors, and more. 800-245-0311; 505-2432-3212 (in NM).

**Advance Solar Hydro Wind Power,** P.O. Box 23, Calpella, CA 95418: Information $1 ◆ Solar, hydro-electric, and wind energy power systems. 707-485-0588.

**Alternative Energy Engineering,** P.O. Box 339, Redway, CA 95560: Catalog $1 ◆ Solar energy equipment. 800-777-6609.

**American Energy Technologies Inc.,** P.O. Box 1865, Green Cove Springs, FL 32043: Free information ◆ Solar energy thermal collectors, absorbers, and systems. 800-874-2190.

**Array Technologies,** 3402 Stanford NE, Albuquerque, NM 87107: Free information ◆ Solar trackers for photo-voltaic arrays. 505-881-7567.

**Backwoods Solar Electric,** 8530 Rapid Lightning Creek, Sandpoint, ID 83864: Catalog $3 ◆ Solar electric-powered appliances and electricity-generating equipment. 208-263-4290.

**Balmar,** 27010 12th Ave., Stanwood, WA 98292: Free information ◆ Wind-driven alternator. 360-629-3210.

**Bergey Windpower Company Inc.,** 2001 Priestly Ave., Norman, OK 73069: Free information ◆ Wind turbines. 405-364-4212.

**Chesapeake Solar,** P.O. Box 732, Hunt Valley, MD 21030: Free information ◆ Solar battery chargers and accessories. 800-346-8724; 410-252-8575 (in MD).

**Dempster Industries Inc.,** P.O. Box 848, Beatrice, NE 68310: Free information ◆ Hand and windmill pumps and parts. 800-234-3367.

**Environmental Solar Systems,** 119 West St., Methuen, MA 01844: Free information ◆ Solar food dryers. 800-934-3848.

**Fanta-Sea Pools,** 1865 Grand Island Blvd., Grand Island, NY 14072: Free information ◆ Solar energy heated swimming pools. 800-845-5500.

**Hamilton-Ferris Company,** P.O. Box 126, Ashland, MA 01721: Free catalog ◆ Solar equipment, wind-water engine-driven systems, alternators, inverter-chargers, monitors, and batteries. 508-881-4602.

**Home Trends,** 1450 Lyell Ave., Rochester, NY 14606: Free catalog ◆ Cleaning supplies, energy-saving devices, lighting equipment, pest controls, brushes, vacuums and accessories, and more. 716-254-6520. home@eznet.net

**Jade Mountain Inc.,** P.O. Box 4616, Boulder, CO 80306: Free catalog ◆ Technological energy-saving and conservation accessories. 800-442-1972; 303-449-6601 (in CO). www.jademountain.com

**Kansas Wind Power,** 13569 214th Rd., Holton, KS 66436: Catalog $4 ◆ Sun ovens, wind generators, composting toilets, tank-less water heaters, air cooler, and solar energy equipment and parts. 913-364-4407.

**Kipp & Zonen,** Division Enraf-Nonius Company, 125 Wilbur Pl., Bohemia, NY 11716: Free information ◆ Solar radiation measurement instrumentation to determine application needs. 800-645-1025.

**Midway Labs Inc.,** 350 N. Ogden Ave., Chicago, IL 60607: Free information ◆ Solar energy electricity-generating components. 312-667-7863.

**Offline Independent Energy Systems,** P.O. Box 231, North Fork, CA 93643: Catalog $3 ◆ Renewable energy systems and supplies. 209-877-7080. www.psnw.com/~ofln

**Photocomm Inc.,** Distribution Division, 7681 E. Gray Rd., Scottsdale, AZ 85260: Catalog $5 ◆ Solar energy modules for homes, recreational vehicles, boats, and cabins. 800-544-6466; 602-948-8003 (in AZ).

**Real Goods,** 555 Leslie St., Ukiah, CA 95482: Free catalog ◆ Solar energy components, and solar educational toys. Also environmental books, games, and other alternative energy products. 800-762-7325. www.realgoods.com

**Refrigeration Research Inc.,** P.O. Box 869, Brighton, MI 48116: Free information ◆ Do-it-yourself solar water heating systems for homes. 810-227-1151.

**Siemens Solar Industries,** P.O. Box 6032, Camarillo, CA 93120: Free information ◆ Solar panels for energy systems. 800-272-6765. www.siemenssolar.com

**Sierra Solar Systems,** 109 Argall Way, Nevada City, CA 95959: Catalog $5 (refundable) ◆ Solar electric energy systems and appliances. 800-51-SOLAR; 530-265-8441. www.sierrasolar.com

**Solar Components Corp.,** 121 Valley St., Manchester, NH 03103: Brochure $1 ◆ Lean-to and free-standing build-it-yourself greenhouse kits and solar energy equipment. 603-668-8186.

**Solar Depot,** 61 Paul Dr., San Rafael, CA 94903: Catalog $4 ◆ Solar electric power systems, water heaters, electric and thermal systems, and other equipment. 415-499-1333. www.solardepot.com

**Solar Electric Inc.,** 5555 Santa Fe St., #J, San Diego, CA 92109: Free information ◆ Solar panels and equipment. 800-842-5678. www.solarelectricinc.com

**Solarex Corp.,** 630 Solarex Ct., Frederick, MD 21701: Free catalog ◆ Solar panels, battery chargers, and other photo-voltaic equipment. 301-698-4200.

**Specialty Concepts Inc.,** 8954 Mason Ave., Chatsworth, CA 91311: Free brochure ◆ Photo-voltaic controls. 818-998-5238.

**The Sun Electric Company,** P.O. Box 1305, Whitefish, MT 59937: Free catalog ◆ Solar energy equipment for recreational vehicles, cabins, or homes. 406-862-5424.

**Sun Solar Products,** 266-12 Middle Island Rd., Medford, NY 11763: Free information ◆ Alternative energy accessories for energy generation, solar components, and other equipment. 516-736-4900.

**Sun-Porch Division,** Vegetable Factory Inc., P.O. Box 368, Westport, CT 06881: Catalog $3 ◆ Solar greenhouses. 203-324-0010.

**Sunelco,** P.O. Box 1499, Hamilton, MT 59840: Catalog $4.95 ◆ Solar modules, controllers, batteries, inverters, water pumps, propane-operated appliances, home power systems, and heating systems for recreational vehicles and cabins. 800-338-6844.

**Sunglo Solar Greenhouses,** 2626 15th Ave. West, Seattle, WA 98119: Free brochure ◆ Solar greenhouses and solariums. 800-647-0606; 206-284-8900 (in WA).

**Sunlight Energy Corp.,** 4411 W. Echo Ln., Glendale, AZ 85302: Free information ◆ Solar battery chargers. 800-338-1781.

**Sunnyside Solar,** RD 4, Box 808, Green River Rd., Brattleboro, VT 05301: Free information ◆ Hydropower equipment and photo-voltaic solar electric systems for remote and non-remote locations. 802-257-1482. www.sunnysidesolar.com

**Sunquest Inc.,** 1555 N. Rankin Ave., Newton, NC 28658: Free information ◆ Solar energy and radiant floor heating systems. 704-465-6805.

**Sunworthy Solar,** 4105 Witty Ln., Hopkinsville, KY 42240: Catalog and design guide $6 ◆ Solar panels and windmills. 502-889-0624.

**Thermo Dynamics Ltd.,** 81 Thornhill Dr., Dartmouth, Nova Scotia, Canada B3B 1R9: Free information ◆ Solar hot water system. 902-468-1001.

**United Solar Systems Corp.,** 9235 Brown Deer Rd., San Diego, CA 92121: Free brochure ◆ Solar electric utility power modules and battery chargers. 800-843-3892. www.ovonic.com/unisolar.htm

**Vanner Power Group,** 4282 Reynolds Dr., Hilliard, OH 43026: Free information ◆ High-powered system for alternative energy power needs. 800-989-2718.

**Windstream Power Systems Inc.,** P.O. Box 1604, Burlington, VT 05402: Free information ◆ Marine wind turbines. 802-658-0075.

**World Power Technologies Inc.,** 19 N. Lake Ave., Duluth, MN 55802: Free brochure ◆ Easy-to-install wind-operated electric generators and solar equipment. 218-722-1492.

**Yankee Environmental Systems Inc.,** 101 Industrial Blvd., Airport Industrial Park, Turners Falls, MA 01376: Free information ◆ Solar radiation measurement systems. 413-863-0200. info@sunlight.yesinc.com

**Zomeworks Corp.,** P.O. Box 25805, Albuquerque, NM 87125: Free information ◆ Passive solar trackers and fixed racks for top-of-pole, side-of-pole, or roof/ground/wall mounts. 800-279-6342.

## SOLARIUMS & SUNROOMS

**Amdega & Machin Conservatories,** 3515 Lakeshore Dr., St. Joseph, MI 49085: Catalog $10 ◆ English-style conservatories constructed in western red cedar or aluminum. 800-922-0110.

**Arctic Glass & Window Outlet,** 565 County Rd. T, Hammond, WI 54015: Catalog $4 ◆ Sunrooms, windows, entryway and patio doors, and skylights. 800-428-9276.

**Florian Greenhouses,** 64 Airport Rd., West Milford, NJ 07480: Catalog $5 ◆ Easy-to-build solariums for do-it-yourselfers. 800-FLORIAN. www.florian-greenhouse.com

**Four Seasons Sunrooms,** 5005 Veterans Memorial Hwy., Holbrook, NY 11741: Free information ◆ Conservatories, sunrooms, patio and deck enclosures, and more. 800-FOURSEASONS; 516-563-4000 (in NY). www.four-seasons-sunrooms.com

**Habitat Solar Rooms,** 21 Elm St., South Deerfield, MA 01373: Brochure $12 ◆ All-cedar kits for solar rooms. 800-992-0121.

**Janco Greenhouses,** 9390 Davis Ave., Laurel, MD 20707: Brochure $5 ◆ Solariums with optional variable pitch roofs. 800-323-6933.

**Lindal Cedar Homes,** P.O. Box 24426, Seattle, WA 98124: Catalog $15 ◆ Sunrooms. 800-426-0536. www.lindal.com

**Southeastern Insulated Glass,** 6477 Peachtree Industrial Blvd., Atlanta, GA 30360: Free information ◆ Greenhouse and sunroom kits, sliding glass doors, and skylights. 800-841-9842; 770-455-8838 (in GA).

**Sturdi-Built Manufacturing Company,** 11304 SW Boones Ferry Rd., Portland, OR 97219: Free catalog ◆ Greenhouses, cold frames, and sunrooms. 800-722-4115; 503-244-4100 (in OR).

**Sunbilt Solar Products,** 109-10 180th St., Jamaica, NY 11433: Free information ◆ Easy-to-build sunrooms. 718-297-6040.

**Sundance Supply,** 1678 Shattuck Ave., Ste. 173, Berkeley, CA 94709: Catalog $2 ◆ Building components for greenhouses, sun rooms, pool enclosures, and skylights. 800-776-2534. www.sundancesupply.com

**Under Glass Manufacturing Corp.,** P.O. Box 798, Lake Katrine, NY 12449: Catalog $3 ◆ Greenhouses and solariums. 914-298-0645.

**Vegetable Factory Inc.,** P.O. Box 368, Westport, CT 06881: Catalog $3 ◆ Insulated winter sun room that converts to a summer screen enclosure.

**Window Quilts,** P.O. Box 975, Brattleboro, VT 05362: Information $1 ◆ Sunrooms. 800-257-4501.

## SOUVENIRS

**Allen-Lewis Manufacturing Company,** P.O. Box 16546, Denver, CO 80216: Free catalog ◆ Souvenirs, carnival and party supplies, fund-raising merchandise, toys and games, T-shirts and sweatshirts, and craft supplies. 800-525-6658.

**Americana Souvenirs & Gifts,** 302 York St., Gettysburg, PA 17325: Free information ◆ Civil War souvenirs and memorabilia. www.americanagifts.com

**Forever Engineering,** 82 Lamark Dr., Amherst, NY 14226: Free brochure ◆ Souvenir trophy hockey pucks and mini-sticks with optional custom printing. 716-868-7790.

**Steve Eagles,** Native American Regalia, 12335 Oregon Wagon Trail, Elbert, CO 80106: Catalog $3 ◆ Native American regalia, arts and crafts, musical instruments, souvenirs, and more. 719-495-0798. SEagles254@.com

## SPELEOLOGY (CAVE EXPLORATION)

**W. Born & Associates,** 2438 Blacklick-Eastern Rd., Millersport, OH 43046: Free information with long SASE ◆ Equipment and supplies for cavers. 614-467-2676.

**Pigeon Mountain Industries,** P.O. Box 803, Lafayette, GA 30728: Free information ◆ Gear and supplies for cavers. 800-282-7673; 706-764-1437 (in GA).

**PMI Petzal Distribution Inc.,** P.O. Box 803, LaFayette, GA 30728: Free list of retail sources ◆ Headlamps. 800-282-7673.

**J.E. Weinel Inc.,** P.O. Box 213, Valencia, PA 16059: Free information with long SASE ◆ Equipment and supplies for caving, climbing, and rappelling. 800-346-7673; 412-898-2335 (in PA).

## SPINNING WHEELS, LOOMS, & CARDERS

**AVL Looms,** 601 Orange St., Chico, CA 95928: Catalog $2 ◆ Looms and supplies. 800-626-9615; 916-893-4915 (in CA).

**Bountiful,** Lois & Bud Scarbrough, P.O. Box 1727, Estes Park, CO 80517: Catalog $5 ◆ Spinning wheels, tapestry looms, books, videos, yarns, parts, and accessories. 970-586-9332.

**Braid-Aid,** 466 Washington St., Pembroke, MA 02359: Catalog $4 ◆ Braided rug kits, braiding supplies, spinning and weaving accessories, and wool by the pound or yard. 781-826-2560.

**Clemes & Clemes Inc.,** 650 San Pablo Ave., Pinole, CA 94564: Free catalog ◆ Spinning wheels, drum carders, wool and cotton carders, drop spindles, and natural and dyed wool. 510-724-2036.

**Country Spun Studio,** RR 1, Box 269, Rochester Mills, PA 15771: Brochure $3 ◆ Handpainted and hand-spun yarns, spinning wheels, books and videos, and accessories. 800-970-9703; 412-286-3255 (in PA).

**Crystal Palace Yarns,** 3006 San Pablo Ave., Berkeley, CA 94702: Free list of retail sources ◆ Yarns, natural fibers, and spinning wheels. 510-548-9988. www.straw.com/cpy/index.html

**The Designery,** P.O. Box 308, Center Sandwich, NH 03227: Catalog $1 ◆ Spinning and weaving supplies, hand-dyed wool, mohair, and yarns. 603-284-6915.

**Earth Guild,** 33 Haywood St., Asheville, NC 28801: Catalog $3 ◆ Basket-making, weaving, spinning, dyeing, pottery, woodcarving, hand and machine knitting, rug-making, netting, and chair-caning supplies. 800-327-8448. www.earthguild.com

**Earthsong Fibers,** 5115 Excelsior Blvd., #428, Minneapolis, MN 55416: Catalog $2 ◆ Fibers, yarns, spinning wheels, looms, and accessories. 800-473-5350; 612-926-3451 (in MN).

**Edgemont Yarn Services,** P.O. Box 205, Washington, KY 41096: Free brochure ◆ Weaving supplies, 2 and 4-harness looms, tabletop looms, loom parts, and rug-making supplies. 800-446-5977.

**Fiber Studio,** 9 Foster Hill Rd., Box 637, Henniker, NH 03242: Spinning fibers catalog $1, yarn samples $4, equipment catalog $1 ◆ Spinning, weaving, and knitting equipment; spinning fibers; and cotton, mohair, wool, alpaca, silk, and linen yarns. 603-428-7830.

**Gilmore Looms,** 1032 N. Broadway, Stockton, CA 95205: Free catalog ◆ Looms and accessories. 209-463-1545.

**Glimakra Looms & Yarns Inc.,** 1338 Ross St., Petaluma, CA 94954: Catalog $2.50 ◆ Weaving equipment, looms, yarns, and lace-making equipment. 800-289-9276; 707-762-3362 (in CA).

**Patrick Green Carders,** 48793 Chilliwack Lake Rd., Chilliwack, British Columbia, Canada V4Z 1A6: Free information ◆ Carders with optional motor units. 604-858-6020.

**Harrisville Designs,** Center Village, Box 806, Harrisville, NH 03450: Yarn catalog $6; loom catalog free ◆ Yarns and looms. 800-338-9415; 603-827-3333 (in NH). www.harrisville.com

**Heritage Looms,** RR 6, Box 731-E, Alvin, TX 77511: Catalog $1.50 ◆ Table looms and weaving supplies. 409-925-4161.

**Hoop 'N Stitch,** 4610 Hixson Pike, Hixson, TX 37343: Free information ◆ Hands-free lap stitching frame with a choice of five sizes. 423-870-8217.

**J-Made Looms,** P.O. Box 452, Oregon City, OR 97045: Catalog $3 ◆ Looms in 45-, 60-, and 72-inch models. 503-631-3973.

**K's Creations,** P.O. Box 161446, Austin, TX 78746: Free information ◆ Adjustable interchangeable lap frames, canvasses, and accessories. 800-727-3769.

**Kokovoko Breeding Farm,** Rt. 3, Box 134, Corinth, KY 41010: Free information ◆ Spinning wheels, accessories, how-to videos, and books. 800-804-5541; 606-234-5707 (in KY). kokovoko@kih.net

**Lacis,** 3163 Adeline St., Berkeley, CA 94703: Catalog $5 ◆ Hairpin lace looms. 510-843-7178. www.lacis.com

**Leesburg Looms & Supply,** 201 N. Cherry St., Van Wert, OH 45891: Free catalog ◆ Easy-to-operate 2- and 4-harness looms. 419-238-2738.

**Louët Sales,** P.O. Box 267, Ogdensburg, NY 13669: Catalog $5 ◆ Books, dyestuffs, yarns and fibers, and spinning, weaving, carding, felting, and lace-making equipment. 315-925-4502. www.louet.com

**Macomber Looms,** P.O. Box 186, York, ME 03909: Catalog $3 ◆ Looms. 207-363-2808.

**Mannings Creative Crafts,** P.O. Box 687, East Berlin, PA 17316: Catalog $1 ◆ Spinning wheels and looms, yarns and spinning fibers, books, dyes, and mordants. 717-624-2223. mannings@sun-link.com

**Mary Lue's Knitting World,** 101 W. Broadway, St. Peter, MN 56082: Free information ◆ Spinning wheels, looms, and accessories. Also yarns and how-to videos. 507-931-3734.

**Mountain Loom Company,** P.O. Box 509, Vader, WA 98593: Free brochure ◆ Sampler, table, pique, tapestry, and floor looms. 800-238-0296. www.mtnloom.com

**Nasco,** 901 Janesville Ave., Fort Atkinson, WI 53538: Free catalog ◆ Weaving supplies, looms, tools, yarns, and needlecraft accessories. 800-558-9595. www.nascofa.com

**Norsk Fjord Fiber,** P.O. Box 271, Lexington, GA 30648: Loom catalog $3, fleece and rovings sample cards $3, Spelsau yarn sample card $3 ◆ Tapestry looms. Also Swedish Gotland fleece, rovings, and yarns. 706-743-5120.

**Norwood Looms,** P.O. Box 167, Freemont, MI 49412: Catalog $2 ◆ Looms, quilting hoops, and frames. 616-924-3901. www.homesteadweaver.com/norwood.html

**Rio Grande Weaver's Supply,** 216 Pueblo Norte, Taos, NM 87571: Catalog $1 ◆ Spinning wheels, looms, and loom kits. Also hand-dyed yarns, dyes, fleece, books, and videos. 505-758-0433.

**Schacht Spindle Company Inc.,** 6101 Ben Pl., Boulder, CO 80301: Catalog $2.50 ◆ Looms and accessories. 800-228-2553.

**Shannock Tapestry Looms,** 10402 NW 11th Ave., Vancouver, WA 98685: Free information ◆ Weaving supplies and tapestry looms with roller beams. 360-573-7264.

**Bonnie Triola,** 343 E. Gore Rd., Erie, PA 16509: Information $10 ◆ Natural fibers, synthetics, blends, discontinued designer yarns, and other yarns. 814-825-7821.

**The Weaver's Loft,** 308 S. Pennsylvania Ave., Centre Hall, PA 16828: Free information ◆ Knitting, weaving, and spinning supplies and yarns. 800-693-7242; 814-364-1433 (in PA). www.knitters-underground.com

**Weaving Works,** 4717 Brooklyn Ave. NE, Seattle, WA 98105: Catalog $4.50 ◆ Looms, spinning wheels, hand and machine-knitting supplies, yarns, and books. 206-524-1221.

**Webs Yarn,** P.O. Box 147, Northampton, MA 01061: Price list $2 ◆ Looms, loom kits, spinning wheels, and weaving and spinning tools. 413-584-2225.

**Woodland Woolworks,** 262 S. Maple St., P.O. Box 400, Yamhill, OR 97148: Catalog $3 ◆ Spinning wheels and hand-spinning supplies. 800-547-3725.

**Wool Room,** 172 Joe's Hill Rd., Brewster, NY 10509: Brochure $1 ◆ Spinning fibers, yarns, and more. 914-279-7627. www.ourworld.compuserve.com/homepage/WoolRoomSue

**The Woolery,** RD 1, Genoa, NY 13071: Catalog $2 ◆ Spinning, weaving, knitting, dye supplies, and books. 315-497-1542. jive@woolery.com

**Yarn Barn,** 930 Massachusetts, Lawrence, KS 66044: Free information ◆ Spinning wheels and looms, parts and accessories, and supplies. 800-468-0035. yarnbarn@idir.net

## SPORTS & NON-SPORTS CARDS

### Non-Sports Cards

**Johnny Adams Jr.,** P.O. Box 8491, Green Bay, WI 54308: Free information with long SASE ◆ Non-sports and sports cards. 414-465-9101.

**Barrington Square Cards,** P.O. Box 310, West Dundee, IL 60118: Free information ◆ Non-sports cards, coins, and comics. 847-426-2020.

**Champion Sports Collectables Inc.,** 702 W. Las Tunas, San Gabriel, CA 91776: Free information ◆ Autographed sports memorabilia, sports and non-sports cards, and supplies. 800-522-4267. www.championcollectables.com

**Chattanooga Coin Company,** P.O. Box 80158, Chattanooga, TN 37414: Free information ◆ Non-sports cards. 800-444-2646.

**Clinton Dean's Figures & Collectibles,** P.O. Box 383, Milford, NH 03055: Free catalog ◆ Character toys and figures, trading cards, toys, and collectibles. 603-673-3290.

**Mile High Comics,** 2151 W. 56th Ave., Denver, CO 80221: Catalog $1 ◆ Movie and TV-related trading cards. 303-455-2659.

**Paul & Judy's Coins & Cards,** P.O. Box 409, Arthur, IL 61911: Free information ◆ Hard-to-find non-sports and sports cards. 217-543-3366. sales@pjcc.com

**Rainbow Card Company,** 223 Wall St., Ste. 189, Huntington, NY 11743: Free catalog ◆ Collectible non-sports and sports cards. 800-437-5213; 516-293-6623 (in NY).

**Sci-Fi Card Company,** 624 Yonge St., Toronto, Ontario, Canada M4Y 1Z8: Free catalog ◆ Non-sports television and movie trading cards. 416-323-0403.

**Sports Memorabilia Etc.,** 11841 Ventura Blvd., Studio City, CA 91604: Free information ◆ Autographed lithographs, signed plates, figurines, plaques, baseball cards, and other collectible cards. 800-995-0650. sports1@earthlink.net

**Unique Dist.,** 110 Denton Ave., New Hyde Park, NY 11040: Free information ◆ Sports and non-sports cards and comics. 800-294-5901; 516-294-5900 (in NY). www.uniquedist.com

**Wex Rex Records & Collectibles,** 280 Worcester Rd., Framingham, MA 01701: Catalog $3 ◆ Non-sports cards, movie and TV show character toys, and collectibles. 508-620-6181.

### Sports Cards

**A.K.A. Sports Cards,** 303 Sheffield Rd., Cherry Hill, NJ 08034: Free information ◆ Collectible baseball, basketball, hockey, and other sports cards. 609-779-6052.

**Johnny Adams Jr.,** P.O. Box 8491, Green Bay, WI 54308: Free information with long SASE ◆ Sports and non-sports cards. 414-465-9101.

**B's Wax Trading Cards & Supplies,** 11 Deer Trail, Tabernacle, NJ 08088: Free catalog ◆ Collectible sports cards and supplies. 609-859-8229. www.wwcd.com/bswax

**B & E Collectibles Inc.,** 950 Broadway, Thornwood, NY 10594: Free information ◆ Hard-to-find sports card singles. 914-769-1304.

**B & O Wholesale,** 2880 N. Dayton-Lakeview Rd., New Carlisle, OH 45344: Free information ◆ Archival and storage supplies. 937-845-3372.

**Ball Four Cards,** 4732 N. Royal Atlanta Dr., Tucker, GA 30084: Free information ◆ Archival and storage supplies. 770-621-0377.

**Barnetts Sports Cards,** P.O. Box 24, Randolph, OH 44265: Free information with long SASE ◆ Hard-to-find sports card singles and sets. 330-325-9511.

**Baseball Card World,** P.O. Box 970, Anderson, IN 46015: Free information with long SASE ◆ Sports card hobby supplies. 800-433-4229.

**Bill's Cards & Supplies,** 25 N. Colonial Dr., Hagerstown, MD 21742: Free information with long SASE ◆ Sports cards and hobby supplies. 301-797-2992. www.cardmall.com/billcard/billcard.htm

**Brigandi Coin Company,** 60 W. 44th St., New York, NY 10036: Free information with long SASE ◆ Sports cards. 800-221-2128.

**Broadway Rick's Strike Zone,** 1840 N. Federal Hwy., Boynton Beach, FL 33435: Free information with long SASE ◆ Autographed sports memorabilia, sports cards, and collectibles. 800-344-9103; 561-364-0453 (in FL).

**Card Collectors Company,** 105 W. 77th St., New York, NY 10024: Catalog $2 ◆ Sports cards and collectibles. 212-873-6999.

**Cardboard Gold,** 1933 E. Pomona St., Santa Ana, CA 92705: Free information ◆ Sports cards collecting supplies. 714-259-0550.

**Cee-Jay Sports Card Company,** Sunset Industrial Park, 52 20th St., Brooklyn, NY 11232: Free information with long SASE ◆ Hard-to-find football, basketball, hockey, golf, and tennis sports card singles and sets. 718-832-5296.

**Champion Sports Collectables Inc.,** 702 W. Las Tunas, San Gabriel, CA 91776: Free information ◆ Autographed sports memorabilia, sports and non-sports cards, and supplies. 800-522-4267. www.championcollectables.com

**Dolloff,** P.O. Box 719, Portsmouth, NH 03802: Free information with long SASE ◆ Basketball, boxing, football, swimming, track and field, and wrestling sports cards. 603-433-3957.

**DR Sports,** 1275 Bloomfield Ave., Bldg. 6, Unit 34, Fairfield, NJ 07004: Free information ◆ Major and minor league baseball card sets. Also other sports cards and figurines, plates, and ceramics and pewter collectibles. 973-227-6547.

**Larry Fritsch Cards Inc.,** 735 Old Wausau Rd., P.O. Box 863, Stevens Point, WI 54481: Catalog $2 (3 issues) ◆ Sports cards. Includes one-of-a-kind collectibles. 715-344-8687.

**Gerry Guenther,** W7521 Patchin Rd., Pardeeville, WI 53954: Free information ◆ Superstar sports cards. 608-742-2201.

**Hall's Nostalgia,** 9 Mystic St., P.O. Box 408, Arlington, MA 02174: Free information ◆ Sports cards. 800-367-4255; 781-646-7757 (in MA).

**Bruce Harris Sportscards,** 1291 Steeple Run Dr., Lawrenceville, GA 30243: Free information ◆ Sports cards. 770-822-0988.

**Bill Henderson's Cards,** 2320 Ruger Ave., Janesville, WI 53545: Free information with long SASE ◆ Rare and hard-to-find sports card singles and sets. 608-755-0922.

**Neil Hoppenworth's Cards,** 3511 Lafayette Rd., P.O. Box 3117, Evansdale, IA 50707: Free information ◆ Vintage sports cards. 319-232-6011.

**Howard's Sports Collectibles,** 128 E. Main St., P.O. Box 84, Leipsic, OH 45856: Catalog $5 ◆ Baseball and football cards in sets or singles. 800-457-9974.

**Jake's House of Cards,** 40 Freeway Dr., Cranston, RI 02920: Free information with long SASE ◆ Baseball cards, from 1948 to 1979. Also other sports cards. 800-892-0024.

**Klassy Kollectibles Inc.,** 137 White Horse Pike, Berlin, NJ 08009: Free information with long SASE ◆ Sports cards singles and sets. 609-767-0250.

**Koinz & Kardz-Madison,** 1101 Stewart St., Madison, WI 53713: Free information with long SASE ◆ Rare and hard-to-find sports card singles and sets. 608-274-5273.

**Greg Manning Sports,** 775 Passaic Ave., West Caldwell, NJ 07006: Free information ◆ Collectible sports cards. 800-221-0243; 201-882-0004 (in NJ).

**Mid-Atlantic Sports Cards,** 22 S. Morton Ave., Morton, PA 19070: Catalog $1 ◆ Posters and hard-to-find sports card singles and sets. 610-544-2171.

**The Minnesota Connection,** 17773 Kenwood Trail, Lakeville, MN 55044: Free information with long SASE ◆ Baseball, football, basketball, and hockey sports cards. 612-892-0406.

**Mark Murphy,** 8 Flying Cloud Rd., Stamford, CT 06902: Free information ◆ Hard-to-find baseball, football, hockey, and basketball cards. 203-348-5050.

**The Nickel Trader,** 3025 Washington Rd., McMurray, PA 15317: Free information with long SASE ◆ Postcards, sports cards, political items, and supplies. 412-941-2338. www.nickeltrader.com

**Paul & Judy's Coins & Cards,** P.O. Box 409, Arthur, IL 61911: Free information ◆ Hard-to-find non-sports and sports cards. 217-543-3366. sales@pjcc.com

**Perfect Image Sports Cards,** 11608 Reistertown Rd., Reistertown, MD 21136: Free information ◆ Baseball, boxing, basketball, football, golf, and hockey sports cards. 800-683-1789.

**Rotman Collectibles,** 4 Brussels St., Worcester, MA 01610: Free information ◆ Sports cards and storage supplies. 508-791-6710.

**Kevin Savage Cards,** c/o Mid-America Sports, 3509 Briarfield Blvd., Maumee, OH 43537: Free information ◆ Collectible sports cards. 419-861-2273.

**The Score Board Inc.,** 1951 Old Cuthbert Rd., Cherry Hill, NJ 08034: Free information ◆ Sports card sets, star cards prior to 1970, commemorative cards prior to 1942, and sports memorabilia. 800-327-4145; 609-354-9000 (in NJ).

**707 Sportscards,** P.O. Box 707, Plumsteadville, PA 18949: Free information ◆ Collectible sports cards. 215-249-0976.

**Sports Collectibles Inc.,** P.O. Box 11171, Chattanooga, TN 37401: Catalog $1 ◆ Sports cards, autographed baseballs, bats, and color photos. 425-265-9366.

**Sports Memorabilia Etc.,** 11841 Ventura Blvd., Studio City, CA 91604: Free information ◆ Autographed lithographs, signed plates, figurines, plaques, baseball cards, and other collectible cards. 800-995-0650. sports1@earthlink.net

**SportsCards Plus,** 28221 Crown Valley Pkwy., Laguna Niguel, CA 92677: Catalog $1 ◆ Sports cards, autographs, and sports memorabilia. 800-350-2273. www.sportscardsplus.com

**Starland Collector's Gallery,** P.O. Box 622, Los Olivos, CA 93441: Catalog $2.50 ◆ Sports cards, movie posters, original comic art, and hard-to-find movies. 805-688-8300.

**T.C. Card Company,** 18 Via Aurelia, Palm Beach Gardens, FL 33418: Free information with long SASE ◆ Sports card singles, sets, and hard-to-find collectibles. 561-624-1909.

**Texas Sportcard Company,** 2816 Center St., Deer Park, TX 77536: Free information with long SASE ◆ Hard-to-find sports card singles and sets. 281-476-9964.

**U.S. Gerslyn Ltd.,** 1100 Port Washington Blvd., Port Washington, NY 11050: Free brochure ◆ Sports card hobby supplies. 516-944-3553.

**Unique Dist.,** 110 Denton Ave., New Hyde Park, NY 11040: Free information ◆ Sports and non-sports cards and comics. 800-294-5901; 516-294-5900 (in NY). www.uniquedist.com

**Brian Wallos & Company,** 3 Kellogg Ct., Unit 15, Edison, NJ 08817: Free information with long SASE ◆ Hard-to-find sports card singles and sets. 908-287-5441.

**West Coast Sports Cards Inc.,** 1808 S. 320th, Federal Way, WA 98003: Free information with long SASE ◆ Rare and hard-to-find sports card singles and sets. 360-941-1986.

**Kit Young Sportscards,** 11535 Sorrento Valley Rd., Ste. 403, San Diego, CA 92121: Catalog $2 ◆ Hard-to-find sports card singles and sets. 619-259-1300.

# SQUARE DANCING

## Amplifiers & Microphones

**Hilton Audio Products,** 1033-E Shary Circle, Concord, CA 94518: Free information ◆ Sound equipment and cue cards for callers. 903-682-8390.

**Random Sound Inc.,** 7317 Harriet Ave. South, Minneapolis, MN 55423: Free catalog ◆ Sound equipment. 612-869-9501.

## Badges & Buckles

**KA-MO Engravers,** P.O. Box 30337, Albuquerque, NM 87190: Free catalog ◆ Badges for square and round dancers. 800-352-5266; 505-883-4963 (in NM).

**J.R. Kush & Company,** 7623 Hesperia St., Reseda, CA 91335: Free information ◆ Handcrafted belt buckles for round and square dancers. 818-344-9671.

**Micro Plastics,** Box 847, Rifle, CO 81650: Free information ◆ Custom club badges. 970-625-1718.

## Books & Videos

**Gold Star Video Productions,** P.O. Box 1057, Sisters, OR 97759: Free information ◆ Video tapes on how-to square or round dance. 800-87-HINGE; 503-549-4302 (in OR).

## Clothing & Shoes

**Andes S/D & Western Apparel,** 2109 Liberty Rd., Eldersburg, MD 21784: Catalog $4 (refundable) ◆ Petticoats, pettipants, dresses, skirts, blouses, matching men's shirts, and scarf ties. 410-795-0808.

**California Ranchwear Inc.,** 14600 S. Main St., Gardena, CA 90248: Free list of retail sources ◆ Square dance clothing and accessories. 310-532-8980.

**CaLyCo Crossing,** 407 Main St., Laurel, MD 20707: Free catalog ◆ Square dance and western-style clothing. 800-627-0412. calycocrossing@calyco.com

**The Catchall,** 2310 Brook Hollow Dr., Wichita Falls, TX 76308: Catalog $2 ◆ Lace-trimmed petticoats and clothing. 940-692-8814. catchall@wf.net

**Coast Shoes Inc.,** 13401 Saticoy, North Hollywood, CA 91605: Free list of retail sources ◆ Square dance shoes. 800-262-7851.

**Doris Crystal Magic Petticoats,** 8331 Pinecrest Dr., Redwood Valley, CA 95470: Free information ◆ Petticoats for square and round dancers. 800-468-6423; 707-485-7448 (in CA).

**Dorothy's Square Dance Shop Inc.,** 3300 Strong Ave., P.O. Box 6004, Kansas City, KS 66106: Free catalog ◆ Clothing for square dancers. 913-262-4240.

**Fashion Magic by Fendler,** 702 Gashey Dr., Havre de Grace, MD 21078: Free list of retail sources ◆ Square dance clothing and accessories. 410-939-1149.

**H Bar C Ranchwear,** 14600 S. Main St., Gardena, CA 90248: Free list of retail sources ◆ Square dance clothing and accessories. 310-532-8980. shootout@earthlink.net

**Honky Tonk Country Western Dance Wear,** 4143 Aveinida De La Plata, Ocean Side, CA 92054: Free information ◆ Square dance clothing and accessories. 800-824-4222; 619-631-0080 (in CA).

**Main-ly Country Western Wear,** 166 Yarmouth Rd., Gray, ME 04039: Catalog $1 (refundable) ◆ Clothing for square dancers. 207-657-3412. afoster1@maine.com

**Nancy's 4-In-One Fashions,** 515 Northridge, Allen, TX 75002: Free information ◆ Square dancing apparel. 888-373-3461. www.sqdance123.com

**Palomino Square Dance,** 1404 Weavers Run Rd., West Point, KY 40177: Free information ◆ Clothing for square dancers. 800-328-3800. www.palominorecords.com

**Promenade Dance Center,** 16210 12th Ave. SW, Burien, WA 98166: Free catalog ◆ Accessories and clothing for square dancers. 888-888-5969.

**Promenade Parade,** 1709 N. Lelia, Guymon, OK 73942: Free catalog ◆ Square dance fashions for men and women. 580-338-2573. www.webtex.com/promenade

**Shirley's Square Dance Shoppe,** Rt. 9-D, Box 423, Hughsonville, NY 12537: Catalog $1 ◆ Patterns, petticoats, and clothing for square dancers. 914-297-8504.

**Meg Simkins,** 119 Allen St., Hampden, MA 01036: Catalog $1 (refundable) ◆ Clothing for square dancers. 413-566-3349.

**Square Dance & Western Wear Fashions Inc.,** 635 E. 47th St., Wichita, KS 67216: Free information ◆ Clothing and shoes. 316-522-6670.

**Square Dance Attire,** 7215 W. Irving Park Rd., Chicago, IL 60634: Free information ◆ Clothing for square dancers. 773-589-9220.

**Stevens Worldwide Inc.,** P.O. Box 112, Mercer, PA 16137: Free catalog ◆ Clogging shoes and supplies. 800-722-8040.

**Tic-Tac-Toes,** P.O. Box 953, Gloversville, NY 12078: Free information ◆ Square dance clothing and accessories. 518-773-8187.

**Western Squares,** 6820 Gravois, St. Louis, MO 63116: Catalog $2 ◆ Men and women's clothing for square dancing. 314-353-7230.

### Records & CDs

**Chaparral Records Inc.,** 1425 Oakhill Dr., Plano, TX 75075: Free catalog ◆ Square dancing records. 972-423-7389.

**Fort Brooke Quartermaster,** Brandon B. Barszcz, P.O. Box 1628, Brandon, FL 33509: Catalog $2.50 ◆ Native American and square dancing cassettes and CDs. Also Celtic folk, Civil War, and Native American music. 813-621-7256.

**Hanhurst's Record Service,** P.O. Box 50, Marlborough, NH 03455: Free information ◆ Square dancing records. 800-445-7398. www.supreme-audio.com

**Palomino Square Dance,** 1404 Weavers Run Rd., West Point, KY 40177: Free information ◆ Records for clogging and square, round, and folk, and solo dancing. 800-328-3800. www.palominorecords.com

**Wagon Wheel Records & Books,** 17191 Corbina Ln., #203, Huntington Beach, CA 92649: Free catalog ◆ Square dancing records and books. 714-846-8169.

## STAINED GLASS & OTHER GLASS CRAFTING SUPPLIES

**AmeriGlas,** P.O. Box 27668, Omaha, NE 68127: Free catalog ◆ Pre-cut kits, books and videos, tools, and supplies. 800-927-7877.

**Anything in Stained Glass,** P.O. Box 444, Rio Grande, NJ 08242: Catalog $3.50 ◆ Glass, supplies, books, and patterns. 609-886-0416.

**Art Glass House Inc.,** 3445 N. Hwy. 1, Cocoa, FL 32926: Free catalog ◆ Stained glass supplies. 800-525-8009; 407-631-4477 (in FL).

**Atlas Art & Stained Glass,** P.O. Box 76084, Oklahoma City, OK 73147: Catalog $3 ◆ Kaleidoscopes, frames, lamp bases, stained glass, jewelry-making, foil-crafting, and other craft supplies. 405-946-1230.

**Big M Stained Glass,** 1171 Andover Park West, Seattle, WA 98188: Catalog $5 ◆ Stained glass supplies. 800-426-8307.

**Cline Glass Inc.,** 1135 SE Grand Ave., Portland, OR 97214: Catalog $5 ◆ Stained glass supplies. 800-547-8417.

**Coran-Sholes,** 509 E. 2nd St., South Boston, MA 02127: Catalog $3 ◆ Stained glass supplies. 617-268-3780.

**Crystalite Corp.,** 8400 Green Meadows Dr., Westerville, OH 43081: Free list of retail sources ◆ Lapidary and glass-working equipment and supplies. 800-777-2894.

**DAB Studio,** P.O. Box 57, 11 Kent Pl., Pompton Plains, NJ 07444: Free catalog ◆ Stained glass windows and decorative accessories. 973-616-7676.

**Delphi Stained Glass,** 3380 E. Jolly Rd., Lansing, MI 48910: Catalog $5 ◆ Stained glass supplies, tools, kits, and books. 800-248-2048. www.delphiglass.com

**Eastern Art Glass,** P.O. Box 9, Wyckoff, NJ 07481: Catalog $2 (refundable) ◆ Stained glass kits and glass etching, engraving, and crafting supplies. 800-872-3458. www.etchworld.com

**Franklin Art Glass,** 222 E. Sycamore St., Columbus, OH 43206: Catalog $5 ◆ Stained glass tools and supplies. 800-848-7683.

**Gemstone Equipment Manufacturing Company,** 750 Easy St., Simi Valley, CA 93065: Free information ◆ Stained glass and lapidary supplies. 800-235-3375; 805-527-6990 (in CA).

**Glass Craft Inc.,** 626 Moss St., Golden, CO 80401: Free catalog ◆ Glass crafting supplies. 303-278-4670.

**Glass Crafters,** 398 Interstate Ct., Sarasota, FL 34240: Catalog $3 ◆ Stained glass and mosaic crafting supplies, tools, accessories, and books. Also Tiffany lamp kits. 800-422-4552. www.glasscrafters.com

**Houston Stained Glass Supply,** 2002 Britmoore, Houston, TX 77043: Free information ◆ Stained glass supplies and beveled glass. 800-231-0148; 713-690-8844 (in TX). www.hsgs.com

**Hudson Glass,** 219 N. Division St., Peekskill, NY 10566: Catalog $3 (refundable) ◆ Stained glass supplies, books, and patterns. 800-431-2964.

**Kingsley North Inc.,** 910 Brown St., Norway, MI 49870: Free catalog ◆ Stained glass and jewelry-making supplies and tools. 800-338-9280. www.kingsleynorth.com

**Nasco,** 901 Janesville Ave., Fort Atkinson, WI 53538: Free catalog ◆ Stained glass supplies. 800-558-9595. www.nascofa.com

**Sunshine Glassworks,** 111 Industrial Pkwy., Buffalo, NY 14227: Catalog $3 ◆ Stained glass supplies and tools. 800-828-7159; 716-668-2918 (in NY).

**Unique Colors,** P.O. Drawer 20, Logansport, LA 71049: Free information ◆ Opaque colors for glass crafting. Also kits, pattern books, and tools. 318-697-4401.

**Wale Apparatus Company Inc.,** 400 Front St., P.O. Box D, Hellertown, PA 18055: Free catalog ◆ Bead-making and glass-working equipment and supplies. 800-334-WALE; 610-838-7047 (in PA).

**Warner-Crivellaro,** 1855 Weaversville Rd., Allentown, PA 18103: Free information ◆ Stained glass supplies and how-to books. 800-523-4242; 610-264-1100 (in PA). www.warner-criv.com

**Whittemore Glass,** Box 2065, Hanover, MA 02339: Catalog $2 ◆ Stained glass kits, tools, patterns, etching, and engraving supplies. 781-871-1790. www.penrose.com/glass

## STAIRLIFTS & ELEVATORS

**Concord Elevator Inc.,** 107 Alfred Kuehne Blvd., Brampton, Ontario, Canada L6T 4K3: Free information ◆ Wheelchair platform lifts, residential elevators, stairlifts, and other lifts. 800-661-5112.

**Econol Lift Corp.,** 2513 Center St., Box 854, Cedar Falls, IA 50613: Free information ◆ Wheelchair and stair-riding lifts, residential elevators, dumbwaiters, and vertical lifts. 319-277-4777.

**Graventa,** P.O. Box 1769, Blaine, WA 98231: Free information ◆ Easy-to-operate portable wheelchair lift for stairs. 800-663-6556. www.graventa.com

**Inclinator Company of America,** P.O. Box 1557, Harrisburg, PA 17105: Free information ◆ Elevators and stairlifts for homes. 800-456-1329.

**The National Wheel-O-Vator Company Inc.,** P.O. Box 348, Roanoke, IL 61561: Free list of retail sources ◆ Wheelchair and side-riding stairlifts. 800-551-9095. www.wheelovator.com

**Waupaca Elevator Company Inc.,** P.O. Box 246, Waupaca, WI 54981: Free list of retail sources ◆ Home elevators. 800-238-8739.

**Whitakers,** 1 Odell Plaza, Yonkers, NY 10703: Free catalog ◆ Motorized stairlifts for homes. 800-44-LIFTS; 800-924-LIFT (in NY).

## STATIONERY & ENVELOPES

**Accountants Supply House,** 301 Grove Rd., Thorofare, NJ 08086: Free catalog ◆ Stationery and envelopes, forms and labels, shipping materials, disk storage cabinets, furniture, office equipment, and other supplies. 800-342-5274.

**American Stationery Company,** 100 Park Ave., Peru, IN 46970: Free catalog ◆ Regular and calligraphy stationery, wedding invitations, note cards, personal memos, envelopes, and postcards. 800-822-2577.

**The American Wedding Album,** American Stationery Company Inc., 300 Park Ave., Peru, IN 46970: Free catalog ◆ Wedding invitations, stationery, and gifts. 800-822-2577.

**Angels Afoot,** P.O. Box 176, Saginaw, MO 64864: Free information ◆ Clothing and note cards with a cat motif. 417-623-2073.

**Artist Roost,** 3520 N. Swan St., Silver City, NM 88061: Free brochure ◆ Aviation art and note cards. 505-538-8814.

**Artistic Greetings Catalog,** P.O. Box 1050, Elmira, NY 14902: Catalog $2 ◆ Personalized stationery and gifts. 800-733-6313. www.artisticgreetings.com

**Beaver Prints,** 305 Main St., Bellwood, PA 16617: Free information ◆ Business cards, matching brochures, stationery, postcards, and more. 814-742-6070.

**The Business Book,** P.O. Box 1393, Hagerstown, MD 21741: Free catalog ◆ Pressure sensitive labels, stampers, personalized business envelopes and stationery, speed letters, memo pads, business cards, forms, greeting cards, books, and other office supplies. 800-558-0220.

**Business Envelopes,** P.O. Box 517, Thorofare, NJ 08086: Free catalog ◆ Business cards, imprinted envelopes, forms, stationery, and labels. 800-275-4400.

**Caprock Business Forms Inc.,** 1211 Ave. F, Lubbock, TX 79401: Free information ◆ Continuous computer forms, letterheads and envelopes, snap-apart sets, manifold books, and scratch pads. 800-666-3322.

**Collage,** P.O. Box 7216, San Francisco, CA 94120: Free information ◆ Writing papers and supplies. 800-926-5524.

**Creations by Elaine,** 6253 W. 74th St., Box 2001, Bedford Park, IL 60499: Free catalog ◆ Wedding invitations and stationery, cake knives and servers, reception and ceremony accessories, and jewelry. 800-323-1208. www.catalogs.order.com/co/index.html

**Culinary Collections,** P.O. Box 1823, Winter Park, FL 32790: Free catalog ◆ Coffee and tea calendars, cookbooks, and stationery. 407-647-6765. www.netcom.com/~sgridley

**Current Inc.,** Express Processing Center, Colorado Springs, CO 80941: Free catalog ◆ Greeting cards, stationery, and gift wrapping. 800-848-2848.

**Day-Timers,** One Day-Timer Plaza, Allentown, PA 18195: Free catalog ◆ Stationery and business cards. 800-225-5005. www.daytimer.com

**Kristin Elliott Inc.,** 6 Opportunity Way, Newburyport, MA 01950: Free catalog ◆ Boxed notes, gift enclosures, Christmas and greeting cards, memo pads, postcards, correspondence cards, and gift wrapping. 800-922-1899; 978-465-1899 (in MA).

**Fine Stationery by Sonya Nussbaum,** P.O. Box 328, Hollywood, SC 29449: Free catalog ◆ Stationery and envelopes. Also note pads and cards. 843-889-3463.

**Fingerhut,** 11 McLeland Rd., St. Cloud, MN 56395: Free catalog ◆ Greeting cards, gift wrapping, stationery, holiday decorations, organizers, and gifts. 800-233-3588. www.fingerhut.com

**Frederick Graphics,** 1 Hillcrest Dr., Holiday Island, AR 72631: Free brochure ◆ Note cards with pet graphics. 501-253-7256.

**Goes Lithographing Company,** 42 W. 61st St., Chicago, IL 60621: Free information ◆ Stationery, envelopes, calendars, calendar pads, certificates, and other printed items. 800-730-4637. www.goeslitho.com

**Grayarc,** P.O. Box 2944, Hartford, CT 06104: Free catalog ◆ Stationery, business cards, forms, labels, envelopes, and office supplies. 800-562-5468.

**Heirloom Editions,** Box 520-B, Rt. 4, Carthage, MO 64836: Catalog $4 ◆ Lithographs, greeting cards, stickers, miniatures, stationery, framed prints, and turn-of-the-century art and paper collectibles. 800-725-0725.

**Hudson Envelope Corp.,** 111 3rd Ave., New York, NY 10003: Free information ◆ Colored envelopes and paper. 212-473-6666.

**Robert James Company Inc.,** P.O. Box 520, Moody, AL 35004: Free information with long SASE ◆ Stationery, furniture, and office supplies. 800-633-8296; 205-640-7081 (in AL).

**Just Between Us,** 41 W. 8th Ave., Oshkosh, WI 54906: Free catalog ◆ Stationery with optional personalization. 800-258-3750. www.mileskimball.com

**Kimmeric Studio,** P.O. Box 10749, Lake Tahoe, CA 96158: Catalog $2 ◆ Postcards, envelopes, and stationery. 530-573-1616.

**Jamie Lee Stationery,** P.O. Box 1855, Bridgeview, IL 60455: Free catalog ◆ Wedding stationery for brides. 800-288-5800.

**Literary Calligraphy,** 5326 White House Rd., Moneta, VA 24121: Catalog $2 ◆ Framed art and stationery. 800-261-6325. susanloy@rev.net

**Main Street Press,** P.O. Box 126, Delafield, WI 53018: Catalog $1 ◆ Wall calendars, boxed greeting cards, note cards and pads, and stationery. 414-646-8511.

**Mattick Business Forms Inc.,** 333 W. Hintz Rd., Wheeling, IL 60090: Free catalog ◆ Stationery, office and business forms, and labels. 847-541-7345.

**Merrimade Inc.,** 275 Billerica Rd., Chelmsford, MA 01824: Free catalog ◆ Stationery and printed items. 800-344-4256.

**Morgan Printing Company,** 2365 Wyandotte Rd., Willow Grove, PA 19090: Free information ◆ Continuous letterheads, labels, and business forms. 800-435-3892.

**NEBS Inc.,** 500 Main St., Groton, MA 01471: Free catalog ◆ Computerized and manual business forms, stationery, labels, checks, business cards, and other supplies. 800-367-6327. www.nebs.com

**New Century Envelope,** P.O. Box 55530, Indianapolis, IN 46205: Free information ◆ Envelopes. 800-234-0666. www.newcenturyenvelope.com

**Papeterie Personalized Paper Products,** 390 Oak Tree Rd., Palisades, NY 10964: Free catalog ◆ Personalized custom stationery, memos, Post-It pads, envelopes, and other related supplies. 914-359-0116.

**Peak Publishing,** P.O. Box V, Flagstaff, AZ 86002: Catalog $2 ◆ Note cards with southwestern scenes. 800-299-4789.

**Pendleton Cowgirl Company,** P.O. Box 19474, Portland, OR 97280: Catalog $2 ◆ Classic western theme T-shirts, lithographs, note cards, and calendars. 503-977-0292.

**Posh Papers,** 532 Elmgrove Ave., Providence, RI 02906: Brochure $1 (refundable) ◆ Personalized handcrafted note cards with envelopes. 401-331-9873.

**Rexcraft,** 1 Stationery Pl., Rexburg, ID 83441: Free catalog ◆ Invitations and stationery, bridal and reception accessories, and thank you cards. 800-635-4653. www.catalog.orders.com

**Shipman Printing Industries,** P.O. Box 157, Niagara Falls, NY 14302: Free information ◆ Forms, letterheads, envelopes, and printed items. 800-462-2114.

**Stationery House,** 1000 Florida Ave., Hagerstown, MD 21740: Free catalog ◆ Business stationery and forms, office supplies, and executive gifts. 301-739-4487.

**Sugar 'n Spice Invitations,** P.O. Box 299, Sugar City, ID 83448: Free catalog ◆ Invitations and stationery, bridal and reception accessories, and thank you cards. 800-535-1002.

**Traditional Papercutting,** Faye & Bernie DuPlessis, 101 Blue Rock Rd., Wilmington, DE 19809: Catalog $2 ◆ Note cards and framed or unframed cuttings. 302-762-8896.

**Triangle Envelope Company,** 325 Hill Ave., Nashville, TN 37210: Free information ◆ Envelopes and stationery. 800-843-9529.

**Victorian Papers,** P.O. Box 411332, Kansas City, MO 61141: Catalog $2 ◆ Greeting and note cards for all occasions, stationery, antique reproductions, replica jewelry, nostalgic toys, and other gifts. 800-800-6647.

**Wholesale Envelopes Inc.,** 2410 Rice St., Lubbock, TX 79415: Free information ◆ Matching envelopes and letterheads. 800-692-4676.

**Write Touch,** The Rytex Company, P.O. Box 68188, Indianapolis, IN 46268: Free catalog ◆ Stationery, writing aids, and gifts. 800-288-6824.

**Yuemei Paper,** 1033 Farmington Ave., Farmington, CT 06032: Free catalog ◆ Handmade papers and silk for fine art and desk top projects, Chinese art supplies, and stationery. 860-674-0128.

## STENCILS

**American Home Stencils,** P.O. Box 32007, Franklin, WI 53132: Catalog $3 ◆ Stencils for decorating. 800-742-4520.

**American Traditional Stencils,** 442 First New Hampshire Tnpk., Northwood, NJ 03261: Catalog $5 ◆ Brass and laser cut stencils. Also paints, brushes, embossing supplies, how-to videos, and books. 603-942-8100. www.amtrad-stencil.com

**Art-2-Go,** 7859 Schenck Rd., Perry, NY 14530: Catalog $3 ◆ Nature and herbal-theme stencils. Also supplies. 716-237-5330.

**Adele Bishop,** 3430 S. Service Rd., Burlington, Ontario, Canada L7N 3I9: Catalog $4 (refundable) ◆ Stencils, stencil paints, brushes, how-to books, and other supplies. 906-681-ROSS.

**Daydreams Stencil Company,** P.O. Box 65, Oregon, WI 53575: Catalog $3 ◆ Folk art stencils. 608-873-3399.

**Decorcal Inc.,** 165 Marine St., Farmingdale, NY 11735: Free catalog ◆ Decorative decals, letter and number stencils, and graphic accessories. 800-645-9868; 516-752-0076 (in NY).

**Dee-signs Ltd.,** Box 490, Rushland, PA 18956: Catalog $5 ◆ Laser-cut stencils. 215-598-3330. www.deesigns.com

**Jan Dressler Stencils,** 253 SW 41st St., Renton, WA 98055: Catalog $5 ◆ Garden scenes, birds, and nature-theme stencils. 425-656-4515. www.dresslerstencils.com

**Epoch Designs,** P.O. Box 4033, Elwyn, PA 19063: Catalog $4.50 ◆ Pre-cut Victorian-style stencils. 610-565-9180.

**Helen Foster Stencils,** 71 Main St., Sanford, ME 04073: Catalog $5 ◆ Pre-cut laser stencils for decorating. 207-490-2625.

**Mary Gannon Stencils,** 830 Malvern HL, Alpharetta, GA 30022: Catalog $5 ◆ Fairies, florals, birds, shells, and other stencil designs.

**Great Tracers,** 3 N. Schoenbeck Rd., Prospect Heights, IL 60070: Brochure $1 ◆ Lettering stencils. 847-255-0436.

**Gail Grisi Stenciling Inc.,** P.O. Box 1263, Haddonfield, NJ 08033: Catalog $2.50 (refundable) ◆ Pre-cut plastic stencils, kits, sponges, acrylic paints, and how-to instructions. 609-354-1757.

**The Mad Stencilist,** P.O. Box 5497, El Dorado Hills, CA 95762: Catalog $5 (refundable) ◆ Pre-cut stencils. 888-882-6232; 916 933 1790 (in CA). www.madstencilist.com

**MB Historic Decor,** P.O. Box 619, Princeton, MA 01541: Catalog $10 ◆ Vermont border stencils. Includes the Moses Eaton collection and floor patterns of New England. 978-464-0162.

**Jeannie Serpa,** Box 672, Jamestown, RI 02835: Catalog $4 ◆ Designer stencils. 800-759-3331. www.jserpa.com/who/who2.htmls

**Southwest Decoratives,** 191 Bighorn Ridge NE, Albuquerque, NM 87122: Catalog $3 ◆ Quilt patterns and kits, applique patterns and kits, cross-stitch charts and kits, and stenciling supplies. 505-856-9585. www.swdecoratives.com

**StenArt Inc.,** P.O. Box 114, Pitman, NJ 08071: Catalog $4.95 ◆ Pre-cut stencils. 609-589-9857.

**The Stencil Collector,** 1723 Tilghman St., Allentown, PA 18104: Catalog $10 ◆ English period design stencils. Also stenciling supplies. 610-433-2105.

**Stencil House of N.H.,** P.O. Box 16109, Hooksett, NH 03306: Brochure $2.50 ◆ Cut and uncut mylar stencils, brushes, paints, stencil adhesive, and brush cleaner. 800-622-9416. stencil@mv.mv.com

**The Stencil Outlet,** P.O. Box 287, Northwood, NH 03261: Catalog $5 ◆ Brass and laser cut stencils. 800-2-STENCIL. www.Amtrad-stencil.com

**The Stencil Shoppe,** 3634 Silverside Rd., Wilmington, DE 19810: Catalog $3.95 ◆ Designer stencils. 800-822-STEN. www.designerstencils.com

**StencilEase Inc.,** P.O. Box 1127, Old Saybrook, CT 06475: Catalog $5 ◆ Stencils, paints, and brushes. 800-334-1776.

**Stencils & Stuff,** 5198 Township Rd. 123, Millersburg, OH 44654: Catalog $3 (refundable) ◆ Florals, borders, other stencils, and paints. 216-893-2499.

**Yowler & Shepp Stencils,** 3529 Main St., Conestoga, PA 17516: Catalog $5 (refundable) ◆ Ribbons and stencils. 717-872-2820.

## STEREOS & CD PLAYERS

### Headphones

**Aiwa America Inc.,** 800 Corporate Dr., Mahwah, NJ 07430: Free information ◆ CD players, sound processors, and headphones. 800-289-2492. www.aiwa.com

**Azden Corp.,** 147 New Hyde Park Rd., Franklin Square, NY 11016: Free information ◆ Camcorders and headphones. 516-328-7500.

**Denon America,** 222 New Rd., Parsippany, NJ 07054: Free information ◆ Headphones, CD players, receivers, amplifiers, and sound processors. 973-575-7810.

**JVC,** 41 Slater Dr., Elmwood Park, NJ 07407: Free information ◆ Headphones, CD players, receivers, and amplifiers. 800-252-5722. www.jvc-america.com

**Nady Systems,** 6701 Bay St., Emeryville, CA 94608: Free information ◆ Headphones and speakers. 510-652-2411. www.nadywireless.com

**Onkyo,** 200 Williams Dr., Ramsey, NJ 07446: Free information ◆ CD players, receivers, amplifiers, universal remotes, and headphones. 201-825-7950.

**Panasonic,** Panasonic Way, Secaucus, NJ 07094: Free list of retail sources ◆ Headphones, receivers, and CD players. 201-348-7000. www.panasonic.com

**Pioneer Technologies,** P.O. Box 1760, Long Beach, CA 90801: Free information ◆ Headphones, speakers, CD players, sound processors, receivers, amplifiers, and decoders. 800-746-6337. www.pioneerelectronics.com

**Recoton,** 2950 Lake Emma Rd., Lake Mary, FL 32746: Free information ◆ Headphones, speakers, video and audio processors, and decoders. 800-223-6009.

**Sony Consumer Products,** 1 Sony Dr., Park Ridge, NJ 07656: Free information ◆ Headphones, speakers, CD players, camcorders, receivers, amplifiers, sound processors, decoders, universal remotes, and other electronics. 201-930-1000. www.sony.com

**Teac,** 7733 Telegraph Rd., Montebello, CA 90640: Free information ◆ CD players, sound processors, and headphones. 213-726-0303. www.teac.com

**Technics,** One Panasonic Way, Secaucus, NJ 07094: Free list of retail sources ◆ Speakers, CD players, headphones, receivers, amplifiers, and sound processors. 201-348-7000. www.panasonic.com

**Yamaha,** P.O. Box 6660, Buena Park, CA 90620: Free list of retail sources ◆ Headphones, speakers, audio and video systems, CD players, and sound processors. 800-492-6242. yamaha-motor.com

### Home-Theater & Surround Sound Systems

**Atlantic Technology,** 343 Vanderbilt Ave., Norwood, MA 02062: Free list of retail sources ◆ Home theater systems and components. 781-762-6300.

**Denon America,** 222 New Rd., Parsippany, NJ 07054: Free information ◆ Surround sound systems. 973-575-7810.

**Division of Video Necessities,** 1546 Coney Island Ave., Brooklyn, NY 11230: Free information ◆ Audio, video, multi-system, and home theater equipment. 800-228-8480.

**Electronic Mailbox,** 10-12 Charles St., Glen Cove, NY 11542: Free information ◆ Camcorder, video, and production accessories. 800-323-2325. www.videoguys.com

**HiFiDirect,** 19 N. 5th Ave., Highland Park, NJ 08904: Free information ◆ Home theater systems. 800-959-HIFI. www.HiFiDirect.com

**Home Theatre Design & Installation,** 190 W. Main St., Somerville, NJ 08876: Free information ◆ Audio/visual receivers, camcorders, speakers, VCRs, projection TVs, and other equipment. 800-676-4434.

**Home Theatre Systems,** Newark Pompton Tnpk., Little Falls, NJ 07424: Free information ◆ Home theater systems. 800-978-7768.

**Klipsch,** Customer Service, 8900 Keystone Crossing, Ste. 1220, Indianapolis, IN 46240: Free list of retail sources ◆ Home theater systems and components. 800-554-7724. www.klipsch.com

**Legacy Audio,** 3023 Sangamon Ave., Springfield, IL 62702: Free catalog ◆ Home theater systems and audio equipment. 800-283-4644. www.legacy-audio.com

**Marine Park Camera & Video Inc.,** 3126 Avenue U, Brooklyn, NY 11229: Free information ◆ Video equipment, home theater systems, VCRs, and camcorders. 800-360-1722; 718-891-1878 (in NY).

**NBO Satellite TV,** 5670-A El Camino Real, Carlsbad, CA 92008: Free catalog ◆ Satellite and big-screen TV systems, surround sound equipment, and accessories. 800-604-2222. www.nbotv.com

**NuReality,** 2907 Daimler St., Santa Ana, CA 92705: Free list of retail sources ◆ Surround sound in 3D for home theater systems. 800-501-8086.

**Parasound Products Inc.,** 950 Battery St., San Francisco, CA 94111: Free information ◆ Home theater systems. 415-397-7100.

**Pioneer Electronics,** 1925 E. Dominguez, Long Beach, CA 90810: Free information ◆ Surround sound systems. 800-421-1404. www.pioneerelectronics.com

**Runco,** 2461 Tripaldi Way, Hayward, CA 94545: Free list of retail sources ◆ Home theater video systems. 510-293-9154.

**Samman's Electronics,** 1166 Hamburg Tnpk., Wayne, NJ 07470: Free information ◆ Video equipment and home theater systems. 800-AU-DIO-93.

**Wholesale Connection,** 361 Charles St., West Hampstead, NY 11552: Free information ◆ Camcorders, other video accessories, and audio, car stereo, and home theater equipment. 800-967-5588.

## Manufacturers

**a/d/s,** 1 Progress Way, Wilmington, MA 01887: Free information ◆ CD players, speakers, receivers, and amplifiers. 978-729-1140.

**Adcom,** 11 Elkins Rd., East Brunswick, NJ 08816: Free information ◆ Amplifiers, CD players, and tuners. 732-390-1130. info@adcom.com

**Aiwa America Inc.,** 800 Corporate Dr., Mahwah, NJ 07430: Free information ◆ CD players, sound processors, and headphones. 800-289-2492. www.aiwa.com

**AudioSource,** 1327 N. Carolan Ave., Burlingame, CA 94010: Free information ◆ Sound processors and audio controllers. 415-348-8114.

**B & K Components Ltd.,** 2100 Old Union Rd., Buffalo, NY 14227: Free list of retail sources ◆ Audio and video control centers, amplifiers, and pre-amplifiers. 800-543-5252.

**Cambridge Soundworks,** 311 Needham St., Newton, MA 02164: Free catalog ◆ Speakers and audio systems. 800-367-4434.

**Canon,** One Canon Plaza, Lake Success, NY 11042: Free list of retail sources ◆ CD players, camcorders, sound processors, and other electronics. 516-488-6700. www.usa.canon.com

**Carver Corp.,** 15300 Woodinville Rd. NE, Ste. A, Woodinville, WA 98072: Free information ◆ Receivers, amplifiers, CD players, tuners, and speakers. 800-521-4333. www.carver.com

**Denon America,** 222 New Rd., Parsippany, NJ 07054: Free information ◆ CD players, receivers, amplifiers, sound processors, and headphones. 973-575-7810.

**Emerson Radio Corp.,** 9 Entin Rd., Parsippany, NJ 07054: Free information ◆ Camcorders, CD and cassette players, and TVs. 201-884-5800.

**Goldstar,** 1000 Sylvan Ave., Englewood, NJ 07632: Free information ◆ CD and cassette players and TVs. 201-816-2000.

**Hitachi Sales Corp.,** Customer Service, 3890 Steve Reynolds Blvd., Norcross, GA 30093: Free information ◆ CD and cassette players, receivers, amplifiers, and TVs. 800-241-6558.

**JVC,** 41 Slater Dr., Elmwood Park, NJ 07407: Free information ◆ Audio and video systems, CD and cassette players, camcorders, receivers, amplifiers, TVs, and headphones. 800-252-5722. www.jvc-america.com

**Harman/Kardon,** 250 Crossways Park Dr., Woodbury, NY 11797: Free information ◆ CD and cassette players, receivers, amplifiers, and projection equipment. 800-645-7484. www.harmankardon.com

**Kenwood,** P.O. Box 22745, Long Beach, CA 90801: Free information ◆ CD and cassette players, TVs, receivers, amplifiers, and sound processors. 310-639-9000. www.kenwood.net

**Marantz America Inc.,** 440 Medinah Rd., Roselle, IL 60172: Free information ◆ Audio and video systems, speakers, CD and cassette players, sound processors, and other electronics. 630-307-3100. www.marantz.com

**McIntosh,** 2 Chambers St., Binghamton, NY 13903: Free information ◆ CD players. 607-723-3512.

**Mitsubishi Electronics,** 5757 Plaza Dr., Cypress, CA 90630: Free information ◆ Audio and video systems, CD and cassette players, camcorders, and TVs. 800-843-2515.

**NAD,** 89 Doug Brown Way, Holliston, MA 01746: Free information ◆ Receivers, amplifiers, CD players, and speakers. 508-429-3600.

**Nakamichi,** 955 Francisco St., Torrance, CA 90502: Free information ◆ Receivers, amplifiers, and CD players. 562-538-8150.

**NEC Technologies,** 1250 N. Arlington Heights Rd., Itasca, IL 60143: Free information ◆ Speakers, CD and cassette players, receivers, amplifiers, TVs, camcorders, sound processors, and other electronics. 800-284-4484. www.nec.com

**Onkyo,** 200 Williams Dr., Ramsey, NJ 07446: Free information ◆ CD players, receivers, amplifiers, universal remotes, and headphones. 201-825-7950.

**Panasonic,** Panasonic Way, Secaucus, NJ 07094: Free list of retail sources ◆ Audio and video systems, CD and cassette players, TVs, camcorders, headphones, and other electronics. 201-348-7000. www.panasonic.com

**Pioneer Technologies,** P.O. Box 1760, Long Beach, CA 90801: Free information ◆ Speakers, receivers, amplifiers, TVs, sound processors, headphones, and cassette, laser disk, and CD players. 800-746-6337. www.pioneerelectronics.com

**Radio Shack,** Division Tandy Corp., One Tandy Center, Fort Worth, TX 76102: Free information ◆ Cassette and CD players, camcorders, universal remotes, computers, and other electronics. 817-390-3011. www.radioshack.com

**RCA Sales Corp.,** Thomson Consumer Electronics, P.O. Box 1976, Indianapolis, IN 46206: Free information ◆ Audio and video systems, cassette and CD players, TVs, camcorders, sound processors, and other electronics. 800-336-1900.

**Recoton,** 2950 Lake Emma Rd., Lake Mary, FL 32746: Free information ◆ Speakers, decoders, audio and video processors, and headphones. 800-223-6009.

**Rotel,** P.O. Box 8, North Reading, MA 01864: Free information ◆ Receivers, amplifiers, CD players, and speakers. 800-370-3740.

**Sansui USA,** 200 Metroplex Dr., Edison, NJ 08817: Free information ◆ Speakers, cassette and CD players, camcorders, receivers, amplifiers, TVs, and sound processors. 732-460-9710.

**Sanyo Fisher,** P.O. Box 2329, Chatsworth, CA 91313: Free information ◆ CD and cassette players, camcorders, TVs, sound processors, universal remotes, and other electronics. 818-998-7322.

**Sharp Electronics,** Sharp Plaza, Mahwah, NJ 07496: Free information ◆ Cassette and CD players, camcorders, TVs, receivers, amplifiers, and other electronics. 800-BE-SHARP. www.sharp-usa.com

**Sherwood,** 14830 Alondra Blvd., La Mirada, CA 90638: Free information ◆ CD players, receivers, amplifiers, and sound processors. 800-962-3203.

**Shure Brothers Inc.,** 222 Hartrey Ave., Evanston, IL 60202: Free information ◆ CD players, sound processors, and other electronics. 800-447-4873.

**Sony Consumer Products,** 1 Sony Dr., Park Ridge, NJ 07656: Free information ◆ Speakers, cassette and CD players, camcorders, receivers, amplifiers, TVs, sound processors, universal remotes, headphones, and other electronics. 201-930-1000. www.sony.com

**Teac,** 7733 Telegraph Rd., Montebello, CA 90640: Free information ◆ Sound processors, headphones, other electronics, and cassette, CD, and laser disk players. 213-726-0303. www.teac.com

**Technics,** One Panasonic Way, Secaucus, NJ 07094: Free list of retail sources ◆ Speakers, CD players, sound processors, receivers, amplifiers, and headphones. 201-348-7000. www.panasonic.com

**Toshiba,** 82 Totowa Rd., Wayne, NJ 07470: Free information ◆ Cassette and CD players, camcorders, sound processors, and TVs. 201-628-8000. www.toshiba.com/tacp

**Yamaha,** P.O. Box 6660, Buena Park, CA 90620: Free list of retail sources ◆ Speakers, receivers, amplifiers, sound processors, headphones, and CD, cassette, and laser disk players. 800-492-6242. www.yamaha-motor.com

## Retailers

**Accessory Source,** 1864 48th St., Brooklyn, NY 11204: Free information ◆ Batteries, videotapes, microphones, editors and mixers, and other equipment. 800-723-6633; 718-435-0343 (in NY).

**Audio Video Center,** 490 2nd Street Pike, Southampton, PA 18966: Free information ◆ Camcorders and audio components. 800-220-6510; 215-942-2242 (in PA).

**AV Distributors,** 10765 Kingspoint, Houston, TX 77075: Free information ◆ Audio, video, stereo equipment, and TVs. 800-843-3697.

**Coast to Coast,** 2570 86th St., Brooklyn, NY 11214: Free information ◆ Camcorders, video editing equipment, receivers, CD players, cassette decks, and other electronics. 800-788-5555. www.coasttocoastcamera.com

**Computability Consumer Electronics,** P.O. Box 17882, Milwaukee, WI 53217: Free catalog ◆ TVs, fax machines, copiers, computers, and audio, video, and stereo equipment. 800-558-0003. www.computability.com/csh.html

**Crutchfield,** 1 Crutchfield Park, Charlottesville, VA 22906: Free catalog ◆ TVs and video, audio, and stereo equipment. 800-955-9009. www.crutchfield.com

**Data Vision,** 445 5th Ave., New York, NY 10016: Free information ◆ Electronics equipment and accessories. 888-888-2087; 212-689-1111 (in NY). www.datavis.com

**Division of Video Necessities,** 1546 Coney Island Ave., Brooklyn, NY 11230: Free information ◆ Audio, video, multi-system, and home theater equipment. 800-228-8480.

**Electronic Wholesalers,** 1166 Hamburg Tnpk., Wayne, NJ 07470: Free information ◆ Receivers, cassette decks, TVs, telephones, laser disk and CD players, and camcorders. 201-696-6531. www.samans.com

**Executive Digital & Imaging Corp.,** 60 Broadway, Brooklyn, NY 11211: Free information ◆ Cameras, camcorders, video equipment, VCRs, and accessories. 888-5-EXECUTIVE.

**Focus Electronics,** 4523 13th Ave., Brooklyn, NY 11219: Free catalog ◆ Appliances, photographic equipment, and audio, stereo, and video equipment. 718-436-4646. www.focususa.com

**Free Trade Photo Video,** 4718 18th Ave., Brooklyn, NY 11204: Free information ◆ Cameras, camcorders, video equipment, VCRs, and accessories. 800-234-8813; 718-633-6890 (in NY). www.freetradephoto.com

**Home Theatre Design & Installation,** 190 W. Main St., Somerville, NJ 08876: Free information ◆ Audio/visual receivers, camcorders, speakers, VCRs, projection TVs, and other equipment. 800-676-4434.

**J & R Music World,** 59-50 Queens-Midtown Expwy., Maspeth, NY 11378: Free catalog ◆ Audio equipment, car and portable stereos, video recorders, telephones, computers, and video and audio tapes. 800-221-8180.

**K.P. Pro Video Inc.,** 87-07 Jamaica Ave., Woodhaven, NY 11421: Free information ◆ Used and new video equipment. 800-670-6555.

**Mission Service Supply,** 4565 Cypress S., West Monroe, LA 71291: Free catalog ◆ TVs and audio, video, stereo equipment, and accessories 800-352-7222; 318-397-2755 (in LA).

**New West Electronics,** 4120 Meridian, Bellingham, WA 98226: Free information ◆ TVs, projection equipment, and audio, video, and stereo equipment. 800-488-8877.

**Olden Video,** 1265 Broadway, New York, NY 10001: Free information ◆ Video equipment, TVs, cassette players, and other electronics. 212-226-3727.

**Percy's Inc.,** 19 Glennie St., Worcester, MA 01605: Free information ◆ Appliances and other electronics. 508-755-5334.

**Planet Electronics,** P.O. Box 251446, West Bloomfield, MI 48325: Free catalog ◆ TVs, video recorders, telephones, tapes, cassettes, and CDs. 800-542-8811.

**S & S Sound City,** 58 W. 45th St., New York, NY 10036: Free information ◆ Audio and video equipment, telephones, office machines, and other electronics. 212-575-0210.

**S.B.H. Enterprises,** 1678 53rd St., Brooklyn, NY 11204: Free information ◆ Audio and video equipment and radar detectors. 800-451-5851; 718-438-1027 (in NY).

**Sound & Cinema,** 15 Minneakoning Rd., Ste. 305, Flemington, NJ 08822: Free information ◆ Audio, video, stereo equipment, and TVs. 888-862-8600.

**The Sound Approach,** 6067 Jericho Tnpk., Commack, NY 11725: Free information ◆ Home electronics and car audio systems. 800-368-2344.

**The Southern Advantage Company,** 8108 Idlewild Rd., #794, Charlotte, NC 28212: Free information ◆ Camcorders, VCRs, home audio equipment, videonics accessories, and other electronics. 800-632-6076. www.southernadvantage.com

**Tri-State Camera,** 650 6th Ave., New York, NY 10011: Free information ◆ Audio and video equipment, camcorders, copiers, fax machines, and other electronics. 800-221-1926; 212-633-2290 (in NY). tscamvid@aol.com

**Uncle's Stereo,** 216 W. 72nd St., New York, NY 10023: Free information ◆ Audio and video equipment and other electronics. 800-978-6253. www.unclestereo.com

**Video Plus,** 6533 Roosevelt Blvd., Philadelphia, PA 19149: Free information ◆ Camcorders, VCRs, home audio equipment, videonics accessories, and other electronics. 800-226-6784.

## Speakers

**a/d/s,** 1 Progress Way, Wilmington, MA 01887: Free information ◆ CD players, speakers, receivers, and amplifiers. 978-729-1140.

**Altec-Lansing,** P.O. Box 277, Milford, PA 18337: Free information ◆ Speakers. 800-258-3288.

**B & W Loudspeakers of America,** 54 Concord St., North Reading, MA 01864: Free brochure ◆ Speakers. 800-370-3740. www.bwspeakers.com

**Bose Express Music,** The Mountain, Framingham, MA 01701: Catalog $6 (refundable) ◆ Speakers. 800-845-BOSE. www.bose.com

**Boston Acoustics,** 300 Jubilee Dr., Peabody, MA 01960: Free information ◆ Speakers. 978-538-5000.

**Energy Loudspeakers,** 3641 NcNicoll Ave., Scarborough, Ontario, Canada M1X 1G5: Free information ◆ Home theater sound systems. 416-321-1800.

**Infinity Systems,** 20630 Nordhoff St., Chatsworth, CA 91311: Free information ◆ Speakers and TVs. 818-553-3332.

**Marantz America Inc.,** 440 Medinah Rd., Roselle, IL 60172: Free information ◆ Audio and video systems, speakers, CD and cassette players, sound processors, and other electronics. 630-307-3100. www.marantz.com

**Nady Systems,** 6701 Bay St., Emeryville, CA 94608: Free information ◆ Speakers and headphones. 510-652-2411. www.nadywireless.com

**NEC Technologies,** 1250 N. Arlington Heights Rd., Itasca, IL 60143: Free information ◆ Speakers, CD and cassette players, receivers, amplifiers, sound processors, and other electronics. 800-284-4484. www.nec.com

**Pioneer Technologies,** P.O. Box 1760, Long Beach, CA 90801: Free information ◆ Speakers, CD players, sound processors, receivers, amplifiers, and headphones. 800-746-6337. www.pioneerelectronics.com

**Polk Audio,** 5601 Metro Dr., Baltimore, MD 21215: Free list of retail sources ◆ Speakers. 800-377-7655. www.polkaudio.com

**Recoton,** 2950 Lake Emma Rd., Lake Mary, FL 32746: Free information ◆ Speakers, audio and video processors, and headphones. 800-223-6009.

**Sansui USA,** 200 Metroplex Dr., Edison, NJ 08817: Free information ◆ Speakers, cassette and CD players, receivers, amplifiers, and sound processors. 732-460-9710.

**Sanyo Fisher,** P.O. Box 2329, Chatsworth, CA 91311: Free information ◆ Speakers, CD and cassette players, sound processors, receivers, amplifiers, and camcorders. 818-998-7322.

**Sony Consumer Products,** 1 Sony Dr., Park Ridge, NJ 07656: Free information ◆ Speakers, audio and video systems, CD players, camcorders, sound processors, and headphones. 201-930-1000. www.sony.com

**Speakerlab Factory,** 6220 Roosevelt Way NE, Seattle, WA 98115: Free information ◆ Speakers and kits, tape decks, receivers, and other electronics. 206-523-2269.

**Technics,** One Panasonic Way, Secaucus, NJ 07094: Free list of retail sources ◆ Speakers, CD players, headphones, receivers, amplifiers, and sound processors. 201-348-7000. www.panasonic.com

**Vandersteen Audio,** 116 W. 4th St., Hanford, CA 93230: Free list of retail sources ◆ Speaker systems. 209-582-0324.

**Yamaha,** P.O. Box 6660, Buena Park, CA 90620: Free list of retail sources ◆ Speakers, CD and laser disk players, receivers, amplifiers, sound processors, and headphones. 800-492-6242. www.yamaha-motor.com

## STICKERS

**Cheri-Oats & Company,** P.O. Box 367, Destrahan, LA 70047: Free information ◆ Wigs, stickers, puppets, and face painting supplies. 504-764-0080. www.mooseburger.com/cheri.htm

**Eastern Emblem,** Box 828, Union City, NJ 07087: Free catalog ◆ T-shirts, jackets, patches, cloisonné pins, decals, and stickers. 800-344-5112.

**Heirloom Editions,** Box 520-B, Rt. 4, Carthage, MO 64836: Catalog $4 ◆ Lithographs, greeting cards, stickers, miniatures, stationery, framed prints, and turn-of-the-century art and paper collectibles. 800-725-0725.

**House-Mouse Designs,** P.O. Box 48, Williston, VT 05495: Free catalog ◆ Christmas cards, note and recipe cards, stickers, and magnets. 800-242-6423. www.house-mouse.com

**T. Myers Magic Inc.,** 1509 Parker Bend, Austin, TX 78734: Free catalog ◆ Balloons and balloon-sculpting supplies. Also clown make-up, stickers, temporary tattoos, and magic. 800-648-6221; 512-263-2375 (in TX). TMyersMagi@aol.com

**Stick-Em Up,** 3942 Valley Ave., Pleasanton, CA 94566: Catalog $2 ◆ Stickers. 510-426-1040.

## STOCK CAR RACING (NASCAR)

**Brickel's Racing Collectibles,** Schoolside Plaza, P.O. Box 205, Leesport, PA 19533: Free catalog ◆ Racing collectibles. 610-926-6719.

**BSR Replicas & Finishes,** 101 Rainbow Way, Fayettevile, GA 30214: Catalog $1 ◆ NASCAR modeling supplies, kits and resin bodies, and decals. 770-719-8195.

**CH Racing Enterprises,** P.O. Box 663, Hamburg, NY 14075: Free brochure ◆ Diecast model NASCAR cars in 1/24 and 1/64 scale, officially licensed NASCAR shirts and other apparel, photos, and books. 716-649-6753. CHRaceEnt@aol.com

**Diversified Electronics Inc.,** 309 Agnew Dr., Ste. C, Forest Park, GA 30050: Free information ◆ Racing radios complete with nicad battery pack, charger, and antenna. 800-669-1522; 404-366-3796 (in GA).

**E.D.P. Products,** P.O. Box 7667, Naples, FL 33941: Free information ◆ Gifts for NASCAR racers and other involved persons. 800-833-0696. mail@edpproducts.com

**Frequency Fan Club,** P.O. Box 610, Milledgeville, GA 31061: Free information ◆ Race scanners, headsets, and accessories. 800-722-3326. www.racescanners.com

**H & L Productions Inc.,** 1425 Oakbrook Dr., Ste. 100, Norcross, GA 30093: Free catalog ◆ NASCAR wearables, collectibles, and other gifts.

**Kathy's Kards,** 7700 E. 42nd Pl., Tulsa, OK 74145: Free information ◆ Miscellaneous NASCAR collectibles and memorabilia. 800-435-3570. www.nascarshop.com

**NASCAR Catalog,** c/o Genesis Direct, 100 Plaza Dr., Secaucus, NJ 07094: Free catalog ◆ NASCAR gifts, model cars, clothing, and more. 800-873-8263. care@GenesisDirect.com

**NASCAR Wearables & Collectibles Catalog,** P.O. Box 2367, Norcross, GA 30091: Free catalog ◆ Official NASCAR wearables and collectibles. 800-987-0606.

**Ole Chevy Store,** Division T & N Manufacturing Company, 2509 S. Cannon Blvd., Kannapolis, NC 28083: Free list ◆ Banks and automotive collectibles. 704-938-2923.

**Racing Fantasies,** 8341 De Soto Ave., Ste. 10, Canoga Park, CA 91304: Free catalog ◆ NASCAR and other racing car gifts and collectibles. 800-376-7386; 818-775-0337 (in CA). www.rfantasies.com

**Redline,** P.O. Box 1629, Secaucus, NJ 07096: Free catalog ◆ Nascar clothing and collectibles. 800-GO-NASCAR. www.nascar.com

**Sparco Motor Sports Inc.,** 6644 San Fernando Rd., Glendale, CA 01201: Free catalog ◆ Driving suits, accessories for drivers, seat accessories, safety gear, and more. 818-502-9160.

**Star Struck,** P.O. Box 308, Bethel, CT 06801: Free catalog ◆ Fitted caps and jerseys with NASCAR logos. 800-908-4637; 877-THE-GAME (in CT). www.starstruck.com

## STONE SCULPTING & CARVING

**Ebersole Lapidary Supply Inc.,** 11417 West Hwy. 54, Wichita, KS 67209: Catalog $5 ◆ Carving materials, beads and bead-stringing supplies, tools, findings, mountings, cabochons and rocks, and jewelry kits. 316-722-4771.

**Gems by Jak,** 113 Sherman St., Ihlen, MN 56140: Free catalog ◆ Indian gifts and catinite for carving. 507-348-8617.

**Montoya/MAS International Inc.,** 435 Southern Blvd., West Palm Beach, FL 33405: Catalog $3 ◆ Carving stone and sculpture tools. 800-682-8665; 561-832-4401 (in FL). home.att.net/~montoya-mas

**Richardson's Recreational Ranch Ltd.,** Gateway Route Box 440, Madras, OR 97741: Free information ◆ Rock and mineral specimens from all over the world, carving materials, and lapidary equipment. 800-433-2680.

**Riviera Lapidary Supply,** 50898 7th St., Box 40, Riviera, TX 78379: Catalog $3 ◆ Carving materials, petrified wood, cabochons, slabs, cabbing rough, gemstones, crystals, beads, and bead-stringing supplies and kits. 512-296-3958.

**Steatite of Southern Oregon Inc.,** 2891 Elk Ln., Grants Pass, OR 97527: Free information ◆ Soapstone for sculpturing and carving. 503-479-3646.

## STOVES & OVENS

**AGA Cookers,** Classic Cookers, RD 3, Box 180-6176, Montpelier, VT 05602: Brochure $2 ◆ Cast-iron stoves with a choice of 3 types of fuel. 800-633-9200. www.agacooker.com

**Aladdin Steel Products Inc.,** 401 N. Wynne St., Colville, WA 99114: Free list of retail sources ◆ Wood, pellet, and gas-burning stoves. Also fireplace inserts. 800-234-2508.

**Barnstable Stove Shop,** Rt. 149, Box 472, West Barnstable, MA 02668: Brochure $1 ◆ Restored antique stoves and parts. 508-362-9913.

**Blaze King Industries,** 400 W. Whitman Dr., P.O. Box 367, College Place, WA 99324: Free list of retail sources ◆ Pellet-burning stoves. 509-522-2730.

**Bryant Stove Inc.,** Box 2048, Thorndike, ME 04986: Free brochure ◆ Antique stoves for coal, gas, wood, wood and gas combination, and electricity. 207-568-3665.

**Charmaster Products Inc.,** 2307 Hwy. 2 West, Grand Rapids, MN 55744: Free brochure ◆ Fireplaces, conversion units, and forced air and hot water wood-burning furnaces. 218-326-6786.

**Country Stoves Inc.,** P.O. Box 987, Auburn, WA 98071: Free information ◆ Wood and gas stoves, fireplaces, and inserts. 206-735-1100.

**Custom Fireplaces,** 1611 E. Spring St., Cookeville, TN 38506: Catalog $4 ◆ Antique-styled electric and gas ranges, coordinated refrigerators, and wall ovens. 615-526-8181.

**Dynamic Cooking Systems,** 5800 Skylab Rd., Huntington Beach, CA 92647: Free catalog ◆ Outdoor gas grills and professional gas ranges for commercial settings. 800-433-8466. www.dcs-range.com

**Earthstone Wood-Fire Ovens,** 1233 N. Highland Ave., Los Angeles, CA 90038: Free brochure ◆ Wood-fired ovens and fireplaces. 800-840-4915.

**Elmira Stove Works,** 595 Colby Dr., Waterloo, Ontario, Canada N2V 1A2: Free catalog ◆ Antique-style kitchen appliances. 800-295-8498. www.elmirastoveworks.com

**Empire Control Systems,** 1918 Freeburg Ave., Belleville, IL 62222: Free brochure ◆ Room heaters, floor furnaces, commercial/industrial unit heaters and duct furnaces, fireplace products, free-standing and semi-enclosed gas stoves, chicken and turkey fryers, and accessories. 800-851-3153; 618-233-7420 (in IL). www.empirecomfort.com

**FiveStar,** P.O. Box 2490, Cleveland, TN 37320: Free brochure ◆ Commercial ranges, cooktops, and range hoods for the home. 800-251-7485.

**Good Time Stove Company,** Rt. 112, P.O. Box 306, Goshen, MA 01032: Free information ◆ Restored ready-to-use antique cooking and heating stoves. 413-268-3677.

**Heartland Appliances,** 5 Hoffman St., Kitchener, Ontario, Canada N2M 3M5: Catalog $2 (request list of retail sources) ◆ Classic cooking stoves with state-of-the-art features. 519-743-8111. www.heartlandapp.com

**Heatilator Inc.,** 1915 W. Saunders St., Mt. Pleasant, IA 52641: Free information ◆ Wood-burning stoves and fireplace inserts. 800-926-4356. www.heatilator.com

**Heating Alternatives,** 1924 Rt. 212, Pleasant Valley, Quakertown, PA 18951: Free catalog ◆ Coal and wood-burning stoves. 800-444-4328; 215-346-7896 (in PA). www.woodheat.com

**The House of Webster,** P.O. Box 9610, Rogers, AR 72757: Catalog $2 ◆ Electric stoves that resemble old-fashioned wood-burning stoves. 501-636-4640. www.houseofwebster.com

**Hutch Manufacturing Company,** 200 Commerce Ave., P.O. Box 350, Loudon, TN 37774: Free information ◆ Catalytic stoves. 800-251-9232.

**Iron Craft,** Old Rt. 28, P.O. Box 351, Ossipee, NH 03864: Catalog $2 ◆ Kettles and grates, enameled cookware, cookstoves, and coal and wood-heating stoves. 603-539-6159.

**J.E.S. Enterprises,** P.O. Box 65, Ventura, CA 93002: Free catalog ◆ Restored electric, gas, coal and wood-burning antique stoves. Also used, new, and restored parts. 805-643-3532.

**Johnny's Appliances & Classic Ranges,** 17549 Sonoma Hwy., P.O. Box 1407, Sonoma, CA 95476: Free information with long SASE ◆ Cooking ranges, from 1900 to 1960. 707-996-9730.

**Jotul USA,** 400 Riverside St., Portland, ME 04104: Free list of retail sources ◆ Wood and gas cast-iron stoves and fireplace inserts. 800-797-5912.

**Kamper's Kettle,** 2165 Bruneau Dr., Boise, ID 83709: Free catalog ◆ Outdoor cooking tables and accessories, ovens, cast-iron cookware, Dutch ovens, accessories, and books and videos on cooking with Dutch ovens. 800-860-1100; 208-377-0344 (in ID). Kampers@RMC.NET

**Mill Creek Antiques,** 109 Newbury, Paxico, KS 66526: Free information ◆ Antique furniture, lighting, and stoves. 913-636-5520.

**Mugnaini Imports,** 340 Aptos Ridge Circle, Watsonville, CA 95076: Brochure $3 ◆ Italian wood-burning oven. 888-887-7206. www.mugnaini.com

**New Buck Corp.,** 1265 Bakersville Hwy., Spruce Pine, NC 28777: Free information ◆ Gas and catalytic wood stoves. Also gas heaters, logs, and wood stove to gas conversion kits. 704-765-6144.

**The Olde Stove Works,** 33507 Thompson Ave., Mission, British Columbia, Canada V2V 2W9: Catalog $7.95 ◆ Country style wood and coal-burning cookstove. 604-826-5669.

**Otis Home Center Inc.,** 312 Armstrong Rd., Rogersville, TN 37857: Catalog $5 ◆ Wood, gas, or electric country-style heating and cooking stoves. 800-743-8133.

**Prestons Household Accessories,** P.O. Box 369, Ossipee, NH 03864: Catalog $3 ◆ Stoves, fireplace accessories, and cast-iron cookware. 603-539-4114.

**Rais & Wittus Inc.,** 23 Hack Green Rd., Pound Ridge, NY 10576: Free catalog ◆ Fireplace stoves for heating and cooking. 914-764-5679.

**Stanley Iron Works,** 64 Taylor St., Nashua, NH 03060: Free information ◆ Antique parlor stoves, gas and wood-gas combination stoves, and coal, gas, and electric conversions of antique stoves. 603-881-8335.

**The Ultimate Cooker,** 803 W. Fairbanks, Winter Park, FL 32789: Free information ◆ Combination grilling and smoking cooker. 407-644-6680.

**Vermont Natural Stoneworks,** Depot St., Box 275, Fair Haven, VT 05743: Free list of retail sources ◆ Tile products that include floors, pet memorials and urns, entryway systems, house and garden markers, instant patios and walkways, and gas stove mats. 802-265-2200. www.sover.net/~stone

**Vogelzang Corp.,** 400 W. 17th St., Holland, MI 49423: Free information ◆ Wood-burning stove conversion kits. 800-222-6950.

**Waterford Irish Stoves Inc.,** 16 Airport Park Rd., Ste. 3, West Lebanon, NH 03784: Free information ◆ Non-catalytic stoves. 603-298-5030.

**Woodstock Soapstone Company Inc.,** 66 Airpark Rd., West Lebanon, NH 03784: Free brochure ◆ Traditional and contemporary-style woodburning stoves. 800-866-4344.

## SUNDIALS

**Armchair Shopper,** P.O. Box 419464, Kansas City, MO 64141: Free catalog ◆ Old-world-style sundials, wind chimes, and lawn ornaments. 816-767-3200.

**Betsy's Place,** 323 Arch St., Philadelphia, PA 19106: Free information ◆ Sundials and stands, brass reproduction door knockers, and trivets. 800-452-3524; 215-922-3536 (in PA).

**Flora Fauna,** P.O. Box 578, Gualala, CA 95445: Free information ◆ Hand-cast solid brass sundials and garden decor. 800-358-9120. flora@mcn.org

**Kenneth Lynch & Sons,** 84 Danbury Rd., Wilton, CT 06897: Catalog $4 ◆ Sundials. 203-762-8363.

**Tom Outhouse,** 2853 Lincoln Hwy. East, Ronks, PA 17572: Free catalog ◆ Antique and polished copper weather vanes with solid brass directional indicators. Also sundials. 800-346-7678.

**Replogle Globes Inc.,** 2801 S. 25th Ave., Broadview, IL 60153: Free catalog ◆ Sundials. 708-343-0900.

**Wind & Weather,** P.O. Box 2320, Mendocino, CA 95460: Free catalog ◆ Sundials, weather vanes, and weather forecasting instruments. 800-922-9463. weather@men.org

## SUNGLASSES & EYE WEAR

**Action Optics,** Division Smith Sport Optics Inc., Box 2999, Ketchum, ID 83340: Free brochure ◆ Polarized sunglasses. 800-654-6428. www.smithsport.com

**Anarchy Eyewear,** 2095 New Hwy., Farmingdale, NY 11735: Free information ◆ Sport sunglasses. 516-752-8900.

**BluBlocker Corp.,** 3350 Palms Centre Dr., Las Vegas, NV 89103: Free brochure ◆ Sunglasses. 800-508-5005.

**Brigade Quartermasters Inc.,** 1025 Cobb International Blvd., Kennesaw, GA 30144: Free catalog ◆ Ski goggles and other eyewear. 800-338-4327. www.actiongear.com

**Fly Industries,** 1560-B Superior Ave., Costa Mesa, CA 92627: Free brochure ◆ UV light-protected sunglasses with hand-finished frames. 714-646-3389. www.flys.com

**Gallagher & Forsythe Ltd.,** 714 Main St., Bldg. 704, Yarmouth Port, MA 02675: Free catalog ◆ Serengeti, Rayban, and Swiss Army sunglasses. 508-362-1366.

**Gatorz Eyewear,** 12925 Brookprinter Pl., Ste. 200, Poway, CA 92064: Free information ◆ Sport sunglasses and goggles. 800-767-4287. www.gatorz.com

**Hidalgo Inc.,** 45 La Buena Vista, Wimberley, TX 78676: Free catalog ◆ Designer sunglasses. 512-847-5571.

**Hobie Sunglasses,** 5866 S. 194th St., Kent, WA 98032: Free information ◆ Polarized sunglasses. 800-554-4335.

**House of Eyes,** 2222 Patterson St., Greensboro, NC 27407: Free information ◆ Designer eye wear. 800-331-4701; 336-852-7107 (in NC).

**Intelligence Research Group,** 1015 Gayley Ave., Ste. 1028, Los Angeles, CA 90024: Free catalog ◆ Technologically advanced sunglasses for eye protection. 800-541-1405.

**JT USA,** 515 Otay Valley Rd., Chula Vista, CA 91911: Free information ◆ Sport sunglasses. 619-421-2660.

**Kaleeb Sunglasses,** 46 Cactus Rd., Levittown, PA 19057: Free brochure ◆ Styled sunglasses. 215-943-9719.

**E.P. Levine Inc.,** 23 Dry Dock Ave., Boston, MA 02210: Free information ◆ Nikon sunglasses. 800-875-3055. www.cameras.com

**Martin Sunglasses,** Jack Martin Company Inc., 9830 Baldwin Pl., El Monte, CA 91731: Free information ◆ Ski goggles and eyewear. 800-767-8555; 213-686-1100 (in CA). martinaccs@aol.com

**Oakley Sunglasses,** 1 Icon, Foothill Ranch, CA 92610: Free information ◆ Eye wear that provides ultraviolet light and injury-causing blue light protection. 714-829-6300. www.oakley.com

**Olympic Optical Company,** P.O. Box 752377, Memphis, TN 38175: Free information ◆ Sunglasses that protect the eyes from ultraviolet light. 800-992-1255.

**Revo Sunglass Inc.,** 1315 Chesapeake Terrace, Sunnyvale, CA 94089: Free information ◆ Sport sunglasses. 800-444-7386.

**Serengeti Eyewear,** 8125 25th Court East, Sarasota, FL 34243: Free information ◆ Designer sunglasses. 800-525-4001. www.h2optix.com

**Smith Sport Optics Inc.,** P.O. Box 2999, Ketchum, ID 83340: Free information ◆ Sport sunglasses and goggles. 208-726-4477. www.smithsport.com

**Spex Amphibious Eye Wear,** P.O. Box 2537, Costa Mesa, CA 92628: Free information ◆ Polarized eyewear with ultraviolet light protection. 714-548-1235.

**Sunglass America,** P.O. Box 147, Hewlett, NY 11557: Catalog $2 (refundable) ◆ Designer sunglasses. 800-424-LENS; 516-791-3400 (in NY). www.pcshades.com

**Sunglass Hut International,** 255 Alhambra Circle, Coral Gables, FL 33124: Free catalog ◆ Eye-protection sunglasses. 800-786-4527. btopal@ibm.net

**Sunglasses U.S.A.,** 469 Sunrise Hwy., Lynbrook, NY 11563: Free catalog ◆ Ray-Ban sunglasses. 800-USA-RAYS.

**SunRay Optical,** 2038 Massachusetts Ave., Cambridge, MA 02140: Free catalog ◆ Custom-made sunglasses. 800-323-2932. genop-co@erols.com

**Ultrasol,** 4040 Spencer St., Ste. J, Torrance, CA 90503: Free brochure ◆ Adjustable and spring-loaded frames with lenses that are 100 percent resistant to UV-A and UV-B radiation. 310-371-7762.

## SURFBOARDS & WINDSURFING

**American Athletic Inc.,** 200 American Ave., Jefferson, IA 50129: Free information ◆ Surfboards and swim rings. 800-247-3978; 515-386-3125 (in IA). www.americanathletic.com

**Body Glove International,** 530 6th St., Hermosa Beach, CA 90254: Free information ◆ Surfboards. 800-678-7873; 310-374-4074 (in CA). www.bodyglove.com

**Skip Hutchison,** Rastaboards Surf-Sail-Snowboards, 4748 NE 11th Ave., Fort Lauderdale, FL 33334: Free information with long SASE ◆ Sailboards, surfboards, and snowboards. 954-491-7992.

**Recreonics Corp.,** 4200 Schmitt Ave., Louisville KY 40213: Free information ◆ Surfboards, swim rings, and diving boards. 800-428-3254.

**Rothhammer International,** P.O. Box 3840, San Luis Obispo, CA 93403: Free information ◆ Surfboards, swim rings, and equipment for divers. 800-235-2156.

**Sailworld-USA,** 112 Oak St., Hood River, OR 97031: Free information ◆ Sails for windsurfing boards. 541-386-9400.

**Tackle Shack,** 7801 66th St. North, Pinellas Park, FL 33781: Free catalog ◆ Windsurfing equipment and clothing. 800-537-6099. www.FunOnWater.com

**Windsurfing Warehouse,** 128 S. Airport Blvd., South San Francisco, CA 94080: Free catalog ◆ Sailboards. 800-628-4599; 415-588-1714 (in CA).

## SURPLUS & LIQUIDATION MERCHANDISE

**American Science & Surplus,** 3605 Howard St., Skokie, IL 60076: Catalog $1 ◆ Surplus science and electro-mechanical supplies, equipment, and kits. 847-982-0870. www.sciplus.com

**Barnes Surplus & John,** Old Hwy. 78 East, Tupelo, MS 38802: Free price list ◆ Surplus merchandise. 601-840-9244.

**Burden's Surplus Center,** P.O. Box 82209, Lincoln, NE 68501: Free catalog ◆ Liquidation merchandise. 800-488-3407.

**COMB Authorized Liquidator,** P.O. Box 29902, Minneapolis, MN 55440: Free catalog ◆ Liquidation merchandise. 800-328-0609.

**Damark International Inc.,** 7101 Winnetka Ave. North, P.O. Box 9437, Minneapolis, MN 55440: Free information ◆ Liquidation of over-production, discontinued, or merchandise obtained through special arrangements with vendors. 800-328-3100. www.damark.com

**ET Supply,** 5055 Exposition Blvd., P.O. Box 78190, Los Angeles, CA 90016: Free catalog ◆ Tools, electro-mechanical equipment, and other surplus items. 213-734-2430.

**Fair Radio Sales Company Inc.,** P.O. Box 1105, Lima, OH 45802: Free information ◆ Industrial and military surplus electronic parts. 419-227-6573. www.alpha.wcoll.com/~fairadio

**Falkner Enterprises,** P.O. Box 1378, Ottumwa, IA 52501: Free catalog ◆ Electronic surplus liquidation. 515-683-7621.

**Harbor Freight Salvage,** 3491 Mission Oaks Blvd., Camarillo, CA 93011: Free catalog ◆ Hardware, tools, and surplus merchandise. 800-444-3353. www.harborfreight.com

**Massachusetts Army & Navy,** 15 Fordham Rd., Boston, MA 02134: Free catalog ◆ Army and navy surplus from around the world. 800-343-7749; 617-783-1250 (in MA).

**Mid-Missouri Surplus,** Russ Hinnard, 780 W. Boyd St., Marshall, MO 65340: Free catalog ◆ New and used military and outdoor gear. 816-886-3585.

**The Original I. Goldberg,** 902 Chestnut St., Philadelphia, PA 19107: Free catalog ◆ Military surplus merchandise. Also footwear, clothing, and camping equipment. 215-925-9393.

**Ruvel & Company Inc.,** 4128 W. Belmont Ave., Chicago, IL 60641: Catalog $2 ◆ Army and navy surplus. 773-286-9494.

**Strand Surplus Center,** 2202 Strand, Galveston, TX 77550: Brochure $1 ◆ All types of equipment that includes many hard-to-find items. 409-762-7397.

**Surplus Center,** P.O. Box 82209, Lincoln, NE 68501: Free catalog ◆ Hydraulics, motors, air compressors, spraying equipment, pumps, and surplus merchandise. 800-488-3407.

**Surplus Shack,** 407 US Rt. 222, Blandon, PA 19510: Free list ◆ Surplus astronomy and optical equipment. 888-88-SHACK; 610-926-9226 (in PA). www.SurplusShack.com

**TAPCO,** P.O. Box 2408, Kennesaw, GA 30144: Free catalog ◆ Military surplus. 800-554-1445.

## SURVEILLANCE & PERSONAL PROTECTION EQUIPMENT

**A.M.C. Sales Inc.,** 193 Vaquero Dr., Boulder, CO 80303: Catalog $5 ◆ Telephone recording adapters, bugging detectors, telephone scramblers, voice changers, and more. 800-926-2488; 303-499-5405 (in CO). www.siteleader.com/catalogdepot/AMCSC-home.html

**American Innovations Inc.,** 119 Rockland Center, Ste. 315, Nanuet, NY 10954: Catalog $6 ◆ Electronics and counter-surveillance equipment. 914-735-6127. www.spysite.com

**CCS International,** 360 Madison Ave., New York, NY 10017: Free information ◆ Video surveillance products. 800-685-6374; 212-557-3040 (in NY). ccsnychq@aol.com

**CIAssociates,** 2801 Shelterwood, Arlington, TX 76016: Catalog $5 ◆ Unique investigative items for professionals and hobbyists.

**Creative Micro Electronics Inc.,** P.O. Box 4477, Englewood, CO 80155: Free catalog ◆ Miniature black-and-white and color video camera modules and equipment. 800-771-1295; 303-771-1288 (in CO).

**Great Southern Security,** 513 Bankhead Hwy., Carrolton, GA 30117: Free information ◆ Electronic protection devices. 800-732-5000. catalog@greatsouthernsecurity.com

**Guardian Personal Security Products,** 21639 N. 14th Ave., Phoenix, AZ 85027: Free information ◆ Pepper spray, stun guns, locksmithing tools, and accessories. 800-527-4434. www.guardianproducts.com

**IEC Surveillance,** P.O. Box 52347, Knoxville, TN 37950: Free catalog with long SASE ◆ Security and control kits. 800-417-6689. www.irmicrolink.com

**Polaris Electronics Industries,** 470 Armour Dr. NE, Atlanta, GA 30324: Free information ◆ Micro-size CCD cameras and wireless monitoring systems. 404-872-0722. www.polarisusa.com

**Protector Enterprises,** P.O. Box 520294, Salt Lake City, UT 84152: Catalog $5 ◆ Spy, counterspy, and protection equipment. 801-487-3823.

**Resources Un-Ltd.,** 300 Bedford St., Manchester, NH 03101: Free information ◆ Surveillance cameras and accessories. 800-810-4070. unltd4u@tiac.net

**Seymor-Radix Inc.,** Box 166055, Irving, TX 75016: Free information ◆ Surveillance and recording devices. 800-594-1047.

**Spy Outlet,** P.O. Box 337, Buffalo, NY 14226: Catalog $5 ◆ Voice changers and scramblers, telephone recorders, bugging detectors, and surveillance and counter-surveillance electronic devices. 716-695-8660. www.spyoutlet.com

**Street Smart Security,** 7147 University Ave., La Mesa, CA 91941: Free information ◆ Remote control receivers for any application. 800-908-4737. www.vanet.com/sss

**Super Circuits,** One Supercircuits Plaza, Leander, TX 78641: Free catalog ◆ Wireless micro-video CCD camera system, security and surveillance equipment, and other mini products. 800-335-9777. www.supercircuits.com

## SWIMMING POOLS & EQUIPMENT

**Allweather Inc.,** 616 Sainte-Famille, Boucherville, Quebec, Canada J4B 4A6: Free information ◆ Alarm that sounds when someone falls into a swimming pool. 800-267-2335. www.allweather.ca

**Aqua Products Inc.,** 25 Rutgers Ave., Cedar Grove, NJ 07009: Free information ◆ Above-ground water pressure-operated pool cleaner. 800-221-1750. www.aqua-products.com

**Aquasol Controllers Inc.,** 2918 Dupree, Houston, TX 77054: Free information ◆ Electronic pool sanitizer and pH monitoring and control equipment. 800-444-0675. www.aquasol.com

**Cover-Pools Inc.,** 66 E. 3335 South, Salt Lake City, UT 84115: Free information ◆ Swimming pool covers. 800-447-2838. www.coverpools.com

**Endless Pools Inc.,** 200 E. Duttons Mill Rd., Aston, PA 19014: Free brochure ◆ Lap pool for swimming in place against a smooth, adjustable current. 800-732-8660. www.endlesspools.com

**Fanta-Sea Pools,** 1865 Grand Island Blvd., Grand Island, NY 14072: Free information ◆ Solar-energy-heated swimming pools. 800-845-5500. www.solarpools.com

**Guardex Pool & Spa Products,** Biolab Inc., 627 E. College Ave., Decatur, GA 30030: Free information ◆ 4-in-1 swimming pool testing kit. 800-959-7946. www.omnipool.com

**Kreepy Krauly USA Inc.,** 403 Sawgrass Corporate Pkwy., Sunrise, FL 33325: Free information ◆ Pool vacuums. 954-846-1250. www.kreepykrauly.com

**Leisure Living Stores,** 415 Pottsville-Minersville Hwy., Minersville, PA 17954: Free catalog ◆ Swimming pool supplies, maintenance aids, and ground equipment. 800-441-7789. www.leisureliving.com

**Meyco Products Inc.,** 225 Park Ave., Hicksville, NY 11801: Free brochure ◆ Swimming pool covers. 800-446-3926; 516-935-0900 (in NY).

**Pool Fence Company,** 1791-907 Blount Rd., Pompano Beach, FL 33069: Free brochure ◆ Swimming pool security fences. 800-992-2206. www.protectachild.com

**Recreonics Corp.,** 4200 Schmitt Ave., Louisville KY 40213: Free information ◆ Swimming pools and supplies. 800-428-3254. www.recreonics.com

**Specialty Pool Products,** 6 Church St., P.O. Box 661, Ellington, CT 06029: Free catalog ◆ Pool accessories and supplies. 800-983-7665. www.poolproducts.com

**Sundance Supply,** 1678 Shattuck Ave., Ste. 173, Berkeley, CA 94709: Catalog $2 ◆ Building components for greenhouses, sun rooms, pool enclosures, and skylights. 800-776-2534. www.sundancesupply.com

**Swimex,** P.O. Box 328, Warren, RI 02885: Free brochure ◆ Compact lap pool for swimming in place, with controls for adjusting water flow. 800-877-7946. www.swimex.com

**Water Warehouse,** 6950 51st St., Kenosha, WI 53144: Free catalog ◆ Swimming pool supplies and maintenance equipment. 800-574-7665. www.waterwarehouse.com

## TABLE TENNIS

**The Athletic Connection,** 1901 Diplomat, Dallas, TX 75234: Free information ◆ Balls, nets, paddles, and tables. 800-527-0871; 972-243-1446 (in TX).

**Bauer Sports,** 150 Ocean Rd., Greenland, NH 03840: Free list of retail sources ◆ Paddles, balls, nets, brackets, and sets. 800-362-3146. www.bauer.com

**Escalade Sports,** P.O. Box 889, Evansville, IN 47706: Free catalog ◆ Tables, paddles, balls, nets, and sets. 800-457-3373; 812-467-1200 (in IN).

**Indian Industries Inc.,** P.O. Box 889, Evansville, IN 47706: Free catalog ◆ Sets. 800-457-3373; 812-467-1200 (in IN).

**Markwort Sporting Goods,** 4300 Forest Park Ave., St. Louis, MO 63108: Catalog $8 (request list of retail sources) ◆ Balls, nets, paddles, and tables. 800-669-6626; 314-652-3757 (in MO).

**Olympia Sports,** P.O. Box 1941, Ann Arbor, MI 48106: Free information ◆ Balls, nets, paddles, and tables. 800-521-2832. www.wolverinesports.com

**Paddle Palace Table Tennis Company,** 8125 SE Glencoe Rd., Portland, OR 97222: Free catalog ◆ Tables, net sets, shoes, paddle cases, paddles, training aids, balls, and other accessories. 800-547-5891; 503-777-2266 (in OR). www.paddlepalace.com

**Saunier-Wilhem Company,** 3216 5th Ave., Pittsburgh, PA 15213: Free catalog ◆ Equipment and accessories for bowling, billiards, darts, table tennis, shuffleboard, and board games. 412-621-4350.

**Spalding Sports Worldwide,** 425 Meadow St., P.O. Box 901, Chicopee, MA 01021: Free list of retail sources ◆ Paddles, balls, nets, brackets, and sets. 800-225-6601. www.spalding.com

**Sportime,** Customer Service, 1 Sportime Way, Atlanta, GA 30340: Free information ◆ Balls, nets, paddles, and tables. 800-444-5700; 770-449-5700 (in GA).

**Sporty's Preferred Living Catalog,** Clermont Airport, Batavia, OH 45103: Free catalog ◆ Folding outdoor table tennis tables. 800-543-8633. www.sportys-catalogs.com

**Tide-Rider Inc.,** P.O. Box 429, Oakdale, CA 95361: Free information ◆ Balls, nets, and paddles. 209-848-4420.

**Wa-Mac Inc.,** 178 Commerce Rd., P.O. Box 128, Carlstadt, NJ 07072: Free information ◆ Paddles, balls, nets, brackets, and sets. 800-447-5673; 201-438-7200 (in NJ).

**World of Leisure Manufacturing Company,** 13504 Phantom St., Victorville, CA 92394: Free list of retail sources ◆ Paddles, balls, nets, brackets, and sets. 619-246-3790.

## TABLECLOTHS, PADS, & OTHER LINENS

**Brown's Country Creations,** 838 E. 385 Rd., Dunnegan, MO 65640: Catalog $2.50 ◆ Place mats, napkins, runners, and other items. 417-326-4880.

**Bucks Trading Post,** 930 Old Bethlehem Pike, Sellersville, PA 18960: Catalog $2 ◆ European lace curtains, matching tablecloths, and doilies. 800-242-0738; 610-453-0623 (in PA).

**Century Table Pad Company,** 1170 Stella St., St. Paul, MN 55108: Free information ◆ Table pads. 800-345-9795.

**Chambers,** Mail Order Dept., P.O. Box 7841, San Francisco, CA 94120: Free catalog ◆ Bed and bath furnishings. 800-334-1254.

**Domestications,** Hanover Direct Pennsylvania, Hanover, PA 17333-0001: Free catalog ◆ Bedding and bath ensembles. 717-633-3333.

**Eldridge Textile Company,** 17 E. 37th St., New York, NY 10016: Catalog $3 (refundable) ◆ Bed, bath, and table linens. 212-576-2991. www.eldridgetextile.com

**Factory Direct Table Pad Company,** 1501 W. Market St., Indianapolis, IN 46222: Free information ◆ Table pads. 800-428-4567. www.tablepads.com

**Genny's Table,** 711 Chuckanut Dr., Bellingham, WA 98226: Free brochure ◆ Judaic-theme tablecloths and wall hangings. 800-903-0357.

**Guardian Custom Products,** P.O. Box A, LaGrange, IN 46761: Free information ◆ Table pads. 800-444-0778. www.guardian-tablepad.com

**Horchow Fine Linen Collection,** P.O. Box 620048, Dallas, TX 75262: Free catalog ◆ Comforters, sheets, pillows, blankets, bed-spreads, throws, and tablecloths. 800-395-5397. www.neimanmarcus.com

**Harris Levy,** 278 Grand St., New York, NY 10002: Free catalog ◆ Table, bed, and bath linens. 800-221-7750; 212-226-3102 (in NY).

**Lifespace Interiors International,** 3946 S. Magnolia Way, Denver, CO 80237: Catalog $4 ◆ Slipcovers, table and other furniture cover-ups, shower curtains, window treatments, and more. 303-759-3024. www.dimensional.com/lifespace-interiors

**Palmetto Linen Company,** 50 Palmetto Bay Rd., Hilton Head, SC 29928: Free information ◆ Sheets, dust ruffles, bath towels, blankets, comforters, pillows, tablecloths, place mats, shower curtains, kitchen towels, and oven gloves. 800-972-7442.

**Pioneer Table Pad Company,** 6520 Carnegie Ave., Gates Mills, OH 44103: Free information ◆ Table pads. 800-541-0271; 440-881-6528 (in OH).

**Rue de France,** 78 Thames St., Newport, RI 02840: Catalog $3 ◆ Pillows, tablecloths, runners, and lace curtains. 800-777-0998.

**Sentry Table Pad Company,** 1170 Stella St., St. Paul, MN 55108: Free information ◆ Table pads. 800-328-7237.

**A Touch of Country,** P.O. Box 653, Palos Heights, IL 60463: Catalog $2 ◆ Table lace. 708-361-0142.

## TAPESTRIES & WALL HANGINGS

**Genny's Table,** 711 Chuckanut Dr., Bellingham, WA 98226: Free brochure ◆ Judaic-theme tablecloths and wall hangings. 800-903-0357.

**Heirloom Tapestries,** Box 539, Dobbins, CA 95935: Catalog $6 ◆ Reproduction museum classic tapestry wall hangings. 800-699-6836. www.tapestries-inc.com

**Oak Tree Furniture Company,** 828 S. Main St., St. Charles, MO 63301: Free information ◆ Afghans. 314-946-8227.

**Peerless Imported Rugs,** 3033 Lincoln Ave., Chicago, IL 60657: Catalog $1 ◆ Hand and machine-woven Oriental rugs, colonial braids, tapestries from Europe, and rag, Navajo, and grass rugs. 800-621-6573.

**Tapestries & Ambience,** 3595 Canton Rd., Ste. A-9, Marietta, GA 30066: Catalog $15 ◆ Authentic European tapestries that can be used as wall hangings. 800-413-3812.

**A Touch of Country,** P.O. Box 653, Palos Heights, IL 60463: Catalog $2 ◆ Tapestry runners. 708-361-0142.

## TATTOOING SUPPLIES & BODY JEWELRY

**American Tattoo Supply Inc.,** P.O. Box 3215, South Farmingdale, NY 11735: Free information ◆ Tattooing equipment. 516-293-4247.

**CLEARCO Tattoo Supplies,** P.O. Box 255025, Sacramento, CA 95865: Catalog $5 ◆ Professional tattoo supplies and equipment.

**Creative Alternatives,** 2904 S. Barnes, Springfield, MO 65804: Brochure $4 ◆ Easy-to-remove waterproof temporary tattoos and face and body painting products. 417-887-8961. www.funtooguy.com

**T. Myers Magic Inc.,** 1509 Parker Bend, Austin, TX 78734: Free catalog ◆ Balloons and balloon-sculpting supplies. Also clown make-up, stickers, temporary tattoos, and magic. 800-648-6221; 512-263-2375 (in TX). TmyersMagi@aol.com

**NDR Tattoo Equipment,** P.O. Box 116, Woodstock, NY 12498: Free information ◆ New and used tattoo equipment and supplies for pet identification. 800-637-3647. www.natidogregistry.com

**Papillon Studio Supply & Manufacturing,** 118 Pearl St., Enfield, CT 06082: Free information ◆ Tattooing equipment. 860-745-9270.

**Pleasurable Piercings Inc.,** 417 Lafayette Ave., Hawthorne, NJ 07506: Catalog $3 (refundable) ◆ Piercing equipment and body jewelry in surgical steel, niobium, and 14k or white gold. 973-238-0305.

**Precision Tattoo Supply,** 2108 S. Alvernon Way, Tucson, AZ 85711: Free catalog ◆ Tattoo machines, needles and accessories, colors and ink cups, design sheets, books and videos, and other supplies. 520-750-1595.

**Spaulding & Rogers Manufacturing,** Rt. 85, New Scotland Rd., Voorheesville, NY 12186: Free catalog ◆ Tattooing equipment and supplies. 518-768-2070. www.spaulding-rogers.com

**Superior Tattoo Equipment,** 1912 West Campbell, Phoenix, AZ 85015: Catalog $2 ◆ Tattooing equipment and kits. 602-433-1888.

**Unimax Supply Company Inc.,** 503 Broadway, New York, NY 10012: Free catalog ◆ Tattoo, piercing, and permanent cosmetic supplies. 800-9-UNIMAX; 212-925-1051 (in NY).

## TAXIDERMY

**Jim Allred Taxidermy,** 216 Sugarloaf Rd., Hendersonville, NC 28792: Free information ◆ Taxidermy supplies. 800-624-7507.

**Blue Ribbon Bases,** 100-K Knickerbocker Ave., Bohemia, NY 11716: Free catalog with long SASE ◆ Walnut and hardwood bases and plaques for mounting projects. 516-589-0707. 888-692-5257.

**Buckey Mannikins,** 2442 S.R. 83, Millersburg, OH 44654: Free catalog ◆ Taxidermy forms.

**Chandler's Taxidermy Supply Inc.,** 1637 Westhaven Blvd., Jackson, MS 39209: Free information ◆ Taxidermy supplies. 800-748-8765.

**Dan Chase Taxidermy Supply,** 13599 Blackwater Rd., Baker, LA 70714: Free catalog ◆ Taxidermy supplies and how-to videos. 800-535-8220.

**Dixieland Taxidermy Supply,** 9605 Hwy. 64, Somerville, TN 38068: Free catalog ◆ Taxidermy supplies. 800-465-2944.

**J.W. Elwood Company,** Elwood Bldg., Omaha, NE 68103: Free catalog ◆ Taxidermy supplies. 800-228-2291.

**Fintastic Fish Mounts,** 3566 Elk Rd., Westbank, British Columbia, Canada V4T 2H4: Free brochure ◆ Fish mounts and trophy reproductions in acrylic. 800-807-6168.

**Foster Taxidermy Supply,** 5124 Troy Hwy., Montgomery, AL 36116: Free catalog ◆ Taxidermy supplies. 800-848-5602.

**Hide & Beak Supply,** 7887 Hwy. 2, Saginaw, MN 55779: Catalog $2 ◆ Taxidermy supplies. 818-729-8452. www.hidebeak.com

**Hionis Taxidermy Supplies,** P.O. Box 766, Concordville, PA 19331: Free information ◆ Taxidermy supplies, tanning equipment, mounts, and more. 800-772-7924; 610-459-8547 (in PA). www.Hionis.com

**Jameson Company Ltd.,** 2200 Terminal Rd., Niles, MI 49120: Free information ◆ Polyurethane molding foam. 616-684-4451.

**Jonas Supply Company,** 2260 Industrial Ln., Broomfield, CO 80020: Free catalog ◆ Taxidermy and tanning supplies. Also true-to-life blended airbrush paints. 800-525-6379. www.jonastaxidermy.com

**McKenzie Taxidermy Supply,** P.O. Box 480, Granite Quarry, NC 28072: Free catalog ◆ Taxidermy supplies. 800-279-7985. mckenziep@infoave.net

**O.H. Mullen Sales Inc.,** 9928 Rd. 171, Oakwood, OH 45873: Free information ◆ Taxidermy supplies. 800-258-6625.

**Panels by Paith,** 2728 Allensville Rd., Roxboro, NC 27573: Free catalog ◆ Plaques, bases, and accessories. 800-677-2484; 336-599-3437 (in NC).

**Archie Phillips Taxidermy,** 200 52nd St., Fairfield, AL 35064: Catalog $2 ◆ Taxidermy supplies. 800-423-8601.

**Rinehart Taxidermy Supply,** 3032 McCormick Dr., P.O. Box 5010, Janesville, WI 53547: Free information ◆ Taxidermy supplies. 800-367-3337; 608-755-5161 (in WI). drinehart@aol.com

**Tohickon Glass Eyes,** 15 Geigel Hill Rd., P.O. Box 15, Erwinna, PA 18920: Free catalog ◆ Glass eyes for taxidermy and woodcarving. 800-441-5983; 610-294-9483 (in PA). www.tohickonglasseyes.com

**Touchstone Taxidermy Supply,** 5011 E. Texas St., Bossier City, LA 71111: Free catalog ◆ Taxidermy supplies. 800-256-4800. members.aol.com/touchtxdmy

**Tru-Form Taxidermy Supplies Inc.,** Mike & Debbie Pere, 4070 Rt. 14 North, Lyons, NY 14489: Free catalog ◆ Taxidermy supplies. 315-946-3012.

**Van Dyke Supply Company,** P.O. Box 278, Woonsocket, SD 57385: Catalog $1 ◆ Taxidermy supplies. 800-843-3320. www.vandyke.com

**Wildlife Artist Supply,** 1306 W. Spring, P.O. Box 967, Monroe, GA 30655: Free information ◆ Airbrush paints and other taxidermy supplies. 800-334-8012; 770-267-8970 (in GA). www.taxidermy.com

# TELEPHONES & ANSWERING MACHINES

## Antique Phones

**Billard's Telephones,** 21710 Regnart Rd., Cupertino, CA 95014: Brochure $1 ◆ Antique telephones and parts. 408-252-2104.

**Chicago Old Telephone Company,** P.O. Box 189, Lemon Springs, NC 28355: Free catalog ◆ Restored telephones that can be plugged into modern systems. 800-843-1320.

**Mahantango Manor,** Box 170, Dalmatia, PA 17017: Catalog $3 ◆ Working replicas of telephones from the 1900s. 800-642-3966.

**Phone Wizard,** P.O. Box 70, Leesburg, VA 22078: Catalog $3 ◆ Restored antique telephones and parts. 703-777-0000.

**Phoneco Inc.,** P.O. Box 70, Galesville, WI 54630: Catalog $3 ◆ Restored antique, novelty, art deco, character, and other telephones. Also parts. 608-582-4124. www.phoneco.inc.com

## Cellular Telephones

**APS Technologies,** 6131 Deramus, P.O. Box 4987, Kansas City, MO 64120: Free catalog ◆ Cordless telephones and accessories. 800-766-8427. www.apstech.com

**AT&T Consumer Products,** 5 Wood Hollow Rd., Parsippany, NJ 07054: Free information ◆ Portable cellular telephones. 800-232-5179.

**Blaupunkt,** 2800 S. 25th Ave., Broadview, IL 60153: Free information ◆ Portable and installation cellular phones. 630-865-5200.

**CellStar Corp.,** 1730 Briercroft Ct., Carrollton, TX 75006: Free information ◆ Cellular phone accessories. 800-766-8283.

**Cellular Phone Accessory Warehouse,** 11741 Valley View St., Ste. I, Cypress, CA 90630: Free catalog ◆ Cellular phones. 800-342-2336.

**Cincinnati Microwave,** One Microwave Plaza, Cincinnati, OH 45249: Free information ◆ Portable cellular phones. 800-543-1608. www.cnmw.com

**Clarion Corp. of America,** 661 W. Redondo Beach Blvd., Gardena, CA 90247: Free information ◆ Installation cellular phones. 800-487-9007.

**Ericsson GE Mobile Communications,** 1 Triangle Dr., Research Triangle Park, NC 27709: Free information ◆ Cellular phones. 800-227-3663.

**Everything Wireless,** 3380 N, 28th Terrace, Hollywood, FL 33020: Free catalog ◆ Cellular telephones, pagers, and accessories. 888-383-7999. www.everythingwireless.com

**Fujitsu America,** 2801 Telecom Pkwy., Richardson, TX 75082: Free information ◆ Portable cellular telephones. 800-955-9926.

**Mitsubishi Electronics,** 5757 Plaza Dr., Cypress, CA 90630: Free information ◆ Portable and installation cellular phones. 800-843-2515.

**Mitsubishi International,** 1500 N. Michael Dr., Ste. B, Wood Dale, IL 60191: Free information ◆ Portable cellular telephones. 630-860-4200.

**Mobile Office Outfitter,** 1048 Serpentine Ln., #308, Pleasanton, CA 94566: Free catalog ◆ Mobile car desks, laptop computer and cellular phone accessories, office supplies, and more. 800-426-3453. www.mobilegear.com

**Motorola Cellular Subscriber Group,** 600 N. US Hwy. 45, Libertyville, IL 60048: Free information ◆ Portable cellular telephones. 800-331-6456.

**NEC America,** 1555 W. Walnut Hill Ln., Irving, TX 75038: Free information ◆ Portable and installation cellular phones. 800-421-2141.

**Newtech Video & Computers,** 350 7th Ave., New York, NY 10001: Free information ◆ Video equipment, computers and peripherals, software, cellular phones, fax machines, and office equipment. 800-554-9747.

**Nokia Mobile Phones Inc.,** 6200 Courtney Campbell Causeway, Ste. 900, P.O. Box 30730, Tampa, FL 33630: Free information ◆ Portable cellular telephones.

**Oki Telecom,** 437 Old Peachtree Rd., Suwanee, GA 30174: Free information ◆ Portable, briefcase, and installation cellular phones. 800-554-3112.

**Panasonic,** Panasonic Way, Secaucus, NJ 07094: Free list of retail sources ◆ Portable and installation cellular phones. 201-348-7000. www.panasonic.com

**Qualcomm Inc.,** 4122 Lusk Blvd., San Diego, CA 92121: Free information ◆ Portable cellular telephones. 800-266-CDMA.

**Radio Shack,** Division Tandy Corp., 1500 One Tandy Center, Fort Worth, TX 76102: Free information ◆ Installation and portable cellular phones. 817-390-3700. www.radioshack.com

**Shure Brothers Inc.,** 222 Hartrey Ave., Evanston, IL 60202: Free information ◆ Hands-free cellular phones. 800-447-4873.

**Uniden,** 4700 Amon Carter Blvd., Fort Worth, TX 76155: Free information ◆ Portable cellular telephones. 800-772-7497.

## Telephones & Answering Machines

**Bernie's Discount Center Inc.,** 821 6th Ave., New York, NY 10001: Catalog $1 (refundable) ◆ Telephones and answering machines, audio and video equipment, large and small kitchen appliances, and personal care appliances. 212-564-8582.

**Crutchfield,** 1 Crutchfield Park, Charlottesville, VA 22906: Free catalog ◆ Fax machines, telephones and answering machines, word processors, copiers, computers, and software. 800-955-9009. www.crutchfield.com

**Electronic Wholesalers,** 1166 Hamburg Tnpk., Wayne, NJ 07470: Free information ◆ Telephones, camcorders, TVs, cassette and disk players, audio equipment, and other electronics. 201-696-6531. www.samans.com

**Hello Direct,** 5893 Rue Ferrari Dr., San Jose, CA 95138: Free catalog ◆ Amplification aids, cellular and paging accessories, telephones and answering machines, and other telephone productivity tools. 800-444-3556. www.hello-direct.com

**J & R Music World,** 59-50 Queens-Midtown Expwy., Maspeth, NY 11378: Free catalog ◆ Telephones, audio equipment, car and portable stereos, video recorders, computers, and other electronics. 800-221-8180.

**Motorola AMSD,** 5401 N. Beech St., Fort Worth, TX 76137: Free list of retail sources ◆ Hand-held miniature answering machine. 800-520-PAGE. focsc1@email.mot.com

**Olden Video,** 1265 Broadway, New York, NY 10001: Free information ◆ Telephones, copiers, and photographic equipment. 212-226-3727.

**Planet Electronics,** P.O. Box 251446, West Bloomfield, MI 48325: Free catalog ◆ Telephones, audio and video equipment, TVs, car and portable stereos, cassette players, video tapes, cassettes, and disks. 800-542-8811.

**S & S Sound City,** 58 W. 45th St., New York, NY 10036: Free information ◆ Audio and video equipment, telephones, office machines, and other electronics. 212-575-0210.

**Sound City,** 45 Indian Lane East, Towaco, NJ 07082: Free information ◆ Audio and video equipment, cassette and CD players, camcorders, TVs, processors, fax machines, telephones, and other electronics. 800-432-0007; 973-263-6060 (in NJ). www.soundcity.com

**Talk-A-Phone,** 5013 N. Kedzie Ave., Chicago, IL 60625: Free brochure ◆ Compliant emergency hands-free telephones. 773-539-1100. www.talkaphone.com

**Telephone Engineering Company,** P.O. Box 72, 786 Main St., Simpson, PA 18407: Free catalog ◆ Rotary and push-button phones, parts, two-line and novelty phones, business telephone systems, and sonic alert telephone ringing signalers. 717-282-5100.

**Temasek Telephone Inc.,** 21 Airport Rd., South San Francisco, CA 94080: Free information ◆ Voice-activated telephones. 800-647-8887.

# TENNIS

## Clothing

**Adidas USA,** 5675 N. Blackstock Rd., Spartanburg, SC 29303: Free list of retail sources ◆ Dresses, sweaters, jackets, caps and sun visors, shirts and tops, shoes and socks, shorts, and warm-up suits. 800-423-4327. www.adidas.com

**Associated Tennis Suppliers,** 200 Waterfront Dr., Pittsburgh, PA 15222: Free catalog ◆ Tennis racquets, supplies, easy-to-use stringing machines, and clothing. 800-866-7071.

**Ball Hopper Products Inc.,** 200 Waterfront Dr., Pittsburgh, PA 15222: Free information ◆ Caps and sun visors, gloves, dresses, jackets, shirts and tops, socks, sweatbands, underwear, and warm-up suits. 800-323-5417; 412-323-9633 (in PA).

**Betlin Manufacturing,** 1445 Marion Rd., Columbus OH 43207: Free information ◆ Tennis jackets, shorts, and warm-up suits. 614-443-0248.

**Converse Inc.,** 1 Fordham Rd., North Reading, MA 01864: Free information ◆ Caps and sun visors, jackets, shirts and tops, socks, sweatbands, and warm-up suits. 800-428-2667; 781-664-1100 (in MA).

**Grass Court Collection,** P.O. Box 972, Hanover, NH 03755: Free catalog ◆ Custom men's clothing for tennis, croquet, lawn bowling, cricket, and squash. 800-829-3412.

**Holabird Sports Discounters,** 9220 Pulaski Hwy., Baltimore, MD 21220: Free catalog ◆ Tennis racquets, shoes, clothes, balls, and bags. 410-687-6400. www.holabirdsports.com

**Las Vegas Discount Golf & Tennis,** 5325 S. Valley View Blvd., Ste. 10, Las Vegas, NV 89109: Free catalog ◆ Equipment, shoes, and clothing for tennis, racquetball, golf, running, and jogging. 702-798-5500. www.lvgolf.com

**Lily's of Beverly Hills,** 4910 W. Rosecrans Ave., Hawthorne, CA 90250: Free information ◆ Dresses, jackets, caps and sun visors, shirts and tops, shorts, sweatbands, and warm-up suits. 800-421-4474.

**Nike Footwear Inc.,** One Bowerman Dr., Beaverton, OR 97005: Free list of retail sources ◆ Jackets, shirts and tops, shoes and socks, shorts, and sweatbands. 800-344-6453. www.nike.com

**Prince Racquet Sports,** 1 Sport Systems Plaza, Bordentown, NJ 08505: Free information ◆ Caps and sun visors, dresses, jackets, shirts and tops, shoes and socks, sweatbands, underwear, and warm-up suits. 800-2-TENNIS; 609-291-5900 (in NJ).

**Professional Golf & Tennis Suppliers,** 7825 Hollywood Blvd., Pembroke Pines, FL 33024: Free catalog with long SASE ◆ Tennis racquets, clothing, shoes, and racquetball equipment. 305-981-7283.

**Puma USA Inc.,** 147 Centre St., Brockton, MA 02403: Free information with long SASE ◆ Dresses, jackets, shirts and tops, socks, sweatbands, sweaters, and warm-up suits. 800-662-7862. www.puma.com

**RayCo Tennis,** P.O. Box 632832, San Diego, CA 92163: Free price list ◆ Strings, shoes, grips, and stringing machines. 800-TENNIS-6. www.tennisrays.com

**Samuels Tennisport,** 7796 Montgomery Rd., Cincinnati, OH 45236: Free information ◆ Tennis, squash, and racquetball racquets and shoes. 216-791-4636. www.nuteknet.com/roots

**Spalding Sports Worldwide,** 425 Meadow St., P.O. Box 901, Chicopee, MA 01021: Free information ◆ Caps and sun visors, gloves, dresses, jackets, shirts and tops, shorts, shoes and socks, sweatbands, underwear, and warm-up suits. 800-225-6601. www.spalding.com

**Sport Casuals,** Box 812313, Boca Raton, FL 33481: Free information ◆ Jackets, shirts and tops, shoes and socks, shorts, sweaters, and warm-up suits. 800-776-7803; 561-997-7723 (in FL).

**The Sporting Look,** 1110 S. Powerline Rd., Deerfield Beach, FL 33442: Catalog $2 ◆ Tennis clothing. 954-570-5386.

**Sportline of Hilton Head Ltd.,** Heritage Plaza, Pope Ave., Hilton Head, SC 29928: Free information ◆ Tennis racquets, shoes, bags, and clothing. 888-996-8855. www.hiltonhead9.com/sportline

**Sports Express,** 5050 F.M. West, Houston, TX 77069: Free information ◆ Tennis racquets, court equipment, grips and wraps, shoes, bags, and clothing. 800-533-6321.

**Sullivan Sports,** P.O. Box 680505, Houston, TX 77268: Free information ◆ Tennis racquets, shoes, bags, and clothing. 800-543-0926.

**Total Sports,** 200 Waterfront Dr., Pittsburgh, PA 15222: Free catalog ◆ Tennis racquet strings, clothing, bags, and court supplies. 800-866-7071.

## Equipment

**Adidas USA,** 5675 N. Blackstock Rd., Spartanburg, SC 29303: Free list of retail sources ◆ Composite graphite tennis racquets. 800-423-4327. www.adidas.com

**American Playground Corp.,** 1801 S. Jackson, P.O. Box 2599, Anderson, IN 46011: Free information ◆ Posts, nets, and other court equipment. 800-541-1602.

**Associated Tennis Suppliers,** 200 Waterfront Dr., Pittsburgh, PA 15222: Free catalog ◆ Tennis racquets, supplies, easy-to-use stringing machines, and clothing. 800-866-7071.

**Austad's Tennis,** Hanover Direct Pennsylvania Inc., Hanover, PA 17333-0001: Free catalog ◆ Equipment for tennis and other sports. 717-633-3333.

**Ball Hopper Products Inc.,** 200 Waterfront Dr., Pittsburgh, PA 15222: Free information ◆ Ball retrievers and balls, posts and nets, practice and stringing machines, strings, and aluminum, boron composite, graphite composite, ceramic, graphite, graphite composite, and wood racquets. 800-323-5417; 412-323-9633 (in PA).

**Cannon Sports,** P.O. Box 11179, Burbank, CA 91510: Free list of retail sources ◆ Posts, nets, balls, ball retrievers, and other court equipment. 800-362-3146.

**Carron Net Company,** 1623 17th St., P.O. Box 177, Two Rivers, WI 54241: Free information ◆ Posts, nets, ball retrievers, practice machines, and other court equipment. 800-558-7768; 414-793-2217 (in WI). sales@carronnet.com

**Century Sports Inc.,** Lakewood Industrial Park, 1995 Rutgers University Blvd., Box 2035, Lakewood, NJ 08701: Free information ◆ Balls, nets, racquet covers, and racquets. 800-526-7548; 732-905-4422 (in NJ).

**Clarke Distributing Company,** 9233 Bryant St., Houston, TX 77075: Catalog $2 ◆ Tennis, golf, soccer equipment, novelties, and gifts. 800-777-3444.

**Croquet International Ltd.,** 7100 Fairway Dr., Palm Beach Gardens, FL 33418: Free catalog ◆ Croquet and tennis sets. 800-533-9061; 561-627-4009 (in FL).

**Dunlop-Slazenger,** 728 N. Pleasantburg Dr., Greenville, SC 29607: Free list of retail sources ◆ Tennis racquets. 864-241-2200. www.dunlopsports.com

**Easton,** 5040 W. Harold Gatty Dr., Salt Lake City, UT 84116: Free list of retail sources ◆ Aluminum, ceramic, graphite, and graphite composite tennis racquets. 801-539-1400.

**Ektelon,** Prince Sports Group, 1 Sportsystem Plaza, Bordentown, NJ 08505: Free information ◆ Tennis equipment. 800-283-2635. www.princetennis.com

**FEMCO Corp.,** 235 Arcadia St., Richmond, VA 23225: Free information ◆ Ball retrievers, nets, posts, practice machines, balls, and stringing supplies. 800-476-5432.

**Gamma Sports,** 200 Waterfront Dr., Pittsburgh, PA 15222: Free information ◆ Tennis racquets. 800-333-0337. www.gammasports.com

**Gared Sports Inc.,** 1107 Mullanphy St., St. Louis, MO 63106: Free information ◆ Tennis equipment. 800-325-2682.

**Goal Oriented Inc.,** 1200 Madison St., Box 592, Denver, CO 80206: Free brochure ◆ Easy-to-setup and take-down short-field tournament goals. 303-393-6040.

**Goal Sporting Goods Inc.,** 37 Industrial Park Rd., P.O. Box 236, Essex, CT 06426: Free catalog ◆ Telescoping, folding, and adjustable goals and nets. 800-334-GOAL. www.goalsports.com

**Golden Shine Inc.,** 4075 E. La Palma Ave., Ste. Q, Anaheim, CA 92807: Free information ◆ Portable easy-to-assemble tennis rebound net, ball machine, and court squeegee. 800-852-8525.

**Guterman International Inc.,** 71 Pullman St., Worcester, MA 01606: Free information ◆ Portable stringers. 800-343-6096; 508-852-8206 (in MA).

**Holabird Sports Discounters,** 9220 Pulaski Hwy., Baltimore, MD 21220: Free catalog ◆ Tennis racquets, shoes, clothes, balls, bags, and other sports equipment. 410-687-6400. www.holabirdsports.com

**Jayfro Corp.,** Unified Sports Inc., 976 Hartford Tnpk., P.O. Box 400, Waterford, CT 06385: Free catalog ◆ Tennis net posts, nets, windscreens, court dividers, and practice tennis standards. 860-447-3001.

**Charlie Johnson's Tennis & Squash Shop,** 2648 Erie Ave., Cincinnati, OH 45208: Free information ◆ Racquets, shoes, strings, and grips. 800-222-1143. cjtennis@cinti.net

**Klipper USA,** 780 Church Rd., Elgin, IL 60123: Free information ◆ Racquet stringer. 847-742-1300.

**Klipspringer USA Inc.,** 780 Church Rd., Elgin, IL 60123: Free brochure ◆ Stringing machines, hand tools, and strings. 800-522-5547; 708-742-1300 (in IL). www.klippersusa.com

**Las Vegas Discount Golf & Tennis,** 5325 S. Valley View Blvd., Ste. 10, Las Vegas, NV 89109: Free catalog ◆ Equipment, shoes, and clothing. 702-798-5500. www.lvgolf.com

**Leisure Marketing Inc.,** 2204 Morris Ave., Ste. 202, Union, NJ 07083: Free information ◆ Aluminum, boron composite, ceramic, graphite, and graphite composite tennis racquets. 908-851-9494.

**Leisure Pro,** 42 W. 18th St., 3rd Floor, New York, NY 10011: Catalog $5 ◆ Racquets, strings, grips, footwear, ball hoppers, and balls. Also backpacking and scuba equipment. 212-645-1234. www.leisure-pro.com

**Lob-Ster Inc.,** 1118 North Ave., Plainfield, NJ 07062: Free brochure ◆ Racquets, ball machines, balls, and other equipment. 800-526-4041; 908-668-1900 (in NJ).

**Markwort Sporting Goods,** 4300 Forest Park Ave., St. Louis, MO 63108: Catalog $8 (request list of retail sources) ◆ Balls, nets, racquet covers, and racquets. 800-669-6626; 314-652-3757 (in MO).

**Maxline,** 18002 Doty Ave., Torrance, CA 90504: Free brochure ◆ Racquet stringing machines. 310-523-4641.

**Memphis Net & Twine Company Inc.,** 2481 Matthews Ave., P.O. Box 80331, Memphis, TN 38108: Free catalog ◆ Cages and backstops, soccer nets, tennis windscreens, pitching machines, protector and miscellaneous nets for other sports, and sports accessories. 800-238-6380. memnet@netten.net

**Midwest Sports & Tennis Supply,** 8740 Montgomery Rd., Cincinnati, OH 45236: Free information ◆ Tennis racquets, shoes for men and women, tennis bags, strings, and court equipment. 800-334-4580.

**Neat Nets Inc.,** P.O. Box 0091, Youngwood, PA 15607: Free brochure ◆ Self-contained retractable net system. 800-257-5250.

**New Tech Tennis,** P.O. Box 201896, Austin, TX 78720: Free catalog ◆ Tennis ball and stringing machines. 800-577-1916; 512-250-8417 (in TX).

**NRC Sports,** 71 Pullman St., Worcester, MA 01606: Free information ◆ Portable stringers and natural gut, synthetic, and nylon strings. 800-243-5033; 508-853-0389 (in MA). guterman-intl@worldnet.att.net

**Olympia Sports,** P.O. Box 1941, Ann Arbor, MI 48106: Free information ◆ Nets, posts, and balls. 800-521-2832. www.wolverinesports.com

**Powers Court,** 40 S. Main St., New City, NY 10956: Free catalog ◆ Racquet stringers, strings, and other equipment. 800-431-2838; 914-634-6969 (in NY).

**Prince Racquet Sports,** 1 Sport Systems Plaza, Bordentown, NJ 08505: Free information ◆ Stringing machines, nylon and synthetic strings, and aluminum, boron composite, ceramic, graphite, graphite composite, and wood tennis racquets. 800-2-TENNIS; 609-291-5900 (in NJ).

**Pro-Kennex,** 9606 Kearny Villa Rd., San Diego, CA 92126: Free information ◆ Tennis racquets. 800-854-1908; 619-271-8390 (in CA).

**Professional Golf & Tennis Suppliers,** 7825 Hollywood Blvd., Pembroke Pines, FL 33024: Free catalog with long SASE ◆ Tennis racquets, clothing and shoes, and racquetball equipment. 305-981-7283.

**Radar Sales,** 5640 International Pkwy., Minneapolis, MN 55428: Free catalog ◆ Radar guns for use in tennis tournaments. 612-533-1100.

**RayCo Tennis,** P.O. Box 632832, San Diego, CA 92163: Free price list ◆ Strings, shoes, grips, and stringing machines. 800-TENNIS-6. www.tennisrays.com

**William Rigley's Tennis,** 25131 Marion Ave., Punta Gorda, FL 33950: Free price list ◆ Racquets, strings, bags, shoes, and accessories. 800-223-1540; 914-637-1487 (in FL). wwrigley@afcon.net

**Samuels Tennisport,** 7796 Montgomery Rd., Cincinnati, OH 45236: Free information ◆ Tennis, squash, and racquetball racquets, equipment, and shoes. 513-791-4636. www.nuteknet.com/roots

**Spalding Sports Worldwide,** 425 Meadow St., P.O. Box 901, Chicopee, MA 01021: Free information ◆ Tennis balls, composite tennis racquets, and nylon, synthetic, and gut strings. 800-225-6601. www.spalding.com

**Sport Casuals,** Box 812313, Boca Raton, FL 33481: Free information ◆ Boron composite, ceramic, graphite, and graphite composite tennis racquets. 800-776-7803; 561-997-7723 (in FL).

**Sportline of Hilton Head Ltd.,** Heritage Plaza, Pope Ave., Hilton Head, SC 29928: Free information ◆ Tennis racquets, shoes, bags, and clothing. 888-996-8855. www.hiltonhead9.com/sportline

**Sports Express,** 5050 F.M. West, Houston, TX 77069: Free information ◆ Tennis racquets, court equipment, grips and wraps, shoes, bags, and clothing. 800-533-6321.

**Sports Tutor,** 2612 W. Burbank Blvd., Burbank, CA 91505: Free brochure ◆ Portable tennis ball machine. 800-448-8867. www.sportstutor.com

**Sullivan Sports,** P.O. Box 680505, Houston, TX 77268: Free information ◆ Tennis racquets and bags, court and training equipment, strings, grips and wraps, shoes, and clothing for men and women. 800-543-0926.

**Total Sports,** 200 Waterfront Dr., Pittsburgh, PA 15222: Free catalog ◆ Tennis racquet strings, clothing, bags, and court supplies. 800-866-7071.

**Wa-Mac Inc.,** 178 Commerce Rd., P.O. Box 128, Carlstadt, NJ 07072: Free information ◆ Tennis balls and aluminum, boron composite, ceramic, graphite, graphite composite, and wood tennis racquets. 800-447-5673; 201-438-7200 (in NJ).

**Wilson Sporting Goods,** 8700 W. Bryn Mawr, Chicago, IL 60631: Free information ◆ Stringing machines and strings, balls, nets, and aluminum, boron composite, ceramic, graphite, graphite composite, and wood tennis racquets. 800-946-6060; 773-714-6400 (in IL). www.wilsonsports.com

**Yamaha Sporting Goods,** 6600 Orangethorpe Ave., Buena Park, CA 90620: Free list of retail sources ◆ Strings and boron composite, ceramic, graphite, and graphite composite tennis racquets. 800-851-6514; 714-522-9011 (in CA). www.yamaha-motor.com

**Yonex Corp.,** 3520 Challenger St., Torrance, CA 90503: Free list of retail sources ◆ Tennis racquets. 800-44-YONEX.

**Zebest Racquet & Golf Sports,** 12790 Hopewell Rd., Alpharetta, GA 30201: Free information ◆ Balls, racquet covers, and racquets. 800-272-7279.

## TERM PAPERS

**Academic Research Inc.,** 240 Park Ave., Rutherford, NJ 02070: Free catalog ◆ Over 20,000 reports and term papers. 201-939-0252.

**Research Assistance,** 11322 Idaho Ave., Los Angeles, CA 90025: Catalog $2 ◆ Over 10,000 term papers. 800-351-0222.

## TETHERBALL

**American Playground Corp.,** 1801 S. Jackson, P.O. Box 2599, Anderson, IN 46011: Free information ◆ Balls, poles, and posts. 800-541-1602.

**Franklin Sports Industries Inc.,** 17 Campanelli Parkway, P.O. Box 508, Stoughton, MA 02072: Free information ◆ Balls and sets. 800-426-7700. www.eisnerbros.com

**General Sportcraft Company,** 140 Woodbine Rd., Bergenfield, NJ 07621: Free information ◆ Balls, poles, posts, and sets. 201-384-4242.

**Indian Industries Inc.,** P.O. Box 889, Evansville, IN 47706: Free catalog ◆ Sets. 800-457-3373; 812-467-1200 (in IN).

**Dick Martin Sports Inc.,** 181 E. Union Ave., P.O. Box 7384, East Rutherford, NJ 07073: Free information ◆ Balls, poles, posts, and sets. 800-221-1993; 201-438-5255 (in NJ).

**Venus Knitting Mills Inc.,** 140 Spring St., Murray Hill, NJ 07974: Free information ◆ Balls, paddles, poles, posts, and sets. 800-955-4200; 908-464-2400 (in NJ).

## THEATRICAL SUPPLIES

### Make-Up

**Abracadabra Magic Shop,** 125 Lincoln Blvd., Middlesex, NJ 08846: Catalog $5 ◆ Costumes, theatrical make-up, and supplies for magicians and clowns. 732-805-0200. umsi@erols.com

**Apples & Company,** 414 Conant Ave., Union, NJ 07083: Free information ◆ Clown-white make-up. 908-353-2193.

**Burpo the Clown,** P.O. Box 299, McMinnville, OR 97128: Free information ◆ Face-painting rubber stamps and supplies. 503-434-1243.

**Cheri-Oats & Company,** P.O. Box 367, Destrahan, LA 70047: Free information ◆ Wigs, stickers, puppets, and face painting supplies. 504-764-0080. www.mooseburger.com/cheri.htm

**Clown Heaven,** 4792 Old State Rd. 37 South, Martinsville, IN 46152: Catalog $3 ◆ Balloons, make-up, puppets, wigs, ministry and gospel items, novelties, magic, clown props, and books. 317-342-6888.

**Costumes by Betty,** 2181 Edgerton St., St. Paul, MN 55117: Catalog $5 (refundable) ◆ Clown costumes, make-up, wigs, and shoes. 612-771-8734. www.clowncostumes.com

**Steve Dawson's Magic Touch Catalog,** 144 N. Milpitas Blvd., Milpitas, CA 95035: Catalog $3 ◆ Magic effects, books, videos, accessories, clown and juggling supplies, and make-up. 408-263-9404.

**Eastern Costume Company,** 510 N. Elm St., Greensboro, NC 27401: Free information ◆ Make-up and theatrical and masquerade costumes. 800-968-8461; 336-379-1026 (in NC).

**Freckles Clown Supplies,** 5509 Roosevelt Blvd., Jacksonville, FL 32244: Catalog $6 ◆ Make-up, costumes, clown supplies, puppets, how-to books on clowning and ballooning, and theatrical supplies. 904-388-5541. www.freckles1.com/index.html

**Graftobian Ltd.,** 510 Tasman St., Madison, WI 53714: Free information ◆ Face-painting supplies. 800-255-0584.

**Bob Kelly Cosmetics Inc.,** 151 W. 46th St., New York, NY 10036: Free catalog ◆ Theatrical make-up kits and instructional videos. 212-819-0030. www.bobkellywigsschool.com

**Lynch's Clown Supplies,** 939 Howard, Dearborn, MI 48124: Catalog $5 ◆ Make-up, costume accessories, and clown equipment. 800-24-LYNCH. www.lynchs.com

**Magic & Fun Shop,** 16872 Hwy. 3, Webster, TX 77598: Free catalog ◆ Jokes, gags, novelties, clown supplies, make-up, magic tricks, and puzzles. 281-332-8142. www.fun-shop.com

**Mecca Magic Inc.,** 49 Dodd St., Bloomfield, NJ 07003: Catalog $10 ◆ Make-up, costumes and wigs, puppets, clown props, magic tricks, and juggling equipment. 201-429-7597. meccamagic@meccamagic.com

**T. Myers Magic Inc.,** 6513 Thomas Springs Rd., Austin, TX 78736: Free catalog ◆ Magic and other supplies for balloon twisters, face paints, clowns, and magicians. 800-288-7925; 512-288-7925 (in TX). www.tmyers.com

**Novelties Unlimited,** 410 W. 21st St., Norfolk, VA 23517: Catalog $5 ◆ Make-up, clown props and gags, magic, balloons, and party decorations. 757-622-0344.

**Ben Nye Makeup,** 5935 Bowcroft St., Los Angeles, CA 90016: Catalog $2.50 ◆ Theatrical make-up. 310-839-1984.

**Potsy & Blimpo Clown Supplies,** P.O. Box 2075, Huntington Beach, CA 92647: Free catalog ◆ Clown make-up, wigs, and props. 800-897-0749; 714-897-0749 (in CA). potsyblimpo@earthlink.net

**Ronjo's Magic & Costumes Inc.,** 4600 Nesconset Hwy., Unit 4, Port Jefferson Station, NY 11776: Catalog $9.95 (receive $25 in coupons) ◆ Magic for amateur and professional magicians, costumes, make-up, and theatrical effects. 516-928-5005. www.conjo.com

**Rubie's Costume Company**, National Sales Office, 999 Gould St., New Hyde Park, NY 11040: Free information ◆ Costumes, make-up, hair goods, and special effects. 516-326-1500.

**Theatrical Light Systems Inc.,** P.O. Box 2646, Huntsville, AL 35804: Free information ◆ Make-up, dimming and lighting control systems, follow spots, and stage equipment. 256-533-7025.

**Tracy Theatre Originals,** 70 High St., Hampton, NH 03842: Free information ◆ Theatrical costumes, props, and make-up. 800-926-8351; 603-926-8315 (in NH). Crfts4stge@aol.com

**Under the Big Top,** P.O. Box 807, Placentia, CA 92670: Catalog $4 ◆ Costumes, clown props, make-up, juggling equipment, and party supplies. 800-995-7727.

**Up, Up & Away,** P.O. Box 159, Beallsville, PA 15313: Catalog $3 ◆ Make-up, props, and clown equipment. 412-769-5447. peacheyk@usaor.net

### Plays

**Samuel French Catalog,** 45 W. 25th St., New York, NY 10010: Catalog $4.50 ◆ Scripts for plays and theatrical productions. 212-206-8990. www.samuelfrench.com

**Samuel French Trade,** 7623 Sunset Blvd., Hollywood, CA 90046: Free catalog ◆ Over 2500 plays. Includes classics made into movies. 213-876-0570. www.samuelfrench.com

## Stage Equipment & Props

**Alcone Company Inc.,** Paramount Theatrical Supplies, 5-49 49th Ave., Long Island City, NY 11101: Catalog $5 ◆ Fabrics, make-up, hardware and rigging, lighting and theatrical equipment, paint, and scenery supplies. 718-361-8373.

**Altman Stage Lighting Company,** 57 Alexander St., Yonkers, NY 10701: Free list of retail sources ◆ Stage lighting equipment. 800-425-8626; 914-476-7987 (in NY). www.altmanltg.com

**Bash Theatrical Lighting Inc.,** 3401 Dell Ave., North Bergen, NJ 07047: Free catalog ◆ New and used lighting, other stage equipment, and accessories. 201-863-3300.

**BMI Supply,** 571 Queensbury Ave., Queensbury, NY 12804: Free information ◆ Theatrical supplies, equipment, and special effects. 800-836-0524. www.bmisupply.com

**Bulbman,** P.O. Box 12280, Reno, NV 89510: Free information ◆ Replacement bulbs for theatrical lighting equipment. 800-648-1163.

**Cinemills Corp.,** 3500 W. Magnolia Blvd., Burbank, CA 91505: Free catalog ◆ Motion picture and television lighting and color filters. 800-325-7674; 800-692-6700 (in CA).

**City Theatrical Inc.,** 752 E. 133rd St., Bronx, NY 10454: Free information ◆ Lighting accessories, fog producer, and more. 800-230-9497.

**Dudley Theatrical,** P.O. Box 519, Walkertown, NC 27051: Free information ◆ Custom drapery, stage fabrics and drops, lighting and dimming systems, scenic paint, foggers, make-up, and more. 336-722-3255.

**Farralane Pro Lighting, Audio & Video Inc.,** 300 Rt. 109, Farmingdale, NY 11735: Catalog $3 ◆ Professional lighting equipment, audio and video systems, and accessories. 800-433-7057; 516-752-9824 (in NY). www.farralane.com

**Florida Magic Company,** P.O. Box 290781, Fort Lauderdale, FL 33329: Free information ◆ Portable AC or battery-operated public address system. 954-473-1902. FlaMagicCo@aol.com

**Gam Products Inc.,** 826 N. Cole Ave., Hollywood, CA 90038: Free catalog ◆ Special effects lighting equipment, 323-461-0200. www.gamonline.com

**Golden Age Productions,** 3130 Castle Cove Ct., Kissimmee, FL 34746: Free information ◆ Hard-to-find props and costume accessories. 800-671-4867.

**Gothic Scenic & Theatrical Paints,** Long Island Paint Company, Box 189, Continental Hill, Glen Cove, NY 11542: Free information ◆ Scenic and theatrical paints. 516-676-6600.

**The Great American Market,** 826 N. Cole Ave., Hollywood, CA 90038: Free catalog ◆ Theatrical stage equipment and supplies. 213-461-0200.

**Jupiter Scenic Inc.,** 603 Commerce Way West, Jupiter, FL 33458: Free information ◆ Scenery drapes and lighting equipment. 561-743-7367.

**Kee Industrial Products Inc.,** 100 Stradtman St., Buffalo, NY 14206: Free information ◆ Hardware for stage platforms, multi-level sets, and backgrounds. 716-896-4949.

**Magic Makers Costumes Inc.,** 940 4th Ave., Ste. 360, Huntington, WV 25701: Free catalog ◆ Costumes, accessories, theatrical props, and special stage effects. 800-233-5810. www.magicmakers.com

**MDG Stage Equipment,** 5639 Christie-Colomb, Montreal, Quebec, Canada H2S 2E8: Free information ◆ Fog generators. 800-663-3020.

**Melco Sound & Services Inc.,** 1400 Wantagh Ave., Wantagh, NY 11793: Free information ◆ Theatrical sound effects on CDs, tapes, and mini-discs. 516-785-6413. melco@juno.com

**Metropolitan Artifacts Inc.,** 4783 Peachtree Rd., Atlanta, GA 30341: Free brochure ◆ Architectural decor and antiques for residential, commercial, and theatrical settings. 770-986-0007.

**Olesen,** Division Entertainment Resources Inc., 1535 Ivar Ave., Hollywood, CA 90028: Free information ◆ Lighting and production supplies. 800-821-1656.

**Peavey Electronics Corp.,** 711 A St., P.O. Box 2898, Meridian, MS 39302: Free information ◆ Lighting equipment. 601-483-5365.

**Pro Sound & Stage Lighting,** Catalog Center, 11711 Monarch St., Garden Grove, CA 92841: Free catalog ◆ Stage, sound, lighting, and video systems. 800-945-9300.

**Production Arts Lighting,** 636 11th Ave., New York, NY 10036: Free catalog ◆ Lighting equipment and controls. 212-489-0312. www.prodart.com

**Rose Brand Fabrics,** 517 W. 35th St., New York, NY 10001: Free catalog ◆ Theatrical fabrics. 800-223-1624; 212-594-7424 (in NY). www.rosebrand.com

**Sitler's Supplies Inc.,** 702 E. Washington, P.O. Box 10, Washington, IA 52353: Free information ◆ Stage, studio, and projector lamps. 800-426-3938.

**The Source Shop,** 18 Mowat Ave., Ste. 103F, Toronto, Ontario, Canada M6K 3E8: Free catalog ◆ Lighting and grip equipment, accessories, and more. 416-588-6712. www.sourceshop.com

**Stage Equipment & Lighting Inc.,** 12231 NE 13th Ct., Miami, FL 33161: Free catalog ◆ Lighting, controls, special effects equipment, and accessories. 305-891-2010.

**StageRight Corp.,** 495 Holley Dr., Clare, MI 48617: Free information ◆ Portable units and extensions for stage assemblies. 800-438-4499.

**Charles H. Stewart & Company,** P.O. Box 187, Somerville, MA 02144: Free information ◆ Scenery backdrops, curtains, scrims, and stage equipment. 617-625-2407.

**Syracuse Scenery & Stage Lighting Company Inc.,** 101 Monarch Dr., Liverpool, NY 13088: Free information ◆ Curtains and other stage fabrics. 800-453-SSSL; 315-453-8096 (in NY). SSSLsales@aol.com

**Theatrical Light Systems Inc.,** P.O. Box 2646, Huntsville, AL 35804: Free information ◆ Dimming and lighting control systems, follow spots, other lighting equipment, and make-up. 256-533-7025.

**Tobins Lake Studios,** 7030 Old US 23, Brighton, MI 48116: Free catalog ◆ Drapes, drops, lighting equipment, and scenery paint. 810-229-6666.

**Tools for Stagecraft,** 713 Quail View Ct., Agoura, CA 91301: Free catalog ◆ Tools and accessories for the theatrical professional. 818-707-2656.

**Tower Lighting Inc.,** 179 Swansea Mall Dr., Swansea, MA 02777: Free catalog ◆ Entertainment lighting equipment. 800-558-6937.

**Tracy Theatre Originals,** 70 High St., Hampton, NH 03842: Free information ◆ Theatrical costumes, props, and make-up. 800-926-8351; 603-926-8315 (in NH). Crfts4stge@aol.com

**Tri-Ess Sciences Inc.,** 1020 W. Chestnut St., Burbank, CA 91506: Catalog $3 ◆ Special effects equipment. 800-274-6910.

**Westgate Enterprises,** 2110 Wilshire Blvd., Santa Monica, CA 90403: Free catalog ◆ Full spectrum color-corrected light bulbs, flood and spot lights, and tubes. 310-477-5891.

# THERMOMETERS

**Abbeon Cal Inc.,** 123 Gray Ave., Santa Barbara, CA 93101: Free catalog ◆ Thermometers, hygrometers, moisture meters, and humidity indicators. 800-922-0977. www.abbeon.com

**Brookstone Company,** Order Processing Center, 1655 Bassford Dr., Mexico, MO 65265: Free catalog ◆ Indoor and outdoor thermometers and other household goods. 800-926-7000.

**Chef's Catalog,** P.O. Box 620048, Dallas, TX 75262: Free catalog ◆ Instant-reading cooking thermometers. 800-338-3232. www.chefscatalog.com

**Polder Thermometers,** 8 Slater St., Port Chester, NY 10573: Free information ◆ Instant-reading cooking thermometers. 914-937-8200.

**Taylor Thermometers,** P.O. Box 1349, Fletcher, NC 28732: Free information ◆ Instant-reading cooking thermometers. 704-684-5178.

**Williams-Sonoma,** Mail Order Dept., P.O. Box 7456, San Francisco, CA 94120: Free catalog ◆ Instant-reading cooking thermometers. 800-541-1262.

## THIMBLES

**Gimbel & Sons Country Store,** 14/16 Commercial St., P.O. Box 57, Boothbay Harbor, ME 04538: Free catalog ◆ Thimbles, collectible crafted porcelains and miniatures, and other gifts. 207-633-5088.

## TICKETS

**Carter Printing,** Box 289, Farmersville, IL 62533: Free information ◆ Raffle tickets. 217-227-4464.

**LMN Printing,** 118 N. Ridgewood Ave., Edgewater, FL 32132: Free price list ◆ Raffle books, tickets, and coupon books. 800-741-5668. www.lmn-printing.com

**Quick Tickets,** 3030 W. Pasadena, Flint, MI 48504: Free information ◆ Tickets. 800-521-1142; 810-732-0770 (in MI).

**Ticket Craft,** 1925 Bellmore Ave., Bellmore, NY 11710: Free catalog ◆ Theater tickets. 800-645-4944; 516-826-1500 (in NY).

## TICKETS (BOX OFFICE MANAGEMENT)

**Center Stage Software,** 1191 Luxton St., Seaside, CA 03955: Free information ◆ Ticket-management software for DOS, Windows 95, and Windows NT. 408-583-0641. www.centerstage.com

**Foothills Software,** 1309 Greenvale Circle, Upland, CA 91784: Free information ◆ IBM-compatible management software for ticketing, reservations, revenue reporting, mailing labels, customer list preparation, and more. 909-946-6956. www.webshingles.com/foothills

**New Concepts Software Inc.,** P.O. Box 357, Roseville, MI 48066: Free information ◆ Computerized box office management system for Windows 95. 810-776-2855. www.ncsoftware.com

**TicketStop Inc.,** 14042 NE 8th St., Ste. 108, Bellevue, WA 98007: Free information ◆ Ticketing and box office management software. 800-961-8111. www.ticketstop.com

## TIMERS

**FarmTek Inc.,** 5113 Heritage Ave., Sachse, TX 75048: Free information ◆ Electronic timing equipment. 800-755-6529.

**U.S. Chess Federation,** 3054 NYS Rt. 9W, New Windsor, NY 12553: Free catalog ◆ Conventional and computer chess sets, books, timers, and competition supplies. 800-388-KING. www.uschess.org

## TOBACCO, PIPES, & CIGARS

### Cigarette Lighters

**The Zippo Store,** 28691 Plymouth Rd., Livonia, MI 48150: Free catalog ◆ Zippo lighters and accessories. 313-762-4895.

### Tobacco, Pipes, & Cigars

**Ale In The Mail,** 121-22 Dupont St., Plainview, NY 11803: Free brochure ◆ Cigars, humidors, and cigar accessories. Also imported and domestic beers and barbecue sauces. 800-708-0024.

**Don Collins Cigars,** P.O. Box 40715, San Juan, PR 00940: Free information ◆ Select cigars. 787-724-0545. www.don-collins.com

**Cornell & Diehl Tobaccos,** P.O. Box 475, Morganton, NC 28680: Free brochure ◆ Over 200 blends of pipe tobacco. 800-433-0080.

**Corona Cigar Company,** 6150 Silver Star Rd., Orlando, FL 32808: Free catalog ◆ Fine cigars, humidors, and accessories. 888-70-CIGARR; 407-522-0006 (in FL). www.coronacigar.com

**Davidoff of Geneva Inc.,** 550 West Ave., Stamford, CT 06902: Free catalog ◆ Cigars and tobacco products. 800-328-4365.

**Famous Smoke Shop Inc.,** 55 W. 39th St., New York, NY 10018: Free catalog ◆ Pipe tobaccos and premium hand-rolled and generic cigars. 800-672-5544.

**Georgetown Tobacco,** 3144 M St. NW, Washington, DC 20007: Catalog $2 ◆ Private tobacco mixtures, pipes, imported and domestic cigars, lighters, and gifts. 800-345-1459. www.gttobacco.com

**Green Mountain Unlimited,** 1463 Graham Farm Circle, Severn, MD 21144: Free brochure ◆ Humidors and Mayorga and La Cosecha cigars. 410-519-7630. www.gmountain.com

**Hiland's Trading Company,** 6917 E. Thomas Rd., Scottsdale, AZ 85251: Free catalog ◆ Premium cigars, pipe tobacco, pipes, and accessories. 800-777-4854.

**Holt's Cigar Company,** 1522 Walnut St., Philadelphia, PA 19102: Free information ◆ Premium cigars. 800-523-1641; 215-732-8500 (in PA).

**J-R Tobacco,** 301 Rt. 10, Whippany, NJ 07981: Free catalog ◆ Imported cigars and pipe tobaccos. 800-JRC-IGAR.

**Las Vegas Cigar Company,** 3755 S. Las Vegas Blvd., Las Vegas, NV 89109: Free brochure ◆ Cigars made with imported tobacco grown using Cuban seed. Available in sampler assortments or boxes of 25 cigars. 800-432-4277.

**Mike's Cigars Inc.,** 1030 Kane Concourse, Bay Harbor, FL 33154: Free information ◆ Premium cigars. 800-962-4427.

**Mom's Cigars,** 172 5th Ave., New York, NY 10010: Free catalog ◆ Handmade long filler imported and domestic premium cigars. 800-831-8893. www.momscigars.com

**My Humidor,** 104 Keyland Ct., Bohemia, NY 11716: Free brochure ◆ Cigar humidors. 888-694-8643; 516-567-3016 (in NY).

**Old Chicago Smoke Shop,** Mail Order Division, 3300 W. Devon, Lincolnwood, IL 60659: Free catalog ◆ Premium cigars and humidors. 800-621-1453.

**Olde World Fine Clays,** 249 South St., Glace Bay, Nova Scotia, Canada B1A 1W6: Free brochure ◆ Hand-rolled clay pipes formed in a solid press mold and burnished with agate. 902-849-1383.

**Iwan Ries & Company,** 19 S. Wabash, 2nd Floor, Chicago, IL 60603: Free catalog ◆ Imported pipes, cigars and tobacco, and accessories. 312-372-1306.

**Nat Sherman Company,** 500 5th Ave., New York, NY 10110: Free catalog ◆ Cigars, pipes, domestic and imported cigarettes, tobaccos, and gifts. 800-MY-CIGAR. www.natsherman.com

**Fred Stoker & Sons Inc.,** P.O. Box 707, Dresden, TN 38225: Catalog $1 ◆ Supplies for smokers, chewing tobaccos, and gifts. 800-243-9377.

**Thompson Cigar Company,** P.O. Box 31274, Tampa, FL 33633: Free catalog ◆ Domestic and imported cigars and smoking accessories. 800-435-0467. www.thompsoncigar.com

## TOLE & DECORATIVE PAINTING

**The Artist's Club,** P.O. Box 8930, Vancouver, WA 98668: Free information ◆ Books and supplies for decorative painters. 800-257-1077.

**Bridgewater Scrollworks,** P.O. Box 585, Osage, MN 56570: Catalog $5 (refundable) ◆ Wood cutouts for tole decoration and crafts. 218-573-3094.

**Stan Brown's Arts & Crafts Inc.,** 13435 NE Whitaker Way, Portland, OR 97230: Catalog $3.50 ◆ Tole and decorative painting supplies. 800-547-5531; 503-257-0559 (in OR). sbrown4207@aol.com

**Cabin Craft Southwest,** 1500 Westpack Way, Euless, TX 76040: Catalog $4 ◆ Tole and decorative painting supplies. Also other craft materials. 800-877-1515. www.flash.net/~cabin

**Cabin Crafters,** 1225 W. 1st St., Nevada, IA 50201: Catalog $4 ◆ Tole and decorative painting supplies. 800-669-3920; 515-382-5406 (in IA).

**Char-Lee Originals,** P.O. Box 606, Somonauk, IL 60552: Catalog $5 ◆ Unpainted resin figures and other ready-to-finish items. 800-242-7533. cloway@prairienet.com

**Chatham Art Distributors,** P.O. Box 3851, Frederick, MD 21705: Free information ◆ Acrylics, brushes, canvasses, oils, milk paint, tin supplies, books, and wood items for decorating. 800-822-4747.

**Chroma Acrylics Inc.,** 205 Bucky Dr., Lititz, PA 17543: Free information ◆ Acrylic polymer emulsion-based gesso for fine, decorative, and wildfowl art. 800-257-8278; 717-626-8866 (in PA). info@chroma-inc.com

**Cridge Inc.,** Box 210, Morrisville, PA 19067: Catalog $2 ◆ Glazed porcelain pieces and ready-to-be-decorated bisque. 215-295-3667.

**Cupboard Distributing,** P.O. Box 148, Urbana, OH 43078: Catalog $2 ◆ Unfinished wood parts for tole and decorative painting, crafts, miniatures, toys, jewelry-making, and woodworking. 937-652-3338. cupboard@foryou.net

**DecoArt,** P.O. Box 370, Stanford, KY 40484: Free list of retail sources ◆ Decorative paints. 606-365-3193. www.decoart.com

**Finishing Touches Crafts,** 5673 E. Shields Ave., Fresno, CA 93727: Free information ◆ Paint products and how-to information for transforming ordinary objects of plaster, wood, paper mache, and metal into works of art. 800-4-DUNCAN.

**Hofcraft,** P.O. Box 72, Grand Haven, MI 49416: Catalog $4 ◆ How-to books and supplies for tole and decorative painting. 800-828-0359. www.hofcraft.com

**Hollins Enterprises Inc.,** P.O. Box 148, Alpha, OH 45301: Catalog $1 ◆ Tole and decorative painting supplies. 937-426-3503.

**Homespun's Woodshed,** P.O. Box 63, Dwight, IL 60420: Free catalog ◆ Custom wood items, cutouts, and other wood surfaces for painting. 800-873-3398; 815-584-2461 (in IL). members.tripod.com/~Homespunwood/index.html

**J.W. etc.,** 2205 1st St., Simi Valley, CA 93065: Free information ◆ Varnish, wood sealer and filler, stains, brush cleanser, and other supplies. 805-526-5066.

**Janovic/Plaza Inc.,** 30-35 Thomson Ave., Long Island City, NY 11101: Catalog $4.95 ◆ Supplies and accessories for art, tole and decorative painting, and other crafts. 800-772-4381. www.janovic.com

**Jo Sonja's Folk Art,** 2136 3rd St., P.O. Box 9080, Eureka, CA 95501: Free brochure ◆ Decorative painting supplies and projects. 888-567-6652.

**Johnson Paint Company Inc.,** 355 Newbury St., Boston, MA 02115: Catalog $1 ◆ Hard-to-find painting supplies, brushes, and tools. 617-536-4838.

**Kerry Specialties,** P.O. Drawer 999, DeLand, FL 32721: Free information ◆ Brushes for tole and decorative painting. 888-738-0029.

**Larson Wood Manufacturing,** P.O. Box 672, Park Rapids, MN 56407: Catalog $2 (refundable) ◆ Country-style mini cutouts, kits and parts, hardware, and supplies. 218-732-9121.

**Perfect Palette,** 5910 N. Lilly Rd., Menenomee Falls, WI 53051: Catalog $1 ◆ Decorative painting and other arts and crafts videos for all skill levels. 800-839-0306.

**Plaid Enterprises,** P.O. Box 7600, Norcross, GA 30091: Free information ◆ Acrylic paints and supplies. 770-923-8200.

**Positively Country,** Fred & Mary O'Neil, W190s7416 Bay Shore Dr., Muskego, WI 53150: Catalog $2 ◆ Unfinished wood items, paints, brushes, and other supplies. 414-679-1573.

**S & G Erectors,** P.O. Box 805, Howell, MI 48844: Free information ◆ Pre-primed ready-to-paint metal wind chimes. 517-546-9240.

**Sandeen's,** 1315 White Bear Ave., St. Paul, MN 55106: Catalog $2 (refundable) ◆ Supplies for folk art crafting, rosemaling, dalmalning, and bauernmalere. Also (separate catalogs, $3 each) supplies for Norwegian stitchery, Danish cross-stitching, and Swedish stitchery. 800-235-1315.

**Sharon & Gayle Publications,** 133 W. 10th St., Covington, KY 41011: Catalog $2 (refundable) ◆ How-to books on decorative art and tole painting. Also pattern packets. 606-291-0784.

**Stone Bridge Collection,** RR 4, Pakenham, Ontario, Canada K0A 2X0: Catalog $3 ◆ Tole and decorative painting supplies. 613-624-5080.

**Sunshine Discount Crafts,** 12335 62nd St. North, Largo, FL 33773: Free catalog ◆ Modeling clays and accessories, art supplies, beads, tole and decorative painting supplies, and more. 800-720-2878. www.sunshinecrafts.com

**Tara Materials Inc.,** P.O. Box 646, Lawrenceville, GA 30246: Free information ◆ Plates for tole art decorating. 770-963-5256.

**Traditional Norwegian Rosemaking,** Pat Virch, 1506 Lynn Ave., Marquette, MI 49855: Catalog $2 ◆ Patterns, books, paints, woodenware, tinware, and supplies for wood and tin decorating. 906-226-3931.

**Vesterheim Sales Shop,** Vesterheim Norwegian-American Museum, 502 W. Water St., Decorah, IA 52101: Free catalog ◆ Books and pattern packets, woodenware, brushes, paints, paper, and supplies. 319-382-9682.

**Viking Woodcrafts Inc.,** 1317 8th St. SE, Waseca, MN 56093: Catalog $10 (refundable) ◆ Ready-to-finish craft items, resin figures, and books. 507-835-8043.

**Western Woodworks,** 1142 Olive Branch Ln., San Jose, CA 95120: Free catalog ◆ Wood surfaces for decorative finishing. 408-997-2356. www.craftnet.org/westwood

**Weston Bowl Mill,** P.O. Box 218, Weston, VT 05161: Catalog $1 ◆ Woodenware for tole and decorative painting. 800-824-6219.

**Wood Cut-Outs Unlimited,** Box 518, Massillon, OH 44648: Catalog $2 (refundable) ◆ Wood items for decorative painting.

**Zims Inc.,** 4370 S. 300 West, Salt Lake City, UT 84107: Catalog $10 (refundable) ◆ Craft and painting supplies. 801-268-9859.

# TOOLS

## Clamps

**Addkison Hardware Company Inc.,** 126 E. Amite St., P.O. Box 102, Jackson, MS 39205: Free information ◆ Power tools and clamps. 800-821-2750. www.addkison.com

**Adjustable Clamp Company,** 417 N. Ashland Ave., Chicago, IL 60622: Catalog $1 ◆ Clamps and work-holding equipment. 312-666-0640.

**Advanced Machinery Imports,** P.O. Box 312, New Castle, DE 19720: Free information ◆ Workshop clamps. 800-220-4264; 302-322-2226 (in DE). woodtech@magpage.com

**American Clamping Corp.,** P.O. Box 399, Batavia, NY 14021: Free information ◆ Woodworking clamps. 800-928-1004.

**Colt Clamp Company Inc.,** 33 Swan St., Batavia, NY 14020: Free catalog ◆ C and bar clamps in screw and eccentric styles. 800-536-8420; 716-343-8622 (in NY).

**Gross Stabil Corp.,** P.O. Box 368, Coldwater, MI 49036: Free list of retail sources ◆ Woodworking clamps. 800-671-0838; 517-279-8040 (in MI).

**Inlet Inc.,** 412 Redhill Ave., Ste. 8, San Anselmo, CA 94960: Free information ◆ Clamps for most workshop needs. 800-786-5665.

**Universal Clamp Corp.,** 15200 Stagg St., Van Nuys, CA 91405: Free information ◆ Lightweight clamps. 818-780-1015.

**Wade Manufacturing Company,** P.O. Box 23666, Portland, OR 97218: Free information ◆ Clamps for woodworking projects. 503-692-5353.

**Wetzler Clamp,** Rt. 611, P.O. Box 175, Mt. Bethel, PA 18343: Free information ◆ Woodworking clamps. 800-451-1852. www.wetzler.com

## Hand & Power Tools

**A & I Supply,** 401 Radio City Dr., North Pekin, IL 61554: Free catalog ◆ Woodworking tools and accessories. 800-260-2647.

**Abbey Tools,** 1173 East St., Anaheim, CA 92805: Free information ◆ Power tools. 800-225-6321.

**Abest Woodworking Machinery,** Division Rudolph Bass Inc., 45 Halliday St., Jersey City, NJ 07304: Free information ◆ Dust collection systems for workshops. 201-433-3800.

**Acme Electric Tools,** P.O. Box 14040, Grand Forks, ND 58208: Catalog $3 ◆ Power tools. 800-358-3096. www.toolcribofthenorth.com

**Addkison Hardware Company Inc.,** 126 E. Amite St., P.O. Box 102, Jackson, MS 39205: Free information ◆ Power tools and clamps. 800-821-2750.

**Airy Sales Corp.,** 1425 S. Allec St., Anaheim, CA 92805: Free list of retail sources ◆ Nailing and stapling tools. 310-926-6192.

**William Alden Woodworking Company,** P.O. Box 4005, Taunton, MA 02780: Free catalog ◆ Power tools and accessories. 800-249-8665. www.williamwalden.com

**Alley Supply Company,** P.O. Box 848, Gardnerville, NV 89410: Catalog $2 ◆ Precision lathes, milling machines, cutter grinders, and other metal-working tools. 702-782-3800.

**American International Tool Industries,** 1116 Park Ave., Cranston, RI 02910: Free information ◆ Paint removal and sanding tools. 800-932-5872; 401-942-7855 (in RI).

**American Machine & Tool Company,** 400 Spring St., P.O. Box 70, Royersford, PA 19468: Free catalog ◆ Woodworking power tools. 800-435-8665.

**Johnson Atelier,** 50 Princeton-Hightstown Rd., Ste. L, Princeton Junction, NJ 08550: Free catalog ◆ Sculpture and casting supplies. Also carving tools for wood and stone. 800-732-7203. jasacs@aol.com

**Bailey's,** P.O. Box 550, Laytonville, CA 95454: Free catalog ◆ Chain saws, bars, files, protective gear, forestry supplies, log splitters, books, other woodsman supplies, and gifts. 707-984-6133. www.bbaileys.com/bbaileys/west.htm

**Berland's House of Tools,** 20254 N. Rand Rd., Palatine, IL 60074: Free catalog ◆ Over 23,000 tools for the trades, hobbyist, and homeowner. 708-627-9090. www.thetoolman.com

**Bethel Mills Lumber Inc.,** N. Main St., Bethel, VT 05032: Free information ◆ Building supplies and tools. 800-234-9951. www.bethelmills.com

**Bishop Cochran,** 4326 SE Woodstock, Portland, OR 97206: Free information ◆ Holding base for Dremel Multi-Pro tool. bishopcochran@IBM.net

**Blue Ridge Machinery & Tools Inc.,** P.O. Box 536, Hurricane, WV 25526: Catalog $1 ◆ Lathes, milling machines, and supplies. 800-872-6500. www.blueridgemachinery.com

**Blume Supply Inc.,** 3316 South Blvd., Charlotte, NC 28209: Free information ◆ Woodworking power tools. 800-288-9200; 704-523-7811 (in NC).

**Bradbury Industries,** 238 Gainsborough Rd., Toronto, Ontario, Canada M4L 3C7: Free information ◆ Tilt-and-lock panel cutting and routing table system. 800-668-1757.

**BrandMark,** 462 Carthage Dr., Beavercreek, OH 45434: Free information ◆ Electric branding irons. 800-323-2570.

**Bridge City Tool Works,** 1104 NE 28th Ave., Portland, OR 97232: Catalog $2 ◆ Precision layout hand tools for avocational woodworking. 800-253-3332. www.bridgecitytools.com

**Brookstone Company,** Order Processing Center, 1655 Bassford Dr., Mexico, MO 65265: Free catalog ◆ Hand tools. 800-926-7000.

**Campbell Hausfeld,** 100 Production Dr., Harrison, OH 45030: Free information ◆ Air compressors, pneumatic tools, and paint sprayers. 800-543-8622; 513-367-4811 (in OH). www.grizzlyimports.com/campair.html

**The Cayce Company,** 221-B Cockeysville Rd., Hunt Valley, MD 21030: Free information ◆ Used tools and equipment. 800-875-0213. www.cayceco.com/index.html

**Chicago Pneumatic Tools,** 825-G Franklin Ct., Marietta, GA 30062: Free information ◆ Woodworking power tools. 800-228-9096. www.chicagopneumatic.com

**CMT Tools,** 310 Mears Blvd., Oldsmar, FL 34677: Free information ◆ 3D-router and carving system. 800-531-5559.

**Coastal The Tool People,** 248 Sisson Ave., Hartford, CT 06105: Free catalog ◆ Power, air-operated, and hand tools. 877-551-8665. www.coastaltool.com

**Colwood Electronics,** 15 Meridian Rd., Eatontown, NJ 07724: Free brochure ◆ All-in-one work station that includes a woodburning and texturizing system and high speed grinding equipment. 908-544-1119. www.woodburning.com

**Conestoga Wood Machinery,** 987 Valley View Rd., New Holland, PA 17557: Free information ◆ Woodworking power tools. 800-445-4669.

**Constantines,** 2050 Eastchester Rd., Bronx, NY 10461: Catalog $1 ◆ Cabinet and furniture wood and veneers, hardware, how-to books, carving tools, and chisels. 800-223-8087; 718-792-1600 (in NY). www.constantines.com

**CP Tools Inc.,** 611 S. Duggan Ave., Azusa, CA 91702: Free information ◆ Woodworking machines. 800-654-7702; 818-815-9897 (in CA).

**Craft Supplies USA,** P.O. Box 50300, Provo, UT 84605: Catalog $2 ◆ Woodturning tools and accessories. 800-551-8876.

**The Cutting Edge,** 7123 Southwest Fwy., Houston, TX 77074: Free catalog ◆ Wood-turning and carving supplies and tools. 713-981-9228. www.cuttingedgetools.com

**Delta International Machinery Corp.,** 246 Alpha Dr., Pittsburgh, PA 15238: Catalog $2 ◆ Woodworking power tools. 800-438-2486.

**DeVilbiss,** 213 Industrial Dr., Jackson, TN 38301: Free brochure ◆ Air compressors, air-operated tools, and accessories. 800-888-2468; 901-423-7931 (in TN).

**Gregory D. Dorrance Company,** 1063 Oak Hill Ave., Attleboro, MA 02703: Free information ◆ Decoy-making and art supplies, tools, and wood for carving. 508-222-6255.

**Dremel Moto-Tool,** P.O. Box 468, Racine, WI 53406: Free information ◆ Hand power tools for modelers and home craftsmen. 414-554-1390. www.dremel.com

**Eastern Tool & Supply Company,** 149 Grand St., New York, NY 10013: Free information ◆ Metal-working tools. 800-221-2679; 212-925-1006 (in NY).

**Ebac Lumber Dryers,** 106 John Jefferson Rd., Ste. 102, Williamsburg, VA 23185: Free information ◆ Easy-to-operate lumber dryers. 800-433-9011. ebacinc@aol.com

**Echo Inc.,** 400 Oakwood Rd., Lake Zurich, IL 60047: Free catalog ◆ Trimmers, blowers, hedge clippers, sprayers, chain saws, and shredders. 800-432-3246.

**EMCO-Maier Corp.,** 2757 Scioto Pkwy., Columbus, OH 43221: Free catalog ◆ Woodworking power tools. 800-521-8289.

**Enco Manufacturing Company,** 5000 W. Bloomingdale Ave., Chicago, IL 60639: Free catalog ◆ Metal-working tools, machinery, and accessories. 800-860-3400; 773-745-1520 (in IL).

**Engraving Arts,** P.O. Box 787, Laytonville, CA 95454: Brochure $1 ◆ Custom branding irons. 800-422-4509.

**The Factory Store,** P.O. Box 503, Agawam, MA 01001: Free information ◆ Power tools and accessories. 800-845-TOOL.

**Falcon-Wood,** Peter & Annette Habieht, 1985 S. Undermountain Rd., Sheffield, MA 01257: Free brochure ◆ Collectible tools. 413-229-7745. peter@oldtools.com

**Falls Run Woodcarving,** 9395 Falls Rd., Girard, PA 16417: Free information ◆ Woodcarving tools. 800-524-9077. www.fallsrun.com

**Farris Machinery,** 1206 Pavilion Dr., Grain Valley, MO 64029: Free information ◆ Woodworking equipment and supplies. 800-872-5489.

**Fein Power Tools Inc.,** 3019 W. Carson St., Pittsburgh, PA 15204: Free brochure ◆ Hand-held detail sander-scraper-saw for restoration projects. 800-441-9878. www.cabinetsupply.com/fein.htm

**Florida Tool,** 1450 S. State Rd. 7, Hollywood, FL 33023: Free information ◆ Woodworking power tools. 800-805-0075. www.fltool.com

**Foley-Belsaw Company,** 6301 Equitable Rd., Kansas City, MO 64120: Free information ◆ Woodworking power tools. 800-821-3452. www.foley-belsaw.com

**Foredom Electric Company,** 16 Stony Hill Rd., Bethel, CT 06801: Free information ◆ Tools for grinding, sawing, drilling, carving, shaping, and polishing. 203-792-8622.

**Forrest Manufacturing Company Inc.,** 461 River Rd., Clifton, NJ 07014: Free information ◆ Table and radial saw blades. 800-733-7111; 973-473-5236 (in NJ).

**Franklin Ace Hardware,** 115 E. 2nd Ave., Franklin, VA 23851: Free information ◆ Woodworking power tools. 800-662-0004. www.franklinace.com

**Freeborn Tool Company Inc.,** P.O. Box 6246, 6202 N. Freya St., Spokane, WA 99207: Free information ◆ Carbide-tipped shaper cutters. 800-523-8988. freeborn@ior.com

**Freud Power Tools,** 218 Feld Ave., High Point, NC 27264: Free catalog ◆ Woodworking power tools. 800-472-7307.

**Frog Tool Company,** 2169 IL Rt. 26, Dixon, IL 61021: Catalog $5 ◆ Woodworking hand tools, books, and finishing materials. 800-648-1270; 815-288-3811 (in IL).

**Gesswein,** Woodworking Products Division, 255 Hancock Ave., Bridgeport, CT 06605: Free information ◆ Woodcarving tools. 800-544-2043.

**Granberg International,** P.O. Box 425, Richmond, CA 94807: Free information ◆ Portable chain saw lumber mill. 510-237-2099. www.medicom.com/granberg

**Griffin Manufacturing Company Inc.,** 1656 Ridge Rd. East, P.O. Box 308, Webster, NY 14580: Free catalog ◆ Cutters, knives, blades, and specialty tools. 716-265-1991.

**Grizzly Imports Inc.,** P.O. Box 2069, Bellingham, WA 98227: Free information ◆ Woodworking power tools. 800-541-5537 (west of the Mississippi); 800-523-4777 (east of the Mississippi).

**Harbor Freight Tools,** 3491 Mission Oaks Blvd., Camarillo, CA 93011: Free catalog ◆ Hardware, power and hand tools, and accessories. 800-444-3353. www.harborfreight.com

**Harris Tools,** 145 Sherman Ave., Jersey City, NJ 07307: Catalog $1 (refundable) ◆ Lapping and sharpening systems. 800-449-7747.

**Hartville Tool & Supply,** 13163 Market Ave. North, Hartville, OH 44632: Free catalog ◆ Woodworking tools. 800-345-2396.

**Harvey Tool,** Box 186, Topsfield, MA 01983: Free catalog ◆ Metalworking tools.

**Hida Japanese Tool Inc.,** 1333 San Pablo Ave., Berkeley, CA 94702: Catalog $4 ◆ Hand-forged tools for delicate work. 800-443-5512.

**Highland Hardware,** 1045 N. Highland Ave. NE, Atlanta, GA 30306: Free catalog ◆ Tools for home craftsmen. 800-241-6748. www.highland-hardware.com

**Hitachi Power Tools U.S.A. Ltd.,** 3850 Steve Reynolds Blvd., Norcross, GA 30093: Free information ◆ Handheld power tools. 800-241-6558.

**Home Lumber Company,** P.O. Box 370, Whitewater, WI 53190: Free information ◆ Portable power tools. 800-262-5482.

**HTC Products,** 120 E. Hudson, P.O. Box 839, Royal Oak, MI 48068: Free catalog ◆ Mobile machine bases to put workshops on wheels. 800-624-2027.

**Christian J. Hummul Company,** P.O. Box 1093, Hunt Valley, MD 21030: Free catalog ◆ Carving tools, artist supplies, and how-to-books. 800-762-0235. www.bcpl.net/~rzajac/index.html

**International Tool Corp.,** 2590 Davie Rd., Davie, FL 33020: Free information ◆ Woodworking machinery. 800-338-3384. www.international.com

**Jamestown Distributors,** P.O. Box 348, Jamestown, RI 02835: Free catalog ◆ Workshop tools. 800-423-0030.

**The Japan Woodworker,** 1731 Clement Ave., Alameda, CA 94501: Catalog $1.50 ◆ Japanese hand tools for craftsmen, carpenters, cabinet makers, and woodcarvers. 800-537-7820. www.japanwoodworker.com

**W.S. Jenks & Son,** 1933 Montana Ave. NE, Washington, DC 20002: Free catalog ◆ Hand and power tools. 202-529-6020. www.wsjenks.com

**Jensen Tools Inc.,** 7815 S. 46th St., Phoenix, AZ 85044: Free catalog ◆ Tools, tool kits, and cases. 800-426-1194; 602-968-6231 (in AZ). www.jensentools.com

**Kasco Woodworking Company Inc.,** 170 W. 600 North, Shelbyville, IN 46176: Free information ◆ Portable band saw mills. 800-458-9129.

**Bob Kaune,** 511 W. 11th, Port Angeles, WA 98362: Catalog $3.50 ◆ Antique and used hand tools for collectors and woodworkers. 360-452-2292. www.olympus.net/bktools

**The Keller Dovetail System,** 1327 I St., Petaluma, CA 94952: Free information ◆ Easy-to-use jig for making angled and curved dovetails, classic and variable spacing, and box joints. 800-995-2456; 707-763-9336 (in CA).

**Kitts Industrial Tools,** 22384 Grand River Ave., Detroit, MI 48219: Free catalog ◆ Precision metalworking tools and supplies. 800-521-6579; 313-538-2585 (in MI).

**Klockit,** P.O. Box 636, Lake Geneva, WI 53147: Free catalog ◆ Woodworking tools, wood finishing supplies, and clock-building equipment. 800-556-2548. www.klockit.com

**Knotts Knives,** 5549 Spinnaker Dr., Salisbury, MD 21801: Free information ◆ Carving tools. 800-388-6759.

**Laguna Tools,** 2265 Laguna Canyon Rd., Laguna Beach, CA 92651: Free information ◆ Space-saving all-in-one shop that includes a table saw, joiner, planer, shaper, mortiser, and sliding table. 800-234-1976. www.lagunatools.com

**Lansky Sharpeners,** P.O. Box 50803, Las Vegas, NV 89016: Free catalog ◆ Knife and tool sharpeners. 702-361-7511. www.customcpu.com/alaskaknife/lansky.htm

**Leatherman Tool Group Inc.,** P.O. Box 20595, Portland, OR 07220: Free information ◆ Compact multi-purpose tools. 503-253-7826. www.leatherman.com

**Leichtung Workshops,** 1108 N. Glenn Rd., Casper, WY 82601: Free catalog ◆ Tools and accessories for gardeners, woodworkers, and hobby do-it-yourselfers. 800-321-6840.

**Leigh Industries Inc.,** P.O. Box 357, Port Coquitlam, British Columbia, Canada V3C 4K6: Free catalog ◆ Dovetailing jigs, cutters, and attachments. 800-663-8932.

**Leisure Time Products,** 2650 Davisson St., River Grove, IL 60171: Free information ◆ Electronic woodburning systems and equipment for carvers, artists, and pyrographers. 708-452-5400. www.fire-art.com

**LeNeave Machinery & Supply Company,** 305 W. Morehead St., Charlotte, NC 28202: Free information ◆ Woodworking power tools. 800-442-2302; 704-376-7421 (in NC).

**Lie-Nielsen Toolworks,** Rt. 1, Warren, ME 04864: Free brochure ◆ Heirloom quality tools. 888-751-2106. www.lie-nielsen.com

**Lobo Power Tools,** 9034 Bermudez St., Pico Rivera, CA 90660: Free information ◆ Woodworking power tools. 310-949-3747.

**MacBeath Hardwood Company,** 930 Ashby Ave., Berkeley, CA 94710: Catalog $2 (refundable with $10 order) ◆ Woodworking tools and supplies. 510-843-4390. www.macbeath.com

**Makita USA Inc.,** 14930 Northam St., La Mirada, CA 90638: Free information ◆ Electric and cordless power tools. 800-462-5482. Makitaapd@aol.com

**Marling Lumber Company,** P.O. Box 7668, Madison, WI 53707: Free information ◆ Woodworking tools. 800-247-7178.

**Mascot Precision Tools,** 750 Washington Ave., Carlstadt, NJ 07072: Free catalog ◆ Precision tools for the hobbyist and craftsman. 800-847-4188. www.w-s-o.com/MascotPrecisionTools/index.htm

**McFeely's Square Drive Screws,** P.O. Box 11169, Lynchburg, VA 24506: Catalog $2 ◆ Woodworking supplies, square drive screws, tools, and other hard-to-find items. 800-443-7937. www.mcfeelys.com

**Mercury Vacuum Presses,** Box 2232, Fort Bragg, CA 95437: Free catalog ◆ Vacuum pressing equipment for veneering and laminating flat and curved panels, vacuum bags, pumps, and clamps. 800-995-4506. www.mcn.org/c/mvp

**Michigan Woodworkers & Supply,** 4133 S. Dort Hwy., Burton, MI 48529: Free catalog ◆ Power tools and accessories, veneers, plywood, and hard, soft, and exotic woods. 800-433-9663.

**Micro-Mark,** 340 Snyder Ave., Berkeley Heights, NJ 07922: Catalog $1 ◆ Miniature tools for hobby craftsmen. 800-225-1066. www.micromark.com

**Miller Woodworking Machinery Inc.,** 1110 E. Quilcene Rd., Quilcene, WA 98376: Free information ◆ Wide belt sanders for the small shop. 360-765-3806.

**Milwaukee Electric Tool Corp.,** 13135 W. Lisbon Rd., Brookfield, WI 53005: Free information ◆ Portable power tools. 414-783-8642. www.mil-electric-tool.com

**Minitech Machinery,** 737 Lambert Dr. NE, Atlanta, GA 30324: Free information ◆ Desktop metalworking machine tools. 800-662-1760. www.minitech.com

**MLCS Tools Ltd.,** P.O. Box 4053, Rydal, PA 19046: Free catalog ◆ Carbide-tipped router bits. 800-533-9298; 215-938-5067 (in PA). www.mlcswoodworking.com

**Mobile Manufacturing Company,** P.O. Box 250, Troutdale, OR 97060: Free brochure ◆ Portable gasoline or electric-powered saw for cutting logs any diameter and lengths up to 60 feet. 503-666-5593.

**Mountain Heritage Crafters,** 601 Quail Dr., Bluefield, VA 24605: Free catalog ◆ Carving tools and how-to books. 540-322-5921. www.mhc-online.com

**Nasco,** 901 Janesville Ave., Fort Atkinson, WI 53538: Free catalog ◆ Woodburning and carving tools, woodcraft supplies, and wood projects. 800-558-9595. www.nascofa.com

**Navesink Electronics,** 820 Nut Swamp Rd., Red Bank, NJ 07701: Free information ◆ Woodburning systems, dust collectors, and carving tools. 732-747-5023. navesink1@aol.com

**Norcraft Custom Brands,** P.O. Box 277, South Easton, MA 02375: Free information ◆ Custom branding irons. 508-238-2163.

**Northern Hydraulics,** P.O. Box 1219, Burnsville, MN 55337: Free catalog ◆ Power tools and accessories. 800-533-5545. www.northern-online.com

**Norwood,** 90 Cartwright Dr., Amherst, NY 14221: Free information ◆ Easy-to-use sawmill. 800-661-7746.

**Nyle Dry Kiln System,** P.O. Box 1107, Bangor, ME 04402: Free information ◆ Easy-to-use lumber dryer. 800-777-NYLE. www.allproducts.com/usa/nyle

**Old World Brush & Tool Company Inc.,** 17 Rio Vista Dr., St. Charles, MO 63303: Free brochure ◆ Specialty brushes, graining tools, how-to videos, and books. 800-821-3314; 314-724-4240 (in MO).

**Packard Woodworks,** P.O. Box 718, Tryon, NC 28782: Free catalog ◆ Wood turning tools and supplies. 800-683-8876.

**Panasonic Cordless Power Tools,** Panasonic Way, Secaucus, NJ 07094: Free information ◆ Handheld cordless power tools. 201-392-6655. www.panasonic.com

**PBL Tools,** P.O. Box 769, Ukiah, CA 95482: Free brochure ◆ Soldering tools. 707-462-7680.

**Penn State Industries,** 2850 Comly Rd., Philadelphia, PA 19154: Free information ◆ Woodworking machines and accessories. 800-377-7297. www.pennstateind.com

**Pfingst & Company Inc.,** 105 Snyder Rd., South Plainfield, NJ 07080: Free catalog ◆ Precision detailing tools for carving, cutting, finishing, and intricate detailing. 908-561-6400.

**Porta-Nails Inc.,** P.O. Box 1257, Wilmington, NC 28402: Free list of retail sources ◆ Woodworking machines. 800-634-9281; 910-762-6334 (in NC). www.porta-nails.com/workshop.html

**Porter-Cable,** P.O. Box 2468, Jackson, TN 38302: Free list of retail sources ◆ Woodworking power tools. 800-487-8665. www.porter-cable.com

**Poulan,** 5020 Flournoy-Lucas Rd., Shreveport, LA 71129: Free information ◆ Electric and gas-operated chain saws. 318-683-3546. www.poulan.com/poulan.html

**Power Tool Specialists,** 3 Craftsman Rd., East Windsor, CT 06088: Free information ◆ Handheld nail gun and portable power tools. 800-243-5114. www.tradesman-rexon.com

**Powermatic Inc.,** 607 Morrison Rd., McMinnville, TN 37110: Free information ◆ Woodworking power tools. 800-248-0144. www.powermatic.com

**Quality Vakuum Products,** 43 Bradford St., Concord, MA 01742: Free brochure ◆ Automatic vacuum pressing and clamping tool. 800-547-5484.

**RBIndustries,** 1801 Vine St., Harrisonville, MO 64071: Free catalog ◆ Woodworking power tools. 800-487-2623. www.rbindustries.com

**Red Hill Corp.,** P.O. Box 4234, Gettysburg, PA 17325: Free catalog ◆ Hot melt glue sticks, glue guns, and sandpaper belts, sheets, and discs. 800-822-4003. www.supergrit.com

**Ridge Carbide Tool Corp.,** 595 New York Ave., P.O. Box 497, Lyndhurst, NJ 07071: Catalog $3 ◆ Custom router bits, saw blades, knives, and shaper cutters. 800-443-0992.

**Ryobi America Corp.,** P.O. Box 1207, Anderson, SC 29622: Free information ◆ Woodworking power tools. 800-525-2579. www.ryobi.com

**S.B. Power Tools,** 4300 W. Peterson Ave., Chicago, IL 60646: Free information ◆ Woodworking power tools. 800-241-3848. www.boschtools.com

**Safranek Enterprises Inc.,** 4005 El Camino Real, Atascadero, CA 93422: Free information ◆ Panel routers and accessories, air-vac clamps, keyhole machines, carbide cutters, and router bits. 800-553-9344.

**Santa Rosa Tool & Supply Inc.,** 1651 Piner Rd., Santa Rosa, CA 95043: Free information ◆ Woodworking power tools. 800-346-0387; 707-545-6460 (in CA).

**Saw Trax Mfg. Company Inc.,** 37900 Hwy. 92, Ste. 220, Acworth, GA 30102: Free information ◆ Industrial panel saw and router. 888-SAW-TRAX; 770-974-0021 (in GA). www.sawtrax.com

**Seco Woodworking Machinery,** 16103 Montoya St., Irwindale, CA 91706: Free information ◆ Tilting spindle shaper. 888-558-4628. www.seco-usa.com

**Seven Corners Hardware Inc.,** 216 W. 7th St., St. Paul, MN 55102: Free catalog ◆ Hand and power tools and supplies. 800-328-0457.

**Shop Outfitters,** 605 S. Adams St., Laramie, WY 82070: Free information ◆ Metalworking tools. 307-745-5999.

**Shop-Task,** P.O. Box 64268, Tacoma, WA 98464: Free catalog ◆ All-in-one home machine shop with mill, lathe, and drill. 800-343-5775.

**Shop-Vac Corp.,** 2323 Reach Rd., Williamsport, PA 17701: Free information ◆ Self-contained portable vacuum cleaner for workshops. 717-326-0502. www.shopvac.com

**Shopsmith Inc.,** 6530 Poe, Dayton, OH 45414: Free information ◆ Multipurpose all-in-one power-woodworking tools. 800-543-7586; 937-898-6070 (in OH). www.shopsmith.com

**Skil-Bosch,** 4300 W. Peterson Ave., Chicago, IL 60646: Free information ◆ Handheld power tools. 800-241-3848. www.skiltool.com

**Smithy,** P.O. Box 1517, Ann Arbor, MI 48106: Free information ◆ Lathe, mill, and drill (3-in-1 powered machine shop). 800-345-6342. www.cskpub.com/catalog_folder/smitty.html

**Stanley Tools,** 600 Myrtle St., New Britain, CT 06050: Free information ◆ Woodworking power tools. 860-225-5111. www.stanleyworks.com

**Star Machine Tools,** 523 Puyallup Ave., Tacoma, WA 98421: Free catalog ◆ Power tools. 253-572-5000. www.forestindustry.com

**Sugino Corp.,** 1700 Penny Ln., Schaumberg, IL 60173: Free information ◆ Lightweight handheld electric woodcarving tool with optional specialized blades. 847-397-9401. www.sugino.com

**Sunhill Machinery,** 500 Andover Park East, Seattle, WA 98188: Free information ◆ Heavy-duty power tools, dust collectors, and accessories. 800-929-4321. www.sunhillnic.com/catalog.htm

**TAIG Tools,** 12419 E. Nightingale Ln., Chandler, AZ 85249: Free information ◆ Four-inch metal cutting lathe and accessories. 602-895-6978.

**Tarheel Filing Company Inc.,** 3400 Lake Woodard Dr., Raleigh, NC 27604: Free information ◆ Power tools. 800-322-6641; 919-231-3323 (in NC).

**Tashiro's Tools,** P.O. Box 3409, Seattle, WA 98114: Free catalog ◆ Japanese tools. 206-621-0199.

**Terrco Inc.,** 222 1st Ave. NW, Watertown, SD 57201: Free catalog ◆ Woodcarving machines. 605-882-3888.

**Timberking Inc.,** P.O. Box 34284, Kansas City, MO 64120: Free information ◆ Portable one-man saw mill. 800-942-4406.

**Tool Crib of the North,** Box 14040, Grand Forks, ND 58208: Free catalog ◆ Hand and power tools. 800-358-3096. www.toolcribofthenorth.com

**Tool Factory Outlet,** P.O. Box 461, Goshen, NY 10924: Free information ◆ Woodworking power tools and accessories. 914-294-7900.

**Tooland Inc.,** 1369 Industrial Rd., San Carlos, CA 94070: Free information ◆ Power tools and accessories. 650-631-9636. www.tooland.com

**Tradesman Power Tools,** 3 Craftsman Rd., East Windsor, CT 06088: Free catalog ◆ Bench and stationary power tools. 800-243-5114.

**Trend-Lines,** 135 American Legion Hwy., Revere, MA 02151: Free catalog ◆ Power and hand tools and accessories. 800-877-7899. www.trendlines.net

**U.S. Cyberlab Inc.,** 14786 Slate Gap Rd., West Fork, AR 72774: Free information ◆ Robotic machine for routing, milling, carving, drilling, and engraving plastic, vinyl, and light metals. 501-839-8293. www.uscyberlab.com

**Vermont American,** 1980 Indian Creek Rd., Lincolnton, NC 28092: Free catalog ◆ Power tool accessories and hand tools. 800-742-3869; 704-735-7464 (in NC). www.vermontamerican.com/toolinfo.htm

**Vintage Tool House,** Box 855, Suffern, NY 10901: Catalog $2 ◆ Antique, used, and new hand tools. 914-352-1347.

**Garrett Wade Company,** 161 6th Ave., New York, NY 10013: Catalog $4 ◆ Hand and power tools for woodworking. 800-221-2942. www.garrettwade.com

**Wahl Clipper Corp.,** 2900 Locust St., Sterling, IL 61081: Free list of retail sources ◆ Lightweight precision drill for fine detailing. 800-435-7748. user5@wahlclipper.com

**Steve Wall Lumber Company,** Box 287, Mayodan, NC 27027: Catalog $1 ◆ Hardwoods and woodworking machinery. 800-633-4062; 910-427-0637 (in NC). www.walllumber.com/

**Walnut Creek Woodworkers Supply Company,** 3601 W. Harry, Wichita, KS 67213: Free catalog ◆ Woodworking tools and accessories. 800-942-0553.

**Ivan Whillock Studio,** 122 NE 1st Ave., Faribault, MN 55021: Free catalog ◆ Woodcarving tools, how-to books, and kits. 800-882-9379; 507-334-8306 (in MN). www.whillock.com

**Wilke Machinery Company,** 3230 Susquehanna Trail, York, PA 17402: Catalog $2 ◆ Woodworking power tools with optional dust collector. 717-764-5000.

**Williams & Hussey Machine Company Inc.,** P.O. Box 1149, Wilton, NH 03086: Free information ◆ Molder-planer for straight, circular, or elliptical moldings. 800-258-1380; 603-654-6828 (in CT). www.williamsnhussey.com

**Wood-Mizer,** 8180 W. 10th St., Indianapolis, IN 46214: Catalog $2 ◆ Portable sawmills and tools. 800-553-0219. www.woodmizer.com

**Woodcraft Supply,** 210 Wood County Industrial Park, P.O. Box 1686, Parkersburg, WV 26102: Free catalog ◆ Woodworking tools, supplies, hardware, and books. 800-535-4482. www.woodcraft.com

**Woodcrafters,** 212 NE 6th Ave., Portland, OR 97232: Free information ◆ Woodcarving tools, knives, power-carving and burning tools, books, carving woods, and supplies. 503-231-0226.

**Woodhaven Tools,** 501 W. 1st Ave., Durant, IA 52747: Free catalog ◆ Woodworking tools. 800-344-6657. www.woodhaven.com

**Woodline Arizona Inc.,** P.O. Box 1530, Payson, AZ 85547: Free information ◆ Industrial quality carbide tipped router bits and shaper cutters. 800-472-6950.

**Woodmaster Tools,** 1431 N. Topping Ave., Kansas City, MO 64120: Free information ◆ Variable feed multi-duty planer, wide-belt sander, and tools. 800-821-6651. sam@woodmastertools.com

**The Woodturners Catalog,** P.O. Box 50300, Provo, UT 84605: Free catalog ◆ Woodturning tools and supplies. 800-551-8876. www.craftusa.com

**The Woodworker's Choice,** 2 The Professional Ave., West Jefferson, NC 28694: Catalog $1 ◆ Woodworking tools and accessories. 800-892-4866. www.1-800-twc-4tools.com

**The Woodworkers' Store,** 4365 Willow Dr., Medina, MN 55340: Free catalog ◆ Hardware, woodworking and finishing supplies, and tools. 800-279-4441. www.woodworkerstore.com

**Woodworkers World,** 1509 Lititz Pike, Lancaster, PA 17601: Free catalog ◆ Woodworking tools and accessories. 800-990-TOOL; 717-299-5264 (in PA).

**WoodWrite Ltd.,** 2121 Abell Ln., Bldg. 1, Sparks, MD 21152: Free information ◆ Mini-lathes. 888-WOODWRITE. www.woodwriteltd.com

### Paint Sprayers

**Fuji Industrial Spray Equipment Ltd.,** 65 Martin Ross Ave., Toronto, Ontario, Canada M3J 2L6: Free information ◆ Compact, portable, and easy-to-control sprayer. www.fujispray.com

**Hydraflow Equipment Company,** 8125 Brentwood Industrial Dr., St. Louis, MO 63144: Free information ◆ High-volume and low-pressure sprayers. 800-444-0423; 314-644-6677 (in MO).

## TOTEM POLES

**The Wood Age,** 5690 Shady Ln., Florence, OR 97439: Free information ◆ Totem poles, custom plaques, and wildlife carvings. 888-4-TOTEMS. woodage@presys.com

## TOWELS

**Chambers,** Mail Order Dept., P.O. Box 7841, San Francisco, CA 94120: Free catalog ◆ Bed and bath linens and furnishings. 800-334-1254.

**Leron,** 750 Madison Ave., New York, NY 10021: Free catalog ◆ Linens, towels, pillows and covers, and imported handkerchiefs with optional monograms for men and women. 212-249-3188.

**Palmetto Linen Company,** 50 Palmetto Bay Rd., Hilton Head, SC 29928: Free information ◆ Sheets and matching dust ruffles, bath towels, blankets, comforters, pillows, tablecloths, place mats, shower curtains, kitchen towels, and oven gloves. 800-972-7442.

## TOY MAKING

**Animal Crackers Patterns,** 1404 Peyton, Los Lunas, NM 87031: Catalog $2 ◆ Kits, supplies, and patterns for easy-to-make stuffed toys, bears, and other animals. 505-865-7218.

**Atlanta Puffections,** P.O. Box 13524, Atlanta, GA 30324: Catalog $1.50 ◆ Easy-to-make stuffed animals. 770-262-7437.

**By Diane,** 1126 Ivon Ave., Endicott, NY 13760: Catalog $3 ◆ Soft toys, puppet kits, bear-making supplies, and patterns for bears, soft toys, and puppets. 607-754-0391.

**Golden Fun,** P.O. Box 3324, Danville, CA 94526: Catalog $1 ◆ Soft toy-making supplies. 888-648-0146.

**Larson Wood Manufacturing,** P.O. Box 672, Park Rapids, MN 56407: Catalog $2 (refundable) ◆ Country-style mini cutouts, kits and parts, hardware, and supplies. 218-732-9121.

**Patterncrafts,** 3919 Van Teylingen, Colorado Springs, CO 80917: Catalog $2 ◆ Patterns for dolls and stuffed animals. 800-414-3888.

**Platypus,** Box 396, Planetarium Station, New York, NY 10024: Free information ◆ Stuffed toy and doll patterns.

## TOY SOLDIERS & MINIATURE FIGURES

**ANI Toy Soldiers,** 628 S. Myrtle Ave., Monrovia, CA 91016: Catalog $5 ◆ Miniature toy soldiers. 818-303-3990.

**Armchair General Ltd.,** 884 Woods Mill Rd., #201, Ballwin, MO 63011: Catalog $2 ◆ Military miniatures and toy soldiers. 800-365-2498. www.armchairgeneral.com

**Armies in Miniature,** 1745 Tradewinds Ln., Newport Beach, CA 92660: List $2 ◆ Miniature military figures. 714-646-4471.

**Artista Accessories,** 1616 S. Franklin St., Philadelphia, PA 19148: Free information with long SASE ◆ O and O27-gauge metal figures and accessories.800-316-2493; 215-467-2493 (in PA).

**Brunton's Barracks,** 415 S. Montezuma St., Prescott, AZ 86303: Free information ◆ Military figures and other miniatures. 520-778-1915.

**Classic Toy Soldier Company,** 11528 Canterbury Circle, Leawood, KS 66211: Brochure $3 ◆ Toy soldiers. 913-451-9458.

**CP Mail Toy Soldiers,** Box 6323, Falls Church, VA 22046: Free information ◆ Toy soldiers. 703-536-3064.

**Cynthia's Country Store,** The Wellington Mall, 12794 W. Forest Hill Blvd., Ste. 15A, West Palm Beach, FL 33414: Catalog $15 ◆ British and other toy soldiers. 561-793-0554.

**Dunken,** Box 95, Calvert, TX 77837: Free catalog ◆ Civil War, World War I and World War II, Napoleonic, German military, and lead soldier molds. 409-364-2020.

**Dutkins' Collectables,** 1019 West Rt. 70, Cherry Hill, NJ 08002: Catalog $4 ◆ Handpainted all-metal toy soldiers and mold kits. 609-428-9559.

**Excalibur Hobbies Ltd.,** 63 Exchange St., Malden, MA 02148: Free information ◆ Old and new toy soldiers, war games, plastic kits, books, and military collectibles. 781-322-2959.

**Gettysburg Miniature Soldiers,** 200 Steinwehr Ave., Gettysburg, PA 17325: Free information with long SASE ◆ American Civil War and British Colonial War miniatures. 717-338-1800.

**Greystone's History & Emporium Gallery,** 461 Baltimore St., Gettysburg, PA 17325: Free brochure ◆ Movies, military documentaries, miniatures, Civil War books, and other collectibles. 717-338-0631. www.greystoneonline.com

**Historical Miniatures,** Box 195, Port Richey, FL 34673: List $1 ◆ Handpainted metal castings, Civil War generals, American and German soldiers from World War II, and other miniatures. 727-868-3150. soldiers@gate.net

**Hornung Art,** 32 E. Charlotte Ave., Cincinnati, OH 45215: Free information ◆ Art, antiques, and miniature figures. 513-761-8518. www.hornungart.com

**In Stock Hobby,** P.O. Box 853, Newton, NJ 07860: Free information ◆ Military miniatures, toy soldiers, plastic and metal models, tools, and supplies. 800-656-5390.

**International Hobby Corp.,** 413 E. Allegheny Ave., Philadelphia, PA 19134: Catalog $4.98 ◆ Battery-powered tools, model airplanes, railroading accessories, and military miniatures. 800-875-1600.

**Michigan Toy Soldier Company,** 405 S. Washington, Royal Oak, MI 48067: Catalog $5 ◆ Historical miniatures, toy soldiers, figure kits, books, videos, and supplies. 248-586-1022. www.michtoy.com

**Military Mites,** Box 2324, Rockville, MD 20847: Catalog $6 ◆ Miniature military figures from the past to the present. 800-296-6483.

**Gary Miller,** 114 Carlsan Pring, Georgetown, KY 40324: Free list with long SASE and two 1st class stamps ◆ Pre and post-war toy soldier sets and singles. 502-863-6343.

**Miniatures,** Box 195, Port Richey, FL 34673: Free list ◆ Handpainted metal toy soldiers. 813-868-3150.

**Modelers Mart,** 1555 Sunshine Dr., Clearwater, FL 34625: Catalog $5 (refundable) ◆ Civil War and other miniature metal figures. 800-223-5260. www.pageworld.com/modelersmart

**Monarch Miniatures Inc.,** P.O. Box 4195, Long Island City, NY 11104: Catalog $6 ◆ Metal figure kits from all historical periods, especially the Civil War.

**Musket Miniatures,** P.O. Box 1976, Broomfield, CO 80038: Catalog $3 ◆ Pewter figures for model railroads and military settings. Alsp cast resin buildings, scenery, and accessories. 303-439-9336.

**Phoenix Model Company,** P.O. Box 15390, Brookville, FL 34609: Catalog $3 ◆ Civil War and other miniature figures. 352-754-8522.

**Red Lancer,** P.O. Box 8056, Mesa, AZ 85214: Catalog $6 ◆ Original 19th-century military art, rare books, Victorian era campaign medals and helmets, old toy soldiers, and collectibles. 602-964-9667.

**The Red Lancers Miniatures,** 14 Broadway, Milton, PA 17847: Catalog $9 ◆ Military miniatures. 717-742-8118.

**Regimental Collectibles,** P.O. Box 685, Sandy, UT 84091: Catalog $3 ◆ Painted and unpainted military miniatures. 801-947-9100.

**Santos Miniatures,** P.O. Box 4062, Harrisburg, PA 17111: Catalog $1 ◆ Military and other miniatures.

**Saratoga Soldier Shop & Military Bookstore,** Curtis Industrial Park, Ballston Spa, NY 12020: Catalog $6 ◆ Miniatures from the Civil War and other eras. 518-885-1497.

**Scotty's Scale Soldiers,** 1008 Adams St., Bay City, MI 48708: Small scale catalog $6; large scale catalog $5; both catalogs $10 ◆ Miniatures, 6mm to 30mm and 54mm to 120mm. 517-892-6177.

**Jack Scruby's Toy Soldiers,** P.O. Box 1809, Atascadero, CA 93423: List $4 ◆ Original and reproduction and handcast toy soldiers. 800-549-1428.

**Sentinel Miniatures,** 4 Broadway, Valhalla, NY 10595: Catalog $9 ◆ Military, historical, and fantasy figure kits. Also die-cast cars and HO and N scale trains. 914-682-3932.

**Stormbird Hobbies,** 11601 4th St. North, St. Petersburg, FL 33716: Free price list with long SASE and two 1st class stamps ◆ Miniature figures, vehicles, and detail sets.

**Stuempfle's Military Miniatures,** 13190 Scott Rd., Waynesboro, PA 17268: Catalog $4 ◆ Military miniatures. 717-765-0201.

**Toy Soldier Company,** 100 Riverside Dr., New York, NY 10024: Catalog $5 ◆ Plastic and lead toy soldiers. 201-792-6665. www.toysoldierco.com

**Toy Soldier Gallery Inc.,** 24 Main St., Highland Falls, NY 12928: Catalog $5 ◆ Toy soldier sets and individual pieces from different historical periods. 800-777-9904.

**VLS Mail Order,** Lone Star Industrial Park, 811 Lone Star Dr., O'Fallon, MO 63366: Catalog $6 ◆ Aircraft and car models, other models, and military miniatures. 314-281-5700. www.vls-vp.com

**Warwick Miniatures Ltd.,** P.O. Box 1498, Portsmouth, NH 03801: Catalog $4 ◆ Imperial toy soldiers from New Zealand and detailed miniatures from historical periods of the United States, England, France, and Germany. 603-431-7139.

## TOYS & GAMES

### Character Toys & Action Figures

**Ancient Idols Collectible Toys,** P.O. Box 245, Whitehall, PA 18052: Catalog $3 ◆ Collectible character and science fiction toys, model kits, puzzles, and games. 610-798-9940. www.ancientidols.com

**Battcave Collectables,** 222 W. Hoyt St., Beatrice, NE 68310: Catalog $3 ◆ Collectible action figure toys. 402-223-3303.

**Benjy's Trains & Toys,** 8715 N. 40th St., Tampa, FL 33604: Free price list with long SASE ◆ Slot cars, accessories, trains, and toys. 813-980-3790.

**Burnus Roadus,** 524 Black Walnut Dr., Rochester, NY 14615: Free list with long SASE ◆ Old to new Road Runner and other collectibles. 716-663-0307.

**Bill & Anne Campbell,** 1221 Littlebrook Ln., Birmingham, AL 35235: Free list ◆ Radio premiums, character toys, and other collectibles. 205-853-8227. billanne@bellsouth.net

**Classic Toys,** 112 Southgate Plaza, Sarasota, FL 34239: Free list with long SASE and two 1st class stamps ◆ Barbie dolls and collectibles, Star Trek and Star Wars classics, Patsy dolls, figurines, and ornaments. 941-365-1121.

**Collectorholics,** 15006 Fuller, Grandview, MO 64030: Catalog $5 ◆ Character TV memorabilia, movie-related toys, and other collectibles. 816-322-0906.

**Collectors Showcase,** 820 Caron Circle NW, Atlanta, GA 30318: Free information ◆ Character toys and memorabilia. 404-792-2929.

**Cotswold Collectibles Inc.,**P.O. Box 716, Freeland, WA 98249: Free catalog ◆ G.I. Joe figures, accessories, uniforms, and vehicles. 360-331-5331. www.whidbey.net/~cotswold

**Clinton Dean's Figures & Collectibles,** P.O. Box 383, Milford, NH 03055: Free catalog ◆ Character toys and figures, trading cards, and other collectibles. 603-673-3290.

**John DiCicco,** 57 Bay View Dr., Shrewsbury, MA 01545: Catalog $2 ◆ Character toys and memorabilia. 508-797-0023.

**The Earth,** 4166 Allendale Dr., #3, Cincinnati, OH 45209: Free information ◆ Stands for Star Wars figures. 513-561-8697. www.theearth.net

**Figures Inc.,** P.O. Box 19842, Johnston, RI 02919: Catalog $2 ◆ TV, movie action, and character toy collectibles. Also other toys. 401-946-5720.

**Fun House Toy Company,** P.O. Box 444, Warrendale, PA 15086: Free catalog with four 1st class stamps ◆ Collectible MARX playsets and plastic figures. Also other vintage collectibles toys. 724-935-1392. www.funhousetoy.com

**Barry Goodman,** P.O. Box 218, Woodbury, NY 11797: Free information with long SASE ◆ Character toys and dolls. 516-338-2701. toysen@aol.com

**Hanger 18 Mail-Order,** Order Dept., 6100 E. 21st St. N., Ste. 200, Wichita, KS 67208: Free information ◆ Collectible action figure and TV character toys. 800-597-3728. hanger18@hanger18toys.com

**Dennis Harry,** 9789 Good Luck Rd., Apt. 8, Lanham, MD 20706: Information $2 (refundable) ◆ Action figures.

**Jim's TV Collectibles,** P.O. Box 4767, San Diego, CA 92164: Catalog TV collectibles $2, TV photos $2 ◆ TV and theatrical collectibles, from the 1950s through 1990s.

**The Joe Depot,** P.O. Box 228, Kulpsville, PA 19443: Catalog $6 ◆ G.I. Joe figures and accessories. 215-721-9749. www.ewtech.com/gijoe

**John's Collectible Toys & Gifts,** 57 Bay View Dr., Shrewsbury, MA 01545: Catalog $2 ◆ Character toys, movie memorabilia, and TV collectibles. 508-797-0023. www.ewtech.com/Johns

**Just Kids Nostalgia,** 310 New York Ave., Huntington, NY 11743: Catalog $5 ◆ Movie and TV character dolls, movie memorabilia, and board games. 516-423-8449. Justkids25@aol.com

**Kadon Enterprises Inc.,** 1227 Lorene Dr., Ste. 16, Pasadena, MD 21122: Free brochure ◆ Puzzles, challenging and historical games, board games, and abstract challenging strategies. 410-437-2163.

**Kimono My House,** 1424 62nd St., Emeryville, CA 94608: Catalog $2 ◆ Godzilla, Ultraman, Kamen Rider, Macross, Astroboy, Sailor Moon, and other Japanese and science-fiction collectibles. 510-654-4627.

**Long Island Train & Hobby Center,** 192 Jericho Tnpk., Mineola, NY 11501: Price list $3 ◆ Collectible toys and character dolls. 516-742-5621.

**Oasis of Quality,** 336 Shamrock Rd., St. Augustine, FL 32086: Free catalog with three 1st class stamps ◆ TV, movie action, and character toy collectibles. 904-797-9745. www.advertisingalliance.com/collect.htm

**Other Worlds Collectibles,** P.O. Box 604596, Bay Terrace, NY 11360: Catalog $5 ◆ Star Trek, Star Wars, Battlestar Galactica, Batman, Superman, and other collectibles. 718-539-9284.

**Outer Limits,** 433 Piaget Ave., Clifton, NJ 07013: Catalog $2 ◆ Science fiction and character toys. 201-340-9393.

**Bob Sellstedt,** 9307 Hillingdon Rd., Woodbury, MN 55125: Price list $2 ◆ Character toys and other collectibles. 612-738-1597.

**Splash Page Comics & Toys,** 1007 E. Patterson, Kirksville, MO 63501: Free information ◆ Character toys and memorabilia. 800-237-PAGE.

**Star Pieces,** 1975 Ripplerock Rd., Fort Mill, SC 29715: Catalog $2 ◆ Star Wars, Star Trek, and other rare action figures. 803-547-4585. STARPIECES@infoavenue.net

**Toy Scouts Inc.,** 137 Casterton Ave., Akron, OH 44303: Catalog $5 ◆ Collectible TV cartoon and comic characters, from 1940 through 1970. 330-836-0668.

**Toys-Toys-Toys,** Jerry & Ellen Harnish, 110 Main St., Bellville, OH 44813: Catalog $2 ◆ Action figures, games, puzzles, dolls, and other toys from the 1950s, 1960s, 1970s, and 1980s. 419-886-4782.

**Toys from Times Past,** 4299 E. Shearer Rd., Rhodes, MI 48652: Free brochure ◆ Action, skill, and animated toys. Also tricks and puzzles. 517-689-4663.

**Wex Rex Records & Collectibles,** 280 Worcester Rd., Framingham, MA 01701: Catalog $3 ◆ Movie and TV show character toys and collectibles. 508-620-6181.

## Educational Toys & Games

**All The Right Stuff,** 4472 White Oak Circle, Kissimmee, FL 34746: Free brochure ◆ Creative toys and gifts, specializing in dinosaurs and space products. 800-799-8697; 407-397-4037 (in FL). www.alltherightstuff.com

**Animal Town,** P.O. Box 757, Greenland, NH 03840: Free catalog ◆ Toys, novelties, games, puzzles, books, and recordings for children. 800-445-8642.

**Aristoplay Games,** 450 S. Wagner Rd., Ann Arbor, MI 48103: Free catalog ◆ Educational games for all ages. 800-634-7738.

**Mary Arnold Toys,** 962 Lexington Ave., New York, NY 10021: Free catalog ◆ Activity play toys for children. 212-744-8510.

**Back to Basics Toys,** 1 Memory Ln., Ridgely, MD 21685: Free catalog ◆ Activity toys and games, backyard games, and sports and family-oriented items. 800-356-5360. www.backtobasicstoys.com

**Barclay School Supplies,** 166 Livingston St., Brooklyn, NY 11201: Catalog $4 ◆ Educational and school supplies and teaching aids. 718-875-2424.

**Binary Arts Corporation,** 1321 Cameron St., Alexandria, VA 22314: Free catalog ◆ Games, puzzles, books, gadgets, and toys. 888-789-9538. www.webgames.com

**Childcraft,** 250 College Park, P.O. Box 1811, Peoria, IL 61656: Free catalog ◆ Educational toys and games for babies and young children. 800-631-5657.

**Constructive Playthings,** 1227 E. 119th St., Grandview, MO 64030: Free catalog ◆ How-to build-them-yourself toys. 800-448-7830; 816-761-5900 (in MO).

**Earthwise Basics,** 8716 Park Lane South, Ste. 3C, Woodhaven, NY 11421: Free brochure ◆ Educational toys for children. 800-791-3957; 718-846-7434 (in NY).

**Edmund Scientific Company,** Edscorp Bldg., Barrington, NJ 08007: Free catalog ◆ Scientific educational items. 609-547-8880. www.edsci.com

**Educational Insights,** 19560 Rancho Way, Dominguez Hills, CA 90220: Free catalog (specify pre-K to age 8 or 8 years and up) ◆ Learning games and toys. 310-637-2131.

**Fun Publishing Company,** 3322 Erie Ave., Cincinnati, OH 45208: Free information ◆ Soft toys for children ages 1 to 3; books for children ages 2 to 4, 5 to 6, kindergarten and 1st grade, and ages 7 and 8; music items for children ages 3 to adults; and special books for teachers. 513-533-3636.

**The Great Kids Company,** P.O. Box 609, Lewisville, NC 27023: Free catalog ◆ Developmental learning materials for early childhood education. 800-582-1493.

**Hand in Hand,** Catalogue Center, 100 Plaza Dr., Secaucus, NJ 07094: Free catalog ◆ Books, toys and games, and products that help nurture, teach, and protect children. 800-872-9745. hihcatalog@aol.com

**Hearth Song,** Mail Processing Center, 6519 N. Galena Rd., P.O. Box 1773, Peoria, IL 61656: Free catalog ◆ Toys and games that provide opportunity for creativity, challenge, discovery, and improving reading skills. 800-325-2502. www.hearthsong.com

**Kapable Kids,** P.O. Box 250, Bohemia, NY 11716: Free catalog ◆ Toys for the developing child. 800-356-1564. www.kapablekids.com

**Miles Kimball Company,** 41 W. 8th Ave., Oshkosh, WI 54906: Free catalog ◆ Children's toys and crafts. 800-546-2255. www.mileskimball.com

**Kimbo Educational,** P.O. Box 477, Long Branch, NJ 07740: Free catalog ◆ Cassettes, CDs, records, videos, read-alongs, and film strips for children. 800-631-2187. www.kimboed.com

**Lilly's Kids,** Lillian Vernon Corp., Virginia Beach, VA 23479: Free catalog ◆ Games, science sets, art activities, backyard and outdoor toys, dolls, animal toys, and rainy day and traveling fun things. 800-285-5555. LVCcustsrv@aol.com

**The Natural Baby Company,** 7835 Freedom Ave. NW, North Canton, OH 44720: Free information ◆ Toys for babies. 800-388-BABY.

**One Step Ahead,** P.O. Box 517, Lake Bluff, IL 60044: Free catalog ◆ Playthings for babies. 800-950-5120. osacatalog@aol.com

**Out of the Woodwork,** 437 Robert E. Lee Dr., Wilmington, NC 28412: Free brochure ◆ Educational puzzles for children. 910-792-6882.

**Papa's Best-Books and Toys,** 1818 South Crystal Springs Rd., Tacoma, WA 98465: Free catalog ◆ Educational books and toys. 888-526-5463; 206-566-1139 (in WA). www.parentsplace.com/shopping/papasbest

**Playfair Toys,** 1690 28th St., Boulder, CO 80301: Catalog $2 ◆ Toys, games, and teaching aids for children. 303-440-7229.

**Right Start Catalog,** Right Start Plaza, 5334 Sterling Center Dr., Westlake Village, CA 91361: Catalog $2 ◆ Infant, toddler, and pre-school toys and games. 800-548-8531.

**S & S Arts & Crafts,** P.O. Box 513, Colchester, CT 06415: Free catalog ◆ Educational games, puzzles, arts and crafts projects, and curriculum products. 800-937-3482. www.snswide.com

**Sensational Beginnings,** 987 Stewart Rd., Monroe, MI 48162: Free catalog ◆ Toys and books for babies and children up to age 4. 800-444-2147.

**Toys to Grow On,** P.O. Box 17, Long Beach, CA 90801: Catalog $1 ◆ Games, backyard, educational, and children's toys. 800-874-4242.

**Troll Learn & Play,** 100 Corporate Dr., Mahwah, NJ 07430: Free catalog ◆ Children's educational toys, books, puzzles, and videos. 800-247-6106.

**U.S. Toy Company Inc.,** 13201 Arrington Rd., Grandview, MO 64030: Catalog $3 ◆ Educational toys and games. 800-448-7830. www.const/play.com

**Web Games,** Binary Arts Corp., 1321 Cameron St., Alexandria, VA 22314: Free catalog ◆ Games, puzzles, books, gadgets, and toys. 888-789-9538. www.webgames.com

**World Book Family Catalog,** 2515 E. 43rd St., P.O. Box 182246, Chattanooga, TN 37422: Free catalog ◆ Learning games, books, toys, and recordings for children. 800-874-5885. www.worldbook.com

**Worldwide Games,** P.O. Box 517, Colchester, CT 06415: Free catalog ◆ Children's puzzles and games. 800-888-0987. www.worldwidegames.com

## Electronic Toys & Games

**Accolade Inc.,** 5300 Stevens Creek Blvd., San Jose, CA 95128: Free information ◆ Video game cassettes. 800-245-7744. www.accolade.com

**BRE Software,** 352 W. Bedford Ave., Ste. 104, Fresno, CA 93711: Free catalog ◆ Video games. 209-432-2684. bre@cybergate.com

**Electronic Arts,** 1450 Fashion Island Blvd., San Mateo, CA 94404: Free information ◆ Video game cassettes. 800-245-4525.

**Impressions Software,** 222 3rd St., Ste. 0234, Cambridge, MA 92142: Free information ◆ Video game cartridges. 800-545-7677.

**Interplay Productions,** 16815 Von Karman Ave., Irvine, CA 92606: Free information ◆ Video game cartridges. 800-461-2752; 714-553-6655 (in CA).

**MicroProse Software Inc.,** 180 Lakefront Dr., Hunt Valley, MD 21030: Free information ◆ Video game cartridges. 800-879-7529.

**Radio Shack,** Division Tandy Corp., 1500 One Tandy Center, Fort Worth, TX 76102: Free information ◆ Electronic teaching toys, musical instruments, radio controlled toys, and electronic chess, strategy, and sports games. 817-390-3700. www.radioshack.com

**Sega of America,** SOA/Parts & Order Dept., P.O. Box 8097, Redwood City, CA 94063: Free information ◆ Video game cassettes. 888-734-2725; 650-508-2800 (in CA).

**Sir-Tech Software,** P.O. Box 245, Ogdensburg, NY 13669: Free information ◆ Video game cassettes. 315-393-6633.

**Spectrum Holobyte,** 2490 Mariner Square Loop, Alameda, CA 94501: Free information ◆ Video game cassettes. 510-522-3584.

**SSI Video Games,** 675 Almanor Ave., Ste. 201, Sunnyvale, CA 94086: Free information ◆ Video game cartridges. 408-737-6800.

**Strategic Simulations Inc.,** c/o Electronic Arts, 1450 Fashion Island Blvd., San Mateo, CA 94404: Free information ◆ Video game cartridges. 800-245-4525.

**Virgin Games,** 18061 Fitch Ave., Irvine, CA 92614: Free information ◆ Video game cartridges. 714-833-8710.

## General Toys & Games

**Action Farm Toys,** 2908 2nd Ave. North, Billings, MT 59101: Free information with long SASE ◆ Limited and collector edition farm toys, farm buildings, cars and trucks, banks, and other collectibles. 406-248-4121.

**Adkins Collectibles Ltd.,** 422 E. Oak St., Oak Creek, WI 53154: Free catalog ◆ Hot Wheels related toys and other collectibles. 414-761-1020. www.AdkinsStore.com

**Al's Farm Toys,** 705 Apache Mall, Rochester, MN 55902: Free catalog ◆ Current and out-of-production farm-related toys, animals, signs, and more. 507-288-1616.

**Allen-Lewis Manufacturing Company,** P.O. Box 16546, Denver, CO 80216: Free catalog ◆ Souvenirs, carnival and party supplies, fund-raising merchandise, toys and games, T-shirts and sweatshirts, and craft supplies. 800-525-6658.

**Ancient Idols Collectible Toys,** P.O. Box 245, Whitehall, PA 18052: Catalog $3 ◆ Collectible character and science fiction toys, model kits, puzzles, and games. 610-798-9940. www.ancientidols.com

**Aristoplay Games,** 450 S. Wagner Rd., Ann Arbor, MI 48103: Free catalog ◆ Educational games for all ages. 800-634-7738.

**Back to Basics Toys,** 1 Memory Ln., Ridgely, MD 21685: Free catalog ◆ Raggedy Ann dolls, Lincoln log building sets, Lionel trains, Tinkertoys, Radio Flyer wagons, Disney classics, science sets, telescopes, Meccano construction sets, sports games, play-in doll houses, and other toys. 800-356-5360. www.backtobasicstoys.com

**By Diane,** 1126 Ivon Ave., Endicott, NY 13760: Catalog $3 ◆ Puppets and soft toys. 607-754-0391.

**Christian Book Distributors,** P.O. Box 7000, Peabody, MA 01961: Free catalog ◆ Religious games for children. 978-977-5050. www.chrbook.com

**Classic Tin Toy Company,** P.O. Box 193, Sheboygan, WI 53082: Free catalog ◆ In-stock and custom replacement plastic toy parts. 414-693-3371.

**Constructive Playthings,** 1227 E. 119th St., Grandview, MO 64030: Free catalog ◆ Toys, novelties, games, puzzles, books, furniture, and sports and fitness equipment. 800-448-7830; 816-761-5900 (in MO).

**Current Inc.,** Express Processing Center, Colorado Springs, CO 80941: Free catalog ◆ Toys, greeting cards, stationery, gift wrapping and decorations, and calendars. 800-848-2848.

**D & K Toy Collectibles Inc.,** 8112 E. Fulton, Ada, MI 49301: Free price list ◆ Collectible toys. 616-676-8876. www.iserv.net/~dktoys

**Dakotah Toys,** Rt. 1, Box 157, Madison, SD 57042: Catalog $3.50 ◆ Parts for farm toys and pedal cars. 605-256-6676.

**Ecobaby,** 1475 N. Cuyamaca, El Cajon, CA 92029: Free catalog ◆ Organic and natural fiber clothes, bedding, toys, and diapering products. 888-ECOBABY; 619-596-7450 (in CA). www.ecobaby.com

**Enchanted Doll House,** Rt. 7A, RR 1, Box 2535, Manchester Center, VT 05255: Catalog $2 ◆ Stuffed animals, dolls, books, toys and games, and miniatures. 802-362-1327.

**52 Girls Collectibles,** P.O. Box 36, Morral, OH 43337: Catalog $3 ◆ Hard-to-find collectible toys and games. 614-465-6062.

**Flying Buffalo Inc.,** P.O. Box 1467, Scottsdale, CA 85252: Free catalog ◆ Player-interactive play-by-mail games. 602-945-6917. www.flyingbuffalo.com

**Games Direct Inc.,** MS112, 820 S. MacArthur Blvd., Ste. 105-112, Coppell, TX 75019: Free catalog ◆ Games and puzzles for teens and grown-ups. 800-344-3328. www.gmsdrct.com

**Games People Played,** P.O. Box 1760, Pinedale, WY 82941: Catalog $4 ◆ Antique replica game boards. 307-367-2502.

**Gordy's,** P.O. Box 201, Sharon Center, OH 44274: Catalog $3 ◆ Collectible toys and figure-related model kits. 330-239-1657. www.gremlins.com/kitbuilders

**Green Mountain Studios,** Rt. 10 North, Box 158, Lyme, NH 03768: Catalog $2 ◆ Toys, novelties, and gifts. 603-795-4398.

**Grumpa's Toys,** 9773 128th Terrace, Largo, FL 33773: Free catalog ◆ Handmade wood toys and furniture. 813-586-3431.

**Hand in Hand,** Catalogue Center, 100 Plaza Dr., Secaucus, NJ 07094: Free catalog ◆ Books, toys, games, car seats, furniture, and bathroom accessories. 800-872-9745. hihcatalog@aol.com

**Heart of America Toys,** 14106 W. 107th St., Lenexa, KS 65215: List $1 (specify interests) ◆ Toys. 913-451-7622.

**House Warmers by Gloria,** 2633 Sunnyview Circle, Appleton, WI 54914: Brochure $3 ◆ Reproduction old-time game boards. 414-749-1447.

**Island Toys,** 307 E. Main St., Ellsworth, ME 04605: Free list with long SASE ◆ Collectible toys. Islandtoys@acadia.net

**Miles Kimball Company,** 41 W. 8th Ave., Oshkosh, WI 54906: Free catalog ◆ Toys and games for children and adults. 800-546-2255. www.mileskimball.com

**Larson Wood Manufacturing,** P.O. Box 672, Park Rapids, MN 56407: Catalog $2 (refundable) ◆ Kits, parts, and supplies for toy-making. 218-732-9121.

**Lilly's Kids,** Lillian Vernon Corp., Virginia Beach, VA 23479: Free catalog ◆ Exclusive and imaginative toys for children. 800-285-5555. LVCcustsrv@aol.com

**Lunar Models,** 302 W. Smith St., Cleburne, TX 76031: Catalog $5 ◆ Science fiction models and figure kits. 817-556-0296.

**M & J Variety,** 802 First Ave., Elizabeth, NJ 07201: Free information ◆ Collectible toys and novelties. 908-820-0082.

**McVay's Old Wood Creations,** P.O. Box 553, Leslie, MI 49251: Brochure $2 ◆ Handmade game boards. 517-589-5312.

**Mobileation,** 445 E. 87th St., Ste 4, New York, NY 10128: Free catalog ◆ Mobile interactive riding toys for children. Includes electric and gasoline-engine cars, battery operated and pedal driven vehicles, ride-on toys for toddlers and infants, tricycles, bikes, scooters, seesaws, build-them-yourself pedal car kits, and handcrafted rocking horses. 888-88-MOBILE; 212-426-8074 (in NY). service@mobileation.com

**Mountain Craft Shop,** American Ridge Rd., New Martinsville, WV 26155: Free brochure ◆ American folk toys. 304-455-3570. www.folktoy.com

**Mueller's Carved Creations,** RD 3, Box 362, Cameron, WV 26033: Free brochure ◆ Handcarved rocking horses in several different sizes. 304-686-3408.

**The Nature Company,** Catalog Division, P.O. Box 188, Florence, KY 41022: Free catalog ◆ Science and nature-oriented items, toys, and novelties. 800-227-1114. www.natureco.com

**Noah's Ark,** 39830 Jackson Rd., Salisbury, MD 21804: Free brochure ◆ One-of-a-kind handcarved and painted wood chess and checker sets, animals, and other original designs. 410-546-9522.

**Oasis of Quality,** 336 Shamrock Rd., St. Augustine, FL 32086: Free catalog with three 1st class stamps ◆ Collectible toys. 904-797-9745. www.advertisingalliance.com/collect.htm

**The Old Game Store,** Rt. 11, Manchester, VT 05254: Free information with long SASE ◆ Games, puzzles, collectible teddy bears, and toys. 802-362-2756.

**Pecos Pine,** 258 A St., Ste. 5, Ashland, OR 97520: Catalog $1 ◆ Handcrafted wood toys and puzzles. 541-535-6606.

**Real Goods,** 555 Leslie St., Ukiah, CA 95482: Free catalog ◆ Solar energy-operating models. 800-762-7325. www.realgoods.com

**Real Toys USA Inc.,** 220 US 64 Hwy., Rutherfordton, NC 28139: Free brochure ◆ Handcrafted wood toys. 800-853-3636; 704-286-1755 (in NC). realtoys@rfci.net

**Rex Games Inc.,** 530 Howard St., Ste. 100, San Francisco, CA 94105: Free brochure ◆ Games, puzzles, and toys that teach and entertain. 800-542-6375; 415-777-2900 (in CA). www.rexgames.com

**Rural America Toy Collectibles,** 2488 Omega Rd., Delhi, IA 52223: Free information with long SASE ◆ Banks, collectibles, and farm toys. 319-926-2479.

**Saunier-Wilhem Company,** 3216 5th Ave., Pittsburgh, PA 15213: Free catalog ◆ Equipment and accessories for bowling, billiards, darts, table tennis, and shuffleboard. Also board games. 412-621-4350.

**Spilsbury Puzzle Company,** 3650 Milwaukee St., P.O. Box 8922, Madison, WI 53708: Free catalog ◆ Puzzles, games, and gifts. 800-772-1760.

**Billy Stefanchuk Toys,** 2445 Ferrier St., Winnipeg, Manitoba, Canada R2V 4P4: List $1 ◆ Collectible toys and display models from 1950 to the present. 204-338-4693.

**Steve's Lost Land of Toys,** 3572 Turner Ct., Fremont, CA 94536: Catalog $3 ◆ Collectible toys. 510-795-0598.

**Surplus Tractor Parts Corp.,** P.O. Box 2125, Fargo, ND 58107: Free catalog ◆ Die-cast replica model autos, trucks, farm tractors, construction equipment, planes, motorcycles, and more. Also shop repair manuals. 800-859-2045; 701-235-7503 (in ND).

**3 Trolls Games & Puzzles,** P.O. Box 4095, South Chelmsford, MA 01824: Free catalog ◆ Games and puzzles. 800-342-6373.

**Toy Parts Peddler,** Box 324, Hancock, MN 56244: Catalog $4.50 ◆ Parts for toy trucks, construction toys, race cars, and other collectibles. 320-392-5375.

**Toys-Toys-Toys,** Jerry & Ellen Harnish, 110 Main St., Bellville, OH 44813: Catalog $2 ◆ Action figures, games, puzzles, dolls, and other items. 419-886-4782.

**Toys by Monica,** Monica Peri, 6424 Louis XIV St., New Orleans, LA 70124: Free information ◆ Handmade original design cloth toys. 504-482-0428. www.craftmall.com/booths/row-h/handmade

**Toys to Grow On,** P.O. Box 17, Long Beach, CA 90801: Catalog $1 ◆ Games, T-shirts, party supplies and backyard, educational, and children's toys. 800-874-4242.

**Troll Learn & Play,** 100 Corporate Dr., Mahwah, NJ 07430: Free catalog ◆ Children's educational toys, books, puzzles, playhouse toys, videos and other recordings, costumes, and T-shirts. 800-247-6106.

**Turn off the TV,** P.O. Box 4162, Bellevue, WA 98009: Free catalog ◆ Family games. 800-949-8688. www.turnoffthetv.com

**U.S. Games Systems Inc.,** 179 Ludlow St., Stanford, CT 06902: Catalog $2 (specify playing cards and games; tarot and cartomancy) ◆ Deluxe double bridge, tarot, cartomancy, historical, and specialty decks. Also regular cards. 800-544-2637.

**Unique Multicultural Playthings,** 1723 Rosewood Ave., Louisville, KY 40204: Free catalog ◆ Jewish books, games, and videos. 502-451-2293.

**Dan Wells Antique Toys,** 7311 Hwy 329, Ste. 601, Westport, KY 40077: Catalog $8 ◆ Antique toys. 502-225-9925.

**Whippoorwill Crafts,** 126 S. Market St., Boston, MA 02109: Free information ◆ Kaleidoscopes, wood boxes and chests, instrumentalist chimes, toys and games, clocks, and imaginative crafts. 800-860-9551; 617-523-5149 (in MA).

**Wisconsin Wagon Company,** 507 Laurel Ave., Janesville, WI 53545: Free brochure ◆ Handcrafted Janesville replica solid oak coaster wagon and Janesville pine and hardwood toddler first riding 3-wheeler, circa 1900-1934. Also scooters, sleds, wheelbarrows, swings, and doll furniture. 608-754-0026.

**Worldwide Games,** P.O. Box 517, Colchester, CT 06415: Free catalog ◆ Casino games, puzzles, outdoor games, kites, and games from world-wide sources. 800-888-0987. www.worldwidegames.com

### Special-Needs Toys & Games

**The Dragonfly Toy Company,** 291 Yale Ave., Winnipeg, MB, Canada R3M 0L4: Free catalog ◆ Toys for children with special play needs. 800-308-2208. www.magic.mb.ca/~dragon

**S & S Arts & Crafts,** P.O. Box 513, Colchester, CT 06415: Free catalog ◆ Educational games, puzzles, arts and crafts projects, and curriculum products. 800-937-3482. www.snswide.com

**Toys for Special Children,** 385 Warburton Ave., Hastings-on-Hudson, NY 10706: Free catalog ◆ Assistive communication devices, specially adapted and activity toys, capability switches, skill builder equipment, computer training devices, and special devices for children with disabilities. 914-478-0960.

**Worldwide Games,** P.O. Box 517, Colchester, CT 06415: Free catalog ◆ Hardwood board games, puzzles, strategy and skill games, outdoor activities, and other games for all ages. 800-888-0987. www.worldwidegames.com

### Water Toys

**American Athletic Inc.,** 200 American Ave., Jefferson, IA 50129: Free information ◆ Surfboards and swim rings. 800-247-3978; 515-386-3125 (in IA). www.americanathletic.com

**Recreonics Corp.,** 4200 Schmitt Ave., Louisville KY 40213: Free information ◆ Surfboards, swim rings, and diving boards. 800-428-3254. www.recreonics.com

**Rothhammer International,** P.O. Box 3840, San Luis Obispo, CA 93403: Free information ◆ Surfboards, swim rings, and equipment for divers. 800-235-2156.

**Sevylor USA,** 6651 E. 26th St., Los Angeles, CA 90040: Free information ◆ Inflatable boats, mattresses, tubes, lounges, balls, and sports recreational products. 213-727-6013.

## TRACK & FIELD SPORTS

### Clothing

**Adidas USA,** 5675 N. Blackstock Rd., Spartanburg, SC 29303: Free list of retail sources ◆ Shoes and clothing. 800-423-4327. www.adidas.com

**The Athletic Connection,** 1901 Diplomat, Dallas, TX 75234: Free information ◆ Crossbars, discuses, hurdles, landing pits, relay batons, starting blocks, shotputs, and poles. 800-527-0871; 972-243-1446 (in TX).

**Betlin Manufacturing,** 1445 Marion Rd., Columbus OH 43207: Free information ◆ Clothing. 614-443-0248.

**Bristol Athletic,** 700-726 Shelby St., Bristol, TN 37621: Free information ◆ Basketball, baseball and softball, football, track, volleyball, and lacrosse uniforms for men, women, and youths. 800-336-8775; 615-968-4140 (in TN).

**Compass Industries,** 104 E. 25th St., New York, NY 10010: Free information ◆ Starter pistols. 800-221-9904.

**Converse Inc.,** 1 Fordham Rd., North Reading, MA 01864: Free information ◆ Shoes. 800-428-2667; 781-664-1100 (in MA).

**Eastbay,** P.O. Box 8066, Wausau, WI 54402: Free catalog ◆ Shoes and clothing. 800-826-2205. www.eastbay.com

**Everlast Sports Manufacturing Corp.,** 750 E. 132nd St., Bronx, NY 10454: Free information ◆ Landing pits. 800-221-8777; 718-993-0100 (in NY).

**Fab Knit Manufacturing Company,** Division Anderson Industries, 1415 N. 4th St., Waco, TX 76707: Free information ◆ Clothing. 800-333-4111; 817-752-2511 (in TX).

**Ivanko Barbell Company,** P.O. Box 1470, San Pedro, CA 90731: Free list of retail sources ◆ Shotputs. 800-247-9044; 310-514-1155 (in CA). www.advmax.com/ivanko

**Markwort Sporting Goods,** 4300 Forest Park Ave., St. Louis, MO 63108: Catalog $8 (request list of retail sources) ◆ Discuses, relay batons, starter pistols, and tape measures. 800-669-6626; 314-652-3757 (in MO).

**New Balance Athletic Shoe Inc.,** 61 N. Deacon St., Boston, MA 02134: Free list of retail sources ◆ Shoes and clothing. 800-622-1218. www.newbalance.com

**Nike Footwear Inc.,** One Bowerman Dr., Beaverton, OR 97005: Free information ◆ Shoes. 800-344-6453. www.nike.com

**JCPenney Catalog,** P.O. Box 675, Milwaukee, WI 53201: Free information ◆ Clothing and accessories. 800-222-6161. www.jcpenney.com/shopping

**Puma USA Inc.,** 147 Centre St., Brockton, MA 02403: Free information with long SASE ◆ Shoes. 800-662-7862. www.puma.com

**Reebok International Ltd.,** 100 Technology Center Dr., Stoughton, MA 02072: Free list of retail sources ◆ Shoes. 800-843-4444.

**Richardson Sports Inc.,** 3490 W. 1st Ave., Eugene, OR 97402: Free information ◆ Discuses, relay batons, and tape measures. 800-545-8686; 541-687-1818 (in OR).

**Venus Knitting Mills Inc.,** 140 Spring St., Murray Hill, NJ 07974: Free information ◆ Clothing. 800-955-4200; 908-464-2400 (in NJ).

### Equipment

**Blazer Manufacturing Company Inc.,** P.O. Box 667, Fremont, NE 68025: Free information ◆ Crossbars, hurdles, discuses, javelins, shotputs, relay batons, tape measures, and starting blocks. 800-322-2731; 402-721-2525 (in NE).

**Cramer Products Inc.,** P.O. Box 1001, Gardner, KS 66030: Free information ◆ Crossbars, hurdles, discuses, javelins, relay batons, starting blocks, and lane markers. 800-345-2231; 913-884-7511 (in KS).

**Gopher Sport,** 2929 Park Dr., Owatonna, MN 55060: Free information ◆ Equipment for basketball, football, soccer, track and field, and other net games. 800-533-0446; 507-451-7470 (in MN).

**Olympia Sports,** P.O. Box 1941, Ann Arbor, MI 48106: Free information ◆ Crossbars, hurdles, hammers, lane markers, relay batons, starter pistols, landing pits, and starting blocks. 800-521-2832. www.wolverinesports.com

## TRAMPOLINES

**American Athletic Inc.,** 200 American Ave., Jefferson, IA 50129: Free information ◆ Trampolines. 800-247-3978; 515-386-3125 (in IA). www.americanathletic.com

**The Athletic Connection,** 1901 Diplomat, Dallas, TX 75234: Free information ◆ Trampolines. 800-527-0871; 972-243-1446 (in TX).

**Austin Athletic Equipment Corp.,** 705 Bedford Ave., Box 423, Bellmore, NY 11710: Free information ◆ Trampolines. 516-785-0100.

**Bollinger Industries,** 602 Fountain Pkwy., Grand Prairie, TX 75050: Free information ◆ Home gymnasiums, trampolines, monitoring aids, and other weight training and body building equipment. 800-527-1166. www.bollinger.com

**Cannon Sports,** P.O. Box 11179, Burbank, CA 91510: Free list of retail sources ◆ Fitness and exercise equipment, monitoring aids, home gymnasiums, weight-lifting equipment, and trampolines. 800-362-3146.

**Dana Playground Equipment Inc.,** 40 E. Southern Ave., Mesa, AZ 85210: Free information ◆ Trampolines and other playground equipment. 800-676-5841. www.danaplayground.com

**JumpKing Trampolines,** 901 W. Miller Rd., Garland, TX 75041: Free catalog ◆ Trampolines. 800-322-2211.

**Spalding Sports Worldwide,** 425 Meadow St., P.O. Box 901, Chicopee, MA 01021: Free list of retail sources ◆ Home gymnasiums, trampolines, monitoring aids, and weight training, body building, and exercise equipment. 800-225-6601. www.spalding.com

**Trampoline World,** P.O. Box 808, Fayetteville, GA 30214: Free catalog ◆ Trampolines. 770-461-9941.

## TRUNK REPAIR

**Antique Trunk Supply Company,** 360 Kenilworth Rd., Bay Village, OH 44140: Catalog $1 ◆ Trunk repair parts and accessories. 440-808-8085.

**Charolette Ford Trunks,** P.O. Box 536, Spearman, TX 79081: Catalog $2.75 ◆ Supplies and tools for restoring trunks. 806-659-3027. www.charolettefordtrunks.com

**Phyllis Kennedy Restoration Hardware,** 10655 Andrade Dr., Zionsville, IN 46077: Catalog $3 ◆ Antique trunk hardware. 317-873-1316. www.kennedyhardware.com

## TVS & VCRS

### Manufacturers

**Brookline Technologies,** 2035 Carriage Hill Rd., Allison Park, PA 15101: Free information ◆ Automatic stabilizer for home video volume control. 800-366-9290.

**Canon,** One Canon Plaza, Lake Success, NY 11042: Free list of retail sources ◆ Cassette players, camcorders, sound processors, and other electronics. 516-488-6700. www.usa.canon.com

**Emerson Radio Corp.,** 9 Entin Rd., Parsippany, NJ 07054: Free information ◆ Camcorders, cassette and CD players, and TVs. 201-884-5800.

**G.E. Appliances,** General Electric Company, Appliance Park, Louisville, KY 40225: Free information ◆ Audio and video equipment, cassette players, camcorders, TVs, and universal remotes. 800-626-2000. www.ge.com

**Goldstar,** 1000 Sylvan Ave., Englewood, NJ 07632: Free information ◆ CD and cassette players and TVs. 201-816-2000.

**Hitachi Sales Corp.,** Customer Service, 3890 Steve Reynolds Blvd., Norcross, GA 30093: Free information ◆ Audio and video equipment, CD and cassette players, camcorders, and TVs. 800-241-6558.

**Infinity Systems,** 20630 Nordhoff St., Chatsworth, CA 91311: Free information ◆ Speakers and TVs. 818-553-3332.

**JVC,** 41 Slater Dr., Elmwood Park, NJ 07407: Free information ◆ Audio and video equipment, CD and cassette players, camcorders, receivers, amplifiers, TVs, and headphones. 800-252-5722. www.jvc-america.com

**Harman/Kardon,** 250 Crossways Park Dr., Woodbury, NY 11797: Free information ◆ Cassette and CD players, receivers, amplifiers, and TVs. 800-645-7484. www.harmankardon.com

**Kenwood,** P.O. Box 22745, Long Beach, CA 90801: Free information ◆ Audio and video equipment, CD and cassette players, receivers, amplifiers, TVs, and sound processors. 310-639-9000. www.kenwood.net

**Mitsubishi Electronics,** 5757 Plaza Dr., Cypress, CA 90630: Free information ◆ Audio and video equipment, CD and cassette players, camcorders, and TVs. 800-843-2515.

**NEC Technologies,** 1250 N. Arlington Heights Rd., Itasca, IL 60143: Free information ◆ Audio and video equipment, CD and cassette players, receivers, amplifiers, TVs, camcorders, sound processors, and other electronics. 800-284-4484. www.nec.com

**Onkyo,** 200 Williams Dr., Ramsey, NJ 07446: Free information ◆ CD players, receivers, amplifiers, universal remotes, and headphones. 201-825-7950.

**Panasonic,** Panasonic Way, Secaucus, NJ 07094: Free list of retail sources ◆ Audio and video systems, CD and cassette players, TVs, camcorders, headphones, and other electronics. 201-348-7000. www.panasonic.com

**Pentax Corp.,** 35 Inverness Dr. East, Englewood, CO 80112: Free information ◆ Cassette players and camcorders. 303-799-8000. www.pentax.com

**Pioneer Technologies,** P.O. Box 1760, Long Beach, CA 90801: Free information ◆ Receivers, amplifiers, TVs, sound processors, headphones, and CD, cassette, and laser disk players. 800-746-6337. www.pioneerelectronics.com

**Radio Shack,** Division Tandy Corp., One Tandy Center, Fort Worth, TX 76102: Free information ◆ Cassette and CD players, camcorders, universal remotes, computers, and other electronics. 817-390-3011. www.radioshack.com

**RCA Sales Corp.,** Thomson Consumer Electronics, P.O. Box 1976, Indianapolis, IN 46206: Free information ◆ Audio and video systems, cassette and CD players, TVs, camcorders, sound processors, and other electronics. 800-336-1900.

**Samsung Opto-Electronics,** 40 Seaview Dr., Secaucus, NJ 07094: Free information ◆ Cassette players and TVs. 800-762-7746. www.simplyamazing.com

**Sansui USA,** 200 Metroplex Dr., Edison, NJ 08817: Free information ◆ CD and cassette players, camcorders, receivers, amplifiers, TVs, and sound processors. 732-460-9710.

**Sanyo Fisher,** P.O. Box 2329, Chatsworth, CA 91313: Free information ◆ Cassette and CD players, camcorders, TVs, sound processors, universal remotes, and other electronics. 818-998-7322.

**Sharp Electronics,** Sharp Plaza, Mahwah, NJ 07496: Free information ◆ Cassette and CD players, camcorders, TVs, receivers, amplifiers, and other electronics. 800-BE-SHARP. www.sharp-usa.com

**Sony Consumer Products,** 1 Sony Dr., Park Ridge, NJ 07656: Free information ◆ Audio and video equipment, cassette and CD players, camcorders, TVs, camcorders, sound processors, universal remotes, headphones, and other electronics. 201-930-1000. www.sony.com

**Teac,** 7733 Telegraph Rd., Montebello, CA 90640: Free information ◆ Sound processors, headphones, other electronics, and CD, cassette, and laser disk players. 213-726-0303. www.teac.com

**Toshiba,** 82 Totowa Rd., Wayne, NJ 07470: Free information ◆ CD and cassette players, camcorders, sound processors, and TVs. 201-628-8000. www.toshiba.com/tacp

**Yamaha,** P.O. Box 6660, Buena Park, CA 90620: Free list of retail sources ◆ Audio and video equipment, speakers, receivers, amplifiers, sound processors, headphones, and cassette, CD, and, laser disk players. 800-492-6242. www.yamaha-motor.com

### Retailers

**Abe's of Maine Camera & Electronics,** 1957 Coney Island Ave., Brooklyn, NY 11223: Free information ◆ Video, camcorder, and photography accessories. 800-531-2237. ABEMAINE@aol.com

**AV Distributors,** 10765 Kingspoint, Houston, TX 77075: Free information ◆ TVs, fax machines, and audio, video, and stereo equipment. 800-843-3697.

**Beach Photo & Video Inc.,** 604 Main St., Daytona Beach, FL 32118: Free information ◆ Video equipment and camcorders. 904-252-0577. www.beachphoto.com

**Bondy Export Corp.,** 40 Canal St., New York, NY 10002: Free information with long SASE ◆ Household appliances, cameras, video and TV equipment, office machines, typewriters, and luggage. 212-925-7785.

**Coast to Coast,** 2570 86th St., Brooklyn, NY 11214: Free information ◆ Camcorders, video editing equipment, receivers, CD players, cassette decks, and other electronics. 800-788-5555. www.coasttocoastcamera.com

**Colonel Video & Audio,** 10765 Kingspoint Dr., Houston, TX 77075: Free information ◆ Video and audio editing equipment, camcorders, and accessories. 713-910-1776.

**Computability Consumer Electronics,** P.O. Box 17882, Milwaukee, WI 53217: Free catalog ◆ TVs, fax machines, copiers, computers, and audio, video, and stereo equipment. 800-558-0003. www.computability.com/csh.html

**Crutchfield,** 1 Crutchfield Park, Charlottesville, VA 22906: Free catalog ◆ Video, audio and stereo equipment, and TVs. 800-955-9009. www.crutchfield.com

**Data Vision,** 445 5th Ave., New York, NY 10016: Free information ◆ Electronics equipment and accessories. 888-888-2087; 212-689-1111 (in NY). www.datavis.com

**Dial-A-Brand Inc.,** 57 S. Main St., Freeport, NY 11520: Free information with long SASE ◆ TVs, appliances, video equipment, and other electronics. 516-378-9694.

**Division of Video Necessities,** 1546 Coney Island Ave., Brooklyn, NY 11230: Free information ◆ Audio, video, multi-system, and home theater equipment. 800-228-8480.

**Electronic Mailbox,** 10-12 Charles St., Glen Cove, NY 11542: Free information ◆ Camcorder, video, and production accessories. 800-323-2325. www.videoguys.com

**Electronic Wholesalers,** 1166 Hamburg Tnpk., Wayne, NJ 07470: Free information ◆ Camcorders, TVs, cassette players, 8mm and beta home decks, receivers, and other electronics. 201-696-6531. www.samans.com

**Executive Digital & Imaging Corp.,** 60 Broadway, Brooklyn, NY 11211: Free information ◆ Cameras, camcorders, video equipment, VCRs, and accessories. 888-5-EXECUTIVE.

**Family Photo & Video,** 1957 Coney Island Ave., Brooklyn, NY 11257: Free information ◆ Cameras, camcorders, video equipment, VCRs, and accessories. 800-405-7468; 718-645-1298 (in NY).

**Farralane Pro Lighting, Audio & Video Inc.,** 300 Rt. 109, Farmingdale, NY 11735: Catalog $3 ◆ Professional lighting equipment, audio and video systems, and accessories. 800-433-7057; 516-752-9824 (in NY). www.farralane.com

**Focus Electronics,** 4523 13th Ave., Brooklyn, NY 11219: Free catalog ◆ Appliances, photographic equipment, other electronics, and audio, stereo, and videoequipment. 718-436-4646. www.focususa.com

**Free Trade Photo Video,** 4718 18th Ave., Brooklyn, NY 11204: Free information ◆ Cameras, camcorders, video equipment, VCRs, and accessories. 800-234-8813; 718-633-6890 (in NY). www.freetradephoto.com

**Genesis Camera Inc.,** 814 W. Lancaster Ave., Bryn Mawr, PA 19010: Free information ◆ Audio, video, and photographic equipment. 800-575-9977; 610-527-5260 (in PA). Genesis@dvol.com

**Home Theater Design & Installation,** 190 W. Main St., Somerville, NJ 08876: Free information ◆ Audio/visual receivers, subwoofers, camcorders, speakers, VCRs, projection TVs, and other equipment. 800-676-4434.

**J & R Music World,** 59-50 Queens-Midtown Expwy., Maspeth, NY 11378: Free catalog ◆ Audio and stereo equipment, video recorders and tapes, telephones, and computers. 800-221-8180.

**K.P. Pro Video Inc.,** 87-07 Jamaica Ave., Woodhaven, NY 11421: Free information ◆ Used and new video equipment. 800-670-6555.

**Marine Park Camera & Video Inc.,** 3126 Avenue U, Brooklyn, NY 11229: Free information ◆ Video equipment, VCRs, and camcorders. 800-360-1722; 718-891-1878 (in NY).

**Mission Service Supply,** 4565 Cypress St., West Monroe, LA 71291: Free catalog ◆ Video systems and accessories. 800-352-7222; 318-397-2755 (in LA).

**New West Electronics,** 4120 Meridian, Bellingham, WA 98226: Free information ◆ Camcorders, cassette and disk players, TVs and monitors, audio components, and speakers. 800-488-8877.

**Olden Video,** 1265 Broadway, New York, NY 10001: Free information ◆ Audio and video equipment, TVs, cassette players, and other electronics. 212-226-3727.

**JCPenney Catalog,** P.O. Box 675, Milwaukee, WI 53201: Free information ◆ Cassette players, TVs, audio and video systems, and other electronics. 800-222-6161. www.jcpenney.com/shopping

**Percy's Inc.,** 19 Glennie St., Worcester, MA 01605: Free information ◆ Appliances and electronics. 508-755-5334.

**Planet Electronics,** P.O. Box 251446, West Bloomfield, MI 48325: Free catalog ◆ TVs, stereo receivers, video recorders, tapes, cassettes, and compact disks. 800-542-8811.

**Porter's Camera Store Inc.,** Box 628, Cedar Falls, IA 50613: Free catalog ◆ Video equipment. 800-553-2001. www.porters.com

**S & S Sound City,** 58 W. 45th St., New York, NY 10036: Free information ◆ Video recorders, CD players, TVs, telephones, and other electronics. 212-575-0210.

**Smile Photo & Video,** 29 W. 35th St., New York, NY 10001: Free information ◆ Photography and video equipment. 212-967-5900.

**Sound & Cinema,** 15 Minneakoning Rd., Ste. 305, Flemington, NJ 08822: Free information ◆ Audio, video, and stereo equipment. Also TVs. 888-862-8600.

**The Sound Approach,** 6067 Jericho Tnpk., Commack, NY 11725: Free information ◆ Home electronics and car audio systems. 800-368-2344.

**Sound City,** 45 Indian Lane East, Towaco, NJ 07082: Free information ◆ Audio and video equipment, cassette and CD players, camcorders, TVs, processors, fax machines, telephones, and other electronics. 800-432-0007; 973-263-6060 (in NJ). www.soundcity.com

**The Southern Advantage Company,** 8108 Idlewild Rd., #794, Charlotte, NC 28212: Free information ◆ Camcorders, VCRs, home audio equipment, videonics accessories, and other electronics. 800-632-6076. www.southernadvantage.com

**Sunshine Camera and Video,** 1562 Coney Island Ave., Brooklyn, NY 11230: Free information ◆ Computers, memory upgrades, fax modems, carrying cases, mouse devices, batteries, video equipment, and other electronics. 800-331-2661; 718-692-4140 (in NY).

**Sunshine Cameras,** 2606 N. Kings Hwy., Myrtle Beach, SC 29577: Free information ◆ Video equipment. 800-845-0693; 803-448-8474 (in SC).

**Tri-State Camera,** 650 6th Ave., New York, NY 10011: Free information ◆ Audio and video equipment, camcorders, copiers, video cassettes, and fax machines. 800-221-1926; 212-633-2290 (in NY). tscamvid@aol.com

**Uncle's Stereo,** 216 W. 72nd St., New York, NY 10023: Free information ◆ Audio and video equipment and other electronics. 800-978-6253. www.unclestereo.com

**Video Plus,** 6533 Roosevelt Blvd., Philadelphia, PA 19149: Free information ◆ Camcorders, VCRs, home audio equipment, videonics accessories, and other electronics. 800-226-6784.

**Worldwide Photo, Video & Electronics,** 203 US Hwy. 22, Greenbrook, NJ 08812: Free information ◆ Cameras, video equipment, camcorders, VCRs, and accessories. 800-617-4686. wpve@aol.com

## Cable TV Equipment

**Advent Electronics,** 10407 Goodrum Rd., Houston, TX 77041: Free catalog ◆ Cable TV and video equipment. 800-677-9994.

**Avalon Technologies,** 9909 Topanga Canyon Blvd., Chatsworth, CA 91311: Free catalog ◆ Cable converters, remote controls, top cases, tools, and accessories. 800-881-7857.

**Basic Electrical Supply & Warehousing Corp.,** P.O. Box 8180, Bartlett, IL 60103: Free information ◆ Cable TV equipment. 800-577-8775.

**Buyer's Associates,** 62 Halstead Pl., East Orange, NJ 07018: Catalog $1 ◆ Converters, descramblers, and video accessories. Also other electronics for the home, car, and recreational vehicles. 201-673-2000.

**Converters Ltd.,** 34 E. Main St., Smithtown, NY 11787: Free information ◆ TV converters with remotes, batteries, and cables. 800-322-9690.

**Electronics Inc.,** 8107 S. High Ave., Oklahoma City, OK 73149: Free brochure ◆ Converters, descramblers, remote controls, and combination units. 405-631-5153.

**Foss Warehouse Distributors,** 285 Schenck St., North Tonawanda, NY 14120: Free information ◆ Cable converters. 800-473-0506. www.fossw.com

**Greenleaf Electronics,** P.O. Box 538, Bensenville, IL 60106: Free information ◆ Cable TV equipment. 630-616-8050.

**Image Electronics,** 100 E. Whitestone, Cedar Park, TX 78613: Free information ◆ Combination converter and descrambler. 800-215-9412; 512-257-2552 (in TX).

**Intek Electronic Systems,** 8111 South I-35, Oklahoma City, OK 73149: Free catalog ◆ Cable TV equipment and accessories. 405-634-1535.

**K.D. Video Inc.,** P.O. Box 43143, Minneapolis, MN 55443: Free catalog ◆ Cable TV descramblers. 800-327-3407.

**KDE Electronics Inc.,** P.O. Box 1494, Addison, IL 60101: Free information ◆ Converters and descramblers. 708-889-0281.

**L & L Electronics Inc.,** 936 Betty Dr., Buffalo Grove, IL 60089: Free catalog ◆ Cable TV equipment. 800-542-9425.

**Mega Electronics,** 21 S. Main St., Winter Garden, FL 34787: Free catalog ◆ Cable TV descramblers and converters. 800-676-6342.

**Midwest Electronics Inc.,** P.O. Box 5000, Carpentersville, IL 60110: Free catalog with long SASE and three 1st class stamps ◆ Cable TV equipment. 800-648-3030. www.midwest-electronics.com

**Modern Communications,** 1528 SW 96th St., Oklahoma City, OK 73159: Free catalog ◆ Cable TV equipment and accessories. 405-691-0594.

**Modern Electronics,** 2609 S. 156th Circle, Omaha, NE 68130: Free catalog ◆ Cable TV equipment. 800-906-6664. www.modernelectronics.com

**ProTech Distributors Inc.,** P.O. Box 7424, Algonquin, IL 60102: Free catalog with long SASE and two 1st class stamps ◆ Cable TV converters and descramblers. 800-818-2282.

**Southern Electronics,** 10097 Cleary Blvd., Ste. 285, Plantation, FL 33324: Free information ◆ Cable descramblers. 888-51-CABLE. www. wahoo.netrunner.net/~southern

**Toni Talli's Original,** P.O. Box 71465, Las Vegas, NV 89170: Free information ◆ Cable television equipment. 702-253-1852.

**Teleview Distributors,** P.O. Box 71465, Las Vegas, NV 89170: Free information ◆ Cable TV equipment. 800-847-3773.

### Satellite Equipment

**R.L. Drake Company,** 230 Industrial Dr., Franklin, OH 45005: Free information ◆ Satellite TV antennas and receivers with optional remote control. 800-937-2534. www.rldrake.com

**Multi-Vision Electronics,** 12105 W. Center Rd., Ste. 364, Omaha, NE 68144: Free catalog ◆ Cable TV descramblers. 800-835-2330.

**Phillips-Tech Electronics,** P.O. Box 8533, Scottsdale, AZ 85252: Free catalog ◆ Satellite TV antennas. 602-269-5974.

**Skyvision Inc.,** 1016 Frontier Dr., Fergus Falls, MN 56537: Free catalog ◆ Satellite TV equipment for do-it-yourself installation and system upgrading. 800-500-9264. www.skyvision.com

**Timberville Electronics,** P.O. Box 202, Timberville, VA 22853: Free information ◆ Satellite TV receivers. 800-825-4641.

**Toshiba America,** P.O. Box 19724, Irvine, CA 92713: Free information ◆ TV satellite receivers and equipment for system upgrading. 800-457-7777. www.toshiba.com

**Universal Antenna Manufacturing,** P.O. Box 338, Ward, AR 72176: Free information ◆ Satellite reflector-type antennas with optional motorized mounts. 800-843-6517; 501-843-6517 (in AR).

**Universal Electronics,** 4555 Grove Rd., Columbus, OH 43232: Free information ◆ Satellite audio receivers. 614-866-4605.

**Xandi Electronics,** P.O. Box 25647, Tempe, AZ 85285: Catalog $2 ◆ Satellite TV receivers, voice disguisers, FM bugs, telephone transmitters, phone snoops, and other easy-to-build kits. 800-336-7389.

## TYPEWRITERS & WORD PROCESSORS

**Bondy Export Corp.,** 40 Canal St., New York, NY 10002: Free information with long SASE ◆ Household appliances, cameras, video equipment, TVs, office machines and typewriters, and luggage. 212-925-7785.

**Crutchfield,** 1 Crutchfield Park, Charlottesville, VA 22906: Free catalog ◆ Word processors, fax machines, telephones and answering machines, computers, and software. 800-955-9009. www.crutchfield.com

**Reliable Home Office,** P.O. Box 1501, Ottawa, IL 61350: Catalog $2 ◆ Word processors, calculators, computer supplies, telephones, and office furniture. 800-326-6230.

**Staples Inc.,** P.O. Box 5173, Westborough, MA 01581: Free catalog ◆ Office supplies, furniture, computer supplies and paper, drafting equipment, fax machines, word processors, and typewriters. 800-333-9328. www.staples.com

## UMBRELLAS

**Essex Manufacturing,** 330 5th Ave., New York, NY 10001: Free information ◆ Golf umbrellas. 800-648-6010; 212-239-0080 (in NY).

**Uncle Sam Umbrella Shop,** 161 W. 57th St., New York, NY 10019: Free catalog ◆ Umbrellas, canes, and walking sticks. 212-247-7163.

## VACUUM CLEANERS

**ABC Vacuum Cleaner Warehouse,** 6720 Burnet Rd., Austin, TX 78757: Free information ◆ Vacuum cleaners. 800-285-8145; 512-459-7643 (in TX). www.abcvacuum.com

**Broan Manufacturing Company,** 926 W. State St., Hartford, WI 53027: Free information ◆ Vacuum cleaner systems. 800-558-1711.

**Central Vac International,** P.O. Box 160, Kimball, NE 69145: Free information ◆ Vacuum cleaner systems. 800-666-3133; 308-235-4139 (in NE). www.centralvac.com

**Dust Boy Inc.,** P.O. Box 278, Arcanum, OH 45304: Free information ◆ Portable and stationary dust collectors. 800-232-3878.

**Home Trends,** 1450 Lyell Ave., Rochester, NY 14606: Free catalog ◆ Cleaning supplies, energy-saving devices, lighting equipment, pest controls, brushes, vacuums and accessories, and more. 716-254-6520. home@eznet.net

**M & S Systems Inc.,** 2861 Congressman Ln., Dallas, TX 75220: Free information ◆ Vacuum cleaner systems. 800-877-6631.

**MidAmerica Vacuum Cleaner Supply Company,** 666 University Ave. West, St. Paul, MN 55104: Catalog $5 ◆ Vacuum cleaners and parts, floor machines, and small kitchen appliances. 612-222-0763.

**NuTone Inc.,** P.O. Box 1580, Cincinnati, OH 45201: Catalog $3 ◆ Vacuum cleaner systems. 800-543-8687. www.nutone.com

**Oneida Air Systems Inc.,** 1005 W. Fayette St., Syracuse, NY 13204: Free brochure ◆ Industrial and for home use bagless dust collection units. 315-476-5151.

**Oreck Corp.,** 100 Plantation Rd., New Orleans, LA 70123: Free catalog ◆ Vacuum cleaners. 800-989-4200. www.oreck.com

**Royal Appliance,** 650 Alpha Dr., Cleveland, OH 44143: Free list of retail sources ◆ Hi-powered upright vacuum cleaner with hose and telescoping wand. 800-321-1134.

**Sew Vac City,** 1667 Texas Ave. South, College Station, TX 77840: Brochure $3 ◆ Sewing machines and vacuum cleaners. 800-338-5672.

**Sewin' in Vermont,** 84 Concord Ave., St. Johnsbury, VT 05819: Free information ◆ Vacuum cleaners and attachments. 800-451-5124; 802-748-3803 (in VT).

**Shop-Vac Corp.,** 2323 Reach Rd., Williamsport, PA 17701: Free information ◆ Wet and dry vacuum cleaners. 717-326-0502. www.shopvac.com

**Vacuflo,** 512 W. Gorgas St., Louisville, OH 44641: Free list of retail sources ◆ Built-in central vacuum cleaner systems. 800-822-8356. www.vacuflo.com

## VIDEO CASSETTES, TAPES, & DISCS

**Artistic Video,** 87 Tyler Ave., Sound Beach, NY 11789: Free catalog ◆ Health and fitness videos. 888-982-4244; 516-744-5999 (in NY). www.nsws.com/TAI-CHI

**Australian Catalogue Company,** 7605 Welborn St., Raleigh, NC 27615: Free catalog ◆ Videos that take you around Australia. 800-808-0938. www.aussiecatalog.com

**Best Film & Video Corp.,** 108 New South Rd., Hicksville, NY 11801: Free information ◆ Special interest and children's videos. 800-527-2189; 516-931-6969 (in NY).

**Myron J. Biggar Group,** P.O. Box 239, 65 S. Broad St., Nazareth, PA 18064: Free brochure ◆ O gauge model railroad videos on layouts, how-to-projects, and other information. 610-759-0406. members.aol.com/Ogaugerwy/OGR.html

**BLT Supplies Inc.,** Mail Order Dept., 35-01 Queens Blvd., Long Island City, NY 11101: Free information ◆ Asian martial arts films. 800-322-2860.

**Brooklyn Botanic Garden,** Attention: Plants & Gardens, 1000 Washington Ave., Brooklyn, NY 11225: Free brochure ◆ Gardening books and videos. 718-941-4044. www.bbg.org

**Calibre Press Inc.,** 666 Dundee Rd., Ste. 1607, Northbrook, IL 60062: Free catalog ◆ Law enforcement and EMS videos, books, and survival equipment. 800-323-0037; 708-498-5680 (in IL). www.calibrepress-catalog.com

**Captioned Films/Videos Program,** National Association of the Deaf, 1447 E. Main St., Spartanburg, SC 29307: Free information ◆ Free loan service of over 4000 films and videos for persons with a hearing loss. 800-237-6213 (voice); 800-237-6819 (TTY). www.cfv.org

**Christian Book Distributors,** P.O. Box 7000, Peabody, MA 01961: Free catalog ◆ Religious videos for children and adults. 978-977-5050. www.chrbook.com

**Classic Cinema,** P.O. Box 18932, Encino, CA 91416: Catalog $5 ◆ Westerns, mysteries, comedies, and drama on video cassettes. 800-94-MOVIE.

**Collage Video Specialties Inc.,** 5390 Main St. NE, Minneapolis, MN 55421: Free catalog ◆ Video and audio exercise and workout cassettes. 800-433-6769.

**Critics' Choice Video,** P.O. Box 749, Itasca, IL 60143: Free catalog ◆ Classics, new releases, special interest, and other subjects on video cassettes. 800-544-9852. www.ccvideo.com

**Defender Industries Inc.,** 42 Great Neck Rd., Waterford, CT 06385: Free catalog ◆ Marine books and videos. 800-435-7180; 860-701-3415 (in CT). defenderus@aol.com

**Direct Video,** P.O. Box 6565, London, Ontario, Canada N5W 5S5: Free catalog ◆ Action and adventure, drama, family and children, horror, musical, mystery and suspense, science fiction, fantasy, and other videos. 800-461-1651; 519-659-3912 (in Canada). www.directvideo.com

**DIY Video Corp.,** Do It Yourself Inc., 117 Creekview Circle, Carboro, NC 27510: Free brochure ◆ Educational how-to home improvement videos. 919-933-8533.

**Double-Time Jazz,** Jamey & Julia Aebersold, P.O. Box 1244, New Albany, IN 47151: Free catalog ◆ Jazz records and videos. 800-293-8528. www.doubletimejazz.com

**Dragon Door Publications,** P.O. Box 4381, St. Paul, MN 55104: Free catalog ◆ Books, videos, audio tapes, and special reports on health, self-defense, and healing systems. 800-899-5111; 651-645-0517 (in MN). www.dragondoor.com

**Englewood Entertainment,** 10917 Winner Rd., Independence, MO 64052: Brochure $1 ◆ Science fiction, horror, and special interest videos. 888-573-5490. www.englewd.com

**Ergo Media,** P.O. Box 2037, Teaneck, NJ 07666: Free catalog ◆ Entertaining and informative programs on different aspects of Jewish life. 800-695-3746. www.jewishvideo.com

**Explorations,** 360 Interlocken Blvd., Ste. 300, Broomfield, CO 80021: Free catalog ◆ Videos, audio recordings, and other products on yoga, meditation, magnetic response, world knowledge, human relations, and more. 800-720-2114.

**Facets Video,** 1517 W. Fullerton Ave., Chicago, IL 60614: Free catalog ◆ Thousands of foreign, classic American, silent, documentary, experimental, cult, music, fine art, and children's videos. Also laser discs and CDs. 800-331-6197. sales@facets.org

**FarPointer Sports Corp.,** P.O. Box 702618, Tulsa, OK 74170: Free information ◆ Books, videos, audio tapes, and software covering training, coaching, motivational and skills improvement, and other sports-related items. 918-587-6477.

**Festival Films,** 6115 Chestnut Terrace, Shorewood, MN 55331: Free catalog ◆ United States and foreign films on video cassettes. Includes the silent era, early feature films, and other classics. 612-470-2172.

**Floyd's Record Shop,** P.O. Drawer 10, Ville Platte, LA 70586: Catalog $1 (refundable) ◆ Cajun and Creole music, books, videos, and T-shirts. 318-363-2184. www.floydsrecords.com

**Foothill Video,** 42257 6th St. West, Bldg. 306, Lancaster, CA 93534: Catalog $5 ◆ Westerns, feature films, serials, and foreign classics on video cassettes. 805-726-7533.

**FORTE Productions,** P.O. Box 325, San Geronimo, CA 94963: Free information ◆ Video instructional series that teaches how to play the piano. 415-488-9446. www.kspace.com/tolchin

**Freestyle Productions,** 675 NW Country View Rd., White Salmon, WA 98672: Free brochure ◆ How-to snowboard and ski videos. 800-805-8580. www.sportsvideo.com

**Full Circle Records,** Gloucester Rd., Blackwood, NJ 08012: Free information ◆ New and used CDs, imported recordings, other records, and videos. 609-227-0662.

**Fusion Video,** 100 Fusion Way, Country Club Hills, IL 60478: Catalog $3.99 ◆ Science fiction videos. 800-959-0061.

**Habari Gani,** African-American Crafts, P.O. Box 468, 132-05 Merrick Blvd., Jamaica, NY 11434: Catalog $1 ◆ Handcarved items from Kenya, Kente cloth from the Ivory Coast, clothing, accessories, craft kits, books, music, videos, beads, feathers, and other supplies. 718-978-7110.

**Gold Medal,** 1 Bennington Ave., Freeport, Long Island, NY 11520: Free catalog ◆ African-American hair products, wigs, videos, music, and more. 800-535-8101.

**Good Music Record Company,** P.O. Box 1935, Ridgely, MD 21681: Free catalog ◆ CDs, cassettes, and videos. 800-538-4200.

**A. Goodman Video Tapes,** P.O. Box 667, Beaumont, CA 92223: Free information ◆ How-to videos on jewelry-making. 800-382-3237.

**GORP,** P.O. Box 3016, Everett, WA 98206: Free catalog ◆ Over 3000 maps, guidebooks, handbooks, videos, CD-ROMs, and more on the outdoors. 888-994-4677. www.gorp.com

**Great Christian Books,** 229 S. Bridge St., P.O. Box 8000, Elkton, MD 21922: Free catalog ◆ Bible video games. 800-775-5422. www.GreatChristianBooks.com

**High View Publications,** P.O. Box 51967, Pacific Grove, CA 93950: Free catalog ◆ Chinese martial arts books and videos. 408-622-0789.

**Historic Aviation,** 1401 Kings Wood Rd., Eagan, MN 55122: Free catalog ◆ Books and videos on the history of commercial airliners, famous men in aviation, nostalgic classics, humor, military action, and other aviation topics. 800-225-5575.

**Home Film Festival,** P.O. Box 2032, Scranton, PA 18501: Catalog $15 ◆ Hard-to-find films, limited release features, Hollywood classics, documentaries, and other videos. 800-258-3456. www.homefilmfestival.com

**The House of Music,** 2057 W. 95th St., Chicago, IL 60643: Free information ◆ Hard-to-find records, tapes, CDs, and videos. 312-239-4114.

**House of Tyrol,** P.O. Box 909, 66 E. Kytle St., Cleveland, GA 30528: Free catalog ◆ Musical cuckoo clocks, crystal, porcelain, lamps, music boxes, other gifts, and travel, folk music from around the world, language, and educational videos. 800-241-5404.

**Infomedia Special Interest Video & CD-ROMs,** 400 Morris Ave., Long Branch, NJ 07740: Catalog $5 ◆ Academic studies, boating and sailing, business and career skills, children's learning, dance performance, documentary exercise and fitness, home improvement, pets, sports, and other special interest videos and CD-ROMs. 800-262-3822.

**International Historic Films Inc.,** Box 29035, Chicago, IL 60629: Catalog $2 ◆ Military, political, and historical documentary films on video cassettes. 312-927-2900.

**Jersey Shore Video,** P.O. Box 293, Whiting, NJ 08759: Free catalog ◆ Verve, Columbia, Epic jazz, RCA living stereo, and rock the house pop titles. 908-350-1446.

**Kimbo Educational,** P.O. Box 477, Long Branch, NJ 07740: Free catalog ◆ Cassettes, CDs, records, videos, read-alongs, and film strips for children. 800-631-2187. www.kimboed.com

**Kino Video,** 333 W. 39th St., Ste. 503, New York, NY 10018: Free catalog ◆ International, foreign, and classic movies from Hollywood's golden era on video cassettes. 800-562-3330; 212-629-6880 (in NY). www.kino.com

**Lark in the Morning,** P.O. Box 1176, Mendocino, CA 95460: Free catalog ◆ Hard-to-find musical instruments, books about music, CDs, cassettes, and videos. 707-964-5569. larkinam@larkinam.com

**Leerburg Video Productions,** P.O. Box 218, Menomonie, WI 54751: Free catalog ◆ Dog training videos. 715-235-6502. Frawley@win.bright.net

**Metropolitan Opera Shop,** Lincoln Center, 135 W. 65th St., New York, NY 10023: Free catalog ◆ Books and classical, concert, operatic, and documentary videos, records, and CDs. 800-453-2258; 212-580-4090 (in NY). www.metguild.com

**Moviecraft Inc.,** P.O. Box 438, Orland Park, IL 60462: Catalog $1 ◆ Old TV shows, rare cartoons, classics, contemporary releases, war newsreels. Propaganda subjects, special interest topics, and feature films. 708-460-9082.

**Movies Unlimited,** 6736 Castor Ave., Philadelphia, PA 19149: Catalog $10.95 ◆ Over 43,000 video titles.

**Music Books Plus,** 23 Hannover Dr., #7, St. Catharines, Ontario, Canada L2W 2A3: Free catalog ◆ Books, instructional videos, audio cassettes, CD-ROMs, computer software, and other music-related items. 800-265-8481.

**Murrays Catamarans,** P.O. Box 490, Carpinteria, CA 93014: Free list of retail sources ◆ Catamarans, factory parts, books, and videos. 800-788-8964. www.murrays.com

**Music Connection,** 430 Market St., Elmwood Park, NJ 07407: Free information ◆ New and used CDs, imported recordings, and videos. 201-797-5212.

**Music for Little People,** P.O. Box 1460, Redway, CA 95560: Free catalog ◆ Famous stories, favorite songs, lullabies, nature stories, folk music, classical music, and other children's music cassettes and videos. 800-346-4445.

**Thomas Nelson Publishers,** P.O. Box 140300, Nashville, TN 37214: Free catalog ◆ Christian books, bibles, audio and video recordings, and music. 800-933-9673. www.nelsonworddirect.com

**The Noontide Press,** P.O. Box 2719, Newport Beach, CA 92659: Free catalog ◆ Books, audio tapes, and videos on social, political, economic, and historical taboos of the modern age. 714-631-1490.

**Opera World,** Box 800, Concord, MA 01742: Free catalog ◆ Videos, laser discs, CDs, and books on the opera. 800-99-OPERA. www.operaworld.com

**PBS Home Video,** Catalog Mail Order Center, P.O. Box 751089, Charlotte, NC 28275: Free catalog ◆ Educational and entertainment videos. 800-645-4PBS. www.pbs.org

**PFS Video Inc.,** P.O. Box 50, Oley, PA 19547: Free information ◆ Martial arts videos on defense techniques. 610-689-5871.

**Pieces of History,** P.O. Box 4470, Cave Creek, AZ 85331: Catalog $2 ◆ Western videos. 602-488-1377.

**The Planetary Society,** 65 N. Catalina Ave., Pasadena, CA 91106: Free brochure ◆ Astronomy books, videos, and slide sets. 626-793-1675.

**Precept Ministries,** P.O. Box 182218, Chattanooga, TN 37422: Free catalog ◆ Religious books, audio cassettes, and videos. 423-894-3277. www.precept.org

**Pro-Action Sports Inc.,** P.O. Box 26657, Los Angeles, CA 90026: Free information ◆ Books and videos on the martial arts. 888-567-7789.

**Pyramid Media,** P.O. Box 1048, Santa Monica, CA 90404: Free information ◆ Videos and software for the educational and healthcare markets. 800-421-2304. www.pyramidmedia.com

**Reader's Digest,** P.O. Box 107, Pleasantville, NY 10571: Free catalog ◆ Videos on travel, nature, drama, movies, children's subjects, how-to-information, sports, and music. 914-241-7445. www.readersdigest.com

**Ridge Runner Music,** 84 York Creek Dr., Driftwood, TX 78619: Catalog $1 ◆ Guitar instruction and entertainment videos. 512-847-8833.

**Roberts Rinehart Publishers,** 6309 Monarch Place Park, Niwote, CO 80503: Free brochure ◆ Videos, CDs, and books about Ireland. 800-352-1985. www.robertsrinehart.com

**Mary Roehr Books & Videos,** 500 Saddlerock Circle, Sedona, AZ 86336: Free catalog ◆ How-to books, videos, and supplies on sewing and tailoring. 800-291-6764.

**Ron's Books,** P.O. Box 714, Harrison, NY 10528: Free information ◆ Books and videos on trains. 914-967-7541.

**Roots & Rhythm Inc.,** P.O. Box 837, El Cerrito, CA 94530: Catalog $5 (specify blues, country, or vintage rock and roll) ◆ Records, tapes, compact disks, music books, and videos. 510-525-1494. roots@hooked.net

**Rose Records,** 214 S. Wabash Ave., Chicago, IL 60604: Free catalog ◆ Classical and opera recordings on long-playing records, CDs, cassettes, and music videos. Includes imports, new releases, and published overstocks. 800-955-ROSE.

**Joseph Russo,** P.O. Box 2422, North Babylon, NY 11703: Free information with long SASE (specify interests) ◆ Past and present rare videos.

**Shokus Video,** P.O. Box 3125, Chatsworth, CA 91313: Catalog $3 (refundable) ◆ Classic TV shows from the 1950s and 1960s. 818-704-0400. www.shokus.com

**Sinister Cinema,** P.O. Box 4369, Medford, OR 97501: Free information ◆ Science fiction, horror, mystery, suspense, fantasy, and other films on video cassettes. 541-773-6860. www.cinemaweb.com/sinister

**Something Weird Video,** P.O. Box 33664, Seattle, WA 98133: Catalog $5 ◆ Rare vintage feature films, shorts, movie trailers, and classic TV commercials, from the 1930s to 1970s. 206-361-3759.

**Sounds True Audio,** 413 S. Arthur Ave., Louisville, CO 80027: Free catalog ◆ Audio and video recordings on personal discovery, relationships, sacred music of the world, homeopathy, psychology, health and healing, and other life-related topics. 800-333-9185. info@soundstrue.com

**Special Products Corp.,** 1081 S. Main St., Ste. 186, Cheshire, CT 06410: Free catalog ◆ Instructional, educational, motivational, and inspirational videos and CD-ROMs. 203-271-0470.

**SportsProducts.com,** P.O. Box 702618, Tulsa, OK 74170: Free information ◆ Sports instructional videos, books, and software for professional and amateur youth coaches and players. 800-926-5892. www.sportsproducts.com

**StageStep,** 2000 Hamilton St., Philadelphia, PA 19130: Free catalog ◆ Dance, theater, film, music, and fitness books, videos, and CDs. 800-523-0960. www.stagestep.com

**Sun Mountain Books,** P.O. Box 743, Virginia City, NV 89440: Catalog $3 (refundable) ◆ Western books, videos, and cassettes.

**Sysko's Books,** 30 W. Main St., P.O. Box 6, Benton, WI 53803: Free catalog ◆ Basketball books and videos. 800-932-2534. www.bbhighway.com/store/Products/catalog.asp

**TAI SENG Video Marketing,** 170 S. Spruce Ave., Ste. 200, South San Francisco, CA 94080: Catalog $7.50 (refundable) ◆ Hong Kong movie videos on VHS, LO, DVO, and VCD. 800-888-3836. www.taiseng.com

**Tara Publications,** P.O. Box 707, Owings Mills, MD 21117: Free catalog ◆ Jewish music books, casettes, CDs, and videos. 800-TARA-400; 410-654-0880 (in MD). www.jewishmusic.com

**TKD Enterprises Inc.,** 1423 18th St., Bettendorf, IA 52722: Free information: Free information ◆ Martial arts books, videos, and shoes. 800-388-5966.

**Unique Multicultural Playthings,** 1723 Rosewood Ave., Louisville, KY 40204: Free catalog ◆ Jewish books, games, and videos. 502-451-2293.

**Unique Publications,** 4201 W. Vanowen Pl., Burbank, CA 91505: Free information ◆ Martial arts videos. 800-332-3330.

**Venture Entertainment Group,** P.O. Box 55113, Sherman Oaks, CA 91413: Free brochure ◆ Children's, fitness, educational, and antiques video tapes. 818-981-7813. www.venture818.com

**Victorian Video Productions,** P.O. Box 1540, Colfax, CA 95713: Free information ◆ How-to videos on textiles, jewelry, bead-crafting, needlework, and other crafts. 800-848-0284. www.victorianvid.com

**Video Opera House,** P.O. Box 800, Concord, MA 01742: Free catalog ◆ Opera, ballet, and classical video recordings. 800-99-OPERA. www.operaworld.com

**Videomaker,** P.O. Box 4591, Chico, CA 95927: Free information ◆ How-to videos on basic video shooting, editing, introduction to desktop videos, lighting techniques, and sound. 916-891-8410.

**Wee Folk Creations,** 18476 Natchez Ave., Prior Lake, MN 55372: Free catalog ◆ How-to videos and books on molding with clay, tools, accessories, and supplies. 888-933-3655. www.weefolk.com

**Whole Person Associates,** 210 W. Michigan, Duluth, MN 55802: Free catalog ◆ Self-improvement books and videos on wellness promotion, stress management, and relaxation. 800-247-6789. www.wholeperson.com

**Wolvering Sports Videos,** P.O. Box 1941, Ann Arbor, MI 48106: Catalog $1 ◆ Sports instructional videos. 313-761-5691.

**Woodworkers' Discount Books & Videos,** 735 Sunrise Ct.. Woodland Park, CO 80863: Free catalog ◆ How-to books and videos on woodworking. 800-378-4060. www.discount-books.com

**Written Heritage,** P.O. Box 1390, Folsom, LA 70437: Free catalog ◆ American Indian (Native American) books and videos. 800-301-8009; 504-796-5433 (in LA). www.whisperingwind.com

**YMAA Publication Center,** 38 Hyde Park Ave., Jamaica Plain, MA 02130: Free catalog ◆ Martial arts books, videos, clothing, and music. 800-669-8892. www.ymaa.com/pubcenter.html

## VIDEO PRODUCTION & TRANSFER SERVICES

**Digital Treasures,** 4250 Executive Square, Ste. 520, La Jolla, CA 92037: Free brochure ◆ Home movies, slides, photos, and other documents converted to videos and CD-ROMs. 800-659-5589; 619-587-0580 (in CA).

**Play it Again Video Productions Inc.,** 295 Reservoir St., Needham, MA 02194: Free information ◆ Home movies, slides, and photos transferred to video cassettes. 800-872-0986; 781-449-3800 (in MA).

**The Transfer Station,** 8523 Reseda Blvd., Northridge, CA 91324: Free information ◆ Film-to-tape and tape-to-tape transfer and conversion services. 800-350-6502; 818-885-6501 (in CA).

## VISION IMPAIRMENT AIDS

**American Council of the Blind,** 1155 15th St. NW, Washington, DC 20005: Free list ◆ Large-print list of low vision aids and large-print publications. 202-467-5081.

**American Printing House for the Blind,** 1839 Frankfort Ave., P.O. Box 6085, Louisville, KY 40206: Free catalog ◆ Braille writing and embossing equipment, electronic devices, low-vision simulation materials, reading readiness products, and educational aids. 800-223-1839; 502-895-2405 (in KY). www.aph.org

**Anything Diabetic,** 7124 N. University Dr., #267, Tamarac, FL 33321: Free catalog ◆ Supplies for diabetics and visually impaired persons. 800-644-7444.

**Duxbury Systems Inc.,** 435 King St., P.O. Box 1504, Littleton, MA 01460: Free brochure ◆ Braille translator software for Windows. 978-486-9766.

**Independent Living Aids/Can-Do Products,** 27 East Mall, Plainview, NY 11803: Free catalog ◆ Writing aids, low-vision and braille items, household items, home health care supplies, mobility equipment, and communication aids. 800-537-2118; 516-752-8080 (in NY).

**Lighthouse Enterprises,** 36-20 Northern Blvd., Long Island City, NY 11101: Free catalog ◆ Assistive aids for people with visual impairments. 800-829-0500.

**LS & S Group Inc.,** P.O. Box 673, Northbrook, IL 60065: Free catalog ◆ Magnifiers, watches, braille computers, gifts, and other products for people with visual impairments. 800-468-4789; 847-498-9777 (in IL).

**Maxi-Aids,** P.O. Box 3209, Farmingdale, NY 11735: Free catalog ◆ Communications devices, eating and kitchen aids, dressing aids, wheelchair accessories, and more. 800-522-6294. sales@maxiaids.com

**Optelec,** 6 Lyberty Way, Westford, MA 01886: Free catalog ◆ Low-vision aids for people with visual impairments. Includes software for magnifying text to large print and an add-on color magnifier for PC computers. 800-828-1056; 978-392-0707 (in MA).

**Science Products,** Box 888, Southeastern, PA 19399: Free catalog ◆ Voice technology equipment and other sensory aids for people with hearing or visual impairments. 800-888-7400; 610-296-2111 (in PA).

## VITAMINS & NUTRITIONAL SUPPLEMENTS

**Akin's Natural Foods Market,** 7807 E. 51st St., Tulsa, OK 74145: Free catalog ◆ Wheat-free groceries, vitamins, and nutritional food supplements. 800-800-3133; 918-663-4137 (in OK). www.akins.com

**Barth's,** P.O. Box 50289, Pompano Beach, FL 33074: Free catalog ◆ Natural vitamin and mineral supplements, cosmetics, health foods, and home health aids. 800-645-2328.

**Bioenergy Nutrients,** 6565 Odell Pl., Boulder, CO 80301: Catalog $1 ◆ Nutritional supplements, homeopathic medicines, antioxidants, and all-natural skin care products. 800-627-7775. www.amiron.com

**Brownville Mills,** Box 145, Brownville, NE 68321: Free price list ◆ Fresh natural foods and vitamins. 800-305-7990; 402-825-4131 (in NE). www.skyport.com/brownvillemills

**Diamond-Herpanacine Associates,** P.O. Box 544, Ambler, PA 19002: Free information ◆ Vitamin preparations. 215-542-2981. herpana@aol.com

**Freeda Vitamins,** 36 E. 41st St., New York, NY 10017: Free catalog ◆ Vitamins and dietary food supplements. 800-777-3737; 212-685-4980 (in NY). www freedvite.com

**Gluten-Free Pantry,** P.O. Box 840, Glastonbury, CT 06033: Free information ◆ Gluten-free vitamins. 800-291-8386. www.glutenfree.com

**Harvest Time Vitamins,** P.O. Box 7241, Bloomfield, CT 06002: Free catalog ◆ Vitamins, herbs, and health supplements. 800-854-7673.

**Health Center for Better Living,** 1414 Rosemary Ln., Naples, FL 33940: Free catalog ◆ Vitamins, and mineral supplements, and other herbal health care products. 800-544-4225.

**Hillestad Corp.,** 178 US Hwy. 51 North, Woodruff, WI 54568: Free catalog ◆ Natural vitamins. 800-535-7742; 715-358-2113 (in WI).

**Indiana Botanic Gardens,** P.O. Box 5, Hammond, IN 46325: Catalog $1 ◆ Vitamins, herbs, spices, and personal care products. 800-644-8327. www.botanichealth.com

**L & H Vitamins Inc.,** 32-33 47th Ave., Long Island City, NY 11101: Free catalog ◆ Vitamins and nutritional supplements, homeopathic medicines, aromatherapy products, and natural health care products. 800-221-1152; 718-937-7400 (in NY). www.justmysizebras.com

**Lee Nutrition,** 290 Main St., Cambridge, MA 02142: Free information ◆ Vitamins and nutritional supplements.

**Mother Nature's General Store,** P.O. Box 1145, Southhampton, PA 18966: Free price list ◆ Herbs, vitamins, and nutritional products. 888-255-2336.

**Nutrition Headquarters,** One Nutrition Plaza, Carbondale, IL 62901: Free catalog ◆ Vitamins and mineral supplements, health and beauty aids, and herbal formulas.

**Nutrition Warehouse,** 106 E. Jericho Tnpk., P.O. Box 311, Mineola, NY 11501: Free catalog ◆ Vitamins and nutritional supplements. 800-645-2929.

**Oleda & Company Inc.,** 6467 Southwest Blvd., Fort Worth, TX 76132: Free catalog ◆ Nutrition, health, and beauty aids. 817-731-1147.

**Pride Vitamins,** 520 Bower Hill Rd., 2nd Floor, Pittsburgh, PA 15228: Free catalog ◆ Vitamins and nutritional supplements. 888-774-3381.

**Puritan's Pride,** 1233 Montauk Hwy., P.O. Box 9001, Oakdale, NY 11769: Free catalog ◆ Natural vitamins, health supplements, and beauty aids. 800-645-1030. www.puritan.com

**Puritan's Pride/Stur-Dee Health Products,** 1233 Montauk Hwy., P.O. Box 9001, Oakdale, NY 11769: Free catalog ◆ Vitamins and health food supplements. 800-645-1030. www.puritan.com

**RVP Health Savings Center,** 3890 Park Central Blvd., North Pompano Beach, FL 33064: Free catalog ◆ Vitamins, natural supplements, cosmetics, and beauty aids. 800-645-2978.

**SDV Vitamins,** P.O. Box 9215, Delray Beach, FL 33482: Free information ◆ Nutritional supplements and vitamins. 800-738-8482.

**Spice Discounters,** P.O. Box 2263, Napa, CA 94558: Free catalog ◆ Herbs, spices, oils, extracts, and vitamins. 800-610-5950. www.spicediscounters.com

**Star Pharmaceuticals/Puritan's Pride,** 1233 Montauk Hwy., P.O. Box 9001, Oakdale, NY 11769: Free catalog ◆ Generic vitamins, nutritional supplements, toiletries, health care products, and pet supplies. 800-274-6400. www.puritan.com

**Sunburst Biorganics,** 832 Merrick Rd., Baldwin, NY 11510: Free catalog ◆ Nutritional supplements and toiletries. 800-645-8448; 516-623-8478 (in NY). www.sunburstbiorganics.com

**Swanson Health Products Inc.,** P.O. Box 6003, Fargo, ND 58108: Free information ◆ Vitamins and food supplements. 800-437-4148.

**Vitamin Direct Inc.,** P.O. Box 1983, San Marcos, CA 92079: Free catalog ◆ Vitamins, minerals, and nutritional supplements. 800-468-4027. vitamins@ix.netcom.com

**Vitamin Power Nutritional Health Products,** P.O. Box 81974, Las Vegas, NV 89180: Catalog $1 ◆ Nutritional health products. 888-297-4640.

**The Vitamin Shoppe,** 4700 Westside Ave., North Bergen, NJ 07047: Free catalog ◆ Vitamins, herbs, homeopathic medicines, and natural cosmetics. 800-223-1216. www.vitaminshoppe.com

**VNF Nutrition,** 246 Rt. 25A, Setauket, NY 11733: Free catalog ◆ Nutritional supplements. 800-681-7099. www.vnfnutrition.com

## VOLLEYBALL

### Clothing

**Action Sport Systems Inc.,** P.O. Box 1442, Morganton, NC 28680: Free information ◆ Uniforms. 800-631-1091; 704-584-8000 (in NC).

**Adidas USA,** 5675 N. Blackstock Rd., Spartanburg, SC 29303: Free list of retail sources ◆ Shoes. 800-423-4327. www.adidas.com

**Bristol Athletic,** 700-726 Shelby St., Bristol, TN 37621: Free information ◆ Basketball, baseball and softball, football, track, volleyball, and lacrosse uniforms for men, women, and youths. 800-336-8775; 615-968-4140 (in TN).

**Champion Products Inc.,** 475 Corporate Square Dr., Winston-Salem, NC 27105: Free information ◆ Uniforms.

**Converse Inc.,** 1 Fordham Rd., North Reading, MA 01864: Free information ◆ Shoes. 800-428-2667; 781-664-1100 (in MA).

**Foot-Joy & Titleist Worldwide,** P.O. Box 965, Fairhaven, MA 02719: Free list of retail sources ◆ Shoes. 888-848-5347. www.titleist.com

**Mizuno Corp.,** 1 Jack Curran Way, Norcross, GA 30071: Free information ◆ Uniforms and shoes. 800-966-1211. www.mizunogolf.com

**Nike Footwear Inc.,** One Bowerman Dr., Beaverton, OR 97005: Free list of retail sources ◆ Shoes. 800-344-6453. www.nike.com

**Puma USA Inc.,** 147 Centre St., Brockton, MA 02403: Free information with long SASE ◆ Shoes. 800-662-7862. www.puma.com

**Spike Nashbar,** 4111 Simon Rd., Youngstown, OH 44512: Free information ◆ Shoes and equipment. 800-774-5348. www.nasbar.com

**Sport Fun Inc.,** 4621 Sperry St., Los Angeles, CA 90039: Free information ◆ Uniforms and shoes. 800-423-2597; 213-245-7530 (in CA).

**Venus Knitting Mills Inc.,** 140 Spring St., Murray Hill, NJ 07974: Free information ◆ Uniforms. 800-955-4200; 908-464-2400 (in NJ).

### Equipment

**Action Sport Systems Inc.,** P.O. Box 1442, Morganton, NC 28680: Free information ◆ Volleyball sets, nets, posts, and standards. 800-631-1091; 704-584-8000 (in NC).

**American Athletic Inc.,** 200 American Ave., Jefferson, IA 50129: Free information ◆ Nets. 800-247-3978; 515-386-3125 (in IA). www.americanathletic.com

**Bauer Sports,** 150 Ocean Rd., Greenland, NH 03840: Free list of retail sources ◆ Nets and balls. 800-362-3146. www.bauer.com

**Carron Net Company,** 1623 17th St., P.O. Box 177, Two Rivers, WI 54241: Free information ◆ Archery, baseball, basketball, gymnasium and climbing, football, racquetball, soccer, tennis, and volleyball equipment. 800-558-7768; 414-793-2217 (in WI). sales@carronnet.com

**Flaghouse Sports Equipment,** 601 Flaghouse Dr., Hasbrouck Heights, NJ 07604: Free catalog ◆ Volleyball equipment. 800-793-7900. www.flaghouse.com

**Franklin Sports Industries Inc.,** 17 Campanelli Pkwy., P.O. Box 508, Stoughton, MA 02072: Free information ◆ Volleyball sets, balls, and nets. 800-426-7700. www.eisnerbros.com

**Gared Sports Inc.,** 1107 Mullanphy St., St. Louis, MO 63106: Free information ◆ Nets, posts, standards, and balls. 800-325-2682.

**General Sportcraft Company,** 140 Woodbine Rd., Bergenfield, NJ 07621: Free information ◆ Nets, posts, standards, balls, and protective gear. 201-384-4242.

**Indian Industries Inc.,** P.O. Box 889, Evansville, IN 47706: Free catalog ◆ Nets and sets. 800-457-3373; 812-467-1200 (in IN).

**Jayfro Corp.,** Unified Sports Inc., 976 Hartford Tnpk., P.O. Box 400, Waterford, CT 06385: Free catalog ◆ Nets, posts, referee stands, and equipment carriers. 860-447-3001.

**Dick Martin Sports Inc.,** 181 E. Union Ave., P.O. Box 7384, East Rutherford, NJ 07073: Free information ◆ Nets, posts, balls, and protective gear. 800-221-1993; 201-453-5255 (in NJ).

**Neat Nets Inc.,** P.O. Box 0091, Youngwood, PA 15607: Free brochure ◆ Self-contained retractable net system. 800-257-5250.

**Spalding Sports Worldwide,** 425 Meadow St., P.O. Box 901, Chicopee, MA 01021: Free list of retail sources ◆ Nets, posts, standards, and balls. 800-225-6601. www.spalding.com

**Spike Nashbar,** 4111 Simon Rd., Youngstown, OH 44512: Free information ◆ Shoes and equipment. 800-774-5348. www.nasbar.com

**Sporting Edge,** 11042 Outpost Dr., North Potomac, MD 20878: Free catalog ◆ Basketball and volleyball equipment. 301-424-2762.

**Sportline of Hilton Head Ltd.,** Heritage Plaza, Pope Ave., Hilton Head, SC 29928: Free information ◆ Volleyballs. 888-996-8855. www.hiltonhead9.com/sportline

**Volleyball One,** 15392 Assembly Ln., Ste. A, Huntington Beach, CA 92649: Catalog $3 (refundable) ◆ Volleyball equipment. 800-950-8844. www.volleyballone.com

**Wilson Sporting Goods,** 8700 W. Bryn Mawr, Chicago, IL 60631: Free information ◆ Balls. 800-946-6060; 773-714-6400 (in IL). www.wilsonsports.com

## WATCHES

**Alpha Omega Fine Watches,** 57 JFK St., Harvard Square, Cambridge, MA 02138: Free information ◆ Watches. 800-447-4367; 617-864-1227 (in MA).

**Bernard Enterprises,** 9330 LBJ Fwy., Ste. 365, Dallas, TX 95243: Free brochure ◆ High-fashion watches for ladies and men. 800-200-2724; 972-480-8283 (in TX).

**Chase-Durer Ltd.,** 270 N. Cannon Dr., Beverly Hills, CA 90210: Free information ◆ Watches for military pilots. 310-550-7280. www.chase-durer.com

**Citizen Watch Company of America,** 1200 Wall St. West, Lyndhurst, NJ 07071: Free information ◆ Professional diving watches and sports, flight, yachting, and windsurfer chronographs. 201-438-8150.

**Grafstein & Company,** Division Capetown Diamonds, 3340 Peachtree Rd. NE, Atlanta, GA 30326: Free brochure ◆ Fine jewelry and watches. 800-442-7866; 404-365-9503 (in GA). www.capetowncorp.com

**Lenox Jewelers,** 2379 Black Rock Tnpk., Fairfield, CT 06430: Free catalog ◆ Watches, figurines, jewelry, porcelain, china, and crystal. 800-243-4473; 203-374-6157 (in CT).

**Lewis & Roberts,** 6400 E. Rogers Circle, Boca Raton, FL 33499: Free catalog ◆ Men and women's watches, jewelry, and gifts. 800-767-5614.

**Alan Marcus & Company,** 815 Connecticut Ave. NW, Washington, DC 20006: Free catalog ◆ Jewelry and Rolex, Patek, Phillippe, Audemars Piguet, Baume Mercier, and Cartier watches. 800-654-7184; 202-331-0671 (in Metro DC).

**National Watch Exchange,** 107 S. 8th St., Philadelphia, PA 19106: Free information ◆ Pre-owned vintage watches. 215-627-7653.

**Oris USA Inc.,** 2 Skyline Dr., Hawthorne, NY 10532: Free information ◆ Classic Swiss watches. 914-347-ORIS.

**Radio-O-Rama,** Mike Stute, 2140 Sequoyah Way, Carrollton, TX 75006: Free catalog ◆ Antique radios and watches from the United States and other worldwide sources. 972-242-1271. www.worldwidewatches.com

**Rolex Watch U.S.A. Inc.,** Rolex Bldg., 665 5th Ave., New York, NY 10022: Free brochure ◆ Rolex watches.

**Ross-Simons Jewelers,** 9 Ross-Simons Dr., Cranston, RI 02920: Free catalog ◆ China, crystal, flatware, silver, watches, figurines, and diamond, gold, pearl, and gemstone jewelry. 800-521-7677; 401-463-3100 (in RI). www.ross-simons.com

**Stocker & Yale Inc.,** 32 Hampshire Rd., Salem, NH 03079: Free brochure ◆ Compasses and authentic United States Army watches. 800-843-8011; 603-893-8778 (in NH).

**Tiffany & Company,** Customer Service, 801 Jefferson Rd., P.O. Box 5477, Parsippany, NJ 07054: Catalog $1 ◆ Jewelry, silver, china, crystal, watches and clocks, and other gifts. 800-452-9146.

**Tourneau,** 488 Madison Ave., New York, NY 10022: Free information ◆ Reconditioned pre-owned Rolex, Patek, Piaget, and other watches. 800-542-2389; 212-758-3671 (in NY).

**Wempe Jewelry,** 700 5th Ave., New York, NY 10019: Free information ◆ Breitling chronograph watches. 212-397-9000.

## WATER PURIFIERS & CHEMICAL TREATMENTS

**Aquathin Corp.,** 950 SW 12th Ave., Pompano Beach, FL 33069: Free information ◆ Portable water purifier. 800-462-7634.

**Aquavitáe,** 1280 Bison, Newport Beach, CA 92660: Free catalog ◆ Water purification system. 800-468-4823.

**Basic Designs,** P.O. Box 1498, St. Cloud, MN 56303: Free list of retail sources ◆ High-flow ceramic water filters. 800-328-3208.

**Climb High Inc.,** 135 Northside Dr., Shelburne, VT 05482: Free catalog ◆ Water purifiers. 802-985-5056. www.climbhigh.com

**Filtration Concepts,** 2226 S. Fairview, Santa Ana, CA 92704: Free brochure ◆ Water recovery systems. 714-850-0123. smcgvirl@ix.netcom.com

**General Ecology Inc.,** 151 Sheree Blvd., Exton, PA 19341: Free list of retail sources ◆ Portable, base camp, and travel-type water purifiers. 800-441-8166. www.general-ecology.com

**Global Water Technology,** Division Village Marine Tec., 2000 W. 135th St., Gardena, CA 90249: Free information ◆ Water purification systems for installation on boats and land. 800-421-4503. www.villagemarine.com

**HRO Systems,** P.O. Box 2560, Gardena, CA 90247: Free brochure ◆ Modular and compact water desalination equipment for boats. 310-327-2600.

**Katadyn USA Inc.,** Suunto USA, 2151 Las Palmas Dr., Ste. G, Carlsbad, CA 92009: Free list of retail sources ◆ Water purification equipment. 800-543-9124.

**Kinetico Water Filters,** P.O. 193, Newbury, OH 44065: Free list of retail sources ◆ Under the counter reverse osmosis water filter system. 800-944-9283.

**Matrix Desalination Inc.,** 3295 SW 11th Ave., Fort Lauderdale, FL 33315: Free information ◆ Desalinization equipment. 954-524-5120.

**Mountain Safety Research,** P.O. Box 24547, Seattle, WA 98124: Free list of retail sources ◆ Portable water purification equipment. 800-877-9677; 206-624-8573 (in WA).

**Natural Lifestyle,** 16 Lookout Dr., Asheville, NC 28804: Free catalog ◆ Water filters, organic foods, macrobiotic specialties, cookware, organic cotton clothes, earth care products, and cookbooks. 704-254-9606.

**PentaPure,** WTC Industries Inc., 14405 21st Ave. North, Minneapolis, MN 55447: Free catalog ◆ Water treatment equipment. 800-637-1244.

**Polar Equipment Inc.,** 12881 Foothill Ln., Saratoga, CA 95070: Free catalog ◆ Liquid iodine treatment for water. 408-867-4576.

**PUR Water Purifiers,** 9300 75th Ave. North, Minneapolis, MN 55428: Free list of retail sources ◆ Self-cleaning water purifier. 800-845-PURE. Millard.Steve@ourwater.com

**Relags USA Inc.,** 1705 14th St., Ste. 119, Boulder, CO 80303: Free catalog ◆ Water treatment filtering aid. 303-440-8047.

**Reverse Osmosis,** 12301 SW 133rd Ct., Miami, FL 33186: Free brochure ◆ Water recovery systems. 305-255-8115.

**Sea Recovery Corp.,** P.O. Box 2560, Gardena, CA 90247: Free brochure ◆ Water recovery systems. 800-354-2000; 310-327-4000 (in CA). www.searecovery.com

**SpectraPure,** 738 S. Perry Ln., Tempe, AZ 85281: Free information ◆ Water purification systems. 800-685-2783. spectra@syspac.com

**SweetWater Inc.,** 4000 1st Ave., Seattle, WA 98134: Free list of retail sources ◆ Water purification systems. 800-557-9338. www.cascadedesigns.com

**Universal Aqua Technologies,** 10555 Norwalk Blvd., Santa Fe Springs, CA 90670: Free brochure ◆ Water recovery systems. 800-777-6939.

**Village Marine Tec.,** 2000 W. 135th St., Gardena, CA 90249: Free brochure ◆ Reverse osmosis water purification systems. 800-421-4503. www.villagemarine.com

**Water Makers Inc.,** 2233 S. Andrews Ave., Fort Lauderdale, FL 33316: Free brochure ◆ Water recovery systems. 954-467-8920.

**Waterwise Inc.,** P.O. Box 494000, Leesburg, FL 34749: Free catalog ◆ Water purification systems for the home and office. 800-874-9028; 352-787-5008 (in FL). www.waterwise.com

## WATER SKIING

### Clothing

**Barefoot International,** 6160 N. 60th St., Milwaukee, WI 53218: Free information ◆ Wet, dry, and barefoot suits. Also ropes and handles. 800-932-0685; 414-466-3668 (in WI).

**Bart's Water Ski Center,** P.O. Box 294, North Webster, IN 46555: Free catalog ◆ Kneeboards, ropes and handles, gloves, water toys, ski boards, wet and dry suits, and T-shirts. 800-348-5016. www.bartsports.com

**Body Glove International,** 530 6th St., Hermosa Beach, CA 90254: Free information ◆ Wet and barefoot suits. 800-678-7873; 310-374-4074 (in CA). www.bodyglove.com

**Connelly Skis Inc.,** P.O. Box 716, Lynnwood, WA 98046: Free information ◆ Water skis, ropes, gloves, vests, trick and boat harnesses, ski racks, and videos. 800-444-7848. www.connellyskis.com

**Harvey's Skin Diving Suits Inc.,** 2505 S. 252nd St., Kent, WA 98032: Free information ◆ Wet and dry suits. 800-347-0054; 206-824-1114 (in WA).

**Overton's Sports Center Inc.,** P.O. Box 8228, Greenville, NC 27835: Free catalog ◆ Water skis, wet and dry suits, ropes, and handles. 800-334-6541. custserv@overtonsonline.com

**Ski Limited,** 7825 South Ave., Youngstown, OH 44512: Free catalog ◆ Vests, ski ropes and handles, and wet, dry, and barefoot suits. 800-477-4040.

**Surfer House,** P.O. Box 726, Lynnwood, WA 98046: Free list of retail sources ◆ Wet and dry suits and clothing for other water sports. 800-444-7848. www.connellyskis.com/SkiWarm

**Thunderwear Inc.,** 1060-C E. Calle Negocio, San Clemente, CA 92672: Free information ◆ Gloves. 800-422-6565.

**Wellington Leisure Products,** P.O. Box 244, Madison, GA 30650: Free information ◆ Water skis, gloves, ropes and handles, kneeboards and ski boards, trick and boat harnesses, videos, and ski racks. 706-342-4915.

**Wiley's Water Ski Shop,** 1417 S. Trenton, Seattle, WA 98108: Free brochure ◆ Drysuits, wetsuits, skis, and accessories. 206-762-4926. www.wileyski.com

**Yamaha Motor Corp.,** P.O. Box 6555, Cypress, CA 90630: Free list of retail sources ◆ Wet suits. 800-526-6650. www.yamahausa.com

### Equipment

**Aamstrand Corp.,** 629 Grove, Manteno, IL 60950: Free information ◆ Water skiing equipment. 800-338-0557; 815-468-2100 (in IL). www.aamstrand.com

**Barefoot International,** 6160 N. 60th St., Milwaukee, WI 53218: Free information ◆ Wet, dry, and barefoot suits. Also ropes and handles. 800-932-0685; 414-466-3668 (in WI).

**Bart's Water Ski Center,** P.O. Box 294, North Webster, IN 46555: Free catalog ◆ Kneeboards, ropes and handles, gloves, water toys, ski boards, wet and dry suits, and T-shirts. 800-348-5016. www.bartsports.com

**Burbank Water Ski Company,** 1861 Victory Pl., Burbank, CA 91504: Free catalog ◆ Water skis, wakeboards, tubes, and accessories. 800-352-0572; 818-848-8808 (in CA).

**Connelly Skis Inc.,** P.O. Box 716, Lynnwood, WA 98046: Free information ◆ Water skis, ropes, gloves, vests, trick and boat harnesses, ski racks, and videos. 800-444-7848. www.connellyskis.com

**Kransco Manufacturing,** 333 Continental Blvd., El Segundo, CA 90245: Free information ◆ Water skis and ski boards.

**Maherajah Water Skis,** 1595 University Rd., Hopland, CA 95449: Free information ◆ Water skis. 707-744-1816.

**Overton's Sports Center Inc.,** P.O. Box 8228, Greenville, NC 27835: Free catalog ◆ Water skis, wet and dry suits, ropes, and handles. 800-334-6541. custserv@overtonsonline.com

**Power-Sail Corp.,** 47 E. Main St., P.O. Box 856, Flemington, NJ 08822: Free brochure ◆ Ascending parachutes for water sports. 800-426-3316; 908-782-9344 (in NJ). www.eclipse.net/~powersail

**Ski Limited,** 7825 South Ave., Youngstown, OH 44512: Free catalog ◆ Vests, ski ropes and handles, and wet, dry, and barefoot suits. 800-477-4040.

**Tackle Shack,** 7801 66th St. North, Pinellas Park, FL 33781: Free catalog ◆ Water skiing equipment. 800-537-6099. www.FunOnWater.com

**Wellington Leisure Products,** P.O. Box 244, Madison, GA 30650: Free information ◆ Water skis, gloves, ropes and handles, kneeboards and ski boards, trick and boat harnesses, videos, and ski racks. 706-342-4915.

**Wiley's Water Ski Shop,** 1417 S. Trenton, Seattle, WA 98108: Free brochure ◆ Drysuits, wetsuits, skis, and accessories. 206-762-4926. www.wileyski.com

## WEATHER FORECASTING

**Abbeon Cal Inc.,** 123 Gray Ave., Santa Barbara, CA 93101: Free catalog ◆ Thermometers, hygrometers, moisture meters, and humidity indicators. 800-922-0977. www.abbeon.com

**Accu-Weather Inc.,** 619 W. College Ave., State College, PA 16801: Free information ◆ IBM compatible, modem-connected on-line weather data base information system. 800-341-1262. www.accuweather.com

**Advanced Receiver Research,** P.O. Box 1242, Burlington, CT 06013: Free information ◆ Weather satellite information-management equipment. 203-584-0776.

**Alden Electronics,** 28 Lord Rd., Ste. 130, Marlborough, MA 01752: Free information ◆ Weather radar equipment, weather graphics systems, and radio facsimile weather chart recorder kits. 800-225-4767. www.alden.com

**Autohelm,** 676 Island Pond Rd., Manchester, NH 03109: Free information ◆ Weather and marine instruments, compasses, autopilots, and navigation and electronic gear. 800-539-5539. www.raymarine.com

**Communications Electronics Inc.,** P.O. Box 1045, Ann Arbor, MI 48106: Free information ◆ Scanners, transceivers, and emergency broadcast, weather station, monitoring, and other electronics. 800-USA-SCAN. www.usascan.com

**C. Crane Company,** 558 10th St., Fortuna, CA 95540: Free catalog ◆ AM/FM radios, long and shortwave equipment, scanners, books, and weather equipment. 800-522-8863.

**Davis Instruments,** 3465 Diablo Ave., Hayward, CA 94545: Free information ◆ Professional weather station for home use and other state-of-the-art instruments. 800-678-3669. www.davisnet.com

**Edmund Scientific Company,** Edscorp Bldg., Barrington, NJ 08007: Free catalog ◆ Weather forecasting instruments, microscopes, magnifiers, magnets, telescopes, binoculars, and other science equipment. 609-547-8880. www.edsci.com

**Fascinating Electronics Inc.,** 31525 Canaan Rd., Deer Island, OR 97054: Free brochure ◆ Full-size weather-monitoring instruments. Available assembled or build-them-yourself kits. 800-683-5487.

**Harrison Astronomy,** 2574 Granville St., Vancouver, British Columbia, Canada V6H 3C8: Free information ◆ Telescopes and accessories, binoculars, microscopes, magnifiers, meteorological instruments, and books. 604-737-4303.

**Hinds Instruments Inc.,** 3175 NW Aloclek Dr., Hillsboro, OR 97124: Free information ◆ Electronic weather data display station that can be linked directly to a computer modem or printer to provide a visible or audible record. 800-688-4463; 503-690-2000 (in OR).

**Innovation Clock-Making Specialties,** 11869 Teale St., Culver City, CA 90230: Free catalog ◆ Clock-making components and weather instruments. 800-421-4445; 562-398-8116 (in CA). www.clockparts.com

**Klockit,** P.O. Box 636, Lake Geneva, WI 53147: Free catalog ◆ Instruments for building weather/time stations, Swiss music box movements, and clock-building parts and supplies. 800-556-2548. www.klockit.com

**Luctor Canada,** Division Emergo Inc., P.O. Box 1330, Brantford, Ontario, Canada N3T 5T6: Free information ◆ Windows 3.1 and 3.11 weather satellite image capture and processing system. 800-668-3224.

**Maximum Inc.,** 30 Barnett Blvd., New Bedford, MA 02745: Free catalog ◆ Instruments for wind, weather, tide, and time measurement with optional digital and analog versions. 781-995-7000. maximum@imtra.com

**Nielsen-Kellerman,** 104 W. 15th St., Chester, PA 19013: Free information ◆ Waterproof pocket wind meter. 800-784-4221. www.nkelectronics.com

**OFS WeatherFAX,** 6404 Lakerest Ct., Raleigh, NC 27612: Free information ◆ PC-based weather satellite image capturing system. 919-847-4545.

**Oregon Scientific,** 18383 SW Boones Ferry Rd., Portland, OR 97224: Free brochure ◆ Weather forecasting and temperature monitoring equipment. 800-869-7779.

**Peet Bros. Company,** 1308 Doris Ave., Ocean, NJ 07712: Free brochure ◆ Home weather stations. 800-USA-PEET. www.peetbros.com

**RainWise Inc.,** 25 Federal St., Bar Harbor, ME 04609: Free catalog ◆ Consumer and industrial meteorological measuring and recording instruments. 800-762-5723. www.rainwise.com

**Sensor Instruments Company Inc.,** 41 Terrill Dr., Concord, NH 03301: Free information ◆ Weather instruments. 800-633-1033.

**SensorMetrics,** P.O. Box 1049, Lakeville, MA 02347: Free information ◆ Temperature, humidity, pressure, wind, solar, rainfall, and other environmental monitoring equipment for display of data on PCs. 508-946-4904.

**Simerl Instruments,** 528 Epping Forest Rd., Annapolis, MD 21401: Free brochure ◆ Weather forecasting instruments. 410-849-8667.

**Software Systems Consulting,** 615 S. El Camino Real, San Clemente, CA 92672: Free catalog ◆ Software interface systems for direct satellite reception. 714-498-5784. www.ssccorp.com

**Spectrum International,** P.O. Box 1084, Concord, MA 01742: Free information ◆ Weather satellite information-management equipment. 978-263-2145.

**Swift Instruments Inc.,** 952 Dorchester Ave., Boston, MA 02125: Free list of retail sources ◆ Telescopes, weather instruments, binoculars, and other optics. 800-446-1115; 617-436-2960 (in MA). www.swift-optics.com

**Texas Weather Instruments Inc.,** 5942 Abrams Rd., Dallas, TX 75231: Free information ◆ Easy-to-operate weather station. 800-284-0245; 214-368-7116 (in TX).

**Vanguard Electronic Labs,** 196-23 Jamaica Ave., Hollis, NY 11423: Free information ◆ Weather satellite information-management equipment. 718-468-2720.

**Vetus-Denouden Inc.,** P.O. Box 8712, Baltimore, MD 21230: Free catalog ◆ Wind and weather forecasting equipment for boats. 410-712-0740. www.vetus.com

**Weather Bureau,** P.O. Box 2797, Ann Arbor, MI 48106: Free information ◆ Scanners, transceivers, emergency broadcast equipment, weather stations and monitoring equipment, and other electronics. 313-996-8888.

**WeatherTrac,** P.O. Box 122, Cedar Falls, IA 50613: Free catalog ◆ Weather forecasting instruments, weather vanes, and educational aids. 800-798-8724.

**What In The World,** P.O. Box 1767, Lake Arrowhead, CA 92352: Free information ◆ Telescopes, cameras, weather stations, binoculars, and accessories. 909-337-5080. www.whatintheworld.com

**Robert E. White Instruments Inc.,** 34 Commercial Wharf, Boston, MA 02110: Free catalog ◆ Electronic equipment for measuring indoor and outdoor temperatures and time of occurrence. 800-992-3045.

**Wind & Weather,** P.O. Box 2320, Mendocino, CA 95460: Free catalog ◆ Barometers, thermometers, hygrometers, psychrometers, wind direction instruments, anemometers, weather vanes, sundials, rain gauges, cloud charts, and books. 800-922-9463. weather@men.org

**YFX/Information by FAX,** Alden Electronics, 28 Lord Rd., Ste. 130, Marlborough, MA 01752: Free information ◆ Weather information system by fax machine. 800-225-4767. www.alden.com

## WEATHER VANES

**A.J.P. Coppersmith & Company,** 20 Industrial Pkwy., Woburn, MA 01801: Catalog $3 ◆ Handcrafted copper, tin, or brass reproduction colonial lanterns, chandeliers, sconces, cupolas, and weather vanes. 800-545-1776.

**Antique Treasures,** 19 Buckingham Plantation Dr., Bluffton, SC 29910: Catalog $3 (request list of retail sources) ◆ Wholesale supplier of home accents in the antique style for dealers only. 800-422-9982. www.antiquehardware.com

**Barnworks Inc.,** 2422 Wildcat Creek Rd., Chapel Hill, NC 27516: Free information ◆ Copper aircraft weather vanes. 800-942-2865. www.barnworks.com

**Berry-Hill Limited,** 75 Burwell Rd., St. Thomas, Ontario, Canada N5P 3R5: Catalog $2 ◆ Weather vanes, canning equipment, cider press, and garden tools. 519-631-0480.

**Cape Cod Cupola Company Inc.,** 78 State Rd., North Dartmouth, MA 02747: Catalog $2 (refundable) ◆ Early American-style weather vanes and cupolas. 508-994-1956.

**Classic Architectural Specialties,** 3223 Canton St., Dallas, TX 75226: Catalog $6 ◆ Weather vanes. 800-662-1221; 214-748-1113 (in TX). www.casdesign.com

**Colonial Casting Company Inc.,** 68 Liberty St., Haverhill, MA 01832: Catalog $3 ◆ Handcrafted lead-free pewter miniature castings, handmade copper weather vanes, and light fixtures. 978-374-8783.

**Colonial Cupolas,** P.O. Box 38, 1816 Nemoke Trail, Haslett, MI 48840: Brochure $3 ◆ Wood cupolas and aluminum or copper weather vanes. Includes build-it-yourself kits. 800-678-1965.

**Copper House,** RFD 1, Box 4, Epsom, NH 03234: Catalog $3 ◆ Hand-hammered copper weather vanes and indoor and outdoor lanterns. 800-281-9798.

**Crosswinds Gallery,** 29 Buttonwood St., Bristol, RI 02809: Free catalog ◆ Cupolas and copper, gold leaf-decorated, aluminum, and wood weather vanes. 800-638-8263. www.crosswinds-gallery.com

**Denninger Weathervanes & Finials,** 77 Whipple Rd., Middletown, NY 10940: Catalog $4 ◆ Redwood cupolas with copper roofs and weather vanes. 914-343-2229. www.denninger.com

**Fischer Artworks,** 5820 W. Rowland Ave., Littleton, CO 80123: Free catalog ◆ Copper and cast-bronze Victorian-style weather vanes. 800-441-9877; 303-948-9877 (in CO).

**Images In Steel,** P.O. Box 288, Clyde Park, MT 59018: Catalog $2 (refundable) ◆ Weather vanes, fireplace screens, furniture, custom designed art, and functional western art handcrafted from plate steel. 800-511-1324; 406-686-4166 (in MT).

**Iron Craft,** Old Rt. 28, P.O. Box 351, Ossipee, NH 03864: Free catalog ◆ Kettles and grates, enamel cookware, butcher aprons, bellows, heating systems for fireplaces, weather vanes, signs, gifts, and cast-iron items. 603-539-6159.

**Marian Ives Weathervanes,** Box 61, Forget Rd., Charlemont, MA 01339: Free brochure ◆ Custom-designed metal weather vanes. 413-339-8534.

**Q.B. Logan,** 270 Rt. 35, Dayton, ME 04005: Free information ◆ Handcarved weather vanes finished in 24K gold leaf over solid mahogany. 207-499-2486.

**Barry Norling Weathervanes,** Beech Hill Rd., RFD 1, Box 5190, Skowhegan, ME 04976: Free brochure ◆ Handcrafted copper weather vanes. 207-474-2738.

**Tom Outhouse,** 2853 Lincoln Hwy. East, Ronks, PA 17572: Free catalog ◆ Antique and polished copper weather vanes with solid brass directional indicators and stainless steel chimney caps. Also cupolas. 800-346-7678.

**Redwood Unlimited,** P.O. Box 2344, Valley Center, CA 92082: Brochure $2 ◆ Weather vanes and post-mounted California redwood, cedar, and pine mailboxes. 800-283-1717.

**Robbins Lighting Inc.,** 124 E. 2nd St., P.O. Box 440, Maryville, MO 56648: Free information ◆ Weather vanes and residential and commercial light protection systems. 800-426-3792. www.robbinslightning.thomasregister.com

**Salt & Chestnut,** Box 41, West Barnstable, MA 02668: Catalog $2 (refundable) ◆ Handcrafted weather vanes. 508-362-6085.

**Travis Tuck,** Metal Sculptor, Box 1832, Martha's Vineyard, MA 02568: Brochure $1 ◆ Sculpted metal weather vanes. 508-693-3914.

**Wagonmaster Antiques,** 409 N. Stark, Bennington, KS 67422: Free information ◆ American eagle-decorated weather vanes. 913-488-2136.

**The Weathervane,** 108 E. Front St., Traverse City, MI 49684: Brochure $1 ◆ Polished copper and antiqued-green weather vanes. 800-332-2460.

**West Coast Weathervanes,** 417 Ingalls St., Santa Cruz, CA 95060: Free information ◆ Handcrafted and limited edition copper weather vanes and finials. 408-425-5505.

**Westwinds Trading Company,** 3540 76th St. SE, Caledonia, MI 49316: Free brochure ◆ Weather vanes, post and mailbox signs, and hitching posts. 800-635-5262.

**Wind & Weather,** P.O. Box 2320, Mendocino, CA 95460: Free catalog ◆ Sundials, weather vanes, and weather forecasting instruments. 800-922-9463. weather@men.org

**Windleaves Weathervanes,** 7560 Morningside Dr., Indianapolis, IN 46240: Free brochure ◆ Weather vanes. 317-251-1381.

## WEDDING INVITATIONS & ACCESSORIES

**The American Wedding Album,** American Stationery Company Inc., 300 Park Ave., Peru, IN 46970: Free catalog ◆ Wedding invitations, stationery, and gifts. 800-822-2577.

**Artistic Judaic Promotions,** 4990 S. Lafayette Ln., Englewood, CO 80110: Free information ◆ Handmade jewelry, Judaica, art, and ketubot. 303-789-3879. ajpi@ixnetcom.com

**Billiann's Bridal,** P.O. Box 35, Atlanta, IN 46031: Catalog $4 ◆ Bridal flowers, other floral arrangements, jewelry, and arranging supplies. 765-292-6388.

**Cedco Publishing Company,** 2955 Kerner Blvd., San Rafael, CA 94901: Free catalog ◆ Books and calendars for children, adults, and recording wedding memories. 800-233-2624. www.cedco.com

**Creations by Elaine,** 6253 W. 74th St., Box 2001, Bedford Park, IL 60499: Free catalog ◆ Wedding invitations and stationery, cake knives and servers, reception and ceremony accessories, and jewelry. 800-323-1208. www.catalogs.order.com/co/index.html

**Custom Glass Etching,** 1139 E. Las Tunas Dr., San Gabriel, CA 91776: Free catalog ◆ Personalized crystal glass awards, gifts, wedding and other gifts, and promotional products. 626-287-3775.

**Dawn Invitations,** 681 Main St., P.O. Box 100, Lumberton, NJ 08048: Free catalog ◆ Wedding invitations and gifts for attendants. 800-528-6677.

**Dewberry Engraving Company,** P.O. Box 2311, Birmingham, AL 35201: Free catalog ◆ Wedding invitations and bridal accessories. 800-633-6050.

**Evangel Wedding Service,** P.O. Box 202, Batesville, IN 47006: Free catalog ◆ Wedding invitations, announcements, programs, napkins, and accessories with a Christian theme. 800-342-4227.

**Forever & Always Company,** 110 W. Manlius St., East Syracuse, NY 13057: Free information ◆ Wedding favors, bridal gifts, and accessories. 800-404-4025. www.foreverandalways.com

**Rolf Gille Import Ltd.,** P.O. Box 747, San Francisco, CA 94101: Free catalog ◆ Bridal supplies. 800-448-9988.

**Green EN,** 2 Hanover Rd., Ste. 1913, Brampton, Ontario, Canada L6S 4H9: Samples and price list $10 ◆ Handmade paper and wedding invitations. 905-789-0313. kant@usa.net

**Heart Thoughts Original Wedding Stationery,** 6200 E. Central, Ste. 100, Wichita, KS 67208: Free catalog ◆ Contemporary, Victorian, and custom wedding invitations. 800-670-4224.

**Heritage Weddings,** P.O. Box 384, Lumberton, NJ 08048: Free catalog ◆ African-American wedding invitations and accessories. 800-892-4297.

**Hollydays Inc.,** Rt. 2, Box 70-21, Lake Providence, LA 71254: Catalog $5 ◆ Flower girl baskets, Protestant and Catholic versions of the bible, ring bearer pillows, purses, and other wedding accessories. 800-256-9792.

**The Judaica Experience,** 210 W. 72nd St., New York, NY 10023: Free catalog ◆ Ketubot, kipot, benchers, invitations, silver, books, and other accessories for Jewish weddings. 800-315-3944; 212-724-2424 (in NY).

**The Ketubah Workshop,** 34 Goddard St., Downsview, Ontario, Canada M3H 5C8: Free catalog ◆ Handpainted ketubahs. 800-867-5997.

**Jamie Lee Stationery,** P.O. Box 1855, Bridgeview, IL 60455: Free catalog ◆ Wedding stationery for brides. 800-288-5800.

**Mail Order Bride,** Association of Bridal Consultants, 200 Chestnutland Rd., New Milford, CT 06776: Free catalog ◆ How-to and what-to-do books and videos for brides before, during, and after the wedding. 800-691-9000; 860-355-0464 (in CT). bridalassn@aol.com

**Now & Forever,** P.O. Box 820, Goshen, CA 92227: Free catalog ◆ Wedding invitations and accessories. 800-521-0584. www.catalog.orders.com

**Peachtree Circle,** 4900 Peachtree Rd., Atlanta, GA 30341: Free brochure ◆ Distinctive gifts for weddings and bridal parties. 770-445-1800. www.mindspring.com/~pcircle

**The Precious Collection,** P.O. Box 22, Quincy, PA 17247: Free catalog ◆ Coordinated wedding invitation ensembles with traditional or contemporary designs. Also wedding ceremony and reception accessories. 800-537-5222. www.catalog.orders.com

**Rexcraft,** 1 Stationery Pl., Rexburg, ID 83441: Free catalog ◆ Invitations and stationery, bridal and reception accessories, and thank you cards. 800-635-4653.catalog.orders.com

**Heath Sedgwick,** P.O. Box 1305, Stony Brook, NY 11790: Catalog $4 ◆ Wedding accessories. 516-751-1129. www.heathsedgwick.com

**Sugar 'n Spice Invitations,** P.O. Box 299, Sugar City, ID 83448: Free catalog ◆ Invitations and stationery, bridal and reception accessories, and thank you cards. 800-535-1002.

**Wedding Treasures,** P.O. Box 22, Quincy, PA 17247: Free catalog ◆ Wedding invitations. 800-537-5222. www.catalog.orders.com

**Weddingware,** P.O. Box 1466, Coshocton, OH 43812: Free catalog ◆ Wedding program covers and invitations. 800-622-4489.

## WELDING & FOUNDRY EQUIPMENT

**Am-Fast Bolt, Nut & Screw Company,** 386 W. Boylston St., Worcester, MA 01606: Free information ◆ Foundry equipment, welding and power machine tools, and machine shop supplies. 508-852-8778.

**Brodhead-Garrett,** 100 Paragon Pkwy., Mansfield, OH 44903: Free information ◆ General workshop supplies and equipment, drafting and design accessories, and tools for graphic arts, wood and metal working, electricity and electronics, and automotive maintenance. 800-321-6730.

**Eastwood Company,** 580 Lancaster Ave., Box 3014, Malvern, PA 19355: Free catalog ◆ Welding and sand blasting equipment, rust removers, body repair tools, pin-striping equipment, and buffing supplies. 800-343-9353. www.ewab.com

**The Lincoln Electric Company,** 22801 St. Clair Ave., Cleveland, OH 44117: Free information ◆ Easy-to-use welding equipment. 216-481-8100. www.lincolnelectric.com

**McKilligan,** 435 Main St., Johnson City, NY 13790: Catalog $5 ◆ Welding, power machine, hand and portable power, and tools for measuring, drafting, and layout design. Also foundry equipment and machine shop supplies. 607-798-9335.

**Pyramid Products Company,** 85357 American Canal Rd., Niland, CA 92257: Information $1 ◆ Foundry equipment and supplies for home and professional metal casting. 760-354-4265.

**Techno-Weld Inc.,** 440 Sedgewick Rd., Summerville, SC 29483: Free information ◆ Aluminum welding kits. 803-875-6555.

## WELLS

**Baker Manufacturing Company,** 133 Enterprise St., Evansville, WI 53536: Free information ◆ Hand pump systems for water wells. 608-882-5100.

**Deeprock Manufacturing Company,** P.O. Box 1, Opelika, AL 36803: Free information ◆ Well-digging equipment. 800-333-7762. www.deeprock.com

## WHEAT WEAVING

**J. Page Basketry,** 820 Albee Rd. West, Nokomis, FL 34275: Catalog $2 (refundable) ◆ Wheat-weaving and pine needle crafting supplies, dried and preserved flowers and herbs, basket-making supplies, and books. 941-485-6730.

## WHEELCHAIRS, TRANSPORTERS, & LIFTS

**Access Industries Inc.,** 4001 E. 138th St., Grandview, MO 64030: Free information ◆ Easy-to-install wheelchair and stairway lifts. 800-925-3100.

**Access to Recreation Inc.,** 8 Sandra Ct., Newbury Park, CA 91320: Free catalog ◆ Pool lifts. 800-634-4351.

**Access Unlimited,** 570 Hance Rd., Binghamton, NY 13903: Free information ◆ Personal transfer lift for automobiles and homes. 800-849-2143. accessun@spectra.net

**Adaptive Solutions/Guldmann,** 7047 Silvermill Dr., Tampa, FL 33635: Free information ◆ Battery-operated lift for wheelchair to bed or bathroom facilities. 800-891-0539; 813-891-1666 (in FL).

**Amigo Mobility International Inc.,** 6693 Dixie Hwy., Bridgeport, MI 48722: Free information ◆ Lightweight take-apart scooter for storage and easy transporting. 800-MY-AMIGO. www.myamigo.com

**Aquatec Bathtub Lift,** PHP-ICM Bldg., 1003 International Dr., Oakdale, PA 15071: Free information ◆ Water pressure-operated portable bathtub lift for the home. 412-695-2122.

**Aquatic Access,** 417 Dorsey Way, Louisville, KY 40223: Free information ◆ In and above-ground lifts for spas and pools. 800-325-5438; 502-425-5817 (in KY).

**Barrier Free Lifts Inc.,** 9230 Prince William St., Manassas, VA 20110: Free information ◆ Battery-operated multi-directional barrier-free ceiling lift. 800-582-8732; 703-361-6531 (in VA). www.bfl-inc.com

**The Braun Corp.,** P.O. Box 310, Winamac, IN 46996: Free information ◆ Van conversion and driving accessories, wheelchair lifts, and other equipment. 800-THE-LIFT; 219-946-6153 (in IN).

**Bruce Medical Supply,** 411 Waverly Oaks Rd., P.O. Box 9166, Waltham, MA 02254: Free catalog ◆ Mobility equipment, health equipment, and supplies for people with physical disabilities. 800-225-8446.

**Bruno Independent Living Aids,** 1780 Executive Dr., P.O. Box 84, Oconomowoc, WI 53066: Free information ◆ Rear-wheel drive and battery-powered scooters, battery-powered stairway elevator system, and wheelchair and scooter lifts for cars, vans, and trucks. 800-882-8183. www.bruno.com

**Burke Inc.,** 1800 Merriam Ln., Kansas City, KS 66106: Free information ◆ Portable, easy-to-operate rear wheel-powered mobility vehicles. 800-255-4147.

**Care Catalog Services,** 1877 NE 7th Ave., Portland, OR 97212: Free catalog ◆ Wheelchairs, wheelchair ramps and parts, urological supplies, and other health care aids. 503-288-8174.

**Columbus McKinnon Corp.,** Medical Products Division, 140 John James Audubon Pkwy., Amherst, NY 14228: Free information ◆ Easy-to-operate mobility and lift system. 800-888-0985. www.cmworks.com

**Concord Elevator Inc.,** 107 Alfred Kuehnw Blvd., Brampton, Ontario, Canada L6T 4K3: Free information ◆ Vertical and inclined wheelchair lifts. 800-661-5112. www.concordelevator.com

**Convaid Products Inc.,** P.O. Box 4209, Palos Verde, CA 90274: Free information ◆ Lightweight compact folding mobility aids for children and adults. 800-552-1020.

**Crow River Industries,** 2800 Northwest Blvd., Minneapolis, MN 55441: Free list of retail sources ◆ All-electric easy-to-operate wheelchair lifts. 800-488-7688.

**Diestco Manufacturing Company,** P.O. Box 6504, Chico, CA 95927: Free information ◆ Collapsible wheelchair canopy covers and other accessories. 800-795-2392. www.diestco.com

**DS Medical,** 1725 Breckinridge Pkwy., Ste. 500, Duluth, GA 30136: Free information ◆ Wheelchair parts and urological, ostomy, and wound care products. 800-722-2604. www.dsmedical.com

**The Electric Cart & Wheelchair Company,** 415 N. Mulberry St., Elizabethtown, KY 42701: Free information ◆ Electric scooters. Also ultralight and pop-a-part electric wheelchairs. 800-227-1919.

**Electric Mobility Corp.,** 1 Mobility Plaza, P.O. Box 156, Sewell, NJ 08080: Free information ◆ Electric scooters, power chairs, water-powered lift for tubs, and other mobility accessories. 800-662-4548. www.electricmobility.com

**Everest & Jennings Inc.,** Attention: Marketing Department, 3601 Rider Trail South, Earth City, MO 63045: Free catalog ◆ Powered wheelchairs, manual rehab wheelchairs, and pediatric models. 800-235-4661.

**Fashion Ease,** Division M & M Health Care, 1541 60th St., Brooklyn, NY 11219: Free catalog ◆ Wheelchair accessories and clothing with Velcro closures. 800-221-8929; 718-871-8188 (in NY). www.fashionease.com

**Frank Mobility Systems,** 1003 International Dr., Oakdale, PA 15071: Free brochure ◆ Adaptive two-person bicycles for physically challenged individuals and an electric-powered motorized accessory that enables wheelchairs to climb steps and stairs with little assistance by an attendant. 724-695-7822. wfrankjun@msn.com

**Freedom Concepts Inc.,** P.O. Box 45117, Winnipeg, Manitoba, Canada R2C 5C7: Free information ◆ Mobility cycles for recreation, therapy, and independence. 800-661-9915. www.freedomconcepts.com

**Freedom Designs Inc.,** 2261 Madera Rd., Simi Valley, CA 93065: Free information ◆ Tilting, tilting and reclining, and reclining transport chairs. 800-331-8551.

**Frog Legs,** P.O. Box 465, Vinton, IA 52349: Free information ◆ Add-on wheels for improving total mobility of wheelchairs and reducing vibrations. 319-472-4972. www.froglegsinc.com

**Gadabout Wheelchairs,** 1165 Portland Ave., Rochester, NY 14621: Free information ◆ Easy-to-store and transport folding wheelchair. 800-338-2110.

**Grant Waterx Corp.,** 144 Prospect St., Stamford, CT 06901: Free information ◆ Pivoting bathtub lift that operates with household water pressure. 800-243-5237. grantairmass@aol.com

**Guardian Products Inc.,** 4175 Guardian St., Simi Valley, CA 93063: Free catalog ◆ Walkers, crutches, canes, home activity aids, beds, lifts, ramps, and transport assistive equipment. 800-255-5022.

**Handicaps Inc.,** 4335 S. Santa Fe Dr., Englewood, CO 80110: Free brochure ◆ Wheelchair lift for vans and motor homes. 800-782-4335; 303-781-2062 (in CO).

**Health Products Express Inc.,** P.O. Box 8, Winthrop, MA 02152: Free catalog ◆ Wheelchairs and accessories. 800-617-5525; 617-846-8924 (in MA).

**T.F. Herceg Inc.,** 982 Pine Island Tnpk., Pine Island, NY 10969: Free information ◆ Remote hand-controlled overhead track and free-standing lifts. 800-724-5305.

**Hoveround,** 2151 Whitfield Industrial Way, Sarasota, FL 34243: Free information ◆ Personal mobility vehicles. 800-771-6565.

**Independent Living Aids/Can-Do Products,** 27 East Mall, Plainview, NY 11803: Free catalog ◆ Self-help products and equipment for individuals with vision impairment and physical disabilities. 800-537-2118; 516-752-8080 (in NY).

**Kid-EZ Chairs,** 732 Cruiser Ln., Belgrade, MT 59714: Free information ◆ Easy-to-fold transfer-adjustable transport chairs, for infants to age 7. 800-388-5278. kidkart@avicom.net

**Kuschall of America,** 708 Via Alondra, Camarillo, CA 93012: Free information ◆ Pediatric wheelchairs. 800-654-4768.

**Lark of America,** P.O. Box 1647, Waukesha, WI 53187: Free information ◆ Easy-to-transport 3-wheel electric scooter. 800-554-3536.

**Levo USA Inc.,** P.O. Box 3869, Peachtree City, GA 30269: Free information ◆ Self-propelled, lightweight, and gas charged assisted standing aid from wheelchairs. 888-LEVO-USA. jamespapac@man.com

**Lifestand,** Independence Providers, P.O. Box 172, Thornwood, NY 10594: Free information ◆ Combination power-assisted standing aid and wheelchair. 800-782-6324. StandUSA@AOL.com

**Mac's Lift Gate Inc.,** 2715 Seabord Ln., Long Beach, CA 90805: Free information ◆ Easy-to-install weather-proof residential lift system. 800-795-6227.

**Medship Direct,** P.O. Box 956848, Duluth, GA 30095: Free catalog ◆ Urological, wound care, ostomy, incontinence, and aids to daily living. Also wheelchair parts. 800-633-1565. www.medshipdirect.com

**Mobilectrics,** 4014 Bardstown Rd., Louisville, KY 40218: Free information ◆ Electric-operated 3-wheel scooters and replacement batteries. 800-876-6846.

**Mobility Options Research Foundation,** P.O. Box 662, Bakersfield, CA 93302: Free information ◆ Children's mobile standers with minimal restraint for maximum freedom. 888-748-3731; 805-328-0438 (in CA).

**The National Wheel-O-Vator Company Inc.,** P.O. Box 348, Roanoke, IL 61561: Free list of retail sources ◆ Wheelchair and side-riding stair lifts. 800-551-9095. www.wheelovator.com

**Natural Access,** P.O. Box 2222, Princeton, NJ 08543: Free brochure ◆ All-terrain wheelchair. 800-411-7789. www.natural-access.com/home

**Open Sesame,** 1933 Davis St., #279, San Leandro, CA 94577: Free information ◆ Remote-controlled door systems that open and close automatically from wheelchairs. 800-673-6911.

**Palmer Industries,** P.O. Box 5707, Endicott, NY 13760: Free brochure ◆ Electric one-hand operated with double and single seats and gear-driven 3-wheelers. 800-847-1304; 607-754-1954 (in NY). www.palmerind.com

**Parkview Pharmacy & Home Health Care Inc.,** 8283 Grove Ave., Ste. 105, Rancho Cucamonga, PA 01730: Free catalog ◆ Canes, walkers, wheelchairs and accessories, and other home health care aids. 800-605-0166. www.parkviewrx.com

**Permobil,** 6B Gill St., Woburn, MA 01801: Free information ◆ Powered wheelchairs and accessories. 888-737-6624.

**Powerlift,** P.O. Box 4390, Georgetown, CA 95634: Free brochure ◆ Dumbwaiters, wheelchair and stairway lifts, and elevators. 800-409-LIFT. www.dumbwaiters.com

**Pride Health Care Inc.,** 182 Susquehanna Ave., Exeter, PA 18643: Free list of retail sources ◆ Scooters and power chairs. 888-655-2677. www.pridehealth.com

**Ranger All Season Corp.,** Box 132, George, IA 51237: Free brochure ◆ Easy-to-disassemble power scooter for transporting in a car. 800-225-3811.

**Redman Power Chairs,** 4790 N. Keet Seel Trail, Tucson, AZ 85749: Free brochure ◆ Power-driven wheelchairs. 800-727-6684. redman2@flashnet.com

**The Ricon Corp.,** 12450 Montague St., Pacoima, CA 91331: Free information ◆ Wheelchair lifts and other mobility aids. 800-322-2884. www.riconcorp.com

**Roamer Technologies Inc.,** 590 Centerville Rd., Ste. 172, Lancaster, PA 17601: Free information ◆ Easy-to-use folding battery-powered gliding chair. 888-544-8566; 717-560-7800 (in PA).

**Rock N' Roll Cycles,** P.O. Box 1558, Levelland, TX 79336: Free information ◆ Single riders, tandems, and hand and foot-powered cycles with optional seat configurations and custom-fitting for individual needs. 800-654-9664. www.rocknrollcycles.com

**Scooter Discounters,** 1945 Winterhaven Dr., Virginia Beach, VA 23456: Free information ◆ Electric scooters, lifts, ramps, and lift recliners. 800-229-1317.

**Scooter T'ote,** Division Thamesford Holdings, 45 Seaview Dr., Port Moody, British Columbia, Canada V3H 1N8: Free brochure ◆ Scooter transporter for cars. 604-931-8168.

**Silcraft Corp.,** 528 Hughes Dr., Traverse City, MI 49686: Free information ◆ Barrier-free roll-in showers, shower and bath accessories, lifts, and transporters. 616-946-4221.

**Stand-Aid of Iowa Inc.,** Box 386, Sheldon, IA 51201: Free information ◆ Equipment to assist in standing and turning a manual wheelchair into a power chair. 800-831-8580; 712-324-2153 (in IA). standaid@rconnect.com

**Stow Away Inc.,** 513 S. Pine St., Chelsea, OK 74016: Free information ◆ Lightweight scooter lifts. 800-221-3433.

**Struck Corp.,** Box 307, Cedarburg, WI 53012: Free information ◆ Lightweight battery-operated scooter for indoor and outdoor use. 414-377-3300.

**SureHands International,** 982 Rt. 1, Pine Island, NY 10969: Free information ◆ Remote overhead track or free-standing movable lift. 800-724-5305. www.surehands.com

**Swift Medical International,** 364 W. Fallbrook Ave., Ste. 101, Fresno, CA 93711: Free information ◆ Urological supplies, ramps, manual and power-operated wheelchairs, bathroom equipment, cushions, and more. 800-659-9207. www.swiftmedical.com

**Teftec Corp.,** 6929 Old Spring Branch Rd., Spring Branch, TX 78070: Free information ◆ Powered wheelchairs with multiple seat options including fixed, adjustable, and power seating compatability. 888-234-1433. teftec@teftec.com

**Thompson Pharmacy & Medical,** 324 S. Union St., Traverse City, MI 49684: Free catalog ◆ Diabetes, health maintenance, home diagnostic, ostomy, and health and pain management aids. Also canes and other mobility equipment. 616-947-4212. thompson@carecenter.com

**Tip Top Mobility Inc.,** P.O. Box 5009, Minot, ND 58702: Free information ◆ Compact and lightweight wheelchair lift for most any vehicle. 800-735-5958. www.minot.com/~tiptop

**Tomco Conversions Inc.,** P.O. Box 30, Wilcox, PA 15870: Free information ◆ All-terrain vehicles and wheelchairs. Also a wheelchair-accessible sidecar for motorcycles. 888-814-5164. www.ncentral.com/~oliver/tomco.htm

**21st Century Scientific Inc.,** 4915 Industrial Way, Coeur d'Alene, ID 83814: Free catalog ◆ Power-operated wheelchairs. 800-448-3680; 208-667-8800 (in ID). www.wheelchairs.com

**Ultimate Home Care Company,** 3250 E. 19th St., Long Beach, CA 90804: Free information ◆ Lightweight folding travel chair that stores in luggage. 800-475-8122.

**Venture Products Inc.,** P.O. Box 148, Orrville, OH 44667: Free brochure ◆ Wheelchair accessible mobile riding garden equipment for the disabled. Provides accessibility, adaptability, and self-sufficiency. 330-683-0075. www.venturepro.com

**Wheelcare Inc.,** 3883-E Via Pescador, Camarillo, CA 93012: Free brochure ◆ Multi-purpose mobility vehicles and powered wheelchairs. 888-910-CARE. www.wheelcare-inc.com

**Wheelchair House,** 1831 E. Mulberry St., Fort Collins, CO 80524: Free information ◆ Custom wheelchair and seating systems, strollers, scooters, bathing and toileting aids, walkers and walking aids, and more. 800-466-7015; 970-482-7116 (in CO).

**Wheelchair Warehouse,** 100 E. Sierra, #3309, Fresno, CA 93710: Free information ◆ Wheelchairs, accessories, and urological supplies. 800-829-0202; 209-436-6147 (in OH).

**Worldwide Engineering Inc.,** 3240 N. Delaware St., Chandler, AZ 85225: Free information ◆ Automatic and semi-automatic folding wheelchair and scooter carrier for automotive vehicles. 800-848-3433. wwmoblift1@aol.com

## WIGS & HATS FOR HAIR LOSS

**Afro World Hair Company,** 7276 Natural Bridge, St. Louis, MO 63121: Free brochure with two 1st class stamps ◆ Toupees, hairpieces, and male wigs in curly, wavy, or African-American styles. 800-325-8067.

**Beauty by Spector Inc.,** One Spector Pl., McKeesport, PA 15134: Catalog $5 ◆ Women's wigs and hairpieces, men's toupees, jewelry, and exotic lingerie. 412-673-3259.

**Beauty Trends,** 14110 NW 57th Ct., Hialeah, FL 33014: Free information ◆ Adolfo, Revlon, and Dolly Parton wigs and add-ons. 800-777-7772.

**Carla Corcini,** P.O. Box 1700, Brockton, MA 02403: Catalog $5 ◆ Exclusive wig styles for women. 800-229-1234.

**Costumes by Betty,** 2181 Edgerton St., St. Paul, MN 55117: Catalog $5 (refundable) ◆ Clown costumes, make-up, wigs, and shoes. 612-771-8734. www.clowncostumes.com

**Louis Feder Company,** 14 E. 38th St., 8th Floor, New York, NY 10016: Women's catalog $10, men's color video $29.95 ◆ Handmade natural-looking hairpieces and wigs for men and women. 212-686-7701.

**Franklin Fashions Corp.,** 75 Holly Hill Ln., Greenwich, CT 06830: Free catalog ◆ Easily styled wigs. 800-556-0034. www.franklinfashions.com

**Gold Medal,** 1 Bennington Ave., Freeport, Long Island, NY 11520: Free catalog ◆ African-American hair products, wigs, videos, music, and more. 800-535-8101.

**Hats For Women With Hair Loss,** P.O. Box 27693, Philadelphia, PA 19118: Free brochure ◆ Hats in many styles and colors for women with hair loss. 215-247-8777.

**Jacquelyn Wigs,** 15 W. 37th St., New York, NY 10018: Catalog $3.50 ◆ Ladies' wigs in human hair, human hair blends, and synthetics. 800-272-2424; 212-302-2266 (in NY).

**Oradell International Corp.,** 3 Harding Pl., Little Ferry, NJ 07643: Free catalog ◆ Women's wigs. 800-223-6588; 201-440-9150 (in NJ).

**Wig America,** 270 Oyster Point Blvd., South San Francisco, CA 94080: Catalog $2 ◆ Wigs and hairpieces for men and women. 800-338-7600.

**The Wig Company,** P.O. Box 12950, Pittsburgh, PA 15241: Free catalog ◆ Women's wigs. 800-456-1788.

**Paula Young Wigs,** P.O. Box 483, Brockton, MA 02403: Free catalog ◆ Wig care supplies and women's wigs. 800-472-4017.

## WIND CHIMES

**AKL Company,** 307 W. Texas, Denison, TX 75020: Free brochure ◆ Wind chimes, assembled or kits. 800-500-5677. www.windancerchimes.com

**Anyone Can Whistle,** 323 Wall St., Kingston, NY 12401: Free catalog ◆ Bird feeders, wind chimes, and other musical gifts. 800-435-8863. anyonecan@chimes.com

**Armchair Shopper,** P.O. Box 419464, Kansas City, MO 64141: Free catalog ◆ Old world-style sundials, wind chimes, and lawn ornaments. 816-767-3200.

**Catskill Mountain Chimes,** P.O. Box 18, Mt. Tremper, NY 12457: Free catalog ◆ Precision tuned wind chimes. 800-868-6964.

**Harmony Hollow,** P.O. Box 1303, Ann Arbor, MI 48106: Free information ◆ Bronze wind bells, brass and aluminum wind chimes, and mobiles. 800-468-2355. www.harmonyhollow.com

**Westminster Chimes,** 408 Front St., Kaslo, British Columbia, Canada V0G 1M0: Free brochure ◆ Wind chimes. 800-667-1184.

## WINE, BEER, & VINEGAR MAKING

**Alfred's Brewing Supply,** P.O. Box 5070, Slidell, LA 70469: Free catalog ◆ Beer, wine, and liqueur making supplies and gourmet foods. 800-641-3757; 504-641-3575 (in LA). www.home-brew.com

**Anderson's Home Brewing,** 430 East US Hwy 6, Valparaiso, IN 46383: Free information ◆ Home-brewing and wine-making ingredients and equipment. 800-673-2384.

**Austin Homebrew Supply,** 306 E. 53rd St., Austin, TX 78751: Free catalog ◆ Home brewing and wine-making equipment, supplies, and ingredients. 800-890-BREW.

**Beer & Wine Hobby,** 180 New Boston St., Woburn, MA 01801: Free catalog ◆ Home brewing and wine-making supplies. 800-523-5423. www.beer-wine.com

**Beer, Beer & More Beer,** 974 D Detroit Ave., Concord, CA 94518: Free catalog ◆ Home brewing supplies. 925-939-2337. www.morebeer.com

**Bierhaus International Inc.,** 3723 W. 12th St., Erie, PA 16505: Free information ◆ Beer-making kits and brewing supplies. 814-833-7747.

**Brew & Grow,** 1824 N. Besly Ct., Chicago, IL 60622: Free information ◆ Home brewing supplies for making beer. Also hydroponic gardening equipment. 312-395-1500.

**Brew Masters Ltd.,** 12266 Wilkins Ave., Rockville, MD 20852: Free catalog ◆ Home-brewing supplies. 800-466-9557; 301-984-9557 (in MD).

**Brew Shop at Cornell's,** 310 White Plains Rd., Eastchester, NY 10707: Free catalog ◆ Home brewing supplies. 800-961-BREW. www.brewshop.com

**The Brewer's Gourmet Inc.,** P.O. Box 6611, Holliston, MA 01746: Free catalog ◆ Beer-making supplies. 800-591-2739.

**Brewers Resource,** 409 Calle San Pablo, Ste. 104, Camarillo, CA 93012: Free catalog ◆ Home-brewing supplies. 800-827-3983. www.brewtek.com

**Brewery,** 2720 University Ave., Minneapolis, MN 55414: Free catalog ◆ Brewer's supplies. 800-234-0685.

**The Brewery Company,** 11 Market St., Potsdam, NY 13676: Free catalog ◆ Beer-brewing kits, equipment, and ingredients. 800-762-2560.

**Canada Homebrew Supply,** 1998 Industrial Blvd., Abilene, TX 79602: Free catalog ◆ Beer and wine-making supplies, kegging equipment, malts, grains, hops, yeasts, and more. 888-839-2739. www.canadahomebrew.com

**The Cellar Homebrew,** P.O. Box 33525, 14411 Greenwood Ave. North, Seattle, WA 98133: Free catalog ◆ Beer and wine-making supplies. 800-342-1871. www.cellar-homebrew.com

**Country Wines & Beer,** 3333 Babcock Blvd., Pittsburgh, PA 15237: Free information ◆ Supplies for the home wine maker and beer brewer. 412-366-0151. www.countrywines.com

**Defalco's Home Brew,** 2415 Robinhood, Houston, TX 77005: Free catalog ◆ Supplies for making beer and wine. 800-216-2739.

**Draftsman Brewing Company,** P.O. Box 546, Mentor, OH 44061: Free catalog ◆ Home brewing supplies. 888-440-BEER; 440-257-5880 (in OH). www.draftsman.com

**Double Springs Homebrew Supply,** 4697 Double Springs Rd., Valley Springs, CA 95252: Free catalog ◆ Homebrew beer kits, wine and liqueur related books, wine-making kits, and supplies. 209-754-4888. www.doublesprings.com

**Fermentap,** P.O. Box 30175, Stockton, CA 95213: Free brochure ◆ Equipment for home beer brewing. 800-942-2750. www.concentric.net/~fermntap/index.html

**Five Star Products and Service,** 6731 East 50th Ave., Commerce City, CO 80222: Free information ◆ Cleaning and sanitizing kits for home brewing equipment. 303-287-0111. www.FiveStarAF.com/Homebrew

**The Grape & Granary,** 1302 E. Tallmadge Ave., Akron, OH 44310: Free catalog ◆ Home brewing supplies and equipment. 800-695-9870. www.grapeandgranary.com

**Great Fermentations California,** 136 Bellam Blvd., San Rafael, CA 94901: Free catalog ◆ Home brewing and wine-making supplies. 800-570-BEER; 888-570-WINE. Greatferm@aol.com

**Heart's Home Beer & Wine Making Supply,** 5824 N. Orange Blossom Trail, Orlando, FL 32810: Free catalog ◆ Beer and wine-making supplies. 800-392-8322; 407-298-4103 (in FL). www.Heartshomebrew.com

**Heartland HomeBrew,** 888 E. Belvidere Rd., #215, Grayslake, IL 60030: Free catalog ◆ Home brewing supplies and equipment. 800-354-4769. heartlandhomebrew@lnd.com

**The Home Brewery,** P.O. Box 730, Ozark, MO 65721: Free catalog ◆ Home brewing supplies. 800-321-2739. www.homebrewery.com

**Homebrew Adventures,** 9240 Albemarle Rd., Charlotte, NC 28227: Free catalog ◆ Canned malts, all-grain mashing equipment, bottling and kegging supplies, specialty malts, wine kits, fruit flavorings, and other supplies. 888-785-7766. www.homebrewadventures.com

**Homebrew Supply of Dallas,** 777 S. Central, Richardson, TX 75080: Free catalog ◆ Home-brewing supplies. 972-234-5922.

**HopTech Homebrewing Supplies,** 3015 Hopyard Rd., Ste. E, Pleasanton, CA 94588: Free catalog ◆ Malts and grains, dry and liquid malt extracts, hops, CO2 extracted hop oils and extracts, natural fruit flavors, and brewing equipment. 800-379-4677. www.hoptech.com

**K & G Cork'n Keg,** P.O. Box 85745, Tucson, AZ 85754: Free catalog ◆ Beer, wine, and cheese-making kits for use at home. 800-743-9970. KGCORKNKEG@AOL.COM

**E.C. Kraus,** P.O. Box 7850, Independence, MO 64054: Free catalog ◆ Home brewing and vinegar-making supplies. 800-841-7404.

**Lake Superior Brewing Company,** 7206 Rix St., Ada, MI 49301: Free catalog ◆ Beer and wine making supplies. 800-745-CORK.

**Liberty Malt Supply,** 1419 1st Ave., Seattle, WA 98101: Free catalog ◆ Brewing supplies and books. 800-990-MALT.

**Maryland Homebrew,** 6770 Oak Hall Ln., Ste. 115, Columbia, MD 21045: Free catalog ◆ Equipment and supplies for home brewing. 888-BREW-NOW; 410-290-3768 (in MD). www.mdhb.com

**Midwest Homebrewing Supplies,** 4528 Excelsior Blvd., Minneapolis, MN 55416: Free catalog ◆ Home brewing supplies and kits. 888-449-BREW. www.midwestsupplies.com

**New Earth Hydroponics & Homebrewing,** 9810 Taylorsville Rd., Louisville, KY 40299: Free catalog ◆ Home-brewing supplies. 800-462-5953; 502-261-0005 (in KY).

**New York HomeBrew,** 33 E. Jericho Tnpk., Mineola, NY 11501: Free catalog ◆ Supplies for brewing beers, ales, stouts, lagers, and making sodas at home. 800-YOO-BREW. www.youbrew.com

**Niagara Tradition,** Niagara Tradition, 1296 Sheridan Dr., Tonawanda, NY 14150: Free information ◆ Home-brewing supplies and kits. 800-283-4418.

**Northern Brewer Ltd.,** 1106 Grand Ave., St. Paul, MN 55105: Free catalog ◆ Home brewing supplies. 800-681-BREW. nbrewer@internet.com

**Oak Barrel Winecraft,** 1443 San Pablo Ave., Berkeley, CA 94702: Free information ◆ Wine, beer, and vinegar-making supplies. 510-849-0400.

**James Page Brewing Company,** 1300 Quincy St. NE, Minneapolis, MN 55413: Free catalog ◆ Home brewing equipment and ingredients. Includes a beginner's kit. 800-234-0685.

**Quoin Beer Dispenser,** 401 Violet St., Golden, CO 80401: Free list of retail sources ◆ Easy-to-use pump and carbon dioxide-free, self-inflating beer dispenser. 303-279-8731. www.partypig.com

**Reno Homebrewer,** 2335A Dickerson Rd., Reno, NV 89503: Free information ◆ Grains, hops, malt extracts, dry and liquid yeats, equipment, and other supplies. 702-329-ALES. WKNN70A@PRODIGY.COM

**River City Homebrewers,** 802 State St., Quincy, IL 62301: Free catalog ◆ Home brewing kits and supplies. 888-LETS-BREW. www.letsbrew.com

**SABCO Industries,** 4511 South Ave., Toledo, OH 43615: Free information ◆ Home brewing systems, home-brew kettles, fermenters, and beverage containers. 419-531-5347. www.kegs.com

**St. Patrick's of Texas Brewers Supply,** 12922 Staton Dr., Austin, TX 78727: Free catalog ◆ Equipment and ingredient kits, extracts, other supplies, and more for home brewing. 512-832-9045. www.stpats.com

**Sebastian Brewers Supply,** 7710 91st Ave., Vero Beach, FL 32958: Free catalog ◆ Home brewing supplies. 800-780-7837.

**Semplex of USA,** P.O. Box 11476, Minneapolis, MN 55411: Free catalog ◆ Home brewing and wine-making supplies. 888-255-7997.

**South Bay Homebrew Supply,** P.O. Box 3798, Torrance, CA 90510: Free catalog ◆ Home-brewing supplies. 800-608-BREW; 310-517-1841 (in CA).

**U-Brew,** 1207 Hwy. 17 South, North Myrtle Beach, SC 29582: Free catalog ◆ Beer and wine kits and supplies. 800-845-4441. www.ubrewit.com

**William's Brewing Company,** P.O. Box 2195, San Leandro, CA 94577: Free catalog ◆ Home brewing supplies. 800-759-6025. www.williamsbrewing.com

**WindRiver Brewing Company,** 7212 Washington Ave. South, Eden Prairie, MN 55344: Free catalog ◆ Home brewing supplies. 800-266-HOPS; 612-942-0589 (in MN). www.windriverbrew.com

**Wine Art,** 5890 N. Keystone Ave., Indianapolis, IN 46220: Free catalog ◆ Wine, beer, and vinegar-making supplies. 800-255-5090; 317-546-9940 (in IN).

**Winemaker's Pantry,** 4599 Park Blvd., Pinellas Park, FL 33781: Free catalog ◆ Home wine-making and beer brewing supplies. 813-546-9117. winemkr@intnet.net

**Worm's Way,** 7850 N. State Rd. 37, Bloomington, IN 47404: Free catalog ◆ Beer-making supplies. 800-274-9676. www.wormsway.com

## WINE CELLARS & RACKS

**Gironde Bros. Inc.,** 3184 NE 12th Ave., Fort Lauderdale, FL 33334: Free brochure ◆ Free-standing wine cellars with automatic temperature and humidity controls. 888-888-0102; 954-564-0006 (in FL).

**International Wine Accessories,** 11020 Audelia Rd., Ste. B-113, Dallas, TX 75243: Free catalog ◆ Refrigerators, thermal doors, wine racks, temperature gauges, and other equipment for building wine cellars. 800-527-4072.

**Kedco Wine Storage Systems,** 564 Smith St., Farmingdale, NY 11735: Free brochure ◆ Credenzas, vaults, wine stewards, and wine storage racks. 800-654-9988; 516-454-7800 (in NY).

**Lift Your Spirits,** 3308 Brownes Creek Rd., Charlotte, NC 28269: Catalog $3 ◆ Wine and bar furnishings and accessories. 704-598-2821.

**Nordicorp Inc.,** 937 E. San Carlos Ave., San Carlos, CA 94070: Free catalog ◆ Wine cellars. 415-592-1818.

**U-Line Corp.,** 8900 N. 55th St., P.O. Box 23220, Milwaukee, WI 53223: Free list of retail sources ◆ Wine cellars and racks. 414-354-0300.

**Vinotemp International,** 17631 S. Susana Rd., Rancho Dominguez, CA 90221: Free catalog ◆ Cellars, walk-in vaults, and racking and cooling systems. 800-777-8466; 310-886-3332 (in CA). www.vinotemp.com

**Vintage Cellars,** 904 Rancheros Dr., Ste. G, San Marcos, CA 92069: Free information ◆ Redwood wine racks, cooling systems, and storage cabinets. 800-876-8789. www.vintagecellars.com

**Wine Appreciation Guild,** 360 Swift Ave., Ste. 34, San Francisco, CA 94080: Free information ◆ Wine cellars, racks, accessories, and books. 800-231-9463.

**Wine Enthusiast,** P.O. Box 39, Pleasantville, NY 10570: Catalog $2 ◆ Crystal, gifts, cellars, vintage keepers, racks, corkscrews, and wine accessories. 800-356-8466.

**Wine Racks Unlimited,** 2121 Ross Ave., Cincinnati, OH 45212: Free list of retail sources ◆ Wine cellars and racks. 800-229-9813.

## WINES & BEERS

**Big Y Wines,** 122 N. King St., Northampton, MA 01060: Free catalog ◆ Imported and domestic beer and wines. 800-474-2449. www.bigywines.com

**Bounty Hunter Rare Wine & Provisions,** 101 S. Coombs, #5, Napa, CA 94559: Catalog $2 ◆ Wines and related life style products. 800-943-9463. www.bountyhunterwine.com

**The Cheese Box,** 801 Wells St., Lake Geneva, WI 53147: Free catalog ◆ Cheese, wine, and other Wisconsin favorites. 800-345-6105; 414-248-3440 (in WI). www.cheesebox.com

**Golden West International,** 2616 Buchanan, San Francisco, CA 94115: Free price list ◆ Fine and rare wines including French and American vintages. 415-931-2300.

**Hagafen Cellars,** P.O. Box 3035, Napa, CA 94558: Free information ◆ Varietal wines for special occasions. 888-HAGAFEN.

**Marin Wine Cellar,** 2138 4th St., San Rafael, CA 94901: Free catalog ◆ Fine and rare wines. 415-456-9463.

**Sam's Wines & Liquors,** 1720 N. Marcey St., Chicago, IL 60614: Free information ◆ Wines and spirits. 800-777-9137; 312-664-4394 (in IL). www.sams-wine.com

**Windsor Vineyards,** P.O. Box 368, Windsor, CA 95492: Free catalog ◆ Personalized holiday labels on favorite wines. Also gourmet foods and wine gifts. 800-333-9987. www.windsorvineyards.com

**Wine Cask,** 813 Anacapa St., Santa Barbara, CA 93101: Free catalog ◆ Wines. 800-436-9463; 805-966-9463 (in CA).

**The Wine Stop,** 1300 Burlingame Ave., Burlingame, CA 94010: Free information ◆ California, imported, and rare wines. 415-342-5858.

## WIRE CRAFTING

**Arizona Gems & Crystals,** 1705 W. 14th Dr., Safford, AZ 85546: Free catalog ◆ Gem tree and wire-crafting supplies, chip beads, other beads and findings, silversmithing and lapidary tools, jewelry-making supplies, and mineral sets. 800-657-6263.

**Bourget Bros.,** 1636 11th St., Santa Monica, CA 90404: Catalog $3 ◆ Silversmithing supplies and copper, gold, and silver wire and sheet. 800-828-3024. www.bourgetbros.com

**Ebersole Lapidary Supply Inc.,** 11417 West Hwy. 54, Wichita, KS 67209: Catalog $5 ◆ Gold and silver sheet and wire and silversmithing supplies. 316-722-4771.

**Herkimer Diamond Mines,** RD 1, P.O. Box 233, Herkimer, NY 13350: Free information ◆ Gem tree and wire crafting supplies, petrified wood, rockhounding equipment, and mineral and rock specimens. 315-866-2011.

**Indian Jewelers Supply Company,** P.O. Box 1774, Gallup, NM 87305: Catalogs $6 ◆ Copper and silver wire and sheet, silversmithing supplies, precious and base metal findings, tools, semi-precious stones, shells, and coral. 505-722-4451.

**Jeanne's Rock & Jewelry,** 5420 Bissonet, Bellaire, TX 77401: Price list $1 ◆ Seashells, petrified wood, gem tree supplies, and rockhounding equipment. 713-664-2988.

**Jems Inc.,** 2293 Aurora Rd., Melbourne, FL 32935: Free price list ◆ Gem trees and wire-crafting supplies, tumbled gemstones, figurines, and jewelry-making supplies. 407-254-5600.

**Laney Company,** 6449 S. 209 East Ave., Broken Arrow, OK 74014: Free information ◆ German silver and gold wire, fancy strip, sheet, findings for silver and goldsmithing, and letters and numbers for trophies, buckles, and other projects. 918-355-1955.

**The NgraveR Company**, 67 Wawecus Hill Rd., Bozrah, CT 06334: Catalog $1 (refundable) ◆ Easy-to-use engraving tools and jewelry-making equipment. 860-823-1533.

**Nonferrous Metals,** P.O. Box 2595, Waterbury, CT 06723: Catalog $3 (refundable) ◆ Plain and ornamental brass, copper, bronze, and nickel-silver wire. 203-264-7255.

**Ross Metals,** 54 W. 47th St., New York, NY 10036: Free information ◆ Findings, gold and silver wire, and spooled chains. 800-654-ROSS; 212-869-3993 (in NY).

**Universal Wirecraft Company,** P.O. Box 20206, Bradenton, FL 34204: Free price list with long SASE ◆ Solderless wirecrafting supplies. 941-745-1219.

**WigJig,** P.O. Box 5306, Arlington, VA 22205: Free information ◆ Accessories for creating solder-free wire designs for chain and necklace components. 800-579-WIRE. www.wigjig.com

## WOOD FINISHING & RESTORING

**Bartley Gel Finishes,** 65 Engerman Ave., Denton, MD 21629: Free information ◆ Easy-to-use wipe-on and wipe-off wood finishes. 800-787-2800.

**Formby's,** c/o Thompson Company, 825 Crossover Ln., Ste. 240C, Memphis, TN 38117: Free information ◆ Furniture refinishing products. 800-FORMBYS. www.thompson.waterseal.com

**Historic Paints Ltd.,** Burr Tavern, Rt. 1, Box 474, East Meredith, NY 13757: Free information ◆ Paints with 18th and 19th-century colors. 607-433-0229.

**Hood Finishing Products Inc.,** P.O. Box 220, Tennent, NJ 07763: Free catalog ◆ Wood finishing and refinishing supplies. 800-229-0934; 732-254-7776 (in NJ).

**Industrial Water-Based Finishes Inc.,** 123 S. Monroe St., Waterloo, WI 53594: Free list of retail sources ◆ Non-flammable water-based finishes. 800-733-1776.

**Klean-Strip,** P.O. Box 1879, Memphis, TN 38101: Free list of retail sources ◆ Solvents, paints, and paint thinners for home restoration and remodeling. 800-235-3546.

**Klockit,** P.O. Box 636, Lake Geneva, WI 53147: Free catalog ◆ Wood kits and parts, decorative wood accessories, finishing supplies, hardware, and clock-making kits and parts. 800-556-2548. www.klockit.com

**Minwax Company Inc.,** 10 Mountainview Rd., Upper Saddle River, NJ 07458: Free list of retail sources ◆ Interior wood finishing products. 201-818-7500.

**Van Dyke's Restorers,** P.O. Box 178, Woonsocket, SD 57385: Free catalog ◆ Supplies for woodworkers and antique restorers. 800-843-3320.

**W-W Finishing Supplies,** 39 Ontario St., Honeoye Falls, NY 14472: Free information ◆ Water-based and other finishing supplies. 716-624-7270.

**Waterlox Chemical & Coatings Corp.,** 9808 Meech Ave., Cleveland, OH 44105: Free information ◆ Tung oil finishes. 800-321-0377; 216-641-4877 (in OH).

**Wayne's Woods Inc.,** 39 N. Plains Industrial Rd., Wallingford, CT 06492: Catalog $2 (refundable) ◆ Refinishing supplies and brass and wood reproduction hardware. 800-793-6208.

**Wise Company,** 6503 St. Claude Ave., P.O. Box 118, Arabi, LA 70032: Catalog $4 ◆ Period and miscellaneous hardware and refinishing products to restore and repair antique furniture. 504-277-7551.

**The Woodworkers' Store,** 4365 Willow Dr., Medina, MN 55340: Free catalog ◆ Hardware, woodworking and finishing supplies, and tools. 800-279-4441. www.woodworkerstore.com

## WOODBURNING EQUIPMENT & SUPPLIES

**B.E.M.I. Publishing Company,** 2650 Davison St., River Grove, IL 60171: Free catalog ◆ Electronic burning systems, patterns, and accessories. 708-452-5551.

**Colwood Electronics,** 15 Meridian Rd., Eatontown, NJ 07724: Free brochure ◆ All-in-one work station that includes woodburning, texturizing system, and high-speed grinding equipment. 908-544-1119. www.woodburning.com

**Eastern Art Glass,** P.O. Box 9, Wyckoff, NJ 07481: Catalog $2 (refundable) ◆ Stained glass kits, glass-etching equipment, glass coloring materials, fabric dyes, mirror-removing and woodburning supplies, and how-to videos. 800-872-3458. www.etchworld.com

**Hot Tools,** Division M.M. Newman Corp., P.O. Box 615, Marblehead, MA 01945: Free catalog ◆ Woodburning tools, accessories, and supplies. 781-639-1000.

**Leisure Time Products,** 2650 Davisson St., River Grove, IL 60171: Free information ◆ Electronic woodburning systems and equipment for carvers, artists, and pyrographers. 708-452-5400. www.fire-art.com

**Nasco,** 901 Janesville Ave., Fort Atkinson, WI 53538: Free catalog ◆ Woodburning and carving tools, woodcraft supplies, and wood projects. 800-558-9595. www.nascofa.com

**Navesink Electronics,** 820 Nut Swamp Rd., Red Bank, NJ 07701: Free information ◆ Woodburning systems, dust collectors, and carving tools. 908-747-5023. navesink1@aol.com

**Wil-Cut Company,** 7113 Spicer Dr., Citrus Heights, CA 95621: Free information ◆ Carving woods and machines, woodburning tools, knives, books, and other supplies. 916-961-5400.

**Woodcrafters,** 212 NE 6th Ave., Portland, OR 97232: Free information ◆ Woodcarving tools, knives, power-carving and burning tools, carving woods, books, and supplies. 503-231-0226.

## WOODWORKING & WOODCARVING

### Parts, Kits & Supplies

**Adams Wood Products Inc.,** 974 Forest Dr., Morristown, TN 37814: Free catalog ◆ Cherry, mahogany, maple, pine, cedar, and oak wood parts. 423-587-2942.

**Anthony Wood Products Inc.,** P.O. Box 1081, Hillsboro, TX 76645: Catalog $3 ◆ Handcrafted Victorian gingerbread. 800-969-2181.

**Armor Crafts,** P.O. Box 445, East Northport, NY 11731: Free catalog ◆ Wood turnings and parts, hardware, lamp parts, electronic music boxes, plans for toys and children's furniture, and movements for restoring mantel, banjo, and grandfather clocks. 800-292-8296.

**Beaver Dam Decoys,** 3311 State Rt. 305, P.O. Box 40, Cortland, OH 44410: Catalog $2 ◆ Decoys, decoy blanks, and carving supplies. 330-637-4007.

**Benny's Woodworks & Tools LLC,** P.O. Box 269, Bell Buckle, TN 37020: Free catalog ◆ Woodworking supplies. 800-255-1335; 931-684-8995 (in TN).

**Big Sky Carvers,** P.O. Box 507, Manhattan, MT 59741: Free catalog ◆ Carved and sanded blanks that are ready for detailing and painting. 800-735-7982.

**Birds in Wood,** P.O. Box 2649, Meriden, CT 06450: Catalog $2 (refundable) ◆ Decoy carving kits and supplies. 203-634-1953.

**Blue Ribbon Bases,** 100-K Knickerbocker Ave., Bohemia, NY 11716: Free catalog with long SASE ◆ Hardwoods for woodcarving. 888-692-5257.

**Buck Run Carving Supplies,** 781 Gully Rd., Aurora, NY 13026: Catalog $2 (refundable) ◆ Woodcarving supplies. 315-364-8414.

**Casey's Wood Products,** P.O. Box 365, Woolrich, ME 04579: Free catalog ◆ Wood parts and supplies. 800-452-2739.

**Cherry Tree Toys,** P.O. Box 369, Belmont, OH 43718: Catalog $1 ◆ Plans, kits, and unfinished hardwood parts for toys. 800-848-4363.

**Cirtain Plywood Inc.,** 677 Galloway Ave., Memphis, TN 38105: Free information ◆ Exotic and domestic premium hardwoods. Also plywood, abrasives, glues, and other supplies. 800-593-3304.

**Classic Designs by Matthew Burak,** P.O. Box 279, Danville, VT 05828: Free brochure ◆ Ready-to-finish mortised hardwood furniture legs. 802-748-9378.

**Cupboard Distributing,** P.O. Box 148, Urbana, OH 43078: Catalog $2 ◆ Unfinished wood parts for crafts, miniatures, toys, jewelry-making, tole and decorative painting, and woodworking. 937-652-3338. cupboard@foryou.net

**Gregory D. Dorrance Company,** 1063 Oak Hill Ave., Attleboro, MA 02703: Free information ◆ Decoy-making and art supplies, tools, and wood for carving. 508-222-6255.

**The Duck Blind,** 8709 Gull Rd., Richland, MI 49083: Free catalog ◆ Carving and art supplies, books, and wood. 800-852-7352.

**Dupli-Tech,** P.O. Box 51, Charleroi, PA 15022: Free brochure ◆ Carving blanks for wildfowl, waterfowl, birds of prey, and song and game birds. 412-483-8883.

**Dux' Dekes Decoy Company,** RD 2, Box 66, Greenwich, NY 12834: Free information ◆ White pine and basswood carving blanks. 800-553-4725; 518-692-7703 (in NY).

**Earth Guild,** 33 Haywood St., Asheville, NC 28801: Catalog $3 ◆ Basket-making, weaving, spinning, dyeing, pottery, woodcarving, hand and machine knitting, rug-making, netting, and chair-caning supplies. 800-327-8448. www.earthguild.com

**Geneva Specialties,** Division Klockit, P.O. Box 636, Lake Geneva, WI 53147: Free catalog ◆ Woodcraft patterns and plans, turned wood parts, and hardware. 800-556-2548. www.klockit.com

**Green Mountain Studios,** Rt. 10 North, Box 158, Lyme, NH 03768: Catalog $2 ◆ Wood turnings and other patterns. 603-795-4398.

**Jennings Decoy Company,** 601 Franklin Ave. NE, St. Cloud, MN 56304: Free catalog ◆ Woodcarving cutouts and kits, tools, and supplies. 800-331-5613.

**J.H. Kline Carving Shop,** P.O. Box 445, Forge Hill Rd., Manchester, PA 17345: Catalog $1 (refundable) ◆ Woodcarving tools and supplies, wood for carving, and patterns for precut wood blanks. 717-266-3501.

**Klockit,** P.O. Box 636, Lake Geneva, WI 53147: Free catalog ◆ Wood kits and parts, decorative wood accessories, finishing supplies, hardware, and clock-making kits and parts. 800-556-2548. www.klockit.com

**Little Mountain Carving Supply,** Rt. 2, Box 1329, Bowling Green Rd., Front Royal, VA 22630: Free catalog ◆ Hard-to-find carving supplies. 703-636-3125.

**MacBeath Hardwood Company,** 930 Ashby Ave., Berkeley, CA 94710: Catalog $2 (refundable with $10 order) ◆ Woodworking tools and supplies. 510-843-4390. www.macbeath.com

**Manasquan Premium Fasteners,** 2391 Cypress St., Manasquan, NJ 08736: Free catalog ◆ Stainless steel screws, nails, joist and framing connectors, staples, and other fasteners. 800-542-1978.

**MDI Woodcarvers Supply,** 228 Main St., Bar Harbor, ME 04609: Free catalog ◆ Woodcarving supplies, books, and tools. 800-866-5728.

**Meisel Hardware Specialties,** P.O. Box 70, Mound, MN 55364: Catalog $2 ◆ Plans for over 1000 woodworking projects for the home hobbyist. 612-471-8550. www.nonni.com/woodhobby

**Midwest Dowel Works Inc.,** 4631 Hutchinson Rd., Cincinnati, OH 45248: Free catalog ◆ Oak, walnut, hickory, maple, cherry, mahogany, and teak dowels, plugs, and pegs. 513-574-8488.

**Mountain Woodcarvers Supplies,** P.O. Box 3485, Estes Park, CO 80517: Catalog $1 ◆ Carving supplies, tools, and books. 800-292-6788; 970-586-8678 (in CO). www.longs-peak.com/highway/carvers

**Nasco,** 901 Janesville Ave., Fort Atkinson, WI 53538: Free catalog ◆ Woodburning and carving tools, woodcraft supplies, and wood projects. 800-558-9595. www.nascofa.com

**Osborne Wood Products,** 8116 Hwy. 123 North, Toccoa, GA 30577: Free information ◆ Easy-to-assemble pencil-post beds. Also turned legs in different styles and wood types. 800-849-8876; 706-886-1065 (in GA).

**Rainbow Woods,** 1480 Bells Berry Rd., Marietta, GA 30066: Free catalog ◆ Hardwood turnings. 800-423-2762.

**Ritter Carvers Inc.,** 640 Bethlehem Pike, Colmar, PA 18915: Free catalog ◆ Woodcarving supplies and tools. 215-997-3395.

**Scherr's Cabinet & Doors,** 5315 Burdick Expwy. East, RR. 5, Box 12, Minot, ND 58701: Brochure $2 ◆ Raised panel doors for cabinets, drawer fronts, and dovetail drawers. 701-839-3384. www.scherrs.com

**Sloan's Woodshop,** 3453 Callis Rd., Lebanon, TN 37090: Free catalog ◆ Wood, accessories, patterns, and books for the scroll saw. 615-453-2222.

**Sugar Pine Woodcarving Supplies,** P.O. Box 859, Lebanon, OR 97355: Free information ◆ Woodcarving supplies. 800-452-2783.

**Tohickon Glass Eyes,** 15 Geigel Hill Rd., P.O. Box 15, Erwinna, PA 18920: Free catalog ◆ Glass eyes for taxidermy and woodcarving. 800-441-5983; 610-294-9483 (in PA). www.tohickonglasseyes.com

**Van Dyke's Restorers,** P.O. Box 178, Woonsocket, SD 57385: Free catalog ◆ Carvings, moldings, and other supplies for woodworkers. 800-843-3320.

**Vintage Wood Works,** Hwy. 34, Box R, Quinlan, TX 75474: Catalog $2 ◆ Victorian-style gingerbread decorative cutouts. 903-356-2158. www.vintagewoodworks.com

**West Coast Wood Craft Supplies,** 1256 Alderney Ct., Oceanside, CA 92054: Catalog $2 ◆ Laser-engraved wood cut-outs. 800-515-9663.

**West Wind Hardwood Inc.,** P.O. Box 2205, Sidney, British Columbia, Canada V8L 3S8: Free catalog ◆ Wood for carving. 800-667-2275.

**Ivan Whillock Studio,** 122 NE 1st Ave., Faribault, MN 55021: Free catalog ◆ Woodcarving tools, supplies, how-to books, and kits. 800-882-9379; 507-334-8306 (in MN). www.whillock.com

**Wil-Cut Company,** 7113 Spicer Dr., Citrus Heights, CA 95621: Free information ◆ Carving woods and machines, woodburning tools, knives, books, and other supplies. 916-961-5400.

**Winfield Collection,** 112 E. Ellen St., Fenton, MI 48430: Catalog $1 ◆ Country woodcraft patterns for folk art, shorebirds, country birds, home and decorative accessories, and toys. 800-946-3435.

**Wood Cut-Outs Unlimited,** Box 518, Massillon, OH 44648: Catalog $2 (refundable) ◆ Wood items for decorative painting.

**Wood-N-Crafts Inc.,** P.O. Box 140, Lakeview, MI 48850: Catalog $2 ◆ Craft and woodworking supplies. 800-444-8075; 517-352-8075 (in MI). www.wood-n-crafts.com

**Wood N' Things Inc.,** 601 E. 44th St., Boise, ID 83714: Free catalog ◆ Carving supplies, tools, woods, and books. 208-375-9663.

**Woodcraft Supply,** 210 Wood County Industrial Park, P.O. Box 1686, Parkersburg, WV 26102: Free catalog ◆ Carving tools, supplies, kits, and books. 800-535-4482. www.woodcraft.com

**Woodcrafters,** 212 NE 6th Ave., Portland, OR 97232: Free information ◆ Woodcarving tools, knives, power carving and burning tools, carving woods, books, and supplies. 503-231-0226.

**Woodcrafts & Supplies,** 405 E. Indiana St., Oblong, IL 62449: Free catalog ◆ Unfinished wood products, hardware, and woodworking and craft supplies. 800-592-4907. woodcraftssupplies.com

**Woodsmith,** 2200 Grand Ave., Des Moines, IA 50312: Free catalog ◆ Woodworking kits and supplies. 800-444-7002.

**The Woodworkers' Store,** 4365 Willow Dr., Medina, MN 55340: Free catalog ◆ Hardware, woodworking and finishing supplies, and tools. 800-279-4441. www.woodworkerstore.com

### Plans

**Accents in Pine,** Box 7387, Gonic, NH 03839: Catalog $2 ◆ Woodcraft patterns for the yard, home, country projects, gifts, and toys. 603-332-4579.

**Armor Crafts,** P.O. Box 445, East Northport, NY 11731: Free catalog ◆ Plans for rocking and riding horses, realistic working automobiles and trucks, and other projects. 800-292-8296.

**Cherry Tree Toys,** P.O. Box 369, Belmont, OH 43718: Catalog $1 ◆ Plans for wooden toys and other projects. 800-848-4363.

**Constantines,** 2050 Eastchester Rd., Bronx, NY 10461: Catalog $1 ◆ Cabinet and furniture wood, veneers, plans, hardware, how-to books, carving tools, chisels, inlay designs, and supplies. 800-223-8087; 718-792-1600 (in NY). www.constantines.com

**Country Designs,** P.O. Box 774, Essex, CT 06426: Catalog $6 ◆ Building plans for barns, sheds, and garages. 860-767-1046.

**Crafters Delight,** P.O. Box 368, Carson City, MI 48811: Catalog $1 ◆ Woodcraft patterns.

**Furniture Designs Inc.,** 1827 Elmdale Ave., Glenview, IL 60025: Catalog $3 ◆ Plans for building furniture. 800-657-7692. www.furnituredesigns.com

**Geneva Specialties,** Division Klockit, P.O. Box 636, Lake Geneva, WI 53147: Free catalog ◆ Woodworking plans for children's furniture, yard ornaments, gun cabinets, and other projects. 800-556-2548. www.klockit.com

**Hammond Barns,** P.O. Box 584, New Castle, IN 47362: Brochure $2 ◆ Plans for storage and tool sheds, workshops, and other structures. 765-529-7822.

**Homestead Design Inc.,** P.O. Box 2010, Port Townsend, WA 98368: Catalog $3 ◆ Plans for small barns, studios, workshops, garden sheds, and country homes.

**U-Bild,** P.O. Box 2383, Van Nuys, CA 91409: Catalog $3.95 ◆ Plans with step-by-step traceable patterns for woodworking and other projects. 800-828-2453.

**Western Wood Products Association,** Yeon Bldg., 522 SW 5th Ave., Dept. PL, Portland, OR 97204: Free list ◆ Consumer and technical information oriented toward do-it-yourself projects and for builders, engineers, and architects. 503-224-3930.

**Winfield Collection,** 112 E. Ellen St., Fenton, MI 48430: Catalog $2 ◆ Country woodcraft patterns for folk art, shorebirds, country birds, home and decorative accessories, and toys. 800-946-3435.

### Sandpaper

**Econ-Abrasives,** P.O. Box 1628, Frisco, TX 75034: Free catalog ◆ Belts, cabinet paper, finishing paper, wet/dry paper, no-load paper, adhesive discs, jumbo cleaning sticks, and other sandpaper supplies. 972-377-9779.

**Industrial Abrasives Company,** 642 N. 8th St., Reading, PA 19612: Free information ◆ Belts, cabinet paper, no load paper, sticky discs, stones, and other sanding materials. 800-428-2222.

**Klingspor's Sanding Catalogue,** P.O. Box 3737, Hickory, NC 28603: Free catalog ◆ Sanding supplies and accessories. 800-228-0000. www.sandingcatalog.com

**Red Hill Corp.,** P.O. Box 4234, Gettysburg, PA 17325: Free catalog ◆ Hot melt glue sticks, glue guns, and sandpaper in belts, sheets, and discs. 800-822-4003. www.supergrit.com

**Sand-Rite Manufacturing Company,** 321 N. Justine St., Chicago, IL 60607: Free information ◆ Graded sandpaper and abrasives in belts, rolls, and sleeves. 800-521-2318.

## WRESTLING

**Adidas USA,** 5675 N. Blackstock Rd., Spartanburg, SC 29303: Free list of retail sources ◆ Shoes. 800-423-4327. www.adidas.com

**Bike Athletic Company,** P.O. Box 666, Knoxville, TN 37901: Free information ◆ Knee pads, braces, and supporters. 800-251-9230. www.bike-athletic.com

**The Brute Group,** 2126 Spring St., P.O. Box 2788, Reading, PA 19609: Free information ◆ Knee pads and braces, mats and mat covers, shoes, supporters, tights and trunks, uniforms, and warm-up suits. 800-486-2788; 610-678-4050 (in PA).

**Cougar Sports,** 6667 W. Old Shakopee Rd., Wilmington, MN 55438: Free information ◆ Knee pads, mouth and teeth protectors, and supporters. 800-445-2664.

**Cramer Products Inc.,** P.O. Box 1001, Gardner, KS 66030: Free information ◆ Knee braces and pads, mouth and teeth protectors, and other equipment. 800-345-2231; 913-884-7511 (in KS).

**Eastbay,** P.O. Box 8066, Wausau, WI 54402: Free catalog ◆ Shoes and clothing. 800-826-2205. www.eastbay.com

**Genesport Industries Ltd.,** Hokkaido Karate Equipment Manufacturing Company, 150 King St., Montreal, Quebec, Canada H3C 2P3: Free information ◆ Knee pads, mouth and teeth protectors, supporters, tights and trunks, and mats. 514-861-1856.

**Cliff Keen Athletic,** 1235 Rosewood, P.O. Box 1447, Ann Arbor, MI 48106: Free information ◆ Knee pads and braces, mat covers, mats, mouth and teeth protectors, shoes, supporters, tights and trunks, uniforms, and warm-up suits. 800-992-0799. www.cliffkeen.com

**Harold Nichols Wrestling Equipment,** P.O. Box 1067, Ames, IA 50014: Free catalog ◆ Wrestling equipment. 515-292-5060.

**Royal Textile Mills Inc.,** P.O. Box 250, Yanceyville, NC 27379: Free information ◆ Knee pads, braces, mouth and teeth protectors, and supporters. 800-334-9361; 336-694-4121 (in NC).

## YARN & SPINNING FIBERS

**Allegro Yarns,** 3535 Pierce St. NE, Minneapolis, MN 55418: Catalog $3 ◆ Yarns, needles, patterns, and kits. 800-547-3808 (evenings).

**Artfibers,** 124 Sutter St., 2nd Floor, San Francisco, CA 94104: Free information ◆ Imported exotic and fashion yarns from Europe. 888-326-1112; 415-956-6319 (in CA).

**Aura Yarns,** Box 602, Derby Line, VT 05830: Free information ◆ Icelandic wool sweater kits, and alpaca, cashmere, mohair, merino, shetland, silk, and cotton yarns. 802-876-2998.

**Ayotte's Designery,** P.O. Box 287, Center Sandwich, NH 03227: Free information with two 1st class stamps ◆ Spinning and weaving supplies, hand-dyed wool, mohair, and other yarns. 603-284-6915.

**Bare Hill Studios,** P.O. Bldg., Rt. 111, Box 327, Harvard, MA 01451: Catalog $5 ◆ Alpaca, cotton, wool, mohair, and synthetic yarns. 978-456-8669.

**Barkim Ltd.,** 47 W. Polk St., Ste. 100, Chicago, IL 60653: Catalog and yarn samples $4 ◆ Sweater kits, books, patterns, and yarns. 888-548-2211. www.barkim.com

**Bartlett Yarns,** Box 36, Harmony, ME 04942: Free brochure with long SASE ◆ Wool yarns for knitting and weaving. 207-683-2251.

**Bendigo Woollen Mills,** P.O. Box 27164, Columbus, OH 43227: Free shade card ◆ Australian cabled wool. 800-829-WOOL.

**Black Sheep Wools,** 12 Perkins St., Lowell, MA 01853: Samples $3 ◆ Natural fiber yarns. 978-937-0320.

**Braid-Aid,** 466 Washington St., Pembroke, MA 02359: Catalog $4 ◆ Braided rug kits, braiding supplies, wool by the pound or yard, and hooking, basket-making, shirret, spinning, and weaving supplies. 781-826-2560.

**Clemes & Clemes Inc.,** 650 San Pablo Ave., Pinole, CA 94564: Free catalog ◆ Spinning wheels, drum carders, wool and cotton carders, drop spindles, and natural and dyed wool. 510-724-2036.

**Cotton Clouds,** 5175 S. 14th Ave., Safford, AZ 85546: Catalog $6.50 ◆ Looms, spinning fibers, kits, books, and 100 percent cotton knitting, weaving, and crochet cone and skein yarns. 800-322-7888; 520-428-5885 (in AZ). www.cottonclouds.com

**Country Spun Studio,** RR 1, Box 269, Rochester Mills, PA 15771: Brochure $3 ◆ Hand-spun yarns, spinning wheels, books and videos, and accessories. 800-970-9703; 412-286-3255 (in PA).

**Crystal Palace Yarns,** 3006 San Pablo Ave., Berkeley, CA 94702: Free brochure and list of retail sources ◆ Yarns, natural fibers, and spinning wheels. 510-548-9988. www.straw.com/cpy/index.html

**Earthsong Fibers,** 5115 Excelsior Blvd., #428, Minneapolis, MN 55416: Catalog $2 ◆ Fibers, yarns, spinning wheels, looms, and accessories. 800-473-5350; 612-926-3451 (in MN).

**Edgemont Yarn Services,** P.O. Box 205, Washington, KY 41086: Free brochure ◆ Cones and skeins of wools in naturals, soft naturals, heavy weights, rug yarn, boucles, wool loops, and piles. 800-446-5977.

**Elann Fiber Company,** Box 257, Eureka, MT 59917: Catalog and samples $4 (refundable) ◆ Kits and an extensive selection of yarn. 800-720-0616. www.elann.com

**Erdal Yarns Ltd.,** 303 5th Ave., Ste. 1104, New York, NY 10016: Free information ◆ Solid and variegated colored yarns. 800-237-6594; 212-725-0162 (in NY). www.erdal.com

**Ernel Yarns,** 1419 Burlingame, Burlingame, CA 94010: Free information ◆ Yarns and kits from Classic Elite, Tiber, and Ale of Norway. Also specialty yarns. 800-343-4874.

**Frederick J. Fawcett Inc.,** 1338 Ross St., Petaluma, CA 94954: Free information ◆ Looms, linen embroidery fabrics, macrame supplies, linen/cotton and wool yarns, and other fibers. 800-289-9276.

**Fiber Loft,** 9 Massachusetts Ave., Harvard, MA 01451: Information $5.25 ◆ Yarns and mill ends for knitters, weavers, and machines. Also silk, angora, ribbon, cashmere, and other fibers. 978-456-8669.

**Fiber Studio,** 9 Foster Hill Rd., Box 637, Henniker, NH 03242: Spinning fibers catalog $1, yarn samples $4, equipment catalog $1 ◆ Spinning, weaving, and knitting equipment and fibers. Also cotton, mohair, wool, alpaca, silk, and linen yarns. 603-428-7830.

**Fingerlakes Yarns,** 1193 Stewarts Corner Rd., Genoa, NY 13071: Free request list of retail sources ◆ Sweater kits and merino, angora, and silk yarns. 800-441-9665.

**Glimakra Looms & Yarns Inc.,** 1338 Ross St., Petaluma, CA 94954: Catalog $2.50 ◆ Weaving equipment, looms, yarns, and lace-making equipment. 800-289-9276; 707-762-3362 (in CA).

**Great Yarns,** Ridgewood Shopping Center, 1208 Ridge Rd., Raleigh, NC 27607: Catalog $2.50 ◆ Yarns. 919-832-3599.

**Martha Hall,** 20 Bartol Island Rd., Freeport, ME 04032: Catalog $2 ◆ Easy-to-knit Maine wool sweater kits and hand-dyed silk, mohair, linen, cotton, cashmere, and alpaca yarn. 800-643-4566.

**Harrisville Designs,** Center Village, Box 806, Harrisville, NH 03450: Yarn catalog $6, free loom catalog ◆ Yarns, looms, and accessories. 800-338-9415; 603-827-3333 (in NH). www.harrisville.com

**Herrschners Inc.,** 2800 Hoover Rd., Stevens Point, WI 54492: Free catalog ◆ Yarns, knitting accessories, and crochet and hooking needle crafts. 800-441-0838. www.herrschners.com

**The Hill Knittery,** 10720 Yonge St., Richmond Hill, Ontario, Canada L4C 3C9: Free information ◆ Yarns, kits, books, and how-to videos. 800-551-KNIT.

**Halcyon Yarn,** 12 School St., Bath, ME 04530: Free information ◆ Yarn and knitting accessories. 800-341-0282. www.halcyonyarn.com

**Imagiknit Ltd.,** 2586 Yonge St., Toronto, Ontario, Canada M4P 2J3: Catalog $4.50 ◆ Yarns, how-to books, and kits. 800-318-9426.

**Judy's Heirloom Sewing,** 13650 E. Zayante Rd., Felton, CA 95018: Catalog $6.50 ◆ Sewing and smocking supplies, fabrics, lace, ribbons, and yarns. 408-335-1050.

**K & J Crafts,** 31351 Feldspar St. NW, Princeton, MN 55371: Free information ◆ Yarns and supplies. 800-325-2385.

**Knit 'N Needle,** 722 W. Center, Duncanville, TX 75116: Free information ◆ Hand and machine yarns, books, and knitting machines. 972-296-4008.

**Krh Knits,** P.O. Box 1587, Avon, CT 06001: Catalog $5 ◆ Knitting machines, how-to information, yarn winders, yarns, fabric paints, finishing tools, crochet accessories, elastic thread, patterns, and notions. 800-248-KNIT.

**La Lana Wools,** North Pueblo Rd., Taos, NM 87571: Sample card $6 ◆ Plant-dyed and hand-spun knitting yarns. 505-758-9631.

**Lion Brand Yarn Company,** 34 W. 15th St., New York, NY 10011: Free information ◆ Yarns. 800-258-YARN.

**Louët Sales,** P.O. Box 267, Ogdensburg, NY 13669: Catalog $5 ◆ Books, dyestuffs, yarns and fibers, and spinning, weaving, carding, felting, and lace-making equipment. 613-925-4502. www.louet.com

**Magic Cabin Dolls,** Prairie Edge Rd., P.O. Box 1996, Peoria, IL 61656: Free information ◆ Natural fiber yarns. 888-623-3655.

**Mannings Creative Crafts,** P.O. Box 687, East Berlin, PA 17316: Catalog $1 ◆ Yarns and spinning fibers, spinning wheels and looms, dyes and mordants, and books. 717-624-2223. mannings@sun-link.com

**Marr Haven,** 772 39th St., Allegan, MI 49010: Free brochure with long SASE ◆ Wool yarn in natural and dyed colors. 800-653-8810; 616-673-8800 (in MI). www.accn.org/~mhyarn

**Mary Maxim Inc.,** 2001 Holland Ave., P.O. Box 5019, Port Huron, MI 48061: Free catalog ◆ Needlecraft kits, yarns, and other supplies. 800-962-9504.

**Morehouse Farm,** RD 2, Box 408, Red Hook, NY 12571: Information $1 with long SASE ◆ Merino wool in natural colors. 914-758-6493.

**Moss Yarns Needlearts,** 225 Pinewood, Hot Springs National Park, AR 71913: Catalog $3 ◆ Needlecraft supplies and imported and domestic yarns. 501-623-5106.

**Nancy's Knitworks,** 1650 W. Wabash, Springfield, IL 62704: Catalog $3 ◆ Yarns. 800-676-9813.

**The Needlework Attic,** 4706 Bethesda Ave., Bethesda, MD 20814: Free information ◆ Knitting yarns and books. 301-652-8688.

**Norsk Fjord Fiber,** P.O. Box 271, Lexington, GA 30648: Loom catalog $3, fleece and rovings sample cards $3, Spelsau yarn sample card $3 ◆ Tapestry looms. Also Swedish Gotland fleece, rovings, and yarns. 706-743-5120.

**Northwest Peddlers,** P.O. Box 70779, Eugene, OR 97401: Free information ◆ Yarns, needlecraft kits, and supplies. 800-764-9276; 541-465-9003 (in OR).

**Ogier Trading Company,** P.O. Box 686, 2385 Carlos St., Moss Beach, CA 94038: Free catalog ◆ Imported yarns, books, and other fiber art supplies. 415-728-8554.

**Personal Threads Boutique,** 8025 W. Dodge Rd., Omaha, NE 68114: Free information ◆ Yarns and needlecraft supplies. 800-306-7733.

**Pieces of String,** 810 22nd Ave. S., Moorhead, MN 56560: Catalog $3 (refundable) ◆ Yarns. 218-233-6670.

**Rio Grande Weaver's Supply,** 216 Pueblo Norte, Taos, NM 87571: Catalog $1 ◆ Spinning wheels, looms, and loom kits. Also hand-dyed rug, tapestry, clothing, and other yarns and dyes, fleeces, books, and videos. 505-758-0433.

**Schoolhouse Press,** 6899 Cary Bluff, Pittsville, WI 54466: Catalog $5 ◆ Supplies for hand knitters, books, videos, wools, needles, and buttons. 715-884-2799.

**Silk City Fibers,** 155 Oxford St., Paterson, NJ 07522: Information $5 ◆ Color-coordinated cone yarns. 201-942-1100.

**Smiley's Yarns,** 92-06 Jamaica Ave., Woodhaven NY 11421: Catalog $2 ◆ Yarns, needles, hooks, books, tools, and other supplies. 718-847-5038.

**Spinner's Hearth,** 7512 Lackey Rd., Vaughn, WA 98394: Catalog and color cards $1.50 and two 1st class stamps ◆ Spinning fibers. 206-884-1500.

**Stitches East,** 55 E. 52nd St., New York, NY 10022: Free information ◆ Knitting and needlepoint supplies, yarns, patterns, needles, and canvases. 212-421-0112.

**Straw into Gold,** 3006 San Pablo Ave., Berkeley, CA 94702: Catalog $2 with long SASE and two 1st class stamps ◆ Ready-to-spin alpaca and books for spinners, weavers, and knitters. 510-548-5241. www.straw.com/sig

**Threads Etc.,** 61568 Eastlake Dr., Bend, OR 97702: Catalog $2 (refundable) ◆ Knitting machines and accessories, yarns, books, patterns, and kits. 800-208-2046; 541-388-2046 (in OR).

**Thumbelina Needlework Shop,** P.O. Box 1065, Solvang, CA 93464: Information $1.75 ◆ Books, fabrics, threads, yarns, and kits. 800-789-4136.

**TLC Yarns,** 32022 8th Ave. South, Roy, WA 98580: Free color card ◆ Wool yarns. 800-382-1820.

**Bonnie Triola,** 343 E. Gore Rd., Erie, PA 16509: Information $10 ◆ Natural fibers, synthetics, blends, discontinued designer yarns, and other yarns. 814-825-7821.

**Unitex Inc.,** 16 Anawan St., Fall River, MA 02721: Free information ◆ Skein, yarn, and ball winders. 508-674-8032.

**The Weaver's Knot Inc.,** 508 Inlet Dr., Seneca, SC 29672: Catalog $1 ◆ Yarns, spinning fibers, looms, and knitting, crochet, and weaving supplies. 800-680-7747; 864-882-1214 (in SC). weaveknot@aol.com

**The Weaver's Loft,** 308 S. Pennsylvania Ave., Centre Hall, PA 16828: Free information ◆ Knitting, weaving and spinning supplies, and yarns. 800-693-7242; 814-364-1433 (in PA). www.knitters-underground.com

**Weaving Works,** 4717 Brooklyn Ave. NE, Seattle, WA 98105: Catalog $4.50 ◆ Looms, spinning wheels, hand and machine knitting supplies, and traditional and fashion yarns. 206-524-1221.

**Web-sters Handspinners, Weavers & Knitters,** 11 N. Main St., Ashland, OR 97520: Free catalog ◆ Designer yarns, books, and tools. 800-482-9801.

**Webs Yarn,** P.O. Box 147, Northampton, MA 01060: Price list $2 ◆ Yarns and weaving and spinning equipment. 413-584-2225.

**Wilde Yarns,** P.O. Box 4662, Philadelphia, PA 19127: Catalog $6 ◆ Yarns for weaving, knitting, handspinning, and more. 215-482-8800.

**WoodsEdge Wools,** P.O. Box 275, Stockton, NJ 08559: Catalog and samples $10 ◆ Raw fleeces, processed fiber, and soft yarns. 609-397-2212.

**The Wool Connection,** 34 E. Main St., Avon, CT 06001: Catalog $3 ◆ Yarns, patterns, kits, and other supplies. 800-933-9665; 860-678-1710 (in CT). www.woolconnection.com

**Wool Room,** 172 Joe's Hill Rd., Brewster, NY 10509: Brochure $1 ◆ Spinning fibers, yarns, and more. 914-279-7627. www.ourworld.compuserve.com/homepage/WoolRoomSue

**Woolgathering,** 750 Calico Ct., Waukesha, WI 53186: Free price list ◆ Rowan yarns, needle point kits, buttons, books, magazines, and sewing notions. 888-248-3225.

**Wooly Knits,** 6728 Lowell Ave., McLean, VA 22101: Catalog $5 (12 issues) ◆ Designer yarns, unusual buttons, and needlework supplies. 703-448-9665. www.woolyknits.com

**Yarn Barn,** 930 Massachusetts, Box 334, Lawrence, KS 66044: Free catalog ◆ Fiber books, patterns, yarns, and more. 800-468-0035. yarnbarn@idir.net

**YLI Corp.,** 161 W. Main St., Rock Hill, SC 29730: Catalog $2.50 ◆ Serging thread in solid colors and variegated color combinations, metallic thread in wool/nylon or nylon mono-filament, and rayon. 800-854-1932.

## YO-YOS

**Brian Dube Inc.,** 520 Broadway, 3rd Floor, New York, NY 10012: Free catalog ◆ Juggling equipment, boomerangs, yo-yo's, and books. 212-941-0060. www.dube.com

**Infinite Illusions,** P.O. Box 2584, Tallahassee, FL 32316: Free information ◆ Juggling supplies, boomerangs, and yo-yo's. 800-548-6724; 904-385-6463 (in FL). www.yoyoguy.com

**Playmaxx Inc.,** 2410 N. Huachuca Dr., Tucson, AZ 85745: Free brochure ◆ Yo-yos, instruction tapes, strings, and replacement axles. 520-623-7085.

**Wooden Monarch Yo-Yos,** P.O. Box 23404, Santa Barbara, CA 93121: Free brochure ◆ Handcrafted light to superweight yo-yos. 805-966-4270. MREID@RAIN.ORG

**The YoYo Store,** 3111 S. Valley View, A-116, Las Vegas, NV 89102: Free catalog ◆ Yo-yos and accessories. 800-638-5483; 702-220-4340 (in NV). www.kitestore.com

## YOGA

**Bheka Yoga Supplies,** P.O. Box 3434, Grass Valley, CA, 95945: Free brochure ◆ Sticky mats, sandbags, neck pillows, cushions, and other yoga supplies. 800-366-4541. www.yogavoices.com/bheka

**Body Bridge by ARCH/EEZ,** 1011 E. Ginter Rd., Tucson, AZ 85706: Free information ◆ Lightweight folding support for body relaxation and posture improvement. 800-326-2724.

**Dharma Crafts,** 405 Waltham St., Ste. 234, Lexington, MA 02173: Catalog $2 ◆ Statues, cushions, ritual objects, benches, books, incense, and meditation supplies. 781-862-9211.

**Fish Crane Yoga Props,** P.O. Box 791029, New Orleans, LA 70179: Free information ◆ Lightweight sticky mats. 800-959-6116.

**Gravity Plus,** P.O. Box 1166, La Jolla, CA 92038: Free catalog ◆ Inversion and back care products. 800-383-8056; 619-454-1626 (in CA). www.gravityplus.com

**Harmony in Design,** 2050 S. Dayton St., Denver, CO 80231: Free catalog ◆ Yoga back bench that provides for different postures to open, stretch, and relax the body. 303-337-7728.

**Himalayan Institute Press,** RR 1, Box 405, Honesdale, PA 18431: Free information ◆ Books and audio tapes on physical, psychological health and well-being, spiritual growth though meditation, and other yoga practices. 800-822-4547. www.himalayaninstitute.org

**H2B Company,** 610 22nd St., Ste. 247, San Francisco, CA 94107: Free catalog ◆ Pillows for relaxation. 800-829-6580.

**Hugger-Mugger Yoga Products,** 31 W. Gregson Ave., Salt Lake City, UT 84115: Free information ◆ Blocks, tapas mats, bolsters, and straps. 800-473-4888; 801-487-4888 (in CA).

**Living Arts,** P.O. Box 2939, Venice, CA 90291: Free information ◆ Yoga videos, accessories, clothing, and books. 800-254-8464. livingarts@aol.com

**Lucidity Institute,** 2555 Park Blvd., Ste 2, Palo Alto, CA 94306: Free catalog ◆ Yoga books, tapes, and biofeedback devices. 800-465-8243. www.lucidity.com

**Mano Creations,** P.O. Box 182, Vernon, British Columbia, Canada V1T 6M2: Catalog $2 (refundable) ◆ Mats, sandbags, blocks, cotton bolsters, wedges, benches, multi-purpose furniture, and other yoga equipment. 604-542-7688.

**Mystic River Video,** 166 Sharon St., Medford, MA 02155: Free information ◆ Yoga video tapes. 781-483-9642.

**Proprioception Inc.,** Box 7612, Ann Arbor, MI 48107: Free information ◆ Straps, slings, tables, wall and ceiling mounts, bars, and other equipment. 800-488-8414.

**Shasta Abbey Buddhist Supplies,** 3724 Summit Dr., Mt. Shasta, CA 96067: Catalog $2 ◆ Buddhist meditation supplies and other accessories. 800-653-3315. www.obcon.org

**Tru Blue Yoga Mats,** P.O. Box 99, Chatham, NJ 07928: Free information ◆ Yoga mats. 201-966-5311.

**White Lotus Yoga Foundation,** 2529 San Marcos Pass, Santa Barbara, CA 93105: Free information ◆ Aerobic yoga workout videos. 800-544-3569; 805-964-1944 (in CA).

**Yoga Mats,** P.O. Box 885044, San Francisco, CA 94188: Free information with long SASE ◆ Handcrafted 100 percent lightweight cotton yoga mats. 800-720-YOGA.

**Yoga Pro Products,** Box 7612, Ann Arbor, MI 48107: Free information ◆ Yoga posture equipment. 800-488-8414.

**Yoga Props,** 3055 23rd St., San Francisco, CA 94110: Catalog $1 ◆ Wall ropes for strengthening and stretching poses. 415-285-YOGA.

**Yoga Zone,** P.O. Box 3908, Milford, CT 06460: Free catalog ◆ Clothing and yoga-inspired products. 800-264-YOGA.

**Yogaware,** 1509 Kearney, Ann Arbor, MI 48104: Free information ◆ Exercise wear and pre-shrunk knit shorts with reinforced leg bands. 313-663-6819.

# ❖ CORPORATE INDEX ❖

## A

## B

## C

## E

## F

## G

## H

## I

## J

## K

## L

## M

## N

## O

## P

## Q



## R

## S

## T

## W

# SUBJECT INDEX

## A



## B

## T

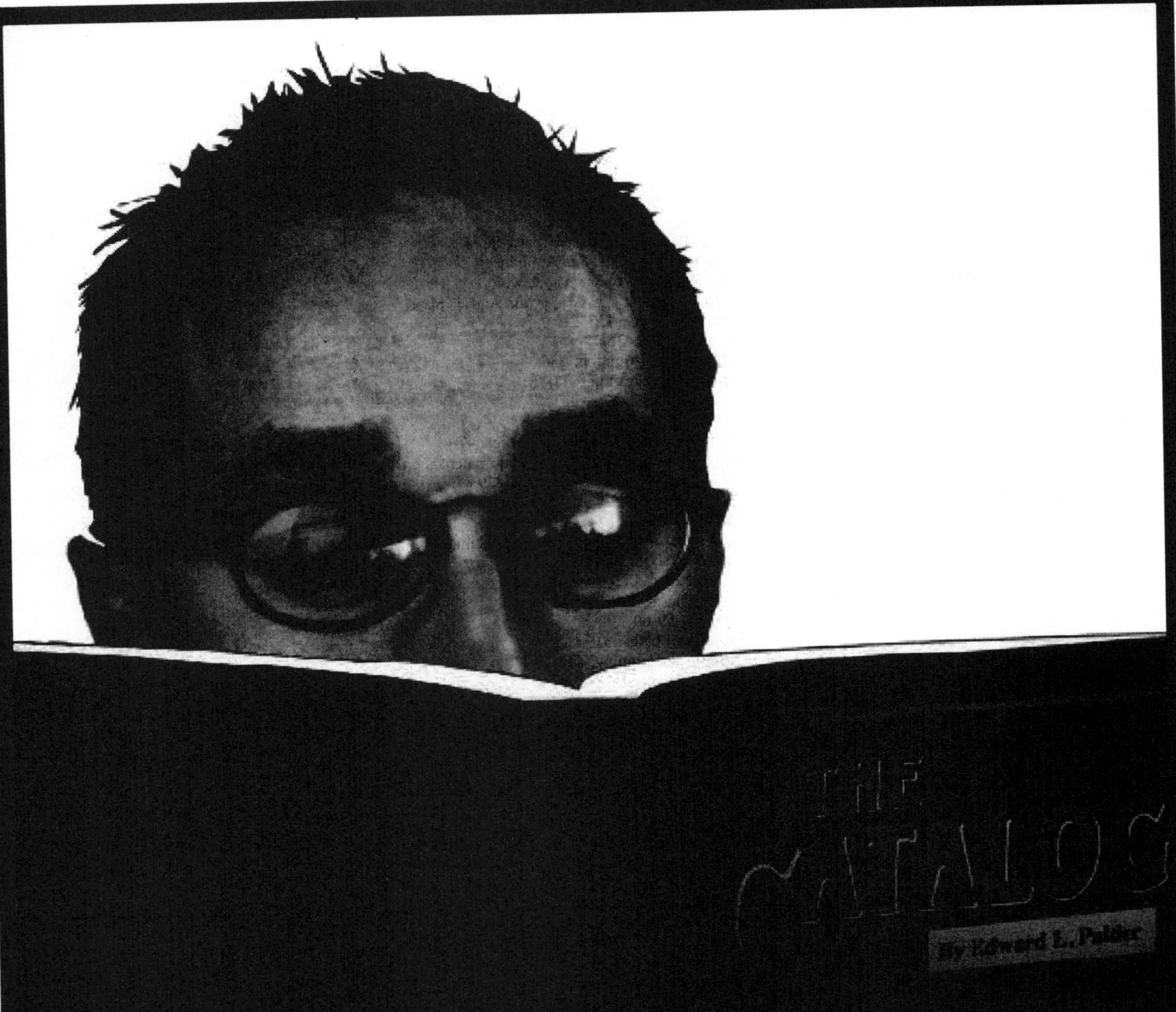
THE CATALOG
By Edward L. Palder

# ❖ HOW TO ORDER ❖

If you cannot find the **Catalog of Catalogs VI** in your local bookstore, you can order the book directly from the publisher or distributor by following the instructions below.

**IN THE UNITED STATES**

Within the United States only the price of the **Catalog of Catalogs VI** is $25.95, plus $4.50 shipping and handling. Maryland residents add 5% sales tax ($1.30). Orders must be prepaid by check, money order, or credit card (Visa or MasterCard). Orders may be placed by phone, fax, or mail by contacting:

Woodbine House
6510 Bells Mill Rd.
Bethesda, MD 20817
Toll-free: 800-843-7323
Phone: 301-897-3570
Fax: 301-897-5838
E-mail: info@woodbinehouse.com

**IN CANADA**

For ordering information, including price and shipping and handling charges, contact:

Monarch Books
5000 Dufferin St.
Downsview, Ontario M3H 5T5
Toll-free: 800-404-7404
Fax: 416-736-1702

**IN EUROPE**

For ordering information, including price and shipping and handling charges, contact:

Gazelle Book Services
Falcon House
Queen Square
Lancaster LA1 1RN
England
Phone: 1-524-68765
Fax: 1-524-63232

**FOR ADDITIONAL INFORMATION**

If you have any questions about ordering the **Catalog of Catalogs VI** that are not answered above, call, write, fax, or e-mail Woodbine House at the address given under "In the United States."

# ❖ HOW TO REPORT OR REQUEST ❖ UPDATED INFORMATION

A new edition of the **Catalog of Catalogs** is published every two years. During the two years between editions, the information in the most recent edition of the **Catalog of Catalogs** is continually being checked, updated, and expanded. Reader feedback is very important in helping to keep the information in the **Catalog of Catalogs** as up-to-date and useful as possible. If you cannot reach a company at the address listed in these pages, please notify the author at:

The Catalog of Catalogs
P.O. Box 6590
Silver Spring, MD 20916-6590
E-mail: catalogs@erols.com

If updated contact information is available, you will receive the new address and/or phone number free of charge. Readers who would like to recommend that a company be included in (or removed from) the next edition of the **Catalog of Catalogs** should also send contact information to the address above. Merchants and manufacturers who would like to suggest that their own company be listed should send a copy of their most recent catalog, brochure, or other print information.

To order the **Catalog of Catalogs,** see page 569. Please do not send orders for the **Catalog of Catalogs** to the address above.